Application

The Letter of the Law

On the Web

These margin features, which are new to this edition, give specific Uniform Resource Locators (URLs), or Internet addresses, concerning topics discussed in the text. You will find over one hundred such references throughout this text. Two examples are shown here.

ON THE WEB
To find state compilations (codes) of statutory laws, go to **www.findlaw.com/casecode/state.html**.

ON THE WEB
Cyberjury has a Web site at which visitors are invited to act as jurors deciding real cases. Go to **www.cyberjury.com**.

The Three Versions of
Business Law Today, Fifth Edition

You now have a choice of three different versions of the Fifth Edition of Business Law Today, depending on your teaching needs.

Business Law Today, Standard Edition: Text & Summarized Cases—Legal. Ethical, Regulatory, and International Environment

- 39 Chapters
- Summarized cases
- Pedagogical features
- A full supplements package

Business Law Today, Comprehensive Edition: Text & Cases—Legal. Ethical, Regulatory, and International Environment

The ideal text for a complete two-semester course in business law and the legal environment. This version includes additional legal environment chapters and those chapters necessary for students taking the CPA exam.

- 43 Chapters
- Actual case excerpts in the words of the court
- Pedagogical features
- A full supplements package

Business Law Today, The Essentials: Text & Summarized Cases—Legal. Ethical, Regulatory, and International Environment

This shorter version is aimed at a one-semester introductory course in business law and the legal environment.

- 23 Chapters
- Paraphrased cases
- Pedagogical features
- A full supplements package

Business Law Today

COMPREHENSIVE EDITION

Text & Cases

Legal, Ethical, Regulatory, and International Environment

FIFTH EDITION

Roger LeRoy Miller
Institute for University Studies
Arlington, Texas

Gaylord A. Jentz
Herbert D. Kelleher
Emeritus Professor in Business Law
MSIS Department
University of Texas at Austin

WEST WEST LEGAL STUDIES IN BUSINESS
Thomson Learning™

Australia • Canada • Denmark • Japan • Mexico • New Zealand • Philippines
Puerto Rico • Singapore • South Africa • Spain • United Kingdom • United States

Publisher/Team Director: Jack Calhoun
Senior Acquisitions Editor: Rob Dewey
Acquisitions Editor: Scott Person
Developmental Editor: Jan Lamar
Senior Marketing Manager: Mike Worls
Production Editor: Bill Stryker
Manufacturing Coordinator: Georgina Calderon
Internal Design: Bill Stryker
Cover Design: Paul Neff Design
Cover Illustrator: Copyright © Theo Rudnak/Stock Illustration Source
Photo Researcher: Megan Ryan
Copy Editor: Patricia Lewis
Indexer: Bob Marsh
Compositor: Parkwood Composition Service
Printer: West Group

Printed in the United States of America
1 2 3 4 5 6 7 8 9 10

International Thomson Publishing Europe
Berkshire House
168-173 High Holborn
London, WC1V7AA, United Kingdom

Nelson ITP, Australia
102 Dodds Street
South Melbourne
Victoria 3205 Australia

Nelson Canada
1120 Birchmount Road
Scarborough, Ontario
Canada M1K 5G4

International Thomson Editores
Seneca, 53
Colonia Polanco
11560 México D.F. México

International Thomson Publishing Asia
60 Alberta Street #15-01
Albert Complex
Singapore 189969

International Thomson Publishing Japan
Hirakawa-cho Kyowa Building, 3F
2-2-1 Hirakawa-cho, Chiyoda-ku
Tokyo 102, Japan

International Thomson Publishing Southern Africa
Building 18, Constantia Square
138 Sixteenth Road, P.O. Box 2459
Halfway House, 1685 South Africa

Library of Congress Cataloging-in-Publication Data
Miller, Roger LeRoy.
Business law today: comprehensive edition: text & cases—
legal, ethical, regulatory, and international environment / Roger LeRoy Miller, Gaylord A. Jentz.—5th ed.
p. cm.
Includes index.
ISBN 0-324-00417-6 (package) (hard cover.: alk. paper)
ISBN 0-324-02222-0 (text)
1. Commercial law—United States. 2. Business law—United States. I. Jentz, Gaylord A. II. Title.
KF888.M553 2000
346.7307—dc21 99–26251
CIP

This book is printed on acid-free paper.

Contents in Brief

Contents

UNIT ONE
The Legal Environment of Business 1

Chapter 10
Agreement and Consideration 257

Chapter 11
Capacity and Legality 284

Chapter 12
Assent and Form 307

Chapter 13
Third Party Rights and Discharge 331

Chapter 14
Breach and Remedies 356

UNIT THREE
Sales and Lease Contracts 379

UNIT FOUR
Negotiable Instruments 491

UNIT SIX Business Organizations 639

Preface to the Instructor

We have always felt that business law and the legal environment should be an exciting, contemporary, and interesting course. *Business Law Today, Comprehensive Edition,* Fifth Edition, we believe, imparts this excitement to your students. We have spent a great deal of effort in giving this book a visual appeal that will encourage students to learn the law. We have also worked hard to make sure that *Business Law Today, Comprehensive Edition,* continues in the established tradition of being the most up-to-date text in the market. The law presented in the Fifth Edition of *Business Law Today, Comprehensive Edition,* includes new statutes and regulations, as well as the most recent developments in case law.

We also believe that a thorough understanding of "black letter law" in the traditional business law topics—contracts, sales, torts, agency, business organizations, and other basic topics—is important. You will find that coverage of traditional business law has not been sacrificed in the process of creating this text. Additionally, *Business Law Today, Comprehensive Edition,* explicitly addresses the American Assembly of Collegiate Schools of Business's (AACSB's) broad array of curriculum requirements. As you will see, many of the features and special pedagogical devices in this text focus on the global, political, ethical, social, environmental, technological, and cultural contexts of business law.

A Flexible Teaching/Learning Package

We realize that different people have different teaching philosophies and learning goals. We believe that the Fifth Edition of *Business Law Today, Comprehensive Edition,* and its extensive supplements offer business law instructors a flexible teaching/learning package. For example, although we have attempted to make the materials flow from chapter to chapter, most of the chapters are self-contained. In other words, you can use the chapters in any order you wish.

Additionally, the extensive number of supplements accompanying *Business Law Today, Comprehensive Edition,* allows instructors to choose those supplements that will most effectively complement classroom instruction. Suggestions on how you can adapt the *Business Law Today, Comprehensive Edition,* teaching/learning package to fit your particular teaching and learning goals are given in the *Instructor's Course Planning Guide.* Furthermore, each chapter of the *Instructor's Manual* contains teaching suggestions, possible discussion questions, and additional information on key statutes or other legal sources that you may wish to use in your classroom. These and numerous other supplementary materials (including printed and multimedia supplements) all contribute to the goal of making *Business Law Today, Comprehensive Edition,* the most flexible teaching/learning package in the market today.

Emphasis on Technology and the Internet

To ensure that *Business Law Today, Comprehensive Edition,* Fifth Edition, is truly up to date and reflects current law to the fullest extent possible, we have added an entirely new chapter titled "Cyberlaw in the Legal Environment" (Chapter 7). The chapter describes how existing laws are being applied to electronic transactions conducted over the Internet and how, in some areas, new laws have been enacted specifically to cover certain aspects of electronic commerce and other activities. In addition to this new chapter, the Fifth Edition has several other components focusing on technology.

BUSINESS LAW TODAY, COMPREHENSIVE EDITION, ON THE WEB

When you visit us at http://blt.westbuslaw.com, you will find, at a minimum, the following:

- Interactive quizzes for most chapters in *Business Law Today, Comprehensive Edition,* Fifth Edition.
- An "Internet Activities Book" containing one or more Internet exercises for most chapters in this text.
- Current legal events updated regularly and keyed to chapters in this text.
- Summaries of new cases from various West legal publications, as well as many other legal publications, all linked to this text.
- Links to other important legal resources available for free on the Web.
- "E-mail the authors" feature.

ONLINE LEGAL RESEARCH GUIDE

With every new book, your students receive a free copy of *Online Legal Research.* This is the most complete brief guide to using the Internet that exists today. It was developed and written especially to accompany *Business Law Today, Comprehensive Edition.* There is even an appendix on how to evaluate information obtained from the Internet.

MULTIMEDIA INTERACTIVE *BUSINESS LAW PARTNER* CD-ROM

With this edition of *Business Law Today, Comprehensive Edition,* your students can explore the law in a practical, interactive way if you order with each copy of the text the *Quicken Business Law Partner* CD-ROM. With each copy of the CD-ROM is the *Multimedia Interactive Guide and Workbook* prepared by Roger LeRoy Miller and Eric William Hollowell. This booklet guides the student to the multimedia part of the CD-ROM. In addition, it presents problems that are linked to the appropriate chapters in *Business Law Today, Comprehensive Edition.* Ask your sales representative how you can bundle this CD-ROM and booklet with each copy of the text.

SPECIAL TECHNOLOGY FEATURES AND PEDAGOGY

The following special features and pedagogy in the Fifth Edition of *Business Law Today, Comprehensive Edition,* are designed to acquaint your students with technological trends in business law, as well as with the broad array of legal resources available on the Web.

- ***Technology and the Law***—The majority of the chapters in the Fifth Edition now contain one of these special features, each of which explores a development in cyberlaw relating to the chapter topic. Virtually all of the technology features in the Fourth Edition have been replaced or rewritten, and many more have been added for the Fifth Edition.
- ***On the Web***—These margin features, which are new to this edition, give specific Uniform Resource Locators (URLs), or Internet addresses, so that students can access online information concerning a topic being discussed in the text.
- ***URLs for Cases***—Whenever possible, we have included URLs that can be used to access the cases presented in the text of *Business Law Today, Comprehensive Edition*. When a URL is available, it appears just below the case citation.
- ***Online Activities***—To familiarize your students with online legal resources and help them learn to navigate the Internet, we have included at the end of every chapter one or more Internet exercises. Some of the exercises refer students to Internet exercises presented in the "Internet Activities Book" on the *Business Law Today, Comprehensive Edition,* Web site at **http://blt.westbuslaw.com**.
- ***Before the Test***—At the end of most chapters, just following the *Online Activities,* students are directed to the *Business Law Today, Comprehensive Edition,* Web site, where they can access twenty interactive questions relating to the topics covered in the chapter.

More on LLCs and LLPs

Because of the growing importance of limited liability companies and limited liability partnerships, we have added an entirely new chapter on "Limited Liability Companies and Partnerships" (Chapter 32). This chapter provides your students with the most current information on these special business organizational forms.

Other Key Features

In addition to the *Technology and the Law* features discussed above, virtually all of the chapters in this text have one or more of the following special sections, which are designed both to instruct and to pique the interest of the business law student. To emphasize critical thinking, many of these features conclude with a question section titled *For Critical Analysis.* These critical-analysis questions, which may serve as a basis for classroom discussion, require the student to reflect on some aspect or implication of the topics discussed in the features.

- ***Landmark in the Law***—This feature, which appears in most of the chapters in this edition, discusses a landmark case, statute, or other law that has had a significant effect on business law.
- ***Business Law in Action***—Nearly every chapter of the text contains one of these features, which present examples of how laws relating to chapter topics are applied to specific situations that have recently arisen in the business arena.
- ***Application***—Almost all of the chapters have an *Application* section, which presents the student with some practical advice on how to apply the law discussed in the chapter to real-world business problems. Each *Application* ends with a "Checklist" for the future businessperson on how to avoid legal problems.

• ***The Letter of the Law***—This feature, which is new to the Fifth Edition, provides students with a glimpse at sometimes humorous, sometimes serious illustrations of how the letter of the law has been phrased, interpreted, or applied. Each feature concludes with a section called *The Bottom Line,* which consists of a statement summarizing the implications of the illustrated topic for businesspersons.

• ***Ethical Issues***—In addition to a chapter on ethics, chapter-ending ethical questions, and the *Ethical Considerations* following many of the cases presented in this text, we have included special features called *Ethical Issues.* These features, which are closely integrated with the text, open with a question addressing an ethical dimension of the topic being discussed. Each *Ethical Issue* has been given a number so that it can be easily located for review or discussion.

• ***International Perspectives***—These features give students an awareness of the global legal environment by indicating how international laws or the laws of other nations deal with specific legal concepts or topics being discussed in the chapter.

A Special Case Format

In each chapter, we present cases that have been selected to illustrate the principles of law discussed in the text. The cases are numbered sequentially for easy referencing in class discussions, homework assignments, and examinations. In choosing the cases to be included in this edition, our goal has been to include the most recent cases from the late 1990s, as well as classic cases in business law.

Each case presented in *Business Law Today, Comprehensive Edition,* follows a basic case format consisting of the following sections:

- Case title and full case citation (including all parallel citations).
- Background and Facts.
- In the Words of the Court.
- Decision and Remedy.

In addition, each case is preceded by either a *Company Profile* providing background information on a party to the case or by a *Historical and [Social or Other] Setting* placing the case in its social, cultural, technological, international, economic, or other relevant setting. Concluding each case is a *For Critical Analysis* section, which consists of a question that requires the student to think critically about a particular issue raised by the case. The section addresses the AACSB's curriculum requirements by focusing on how particular aspects of the dispute or the court's decision relate to ethical, international, technological, cultural, or other types of issues.

Other Special Pedagogical Devices

We have included in *Business Law Today, Comprehensive Edition,* a number of additional pedagogical devices, including those discussed below.

SPECIAL PEDAGOGICAL DEVICES IN THE TEXT

- *Learning Objectives.*
- *Contents* (an outline of the chapter's first-level and second-level headings).
- Margin definitions.
- Margin *On the Web* features directing students to relevant Web sites.
- Highlighted and numbered examples illustrating legal principles.
- Quotations.

- Exhibits and forms (about one hundred).
- Photographs (with critical-thinking questions).
- Judiciously selected cartoons.

Chapter-Ending Pedagogy

- *Key Terms* (with appropriate page references).
- *Chapter Summary* (in graphic format with page references).
- *For Review* (a series of brief review questions).
- *Questions and Case Problems* (including hypotheticals and case problems; many of the case problems are based on cases from the late 1990s).
- *A Question of Ethics and Social Responsibility.*
- *For Critical Analysis.*
- *Online Activities.*
- *Before the Test* (online chapter-by-chapter quizzes).

Unit-Ending Pedagogy—Cumulative Business Hypotheticals

Each unit in *Business Law Today, Comprehensive Edition*, Fifth Edition, concludes with a section that introduces a hypothetical business firm and then asks a series of questions about how the law applies to various actions taken by the firm. To answer the questions, the student must apply the laws discussed throughout the unit. Suggested answers to the unit-ending cumulative questions are included in the *Answers Manual.* Each of these sections has been newly created for the Fifth Edition.

Unit-Ending Pedagogy—Extended Case Studies

New to the Fifth Edition is a special, two-page feature called *Extended Case Study: The Law in Context.* This feature, which appears just following the *Cumulative Business Hypothetical* at the end of each unit, focuses on a specific court case relating to a topic covered in the unit. Each feature opens with an introductory section, which discusses the background and significance of the case being presented. Then we present excerpts from the court's majority opinion and, when one exists, from a dissenting opinion in the case. These excerpts are followed by a section titled *Media Coverage,* which presents excerpts from a news article discussing the case. In the *Going Online* section that follows, the student is directed to one or more Web sites at which the case itself or further information on the case can be found. The feature concludes with a series of questions, under the heading *Questions for Analysis,* that prompt the student to think critically about the legal, ethical, economic, international, or general business implications of the case.

Appendices

To help students learn how to find and analyze case law, we have included a special appendix at the end of Chapter 1. There your students will find information, including an exhibit, on how to read case citations, how to locate cases in case reporters, and what the different components of URLs (Internet addresses) mean. The appendix to Chapter 1 also presents an annotated sample court case to help your students understand how to read and understand the cases presented within this text.

Because the majority of students keep their business law texts as a reference source, we have included at the end of the book the following full set of appendices (Appendix E and Appendix G are new to the Fifth Edition):

A. The Constitution of the United States.
B. The Uniform Commercial Code, including the 1994 revised version of Article 8.
C. The Uniform Partnership Act.
D. The Revised Model Business Corporation Act (Excerpts).
E. The Uniform Limited Liability Company Act (Excerpts).
F. The Restatement (Second) of Torts (Excerpts).
G. The Restatement (Third) of Torts: Products Liability (Excerpts).
H. The Sherman Antitrust Act of 1890 (Excerpts).
I. The Securities Act of 1933 (Excerpts).
J. The Securities Exchange Act of 1934 (Excerpts).
K. Title VII of the Civil Rights Act of 1964 (Excerpts).
L. The Americans with Disabilities Act of 1990 (Excerpts).
M. The Civil Rights Act of 1991 (Excerpts).
N. The United Nations Convention on Contracts for the International Sale of Goods (Excerpts)
O. Spanish Equivalents for Important Legal Terms in English.

Supplemental Teaching Materials

This edition of *Business Law Today, Comprehensive Edition,* is accompanied by a vastly expanded number of teaching and learning supplements. Individually and in conjunction with a number of our colleagues, we have developed supplementary teaching materials that we believe are the best available today. Each component of the supplements package is listed below.

Printed Supplements

- *Instructor's Course Planning Guide.*
- *Instructor's Manual.*
- *Study Guide.*
- A comprehensive *Test Bank.*
- *Answers Manual.*
- *Instructor's Manual* for the *Drama of the Law* video series.
- *Case Printouts* (including printouts of cases referred to in selected features).
- *Handbook on Critical Thinking and Writing.*
- *Handbook of Landmark Cases and Statutes in Business Law.*
- *A Guide to Personal Law.*
- *Lecture Outline System.*
- *Online Legal Research.*
- *Multimedia Interactive Guide and Workbook for* Quicken Business Law Partner *CD-ROM*
- *Law and Women's Issues.*
- Regional Reporters.
- *Business Law and the CPA Exam.*

Software and Video Supplements

- Thomson Learning Testing Tools—including Testing Tools Test, Testing Tools Manager, and Testing Tools Online.
- Computerized *Instructor's Manual.*
- Computerized *Answers Manual.*
- *Quicken Business Law Partner* CD-ROM.
- Interactive Software—Contracts and Sales.

- "You Be the Judge" software.
- Case-Problem Cases on Diskette.
- PowerPoint Slides.
- Transparency Acetates.
- Westlaw®.
- West's Business Law and Legal Environment Audiocassette Library.
- Videocassettes, including new videos on specific legal applications. (For further information on video supplements, access the *Business Law Today, Comprehensive Edition,* Web site at http://blt.westbuslaw.com.)

For Users of the Fourth Edition

We thought that those of you who have been using *Business Law Today, Comprehensive Edition,* would like to know some of the major changes that have been made for the Fifth Edition. The book is basically the same, but we think that we have improved it greatly, thanks in part to the many letters, telephone calls, and reviews that we have received.

New Chapters and Organizational Changes

- An entirely new chapter on cyberlaw, titled "Cyberlaw in the Legal Environment" (Chapter 7) has been added for the Fifth Edition. The chapter focuses on how cyberspace is affecting business practices and the legal environment in a number of areas. Topics covered in the chapter include court practices and procedures, jurisdictional issues, free speech, cyber crimes, cyber torts, virtual property rights, e-commerce, e-money, and marketing on the Internet.
- A newly created chapter titled "Limited Liability Companies and Partnerships" (Chapter 32), expands the Fourth Edition's coverage of limited liability companies and partnerships, and incorporates the materials on limited partnerships that were previously presented within the chapter on partnerships.
- The materials on private franchises and special business forms (joint ventures, business trusts, and others) now appear in a separate chapter at the end of the business organizations unit as Chapter 33, "Special Business Forms and Private Franchises."
- The chapter titled "Ethics and Social Responsibility," which was placed as Chapter 4 in the Fourth Edition, has been repositioned for the Fifth Edition so that it follows the chapters on torts, criminal law, and cyberlaw; it now appears as Chapter 8, concluding Unit One of the text.

New Features and Pedagogy

- *The Letter of the Law.*
- *Ethical Issues* (these replace the Fourth Edition's Ethical Perspectives).
- *Extended Case Study: The Law in Context* (at the end of each unit).
- *On the Web* margin notes.
- Internet URLs for cases presented in the text.
- *Online Activities* (at the end of each chapter).
- *Before the Test* (at the end of most chapters—online chapter quizzes).
- Highlighted and numbered examples.

Significantly Revised Chapters

Every chapter of the Fifth Edition has been revised as necessary to incorporate new developments in the law or to streamline the presentations. A number of new trends in business law are addressed in the special features of the Fifth Edition. Other major changes and additions made for this edition include the following:

- Chapter 2 (Constitutional Law) now contains an expanded discussion of federalism and the balance of powers. The subsections on the constitutional protections in criminal proceedings were moved to Chapter 6 and are now discussed in the context of criminal law.
- Chapter 5 (Business Torts and Intellectual Property) now includes a discussion of the Trademark Dilution Act of 1995, the Digital Millennium Copyright Act of 1998, and state food-disparagement statutes (including a discussion of the case brought against Oprah Winfrey for trade libel).
- Chapter 6 (Criminal Law) includes a discussion of the Economic Espionage Act of 1996, which criminalized the theft of trade secrets, and a fuller discussion of the distinction between criminal and civil law. Sections on white-collar crimes and corporate criminal liability were also added to the chapter.
- Chapter 18 (Warranties and Product Liability) contains a new section on the *Restatement (Third) of Torts: Products Liability* and incorporates provisions from this new *Restatement* in the discussion of strict product liability.
- Chapter 23 (Creditors' Rights and Bankruptcy) reflects the 1998 adjustments to dollar amounts for exempted property and distributions under the Bankruptcy Code.
- Chapter 31 (Investor Protection) includes a discussion of the "Plain English" requirements of the Securities and Exchange Commission (SEC) and examines the reversal by the SEC of its earlier rulings on shareholder agenda proposals relating to equal employment opportunity.
- Chapter 35 (Antitrust Law) discusses, in an *Ethical Issue,* the Curt Flood Act of 1998, which modified professional baseball's exempt status under antitrust laws. A technology feature discusses the case brought by the Justice Department against Microsoft Corporation.
- The chapters on employment (Chapters 37 and 38) incorporate references to the latest developments in the areas of labor and employment law, including 1998 decisions by the United States Supreme Court.

WHAT ELSE IS NEW?

In addition to the changes noted above, you will find a number of other new items or features in *Business Law Today, Comprehensive Edition,* Fifth Edition, as listed below.

- **New Cases and Case Problems**—Numerous new cases were added for the Fifth Edition, including at least thirty-eight cases decided in 1998. Additionally, virtually every chapter has one new case problem dating from the late 1990s. As mentioned earlier in this preface, all of the unit-ending hypothetical questions are new.
- **New Exhibits**—We have modified exhibits contained in the Fourth Edition of *Business Law Today, Comprehensive Edition,* Fifth Edition, whenever necessary to achieve greater clarity or accuracy. In addition, new exhibits have been added for this edition, including a series of Web home pages (in Chapter 7); Exhibit 32–2, a two-page exhibit comparing business organizational forms (sole proprietorships, partnerships, corporations, limited partnerships, limited liability companies, and limited liability partnerships) with respect to how they are formed, the liability of the owners, and other characteristics; and Exhibit 42–3 (John Lennon's will).
- **New Appendices**—Appendix E, "The Uniform Limited Liability Company Act (Excerpts)," and Appendix G, "The Restatement (Third) of Torts: Products Liability (Excerpts)," are both new to the Fifth Edition. Additionally, the Uniform

Commercial Code is presented in its entirety in Appendix B. Appendix B also now includes the 1994 revised version of Article 8.

NEW SUPPLEMENTS

- *Online Legal Research.*
- *A Guide to Personal Law* (now offered separately from the text).
- *Multimedia Interactive Guide and Workbook to* Quicken Business Law Partner *CD-ROM.*
- PowerPoint Slides.
- *Quicken Business Law Partner* CD-ROM.
- *Law and Women's Issues.*
- A greatly enhanced Web site at http://blt.westbuslaw.com.

Acknowledgments

Numerous careful and conscientious users of *Business Law Today, Comprehensive Edition,* were kind enough to help us revise the book. In addition, the staff at West Publishing Company went out of its way to make sure that this edition came out early and in accurate form. Our editors, Rob Dewey and Scott Person, gave us countless new ideas, many of which have been incorporated into this new edition. Our fearless and tireless Webmaster, Kurt Gerdenich, guided us throughout the project so that we ended up with the most advanced and useful Web site around. We learned much from our marketing manager, Mike Worls, and we keep on learning from his in-field experiences. We thank also Kristen Meere, who mans the "hotline" and who relays new issues and ideas to us all of the time. We have enjoyed the support and respect of "the Chief" Bob Lynch for years. We hope to continue to satisfy his demands. Our production manager and designer, Bill Stryker, made sure that we came out with an error-free, visually attractive edition. We will always be in his debt. Finally, we continue to be the grateful beneficiaries of the great work of our long-time developmental editor, Jan Lamar. She continues to deserve our thanks for her efforts in coordinating reviews and in guaranteeing the timely and accurate publication of all supplemental materials. Finally, we wish to thank Megan Ryan, our production editor for all of the supplements, for the great job she has done.

We must especially thank William Eric Hollowell, co-author of the *Instructor's Manual, Study Guide, Test Bank, Online Legal Research* guide, and *Multimedia Interactive Guide and Workbook,* for his excellent research efforts. We also wish to thank Lavina Leed Miller, who provided expert research, editing, and proofing services for this project. Additional proofing was done by Suzie Franklin DeFazio and Roxanna Lee. We were again fortunate to have the indexing services of Bob Marsh. Our appreciation also goes to Suzanne Jasin for her many special efforts on the projects. In addition, our gratitude goes to Xiaochun Jin for her proofing and for making sure that the work flowed smoothly through Austin.

ACKNOWLEDGMENTS

John J. Balek
Morton College, Illinois
Brad Botz
Garden City Community College, Kansas
Lee B. Burgunder
California Polytechnic University—San Luis Obispo
Dale Clark
Corning Community College, New York
Patricia L. DeFrain
Glendale College, California
Joe D. Dillsaver
Northeastern State University, Oklahoma
Larry R. Edwards
Tarrant County Junior College, South Campus, Texas
George E. Eigsti
Kansas City, Kansas, Community College
Jerry Furniss
University of Montana

ACKNOWLEDGMENTS, Continued

Nancy L. Hart
Midland College, Texas
Janine S. Hiller
Virginia Polytechnic Institute & State University
Sarah Weiner Keidan
Oakland Community College, Michigan
Bradley T. Lutz
Hillsborough Community College, Florida
John D. Mallonee
Manatee Community College, Florida
James K. Miersma
Milwaukee Area Technical Institute, Wisconsin
Jim Lee Morgan
West Los Angeles College
Jack K. Morton
University of Montana
Solange North
Fox Valley Technical Institute, Wisconsin
Robert H. Orr
Florida Community College at Jacksonville
George Otto
Truman College, Illinois
William M. Rutledge
Macomb Community College, Michigan
Anne W. Schacherl
Madison Area Technical College, Wisconsin
Edward F. Shafer
Rochester Community College, Minnesota
Lou Ann Simpson
Drake University, Iowa
James E. Walsh, Jr.
Tidewater Community College, Virginia
Edward L. Welsh, Jr.
Phoenix College
Clark W. Wheeler
Santa Fe Community College, Florida
James L. Wittenbach
University of Notre Dame
Joseph Zavaglia, Jr.
Brookdale Community College, New Jersey

ACKNOWLEDGMENTS FOR THE SECOND EDITION

Merlin Bauer
Mid State Technical College, Wisconsin
Fred Ittner
College of Alameda, California
Susan S. Jarvis
University of Texas, Pan American, Texas
Beverly McCormick
Morehead State University, Kentucky
Robert H. Orr
Florida Community College at Jacksonville
Donald L. Petote
Genessee Community College, New York
Anne W. Schacherl
Madison Area Technical College, Wisconsin

ACKNOWLEDGMENTS FOR THE THIRD EDITION

Daryl Barton
Eastern Michigan University
Jere L. Crago
Delgado Community College, Louisiana
Tony Enerva
Lakeland Community College, Ohio
Richard N. Kleeberg
Solano Community College, California
Darlene Mallick
Anne Arundel Community College, Maryland
Susan J. Mitchell
Des Moines Area Community College, Iowa
Thomas L. Palmer
Northern Arizona University
Francis D. Polk
Ocean County College, New Jersey

ACKNOWLEDGMENTS FOR THE FOURTH EDITION

Lorraine K. Bannai
Western Washington University
Claude W. Dotson
Northwest College, Wyoming
Jacolin Eichelberger
Hillsborough Community College, Florida
Phil Harmeson
University of South Dakota
William J. McDevitt
Saint Joseph's University, Pennsylvania
John W. McGee
Aims Community College, Colorado
Joseph D. Marcus
Prince George's Community College, Maryland
Woodrow J. Maxwell
Hudson Valley Community College, New York
Susan J. Mitchell
Des Moines Area Community College, Iowa
Martha Wright Sartoris
North Hennepin Community College, Minnesota

ACKNOWLEDGMENTS FOR THE FIFTH EDITION

Marlene E. Barken
Ithaca College, New York
Donna E. Becker
Frederick Community College, Maryland
Teresa Brady
Holy Family College, Philadelphia
Sandra J. Defebaugh
Eastern Michigan University
Julia G. Derrick
Brevard Community College, Florida
Florence E. Elliott-Howard
Stephen F. Austin State University, Texas
Benjamin C. Fassberg
Prince George's Community College, Maryland
Elizabeth J. Guerriero
Northeast Louisiana University

Jack E. Karns
East Carolina University, North Carolina
Gregory Rabb
Jamestown Community College, New York
Hugh Rode
Utah Valley State College
Denise Smith
Missouri Western State College
Hugh M. Spall
Central Washington University
James D. Van Tassel
Mission College, California
Frederick J. Walsh
Franklin Pierce College, New Hampshire
Kay O. Wilburn
The University of Alabama at Birmingham

We know that we are not perfect. If you or your students find something you don't like or want us to change, write to us. That is how we can make *Business Law Today, Comprehensive Edition,* an even better book in the future.

Roger LeRoy Miller
Gaylord A. Jentz

Dedication

To Larry Mayle,
who just keeps going and going.
Thanks for years of friendship.
R.L.M.

To my wife, JoAnn; to my children, Kathy, Gary, Lori, and Rory; and to my grandchildren, Erin, Megan, Eric, Emily, Michelle, Javier, Carmen, and Steve.
G.A.J.

UNIT ONE

The Legal Environment of Business

CHAPTER 1

The Legal & International Environment

> "The law is of as much interest to the layman as it is to the lawyer."
>
> Lord Balfour, 1848–1930
> (British prime minister, 1902–1905)

CONTENTS

LEARNING OBJECTIVES

After reading this chapter, you should be able to:

1. Explain what is generally meant by the term *law.*
2. Describe the origins and importance of the common law tradition.
3. Identify the four major sources of American law.
4. List some important classifications of law.
5. Distinguish between national law and international law.

Lord Balfour's assertion in the quotation above emphasizes the underlying theme of every page in this book—that law is of interest to all persons, not just to lawyers. Those entering the world of business will find themselves subject to numerous laws and government regulations. A basic knowledge of these laws and regulations is beneficial—if not essential—to anyone contemplating a successful career in the business world of today.

In this introductory chapter, we first look at the nature of law and at some concepts that have significantly influenced how jurists and scholars view the nature and function of law. We then examine the common law tradition of the United States, as well as some of the major sources and classifications of American law. The chapter concludes with a discussion of the global legal environment, which frames many of today's business transactions.

The Nature of Law

There have been and will continue to be different definitions of law. The Greek philosopher Aristotle (384–322 B.C.E.) saw law as a "pledge that citizens of a state will do justice to one another." Aristotle's mentor, Plato (427–347 B.C.E.), believed that law was a form of social control. The Roman orator and politician Cicero (106–43 B.C.E.) contended that law was the agreement of reason and nature, the distinction between the just and the unjust. The British jurist Sir William Blackstone (1723–1780) described law as "a rule of civil conduct prescribed by the supreme power in a state, commanding what is right, and prohibiting what is wrong." In America, the eminent jurist Oliver Wendell Holmes, Jr. (1841–1935), contended that law was a set of rules that allowed one to predict how a court would resolve a particular dispute—"the prophecies of what the courts will do in fact, and nothing more pretentious, are what I mean by the law."

• **LAW**
A body of enforceable rules governing relationships among individuals and between individuals and their society.

• **JURISPRUDENCE**
The science or philosophy of law.

"There is in fact a true law—namely, right reason—which is in accordance with nature [and] applies to all men and is unchangeable and eternal."
CICERO, 106–43 B.C.E.
(Roman statesman and orator)

Although these definitions vary in their particulars, they all are based on the following general observation: **law** consists of enforceable rules governing relationships among individuals and between individuals and their society. In the study of law, often referred to as **jurisprudence,** this very broad statement concerning the nature of law is the point of departure for all legal scholars and philosophers. We look here at three of the most influential schools of legal thought, or philosophies of law: the natural law tradition, legal positivism, and legal realism.

THE NATURAL LAW TRADITION

The oldest and one of the most significant schools of jurisprudence is the natural law tradition, which dates back to ancient Greece and Rome. **Natural law** denotes a system of moral and ethical principles that are inherent in human nature and that can be discovered by humans through the use of their natural intelligence, or reason. The Greek philosopher Aristotle distinguished between natural law (which applies universally to all humankind) and **positive law** (the conventional, or written, law of a particular society at a particular point in time). In essence, the natural law tradition presupposes that the legitimacy of positive, or conventional, law derives from natural law. Whenever positive law conflicts with natural law, positive law loses its legitimacy and should be changed.

• **NATURAL LAW**
The belief that government and the legal system should reflect universal moral and ethical principles that are inherent in human nature. The natural law school is the oldest and one of the most significant schools of legal thought.

• **POSITIVE LAW**
The body of conventional, or written, law of a particular society at a particular point in time.

• **EXAMPLE 1.1** A law prohibiting murder reflects not only the values accepted by a particular society at a particular time (positive law) but also a universally accepted precept that murder is wrong (natural law). To murder someone is thus a violation of natural law. If a law allowed persons to murder each other, that law would be wrong, because it did not accord with natural law. In a sense, the natural law tradition encourages individuals to disobey conventional, or written, laws if those individuals believe that the laws are in conflict with natural law.•

LEGAL POSITIVISM

• **LEGAL POSITIVISM**
A school of legal thought centered on the assumption that there is no law higher than the laws created by the government. Laws must be obeyed, even if they are unjust, to prevent anarchy.

Another school of legal thought is known as **legal positivism.** Legal positivists believe that there can be no higher law than a nation's positive laws—the laws created by a particular society at a particular point in time. Essentially, from the positivist perspective, the law is the law and must be obeyed on pain of punishment. Whether a particular law is bad or good is irrelevant. The merits or demerits of a given law can be discussed, and laws can be changed in an orderly manner through a legitimate lawmaking process. As long as a law exists, however, that law must be obeyed. If people felt justified in disobeying particular laws just because they did not feel the laws were just, anarchy would ensue.

LEGAL REALISM

• **LEGAL REALISM**
A school of legal thought of the 1920s and 1930s that generally advocated a less abstract and more realistic approach to the law, an approach that takes into account customary practices and the circumstances in which transactions take place. The school left a lasting imprint on American jurisprudence.

Legal realism, which became a popular school of legal thought in the 1920s and 1930s, left a strong imprint on American jurisprudence. Contrary to the dominant legal thinking of their time, the legal realists believed that the law could not—and should not—be an abstract body of rules applied uniformly to cases with similar circumstances. According to the legal realists, impartial and uniform application of the law is not possible. After all, judges are human beings with unique personalities, value systems, and intellects. Given this obvious fact, it would be impossible for any two judges to engage in an identical reasoning process when evaluating the same case.

The legal realists argued that each case also involves a unique set of circumstances—no two cases, no matter how similar, are ever exactly the same. Therefore, judges should take into account the specific circumstances of each case, rather than rely on some abstract rule that might not relate to those particular circumstances. When making decisions, judges should also consider extra-legal sources, such as economic and sociological data, to the extent that such sources could illuminate the circumstances and issues involved in specific cases. In other words, the law should take social and economic realities into account.

United States Supreme Court Justice Oliver Wendell Holmes, Jr. (1841–1935), and Karl Llewellyn (1893–1962) were both influential proponents of legal realism. Llewellyn is best known for his dominant role in drafting the Uniform Commercial Code (UCC), a set of rules for commercial transactions that will be discussed later in this chapter. The UCC reflects the influence of legal realism in its emphasis on practicality, flexibility, reasonability, and customary trade practices.

The Common Law Tradition

How jurists view the law is particularly important in a legal system in which judges play a paramount role, as they do in the American legal system. Because of our colonial heritage, much of American law is based on the English legal system. A knowledge of this tradition is necessary to an understanding of the nature of our legal system today.

EARLY ENGLISH COURTS OF LAW

In 1066, after the Normans conquered England, William the Conqueror and his successors began the process of unifying the country under their rule. One of the means they used to this end was the establishment of the king's courts, or *curiae regis*. Before the Norman Conquest, disputes had been settled according to the local legal customs and traditions in various regions of the country. The king's courts sought to establish a uniform set of rules for the country as a whole. What evolved in these courts was the beginning of the **common law**—a body of general rules that prescribed social conduct and that was applied throughout the entire English realm.

• **COMMON LAW**
That body of law developed from custom or judicial decisions in English and U.S. courts, not attributable to a legislature.

Courts developed the common law rules from the principles underlying judges' decisions in actual legal controversies. Judges attempted to be consistent, and when-

THE COURT OF CHANCERY IN THE REIGN OF GEORGE I. EARLY ENGLISH COURT DECISIONS FORMED THE BASIS OF WHAT TYPE OF LAW?

• **PRECEDENT**
A court decision that furnishes an example or authority for deciding subsequent cases involving identical or similar facts.

• ***STARE DECISIS***
A common law doctrine under which judges are obligated to follow the precedents established in prior decisions.

• **BINDING AUTHORITY**
Any source of law that a court must follow when deciding a case. Binding authorities include constitutions, statutes, and regulations that govern the issue being decided, as well as court decisions that are controlling precedents within the jurisdiction.

ever possible, they based their decisions on the principles suggested by earlier cases. They sought to decide similar cases in a similar way and considered new cases with care, because they knew that their decisions would make new law. Each interpretation became part of the law on the subject and served as a legal **precedent**—that is, a decision that furnished an example or authority for deciding subsequent cases involving similar legal principles or facts.

In the early years of the common law, there was no single place or publication in which court opinions, or written decisions, could be found. In the late thirteenth and early fourteenth centuries, however, portions of significant decisions of each year were gathered together and recorded in *Year Books*. The *Year Books* were useful references for lawyers and judges. In the sixteenth century, the *Year Books* were discontinued, and other reports of cases became available. (See the appendix to this chapter for a discussion of how cases are reported, or published, in the United States today.)

STARE DECISIS

The practice of deciding new cases with reference to former decisions, or precedents, eventually became a cornerstone of the English and American judicial systems. The practice forms a doctrine called ***stare decisis***[1] ("to stand on decided cases"). The doctrine means that once a court has set forth a principle of law as being applicable to a certain set of facts, that court and courts of lower rank will adhere to that principle and apply it in future cases involving similar fact patterns.

• **EXAMPLE 1.2** Suppose that the lower state courts in California have reached conflicting conclusions on whether drivers are liable for accidents they cause while merging into freeway traffic, even though the drivers looked and did not see any oncoming traffic and even though witnesses (passengers in their cars) testified to that effect. To settle the law on this issue, the California Supreme Court decides to review a case involving this fact pattern. The court rules that in such a situation, the driver who is merging into traffic is liable for any accidents caused by the driver's failure to yield to freeway traffic—regardless of whether the driver looked carefully and did not see an approaching vehicle. The California Supreme Court's decision on the matter will influence the outcome of all future cases on this issue brought before the California state courts.•

Similarly, a decision on a given issue by the United States Supreme Court (the nation's highest court) is binding on all inferior courts. Controlling precedents in a jurisdiction are referred to as **binding authorities,** as are statutes or other laws that must be followed.

The doctrine of *stare decisis* helps the courts to be more efficient, because if other courts have carefully reasoned through a similar case, their legal reasoning and opinions can serve as guides. *Stare decisis* also makes the law more stable and predictable. If the law on a given subject is well settled, someone bringing a case to court can usually rely on the court to make a decision based on what the law has been.

Departures from Precedent Sometimes a court will depart from the rule of precedent if it decides that a given precedent should no longer be followed. If a court decides that a precedent is simply incorrect or that technological or social changes have rendered the precedent inapplicable, the court might rule contrary to the precedent. Cases that overturn precedent often receive a great deal of publicity.

1. Pronounced *ster*-ay dih-*si*-ses.

ON THE WEB

To learn how the Supreme Court justified its departure from precedent in the 1954 *Brown* decision, you can access the Court's opinion online at www.findlaw.com.

• **EXAMPLE 1.3** In *Brown v. Board of Education of Topeka,*[2] the United States Supreme Court expressly overturned precedent when it concluded that separate educational facilities for whites and blacks, which had been upheld as constitutional in numerous previous cases,[3] were inherently unequal. The Supreme Court's departure from precedent in *Brown* received a tremendous amount of publicity as people began to realize the ramifications of this change in the law. •

When There Is No Precedent Sometimes there is no precedent within a jurisdiction on which to base a decision, or there are conflicting precedents. A court then may look to precedents set in other jurisdictions for guidance. Such precedents, because they are not binding on the court, are referred to as **persuasive authorities.** A court may also consider a number of factors, including legal principles and policies underlying previous court decisions or existing statutes, fairness, social values and customs, public policy, and data and concepts drawn from the social sciences.

• **PERSUASIVE AUTHORITY**
Any legal authority or source of law that a court may look to for guidance but on which it need not rely in making its decision. Persuasive authorities include cases from other jurisdictions and secondary sources of law.

International Perspective • The "Americanization" of Israeli Law

In the past, all Israeli courts generally adhered to the doctrine of *stare decisis* and only rarely departed from precedent. Recently, however, the Israeli parliament released the supreme court in Israel (but not the lower courts) from this obligation. The parliament concluded that, given the nation's cultural diversity and the security threats it faces in the Middle East, the high court should be given more flexibility to adapt the law to changing circumstances. Since then, the Israeli supreme court has turned for guidance to other nations' laws, including U.S. laws and court decisions. For example, in a recent case the court held that Israel's all-male air force academy could not deny admission to a female applicant—a decision that was strikingly similar to that taken by U.S. courts on similar issues.

Many Israelis believe that the supreme court's application of American legal principles threatens their culture by, among other things, giving the rights of the individual more weight on the scales of justice than the rights of the community. Traditionally, Israel placed significant restrictions on speech, including prohibitions against "hate speech," in the interest of protecting the welfare and security of the community. In contrast, courts in the United States have been reluctant to impose any restrictions on the right to freely express opinions, even if they qualify as "hate speech" (see Chapter 2).

FOR CRITICAL ANALYSIS
Would the United States be better or worse off if the United States Supreme Court, like Israel's highest court, could look to other nations' laws for guidance?

EQUITABLE REMEDIES AND COURTS OF EQUITY

In law, a **remedy** is the means given to a party to enforce a right or to compensate for the violation of a right. • **EXAMPLE 1.4** Suppose that Shem is injured because of Rowan's wrongdoing. A court may order Rowan to compensate Shem for the harm by paying Shem a certain amount of money. •

• **REMEDY**
The relief given to an innocent party to enforce a right or compensate for the violation of a right.

In the early king's courts of England, the kinds of remedies that could be granted were severely restricted. If one person wronged another, the king's courts could award as compensation either money or property, including land. These courts became known as *courts of law,* and the remedies were called *remedies at law.* Even though this system introduced uniformity in the settling of disputes, when plaintiffs

2. 347 U.S. 483, 74 S.Ct. 686, 98 L.Ed. 873 (1954). (See the appendix at the end of this chapter for an explanation of how to read legal citations.)
3. See *Plessy v. Ferguson,* 163 U.S. 537, 16 S.Ct. 1138, 41 L.Ed. 256 (1896).

wanted a remedy other than economic compensation, the courts of law could do nothing, so "no remedy, no right."

Remedies in Equity Equity is that branch of unwritten law, founded in justice and fair dealing, that seeks to supply a fairer and more adequate remedy than any remedy available at law. In medieval England, when individuals could not obtain an adequate remedy in a court of law, they petitioned the king for relief. Most of these petitions were decided by an adviser to the king called the *chancellor.* The chancellor was said to be the "keeper of the king's conscience." When the chancellor thought that the claim was a fair one, new and unique remedies were granted. In this way, a new body of rules and remedies came into being, and eventually formal *chancery courts,* or *courts of equity,* were established. The remedies granted by these courts were called *remedies in equity.* Thus, two distinct court systems were created, each having a different set of judges and a different set of remedies.

• **PLAINTIFF**
One who initiates a lawsuit.

• **DEFENDANT**
One against whom a lawsuit is brought; the accused person in a criminal proceeding.

Plaintiffs (those bringing lawsuits) had to specify whether they were bringing an "action at law" or an "action in equity," and they chose their courts accordingly. • EXAMPLE 1.5 A plaintiff might ask a court of equity to order a **defendant** (a person against whom a lawsuit is brought) to perform within the terms of a contract. A court of law could not issue such an order, because its remedies were limited to payment of money or property as compensation for damages. A court of equity, however, could issue a decree for *specific performance*—an order to perform what was promised. A court of equity could also issue an *injunction,* directing a party to do or refrain from doing a particular act. In certain cases, a court of equity could allow for the *rescission* (cancellation) of the contract so that the parties would be returned to the positions that they held prior to the contract's formation. • Equitable remedies will be discussed in greater detail in Chapter 14.

¡REMEMBER! Even though, in most states, courts of law and equity have merged, the principles of equity still apply.

The Merging of Law and Equity Today, in most states, the courts of law and equity are merged, and thus the distinction between the two courts has largely disappeared. A plaintiff may now request both legal and equitable remedies in the same action, and the trial court judge may grant either form—or both forms—of relief. The merging of law and equity, however, does not diminish the importance of distinguishing legal remedies from equitable remedies. To request the proper remedy, one must know what remedies are available for the specific kinds of harms suffered. Today, as a rule, courts will grant an equitable remedy only when the remedy at law (money damages) is inadequate. Exhibit 1–1 summarizes the procedural differences (applicable in most states) between an action at law and an action in equity.

• **EQUITABLE PRINCIPLES AND MAXIMS**
General propositions or principles of law that have to do with fairness (equity).

Equitable Principles and Maxims Over time, a number of **equitable principles and maxims** evolved that have since guided the courts in deciding whether plaintiffs

EXHIBIT 1–1 • Procedural Differences between an Action at Law and an Action in Equity

PROCEDURE	ACTION AT LAW	ACTION IN EQUITY
Initiation of lawsuit	By filing a complaint	By filing a petition
Decision	By jury or judge	By judge (no jury)
Result	Judgment	Decree
Remedy	Monetary damages	Injunction, specific performance, or rescission

should be granted equitable relief. Because of their importance, both historically and in our judicial system today, these principles and maxims are set forth in the following *Landmark in the Law.*

Landmark in the Law • EQUITABLE PRINCIPLES AND MAXIMS

In medieval England, courts of equity had the responsibility of using discretion in supplementing the common law. Even today, when the same court can award both legal and equitable remedies, such discretion is exercised. Courts often invoke equitable principles and maxims when making their decisions. Here are some of the more significant equitable principles and maxims:

1. *Whoever seeks equity must do equity.* (Anyone who wishes to be treated fairly must treat others fairly.)
2. *Where there is equal equity, the law must prevail.* (The law will determine the outcome of a controversy in which the merits of both sides are equal.)
3. *One seeking the aid of an equity court must come to the court with clean hands.* (Plaintiffs must have acted fairly and honestly.)
4. *Equity will not suffer a wrong to be without a remedy.* (Equitable relief will be awarded when there is a right to relief and there is no adequate remedy at law.)
5. *Equity regards substance rather than form.* (Equity is more concerned with fairness and justice than with legal technicalities.)
6. *Equity aids the vigilant, not those who rest on their rights.* (Equity will not help those who neglect their rights for an unreasonable period of time.)

• **STATUTE OF LIMITATIONS**
A federal or state statute setting the maximum time period during which a certain action can be brought or certain rights enforced.

The last maxim has become known as the *equitable doctrine of laches.* The doctrine arose to encourage people to bring lawsuits while the evidence was fresh; if they failed to do so, they would not be allowed to bring a lawsuit. What constitutes a reasonable time, of course, varies according to the circumstances of the case. Time periods for different types of cases are now usually fixed by **statutes of limitations.** After the time allowed under a statute of limitations has expired, no action can be brought, no matter how strong the case was originally.

FOR CRITICAL ANALYSIS
Do you think that the government should establish, through statutes of limitations, the time limits within which different types of lawsuits can be brought?

Sources of American Law

• **PRIMARY SOURCE OF LAW**
A document that establishes the law on a particular issue, such as a constitution, a statute, an administrative rule, or a court decision.

There are numerous sources of American law. **Primary sources of law,** or sources that establish the law, include the following:

1. The U.S. Constitution and the constitutions of the various states.
2. Statutes, or laws, passed by Congress and by state legislatures.
3. Regulations created by administrative agencies, such as the federal Food and Drug Administration.
4. Case law (court decisions).

We describe each of these important primary sources of law in the following pages.

• **SECONDARY SOURCE OF LAW**
A publication that summarizes or interprets the law, such as a legal encyclopedia, a legal treatise, or an article in a law review.

Secondary sources of law are books and articles that summarize and clarify the primary sources of law. Legal encyclopedias, compilations (such as *Restatements of the Law*—to be discussed later in this chapter), official comments to statutes, treatises, articles in law reviews published by law schools, and articles in other legal journals are examples of secondary sources of law. Courts often refer to secondary sources of law for guidance in interpreting and applying the primary sources of law discussed here.

ON THE WEB

The National Constitution Center provides extensive information on the Constitution, including its history and current debates over constitutional provisions, at members.constitutioncenter.org.

CONSTITUTIONAL LAW

The federal government and the states have separate written constitutions that set forth the general organization, powers, and limits of their respective governments. **Constitutional law** is the law as expressed in these constitutions.

• **CONSTITUTIONAL LAW**
Law based on the U.S. Constitution and the constitutions of the various states.

The U.S. Constitution is the supreme law of the land. As such, it is the basis of all law in the United States. A law in violation of the Constitution, no matter what its source, will be declared unconstitutional and will not be enforced. Because of its paramount importance in the American legal system, we discuss the Constitution at length in Chapter 2 and present the complete text of the U.S. Constitution in Appendix A.

The Tenth Amendment to the U.S. Constitution, which defines the powers and limitations of the federal government, reserves all powers not granted to the federal government to the states. Each state in the union has its own constitution. Unless they conflict with the U.S. Constitution or a federal law, state constitutions are supreme within their respective borders.

YOUNG STUDENTS VIEW THE U.S. CONSTITUTION ON DISPLAY IN WASHINGTON, D.C. CAN A LAW BE IN VIOLATION OF THE CONSTITUTION AND STILL BE ENFORCED? WHY OR WHY NOT?

STATUTORY LAW

Statutes enacted by legislative bodies at any level of government make up another source of law, which is generally referred to as **statutory law.**

• **STATUTORY LAW**
The body of law enacted by legislative bodies (as opposed to constitutional law, administrative law, or case law).

Federal Statutes Federal statutes are laws that are enacted by the U.S. Congress. As mentioned, any law—including a federal statute—that violates the U.S. Constitution will be held unconstitutional.

Federal statutes that affect business operations include laws regulating the purchase and sale of securities (corporate stocks and bonds—discussed in Chapter 31), consumer protection statutes (discussed in Chapter 33), and statutes prohibiting employment discrimination (discussed in Chapter 36). Whenever a particular statute is mentioned in this text, we usually provide a footnote showing its **citation** (a reference to a publication in which a legal authority—such as a statute or a court decision—or other source can be found). In the appendix following this chapter, we explain how you can use these citations to find statutory law.

• **CITATION**
A reference to a publication in which a legal authority—such as a statute or a court decision—or other source can be found.

State and Local Statutes and Ordinances State statutes are laws enacted by state legislatures. Any state law that is found to conflict with the U.S. Constitution, with federal laws enacted by Congress, or with the state's constitution will be deemed unconstitutional. Statutory law also includes the ordinances passed by cities and counties, none of which can violate the U.S. Constitution, the relevant state constitution, or federal or state laws.

ON THE WEB
To find state compilations (codes) of statutory laws, go to www.findlaw.com/casecode/state.html.

State statutes include state criminal statutes (discussed in Chapter 6), state corporation statutes (discussed in Chapters 27 through 31), state deceptive trade practices acts (referred to in Chapter 36), state laws governing wills and trusts (discussed in Chapter 42), and state versions of the Uniform Commercial Code (to be discussed shortly). Local ordinances include zoning ordinances and local laws regulating housing construction and such things as the overall appearance of a community.

A HOUSING DEVELOPMENT IS UNDER CONSTRUCTION. WHAT TYPES OF LAW GOVERN THE WAY HOUSES ARE CONSTRUCTED?

A federal statute, of course, applies to all states. A state statute, in contrast, applies only within the state's borders. State laws thus vary from state to state.

Uniform Laws The differences among state laws were particularly notable in the 1800s, when conflicting state statutes frequently made the rapidly developing trade and commerce among the states very difficult. To counter these problems, a group of legal scholars and lawyers formed the National Conference of Commissioners (NCC) on Uniform State Laws in 1892 to draft uniform ("model") statutes for adoption by the states. The NCC still exists today and continues to issue uniform statutes.

ON THE WEB

You can find links to most uniform laws online at www.lawsource.com.

Adoption of a uniform law is a state matter, and a state may reject all or part of the statute or rewrite it as the state legislature wishes. Hence, even when a uniform law is said to have been adopted in many states, those states' laws may not be entirely "uniform." Once adopted by a state legislature, a uniform act becomes a part of the statutory law of that state.

¡BE CAREFUL!

Even though uniform laws are intended to be adopted without changes, states often modify them to suit their particular needs.

The earliest uniform law, the Uniform Negotiable Instruments Law, was completed by 1896 and was adopted in every state by the early 1920s (although not all states used exactly the same wording). Over the following decades, other acts were drawn up in a similar manner. In all, over two hundred uniform acts have been issued by the NCC since its inception. The most ambitious uniform act of all, however, was the Uniform Commercial Code.

ON THE WEB

The UCC is available online at www.law.cornell.edu/topics/sales.html.

The Uniform Commercial Code (UCC) The Uniform Commercial Code (UCC), which was created through the joint efforts of the NCC and the American Law Institute,[4] was first issued in 1952. The UCC has been adopted in all fifty states,[5] the District of Columbia, and the Virgin Islands. The UCC facilitates commerce among the states by providing a uniform, yet flexible, set of rules governing commercial transactions. The UCC assures businesspersons that their contracts, if validly entered into, normally will be enforced.

Because of its importance in the area of commercial law, we cite the UCC frequently in this text. We also present the latest version of the UCC in its entirety in Appendix B. (For a discussion of the creation of the UCC, see the *Landmark in the Law* in Chapter 15.)

ADMINISTRATIVE LAW

An important source of American law consists of **administrative law**—the rules, orders, and decisions of administrative agencies. An **administrative agency** is a federal, state, or local government agency established to perform a specific function. Rules issued by various administrative agencies now affect virtually every aspect of a business's operation, including the firm's capital structure and financing, its hiring and firing procedures, its relations with employees and unions, and the way it manufactures and markets its products.

• **ADMINISTRATIVE LAW**
The body of law created by administrative agencies (in the form of rules, regulations, orders, and decisions) in order to carry out their duties and responsibilities.

• **ADMINISTRATIVE AGENCY**
A federal or state government agency established to perform a specific function. Administrative agencies are authorized by legislative acts to make and enforce rules to administer and enforce the acts.

At the national level, numerous **executive agencies** exist within the cabinet departments of the executive branch. For example, the Food and Drug Administration is within the Department of Health and Human Services. Executive agencies are subject to the authority of the president, who has the power to appoint and remove officers of federal agencies. There are also major **independent regulatory agencies** at

• **EXECUTIVE AGENCY**
An administrative agency within the executive branch of government. At the federal level, executive agencies are those within the cabinet departments.

• **INDEPENDENT REGULATORY AGENCY**
An administrative agency that is not considered part of the government's executive branch and is not subject to the authority of the president. Independent agency officials cannot be removed without cause.

4. This institute was formed in the 1920s and consists of practicing attorneys, legal scholars, and judges.
5. Louisiana has adopted only Articles 1, 3, 4, 5, 7, 8, and 9.

ON THE WEB

The *United States Government Manual* describes the origins, purposes, and administrators of every federal department and agency. You can access this publication online at www.access.gpo.gov/nara/nara001.html.

the federal level, including the Federal Trade Commission, the Securities and Exchange Commission, and the Federal Communications Commission. The president's power is less pronounced in regard to independent agencies, whose officers serve for fixed terms and cannot be removed without just cause.

There are administrative agencies at the state and local levels as well. Commonly, a state agency (such as a state pollution-control agency) is created as a parallel to a federal agency (such as the Environmental Protection Agency). Just as federal statutes take precedence over conflicting state statutes, so do federal agency regulations take precedence over conflicting state regulations. Because the rules of state and local agencies vary widely, we focus here exclusively on federal administrative law.

The Letter of the Law SAY WHAT?

The language of statutory and administrative law can sometimes be a "tangled web" indeed. Suppose, for example, that you were on the board of directors of a charitable corporation and wanted to find out, for tax purposes, whether your organization qualified as a "private foundation." If you consulted Section 509(a) of the Internal Revenue Code, which deals with the definition of a private foundation, you would probably be mystified by the following statement: "For purposes of paragraph (3), an organization described in paragraph (2) shall be deemed to include an organization described in Section 501(c)(4), (5), or (6), which would be described in paragraph (2) if it were an organization described in section 501(c)(3)."

THE BOTTOM LINE

Any person needing to understand a statute or a regulation relevant to his or her business should seek legal advice.

VOLUMES AND FORMS RELATING TO THE INTERNAL REVENUE CODE ARE DISPLAYED. WHY IS THE LANGUAGE OF THE LAW A "TANGLED WEB"?

Agency Creation Because Congress cannot possibly oversee the actual implementation of all the laws it enacts, it must delegate such tasks to others, particularly when the issues relate to highly technical areas, such as air and water pollution. Congress creates an administrative agency by enacting **enabling legislation,** which specifies the name, composition, purpose, and powers of the agency being created.

• **ENABLING LEGISLATION**
A statute enacted by Congress that authorizes the creation of an administrative agency and specifies the name, composition, purpose, and powers of the agency being created.

• EXAMPLE 1.6 The Federal Trade Commission (FTC) was created in 1914 by the Federal Trade Commission Act.[6] This act prohibits unfair and deceptive trade practices. It also describes the procedures the agency must follow to charge persons or organizations with violations of the act, and it provides for judicial review (review by the courts) of agency orders. Other portions of the act grant the agency powers to "make rules and regulations for the purpose of carrying out the Act," to conduct investigations of business practices, to obtain reports from interstate corporations concerning their business practices, to investigate possible violations of the act, to publish findings of its investigations, and to recommend new legislation. The act also empowers the FTC to hold trial-like hearings and to **adjudicate** (resolve judicially) certain kinds of trade disputes that involve FTC regulations. •

• **ADJUDICATE**
To render a judicial decision. In the administrative process, the proceeding in which an administrative law judge hears and decides on issues that arise when an administrative agency charges a person or a firm with violating a law or regulation enforced by the agency.

6. 15 U.S.C. Sections 45–58.

• **ADMINISTRATIVE PROCESS**
The procedure used by administrative agencies in the administration of law.

• **RULEMAKING**
The process undertaken by an administrative agency when formally adopting a new regulation or amending an old one. Rulemaking involves notifying the public of a proposed rule or change and receiving and considering the public's comments.

Note that the FTC's grant of power incorporates functions associated with the legislative branch of government (rulemaking), the executive branch (investigation and enforcement), and the judicial branch (adjudication). Taken together, these functions constitute what has been termed **administrative process,** which is the administration of law by administrative agencies.

Rulemaking One of the major functions of an administrative agency is **rulemaking**—creating or modifying rules, or regulations, pursuant to its enabling legislation. The Administrative Procedure Act of 1946[7] imposes strict procedural requirements that agencies must follow in their rulemaking and other functions.

The most common rulemaking procedure involves three steps. First, the agency must give public notice of the proposed rulemaking proceedings, where and when the proceedings will be held, the agency's legal authority for the proceedings, and the terms or subject matter of the proposed rule. The notice must be published in the *Federal Register,* a daily publication of the U.S. government. Second, following this notice, the agency must allow ample time for interested parties to comment in writing on the proposed rule. After the comments have been received and reviewed, the agency takes them into consideration when drafting the final version of the regulation. The third and final step is the drafting of the final version and the publication of the rule in the *Federal Register.* (See the appendix at the end of this chapter for an explanation of how to find agency regulations.)

ON THE WEB
You can access the *Federal Register* online at www.access.gpo.gov/su_docs/aces/aces140.html.

Investigation and Enforcement Agencies have both investigatory and prosecutorial powers. An agency can request individuals or organizations to hand over specified books, papers, records, or other documents. In addition, agencies may conduct on-site inspections, although a search warrant is normally required for such inspections. Sometimes the search of a home, an office, or a factory is the only means of obtaining evidence needed to prove a regulatory violation. Agencies investigate a wide range of activities, including coal mining, automobile manufacturing, and the industrial discharge of pollutants into the environment.

Adjudication After conducting its own investigation of a suspected rule violation, an agency may decide to take action against a specific party. The action may involve a trial-like hearing before an **administrative law judge (ALJ).** The ALJ may compel the charged party to pay fines or may forbid the party to carry on some specified activity. Either side may appeal the ALJ's decision to the commission or board that governs the agency. If the party fails to get relief there, appeal can be made to a federal court.

• **ADMINISTRATIVE LAW JUDGE (ALJ)**
One who presides over an administrative agency hearing and who has the power to administer oaths, take testimony, rule on questions of evidence, and make determinations of fact.

ETHICAL ISSUE 1.1 ***Do administrative agencies exercise too much authority?*** Administrative agencies, such as the FTC, combine functions normally divided among the three branches of government into a single governmental entity. The broad range of authority that agencies exercise sometimes poses questions of fairness. After all, agencies create rules that are as legally binding as the laws passed by Congress—the only federal government institution authorized by the Constitution to make laws. To be sure, arbitrary rulemaking by agencies is checked by the procedural requirements set forth in the Administrative Procedure Act (APA), as well as by the courts, to which agency decisions may be appealed. Yet some people claim that these checks are not enough.

7. 5 U.S.C. Sections 551–706.

Consider that in addition to *legislative rules,* which are subject to the procedural requirements of the APA, agencies also create *interpretive rules*—rules that specify how the agency will interpret and apply its regulations. The APA does not apply to interpretative rulemaking. Additionally, although a firm that challenges an agency's rule may be able to appeal the agency's decision in the matter to a court, the policy of the courts is generally to defer to agency rules, including interpretative rules, and to agency decisions.

CASE LAW AND COMMON LAW DOCTRINES

The body of law that was first developed in England and that is still used today in the United States consists of the rules of law announced in court decisions. These rules of law include interpretations of constitutional provisions, of statutes enacted by legislatures, and of regulations created by administrative agencies. Today, this body of law is referred to variously as the common law, judge-made law, or **case law.**

• **CASE LAW**
The rules of law announced in court decisions. Case law includes the aggregate of reported cases that interpret judicial precedents, statutes, regulations, and constitutional provisions.

The common law—the doctrines and principles embodied in case law—governs all areas not covered by statutory law (or agency regulations issued to implement various statutes). • **EXAMPLE 1.7** In disputes concerning contracts for the sale of goods, the Uniform Commercial Code (statutory law) applies when one of its provisions supersedes the common law of contracts. Similarly, in a dispute concerning a particular employment practice, if a statute regulates that practice, the statute will apply rather than the common law doctrine governing employment relationships that applied prior to the enactment of the statute. •

The Relationship between the Common Law and Statutory Law The body of statutory law has expanded greatly since the beginning of this nation, and this expansion has resulted in a proportionate reduction in the applicability of common law doctrines. Nonetheless, there is a significant overlap between statutory law and the common law, and thus common law doctrines remain a significant source of legal authority.

Many statutes essentially codify existing common law rules, and thus the courts, in interpreting the statutes, often rely on the common law as a guide to what the legislators intended. Additionally, how the courts interpret a particular statute determines how that statute will be applied. • **EXAMPLE 1.8** If you wanted to learn about the coverage and applicability of a particular statute, for example, you would, of course, need to locate the statute and study it. You would also need to see how the courts in your jurisdiction have interpreted the statute—in other words, what precedents have been established in regard to that statute. Often, the applicability of a newly enacted statute does not become clear until a body of case law develops to clarify how, when, and to whom the statute applies. •

¡BE AWARE!
Restatements of the Law are authoritative sources, but they do not have the force of law.

ON THE WEB
You can learn more about the American Law Institute and its projects and publications by accessing its Web site at **www.ali.org**.

Restatements of the Law The American Law Institute (ALI) drafted and published compilations of the common law called *Restatements of the Law,* which generally summarize the common law rules followed by most states. There are *Restatements of the Law* in many areas of the law, including contracts, torts, agency, trusts, property, restitution, security, judgments, and conflict of laws. The *Restatements,* like other secondary sources of law, do not in themselves have the force of law but are an important source of legal analysis and opinion on which judges often rely in making their decisions.

The ALI periodically revises the *Restatements,* and many of the *Restatements* are now in their second or third editions. For instance, as you will read in Chapter 18, the ALI has recently published the first volume of the third edition of the *Restatement of the Law of Torts*.

We refer to the *Restatements* frequently in subsequent chapters of this text, indicating in parentheses the edition to which we are referring. For example, we refer to the second edition of the *Restatement of the Law of Contracts* simply as the *Restatement (Second) of Contracts*.

Classifications of Law

• **SUBSTANTIVE LAW**
Law that defines, describes, regulates, and creates legal rights and obligations.

• **PROCEDURAL LAW**
Law that establishes the methods of enforcing the rights established by substantive law.

The huge body of the law may be broken down according to several classification systems. For example, one classification system divides law into **substantive law** (all laws that define, describe, regulate, and create legal rights and obligations) and **procedural law** (all laws that establish the methods of enforcing the rights established by substantive law). Other classification systems divide law into federal law and state law, private law (dealing with relationships between persons) and public law (addressing the relationship between persons and their government), and so on.

We look below at two broad classifications. One divides the law into criminal and civil law; the other divides the law into national law and international law. Following that, we mention an emerging body of law regulating transactions in cyberspace, informally characterized as "cyberlaw."

Civil Law and Criminal Law

• **CIVIL LAW**
The branch of law dealing with the definition and enforcement of all private or public rights, as opposed to criminal matters.

Civil law spells out the rights and duties that exist between persons and between persons and their governments, and the relief available when a person's rights are violated. Typically, in a civil case, a private party sues another private party (although the government can also sue a party for a civil law violation) to make that other party comply with a duty or pay for the damage caused by the failure to comply with a duty. • EXAMPLE 1.9 If a seller fails to perform a contract with a buyer, the buyer may bring a lawsuit against the seller. The purpose of the lawsuit will be either to compel the seller to perform as promised or, more commonly, to obtain money damages for the seller's failure to perform. • Much of the law that we discuss in this text is civil law. Contract law, for example, which we discuss in Chapters 9 through 14, is civil law. The whole body of tort law (see Chapters 4 and 5), is civil law.

• **CRIMINAL LAW**
Law that defines and governs actions that constitute crimes. Generally, criminal law has to do with wrongful actions committed against society for which society demands redress.

Criminal law has to do with a wrong committed against society for which society demands redress (see Chapter 6). Criminal acts are proscribed by local, state, or federal government statutes. Criminal defendants are thus prosecuted by public officials, such as a district attorney (D.A.), on behalf of the state, not by their victims or other private parties. Whereas in a civil case the object is to obtain remedies (such as money damages) to compensate the injured party, in a criminal case the object is to punish the wrongdoer in an attempt to deter others from similar actions. Penalties for violations of criminal statutes consist of fines and/or imprisonment—and, in some cases, death.

National and International Law

Although the focus of this book is U.S. business law, increasingly businesspersons in this country engage in transactions that extend beyond our national borders. In these situations, the laws of other nations or the laws governing relationships among nations may come into play. For this reason, those who pursue a career in business today should have an understanding of the global legal environment.

ON THE WEB

The Library of Congress offers extensive information on national and international law at law.house.gov.

Technology and Online Legal Research

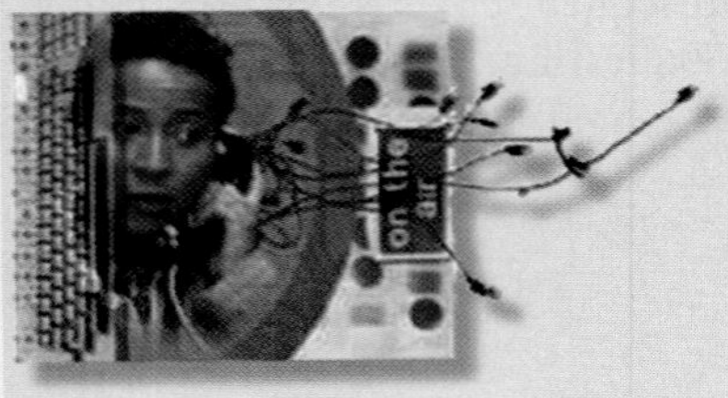

Technology is changing the ways in which lawyers, law students, and others conduct legal research. In the past, researchers painstakingly had to examine dozens, if not hundreds, of different printed volumes containing court decisions, federal statutes, state statutes, and regulations from administrative agencies. Today, much legal research can be done online quickly and easily, and without having to leave one's office or home.

ONLINE INFORMATION SOURCES

Anybody with a computer, modem, and a way to access the Internet can obtain certain legal documents online at no cost. The Web sites given in the margins of the chapters of this text and in the various technology features, as well as those found at the Web site accompanying this text at **http://blt.westbuslaw.com**, will direct you to many of the legal resources that are now online.

These resources include Supreme Court decisions, which are available online within hours after they are announced, as well as the decisions of the federal appellate courts (and some of the federal trial courts). Increasingly, state courts are posting information about their schedules and procedures online, and some courts publish recently decided cases on their Web pages. Online resources also include federal and state statutes and administrative regulations, the federal Constitution, state constitutions, laws and constitutions governing other nations, proposed legislation being considered by Congress, congressional proceedings, law reviews and other journals and publications discussing legal issues, forms to use for certain legal transactions, and so on—the list gets longer virtually every day.

FEE-BASED COMMERCIAL SERVICES

Although there is much information available on the Web for free, for in-depth legal research many legal professionals or law students prefer to use fee-based commercial services, such as Lexis® (at **www.lexis.com**) and Westlaw® (at **www.westlaw.com**). This is because these services offer extensive legal databases, efficient internal search engines, and editorial enhancements. Westlaw®, for example, has more than ten thousand databases covering all areas of the law. You can access federal and state statutes, court cases, administrative regulations, specialized databases (such as for bankruptcy), legal texts and periodicals, public records, and other legal, business, and financial information.

Westlaw® also offers numerous editorial enhancements. For example, if your search results include a statute or an agency rule, you can check for any recent changes with the "Update" service, which, among other things, lets you know if the statute or rule that you are viewing has been amended or repealed. Other special features allow you to learn about the history of a particular case (its progression through the court system—from the trial court through appellate courts, for example) and to find cases or other legal sources that have cited the case.

An especially useful feature of Westlaw® is KeyCite, which lets you know whether the ruling in a particular case still represents "good law." KeyCite "flags" indicate when there is case history that should be investigated. Depending on the color of the flag, you are warned that a case is not good law for at least one of its points, that the case has some negative history but its holding has not been reversed, or that the case has been overruled.

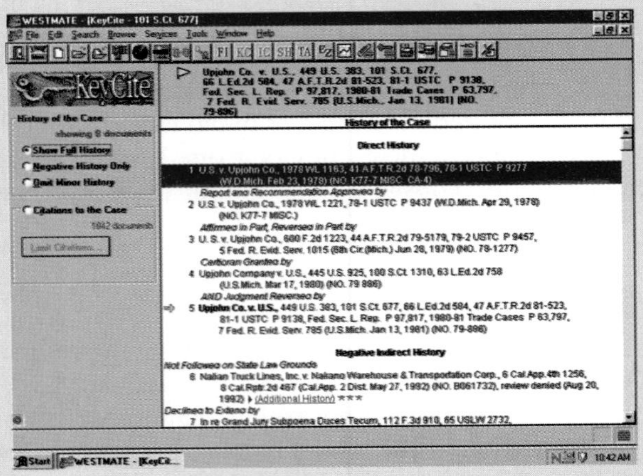

A KEYCITE PAGE APPEARS ON WESTLAW®. WHY IS THIS FEATURE ESPECIALLY USEFUL?

FOR CRITICAL ANALYSIS

Describe what a law library might consist of in the future.

INTERNET CONNECT

• **NATIONAL LAW**
Law that pertains to a particular nation (as opposed to international law).

National Law The law of a particular nation, such as the United States or Sweden, is **national law.** National law, of course, varies from country to country, because each country's law reflects the interests, customs, activities, and values that are unique to that nation's culture. Even though the laws and legal systems of various countries differ substantially, broad similarities do exist.

• **CIVIL LAW SYSTEM**
A system of law derived from that of the Roman Empire and based on a code rather than case law; the predominant system of law in the nations of continental Europe and the nations that were once their colonies. In the United States, Louisiana, because of its historical ties to France, has in part a civil law system.

Basically, there are two legal systems in today's world. One of these systems is the common law system of England and the United States, which we have already discussed. The other system is based on Roman civil law, or "code law." The term *civil law,* as used here, refers not to civil as opposed to criminal law but to codified law—an ordered grouping of legal principles enacted into law by a legislature or governing body. In a **civil law system,** the primary source of law is a statutory code, and case precedents are not judicially binding, as they normally are in a common law system. Although judges in a civil law system commonly refer to previous decisions as sources of legal guidance, they are not bound by precedent; in other words, the doctrine of *stare decisis* does not apply.

Exhibit 1–2 lists the countries that today follow either the common law system or the civil law system. Generally, those countries that were once colonies of Great Britain retained their English common law heritage after they achieved their independence. Similarly, the civil law system, which is followed in most of the continental European countries, was retained in the Latin American, African, and Asian countries that were once colonies of the continental European nations. Japan and South Africa also have civil law systems, and ingredients of the civil law system are found in the Islamic courts of predominantly Muslim countries. In the United States, the state of Louisiana, because of its historical ties to France, has in part a civil law system. The legal systems of Puerto Rico, Québec, and Scotland are similarly characterized as having elements of the civil law system.

• **INTERNATIONAL LAW**
The law that governs relations among nations. National laws, customs, treaties, and international conferences and organizations are generally considered to be the most important sources of international law.

International Law In contrast to national law, international law applies to more than one nation. **International law** can be defined as a body of written and unwritten laws observed by independent nations and governing the acts of individuals as well as governments. International law is an intermingling of rules and constraints derived from a variety of sources, including the laws of individual nations, the customs that have evolved among nations in their relations with one another, and treaties and international organizations. In essence, international law is the result of centuries-old attempts to reconcile the traditional need of each nation to be the final authority over its own affairs with the desire of nations to benefit economically from trade and harmonious relations with one another.

EXHIBIT 1–2 • The Legal Systems of Nations

CIVIL LAW		COMMON LAW	
Argentina	Indonesia	Australia	Nigeria
Austria	Iran	Bangladesh	Singapore
Brazil	Italy	Canada	United Kingdom
Chile	Japan	Ghana	United States
China	Mexico	India	Zambia
Egypt	Poland	Israel	
Finland	South Korea	Jamaica	
France	Sweden	Kenya	
Germany	Tunisia	Malaysia	
Greece	Venezuela	New Zealand	

The key difference between national law and international law is the fact that national law can be enforced by government authorities. If a nation violates an international law, however, the most that other countries or international organizations can do (if persuasive tactics fail) is resort to coercive actions against the violating nation. Coercive actions range from severance of diplomatic relations and boycotts to, at the last resort, war. We examine the laws governing international business transactions in later chapters (including parts of Chapters 15 through 18, which cover contracts for the sale of goods, and all of Chapter 43).

CYBERLAW

Increasingly, traditional laws are being adapted and applied to new legal issues stemming from the use of a new medium—the Internet—to conduct business transactions. Additionally, new laws are being created to deal specifically with such issues. Frequently, people use the term **cyberlaw** to designate the emerging body of law (consisting of court decisions, newly enacted or amended statutes, and so on) that governs cyberspace transactions. Note that cyberlaw is not really a classification of law; rather, it is an informal term used to describe how traditional classifications of law, such as civil law and criminal law, are being applied to online activities.

Anyone preparing to enter today's business world will find it useful to know how old and new laws are being applied to activities conducted online, such as advertising, contracting, banking, filing documents with the courts or government agencies, employment relations, and a variety of other transactions. For that reason, Chapter 7 of this text is devoted entirely to this topic. Special features throughout the text also focus on how technology, and particularly the use of the Internet, is transforming the business world.

ON THE WEB

A good site for updates on how the laws are being applied to cyberspace transactions is the Law Journal EXTRA! Web site at www.ljx.com.

• CYBERLAW
An informal term used to refer to all laws governing electronic communications and transactions, particularly those conducted via the Internet.

APPLICATION
Law and the Businessperson: How to Choose and Use a Lawyer*

If you are contemplating a career in the business world, sooner or later you will probably face the question, "Do I need a lawyer?" The answer to this question will likely be "Yes," at least at some time during your career. Even individuals who have gone on to law school and later entered into a business often hire an outside lawyer to help them with their legal problems. Today, it is virtually impossible for nonexperts to keep up with the myriad rules and regulations that govern the way in which business can be conducted in the United States. It is also increasingly possible for businesspersons to incur penalties for violating laws or regulations of which they are totally unaware.

Although lawyers may seem expensive—anywhere from $75 to $400 per hour—the cautious businessperson will make sure that he or she is not "penny wise and pound foolish." The consultation fee paid to an attorney may be a drop in the bucket compared with the potential liability facing a businessperson.

SELECTING AN ATTORNEY

In selecting an attorney, you can ask friends, relatives, or business associates to recommend someone. Alternatively, you can call the local or state bar association to obtain the names of several lawyers. You can also go to your local library to look at *West's Legal Directory* (or access it online at www.westbuslaw.com—click on "About This Site/Site Map" to find the directory), which includes professional biographies of most of the attorneys engaged in private practice throughout the country. The directory also lists areas of concentration, as well as bank references and representative clients. Some legal aid programs have staff attorneys, and others may refer you to volunteers. You also might investigate legal clinics and prepaid legal service plans.

At your initial meeting with the attorney you have

*This *Application* is not meant to substitute for the services of an attorney who is licensed to practice law in your state.

APPLICATION CONTINUED

selected, you should have a written list of your questions in hand, and perhaps a summary of the problem for which you need legal advice. Attach to your list copies of any relevant documents that you can leave with the lawyer. In fact, it is a good idea to drop off your list of questions and copies of related documents at the attorney's office *before* the meeting, with a note attached indicating that the material is for your scheduled meeting on (give the date and time). This way, the lawyer will have some time to think about your situation and prepare for the meeting. While at the meeting, ask about legal fees, discuss the legal problem you are facing (remember that virtually everything that you say to your attorney is protected by the attorney-client privilege of confidentiality), and clarify the scope of what you want the lawyer to do for you.

EVALUATING YOUR ATTORNEY

Ask yourself the following questions after your first meeting: Did the attorney seem knowledgeable about what is needed to address your concerns? Did he or she seem willing to investigate the law and the facts further to ensure an accurate understanding of your legal situation? Did you communicate well with each other? Did the attorney perceive what issues were of foremost concern to you and address those issues to your satisfaction? Did the attorney "speak your language" when explaining the legal implications of those issues?

Continue to evaluate the relationship as it continues. For many businesspersons, relationships with attorneys last for decades. Make sure that your relationship with your attorney will be a fruitful one.[a]

CHECKLIST FOR CHOOSING AND USING A LAWYER

1. If you ever think that you need legal advice, you probably do.
2. When choosing an attorney, try to get recommendations from friends, relatives, or business associates who have had long-standing relationships with their attorneys. If that fails, check with your local or state bar association or check *West's Legal Directory.*
3. When you initially consult with an attorney, have with you a written list of questions to which you want answers, perhaps a summary of your problem, and copies of relevant documents.
4. Do not hesitate to ask about the legal fees that your attorney will charge and clarify the scope of the work to be undertaken by the attorney. Ask whatever questions are necessary to ensure that you understand what your legal options are. Do not worry about appearing stupid.

a. With appreciation to James D. Van Tassel at Mission College, California, for his helpful suggestions on this topic.

Key Terms

adjudicate 12
administrative agency 11
administrative law 11
administrative law judge (ALJ) 13
administrative process 13
binding authority 5
case law 14
citation 10
civil law 15
civil law system 17
common law 4
constitutional law 9
criminal law 15
cyberlaw 18
defendant 7
enabling legislation 12
equitable principles and maxims 7
executive agency 11
independent regulatory agency 11
international law 17
jurisprudence 3
law 3
legal positivism 3
legal realism 4
national law 17
natural law 3
persuasive authority 6
plaintiff 7
positive law 3
precedent 5
primary source of law 8
procedural law 15
remedy 6
rulemaking 13
secondary source of law 8
stare decisis 5
statute of limitations 8
statutory law 10
substantive law 15

Chapter Summary • The Legal and International Environment

The Nature of Law (See pages 1–4.)	Law can be defined as a body of rules of conduct with legal force and effect, prescribed by the controlling authority (the government) of a society. Three important schools of legal thought, or legal philosophies, are the following: 1. *Natural law tradition*—One of the oldest and most significant schools of legal thought. Those who believe in natural law hold that there is a universal law applicable to all human beings and that this law is of a higher order than positive, or conventional, law. 2. *Legal positivism*—A school of legal thought centered on the assumption that there is no law higher than the laws created by the government. Laws must be obeyed, even if they are unjust, to prevent anarchy. 3. *Legal realism*—A popular school of legal thought during the 1920s and 1930s that left a lasting imprint on American jurisprudence. Legal realists generally advocated a less abstract and more realistic approach to the law, an approach that would take into account customary practices and the circumstances in which transactions take place.
The Common Law Tradition (See pages 4–8.)	1. *Common law*—Law that originated in medieval England with the creation of the king's courts, or *curiae regis,* and the development of a body of rules that were common to (or applied throughout) the land. 2. *Stare decisis*—A doctrine under which judges "stand on decided cases"—or follow the rule of precedent—in deciding cases. *Stare decisis* is the cornerstone of the common law tradition. 3. *Remedies*— a. Remedies at law—Money or something else of value. b. Remedies in equity—Remedies that are granted when the remedies at law are unavailable or inadequate. Equitable remedies include specific performance, an injunction, and contract rescission (cancellation).
Sources of American Law (See pages 8–15.)	1. *Constitutional law*—The law as expressed in the U.S. Constitution and the various state constitutions. The U.S. Constitution is the supreme law of the land. State constitutions are supreme within state borders to the extent that they do not violate the U.S. Constitution or a federal law. 2. *Statutory law*—Laws or ordinances created by federal, state, and local legislatures and governing bodies. None of these laws can violate the U.S. Constitution or the relevant state constitutions. Uniform laws, when adopted by a state legislature, become statutory law in that state. 3. *Administrative law*—The rules, orders, and decisions of federal or state government administrative agencies. Federal administrative agencies are created by enabling legislation enacted by the U.S. Congress. Agency functions include rulemaking, investigation and enforcement, and adjudication. 4. *Case law and common law doctrines*—Judge-made law, including interpretations of constitutional provisions, of statutes enacted by legislatures, and of regulations created by administrative agencies. The common law—the doctrines and principles embodied in case law—governs all areas not covered by statutory law (or agency regulations issued to implement various statutes).
Classifications of Law (See pages 15–19.)	The law may be broken down according to several classification systems, such as substantive or procedural law, federal or state law, and private or public law. Two broad classifications are civil and criminal law, and national and international law. Cyberlaw is not really a classification of law but a term that is applied to the growing body of case law and statutory law that applies to Internet transactions.

For Review

1. What is the common law tradition?
2. What is a precedent? When might a court depart from precedent?
3. What is the difference between remedies at law and remedies in equity?
4. What is the Uniform Commercial Code?
5. What are some important differences between civil law and criminal law?

Questions and Case Problems

1–1. Philosophy of Law. After World War II, which ended in 1945, an international tribunal of judges convened at Nuremberg, Germany. The judges convicted several Nazi war criminals of "crimes against humanity." Assuming that the Nazis who were convicted had not disobeyed any law of their country and had merely been following their government's (Hitler's) orders, what law had they violated? Explain.

1–2. Legal Systems. What are the key differences between a common law system and a civil law system? Why do some countries have common law systems and others have civil law systems?

1–3. Reading Citations. Assume that you want to read the entire court opinion in the case of *Childress v. City of Richmond, Va.,* 134 F.3d 1205 (4th Cir. 1998). The case deals with the question of whether a police department discriminated against certain employees in violation of a federal law prohibiting employment discrimination (Title VII of the Civil Rights Act of 1964). Read the section entitled "Finding Case Law" in the appendix that follows this chapter, and then explain specifically where you would find the court's opinion.

1–4. Sources of American Law. This chapter discussed a number of sources of American law. Which source of law takes priority in the following situations, and why?

(a) A federal statute conflicts with the U.S. Constitution.
(b) A federal statute conflicts with a state constitution.
(c) A state statute conflicts with the common law of that state.
(d) A state constitutional amendment conflicts with the U.S. Constitution.
(e) A federal administrative regulation conflicts with a state constitution.

1–5. *Stare Decisis.* In the text of this chapter, we stated that the doctrine of *stare decisis* "became a cornerstone of the English and American judicial systems." What does *stare decisis* mean, and why has this doctrine been so fundamental to the development of our legal tradition?

1–6. Court Opinions. Read through the section entitled "Case Titles and Terminology" in the appendix following this chapter. What is the difference between a concurring opinion and a majority opinion? Between a concurring opinion and a dissenting opinion? Why do judges and justices write concurring and dissenting opinions, given the fact that these opinions will not affect the outcome of the case at hand, which has already been decided by majority vote?

1–7. Statute of Limitations. The equitable principle "Equity aids the vigilant, not those who rest on their rights" means that courts will not aid those who do not pursue a cause of action while the evidence is fresh and while the true facts surrounding the issue can be discovered. State statutes of limitations are based on this principle. Under Article 2 of the Uniform Commercial Code, which has been adopted by virtually all of the states, the statute of limitations governing sales contracts states that parties must bring an action for the breach of a sales contract within four years, although the parties (the seller and the buyer) can reduce this period by agreement to only one year. Which party (the seller or the buyer) would benefit more by a one-year period, and which would benefit more by a four-year period? Discuss.

1–8. Binding versus Persuasive Authority. A county court in Illinois is deciding a case involving an issue that has never been addressed before in that state's courts. The Iowa Supreme Court, however, recently decided a case involving a very similar fact pattern. Is the Illinois court obligated to follow the Iowa Supreme Court's decision on the issue? If the United States Supreme Court had decided a similar case, would that decision be binding on the Illinois court? Explain.

A QUESTION OF ETHICS AND SOCIAL RESPONSIBILITY

1–9. On July 5, 1884, Dudley, Stephens, and Brooks—"all able-bodied English seamen"—and an English teen-age boy were cast adrift in a lifeboat following a storm at sea. They had no water with them in the boat, and all they had for sustenance were two one-pound tins of turnips. On July 24, Dudley proposed that one of the four in the lifeboat be sacrificed to save the others. Stephens agreed with Dudley, but Brooks refused to consent—and the boy was never asked for his opinion. On July 25, Dudley killed the boy, and the three men then fed on the boy's body and blood. Four days later, the men were rescued by a passing vessel. They were taken to England and tried for the murder of the boy. If the men had not fed on the boy's body, they would probably have died of starvation within the four-day period. The boy, who was in a much weaker condition, would likely have died before the rest. [*Regina v. Dudley and Stephens*, 14 Q.B.D. (Queen's Bench Division, England) 273 (1884)]

1. The basic question in this case is whether the survivors should be subject to penalties under English criminal law, given the men's unusual circumstances. You be the judge, and decide the issue. Give the reasons for your decisions.
2. Should judges ever have the power to look beyond the written "letter of the law" in making their decisions? Why or why not?

FOR CRITICAL ANALYSIS

1–10. Courts of equity tend to follow general rules or maxims rather than common law precedents, as courts of law do. Some of these maxims were listed in this chapter's *Landmark in the Law.* Why would equity courts give credence to such general maxims rather than to a hard-and-fast body of law?

Online Activities

ONLINE EXERCISE 1–1

Go to the "Internet Activities Book" on the Web site that accompanies this text, the URL for which is **http://blt.westbuslaw.com**. Select the following activity, and perform the exercise according to the instructions given there:

Activity 1–1: Internet Sources of Law

Internet sites tend to come and go, and there is no guarantee that a site included in one of the *Online Exercises* or referred to elsewhere in this text will be there by the time this book is in print. We have tried, though, to include sites that have so far proved to be fairly stable. If you do have difficulty reaching a site (that is, if your destination is "Not Found" or has "No DNS Entry"), do not immediately assume that the site does not exist. First, recheck the URL shown in your browser. Remember, you have to type the URLs exactly as written: upper case and lower case are important. If it appears that the URL has been keyed in correctly, then try the following technique: delete all of the information to the right of the forward slash that is farthest to the right and press enter.

For example, suppose that you are trying to reach the following site: **lawlib.wuacc.edu/washlaw/washlaw.html**. First, check the URL as you keyed it in. Then try deleting the final "washlaw.html" from the URL and press enter. If you still have problems, delete "washlaw," which is now the farthest to the right. Eventually, you will get back to the home page and can again start your search.

Note that in the *On the Web* margin features within this text, we have added punctuation (such as a period, comma, colon, or semicolon) immediately following the Web site URLs when this is necessary for grammatical purposes. Be aware that this punctuation is not part of the URL and should not be included when you key in the URL while online.

Before the Test

Go to the *Business Law Today* home page at **http://blt.westbuslaw.com**. Click on TestTutor.® You will find twenty interactive questions relating to this chapter.

CHAPTER 1 Appendix

Finding and Analyzing the Law

The statutes, agency regulations, and case law referred to in this text establish the rights and duties of businesspersons engaged in various types of activities. The cases presented within the following chapters provide you with concise, real-life illustrations of how the courts interpret and apply these laws. Because of the importance of knowing how to find statutory, administrative, and case law, this appendix offers a brief introduction to how these laws are published and to the legal "shorthand" employed in referencing these legal sources.

Finding Statutory and Administrative Law

When Congress passes laws, they are collected in a publication titled *United States Statutes at Large*. When state legislatures pass laws, they are collected in similar state publications. Most frequently, however, laws are referred to in their codified form—that is, the form in which they appear in the federal and state codes.

> **ON THE WEB**
> *The Bluebook: A Uniform System of Citation* offers detailed information on the format for citations to legal sources. The "Bluebook" is now online at www.law.cornell.edu/citation/citation.table.html.

In these codes, laws are compiled by subject. The *United States Code* (U.S.C.) arranges all existing federal laws of a public and permanent nature by subject. Each of the fifty subjects into which the U.S.C. arranges the laws is given a title and a title number. For example, laws relating to commerce and trade are collected in Title 15, which is titled "Commerce and Trade." Titles are subdivided by sections. A citation to the U.S.C. includes title and section numbers. Thus, a reference to "15 U.S.C. Section 1" means that the statute can be found in Section 1 of Title 15. ("Section" may also be designated by the symbol §, and "Sections" by §§.)

Sometimes a citation includes the abbreviation *et seq.*—as in "15 U.S.C. Sections 1 *et seq.*" The term is an abbreviated form of *et sequitur,* which in Latin means "and the following"; when used in a citation, it refers to sections that concern the same subject as the numbered section and follow it in sequence.

> **ON THE WEB**
> You can search the *United States Code* online at gpo.ucop.edu/search/uscode.html.

State codes follow the U.S.C. pattern of arranging law by subject. The state codes may be called codes, revisions, compilations, consolidations, general statutes, or statutes, depending on the preference of the states. In some codes, subjects are designated by number. In others, they are designated by name. For example, "13 Pennsylvania Consolidated Statutes Section 1101" means the statute can be found in Title 13, Section 1101, of the Pennsylvania code. "California Commercial Code Section 1101" means the statute can be found under the subject heading "Commercial Code" of the California code in Section 1101. Abbreviations may be used. For example, "13 Pennsylvania Consolidated Statutes Section 1101" may be

> **ON THE WEB**
> The *Code of Federal Regulations* is online at www.access.gpo.gov/nara/cfr/index.html.

abbreviated "13 Pa. C.S. § 1101," and "California Commercial Code Section 1101" may be abbreviated "Cal. Com. Code § 1101."

Rules and regulations adopted by federal administrative agencies are compiled in the *Code of Federal Regulations* (C.F.R.). Like the U.S.C., the C.F.R. is divided into fifty titles. Rules within each title are assigned section numbers. A full citation to the C.F.R. includes title and section numbers. For example, a reference to "17 C.F.R. Section 230.504" means that the rule can be found in Section 230.504 of Title 17.

Commercial publications of these laws and regulations are available and are widely used. For example, West Group publishes the *United States Code Annotated* (U.S.C.A.). The U.S.C.A. contains the complete text of laws included in the U.S.C., as well as notes of court decisions that interpret and apply specific sections of the statutes, plus the text of presidential proclamations and executive orders. The U.S.C.A. also includes research aids, such as cross-references to related statutes, historical notes, and library references. A citation to the U.S.C.A. is similar to a citation to the U.S.C.: "15 U.S.C.A. Section 1."

Finding Case Law

Before discussing the case reporting system, we need to look briefly at the court system (which will be discussed in detail in Chapter 3). There are two types of courts in the United States, federal courts and state courts. Both the federal and state court systems consist of several levels, or tiers, of courts. *Trial courts,* in which evidence is presented and testimony given, are on the bottom tier (which also includes lower courts handling specialized issues). Decisions from a trial court can be appealed to a higher court, which commonly would be an intermediate *court of appeals,* or an *appellate court.* Decisions from these intermediate courts of appeals may be appealed to an even higher court, such as a state supreme court or the United States Supreme Court.

State Court Decisions

> **ON THE WEB**
> You can find information on state courts, including whether they publish any of their decisions online, at the Center for Information Law and Policy's State Court Locator. Go to www.cilp.org/tblhome.html.

Most state trial court decisions are not published. Except in New York and a few other states that publish selected opinions of their trial courts, decisions from the state trial courts are merely filed in the office of the clerk of the court, where the decisions are available for public inspection. Written decisions of the appellate, or reviewing, courts, however, are published and distributed. The reported appellate decisions are published in volumes called *reports* or *reporters,* which are numbered consecutively. State appellate court decisions are found in the state reporters of that particular state.

Additionally, state court opinions appear in regional units of the *National Reporter System,* published by West Group. Most lawyers and libraries have the West reporters because they report cases more quickly and are distributed more widely than the state-published reports. In fact, many states have eliminated their own reporters in favor of West's National Reporter System. The National Reporter System divides the states into the following geographical areas: *Atlantic* (A. or A.2d), *South Eastern* (S.E. or S.E.2d), *South Western* (S.W. or S.W.2d), *North Western* (N.W. or N.W.2d), *North Eastern* (N.E. or N.E.2d), *Southern* (So. or So.2d), and *Pacific* (P. or P.2d). (The *2d* in the abbreviations refers to *Second Series.* In the near future, the designation *3d,* for *Third Series,* will be used for some of the regional reporters.) The states included in each of these regional divisions are indicated in Exhibit 1A–1, which illustrates West's National Reporter System.

EXHIBIT 1A-1 • National Reporter System—Regional/Federal

Regional Reporters	Coverage Beginning	Coverage
Atlantic Reporter (A. or A.2d)	1885	Connecticut, Delaware, Maine, Maryland, New Hampshire, New Jersey, Pennsylvania, Rhode Island, Vermont, and District of Columbia.
North Eastern Reporter (N.E. or N.E.2d)	1885	Illinois, Indiana, Massachusetts, New York, and Ohio.
North Western Reporter (N.W. or N.W.2d)	1879	Iowa, Michigan, Minnesota, Nebraska, North Dakota, South Dakota, and Wisconsin.
Pacific Reporter (P. or P.2d)	1883	Alaska, Arizona, California, Colorado, Hawaii, Idaho, Kansas, Montana, Nevada, New Mexico, Oklahoma, Oregon, Utah, Washington, and Wyoming.
South Eastern Reporter (S.E. or S.E.2d)	1887	Georgia, North Carolina, South Carolina, Virginia, and West Virginia.
South Western Reporter (S.W. or S.W.2d)	1886	Arkansas, Kentucky, Missouri, Tennessee, and Texas.
Southern Reporter (So. or So.2d)	1887	Alabama, Florida, Louisiana, and Mississippi.
Federal Reporters		
Federal Reporter (F., F.2d, or F.3d)	1880	U.S. Circuit Court from 1880 to 1912; U.S. Commerce Court from 1911 to 1913; U.S. District Courts from 1880 to 1932; U.S. Court of Claims (now called U.S. Court of Federal Claims) from 1929 to 1932 and since 1960; U.S. Court of Appeals since 1891; U.S. Court of Customs and Patent Appeals since 1929; U.S. Emergency Court of Appeals since 1943.
Federal Supplement (F.Supp.)	1932	U.S. Court of Claims from 1932 to 1960; U.S. District Courts since 1932; and U.S. Customs Court since 1956.
Federal Rules Decisions (F.R.D.)	1939	U.S. District Courts involving the Federal Rules of Civil Procedure since 1939 and Federal Rules of Criminal Procedure since 1946.
Supreme Court Reporter (S.Ct.)	1882	U.S. Supreme Court since the October term of 1882.
Bankruptcy Reporter (Bankr.)	1980	Bankruptcy decisions of U.S. Bankruptcy Courts, U.S. District Courts, U.S. Courts of Appeals, and U.S. Supreme Court.
Military Justice Reporter (M.J.)	1978	U.S. Court of Military Appeals and Courts of Military Review for the Army, Navy, Air Force, and Coast Guard.

NATIONAL REPORTER SYSTEM MAP

After appellate decisions have been published, they are normally referred to (cited) by the name of the case; the volume, name, and page number of the state's official reporter (if different from West's National Reporter System); the volume, unit, and page number of the *National Reporter;* and the volume, name, and page number of any other selected reporter. This information is included in the *citation.* (Citing a reporter by volume number, name, and page number, in that order, is common to all citations.) When more than one reporter is cited for the same case, each reference is called a *parallel citation.* For example, consider the following case: *State v. Ollens,* 89 Wash.App. 437, 949 P.2d 407 (1998). We see that the opinion in this case may be found in Volume 89 of the official *Washington Appellate Reports,* on page 437. The parallel citation is to Volume 949 of the *Pacific Reporter, Second Series,* page 407. In presenting appellate opinions in this text, in addition to the reporter, we give the name of the court hearing the case and the year of the court's decision.

A few of the states—including those with intermediate appellate courts, such as California, Illinois, and New York—have more than one reporter for opinions given by courts within their states. Sample citations from these courts, as well as others, are listed and explained in Exhibit 1A–2.

FEDERAL COURT DECISIONS

Federal district court decisions are published unofficially in West's *Federal Supplement* (F.Supp.), and opinions from the circuit courts of appeals (federal reviewing courts) are reported unofficially in West's *Federal Reporter* (F., F.2d, or F.3d). Cases concerning federal bankruptcy law are published unofficially in West's *Bankruptcy Reporter* (Bankr.). The official edition of United States Supreme Court decisions is the *United States Reports* (U.S.), which is published by the federal government. Unofficial editions of Supreme Court cases include West's *Supreme Court Reporter* (S.Ct.) and the *Lawyers' Edition of the Supreme Court Reports* (L.Ed. or L.Ed.2d). Sample citations for federal court decisions are also listed and explained in Exhibit 1A–2.

> **ON THE WEB**
> To find Supreme Court opinions and opinions issued by the federal appellate courts, a good starting point is FindLaw's site at www.findlaw.com.

UNPUBLISHED OPINIONS

Many court opinions that are not yet published or that are not intended for publication can be accessed through Westlaw® (abbreviated in citations as "WL"), which was described earlier in this chapter in the feature *Technology and Online Legal Research.* In cases cited in this text, when no cite to a published reporter is available we give the WL citation (see Exhibit 1A–2 for an example).

OLD CASE LAW

On a few occasions, this text cites opinions from old, classic cases dating to the nineteenth century or earlier; some of these are from the English courts. The citations to these cases appear not to conform to the descriptions given above, because the reporters in which they were published have since been replaced.

Reading and Understanding Case Law

The cases in this text have been condensed from the full text of the courts' opinions and paraphrased by the authors. For those wishing to review court cases for future

EXHIBIT 1A-2 • How to Read Case Citations

State Courts

225 Neb. 290, 583 N.W.2d 611 (1998)[a]

N.W. is the abbreviation for West's publication of state court decisions rendered in the *North Western Reporter* of the National Reporter System. *2d* indicates that this case was included in the *Second Series* of that reporter. The number 583 refers to the volume number of the reporter; the number 611 refers to the first page in that volume on which this case can be found.

Neb. is an abbreviation for *Nebraska Reports*, Nebraska's official reports of the decisions of its highest court, the Nebraska Supreme Court.

62 Cal.App.4th 186, 72 Cal.Rptr.2d 543 (1998)

Cal.Rptr. is the abbreviation for West's unofficial reports—titled *California Reporter*—of the decisions of California courts.

85 N.Y.2d 549, 650 N.E.2d 829, 626 N.Y.S.2d 982 (1995)

N.Y.S. is the abbreviation for West's unofficial reports—titled *New York Supplement*—of the decisions of New York courts.

N.Y. is the abbreviation for *New York Reports*, New York's official reports of the decisions of its court of appeals. The New York Court of Appeals is the state's highest court, analogous to other states' supreme courts. In New York, a supreme court is a trial court.

89 Wa.App. 437, 949 P.2d 407 (1998)

Wa.App. is the abbreviation for *Washington Appellate Reports*, Washington's official reports of the decisions of its court of appeals.

Federal Courts

___ U.S. ___, 118 S.Ct. 2196, 141 L.Ed.2d 540 (1998)

L.Ed. is an abbreviation for *Lawyers' Edition of the Supreme Court Reports*, an unofficial edition of decisions of the United States Supreme Court.

S.Ct. is the abbreviation for West's unofficial reports—titled *Supreme Court Reporter*—of decisions of the United States Supreme Court.

U.S. is the abbreviation for *United States Reports*, the official edition of the decisions of the United States Supreme Court. Volume and page numbers are not included in this citation because they have not yet been assigned.

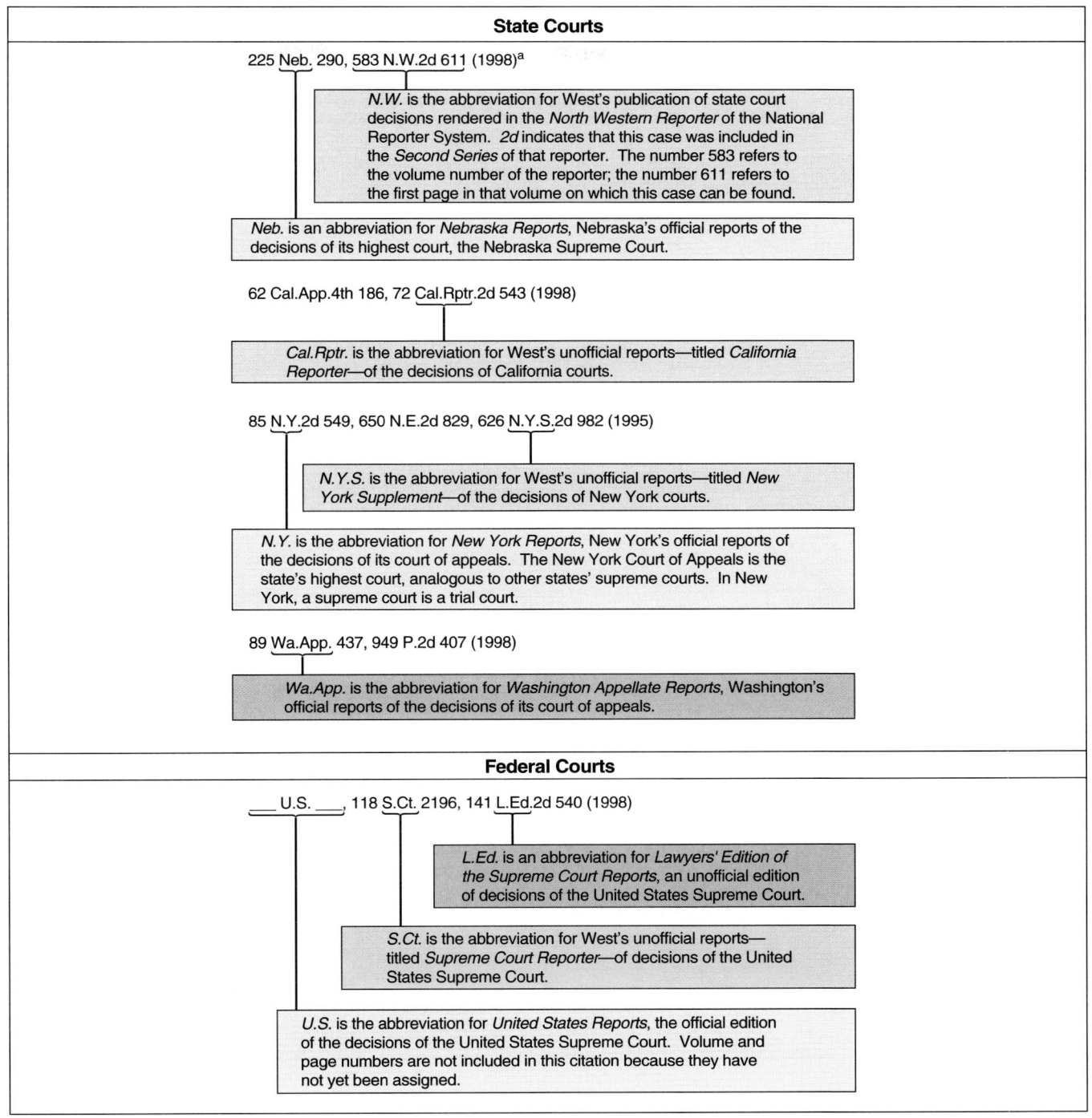

a. The case names have been deleted from these citations to emphasize the publications. It should be kept in mind, however, that the name of a case is as important as the specific page numbers in the volumes in which it is found. If a citation is incorrect, the correct citation may be found in a publication's index of case names. The date of a case is also important because, in addition to providing a check on error in citations, the value of a recent case as an authority is likely to be greater than that of earlier cases.

EXHIBIT 1A-2 • How to Read Case Citations—Continued

Federal Courts (continued)

153 F.3d 1305 (5th Cir. 1998)

5th Cir. is an abbreviation denoting that this case was decided in the United States Court of Appeals for the Fifth Circuit.

990 F.Supp. 657 (E.D.Ark. 1998)

E.D.Ark. is an abbreviation indicating that the United States District Court for the Eastern District of Arkansas decided this case.

English Courts

9 Exch. 341, 156 Eng.Rep. 145 (1854)

Eng.Rep. is an abbreviation for *English Reports, Full Reprint,* a series of reports containing selected decisions made in English courts between 1378 and 1865.

Exch. is an abbreviation for *English Exchequer Reports,* which included the original reports of cases decided in England's Court of Exchequer.

Statutory and Other Citations

18 U.S.C. Section 1961(1)(A)

U.S.C. denotes *United States Code*, the codification of *United States Statutes at Large*. The number 18 refers to the statute's U.S.C. title number and 1961 to its section number within that title. The number 1 refers to a subsection within the section and the letter A to a subdivision within the subsection.

UCC 2–206(1)(b)

UCC is an abbreviation for *Uniform Commercial Code*. The first number 2 is a reference to an article of the UCC and 206 to a section within that article. The number 1 refers to a subsection within the section and the letter b to a subdivision within the subsection.

Restatement (Second) of Torts, Section 568

Restatement (Second) of Torts refers to the second edition of the American Law Institute's *Restatement of the Law of Torts*. The number 568 refers to a specific section.

17 C.F.R. Section 230.505

C.F.R. is an abbreviation for *Code of Federal Regulations,* a compilation of federal administrative regulations. The number 17 designates the regulation's title number, and 230.505 designates a specific section within that title.

EXHIBIT 1A-2 • How to Read Case Citations—Continued

Westlaw® Citations

1998 WL 12345

WL is an abbreviation for Westlaw®. The number 1998 is the year of the document that can be found with this citation in the Westlaw® database. The number 12345 is a number assigned to a specific document. A higher number indicates that a document was added to the Westlaw® database later in the year.

Uniform Resource Locators[b]

www.westlaw.com

The suffix *com* is the top-level domain (TLD) for this Web site. The TLD *com* is an abbreviation for "commercial," which means that a for-profit entity hosts (maintains or supports) this Web site.

westlaw is the host name—the part of the domain name selected by the organization that registered the name. In this case, West Group registered the name. This Internet site is the Westlaw database on the Web.

www is an abbreviation for "World Wide Web." The Web is a system of Internet servers[c] that support documents formatted in *HTML* (hypertext markup language). HTML supports links to text, graphics, and audio and video files.

www.uscourts.gov

This is "The Federal Judiciary Home Page." The host is the Administrative Office of the U.S. Courts. The TLD *gov* is an abbreviation for "government." This Web site includes information and links from, and about, the federal courts.

www.law.cornell.edu/index.html

This part of an URL points to a Web page or file at a specific location within the host's domain. This page, at this Web site, is a menu with links to documents within the domain and to other Internet resources.

This is the host name for a Web site that contains the Internet publications of the Legal Information Institute (LII), which is a part of Cornell Law School. The LII site includes a variety of legal materials and links to other legal resources on the Internet. The TLD *edu* is an abbreviation for "educational institution" (a school or a university).

www.ipl.org.ref./RR

RR is an abbreviation for this Web site's "Ready Reference Collection," which contains links to a variety of Internet resources.

ref is an abbreviation for "Internet Public Library Reference Center," which is a map of the topics into which the links at this Web site have been categorized.

ipl is an abbreviation for Internet Public Library, which is an online service that provides reference resources and links to other information services on the Web. The IPL is supported chiefly by the School of Information at the University of Michigan. The TLD *org* is an abbreviation for "organization (nonprofit)."

b. The basic form for a URL is "service://hostname/path." The Internet service for all of the URLs in this text is *http* (hypertext transfer protocol). Most Web browsers will add this prefix automatically when a user enters a host name or a hostname/path.

c. A *server* is hardware that manages the resources on a network. For example, a network server is a computer that manages the traffic on the network, and a print server is a computer that manages one or more printers.

research projects or to gain additional legal information, the following sections will provide useful insights into how to read and understand case law.

CASE TITLES AND TERMINOLOGY

The title of a case, such as *Adams v. Jones,* indicates the names of the parties to the lawsuit. The *v.* in the case title stands for *versus,* which means "against." In the trial court, Adams was the plaintiff—the person who filed the suit. Jones was the defendant. If the case is appealed, however, the appellate court will sometimes place the name of the party appealing the decision first, so that the case may be called *Jones v. Adams.* Because some reviewing courts retain the trial court order of names, it is often impossible to distinguish the plaintiff from the defendant in the title of a reported appellate court decision. You must carefully read the facts of each case to identify each party.

The following terms and phrases are frequently encountered in court opinions and legal publications. Because it is important to understand what is meant by these terms and phrases, we define and discuss them here.

Plaintiffs and Defendants As mentioned in Chapter 1, the plaintiff in a lawsuit is the party that initiates the action. The defendant is the party against which a lawsuit is brought. Lawsuits frequently involve more than one plaintiff and/or defendant.

Appellants and Appellees The *appellant* is the party that appeals a case to another court or jurisdiction from the court or jurisdiction in which the case was originally brought. Sometimes, an appellant that appeals a judgment is referred to as the *petitioner.* The *appellee* is the party against which the appeal is taken. Sometimes, the appellee is referred to as the *respondent.*

Judges and Justices The terms *judge* and *justice* are usually synonymous and represent two designations given to judges in various courts. All members of the United States Supreme Court, for example, are referred to as justices. And justice is the formal title usually given to judges of appellate courts, although this is not always the case. In New York, a justice is a judge of the trial court (which is called the Supreme Court), and a member of the Court of Appeals (the state's highest court) is called a judge. The term *justice* is commonly abbreviated to J., and *justices* to JJ. A Supreme Court case might refer to Justice O'Connor as O'Connor, J., or to Chief Justice Rehnquist as Rehnquist, C.J.

Decisions and Opinions Most decisions reached by reviewing, or appellate, courts are explained in written *opinions.* The opinion contains the court's reasons for its decision, the rules of law that apply, and the judgment. When all judges or justices unanimously agree on an opinion, the opinion is written for the entire court and can be deemed a *unanimous opinion.* When there is not a unanimous opinion, a *majority opinion* is written, outlining the views of the majority of the judges or justices deciding the case.

Often, a judge or justice who feels strongly about making or emphasizing a point that was not made or emphasized in the unanimous or majority opinion will write a *concurring opinion.* That means the judge or justice agrees (concurs) with the judgment given in the unanimous or majority opinion but for different reasons. In other than unanimous opinions, a *dissenting opinion* is usually written by a judge or justice who does not agree with the majority. The dissenting opinion is important because it may form the basis of the arguments used years later in overruling the precedential majority opinion. Occasionally, a court issues a *per curiam* (Latin for "of the court") opinion, and there is no indication of which judge or justice authored the opinion.

A Sample Court Case

To illustrate how to read and analyze a court opinion, we have annotated an actual case that was heard by the Supreme Court of the United States. The lawsuit was initiated by Sidney Abbott, who filed a discrimination suit, claiming that she was treated differently on the basis of her disability.

You will note that triple asterisks (* * *) and quadruple asterisks (* * * *) frequently appear within the opinion. The triple asterisks indicate that we have deleted a few words or sentences from the opinion for the sake of readability or brevity. Quadruple asterisks mean that an entire paragraph (or more) has been omitted. Also, when the opinion cites another case or legal source, the citation to the referenced cases or sources has been omitted to save space and to improve the flow of the text. These editorial practices are continued in the other court opinions presented in this text. In addition, whenever a case opinion presented in this text includes a term or a phrase that may not be readily understandable, we have added a bracketed definition or paraphrase of the term or phrase. In the sample case in Exhibit 1A–3, important sections, terms, and phrases are defined or discussed in the margins.

THE SUPREME COURT BUILDING IN WASHINGTON, D.C.

EXHIBIT 1A–3 • A Sample Court Case

Bragdon v. Abbott

Supreme Court of the United States, 1998.
___ U.S. ___ ,
118 S.Ct. 2196,
141 L.Ed.2d 540.
supct.law.cornell.edu/supct/html/97-156.ZS.html[a]

> The first part of this opinion identifies the statute that the Court is being asked to interpret and apply in this case. This paragraph also sets out the issue that the Court will address under that statute.

Justice *KENNEDY* delivered the opinion of the Court.

> A writ from a higher court (in this case, the United States Supreme Court) asking a lower court (here, the U.S. Court of Appeals for the First Circuit) for the record of a case for review.

We address in this case the application of the Americans with Disabilities Act of 1990 **(ADA)** to persons infected with the human immunodeficiency virus (HIV). We granted ***certiorari*** to review * * * whether HIV infection is a disability under the ADA when the infection has not yet progressed to the socalled symptomatic phase * * * .

* * * *

> The party who is asked to respond in an appeal.

> The party who initiates an appeal by filing a petition with a higher court.

> This part of the opinion summarizes the facts of the case. The facts include the identities of the petitioner (the party initiating the appeal) and the respondent (the party against whom the appeal is brought), the reason for the original suit, and the judgments of the lower courts.

Respondent Sidney Abbott has been infected with HIV since 1986. When the incidents we recite occurred, her infection had not manifested its most serious symptoms. On September 16, 1994, she went to the office of **petitioner** Randon Bragdon in Bangor, Maine, for a dental appointment. She disclosed her HIV infection on the patient registration form. Petitioner completed a dental examination, discovered a cavity, and informed respondent of his policy against filling cavities of HIV-infected patients. He offered to perform the work at a hospital with no added fee for his services, though respondent would be responsible for the cost of using the hospital's facilities. Respondent declined.

Respondent sued petitioner * * * , alleging discrimination on the basis of her disability. * * *

* * * *

A

> The trial court's decision.

* * * The District Court ruled in favor of [Abbott], holding that respondent's HIV infection satisfied the ADA's definition of disability. * * *

B

> The appellate court's decision.

The Court of Appeals affirmed. * * *

* * * *

* * * The [ADA] defines disability as:

" * * * a physical or mental impairment that substantially limits one or more of the major life activities of such individual * * * ."

> The Supreme Court sets out the three steps that the Court will use to analyze the facts.

Our consideration of [this] definition proceeds in three steps. First, we consider whether respondent's HIV infection was a physical impairment. Second, we identify the life activity upon which respondent relies (reproduction and child bearing) and determine whether it constitutes a major life activity under the ADA. Third, * * * we ask whether the impairment substantially limited the major life activity. * * *

* * * *

a. This site is part of the Supreme Court Collection of cases maintained by the Legal Information Institute, which is part of Cornell Law School.

The first step in the inquiry * * * requires us to determine whether respondent's condition constituted a physical impairment. * * * The [applicable administrative agency] regulations * * * define "physical * * * impairment" to mean:

"any physiological disorder or condition * * * affecting * * * the following body systems: * * * hemic and lymphatic * * * ."

* * * *

The Supreme Court's conclusion on the first part of the definition that will determine the issue the Court has been asked to decide.

* * * [I]nfection with HIV causes immediate abnormalities in a person's blood, and the infected person's white cell count continues to drop throughout the course of the disease, * * * when the attack is concentrated in the lymph nodes. In light of these facts, HIV infection must be regarded as a physiological disorder with a constant and detrimental effect on the infected person's hemic and lymphatic systems from the moment of infection. HIV infection satisfies the * * * definition of a physical impairment during every stage of the disease.

The statute is not operative * * * unless the impairment affects a major life activity. * * *

* * * *

The Supreme Court's conclusion on the second part of the definition.

We have little difficulty concluding that it [does]. * * * Reproduction falls well within the phrase "major life activity." Reproduction and the sexual dynamics surrounding it are central to the life process itself.

* * * *

The final element of the disability definition is whether respondent's physical impairment was a substantial limit on the major life activity she asserts. * * *

The Supreme Court's conclusion on the third part of the definition.

Our evaluation of the medical evidence leads us to conclude that respondent's infection substantially limited her ability to reproduce in two independent ways. First, a woman infected with HIV who tries to conceive a child imposes on the man a significant risk of becoming infected. * * *

Second, an infected woman risks infecting her child during gestation and childbirth * * * .

* * * *

* * * The laws of some States, moreover, forbid persons infected with HIV from having sex with others, regardless of consent.

* * * *

The judgment of the appellate court is affirmed.

The determination of the Court of Appeals that respondent's HIV infection was a disability under the ADA is affirmed. The * * * case is **remanded** for further proceedings consistent with this opinion.

Remand means to send back. This is the act of an appellate court to a lower court when it orders the lower court to take further action.

CHAPTER 2 Constitutional Law

"The United States Constitution has proved itself the most marvelously elastic compilation of rules of government ever written."

Franklin D. Roosevelt, 1882–1945
(Thirty-second president of the United States, 1933–1945)

CONTENTS

LEARNING OBJECTIVES

After reading this chapter, you should be able to:

1. Describe the form of government created by the U.S. Constitution.
2. Explain the relationship between the national government and state governments as set forth in the Constitution.
3. Identify the constitutional basis for the regulatory power of the federal government.
4. Summarize the fundamental rights protected by the First Amendment.
5. Give some examples of how other constitutional protections affect business.

The U.S. Constitution is brief.[1] It consists of only about seven thousand words, which is less than one-third of the number of words in the average state constitution. Perhaps its brevity explains why it has proved to be so "marvelously elastic," as Franklin Roosevelt pointed out in the above quotation, and why it has survived for over two hundred years—longer than any other written constitution in the world.

Laws that govern business have their origin in the lawmaking authority granted by this document, which is the supreme law in this country. As mentioned in Chapter 1, neither Congress nor any state may pass a law that conflicts with the Constitution.

In this chapter, we first look at some basic constitutional concepts and clauses and their significance for business. Then we examine how certain fundamental freedoms guaranteed by the Constitution affect businesspersons and the workplace.

1. See Appendix A for the full text of the U.S. Constitution.

The Constitutional Powers of Government

Following the Revolutionary War, the states created a *confederal* form of government. The Articles of Confederation, which went into effect in 1781, established a confederation of independent states and a central (national) government that could exercise only very limited powers. The sovereign power, or supreme authority to govern, rested largely with the states. The limitation on the central government's powers reflected a basic tenet of the American Revolution—that a national government should not have unlimited power that could be used to tyrannize over the states.

The confederation, however, faced serious problems. For one thing, laws passed by the various states hampered national commerce and foreign trade by preventing the free movement of goods and services. By 1784, the nation faced a serious economic depression. Many who could not afford to pay their debts were thrown into "debtors' prisons." By 1786, a series of uprisings by farmer debtors were difficult to control because the national government did not have the authority to demand revenues (by levying taxes, for example) to support a militia.

Because of these problems, a national convention was called to amend the Articles of Confederation. Instead of amending the articles, however, the delegates to the convention wrote the U.S. Constitution, which, after its ratification by the states in 1789, became the basis for an entirely new form of government. Many of the provisions of the Constitution, including those discussed in the following pages, were shaped by the delegates' experiences during the confederal era (1781–1789).

Federalism and the Separation of Powers

ON THE WEB

To learn the founders' views on federalism, a good source is *The Federalist Papers,* a series of essays authored by Alexander Hamilton, James Madison, and John Jay. You can access these essays online at www.law.emory.edu/FEDERAL.

The new government created by the Constitution reflected a series of compromises made by delegates to the convention on various issues. Some delegates wanted sovereign power to remain with the states; others wanted the national government alone to exercise sovereign power. The end result was a compromise—a **federal form of government** in which the national government and the states *share* sovereign power. The Constitution expressly delegated certain powers to the national government and reserved all other powers to the states. The relationship between the national government and the state governments is a partnership. Neither partner is superior to the other except within the particular area of exclusive authority granted to it under the Constitution.

• **FEDERAL FORM OF GOVERNMENT** A system of government in which the states form a union and the sovereign power is divided between a central government and the member states.

• **CHECKS AND BALANCES** The national government is composed of three separate branches: the executive, the legislative, and the judicial branches. Each branch of the government exercises a check on the actions of the others.

To prevent the possibility that the national government might use its power arbitrarily, the Constitution divided the national government's powers among the three branches of government. The legislative branch makes the laws, the executive branch enforces the laws, and the judicial branch interprets the laws. Each branch performs a separate function, and no branch may exercise the authority of another branch. Additionally, a system of **checks and balances** allows each branch to limit the actions of the other two branches, thus preventing any one branch from exercising too much power. Some examples of these checks and balances are the following:

1. The legislative branch (Congress) can enact a law, but the executive branch (the president) has the constitutional authority to veto that law.
2. The executive branch is responsible for foreign affairs, but treaties with foreign governments require the advice and consent of the Senate.

❸ Congress determines the jurisdiction of the federal courts and the president appoints federal judges, with the advice and consent of the Senate, but the judicial branch has the power to hold actions of the other two branches unconstitutional.[2]

ETHICAL ISSUE 2.1 ***Should nine unelected justices make the law?*** The checks and balances built into the Constitution were designed to keep any one branch of government from exercising too much power. Among these checks is the judiciary's power to hold unconstitutional the laws and actions of the other two branches. Yet some claim that this power gives federal judges, particularly the justices who sit on the United States Supreme Court, too much control over national laws and policies, the making of which the framers of the Constitution entrusted to Congress. Because members of Congress are elected, the people have some say in the lawmaking process. But the people have little say in the decisions made by federal judges, who are not elected but appointed—albeit with the advice and consent of the Senate, an elected body. In the early years of the nation, there was little concern about the Supreme Court wielding too much power. In fact, Alexander Hamilton spoke of the judicial branch (the Supreme Court) as "the least dangerous branch" of government because the Court had no enforcement powers and—in those days—little stature in the eyes of the public. Today, although it still has no enforcement powers, its stature in the eyes of the public allows it to influence national affairs to an extent that the founders could not possibly have foreseen.

THE COMMERCE CLAUSE

To prevent states from establishing laws and regulations that would interfere with trade and commerce among the states, the Constitution expressly delegated to the national government the power to regulate interstate commerce. Article I, Section 8, of the U.S. Constitution expressly permits Congress "[t]o regulate Commerce with foreign Nations, and among the several States, and with the Indian Tribes." This clause, referred to as the **commerce clause,** has had a greater impact on business than any other provision in the Constitution.

• **COMMERCE CLAUSE**
The provision in Article I, Section 8, of the U.S. Constitution that gives Congress the power to regulate interstate commerce.

For some time, the commerce power was interpreted as being limited to *interstate* commerce (commerce among the states) and not applicable to *intrastate* commerce (commerce within the states). In 1824, however, in *Gibbons v. Ogden* (see the *Landmark in the Law*), the United States Supreme Court held that commerce within states could also be regulated by the national government as long as the commerce *substantially affected* commerce involving more than one state.

"We are under a Constitution, but the Constitution is what judges say it is."
CHARLES EVANS HUGHES, 1862–1948 (American jurist)

The Breadth of the Commerce Clause In *Gibbons v. Ogden,* the commerce clause was expanded to regulate activities that "substantially affect interstate commerce." As the nation grew and faced new kinds of problems, the commerce clause became a vehicle for the additional expansion of national-government regulatory powers. Even activities that seemed purely local came under the regulatory reach of the national government if those activities were deemed to substantially affect interstate commerce. • **EXAMPLE 2.1** In 1942, in *Wickard v. Filburn,*[3] the Supreme Court held that wheat production by an individual farmer intended wholly for consumption on

2. See the *Landmark in the Law* in Chapter 3 on *Marbury v. Madison,* 5 U.S. (1 Cranch) 137, 2 L.Ed. 60 (1803), a case in which the doctrine of judicial review was clearly enunciated by Chief Justice John Marshall.
3. 317 U.S. 111, 63 S.Ct. 82, 87 L.Ed. 122 (1942).

Landmark in the Law • *GIBBONS v. OGDEN* (1824)

The commerce clause, which is found in Article I, Section 8, of the U.S. Constitution, gives Congress the power "to regulate Commerce with foreign Nations, and among the several States, and with the Indian Tribes." What exactly does "to regulate commerce" mean? What does "commerce" entail? These questions came before the United States Supreme Court in 1824 in the case of *Gibbons v. Ogden*.[a]

The background of the case was as follows. Robert Fulton, inventor of the steamboat, and Robert Livingston, who was then American minister to France, secured a monopoly on steam navigation on the waters in the state of New York from the New York legislature in 1803. Fulton and Livingston licensed Aaron Ogden, a former governor of New Jersey and a U.S. senator, to operate steam-powered ferryboats between New York and New Jersey. Thomas Gibbons, who had obtained a license from the U.S. government to operate boats in interstate waters, competed with Ogden without New York's permission. Ogden sued Gibbons. The New York state courts granted Ogden an injunction, prohibiting Gibbons from operating in New York waters. Gibbons appealed the decision to the United States Supreme Court.

Sitting as chief justice on the Supreme Court was John Marshall, an advocate of a strong national government. In his decision, Marshall defined the word *commerce* as used in the commerce clause to mean all commercial intercourse—that is, all business dealings that affect more than one state. The Court ruled against Ogden's monopoly, reversing the injunction against Gibbons. Marshall used this opportunity not only to expand the definition of commerce but also to validate and increase the power of the national legislature to regulate commerce. Said Marshall, "What is this power? It is the power . . . to prescribe the rule by which commerce is to be governed." Marshall held that the power to regulate interstate commerce was an exclusive power of the national government and that this power included the power to regulate any intrastate commerce that substantially affects interstate commerce.

FOR CRITICAL ANALYSIS
What might have resulted if the Court had held otherwise—that the national government did *not* have the exclusive power to regulate interstate commerce?

a. 22 U.S. (9 Wheat.) 1, 6 L.Ed. 23 (1824).

his own farm was subject to federal regulation. The Court reasoned that the home consumption of wheat reduced the demand for wheat and thus could have a substantial effect on interstate commerce. •

By 1980, the Court acknowledged, in *McLain v. Real Estate Board of New Orleans, Inc.*,[4] that the commerce clause had "long been interpreted to extend beyond activities actually in interstate commerce to reach other activities, while wholly local in nature, which nevertheless substantially affect interstate commerce."

Today, at least theoretically, the power over commerce authorizes the national government to regulate every commercial enterprise in the United States. Federal (national) legislation governs virtually every major activity conducted by businesses—from hiring and firing decisions, to workplace safety, to competitive practices, to how they compete for business, to how they finance their enterprises.

Only rarely has the Supreme Court limited the regulatory reach of the national government under the commerce power. One of these occasions was in 1995, when the Court held—for the first time in sixty years—that Congress had exceeded its regulatory authority under the commerce clause when it passed the Gun-Free School Zones Act in 1990. The Court stated that the act, which banned the possession of

¡RECALL!
Any law in violation of the U.S. Constitution will not be enforced.

4. 444 U.S. 232, 100 S.Ct. 502, 62 L.Ed.2d 441 (1980).

guns within one thousand feet of any school, was unconstitutional because it attempted to regulate an area that had "nothing to do with commerce."[5] The following landmark case involves an earlier challenge to the scope of the national government's constitutional authority to regulate local activities.

5. 514 U.S. 549, 115 S.Ct. 1624, 131 L.Ed.2d 626 (1995).

CASE 2.1 Heart of Atlanta Motel v. United States

Supreme Court of the United States, 1964.
379 U.S. 241,
85 S.Ct. 348,
13 L.Ed. 2d 258.
supct.law.cornell.edu/supct/cases/name.htm[a]

HISTORICAL AND SOCIAL SETTING *In the first half of the twentieth century, state governments sanctioned segregation on the basis of race. In 1954, the United States Supreme Court decided that racially segregated school systems violated the Constitution. In the following decade, the Court ordered an end to racial segregation imposed by the states in other public facilities, such as beaches, golf courses, buses, parks, auditoriums, and courtroom seating. Privately owned facilities that excluded or segregated African Americans and others on the basis of race were not subject to the same constitutional restrictions, however. Congress passed the Civil Rights Act of 1964 to prohibit racial discrimination in "establishments affecting interstate commerce." These facilities included "places of public accommodation."*

a. This is the "Historic Supreme Court Decisions—by Party Name" page within the "Caselists" collection of the Legal Information Institute available at its site on the Web. Click on the "H" link or scroll down the list of cases to the entry for the *Heart of Atlanta* case. Click on the case name. When the link opens, click on one of the choices to read the "Syllabus," the "Full Decision," or the "Edited Decision."

BACKGROUND AND FACTS The owner of the Heart of Atlanta Motel, in violation of the Civil Rights Act of 1964, refused to rent rooms to African Americans. The motel owner brought an action in a federal district court to have the act declared unconstitutional, alleging that Congress had exceeded its constitutional authority to regulate commerce by enacting the act. The owner argued that his motel was not engaged in interstate commerce but was "of a purely local character." The motel, however, was accessible to state and interstate highways. The owner advertised nationally, maintained billboards throughout the state, and accepted convention trade from outside the state (75 percent of the guests were residents of other states). The court sustained the constitutionality of the act and enjoined (prohibited) the owner from discriminating on the basis of race. The owner appealed. The case ultimately went to the United States Supreme Court.

IN THE WORDS OF THE COURT . . .
Mr. Justice *CLARK* delivered the opinion of the Court.

* * * *

While the Act as adopted carried no congressional findings, the record of its passage through each house is replete with evidence of the burdens that discrimination by race or color places upon interstate commerce * * * . This testimony included the fact that our people have become increasingly mobile with millions of all races traveling from State to State; that Negroes in particular have been the subject of discrimination in transient accommodations, having to travel great distances to secure the same; that often they have been unable to obtain accommodations and have had to call upon friends to put them up overnight. * * * These exclusionary practices were found to be nationwide, the Under Secretary of Commerce testifying that there is "no question that this discrimination in the North still exists to a large degree" and in the West and Midwest as well * * * . This testimony indicated a qualitative as well as quantitative effect on interstate travel by Negroes. The former was the obvious impairment of the Negro traveler's pleasure and convenience that resulted when he continually was uncertain of finding lodging. As for the latter, there was evidence that this uncertainty stemming from racial discrimination had the effect of discouraging travel on the part of a

CASE 2.1—Continued

substantial portion of the Negro community * * * . We shall not burden this opinion with further details since the voluminous testimony presents overwhelming evidence that discrimination by hotels and motels impedes interstate travel.

* * * *

It is said that the operation of the motel here is of a purely local character. But, assuming this to be true, "if it is interstate commerce that feels the pinch, it does not matter how local the operation that applies the squeeze." * * * Thus the power of Congress to promote interstate commerce also includes the power to regulate the local incidents thereof, including local activities in both the States of origin and destination, which might have a substantial and harmful effect upon that commerce.

DECISION AND REMEDY The United States Supreme Court upheld the constitutionality of the Civil Rights Act of 1964. The power of Congress to regulate interstate commerce permitted the enactment of legislation that could halt local discriminatory practices.

FOR CRITICAL ANALYSIS—Political Consideration *Suppose that only 5 percent of the motel's guests—or even 2 or 1 percent—were from out of state. In such a situation, would the Court still have been justified in regulating the motel's activities?*

• **POLICE POWERS**
Powers possessed by states as part of their inherent sovereignty. These powers may be exercised to protect or promote the public order, health, safety, morals, and general welfare.

ON THE WEB
An ongoing debate in our federal system is whether the national government exercises too much regulatory control over intrastate affairs. To find current articles on this topic, go to www.vote-smart.org/issues/FEDERALISM_STATES_RIGHTS.

The Regulatory Powers of the States As part of their inherent sovereignty, state governments have the authority to regulate affairs within their borders. State regulatory powers are often referred to as **police powers.** The term does not relate solely to criminal law enforcement but also to the right of state governments to regulate private activities to protect or promote the public order, health, safety, morals, and general welfare. Fire and building codes, antidiscrimination laws, parking regulations, zoning restrictions, licensing requirements, and thousands of other state statutes covering virtually every aspect of life have been enacted pursuant to a state's police powers.

Generally, laws enacted pursuant to a state's police powers carry a strong presumption of validity. If a state law substantially burdens interstate commerce, however, it will be held to violate the commerce clause of the Constitution—which authorizes only the national government to regulate trade and commerce among the states. When state regulations impinge on interstate commerce, courts must balance the state's interest in the merits and purposes of the regulation against the burden placed on interstate commerce.

• **EXAMPLE 2.2** In *Raymond Motor Transportation, Inc. v. Rice,*[6] the issue concerned Wisconsin administrative regulations that limited the length of trucks traveling on its highways. The United States Supreme Court weighed the burden on interstate commerce against the benefits created by the regulations and concluded that the challenged regulations "place a substantial burden on interstate commerce and they cannot be said to make more than the most speculative contribution to highway safety." • (For another example of how state laws can violate the commerce clause, see this chapter's *Technology and the "Dormant" Commerce Clause* on page 41.) Because courts balance the interests involved, it is extremely difficult to predict the outcome in a particular case.

Local governments, including cities, also exercise police powers. Local governments derive their authority to regulate their communities from the state, because they are creatures of the state. In other words, they cannot come into existence unless authorized by the state to do so. The following case concerns whether it is reasonable for a local government to impose a duty on property owners to keep clear the strips of government-owned land between the streets and the adjoining property.

6. 434 U.S. 429, 98 S.Ct. 787, 54 L.Ed.2d 664 (1978).

HAZARDOUS WASTE IS DEPOSITED AT A BURIAL SITE. CAN THE STATE IN WHICH THIS SITE IS LOCATED REGULATE THIS ACTIVITY? IF SO, AND IF THOSE REGULATIONS IMPINGE ON INTERSTATE COMMERCE, WILL THEY BE HELD UNCONSTITUTIONAL?

CASE 2.2 J. E. Goodenow v. City Council of Maquoketa, Iowa

Supreme Court of Iowa, 1998.
574 N.W.2d 18.
www.iowabar.org/IowaSupremeCourt.nsf[a]

HISTORICAL AND ENVIRONMENTAL SETTING *The ditches that line roads are generally designed to channel water that runs off those right-of-ways during storms and other severe weather. At one time, those who lived in a community maintained the right-of-ways that ran through it and kept them clear. As cities developed, the bulk of the work was given to local government departments, but the owners of the adjoining property were sometimes expected to clear the ditches. Steep, rolling ditches cannot be mowed with a push mower or riding mower, but require a rotary mower or a sickle bar attached to a utility tractor and heavy-duty weed eaters. This equipment can cost tens of thousands of dollars to buy and hundreds of dollars a month in man-hours to use.*

a. This is a page within a collection of Iowa state court cases made available on the Web by the Iowa State Bar Association. Click on the "Date" link. When the "Date" page opens, scroll down the list to the *Goodenow* case, which was decided on January 21, 1998. Click on the number preceding the date to access the opinion.

BACKGROUND AND FACTS Two-thirds of the Goodenow family farm is located within the city limits of Maquoketa, Iowa. At one time, the city mowed all of its right-of-ways, including the grass and weeds between its streets and the edge of the Goodenow property (and the property of other landowners). This included the hard-to-mow ditches that border the Goodenow farm. When the city enacted an ordinance to require the owners of the adjoining property to mow these strips, the owners of the Goodenow farm did not comply. Instead, they appealed to the city council, which refused to exempt them from the ordinance. John Goodenow, and others, filed a petition in an Iowa state court against the city, and others, asking the court to prevent enforcement of the ordinance. The court issued a summary judgment in favor of the defendants. The plaintiffs appealed.

CASE 2.2—Continued

IN THE WORDS OF THE COURT . . .
McGIVERIN, Chief Justice.

* * * *

* * * We believe that the [ordinance is] designed to maintain the height of weeds and grasses along the boulevard of city streets to ensure adequate view of the road and access thereto, especially at or near intersections, and to prevent vegetation from becoming unsightly and unsafe to the public. * * * In other words the statute was enacted for the public safety, which has always been regarded as a proper subject of police power. * * *

We further note that [a] law does not become unconstitutional because it works a hardship. Additionally, the fact that one must make substantial expenditures to comply with regulatory statutes does not raise constitutional barriers.

We therefore conclude that * * * the Maquoketa city ordinances promote and protect the public health, safety, and welfare of persons who travel the city streets, and that the enactments are reasonably related to achieving those goals. The enactments thus constitute valid exercises of police power * * * .

DECISION AND REMEDY The Supreme Court of Iowa affirmed the decision of the lower court. The state supreme court held that the ordinance constituted a valid exercise of police power.

FOR CRITICAL ANALYSIS—Social Consideration *Should all citizens be considered obligated to render some unpaid service to their states?*

THE SUPREMACY CLAUSE

Article VI of the Constitution provides that the Constitution, laws, and treaties of the United States are "the supreme Law of the Land." This article, commonly referred to as the **supremacy clause,** is important in the ordering of state and federal relationships. When there is a direct conflict between a federal law and a state law, the state law is rendered invalid. Because some powers are concurrent (shared by the federal government and the states), however, it is necessary to determine which law governs in a particular circumstance.

• **SUPREMACY CLAUSE**
The provision in Article VI of the Constitution that provides that the Constitution, laws, and treaties of the United States are "the supreme Law of the Land." Under this clause, state and local laws that directly conflict with federal law will be rendered invalid.

When Congress chooses to act exclusively in a concurrent area, it is said to have *preempted* the area. In this circumstance, a valid federal statute or regulation will take precedence over a conflicting state or local law or regulation on the same general subject. Congress, however, rarely makes clear its intent to preempt an entire subject area against state regulation; consequently, the courts must determine whether Congress intended to exercise exclusive dominion over a given area. Consideration of **preemption** often occurs in the commerce clause context.

• **PREEMPTION**
A doctrine under which certain federal laws preempt, or take precedence over, conflicting state or local laws.

No single factor is decisive as to whether a court will find preemption. Generally, congressional intent to preempt will be found if a federal law regulating an activity is so pervasive, comprehensive, or detailed that the states have no room to regulate in that area. Also, when a federal statute creates an agency—such as the National Labor Relations Board—to enforce the law, matters that may come within the agency's jurisdiction will likely preempt state laws.

THE TAXING AND SPENDING POWERS

Article I, Section 8, provides that Congress has the "Power to lay and collect Taxes, Duties, Imposts, and Excises." Section 8 further provides that "all Duties, Imposts and Excises shall be uniform throughout the United States." The requirement of uni-

Technology and the "Dormant" Commerce Clause

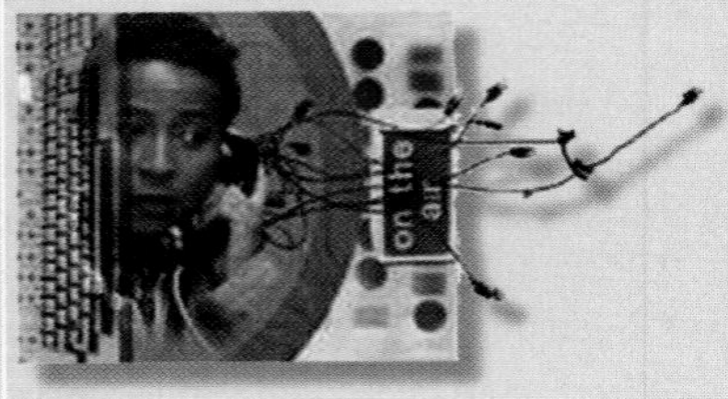

The commerce clause of the U.S. Constitution expressly authorizes the national government to regulate interstate commerce. The Supreme Court has interpreted the commerce clause to mean that the national government has the *exclusive* authority to regulate commerce that substantially affects trade and commerce among the states. This express grant of authority to the national government, which is often referred to as the "positive" aspect of the commerce clause, implies a negative aspect of the clause—that the states do *not* have the authority to regulate interstate commerce. This negative aspect of the commerce clause is often referred to as the "dormant" (implied) commerce clause.

The dormant commerce clause comes into play when state regulations impinge on interstate commerce. As mentioned elsewhere, states have the authority to regulate commerce and other activities within their borders, and usually the courts will balance the state's interest in regulating a certain matter—such as the length of trucks or trains traveling on its highways—against the burden that the state's regulation places on interstate commerce. An emerging issue has to do with state attempts to regulate Internet transactions.

The Internet used to be referred to as the "Information Superhighway." This rather inaccurate comparison of the Internet to a highway helps to explain how the commerce clause might apply in cyberspace. The Internet—today's superhighway—is used to transport speech and information all over the world. Is cyberspace activity therefore interstate commerce? Does the commerce clause restrict states from interfering with cyberspace activity?

According to at least one court, the answer to both of these questions is "Yes." The case involved a state statute that required state libraries to filter the data their patrons could access over the Internet from the libraries' computers. The court viewed the case through the lens of the commerce clause and held that the statute was unconstitutional. The court reasoned that "the burdens on interstate commerce resulting from the [statute] clearly exceed any local benefit derived from it. . . . [T]he Internet is one of those areas of commerce that must be marked off as a national preserve to protect users from inconsistent legislation that, taken to its most extreme, could paralyze development of the Internet altogether."[a]

FOR CRITICAL ANALYSIS

Given that the Internet is a global network, could this same reasoning be applied to attempts by national governments to regulate this new "area of commerce"?

a. *American Library Association v. Pataki,* 969 F.Supp. 160 (S.D.N.Y. 1997).

INTERNET CONNECT

formity refers to uniformity among the states, and thus Congress may not tax some states while exempting others.

Traditionally, if Congress attempted to regulate indirectly, by taxation, an area over which it had no authority, the tax would be invalidated by the courts. Today, however, if a tax measure bears some reasonable relationship to revenue production, it is generally held to be within the national taxing power. Moreover, the expansive interpretation of the commerce clause almost always provides a basis for sustaining a federal tax.

Under Article I, Section 8, Congress has the power "to pay the Debts and provide for the common Defence and general welfare of the United States." Through the spending power, Congress disposes of the revenues accumulated from the taxing power. Congress can spend revenues not only to carry out its enumerated powers but also to promote any objective it deems worthwhile, so long as it does not violate the Constitution or its amendments. For example, Congress could not condition welfare payments on the recipients' political views. The spending power necessarily involves policy choices, with which taxpayers may disagree.

Business and the Bill of Rights

• **BILL OF RIGHTS**
The first ten amendments to the U.S. Constitution.

ON THE WEB
To learn about some current issues involving the rights and liberties contained in the Bill of Rights, go to the Web site of the American Civil Liberties Union at www.aclu.org.

¡BE CAREFUL!
Although most of these rights apply to actions of the states, some of them apply only to actions of the federal government.

The importance of a written declaration of the rights of individuals eventually caused the first Congress of the United States to submit twelve amendments to the Constitution to the states for approval. The first ten of these amendments, commonly known as the **Bill of Rights,** were adopted in 1791 and embody a series of protections for the individual against various types of interference by the federal government.[7] Some constitutional protections apply to business entities as well. For example, corporations exist as separate legal entities, or legal persons, and enjoy many of the same rights and privileges as natural persons do. Summarized here are the protections guaranteed by these ten amendments (see the Constitution in Appendix A for the complete text of each amendment):

1. The First Amendment guarantees the freedoms of religion, speech, and the press and the rights to assemble peaceably and to petition the government.
2. The Second Amendment guarantees the right to keep and bear arms.
3. The Third Amendment prohibits, in peacetime, the lodging of soldiers in any house without the owner's consent.
4. The Fourth Amendment prohibits unreasonable searches and seizures of persons or property.
5. The Fifth Amendment guarantees the rights to indictment by grand jury, to due process of law, and to fair payment when private property is taken for public use. The Fifth Amendment also prohibits compulsory self-incrimination and double jeopardy (trial for the same crime twice).
6. The Sixth Amendment guarantees the accused in a criminal case the right to a speedy and public trial by an impartial jury and with counsel. The accused has the right to cross-examine witnesses against him or her and to solicit testimony from witnesses in his or her favor.
7. The Seventh Amendment guarantees the right to a trial by jury in a civil case involving at least twenty dollars.[8]
8. The Eighth Amendment prohibits excessive bail and fines, as well as cruel and unusual punishment.
9. The Ninth Amendment establishes that the people have rights in addition to those specified in the Constitution.
10. The Tenth Amendment establishes that those powers neither delegated to the federal government nor denied to the states are reserved for the states.

As originally intended, the Bill of Rights limited only the powers of the national government. Over time, however, the Supreme Court "incorporated" most of these rights into the protections against state actions afforded by the Fourteenth Amendment to the Constitution. That amendment, passed in 1868 after the Civil War, provides in part that "[n]o State shall . . . deprive any person of life, liberty, or property, without due process of law." Starting in 1925, the Supreme Court began to define various rights and liberties guaranteed in the national Constitution as constituting "due process of law," which was required of state governments under the Fourteenth Amendment. Today, most of the rights and liberties set forth in the Bill of Rights apply to state governments as well as the national government.

7. One of these proposed amendments was ratified 203 years later (in 1992) and became the Twenty-seventh Amendment to the Constitution. See Appendix A.
8. Twenty dollars was forty days' pay for the average person when the Bill of Rights was written.

POLICE SEARCH A CRACK HOUSE IN FLORIDA. DO THE OWNERS AND OCCUPANTS OF SUCH HOUSES RECEIVE PROTECTION FROM UNREASONABLE SEARCHES AND SEIZURES UNDER THE U.S. CONSTITUTION? SHOULD THEY?

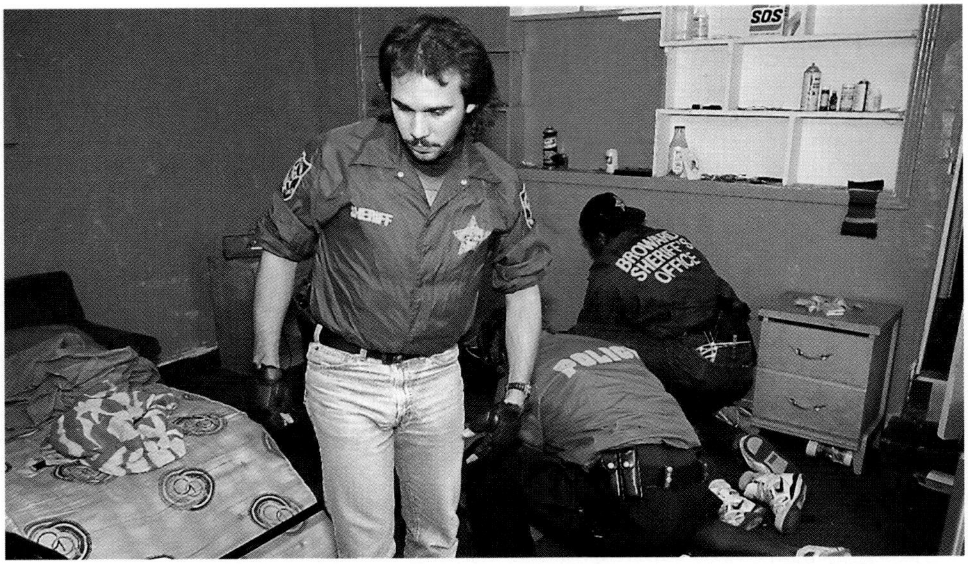

"It is by the goodness of God that in our country we have three unspeakably precious things: freedom of speech, freedom of conscience, and the prudence never to practice either of them."

MARK TWAIN (SAMUEL CLEMENS), 1835–1910
(American author and humorist)

We will look closely at several of the amendments in the above list in Chapter 6, in the context of criminal law and procedures. Here we examine two important guarantees of the First Amendment—freedom of speech and freedom of religion. These and other First Amendment freedoms (of the press, assembly, and petition) have all been applied to the states through the due process clause of the Fourteenth Amendment. As you read through the following pages, keep in mind that none of these (or other) constitutional freedoms confers an absolute right. Ultimately, it is the United States Supreme Court, as the final interpreter of the Constitution, that gives meaning to these rights and determines their boundaries.

THE FIRST AMENDMENT—FREEDOM OF SPEECH

Freedom of speech is the most prized freedom that Americans have. Indeed, it forms the basis for our democratic form of government, which could not exist if people could not express freely their political opinions and criticize government actions or policies. Because of its importance, the courts traditionally have protected this right to the fullest extent possible.

• **SYMBOLIC SPEECH**
Nonverbal expressions of beliefs. Symbolic speech, which includes gestures, movements, and articles of clothing, is given substantial protection by the courts.

The courts also protect **symbolic speech**—gestures, movements, articles of clothing, and other forms of nonverbal expressive conduct. For example, the Supreme Court has held that the burning of the American flag to protest government policies is a constitutionally protected form of expression.[9] Similarly, the Court has ruled that the placing of a burning cross in another's front yard as a gesture of hate is protected under the First Amendment.[10] In the interests of curbing violence in our society, many Americans have concluded that the courts should give more weight to community interests when deciding cases involving free speech and other First Amendment freedoms. (See this chapter's *Business Law in Action* for a discussion of this issue.)

Corporate Political Speech Political speech by corporations also falls within the protection of the First Amendment. • EXAMPLE 2.3 In *First National Bank of Boston v. Bellotti,* national banking associations and business corporations sought

9. See *Texas v. Johnson,* 491 U.S. 397, 109 S.Ct. 2533, 105 L.Ed.2d 342 (1989).
10. *R.A.V. v. City of St. Paul, Minnesota,* 505 U.S. 377, 112 S.Ct. 2538, 120 L.Ed.2d 305 (1992).

Business Law in Action • INDIVIDUAL RIGHTS VERSUS COMMUNITY INTERESTS

Traditionally, the courts have given the fullest protection possible to free speech and other First Amendment freedoms, even when the result is to allow "hate speech" or "hate crimes" that interfere with the security and welfare of a community. For example, the Minnesota Supreme Court recently concluded that even though a man rode a horse through a gay pride parade and shouted anti-gay slogans, he cannot be prosecuted under a Minnesota "hate crime" statute because the statute violates the First Amendment.[a] The statute criminalized "harassing conduct" that caused a victim to feel "oppressed, persecuted or intimidated." The court concluded that the statute sweeps too broadly because it also criminalizes protected "expressive activity," such as an employer who chastises a worker for tardiness or a law professor who drills a student with the Socratic method.

In a few cases, however, the courts have shown a willingness to take community concerns into consideration when deciding First Amendment cases. For example, the Supreme Court of California recently concluded that the First Amendment right to "peaceably assemble" does not outweigh the community's interests in curbing gang-related violence.[b] According to that court, gang members can be enjoined (prevented) from associating with each other under a Los Angeles "public nuisance" ordinance even though they have not been convicted of a crime.

The Supreme Court of Illinois also recently upheld a Chicago ordinance designed to prevent gangs from loitering on the streets. The ordinance stated that "[w]henever a police officer observes a person who he reasonably believes to be a criminal street gang member loitering in any public place with one or more other persons, he shall order all such persons to disperse and remove themselves from the area."[c]

FOR CRITICAL ANALYSIS

Should ordinances prohibiting gangs from assembling on streets be permissible restraints on First Amendment freedoms?

a. *State v. Machholz,* 574 N.W.2d 415 (Minn. 1998).

b. *People ex rel. Gallo v. Acuna,* 14 Cal.4th 1090, 929 P.2d 596, 60 Cal.Rptr.2d 277 (1997).

c. *Chicago v. Morales,* 177 Ill.2d 440, 687 N.E.2d 53, 227 Ill.Dec. 130 (1997).

¡ REMEMBER!
The First Amendment guarantee of freedom of speech only applies to *government* restrictions on speech.

United States Supreme Court review of a Massachusetts statute that prohibited corporations from making political contributions or expenditures that individuals were permitted to make. The Court ruled that the Massachusetts law was unconstitutional because it violated the right of corporations to freedom of speech.[11] • Similarly, the Court has held that a law forbidding a corporation from using bill inserts to express its views on controversial issues violates the First Amendment.[12] Although in 1990 a more conservative Supreme Court reversed this trend somewhat,[13] corporate political speech continues to be given significant protection under the First Amendment.

Commercial Speech—Advertising The courts also give substantial protection to "commercial" speech, which consists of speech and communications—primarily advertising—made by business firms. The protection given to commercial speech under the First Amendment is not as extensive as that afforded to noncommercial speech, however. A state may restrict certain kinds of advertising, for example, in

11. 435 U.S. 765, 98 S.Ct. 1407, 55 L.Ed.2d 707 (1978).

12. *Consolidated Edison Co. v. Public Service Commission,* 447 U.S. 530, 100 S.Ct. 2326, 65 L.Ed.2d 319 (1980).

13. See *Austin v. Michigan Chamber of Commerce,* 494 U.S. 652, 110 S.Ct. 1391, 108 L.Ed.2d 652 (1990), in which the Court upheld a state law prohibiting corporations from using general corporate funds for independent expenditures in state political campaigns.

the interest of protecting consumers from being misled by the advertising practices. States also have a legitimate interest in the beautification of roadsides, and this interest allows states to place restraints on billboard advertising.

Generally, a restriction on commercial speech will be considered valid as long as it meets the following three criteria: (1) it must seek to implement a substantial government interest, (2) it must directly advance that interest, and (3) it must go no further than necessary to accomplish its objective. At issue in the following case was whether a government agency's decision to prohibit the inclusion of a certain illustration on beer labels unconstitutionally restricted commercial speech.

CASE 2.3 Bad Frog Brewery, Inc. v. New York State Liquor Authority

U.S. Court of Appeals,
Second Circuit, 1998.
134 F.3d 87.
www.tourolaw.edu/2ndCircuit/January98/97-79490.html[a]

HISTORICAL AND CULTURAL SETTING *Hand gestures signifying insults have been in use throughout the world for centuries. Hand gestures regarded as insults in some countries include an extended right thumb, an extended little finger, raised index and middle fingers, and gestures effected with two hands. A gesture using the extended middle finger of either hand (sometimes referred to as "giving the finger" or "flipping the bird") is generally acknowledged to convey an obscene, offensive message: a suggestion to have intercourse with one's self. This gesture is said to have been used by Diogenes (a Greek philosopher in the fourth century* B.C.E. *who was known for his disregard of social niceties) to insult Demosthenes (a Greek statesman and contemporary of Diogenes).*[b]

BACKGROUND AND FACTS Bad Frog Brewery, Inc., makes and sells alcoholic beverages. Some of the beverages feature labels that display a drawing of a frog making the gesture generally known as "giving the finger." Bad Frog's authorized New York distributor, Renaissance Beer Company, applied to the New York State Liquor Authority (NYSLA) for brand label approval, as required by state law before the beer could be sold in New York. The NYSLA denied the application, in part because "the label could appear in grocery and convenience stores, with obvious exposure on the shelf to children of tender age." Bad Frog filed a suit in a federal district court against the NYSLA, asking for, among other things, an injunction against the denial of Bad Frog's application. The court granted a summary judgment in favor of the NYSLA. Bad Frog appealed to the U.S. Court of Appeals for the Second Circuit.

DIFFERENT LABELS ON BEER BOTTLES ARE DISPLAYED. CAN A BREWERY USE ANY TYPE OF LABEL ON ITS BEER? IF NOT, WHAT ARE THE CONSTRAINTS?

a. This page is part of a Web site maintained by the Touro College Jacob D. Fuchsberg Law Center in Huntington, New York.
b. Betty J. Bauml and Franz H. Bauml, *Dictionary of Worldwide Gestures,* 2d ed. (Lanham, Md.: Scarecrow Press, 1997), p. 159.

IN THE WORDS OF THE COURT . . .
JON O. NEWMAN, Circuit Judge:

* * * *

* * * [T]o support its asserted power to ban Bad Frog's labels [NYSLA advances] * * * the State's interest in "protecting children from vulgar and profane advertising" * * * .

CASE 2.3—Continued

[This interest is] substantial * * * . States have a compelling interest in protecting the physical and psychological well-being of minors * * * .

* * * *

* * * NYSLA endeavors to advance the state interest in preventing exposure of children to vulgar displays by taking only the limited step of barring such displays from the labels of alcoholic beverages. In view of the wide currency of vulgar displays throughout contemporary society, including comic books targeted directly at children, barring such displays from labels for alcoholic beverages cannot realistically be expected to reduce children's exposure to such displays to any significant degree.

* * * If New York decides to make a substantial effort to insulate children from vulgar displays in some significant sphere of activity, at least with respect to materials likely to be seen by children, NYSLA's label prohibition might well be found to make a justifiable contribution to the material advancement of such an effort, but its currently isolated response to the perceived problem, applicable only to labels on a product that children cannot purchase, does not suffice. * * * [A] state must demonstrate that its commercial speech limitation is part of a substantial effort to advance a valid state interest, not merely the removal of a few grains of offensive sand from a beach of vulgarity.

* * * *

* * * Even if we were to assume that the state materially advances its asserted interest by shielding children from viewing the Bad Frog labels, it is plainly excessive to prohibit the labels from all use, including placement on bottles displayed in bars and taverns where parental supervision of children is to be expected. Moreover, to whatever extent NYSLA is concerned that children will be harmfully exposed to the Bad Frog labels when wandering without parental supervision around grocery and convenience stores where beer is sold, that concern could be less intrusively dealt with by placing restrictions on the permissible locations where the appellant's products may be displayed within such stores.

DECISION AND REMEDY The U.S. Court of Appeals for the Second Circuit reversed the judgment of the district court and remanded the case for the entry of a judgment in favor of Bad Frog. The NYSLA's ban on the use of the labels lacked a "reasonable fit" with the state's interest in shielding minors from vulgarity, and the NYSLA did not adequately consider alternatives to the ban.

FOR CRITICAL ANALYSIS—Political Consideration *Whose interests are advanced by the banning of certain types of advertising?*

Unprotected Speech The United States Supreme Court has made it clear that certain types of speech will not be given any protection under the First Amendment. Speech that harms the good reputation of another, or defamatory speech (see Chapter 4), will not be protected. Speech that violates criminal laws (such as threatening speech) is not constitutionally protected. Other unprotected speech includes "fighting words," or words that are likely to incite others to respond violently.

The Supreme Court has also held that obscene speech is not protected by the First Amendment. The Court has grappled from time to time with the problem of trying to establish an objective definition of obscene speech. In a 1973 case, *Miller v. California,*[14] the Supreme Court created a test for legal obscenity, which involved a set of requirements that must be met for material to be legally obscene. Under this test, material is obscene if (1) the average person finds that it violates contemporary

14. 413 U.S. 15, 93 S.Ct. 2607, 37 L.Ed.2d 419 (1973).

community standards; (2) the work taken as a whole appeals to a prurient interest in sex; (3) the work shows patently offensive sexual conduct; and (4) the work lacks serious redeeming literary, artistic, political, or scientific merit.

Because community standards vary widely, the *Miller* test has had inconsistent applications, and obscenity remains a constitutionally unsettled issue. Numerous state and federal statutes make it a crime to disseminate obscene materials, however, and such laws have often been upheld by the Supreme Court, including laws prohibiting the sale and possession of child pornography.[15]

Increasingly, the courts are protecting employees against obscene, lewd, or pornographic speech or images in the workplace by holding that such speech constitutes sexual harassment (see Chapter 38). In recent years, obscenity issues have also arisen in relation to materials available on the Internet (this topic is discussed in Chapter 7).

ESTABLISHMENT CLAUSE
The provision in the First Amendment to the Constitution that prohibits Congress from creating any law "respecting an establishment of religion."

FREE EXERCISE CLAUSE
The provision in the First Amendment to the Constitution that prohibits Congress from making any law "prohibiting the free exercise" of religion.

THE FIRST AMENDMENT—FREEDOM OF RELIGION

The First Amendment states that the government may neither establish any religion nor prohibit the free exercise of religious practices. The first part of this constitutional provision is referred to as the **establishment clause,** and the second part is known as the **free exercise clause.** Government action, both federal and state, must be consistent with this constitutional mandate.

15. For example, see *Osborne v. Ohio,* 495 U.S. 103, 110 S.Ct. 1691, 109 L.Ed.2d 98 (1990).

International Perspective • CHURCH AND STATE UNDER ISLAMIC LAW

Today, Muslims constitute over one-half of the population in thirty-five nations, a significant portion of the population in twenty-one other nations, and nearly one-fourth of the global population. The Muslim faith (Islam) is one of the great religions of the world. Increasingly, American businesspersons deal with Muslims in the international marketplace. Yet Americans who would like to understand Islamic law often find it difficult to do so.

This is not really surprising, given the American legal tradition in which church and state are separate entities. Indeed, for many Americans the idea of a state-sponsored religion is regarded as somehow inherently evil. Islamic law, in contrast, does not provide for the separation of church and state—law and religion are one and the same concept. The Islamic religion controls Islamic law and regulates all public and private matters. The governments of Islamic nations, such as Iraq, are to a large extent "theocracies" that govern in accordance with religious principles. This lack of any separation between church and state is perhaps the most difficult aspect of Islamic law for Americans to grasp.

ISLAMIC LAW DOES NOT PROVIDE FOR THE SEPARATION OF CHURCH AND STATE. ARE THERE ASPECTS OF RELIGION THAT PERMEATE THE AMERICAN POLITICAL AND LEGAL SYSTEM?

FOR CRITICAL ANALYSIS
Is the union of religion and law incompatible with a democratic form of government?

The Establishment Clause The establishment clause prohibits the government from establishing a state-sponsored religion, as well as from passing laws that promote (aid or endorse) religion or that show a preference for one religion over another. The establishment clause does not require a complete separation of church and state, however. On the contrary, it requires the government to accommodate religions.[16]

The establishment clause covers all conflicts about such matters as the legality of state and local government support for a particular religion, government aid to religious organizations and schools, the government's allowing or requiring school prayers, and the teaching of evolution versus fundamentalist theories of creation. The Supreme Court has held that to be constitutional, a government law or policy must be secular in aim, must not have the primary effect of advancing or inhibiting religions, and must not create "an excessive government entanglement with religion."[17] Generally, federal or state regulation that does not promote religion or place a significant burden on religion is constitutional even if it has some impact on religion.

• **EXAMPLE 2.4** "Sunday closing laws" make the performance of some commercial activities on Sunday illegal. These statutes, also known as "blue laws" (from the color of the paper on which an early Sunday law was written), have been upheld on the ground that it is a legitimate function of government to provide a day of rest. The United States Supreme Court has held that the closing laws, although originally of a religious character, have taken on the secular purpose of promoting the health and welfare of workers.[18] Even though Sunday closing laws admittedly make it easier for Christians to attend religious services, the Court has viewed this effect as an incidental, not a primary, purpose of Sunday closing laws. •

ETHICAL ISSUE 2.2 ***Do religious displays on public property violate the establishment clause?*** The thorny issue of whether religious displays on public property violate the establishment clause often arises during the holiday season. Time and again, the courts have wrestled with this issue, but it has never been resolved in a way that satisfies everyone. In a 1984 case, the United States Supreme Court decided that a city's official Christmas display, which included a crèche (Nativity scene), did not violate the establishment clause because it was just one part of a larger holiday display that featured secular symbols, such as reindeer and candy canes.[19] In a later case, the Court held that the presence of a crèche within a county courthouse violated the establishment clause because it was not in close proximity to nonreligious symbols, including a Christmas tree, which were located outside, on the building's steps. The presence of a menorah (a nine-branched candelabrum used in celebrating Chanukah) on the building's steps, however, did not violate the establishment clause because the menorah was situated in close proximity to the Christmas tree.[20] The courts continue to apply this reasoning in cases involving similar issues.

The Free Exercise Clause The free exercise clause guarantees that a person can hold any religious belief that he or she wants; or a person can have no religious belief.

16. *Zorach v. Clauson,* 343 U.S. 306, 72 S.Ct. 679, 96 L.Ed. 954 (1952).
17. *Lemon v. Kurtzman,* 403 U.S. 602, 91 S.Ct. 2105, 29 L.Ed.2d 745 (1971).
18. *McGowan v. Maryland,* 366 U.S. 420, 81 S.Ct. 1101, 6 L.Ed.2d 393 (1961).
19. *Lynch v. Donnelly,* 465 U.S. 668, 104 S.Ct. 1355, 79 L.Ed.2d 604 (1984).
20. See, for example, *County of Allegheny v. American Civil Liberties Union,* 492 U.S. 573, 109 S.Ct. 3086, 106 L.Ed.2d 472 (1989).

When religious *practices* work against public policy and the public welfare, however, the government can act. For example, regardless of a child's or parent's religious beliefs, the government can require certain types of vaccinations. Similarly, although children of Jehovah's Witnesses are not required to say the Pledge of Allegiance at school, their parents cannot prevent them from accepting medical treatment (such as blood transfusions) if in fact their lives are in danger. Additionally, public school students can be required to study from textbooks chosen by school authorities.

For business firms, an important issue involves the accommodation that businesses must make for the religious beliefs of their employees. For example, if an employee's religion prohibits him or her from working on a certain day of the week or at a certain type of job, the employer must make a reasonable attempt to accommodate these religious requirements. Employers must reasonably accommodate an employee's religious beliefs even if the beliefs are not based on the tenets or dogma of particular church, sect, or denomination. The only requirement is that the belief be religious in nature and sincerely held by the employee. (We will look further at this issue in Chapter 38, in the context of employment discrimination.)

The Letter of the Law — Accommodating Snake Bites?

Title VII of the 1964 Civil Rights Act, which prohibits employment discrimination (see Chapter 35), requires employers to accommodate the religious needs of their workers. But to what extent must employers do so? There are no hard-and-fast answers to this question. For example, in one case a worker became ill after being bitten by a snake during a religious snake-handling service. The employee requested a leave of absence, but he refused to obtain the required physician's note because his religious beliefs precluded medical treatment. The employer granted the worker a leave of absence after the first snake bite but fired the worker after he took subsequent unexcused leaves for other snake bites.

The employer should have known better, at least according to the federal district court that heard the case brought by the employee for religious discrimination. The court held that the employer failed to accommodate the employee's religious beliefs and awarded the employee $20,500 in damages.[a]

THE BOTTOM LINE

Employers are advised not to jump to conclusions about what might or might not be a religious belief that requires reasonable accommodation.

a. *The National Law Journal,* March 16, 1998, p. A19.

Due Process and Equal Protection

Two other constitutional guarantees of great significance to Americans are mandated by the due process clauses of the Fifth and Fourteenth Amendments and the equal protection clause of the Fourteenth Amendment.

Due Process

• **DUE PROCESS CLAUSE**
The provisions of the Fifth and Fourteenth Amendments to the Constitution that guarantee that no person shall be deprived of life, liberty, or property without due process of law. Similar clauses are found in most state constitutions.

Both the Fifth and the Fourteenth Amendments provide that no person shall be deprived "of life, liberty, or property, without due process of law." The **due process clause** of each of these constitutional amendments has two aspects—procedural and substantive.

Procedural Due Process Procedural due process requires that any government decision to take life, liberty, or property must be made fairly. For example, fair proce-

"What is due process of law depends on circumstances. It varies with the subject-matter and necessities of the situation."

OLIVER WENDELL HOLMES, JR., 1841–1935
(Associate justice of the United States Supreme Court, 1902–1932)

dures must be used in determining whether a person will be subjected to punishment or have some burden imposed on him or her. Fair procedure has been interpreted as requiring that the person have at least an opportunity to object to a proposed action before a fair, neutral decision maker (which need not be a judge). Thus, for example, if a driver's license is construed as a property interest, some sort of opportunity to object to its suspension or termination by the state must be provided.

Substantive Due Process Substantive due process focuses on the content, or substance, of legislation. If a law or other governmental action limits a *fundamental right,* it will be held to violate substantive due process unless it promotes a compelling or overriding state interest. Fundamental rights include interstate travel, privacy, voting, and all First Amendment rights. Compelling state interests could include, for example, the public's safety. • EXAMPLE 2.5 Laws designating speed limits may be upheld even though they affect interstate travel, if they are shown to reduce highway fatalities, because the state has a compelling interest in protecting the lives of its citizens. •

In situations not involving fundamental rights, a law or action does not violate substantive due process if it rationally relates to any legitimate governmental end. It is almost impossible for a law or action to fail the "rationality" test. Under this test, virtually any business regulation will be upheld as reasonable—the United States Supreme Court has sustained insurance regulations, price and wage controls, banking controls, and controls of unfair competition and trade practices against substantive due process challenges.

• EXAMPLE 2.6 If a state legislature enacted a law imposing a fifteen-year term of imprisonment without a trial on all businesspersons who appeared in their own television commercials, the law would be unconstitutional on both substantive and procedural grounds. Substantive review would invalidate the legislation because it abridges freedom of speech. Procedurally, the law is unfair because it imposes the penalty without giving the accused a chance to defend his or her actions. • The lack of procedural due process will cause a court to invalidate any statute or prior court decision. Similarly, a denial of substantive due process requires courts to overrule any state or federal law that violates the Constitution. In the following case, the court considered whether the retroactive application of a statute violated a defendant's due process rights.

CASE 2.4 Shadburne-Vinton v. Dalkon Shield Claimants Trust

United States Court of Appeals,
Fourth Circuit, 1995.
60 F.3d 1071.
www.law.emory.edu/4circuit/july95/index.html[a]

HISTORICAL AND TECHNOLOGICAL SETTING *An intrauterine device (IUD) is a contraceptive device made of plastic and sometimes containing copper. Today, IUDs are generally reliable, although some women experience painful periods, and there is a risk of pelvic infection. In the 1980s, however, the Dalkon Shield IUD, manufactured by the A. H. Robins Company, was believed to have caused much more serious injuries to many of the women who used it.*

BACKGROUND AND FACTS Susan Shadburne-Vinton used a Dalkon Shield IUD from 1974 through 1976. Claiming that the IUD had rendered her infertile and caused her to develop multiple sclerosis, Shadburne-Vinton filed suit against the A. H. Robins Company in a federal district court in 1983. The court dismissed her suit under an Oregon statute that limited the time for filing such suits to "not later than eight years" after the date on which a product was purchased. Shadburne-Vinton appealed, but the appeal was suspended when Robins filed for bankruptcy. During the suspension, the Oregon legislature amended the statute to exclude IUD manufacturers. The

(Continued)

a. This is a page within the Web site of the Emory University School of Law that lists the published opinions of the U.S. Court of Appeals for the Fourth Circuit for July 1995. Scroll down the list of cases to the *Shadburne-Vinton* case. Click on the case name to access the opinion.

CASE 2.4—Continued

amendment expressly stated that it applied retroactively. When Shadburne-Vinton's case went forward, the Dalkon Shield Claimants Trust (which substituted for Robins as a result of the bankruptcy proceeding) argued that retroactive application of the amendment to the statute would violate the trust's due process rights. The court agreed and issued a judgment in favor of the trust. Shadburne-Vinton appealed.

IN THE WORDS OF THE COURT . . .
CHAPMAN, Senior Circuit Judge:

* * * *

* * * [T]he Due Process Clause of the Fifth Amendment allows retroactive application of either federal or state statutes as long as the statute serves a legitimate legislative purpose that is furthered by rational means. * * *

* * * *

* * * [W]e must determine whether the Oregon statute * * * , which expressly states that it applies retroactively, serves a legitimate legislative purpose that is furthered by rational means. After extensive hearings on the legislation, the Oregon legislature determined that retroactive application of the Special IUD Statute was fair and equitable to all parties involved. Because many of the women suffered injuries from the IUD in the early to mid-1970s, and the link between the IUD and the injuries it caused was not discovered until the early 1980s, the unamended statute * * * barred the claims of many women. The Oregon Legislature determined that the Special IUD Statute was necessary to provide these claimants with a fair opportunity to litigate their claims.

DECISION AND REMEDY The U.S. Court of Appeals for the Fourth Circuit concluded that the statute did not violate the due process clause of the Fifth Amendment and reversed the lower court's ruling.

FOR CRITICAL ANALYSIS—**Political Consideration**
In whose best interest is it to set a time limit within which a lawsuit must be brought?

Equal Protection

• **EQUAL PROTECTION CLAUSE**
The provision in the Fourteenth Amendment to the Constitution that guarantees that no state will "deny to any person within its jurisdiction the equal protection of the laws." This clause mandates that the state governments treat similarly situated individuals in a similar manner.

Under the Fourteenth Amendment, a state may not "deny to any person within its jurisdiction the equal protection of the laws." The United States Supreme Court has used the due process clause of the Fifth Amendment to make the **equal protection clause** applicable to the federal government as well. Equal protection means that the government must treat similarly situated individuals in a similar manner.

Both substantive due process and equal protection require review of the substance of the law or other governmental action rather than review of the procedures used. When a law or action limits the liberty of all persons to do something, it may violate substantive due process; when a law or action limits the liberty of some persons but not others, it may violate the equal protection clause. • **EXAMPLE 2.7** If a law prohibits all persons from buying contraceptive devices, it raises a substantive due process question; if it prohibits only unmarried persons from buying the same devices, it raises an equal protection issue. •

Basically, in determining whether a law or action violates the equal protection clause, a court will consider questions similar to those previously noted as applicable in a substantive due process review. Under an equal protection inquiry, when a law or action distinguishes between or among individuals, the basis for the distinction—that is, the classification—is examined. Depending on the classification, the courts apply different levels of scrutiny, or "tests," to determine whether the law or action violates the equal protection clause.

Minimal Scrutiny—The "Rational Basis" Test Generally, laws regulating economic and social matters are presumed to be valid and are subject to only minimal scrutiny. A classification will be considered valid if there is any conceivable "rational basis" on which the classification might relate to any legitimate government interest. It is almost impossible for a law or action to fail the rational basis test.

• **EXAMPLE 2.8** A city ordinance that in effect prohibits all pushcart vendors except a specific few from operating in a particular area of the city will be upheld if the city proffers a rational basis—perhaps regulation and reduction of traffic in the particular area—for the ordinance. In contrast, a law that provides unemployment benefits only to people over six feet tall would violate the guarantee of equal protection. There is no rational basis for determining the distribution of unemployment compensation on the basis of height. Such a distinction could not further any legitimate government objective.•

In the following case, the court applied the rational basis test to consider the constitutionality of a government-imposed dress code for cab drivers.

CASE 2.5 Bah v. City of Atlanta

United States Court of Appeals,
Eleventh Circuit, 1997.
103 F.3d 964.
www.law.emory.edu/11circuit/jan97/96-8095.opa.html[a]

HISTORICAL AND SOCIAL SETTING *In the first third of the twentieth century, dress codes were imposed in a variety of occupations. When particular clothing was not expressly required, there were social norms that dictated appropriate dress. Suits were often considered proper attire for men, for example, even in casual situations. After World War II, men began to stop wearing hats. This started a trend toward more casual dress. In the 1960s, the trend accelerated, with an explosion of flamboyant, individual styles of dress and casual clothes, such as denim. By the 1990s, the diverse cultural background of Americans was influencing this fashion mix.*

a. This is a page within an online library of court decisions maintained by the Hugh F. Macmillan Law Library at Emory University School of Law in Atlanta, Georgia.

BACKGROUND AND FACTS The Atlanta City Council adopted a dress code for cab drivers that required them, while driving a cab, to wear "shoes which entirely cover the foot (no sandals) and dark pants to ankle length or dark skirt or dress and solid white or light blue shirt or solid white or light blue blouse with sleeves and folded collar. * * * If a hat is worn, it shall be a base-ball style cap with an Atlanta or taxicab theme."[b] Mohamed Bah, a cab driver, was cited for violating the code and filed a suit in a federal district court against the city. Bah contended in part that the code violated the equal protection clause and asked the court to enjoin its enforcement. The city offered several reasons for the code, including "public safety," "identification of gypsy taxicab drivers," and "promoting a safe image." The court issued the injunction. The city appealed to the U.S. Court of Appeals for the Eleventh Circuit.

b. Atlanta Code of Ordinances Section 14-8005(d)(2). The Atlanta Code of Ordinances was renumbered in 1996. This is the prior number for this section, which is the number that the court cited in this case.

IN THE WORDS OF THE COURT . . .

PER CURIAM [by the whole court]:

* * * *

* * * Bah does not contend * * * that the dress code burdens a fundamental right or targets a suspect class. Both Bah and the City agree that rational basis is the appropriate level of scrutiny.

(Continued)

CASE 2.5—Continued

[Other courts have stated that in] a rational basis analysis, the legislative enactment carries a "strong presumption of validity." Review of enactments must be a "paradigm of judicial restraint." "[T]hose attacking the rationality of the legislative classification have the burden to negative every conceivable basis which might support it." * * *

Following these decisional directives, we readily conclude that the district court erred in finding that the dress code is not rationally related to a legitimate government interest. * * * .

[E]ven if the district court was correct in rejecting the two reasons it discussed—public safety and identification of gypsy taxicab drivers—there is another reason for the dress code that is rationally related to a legitimate government interest. As the City explained in the district court and this Court, the dress code is rationally related to its legitimate interest in promoting a safe image. Drivers of vehicles for hire, particularly taxicab drivers, are often among the first people that out-of-town visitors encounter. Such visitors often find themselves getting into a vehicle for hire driven by a total stranger, sometimes at night and sometimes while they are alone. It is in the City's interest to promote a safe appearance and image, and a rational way to do that is by prescribing that its self-styled "ambassadors" wear innocuous, conventional, relatively uniform clothing.

DECISION AND REMEDY The U.S. Court of Appeals for the Eleventh Circuit reversed the decision of the lower court and remanded the case. The appellate court held that the dress code was rationally related to a legitimate government objective and thus did not violate the equal protection clause.

FOR CRITICAL ANALYSIS—Social Consideration *Would it be constitutional to impose a dress code on others who are licensed by the city and who deal with out-of-town visitors—food servers, bellhops, and outdoor vendors, for example?*

Intermediate Scrutiny A harder standard to meet, that of "intermediate scrutiny," is applied in cases involving discrimination based on gender or legitimacy. Laws using these classifications must be substantially related to important government objectives. • **EXAMPLE 2.9** An important government objective is preventing illegitimate teenage pregnancies. Because males and females are not similarly situated in this circumstance—only females can become pregnant—a law that punishes men but not women for statutory rape will be upheld. A state law requiring illegitimate children to bring paternity suits within six years of their births, however, will be struck down if legitimate children are allowed to seek support from their parents at any time. •

Strict Scrutiny The most difficult standard to meet is that of "strict scrutiny." Very few cases survive strict-scrutiny analysis. Strict scrutiny is applied when a law or action inhibits some persons' exercise of a fundamental right or is based on a suspect trait (such as race, national origin, or citizenship status). Strict scrutiny means that the court will examine the law or action involved very closely, and the law or action will be allowed to stand only if it is *necessary to promote a compelling state interest.*

• **EXAMPLE 2.10** Suppose that a city gives preference to minority applicants in awarding construction contracts. Because the policy is based on suspect traits (race and national origin), it will violate the equal protection clause *unless* it is necessary to promote a compelling state interest. Courts have often held that states have a compelling interest in remedying past unconstitutional or illegal discrimination. The Supreme Court has declared, however, that such programs must be narrowly tailored. In other words, the city must identify the past unconstitutional or illegal discrimination against minority construction firms that it is attempting to correct, go no further than necessary to correct the problem, and change or drop its program once it has succeeded in correcting the problem.[21] •

Privacy Rights

Today, virtually all institutions and professionals with which an individual has dealings—including schools, physicians and dentists, insurance companies, mail-order houses, banking institutions, credit-card companies, and mortgage firms—obtain information about that individual and store it in their computer files. In addition,

21. *Adarand Constructors, Inc. v. Peña,* 515 U.S. 200, 115 S.Ct. 2097, 132 L.Ed.2d 158 (1995).

EXHIBIT 2–1 • Federal Legislation Relating to Privacy

TITLE	PROVISIONS CONCERNING PRIVACY
Freedom of Information Act (1966)	Provides that individuals have a right to obtain access to information about them collected in government files.
Fair Credit Reporting Act (1970)	Provides that consumers have the right to be informed of the nature and scope of a credit investigation, the kind of information that is being compiled, and the names of the firms or individuals who will be receiving the report.
Crime Control Act (1973)	Safeguards the confidentiality of information amassed for certain state criminal systems.
Family and Educational Rights and Privacy Act (1974)	Limits access to computer-stored records of education-related evaluations and grades in private and public colleges and universities.
Privacy Act (1974)	Protects the privacy of individuals about whom the federal government has information. Specifically, the act provides as follows: 1. Agencies originating, using, disclosing, or otherwise manipulating personal information must ensure the reliability of the information and provide safeguards against its misuse. 2. Information compiled for one purpose cannot be used for another without the concerned individual's permission. 3. Individuals must be able to find out what data concerning them are being compiled and how the data will be used. 4. Individuals must be given a means by which to correct inaccurate data.
Tax Reform Act (1976)	Preserves the privacy of personal financial information.
Right to Financial Privacy Act (1978)	Prohibits financial institutions from providing the federal government with access to customers' records unless a customer authorizes the disclosure.
Electronic Fund Transfer Act (1978)	Prohibits the use of a computer without authorization to retrieve data in a financial institution's or consumer reporting agency's files.
Cable Communications Policy Act (1984)	Regulates access to information collected by cable service operators on subscribers to cable services.
Electronic Communications Privacy Act (1986)	Prohibits the interception of information communicated by electronic means.

numerous government agencies, such as the Census Bureau, the Social Security Administration, and the Internal Revenue Service, collect and store data concerning individuals' incomes, expenses, marital status, and other personal history and habits. Any time an individual applies for a driver's license, a credit card, or even telephone service, information concerning that individual is gathered and stored. Frequently, this personal information finds its way to credit bureaus, marketing departments and firms, or other organizations without the permission or even the knowledge of the individuals concerned.

Although there is no specific guarantee of a right to privacy in the Constitution, such a right has been derived from guarantees found in the First, Third, Fourth, Fifth, and Ninth Amendments. Furthermore, a personal right to privacy has been held to be so fundamental as to be applicable at both the state and the federal levels. Additionally, invasion of another's privacy is a civil wrong (see Chapter 4), and over the last several decades legislation has been passed at the federal level to protect the privacy of individuals in several areas of concern (see Exhibit 2–1). In the business context, issues of privacy often arise in the employment context, a topic we will cover in detail in Chapter 37.

An area of pressing concern today is how to secure privacy rights in an online world. We will discuss this important topic in Chapter 7.

Key Terms

Bill of Rights 43

checks and balances 35

commerce clause 36

due process clause 50

equal protection clause 52

establishment clause 48

federal form of government 35

free exercise clause 48

police powers 39

preemption 41

supremacy clause 41

symbolic speech 44

Chapter Summary • Constitutional Law

The Constitutional Powers of Government (See pages 35–36.)	The U.S. Constitution established a federal form of government, in which government powers are shared by the national government and the state governments. At the national level, government powers are divided among the legislative, executive, and judicial branches.
The Commerce Clause (See pages 36–41.)	1. *The breadth of the commerce clause*—The commerce clause expressly permits Congress to regulate commerce. Over time, courts expansively interpreted this clause, and today the commerce power authorizes the national government, at least theoretically, to regulate every commercial enterprise in the United States. 2. *The regulatory powers of the states*—Under their police powers, state governments may regulate private activities to protect or promote the public order, health, safety, morals, and general welfare. If state regulations substantially interfere with interstate commerce, they will be held to violate the commerce clause of the U.S. Constitution.
The Supremacy Clause (See page 41.)	The U.S. Constitution provides that the Constitution, laws, and treaties of the United States are "the supreme Law of the Land." Whenever a state law directly conflicts with a federal law, the state law is rendered invalid.

Chapter Summary • Constitutional Law, Continued

The Taxing and Spending Powers (See pages 41–42.)	The U.S. Constitution gives Congress the power to impose uniform taxes throughout the United States and to spend revenues accumulated from the taxing power. Congress can spend revenues to promote any objective it deems worthwhile, so long as it does not violate the Bill of Rights.
Business and the Bill of Rights (See pages 43–50.)	The Bill of Rights, which consists of the first ten amendments to the U.S. Constitution, was adopted in 1791 and embodies a series of protections for individuals—and in some cases, business entities—against various types of interference by the federal government. Freedoms guaranteed by the First Amendment that affect businesses include the following: 1. *Freedom of speech*—Speech, including symbolic speech, is given the fullest possible protection by the courts. Corporate political speech and commercial speech also receive substantial protection under the First Amendment. Certain types of speech, such as defamatory speech and lewd or obscene speech, are not protected under the First Amendment. 2. *Freedom of religion*—Under the First Amendment, the government may neither establish any religion (the establishment clause) nor prohibit the free exercise of religion (the free exercise clause).
Due Process and Equal Protection (See pages 50–55.)	1. *Due process*—Both the Fifth and the Fourteenth Amendments provide that no person shall be deprived of "life, liberty, or property, without due process of law." Procedural due process requires that any government decision to take life, liberty, or property must be made fairly, using fair procedures. Substantive due process focuses on the content of legislation. Generally, a law that is not compatible with the Constitution violates substantive due process unless the law promotes a compelling state interest, such as public safety. 2. *Equal protection*—Under the Fourteenth Amendment, a state may not "deny to any person within its jurisdiction the equal protection of the laws." A law or action that limits the liberty of some persons but not others may violate the equal protection clause. Such a law may be deemed valid, however, if there is a rational basis for the discriminatory treatment of a given group or if the law substantially relates to an important government objective.
Privacy Rights (See pages 55–56.)	There is no specific guarantee of a right to privacy in the Constitution, but such a right has been derived from guarantees found in other constitutional amendments.

For Review

❶ What is the basic structure of the U.S. government?
❷ What constitutional clause gives the federal government the power to regulate commercial activities among the various states?
❸ What constitutional clause allows laws enacted by the federal government to take priority over conflicting state laws?
❹ What is the Bill of Rights? What freedoms are guaranteed by the First Amendment?
❺ Where in the Constitution can the due process clause be found?

Questions and Case Problems

2–1. Government Powers. The framers of the Constitution feared the twin evils of tyranny and anarchy. Discuss how specific provisions of the Constitution and the Bill of Rights reflect these fears and protect against both of these extremes.

2–2. Commercial Speech. A mayoral election is about to be held in a large U.S. city. One of the candidates is Luis Delgado, and his campaign supporters wish to post campaign signs on lampposts and utility posts throughout the city. A city ordinance, however, prohibits the posting of any signs on public property. Delgado's supporters contend that the city ordinance is unconstitutional, because it violates their rights to free speech. What factors might a court consider in determining the constitutionality of this ordinance?

2–3. Commerce Clause. Suppose that Georgia enacts a law requiring the use of contoured rear-fender mudguards on trucks and trailers operating within its state lines. The statute further makes it illegal for trucks and trailers to use straight mudguards. In thirty-five other states, straight mudguards are legal. Moreover, in the neighboring state of Florida, straight mudguards are explicitly required by law. There is some evidence suggesting that contoured mudguards might be a little safer than straight mudguards. Discuss whether this Georgia statute would violate the commerce clause of the U.S. Constitution.

2–4. Freedom of Religion. A business has a backlog of orders, and to meet its deadlines, management decides to run the firm seven days a week, eight hours a day. One of the employees, Marjorie Tollens, refuses to work on Saturday on religious grounds. Her refusal to work means that the firm may not meet its production deadlines and may therefore suffer a loss of future business. The firm fires Tollens and replaces her with an employee who is willing to work seven days a week. Tollens claims that her employer, in terminating her employment, violated her constitutional right to the free exercise of her religion. Do you agree? Why or why not?

2–5. Equal Protection. In 1988, the Nebraska legislature enacted a statute that required any motorcycle operator or passenger on Nebraska's highways to wear a protective helmet. Eugene Robotham, a licensed motorcycle operator, sued the state of Nebraska to block enforcement of the law. Robotham asserted, among other things, that the statute violated the equal protection clause, because it placed requirements on motorcyclists that were not imposed on other motorists. Will the court agree with Robotham that the law violates the equal protection clause? Why or why not? [*Robotham v. State,* 241 Neb. 379, 488 N.W.2d 533 (1992)]

2–6. Commerce Clause. Taylor owned a bait business in Maine and arranged to have live baitfish imported into the state. The importation of the baitfish violated a Maine statute. Taylor was charged with violating a federal statute that makes it a federal crime to transport fish in interstate commerce in violation of state law. Taylor moved to dismiss the charges on the ground that the Maine statute unconstitutionally burdened interstate commerce. Maine intervened to defend the validity of its statute, arguing that the law legitimately protected the state's fisheries from parasites and nonnative species that might be included in shipments of live baitfish. Were Maine's interests in protecting its fisheries from parasites and nonnative species sufficient to justify the burden placed on interstate commerce by the Maine statute? Discuss. [*Maine v. Taylor,* 477 U.S. 131, 106 S.Ct. 2440, 91 L.Ed.2d 110 (1986)]

2–7. Freedom of Religion. Isaiah Brown was the director of the information services department for Polk County, Iowa. During department meetings in his office, he allowed occasional prayers and, in addressing one meeting, referred to Bible passages related to sloth and "work ethics." There was no apparent disruption of the work routine, but the county administrator reprimanded Brown. Later, the administrator ordered Brown to remove from his office all items with a religious connotation. Brown sued the county, alleging that the reprimand and the order violated, among other things, the free exercise clause of the First Amendment. Could the county be held liable for violating Brown's constitutional rights? Discuss. [*Brown v. Polk County, Iowa,* 61 F.3d 650 (8th Cir. 1995)]

2–8. Equal Protection. With the objectives of preventing crime, maintaining property values, and preserving the quality of urban life, New York City enacted an ordinance to regulate the locations of commercial establishments that featured adult entertainment. The ordinance expressly applied to female, but not male, topless entertainment. Adele Buzzetti owned the Cozy Cabin, a New York City cabaret, that featured female topless dancers. Buzzetti and an anonymous dancer filed a suit in a federal district court against the city, asking the court to block the enforcement of the ordinance. The plaintiffs argued in part that the ordinance violated the equal protection clause. Under the equal protection clause, what standard applies to the court's consideration of this ordinance? Under this test, how should the court rule? Why? [*Buzzetti v. City of New York,* 140 F.3d 134 (2d Cir. 1998)]

2–9. Free Speech. The City of Tacoma, Washington, enacted an ordinance that prohibited the playing of car sound systems at a volume that would be "audible" at a distance greater than fifty feet. Dwight Holland was arrested and convicted for violating the ordinance. The conviction was later dismissed but Holland filed a civil suit in a Washington state court against the city. He claimed in part that the ordinance violated his freedom of speech under the First Amendment. On what basis might the court conclude that this ordinance is constitutional? (Hint: In playing a sound system, was Holland actually expressing himself?) [*Holland v. City of Tacoma,* 90 Wash.App. 533, 954 P.2d 290 (1998)]

A QUESTION OF ETHICS AND SOCIAL RESPONSIBILITY

2–10. Carol Elewski, a resident of Syracuse, New York, brought an action to enjoin (prevent) the city from displaying a crèche in a city park during the holidays. The crèche, accompanied by a religious banner, was situated at the foot of a decorated evergreen tree and surrounded by sawhorse barricades containing the names of the mayor and a municipal agency. The downtown merchants supported the display to attract shoppers. There were secular decorations in neighboring areas of the park, and a menorah was displayed in another city park located a block away. In view of these facts, consider the following questions. [*Elewski v. City of Syracuse,* 123 F.3d 51 (2d Cir. 1997)]

1. Does the display of the crèche and the religious banner on city property violate the establishment clause? How might the precedents established by the Supreme Court on this issue (see *Ethical Issue 2.2*) apply to this set of facts?
2. Are the crèche and the menorah in close enough proximity to be considered part of one "display"?
3. How can a city avoid the appearance of endorsing one religion over another if it includes symbols from some religions—but not all religions—in its seasonal displays?

FOR CRITICAL ANALYSIS

2–11. In recent years, many people have criticized the film and entertainment industries for promoting violence by exposing the American public, and particularly American youth, to extremely violent films and song lyrics. Do you think that the right to free speech can (or should) be traded off to reduce violence in America?

Online Activities

ONLINE EXERCISE 2–1

The Center for Democracy and Technology (CDT) is a nonprofit organization dedicated to promoting civil liberties on the Internet. One of CDT's major concerns is the lack of privacy or possible invasions of privacy that can occur on the Internet. Access the CDT's Web site at

www.cdt.org

and then do the following:

- Select CDT's "Guide to Online Privacy," and browse through the contents of that page. Describe at least three of CDT's recommendations for how you can maintain the privacy of Internet communications.
- Take the "Privacy Quiz." List three of the questions included in the quiz, and give the correct answers to each question.

ONLINE EXERCISE 2–2

Go to

www.freedomforum.org/first/welcome.asp.

This is the Web site of Vanderbilt University's Freedom Forum First Amendment Center. Select one of the First Amendment cases described at this site, and answer the following questions about the case:

- What First Amendment issue was involved in the case?
- How and why did the case arise? (Summarize briefly the "facts" of the case.)
- What court decided the case? When?
- What did the court decide, and why?

Before the Test

Go to the *Business Law Today* home page at http://blt.westbuslaw.com. Click on TestTutor.® You will find twenty interactive questions relating to this chapter.

CHAPTER 3

Courts & Procedures

> "The Judicial Department comes home in its effects to every man's fireside: it passes on his property, his reputation, his life, his all."
>
> John Marshall, 1755–1835
> (Chief justice of the United States Supreme Court, 1801–1835)

CONTENTS

LEARNING OBJECTIVES

After reading this chapter, you should be able to:

1. Explain the concepts of jurisdiction and venue.
2. State the requirements for federal jurisdiction.
3. Identify the basic components of the federal and state court systems.
4. Compare and contrast the functions of trial courts and appellate courts.
5. Discuss the various ways in which disputes can be resolved outside the court system.

As Chief Justice John Marshall remarked in the above quotation, ultimately, we are all affected by what the courts say and do. This is particularly true in the business world—nearly every businessperson faces either a potential or an actual lawsuit at some time or another in his or her career. For this reason, anyone contemplating a career in business will benefit from an understanding of American court systems, including the mechanics of lawsuits.

In this chapter, after examining the judiciary's overall role in the American governmental scheme, we discuss some basic requirements that must be met before a party may bring a lawsuit before a particular court. We then look at the court systems of the United States in some detail and, to clarify judicial procedures, follow a hypothetical case through a state court system. Even though there are fifty-two court systems—one for each of the fifty states, one for the District of Columbia, plus a federal system—similarities abound. Keep in mind that the federal courts are not superior to the state courts; they are simply an independent system of courts, which derives its authority from

Article III, Section 2, of the U.S. Constitution. The chapter concludes with an overview of some alternative methods of settling disputes.

Note that technological developments are affecting court procedures just as they are affecting all other areas of the law. This important topic will be explored in detail in Chapter 7.

The Judiciary's Role in American Government

As you learned in Chapter 1, the body of American law is vast and complex. It includes the federal and state constitutions, statutes passed by legislative bodies, administrative law, and the case decisions and legal principles that form the common law. These laws would be meaningless, however, without the courts to interpret and apply them. This is the essential role of the judiciary—the courts—in the American governmental system: to interpret and apply the law.

As the branch of government entrusted with interpreting the laws, the judiciary can decide, among other things, whether the laws or actions of the other two branches are constitutional. The process for making such a determination is known as **judicial review.** The power of judicial review enables the judicial branch to act as a check on the other two branches of government, in line with the checks-and-balances system established by the U.S. Constitution.

• **JUDICIAL REVIEW**
The process by which a court decides on the constitutionality of legislative enactments and actions of the executive branch.

The power of judicial review was not mentioned in the Constitution, but the concept was not new at the time the nation was founded. Indeed, prior to 1789 state courts had already overturned state legislative acts that conflicted with state constitutions. Additionally, many of the founders expected the United States Supreme Court to assume a similar role with respect to the federal Constitution. Alexander Hamilton and James Madison both emphasized the importance of judicial review in their essays urging the adoption of the new Constitution.

"I am unaware that any nation of the globe has hitherto organized a judicial power in the same manner as the Americans . . . . A more imposing judicial power was never constituted by any people."

ALEXIS DE TOCQUEVILLE, 1805–1859
(French historian and statesman)

The doctrine of judicial review was not legally established, however, until 1803, when the United States Supreme Court rendered its decision in *Marbury v. Madison.*[1] In that case, the Supreme Court stated, "It is emphatically the province and duty of the Judicial Department to say what the law is. . . . If two laws conflict with each other, the courts must decide on the operation of each. . . . So if the law be in opposition to the Constitution . . . [t]he Court must determine which of these conflicting rules governs the case. This is the very essence of judicial duty." Since the *Marbury v. Madison* decision, details of which are offered in the *Landmark in the Law* below, the power of judicial review has remained unchallenged. Today, this power is exercised by both federal and state courts.

1. 5 U.S. (1 Cranch) 137, 2 L.Ed. 60 (1803).

Landmark in the Law • *MARBURY v. MADISON* (1803)

In the edifice of American law, the *Marbury v. Madison* decision in 1803 can be viewed as the keystone of the constitutional arch. The facts of the case were as follows. John Adams, who had lost his bid for reelection to Thomas Jefferson in 1800, feared the Jeffersonians' antipathy toward business and toward a strong central government. Adams thus worked feverishly to "pack" the judiciary with loyal Federalists (those who believed in a strong national government) by appointing what came to be called "midnight judges" just before Jefferson took office. All of the fifty-nine judicial appointment letters had to be certified and delivered, but Adams's secretary of state (John Marshall) had only succeeded in delivering forty-two of them by the time Jefferson took over as president. Jefferson, of course, refused to order his secretary of state, James Madison, to deliver the remaining commissions.

William Marbury and three others to whom the commissions had not been delivered sought a writ of *mandamus* (an order directing a government official to fulfill a duty) from the United States Supreme Court, as authorized by Section 13 of the Judiciary Act of 1789. As fate would have it, John Marshall had stepped down as Adams's secretary of state only to become chief justice of the Supreme Court. Marshall faced a dilemma: If he ordered the commissions delivered, the new secretary of state (Madison) could simply refuse to deliver them—and the Court had no way to compel action, because it had no police force. At the same time, if Marshall simply allowed the new administration to do as it wished, the Court's power would be severely eroded.

Marshall masterfully fashioned a decision that did not require anyone to do anything but at the same time enlarged the power of the Supreme Court. He stated that the highest court did not have the power to issue a writ of *mandamus* in this particular case. Marshall pointed out that although the Judiciary Act of 1789 specified that the Supreme Court could issue writs of *mandamus* as part of its original jurisdiction, Article III of the Constitution, which spelled out the Court's original jurisdiction, did not mention writs of *mandamus*. Because Congress did not have the right to expand the Supreme Court's jurisdiction, this section of the Judiciary Act of 1789 was unconstitutional—and thus void. The decision still stands today as a judicial and political masterpiece.

JAMES MADISON. IF MADISON HAD DELIVERED THE COMMISSIONS OF THE FEDERALIST JUDGES, WOULD THE U.S. SUPREME COURT TODAY HAVE THE POWER OF JUDICIAL REVIEW?

FOR CRITICAL ANALYSIS What might result if the courts could not exercise the power of judicial review?

Basic Judicial Requirements

Before a lawsuit can be brought before a court, certain requirements must first be met. These requirements relate to jurisdiction, venue, and standing to sue. We examine each of these important concepts here.

JURISDICTION

In Latin, *juris* means "law," and *diction* means "to speak." Thus, "the power to speak the law" is the literal meaning of the term **jurisdiction.** Before any court can hear a case, it must have jurisdiction over the person against whom the suit is brought or over the property involved in the suit. The court must also have jurisdiction over the subject matter.

• **JURISDICTION**
The authority of a court to hear and decide a specific action.

Jurisdiction over Persons Generally, a court can exercise personal jurisdiction (*in personam* jurisdiction) over residents of a certain geographical area. A state trial court, for example, normally has jurisdictional authority over residents of a particular area of the state, such as a county or district. A state's highest court (often called the state supreme court)[2] has jurisdictional authority over all residents within the state.

In some cases, under the authority of a state **long arm statute,** a court can exercise personal jurisdiction over nonresident defendants as well. Before a court can exercise jurisdiction over a nonresident under a long arm statute, though, it must be demonstrated that the nonresident had sufficient contacts, or *minimum contacts,*

• **LONG ARM STATUTE**
A state statute that permits a state to obtain personal jurisdiction over nonresident defendants. A defendant must have certain "minimum contacts" with that state for the statute to apply.

2. As will be discussed shortly, a state's highest court is often referred to as the state supreme court, but there are exceptions. For example, in New York, the supreme court is a trial court.

with the state to justify the jurisdiction.[3] • **EXAMPLE 3.1** If an individual has committed a wrong within the state, such as causing an automobile injury or selling defective goods, a court can usually exercise jurisdiction even if the person causing the harm is located in another state. Similarly, a state may exercise personal jurisdiction over a nonresident defendant who is sued for breaching a contract that was formed within the state.•

In regard to corporations, the minimum-contacts requirement is usually met if the corporation does business within the state. • **EXAMPLE 3.2** Suppose that a corporation incorporated under the laws of Maine and headquartered in that state has a branch office or manufacturing plant in Georgia. Does this corporation have sufficient minimum contacts with the state of Georgia to allow a Georgia court to exercise jurisdiction over the Maine corporation? Yes, it does. If the Maine corporation advertises and sells its products in Georgia, those activities may also suffice to meet the minimum-contacts requirement.•

In the following case, the issue was whether phone calls and letters constituted sufficient minimum contacts to give a court jurisdiction over a nonresident defendant.

3. The minimum-contacts standard was established in *International Shoe Co. v. State of Washington*, 326 U.S. 310, 66 S.Ct. 154, 90 L.Ed. 95 (1945).

CASE 3.1 Cole v. Mileti

United States Court of Appeals,
Sixth Circuit, 1998.
133 F.3d 433.
www.law.emory.edu/6circuit/jan98/index.html[a]

HISTORICAL AND ECONOMIC SETTING *A movie production company is expensive to operate. Over the several years it can take to produce a film, there are many expenses, including maintaining an office and hiring professionals of all kinds. Newcomers to the industry make many of the same wrong moves that are the pitfalls of all businesses. For a novice producer or investor, there is the uncertainty of not knowing what you are doing and the danger of being out-negotiated by those who prey on a novice's ignorance. Finally, once a film is made, there is the audience, which may not choose to see it.*

a. This is a page, at the Web site of the Emory University School of Law, that lists the published opinions of the U.S. Court of Appeals for the Sixth Circuit for January 1998. Scroll down the list of cases to the *Cole* case. To access the opinion, click on the case name.

BACKGROUND AND FACTS Nick Mileti, a resident of California, co-produced a movie called *Streamers* and organized a corporation, Streamers International Distributors, Inc., to distribute the film. Joseph Cole, a resident of Ohio, bought two hundred shares of Streamers stock. Cole also lent the firm $475,000, which he borrowed from Equitable Bank of Baltimore. The film was unsuccessful. Mileti agreed to repay Cole's loan in a contract arranged through phone calls and correspondence between California and Ohio. When Mileti did not repay the loan, the bank sued Cole, who in turn filed a suit against Mileti in a federal district court in Ohio. The court entered a judgment against Mileti. He appealed to the U.S. Court of Appeals for the Sixth Circuit, arguing in part that the district court's exercise of jurisdiction over him was unfair.

IN THE WORDS OF THE COURT . . .
MERRITT, Circuit Judge.

* * * *

* * * [There is] a three-part test to determine whether specific jurisdiction exists over a nonresident defendant like Mileti. First, the defendant must purposefully avail himself of the privilege of conducting activities within the forum state; second, the cause of action must arise from the defendant's activities there; and third, the acts of the defendant or consequences caused by the defendant must have a substantial enough connection with the forum state to make its exercise of jurisdiction over the defendant fundamentally fair.

CASE 3.1—Continued

If, as here, a nonresident defendant transacts business by negotiating and executing a contract via telephone calls and letters to an Ohio resident, then the defendant has purposefully availed himself of the forum by creating a continuing obligation in Ohio. Furthermore, if the cause of action is for breach of that contract, as it is here, then the cause of action naturally arises from the defendant's activities in Ohio. Finally, when we find that a defendant like Mileti purposefully availed himself of the forum and that the cause of action arose directly from that contact, we presume the specific assertion of personal jurisdiction was proper.

DECISION AND REMEDY The U.S. Court of Appeals for the Sixth Circuit held that the district court could exercise personal jurisdiction over Mileti. The appellate court reasoned that a federal district court in Ohio can exercise personal jurisdiction over a resident of California who does business in Ohio via phone calls and letters.

FOR CRITICAL ANALYSIS—Economic Consideration *Why might a defendant prefer to be sued in one state rather than in another?*

Jurisdiction over Property A court can also exercise jurisdiction over property that is located within its boundaries. This kind of jurisdiction is known as *in rem* jurisdiction, or "jurisdiction over the thing." • **EXAMPLE 3.3** Suppose that a dispute arises over the ownership of a boat in dry dock in Fort Lauderdale, Florida. The boat is owned by an Ohio resident, over whom a Florida court cannot normally exercise personal jurisdiction. The other party to the dispute is a resident of Nebraska. In this situation, a lawsuit concerning the boat could be brought in a Florida state court on the basis of the court's *in rem* jurisdiction. •

Jurisdiction over Subject Matter Jurisdiction over subject matter is a limitation on the types of cases a court can hear. In both the federal and state court systems, there are courts of *general* (unlimited) *jurisdiction* and courts of *limited jurisdiction*. An example of a court of general jurisdiction is a state trial court or a federal district court. An example of a state court of limited jurisdiction is a probate court. **Probate courts** are state courts that handle only matters relating to the transfer of a person's assets and obligations after that person's death, including matters relating to the custody and guardianship of children. An example of a federal court of limited subject-matter jurisdiction is a bankruptcy court. **Bankruptcy courts** handle only bankruptcy proceedings, which are governed by federal bankruptcy law (discussed in Chapter 23). In contrast, a court of general jurisdiction can decide a broad array of cases.

• **PROBATE COURT**
A state court of limited jurisdiction that conducts proceedings relating to the settlement of a deceased person's estate.

• **BANKRUPTCY COURT**
A federal court of limited jurisdiction that handles only bankruptcy proceedings. Bankruptcy proceedings are governed by federal bankruptcy law.

A court's jurisdiction over subject matter is usually defined in the statute or constitution creating the court. In both the federal and state court systems, a court's subject-matter jurisdiction can be limited not only by the subject of the lawsuit but also by the amount of money in controversy, by whether a case is a felony (a more serious type of crime) or a misdemeanor (a less serious type of crime), or by whether the proceeding is a trial or an appeal.

Original and Appellate Jurisdiction The distinction between courts of original jurisdiction and courts of appellate jurisdiction normally lies in whether the case is being heard for the first time. Courts having original jurisdiction are courts of the first instance, or trial courts—that is, courts in which lawsuits begin, trials take place, and evidence is presented. In the federal court system, the *district courts* are trial courts. In the various state court systems, the trial courts are known by various names, as will be discussed shortly.

The Letter of the Law — THE (POETIC) LANGUAGE OF THE LAW

Not all judges couch their legal reasoning in lengthy, ponderous, complicated opinions filled with Latin phrases and terms that only lawyers can understand. In fact, several judges over the years have peppered their opinions with humor and flights of fancy that entertain their readers. One bankruptcy judge, A. Jay Cristol, even wrote his entire opinion in the form of a poem. In the poem, the judge first decided to dismiss the case, based on the conclusion that it would constitute an abuse of bankruptcy law to let the debtor avoid his debts. During his poetic travels, however, he considered the debtor's plight and decided to allow the debtor to obtain bankruptcy relief.[a] (The judge's poem is online at www.netside.net/~drose/lexloco.html#Cofield.)

a. *In re Robin E. Love,* 61 Bankr. 558 (S.D.Fla. 1986). (*In re* is one of the terms used in cases that typically involve only one party, as in bankruptcy cases—see Chapter 23.)

THE BOTTOM LINE

Increasingly, judges are being encouraged to use "plain language" and "simple English" in their opinions so that laypersons (and even other lawyers) can understand them. Notably, Judge Cristol's opinion clearly indicated his thoughts on the options available to him as well as his decision in the matter.

The key point here is that normally, any court having original jurisdiction is known as a trial court. Courts having appellate jurisdiction act as reviewing courts, or appellate courts. In general, cases can be brought before appellate courts only on appeal from an order or a judgment of a trial court or other lower court.

Jurisdiction of the Federal Courts Because the federal government is a government of limited powers, the jurisdiction of the federal courts is limited. Article III of the U.S. Constitution establishes the boundaries of federal judicial power. Section 2 of Article III states that "[t]he judicial Power shall extend to all Cases, in Law and Equity, arising under this Constitution, the Laws of the United States, and Treaties made, or which shall be made, under their Authority."

Whenever a plaintiff's cause of action is based, at least in part, on the U.S. Constitution, a treaty, or a federal law, then a **federal question** arises, and the case comes under the judicial power of the federal courts. Any lawsuit involving a federal question can originate in a federal court. People who claim that their constitutional rights have been violated can begin their suits in a federal court.

• **FEDERAL QUESTION**
A question that pertains to the U.S. Constitution, acts of Congress, or treaties. A federal question provides a basis for federal jurisdiction.

• **DIVERSITY OF CITIZENSHIP**
Under Article III, Section 2, of the Constitution, a basis for federal district court jurisdiction over a lawsuit between (1) citizens of different states, (2) a foreign country and citizens of a state or of different states, or (3) citizens of a state and citizens or subjects of a foreign country. The amount in controversy must be more than $75,000 before a federal district court can take jurisdiction in such cases.

Federal district courts can also exercise original jurisdiction over cases involving **diversity of citizenship.** Such cases may arise between (1) citizens of different states, (2) a foreign country and citizens of a state or of different states, or (3) citizens of a state and citizens or subjects of a foreign country. The amount in controversy must be more than $75,000 before a federal court can take jurisdiction in such cases. For purposes of diversity jurisdiction, a corporation is a citizen of both the state in which it is incorporated and the state in which its principal place of business is located. A case involving diversity of citizenship can be filed in the appropriate federal district court, or, if the case starts in a state court, it can sometimes be transferred to a federal court. A large percentage of the cases filed in federal courts each year are based on diversity of citizenship.

Note that in a case based on a federal question, a federal court will apply federal law. In a case based on diversity of citizenship, however, a federal court will apply the relevant state law (which is often the law of the state in which the court sits).

Exclusive versus Concurrent Jurisdiction When both federal and state courts have the power to hear a case, as is true in suits involving diversity of citizenship,

• **CONCURRENT JURISDICTION** Jurisdiction that exists when two different courts have the power to hear a case. For example, some cases can be heard in a federal or a state court.

• **EXCLUSIVE JURISDICTION** Jurisdiction that exists when a case can be heard only in a particular court or type of court.

concurrent jurisdiction exists. When cases can be tried only in federal courts or only in state courts, exclusive jurisdiction exists. Federal courts have **exclusive jurisdiction** in cases involving federal crimes, bankruptcy, patents, and copyrights; in suits against the United States; and in some areas of admiralty law (law governing transportation on the seas and ocean waters). States also have exclusive jurisdiction in certain subject matters—for example, in divorce and adoption. The concepts of concurrent and exclusive jurisdiction are illustrated in Exhibit 3–1.

VENUE

• **VENUE** The geographical district in which an action is tried and from which the jury is selected.

Jurisdiction has to do with whether a court has authority to hear a case involving specific persons, property, or subject matter. **Venue**[4] is concerned with the most appropriate location for a trial. Two state courts (or two federal courts) may have the authority to exercise jurisdiction over a case, but it may be more appropriate or convenient to hear the case in one court than in the other.

Basically, the concept of venue reflects the policy that a court trying a suit should be in the geographical neighborhood (usually the county) in which the incident leading to the lawsuit occurred or in which the parties involved in the lawsuit reside. Pretrial publicity or other factors, though, may require a change of venue to another community, especially in criminal cases in which the defendant's right to a fair and impartial jury has been impaired. • **EXAMPLE 3.4** A change of venue from Oklahoma City to Denver, Colorado, was ordered for the trials of Timothy McVeigh and Terry Nichols, who had been indicted in connection with the 1995 bombing of the Alfred P. Murrah Federal Building in Oklahoma City. •

STANDING TO SUE

• **STANDING TO SUE** The requirement that an individual must have a sufficient stake in a controversy before he or she can bring a lawsuit. The plaintiff must demonstrate that he or she either has been injured or threatened with injury.

Before a person can bring a lawsuit before a court, the party must have **standing to sue,** or a sufficient "stake" in a matter to justify seeking relief through the court sys-

4. Pronounced *ven*-yoo.

EXHIBIT 3–1 • Exclusive and Concurrent Jurisdiction

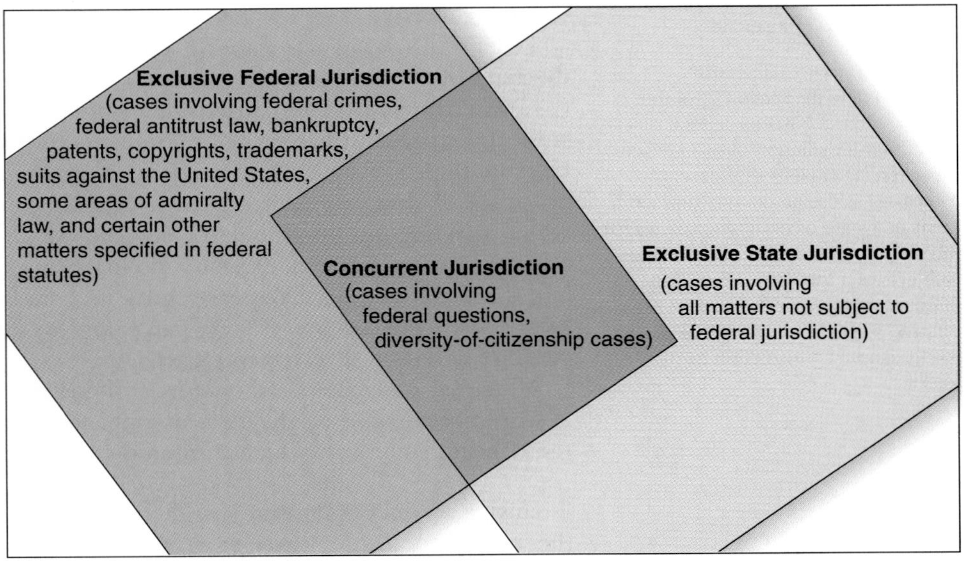

tem. In other words, a party must have a legally protected and tangible interest at stake in the litigation in order to have standing. The party bringing the lawsuit must have suffered a harm, or have been threatened by a harm, as a result of the action about which he or she complained. At times, a person will have standing to sue on behalf of another person. • **EXAMPLE 3.5** Suppose that a child suffered serious injuries as a result of a defectively manufactured toy. Because the child is a minor, a lawsuit could be brought on his or her behalf by another person, such as the child's parent or legal guardian. •

• **JUSTICIABLE CONTROVERSY**
A controversy that is not hypothetical or academic but real and substantial; a requirement that must be satisfied before a court will hear a case.

Standing to sue also requires that the controversy at issue be a **justiciable[5] controversy**—a controversy that is real and substantial, as opposed to hypothetical or academic. • **EXAMPLE 3.6** In the above example, the child's parent could not sue the toy manufacturer merely on the ground that the toy was defective. The issue would become justiciable only if the child had actually been injured due to the defect in the toy as marketed. In other words, the parent normally could not ask the court to determine, for example, what damages might be obtained if the child had been injured, because this would be merely a hypothetical question. •

Meeting standing requirements is not always easy. In the following case, for example, an environmental organization sued a company for allegedly discharging pollutants into waterways beyond the amount allowed by the Environmental Protection Agency. At issue in the case was whether the organization had standing to sue under federal environmental laws.

5. Pronounced jus-*tish*-uh-bul.

CASE 3.2 Friends of the Earth, Inc. v. Crown Central Petroleum Corp.

United States Court of Appeals,
Fifth Circuit, 1996.
95 F.3d 358.
www.ca5.uscourts.gov/oparchdt.cfm?Year-1996[a]

HISTORICAL AND ENVIRONMENTAL SETTING *In the early 1970s, the Sierra Club, a conservation organization, challenged the Environmental Protection Agency's approval of locating a ski complex near a national wilderness area. The court refused to consider the challenge on the ground that the Sierra Club did not show that it had standing to bring the suit. The United States Supreme Court upheld this decision.[b] The Sierra Club amended its complaint to allege that some of its members used, hiked in, and enjoyed the wilderness area that the development threatened. It also alleged that the ski complex compromised these members' enjoyment of the area. The court then agreed to hear the case. In 1972, Congress incorporated this same test for standing into the Federal Water Pollution Control Act.*

BACKGROUND AND FACTS Crown Central Petroleum Corporation does business as La Gloria Oil & Gas Company. Under a permit issued by the Environmental Protection Agency (EPA), La Gloria's oil refinery discharges storm-water run-off into Black Fork Creek. Black Fork Creek flows into Prairie Creek, which flows into the Neches River, which flows into Lake Palestine eighteen miles downstream. Friends of the Earth, Inc. (FOE), is a not-for-profit corporation dedicated to the protection of the environment. FOE filed a suit in a federal district court against La Gloria under the Federal Water Pollution Control Act.[c] FOE claimed that La Gloria had violated its EPA permit and that this conduct had directly affected "the health, economic, recreational, aesthetic and environmental interests of FOE's members" who used the lake. La Gloria filed a motion for summary judgment, arguing that FOE lacked standing to bring the suit. The court granted the motion, and FOE appealed.

a. This is the "Opinions Archive by Date Released" page within the Web site of the U.S. Courts of the Fifth Judicial Circuit. Click on "1996." When the link opens, click on "September." When that link opens, click on "September 3." From the list of cases that appears, click on the appropriate case name to access the opinion.

b. *Sierra Club v. Morton,* 405 U.S. 727, 92 S.Ct. 1361, 31 L.Ed.2d 636 (1972).

c. 33 U.S.C. Sections 1251–1387.

CASE 3.2—Continued

IN THE WORDS OF THE COURT . . .
PATRICK E. HIGGINBOTHAM, Circuit Judge:

* * * *

To demonstrate that FOE's members have standing, FOE must show that * * * the injury is "fairly traceable" to the defendant's actions * * * .

* * * *

* * * FOE offered no competent evidence that La Gloria's discharges have made their way to Lake Palestine or would otherwise affect Lake Palestine. * * * FOE and its members relied solely on the truism that water flows downstream and inferred therefrom that any injury suffered downstream is "fairly traceable" to unlawful discharges upstream. At some point this common sense observation becomes little more than surmise. At that point certainly the requirements [for standing] are not met.

DECISION AND REMEDY The U.S. Court of Appeals for the Fifth Circuit affirmed the lower court's decision. FOE lacked standing to bring a suit against La Gloria.

FOR CRITICAL ANALYSIS—Social Consideration *What might result if the courts did not impose the requirement of standing to sue?*

The State and Federal Court Systems

"The perfect judge fears nothing—he could go front to front before God."

WALT WHITMAN,
1819–1892
(American poet)

As mentioned earlier in this chapter, each state has its own court system. Additionally, there is a system of federal courts. Although state court systems differ, Exhibit 3–2 illustrates the basic organizational structure characteristic of the court systems in many states. The exhibit also shows how the federal court system is structured. We turn now to an examination of these court systems, beginning with the state courts.

STATE COURT SYSTEMS

Typically a state court system will include several levels, or tiers, of courts. As indicated in Exhibit 3–2, state courts may include (1) trial courts of limited jurisdiction, (2) trial courts of general jurisdiction, (3) appellate courts, and (4) the state's highest court (often called the state supreme court). Judges in the state court system are usually elected by the voters for a specified term.

Generally, any person who is a party to a lawsuit has the opportunity to plead the case before a trial court and then, if he or she loses, before at least one level of appellate court. Finally, if a federal statute or federal constitutional issue is involved in the decision of the state supreme court, that decision may be further appealed to the United States Supreme Court.

ON THE WEB

You can find information on state courts by using the Center for Information Law and Policy's State Court Locator. Go to **www.cilp.org/tblhome.html**.

Trial Courts Trial courts are exactly what their name implies—courts in which trials are held and testimony taken. State trial courts have either general or limited jurisdiction. Trial courts that have general jurisdiction as to subject matter may be called county, district, superior, or circuit courts.[6] The jurisdiction of these courts is often determined by the size of the county in which the court sits. State trial courts of general jurisdiction have jurisdiction over a wide variety of subjects, including both civil disputes and criminal prosecutions. In some states, trial courts of general jurisdiction may hear appeals from courts of limited jurisdiction.

6. The name in Ohio is court of common pleas; the name in New York is supreme court.

EXHIBIT 3–2 • Federal Courts and State Court Systems

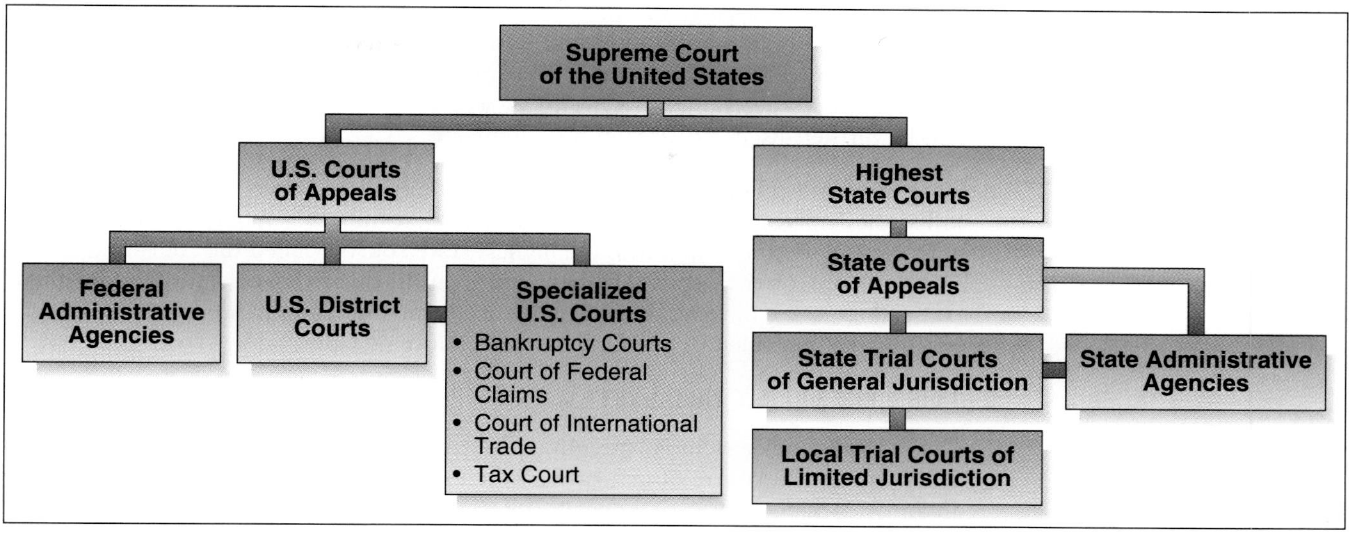

• **SMALL CLAIMS COURTS**
Special courts in which parties may litigate small claims (usually, claims involving $5,000 or less). Attorneys are not required in small claims courts, and in many states attorneys are not allowed to represent the parties.

Some courts of limited jurisdiction are called special inferior trial courts or minor judiciary courts. **Small claims courts** are inferior trial courts that hear only civil cases involving claims of less than a certain amount, such as $5,000 (the amount varies from state to state). Suits brought in small claims courts are generally conducted informally, and lawyers are not required. In a minority of states, lawyers are not even allowed to represent people in small claims courts for most purposes. Another example of an inferior trial court is a local municipal court that hears mainly traffic cases. Decisions of small claims courts and municipal courts may be appealed to a state trial court of general jurisdiction.

Other courts of limited jurisdiction as to subject matter include domestic relations courts, which handle only divorce actions and child-custody cases, and probate courts, as mentioned earlier.

Courts of Appeals Every state has at least one court of appeals (appellate court, or reviewing court), which may be an intermediate appellate court or the state's highest court. About three-fourths of the states have intermediate appellate courts. Generally, courts of appeals do not conduct new trials, in which evidence is submitted to the court and witnesses are examined. Rather, an appellate court panel of three or more judges reviews the record of the case on appeal, which includes a transcript of the trial proceedings, and the panel determines whether the trial court committed an error.

Usually, appellate courts do not look at questions of *fact* (such as whether a party did, in fact, commit a certain action, such as burning a flag) but at questions of *law* (such as whether the act of flag-burning is a form of speech protected by the First Amendment to the Constitution). Only a judge, not a jury, can rule on questions of law. Appellate courts normally defer to a trial court's findings on questions of fact because the trial court judge and jury were in a better position to evaluate testimony—by directly observing witnesses' gestures, demeanor, and nonverbal behavior during the trial. At the appellate level, the judges review the written transcript of the trial, which does not include these nonverbal elements.

An appellate court will challenge a trial court's finding of fact only when the finding is clearly erroneous (that is, when it is contrary to the evidence presented at trial) or when there is no evidence to support the finding. • **EXAMPLE 3.7** If a jury concluded that a manufacturer's product harmed the plaintiff but no evidence was submitted to the court to support that conclusion, the appellate court would hold that the trial court's decision was erroneous. The options exercised by appellate courts will be further discussed later in this chapter. •

¡BE CAREFUL! The decisions of a state's highest court are final on questions of state law.

State Supreme (Highest) Courts The highest appellate court in a state is usually called the supreme court but may be called by some other name. For example, in both New York and Maryland, the highest state court is called the court of appeals. The decisions of each state's highest court on all questions of state law are final. Only when issues of federal law are involved can a decision made by a state's highest court be overruled by the United States Supreme Court.

THE FEDERAL COURT SYSTEM

The federal court system is basically a three-tiered model consisting of (1) U.S. district courts (trial courts of general jurisdiction) and various courts of limited jurisdiction, (2) U.S. courts of appeals (intermediate courts of appeals), and (3) the United States Supreme Court.

Unlike state court judges, who are usually elected, federal court judges—including the justices of the Supreme Court—are appointed by the president of the United States and confirmed by the U.S. Senate. All federal judges receive lifetime appointments (because under Article III they "hold their offices during Good Behavior").

ON THE WEB

If you are interested in learning about the federal court system generally, go to the home page of the federal courts at www.uscourts.gov. At this site, you can even follow the "path" of a case as it moves through the federal court system.

U.S. District Courts At the federal level, the equivalent of a state trial court of general jurisdiction is the district court. There is at least one federal district court in every state. The number of judicial districts can vary over time, primarily owing to population changes and corresponding caseloads. Currently, there are ninety-four federal judicial districts.

U.S. district courts have original jurisdiction in federal matters. Federal cases typically originate in district courts. There are other courts with original, but special (or limited), jurisdiction, such as the federal bankruptcy courts and others shown in Exhibit 3–2.

U.S. Courts of Appeals In the federal court system, there are thirteen U.S. courts of appeals—also referred to as U.S. circuit courts of appeals. The federal courts of appeals for twelve of the circuits, including the U.S. Court of Appeals for the District of Columbia Circuit, hear appeals from the federal district courts located within their respective judicial circuits. The Court of Appeals for the Thirteenth Circuit, called the Federal Circuit, has national appellate jurisdiction over certain types of cases, such as cases involving patent law and cases in which the U.S. government is a defendant.

The decisions of the circuit courts of appeals are final in most cases, but appeal to the United States Supreme Court is possible. Exhibit 3–3 shows the geographical boundaries of U.S. circuit courts of appeals and the boundaries of the U.S. district courts within each circuit.

"We are not final because we are infallible, but we are infallible only because we are final."

ROBERT H. JACKSON, 1892–1954 (Associate justice of the United States Supreme Court, 1941–1954)

The United States Supreme Court The highest level of the three-tiered model of the federal court system is the United States Supreme Court. According to the language of Article III of the U.S. Constitution, there is only one national Supreme Court. All other courts in the federal system are considered "inferior." Congress is empowered

EXHIBIT 3–3 • U.S. Courts of Appeals and U.S. District Courts

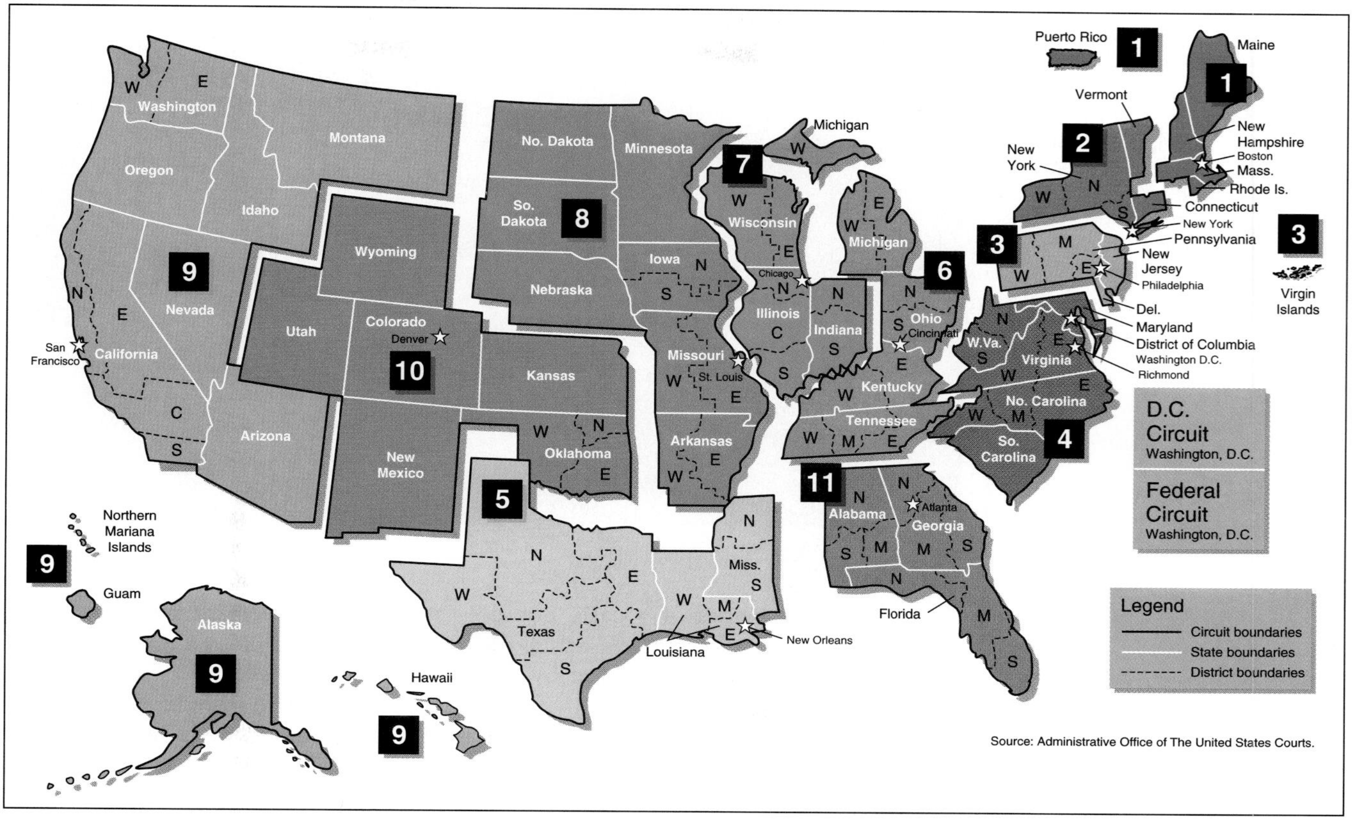

Source: Administrative Office of The United States Courts.

to create other inferior courts as it deems necessary. The inferior courts that Congress has created include the second tier in our model—the U.S. courts of appeals—as well as the district courts and any other courts of limited, or specialized, jurisdiction.

The United States Supreme Court consists of nine justices. Although the United States Supreme Court has original, or trial, jurisdiction in rare instances (set forth in Article III, Section 2), most of its work is as an appeals court. The Supreme Court can review any case decided by any of the federal courts of appeals, and it also has appellate authority over some cases decided in the state courts.

To bring a case before the Supreme Court, a party requests the Court to issue a writ of *certiorari.* A **writ of *certiorari*[7]** is an order issued by the Supreme Court to a lower court requiring the latter to send it the record of the case for review. The Court will not issue a writ unless at least four of the nine justices approve of it. This is called the **rule of four.** Whether the Court will issue a writ of *certiorari* is entirely within its discretion. The Court is not required to issue one, and most petitions for writs are denied. (Thousands of cases are filed with the Supreme Court each year, yet it hears, on average, less than one hundred of these cases.[8]) A denial is not a

• **WRIT OF *CERTIORARI***
A writ from a higher court asking the lower court for the record of a case.

• **RULE OF FOUR**
A rule of the United States Supreme Court under which the Court will not issue a writ of *certiorari* unless at least four justices approve of the decision to issue the writ.

ON THE WEB

An excellent online source for Supreme Court opinions since 1893 is FindLaw's site at

www.findlaw.com.

Click on "Supreme Court Opinions" in the "Law: Cases and Code" category.

7. Pronounced sur-shee-uh-*rah*-ree.

8. From the mid-1950s through the early 1990s, the Supreme Court reviewed more cases per year than it has in the last few years. In the Court's 1982–1983 term, for example, the Court issued opinions in 151 cases. In contrast, since the mid-1990s, the Court has issued opinions in only about 80 to 90 cases each term.

THE JUSTICES OF THE U.S. SUPREME COURT ARE, SEATED LEFT TO RIGHT, ANTONIN SCALIA, JOHN PAUL STEVENS, CHIEF JUSTICE WILLIAM H. REHNQUIST, SANDRA DAY O'CONNOR, AND ANTHONY M. KENNEDY; AND STANDING LEFT TO RIGHT, RUTH BADER GINSGURG, DAVID H. SOUTER, CLARENCE THOMAS, AND STEPHEN BREYER. DOES THE FACT THAT THESE JUSTICES ARE APPOINTED FOR LIFE HAVE ANY EFFECT ON THE DECISIONS THEY REACH IN THE CASES THEY HEAR?

decision on the merits of a case, nor does it indicate agreement with the lower court's opinion. Furthermore, a denial of the writ has no value as a precedent.

Typically, the petitions granted by the Court involve cases that raise important constitutional questions or cases that conflict with other state or federal court decisions. Similarly, if federal appellate courts are rendering inconsistent opinions on an important issue, the Supreme Court may review the case and issue a decision to define the law on the matter.

Following a State Court Case

To illustrate the procedures that would be followed in a civil lawsuit brought in a state court, we present a hypothetical case and follow it through the state court system. The case involves an automobile accident in which Kevin Anderson, driving a Mercedes, struck Lisa Marconi, driving a Ford Taurus. The accident occurred at the intersection of Wilshire Boulevard and Rodeo Drive in Beverly Hills, California. Marconi suffered personal injuries, incurring medical and hospital expenses as well as lost wages for four months. Anderson and Marconi are unable to agree on a settlement, and Marconi sues Anderson. Marconi is the plaintiff, and Anderson is the defendant. Both are represented by lawyers.

• **LITIGATION**
The process of resolving a dispute through the court system.

During each phase of the **litigation** (the process of working a lawsuit through the court system), Marconi and Anderson will be required to observe strict procedural requirements. A large body of law—procedural law—establishes the rules and standards for determining disputes in courts. Procedural rules are very complex, and they vary from court to court. There is a set of federal rules of procedure and various sets of rules for state courts. Additionally, the applicable procedures will depend on whether the case is a civil or criminal proceeding. Generally, the Marconi-Anderson civil lawsuit will involve the procedures discussed in the following subsections. Keep in mind that attempts to settle the case may be ongoing throughout the trial.

ETHICAL ISSUE 3.1 ***Are confidential settlement agreements contrary to the public interest?*** One of the major advantages of a settlement agreement, aside from avoiding litigation costs, is confidentiality. A defendant manufacturer, for example, might place a high value on keeping allegations that its product is defective from reaching the public or other potential plaintiffs. In the past, the courts tended to approve settlement agreements, including confidentiality provisions, with few objections. This tradition is now changing. Increasingly, "sunshine in government" or "sunshine in litigation" laws and court rules are imposing requirements on the courts that make it difficult for parties to obtain a court's consent to a confidentiality agreement. This is particularly true when the agreement relates to disputes concerning products or practices that may be harmful to the public. Clearly, shielding the public from knowledge of harmful products or services by means of confidentiality agreements may not be in the public interest. Yet limiting the availability of confidentiality agreements may not be in the public interest, either, because it makes settlements less attractive for many litigants. As a result, more cases will go to trial and an already strained court system will be even more heavily burdened.

• **PLEADINGS**
Statements made by the plaintiff and the defendant in a lawsuit that detail the facts, charges, and defenses involved in the litigation; the complaint and answer are part of the pleadings.

• **COMPLAINT**
The pleading made by a plaintiff alleging wrongdoing on the part of the defendant; the document that, when filed with a court, initiates a lawsuit.

• **SUMMONS**
A document informing a defendant that a legal action has been commenced against him or her and that the defendant must appear in court on a certain date to answer the plaintiff's complaint. The document is delivered by a sheriff or any other person so authorized.

• **DEFAULT JUDGMENT**
A judgment entered by a court against a defendant who has failed to appear in court to answer or defend against the plaintiff's claim.

• **ANSWER**
Procedurally, a defendant's response to the plaintiff's complaint.

• **COUNTERCLAIM**
A claim made by a defendant in a civil lawsuit against the plaintiff. In effect, the defendant is suing the plaintiff.

• **REPLY**
Procedurally, a plaintiff's response to a defendant's answer.

THE PLEADINGS

The complaint and answer (and the counterclaim and reply)—all of which are discussed below—taken together are called the **pleadings.** The pleadings inform each party of the claims of the other and specify the issues (disputed questions) involved in the case.

The Plaintiff's Complaint Marconi's suit against Anderson commences when her lawyer files a **complaint** with the appropriate court. The complaint contains a statement alleging (asserting to the court, in a pleading) the facts necessary for the court to take jurisdiction, a brief summary of the facts necessary to show that the plaintiff is entitled to a remedy, and a statement of the remedy the plaintiff is seeking. Exhibit 3–4 illustrates how the complaint might read in the Marconi-Anderson case. Complaints may be lengthy or brief, depending on the complexity of the case.

After the complaint has been filed, the sheriff, a deputy of the county, or another *process server* (one who delivers a complaint and summons) serves a **summons** and a copy of the complaint on defendant Anderson. The summons notifies Anderson that he must file an answer to the complaint with both the court and the plaintiff's attorney within a specified time period (usually twenty to thirty days). The summons also informs Anderson that failure to answer may result in a **default judgment** for the plaintiff, meaning the plaintiff will be awarded the damages alleged in her complaint.

The Defendant's Answer The defendant's **answer** either admits the statements or allegations set forth in the complaint or denies them and outlines any defenses that the defendant may have. If Anderson admits to all of Marconi's allegations in his answer, the court will enter a judgment for Marconi. If Anderson denies any of Marconi's allegations, the litigation will go forward.

Anderson can deny Marconi's allegations and set forth his own claim that Marconi was in fact negligent and therefore owes him money for damages to his Mercedes. This is appropriately called a **counterclaim.** If Anderson files a counterclaim, Marconi will have to answer it with a pleading, normally called a **reply,** which has the same characteristics as an answer.

EXHIBIT 3–4 • Example of a Typical Complaint

IN THE LOS ANGELES MUNICIPAL COURT
FOR THE LOS ANGELES JUDICIAL DISTRICT

CIVIL NO. 8–1026

Lisa Marconi
Plaintiff

v.

COMPLAINT

Kevin Anderson
Defendant

Comes now the plaintiff and for her cause of action against the defendant alleges and states as follows:

1. The jurisdiction of this court is based on Section 86 of the California Civil Code.
2. This action is between plaintiff, a California resident living at 1434 Palm Drive, Anaheim, California, and defendant, a California resident living at 6950 Garrison Avenue, Los Angeles, California.
3. On September 10, 1999, plaintiff, Lisa Marconi, was exercising good driving habits and reasonable care in driving her car through the intersection of Rodeo Drive and Wilshire Boulevard when defendant, Kevin Anderson, negligently drove his vehicle through a red light at the intersection and collided with plaintiff's vehicle. Defendant was negligent in the operation of the vehicle as to:
   a. Speed,
   b. Lookout,
   c. Management and control.
4. As a result of the collision plaintiff suffered severe physical injury that prevented her from working and property damage to her car. The costs she incurred included $10,000 in medical bills, $9,000 in lost wages, and $5,000 for automobile repairs.

WHEREFORE, plaintiff demands judgment against the defendant for the sum of $24,000 plus interest at the maximum legal rate and the costs of this action.

By *Roger Harrington*
Roger Harrington
Attorney for the Plaintiff
800 Orange Avenue
Anaheim, CA 91426

Anderson can also admit the truth of Marconi's complaint but raise new facts that may result in dismissal of the action. This is called raising an affirmative defense. For example, Anderson could assert the expiration of the time period under the relevant statute of limitations (a state or federal statute that sets the maximum time period during which a certain action can be brought or rights enforced) as an affirmative defense.

Business Law in Action • Evidence Spoliation

Omnia praesumuntur contra spoliatorem (Latin for "all things are presumed against the destroyer") is an age-old legal maxim. It means that when a party loses or destroys evidence relating to a lawsuit, the presumption arises that the evidence was harmful to the "spoliator"—the party that lost or destroyed the evidence. Courts in most states hold that the jury may—but is not compelled to—infer or presume that any evidence that has been destroyed would have been adverse to the spoliator.

Courts can also impose more severe sanctions—including fines, the dismissal of a lawsuit, or the entry of a default judgment for the opposing party—for evidence spoliation. Traditionally, courts have imposed these harsher sanctions only when evidence is *intentionally* destroyed. Increasingly, however, even parties that accidentally destroy or inadvertently fail to preserve relevant evidence may face similar sanctions. In one case, for example, the plaintiff, Jordan Miller, purchased a Cessna twin-engine airplane from Mid-Continent Aircraft Service and Jet Center Tulsa, Inc. (collectively, MCAS). When landing the aircraft after his first flight, the left landing gear collapsed, causing major damage to the airplane. A Federal Aviation Administration (FAA) investigator who inspected the airplane shortly after the crash reported that the landing gear was defective. Inspectors for Miller's insurance company concluded likewise.

When Miller sued MCAS to recover damages, MCAS requested that it be allowed to inspect the defective landing gear. As it turned out, the various companies involved in making repairs to the plane had either lost or destroyed all but one of the component parts of the left landing gear. Notwithstanding the FAA inspector's report, the insurance company's findings, and testimony from those repairing the plane, the court dismissed Miller's case. To allow the case to go forward, stated the court, would be prejudicial to MCAS because it could not conduct its own inspection of the gear.[a]

Notably, the spoliation of evidence can give rise not only to court sanctions but also, in some states, to tort lawsuits. (As will be discussed in Chapter 4, under tort law, a party who suffers harm as a result of another's wrongful act, or *tort,* may sue to obtain money damages.) Some of these states limit the tort to the intentional destruction of evidence. Others, however, allow private actions against spoliators even though the spoliation may have been accidental.

Avoiding court-imposed sanctions or tort liability for evidence spoliation is particularly challenging with respect to electronic evidence, including e-mail. As discussed in this chapter's feature *Technology and E-Mailed Smoking Guns,* if a firm retains back-up copies of all e-mail messages, it may face significant time costs in sorting through those messages to satisfy a request for documents during discovery. At the same time, if it deletes (destroys) e-mail that could be crucial evidence in bringing or defending against a lawsuit, it may face significant sanctions.

a. *Miller v. Mid-Continent Aircraft Service, Inc.,* 139 F.3d 912 (10th Cir. 1998).

A MAN SHREDS A DOCUMENT WITH THE HELP OF A DOCUMENT SHREDDER. WHAT OTHER ACTIONS, BESIDES SHREDDING DOCUMENTS, MIGHT BE INVOLVED IN EVIDENCE SPOLIATION?

One of the murkier aspects of spoliation law is determining when the obligation to preserve evidence arises. Clearly, once a summons has been served on a defendant, the defendant is obligated to preserve all evidence relevant to the plaintiff's claim. Beyond this requirement, however, there are few guidelines, and generally the courts decide the issue on a case-by-case basis. As a practical matter, any businessperson today should seek legal advice when establishing a document-retention policy, with respect to both paper and electronic documents.

FOR CRITICAL ANALYSIS

Is it fair to impose severe sanctions, such as the dismissal of a case, on those who inadvertently lose or destroy evidence relevant to a lawsuit?

• **MOTION TO DISMISS**
A pleading in which a defendant asserts that the plaintiff's claim fails to state a cause of action (that is, has no basis in law) or that there are other grounds on which a suit should be dismissed.

Motion to Dismiss A **motion to dismiss** requests the court to dismiss the case for stated reasons. The motion to dismiss is often made by a defendant before filing an answer to the plaintiff's complaint. Grounds for dismissal of a case include improper delivery of the complaint and summons, improper venue, and the plaintiff's failure to state a claim for which a court could grant relief (a remedy). For example, if Marconi had suffered no injuries or losses as a result of Anderson's negligence, Anderson could move to have the case dismissed because Marconi had not stated a claim for which relief could be granted.

If the judge grants the motion to dismiss, the plaintiff generally is given time to file an amended complaint. If the judge denies the motion, the suit will go forward, and the defendant must then file an answer. Note that if Marconi wishes to discontinue the suit because, for example, an out-of-court settlement has been reached, she can likewise move for dismissal. The court can also dismiss the case on its own motion. (Occasionally, a judge will dismiss a case to sanction a party for failing to preserve evidence relevant to the litigation. See this chapter's *Business Law in Action* for a discussion of this issue.)

PRETRIAL MOTIONS

Either party may attempt to get the case dismissed before trial through the use of various pretrial motions. We have already mentioned the motion to dismiss. Two other important pretrial motions are the motion for judgment on the pleadings and the motion for summary judgment.

• **MOTION FOR JUDGMENT ON THE PLEADINGS**
A motion by either party to a lawsuit at the close of the pleadings requesting the court to decide the issue solely on the pleadings without proceeding to trial. The motion will be granted only if no facts are in dispute.

At the close of the pleadings, either party may make **a motion for judgment on the pleadings,** or on the merits of the case. The judge will grant the motion only when there is no dispute over the facts of the case and the only issue to be resolved is a question of law. In deciding on the motion, the judge may only consider the evidence contained in the pleadings.

• **MOTION FOR SUMMARY JUDGMENT**
A motion requesting the court to enter a judgment without proceeding to trial. The motion can be based on evidence outside the pleadings and will be granted only if no facts are in dispute.

In contrast, in a **motion for summary judgment** the court may consider evidence outside the pleadings, such as sworn statements (affidavits) by parties or witnesses or other documents relating to the case. A motion for summary judgment can be made by either party. As with the motion for judgment on the pleadings, a motion for summary judgment will be granted only if there are no genuine questions of fact and the only question is a question of law.

Deciding whether a certain issue presents a question of fact or a question of law is not always easy, and judges sometimes disagree on whether summary judgment is appropriate in a given case. The following case illustrates this point.

CASE 3.3 Metzgar v. Playskool, Inc.

United States Court of Appeals,
Third Circuit, 1994.
30 F.3d 459.
www.law.vill.edu/Fed-Ct/Circuit/3d/July94.html[a]

COMPANY PROFILE *Hasbro, Inc., is the world's largest toy maker. Hasbro manufactures and sells many of the most famous, biggest-selling toys—including games, puzzles, and baby items—on the U.S. and world markets. Hasbro products include Cabbage Patch Kids, G.I. Joe, Lincoln Logs, Mr. Potato Head, Monopoly, Scrabble, Trivial Pursuit, Twister, and Yahtzee. Hasbro brand names include Hasbro, Kenner, Milton Bradley, Parker Brothers, Tonka, and Playskool.*

a. This is the "July Decisions" page within the collection of "1994 Decisions" of the U.S. Court of Appeals for the Third Circuit available at the Web site of the Center for Information Law and Policy. This Web site is a joint initiative of the Villanova University School of Law and the Illinois Institute of Technology's Chicago-Kent College of Law. Scroll down the list of cases to the entry for the *Metzgar* case. Click on the appropriate link to read or download the case.

CASE 3.3—Continued

BACKGROUND AND FACTS Ronald Metzgar placed his fifteen-month-old son Matthew, awake and healthy, in his playpen. Ronald left the room for five minutes and on his return found Matthew lifeless. A purple toy block had lodged in the boy's throat, choking him to death. Ronald called 911, but efforts to revive Matthew were to no avail. There was no warning of a choking hazard on the box containing the block. Matthew's parents sued Playskool, Inc., the manufacturer of the block, and others in a federal district court. They alleged, among other things, negligence[b] in failing to warn of the hazard of the block. Playskool filed a motion for summary judgment, arguing that the danger of a young child choking on a small block was obvious. The court entered a summary judgment in favor of Playskool. The parents appealed.

b. Negligence is a failure to use the standard of care that a reasonable person would exercise in similar circumstances. See Chapter 4.

IN THE WORDS OF THE COURT . . .
MANSMANN, Circuit Judge.

* * * *

* * * For a risk to be deemed obvious for purposes of a failure to warn claim, * * * there must be general consensus within the relevant community. We cannot see how the purple Playskool block can be deemed as a matter of law an obvious safety hazard in the eyes of the relevant community, when Playskool itself believed the block was safe for its intended use. Furthermore, Matthew's parents * * * testified that they did not believe that the product posed an obvious threat of asphyxiation to Matthew. Moreover, the defendant did not proffer any evidence tending to show that the danger of asphyxiation was obvious.

Under a negligence theory, although a failure to warn claim may be defeated if the risk was obvious or known, the question of obviousness is more properly submitted to a jury than disposed on motion for summary judgment. The court's role in deciding a motion for summary judgment is merely to decide whether there is a genuine issue of material fact for trial. The district court's dismissal of Metzgars' negligence claim on the basis of its determination that the danger to Matthew was obvious was tantamount to holding that no reasonable jury could conclude otherwise. Based on the evidence of record, we cannot agree.

DECISION AND REMEDY The U.S. Court of Appeals for the Third Circuit held that the question of the obviousness in this case was not a proper subject for summary judgment and remanded the case for a trial.

FOR CRITICAL ANALYSIS—Social Consideration
When a case requires a determination of such matters as community standards, summary judgment is not considered appropriate. Such matters are given to juries to determine. Why?

DISCOVERY

• **DISCOVERY**
A phase in the litigation process during which the opposing parties may obtain information from each other and from third parties prior to trial.

Before a trial begins, each party can use a number of procedural devices to obtain information and gather evidence about the case from the other party or from third parties. The process of obtaining such information is known as **discovery.** Discovery includes gaining access to witnesses, documents, records, and other types of evidence.

The Federal Rules of Civil Procedure and similar rules in the states set forth the guidelines for discovery activity. The rules governing discovery are designed to make sure that a witness or a party is not unduly harassed, that privileged material (communications that need not be presented in court) is safeguarded, and that only matters relevant to the case at hand are discoverable.

Discovery prevents surprises at trial by giving parties access to evidence that might otherwise be hidden. This allows both parties to learn as much as they can about what to expect at a trial before they reach the courtroom. It also serves to narrow the issues so that trial time is spent on the main questions in the case. Currently, the trend is toward allowing more discovery and thus fewer surprises.[9]

Depositions and Interrogatories Discovery can involve the use of depositions or interrogatories, or both. **Depositions** are sworn testimony by a party to the lawsuit or any witness. The person being deposed (the deponent) answers questions asked by the attorneys, and the questions and answers are recorded by an authorized court official and sworn to and signed by the deponent. (Occasionally, written depositions are taken when witnesses are unable to appear in person.) The answers given to depositions will, of course, help the attorneys prepare their cases. They can also be used in court to impeach (challenge the credibility of) a party or a witness who changes testimony at the trial. In addition, the answers given in a deposition can be used as testimony if the witness is not available at trial.

• **DEPOSITION**
The testimony of a party to a lawsuit or a witness taken under oath before a trial.

Interrogatories are written questions for which written answers are prepared and then signed under oath. The main difference between interrogatories and written depositions is that interrogatories are directed to a party to the lawsuit (the plaintiff or the defendant), not to a witness, and the party can prepare answers with the aid of an attorney. The scope of interrogatories is broader, because parties are obligated to answer questions, even if it means disclosing information from their records and files.

• **INTERROGATORIES**
A series of written questions for which written answers are prepared and then signed under oath by a party to a lawsuit, usually with the assistance of the party's attorney.

Other Information A party can serve a written request to the other party for an admission of the truth of matters relating to the trial. Any matter admitted under such a request is conclusively established for the trial. For example, Marconi can ask Anderson to admit that he was driving at a speed of forty-five miles an hour. A request for admission saves time at trial, because the parties will not have to spend time proving facts on which they already agree.

A party can also gain access to documents and other items not in his or her possession in order to inspect and examine them. Likewise, a party can gain "entry upon land" to inspect the premises. Anderson's attorney, for example, normally can gain permission to inspect and duplicate Marconi's car repair bills. This chapter's feature *Technology and E-Mailed "Smoking Guns"* indicates some of the problems businesspersons face when requests for e-mailed documents are submitted during discovery.

When the physical or mental condition of one party is in question, the opposing party can ask the court to order a physical or mental examination. If the court is willing to make the order, which it will do only if the need for the information outweighs the right to privacy of the person to be examined, the opposing party can obtain the results of the examination.

ON THE WEB
One of the first court decisions containing hyperlinks to exhibits, *C.L.I.C. Electronics International v. Casio, Inc.*, is online at www.fedjudge.org.

PRETRIAL CONFERENCE

Either party or the court can request a pretrial conference, or hearing. Usually, the hearing consists of an informal discussion between the judge and the opposing attorneys after discovery has taken place. The purpose of the hearing is to explore the possibility of a settlement without trial and, if this is not possible, to identify the matters that are in dispute and to plan the course of the trial.

ON THE WEB
Cyberjury has a Web site at which visitors are invited to act as jurors deciding real cases. Go to www.cyberjury.com.

9. This is particularly evident in the 1993 revision of the Federal Rules of Civil Procedure. The revised rules provide that each party must disclose to the other, on an ongoing basis, the types of evidence that will be presented at trial, the names of witnesses that may or will be called, and so on.

¡TAKE NOTE!
A prospective juror cannot be excluded solely on the basis of his or her race or gender.

JURY SELECTION

A trial can be held with or without a jury. If there is no jury, the judge determines the truth of the facts alleged in the case. The Seventh Amendment to the U.S. Constitution guarantees the right to a jury trial for cases in federal courts when the amount in controversy exceeds $20. Most states have similar guarantees in their own constitutions (although the threshold dollar amount is higher than $20). The right to a trial by jury does not have to be exercised, and many cases are tried without a jury. In most states and in federal courts, one of the parties must request a jury, or the right is presumed to be waived.

• ***VOIR DIRE***
French verbs that mean, literally, "to see" and "to speak." In jury trials, the phrase refers to the process in which the attorneys question prospective jurors to determine whether they are biased or have any connection with a party to the action or with a prospective witness.

Before a jury trial commences, a jury must be selected. The jury-selection process is known as ***voir dire.***[10] In most jurisdictions, *voir dire* consists of oral questions that attorneys for the plaintiff and the defendant ask a group of prospective jurors (one at a time) to determine whether a potential jury member is biased or has any connection with a party to the action or with a prospective witness.

During *voir dire,* a party may challenge a certain number of prospective jurors *peremptorily*—that is, ask that an individual not be sworn in as a juror without providing any reason. Alternatively, a party may challenge a prospective juror *for cause*—that is, provide a reason why an individual should not be sworn in as a juror. If the judge grants the challenge, the individual is asked to step down. A prospective juror may not be excluded from the jury by the use of discriminatory challenges, however, such as those based on racial criteria[11] or gender.[12]

ETHICAL ISSUE 3.2 ***Are jurors underpaid for their services?*** When David Olson was selected as a juror in the Minnesota trial against the major tobacco companies, little did he realize the consequences he would pay for fulfilling his civic duty. For the four months he served on the jury (before the case was settled, in early 1998), he was paid $30 a day by the court and nothing by his employer. A single father with two children, Olson ended up defaulting on credit-card payments, struggling to obtain food for his family, and refinancing his home to avoid losing it. Yet Olson's $30 a day was in the upper range ($30 to $40 per day) of juror fees paid by state courts. Some states pay much less—Texas, for example, pays only $6 per day. Although some programs are under way to increase juror pay in long trials, most jurors in U.S. courtrooms continue to experience what one economist has referred to as the only remaining form of involuntary servitude in the United States.

AT THE TRIAL

At the beginning of the trial, the attorneys present their opening arguments, setting forth the facts that they expect to provide during the trial. Then the plaintiff's case is presented. In our hypothetical case, Marconi's lawyer would introduce evidence

10. Pronounced vwahr *deehr.* Literally, these French verbs mean "to see, to speak." During the *voir dire* phase of litigation, attorneys do in fact see the prospective jurors speak. In legal language, however, the phrase refers to the process of interrogating prospective jurors to learn about their backgrounds, attitudes, and so on.

11. *Batson v. Kentucky,* 476 U.S. 79, 106 S.Ct. 1712, 90 L.Ed.2d 69 (1986).

12. *J.E.B. v. Alabama ex rel. T.B.,* 511 U.S. 127, 114 S.Ct. 1419, 128 L.Ed.2d 89 (1994). (*Ex rel.* is Latin for *ex relatione.* The phrase refers to an action brought on behalf of the state, by the attorney general, at the instigation of an individual who has a private interest in the matter.)

Technology and E-Mailed "Smoking Guns"

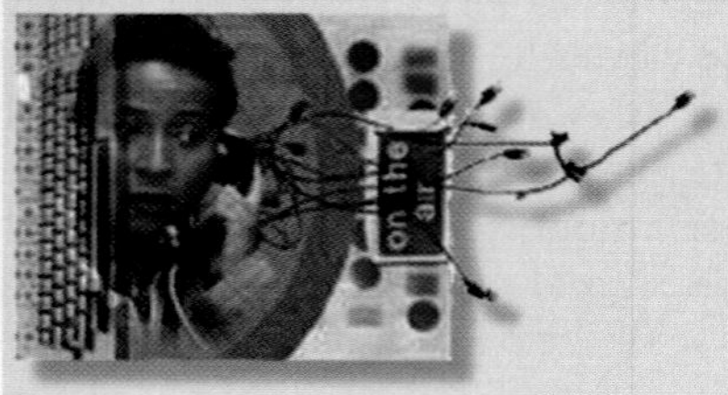

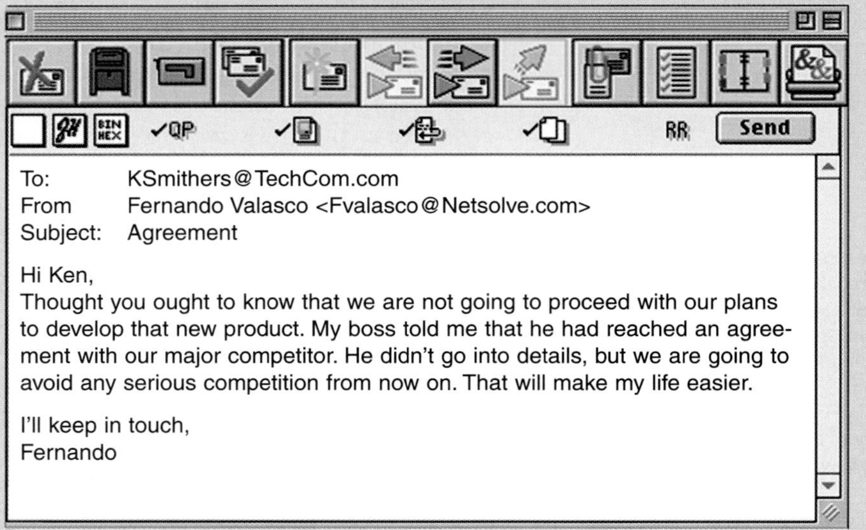
✓QP
RR
Send
To: KSmithers@TechCom.com
From Fernando Valasco <Fvalasco@Netsolve.com>
Subject: Agreement
Hi Ken,
Thought you ought to know that we are not going to proceed with our plans to develop that new product. My boss told me that he had reached an agreement with our major competitor. He didn't go into details, but we are going to avoid any serious competition from now on. That will make my life easier.
I'll keep in touch,
Fernando

An e-mail message between co-workers is revealed. Are e-mail messages truly private? How might this e-mail become a problem later on?

E-mail offers numerous benefits. Because of its speed, relative inexpensiveness, and ease of use, it is rapidly replacing hard copy as a means of communication within and between business firms. For all its benefits, however, e-mail can also lead to litigation nightmares when e-mailed documents are requested during discovery. The reasons for this include common misperceptions about the nature of e-mail and the sheer volume of e-mail messages being sent and received by firms today.

Common Misperceptions about E-Mail

A common misperception about e-mail is that such messages are private. Those sending e-mail thus tend to be more casual—and often more candid—in these communications than they would be if they were writing similar thoughts in interoffice memos or business correspondence using company letterhead. Informal comments made via e-mail, however, can come back to haunt the sender years later, as many firms are learning. For example, e-mail messages exchanged years ago by Microsoft Corporation executives became, for the Department of Justice (DOJ), "smoking guns" (evidence supporting the DOJ's

"Proceed. You have my biased attention."

Learned Hand,
1872–1961
(American jurist)

• **MOTION FOR A DIRECTED VERDICT**
In a jury trial, a motion for the judge to take the decision out of the hands of the jury and direct a verdict for the moving party on the ground that the other party has not produced sufficient evidence to support his or her claim.

• **AWARD**
The amount of money awarded to a plaintiff in a civil lawsuit as damages.

(relevant documents, exhibits, and the testimony of witnesses) to support Marconi's position. The defendant has the opportunity to challenge any evidence introduced and to cross-examine any of the plaintiff's witnesses.

At the end of the plaintiff's case, the defendant's attorney has the opportunity to ask the judge to direct a verdict for the defendant on the ground that the plaintiff has presented no evidence that would justify the granting of the plaintiff's remedy. This is called a **motion for a directed verdict** (known in federal courts as a *motion for judgment as a matter of law*). If the motion is not granted (it seldom is), the defendant's attorney then presents the evidence and witnesses for the defendant's case. The defendant's attorney may also make a motion for a directed verdict. The plaintiff's attorney can challenge any evidence introduced and cross-examine the defendant's witnesses.

After the defense concludes its presentation, the attorneys give their closing arguments, each urging a verdict in favor of his or her client. The judge instructs the jury in the law that applies to the case (these instructions are often called *charges*), and the jury retires to the jury room to deliberate a verdict. In the Marconi-Anderson case, the jury will not only decide for the plaintiff or for the defendant but, if it finds for the plaintiff, will also decide on the amount of the **award** (the money to be paid to her).

Technology and E-Mailed "Smoking Guns," Continued

position) in the department's suit against Microsoft for anticompetitive business practices. The DOJ claimed that the e-mail tended to show that Microsoft deliberately tried to monopolize access to the Internet.[a]

Another common misperception is that e-mail lacks permanence because it can be so easily deleted. In fact, the e-mail is not really deleted from the computer's hard drive just by a click of the mouse; rather, the delete command clears space on the hard drive that can be overwritten when the computer needs that space. Until the message is overwritten, it can be retrieved by an opponent in a lawsuit during discovery. Furthermore, copies of the e-mail message exist not only in the sender's hard drive but also in the hard drives of any recipients of the message, as well as in any servers through which the e-mail might have been routed. Finally, many businesses routinely back up computer information, and back-up tapes may contain e-mail that has been sent to the electronic trash bin.

a. This case is discussed in detail in Chapter 32, in the context of antitrust law, which deals with anticompetitive business practices.

E-Mail Management Policies

To curb potential litigation problems stemming from the use of e-mail, some firms simply delete e-mail after a specified period, such as two weeks or thirty days, and do not include e-mail on their routine back-ups. Other businesses keep back-up copies of their e-mail forever, in the event they may need access to those messages at some future time (to defend against a lawsuit, for example). Still other companies print out or make back-up copies of important e-mail and trash the rest, just as they do with paper documents; this is perhaps the most prudent approach.

Creating an effective e-mail management policy has now become a priority for many firms due to the sheer volume of their e-mail exchanges. According to a Gallup poll conducted in May 1998, the typical office worker sends and receives an average of sixty e-mail messages each day. That means that a company with, say, four thousand workers sends and receives, on average, a staggering 240,000 e-mail messages per day, or 1.2 million per week. If the company were to keep all e-mail on back-up storage devices, in the event of a lawsuit it could face a nightmare indeed. In one case, for example, the court ordered a defendant to review and produce about 30 million pages of e-mail stored on back-up tapes (at a cost of between $50,000 and $70,000).[b]

FOR CRITICAL ANALYSIS

Would it ever be advantageous to a firm to retain all e-mail on back-up tapes indefinitely?

b. *In re Brand Name Prescription Drugs Antitrust Litigation,* 1995 WL 360526 (N.D.Ill. 1995).

Posttrial Motions

• **MOTION FOR JUDGMENT *N.O.V.*** A motion requesting the court to grant judgment in favor of the party making the motion on the ground that the jury verdict against him or her was unreasonable and erroneous.

After the jury has rendered its verdict, either party may make a posttrial motion. If Marconi wins, and Anderson's attorney has previously moved for a directed verdict, Anderson's attorney may make a **motion for judgment *n.o.v.*** (from the Latin *non obstante veredicto*, which means "notwithstanding the verdict"—called a *motion for judgment as a matter of law* in the federal courts) in Anderson's favor on the ground that the jury verdict in favor of Marconi was unreasonable and erroneous. If the judge decides that the jury's verdict was reasonable in light of the evidence presented at trial, the motion will be denied. If the judge agrees with Anderson's attorney, then he or she will set the jury's verdict aside and enter a judgment in favor of Anderson.

• **MOTION FOR A NEW TRIAL** A motion asserting that the trial was so fundamentally flawed (because of error, newly discovered evidence, prejudice, or other reason) that a new trial is necessary to prevent a miscarriage of justice.

Alternatively, Anderson could make a **motion for a new trial,** requesting the judge to set aside the adverse verdict and to hold a new trial. The motion will be granted if the judge is convinced, after looking at all the evidence, that the jury was in error but does not feel it is appropriate to grant judgment for the other side. A new trial may also be granted on the ground of newly discovered evidence, misconduct by the participants or the jury during the trial, or error by the judge.

In the following case, the defendants filed a motion for a new trial based on the plaintiff's attorney's "improper and inflammatory" remarks.

CASE 3.4 LeBlanc v. American Honda Motor Co.

Supreme Court of New Hampshire, 1997.
141 N.H. 579,
688 A.2d 556.
www.state.nh.us/courts/supreme/opinions/9701/honda.htm[a]

HISTORICAL AND SOCIAL SETTING *One of the principles on which the United States was founded is that all persons are created equal and are entitled to have their individual dignity respected. This guarantee is in our federal and state constitutions, and there have been continual efforts by legislative enactments and judicial decisions to purge our society of racial and other prejudices. Despite these efforts, such biases still appear to influence decisions by many people who would deny equal respect to those of us of a different race, religion, or ethnic origin.*

a. This is a page within the collection of New Hampshire Supreme Court opinions available at the Web site of the New Hampshire state government.

BACKGROUND AND FACTS While riding on a snowmobile, Thomas LeBlanc was injured when the snowmobile collided with an off-road vehicle manufactured by American Honda Motor Company (a subsidiary of a Japanese corporation). LeBlanc sued Honda and the driver in a New Hampshire state court. During the trial, LeBlanc's lawyer, Vincent Martina, asked Honda's expert witness if he had ever wondered why the Honda vehicle was "red, white, and blue, the color of the American flag?". During his closing argument, Martina told the jury that the case was not about "Pearl Harbor or the Japanese prime minister saying Americans are lazy and stupid. * * * What this case is about is not American xenophobia; it's about corporate greed." When the jury returned a verdict in favor of LeBlanc, Honda filed a motion for a new trial, which the court denied. Honda appealed to the Supreme Court of New Hampshire, arguing in part that Martina's remarks so tainted the proceedings as to deprive Honda of a fair trial.

IN THE WORDS OF THE COURT . . .
BROCK, Chief Justice.

* * * *

* * * To justify a [new trial], remarks or * * * conduct must be more than merely inadmissible; they must constitute an irreparable injustice * * * .

* * * *

* * * [A] new trial may be warranted where counsel attempts to appeal to the sympathies, passions, and prejudices of jurors grounded in race or nationality, by reference to the opposing party's religious beliefs or lack thereof, or by reference to a party's social or economic condition or status. Such an appeal was attempted in this case.

* * * It is true that counsel's closing reference was brief. At the same time, when an elephant has passed through the courtroom one does not need a forceful reminder.

DECISION AND REMEDY The Supreme Court of New Hampshire reversed the decision in favor of LeBlanc and remanded the case for a new trial. The court held that remarks made during a trial to cultivate in the jury a racial and national bias constitute sufficient grounds for a new trial.

FOR CRITICAL ANALYSIS—Social Consideration *If a trial judge tells a jury to ignore a lawyer's remarks, it is presumed that the jury does not consider them. Do you think that is a valid presumption?*

The Appeal

Assume here that any posttrial motion is denied, and Anderson appeals the case. (If Marconi wins but receives a smaller money award than she sought, she can appeal also.) A notice of appeal must be filed with the clerk of the trial court within a prescribed time. Anderson now becomes the appellant, or petitioner, and Marconi becomes the appellee, or respondent.

Filing the Appeal Anderson's attorney files with the appellate court the record on appeal, which includes the pleadings, the trial transcript, the judge's ruling on motions made by the parties, and other trial-related documents. Anderson's attorney will also file with the reviewing court a condensation of the record, known as an abstract, which is filed with the reviewing court along with the brief. The **brief** is a formal legal document outlining the facts and issues of the case, the judge's rulings or jury's findings that should be reversed or modified, the applicable law, and arguments on Anderson's behalf (citing applicable statutes and relevant cases as precedents).

• **BRIEF**
A formal legal document submitted by the attorney for the appellant or the appellee (in answer to the appellant's brief) to an appellate court when a case is appealed. The appellant's brief outlines the facts and issues of the case, the judge's rulings or jury's findings that should be reversed or modified, the applicable law, and the arguments on the client's behalf.

Marconi's attorney will file an answering brief. Anderson's attorney can file a reply to Marconi's brief, although it is not required. The reviewing court then considers the case.

Appellate Review As mentioned earlier, a court of appeals does not hear evidence. Rather, it reviews the record for errors of law. Its decision concerning a case is based on the record on appeal, the abstracts, and the attorneys' briefs. The attorneys can present oral arguments, after which the case is taken under advisement. In general, appellate courts do not reverse findings of fact unless the findings are unsupported or contradicted by the evidence.

If the reviewing court believes that an error was committed during the trial or that the jury was improperly instructed, the judgment will be *reversed.* Sometimes the case will be *remanded* (sent back to the court that originally heard the case) for a new trial. • **EXAMPLE 3.8** A case may be remanded for several reasons. For instance, if the appellate court decided that a judge improperly granted summary judgment, the case would be remanded for trial. If an appellate court decided that the trial jury's award of damages was too high, the case would be remanded with instructions to reduce the damages award.• In most cases, the judgment of the lower court is *affirmed,* resulting in the enforcement of the court's judgment or decree.

If the reviewing court is an intermediate appellate court, the losing party normally may appeal to the state supreme court (the highest state court). Such a petition corresponds to a petition for a writ of *certiorari* in the United States Supreme Court. If the petition is granted, new briefs must be filed before the state supreme court, and the attorneys may be allowed or requested to present oral arguments. Like the intermediate appellate courts, the supreme court may reverse or affirm the appellate court's decision or remand the case. At this point, unless a federal question is at issue, the case has reached its end.

Alternative Dispute Resolution

Because the number of court cases filling the **dockets** (court schedules listing the cases to be heard) grows every year and the cost of litigation continues to increase, more and more businesspersons, consumers, and others are turning to **alternative dispute resolution** (**ADR**) as a means of settling their disputes.

• **DOCKET**
The list of cases entered on a court's calendar and thus scheduled to be heard by the court.

• **ALTERNATIVE DISPUTE RESOLUTION (ADR)**
The resolution of disputes in ways other than those involved in the traditional judicial process. Negotiation, mediation, and arbitration are examples of ADR methods.

Methods of ADR range from neighbors sitting down over a cup of coffee in an attempt to work out their differences to huge multinational corporations agreeing to resolve a dispute through a formal hearing before a panel of experts. The great advantage of ADR is its flexibility. Normally, the parties themselves can control how the dispute will be settled, what procedures will be used, and whether the decision reached (either by themselves or by a neutral third party) will be legally binding or nonbinding.

Today, approximately 95 percent of cases are settled before trial through some form of ADR. Indeed, the majority of the states either require or encourage parties

ON THE WEB
Information on the rules and procedures used in mediation and arbitration can be accessed at www.legal.gsa.gov/legal89.htm.

to undertake ADR prior to trial. Several federal courts have instituted ADR programs as well. In the following pages, we examine various forms of ADR. Keep in mind, though, that ADR is an ongoing experiment. In other words, new methods of ADR—or new combinations of existing methods—are continuously being devised and employed.

NEGOTIATION

• **NEGOTIATION**
A process in which parties attempt to settle their dispute informally, with or without attorneys to represent them.

One of the simplest forms of ADR is **negotiation,** a process in which the parties attempt to settle their dispute informally, with or without attorneys to represent them. Attorneys frequently advise their clients to negotiate a settlement voluntarily before they proceed to trial.

Negotiation traditionally involves just the parties themselves and (typically) their attorneys. The attorneys, though, are advocates—they are obligated to put their clients' interests first. Often, parties find it helpful to have the opinion and guidance of a neutral (unbiased) third party when deciding whether or how to negotiate a settlement of their dispute. The methods of ADR discussed next all involve neutral third parties.

MEDIATION

• **MEDIATION**
A method of settling disputes outside of court by using the services of a neutral third party, who acts as a communicating agent between the parties and assists the parties in negotiating a settlement.

In the **mediation** process, the parties themselves attempt to negotiate an agreement, but with the assistance of a neutral third party, a mediator. In mediation, the mediator talks with the parties separately as well as jointly. The mediator emphasizes points of agreement, helps the parties evaluate their positions, and proposes solutions. The mediator, however, does not make a decision on the matter being disputed. The mediator, who need not be a lawyer, usually charges a fee for his or her services (which can be split between the parties). States that require parties to undergo ADR before trial often offer mediation as one of the ADR options or (as in Florida) the only option.

Because mediation is not adversarial in nature, the process tends to reduce the antagonism between the disputants and to allow them to resume their former relationship. For this reason, mediation is often the preferred form of ADR for disputes involving business parties, employers and employees, or other parties involved in long-term relationships.

A recent development in ADR is combining characteristics of mediation with those of arbitration (to be discussed next). In *binding mediation,* for example, the parties agree that if they cannot come to an agreement, the mediator can make a legally binding decision on the issue. In *mediation-arbitration,* or "med-arb," the parties agree to first attempt to settle their dispute through mediation. If no settlement is reached, the dispute will be arbitrated.

ARBITRATION

• **ARBITRATION**
The settling of a dispute by submitting it to a disinterested third party (other than a court), who renders a decision that is (most often) legally binding.

A more formal method of ADR is **arbitration,** in which an arbitrator (a neutral third party or a panel of experts) hears a dispute and renders a decision. The key difference between arbitration and the forms of ADR just discussed is that in arbitration, the parties typically agree that the third party's decision will be *legally binding.* Parties can also agree to *nonbinding* arbitration, however. Additionally, when a court refers a case for arbitration, the arbitrator's decision is not binding on the par-

¡KEEP IN MIND! Litigation—even of a dispute over whether a particular matter should be submitted to arbitration—can be time consuming and expensive.

ties. If the parties do not agree with the arbitrator's decision, they can go forward with the lawsuit.

In some respects, formal arbitration resembles a trial, although usually the procedural rules are much less restrictive than those governing litigation. In the typical hearing format, the parties present opening arguments to the arbitrator and state what remedies should or should not be granted. Evidence is then presented, and witnesses may be called and examined by both sides. The arbitrator then renders a decision, which is called an *award.*

An arbitrator's award is usually the final word on the matter. Although the parties may appeal an arbitrator's decision, a court's review of the decision will be much more restricted in scope than an appellate court's review of a trial court's decision. The general view is that because the parties were free to frame the issues and set the powers of the arbitrator at the outset, they cannot complain about the results. The award will only be set aside if the arbitrator's conduct or "bad faith" substantially prejudiced the rights of one of the parties, if the award violates an established public policy, or if the arbitrator exceeded his or her powers (arbitrated issues that the parties did not agree to submit to arbitration).

• **ARBITRATION CLAUSE**
A clause in a contract that provides that, in case of a dispute, the parties will submit the dispute to arbitration rather than litigate the dispute in court.

Arbitration Clauses and Statutes Virtually any commercial matter can be submitted to arbitration. Frequently, parties include an **arbitration clause** in a contract (a written agreement—see Chapter 9), which provides that any dispute that arises under the contract will be resolved through arbitration rather than through the court system. Parties can also agree to arbitrate a dispute after a dispute arises.

Most states have statutes (often based in part on the Uniform Arbitration Act of 1955) under which arbitration clauses will be enforced, and some state statutes compel arbitration of certain types of disputes, such as those involving public employees. At the federal level, the Federal Arbitration Act (FAA), enacted in 1925, enforces arbitration clauses in contracts involving maritime activity and interstate commerce. Because of the breadth of the commerce clause (see Chapter 2), arbitration agreements involving transactions only slightly connected to the flow of interstate commerce may fall under the FAA.

Arbitrability When a dispute arises as to whether or not the parties have agreed in an arbitration clause to submit a particular matter to arbitration, one party may file suit to compel arbitration. The court before which the suit is brought will not decide the basic controversy but must decide the issue of arbitrability—that is, whether the matter is one that must be resolved through arbitration.

Even when a claim involves a violation of a statute passed to protect a certain class of people (such as investors), a court may determine that the parties must nonetheless abide by their agreement to arbitrate the dispute. Usually, a court will allow the claim to be arbitrated if the court, in interpreting the statute, can find no legislative intent to the contrary. • **EXAMPLE 3.9** In *Shearson/American Express, Inc. v. McMahon,*[13] a case decided by the United States Supreme Court in 1987, customers of a brokerage firm alleged that the firm had engaged in fraudulent trading on their accounts in violation of two federal acts—the Racketeer Influenced and Corrupt Organizations Act (see Chapter 5) and the Securities Exchange Act of 1934 (see Chapter 29). When the customers sued the firm, the firm moved to compel arbitration of the claims in accordance with an arbitration clause in the contract. The Court found that when Congress enacted these federal acts, it did not intend to bar

13. 482 U.S. 220, 107 S.Ct. 2332, 96 L.Ed.2d 185 (1987).

enforcement of all predispute arbitration agreements, and thus the claims were arbitrable. ●

Subsequent to the *Shearson* case, the Court faced a similar question: Should claims involving alleged violations of federal statutes protecting employees from employment discrimination also be arbitrable? The Court answered this question in the following landmark case.

CASE 3.5 Gilmer v. Interstate/Johnson Lane Corp.

Supreme Court of the United States, 1991.
500 U.S. 20,
111 S.Ct. 1647,
114 L.Ed.2d 26.
supct.law.cornell.edu/supct/html/90-18.ZS.html[a]

HISTORICAL AND SOCIAL SETTING *In the nineteenth century, some judges would give little respect to the decisions of private arbitrators. These judges may not have wanted competition for the power to decide cases. In 1925, Congress ordered federal courts to respect the decisions of arbitrators. Today, courts generally enforce arbitration awards without reexamining their correctness. At times, though, it may not be clear whether a certain dispute is arbitrable.*

a. This is a page within the "Historic Supreme Court Decisions" collection of the Legal Information Institute (LII) and Project Hermes available at the LII site on the Web. Read the opinion at this page or click on a link to take advantage of one of the other options.

BACKGROUND AND FACTS Interstate/Johnson Lane Corporation required some of its employees, including Robert Gilmer, to register as securities representatives with the New York Stock Exchange (NYSE). The registration application included an agreement to arbitrate when NYSE rules required it. One of the rules requires the arbitration of any controversy arising out of a registrant's termination of employment. Interstate terminated Gilmer's employment. Gilmer, who was sixty-two years old when he was terminated, filed a suit in a federal district court, alleging that he had been discharged in violation of the Age Discrimination in Employment Act (ADEA) of 1967. (This act prohibits employers from discriminating against older employees—see Chapter 38.) Interstate asked the court to order the arbitration of Gilmer's claim, according to the agreement in Gilmer's registration application with the NYSE. The court denied the employer's request, but on appeal, the appellate court ordered the arbitration. Gilmer appealed to the United States Supreme Court.

IN THE WORDS OF THE COURT . . .
Justice *WHITE* delivered the opinion of the Court.

* * * *

* * * [P]rovisions [of the Federal Arbitration Act (FAA)] manifest a "liberal federal policy favoring arbitration agreements."

* * * *

* * * "[H]aving made the bargain to arbitrate, the party should be held to it unless Congress itself has evinced an intention to preclude a waiver of judicial remedies for the statutory rights at issue." * * * If such an intention exists, it will be discoverable in the text of the ADEA, its legislative history, or an "inherent conflict" between arbitration and the ADEA's underlying purposes. * * *

* * * *

* * * [T]he ADEA is designed not only to address individual grievances, but also to further important social policies. We do not perceive any inherent inconsistency between those policies, however, and enforcing agreements to arbitrate age discrimination claims. * * *

* * * An individual ADEA claimant subject to an arbitration agreement will still be free to file a charge with the EEOC * * * .

* * * Congress * * * did not explicitly preclude arbitration or other nonjudicial resolution of claims, even in its recent amendments to the ADEA. * * * In addition, * * * arbitration agreements, "* * * serve to advance the objective of allowing [claimants] a broader right to select the forum for resolving disputes, whether it be judicial or otherwise."

CASE 3.5—Continued

DECISION AND REMEDY The United States Supreme Court held that the arbitration of an age discrimination claim can be compelled. The Court affirmed the order requiring the parties to arbitrate the claim.

FOR CRITICAL ANALYSIS—Ethical Consideration *The decision to compel arbitration may seem to contradict the public policy enunciated in such statutes as the ADEA. For what practical reason might courts favor the arbitration of disputes, even in the employment context?*

OTHER TYPES OF ADR

The three forms of ADR just discussed are the oldest and traditionally the most commonly used forms. In recent years, a variety of new types of ADR have emerged, some of which were mentioned earlier in the discussion of mediation. Other ADR forms that are used today are sometimes referred to as "assisted negotiation" because they involve a third party in what is essentially a negotiation process. For example, in **early neutral case evaluation,** the parties select a neutral third party (generally an expert in the subject matter of the dispute) to evaluate their respective positions. The parties explain their positions to the case evaluator in any manner they choose. The case evaluator then assesses the strengths and weaknesses of the parties' positions, and this evaluation forms the basis of negotiating a settlement.

• **EARLY NEUTRAL CASE EVALUATION**
A form of alternative dispute resolution in which a neutral third party evaluates the strengths and weakness of the disputing parties' positions; the evaluator's opinion forms the basis for negotiating a settlement.

Another form of assisted negotiation that is often used by business parties is the **mini-trial,** in which each party's attorney briefly argues the party's case before representatives of each firm who have the authority to settle the dispute. Typically, a neutral third party (usually an expert in the area being disputed) acts as an adviser. If the parties fail to reach an agreement, the adviser renders an opinion as to how a court would likely decide the issue. The proceeding assists the parties in determining whether they should negotiate a settlement of the dispute or take it to court.

• **MINI-TRIAL**
A private proceeding in which each party to a dispute argues its position before the other side and vice versa. A neutral third party may be present and act as an adviser if the parties fail to reach an agreement.

Today's courts are also experimenting with a variety of ADR alternatives to speed up (and reduce the cost of) justice. Numerous federal courts now hold **summary jury trials (SJTs),** in which the parties present their arguments and evidence and the jury renders a verdict. The jury's verdict is not binding, but it does act as a guide to both sides in reaching an agreement during the mandatory negotiations that immediately follow the trial. Other alternatives being employed by the courts include summary procedures for commercial litigation and the appointment of special masters to assist judges in deciding complex issues.

• **SUMMARY JURY TRIAL (SJT)**
A method of settling disputes used in many federal courts in which a trial is held, but the jury's verdict is not binding. The verdict acts only as a guide to both sides in reaching an agreement during the mandatory negotiations that immediately follow the summary jury trial.

PROVIDERS OF ADR SERVICES

ADR services are provided by both government agencies and private organizations. A major provider of ADR services is the American Arbitration Association (AAA). Most of the nation's largest law firms are members of this nonprofit association. Founded in 1926, the AAA now settles about seventy thousand disputes a year in its numerous offices around the country. Cases brought before the AAA are heard by an expert or a panel of experts in the area relating to the dispute and are usually settled quickly. Generally, about half of the panel members are lawyers. To cover its costs, the AAA charges a fee, paid by the party filing the claim. In addition, each party to the dispute pays a specified amount for each hearing day, as well as a special additional fee for cases involving personal injuries or property loss.

ON THE WEB
To obtain information on the services offered by the American Arbitration Association, go to its Web site at www.adr.org.

Hundreds of for-profit firms around the country also provide various forms of dispute-resolution services. Typically, these firms hire retired judges to conduct arbitration hearings or otherwise assist parties in settling their disputes. The judges follow procedures similar to those of the federal courts and use similar rules. Usually, each party to the dispute pays a filing fee and a designated fee for a hearing session or conference.

International Perspective • ADR IN JAPAN AND CHINA

The United States is not the only country that encourages mediation, arbitration, and other forms of ADR. Japan, for example, has recently authorized the establishment of neutral panels to act as mediators in product liability suits (suits brought by plaintiffs who have allegedly been injured by a seller's defective product—see Chapter 18). Several industries, including those that manufacture and sell housing materials, automobiles, and appliances, have set up such panels, which follow guidelines published by the Japanese Ministry of International Trade and Industry. Since the mid-1990s, China also has made it simpler for disputes to be settled through ADR. Under Chinese law, although most disputes can be arbitrated, family matters (such as those relating to marriage, adoption, and financial support) cannot be submitted for arbitration. Such disputes are handled by the relevant administrative agencies of the Chinese government.

FOR CRITICAL ANALYSIS

Do you see any reason why certain types of disputes, such as those involving family matters, should not be decided by arbitration?

APPLICATION Law and the Businessperson: To Sue or Not to Sue*

Wrongs are committed every minute of every day in the United States. These wrongs may be committed inadvertently or intentionally. Sometimes, businesspersons believe that wrongs have been committed against them by other businesspersons, by consumers, or by the local, state, or federal government. If you are deciding whether or not to sue for a wrong that has been committed against you or your business, you must consider many issues.

THE QUESTION OF COST

Competent legal advice is not inexpensive. Good commercial business law attorneys charge $75 to $400 an hour, plus expenses. It is almost always worthwhile to make an initial visit to an attorney who has skills in the area in which you are going to sue to get an estimate of the expected costs of pursuing a redress for your grievance. You may be charged for the initial visit as well.

Note that less than 10 percent of all corporate lawsuits end up in trial—the rest are settled beforehand. You may end up settling for far less than you thought you were "owed" simply because of the length of time it takes your attorney to bring your case to trial and to finish the trial. And then you might not win, anyway!

Basically, then, you must do a cost-benefit analysis to determine whether you should sue. Your attorney can give you the costs, and you can "guesstimate" the benefits. You do this by multiplying the probable size of the award by the probability of obtaining that award.

THE ALTERNATIVES BEFORE YOU

Another method of settling your grievance is by alternative dispute resolution (ADR). Negotiation, mediation, arbitration, and other ADR forms are becoming increasingly attractive alternatives to court litigation, because they usually yield quick results at a comparatively low cost. Most disputes relating to business can be mediated or arbitrated through the American Arbitration Association (AAA), and there are numerous other ADR centers as well. You can obtain information on ADR from the AAA, courthouses, chambers of commerce, law firms, state bar associations, or the American Bar Association. The latter is located at 750 N. Lake Shore Dr., Chicago, IL 60611, and can be accessed online at **www.abanet.org**. The Yellow Pages in large metropolitan areas usually list agencies and firms that could help you settle your dispute out of court; look under "Mediation" or "Social Service Agencies."

CHECKLIST FOR DECIDING WHETHER TO SUE

1. Are you prepared to pay for going to court? Make this decision only after you have consulted an attorney to get an estimate of the costs of litigating the dispute.
2. Do you have the patience to follow a court case through the judicial system, even if it takes several years?
3. Is there a way for you to settle your grievance without going to court? Even if the settlement is less than you think you are owed—in net terms corrected for future expenses, lost time, and frustration—you may be better off settling now for the smaller figure.
4. Can you use some form of alternative dispute resolution? Before you say no, investigate these alternatives—they are usually cheaper and quicker to use than the standard judicial process.

*This *Application* is not meant to substitute for the services of an attorney who is licensed to practice law in your state.

Key Terms

Chapter Summary • Courts and Procedures

The Judiciary's Role in American Government (See pages 61–62.)	The role of the judiciary—the courts—in the American governmental system is to interpret and apply the law. Through the process of judicial review—determining the constitutionality of laws—the judicial branch acts as a check on the executive and legislative branches of government. The power of judicial review was established by Chief Justice John Marshall in *Marbury v. Madison* (1803).
Basic Judicial Requirements (See pages 62–68)	1. *Jurisdiction*—Before a court can hear a case, it must have jurisdiction over the person against whom the suit is brought or the property involved in the suit, as well as jurisdiction over the subject matter. a. Limited versus general jurisdiction—Limited jurisdiction exists when a court is limited to a specific subject matter, such as probate or divorce. General jurisdiction exists when a court can hear any kind of case. b. Original versus appellate jurisdiction—Original jurisdiction exists with courts that have authority to hear a case for the first time (trial courts). Appellate jurisdiction exists with courts of appeals, or reviewing courts; generally, appellate courts do not have original jurisdiction. c. Federal jurisdiction—Arises (1) when a federal question is involved (when the plaintiff's cause of action is based, at least in part, on the U.S. Constitution, a treaty, or a federal law) or (2) when a case involves diversity of citizenship (citizens of different states, for example) and the amount in controversy exceeds $75,000.

Chapter Summary • Courts and Procedures, Continued

Basic Judicial Requirements—continued	d. Concurrent versus exclusive jurisdiction—Concurrent jurisdiction exists when two different courts have authority to hear the same case. Exclusive jurisdiction exists when only state courts or only federal courts have authority to hear a case. 2. *Venue*—Venue has to do with the most appropriate location for a trial, which is usually the geographical area in which the event leading to the dispute took place or where the parties reside. 3. *Standing to sue*—A requirement that a party must have a legally protected and tangible interest at stake sufficient to justify seeking relief through the court system. The controversy at issue must also be a justiciable controversy—one that is real and substantial, as opposed to hypothetical or academic.
The State and Federal Court Systems (See pages 68–72)	1. *Trial courts*—Courts of original jurisdiction, in which legal actions are initiated. a. State—Courts of general jurisdiction can hear any case; courts of limited jurisdiction include divorce courts, probate courts, traffic courts, small claims courts, and so on. b. Federal—The federal district court is the equivalent of the state trial court. Federal courts of limited jurisdiction include the U.S. Tax Court, the U.S. Bankruptcy Court, and the U.S. Court of Federal Claims. 2. *Intermediate appellate courts*—Courts of appeals, or reviewing courts; generally without original jurisdiction. Many states have an intermediate appellate court; in the federal court system, the U.S. circuit courts of appeals are the intermediate appellate courts. 3. *Supreme (highest) courts*—Each state has a supreme court, although it may be called by some other name, from which appeal to the United States Supreme Court is only possible if a federal question is involved. The United States Supreme Court is the highest court in the federal court system and the final arbiter of the Constitution and federal law.
Following a State Court Case (See pages 72–83.)	Rules of procedure prescribe the way in which disputes are handled in the courts. Rules differ from court to court, and separate sets of rules exist for federal and state courts, as well as for criminal and civil cases. A sample civil court case in a state court would involve the following procedures: 1. *The pleadings*— a. Complaint—Filed by the plaintiff with the court to initiate the lawsuit; served with a summons on the defendant. b. Answer—Admits or denies allegations made by the plaintiff; may assert a counterclaim or an affirmative defense. c. Motion to dismiss—A request to the court to dismiss the case for stated reasons, such as the plaintiff's failure to state a claim for which relief can be granted. 2. *Pretrial motions (in addition to the motion to dismiss)*— a. Motion for judgment on the pleadings—May be made by either party; will be granted if the parties agree on the facts and the only question is how the law applies to the facts. The judge bases the decision solely on the pleadings. b. Motion for summary judgment—May be made by either party; will be granted if the parties agree on the facts. The judge applies the law in rendering a judgment. The judge can consider evidence outside the pleadings when evaluating the motion. 3. *Discovery*—The process of gathering evidence concerning the case. Discovery involves depositions (sworn testimony by a party to the lawsuit or any witness), interrogatories (written questions and answers to these questions made by parties to the action with the aid of their attorneys), and various requests (for admissions, documents, medical examination, and so on).

Chapter Summary • Courts and Procedures, Continued

Following a State Court Case—continued	4. *Pretrial conference*—Either party or the court can request a pretrial conference to identify the matters in dispute after discovery has taken place and to plan the course of the trial. 5. *Trial*—Following jury selection (*voir dire*), the trial begins with opening statements from both parties' attorneys. The following events then occur: a. The plaintiff's introduction of evidence (including the testimony of witnesses) supporting the plaintiff's position. The defendant's attorney can challenge evidence and cross-examine witnesses. b. The defendant's introduction of evidence (including the testimony of witnesses) supporting the defendant's position. The plaintiff's attorney can challenge evidence and cross-examine witnesses. c. Closing arguments by attorneys in favor of their respective clients, the judge's instructions to the jury, and the jury's verdict. 6. *Posttrial motions*— a. Motion for judgment *n.o.v.* ("notwithstanding the verdict")—Will be granted if the judge is convinced that the jury was in error. b. Motion for a new trial—Will be granted if the judge is convinced that the jury was in error; can also be granted on the grounds of newly discovered evidence, misconduct by the participants during the trial, or error by the judge. 7. *Appeal*—Either party can appeal the trial court's judgment to an appropriate court of appeals. After reviewing the record on appeal, the abstracts, and the attorneys' briefs, the appellate court holds a hearing and renders its opinion.
Alternative Dispute Resolution (ADR) (See pages 83–88.)	1. *Negotiation*—The parties come together, with or without attorneys to represent them, and try to reach a settlement without the involvement of a third party. 2. *Mediation*—The parties themselves reach an agreement with the help of a neutral third party, called a mediator, who proposes solutions. At the parties' request, a mediator may make a legally binding decision. 3. *Arbitration*—A more formal method of ADR in which the parties submit their dispute to a neutral third party, the arbitrator, who renders a decision. The decision may or may not be legally binding, depending on the circumstances. 4. *Early neutral case evaluation*—A private proceeding in which the parties argue their respective cases before a neutral third party, whose decision becomes the basis for negotiating a settlement. 5. *Mini-trial*—A private proceeding in which each party's attorney argues the party's case before the other party. Often, a neutral third party renders an opinion on how a court would likely decide the issue. 6. *Summary jury trial (SJT)*—A kind of trial employed by numerous federal courts in which litigants present their arguments and evidence and the jury renders a nonbinding verdict. The verdict guides the parties in reaching an agreement during the mandatory negotiations that immediately follow the trial. 7. *Providers of ADR services*—The leading nonprofit provider of ADR services is the American Arbitration Association. Hundreds of for-profit firms also provide ADR services.

For Review

1. What is judicial review? How and when was the power of judicial review established?
2. Before a court can hear a case, it must have jurisdiction. Over what must it have jurisdiction? In what circumstances does a federal court have jurisdiction?
3. What is the difference between a trial court and an appellate court?
4. In a lawsuit, what are the pleadings? What is discovery?
5. Name five methods of alternative dispute resolution (ADR). What advantages does ADR offer to the parties?

Questions and Case Problems

3–1. Appellate Process. If a judge enters a judgment on the pleadings, the losing party can usually appeal but cannot present evidence to the appellate court. Does this seem fair? Explain.

3–2. Arbitration. In an arbitration proceeding, the arbitrator need not be a judge or even a lawyer. How, then, can the arbitrator's decision have the force of law and be binding on the parties involved?

3–3. Appellate Process. Sometimes on appeal there are questions concerning whether the facts presented in the trial court support the conclusion reached by the judge or the jury. An appellate court, however, normally defers to the trial court's decision with regard to the facts. Can you see any reason for this?

3–4. Jurisdiction. Marya Callais, a citizen of Florida, was walking near a busy street in Tallahassee one day when a large crate flew off a passing truck and hit her, resulting in numerous injuries to Callais. She incurred a great deal of pain and suffering plus numerous medical expenses, and she could not work for six months. She wishes to sue the trucking firm for $300,000 in damages. The firm's headquarters are in Georgia, although the company does business in Florida. In what court may Marya bring suit—a Florida state court, a Georgia state court, or a federal court? What factors might influence her decision?

3–5. Jurisdiction. Shem and Nadine Maslov, who live in Massachusetts, saw an advertisement in the *Boston Globe* for vacationers that was sponsored by a national hotel chain: "Stay in Maximum Inns' beachfront hotel in Puerto Rico for one week for only $800; continental breakfast included." The Maslovs decided to accept the offer and spent a week at the hotel. On the last day, Nadine fell on a wet floor in the hotel lobby and sustained multiple fractures to her left ankle and hip. Because of her injuries, which were subsequently complicated by infections, she was unable to work at her job as an airline flight attendant for ten months. The hotel chain does not do business in Massachusetts. If Nadine sues Maximum Inns in a Massachusetts state court, can the court exercise jurisdiction over Maximum Inns? What factors should the court consider in deciding this jurisdictional issue?

3–6. Arbitration. Gates worked for Arizona Brewing Co. A contract between Gates's employer and the union to which Gates belonged stated that the employer and the union were to try to settle their differences, but if the parties could not reach a settlement, the matter was to be decided by arbitration. Gates brought a lawsuit against his employer (instead of submitting the dispute to arbitration) to recover wages. The employer argued that Gates could not bring a lawsuit until after arbitration had occurred. Gates claimed that the arbitration clause was void under an Arizona arbitration statute, which stated that "this act shall not apply to collective [bargained] contracts between employers and . . . associations of employ[ees]." Must Gates undergo arbitration before bringing a lawsuit? Explain. [*Gates v. Arizona Brewing Co.,* 54 Ariz. 266, 95 P.2d 49 (1939)]

3–7. Arbitration. Randall Fris worked as a seaman on an Exxon Shipping Co. oil tanker for eight years without incident. One night, he boarded the ship for duty while intoxicated, in violation of company policy. This policy also allowed Exxon to discharge employees who were intoxicated and thus unfit for work. Exxon discharged Fris. Under a contract with Fris's union, the discharge was submitted to arbitration. The arbitrators ordered Exxon to reinstate Fris on an oil tanker. Exxon filed a suit against the union, challenging the award as contrary to public policy, which opposes having intoxicated persons operate seagoing vessels. Can a court set aside an arbitration award on the ground that the award violates public policy? Should the court set aside the award in this case? Explain. [*Exxon Shipping Co. v. Exxon Seamen's Union,* 11 F.3d 1189 (3d Cir. 1993)]

3–8. Procedure. Washoe Medical Center, Inc., admitted Shirley Swisher for the treatment of a fractured pelvis. During her stay, Swisher suffered a fatal fall from her hospital bed. Gerald Parodi, the administrator of her estate, and others filed an action against Washoe in which they sought damages for the alleged lack of care in treating Swisher. During *voir dire,* when the plaintiffs' attorney returned a few minutes late from a break, the trial judge led the prospective jurors in a standing ovation. The judge joked with one of the prospective jurors, whom he had known in college, about the judge's fitness to serve as a judge and personally endorsed another prospective juror's business. After the trial, the jury returned a verdict in favor of Washoe. The plaintiffs appealed, arguing that the tone set by the judge during *voir dire* prejudiced their right to a fair trial. Should the appellate court agree? Why or why not? [*Parodi v. Washoe Medical Center, Inc.*, 111 Nev. 365, 892 P.2d 588 (1995)]

3–9. Jurisdiction. George Rush, a New York resident and columnist for the New York *Daily News*, wrote a critical column about Berry Gordy, the founder and former president of Motown Records. Gordy, a California resident, filed suit in a California state court against Rush and the newspaper (the defendants), alleging defamation (a civil wrong, or tort, that occurs when the publication of false statements harms a person's good reputation). Most of the newspaper's subscribers are in the New York area, and the paper covers mostly New York events. Thirteen copies of its daily edition are distributed to California subscribers, however, and the paper does cover events that are of nationwide interest to the entertainment industry. Because of its focus on entertainment, the newspaper also routinely sends reporters to California to gather news from California sources. Can a California state court exercise personal jurisdiction over the New York defendants in this case? What factors will the court consider in deciding this question? If you were the judge, how would you decide the issue, and why? Discuss fully. [*Gordy v. Daily News, L.P.*, 95 F.3d 829 (9th Cir. 1996)]

3–10. Jurisdiction. George Noonan, a Boston police detective and a devoted nonsmoker, has spent most of his career educating Bostonians about the health risks of tobacco use. In 1992, an ad for Winston cigarettes featuring Noonan's image appeared in several French magazines. Some of the magazines were on sale at newsstands in Boston. Noonan filed a suit in a federal district court against The Winston Co., Lintas:Paris (the French ad agency that created the ads), and others. Lintas:Paris and the other French defendants claimed that they did not know the magazines would be sold in Boston and filed a motion to dismiss the suit for lack of personal jurisdiction. Does the court have jurisdiction? Why or why not? [*Noonan v. The Winston Co.*, 135 F.3d 85 (1st Cir. 1998)]

A QUESTION OF ETHICS AND SOCIAL RESPONSIBILITY

3–11. Linda Bender brought an action in a federal court against her supervisor at A. G. Edwards & Sons, Inc., a stockbrokerage firm (the defendants). Bender alleged sexual harassment in violation of Title VII of the Civil Rights Act of 1964, which prohibits, among other things, employment discrimination based on gender. In her application for registration as a stockbroker, Bender had agreed to arbitrate any disputes with her employer. The defendants moved to compel arbitration. The district court judge denied the motion, holding that Bender could not be forced to waive her right to adjudicate Title VII claims in federal court. The appellate court reversed, ruling that Title VII claims are arbitrable. The court held that compelling Bender to submit her claim for arbitration did not deprive her of the right to a judicial forum, because if the arbitration proceedings were somehow legally deficient, she could still take her case to a federal court for review. [*Bender v. A. G. Edwards & Sons, Inc.*, 971 F.2d 698 (11th Cir. 1992)]

1. Does the right to a postarbitration judicial forum equate to the right to initial access to a judicial forum in employment disputes?
2. Should the fact that reviewing courts rarely set aside arbitrators' awards have any bearing on the arbitrability of certain types of claims, such as those brought under Title VII?

FOR CRITICAL ANALYSIS

3–12. American courts are forums for adversarial justice, in which attorneys defend the interests of their respective clients before the court. This means that an attorney may end up claiming before a court that his or her client is innocent, even though the attorney knows that the client acted wrongfully. Is it ethical for attorneys to try to "deceive" the court in these situations? Can the adversarial system of justice really lead to "truth"?

Online Activities

ONLINE EXERCISE 3–1

The United States Supreme Court plays a vital role in the American system of government. To inform the public of its origins, its significance, and its procedures, the Court published a pamphlet that is now online at

www.usscplus.com/info/index.htm.

Go to this site and click on the box titled "The Court and Constitutional Interpretation" in the left-hand margin of the screen. Read through this page, and then answer the following questions:

- How does the Court describe its basic function in the American system of government?
- Why does the Court consider itself to be a uniquely American institution?
- What basic arguments did Alexander Hamilton and James Madison offer in support of the concept of judicial review?
- When did the Supreme Court first clarify that its authority is limited to deciding actual cases and controversies?
- When the Supreme Court rules on a constitutional issue, is that decision necessarily final? Can it ever be changed? If so, how?
- When the Supreme Court renders an interpretation of a statute passed by Congress, is that decision necessarily final? Explain.

Before the Test

Go to the *Business Law Today* home page at http://blt.westbuslaw.com. Click on TestTutor.® You will find twenty interactive questions relating to this chapter.

CHAPTER 4 Torts

> "Tort more or less means 'wrong' . . . . One of my friends [in law school] said that Torts is the course which proves that your mother was right."
>
> Scott Turow, 1949–
> (American lawyer and author)

CONTENTS

LEARNING OBJECTIVES

After reading this chapter, you should be able to:

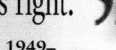

1. Explain how torts and crimes differ.
2. State the purpose of tort law.
3. Identify some intentional torts against persons and property.
4. Name the four elements of negligence.
5. Define strict liability, and list some circumstances in which it will be applied.

As Scott Turow's statement in the above quotation indicates, **torts** are wrongful actions.[1] Through tort law, society compensates those who have suffered injuries as a result of the wrongful conduct of others. Although some torts, such as assault and trespass, originated in the English common law, the field of tort law continues to expand as new ways to commit wrongs are discovered and new conceptions of what is right and wrong in a social or business context emerge.

Tort law covers a wide variety of injuries. Society recognizes an interest in personal physical safety, and tort law provides remedies for acts that cause physical injury or that interfere with physical security and freedom of movement. Society recognizes an interest in protecting real and personal property, and tort law provides remedies for acts that cause destruction or damage to property. Society also recognizes an interest in protecting certain intangible interests, such as personal privacy, family relations, reputation, and dignity, and tort law provides remedies for invasion of these protected interests.

● **TORT**
A civil wrong not arising from a breach of contract. A breach of a legal duty that proximately causes harm or injury to another.

1. The term *tort* is French for "wrong."

Certain torts normally occur only in the business context. The important area of business torts will be treated in Chapter 5. In this chapter, we discuss torts that can occur in any context, including the business environment. In fact, as you will see in later chapters of this book, many of the lawsuits brought by or against business firms are based on the tort theories discussed in this chapter.

The Restatement (Third) of Torts

In deciding tort cases, courts frequently refer to the second edition of the *Restatement of the Law of Torts,* commonly referred to as the *Restatement (Second) of Torts.* As discussed in Chapter 1, although the *Restatements of the Law* are secondary sources of law, they are valuable summaries of common law principles, and judges often rely on them when making decisions. The American Law Institute (ALI), which drafts and publishes the *Restatements,* is currently revising the *Restatement (Second) of Torts.*

To date, the only published portion of the revision concerns product liability law (mentioned later in this chapter). Because of its importance to the legal community, the *Restatement (Third) of Torts: Products Liability* is discussed in detail in Chapter 18 in the context of product liability law.

> **ON THE WEB**
> You can keep abreast of recent and planned revisions of the *Restatements of the Law* by accessing the American Law Institute's Web site at www.ali.org.

The Basis of Tort Law

Two notions serve as the basis of all torts: wrongs and compensation. Tort law recognizes that some acts are wrong because they cause injuries to others. Of course, a tort is not the only type of wrong that exists in the law; crimes also involve wrongs. A crime, however, is an act so reprehensible that it is considered a wrong against the state or against society as a whole, as well as against the individual victim. Therefore, the *state* prosecutes and punishes (through fines and/or imprisonment—and possibly death) persons who commit criminal acts. A tort action, in contrast, is a civil action in which one person brings a personal suit against another to obtain compensation (money **damages**) or other relief for the harm suffered.

• **DAMAGES**
Money sought as a remedy for a breach of contract or a tortious action.

Some torts provide a basis for a criminal prosecution as well as a tort action. We discuss how the same act can give rise to liability under both tort law and criminal law in Chapter 6.

Intentional Torts against Persons

• **INTENTIONAL TORT**
A wrongful act knowingly committed.

• **TORTFEASOR**
One who commits a tort.

An **intentional tort,** as the term implies, requires *intent.* The **tortfeasor** (the one committing the tort) must intend to commit an act, the consequences of which interfere with the personal or business interests of another in a way not permitted by law. An evil or harmful motive is not required—in fact, the actor may even have a beneficial motive for committing what turns out to be a tortious act. In tort law, intent only means that the actor intended the consequences of his or her act or knew with substantial certainty that certain consequences would result from the act. The law generally assumes that individuals intend the *normal* consequences of their actions. Thus, forcefully pushing another—even if done in jest and without any evil motive—is an intentional tort (if injury results), because the object of a strong push can ordinarily be expected to go flying.

This section discusses intentional torts against persons, which include assault and battery, false imprisonment, infliction of emotional distress, defamation, invasion of the right to privacy, and misrepresentation.

Assault and Battery

• **ASSAULT**
Any word or action intended to make another person fearful of immediate physical harm; a reasonably believable threat.

• **BATTERY**
The unprivileged, intentional touching of another.

Any intentional, unexcused act that creates in another person a reasonable apprehension or fear of immediate harmful or offensive contact is an **assault.** Apprehension is not the same as fear. If a contact is such that a reasonable person would want to avoid it, and if there is a reasonable basis for believing that the contact will occur, then the plaintiff suffers apprehension whether or not he or she is afraid. The interest protected by tort law concerning assault is the freedom from having to expect harmful or offensive contact. The occurrence of apprehension is enough to justify compensation.

The *completion* of the act that caused the apprehension, if it results in harm to the plaintiff, is a **battery,** which is defined as an unexcused and harmful or offensive physical contact *intentionally* performed. For example, suppose that Ivan threatens Jean with a gun, then shoots her. The pointing of the gun at Jean is an assault; the firing of the gun (if the bullet hits Jean) is a battery. The interest protected by tort law concerning battery is the right to personal security and safety. The contact can be harmful, or it can be merely offensive (such as an unwelcome kiss). Physical injury need not occur. The contact can involve any part of the body or anything attached to it—for example, a hat or other item of clothing, a purse, or a chair or an automobile in which one is sitting. Whether the contact is offensive or not is determined by the *reasonable person* standard.[2] The contact can be made by the defendant or by some force the defendant sets in motion—for example, a rock thrown, food poisoned, or a stick swung.

Compensation If the plaintiff shows that there was contact, and the jury agrees that the contact was offensive, the plaintiff has a right to compensation. There is no need to show that the defendant acted out of malice; the person could have just been joking or playing around. The underlying motive does not matter, only the intent to bring about the harmful or offensive contact to the plaintiff. In fact, proving a motive is never necessary (but is sometimes relevant). A plaintiff may be compensated for the emotional harm or loss of reputation resulting from a battery, as well as for physical harm.

• **DEFENSE**
That which a defendant offers and alleges in an action or suit as a reason why the plaintiff should not recover or establish what he or she seeks.

Defenses to Assault and Battery A number of legally recognized **defenses** (reasons why plaintiffs should not obtain what they are seeking) can be raised by a defendant who is sued for assault or battery, or both:

1. *Consent.* When a person consents to the act that damages him or her, there is generally no liability (legal responsibility) for the damage done.
2. *Self-defense.* An individual who is defending his or her life or physical well-being can claim self-defense. In situations of both *real* and *apparent* danger, a person may use whatever force is *reasonably* necessary to prevent harmful contact.
3. *Defense of others.* An individual can act in a reasonable manner to protect others who are in real or apparent danger.
4. *Defense of property.* Reasonable force may be used in attempting to remove intruders from one's home, although force that is likely to cause death or great bodily injury can never be used just to protect property.

¡BE AWARE!
Some of these same defenses can be raised by a defendant who is sued for other torts.

2. The reasonable person standard is an objective test of how a reasonable person would have acted under the same circumstances. See "The Duty of Care and Its Breach" later in this chapter.

FALSE IMPRISONMENT

False imprisonment is defined as the intentional confinement or restraint of another person's activities without justification. False imprisonment interferes with the freedom to move without restraint. The confinement can be accomplished through the use of physical barriers, physical restraint, or threats of physical force. Moral pressure or threats of future harm do not constitute false imprisonment. It is essential that the person being restrained not comply with the restraint willingly.

Businesspersons are often confronted with suits for false imprisonment after they have attempted to confine a suspected shoplifter for questioning. Under the "privilege to detain" granted to merchants in some states, a merchant can use the defense of *probable cause* to justify delaying a suspected shoplifter. Probable cause exists when the evidence to support the belief that a person is guilty outweighs the evidence against that belief. The detention, however, must be conducted in a *reasonable* manner and for only a *reasonable* length of time. At issue in the following case was whether a store's detention of a suspected shoplifter was reasonable.

CASE 4.1 Wal-Mart Stores, Inc. v. Resendez

Supreme Court of Texas, 1998.
962 S.W.2d 539.
www.supreme.courts.state.tx.us/scopn.htm[a]

COMPANY PROFILE *Wal-Mart Stores, Inc., is the world's leading retail firm—larger than J. C. Penney Company, Kmart Corporation, and Sears, Roebuck and Company combined. Wal-Mart is also the second largest grocer and the second largest chain of warehouse stores in the United States. With more than 3,400 Wal-Mart stores, Sam's Club membership-only warehouse stores, and Wal-Mart Supercenter stores, the company accounts for 15 percent of U.S. general merchandise, apparel, and furniture sales.*

a. The opinion in this case can be downloaded from this page within the Web site "Texas Judiciary Online," the home page of the Texas state courts. The case's date, which is needed to download the case, is February 13, 1998.

BACKGROUND AND FACTS In a Wal-Mart store, Raul Salinas, a store security guard, saw Lucia Resendez, a customer, eating from a bag of peanuts marked with a Wal-Mart price sticker. Salinas saw Resendez discard the empty bag in the store. After she left, he determined that she had not paid for a bag of peanuts. He followed her into the parking lot and accused her of taking the peanuts without paying. She protested that she had purchased them the day before at another Wal-Mart store and said that she could provide the receipt. They went back into the store, where she was detained. Less than fifteen minutes later, a police officer arrived and arrested her. She was convicted of misdemeanor theft. When the conviction was overturned on appeal, Resendez filed a suit in a Texas state court against Wal-Mart, alleging, among other things, false imprisonment. The court entered a judgment in Resendez's favor, which the state intermediate appellate court affirmed. Wal-Mart appealed to the Texas Supreme Court.

IN THE WORDS OF THE COURT . . .
PER CURIAM [by the whole court]:

* * * *

* * * [Under a state statute, the] "shopkeeper's privilege" expressly grants an employee the authority of law to detain a customer to investigate the ownership of property in a reasonable manner and for a reasonable period of time if the employee has a reasonable belief that the customer has stolen or is attempting to steal store merchandise.

CASE 4.1—Continued

There was no evidence to support the contention that the detention occurred for an unreasonable period of time. * * * [T]he ten to fifteen minute detention in this case was not unreasonable * * * . Also, no evidence exists that the detention occurred in an unreasonable manner. The only question is whether it was reasonable for Salinas to believe that Resendez had stolen the peanuts. It was.

* * * Based upon the undisputed facts—Resendez * * * was * * * seen eating from a bag of peanuts marked with a Wal-Mart price sticker, and she did not pay for the peanuts on leaving the store—probable cause existed to believe that the peanuts were stolen property. * * * [T]he undisputed facts of this case establish that Salinas had the authority of law to detain Resendez and therefore she was not falsely imprisoned.

* * * *

* * * The [shopkeeper's] privilege does not require the detainer to confirm or refute the detainee's claims, nor does it prevent the detainer from holding the suspected shoplifter for a reasonable time in order to deliver her to the police.

DECISION AND REMEDY The Texas Supreme Court reversed the decision of the lower court and entered a judgment for Wal-Mart. The state supreme court held that Wal-Mart detained Resendez for a reasonable period of time, in a reasonable manner, and under a reasonable belief that she had stolen store merchandise.

FOR CRITICAL ANALYSIS—Social Consideration *What might be the result for society if businesses were held liable every time they detained a customer?*

INFLICTION OF EMOTIONAL DISTRESS

The tort of *infliction of emotional distress* can be defined as an intentional act that amounts to extreme and outrageous conduct resulting in severe emotional distress to another.[3] • **EXAMPLE 4.1** A prankster telephones an individual and says that the individual's spouse has just been in a horrible accident. As a result, the individual suffers intense mental pain or anxiety. The caller's behavior is deemed to be extreme and outrageous conduct that exceeds the bounds of decency accepted by society and is therefore **actionable** (capable of serving as the ground for a lawsuit).•

• **ACTIONABLE**
Capable of serving as the basis of a lawsuit. An actionable claim can be pursued in a lawsuit or other court action.

The tort of infliction of emotional distress poses several problems for the courts. One problem is the difficulty of proving the existence of emotional suffering. For this reason, some courts require that the emotional distress be evidenced by some physical symptom or illness or some emotional disturbance that can be documented by a psychiatric consultant or other medical professional.

Another problem is that emotional distress claims must be subject to some limitation, or they could flood the courts with lawsuits. A society in which individuals are rewarded if they are unable to endure the normal emotional stresses of day-to-day living is obviously undesirable. Therefore, the law usually holds that indignity or annoyance alone is not enough to support a lawsuit based on infliction of emotional distress. Repeated annoyances (such as those experienced by a person who is being stalked), however, coupled with threats, are enough. In the business context, the repeated use of extreme methods to collect a delinquent account may be actionable.

In the following case, the court looks at one of the requirements that plaintiffs must meet to establish an emotional distress claim.

3. *Restatement (Second) of Torts,* Section 46, Comment d.

CASE 4.2 Roach v. Stern

Supreme Court of New York,
Appellate Division,
Second Department, 1998.
675 N.Y.S.2d 133.

HISTORICAL AND SOCIAL SETTING *What some persons may consider extreme and outrageous, others may consider humorous or insightful. Never has this been truer than in the case of Howard Stern. Stern is a talk-show host whose style is to ask irreverent questions and make off-color jokes. The subjects of his interviews—and the objects of his comments—include celebrities and less well-known personalities with offbeat interests.* The Howard Stern Show *is broadcast on radio and on television. The show is popular—the radio broadcasts alone have more than 16 million weekly listeners. Stern's style can be controversial, however. Over the years, the Federal Communications Commission has fined his employer, Infinity Broadcasting, Inc., more than $2 million for indecency.*

BACKGROUND AND FACTS Deborah Roach—known as "Debbie Tay"—was a perennial guest on *The Howard Stern Show,* on which she discussed her purported sexual encounters with female aliens. Tay used the notoriety to launch her own cable television show. After her death from a drug overdose at the age of twenty-seven, her sister Melissa Driscol had the body cremated and gave a portion of the remains to Tay's friend Chaunce Hayden. Shortly afterward, Tay's brother Jeff Roach learned that Hayden was to appear on Stern's show and asked the producer to cancel the appearance. Hayden went on as planned, and during his appearance, the participants in the program handled and joked about Tay's remains. For example, Stern held up bone fragments while he guessed whether they came from Tay's skull or ribs. Tay's brother and sister filed a suit in a New York state court against Stern and others, seeking $8 million in damages for, among other things, intentional infliction of emotional distress. The defendants filed a motion to dismiss, contending that the conduct at issue was not particularly shocking, in light of Stern's reputation for vulgar humor and Tay's actions during her guest appearances on his show. The court granted the motion, and the plaintiffs appealed.

IN THE WORDS OF THE COURT . . .
MEMORANDUM BY THE COURT.

* * * *

* * * In order to impose liability for this intentional tort, the conduct complained of must be so outrageous in character, and so extreme in degree, as to go beyond all possible bounds of decency, and to be regarded as atrocious, and utterly intolerable in a civilized community. The element of outrageous conduct is rigorous, and difficult to satisfy, and its purpose is to filter out trivial complaints and assure that the claim of severe emotional distress is genuine. * * *

Upon our review of the allegations in the case at bar, we conclude that the Supreme Court erred in determining that the element of outrageous conduct was not satisfied * * * . Although the defendants contend that the conduct at issue was not particularly shocking, in light of Stern's reputation for vulgar humor and Tay's actions during her guest appearances on his program, a jury might reasonably conclude that the manner in which Tay's remains were handled, for entertainment purposes and against the express wishes of her family, went beyond the bounds of decent behavior.

We further conclude that the remaining elements necessary to establish a cause of action to recover damages for the intentional infliction of emotional distress were also sufficiently pleaded in the complaint.

DECISION AND REMEDY The state intermediate appellate court reversed the decision of the lower court and remanded the case for trial. The court held that a jury could reasonably conclude the manner in which Tay's remains were handled could constitute intentional infliction of emotional distress.

FOR CRITICAL ANALYSIS—Social Consideration
What would be the result for society if broadcasters such as Howard Stern were never held liable for any distress caused by their broadcasts?

DEFAMATION

• **DEFAMATION**
Anything published or publicly spoken that causes injury to another's good name, reputation, or character.

• **SLANDER**
Defamation in oral form.

• **LIBEL**
Defamation in writing or other form (such as in a videotape) having the quality of permanence.

Defamation of character involves wrongfully hurting a person's good reputation. The law has imposed a general duty on all persons to refrain from making false, defamatory statements about others. Breaching this duty orally involves the tort of **slander;** breaching it in writing involves the tort of **libel.** The tort of defamation also arises when a false statement is made about a person's product, business, or title to property. We deal with these torts in the following chapter.

The common law defines four types of false utterances that are considered slander *per se* (meaning that no proof of injury or harm is required for these false utterances to be actionable):

1. A statement that another has a loathsome communicable disease.
2. A statement that another has committed improprieties while engaging in a profession or trade.
3. A statement that another has committed or has been imprisoned for a serious crime.
4. A statement that an unmarried woman is unchaste.

"Reputation, reputation, reputation! Oh, I have lost my reputation! I have lost the immortal part of myself, and what remains is bestial."

WILLIAM SHAKESPEARE, 1564–1616
(English dramatist and poet)

The Publication Requirement The basis of the tort of defamation is the publication of a statement or statements that hold an individual up to contempt, ridicule, or hatred. *Publication* here means that the defamatory statements are communicated to persons other than the defamed party. • EXAMPLE 4.2 If Thompson writes Andrews a private letter accusing him of embezzling funds, the action does not constitute libel. If Peters calls Gordon dishonest, unattractive, and incompetent when no one else is around, the action does not constitute slander. In neither case was the message communicated to a third party. •

The courts have generally held that even dictating a letter to a secretary constitutes publication, although the publication may be privileged (privileged communications will be discussed shortly). Moreover, if a third party overhears defamatory statements by chance, the courts usually hold that this also constitutes publication. Defamatory statements made via the Internet are also actionable (see Chapter 7). Note further that any individual who republishes or repeats defamatory statements is liable even if that person reveals the source of such statements.

"Truth is generally the best vindication against slander."

ABRAHAM LINCOLN, 1809–1865
(Sixteenth president of the United States, 1861–1865)

Defenses against Defamation Truth is normally an absolute defense against a defamation charge. In other words, if the defendant in a defamation suit can prove that his or her allegedly defamatory statements were true, the defendant will not be liable.

• **PRIVILEGE**
In tort law, the ability to act contrary to another person's right without that person's having legal redress for such acts. Privilege may be raised as a defense to defamation.

Another defense that is sometimes raised is that the statements were **privileged** communications, and thus the defendant is immune from liability. Privileged communications are of two types: absolute and qualified. Only in judicial proceedings and certain legislative proceedings is *absolute* privilege granted. For example, statements made in the courtroom by attorneys and judges during a trial are absolutely privileged. So are statements made by legislators during congressional floor debate, even if the legislators make such statements maliciously—that is, knowing them to be untrue. An absolute privilege is granted in these situations because judicial and legislative personnel deal with matters that are so much in the public interest that the parties involved should be able to speak out fully and freely without restriction.

In general, false and defamatory statements that are made about *public figures* (those who exercise substantial governmental power and any persons in the public limelight) and that are published in the press are privileged if they are made without

• **ACTUAL MALICE**
Real and demonstrable evil intent. In a defamation suit, a statement made about a public figure normally must be made with actual malice (with either knowledge of its falsity or a reckless disregard of the truth) for liability to be incurred.

actual malice.[4] To be made with actual malice, a statement must be made *with either knowledge of falsity or a reckless disregard of the truth*. Statements made about public figures, especially when they are made via a public medium, are usually related to matters of general public interest; they are made about people who substantially affect all of us. Furthermore, public figures generally have some access to a public medium for answering disparaging (belittling, discrediting) falsehoods about themselves; private individuals do not. For these reasons, public figures have a greater burden of proof in defamation cases (they must prove actual malice) than do private individuals.

The court in the following case considered whether the actual-malice requirement had been met in a set of circumstances involving the *National Enquirer's* "exclusive interview" with Clint Eastwood.

4. *New York Times Co. v. Sullivan*, 376 U.S. 254, 84 S.Ct. 710, 11 L.Ed.2d 686 (1964).

CASE 4.3 Eastwood v. National Enquirer, Inc.

United States Court of Appeals,
Ninth Circuit, 1997.
123 F.3d 1249.
www.vcilp.org/Fed-Ct/Circuit/9th/August97.html[a]

HISTORICAL AND SOCIAL SETTING *Establishing damages in a defamation suit can be difficult. How can a celebrity, for example, demonstrate that his or her reputation was damaged? Sometimes, a celebrity can succeed by showing that a defamatory statement created a false public impression. For example, singer Tom Waits was awarded damages on evidence that a commercial featuring an imitation of his voice created a public impression that he was a hypocrite for endorsing Doritos.*[b] *When a statement is made in a national publication, evidence of the publication's readership and the celebrity's image may be enough.*[c]

a. This page is a list of cases decided by the U.S. Court of Appeals for the Ninth Circuit in August 1997. Scroll down the list to the *Eastwood* case and click on the case name to access the opinion. This Web page is a part of the Web site maintained by the Center for Information Law and Policy at the Villanova University School of Law.
b. *Waits v. Frito-Lay, Inc.*, 978 F.2d 1093 (9th Cir. 1992).

BACKGROUND AND FACTS Cameron Docherty, a freelance writer, sold a purported interview with Clint Eastwood to *Today*, a British tabloid. Steve Plamann, an editor with the *National Enquirer*, saw the article in *Today* and contacted Docherty, who owned the piece. After a cursory check of Docherty's reputation, the *Enquirer* published the article as an "Exclusive Interview." The story included the by-line of Don Gentile, an *Enquirer* assistant editor, and such phrases as "[Eastwood] said with a chuckle." Eastwood filed a suit in a federal district court against the *Enquirer*. He contended in part that by using the label "exclusive," the *Enquirer* suggested he had granted it an interview. This, he charged, damaged his reputation. The *Enquirer* explained that it used the label "*Enquirer* Interview" when an interview was given to the *Enquirer* directly and "Exclusive Interview" when it was not. The jury returned a verdict in Eastwood's favor and awarded him $150,000 in damages. The *Enquirer* appealed the verdict and the award.

c. See, for example, *Carol Burnett v. National Enquirer, Inc.*, 144 Cal.App.3d 991, 193 Cal.Rptr. 206 (1983).

IN THE WORDS OF THE COURT . . .
KOZINSKI, Circuit Judge.

* * * *

Did the *Enquirer* editors mislabel the interview as having been given to them by Clint Eastwood? The interview is marked "Exclusive" * * * . The *Enquirer* gave the by-line * * * to Don Gentile * * * . It inserted scene-setting phrases. It quoted Eastwood in the "simple past" tense; using "Eastwood has said" instead of "Eastwood said" would have informed readers that the statement was not directed

CASE 4.3—Continued

to the article's purported author. (For that matter, using "Eastwood told freelance writer Cameron Docherty" would have eliminated any ambiguity whatever.) * * *

* * * [W]e look to the totality of the *Enquirer's* presentation of the interview and find that the editors falsely suggested to the ordinary reader of their publication * * * that Eastwood had willingly chatted with someone from the *Enquirer.*

* * * [W]e [also] find the editors knew or should have known that their statements would be misleading.

* * * [W]e do not believe the absence of the phrase "*Enquirer* Interview" would inform the average reader * * * that the subject had not spoken to the *Enquirer,* or that the editors could have believed their code sufficient for that purpose. Rather, we find, from the totality of their choices, that the editors intended to convey the impression—known by them to be false—that Eastwood willfully submitted to an interview by the *Enquirer.* This intentional conduct satisfies the "actual malice" standard, permitting a verdict for Eastwood.

DECISION AND REMEDY The U.S. Court of Appeals for the Ninth Circuit affirmed the verdict and the award of the lower court. The court held that the Enquirer's conduct constituted defamation.

FOR CRITICAL ANALYSIS—Cultural Consideration *Why do journalists check, or at least make a pretense of checking, the reliability of a source before publishing a story?*

INVASION OF THE RIGHT TO PRIVACY

A person has a right to solitude and freedom from prying public eyes—in other words, to privacy. Four acts qualify as an invasion of that privacy:

1. *The use of a person's name, picture, or other likeness for commercial purposes without permission.* This tort, which is usually referred to as the tort of appropriation, will be examined in the next chapter.
2. *Intrusion in an individual's affairs or seclusion.* For example, invading someone's home or illegally searching someone's briefcase is an invasion of privacy. The tort has been held to extend to eavesdropping by wiretap, the unauthorized scanning of a bank account, compulsory blood testing, and window peeping.
3. *Publication of information that places a person in a false light.* This could be a story attributing to the person ideas not held or actions not taken by the person. (Publishing such a story could involve the tort of defamation as well.)
4. *Public disclosure of private facts about an individual that an ordinary person would find objectionable.* A newspaper account of a private citizen's sex life or financial affairs could be an actionable invasion of privacy.

As discussed in Chapter 2, the Supreme Court has held that a fundamental right to privacy is also implied by various amendments to the U.S. Constitution. This right protects individuals against government intrusion into their lives. The tort of invasion of privacy protects people against intrusions by other persons. A growing concern is how persons can protect against undue intrusion by others into their private lives when using the Internet—a topic discussed in the feature *Technology and the Protection of Privacy Rights.*

MISREPRESENTATION (FRAUD)

A misrepresentation leads another to believe in a condition that is different from the condition that actually exists. This is often accomplished through a false or an incor-

Technology and the Protection of Privacy Rights

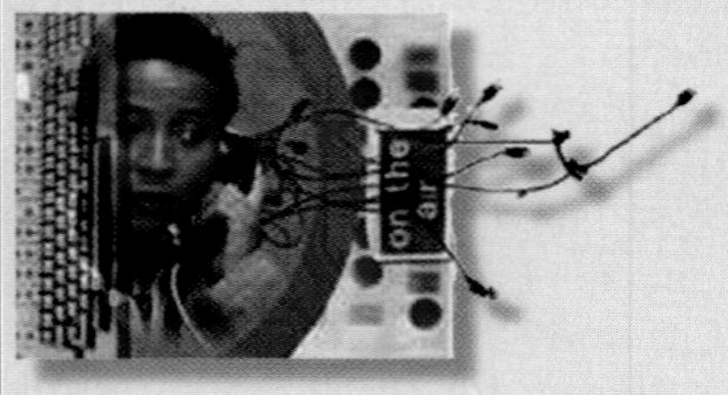

In most cases, a person who surfs the Web does not do so anonymously. When the surfer visits a Web site, the site's operator knows where the surfer came from, the kind of computer the surfer has, the surfer's Internet service provider, and other details. The surfer may give his or her e-mail address to the operator. With this information, and a search of other databases and sites on the Internet, a person might be able to follow the surfer's online activities without his or her knowledge.

Why should the surfer care? If you were the surfer, you would have no control over the use of this information. If you visit a number of sites concerning auto races, for example, you could become the recipient of "junk" e-mail (spam), or even junk regular mail, about auto racing and fast cars. This may not seem serious. If those visits are used as a reason to classify you as a risky driver and raise your auto insurance rates, however, you might want to protest.

Steps to take to protect your privacy online and prevent falling victim to cyber torts include the use of encryption and digital signatures (discussed in Chapter 7). At best, e-mail should be encrypted. At least, e-mail should not contain any statements that its sender would not want to see on the front page of a newspaper. Personal information should not be posted online. Other steps to take include making sure that when you contract with an Internet service provider (ISP) you become aware of the ISP's policies regarding privacy. Some ISPs remove users from unwanted e-mail lists, prevent the release of a user's e-mail address, block ads, and stop "cookies"—messages given to a browser, and stored in a file on the browser, to identify the user to the server. (Use the "Find" feature on a computer to find and delete the cookies file.)

What about legal options? There is not a comprehensive law that protects privacy. For invasions by private parties (not the government), there is some common law protection. There is some protection against government invasions of privacy under the Constitution (see Chapter 2). There are also a variety of statutes that provide protection in specific cases. For example, the Electronic Communications Privacy Act (ECPA) of 1986 requires the government to obtain a search warrant or a subpoena before soliciting otherwise private information. In a recent case, the court blocked the discharge of a Navy officer on the ground that the Navy did not comply with the ECPA when it obtained from an Internet service provider the officer's e-mail user identity.[a]

FOR CRITICAL ANALYSIS

What can (or should) the government do to protect individual privacy rights on the Internet?

a. *McVeigh v. Cohen,* 983 F.Supp. 215 (D.D.C. 1998).

INTERNET CONNECT

rect statement. Misrepresentations may be innocently made by someone who is unaware of the existing facts, but the tort of **fraudulent misrepresentation,** or fraud, involves intentional deceit for personal gain. The tort includes several elements:

1. Misrepresentation of facts or conditions with knowledge that they are false or with reckless disregard for the truth.
2. Intent to induce another to rely on the misrepresentation.
3. Justifiable reliance by the deceived party.
4. Damages suffered as a result of the reliance.
5. Causal connection between the misrepresentation and the injury suffered.

• **FRAUDULENT MISREPRESENTATION**
Any misrepresentation, either by misstatement or omission of a material fact, knowingly made with the intention of deceiving another and on which a reasonable person would and does rely to his or her detriment.

• **PUFFERY**
A salesperson's often exaggerated claims concerning the quality of property offered for sale. Such claims involve opinions rather than facts and are not considered to be legally binding promises or warranties.

For fraud to occur, more than mere **puffery,** or *seller's talk,* must be involved. Fraud exists only when a person represents as a fact something he or she knows is untrue. For example, it is fraud to claim that a building does not leak when one knows it does. Facts are objectively ascertainable, whereas seller's talk is not. "I am the best accountant in town" is seller's talk. The speaker is not trying to represent something as fact, because the term *best* is a subjective, not an objective, term.[5]

Normally, the tort of misrepresentation or fraud occurs only when there is reliance on a *statement of fact*. Sometimes, however, reliance on a *statement of opinion* may involve the tort of misrepresentation if the individual making the statement of opinion has a superior knowledge of the subject matter. For example, when a lawyer makes a statement of opinion about the law in a state in which the lawyer is licensed to practice, a court would construe reliance on such a statement to be equivalent to reliance on a statement of fact. We examine fraudulent misrepresentation in further detail in Chapter 12, in the context of contract law.

Intentional Torts against Property

Intentional torts against property include trespass to land, trespass to personal property, and conversion. These torts are wrongful actions that interfere with individuals' legally recognized rights with regard to their land or personal property. The law distinguishes real property from personal property (see Chapters 40 and 41). *Real property* is land and things "permanently" attached to the land. *Personal property* consists of all other items, which are basically movable. Thus, a house and lot are real property, whereas the furniture inside a house is personal property. Money and stocks and bonds are also personal property.

Trespass to Land

• **TRESPASS TO LAND**
The entry onto, above, or below the surface of land owned by another without the owner's permission or legal authorization.

A **trespass to land** occurs whenever a person, without permission, enters onto, above, or below the surface of land that is owned by another; causes anything to enter onto the land; remains on the land; or permits anything to remain on it. Actual harm to the land is not an essential element of this tort because the tort is designed to protect the right of an owner to exclusive possession of his or her property. Common types of trespass to land include walking or driving on the land, shooting a gun over the land, throwing rocks at a building that belongs to someone else, building a dam across a river and thus causing water to back up on someone else's land, and placing part of one's building on an adjoining landowner's property.

A SIGN WARNS TRESPASSERS. SHOULD A TRESPASSER BE ALLOWED TO RECOVER FROM A LANDOWNER FOR INJURIES SUSTAINED ON THE PREMISES?

Trespass Criteria, Rights, and Duties Before a person can be a trespasser, the owner of the real property (or other person in actual and exclusive possession of the property) must establish that person as a trespasser. For example, "posted" trespass signs expressly establish as a trespasser a person who ignores these signs and enters onto the property. A guest in your home is not a trespasser—unless he or she has been asked to leave but refuses. Any person who enters onto your property to commit an illegal act (such as a thief entering a lumberyard at night to steal lumber) is established impliedly as a trespasser, without posted signs.

At common law, a trespasser is liable for damages caused to the property and generally cannot hold the owner liable for injuries sustained on the premises. This common law rule is being abandoned in many jurisdictions in favor of a "reasonable duty of care" rule that varies depending on the status of the parties; for example, a

5. In contracts for the sale of goods, Article 2 of the Uniform Commercial Code distinguishes, for warranty purposes, between statements of opinion ("puffery") and statements of fact. See Chapter 18 for a further discussion of this issue.

landowner may have a duty to post a notice that the property is patrolled by guard dogs. Futhermore, under the "attractive nuisance" doctrine, children do not assume the risks of the premises if they are attracted to the premises by some object, such as a swimming pool, an abandoned building, or a sand pile. Trespassers normally can be removed from the premises through the use of reasonable force without the owner's being liable for assault and battery.

Defenses against Trespass to Land Trespass to land involves wrongful interference with another person's real property rights. If it can be shown that the trespass was warranted, however, as when a trespasser enters to assist someone in danger, a defense exists. Another defense exists when the trespasser can show that he or she had a license to come onto the land. A *licensee* is one who is invited (or allowed to enter) onto the property of another for the licensee's benefit. A person who enters another's property to read an electric meter, for example, is a licensee. When you purchase a ticket to attend a movie or sporting event, you are licensed to go onto the property of another to view that movie or event. Note that licenses to enter upon another's property are *revocable* by the property owner. If a property owner asks a meter reader to leave and the meter reader refuses to do so, the meter reader at that point becomes a trespasser.

TRESPASS TO PERSONAL PROPERTY

• **TRESPASS TO PERSONAL PROPERTY**
The unlawful taking or harming of another's personal property; interference with another's right to the exclusive possession of his or her personal property.

Whenever any individual unlawfully harms the personal property of another or otherwise interferes with the personal property owner's right to exclusive possession and enjoyment of that property, **trespass to personal property**—also called *trespass to personalty*[6]—occurs. If a student takes another student's business law book as a practical joke and hides it so that the owner is unable to find it for several days prior to a final examination, the student has engaged in a trespass to personal property.

If it can be shown that trespass to personal property was warranted, then a complete defense exists. Most states, for example, allow automobile repair shops to hold a customer's car (under what is called an *artisan's lien,* discussed in Chapter 23) when the customer refuses to pay for repairs already completed.

CONVERSION

• **CONVERSION**
The wrongful taking or retaining possession of a person's personal property and placing it in the service of another.

Whenever personal property is wrongfully taken from its rightful owner or possessor and placed in the service of another, the act of **conversion** occurs. Conversion is defined as any act depriving an owner of personal property without that owner's permission and without just cause. When conversion occurs, the lesser offense of trespass to personal property usually occurs as well. If the initial taking of the property was unlawful, there is trespass; retention of that property is conversion. If the initial taking of the property was permitted by the owner or for some other reason is not a trespass, failure to return it may still be conversion. Conversion is the civil side of crimes related to theft. A store clerk who steals merchandise from the store commits a crime and engages in the tort of conversion at the same time.

Even if a person mistakenly believed that he or she was entitled to the goods, a tort of conversion may occur. In other words, good intentions are not a defense against conversion; in fact, conversion can be an entirely innocent act. Someone who buys stolen goods, for example, is guilty of conversion even if he or she did not know that the goods were stolen. If the true owner brings a tort action against the

6. Pronounced *per*-sun-ul-tee.

¡KEEP IN MIND!
In tort law, the underlying motive for an act does not matter. What matters is the intent to do the act that results in the tort.

buyer, the buyer must either return the property to the owner or pay the owner the full value of the property, despite having already paid money to the thief.

A successful defense against the charge of conversion is that the purported owner does not in fact own the property or does not have a right to possess it that is superior to the right of the holder. Necessity is another possible defense against conversion. • EXAMPLE 4.3 If Abrams takes Mendoza's cat, Abrams is guilty of conversion. If Mendoza sues Abrams, Abrams must return the cat or pay damages. If, however, the cat has rabies and Abrams took the cat to protect the public, Abrams has a valid defense—necessity (and perhaps even self-defense, if he can prove that he was in danger because of the cat).•

Unintentional Torts (Negligence)

• **NEGLIGENCE**
The failure to exercise the standard of care that a reasonable person would exercise in similar circumstances.

ON THE WEB
To obtain information on negligence law and cases, go to the Web site of Law Journal EXTRA! at **www.ljx.com:80/practice/negligence**.

The tort of **negligence** occurs when someone suffers injury because of another's failure to live up to a required *duty of care*. In contrast to intentional torts, in torts involving negligence, the tortfeasor neither wishes to bring about the consequences of the act nor believes that they will occur. The actor's conduct merely creates a *risk* of such consequences. If no risk is created, there is no negligence.

Many of the actions discussed in the section on intentional torts constitute negligence if the element of intent is missing. • EXAMPLE 4.4 If Juarez intentionally shoves Natsuyo, who falls and breaks an arm as a result, Juarez will have committed the intentional tort of assault and battery. If Juarez carelessly bumps into Natsuyo, however, and she falls and breaks an arm as a result, Juarez's action will constitute negligence. In either situation, Juarez has committed a tort.•

"To answer your question. Yes, if you shoot an arrow into the air and it falls to earth you should know not where, you could be liable for any damage it may cause."

In examining a question of negligence, one should ask four questions:

1. Did the defendant owe a duty of care to the plaintiff?
2. Did the defendant breach that duty?
3. Did the plaintiff suffer a legally recognizable injury as a result of the defendant's breach of the duty of care?
4. Did the defendant's breach cause the plaintiff's injury?

Each of these elements of negligence is discussed in this section.

THE DUTY OF CARE AND ITS BREACH

• **DUTY OF CARE**
The duty of all persons, as established by tort law, to exercise a reasonable amount of care in their dealings with others. Failure to exercise due care, which is normally determined by the "reasonable person standard," constitutes the tort of negligence.

The concept of a **duty of care** arises from the notion that if we are to live in society with other people, some actions can be tolerated and some cannot; some actions are right and some are wrong; and some actions are reasonable and some are not. The basic principle underlying the duty of care is that people are free to act as they please so long as their actions do not infringe on the interests of others.

When someone fails to comply with the duty of exercising reasonable care, a potentially tortious act may have been committed. Failure to live up to a standard of care may be an act (setting fire to a building) or an omission (neglecting to put out a campfire). It may be a careless act or a carefully performed but nevertheless dangerous act that results in injury. Courts consider the nature of the act (whether it is outrageous or commonplace), the manner in which the act is performed (cautiously versus heedlessly), and the nature of the injury (whether it is serious or slight) in determining whether the duty of care has been breached.

• **REASONABLE PERSON STANDARD**
The standard of behavior expected of a hypothetical "reasonable person." The standard against which negligence is measured and that must be observed to avoid liability for negligence.

The Reasonable Person Standard Tort law measures duty by the **reasonable person standard.** In determining whether a duty of care has been breached, the courts ask how a reasonable person would have acted in the same circumstances. The reasonable person standard is said to be (though in an absolute sense it cannot be) objective. It is not necessarily how a particular person would act. It is society's judgment on how people *should* act. If the so-called reasonable person existed, he or she would be careful, conscientious, even tempered, and honest. This hypothetical reasonable person is frequently used by the courts in decisions relating to other areas of law as well.

That individuals are required to exercise a reasonable standard of care in their activities is a pervasive concept in business law, and many of the issues dealt with in subsequent chapters of this text have to do with this duty. What constitutes reasonable care varies, of course, with the circumstances.

ETHICAL ISSUE 4.1 ***Does a person's duty of care include a duty to come to the aid of a stranger in peril?*** Suppose that you are walking down a city street and notice that a pedestrian is about to step directly in front of an oncoming bus. Do you have a legal duty to warn that individual? No. Although most people would probably concede that in this situation, the observer has an *ethical* or *moral* duty to warn the other, tort law does not impose a general duty to rescue others in peril. People involved in special relationships, however, have been held to have a duty to rescue other parties within the relationship. A married person, for example, has a duty to rescue his or her child or spouse if either is in danger. Other special relationships, such as those between teachers and students or hiking and hunting partners, may also give rise to a duty to rescue. In addition, if a person who has no duty to rescue undertakes to rescue another, then the rescuer is charged with a duty to follow through with due care on the rescue attempt.

ON THE WEB

At the Web site of the Law Offices of Herbert Monheit you can find information on premises liability as well as other types of tort liability. You can access this site at **www.civilrights.com/areasofpractice.html**.

• **BUSINESS INVITEES**
Those people, such as customers or clients, who are invited onto business premises by the owner of those premises for business purposes.

The Duty of Landowners Landowners are expected to exercise reasonable care to protect from harm persons coming onto their property. As mentioned earlier, in some jurisdictions, landowners are held to owe a duty to protect even trespassers against certain risks. Landowners who rent or lease premises to tenants (see Chapter 41) are expected to exercise reasonable care to ensure that the tenants and their guests are not harmed in common areas, such as stairways, entryways, laundry rooms, and the like.

Retailers and other firms that explicitly or implicitly invite persons to come onto their premises are usually charged with a duty to exercise reasonable care to protect those persons, who are considered **business invitees.** For example, if you entered a supermarket, slipped on a wet floor, and sustained injuries as a result, the owner of the supermarket would be liable for damages if when you slipped there was no sign warning that the floor was wet. A court would hold that the business owner was negligent because the owner failed to exercise a reasonable degree of care in protecting the store's customers against foreseeable risks about which the owner knew or *should have known.* That a patron might slip on the wet floor and be injured as a result was a foreseeable risk, and the owner should have taken care to avoid this risk or to warn the customer of it. The landowner also has a duty to discover and remove any hidden dangers that might injure a customer or other invitee. (For a discussion of whether the owner of a golf course has a duty to protect invitees against lightning strikes, see this chapter's *The Letter of the Law.*)

The Letter of the Law — GOLF CLUBS, LIGHTNING, AND LIABILITY

Certain events, such as lightning bolts, are often referred to as "acts of God" because they are beyond the power of humans to control. Do owners of golf courses nonetheless have a duty to protect golfers against the risk of lightning strikes? This question recently came before a court in New Jersey when Spencer Maussner, after being struck by lightning and injured while on a golf course owned by the Atlantic City Country Club, sued the club for damages. The trial court found that the proximate cause of the injury was "first of all, an act of God, the lightning" and second, the plaintiff's "own activities in exposing himself to the possibility of being struck by lightning." On appeal, however, the reviewing court held that because the golf course normally monitored the weather and warned golfers when lightning was in the vicinity, it had established a duty of reasonable care to golfers to protect them against this risk. It breached this duty by failing to follow its normal procedures in Maussner's case and thus could be held liable for Maussner's injuries.

THE BOTTOM LINE

Business owners should never assume that they can escape liability for injuries sustained by invitees who come onto their premises.

Some risks, of course, are so obvious that the owner need not warn of them. For instance, a business owner does not need to warn customers to open a door before attempting to walk through it. Other risks, however, even though they may seem obvious to a business owner, may not be so in the eyes of another, such as a child. For example, a hardware store owner may not think it is necessary to warn customers that a stepladder leaning against the back wall of the store could fall down and harm them. It is possible, though, that a child could tip the ladder over and be hurt as a result and that the store could be held liable.

In the following case, the court had to decide whether a supermarket owner should be held liable for a customer's injuries on the premises.

CASE 4.4 Dumont v. Shaw's Supermarkets, Inc.

Supreme Judicial Court of Maine, 1995.
664 A.2d 846.

HISTORICAL AND POLITICAL SETTING *For more than two decades, the states have been changing their tort laws to reduce what some consider to be excessive advantages given to plaintiffs. In the mid-1970s, for example, some states set limits on the amounts of recovery allowed in medical malpractice cases. In the 1980s, the focus was on reducing liability in cases involving product liability (see Chapter 18). In the 1990s, the debate concerned other liability issues, lawyers' fees, and the "loser pays" concept. Due in part to these efforts by the states, the number of filings of tort lawsuits has decreased by 6 percent since 1991.*

BACKGROUND AND FACTS At Shaw's Supermarkets, Inc., chocolate-covered peanuts are sold in bulk with other unpackaged, unwrapped candy in bins next to the produce section. Shaw's is aware that self-serve, small, loose, slippery items create a hazard for customers, who may slip and fall if they step on them. Shaw's places mats next to some of the produce and in other locations, but Shaw's does not place mats on the floor next to the candy bins. While shopping at Shaw's, Shirley Dumont slipped on a chocolate-covered peanut, fell, and was injured. Dumont sued Shaw's in a Maine state court, alleging negligence. The court ruled that Dumont could recover only if she proved that Shaw's caused the candy to be on the floor, that Shaw's knew that the candy was on the floor, or that the candy was on the floor for such a length of time that Shaw's should have known it was there. Because Dumont proved none of these things, the court entered a judgment in favor of Shaw's. Dumont appealed to the state's highest court, the Supreme Judicial Court of Maine.

IN THE WORDS OF THE COURT . . .
GLASSMAN, Justice.

* * * *

* * * [T]he plaintiff presented evidence * * * that there existed a foreseeable risk of a recurrent condition and that Shaw's did not exercise reasonable care in failing to place mats next to the bulk candy display. Shaw's was aware that items with similar characteristics to the chocolate-covered peanuts created an increased hazard to customers and had placed mats on the floor to mitigate the risk.

* * * In those circumstances, a store owner may be chargeable with constructive notice[a] of the existence of the specific condition at issue.

* * * [A] store owner who is aware of the existence of a recurrent condition that poses a potential danger to invitees may not ignore that knowledge and fail reasonably to respond to the foreseeable danger of the likelihood of a recurrence of the condition.

DECISION AND REMEDY The Supreme Judicial Court of Maine held that it is not necessary to prove that a store owner had actual notice of a specific condition giving rise to an injury. The court vacated the lower court's judgment and remanded the case for further proceedings.

a. Notice that is implied or imposed by law, as opposed to actual notice.

FOR CRITICAL ANALYSIS—Social Consideration *Does the principle applied in this case make a store owner the "absolute insurer" of the store's customers? In other words, is a store owner liable for injuries to customers on the premises even if the owner has taken precautions that are reasonably necessary to protect those customers?*

The Duty of Professionals If an individual has knowledge, skill, or intelligence superior to that of an ordinary person, the individual's conduct must be consistent with that status. Professionals—including physicians, dentists, psychiatrists, architects, engineers, accountants, lawyers, and others—are required to have a standard minimum level of special knowledge and ability. Therefore, in determining what constitutes reasonable care in the case of professionals, their training and expertise is taken into account. In other words, an accountant cannot defend against a lawsuit for negligence by stating, "But I was not familiar with that principle of accounting."

If a professional violates his or her duty of care toward a client, the professional may be sued for **malpractice.** For example, a patient might sue a physician for *medical malpractice.* A client might sue an attorney for *legal malpractice.*

> **ON THE WEB**
> Standards established by professional associations play an important role in determining the minimum standard of care expected of members of those associations. You can locate the professional standards for various organizations at www.lib.uwaterloo.ca/society/standards.html.

• **MALPRACTICE**
Professional misconduct or the lack of the requisite degree of skill as a professional. Negligence—the failure to exercise due care—on the part of a professional, such as a physician, is commonly referred to as malpractice.

The Injury Requirement and Damages

For a tort to have been committed, the plaintiff must have suffered a *legally recognizable* injury. To recover damages (receive compensation), the plaintiff must have suffered some loss, harm, wrong, or invasion of a protected interest. Essentially, the purpose of tort law is to compensate for legally recognized injuries resulting from wrongful acts. If no harm or injury results from a given negligent action, there is nothing to compensate—and no tort exists.

• **Example 4.5** If you carelessly bump into a passerby, who stumbles and falls as a result, you may be liable in tort if the passerby is injured in the fall. If the person is unharmed, however, there normally could be no suit for damages, because no injury was suffered. Although the passerby might be angry and suffer emotional distress, few courts recognize negligently inflicted emotional distress as a tort unless it results in some physical disturbance or dysfunction.•

As already mentioned, the purpose of tort law is not to punish people for tortious acts but to compensate the injured parties for damages suffered. Occasionally, however, damages awarded in tort lawsuits include both **compensatory damages** (which are intended to reimburse a plaintiff for actual losses—to make the plaintiff whole) and **punitive damages** (which are intended to punish the wrongdoer and deter others from similar wrongdoing). The damages awarded do not depend on whether the tort was intentional or negligent, although punitive damages are awarded more often in cases involving intentional torts.

• **COMPENSATORY DAMAGES**
A money award equivalent to the actual value of injuries or damages sustained by the aggrieved party.

• **PUNITIVE DAMAGES**
Money damages that may be awarded to a plaintiff to punish the defendant and deter future similar conduct.

International Perspective • TORT LIABILITY IN EUROPE

In contrast to U.S. courts, courts in Europe generally limit damages to compensatory damages, and punitive damages are virtually unheard of in European countries such as Germany. Even when plaintiffs do win compensatory damages, generally the amount they receive is much less than it would be in a similar case brought in the United States. In part, this is because governments in Europe usually provide for health care and have relatively generous Social Security payments. Yet it is also because European courts tend to view the duty of care and the concept of risk differently than U.S. courts do. In the United States, if a swimmer is injured while falling off a high diving board, a court may decide that the pool owner should be held liable, given that such falls are a foreseeable risk. If punitive damages are awarded, they could total millions of dollars. In a similar situation in Europe, a court might hold that the plaintiff, not the pool owner, was responsible for the injury.

FOR CRITICAL ANALYSIS
Punitive damages are an important element in American tort litigation. Why is this? What do awards of punitive damages achieve?

Causation

Another element necessary to a tort is *causation.* If a person fails in a duty of care and someone suffers injury, the wrongful activity must have caused the harm for a tort to have been committed.

"There's no limit to how complicated things can get, on account of one thing always leading to another."

E. B. WHITE, 1899–1985
(American author)

• **CAUSATION IN FACT**
An act or omission without which an event would not have occurred.

• **PROXIMATE CAUSE**
Legal cause; exists when the connection between an act and an injury is strong enough to justify imposing liability.

Causation in Fact and Proximate Cause In deciding whether there is causation, the court must address two questions:

1. *Is there causation in fact?* Did the injury occur because of the defendant's act, or would it have occurred anyway? If an injury would not have occurred without the defendant's act, then there is causation in fact. **Causation in fact** can usually be determined by the use of the *but for* test: "but for" the wrongful act, the injury would not have occurred. Theoretically, causation in fact is limitless. One could claim, for example, that "but for" the creation of the world, a particular injury would not have occurred. Thus, as a practical matter, the law has to establish limits, and it does so through the concept of proximate cause.
2. *Was the act the proximate cause of the injury?* **Proximate cause,** or legal cause, exists when the connection between an act and an injury is strong enough to justify imposing liability. • EXAMPLE 4.6 Ackerman carelessly leaves a campfire burning. The fire not only burns down the forest but also sets off an explosion in a nearby chemical plant that spills chemicals into a river, killing all the fish for a hundred miles downstream and ruining the economy of a tourist resort. Should Ackerman be liable to the resort owners? To the tourists whose vacations were ruined? These are questions of proximate cause that a court must decide. •

Probably the most cited case on proximate cause is the *Palsgraf* case discussed in the following *Landmark in the Law.* The question before the court was as follows: Does a defendant's duty of care extend only to those who may be injured as a result of a foreseeable risk, or does it extend also to a person whose injury could not reasonably be foreseen?

Landmark in the Law •

PALSGRAF v. LONG ISLAND RAILROAD CO. (1928)

In 1928, the New York Court of Appeals (that state's highest court) issued its decision in *Palsgraf v. Long Island Railroad Co.,*[a] a case that has become a landmark in negligence law with respect to proximate cause.

The facts of the case were as follows. The plaintiff, Palsgraf, was waiting for a train on a station platform. A man carrying a small package wrapped in newspaper was rushing to catch a train that had begun to move away from the platform. As the man attempted to jump aboard the moving train, he seemed unsteady and about to fall. A railroad guard on the train car reached forward to grab him, and another guard on the platform pushed him from behind to help him board the train. In the process, the man's package fell on the railroad tracks and exploded, because it contained fireworks. The repercussions of the explosion caused scales at the other end of the train platform to fall on Palsgraf, who was injured as a result. She sued the railroad company for damages in a New York state court.

At the trial, the jury found that the railroad guards were negligent in their conduct. On appeal, the question before the New York Court of Appeals was whether the conduct of the railroad guards was the proximate cause of Palsgraf's injuries. In other words, did the guards' duty of care extend to Palsgraf, who was outside the zone of danger and whose injury could not reasonably have been foreseen?

The court stated that the question of whether the guards were negligent *with respect to Palsgraf* depended on whether her injury was *reasonably foreseeable* to the railroad guards. Although the guards may have acted negligently with respect to the man boarding the train,

a. 248 N.Y. 339, 162 N.E. 99 (1928).

FOR CRITICAL ANALYSIS
If the guards knew that the package contained fireworks, would the court have ruled otherwise? Would it matter that the guards were motivated by a desire to help the man board the train and not by a desire to harm anyone?

this has no bearing on the question of their negligence with respect to Palsgraf. This is not a situation in which a person commits an act so potentially harmful (for example, firing a gun at a building) that he or she would be held responsible for any harm that resulted. The court stated that here, "by concession, there was nothing in the situation to suggest to the most cautious mind that the parcel wrapped in newspaper would spread wreckage through the station." The court thus concluded that the railroad guards were not negligent with respect to Palsgraf and not liable for her injuries.

¡NOTE! Proximate cause can be thought of as a question of social policy. Should the defendant be made to bear the loss instead of the plaintiff?

Foreseeability Since the *Palsgraf* case, the courts have used *foreseeability* as the test for proximate cause. The railroad guards were negligent, but the railroad's duty of care did not extend to Palsgraf, because her injury was unforeseeable. If the victim of the harm or the consequences of the harm done are unforeseeable, there is no proximate cause. Of course, it is foreseeable that people will stand on railroad platforms and that objects attached to the platforms will fall as the result of explosions nearby; however, this is not a chain of events against which a reasonable person would usually guard.

It is difficult to predict when a court will say that something is foreseeable and when it will say that something is not. How far a court stretches foreseeability is determined in part by the extent to which the court is willing to stretch the defendant's duty of care. (See this chapter's *Business Law in Action* for a further discussion of this topic.)

A BUNGEE JUMPER LEAPS FROM A PLATFORM. IF THE JUMPER IS INJURED AND SUES THE OPERATOR OF THE JUMP FOR NEGLIGENCE, WHAT DEFENSES MIGHT THE OPERATOR USE TO AVOID LIABILITY?

Superseding Cause An independent intervening force may break the connection between a wrongful act and an injury to another. If so, it acts as a *superseding cause*—that is, the intervening force or event sets aside, or replaces, the original wrongful act as the cause of the injury. • **EXAMPLE 4.7** Suppose that Derrick keeps a can of gasoline in the trunk of his car. The presence of the gasoline creates a foreseeable risk and is thus a negligent act. If Derrick's car skids and crashes into a tree, causing the gasoline can to explode, Derrick would be liable for injuries sustained by passing pedestrians because of his negligence. If the explosion had been caused by lightning striking the car, however, the lightning would supersede Derrick's original negligence as a cause of the damage, because the lightning was not foreseeable. •

In negligence cases, the negligent party will often attempt to show that some act has intervened after his or her action and that this second act was the proximate cause of injury. Typically, in cases in which an individual takes a defensive action, such as swerving to avoid an oncoming car, the original wrongdoer will not be relieved of liability even if the injury actually resulted from the attempt to escape harm. The same is true under the "danger invites rescue" doctrine. Under this doctrine, if Lemming commits an act that endangers Salter and Yokem sustains an injury trying to protect Salter, then Lemming will be liable for Yokem's injury, as well as for any injuries Salter may sustain. Rescuers can injure themselves, or the person rescued, or even a stranger, but the original wrongdoer will still be liable.

DEFENSES TO NEGLIGENCE

Defendants often defend against negligence claims by asserting that the plaintiffs failed to prove the existence of one or more of the required elements for negligence.

Business Law in Action • How Far Should Foreseeability Extend?

Foreseeability is an important element in tort law because it establishes an outer limit on the duty of care. In a tort case, the defendant's duty of care is usually held to extend only to those who might foreseeably be harmed or placed at risk by the defendant's action. If a defendant could not reasonably foresee that his or her actions would place the plaintiff at risk, then it would be unfair to hold the defendant liable for the plaintiff's injury.

Deciding whether a given risk is reasonably foreseeable is not easy, and it is difficult to predict how the courts might hold in particular cases. Consider an example. On the evening of March 28, 1990, Tonya Brown was using a pay telephone located on the corner of a busy intersection in the city of Flint, Michigan. Tonya Brown's friend, Anita Addison, stood nearby. Suddenly, a car driven by Ruby Greer veered out of control as she attempted to make a left turn and crashed into both girls at the phone booth, causing Brown to lose both legs and Addison to suffer permanent brain damage. Brown and Addison's guardian (on behalf of Addison) sued Michigan Bell Telephone, Inc., for damages.

The plaintiffs argued that Michigan Bell should have foreseen the possibility of a car veering off the road near that busy intersection and that Michigan Bell should therefore have placed its phone booth in a "safer" area. Michigan Bell contended that this accident was in no way foreseeable. The telephone company pointed out that Ruby Greer had never driven a car before, had no driver's license, was high on crack cocaine, and was in a frightened state—she was fleeing the scene of a nearby robbery. Michigan Bell also pointed out that its phone booth at that intersection had never before been hit by a car. Nonetheless, a Michigan appellate court concluded that the accident was foreseeable and therefore the defendant owed a duty of care (and monetary damages for violating that duty of care) to the plaintiffs.[a]

Plaintiffs who crash into utility poles near roadways have made similar claims. In 1998, the Supreme Court of Mississippi held that Mississippi Power and Light Company could be held liable for the injuries suffered by a plaintiff whose car ran off the road and hit an electrical utility pole. Even though the driver had been drinking, the court held that the utility company should have foreseen that, for whatever reason, drivers may veer off the road and hit utility poles that are placed too close to roadways.[b]

FOR CRITICAL ANALYSIS

In regard to the Michigan Bell *case, the defendant telephone company was much "wealthier" than the driver of the car that crashed into the phone booth (who was, according to the court, "impecunious"—meaning that she had no money). Should wealth ("deep pockets") enter into the picture when making decisions regarding tort liability?*

a. *Brown v. Michigan Bell Telephone, Inc.*, 225 Mich.App. 617, 572 N.W.2d 33 (1998).
b. *Mississippi Power & Light Co. v. Lumpkin*, 1998 WL 80164 (Miss. 1998).

¡NOTE!
The concept of superseding cause is not a question of physics but is, like proximate cause, a question of responsibility.

A defendant may also assert that an intervening force should be deemed a superseding cause, thus relieving the defendant of liability. Additionally, there are three basic *affirmative* defenses in negligence cases (defenses that defendants can use to avoid liability even if the facts are as the plaintiffs state). These defenses are (1) assumption of risk, (2) contributory negligence, and (3) comparative negligence.

• **ASSUMPTION OF RISK**
A doctrine whereby a plaintiff may not recover for injuries or damages suffered from risks he or she knows of and assents to. A defense against negligence that can be used when the plaintiff has knowledge of and appreciates a danger and voluntarily exposes himself or herself to the danger.

Assumption of Risk A plaintiff who voluntarily enters into a risky situation, knowing the risk involved, will not be allowed to recover. This is the defense of **assumption of risk.** The requirements of this defense are (1) knowledge of the risk and (2) voluntary assumption of the risk.

The risk can be assumed by express agreement, or the assumption of risk can be implied by the plaintiff's knowledge of the risk and subsequent conduct. For example, a driver entering a race knows that there is a risk of being killed or injured in a crash. Of course, the plaintiff does not assume a risk different from or greater than the risk normally carried by the activity. In our example, the race driver would not assume the risk that the banking in the curves of the racetrack will give way during the race because of a construction defect.

Risks are not deemed to be assumed in situations involving emergencies. Neither are they assumed when a statute protects a class of people from harm and a member of the class is injured by the harm. For example, employees are protected by statute from harmful working conditions and therefore do not assume the risks associated with the workplace. If an employee is injured, he or she will generally be compensated regardless of fault under state workers' compensation statutes (discussed in Chapter 37).

In the following case, the plaintiff suffered an injury to his pitching arm in a simulated baseball game during a tryout for a major league team. The issue before the court was whether the plaintiff had assumed the risk of the injury, thus precluding him from recovery.

CASE 4.5 Wattenbarger v. Cincinnati Reds, Inc.

California Court of Appeal, Third District, 1994.
28 Cal.App.4th 746,
33 Cal.Rptr.2d 732.

HISTORICAL AND CULTURAL SETTING *Despite the legend of Abner Doubleday's invention of baseball, most sports historians agree that the game was not the invention of just a single person. Instead, baseball evolved in the nineteenth century from a number of ball-and-stick games (including a game called "base ball") that had been popular earlier in Great Britain and colonial America. Segregated until John (Jackie) Robinson integrated the Brooklyn Dodgers in 1947, baseball teams today can include players of all ethnic, cultural, and national backgrounds.*

BACKGROUND AND FACTS In June 1990, in Lodi, California, seventeen-year-old Jeffrey Wattenbarger tried out for the position of pitcher for the Cincinnati Reds. During the tryouts, Wattenbarger's shoulder popped. It occurred on his third pitch to a batter during a simulated game. He stepped off the mound and told the representatives of the Reds. Hearing no response, Wattenbarger stepped back onto the mound and threw another pitch. He immediately experienced severe pain. Later, it was discovered that a portion of the bone and tendons had pulled away sometime during Wattenbarger's pitching, and he underwent an operation on the arm. Seeking damages for the injury, Wattenbarger brought an action in a California state court against the Reds, claiming they had been negligent in allowing him to throw the fourth pitch. The Reds asserted, among other things, the defense of assumption of risk—that is, that Wattenbarger, by participating in the tryout, had assumed the risk of injury—and filed a motion for summary judgment. The court granted the motion, and Wattenbarger appealed to a state appellate court.

IN THE WORDS OF THE COURT . . .
PUGLIA, Presiding Justice.

* * * *

* * * [A]ssumption of risk occurs where a plaintiff voluntarily participates in a sporting event or activity involving certain inherent risks. * * *

* * * *

Had plaintiff stopped after his third pitch of the simulated game, we would have no difficulty finding * * * assumption of risk a bar to recovery. * * *

However, the incident did not end with the third pitch. * * * [W]hen plaintiff * * * informed the Reds' personnel his arm had "popped," he was seeking guidance as to how to proceed. Hearing nothing to countermand the original instruction to pitch, * * * plaintiff threw another pitch, thereby causing further injury.

(Continued)

CASE 4.5—Continued

* * * *

* * * [D]efendants were not co-participants in the sport or activity but were instead in control of it. Defendants decided what would be done and when. They controlled the simulated game * * * .

Under these circumstances, defendants owed a duty to plaintiff and the other participants not to increase the risks * * * .

DECISION AND REMEDY Concluding that there were factual issues to be resolved at trial, the California Court of Appeal remanded the case to the lower court for further proceedings.

FOR CRITICAL ANALYSIS—Cultural Consideration *Baseball team managers are aware that young potential players, such as Wattenbarger, sometimes face significant cultural pressure to succeed in the sport. How does this knowledge affect baseball managers' duty of care during tryouts?*

Contributory Negligence All individuals are expected to exercise a reasonable degree of care in looking out for themselves. In a few jurisdictions, recovery for injury resulting from negligence is prevented if the plaintiff was also negligent (failed to exercise a reasonable degree of care). This is the defense of **contributory negligence.** Under the common law doctrine of contributory negligence, no matter how insignificant the plaintiff's negligence is relative to the defendant's negligence, the plaintiff will be precluded from recovering any damages.

• **CONTRIBUTORY NEGLIGENCE** A theory in tort law under which a complaining party's own negligence contributed to or caused his or her injuries. Contributory negligence is an absolute bar to recovery in a minority of jurisdictions.

An exception to the doctrine of contributory negligence may apply if the defendant failed to take advantage of an opportunity to avoid causing the damage. Under the "last clear chance" rule, the plaintiff may recover full damages despite his or her own negligence. (Note that in those states that have adopted the comparative negligence rule, discussed next, the last clear chance doctrine does not apply.) • **EXAMPLE 4.8** Murphy is walking across the street against the light, and Lewis, a motorist, sees her in time to avoid hitting her but hits her anyway. In this situation, Lewis (the defendant) is not permitted to use Murphy's (the plaintiff's) prior negligence as a defense. The defendant negligently missed the opportunity to avoid injuring the plaintiff. •

Comparative Negligence The majority of states now allow recovery based on the doctrine of **comparative negligence.** This doctrine enables both the plaintiff's and the defendant's negligence to be computed and the liability for damages distributed accordingly. Some jurisdictions have adopted a "pure" form of comparative negligence that allows the plaintiff to recover, even if the extent of his or her fault is greater than that of the defendant. For example, if the plaintiff was 80 percent at fault and the defendant 20 percent at fault, the plaintiff may recover 20 percent of his or her damages. Many states' comparative negligence statutes, however, contain a "50 percent" rule by which the plaintiff recovers nothing if he or she was more than 50 percent at fault.

• **COMPARATIVE NEGLIGENCE** A theory in tort law under which the liability for injuries resulting from negligent acts is shared by all persons who were guilty of negligence (including the injured party), on the basis of each person's proportionate carelessness.

SPECIAL NEGLIGENCE DOCTRINES AND STATUTES

There are a number of special doctrines and statutes relating to negligence. We examine a few of them here.

Res Ipsa Loquitur Generally, in lawsuits involving negligence, the plaintiff has the burden of proving that the defendant was negligent. In certain situations, when negligence is very difficult or impossible to prove, the courts may infer that negligence has occurred, in which case the burden of proof rests on the defendant—to prove he

• *RES IPSA LOQUITUR*
A doctrine under which negligence may be inferred simply because an event occurred, if it is the type of event that would not occur in the absence of negligence. Literally, the term means "the facts speak for themselves."

or she was *not* negligent. The inference of the defendant's negligence is known as the doctrine of ***res ipsa loquitur,***[7] which translates as "the facts speak for themselves."

This doctrine is applied only when the event creating the damage or injury is one that ordinarily does not occur in the absence of negligence. For example, if a person undergoes knee surgery and following the surgery has a severed nerve in the knee area, that person can sue the surgeon under a theory of *res ipsa loquitur.* In this case, the injury would not have occurred but for the surgeon's negligence.[8] For the doctrine of *res ipsa loquitur* to apply, the event must have been within the defendant's power to control, and it must not have been due to any voluntary action or contribution on the part of the plaintiff.

• NEGLIGENCE *PER SE*
An action or failure to act in violation of a statutory requirement.

Negligence *Per Se* Certain conduct, whether it consists of an action or a failure to act, may be treated as **negligence *per se*** (*per se* means "in or of itself"). Negligence *per se* may occur if an individual violates a statute or an ordinance providing for a criminal penalty and that violation causes another to be injured. The injured person must prove (1) that the statute clearly sets out what standard of conduct is expected, when and where it is expected, and of whom it is expected; (2) that he or she is in the class intended to be protected by the statute; and (3) that the statute was designed to prevent the type of injury that he or she suffered. The standard of conduct required by the statute is the duty that the defendant owes to the plaintiff, and a violation of the statute is the breach of that duty.

ON THE WEB
To find state statutes, including Good Samaritan and dram shop statutes, go to
www.findlaw.com/casecode/state.html.

• **EXAMPLE 4.9** A statute may require a landowner to keep a building in a safe condition and may also subject the landowner to a criminal penalty, such as a fine, if the building is not kept safe. The statute is meant to protect those who are rightfully in the building. Thus, if the owner, without a sufficient excuse, violates the statute and a tenant is thereby injured, then a majority of courts will hold that the owner's unexcused violation of the statute conclusively establishes a breach of a duty of care—that is, that the owner's violation is negligence *per se.*•

• GOOD SAMARITAN STATUTES
State statutes that provide that persons who provide emergency services to, or rescue, others in peril—unless they do so recklessly, thus causing further harm—cannot be sued for negligence.

• DRAM SHOP ACTS
State statutes that impose liability on the owners of bars and taverns, as well as those who serve alcoholic drinks to the public, for injuries resulting from accidents caused by intoxicated persons when the sellers or servers of alcoholic drinks contributed to the intoxication.

Special Negligence Statutes A number of states have enacted statutes prescribing duties and responsibilities in certain circumstances. For example, most states now have what are called **Good Samaritan statutes.** Under these statutes, persons who are aided voluntarily by others cannot turn around and sue the "Good Samaritans" for negligence. These laws were passed largely to protect physicians and medical personnel who voluntarily render their services in emergency situations to those in need, such as individuals hurt in car accidents.

Many states have also passed **dram shop acts,** under which a tavern owner or bartender may be held liable for injuries caused by a person who became intoxicated while drinking at the bar or who was already intoxicated when served by the bartender. In some states, statutes impose liability on *social hosts* (persons hosting parties) for injuries caused by guests who became intoxicated at the hosts' homes. Under these statutes, it is unnecessary to prove that the tavern owner, bartender, or social host was negligent.

ETHICAL ISSUE 4.2 ***Should social hosts be liable for injuries caused by intoxicated guests?*** Many people question the fairness of imposing liability on social hosts for injuries causes by intoxicated guests. Currently, nearly half of the states allow plaintiffs injured in car accidents to sue social hosts—those who served alcoholic beverages to the defendants. Some courts fashion the definition of "social host" broadly. For example, in

7. Pronounced *rihz ihp*-suh *low*-kwuh-duhr.
8. *Edwards v. Boland,* 41 Mass.App.Ct. 375, 670 N.E.2d 404 (1996).

a New York case the court held that the father of a minor who hosted a "bring your own keg" party could be held liable for injuries caused by an intoxicated guest.[9] In some states and jurisdictions, however, courts refuse to hold social hosts liable in these situations. In one case, the Illinois Supreme Court declared that it would not open that "Pandora's Box of unlimited liability" in which plaintiffs' attorneys could "drag into court any and all adults who may qualify as a social host." The court declared that the victims of drunk driving "have always had, and will continue to have, a civil remedy. They can sue the drunk driver, who is undoubtedly at fault."[10]

Strict Liability

• **STRICT LIABILITY**
Liability regardless of fault. In tort law, strict liability is imposed on a merchant who introduces into commerce a good that is unreasonably dangerous when in a defective condition.

Another category of torts is called **strict liability,** or *liability without fault.* Intentional torts and torts of negligence involve acts that depart from a reasonable standard of care and cause injuries. Under the doctrine of strict liability, liability for injury is imposed for reasons other than fault. Strict liability for damages proximately caused by an abnormally dangerous or exceptional activity is one application of this doctrine. Courts apply the doctrine of strict liability in such cases because of the extreme risk of the activity. Even if blasting with dynamite is performed with all reasonable care, there is still a risk of injury. Balancing that risk against the potential for harm, it seems reasonable to ask the person engaged in the activity to pay for injuries caused by that activity. Although there is no fault, there is still responsibility because of the dangerous nature of the undertaking.

There are other applications of the strict liability principle. Persons who keep dangerous animals, for example, are strictly liable for any harm inflicted by the animals. A significant application of strict liability is in the area of *product liability*—liability of manufacturers and sellers for harmful or defective products. Liability here is a matter of social policy and is based on two factors: (1) the manufacturing company can better bear the cost of injury, because it can spread the cost throughout society by increasing prices of goods and services, and (2) the manufacturing company is making a profit from its activities and therefore should bear the cost of injury as an operating expense. We will discuss product liability in greater detail in Chapter 18.

9. *Rust v. Reyer,* 693 N.E.2d 1074, 670 N.Y.S.2d 822 (1998).
10. *Charles v. Seigfried,* 165 Ill.2d 482, 651 N.E.2d 154, 209 Ill.Dec. 226 (1995).

Application: Law and the Retailer*

Retailers are faced with potential legal problems every day. They face a potential lawsuit not only every time a customer steps onto their property but also whenever a customer purchases a product from them. Here we consider only a few areas in which knowledge of the law can help a retailer prevent a legal problem.

*This *Application* is not meant to substitute for the services of an attorney who is licensed to practice law in your state.

Negligence

Negligence is an important area in tort law. Any retail business firm, whether it is a shoe store or a hamburger stand, must take reasonable care—not be negligent—in providing a safe environment in which the customer can examine products or purchase goods and services. The courts tend to conclude that "the customer is always right." Therefore, if you are a retailer, to assume that your customers will take reasonable care in their behavior or in the management of their small children while on your premises is to invite disaster. In con-

APPLICATION CONTINUED

trast, if you assume that any person on the premises may show a complete lack of common sense, you are going a long way toward preventing a lawsuit for negligence.

For example, even though it might be obvious that an employee is washing a section of the salesroom floor, there should be signs posted that warn the customer that the employee is doing so. Also, if your premises include a parking lot used by customers, the parking lot should be periodically inspected to make sure that there are no hazards, such as potholes, that might cause a customer to be injured. Again, even if a risk appears "obvious," the retailer should take steps to remove the risk.

HANDLING SHOPLIFTERS

To what extent can you, the businessperson, detain a suspected shoplifter without being successfully sued for false imprisonment, invasion of privacy, or some other charge, such as defamation or infliction of emotional distress? Suspected shoplifters can be accused and temporarily detained if certain reasonable procedures are used. These procedures differ, depending on the jurisdiction. The word to remember is *reasonable.* Keeping a suspected shoplifter in a locked storeroom for two hours because the manager has not yet got around to contacting the police would usually not be considered reasonable if the individual in question sued for false imprisonment.

When apprehending and questioning a suspected shoplifter, choose your words carefully. Using abusive or accusatory words or otherwise subjecting the person to indignity may result in a lawsuit. In one case, for example, the words "a big fat woman like you" served as the basis for the tort of infliction of emotional distress.[a] If you think someone has shoplifted, act on your suspicion before the suspect leaves the store. Usually, the courts will allow detention only if the suspected shoplifter is still on your premises.

CHECKLIST FOR THE RETAILER

1. Obtain adequate liability insurance coverage, if possible.
2. Always assume that the worst can happen; post warnings near all potential hazards no matter how obvious they may seem.
3. Always provide immediate medical care to an individual injured while on your premises.
4. Even for the most minor negligence lawsuit, hire an attorney and be willing to consider an out-of-court settlement (even if you believe that the customer was 100 percent at fault).
5. Employees who handle shoplifters should be appropriately trained in the proper procedure for apprehending and detaining someone suspected of shoplifting. Print out a short list of rules and have it checked by a local attorney familiar with recent court decisions in your area.

a. *Haile v. New Orleans Railway & Light Co.,* 135 La. 229, 65 So. 225 (1914). According to tort scholar William Prosser, this is the mildest insult for which recovery on the ground of infliction of emotional distress has been allowed. See W. Page Keeton et al., *Prosser and Keeton on Torts,* 5th ed. (St. Paul: West Publishing Co., 1984), p. 58.

Key Terms

actionable 99
actual malice 102
assault 97
assumption of risk 114
battery 97
business invitee 109
causation in fact 112
comparative negligence 116
compensatory damages 111
contributory negligence 116
conversion 106
damages 96
defamation 101
defense 97
dram shop act 117
duty of care 108
fraudulent misrepresentation 104
Good Samaritan statute 117
intentional tort 96
libel 101
malpractice 111
negligence 107
negligence *per se* 117
privilege 101
proximate cause 112
puffery 104
punitive damages 111
reasonable person standard 108
res ipsa loquitur 117
slander 101
strict liability 118
tort 95
tortfeasor 96
trespass to land 105
trespass to personal property 106

Chapter Summary • Torts

Intentional Torts against Persons (See pages 96–105.)	1. *Assault and battery*—An assault is an unexcused and intentional act that causes another person to be apprehensive of immediate harm. A battery is an assault that results in physical contact. 2. *False imprisonment*—The intentional confinement or restraint of another person's movement without justification. 3. *Infliction of emotional distress*—An intentional act that amounts to extreme and outrageous conduct resulting in severe emotional distress to another. 4. *Defamation (libel or slander)*—A false statement of fact, not made under privilege, that is communicated to a third person and that causes damage to a person's reputation. For public figures, the plaintiff must also prove actual malice. 5. *Invasion of the right to privacy*—The use of a person's name or likeness for commercial purposes without permission, wrongful intrusion into a person's private activities, publication of information that places a person in a false light, or disclosure of private facts that an ordinary person would find objectionable. 6. *Misrepresentation (fraud)*—A false representation made by one party, through misstatement of facts or through conduct, with the intention of deceiving another and on which the other reasonably relies to his or her detriment.
Intentional Torts against Property (See pages 105–107.)	1. *Trespass to land*—The invasion of another's real property without consent or privilege. Specific rights and duties apply once a person is expressly or impliedly established as a trespasser. 2. *Trespass to personal property*—Unlawfully damaging or interfering with the owner's right to use, possess, or enjoy his or her personal property. 3. *Conversion*—A wrongful act in which personal property is taken from its rightful owner or possessor and placed in the service of another.
Unintentional Torts—Negligence (See pages 107–118.)	1. *Negligence*—The careless performance of a legally required duty or the failure to perform a legally required act. Elements that must be proved are that a legal duty of care exists, that the defendant breached that duty, and that the breach caused damage or injury to another. 2. *Defenses to negligence*—The basic affirmative defenses in negligence cases are (a) assumption of risk, (b) contributory negligence, and (c) comparative negligence. 3. *Special negligence doctrines and statutes*— a. *Res ipsa loquitur*—A doctrine under which a plaintiff need not prove negligence on the part of the defendant because "the facts speak for themselves." b. Negligence *per se*—A type of negligence that may occur if a person violates a statute or an ordinance providing for a criminal penalty and the violation causes another to be injured. c. Special negligence statutes—State statutes that prescribe duties and responsibilities in certain circumstances. Dram shop acts and Good Samaritan statutes are examples of special negligence statutes.
Strict Liability (See page 118.)	Under the doctrine of strict liability, a person may be held liable, regardless of the degree of care exercised, for damages or injuries caused by his or her product or activity. Strict liability includes liability for harms caused by abnormally dangerous activities, by wild animals, and by defective products (product liability).

For Review

❶ What is the function of tort law?
❷ What must a public figure prove to succeed in a defamation suit?
❸ What are the four elements of negligence?
❹ What defenses are available in an action for negligence?
❺ What is strict liability? In what circumstances might this doctrine be applied?

Questions and Case Problems

4–1. Defenses to Negligence. Corinna was riding her bike on a city street. While she was riding, she frequently looked behind her to verify that the books that she had fastened to the rear part of her bike were still attached. On one occasion while she was looking behind her, she failed to notice a car that was entering an intersection just as she was crossing it. The car hit her, causing her to sustain numerous injuries. Three eyewitnesses stated that the driver of the car had failed to stop at the stop sign before entering the intersection. Corinna sued the driver of the car for negligence. What defenses might the defendant driver raise in this lawsuit? Discuss fully.

4–2. Liability to Business Invitees. Kim went to Ling's Market to pick up a few items for dinner. It was a rainy, windy day, and the wind had blown water through the door of Ling's Market each time the door opened. As Kim entered through the door, she slipped and fell in the approximately one-half inch of rainwater that had accumulated on the floor. The manager knew of the weather conditions but had not posted any sign to warn customers of the water hazard. Kim injured her back as a result of the fall and sued Ling's for damages. Can Ling's be held liable for negligence in this situation? Discuss.

4–3. Negligence. In which of the following situations will the acting party be liable for the tort of negligence? Explain fully.

(a) Mary goes to the golf course on Sunday morning, eager to try out a new set of golf clubs she has just purchased. As she tees off on the first hole, the head of her club flies off and injures a nearby golfer.
(b) Mary's doctor gives her some pain medication and tells her not to drive after she takes it, as the medication induces drowsiness. In spite of the doctor's warning, Mary decides to drive to the store while on the medication. Owing to her lack of alertness, she fails to stop at a traffic light and crashes into another vehicle, in which a passenger is injured.

4–4. Causation. Ruth carelessly parks her car on a steep hill, leaving the car in neutral and failing to engage the parking brake. The car rolls down the hill, knocking down an electric line. The sparks from the broken line ignite a grass fire. The fire spreads until it reaches a barn one mile away. The barn houses dynamite, and the burning barn explodes, causing part of the roof to fall on and injure a passing motorist, Jim. Can Jim recover from Ruth? Why or why not?

4–5. Trespass to Land. During a severe snowstorm, Yoshiko parked his car in a privately owned parking lot. The car was later towed from the lot, and Yoshiko had to pay $100 to the towing company to recover his car. Yoshiko sued the owner of the parking lot, Icy Holdings, Inc., to get back the $100 he had paid. Icy Holdings claimed that notwithstanding the severe snowstorm, Yoshiko's parking of his car on its property constituted trespass, and therefore Icy Holdings did not act wrongfully in having the car towed off the lot. Discuss whether Yoshiko can recover his $100.

4–6. Tort Theories. The Yommers operated a gasoline station. In December 1967, the McKenzies, their neighbors, noticed a smell in their well water, which proved to be caused by gasoline in the water. The McKenzies complained to the Yommers, who arranged to have one of their underground storage tanks replaced. Nevertheless, the McKenzies were unable to use their water for cooking or bathing until they had a filter and water softener installed. At the time of the trial, in December 1968, they were still bringing in drinking water from an outside source. The McKenzies sued the Yommers for damages. The Yommers claimed that the McKenzies had not proved that there was any intentional wrongdoing or negligence on the part of the Yommers, and therefore they should not be held liable. Under what theory might the McKenzies recover damages even in the absence of any negligence on the Yommers' part? Explain. [*Yommer v. McKenzie,* 255 Md. 220, 257 A.2d 138 (1969)]

4–7. Negligence *Per Se*. A North Carolina Department of Transportation regulation prohibits the placement of telephone booths within public rights of way. Despite this regulation, GTE South, Inc., placed a booth in the right of way near the intersection of Hillsborough and Sparger Roads in Durham County. Laura Baldwin was using the booth when an accident at the intersection caused a dump truck to cross the right of way and smash into the booth. To recover for her injuries, Baldwin filed a suit in a North Carolina state court against GTE and others. Was Baldwin within the class of persons protected by the regulation? If so, did GTE's placement of the booth constitute negligence *per se*? [*Baldwin v. GTE South, Inc.,* 335 N.C. 544, 439 S.E.2d 108 (1995)]

4–8. Duty of Care. As pedestrians exited at the close of an arts and crafts show, Jason Davis, an employee of the show's producer, stood near the exit. Suddenly and without warning, Davis turned around and collided with Yvonne Esposito, an eighty-year-old woman. Esposito was knocked to the ground, fracturing her hip. After hip-replacement surgery, she was left with a permanent physical impairment. Esposito filed a suit in a federal district court against Davis and others, alleging negligence. What are the factors that indicate whether or not Davis owed Esposito a duty of care? What do those factors indicate in these circumstances? [*Esposito v. Davis,* 47 F.3d 164 (5th Cir. 1995)]

4–9. Duty to Business Invitees. Flora Gonzalez visited a Wal-Mart store. While walking in a busy aisle from the store's cafeteria toward a refrigerator, Gonzalez stepped on some macaroni that came from the cafeteria. She slipped and fell, sustaining injuries to her back, shoulder, and knee. She filed a suit in a Texas state court against Wal-Mart, alleging that the store was negligent. She presented evidence that the macaroni had "a lot of dirt" and tracks through it and testified that the macaroni "seemed like it had been there awhile." What duty does a business have to protect its patrons from dangerous conditions? In Gonzalez's case, should Wal-Mart be held liable for a breach of that duty? Why or why not? [*Wal-Mart Stores, Inc. v. Gonzalez,* 968 S.W.2d 934 (Tex.Sup. 1998)]

4–10. Duty of Landowners. The Oklahoma State Board of Cosmetology inspected the equipment of the Poteau Beauty College and found it to be in satisfactory condition. A month later, Marilyn Sue Weldon, a student at Poteau, was injured when a salon chair failed to work properly. Weldon had washed the hair of a woman with the chair in a reclining position. The chair did not spring back, and due to a previous injury, the client had to be helped into an upright position. The chair was close to a manicure table, and in maneuvering around the table, Weldon twisted her back. Weldon filed a suit in an Oklahoma state court against Charles Dunn and other owners of Poteau, claiming in part that the college was negligent. Assuming that Weldon was a business invitee, what duty did Poteau, as the owner of the premises, owe to her? On what basis might the court rule that Poteau was not liable? [*Weldon v. Dunn,* 962 P.2d 1273 (Okla.Sup. 1998)]

A QUESTION OF ETHICS AND SOCIAL RESPONSIBILITY

4–11. Patsy Slone, while a guest at the Dollar Inn, a hotel, was stabbed in the thumb by a hypodermic needle concealed in the tube of a roll of toilet paper. Slone, fearing that she might have been exposed to the virus that causes acquired immune deficiency syndrome (AIDS), sued the hotel for damages to compensate her for the emotional distress she suffered after the needle stab. An Indiana trial court held for Slone and awarded her $250,000 in damages. The hotel appealed, and one of the issues before the court was whether Sloane had to prove that she was actually exposed to AIDS to recover for emotional distress. The appellate court held that she did not and that her fear of getting AIDS was reasonable in these circumstances. [*Slone v. Dollar Inn, Inc.,* 395 N.E.2d 185 (Ind.App. 1998)]

1. Should the plaintiff in this case have been required to show that she was actually exposed to the AIDS virus in order to recover for emotional distress? Should she have been required to show that she actually acquired the AIDS virus as a result of the needle stab?
2. In some states, plaintiffs are barred from recovery in emotional distress cases unless the distress is evidenced by some kind of physical illness. Is this fair?

FOR CRITICAL ANALYSIS

4–12. What general principle underlies the common law doctrine that business owners have a duty of care toward their customers? Does the duty of care unfairly burden business owners? Why or why not?

Online Activities

ONLINE EXERCISE 4–1

Go to FindLaw's database of Supreme Court cases at

www.findlaw.com/casecode/supreme.html.

Select Supreme Court decisions "by year," access the list of 1996 cases, and click on *BMW of North America v. Gore.* Read the summary of the case, scan through the words of the Court, and then answer the following questions:

- Why did the plaintiff bring this lawsuit against BMW?
- Why is this issue significant in tort litigation?
- What was the Supreme Court's decision in the matter?
- In your opinion, was the Supreme Court's ruling fair? Why or why not?

Before the Test

Go to the *Business Law Today* home page at http://blt.westbuslaw.com. Click on TestTutor.® You will find twenty interactive questions relating to this chapter.

CHAPTER 5 Business Torts & Intellectual Property

"The language of the law must not be foreign to the ears of those who are to obey it."

Learned Hand, 1872–1961
(American jurist)

CONTENTS

LEARNING OBJECTIVES

After reading this chapter, you should be able to:

1. Explain the circumstances in which a party will be held liable for the tort of wrongful interference.
2. Indicate how the tort of appropriation occurs.
3. Summarize the laws protecting trademarks, patents, and copyrights.
4. Describe how trade secrets are protected by the law.
5. Point out how the Racketeer Influenced and Corrupt Organizations Act is applied in civil cases.

Our economic system of free enterprise is based on the ability of persons, acting either as individuals or as business firms, to compete freely for customers. Businesses may, generally speaking, engage in whatever is reasonably necessary to obtain a fair share of a market or to recapture a share that has been lost. They are not allowed to use the motive of complete elimination of competition to justify certain business activities, however. Those who enter into business should be acquainted with the point at which zealous competition might be construed by a court of law to cross over into tortious interference with the business rights of others. As the opening quotation indicates, businesspersons need to know what the law is if they are to obey it.

• **BUSINESS TORT**
The wrongful interference with another's business rights.

• **INTELLECTUAL PROPERTY**
Property resulting from intellectual, creative processes.

Business torts are defined as wrongful interference with another's business rights. Included in business torts are such vaguely worded common law concepts as *unfair competition* and *interfering with the business relations of others.* Many of the torts that were discussed in the previous chapter, including defamation, also occur in the business context.

Of significant concern to businesspersons is the need to protect their rights in **intellectual property.** Intellectual property is any property resulting from intellectual, creative processes—the products of an individual's mind. Although it is an abstract term for an abstract concept, intellectual property is nonetheless wholly familiar to virtually everyone. The information contained in books and computer files is intellectual property. The software you use, the movies you see, and the music you listen to are all forms of intellectual property. In fact, in today's information age, it should come as no surprise that the value of the world's intellectual property now exceeds the value of physical property, such as machines and houses.

In this chapter, we examine business torts and the protection given to intellectual property rights under trademark, patent, copyright, and other laws. We also look at how the Racketeer Influenced and Corrupt Organizations Act (known more popularly as RICO) has been applied to fraudulent business activities.

Wrongful Interference

ON THE WEB

You can find cases and articles on torts, including business torts, in the tort law library at the Internet Law Library's Web site. Go to law.house.gov/110.htm.

Business torts involving wrongful interference are generally divided into two categories: wrongful interference with a contractual relationship and wrongful interference with a business relationship.

WRONGFUL INTERFERENCE WITH A CONTRACTUAL RELATIONSHIP

Tort law relating to *intentional interference with a contractual relationship* has expanded greatly in recent years. A landmark case involved an opera singer, Joanna Wagner, who was under contract to sing for a man named Lumley for a specified period of years. A man named Gye, who knew of this contract, nonetheless "enticed" Wagner to refuse to carry out the agreement, and Wagner began to sing for Gye. Gye's action constituted a tort because it wrongfully interfered with the contractual relationship between Wagner and Lumley.[1] (Of course, Wagner's refusal to carry out the agreement also entitled Lumley to sue Wagner for breach of contract.)

Three elements are necessary for wrongful interference with a contractual relationship to occur:

1. A valid, enforceable contract must exist between two parties.
2. A third party must know that this contract exists.
3. The third party must *intentionally* cause either of the two parties to breach the contract.

¡REMEMBER!
It is the intent to do an act that is important in tort law, not the motive behind the intent.

The contract may be between a firm and its employees or a firm and its customers. Sometimes a competitor of a firm draws away one of the firm's key employees. If the original employer can show that the competitor induced the breach—that is, that the former employee would not otherwise have broken the contract—damages can be recovered from the competitor.

The following case illustrates the elements of the tort of wrongful interference with a contractual relationship in the context of an agreement not to compete (see Chapter 11).

1. *Lumley v. Gye,* 118 Eng.Rep. 749 (1853).

CASE 5.1 Kallok v. Medtronic, Inc.

Supreme Court of Minnesota, 1998.
573 N.W.2d 356.
www.courts.state.mn.us/library/archive/sctjl.html[a]

COMPANY PROFILE *Medtronic, Inc., is the world's leading manufacturer of implantable biomedical devices. The company was started in 1949 by Earl Bakken, who was then a graduate student at the University of Minnesota, and Palmer Hermundslie, who worked in a lumberyard. The company's initial focus was the repair of hospital laboratory equipment. Today, Medtronic's most important products relate to cardiovascular and neurological health. It makes the most-often-prescribed heart pacemakers, as well as heart valves, implantable neurostimulation and drug-delivery systems, catheters used in angioplasties, and other products. Medtronic sells these products in more than 120 countries.*

a. This page lists, in alphabetical order, Minnesota Supreme Court opinions and orders that have been issued since May 2, 1996, with first party names beginning with the letter J, K, or L. Scroll down the list to the *Kallok* case and click on the docket number to access the opinion. This page is part of the Web site for the "Minnesota State Court System" maintained by the Minnesota state government.

BACKGROUND AND FACTS Michael Kallok signed a series of noncompete agreements when he worked for Medtronic, Inc., a medical device manufacturer. The agreements restricted his ability to work for Medtronic's competitors, including Angeion Corporation. When Kallok later approached Angeion for a job, he told it about the agreements. Angeion consulted with its attorneys, who advised that Kallok would not breach the agreements by accepting a job with Angeion. Angeion did not tell the attorneys all of the details of the agreements, however. After Kallok resigned to work for Angeion, he and Angeion filed a suit in a Minnesota state court against Medtronic, asserting that the noncompete agreements were unenforceable. Medtronic counterclaimed, alleging wrongful interference by Angeion. Angeion argued that its hiring of Kallok was justified because it consulted attorneys first. The court held Angeion liable and, among other things, awarded Medtronic damages. The plaintiffs appealed. The state intermediate appellate court took away the award. Medtronic appealed to the Minnesota Supreme Court.

IN THE WORDS OF THE COURT . . .
ANDERSON, Justice.

* * * *

Medtronic easily established the * * * elements [of a cause of action for tortious interference with a contractual relationship]. First, as Kallok signed valid noncompete agreements, it is evident that a contract existed between him and Medtronic. Second, Angeion knew of the existence of Kallok's noncompete agreements before it hired him. * * * Third, * * * Angeion * * * procured the breach of his noncompete agreements by offering him the * * * position that he eventually accepted.

* * * Angeion, however, asserts that * * * its actions were justified because it consulted with its outside legal counsel before hiring Kallok * * * . We conclude that Angeion's argument lacks merit.

* * * Angeion did not fully inform its outside counsel about Kallok's background at Medtronic or the intricacies of his noncompete agreements. Had Angeion candidly provided its attorneys with all relevant information * * * Angeion would have understood that hiring Kallok would cause him to breach his noncompete agreements with Medtronic. * * *

* * * *

* * * As a result, Medtronic was forced into court to protect the legitimate interest embodied in Kallok's noncompete agreements. * * * We hold that the [trial] court * * * correctly allowed Medtronic to recover from Angeion the * * * expenses it incurred in enforcing its noncompete agreements with Kallok.

(Continued)

CASE 5.1—Continued

DECISION AND REMEDY The Minnesota Supreme Court reversed the decision of the lower court. The state supreme court reinstated Medtronic's award of damages for Angeion's interference with the noncompete agreements between Medtronic and Kallok.

FOR CRITICAL ANALYSIS—Social Consideration *What might be the result for society if there were no cause of action for wrongful interference with a contractual relationship?*

WRONGFUL INTERFERENCE WITH A BUSINESS RELATIONSHIP

• **PREDATORY BEHAVIOR** Business behavior, such as the entry into business, that is undertaken with the intention of unlawfully driving competitors out of the market.

"Anyone can win unless there happens to be a second entry."
GEORGE ADE, 1866–1944 (American humorist)

Businesspersons devise countless schemes to attract customers, but they are forbidden by the courts to interfere unreasonably with another's business in their attempts to gain a share of the market. There is a difference between competitive methods and **predatory behavior**—actions undertaken with the intention of unlawfully driving competitors completely out of the market.

The distinction usually depends on whether a business is attempting to attract customers in general or to solicit only those customers who have shown an interest in a similar product or service of a specific competitor. If a shopping center contains two shoe stores, an employee of Store A cannot be positioned at the entrance of Store B for the purpose of diverting customers to Store A. This type of activity constitutes the tort of wrongful interference with a business relationship, which is commonly considered to be an unfair trade practice. If this type of activity were permitted, Store A would reap the benefits of Store B's advertising.

DEFENSES TO WRONGFUL INTERFERENCE

¡REMEMBER! What society and the law consider permissible often depends on the circumstances.

A person will not be liable for the tort of wrongful interference with a contractual or business relationship if it can be shown that the interference was justified, or permissible. Bona fide competitive behavior is a permissible interference even if it results in the breaking of a contract. • EXAMPLE 5.1 If Antonio's Meats advertises so effectively that it induces Beverly's Restaurant Chain to break its contract with Otis Meat Company, Otis Meat Company will be unable to recover against Antonio's Meats on a wrongful interference theory. After all, the public policy that favors free competition in advertising outweighs any possible instability that such competitive activity might cause in contractual relations.•

Appropriation

• **APPROPRIATION** In tort law, the use by one person of another person's name, likeness, or other identifying characteristic without permission and for the benefit of

The use by one person of another person's name, likeness, or other identifying characteristic, without permission and for the benefit of the user, constitutes the tort of **appropriation.** Under the law, an individual's right to privacy includes the right to the exclusive use of his or her identity.

• EXAMPLE 5.2 Vanna White, the hostess of the popular television game show *Wheel of Fortune,* brought a case against Samsung Electronics America, Inc. Without White's permission, Samsung included in an advertisement for Samsung videocassette recorders (VCRs) a depiction of a robot dressed in a wig, gown, and jewelry, posed in a setting that resembled the *Wheel of Fortune* set, in a stance for which White is famous. The court held in White's favor, holding that the tort of appropriation does not require the use of a celebrity's name or likeness. The court

ON THE WEB

Law firms' Web sites are good sources for information on various areas of the law, including business torts. FindLaw provides a list of law firm Web sites at www.firms.findlaw.com.

stated that Samsung's robot ad left "little doubt" as to the identity of the celebrity whom the ad was meant to depict.[2] •

Often, cases alleging appropriation require the courts to balance a celebrity's right to the exclusive use of his or her identity against the First Amendment right to freedom of speech. • **EXAMPLE 5.3** In one case, a California newspaper reproduced in poster form various pages from its newspapers that contained a photograph and artist's rendition of Joe Montana, the then famous professional football player. In Montana's suit against the newspaper for the commercial misappropriation of his name, photograph, and likeness, however, the court held that the defendant newspaper's reproduction and sale of the posters was protected speech under the First Amendment.[3] •

Other sports-related commercial misappropriation cases have involved the rights of those who invest time and money in the creation and broadcast of sports events. In the following case, the court considered whether the transmission of real-time information about National Basketball Association games in progress via America Online constituted commercial misappropriation.

2. *White v. Samsung Electronics America, Inc.*, 971 F.2d 1395 (9th Cir. 1992).
3. *Montana v. San Jose Mercury News, Inc.*, 34 Cal.App.4th 790, 40 Cal.Rptr.2d 639 (1995).

CASE 5.2 National Basketball Association v. Sports Team Analysis and Tracking Systems, Inc.

United States Court of Appeals,
Second Circuit, 1997.
105 F.3d 841.
www.law.pace.edu/lawlib/legal/us-legal/judiciary/second-circuit/test3/96-7975.opn.html[a]

HISTORICAL AND ECONOMIC SETTING *The commercial value and appeal of National Basketball Association (NBA) games can be attributed to years of successful promotion. NBA games reach the peak of their value while they are being played. In the mid-1990s, 80 percent of NBA revenues were derived from the sale of broadcast distribution licenses and admission fees to the arenas. The NBA licenses rights to real-time game data to select local, regional, and national media, including television and radio broadcasters, a satellite service, and a company that provides audio descriptions of games via an 800 number.*

a. This is the "Decisions for January 1997" page within the collection of opinions of the U.S. Court of Appeals for the Second Circuit available at the Web site of the Pace University School of Law.

BACKGROUND AND FACTS Sports Team Analysis and Tracking Systems, Inc. (STATS), provides information about sports to the media—including ESPN and NBC Sports—and to the public. One of STATS's methods was to disseminate real-time information about NBA games in progress via its Web site on America Online, Inc. (AOL). Users who accessed the site saw point-by-point changes in scores, game time remaining, and such player and team statistics as field goals, free throws, rebounds, three-point shots, total points, and minutes played. The information was updated as frequently as every fifteen seconds. STATS did not have the NBA's permission to transmit this information, however. The NBA and NBA Properties, Inc., filed a suit in a federal district court against STATS and others, alleging, in part, commercial misappropriation. The defendants argued that because they did not replicate entire broadcasts of NBA games, they were doing nothing wrong.

IN THE WORDS OF THE COURT . . .
PRESKA, District Judge:

* * * *

Defendants would * * * strictly limit misappropriation to "entire act" replications. * * * [This] would allow parties to escape liability simply by choosing to

(Continued)

CASE 5.2—Continued

omit some peripheral aspect of the event, thus conveying something less than the entire act. Equity will not stand for such a result * * * .

* * * *

By disseminating to fans the changing scores and leads and other information on a real-time basis, defendants have appropriated the essence of NBA's most valuable property—the excitement and entertainment of a game in progress.

DECISION AND REMEDY The court held that STATS's transmission of real-time NBA game information on AOL constituted commercial misappropriation and ordered STATS to stop.

FOR CRITICAL ANALYSIS—Social Consideration *Do you believe that real-time broadcasts of NBA games via the Internet will ever become a substitute for attending the games or watching them on television?*

Defamation in the Business Context

As discussed in Chapter 4, the tort of defamation occurs when an individual makes a false statement that injures another's reputation. Defamation may take the form of libel (defamatory statements in written or printed form) or slander (defamatory statements made orally). Defamation becomes a business tort when the defamatory matter injures someone in a profession, business, or trade or when it adversely affects a business entity in its credit rating and other dealings.

In recent years, questions have arisen about the potential liability of online computer information services for defamatory statements made in sources included in their databases. This important issue will be discussed in Chapter 7.

Disparagement of Property

• **DISPARAGEMENT OF PROPERTY** An economically injurious falsehood made about another's product or property. A general term for torts that are more specifically referred to as slander of quality or slander of title.

Disparagement of property occurs when economically injurious falsehoods are made not about another's reputation but about another's product or property. Disparagement of property is a general term for torts that can be more specifically referred to as *slander of quality* or *slander of title.*

Slander of Quality

• **SLANDER OF QUALITY (TRADE LIBEL)** The publication of false information about another's product, alleging that it is not what its seller claims.

Publication of false information about another's product, alleging that it is not what its seller claims, constitutes the tort of **slander of quality,** or **trade libel.** The plaintiff must prove that actual damages proximately resulted from the slander of quality. In other words, the plaintiff must show not only that a third person refrained from dealing with the plaintiff because of the improper publication but also that there were associated damages. The economic calculation of such damages—they are, after all, conjectural—is often extremely difficult.

"Hurl your calumnies boldly; something is sure to stick."
FRANCIS BACON, 1561–1626
(English philosopher and statesman)

An improper publication may be both a slander of quality and a defamation. For example, a statement that disparages the quality of a product may also, by implication, disparage the character of the person who would sell such a product. In one case, for instance, the claim that a product that was marketed as a sleeping aid contained "habit-forming drugs" was held to constitute defamation.[4]

4. *Harwood Pharmacal Co. v. National Broadcasting Co.,* 9 N.Y.2d 460, 174 N.E.2d 602, 214 N.Y.S.2d 725 (1961).

OPRAH WINFREY GREETS THE PRESS FOLLOWING THE RULING IN THE DEFAMATION SUIT AGAINST HER. DOES A PERSON OF WINFREY'S STATURE HAVE AN ETHICAL DUTY TO AVOID EVEN THE APPEARANCE OF DISPARAGING OTHERS' PRODUCTS?

Trademark law (to be discussed shortly) has, to some extent, made it easier for companies to sue other companies on the basis of purported false advertising. In the past, courts often ruled that companies could be liable for false advertising only when they misrepresented their own products. It mattered little what such companies claimed about their competitors' brands, particularly in so-called comparative advertisements. Today, false or misleading statements about another firm's products are actionable.

During the 1990s, at least thirteen states enacted special statutes to protect against disparagement of perishable food products. Food producers began to push for such laws, often called veggie-libel laws, in 1991 after Washington state apple growers, using traditional libel and product-disparagement laws, failed to win a lawsuit against CBS News for a *60 Minutes* broadcast on the growth regulator Alar. These food-disparagement statutes have caused substantial controversy because, among other things, they make it easier for plaintiffs to get to court. Unlike traditional trade libel law, which allows a company to sue for libel only if the company's particular brand or product has been defamed, the statutes permit any company within a food-related industry to sue a party that has disparaged a food product.

ETHICAL ISSUE 5.1 ***Are food-disparagement laws against the public interest?*** Food-disparagement laws received national media attention when a group of Texas cattle ranchers sued talk-show host Oprah Winfrey for saying on one of her shows that the fear of "mad cow" disease "stopped her cold from eating a hamburger." The ranchers claimed that Winfrey had defamed their product, beef, in violation of the Texas food-disparagement statute. In 1998, the federal judge hearing the case held that the cattle ranchers had failed to make a case under the Texas statute, but it did not hold the statute unconstitutional—as Winfrey (and many others) had hoped it would. Food-disparagement statutes have been hailed by some as a necessary protection for food producers, who are particularly vulnerable to false or misleading statements made about food products. Critics of such statutes, however, claim that their effect is to "chill" free speech and would like to see them held unconstitutional as violations of the First Amendment.

SLANDER OF TITLE

When a publication denies or casts doubt on another's legal ownership of any property, and when this results in financial loss to that property's owner, the tort of **slander of title** may exist. Usually, this is an intentional tort in which someone knowingly publishes an untrue statement about property with the intent of discouraging a third person from dealing with the person slandered. For example, it would be difficult for a car dealer to attract customers after competitors published a notice that the dealer's stock consisted of stolen autos.

• **SLANDER OF TITLE**
The publication of a statement that denies or casts doubt on another's legal ownership of any property, causing financial loss to that property's owner.

Intellectual Property Protection

The need to protect creative works was voiced by the framers of the U.S. Constitution over two hundred years ago: Article I, Section 8, of the Constitution authorized Congress "[t]o promote the Progress of Science and useful Arts, by securing for limited Times to Authors and Inventors the exclusive Right to their respective Writings and Discoveries." Laws protecting patents, trademarks, and copyrights are explicitly designed to protect and reward inventive and artistic creativity.

An understanding of intellectual property law is important because intellectual property has taken on increasing significance, not only in the United States but globally as well. Today, ownership rights in intangible intellectual property are more important to the prosperity of many U.S. companies than are their tangible assets. Protecting these assets in today's online world has proved particularly challenging (see Chapter 7 for a further discussion of this issue).

Trademarks and Related Property

A **trademark** is a distinctive mark, motto, device, or emblem that a manufacturer stamps, prints, or otherwise affixes to the goods it produces so that they may be identified on the market and their origin vouched for. At common law, the person who used a symbol or mark to identify a business or product was protected in the use of that trademark. Clearly, if one used the trademark of another, it would lead consumers to believe that one's goods were made by the other. The law seeks to avoid this kind of confusion. In the following famous case concerning Coca-Cola, the defendants argued that the Coca-Cola trademark was entitled to no protection under the law, because the term did not accurately represent the product.

• **TRADEMARK**
A distinctive mark, motto, device, or emblem that a manufacturer stamps, prints, or otherwise affixes to the goods it produces so that they may be identified on the market and their origins made known. Once a trademark is established (under the common law or through registration), the owner is entitled to its exclusive use.

CASE 5.3 The Coca-Cola Co. v. Koke Co. of America

Supreme Court of the United States, 1920.
254 U.S. 143,
41 S.Ct. 113,
65 L.Ed. 189.
www.findlaw.com/casecode/supreme.html[a]

COMPANY PROFILE *John Pemberton, an Atlanta pharmacist, invented a caramel-colored, carbonated soft drink in 1886. His bookkeeper, Frank Robinson, named the beverage Coca-Cola after two of the ingredients, coca leaves and kola nuts. Asa Candler bought the Coca-Cola Company in 1891, and within seven years, he made the soft drink available in all of the United States, as well as in parts of Canada and Mexico. Candler continued to sell Coke aggressively and to open up new markets, reaching Europe before 1910. In doing so, however, he attracted numerous competitors, some of whom tried to capitalize directly on the Coke name.*

a. This is the "U.S. Supreme Court Opinions" page within the Web site of the "Findlaw Internet Legal Resources" database. This page provides several options for accessing an opinion. Because you know the citation for this case, you can go to the "Citation Search" box, type in the appropriate volume and page numbers for the *United States Reports* ("254" and "143," respectively, for the *Coca-Cola* case), and click on "Get It."

BACKGROUND AND FACTS The Coca-Cola Company brought an action in a federal district court to enjoin other beverage companies from using the words "Koke" and "Dope" for the defendants' products. The defendants contended that the Coca-Cola trademark was a fraudulent representation and that Coca-Cola was therefore not entitled to any help from the courts. By use of the Coca-Cola name, the defendants alleged, the Coca-Cola Company represented that the beverage contained cocaine (from coca leaves). The district court granted the injunction, but the federal appellate court reversed. The Coca-Cola Company appealed to the United States Supreme Court.

IN THE WORDS OF THE COURT . . .
Mr. Justice *HOLMES* delivered the opinion of the court.

* * * *

* * * Before 1900 the beginning of [Coca-Cola's] good will was more or less helped by the presence of cocaine, a drug that, like alcohol or caffein or opium, may be described as a deadly poison or as a valuable item of the pharmacopœa according to the rhetorical purposes in view. * * * [A]fter the Food and Drug Act of June 30, 1906, if not earlier, long before this suit was brought, it was eliminated from the plaintiff's compound. * * *

CASE 5.3—Continued

* * * Since 1900 the sales have increased at a very great rate corresponding to a like increase in advertising. The name now characterizes a beverage to be had at almost any soda fountain. It means a single thing coming from a single source, and well known to the community. It hardly would be too much to say that the drink characterizes the name as much as the name the drink. In other words Coca-Cola probably means to most persons the plaintiff's familiar product to be had everywhere rather than a compound of particular substances. * * * [B]efore this suit was brought the plaintiff had advertised to the public that it must not expect and would not find cocaine, and had eliminated everything tending to suggest cocaine effects except the name and the picture of the leaves and nuts, which probably conveyed little or nothing to most who saw it. It appears to us that it would be going too far to deny the plaintiff relief against a palpable fraud because possibly here and there an ignorant person might call for the drink with the hope for incipient cocaine intoxication. The plaintiff's position must be judged by the facts as they were when the suit was begun, not by the facts of a different condition and an earlier time.

DECISION AND REMEDY The United States Supreme Court upheld the district court's injunction. The competing beverage companies were enjoined from calling their products "Koke." The Court did not prevent them, however, from calling their products "Dope."

FOR CRITICAL ANALYSIS—Social Consideration *How can a court determine when a particular nickname for a branded product has entered into common use?*

"The protection of trademarks is the law's recognition of the psychological function of symbols. If it is true that we live by symbols, it is no less true that we purchase goods by them."

FELIX FRANKFURTER, 1882–1965
(Associate justice of the United States Supreme Court, 1939–1962)

ON THE WEB

You can find answers to frequently asked questions (FAQs) about trademark and patent law, as well as a host of other information, at the Web site of the U.S. Patent and Trademark Office. Go to www.uspto.gov.

Statutory Protection of Trademarks Statutory protection of trademarks and related property is provided at the federal level by the Lanham Trade-Mark Act of 1946.[5] The Lanham Act was enacted in part to protect manufacturers from losing business to rival companies that used confusingly similar trademarks. The Lanham Act incorporates the common law of trademarks and provides remedies for owners of trademarks who wish to enforce their claims in federal court. Many states also have trademark statutes.

In 1995, Congress amended the Lanham Act by passing the Federal Trademark Dilution Act,[6] which extended the protection available to trademark owners by creating a federal cause of action for trademark *dilution.* Until the passage of this amendment, federal trademark law only prohibited the unauthorized use of the same mark on competing—or on noncompeting but "related"—goods or services when such use would likely confuse consumers as to the origin of those goods and services. Trademark dilution laws, which about half of the states have also enacted, protect "distinctive" or "famous" trademarks (such as Jergens, McDonald's, RCA, and Macintosh) from certain unauthorized uses of the marks *regardless* of a showing of competition or a likelihood of confusion.

A famous mark may be diluted not only by the use of an *identical* mark but also by the use of a *similar* mark. • EXAMPLE 5.4 A case was brought by Ringling Bros.–Barnum & Bailey, Combined Shows, Inc., against the state of Utah. Ringling Bros. claimed that Utah's use of the slogan "The Greatest Snow on Earth"—to attract visitors to the state's recreational and scenic resorts—diluted the distinctiveness of the circus's famous trademark, "The Greatest Show on Earth." Utah moved to dismiss the suit, arguing that the 1995 provisions only protect owners of famous trademarks against the unauthorized use of identical marks. A federal court disagreed and refused to grant Utah's motion to dismiss the case.[7] •

5. 15 U.S.C. Sections 1051–1128.
6. 15 U.S.C. Section 1125.
7. *Ringling Bros.–Barnum & Bailey, Combined Shows, Inc. v. Utah Division of Travel Development,* 935 F.Supp. 736 (E.D.Va. 1996).

ON THE WEB

To access the federal database of registered trademarks, go to **www.uspto.gov/tmdb/index.html**.

Trademark Registration Trademarks may be registered with the state or with the federal government. To register for protection under federal trademark law, a person must file an application with the U.S. Patent and Trademark Office in Washington, D.C. Under current law, a mark can be registered (1) if it is currently in commerce or (2) if the applicant intends to put the mark into commerce within six months.

Under extenuating circumstances, the six-month period can be extended by thirty months, giving the applicant a total of three years from the date of notice of trademark approval to make use of the mark and file the required use statement. Registration is postponed until actual use of the mark. Nonetheless, during this waiting period, any applicant can legally protect his or her trademark against a third party who previously has neither used the mark nor filed an application for it. Registration is renewable between the fifth and sixth years after the initial registration and every ten years thereafter (every twenty years for trademarks registered before 1990).

Trademark Infringement Registration of a trademark with the U.S. Patent and Trademark Office gives notice on a nationwide basis that the trademark belongs exclusively to the registrant. The registrant is also allowed to use the symbol ® to indicate that the mark has been registered. Whenever that trademark is copied to a substantial degree or used in its entirety by another, intentionally or unintentionally, the trademark has been *infringed* (used without authorization). When a trademark has been infringed, the owner of the mark has a cause of action against the infringer. A person need not have registered a trademark in order to sue for trademark infringement, but registration does furnish proof of the date of inception of the trademark's use. (For a discussion of whether "framing" another's Web page constitutes trademark infringement, see this chapter's *Technology and Online Trademark Infringement.*)

Distinctiveness of Mark The Lanham Act states, "No trademark by which the goods of the applicant may be distinguished from the goods of others shall be refused registration."[8] Only those trademarks that are deemed sufficiently distinctive from all competing trademarks will be protected, however. The trademarks must be sufficiently distinct to enable consumers to identify the manufacturer of the goods easily and to differentiate among competing products.

Strong Marks. Fanciful, arbitrary, or suggestive trademarks are generally considered to be the most distinctive (strongest) trademarks, because they are normally taken from outside the context of the particular product and thus provide the best means of distinguishing one product from another.

A BILLBOARD AND THEATER MARQUEE IN NEW YORK CITY. WHY ARE TRADEMARKS PROTECTED BY THE LAW?

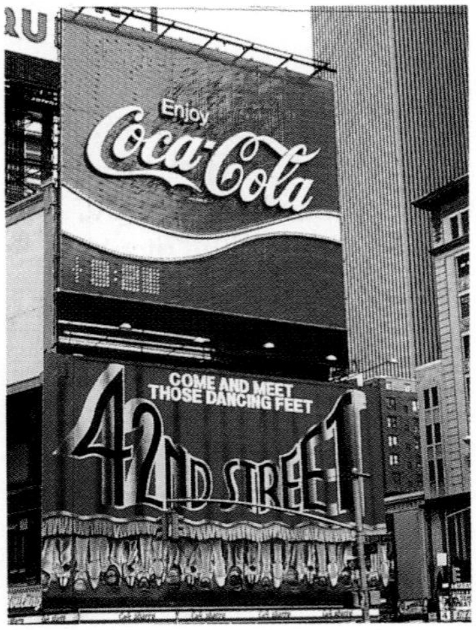

• EXAMPLE 5.5 Fanciful trademarks include invented words, such as "Xerox" for one manufacturer's copiers and "Kodak" for another company's photographic products. Arbitrary trademarks include actual words that have no literal connection to the product, such as "English Leather" used as a name for an after-shave lotion (and not for leather processed in England). Suggestive trademarks are those that suggest something about a product without describing the product directly. For example, "Dairy Queen" suggests an association between its products and milk, but it does not directly describe ice cream. •

Secondary Meaning. Descriptive terms, geographical terms, and personal names are not inherently distinctive and do not receive protection under the law until they acquire a secondary meaning. A secondary meaning may arise when customers begin to associate a specific term or phrase, such as "London Fog," with specific trademarked items (coats with "London Fog" labels). Whether a secondary meaning becomes attached to

8. 15 U.S.C. Section 1052.

Technology and Online Trademark Infringement

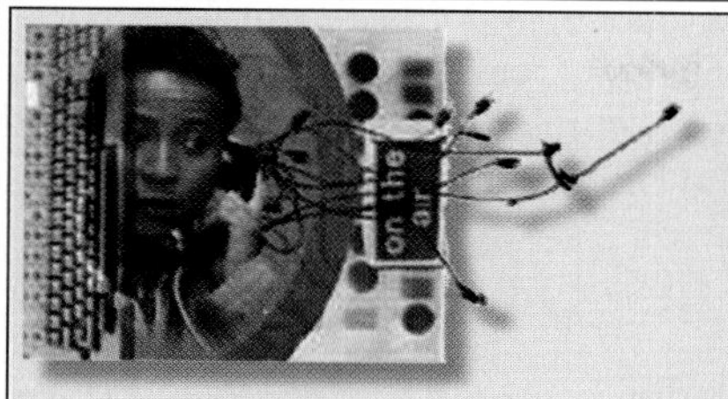

When a user clicks on an icon or on highlighted text that is programmed to be a hypertext link, the user's computer is immediately linked to a new online location. The link may lead to another point within the same site or to a different, unrelated site somewhere else in cyberspace. Sometimes, a site owner may ask the permission of other owners to link to their sites, but this is not normally done. Linking by underlining the name of a linked site is legal and does not require permission. Linking is considered one of the primary factors in the success of Internet commerce, and is part of the revolution of the new technology.

Site owners are less agreeable to framing, however. If the linking site is a framing site, the pages of the linked site will appear in a window of the original site. With frames, a single site can let users view several sites simultaneously. The law is just emerging on this issue, but site owners, before framing another's Web pages, should obtain consent if a link falsely implies an affiliation between the sites, if a link uses the linked site's logo or trademark, if an imaged link is used, if the link is "deep" (to internal pages), or if a frame modifies or distorts the linked site.[a] Also, consent should be obtained if the linked site requests or requires it, or if the link diverts advertising revenue from the linked site. To avoid liability for trademark (or possibly copyright) infringement, a linking site should include a disclaimer.

With linking and framing, any site owner can divert traffic from another site. This may be desired because search engines base their results on the number of hits (visits to a site). More hits can mean more advertising revenue and more sales. An owner may even appropriate a competitor's content and hide it, so that an unsuspecting user is transported to the appropriator's site even though he or she cannot see the appropriated material. This is a violation of trademark law (and copyright law).

a. For example, Ticketmaster recently filed a complaint against Microsoft in a federal district court, alleging that Microsoft Network's unauthorized links to interior pages of Ticketmaster's site constituted trademark infringement and unfair competition. Ticketmaster argued that its Web site is the same as a trademark and that it should be allowed to control the way in which others use it. Even if this case is settled, the issue will likely come up again.

FOR CRITICAL ANALYSIS

Do new types of legal issues posed by technology, such as the Internet, require new laws or just new adaptations of old laws?

a term or name usually depends on how extensively the product is advertised, the market for the product, the number of sales, and other factors. Once a secondary meaning is attached to a term or name, a trademark is considered distinctive and is protected.

In the following landmark case, the Supreme Court addressed the issue of whether a *color* can be trademarked on the basis that it has acquired a secondary meaning.

CASE 5.4 Qualitex Co. v. Jacobson Products Co.

Supreme Court of the United States, 1995.
514 U.S. 159,
115 S.Ct. 1300,
131 L.Ed.2d 248.
supct.law.cornell.edu/supct/html/93-1577.ZS.html[a]

a. This is a page within the "Historic Supreme Court Decisions" collection of the Legal Information Institute (LII) and Project Hermes available at the LII site on the Web. Read the opinion beginning with the syllabus on this Web page or click on a link to take advantage of one of the other options.

HISTORICAL AND SOCIAL SETTING *For centuries, color has been used to represent affiliations and loyalties and to symbolize various moods and qualities. For example, churches use vestments of different colors for different religious holidays, such as white for Easter. Certain colors are associated with particular political organizations—green with environmental groups, for example. Other colors add distinctive identifying qualities to commercial products, such as the purple and orange of FedEx.*

(Continued)

CASE 5.4—Continued

BACKGROUND AND FACTS Since the 1950s, the Qualitex Company has manufactured Sun Glow press pads, which are used in dry cleaning and laundry establishments. The pads are a distinctive green-gold color. In 1989, the Jacobson Products Company began to sell its own press pads, which are a similar green-gold color. Qualitex brought an action against Jacobson in a federal district court, alleging, among other things, trademark infringement. The court entered a judgment in favor of Qualitex, and Jacobson appealed. The appellate court ruled in favor of Jacobson, and Qualitex appealed to the United States Supreme Court.

IN THE WORDS OF THE COURT . . .
Justice *BREYER* delivered the opinion of the Court.

* * * *

* * * [The Lanham Act] says that trademarks "includ[e] any word, name, symbol, or device, or any combination thereof." Since human beings might use as a "symbol" or "device" almost anything at all that is capable of carrying meaning, this language, read literally, is not restrictive. The courts and the Patent and Trademark Office have authorized for use as a mark a particular shape (of a Coca-Cola bottle), a particular sound (of NBC's three chimes), and even a particular scent (of plumeria blossoms on sewing thread). If a shape, a sound, and a fragrance can act as symbols why, one might ask, can a color not do the same?

A color is also capable of satisfying the more important part of the [Lanham Act] definition of a trademark, which requires that a person "us[e]" or "inten[d] to use" the mark "to identify and distinguish his or her goods, including a unique product, from those manufactured or sold by others and to indicate the source of the goods, even if that source is unknown." * * * [O]ver time, customers may come to treat a particular color on a product or its packaging * * * as signifying a brand. And, if so, that color would have come to identify and distinguish the goods * * * much in the way that descriptive words on a product * * * can come to indicate a product's origin. * * * Again, one might ask, if trademark law permits a descriptive word with secondary meaning to act as a mark, why would it not permit a color, under similar circumstances, to do the same?

DECISION AND REMEDY The United States Supreme Court reversed the ruling of the appellate court and held that color alone can qualify for trademark protection.

FOR CRITICAL ANALYSIS—Technological Consideration *The Court pointed out that there is "no competitive need in the press pad industry for the green-gold color, since other colors are equally usable." If, however, a color were essential to a product's use or purpose, should that color be given trademark protection? Why or why not?*

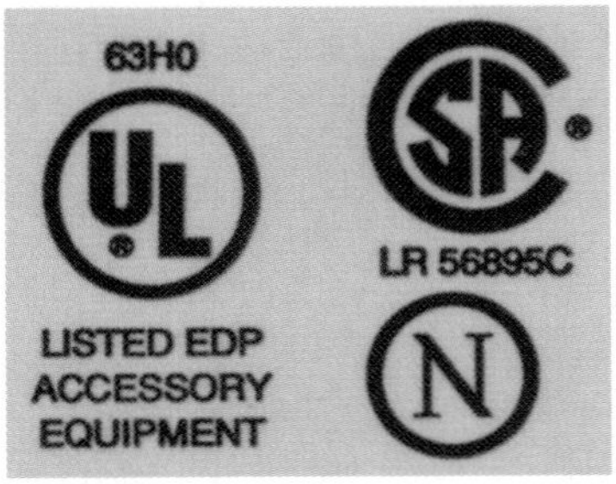

A "UL" CERTIFICATION MARK. HOW DOES A CERTIFICATION MARK DIFFER FROM A TRADEMARK?

Generic Terms. Generic terms, such as *bicycle* or *computer,* receive no protection, even if they acquire secondary meanings. A particularly thorny problem arises when a trademark acquires generic use. For example, *aspirin* and *thermos* were originally trademarked products, but today the words are used generically. Other examples are *escalator, trampoline, raisin bran, dry ice, lanolin, linoleum, nylon,* and *corn flakes.* Even so, the courts will not allow another firm to use those marks in such a way as to deceive a potential consumer.

Service, Certification, and Collective Marks

A **service mark** is similar to a trademark but is used to distinguish the services of one person or company from those of another. For example, each airline has a particular mark or symbol associated with its name. Titles and character names used in radio and television are frequently registered as service marks.

• **SERVICE MARK**
A mark used in the sale or the advertising of services, such as to distinguish the services of one person from the services of others. Titles, character names, and other distinctive features of radio and television programs may be registered as service marks.

Other marks protected by law include certification marks and collective marks. A *certification mark* is used by one or more persons other than the owner to certify the region, materials, mode of manufacture, quality, or accuracy of the owner's goods or services. When used by members of a cooperative, association, or other organization, it is referred to as a *collective mark*. • **EXAMPLE 5.6** Certification marks include such marks as "Good Housekeeping Seal of Approval" and "UL Tested." Collective marks appear at the ends of the credits of movies to indicate the various associations and organizations that participated in the making of the movies. The union marks found on the tags of certain products are also collective marks.•

• **TRADE NAME**
A term that is used to indicate part or all of a business's name and that is directly related to the business's reputation and goodwill. Trade names are protected under the common law (and under trademark law, if the name is the same as the firm's trademarked property).

Trade Names Trademarks apply to *products*. The term **trade name** is used to indicate part or all of a business's name, whether the business is a sole proprietorship, a partnership, or a corporation. Generally, a trade name is directly related to a business and its goodwill. Trade names may be protected as trademarks if the trade name is the same as the company's trademarked product—for example, Coca-Cola. Unless also used as a trademark or service mark, a trade name cannot be registered with the federal government. Trade names are protected under the common law, however. As with trademarks, words must be unusual or fancifully used if they are to be protected as trade names. The word *Safeway*, for example, was held by the courts to be sufficiently fanciful to obtain protection as a trade name for a food-store chain.[9]

• **TRADE DRESS**
The image and overall appearance of a business—for example, the distinctive decor, menu, layout, and style of service of a particular restaurant. Basically, trade dress is subject to the same protection as trademarks.

Trade Dress The term **trade dress** refers to the image and overall appearance of a business. For example, the distinctive decor, menu, layout, and style of service of a particular restaurant may be regarded as the restaurant's trade dress. Similarly, if a golf course is distinguished from other golf courses by prominent features, those features may be considered the golf course's trade dress. Basically, trade dress is subject to the same protection as trademarks. In cases involving trade dress infringement, as in trademark infringement cases, a major consideration is whether consumers are likely to be confused by the allegedly infringing use.

PATENTS

• **PATENT**
A government grant that gives an inventor the exclusive right or privilege to make, use, or sell his or her invention for a limited time period.

A **patent** is a grant from the government that gives an inventor the exclusive right to make, use, and sell an invention for a period of twenty years from the date of filing the application for a patent. Patents for a fourteen-year period are given for designs, as opposed to inventions. For either a regular patent or a design patent, the applicant must demonstrate to the satisfaction of the U.S. Patent and Trademark Office that the invention, discovery, process, or design is genuine, novel, useful, and not obvious in light of current technology. A patent holder gives notice to all that an article or design is patented by placing on it the word *Patent* or *Pat.* plus the patent number. In contrast to patent law in other countries, in the United States patent protection is given to the first person to invent a product or process, even though someone else may have been the first to file for a patent on that product or process.

"The patent system . . . added the fuel of interest to the fire of genius."

ABRAHAM LINCOLN, 1809–1865
(Sixteenth president of the United States, 1861–1865)

At one time, it was difficult for developers and manufacturers of software to obtain patent protection because many software products simply automate procedures that can be performed manually. In other words, the computer programs do not meet the "novel" and "not obvious" requirements previously mentioned. Also, the basis for software is often a mathematical equation or formula, which is not patentable. In 1981, the United States Supreme Court held that it is possible, however, to obtain a patent for a *process* that incorporates a computer program—providing, of course, that

9. *Safeway Stores v. Suburban Foods*, 130 F.Supp. 249 (E.D.Va. 1955).

ON THE WEB

For information on patent law and links to related Web sites, go to the Web site of the U.S. Patent and Trademark Office at
www.uspto.gov.

Other good online sources for information on patents can be found at
www.patents.com
and
www.ljx.com/patent.

the process itself is patentable.[10] Subsequently, many patents have been issued for software-related inventions.

If a firm makes, uses, or sells another's patented design, product, or process without the patent owner's permission, it commits the tort of patent infringement. Patent infringement may exist even though the patent owner has not put the patented product in commerce. Patent infringement may also occur even though not all features or parts of an invention are copied. (With respect to a patented process, however, all steps or their equivalent must be copied for infringement to exist.)

Often, litigation for patent infringement is so costly that the patent holder will instead offer to sell to the infringer a license to use the patented design, product, or process. Indeed, in many cases the costs of detection, prosecution, and monitoring are so high that patents are valueless to their owners; the owners cannot afford to protect them.

COPYRIGHTS

• **COPYRIGHT**
The exclusive right of "authors" to publish, print, or sell an intellectual production for a statutory period of time. A copyright has the same monopolistic nature as a patent or trademark, but it differs in that it applies exclusively to works of art, literature, and other works of authorship (including computer programs).

A **copyright** is an intangible property right granted by federal statute to the author or originator of certain literary or artistic productions. Currently, copyrights are governed by the Copyright Act of 1976,[11] as amended. Works created after January 1, 1978, are automatically given statutory copyright protection for the life of the author plus 70 years. For copyrights owned by publishing houses, the copyright expires 95 years from the date of publication or 120 years from the date of creation, whichever is first. For works by more than one author, the copyright expires 70 years after the death of the last surviving author.[12]

Copyrights can be registered with the U.S. Copyright Office in Washington, D.C. A copyright owner no longer needs to place a © or *Copr.* or *Copyright* on the work, however, to have the work protected against infringement. Chances are that if somebody created it, somebody owns it.

ON THE WEB

For information on copyrights, go to the U.S. Copyright Office at
lcweb.loc.gov/copyright.

What Is Protected Expression? Works that are copyrightable include books, records, films, artworks, architectural plans, menus, music videos, product packaging, and computer software. To obtain protection under the Copyright Act, a work must be original and fall into one of the following categories: (1) literary works; (2) musical works; (3) dramatic works; (4) pantomimes and choreographic works; (5) pictorial, graphic, and sculptural works; (6) films and other audiovisual works; and (7) sound recordings. To be protected, a work must be "fixed in a durable medium" from which it can be perceived, reproduced, or communicated. Protection is automatic. Registration is not required.

¡BE CAREFUL!
If a creative work does not fall into a certain category, it may not be copyrighted, but it may be protected by other intellectual property law.

Section 102 of the Copyright Act specifically excludes copyright protection for any "idea, procedure, process, system, method of operation, concept, principle, or discovery, regardless of the form in which it is described, explained, illustrated, or embodied." Note that it is not possible to copyright an *idea*. The underlying ideas embodied in a work may be freely used by others. What is copyrightable is the particular way in which an idea is *expressed*. Whenever an idea and an expression are inseparable, the expression cannot be copyrighted. Generally, anything that is not an original

10. *Diamond v. Diehr*, 450 U.S. 175, 101 S.Ct. 1048, 67 L.Ed.2d 155 (1981).11. 17 U.S.C. Sections 101 *et seq*.
11. 17 U.S.C. Sections 101 *et seq*.
12. These time periods relect the extensions set forth in the Sonny Bono Copyright Term Extension Act of 1988.

expression will not qualify for copyright protection. Facts widely known to the public are not copyrightable. Page numbers are not copyrightable, because they follow a sequence known to everyone. Mathematical calculations are not copyrightable.

Compilations of facts, however, are copyrightable. Section 103 of the Copyright Act defines a compilation as "a work formed by the collection and assembling of preexisting materials of data that are selected, coordinated, or arranged in such a way that the resulting work as a whole constitutes an original work of authorship." The key requirement in the copyrightability of a compilation is originality. • EXAMPLE 5.7 The White Pages of a telephone directory do not qualify for copyright protection when the information that makes up the directory (names, addresses, and telephone numbers) is not selected, coordinated, or arranged in an original way.[13] In one case, even the Yellow Pages of a telephone directory did not qualify for copyright protection.[14] •

ETHICAL ISSUE 5.2 ***Should copyright protection extend to "reimported" goods?*** Cases involving claims of copyright infringement can sometimes involve questions of fairness. One such question that reached the United States Supreme Court involved L'anza Research International, Inc., a company that sells hair-care products. L'anza sells its products in the United States only to distributors who agree to resell the products in certain geographic areas to authorized retailers. L'anza also sells its products in foreign markets but for lower prices—because it does little advertising abroad. At one point, an American firm purchased L'anza hair products abroad from a L'anza distributor, "reimported" the goods into the United States, and sold them at discount prices to unauthorized retailers. L'anza claimed that this activity infringed on its exclusive rights under the Copyright Act to reproduce and distribute the copyrighted material (the labels on the products) in the United States. According to the United States Supreme Court, however, no infringement occurred. The Court stated that under the "first-sale" doctrine, which is codified in the Copyright Act, the purchaser of copyrighted material is entitled, without the permission of the copyright owner, to sell or otherwise dispose of the purchased copyrighted materials, imported or not.[15]

Copyright Protection for Software In 1980, Congress passed the Computer Software Copyright Act, which amended the Copyright Act of 1976 to include computer programs in the list of creative works protected by federal copyright law. The 1980 statute, which classifies computer programs as "literary works," defines a computer program as a "set of statements or instructions to be used directly or indirectly in a computer in order to bring about a certain result."

Because of the unique nature of computer programs, the courts have had many problems in applying and interpreting the 1980 act. In a series of cases decided in the 1980s, the courts held that copyright protection extended not only to those parts of a computer program that can be read by humans, such as the "high-level" language of a source code, but also to the binary-language object code of a computer program,

13. *Feist Publications, Inc. v. Rural Telephone Service Co.,* 499 U.S. 340, 111 S.Ct. 1282, 113 L.Ed.2d 358 (1991).
14. *Bellsouth Advertising & Publishing Corp. v. Donnelley Information Publishing, Inc.,* 999 F.2d 1436 (11th Cir. 1993).
15. *Quality King Distributors, Inc. v. L'anza Research International, Inc.,* __U.S.__, 118 S.Ct. 1125, 140 L.Ed.2d 254 (1998).

which is readable only by the computer.[16] Additionally, such elements as the overall structure, sequence, and organization of a program were deemed copyrightable.[17]

By the early 1990s, the issue had evolved into whether the "look and feel"—the general appearance, command structure, video images, menus, windows, and other screen displays—of computer programs should also be protected by copyright. Although the courts have disagreed on this issue, the tendency has been not to extend copyright protection to look-and-feel aspects of computer programs. • **EXAMPLE 5.8** In 1995 the Court of Appeals for the First Circuit held that Lotus Development Corporation's menu command hierarchy for its Lotus 1-2-3 spreadsheet is not protectable under the Copyright Act. The court deemed that the menu command hierarchy is a "method of operation," and Section 102 of the Copyright Act specifically excludes methods of operation from copyright protection.[18] The decision was affirmed by the United States Supreme Court in 1996.[19] •

> **ON THE WEB**
> You can find a host of information on copyright law, including the Copyright Act and significant United States Supreme Court cases in the area of copyright law, at supct.law.cornell.edu/supct/cases/copyrt.htm.

Copyright Infringement Whenever the form or expression of an idea is copied, an infringement of copyright occurs. The reproduction does not have to be exactly the same as the original, nor does it have to reproduce the original in its entirety.

Penalties or remedies can be imposed on those who infringe copyrights. These range from actual damages (damages based on the actual harm caused to the copyright holder by the infringement) or statutory damages (damages provided for under the Copyright Act, not to exceed $100,000) to criminal proceedings for willful violations (which may result in fines and/or imprisonment).

An exception to liability for copyright infringement is made under the "fair use" doctrine. In certain circumstances, a person or organization can reproduce copyrighted material without paying royalties (fees paid to the copyright holder for the privilege of reproducing the copyrighted material). Section 107 of the Copyright Act provides as follows:

> [T]he fair use of a copyrighted work, including such use by reproduction in copies or phonorecords or by any other means specified by [Section 106 of the Copyright Act,] for purposes such as criticism, comment, news reporting, teaching (including multiple copies for classroom use), scholarship, or research, is not an infringement of copyright. In determining whether the use made of a work in any particular case is a fair use the factors to be considered shall include—
>
> (1) the purpose and character of the use, including whether such use is of a commercial nature or is for nonprofit educational purposes;
> (2) the nature of the copyrighted work;
> (3) the amount and substantiality of the portion used in relation to the copyrighted work as a whole; and
> (4) the effect of the use upon the potential market for or value of the copyrighted work.

Because these guidelines are very broad, the courts determine whether a particular use is fair on a case-by-case basis. Thus, anyone reproducing copyrighted material may be subject to a violation.

The following case indicates what must be proved to win a case involving charges of copyright infringement of a musical work.

---

16. See *Stern Electronics, Inc. v. Kaufman*, 669 F.2d 852 (2d Cir. 1982); and *Apple Computer, Inc. v. Franklin Computer Corp.*, 714 F.2d 1240 (3d Cir. 1983).
17. *Whelan Associates, Inc. v. Jaslow Dental Laboratory, Inc.*, 797 F.2d 1222 (3d Cir. 1986).
18. *Lotus Development Corp. v. Borland International, Inc.*, 49 F.3d 807 (1st Cir. 1995).
19. *Lotus Development Corp. v. Borland International, Inc.*, 517 U.S. 843, 116 S.Ct. 804, 113 L.Ed.2d 610 (1996). This issue may again come before the Supreme Court for a decision, because only eight justices heard the case, and there was a tied vote; the effect of the tie was to affirm the lower court's decision.

CASE 5.5 Repp v. Webber

United States Court of Appeals, Second Circuit, 1997.
132 F.3d 882.
www.tourolaw.edu/2ndCircuit/December97/[a]

HISTORICAL AND CULTURAL SETTING *Musical works fall within the category of works of authorship that can be protected by copyright. A protected musical work can consist of lyrics or music alone, or of both lyrics and music, as in a song. A musical work can exist in a number of different forms, including a tape, a compact disk, and sheet music. To determine whether a copyright of a musical work has been infringed, an expert might dissect the works into musical phrases and compare those phrases to other works by the same, or other, composers. Pitch and rhythm—the elements of a melody—might also be dissected and compared. Harmony—the chordal elements that support the melody—can also be an important element in comparing pop compositions.*

a. This is the "Decisions for December 1997" page within the collection of opinions of the U.S. Court of Appeals for the Second Circuit. Scroll down the list of cases to the entry for the *Repp* case. Click on the case name to read the court's opinion.

BACKGROUND AND FACTS Over a period of thirty years, Ray Repp wrote and published more than 120 musical compositions, including the song "Till You," which was registered with the U.S. Copyright Office in 1978. Repp included "Till You" on his album "Benedicamus" and in two books of sheet music, and performed the song in over two hundred concerts. Andrew Lloyd Webber, the composer of such musicals as *Cats* and *Evita,* wrote the musical *Phantom of the Opera* in 1983 and 1984. Claiming that "Phantom Song," one of the songs in *Phantom of the Opera,* infringed on the copyright of "Till You," Repp and others filed a suit in a federal district court against Lloyd Webber and others. Lloyd Webber responded that he never heard of Repp or "Till You" and that "Phantom Song" was an "independent creation." Musical experts offered conflicting testimony about the similarity of the songs' melodies, harmonics, and phrases. Despite this conflict, the court stated that "the two songs do not share a striking similarity" and issued a summary judgment for Lloyd Webber. The court added that Repp failed to show "Phantom Song" was not created independently. Repp appealed to the U.S. Court of Appeals for the Second Circuit.

IN THE WORDS OF THE COURT . . .
MINER, Circuit Judge:

* * * *

While there was little, if any, evidence demonstrating access, there was considerable evidence that "Phantom Song" is so strikingly similar to "Till You" as to preclude the possibility of independent creation and to allow access to be inferred without direct proof. * * * Two highly qualified experts * * * gave unequivocal opinions based on musicological analyses. * * *

* * * The issue of "striking similarity," by virtue of the supported opinions of the experts * * * was shown to be a genuine issue of material fact. Access to the music of Repp being an essential element of his case, it cannot be said that there is an absence of evidence to support proof of that element through the inference generated by the striking similarity of the two pieces.

* * * *

* * * The plaintiffs here have established a *prima facie* case of access through striking similarity * * * . Whether the evidence of independent creation here is sufficient to rebut the *prima facie* case established in this action is a question for the factfinder * * * .

DECISION AND REMEDY The U.S. Court of Appeals reversed the decision of the lower court and remanded the case. Because the issues of "striking similarity" and "independent creation" were disputed, there was a genuine dispute about the material facts and summary judgment was not appropriate.

(Continued)

CASE 5.5—Continued

FOR CRITICAL ANALYSIS—Cultural Consideration
Considering that there are a limited number of musical notes and a limited number of works into which those notes can be composed, should the fact that infringement might be "subconscious" affect liability in a copyright suit?

TRADE SECRETS

Some business processes and information that are not or cannot be patented, copyrighted, or trademarked are nevertheless protected against appropriation by a competitor as trade secrets. **Trade secrets** consist of customer lists, plans, research and development, pricing information, marketing techniques, production techniques, and generally anything that makes an individual company unique and that would have value to a competitor.

• **TRADE SECRETS**
Information or processes that give a business an advantage over competitors who do not know the information or processes.

Until recently, virtually all law with respect to trade secrets was common law. In an effort to reduce the unpredictability of the common law with respect to trade secrets, a model act, the Uniform Trade Secrets Act, was presented to the states in 1979 for adoption. Parts of it have been adopted in over twenty states. Typically, a state that has adopted parts of the act has adopted only those parts that encompass its own existing common law. In 1996, Congress passed the Economic Espionage Act, which made the theft of trade secrets a federal crime. We will examine the provisions and significance of this act in Chapter 6, in the context of crimes related to business.

Unlike copyright and trademark protection, protection of trade secrets extends both to ideas and to their expression. (For this reason, and because a trade secret involves no registration or filing requirements, trade secret protection may be well suited for software.) Of course, the secret formula, method, or other information must be disclosed to some persons, particularly to key employees. Businesses generally attempt to protect their trade secrets by having all employees who use the process or information agree in their contracts, or in confidentiality agreements, never to divulge it.

INTERNATIONAL PROTECTION

For many years, the United States has been a party to various international agreements relating to intellectual property rights. For example, the Paris Convention of 1883, to which about ninety countries are signatory, allows parties in one country to file for patent and trademark protection in any of the other member countries. Other international agreements include the Berne Convention and the TRIPS agreement.

The Berne Convention Under the Berne Convention of 1886, an international copyright agreement, if an American writes a book, his or her copyright in the book must be recognized by every country that has signed the convention. Also, if a citizen of a country that has not signed the convention first publishes a book in a country that has signed, all other countries that have signed the convention must recognize that author's copyright. Copyright notice is not needed to gain protection under the Berne Convention for works published after March 1, 1989.

ON THE WEB
The Web site of Cornell University's Legal Information Institute includes the texts of the Berne Convention and other international treaties on copyright issues at **www.law.cornell.edu/topics/copyright.html**.

These and other international agreements have given some protection to intellectual property on a worldwide level. None of them, however, has been as significant and far reaching in scope as the agreement on Trade-Related Aspects of Intellectual Property Rights, or, more simply, TRIPS.

The TRIPS Agreement The TRIPS agreement was signed by representatives from over one hundred nations in 1994. The agreement established, for the first time, standards for the international protection of intellectual property rights, including patents, trademarks, and copyrights for movies, computer programs, books, and music.

Prior to the agreement, one of the difficulties faced by U.S. sellers of intellectual property in the international market was either the lack of protection of intellectual property rights under other countries' laws or the lack of enforcement of those laws that do exist. To address this problem, the TRIPS agreement provides that each member country must include in its domestic laws broad intellectual property rights and effective remedies (including civil and criminal penalties) for violations of those rights.

Generally, the TRIPS agreement provides that each member nation must not discriminate (in terms of the administration, regulation, or adjudication of intellectual property rights) against foreign owners of such rights. In other words, a member nation cannot give its own nationals (citizens) favorable treatment without offering the same treatment to nationals of all member countries. For example, if a U.S. software manufacturer brings a suit for the infringement of intellectual property rights under a member nation's national laws, the U.S. manufacturer is entitled to receive the same treatment as a domestic manufacturer. Each member nation must also ensure that legal procedures are available for parties who wish to bring actions for infringement of intellectual property rights. Additionally, in a related document, a mechanism was established for settling disputes among member nations.

Particular provisions of the TRIPS agreement refer to patent, trademark, and copyright protection for intellectual property. The agreement specifically provides copyright protection for computer programs by stating that compilations of data, databases, or other materials are "intellectual creations" and that they are to be protected as copyrightable works. Other provisions relate to trade secrets and the rental of computer programs and cinematographic works.

International Perspective • THE PROBLEM OF SOFTWARE PIRACY

Highly skilled programmers must expend thousands of hours of labor to create a commercially successful software program. Each copy of the program may sell for hundreds of dollars. Consequently, there is a tremendous incentive for individuals and companies to purchase a single copy of the program and then make duplicates—to give or sell to others or to distribute to employees within the company. The popularity of such practices in companies throughout Europe and Asia has proved particularly costly for U.S. software manufacturers. Over 90 percent of the software in Pakistan, Russia, and China, for example, consists of pirated (illegal) copies. For Brazil, Malaysia, and Mexico, the figures are slightly lower, but they still exceed 80 percent. In the United States, an estimated 35 percent of the software in use has been pirated. The development of electronic networks makes it even easier to copy software illegally. Anyone with a computer and a modem can now transmit copies of computer programs to others over the Internet.

FOR CRITICAL ANALYSIS

Is there any practical way to prevent software piracy via the Internet?

RICO

Increasingly in recent years, businesses have been sued for fraudulent or other tortious activities under the Racketeer Influenced and Corrupt Organizations Act.[20] The act, which is commonly known as RICO, was passed by Congress in 1970 as part of the Organized Crime Control Act. The purpose of the act was to curb the apparently increasing entry of organized crime into the legitimate business world. Today, however, as will be discussed shortly, RICO is often applied to actions that have little to do with organized crime.

20. 18 U.S.C. Sections 1961–1968.

ACTIVITIES PROHIBITED BY RICO

¡BE AWARE!
RICO is often applied in cases that have little to do with what is traditionally thought of as organized crime.

Under RICO, it is a federal crime (1) to use income obtained from racketeering activity to purchase any interest in an enterprise, (2) to acquire or maintain an interest in an enterprise through racketeering activity, (3) to conduct or participate in the affairs of an enterprise through racketeering activity, or (4) to conspire to do any of the preceding activities.

Racketeering activity is not a new type of substantive crime created by RICO; rather, RICO incorporates by reference twenty-six separate types of federal crimes and nine types of state felonies[21] and states that if a person commits two of these offenses, he or she is guilty of "racketeering activity." The act provides for both criminal liability (to be discussed in the following chapter) and civil liability.

CIVIL LIABILITY UNDER RICO

The penalties for violations of the RICO statute are harsh. In the event of a violation, the statute permits the government to seek civil penalties, including the divestiture of a defendant's interest in a business (called forfeiture) or the dissolution of the business. Perhaps the most controversial aspect of RICO is that in many cases, private individuals are allowed to recover three times their actual losses (treble damages), plus attorneys' fees, for business injuries caused by a violation of the statute.

The broad language of RICO has allowed it to be applied in cases that have nothing to do with organized crime, and an aggressive prosecuting attorney may attempt to show that any business fraud constitutes "racketeering activity." In its 1985 decision in *Sedima, S.P.R.L. v. Imrex Co.*,[22] the United States Supreme Court interpreted RICO broadly and set a significant precedent for subsequent applications of the act. Plaintiffs have used the RICO statute in numerous commercial fraud cases because of the inviting prospect of being awarded treble damages if they win. (See this chapter's *Business Law in Action* for a discussion of the extent of civil liability under RICO.)

21. See 18 U.S.C. Section 1961(1)(A).
22. 473 U.S. 479, 105 S.Ct. 3275, 87 L.Ed.2d 346 (1985).

Business Law in Action • DAMAGES UNDER CIVIL RICO CAN BE STEEP

The loosely worded language of the Racketeer Influenced and Corrupt Organizations Act (RICO) of 1970 has allowed it to become a controversial litigation tool. Today, the act's scope and applicability seem to be limited only by the imaginations of trial attorneys. Plaintiffs bring lawsuits under civil RICO for garden-variety fraud. Tenants sue "racketeer" landlords. Indeed, recently even abortion protesters were held to have violated RICO. The most frequent targets of civil RICO lawsuits are insurance companies, employment agencies, commercial banks, and stockbrokerage firms.

One of the reasons for the extensive use of RICO is, of course, the lure of treble damages. Damages awarded to successful plaintiffs in RICO cases are trebled, and attorneys' fees (which can be costly) are also awarded. At least one court has held that in addition to treble damages and attorneys' fees, plaintiffs may also be awarded punitive damages under state law for the same conduct that violated RICO. That court was the Ninth Circuit Court of Appeals, which was reviewing a case that had been brought under RICO by victims of an alleged insurance scam against an insurance company.

The trial court found for the plaintiffs, and the jury awarded the plain-

Business Law in Action • *Continued*

tiffs $259,366 in actual damages (trebled to $778,098), $87,000 in damages for the plaintiffs' state law claims of fraud and negligent misrepresentation, and $500,000 in punitive damages, available under state law. After the trial, the court awarded the plaintiffs nearly $522,000 in attorneys' fees and other costs.

The insurance company appealed, contending, among other things, that treble damages are "punitive" in themselves and that other federal appellate courts have held, in cases brought under antitrust laws (see Chapter 32), that a plaintiff cannot receive both treble antitrust damages and state law punitive damages from the same course of conduct. The court, however, refused to extend the logic of the antitrust cases to RICO damages awards. To do so, stated the court, would be to "ignore the text of RICO itself, which states: 'Nothing in this title shall supersede any provision of Federal, State, or other law imposing criminal penalties or affording civil remedies in addition to those provided for in this title.'"[a]

FOR CRITICAL ANALYSIS

The United States Supreme Court has consistently struck down the efforts of some lower courts to narrow the scope of RICO. In light of the Supreme Court's decisions, is there any way RICO's scope can be narrowed? If so, how?

a. *Neibel v. Trans World Assurance Co.*, 108 F.3d 1123 (9th Cir. 1997).

APPLICATION Law and the Businessperson: Creating & Protecting Your Trademark*

Imagine the following scenario: You have decided to turn your hobby of recording alternative music into a bona fide business. You pick a name for your company—Cruising—and incorporate the company in your state. The secretary of state approves the name because no one else in your state has incorporated under that name or one that could be confused with it. You open for business, and the name Cruising appears in your ads and brochures and in the Yellow Pages. You put out your first CD using the Cruising label. Then you receive a letter in the mail from Tom Cruise's attorneys informing you that Cruising is a federally registered trademark used for all of Tom Cruise's enterprises, and in fact he may someday have a CD label. If you attempt to fight Tom Cruise's attorneys, you will probably lose.

*This *Application* is not meant to substitute for the services of an attorney who is licensed to practice law in your state.

A Trademark Is Not the Same as a Trade Name

When you incorporated in your state, the secretary of state only approved your company's name, Cruising, as a trade name—the formal name for your business that you can use on checks, invoices, and letterhead stationery. You have permission to use Cruising as a trade name only in your state. A trademark (or a service mark) is the word, phrase, slogan, design, or symbol that identifies a specific product brand that you use to market products. If you decide to use your business (trade) name as a trademark, then you need to follow the principles of trademark law. The general rule is that you cannot use a trademark that might lead a customer to think that your product was produced by someone else.

Who Owns a Trademark?

Generally, the first business to use a trademark owns it. The way to qualify as a first user is to be the first company to actually use the trademark in the marketplace or to register the trademark with the U.S. Patent and Trademark Office. First use sometimes takes precedence over federal registration. If Tom Cruise had not registered Cruising as a trademark until two years after you started selling Cruising-labeled CDs throughout the United States, you would probably win your trademark dispute.

Doing a Trademark Search

After you have decided on a trademark, you need to do a search to find out if the trademark is confusingly similar to existing trademarks. You can look at the federal trademark

APPLICATION CONTINUED

register (you can search the federal database of registered trademarks by going to www.uspto.gov/tmdb/index.html), as well as the trademark register in your state (which you may be able to access online). You can examine the Yellow Pages in your area of business (you can search the Yellow Pages online at various sites, including yp.ameritech.net). Finally, you can hire a trademark search firm to do the search for you. You can find information on what a trademark search might cost by going online to Thomson & Thomson at www.thomson-thomson.com or to Curt Harrington's law offices at warrior.com/tmsearch.

Once you have done an appropriate trademark search and you have not found another trademark that would be confusingly similar to yours, you are probably entitled to register the mark with the U.S. Patent and Trademark Office. Normally, you have to start using the trademark within six months within your state or across state, international, or territorial lines.

CHECKLIST FOR THE BUSINESSPERSON

1. Remember that a trade name authorized for use by a secretary of state is not the same as a trademark.
2. When deciding on a trademark, be sure that it is not confusingly similar to an existing trademark.
3. There are two ways to own a trademark—being the first to use a trademark or registering the trademark with the U.S. Patent and Trademark Office.
4. Remember that in trademark disputes, first use of a trademark sometimes takes precedence over federal registration.

Key Terms

appropriation 126
business tort 124
copyright 136
disparagement of property 128
intellectual property 124
patent 135
predatory behavior 126
service mark 135
slander of quality (trade libel) 128
slander of title 129
trade dress 135
trade name 135
trade secret 140
trademark 130

Chapter Summary • Business Torts and Intellectual Property

Wrongful Interference (See pages 124–126.)	1. *Wrongful interference with a contractual relationship*—A third party's intentional interference with a valid, enforceable contract that causes one of the contracting parties to breach the contract. 2. *Wrongful interference with a business relationship*—The unreasonable interference by one party with another's established business relationship.
Appropriation (See pages 126–128.)	The use by one person of another's name, likeness, or other identifying characteristic, without permission and for the benefit of the user.
Defamation in the Business Context (See page 128.)	A false statement that injures someone in a profession, business, or trade or that adversely affects a business entity in its credit rating and other dealings.
Disparagement of Property (See pages 128–129.)	Slanderous or libelous statements made about another's product or property; more specifically referred to as slander of quality (trade libel) or slander of title.
Intellectual Property Protection (See pages 129–141.)	1. *Trademark infringement and infringement of related property*—Occurs when one uses the protected trademark, service mark, trade name, or trade dress of another without permission when marketing goods or services.

Chapter Summary, Continued

Intellectual Property Protection —continued	2. *Patent infringement*—Occurs when one uses or sells another's patented design, product, or process without the patent owner's permission. Computer software may be patented. 3. *Copyright infringement*—Occurs whenever the form or expression of an idea is copied without the permission of the copyright holder. An exception applies if the copying is deemed a "fair use." The Computer Software Copyright Act of 1980 specifically includes software among the kinds of intellectual property covered by copyright law. 4. *Trade secrets*—Customer lists, plans, research and development, pricing information, and so on are protected under the common law and, in some states, under statutory law against misappropriation by competitors. 5. *International protection*—International protection for intellectual property exists under various international agreements. A landmark agreement is the 1994 agreement on Trade-Related Aspects of Intellectual Property Rights (TRIPS), which provides for enforcement procedures in all countries signatory to the agreement.
RICO (See pages 141–143.)	The Racketeer Influenced and Corrupt Organizations Act (RICO) of 1970 makes it a federal crime (1) to use income obtained from racketeering activity to purchase any interest in an enterprise, (2) to acquire or maintain an interest in an enterprise through racketeering activity, (3) to conduct or participate in the affairs of an enterprise through racketeering activity, or (4) to conspire to do any of the preceding activities. The broad language of RICO has allowed it to be applied in cases that have little or nothing to do with organized crime.

For Review

1. What elements are necessary to establish the existence of wrongful interference with a contractual or business relationship?
2. How might the tort of defamation occur in the business context?
3. What is intellectual property? How does the law protect intellectual property?
4. What is a trade secret? How are trade secrets protected by law?
5. What is RICO? What activities are prohibited by this act?

Questions and Case Problems

5–1. Copyright Infringement. In which of the following situations would a court likely hold Maruta liable for copyright infringement?

(a) At the library, Maruta photocopies ten pages from a scholarly journal relating to a topic on which she is writing a term paper.

(b) Maruta makes leather handbags and sells them in her small leather shop. She advertises her handbags as "Vutton handbags," hoping that customers might mistakenly assume that they were made by Vuitton, the well-known maker of high-quality luggage and handbags.

(c) Maruta owns a video store. She purchases the latest videos from various video manufacturers but buys only one copy of each video. Then, using blank videotapes, she makes copies to rent or sell to her customers.

(d) Maruta teaches Latin American history at a small university. She has a videocassette recorder (VCR) and frequently tapes television programs relating to Latin America. She then takes the videos to her classroom so that her students can watch them.

5–2. Wrongful Interference. Jennings owns a bakery shop. He has been trying to obtain a long-term contract with the owner of

Julie's Tea Salon for some time. Jennings starts a local advertising campaign on radio and television and in the newspaper. The campaign is so persuasive that Julie decides to break the contract she has had for some time with Orley's Bakery so that she can patronize Jennings's bakery. Is Jennings liable to Orley's Bakery for the tort of wrongful interference with a contractual relationship? Is Julie liable for this tort? For anything?

5–3. Patent Infringement. John and Andrew Doney invented a hard-bearing device for balancing rotors. Although they registered their invention with the U.S. Patent and Trademark Office, it was never used as an automobile wheel balancer. Some time later, Exetron Corp. produced an automobile wheel balancer that used a hard-bearing device with a support plate similar to that of the Doneys. Given the fact that the Doneys had not used their device for automobile wheel balancing, does Exetron's use of a similar hard-bearing device infringe on the Doneys' patent?

5–4. Copyright Infringement. Max plots a new Batman adventure and carefully and skillfully imitates the art of DC Comics to create an authentic-looking Batman comic. Max is not affiliated with the owners of the copyright to Batman. Can Max publish the comic without infringing on the owners' copyright?

5–5. Business Tort Theories. After a careful study and analysis, Green Top Airlines decides to expand its operations into Harbor City. Green Top acquires the necessary regulatory authorizations and licenses, negotiates a lease at the airport terminal, and makes substantial capital expenditures renovating airport gates. Immediately thereafter, Red Stripe Airlines, Green Top's major competitor, also undertakes operations in Harbor City, even though (1) Harbor City is nowhere near any of Red Stripe's major existing routes and (2) Red Stripe will lose money by servicing Harbor City. Green Top claims that Red Stripe's entry into Harbor City constitutes a tort. Discuss fully Green Top's claim.

5–6. Wrongful Interference. Bombardier Capital, Inc., provides financing to boat and recreational vehicle dealers. Bombardier's credit policy requires dealers to forward immediately to Bombardier the proceeds of boat sales. When Howard Mulcahey, Bombardier's vice president of sales and marketing, learned that a dealer was not complying with this policy, he told Frank Chandler, Bombardier's credit director, of his concern. Before Chandler could obtain the proceeds, Mulcahey falsely told Jacques Gingras, Bombardier's president, that Chandler was, among other things, trying to hide the problem. On the basis of Mulcahey's statements, Gingras fired Chandler and put Mulcahey in charge of the credit department. Under what business tort theory discussed in this chapter might Chandler recover damages from Mulcahey? Explain. [*Chandler v. Bombardier Capital, Inc.*, 44 F.3d 80 (2d Cir. 1994)]

5–7. RICO. During the 1980s, the Mutual Trading Corp. (MTC) bought and sold tires made by the Uniroyal Goodrich Tire Co. In the 1990s, Uniroyal discovered that MTC had perpetrated at least four separate schemes to swindle money from Uniroyal. As part of one scheme, for example, MTC had submitted fraudulent claims for reimbursement for amounts it had refunded to customers in Saudi Arabia. As part of another scheme, MTC had obtained from Uniroyal twice as much for its advertising costs in Nigeria as the parties had previously agreed. Uniroyal filed a suit against MTC and others in a federal district court, alleging, among other things, that these schemes violated RICO. MTC responded in part that the allegations depicted only a single scheme perpetrated on a single victim and that thus there was no "pattern of racketeering activity." What constitutes a "pattern" of activity to satisfy RICO? Is RICO satisfied in this case? [*Uniroyal Goodrich Tire Co. v. Mutual Trading Corp.*, 63 F.3d 516 (7th Cir. 1995)]

5–8. Copyright Infringement. James Smith, the owner of Michigan Document Services, Inc. (MDS), a commercial copyshop, concluded that it was unnecessary to obtain the copyright owners' permission to reproduce copyrighted materials in course packs. Smith publicized his conclusion, claiming that professors would not have to worry about any delay in production at his shop. MDS then compiled, bound, and sold course packs to students at the University of Michigan without obtaining the permission of copyright owners. Princeton University Press and two other publishers filed a suit in a federal district court against MDS, alleging copyright infringement. MDS claimed that its course packs were covered under the fair use doctrine. Were they? Explain. [*Princeton University Press v. Michigan Document Services, Inc.*, 99 F.3d 1381 (6th Cir. 1996)]

5–9. Trademarks. Sara Lee Corp. manufactures pantyhose under the L'eggs trademark. Originally, L'eggs were sold in egg-shaped packaging, a design that Sara Lee continues to use with its product. Sara Lee's only nationwide competitor in the same pantyhose markets is Kayser-Roth Corp. When Kayser-Roth learned of Sara Lee's plan to introduce L'eggs Everyday, a new line of hosiery, Kayser-Roth responded by simultaneously introducing a new product, Leg Looks. Sara Lee filed a complaint in a federal district court against Kayser-Roth, asserting that the name Leg Looks infringed on the L'eggs mark. Does Kayser-Roth's Leg Looks infringe on Sara Lee's L'eggs? Why or why not? [*Sara Lee Corp. v. Kayser-Roth Corp.*, 81 F.3d 455 (4th Cir. 1996)]

5–10. Trademark Infringement. Elvis Presley Enterprises, Inc. (EPE), owns all of the trademarks of the Elvis Presley estate. None of these marks is registered for use in the restaurant business. Barry Capece registered "The Velvet Elvis" as a service mark for a restaurant and tavern with the U.S. Patent and Trademark Office. Capece opened a nightclub called "The Velvet Elvis" with a menu, décor, advertising, and promotional events that evoked Elvis Presley and his music. EPE filed a suit in a federal district court against Capece and others, claiming, among other things, that "The Velvet Elvis" service mark infringed on EPE's trademarks. During the trial, witnesses testified that they thought the bar was associated with Elvis Presley. Should Capece be ordered to stop using "The Velvet Elvis" mark? Why or why not? [*Elvis Presley Enterprises, Inc. v. Capece*, 141 F.3d 188 (5th Cir. 1998)]

A QUESTION OF ETHICS AND SOCIAL RESPONSIBILITY

5–11. Texaco, Inc., conducts research to develop new products and technology in the petroleum industry. As part of the research, Texaco employees routinely photocopy articles from scientific and medical journals without the permission of the copyright holders. The publishers of the journals brought a copyright infringement action against Texaco in a federal district court. The court ruled that the copying was not a fair use. The U.S. Court of Appeals for the Second Circuit affirmed this ruling "primarily because the dominant purpose of the use is 'archival'—to assemble a set of papers for future reference, thereby serving the same purpose for which additional subscriptions are normally sold, or . . . for which photocopying licenses may be obtained." [*American Geophysical Union v. Texaco, Inc.*, 37 F.3d 881(2d Cir. 1994)]

1. Do you agree with the court's decision that the copying was not a fair use? Why or why not?
2. Do you think that the law should impose a duty on every person to obtain permission to photocopy or reproduce any article under any circumstance? What would be some of the implications of such a duty for society? Discuss fully.

FOR CRITICAL ANALYSIS

5–12. Patent protection in the United States is granted to the first person to invent a given product or process, even though another person might be the first to file for a patent on the same product or process. What are the advantages of this patenting procedure? Can you think of any disadvantages? Explain.

Online Activities

ONLINE EXERCISE 5-1

Go to "The Trade Secrets Home Page (TM)," a Web site maintained by attorney R. Mark Halligan, at

www.execpc.com/~mhallign.

Select the category "Summary/Intellectual Property Cases/Internet." Scan through the cases described on this page, and then select three cases for closer scrutiny. Answer the following questions about each of the cases that you selected:

- What type of intellectual property was involved in the case (patents, trademarks, trade names, copyrights, trade secrets, and so on)?
- Who were the plaintiff(s) and defendant(s) in the suit, and why was the suit initiated?
- What allegations were made by the plaintiff(s)? What arguments were raised by the defendants?
- When was the case decided, and what court rendered the decision?
- What did the court decide, and why?

Before the Test

Go to the *Business Law Today* home page at http://blt.westbuslaw.com. Click on TestTutor.® You will find twenty interactive questions relating to this chapter.

CHAPTER 6

Criminal Law

"No State shall . . . deprive any person of life, liberty, or property without due process of law, nor deny to any person within its jurisdiction the equal protection of the laws."

Fourteenth Amendment to the U.S. Constitution, July 28, 1868

CONTENTS

LEARNING OBJECTIVES

After reading this chapter, you should be able to:

1. Explain the difference between criminal offenses and other types of wrongful conduct.
2. Indicate the essential elements of criminal liability.
3. Describe the constitutional safeguards that protect the rights of persons accused of crimes.
4. Identify and define the crimes that affect business.
5. Summarize the defenses to criminal liability.

Various sanctions are used to bring about a society in which individuals engaging in business can compete and flourish. These sanctions include damages for various types of tortious conduct (as discussed in the preceding chapters), damages for breach of contract (to be discussed in Chapter 14), and the equitable remedies discussed in Chapter 1. Additional sanctions are imposed under criminal law. Many statutes regulating business provide for criminal as well as civil sanctions. Therefore, criminal law joins civil law as an important element in the legal environment of business.

In this chapter, following a brief summary of the major differences between criminal and civil law, we look at how crimes are classified and what elements must be present for criminal liability to exist. We then focus on crimes affecting business and the defenses that can be raised to avoid liability for criminal actions. In the remainder of the chapter, we examine criminal procedural law, which attempts to ensure that a criminal defendant's right to "due process of law" (see the above quotation) is enforced.

Civil Law and Criminal Law

Remember from Chapter 1 that *civil law* spells out the duties that exist between persons or between citizens and their governments, excluding the duty not to commit crimes. Contract law, for example, is part of civil law. The whole body of tort law, which deals with the infringement by one person on the legally recognized rights of another, is also an area of civil law.

• **CRIME**
A wrong against society proclaimed in a statute and, if committed, punishable by society through fines, removal from public office, and/or imprisonment—and, in some cases, death.

Criminal law, in contrast, has to do with crime. A **crime** can be defined as a wrong against society proclaimed in a statute and, if committed, punishable by society through fines and/or imprisonment—and, in some cases, death. As mentioned in Chapter 1, because crimes are *offenses against society as a whole,* they are prosecuted by a public official, such as a district attorney (D.A.), not by victims.

Key Differences between Civil Law and Criminal Law

Because the state has extensive resources at its disposal when prosecuting criminal cases, there are numerous procedural safeguards to protect the rights of defendants. One of these safeguards is the higher standard of proof that applies in a criminal case. As you can see in Exhibit 6–1, which summarizes some of the key differences between civil law and criminal law, in a civil case the plaintiff usually must prove his or her case by a *preponderance of the evidence.* Under this standard, the plaintiff must convince the court that, based on the evidence presented by both parties, it is more likely than not that the plaintiff's allegation is true.

• **BEYOND A REASONABLE DOUBT**
The standard of proof used in criminal cases. If there is any reasonable doubt that a criminal defendant did not commit the crime with which he or she has been charged, then the verdict must be "not guilty."

In a criminal case, in contrast, the state must prove its case **beyond a reasonable doubt.** Every juror in a criminal case must be convinced, beyond a reasonable doubt, of the defendant's guilt. The higher standard of proof in criminal cases reflects a fundamental social value—a belief that it is worse to convict an innocent individual than to let a guilty person go free. We will look at other safeguards later in the chapter, in the context of criminal procedure.

Civil Liability for Criminal Acts

Those who commit crimes may be subject to both civil and criminal liability. • **Example 6.1** Joe is walking down the street, minding his own business, when

EXHIBIT 6–1 • Civil and Criminal Law Compared

ISSUE	CIVIL LAW	CRIMINAL LAW
Area of concern	Rights and duties between individuals	Offenses against society as a whole
Wrongful act	Harm to a person	Violation of a statute that prohibits some type of activity
Party who brings suit	Person who suffered harm	The state
Standard of proof	Preponderance of the evidence	Beyond a reasonable doubt
Remedy	Damages to compensate for the harm, or a decree to achieve an equitable result	Punishment (fine, removal from public office, imprisonment, or death)

suddenly a person attacks him. In the ensuing struggle, the attacker stabs Joe several times, seriously injuring him. A police officer restrains and arrests the wrongdoer. In this situation, the attacker may be subject both to criminal prosecution by the state and to a tort lawsuit brought by Joe.• Exhibit 6–2 illustrates how the same wrongful act can result in both a civil (tort) action and a criminal action against the wrongdoer.

Classification of Crimes

• **FELONY**
A crime—such as arson, murder, rape, or robbery—that carries the most severe sanctions, which range from one year in a state or federal prison to the death penalty.

Depending on their degree of seriousness, crimes are classified as felonies or misdemeanors. **Felonies** are serious crimes punishable by death or by imprisonment in a federal or state penitentiary for more than a year. The Model Penal Code[1] provides for four degrees of felony: (1) capital offenses, for which the maximum penalty is death; (2) first degree felonies, punishable by a maximum penalty of life imprisonment; (3) second degree felonies, punishable by a maximum of ten years' imprisonment; and (4) third degree felonies, punishable by a maximum of five years' imprisonment.

1. The American Law Institute issued the Official Draft of the Model Penal Code in 1962. The Model Penal Code is not a uniform code. Uniformity of criminal law among the states is not as important as uniformity in other areas of the law. Types of crimes vary with local circumstances, and it is appropriate that punishments vary accordingly. The Model Penal Code contains four parts: (1) general provisions, (2) definitions of special crimes, (3) provisions concerning treatment and corrections, and (4) provisions on the organization of correction.

EXHIBIT 6–2 • Tort Lawsuit and Criminal Prosecution for the Same Act

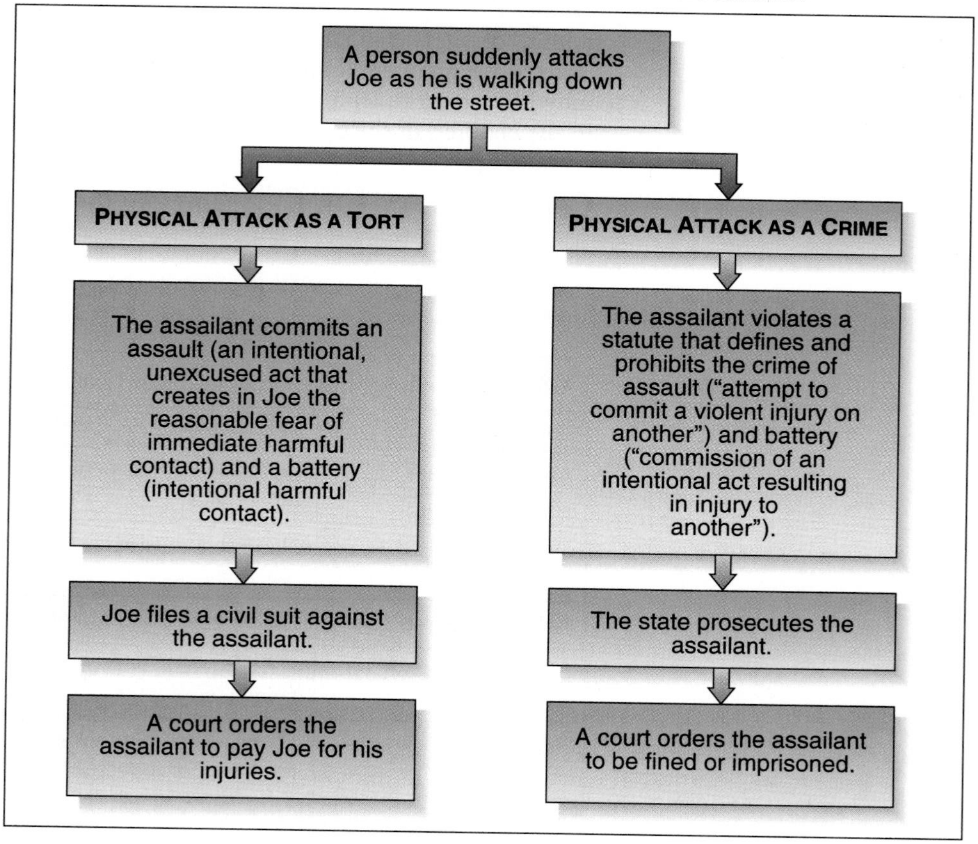

• MISDEMEANOR
A lesser crime than a felony, punishable by a fine or incarceration in a jail for up to one year.

Under federal law and in most states, any crime that is not a felony is considered a **misdemeanor.** Misdemeanors are crimes punishable by a fine or by confinement for up to a year. If incarcerated (imprisoned), the guilty party goes to a local jail instead of a prison. Disorderly conduct and trespass are common misdemeanors. Some states have different classes of misdemeanors. For example, in Illinois misdemeanors are either Class A (confinement for up to a year), Class B (not more than six months), or Class C (not more than thirty days). Whether a crime is a felony or a misdemeanor can also determine whether the case is tried in a magistrate's court (for example, by a justice of the peace) or in a general trial court.

• PETTY OFFENSE
In criminal law, the least serious kind of criminal offense, such as a traffic or building-code violation.

In most jurisdictions, **petty offenses** are considered to be a subset of misdemeanors. Petty offenses are minor violations, such as driving under the influence of alcohol or violations of building codes. Even for petty offenses, however, a guilty party can be put in jail for a few days, fined, or both, depending on state or local law.

Criminal Liability

Two elements must exist simultaneously for a person to be convicted of a crime: (1) the performance of a prohibited act and (2) a specified state of mind or intent on the part of the actor. Every criminal statute prohibits certain behavior. Most crimes require an act of *commission;* that is, a person must *do* something in order to be accused of a crime.[2] In some cases, an act of *omission* can be a crime, but only when a person has a legal duty to perform the omitted act. Failure to file a tax return is an example of an omission that is a crime.

The *guilty act* requirement is based on one of the premises of criminal law—that a person is punished for harm done to society. Thinking about killing someone or about stealing a car may be wrong, but the thoughts do no harm until they are translated into action. Of course, a person can be punished for attempting murder or robbery, but normally only if he or she took substantial steps toward the criminal objective.

A *wrongful mental state*[3] is as necessary as a wrongful act in establishing criminal liability. What constitutes such a mental state varies according to the wrongful action. For murder, the act is the taking of a life, and the mental state is the intent to take life. For theft, the guilty act is the taking of another person's property, and the mental state involves both the knowledge that the property belongs to another and the intent to deprive the owner of it.

Criminal liability typically arises for actions that violate state criminal statutes. Federal criminal jurisdiction is limited to crimes that occur outside the jurisdiction of any state, crimes involving interstate commerce or communications, crimes that interfere with the operation of the federal government or its agents, and crimes directed at citizens or property located outside the United States. Federal jurisdiction also exists if a federal law or a federal government agency (such as the U.S. Department of Justice or the federal Environmental Protection Agency) defines a certain type of action as a crime. Today, businesspersons are subject to criminal penalties under numerous federal laws and regulations. We will examine many of these laws in later chapters of this text.

ON THE WEB
Many state criminal codes are now online. To find your state's code, go to
www.findlaw.com
and select "State" under the link to "Laws: Cases and Codes."

Regardless of the type of criminal activity involved, generally the rule is that without the intent required by law for a particular crime, there is no crime. At issue in the following case is whether the required intent for a crime was present.

2. Called the *actus reus* (pronounced *ak*-tuhs *ray*-uhs), or "guilty act."
3. Called the *mens rea* (pronounced mehns *ray*-uh), or "evil intent."

CASE 6.1 In re Gavin T.

California Court of Appeal,
First District, Division 5, 1998.
66 Cal.App.4th 238,
77 Cal.Rptr.2d 701.

HISTORICAL AND SOCIAL SETTING *Many observers believe that public education deteriorated between the 1950s and the 1990s. Some commentators blame this deterioration on changing achievement standards. Others fault a societal mistrust of institutional authority in general. Suggestions for improving education and the educational environment also range across a wide spectrum. Despite these differences, however, a safe environment is generally considered a necessity for a quality education. A safe environment might be defined as one in which there is little crime or unruly behavior. Discipline is seen as a key to creating a safe environment.*

BACKGROUND AND FACTS On the grounds of a school, Gavin T., a fifteen-year-old student, was eating lunch. He threw a half-eaten apple toward the outside wall of a classroom some distance away. The apple sailed through a slowly closing door and struck a teacher who was in the room. The teacher was knocked to the floor and lost consciousness for a few minutes. Gavin was charged, in a California state court, with assault by "any means of force likely to produce great bodily injury." The court found that he did not intend to hit the teacher but only intended to see the apple splatter against the outside wall. To send a "message" to his classmates that his actions were wrong, however, the court convicted him of the charge. Gavin appealed.

IN THE WORDS OF THE COURT . . .
PETERSON, Presiding Justice.

* * * *

* * * [I]t is black letter law that one cannot unintentionally commit the crime of assault. In order to be found guilty of a criminal assault, one must have either the intent to batter, hit, strike, or wrongfully touch a victim; or one must have a general criminal intent to do an act which is inherently dangerous to human life—such as firing a cannon at an inhabited castle, or driving an elephant into a crowded judicial conference.

* * * *

Here, there was * * * no evidence that appellant intended to strike the teacher with a discarded apple core; and all the evidence and circumstances showed the contrary. In the absence of any sufficient evidence of an intent to touch or strike the victim, the [lower] court rightly found appellant had no such intent, and that he merely intended to watch the discarded apple splatter against the wall. Such an urge may have been juvenile and, therefore, rather appropriate to appellant's age; but it did not constitute a criminal intent to batter the victim or a general criminal intent to act in a manner inherently dangerous to human life.

DECISION AND REMEDY The state intermediate appellate court vacated the order of the lower court and remanded the case with instructions to dismiss it. The appellate court held that a defendant cannot be convicted of assault without having had the intent to commit the crime.

FOR CRITICAL ANALYSIS—Ethical Consideration
If the lower court's "message" to Gavin and his classmates was that reckless behavior would not be condoned, what was the appellate court's message to the lower court?

Corporate Criminal Liability

At one time, it was thought that a corporation could not incur criminal liability because, although a corporation is a legal person, it can act only through its agents (corporate directors, officers, and employees). Therefore, the corporate entity itself could not "intend" to commit a crime. Under modern criminal law, however, a corporation may be held liable for crimes. Obviously, corporations cannot be imprisoned, but they can be fined or denied certain legal privileges (such as a license). Today, corporations are normally liable for the crimes committed by their agents and employees within the course and scope of their employment.

Corporate directors and officers are personally liable for the crimes they commit, regardless of whether the crimes were committed for their personal benefit or on the corporation's behalf. Additionally, corporate directors and officers may be held liable for the actions of employees under their supervision. Under what has become known as the "responsible corporate officer" doctrine, a court may impose criminal liability on a corporate officer regardless of whether he or she participated in, directed, or even knew about a given criminal violation.

• **EXAMPLE 6.2** In *United States v. Park,*[4] the chief executive officer of a national supermarket chain was held personally liable for sanitation violations in corporate warehouses, in which the food was exposed to contamination by rodents. The court imposed personal liability on the corporate officer not because he intended the crime or even knew about it. Rather, liability was imposed because the officer was in a "responsible relationship" to the corporation and had the power to prevent the violation. • Since the *Park* decision, courts have applied this "responsible corporate officer" doctrine on a number of occasions to hold corporate officers liable for their employees' statutory violations.

Crimes Affecting Business

A number of crimes that affect business may or may not be committed by businesspersons. Typically, they are crimes against business property. Such crimes include robbery, burglary, larceny, obtaining goods by false pretenses, receiving stolen goods, arson, and forgery—all of which we examine here. Other crimes affecting business fall into the category of "white-collar" crimes—crimes that are normally committed only by businesspersons within the business context. We will discuss these types of crimes in the next section.

ROBBERY

• **ROBBERY**
The act of forcefully and unlawfully taking personal property of any value from another; force or intimidation is usually necessary for an act of theft to be considered a robbery.

At common law, **robbery** was defined as forcefully and unlawfully taking personal property of any value from another. The use of force or intimidation is usually necessary for an act of theft to be considered a robbery. Thus, picking pockets is not robbery, because the action is unknown to the victim. Typically, states have more severe penalties for *aggravated* robbery—robbery with the use of a deadly weapon.

BURGLARY

• **BURGLARY**
The unlawful entry or breaking into a building with the intent to commit a felony. (Some state statutes expand this to include the intent to commit any crime.)

At common law, **burglary** was defined as breaking and entering the dwelling of another at night with the intent to commit a felony. Originally, the definition was aimed at protecting an individual's home and its occupants. Most state statutes have eliminated some of the requirements found in the common law definition. The time at which the breaking and entering occurs, for example, is usually immaterial. State statutes frequently omit the element of breaking, and some states do not require that the building be a dwelling. Aggravated burglary, which is defined as burglary with the use of a deadly weapon, burglary of a dwelling, or both, incurs a greater penalty.

4. 421 U.S. 658, 95 S.Ct. 1903, 44 L.Ed.2d 489 (1975).

Larceny

• **LARCENY**
The wrongful taking and carrying away of another person's personal property with the intent to permanently deprive the owner of the property. Some states classify larceny as either grand or petit, depending on the property's value.

Any person who wrongfully or fraudulently takes and carries away another person's personal property is guilty of **larceny.** Larceny includes the fraudulent intent to deprive an owner permanently of property. Many business-related larcenies entail fraudulent conduct. Whereas robbery involves force or fear, larceny does not. Therefore, picking pockets is larceny. Similarly, taking company products and supplies home for personal use, if one is not authorized to do so, is larceny.

As society becomes more complex, the question often arises as to what is property. In most states, the definition of property that is subject to larceny statutes has expanded. Stealing computer programs may constitute larceny even though the "property" consists of magnetic impulses. Stealing computer time can also constitute larceny. So, too, can the theft of natural gas. Trade secrets can be subject to larceny statutes. Intercepting cellular phone calls to obtain another's phone card number—and then using that number to place long-distance calls, often overseas—is a form of property theft. These types of larceny are covered by "theft of services" statutes in many jurisdictions.

The common law distinguishes between grand and petit larceny depending on the value of the property taken. Many states have abolished this distinction, but in those that have not, grand larceny is a felony and petit larceny, a misdemeanor.

Obtaining Goods by False Pretenses

It is a criminal act to obtain goods by means of false pretenses—for example, buying groceries with a check, knowing that one has insufficient funds to cover it. Statutes dealing with such illegal activities vary widely from state to state.

Receiving Stolen Goods

It is a crime to receive stolen goods. The recipient of such goods need not know the true identity of the owner or the thief. All that is necessary is that the recipient knows or should have known that the goods are stolen, which implies an intent to deprive the owner of those goods.

Arson

• **ARSON**
The intentional burning of another's dwelling. Some statutes have expanded this to include any real property regardless of ownership and the destruction of property by other means—for example, by explosion.

"A large number of houses deserve to be burnt."
H.G. Wells, 1866–1946
(English author)

The willful and malicious burning of a building (and in some states, personal property) owned by another is the crime of **arson.** At common law, arson applied only to burning down another person's house. The law was designed to protect human life. Today, arson statutes have been extended to cover the destruction of any building, regardless of ownership, by fire or explosion.

Every state has a special statute that covers a person's burning a building for the purpose of collecting insurance. If Smith owns an insured apartment building that is falling apart and sets fire to it himself or pays someone else to do so, he is guilty not only of arson but also of defrauding insurers, which is an attempted larceny. Of course, the insurer need not pay the claim when insurance fraud is proved.

Forgery

• **FORGERY**
The fraudulent making or altering of any writing in a way that changes the legal rights and liabilities of another.

The fraudulent making or altering of any writing in a way that changes the legal rights and liabilities of another is **forgery.** If, without authorization, Severson signs Bennett's name to the back of a check made out to Bennett, Severson is committing forgery. Forgery also includes changing trademarks, falsifying public records, counterfeiting, and altering a legal document.

White-Collar Crimes

• **WHITE-COLLAR CRIME**
Nonviolent crime committed by individuals or corporations to obtain a personal or business advantage.

Many of the crimes discussed in the following pages are commonly referred to as **white-collar crimes.** Although there is no official definition of white-collar crime, the term is popularly used to mean an illegal act or series of acts committed by an individual or business entity using some nonviolent means. Usually, this kind of crime is committed in the course of a legitimate occupation. Corporate crimes fall into this category.

EMBEZZLEMENT

• **EMBEZZLEMENT**
The fraudulent appropriation of funds or other property by a person to whom the funds or property has been entrusted.

When a person entrusted with another person's property or money fraudulently appropriates it, **embezzlement** occurs. Typically, embezzlement involves an employee who steals funds. Banks face this problem, and so do a number of businesses in which corporate officers or accountants "jimmy" the books to cover up the fraudulent conversion of funds for their own benefit. Embezzlement is not larceny, because the wrongdoer does not physically take the property from the possession of another, and it is not robbery, because force or fear is not used.

It does not matter whether the accused takes the funds from the victim or from a third person. If, as the financial officer of a large corporation, Saunders pockets a certain number of checks from third parties that were given to her to deposit into the corporate account, she is embezzling.

Ordinarily, an embezzler who returns what has been taken will not be prosecuted, because the owner usually will not take the time to make a complaint, give depositions, and appear in court. That the accused intended eventually to return the embezzled property, however, does not constitute a sufficient defense to the crime of embezzlement. The role of intention in establishing whether embezzlement has occurred is emphasized in the following case.

CASE 6.2 United States v. Faulkner

United States Court of Appeals,
Ninth Circuit, 1981.
638 F.2d 129.

HISTORICAL AND SOCIAL SETTING *At one time, the law generally divided theft into three separate crimes—larceny, false pretenses, and embezzlement. Statutes prohibiting embezzlement often listed the kinds of persons who might have lawful possession of another's property (store clerks, bank employees, merchants, and so on) and provided that any such person who fraudulently converted the property to his or her own use was guilty of embezzlement. Today, in those jurisdictions that have enacted new criminal codes, the three separate crimes have been replaced with a single crime. With regard to the once-separate crime of embezzlement, these statutes may simply provide that one who is in lawful possession of another's property and intends to convert it to his or her own use is guilty.*

BACKGROUND AND FACTS Faulkner, a truck driver, was hauling a load of refrigerators from San Diego to New York for the trucking company that employed him. He departed from his assigned route and stopped in Las Vegas, where he attempted to display and sell some of the refrigerators to a firm. Although the refrigerators never left the truck, to display them he had to break the truck's seals, enter the cargo department, and open two refrigerator cartons. The store owner refused to purchase the appliances, and when Faulkner left the store, he was arrested. He was later convicted under federal law for the embezzlement of an interstate shipment. Faulkner appealed, claiming that there were no grounds for the charge, because he had never removed any equipment from the truck.

(Continued)

CASE 6.2—Continued

IN THE WORDS OF THE COURT . . .
SKOPIL, Circuit Judge:

* * * *

The stealing or unlawful taking contemplated by the statute consists of taking over possession and control with intent to convert to the use of the taker. The statute does not require physical removal of the goods, nor even asportation in the common law larceny sense.

The felonious intent required by the statute consists of the intent to appropriate or convert the property of the owner. An intent to return the property does not exculpate the defendant.

We hold that there was sufficient evidence establishing the requisite act and intent. Faulkner exercised dominion and control over the refrigerators by leaving his assigned route to go to Urbauer's store and negotiate a sale. * * * The jury could therefore find that Faulkner had assumed possession and control of the goods. These facts also permitted the jury to conclude that Faulkner intended to convert the goods to his own use. It was not necessary that Faulkner remove the goods from the truck, nor complete the sale.

DECISION AND REMEDY The U.S. Court of Appeals for the Ninth Circuit affirmed the judgment of the trial court.

FOR CRITICAL ANALYSIS—Social Consideration *By definition, a crime involves both intent and a criminal act. What criminal act did Faulkner commit?*

MAIL AND WIRE FRAUD

One of the most potent weapons against white-collar criminals is the Mail Fraud Act of 1990.[5] Under this act, it is a federal crime (mail fraud) to use the mails to defraud the public. Illegal use of the mails must involve (1) mailing or causing someone else to mail a writing—something written, printed, or photocopied—for the purpose of executing a scheme to defraud and (2) a contemplated or an organized scheme to defraud by false pretenses. If, for example, Johnson advertises by mail the sale of a cure for cancer that he knows to be fraudulent because it has no medical validity, he can be prosecuted for fraudulent use of the mails.

Federal law also makes it a crime (wire fraud) to use wire (for example, the telephone), radio, or television transmissions to defraud.[6] Violators may be fined up to $1,000, imprisoned for up to five years, or both. If the violation affects a financial institution, the violator may be fined up to $1 million, imprisoned for up to thirty years, or both.

COMPUTER CRIME

• **COMPUTER CRIME**
Any act that is directed against computers and computer parts, that uses computers as instruments of crime, or that involves computers and constitutes abuse.

The American Bar Association defines **computer crime** as any act that is directed against computers and computer parts, that uses computers as instruments of crime, or that involves computers and constitutes abuse. A variety of different types of crime can be committed with or against computers.

Types of Computer Crimes Many computer crimes fall into the broad category of financial crimes. Computer networks provide opportunities for employees and others to commit crimes that can involve serious economic losses. For example, employees of a company's accounting department can transfer funds among accounts with little effort and often with less risk than that involved in transactions evidenced by paper-

5. 18 U.S.C. Sections 1341–1342.
6. 18 U.S.C. Section 1343.

A BUSINESSPERSON WORKS WITH A COMPUTER. IF THE WORK BEING DONE IS COPIED BY ANOTHER EMPLOYEE WITHOUT PERMISSION AND GIVEN TO A BUSINESS COMPETITOR, WHAT CRIME HAS BEEN COMMITTED?

¡BE AWARE! Technological change is one of the primary factors that lead to new types of crime.

work. Not only is the potential for crime in the area of financial transactions great, but also most monetary losses from computer crime are suffered in this area.

The theft of computer equipment and the theft of goods with the aid of computers (such as by manipulating inventory records to cover the theft of goods) are subject to the same criminal and tort laws as thefts of other physical property. In many jurisdictions, the unauthorized use of computer data or services is considered larceny. Other computer crimes include vandalism and destructive programming. A knowledgeable individual, such as an angry employee whose job has just been terminated, can do a considerable amount of damage to computer data and files. Destructive programming in the form of "viruses" presents an ongoing problem for businesspersons and other computer users.

A major problem for businesspersons today, as discussed in Chapter 5, is software piracy. Under most state laws, software piracy is classified as a crime. At the federal level, the laws protecting intellectual property (such as patent and copyright laws—see Chapter 5) also cover computer programs.

Prosecuting Computer Crime Several states have laws specifically addressing the problem of computer crime. At the federal level, the Counterfeit Access Device and Computer Fraud and Abuse Act of 1984, as amended, prohibits unauthorized access to certain types of information, such as restricted government information, information contained in a financial institution's financial records, and information contained in a consumer reporting agency's files on consumers. Penalties for violations include up to five years' imprisonment and a fine of up to $250,000 or twice the amount that was gained by the thief or lost by the victim as a result of the crime.

Another federal statute, the Electronic Fund Transfer Act (EFTA) of 1978, makes the unauthorized access to an electronic fund transfer system a crime. Unauthorized users of such systems are subject to criminal sanctions, including a $10,000 fine and ten years' imprisonment. (See Chapter 21 for a more detailed discussion of how the EFTA regulates electronic fund transfers.)

One of the problems presented by computer crime is its relative invisibility. Even when it is apparent that a computer crime has occurred, tracing the crime to the individual who committed it can be difficult, because the individual's identity is hidden by the "faceless" nature of computer networks, particularly the Internet. Another problem is that the law is always a step or two behind technological developments, and thus traditional laws may not always apply to activities conducted using computers. This is particularly true in today's online world—as you will read in Chapter 7.

BRIBERY

"[It is] very much better to bribe a person than kill him."
SIR WINSTON CHURCHILL, 1874–1965
(British prime minister, 1940–1945, 1951–1955)

Basically, three types of bribery are considered crimes: bribery of public officials, commercial bribery, and bribery of foreign officials. The attempt to influence a public official to act in a way that serves a private interest is a crime. As an element of this crime, intent must be present and proved. The bribe can be anything the recipient considers to be valuable. Realize that *the crime of bribery occurs when the bribe is offered.* It does not matter whether the person to whom the bribe is offered accepts the bribe or agrees to perform whatever action is desired by the person offering the bribe. *Accepting a bribe* is a separate crime.

Typically, people make commercial bribes to obtain proprietary information, cover up an inferior product, or secure new business. Industrial espionage sometimes involves commercial bribes. For example, a person in one firm may offer an employee in a competing firm some type of payoff in exchange for trade secrets or pricing schedules. So-called kickbacks, or payoffs for special favors or services, are a form of commercial bribery in some situations.

Bribing foreign officials to obtain favorable business contracts is a crime. The Foreign Corrupt Practices Act of 1977, which is presented as a *Landmark in the Law* in Chapter 8, was passed to curb the use of bribery by American businesspersons in securing foreign contracts.

BANKRUPTCY FRAUD

Today, federal bankruptcy law (see Chapter 23) allows individuals and businesses to be relieved of oppressive debt through bankruptcy proceedings. Numerous white-collar crimes may be committed during the many phases of a bankruptcy proceeding. A creditor, for example, may file a false claim against the debtor, which is a crime. Also, a debtor may fraudulently transfer assets to favored parties before or after the petition for bankruptcy is filed. For example, a company-owned automobile may be "sold" at a bargain price to a trusted friend or relative. Closely related to the crime of fraudulent transfer of property is the crime of fraudulent concealment of property, such as hiding gold coins.

MONEY LAUNDERING

The profits from illegal activities amount to billions of dollars a year, particularly the profits from illegal drug transactions and, to a lesser extent, from racketeering, prostitution, and gambling. Under federal law, banks, savings and loan associations, and other financial institutions are required to report currency transactions of over $10,000. Consequently, those who engage in illegal activities face difficulties in depositing their cash profits from illegal transactions.

As an alternative to simply placing cash from illegal transactions in bank deposits, wrongdoers and racketeers have invented ways to launder "dirty" money to make it "clean." This **money laundering** is done through legitimate businesses.

• **MONEY LAUNDERING**
Falsely reporting income that has been obtained through criminal activity as income obtained through a legitimate business enterprise—in effect, "laundering" the "dirty money."

• **EXAMPLE 6.3** A successful drug dealer might become a partner with a restaurateur. Little by little, the restaurant shows an increasing profit. As a shareholder or partner in the restaurant, the wrongdoer is able to report the "profits" of the restaurant as legitimate income on which federal and state taxes are paid. The wrongdoer can then spend those monies without worrying about whether his or her lifestyle exceeds the level possible with his or her reported income. •

The Federal Bureau of Investigation estimates that organized crime alone has invested tens of billions of dollars in as many as a hundred thousand business establishments in the United States for the purpose of money laundering. Globally, it is estimated that more than $500 billion in illegal money moves through the world banking system every year.

INSIDER TRADING

An individual who obtains "inside information" about the plans of large corporations can often make stock-trading profits by using such information to guide decisions relating to the purchase or sale of corporate securities. **Insider trading** is a violation of securities law and will be considered more fully in Chapter 31. At this point, it may be said that one who possesses inside information and who has a duty not to disclose it to outsiders may not profit from the purchase or sale of securities based on that information until the information is available to the public.

• **INSIDER TRADING**
The purchase or sale of securities on the basis of "inside information" (information that has not been made available to the public).

THE THEFT OF TRADE SECRETS

As discussed in Chapter 5, trade secrets constitute a form of intellectual property that for many businesses can be extremely valuable. The Economic Espionage Act of 1996[7] made the theft of trade secrets a federal crime. The act also made it a federal crime to buy or possess trade secrets of another person, knowing that the trade secrets were stolen or otherwise acquired without the owner's authorization.

The act defines a trade secret to incorporate the new methods of creating and storing trade secrets that technology has made possible:

> [T]he term "trade secret" means all forms and types of financial, business, scientific, technical, economic, or engineering information, including patterns, plans, compilations, program devices, formulas, designs, prototypes, methods, techniques, processes, procedures, programs or codes, whether tangible or intangible, and whether or how stored, compiled, or memorialized physically, electronically, graphically, photographically, or in writing if
>
> (A) the owner thereof has taken reasonable measures to keep such information secret; and
> (B) the information derives independent economic value, actual or potential, from not being generally known to, and not being readily ascertainable through proper means by the public.

Violations of the act can result in steep penalties. The act provides that an individual who violates the act can be imprisoned for up to ten years and fined up to $500,000. If a corporation or other organization violates the act, it can be fined up to $5 million. Additionally, the law provides that any property acquired as a result of the violation and any property used in the commission of the violation is subject to criminal forfeiture—meaning that the government can take the property. A theft of trade secrets conducted via the Internet, for example, could result in the forfeiture of every computer, printer, or other device used to commit or facilitate the violation.

CRIMINAL RICO VIOLATIONS

The Racketeer Influenced and Corrupt Organizations Act (RICO) was passed in an attempt to prevent the use of legitimate business enterprises as shields for racketeering activity and to prohibit the purchase of any legitimate business interest with illegally obtained funds (see the discussion of RICO in Chapter 5).

Most of the criminal RICO offenses have little, if anything, to do with normal business activities, for they involve gambling, arson, and extortion. Securities fraud (involving the sale of stocks and bonds), as well as mail fraud, wire fraud, welfare fraud, embezzlement, and numerous other crimes defined by state or federal statutes, however, are also criminal RICO violations, and RICO has become an effective tool in attacking these white-collar crimes in recent years.

Under criminal provisions of RICO, any individual found guilty of a violation is subject to a fine of up to $25,000 per violation, imprisonment for up to twenty years, or both. Additionally, the RICO statute provides that those who violate RICO may be required to *forfeit* (give up) any assets, in the form of property or cash, that were acquired as a result of the illegal activity or that were "involved in" or an "instrumentality of" the activity.

Defenses to Criminal Liability

Among the most important defenses to criminal liability are infancy, intoxication, insanity, mistake, consent, duress, justifiable use of force, entrapment, and the statute of limitations. Many of these defenses involve assertions that the intent requirement for criminal liability is lacking. Also, in some cases, defendants are

7. 18 U.S.C. 1831–1839.

given immunity and thus relieved, at least in part, of criminal liability for crimes they committed. We look at each of these defenses here.

Note that procedural violations (such as obtaining evidence without a valid search warrant—criminal procedure will be discussed later in this chapter) may operate as defenses also—because evidence obtained in violation of a defendant's constitutional rights normally may not be admitted in court. If the evidence is suppressed, then there may be no basis for prosecuting the defendant.

ON THE WEB

You can gain some insights into criminal law and procedures, including some of the defenses that can be raised to avoid criminal liability, by looking at some of the famous criminal law cases included on Court TV's Web site. Go to www.courttv.com/index.html.

INFANCY

The term *infant,* as used in the law, refers to any person who has not yet reached the age of majority (see Chapter 11). In all states, certain courts handle cases involving children who are alleged to have violated the law. In some states, juvenile courts handle children's cases exclusively. In other states, however, courts that handle children's cases may also have jurisdiction over other matters.

Originally, juvenile court hearings were informal, and lawyers were rarely present. Since 1967, however, when the United States Supreme Court ordered that a child charged with delinquency must be allowed to consult with an attorney before being committed to a state institution,[8] juvenile court hearings have become more formal. In some states, a child will be treated as an adult and tried in a regular court if he or she is above a certain age (usually fourteen) and is guilty of a felony, such as rape or murder.

INTOXICATION

The law recognizes two types of intoxication, whether from drugs or from alcohol: *involuntary* and *voluntary.* Involuntary intoxication occurs when a person either is physically forced to ingest or inject an intoxicating substance or is unaware that a substance contains drugs or alcohol. Involuntary intoxication is a defense to a crime if its effect was to make a person incapable of obeying the law or incapable of understanding that the act committed was wrong. There is controversy as to whether voluntary intoxication is a defense when the defendant was *extremely* intoxicated when committing the wrong. In the following case, the United States Supreme Court had to decide whether a state law banning the introduction at trial of evidence of intoxication violated the defendant's constitutional right to due process of law.

8. *In re Gault,* 387 U.S. 1, 87 S.Ct. 1428, 18 L.Ed.2d 527 (1967).

CASE 6.3 Montana v. Egelhoff

Supreme Court of the United States, 1996.
518 U.S. 37,
116 S.Ct. 2013,
135 L.Ed.2d 361.
supct.law.cornell.edu/supct/html/95-566.ZS.html[a]

HISTORICAL AND SOCIAL SETTING Using voluntary drug or alcohol intoxication as a defense is based on the theory that extreme levels of intoxication may negate the state of mind that a crime requires. Many courts are reluctant to allow voluntary intoxication as a defense to a crime, however. After all, the defendant, by definition, voluntarily chose to put himself or herself into an intoxicated state.

a. This is a page within the "Historic Supreme Court Decisions" collection of the Legal Information Institute (LII) and Project Hermes available at the LII site on the Web. Read the opinion beginning with the syllabus on this page or click on a link to take advantage of one of the other options.

BACKGROUND AND FACTS James Egelhoff was charged in a Montana state court with two counts of deliberate homicide. Egelhoff claimed that he had been intoxicated at the time the incident occurred and therefore he lacked the mental state required for commission of the crime of murder. Under a

CASE 6.3—Continued

state statute, the jury was told not to consider his intoxication in determining whether he had lacked the required mental state. The jury found him guilty, and he appealed. The Montana Supreme Court reversed, reasoning that a defendant has a right, under the Constitution's due process clause, to have a jury consider evidence of voluntary intoxication in deciding whether he or she had the requisite mental state. The state appealed to the United States Supreme Court.

IN THE WORDS OF THE COURT . . .

Justice *SCALIA* announced the judgment of the Court * * * .

* * * *

* * * [The] stern rejection of inebriation as a defense became a fixture of early American law * * * .

* * * *

* * * Over the course of the 19th century, courts carved out an exception * * * .

* * * *

* * * [O]ne-fifth of the States either never adopted the [exception] or have recently abandoned it.

* * * [P]rohibiting consideration of voluntary intoxication in the determination of *mens rea* * * * has considerable justification * * * . [For example, d]isallowing consideration of voluntary intoxication has the effect of increasing the punishment for all unlawful acts committed in that state, and thereby deters drunkenness or irresponsible behavior while drunk. * * *

* * * *

* * * [T]he rule allowing a jury to consider evidence of a defendant's voluntary intoxication where relevant to *mens rea* * * * has not received sufficiently uniform and permanent allegiance to qualify as fundamental, especially since it displaces a lengthy common-law tradition which remains supported by valid justifications today.

DECISION AND REMEDY The Supreme Court held that Montana's ban did not violate the Constitution's due process clause. The Court reversed the state supreme court's decision.

FOR CRITICAL ANALYSIS—Social Consideration *Do you agree that disallowing voluntary intoxication as a defense "deters drunkenness or irresponsible behavior while drunk"? Why or why not?*

INSANITY

"Insanity is often the logic of an accurate mind overtaxed."

OLIVER WENDELL HOLMES, JR., 1841–1935
(Associate justice of the United States Supreme Court, 1902–1932)

Just as a child is often judged incapable of the state of mind required to commit a crime, so also may be someone suffering from a mental illness. Thus, insanity may be a defense to a criminal charge. The courts have had difficulty deciding what the test for legal insanity should be, and psychiatrists as well as lawyers are critical of the tests used. Almost all federal courts and some states use the relatively liberal standard set forth in the Model Penal Code:

> A person is not responsible for criminal conduct if at the time of such conduct as a result of mental disease or defect he lacks substantial capacity either to appreciate the wrongfulness of his conduct or to conform his conduct to the requirements of the law.

Some states use the *M'Naghten* test,[9] under which a criminal defendant is not responsible if, at the time of the offense, he or she did not know the nature and quality of the act or did not know that the act was wrong. Other states use the irresistible-impulse test. A person operating under an irresistible impulse may know an act is wrong but cannot refrain from doing it.

MISTAKE

¡COMPARE! "Ignorance" is a lack of information. "Mistake" is a confusion of information.

Everyone has heard the saying, "Ignorance of the law is no excuse." Ordinarily, ignorance of the law or a mistaken idea about what the law requires is not a valid defense. In some states, however, that rule has been modified. Criminal defendants who claim that they honestly did not know that they were breaking a law may have a valid defense if (1) the law was not published or reasonably made known to the public or (2) the defendant relied on an official statement of the law that was erroneous.

A *mistake of fact,* as opposed to a *mistake of law,* operates as a defense if it negates the mental state necessary to commit a crime. • **EXAMPLE 6.4** If Oliver Wheaton mistakenly walks off with Julie Tyson's briefcase because he thinks it is his, there is no theft. Theft requires knowledge that the property belongs to another. (If Wheaton's act causes Tyson to incur damages, however, Wheaton may be subject to tort liability for trespass to personalty or conversion.) •

CONSENT

• **CONSENT** Voluntary agreement to a proposition or an act of another. A concurrence of wills.

What if a victim consents to a crime or even encourages the person intending a criminal act to commit it? The law allows **consent** as a defense if the consent cancels the harm that the law is designed to prevent. In each case, the question is whether the law forbids an act that was committed against the victim's will or forbids the act without regard to the victim's wish. The law forbids murder, prostitution, and drug use regardless of whether the victim consents to it. Also, if the act causes harm to a third person who has not consented, there is no escape from criminal liability. Consent or forgiveness given after a crime has been committed is not really a defense, though it can affect the likelihood of prosecution. Consent operates as a defense most successfully in crimes against property.

DURESS

• **DURESS** Unlawful pressure brought to bear on a person, causing the person to perform an act that he or she would not otherwise perform.

Duress exists when the *wrongful threat* of one person induces another person to perform an act that he or she would not otherwise perform. In such a situation, duress is said to negate the mental state necessary to commit a crime. For duress to qualify as a defense, the following requirements must be met:

1. The threat must be of serious bodily harm or death.
2. The harm threatened must be greater than the harm caused by the crime.
3. The threat must be immediate and inescapable.
4. The defendant must have been involved in the situation through no fault of his or her own.

JUSTIFIABLE USE OF FORCE

• **SELF-DEFENSE** The legally recognized privilege to protect one's self or property against injury by another. The privilege of self-defense protects only acts that are reasonably necessary to protect oneself, one's property, or another person.

Probably the most well-known defense to criminal liability is **self-defense.** Other situations, however, also justify the use of force: the defense of one's dwelling, the

9. A rule derived from *M'Naghten's Case,* 8 Eng.Rep. 718 (1843).

defense of other property, and the prevention of a crime. In all of these situations, it is important to distinguish between the use of deadly and nondeadly force. *Deadly force* is likely to result in death or serious bodily harm. *Nondeadly force* is force that reasonably appears necessary to prevent the imminent use of criminal force.

Generally speaking, people can use the amount of nondeadly force that seems necessary to protect themselves, their dwellings, or other property or to prevent the commission of a crime. Deadly force can be used in self-defense if there is a *reasonable belief* that imminent death or grievous bodily harm will otherwise result, if the attacker is using unlawful force (an example of lawful force is that exerted by a police officer), and if the defender has not initiated or provoked the attack. Deadly force normally can be used to defend a dwelling only if the unlawful entry is violent and the person believes deadly force is necessary to prevent imminent death or great bodily harm or—in some jurisdictions—if the person believes deadly force is necessary to prevent the commission of a felony (such as arson) in the dwelling.

ENTRAPMENT

• **ENTRAPMENT**
In criminal law, a defense in which the defendant claims that he or she was induced by a public official—usually an undercover agent or police officer—to commit a crime that he or she would otherwise not have committed.

Entrapment is a defense designed to prevent police officers or other government agents from encouraging crimes in order to apprehend persons wanted for criminal acts. In the typical entrapment case, an undercover agent *suggests* that a crime be committed and somehow pressures or induces an individual to commit it. The agent then arrests the individual for the crime.

For entrapment to be considered a defense, both the suggestion and the inducement must take place. The defense is intended not to prevent law enforcement agents from setting a trap for an unwary criminal but rather to prevent them from pushing the individual into it. The crucial issue is whether a person who committed a crime was predisposed to commit the crime or did so because the agent induced it.

STATUTE OF LIMITATIONS

With some exceptions, such as for the crime of murder, statutes of limitations apply to crimes just as they do to civil wrongs. In other words, criminal cases must be prosecuted within a certain number of years. If a criminal action is brought after the statutory time period has expired, the accused person can raise the statute of limitations as a defense.

IMMUNITY

At times, the state may wish to obtain information from a person accused of a crime. Accused persons are understandably reluctant to give information if it will be used to prosecute them, and they cannot be forced to do so. The privilege against self-incrimination is granted by the Fifth Amendment to the Constitution, which reads, in part, "nor shall [any person] be compelled in any criminal case to be a witness against himself." In cases in which the state wishes to obtain information from a person accused of a crime, the state can grant *immunity* from prosecution or agree to prosecute for a less serious offense in exchange for the information. Once immunity is given, the person can no longer refuse to testify on Fifth Amendment grounds, because he or she now has an absolute privilege against self-incrimination.

• **PLEA BARGAINING**
The process by which a criminal defendant and the prosecutor in a criminal case work out a mutually satisfactory disposition of the case, subject to court approval; usually involves the defendant's pleading guilty to a lesser offense in return for a lighter sentence.

Often a grant of immunity from prosecution for a serious crime is part of the **plea bargaining** between the defendant and the prosecuting attorney. The defendant may be convicted of a lesser offense, while the state uses the defendant's testimony to prosecute accomplices for serious crimes carrying heavy penalties.

Constitutional Safeguards and Criminal Procedures

Criminal law brings the power of the state, with all its resources, to bear against the individual. Criminal procedures are designed to protect the constitutional rights of individuals and to prevent the arbitrary use of power on the part of the government.

The U.S. Constitution provides specific safeguards for those accused of crimes. Most of these safeguards protect individuals against state government actions, as well as federal government actions, by virtue of the due process clause of the Fourteenth Amendment. These safeguards are set forth in the Fourth, Fifth, Sixth, and Eighth Amendments.

FOURTH AMENDMENT PROTECTIONS

The Fourth Amendment protects the "right of the people to be secure in their persons, houses, papers, and effects." Before searching or seizing private property, law enforcement officers must obtain a **search warrant**—an order from a judge or other public official authorizing the search or seizure.

• **SEARCH WARRANT**
An order granted by a public authority, such as a judge, that authorizes law enforcement personnel to search particular premises or property.

• **PROBABLE CAUSE**
Reasonable grounds to believe the existence of facts warranting certain actions, such as the search or arrest of a person.

Search Warrants and Probable Cause To obtain a search warrant, the officers must convince a judge that they have reasonable grounds, or **probable cause,** to believe a search will reveal a specific illegality. Probable cause requires law enforcement officials to have trustworthy evidence that would convince a reasonable person that the proposed search or seizure is more likely justified than not. Furthermore, the Fourth Amendment prohibits general warrants. It requires a particular description of that which is to be searched or seized. General searches through a person's belongings are impermissible. The search cannot extend beyond what is described in the warrant.

There are exceptions to the requirement of a search warrant, as when it is likely that the items sought will be removed before a warrant can be obtained. For example, if a police officer has probable cause to believe an automobile contains evidence of a crime and it is likely that the vehicle will be unavailable by the time a warrant is obtained, the officer can search the vehicle without a warrant.

ON THE WEB
You can learn about some of the constitutional questions raised by various criminal laws and procedures by going to the Web site of the American Civil Liberties Union at www.aclu.org.

Searches and Seizures in the Business Context Constitutional protection against unreasonable searches and seizures is important to businesses and professionals. As federal and state regulation of commercial activities increased, frequent and unannounced government inspections were conducted to ensure compliance with the regulations. Such inspections were at times extremely disruptive. In *Marshall v. Barlow's, Inc.,*[10] the United States Supreme Court held that government inspectors do not have the right to enter business premises without a warrant, although the standard of probable cause is not the same as that required in nonbusiness contexts. The existence of a general and neutral enforcement plan will justify issuance of the warrant.

Lawyers and accountants frequently possess the business records of their clients, and inspecting these documents while they are out of the hands of their true owners also requires a warrant. No warrant is required, however, for seizures of spoiled or contaminated food. Nor are warrants required for searches of businesses in such highly regulated industries as liquor, guns, and strip mining. General manufacturing is not considered to be one of these highly regulated industries, however.

10. 436 U.S. 307, 98 S.Ct. 1816, 56 L.Ed.2d 305 (1978).

• **SELF-INCRIMINATION**
The giving of testimony that may subject the testifier to criminal prosecution. The Fifth Amendment to the Constitution protects against self-incrimination by providing that no person "shall be compelled in any criminal case to be a witness against himself."

Of increasing concern to many employers is how to maintain a safe and efficient workplace without jeopardizing the Fourth Amendment rights of employees "to be secure in their persons." Requiring employees to undergo random drug tests, for example, may be held to violate the Fourth Amendment. In Chapter 37, we discuss Fourth Amendment issues in the employment context, as well as the privacy rights of employees in general, in detail.

FIFTH AMENDMENT PROTECTIONS

The Fifth Amendment offers significant protections for accused persons. One is the requirement that no one can be deprived of "life, liberty, or property without due process of law." Two other important Fifth Amendment provisions protect persons against double jeopardy and self-incrimination.

Due Process of Law Remember from Chapter 2 that *due process of law* has both procedural and substantive aspects. Procedural due process requirements underlie criminal procedures. Basically, the law must be carried out in a fair and orderly way. In criminal cases, due process means that defendants should have an opportunity to object to the charges against them before a fair, neutral decision maker, such as a judge. Defendants must also be given the opportunity to confront and cross-examine witnesses and accusers and to present their own witnesses.

• **DOUBLE JEOPARDY**
A situation occurring when a person is tried twice for the same criminal offense; prohibited by the Fifth Amendment to the Constitution.

Double Jeopardy The Fifth Amendment also protects persons from **double jeopardy** (being tried twice for the same criminal offense). The prohibition against double jeopardy means that once a criminal defendant is acquitted (found "not guilty") of a particular crime, the government may not reindict the person and retry him or her for the same crime. The prohibition against double jeopardy does not preclude the crime victim from bringing a civil suit against the same person to recover damages, however. For example, a person found "not guilty" of assault and battery in a criminal case may be sued by the victim in a civil tort case for damages. Additionally, a state's prosecution of a crime will not prevent a separate federal prosecution relating to the same activity, and vice versa. For example, a person who is prosecuted for assault and battery in a state court may be prosecuted in a federal court for civil rights violations resulting from the same action.

¡BE AWARE!
The Fifth Amendment protection against self-incrimination does not cover partnerships or corporations.

Self-Incrimination The Fifth Amendment guarantees that no person "shall be compelled in any criminal case to be a witness against himself." Thus, in any criminal proceeding, an accused person cannot be compelled to give testimony that might subject him or her to any criminal prosecution.

The Fifth Amendment's guarantee against **self-incrimination** extends only to natural persons. Because a corporation is a legal entity and not a natural person, the privilege against self-incrimination does not apply to it. Similarly, the business records of a partnership do not receive Fifth Amendment protection.[11] When a partnership is required to produce these records, it must give the information even if it incriminates the persons who constitute the business entity. Sole proprietors and sole practitioners (those who fully own their businesses) who have not incorporated cannot be compelled to produce their business records. These individuals have full protection against self-incrimination, because they function in only one capacity; there is no separate business entity (see Chapter 25).

11. The privilege has been applied to some small family partnerships. See *United States v. Slutsky*, 352 F.Supp. 1005 (S.D.N.Y. 1972).

International Perspective • THE FIFTH AMENDMENT AND FOREIGN GOVERNMENTS

The Fifth Amendment allows defendants or witnesses in criminal cases to refuse to answer certain questions if their answers may be self-incriminating and lead to future government prosecutions against them. But what if a person fears that a foreign government may bring a criminal prosecution against him or her as a result of statements made in a U.S. legal proceeding? Can that person "take the Fifth"? This question recently came before the United States Supreme Court in *United States v. Balsys.*[a] The case involved a resident alien, Aloyzas Balsys, who was requested to testify before the Justice Department's Office of Special Investigations (OSI). The OSI sought to determine whether Balsys had lied on his immigration application about his activities during World War II. Balsys asserted the Fifth Amendment privilege against self-incrimination, contending that compliance with the OSI's request could subject him to prosecution for war crimes by foreign governments, such as Germany or Israel. The Supreme Court held that Balsys's concern with foreign prosecution was beyond the scope of the Fifth Amendment, which applied only to possible federal or state government prosecutions in the United States. Therefore, Balsys could not avoid complying with the OSI's request on Fifth Amendment grounds.

a. 524 U.S. 666, 118 S.Ct. 2218, 141 L.Ed.2d 575 (1998).

FOR CRITICAL ANALYSIS
How would you argue in support of the Supreme Court's conclusion in this case?

PROTECTIONS UNDER THE SIXTH AMENDMENT AND EIGHTH AMENDMENT

The Sixth Amendment guarantees several important rights for criminal defendants: the right to a speedy trial, the right to a jury trial, the right to a public trial, the right to confront witnesses, and the right to counsel. The Eighth Amendment prohibits excessive bails and fines, and cruel and unusual punishment.

ETHICAL ISSUE 6.1 ***Can asset forfeitures violate the Eighth Amendment?*** Questions of fairness often arise in asset forfeiture proceedings under RICO or other laws because sometimes the punishment (the value of the assets forfeited) can be grossly disproportionate to the crime. For example, suppose that a U.S. citizen boards an international flight carrying $357,144 but does not declare that he or she is carrying that amount (in violation of a federal law that requires the reporting of any transport of more than $10,000 in U.S. currency). Should the entire amount ($357,144) be subject to forfeiture, even though the funds were legally acquired and were being transported to pay a legal debt? If so, would the forfeiture violate the "excessive fines" clause of the Eighth Amendment? In 1998, addressing this issue for the first time, the United States Supreme Court gave some guidance to the lower courts on this issue. The Court held that "a punitive forfeiture violates the Excessive Fines Clause if it is grossly disproportional to the gravity of a defendant's offense."[12]

"A search is not to be made legal by what it turns up."

ROBERT H. JACKSON, 1892–1954
(Associate justice of the United States Supreme Court, 1941–1954)

THE EXCLUSIONARY RULE AND THE *MIRANDA* RULE

Two other procedural protections for criminal defendants are the exclusionary rule and the *Miranda* rule.

The Exclusionary Rule Under what is known as the **exclusionary rule,** all evidence obtained in violation of the constitutional rights spelled out in the Fourth, Fifth, and

• **EXCLUSIONARY RULE**
In criminal procedure, a rule under which any evidence that is obtained in violation of the accused's constitutional rights guaranteed by the Fourth, Fifth, and Sixth Amendments, as well as any evidence derived from illegally obtained evidence, will not be admissible in court.

12. *United States v. Bajakajian,* ___ U.S. ___, 118 S.Ct. 2028, 141 L.Ed.2d 314 (1998).

POLICE OFFICERS TAKE A SUSPECT INTO CUSTODY. WHY MUST A CRIMINAL SUSPECT BE INFORMED OF HIS OR HER LEGAL RIGHTS?

Sixth Amendments normally must be excluded from the trial, as well as all evidence derived from the illegally obtained evidence. Illegally obtained evidence is known as the "fruit of the poisonous tree." For example, if a confession is obtained after an illegal arrest, the arrest is "the poisonous tree," and the confession, if "tainted" by the arrest, is the "fruit."

The purpose of the exclusionary rule is to deter police from conducting warrantless searches and other misconduct. The rule is sometimes criticized because it can lead to injustice. Many a defendant has "gotten off on a technicality" because law enforcement personnel failed to observe procedural requirements. Even though a defendant may be obviously guilty, if the evidence of that guilt is obtained improperly (without a valid search warrant, for example), it normally cannot be used against the defendant in court.

The *Miranda* Rule In *Miranda v. Arizona,* the United States Supreme Court established the rule that individuals who are arrested must be informed of certain constitutional rights, including their Fifth Amendment right to remain silent and their Sixth Amendment right to counsel. If the arresting officers fail to inform a criminal suspect of these constitutional rights, any statements the suspect makes normally will not be admissible in court. Because of its importance in criminal procedure, the *Miranda* case is presented as this chapter's *Landmark in the Law.*

¡ NOTE!

A person may be convicted despite police misconduct, because knowledge of facts obtained independently of the misconduct are admissible.

Over time, several exceptions to the *Miranda* rule have been created. A 1968 federal law provides that in federal cases, a voluntary confession may be used in evidence even if the accused was not informed of his or her rights. The United States Supreme Court has carved out other exceptions. In 1984, for example, the Court recognized a "public safety" exception to the *Miranda* rule. The need to protect the public warranted the admissibility of statements made by the defendant (in this case, indicating where he placed the gun) as evidence in a trial, even when the defendant had not been informed of his *Miranda* rights.[13] Today, juries are able to consider confessions, even if they are not voluntary.

13. *New York v. Quarles,* 467 U.S. 649, 104 S.Ct. 2626, 81 L.Ed.2d 550 (1984).

Landmark in the Law • *MIRANDA v. ARIZONA* (1966)

The United States Supreme Court's decision in *Miranda v. Arizona*[a] has been cited in more court decisions than any other case in the history of American law. Through television shows and other media, the case has also become familiar to most of America's adult population. The case arose after Ernesto Miranda was arrested in his home, on March 13, 1963, for the kidnapping and rape of an eighteen-year-old woman. Miranda was taken to a Phoenix, Arizona, police station and questioned by two police officers. Two hours later, the officers emerged from the interrogation room with a written confession signed by Miranda. The confession was admitted into evidence at the trial, and Miranda was convicted and sentenced to prison for twenty to thirty years.

¡ REMEMBER!

Once a suspect has been informed of his or her rights, anything that person says can be used as evidence in a trial.

ON THE WEB

If you are interested in reading the Supreme Court's opinion in *Miranda v. Arizona,* go to www.law.cornell.edu/supct.

Miranda appealed the decision, claiming that he had not been informed of his constitutional rights. He did not claim that he was innocent of the crime or that his confession was false or made under duress. He only claimed that he would not have confessed to the crime if he had been advised of his right to remain silent and to have an attorney. Nonetheless, the Supreme Court of Arizona held that Miranda's constitutional rights had not been violated and affirmed his conviction. In forming its decision, the court emphasized the fact that Miranda had not specifically requested an attorney. The *Miranda* case was subsequently consolidated with three other cases involving similar issues and reviewed by the United States Supreme Court.

In its decision, the Supreme Court stated that whenever an individual is taken into custody, "the following measures are required: He must be warned prior to any questioning that he has the right to remain silent, that anything he says can be used against him in a court of law, that he has the right to the presence of an attorney, and that if he cannot afford an attorney one will be appointed for him prior to any questioning if he so desires." If the accused waives his or her rights to remain silent and to have counsel present, the government must be able to demonstrate that the waiver was made knowingly, intelligently, and voluntarily.

Today, both on television and in the real world, police officers routinely advise suspects of their "*Miranda* rights" on arrest. When Ernesto Miranda himself was later murdered, the suspected murderer was "read his *Miranda* rights."

a. 384 U.S. 436, 86 S.Ct. 1602, 16 L.Ed.2d 694 (1966).

FOR CRITICAL ANALYSIS
Why should defendants who have admitted that they are guilty be allowed to avoid criminal liability because of procedural violations?

Criminal Process

ON THE WEB
An excellent site for information on the criminal justice system is tqd.advanced.org/2760/homep.htm.

Here, you can follow a fictional criminal case through the courts, find a glossary of terms used in criminal law, view actual forms that are filled out during the course of an arrest, and learn about some controversial issues in criminal law.

As mentioned, a criminal prosecution differs significantly from a civil case in several respects. These differences reflect the desire to safeguard the rights of the individual against the state. Exhibit 6–3 summarizes the major steps in processing a criminal case. We discuss below in more detail three phases of the criminal process—arrest, indictment or information, and trial.

ARREST

Before a warrant for arrest can be issued, there must be probable cause for believing that the individual in question has committed a crime. As discussed earlier, *probable cause* can be defined as a substantial likelihood that the person has committed or is about to commit a crime. Note that probable cause involves a likelihood, not just a possibility. Arrests may sometimes be made without a warrant if there is no time to get one, as when a police officer observes a crime taking place, but the action of the arresting officer is still judged by the standard of probable cause.

INDICTMENT OR INFORMATION

Individuals must be formally charged with having committed specific crimes before they can be brought to trial. If issued by a grand jury, this charge is called an **indictment.**[14] A **grand jury** usually consists of a greater number of jurors than the ordinary trial jury. A grand jury does not determine the guilt or innocence of an accused party; rather, its function is to determine, after hearing the state's evidence, whether a reasonable basis (probable cause) exists for believing that a crime has been committed and whether a trial ought to be held.

Usually, grand juries are called in cases involving serious crimes, such as murder. For lesser crimes, an individual may be formally charged with a crime by what is called an **information,** or criminal complaint. An information will be issued by a magistrate (a public official vested with judicial authority) if the magistrate determines that there is sufficient evidence to justify bringing the individual to trial.

• **INDICTMENT**
A charge by a grand jury that a named person has committed a crime.

• **GRAND JURY**
A group of citizens called to decide, after hearing the state's evidence, whether a reasonable basis (probable cause) exists for believing that a crime has been committed and whether a trial ought to be held.

• **INFORMATION**
A formal accusation or complaint (without an indictment) issued in certain types of actions (usually criminal actions involving lesser crimes) by a law officer, such as a magistrate.

TRIAL

At a criminal trial, the accused person does not have to prove anything; the entire burden of proof is on the prosecutor (the state). As mentioned earlier, the prosecution must show that, based on all the evidence presented, the defendant's guilt is estab-

14. Pronounced in-*dyte*-ment.

lished *beyond a reasonable doubt.* If there is any reasonable doubt that a criminal defendant did not commit the crime with which he or she has been charged, then the verdict must be "not guilty." Note that giving a verdict of "not guilty" is not the same as stating that the defendant is innocent; it merely means that not enough evidence was properly presented to the court to prove guilt beyond all reasonable doubt.

EXHIBIT 6–3 • Major Steps in Processing a Criminal Case

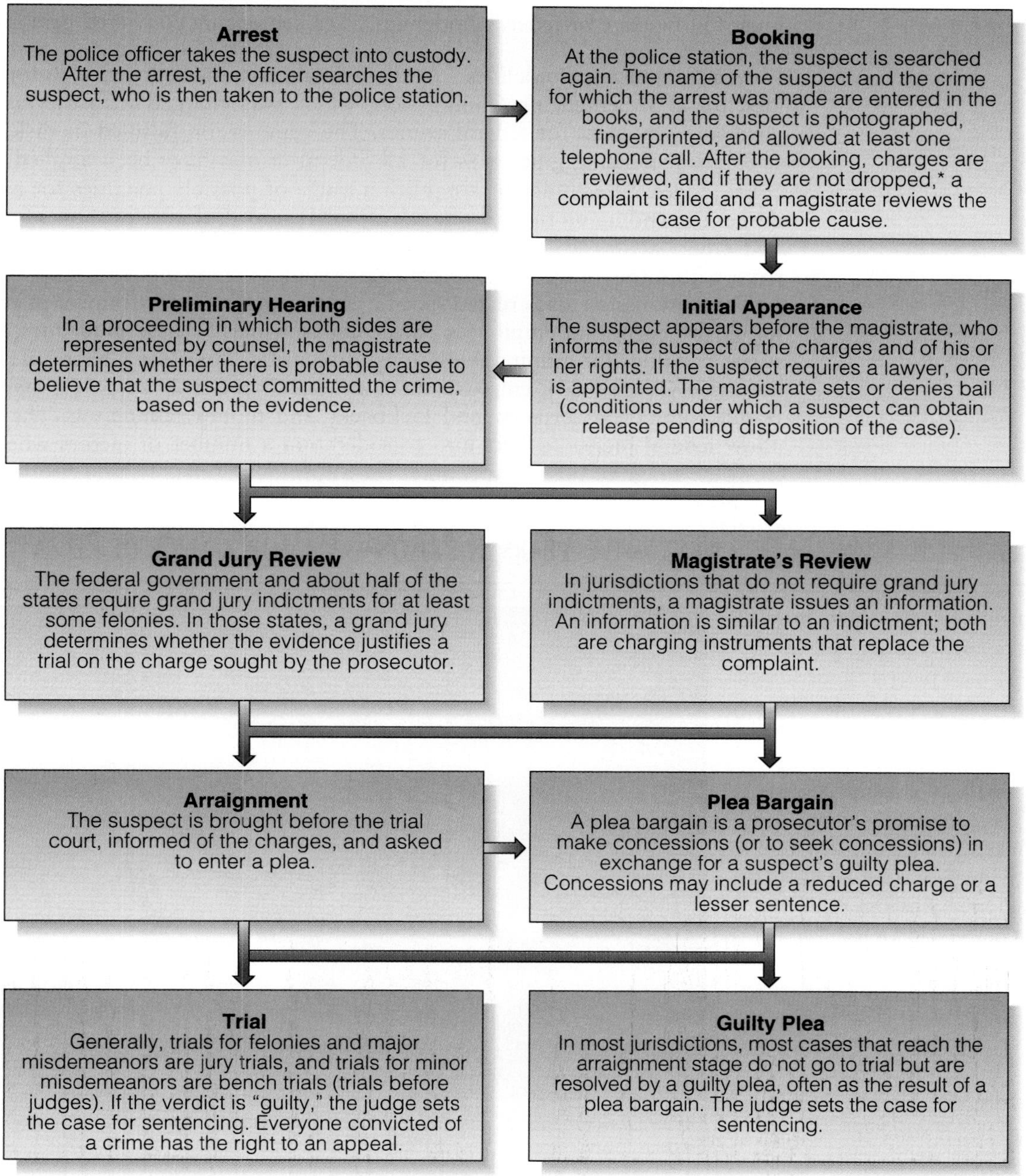

Arrest
The police officer takes the suspect into custody. After the arrest, the officer searches the suspect, who is then taken to the police station.
Booking
At the police station, the suspect is searched again. The name of the suspect and the crime for which the arrest was made are entered in the books, and the suspect is photographed, fingerprinted, and allowed at least one telephone call. After the booking, charges are reviewed, and if they are not dropped,* a complaint is filed and a magistrate reviews the case for probable cause.
Initial Appearance
The suspect appears before the magistrate, who informs the suspect of the charges and of his or her rights. If the suspect requires a lawyer, one is appointed. The magistrate sets or denies bail (conditions under which a suspect can obtain release pending disposition of the case).
Preliminary Hearing
In a proceeding in which both sides are represented by counsel, the magistrate determines whether there is probable cause to believe that the suspect committed the crime, based on the evidence.
Grand Jury Review
The federal government and about half of the states require grand jury indictments for at least some felonies. In those states, a grand jury determines whether the evidence justifies a trial on the charge sought by the prosecutor.
Magistrate's Review
In jurisdictions that do not require grand jury indictments, a magistrate issues an information. An information is similar to an indictment; both are charging instruments that replace the complaint.
Arraignment
The suspect is brought before the trial court, informed of the charges, and asked to enter a plea.
Plea Bargain
A plea bargain is a prosecutor's promise to make concessions (or to seek concessions) in exchange for a suspect's guilty plea. Concessions may include a reduced charge or a lesser sentence.
Trial
Generally, trials for felonies and major misdemeanors are jury trials, and trials for minor misdemeanors are bench trials (trials before judges). If the verdict is "guilty," the judge sets the case for sentencing. Everyone convicted of a crime has the right to an appeal.
Guilty Plea
In most jurisdictions, most cases that reach the arraignment stage do not go to trial but are resolved by a guilty plea, often as the result of a plea bargain. The judge sets the case for sentencing.

* At any point in the processing of a criminal case, charges may be reduced or dismissed.

Courts have complex rules about what types of evidence may be presented and how the evidence may be brought out in criminal cases, especially in jury trials. These rules are designed to ensure that evidence in trials is relevant, reliable, and not prejudicial against the defendant.

SENTENCING GUIDELINES

Traditionally, persons who had committed the same crime might have received very different sentences, depending on the judge hearing the case, the jurisdiction in which it was heard, and many other facts. Today, however, court judges typically must follow state or federal guidelines when sentencing convicted persons.

Federal Sentencing Guidelines At the federal level, the Sentencing Reform Act created the U.S. Sentencing Commission, which was charged with the task of standardizing sentences for federal crimes. The commission fulfilled its task, and since 1987 its sentencing guidelines for all federal crimes have been applied by federal court judges. The guidelines establish a range of possible penalties for each federal crime. Depending on the defendant's criminal record, the seriousness of the offense, and other factors specified in the guidelines, federal judges must select a sentence from within this range when sentencing criminal defendants.

The commission also created specific guidelines for the punishment of crimes committed by corporate employees (white-collar crimes). These guidelines established stiffer penalties for criminal violations of securities laws (see Chapter 31), antitrust laws (see Chapter 35), employment laws (see Chapters 37 and 38), mail and wire fraud, commercial bribery, and kickbacks and money laundering. The guidelines allow federal judges to take into consideration a number of factors when selecting from the range of possible penalties for a specified crime. These factors include the

ON THE WEB

The U.S. Sentencing Guidelines can be found online at www.ussc.gov.

The Letter of the Law — TWENTY-FIVE YEARS IN PRISON—ALL FOR A SLICE OF PIZZA

As mentioned elsewhere, many states, as well as the federal government, have passed "three strikes and you're out" laws. Although the purpose of these laws may be laudatory, they can lead to extreme situations. In January 1995, Jerry Dewayne Williams was convicted of felony petty theft for stealing a slice of pizza from a group of children on a pier in Redondo Beach, California. Because Williams had prior convictions for robbery and other felonies, he was sentenced to twenty-five years in prison for the theft of the slice of pizza![a]

THE BOTTOM LINE

The law is the law.

a. "Theft of Pizza Slice Nets a 25-Year Term," *The New York Times,* March 5, 1995, p. 11.

JERRY DEWAYNE WILLIAMS (RIGHT). SHOULD CRIMES LIKE WILLIAMS'S BE EXCEPTED FROM "THREE STRIKES" LAWS?

defendant company's history of past violations, the extent of management's cooperation with federal investigators, and the extent to which the firm has undertaken specific programs and procedures to prevent criminal activities by its employees.

"Three Strikes" Laws Many states have enacted "three strikes and you're out" legislation. Typically, this legislation states that any "career" criminal who already has two violent felony convictions on his or her record will go to jail (in some states, for life and without parole) if convicted of a third similar felony. A federal crime bill enacted in 1994 adopted this provision as well. A California law, enacted in 1994, requires longer prison sentences for felons who have had at least one prior conviction for a serious or violent felony.

APPLICATION

Law and the Businessperson: Protecting against Electronic Crime*

In addition to protecting their physical property, businesspersons today also are concerned about protecting their intangible property—such as computer data or files—from outside access. U.S. business firms lose millions of dollars to industrial espionage and sabotage every year. Once a computer system has been corrupted, it can be difficult to recover. To prevent losses through computer systems, some firms hire experts to improve the security of the systems.

Security measures that can protect against cyber crimes include data encryption, which is essential to doing business in cyberspace. The Data Encryption Standard (DES) is an encryption code that uses what is referred to as a 56-bit key size. The National Institute of Standards and Technology (NIST), which is part of the U.S. Department of Commerce, adopted the 56-bit standard in 1977.

As of the time of this writing, it had been shown that a medium-sized computer could break a 56-bit key code within a few hours. For this reason, it was recommended that a business firm use Triple DES, which involves three different DES operations to encrypt and decode. NIST is currently accepting proposals for the next generation code, Advanced Encryption Standard (AES), to be formally adopted by 2001.

Other steps to guard against cyber crimes include using digital signatures (discussed later in the text) and protecting a computer with passwords. Passwords should be nonsensical, and they should be changed often. E-mail that is not encrypted should not contain information that its sender or receiver would want to keep secret. Personal, private, and confidential information should not be posted on a Web site or to a Usenet newsgroup.

CHECKLIST FOR THE BUSINESSPERSON

1. Consider encrypting computer data before transmitting the data to another party.
2. Consider using digital signatures.
3. Protect against unauthorized computer access by using passwords and changing them often.
4. Do not e-mail sensitive or confidential messages unless they are encrypted.
5. Do not post personal or confidential information on a Web site.

*This *Application* is not meant to substitute for the services of an attorney who is licensed to practice law in your state.

Key Terms

arson 154
beyond a reasonable doubt 149
burglary 153
computer crime 156
consent 162
crime 149
double jeopardy 165
duress 162
embezzlement 155
entrapment 163
exclusionary rule 166
felony 150
forgery 154
grand jury 168
indictment 168
information 168
insider trading 158
larceny 154
misdemeanor 151
money laundering 158
petty offense 151
plea bargaining 163
probable cause 164
robbery 153
search warrant 164
self-defense 162
self-incrimination 165
white-collar crime 155

Chapter Summary • Criminal Law

Civil Law and Criminal Law (See pages 149–150.)	1. *Civil law*—Spells out the duties that exist between persons or between citizens and their governments, excluding the duty not to commit crimes. 2. *Criminal law*—Has to do with crimes, which are defined as wrongs against society proclaimed in statutes and, if committed, punishable by society through fines, removal from public office, and/or imprisonment—and, in some cases, death. Because crimes are *offenses against society as a whole,* they are prosecuted by a public official, not by victims. 3. *Key differences*—An important difference between civil and criminal law is that the standard of proof is higher in criminal cases (see Exhibit 6–1 for other differences between criminal and civil laws). 4. *Civil liability for criminal acts*—A criminal act may give rise to both criminal liability and tort liability (see Exhibit 6–2 for an example of criminal and tort liability for the same act).
Classification of Crimes (See pages 150–151.)	1. *Felonies*—Serious crimes punishable by death or by imprisonment in a penitentiary for more than one year. 2. *Misdemeanors*—Under federal law and in most states, any crime that is not a felony.
Criminal Liability (See pages 151–152.)	1. *Guilty act*—In general, some form of harmful act must be committed for a crime to exist. 2. *Intent*—An intent to commit a crime, or a wrongful mental state, is required for a crime to exist.
Corporate Criminal Liability (See pages 152–153.)	1. *Liability of corporations*—Corporations normally are liable for the crimes committed by their agents and employees within the course and scope of their employment. Corporations cannot be imprisoned, but they can be fined or denied certain legal privileges. 2. *Liability of corporate officers and directors*—Corporate directors and officers are personally liable for the crimes they commit and may be held liable for the actions of employees under their supervision.
Crimes Affecting Business (See pages 153–154.)	1. *Robbery*—The forceful and unlawful taking of personal property of any value from another. 2. *Burglary*—At common law, defined as breaking and entering the dwelling of another at night with the intent to commit a felony. State statutes now vary in their definitions of burglary.

Chapter Summary • Criminal Law, Continued

Crimes Affecting Business—continued	3. *Larceny*—The wrongful or fraudulent taking and carrying away of another's personal property with the intent to deprive the owner permanently of the property. 4. *Obtaining goods by false pretenses*—An example of this crime is cashing a check knowing that there are insufficient funds in the bank to cover it. 5. *Receiving stolen goods*—This is a crime if the recipient knew or should have known that the goods were stolen. 6. *Forgery*—The fraudulent making or altering of any writing in a way that changes the legal rights and liabilities of another. 7. *Arson*—The willful and malicious burning of a building or (in some states) personal property owned by another.
White-Collar Crimes (See pages 155–159.)	1. *Embezzlement*—The fraudulent appropriation of another person's property or funds by a person to whom the property or funds were entrusted. 2. *Mail and wire fraud*—Using the mails, wires, radio, or television to defraud the public. 3. *Computer crime*—Any act that is directed against computers and computer parts, that uses computers as instruments of crime, or that involves computers and constitutes abuse. Computer crime includes financial crimes that involve computers; theft of computer software, equipment, data, or services; and vandalism and destructive programming of computers. Some federal and state laws have been enacted specifically to deal with computer crimes. 4. *Bribery*—Includes bribery of public officials, commercial bribery, and bribery of foreign officials. The crime of bribery is committed when the bribe is tendered. 5. *Bankruptcy fraud*—Encompasses crimes committed in connection with bankruptcy proceedings, including false claims of creditors and fraudulent transfers of assets by debtors. 6. *Money laundering*—Establishing legitimate enterprises through which "dirty" money (obtained through criminal activities) can be "laundered." 7. *Insider trading*—The buying or selling of corporate securities by a person in possession of material nonpublic information in violation of securities laws. 8. *Theft of trade secrets*—The theft of another's trade secrets was made a crime by the federal Economic Espionage Act of 1996. 9. *Criminal RICO violations*—Include the use of legitimate business enterprises to shield racketeering activity, securities fraud, and mail fraud.
Defenses to Criminal Liability (See pages 159–163.)	1. *Infancy.* 2. *Intoxication.* 3. *Insanity.* 4. *Mistake.* 5. *Consent.* 6. *Duress.* 7. *Justifiable use of force.* 8. *Entrapment.* 9. *Statute of limitations.* 10. *Immunity.*
Constitutional Safeguards and Criminal Procedures (See pages 164–168.)	1. *Fourth Amendment*—Provides protection against unreasonable searches and seizures and requires that no warrants for a search or an arrest can be issued without probable cause. 2. *Fifth Amendment*—Requires due process of law, prohibits double jeopardy, and protects against self-incrimination. 3. *Sixth Amendment*—Provides guarantees of a speedy trial, a trial by jury, a public trial, the right to confront witnesses, and the right to counsel. 4. *Eighth Amendment*—Prohibits excessive bail and fines, and cruel and unusual punishment.

Chapter Summary • Criminal Law, Continued

Constitutional Safeguards and Criminal Procedures—continued	5. *Exclusionary rule*—A criminal procedural rule that prohibits the introduction at trial of all evidence obtained in violation of constitutional rights, as well as any evidence derived from the illegally obtained evidence. 6. *Miranda rule*—A rule set forth by the Supreme Court in *Miranda v. Arizona* that individuals who are arrested must be informed of certain constitutional rights, including their right to counsel.
Criminal Process (See pages 168–171.)	1. *Arrest, indictment, and trial*—Procedures governing arrest, indictment, and trial for a crime are designed to safeguard the rights of the individual against the state. See Exhibit 6–3 for the steps involved in prosecuting a criminal case. 2. *Sentencing guidelines*—Both the federal government and the states have established sentencing laws or guidelines. The federal sentencing guidelines indicate a range of penalties for each federal crime; federal judges must abide by these guidelines when imposing sentences on those convicted of federal crimes. "Three strikes" laws have been passed by many states as well as the federal government.

For Review

1. What is the difference between criminal law and civil law?
2. What two elements must exist before a person can be held liable for a crime? Can a corporation be liable for crimes?
3. List and describe five crimes affecting business. Give five examples of white-collar crimes.
4. What defenses might be raised by criminal defendants to avoid liability for criminal acts?
5. What constitutional safeguards exist to protect persons accused of crimes? What are the basic steps in the criminal process?

Questions and Case Problems

6–1. Criminal versus Civil Trials. In criminal trials, the defendant must be proved guilty beyond a reasonable doubt, whereas in civil trials, the defendant need only be proved guilty by a preponderance of the evidence. Discuss why a higher standard of proof is required in criminal trials.

6–2. Types of Crimes. The following situations are similar (all involve the theft of Makoto's television set), yet they represent three different crimes. Identify the three crimes, noting the differences among them.

(a) While passing Makoto's house one night, Sarah sees a portable television set left unattended on Makoto's lawn. Sarah takes the television set, carries it home, and tells everyone she owns it.

(b) While passing Makoto's house one night, Sarah sees Makoto outside with a portable television set. Holding Makoto at gunpoint, Sarah forces him to give up the set. Then Sarah runs away with it.

(c) While passing Makoto's house one night, Sarah sees a portable television set in a window. Sarah breaks the front-door lock, enters, and leaves with the set.

6–3. Types of Crimes. Which, if any, of the following crimes necessarily involve illegal activity on the part of more than one person?

(a) Bribery.
(b) Forgery.
(c) Embezzlement.
(d) Larceny.
(e) Receiving stolen property.

6–4. Double Jeopardy. Armington, while robbing a drugstore, shot and seriously injured a drugstore clerk, Jennings.

Armington was subsequently convicted in a criminal trial of armed robbery and assault and battery. Jennings later brought a civil tort suit against Armington for damages. Armington contended that he could not be tried again for the same crime, as that would constitute double jeopardy, which is prohibited by the Fifth Amendment to the Constitution. Is Armington correct? Explain.

6–5. Receiving Stolen Property. Rafael stops Laura on a busy street and offers to sell her an expensive wristwatch for a fraction of its value. After some questioning by Laura, Rafael admits that the watch is stolen property, although he says he was not the thief. Laura pays for and receives the wristwatch. Has Laura committed any crime? Has Rafael? Explain.

6–6. Embezzlement. Slemmer, who had been a successful options trader, gave lectures to small groups about stock options. Several persons who attended his lectures decided to invest in stock options and have Slemmer advise them. They formed an investment club called Profit Design Group (PDG). Slemmer set up an account for PDG with a brokerage firm. Slemmer had control of the PDG account and could make decisions on which stock options to buy or sell. He was not authorized to withdraw money from the account for his own benefit. Nonetheless, he withdrew money from the PDG account to make payments on personal loans. Slemmer made false representations to the members of PDG, and he eventually lost all the money in their account. A jury found him guilty of first degree theft by embezzlement. Slemmer objected to the trial court's failure to instruct the jury that an intent to permanently deprive was an element of the crime charged. Is intent to permanently deprive another of property a required element for the crime of embezzlement? Discuss fully. [*State v. Slemmer,* 48 Wash.App. 48, 738 P.2d 281 (1987)]

6–7. Self-Defense. Bernardy came to the defense of his friend Harrison in a fight with Wilson. Wilson started the fight, and after Harrison knocked Wilson down, Bernardy (who was wearing tennis shoes) kicked Wilson several times in the head. Bernardy stated that he did so because he believed an onlooker, Gowens, would join forces with Wilson against Harrison. Bernardy maintained that his use of force was justifiable because he was protecting another (Harrison) from injury. Discuss whether Bernardy's use of force to protect Harrison from harm was justified. [*State v. Bernardy,* 25 Wash.App. 146, 605 P.2d 791 (1980)]

6–8. Criminal Liability. In January 1988, David Ludvigson was hired as chief executive officer of Leopard Enterprises, a group of companies that owned funeral homes and cemeteries in Iowa and sold "pre-need" funeral contracts. Under Iowa law, 80 percent of monies obtained under such a contract must be set aside in trust until the death of the person for whose benefit the funds were paid. Shortly after Ludvigson was hired, the firm began having financial difficulties. Ludvigson used money from these contracts to pay operating expenses until the company went bankrupt and was placed in receivership. Ludvigson was charged and found guilty on five counts of second degree theft stemming from the misappropriation of these funds. He appealed, alleging, among other things, that because none of the victims whose trust funds were used to cover operating expenses was denied services, no injury was done and thus no crime was committed. Will the court agree with Ludvigson? Explain. [*State v. Ludvigson,* 482 N.W.2d 419 (Iowa 1992)]

6–9. Defenses to Criminal Liability. The Child Protection Act of 1984 makes it a crime to receive knowingly through the mails sexually explicit depictions of children. After this act was passed, government agents found Keith Jacobson's name on a bookstore's mailing list. (Jacobson previously had ordered and received from a bookstore two *Bare Boys* magazines containing photographs of nude preteen and teenage boys.) To test Jacobson's willingness to break the law, government agencies sent mail to him, through five fictitious organizations and a bogus pen pal, over a period of two and a half years. Many of these "organizations" claimed that they had been founded to protect sexual freedom, freedom of choice, and so on. Jacobson eventually ordered a magazine. He testified at trial that he ordered the magazine because he was curious about "all the trouble and the hysteria over pornography and I wanted to see what the material was." When the magazine was delivered, he was arrested for violating the 1984 act. What defense discussed in this chapter might Jacobson raise to avoid criminal liability under the act? Explain fully. [*Jacobson v. United States,* 503 U.S. 540, 112 S.Ct. 1535, 118 L.Ed.2d 174 (1992)]

6–10. Searches and Seizures. The city of Ferndale enacted an ordinance regulating massage parlors. Among other things, the ordinance provided for periodic inspections of the establishments by "[t]he chief of police or other authorized inspectors from the City." Operators and employees of massage parlors in Ferndale filed a suit in a Michigan state court against the city. The plaintiffs pointed out that the ordinance did not require a warrant to conduct a search and argued in part that this was a violation of the Fourth Amendment. On what ground might the court uphold the ordinance? Do massage parlors qualify on this ground? Why or why not? [*Gora v. City of Ferndale,* 456 Mich. 704, 576 N.W.2d 141 (1998)]

A QUESTION OF ETHICS AND SOCIAL RESPONSIBILITY

6–11. A troublesome issue concerning the constitutional privilege against self-incrimination has to do with "jail plants"—that is, placing undercover police officers in cells with criminal suspects to gain information from the suspects. For example, in one case the police placed an undercover agent, Parisi, in a jail cell block with Lloyd Perkins, who had been imprisoned on charges unrelated to the murder that Parisi was investigating. When Parisi asked Perkins if he had ever killed anyone, Perkins made statements implicating himself in the murder. Perkins was then charged with the murder. [*Illinois v. Perkins,* 496 U.S. 914, 110 S.Ct. 2394, 110 L.Ed.2d 243 (1990)]

1. Review the discussion of *Miranda v. Arizona* in this chapter's *Landmark in the Law.* Should Perkins's statements be suppressed—that is, not be treated as admissible evidence at trial—because he was not "read his rights," as required by the *Miranda* decision, prior to making his self-incriminating statements? Does *Miranda* apply to Perkins's situation?
2. Do you think that it is fair for the police to resort to trickery and deception to bring those who have committed crimes to justice? Why or why not? What rights or public policies must be balanced in deciding this issue?

FOR CRITICAL ANALYSIS

6–12. Do you think that criminal procedure in this country is weighted too heavily in favor of accused persons? Can you think of a fairer way to balance the constitutional rights of accused persons against the right of society to be protected against criminal behavior? Explain.

Online Activities

ONLINE EXERCISE 6–1

Go to the following Web site, which shows a federal court's "Change of Venue Order" in a criminal case:

www.courttv.com/casefiles/oklahoma/documents/venue.html.

Read through the order, and answer the following questions:

- Who were the defendants in this case, and with what crimes were they charged?
- What was the original venue for the trial?
- Who requested a change of venue, and why?
- What constitutional provisions did the court cite as relevant to the request for a change of venue?
- According to the federal procedural rule that is based on these constitutional provisions, in what circumstances will a change of venue be permitted?
- Why did the court grant a change of venue?

Before the Test

Go to the *Business Law Today* home page at http://blt.westbuslaw.com. Click on TestTutor.® You will find twenty interactive questions relating to this chapter.

CHAPTER 7

Cyberlaw in the Legal Environment

"The Internet, by virtue of its ability to mesh what will be hundreds of millions of people together, . . . is . . . a profoundly different capability that by and large human beings have not had before."

Tony Rutkowski, 1943–
(Executive director of the Internet Society, 1994–1996)

CONTENTS

LEARNING OBJECTIVES

After reading this chapter, you should be able to:

1. Describe the circumstances in which a court can exercise jurisdiction over a party who conducts business over the Internet.
2. Discuss the limits that the Constitution imposes on government restrictions of Web site access and content.
3. Give examples of laws that can be applied to criminal and tortious acts in cyberspace.
4. Indicate what legal protection exists for trademarks, copyrights, and other intellectual property existing in digital form.
5. Identify the legal framework for transacting business in cyberspace.

Technology affects business practices and, for this reason, can affect business law. Cyberspace, the Internet, and the World Wide Web represent the latest in technological developments. In general, the law is attempting to catch up with, to paraphrase the opening quotation, these profoundly different capabilities that we have not had before.

There are three aspects to this new technology that are affecting the law. First, the new technology represents mass communication on an unprecedented scale. Geographical limits do not apply. Any person or business with a computer has a potential worldwide audience. Second, this mass communication does not originate from a few central locations. Physical and political limits do not apply. Third, information on the Internet is highly changeable. A database can be easily downloaded and its data changed and passed on without detection.

These factors challenge the traditional governmental means for controlling the use and communication of information. In fact, they imply that complete government monitoring and control of cyberspace is impractical, unrealistic, and probably impossible. Some observers argue that the law does not, or should not, apply in cyberspace. Others think that the law is responding too slowly to technological developments. Still others contend that it is not necessary to change the law to respond to the developments. How the law is currently dealing with these factors is the subject of this chapter.

The Courts

The courts are overloaded. Court dockets are packed, record-keeping facilities are bulging, judges are overwhelmed—and still more plaintiffs are filing more suits. Technological developments, including the Internet, promise to relieve some of this burden, providing that the courts, the parties, and their attorneys are willing to use technology. One problem that the new technology has caused and cannot solve, however, is the threshold issue of jurisdiction. We discuss both of these topics in the following sections.

Changes in Practices and Procedures

In the filing of pleadings and other documents, and in the issuance of decisions and opinions, courts will switch from the use of paper to the use of electronic means. Technology can save judges, lawyers, litigants, and court personnel time and overhead. Technology can reduce storage space, paperwork, and drudgery, and it can speed up legal research.

Electronic Filing Filing documents with a court by electronic means may involve a transfer over the Internet, a transmission through an electronic mail (e-mail) system, or a delivery of a computer disk.[1] The Judicial Conference of the United States has established technical standards and guidelines for electronic filing in federal courts. As of this writing, more than a dozen federal courts allow online filing of pleadings. They do not all currently use the same methods, but that will change when it becomes clear which approach and which technology works best.

State and local courts also are setting up electronic court filing systems in whole, or at least in part. Electronic filing projects are being developed in several states, including Kansas and Virginia. In Utah, the courts use an electronic filing system for criminal cases. A court in Michigan encourages attorneys to file briefs as attachments to e-mail messages. In California, Florida, and other states, some court clerks offer docket information and other searchable databases online.

These examples indicate that the courts have just begun to exploit the cost-saving and information-sharing features of the Internet. The Administrative Office of the U.S. Courts is looking for a new electronic case-management system. The new system will be set up in most federal courts. The system will provide electronic filing and document management capabilities, as well case-management features (details

1. *Yukiyo, Ltd. v. Watanabe,* 111 F.3d 883 (Fed.Cir. 1997). In this case the appellant filed a brief on CD-ROM using an Internet browser interface. Every citation was in the form of a hyperlink. The brief also contained the entire trial record, including a transcript, and an audio-video appendix with deposition testimony. For an example of a hyperlinked court opinion, see the decision in *C.L.I.C. Electronics International, Inc. v. Casio, Inc.,* 975 F.Supp. 1343 (M.D.Fla. 1997), at **www.fedjudge.org/96-929.htm**.

> **ON THE WEB**
> The Washtenaw County Trial Court in Michigan provides an excellent example of what a court can do at a site on the Web at www.co.washtenaw.mi.us/depts/courts/index.htm.

about cases that would normally be in paper files, appointment books, accounting systems, and personal computers).

Courts Online Most courts have sites on the Web. Of course, it is up to each court to decide what to make available at its site. Some courts display only the names of court personnel and office phone numbers. Others add court rules and forms. Some include judicial decisions, although generally the sites do not feature archives of old decisions. Instead, the time within which decisions are available online is limited. For example, California keeps opinions online for only sixty days.[2] The official opening Web page for the opinions of the California state courts at www.courtinfo.ca.gov/opinions is illustrated in Exhibit 7–1.

• VIRTUAL COURTROOM
A courtroom that is conceptual and not physical. In the context of cyberspace, a virtual courtroom could be a location on the Internet at which judicial proceedings take place.

Someday, we may see the use of **virtual courtrooms,** in which judicial proceedings take place only on the Internet. The parties to a case could meet online to make their arguments and present their evidence. This might be done with e-mail submissions, through video cameras, in designated "chat" rooms, at closed sites, or through the use of any other Internet facility. These courtrooms could be efficient and economical. Will we also see the use of virtual lawyers, judges, or juries—computers or software replacing court personnel? How would this affect the application of the law? Would removing the "human" aspect of justice make radical changes to the legal system we know? These are questions for the future.

2. Older judicial opinions are available at other sites. As of this writing, however, except for the decisions of the United States Supreme Court and some opinions in classic cases, there are not many court decisions available that predate the 1990s.

EXHIBIT 7–1 • Opening Web Page for California Court Opinions

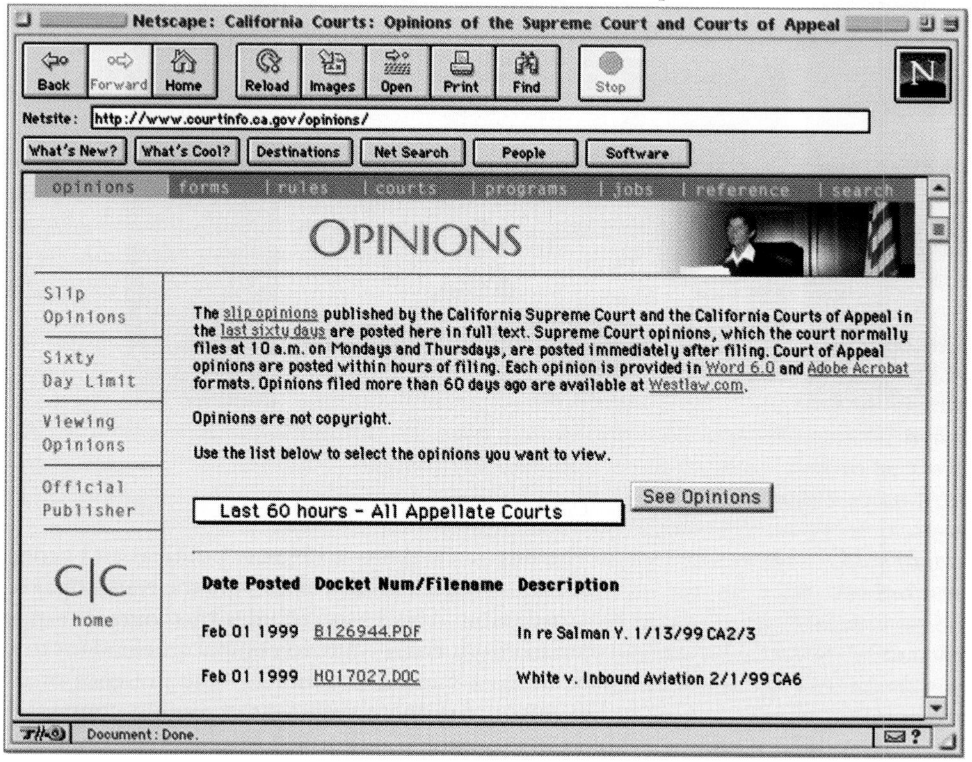

Technology and State Court Trials

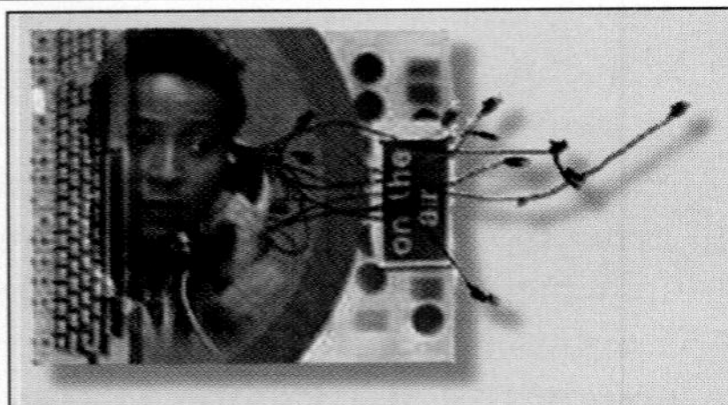

Most states permits cameras to broadcast state court trials, but it is up to each individual judge to decide whether to allow a particular trial to be broadcast. (Cameras are not allowed in federal courts.) Court Television Network (Court TV) is a round-the-clock, cable, legal news network dedicated to reporting on the U.S. judicial systems. Court TV's programming includes the broadcast of state court trials. Court TV broadcasts civil and criminal trials, live and on videotape. Attorneys supplement the broadcasts with commentary to explain the proceedings to the more than thirty-three million viewers of the network.

Begun in 1991, Court TV is owned by Liberty Programming Corporation, National Broadcasting Corporation, and Time Warner, Inc. In determining what trials to broadcast, the network considers "how important and interesting the issues in the case are; the newsworthiness of the case and the people involved; the quality and educational value of the trial; and the expected length of the trial."[a]

Court TV Online, at courttv.com, is a Web site that features Court TV program guides, as well as updates on Court TV trials and other aspects of the law. The site contains court documents, transcripts of legal proceedings, legal news, and discussion groups about the law. The site includes streaming video clips, which are updated daily. The video clips include background information on the broadcast trials, highlights of the attorneys' opening statements, important testimony, the attorneys' closing arguments, and the trial verdicts. Links to the clips are included in the daily trial updates.

Court TV also sponsors Citizens for Court TV, an effort to encourage viewers to lobby for more broadcast coverage of the trials in their communities and in the federal courts.

THE HOME PAGE OF COURT TV ONLINE. WHY DOES COURT TV LOBBY TO HAVE MORE TRIALS OPEN TO LIVE COVERAGE?

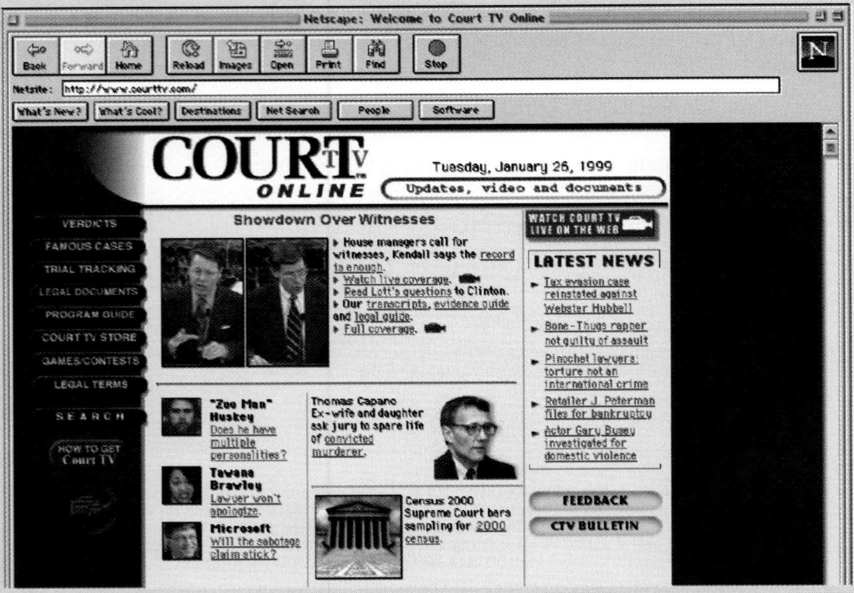

FOR CRITICAL ANALYSIS

Why would a judge choose not to authorize the broadcast of a particular trial?

a. This statement was made on the Web page at courttv.com/about.

JURISDICTION IN CYBERSPACE

The Internet's ability to bypass political and geographical boundaries makes it revolutionary. This ability undercuts the traditional basis for a court to assert personal jurisdiction. This basis includes the contacts a party has with a court's geographic jurisdiction. For a court to compel a defendant to come before the court, there must be at least minimum contacts—the presence of a salesperson within the state, for example. Are there sufficient minimum contacts if the only connection to a jurisdiction is an ad on the Web originating from a remote location?

● **EXAMPLE 7.1** Adam lives in Florida. Carol, who lives in New York and has never been to Florida or done business with anyone in Florida, advertises her business on the Web. Carol's home page has received hundreds of "hits" by residents of Florida. Adam files a suit against Carol in a Florida state court. Can the court compel Carol to appear?

On the one hand, it could be argued that Carol knows (or should know) that her Web site could be accessed by residents of Florida, and by advertising her business on the Web, she should reasonably expect to be called into court there. If this reasoning is applied, then setting up a Web site could subject the owner to a suit anywhere that the site can be accessed. Some courts have upheld exercises of jurisdiction on the basis of the accessibility of a Web page.[3]

On the other hand, it could be argued that it is not possible for Carol to set up a Web page that excludes residents of Florida (or of any other specific jurisdiction). With this in mind, it would seem unreasonable and unfair to subject Carol to the possible personal jurisdiction of every court in the United States and maybe the world. For this reason, some courts have concluded that without more, a presence on the Web is not enough to support jurisdiction over nonresident defendants.[4] ●

Recently, a new standard is becoming generally accepted for evaluating the exercise of jurisdiction based on contacts over the Internet. This standard is a "sliding scale." On this scale, a court's exercise of personal jurisdiction depends on the amount of business that an individual or firm transacts over the Internet. The standard is explained more fully in the following case.

3. See, for example, *Minnesota v. Granite Gates Resorts, Inc.*, 568 N.W.2d 715 (Minn.App. 1997).
4. See, for example, *Weber v. Jolly Hotels*, 977 F.Supp. 327 (D.N.J. 1997).

CASE 7.1 Zippo Manufacturing Co. v. Zippo Dot Com, Inc.

United States District Court,
Western District of Pennsylvania, 1997.
952 F.Supp. 1119.
zeus.bna.com/e-law/cases/zippo.html[a]

HISTORICAL AND TECHNOLOGICAL SETTING

*In a case decided before 1960, the United States Supreme Court noted that "[a]s technological progress has increased the flow of commerce between States, the need for jurisdiction has undergone a similar increase."[b] Twenty-seven years later, the Court observed that jurisdiction could not be avoided "merely because the defendant did not physically enter the forum state. * * * [I]t is an inescapable fact of modern commercial life that a substantial amount of commercial business is transacted solely by mail and wire communications across state lines."[c] The Internet makes it possible to do business anywhere in the world entirely from a desktop.*

a. This is a page at the "Electronic Commerce & Law Report" maintained by the Bureau of National Affairs, Inc.
b. *Hanson v. Denckla*, 357 U.S. 235, 78 S.Ct. 1228, 2 L.Ed.2d 1283 (1958).
c. *Burger King Corp. v. Rudzewicz*, 471 U.S. 462, 105 S.Ct. 2174, 85 L.Ed.2d 528 (1985).

BACKGROUND AND FACTS

Zippo Manufacturing Company (ZMC) makes, among other things, "Zippo" lighters. Zippo Dot Com, Inc. (ZDC), operates a Web page and an Internet subscription news service. ZDC has the exclusive right to use the domain names "zippo.com," "zippo.net," and "zipponews.com." ZMC is based in Pennsylvania. ZDC is based in California, and its contacts with Pennsylvania have occurred almost exclusively over the Internet. Two percent of its subscribers (3,000 of 140,000) are Pennsylvania residents who contracted over the Internet to receive its service. Also, ZDC has agreements with seven ISPs in Pennsylvania to permit their subscribers to access the service. ZMC filed a suit in

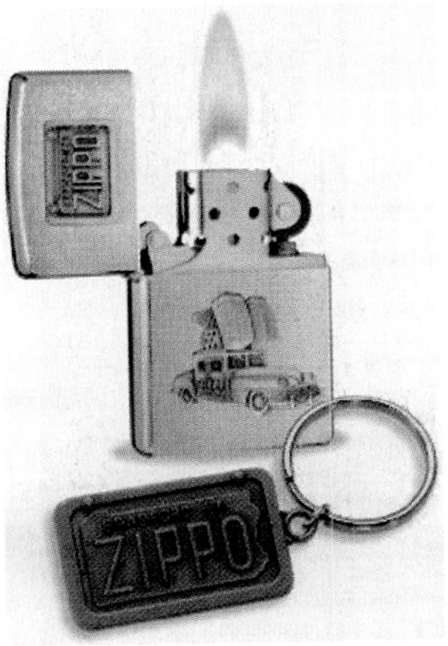

(Continued)

CASE 7.1—Continued

a federal district court against ZDC, alleging trademark infringement and other claims, based on ZDC's use of the word "Zippo." ZDC filed a motion to dismiss for lack of personal jurisdiction.

IN THE WORDS OF THE COURT . . .
McLAUGHLIN, District Judge.

* * * *

* * * [T]he likelihood that personal jurisdiction can be constitutionally exercised is directly proportionate to the nature and quality of commercial activity that an entity conducts over the Internet. * * * At one end of the spectrum are situations where a defendant clearly does business over the Internet. If the defendant enters into contracts with residents of a foreign jurisdiction that involve the knowing and repeated transmission of computer files over the Internet, personal jurisdiction is proper. At the opposite end are situations where a defendant has simply posted information on an Internet Web site which is accessible to users in foreign jurisdictions. A passive Web site that does little more than make information available to those who are interested in it is not grounds for the exercise of personal jurisdiction. The middle ground is occupied by interactive Web sites where a user can exchange information with the host computer. In these cases, the exercise of jurisdiction is determined by examining the level of interactivity and commercial nature of the exchange of information that occurs on the Web site.

* * * *

* * * We are being asked to determine whether [ZDC's] conducting of electronic commerce with Pennsylvania residents constitutes * * * doing business in Pennsylvania. We conclude that it does. [ZDC] has contracted with approximately 3,000 individuals and seven Internet access providers in Pennsylvania. The intended object of these transactions has been the downloading of the electronic messages that form the basis of this suit in Pennsylvania.

DECISION AND REMEDY The court held that it has jurisdiction over parties who conduct substantial business in its jurisdiction exclusively over the Internet. The court concluded that ZDC fits this description and denied the motion to dismiss.

FOR CRITICAL ANALYSIS—Political Consideration
To what extent should a person who sends e-mail over the Internet be subject to jurisdiction in states or countries other than his or her own?

The Constitution

"The interest in encouraging freedom of expression in a democratic society outweighs any theoretical but unproven benefit of censorship."

JOHN PAUL STEVENS,
1920–
(Associate justice of the United States Supreme Court, 1975–)

To date, most of the Internet and new technology issues raised under the Constitution involve regulations of the freedom of speech. Legal challenges to laws that attempt to inhibit speech have generally been most successful when based on the commerce clause or the First Amendment. (For a discussion of the commerce clause, see Chapter 2.)

The problem is related to the unique feature of the Internet—its ability to cross political and geographic borders—and the inability of current technology to effectively filter out what legislators and government regulators would like to block. The issues are not unique to the United States. China and some European countries, among other nations, also attempt to block what their governments believe is bad for their citizens.

One of the basic questions concerns how much freedom of speech we are willing to sacrifice to allow the government to further a particular value, such as shielding children from certain material or preventing terrorism and crime. Phrased another way, how much of any value are we willing to sacrifice to protect our freedom of speech? There is no clear, definite answer to this question. Generally, the courts hold that speech may be restricted to serve a *compelling interest* but only if the restriction is the *least restrictive means* of doing so. (See Chapter 2 for definitions of these italicized terms and for a fuller discussion of freedom of speech.)

IS AN ENCRYPTION CODE SPEECH?

Privacy is one of the primary worries of most of those who use the Internet. It is possible to "eavesdrop" on Internet communications. The wrong person might learn your credit-card number when you enter it to make an online purchase. Your Social Security number might be revealed when it is passed through cyberspace. Details of your business transactions or personal details of your private life might be revealed to persons to whom you would not otherwise give such information.

• **ENCRYPTION**
The process by which a message (plaintext) is transformed into something (ciphertext) that the sender and receiver intend third parties not to understand.

Encryption is the process by which a message (plaintext) is transformed into something (ciphertext) that the sender and receiver intend third parties not to understand. Decryption is the process of transforming ciphertext into plaintext. An encryption code is a program used in encryption software to transform plaintext into ciphertext and vice versa. This software includes source codes, object codes, applications software, and system software.

Law enforcement authorities are afraid that the wrong persons, including international terrorists, will take advantage of Internet security to engage in illegal activities. For this reason, U.S. Department of Commerce regulations prohibit the export of encryption code.[5] (The export of cryptography is also a violation of a federal criminal statute that is discussed later in this chapter.) This prohibition has been challenged in a few cases on the ground that an encryption code is speech and therefore protected by the First Amendment. That would mean that the regulations banning its export are unconstitutional.[6] In a recent case, however, a federal district court held that an encryption code is not speech, because its purpose is to "transfer functions, not to communicate ideas."[7]

RESTRICTING THE CONTENTS OF WEB SITES

The Communications Decency Act (CDA) of 1996 sought to protect minors from harmful material on the Internet by taking a broad approach. The CDA made it a crime to make available to minors online any "obscene or indecent" message that "depicts or describes, in terms patently offensive as measured by contemporary community standards, sexual or excretory activities or organs."[8]

The United States Supreme Court disapproved of this approach and ruled that portions of the act were unconstitutional.[9] The Court said that "[t]he general, undefined terms 'indecent' and 'patently offensive' cover large amounts of nonpornographic material with serious educational or other value. Moreover, the 'community standards' criterion as applied to the Internet means that any communication avail-

5. 15 C.F.R. Part 772.
6. See, for example, *Bernstein v. U.S. Department of State*, 974 F.Supp. 1288 (N.D.Cal. 1997).
7. *Junger v. Daley*, 8 F.Supp.2d 708 (N.D.Ohio 1998).
8. 47 U.S.C. Section 223(a)(1)(B)(ii).
9. *Reno v. American Civil Liberties Union*, 521 U.S. 844, 117 S.Ct. 2329, 138 L.Ed.2d 874 (1997).

A CHILD USES A COMPUTER IN A PUBLIC PLACE. TO WHAT EXTENT CAN PUBLIC INSTITUTIONS BLOCK ACCESS TO OBJECTIONABLE MATERIALS ON THE INTERNET?

ON THE WEB

According to a page within the Web site of Lehigh University, "citizens of the electronic community of learners" have fundamental rights that include a right of access to information resources. These rights are declared in the "Bill of Rights for Electronic Learners" at **www.lehigh.edu/www/www-data/bill-of-rights/top.html**.

able to a nationwide audience will be judged by the standards of the community most likely to be offended by the message."

Congress made a further attempt to regulate Internet speech in 1998. Included in the federal budget bill passed in that year was the Child Online Protection Act, which became known as CDA II. The act imposed criminal penalties on those who distribute material that is "harmful to minors" without using some kind of age-verification system to separate adult and minor users. Like the CDA of 1996, the new law was immediately challenged in court by civil rights groups.

Are there forms of speech that the government can effectively restrict online? On the Internet, extreme hate speech is known as **cyber hate speech.** Racist materials and Holocaust denials on the Web, for example, are cyber hate speech. Can the federal government restrict this type of speech? Should it? Are there other forms of speech that the government should restrict?[10] Content restrictions generally amount to censorship and can be difficult to enforce. In cyberspace, they are almost impossible to enforce.

• **CYBER HATE SPEECH** Extreme hate speech on the Internet. Racist materials and Holocaust denials disseminated on the Web are examples.

Even if it were possible to enforce content restrictions online, U.S. federal law (or the law of any single nation) is only "local" law in cyberspace—less than half of the users of the Internet are in the United States. This highlights one of the criticisms of restricting online content at its source. Such restrictions are out of step with the revolutionary nature of the Internet. Any source of content may be in a different jurisdiction than those who view it. Information may be legal in some jurisdictions and not in others.

BLOCKING ACCESS TO WEB SITES

An alternative to regulating the content of Web sites is to block access to them. An employer may want to limit what his or her employees can do in cyberspace during

10. The content of some speech is regulated to a certain extent by tort law, copyright law, and other laws. See, for example, the discussions of defamation, cyber fraud, and copyright infringement later in this chapter and in Chapters 4 and 5.

• **FILTERING SOFTWARE**
A computer program that includes a pattern through which data are passed. When designed to block access to certain Web sites, the pattern blocks the retrieval of a site whose URL or key words are on a list within the program.

• **TAG**
A key word in a document that can serve as an index reference to the document. On the Web, search engines return results based, in part, on the tags in Web documents.

working hours. A parent may wish to block what his or her child views on the Internet. **Filtering software,** or filters, can prevent certain persons from viewing certain Web sites at certain times by responding to a site's uniform resource locator (URL), or Internet address, or its **tags,** or key words. This technology is at the core of the current debate on the control and regulation of information on the Internet.

There are questions about the software and whether it effectively does what it claims to do. There are questions about the tags: What should they consist of, and who should decide which sites have which tags? Using filters to control the accessibility of information on the Internet also raises questions about the relationship of technology to law. Because the First Amendment is aimed at curtailing the government's power to censor speech, the fundamental question is whether the law should apply in cyberspace, and if so, how it should operate.

The debate centers on the use of filters by government employers, public schools, and public libraries. In its opinion in the *Reno v. American Civil Liberties Union* case noted above, the United States Supreme Court seemed to approve of the use of filters as a "less restrictive alternative." But is it constitutional for a public library to install filtering software on its public access computers? The court addressed this issue in the following case.

CASE 7.2 Mainstream Loudoun v. Board of Trustees of the Loudoun County Library

United States District Court,
Eastern District of Virginia, 1998.
2 F.Supp.2d 783.
www.techlawjournal.com/courts/loudon/80407mem.htm[a]

HISTORICAL AND TECHNOLOGICAL SETTING *One of the costly features of a library has always been the amount of time and financial resources required to expand its collection. Unlike a collection of individual books, the Internet is a single, linked system. The Internet might be compared to a set of encyclopedias. With access to the Internet, a user has access to all Internet publications instantly. Unlike looking for and buying a book, it does not take any appreciable amount of time or resources to view a particular Internet publication. In effect, by accessing the Internet, a user has bought everything on it. The United States Supreme Court has described the Internet as a "vast library including millions of readily available and indexed publications," the content of which "is as diverse as human thought."*[b]

a. This Web site is called "Tech Law Journal" ("News, records, and analysis of legislation, litigation, and regulation affecting the computer and Internet industry"), which claims not to be affiliated with "any company, interest group, political party, or other political entity."

BACKGROUND AND FACTS The Board of Trustees of the Loudoun County Library in Virginia opted to provide Internet access for its patrons. The board also adopted a "Policy on Internet Sexual Harassment." This required that Web site blocking software be installed on all library computers to "a. block child pornography and obscene material (hard core pornography)" and "b. block material deemed harmful to juveniles under applicable Virginia statutes and legal precedents (soft core pornography)." Mainstream Loudoun, an association of individuals, claimed that this policy blocked their access to such sites as the Quaker Home Page. Mainstream filed a suit in a federal district court against the board, alleging that this was an unconstitutional restriction on their right to access protected speech on the Internet. The board filed a motion for summary judgment.

b. *Reno v. American Civil Liberties Union,* 521 U.S. 844, 117 S.Ct. 2329, 138 L.Ed.2d 874 (1997).

IN THE WORDS OF THE COURT . . .
BRINKEMA, District Judge.

* * * *

* * * [T]he First Amendment applies to, and limits, the discretion of a public library to place content-based restrictions on access to constitutionally protected materials within its collection. * * *

(Continued)

CASE 7.2—Continued

* * * *

* * * [C]ontent-based restrictions on speech must be justified by a compelling governmental interest and must be narrowly tailored to achieve that end. * * *

This * * * does not obligate defendants to act as unwilling conduits of information, because the Library Board need not provide access to the Internet at all. Having chosen to provide access, however, the Library Board may not thereafter selectively restrict certain categories of Internet speech because it disfavors their content. * * *

* * * *

* * * [E]ven when government regulation of content is undertaken for a legitimate purpose, whether it be to prevent the communication of obscene speech or materials harmful to children, the means it uses must be a reasonable response to the threat which will alleviate the harm in a direct and material way. Plaintiffs have adequately alleged a lack of such reasonable means here.

DECISION AND REMEDY The court held that the First Amendment limits the decisions of a public library on whether to restrict its patrons' access to information on the Internet. The court denied the board's motion for summary judgment.

FOR CRITICAL ANALYSIS—Political Consideration *Should libraries and other public institutions be obligated to offer Internet access to the public?*

International Perspective • CONTROLLING INTERNET ACCESS AND CONTENT

The freedom of expression includes the right "to receive and impart information and ideas without interference by public authority and regardless of borders," according to Article 10 of the European Convention for the Protection of Human Rights and Fundamental Freedoms. In theory, international law claims to value this freedom. In practice, many countries attempt to undercut it.

Governments all over the globe attempt to impose restrictions on Internet access and content. These limits are sometimes imposed for reasons of political control. Some governments, including those of India and Saudi Arabia, attempt to control the political effect that communications over the Internet might have on their citizens by charging high prices for access or by limiting access to certain groups. Other governments, such as those of China, Singapore, and Iran, target the flow of information itself by trying to censor pro-democracy discussions and human rights education.

One of the main targets of the political censors are the Usenet groups (newsgroups), because of their potential for increasing the political participation of their members. Other targets include general business information services and news services, which are sometimes subject to censorship before subscribers can access them. Censorship can be accomplished by requiring that all data be routed through government-owned telephone companies. This routing illustrates a second reason for government control of the Internet: economic gain.

FOR CRITICAL ANALYSIS
Should there be an internationally recognized right of access to the Internet?

Cyber Crimes

• **CYBER CRIME**
A crime that occurs online, in the virtual community of the Internet, as opposed to the physical world.

A **cyber crime** is a crime that occurs in the virtual community of the Internet. Some of these crimes are discussed in the following subsections.

The "location" of cyber crime—cyberspace—raises new issues in the investigation and prosecution of perpetrators and crimes. It is the unique nature of the Internet that causes one of the toughest problems in enforcing laws against cyber crimes: the issue of jurisdiction. • EXAMPLE 7.2 A person who commits an act against a business in California, where the act is a cyber crime, might never have set foot in California but instead might reside in New York, or even in Canada, where the act may not be a crime. If the crime were committed via e-mail, would the e-mail constitute sufficient "minimum contacts" for the victim's state to exercise jurisdiction? •

Other difficulties include identifying the perpetrators. Cyber criminals do not leave physical traces, such as fingerprints or DNA samples, as evidence of their crimes. Even electronic "footprints" can be hard to find and follow. For example, e-mail may be sent through a remailer, an online service that guarantees that a message cannot be traced to its source.

CYBER STALKING

California enacted the first stalking law in 1990, in response to the contemporary murders of six women—including Rebecca Schaeffer, a television star—by the men who had harassed them. The law made it a crime to harass or follow a person while making a "credible threat" that put that person in reasonable fear for his or her safety or the safety of the person's immediate family.[11] Most other states have also enacted stalking laws.

• **CYBER STALKER**
A person who commits the crime of stalking in cyberspace. Generally, stalking consists of harassing a person and putting that person in reasonable fear for his or her safety or the safety of the person's immediate family.

Generally speaking, the laws in about half of the states require a physical act (following the victim). **Cyber stalkers**—stalkers who commit their crimes in cyberspace—find their victims through Internet relay chat (or live chat), Usenet newsgroups or other bulletin boards, and e-mail connections. None of these communications requires that a stalker physically "follow" his or her prey. For this reason, these statutes do not apply in the virtual community. About three-quarters of the laws in the other states *could* apply in cyberspace, because those statutes deem tools of harassment to include written communications (e-mail) or telephones (Internet connections).

As of this writing, seven states have statutes that specifically address stalking by computer, or cyber stalking. It is also a federal crime to harass someone by means of interstate "telecommunications devices."[12] Some of the state statutes are based on California's law and require a "credible threat." Others require only an intention to harass, annoy, or alarm.[13]

CYBER THEFT

In cyberspace, thieves are not subject to the physical limitations of the "real" world. A thief can steal data stored in a networked computer with dial-in access from anywhere on the globe. Only the speed of the connection and the thief's computer equipment limit the quantity of data that can be stolen.

For this reason, laws written to protect physical property are difficult to apply in cyberspace. For example, the federal statute that bans the interstate transportation of stolen property refers to "goods, wares and merchandise."[14] At least one court has held that this does not to apply to intangible property such as computer data.[15]

11. Cal. Penal Code Section 646.9.
12. 47 U.S.C. Section 223 (1)(A) and (B). See also 18 U.S.C Section 875. Another possibility was indicated in 1998, when a former University of California student was convicted under federal civil rights law for sending hate e-mail to Asian students.
13. See, for example, Conn. General Statutes Sections 53a-182b and 53a-183.
14. 18 U.S.C. Section 2314.
15. *United States v. Brown*, 925 F.2d 1301, 1308 (10th Cir. 1991).

Another federal statute makes it illegal to threaten physical violence to property.[16] A threat to delete files may not qualify.

To address abuses that stem from the misuse of new technology, Congress amended the Counterfeit Access Device and Computer Fraud and Abuse Act of 1984 with the National Information Infrastructure Protection Act of 1996.[17] The 1996 act provides, among other things, that a person who accesses a computer online, without authority, to obtain classified, restricted, or protected data, or attempts to do so, is subject to criminal prosecution. These data could include financial and credit records, medical records, legal files, military and national security files, and other confidential information in government or private computers. The crime has two elements: accessing a computer without authority and taking the data.

This theft is a felony if it is committed for a commercial purpose or for private financial gain, or if the value of the stolen data (or computer time) exceeds $5,000. Penalties include fines and imprisonment for up to twenty years. A victim of computer theft can also bring a civil suit against the violator to obtain damages, an injunction, and other relief.

Persons who use one computer to break into another are sometimes referred to as **hackers.** Hackers who break into computers without authorization commit cyber theft. Often, their principal aim is to prove how smart they are by gaining access to others' password-protected computers and causing random data errors or making unpaid-for telephone calls.[18] Such crimes should not be taken lightly, but from a larger perspective, they might be considered the equivalent of new-tech car theft.

• **HACKER**
A person who uses one computer to break into another. Professional computer programmers refer to such persons as "crackers."

• **CYBER TERRORIST**
A hacker whose purpose is to exploit a target computer for a serious impact, such as the corruption of a program to sabotage a business.

ON THE WEB

The Computer Crime and Intellectual Property Section (CCIPS) of the U.S. Department of Justice is implementing a comprehensive program to address the growing global computer crime problem. Information on this topic, with links to other resources, is on the CCIPS Web page at www.usdoj.gov/criminal/cybercrime/index.html.

CYBER TERRORISM

Cyber terrorists are hackers who aim not to gain attention but to remain undetected in order to exploit computers for a more serious impact. Just as a "real" terrorist might explode a bomb to shut down an embassy, a cyber terrorist might explode a "logic bomb" to shut down a central computer. Other goals might include a wholesale theft of data, such as a merchant's customer files, or the monitoring of a computer to discover a business firm's plans and transactions. A cyber terrorist might want to insert false codes or data. For example, the processing control system of a food manufacturer could be changed to alter the levels of ingredients so that consumers of the food would become ill.

Cyber Torts

In the area of torts, as in other areas of the law affected by the new technology, there are more questions than there are answers. One of the foremost issues is the question of who should be held liable for a **cyber tort** (a tort committed in cyberspace). For example, who should be held liable when someone in a newsgroup posts a defamatory **flame** (an online message in which one party attacks another in harsh, often personal terms)? Should an Internet service provider (ISP) be liable for the remark if the ISP was unaware that it was being made? Who should be held liable for an employee's defamatory remark on a company bulletin board?

Other questions involve issues of proof. How, for example, can it be proved that an online defamatory remark was "published" (which requires that a third party see

• **CYBER TORT**
A tort committed in cyberspace.

• **FLAME**
An online message in which one party attacks another in harsh, often personal terms.

16. 18 U.S.C. Section 1951(a).
17. 18 U.S.C. Section 1030.
18. The total cost of crime on the Internet is estimated to be several billion dollars, but two-thirds of that total is said to consist of unpaid-for toll calls.

or hear it)? How can the identity of the person who made the remark be discovered? Can an ISP be forced to reveal the source of an anonymous comment? Answers to some of these questions are explored in the following sections.

DEFAMATION ONLINE: WHO IS LIABLE?

Online forums allow anyone—customers, employees, or crackpots—to complain about a business firm. The complaint could concern the firm's personnel, policies, practices, or products, and it might have an impact on the business of the firm. This is possible whether or not the complaint is justified and whether or not it is true.

If a statement is not true, it may constitute defamation. Defamation is any published or publicly spoken false statement that causes injury to another's good name, reputation, or character. Like other torts, defamation is governed by state law, and the elements of the tort can vary from state to state. As discussed in Chapter 4, generally a plaintiff must show that a statement was false, was not subject to a privilege, was communicated to a third person, and resulted in damage to the plaintiff. A public figure must also show that the statement was made with actual malice.

Newspapers, magazines, and television and radio stations may be held liable for defamatory remarks that they disseminate, even if those remarks are prepared or created by others. Under the Communications Decency Act of 1996, however, Internet service providers (ISPs), or "interactive computer service providers," are not liable with respect to such material.[19] An ISP typically provides access to the Internet through a local phone number and may provide other services, including access to databases available only to the ISP's subscribers. One of the most well known ISPs is America Online, Inc. (AOL).

As of this writing, there is no proved case of an untrue, negative posting on the Internet ruining a business. Defamation suits involving online statements have not yet resulted in decisions in U.S. courts that plaintiffs were defamed and are entitled to a remedy. The courts have focused chiefly on such issues as determining who would be held liable, which was the issue in the following case.

19. 47 U.S.C. Section 230.

CASE 7.3 Blumenthal v. Drudge

United States District Court,
District of Columbia, 1998.
992 F.Supp. 44.
www.courttv.com/legaldocs/cyberlaw/drudge2.html[a]

COMPANY PROFILE *Founded in 1985, America Online, Inc. (AOL), operates two global Internet online services: AOL Interactive Services and CompuServe Interactive Services. This makes AOL the world's largest interactive computer service, or Internet service provider. As many as fifty million subscribers or other users use AOL as a conduit to receive and disseminate huge quantities of information over its computer network. In 1998, AOL merged with Netscape. AOL's Web site is at* www.aol.com.

a. This site is Court TV Online's "Technology and Computers" section in its "Legal Documents" collection.

MATT DRUDGE. WHY WOULD A PLAINTIFF WHO ACCUSES A REPORTER OF DEFAMATION ALSO WANT TO SUE THE REPORTER'S PUBLISHER?

(Continued)

CASE 7.3—Continued

BACKGROUND AND FACTS Under a licensing agreement with America Online, Inc. (AOL), the *Drudge Report,* an online political publication, was made available free to all AOL subscribers. According to the agreement, AOL could remove content that it determined was in violation of AOL's "standard terms of service." One issue of the *Drudge Report* contained an article charging that Sidney Blumenthal, an assistant to the president of the United States, "has a spousal abuse past that has been effectively covered up." Blumenthal's spouse, Jacqueline Blumenthal, also worked in the White House as the director of a presidential commission. When the *Report's* editor, Matt Drudge, learned that the article was false, he printed a retraction and publicly apologized to the Blumenthals. The Blumenthals filed a suit in a federal district court against Drudge, AOL, and others, alleging in part that the original remarks were defamatory. AOL filed a motion for summary judgment.

IN THE WORDS OF THE COURT . . .
PAUL L. FRIEDMAN, District Judge.

* * * *

* * * AOL was nothing more than a provider of an interactive computer service on which the *Drudge Report* was carried, and Congress has said quite clearly [in the Communications Decency Act (CDA) of 1996] that such a provider shall not be treated as a "publisher or speaker" and therefore may not be held liable in tort.

* * * *

Plaintiffs make the additional argument, however, that * * * Drudge was not just an anonymous person who sent a message over the Internet through AOL. He is a person with whom AOL contracted, whom AOL paid * * * and whom AOL promoted to its subscribers and potential subscribers as a reason to subscribe to AOL. * * *

* * * *

If it were writing on a clean slate, this Court would agree with plaintiffs. * * * But Congress has made a different policy choice by providing immunity even where the interactive service provider has an active, even aggressive role in making available content prepared by others. * * * Congress has conferred immunity from tort liability as an incentive to Internet service providers to self-police the Internet for obscenity and other offensive material, even where the self-policing is unsuccessful or not even attempted.

DECISION AND REMEDY The court granted AOL's motion for summary judgment. The court held that under the CDA, an Internet service provider (ISP) is not liable for failing to edit, withhold, or restrict access to defamatory remarks which it disseminates but which it did not create.

FOR CRITICAL ANALYSIS—Technological Consideration *What other reasons might have led Congress to exempt ISPs from liability for defamation?*

IS SPAMMING TRESPASSING?

• **SPAM**
Bulk, unsolicited ("junk") e-mail.

Spam is "junk" e-mail—bulk, unsolicited e-mail—or junk newsgroup postings.[20] Typical spam consists of a product ad sent to all of the users on an e-mailing list or all of the members of a newsgroup.

Because spam can waste user time and network bandwidth (the amount of data that can be transmitted within a certain time), some individuals and organizations are

20. The term *spam* is said to come from a Monty Python song with the lyrics, "Spam spam spam spam, spam spam spam spam, lovely spam, wonderful spam." Like these lyrics, spam online is often considered to be a repetition of worthless text.

> **ON THE WEB**
> The Federal Trade Commission makes its consumer publications, including "Trouble @ the In-Box," which concerns "junk" e-mail, available at
> www.ftc.gov.

attempting to inhibit its use. The Internet is a public forum, however. Under the First Amendment (see Chapter 2), this limits what can be done to restrict the use of spam.

ETHICAL ISSUE 7.1 ***Should a business advertise itself via unsolicited e-mail?*** E-mail can be an effective tool for showcasing a business's goods and services, getting information to those who ask for it, and giving customers an easy way to place an order. E-mail that is not solicited can have a negative impact, however. A few states, such as Washington, prohibit unsolicited e-mail that has the purpose of promoting goods, services, or real estate for sale or lease. Where it is not banned, some professionals, such as lawyers, may be subject to codes of ethics that restrict its use. Even when it is not restricted, it is generally considered a violation of Netiquette, the Internet's unwritten code of conduct. The first rule of Netiquette is that e-mail ads should be directed only to existing customers or persons, such as subscribers, who ask to receive it. Netiquette also provides that a business should not spam the members of a newsgroup or post messages to other users who may not be interested in what the business is promoting. When in doubt about what is possible, a business should check with its Internet service provider.

In the following anti-spam case, an Internet service provider (ISP) argued that spamming is trespassing. Would the court accept this argument and block the sending of unsolicited ads to the ISP's subscribers?

CASE 7.4 CompuServe, Inc. v. Cyber Promotions, Inc.

United States District Court,
Southern District of Ohio, 1997.
962 F.Supp. 1015.
www.leepfrog.com/E-Law/Cases/CompuServe_v_Cyber_Promo.html[a]

HISTORICAL AND SOCIAL SETTING *Cyber Promotions, Inc., is in the business of sending unsolicited e-mail ads, or spam, to Internet users. Cases brought by Internet service providers (ISPs) against Cyber Promotions have generally had results that are unfavorable to the firm. For example, a federal district court in one case, and a California state court in another, dismissed claims against the firm only after it agreed to stop sending spam to certain ISPs' subscribers. Spam was also the subject of the first case brought before the Virtual Magistrate Project, an Internet arbitration service (arbitration is discussed in Chapter 3). In that case, EMail America, an online marketer, posted an ad on America Online (AOL). When an AOL subscriber objected, the Virtual Magistrate recommended that AOL remove the ad.*

a. This page is at the E-LAW Web Page site, "the home page of David J. Loundy, an attorney and author."

BACKGROUND AND FACTS Through a nationwide computer network, CompuServe, Inc., operates a communication service that includes e-mail for CompuServe subscribers. E-mail sent to the subscribers is processed and stored on CompuServe's equipment. CompuServe subscribers complained to the service about Cyber Promotions's ads, and many canceled their subscriptions. Handling the ads also placed a tremendous burden on CompuServe's equipment. CompuServe told Cyber Promotions to stop using CompuServe's equipment to process and store the ads—in effect, to stop sending the ads to CompuServe subscribers. Ignoring the demand, Cyber Promotions stepped up the volume of its ads. After CompuServe attempted unsuccessfully to block the flow with screening software, it filed a suit against Cyber Promotions in a federal district court, seeking an injunction on the ground that the ads constituted trespass to personal property.

IN THE WORDS OF THE COURT . . .
GRAHAM, District Judge.

* * * *

* * * [An] actor may commit a trespass by an act which brings him [or her] into an intended physical contact with a chattel [property] in the possession of another[.]

(Continued)

CASE 7.4—Continued

* * * It is undisputed that plaintiff has a possessory interest in its computer systems. Further, defendants' contact with plaintiff's computers is clearly intentional. Although electronic messages may travel through the Internet over various routes, the messages are affirmatively directed to their destination.

* * * *

* * * Harm to the personal property or diminution of its quality, condition, or value as a result of defendants' use can also be the predicate for liability. * * * To the extent that defendants' multitudinous electronic mailings demand the disk space and drain the processing power of plaintiff's computer equipment, those resources are not available to serve CompuServe subscribers. Therefore, the value of that equipment to CompuServe is diminished even though it is not physically damaged by defendants' conduct.

* * * *

Many subscribers have terminated their accounts specifically because of the unwanted receipt of bulk e-mail messages. Defendants' intrusions into CompuServe's computer systems, insofar as they harm plaintiff's business reputation and goodwill with its customers, are actionable.

DECISION AND REMEDY The court held that spamming is trespassing. The court issued an injunction, ordering Cyber Promotions to stop sending its ads to e-mail addresses maintained by CompuServe.

FOR CRITICAL ANALYSIS—Social Consideration *Are there points, in addition to those discussed by the court in this case, that would support tort causes of action against parties who send computer viruses into cyberspace?*

Virtual Property

• VIRTUAL PROPERTY
Property that, in the context of cyberspace, is conceptual, as opposed to physical. Intellectual property that exists on the Internet is virtual property.

The legal issues relating to **virtual property**—property in cyberspace—are essentially legal questions involving intellectual property. As discussed in Chapter 5, intellectual property consists of trademarks, patents, copyrights, and trade secrets. Legal protection for these forms of property makes it possible to market goods and services profitably, which provides an incentive to market competitive goods and services.

In the context of cyberspace, a fundamental issue has to do with the degree of legal protection that should be given to virtual property. If the protection is inadequate, the incentive to make new works available online will be reduced. If the protection is too strict, the free flow and fair use of data will be impaired.

Cyber Marks

• CYBER MARK
A trademark in cyberspace.

In cyberspace, trademarks are sometimes referred to as **cyber marks.** An early legal issue relating to cyber marks concerned the rights of a mark's owner to use it as part of a domain name (an Internet address). The question was whether *cybersquatting* (registering another party's mark as a domain name and offering to forfeit it for a sum of money) constituted a commercial use of the mark so as to violate federal law. Generally, the courts have held that cybersquatting does violate the law.[21]

As the dust settles around this once contentious issue, cyber mark questions that courts are more likely to confront in the future revolve around other uses and abuses of those marks. Some questions are not new, but the context of cyberspace requires new answers. Other questions, however, are as new as the technological ability to

21. See, for example, *Panavision International, L.P. v. Toeppen*, 141 F.3d 1316 (9th Cir. 1998).

create hypertext links and frames (see the *Technology and Online Trademark Infringement* feature in Chapter 5) and to imbed hidden code called *meta tags* in Web sites.

• **META TAGS**
Words inserted into a Web site's key words field to increase the site's appearance in search engine results.

Meta Tags Search engines compile their results by looking through a Web site's key words field. **Meta tags** are words that are inserted in this field to increase a site's appearance in search engine results, even if the site has nothing to do with the inserted words. Using this same technique, one site may appropriate the key words of other sites with more frequent hits, so that the appropriating site appears in the same search engine results as the more popular site. One use of meta tags was at issue in the following case.

CASE 7.5 Playboy Enterprises, Inc. v. Welles

United States District Court,
Southern District of California, 1998.
7 F.Supp.2d 1098.
www.Loundy.com/CASES/Playboy_v_Wells.html[a]

COMPANY PROFILE *Playboy Enterprises, Inc. (PEI), is an international publishing and entertainment company. Since 1953, PEI has published* Playboy *magazine, a popular magazine with approximately ten million readers each month. PEI also publishes numerous specialty magazines and other publications. In addition, PEI produces television programming for cable and satellite transmission, and sells and licenses other goods and services. PEI bestows on its models, who appear in the magazine, such titles as "Playmate of the Month" and "Playmate of the Year." PEI encourages its models to identify themselves and to use their titles for their self-promotion and the promotion of its magazines and other goods and services.*

a. This is a different URL for a page within the E-LAW site described in a footnote to Case 7.4 as "the home page of David J. Loundy, an attorney and author."

BACKGROUND AND FACTS Playboy Enterprises, Inc. (PEI), maintains Web sites to promote *Playboy* magazine and PEI models. PEI's trademarks include the terms "Playboy," "Playmate," and "Playmate of the Year." Terri Welles is a self-employed model and spokesperson, who was featured as the "Playmate of the Year" in June 1981. Welles maintains a Web site titled "Terri Welles—Playmate of the Year 1981." As meta tags, Welles's site uses the terms "Playboy" and "Playmate," among others. PEI asked Welles to stop using these terms, but she refused. PEI filed a suit in a federal district court against Welles, asking the court to order her to, among other things, stop using those terms as meta tags. PEI argued, in part, that this constituted trademark infringement under the Lanham Act (see Chapter 5). Welles responded in part that her use of the terms is a "fair use," because she was and is the "Playmate of the Year 1981."

IN THE WORDS OF THE COURT . .
GRAHAM, District Judge.

* * * *

In a case where the mark is used only to describe the goods or services of [a] party, or their geographic origin, trademark law recognizes a "fair use" defense. * * *

* * * *

It is clear that defendant is selling Terri Welles and only Terri Welles on the website. There is no overt attempt to confuse the websurfer into believing that her site is a Playboy-related website. In this case, then, defendant's use of the term Playmate of the Year 1981 is descriptive of and used fairly and in good faith only to describe [herself]. * * *

With respect to the meta tags, the court finds there to be no trademark infringement where defendant has used plaintiff's trademarks in good faith to index the content of

(Continued)

CASE 7.5—Continued

her website. * * * Much like the subject index of a card catalog, the meta tags give the websurfer using a search engine a clearer indication of the content of a website. The use of the term Playboy is not an infringement because it references not only her identity as a "Playboy Playmate of the Year 1981," but it may also reference the legitimate editorial uses of the term Playboy contained in the text of defendant's website.

DECISION AND REMEDY The court held that a party can use another's trademarks as meta tags when those marks describe the party who uses them. The court ruled that Welles was entitled to the "fair use" of the "Playboy" and "Playmate" marks as meta tags.

FOR CRITICAL ANALYSIS—Technological Consideration *Why would PEI encourage its models to use its marks outside cyberspace but attempt to block such uses within cyberspace?*

Dilution As discussed in Chapter 5, trademark *dilution* occurs when a trademark is used, without authorization, in a way that diminishes the distinctive quality of the mark. Unlike trademark infringement, a dilution cause of action does not require proof that consumers are likely to be confused by a connection between the unauthorized use and the mark. For this reason, the products involved do not have to be similar. In the first case alleging dilution on the Web, a court precluded the use of "candyland.com" as the URL for an adult site, in a suit by the maker of the "Candyland" children's game and owner of the "Candyland" mark.[22]

A dilution case does require, however, that a mark be famous when the dilution occurs. ● **EXAMPLE 7.3** Gateway 2000 has been making personal computers since 1985 and owns the mark "Gateway 2000." In 1988, Gateway.com, Inc., an entirely different company, began to use "gateway.com" as part of its URL and registered it as a domain name in 1990. Gateway 2000 later filed a suit to block the use of "gateway" on the ground of dilution. The court refused to grant the request, concluding that Gateway 2000 could not prove that its name was famous at the time when Gateway.com chose "gateway" as a domain name. ●

In another interesting case, a court issued an injunction on the ground that spamming under another's logo is trademark dilution.[23] In that case, Hotmail, Inc., provided e-mail services and worked to dissociate itself from spam. Van$ Money Pie, Inc., and others spammed thousands of e-mail customers, using the free e-mail service Hotmail as a return address. The court ordered the defendants to stop.

Licensing One of the ways to make use of another's mark (or another's copyright, patent, or trade secret), while avoiding litigation, is to obtain a license to do so. A license in this context is essentially an agreement to permit the use of a mark for certain purposes. A licensee (the party obtaining the license) might be allowed to use the mark of the licensor (the party issuing the license) as part of the name of its company, or as part of its domain name, without otherwise using the mark on any products or services.

A licensee must not break the terms of the license, however, or litigation could ensue and liability may result. ● **EXAMPLE 7.4** In the first case involving a trademark license in cyberspace, the licensee took advantage of its licensor's increasingly famous mark to make its Web site look more like the licensor's. Alleging a violation of the licensing agreement, the licensor sued. The court granted the licensor's motion

22. *Hasbro, Inc. v. Internet Entertainment Group, Ltd.*, 1996 WL 84853 (W.D.Wash. 1996).
23. *Hotmail Corp. v. Van$ Money Pie, Inc.*, 1998 WL 388389 (N.D.Cal. 1998).

for a preliminary injunction, holding that the licensee likely breached the license and infringed the mark.[24]

Patents Online

There are four noteworthy aspects to patents and the new technology. First is the rapidly increasing number of patents that the U.S. Patent and Trademark Office (USPTO) has granted in recent years. Software patents number in the thousands, with more than ten thousand applications pending. Software technology has progressed quickly. This points to another important feature of the new technology that relates to patents.

Software developers use combinations of previous software to create new products and processes. This practice has led to uncertainty and controversy about the ownership and the use of patent rights to the hybrid products. One way to prevent legal problems in this regard is for a software developer or maker to obtain licenses for others' products and to issue licenses for its own.

The third aspect to patents related to the new technology concerns one of the most important reasons that a patent is granted. A developer obtains a patent to prevent others from patenting the same product or process. When more than one party is developing the same product or process, the first party to obtain a patent is the party who gets the protection. Even before a patent is obtained, however, the disclosure of a product or process can block others from obtaining a patent for it. For this reason, those who reveal their inventions to the public are rewarded. It is a practice in the software industry to keep technology secret, but this is risky. A developer could lose all rights to a product by keeping it secret.

Finally, a significant development relating to patents is the availability online of the world's patent databases. The USPTO provides at its Web site (www.uspto.gov) searchable databases covering U.S. patents granted since 1976, as well as AIDS-related patents issued by U.S., Japanese, and European patent offices. The European Patent Office maintains at its Web site (www.european-patent-office.org) databases covering all patent documents in sixty-five nations and the legal status of patents in twenty-two of those countries.

Copyrights in Digital Information

Copyright law is probably the most important form of intellectual property protection on the Internet. This is because much of the material on the Internet consists of works of authorship (including multimedia presentations, software, and database information). These works are the traditional focus of copyright law. Copyright law is also important because the nature of the Internet requires that data be "copied" to be transferred online. Copies are a significant part of the traditional controversies arising in this area of the law.

Does Old Copyright Law Cover Works in New Electronic Forms? Remember from the discussion of copyright law in Chapter 5 that copyright law is concerned chiefly with the creation, distribution, and sale of protected works of authorship. When Congress drafted the principal U.S. law governing copyrights, the Copyright Act of 1976, cyberspace did not exist for most of us. The threat to copyright owners was not posed by computer technology but by unauthorized tangible copies of works and the sale of rights to movies, television, and other media.

24. *Digital Equipment Corp. v. AltaVista Technology, Inc.*, 960 F.Supp. 456 (D.Mass. 1997).

Some of the issues that were unimagined when the Copyright Act was drafted have posed thorny questions for the courts. For example, to sell a copy of a work, permission of the copyright holder is necessary. Because of the nature of cyberspace, however, one of the early controversies was determining at what point an intangible, electronic "copy" of a work has been made. The courts have held that loading a file or program into a computer's random access memory, or RAM, constitutes the making of a "copy" for purposes of copyright law.[25] RAM is a portion of a computer's memory into which a file, for example, is loaded so that it can be accessed (read or written over).

Others rights, including those relating to the revision of "collective works" such as magazines, were acknowledged thirty years ago but were considered to have only limited economic value. Today, technology has made some of those rights vastly more significant. Does the old law apply to these rights? That was one of the questions in the following case.

25. *MAI Systems Corp. v. Peak Computer, Inc.*, 991 F.2d 511 (9th Cir. 1993).

CASE 7.6 Tasini v. New York Times Co.

United States District Court,
Southern District of New York, 1997.
972 F.Supp. 804.
www.ljextra.com/copyright/tasini.html[a]

HISTORICAL AND TECHNOLOGICAL SETTING *In the early 1980s, the New York Times Company and other publishers of periodicals began to sell the contents of their publications to e-publishers, including Lexis/Nexis, a division of Reed Elsevier, Inc. Lexis/Nexis, for example, has carried online the articles appearing in the* New York Times *since 1983. UMI Company has distributed "*The New York Times *OnDisc," a text-based CD-ROM, since 1992, and the* New York Times Magazine *and* Book Review *have been available on an image-based CD-ROM since 1990.*

a. This opinion is reproduced in a Law Journal Extra! database, in a section titled "Copyright." This site is owned by American Lawyer Media, Inc.

BACKGROUND AND FACTS Magazines and newspapers, including the *New York Times,* buy and publish articles written by freelance writers. Besides circulating hard copies of their periodicals, these publishers sell the contents to e-publishers for inclusion in online and other electronic databases. Jonathan Tasini and other freelance writers filed a suit in a federal district court against the New York Times Company and other publishers, including the e-publishers, contending that the e-publication of the articles violated the Copyright Act. The publishers responded, among other things, that the Copyright Act gave them a right to produce "revisions" of their publications. The writers argued that the Copyright Act did not cover electronic "revisions." The publishers filed a motion for summary judgment.

IN THE WORDS OF THE COURT . . .
GRAHAM, District Judge.

* * * *

* * * [T]o the extent that the electronic reproductions qualify as revisions under [the Copyright Act] the defendant publishers were entitled to authorize the electronic defendants to create those revisions.

* * * *

* * * If the disputed periodicals manifest an original selection or arrangement of materials, and if that originality is preserved electronically, then the electronic reproductions can be deemed permissible revisions of the publisher defendants' collective works. * * *

CASE 7.6—Continued

* * * *

One of the defining original aspects of the publisher defendants' periodicals is the selection of articles included in those works. * * *

* * * *

* * * By retaining the publisher defendants' original selection of articles, * * * the electronic defendants have managed to retain one of the few defining original elements of the publishers' collective works. * * * For the purposes of [the Copyright Act] then, defendants have succeeded at creating * * * revision[s] of those collective works.

DECISION AND REMEDY The court held that publishers can put the contents of their periodicals into e-databases and onto CD-ROMs without securing the permission of the writers whose contributions are included in the periodicals. The court granted the publishers' motion for summary judgment.

FOR CRITICAL ANALYSIS—Political Consideration *When technology creates a situation in which rights such as those in this case are more valuable than originally anticipated, should the law be changed to redistribute the economic benefit of those rights?*

International Perspective • EUROPEAN LEGAL PROTECTION FOR DATABASES

In 1996, the European Union (EU) issued an important directive titled "Directive 96/9/EC of the European Parliament and of the Council of 11 March 1996 on the Legal Protection of Databases." This directive took effect in 1998. Its objective "is to afford an appropriate and uniform level of protection of databases as a means to secure the remuneration of the maker of the database."[a]

The directive created Europe-wide copyright protection for databases that might not otherwise had have this protection because the law in the country in which the database was created did not provide it.[b] This might have occurred when a database was a compilation of factual items even when their selection or arrangement was a unique, intellectual creation of the author.

One of the most important provisions of the directive is Article 7 ("Object of protection"). Article 7 provides that the maker of a database is protected if he or she can show a substantial investment in obtaining, verifying, or presenting the contents. The protection lasts for at least fifteen years from the date of the completion of the database.

Another important provision is Article 10 ("Term of protection"). Article 10 states that, when a database is made available to the public, the fifteen-year protection period runs "from the first of January of the year following the date when the database was first made available to the public." Article 10 also provides that the period of protection can be extended if the maker can show that additional work on the database is done during the current fifteen-year period.

a. OJ L 77/20 of 27.3.1996 [Official Journal of the European Communities, no. L 77, page 20, March 27, 1996]. To read this directive, see, within a Web site of the European Commission, **www2.echo.lu/legal/en/ipr/database/database.html**.

b. Other EU directives cover other aspects of copyright protection. These include Council Directive 91/250/EEC on computer programs, OJ L 122/42 of 17.5.1991; Council Directive 92/100/EEC on rental and lending rights in the area of intellectual property, OJ L 346/61 of 27.11.1992; Council Directive 93/83 on satellite broadcasting and cable retransmission, OJ L 248/15 of 6.10.1993; and Council Directive 93/98 on the term of copyright protection, OJ L 290/9 of 24.11.1993.

FOR CRITICAL ANALYSIS
Why is it necessary to provide uniform, international legal protection for databases?

Is a New Copyright Law Needed? One of the main problems for the international online community is that copyright protection varies between jurisdictions. For example, in the United States, for U.S. authors, there is no recognition of what are called *moral rights*. **Moral rights** include the rights of an author to proclaim or disclaim authorship, and to object to any change to the author's work that would injure his or her reputation. These rights are considered to be personal to the author, and they cannot be taken away or abridged. Other countries, such as France, recognize and enforce these rights. In Great Britain, an author of a copyrighted work is entitled to be identified as the author. This is called a paternity right.

• **MORAL RIGHTS**
The rights of an author to proclaim or disclaim authorship, and to object to any change to the author's work that would injure his or her reputation. These rights are personal to the author and cannot be taken away or abridged.

The existence of these and other rights brings up a number of questions. Should we adopt these rights in the United States? Should they be adopted in all countries? These questions point to another fundamental issue: Should there be a different copyright law solely for cyberspace? If so, what rights should it include?

In 1996, the United States signed the World Intellectual Property Organization (WIPO) Copyright Treaty, a special agreement under the Berne Convention. (The WIPO Copyright Treaty and the Berne Convention are discussed in Chapter 5.) Special provisions of the WIPO treaty relate to rights in digital data. The treaty strengthens some rights for copyright owners, in terms of their application in cyberspace, but leaves other questions unresolved. For example, the treaty does not make clear what, for purposes of international law, constitutes the making of a "copy" in electronic form. The United States implemented the the terms of the WIPO treaty in the Digital Millennium Copyright Act of 1998, which is the subject of the following *Landmark in the Law.*

ON THE WEB
The World Intellectual Property Organization offers information on the background of intellectual property, including copyrights, and its international protection at **www.wipo.org/eng/newindex/intellct.htm**.

Landmark in the Law • THE DIGITAL MILLENNIUM COPYRIGHT ACT OF 1998

The United States leads the world in the production of creative products, including books, films, videos, recordings, and software. In fact, the creative industries are more important to the U.S. economy than the more traditional product industries are. The value of the export of U.S. creative products, for example, surpasses that of every other U.S. industry. Creative industries are growing at nearly three times the rate of the economy as a whole.

Technology, particularly the Internet, offers new outlets for these products. It also makes them easier to steal. Copyrighted works can be pirated and distributed around the world quickly and efficiently. To curb this crime, the World Intellectual Property Organization (WIPO) enacted two treaties in 1996 to upgrade global standards of copyright protection, particularly for the Internet.

In 1998, Congress implemented the provisions of these treaties to update U.S. copyright law. Besides standing as a beacon to the rest of the world, because of the leading position of the United States in the creative industries, this action is a landmark step in the protection of copyright. Among other things, the new law—the Digital Millennium Copyright Act of 1998[a]—created civil and criminal penalties for anyone who circumvents encryption software or other technological anti-piracy protection. Also prohibited are the manufacture, import, sale, or distribution of devices or services for circumvention.

There are exceptions to fit the needs of libraries, scientists, universities, and others. In general, the new law does not restrict the "fair use" of circumvention for educational and other noncommercial purposes. For example, circumvention is allowed to test computer security, to conduct encryption research, to protect personal privacy, or to allow parents to

a. As of this writing, access to the text of the new law is possible at **lcweb.loc.gov/copyright/penleg.html**. Click on the title of the bill. When a new page opens, click on the number that corresponds to the "enrolled bill."

monitor their children's journeys over the Internet. The exceptions are to be reconsidered every three years.

An Internet service provider (ISP) is not liable for any copyright infringement by its customer if the ISP is unaware of the subscriber's violation. An ISP may be held liable only after learning of the violation and failing to take action to shut the subscriber down. A copyright holder has to act promptly, however, by pursuing a claim in court, or the subscriber has the right to be restored to online access.

FOR CRITICAL ANALYSIS
How will the Digital Millennium Copyright Act of 1998 spur the growth of commerce online?

TRADE SECRETS IN CYBERSPACE

The nature of the new technology—the versatility of e-mail in particular—undercuts a business firm's ability to protect its confidential information, including trade secrets (trade secrets are defined and discussed in more detail in Chapter 5).[26] For example, a dishonest employee could transmit trade secrets in a company's computer to anyone via an e-mail connection on the Internet. "Anyone" could be a thief, a competitor, or a future employer. If e-mail is not an option, the employee might walk out with the information on a computer disk. Even honest employees can make mistakes, sending confidential data to the wrong e-mail address—a competitor, for example, instead of a client—or losing a disk on a business trip.

An illustration of what a departing employee might do is provided by a criminal case that involved two competing software developers, Borland International, Inc., and Symantec. Eugene Wang, a Borland vice president, expressed dissatisfaction with his job and quit. Other Borland officers reviewed Wang's e-mail files and found messages to Gordon Eubanks, Symantec's president and chief executive officer. Believing that the messages contained trade secrets and other confidential information, Borland filed a civil suit to recover damages and also notified the police. After an investigation, criminal charges, including the theft of trade secrets, were filed against both Wang and Eubanks.[27]

E-Commerce

• E-COMMERCE
Business transacted in cyberspace.

• E-CONTRACT
A contract that is entered into in cyberspace and is evidenced only by electronic impulses (such as those that make up a computer's memory), rather than, for example, a typewritten form.

The increasing use of the Internet to do business brings to light at least two important concerns to persons who engage in commerce online, or **e-commerce,** and agree to **e-contracts.** There is some concern about the limits of current Internet technology to guarantee the security of e-commerce. There is also concern about the limits of the legal framework to guarantee the enforcement of e-contracts.

In the following sections, we discuss these concerns in the context of the following types of Internet business transactions: contracting in cyberspace, making payments and investing online, and marketing on the Internet.

CONTRACTING IN CYBERSPACE

Over the last ten years, the new technology has transformed society and is defining new ways of doing business. This revolution in technology has even changed the

26. Note that in a recent case, it was indicated that customers' e-mail addresses may constitute trade secrets. See *T-N-T Motorsports, Inc. v. Hennessey Motorsports, Inc.*, 965 S.W.2d 18 (Tex.App.—Hous. [1 Dist.] 1998), rehearing overruled (1998), petition dismissed (1998).

27. *People v. Eubanks*, 14 Cal.4th 580, 14 Cal.4th 1282D, 927 P.2d 310, 59 Cal.Rptr.2d 200 (1996), as modified on denial of rehearing (1997). The charges were dismissed after Borland paid a substantial part of the cost of the criminal investigation. The California Supreme Court felt that Borland's payment made it unlikely that the defendants would receive fair treatment.

"We've proven that the World Wide Web can draw a lot of people. Now we have to make some money at it."

RICHARD PITT, 1943–
(Co-proprietor of Wimsey Information Services, Inc., 1993–1995)

nature of many of the goods and services that are the subjects of e-commerce and e-contracts.

A significant issue is how the law should be adapted to reflect business practices regarding such cyberspace agreements as Web site click-on agreements, software licenses (licensing agreements were discussed earlier in this chapter), e-data interchange, and online sales. Some aspects of these agreements are discussed in the *Technology and Online Offers* feature in Chapter 15. Other aspects are discussed in the following subsections.

Article 2B of the Uniform Commercial Code The Uniform Commercial Code (UCC) is a uniform state law that reflects business practices and social changes. (The UCC is mentioned briefly in Chapter 1 and discussed in detail in Chapters 15 through 22.) To reflect current and future business conditions, the UCC needs to change to provide a legal framework for e-contracts and contracts related to software, information databases, and other aspects of the new technology.

The National Conference of Commissioners (NCC) on Uniform State Laws is aware of this need. To partially meet it, the NCC is in the process of drafting UCC Article 2B, which deals with licensing. The proposed Article 2B consists of seven parts: (1) General Provisions, (2) Formation, (3) Construction, (4) Warranties, (5) Transfer of Interests and Rights, (6) Performance, and (7) Remedies.

Article 2B's outline and some of Article 2B's legal principles parallel those of UCC Article 2 (see Chapters 15 through 18). For example, the terms of an Article 2 sales contract and an Article 2B licensing agreement include the express terms, as well as the terms arising from the *course of performance,* the *course of dealing,* and the *usage of trade.* (These italicized legal terms are defined in Chapter 15.) Both articles give these concepts the same priority: express terms take precedence over the course of performance, followed by the course of dealing and the usage of trade.[28]

Article 2B goes beyond Article 2, however, to define, among other things, an *electronic transaction* as a contract in which humans may not review the messages. An *electronic agent* is a "computer program or other electronic or automated means used, selected, or programmed by a party to initiate or respond to electronic messages or performances in whole, or in part, without review by an individual."[29] (For more information on electronic agents, see the feature *Technology and "Intelligent Agents"* in Chapter 24.)

Some observers believe that, by providing a legal framework for the new technological age, Article 2B may become the most significant law of the new century. Our economy is now centered on information products and services. Article 2B will provide uniform legal rules for some of this commerce, which in turn will encourage its further development.

ON THE WEB

The most recent drafts of Article 2B of the Uniform Commercial Code and the Uniform Electronic Transactions Act can be found at **www.law.upenn.edu/bll/ulc/ulc.htm**.

The Uniform Electronics Transactions Act The National Conference of Commissioners (NCC) on Uniform State Laws is also in the process of drafting the Uniform Electronics Transactions Act (UETA). The goal of the UETA is to support the enforcement of e-contracts. For example, the UETA defines *record* as "information that is inscribed on a tangible medium or that is stored in an electronic or other medium and is retrievable in perceivable form."[30] In other words, a contract could be in any medium the parties want, including an electronic form.

28. Proposed UCC 2B–302.
29. Proposed UCC 2B–102(a).
30. Proposed UETA 102(15).

Other Issues As already indicated, one of the foremost issues in the area of contract law in cyberspace is the enforceability of an e-contract. Does a business deal agreed to online meet the legal requirements for a contract (see Chapter 9)? For example, does an e-contract fulfill the requirement of a "writing"? How can a party to the agreement verify that the other party "signed" this "writing"? These issues are discussed in the *Technology and the Electronic Signatures* feature in Chapter 12 and in the *Application* feature at the end of this chapter.

E-MONEY

The technological revolution is changing the nature of financial services, including banking and investing, in fundamental ways. Traditional concepts of branches, networks, and payment systems do not apply in cyberspace. A bank or an investment broker with a home office in Kansas, for example, can do business with a customer anywhere in the world. In fact, an online financial institution does not even need a physical office—a Web page is enough.

One of the most important ways in which new technology is changing the nature of financial services is the way in which payments are made. Electronic money, or **e-money,** includes a number of alternatives to traditional means of payment. From a consumer's point of view, these alternatives include prepaid funds recorded on the consumer's personal computer or on a card.

• **E-MONEY**
Prepaid funds recorded on a computer or a card (such as a *smart card*).

Card-based e-money is of two types. One type involves recording a balance of funds on a magnetic stripe on a card that is debited by a computer terminal on each use. The second type uses a microprocessor chip embedded in a so-called **smart card.** A smart card is safer and more versatile than a magnetic-stripe card. A smart card can be encrypted to protect the value on the card from theft. Also, a smart card can function simultaneously as a credit card, a debit card, a stored value card, and a personal information card, such as a driver's license.

• **SMART CARD**
Prepaid funds recorded on a microprocessor chip embedded on a card. One type of *e-money.*

Is E-Money a "Private" Means of Payment? Current technology allows e-money to be used in a variety of ways. E-money can be used like cash, in which no personally identifiable records are created. It can also be used as part of a system that identifies and keeps information about every transaction of every consumer. The use of this information is a concern.

As of this writing, the federal government is encouraging the financial industry, like other businesses in cyberspace, to come up with a scheme to regulate its use of this information itself. Financial institutions are being encouraged to tell consumers of the institutions' policies regarding the information that is kept about their customers. Financial institutions are also being urged to give consumers choices as to what is done with the information, to allow consumers to correct inaccuracies, and to take steps to keep the information secure. In mid-1998, the Federal Trade Commission (FTC) announced that, unless cyberspace businesses showed by the end of the year an effective self-regulation plan to ensure privacy online, the FTC would seek a new law to require these practices.

Presently, it is not clear which, if any, laws apply to the security of e-money payment information. The Federal Reserve has decided not to impose Regulation E, which governs certain electronic funds transfers, on e-money transactions. (Regulation E is discussed in Chapter 21.) Federal laws prohibiting unauthorized access to electronic communications might apply, however. For example, the Electronic Communications Privacy Act of 1986 prohibits any person from knowingly divulging to any other person the contents of an electronic communication while that communication is in transmission or in electronic storage.

What Happens If an E-Money Issuer Goes Broke? There is no actual "cash," or "legal tender," on a smart card, just as there is no actual currency in a checkbook. Instead, the balance of funds recorded on a smart card (or in a checkbook) represents a balance of funds deposited with a financial institution. The Federal Deposit Insurance Corporation (FDIC) insures deposits in most bank accounts. Subject to certain limits, the FDIC guarantees to pay a bank's customer the amount in his or her deposit account if the bank becomes insolvent.

Does e-money qualify as a "deposit"? The FDIC has said that most forms of e-money do not qualify as deposits and thus are not covered by deposit insurance. If a bank becomes insolvent, an e-money holder would then be in the position of a general creditor. This means that he or she would be entitled to reimbursement only after nearly everyone else who is owed money is paid (except, of course, for other e-money holders and other general creditors). At that point, there may not be any funds left. (For more discussion of the priority of creditors when a debtor is insolvent, see Chapter 23.)

Are New Laws Needed to Cover E-Money? There are some existing laws that extend to e-money and e-money transactions. • **EXAMPLE 7.5** The Federal Trade Commission Act (discussed in Chapter 33) prohibits unfair or deceptive practices in, or affecting, commerce.[31] Under this law, e-money issuers who misrepresent the value of their products, or make other misrepresentations on which e-money consumers rely to their detriment, may be liable for engaging in deceptive practices.•

General common law principles also apply. For example, the rights and liabilities of e-money issuers and consumers are subject to the law of contracts (see Chapters 9 through 14). This means that the parties' relationships are affected by the terms of the contracts to which they agree. On the whole, however, it is unclear how existing laws will apply to e-money.

Even without legal protection, e-money payment systems could be safer than currency and checks. Encryption (discussed earlier in this chapter) may solve some of the problems associated with e-money and with unprotected online exchanges. For example, the theft of encrypted e-money would be a waste of time because without the code a thief could not use the money. The failure of a merchant to give a customer a receipt may not matter if the e-money payment system provides proof of a transaction. Digital signatures (discussed in Chapter 12) could eliminate problems associated with forged and bounced checks. Digital signatures can also increase the enforceability of contracts entered into online.

Marketing on the Internet: Consumers Beware

On the Web, advertising is everywhere. It is a source for the funds that pay the Internet servers and others who maintain the connections in cyberspace. It presents opportunities for consumers and merchants around the world. It also presents a challenge for those charged with protecting consumers from dishonest sellers: How can the law be administered without stifling the potential of the Internet?

Fraud, deception, misleading information—despite new advances, some things never change. Apparently, there will always be those who would take advantage of others, and cyberspace provides new opportunities for wrongdoers in all aspects of virtual commerce, including marketing. On the Web, users need to be watchful to avoid becoming victims. Here, we point out three situations in which consumers and businesses need to be careful.

31. 15 U.S.C. Sections 41–58.

Getting Up Close and Personal Information about consumers can be used to aim advertising at those persons who might be most interested in what is being sold. It is not illegal to attempt to target only those consumers who might buy what a merchant is selling.

As explained in the *Technology and the Protection of Privacy Rights* feature in Chapter 4, information can be gathered about a Web surfer without his or her permission, or even knowledge. The surfer has limited control over the use of this information. To some observers, this does not seem threatening, especially if the data are used only to direct an ad to those surfers who are most likely to find it informative. To others, however, it is perceived as an invasion of privacy and a potential basis for a lawsuit.

Data about users can also be compiled with their awareness and consent. Nearly all commercial Web sites, for example, collect information about their visitors and members, and most do so with those users' knowledge. Few of these sites have a privacy policy, however, and many do not provide details about what they do with the data.

• EXAMPLE 7.6 One commercial site that collects information about its members is GeoCities, a provider of free home pages and e-mail addresses. GeoCities has more than one million members and hosts one of the five most frequently visited sites on the Web (at www.geocities.com). At one time, GeoCities told new members that it would not share the information that it collects with anyone without the permission of the persons from whom it was collected but would "use it to gain a better understanding of who is visiting GeoCities."

In 1998, the Federal Trade Commission (FTC) charged to the contrary. In the first case involving Internet privacy, the FTC claimed that GeoCities "misrepresent[ed] the purposes for which it collect[ed] personal identifying information from children and adults." On its registration form, GeoCities treated the failure of a member or visitor to click on a box that would let the user opt out of marketing offers as "permission" to share the information. Those who did not click on the box were considered to have opted in. The FTC also claimed that GeoCities sold the data to third parties "who used [the information] to target members solicitations beyond those agreed to by the member."

Without admitting any wrongdoing, GeoCities agreed to change its policies on disclosing user information (see a copy of the agreement at www.ftc.gov/os/1998/9808/geo-ord.htm). Among other changes, the company now posts a detailed privacy policy outlining how the information is used (the statement begins on the Web page at www.geocities.com/main/info/company/privacy.html). Users can also access and remove their information.•

Keeping Up to Date In any market, the prices and the availability of products change quickly. This is as true in cyberspace as it is at your local mall. Even with the global reach of the Internet, what is a glut on a Web market one day can be a scarcity the next. Partly for this reason, one of the most important details to watch for is the date of the content placed on a particular Web site.

It is equally as important for those who host pages on the Web to make sure that their content is current. Merchants should take special care to change their publicized prices to avoid penalties and potential lawsuits. • EXAMPLE 7.7 An airline was fined $14,000 for failing to change expired fare information. A bank or other financial institution may be subject to liability if it displays expired interest rate information on its site.•

One step to take to guard against liability for dated information is to include on the site a disclaimer page. Because a visitor may bypass a home page and go directly to an inner page, the disclaimer should be linked to all pages on the site.

Opportunities Too Good to Be True No one knows the full extent of cyber fraud (fraud committed on the Internet). Indications are that cyber fraud is increasing with the rising use of the Internet. Scams that were once conducted solely by mail or phone can now be found online, and new technology is contributing to more creative ways to commit fraud.

Cyber fraud takes many forms. • EXAMPLE 7.8 Products and services that are offered on the Web and for which fees are collected, but which are misrepresented or never delivered, represent common forms of cyber fraud. Cyber fraud also includes bogus bidding in Web auctions, empty promises of huge profits for investing in business "opportunities," schemes in which profits are made from recruiting others instead of from sales of goods or services, and so on.•

The unique nature of the Internet makes it easy for cyber wrongdoers to hide their identities and locations. Attractive, impressive Web sites can be set up for a small price. For a similarly low cost, e-mail can be sent to hundreds of thousands of users. In newsgroups and chat rooms, phony tips concerning fraudulent investments can be posted. Return addresses can be falsified or omitted. A wrongdoer can operate from anywhere in the world.

Besides the difficulty of identifying and finding cyber wrongdoers, it can be difficult to bring legal actions against them. When they are located in other states or countries, there are questions involving jurisdiction (see the discussion of jurisdiction earlier in this chapter). In other places, it can be complicated to obtain search warrants and to seize evidence and the proceeds of criminal activity. Anywhere, it can be expensive to maintain legal proceedings.

Despite these limitations, most state and federal laws that apply to unfair and deceptive acts and practices also apply to cyber fraud. State consumer fraud and false advertising laws are based on Section 5 of the Federal Trade Commission Act, which is discussed in Chapter 36.

APPLICATION Law and the Businessperson: Forming E-Contracts*

As indicated earlier in this chapter, the increasing use of the Internet to do business highlights the concern about the limits of current Internet technology to guarantee the security of e-commerce. There is also concern about the limits of the legal framework to guarantee the enforcement of e-contracts.

*This *Application* is not meant to substitute for the services of an attorney who is licensed to practice law in your state.

To use the Internet to communicate with suppliers and customers, a business firm needs to be sure of the identity of the party at the other end of the transaction. Currently, a business verifies identities with passwords, electronic signatures, and Internet protocol (IP) addresses.

A password consists of characters that allow access to a file or a computer. An electronic signature is any identifier, such as letters or symbols, that is transmitted online or by similar means with the intent of the party who transmits it to certify a writing. An IP address describes the format of data, including such details as the speed of transmission, required to communicate with a computer on the Internet.

Other technology is being developed to ensure a more effective system of digital identification. To protect privacy and ensure the security of Internet transactions, some firms use encryption software. For example, a digital signature is an electronic signature that uses a security measure, such as encryption software, to ensure the signature's authenticity. Another security measure is the use of a firewall. A firewall is a program designed to examine e-messages and block those that do not meet security requirements.

APPLICATION CONTINUED

A party to a business deal also wants to know that any agreement made online is binding. In the United States, the federal government and the National Conference of Commissioners on Uniform State Laws are in the process of developing uniform laws to facilitate e-commerce and enforce e-contracts. Internationally, the United Nations Commission on International Trade Law (UNCITRAL) has completed a model law that relates to e-contracts. The International Chamber of Commerce has also issued model e-commerce guidelines.

CHECKLIST FOR FORMING E-CONTRACTS

1. As a basic precaution, use passwords, electronic signatures (digital signatures, if possible), and Internet protocol (IP) addresses.
2. Use encryption software.
3. Install firewalls in your computer system.

Key Terms

cyber crime 186
cyber hate speech 184
cyber mark 192
cyber stalker 187
cyber terrorist 188
cyber tort 188
e-commerce 199
e-contract 199
e-money 201
encryption 183
filtering software 185
flame 188
hacker 188
meta tags 193
moral rights 198
smart card 201
spam 190
tag 185
virtual courtroom 179
virtual property 192

Chapter Summary • Cyberlaw in the Legal Environment

The Courts (See pages 178–182.)	1. *Practices and procedures*—Technology can relieve the burden of the courts by reducing storage space and paperwork, and speeding up legal research. Many courts accept legal papers and issue opinions online. 2. *Jurisdiction*—Generally, a court's exercise of personal jurisdiction based on contacts over the Internet depends on the amount of business that is transacted online: (1) substantial business warrants jurisdiction; (2) some interactivity through a Web site may or may not support jurisdiction; and (3) passive advertising does not support jurisdiction.
The Constitution (See pages 182–186.)	1. *Encryption*—Federal regulations and a criminal statute prohibit the export of encryption codes. In a challenge to this prohibition, one court held the regulations unconstitutional on the ground that an encryption code is speech protected by the First Amendment. A different court held that an encryption code is not protected speech. 2. *Restrictions on the content of Web sites*—These generally amount to censorship and can be difficult to enforce, because of jurisdiction problems and because what is acceptable differs among communities. 3. *Blocking access to Web sites*—The First Amendment may limit the decision of a public entity to restrict its patrons' access to information on the Internet.

Chapter Summary • Cyberlaw in the Legal Environment, Continued

Cyber Crimes (See pages 186–188.)	1. *Cyber stalking*—Harassing someone by computer. 2. *Cyber theft*—Accessing a computer without authority and taking the data is a felony under the National Infrastructure Protection Act of 1996. 3. *Cyber terrorism*—Exploiting a computer for a serious impact, such as inserting false codes or data.
Cyber Torts (See pages 188–192.)	1. *Defamation*—Under the Communications Decency Act of 1996, an Internet service provider is not liable for failing to edit, withhold, or restrict access to defamatory remarks it disseminated but did not create. 2. *Spamming*—Sending bulk, unsolicited e-mail can constitute trespassing.
Virtual Property (See pages 192–199.)	1. *Cyber marks*—Trademark infringement may occur in cyberspace if (1) another site's key words are used improperly as meta tags; (2) the quality of another's mark is diluted by improper use; (3) another's mark is used without a license; or (4) a licensing agreement is broken. (Trademark infringement can also occur with certain uses of hypertext links and framing technology—see the feature in Chapter 5 entitled *Technology and Online Trademark Infringement.*) 2. *Patents*—Patent infringement of a cyberspace product or process may occur if a user, including a software developer, fails to obtain a license to use the item. 3. *Copyrights*—Under U.S. copyright law, loading a computer program or data into the RAM of a computer is making a "copy." (International law does not clearly resolve this issue.) The Digital Millennium Copyright Act of 1998 created civil and criminal penalties for anyone who circumvents encryption software or other technological antipiracy protection. 4. *Trade secrets*—Communicating trade secrets via new technology without authorization may be a violation of criminal and civil laws.
E-Commerce (See pages 199–205.)	1. *Contracts*—Article 2B of the UCC and the Uniform Electronic Transactions Act may provide a legal framework for an economy centered on the licensing of information products and services. 2. *E-money*—The Electronic Communications Privacy Act, which prohibits a person from revealing the contents of an electronic communication without authority, may protect the security of e-money payment information. Other laws (such as the Federal Trade Commission Act) may also cover e-money and e-money transactions. E-money is not covered by bank deposit insurance, however. 3. *Marketing*—State and federal laws that regulate fraud and deception by other means prohibit those same acts in cyberspace.

For Review

❶ What factors determine whether a court can exercise jurisdiction over a business that advertises on the Web?

❷ What constitutional clause limits the government in restricting the contents of, and blocking access to, Web sites?

❸ What laws apply to a party who makes defamatory statements online?

❹ What legal protection does an owner of intellectual property in digital form have against a cyber pirate?

❺ What laws and regulations impose limits on business transactions over the Internet?

Questions and Case Problems

7–1. Technology and the Law. Some observers believe that the law should not apply in cyberspace because they think that it inhibits the Internet's development. In what ways is the law facilitating the development of technology in cyberspace?

7–2. Freedom of Speech. Jill is a professor who teaches a business law course. Jill maintains a Web site that contains background material for the class sessions. This material includes student research papers, which are submitted in advance of the classes at which they are discussed. In preparation for a class discussion on computers and the law, Mark, one of Jill's students, submits a paper that includes encryption programs he wrote to show how computers work. Jill posts this paper on her Web site. Is this post an "export"? Assuming that it is, what arguments could you make that it is protected by the First Amendment? What arguments could you make that it is not so protected?

7–3. Electronic Filing. Like other courts, the Washington County courts thoroughly document their proceedings. Even oral proceedings are transcribed so that the written records are complete. The courts make use of copy machines, word processors, and computers (for legal research). The basic functions of filing, storing, locating, updating, searching, and cross-referencing court documents are still done manually, however. What advantages would the Washington County courts realize if they were to switch to an electronic filing system?

7–4. Jurisdiction. Cybersell AZ is an Arizona company that provides Internet marketing services. Cybersell AZ applied with the U.S. Patent and Trademark Office (USPTO) to register "Cybersell" as a service mark. Before the application was granted, unrelated parties formed Cybersell, Inc., a Florida corporation (Cybersell FL), to provide consulting services for marketing on the Internet. Cybersell FL put up a Web site using the name "Cybersell," but its interactivity was limited to taking a surfer's name and address. No one in Arizona contacted Cybersell FL, or even hit on its Web page, before the USPTO granted Cybersell AZ's service mark application. Cybersell AZ then told Cybersell FL to stop using "Cybersell" and filed a suit in a federal district court in Arizona against Cybersell FL, alleging, among other things, trademark infringement. Cybersell FL filed a motion to dismiss for lack of jurisdiction. How should the court rule? Why? [*Cybersell, Inc., an Arizona Corporation v. Cybersell, Inc., a Florida Corporation,* 130 F.3d 414 (9th Cir. 1997)]

7–5. Freedom of Speech. The Commonwealth (state) of Virginia enacted a statute to restrict the ability of state employees to access sexually explicit material on state-owned or leased computers. Melvin Urofsky and other professors at colleges and universities in Virginia felt that the statute interfered with their teaching. For example, Urofsky was reluctant to have students do certain online research assignments. Urofsky and others filed a suit in a federal district court against Virginia Governor George Allen and others, contending that the statute violated their First Amendment right to free speech. Both sides filed motions for summary judgment. Why would the court grant the professors' motion? Why would the court rule in the Commonwealth's favor? [*Urofsky v. Allen,* 995 F.Supp. 634 (E.D.Va. 1998)]

7–6. Defamation. An unidentified person posted messages on America Online, Inc. (AOL), advertising for sale t-shirts and other items with offensive slogans related to the 1995 bombing of the federal building in Oklahoma City. Buyers were instructed to call the business phone number of Ken Zeran, who knew nothing about the ad. Zeran received a high volume of calls, consisting of derogatory messages and death threats. He called AOL and was assured that the messages would be removed. The postings remained up for five days, however, during which time the angry calls to Zeran intensified. Zeran filed a suit in a federal district court against AOL, arguing in part that AOL was liable for unreasonably delaying in removing the defamatory messages. Why would the court rule in AOL's favor? [*Zeran v. America Online, Inc.,* 129 F.3d 327 (4th Cir. 1997)]

7–7. Cyber Marks. Playboy Enterprises, Inc. (PEI), owns the rights to the cyber marks "Playboy," "Playboy magazine," and "Playmate." Without authorization, Calvin Designer Label used the terms as meta tags for its Web sites on the Internet. As tags, the terms were invisible to viewers (in black type on a black background), but they caused the Web sites to be returned at the top of the list of a search engine query for "Playboy" or "Playmate." PEI filed a suit in a federal district court against Calvin Designer Label, alleging, among other things, trademark infringement. Should the court order the defendants to stop using the terms as tags? Why or why not? [*Playboy Enterprises, Inc. v. Calvin Designer Label,* 985 F.Supp. 1220 (N.D.Cal. 1997)]

7–8. Copyrights. Webbworld operates a Web site called Neptics, Inc. The site accepts downloads of certain images from third parties and makes these images available to any user who accesses the site. Before being allowed to view the images, however, the user must pay a subscription fee of $11.95 per month. Over a period of several months, images were available that were originally created by or for Playboy Enterprises, Inc. (PEI). The images were displayed at Neptics's site without PEI's permission. PEI filed a suit in a federal district court against Webbworld, alleging copyright infringement. Webbworld argued in part that it should not be held liable because, like an Internet service provider that provides access to the Internet, it did not create or control the content of the information available to its subscribers. Do you agree with Webbworld? Why or why not? [*Playboy Enterprises, Inc. v. Webbworld,* 968 F.Supp. 1171 (N.D.Tex. 1997)]

A QUESTION OF ETHICS AND SOCIAL RESPONSIBILITY

7–9. Storm Impact, Inc., produces software, including the games TaskMaker and MacSki. To market upgraded versions of the games, Storm distributed them as shareware with locks built into the programs. A user could sample the unlocked portions at no charge and then buy a key, in the form of a floppy disk and registration number, to use the whole program. A legend expressly encouraged users to give unaltered copies to others but prohibited users from charging others for the shareware. Software of the Month Club (SOMC) provides collections of new shareware to its members for a $24.95 per month fee. When Storm's games were included in one of SOMC's collections, Storm filed a suit in a federal district court against SOMC, alleging, among other things, copyright infringement. SOMC argued that its copying and distribution of the games constituted a "fair use." The court held that SOMC had infringed Storm's copyrights and awarded Storm $20,000 in damages. [*Storm Impact, Inc. v. Software of the Month Club,* 13 F.Supp.2d 782, 1998 WL 466855 (N.D.Ill. 1998)]

1. SOMC claimed that by endorsing and distributing shareware, it was performing a service for the creators, much like a book reviewer does for a book. Do you agree? Why or why not? How might SOMC have avoided this suit? (To fully answer these questions, you may need to review the "fair use" doctrine discussed in Chapter 5.)
2. Should the fact that SOMC was charging for something that was otherwise free on the Internet affect the outcome in this suit? Should Storm's restriction on charging for its shareware affect the result? Why or why not? What are the implications of the holding in this case for other shareware distributors?

FOR CRITICAL ANALYSIS

7–10. It has been said that, regardless of what the law requires, the best way for a party to pursue a remedy for defamation is to demand a public retraction. Why might this be good advice? Would a retraction on the Internet be an effective remedy for an instance of defamation on the Internet? Why or why not?

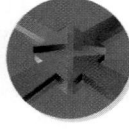

Online Activities

ONLINE EXERCISE 7–1

Go to www.maricopa.gov/supcrt/supcrt.html, the Web site of the Superior Court of Arizona, Maricopa County. Click on some of the links to determine what is available at this site and then answer the following questions:

- What help is provided for nonlawyers who have cases to bring to the court?
- What information is available regarding trials and court hearings taking place?
- On the "Law Library" page, click on the "Bibliographies and Research" link. What material is available concerning electronic filing with courts and other electronic access issues?
- What links at this site might you follow to determine whether your local court is online?
- What might be added to this site to improve it?

ONLINE EXERCISE 7–2

The Copyright Web site provides basic information concerning copyrights. Access this site at www.benedict.com, click on "Let's Go!," and then do the following:

- Click on the "Edge: Internet and Software" title, icon (the razor blade), or pull-down menu, and browse through some of the links on the "Edge" page. According to these sources, how much of what is on the Web is protected by copyright law? If you publish on the Web, what can you take from others' Web sites to include on your page?
- On the "Edge" page, click on the "Controlling Software" link. According to this source, what right does the owner of copyrighted software have to prevent the public from using the software without payment? Can the owner distribute the software for free and without restrictions? Why might an owner who is willing to distribute software for free not want to do so without imposing restrictions?

Before the Test

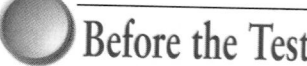

Go to the *Business Law Today* home page at http://blt.westbuslaw.com. Click on TestTutor.® You will find twenty interactive questions relating to this chapter.

CHAPTER 8

Ethics & Social Responsibility

"New occasions teach new duties."

James Russell Lowell, 1819–1891
(American editor, poet, and diplomat)

CONTENTS

LEARNING OBJECTIVES

After reading this chapter, you should be able to:

1. Define business ethics and its relationship to personal ethics.
2. Explain the relationship between the law and ethics.
3. Compare and contrast duty-based ethics and utilitarian ethics.
4. Identify the various groups to whom corporations are perceived to owe duties.
5. Discuss some of the difficulties involved in measuring corporate social responsibility.

Business owners and managers traditionally have had to ensure that their profit-making activities do not exceed the ethical boundaries established by society. In the past, though, these boundaries were often regarded as being coterminous with the law—that is, if something was legal, it was ethical. Shady business dealings were regarded as "just business" more often than not.

In the last few decades, however, the ethical boundaries within which business firms must operate have narrowed significantly. As indicated in the chapter-opening quotation, "New occasions teach new duties," and in the rights-conscious world of today a business firm that decides it has no duties other than those prescribed by law may find it difficult to survive. If a firm's behavior is perceived as unethical—even though it may be legal—that firm may suffer negative publicity, boycotts, and lost profits.

In preparing for a career in business, you will find that a background in business ethics and a commitment to ethical behavior is just as important as a knowledge of the specific laws that you will read about in this text. In this chapter, we first examine the nature of business ethics and some of the sources of ethical standards that have guided others in their business decision making. We then look at some of the obstacles to ethical behavior faced by businesspersons. In the remaining pages of the chapter, which deal with corporate social responsibility, we explore the following question: How can businesspersons act in an ethically responsible manner and at the same time make profits for their firms or their firms' owners?

The Nature of Business Ethics

• **ETHICS**
Moral principles and values applied to social behavior.

To understand the nature of business ethics, we need to define what is meant by ethics generally. **Ethics** can be defined as the study of what constitutes right or wrong behavior. It is the branch of philosophy that focuses on morality and the way in which moral principles are applied to daily life. Ethics has to do with questions relating to the fairness, justness, rightness, or wrongness of an action. What is fair? What is just? What is the right thing to do in this situation?—these are essentially ethical questions.

Often, moral principles serve as the guiding force in an individual's personal ethical system. Although the terms *ethical* and *moral* are often used interchangeably, the terms refer to slightly different concepts. Whereas ethics has to do with the philosophical, rational basis for morality, morals are often defined as universal rules or guidelines (such as those rooted in religious precepts) that determine our actions and character.

Defining Business Ethics

• **BUSINESS ETHICS**
Ethics in a business context; a consensus of what constitutes right or wrong behavior in the world of business and the application of moral principles to situations that arise in a business setting.

Business ethics focuses on what constitutes ethical behavior in the world of business. Personal ethical standards, of course, play an important role in determining what is or is not ethical, or appropriate, business behavior. Business activities are just one part of the human enterprise, and the ethical standards that guide our behavior as, say, mothers, fathers, or students apply equally well to our activities as businesspersons. Businesspersons, though, often must address more complex ethical issues and conflicts in the workplace than they do in their personal lives—as you will learn in this chapter and throughout this book.

Business Ethics and the Law

Because the law reflects and codifies a society's ethical values, many of our ethical decisions are made for us—by our laws. Nevertheless, simply obeying the law does not fulfill all ethical obligations. In the interest of preserving personal freedom, as well as for practical reasons, the law does not—and cannot—codify all ethical requirements. No law says, for example, that it is *illegal* to lie to one's family, but it may be *unethical* to do so.

Likewise, in the business world, numerous actions might be unethical but not necessarily illegal. Even though it may be convenient for businesspersons to satisfy themselves by mere compliance with the law, such an approach may not always yield ethical outcomes. For example, a pharmaceutical company may be banned from marketing a particular drug in the United States because of the drug's adverse side effects. Yet no law prohibits the company from selling the drug in foreign markets—even though some consumers in those markets may suffer serious health problems as a result of using the drug. At issue here is not whether it would be legal to market the drug in other countries but whether it would *ethical* to do so.

In short, the law has its limits—it cannot make all our ethical decisions for us. When it does not, ethical standards must guide the decision-making process.

Sources of Ethical Standards

Religious and philosophical inquiry into the nature of "the good" is an age-old pursuit. Broadly speaking, though, ethical reasoning relating to business traditionally has been characterized by two fundamental approaches. One approach defines ethical behavior in terms of *duty*. The other approach determines what is ethical in terms of the *consequences*, or outcome, of any given action. We examine each of these approaches here.

Duty-Based Ethics

Is it wrong to cheat on an examination, if nobody will ever know that you cheated and if it helps you get into law school so that you can eventually volunteer your legal services to the poor and needy? Is it wrong to lie to your parents if the lie harms nobody but helps to keep family relations congenial? These kinds of ethical questions implicitly weigh the "end" of an action against the "means" used to attain that end. If you believe that you have an ethical *duty* not to lie or cheat, however, then lying and cheating can never be justified by the consequences, no matter how benevolent or desirable those consequences may be. Duty-based ethics may be based on religious precepts or philosophical reasoning.

Religion Duty-based ethical standards are often derived from moral principles rooted in religious sources. For example, in the Judeo-Christian tradition, the Ten Commandments of the Old Testament establish rules for moral action. Other religions have their own sources of revealed truth—such as the Koran in the Muslim world. Within the confines of their influence, moral principles are universal and *absolute*—they are not to be questioned. • **EXAMPLE 8.1** Consider one of the Ten Commandments: "Thou shalt not steal." This is an absolute mandate. Even a benevolent motive for stealing (such as Robin Hood's) cannot justify the act, because the act itself is inherently immoral and thus wrong. When an act is prohibited by religious teachings that serve as the foundation of a person's moral or ethical standards, the act is unethical for that person and should not be undertaken, regardless of its consequences.•

Ethical standards based on religious teachings also may involve an element of compassion. Therefore, even though it might be profitable for a firm to lay off a less productive employee, if that employee were to find it difficult to find employment elsewhere and his or her family were to suffer as a result, this potential suffering would be given substantial weight by the decision makers. Compassionate treatment of others is also mandated—to a certain extent, at least—by the Golden Rule of the ancients ("Do unto others as you would have them do unto you"), which has been adopted by most religions.

Kantian Philosophy Ethical standards based on a concept of duty may also be derived solely from philosophical principles. Immanuel Kant (1724–1804), for example, identified some general guiding principles for moral behavior based on what he believed to be the fundamental nature of human beings. Kant held that it is rational to assume that human beings are qualitatively different from other physical objects occupying space. Persons are endowed with moral integrity and the capacity to reason and conduct their affairs rationally. Therefore, their thoughts and actions should be respected. When human beings are treated merely as a means to an end, they are being treated as the equivalent of objects and are being denied their basic humanity.

A central postulate in Kantian ethics is that individuals should evaluate their actions in light of the consequences that would follow if everyone in society acted in the same way. This **categorical imperative** can be applied to any action. For example, say that you are deciding whether to cheat on an examination. If you have adopted Kant's categorical imperative, you will decide not to cheat, because if everyone cheated, the examination would be meaningless.

• **CATEGORICAL IMPERATIVE**
A concept developed by the philosopher Immanuel Kant as an ethical guideline for behavior. In deciding whether an action is right or wrong, or desirable or undesirable, a person should evaluate the action in terms of what would happen if everybody else in the same situation, or category, acted the same way.

• **UTILITARIANISM**
An approach to ethical reasoning in which ethically correct behavior is not related to any absolute ethical or moral values but to an evaluation of the consequences of a given action on those who will be affected by it. In utilitarian reasoning, a "good" decision is one that results in the greatest good for the greatest number of people affected by the decision.

• **COST-BENEFIT ANALYSIS**
A decision-making technique that involves weighing the costs of a given action against the benefits of the action.

OUTCOME-BASED ETHICS

"Thou shalt act so as to generate the greatest good for the greatest number." This is a paraphrase of the major premise of the utilitarian approach to ethics. **Utilitarianism** is a philosophical theory first developed by Jeremy Bentham (1748–1832) and then advanced, with some modifications, by John Stuart Mill (1806–1873)—both British philosophers. In contrast to duty-based ethics, utilitarianism is outcome oriented. It focuses on the consequences of an action, not on the nature of the action itself or on any set of preestablished moral values or religious beliefs.

Under a utilitarian model of ethics, an action is morally correct, or "right," when, among the people it affects, it produces the greatest amount of good for the greatest number. When an action affects the majority adversely, it is morally wrong. Applying the utilitarian theory thus requires (1) a determination of which individuals will be affected by the action in question; (2) a **cost-benefit analysis**—an assessment of the negative and positive effects of alternative actions on these individuals; and (3) a choice among alternative actions that will produce maximum societal utility (the greatest positive benefits for the greatest number of individuals).

Utilitarianism is often criticized because it tends to focus on society as a whole rather than on individual human rights. For example, from a utilitarian standpoint, it might be ethically acceptable to test drugs or medicines on human beings because presumably a majority of the population would benefit from the experiments. If, however, one accepts the principle that each individual has basic human rights (to life, freedom, and the pursuit of happiness), then an action that deprives an individual or group of individuals of these rights—even for the greater good of society—is ethically unacceptable. No amount of cost-benefit analysis can justify the action.

APPLYING ETHICAL STANDARDS

¡BE CAREFUL!
Ethical concepts about what is right and what is wrong can change.

Consider the following example: A corporation that markets baby formula in developing countries has learned that mothers in those countries often mix the formula with impure water, to make the formula go further. As a result, babies are suffering from malnutrition, diarrhea, and in some instances, even death. What is the corporation's ethical responsibility in this situation? Should it withdraw the product from those markets (and lose profits), or should it conduct a cost-benefit analysis and let the decision be guided by the results?

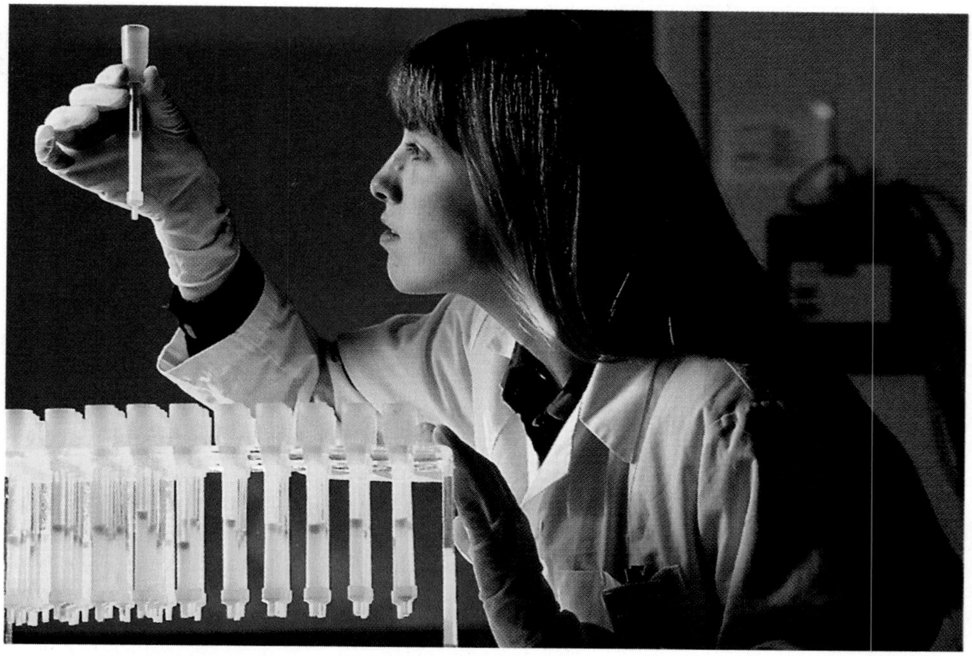

A LAB WORKER CONDUCTS RESEARCH FOR THE DEVELOPMENT OF A DRUG. IF THE DRUG PROVES BENEFICIAL TO MOST PEOPLE BUT ADVERSE TO A FEW, WOULD IT, UNDER A UTILITARIAN MODEL OF ETHICS, BE MARKETED?

If the corporation's decision makers felt that they had an absolute duty not to harm others, then the only ethical response would be to withdraw the product from those markets. If the decision makers approached the problem from a utilitarian perspective, they would engage in a cost-benefit analysis. The cost of the action (the suffering and death of babies) would be weighed against its benefit (the availability of the formula to mothers). Having the formula available frees mothers from the task of breastfeeding and thus allows them to earn money to help raise their incomes and standards of living. The question in a utilitarian analysis would focus on whether the benefit outweighed the cost—not the inherent rightness or wrongness of the action.

In fact, this scenario is not hypothetical. In the 1970s, the Nestlé Company concluded, on the basis of a cost-benefit analysis, that it was ethically justified in continuing to market its baby formula in developing countries. Other companies marketing infant formula in those areas, in contrast, reached a different decision: they pulled out of those markets. Nestlé was severely criticized for its behavior. The company's opponents were outraged, not because the formula had been marketed initially but because of Nestlé's decision to continue marketing the formula based on its cost-benefit analysis.

Obstacles to Ethical Business Behavior

People sometimes behave unethically in the business context, just as they do in their private lives. Some businesspersons knowingly engage in unethical behavior because they think that they can "get away with it"—that no one will ever learn of their unethical actions. Examples of this kind of unethical behavior include padding expense accounts, casting doubts on the integrity of a rival co-worker to gain a job promotion, stealing company supplies or equipment, and so on. Obviously, these acts are unethical, and many of them are illegal as well.

ON THE WEB
The Web site of DePaul University's Institute for Business and Professional Ethics includes several examples of the types of ethical issues that can arise in the business context. Go to
condor.depaul.edu/ethics/biz17.html.

In other situations, businesspersons who would choose to act ethically may be deterred from doing so because of situational circumstances or external pressures. We look here at how both the corporate environment and the conduct of management can sometimes act as deterrents to ethical behavior.

ETHICS AND THE CORPORATE ENVIRONMENT

Some contend that the nature of the corporate structure itself acts as a deterrent to ethically responsible behavior. We examine the corporate structure in detail in Chapters 27 and 28. Briefly, a corporation is structured as follows: The owners of the corporation are the shareholders—those who purchase shares of stock in the company. The shareholders, however, do not run the corporation. Rather, they elect a board of directors and entrust those directors with the responsibility of directing and overseeing the corporate enterprise. The directors, in turn, hire officers and managers to handle the day-to-day business activities of the firm. A shareholder may also be a director, and a director may also be a corporate officer—the president or chief executive officer, for example.

Ethics and Collective Decision Making The corporate setting complicates ethical decision making because (normally) no one person makes a corporate decision. If you are an officer or manager of a large corporation, for example, you may find that the decision as to what is right or wrong for the corporation is not yours to make. Corporate officers and managers, of course, do make decisions that affect the corporation, and your input may weigh in the decision. The ultimate decision makers, however, are the members of the board of directors, who must make decisions as a group.

Collective decision making, because it places emphasis on consensus and unity of opinion, also tends to hinder individual ethical assertiveness. For example, suppose that a director has ethical misgivings about a planned corporate venture that promises to be highly profitable. If the other directors have no such misgivings, the director who does may be swayed by the enthusiasm of the others for the project and downplay his or her own criticisms.

Diminished Personal Accountability To some extent, the corporate collectivity may shield corporate personnel from both personal exposure to the consequences of their decisions and personal accountability for those decisions. • **EXAMPLE 8.2** Suppose that a corporate board decides to market a new product that results in several consumers' deaths. Those who made the decision do not witness or deal directly with these consequences. Furthermore, just as normally no one individual is responsible for a corporate decision, so normally no one person is held accountable for the decision. (In recent years, though, the courts have been increasingly willing to look behind the "corporate veil" and hold individual corporate actors liable, or legally responsible, for actions resulting in harm to others.) •

¡NOTE!
A business that examines its conduct, and the conduct of its managers and employees, can prevent unethical and illegal acts.

ETHICS AND MANAGEMENT

Much unethical business behavior occurs simply because it is not always clear what ethical standards and behaviors are appropriate or acceptable in a given context. Although most firms now issue ethical policies or codes of conduct, these policies and codes are not always effective in creating an ethical workplace. At times, this is because a firm's ethical policies are not communicated clearly to employees or do not bear on the real ethical issues confronting decision makers. Additionally, particularly in a large corporation, unethical behavior in one corporate department may simply escape the attention of those in control of the corporation or the corporate officials responsible for implementing and monitoring the company's ethics program.

Another deterrent to ethical behavior exists when corporate management, by its own conduct, indicates that ethical considerations take second place. • EXAMPLE 8.3 If management makes no attempt to deter unethical behavior—by reprimanding or firing employees, for example—it will be clear to employees that management is not all that serious about ethics. Likewise, if a company doles out promotions or salary increases to those who obviously engage in unethical tactics to increase the firm's profits, then employees who do not resort to such tactics will be at a disadvantage. An employee in this situation may decide that because "everyone else does it," he or she might as well do so also.•

Of course, an even stronger deterrent to ethical behavior occurs when employers engage in blatantly unethical or illegal conduct and expect their employees to do so as well. An employee in this situation faces two options, neither of which is satisfactory: (1) participate in the conduct or (2) "blow the whistle" on—inform authorities of—the employer's actions and risk being fired. (See Chapter 37 for a more detailed discussion of "whistleblowing.")

Corporate Social Responsibility

We now return to the question posed in this chapter's introduction: How can businesspersons act in an ethically responsible manner and at the same time make profits for their firms or their firms' owners? This question is at the heart of the debate surrounding the concept of **corporate social responsibility**—the idea that corporations can and should act ethically and be accountable to society for their actions. No one contests the claim that corporations have duties to their shareholders, employers, and product users (consumers). Many of these duties are written into law—that is, they are legal duties. The question of corporate social responsibility concerns the extent to which a corporation has ethical duties to various groups in society that go beyond its legally prescribed duties.

• **CORPORATE SOCIAL RESPONSIBILITY**
The concept that corporations can and should act ethically and be accountable to society for their actions.

To understand the debate over corporate social responsibility, consider a hypothetical firm: the Farris Company. This firm markets its products, primarily paints and glues, throughout the world. The company is facing a financial crisis and must find a way to increase its profits if it is to survive. In so doing, however, Farris will need to take into account the ethical ramifications of any decisions it makes. In the following pages, we examine some of the problematic aspects of a corporation's responsibilities in regard to shareholders, employees, consumers, the community, and society. As you will see, corporations such as the Farris Company face difficult choices in trying to be ethically responsible.

> **ON THE WEB**
> Numerous online groups focus on the activities of various corporations from the perspective of corporate social responsibility. A good starting point for locating these kinds of Web sites is Beobab's Corporate Power Information Center at **www.beobabcomputing.com**.

DUTY TO SHAREHOLDERS

Corporate directors and officers have a duty to act in the shareholders' interest. Because of the nature of the relationship between corporate directors and officers and the shareholder-owners, the law holds directors and officers to a high standard of care in business decision making (see Chapter 28).

Traditionally, it was perceived that this duty to shareholders took precedence over all other corporate duties and that the primary goal of corporations should be profit maximization. Milton Friedman, the Nobel Prize–winning economist and a

ON THE WEB
You can find articles on issues relating to shareholders and corporate accountability at the Corporate Governance Web site. Go to
www.corpgov.net.

proponent of the profit-maximization view, saw "one and only one" social responsibility of a corporation: "to use its resources and engage in activities designed to increase its profits, so long as it stays within the rules of the game."[1] The "rules of the game" were the "basic rules of society, both those embodied in law and those embodied in ethical custom."[2]

Those who support the profit-maximization view of social responsibility contend that the duty to maximize profits must outweigh any other duty when duties conflict—to the extent, of course, that in maximizing shareholders' profits a firm does not violate the "basic rules of society." The question here is, what are these basic rules?

• **EXAMPLE 8.4** Suppose that our hypothetical firm, the Farris Company, has suffered a setback because the U.S. government banned the sale of one of its paint thinners. The paint thinner, if allowed to touch the skin of some users, can cause severe irritation, and many consumers have complained of such problems. The product is not banned in foreign markets, though, and thus Farris faces an ethical question: Should it continue marketing the product in other countries? Certainly, it would benefit the shareholders to do so, but would such an action violate society's basic rules and ethical customs? Even if the action violated the ethical rules of even a small minority of Americans, that small minority, through activism and publicity, could harm Farris's reputation as an ethically responsible corporation.•

DUTY TO EMPLOYEES

ON THE WEB
You can find the complete text of the major federal laws prohibiting employment discrimination, including the ADEA, at the Web site of the Equal Employment Opportunity Commission. Go to
www.eeoc.gov.

As you will read in Chapters 37 and 38, by law employers are required to provide a safe workplace, to pay a minimum wage, and to provide equal employment opportunities for all potential and existing employees. There are many "gray areas" in the law, however, and it is not always clear to employers just how the law will apply to a certain set of circumstances. • **EXAMPLE 8.5** Under federal laws employers must "reasonably accommodate" the religious needs of their employees and the needs of employees or job applicants with disabilities—unless to do so creates an "undue hardship" for the employer. No law, however, spells out exactly what "reasonable accommodation" means or the point at which an employer experiences "undue hardship." Generally, the courts decide these issues on a case-by-case basis.•

When facing legal uncertainties such as these, business decision makers need to proceed with caution and evaluate the action and its consequences from an ethical perspective. Generally, if a company can demonstrate that it acted responsibly and in good faith in the circumstances, it has a better chance of defending its action successfully in court or before an administrative law judge.

We look next at some employment decisions facing employers in which ethical considerations often come into play. (You will read about other ethical issues that arise in the employment context in Chapters 37 and 38.)

Sexual Harassment in the Workplace An ongoing problem for employers is how to prevent sexual harassment from occurring in the workplace. This is particularly true with respect to "hostile-environment harassment," which occurs when an employee is subjected to sexual conduct or comments that he or she perceives as offensive. Generally, employers are expected to take immediate and appropriate cor-

1. *Capitalism and Freedom* (Chicago: University of Chicago Press, 1962), p. 133.
2. Milton Friedman, "Does Business Have Social Responsibility?" *Bank Administration,* April 1971, pp. 13–14.

The Letter of the Law — NO REAL DAMAGES, BUT PUNISHMENT NONETHELESS

The Seventh Circuit Court of Appeals recently reviewed a sexual-harassment case in which the jury awarded the plaintiff punitive damages of $15,000 but no back pay or compensatory damages. On appeal, the defendant company argued that punitive damages could not be awarded when the jury determined that the plaintiff did not suffer any injury to be compensated (by compensatory damages). The appellate court, however, held that the award had "no legal flaws" and affirmed the jury's decision. The appellate court stated that although state law did not allow punitive damages without a compensatory award, under a federal law prohibiting racial discrimination a jury could award punitive damages even though it does not award compensatory damages. The court pointed out that even persons who do no more than read newspaper advertisements that depict racially unbalanced groups of models may be entitled to punitive damages. The court decided to extend this principle to the federal law prohibiting gender-based discrimination (including sexual harassment) as well.[a]

THE BOTTOM LINE

When the letter of the law is silent or ambiguous on a particular issue, judges determine how the law will be applied.

a. *Timm v. Progressive Steel Treating, Inc.*, 137 F.3d 1008 (7th Cir. 1998).

ON THE WEB

To learn about the United States Supreme Court's recent views on sexual harassment, access the Supreme Court opinions at

www.findlaw.com

and browse through the following two cases decided by the Court in 1998: *Burlington Industries v. Ellerth* and *Faragher v. City of Boca Raton.*

rective action in response to employees' complaints of sexual harassment or abuse. If they do not, they may face costly damages in a subsequent lawsuit. Yet taking immediate corrective action—such as firing an employee for harassing behavior—may lead to other problems.

• **EXAMPLE 8.6** Suppose that an employee complains to her supervisor that a co-worker is sexually harassing her—physically touching her in objectionable ways, making lewd comments to her, and so on. The company immediately investigates the claim, and on finding that it is somewhat substantiated, promptly fires the harassing employee. In taking this action, the company assumes that it is acting responsibly. The fired employee, however, then sues the firm for *wrongful discharge* (firing an employee without good cause or for discriminatory reasons—see Chapter 37). Will the fired employee win the lawsuit? Perhaps. Under some state laws and employment agreements, employers are prohibited from firing employees without "just cause," and particular incidents of sexual harassment may or may not constitute just cause for firing the purported harasser. •

In an attempt to protect their employees from harassment—and shield themselves from liability (see, for example, this chapter's *The Letter of the Law*)—most large companies today, as well as many smaller ones, have implemented harassment policies. These policies typically establish procedures that employees can follow if they feel they are being harassed by supervisors or co-workers. The policies also instruct management and supervisory personnel on the proper corrective actions to take in response to employees' complaints. For most situations, corrective actions involve a series of steps. Initially, the harassing employee is informed of the problem and asked to cease the offensive behavior. If the behavior continues, then the employee may be placed on probation. Finally, if the problem recurs, the employee will be fired. A company that can demonstrate that it established and followed such procedures may be able to avoid liability for either sexual harassment or wrongful discharge.

The following case illustrates what can result when an employer maintains and distributes a sexual-harassment policy and reporting procedures, and a harassed employee delays in using them.

CASE 8.1 Montero v. AGCO Corp.

United States District Court,
Eastern District of California, 1998.
19 F.Supp.2d 1143.

HISTORICAL AND SOCIAL SETTING *Title VII of the Civil Rights Act of 1964 prohibits employment discrimination on the basis of "sex," or gender. This discrimination includes acts or comments that create a hostile working environment, which is a situation that a reasonable person would find offensive. Courts have often been asked to determine whether particular acts or comments are extreme enough to create a hostile environment. What has been rarely at issue is what defense employers might use to avoid liability for the wrongful behavior of their employees. (It was long ago held that an employer is not "automatically" liable.[a]) Recently, the United States Supreme Court set out two elements of such a defense. The Court indicated that an employer might avoid liability if it has established a harassment policy and complaint procedures and employees alleging harassment failed to follow those procedures.[b]*

a. *Meritor Savings Bank, FSB v. Vinson,* 477 U.S. 57, 106 S.Ct. 2399, 91 L.Ed.2d 49 (1986).

BACKGROUND AND FACTS AGCO Corporation's employee policies include provisions against sexual harassment and procedures for reporting and handling allegations of harassment. Shortly after being hired by AGCO, Carrie Ann Montero was subjected to sexual harassment by Glenn Carpenter, a warehouse manager, and Russ Newman, a warehouse supervisor. Although Montero knew of AGCO's harassment policies, she did not report the sexual harassment for nearly two years. When she did report it, AGCO immediately began an investigation. Carpenter was discharged, and Newman was disciplined. Montero took a short leave of absence, after which she did not return to work, despite encouragement from AGCO executives. Montero filed a suit in a federal district court against AGCO and others, alleging, in part, violations of Title VII. AGCO filed a motion for summary judgment on the Title VII charge.

b. *Faragher v. City of Boca Raton,* ___ U.S. ___, 118 S.Ct. 2275, 141 L.Ed.2d 662 (1998).

IN THE WORDS OF THE COURT . . .
DAMRELL, District J.

* * * *

* * * [An] employer may raise an affirmative defense [against charges of sexual harassment]. * * * The defense comprises two necessary elements: (a) that the employer exercised reasonable care to prevent and correct promptly any sexually harassing behavior, and (b) that the plaintiff employee unreasonably failed to take advantage of any preventive or corrective opportunities provided by the employer or to avoid harm otherwise.

* * * *

* * * AGCO exercised reasonable care to prevent sexual harassment by maintaining and distributing a policy prohibiting sexual harassment and by providing a mechanism for employees to report such conduct directly to the Human Resources Department. Moreover, AGCO immediately investigated plaintiff's complaints and acted to correct the same. Conversely, plaintiff unreasonably failed to take advantage of the preventive and corrective opportunities provided by AGCO or to otherwise avoid harm.

DECISION AND REMEDY The court issued a summary judgment in AGCO's favor regarding the Title VII claim. The court held that an employer's policy and procedure concerning sexual harassment, and an employee's delay in using the procedure, can constitute a defense to a charge of harassment.

FOR CRITICAL ANALYSIS—Economic Consideration *What might have been the result in this case if AGCO had not had a sexual-harassment policy and reporting procedure?*

Corporate Restructuring and Employee Welfare Suppose that our hypothetical firm, the Farris Company, decided to reduce its costs by downsizing and restructuring its operations. Among other things, this would allow Farris to cut back on its overhead by consolidating various supervisory and managerial positions. Yet which employees should Farris retain, and which employees should Farris let go? Should the firm retain its highly paid employees who have worked for—and received annual

Business Law in Action • PROTECTION FOR OLDER WORKERS

The Age Discrimination in Employment Act (ADEA) of 1967, as amended by the Older Workers Benefit Protection Act (OWBPA) of 1990, allows employers to obtain releases from employees—contracts in which the employees agree not to bring legal proceedings against the employers under the ADEA—in return for receiving severance benefits. The OWBPA sets forth specific requirements that employers must meet when drafting such contracts, however. An employee, for example, must sign the release "knowingly and voluntarily" and must be given forty-five days to decide whether to sign the release.

Whether Sears Roebuck & Company had violated the OWBPA was at issue in a recent case brought by a former Sears employee, Thomas Long. Long had worked for Sears for thirty years when he and several other employees in the Home Improvement Products and Services (HIPS) division of Sears were told that the company was permanently disbanding the HIPS division. Sears promised HIPS employees that it would try to transfer them to other positions with the company and that preference would be given to long-term HIPS employees with satisfactory performance ratings. Those employees who were not transferred would be laid off, as Long ultimately was, even though he had actively sought a transfer within Sears.

Long was offered a severance package, including $39,000 in severance benefits, in return for signing a release in which he agreed to waive all claims against Sears under the ADEA. Although Long accepted the benefits and signed the release, he later sued Sears for age discrimination and for violating the OWBPA. Long claimed that following his layoff, Sears retrained younger employees with less seniority to work in other departments, and, contrary to its representations, Sears did not permanently disband its HIPS division. Long also claimed that he had not knowingly or voluntarily signed the release; rather, he had been pressured by his supervisor into signing it.

A central issue before the court was whether Long had to "tender back" the $39,000 in order to be able to bring an action against Sears or whether Long could go forward with the suit and simply deduct the $39,000 from any damage award he received. Ultimately, a federal appellate court held against the "tender-back" requirement. The court held that to apply the requirement in such circumstances would mean that "[n]o matter how egregiously releases might violate the requirements of the [OWBPA], employees would be precluded from challenging them unless they somehow . . . come up with the money they were given when allegedly forced into retirement." In the appellate court's eyes, employees whose releases were defective under the OWBPA would, in effect, be "no better off than before the OWBPA was enacted."[a]

AN ELDERLY EMPLOYEE WORKS AT A FAST FOOD RESTAURANT. WHAT LAWS PROTECT OLDER WORKERS FROM DISCRIMINATION?

FOR CRITICAL ANALYSIS

When an older employee, such as Long, is laid off, does that person have any real choice when deciding whether or not to accept severance pay and sign a required release?

a. *Long v. Sears Roebuck & Co.*, 105 F.3d 1529 (3d Cir. 1997).

ON THE WEB
You can find links to numerous Web sites focusing on employment benefits, including the federal law governing employer-provided pension plans, at **www.benefitslink.com**.

raises from—the firm for years? Alternatively, in the interests of cutting costs, should it retain (or hire) younger, less experienced persons at lower salaries?

The firm would not necessarily be acting illegally if it pursued the second option. Unless a fired employee can prove that the employer has breached an employment contract or violated the Age Discrimination in Employment Act (ADEA) of 1967, the employee normally will not have a cause of action against the employer. The ADEA prohibits discrimination against workers forty years old and older on the basis of their age (see this chapter's *Business Law in Action* for a further discussion of age discrimination). Farris, though, can always say that lack of performance or ability, not age, was the deciding factor. The question here is whether such an action would be ethical.

In deciding this issue, remember that Farris must keep its eye on its profit margin. If it does not, the firm may fail, and the shareholders will lose their investments. Furthermore, why should the firm retain highly paid employees if it can obtain essentially the same work output for a lower price by retaining its less highly paid employees? Does Farris owe an ethical duty to its employees who have served the firm loyally over a long period of time? Most people would say yes. Should this duty take precedence over Farris's duty to the firm's owners to maintain or increase the profitability of the firm? Would your answer be the same if the firm faced imminent bankruptcy if it could not lower its operating costs? What if long-time employees were willing to take a slight reduction in pay to help the firm through its financial difficulties? What if they were not?

In the following case, an employer was confronted with a dwindling market and decreasing sales. The employer decided to reduce its costs of doing business by eliminating some of its obligations to its employees.

CASE 8.2 Varity Corp. v. Howe

Supreme Court of the United States, 1996.
516 U.S. 489,
116 S.Ct. 1065,
134 L.Ed.2d 130.
laws.findlaw.com/US/000/U10206.html[a]

HISTORICAL AND ECONOMIC SETTING *Since 1950, the number of U.S. farms has declined as small farms have been driven out of business by corporate agribusinesses with assets that small farmers cannot match. Between 1980 and 1996, the number of farms decreased by over 14 percent, to less than 2 million, even as the average acreage per farm increased by 10 percent, to nearly 470 acres. Agribusinesses require fewer workers than do small farms, and thus, the total farm population also decreased by 24 percent in the 1980s. Fewer farmers means a smaller market for those who cater to it.*

BACKGROUND AND FACTS Varity Corporation manufactures and sells farm implements. In 1986, Varity set up a subsidiary, Massey Combines Corporation (MCC), to market its self-propelled combines and four-wheel-drive tractors. The sales of both products were at an all-time low. Varity convinced current and former employees who were, or had been, involved with the products to accept a transfer of their jobs and retirement benefit plans to MCC. Varity did not tell those employees that it expected MCC to fail. Within two years, MCC failed. Among other consequences, some retirees stopped receiving benefits. The retirees and other ex-employees sued Varity in a federal district court under the Employee Retirement Income Security Act of 1974 (ERISA).[b] They claimed that Varity owed them a fiduciary duty, which it had breached.[c] The court ruled in their favor, and the U.S. Court of Appeals for the Eighth Circuit affirmed the decision. Varity then appealed to the United States Supreme Court.

a. This is a page within the Web site of FindLaw. In addition to its own databases, FindLaw provides links to other legal resources on the Internet.

b. 29 U.S.C. Sections 1001–1461. See Chapter 37.

c. A fiduciary is a party who, because of something that he or she has undertaken to do, has a duty to act primarily for another's benefit.

CASE 8.2—Continued

IN THE WORDS OF THE COURT . . .
JUSTICE BREYER delivered the opinion of the Court.

* * * *

* * * ERISA requires a "fiduciary" to "discharge his duties with respect to a plan solely in the interest of the participants and beneficiaries." To participate knowingly and significantly in deceiving a plan's beneficiaries in order to save the employer money at the beneficiaries' expense, is not to act "solely in the interest of the participants and beneficiaries." As other courts have held, "[l]ying is inconsistent with the duty of loyalty owed by all fiduciaries * * * ."

DECISION AND REMEDY The United States Supreme Court affirmed the decision of the lower court. Varity breached its fiduciary duty to its employees with respect to their retirement benefits.

FOR CRITICAL ANALYSIS—Ethical Consideration *Should a company continue to market a slow-selling line of products for the sole purpose of employing those who work on the products?*

DUTY TO CONSUMERS

"A man cannot shift his misfortunes to his neighbor's shoulders."
OLIVER WENDELL HOLMES, JR., 1841–1935
(Associate justice of the United States Supreme Court, 1902–1932)

Clearly, a corporation has a duty to the users of its products. This is not just an ethical duty but a legal one as well—as you will read in later chapters of this book. Sometimes, though, firms find it difficult to know exactly how the law will apply to certain uses, or misuses, of their products. Another issue with respect to corporate social responsibility has to do with the extent to which a corporation has an ethical duty beyond those duties mandated by law.

Foreseeable Product Misuses Generally, whenever a corporation markets a product, the law imposes a duty on the firm to warn consumers, among other things, of the harms that can result from *foreseeable* misuses. When a risk is "open and obvious," however, courts tend to hold that no warning is necessary. Sharp knives, for example, can obviously injure their users. Courts normally decide whether a particular risk is "open and obvious" on a case-by-case basis, and courts often disagree on whether certain types of risks are open and obvious. Businesspersons thus find it difficult to predict how a court might rule in deciding whether a particular risk is open and obvious or whether consumers should be warned of that risk.

The following case involves an allegation that the warning on an aerosol can of butane failed to warn consumers of the danger of inhaling the contents of the can.

ON THE WEB
The U.S. Consumer Gateway discusses some of the most important consumer issues and offers links to other consumer sites. Go to www.consumer.gov.

CASE 8.3 Pavlik v. Lane Ltd./Tobacco Exporters International

United States Court of Appeals,
Third Circuit, 1998.
135 F.3d 876.
www.law.vill.edu/Fed-Ct/Circuit/3d/February98.html[a]

a. This is the "February Decisions" page within the collection of "1998 Decisions" of the U.S. Court of Appeals for the Third Circuit available at the Web site of the Center for Information Law and Policy. Scroll down the list of cases to the entry for the *Pavlik* case. Click on the link to access the opinion.

HISTORICAL AND CULTURAL SETTING *It is human nature to play Monday morning quarterback—to second guess the choices that others make after the consequences of those choices become fact. Sometimes, such hindsight consists of superimposing what one person believes is common knowledge onto another's set of beliefs and assumptions. This can occur when adults assume that children know what adults know—that an oven is hot, for*

(Continued)

CASE 8.3—Continued

example. A child has to be warned that an oven is hot, and even then he or she may not appreciate the danger, or the seriousness of the danger, depending on the context of the warning. Judges, in particular, have to avoid the temptation to impose their own assumptions about what is common knowledge onto the parties in the cases that come before them.

BACKGROUND AND FACTS Butane is a fuel for cigarette lighters. Zeus brand butane is distributed in small aerosol cans by Lane Limited/Tobacco Exporters International (Lane). On each can is the warning "DO NOT BREATHE SPRAY." Twenty-year-old Stephen Pavlik died from intentionally inhaling the contents of one of the cans. His father, George Pavlik, filed a suit in a federal district court against Lane and others, claiming in part that the statement on the can did not adequately warn users of the hazards of butane inhalation. The court issued a summary judgment in the defendants' favor, reasoning in part that Stephen must have been aware of the dangers of inhaling butane and that a more specific warning would not have affected his conduct. George Pavlik appealed to the U.S. Court of Appeals for the Third Circuit.

IN THE WORDS OF THE COURT . . .
BECKER, Chief Judge.

* * * *

* * * [A]n otherwise properly designed product may still be unreasonably dangerous (and therefore "defective") for strict liability purposes if the product is distributed without sufficient warnings to apprise the ultimate user of the latent dangers in the product.

* * * *

* * * [W]e have serious doubts that the Zeus warning sufficiently warns users of the potentially fatal consequences of butane inhalation, and we are not convinced of its adequacy * * * . More specifically, the "DO NOT BREATHE SPRAY" warning appears to give the user no notice of the serious nature of the danger posed by inhalation, intentional or otherwise, and no other language on the Zeus can does so. Yet, we similarly cannot find that such a directive is inadequate as a matter of law, and so we must leave the question for the jury.

DECISION AND REMEDY The U.S. Court of Appeals for the Third Circuit held that it was not clear that Stephen was fully aware of the dangers of inhaling butane, based on the label on the Zeus cans. The court reversed the judgment of the lower court and remanded the case for trial.

FOR CRITICAL ANALYSIS—Cultural Consideration *Would it have made any difference to the outcome in this case if Stephen's parents had warned him of the dangers of inhaling butane?*

Unforeseeable Product Misuses Sometimes, unforeseeable product misuses pose ethical dilemmas for manufacturers. • **EXAMPLE 8.7** Suppose that the Farris Company learns that one of its products—glue—is being inhaled by thousands of children in several Latin American countries. The health consequences of this misuse can include future kidney disease and brain damage. Consumer activists have launched a media campaign against Farris, accusing it of being unethical by marketing its glue in those countries when such harms result. What is Farris's responsibility in this situation? On the one hand, it has not violated any law and to cease selling the product in those areas would significantly cut into its profits. On the other hand, suspending sales would reduce the suffering of children, and if Farris ignores the public outcry, the continued adverse publicity could also cause the firm to lose sales—and thus profits. Farris's solution will rest on the "ethical weight" it attaches to each of these factors.[3] •

3. When the H. B. Fuller Company faced this situation a few years ago, its solution was to suspend sales of its glues in some Latin American countries but not others. Fuller's critics contended that it should have suspended sales in all of the Latin American countries in which the product was being misused.

ETHICAL ISSUE 8.1 ***Do firms have a duty to prevent criminal misuses of their products?*** Should pesticide manufacturers be held liable when their products are used to create bombs that cause destruction? Should service stations be held liable for selling gasoline to purchasers who then use the gas to set buildings on fire? Such questions have come before the courts on several occasions. In a recent Colorado case, for example, the plaintiff was injured when, after an argument with a man, the man went to a gas station, bought a cupful of gasoline, threw it on the plaintiff, and set her on fire. The plaintiff argued that the defendant gas station was negligent because it should have foreseen, based on the man's behavior and appearance, that selling him a cupful of gas could create a risk that he might harm someone with it. Routinely, the courts have held that such criminal uses of products are unforeseeable misuses for which the manufacturers of the products cannot be held liable. In the Colorado case, a Colorado appellate court also reached this conclusion. The court stated that the risk that a purchaser of gasoline would intentionally throw it on a victim and set the victim on fire was not reasonably foreseeable.[4]

DUTY TO THE COMMUNITY

In some circumstances, the community in which a business enterprise is located has a substantial stake in the firm. Assume, for example, that the Farris Company employs two thousand workers at one of its plants. If the company decides that it would be profitable to close the plant or move it to another location, the employees—and the community—would suffer as a result. Today, to be considered socially responsible, a corporation must take both employees' needs and community needs into consideration when making such a decision.

DUTY TO SOCIETY

"Responsibility walks hand in hand with capacity and power."
JOSIAH G. HOLLAND, 1819–1881
(American author and editor)

Perhaps the most disputed area in the controversy surrounding corporate social responsibility is the nature of a corporation's duty to society at large. Generally, the question turns less on whether corporations owe a duty to society than on how that duty can best be fulfilled.

Profit Maximization Those who contend that corporations should attend to the goal of profit maximization would argue that it is by generating profits that a firm can best contribute to society. Society benefits by profit-making activities, because profits can only be realized when a firm markets products or services that are desired by society. These products and services enhance the standard of living, and the profits accumulated by successful business firms generate national wealth. Our laws and court decisions promoting trade and commerce reflect the public policy that the fruits of commerce (income and wealth) are desirable and good. Because our society values income and wealth as ethical goals, corporations, by contributing to income and wealth, automatically are acting ethically.

Furthermore, profit maximization results in the efficient allocation of resources. Capital, labor, raw materials, and other resources are directed to the production of

4. *Walcott v. Total Petroleum, Inc.*, 964 P.2d 609 (Colo.App. 1998).

those goods and services most desired by society. If capital were directed toward a social goal instead of being reinvested in the corporation, the business operation would become less efficient. For example, if an automobile company contributes $1 million annually to the United Way, that contribution represents $1 million that is not reinvested in making better and safer cars.

Those arguing for profit maximization as a corporate goal also point out that it would be inappropriate to use the power of the corporate business world to fashion society's goals by promoting social causes. Determinations as to what exactly is in society's best interest are essentially political questions, and therefore the public, through the political process, should have a say in making those determinations. The legislature—not the corporate boardroom—is thus the appropriate forum for such decisions.

Critics of Profit Maximization Critics of the profit-maximization view believe that corporations should become actively engaged in seeking and furthering solutions to social problems. Because so much of the wealth and power of this country is controlled by business, business in turn has a responsibility to society to use that wealth and power in socially beneficial ways. Corporations should therefore promote human rights, strive for equal treatment of minorities and women in the workplace, take care to preserve the environment, and generally not profit from activities that society has deemed unethical. The critics also point out that it is ethically irresponsible to leave decisions concerning social welfare up to the government, because many social needs are not being met sufficiently through the political process.

Measuring Corporate Social Responsibility

Measuring corporate social responsibility is difficult because depending on whose yardstick one uses, the answer differs. Traditionally, corporate philanthropy has been used to measure social responsibility. Today, many feel that being ethically responsible involves much more than simply donating funds to charitable causes.

Corporate Philanthropy

"Next to doing the right thing, the most important thing is to let people know you are doing the right thing."

JOHN D. ROCKEFELLER, 1839–1897 (Industrialist and philanthropist)

Since the nineteenth century and the emergence of large business enterprises in America, corporations have generally contributed some of their shareholders' wealth to meet social needs. Frequently, corporations establish separate nonprofit foundations for this purpose. For example, Honda, Inc., created the American Honda Education Corporation, through which it donated $40 million over a ten-year period to launch and support the Eagle Rock School in Estes Park, Colorado. This school and educator training center gives preference to students who have not been able to succeed in the more rigid, highly structured public school systems. Today, virtually all major corporations routinely donate to hospitals, medical research, the arts, universities, and programs that benefit society.

Corporate Process

Increasingly, corporations are being judged less on the basis of their philanthropic activities than on their practices, or corporate process. Corporate process, in this

BEN AND JERRY, OF BEN AND JERRY'S ICE CREAM, AT THE ONE WORLD, ONE HEART FESTIVAL IN NEW YORK CITY. ACCORDING TO BEN, "BUSINESS HAS A RESPONSIBILITY TO GIVE BACK TO THE COMMUNITY." DOES GIVING BACK TO THE COMMUNITY CONFLICT WITH OTHER CORPORATE PURPOSES? IF SO, CAN A BALANCE BE STRUCK? HOW?

"The highest morality almost always is the morality of process."

ALEXANDER M. BICKEL, 1924–1974 (Rumanian-American legal scholar)

sense, refers to how a corporation conducts its affairs at all levels of operation. Does it establish and effectively implement ethical policies and take those policies seriously? Does it deal ethically with its shareholders? Does it consider the needs of its employees—for day-care facilities or flexible working hours, for example? Does it promote equal opportunity in the workplace for women, minority groups, and persons with disabilities? Do the corporation's suppliers, particularly those from developing countries, protect the human rights of their employees (provide for safety in the workplace or pay a decent wage, for example)? Does the corporation investigate complaints about its products promptly and, if necessary, take action to improve them?

For many, the answers to these and similar questions are the key factors in determining whether a corporation is socially responsible. From this perspective, no matter how much a corporation may contribute to worthy causes, it will not be socially responsible if it fails to observe ethical standards in its day-to-day activities.

IT PAYS TO BE ETHICAL

¡ REMEMBER!
There is a constant tension among ethics, social forces, profits, and the law.

Most corporations today have learned that it pays to be ethically responsible—even if it means less profits in the short run (and it often does). Today's corporations are subject to more intensive scrutiny—both by government agencies and the public—than they ever were in the past. If a corporation fails to conduct its operations ethically or respond quickly to an ethical crisis, its goodwill and reputation (and thus future profits) will likely suffer as a result. For this reason, many firms today, instead of aiming for *maximum profits,* aim for *optimum profits*—profits that can be realized while staying within legal and ethical limits. Notice how PriceCostco's Code of Ethics (see the fold-out exhibit in this chapter) stresses both legal and ethical duties.

There are other reasons as well for a corporation to behave ethically. Companies that demonstrate a commitment to ethical behavior—by implementing ethical programs, complying with environmental regulations, and promptly investigating product complaints, for example—often receive more lenient treatment from government agencies or the courts. Furthermore, by keeping their own houses in order, corporations may be able to avoid the necessity for the government to do so—through new laws and regulations.

Additionally, investors may shy away from a corporation's stock if the corporation is perceived to be socially irresponsible. Since the 1970s, certain investment funds have guaranteed to the purchasers of their shares that they will only invest in companies that are socially responsible. These "ethical" investment funds base their investments on various ethical criteria. For example, some funds invest money only in corporations that are "environmentally kind"; others invest only in corporations that ensure fair treatment for their employees or the employees of their suppliers in foreign countries.

Ethics in the Global Context

Given the varied cultures and religions of the world's nations, one should not be surprised that frequent conflicts in ethics arise between foreign and U.S. businesspersons. • EXAMPLE 8.8 In Islamic (Muslim) countries the consumption of alcohol and certain foods is forbidden by the Koran (the sayings of the prophet Mohammed, which lie at the heart of Islam and Islamic law). It would be thoughtless and imprudent to invite a Saudi Arabian business contact out for a drink. •

The role played by women in other countries also may present some difficult ethical problems for firms doing business internationally. Equal employment opportunity is a fundamental public policy in the United States, and Title VII of the Civil Rights Act of 1964 prohibits discrimination against women in the employment context (see Chapter 38). Some other countries, however, offer little protection for women against gender discrimination in the workplace, including sexual harassment.

> **ON THE WEB**
> Global Exchange offers information on global business activities, including some of the ethical issues stemming from such activities, at www.globalexchange.org.

We look here at how laws governing workers in other countries, particularly in the developing countries, have created some especially difficult ethical problems for U.S. sellers of goods manufactured in foreign countries. We also examine some of the ethical ramifications of a U.S. law that prohibits American businesspersons from bribing foreign officials to obtain favorable business contracts.

MONITORING THE EMPLOYMENT PRACTICES OF FOREIGN SUPPLIERS

Suppose that the Farris Company, to save costs, contracts with companies in developing nations to manufacture some of its products, because the wage rates in those nations are significantly lower than in the United States. Further suppose that one of the foreign companies exploits its workers—it hires women and children at below-minimum-wage rates and requires its employees to work long hours in a workplace full of health hazards. Additionally, the company's supervisors routinely engage in workplace conduct that is offensive to women.

What is the Farris Company's ethical responsibility in this situation? Should it refuse to deal with these suppliers (and sacrifice profits)? Should it use these suppliers' services but only on the condition that the suppliers allow Farris employees to monitor the suppliers' workplaces to make sure that the workers are not being mistreated?

> **¡REMEMBER!**
> Changing ethical notions about social responsibility often motivate lawmakers to enact or repeal laws.

At one time, society's concept of ethical business behavior did not include concerns over other nations' employment laws and practices. Today, however, the situation has changed. Few activities of business firms go overlooked by interest groups supporting human rights on a worldwide level. If a firm such as Farris fails to take steps to protect foreign workers' rights, its reputation as an ethically responsible firm may be damaged—and its profits significantly affected—by the adverse publicity sponsored by such interest groups. (For a further discussion of this issue, see this chapter's feature *Technology and Corporate Social Responsibility.*)

International Perspective •

INTERNATIONAL STANDARDS FOR SOCIAL ACCOUNTABILITY

The International Standards Organization (ISO) has created standards for environmental auditing that have been widely adopted by corporate managers around the world. When such standards are issued or revised, they are given a number, such as ISO14001. Recently, the Council on Economic Priorities Accreditation Agency (CEPAA) used the ISO's model for its new human rights standards, called Social Accountability 8000 (SA8000). These standards call on corporate leaders to restrict child labor and forced labor, limit workweeks to forty-eight hours, respect workers' rights to form unions, provide safe working conditions, and pay wages that meet basic needs. By adopting these standards and agreeing to "Social Accountability audits," firms can demonstrate their commitment to international human rights and help to dispel stories that they make profits by using "sweatshop labor."

FOR CRITICAL ANALYSIS

Can an American corporation be *compelled* to respect the human rights of workers in factories located in other nations?

The Foreign Corrupt Practices Act

Another ethical problem in international business dealings has to do with the legitimacy of certain side payments to government officials. In the United States, the majority of contracts are formed within the private sector. In many foreign countries, however, decisions on most major construction and manufacturing contracts are made by government officials because of extensive government regulation and control over trade and industry. Side payments to government officials in exchange for favorable business contracts are not unusual in such countries, nor are they considered to be unethical. In the past, U.S. corporations doing business in developing countries largely followed the dictum, "When in Rome, do as the Romans do."

In the 1970s, however, the U.S. press, and government officials as well, uncovered a number of business scandals involving large side payments by American corporations to foreign representatives for the purpose of securing advantageous international trade contracts. In response to this unethical behavior, Congress passed the Foreign Corrupt Practices Act (FCPA) in 1977, which prohibits American businesspersons from bribing foreign officials to secure advantageous contracts. The act, which is the subject of the *Landmark in the Law* that follows, made it difficult for American companies to compete as effectively as they otherwise might have in the global marketplace.

Other Nations Denounce Bribery

For twenty years, the FCPA was the only law of its kind in the world, despite attempts by U.S. political leaders to convince other nations to pass similar legislation. That situation is now changing. In 1997, the Organization for Economic Cooperation and Development, to which twenty-six of the world's leading industrialized nations belong, signed a convention (treaty) that made the bribery of foreign public officials a serious crime. Each signatory is obligated to enact legislation within its nation in accordance with the treaty. The agreement will not only improve the ethical climate in international trade but also level the playing field for U.S businesspersons.

Technology and Corporate Social Responsibility

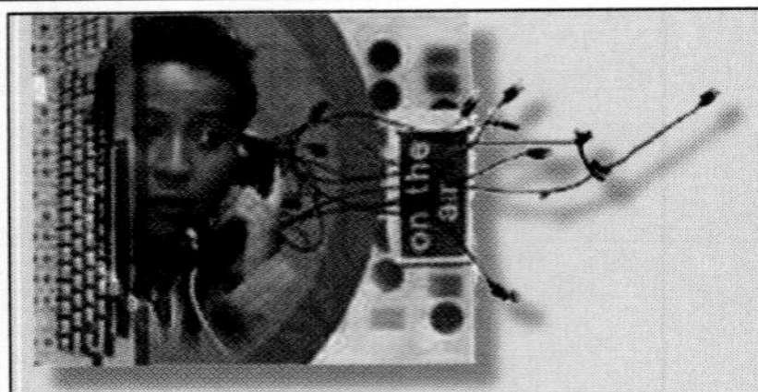

In recent years, the Internet has made it possible for business conduct to come under closer public scrutiny than ever before. Human rights activists and other interest groups concerned with unethical business behavior no longer have to spend years getting organized and soliciting funds to pay for their operating expenses, for distributing literature, and for costly media ads exposing unethical business practices. Today, such groups can plead their causes on the Internet. They can publish online, at virtually no cost, reports about unethical business practices. They can invite other Internet users to donate to their causes or join in their missions in other ways—by telephoning or sending letters to a company, for example, as part of a pressure campaign against the firm to cease its unethical behavior. Indeed, many sites invite users to simply print out letters that have already been drafted, sign the letters, and send them to the targeted firm.

Consider the activities of just one of these online groups—Corporate Watch (at www.corpwatch.org). Corporate Watch delves into American companies' global activities and gives online reports of what it finds. Recent reports at Corporate Watch's Web site, for example, included those titled "Nike Raises Wages for Indonesian Workers," "Italy: Benetton Implicated in Child Labour Scandal," "Indigenous Groups Get Suit Reinstated against Texaco for Rainforest Destruction," and "Action Update: Firings Halted at L. V. Myles."

AN OIL PRODUCTION FACILITY BEING DEVELOPED IS CAUSING DEFORESTATION IN THE AMAZON JUNGLE IN PERU. DO FIRMS HAVE THE SAME ETHICAL RESPONSIBILITIES WHEN THEY DO BUSINESS IN DEVELOPING COUNTRIES AS WHEN THEY DO BUSINESS IN DEVELOPED COUNTRIES?

Corporate Watch, like several other online "corporate watchers," pays special attention not only to environmental issues but also to the welfare of workers in factories located abroad that produce or assemble goods for American companies. For example, L. V. Myles, a factory located in Port-au-Prince, Haiti, assembles clothing for several U.S. firms, including the Disney Company. According to Corporate Watch, workers at the factory were paid about half of the basic living wage, and women were allegedly subjected to sexual harassment from their supervisors. When a flier protesting the abusive working conditions was circulated throughout the factory, the management responded by firing a number of workers who were suspected of being responsible for the flier. The management ceased firing workers, however, after it was bombarded with faxes, letters, and telephone calls from concerned U.S. citizens, who were alerted to the situation by Corporate Watch and other online corporate "watchers."

FOR CRITICAL ANALYSIS

Using the Internet, a small handful of activists can bring significant pressure to bear on a corporation that, in the opinion of those activists, is acting unethically. What are the implications of this development for corporate ethical decision making?

Landmark in the Law • THE FOREIGN CORRUPT PRACTICES ACT OF 1977

The Foreign Corrupt Practices Act (FCPA) of 1977 is divided into two major parts. The first part applies to all U.S. companies and their directors, officers, shareholders, employees, and agents. This part of the FCPA prohibits the bribery of most officials of foreign governments if the purpose of the payment is to get the official to act in his or her official capacity to provide business opportunities.

The FCPA does not prohibit payment of substantial sums to minor officials whose duties are ministerial. These payments are often referred to as "grease," or facilitating payments. They are meant to ensure that administrative services that might otherwise be performed at a slow pace are sped up. Thus, for example, if a firm makes a payment to a minor official to speed up an import licensing process, the firm has not violated the FCPA. Generally, the act, as amended, permits payments to foreign officials if such payments are lawful within the foreign country. The act also does not prohibit payments to private foreign companies or other third parties unless the American firm knows that the payments will be passed on to a foreign government in violation of the FCPA.

The second part of the FCPA is directed toward accountants, because in the past bribes were often concealed in corporate financial records. All companies must keep detailed records that "accurately and fairly" reflect the company's financial activities. In addition, all companies must have an accounting system that provides "reasonable assurance" that all transactions entered into by the company are accounted for and legal. These requirements assist in detecting illegal bribes. The FCPA further prohibits any person from making false statements to accountants or false entries in any record or account.

In 1988, the FCPA was amended to provide that business firms that violated the act may be fined up to $2 million. Individual officers or directors who violate the FCPA may be fined up to $100,000 (the fine cannot be paid by the company) and may be imprisoned for up to five years.

FOR CRITICAL ANALYSIS

The FCPA did not change international trade practices in other countries, but it effectively tied the hands of American firms trying to secure foreign contracts. In passing the FCPA, did Congress give too much weight to ethics and too little weight to international economic realities?

APPLICATION Law & the Manager: How to Create an Ethical Workplace*

The most important factor in creating and maintaining an ethical workplace is the attitude of top management. If you are a manager, rest assured that unless you are totally committed to this goal, you will not succeed in achieving it. In addition to your conduct, two other factors help to create an ethical workplace environment: a written code of ethics, or policy statement, and the effective communication of the firm's ethical policies to employees.

*This *Application* is not meant to substitute for the services of an attorney who is licensed to practice law in your state.

THE ROLE OF MANAGEMENT

Surveys of business executives indicate that management's behavior, more than anything else, sets the ethical tone of a firm. If an employee persists in unethical behavior, you should consider discharging the employee as a clear example to other employees that you will not tolerate unethical behavior. Although this may seem harsh, business managers have found that discharging even one employee for ethical reasons has had a tremendous impact as a deterrent to unethical behavior in the workplace. Additionally, you should ensure that your firm's production or marketing goals are realistic. If a sales quota, for example, can only be met through high-pressure, unethical sales tactics, employees trying to act "in

APPLICATION CONTINUED

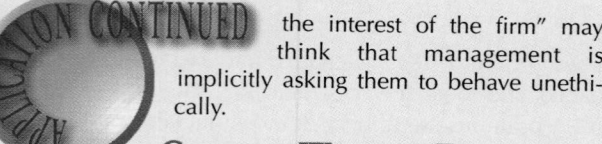

the interest of the firm" may think that management is implicitly asking them to behave unethically.

CREATE A WRITTEN ETHICAL CODE

A written ethics code or policy statement helps to make clear to employees how they are expected to relate to their supervisors or managers, to consumers, to suppliers, and to other employees. Above all, it is important to state explicitly what your firm's ethical priorities are. For example, in 1982 Johnson & Johnson (J&J) was confronted with the Tylenol crisis (Tylenol "spiked" with cyanide had caused the deaths of several persons in Chicago). Top management at J&J was able to act swiftly and ethically, because the company had made its goals clear in its ethical code. Its first priority was the welfare of those who used its product; hence, the firm decided to withdraw thirty-one million bottles of Tylenol from the market, at a cost of about $100 million.

COMMUNICATE ETHICAL STANDARDS TO EMPLOYEES

For an ethical code to be effective, its provisions must be clearly communicated to employees. A good way to do this is by implementing an ethics training program, in which management discusses with employees—face to face—the firm's policies and the importance of ethical conduct. Some firms hold periodic ethics seminars to allow employees to discuss openly any ethical problems that they may be experiencing and how the firm's ethical policies apply to those specific problems. Generally, the smaller the group, the more effective these discussions are. It is important that employees know that the ethical program is a "two-way street." That is, management must make it clear that feedback from employees and their ethical concerns are a top priority.

Another effective technique is to evaluate periodically the ethical performance of each individual employee. One company, for example, hands out to its employees each week an ethical checklist to fill out and return to their supervisors. This practice serves two purposes: first, employees realize that ethics matters; and second, employees are given an opportunity to reflect on how well they have measured up in terms of ethical performance.

CHECKLIST FOR CREATING AN ETHICAL WORKPLACE

1. Make sure that management is committed to ethical behavior and sets an ethical example.
2. Create, print, and distribute an ethical code clearly stating your firm's ethical goals and priorities, as well as what behavior is expected of employees in their areas of responsibility.
3. Implement an ethics training program to communicate your firm's ethical policies to employees.
4. Hold seminars or small-group meetings in which ethical policies and performance can be discussed on an ongoing basis.
5. Devise a method, such as an ethical checklist, for evaluating the ethical performance of each individual employee.

Key Terms

business ethics 210
categorical imperative 212
corporate social responsibility 215
cost-benefit analysis 212
ethics 210
utilitarianism 212

Chapter Summary • Ethics and Social Responsibility

The Nature of Business Ethics (See pages 210–211.)	Ethics can be defined as the study of what constitutes right or wrong behavior. Business ethics focuses on how moral and ethical principles are applied in the business context. The law reflects society's convictions on what constitutes right or wrong behavior. The law has its limits, though, and some actions may be legal yet not be ethical.
Sources of Ethical Standards (See pages 211–213.)	1. *Duty-based ethics*—Ethics based on religious beliefs and philosophical reasoning, such as that of Immanuel Kant. 2. *Outcome-based ethics (utilitarianism)*—Ethics based on philosophical reasoning, such as that of John Stuart Mill.

Chapter Summary • Ethics and Social Responsibility, Continued

Obstacles to Ethical Business Behavior (See pages 213–215.)	1. *The corporate structure*— a. Collective decision making tends to deter individual ethical assertiveness. b. The corporate structure tends to shield corporate actors from personal responsibility and accountability. 2. *Management*— a. Uncertainty on the part of employees as to what kind of behavior is expected of them makes it difficult for them to behave ethically. b. Unethical conduct by management shows employees that ethical behavior is not a priority.
Corporate Social Responsibility (See pages 215–224.)	Corporate social responsibility rests on the assumption that corporations should conduct their affairs in a socially responsible manner. Corporations are perceived to hold duties to the following groups: 1. *Shareholders*—Because the shareholders are the owners of the corporation, directors and officers have a duty to act in the shareholders' interest (maximize profits). 2. *Employees*—Employers have numerous legal duties to employees, including the duty to provide employees with a safe workplace and to refrain from discriminating against employees on the basis of race, color, national origin, gender, religion, age, or disability. 3. *Consumers*—Corporate directors and officers have a legal duty to the users of their products. Controversy exists over the point at which corporate responsibility for consumer safety ends and consumer responsibility begins. 4. *The community*—Most people hold that a corporation has a duty to the community in which it operates. The corporation should consider the needs of the community when making decisions that substantially affect the welfare of the community. 5. *Society*—Most people hold that a corporation has a duty to society in general, but they differ in their ideas on how corporations can best fulfill this duty. One view is that corporations serve society's needs most effectively by maximizing profits because profits generally increase national wealth and social welfare. Another view holds that corporations, because they control so much of the country's wealth and power, should use that wealth and power in socially beneficial ways and not engage in actions that society deems unethical.
Measuring Corporate Social Responsibility (See pages 224–226.)	It is difficult to measure corporate social responsibility because different yardsticks are used. Traditionally, corporate philanthropy has been used as a means of measuring corporate social responsibility. Increasingly, corporate process—how a corporation conducts its business on a day-to-day basis—is a key factor in determining whether a corporation is socially responsible.
Ethics in the Global Context (See pages 226–229.)	There are many cultural, religious, and legal differences among nations. Notable differences relate to the role of women in society, employment laws governing workplace conditions, and the practice of giving side payments to foreign officials to secure favorable contracts.

For Review

❶ What is ethics? What is business ethics? What are some sources of ethical standards?

❷ What are some of the obstacles to ethical business behavior?

❸ To what groups does a corporation owe duties? Why do these duties sometimes come into conflict?

❹ What is the difference between maximum profits and optimum profits?

❺ What are some of the yardsticks by which corporate social responsibility is measured?

Questions and Case Problems

8–1. Business Ethics. Some business ethicists maintain that whereas personal ethics has to do with right or wrong behavior, business ethics is concerned with appropriate behavior. In other words, ethical behavior in business has less to do with moral principles than with what society deems to be appropriate behavior in the business context. Do you agree with this distinction? Do personal and business ethics ever overlap? Should personal ethics play any role in business ethical decision making?

8–2. Corporate Social Responsibility. Assume that you are a high-level manager for a shoe manufacturer. You know that your firm could increase its profit margin by producing shoes in Indonesia, where you could hire women for $100 a month to assemble them. You also know, however, that a competing shoe manufacturer recently was accused by human rights advocates of engaging in exploitative labor practices because the manufacturer sold shoes made by Indonesian women for similarly low wages. You personally do not believe that paying $100 a month to Indonesian women is unethical, because you know that in that country, $100 a month is a better-than-average wage rate. Assuming that the decision is yours to make, should you have the shoes manufactured in Indonesia and make higher profits for your company? Should you instead avoid the risk of negative publicity and the consequences of that publicity for the firm's reputation and subsequent profits? Are there other alternatives? Discuss fully.

8–3. Corporate Social Responsibility. In recent years, human rights groups, environmental activists, and other interest groups concerned with unethical business practices have conducted publicity campaigns against various corporations that those groups feel have engaged in unethical practices. Do you believe that a small group of well-organized activists should dictate how a major corporation should conduct its affairs? Discuss fully.

8–4. Duty to Consumers. Two eight-year-old boys, Douglas Bratz and Bradley Baughn, were injured while riding a mini-trail bike manufactured by Honda Motor Co. Bratz, who was driving the bike while Baughn rode as a passenger behind him, ran three stop signs and then collided with a truck. Bratz did not see the truck because, at the time of the accident, he was looking behind him at a girl chasing them on another mini-trail bike. Bratz wore a helmet, but it flew off on impact because it was unfastened. Baughn was not wearing a helmet. The owner's manual for the mini-trail bike stated in bold print that the bike was intended for off-the-road use only and urged users to "Always Wear a Helmet." A prominent label on the bike itself also warned that the bike was for off-the-road use only and that it should not be used on public streets or highways. In addition, Bratz's father had repeatedly told the boy not to ride the bike in the street. The parents of the injured boys sued Honda, alleging that the mini-trail bike was unreasonably dangerous. Honda claimed it had sufficiently warned consumers of potential dangers that could result if the bike was not used as directed. Should Honda be held responsible for the boys' injuries? Why or why not? [*Baughn v. Honda Motor Co.*, 107 Wash.2d 127, 727 P.2d 655 (1986)]

8–5. Duty to Employees. In 1984, General Telephone Co. of Illinois, Inc. (GTE), for reasons of efficiency, decided to consolidate its nationwide operations and eliminate unnecessary job positions. One of the positions eliminated was held by John Burnell, a fifty-two-year-old employee who had worked for GTE for thirty-four years and had always received "above average" performance ratings. GTE offered Burnell the choice of either accepting another position within the firm at the same salary or accepting early retirement with a salary continuation for a certain period of time. Burnell did not want to retire, but he was afraid that if he did accept the other position and if the other position was later eliminated, he might not then have the choice of early retirement with the same separation benefit. Because he received no assurances that the other job would be secure in the future, he accepted the early-retirement alternative. Burnell later alleged that he had been "constructively discharged"—that is, that GTE had made his working conditions so intolerable that he was forced to resign. Had GTE constructively discharged Burnell? Can GTE's actions toward Burnell be justified from an ethical standpoint? Discuss. [*Burnell v. General Telephone Co. of Illinois, Inc.*, 181 Ill.App.3d 533, 536 N.E.2d 1387, 130 Ill.Dec. 176 (1989)]

8–6. Duty to Consumers. Beverly Landrine's infant daughter died after the baby swallowed a balloon while playing with a doll known as "Bubble Yum Baby." When a balloon was inserted into the doll's mouth and the doll's arm was pumped, thereby inflating the balloon, the doll simulated the blowing of a bubble gum bubble. The balloon was made by Perfect Product Co. and distributed by Mego Corp. Landrine brought a suit against the manufacturer and distributor, alleging that the balloon was defectively made or inherently unsafe when used by children and that Perfect had failed to warn of the danger associated with the balloon's use. Discuss whether the producer and distributor of the balloon should be held liable for the harm caused by its product. [*Landrine v. Mego Corp.*, 95 A.D.2d 759, 464 N.Y.S.2d 516 (1983)]

8–7. Duty to Consumers. The Seven-Up Co., as part of a marketing scheme, placed two glass bottles of "Like" cola on the front entrance of the Gruenemeier residence. Russell Gruenemeier, a nine-year-old boy, began playing while holding one of the bottles. He tripped and fell, and the bottle broke, severely cutting his right eye and causing him to eventually lose his eyesight in the eye. Russell's mother brought an action against the Seven-Up Co. for damages, claiming that the cause of Russell's injury was Seven-Up's negligence. She claimed that the company was negligent because it placed potentially dangerous instrumentalities—glass bottles—within the reach of small children and that the firm should have used unbreakable bottles for its marketing scheme. Are glass bottles so potentially dangerous that the Seven-Up Co. should be held liable for the boy's harm? If you were the judge, how would you decide the issue? [*Gruenemeier v. Seven-Up Co.,* 229 Neb. 267, 426 N.W.2d 510 (1988)]

8–8. Duty to Consumers. The father of an eleven-year-old child sued the manufacturer of a jungle gym because the manufacturer had failed to warn users of the equipment that they might fall off the gym and get hurt, as the boy did in this case. The father also claimed that the jungle gym was unreasonably dangerous because, as his son began to fall and reached frantically for a bar to grasp, there was no bar within reach. The father based his argument in part on a previous case involving a plaintiff who was injured as a result of somersaulting off a trampoline. In that case [*Pell v. Victor J. Andrew High School,* 123 Ill.App.3d 423, 462 N.E.2d 858, 78 Ill.Dec. 739 (1984)], the court had held that the trampoline's manufacturer was liable for the plaintiff's injuries because it had failed to warn of the trampoline's propensity to cause severe spinal cord injuries if it was used for somersaulting. Should the court be convinced by the father's arguments? Why or why not? [*Cozzi v. North Palos Elementary School District No. 117,* 232 Ill.App.3d 379, 597 N.E.2d 683, 173 Ill.Dec. 709 (1992)]

8–9. Duty to Employees. Matt Theurer, an eighteen-year-old high school senior, worked part-time at a McDonald's restaurant in Oregon. Theurer volunteered to work an extra shift one day, in addition to his regular shifts (one preceding and one following the extra shift). After working about twelve hours during a twenty-four-hour period, Theurer told the manager that he was tired and asked to be excused from his next regularly scheduled shift so that he could rest. The manager agreed. While driving home from work, Theurer fell asleep at the wheel and crashed into a van driven by Frederic Faverty. Theurer died, and Faverty was severely injured. Faverty sued McDonald's, alleging, among other things, that McDonald's was negligent in permitting Theurer to drive a car when it should have known that Theurer was too tired to drive safely. Do employers have a duty to prevent fatigued employees from driving home from work? Should such a duty be imposed on them? How should the court decide this issue? How would you decide the issue if you were the judge? [*Faverty v. McDonald's Restaurants of Oregon, Inc.,* 133 Or.App. 514, 892 P.2d 703 (1994)]

8–10. Duty to Consumers. Isuzu Motors America, Inc., does not warn its customers of the danger of riding unrestrained in the cargo beds of its pickup trucks. Seventeen-year-old Donald Josue was riding unrestrained in the bed of an Isuzu truck driven by Iaone Frias. When Frias lost control of the truck, it struck a concrete center divider. Josue was ejected and his consequent injuries rendered him a paraplegic. Josue filed a suit in a Hawaii state court against Isuzu, asserting a variety of legal claims based on its failure to warn of the danger of riding in the bed of the truck. Should Isuzu be held liable for Josue's injuries? Why or why not? [*Josue v. Isuzu Motors America, Inc.,* 87 Haw. 413, 958 P.2d 535 (1998)]

A QUESTION OF ETHICS AND SOCIAL RESPONSIBILITY

8–11. Hazen Paper Co. manufactured paper and paperboard for use in such products as cosmetic wrap, lottery tickets, and pressure-sensitive items. Walter Biggins, a chemist hired by Hazen in 1977, developed a water-based paper coating that was both environmentally safe and of superior quality. By the mid-1980s, the company's sales had increased dramatically as a result of its extensive use of "Biggins Acrylic." Because of this, Biggins thought he deserved a substantial raise in salary, and from 1984 to 1986, Biggins's persistent requests for a raise became a bone of contention between him and his employers. Biggins ran a business on the side, which involved cleaning up hazardous wastes for various companies. Hazen told Biggins that unless he signed a "confidentiality agreement" promising to restrict his outside activities during the time he was employed by Hazen and for a limited time afterward, he would be fired. Biggins said he would sign the agreement only if Hazen raised his salary to $100,000. Hazen refused to do so, fired Biggins, and hired a younger man to replace him. At the time of his discharge in 1986, Biggins was sixty-two years old, had worked for the company nearly ten years, and was just a few weeks away from being entitled to pension rights worth about $93,000. In view of these circumstances, evaluate and answer the following questions. [*Hazen Paper Co. v. Biggins,* 507 U.S. 604, 113 S.Ct. 1701, 123 L.Ed.2d 338 (1993)]

1. Did the company owe an ethical duty to Biggins to increase his salary, given the fact that its sales increased dramatically as a result of Biggins's efforts and ingenuity in developing the coating? If you were one of the company's executives, would you have raised Biggins's salary? Why or why not?
2. Generally, what public policies come into conflict in cases involving employers who, for reasons of cost and efficiency of operations, fire older, higher-paid workers and replace them with younger, lower-paid workers? If you were an employer facing the need to cut back on personnel to save costs, what would you do, and on what ethical premises would you justify your decision?

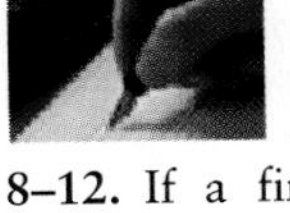

FOR CRITICAL ANALYSIS

8–12. If a firm engages in "ethically responsible" behavior solely for the purpose of gaining profits from the goodwill it generates, the "ethical" behavior is essentially a means toward a self-serving end (profits and the accumulation of wealth). In this situation, is the firm acting unethically in any way? Should motive or conduct carry greater weight on the ethical scales in this situation?

Online Activities

• **ONLINE EXERCISE 8–1**

Go to the "Internet Activities Book" posted on the Web site accompanying this text, the URL for which is http://blt.westbuslaw.com. Select the following activity, and perform the exercise according to the instructions given there:

Activity 8–1: Ethics in Business

Before the Test

Go to the *Business Law Today* home page at http://blt.westbuslaw.com. Click on TestTutor.® You will find twenty interactive questions relating to this chapter.

Unit One • Cumulative Business Hypothetical

CompTac, Inc., which is headquartered in San Francisco, California, is one of the leading software manufacturers in the United States. The company invests millions of dollars in researching and developing new software applications and computer games that are sold worldwide. It also has a large service department and has taken great pains to offer its customers excellent support services.

1. CompTac routinely purchases some of the materials necessary to produce its computer games from a New York firm, Electrotex, Inc. A dispute arises between the two firms, and CompTac wants to sue Electrotex for breach of contract. Can CompTac bring the suit in a California state court? Can CompTac bring the suit in a federal court? Explain.
2. A customer at one of CompTac's retail stores stumbles over a crate in the parking lot and breaks her leg. The crate had just moments before fallen off a CompTac truck that was delivering goods from a CompTac warehouse to the store. The customer sues CompTac, alleging negligence. Will she succeed in her suit? Why or why not?
3. Roban Electronics, a software manufacturer and one of CompTac's major competitors, has been trying to convince one of CompTac's key employees, Jim Baxter, to come to work for Roban. Roban knows that Baxter has a written employment contract with CompTac, which Baxter would breach if he left CompTac before the contract expired. Baxter goes to work for Roban, and the departure of its key employee causes CompTac to suffer substantial losses due to delays in completing new software. Can CompTac sue Roban to recoup some of these losses? If so, on what ground?
4. One of CompTac's employees in its accounting division, Alan Green, has a gambling problem. To repay a gambling debt of $10,000, Green decides to "borrow" some money from CompTac to cover the debt. Using his "hacking" skills and his knowledge of CompTac account numbers, Green electronically transfers CompTac funds into his personal checking account. A week later, he is luckier at gambling and uses the same electronic procedures to transfer funds from his personal checking account to the relevant CompTac account. Has Green committed any crimes? If so, what are they?
5. One of CompTac's best-selling products is a computer game that involves some extremely violent actions. Groups of parents, educators, and consumer activists have bombarded CompTac with letters and e-mail messages requesting the company to discontinue its sales of the product. CompTac executives are concerned with the public outcry, but at the same time they realize that the game is CompTac's major source of profits. If it ceased marketing the game, the company could go bankrupt. If you were a CompTac decision maker, what would your decision be in this situation? How would you justify your decision from an ethical perspective?

UNIT ONE • EXTENDED CASE STUDY: THE LAW IN CONTEXT

National Endowment for the Arts v. Finley

In Chapter 2, we discussed the protection given to freedom of speech under the First Amendment to the Constitution. In this extended case study, we examine National Endowment for the Arts v. Finley,[1] *a recent and controversial Supreme Court decision on an issue involving free speech.*

CASE BACKGROUND

The National Foundation on the Arts and Humanities Act (AHA) of 1965 authorizes the National Endowment for the Arts (NEA) to award financial grants to support the arts. The 1965 law gives the NEA substantial discretion in awarding grants. Congress amended the AHA in 1990 in response to the public outcry over certain NEA–funded exhibits in 1989, including a retrospective by photographer Robert Mapplethorpe. Many people, including several members of Congress, condemned Mapplethorpe's work as pornographic. The 1990 amendment to the AHA directs the NEA chairperson to ensure that "artistic excellence and artistic merit are the criteria by which [grant] applications are judged, taking into consideration general standards of decency and respect for the diverse beliefs and values of the American public." The addition of "general standards of decency" as a factor that may be considered by the NEA in giving grants was the target of considerable criticism by many artists.

Karen Finley and other artists who were denied grants filed a suit in a federal district court against the NEA, asserting, among other things, that the statute violated the First Amendment. The court ruled that the statute was unconstitutional. The U.S. Court of Appeals for the Ninth Circuit upheld this ruling, and the NEA appealed to the United States Supreme Court. We present below excerpts from the majority opinion in the case, which announced the law on the matter, as well as excerpts from a dissenting opinion.

1. __U.S.___, 118 S.Ct. 2168, 141 L.Ed.2d 500 (1998).

MAJORITY OPINION

Justice *O'CONNOR* delivered the opinion of the Court.

* * * *[a]

Respondents [Finley and the other artists] argue that the provision is * * * [an] example of viewpoint discrimination because it rejects any artistic speech that either fails to respect mainstream values or offends standards of decency. The premise of respondents' claim is that [the AHA] constrains the agency's ability to fund certain categories of artistic expression. The NEA, however, reads the provision as merely hortatory [highly recommended], and contends that it stops well short of an absolute restriction. [The AHA] adds "considerations" to the grant-making process; it does not preclude awards to projects that might be deemed "indecent" or "disrespectful," nor place conditions on grants, or even specify that those factors must be given any particular weight in reviewing an application. * * *

Furthermore, * * * the political context surrounding the adoption of the "decency and respect" clause is inconsistent with respondents' assertion that the provision compels the NEA to deny funding on the basis of viewpoint discriminatory criteria. The legislation was a bipartisan proposal introduced as a counterweight to amendments aimed at eliminating the NEA's funding or substantially constraining its grant-making authority. * * *

That [the AHA] admonishes the NEA merely to take "decency and respect" into consideration, and that the legislation was aimed at reforming procedures rather than precluding speech, undercut respondents' argument that the provision inevitably will be utilized as a tool for invidious viewpoint discrimination. * * *

* * * As respondents' own arguments demonstrate, the considerations that the provision introduces, by their nature, do not engender the kind of directed viewpoint discrimination that would prompt this Court to invalidate a statute on its face. Respondents assert, for example, that "[o]ne would be hard-pressed to find two people in the United States who could agree on what the 'diverse beliefs and values of the American public' are, much less on whether a particular work of art 'respects' them," and they claim that " '[d]ecency' is likely to mean something very different to a septuagenarian in

a. The asterisks mean that material has been deleted.

Tuscaloosa and a teenager in Las Vegas." The NEA likewise views the considerations enumerated in [the AHA] as susceptible to multiple interpretations. Accordingly, the provision does not introduce considerations that, in practice, would effectively preclude or punish the expression of particular views. * * *

* * * *

* * * Any content-based considerations that may be taken into account in the grant-making process are a consequence of the nature of arts funding. The NEA has limited resources and it must deny the majority of the grant applications that it receives, including many that propose "artistically excellent" projects. The agency may decide to fund particular projects for a wide variety of reasons, such as the technical proficiency of the artist, the creativity of the work, the anticipated public interest in or appreciation of the work, the work's contemporary relevance, its educational value, its suitability for or appeal to special audiences (such as children or the disabled), its service to a rural or isolated community, or even simply that the work could increase public knowledge of an art form.

DISSENTING OPINION

Justice *SOUTER*, dissenting.

* * * *

If there is a bedrock principle underlying the First Amendment, it is that the government may not prohibit the expression of an idea simply because society finds the idea itself offensive or disagreeable. * * *

* * * *

* * * Boiled down to its practical essence, the [decency and respect provision] obviously means that art that disrespects the ideology, opinions, or convictions of a significant segment of the American public is to be disfavored, whereas art that reinforces those values is not. * * * Nothing could be more viewpoint based than that. * * *

MEDIA COVERAGE

The Court's ruling in this case was both praised and criticized. Here we present excerpts from an article by Jacqueline Trescott that appeared in the *Washington Post* on June 26, 1998 (p. A15).

"Representatives of arts groups yesterday said they were deeply disturbed that the U.S. Supreme Court in its decision yesterday failed to understand "the chilling effect" of congressional wrangling over artistic freedom and public funding of the arts.

. . . .

But officials at the center of the storm, which has overshadowed debate about the direction of the NEA and forced reorganization of its tasks, were relieved and enthusiastic.

. . . .

The decision brought to a close eight years of legal battles about restrictions on artistic freedom. The mix of arts and politics had long caused disputes, and the arts endowment, since its creation in 1965, had often been at the center.

. . . .

Since [1990] a number of grants have put the agency in hot water, supplying its opponents with new reasons to call for drastic cuts and even elimination. In 1996, Congress ordered that the NEA can no longer make grants to individual artists, except for literature fellows and jazz and folk artists.

. . . .

Those who have fought hard to end federal funding for the arts interpreted the ruling as a new window for more congressional restrictions. . . .

In the opinion of activists and lawyers who represent the artistic community, the court decision almost guarantees the continuation of the chilling effect."

GOING ONLINE

The *Business Law Today,* Fifth Edition, Web site, at **http://blt.westbuslaw.com**, provides a link through which you can access other Supreme Court opinions in First Amendment cases. Supreme Court cases are also online at a number of other sites, including **www.findlaw.com**.

QUESTIONS FOR ANALYSIS

1. **Law.** What was the major argument of the plaintiffs? Why did the Court conclude that the plaintiffs' argument was invalid?
2. **Law.** Would the result in this case have been different if the plaintiffs had shown that the NEA denied their requests for grants in an attempt to suppress unpopular views?
3. **Ethics.** What is the ethical basis for the requirement that the government consider "decency and respect" in awarding a grant for artistic work?
4. **International Dimensions.** What is the impact on an artist in any society when his or her work is supported solely on the basis of "decency and respect" for the society in which it is created?
5. **Implications for the Business Manager.** Can new ideas, particularly ideas that defy contemporary tastes, beliefs, or values, lead to innovation in business? What are the pros and cons of having the government pay to foster new ideas?

UNIT TWO Contracts

CHAPTER 9

Nature & Classification

"The social order rests upon the stability and predictability of conduct, of which keeping promises is a large item."

Roscoe Pound, 1870–1964
(American jurist)

CONTENTS

LEARNING OBJECTIVES

After reading this chapter, you should be able to:

1. Explain the function of contract law.
2. Define the term *contract,* and list the basic elements that are required for contract formation.
3. Discuss the objective theory of contracts.
4. Identify the various types of contracts.
5. Outline the rules that govern the courts' interpretation of contracts.

As Roscoe Pound—an eminent jurist—observed in the above quotation, "keeping promises" is important to a stable social order. Contract law deals with, among other things, the formation and keeping of promises. A **promise** is a declaration that something either will or will not happen in the future.

Like other types of law, contract law reflects our social values, interests, and expectations at a given point in time. It shows, for example, what kinds of promises our society thinks should be legally binding. It shows what excuses our society accepts for breaking such promises. Additionally, it shows what promises are considered to be contrary to public policy, or against the interests of society, and therefore legally void. Also, if it was made by a child or a mentally incompetent person, or on the basis of false information, a question will arise as to whether the promise should be enforced. Resolving such questions is the essence of contract law.

• **PROMISE**
A declaration that something either will or will not happen in the future.

> **ON THE WEB**
> You can keep abreast of recent and planned revisions of the *Restatements of the Law* by accessing the American Law Institute's Web site at www.ali.org.

In the business world, questions and disputes concerning contracts arise daily. Although aspects of contract law vary from state to state, much of it is based on the common law. In 1932, the American Law Institute compiled the *Restatement of the Law of Contracts*. This work is a nonstatutory, authoritative exposition of the present law on the subject of contracts and is currently in its second edition (although a third edition is in the process of being drafted). Throughout the following chapters on contracts, we will refer to the second edition of the *Restatement of the Law of Contracts* as simply the *Restatement (Second) of Contracts*.

The Uniform Commercial Code (UCC), which governs contracts and other transactions relating to the sale of goods, occasionally departs from common law contract rules. Generally, the different treatment of contracts falling under the UCC stems from the general policy of encouraging commerce. The ways in which the UCC changes common law contract rules will be discussed extensively in later chapters. In this unit covering the common law of contracts (Chapters 9 through 14), we only indicate briefly or in footnotes those common law rules that have been altered significantly by the UCC for sales contracts.

The Function of Contracts

No aspect of modern life is entirely free of contractual relationships. You acquire rights and obligations, for example, when you borrow funds, when you buy or lease a house, when you procure insurance, when you form a business, when you purchase goods or services—the list goes on. Contract law is designed to provide stability and predictability for both buyers and sellers in the marketplace.

Contract law assures the parties to private agreements that the promises they make will be enforceable. Clearly, many promises are kept because of a moral obligation to do so or because keeping a promise is in the mutual self-interest of the parties involved, not because the **promisor** (the person making the promise) or the **promisee** (the person to whom the promise is made) is conscious of the rules of contract law. Nevertheless, the rules of contract law are often followed in business agreements to avoid potential problems.

• **PROMISOR**
A person who makes a promise.

• **PROMISEE**
A person to whom a promise is

By supplying procedures for enforcing private agreements, contract law provides an essential condition for the existence of a market economy. Without a legal framework of reasonably assured expectations within which to plan and venture, businesspersons would be able to rely only on the good faith of others. Duty and good faith are usually sufficient, but when dramatic price changes or adverse economic factors make it costly to comply with a promise, these elements may not be enough. Contract law is necessary to ensure compliance with a promise or to entitle the innocent party to some form of relief.

> **ON THE WEB**
> An extensive definition of the term *contract* is offered by the 'Lectric Law Library at www.lectlaw.com/def/c123.htm.

Definition of a Contract

A **contract** is an agreement that can be enforced in court. It is formed by two or more parties who agree to perform or to refrain from performing some act now or in the future. Generally, contract disputes arise when there is a promise of future performance. If the contractual promise is not fulfilled, the party who made it is subject to the sanctions of a court (see Chapter 14). That party may be required to pay money damages for failing to perform the contractual promise; in limited instances, the party may be required to perform the promised act.

• **CONTRACT**
An agreement that can be enforced in court; formed by two or more competent parties who agree, for consideration, to perform or to refrain from performing some legal act now or in the future.

• **OBJECTIVE THEORY OF CONTRACTS** A theory under which the intent to form a contract will be judged by outward, objective facts (what the party said when entering into the contract, how the party acted or appeared, and the circumstances surrounding the transaction) as interpreted by a reasonable person, rather than by the party's own secret, subjective intentions.

In determining whether a contract has been formed, the element of intent is of prime importance. In contract law, intent is determined by what is referred to as the **objective theory of contracts,** not by the personal or subjective intent, or belief, of a party. The theory is that a party's intention to enter into a contract is judged by outward, objective facts as interpreted by a reasonable person, rather than by the party's own secret, subjective intentions. Objective facts include (1) what the party said when entering into the contract, (2) how the party acted or appeared, and (3) the circumstances surrounding the transaction. As will be discussed later in this chapter, in the section on express versus implied contracts, intent to form a contract may be manifested not only in words, oral or written, but also by conduct.

International Perspective • HOW INTENT TO FORM A CONTRACT IS MEASURED IN OTHER COUNTRIES

U.S. courts routinely adhere to the objective theory of contracts. Courts in some nations, however, give more weight to subjective intentions. Under French law, for example, when there is a conflict between an objective interpretation and a subjective interpretation of a contract, the French civil law code prefers the subjective construction. Other nations that have civil law codes take this same approach. French courts, nonetheless, will look to writings and other objective evidence to determine a party's subjective intent. In operation, the difference between the French and U.S. approaches is therefore perhaps not as significant as it may seem at first blush.

FOR CRITICAL ANALYSIS
What problems may arise when a court attempts to look at the subjective basis of a contract?

Requirements of a Contract

The following list describes the requirements of a contract. Each item will be explained more fully in the chapter indicated. Although we pair these requirements in subsequent chapters (for example, agreement and consideration are treated in Chapter 10), it is important to stress that each requirement is separate and independent. They are paired merely for reasons of space.

1. ***Agreement.*** An agreement includes an offer and an acceptance. One party must offer to enter into a legal agreement, and another party must accept the terms of the offer (Chapter 10).
2. ***Consideration.*** Any promises made by parties must be supported by legally sufficient and bargained-for consideration (something of value received or promised, to convince a person to make a deal) (Chapter 10).
3. ***Contractual capacity.*** Both parties entering into the contract must have the contractual capacity to do so; the law must recognize them as possessing characteristics that qualify them as competent parties (Chapter 11).
4. ***Legality.*** The contract's purpose must be to accomplish some goal that is legal and not against public policy (Chapter 11).
5. ***Genuineness of assent.*** The apparent consent of both parties must be genuine (Chapter 12).
6. ***Form.*** The contract must be in whatever form the law requires; for example, some contracts must be in writing to be enforceable (Chapter 12).

The first four items in this list are formally known as the elements of a contract. The last two are possible defenses to the formation or the enforcement of a contract.

ON THE WEB
For another perspective on the requirements for a valid contract, go to the Web site of The Law Office at www.thelawoffice.com.

Freedom of Contract and Freedom from Contract

As a general rule, the law recognizes everyone's ability to enter freely into contractual arrangements. This recognition is called *freedom of contract,* a freedom protected by the U.S. Constitution in Article I, Section 10. Because freedom of contract is a fundamental public policy of the United States, courts rarely interfere with contracts that have been voluntarily made.

Of course, as in other areas of the law, there are many exceptions to the general rule that contracts voluntarily negotiated will be enforced. For example, illegal bargains, agreements that unreasonably restrain trade, and certain unfair contracts made between one party with a great amount of bargaining power and another with little power are generally not enforced. In addition, certain contracts with consumers, as well as certain clauses within those contracts, may not be enforceable if they are contrary to public policy, fairness, and justice (see Chapter 11 for a discussion of contracts contrary to public policy). These exceptions provide freedom from contract for persons who may have been forced into making contracts unfavorable to themselves. (See this chapter's *Business Law in Action* for a discussion of whether an exception should be made for surrogate-parenting contracts.)

> **ON THE WEB**
>
> The Web sites of various law firms are often good sources of information on contract law. To find the names of law firms in this area, go to FindLaw's site at **firms.findlaw.com/firms/pract15.html**.

Types of Contracts

There are numerous types of contracts. The categories into which contracts are placed involve legal distinctions as to formation, enforceability, or performance. The best method of explaining each type of contract is to compare one type with another.

Bilateral versus Unilateral Contracts

Every contract involves at least two parties. The **offeror** is the party making the offer. The **offeree** is the party to whom the offer is made. The offeror always promises to do or not to do something and thus is also a promisor. Whether the contract is classified as *unilateral* or *bilateral* depends on what the offeree must do to accept the offer and to bind the offeror to a contract.

• **OFFEROR**
A person who makes an offer.

• **OFFEREE**
A person to whom an offer is made.

Bilateral Contracts If to accept the offer the offeree must only promise to perform, the contract is a **bilateral contract.** Hence, a bilateral contract is a "promise for a promise." An example of a bilateral contract is a contract in which one person agrees to buy another person's automobile for a specified price. No performance, such as the payment of money or delivery of goods, need take place for a bilateral contract to be formed. The contract comes into existence at the moment the promises are exchanged.

• **BILATERAL CONTRACT**
A type of contract that arises when a promise is given in exchange for a return promise.

Unilateral Contracts If the offer is phrased so that the offeree can accept only by completing the contract performance, the contract is a **unilateral contract.** Hence, a unilateral contract is a "promise for an act."

• **UNILATERAL CONTRACT**
A contract that results when an offer can only be accepted by the offeree's performance.

• **EXAMPLE 9.1** Joe says to Celia, "If you walk across the Brooklyn Bridge, I'll give you $10." Joe promises to pay only if Celia walks the entire span of the bridge. Only on Celia's complete crossing does she fully accept Joe's offer to pay $10. If she chooses not to undertake the walk, there are no legal consequences. •

Contests, lotteries, and other prize-winning competitions are also examples of offers for unilateral contracts. If a person complies with the rules of the contest—

Business Law in Action • CONTRACT LAW AND PARENTAL RIGHTS

The doctrine of freedom of contract is wide reaching. Nonetheless, courts routinely invalidate contracts that are against public policy. A contract area of increasing concern for today's courts involves surrogate-parenting contracts.

In a surrogate-parenting contract, a woman might agree with a couple to be artificially inseminated with the man's sperm and to be the "gestational" mother. The typical contract might pay the surrogate mother $10,000 "for services rendered in conceiving, carrying, and giving birth." The surrogate agrees to let the biological father assume custody after the child is born. Such agreements typically provide that if the biological (surrogate) mother changes her mind, she forfeits any contractual rights to payment and must reimburse the biological father for all fees and expenses paid—for example, fees for medical treatment, hospital costs, and so on.

ARE SURROGATE-PARENTING CONTRACTS CONTRARY TO PUBLIC POLICY?

Do such contracts amount to "baby selling," and should they be deemed unenforceable as contrary to public policy? Furthermore, if a surrogate-parenting contract is breached or held to be unenforceable, who should have custody of the child who was born as a result of the contract? These significant questions, which first began to be litigated in the 1980s,[a] continue to come before the courts.

In a recent case, a Massachusetts court ruled that there was nothing inherently against public policy in an agreement that allows an informed woman to agree to conceive artificially and bear a child whose biological father is the husband of an infertile wife. But, said the court, the surrogate mother is not bound by her consent to give custody of the child to the biological father until after a suitable period has passed after the birth. Then such a contract could be enforceable. In this particular case, the surrogate mother changed her mind prior to the birth and was therefore deemed not bound by the contract.[b]

BIOTECHNOLOGY AND CUSTODY ISSUES

In a widely publicized California case, the Fourth District Court of Appeal had to resolve a much more complicated issue. John and Luanne Buzzanca could not conceive a child. They decided to have one conceived for them using anonymous donations of egg and sperm, in which the fertile egg was artificially placed in a gestational surrogate whom they hired to carry the baby. The surrogate agreed to accept $10,000 and to give custody of the future baby to the Buzzancas.

Before the baby was born, however, John Buzzanca filed for divorce. He claimed that he was not liable for child support and that in any event Luanne was not the baby's legal mother. At trial, Mr. Buzzanca prevailed. On appeal, however, the reviewing court unanimously held that Luanne was the child's legal mother and that John was the legal father and had to pay child support, in spite of the fact that he had no genetic ties to the child. Basically, the court ruled that the state had a compelling interest in establishing paternity for all children. Absent the Buzzancas' desire to have a child, the baby would have never been born.[c]

FOR CRITICAL ANALYSIS

Why might a judge examine the economic position of the gestational surrogate to determine whether she entered into this surrogate contract freely?

a. See, for example, *In re Baby M,* 217 N.J.Super. 313, 525 A.2d 1128 (1987).

b. *R.R. v. M.H.,* 426 Mass. 501, 689 N.E.2d 790 (Mass. 1998).

c. *In re Marriage of Buzzanca,* 61 Cal.App.4th 1410, 72 Cal. Rptr. 2d 280 (1998).

such as by submitting the right lottery number at the right place and time—a unilateral contract is formed, binding the organization offering the prize to a contract to perform as promised in the offer.

Revocation of Offers for Unilateral Contracts A problem arises in unilateral contracts when the promisor attempts to *revoke* (cancel) the offer after the promisee has begun performance but before the act has been completed. • **EXAMPLE 9.2** Suppose that Roberta offers to buy Ed's sailboat, moored in San Francisco, on delivery of the boat to Roberta's dock in Newport Beach, three hundred miles south of San Francisco. Ed rigs the boat and sets sail. Shortly before his arrival at Newport Beach, Ed receives a radio message from Roberta withdrawing her offer. Roberta's offer is an offer for a unilateral contract, and only Ed's delivery of the sailboat at her dock is an acceptance.•

In contract law, offers are normally *revocable* (capable of being taken back, or canceled) until accepted. Under the traditional view of unilateral contracts, Roberta's revocation would terminate the offer. Because of the harsh effect on the offeree of the revocation of an offer to form a unilateral contract, the modern-day view is that once performance has been *substantially* undertaken, the offeror cannot revoke the offer. Thus, in our example, even though Ed has not yet accepted the offer by complete performance, Roberta is prohibited from revoking it. Ed can deliver the boat and bind Roberta to the contract.

EXPRESS VERSUS IMPLIED CONTRACTS

• **EXPRESS CONTRACT**
A contract in which the terms of the agreement are fully and explicitly stated in words, oral or written.

• **IMPLIED-IN-FACT CONTRACT**
A contract formed in whole or in part from the conduct of the parties (as opposed to an express contract).

"Outward actions are a clue to hidden secrets."
(LEGAL MAXIM)

WHAT DETERMINES WHETHER A CONTRACT FOR ACCOUNTING, TAX PREPARATION, OR ANY OTHER SERVICE IS AN EXPRESS CONTRACT OR AN IMPLIED-IN-FACT CONTRACT?

An **express contract** is one in which the terms of the agreement are fully and explicitly stated in words, oral or written. A signed lease for an apartment or a house is an express written contract. If a classmate accepts your offer to sell your textbooks from last semester for $50, an express oral contract has been made.

A contract that is implied from the conduct of the parties is called an **implied-in-fact contract,** or an implied contract. This type of contract differs from an express contract in that the *conduct* of the parties, rather than their words, creates and defines at least some of the terms of the contract. • EXAMPLE 9.3 Suppose that you need an accountant to fill out your tax return this year. You look through the Yellow Pages and find an accounting firm located in your neighborhood. You drop by the firm's office, explain your problem to an accountant, and learn what fees will be charged. The next day you return, giving the receptionist all of the necessary information and documents, such as canceled checks, W-2 forms, and so on. You

say nothing expressly to the receptionist; rather, you walk out the door. In this situation, you have entered into an implied-in-fact contract to pay the accountant the usual and reasonable fees for the accounting services. The contract is implied by your conduct. The accountant expects to be paid for completing your tax return. By bringing in the records the accountant will need to do the work, you have implied an intent to pay for the services. •

The following three steps establish an implied-in-fact contract:

1. The plaintiff furnished some service or property.
2. The plaintiff expected to be paid for that service or property, and the defendant knew or should have known that payment was expected (by using the objective-theory-of-contracts test, discussed previously).
3. The defendant had a chance to reject the services or property and did not.

A statement can sometimes create an implied contract term. The following case involves such a statement.

CASE 9.1 McIlravy v. Kerr-McGee Corp.

United States Court of Appeals,
Tenth Circuit, 1997.
119 F.3d 876.
www.law.emory.edu/10circuit/july97/[a]

HISTORICAL AND SOCIAL SETTING *"At-will" employment is employment that can be terminated at any time, for any reason, by the employer or the employee. Employment is generally considered to be "at will" unless there is a contract that provides otherwise. Some state courts have ruled that employee handbooks constitute implied contracts of employment if the handbooks contain statements that the employees will be terminated only for "good cause." If the handbooks spell out procedures to be followed in cases of discharge the courts have held that employers are bound to those statements.*

a. This is a page at the Web site of the Emory University School of Law that lists the published opinions of the U.S. Court of Appeals for the Tenth Circuit for July 1997. The *McIlravy* case is listed as *Allen v. Kerr-McGee Corp.* Scroll down the list to the *Allen* case. To access the opinion, click on the case name.

BACKGROUND AND FACTS In 1976, Kerr-McGee Corporation issued an employee handbook that listed examples of misconduct that could result in discipline or discharge and spelled out specific procedures that would be used in those instances. This handbook was in effect when LeRoy McIlravy began working for Kerr-McGee. In 1992, as part of a reduction in Kerr-McGee's work force, McIlravy was laid off. He and other former employees filed a suit in a federal district court against Kerr-McGee, contending, among other things, that the handbook implied that employees would not be dismissed without "cause." The plaintiffs argued that Kerr-McGee breached this implied term when it discharged them. On this issue, Kerr-McGee filed a motion for summary judgment. The court granted the motion, and the plaintiffs appealed.

IN THE WORDS OF THE COURT . . .
BROWN, District Judge.

* * * *

* * * It is true that the general presumption * * * is that employees serve at the will of their employers. * * * An employee handbook may alter the presumption, however, if its terms reasonably create an expectation on the part of an employee that the company will not discharge him without cause.

* * * Nowhere in the 1976 [handbook] was it made clear that the company was not bound by the procedures in the handbook or that despite the general application of such policies the company intended to retain the absolute right to discharge employees at any time with or without cause. Taken as a whole, the 1976 [handbook is] sufficiently ambiguous that [it] could be said to have reasonably created expectations on plaintiffs' part that the company had promised not to discharge employees absent cause for the dismissal.

CASE 9.1—Continued

DECISION AND REMEDY The U.S. Court of Appeals for the Tenth Circuit held that the statements in the handbook create an implied contract term. The court reversed the decision of the lower court and remanded the case to determine whether the employer had followed the procedures for discharge specified in the handbook.

FOR CRITICAL ANALYSIS—Economic Consideration *What costs might an employer face if its employee handbook is considered an employment contract?*

QUASI CONTRACTS—CONTRACTS IMPLIED IN LAW

• **QUASI CONTRACT**
A fictional contract imposed on parties by a court in the interests of fairness and justice; usually, quasi contracts are imposed to avoid the unjust enrichment of one party at the expense of another.

Quasi contracts, or contracts *implied in law,* are wholly different from actual contracts. Express contracts and implied-in-fact contracts are actual, or true, contracts. Quasi contracts, as the term suggests, are not true contracts. They do not arise from any agreement, express or implied, between the parties themselves. Rather, quasi contracts are fictional contracts imposed on parties by courts in the interests of fairness and justice. Quasi contracts are therefore equitable, rather than contractual, in nature. Usually, quasi contracts are imposed to avoid the *unjust enrichment* of one party at the expense of another.

"A legal fiction is always consistent with equity."
(LEGAL MAXIM)

• EXAMPLE 9.4 Suppose that a vacationing doctor is driving down the highway and comes upon Emerson, who is lying unconscious on the side of the road. The doctor renders medical aid that saves Emerson's life. Although the injured, unconscious Emerson did not solicit the medical aid and was not aware that the aid had been rendered, Emerson received a valuable benefit, and the requirements for a quasi contract were fulfilled. In such a situation, the law normally will impose a quasi contract, and Emerson will have to pay the doctor for the reasonable value of the medical services rendered. •

A WORKER TAKES APART MACHINERY. IF THE WORKER MAKES A DESIGN MODIFICATION THAT THE MANUFACTURER INCORPORATES INTO LATER MODELS OF THE MACHINE, WITHOUT A CONTRACT, SHOULD THE WORKER BE COMPENSATED?

Limitations on Quasi-Contractual Recovery Although quasi contracts exist to prevent unjust enrichment, situations exist in which the party who obtains a benefit will not be deemed to have been unjustly enriched by that benefit. Basically, the quasi-contractual principle cannot be invoked by the party who has conferred a benefit on someone else unnecessarily or as a result of misconduct or negligence.

• EXAMPLE 9.5 You take your car to the local car wash and ask to have it run through the washer and to have the gas tank filled. While your car is being washed, you go to a nearby shopping center for two hours. In the meantime, one of the workers at the car wash has mistakenly believed that your car is the one that he is supposed to hand wax. When you come back, you are presented with a bill for a full tank of gas, a wash job, and a hand wax. Clearly, a benefit has been conferred on you, but this benefit has been conferred because of a mistake by the car wash employee. You have not been *unjustly* enriched under these circumstances. People cannot normally be forced to pay for benefits "thrust" on them. •

ETHICAL ISSUE 9.1 ***Why should contracts be implied in law?*** Quasi contracts, or contracts implied in law, arise to establish justice and fairness. The term *quasi contract* is misleading, because a quasi contract is not really a contract at all. It does not arise from any agreement between two individuals. Rather, a court imposes a quasi contract on the parties when justice so requires to prevent unjust enrichment. The doctrine of unjust enrichment is based on the theory that individuals should not be allowed to profit or enrich themselves inequitably at the expense of others. This belief is fundamental in our society and is clearly inspired by ethical considerations.

When a Contract Already Exists The doctrine of quasi contract generally cannot be used when an actual contract covers the area in controversy. This is because a remedy already exists if a party is unjustly enriched as a result of a breach of contract: the nonbreaching party can sue the breaching party for breach of contract. No quasi contract need be imposed by the court in this instance to achieve justice. The following case involves this issue. A party sought to recover in quasi contract even though an express contract covering the area in controversy already existed.

CASE 9.2 Industrial Lift Truck Service Corp. v. Mitsubishi International Corp.

Appellate Court of Illinois,
First District, Fourth Division, 1982.
104 Ill.App.3d 357,
432 N.E.2d 999,
60 Ill.Dec. 100.

HISTORICAL AND SOCIAL SETTING *Quasi contracts have sometimes been applied in contractual contexts. These contexts, however, usually involve contracts that are unenforceable. A contract may be unenforceable because its terms are too indefinite, because each party has a different reasonable understanding of the agreement, because of lack of consideration, or because the agreement is illegal. A contract may also be unenforceable because it is not in the correct form; because it involves fraud, duress, mistake, or incapacity; or because of other circumstances that allow a contract to be avoided. In none of the situations in which the doctrine of quasi contract is applied, however, is there an enforceable contract covering the area in controversy.*

BACKGROUND AND FACTS In 1973 and again in 1976, an agreement was executed between Industrial Lift Truck Service Corporation (IL) and Mitsubishi International Corporation calling for IL to purchase forklift trucks from Mitsubishi and to use its best efforts to sell and service the trucks. The agreement also allowed Mitsubishi to terminate the agreement without just cause by giving ninety days' notice. From 1973 to 1977, IL allegedly became the nation's largest dealer of Mitsubishi forklift trucks. During this period, IL made design changes in the trucks to better suit the American market. Mitsubishi did not request these changes but later incorporated them into the trucks it sold to other dealers. In 1978, Mitsubishi terminated the agreement. IL sued Mitsubishi in an Illinois state court under quasi-contractual principles to recover the benefits conferred on Mitsubishi by the design changes. The suit was dismissed, and IL appealed.

IN THE WORDS OF THE COURT . . .
LINN, Justice.

* * * *

A contract implied in law, or a quasi-contract, is fictitious and arises by implication of law wholly apart from the usual rules relating to contract. * * * One party performs a service that benefits another. The benefiting party has not requested the service but accepts the benefit. Circumstances indicate that the services were not intended to be gratuitous. As a result, the law will sometimes impose a duty on the benefiting party to pay for the services rendered despite the lack of a contract. * * *

* * * The general rule is that no quasi-contractual claim can arise when a contract exists between the parties concerning the same subject matter on which the quasi-contractual claim rests.

* * * *

* * * When the [design] changes were made, plaintiff knew the risk involved. It knew the contract could be terminated as it was terminated, and thus knew when it made the changes that it might not be compensated under the contract to the extent it hoped to be compensated. * * * In essence, plaintiff is seeking to use quasi-contract as a means to circumvent the realities of a contract freely entered into.

* * * *

CASE 9.2—Continued

The contract defined the entire relationship of the parties with respect to its general subject matter—the sale and servicing of defendant's products. * * * Defendant had a right to assume, absent a valid amendment to the agreement, that it should not have to compensate plaintiff for any acts done in relation to the subject matter of the contract except pursuant to the contract terms.

DECISION AND REMEDY The existence of the specific contract barred the plaintiff's action in quasi contract, and the Appellate Court of Illinois held that the plaintiff's action in quasi contract was properly dismissed.

FOR CRITICAL ANALYSIS—Ethical Consideration *Is it fair, in a case such as the one presented here, for the court to hold that quasi-contractual recovery is unavailable if an existing contract covers the disputed area?*

FORMAL VERSUS INFORMAL CONTRACTS

• **FORMAL CONTRACT**
A contract that by law requires for its validity a specific form, such as executed under seal.

Formal contracts require a special form or method of creation (formation) to be enforceable. They include (1) contracts under seal, (2) recognizances, (3) negotiable instruments, and (4) letters of credit.[1] *Contracts under seal* are formalized writings with a special seal attached.[2] The significance of the seal has lessened, although about ten states require no consideration when a contract is under seal. A *recognizance* is an

1. *Restatement (Second) of Contracts,* Section 6.
2. A seal may be actual (made of wax or some other durable substance), impressed on the paper, or indicated simply by the word seal or the letters *L.S.* at the end of the document. *L.S.* stands for *locus sigilli* and means "the place for the seal."

Technology and Contract Forms

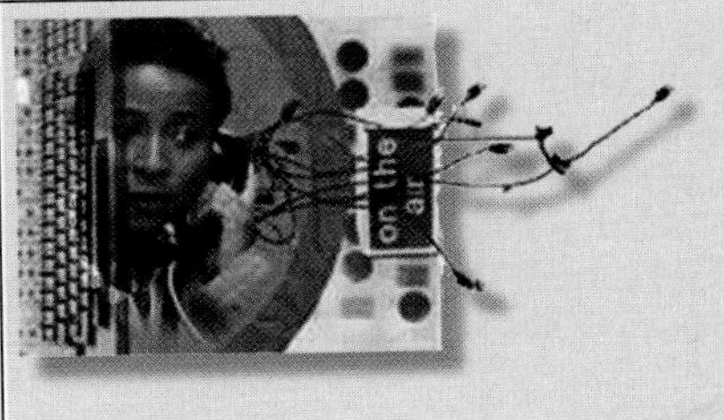

Before the printing press, every contract form had to be handwritten. Since the advent of printing, in contrast, most standard contract forms have been readily available at low cost. The introduction of computers into legal practice obviated the need to use preprinted forms and further allowed attorneys to customize contract forms for each given situation. This procedure has been both simplified and expanded by the inclusion of contract forms on simple-to-use CD-ROMs, such as Quicken's *Business Law Partner* (a copy of which is included in the inside back cover of this text).

Now the Internet has made available an even larger variety of contract forms, as well as other legal and business forms. For example, over five thousand forms are available at www.legal-businessforms.com. Sources for the forms include the American Law Institute and the American Bar Association, as well as various firms, government entities, and bar associations. At that site, you can preview the forms you need. If you want to download an entire form, you have to pay a fee ranging from $10 to $45.

Another source for forms is the 'Lectric Law Library's collection of forms at www.lectlaw.com/form.html. In addition to actual forms, there are comments on how the forms should be used and filled out. The site includes forms for the assignment of a contract, a contract for sale of a motor vehicle, and many others.

At www.legaldocs.com you will find an electronic forms book that offers hundreds of standardized legal forms, some of which are free.

Finally, at www.findlaw.com/16forms/index.html you will find hyperlinks to other online collections of contract forms.

FOR CRITICAL ANALYSIS
Does the availability of contract forms on the Internet obviate the need to use an attorney?

¡KEEP IN MIND! Not every contract is a document with the word "Contract" printed in block letters at the top. A contract can be expressed in a letter, a memo, or another document.

acknowledgment in court by a person that he or she will perform some specified obligation or pay a certain sum if he or she fails to perform. One form of recognizance is the surety bond.[3] Another is the personal recognizance bond used as bail in a criminal matter. As will be discussed at length in subsequent chapters, *negotiable instruments* include checks, notes, drafts, and certificates of deposit; letters of credit are agreements to pay contingent on the purchaser's receipt of invoices and bills of lading (documents evidencing receipt of, and title to, goods shipped).

• **INFORMAL CONTRACT** A contract that does not require a specified form or formality in order to be valid.

Informal contracts (also called *simple contracts*) include all other contracts. No special form is required (except for certain types of contracts that must be in writing), as the contracts are usually based on their substance rather than on their form. Typically, businesspersons put their contracts in writing to ensure that there is some proof of a contract's existence should problems arise. (Standard contract forms are now available online at numerous Web sites—see this chapter's feature *Technology and Contract Forms* for information on some of these sites.)

EXECUTED VERSUS EXECUTORY CONTRACTS

• **EXECUTED CONTRACT** A contract that has been completely performed by both parties.

• **EXECUTORY CONTRACT** A contract that has not as yet been fully performed.

Contracts are also classified according to their state of performance. A contract that has been fully performed on both sides is called an **executed contract.** A contract that has not been fully performed on either side is called an **executory contract.** If one party has fully performed but the other has not, the contract is said to be executed on the one side and executory on the other, but the contract is still classified as executory.

• **EXAMPLE 9.6** Assume that you agree to buy ten tons of coal from Western Coal Company. Further assume that Western has delivered the coal to your steel mill, where it is now being burned. At this point, the contract is an executory contract—it is executed on the part of Western and executory on your part. After you pay Western for the coal, the contract will be executed on both sides. •

VALID, VOID, VOIDABLE, AND UNENFORCEABLE CONTRACTS

• **VALID CONTRACT** A contract that results when the elements necessary for contract formation (agreement, consideration, legal purpose, and contractual capacity) are present.

• **VOID CONTRACT** A contract having no legal force or binding effect.

• **VOIDABLE CONTRACT** A contract that may be legally avoided (canceled, or annulled) at the option of one or both of the parties.

A **valid contract** has the elements necessary for contract formation. Those elements consist of (1) an agreement (offer and an acceptance) (2) supported by legally sufficient consideration (3) for a legal purpose and (4) made by parties who have the legal capacity to enter into the contract. As mentioned, we will discuss each of these elements in the following chapters.

A **void contract** is no contract at all. The terms *void* and *contract* are contradictory. A void contract produces no legal obligations on the part of any of the parties. For example, a contract can be void because one of the parties was adjudged by a court to be legally insane (and thus lacked the legal capacity to enter into a contract) or because the purpose of the contract was illegal.

A **voidable contract** is a *valid* contract but one that can be avoided at the option of one or both of the parties. The party having the option can elect either to avoid any duty to perform or to *ratify* (make valid) the contract. If the contract is avoided, both parties are released from it. If it is ratified, both parties must fully perform their respective legal obligations.

As a general rule, contracts made by minors are voidable at the option of the minor (see Chapter 11). Contracts entered into under fraudulent conditions are voidable at the option of the defrauded party. In addition, contracts entered into under legally defined duress or undue influence are voidable (see Chapter 12).

3. An obligation of a party who guarantees that he or she will pay a second party if a third party does not perform.

• **UNENFORCEABLE CONTRACT**
A valid contract rendered unenforceable by some statute or law.

An **unenforceable contract** is one that cannot be enforced because of certain legal defenses against it. It is not unenforceable because a party failed to satisfy a legal requirement of the contract; rather, it is a valid contract rendered unenforceable by some statute or law. For example, certain contracts must be in writing (see Chapter 12), and if they are not, they will not be enforceable except in certain exceptional circumstances.

Interpretation of Contracts

Common law rules of contract interpretation have evolved over time to provide the courts with guidelines for determining the meaning of contracts.

THE PLAIN MEANING RULE

¡NOTE!
No one can avoid a contract by claiming that he or she did not read it. A contract is interpreted as if each party read every word carefully.

When the writing is clear and unequivocal, a court will enforce it according to its plain terms (what is clearly stated in the contract), and there is no need for the court to interpret the language of the contract. The meaning of the terms must be determined from *the face of the instrument*—from the written document alone. This is sometimes referred to as the *plain meaning rule.* Under this rule, if a contract's words appear to be clear and unambiguous, a court cannot consider *extrinsic evidence,* which is any evidence not contained in the document itself. Admissibility of extrinsic evidence can significantly affect how a court may interpret ambiguous contractual provisions and thus the outcome of litigation.

OTHER RULES OF INTERPRETATION

"How many a dispute could have been deflated into a single paragraph if the disputants had dared define their terms."
ARISTOTLE, 384–322 B.C.E.
(Greek philosopher)

When the writing contains ambiguous or unclear terms, a court will interpret the language to give effect to the parties' intent as *expressed in their contract.* This is the primary purpose of the rules of interpretation—to determine the parties' intent from the language used in their agreement and to give effect to that intent. A court normally will not make or remake a contract, nor will it normally interpret the language according to what the parties *claim* their intent was when they made it. The following rules are used by the courts in interpreting ambiguous contractual terms:

1. Insofar as possible, a reasonable, lawful, and effective meaning will be given to all of a contract's terms.
2. A contract will be interpreted as a whole; individual, specific clauses will be considered subordinate to the contract's general intent. All writings that are a part of the same transaction will be interpreted together.
3. Terms that were the subject of separate negotiation will be given greater consideration than standardized terms and terms that were not negotiated separately.
4. A word will be given its ordinary, commonly accepted meaning, and a technical word or term will be given its technical meaning, unless the parties clearly intended something else.
5. Specific and exact wording will be given greater consideration than general language.
6. Written or typewritten terms prevail over preprinted terms.
7. Because a contract should be drafted in clear and unambiguous language, a party that uses ambiguous expressions is held to be responsible for the ambiguities. Thus, when the language has more than one meaning, it will be interpreted against the party that drafted the contract.
8. Evidence of trade usage, prior dealing, and course of performance may be admitted to clarify the meaning of an ambiguously worded contract. (We define and dis-

cuss these terms in Chapter 15.) What each of the parties does pursuant to the contract will be interpreted as consistent with what the other does and with any relevant usage of trade and course of dealing or performance. Express terms (terms expressly stated in the contract) are given the greatest weight, followed by course of performance, course of dealing, and custom and usage of trade—in that order. When considering custom and usage, a court will look at the trade customs and usage common to the particular business or industry and to the locale in which the contract was made or is to be performed.

ETHICAL ISSUE 9.2 ***Why do courts interpret vague or ambiguous contract terms against the party that drafted the contract?*** Point number 7 in the above list—that a party that uses ambiguous language will be held responsible for the ambiguities—expresses the ethical conviction that those who draft contracts should not be allowed to reap benefits from vague language. Often, the party responsible for drafting a contract has superior bargaining power relative to the other party. For example, if a person wants to obtain life or health insurance, that person must either accept the terms of the insurance company's policy, as drafted, or not obtain insurance coverage from that company. (Of course, the person can shop around for a policy with terms that are acceptable.) Insurance contracts are essentially adhesion contracts. An adhesion contract is a contract drafted by the dominant party and then presented to the other (adhering) party on a "take it or leave it" basis (see Chapter 11). If an insurance policy contains an ambiguous clause, the insurance company could, by interpreting the clause in its favor, deny coverage to the policyholder in the event of a claim. To prevent such unfairness, the courts interpret vague or ambiguous statements against the party that drafted the contract.

Plain Language Laws

> **¡DON'T FORGET!** Most law, like most contracts, can be expressed in ordinary English.

To avoid disputes over contract interpretation, business managers should make sure that their intentions are clearly expressed in their contracts. Careful drafting of contracts not only helps prevent potential disputes over the meaning of certain terms but also may be crucial if the firm brings or needs to defend against a lawsuit for breach of contract.

In the interests of helping consumers, as well as easing the work of the courts, the federal and state governments have been active in the push for more clearly written legal contracts by enacting "plain language laws." These laws, which are the subject of this chapter's *Landmark in the Law*, deal with private contracts in their entirety. Plain language laws attempt to reach a broad variety of consumer agreements relating to personal, family, and household matters, including residential leases.

Landmark in the Law • PLAIN LANGUAGE LAWS

Plain language is increasingly being required in contracts, and for a good reason: parties to contracts cannot genuinely assent to contractual terms that they do not understand. Compare, for example, the following words from a Citibank loan agreement:

> In the event of default in the payment of this or any other Obligation or the performance or observance of any term or covenant contained herein or in any note or other contract or agreement evidencing or relating to any Obligation or any Collateral on the Borrower's part to be performed or observed . . .

with this phrase: "If I don't pay an installment on time . . ."[a]

The difference is obvious: one statement is in "legalese," and the other is in "plain English." Citibank's use of the plain language version in loan agreements has led to fewer *defaults* (failures to make payments on time) by borrowers.

Today, the federal government and a majority of the states regulate legal writing through "plain language laws." The New York law, which has strongly influenced the plain language laws adopted by other states, illustrates how such statutes address the language problem. In New York, an agreement must be (1) "written in a clear and coherent manner using words with common and everyday meanings" and (2) "appropriately divided and captioned by its various sections."[b]

If a party to a contract, such as an insurance company, violates a plain language statute, the contract may be void—unless it can be shown that the party made a good faith effort to comply with the statute. Some state statutes even allow proposed contracts to be submitted to the state attorney general, whose approval then eliminates any liability for damages because of supposed violation of the plain language statute.

In response to plain language laws, the legal profession has attempted to abandon the traditional preference for often turgid and verbose language in favor of clear and easily understandable legal writing. The Securities and Exchange Commission (see Chapter 31) has published a "Plain English Handbook" to guide businesspersons who create documents to be filed with the commission. (The handbook is a good source for anyone interested in writing in plain English. It defines what plain English is—and is not—and offers some tips on how to write clearly.)

Judges and clients also are pressuring lawyers to make legal concepts and documents more comprehensible. At one point during the O. J. Simpson murder trial in 1994–1995, for example, the judge ordered the defense attorneys to redraft what the judge called an "incoherent" motion relating to certain evidence in the case. In some areas, judges themselves are being asked to write their opinions more clearly. Recently, for example, the chief judge of New York's highest court encouraged judges in the New York court system to hand down clearly written rulings so that other judges, lawyers, lawmakers, and the taxpayers who pay judicial salaries know what the decisions mean.[c]

FOR CRITICAL ANALYSIS
Are there any potential hazards in "translating" legalese into plain English?

a. As quoted in Scott J. Burnham, "The Hazards of Using Plain English: A New Look at Contracts," *The Compleat Lawyer*, Summer 1991, pp. 46–47.

b. N.Y. Gen. Oblig. Law, Section 5–702.

c. *The National Law Journal*, February 9, 1998, p. A23.

APPLICATION

Law & the Employer: Avoiding Unintended Employment Contracts*

Employers have learned many lessons from court decisions. In recent years, for example, the message has been becoming clear that promises made in an employment manual may create an implied-in-fact employment contract (see, for example, *Case 9.1* in this chapter). If an employment handbook contains a statement that employees will be fired only for specific causes, the employer may be held to that "promise." Even if, by state law, employment is "at will"—that is, the employer is allowed to hire and fire employees at will, with or without cause—the at-will doctrine will not apply if the terms of employment are subject to a contract between the employer and employee. If a court holds that an implied employment contract exists—on the basis of promises made in an employment manual in effect—the employment is no longer at will. The employer will be bound by the contract and liable for damages for breaching the contract.

Employers who wish to avoid potenal liability for breaching unintended employment contracts should therefore make it clear to employees that the policies expressed in an employment manual are not to be interpreted as contractual promises. An effective way to do this is to inform employees, when initially giving them the handbook or discussing its contents with them, that the handbook is not intended as a contract and to include a disclaimer to that effect in the employment application. The disclaimer might read as follows: "I understand and agree that, if hired, my employment is for no definite period and may be terminated at any time without any prior notice." The employer should make the disclaimer clear and prominent so that the applicant cannot later claim that it was the employer's fault that the employee did not see the disclaimer. A disclaimer will be clear and prominent if it is set off from the surrounding text by the use of larger type, a different color, all capital letters, or some other device that calls the reader's attention to it.

In the handbook, the employer should avoid making definite promises that employees will be fired only for cause, that they will not be fired after they have worked for a certain length of time except for certain reasons, or the like. The handbook itself should include a clear and prominent disclaimer of contractual liability for its contents.

*This *Application* is not meant to substitute for the services of an attorney who is licensed to practice law in your state.

CHECKLIST FOR THE EMPLOYER

1. Inform new employees that statements in an employment handbook are not intended as contractual terms.
2. Include a clear and prominent disclaimer to this effect in employment applications.
3. Avoid including in the handbook any definite promises relating to job security, and include a clear and prominent disclaimer of contractual liability for any statements made within the handbook.
4. Last but not least: check with your attorney concerning your state's employment laws.

Key Terms

bilateral contract 241
contract 239
executed contract 248
executory contract 248
express contract 243
formal contract 247
implied-in-fact contract 243
informal contract 248
objective theory of contracts 240
offeree 241
offeror 241
promise 238
promisee 239
promisor 239
quasi contract 245
unenforceable contract 249
unilateral contract 241
valid contract 248
void contract 248
voidable contract 248

Chapter Summary • Nature and Classification

The Function of Contracts (See page 239.)	Contract law establishes what kinds of promises will be legally binding and supplies procedures for enforcing legally binding promises, or agreements.
Requirements of a Contract (See page 240.)	1. *Elements of a valid contract*—Agreement, consideration, contractual capacity, and legality. 2. *Possible defenses to the enforcement of a contract*—Genuineness of assent and form.
Types of Contracts (See pages 241–249.)	1. *Bilateral*—A promise for a promise. 2. *Unilateral*—A promise for an act (acceptance is the completed—or substantial—performance of the contract by the offeree). 3. *Express*—Formed by words (oral, written, or a combination). 4. *Implied in fact*—Formed at least in part by the conduct of the parties. 5. *Quasi contract (contract implied in law)*—Imposed by law to prevent unjust enrichment. 6. *Formal*—Requires a special form for creation. 7. *Informal*—Requires no special form for creation. 8. *Executed*—A fully performed contract. 9. *Executory*—A contract not yet fully performed. 10. *Valid*—The contract has the necessary contractual elements of offer and acceptance, consideration, parties with legal capacity, and having been made for a legal purpose. 11. *Void*—No contract exists, or there is a contract without legal obligations. 12. *Voidable*—A party has the option of avoiding or enforcing the contractual obligation. 13. *Unenforceable*—A contract exists, but it cannot be enforced because of a legal defense.
Interpretation of Contracts (See pages 249–251.)	When the terms of a contract are unambiguous, a court will enforce the contract according to its plain terms, the meaning of which must be determined from the written document alone. (Plain language laws enacted by the federal government and the majority of the states require contracts to be clearly written and easily understandable.) When the terms of a contract are ambiguous, the following rules are used by the courts in interpreting the terms: 1. A reasonable, lawful, and effective meaning will be given to all contract terms. 2. A contract will be interpreted as a whole, specific clauses will be considered subordinate to the contract's general intent, and all writings that are a part of the same transaction will be interpreted together. 3. Terms that were negotiated separately will be given greater consideration than standardized terms and terms not negotiated separately. 4. Words will be given their commonly accepted meanings and technical words their technical meanings, unless the parties clearly intended otherwise. 5. Specific wording will be given greater consideration than general language. 6. Written or typewritten terms prevail over preprinted terms. 7. A party that uses ambiguous expressions is held to be responsible for the ambiguities. 8. Evidence of prior dealing, course of performance, or usage of trade is admissible to clarify an ambiguously worded contract. In these circumstances, express terms are given the greatest weight, followed by course of performance, course of dealing, and custom and usage of trade—in that order.

For Review

1. What is a contract? What is the objective theory of contracts?
2. What are the four basic elements necessary to the formation of a valid contract?
3. What is the difference between an implied-in-fact contract and an implied-in-law contract (quasi contract)?
4. What is a void contract? How does it differ from a voidable contract? What is an unenforceable contract?
5. What rules guide the courts in interpreting contracts?

Questions and Case Problems

9–1. Express versus Implied Contracts. Suppose that McDougal, a local businessperson, is a good friend of Krunch, the owner of a local candy store. Every day on his lunch hour McDougal goes into Krunch's candy store and spends about five minutes looking at the candy. After examining Krunch's candy and talking with Krunch, McDougal usually buys one or two candy bars. One afternoon, McDougal goes into Krunch's candy shop, looks at the candy, and picks up a $1 candy bar. Seeing that Krunch is very busy, he waves the candy bar at Krunch without saying a word and walks out. Is there a contract? If so, classify it within the categories presented in this chapter.

9–2. Contractual Promises. Rosalie, a wealthy widow, invited an acquaintance, Jonathan, to her home for dinner. Jonathan accepted the offer and, eager to please her, spent lavishly in preparing for the evening. His purchases included a new blazer, new shoes, an expensive floral arrangement, and champagne. On the appointed evening, Jonathan arrived at Rosalie's house only to find that she had left for the evening. Jonathan wants to sue Rosalie to recover some of his expenses. Can he? Why or why not?

9–3. Contract Classification. Jennifer says to her neighbor, Gordon, "Upon completion of mowing my lawn, I'll pay you $25." Gordon orally accepts her offer. Is there a contract? Is Jennifer's offer intended to create a bilateral or a unilateral contract? What is the legal significance of the distinction?

9–4. Contract Classification. High-Flying Advertising, Inc., contracted with Big Burger Restaurants to fly an advertisement above the Connecticut beaches. The advertisement offered $5,000 to any person who could swim from the Connecticut beaches to Long Island across the Long Island Sound in less than a day. McElfresh saw the streamer and accepted the challenge. He started his marathon swim that same day at 10 A.M. After he had been swimming for four hours and was about halfway across the sound, McElfresh saw another plane pulling a streamer that read, "Big Burger revokes." Is there a contract between McElfresh and Big Burger? If there is a contract, what type(s) of contract is (are) formed?

9–5. Equitable Doctrines. Ashton Co., which was engaged in a construction project, leased a crane from Artukovich & Sons, Inc., and hired the Reliance Truck Co. to deliver the crane to the construction site. Reliance, while the crane was in its possession and without permission from either Ashton or Artukovich, used the crane to install a transformer for a utility company, which paid Reliance for the job. Reliance then delivered the crane to the Ashton construction site at the appointed time of delivery. When Artukovich learned of the unauthorized use of the crane by Reliance, it sued Reliance for damages. What equitable doctrine could be used as a basis for awarding damages to Artukovich? [*Artukovich & Sons, Inc. v. Reliance Truck Co.*, 126 Ariz. 246, 614 P.2d 327 (1980)]

9–6. Bilateral versus Unilateral Contracts. William Greene began working for Grant Building, Inc., in 1959. Greene allegedly agreed to work at a pay rate below union scale in exchange for a promise that Grant would employ him "for life." In 1975, Oliver Realty, Inc., took over the management of Grant Building. Oliver Realty's president assured former Grant employees that existing employment contracts would be honored. During that same year, Greene explained the terms of his agreement to an Oliver Realty supervisor. The supervisor stated that he would look into the matter but never got back to Greene. After twenty-four years of service, Greene was fired by the new owners of the business. Greene sued Oliver Realty for breach of a unilateral contract. Discuss fully whether Greene and Oliver Realty had a unilateral contract. [*Greene v. Oliver Realty, Inc.*, 363 Pa.Super. 534, 526 A.2d 1192 (1987)]

9–7. Recovery for Services Rendered. Sosa Crisan, an eighty-seven-year-old widow, collapsed while shopping at a local grocery store. The Detroit police took her to the Detroit city hospital by ambulance. She was admitted to the hospital and remained there for fourteen days. Then she was transferred to another hospital, where she died some eleven months later. Crisan had never regained consciousness after her collapse at the grocery store. After she died, the city of Detroit sued her estate to recover the expenses of both the ambulance that took her to the Detroit city hospital and her Detroit city hospital stay. Is there a contract between Sosa Crisan and the Detroit city hospital? If so, how much can the hospital recover? [*In re Estate of Crisan*, 362 Mich. 569, 107 N.W.2d 907 (1961)]

9–8. Bilateral versus Unilateral Contracts. Nichols is the principal owner of Samuel Nichols, Inc., a real estate firm. Nichols signed an exclusive brokerage agreement with Molway to find a purchaser for Molway's property within ninety days. This type of agreement entitles the broker to a commission if the property is sold to any purchaser to whom the property is shown during the ninety-day period. Molway tried to cancel the brokerage agreement before the ninety-day term had expired. Nichols had already advertised the property, put up a "for sale" sign, and shown the property to prospective buyers. Molway claimed that the brokerage contract was unilateral and that she could cancel the contract at any time before Nichols found a buyer. Nichols claimed the contract was bilateral and that Molway's cancellation breached the contract. Discuss who should prevail at trial. [*Samuel Nichols, Inc. v. Molway,* 25 Mass.App. 913, 515 N.E.2d 598 (1987)]

9–9. Recovery for Services Rendered. After Walter Washut had suffered a heart attack and could no longer take care of himself, he asked Eleanor Adkins, a friend who had previously refused Washut's proposal to marry him, to move to his ranch. For the next twelve years, Adkins lived with Washut, although she retained ownership of her own house and continued to work full-time at her job. Adkins took care of Washut's personal needs, cooked his meals, cleaned and maintained his house, cared for the livestock, and handled other matters for Washut. According to Adkins, Washut told her on numerous occasions that "everything would be taken care of" and that she would never have to leave the ranch. After Washut's death, Adkins sought to recover in quasi contract for the value of the services she had rendered to Washut. Adkins stated in her deposition that she performed the services because she loved Washut, not because she expected to be paid for them. What will the court decide, and why? [*Adkins v. Lawson,* 892 P.2d 128 (Wyo. 1995)]

9–10. Interpretation of Contracts. Jerilyn Dawson hired Michael Shaw of the law firm of Jones, Waldo, Holbrook, and McDonough to represent her in her divorce. Dawson signed an agreement to pay the attorney's fees. The agreement did not include an estimate of how much the divorce would cost. When Dawson failed to pay, the firm filed a suit in a Utah state court to collect, asking for an award of more than $43,000. During the trial, Shaw testified that he had told Dawson the divorce would cost "something in the nature of $15,000 to $18,000." The court awarded the firm most—but not all—of what it sought. Both parties appealed: Dawson contended that the award was too high, and the firm complained that it was too low. What rule of interpretation discussed in this chapter might the appellate court apply in deciding the appropriate amount of damages in this case? If this rule is applied, what will the court likely decide? Explain. [*Jones, Waldo, Holbrook & McDonough v. Dawson,* 923 P.2d 1366 (Utah 1996)]

A QUESTION OF ETHICS AND SOCIAL RESPONSIBILITY

9–11. In 1982, in the closing days of Minnesota's gubernatorial campaign, Dan Cohen offered a reporter from the *Minneapolis Star and Tribune* some documents—copies of two public court records of a rival party's candidate for lieutenant governor—if the reporter promised not to reveal the source of the information. The reporter promised to keep the source confidential. The editor of the *Tribune,* however, in spite of the reporter's objections, decided to name Cohen as the source of the information so as not to mislead the public into thinking that the information came from an unbiased source. On the day the newspaper article was published, Cohen was fired by his employer. Cohen sued the newspaper's owner, Cowles Media Co., for breach of contract. Given these facts, discuss the following questions. [*Cohen v. Cowles Media Co.,* 501 U.S. 663, 111 S.Ct. 2513, 115 L.Ed.2d 586 (1991)]

1. Should the editor's ethical duty to provide the reading public with unbiased news coverage have overridden the editor's ethical duty to honor the reporter's promise to Cohen?
2. Did the reporter's promise to keep Cohen's identity confidential create solely an ethical obligation, or did it create an enforceable contract?
3. If the court decides that an enforceable contract was formed between Cohen and the reporter, would the decision be counter to society's valuation—as expressed in the First Amendment to the Constitution—that freedom of the press should not be constrained?

FOR CRITICAL ANALYSIS

9–12. Review the list of basic requirements for contract formation given at the beginning of this chapter. In view of those requirements, analyze the relationship entered into when a student enrolls in a college or university. Has a contract been formed? If so, is it a bilateral contract or a unilateral contract? Discuss.

Online Activities

ONLINE EXERCISE 9-1

Access the Web site of the 'Lectric Law Library's business forms collection at

www.lectlaw.com/form.

Scroll down the list of forms to "Employment Agreement." Read through the provisions of this standard-form contract. Then select the form titled "Agreement between Owner and Contractor." Read through this standard-form contract also, and then answer the following questions:

- Identify the provisions in both agreements that are similar. (Hint: Both agreements require the names of the parties; what else do they have in common?)
- Will each of these "form contracts," when filled out and signed by the parties, constitute a valid contract? Explain.
- List four provisions in each contract that constitute the *terms* of the contract.

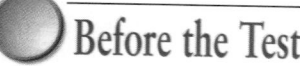

Before the Test

Go to the *Business Law Today* home page at http://blt.westbuslaw.com. Click on TestTutor.® You will find twenty interactive questions relating to this chapter.

CHAPTER 10 Agreement & Consideration

> "It is necessity that makes laws."
>
> Voltaire, 1749–1832
> (French philosopher and writer)

CONTENTS

LEARNING OBJECTIVES

After reading this chapter, you should be able to:

1. Identify the elements of contractual agreement.
2. State the requirements of an offer.
3. Describe how an offer can be accepted.
4. List and define the elements of consideration.
5. Explain the circumstances in which a promise will be enforced despite a lack of consideration.

Voltaire's statement that it is "necessity that makes laws" is certainly true in regard to contracts. In Chapter 9, we pointed out that promises and agreements, and the knowledge that certain of those promises and agreements will be legally enforced, are essential to civilized society. The homes we live in, the food we eat, the clothes we wear, the cars we drive, the books we read, the videos and recordings we watch and listen to—all of these have been purchased through contractual agreements. Contract law developed over time, through the common law tradition, to meet society's need to know with certainty what kinds of promises, or contracts, will be enforced and the point at which a valid and binding contract is formed.

For a contract to be considered valid and enforceable, the requirements listed in Chapter 9 must be met. In this chapter, we look closely at two of these requirements, *agreement* and *consideration.* As you read through this chapter, keep in mind that the contract requirements of agreement and consideration apply to all contracts, regardless of whether they are formed in the traditional way (through the exchange of paper documents) or online (through the exchange of electronic messages or documents).

Agreement

• **AGREEMENT**
A meeting of two or more minds in regard to the terms of a contract; usually broken down into two events—an offer by one party to form a contract, and an acceptance of the offer by the person to whom the offer is made.

An essential element for contract formation is **agreement**—the parties must agree on the terms of the contract. Ordinarily, agreement is evidenced by two events: an *offer* and an *acceptance*. One party offers a certain bargain to another party, who then accepts that bargain.

Because words often fail to convey the precise meaning intended, the law of contracts generally adheres to the *objective theory of contracts,* as discussed in Chapter 9. Under this theory, a party's words and conduct are held to mean whatever a reasonable person in the offeree's position would think they meant. The court will give words their usual meanings even if "it were proved by twenty bishops that [the] party . . . intended something else."[1]

REQUIREMENTS OF THE OFFER

• **OFFER**
A promise or commitment to perform or refrain from performing some specified act in the future.

An **offer** is a promise or commitment to perform or refrain from performing some specified act in the future. As discussed in Chapter 9, the party making an offer is called the *offeror,* and the party to whom the offer is made is called the *offeree.*

Three elements are necessary for an offer to be effective:

1. There must be a serious, objective intention by the offeror.
2. The terms of the offer must be reasonably certain, or definite, so that the parties and the court can ascertain the terms of the contract.
3. The offer must be communicated to the offeree.

Once an effective offer has been made, the offeree's acceptance of that offer creates a legally binding contract (providing the other essential elements for a valid and enforceable contract are present).

Intention The first requirement for an effective offer to exist is a serious, objective intention on the part of the offeror. Intent is not determined by the *subjective* intentions, beliefs, or assumptions of the offeror. Rather, it is determined by what a reasonable person in the offeree's position would conclude the offeror's words and actions meant. Offers made in obvious anger, jest, or undue excitement do not meet the serious-and-objective-intent test. Because these offers are not effective, an offeree's acceptance does not create an agreement.

• **EXAMPLE 10.1** You and three classmates ride to school each day in Julio's new automobile, which has a market value of $18,000. One cold morning the four of you get into the car, but Julio cannot get it started. He yells in anger, "I'll sell this car to anyone for $500!" You drop $500 in his lap. A reasonable person, taking into consideration Julio's frustration and the obvious difference in value between the car's market price and the purchase price, would declare that Julio's offer was not made with serious and objective intent and that you do not have an agreement. The concept of intention can be further explained by distinctions between offers and nonoffers. •

ON THE WEB
The Legal Information Institute at Cornell University is an excellent source for legal information, including information on contract law. To access the institute's site, go to **www.law.cornell.edu/topics/contracts.html**.

"[Contracts] must not be the sports of an idle hour, mere matters of pleasantry and badinage, never intended by the parties to have any serious effect whatever."

WILLIAM STOWELL, 1745–1836 (English jurist)

Expressions of Opinion. An expression of opinion is not an offer. It does not evidence an intention to enter into a binding agreement. • **EXAMPLE 10.2** In *Hawkins v.*

1. Judge Learned Hand in *Hotchkiss v. National City Bank of New York,* 200 F. 287 (2d Cir. 1911), aff'd 231 U.S. 50, 34 S.Ct. 20, 58 L.Ed. 115 (1913). (The term *aff'd* is an abbreviation for *affirmed;* an appellate court can affirm a lower court's judgment, decree, or order, thereby declaring that it is valid and must stand as rendered.)

¡ BE CAREFUL!
An opinion is not an offer and not a contract term. Goods or services can be "perfect" in one party's opinion and "poor" in another's.

McGee,[2] Hawkins took his son to McGee, a doctor, and asked McGee to operate on the son's hand. McGee said that the boy would be in the hospital three or four days and that the hand would *probably* heal a few days later. The son's hand did not heal for a month, but nonetheless the father did not win a suit for breach of contract. The court held that McGee did not make an offer to heal the son's hand in three or four days. He merely expressed an opinion as to when the hand would heal. •

Statements of Intention. A statement of an *intention* to do something in the future is not an offer. • **EXAMPLE 10.3** If Ari says "I *plan* to sell my stock in Novation, Inc., for $150 per share," a contract is not created if John "accepts" and tenders the $150 per share for the stock. Ari has merely expressed his intention to enter into a future contract for the sale of the stock. If John accepts and tenders the $150 per share, no contract is formed, because a reasonable person would conclude that Ari was only *thinking about* selling his stock, not promising to sell it. •

Preliminary Negotiations. A request or invitation to negotiate is not an offer; it only expresses a willingness to discuss the possibility of entering into a contract. Examples are statements such as "Will you sell Forest Acres?" and "I wouldn't sell my car for less than $1,000." A reasonable person in the offeree's position would not conclude that such a statement evidenced an intention to enter into a binding obligation. Likewise, when the government and private firms need to have construction work done, contractors are invited to submit bids. The *invitation* to submit bids is not an offer, and a contractor does not bind the government or private firm by submitting a bid. (The bids that the contractors submit are offers, however, and the government or private firm can bind the contractor by accepting the bid.)

In the following classic case, the court addressed the question of whether a letter informing several people that a cottage was for sale was an offer or merely a preliminary negotiation.

2. 84 N.H. 114, 146 A. 641 (1929).

CASE 10.1 Mellen v. Johnson

Supreme Judicial Court of Massachusetts, 1948.
322 Mass. 236,
76 N.E.2d 658.

HISTORICAL AND ENVIRONMENTAL SETTING *Nahant, Massachusetts, is one of the small communities on the North Shore of Greater Boston Harbor. An area of rugged coast and ocean beaches, the North Shore has been a desirable place to live since the Puritans landed in Salem in 1628. The area's many rivers and marshes supply the region with drinking water. Plum Island includes an important wildlife refuge. The fish population has been decimated, but lobsters and clams abound. Residents say no place is as perfect or as pristine.*[a] *As for Nahant, even in years in which other North Shore communities saw declines in the prices of housing, Nahant saw increases.*

BACKGROUND AND FACTS Johnson, who owned a three-bedroom cottage in Nahant, Massachusetts, sent a letter to Mellen saying that he was putting the cottage on the market. Earlier, Mellen had expressed an interest in purchasing the cottage. The letter indicated that several other people, who had also expressed an interest in purchasing the property, were being informed by letter of its availability at the same time. Mellen, interpreting the letter as an offer, promptly accepted. Johnson sold the property to a higher bidder, and Mellen sued Johnson in a Massachusetts state court. The court found that the letter was an offer and ordered Johnson to convey the property to Mellen on Mellen's payment of the purchase price. Johnson appealed.

a. Beth Daley, "South vs. North," *The Boston Globe,* September 3, 1995, p. 1.

(Continued)

CASE 10.1—Continued

IN THE WORDS OF THE COURT . . .
WILKINS, Justice.

* * * *

The letter of March 27 was not an offer. It expressed "a desire to dispose of" the property. It announced that the agent was "writing the several people, including yourself, who have previously expressed an interest in the property." Its conclusion, in part, was, "I will be interested in hearing further from you if you have any interest in this property, for as I said before, I am advising those who have asked for an opportunity to consider it." The recipient could not reasonably understand this to be more than an attempt at negotiation. It was a mere request or suggestion that an offer be made to the defendant.

DECISION AND REMEDY The Supreme Judicial Court of Massachusetts reversed the decision of the trial court and dismissed Mellen's complaint.

FOR CRITICAL ANALYSIS—Social Consideration *How can the kind of confusion that arose in this case be prevented? Is it enough to say to prospective purchasers that other parties have also been informed that certain property is for sale?*

¡KEEP IN MIND! Advertisements are not binding, but they cannot be deceptive.

Advertisements, Catalogues, and Circulars. In general, advertisements, mail-order catalogues, price lists, and circular letters (meant for the general public) are treated not as offers to contract but as invitations to negotiate.[3] • **EXAMPLE 10.4** Suppose that you put an ad in the classified section of your local newspaper offering to sell your guitar for $75. Seven people call and "accept" your "offer" before you can remove the ad from the newspaper. If the ad were truly an offer, you would be bound by seven contracts to sell your guitar. Because *initial* advertisements are treated as *invitations* to make offers rather than offers, however, you would have seven offers to choose from, and you could accept the best one without incurring any liability for the six you rejected. On some occasions, though, courts have construed advertisements to be offers because the ads contained definite terms that invite acceptance (such as an ad offering a reward for the return of a lost dog).[4] •

Price lists are another form of invitation to negotiate or trade. A seller's price list is not an offer to sell at that price; it merely invites the buyer to offer to buy at that price. In fact, the seller usually puts "prices subject to change" on the price list. Only in rare circumstances will a price quotation be construed as an offer.[5]

Auctions. In an auction, a seller "offers" goods for sale through an auctioneer. This is not, however, an offer for purposes of contract. The seller is really only expressing a willingness to sell. Unless the terms of the auction are explicitly stated to be *without reserve,* the seller (through the auctioneer) may withdraw the goods at any time before the auctioneer closes the sale by announcement or by fall of the hammer. The seller's right to withdraw the goods characterizes an auction with reserve; all auctions are assumed to be of this type unless a clear statement to the contrary is made.[6] At auctions without reserve, the goods cannot be withdrawn and must be sold to the highest bidder.

---

3. *Restatement (Second) of Contracts,* Section 26, Comment b.
4. See, for example, *Lefkowitz v. Great Minneapolis Surplus Store, Inc.,* 251 Minn. 188, 86 N.W.2d 689 (1957).
5. See, for example, *Fairmount Glass Works v. Grunden-Martin Woodenware Co.,* 106 Ky. 659, 51 S.W. 196 (1899).
6. See UCC 2–328.

AN AUCTION IN PROGRESS AT CHRISTIE'S IN LONDON. WHEN A SELLER PUTS UP GOODS FOR A BID IN AN AUCTION WITH RESERVE, HAS THE SELLER MADE AN OFFER FOR PURPOSES OF CONTRACT LAW? WHY OR WHY NOT?

In an auction with reserve, there is no obligation to sell, and the seller may refuse the highest bid. The bidder is actually the offeror. Before the auctioneer strikes the hammer, which constitutes acceptance of the bid, a bidder may revoke his or her bid, or the auctioneer may reject that bid or all bids. Typically, an auctioneer will reject a bid that is below the price the seller is willing to accept. When the auctioneer accepts a higher bid, he or she rejects all previous bids. Because rejection terminates an offer (as will be pointed out later), those bids represent offers that have been terminated. Thus, if the highest bidder withdraws his or her bid before the hammer falls, none of the previous bids is reinstated. If the bid is not withdrawn or rejected, the contract is formed when the auctioneer announces, "Going once, going twice, sold!" (or something similar) and lets the hammer fall.

In auctions with reserve, the seller may reserve the right to confirm or reject the sale even after the "hammer has fallen." In this situation, the seller is obligated to notify those attending the auction that sales of goods made during the auction are not final until confirmed by the seller. The following case illustrates this point.

CASE 10.2 Lawrence Paper Co. v. Rosen & Co.

United States Court of Appeals,
Sixth Circuit, 1991.
939 F.2d 376.

HISTORICAL AND SOCIAL SETTING *More than two hundred years ago, it was established at common law that when an auctioneer says, "What am I bid?" the auctioneer is not making an offer to sell but is inviting offers to buy, which the auctioneer is free to accept or reject. More than one hundred years ago, it was established that in some cases, even if an auctioneer announces, "I will sell to the highest bidder," the statement still does not constitute an offer. These common law rules relating to auctions plus auctions "without reserve" were adopted by the Uniform Commercial Code, which has governed most sales of goods since the 1950s. It is also generally held that when a seller reserves the right to refuse to accept a bid, a binding sale is not made until the seller accepts the bid.*

BACKGROUND AND FACTS This dispute arose when some equipment, which had been used as security for a loan obtained by North Coast Corrugator Company from

(Continued)

CASE 10.2—Continued

Ameritrust Company, was sold at auction to satisfy North Coast's debt to Ameritrust. Ameritrust Company employed Rosen & Company to conduct the sale. Included in Rosen's extensive advertisements of the sale was the announcement that the sale was subject to confirmation by Ameritrust. The auctioneer made a similar announcement at the time of the sale. Sixty bidders attended the auction. The auctioneer first offered the equipment in bulk, but only one bid—from Alpine Company for $50,000 was received. Then the equipment was offered piecemeal, and total bids of $139,000 were received. Two bids from Lawrence Paper Company and American Corrugated Machine Corporation (ACMC) were accepted, and both companies submitted checks for 25 percent of their bid totals, as requested. After the auction, Alpine offered $175,000 for the equipment, and Ameritrust sold the entire lot to Alpine. Lawrence and ACMC sued in a federal district court for breach of contract. The trial judge dismissed the suit, and the plaintiffs appealed.

IN THE WORDS OF THE COURT . . .

BERTELSMAN, District Judge:

* * * Rosen & Company advertised the sale extensively in newspapers, trade journals, and a catalog which was prepared especially for the sale. On the cover page of the mail catalog, the terms of this particular auction were printed and included: "* * * Sale subject to confirmation of the Secured Party." * * * Terms and conditions that were announced [orally at the auction] and are relevant to the instant case include the following: "Be advised any and all sales are subject to confirmation by the Secured Party * * * ."

* * * *

[The trial court judge] based his dismissal of the complaint on his finding that the auction sale was "clearly with reserve" and that the sale was, as a matter of law, "subject to * * * the confirmation of the secured party * * * ." In his view, there was no acceptance of the bid, because the sale was not confirmed by the secured party. Therefore, he held there was no binding contract and the sellers were free to accept the subsequent offer. We agree and affirm.

* * * *

* * * [W]here a sale is with reserve and subject to "confirmation" by the seller, the bids are subject to rejection after the sale, even though accepted by the auctioneer.

DECISION AND REMEDY The U.S. Court of Appeals for the Sixth Circuit affirmed the trial court's decision. A contract did not exist between the plaintiffs and Rosen as a result of the auctioneer's acceptance of the plaintiffs' bids because the seller had notified the plaintiffs that any sale was not final until confirmed by the seller.

FOR CRITICAL ANALYSIS—Ethical Consideration *Are auctions with reserve unfair to the bidders, whose bids and partial payments toward the purchase prices of the items being sold may be freely ignored later by the seller?*

ON THE WEB

The Web sites of various law firms are often good sources of information on contract law. To find the names of law firms in this area, go to FindLaw's site at **firms.findlaw.com/firms/pract15.html**.

Agreements to Agree. Traditionally, agreements to agree—that is, agreements to agree to the material terms of a contract at some future date—were not considered to be binding contracts. The modern view, however, is that agreements to agree may be enforceable agreements (contracts) if it is clear that the parties intend to be bound by the agreements. In other words, under the modern view the emphasis is on the parties' intent rather than on form.

• **EXAMPLE 10.5** When the Pennzoil Company discussed with the Getty Oil Company the possible purchase of Getty's stock, a memorandum of agreement was drafted to reflect the terms of the conversations. After more negotiations over the price, both companies issued press releases announcing an agreement in principle on the terms of the memorandum. The next day, Texaco, Inc., offered to buy all Getty's stock at a higher price. The day after that, Getty's board of directors voted to accept

Texaco's offer, and Texaco and Getty signed a merger agreement. When Pennzoil sued Texaco for tortious interference with its "contractual" relationship with Getty, a jury concluded that Getty and Pennzoil had intended to form a binding contract before Texaco made its offer, with only the details left to be worked out. Texaco was held liable for wrongfully interfering with this contract.[7] • (For a further discussion of when agreements to agree may constitute enforceable contracts, see this chapter's *Business Law in Action* on pages 264–265.)

ON THE WEB

To view the terms of a sample contract, go to the "forms" pages of the 'Lectric Law Library at www.lectlaw.com/form.

Definiteness The second requirement for an effective offer involves the definiteness of its terms. An offer must have reasonably definite terms so that a court can determine if a breach has occurred and give an appropriate remedy.[8]

An offer may invite an acceptance to be worded in such specific terms that the contract is made definite. • **EXAMPLE 10.6** Suppose that Marcus Business Machines contacts your corporation and offers to sell "from one to ten MacCool copying machines for $1,600 each; state number desired in acceptance." Your corporation agrees to buy two copiers. Because the quantity is specified in the acceptance, the terms are definite, and the contract is enforceable. •

If some terms are not specified in the words of a document, a court may nonetheless find that an enforceable contract exists if the terms can be made definite in light of the surrounding circumstances. The following case illustrates this point.

7. *Texaco, Inc. v. Pennzoil Co.*, 729 S.W.2d 768 (Tex.App—Houston [1st Dist.] 1987, writ ref'd n.r.e.). (Generally, a complete Texas court of appeals citation includes the writ-of-error history showing the Texas Supreme Court's disposition of the case. In this case, *writ ref'd n.r.e.* is an abbreviation for "writ refused, no reversible error," which means that Texas's highest court refused to grant the appellant's request to review the case, because the court did not consider there to be any reversible error.)

8. *Restatement (Second) of Contracts*, Section 33. The UCC has relaxed the requirements regarding the definiteness of terms in contracts for the sale of goods. See UCC 2–204(3).

CASE 10.3 R. K. Chevrolet, Inc. v. Hayden

Supreme Court of Virginia, 1997.
253 Va. 50,
480 S.E.2d 477.
www.courts.state.va.us/opin.htm[a]

HISTORICAL AND SOCIAL SETTING *Employment contracts are often considered to be a disadvantage to an employer. Such contracts sometimes work to an employer's advantage, however. An employer invests time and money in hiring and training its employees. An employment contract helps to ensure that the employer will get something in return for this investment. Also, employment often gives employees access to confidential information. This is particularly true of business managers. A contract can help to ensure that this confidential information will not be disclosed to unauthorized persons.*

a. This page, which is part of a Web site maintained by the state of Virginia, includes links to, among other things, some of the "Opinions of the Supreme Court of Virginia." Under that heading, click on the box for the format in which you want to view the opinion. From that page, scroll down the list of cases to the *R. K. Chevrolet v. Hayden* case and click on the number (906943) to download the opinion.

BACKGROUND AND FACTS R. K. Chevrolet, Inc., an automobile dealership, employed James Hayden as an assistant manager in its used-car department. Hayden's father owned and operated Coastal Chevrolet, one of R. K. Chevrolet's competitors. In May 1992, after Hayden had worked for R. K. Chevrolet for more than a year, he signed the following document:

> Contract Between James J. Hayden & R. K. Chevrolet, GEO
> May 12, 1992
> I, James J. Hayden, willingly enter into a two year contract of employment with R. K. Chevrolet, Inc., GEO. The only reason allowable for Mr. Hayden to leave in this time frame, under this contract, is the untimely death of his father. Therefore, with the above exception, James J. Hayden agrees to work continuously at R. K. Chevrolet, Inc., GEO for at least two years in good faith.

Nine months later, Hayden quit without notice. After his departure, R. K. Chevrolet did not realize anticipated profits

(Continued)

CASE 10.3—Continued

of $348,832 in its used-car department. The dealer filed a suit in a Virginia state court against Hayden, seeking, among other things, damages for breach of contract. Hayden argued that there was no contract because, in part, the terms were too indefinite. The court ruled in Hayden's favor. The dealer appealed.

IN THE WORDS OF THE COURT . . .
STEPHENSON, Justice.

* * * *

* * * Even if some terms of a contract are uncertain, it may be read in the light of the surrounding circumstances, and, if from such reading, its meaning may be determined, the contract will be enforced. * * *

The trial court concluded that a number of terms were missing from the alleged contract. The court stated that "[t]he document is dated on May the 12th of 1992, but it does not say that it will continue until May the 12th of 1994." The document does state, however, that Hayden agreed to work continuously at R.K. "for at least two years." We think a jury, in the light of the surrounding circumstances, reasonably could conclude that the two-year period commenced on the date the document was executed.

The trial court also stated that there was nothing in the document to indicate what Hayden's position would be. Hayden, however, signed the document as the used car manager, and it is clear from the evidence adduced that he intended to serve in that capacity for the two-year term.

The court further noted that the document did not specify the amount of time Hayden was to work. Again, Hayden was already working as the used car manager when he signed the document, and a jury reasonably could find that he would continue to work the hours in a day and the days in a week that he had been working.

Finally, the trial court stated that the document made no mention of what Hayden's compensation would be. From the surrounding circumstances, however, a jury reasonably could have concluded that Hayden's salary would be that which he was receiving at the time he signed the document.

DECISION AND REMEDY The Supreme Court of Virginia held that the terms were sufficiently definite to create an enforceable contract. The court reversed the decision of the lower court and remanded the case for a new trial.

FOR CRITICAL ANALYSIS—Ethical Consideration *Are there any circumstances in which an employer might agree to allow an employee to break an employment contract?*

Business Law in Action • WHEN YOU HAVE MADE A DEAL, IS IT REALLY A DEAL?

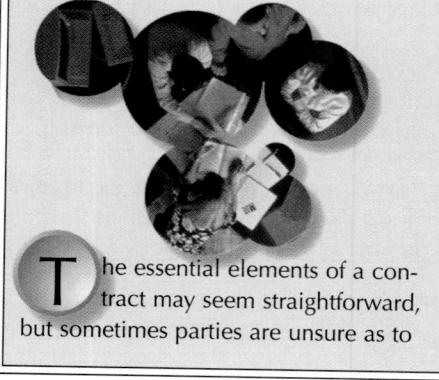

The essential elements of a contract may seem straightforward, but sometimes parties are unsure as to whether they have formed an enforceable contract or simply an "agreement to agree" in the future. For example, suppose that at some point during protracted contract negotiations, but before a formal contract is drawn up, the parties proclaim that they have "made a deal." Does their agreement mean that an enforceable contract has been formed even though the parties have not signed a formal contract? Or does their agreement simply mean that they have agreed to agree to a contract in the future?

How a court might interpret such a situation can, of course, have significant consequences for the parties—as Texaco Oil Company learned in 1987. As discussed elsewhere, Texaco had to pay damages in the millions of dollars when a court held that Texaco had tortiously interfered with a "contract"

Business Law in Action • CONTINUED

between two other oil companies, even though those companies had not yet finalized their deal in a formal contract.

TYPES OF PRELIMINARY AGREEMENTS

A decision by the U.S. Court of Appeals for the Second Circuit set forth some helpful guidelines on this issue. In doing so, the court distinguished between two types of preliminary agreements. A Type I preliminary agreement is one in which all essential terms have been agreed on—no disputed issues remain to be resolved. The formal contract to follow is simply that—a writing to satisfy formalities. According to the court, in this situation a formal contract is not necessary to create a binding agreement, which has already been created.

Type II preliminary agreements are all other preliminary agreements in which open terms still exist. All that the parties are doing is agreeing to continue negotiations in good faith to work out the remaining terms. Type II preliminary agreements are therefore not binding. The only obligation of the parties is to continue negotiating in good faith in an attempt to resolve open terms, but such a resolution is not legally required.[a]

AN EXAMPLE OF A TYPE II PRELIMINARY AGREEMENT

Important factors in determining whether a Type I or a Type II preliminary agreement has been reached are whether there was a "meeting of the minds" between the parties as to the essential terms of the future contract and whether the parties intended to be bound by their agreement. The court's evaluation of these factors played a key role in the outcome of a recent case brought by Fox News Network against Time Warner. A few years prior to the lawsuit, Time Warner and Turner Broadcasting had decided to merge. They knew that the Federal Trade Commission would require them to carry an additional affiliated cable news network in order to receive merger approval. Time Warner started negotiations with Fox News and MSNBC (a joint venture of Microsoft and NBC), ultimately choosing the latter. Fox sued Time Warner, claiming that such statements as "We are in agreement," "We will certainly reach agreement," and "All the details are set" made by Time Warner during the contract negotiations indicated that the parties agreed on the terms of a contract and intended to be bound by those terms.

The federal district court hearing the case did not agree with Fox. The court stated that the parties "never reached—or even approached—agreement on the essentials to a contractual relationship." According to the court, Fox should have known better than to rely on statements made by Time Warner during the preliminary negotiations. "These were not Adam-and-Eve-like innocents slipping naked into the cable television and broadcast jungle to negotiate with each other and the serpent," said the court. Rather, "They were hard bitten executives steeled in such hagglings. . . . The 'morals of the marketplace' controlled." The law was not violated.[b]

FOR CRITICAL ANALYSIS

In deciding whether an agreement to agree or an enforceable contract has been formed, why should it matter whether the parties are "hard bitten executives steeled in such hagglings" or relatively inexperienced businesspersons?

a. *Shann v. Dunk,* 84 F.3d 73 (2d Cir. 1996).

b. *Fox News Network, L.L.C. v. Time Warner, Inc.,* 1997 WL 271720 (E.D.N.Y. 1997).

Communication A third requirement for an effective offer is communication—the offer must be communicated to the offeree. • EXAMPLE 10.7 Suppose that Tolson advertises a reward for the return of her lost cat. Dirlik, not knowing of the reward, finds the cat and returns it to Tolson. Ordinarily, Dirlik cannot recover the reward, because an essential element of a reward contract is that the one who claims the reward must have known it was offered. A few states would allow recovery of the reward, but not on contract principles—Dirlik would be allowed to recover on the basis that it would be unfair to deny him the reward just because he did not know about it. • The following case is one of the classic reward suits in common law.

CASE 10.4 Glover v. Jewish War Veterans of the United States, Post No. 58

Municipal Court of Appeals for the District of Columbia, 1949.
68 A.2d 233.

HISTORICAL AND SOCIAL SETTING *Rewards have been offered for the capture of criminals since the days of the Old West. Such rewards gave rise to the bounty hunters who tried to make a living by finding alleged criminals. After World War II, which ended in 1945, the professional bounty-hunting business had died, but some rewards continued to be given. The purpose of these rewards remained the same as in the Old West—to provide incentives for persons to make an extra effort to find those accused of committing crimes.*

BACKGROUND AND FACTS The Jewish War Veterans of the United States placed in the newspaper an offer of a reward of $500 "to the person or persons furnishing information resulting in the apprehension and conviction of the persons guilty of the murder of Maurice L. Bernstein." Mary Glover gave police information that led to the arrest and conviction of the murderers, not knowing that a reward had been offered and not learning of it until the next day. In an action brought before a District of Columbia trial court, the court held that no contract existed because Mary Glover did not know about the reward at the time she gave the police the information. Glover appealed.

IN THE WORDS OF THE COURT . . .
CLAGETT, Associate Judge.

* * * *

* * * [T]*here can be no contract unless the claimant when giving the desired information knew of the offer of the reward and acted with the intention of accepting such offe*r [emphasis added]; otherwise the claimant gives the information not in the expectation of receiving a reward but rather out of a sense of public duty or other motive unconnected with the reward.

We have considered the reasoning in [the minority of] state decisions following the contrary rule. Mostly, as we have said, they involve rewards offered by governmental bodies and in general are based upon the theory that the government is benefited equally whether or not the claimant gives the information with knowledge of the reward and that therefore the government should pay in any event. We believe that the rule adopted * * * in the majority of cases is the better reasoned rule and therefore we adopt it. We believe furthermore that this rule is particularly applicable in the present case since the claimant did not herself contact the authorities and volunteer information but gave information only upon questioning by the police officers and did not claim any knowledge of the guilt or innocence of the criminal but only knew where he probably could be located.

DECISION AND REMEDY The Municipal Court of Appeals for the District of Columbia affirmed the trial court's judgment. The Jewish War Veterans did not have to pay the reward to Glover. No contract existed, because Glover's performance had not been induced by the offer, of which she had had no knowledge.

FOR CRITICAL ANALYSIS—Political Consideration *With respect to rewards offered by the government, should it be assumed by the government that members of the public have knowledge of government actions and that members of the public should receive government rewards without further proof of knowledge?*

TERMINATION OF THE OFFER

The communication of an effective offer to an offeree gives the offeree the power to transform the offer into a binding, legal obligation (a contract) by an acceptance. This power of acceptance, however, does not continue forever. It can be terminated by action of the parties or by operation of law.

MISSING TEEN
name
Sarah Bown
White Female
14 years old
Date of Birth: 8/16/72
Height: 5'-8"
Last Seen:
5300 North Lamar Blvd.
at North Loop
in the vicinity of
McCallum High School
Monday afternoon 2/23
Reward for information leading to
the location of this child.
Call 474-2286
or 343-5080

A POSTER OFFERS A REWARD. HOW CAN THIS OFFER BE REVOKED?

Termination by Action of the Parties An offer can be terminated by the action of the parties in any of three ways: by revocation, by rejection, or by counteroffer.

Revocation of the Offer. The offeror's act of withdrawing an offer is referred to as **revocation.** Unless an offer is irrevocable, the offeror usually can revoke the offer (even if he or she has promised to keep the offer open), as long as the revocation is communicated to the offeree before the offeree accepts. Revocation may be accomplished by express repudiation of the offer (for example, with a statement such as "I withdraw my previous offer of October 17") or by performance of acts inconsistent with the existence of the offer, which are made known to the offeree.

• **REVOCATION**
In contract law, the withdrawal of an offer by an offeror; unless the offer is irrevocable, it can be revoked at any time prior to acceptance without liability.

• EXAMPLE 10.8 Geraldine offers to sell some land to Gary. A week passes, and Gary, who has not yet accepted the offer, learns from his friend Konstantine that Geraldine has in the meantime sold the property to Nunan. Gary's knowledge of Geraldine's sale of the land to Nunan, even though Gary learned of it through a third party, effectively revokes Geraldine's offer to sell the land to Gary. Geraldine's sale of the land to Nunan is inconsistent with the continued existence of the offer to Gary, and thus the offer to Gary is revoked. •

The general rule followed by most states is that a revocation becomes effective when the offeree or offeree's agent (a person who acts on behalf of another) actually receives it. Therefore, a letter of revocation mailed on April 1 and delivered at the offeree's residence or place of business on April 3 becomes effective on April 3.

An offer made to the general public can be revoked in the same manner the offer was originally communicated. • EXAMPLE 10.9 Suppose that a department store offers a $10,000 reward to anyone giving information leading to the apprehension of the persons who burglarized its downtown store. The offer is published in three local papers and four papers in neighboring communities. To revoke the offer, the store must publish the revocation in all seven papers for the same number of days it published the offer. The revocation is then accessible to the general public, and the offer is revoked even if some particular offeree does not know about the revocation. •

Irrevocable Offers. Although most offers are revocable, some can be made irrevocable. Increasingly, courts refuse to allow an offeror to revoke an offer when the offeree has changed position because of justifiable reliance on the offer (under the doctrine of detrimental reliance, or promissory estoppel, discussed later in the chapter). In some circumstances, "firm offers" made by merchants may also be considered irrevocable. We discuss these offers in Chapter 15.

• **OPTION CONTRACT**
A contract under which the offeror cannot revoke his or her offer for a stipulated time period, and the offeree can accept or reject the offer during this period without fear that the offer will be made to another person. The offeree must give consideration for the option (the irrevocable offer) to be enforceable.

Another form of irrevocable offer is an option contract. An **option contract** is created when an offeror promises to hold an offer open for a specified period of time in return for a payment (consideration) given by the offeree. An option contract takes away the offeror's power to revoke an offer for the period of time specified in the option. If no time is specified, then a reasonable period of time is implied. • EXAMPLE 10.10 Suppose that you are in the business of writing movie scripts. Your agent contacts the head of development at New Line Cinema and offers to sell New Line your new movie script. New Line likes your script and agrees to pay you $5,000 for a six-month option. In this situation, you (through your agent) are the offeror, and New Line is the offeree. You cannot revoke your offer to sell New Line your script for the next six months. If after six months no contract has been formed, however, New Line loses the $5,000, and you are free to sell the script to another firm. •

Option contracts are also frequently used in conjunction with the sale of real estate. • EXAMPLE 10.11 You might agree with a landowner to lease a home and include in the lease contract a clause stating that you will pay $2,000 for an option to purchase the home within a specified period of time. If you decide not to purchase the home after the specified period has lapsed, you forfeit the $2,000, and the landlord is free to sell the property to another buyer.•

¡BE CAREFUL! The way in which a response to an offer is phrased can determine whether the offer is accepted or rejected.

Rejection of the Offer by the Offeree. The offer may be rejected by the offeree, in which case the offer is terminated. Any subsequent attempt by the offeree to accept will be construed as a new offer, giving the original offeror (now the offeree) the power of acceptance. A rejection is ordinarily accomplished by words or by conduct evidencing an intent not to accept the offer.

As with revocation, rejection of an offer is effective only when it is actually received by the offeror or the offeror's agent. • EXAMPLE 10.12 Suppose that Growgood Farms mails a letter to Campbell Soup Company offering to sell carrots at ten cents a pound. Campbell Soup Company could reject the offer by sending or faxing a letter to Growgood Farms expressly rejecting the offer, or by mailing the offer back to Growgood, evidencing an intent to reject it. Alternatively, Campbell could offer to buy the carrots at eight cents per pound (a counteroffer), necessarily rejecting the original offer.•

Merely inquiring about the offer does not constitute rejection. • EXAMPLE 10.13 A friend offers to buy your CD-ROM library for $300. You respond, "Is this your best offer?" or "Will you pay me $375 for it?" A reasonable person would conclude that you did not reject the offer but merely made an inquiry for further consideration of the offer. You can still accept and bind your friend to the $300 purchase price. When the offeree merely inquires as to the firmness of the offer, there is no reason to presume that he or she intends to reject it.•

• **COUNTEROFFER**
An offeree's response to an offer in which the offeree rejects the original offer and at the same time makes a new offer.

Counteroffer by the Offeree. A **counteroffer** is a rejection of the original offer and the simultaneous making of a new offer. • EXAMPLE 10.14 Suppose that Burke offers to sell his home to Lang for $170,000. Lang responds, "Your price is too high. I'll offer to purchase your house for $165,000." Lang's response is termed a counteroffer because it rejects Burke's offer to sell at $170,000 and creates a new offer by Lang to purchase the home at a price of $165,000.•

• **MIRROR IMAGE RULE**
A common law rule that requires, for a valid contractual agreement, that the terms of the offeree's acceptance adhere exactly to the terms of the offeror's offer.

At common law, the **mirror image rule** requires that the offeree's acceptance match the offeror's offer exactly. In other words, the terms of the acceptance must "mirror" those of the offer. If the acceptance materially changes or adds to the terms of the original offer, it will be considered not an acceptance but a counteroffer—which, of course, need not be accepted. The original offeror can, however, accept the terms of the counteroffer and create a valid contract.[9]

Termination by Operation of Law The offeree's power to transform an offer into a binding, legal obligation can be terminated by operation of the law if any of four conditions occur: lapse of time, destruction of the specific subject matter, death or incompetence of the offeror or offeree, or supervening illegality of the proposed contract.

Lapse of Time. An offer terminates automatically by law when the period of time *specified in the offer* has passed. If the offer states that it will be left open until a particular date, then the offer will terminate at midnight on that day. If the offer

9. The mirror image rule has been greatly modified in regard to sales contracts. Section 2–207 of the UCC provides that a contract is formed if the offeree makes a definite expression of acceptance (such as signing the form in the appropriate location), even though the terms of the acceptance modify or add to the terms of the original offer (see Chapter 15).

states that it will be left open for a number of days, such as ten days, this time period normally begins to run when the offer is actually received by the offeree, not when it is formed or sent. When the offer is delayed (through the misdelivery of mail, for example), the period begins to run from the date the offeree would have received the offer, but only if the offeree knows or should know that the offer is delayed.[10]

• EXAMPLE 10.15 Suppose that Beth offers to sell her boat to Jonah, stating that the offer will remain open until May 20. Unless Jonah accepts the offer by midnight on May 20, the offer will lapse (terminate). Now suppose that Beth writes a letter to Jonah, offering to sell him her boat if Jonah accepts the offer within twenty days of the letter's date, which is May 1. Jonah must accept within twenty days after May 1, or the offer will terminate. The same rule would apply even if Beth had used improper postage when mailing the offer to Jonah, and Jonah received the letter ten days after May 1, not knowing of the improper mailing. If, however, Jonah knew about the improper mailing, the offer would lapse twenty days after the day Jonah ordinarily would have received the offer had Beth used proper postage.•

If no time for acceptance is specified in the offer, the offer terminates at the end of a *reasonable* period of time. A reasonable period of time is determined by the subject matter of the contract, business and market conditions, and other relevant circumstances. An offer to sell farm produce, for example, will terminate sooner than an offer to sell farm equipment, because farm produce is perishable and subject to greater fluctuations in market value.

Destruction of the Subject Matter. An offer is automatically terminated if the specific subject matter of the offer is destroyed before the offer is accepted. For example, if Bekins offers to sell his prize cow to Yatsen, but the cow dies before Yatsen can accept, the offer is automatically terminated.

Death or Incompetence of the Offeror or Offeree. An offeree's power of acceptance is terminated when the offeror or offeree dies or is deprived of legal capacity to enter into the proposed contract, *unless the offer is irrevocable.*[11] An offer is personal to both parties and normally cannot pass to the decedent's heirs, guardian, or estate. This rule applies whether or not the one party had notice of the death or incompetence of the other party.

Supervening Illegality of the Proposed Contract. A statute or court decision that makes an offer illegal will automatically terminate the offer. • EXAMPLE 10.16 If Acme Finance Corporation offers to lend Jack $20,000 at 15 percent annually, and a state statute is enacted prohibiting loans at interest rates greater than 12 percent before Jack can accept, the offer is automatically terminated. (If the statute is enacted after Jack accepts the offer, a valid contract is formed, but the contract may still be unenforceable—see Chapter 11.)•

ACCEPTANCE

• **ACCEPTANCE**
A voluntary act by the offeree that shows assent, or agreement, to the terms of an offer; may consist of words or conduct.

An **acceptance** is a voluntary act by the offeree that shows assent, or agreement, to the terms of an offer. The offeree's act may consist of words or conduct. The acceptance must be unequivocal and must be communicated to the offeror.

10. *Restatement (Second) of Contracts,* Section 49.
11. *Restatement (Second) of Contracts,* Section 48. If the offer is irrevocable, it is not terminated when the offeror dies. Also, if the offer is such that it can be accepted by the performance of a series of acts, and those acts began before the offeror died, the offeree's power of acceptance is not terminated.

"It's a deal, but just to be on the safe side let's have our lawyers look at this handshake."

ON THE WEB

The Law Office Consumer Guide offers information on the requirements for contract formation—including offer and acceptance—at **www.thelawoffice.com**.

Who Can Accept? Generally, a third person cannot substitute for the offeree and effectively accept the offer. After all, the identity of the offeree is as much a condition of a bargaining offer as any other term contained therein. Thus, except in special circumstances, only the person to whom the offer is made or that person's agent can accept the offer and create a binding contract. For example, Lottie makes an offer to Paul. Paul is not interested, but Paul's friend José accepts the offer. No contract is formed.

Unequivocal Acceptance To exercise the power of acceptance effectively, the offeree must accept unequivocally. This is the *mirror image rule* previously discussed. If the acceptance is subject to new conditions or if the terms of the acceptance materially change the original offer, the acceptance may be deemed a counteroffer that implicitly rejects the original offer.

Certain terms, when added to an acceptance, will not qualify the acceptance sufficiently to constitute rejection of the offer. • **EXAMPLE 10.17** Suppose that in response to a person offering to sell a painting by a well-known artist, the offeree replies, "I accept; please send a written contract." The offeree is requesting a written contract but is not making it a condition for acceptance. Therefore, the acceptance is effective without the written contract. If the offeree replies, "I accept *if* you send a written contract," however, the acceptance is expressly conditioned on the request for a writing, and the statement is not an acceptance but a counteroffer. (Notice how important each word is!)[12] •

¡DON'T FORGET!
When an offer is rejected, it is terminated.

12. As noted in footnote 9, in regard to sales contracts, the UCC provides that an acceptance may still be effective even if some terms are added. The new terms are simply treated as proposals for additions to the contract, unless both parties are merchants—in which case the additional terms (with some exceptions) become part of the contract [UCC 2–207(2)].

Silence as Acceptance Ordinarily, silence cannot constitute acceptance, even if the offeror states, "By your silence and inaction, you will be deemed to have accepted this offer." This general rule applies because an offeree should not be put under a burden of liability to act affirmatively in order to reject an offer. No consideration—that is, nothing of value—has passed to the offeree to impose such a liability.

In some instances, however, the offeree does have a duty to speak, in which case his or her silence or inaction will operate as an acceptance. Silence may be an acceptance when an offeree takes the benefit of offered services even though he or she had an opportunity to reject them and knew that they were offered with the expectation of compensation. • EXAMPLE 10.18 Suppose that Jameson watches while a stranger mows her lawn, even though the stranger has not been asked to mow the lawn. Jameson knows the stranger expects to be paid and does nothing to stop him. Here, Jameson's silence constitutes an acceptance, and an implied-in-fact contract is created. Jameson is bound to pay a reasonable value for the stranger's work.•

Silence can also operate as acceptance when the offeree has had prior dealings with the offeror. If a merchant, for example, routinely receives shipments from a supplier and in the past has always notified the supplier of rejection of defective goods, then silence constitutes acceptance. Also, if a person solicits an offer specifying that certain terms and conditions are acceptable, and the offeror makes the offer in response to the solicitation, the offeree has a duty to reject—that is, a duty to tell the offeror that the offer is not acceptable. Failure to reject (silence) would operate as an acceptance.

¡REMEMBER! A bilateral contract is a promise for a promise, and a unilateral contract is performance for a promise.

Communication of Acceptance Whether the offeror must be notified of the acceptance depends on the nature of the contract. In a bilateral contract, communication of acceptance is necessary, because acceptance is in the form of a promise (not performance), and the contract is formed when the promise is made (rather than when the act is performed). Communication of acceptance is not necessary, however, if the offer dispenses with the requirement. Also, if the offer can be accepted by silence, no communication is necessary.[13]

Because in a unilateral contract the full performance of some act is called for, acceptance is usually evident, and notification is therefore unnecessary. Exceptions do exist, however. When the offeror requests notice of acceptance or has no adequate means of determining whether the requested act has been performed, or when the law requires such notice of acceptance, then notice is necessary.[14]

Mode and Timeliness of Acceptance The general rule is that acceptance in a bilateral contract is timely if it is effected within the duration of the offer. Problems arise, however, when the parties involved are not dealing face to face. In such situations, the offeree may use an authorized mode of communication. Acceptance takes effect, thus completing formation of the contract, at the time the offeree sends or delivers the communication via the mode expressly or impliedly authorized by the offeror. This is the so-called **mailbox rule,** also called the "deposited acceptance rule," which the majority of courts uphold. Under this rule, if the authorized mode of communication is the mail, then an acceptance becomes valid

• **MAILBOX RULE**
A rule providing that an acceptance of an offer becomes effective on dispatch (on being placed in an official mailbox), if mail is, expressly or impliedly, an authorized means of communication of acceptance to the offeror.

13. Under the UCC, an order or other offer to buy goods that are to be promptly shipped may be treated as either a bilateral or a unilateral offer and can be accepted by a promise to ship or by actual shipment. See UCC 2–206(1)(b).
14. UCC 2–206(2).

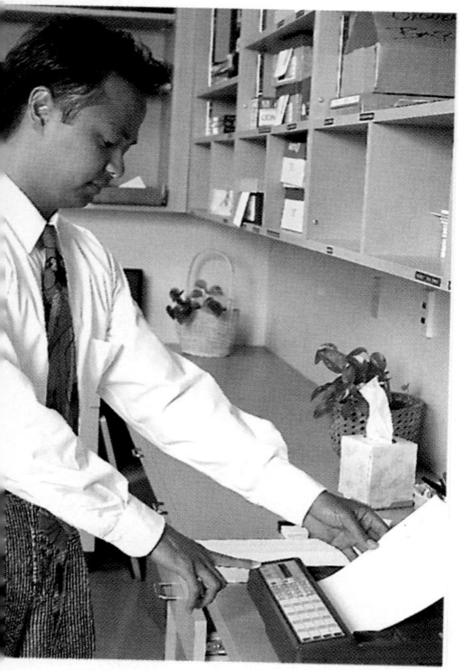

If an offeror expressly authorizes acceptance of his or her offer by first-class mail or express delivery, can the offeree accept by a faster means, such as by fax or e-mail?

when it is dispatched (placed in the control of the U.S. Postal Service)—*not* when it is received by the offeror.

The mailbox rule was formed to prevent the confusion that arises when an offeror sends a letter of revocation but, before this letter is received by the offeree, the offeree sends a letter of acceptance. Thus, whereas a revocation becomes effective only when it is *received* by the offeree, an acceptance becomes effective on *dispatch* (even if it is never received), provided that an *authorized* means of communication is used.

Authorized means can be either expressly authorized—that is, expressly stipulated in the offer—or impliedly authorized by facts or law.[15] When an offeror specifies how acceptance should be made (for example, by first-class mail or express delivery), *express authorization* is said to exist. Moreover, both the offeror and the offeree are bound in contract the moment that such means of acceptance are employed.

Most offerors do not specify expressly the means by which the offeree is to accept. Thus, the common law recognizes the following implied authorized means of acceptance:[16]

1. The choice of a particular means by the offeror in making the offer implies that the offeree is authorized to use the same or a faster means for acceptance.
2. When two parties are at a distance, mailing is impliedly authorized.

There are three basic exceptions to the rule that a contract is formed when acceptance is sent by authorized means:

1. If the acceptance is not properly dispatched (if a letter is incorrectly addressed, for example, or is without the proper postage), in most states it will not be effective until it is received by the offeror.
2. The offeror can specifically condition his or her offer on the receipt of an acceptance by a certain time, in which case, to be effective, the acceptance must be received prior to the end of the time period.
3. Sometimes an offeree sends a rejection first, then later changes his or her mind and sends an acceptance. Obviously, this chain of events could cause confusion and even detriment to the offeror, depending on whether the rejection or the acceptance arrived first. In such situations, the law cancels the rule of acceptance on dispatch, and the first communication received by the offeror determines whether a contract is formed. If the rejection comes first, there is no contract.[17]

An acceptance given by means not expressly or impliedly authorized is not effective until it is received by the offeror.

Note that technology, particularly the Internet, has all but eliminated the need for the mailbox rule because online acceptances typically are communicated instantaneously to the offeror. (See Chapter 15's *Technology and Online Offers* for an examination of online contract formation in the context of sales law.)

---

15. *Restatement (Second) of Contracts,* Section 30, provides that an offer invites acceptance "by any medium reasonable in the circumstances," unless the offer is specific about the means of acceptance. Under Section 65, a medium is reasonable if it is one used by the offeror or one customary in similar transactions, unless the offeree knows of circumstances that would argue against the reasonableness of a particular medium (the need for speed because of rapid price changes, for example).
16. Note that UCC 2–206(1)(a) states specifically that an acceptance of an offer for the sale of goods can be made by any medium that is *reasonable* under the circumstances.
17. *Restatement (Second) of Contracts,* Section 40.

Consideration and Its Requirements

• **CONSIDERATION**
Generally, the value given in return for a promise. The consideration, which must be present to make the contract legally binding, must result in a detriment to the promisee (something of legally sufficient value and bargained for) or a benefit to the promisor.

In every legal system, some promises will be enforced, and some promises will not be enforced. The simple fact that a party has made a promise, then, does not mean the promise is enforceable. Under the common law, a primary basis for the enforcement of promises is consideration. **Consideration** is usually defined as the value given in return for a promise. We look here at the basic elements of consideration and then at some other contract doctrines relating to consideration.

ELEMENTS OF CONSIDERATION

Often, consideration is broken down into two parts: (1) something of *legally sufficient value* must be given in exchange for the promise, and (2) there must be a *bargained-for* exchange.

Legal Value The "something of legally sufficient value" may consist of (1) a promise to do something that one has no prior legal duty to do (to pay money on receipt of certain goods, for example), (2) the performance of an action that one is otherwise not obligated to undertake (such as providing accounting services), or (3) the refraining from an action that one has a legal right to undertake. Generally, to be legally sufficient, consideration must be either *detrimental to the promisee* (the one receiving the promise) or *beneficial to the promisor* (the one making the promise).

• EXAMPLE 10.19 Jerry says to his son, "When you finish painting the garage, I will pay you $100." Jerry's son paints the garage. The act of painting the garage is the consideration that creates Jerry's contractual obligation to pay his son $100. In this situation, the consideration is both detrimental to the promisee (the son) and beneficial to the promisor (Jerry). Jerry's garage was painted, and his son undertook an action that the son was not otherwise legally obligated to undertake.•

What if, in return for a promise to pay, a person forbears to pursue harmful habits, such as the use of tobacco and alcohol? Does such forbearance represent a legal detriment to the promisee and thus create consideration for the contract, or does it in fact benefit the promisee and thus not create consideration for the contract? This was the issue before the court in *Hamer v. Sidway,* a classic case concerning consideration that we present as this chapter's *Landmark in the Law.*

Landmark in the Law •

HAMER v. SIDWAY (1891)

In *Hamer v. Sidway,*[a] the issue before the court arose from a contract created in 1869 between William Story, Sr., and his nephew, William Story II. The uncle promised his nephew that if the nephew refrained from drinking alcohol, using tobacco, and playing billiards and cards for money until he reached the age of twenty-one, the uncle would pay him $5,000. The nephew, who indulged occasionally in all of these "vices," agreed to refrain from them and did so for the next six years. Following his twenty-first birthday in 1875, the nephew wrote to his uncle that he had performed his part of the bargain and was thus entitled to the promised $5,000. A few days later, the uncle wrote the nephew a letter stating, "[Y]ou shall have the five thousand dollars, as I promised you." The uncle said that the money was in the bank, and that the nephew could "consider this money on interest."

a. 124 N.Y. 538, 27 N.E. 256 (1891).

(Continued)

The nephew left the money in the care of his uncle, who held it for the next twelve years. When the uncle died in 1887, however, the executor of the uncle's estate refused to pay the $5,000 claim brought by Hamer, a third party to whom the promise had been *assigned.* (The law allows parties to assign, or transfer, rights in contracts to third parties; see Chapter 13.) The executor, Sidway, contended that the contract was invalid because there was insufficient consideration to support it. He argued that neither a benefit to the promisor (the uncle) nor a detriment to the promisee (the nephew) existed in this case. The uncle had received nothing, and the nephew had actually benefited by fulfilling the uncle's wishes. Therefore, no contract existed.

Although a lower court upheld Sidway's position, the New York Court of Appeals reversed and ruled in favor of the plaintiff, Hamer. "The promisee used tobacco, occasionally drank liquor, and he had a legal right to do so," the court stated. "That right he abandoned for a period of years upon the strength of the promise of the testator [one who makes a will] that for such forbearance he would give him $5,000. We need not speculate on the effort which may have been required to give up the use of those stimulants. It is sufficient that he restricted his lawful freedom of action within certain prescribed limits upon the faith of his uncle's agreement."

FOR CRITICAL ANALYSIS
How might one argue that this contract also benefited the promisor (Story, Sr.)?

"Man is an animal that makes bargains; no other animal does this—one dog does not change a bone with another."

ADAM SMITH,
1723–1790
(Scottish political economist and philosopher)

Bargained-for Exchange The second element of consideration is that it must provide the basis for the bargain struck between the contracting parties. The consideration given by the promisor must induce the promisee to incur a legal detriment either now or in the future, and the detriment incurred must induce the promisor to make the promise. This element of bargained-for exchange distinguishes contracts from gifts.

• EXAMPLE 10.20 Suppose that Jerry says to his son, "In consideration of the fact that you are not as wealthy as your brothers, I will pay you $500." This promise is not enforceable, because Jerry's son has not given any return consideration for the $500 promised.[18] The son (the promisee) incurs no legal detriment; he does not have to promise anything or undertake (or refrain from undertaking) any action to receive the $500. Here, Jerry has simply stated his motive for giving his son a gift. The fact that the word *consideration* is used does not, alone, mean that consideration has been given. •

18. See *Fink v. Cox,* 18 Johns. 145, 9 Am.Dec. 191 (N.Y. 1820).

International Perspective • CONSIDERATION IN GERMANY

Many of the principles of contract law are common around the globe. There are some differences, however, including differences in what constitutes consideration for contractual purposes. In the United States, as just discussed, consideration is a required element for a valid contract. Promises to make gifts are normally not enforceable, because the donee does not give consideration for the gift. In Germany, in contrast, the exchange of consideration is not required for a contract to be legally binding.

FOR CRITICAL ANALYSIS
Do you think that promises to make gifts should be enforceable in the United States? Why or why not?

LEGAL SUFFICIENCY AND ADEQUACY OF CONSIDERATION

ON THE WEB

The Web site of the New Hampshire Consumer's Sourcebook provides information on contract law from a consumer's perspective. You can access this site at www.state.nh.us/oag/cpb.html.

Legal sufficiency of consideration involves the requirement that consideration be something of value in the eyes of the law. Adequacy of consideration involves "how much" consideration is given. Essentially, adequacy of consideration concerns the fairness of the bargain. On the surface, fairness would appear to be an issue when the values of items exchanged are unequal. In general, however, courts do not question the adequacy of consideration if the consideration is legally sufficient. Under the doctrine of freedom of contract, parties are usually free to bargain as they wish. If people could sue merely because they had entered into an unwise contract, the courts would be overloaded with frivolous suits.

In extreme cases, however, a court of law may look to the amount or value (the adequacy) of the consideration, because apparently inadequate consideration can indicate that fraud, duress, or undue influence was involved or that a gift was made (if a father "sells" a $100,000 house to his daughter for only $1, for example). Additionally, in cases in which the consideration is grossly inadequate, the courts may declare the contract unenforceable on the ground that it is unconscionable[19]—that is, generally speaking, it is so one sided under the circumstances as to be overly unfair. (Unconscionability is discussed further in Chapter 11.)

¡BE AWARE!

A consumer's signature on a contract does not always guarantee that the contract will be enforced. Ultimately, the terms must be fair.

CONTRACTS THAT LACK CONSIDERATION

Sometimes, one of the parties (or both parties) to a contract may think that they have exchanged consideration when in fact they have not. Here we look at some situations in which the parties' promises or actions do not qualify as contractual consideration.

Preexisting Duty Under most circumstances, a promise to do what one already has a legal duty to do does not constitute legally sufficient consideration, because no legal detriment is incurred.[20] The preexisting legal duty may be imposed by law or may arise out of a previous contract. A sheriff, for example, cannot collect a reward for information leading to the capture of a criminal if the sheriff already has a legal duty to capture the criminal. Likewise, if a party is already bound by contract to perform a certain duty, that duty cannot serve as consideration for a second contract.

• **EXAMPLE 10.21** Suppose that Bauman-Bache, Inc., begins construction on a seven-story office building and after three months demands an extra $75,000 on its contract. If the extra $75,000 is not paid, it will stop working. The owner of the land, having no one else to complete construction, agrees to pay the extra $75,000. The agreement is not enforceable, because it is not supported by legally sufficient consideration; Bauman-Bache had a preexisting contractual duty to complete the building. •

Unforeseen Difficulties. The rule regarding preexisting duty is meant to prevent extortion and the so-called holdup game. What happens, though, when an honest contractor, who has contracted with a landowner to build a house, runs into extraordinary difficulties that were totally unforeseen at the time the contract was formed? In the interests of fairness and equity, the courts sometimes allow exceptions to the preexisting duty rule. In the example just mentioned, if the landowner agrees to pay extra compensation to the contractor for overcoming the unforeseen difficulties (such as having to use dynamite and special equipment to remove an unexpected

19. Pronounced un-*kon*-shun-uh-bul.

20. See *Foakes v. Beer,* 9 App.Cas. 605 (1884).

rock formation in order to build a basement), the court may refrain from applying the preexisting duty rule and enforce the agreement. When the "unforeseen difficulties" that give rise to a contract modification are the types of risks ordinarily assumed in business, however, the courts will usually assert the preexisting duty rule.[21]

Rescission and New Contract. The law recognizes that two parties can mutually agree to rescind their contract, at least to the extent that it is executory (still to be carried out). **Rescission**[22] is defined as the unmaking of a contract so as to return the parties to the positions they occupied before the contract was made. When rescission and the making of a new contract take place at the same time, the courts frequently are given a choice of applying the preexisting duty rule or allowing rescission and letting the new contract stand.

• **RESCISSION**
A remedy whereby a contract is canceled and the parties are returned to the positions they occupied before the contract was made; may be effected through the mutual consent of the parties, by their conduct, or by court decree.

Past Consideration Promises made in return for actions or events that have already taken place are unenforceable. These promises lack consideration in that the element of bargained-for exchange is missing. In short, you can bargain for something to take place now or in the future but not for something that has already taken place. Therefore, **past consideration** is no consideration.

• **PAST CONSIDERATION**
An act done before the contract is made, which ordinarily, by itself, cannot be consideration for a later promise to pay for the act.

• **EXAMPLE 10.22** Suppose that Elsie, a real estate agent, does her friend Judy a favor by selling Judy's house and not charging any commission. Later, Judy says to Elsie, "In return for your generous act, I will pay you $3,000." This promise is made in return for past consideration and is thus unenforceable; in effect, Judy is stating her intention to give Elsie a gift. •

Illusory Promises If the terms of the contract express such uncertainty of performance that the promisor has not definitely promised to do anything, the promise is said to be *illusory*—without consideration and unenforceable. • **EXAMPLE 10.23** The president of Tuscan Corporation says to his employees, "All of you have worked hard, and if profits continue to remain high, a 10 percent bonus at the end of the year will be given—if management thinks it is warranted." This is an *illusory promise,* or no promise at all, because performance depends solely on the discretion of the president (the management). There is no bargained-for consideration. The statement declares merely that management may or may not do something in the future. •

Option-to-cancel clauses in contracts for specified time periods sometimes present problems in regard to consideration. • **EXAMPLE 10.24** Abe contracts to hire Chris for one year at $5,000 per month, reserving the right to cancel the contract at any time. On close examination of these words, you can see that Abe has not actually agreed to hire Chris, as Abe could cancel without liability before Chris started performance. Abe has not given up the opportunity of hiring someone else. This contract is therefore illusory. Now suppose that Abe contracts to hire Chris for a one-year period at $5,000 per month, reserving the right to cancel the contract at any time after Chris has begun performance by giving Chris thirty days' notice. Abe, by saying that he will give Chris thirty days' notice, is relinquishing the opportunity (legal right) to hire someone else instead of Chris for a thirty-day period. If Chris works for one month, at the end of which Abe gives him thirty days' notice, Chris has a valid and enforceable contractual claim for $10,000 in salary. •

21. Note that under the UCC, any agreement modifying a contract within Article 2 on Sales needs no consideration to be binding. See UCC 2–209(1).
22. Pronounced reh-*sih*-zhen.

SETTLEMENT OF CLAIMS

Businesspersons or others can settle legal claims in several ways. It is important to understand the nature of consideration given in these kinds of settlement agreements, or contracts. A common means of settling a claim is through an *accord and satisfaction,* in which a debtor offers to pay a lesser amount than the creditor purports to be owed. Two other methods that are commonly used to settle claims are the release and the covenant not to sue.

• **ACCORD AND SATISFACTION**
A common means of settling a claim, in which a debtor offers to pay a lesser amount than the creditor purports to be owed. The creditor's acceptance of the offer creates an accord (agreement), and when the accord is executed, satisfaction occurs.

Accord and Satisfaction The concept of **accord and satisfaction** deals with a debtor's offer of payment and a creditor's acceptance of a lesser amount than the creditor originally purported to be owed. The *accord* is defined as the agreement under which one of the parties undertakes to give or perform, and the other to accept, in satisfaction of a claim, something other than that on which the parties originally agreed. *Satisfaction* may take place when the accord is executed. Accord and satisfaction deal with an attempt by the obligor to extinguish an obligation. A basic rule is that there can be no satisfaction unless there is first an accord.

For accord and satisfaction to occur, the amount of the debt *must be in dispute.* If a debt is *liquidated,* accord and satisfaction cannot take place. A liquidated debt is one whose amount has been ascertained, fixed, agreed on, settled, or exactly determined. A loan contract, for example, in which the borrower agrees to pay a stipulated amount every month until the amount of the loan is paid, is a liquidated debt. In the majority of states, acceptance of (an accord for) a lesser sum than the entire amount of a liquidated debt is not satisfaction, and the balance of the debt is still legally owed. The rationale for this rule is that no consideration is given by the debtor to satisfy the obligation of paying the balance to the creditor—because the debtor has a preexisting legal obligation to pay the entire debt.

An *unliquidated debt* is the opposite of a liquidated debt. Here, reasonable persons may differ over the amount owed. It is not settled, fixed, agreed on, ascertained, or determined. In these circumstances, acceptance of payment of the lesser sum operates as a satisfaction, or discharge, of the debt. One argument to support this rule is that the parties give up a legal right to contest the amount in dispute, and thus consideration is given.

• **RELEASE**
A contract in which one party forfeits the right to pursue a legal claim against the other party.

Release A **release** is a contract in which one party forfeits the right to pursue a legal claim against the other party. Releases will generally be binding if they are (1) given in good faith, (2) stated in a signed writing (required by many states), and (3) accompanied by consideration.[23] Clearly, persons are better off if they know the extent of their injuries or damages before signing releases.

• **EXAMPLE 10.25** Suppose that you are involved in an automobile accident caused by Raoul's negligence. Raoul offers to give you $1,000 if you will release him from further liability resulting from the accident. You believe that this amount will cover your damages, so you agree to and sign the release. Later you discover that it will cost $1,200 to repair your car. Can you collect the balance from Raoul? The answer is normally no; you are limited to the $1,000 in the release. Why? Because a valid contract existed. You and Raoul both assented to the bargain (hence, agreement existed), and sufficient consideration was present. Your consideration for the contract was the legal detriment you suffered (by releasing Raoul from liability, you

23. Under the UCC, a written, signed waiver or renunciation by an aggrieved party discharges any further liability for a breach, even without consideration [UCC 1–107].

forfeited your right to sue to recover damages, should they be more than $1,000). This legal detriment was induced by Raoul's promise to give you the $1,000. Raoul's promise was, in turn, induced by your promise not to pursue your legal right to sue him for damages. •

• **COVENANT NOT TO SUE**
An agreement to substitute a contractual obligation for some other type of legal action based on a valid claim.

Covenant Not to Sue A **covenant not to sue,** unlike a release, does not always bar further recovery. The parties simply substitute a contractual obligation for some other type of legal action based on a valid claim. Suppose (following the earlier example) that you agree with Raoul not to sue for damages in a tort action if he will pay for the damage to your car. If Raoul fails to pay, you can bring an action for breach of contract.

Promises Enforceable without Consideration—Promissory Estoppel

• **PROMISSORY ESTOPPEL**
A doctrine that applies when a promisor makes a clear and definite promise on which the promisee justifiably relies; such a promise is binding if justice will be better served by the enforcement of the promise.

• **ESTOPPED**
Barred, impeded, or precluded.

Sometimes individuals rely on promises, and such reliance may form a basis for contract rights and duties. Under the doctrine of **promissory estoppel** (also called *detrimental reliance*), a person who has reasonably relied on the promise of another can often hope to obtain some measure of recovery. When the doctrine of promissory estoppel is applied, the promisor (the offeror) is **estopped** (barred, or impeded) from revoking the promise. For the doctrine of promissory estoppel to be applied, the following elements are required:

1. There must be a clear and definite promise.
2. The promisee must justifiably rely on the promise.
3. The reliance normally must be of a substantial and definite character.
4. Justice will be better served by the enforcement of the promise.

• **EXAMPLE 10.26** Your uncle tells you, "I'll pay you $150 a week so you won't have to work anymore." In reliance on your uncle's promise, you quit your job, but your uncle refuses to pay you. Under the doctrine of promissory estoppel, you may be able to enforce such a promise.[24] Now your uncle makes a promise to give you $10,000 with which to buy a car. If you buy the car and he does not pay you, you may once again be able to enforce the promise under this doctrine. •

ETHICAL ISSUE 10.1 ***Should social promises be enforced under the doctrine of promissory estoppel?*** Suppose that a bride-to-be spends thousands of dollars preparing for a wedding, only to be stranded by the groom at the altar. In such a case, is the groom's promise of marriage enforceable? In other words, because of the detrimental reliance, would a court impose a contractual relationship on the parties so that the bride-to-be could collect damages for breach of a "contract"? A number of plaintiffs over the years have tried to collect damages in similar cases, but to no avail. Recently, for example, a college freshman whose boyfriend broke their prom date sued the boyfriend for the cost of her unused prom dress. A Minnesota state court, however, dismissed the case, suggesting that "[w]hether the defendant has a social or moral duty to help the plaintiff with her prom costs is a question for the likes of Emily Post or Miss Manners, not for courts of this state." As discussed in Chapter 9, contract law reflects society's decisions on what promises will be enforced and what promises will not. Clearly, society has determined that social agreements such as those just mentioned do not fall into the category of promises that should be enforceable.[25]

24. *Ricketts v. Scothorn,* 57 Neb. 51, 77 N.W. 365 (1898).
25. *The National Law Journal,* June 22, 1998, p. A23

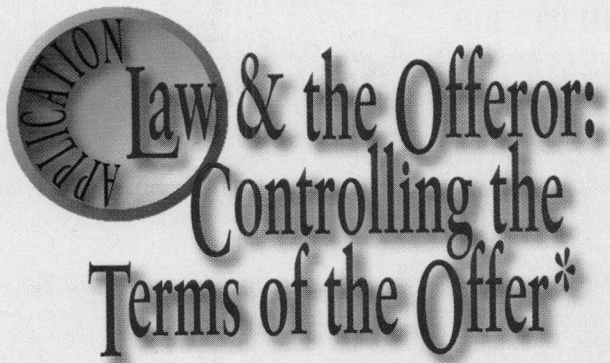

APPLICATION Law & the Offeror: Controlling the Terms of the Offer*

The courts normally attempt to "save" contracts whenever possible, but sometimes it is simply impossible to do so. Two common reasons why contracts fail is because (1) the terms of the offer were too unclear or indefinite to constitute a binding contract on the offer's acceptance and (2) the acceptance was not timely. If you are an offeror, you can control both of these factors: you can determine what the terms of the future contract will be, as well as the time and mode of acceptance.

INCLUDE CLEAR AND DEFINITE TERMS

If a contract's terms are too unclear or indefinite, the contract will fail. Unless a court can ascertain what exactly the rights and duties of the parties are under a particular contract, the court cannot enforce those rights and duties. Therefore, as an offeror, make sure that the terms of your offer are sufficiently definite to constitute a binding contract if the offer is accepted. A statement such as "Quantity to be determined later" may allow the offeree, after acceptance, to claim that a contract was never formed, because the quantity term was not specified.

Another reason why an offeror, in drafting the offer, should make sure that the offer's terms are clear and definite is that if a contract results, any ambiguous provision may be interpreted against the party that drafted the contract (see Chapter 9).

SPECIFY THE TIME AND MODE OF ACCEPTANCE

Problems concerning contract formation also arise when it is unclear whether an acceptance is effective. To avoid such problems, you should take some precautions when phrasing the offer. Whether your offer is made via the Internet, fax, express delivery, or mail, you can specify that the offer must be accepted (or even that the acceptance must be received by you) by a certain time, and if it is not, the offer will terminate. Similarly, you can specify the mode of acceptance. In online offers, you can indicate that to accept the offer, the user must click on a certain box on the screen. If you make an offer and want the acceptance to be faxed to you, make sure that you clearly indicate that the acceptance must be faxed to you at a given fax number by a specific time or it will not be effective.

CHECKLIST FOR THE OFFEROR

1. Make sure that the terms of the offer are sufficiently clear and definite to allow both the parties and a court to determine the specific rights and obligations of the parties. Otherwise, the contract may fail for indefiniteness.
2. Specify in the offer the date on which the offer will terminate and the authorized mode of acceptance. For example, you can indicate that an acceptance, to be effective, must be faxed to you at a specific fax number by a specific time or date.

*This *Application* is not meant to substitute for the services of an attorney who is licensed to practice law in your state.

Key Terms

acceptance 269
accord and satisfaction 277
agreement 258
consideration 273
counteroffer 268
covenant not to sue 278
estopped 278
mailbox rule 271
mirror image rule 268
offer 258
option contract 267
past consideration 276
promissory estoppel 278
release 277
rescission 276
revocation 267

Chapter Summary • Agreement and Consideration

AGREEMENT	
Requirements of the Offer (See pages 258–266.)	1. *Intent*—There must be a serious, objective intention by the offeror to become bound by the offer. Nonoffer situations include (a) expressions of opinion; (b) statements of intention; (c) preliminary negotiations; (d) generally, advertisements, catalogues, price lists, and circulars; (e) solicitations for bids made by an auctioneer; and (f) traditionally, agreements to agree in the future. 2. *Definiteness*—The terms of the offer must be sufficiently definite to be ascertainable by the parties or by a court. 3. *Communication*—The offer must be communicated to the offeree.
Termination of the Offer (See pages 266–269.)	1. *By action of the parties*— a. Revocation—Unless the offer is irrevocable, it can be revoked at any time before acceptance without liability. Revocation is not effective until received by the offeree or the offeree's agent. Some offers, such as the merchant's firm offer and option contracts, are irrevocable. b. Rejection—Accomplished by words or actions that demonstrate a clear intent not to accept the offer; not effective until received by the offeror or the offeror's agent. c. Counteroffer—A rejection of the original offer and the making of a new offer. 2. *By operation of law*— a. Lapse of time—The offer terminates (a) at the end of the time period specified in the offer or (b) if no time period is stated in the offer, at the end of a reasonable time period. b. Destruction of the specific subject matter of the offer—Automatically terminates the offer. c. Death or incompetence—Terminates the offer unless the offer is irrevocable. d. Illegality—Supervening illegality terminates the offer.
Acceptance (See pages 269–272.)	1. Can be made only by the offeree or the offeree's agent. 2. Must be unequivocal. Under the common law (mirror image rule), if new terms or conditions are added to the acceptance, it will be considered a counteroffer. 3. Acceptance of a unilateral offer is effective on full performance of the requested act. Generally, no communication is necessary. 4. Acceptance of a bilateral offer can be communicated by the offeree by any authorized mode of communication and is effective on dispatch. Unless the mode of communication is expressly specified by the offeror, the following methods are impliedly authorized: a. The same mode used by the offeror or a faster mode. b. Mail, when the two parties are at a distance. c. In sales contracts, by any reasonable medium.
CONSIDERATION	
Elements of Consideration (See pages 273–274.)	Consideration is broken down into two parts: (1) something of *legally sufficient value* must be given in exchange for the promise, and (2) there must be a *bargained-for exchange*. To be legally sufficient, consideration must involve a legal detriment to the promisee, a legal benefit to the promisor, or both. One incurs a legal detriment by doing (or refraining from doing) something that one had no prior legal duty to do (or to refrain from doing).

Chapter Summary • Agreement and Consideration, Continued

Legal Sufficiency and Adequacy of Consideration (See page 275.)	Legal sufficiency of consideration relates to the first element of consideration just mentioned—something of legal value must be given in exchange for a promise. Adequacy of consideration relates to "how much" consideration is given and whether a fair bargain was reached. Courts will inquire into the adequacy of consideration (if the consideration is legally sufficient) only when fraud, undue influence, duress, or unconscionability may be involved.
Contracts That Lack Consideration (See pages 275–276.)	Consideration is lacking in the following situations: 1. *Preexisting duty*—Consideration is not legally sufficient if one is either by law or by contract under a *preexisting duty* to perform the action being offered as consideration for a new contract. 2. *Past consideration*—Actions or events that have already taken place do not constitute legally sufficient consideration. 3. *Illusory promises*—When the nature or extent of performance is too uncertain, the promise is rendered illusory (without consideration and unenforceable).
Settlement of Claims (See pages 277–278.)	1. *Accord and satisfaction*—An *accord* is an agreement in which a debtor offers to pay a lesser amount than the creditor purports to be owed. *Satisfaction* may take place when the accord is executed. 2. *Release*—An agreement by which, for consideration, a party is barred from further recovery beyond the terms specified in the release. 3. *Covenant not to sue*—An agreement not to sue on a present, valid claim.
Promises Enforceable without Consideration—Promissory Estoppel (See page 278.)	The equitable doctrine of promissory estoppel applies when a promisor reasonably expects a promise to induce definite and substantial action or forbearance by the promisee, and the promisee does act in reliance on the promise. Such a promise is binding if injustice can be avoided only by enforcement of the promise. Also known as the doctrine of detrimental reliance.

For Review

❶ What elements are necessary for an effective offer? What are some examples of nonoffers?

❷ In what circumstances will an offer be irrevocable?

❸ What are the elements that are necessary for an effective acceptance?

❹ What is consideration? What is required for consideration to be legally sufficient?

❺ In what circumstances might a promise be enforced despite a lack of consideration?

Questions and Case Problems

10–1. Offer. Chernek, the sole owner of a small business, has a large piece of used farm equipment for sale. He offers to sell the equipment to Bollow for $10,000. Discuss the legal effects of the following events on the offer.

(a) Chernek dies prior to Bollow's acceptance, and at the time she accepts Bollow is unaware of Chernek's death.

(b) The night before Bollow accepts, a fire destroys the equipment.

(c) Bollow pays $100 for a thirty-day option to purchase the equipment. During this period Chernek dies, and Bollow accepts the offer, knowing of Chernek's death.

(d) Bollow pays $100 for a thirty-day option to purchase the equipment. During this period Bollow dies, and Bollow's estate accepts Chernek's offer within the stipulated time period.

10–2. Offers versus Nonoffers. On June 1, Jason placed an ad in a local newspaper, to be run on the following Sunday, June 5, offering a reward of $100 to anyone who found his wallet. When his wallet had not been returned by June 12, he purchased another wallet and took steps to obtain duplicates of his driver's license, credit cards, and other items that he had lost. On June 15, Sharith, who had seen Jason's ad in the paper, found Jason's wallet, returned it to Jason, and asked for the $100. Is Jason obligated to pay Sharith the $100? Why or why not?

10–3. Offer and Acceptance. Carrie offered to sell a set of legal encyclopedias to Antonio for $300. Antonio said that he would think about her offer and let her know his decision the next day. Norvel, who had overheard the conversation between Carrie and Antonio, said to Carrie, "I accept your offer" and gave her $300. Carrie gave Norvel the books. The next day, Antonio, who had no idea that Carrie had already sold the books to Norvel, told Carrie that he accepted her offer. Has Carrie breached a valid contract with Antonio? Explain.

10–4. Consideration. Ben hired Lewis to drive his racing car in a race. Tuan, a friend of Lewis, promised to pay Lewis $3,000 if he won the race. Lewis won the race, but Tuan refused to pay the $3,000. Tuan contended that no legally binding contract had been formed, because he had received no consideration from Lewis for his promise to pay the $3,000. Lewis sued Tuan for breach of contract, arguing that winning the race was the consideration given in exchange for Tuan's promise to pay the $3,000. What rule of law discussed in this chapter supports Tuan's claim? Explain.

10–5. Acceptance. On Saturday, Arthur mailed Tanya an offer to sell his car to her for $2,000. On Monday, having changed his mind and not having heard from Tanya, Arthur sent her a letter revoking his offer. On Wednesday, before she had received Arthur's letter of revocation, Tanya mailed a letter of acceptance to Arthur. When Tanya demanded that Arthur sell his car to her as promised, Arthur claimed that no contract existed because he had revoked his offer prior to Tanya's acceptance. Is Arthur correct? Explain.

10–6. Promissory Estoppel. Red Owl Stores, Inc., induced the Hoffmans to give up their current business and run a Red Owl franchise. Although no contract was ever signed, the Hoffmans incurred numerous expenses in reliance on Red Owl's representations. When the deal ultimately fell through because of Red Owl's failure to keep its promise concerning the operation of the franchise agency store, the Hoffmans brought suit to recover their losses under the doctrine of promissory estoppel. What is this doctrine, and what elements must exist before it will be applied by the court? Will the Hoffmans likely succeed in their suit? Discuss fully. [*Hoffman v. Red Owl Stores, Inc.,* 26 Wis.2d 683, 133 N.W.2d 267 (1965)]

10–7. Offers versus Nonoffers. The Olivers were planning to sell some of their ranch land and mentioned this fact to Southworth, a neighbor. Southworth expressed interest in purchasing the property and later notified the Olivers that he had the money available to buy it. The Olivers told Southworth they would let him know shortly about the details concerning the sale. The Olivers later sent a letter to Southworth—and (unknown to Southworth) to several other neighbors—giving information about the sale, including the price, the location of the property, and the amount of acreage involved. When Southworth received the letter, he sent a letter to the Olivers "accepting" their offer. The Olivers stated that the information letter had not been intended as an "offer" but merely as a starting point for negotiations. Southworth brought suit against the Olivers to enforce the "contract." Did a contract exist? Why or why not? Explain fully. [*Southworth v. Oliver,* 284 Or. 361, 587 P.2d 994 (1978)]

10–8. Offer and Acceptance. James sent invitations to a number of potential buyers to submit bids for some timber he wanted to sell. Two bids were received as a result, the highest one submitted by Eames. James changed his mind about selling the timber and did not accept Eames's bid. Eames claimed that a contract for sale existed and sued James for breach. Did a contract exist? Explain. [*Eames v. James,* 452 So.2d 384 (La.App.3d 1984)]

10–9. Accord and Satisfaction. John and Alan Padgett sold their business, Econotax, Inc., to Taxpro, Inc. The terms of the sale required Taxpro to take over the Padgetts' payments to Wanda Austin under a promissory note as part of the price. When Austin died, James Austin inherited the right to payment. A dispute arose over the exact amount owed. Taxpro sent Austin three checks and a new promissory note as a proposed settlement, asking Austin to sign and return the note to accept the settlement. Austin cashed the checks but did not return the note. Instead, he filed a suit in a Mississippi state court against the Padgetts. The Padgetts sued Taxpro. Did Austin's cashing the checks and keeping the note constitute an accord and satisfaction? Why or why not? [*Austin v. Padgett,* 678 So.2d 1002 (Miss. 1996)]

10–10. Intention. For an employee convention, Nationwide Mutual Insurance Co. created a committee, whose members included Mary Peterson, to select a theme. The committee announced a contest for theme suggestions: "Here's what you could win: His and Hers Mercedes. An all-expense-paid trip for two around the world. Additional prizes to be announced. (All prizes subject to availability)." David Mears submitted the theme "At the Top and Still Climbing." At a dinner of Nationwide employees, Peterson told Mears that he had won two Mercedes. Mears and others who heard this believed that he had won the cars. Nationwide never gave him the cars, however, and he filed a suit in a federal district court, alleging breach of contract. At the trial, Peterson claimed that she spoke with a facetious tone and, in reality, had no intention of awarding the cars. Is Mears entitled to the cars? Why or why not? [*Mears v. Nationwide Mutual Insurance Co.,* 91 F.3d 1118 (8th Cir. 1996)]

A QUESTION OF ETHICS AND SOCIAL RESPONSIBILITY

10–11. E. S. Herrick Company grows and sells blueberries. Maine Wild Blueberry Company agreed to buy all of Herrick's 1990 crop under a contract that left the price unliquidated.

Herrick delivered the berries, but a dispute arose over the price. Maine Wild sent Herrick a check with a letter that stated the check was the "final settlement." Herrick cashed the check but filed a suit in a Maine state court against Maine Wild, on the ground of breach of contract, alleging that the buyer owed more. Given these facts, consider the following questions. [*E. S. Herrick Co. v. Maine Wild Blueberry Co.*, 670 A.2d 944 (Me. 1996)]

1. What will the court likely decide in this case? Why?
2. Generally, what are the ethical underpinnings of the legal concept of accord and satisfaction? Why does this concept only apply to unliquidated debts?

FOR CRITICAL ANALYSIS

10–12. Under what circumstances should courts examine the adequacy of consideration?

Online Activities

ONLINE EXERCISE 10–1

Go to the "Internet Activities Book" posted on the Web site accompanying this text, the URL for which is http://blt.westbuslaw.com. Select the following activities, and perform the exercises according to the instructions given there:

Activity 10–1: Acceptance and Digital Signatures
Activity 10–2: Promissory Estoppel

Before the Test

Go to the *Business Law Today* home page at http://blt.westbuslaw.com. Click on TestTutor.® You will find twenty interactive questions relating to this chapter.

CHAPTER 11 Capacity & Legality

> "Liberty of contract is not an absolute concept. It is relative to many conditions of time and place and circumstance."
>
> Benjamin Cardozo, 1870–1938
> (Associate justice of the United States Supreme Court, 1932–1938)

CONTENTS

LEARNING OBJECTIVES

After reading this chapter, you should be able to:

1. Explain the contractual rights and obligations of minors.
2. Indicate how intoxication affects contractual liability.
3. Outline the effects of mental incompetency on contractual liability.
4. Give examples of some contracts that are contrary to state or federal statutes.
5. Discuss why certain types of contracts and clauses are contrary to public policy.

Courts generally want contracts to be enforceable, and much of the law is made to aid in the enforceability of contracts. Nonetheless, as indicated in the opening quotation, "liberty of contract" is not absolute. In other words, not all people can make legally binding contracts at all times. Contracts entered into by persons lacking the capacity to do so may be unenforceable. Similarly, contracts calling for the performance of an illegal act are illegal and thus void—they are not contracts at all. In this chapter, we examine contractual capacity and some aspects of illegal bargains.

Contractual Capacity

• **CONTRACTURAL CAPACITY**
The threshold mental capacity required by law for a party who enters into a contract to be bound by that contract.

Contractual capacity is the legal ability to enter into a contractual relationship. Courts generally presume the existence of contractual capacity, but there are some situations in which capacity is lacking or may be questionable. A person *adjudged by a court* to be mentally incompetent, for example, cannot form a legally binding contract with another party. In other situations, a party may have the capacity to enter into a valid contract but also have the right to avoid liability under it. For example, minors—or *infants,* as they are commonly referred to legally—usually are not legally bound by contracts. In this section, we look at the effect of youth, intoxication, and mental incompetence on contractual capacity.

MINORS

ON THE WEB

For articles from *West's Encyclopedia of American Law* on contractual capacity with respect to minors, intoxicated persons, and mentally incompetent persons, go to www.wld.com/conbus/weal/wcontra2.htm.

Today, in virtually all states, the *age of majority* (when a person is no longer a minor) for contractual purposes is eighteen years for both sexes. (The age of majority may still be twenty-one for other purposes, however, such as the purchase and consumption of alcohol.) In addition, some states provide for the termination of minority on marriage. Subject to certain exceptions, the contracts entered into by a minor are voidable at the option of that minor.

The general rule is that a minor can enter into any contract an adult can, provided that the contract is not one prohibited by law for minors (for example, the sale of alcoholic beverages or tobacco). Although minors have the right to avoid their contracts, there are exceptions (to be discussed later).

• **DISAFFIRMANCE**
The legal avoidance, or setting aside, of a contractual obligation.

Disaffirmance For a minor to exercise the option to avoid a contract, he or she need only manifest an intention not to be bound by it. The minor "avoids" the contract by disaffirming it. The technical definition of **disaffirmance** is the legal avoidance, or setting aside, of a contractual obligation. Words or conduct may serve to express this intent. The contract can ordinarily be disaffirmed at any time during minority or for a reasonable time after the minor comes of age. In some states, however, when there is a contract for the sale of land by a minor, the minor cannot disaffirm the contract until he or she reaches the age of majority. When a minor disaffirms a contract, all property that he or she has transferred to the adult as consideration can be recovered, even if it is then in the possession of a third party.[1]

Disaffirmance must be timely. If, for example, an individual wishes to disaffirm an executed contract made as a minor but fails to do so until two years after he or she has reached the age of majority, a court will likely hold that the contract has been ratified (see the discussion of ratification below). Additionally, if a minor disaffirms a contract, he or she must disaffirm the *entire* contract. The minor cannot decide to keep part of the goods contracted for and return the remainder.

Note that an adult who enters into a contract with a minor cannot avoid his or her contractual duties on the ground that the minor can do so. Unless the minor exercises the option to disaffirm the contract, the adult party normally is bound by it.

1. The Uniform Commercial Code, in Section 2–403(1), allows an exception if the third party is a "good faith purchaser for value." See Chapter 16.

International Perspective • MINORS AND LEGAL CAPACITY IN GREAT BRITAIN

Like courts in the United States, courts in Great Britain may permit minors' contracts to be avoided on the ground that minors lack contractual capacity. Great Britain, however, has no single, fixed age limit for lack of capacity. British courts deal with contracts on a case-by-case basis. In deciding whether a minor can avoid a particular contract, a British court will consider a number of factors, including the specific circumstances of the case, the nature of the item contracted for, and the psychological maturity of the minor.

FOR CRITICAL ANALYSIS

What benefit is there to the U.S. system, which lacks flexibility with respect to the contractual capacity of minors?

A Minor's Obligations on Disaffirmance. All state laws permit minors to disaffirm contracts (with certain exceptions—to be discussed shortly), including executed contracts. States differ, however, on the extent of a minor's obligations on disaffirmance. Courts in a majority of states hold that the minor need only return the goods (or other consideration) subject to the contract, provided the goods are in the minor's possession or control. • **EXAMPLE 11.1** Jim Garrison, a seventeen-year-old, purchases a computer from Radio Shack. While transporting the computer to his home, Garrison, through no fault of his own, is involved in a car accident. As a result of the accident, the plastic casing of the computer is broken. The next day, he returns the computer to Radio Shack and disaffirms the contract. Under the majority view, this return fulfills Garrison's duty even though the computer is now damaged. Garrison is entitled to get a refund of the purchase price (if paid in cash) or to be relieved of any further obligations under an agreement to purchase the computer on credit.•

A growing number of states, either by statute or by court decision, place an additional duty on the minor—the duty to restore the adult party to the position he or she held before the contract was made. In the example just given, Garrison would be required not only to return the computer but also to pay Radio Shack for damages to the computer.

In the following classic case, a minor's father brought an action on behalf of his son to disaffirm the minor's purchase of an automobile and to recover the funds paid for the car from a seller who knew that the purchaser was a minor when the contract was made.

CASE 11.1 Quality Motors, Inc. v. Hays

Supreme Court of Arkansas, 1949.
216 Ark. 264,
225 S.W.2d 326.

HISTORICAL AND ECONOMIC SETTING *In 1949, a business recession produced a decline in the cost of living. United Automobile Workers at General Motors plants accepted a slight wage cut, after they had obtained a wage increase the year before. Unemployment jumped more than two percentage points, while prices of shares on the stock market fell more than 10 percent. The cost of housing and health care rose, while other consumer prices fell. A gallon of gasoline cost 21 cents. A new Cadillac cost $5,000. The average steelworker, after taxes, made $3,000 a year, and the average high school teacher made $4,700 a year. The typical car salesperson made, after taxes, $8,000 annually.*

BACKGROUND AND FACTS Sixteen-year-old Johnny Hays went to Quality Motors, Inc., to purchase a car. The salesperson refused to sell the car unless the purchase was made by an adult, so Johnny left and later returned with a

CASE 11.1—Continued

young man of twenty-three. Hays paid for the car, and a bill of sale was made out to the twenty-three-year-old. The salesperson then drove the two boys into town to a notary public, the young man transferred the title to the car to Johnny, and the salesperson delivered the car to Johnny. Johnny's father attempted to return the car to Quality Motors for a full refund, but Quality Motors refused it. Subsequently, Johnny wrecked the car in an accident. Johnny, through his father, brought suit in an Arkansas state court to disaffirm the contract and recover the purchase price. The trial court ordered the purchase price to be refunded to Hays on his return of the car to Quality Motors. Quality Motors appealed.

IN THE WORDS OF THE COURT . . .
DUNAWAY, Justice.

* * * *

The law is well settled in Arkansas that an infant may disaffirm his contracts, except those made for necessaries, without being required to return the consideration received, except such part as may remain in specie [cash] in his hands. * * *

* * * *

Appellant knowingly and through a planned subterfuge sold an automobile to a minor. It then refused to take the car back. Even after the car was wrecked once, it was in appellant's place of business, and appellant was still resisting disaffirmance of the contract. The loss which appellant has suffered is the first result of its own acts.

DECISION AND REMEDY The Supreme Court of Arkansas affirmed the lower court's decree. Hays was allowed to disaffirm the contract and return the car without liability for damages.

FOR CRITICAL ANALYSIS—Cultural Consideration *What societal values have led to laws governing disaffirmance that weigh so heavily in favor of minors?*

Disaffirmance and Misrepresentation of Age. Suppose that a minor tells a seller she is twenty-one years old when she is really seventeen. Ordinarily, the minor can disaffirm the contract even though she has misrepresented her age. Moreover, the minor is not liable in certain jurisdictions for the tort of fraud for such misrepresentation, the rationale being that such a tort judgment might indirectly force the minor to perform the contract.

Many jurisdictions, however, do find circumstances under which a minor can be bound by a contract when the minor has misrepresented his or her age. First, several states have enacted statutes for precisely this purpose. In these states, misrepresentation of age is enough to prohibit disaffirmance. Other statutes prohibit disaffirmance by a minor who has engaged in business as an adult.

Second, some courts refuse to allow minors to disaffirm executed (fully performed) contracts unless they can return the consideration received. The combination of the minors' misrepresentations and their unjust enrichment has persuaded these courts to *estop* (prevent) minors from asserting contractual incapacity.

Third, some courts allow a misrepresenting minor to disaffirm the contract, but they hold the minor liable for damages in tort. Here, the defrauded party may sue the minor for misrepresentation or fraud. A split in authority exists on this point, because some courts, as previously noted, have recognized that allowing a suit in tort is equivalent to the indirect enforcement of the minor's contract.

• **NECESSARIES**
Necessities required for life, such as food, shelter, clothing, and medical attention; may include whatever is believed to be necessary to maintain a person's standard of living or financial and social status.

Liability for Necessaries, Insurance, and Loans. A minor who enters into a contract for necessaries may disaffirm the contract but remains liable for the reasonable value of the goods used. **Necessaries** are basic needs, such as food, clothing, shelter,

TWO YOUNG MEN DISCUSS THE SALE OF A CAR. WHEN A MINOR DISAFFIRMS A CONTRACT, SUCH AS A CONTRACT TO BUY A CAR, MOST STATES REQUIRE THE MINOR TO RETURN ONLY WHATEVER CONSIDERATION HE OR SHE RECEIVED, IF IT IS WITHIN HIS OR HER CONTROL. WHY DO SOME STATES REQUIRE MORE?

¡BE AWARE!

A minor's station in life (financial and social status, lifestyle, and so on) is important in determining whether an item is a necessary or a luxury. For example, clothing is a necessary, but if a minor from a low-income family contracts for the purchase of a $2,000 coat, a court may deem the coat a luxury. In this situation, the contract would not be for "necessaries."

and medical services, at a level of value required to maintain the minor's standard of living or financial and social status. Thus, what will be considered a necessary for one person may be a luxury for another. Additionally, what is considered a necessary depends on whether the minor is under the care or control of his or her parents, who are required by law to provide necessaries for the minor. If a minor's parents provide the minor with shelter, for example, then a contract to lease shelter (such as an apartment) normally will not be classified as a contract for necessaries.

Generally, then, to qualify as a contract for necessaries, (1) the item contracted for must be necessary to the minor's existence, (2) the value of the necessary item may be up to a level required to maintain the minor's standard of living or financial and social status, and (3) the minor must not be under the care of a parent or guardian who is required to supply this item. Unless these three criteria are met, the minor can disaffirm the contract *without* being liable for the reasonable value of the goods used.

Traditionally, insurance has not been viewed as a necessary, so minors can ordinarily disaffirm their insurance contracts and recover all premiums paid. Some jurisdictions, however, prohibit the right to disaffirm insurance contracts—for example, when minors contract for life insurance on their own lives. Financial loans are seldom considered to be necessaries, even if the minor spends the money borrowed on necessaries. If, however, a lender makes a loan to a minor for the express purpose of enabling the minor to purchase necessaries, and the lender personally makes sure the money is so spent, the minor normally is obligated to repay the loan.

• **RATIFICATION**
The act of accepting and giving legal force to an obligation that previously was not enforceable.

Ratification In contract law, **ratification** is the act of accepting and giving legal force to an obligation that previously was not enforceable. A minor who has reached the age of majority can ratify a contract expressly or impliedly.

Express ratification occurs when the minor expressly states, orally or in writing, that he or she intends to be bound by the contract. Implied ratification exists when the conduct of the minor is inconsistent with disaffirmance (as when the minor enjoys the benefits of the contract) or when the minor fails to disaffirm an executed (fully performed) contract within a reasonable time after reaching the age of major-

> **ON THE WEB**
> For an example of state statutory provisions governing the emancipation of minors, you can view Wyoming's statutory provisions on this topic at **legisweb.state.wy.us/titles/98titles/sub14.htm**.

ity. If the contract is still executory (not yet performed or only partially performed), however, failure to disaffirm the contract will not necessarily imply ratification.

Generally, the courts base their determination on whether the minor, after reaching the age of majority, has had ample opportunity to consider the nature of the contractual obligations he or she entered into as a minor and the extent to which the adult party to the contract has performed.

Parents' Liability As a general rule, parents are not liable for the contracts made by minor children acting on their own, except for contracts for necessaries, which the parents are legally required to provide. This is why businesses ordinarily require parents to cosign any contract made with a minor. The parents then become personally obligated under the contract to perform the conditions of the contract, even if their child avoids liability.

Generally, a minor is held personally liable for the torts he or she commits. Therefore, minors cannot disaffirm their liability for their tortious conduct. The parents of the minor can *also* be held liable under certain circumstances. For example, if the minor commits a tort under the direction of a parent or while performing an act requested by a parent, the injured party can hold the parent liable. In addition, parents are liable in many states up to a statutory amount for malicious torts committed by a minor child living in their home.

• **EMANCIPATION**
In regard to minors, the act of being freed from parental control; occurs when a child's parent or legal guardian relinquishes the legal right to exercise control over the child. Normally, a minor who leaves home to support himself or herself is considered emancipated.

Emancipation The release of a minor by his or her parents is known as emancipation. **Emancipation** occurs when a child's parent or legal guardian relinquishes the legal right to exercise control over the child. Normally, a minor who leaves home to support himself or herself is considered emancipated. Several jurisdictions permit minors to petition a court for emancipation themselves. For business purposes, a minor may petition a court to be treated as an adult. If the court grants the minor's request, it removes the minor's lack of contractual capacity and right of disaffirmance for those contracts entered into in conducting the business.

INTOXICATED PERSONS

Another situation in which contractual capacity becomes an issue is when a contract is formed by a person who claims to have been intoxicated at the time the contract was made. The general rule is that if a person who is sufficiently intoxicated to lack mental capacity enters into a contract, the contract is voidable at the option of the intoxicated person. This is true even if the intoxication was purely voluntary. For the contract to be voidable, it must be proved that the intoxicated person's reason and judgment were impaired to the extent that he or she did not comprehend the legal consequences of entering into the contract. In addition, in the majority of states, the person claiming intoxication must be able to return whatever consideration he or she received in order to avoid the contract. If the person was intoxicated but understood these legal consequences, the contract is enforceable.

Simply because the terms of the contract are foolish or are obviously favorable to the other party does not mean the contract is voidable (unless the other party fraudulently induced the person to become intoxicated). Problems often arise in determining whether a party was sufficiently intoxicated to avoid legal duties. Generally, contract avoidance on the ground of intoxication is rarely permitted.

The following case involves an unusual business transaction in which boasts and dares "after a few drinks" resulted in a contract to sell certain property. The issue before the court was whether the seller was sufficiently intoxicated to render the contract voidable at the seller's option.

CASE 11.2 Lucy v. Zehmer

Supreme Court of Appeals of Virginia, 1954.
196 Va. 493,
84 S.E.2d 516.

HISTORICAL AND SOCIAL SETTING *In part because intoxication is usually self-induced, the emphasis in cases that concern lack of capacity on the ground of intoxication is sometimes different from the emphasis in cases that concern lack of capacity on other grounds. Particularly in older cases, there is often a discussion of the parties' morals. Rather than focusing on whether the person was sober enough to understand what he or she was doing, the issue was whether the law should allow someone who becomes intoxicated voluntarily to avoid the consequences of his or her behavior. At least one court at the turn of the century held that intoxication is never a defense.*[a]

BACKGROUND AND FACTS Lucy and Zehmer had known each other for fifteen or twenty years. For some time, Lucy had been wanting to buy Zehmer's farm. Zehmer had always told Lucy that he was not interested in selling. One night, Lucy stopped in to visit with the Zehmers at a restaurant they operated. Lucy said to Zehmer, "I bet you wouldn't take $50,000 for that place." Zehmer replied, "Yes, I would, too; you wouldn't give fifty." Throughout the evening, the conversation returned to the sale of the farm. At the same time, the parties were drinking whiskey. Eventually, Zehmer wrote up an agreement, on the back of a restaurant check, for the sale of the farm, and he asked his wife to sign it—which she did. When Lucy brought an action in a Virginia state court to enforce the agreement, Zehmer argued that he had been "high as a Georgia pine" at the time and that the offer had been made in jest: "two doggoned drunks bluffing to see who could talk the biggest and say the most." Lucy claimed that he had not been intoxicated and did not think Zehmer had been, either, given the way Zehmer handled the transaction. The trial court ruled in favor of the Zehmers, and Lucy appealed.

a. *Cook v. Bagnell Timber Co.*, 78 Ark. 47, 94 S.W. 695 (1906).

IN THE WORDS OF THE COURT . . .
BUCHANAN, J. [Justice] delivered the opinion of the court.

* * * *

The appearance of the contract, the fact that it was under discussion for forty minutes or more before it was signed; Lucy's objection to the first draft because it was written in the singular, and he wanted Mrs. Zehmer to sign it also; the rewriting to meet that objection and the signing by Mrs. Zehmer; the discussion of what was to be included in the sale, the provision for the examination of the title, the completeness of the instrument that was executed, the taking possession of it by Lucy with no request or suggestion by either of the defendants that he give it back, are facts which furnish persuasive evidence that the execution of the contract was a serious business transaction rather than a casual, jesting matter as defendants now contend.

* * * *

In the field of contracts, as generally elsewhere, "*We must look to the outward expression of a person as manifesting his intention rather than to his secret and unexpressed intention.* [Emphasis added.] 'The law imputes to a person an intention corresponding to the reasonable meaning of his words and acts.' "

DECISION AND REMEDY The Supreme Court of Virginia determined that the writing was an enforceable contract and reversed the ruling of the lower court. The Zehmers were required by court order to carry through with the sale of the farm to the Lucys.

FOR CRITICAL ANALYSIS—Cultural Consideration *How does the court's decision in this case relate to the objective theory of contracts discussed in Chapter 9?*

MENTALLY INCOMPETENT PERSONS

If a person has been adjudged mentally incompetent by a court of law and a guardian has been appointed, any contract made by the mentally incompetent person is *void*—no contract exists. Only the guardian can enter into a binding contract on behalf of the mentally incompetent person.

If a mentally incompetent person not previously so adjudged by a court enters into a contract, the contract may be *voidable* if the person does not know he or she is entering into the contract or lacks the mental capacity to comprehend its nature, purpose, and consequences. In such situations, the contract is voidable at the option of the mentally incompetent person but not the other party. The contract may then be disaffirmed or ratified. To disaffirm the contract, the person claiming mental incompetence must return whatever consideration he or she has received. Ratification must occur after the person has regained mental competence or after a guardian is appointed and ratifies the contract. Like minors and intoxicated persons, mentally incompetent persons are liable for the reasonable value of any necessaries they receive.

A contract entered into by a mentally incompetent person (but not previously so adjudged by a court) may also be deemed valid and enforceable if the contract was formed during a lucid interval. For such a contract to be valid, it must be shown that the person was able to comprehend the nature, purpose, and consequences of the contract *at the time the contract was formed.*

"Public policy is in its nature so uncertain and fluctuating, varying with the habits of the day, . . . that it is difficult to determine its limits with any degree of exactness."

JOSEPH STORY,
1779–1845
(Associate justice of the United States Supreme Court, 1811–1845)

ETHICAL ISSUE 11.1 ***Do businesspersons have a duty to determine the mental competence of their customers?*** Now and then, cases come before the courts that raise the question of whether businesspersons have a duty to ascertain the mental competence of customers, particularly elderly persons, before doing business with them. A question of this kind came before the Texas Supreme Court in relation to a stockbroker's services to an elderly woman. The stockbroker had helped a ninety-one-year-old woman, Beatrice Clark Cairns, who was in failing health, transfer securities worth more than $300,000 to her nephew, Carlton Anness. Two of Cairns's nieces were concerned that Anness was taking advantage of their aunt, and later, after Cairns's death, one of the nieces sued the stockbroker for negligence, seeking both actual and punitive damages. The Texas Supreme Court pointed out that to be negligent, one must have breached a duty (see Chapter 4), so the issue turned on whether the stockbroker owed a duty to Cairns to determine her competence. The court declined to recognize such a duty, holding that "the rights of incompetents of whatever age are adequately protected by the rule that voids transactions in which they are involved in some circumstances and by the availability of guardianships."[2]

Legality

To this point, we have discussed three of the requirements for a valid contract to exist—agreement, consideration, and contractual capacity. Now we examine a fourth—legality. For a contract to be valid and enforceable, it must be formed for a legal purpose. A contract to do something that is prohibited by federal or state

2. *Edward D. Jones & Co. v. Fletcher,* 975 S.W.2d 539 (Tex. 1998).

statutory law is illegal and, as such, void from the outset and thus unenforceable. Additionally, a contract to commit a tortious act or to commit an action that is contrary to public policy is illegal and unenforceable.

Contracts Contrary to Statute

Statutes sometimes prescribe the terms of contracts. In some instances, the laws are specific, even providing for the inclusion of certain clauses and their wording. Other statutes prohibit certain contracts on the basis of their subject matter, the time at which they are entered into, or the status of the contracting parties. We examine here several ways in which contracts may be contrary to a statute and thus illegal.

• **USURY** Charging an illegal rate of interest.

Usury Virtually every state has a statute that sets the maximum rate of interest that can be charged for different types of transactions, including ordinary loans. A lender who makes a loan at an interest rate above the lawful maximum commits **usury.** The maximum rate of interest varies from state to state.

Although usury statutes place a ceiling on allowable rates of interest, exceptions have been made to facilitate business transactions. For example, many states exempt corporate loans from the usury laws. In addition, almost all states have adopted special statutes allowing much higher interest rates on small loans to help those borrowers who need funds and who could not otherwise obtain loans.

The effects of a usurious loan differ from state to state. A number of states allow the lender to recover only the principal of a loan along with interest up to the legal maximum. In effect, the lender is denied recovery of the excess interest. In other states, the lender can recover the principal amount of the loan but not the interest. In a few states, a usurious loan is a void transaction, and the lender cannot recover either the principal or the interest.

Gambling In general, gambling contracts are illegal and thus void. All states have statutes that regulate gambling—defined as any scheme that involves the distribution of property by chance among persons who have paid valuable consideration for the opportunity (chance) to receive the property.[3] Gambling is the creation of risk for the purpose of assuming it.

In some states, such as Nevada and New Jersey, casino gambling is legal. In other states, certain other forms of gambling are legal. California, for example, has not defined draw poker as a crime, although criminal statutes prohibit numerous other types of gambling games. Several states allow horse racing, and about half of the states have recognized the substantial revenues that can be obtained from gambling and have legalized state-operated lotteries, as well as lotteries (such as bingo) arranged for charitable purposes. Many states also allow gambling on Indian reservations. (For a discussion of some of the legal challenges presented by gambling via the Internet, see the feature *Technology and Online Gambling Operations.*)

¡REMEMBER! Virtually everyone is liable for his or her own torts, and this responsibility cannot be contracted away.

Sometimes it is difficult to distinguish a gambling contract from the risk sharing inherent in almost all contracts. • **EXAMPLE 11.2** Suppose that Isaacson takes out a life insurance policy on Donohue, naming himself as beneficiary under the policy. At first glance, this may seem entirely legal; but further examination shows that Isaacson is simply gambling on how long Donohue will live. To prevent that type of practice, insurance contracts can be entered into only by someone with an *insurable interest* (see Chapter 42). •

3. See *Wishing Well Club v. Akron,* 66 Ohio Law Abs. 406, 112 N.E.2d 41 (1951).

ADULTS GAMBLE AT A CASINO. WOULD THIS SAME ACTIVITY BE ILLEGAL IF IT WERE CONDUCTED ONLINE? IF SO, COULD IT BE PREVENTED? HOW?

Sabbath (Sunday) Laws Statutes called Sabbath (Sunday) laws prohibit the formation or performance of certain contracts on a Sunday. Under the common law, such contracts are legal in the absence of this statutory prohibition. Under some state and local laws, all contracts entered into on a Sunday are illegal. Laws in other states or municipalities prohibit only the sale of certain types of merchandise, such as alcoholic beverages, on a Sunday.

As noted in Chapter 2, these laws, which date back to colonial times, are often called **blue laws.** Blue laws get their name from the blue paper on which New Haven, Connecticut, printed its new town ordinance in 1781. The ordinance prohibited all work on Sunday and required all shops to close on the "Lord's Day." A number of states and municipalities enacted laws forbidding the carrying on of "all secular labor and business on the Lord's Day." Exceptions to Sunday laws permit contracts for necessities (such as food) and works of charity. Additionally, a fully performed (executed) contract that was entered into on a Sunday normally cannot be rescinded (canceled).

• **BLUE LAWS**
State or local laws that prohibit the performance of certain types of commercial activities on Sunday.

Sunday laws are often not enforced, and some of these laws have been held to be unconstitutional on the ground that they are contrary to the freedom of religion. Nonetheless, as a precaution, business owners contemplating doing business in a particular locality should check to see if any Sunday statutes or ordinances will affect their business activities.

ON THE WEB

If you are interested in reading the first "Sunday law" in colonial America and learning about some of the punishments meted out in those days for failing to obey such laws, go to **www.tagnet.org/crsda/first.htm**.

Licensing Statutes All states require that members of certain professions obtain licenses allowing them to practice. Physicians, lawyers, real estate brokers, architects, electricians, and stockbrokers are but a few of the people who must be licensed. Some licenses are obtained only after extensive schooling and examinations, which indicate to the public that a special skill has been acquired. Others require only that the particular person be of good moral character.

¡CONTRAST!

When a minor avoids a contract, the minor has to return the consideration only if he or she still possesses or has control over it.

Generally, business licenses provide a means of regulating and taxing certain businesses and protecting the public against actions that could threaten the general

Technology and Online Gambling Operations

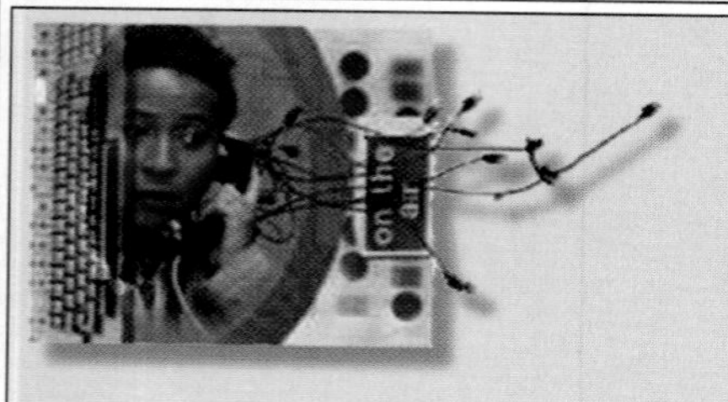

In the typical physical world, gambling contracts are usually illegal, except when sanctioned by the state in the form of lotteries, off-track betting, and so on. Today, however, virtually any person, even a fourteen-year-old with a credit card, can play blackjack or other gambling games on the Internet. If a state resident places bets on an online gambling site, do the laws of that state apply? If the bet would be illegal under state law, is there anything the state can do about it? Given that annual expenditures on gambling are estimated to be between $100 billion and $500 billion a year,[a] the questions raised by online gambling are certainly not about to go away.

Who Has Jurisdiction?

In most states, gambling contracts are illegal and thus void. But state laws generally govern only activities within a state's borders. Texas, for example, has no constitutional authority to regulate gambling activities in New Jersey or Nevada, and no state government has jurisdiction over activities that take place in other countries. As you learned in Chapter 3, under certain conditions the federal courts can exercise jurisdiction based on diversity of citizenship between the parties. Also, under certain conditions, a state court can exercise jurisdiction over an out-of-state party that has a threshold level of contacts ("minimum contacts") with the state.

As noted in Chapter 7, jurisdictional issues become complicated when they concern parties involved in Internet transactions. Certainly, this is true with respect to online gambling. Consider a lawsuit brought by a Texas resident to recover winnings from games he had played on his computer in Texas. The Web server and the corporate defendant were in California. The gambling corporation had no sales force or employees in Texas. Under traditional jurisdictional concepts, the California company probably would not have had sufficient contacts (minimum contacts) with the state of Texas to allow a Texas court to exercise jurisdiction over the California defendant. In this case, however, the court held that the company had sufficient minimum contacts with Texas. The company advertised its virtual casino over the Internet and therefore knew that residents of all states, including Texas, would see the advertisements.[b]

Going Offshore

Billions of dollars of Internet gambling are conducted through gambling entities residing in offshore locations, such as the Cayman Islands, Finland, or Iceland. Suppose that a Missouri resident logs on the Internet, pulls up a gambling site, and places a bet using his or her credit card. The home Web site server of the gambling company is on the Caribbean Island of Grenada. Interacting electronic links between the home server and the Missouri gambler may go through Asian or African countries. While the transaction is physically illegal in Missouri, that state cannot pass a law banning gambling operations in other jurisdictions. The issue is particularly bothersome when the gambling entity is operating legally where its home server is located.

Until 1998, no court ever held that U.S. law prohibits online betting. Indeed, in January 1998 a Justice Department spokesman, John Hussall, stated, "We have no jurisdiction [to prosecute offshore Internet gambling operators]. The offense has not been made on U.S. soil." In fact, in 1997 Missouri Attorney General Jay Nixon had brought the first criminal indictment of an online gambling operation. The complaint charged Michael Simone and his Philadelphia-based Interactive Gaming & Communications Corporation with running illegal Internet gambling operations. The company had accepted bets from Missourians.[c] State governments are also considering laws such as that passed by the state of Nevada, which bars residents from placing or accepting bets over the Internet.[d]

However hard federal and state law enforcement authorities try to crack down on Internet casino operators, service providers, players, credit-card companies, and banks, the results will eventually be discouraging. Anybody anywhere with very little investment can buy a server and create a Web page. The use of Internet currencies, such as DigiCash and CyberCash, further enhances the lure of Internet gambling because gamblers can remain anonymous.

For Critical Analysis

Are the contract issues any different whether one engages in illegal gambling in person, over the phone, or via the Internet?

a. Richard Raysman and Peter Brown, "Cyber-Casinos: Gambling Meets the Internet," *The New York Law Journal,* August 12, 1997, p. 1.

b. *Thompson v. Handa-Lopez, Inc.,* 998 F.Supp. 738 (W.D.Tex. 1998).

c. *Missouri v. Interactive Gaming & Communications Corporation,* Case No. 197CF0014(2) (Cir.Ct., Green County, Mo., filed June 26, 1997); unpublished opinion.

d. N.R.S. Ch. 465, Section 9.

welfare. For example, in nearly all states, a stockbroker must be licensed and must file a bond with the state to protect the public from fraudulent transactions in stock. Similarly, a plumber must be licensed and bonded to protect the public against incompetent plumbers and to protect the public health. Only persons or businesses possessing the qualifications and complying with the conditions required by statute are entitled to licenses. Typically, for example, an owner of a saloon or tavern is required to sell food as a condition of obtaining a license to sell liquor for consumption on the premises.

When a person enters into a contract with an unlicensed individual, the contract may still be enforceable, depending on the nature of the licensing statute. Some states expressly provide that the lack of a license in certain occupations bars the enforcement of work-related contracts. If the statute does not expressly state this, one must look to the underlying purpose of the licensing requirements for a particular occupation. If the purpose is to protect the public from unauthorized practitioners, a contract involving an unlicensed individual is illegal and unenforceable. If, however, the underlying purpose of the statute is to raise government revenues, a contract with an unlicensed practitioner is enforceable—although the unlicensed person is usually fined.

CONTRACTS CONTRARY TO PUBLIC POLICY

Although contracts involve private parties, some are not enforceable because of the negative impact they would have on society. These contracts are said to be *contrary to public policy.* Examples include a contract to commit an immoral act (such as a surrogate-parenting contract, which several courts and state statutes equate with "baby selling") and a contract that prohibits marriage. • **EXAMPLE 11.3** Everett offers a young man $500 if he refrains from marrying Everett's daughter. If the young man accepts, no contract is formed (the contract is void) because it is contrary to public policy. Thus, if the man marries Everett's daughter, Everett cannot sue him for breach of contract. Business contracts that may be contrary to public policy include contracts in restraint of trade and unconscionable contracts or clauses. •

Contracts in Restraint of Trade Contracts in restraint of trade (anticompetitive agreements) usually adversely affect the public policy that favors competition in the economy. Typically, such contracts also violate one or more federal or state statutes.[4] An exception is recognized when the restraint is reasonable and it is *ancillary to* (is a subsidiary part of) a contract, such as a contract for the sale of a business or an employment contract. Many such exceptions involve a type of restraint called a *covenant not to compete,* or a restrictive covenant.

Covenants Not to Compete. Covenants not to compete are often contained in contracts concerning the sale of an ongoing business. A covenant not to compete is created when a seller agrees not to open a new store in a certain geographical area surrounding the old store. Such an agreement, when it is ancillary to a sales contract and reasonable in terms of time and geographic area, enables the seller to sell, and the purchaser to buy, the "goodwill" and "reputation" of an ongoing business. If, for example, a well-known merchant sells his or her store and opens a competing business a block away, many of the merchant's customers will likely do business at

4. Such as the Sherman Antitrust Act, the Clayton Act, and the Federal Trade Commission Act (see Chapter 35).

the new store. This renders valueless the good name and reputation sold to the other merchant for a price. If a covenant not to compete was not ancillary to a sales agreement, however, it would be void, because it unreasonably restrains trade and is contrary to public policy.

Agreements not to compete can also be contained in employment contracts. It is common for many people in middle-level and upper-level management positions to agree not to work for competitors or not to start a competing business for a specified period of time after terminating employment. Such agreements are generally legal so long as the specified period of time is not excessive in duration and the geographical restriction is reasonable. Basically, the restriction on competition must be reasonable—that is, not any greater than necessary to protect a legitimate business interest. The following case illustrates this point.

CASE 11.3 Brunswick Floors, Inc. v. Guest

Court of Appeals of Georgia, 1998.
506 S.E.2d 670.

HISTORICAL AND SOCIAL SETTING *The value of a business depends on the goodwill between key employees and customers. To enhance this value, a business will invest its key employees with training, experience, customer lists, trade secrets, and other valuable information. It can be devastating when a key employee quits, or is fired, and goes into business to compete with his or her former employer. A covenant not to compete can protect goodwill, and other assets, by at least prohibiting an employee from stealing customers. A covenant not to compete is enforceable if its provisions are reasonable, if it is part of a valid contract, and if it is related to the protection of a legitimate interest. As much as a business might wish, however, legitimate interests do not include preventing competition.*

BACKGROUND AND FACTS Brian Guest was a floor covering installer for Brunswick Floors, Inc. Guest signed a covenant not to compete that prohibited him for two years after termination of employment from engaging in the floor covering business in virtually any way, within an eighty-mile radius of Brunswick's location. After Guest quit Brunswick, he went to work as an independent flooring contractor. Brunswick filed a suit in a Georgia state court against Guest based on the covenant not to compete. The court ruled in part that the covenant unduly restricted Guest's right to earn a living. Brunswick appealed.

IN THE WORDS OF THE COURT . . .
RUFFIN, Judge.

* * * *

* * * [A]n employer is permitted to include in * * * a covenant [not to compete] the territory in which the employee has in fact performed work, thus protecting itself from the unfair appropriation of good will and information acquired in the course of that work. In contrast, [a] restriction relating to the area in which the employer does business is generally unenforceable due to overbreadth, unless the employer can show a legitimate business interest that will be protected by such an expansive geographic description.

In this case, the covenant restricts Guest from working within an 80 mile radius of Brunswick Floors' location * * * . The 80 mile radius relates to the area in which the employer, Brunswick Floors, and not the employee, Guest, did business. * * *

[Robert] Blake [the president of Brunswick] testified that "if our employees start * * * working for our competitors, then certainly our market share would face, you know, diminishing status." Avoidance of competition, however, is not a legitimate business interest.

Brunswick Floors contends the training and money expended on Guest legitimizes their interest. * * * Here, Guest's minimal training does not outweigh the

CASE 11.3—Continued

substantial harm imposed by prohibiting him from installing carpet in an 80 mile radius. Thus, we find this to be an overbroad territorial limitation.

We also find the scope of activity prohibited in the non-compete provision is overbroad. * * * This imposes a greater limitation on the employee than is necessary because [Guest] is prohibited from being an officer or director or owning stock in other companies, activities which are very different from [his] work as [a floor covering installer].

DECISION AND REMEDY The Court of Appeals of Georgia held that a covenant not to compete is unenforceable if it bars an employee from engaging in the employer's business in virtually any way within the area in which the employer does business. The court affirmed the decision of the lower court.

FOR CRITICAL ANALYSIS—Technological Consideration *Should these same limits apply to employers who do business only on the Internet?*

Reformation of an Illegal Covenant Not to Compete. On occasion, when a covenant not to compete is unreasonable in time or geographic area, the court may *reform* the covenant, converting its terms into reasonable ones. Instead of declaring the covenant illegal and unenforceable, the court applies the rule of reasonableness and changes the contract so that its basic, original intent can be enforced. This presents a problem, however, in that the judge becomes a party to the contract. Consequently, contract **reformation** is usually carried out by a court only when necessary to prevent undue burdens or hardships. (See this chapter's *Business Law in Action* for a further discussion of how the courts treat covenants not to compete.)

• **REFORMATION**
A court-ordered correction of a written contract so that it reflects the true intentions of the parties.

Unconscionable Contracts or Clauses Ordinarily, a court does not look at the fairness or equity of a contract; for example, a court normally will not inquire into the adequacy of consideration. Persons are assumed to be reasonably intelligent, and the court does not come to their aid just because they have made unwise or foolish bargains. In certain circumstances, however, bargains are so oppressive that the courts relieve innocent parties of part or all of their duties. Such a bargain is called an **unconscionable contract** (or **unconscionable clause**). Both the Uniform Commercial Code (UCC) and the Uniform Consumer Credit Code (UCCC) embody the unconscionability concept—the former with regard to the sale of goods and the latter with regard to consumer loans and the waiver of rights.[5]

• **UNCONSCIONABLE CONTRACT (OR UNCONSCIONABLE CLAUSE)**
A contract or clause that is void on the basis of public policy because one party, as a result of his or her disproportionate bargaining power, is forced to accept terms that are unfairly burdensome and that unfairly benefit the dominating party.

Procedural Unconscionability. Procedural unconscionability has to do with how a term becomes part of a contract and relates to factors bearing on a party's lack of knowledge or understanding of the contract terms because of inconspicuous print, unintelligible language ("legalese"), lack of opportunity to read the contract, lack of opportunity to ask questions about its meaning, and other factors. Procedural unconscionability sometimes relates to purported lack of voluntariness because of a disparity in bargaining power between the two parties. Contracts entered into because of one party's vastly superior bargaining power may be deemed unconscionable. These situations usually involve an **adhesion contract,** which is a contract drafted by the dominant party and then presented to the other—the adhering party—on a "take it or leave it" basis.[6]

• **ADHESION CONTRACT**
A "standard-form" contract, such as that between a large retailer and a consumer, in which the stronger party dictates the terms.

5. See, for example, UCC Sections 2–302 and 2–719 (see Chapters 15 and 17, respectively) and UCCC Sections 5.108 and 1.107.

6. See, for example, *Henningsen v. Bloomfield Motors, Inc.*, 32 N.J. 358, 161 A.2d 69 (1960).

Business Law in Action • When Are Covenants Not to Compete Reasonable?

In today's complicated, technological business world, knowledge learned on the job, including trade secrets, has become a valuable commodity. To prevent this knowledge from falling into the hands of competitors, more and more employers are requiring their employees to sign covenants not to compete. The increasing number of lawsuits over noncompete clauses in employment contracts have caused numerous courts to reconsider the reasonableness of these covenants.

In one case, for example, all of the workers for the British brokerage firm Exco PLC, located in New Jersey, had to sign agreements not to work for competitors after their employment with Exco terminated. When eight employees quit Exco and joined a rival firm in New York, Exco sued to enforce the noncompete covenants. The state judge hearing the case sided with the employees. The noncompete clauses stated that Exco employees could not work for one year with any competitors located within one hundred miles of New York City. The judge held that this clause was too broad, because for some highly technical jobs in the brokerage industry (such as trading interest-rate options), New York City is one of the few places the employees could get a job.[a]

Exco's experience is being mirrored throughout the United States. Miami attorney James Gale, who has litigated noncompete clauses in courts throughout the country, has concluded that the farther you go west of the Mississippi River, the harder it is to enforce a covenant not to compete.[b] Because of this, some savvy employees have changed their residence to avoid compliance with the terms of noncompete agreements. For example, when a top executive of a Minnesota health-care company was offered a chance to work at a competing firm, he rented an apartment in California, got a California driver's license, and then sued as a California resident to avoid the noncompete clause in his employment contract with the Minnesota company. Because noncompete agreements are illegal in California, the ploy worked.[c]

a. Noam Neusner, "As 'Non-Compete' Clauses Proliferate, So Do Lawsuits over Them," *International Herald Tribune*, May 5, 1997, p. 13.
b. Janet Novack, "Just a Piece of Paper?", *Forbes*, May 5, 1997, p. 156.
c. *Ibid.*

In contrast, Florida is more "employer friendly" with respect to noncompete agreements. Under Florida statutory law, judges may modify unreasonable restrictions as to time and place in such covenants, and then enforce them—rather than void the contracts. Florida law also allows the courts to enforce noncompete clauses that protect "legitimate business interests," which have been interpreted to include more than just trade secrets. According to the relevant Florida statute, the "use of specific trade secrets, customer lists, or direct solicitation of existing customers shall be presumed to be an irreparable injury" to the employer "and may be specifically enjoined."[d] Also, if an employee has obtained extraordinary training (through classes or seminars, for example) in addition to on-the-job training, this may qualify as a legtimate business interest that can be protected by a covenant not to compete.[e]

FOR CRITICAL ANALYSIS

What ethical reasons are there for enforcing covenants not to compete?

d. Chapter 90–216, Section 1, Florida Statutes (1990).
e. See the *Question of Ethics and Social Responsibility* at the end of this chapter for a recent Florida case applying this law.

Substantive Unconscionability. Substantive unconscionability characterizes those contracts, or portions of contracts, that are oppressive or overly harsh. Courts generally focus on provisions that deprive one party of the benefits of the agreement or leave that party without remedy for nonperformance by the other. For example, suppose that a welfare recipient with a fourth-grade education agrees to purchase a refrigerator for $2,000 and signs a two-year installment contract. The same type of refrigerator usually sells for $400 on the market. Some courts have held this type of contract to be unconscionable, despite the general rule that the courts will not inquire into the adequacy of the consideration, because the contract terms are so oppressive as to "shock the conscience" of the court.[7]

¡BE CAREFUL!

In some states, such as Texas, an employee must receive some benefit for a covenant not to compete to be imposed on him or her. This is true even if the covenant is reasonable as to time and area. If the employee receives no benefit, the covenant will be deemed void.

Exculpatory Clauses Often closely related to the concept of unconscionability are **exculpatory clauses,** defined as clauses that release a party from liability in the event of monetary or physical injury, *no matter who is at fault.* Indeed, some courts refer to such clauses in terms of unconscionability. Suppose, for example, that Madison Manufacturing Company hires a laborer and has him sign a contract containing the following clause:

• **EXCULPATORY CLAUSE**
A clause that releases a contractual party from liability in the event of monetary or physical injury, no matter who is at fault.

> Said employee hereby agrees with employer, in consideration of such employment, that he will take upon himself all risks incident to his position and will in no case hold the company liable for any injury or damage he may sustain, in his person or otherwise, by accidents or injuries in the factory, or which may result from defective machinery or carelessness or misconduct of himself or any other employee in service of the employer.

This contract provision attempts to remove Madison's potential liability for injuries occurring to the employee, and it would usually be held contrary to public policy.[8] Additionally, exculpatory clauses found in agreements to lease commercial property are, in the majority of cases, held to be contrary to public policy, and such clauses are almost universally held to be illegal and unenforceable when they are included in residential property leases.

ETHICAL ISSUE 11.2 ***Should exculpatory clauses in employment contracts with independent contractors be enforced?*** The law often takes a dubious view of exculpatory agreements, particularly in employment contracts involving a disparity in bargaining power between the parties. An exculpatory clause that attempts to exempt an employer from all liability for negligence toward its employees normally is held to be against public policy and thus void. Should this "freedom *from* contract" be extended to independent contractors as well as employees? (An independent contractor is a worker who is hired to undertake a specific function and who is not classified as an employee—see Chapter 24.) At least one court has concluded that it should be. The court drew this conclusion largely because of the disparity in bargaining power between the plaintiff (a newspaper carrier who was injured when she fell on some ice outside the newspaper's distribution facility) and the defendant (Knight Ridder, a major newspaper publisher). The court found that the disparity in bargaining power in this case was comparable to—if not greater than—that between most employers and employees. Therefore, the court would not allow Knight Ridder to avoid liability on the basis of a contract signed with the carrier that included a clause relieving Knight Ridder of any liability in the event of an accident.[9]

Generally, an exculpatory clause will not be enforced if the party seeking its enforcement is involved in a business that is important to the public interest. These businesses include public utilities, common carriers, and banks. Because of the essential nature of these services, the companies offering them have an advantage in bargaining strength and could insist that anyone contracting for their services agree not to hold them liable. This would tend to relax their carefulness and increase the

7. See, for example, *Jones v. Star Credit Corp.*, 59 Misc.2d 189, 298 N.Y.S.2d 264 (1969). This case is presented in Chapter 15 as Case 15.3.
8. For a case with similar facts, see *Little Rock & Fort Smith Railway Co. v. Eubanks,* 48 Ark. 460, 3 S.W. 808 (1887). In such a case, the exculpatory clause may also be illegal on the basis of a violation of a state workers' compensation law.
9. *Bunia v. Knight Ridder,* 544 N.W.2d 60 (Minn.App. 1996).

number of injuries. Imagine the results, for example, if all exculpatory clauses in contracts between airlines and their passengers were enforced.

Exculpatory clauses may be enforced, however, when the parties seeking their enforcement are not involved in businesses considered important to the public interest. These businesses have included health clubs, amusement parks, horse-rental concessions, golf-cart concessions, and skydiving organizations. Because these services are not essential, the firms offering them are sometimes considered to have no relative advantage in bargaining strength, and anyone contracting for their services is considered to do so voluntarily.

The Effect of Illegality

In general, an illegal contract is void: the contract is deemed never to have existed, and the courts will not aid either party. In most illegal contracts, both parties are considered to be equally at fault—*in pari delicto*. If the contract is executory (not yet fulfilled), neither party can enforce it. If it is executed, there can be neither contractual nor quasi-contractual recovery.

That one wrongdoer in an illegal contract is unjustly enriched at the expense of the other is of no concern to the law—except under certain circumstances (to be discussed shortly). The major justification for this hands-off attitude is that it is improper to place the machinery of justice at the disposal of a plaintiff who has broken the law by entering into an illegal bargain. Another justification is the hoped-for deterrent effect of this general rule. A plaintiff who suffers a loss because of an illegal bargain should presumably be deterred from entering into similar illegal bargains in the future.

There are exceptions to the general rule that neither party to an illegal bargain can sue for breach and neither can recover for performance rendered. We look at these exceptions here.

Justifiable Ignorance of the Facts When one of the parties to a contract is relatively innocent (has no knowledge or any reason to know that the contract is illegal), that party can often obtain restitution or recovery of benefits conferred in a partially executed contract. The courts do not enforce the contract but do allow the parties to return to their original positions.

It is also possible for an innocent party who has fully performed under the contract to enforce the contract against the guilty party. If a party engages in an illegal act (such as selling certain goods in violation of the law) and contracts with a trucking firm to deliver the goods for $1,000, for example, the trucking firm, as an innocent party, will be entitled to collect the $1,000 once the delivery is made.

Members of Protected Classes When a statute protects a certain class of people, a member of that class can enforce an illegal contract even though the other party cannot. For example, there are statutes that prohibit certain employees (such as flight attendants) from working more than a specified number of hours per month. These employees thus constitute a class protected by statute. An employee who is required to work more than the maximum can recover for those extra hours of service.

• BLUE SKY LAWS
State laws that regulate the offer and sale of securities.

Another example of statutes designed to protect a particular class of people are **blue sky laws,** which are state laws that regulate and supervise investment companies for the protection of the public. (The phrase *blue sky laws* dates to a 1917 decision by the United States Supreme Court in which the Court declared that the purpose of such laws was to prevent "speculative schemes which have no more basis than so many feet of 'blue sky.'")[10] These laws are intended to stop the sale of stock

10. *Hall v. Geiger-Jones Co.,* 242 U.S. 539, 37 S.Ct. 217, 61 L.Ed. 480 (1917).

in fly-by-night concerns, such as visionary oil wells and distant and perhaps nonexistent gold mines. Investors are protected as a class and can sue to recover the purchase price of stock issued in violation of such laws.

Most states also have statutes regulating the sale of insurance. If an insurance company violates a statute when selling insurance, the purchaser can nevertheless enforce the policy and recover from the insurer.

Withdrawal from an Illegal Agreement If the illegal part of a bargain has not yet been performed, the party tendering performance can withdraw from the bargain and recover the performance or its value. • EXAMPLE 11.4 Suppose that Martha and Andy decide to wager (illegally) on the outcome of a boxing match. Each deposits money with a stakeholder, who agrees to pay the winner of the bet. At this point, each party has performed part of the agreement, but the illegal part of the agreement will not occur until the money is paid to the winner. Before such payment occurs, either party is entitled to withdraw from the agreement by giving notice to the stakeholder of his or her withdrawal. •

Fraud, Duress, or Undue Influence Whenever a plaintiff has been induced to enter into an illegal bargain as a result of fraud, duress, or undue influence, he or she can either enforce the contract or recover for its value.

APPLICATION

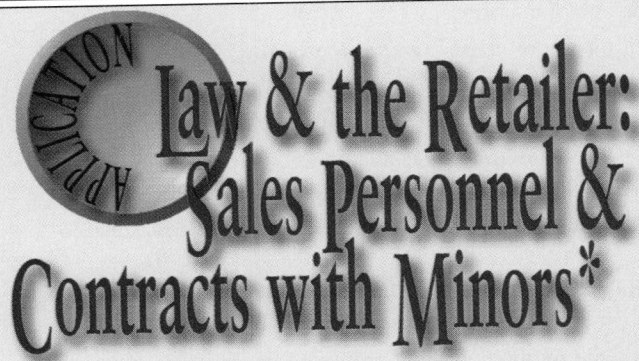

Law & the Retailer: Sales Personnel & Contracts with Minors*

Sales personnel, particularly those who are paid on a commission basis, are often eager to make contracts. Sometimes, however, these salespersons must deal with minors and intoxicated persons, both of whom have limited contractual capacity. Therefore, if you are a retailer, you should make sure that your employees are acquainted with the law governing minors and intoxicated persons.

If in your business you sell consumer durables, such as furniture or automobiles, your sales personnel must be careful in forming contracts with minors and should heed the adage, "When in doubt, check." Remember that a contract signed by a minor (unless it is for necessaries) normally is voidable, and the minor may exercise the option to disaffirm the contract. Employees should demand proof of legal age of a customer when they have any doubt concerning the customer's age.

In addition, because the law governing minors' rights varies substantially from state to state, you should check with your attorney concerning the laws governing disaffirmance in your state. You and those you hire to sell your products should know, for example, what the consequences will be if a minor has misrepresented his or her age when forming a sales contract. Similarly, you need to find out whether and in what circumstances a minor, on disaffirming a contract, can be required to pay for damage to goods sold under the contract.

Little need be said about a salesperson's dealings with obviously intoxicated persons. If the customer, despite intoxication, understands the legal consequences of the contract being signed, the contract is enforceable. Nonetheless, it may be extremely difficult to establish that the intoxicated customer understood the consequences of entering into the contract if the customer claims that he or she did not understand those consequences. Therefore, the best advice is, "When in doubt, don't." In other words, if you suspect a customer may be intoxicated, do not sign a contract with him or her.

CHECKLIST FOR THE SALESPERSON

1. When in doubt about the age of a customer to whom you are about to sell major consumer durable goods or anything other than necessities, require legal proof of age.
2. If such proof is not forthcoming, require that a parent or guardian sign the contract.
3. Check with an attorney about the laws governing minors' contracts in your state.
4. Do not sign contracts with intoxicated customers.

*This *Application* is not meant to substitute for the services of an attorney who is licensed to practice law in your state.

Key Terms

Chapter Summary • Capacity and Legality

CONTRACTUAL CAPACITY	
Minors (See pages 285–289.)	A minor is a person who has not yet reached the age of majority. In most states, the age of majority is eighteen for contract purposes. Contracts with minors are voidable at the option of the minor. 1. *Disaffirmance*—Defined as the legal avoidance of a contractual obligation. a. Can take place (in most states) at any time during minority and within a reasonable time after the minor has reached the age of majority. b. If a minor disaffirms a contract, the entire contract must be disaffirmed. c. When disaffirming executed contracts, the minor has a duty to return received goods if they are still in the minor's control or (in some states) to pay their reasonable value. d. A minor who has committed an act of fraud (such as misrepresentation of age) will be denied the right to disaffirm by some courts. e. A minor may disaffirm a contract for necessaries but remains liable for the reasonable value of the goods. 2. *Ratification*—Defined as the acceptance, or affirmation, of a legal obligation; may be express or implied. a. Express ratification—Exists when the minor, through a writing or an oral agreement, explicitly assumes the obligations imposed by the contract. b. Implied ratification—Exists when the conduct of the minor is inconsistent with disaffirmance or when the minor fails to disaffirm an executed contract within a reasonable time after reaching the age of majority. 3. *Parents' liability*—Generally, except for contracts for necessaries, parents are not liable for the contracts made by minor children acting on their own, nor are parents liable for minors' torts except in certain circumstances. 4. *Emancipation*—Occurs when a child's parent or legal guardian relinquishes the legal right to exercise control over the child. Normally, a minor who leaves home to support himself or herself is considered emancipated. In some jurisdictions, minors themselves are permitted to petition for emancipation for limited purposes.
Intoxicated Persons (See pages 289–290.)	1. A contract entered into by an intoxicated person is voidable at the option of the intoxicated person if the person was sufficiently intoxicated to lack mental capacity, even if the intoxication was voluntary. 2. A contract with an intoxicated person is enforceable if, despite being intoxicated, the person understood the legal consequences of entering into the contract.

Chapter Summary • Capacity and Legality, Continued

Mentally Incompetent Persons (See page 291.)	1. A contract made by a person adjudged by a court to be mentally incompetent is void. 2. A contract made by a mentally incompetent person not adjudged by a court to be mentally incompetent is voidable at the option of the mentally incompetent person.
LEGALITY	
Contracts Contrary to Statute (See pages 292–295.)	1. *Usury*—Occurs when a lender makes a loan at an interest rate above the lawful maximum. The maximum rate of interest varies from state to state. 2. *Gambling*—Gambling contracts that contravene (go against) state statutes are deemed illegal and thus void. 3. *Sabbath (Sunday) laws*—Laws prohibiting the formation or the performance of certain contracts on Sunday. Such laws vary widely from state to state, and many states do not enforce them. 4. *Licensing statutes*—Contracts entered into by persons who do not have a license, when one is required by statute, will not be enforceable unless the underlying purpose of the statute is to raise government revenues (and not to protect the public from unauthorized practitioners).
Contracts Contrary to Public Policy (See pages 295–300.)	1. *Contracts in restraint of trade*—Contracts to reduce or restrain free competition are illegal. Most such contracts are now prohibited by statutes. An exception is a *covenant not to compete.* It is usually enforced by the courts if the terms are ancillary to a contract (such as a contract for the sale of a business or an employment contract) and are reasonable as to time and area of restraint. Courts tend to scrutinize covenants not to compete closely. If a covenant is overbroad, a court may either reform the covenant to fall within reasonable constraints and then enforce the reformed contract or declare the covenant void and thus unenforceable. 2. *Unconscionable contracts and clauses*—When a contract or contract clause is so unfair that it is oppressive to one party, it can be deemed unconscionable; as such, it is illegal and cannot be enforced. 3. *Exculpatory clauses*—An exculpatory clause is a clause that releases a party from liability in the event of monetary or physical injury, no matter who is at fault. In certain situations, exculpatory clauses may be contrary to public policy and thus unenforceable.
Effect of Illegality (See pages 300–301.)	In general, an illegal contract is void, and the courts will not aid either party when both parties are considered to be equally at fault *(in pari delicto).* If the contract is executory, neither party can enforce it. If the contract is executed, there can be neither contractual nor quasi-contractual recovery. Exceptions (situations in which recovery is allowed): 1. When one party to the contract is relatively innocent. 2. When one party to the contract is a member of a group of persons protected by statute. 3. When either party seeks to recover consideration given for an illegal contract before the illegal act is performed. 4. When one party was induced to enter into an illegal bargain through fraud, duress, or undue influence.

For Review

1. Generally, a minor can disaffirm any contract. What are some exceptions to this rule?
2. Under what circumstances does intoxication make a contract voidable?
3. Does mental incompetence necessarily render a contract void?
4. Under what circumstances will a covenant not to compete be enforceable? When will such covenants not be enforced?
5. What is an exculpatory clause? In what circumstances might exculpatory clauses be enforced? When will they not be enforced?

Questions and Case Problems

11–1. Contracts by Minors. Kalen is a seventeen-year-old minor who has just graduated from high school. He is attending a university two hundred miles from home and has contracted to rent an apartment near the university for one year at $500 per month. He is working at a convenience store to earn enough income to be self-supporting. After living in the apartment and paying monthly rent for four months, a dispute arises between him and the landlord. Kalen, still a minor, moves out and returns the key to the landlord. The landlord wants to hold Kalen liable for the balance of the payments due under the lease. Discuss fully Kalen's liability in this situation.

11–2. Covenants Not to Compete. Joseph, who owns the only pizza parlor in Middletown, learns that Giovanni is about to open a competing pizza parlor in the same small town, just a few blocks from Joseph's restaurant. Joseph offers Giovanni $10,000 in return for Giovanni's promise not to open a pizza parlor in the Middletown area. Giovanni accepts the $10,000 but goes ahead with his plans, in spite of the agreement. When Giovanni opens his restaurant for business, Joseph sues to enjoin (prevent) Giovanni's continued operation of his restaurant or to recover the $10,000. The court denies recovery. On what basis?

11–3. Intoxication. After Katie has several drinks one night, she sells Emily a valuable fur stole for $10. The next day, Katie offers the $10 to Emily and requests the return of her stole. Emily refuses, claiming that they had a valid contract of sale. Katie explains that she was intoxicated at the time the bargain was made, and thus the contract is voidable at her option. Who is right? Explain.

11–4. Mental Incompetence. Jermal has been the owner of a car dealership for a number of years. One day, Jermal sold one of his most expensive cars to Kessler. At the time of the sale, Jermal thought Kessler acted in a peculiar manner, but he gave the matter no further thought until four months later, when Kessler's court-appointed guardian appeared at Jermal's office, tendered back the car, and demanded Kessler's money back. The guardian informed Jermal that Kessler had been adjudicated mentally incompetent two months earlier by a proper court.

(a) Discuss the rights of the parties in this situation.
(b) If Kessler had been adjudicated mentally incompetent before the contract was formed, what would be the legal effect of the contract?

11–5. Licensing Statutes. State X requires that persons who prepare and serve liquor in the form of drinks at commercial establishments be licensed by the state to do so. The only requirement for obtaining a yearly license is that the person be at least twenty-one years old. Mickey, aged thirty-five, is hired as a bartender for the Southtown Restaurant. Gerald, a staunch alumnus of a nearby university, brings twenty of his friends to the restaurant to celebrate a football victory one afternoon. Gerald orders four rounds of drinks, and the bill is nearly $200. Gerald learns that Mickey has failed to renew his bartender's license, and Gerald refuses to pay, claiming that the contract is unenforceable. Discuss whether Gerald is correct.

11–6. Contracts by Minors. In 1982, Webster Street Partnership, Ltd. (Webster), entered into a lease agreement with Matthew Sheridan and Pat Wilwerding. Webster was aware that both Sheridan and Wilwerding were minors. Both tenants were living away from home, apparently with the understanding that they could return home at any time. Sheridan and Wilwerding paid the first month's rent but then failed to pay the rent for the next month and vacated the apartment. Webster sued them for breach of contract. They claimed that the lease agreement was voidable because they were minors. Who will win, and why? [*Webster Street Partnership, Ltd. v. Sheridan,* 220 Neb. 9, 368 N.W.2d 439 (1985)]

11–7. Unconscionability. Carolyn Murphy was a welfare recipient with four minor children. After seeing Brian McNamara's advertisement for "rent to own" televisions, Murphy signed a lease agreement with McNamara for a twenty-five-inch Philco color TV at $16 per week. The lease payments were to run for seventy-eight weeks, after which Murphy would become the owner. At no time did McNamara tell Murphy that the total lease payments amounted to $1,268, including the delivery charge. The retail sale price of the set was $499. Murphy had paid about $436 when she read a newspaper article criticizing the lease plan. When she learned that she was required to pay $1,268, Murphy stopped making payments. McNamara's employees attempted to take possession of the TV and made threats through telephone and written communications. Murphy filed suit, alleging, among other things, that the contract terms were unconscionable. Discuss her allegation and whether a court might find the contract unconscionable. [*Murphy v. McNamara,* 36 Conn.Supp. 183, 416 A.2d 170 (1979)]

11–8. Usury. Tony's Tortilla Factory, Inc., had two checking accounts with First Bank. Due to financial difficulties, Tony's wrote a total of 2,165 checks (totaling $88,000) for which there were insufficient funds in the accounts. First Bank paid the overdrawn checks but imposed an "NSF" (nonsufficient funds) fee of $20 for each check paid. The owners of Tony's sued First Bank and one of its officers, alleging, among other things, that the $20-per-check fee was essentially "interest" charged by the bank for Tony's use of the bank's funds (the funds the bank advanced to cover the bad checks); because the rate of "interest" charged by the bank ($20 per check) exceeded the rate allowed by law, it was usurious. First Bank claimed that its NSF fees were not interest but fees charged to cover its costs in processing checks drawn on accounts with insufficient funds. How should the court decide this issue? Discuss fully. [*First Bank v. Tony's Tortilla Factory, Inc.*, 877 S.W.2d 285 (Tex. 1994)]

11–9. Gambling Contracts. No law prohibits citizens in a state that does not sponsor a state-operated lottery from purchasing lottery tickets in a state that does have such a lottery. Because Georgia did not have a state-operated lottery, Talley and several other Georgia residents allegedly agreed to purchase a ticket in a lottery sponsored by Kentucky and to share the proceeds if they won. They did win, but apparently Talley had difficulty collecting his share of the proceeds. In Talley's suit to obtain his share of the funds, a Georgia trial court held that the "gambling contract" was unenforceable because it was contrary to Georgia's public policy. On appeal, how should the court rule on this issue? Discuss. [*Talley v. Mathis*, 265 Ga. 179, 453 S.E.2d 704 (1995)]

11–10. Minority. Sergei Samsonov is a Russian and one of the top hockey players in the world. When Samsonov was seventeen years old, he signed a contract to play hockey for two seasons with the Central Sports Army Club, a Russian club known by the abbreviation CSKA. Before the start of the second season, Samsonov learned that because of a dispute between CSKA coaches, he would not be playing in Russia's premier hockey league. Samsonov hired Athletes and Artists, Inc. (A&A), an American sports agency, to make a deal with a U.S. hockey team. Samsonov signed a contract to play for the Detroit Vipers (whose corporate name was, at the time, Arena Associates, Inc.). Neither A&A nor Arena knew about the CSKA contract. CSKA filed a suit in a federal district court against Arena and others, alleging, among other things, wrongful interference with a contractual relationship. What effect will Samsonov's age have on the outcome of this suit? [*Central Sports Army Club v. Arena Associates, Inc.*, 952 F.Supp. 181 (S.D.N.Y. 1997)]

A QUESTION OF ETHICS AND SOCIAL RESPONSIBILITY

11–11. Nancy Levy worked for Health Care Financial Enterprises, Inc., and signed a noncompete agreement in June 1992. When Levy left Health Care and opened up her own similar business in 1993, Health Care brought a court action in a Florida state court to enforce the covenant not to compete. The trial court concluded that the noncompete agreement prevented Levy from working in too broad a geographical area and thus refused to enforce the agreement. A Florida appellate court, however, reversed the trial court's ruling and remanded the case with instructions that the trial court modify the geographical area to make it reasonable and then enforce the covenant. [*Health Care Financial Enterprises, Inc. v. Levy*, 715 So.2d 341 (Fla.App.4th 1998)]

1. At one time in Florida, under the common law, noncompete covenants were illegal, although modern Florida statutory law now allows such covenants to be enforced. Generally, what interests are served by refusing to enforce covenants not to compete? What interests are served by allowing them to be enforced?
2. What argument could be made in support of reforming (and then enforcing) illegal covenants not to compete? What argument could be made against this practice?

FOR CRITICAL ANALYSIS

11–12. Do you think that the advent of legalized forms of gambling, such as state-operated lotteries, is consistent with a continued public policy against the enforcement of gambling contracts? Why or why not?

Online Activities

ONLINE EXERCISE 11-1

Go to the following Web page, which presents a provision in the Indiana Code governing a minor's misrepresentation of age:

www.law.indiana.edu/codes/in/28/ch-28-1-26.5 html.

Read through this provision and then "translate" it into "plain English." (For guidance on "plain English" legal writing, read through Chapters 1 and 6 of the Security and Exchange Commission's handbook on the use of plain English, which is online at www.sec.gov/consumer/plaine.htm.)

ONLINE EXERCISE 11–2

Go to the the "Internet Activities Book" on the Web site that accompanies this text, the URL for which is http://blt.westbuslaw.com. Select the following activity, and perform the exercise according to the instructions given there:

Activity 11–1: State Laws Relating to Contracting Capacity

Before the Test

Go to the *Business Law Today* home page at http://blt.westbuslaw.com. Click on TestTutor.® You will find twenty interactive questions relating to this chapter.

CHAPTER 12

Assent & Form

"Law is a pledge that the citizens of a state will do justice to one another."

Aristotle, 384–322 B.C.E.
(Greek philosopher)

CONTENTS

LEARNING OBJECTIVES

After reading this chapter, you should be able to:

1. Distinguish between a mistake of value or quality and a mistake of fact.
2. Describe fraudulent misrepresentation and its elements.
3. Discuss the effects of undue influence and duress on contract enforceability.
4. Identify the types of contracts that must be in writing to be enforceable.
5. State the parol evidence rule, and indicate when parol evidence will be admissible.

An otherwise valid contract may still be unenforceable if the parties have not genuinely assented to its terms. As mentioned in Chapter 9, lack of genuine assent is a *defense* to the enforcement of a contract. As Aristotle stated in the above quotation, the law seeks to ensure that "the citizens of a state will do justice to one another." If the law were to enforce contracts not genuinely assented to by the contracting parties, injustice would result. The first part of this chapter focuses on the kinds of factors that indicate whether genuineness of assent to a contract may be lacking.

A contract that is otherwise valid may also be unenforceable if it is not in the proper form. For example, if a contract is required by law to be in writing and there is no written evidence of the contract, it may not be enforceable. In the second part of this chapter, we examine the kinds of contracts that require a writing under what is called the *Statute of Frauds*. The chapter concludes with a discussion of the parol evidence rule, under which courts determine the admissibility at trial of evidence extraneous (external) to written contracts.

Genuineness of Assent

Genuineness of assent may be lacking because of mistake, fraudulent misrepresentation, undue influence, or duress. Generally, a party who demonstrates that he or she did not genuinely assent to the terms of a contract can choose either to carry out the contract or to rescind (cancel) it, and thus avoid the entire transaction.

MISTAKES

We all make mistakes, and it is not surprising that mistakes are made when contracts are created. In certain circumstances, contract law allows a contract to be avoided on the basis of mistake. Realize, though, that the concept of mistake in contract law has to do with mistaken assumptions relating to contract formation. For example, if you send your monthly bank loan payment to your plumber "by mistake," that is a kind of mistake totally different from the kind of mistake that we are discussing here. In contract law, a mistake may be a defense to the enforcement of a contract if it can be proved that the parties entered into the contract under different assumptions relating to the subject matter of the contract.

"Mistakes are the inevitable lot of mankind."

SIR GEORGE JESSEL, 1824–1883 (English jurist)

Courts have considerable difficulty in specifying the circumstances that justify allowing a mistake to invalidate a contract. Generally, though, courts distinguish between *mistakes as to judgment of market value or conditions* and *mistakes as to fact.* Only the latter normally have legal significance.

● **EXAMPLE 12.1** Jud Wheeler contracts to buy ten acres of land because he believes that he can resell the land at a profit to Bart. Can Jud escape his contractual obligations if it later turns out that he was mistaken? Not likely. Jud's overestimation of the value of the land or of Bart's interest in it is an ordinary risk of business for which a court will not normally provide relief. Now suppose that Jud purchases a painting of a landscape from Roth's Gallery. Both Jud and Roth believe that the painting is by the artist Van Gogh. Jud later discovers that the painting is a very clever fake. Because neither Jud nor Roth was aware of this fact when they made their deal, Jud can normally rescind the contract and recover the purchase price of the painting. ●

Mistakes occur in two forms—*unilateral* and *bilateral (mutual).* A unilateral mistake is made by only one of the contracting parties; a mutual mistake is made by both.

Unilateral Mistakes A unilateral mistake occurs when only one party is mistaken as to a *material fact*—that is, a fact important to the subject matter of the contract. Generally, a unilateral mistake does not afford the mistaken party any right to relief from the contract. In other words, the contract normally is enforceable against the mistaken party. ● **EXAMPLE 12.2** Ellen intends to sell her motor home for $17,500. When she learns that Chin is interested in buying a used motor home, she types a letter offering to sell her vehicle to him. When typing the letter, however, she mistakenly keys in the price of $15,700. Chin writes back, accepting Ellen's offer. Even though Ellen intended to sell her motor home for $17,500, she has made a unilateral mistake and is bound by contract to sell the vehicle to Chin for $15,700. ●

¡BE CAREFUL!
What a party to a contract knows or should know can determine whether the contract is enforceable.

There are at least two exceptions to this rule.[1] First, if the *other* party to the contract knows or should have known that a mistake of fact was made, the contract may not be enforceable. In the above example, if Chin knew that Ellen intended to sell her motor home for $17,500, then Ellen's unilateral mistake (stating $15,700 in her offer) may render the resulting contract unenforceable. The second exception arises when a unilateral

1. *The Restatement (Second) of Contracts,* Section 153, liberalizes the general rule to take into account the modern trend of allowing avoidance in some circumstances even though only one party has been mistaken.

mistake of fact was due to a mathematical mistake in addition, subtraction, division, or multiplication and was made inadvertently and without gross (extreme) negligence. If a contractor's bid was low because he or she made a mistake in addition when totaling the estimated costs, any contract resulting from the bid normally may be rescinded. Of course, in both situations, the mistake must still involve some *material* fact.

Mutual Mistakes When both parties are mistaken about the same material fact, the contract can be rescinded by either party.[2] Note that, as with unilateral mistakes, the mistake must be about a *material fact* (one that is important and central to the contract—as was the "Van Gogh" painting in Example 12.1). If, instead, a mutual mistake concerns the market value or quality of the object of the contract, the contract normally can be enforced by either party. This rule is based on the theory that both parties assume certain risks when they enter into a contract. Without this rule, almost any party who did not receive what he or she considered a fair bargain could argue bilateral mistake.

A word or term in a contract may be subject to more than one reasonable interpretation. In that situation, if the parties to the contract attach materially different meanings to the term, their mutual misunderstanding may allow the contract to be rescinded. The following classic case on mutual mistake involved a ship called the *Peerless* that was to sail from Bombay with certain cotton goods on board. More than one ship called the *Peerless* sailed from Bombay that winter, however.

2. *Restatement (Second) of Contracts,* Section 152.

CASE 12.1 Raffles v. Wichelhaus

Court of Exchequer, England, 1864.
159 Eng.Rep. 375.
www.courtservice.gov.uk/qbdind.htm[a]

HISTORICAL AND POLITICAL SETTING *Before the Civil War, the states in the southern United States were largely agricultural. By the mid-nineteenth century, the staple of this agricultural area had become cotton. Cotton was important to the economy of the South and to the economy of the European textile industry, which by 1860 was booming. In the 1860s, when the southern states seceded from the United States to form the Confederate States, the United States announced a blockade of southern ports. The states of the Confederacy knew that cotton was important to the European economy, and they were confident that Europe would exert pressure on the United States to lift the blockade. Instead, to obtain cotton, European merchants turned to other sources, including India.*

a. As of this writing, this opinion is not available free on the Internet. Recent opinions of the High Court, Queen's Bench Division (into which the Court of Exchequer was merged in 1881) can be found, however, at this page within "The Court Service Web Site" maintained by the United Kingdom.

BACKGROUND AND FACTS Wichelhaus purchased a shipment of cotton from Raffles to arrive on a ship called the *Peerless* from Bombay, India. Wichelhaus meant a ship called the *Peerless* sailing from Bombay in October; Raffles meant another ship called the *Peerless* sailing from Bombay in December. When the goods arrived on the December *Peerless,* Raffles delivered them to Wichelhaus. By that time, however, Wichelhaus was no longer willing to accept them.

IN THE WORDS OF THE COURT . . .
PER CURIAM [an opinion by the entire court].

* * * *

There is nothing on the face of the contract to show that any particular ship called the "Peerless" was meant; but the moment it appears that two ships called the "Peerless" were about to sail from Bombay there is a latent ambiguity * * * . That being so, there was no consensus * * * , and therefore no binding contract.

(Continued)

CASE 12.1—Continued

DECISION AND REMEDY The judgment was for the defendant, Wichelhaus. The court held that no mutual assent existed, because each party attached a materially different meaning to an essential term of the written contract—that is, a mutual mistake of fact had occurred.

FOR CRITICAL ANALYSIS—Social Consideration *What policy considerations underlie the general rule that contracts involving mutual mistakes of fact may be rescinded, whereas contracts involving unilateral mistakes of fact (with the exceptions discussed earlier) may not be?*

"It was beautiful and simple as all truly great swindles are."

O. HENRY, 1862–1910 (American author)

FRAUDULENT MISREPRESENTATION

Although fraud is a tort, the presence of fraud also affects the genuineness of the innocent party's consent to a contract. When an innocent party consents to a contract with fraudulent terms, the contract usually can be avoided, because he or she has not *voluntarily* consented to the terms.[3] Normally, the innocent party can either rescind (cancel) the contract and be restored to his or her original position or enforce the contract and seek damages for injuries resulting from the fraud.

Typically, there are three elements of fraud:

1. A misrepresentation of a material fact must occur.
2. There must be an intent to deceive.
3. The innocent party must justifiably rely on the misrepresentation.

¡REMEMBER! To collect damages in almost any lawsuit, there must be some sort of injury.

Additionally, to collect damages, a party must have been injured as a result of the misrepresentation.

Misrepresentation Must Occur The first element of proving fraud is to show that misrepresentation of a material fact has occurred. This misrepresentation can take the form of words or actions. For example, an art gallery owner's statement "This painting is a Picasso" is a misrepresentation of fact if the painting was done by another artist.

A statement of opinion is generally not subject to a claim of fraud. For example, claims such as "This computer will never break down" and "This car will last for years and years" are statements of opinion, not fact, and contracting parties should recognize them as such and not rely on them. A fact is objective and verifiable; an opinion is usually subject to debate. Therefore, a seller is allowed to "huff and puff his wares" without being liable for fraud. In certain cases, however, particularly when a naïve purchaser relies on an expert's opinion, the innocent party may be entitled to rescission or reformation (an equitable remedy granted by a court in which the terms of a contract are altered to reflect the true intentions of the parties).

In the following classic case, the court addressed the issue of whether statements made by instructors at a dancing school to one of the school's dance students qualified as statements of opinion or statements of fact.

3. *Restatement (Second) of Contracts,* Sections 163 and 164.

CASE 12.2 Vokes v. Arthur Murray, Inc.

District Court of Appeal of Florida, Second District, 1968. 212 So.2d 906.

HISTORICAL AND SOCIAL SETTING *In the seventeenth century, in some of the new American colonies, the law prohibited professional performances of music. By the time of the Revolutionary War, however, the bans had generally been lifted, and the nineteenth century saw the founding of opera companies, city orchestras, and music schools. In the South, gospel music gave birth to the blues,*

CASE 12.2—Continued

which in turn gave birth to ragtime and jazz. With the development of radio and the recording industries in the first decades of the twentieth century, music became available to an ever-growing American audience, and social dancing became increasingly popular. With the popularity of social dancing came dancing schools.

BACKGROUND AND FACTS Audrey Vokes was a fifty-one-year-old widow. While she was attending a dance party at Davenport's School of Dancing, an Arthur Murray dancing school, an instructor sold her eight half-hour dance lessons for the sum of $14.50. Thereafter, over a period of less than sixteen months, she was sold a total of fourteen dance courses, which amounted to 2,302 hours of dancing lessons for a total cash outlay of $31,090.45. All of these lessons were sold to her by salespersons who continually assured her that she was very talented, that she was progressing in her lessons, that she had great dance potential, and that they were "developing her into a beautiful dancer." Vokes contended that, in fact, she was not progressing in her dancing ability, had no "dance aptitude," and had difficulty even "hearing the musical beat." She filed suit against the school in a Florida state court, seeking rescission of her contract on the ground of fraudulent misrepresentation. When the trial court dismissed her complaint, she appealed.

IN THE WORDS OF THE COURT . . .
PIERCE, Judge.

* * * *

[The dance contracts] were procured by defendant Davenport and Arthur Murray, Inc., by false representations to her that she was improving in her dancing ability, that she had excellent potential, that she was responding to instructions in dancing grace, and that they were developing her into a beautiful dancer, whereas in truth and in fact she did not develop in her dancing ability, she had no "dance aptitude," and in fact had difficulty in "hearing the musical beat." * * *

* * * *

It is true that generally a misrepresentation, to be actionable, must be one of fact rather than of opinion. * * * A statement of a party having * * * superior knowledge may be regarded as a statement of fact although it would be considered as opinion if the parties were dealing on equal terms.

It could be reasonably supposed here that defendants had "superior knowledge" as to whether plaintiff had "dance potential" * * * .

DECISION AND REMEDY The Florida appellate court reinstated Vokes's complaint, which had originally been dismissed from the trial court, and remanded the case to the trial court to allow Vokes to prove her case.

FOR CRITICAL ANALYSIS—Social Consideration
If the law imposed liability for fraudulent misrepresentation on all persons who make false statements of opinion (such as "This car is the best on the road"), as well as on those persons who make false statements of fact (such as "This car has only been driven twelve thousand miles"), would society benefit? Explain.

"Ignorance of the law is no excuse in any country. If it were, the laws would lose their effect, because ignorance can always be pretended."

THOMAS JEFFERSON, 1743–1826
(Third president of the United States, 1801–1809)

Misrepresentation by Conduct. Misrepresentation can occur by conduct, as well as through express oral or written statements. For example, if a seller, by his or her actions, prevents a buyer from learning of some fact that is material to the contract, such an action constitutes misrepresentation by conduct.[4] • **EXAMPLE 12.3** Cummings contracts to purchase a racehorse from Garner. The horse is blind in one eye, but when Garner shows the horse, he skillfully conceals this fact by keeping the horse's head turned so that Cummings does not see the defect. The concealment constitutes fraud. • Another example of misrepresentation by conduct is the false denial of knowledge or information concerning facts that are material to the contract when such knowledge or information is requested.

4. *Restatement (Second) of Contracts,* Section 160.

WORKERS EXCAVATE A SITE AND BURY A SEWER LINE. WOULD THE PARTY WHO CONTRACTED FOR THIS WORK BE LIABLE FOR FRAUD IF THE PARTY KNEW, OR SHOULD HAVE KNOWN, THAT SUBSOIL CONDITIONS COULD INCREASE THE EXPENSE OF THE WORK AND FAILED TO DISCLOSE THIS TO THE BIDDERS?

Misrepresentation of Law. Misrepresentation of law does not *ordinarily* entitle a party to be relieved of a contract. • EXAMPLE 12.4 Debbie has a parcel of property that she is trying to sell to Barry. Debbie knows that a local ordinance prohibits building anything higher than three stories on the property. Nonetheless, she tells Barry, "You can build a condominium fifty stories high if you want to." Barry buys the land and later discovers that Debbie's statement is false. Normally, Barry cannot avoid the contract, because under the common law, people are assumed to know state and local laws.• Exceptions to this rule occur, however, when the misrepresenting party is in a profession known to require greater knowledge of the law than the average citizen possesses.

Misrepresentation by Silence. Ordinarily, neither party to a contract has a duty to come forward and disclose facts, and a contract normally will not be set aside because certain pertinent information has not been volunteered. • EXAMPLE 12.5 Suppose that you are selling a car that has been in an accident and has been repaired. You do not need to volunteer this information to a potential buyer. If, however, the purchaser asks you if the car has had extensive body work and you lie, you have committed a fraudulent misrepresentation.•

Generally, if a serious defect or a *serious* potential problem is known to the seller but cannot reasonably be suspected to be known by the buyer, the seller may have a duty to speak. • EXAMPLE 12.6 Suppose that a city fails to disclose to bidders for sewer-construction contracts the fact that subsoil conditions will cause great expense in constructing the sewer. In this situation, the city has committed fraud.[5]• Also, when the parties are in a fiduciary relationship (one of trust, such as partners, physician and patient, or attorney and client), there is a duty to disclose material facts; failure to do so may constitute fraud. (See this chapter's *Business Law in*

5. *City of Salinas v. Souza & McCue Construction Co.*, 66 Cal.2d 217, 424 P.2d 921, 57 Cal.Rptr. 337 (1967). Normally, the seller must disclose only "latent" defects—that is, defects that would not readily be discovered. Thus, termites in a house would not be a latent defect, because a buyer could normally discover their presence.

Action for a discussion of whether an employer has a duty to disclose pertinent information concerning a company's financial situation to a potential employee.)

● ***SCIENTER***
Knowledge by the misrepresenting party that material facts have been falsely represented or omitted with an intent to deceive.

Intent to Deceive The second element of fraud is knowledge on the part of the misrepresenting party that facts have been misrepresented. This element, normally called ***scienter,***[6] or "guilty knowledge," generally signifies that there was an intent to deceive. *Scienter* clearly exists if a party knows that a fact is not as stated. *Scienter* also exists if a party makes a statement that he or she believes not to be true or makes a statement recklessly, without regard to whether it is true or false. Finally, this element is met if a party says or implies that a statement is made on some basis, such as personal knowledge or personal investigation, when it is not.

● **EXAMPLE 12.7** Suppose that Rolando, when selling a house to Cariton, tells Cariton that the plumbing pipe is of a certain quality. Rolando knows nothing about the quality of the pipe but does not believe it to be what she is representing it to be (and in fact it is not what she says it is). Rolando's statement induces Cariton to buy the house. Rolando's statement is a fradulent misrepresentation, because Rolando

6. Pronounced sy-*en*-ter.

Business Law in Action • "SILENT FRAUD" IN THE EMPLOYMENT CONTEXT

The concept of "silent fraud" dates back to at least 1886. In that year, the Michigan Supreme Court held that "[a] fraud arising from the suppression of the truth is as prejudicial as that which springs from the assertion of a falsehood, and courts have not hesitated to sustain recoveries where the truth has been suppressed with the intent to defraud."[a]

One of the problems with claims of silent fraud is that it is not always clear what information a party to a contract is required to disclose to the other party. For example, does a company have a duty to disclose to prospective employees the most current information concerning the financial health of the company?

This question arose in a recent case brought by R. Michael Hord against the Environmental Research Institute of Michigan (ERIM). When Hord was interviewed for a position with ERIM, he was told by company representatives that they would be able to fund long-term projects. During the interview, they gave Hord a copy of the company's financial statement, showing profitable operations. The statement they showed Hord, however, was not the most recent one—which showed losses. A year later, Hord was laid off because ERIM had suffered financial losses. Hord subsequently sued ERIM for fraudulent misrepresentation and "silent fraud."

A Michigan trial court jury held in favor of Hord, and the verdict was upheld on appeal. The appellate court stated that ERIM's act of giving Hord an out-of-date operating summary financial statement, when a more recent one was readily available, "constituted an endorsement of [ERIM's] current financial strength. This was obviously a material misrepresentation, and the act of giving the operating summary to [Hord] during a job interview allowed the jury to infer that [ERIM] intended that Hord act on it."[b]

During job interviews, in order to lure qualified employees, prospective employers often "promise the moon" and paint their companies' prospects as bright. Employers must be careful, though, to avoid any conduct that could be interpreted by a court as intentionally deceptive. Additionally, when a job candidate requests information about a company's financial health, the employer must respond truthfully.[c]

FOR CRITICAL ANALYSIS

What if ERIM assumed that its current financial situation was only temporary? Should this assumption be given any weight by the court in evaluating the "silent fraud" claim?

a. *Tompkins v. Hollister,* 60 Mich. 470, 27 N.W. 651 (1886).

b. *Hord v. Environmental Research Institute of Michigan,* 228 Mich.App. 638, 579 N.W.2d 133 (1998).

c. See, for example, *Clement-Rowe v. Michigan Health Care Corp.,* 212 Mich.App. 503, 538 N.W.2d 20 (1995).

does not believe that what she says is true and because she knows that she does not have any basis for making the statement. Cariton can avoid the contract. •

¡REMEMBER!
An opinion is not a contract offer, not a contract term, and not fraud.

Reliance on the Misrepresentation The third element of fraud is *justifiable reliance* on the misrepresentation of fact. The deceived party must have a justifiable reason for relying on the misrepresentation, and the misrepresentation must be an important factor (but not necessarily the sole factor) in inducing the party to enter into the contract.

Reliance is not justified if the innocent party knows the true facts or relies on obviously extravagant statements. • EXAMPLE 12.8 If a used-car dealer tells you, "This old Cadillac will get over sixty miles to the gallon," you normally would not be justified in relying on this statement. Suppose, however, that Merkel, a bank director, induces O'Connell, a co-director, to sign a statement that the bank's assets will satisfy its liabilities by telling O'Connell, "We have plenty of assets to satisfy our creditors." This statement is false. If O'Connell knows the true facts, or, as a bank director should know the true facts, he is not justified in relying on Merkel's statement. If O'Connell does not know the true facts, however, *and has no way of finding them out,* he may be justified in relying on the statement. •

Injury to the Innocent Party Most courts do not require a showing of injury when the action is to *rescind* (cancel) the contract—these courts hold that because rescission returns the parties to the positions they held before the contract was made, a showing of injury to the innocent party is unnecessary.[7]

For a person to recover damages caused by fraud, however, proof of an injury is universally required. The measure of damages is ordinarily equal to the property's value had it been delivered as represented, less the actual price paid for the property. In actions based on fraud, courts often award *punitive,* or *exemplary, damages*—which are granted to a plaintiff over and above the proved, actual compensation for the loss. As pointed out in Chapter 4, punitive damages are based on the public-policy consideration of punishing the defendant or setting an example to deter similar wrongdoing by others.

7. See, for example, *Kaufman v. Jaffe,* 244 App.Div. 344, 279 N.Y.S. 392 (1935).

The Letter of the Law PROMISES, PROMISES

At one time, "breach of promise" suits allowed plaintiffs to recover under the common law (and under some state statutes) for breach of promises of love and affection. Such suits, however, were largely banned long ago by "anti-heart-balm" statutes, which expressed a public policy against litigating affairs of the heart. Nonetheless, old laws allowing "breach of promise" suits are still on the books in some states.

For example, in a case brought in a Kentucky state court, Suzanne Barkes sought damages from her former fiancé, Alvin Gilbert, on the ground that he breached his promise to marry her. Barkes had apparently quit her job, sold her house, and moved into Gilbert's home in reliance on Gilbert's promise of marriage—only to be "dumped" by Gilbert when the relationship deteriorated. The trial court dismissed the case, but an appellate court held that the suit could go forward. The appellate judges concluded that even though Barkes would probably not win her case, such suits were permitted under an antiquated state statute.[a]

THE BOTTOM LINE

For some judges, the law is the law, even if it happens to be embodied in an antiquated statute.

a. As reported in *Lawyers Weekly USA,* June 2, 1997, p. 19.

UNDUE INFLUENCE

Undue influence arises from relationships in which one party can greatly influence another party, thus overcoming that party's free will. Minors and elderly people, for example, are often under the influence of guardians. If a guardian induces a young or elderly ward (a person placed by a court under the care of a guardian) to enter into a contract that benefits the guardian, the guardian may have exerted undue influence.

Undue influence can arise from a number of confidential relationships or relationships founded on trust, including attorney-client, physician-patient, guardian-ward, parent-child, husband-wife, and trustee-beneficiary relationships. The essential feature of undue influence is that the party being taken advantage of does not, in reality, exercise free will in entering into a contract. A contract entered into under excessive or undue influence lacks genuine assent and is therefore voidable.[8]

DURESS

Assent to the terms of a contract is not genuine if one of the parties is forced into the agreement. Forcing a party to enter into a contract because of the fear created by threats is legally defined as *duress*.[9] In addition, blackmail or extortion to induce consent to a contract constitutes duress. Duress is both a defense to the enforcement of a contract and a ground for rescission, or cancellation, of a contract. Therefore, a party who signs a contract under duress can choose to carry out the contract or to avoid the entire transaction. (The wronged party usually has this choice in cases in which assent is not real or genuine.)

Economic need is generally not sufficient to constitute duress, even when one party exacts a very high price for an item the other party needs. If the party exacting the price also creates the need, however, economic duress may be found. • **EXAMPLE 12.9** The Internal Revenue Service (IRS) assessed a large tax and penalty against Weller. Weller retained Eyman to resist the assessment. Two days before the deadline for filing a reply with the IRS, Eyman declined to represent Weller unless Weller agreed to pay a very high fee for Eyman's services. The agreement was held to be unenforceable.[10] Although Eyman had threatened only to withdraw his services, something that he was legally entitled to do, he was responsible for delaying his withdrawal until the last two days. Because Weller was forced into either signing the contract or losing his right to challenge the IRS assessment, the agreement was secured under duress. •

The Statute of Frauds—Requirement of a Writing

• **STATUTE OF FRAUDS**
A state statute under which certain types of contracts must be in writing to be enforceable.

Today, every state has a statute that stipulates what types of contracts must be in writing. In this text, we refer to such statutes as the **Statute of Frauds.** The primary purpose of the statute is to ensure that there is reliable evidence of the existence and terms of certain classes of contracts deemed historically to be important or complex. Although the statutes vary slightly from state to state, the following types of contracts are normally required to be in writing or evidenced by a written memorandum:

1. Contracts involving interests in land.
2. Contracts that cannot by their terms be performed within one year from the date of formation.

8. *Restatement (Second) of Contracts*, Section 177.
9. *Restatement (Second) of Contracts*, Sections 174 and 175.
10. *Thompson Crane & Trucking Co. v. Eyman*, 123 Cal.App.2d 904, 267 P.2d 1043 (1954).

3. Collateral contracts, such as promises to answer for the debt or duty of another.
4. Promises made in consideration of marriage.
5. Contracts for the sale of goods priced at $500 or more.

Agreements or promises that fit into one or more of these categories are said to "fall under" or "fall within" the Statute of Frauds.

Certain exceptions are made to the applicability of the Statute of Frauds in some circumstances. These exceptions are discussed later in this section.

The actual name of the Statute of Frauds is misleading, because it does not apply to fraud. Rather, the statute denies enforceability to certain contracts that do not comply with its requirements. The name derives from an English act passed in 1677, which is presented here as this chapter's *Landmark in the Law.*

Landmark in the Law • THE STATUTE OF FRAUDS

On April 12, 1677, the English Parliament passed "An Act for the Prevention of Frauds and Perjuries." Four days later, the act was signed by King Charles II and became the law of the land. The act contained twenty-five sections and required that certain types of contracts, if they were to be enforceable by the courts, would henceforth have to be in writing or evidenced by a written memorandum.[a]

The British act was created specifically to prevent the further perpetration of the many frauds that had been brought about through the perjured testimony of witnesses in cases involving breached oral agreements, for which no written evidence existed. Although in the early history of common law in England, oral contracts were generally not enforced by the courts, they began to be enforced in the fourteenth century in certain *assumpsit actions.*[b] These actions, to which the origins of modern contract law are traced, allowed a party to sue and obtain relief in cases in which a promise or contract had been breached. Enforcement of oral promises in actions in *assumpsit* became a common practice in the king's courts during the next two centuries.

KING CHARLES II, UNDER WHOSE REIGN PARLIAMENT ENACTED THE STATUTE OF FRAUDS. WHAT REASONS SUPPORT THE APPLICATION OF THE STATUTE TODAY?

Because courts enforced oral contracts on the strength of oral testimony by witnesses, it was not too difficult to evade justice by alleging that a contract had been breached and then procuring "convincing" witnesses to support the claim. The possibility of fraud in such actions was enhanced by the fact that in seventeenth-century England, courts did not allow oral testimony to be given by the parties to a lawsuit—or by any parties with an interest in the litigation, such as husbands or wives. Defense against actions for breach of contract was thus limited to written evidence and the testimony given by third parties.

Essentially, the Statute of Frauds offers a defense against oral contracts that fall under the statute. If a contract is oral when it is required to be in writing, it will not, as a rule, be enforced by the courts.

FOR CRITICAL ANALYSIS
How does the Statute of Frauds benefit society economically—that is, in terms of the costs associated with litigation?

a. These contracts are discussed in the text of this chapter.

b. *Assumpsit* is Latin for "he undertook" or "he promised." The emergence of remedies given on the basis of breached promises and duties dates to these actions. One of the earliest occurred in 1370, when the court allowed an individual to sue a person who, in trying to cure the plaintiff's horse, had acted so negligently that the horse died. Another such action was permitted in 1375, when a plaintiff obtained relief for having been maimed by a surgeon hired to cure him.

EXHIBIT 12–1 • The One-Year Rule

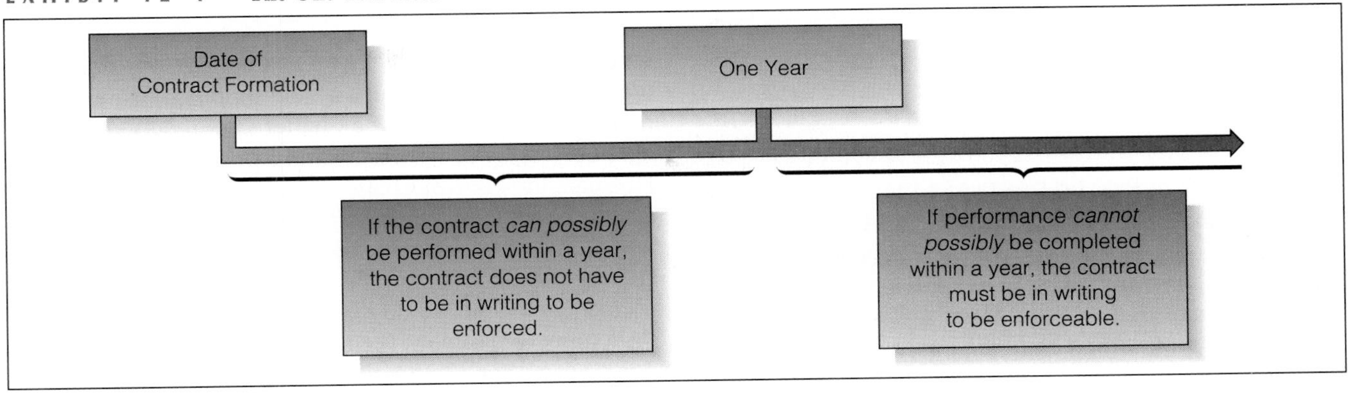
Date of
Contract Formation
One Year
If the contract *can possibly* be performed within a year, the contract does not have to be in writing to be enforced.
If performance *cannot possibly* be completed within a year, the contract must be in writing to be enforceable.

CONTRACTS INVOLVING INTERESTS IN LAND

Land is a form of *real property,* which includes not only land but all physical objects that are permanently attached to the soil, such as buildings, plants, trees, and the soil itself. Under the Statute of Frauds, a contract involving an *interest* in land, to be enforceable, must be evidenced by a writing.[11] If Carol, for example, contracts orally to sell Seaside Shelter to Axel but later decides not to sell, Axel cannot enforce the contract. Similarly, if Axel refuses to close the deal, Carol cannot force Axel to pay for the land by bringing a lawsuit. The Statute of Frauds is a *defense* to the enforcement of this type of oral contract.

A contract for the sale of land ordinarily involves the entire interest in the real property, including buildings, growing crops, vegetation, minerals, timber, and anything else affixed to the land. Therefore, a *fixture* (personal property so affixed or so used as to become a part of the realty—see Chapter 41) is treated as real property.

The Statute of Frauds requires written contracts not just for the sale of land but also for the transfer of other interests in land, such as mortgages and leases. We describe these other interests in Chapter 41.

THE ONE-YEAR RULE

Contracts that cannot, *by their own terms,* be performed within one year from the day after the contract is formed must be in writing to be enforceable. Because disputes over such contracts are unlikely to occur until some time after the contracts are made, resolution of these disputes is difficult unless the contract terms have been put in writing. The one-year period begins to run *the day after the contract is made.* Exhibit 12–1 illustrates the one-year rule.

Normally, the test for determining whether an oral contract is enforceable under the one-year rule of the Statute of Frauds is not whether the agreement is *likely* to be performed within one year from the date of contract formation but whether performance within a year is *possible.* When performance of a contract is objectively impossible during the one-year period, the oral contract will be unenforceable. In the following case, the question before the court was whether an oral contract for lifetime employment was enforceable.

11. In some states, the contract will be enforced, however, if each party admits to the existence of the oral contract in court or admits to its existence during discovery before trial (see Chapter 3).

CASE 12.3 McInerney v. Charter Golf, Inc.

Supreme Court of Illinois, 1997.
176 Ill.2d 482,
680 N.E.2d 1347,
223 Ill.Dec. 911.
www.state.il.us/court/supremes/80248.txt[a]

HISTORICAL AND SOCIAL SETTING *The purpose of the English Statute of Frauds was to prohibit "many fraudulent practices, which are commonly endeavored to be upheld by perjury and subordination of perjury." The many statutes of frauds in the United States seek to do the same by barring lawsuits based on nothing more than loose verbal statements. The one-year provision recognizes that with the passage of time evidence becomes stale and memories fade. This provision functions as an evidentiary safeguard. It protects not just the parties to a contract but also a court from charlatans, liars, and the problems of proof accompanying oral contracts.*

a. This is a page within a Web site maintained by the state of Illinois that includes some of the recent "Opinions of the Illinois Supreme and Appellate Courts."

BACKGROUND AND FACTS Charter Golf, Inc., manufactures and sells golf apparel and supplies. Dennis McInerney had worked as a Charter sales representative for about a year when he was offered a position with Hickey-Freeman, Inc., one of Charter's competitors. Jerry Montiel, Charter's president, urged McInerney to turn down the offer and promised to guarantee him a 10 percent commission "for the remainder of his life." Montiel also promised McInerney that he would be subject to discharge only for dishonesty or disability. McInerney accepted Montiel's offer. Three years later, Charter fired McInerney. McInerney filed a suit in an Illinois state court against Charter, alleging breach of contract. Charter argued in part that Montiel's oral promises were not enforceable because they were not capable of being performed within one year. The trial court ruled in favor of Charter, and the state intermediate appellate court affirmed. McInerney appealed to the Supreme Court of Illinois.

IN THE WORDS OF THE COURT . . .
Justice *HEIPLE* delivered the opinion of the court:

* * * *

* * * A "lifetime" employment contract is, in essence, a permanent employment contract. Inherently, it anticipates a relationship of long duration—certainly longer than one year. In the context of an employment-for-life contract, we believe that the better view is to treat the contract as one not to be performed within the space of one year from the making thereof. To hold otherwise would eviscerate the policy underlying the statute of frauds and would invite confusion, uncertainty and outright fraud. Accordingly, we hold that a writing is required for the fair enforcement of lifetime employment contracts.

* * * * *

In sum, though an employee's promise to forgo another job opportunity in exchange for a guarantee of lifetime employment is consideration to support the formation of a contract, the statute of frauds requires that contracts for lifetime employment be in writing.

DECISION AND REMEDY The Supreme Court of Illinois affirmed the lower court's decision. The state supreme court held that an employer's promise of lifetime employment in exchange for an employee's promise to forgo a job opportunity needs to be in writing to satisfy the Statute of Frauds.

FOR CRITICAL ANALYSIS—Social Consideration *If the Statute of Frauds were repealed—as it has been in some countries—what might be the effect on the results in cases such as McInerney's?*

Collateral Promises

• **COLLATERAL PROMISE**
A secondary promise that is ancillary (subsidiary) to a principal transaction or primary contractual relationship, such as a promise made by one person to pay the debts of another if the latter fails to perform. A collateral promise normally must be in writing to be enforceable.

A **collateral promise,** or secondary promise, is one that is ancillary (subsidiary) to a principal transaction or primary contractual relationship. In other words, a collateral promise is one made by a third party to assume the debts or obligations of a primary party to a contract if that party does not perform. Any collateral promise of this nature falls under the Statute of Frauds and therefore must be in writing to be enforceable. To understand this concept, it is important to distinguish between primary and secondary promises and obligations.

Primary versus Secondary Obligations Suppose that Kenneth orally contracts with Joanne's Floral Boutique to send his mother a dozen roses for Mother's Day. Kenneth promises to pay the boutique when he receives the bill for the flowers. Kenneth is a direct party to this contract and has incurred a *primary* obligation under the contract. Because he is a party to the contract and has a primary obligation to Joanne's Floral Boutique, this contract does not fall under the Statute of Frauds and does not have to be in writing to be enforceable. If Kenneth fails to pay the florist and the florist sues him for payment, Kenneth cannot raise the Statute of Frauds as a defense. He cannot claim that the contract is unenforceable because it was not in writing.

Now suppose that Kenneth's mother borrows $1,000 from the Medford Trust Company on a promissory note payable six months later. Kenneth promises the bank officer handling the loan that he will pay the $1,000 *if his mother does not pay the loan on time*. Kenneth, in this situation, becomes what is known as a *guarantor* on the loan. That is, he is guaranteeing to the bank (the creditor) that he will pay the loan if his mother fails to do so. This kind of collateral promise, in which the guarantor states that he or she will become responsible only if the primary party does not perform, must be in writing to be enforceable. We return to the concept of guaranty and the distinction between primary and secondary obligations in Chapter 23, in the context of creditors' rights.

An Exception—The "Main Purpose" Rule An oral promise to answer for the debt of another is covered by the Statute of Frauds *unless* the guarantor's purpose in accepting secondary liability is to secure a personal benefit. Under the "main purpose" rule, this type of contract need not be in writing.[12] The assumption is that a court can infer from the circumstances of a case whether a "leading objective" of the promisor was to secure a personal benefit.

• **Example 12.10** Oswald contracts with Machine Manufacturing Company to have some machines custom-made for Oswald's factory. She promises Allrite Materials Supply Company, Machine Manufacturing's supplier, that if Allrite continues to deliver materials to Machine Manufacturing, she will guarantee payment. This promise need not be in writing, even though the effect may be to pay the debt of another, because Oswald's main purpose is to secure a benefit for herself.[13] •

Another typical application of the so-called main purpose doctrine is the situation in which one creditor guarantees the debtor's debt to another creditor to forestall litigation. This allows the debtor to remain in business long enough to generate profits sufficient to pay *both* creditors. In this situation, the guaranty does not need to be in writing to be enforceable.

12. *Restatement (Second) of Contracts,* Section 116.
13. See *Kampman v. Pittsburgh Contracting and Engineering Co.,* 316 Pa. 502, 175 A. 396 (1934).

Schwadron/Cartoonists & Writers Syndicate.

"And do you, Bob, agree to the wording of Alice's pre-nuptial agreements, and do you, Alice, agree to the wording of Bob's?"

Promises Made in Consideration of Marriage

• **PRENUPTIAL AGREEMENT**
An agreement made before marriage that defines each partner's ownership rights in the other partner's property. Prenuptial agreements must be in writing to be enforceable.

A unilateral promise to pay a sum of money or to give property in consideration of marriage must be in writing. If Mr. Baumann promises to pay Joe Villard $10,000 if Villard marries Baumann's daughter, the promise must be in writing to be enforceable. The same rule applies to **prenuptial agreements**—agreements made before marriage (also called *antenuptial agreements*) that define each partner's ownership rights in the other partner's property. For example, a prospective wife or husband may wish to limit the amount the prospective spouse could obtain if the marriage ended in divorce. Prenuptial agreements made in consideration of marriage must be in writing to be enforceable.

Generally, courts tend to give more credence to prenuptial agreements that are accompanied by consideration. • **Example 12.11** Maureen, who has little money, marries Kaiser, who has a net worth of $300 million. Kaiser has several children, and he wants them to receive most of his wealth on his death. Prior to their marriage, Maureen and Kaiser draft and sign a prenuptial agreement in which Kaiser promises to give Maureen $100,000 per year for the rest of her life should they divorce. As consideration for her consenting to this amount, Kaiser offers Maureen $500,000. If Maureen consents to the agreement and accepts the $500,000, very likely a court would hold this to be a valid prenuptial agreement should the agreement ever be contested. •

ETHICAL ISSUE 12.1 ***Should prenuptial agreements be enforced if one party did not have advice of counsel?*** Cases occasionally come before the courts in which a party to a prenuptial agreement claims that the agreement should not be enforced for one reason or another. One reason that is sometimes given is that the party was not advised to obtain an attorney's advice before signing the agreement. In a recent case, for example, a woman challenged the enforceability of a prenuptial agreement on the ground that her husband's lawyer, who was hired to draft the agreement, did not advise her to have it reviewed by her own attorney. The Supreme Court of North Dakota held that the agreement may be unenforceable. The court joined a number of other jurisdictions in concluding that advice of independent counsel is a significant factor in determining whether a party signed a prenuptial agreement voluntarily.[14]

CONTRACTS FOR THE SALE OF GOODS

ON THE WEB

The online version of UCC Section 2–201 on the Statute of Frauds includes links to definitions of certain terms used in the section. To access this site, go to www.law.cornell.edu/ucc/2/2-201.html.

The Uniform Commercial Code (UCC) contains Statute of Frauds provisions that require written evidence of a contract. Section 2–201 contains the major provision, which generally requires a writing or memorandum for the sale of goods priced at $500 or more. A writing that will satisfy the UCC requirement need only state the quantity term; other terms agreed on need not be stated "accurately" in the writing, as long as they adequately reflect both parties' intentions. The contract will not be enforceable, however, for any quantity greater than that set forth in the writing. In addition, the writing must be signed by the person against whom enforcement is sought. Beyond these two requirements, the writing need not designate the buyer or the seller, the terms of payment, or the price.

International Perspective • THE STATUTE OF FRAUDS AND INTERNATIONAL SALES CONTRACTS

As you will read in Chapter 15, the Convention on Contracts for the International Sale of Goods (CISG) provides rules that govern international sales contracts between countries that have ratified the convention (agreement). Article 11 of the CISG does not incorporate any Statute of Frauds provisions. Rather, it states that a "contract for sale need not be concluded in or evidenced by writing and is not subject to any other requirements as to form."

Article 11 accords with the legal customs of most nations, in which contracts no longer need to meet certain formal or writing requirements to be enforceable. Ironically, even England, the nation that created the original Statute of Frauds in 1677, has repealed all of it except the provisions relating to collateral promises and to transfers of interests in land. Many other countries that once had such statutes have also repealed all or parts of them. Civil law countries, such as France, never have required certain types of contracts to be in writing.

FOR CRITICAL ANALYSIS

If there were no Statute of Frauds and if a dispute arose concerning an oral agreement, how would the parties substantiate their respective positions?

EXCEPTIONS TO THE STATUTE OF FRAUDS

Exceptions to the applicability of the Statute of Frauds are made in certain situations. We describe those situations here.

Partial Performance In cases involving contracts relating to the transfer of interests in land, if the purchaser has paid part of the price, taken possession, and made valuable improvements to the property, and if the parties cannot be returned to their status quo prior to the contract, a court may grant *specific performance* (performance of the contract according to its precise terms). Whether the courts will enforce an oral contract for an interest in land when partial performance has taken place is

14. *Estate of Lutz,* 563 N.W.2d 90 (N.Dak. 1997).

usually determined by the degree of injury that would be suffered if the court chose *not* to enforce the oral contract. In some states, mere reliance on certain types of oral contracts is enough to remove them from the Statute of Frauds.

Under the UCC, an oral contract for goods priced at $500 or more is enforceable to the extent that a seller accepts payment or a buyer accepts delivery of the goods.[15] For example, if Ajax Corporation ordered by telephone twenty crates of bleach from Cloney, Inc., and repudiated the contract after ten crates had been delivered and accepted, Cloney could enforce the contract to the extent of the ten crates accepted by Ajax.

Admissions In some states, if a party against whom enforcement of an oral contract is sought "admits" in pleadings, testimony, or otherwise in court proceedings that a contract for sale was made, the contract will be enforceable.[16] A contract subject to the UCC will be enforceable, but only to the extent of the quantity admitted.[17] Thus, if the president of Ajax Corporation admits under oath that an oral agreement was made with Cloney, Inc., for the twenty crates of bleach, the agreement will be enforceable to that extent.

> **ON THE WEB**
> For information on the *Restatements of the Law,* including the *Restatement (Second) of Contracts,* go to the American Law Institute's Web site at www.ali.org.

Promissory Estoppel In some states, an oral contract that would otherwise be unenforceable under the Statute of Frauds may be enforced under the doctrine of promissory estoppel, or detrimental reliance. Recall from Chapter 10 that if a promisor makes a promise on which the promisee justifiably relies to his or her detriment, a court may *estop* (prevent) the promisor from denying that a contract exists. Section 139 of the *Restatement (Second) of Contracts* provides that in these circumstances, an oral promise can be enforceable notwithstanding the Statute of Frauds if the reliance was foreseeable to the person making the promise and if injustice can be avoided only by enforcing the promise.

ETHICAL ISSUE 12.2 ***Does the Statute of Frauds cause more injustice than it prevents?*** Since its inception three hundred years ago, the Statute of Frauds has been criticized by some because, although it was created to protect the innocent, it can also be used as a technical defense by a party who has breached a genuine, mutually agreed-on oral contract—if the contract falls within the Statute of Frauds. For this reason, some legal scholars believe the act has caused more fraud than it has prevented. Thus, exceptions are sometimes made, such as under the doctrine of promissory estoppel. To be sure, enforcing an oral contract on the basis of a party's reliance arguably undercuts the essence of the Statute of Frauds, yet this exception is made to prevent the statute—which was created to prevent injustice—from being used to promote injustice. Nevertheless, the doctrine of promissory estoppel is controversial, as is the Statute of Frauds itself.

Special Exceptions under the UCC Special exceptions to the applicability of the Statute of Frauds apply to sales contracts. Oral contracts for customized goods may be enforced in certain circumstances. Another exception has to do with oral contracts between merchants that have been confirmed in writing. We will examine these exceptions in Chapter 15.

---

15. UCC 2–201(3)(c). See Chapter 15.
16. *Restatement (Second) of Contracts,* Section 133.
17. UCC 2–201(3)(b). See Chapter 15.

The Statute of Frauds—Sufficiency of the Writing

ON THE WEB

If you are interested in learning about the American Bar Association's "Digital Signature Guidelines," go to www.abanet.org/scitech/ec/isc/dsg.toc.html.

A written contract will satisfy the writing requirement of the Statute of Frauds. A *written memorandum* (written evidence of the oral contract) signed by the party against whom enforcement is sought will also satisfy the writing requirement.[18] The signature need not be placed at the end of the document but can be anywhere in the writing; it can even be initials rather than the full name. (A major concern in today's world is how "signatures" can be created and verified on electronic contracts and other documents—see this chapter's *Technology and Electronic Signatures* for a discussion of this issue.)

A writing can consist of any confirmation, invoice, sales slip, check, or fax—or such items in combination. The written contract need not consist of a single document to constitute an enforceable contract. One document may incorporate another document by expressly referring to it. Several documents may form a single contract

18. As mentioned earlier, under the UCC Statute of Frauds, a writing is only required for contracts for the sale of goods priced at $500 or more. See Chapter 15.

Technology and Electronic Signatures

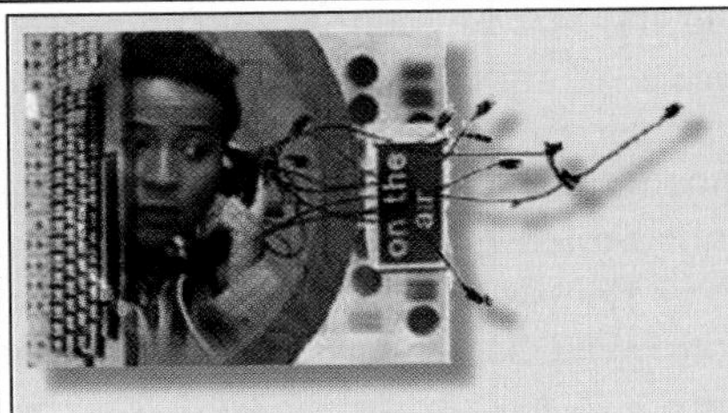

Before the days when most people could write, they signed documents with an "X." Then came the handwritten signature, followed by typed signatures, printed signatures, and, most recently, digital signatures that are transmitted electronically. Throughout the evolution of signature technology, debates over what constitutes a valid signature have occurred, and with good reason: without some consensus on what constitutes a valid signature, little business or legal work could be accomplished. Generally, any contract or other legally binding document requires the signatures of the parties involved. As discussed elsewhere in this chapter, contracts required to be in writing by the Statute of Frauds also must meet certain signature requirements.

Today, there are numerous technologies that allow electronic documents to be signed. Indeed, most states have passed legislation—or will do so relatively soon—dealing with such electronic signatures. As of 1999, thirty-eight states had digital signature laws on the books. For example, in 1997 California adopted legislation that allows any technology to be used that satisfies existing signature requirements governing the filing of documents with the state agency. So, any company using technology that captures and encrypts a handwritten signature using a special pen attached to a computer would satisfy the new California legislation.

Some argue that an electronic signature should be deemed valid only if a public-private/dual-key encryption system is used. In such a system, a person attaches a digital signature to a document using a private key, or code. The key has a publicly available counterpart. Anyone can use it with the appropriate software to verify that the digital signature was made using the private key. A legally recognized certification authority, or "cyber notary," issues the key pair, identifies the owner of the keys, and certifies the validity of the public key. The cyber notary also serves as a repository for public keys. Cyber notaries already exist, but they do not operate within any existing legal framework because they are so new.

The National Conference of Commissioners (NCC) on Uniform State Laws and the American Law Institute (ALI) have recommended that some verification procedure for digital signatures be included in future uniform state laws, particularly in the newly drafted Article 2B of the Uniform Commercial Code.

FOR CRITICAL ANALYSIS

How could a party to a contract know whether the digital signature of the other party was used by someone else, such as an imposter who misappropriated the private key?

INTERNET CONNECT

if they are physically attached, by staple, paper clip, or glue. Several documents may form a single contract even if they are only placed in the same envelope.

• **EXAMPLE 12.12** Sam orally agrees to sell to Terry some land next to a shopping mall. Sam gives to Terry an unsigned memo that contains a legal description of the property, and Terry gives to Sam an unsigned first draft of their contract. Sam writes a signed letter to Terry that refers to the memo and to the first and final drafts of the contract. Terry sends to Sam an unsigned copy of the final draft of the contract with a signed check stapled to it. Together, the documents can constitute a writing sufficient to satisfy the Statute of Frauds and bind both parties to the terms of the contract as evidenced by the writings. •

A memorandum evidencing the oral contract need only contain the essential terms of the contract. Under most provisions of the Statute of Frauds, the writing must name the parties, subject matter, consideration, and quantity. With respect to contracts for the sale of land, some states require that the memorandum also state the essential terms of the contract, such as location and price, with sufficient clarity to allow the terms to be determined from the memo itself, without reference to any outside sources.[19] Under the UCC, in regard to the sale of goods, the writing need only name the quantity term and be signed by the party against whom enforcement is sought.

Because only the party against whom enforcement is sought need have signed the writing, a contract may be enforceable by one of its parties but not by the other. • **EXAMPLE 12.13** Rock orally agrees to buy Devlin's lake house and lot for $150,000. Devlin writes Rock a letter confirming the sale by identifying the parties and the essential terms of the sales contract—price, method of payment, and legal address—and signs the letter. Devlin has made a written memorandum of the oral land contract. Because she signed the letter, she normally can be held to the oral contract by Rock. Rock, however, because he has not signed or entered into a written contract or memorandum, can plead the Statute of Frauds as a defense, and Devlin cannot enforce the contract against him. • The following classic case illustrates what may be considered a "signed writing" by the court.

19. *Rhodes v. Wilkins*, 83 N.M. 782, 498 P.2d 311 (1972).

CASE 12.4 Drury v. Young

Court of Appeals of Maryland, 1882.
58 Md. 546.

HISTORICAL AND ECONOMIC SETTING *Changes in the weather have sometimes affected U.S. harvests dramatically. In 1880, U.S. wheat production was up more than 200 percent over production a dozen years before. Due in part to this greater quantity of wheat on the market, the price was down nearly 30 percent. Corn production was so high, and prices so low, that many corn farmers burned corn for fuel because it was cheaper than shipping the crop to market. The next year, drought struck the United States, and harvests were poor. This caused prices to rise in 1882. At the time, one popular dish was sliced tomatoes with sugar and vinegar.*

BACKGROUND AND FACTS The plaintiff, Young, formed an oral agreement with the defendant, Drury, to buy several carloads of tomatoes. Afterward, Drury wrote a memorandum concerning the agreement and all its terms for his own records and put it in his safe. The memo, which Drury did not sign, was created on Drury's letterhead (which is a sufficient signing in the eyes of the court) and contained Young's name in the text. Subsequently, Drury wrote a letter to Young stating he was not going to sell Young the tomatoes as agreed. When Young sued Drury in a Maryland state court for breach of contract, Drury used the Statute of Frauds as a defense. The trial court held in Young's favor, claiming that Drury's memo (even if it was never delivered to Young), combined with the subsequent letter, satisfied the writing requirement of the Statute of Frauds. Drury appealed. Ultimately, the Court of Appeals of Maryland (that state's highest court) reviewed the case.

IN THE WORDS OF THE COURT . . .

CASE 12.4—Continued

STONE, J. delivered the opinion of the court.

* * * *

Now the Statute [of Frauds] is entirely silent on the question of the delivery of the note or memorandum of the bargain, and its literal requirements are fulfilled by the existence of the note or memorandum of the bargain, signed by the party to be charged thereby. The Statute itself deals exclusively with the existence and not with the custody of the paper.

* * * *

If the * * * memorandum was insufficient of itself, the * * * letter addressed by defendants to plaintiff, and which sufficiently refers in its terms to the former note or memorandum, would certainly be sufficient when taken in connection with it, to take this case out of the Statute * * * .

DECISION AND REMEDY The Court of Appeals of Maryland affirmed the trial court's decision.

FOR CRITICAL ANALYSIS—Technological Consideration *How does the existence of electronic mail (e-mail) affect the writing requirements under the Statute of Frauds?*

The Parol Evidence Rule

• **PAROL EVIDENCE RULE**
A substantive rule of contracts, as well as a procedural rule of evidence, under which a court will not receive into evidence the parties' prior negotiations, prior agreements, or contemporaneous oral agreements if that evidence contradicts or varies the terms of the parties' written contract.

The **parol evidence rule** prohibits the introduction at trial of evidence of the parties' prior negotiations, prior agreements, or contemporaneous oral agreements if that evidence contradicts or varies the terms of written contracts. The written contract is ordinarily assumed to be the complete embodiment of the parties' agreement. Because of the rigidity of the parol evidence rule, however, courts make several exceptions:

¡NOTE! The parol evidence rule and its exceptions relate to the rules concerning the interpretation of contracts.

1. Evidence of a *subsequent modification* of a written contract can be introduced in court. Keep in mind that the oral modifications may not be enforceable if they come under the Statute of Frauds—for example, if they increase the price of the goods for sale to $500 or more or increase the term for performance to more than one year. Also, oral modifications will not be enforceable if the original contract provides that any modification must be in writing.[20]
2. Oral evidence can be introduced in all cases to show that the contract was voidable or void (for example, induced by mistake, fraud, or misrepresentation). In this situation, if deception led one of the parties to agree to the terms of a written contract, oral evidence indicating fraud should not be excluded. Courts frown on bad faith and are quick to allow the introduction at trial of parol evidence when it establishes fraud.
3. When the terms of a written contract are ambiguous, evidence is admissible to show the meaning of the terms.
4. Evidence is admissible when the written contract is incomplete in that it lacks one or more of the essential terms. The courts allow evidence to "fill in the gaps" in the contract.
5. Under the UCC, evidence can be introduced to explain or supplement a written contract by showing a prior dealing, course of performance, or usage of trade.[21] We discuss these terms in further detail in Chapter 15, in the context of sales contracts.

20. UCC 2–209(2), (3). See Chapter 15.
21. UCC 1–205, 2–202. See Chapter 15.

Here, it is sufficient to say that when buyers and sellers deal with each other over extended periods of time, certain customary practices develop. These practices are often overlooked in the writing of the contract, so courts allow the introduction of evidence to show how the parties have acted in the past. Usage of trade—practices and customs generally followed in a particular industry—also can shed light on the meaning of certain contract provisions, and thus evidence of trade usage may be admissible.

6 The parol evidence rule does not apply if the existence of the entire written contract is subject to an orally agreed-on condition. Proof of the condition does not alter or modify the written terms but affects the *enforceability* of the written contract. • **EXAMPLE 12.14** Jelek agrees to purchase Armand's car for $4,000, but only if Jelek's mechanic, Frank, inspects the car and approves of the purchase. Armand agrees to this condition, but because he is leaving town for the weekend and Jelek wants to use the car (if he buys it) before Armand returns, Jelek drafts a contract of sale, and they both sign it. Frank, the mechanic, does not approve of the purchase, and when Jelek does not buy the car, Armand sues him, alleging that he breached the contract. In this case, Jelek's oral agreement did not alter or modify the terms of the written agreement but concerned whether or not the contract existed at all. •

7 When an *obvious* or *gross* clerical (or typographic) error exists that clearly would not represent the agreement of the parties, parol evidence is admissible to correct the error. • **EXAMPLE 12.15** Sharon agrees to lease 1,000 square feet of office space at the current monthly rate of $3 per square foot from Stone Enterprises. The signed written lease provides for a monthly lease payment of $300 rather than the $3,000 agreed to by the parties. Because the error is obvious, Stone Enterprises would be allowed to admit parol evidence to correct the mistake. •

• **INTEGRATED CONTRACT**
A written contract that constitutes the final expression of the parties' agreement. If a contract is integrated, evidence extraneous to the contract that contradicts or alters the meaning of the contract in any way is inadmissible.

The determination of whether evidence will be allowed basically depends on whether the written contract is intended to be a complete and final embodiment of the terms of the agreement. If it is so intended, it is referred to as an **integrated contract,** and extraneous evidence is excluded. If it is only partially integrated, evidence of consistent additional terms is admissible to supplement the written agreement.[22]

22. *Restatement (Second) of Contracts,* Section 216.

APPLICATION

Law and the Businessperson: the Problem with Oral Contracts*

*This *Application* is not meant to substitute for the services of an attorney who is licensed to practice law in your state.

As a general rule, most business contracts should be in writing even when they fall outside of the Statute of Frauds. Businesspersons frequently make oral contracts over the telephone, however, particularly when the parties have done business with each other in the past.

Any time an oral contract is made, it is advisable for one of the parties to send either a written memorandum or a confirmation of the oral agreement by fax or e-mail to the other party. This accomplishes two purposes: (1) it demonstrates a party's clear intention to form a contract, and (2) it provides the terms of the contract as that party understood them. If the party receiving the memorandum or confirmation then disagrees with the terms as described, the issue can be addressed before performance begins.

What about the sale of goods between merchants? Under the UCC, written confirmation received by one merchant removes the Statute of Frauds requirement of a writing unless the merchant receiving the confirmation objects in writing

APPLICATION CONTINUED within ten days of its receipt. This law (discussed in Chapter 15) points out clearly the need for the merchant receiving the confirmation to review it carefully to ascertain that the confirmation conforms to the oral contract. If the writing does not so conform, the merchant can object in writing (the Statute of Frauds still applies), and the parties can resolve misunderstandings without legal liability. If the merchant fails to object, the written confirmation can be used as evidence to prove the terms of the oral contract. Note, however, that this ten-day rule does not apply to contracts for interests in realty or for services.

CHECKLIST FOR ORAL CONTRACTS

1. When feasible, use written contracts.
2. If you enter into an oral contract over the telephone, fax or e-mail a written confirmation outlining your understanding of the oral contract.
3. If you receive the other party's written or faxed confirmation, read it carefully to make sure that its terms agree with what you believed was already agreed on in the oral contract.
4. If you have any objections, notify the other party of these objections, in writing, within ten days.

Key Terms

collateral promise 319
integrated contract 326
parol evidence rule 325
prenuptial agreement 320
scienter 313
Statute of Frauds 315

Chapter Summary • Assent and Form

GENUINENESS OF ASSENT	
Mistakes (See pages 308–310.)	1. *Unilateral*—Generally, the mistaken party is bound by the contract *unless* (a) the other party knows or should have known of the mistake or (b) the mistake is an inadvertent mathematical error—such as an error in addition or subtraction—committed without gross negligence. 2. *Bilateral (mutual)*—When both parties are mistaken about the same material fact, such as identity, either party can avoid the contract. If the mistake concerns value or quality, either party can enforce the contract.
Fraudulent Misrepresentation (See pages 310–314.)	When fraud occurs, usually the innocent party can enforce or avoid the contract. The elements necessary to establish fraud are as follows: 1. A misrepresentation of a material fact must occur. 2. There must be an intent to deceive. 3. The innocent party must justifiably rely on the misrepresentation.
Undue Influence (See page 315.)	Undue influence arises from special relationships, such as fiduciary or confidential relationships, in which one party's free will has been overcome by the undue influence exerted by the other party. Usually, the contract is voidable.
Duress (See page 315.)	Duress is defined as the tactic of forcing a party to enter a contract under the fear of a threat—for example, the threat of violence or serious economic loss. The party forced to enter the contract can rescind the contract.

Chapter Summary • Assent and Form, Continued

FORM	
The Statute of Frauds—The Requirement of a Writing (See pages 315–322.)	*Applicability*—The following types of contracts fall under the Statute of Frauds and must be in writing to be enforceable: 1. *Contracts involving interests in land*—The statute applies to any contract for an interest in realty, such as a sale, a lease, or a mortgage. 2. *Contracts whose terms cannot be performed within one year*—The statute applies only to contracts objectively impossible to perform fully within one year from (the day after) the contract's formation. 3. *Collateral promises*—The statute applies only to express contracts made between the guarantor and the creditor whose terms make the guarantor secondarily liable. *Exception:* the "main purpose" rule. 4. *Promises made in consideration of marriage*—The statute applies to promises to pay money or give property in consideration of a promise to marry and to prenuptial agreements made in consideration of marriage. 5. *Contracts for the sale of goods priced at $500 or more*—Under the UCC Statute of Frauds provision in UCC 2–201. *Exceptions*—Partial performance, admissions, and promissory estoppel.
The Statute of Frauds—Sufficiency of the Writing (See pages 323–325.)	To constitute an enforceable contract under the Statute of Frauds, a writing must be signed by the party against whom enforcement is sought, must name the parties, must identify the subject matter, and must state with reasonable certainty the essential terms of the contract. In a sale of land, the price and a description of the property may need to be stated with sufficient clarity to be determined without reference to outside sources. Under the UCC, a contract for a sale of goods is not enforceable beyond the quantity of goods shown in the contract.
Parol Evidence Rule (See pages 325–326.)	The parol evidence rule prohibits the introduction at trial of evidence of the parties' prior negotiations, prior agreements, or contemporaneous oral agreements that contradicts or varies the terms of written contracts. The written contract is assumed to be the complete embodiment of the parties' agreement. Exceptions are made in the following circumstances: 1. To show that the contract was subsequently modified. 2. To show that the contract was voidable or void. 3. To clarify the meaning of ambiguous terms. 4. To clarify the terms of the contract when the written contract lacks one or more of its essential terms. 5. Under the UCC, to explain the meaning of contract terms in light of a prior dealing, course of performance, or usage of trade. 6. To show that the entire contract is subject to an orally agreed-on condition. 7. When an obvious clerical or typographic error was made.

For Review

❶ In what types of situations might genuineness of assent to a contract's terms be lacking?
❷ What is the difference between a mistake of value or quality and a mistake of fact?
❸ What elements must exist for fraudulent misrepresentation to occur?
❹ What contracts must be in writing to be enforceable?
❺ What is parol evidence? When is it admissible to clarify the terms of a written contract?

Questions and Case Problems

12–1. Genuineness of Assent. Jerome is an elderly man who lives with his nephew, Philip. Jerome is totally dependent on Philip's support. Philip tells Jerome that unless Jerome transfers a tract of land he owns to Philip for a price 30 percent below market value, Philip will no longer support and take care of him. Jerome enters into the contract. Discuss fully whether Jerome can set aside this contract.

12–2. Collateral Promises. Gemma promises a local hardware store that she will pay for a lawn mower that her brother is purchasing on credit if the brother fails to pay the debt. Must this promise be in writing to be enforceable? Why or why not?

12–3. One-Year Rule. On January 1, Dominic, for consideration, orally promised to pay Francis $300 a month for as long as Francis lived, with the payments to be made on the first day of every month. Dominic made the payments regularly for nine months and then made no further payments. Francis claimed that Dominic had breached the oral contract and sued Dominic for damages. Dominic contended that the contract was unenforceable because, under the Statute of Frauds, contracts that cannot be performed within one year must be in writing. Discuss whether Dominic will succeed in this defense.

12–4. Fraudulent Misrepresentation. Larry offered to sell Stanley his car and told Stanley that the car had been driven only 25,000 miles and had never been in an accident. Stanley hired Cohen, a mechanic, to appraise the condition of the car, and Cohen said that the car probably had at least 50,000 miles on it and probably had been in an accident. In spite of this information, Stanley still thought the car would be a good buy for the price, so he purchased it. Later, when the car developed numerous mechanical problems, Stanley sought to rescind the contract on the basis of Larry's fraudulent misrepresentation of the auto's condition. Will Stanley be able to rescind his contract? Discuss.

12–5. Collateral Promises. Jeffrey took his mother on a special holiday to Mountain Air Resort. Jeffrey was a frequent patron of the resort and was well known by its manager. The resort required of each of its patrons a large deposit to ensure payment of the room rental. Jeffrey asked the manager to waive the requirement for his mother and told the manager that if his mother for any reason failed to pay the resort for her stay there, he would cover the bill. Relying on Jeffrey's promise, the manager waived the deposit requirement for Jeffrey's mother. After she returned home from her holiday, Jeffrey's mother refused to pay the resort bill. The resort manager tried to collect the sum from Jeffrey, but Jeffrey also refused to pay, stating that his promise was not enforceable under the Statute of Frauds. Is Jeffrey correct? Explain.

12–6. Genuineness of Assent. Steven Lanci was involved in an automobile accident with an uninsured motorist. Lanci was insured with Metropolitan Insurance Co., although he did not have a copy of the insurance policy. Lanci and Metropolitan entered settlement negotiations, during which Lanci told Metropolitan that he did not have a copy of his policy. Ultimately, Lanci agreed to settle all claims for $15,000, noting in a letter to Metropolitan that $15,000 was the "sum you have represented to be the . . . policy limits applicable to this claim." After signing a release, Lanci learned that the policy limits were actually $250,000, and he refused to accept the settlement proceeds. What defense could Lanci assert to avoid his obligations under the release (contract)? Explain. [*Lanci v. Metropolitan Insurance Co.*, 388 Pa.Super. 1, 564 A.2d 972 (1989)]

12–7. One-Year Rule. Fernandez orally promised Pando that if Pando helped her win the New York state lottery, she would share the proceeds equally with him. Pando agreed to purchase the tickets in Fernandez's name, select the lottery numbers, and pray for the divine intervention of a saint to help them win. Fernandez won $2.8 million in the lottery, which was to be paid over a ten-year period. When Fernandez failed to share the winnings equally, Pando sued for breach of her contractual obligation. Fernandez countered that their contract was unenforceable under the Statute of Frauds, because the contract could not be performed within one year. Could the contract be performed within one year? Explain. [*Pando by Pando v. Fernandez*, 127 Misc.2d 224, 485 N.Y.S.2d 162 (1984)]

12–8. Genuineness of Assent. Linda Lorenzo purchased Lurlene Noel's home in 1988 without having it inspected. The basement started leaking in 1989. In 1991, Lorenzo had the paneling removed from the basement walls and discovered that the walls were bowed inward and cracked. Lorenzo then had a civil engineer inspect the basement walls, and he found that the cracks had been caulked and painted over before the paneling was installed. He concluded that the "wall failure" had existed "for at least thirty years" and that the basement walls were "structurally unsound." Does Lorenzo have a cause of action against Noel? If so, on what ground? Discuss. [*Lorenzo v. Noel,* 206 Mich.App. 682, 522 N.W.2d 724 (1994)]

12–9. The Parol Evidence Rule. Glenn Grove bought a 1936 Pontiac from Bernard Stanfield. Stanfield signed the certificate of title, which stated that the car was sold for $1,000. No other terms of sale were mentioned in the certificate, and none were incorporated by reference. Three years later, Stanfield filed a suit against Grove in a Missouri state court, claiming that Grove still owed $9,000 on the price of the car. At the trial, Stanfield testified that he and Grove had an oral agreement by which Grove was to pay $1,000 for the "title document" and $9,000 for the actual car. The court entered a judgment in Stanfield's favor. What will happen on appeal? Explain. [*Stanfield v. Grove,* 924 S.W.2d 611 (Mo.App.Div.4 1996)]

12–10. Misrepresentation. W. B. McConkey owned commercial property, including a building, that, as McConkey knew, had experienced flooding problems for years. McConkey painted the building, replaced damaged carpeting, and sold the property to M&D, Inc., on an "as is" basis. M&D did not ask whether there were flooding problems, and McConkey said nothing about them. M&D leased the property to Donmar, Inc., to operate a pet supplies store. Two months after the store opened, the building flooded following heavy rain. M&D and Donmar filed a suit in a Michigan state court against McConkey and others, claiming in part that McConkey had committed misrepresentation by silence. Based on this claim, will the court hold McConkey liable? Why or why not? [*M&D, Inc. v. McConkey,* 585 N.W.2d 33 (Mich.App. 1998)]

A QUESTION OF ETHICS AND SOCIAL RESPONSIBILITY

12–11. Mark Van Wagoner, an attorney experienced in real estate transactions, and his wife, Kathryn, were interested in buying certain property being sold by Carol Klas for her former husband, John Klas. When the Van Wagoners asked Carol Klas if there had been any appraisals of the property, she replied that there had been several appraisals, ranging from $175,000 to $192,000. (At trial, Carol claimed that she understood the term *appraisal* to mean any opinion as to the market value of the house.) The Van Wagoners did not request a written appraisal of the property until after signing an agreement to purchase the property for $175,000. Carol Klas then provided them with a written appraisal that listed the house's value as $165,000. When the Van Wagoners refused to go through with the deal, John Klas brought suit to recover the difference between the agreement price and the price for which the house was later sold. In view of these facts, answer the following questions. [*Klas v. Van Wagoner,* 829 P.2d 135 (Utah App.1992)]

1. The Van Wagoners claimed that the contract should be rescinded on the basis of their mistaken assumption as to the value of the house. What kind of mistake was made in this situation (mutual or unilateral, mistake of value or mistake of fact)? How should the court rule on this issue?
2. Mark Van Wagoner was an attorney experienced in real estate transactions. Should the court take this fact into consideration when making its decision?
3. Generally, what ethical principles, as expressed in public policies, are in conflict here and in similar situations in which parties enter into a contract with mistaken assumptions?

FOR CRITICAL ANALYSIS

12–12. Describe the types of individuals who might be capable of exerting undue influence on others.

Online Activities

ONLINE EXERCISE 12-1

Go to the "Internet Activities Book" on the Web site that accompanies this text, the URL for which is http://blt.westbuslaw.com. Select the following activity, and perform the exercise according to the instructions given there:

Activity 12–1: Fraud and Unconscionability

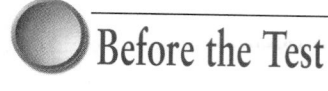

Before the Test

Go to the *Business Law Today* home page at http://blt.westbuslaw.com. Click on TestTutor.® You will find twenty interactive questions relating to this chapter.

CHAPTER 13 Third Party Rights & Discharge

"The laws of a state change with the changing times."

Aeschylus, 525–456 B.C.E.
(Greek dramatist)

CONTENTS

LEARNING OBJECTIVES

After reading this chapter, you should be able to:

1. Identify noncontracting parties who have rights under a contract.
2. Discuss assignments of contract rights, and describe what rights can or cannot be assigned.
3. Explain what a contract condition is and the different kinds of conditions that may exist.
4. Indicate how contract obligations are commonly discharged.
5. Differentiate between complete and substantial performance of a contract, and indicate when a breach of contract occurs.

PRIVITY OF CONTRACT
The relationship that exists between the promisor and the promisee of a contract.

Because a contract is a private agreement between the parties who have entered into it, it is fitting that these parties alone should have rights and liabilities under the contract. This concept is referred to as **privity of contract,** and it establishes the basic principle that third parties have no rights in contracts to which they are not parties.

You are probably convinced by now that for every rule of contract law there seems to be an exception. As times change, so must the laws, as indicated in the opening quotation. When justice cannot be served by adherence to a rule of law, exceptions to the rule must be made. In this chapter, we look at some exceptions to the rule of privity of contract. We also examine how a contract is *discharged*. Normally, contract discharge is accomplished when both parties have performed the acts promised in the contract. In the latter part of this chapter, we look at the degree of performance required to discharge a contractual obligation, as well as at some other ways in which contract discharge can occur.

Assignments and Delegations

When third parties acquire rights or assume duties arising from contracts to which they were not parties, the rights are transferred to them by *assignment,* and the duties are transferred by *delegation.* Assignment and delegation occur after the original contract is made, when one of the parties transfers to another party a right or obligation arising from the contract.

ASSIGNMENTS

• **ASSIGNMENT**
The act of transferring to another all or part of one's rights arising under a contract.

In a bilateral (mutual) contract, the two parties have corresponding rights and duties. One party has a right to require the other to perform some task, and the other has a duty to perform it. The transfer of *rights* to a third person is known as an **assignment.** When rights under a contract are assigned unconditionally, the rights of the *assignor* (the party making the assignment) are extinguished.[1] The third party (the *assignee,* or party receiving the assignment) has a right to demand performance from the other original party to the contract (the *obligor*). Exhibit 13–1 illustrates assignment relationships.

• **EXAMPLE 13.1** Brent owes Alex $1,000, and Alex assigns to Carmen the right to receive the $1,000. Here, a valid assignment of a debt exists. Once Alex has assigned to Carmen his rights under the original contract with Brent, Carmen can enforce the contract against Brent if Brent fails to perform. •

The assignee takes only those rights that the assignor originally had. Furthermore, the assignee's rights are subject to the defenses that the obligor has

1. *Restatement (Second) of Contracts,* Section 317.

EXHIBIT 13–1 • Assignment Relationships

In the assignment relationship illustrated here, Alex assigns his *rights* under a contract that he made with Brent to a third party, Carmen. Alex thus becomes the *assignor* and Carmen the *assignee* of the contractual rights. Brent, the *obligor* (the party owing performance under the contract), now owes performance to Carmen instead of Alex. Alex's original contract rights are extinguished after assignment.

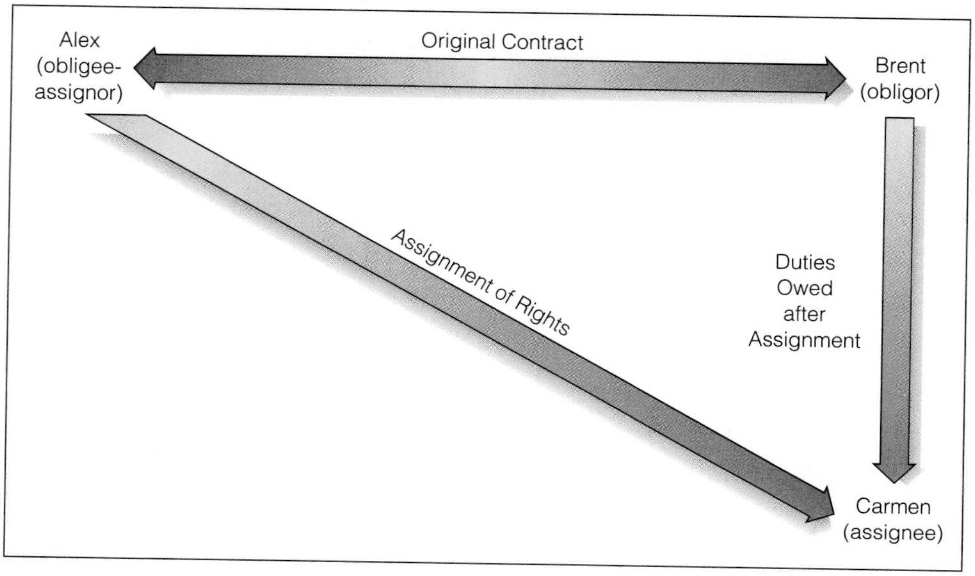

ON THE WEB

You can find a summary of the law governing assignments, as well as "SmartAgreement" forms that you can use for various types of contracts, at www.smartagreements.com/genl/1p75.htm.

against the assignor. • **EXAMPLE 13.2** Brent owes Alex $1,000 under a contract in which Brent agreed to buy Alex's computer work station. Alex assigns his right to receive the $1,000 to Carmen. Brent, in deciding to purchase the work station, relied on Alex's fraudulent misrepresentation that the computer's hard drive had a storage capacity of twelve gigabytes. When Brent discovered that the computer could store only six megabytes, he told Alex that he was going to return the work station to him and cancel the contract. Even though Alex had assigned his "right" to receive the $1,000 to Carmen, Brent need not pay Carmen the $1,000—Brent can raise the defense of Alex's fraudulent misrepresentation to avoid payment. •

Assignments are important because they are involved in much business financing. Lending institutions, for example, such as banks, frequently assign the rights to receive payments under their loan contracts to other firms, which pay for those rights. If you obtain a loan from your local bank to purchase a car, you might later receive in the mail a notice stating that your bank has transferred (assigned) its rights to receive payments on the loan to another firm and that, when the time comes to repay your loan, you must make the payments to that other firm.

Lenders that make *mortgage loans* (loans to allow prospective home buyers to purchase land or a home) often assign their rights to collect the mortgage payments to a third party, such as GMAC Mortgage Corporation. Following an assignment, the home buyer is notified that he or she must make future payments not to the lender that loaned him or her the funds but to the third party. Millions of dollars change hands daily in the business world in the form of assignments of rights in contracts. If it were not possible to transfer (assign) contractual rights, many businesses could not continue to operate.

Rights That Cannot Be Assigned As a general rule, all rights can be assigned. Exceptions are made, however, in the following special circumstances:

1. If a statute expressly prohibits assignment, the particular right in question cannot be assigned. • **EXAMPLE 13.3** Marn is a new employee of CompuFuture, Inc. CompuFuture is an employer under workers' compensation statutes (see Chapter 34) in this state, and thus Marn is a covered employee. Marn has a relatively high-risk job. In need of a loan, Marn borrows some money from Stark, assigning to Stark all workers' compensation benefits due her should she be injured on the job. The assignment of *future* workers' compensation benefits is prohibited by state statute, and thus such rights cannot be assigned. •
2. When a contract is for personal services, the rights under the contract normally cannot be assigned unless all that remains is a money payment.[2] • **EXAMPLE 13.4** Brent signs a contract to be a tutor for Alex's children. Alex then attempts to assign to Carmen his right to Brent's services. Carmen cannot enforce the contract against Brent. Brent may not like Carmen's children or may for some other reason not want to tutor them. Because personal services are unique to the person rendering them, rights to receive personal services cannot be assigned. •
3. A right cannot be assigned if assignment will materially increase or alter the risk or duties of the obligor.[3] • **EXAMPLE 13.5** Alex has a hotel, and to insure it he takes out a policy with Northwest Insurance Company. The policy insures against fire, theft, floods, and vandalism. Alex attempts to assign the insurance policy to Carmen, who also owns a hotel. The assignment is ineffective because it may sub-

2. *Restatement (Second) of Contracts,* Sections 317 and 318.
3. See UCC 2–210(2).

AN ADULT TUTORS CHILDREN. CAN PERSONAL SERVICES SUCH AS TUTORING CHILDREN BE ASSIGNED? WHY OR WHY NOT?

stantially alter the insurance company's duty of performance and the risk that the company undertakes. An insurance company evaluates the particular risk of a certain party and tailors its policy to fit that risk. If the policy is assigned to a third party, the insurance risk is materially altered.•

4. If a contract stipulates that the right cannot be assigned, then *ordinarily* it cannot be assigned. • **EXAMPLE 13.6** Brent agrees to build a house for Alex. The contract between Brent and Alex states, "This contract cannot be assigned by Alex without Brent's consent. Any assignment without such consent renders this contract void, and all rights hereunder will thereupon terminate." Alex then assigns his rights to Carmen, without first obtaining Brent's consent. Carmen cannot enforce the contract against Brent.•

There are several exceptions to the fourth rule. These exceptions are as follows:

1. A contract cannot prevent an assignment of the right to receive money. This exception exists to encourage the free flow of money and credit in modern business settings.
2. The assignment of ownership rights in real estate often cannot be prohibited, because such a prohibition is contrary to public policy in most states. Prohibitions of this kind are called restraints against **alienation** (the voluntary transfer of land ownership).
3. The assignment of negotiable instruments (see Chapter 19) cannot be prohibited.
4. In a contract for the sale of goods, the right to receive damages for breach of contract or for payment of an account owed may be assigned even though the sales contract prohibits such assignment.[4]

• **ALIENATION**
A term used to define the process of transferring land out of one's possession (thus "alienating" the land from oneself).

In the following case, the central issue was whether a contract that contained a covenant not to compete could be assigned.

4. UCC 2–210(2).

CASE 13.1 Reynolds and Reynolds Co. v. Hardee

United States District Court,
Eastern District of Virginia, 1996.
932 F.Supp. 149.

COMPANY PROFILE *There is a $23 billion market in North America for business forms and related services. Reynolds and Reynolds Company provides business forms and electronic-document management systems for general and specialized business markets. Reynolds's products include traditional business forms, laser-print products, labels, digital printing, and mailers. Reynolds's services include document management, storage, and distribution. These products and services help business firms with accounting, inventory control, and sales. Reynolds's customers include 110 of the "Fortune 500" companies.*

BACKGROUND AND FACTS Thomas Hardee worked for Jordan Graphics, Inc., as a sales representative under an employment contract that included a covenant not to compete. Reynolds and Reynolds Company contracted to buy most of Jordan's assets. On the day of the sale, Jordan terminated Hardee's employment. Reynolds offered Hardee a new contract that contained a more restrictive covenant not to compete. Hardee rejected the offer and began selling in competition with Reynolds. Reynolds filed a suit in a federal district court against Hardee, seeking, among other things, to enforce the covenant not to compete that was in the contract between Hardee and Jordan. Hardee filed a motion to dismiss the case, asserting that Reynolds was not an assignee of that contract and could not enforce it.

IN THE WORDS OF THE COURT . . .
REBECCA BEACH SMITH, District Judge.

* * * *

* * * [C]ontracts for personal services are not assignable, unless both parties agree to the assignment. Defendant's [Hardee's] Employment Agreement with Jordan [was] clearly a contract for personal services, based on trust and confidence. Defendant's position involved direct sales to clients; he acted as Jordan's agent in its dealings with customers. A person in such a position must necessarily obtain the trust and confidence of his or her employer. Defendant also placed considerable trust in Jordan by even agreeing to the non-compete clause, namely trusting that Jordan would not fire him and then invoke the covenant not to compete.

* * * *

* * * Without question, an employment contract of the sort involved in this case is not assignable * * * .

DECISION AND REMEDY The court found that Reynolds was not an assignee of the contract between Hardee and Jordan and thus could not enforce it. The court dismissed this part of Reynolds's claim.

FOR CRITICAL ANALYSIS—Social Consideration
What interests must a court balance when deciding whether a covenant not to compete is assignable?

Notice of Assignment Once a valid assignment of rights has been made to a third party, the third party should notify the obligor of the assignment (for example, in Exhibit 13–1, Carmen should notify Brent). Giving notice is not legally necessary to establish the validity of the assignment, because an assignment is effective immediately, whether or not notice is given. Two major problems arise, however, when notice of the assignment is *not* given to the obligor:

1. If the assignor assigns the same right to two different persons, the question arises as to which one has priority—that is, which one has the right to the performance by the obligor. Although the rule most often observed in the United States is that the first assignment in time is the first in right, some states follow the English rule, which basically gives priority to the first assignee who gives notice. • **EXAMPLE 13.7** Brent owes Alex $1,000 on a contractual obligation. On May 1, Alex assigns this

monetary claim to Carmen. Carmen gives no notice of the assignment to Brent. On June 1, for services Dorman has rendered to Alex, Alex assigns the same monetary claim (to collect $1,000 from Brent) to Dorman. Dorman immediately notifies Brent of the assignment. In the majority of states, Carmen would have priority, because the assignment to Carmen was first in time. In some states, however, Dorman would have priority, because Dorman gave first notice. •

2. Until the obligor has notice of assignment, the obligor can discharge his or her obligation by performance to the assignor, and performance by the obligor to the assignor constitutes a discharge to the assignee. Once the obligor receives proper notice, only performance to the assignee can discharge the obligor's obligations. • EXAMPLE 13.8 In the above example, Alex assigns to Carmen his right to collect $1,000 from Brent. Carmen does not give notice to Brent. Brent subsequently pays Alex the $1,000. Although the assignment was valid, Brent's payment to Alex was a discharge of the debt, and Carmen's failure to give notice to Brent of the assignment caused her to lose the right to collect the money from Brent. If Carmen had given Brent notice of the assignment, however, Brent's payment to Alex would not have discharged the debt. •

DELEGATIONS

• **DELEGATION OF DUTIES**
The act of transferring to another all or part of one's duties arising under a contract.

Just as a party can transfer rights to a third party through an assignment, a party can also transfer duties. Duties are not assigned, however; they are *delegated.* Normally, a **delegation of duties** does not relieve the party making the delegation (the *delegator*) of the obligation to perform in the event that the party to whom the duty has been delegated (the *delegatee*) fails to perform. No special form is required to create a valid delegation of duties. As long as the delegator expresses an intention to make the delegation, it is effective; the delegator need not even use the word *delegate.* Exhibit 13–2 graphically illustrates delegation relationships.

Duties That Cannot Be Delegated As a general rule, any duty can be delegated. There are, however, some exceptions to this rule. Delegation is prohibited in the following circumstances:

1. When performance depends on the personal skill or talents of the obligor.
2. When special trust has been placed in the obligor.
3. When performance by a third party will vary materially from that expected by the obligee (the one to whom performance is owed) under the contract.
4. When the contract expressly prohibits delegation.

The following examples will help to clarify the kinds of duties that can and cannot be delegated:

1. Brent contracts with Alex to tutor Alex in the various aspects of financial underwriting and investment banking. Brent, an experienced businessperson known for his expertise in finance, delegates his duties to a third party, Carmen. This delegation is ineffective, because Brent contracted to render a service that is founded on Brent's *expertise,* and the delegation changes Alex's expectancy under the contract.
2. Brent contracts with Alex *personally* to mow Alex's lawn during June, July, and August. Then Brent decides that he would rather spend the summer at the beach. Brent delegates his lawn-mowing duties to Carmen, who is in the business of mowing lawns and doing other landscaping work to earn income to pay for college. The delegation is not effective, no matter how competent Carmen is, without Alex's consent. The contract was for *personal* performance.

EXHIBIT 13–2 • Delegation Relationships

In the delegation relationship illustrated here, Brent delegates his *duties* under a contract that he made with Alex to a third party, Carmen. Brent thus becomes the *delegator* and Carmen the *delegatee* of the contractual duties. Carmen now owes performance of the contractual duties to Alex. Note that a delegation of duties does not normally relieve the delegator (Brent) of liability if the delegatee (Carmen) fails to perform the contractual duties.

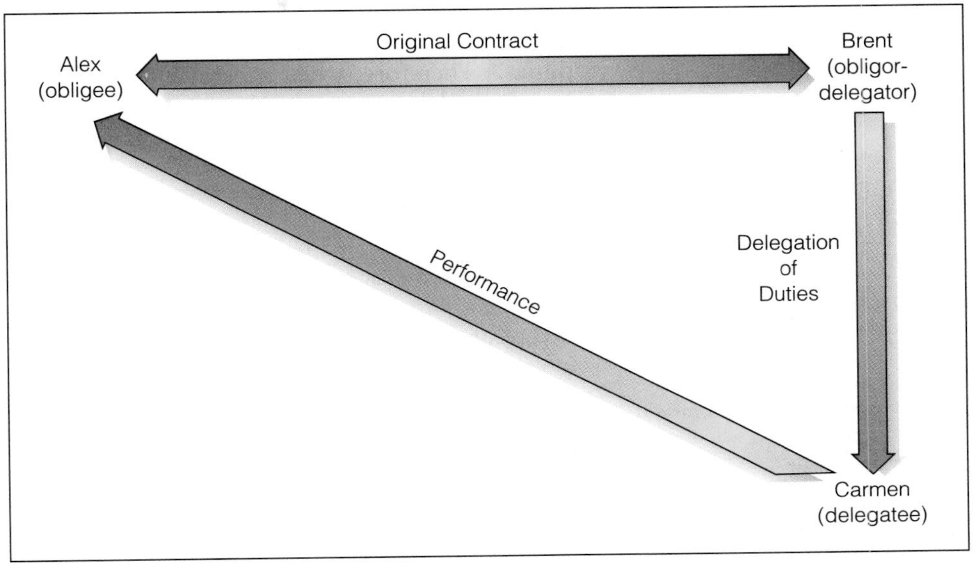

❸ Brent contracts with Alex to pick up and deliver heavy construction machinery to Alex's property. Brent delegates this duty to Carmen, who is in the business of delivering heavy machinery. This delegation is effective. The performance required is of a routine and nonpersonal nature, and the delegation does not change Alex's expectancy under the contract.

Effect of a Delegation If a delegation of duties is enforceable, the *obligee* (the one to whom performance is owed) must accept performance from the delegatee (the one to whom the duties are delegated). • **EXAMPLE 13.9** In the third example in the above list, Brent delegates his duty (to pick up and deliver heavy construction machinery to Alex's property) to Carmen. In that situation, Alex (the obligee) must accept performance from Carmen (the delegatee), because the delegation was effective. The obligee can legally refuse performance from the delegatee only if the duty is one that cannot be delegated. •

A valid delegation of duties does not relieve the delegator of obligations under the contract.[5] In the above example, if Carmen (the delegatee) fails to perform, Brent (the delegator) is still liable to Alex (the obligee). The obligee can also hold the delegatee liable if the delegatee made a promise of performance that will directly benefit the obligee. In this situation, there is an "assumption of duty" on the part of the delegatee, and breach of this duty makes the delegatee liable to the obligee. For example, if Carmen (the delegatee) promises Brent (the delegator), in a contract, to pick up and deliver the construction equipment to Alex's property but fails to do so, Alex (the obligee) can sue Brent, Carmen, or both. Although there are many exceptions, the general rule today is that the obligee can sue both the delegatee and the delegator.

5. *Crane Ice Cream Co. v. Terminal Freezing & Heating Co.*, 147 Md. 588, 128 A. 280 (1925).

¡COMPARE!
In an assignment, the assignor's original contract rights are extinguished after assignment. In a delegation, the delegator remains liable for performance under the contract if the delegatee fails to perform.

"Assignment of All Rights"

Sometimes, a contract provides for an "assignment of all rights." The traditional view was that under this type of assignment, the assignee did not assume *any* duties. This view was based on the theory that the assignee's agreement to accept the benefits of the contract was not sufficient to imply a promise to assume the duties of the contract.

Modern authorities, however, take the view that the probable intent in using such general words is to create both an assignment of rights and an assumption of duties.[6] Therefore, when general words are used (for example, "I assign the contract" or "all my rights under the contract"), the contract is construed as implying both an assignment of rights and an assumption of duties.

Third Party Beneficiaries

• **THIRD PARTY BENEFICIARY**
One for whose benefit a promise is made in a contract but who is not a party to the contract.

• **INTENDED BENEFICIARY**
A third party for whose benefit a contract is formed; an intended beneficiary can sue the promisor if such a contract is breached.

ON THE WEB
A *New York Law Journal* article discussing *Lawrence v. Fox* and other leading decisions from the New York Court of Appeals is online at www.nylj.com/links/150sterk.html.

As mentioned earlier in this chapter, to have contractual rights, a person normally must be a party to the contract. In other words, privity of contract must exist. An exception to the doctrine of privity exists when the original parties to the contract intend at the time of contracting that the contract performance directly benefit a third person. In this situation, the third person becomes a **third party beneficiary** of the contract. As an **intended beneficiary** of the contract, the third party has legal rights and can sue the promisor directly for breach of the contract.

Who, though, is the promisor? In bilateral contracts, both parties to the contract are promisors, because they both make promises that can be enforced. In third party beneficiary contracts, courts will determine the identity of the promisor by asking which party made the promise that benefits the third party—the answer indicates which person is the promisor. Allowing a third party to sue the promisor directly in effect circumvents the "middle person" (the promisee) and thus reduces the burden on the courts. Otherwise, a third party would sue the promisee, who would then sue the promisor.

A classic case in the area of third party beneficiary contracts is *Lawrence v. Fox*—a case decided in 1859. In *Lawrence,* which is presented below as this chapter's *Landmark in the Law,* the court set aside the traditional requirement of privity and allowed a third party to bring a suit directly against the promisor. At the time, this was a novel idea and represented a radical departure from contract law. Prior to that time, contractual liability had always been limited to the parties to the contract.

6. See UCC 2–210(1), (4); *Restatement (Second) of Contracts,* Section 328.

Landmark in the Law •

LAWRENCE v. FOX (1859)

In 1859, the New York Court of Appeals (that state's highest court) decided a case, *Lawrence v. Fox,*[a] involving the following facts: Holly had borrowed $300 from Lawrence. Shortly thereafter, Holly loaned $300 to Fox, who in return promised Holly that he would pay Holly's debt to Lawrence on the following day. When Lawrence failed in his attempts to obtain the $300 from Fox, he sued Fox to recover the money. The issue before the court was whether Lawrence, who was not a party to the Holly-Fox contract, could sue Fox directly to recover the $300. The court held that Lawrence could do so. It was manifestly

a. 20 N.Y. 268 (1859).

"just," declared the court, to allow Lawrence to recover the money from Fox. The principle of law enunciated was that "[in the case of] a promise made for the benefit of another, he for whose benefit it is made may bring an action for its breach."

Why didn't Lawrence sue Holly directly, rather than pursue the unusual route of suing Fox, which meant that his chances at recovery were much slimmer? According to one scholar, the answer to this question is that the "Holly" in this case was probably Merwin Spencer Hawley. Both Hawley and the defendant, Arthur Wellesley Fox, were prominent members of the Buffalo, New York, business community. Evidence at trial suggested that the debt Hawley owed Lawrence was a gambling debt. Because gambling was illegal under New York law, Lawrence could not recover from Hawley directly in court, as the contract would have been deemed illegal.[b]

Although privity of contract remained the guiding principle until after the turn of the century, in two leading cases decided in 1916[c] and 1918,[d] the New York Court of Appeals cited *Lawrence v. Fox* in justifying its departure from the principle of privity of contract. Since then, the third party beneficiary rule has been continuously expanded in scope.

FOR CRITICAL ANALYSIS
What argument could be made in favor of not abandoning the concept of privity of contract in any circumstances?

b. See Antony Jon Waters, "The Property in the Promise: A Study of the Third Party Beneficiary Rule," 98 *Harvard Law Review* 1109, 1168 (1985).
c. *MacPherson v. Buick Motor Co.*, 217 N.Y. 382, 111 N.E. 1050 (1916).
d. *Seaver v. Ransom*, 224 N.Y. 233, 120 N.E. 639 (1918).

Types of Intended Beneficiaries

The law distinguishes between *intended* beneficiaries and *incidental* beneficiaries. Only intended beneficiaries acquire legal rights in a contract. One type of intended beneficiary is a *creditor beneficiary.* A creditor beneficiary is one who, like Lawrence in the case discussed in this chapter's *Landmark in the Law,* benefits from a contract in which one party (the promisor) promises another party (the promisee) to pay a debt that the promisee owes to a third party (the creditor beneficiary). As an intended beneficiary, the creditor beneficiary can sue the promisor directly to enforce the contract.

Another type of intended beneficiary is a *donee* beneficiary. When a contract is made for the express purpose of giving a *gift* to a third party, the third party (the donee beneficiary) can sue the promisor directly to enforce the promise.[7] The most common donee beneficiary contract is a life insurance contract. • **EXAMPLE 13.10** Akins (the promisee) pays premiums to Standard Life, a life insurance company, and Standard Life (the promisor) promises to pay a certain amount of money on Akins's death to anyone Akins designates as a beneficiary. The designated beneficiary is a donee beneficiary under the life insurance policy and can enforce the promise made by the insurance company to pay him or her on Akins's death. •

As the law concerning third party beneficiaries evolved, numerous cases arose in which the third party beneficiary did not fit readily into either category—creditor beneficiary or donee beneficiary. Thus, the modern view, and the one adopted by the *Restatement (Second) of Contracts,* does not draw such clear lines and distinguishes only between intended beneficiaries (who can sue to enforce contracts made for their benefit) and incidental beneficiaries (who cannot sue, as will be discussed shortly).

Can an intended beneficiary recover on the basis of a contract between an attorney and client for legal services, if a transfer of property from the client to the beneficiary fails due to the attorney's negligence? That was the issue in the following case.

7. *Seaver v. Ransom,* 224 N.Y. 233, 120 N.E. 639 (1918).

CASE 13.2 Holsapple v. McGrath

Supreme Court of Iowa, 1994.
521 N.W.2d 711.
www.iowabar.org/IowaSupremeCourt.nsf[a]

HISTORICAL AND ENVIRONMENTAL SETTING *The two great rivers of the central United States, the Mississippi and the Missouri, border the state of Iowa. The state contains a quarter of the finest, richest soil in the country. With 90 percent of this land farmed, Iowa farmers lead the nation in the production of corn, as well as providing much of our cattle, hogs, and other livestock. Three-quarters of the state's residents work in agriculture-related industries.*

a. On this page, click on the "Date" link. When the "Date" page opens, click on the "Search" link. On that page, in the "Search for the following words" box, enter "Holsapple" and click "Search." From the search results, click on the link for the opinion dated "09/21/94." This database is maintained by the Iowa State Bar Association.

BACKGROUND AND FACTS Don and Beulah DeVoss hired attorney James McGrath to handle the transfer of title to a farm they wished to give to Bobby and Barbara Holsapple. The transfer failed because McGrath did not have the new deed notarized. The DeVosses died before a corrected deed could be signed. The Holsapples filed a suit in an Iowa state court against McGrath, alleging negligence. McGrath filed a motion to dismiss for failure to state a claim, which the court granted on the ground that the Holsapples were not parties to the lawyer-client relationship between McGrath and the DeVosses and thus McGrath owed them no duty. The Holsapples appealed to the Supreme Court of Iowa.

IN THE WORDS OF THE COURT . . .
LARSON, Justice.

* * * *

* * * [First, a cause of action will arise only when] a plaintiff [is] a specifically identifiable beneficiary as expressed [by the grantor]. Thus, more than an unrealized expectation of benefits must be shown; a plaintiff must show that the * * * grantor attempted to put the donative wishes into effect and failed to do so only because of the intervening negligence of a lawyer. * * *

Second, a cause of action ordinarily will arise only when as a direct result of the lawyer's professional negligence * * * the [benefit] is * * * lost * * * .

* * * The plaintiffs' petition alleged both elements, and it was error for the district court to dismiss it.

DECISION AND REMEDY The Supreme Court of Iowa reversed the decision of the lower court and remanded the case.

FOR CRITICAL ANALYSIS—Social Consideration *What are the policy reasons for allowing intended beneficiaries to enforce contracts made between other parties for their benefit (or, as in the* Holsapple *case, to sue for negligence in the execution of such a contract)?*

When the Rights of an Intended Beneficiary Vest

An intended third party beneficiary cannot enforce a contract against the original parties until the rights of the third party have *vested,* which means the rights have taken effect and cannot be taken away. Until these rights have vested, the original parties to the contract—the promisor and the promisee—can modify or rescind the contract without the consent of the third party. When do the rights of third parties vest? Generally, the rights vest when one of the following occurs:

1. When the third party demonstrates manifest assent to the contract, such as sending a letter or note acknowledging awareness of and consent to a contract formed for his or her benefit.

2. When the third party materially alters his or her position in detrimental reliance on the contract.
3. When the conditions for vesting mature. For example, the rights of a beneficiary under a life insurance policy vest when the insured person dies.

If the contract expressly reserves to the contracting parties the right to cancel, rescind, or modify the contract, the rights of the third party beneficiary are subject to any changes that result. In such a situation, the vesting of the third party's rights does not terminate the power of the original contracting parties to alter their legal relationships.[8]

INCIDENTAL BENEFICIARIES

• **INCIDENTAL BENEFICIARY**
A third party who incidentally benefits from a contract but whose benefit was not the reason the contract was formed; an incidental beneficiary has no rights in a contract and cannot sue to have the contract enforced.

The benefit that an **incidental beneficiary** receives from a contract between two parties is unintentional. Therefore, an incidental beneficiary cannot enforce a contract to which he or she is not a party. • EXAMPLE 13.11 Jules contracts with Vivian to build a cottage on Vivian's land. Vivian's plans specify that Super Insulation Company's insulation materials must be used in constructing the house. In this situation, Super Insulation Company is an *incidental beneficiary.* If Jules and Vivian decide to cancel the contract, Super Insulation Company cannot sue to enforce it.•

International Perspective • THE RULE OF PRIVITY APPLIES IN OTHER COUNTRIES

Among the common law countries, the third party beneficiary rule is unique to the United States. In all other common law countries, privity of contract is required before a party can sue to have a contract enforced—unless a statutory exception exists to counter common law.

FOR CRITICAL ANALYSIS

Can you think of any reason why U.S. courts allow exceptions to the privity requirement with respect to third party beneficiaries, while other common law countries do not?

INTENDED VERSUS INCIDENTAL BENEFICIARIES

In determining whether a third party beneficiary is an intended or an incidental beneficiary, the courts generally use the *reasonable person* test. That is, a beneficiary will be considered an intended beneficiary if a reasonable person in the position of the beneficiary would believe that the promisee *intended* to confer on the beneficiary the right to bring suit to enforce the contract. In determining whether a party is an intended or an incidental beneficiary, the courts also look at a number of other factors. The presence of one or more of the following factors strongly indicates that the third party is an intended (rather than an incidental) beneficiary to the contract:

1. Performance is rendered directly to the third party.
2. The third party has the right to control the details of performance.
3. The third party is expressly designated as a beneficiary in the contract.

8. Defenses raised against third party beneficiaries are given in *Restatement (Second) of Contracts,* Section 309.

Contract Discharge

• **DISCHARGE**
The termination of an obligation. In contract law, discharge occurs when the parties have fully performed their contractual obligations or when events, conduct of the parties, or operation of the law releases the parties from performance.

• **PERFORMANCE**
In contract law, the fulfillment of one's duties arising under a contract with another; the normal way of discharging one's contractual obligations.

• **CONDITION**
A qualification, provision, or clause in a contractual agreement, the occurrence of which creates, suspends, or terminates the obligations of the contracting parties.

• **CONDITION PRECEDENT**
In a contractual agreement, a condition that must be met before a party's promise becomes absolute.

• **CONDITION SUBSEQUENT**
A condition in a contract that, if not fulfilled, operates to terminate a party's absolute promise to perform.

The most common way to **discharge,** or terminate, one's contractual duties is by the **performance** of those duties. The duty to perform under a contract may be *conditioned* on the occurrence or nonoccurrence of a certain event, or the duty may be *absolute.* In addition to performance, there are numerous other ways in which a contract can be discharged, including discharge by agreement of the parties and discharge by operation of law.

Conditions of Performance

In most contracts, promises of performance are not expressly conditioned or qualified. Instead, they are *absolute promises.* They must be performed, or the party promising the act will be in breach of contract. • EXAMPLE 13.12 JoAnne contracts to sell Alfonso a painting for $10,000. The parties' promises are unconditional: JoAnne's transfer of the painting to Alfonso and Alfonso's payment of $10,000 to JoAnne. The payment does not have to be made if the painting is not transferred. •

In some situations, however, contractual promises are conditioned. A **condition** is a possible future event, the occurrence or nonoccurrence of which will trigger the performance of a legal obligation or terminate an existing obligation under a contract. If the condition is not satisfied, the obligations of the parties are discharged. • EXAMPLE 13.13 Suppose that Alfonso, in the above example, offers to purchase JoAnne's painting only if an independent appraisal indicates that it is worth at least $10,000. JoAnne accepts Alfonso's offer. Their obligations (promises) are conditioned on the outcome of the appraisal. Should this condition not be satisfied (for example, if the appraiser deems the value of the painting to be only $5,000), their obligations to each other are discharged and cannot be enforced. •

We look here at three types of conditions that can be present in any given contract: conditions precedent, conditions subsequent, and concurrent conditions.

Conditions Precedent A condition that must be fulfilled before a party's promise becomes absolute is called a **condition precedent.** The condition precedes the absolute duty to perform. • EXAMPLE 13.14 In the JoAnne-Alfonso example just given, Alfonso's promise is subject to the condition precedent that the appraised value of the painting be at least $10,000. Until the condition is fulfilled, Alfonso's promise is not absolute. Insurance contracts frequently specify that certain conditions, such as passing a physical examination, must be met before the insurance company will be obligated to perform under the contract. •

Conditions Subsequent When a condition operates to terminate a party's absolute promise to perform, it is called a **condition subsequent.** The condition follows, or is subsequent to, the absolute duty to perform. If the condition occurs, the party need not perform any further. • EXAMPLE 13.15 A law firm hires Julia Darby, a recent law school graduate and a newly licensed attorney. Their contract provides that the firm's obligation to continue employing Darby is discharged if Darby fails to maintain her license to practice law. This is a condition subsequent, because a failure to maintain the license would discharge a duty that has already arisen.[9] •

9. The difference between conditions precedent and conditions subsequent is relatively unimportant from a substantive point of view but very important procedurally. Usually, the plaintiff must prove conditions precedent, because normally it is he or she who claims that there is a duty to be performed. Similarly, the defendant must normally prove conditions subsequent, because usually it is he or she who claims that a duty no longer exists.

AN APPRAISER EXAMINES A PAINTING BY THE ARTIST HENRI MATISSE. IF A PARTY AGREES TO BUY A PAINTING ON THE CONDITION THAT THE WORK'S VALUE BE A CERTAIN MINIMUM AS DETERMINED BY AN INDEPENDENT APPRAISAL AND THE APPRAISAL SETS THE VALUE AT LESS THAN THE MINIMUM, WHAT HAPPENS TO THE AGREEMENT TO BUY THE WORK?

Generally, conditions precedent are common; conditions subsequent are rare. The *Restatement (Second) of Contracts* deletes the terms *condition subsequent* and *condition precedent* and refers to both simply as "conditions."[10]

• **CONCURRENT CONDITIONS**
Conditions that must occur or be performed at the same time; they are mutually dependent. No obligations arise until these conditions are simultaneously performed.

Concurrent Conditions When each party's absolute duty to perform is conditioned on the other party's absolute duty to perform, there are **concurrent conditions.** These conditions exist only when the parties expressly or impliedly are to perform their respective duties *simultaneously.* • **EXAMPLE 13.16** If a buyer promises to pay for goods when they are delivered by the seller, each party's absolute duty to perform is conditioned on the other party's absolute duty to perform. The buyer's duty to pay for the goods does not become absolute until the seller either delivers or attempts to deliver the goods. Likewise, the seller's duty to deliver the goods does not become absolute until the buyer pays or attempts to pay for the goods. Therefore, neither can recover from the other for breach without first tendering performance. •

DISCHARGE BY PERFORMANCE

• **TENDER**
An unconditional offer to perform an obligation by a person who is ready, willing, and able to do so.

The contract comes to an end when both parties fulfill their respective duties by performance of the acts they have promised. Performance can also be accomplished by tender. **Tender** is an unconditional offer to perform by a person who is ready, willing, and able to do so. Therefore, a seller who places goods at the disposal of a buyer has tendered delivery and can demand payment according to the terms of the agreement. A buyer who offers to pay for goods has tendered payment and can demand delivery of the goods.

Once performance has been tendered, the party making the tender has done everything possible to carry out the terms of the contract. If the other party then refuses to perform, the party making the tender can consider the duty discharged and sue for **breach of contract.**

• **BREACH OF CONTRACT**
The failure, without legal excuse, of a promisor to perform the obligations of a contract.

10. *Restatement (Second) of Contracts,* Section 224.

Business Law in Action • When Performance Is Due on a Legal Holiday

Today, much business is conducted on weekends and even during legal holidays, such as the Fourth of July. This change in the business environment in America has led at least one judge to rule against a plaintiff who chose to transact its business the first business day after a legal holiday.

The case in question involved an agreement (called a warrant) that entitled Swiss Bank Corporation to purchase one million shares of stock in Dresser Industries, Inc., at a specified price. The warrant provided that it could be exercised at any time "prior to five years from the Closing Date." Five years from the closing date happened to fall on Good Friday, which is a legal holiday in the state of Delaware. All stock exchanges on that day were closed, and therefore Dresser's stock could not be traded. The main office of Dresser was also closed on Good Friday.

Swiss Bank therefore chose to wait until the Monday after Good Friday to deliver the necessary documents and funds to purchase Dresser's stock. Dresser, however, refused to accept Swiss Bank's tender of the documents and funds, arguing that the time for performance had lapsed. Because the price of Dresser's stock was higher than the contract purchase price by Swiss Bank, the bank lost out on several million dollars by Dresser's refusal to sell the shares to the bank at the contract price.

In Swiss Bank's subsequent suit against Dresser for breach of contract, a federal appellate court affirmed the trial court's dismissal of the case. The appellate court pointed out that Swiss Bank had never attempted to purchase the Dresser stock prior to the final date, had never indicated to Dresser that it wanted to purchase the shares on the final exercise date, and did not even attempt to delivery the documents and funds on Good Friday. The court noted that nothing in the contract made delivery conditional on Dresser's office being open. All the contract required was the "receipt" of the documents, plus the funds. Therefore, Swiss Bank could have arranged to have the documents and funds "received" by Dresser by simply mailing them to Dresser (because the U.S. Postal Service delivered the mail on Good Friday) or having them delivered by a private courier service, such as FedEx. Barring that, the court noted that Saturday was still available and that "conduct of business of all kinds" on Saturdays "has long been lawful and commonplace."[a]

The moral of this story is, of course, that if you wait until the last minute, problems may arise. It is always preferred to tender performance prior to a contractual date, and certainly not afterward.

FOR CRITICAL ANALYSIS

What if Swiss Bank had argued that it simply assumed that Dresser would have been closed for the three-day holiday weekend?

a. *Swiss Bank Corporation v. Dresser Industries Inc.*, 141 F.3d 689 (7th Cir. 1998).

(Note that tender must be timely—that is, performance must be tendered within the time period designated in the contract. See this chapter's *Business Law in Action* for a discussion of a case in which the final date for contract performance fell on a legal holiday.)

"The law is not exact upon the subject, but leaves it open to a good man's judgment."

HUGO GROTIUS, 1583–1645 (Dutch jurist, political leader, and theologian)

Complete versus Substantial Performance Normally, conditions expressly stated in the contract must fully occur in all aspects for *complete performance* (strict performance) of the contract to occur. Any deviation breaches the contract and discharges the other party's obligations to perform. Although in most contracts the parties fully discharge their obligations by complete performance, sometimes a party fails to fulfill all of the duties or completes the duties in a manner contrary to the terms of the contract. The issue then arises as to whether the performance was nonetheless sufficiently substantial to discharge the contractual obligations.

To qualify as *substantial performance,* the performance must not vary greatly from the performance promised in the contract, and it must create substantially the same benefits as those promised in the contract. If performance is substantial, the

> **ON THE WEB**
> For a summary of how contracts may be discharged and other principles of contract law, go to
> www.lawyers.com/site/aboutlaw/contract.html#contract10.

other party's duty to perform remains absolute (less damages, if any, for the minor deviations).

• **EXAMPLE 13.17** A couple contracts with a construction company to build a house. The contract specifies that Brand X plasterboard be used for the walls. The builder cannot obtain Brand X plasterboard, and the buyers are on holiday in the mountains of Peru and virtually unreachable. The builder decides to install Brand Y instead, which he knows is identical in quality and durability to Brand X plasterboard. All other aspects of construction conform to the contract. Does this deviation constitute a breach of contract? Can the buyers avoid their contractual obligation to pay the builder because Brand Y plasterboard was used instead of Brand X? Very likely, a court would hold that the builder had substantially performed his end of the bargain, and therefore the couple will be obligated to pay the builder. •

What if the plasterboard substituted for Brand X was not of the same quality as Brand X, reducing the value of the house by $1,000? Again, a court would likely hold that the contract was substantially performed and that the contractor should be paid the price agreed on in the contract, less that $1,000.

DIFFERENT BRANDS OF CONSTRUCTION SUPPLIES DISPLAYED AT A SITE. IF A CONTRACT FOR THE CONSTRUCTION OF A BUILDING OR HOUSE SPECIFIES A PARTICULAR BRAND, CAN A PRODUCT OF A DIFFERENT BRAND OF COMPARABLE QUALITY BE SUBSTITUTED?

ETHICAL ISSUE 13.1 ***What if construction contracts could not be discharged by substantial performance?*** The doctrine of substantial performance, which often applies in construction contracts, is rooted in considerations of fairness. For example, in a classic case on this issue, a contractor was instructed by the landowner to use a certain type of wrought-iron pipe "of Reading manufacture." The contractor installed pipe that was not manufactured by Reading but that was of the same quality, appearance, value, and cost as Reading pipe. In the litigation that followed, New York's highest court held that the contractor had substantially performed the contract.[11] Generally, the courts recognize that it is often impossible for a building contractor to perform completely each and every particular requirement of a construction contract. Therefore, demanding complete performance of every construction contract could result in unfairness. Furthermore, as a practical matter, if courts routinely held that only complete (strict) performance could discharge contractual obligations, the construction industry would likely come to a standstill.

Performance to the Satisfaction of Another Contracts often state that completed work must personally satisfy one of the parties or a third person. The question is whether this satisfaction becomes a condition precedent, requiring actual personal satisfaction or approval for discharge, or whether the test of satisfaction is performance that would satisfy a *reasonable person* (substantial performance).

When the subject matter of the contract is personal, a contract to be performed to the satisfaction of one of the parties is conditioned, and performance must actually satisfy that party. For example, contracts for portraits, works of art, and tailoring are considered personal. Therefore, only the personal satisfaction of the party fulfills the condition—unless a jury finds the party is expressing dissatisfaction only to avoid payment or otherwise is not acting in good faith.

Contracts that involve mechanical fitness, utility, or marketability need only be performed to the satisfaction of a reasonable person unless they *expressly state otherwise*. When such contracts require performance to the satisfaction of a third

11. For a classic case on substantial performance, see *Jacobs & Young, Inc. v. Kent,* 230 N.Y. 239, 129 N.E. 889 (1921).

party (for example, "to the satisfaction of Robert Ames, the supervising engineer"), the courts are divided. A majority of courts require the work to be satisfactory to a reasonable person, but some courts hold that the personal satisfaction of the third party designated in the contract (Robert Ames, in this example) must be met. Again, the personal judgment must be made honestly, or the condition will be excused.

"Men do less than they ought, unless they do all that they can."
THOMAS CARLYLE,
1795–1881
(Scottish historian and essayist)

Material Breach of Contract When a breach of contract is *material*[12]—that is, when performance is not deemed substantial—the nonbreaching party is excused from the performance of contractual duties and has a cause of action to sue for damages caused by the breach. If the breach is *minor* (not material), the nonbreaching party's duty to perform may sometimes be suspended until the breach is remedied, but the duty is not entirely excused. Once the minor breach is cured, the nonbreaching party must resume performance of the contractual obligations that had been undertaken.

A breach entitles the nonbreaching party to sue for damages, but only a material breach discharges the nonbreaching party from the contract. The policy underlying these rules is that contracts should go forward when only minor problems occur, but contracts should be terminated if major problems arise.[13]

Does preventing an employee from working constitute a breach of contract if the employer continues to pay her salary? That was the issue in the following case.

12. *Restatement (Second) of Contracts*, Section 241.
13. See UCC 2–612, which deals with installment contracts for the sale of goods.

CASE 13.3 Van Steenhouse v. Jacor Broadcasting of Colorado, Inc.

Supreme Court of Colorado, 1998.
958 P.2d 464.

HISTORICAL AND SOCIAL SETTING *The nature of television and radio broadcasting has changed dramatically in the 1990s. Unlike previous decades, the most popular shows in the media today are news programs and talk shows. Also unlike previous decades, competition has proliferated with the expansion of cable and satellite television and the development of the World Wide Web. As a consequence, broadcasters are constantly looking to increase the sizes of their audiences by adding or dropping programs based on their popularity at the moment.*

BACKGROUND AND FACTS Jacor Broadcasting of Colorado, Inc., owns and operates Newsradio 85 KOA. In June 1991, Andrea Van Steenhouse signed a three-year agreement to perform as a radio talk-show host for KOA. She was to receive a base salary and a performance bonus, depending on how many people tuned into her show. In January 1994, Jacor replaced her show with Rush Limbaugh's program. Jacor paid Van Steenhouse her base salary for the rest of the term of their agreement but did not employ her as a talk-show host. Van Steenhouse filed a suit in a Colorado state court against Jacor and others, claiming, among other things, breach of contract. The court ruled that Jacor materially breached the contract and awarded Van Steenhouse an amount representing the bonus she could have received if she had not been taken off the air. The state intermediate appellate court affirmed the judgment. Jacor appealed to the Supreme Court of Colorado.

IN THE WORDS OF THE COURT . . .
Chief Justice *VOLLACK* delivered the Opinion of the Court.

* * * *

Ordinarily, an employment agreement does not obligate an employer to furnish work for an employee. However, such an obligation may be inferred depending on the circumstances under which the agreement for employment is made or the nature of the employment. In particular, an obligation to furnish work arises if the

CASE 13.3—Continued

employee materially benefits from performing the duties described in the agreement * * * . [W]hen an employer fails to furnish the kind of work specified in an employment agreement, the employee has a cause of action for breach of contract.

* * * *

* * * [I]n this case * * * Jacor breached the Agreement by depriving Van Steenhouse of the opportunity to perform as a talk show host on KOA. * * * As a result, Van Steenhouse lost the opportunity to build and maintain her professional marketability. In addition, Van Steenhouse lost the opportunity to earn a 1994 performance bonus.

Jacor deprived Van Steenhouse of these benefits by refusing to broadcast her show [as] specified by the clear terms of the Agreement. Accordingly, we hold that Van Steenhouse stated a valid claim for breach of contract.

DECISION AND REMEDY The Supreme Court of Colorado held that an employee's claim for breach of contract can be based solely on an employer's failure to provide an opportunity to work. The court affirmed this part of the lower court's decision.

FOR CRITICAL ANALYSIS—Social Consideration *If courts routinely held that only performance could discharge employment contracts, how would this affect employment relations?*

Anticipatory Repudiation of a Contract Before either party to a contract has a duty to perform, one of the parties may refuse to perform his or her contractual obligations. This is called **anticipatory repudiation.**[14] When anticipatory repudiation occurs, it is treated as a material breach of contract, and the nonbreaching party is permitted to bring an action for damages immediately, even though the scheduled time for performance under the contract may still be in the future.[15] Until the nonbreaching party treats this early repudiation as a breach, however, the breaching party can retract his or her anticipatory repudiation by proper notice and restore the parties to their original obligations.[16]

• **ANTICIPATORY REPUDIATION** An assertion or action by a party indicating that he or she will not perform an obligation that the party is contractually obligated to perform at a future time.

There are two reasons for treating an anticipatory repudiation as a present, material breach. First, the nonbreaching party should not be required to remain ready and willing to perform when the other party has already repudiated the contract. Second, the nonbreaching party should have the opportunity to seek a similar contract elsewhere and may have the duty to do so to minimize his or her loss.

Quite often, an anticipatory repudiation occurs when a sharp fluctuation in market prices creates a situation in which performance of the contract would be extremely unfavorable to one of the parties. • **EXAMPLE 13.18** Shasta Manufacturing Company contracts to manufacture and sell 100,000 personal computers to New Age, Inc., a computer retailer with 500 outlet stores. Delivery is to be made two months from the date of the contract. One month later, three suppliers of computer parts raise their prices to Shasta. Because of these higher prices, Shasta stands to lose $500,000 if it sells the computers to New Age at the contract price. Shasta writes to New Age, informing New Age that it cannot deliver the 100,000 computers at the agreed-on contract price. Even though you might sympathize with Shasta, its letter is an anticipatory repudiation of the contract, allowing New Age the option of treating

¡REMEMBER! The risks that prices will fluctuate and values will change are ordinary business risks for which the law does not provide relief.

14. *Restatement (Second) of Contracts*, Section 253, and UCC 2–610.
15. The doctrine of anticipatory repudiation first arose in the landmark case of *Hochster v. De La Tour*, 2 Ellis and Blackburn Reports 678 (1853), when the English court recognized the delay and expense inherent in a rule requiring a nonbreaching party to wait until the time of performance before suing on an anticipatory repudiation.
16. See UCC 2–611.

the repudiation as a material breach and proceeding immediately to pursue remedies, even though the contract delivery date is still a month away.[17] •

Discharge by Agreement

"Agreement makes law."
(LEGAL MAXIM)

Any contract can be discharged by the agreement of the parties. The agreement can be contained in the original contract, or the parties can form a new contract for the express purpose of discharging the original contract.

Discharge by Rescission As discussed in an earlier chapter, rescission is the process in which the parties cancel the contract and are returned to the positions they occupied prior to the contract's formation. For *mutual rescission* to take place, the parties must make another agreement that also satisfies the legal requirements for a contract—there must be an *offer,* an *acceptance,* and *consideration.* Ordinarily, if the parties agree to rescind the original contract, their promises not to perform those acts promised in the original contract will be legal consideration for the second contract.

Mutual rescission can occur in this manner when the original contract is executory on both sides (that is, neither party has completed performance). The agreement to rescind an executory contract is generally enforceable, even if it is made orally and even if the original agreement was in writing.[18] When one party has fully performed, however, an agreement to rescind the original contract is not usually enforceable unless additional consideration is given or restitution is made.[19]

• **NOVATION**
The substitution, by agreement, of a new contract for an old one, with the rights under the old one being terminated. Typically, there is a substitution of a new person who is responsible for the contract and the removal of the original party's rights and duties under the contract.

Discharge by Novation The process of **novation** substitutes a third party for one of the original parties. Essentially, the parties to the original contract and one or more new parties all get together and agree to the substitution. The requirements of a novation are as follows:

1. The existence of a previous, valid obligation.
2. Agreement by all of the parties to a new contract.
3. The extinguishing of the old obligation (discharge of the prior party).
4. A new, valid contract.

An important distinction between an assignment or delegation and a novation is that a novation involves a new contract, and an assignment or delegation involves the old contract.

• **Example 13.19** Suppose that you contract with A. Logan Enterprises to sell it your office-equipment business. Logan later learns that it should not expand at this time but knows of another party, MBI Corporation, that is interested in purchasing your business. All three of you get together and agree to a novation. As long as the new contract is supported by consideration, the novation discharges the original contract between you and Logan and replaces it with the new contract between you and MBI Corporation. Logan prefers the novation to an assignment because it discharges all the contract liabilities stemming from its contract with you. If an installment sales contract had been involved, requiring twelve monthly payments, and Logan had merely assigned the contract (assigned its rights and delegated its duties

17. Another illustration can be found in *Reliance Cooperage Corp. v. Treat,* 195 F.2d 977 (8th Cir. 1952).
18. Agreements to rescind contracts involving transfers of realty, however, must be evidenced by a writing. Another exception has to do with the sale of goods under UCC 2–209, when the sales contract requires written rescission.
19. Under UCC 2–209(1), however, no consideration is needed to modify a contract for a sale of goods. See Chapter 15. Also see UCC 1–107.

under the contract) to MBI Corporation, Logan would have remained liable to you for the payments if MBI Corporation defaulted. •

Discharge by Accord and Satisfaction As discussed in Chapter 10, in an *accord and satisfaction,* the parties agree to accept performance different from the performance originally promised. An *accord* is defined as an executory contract (one that has not yet been performed) to perform some act in order to satisfy an existing contractual duty that is not yet discharged.[20] A *satisfaction* is the performance of the accord agreement. An *accord* and its *satisfaction* discharge the original contractual obligation.

Once the accord has been made, the original obligation is merely suspended until the accord agreement is fully performed. If it is not performed, the party to whom performance is owed can bring an action on the original obligation or for breach of the accord. • **EXAMPLE 13.20** Shea obtains a judgment against Marla for $4,000. Later, both parties agree that the judgment can be satisfied by Marla's transfer of her automobile to Shea. This agreement to accept the auto in lieu of $4,000 in cash is the accord. If Marla transfers her automobile to Shea, the accord agreement is fully performed, and the $4,000 debt is discharged. If Marla refuses to transfer her car, the accord is breached. Because the original obligation is merely suspended, Shea can bring an action to enforce the judgment for $4,000 in cash or bring an action for breach of the accord. •

DISCHARGE BY OPERATION OF LAW

"Law is a practical matter."
ROSCOE POUND,
1870–1964
(American jurist)

Under some circumstances, contractual duties may be discharged by operation of law. These circumstances including the running of the relevant statute of limitations, material alteration of the contract, bankruptcy, and impossibility of performance.

Contract Alteration To discourage parties from altering written contracts, the law operates to allow an innocent party to be discharged when one party has materially altered a written contract without the knowledge or consent of the other party. For example, if a party alters a material term of the contract—such as the quantity term or price term—without the knowledge or consent of the other party, the party who was unaware of the alteration can treat the contract as discharged or terminated.

Statutes of Limitations As mentioned earlier in this text, statutes of limitations limit the period during which a party can sue on a particular cause of action. After the applicable limitations period has passed, a suit can no longer be brought. For example, the limitations period for bringing suits for breach of oral contracts is usually two to three years: for written contracts, four to five years; and for recovery of amounts awarded in judgment, ten to twenty years, depending on state law. Suits for breach of a contract for the sale of goods must be brought within four years after the cause of action has accrued. By original agreement, the parties can reduce this four-year period to a one-year period. They cannot, however, extend it beyond the four-year limitation period.

Bankruptcy A proceeding in bankruptcy attempts to allocate the assets the debtor owns to the creditors in a fair and equitable fashion. Once the assets have been allocated, the debtor receives a *discharge in bankruptcy*—see Chapter 23. A discharge in bankruptcy will ordinarily bar enforcement of most of a debtor's contracts by the creditors.

20. *Restatement (Second) of Contracts,* Section 281.

• **IMPOSSIBILITY OF PERFORMANCE** A doctrine under which a party to a contract is relieved of his or her duty to perform when performance becomes objectively impossible or totally impracticable (through no fault of either party).

When Performance Is Impossible After a contract has been made, performance may become impossible in an objective sense. This is known as **impossibility of performance** and may discharge a contract.[21]

Objective Impossibility. *Objective impossibility* ("It can't be done") must be distinguished from subjective impossibility ("I'm sorry, I simply can't do it"). Examples of subjective impossibility include contracts in which goods cannot be delivered on time because of a freight car shortage[22] and contracts in which funds cannot be paid on time because the bank is closed.[23] In effect, the nonperforming party is saying, "It is impossible for *me* to perform," rather than "It is impossible for *anyone* to perform." Accordingly, such excuses do not discharge a contract, and the nonperforming party is normally held in breach of contract. Four basic types of situations will generally qualify as grounds for the discharge of contractual obligations based on impossibility of performance:[24]

¡NOTE! The doctrine of commercial impracticability does not provide relief from such events as ordinary price increases or easily predictable changes in the weather.

1. ***When a party whose personal performance is essential to the completion of the contract dies or becomes incapacitated prior to performance.*** • **EXAMPLE 13.21** Fred, a famous dancer, contracts with Ethereal Dancing Guild to play a leading role in its new ballet. Before the ballet can be performed, Fred becomes ill and dies. His personal performance was essential to the completion of the contract. Thus, his death discharges the contract and his estate's liability for his nonperformance.•
2. ***When the specific subject matter of the contract is destroyed.*** • **EXAMPLE 13.22** A-1 Farm Equipment agrees to sell Gudgel the green tractor on its lot and promises to have it ready for Gudgel to pick up on Saturday. On Friday night, however, a truck veers off the nearby highway and smashes into the tractor, destroying it beyond repair. Because the contract was for this specific tractor, A-1's performance is rendered impossible owing to the accident.•
3. ***When a change in the law renders performance illegal.*** An example is a contract to build an apartment building, when the zoning laws are changed to prohibit the construction of residential rental property at this location. This change renders the contract impossible to perform.
4. ***When performance becomes commercially impracticable.*** The inclusion of this type of "impossibility" as a basis for contract discharge results from a growing trend to allow parties to discharge contracts in which the originally contemplated performance turns out to be much more difficult or expensive than anticipated. In such situations, courts may excuse parties from their performance obligations under the doctrine of *commercial impracticability*. For example, in one case, a court held that a contract could be discharged because a party would have to pay ten times more than the original estimate to excavate a certain amount of gravel.[25]

A PRODUCTION LINE IN A COMMERCIAL BAKERY. IF A FIRE INCAPACITATED THE BAKERY'S OVEN, WOULD THE BAKERY BE EXCUSED FROM PERFORMING ITS CONTRACTS UNTIL THE OVEN WAS FIXED? IF A CONTRACT INVOLVED A SPECIAL HOLIDAY ORDER AND THE OVEN COULD NOT BE FIXED UNTIL AFTER THE HOLIDAY, WOULD THE CONTRACT BE DISCHARGED?

ETHICAL ISSUE 13.2 ***Should the courts allow the defense of impossibility of performance to be used more often?*** The doctrine of impossibility is applied only when the parties could not have reasonably foreseen, at the time the contract was formed, the event or events that rendered performance impossible. In some cases, it would seem that the courts go too far in holding that certain events or conditions should have been

21. *Restatement (Second) of Contracts*, Section 261.
22. *Minneapolis v. Republic Creosoting Co.*, 161 Minn. 178, 201 N.W. 414 (1924).
23. *Ingham Lumber Co. v. Ingersoll & Co.*, 93 Ark. 447, 125 S.W. 139 (1910).
24. *Restatement (Second) of Contracts*, Sections 262–266, and UCC 2–615.
25. *Mineral Park Land Co. v. Howard*, 172 Cal. 289, 156 P. 458 (1916).

foreseen by the parties, thus precluding parties from avoiding contractual obligations under the doctrine of impossibility of performance. Yet even though the courts rarely excuse parties from performance under the doctrine of impossibility, they allow parties to raise this defense more often than they once did. Indeed, until the latter part of the nineteenth century courts were reluctant to discharge a contract even when it appeared that performance was literally impossible. Generally, the courts must balance the freedom of parties to contract as they will (and assume the risks involved) against the injustice that may result when certain contractual obligations are enforced. If the courts allowed parties to raise impossibility of performance as a defense to contractual obligations more often, freedom of contract would suffer.

Temporary Impossibility. An occurrence or event that makes performance temporarily impossible operates to suspend performance until the impossibility ceases. Then, ordinarily, the parties must perform the contract as originally planned. If, however, the lapse of time and the change in circumstances surrounding the contract make it substantially more burdensome for the parties to perform the promised acts, the contract is discharged.

• **EXAMPLE 13.22** The leading case on the subject, *Autry v. Republic Productions,*[26] involved an actor who was drafted into the army in 1942. Being drafted rendered the actor's contract temporarily impossible to perform, and it was suspended until the end of the war. When the actor got out of the army, the purchasing power of the dollar had so changed that performance of the contract would have been substantially burdensome to him. Therefore, the contract was discharged. •

26. 30 Cal.2d 144, 180 P.2d 888 (1947).

Key Terms

alienation 334

anticipatory repudiation 347

assignment 332

breach of contract 343

concurrent condition 343

condition 342

condition precedent 342

condition subsequent 342

delegation of duties 336

discharge 342

impossibility of performance 350

incidental beneficiary 341

intended beneficiary 338

novation 348

performance 342

privity of contract 331

tender 343

third party beneficiary 338

Chapter Summary • Third Party Rights and Discharge

THIRD PARTY RIGHTS	
Assignment (See pages 332–336.)	1. An assignment is the transfer of rights under a contract to a third party. The person assigning the rights is the *assignor,* and the party to whom the rights are assigned is the *assignee.* The assignee has a right to demand performance from the other original party to the contract. 2. Generally, all rights can be assigned, except in the following circumstances:

Chapter Summary • Third Party Rights and Discharge, Continued

Assignment—continued	a. When assignment is expressly prohibited by statute (for example, workers' compensation benefits). b. When a contract calls for the performance of personal services. c. When the assignment will materially increase or alter the risks or duties of the *obligor* (the party that is obligated to perform). d. When the contract itself stipulates that the rights cannot be assigned (with some exceptions). 3. Notice of the assignment should be given by the assignee to the obligor. a. If the assignor assigns the same right to two different persons, generally the first assignment in time is the first in right, although in some states the first assignee to give notice takes priority. b. Until the obligor is notified of the assignment, the obligor can tender performance to the assignor; and if performance is accepted by the assignor, the obligor's duties under the contract are discharged without benefit to the assignee.
Delegation (See pages 336–338.)	1. A delegation is the transfer of duties under a contract to a third party (the *delegatee*), who then assumes the obligation of performing the contractual duties previously held by the one making the delegation (the *delegator*). 2. As a general rule, any duty can be delegated, except in the following circumstances: a. When performance depends on the personal skill or talents of the obligor. b. When special trust has been placed in the obligor. c. When performance by a third party will vary materially from that expected by the obligee (the one to whom the duty is owed) under the contract. d. When the contract expressly prohibits delegation. 3. A valid delegation of duties does not relieve the delegator of obligations under the contract. If the delegatee fails to perform, the delegator is still liable to the obligee. 4. An "assignment of all rights" or an "assignment of contract" is often construed to mean that both the rights and duties arising under the contract are transferred to a third party.
Third Party Beneficiaries (See pages 338–341.)	A third party beneficiary contract is one made for the purpose of benefiting a third party. 1. *Intended beneficiary*—One for whose benefit a contract is created. When the promisor (the one making the contractual promise that benefits a third party) fails to perform as promised, the third party can sue the promisor directly. Examples of third party beneficiaries are creditor and donee beneficiaries. 2. *Incidental beneficiary*—A third party who indirectly (incidentally) benefits from a contract but for whose benefit the contract was not specifically intended. Incidental beneficiaries have no rights to the benefits received and cannot sue to have the contract enforced.
CONTRACT DISCHARGE	
Conditions of Performance (See pages 342–343.)	Contract obligations may be subject to the following types of conditions: 1. *Condition precedent*—A condition that must be fulfilled before a party's promise becomes absolute. 2. *Condition subsequent*—A condition that, if not fulfilled, operates to terminate a party's absolute promise to perform. 3. *Concurrent conditions*—In which case each party's absolute duty to perform is conditioned on the other party's absolute duty to perform.

Chapter Summary • Third Party Rights and Discharge, Continued

Discharge by Performance (See pages 343–348.)	A contract may be discharged by complete (strict) or by substantial performance. In some cases, performance must be to the satisfaction of another. Totally inadequate performance constitutes a material breach of contract. An anticipatory repudiation of a contract allows the other party to sue immediately for breach of contract.
Discharge by Agreement (See pages 348–349.)	Parties may agree to discharge their contractual obligations in several ways: 1. *By rescission*—The parties mutually agree to rescind (cancel) the contract. 2. *By novation*—A new party is substituted for one of the primary parties to a contract. 3. *By accord and satisfaction*—The parties agree to render and accept performance different from that on which they originally agreed.
Discharge by Operation of Law (See pages 349–351.)	Parties' obligations under contracts may be discharged by operation of law owing to one of the following: 1. Contract alteration. 2. Statutes of limitations. 3. Bankruptcy. 4. Impossibility of performance.

For Review

1 What is the difference between an assignment and a delegation?

2 State what rights can be assigned despite a contract clause expressly prohibiting assignment.

3 What factors indicate that a third party beneficiary is an intended beneficiary?

4 How are most contracts discharged?

5 What is a contractual condition, and how might a condition affect contractual obligations?

Questions and Case Problems

13–1. Substantial Performance. Complete performance is full performance according to the terms of a contract. Discuss the effect on the parties if there is less than full performance.

13–2. Third Party Beneficiaries. Wilken owes Rivera $2,000. Howie promises to Wilken that he will pay Rivera the $2,000 in return for Wilken's promise to give Howie's children guitar lessons. Is Rivera an intended beneficiary of the Howie-Wilken contract? Explain.

13–3. Assignments. Aron is a student attending college. He signs a one-year lease agreement that runs from September 1 to August 31. The lease agreement specifies that the lease cannot be assigned without the landlord's consent. In late May, Aron decides not to go to summer school and assigns the balance of the lease (three months) to a close friend, Erica. The landlord objects to the assignment and denies Erica access to the apartment. Aron claims that Erica is financially sound and should be allowed the full rights and privileges of an assignee. Discuss fully whether the landlord or Aron is correct.

13–4. Novation versus Accord and Satisfaction. Doug owes creditor Cartwright $1,000, which is due and payable on June 1. Doug has a car accident, misses several months of work, and consequently does not have the funds to pay Cartwright on June 1. Doug's father, Bert, offers to pay Cartwright $1,100 in four equal installments if Cartwright will discharge Doug from any further liability on the debt. Cartwright accepts. Is the transaction a novation, or is it an accord and satisfaction? Explain.

13–5. Impossibility of Performance. Millie contracted to sell Frank 1,000 bushels of corn to be grown on Millie's farm. Owing to drought conditions during the growing season, Millie's yield was much less than anticipated, and she could deliver only 250 bushels to Frank. Frank accepted the lesser amount but sued Millie for breach of contract. Can Millie defend successfully on the basis of objective impossibility of performance? Explain.

13–6. Third Party Beneficiaries. Rensselaer Water Co. was under contract to the city of Rensselaer, New York, to provide water to the city, including water at fire hydrants. A warehouse owned by H. R. Moch Co. was totally destroyed by a fire that could not be extinguished because of inadequate water pressure at the fire hydrants. Moch brought suit against Rensselaer Water Co. for damages, claiming that Moch was a third party beneficiary to the city's contract with the water company. Will Moch be able to recover damages from the water company on the basis that the water company breached its contract with the city? Explain. [*H. R. Moch Co. v. Rensselaer Water Co.,* 247 N.Y. 160, 159 N.E. 896 (1928)]

13–7. Conditions Precedent. Larry McLanahan's 1985 Lamborghini was stolen, and by the time McLanahan recovered the car, it had been extensively damaged. The car was insured by Farmers Insurance Co. of Washington under a policy providing comprehensive coverage, including theft. A provision in the policy stated that the coverage for theft damages was subject to certain terms and conditions, including the condition that any person claiming coverage under the policy must allow Farmers "to inspect and appraise the damaged vehicle before its repair or disposal." McLanahan, without notifying Farmers and without giving Farmers an opportunity to inspect the vehicle, sold the car to a wholesale car dealer. Farmers then denied coverage, and McLanahan brought suit to recover for the damages caused to his car by the theft. Did McLanahan have a valid claim against the insurance company? Explain. [*McLanahan v. Farmers Insurance Co. of Washington,* 66 Wash.App. 36, 831 P.2d 160 (1992)]

13–8. Third Party Beneficiaries. When Charles and Judy Orr were divorced in 1970, their divorce agreement included a provision that Charles would pay for the college or professional school education of the couple's two children, then minors. In 1990, when Charles's daughter Jennifer was attending college, Charles refused to pay her college tuition. Can Jennifer, who was not a party to her parents' divorce agreement, bring a court action to compel her father to pay her college expenses? Discuss fully. [*Orr v. Orr,* 228 Ill.App.3d 234, 592 N.E.2d 553, 170 Ill.Dec. 117 (1992)]

13–9. Assignments. Joseph LeMieux, of Maine, won $373,000 in a lottery operated by the Tri-State Lotto Commission. The lottery is sponsored by the three northern New England states and is administered in Vermont. Per its usual payment plan, Tri-State was to pay the $373,000 to LeMieux in equal annual installments over a twenty-year period. LeMieux assigned his rights to the lottery installment payments for the years 1996 through 2006 to Singer Freidlander Corp. for the sum of $80,000. LeMieux and Singer Freidlander (the plaintiffs) sought a declaratory judgment from a court authorizing the assignment agreement between them despite Tri-State's regulation barring the assignment of lottery proceeds. The trial court granted Tri-State's motion for summary judgment. On appeal, the plaintiffs argued that Tri-State's regulation was invalid. Is it? Discuss. [*LeMieux v. Tri-State Lotto Commission,* 666 A.2d 1170 (Vt. 1995)]

13–10. Conditions. Heublein, Inc., manufactures wines and distilled spirits. Tarrant Distributors, Inc., agreed to distribute Heublein brands. When problems arose, the parties entered mediation. Under a settlement agreement, Heublein agreed to pay Tarrant the amount of its "net loss" as determined by Coopers & Lybrand, an accounting firm, according to a specified formula. The parties agreed that Coopers & Lybrand's calculation would be "final and binding." Heublein disagreed with Coopers & Lybrand's calculation, however, and refused to pay. The parties asked a federal district court to rule on the dispute. Heublein argued that the settlement agreement included an implied condition precedent that Coopers & Lybrand would correctly apply the specified formula before Heublein was obligated to pay. Tarrant pointed to the clause that the calculation would be "final and binding." With whom will the court agree, and why? [*Tarrant Distributors, Inc. v. Heublein, Inc.,* 127 F.3d 375 (5th Cir. 1997)]

A QUESTION OF ETHICS AND SOCIAL RESPONSIBILITY

13–11. Bath Iron Works (BIW) offered a job to Thomas Devine, contingent on Devine's passing a drug test. The testing was conducted by NorDx, a subcontractor of Roche Biomedical Laboratories. When NorDx found that Devine's urinalysis showed the presence of opiates, a result confirmed by Roche, BIW refused to offer Devine permanent employment. Devine claimed that the ingestion of poppy seeds can lead to a positive result and that he tested positive for opiates only because of his daily consumption of poppy seed muffins. In Devine's suit against Roche, Devine argued, among other things, that he was a third party beneficiary of the contract between his employer (BIW) and NorDx (Roche). Given this factual background, consider the following questions. [*Devine v. Roche Biomedical Laboratories,* 659 A.2d 868 (Me. 1995)]

1. Is Devine an intended third party beneficiary of the BIW-NorDx contract? In deciding this issue, should the court focus on the nature of the promises made in the contract itself or on the consequences of the contract for Devine, a third party?
2. Should employees whose job security and reputation have suffered as a result of false test results be allowed to sue the drug-testing labs for the tort of negligence? In such situations, do drug-testing labs have a duty to the employees to exercise reasonable care in conducting the tests?

FOR CRITICAL ANALYSIS

13–12. The concept of substantial performance permits a party to be discharged from a contract even though the party has not fully performed his or her obligations according to the contract's terms. Is this fair? What policy interests are at issue here?

Online Activities

ONLINE EXERCISE 13–1

Go to the "Internet Activities Book" on the Web site that accompanies this text, the URL for which is http://blt.westbuslaw.com. Select the following activity, and perform the exercise according to the instructions given there:

Activity 13–1: Third Party Beneficiaries

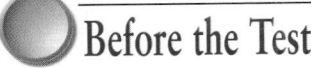

Before the Test

Go to the *Business Law Today* home page at http://blt.westbuslaw.com. Click on TestTutor.® You will find twenty interactive questions relating to this chapter.

CHAPTER 14

Breach & Remedies

"Men keep their engagements when it is to the advantage of both not to break them."

Solon, sixth century B.C.E.
(Athenian legal reformer)

CONTENTS

LEARNING OBJECTIVES

After reading this chapter, you should be able to:

1. Define the different types of damages that may be obtainable on the breach of a contract.
2. Describe the types of situations in which mitigation of damages will be required.
3. Distinguish between liquidated damages and penalties.
4. List the equitable remedies that may be granted by courts, and indicate when they will be granted.
5. Explain the common law doctrine of election of remedies.

As the Athenian political leader Solon instructed centuries ago, a contract will not be broken so long as "it is to the advantage of both" parties to fulfill their contractual obligations. Normally, the reason a person enters into a contract with another is to secure an advantage. When it is no longer advantageous for a party to fulfill his or her contractual obligations, breach of contract may result. As discussed in Chapter 13, a *breach of contract* occurs when a party fails to perform part or all of the required duties under a contract.[1] Once a party fails to perform or performs inadequately, the other party—the nonbreaching party—can choose one or more of several remedies.

The most common remedies available to a nonbreaching party under contract law include damages, rescission and restitution, specific performance, and reformation. As discussed in Chapter 1, courts distinguish between *remedies at law* and *remedies in equity.* Today, the

1. *Restatement (Second) of Contracts,* Section 235(2).

remedy at law is normally money damages. We discuss this remedy in the first part of this chapter. Equitable remedies include rescission and restitution, specific performance, and reformation, all of which we examine later in the chapter. Usually, a court will not award an equitable remedy unless the remedy at law is inadequate. In the final pages of this chapter, we look at some special legal doctrines and concepts relating to remedies.

Damages

¡REMEMBER!
The terms of a contract must be sufficiently definite for a court to determine the amount of damages to award.

A breach of contract entitles the nonbreaching party to sue for money damages. As you read in Chapter 4, damages are designed to compensate a party for harm suffered as a result of another's wrongful act. In the context of contract law, damages are designed to compensate the nonbreaching party for the loss of the bargain. Often, courts say that innocent parties are to be placed in the position they would have occupied had the contract been fully performed.[2]

TYPES OF DAMAGES

There are basically four kinds of damages: compensatory, consequential, punitive, and nominal damages.

The Letter of the Law — THE SPY WHO WAS LEFT OUT IN THE COLD

In a suit against the U.S. government for breach of contract, Boris Korczak sought compensation for services that he had allegedly performed for the Central Intelligence Agency (CIA) from 1973 to 1980. Korczak claimed that the government had failed to pay him an annuity and other compensation required by a secret oral agreement with the CIA. The federal trial court dismissed Korczak's claim, and Korczak appealed the decision to the U.S. Court of Appeals for the Federal Circuit. At issue on appeal was whether a Supreme Court case decided in 1875, *Totten v. United States*,[a] remained the controlling precedent in this area. In *Totten*, the plaintiff alleged that he had formed a secret contract with President Lincoln to collect information on the Confederate army during the Civil War. When the plaintiff sued the government for compensation for his services, the Supreme Court held that to enforce such agreements could result in the disclosure of information that "might compromise or embarrass our government" or cause other "serious detriment" to the public. In Korczak's case, the federal appellate court held that *Totten* was still good law. Said the court, "*Totten*, despite its age, is the last pronouncement on this issue by the Supreme Court. . . . We are duty bound to follow the law given us by the Supreme Court unless and until it is changed."[b]

THE BOTTOM LINE

Supreme Court precedents, no matter how old, remain controlling until they are overruled by a subsequent decision of the Supreme Court, by a constitutional amendment, or by congressional legislation.

a. 92 U.S. 105 (1875).

b. *Korczak v. United States*, 124 F.3d 227 (Fed.Cir. 1997).

Compensatory Damages As discussed in Chapter 4, *compensatory damages* compensate an injured party for injuries or damages actually sustained by that party. The nonbreaching party must prove that the actual damages arose directly from the loss of the bargain caused by the breach of contract. The amount of compensatory damages is the difference between the value of the breaching party's promised performance under the contract and the value of his or her actual performance. This amount is reduced by any loss that the injured party has avoided, however.

2. *Restatement (Second) of Contracts*, Section 347, and UCC 1–106(1).

"The duty to keep a contract at common law means a prediction that you must pay damages if you do not keep it—and nothing else."

OLIVER WENDELL HOLMES, JR., 1841–1935
(Associate justice of the United States Supreme Court, 1902–1932)

• **EXAMPLE 14.1** You contract with Marinot Industries to perform certain personal services exclusively for Marinot during August for a payment of $3,500. Marinot cancels the contract and is in breach. You are able to find another job during August but can only earn $1,000. You normally can sue Marinot for breach and recover $2,500 as compensatory damages. You may also recover from Marinot the amount that you spent to find the other job. • Expenses that are directly incurred because of a breach of contract—such as those incurred to obtain performance from another source—are called *incidental damages.*

The measurement of compensatory damages varies by type of contract. Certain types of contracts deserve special mention—contracts for the sale of goods, contracts for the sale of land, and construction contracts.

ON THE WEB

For a summary of how contracts may be breached and other information on contract law, go to www.lawyers.com/site/aboutlaw/contract.html#contract10.

Sale of Goods. In a contract for the sale of goods, the usual measure of compensatory damages is an amount equal to the difference between the contract price and the market price.[3] • **EXAMPLE 14.2** MediQuick Laboratories contracts with Cal Computer Industries to purchase ten Model X-15 computer work stations for $8,000 each. If Cal Computer fails to deliver the ten work stations, and the current market price of the workstations is $8,150, MediQuick's measure of damages is $1,500 (10 × $150). In cases in which the buyer breaches and the seller has not yet produced the goods, compensatory damages normally equal the lost profits on the sale rather than the difference between the contract price and the market price. •

Sale of Land. The measure of damages in a contract for the sale of land is ordinarily the same as it is for contracts involving the sale of goods—that is, the difference between the contract price and the market price of the land. The majority of states follow this rule regardless of whether it is the buyer or the seller who breaches the contract.

Construction Contracts. With construction contracts, the measure of damages often varies depending on which party breaches and at what stage the breach occurs. See Exhibit 14–1 for illustrations.

• **CONSEQUENTIAL DAMAGES**
Special damages that compensate for a loss that does not directly or immediately result from the breach (for example, lost profits). The special damages must have been reasonably foreseeable at the time the breach or injury occurred in order for the plaintiff to collect them.

Consequential Damages Foreseeable damages that result from a party's breach of contract are referred to as **consequential damages,** or *special damages.* Consequential damages differ from compensatory damages in that they are caused by special cir-

3. That is, the difference between the contract price and the market price at the time and place at which the goods were to be delivered or tendered. See UCC 2–708, 2–713, and 2–715(1) (discussed in Chapter 17).

EXHIBIT 14–1 • Measurement of Damages—Breach of Construction Contracts

PARTY IN BREACH	TIME OF BREACH	MEASUREMENT OF DAMAGES
Owner	Before construction begins	Profits (contract price less cost of materials and labor)
Owner	After construction begins	Profits plus costs incurred up to time of breach
Owner	After construction is completed	Contract price
Contractor	Before construction is completed	Generally, all costs incurred by owner to complete construction

cumstances beyond the contract itself. When a seller does not deliver goods, knowing that a buyer is planning to resell those goods immediately, consequential damages are awarded for the loss of profits from the planned resale.

• **EXAMPLE 14.3** Gilmore contracts to have a specific item shipped to her—one that she desperately needs to repair her printing press. In contracting with the shipper, Gilmore tells the shipper that she must receive the item by Monday or she will not be able to print her paper and will lose $750. If the shipper is late, Gilmore normally can recover the consequential damages caused by the delay (that is, the $750 in losses).•

¡NOTE! A seller who does not wish to take on the risk of consequential damages can limit the buyer's remedies.

For a nonbreaching party to recover consequential damages, the breaching party must know (or have reason to know) that special circumstances will cause the nonbreaching party to suffer an additional loss.[4] This rule was enunciated in *Hadley v. Baxendale*, a case decided in England in 1854 and presented below as this chapter's *Landmark in the Law*. Today, the rule still applies. When damages are awarded, compensation is given only for those injuries that the defendant *could reasonably have foreseen* as a probable result of the usual course of events following a breach. If the injury complained of is outside the usual and foreseeable course of events, the plaintiff must show specifically that the defendant had reason to know the facts and foresee the injury.

4. UCC 2–715(2). See Chapter 17.

Landmark in the Law • HADLEY V. BAXENDALE (1854)

A landmark case in establishing the rule that notice of special ("consequential") circumstances must be given if consequential damages are to be recovered is *Hadley v. Baxendale*,[a] decided in 1854. This case involved a broken crankshaft used in a flour mill run by the Hadley family in Gloucester, England. The crankshaft attached to the steam engine in the mill broke, and the shaft had to be sent to a foundry located in Greenwich so that a new shaft could be made to fit the other parts of the engine.

The Hadleys hired Baxendale, a common carrier, to transport the shaft from Gloucester to Greenwich. Baxendale received payment in advance and promised to deliver the shaft the following day. It was not delivered for several days, however. As a consequence, the mill was closed during those days because the Hadleys had no extra crankshaft on hand to use. The Hadleys sued Baxendale to recover the profits they lost during that time. Baxendale contended that the loss of profits was "too remote."

In the mid-1800s, it was common knowledge that large mills, such as that run by the Hadleys, normally had more than one crankshaft in case the main one broke and had to be repaired, as it did in this case. It is against this background that the parties argued their respective positions on whether the damages resulting from loss of profits while the crankshaft was out for repair were "too remote" to be recoverable.

The crucial issue before the court was whether the Hadleys had informed the carrier, Baxendale, of the special circumstances surrounding the crankshaft's repair, particularly of the fact that the mill would have to shut down while the crankshaft was being repaired. If Baxendale had been notified of this circumstance at the time the contract was formed, then the remedy for breaching the contract would have been the amount of damages that would reasonably follow from the breach—including the Hadleys' lost profits. In the court's opinion, however, the only circumstances communicated by the Hadleys to Baxendale at the time the contract was made were that the item to be transported was a broken crankshaft of a mill and that the Hadleys were the owners and operators of that mill. The court concluded that these circumstances did not reasonably indicate that the mill would have to stop operations if the delivery of the crankshaft was delayed.

FOR CRITICAL ANALYSIS If it had not been the custom in the mid-1800s for mills to have extra crankshafts on hand, how would this circumstance have affected the court's ruling?

a. 9 Exch. 341, 156 Eng.Rep. 145 (1854).

Punitive Damages Recall from Chapter 4 that punitive damages are designed to punish a wrongdoer and set an example to deter similar conduct in the future. Punitive damages, which are also referred to as *exemplary damages,* are generally not recoverable in an action for breach of contract. Such damages have no legitimate place in contract law because they are, in essence, penalties, and a breach of contract is not unlawful in a criminal sense. A contract is simply a civil relationship between the parties. The law may compensate one party for the loss of the bargain—no more and no less.

In a few situations, a person's actions can cause both a breach of contract and a tort. For example, the parties can establish by contract a certain reasonable standard or duty of care. Failure to live up to that standard is a breach of contract, and the act itself may constitute negligence. An intentional tort (such as fraud) may also be tied to a breach of contract. In such a situation, it is possible for the nonbreaching party to recover punitive damages for the tort in addition to compensatory and consequential damages for the breach of contract.

"Nominal damages are, in effect, only a peg to hang costs on."
SIR WILLIAM HENRY MAULE, 1788–1858 (British jurist)

Nominal Damages Damages that are awarded to an innocent party when only a technical injury is involved and no actual damage (no financial loss) has been suffered are called **nominal damages.** Nominal damage awards are often small, such as one dollar, but they do establish that the defendant acted wrongfully.

• **NOMINAL DAMAGES**
A small monetary award (often one dollar) granted to a plaintiff when no actual damage was suffered.

• **EXAMPLE 14.4** Parrott contracts to buy potatoes at fifty cents a pound from Lentz. Lentz breaches the contract and does not deliver the potatoes. Meanwhile, the price of potatoes falls. Parrott is able to buy them in the open market at half the price he agreed to pay Lentz. Parrott is clearly better off because of Lentz's breach. Thus, in a suit for breach of contract, Parrott may be awarded only nominal damages for the technical injury he sustained, as no monetary loss was involved. Most lawsuits for nominal damages are brought as a matter of principle under the theory that a breach has occurred and some damages must be imposed regardless of actual loss. •

• **MITIGATION OF DAMAGES**
A rule requiring a plaintiff to have done whatever was reasonable to minimize the damages caused by the defendant.

MITIGATION OF DAMAGES

In most situations, when a breach of contract occurs, the injured party is held to a duty to mitigate, or reduce, the damages that he or she suffers. Under this doctrine of **mitigation of damages,** the required action depends on the nature of the situation. For example, some states require a landlord to use reasonable means to find a new tenant if a tenant abandons the premises and fails to pay rent. If an acceptable tenant becomes available, the landlord is required to lease the premises to the tenant to mitigate the damages recoverable from the former tenant. The former tenant is still liable for the difference between the amount of the rent under the original lease and the rent received from the new tenant. If the landlord has not used the reasonable means necessary to find a new tenant, presumably a court can reduce any award made to the landlord by the amount of rent he or she could have received had such reasonable means been used.

SHIRLEY MACLAINE PARKER IS AN ACCLAIMED ARTIST. WHAT MUST AN ARTIST DO TO MITIGATE HIS OR HER DAMAGES CAUSED BY A BROKEN CONTRACT?

In the majority of states, wrongfully terminated employees have a duty to mitigate damages suffered by their employers' breach. (This is true even for victims of employment discrimination—see this chapter's Business *Law in Action* for an illustration of this principle.) The damages they will be awarded are their salaries less the incomes they would have received in similar jobs obtained by reasonable means. It is the employer's burden to prove the existence of such jobs and to prove that the

Business Law in Action • Even Victims of Employment Discrimination Must Try to Mitigate Damages

American employees are protected in their employment under a variety of laws, such as Title VII of the Civil Rights Act of 1964, the Age Discrimination in Employment Act of 1967, and the Americans with Disabilities Act of 1990. Employees who are fired in violation of one of these acts typically are awarded damages to compensate the employee for lost wages. In some cases of intentional discrimination against employees, punitive damages may be awarded as well. There is a presumption, nonetheless, that even a person who has been wrongfully terminated must attempt to mitigate damages by seeking alternative, comparable employment. The U.S. Court of Appeals for the Second Circuit confirmed this principle in the case of *Greenway v. Buffalo Hilton Hotel.*[a]

That case was brought by Danny Greenway against his former employer, the Buffalo Hilton Hotel. Earlier, when Greenway was hired by the hotel to be a bartender, he did not reveal to his employer that he had tested positive for HIV, the virus that causes AIDS. Five years later, when he took a disability leave, he informed his employer that he was HIV positive. He returned to work but was disciplined on numerous occasions and was ultimately fired.

At trial, Greenway succeeded in convincing the court that he was fired in violation of the Americans with Disabilities Act (ADA) of 1990, and the jury awarded him $1.4 million. That amount included compensatory damages for back pay, front pay (lost future wages), and future medical costs (for health insurance, medication, and the like) that would have been covered by Hilton's group insurance policy had Greenway not been fired. The amount also included $1 million in punitive damages. Following the trial, the trial court judge reduced the punitive damages award to $200,000 and modified other damages, reducing the total amount awarded to approximately $771,000.

On appeal, the Second Circuit upheld the trial jury's finding that the hotel had violated the ADA but held that Greenway was not entitled to receive damages for front pay, future health insurance premiums, or future medication costs. Why? Because Greenway had failed to mitigate his damages by seeking other permanent employment. Greenway worked for six months at a temporary agency. After that, he made no effort whatsoever to find suitable employment as a bartender. The court noted that under a number of case precedents, victims of employment discrimination have been required to mitigate their damages.[b]

FOR CRITICAL ANALYSIS

If the wrongfully discharged employee does seek employment but fails to find any, why does the burden then fall on the former employer to prove that suitable employment was nonetheless available?

a. 143 F.3d 47 (1998).

b. Among other cases, the court cited *Ford Motor Company v. EEOC,* 458 U.S. 219, 102 S.Ct 3057, 73 L.Ed.2d 721 (1982); and *Dailey v. Societe Generale,* 108 F.3d 451 (2d Cir. 1997).

employee could have been hired. An employee is, of course, under no duty to take a job that is not of the same type and rank. This concept is illustrated in the following case.

CASE 14.1 Parker v. Twentieth Century-Fox Film Corp.

Supreme Court of California, 1970.
3 Cal.3d 176,
474 P.2d 689,
89 Cal.Rptr. 737.

COMPANY PROFILE *Daryl Zanuck and Joseph Schenk formed the Twentieth Century Company in 1933 to make movies. Two years later, they merged with the Fox Film Company, which had been founded by William Fox, and became Twentieth Century-Fox Film Corporation. Today, Twentieth Century-Fox produces movies and television shows as part of the News Corporation Limited, which is headquartered in Australia. The News Corporation also has interests in the production and distribution of newspapers, magazines, books, television programs, and films in Great Britain, Hong Kong, New Zealand, and other countries.*

(Continued)

CASE 14.1—Continued

BACKGROUND AND FACTS Twentieth Century-Fox Film Corporation planned to produce a musical, *Bloomer Girl,* and contracted with Shirley MacLaine Parker to play the leading female role. According to the contract, Fox was to pay Parker $53,571.42 per week for fourteen weeks, for a total of $750,000. Fox later decided not to produce *Bloomer Girl* and tried to substitute another contract for the existing contract. Under the terms of this second contract, Parker would play the leading role in a Western movie for the same amount of money guaranteed by the first contract. Fox gave Parker one week in which to accept the new contract. Parker filed suit in a California state court against Fox to recover the amount of compensation guaranteed in the first contract because, she maintained, the two roles were not at all equivalent. The *Bloomer Girl* production was a musical, to be filmed in California, and it could not be compared with a "Western-type" production that Fox tentatively planned to produce in Australia. When the trial court held for Parker, Fox appealed. Ultimately, the California Supreme Court reviewed the case.

IN THE WORDS OF THE COURT . . .
BURKE, Justice.

* * * *

The general rule is that the measure of recovery by a wrongfully discharged employee is the amount of salary agreed upon for the period of service, less the amount which the employer affirmatively proves the employee has earned or with reasonable effort might have earned from other employment. However, before projected earnings from other employment opportunities not sought or accepted by the discharged employee can be applied in mitigation, the employer must show that the other employment was comparable, or substantially similar, to that of which the employee has been deprived * * * .

* * * *

* * * The mere circumstance that *Bloomer Girl* was to be a musical review calling upon plaintiff's talents as a dancer as well as an actress, and was to be produced in the City of Los Angeles, whereas *Big Country* was a straight dramatic role in a 'Western Type' story taking place in an opal mine in Australia, demonstrates the difference in kind between the two employments; the female lead as a dramatic actress in a western style motion picture can by no stretch of imagination be considered the equivalent of or substantially similar to the lead in a song-and-dance production.

DECISION AND REMEDY The Supreme Court of California affirmed the trial court's ruling. Parker could not be required to accept Fox's offer of the western-movie contract to mitigate the damages she incurred as a result of the breach of contract.

FOR CRITICAL ANALYSIS—International Consideration *Many legal systems, including that of France, have no clear requirement that damages must be mitigated. Can justice be better served by requiring that damages be mitigated? If so, how?*

• **LIQUIDATED DAMAGES**
An amount, stipulated in the contract, that the parties to a contract believe to be a reasonable estimation of the damages that will occur in the event of a breach.

• **PENALTY**
A sum inserted into a contract, not as a measure of compensation for its breach but rather as punishment for a default. The agreement as to the amount will not be enforced, and recovery will be limited to actual damages.

Liquidated Damages versus Penalties

A **liquidated damages** provision in a contract specifies that a certain dollar amount is to be paid in the event of a future default or breach of contract. (*Liquidated* means determined, settled, or fixed.) Liquidated damages differ from penalties. A **penalty** specifies a certain amount to be paid in the event of a default or breach of contract and is designed to penalize the breaching party. Liquidated damages provisions normally are enforceable. In contrast, if a court finds that a provision is a penalty provision, the agreement as to the amount will not be enforced, and recovery will be limited to actual damages.[5]

5. This is also the rule under the Uniform Commercial Code. See UCC 2–718(1).

To determine whether a particular provision is for liquidated damages or for a penalty, the court must answer two questions: First, at the time the contract was formed, was it difficult to estimate the potential damages that would be incurred if the contract was not performed on time? Second, was the amount set as damages a reasonable estimate of those potential damages and not excessive?[6] If the answers to both questions are yes, the provision normally will be enforced. If either answer is no, the provision will normally not be enforced. In a construction contract, it is difficult to estimate the amount of damages that might be caused by a delay in completing construction, so liquidated damages clauses are often used.

ETHICAL ISSUE 14.1 ***Should disproportionately high "late fees" on monthly bills be considered "penalties"?*** Nearly every service provider has to deal with the issue of late payments from its subscribers. One way that some companies have dealt with this problem is to charge a "late fee." But what if the late fee is significantly higher than the actual loss incurred by a company due to a late payment? In this situation, can customers sue the company under the common law rules governing liquidated damages versus penalties? At least one court has answered that question in the affirmative. The case involved a subscriber contract between a cable TV company in Baltimore, Maryland, and its customers. The contract provided that whenever a payment was late, the customer would be charged $5. In fact, the cable company lost, on average, only 38 cents when someone paid his or her bill late. In a class-action suit against the company, the customers alleged that late fees constitute a form of liquidated damages but that "grossly excessive" fees constitute penalties. A Maryland state trial court agreed, concluding that the "cable company's late fee is exorbitant, bears no reasonable relation to the real cost of handling and collecting the late payment, and constitutes a tool of profit for the collection of additional revenues." The court ordered the company to pay $5.4 million in damages.[7]

Rescission and Restitution

• **RESTITUTION**
An equitable remedy under which a person is restored to his or her original position prior to loss or injury, or placed in the position he or she would have been in had the breach not occurred.

¡CONTRAST!
The advantages of obtaining restitution instead of damages include the possibility of recovering specific property, the possibility of making a recovery when damages cannot be proved, and the possibility of obtaining a greater award.

As discussed in Chapter 13, rescission is essentially an action to undo, or cancel, a contract—to return nonbreaching parties to the positions that they occupied prior to the transaction. When fraud, mistake, duress, or failure of consideration is present, rescission is available. The failure of one party to perform under a contract entitles the other party to rescind the contract.[8] The rescinding party must give prompt notice to the breaching party. Furthermore, both parties must make **restitution** to each other by returning goods, property, or funds previously conveyed.[9] If the physical property or goods can be returned, they must be. If the property or goods have been consumed, restitution must be made in an equivalent dollar amount.

Essentially, restitution refers to the recapture of a benefit conferred on the defendant through which the defendant has been unjustly enriched. • **EXAMPLE 14.5**

6. *Restatement (Second) of Contracts,* Section 356(1).
7. *Burch v. United Cable Television of Baltimore Limited Partnership,* Baltimore City (Maryland) Circuit Court, September 16, 1997, as cited in *Lawyers Weekly USA,* October 20, 1997, pp. 9–10.
8. The rescission discussed here refers to *unilateral* rescission, in which only one party wants to undo the contract. In *mutual* rescission, both parties agree to undo the contract. Mutual rescission discharges the contract; unilateral rescission is generally available as a remedy for breach of contract.
9. *Restatement (Second) of Contracts,* Section 370.

WHEN IS SPECIFIC PERFORMANCE THE APPROPRIATE REMEDY FOR A BREACH OF CONTRACT?

Andrea pays $10,000 to Myles in return for Myles's promise to design a house for her. The next day, Myles calls Andrea and tells her that he has taken a position with a large architectural firm in another state and cannot design the house. Andrea decides to hire another architect that afternoon. Andrea can require restitution of $10,000, because Myles has received an unjust benefit of $10,000.•

Specific Performance

• **SPECIFIC PERFORMANCE** An equitable remedy requiring exactly the performance that was specified in a contract; usually granted only when money damages would be an inadequate remedy and the subject matter of the contract is unique (for example, real property).

The equitable remedy of **specific performance** calls for the performance of the act promised in the contract. This remedy is often attractive to a nonbreaching party, because it provides the exact bargain promised in the contract. It also avoids some of the problems inherent in a suit for money damages. First, the nonbreaching party need not worry about collecting the judgment.[10] Second, the nonbreaching party need not look around for another contract. Third, the actual performance may be more valuable than the money damages. Although the equitable remedy of specific performance is often preferable to other remedies, normally it is not granted unless the party's legal remedy (money damages) is inadequate and the subject matter of the contract is unique.[11]

Contracts for the sale of goods that are readily available on the market, for instance, rarely qualify for specific performance. Money damages ordinarily are adequate in such situations, because substantially identical goods can be bought or sold in the market. If the goods are unique, however, a court of equity will decree specific performance. For example, paintings, sculptures, and rare books and coins are often unique, and money damages will not enable a buyer to obtain substantially identical

"Specific performance is a remedy of grace and not a matter of right, and the test of whether or not it should be granted depends on the particular circumstances of each case."

GEORGE BUSHNELL, 1887–1965
(American jurist)

10. Courts dispose of cases, after trials, by entering judgments. A judgment may order the losing party to pay money damages to the winning party. Collection of judgments, however, poses problems—such as when the judgment debtor is insolvent (cannot pay his or her bills when they become due) or has only a small net worth, or when the debtor's assets cannot be seized, under exemption laws, by a creditor to satisfy a debt (see Chapter 23).

11. *Restatement (Second) of Contracts,* Section 359.

substitutes on the market. The same principle applies to contracts relating to sales of land or interests in land, because each parcel of land is unique by legal description.

Courts refuse to grant specific performance of contracts for personal services. This is because to order a party to perform personal services against his or her will amounts to a type of involuntary servitude, which is contrary to the public policy expressed in the Thirteenth Amendment to the Constitution. Moreover, the courts do not want to monitor personal-services contracts. • EXAMPLE 14.6 If you contract with a brain surgeon to perform brain surgery on you and the surgeon refuses to perform, the court would not compel (and you certainly would not want) the surgeon to perform under these circumstances. There is no way the court can assure meaningful performance in such a situation.[12] •

International Perspective • SPECIFIC PERFORMANCE IN GERMANY

In the United States, the general rule is that the equitable remedy of specific performance will be granted only if the remedy at law (money damages) is inadequate and the subject matter of the contract is unique. In Germany, however, the typical remedy for a breach of contract is specific performance. In other words, a German court normally would order the breaching party to go forward and perform the contract. German courts will award damages for breach of contract in some circumstances, but damages are available only after notice and other procedures have been employed to seek performance.

FOR CRITICAL ANALYSIS

If U.S. courts commonly granted the remedy of specific performance, as German courts do, would parties be less likely to breach their contracts?

Reformation

When the parties have imperfectly expressed their agreement in writing, the equitable remedy of *reformation* allows the contract to be rewritten to reflect the parties' true intentions. This remedy applies most often when fraud or mutual mistake has occurred. • EXAMPLE 14.7 If Keshan contracts to buy a forklift from Shelley but the written contract refers to a crane, a mutual mistake has occurred. Accordingly, a court could reform the contract so that the writing conforms to the parties' original intention as to which piece of equipment is being sold. •

Two other examples deserve mention. The first involves two parties who have made a binding oral contract. They further agree to reduce the oral contract to writing, but in doing so, they make an error in stating the terms. Universally, the courts allow into evidence the correct terms of the oral contract, thereby reforming the written contract.

The second example has to do with written covenants not to compete. As discussed in Chapter 11, if a covenant not to compete is for a valid and legitimate purpose (such as the sale of a business) but the area or time restraints of the covenant are unreasonable, some courts reform the restraints by making them reasonable and enforce the entire contract as reformed. Other courts throw the entire restrictive covenant out as illegal.

12. Similarly, courts often refuse to order specific performance of construction contracts, because courts are not set up to operate as construction supervisors or engineers.

Recovery Based on Quasi Contract

¡DON'T FORGET!
The function of a quasi contract is to impose a legal obligation on a party who made no actual promise.

Recall from Chapter 9 that a quasi contract is not a true contract but a fictional contract that is imposed on the parties to obtain justice and prevent unjust enrichment. Hence, a quasi contract becomes an equitable basis for relief. Generally, when one party confers a benefit on another, justice requires that the party receiving the benefit pay a reasonable value for it so as not to be unjustly enriched at the other party's expense.

Quasi-contractual recovery is useful when one party has partially performed under a contract that is unenforceable. It can be an alternative to suing for damages, and it allows the party to recover the reasonable value of the partial performance. For quasi-contractual recovery to occur, the party seeking recovery must show the following:

1. A benefit was conferred on the other party.
2. The party conferring the benefit did so with the expectation of being paid.
3. The party seeking recovery did not act as a volunteer in conferring the benefit.
4. Retaining the benefit without paying for it would result in an unjust enrichment of the party receiving the benefit.

"What burns me up is that the answer is right here somewhere, staring us in the face."

> **ON THE WEB**
> Cornell University's Legal Information Institute offers a menu of sources on contract law at www.law.cornell.edu. When you access this site, scroll down the page to "Contracts."

• **EXAMPLE 14.8** Ericson contracts to build two oil derricks for Petro Industries. The derricks are to be built over a period of three years, but the parties do not create a written contract. Enforcement of the contract will therefore be barred by the Statute of Frauds.[13] Ericson completes one derrick, and then Petro Industries informs him that it will not pay for the derrick. Ericson can sue in quasi contract because all of the conditions just mentioned for quasi-contractual recovery have been fulfilled. Ericson should be able to recover the reasonable value of the oil derrick (under the theory of *quantum meruit*[14]—"as much as he deserves"). The reasonable value is ordinarily equal to the fair market value.•

The following case involved a question of the calculation of the amount of a recovery under the theory of *quantum meruit.*

13. Contracts that by their terms cannot be performed within one year must be in writing to be enforceable. See Chapter 12.

14. Pronounced *kwahn*-tuhm *mehr*-oo-wuht.

CASE 14.2 Maglica v. Maglica

California Court of Appeal, Fourth District, Division 3, 1998.
66 Cal.App.4th 442,
66 Cal.App.4th 1367C,
78 Cal.Rptr.2d 101.

HISTORICAL AND SOCIAL SETTING *The absence of a contract does not preclude recovery in* quantum meruit. *"The measure of recovery in* quantum meruit *is the reasonable value of the services rendered provided they were of direct benefit to the defendant."*[a] *The underlying idea behind* quantum meruit *is the law's distaste for unjust enrichment. If a person receives a benefit that he or she may not justly retain, the person should return whatever was received or pay for it. The idea that one must be benefited by the goods or services bestowed is thus an essential element to recovery in* quantum meruit. *Courts have always required that a plaintiff must have bestowed a benefit on the defendant in order to recover in* quantum meruit.

a. *Palmer v. Gregg,* 65 Cal.2d 657, 422 P.2d 985, 56 Cal.Rptr. 97 (1967).

BACKGROUND AND FACTS Anthony Maglica founded a machine shop business called Mag Instrument in 1955. In 1971, he and Claire Halasz began to live together, holding themselves out as husband and wife, but they never actually married. Claire worked with Anthony to build Mag Instrument, although when it was incorporated in 1974, all shares were issued to Anthony. Anthony, as president, and Claire, as secretary, were paid equal salaries. In 1978, the business began manufacturing flashlights, and thanks to ideas and hard work on Claire's part, the business boomed. The couple separated in 1992, and Claire filed a suit in a California state court against Anthony, seeking a recovery, among other grounds, in *quantum meruit.* The jury awarded Claire $84 million, based on the business's benefit from her services. Anthony appealed.

IN THE WORDS OF THE COURT . . .
SILLS, Presiding Justice.

* * * *

* * * [T]he threshold requirement [under *quantum meruit*] that there be a benefit from the services can lead to confusion, as it did in the case before us. It is one thing to require that the defendant be benefited by services, it is quite another to measure the reasonable value of those services by the value by which the defendant was "benefited" as a result of them. Contract price and the reasonable value of services rendered are two separate things; sometimes the reasonable value of services exceeds a contract price. And sometimes it does not.

* * * Resulting benefit is an open-ended standard, which * * * can result in the plaintiff obtaining recovery amounting to *de facto* ownership in a business all out

(Continued)

CASE 14.2—Continued

of reasonable relation to the value of services rendered. After all, a particular service timely rendered can have * * * disproportionate value to what it would cost on the open market.

* * * *

* * * Allowing recovery based on resulting benefit would mean the law imposes an exchange of equity for services, and that can result in a windfall—as in the present case * * * . To impose such a measure of recovery would make a deal for the parties that they did not make themselves. * * * [Courts cannot] use *quantum meruit* to impose a highly generous and extraordinary contract that the parties did not make.

DECISION AND REMEDY The state intermediate appellate court reversed the lower court's decision and remanded the case to the trial court for a recalculation of the award. The appellate court held that Claire could recover for the value of her services, but she could not recover for the benefit conferred on the business.

FOR CRITICAL ANALYSIS—Economic Consideration *Should the result be the same in a case involving a business firm such as the Walt Disney Company and an idea such as Mickey Mouse?*

Election of Remedies

¡BE AWARE! Which remedy a plaintiff elects depends on the subject of the contract, the defenses of the breaching party, the advantages that might be gained in terms of tactics against the defendant, and what the plaintiff can prove with respect to the remedy sought.

In many cases, a nonbreaching party has several remedies available. Because the remedies may be inconsistent with one another, the common law of contracts requires the party to choose which remedy to pursue. This is called *election of remedies*. The purpose of the doctrine of election of remedies is to prevent double recovery.

• **EXAMPLE 14.9** Suppose that Jefferson agrees to sell his land to Adams. Then Jefferson changes his mind and repudiates the contract. Adams can sue for compensatory damages or for specific performance. If she receives damages as a result of the breach, she should not also be granted specific performance of the sales contract, because that would mean she would unfairly end up with both the land and damages. The doctrine of election of remedies requires Adams to choose the remedy she wants, and it eliminates any possibility of double recovery. •

In contrast, remedies under the UCC are *cumulative*. They include all of the remedies available under the UCC for breach of a sales or lease contract.[15]

In the following case, the frustrated sellers of a house were apparently attempting to avoid the doctrine of election of remedies in order to, as the old saying goes, "have their cake and eat it, too."

15. See UCC 2–703 and 2–711.

CASE 14.3 Palmer v. Hayes

Court of Appeals of Utah, 1995.
892 P.2d 1059.

HISTORICAL AND ECONOMIC SETTING *Real estate transactions have long involved the same steps as those that shape a deal today. A transaction starts with a seller who wants to sell and a buyer who wants to buy. The buyer might make a bid on the property. This bid usually takes the form of a proposed contract of sale and includes a deposit of a percentage of the price offered for the property. If a seller accepts a buyer's proposal, the buyer is bound to it.*

BACKGROUND AND FACTS Kenneth and Rebecca Palmer wanted to sell their house. Edward and Stephanie Hayes signed a proposed contract of sale, under which they agreed to give the Palmers' real estate agent, Maple Hills

CASE 14.3—Continued

Realty, $2,000 as a deposit on the house. The agreement provided that in the event of default, the Palmers could either keep the deposit or sue to enforce their rights. The Palmers accepted the Hayeses' offer and signed the contract. Before the property changed hands, however, the Hayeses changed their minds and asked for the return of their deposit. The Palmers refused and filed a suit against the Hayeses in a Utah state court, seeking damages. The Hayeses filed a motion for summary judgment on the ground that, by not releasing the deposit, the Palmers had elected their remedy. The court ruled in favor of the Hayeses on this point, and the Palmers appealed.

IN THE WORDS OF THE COURT . . .
BENCH, Judge:

* * * *

* * * [A] seller's failure to offer to return earnest money deposits precludes the seller from pursuing other remedies.

* * * [B]efore a seller may pursue a remedy other than liquidated damages, the seller must release any claim to the deposit money.

* * * The Palmers therefore needed only to indicate to Maple Hills Realty, in writing, that they released the deposit money to the Hayeses. Then they could have proceeded with their suit for damages. * * *

* * * [B]y failing to release the deposit money, the Palmers elected to retain it as liquidated damages.

DECISION AND REMEDY The Court of Appeals of Utah, concluding that the Palmers had elected the remedy of liquidated damages, affirmed the lower court's ruling.

FOR CRITICAL ANALYSIS—Economic Consideration
What are the reasons for applying the doctrine of election of remedies to preclude sellers who keep deposits from suing for damages?

Provisions Limiting Remedies

¡RECALL!
Exculpatory clauses may be held unconscionable, depending on the relative bargaining positions of the parties and the importance to the public interest of the business seeking to enforce the clause.

A contract may include provisions stating that no damages can be recovered for certain types of breaches or that damages must be limited to a maximum amount. The contract may also provide that the only remedy for breach is replacement, repair, or refund of the purchase price. Provisions stating that no damages can be recovered are called *exculpatory clauses* (see Chapter 11). Provisions that affect the availability of certain remedies are called *limitation-of-liability clauses.*

Whether these contract provisions and clauses will be enforced depends on the type of breach that is excused by the provision. For example, a provision excluding liability for fraudulent or intentional injury will not be enforced. Likewise, a clause excluding liability for illegal acts or violations of law will not be enforced. A clause excluding liability for negligence may be enforced in some cases. When an exculpatory clause for negligence is contained in a contract made between parties who have roughly equal bargaining positions, the clause usually will be enforced.

The UCC provides that in a contract for the sale of goods, remedies can be limited.[16] We will examine the UCC's provisions on limited remedies in Chapter 17, in the context of the remedies available on the breach of a sales contract.

16. UCC 2–719.

APPLICATION

Law & the Contractor: When You Cannot Perform*

Not every contract can be performed. If you are a contractor, you may take on a job that, for one reason or another, you cannot or do not wish to perform. Simply walking away from the job and hoping for the best is not normally the most effective way to avoid litigation—which can be costly, time consuming, and emotionally draining. Instead, you should consider avoidance of litigation through *compromise.*

For example, suppose that you are a building contractor and you sign a contract to build a home for the Andersons. Performance is to begin on June 15. On June 1, Central Enterprises offers you a position that will yield you two and a half times the amount of net income you could earn as an independent builder. To take the job, you have to start on June 15. You cannot be in two places at the same time, so to accept the new position you must breach the contract with the Andersons.

*This *Application* is not meant to substitute for the services of an attorney who is licensed to practice law in your state.

What to do? One option is to subcontract the work to another builder and oversee the work yourself to make sure it conforms to the contract. Another option is to negotiate with the Andersons for a release. You can offer to find another qualified builder who will build a house of the same quality at the same price. Alternatively, you can offer to pay any additional costs if another builder takes the job and is more expensive. In any event, this additional cost would be the measure of damages that a court would impose on you if the Andersons sued you for breach of contract and the Andersons prevailed. Thus, by making the offer, you might be able to avoid the expense of litigation—if the Andersons accept your offer.

Often, parties are reluctant to propose compromise settlements because they fear that what they say will be used against them in court if litigation ensues. The general rule, however, is that offers for settlement cannot be used in court to prove that you are liable for a breach of contract.

Checklist for the Contractor Who Cannot Perform

1. Consider a compromise.
2. Subcontract out the work and oversee it.
3. Offer to find an alternative contractor to fulfill your obligation.
4. Make a cash offer to "buy" a release from your contract. If anything other than an insignificant amount of money is involved, however, work with an attorney in making the offer.

Key Terms

consequential damages 358
liquidated damages 362
mitigation of damages 360
nominal damages 360
penalty 362
restitution 363
specific performance 364

Chapter Summary • Breach and Remedies

COMMON REMEDIES AVAILABLE TO NONBREACHING PARTY	
Damages (See pages 357–363.)	The legal remedy designed to compensate the nonbreaching party for the loss of the bargain. By awarding money damages, the court tries to place the parties in the positions that they would have occupied had the contract been fully performed. The nonbreaching party frequently has a duty to *mitigate* (lessen or reduce) the damages incurred as a result of the contract's breach. There are five broad categories of damages:

Chapter Summary • Breach and Remedies, Continued

Damages—continued	1. *Compensatory damages*—Damages that compensate the nonbreaching party for injuries actually sustained and proved to have arisen directly from the loss of the bargain resulting from the breach of contract. a. In breached contracts for the sale of goods, the usual measure of compensatory damages is an amount equal to the difference between the contract price and the market price. b. In breached contracts for the sale of land, the measure of damages is ordinarily the same as in contracts for the sale of goods. c. In breached construction contracts, the measure of damages depends on which party breaches and at what stage of construction the breach occurs. 2. *Consequential damages*—Damages resulting from special circumstances beyond the contract itself; the damages flow only from the consequences of a breach. For a party to recover consequential damages, the damages must be the foreseeable result of a breach of contract, and the breaching party must have known at the time the contract was formed that special circumstances existed that would cause the nonbreaching party to incur additional loss on breach of the contract. Also called *special damages.* 3. *Punitive damages*—Damages awarded to punish the breaching party. Usually not awarded in an action for breach of contract unless a tort is involved. 4. *Nominal damages*—Damages small in amount (such as one dollar) that are awarded when a breach has occurred but no actual damages have been suffered. Awarded only to establish that the defendant acted wrongfully. 5. *Liquidated damages*—Damages that may be specified in a contract as the amount to be paid to the nonbreaching party in the event the contract is breached in the future. Clauses providing for liquidated damages are enforced if the damages were difficult to estimate at the time the contract was formed and if the amount stipulated is reasonable. If construed to be a penalty, the clause will not be enforced.
Rescission and Restitution (See page 363–364.)	1. *Rescission*—A remedy whereby a contract is canceled and the parties are restored to the original positions that they occupied prior to the transaction. Available when fraud, a mistake, duress, or failure of consideration is present. The rescinding party must give prompt notice of the rescission to the breaching party. 2. *Restitution*—When a contract is rescinded, both parties must make restitution to each other by returning the goods, property, or funds previously conveyed. Restitution prevents the unjust enrichment of parties.
Specific Performance (See pages 364–365.)	An equitable remedy calling for the performance of the act promised in the contract. This remedy is available only in special situations—such as those involving contracts for the sale of unique goods or land—and when monetary damages would be an inadequate remedy. Specific performance is not available as a remedy in breached contracts for personal services.
Reformation (See page 365.)	An equitable remedy allowing a contract to be "reformed," or rewritten, to reflect the parties' true intentions. Available when an agreement is imperfectly expressed in writing.
Recovery Based on Quasi Contract (See pages 366–368.)	An equitable theory imposed by the courts to obtain justice and prevent unjust enrichment in a situation in which no enforceable contract exists. The party seeking recovery must show the following: 1. A benefit was conferred on the other party. 2. The party conferring the benefit did so with the expectation of being paid. 3. The benefit was not volunteered.

Chapter Summary • Breach and Remedies, Continued

Recovery Based on Quasi Contract—continued	4. Retaining the benefit without paying for it would result in the unjust enrichment of the party receiving the benefit.
CONTRACT DOCTRINES RELATING TO REMEDIES	
Election of Remedies (See pages 368–369.)	A common law doctrine under which a nonbreaching party must choose one remedy from those available. This doctrine prevents double recovery. Under the UCC, in contracts for the sale of goods, remedies are cumulative.
Provisions Limiting Remedies (See page 369.)	A contract may provide that no damages (or only a limited amount of damages) can be recovered in the event the contract is breached. Clauses excluding liability for fraudulent or intentional injury or for illegal acts cannot be enforced. Clauses excluding liability for negligence may be enforced if both parties hold roughly equal bargaining power. Under the UCC, in contracts for the sale of goods, remedies may be limited.

For Review

1. What is the difference between compensatory damages and consequential damages? What are nominal damages, and when might they be awarded by a court?
2. What is the usual measure of damages on a breach of contract for a sale of goods?
3. Under what circumstances will the remedy of rescission and restitution be available?
4. When might specific performance be granted as a remedy?
5. What is the rationale underlying the doctrine of election of remedies?

Questions and Case Problems

14–1. Liquidated Damages. Carnack contracts to sell his house and lot to Willard for $100,000. The terms of the contract call for Willard to pay 10 percent of the purchase price as a deposit toward the purchase price, or as a down payment. The terms further stipulate that should the buyer breach the contract, the deposit will be retained by Carnack as liquidated damages. Willard pays the deposit, but because her expected financing of the $90,000 balance falls through, she breaches the contract. Two weeks later, Carnack sells the house and lot to Balkova for $105,000. Willard demands her $10,000 back, but Carnack refuses, claiming that Willard's breach and the contract terms entitle him to keep the deposit. Discuss who is correct.

14–2. Election of Remedies. Perez contracts to buy a new Oldsmobile from Central City Motors, paying $2,000 down and agreeing to make twenty-four monthly payments of $350 each. He takes the car home and, after making one payment, learns that his Oldsmobile has a Chevrolet engine in it rather than the famous Olds Super V-8 engine. Central City never informed Perez of this fact. Perez immediately notifies Central City of his dissatisfaction and returns the car to Central City. Central City accepts the car and returns to Perez the $2,000 down payment plus the one $350 payment. Two weeks later Perez, without a car and feeling angry, files a suit against Central City, seeking damages for breach of warranty and fraud. Discuss the effect of Perez's actions.

14–3. Specific Performance. In which of the following situations might a court grant specific performance as a remedy for the breach of the contract?

(a) Tarrington contracts to sell her house and lot to Rainier. Then, on finding another buyer willing to pay a higher purchase price, she refuses to deed the property to Rainier.

(b) Marita contracts to sing and dance in Horace's nightclub for one month, beginning June 1. She then refuses to perform.

(c) Juan contracts to purchase a rare coin from Edmund, who is breaking up his coin collection. At the last minute, Edmund decides to keep his coin collection intact and refuses to deliver the coin to Juan.

(d) There are three shareholders of Astro Computer Corp.: Coase, who owns 48 percent of the stock; De Valle, who owns 48 percent; and Cary, who owns 4 percent. Cary contracts to sell his 4 percent to De Valle but later refuses to transfer the shares to him.

14–4. Measure of Damages. Johnson contracted to lease a house to Fox for $700 a month, beginning October 1. Fox stipulated in the contract that before he moved in, the interior of the house had to be completely repainted. On September 9, Johnson hired Keever to do the required painting for $1,000. He told Keever that the painting had to be finished by October 1 but did not explain why. On September 28, Keever quit for no reason, having completed approximately 80 percent of the work. Johnson then paid Sam $300 to finish the painting, but Sam did not finish until October 4. Fox, when the painting had not been completed as stipulated in his contract with Johnson, leased another home. Johnson found another tenant who would lease the property at $700 a month, beginning October 15. Johnson then sued Keever for breach of contract, claiming damages of $650. This amount included the $300 Johnson paid Sam to finish the painting and $350 for rent for the first half of October, which Johnson had lost as a result of Keever's breach. Johnson had not yet paid Keever anything for Keever's work. Can Johnson collect the $650 from Keever? Explain.

14–5. Measure of Damages. Ben owns and operates a famous candy store. He makes most of the candy sold in the store, and business is particularly heavy during the Christmas season. Ben contracts with Sweet, Inc., to purchase ten thousand pounds of sugar, to be delivered on or before November 15. Ben informs Sweet that this particular order is to be used for the Christmas season business. Because of production problems, the sugar is not tendered to Ben until December 10, at which time Ben refuses the order because it is so late. Ben has been unable to purchase the quantity of sugar needed to meet the Christmas orders and has had to turn down numerous regular customers, some of whom have indicated that they will purchase candy elsewhere in the future. The sugar that Ben has been able to purchase has cost him ten cents per pound above Sweet's price. Ben sues Sweet for breach of contract, claiming as damages the higher price paid for the sugar from others, lost profits from this year's lost Christmas sales, future lost profits from customers who have indicated that they will discontinue doing business with him, and punitive damages for failure to meet the contracted-for delivery date. Sweet claims Ben is limited to compensatory damages only. Discuss who is correct and why.

14–6. Consequential Damages. Kerr Steamship Co. delivered to Radio Corp. of America (RCA) a twenty-nine-word, coded message to be sent to Kerr's agent in Manila. The message included instructions on loading cargo onto one of Kerr's vessels. Kerr's profits on the carriage of the cargo were to be about $6,600. RCA mislaid and never sent the coded message, and the cargo was shipped by another carrier. Kerr sued RCA for the $6,600 in profits that it lost because RCA failed to send the message. Can Kerr recover? Explain. [*Kerr Steamship Co. v. Radio Corp. of America,* 245 N.Y. 284, 157 N.E. 140 (1927)]

14–7. Limitation of Liability. Westinghouse Electric Corp. entered into a contract with New Jersey Electric to manufacture and install a turbine generator for producing electricity. The contract price was over $10 million. The parties engaged in three years of negotiations and bargaining before they agreed on a suitable contract. The ultimate contract provided, among other things, that Westinghouse would not be liable for any injuries to the property belonging to the utility or to its customers or employees. Westinghouse warranted only that it would repair any defects in workmanship and materials appearing within one year of installation. After installation, part of New Jersey Electric's plant was damaged, and several of its employees were injured because of a defect in the turbine. New Jersey Electric sued Westinghouse, claiming that Westinghouse was liable for the damages because the exculpatory provisions in the contract were unconscionable. What was the result? [*Royal Indemnity Co. v. Westinghouse Electric Corp.,* 385 F.Supp. 520 (S.D.N.Y. 1974)]

14–8. Liquidated Damages versus Penalties. The Ivanovs, who were of Russian origin, agreed to purchase the Sobels' home for $300,000. A $30,000 earnest money deposit was placed in the trust account of Kotler Realty, Inc., the broker facilitating the transaction. Tiasia Buliak, one of Kotler's salespersons, negotiated the sale because she spoke fluent Russian. To facilitate the closing without the Ivanovs' having to be present, Buliak suggested they form a Florida corporation, place the balance of the cash necessary to close the sale in a corporate account, and give her authority to draw checks against it. The Ivanovs did as Buliak had suggested. Before the closing date of the sale, Buliak absconded with all of the closing money, which caused the transaction to collapse. Subsequently, because the Ivanovs had defaulted, Kotler Realty delivered the $30,000 earnest money deposit in its trust account to the Sobels. The Ivanovs then sued the Sobels, seeking to recover the $30,000. Was the clause providing that the seller could retain the earnest money if the buyer defaulted an enforceable liquidated damages clause or an unenforceable penalty clause? Discuss. [*Ivanov v. Sobel,* 654 So.2d 991 (Fla.App.3d 1995)]

14–9. Mitigation of Damages. Charles Kloss had worked for Honeywell, Inc., for over fifteen years when Honeywell decided to transfer the employees at its Ballard facility to its Harbour Pointe facility. Honeywell planned to hire a medical person at the Harbour Pointe facility and promised Kloss that if he completed a nursing program and became a registered nurse (RN), the company would hire him for the medical position. When Kloss graduated from his RN program, however, Honeywell did not assign him to a nursing or medical position. Instead, the company gave Kloss a job in its maintenance department. Shortly thereafter, Kloss left the company and eventually sued Honeywell for damages (lost wages) resulting from Honeywell's breach of the employment contract. One of the issues facing the court was whether Kloss, by voluntarily leaving the maintenance job at Honeywell, had failed to mitigate his damages. How should the court rule on this issue? Discuss. [*Kloss v. Honeywell, Inc.,* 77 Wash.App. 294, 890 P.2d 480 (1995)]

14–10. Mitigation of Damages. Patricia Fair worked in a Red Lion restaurant. The employee manual provided that "[d]uring a medical leave of absence, every effort will be made to keep a position available for the employee's return." After sustaining an injury that was unrelated to her work, Fair was given a month's medical leave. On her return, she asked for, and was granted, additional time to submit a physician's release to return to work. She provided the release within the extra time, but before she went back to work she was terminated, effective as of her original return date. When she attempted to resolve the matter, Red Lion offered to reinstate her in her old job. Her response was to set several conditions for a return, including a different job. Red Lion said no, and Fair did not return. Fair filed a suit in a Colorado state court against Red Lion, alleging in part breach of contract. Red Lion argued that by rejecting its offer of reinstatement, Fair failed to mitigate her damages. Assuming that Red Lion was in breach of contract, did Fair fail to mitigate her damages? Explain. [*Fair v. Red Lion Inn, L.P.*, 943 P.2d 431 (Colo. 1997)]

A QUESTION OF ETHICS AND SOCIAL RESPONSIBILITY

14–11. In 1984, Robert Ryan, a widower with a ninth-grade education, fell behind in his mortgage payments and faced foreclosure (a proceeding in which a lender either takes title to or forces the sale of the debtor's property in satisfaction of the debt). Norman Weiner told Ryan that he could loan him funds to help him keep his house if Ryan signed over the deed to the house as "security" for the loan. When Weiner left, he took Ryan's deed to the property with him for "safekeeping." The next day, Ryan signed several papers without reading them, believing that he was signing loan documents, because he trusted Weiner. In fact, he had signed documents that conveyed ownership of his house to Weiner. Weiner brought the mortgage payments up to date, continued to make the payments on the house, and paid for utilities and services necessary to maintain the house. Ryan continued to live in the house and made monthly payments to Weiner. The payments steadily increased from $100 to $310 a month. During that time, the mortgage payments increased also, from $93 in 1984 to $120 in 1991. In May 1991, Ryan concluded that he had paid off his mortgage and also his "loan" from Weiner and refused to make further payments. When Weiner initiated legal proceedings to evict Ryan, Ryan sought to rescind his transfer of the property to Weiner. Based on these facts, answer the following questions. [*Ryan v. Weiner*, 610 A.2d 1377 (Del. 1992)]

1. In view of the fact that Ryan voluntarily signed a document (contract) conveying his property to Weiner, should he be allowed to rescind that contract? What public policies are in conflict here?
2. When the equitable remedy of rescission and restitution is granted, the parties are restored to their status quo prior to the contract's formation. Is it possible in this case to restore the parties to their status quo prior to the 1984 transaction? Discuss.

FOR CRITICAL ANALYSIS

14–12. Review the discussion of the doctrine of election of remedies in this chapter. What are some of the advantages and disadvantages of this doctrine?

Online Activities

ONLINE EXERCISE 14–1

Go to the "Internet Activities Book" on the Web site that accompanies this text, the URL for which is http://blt.westbuslaw.com. Select the following activity, and perform the exercise according to the instructions given there:

Activity 14–1: Contract Damages and Contract Theory

Before the Test

Go to the *Business Law Today* home page at http://blt.westbuslaw.com. Click on TestTutor.® You will find twenty interactive questions relating to this chapter.

Unit Two • Cumulative Business Hypothetical

Alberto Corelli offers to purchase for $2,500 a painting titled Moonrise *from Tara Shelley, an artist whose works have been causing a stir in the art world. Shelley accepts Corelli's offer. Assuming that the contract has met all of the requirements for a valid contract, answer the questions raised in each of the following questions.*

1 Corelli was a minor when he purchased the painting. Is the contract void? Is it voidable? What is the difference between these two concepts? A month after his eighteenth birthday, Corelli decides that he would rather have the $2,500 instead of the painting. He informs Shelley that he is disaffirming the contract and requests that Shelley return the $2,500 to him. When Shelley refuses to do so, Corelli brings a court action to recover the $2,500. What will the court likely decide in this situation? Why?

2 Both parties are adults, the contract is oral, and the painting is still in progress. Corelli pays Shelley the $2,500 in return for Shelley's promise to deliver the painting to his home when it is finished. A week or so later, after Shelley finishes the painting, a visitor to her gallery offers her $3,500 for it. Shelley sells the painting to the visitor and sends Corelli a signed letter explaining that she is "canceling" their contract for the *Moonrise* painting. Corelli sues Shelley to enforce the contract. Is the contract enforceable? Explain.

3 Both parties are adults, and the contract, which is in writing, states that Corelli will pay Shelley the $2,500 the following day. In the meantime, Shelley allows Corelli to take the painting home with him. The next day, Corelli's son returns the painting to Shelley, stating that he is canceling the contract. He explains that his father has been acting strangely lately, that he seems to be mentally incompetent at times, and that he clearly was not acting rationally when he bought the painting, which he could not afford. Is the contract enforceable? Discuss fully.

4 Both parties are adults, and the contract is in writing. The contract calls for Shelley to deliver the painting to Corelli's gallery in two weeks. Corelli has already arranged to sell the painting to a third party for $4,000, for a $1,500 profit, but it must be available for the third party in two weeks or the sale will not go through. Shelley knows this but does not deliver the painting at the time promised. Corelli sues Shelley for $1,500 in damages. Shelley claims that performance was impossible because her mother fell seriously ill and required Shelley's care. Who will win this lawsuit, and why?

5 After Shelley has agreed to sell Corelli the painting, he takes it home, promising to pay her the $2,500 the following day. That night, he has second thoughts about the value of the painting. The next day, he writes a letter to Shelley, stating that she overpriced the painting and that he is enclosing a check for $1,500 as "payment in full" for it. He delivers the letter to Shelley. Later that day, Shelley endorses the check and deposits it into her account. The day after that, she writes to Corelli stating that if he refuses to pay her the additional $1,000, she will sue him. Would Shelley succeed in a suit against Corelli for the remainder of the purchase price? Explain.

UNIT TWO • EXTENDED CASE STUDY: THE LAW IN CONTEXT

Chock Full O' Nuts Corp. v. Tetley, Inc.

In Chapter 9, we discussed the common law principles of contract interpretation. In this extended case study, we examine Chock Full O' Nuts Corp. v. Tetley, Inc.,[1] *a recent decision involving the interpretation of a contract provision.*

CASE BACKGROUND

Tetley, Inc., owned and operated a plant to process and package instant coffee in Linden, New Jersey. In 1989, Tetley sold its instant coffee business, including its list of customers and the Linden plant, to Chock Full O' Nuts Corporation. As part of the deal, Chock assumed Tetley's liability under a pension plan that was underfunded by about $1.6 million. The contract provided that if, before October 30, 1994, Chock chose to "close the Business" and terminate the pension plan, Tetley would pay Chock the lesser of this amount or the amount by which the plan was deficient on September 1, 1994. The contract defined "the Business" as "processing and packaging in Linden, New Jersey, and selling instant coffee."

Chock experienced high production costs at the plant. In early 1994, Chock told Tetley that Chock intended to close the Linden plant by July 9, terminate the pension plan by October 8, and transfer its instant coffee operation to Mexico. Chock also told Tetley that the pension plan was short by about $1.6 million, which Tetley was expected to pay. Chock closed the plant in July but continued to sell the plant's inventory after October 30. To customers that Chock obtained from Tetley in 1989, Chock continued to sell instant coffee produced in Mexico. Tetley refused to pay the pension plan's deficiency, contending that Chock had failed to "close the Business" by October 30. Chock filed a suit for breach of contract against Tetley. Tetley filed a motion for summary judgment, which the court granted, and Chock appealed.

1. 152 F.3d 202 (2d Cir. 1998).

MAJORITY OPINION

LEVAL, Circuit Judge:

* * * *

It is undisputed that Chock was required to "close the Business" before October 30 to trigger Tetley's liability. In light of the contract's definition of "the Business" as "processing and packaging in Linden, New Jersey, and selling instant coffee," three plausible interpretations of the phrase "close the Business" have been advanced.

Under the first interpretation, in order to trigger Tetley's liability, Chock was required to close the Linden plant and stop selling instant coffee regardless where produced, since "the Business" includes "selling instant coffee." Neither the source of the coffee nor the identity of the buyers would be material. Under the second interpretation, Chock was required to close the plant and stop selling instant coffee to customers it had obtained from Tetley. On this view, the "Business" purchased by Chock under the contract was Tetley's business of processing, packaging, and selling instant coffee. Given that Chock had an instant coffee business before entering into the contract, the contract could be read as requiring only that Chock "close" that which it bought from Tetley—including the plant in Linden and the business of selling instant coffee to customers acquired from Tetley. Finally, under the third interpretation, the Business included sales of instant coffee only to the extent it was processed at the Linden plant, and Chock could close the Business by closing the plant and ceasing to sell that instant coffee.

It is undisputed that Chock failed to satisfy any of these three alternative conditions * * * . Unless Chock identified some other plausible interpretation of the contract, summary judgment in favor of Tetley was appropriate.

Chock maintains the contract is susceptible of such an interpretation, under which it could "close the Business" by closing the Linden plant, notwithstanding its subsequent sales of Linden-produced instant coffee to liquidate its inventory. The [lower] court rejected this interpretation on the ground that the definition of "the Business" unambiguously included "selling instant coffee." We agree.

In making this argument, Chock is undertaking to rewrite the contract. The contract did not require Chock to close the plant; it required Chock to close "the Business," and "the Business" included the selling of instant coffee. Where the definition of the Business included the selling of instant coffee, and Chock continued to sell instant coffee after the specified date, we cannot agree that it had "closed" the Business. Closing the plant did not satisfy the contract's requirement.

DISSENTING OPINION

BRIEANT, District Judge, dissenting:

* * * *

The crucial phrase "elect to close the business" is not defined in the agreement. Tetley has advanced three possible interpretations of that phrase, and Chock has advanced a fourth. * * *

I have a fifth possible interpretation: the licensed New York attorney retained by Chock to draft the agreement * * * failed to distinguish between closing "the Business" and closing "the manufacturing facility at Linden, New Jersey." The latter was the true [intention] of the parties, and this may be ascertained by a court from all of the surrounding facts and circumstances known to the parties at the time they contracted, including their purposes in contracting and the benefits sought by each. * * *

* * * *

If "close the Business" in the context of this case means anything more than closing the manufacturing facility at Linden, New Jersey, the contract as written is so much gibberish and does not reflect the objective intentions of the parties.

MEDIA COVERAGE

The court's ruling in this case was criticized. Here we present excerpts from an article by Robert Feldman, titled "The Triumph of Interpretation over Form and Substance," that appeared in *Corporate Legal Times,* November 1998 (Vol. 8, No. 84), p. 9.

"Has Chock closed the "business"? A recital in the contract between these two defines the business: "[Tetley] is engaged in the business of processing and packaging in Linden, N.J., and selling instant coffee (the 'business')." . . .

Under [one] interpretation, "closing" referred to closing the plant and ceasing to sell the coffee produced there. Chock continues to sell off inventory after the drop-dead date. It is this . . . interpretation that the majority [of the court] . . . finds to be the most plausible. It does not find fault in the drafting of the contract language. It notes that Chock could have controlled the sell-off by appropriate planning. . . .

If, says [a dissenting judge], "close the Business" in this context means anything more than closing the manufacturing facility, the "contract as written is so much gibberish and does not reflect the objective intentions of the parties."

Look at the definition of "Business" again. Note that the business is a bit of this "and" that "and" that. If we wanted this suit to come out the other way, we could simply point to the "ands." Pontificate on the conjunctive: A failure to do any one of the three enumerated activities means Business is no longer being conducted."

GOING ONLINE

The *Business Law Today,* Fifth Edition, Web site, at http://blt.westbuslaw.com, provides a link through which you can access other court opinions in contract cases. Also, Hieros Gamos at www.hg.org/hg2.html provides links to online resources for contracts cases. From Hieros Gamos's Topics Index, click on the letter "C," and from the list of topics at that letter, click on "Contract Law."

QUESTIONS FOR ANALYSIS

1. **Law.** What was the major argument of the plaintiffs? Why did the court conclude that the plaintiffs' argument was invalid?
2. **Law.** Would the result in this case have been different if Tetley's attorney, who drafted the parties' agreement, had included in the contract a reference to closing "the Plant" rather than a reference to closing "the Business"?
3. **Ethics.** What is the ethical basis for the requirement that a court interpret the language of a contract to give effect to the parties' intent as expressed in their contract?
4. **International Dimensions.** What is the impact on a business of closing a plant in the United States and moving its operations to another country?
5. **Implications for the Business Manager.** How is the language of the contract in this case of particular interest to those who may in the future deal with issues relating to the closing of a business?

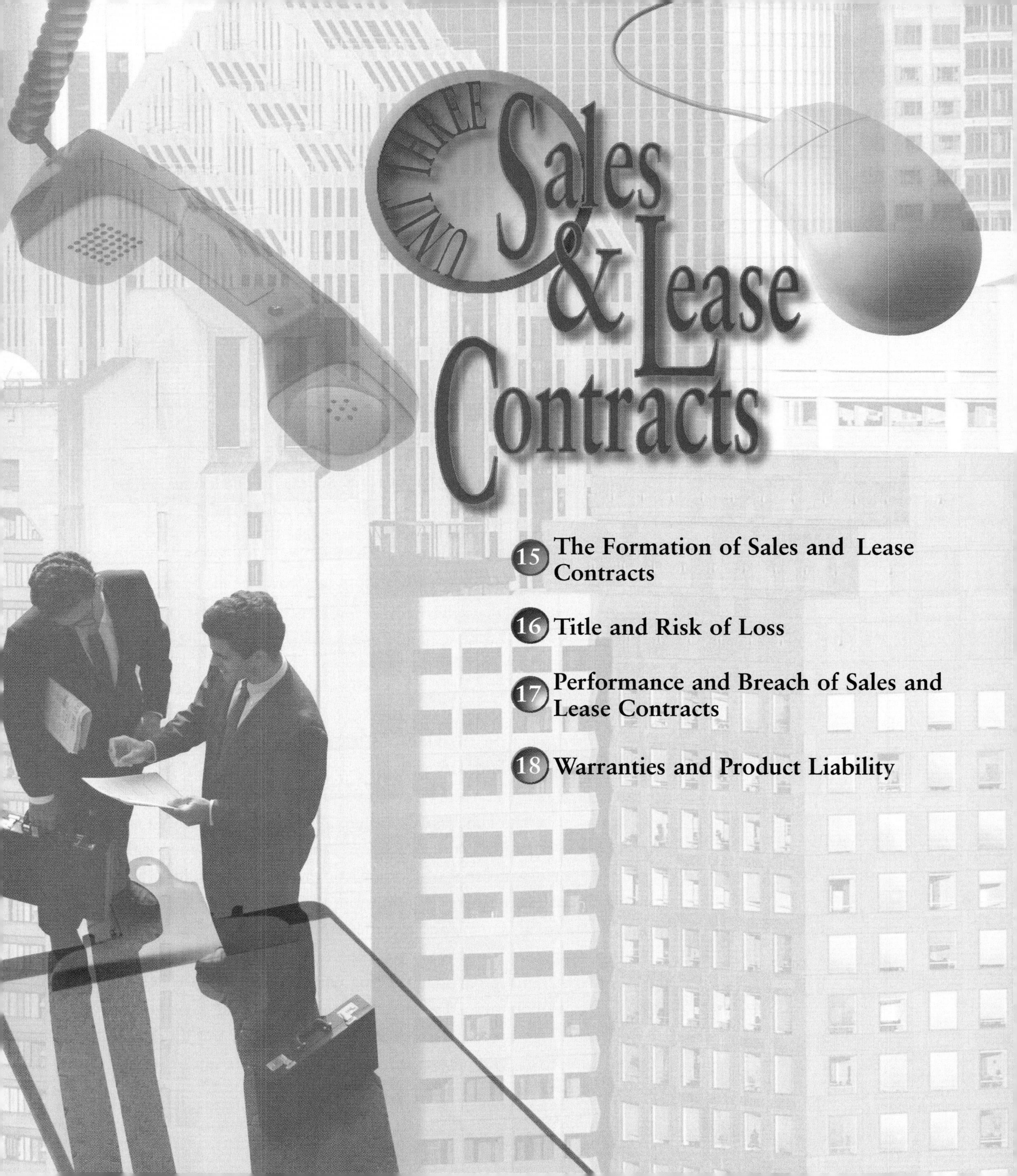

UNIT THREE

Sales & Lease Contracts

CHAPTER 15 The Formation of Sales & Lease Contracts

"The great object of the law is to encourage commerce."

J. Chambre, 1739–1823
(British jurist)

CONTENTS

LEARNING OBJECTIVES

After reading this chapter, you should be able to:

1. Discuss the scope of the UCC's Article 2 (on sales of goods) and Article 2A (on leases of goods).
2. Indicate the ways in which the UCC changes the common law of contracts with respect to contract formation.
3. Describe how the UCC attempts to avoid the "battle of the forms."
4. Identify some rules that apply only to contracts between merchants.
5. Compare the law governing domestic sales contracts with the law governing contracts for the international sale of goods.

When we turn to sales and lease contracts, we move away from common law principles and into the area of statutory law. State statutory law governing sales and lease transactions is based on the Uniform Commercial Code (UCC). Recall from Chapter 1 that the UCC is one of many uniform (model) acts drafted by the National Conference of Commissioners on Uniform State Laws and submitted to the states for adoption. Once a state legislature has adopted a uniform act, the act becomes statutory law in that state.

The opening quotation states that the object of the law is to encourage commerce. This is particularly true with respect to the UCC. The UCC facilitates commercial transactions by making the laws governing sales and lease contracts uniform, clearer, simpler, and more readily applicable to the numerous difficulties that can arise during such transactions.

We open this chapter with a discussion of the general coverage of the UCC and its significance as a legal landmark. We then look at the scope of the UCC's Article 2 (on sales) and Article 2A (on leases) as a background to the focus of this chapter, which is the formation of contracts for the sale and lease of goods. Because international sales transactions are increasingly commonplace in the business world, the chapter concludes with an examination of the United Nations Convention on Contracts for the International Sale of Goods (CISG), which governs international sales contracts.

The Scope of the UCC

"When there's no law, there's no bread."

BENJAMIN FRANKLIN, 1706–1790
(American diplomat, author, and scientist)

The UCC attempts to provide a consistent and integrated framework of rules to deal with all phases ordinarily arising in a commercial sales transaction from start to finish. For example, consider the following events, all of which may be involved in a single sales transaction:

1. ***A contract for the sale or lease of goods is formed and executed.*** Article 2 and Article 2A of the UCC provide rules governing all the facets of this transaction.
2. ***The transaction may involve a payment—by check, electronic fund transfer, or other means.*** Article 3 (on negotiable instruments), Article 4 (on bank deposits and collections), Article 4A (on fund transfers), and Article 5 (on letters of credit) cover this part of the transaction.
3. ***If the goods purchased are shipped or stored, they may be covered by a bill of lading or a warehouse receipt.*** Article 7 (on documents of title) deals with this subject.
4. ***The transaction may involve the demand by a seller or lender for some form of security for a remaining balance owed.*** Article 9, on secured transactions, covers this part of the transaction.

Two articles of the UCC seemingly do not address the "ordinary" commercial sales transaction. Article 6, on bulk transfers, has to do with merchants who sell off the major part of their inventory. Such bulk sales are not part of the ordinary course of business. Article 8, which covers investment securities, deals with transactions involving negotiable securities (stocks and bonds), transactions that do not involve the sale of goods. The subject matter of Articles 6 and 8, however, was considered by the UCC's drafters to be related *sufficiently* to commercial transactions to warrant its inclusion in the UCC. The most recent version of the UCC is included as Appendix B in this text.

¡BE CAREFUL! Although the UCC has been widely adopted without many changes, states have modified some of the details to suit their particular needs.

The UCC has been adopted in whole or in part by all of the states. Because of its importance in the area of commercial transactions, we present the UCC as this chapter's *Landmark in the Law.*

Landmark in the Law • THE UNIFORM COMMERCIAL CODE

Of all the attempts in the United States to produce a uniform body of laws relating to commercial transactions, none has been as comprehensive or successful as the Uniform Commercial Code (UCC). The UCC was the brain child of William A. Schnader, president of the National Conference of Commissioners on Uniform State Laws (NCC). The drafting of the UCC began in 1945. The most significant individual involved in the project was its chief editor, Karl N. Llewellyn, of the Columbia University Law School. Llewellyn's intellect, continuous efforts, and ability to compromise made the first version of the UCC (1949) a legal landmark. Over the next several years, the UCC was substantially accepted by virtually every state in the Union.

(Continued)

Various articles and sections of the UCC are periodically changed or supplemented to clarify certain rules or to establish new rules when changes in business customs render the existing UCC provisions inapplicable. For example, because of the increasing importance of leases of goods in the commercial context, Article 2A, governing leases, was added to the UCC and is being revised. To clarify the rights of parties to commercial fund transfers, particularly electronic fund transfers, Article 4A was issued. Articles 3 and 4, on negotiable instruments and banking relationships, underwent a significant revision in the 1990s. Because of other changes in business and in the law, the NCC has recommended the repeal of Article 6 (on bulk transfers), offering a revised Article 6 to those states that prefer not to repeal it.

Currently, the NCC is in the process of revising Article 2 (on sales transactions) and Article 9 (covering secured transactions), and of adding a new article—Article 2B on Software Contracts and Licenses of Information—to clarify the law in regard to new business practices in these areas that have emerged in recent years.

FOR CRITICAL ANALYSIS
What are the benefits of having uniform laws among the states in regard to commercial transactions?

The Scope of Article 2—Sales

• SALES CONTRACT
A contract for the sale of goods under which the ownership of goods is transferred from a seller to a buyer for a price.

Article 2 of the UCC governs **sales contracts,** or contracts for the sale of goods. To facilitate commercial transactions, Article 2 modifies some of the common law contract requirements that were summarized in Chapter 9 and discussed in detail in Chapters 10 through 14. To the extent that it has not been modified by the UCC, however, the common law of contracts also applies to sales contracts. In general, the rule is that when a UCC provision addresses a certain issue, the UCC governs; when the UCC is silent, the common law governs.

In regard to Article 2, you should keep in mind two things. First, Article 2 deals with the sale of *goods;* it does not deal with real property (real estate), services, or intangible property such as stocks and bonds. Thus, if the subject matter of a dispute is goods, the UCC governs. If it is real estate or services, the common law applies. The relationship between general contract law and the law governing sales of goods is illustrated in Exhibit 15–1. Second, in some cases, the rules may vary quite a bit, depending on whether the buyer or the seller is a merchant. We look now at how the UCC defines three important terms: *sale, goods,* and *merchant status.*

WHAT IS A SALE?

• SALE
The passing of title to property from the seller to the buyer for a price.

The UCC defines a **sale** as "the passing of title from the seller to the buyer for a price" [UCC 2–106(1)]. The price may be payable in money or in other goods, services, or realty (real estate).

WHAT ARE GOODS?

• TANGIBLE PROPERTY
Property that has physical existence and can be distinguished by the senses of touch, sight, and so on. A car is tangible property; a patent right is intangible property.

To be characterized as a *good,* the item of property must be *tangible,* and it must be *movable.* **Tangible property** has physical existence—it can be touched or seen. Intangible property—such as corporate stocks and bonds, patents and copyrights, and ordinary contract rights—have only conceptual existence and thus do not come under Article 2. A movable item can be carried from place to place. Hence, real estate is excluded from Article 2.

Two areas of dispute arise in determining whether the object of the contract is goods and thus whether Article 2 is applicable. One problem has to do with *goods associated with real estate,* such as crops or timber, and the other concerns contracts involving a combination of *goods and services.*

EXHIBIT 15–1 • Law Governing Contracts

This exhibit graphically illustrates the relationship between general contract law and the law governing contracts for the sale of goods. Contracts for the sale of goods are not governed exclusively by Article 2 of the Uniform Commercial Code but also by general contract law whenever it is relevant and has not been modified by the UCC.

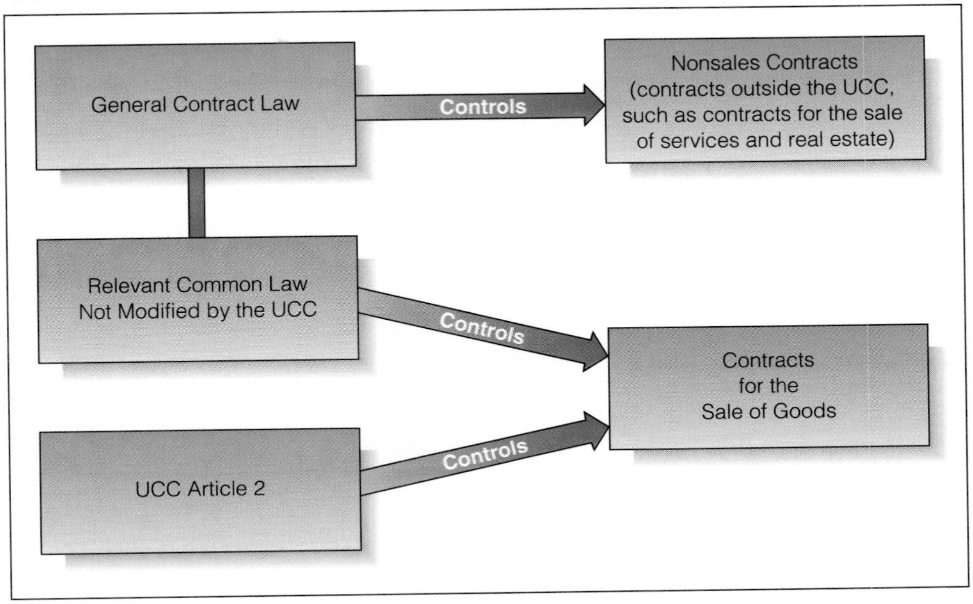

ON THE WEB

To view the UCC provisions discussed in this chapter, go to www.law.cornell.edu/uniform.

Goods Associated with Real Estate Goods associated with real estate often fall within the scope of Article 2. Section 2–107 provides the following rules:

1. A contract for the sale of minerals or the like (including oil and gas) or a structure (such as a building) is a contract for the sale of goods if *severance, or separation, is to be made by the seller.* If the *buyer* is to sever (separate) the minerals or structure from the land, the contract is considered to be a sale of real estate governed by the principles of real property law, not the UCC.
2. A sale of growing crops or timber to be cut is considered to be a contract for the sale of goods *regardless of who severs them.*
3. Other "things attached" to realty but capable of severance without material harm to the land are considered goods *regardless of who severs them.*[1] "Things attached" that are severable without harm to realty could include such items as a heater, a window air conditioner in a house, and counters and stools in a restaurant. Thus, removal of one of these things would be considered a sale of goods. The test is whether removal will cause substantial harm to the real property to which the item is attached.

Goods and Services Combined In cases in which goods and services are combined, courts disagree. For example, is the blood furnished to a patient during an operation a "sale of goods" or the "performance of a medical service"? Some courts say it is a good; others say it is a service. Similarly, contracts to sell and install software

1. The UCC avoids the term *fixtures* here because of the numerous definitions of the word. A fixture is anything so firmly or permanently attached to land or to a building as to become a part of it. Once personal property becomes a fixture, it is governed by real estate law. See Chapter 41.

SUNFLOWERS IN BLOOM. DOES ARTICLE 2 APPLY TO THE SALE OF SUNFLOWER SEEDS TO A SNACK FOODS COMPANY?

have posed the question of whether such contracts are primarily contracts for the sale of goods or contracts for the sale of services.[2] Because the UCC does not provide the answers to such questions, the courts try to determine which factor is predominant—the good or the service.

The UCC does stipulate, however, that serving food or drink to be consumed either on or off restaurant premises is a "sale of goods," at least for the purpose of an implied warranty of merchantability (to be explained in Chapter 18) [UCC 2–314(1)]. Other special transactions are also explicitly characterized as sales of goods by the UCC, including sales of unborn animals and rare coins. Whether the transaction in question involves the sale of goods or services is important, because the majority of courts treat services as being excluded by the UCC. If the transaction is not covered by the UCC, then UCC provisions, including those relating to implied warranties, would not apply.

WHO IS A MERCHANT?

Article 2 governs the sale of goods in general. It applies to sales transactions between all buyers and sellers. In a limited number of instances, however, the UCC presumes that in certain phases of sales transactions involving merchants, special business standards ought to be imposed because of the merchants' relatively high degree of commercial expertise.[3] Such standards do not apply to the casual or inexperienced seller or buyer ("consumer"). Section 2–104 defines three ways in which merchant status can arise:

> **ON THE WEB**
> Cornell University's Legal Information Institute offers online access to the UCC as enacted in several of the states at www.law.cornell.edu/statutes.html#state.

2. See, for example, *Richard Haney Ford v. Ford Dealer Computer Services,* 218 Ga.App. 315, 461 S.E.2d 282 (1995).

3. The provisions that apply only to merchants deal principally with the Statute of Frauds, firm offers, confirmatory memoranda, warranties, and contract modification. These special rules reflect expedient business practices commonly known to merchants in the commercial setting. They will be discussed later in this chapter.

1. A merchant is a person *who deals in goods of the kind* involved in the sales contract. Thus, a retailer, a wholesaler, or a manufacturer is a merchant of those goods sold in the business. A merchant for one type of goods is not necessarily a merchant for another type. For example, a sporting-equipment retailer is a merchant when selling tennis equipment but not when selling a used computer.
2. A merchant is a person who, by occupation, holds himself or herself out as having knowledge and skill unique to the practices or goods involved in the transaction. This broad definition may include banks or universities as merchants.
3. A person who *employs a merchant as a broker, agent, or other intermediary* has the status of merchant in that transaction. Hence, if a "gentleman farmer" who ordinarily does not run the farm hires a broker to purchase or sell livestock, the farmer is considered a merchant in the transaction.

• **MERCHANT**
A person who is engaged in the purchase and sale of goods. Under the UCC, a person who deals in goods of the kind involved in the sales contract or who holds himself or herself out as having skill or knowledge peculiar to the practice or use of the goods being purchased or sold. For definitions, see UCC 2–104.

In summary, a person is a **merchant** when he or she, acting in a mercantile capacity, possesses or uses an expertise specifically related to the goods being sold. This basic distinction is not always clear-cut. For example, courts in most states have determined that farmers may be merchants if they sell products or livestock on a regular basis, while courts in other states have determined that it was not within the contemplation of the drafters of the UCC to include farmers as merchants.

The Scope of Article 2A—Leases

In the past few decades, leases of personal property (goods) have become increasingly common. Article 2A of the UCC was created to fill the need for uniform guidelines in this area. Article 2A covers any transaction that creates a lease of goods, as well as subleases of goods [UCC 2A–102, 2A–103(k)]. Article 2A is essentially a repetition of Article 2, except that it applies to leases of goods, rather than sales of goods, and thus varies to reflect differences between sale and lease transactions. (Note that Article 2A is not concerned with leases of real property, such as land or buildings. The laws governing these types of transactions will be examined in Chapter 41.)

Definition of a Lease

• **LEASE AGREEMENT**
In regard to the lease of goods, an agreement in which one person (the lessor) agrees to transfer the right to the possession and use of property to another person (the lessee) in exchange for rental payments.

• **LESSOR**
A person who sells the right to the possession and use of goods to another in exchange for rental payments.

• **LESSEE**
A person who acquires the right to the possession and use of another's goods in exchange for rental payments.

Article 2A defines a **lease agreement** as a lessor and lessee's bargain with respect to the lease of goods, as found in their language and as implied by other circumstances, including course of dealing and usage of trade or course of performance [UCC 2A–103(k)]. A **lessor** is one who sells the right to the possession and use of goods under a lease [UCC 2A–103(p)]. A **lessee** is one who acquires the right to the possession and use of goods under a lease [UCC 2A–103(o)]. Article 2A applies to all types of leases of goods, including commercial leases and consumer leases. Special rules apply to certain types of leases, however, including consumer leases and finance leases.

Consumer Leases

A *consumer lease* involves three elements: (1) a lessor who regularly engages in the business of leasing or selling, (2) a lessee (except an organization) who leases the goods "primarily for a personal, family, or household purpose," and (3) total lease payments that are less than a dollar amount set by state statute [UCC 2A–103(1)(e)]. In the interest of providing special protection for consumers, certain provisions of

Article 2A apply only to consumer leases. For example, one provision states that a consumer may recover attorneys' fees if a court finds that a term in a consumer lease contract is unconscionable [UCC 2A–108(4)(a)].

FINANCE LEASES

A *finance lease* involves a lessor, a lessee, and a supplier. The lessor buys or leases goods from a supplier and leases or subleases them to the lessee [UCC 2A–103(g)]. Typically, in a finance lease, the lessor is simply financing the transaction. • **EXAMPLE 15.1** Suppose that Marlin Corporation wants to lease a crane for use in its construction business. Marlin's bank agrees to purchase the equipment from Jennco, Inc., and lease the equipment to Marlin. In this situation, the bank is the lessor-financer, Marlin is the lessee, and Jennco is the supplier. •

Article 2A, unlike ordinary contract law, makes the lessee's obligations under a commercial finance lease irrevocable and independent from the financer's obligations [UCC 2A–407]. That is, the lessee must perform whether or not the financer performs. The lessee also must look almost entirely to the supplier for warranties.

The Formation of Sales and Lease Contracts

In regard to the formation of sales and lease contracts, the UCC modifies the common law in several ways. We look here at how Article 2 and Article 2A of the UCC modify common law contract rules. Remember, parties to sales contracts are free to establish whatever terms they wish. The UCC comes into play only when the parties have not, in their contract, provided for a contingency that later gives rise to a dispute. The UCC makes this clear time and again by its use of such phrases as "unless the parties otherwise agree" or "absent a contrary agreement by the parties."

OFFER

¡NOTE! Under the UCC, it is the actions of the parties that determine whether they intended to form a contract.

In general contract law, the moment a definite offer is met by an unqualified acceptance, a binding contract is formed. In commercial sales transactions, the verbal exchanges, the correspondence, and the actions of the parties may not reveal exactly when a binding contractual obligation arises. The UCC states that an agreement sufficient to constitute a contract can exist even if the moment of its making is undetermined [UCC 2–204(2), 2A–204(2)].

Open Terms Remember from Chapter 10 that under the common law of contracts, an offer must be definite enough for the parties (and the courts) to ascertain its essential terms when it is accepted. In contrast to the common law, the UCC states that a sales or lease contract will not fail for indefiniteness even if one or more terms are left open as long as (1) the parties intended to make a contract and (2) there is a reasonably certain basis for the court to grant an appropriate remedy [UCC 2–204(3), 2A–204(3)].

• **EXAMPLE 15.2** Mike agrees to lease from CompuQuik a highly specialized computer work station. Mike and one of CompuQuick's sales representatives sign a lease agreement that leaves some of the details blank, to be "worked out" the following week, when the leasing manager will be back from her vacation. In the meantime, CompuQuick obtains the necessary equipment from one of its suppliers and spends several days modifying the equipment to suit Mike's needs. When the leasing manager returns, she calls Mike and tells him that his work station is ready. Mike says he is no longer interested in the work station, as he has arranged to lease the same type of equipment for a lower price from another firm. CompuQuik sues Mike to recover its costs in obtaining and modifying the equipment, and one of the issues before the court is whether the parties had an enforceable contract. The court will likely hold that they did, based on their intent and conduct, despite the "blanks" in their written agreement.•

Although the UCC has radically lessened the requirement of definiteness of terms, keep in mind that the more terms left open, the less likely it is that a court will find that the parties intended to form a contract. (This is also true with respect to online contracts—see this chapter's *Technology and Online Offers* for some suggestions on how online sellers can protect themselves against potential problems by including specific terms and provisions in their offers.)

Open Price Term. If the parties have not agreed on a price, the court will determine a "reasonable price at the time for delivery" [UCC 2–305(1)]. If either the

THE PAGE FOR DOWNLOADING PALM PILOT GAME SOFTWARE FROM THE WEB SITE OF 3COM IS DISPLAYED. DOES CLICKING ON THE "I AGREE" LINK LEGALLY CONSTITUTE THE ACCEPTANCE OF AN OFFER?

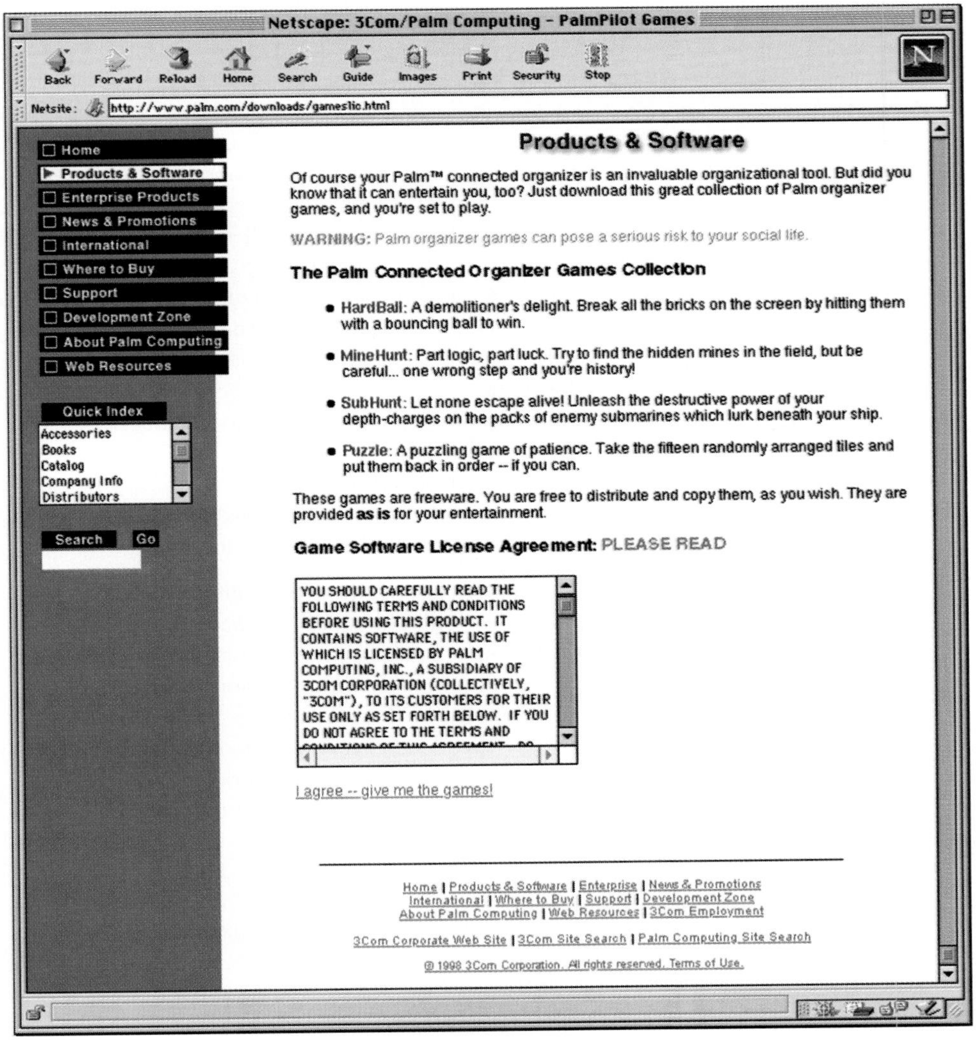

Technology and Online Offers

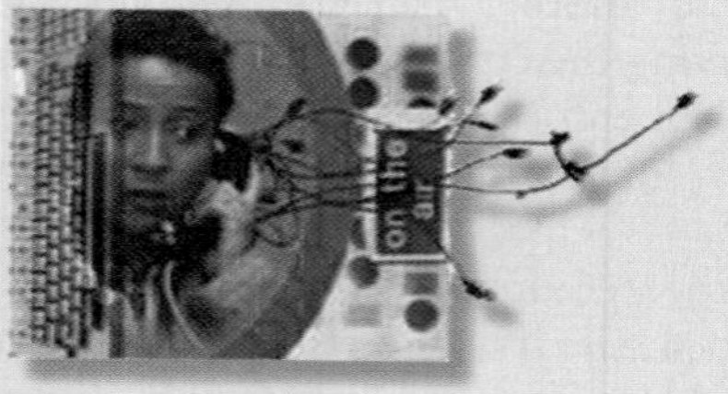

Today, numerous sales contracts are being formed online. Consumers can make online purchases of books, compact discs, software, and computers. Although the medium through which sales contracts are generated has changed, the age-old problems attending contract formation have not. Disputes concerning contracts formed online continue to center around contract terms and whether the parties voluntarily assented to those terms. Sellers doing business via the Internet can protect themselves against contract disputes and legal liability by creating offers that clearly spell out the terms that will govern their transactions if the offers are accepted.

Online offers should not be casually drafted. Rather, they must be carefully constructed and address all key terms and conditions so that, on their acceptance, the resulting contract clearly spells out the obligations of the parties. All important terms should be conspicuous and easily viewed by potential buyers. The seller's Web site should include a hypertext link to a page containing the full contract so that potential buyers are made aware of the terms to which they are assenting. Provisions that should be included in the offer (contract) include at least the following:

- A provision specifying the remedies available to the buyer if the goods turn out to be defective or if the contract is otherwise breached (any limitation of remedies should be clearly spelled out).
- A forum-selection clause (indicating the forum, or location, for the resolution of any dispute that may arise under the contract). This clause will help to avert future jurisdictional problems, which often arise in online transactions, and ensure that the seller will not be required to appear in court in a distant state.
- The statute of limitations governing the transaction (that is, the time period within which a legal action can be brought over a dispute concerning the contract).
- A clause that clearly indicates the buyer's agreement to the terms of the offer.
- A provision specifying how payment for the goods and of any applicable taxes must be made.
- A statement of the seller's refund and return policies.
- Disclaimers of liability for certain uses of the goods. For example, an online seller of business forms may add a disclaimer that the seller does not accept responsibility for the buyer's reliance on the form rather than on an attorney's advice.
- How the information gathered about the buyer will be used by the seller.

In terms of how the contract must be displayed online, generally it must be in a readable format such as 12-point typeface. All provisions should be reasonably clear. For example, if a seller is offering certain goods priced according to a complex price schedule, that schedule must be fully provided and explained.

Finally, an online offer should include some mechanism by which the customer may accept the offer. Typically, online sellers include boxes containing the words "I agree" or "I accept the terms of the offer" that offerees can click on to indicate acceptance. To be sure, electronic "click-on" acceptances have raised several legal issues. One issue is whether the agreement meets the signature requirements of the Statute of Frauds—because a point-and-click agreement is not actually signed by the recipient. A similar issue arises with agreements that are included in virtually all shrink-wrapped software. When the purchaser opens the software package, he or she agrees to abide by the terms of the limited license agreement.

Increasingly, the courts are holding that limited licenses included with shrink-wrapped software, as well as their equivalents on the Internet ("click-on" acceptances), are binding on the buyer. Section 2–204 of the UCC provides that any contract for the sale of goods "may be made in any manner sufficient to show agreement, including conduct by both parties which recognizes the existence of a contract." Thus, a buyer's failure to object to terms contained within a shrink-wrapped software package (or an online offer) may constitute an acceptance of the terms by conduct.[a]

FOR CRITICAL ANALYSIS

Are there any significant differences between the types of terms and provisions that should be included in online offers as opposed to traditional (offline) offers?

a. See, for example, *ProCD, Inc. v. Zeidenberg*, 86 F.3d 1447 (7th Cir. 1996); and *Hill v. Gateway 2000, Inc.*, 105 F.3d 1147 (7th Cir. 1997).

INTERNET CONNECT

buyer or the seller is to determine the price, the price is to be fixed in good faith [UCC 2–305(2)].

Sometimes the price fails to be fixed through the fault of one of the parties. In that situation, the other party can treat the contract as canceled or fix a reasonable price. • **EXAMPLE 15.3** Johnson and Merrick enter into a contract for the sale of unfinished wooden doors and agree that Johnson will determine the price. Johnson refuses to fix the price. Merrick can either treat the contract as canceled or set a reasonable price [UCC 2–305(3)].•

ETHICAL ISSUE 15.1 ***Should merchants be required to act in good faith?*** This question was among many others facing the drafters of the UCC. Their answer to the question was a resounding "Yes." UCC 1–203 states, "Every contract or duty within this act imposes an obligation of good faith in its performance or enforcement." The problem, of course, lay in the difficulty of defining good faith in a meaningful way. The UCC resolved the problem by stating that good faith in the case of a merchant is defined to mean honesty in fact and the observance of reasonable commercial standards of fair dealing in the trade [UCC 2–103(1)(b)]. Thus, the concepts of *good faith* and *commercial reasonableness* permeate the UCC. As you just read, if the buyer or the seller is to determine the price, the UCC requires that the price be determined in good faith. This is but one of many UCC provisions requiring good faith in the formation and performance of sales contracts. The concept of commercial reasonableness also underlies numerous UCC provisions. A merchant is expected to act in a reasonable manner according to reasonable commercial customs. The importance of commercial reasonableness as a component of good faith is underscored by the appearance of the word *reasonable* about ninety times in Article 2.

¡CONTRAST!

The common law requires that the parties make their terms definite before they have a contract. The UCC applies general commercial standards to make the terms of a contract definite.

Open Payment Term. When parties do not specify payment terms, payment is due at the time and place at which the buyer is to receive the goods [UCC 2–310(a)]. The buyer can tender payment using any commercially normal or acceptable means, such as a check or credit card. If the seller demands payment in cash, however, the buyer must be given a reasonable time to obtain it [UCC 2–511(2)]. This is especially important when the contract states a definite and final time for performance.

Open Delivery Term. When no delivery terms are specified, the buyer normally takes delivery at the seller's place of business [UCC 2–308(a)]. If the seller has no place of business, the seller's residence is used. When goods are located in some other place and both parties know it, delivery is made there. If the time for shipment or delivery is not clearly specified in the sales contract, the court will infer a "reasonable" time for performance [UCC 2–309(1)].

Duration of an Ongoing Contract. A single contract might specify successive performances but not indicate how long the parties are required to deal with each other. Although either party may terminate the ongoing contractual relationship, principles of good faith and sound commercial practice call for reasonable notification before termination so as to give the other party reasonable time to seek a substitute arrangement [UCC 2–309(2), (3)].

Options and Cooperation Regarding Performance. When specific shipping arrangements have not been made but the contract contemplates shipment of the goods, the seller has the right to make these arrangements in good faith, using commercial reasonableness in the situation [UCC 2–311].

When terms relating to the assortment of goods are omitted from a sales contract, the *buyer* can specify the assortment. • EXAMPLE 15.4 Petry Drugs, Inc., agrees to purchase one thousand toothbrushes from Marconi's Dental Supply. The toothbrushes come in a variety of colors, but the contract does not specify color. Petry, the buyer, has the right to take six hundred blue toothbrushes and four hundred green ones if it wishes. Petry, however, must exercise good faith and commercial reasonableness in making its selection [UCC 2–311]. •

• **REQUIREMENTS CONTRACT**
An agreement in which a buyer agrees to purchase and the seller agrees to sell all or up to a stated amount of what the buyer needs or requires.

Open Quantity Term. Normally, if the parties do not specify a quantity, a court will have no basis for determining a remedy. The UCC recognizes two exceptions in requirements and output contracts [UCC 2–306(1)]. In a **requirements contract,** the buyer agrees to purchase and the seller agrees to sell all or up to a stated amount of what the buyer *needs* or *requires.* There is implicit consideration in a requirements contract, for the buyer gives up the right to buy from any other seller, and this forfeited right creates a legal detriment. Requirements contracts are common in the business world and are normally enforceable. If, however, the buyer promises to purchase only if the buyer *wishes* to do so, or if the buyer reserves the right to buy the goods from someone other than the seller, the promise is illusory (without consideration) and unenforceable by either party.

• **OUTPUT CONTRACT**
An agreement in which a seller agrees to sell and a buyer agrees to buy all or up to a stated amount of what the seller produces.

In an **output contract,** the seller agrees to sell and the buyer agrees to buy all or up to a stated amount of what the seller *produces.* Again, because the seller essentially forfeits the right to sell goods to another buyer, there is implicit consideration in an output contract.

The UCC imposes a *good faith limitation* on requirements and output contracts. The quantity under such contracts is the amount of requirements or the amount of output that occurs during a *normal* production year. The actual quantity purchased or sold cannot be unreasonably disproportionate to normal or comparable prior requirements or output [UCC 2–306].

ETHICAL ISSUE 15.2 ***Why is good faith particularly important in performing requirements and output contracts?*** The obligation of good faith is particularly important in requirements and output contracts because these types of contracts have a great potential for abuse. For example, suppose that Tarpec Corporation contracts with Elfax, Inc., to purchase all of the electrical cable Tarpec needs for a three-year period. A year after the contract is formed, the market price of electrical cable doubles. Tarpec, claiming that its needs are now equivalent to the entire output of Elfax, buys all of Elfax's output at the contract price and then resells the cable that it does not use at the now higher market price. Under the UCC, this type of unethical behavior is prohibited. Even though contracts that call for the buyer to purchase all of his or her needs from the seller are explicitly authorized under the UCC, such contracts are construed to involve *actual* requirements that may occur in good faith.

• **FIRM OFFER**
An offer (by a merchant) that is irrevocable without consideration for a stated period of time or, if no definite period is stated, for a reasonable time (neither period to exceed three months). A firm offer by a merchant must be in writing and must be signed by the offeror.

Merchant's Firm Offer Under regular contract principles, an offer can be revoked at any time before acceptance. The major common law exception is an *option contract* (discussed in Chapter 10), in which the offeree pays consideration for the offeror's irrevocable promise to keep the offer open for a stated period. The UCC creates a second exception for firm offers made by a merchant to sell, buy, or lease goods. A **firm offer** arises when a merchant-offeror gives *assurances* in a *signed writing* that the offer will remain open. The merchant's firm offer is irrevocable without the necessity of consideration[4] for the stated period or, if no definite period is stated, a reasonable period (neither period to exceed three months) [UCC 2–205, 2A–205].

It is necessary that the offer be both *written* and *signed* by the offeror.[5] When a firm offer is contained in a form contract prepared by the offeree, the offeror must also sign a separate firm offer assurance. This requirement ensures that the offeror will be made aware of the offer. If the firm offer is buried amid copious language in one of the pages of the offeree's form contract, the offeror may inadvertently sign the contract without realizing that there is a firm offer, thus defeating the purpose of the rule—which is to give effect to a merchant's deliberate intent to be bound to a firm offer.

International Perspective • FIRM OFFERS UNDER THE CISG

As just mentioned, under the UCC a merchant's firm offer is irrevocable, even without consideration, if the offer gives assurances in a signed writing that the offer will remain open. The United Nations Convention on Contracts for the International Sale of Goods (CISG), which will be discussed later in this chapter, takes a different approach in regard to international sales contracts. Article 16(2) of the CISG provides that an offer will be irrevocable if the merchant-offeror simply states orally that the offer is irrevocable or if the offeree reasonably relies on the offer as being irrevocable. In either of these situations, the offer will be irrevocable even without a writing and without consideration.

FOR CRITICAL ANALYSIS
What are the advantages and disadvantages of the CISG's provisions on firm offers relative to the UCC's provisions?

ACCEPTANCE

¡BE AWARE!
The UCC's rules on means of acceptance illustrate the UCC's flexibility. The rules have been adapted to new forms of communication, such as faxes and online communications.

The following sections examine the UCC's provisions governing acceptance. As you will see, acceptance of an offer to buy, sell, or lease goods generally may be made in any reasonable manner and by any reasonable means.

Methods of Acceptance The general common law rule is that an offeror can specify, or authorize, a particular means of acceptance, making that means the only one effective for contract formation. Even an unauthorized means of communication is effective, however, as long as the acceptance is received by the specified deadline. • **EXAMPLE 15.5** Suppose that an offer states, "Answer by fax within five days." If the offeree sends a letter, and the offeror receives it within five days, a valid contract is formed. •

Any Reasonable Means. When the offeror does not specify a means of acceptance, the UCC provides that acceptance can be made by any means of communication reasonable under the circumstances [UCC 2–206(1), 2A–206(1)]. This broadens the common law rules concerning authorized means of acceptance. (For a review of the requirements relating to mode and timeliness of acceptance, see Chapter 10.)

• **EXAMPLE 15.6** Anodyne Corporation writes Bethlehem Industries a letter offering to lease $1,000 worth of postage meters. The offer states that Anodyne will keep

4. If the offeree pays consideration, then an option contract (not a merchant's firm offer) is formed.

5. "Signed" includes any symbol executed or adopted by a party with a present intention to authenticate a writing [UCC 1–201(39)]. A complete signature is not required. Therefore, initials, a thumbprint, a trade name, or any mark used in lieu of a written signature will suffice, regardless of its location on the document.

the offer open for only ten days from the date of the letter. Before the ten days have lapsed, Bethlehem sends Anodyne an acceptance by fax. Is a valid contract formed? The answer is yes, because acceptance by fax is a commercially reasonable medium of acceptance under the circumstances. Acceptance would be effective on Bethlehem's transmission of the fax, which occurred before the offer lapsed.●

Promise to Ship or Prompt Shipment. The UCC permits a seller to accept an offer to buy goods for current or prompt shipment by either a prompt *promise* to ship the goods to the buyer or the *prompt shipment* of conforming goods (that is, goods that accord with the contract's terms) to the buyer [UCC 2–206(1)(b)]. The seller's prompt shipment of *nonconforming goods* in response to the offer constitutes both an acceptance (a contract) and a *breach* of that contract.

• **SEASONABLY**
Within a specified time period, or, if no period is specified, within a reasonable time.

This rule does not apply if the seller **seasonably** (within a reasonable amount of time) notifies the buyer that the nonconforming shipment is offered only as an *accommodation,* or as a favor. The notice of accommodation must clearly indicate to the buyer that the shipment does not constitute an acceptance and that, therefore, no contract has been formed.

● **EXAMPLE 15.7** McFarrell Pharmacy orders five cases of Johnson & Johnson 3×5-inch gauze pads from Halderson Medical Supply, Inc. If Halderson ships five cases of Xeroform 3×5-inch gauze pads instead, the shipment acts as both an acceptance of McFarrell's offer and a *breach* of the resulting contract. McFarrell may sue Halderson for any appropriate damages. If, however, Halderson notifies McFarrell that the Xeroform gauze pads are being shipped *as an accommodation*—because Halderson has only Xeroform pads in stock—the shipment will not constitute an acceptance but a counteroffer. A contract will be formed only if McFarrell accepts the Xeroform gauze pads.●

Notice of Acceptance As noted in Chapter 10, notice of acceptance is not an issue in *bilateral* contracts, because such contracts are formed by an exchange of promises. In other words, a bilateral contract is formed when the promise is made. In contrast, unilateral contracts invite acceptance by performance. Under the common law, because acceptance (performance) of a unilateral contract was usually evident, the offeree normally was not required to notify the offeror of the acceptance. The UCC changes this common law rule. According to the UCC, when "the beginning of requested performance is a reasonable mode of acceptance[,] an offeror who is not notified of acceptance within a reasonable time may treat the offer as having lapsed before acceptance" [UCC 2–206(2), 2A–206(2)].

Additional Terms Under the common law, if Alderman makes an offer to Beale, and Beale in turn accepts but in the acceptance makes some slight modification to the terms of the offer, there is no contract. The so-called *mirror image rule,* which requires that the terms of the acceptance exactly match those of the offer (see Chapter 10), makes Beale's action a rejection of—and a counteroffer to—Alderman's offer. In the sale of goods, this rule often results in the so-called *battle of the forms.*

● **EXAMPLE 15.8** A buyer negotiates with a seller over the phone to purchase digital video disc (DVD) players. The parties agree to all of the specific terms of the sale—price, quantity, delivery date, and so on. The buyer then offers to buy the DVD players, using its standard purchase order form, and sends the form to the seller. At the same time, the seller accepts the offer, using its standard sales form. Because the parties presume that they have reached an agreement, discrepancies in the terms and conditions contained in their respective forms may go unnoticed. (See Exhibit 15–2 for an illustration of the kinds of terms and conditions that may be included in a standard purchase order form.) If a dispute arises, however, the

EXHIBIT 15–2 • An Example of Terms and Conditions in a Purchase Order

STANDARD TERMS AND CONDITIONS

IBM EXPRESSLY LIMITS ACCEPTANCE TO THE TERMS SET FORTH ON THE FACE AND REVERSE SIDE OF THIS PURCHASE ORDER AND ANY ATTACHMENTS HERETO:

PURCHASE ORDER CONSTITUTES COMPLETE AGREEMENT This Purchase order, including the terms and conditions on the face and reverse side hereof and any attachments hereto, contains the complete and final agreement between International Business Machines Corporation (IBM) and Seller. Reference to Seller's bids or proposals, if noted on this order, shall not affect terms and conditions hereof, unless specifically provided to the contrary herein, and no other agreement or quotation in any way modifying any of said terms and conditions will be binding upon IBM unless made in writing and signed by IBM's authorized representative.

ADVERTISING Seller shall not, without first obtaining the written consent of IBM, in any manner advertise, publish or otherwise disclose the fact that Seller has furnished, or contracted to furnish to IBM, the material and/or services ordered hereunder.

APPLICABLE LAW The agreement arising pursuant to this order shall be governed by the laws of the State of New York. No rights, remedies and warranties available to IBM under this contract or by operation of law are waived or modified unless expressly waived or modified by IBM in writing.

CASH DISCOUNT OR NET PAYMENT PERIOD Calculations will be from the date an acceptable invoice is received by IBM. Any other arrangements agreed upon must appear on this order and on the invoice.

CONFIDENTIAL INFORMATION Seller shall not disclose to any person outside of its employ, or use for any purpose other than to fulfill its obligations under this order, any information received from IBM pursuant to this order, which has been disclosed to Seller by IBM in confidence, except such information which is otherwise publicly available or is publicly disclosed by IBM subsequent to Seller's receipt of such information or is rightfully received by Seller from a third party. Upon termination of this order, Seller shall return to IBM upon request all drawings, blueprints, descriptions or other material received from IBM and all materials containing said confidential information. Also, Seller shall not disclose to IBM any information which Seller deems to be confidential, and it is understood that any information received by IBM, including all manuals, drawings and documents will not be of a confidential nature or restrict, in any manner, the use of such information by IBM. Seller agrees that any legend or other notice on any information supplied by Seller, which is inconsistent with the provisions of this article, does not create any obligation on the part of IBM.

GIFTS Seller shall not make or offer gifts or gratuities of any type to IBM employees or members of their families. Such gifts or offerings may be construed as Seller's attempt to improperly influence our relationship.

IBM PARTS All parts and components bailed by IBM to Seller for incorporation in work being performed for IBM shall be used solely for such purposes.

OFF-SPECIFICATION Seller shall obtain from IBM written approval of all off-specification work.

PACKAGES Packages must bear IBM's order number and show gross, tare and net weights and/or quantity.

PATENTS Seller will settle or defend, at Seller's expense (and pay any damages, costs or fines resulting from), all proceedings or claims against IBM, its subsidiaries and affiliates and their respective customers, for infringement, or alleged infringement, by the goods furnished under this order, or any part or use thereof of patents (including utility models and registered designs) now or hereafter granted in the United States or in any country where Seller, its subsidiaries or affiliates, heretofore has furnished similar goods. Seller will, at IBM's request, identify the countries in which Seller, its subsidiaries or affiliates, heretofore has furnished similar goods.

PRICE If price is not stated on this order, Seller shall invoice at lowest prevailing market price.

QUALITY Material is subject to IBM's inspection and approval within a reasonable time after delivery. If specifications are not met, material may be returned at Seller's expense and risk for all damages incidental to the rejection. Payment shall not constitute an acceptance of the material nor impair IBM's right to inspect or any of its remedies.

SHIPMENT Shipment must be made within the time stated on this order, failing which IBM reserves the right to purchase elsewhere and charges Seller with any loss incurred, unless delay in making shipment is due to unforeseeable causes beyond the control and without the fault or negligence of Seller.

SUBCONTRACTS Seller shall not subcontract or delegate its obligations under this order without the written consent of IBM. Purchase of parts and materials normally purchased by Seller or required by this order shall be construed as subcontracts or delegations.

(NON-U.S. LOCATIONS ONLY) Seller further agrees that during the process of bidding or production of goods and services hereunder, it will not re-export or divert to others any IBM specifications, drawing or other data, or any product of such data.

TAXES Unless otherwise directed, Seller shall pay all sales and use taxes imposed by law upon or on account of this order. Where appropriate, IBM will reimburse Seller for this expense.

TOOLS IBM owned tools held by Seller are to be used only for making parts for IBM. Tools of any kind held by Seller for making IBM's parts must be repaired and renewed by Seller at Seller's expense.

TRANSPORTATION
Routing—As indicated in transportation routing guidelines on face of this order.
F.O.B.—Unless otherwise specified, ship collect, F.O.B. origin.
Prepaid Transportation (when specified)—Charges must be supported by a paid freight bill or equivalent.
Cartage) No charge allowed
Premium Transportation) unless authorized
Insurance) by IBM
Consolidation—Unless otherwise instructed, consolidate all daily shipments to one destination on one bill of lading.

COMPLIANCE WITH LAWS AND REGULATIONS Seller shall at all times comply with all applicable Federal, State and local laws, rules and regulations.

EQUAL EMPLOYMENT OPPORTUNITY There are incorporated in this order the provisions of Executive Order 11246 (as amended) of the President of the United States on Equal Employment Opportunity and the rules and regulations issued pursuant thereto with which the Seller represents that he will comply, unless exempt.

EMPLOYMENT AND PROCUREMENT PROGRAMS There are incorporated in this order the following provisions as they apply to performing work under Government procurement contracts: Utilization of Small Business Concerns (if in excess of $10,000) (Federal Procurement Regulation (FPR) 1-1.710-3(a)); Small Business Subcontracting Program (if in excess of $500,000) (FPR 1-1.710-3 (b)); Utilization of Labor Surplus Area Concerns (if in excess of $10,000) (FPR 1-1.805-3(a)); Labor Surplus Area Subcontracting Program (if in excess of $500,000) (FPR 1-1.805-3 (b)); Utilization of Minority Enterprises (if in excess of $10,000) (FPR 1-1.1310-2 (a)); Minority Business Enterprises Subcontracting Program (if in excess of $50,000) (FPR 1-1.1310-2(b)); Affirmative Action for Handicapped Workers (if $2,500 or more) (41 CFR 60-741.4); Affirmative Action for Disabled Veterans and Veterans of the Vietnam Era (if $10,000 or more) (41 CFR 60-250.4); Utilization of Small Business Concerns and Small Business Concerns Owned and Controlled by Socially and Economically Disadvantaged Individuals (if in excess of $10,000) (44 Fed. Reg. 23610 (April 20, 1979)); Small Business and Small Disadvantaged Business Subcontracting Plan (if in excess of $500,000) (44 Fed. Reg. 23610 (April 20, 1979)).

WAGES AND HOURS Seller warrants that in the performance of this order Seller has complied with all of the provisions of the Fair Labor Standards Act of 1938 of the United States as amended.

WORKERS' COMPENSATION, EMPLOYERS' LIABILITY INSURANCE If Seller does not have Workers' Compensation or Employer's Liability Insurance, Seller shall indemnify IBM against all damages sustained by IBM resulting from Seller's failure to have such insurance.

Source: Reprinted with the permission of the IBM Corp. © 1985. Copyright: IBM.

¡DON'T FORGET! The UCC recognizes that a proposed deal is a contract if, in commercial understanding, the deal has been closed.

discrepancies become significant, and a "battle of the forms" begins, in which each party claims that its form represents the true terms of the agreement. •

Under the common law, the courts tended to resolve this difficulty by holding that no contract was formed, because the last form to be sent was not an acceptance but a counteroffer. To avoid the battle of the forms, the UCC dispenses with the mirror image rule. The UCC generally takes the position that if the offeree's response indicates a *definite* acceptance of the offer, a contract is formed even if the acceptance includes additional or different terms from those contained in the offer [UCC 2–207(1)]. What happens to these additional terms? The answer to this question depends, in part, on whether the parties are nonmerchants or merchants.

One Party or Both Parties Are Nonmerchants. If one (or both) of the parties is a *nonmerchant,* the contract is formed according to the terms of the original offer submitted by the original offeror and not according to the additional terms of the acceptance [UCC 2–207(2)]. • **EXAMPLE 15.9** Tolsen offers in writing to sell his personal computer and color printer and scanner to Valdez for $1,500. Valdez faxes a reply to Tolsen in which Valdez states, "I accept your offer to purchase your computer, color printer, and scanner for $1,500. I *would like* two extra sets of color toner for the printer to be included in the purchase price." Valdez has given Tolsen a definite expression of acceptance (creating a contract), even though Valdez's acceptance also suggests an added term for the offer. Because Tolsen is not a merchant, the additional term is merely a proposal (suggestion), and Tolsen is not legally obligated to comply with that term. •

Both Parties Are Merchants. In contracts *between merchants* (that is, when both parties to the contract are merchants), the additional terms automatically become part of the contract unless (1) the original offer expressly limits acceptance to the terms of the offer, (2) the new or changed terms *materially* alter the contract, or (3) the offeror objects to the new or changed terms within a reasonable period of time [UCC 2–207(2)].

What constitutes a material alteration is frequently a question of fact that only a court can decide. Generally, if the modification involves no unreasonable element of surprise or hardship for the offeror, the court will hold that the modification did not materially alter the contract. The issue in the following case was whether a party was bound to conditions of sale included in a confirmation form sent after a phone order.

CASE 15.1 Tupman Thurlow Co. v. Woolf International Corp.

Appeals Court of Massachusetts, 1997.
43 Mass.App. 334,
682 N.E.2d 1378.

HISTORICAL AND SOCIAL SETTING *When the first cases arose under the UCC, some merchant-litigants contended that UCC 2–207 gave them the freedom to ignore, for example, a confirmation form if its terms did not match the original order. They argued that if they (the offerors) did not expressly agree to the terms, the terms were not part of their agreements. In the leading case on this issue, the court concluded that if this were the result, "the statute would lead to an absurdity," because there would be no reason for an offeror to agree to the new terms. Instead, the court held that if an offeror receives a response that includes new terms and the offeror goes ahead with the deal, the new terms are part of the contract.*[a] *This rule applies, however, only if the new terms are presented before the goods are accepted.*

BACKGROUND AND FACTS Woolf International, Inc., and Tupman Thurlow Company are meat wholesalers. Over a two-year period, Woolf bought meat from Tupman sixty-four times. Woolf ordered the meat by phone, and Tupman

a. *Roto-Lith, Ltd. v. F.P. Bartlett & Co.,* 297 F.2d 497 (1st Cir. 1962).

CASE 15.1—Continued

mailed a confirmation form. After delivery, Tupman sent an invoice, which Woolf paid. The confirmation form and the invoice set out the same conditions of sale, including a clause requiring arbitration, in New York, of any dispute. On Woolf's sixty-fifth order, Tupman delivered $45,792 worth of meat, but Woolf did not pay. Tupman initiated arbitration proceedings. Woolf refused to participate, claiming that there was no agreement to arbitrate. The arbitrator ruled otherwise and awarded Tupman damages. A New York state court affirmed the award, and Tupman filed a petition in a Massachusetts state court to enforce the judgment. The Massachusetts court concluded that Woolf was bound by the New York judgment. Woolf appealed.

IN THE WORDS OF THE COURT . . .

PERRETA, Justice.

* * * *

* * * [W]hether the conditions of sale became part of their agreement is controlled by Section 2–207(2) of the Uniform Commercial Code. As here relevant and as between merchants, that provision makes additional terms which are included in a written confirmation part of the parties' contract unless "they materially alter it."

* * * *

* * * Massachusetts law would require enforcement of the arbitration provision on the basis that it was set out in the order confirmation forms which were received prior to the delivery of the goods.

* * * Woolf never refuted the facts that the arbitration provision was set out on Tupman's order confirmation forms which preceded delivery of the order, that the conditions of sale were set out on the confirmation forms as well as the invoices, that Tupman followed this procedure in every transaction with Woolf, and that Woolf had a long history of dealings with Tupman. * * *

On the undisputed facts, we conclude that Woolf was * * * bound under Massachusetts law by the conditions of sale appearing on the order confirmation forms and invoices.

DECISION AND REMEDY The Appeals Court of Massachusetts affirmed the lower court's decision. The appellate court held that a buyer can be held to an arbitration clause contained in a confirmation form sent by the seller following a phone order. Woolf was bound by the conditions of sale on the confirmation form.

FOR CRITICAL ANALYSIS—Social Consideration *Woolf argued in part that it had never read the invoices. Why didn't the court rule in Woolf's favor on this basis?*

Conditioned on Offeror's Assent. Regardless of merchant status, the UCC provides that the offeree's expression cannot be construed as an acceptance if additional or different terms in the acceptance are expressly conditioned on the offeror's assent to the additional or different terms [UCC 2–207(1)]. • **EXAMPLE 15.10** Philips offers to sell Hundert 650 pounds of turkey thighs at a specified price and with specified delivery terms. Hundert responds, "I accept your offer for 650 pounds of turkey thighs *on the condition that you give me ninety days to pay for them.*" Hundert's response will be construed not as an acceptance but as a counteroffer, which Philips may or may not accept. •

Additional Terms May Be Stricken. The UCC provides yet another option for dealing with conflicting terms in the parties' writings. Section 2–207(3) states that conduct by both parties that recognizes the existence of a contract is sufficient to establish a contract for the sale of goods even though the writings of the parties do

Business Law in Action • The "Knock-Out Rule" of UCC 2–207(3)

The drafters of UCC Section 2–207 attempted to avoid the "battle of the forms" by providing that a contract can be formed even though the acceptance includes additional terms. Nonetheless, the battle continues in earnest. Indeed, one of the results of Section 2–207 is that buyers and sellers go to great lengths to draft their acceptances as "offers" or "counteroffers" (instead of acceptances) so that their terms will control the resulting contracts. This is because under UCC 2–207(2), additional terms in an acceptance, if they materially alter the contract, do not become a part of the contract—the terms of the offer control. Whether a form is defined as an acceptance or an offer can thus have significant legal consequences for the parties.

Some courts have taken a different approach in resolving contract disputes when the parties are in fundamental disagreement over a material term. Rather than looking to UCC 2–207(2), they apply the rule expressed in UCC 2–207(3). As mentioned elsewhere, UCC 2–207(3) provides that when the parties' conduct and communications clearly indicate that a contract was formed, any conflicting material terms may simply be stricken from the contract. This rule is sometimes referred to, aptly enough, as the "knock-out rule." The Supreme Court of Rhode Island chose to use this approach in a case involving conflicting terms relating to the time for delivery.

The case involved a contract between R. J. Sanders, Inc., an installer of large heating systems, and Superior Boiler Works, Inc., a manufacturer of commercial boilers. Sanders had a contract with the government to install a heating system in a federal prison camp being built in West Virginia. Sanders contracted with Superior to provide the necessary boilers. A number of forms—including purchase orders, amended purchase orders, proposals containing specifications and price quotes, memoranda confirming telephone conversations, and sales orders—were exchanged between the parties. The problem was, although it was clear that the parties had formed a contract, the forms indicated that they had never agreed on the time for delivery. Sanders, who had to complete his work on the prison camp's heating system by a certain date, could not do so because Superior could not complete the boilers in time. As a result, Sanders rented temporary boilers to install and then sued Superior for damages.

When the case reached the Rhode Island Supreme Court, the court concluded that "both prudence and the weight of authority favor adoption of the knock-out rule as the law of this jurisdiction." The court thus struck the delivery term from the contract entirely, stating that the subsequent "gap" in the contract would be filled by the UCC's gap-filling provision concerning the time for delivery—UCC 2–309(1). Under this provision, the time for shipment or delivery, if not agreed on by the parties, "shall be a reasonable time."[a]

One of the goals in the proposed revision of Article 2 of the UCC is to redesign UCC 2–207 so that the battle of the forms can be avoided. Some have suggested that this section should be revised so that it focuses less on contract formation (offer-acceptance) and more on the approach currently provided under UCC 2–207(3)—that the terms of a contract are only those on which the parties have agreed. To be sure, this could mean that parties may end up with a contract containing a UCC gap-filling term to which neither party agrees. Yet, as the Rhode Island court explained, "the offeror and the offeree both have the power to protect any term they deem critical by expressly making acceptance conditional on assent to that term."

FOR CRITICAL ANALYSIS

What argument could be made in support of a requirement that a definite expression of acceptance by the offeree will always result in a contract on the offeror's terms unless *the offeree specifically conditions the acceptance on the offeror's assent to additional or different terms?*

a. *Superior Boiler Works, Inc. v. R. J. Sanders, Inc.,* 711 A.2d 625 (R.I. 1998).

not otherwise establish a contract. In this situation, "the terms of the particular contract will consist of those terms on which the writings of the parties agree, together with any supplementary terms incorporated under any other provisions of this Act." In a dispute over contract terms, this provision allows a court simply to strike from the contract those terms on which the parties do not agree. (See this chapter's *Business Law in Action* for an application of this UCC provision.)

CONSIDERATION

The common law rule that a contract requires consideration also applies to sales and lease contracts. Unlike the common law, however, the UCC does not require a contract modification to be supported by new consideration. An agreement modifying a contract for the sale or lease of goods "needs no consideration to be binding" [UCC 2–209(1), 2A–208(1)].

Modifications Must Be Made in Good Faith Of course, contract modification must be sought in good faith [UCC 1–203]. • **EXAMPLE 15.11** Allied, Inc., agrees to lease a new recreational vehicle (RV) to Louise for a stated price. Subsequently, a sudden shift in the market makes it difficult for Allied to lease the new RV to Louise at the contract price without suffering a loss. Allied tells Louise of the situation, and Louise agrees to pay an additional sum for the lease of the RV. Later Louise reconsiders and refuses to pay more than the original price. Under the UCC, Louise's promise to modify the contract needs no consideration to be binding. Hence, Louise is bound by the modified contract. •

In this example, a shift in the market is a *good faith* reason for contract modification. What if there really was no shift in the market, however, and Allied knew that Louise needed to lease the new RV immediately but refused to deliver it unless Louise agreed to pay an additional sum of money? This sort of extortion of a modification without a legitimate commercial reason would be ineffective, because it would violate the duty of good faith. Allied would not be permitted to enforce the higher price.

When Modification without Consideration Requires a Writing In some situations, modification of a sales or lease contract without consideration must be in writing to be enforceable. If the contract itself prohibits any changes to the contract unless they are in a signed writing, for example, then only those changes agreed to in a signed writing are enforceable. If a consumer (nonmerchant buyer) is dealing with a merchant and the merchant supplies the form that contains a prohibition against oral modification, the consumer must sign a separate acknowledgment of such a clause [UCC 2–209(2), 2A–208(2)].

Additionally, any modification that brings a sales contract under the Statute of Frauds must usually be in writing to be enforceable. Thus, if an oral contract for the sale of goods priced at $400 is modified so that the contract goods are now priced at $600, the modification must be in writing to be enforceable [UCC 2–209(3)]. If, however, the buyer accepts delivery of the goods after the modification, he or she is bound to the $600 price [UCC 2–201(3)(c)]. (Unlike Article 2, Article 2A does not say whether a lease as modified needs to satisfy the Statute of Frauds.)

STATUTE OF FRAUDS

¡BE AWARE!
It has been proposed that the UCC be revised to eliminate the Statute of Frauds.

The UCC contains Statute of Frauds provisions covering sales and lease contracts. Under these provisions, sales contracts for goods priced at $500 or more and lease contracts requiring payments that are $1,000 or more must be in writing to be enforceable [UCC 2–201(1), 2A–201(1)].

Sufficiency of the Writing The UCC has greatly relaxed the requirements for the sufficiency of a writing to satisfy the Statute of Frauds. A writing or a memorandum will be sufficient as long as it indicates that the parties intended to form a contract and as long as it is signed by the party (or agent of the party) against whom enforcement is

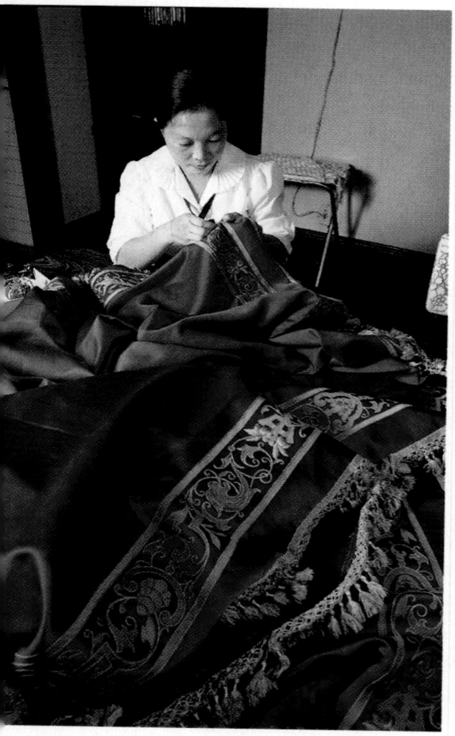

A SEAMSTRESS STITCHES SPECIALLY DESIGNED DRAPERY. UNDER WHAT CIRCUMSTANCES WOULD AN ORAL CONTRACT FOR THESE GOODS BE ENFORCEABLE?

sought. The contract normally will not be enforceable beyond the quantity of goods shown in the writing, however. All other terms can be proved in court by oral testimony. For leases, the writing must reasonably identify and describe the goods leased and the lease term.

Written Confirmation between Merchants Once again, the UCC provides a special rule for merchants. Merchants can satisfy the requirements of a writing for the Statute of Frauds if, after the parties have agreed orally, one of the merchants sends a signed written confirmation to the other merchant. The communication must indicate the terms of the agreement, and the merchant receiving the confirmation must have reason to know of its contents. Unless the merchant who receives the confirmation gives written notice of objection to its contents within ten days after receipt, the writing is sufficient against the receiving merchant, even though he or she has not signed anything [UCC 2–201(2)].[6]

• EXAMPLE 15.12 Alfonso is a merchant buyer in Cleveland. He contracts over the telephone to purchase $4,000 worth of spare aircraft parts from Goldster, a New York City merchant seller. Two days later, Goldster sends written confirmation detailing the terms of the oral contract, and Alfonso subsequently receives it. If Alfonso does not give Goldster written notice of objection to the contents of the written confirmation within ten days of receipt, Alfonso cannot raise the Statute of Frauds as a defense against the enforcement of the oral contract.•

Exceptions The UCC defines three exceptions to the writing requirements of the Statute of Frauds. An oral contract for the sale of goods priced at $500 or more or the lease of goods involving total payments of $1,000 or more will be enforceable despite the absence of a writing in the circumstances discussed in the following subsections [UCC 2–201(3), 2A–201(4)]. These exceptions and other ways in which sales law differs from general contract law are summarized in Exhibit 15–3.

Specially Manufactured Goods. An oral contract is enforceable if it is for (1) goods that are specially manufactured for a particular buyer or specially manufactured or obtained for a particular lessee, (2) these goods are not suitable for resale or lease to others in the ordinary course of the seller's or lessor's business, and (3) the seller or lessor has substantially started to manufacture the goods or has made commitments for the manufacture or procurement of the goods. In this situation, once the seller or lessor has taken action, the buyer or lessee cannot repudiate the agreement claiming the Statute of Frauds as a defense.

• EXAMPLE 15.13 Womach orders custom-made draperies for her new boutique. The price is $1,000, and the contract is oral. When the merchant seller manufactures the draperies and tenders delivery to Womach, Womach refuses to accept them even though the quality of the work is satisfactory and the job has been completed on time. Womach claims that she is not liable because the contract was oral. Clearly, if the unique style and color of the draperies makes it improbable that the seller can find another buyer, Womach is liable to the seller. Note that the seller must have made a substantial beginning in manufacturing the specialized item prior to the buyer's repudiation. (Here, the manufacture was completed.) Of course, the court must still be convinced by evidence of the terms of the oral contract.•

6. According to the Comments accompanying UCC 2A–201 (Article 2A's Statute of Frauds), the "between merchants" provision was not included because the number of such transactions involving leases, as opposed to sales, was thought to be modest.

EXHIBIT 15–3 • Major Differences between Contract Law and Sales Law

	CONTRACT LAW	SALES LAW
Contract Terms	Contract must contain all material terms.	Open terms are acceptable if parties intended to form a contract, but contract not enforceable beyond quantity term.
Acceptance	Mirror image rule applies. If additional terms are added in acceptance, counteroffer is created.	Additional terms will not negate acceptance unless acceptance is made expressly conditional on assent to the additional terms.
Contract Modification	Requires consideration.	Does not require consideration.
Irrevocable Offers	Option contracts (with consideration).	Merchants' firm offers (without consideration).
Statute of Frauds Requirements	All material terms must be included in the writing.	Writing required only in sale of goods priced at $500 or more but not enforceable beyond quantity specified. *Exceptions:* 1. Contracts for specially manufactured goods. 2. Contracts admitted to by party against whom enforcement is sought. 3. Contracts will be enforced to extent goods delivered or paid for. 4. A contract between merchants is enforceable if a merchant fails to object in writing to a confirming memorandum within ten days of its receipt.

¡ REMEMBER!
An admission can be made in documents revealed during discovery, including internal memos and employee reports.

Admissions. An oral contract for the sale or lease of goods is enforceable if the party against whom enforcement of a contract is sought admits in pleadings, testimony, or other court proceedings that a contract for sale was made. In this situation, the contract will be enforceable even though it was oral, but enforceability will be limited to the quantity of goods admitted.

• **EXAMPLE 15.14** Lane and Sugg negotiate an agreement over the telephone. During the negotiations, Lane requests a delivery price for five hundred gallons of gasoline and a separate price for seven hundred gallons of gasoline. Sugg replies that the price would be the same, $1.10 per gallon. Lane orally orders five hundred gallons. Sugg honestly believes that Lane ordered seven hundred gallons and tenders that amount. Lane refuses the shipment of seven hundred gallons, and Sugg sues for breach. In his pleadings and testimony, Lane admits that an oral contract was made, but only for five hundred gallons. Because Lane admits the existence of the oral contract, Lane cannot plead the Statute of Frauds as a defense. The contract is enforceable, however, only to the extent of the quantity admitted (five hundred gallons). •

Partial Performance. An oral contract for the sale or lease of goods is enforceable if payment has been made and accepted or goods have been received and accepted. This is the "partial performance" exception. The oral contract will be enforced at least to the extent that performance *actually* took place.

• **EXAMPLE 15.15** Suppose that Jeffrey Allan orally contracts to lease to Opus Enterprises a thousand chairs at $2 each to be used during a one-day concert. Before delivery, Opus sends Allan a check for $1,000, which Allan cashes. Later, when Allan attempts to deliver the chairs, Opus refuses delivery, claiming the Statute of Frauds as a defense, and demands the return of his $1,000. Under the UCC's partial performance rule, Allan can enforce the oral contract by tender of delivery of five hundred chairs for the $1,000 accepted. Similarly, if Opus had made no payment but had accepted the delivery of five hundred chairs from Allan, the oral contract would have been enforceable against Opus for $1,000, the lease price of the five hundred chairs delivered. •

PAROL EVIDENCE

If the parties to a contract set forth its terms in a confirmatory memorandum (a writing expressing offer and acceptance of the deal) or in a writing intended as their final expression, the terms of the contract cannot be contradicted by evidence of any prior agreements or contemporaneous oral agreements. The terms of the contract may, however, be explained or supplemented by *consistent additional terms* or by *course of dealing, usage of trade, or course of performance* [UCC 2–202, 2A–202].

Consistent Additional Terms If the court finds an ambiguity in a writing that is supposed to be a complete and exclusive statement of the agreement between the parties, it may accept evidence of consistent additional terms to clarify or remove the ambiguity. The court will not, however, accept evidence of contradictory terms. This is the rule under both the UCC and the common law of contracts.

Course of Dealing and Usage of Trade Under the UCC, the meaning of any agreement, evidenced by the language of the parties and by their actions, must be interpreted in light of commercial practices and other surrounding circumstances. In interpreting a commercial agreement, the court will assume that the course of prior dealing between the parties and the usage of trade were taken into account when the agreement was phrased.

• **COURSE OF DEALING**
Prior conduct between parties to a contract that establishes a common basis for their understanding.

A **course of dealing** is a sequence of previous actions and communications between the parties to a particular transaction that establishes a common basis for their understanding [UCC 1–205(1)]. A course of dealing is restricted to the sequence of actions and communications between the parties that has occurred prior to the agreement in question. The UCC states, "A course of dealing between the parties and any usage of trade in the vocation or trade in which they are engaged or of which they are or should be aware give particular meaning to [the terms of the agreement] and supplement or qualify the terms of [the] agreement" [UCC 1–205(3)].

• USAGE OF TRADE
Any practice or method of dealing having such regularity of observance in a place, vocation, or trade as to justify an expectation that it will be observed with respect to the transaction in question.

Usage of trade is defined as any practice or method of dealing having such regularity of observance in a place, vocation, or trade as to justify an expectation that it will be observed with respect to the transaction in question [UCC 1–205(2)]. Further, the express terms of an agreement and an applicable course of dealing or usage of trade will be construed to be consistent with each other whenever reasonable. When such a construction is *unreasonable,* however, the express terms in the agreement will prevail [UCC 1–205(4)]. In the following classic case, the issue concerned whether evidence of usage and custom in the trade could be used to explain the meaning of the quantity figures specified by the parties when the contract was formed.

CASE 15.2 Heggblade-Marguleas-Tenneco, Inc. v. Sunshine Biscuit, Inc.

California Court of Appeal, Fifth District, 1976.
59 Cal.App.3d 948,
131 Cal.Rptr. 183.

HISTORICAL AND SOCIAL SETTING *George Crumb cooked the first known potato chips at the Moon Lake Lodge in Saratoga, New York, in 1853. Generally unknown outside the northeastern United States for nearly seventy years, potato chips began to become popular in other areas of the country in the 1920s. After 1945, their popularity soared, particularly with the creation of California dip, which was perfect for the casual entertaining that was part of the growing middle-class, suburban lifestyle. In the late 1960s and early 1970s, however, it became fashionable among some groups to reject all things perceived to be middle class or suburban. This may have contributed to a decline in the demand for potato chips during those years.*

BACKGROUND AND FACTS In 1970, Heggblade-Marguleas-Tenneco, Inc. (HMT), contracted with Sunshine Biscuit, Inc., to supply potatoes to be used in the 1971 production of snack foods. HMT had never marketed processing potatoes before. The quantity mentioned in its contract negotiations was 100,000 sacks of potatoes. The parties agreed that the amount of potatoes to be supplied would vary somewhat with Sunshine Biscuit's needs. Subsequently, a decline in demand for Sunshine Biscuit's products severely reduced its need for potatoes. Sunshine Biscuit was able to take only 60,105 sacks out of the 100,000 previously estimated. HMT filed suit against Sunshine Biscuit in a California state court. Sunshine Biscuit attempted to introduce evidence that it is customary in the potato-processing industry for the number of potatoes specified in sales contracts to be reasonable estimates rather than exact numbers that a buyer intends to purchase. The trial court held for Sunshine Biscuit, and HMT appealed.

IN THE WORDS OF THE COURT . . .
FRANSON, Acting Presiding Justice.

* * * *

[UCC 2–202] states [that evidence of prior agreements or contemporaneous oral agreements that contradict a written contract is inadmissible, but] permits a trade usage to be put in evidence "as an instrument of interpretation." The Uniform Commercial Code comment to subdivision (a) of section [2-202] states that evidence of trade usage is admissible "* * * in order that the true understanding of the parties as to the agreement may be reached. Such writings are to be read on the assumption that * * * the usages of trade were taken for granted when the document was phrased. Unless carefully negated they have become an element of the meaning of the words used. * * * "

* * * *

* * * Because potatoes are a perishable commodity and their demand is dependent upon a fluctuating market, and because the marketing contracts are signed eight

(Continued)

CASE 15.2—Continued

or nine months in advance of the harvest season, common sense dictates that the quantity would be estimated by both the grower and processor. Thus, it cannot be said as a matter of law that HMT was ignorant of the trade custom.

DECISION AND REMEDY The Court of Appeal of California affirmed the trial court's judgment. Sunshine Biscuit did not have to pay HMT for the difference between the 100,000 sacks of potatoes it estimated it would need and the 60,105 sacks of potatoes it actually purchased.

FOR CRITICAL ANALYSIS—Ethical Consideration *If HMT had not been aware of the prevailing customs in the potato-processing trade, would evidence of those customs still be admissible? Should it be?*

• **COURSE OF PERFORMANCE** The conduct that occurs under the terms of a particular agreement; such conduct indicates what the parties to an agreement intended it to mean.

"Merchants know perfectly well what they mean when they express themselves, not in the language of lawyers, but in the language of courteous mercantile communication."

LORD CAIRNS, 1819–1885 (British jurist)

Course of Performance A **course of performance** is the conduct that occurs under the terms of a particular agreement. Presumably, the parties themselves know best what they meant by their words, and the course of performance actually undertaken under their agreement is the best indication of what they meant [UCC 2–208(1), 2A–207(1)].

• **EXAMPLE 15.16** Janson's Lumber Company contracts with Barrymore to sell Barrymore a specified number of "two-by-fours." The lumber in fact does not measure 2 inches by 4 inches but rather 1⅞ inches by 3¾ inches. Janson's agrees to deliver the lumber in five deliveries, and Barrymore, without objection, accepts the lumber in the first three deliveries. On the fourth delivery, however, Barrymore objects that the two-by-fours do not measure 2 inches by 4 inches. The course of performance in this transaction—that is, the fact that Barrymore accepted three deliveries without objection under the agreement—is relevant in determining that here the term "two-by-four" actually means "1⅞ by 3¾." Janson's can also prove that two-by-fours need not be exactly 2 inches by 4 inches by applying usage of trade, course of prior dealing, or both. Janson's can, for example, show that in previous transactions, Barrymore took 1⅞-inch-by-3¾-inch lumber without objection. In addition, Janson's can show that in the lumber trade, two-by-fours are commonly 1⅞ inches by 3¾ inches. •

Rules of Construction The UCC provides *rules of construction* for interpreting contracts. Express terms, course of performance, course of dealing, and usage of trade are to be construed together when they do not contradict one another. When such a construction is unreasonable, however, the following order of priority controls: (1) express terms, (2) course of performance, (3) course of dealing, and (4) usage of trade [UCC 1–205(4), 2–208(2), 2A–207(2)].

UNCONSCIONABILITY

As discussed in Chapter 11, an unconscionable contract is one that is so unfair and one sided that it would be unreasonable to enforce it. The UCC allows the court to evaluate a contract or any clause in a contract, and if the court deems it to have been unconscionable at the time it was made, the court can (1) refuse to enforce the contract, (2) enforce the remainder of the contract without the unconscionable clause, or (3) limit the application of any unconscionable clauses to avoid an unconscionable result [UCC 2–302, 2A–108].

The inclusion of Sections 2–302 and 2A–108 in the UCC reflects an increased sensitivity to certain realities of modern commercial activities. Classical contract theory holds that a contract is a bargain in which the terms have been worked out freely between parties that are equals. In many modern commercial transactions, this premise is invalid. Standard-form contracts and leases are often signed by consumer-buyers who understand few of the terms used and who often do not even read them. Virtually all of the terms are advantageous to the party supplying the standard-form contract. The UCC's unconscionability provisions give the courts a powerful weapon for policing such transactions, as the next case illustrates.

CASE 15.3 Jones v. Star Credit Corp.

Supreme Court of New York, Nassau County, 1969.
59 Misc. 2d 189,
298 N.Y.S.2d 264.

HISTORICAL AND ECONOMIC SETTING *In the sixth century, under Roman civil law, the rescission of a contract was allowed when the court determined that the market value of the goods that were the subject of the contract equaled less than half the contract price. This same ratio has appeared over the last thirty years in many cases in which courts have found contract clauses to be unconscionable under UCC 2–302 on the ground that the price was excessive. In a Connecticut case, for example, the court held that a contract requiring a welfare recipient to make payments totaling $1,248 for a television set that retailed for $499 was unconscionable.[a] The seller had not told the buyer the full purchase price. Most of the litigants who have used UCC 2–302 successfully have been consumers who are poor or otherwise at a disadvantage. In one New York case, for example, the court held that a contract requiring a Spanish-speaking consumer to make payments totaling nearly $1,150 for a freezer that wholesaled for less than $350 was unconscionable.[b] The contract was in English, and the salesperson did not translate or explain it.*

BACKGROUND AND FACTS The Joneses, the plaintiffs, were welfare recipients who agreed to purchase a freezer for $900 as the result of a salesperson's visit to their home. Tax and financing charges raised the total price to $1,234.80. At trial, the freezer was found to have a maximum retail value of approximately $300. The plaintiffs, who had made payments totaling $619.88, brought a suit in a New York state court to have the purchase contract declared unconscionable under the UCC.

a. *Murphy v. McNamara*, 36 Conn.Supp. 183, 416 A.2d 170 (1979).

b. *Frostifresh Corp. v. Reynoso*, 52 Misc.2d 26, 274 N.Y.S.2d 757 (Dist. 1966); rev'd on issue of relief, 54 Misc.2d 119, 281 N.Y.S.2d 946 (Sup. 1967).

IN THE WORDS OF THE COURT . . .
Sol M. WACHTLER, Justice.

* * * *

* * * [Section 2-302 of the UCC] authorizes the court to find, as a matter of law, that a contract or a clause of a contract was "unconscionable at the time it was made," and upon so finding the court may refuse to enforce the contract, excise the objectionable clause or limit the application of the clause to avoid an unconscionable result. * * *

* * * *

* * * The question which presents itself is whether or not, under the circumstances of this case, the sale of a freezer unit having a retail value of $300 for $900 ($1,439.69 including credit charges and $18 sales tax) is unconscionable as a matter of law. * * *

* * * [T]he mathematical disparity between $300, which presumably includes a reasonable profit margin, and $900, which is exorbitant on its face, carries the greatest weight. Credit charges alone exceed by more than $100 the retail value of the freezer. * * * The very limited financial resources of the purchaser, known to the sellers at the time of the sale, is entitled to weight in the balance. * * *

* * * *

* * * [T]he defendant has already been amply compensated. In accordance with the statute, the application of the payment provision should be limited to amounts

(Continued)

CASE 15.3—Continued

already paid by the plaintiffs and the contract be reformed and amended by changing the payments called for therein to equal the amount of payment actually so paid by the plaintiffs.

DECISION AND REMEDY The New York trial court entered a judgment for the plaintiffs. The contract was reformed so that they were required to make no further payments.

FOR CRITICAL ANALYSIS—Ethical Consideration *What if the plaintiffs had made payments totaling $300—the retail value of the freezer? Would the court regard that $300 as "payment in full"? Should the court consider the seller's interests in a case such as this one, in which the seller was deemed to have acted unconscionably?*

Contracts for the International Sale of Goods

ON THE WEB

The full text of the CISG is available online at the Pace University School of Law's Institute of International Commercial Law. Go to cisgw3.law.pace.edu.

International sales contracts between firms or individuals located in different countries are governed by the 1980 United Nations Convention on Contracts for the International Sale of Goods (CISG)—if the countries of the parties to the contract have ratified the CISG (and if the parties have not agreed that some other law will govern their contract). As of 1999, fifty-three countries had ratified or acceded to the CISG, including the United States, Canada, Mexico, some Central and South American countries, and most of the European nations.

APPLICABILITY OF THE CISG

Essentially, the CISG is to international sales contracts what Article 2 of the UCC is to domestic sales contracts. As discussed in this chapter, in domestic transactions the UCC applies when the parties to a contract for a sale of goods have failed to specify in writing some important term concerning price, delivery, or the like. Similarly, whenever the parties subject to the CISG have failed to specify in writing

A PRODUCTION LINE IN A GLOBE FACTORY. IF, IN THE UNITED STATES, A CONTRACT FOR A SALE OF GLOBES IS NOT IN WRITING, IS IT ENFORCEABLE? IS A CONTRACT FOR AN INTERNATIONAL SALE OF THE GLOBES ENFORCEABLE IF IT IS NOT IN WRITING?

the precise terms of a contract for the international sale of goods, the CISG will be applied. Although the UCC applies to consumer sales, the CISG does not, and neither applies to contracts for services.

Businesspersons must take special care when drafting international sales contracts to avoid problems caused by distance, including language differences and different national laws. The fold-out exhibit contained within this chapter, which shows an actual international sales contract used by Starbucks Coffee Company, illustrates many of the special terms and clauses that are typically contained in international contracts for the sale of goods. Annotations in the exhibit explain the meaning and significance of specific clauses in the contract. (See Chapter 43 for a discussion of other laws that frame global business transactions.)

A Comparison of CISG and UCC Provisions

The provisions of the CISG, although similar for the most part to those of the UCC, differ from them in some respects. We have already mentioned some of these differences. In the *International Perspective* in Chapter 12, for example, we pointed out that the CISG does not include the requirements imposed by the UCC's Statute of Frauds. Rather, Article 11 of the CISG states that an international sales contract "need not be concluded in or evidenced by writing and is not subject to any other requirements as to form." Other differences between the UCC and the CISG were indicated in this chapter's *International Perspective* discussing firm offers.

With respect to contract formation, some other differences between the CISG and the UCC merit attention. First, under the UCC, if the price term is left open, the court will determine "a reasonable price at the time for delivery" [UCC 2–305(1)]. Under the CISG, however, the price term must be specified, or at least provisions for its specification must be included in the agreement; otherwise, normally no contract will exist.

Second, like UCC 2–207, the CISG provides that a contract can be formed even though the acceptance contains additional terms, unless the additional terms materially alter the contract. The definition of a "material alteration" under the CISG, however, involves virtually any differences in terms. In its effect, then, the CISG requires that the terms of the acceptance mirror those of the offer.

Third, under the UCC, an acceptance is effective on dispatch. Under the CISG, however, a contract is created not at the time the acceptance is transmitted but only on its receipt by the offeror. (The offer becomes irrevocable, however, when the acceptance is sent.) Additionally, in contrast to the UCC, the CISG provides that acceptance by performance does not require that the offeror be notified of the performance.

In the following chapters, we continue to point out differences between the CISG and the UCC as they relate to the topics covered. These topics include risk of loss, performance, remedies, and warranties.

Key Terms

course of dealing 400
course of performance 402
firm offer 390
lease agreement 385
lessee 385
lessor 385
merchant 385
output contract 390
requirements contract 390
sale 382
sales contract 382
seasonably 392
tangible property 382
usage of trade 401

Chapter Summary • The Formation of Sales and Lease Contracts

The Scope of the UCC (See pages 381–382.)	The UCC attempts to provide a consistent, uniform, and integrated framework of rules to deal with all phases *ordinarily arising* in a commercial sales or lease transaction, including contract formation, passage of title and risk of loss, performance, remedies, payment for goods, warehoused goods, and secured transactions. If there is a conflict between a common law rule and the UCC, the UCC controls.
The Scope of Article 2—Sales (See pages 382–385.)	Article 2 governs contracts for the sale of goods (tangible, movable personal property). The common law of contracts also applies to sales contracts to the extent that the common law has not been modified by the UCC.
The Scope of Article 2A—Leases (See pages 385–386.)	Article 2A governs contracts for the lease of goods. Article 2A is essentially a repetition of Article 2, except that it applies to leases, instead of sales, of goods and thus varies to reflect differences between sale and lease transactions.
Offer and Acceptance (See pages 386–396.)	1. *Offer—* a. Not all terms have to be included for a contract to be formed (only the subject matter and quantity term must be specified). b. The price does not have to be included for a contract to be formed. c. Particulars of performance can be left open. d. A written and signed offer by a *merchant,* covering a period of three months or less, is irrevocable without payment of consideration. 2. *Acceptance—* a. Acceptance may be made by any reasonable means of communication; it is effective when dispatched. b. The acceptance of a unilateral offer can be made by a promise to ship or by prompt shipment of conforming goods, or by prompt shipment of nonconforming goods if not accompanied by a notice of accommodation. c. Acceptance by performance requires notice within a reasonable time; otherwise, the offer can be treated as lapsed. d. A definite expression of acceptance creates a contract even if the terms of the acceptance vary from those of the offer unless the varied terms in the acceptance are expressly conditioned on the offeror's assent to the varied terms.
Consideration (See page 397.)	A modification of a contract for the sale of goods does not require consideration.
Requirements under the Statute of Frauds (See pages 397–400.)	1. All contracts for the sale of goods priced at $500 or more must be in writing. A writing is sufficient as long as it indicates a contract between the parties and is signed by the party against whom enforcement is sought. A contract is not enforceable beyond the quantity shown in the writing. 2. When written confirmation of an oral contract *between merchants* is not objected to in writing by the receiver within ten days, the contract is enforceable. 3. Exceptions to the requirement of a writing exist in the following situations: a. When the oral contract is for specially manufactured goods not suitable for resale to others, and the seller has substantially started to manufacture the goods. b. When the defendant admits in pleadings, testimony, or other court proceedings that an oral contract for the sale of goods was made. In this case, the contract will be enforceable to the extent of the quantity of goods admitted.

Chapter Summary • The Formation of Sales and Lease Contracts, Continued

Requirements under the Statute of Frauds—continued	c. The oral agreement will be enforceable to the extent that payment has been received and accepted by the seller or to the extent that the goods have been received and accepted by the buyer.
Parol Evidence Rule (See pages 400–402.)	1. The terms of a clearly and completely worded written contract cannot be contradicted by evidence of prior agreements or contemporaneous oral agreements. 2. Evidence is admissible to clarify the terms of a writing in the following situations: a. If the contract terms are ambiguous. b. If evidence of course of dealing, usage of trade, or course of performance is necessary to learn or to clarify the intentions of the parties to the contract.
Unconscionability (See pages 402–404.)	An unconscionable contract is one that is so unfair and one sided that it would be unreasonable to enforce it. If the court deems a contract to have been unconscionable at the time it was made, the court can (1) refuse to enforce the contract, (2) refuse to enforce the unconscionable clause of the contract, or (3) limit the application of any unconscionable clauses to avoid an unconscionable result.
Contracts for the International Sale of Goods (See pages 404–405.)	International sales contracts are governed by the United Nations Convention on Contracts for the International Sale of Goods (CISG)—if the countries of the parties to the contract have ratified the CISG (and if the parties have not agreed that some other law will govern their contract). Essentially, the CISG is to international sales contracts what Article 2 of the UCC is to domestic sales contracts. Whenever parties who are subject to the CISG have failed to specify in writing the precise terms of a contract for the international sale of goods, the CISG will be applied.

For Review

1 Describe the scope and coverage of Article 2 and Article 2A of the UCC.

2 What is a merchant's firm offer?

3 If an offeree includes additional or different terms in an acceptance, will a contract result? If so, what happens to these terms?

4 Article 2 and Article 2A of the UCC both define three exceptions to the writing requirements of the Statute of Frauds. What are these three exceptions?

5 What law governs contracts for the international sale of goods?

Questions and Case Problems

15–1. Terms of the Offer. The UCC changes the effect of the common law of contracts in several ways. For instance, at common law, an offer must be definite enough for the parties to ascertain its essential terms when it is accepted. What happens under the UCC if some of an offer's terms—the price term, for example—are left open? What if the quantity term is left open?

15–2. Statute of Frauds. Fresher Foods, Inc., orally agreed to purchase from Dale Vernon, a farmer, one thousand bushels of corn for $1.25 per bushel. Fresher Foods paid $125 down and agreed to pay the remainder of the purchase price on delivery, which was scheduled for one week later. When Fresher Foods tendered the balance of $1,125 on the scheduled day of delivery and requested the corn, Vernon refused to deliver it. Fresher Foods sued Vernon for damages, claiming that Vernon had breached their oral contract. Can Fresher Foods recover? If so, to what extent?

15–3. Merchant's Firm Offer. On September 1, Jennings, a used-car dealer, wrote a letter to Wheeler in which he stated, "I have a 1955 Thunderbird convertible in mint condition that I will sell you for $13,500 at any time before October 9. [signed]

Peter Jennings." By September 15, having heard nothing from Wheeler, Jennings sold the Thunderbird to another party. On September 29, Wheeler accepted Jennings's offer and tendered the $13,500. When Jennings told Wheeler he had sold the car to another party, Wheeler claimed Jennings had breached their contract. Is Jennings in breach? Explain.

15–4. Accommodation Shipments. M. M. Salinger, Inc., a retailer of television sets, orders one hundred Model Color-X sets from manufacturer Fulsom. The order specifies the price and that the television sets are to be shipped via Interamerican Freightways on or before October 30. Fulsom receives the order on October 5. On October 8, Fulsom writes Salinger a letter indicating that it has received the order and that it will ship the sets as directed, at the specified price. Salinger receives this letter on October 10. On October 28, Fulsom, in preparing the shipment, discovers it has only ninety Color-X sets in stock. Fulsom ships the ninety Color-X sets and ten television sets of a different model, stating clearly on the invoice that the ten sets are being shipped only as an accommodation. Salinger claims that Fulsom is in breach of contract. Fulsom claims that there was not an acceptance, and therefore no contract was formed. Explain who is correct, and why.

15–5. Statute of Frauds. Loeb & Co. entered into an oral agreement with Schreiner, a farmer, in which Schreiner agreed to sell Loeb 150 bales of cotton, each weighing 480 pounds. Shortly thereafter, Loeb sent Schreiner a letter confirming the terms of the oral contract. Schreiner neither acknowledged receipt of the letter nor objected to its terms. When delivery came due, Schreiner ignored the oral agreement and sold his cotton on the open market, because the price of cotton had more than doubled (from 37 cents to 80 cents per pound) since the oral agreement had been made. In the lawsuit by Loeb & Co. against Schreiner, did Loeb recover? Explain. [*Loeb & Co. v. Schreiner,* 294 Ala. 722, 321 So.2d 199 (1975)]

15–6. Additional Terms in Acceptance. The Carpet Mart, a carpet dealer, telephoned an order (offer) for carpet to Collins & Aikman Corp., a carpet manufacturer. Collins & Aikman then sent Carpet Mart an acknowledgment form (acceptance), which specified the quantity and price agreed to in the telephone conversation. The reverse side of the printed acknowledgment form stated that Collins & Aikman's acceptance was subject to the buyer's agreement to submit all disputes to arbitration. Collins & Aikman shipped the carpet to Carpet Mart, which received the acknowledgment form and shipment without objection. Later, a dispute arose, and Carpet Mart brought a civil suit against Collins & Aikman, claiming misrepresentation as to the quality of the carpet. Collins & Aikman filed a motion to compel arbitration. Will the court enforce the arbitration clause? Discuss. [*Dorton v. Collins & Aikman Corp.,* 453 F.2d 1161 (6th Cir. 1972)]

15–7. Merchant Status. Albert Reifschneider was raised on a farm and had been in the business of selling corn and in the business of selling other crops under futures contracts (contracts for goods to be harvested in the future) for twenty years. In April 1988, Reifschneider orally agreed to sell Colorado-Kansas Grain Co. 12,500 bushels of corn after the harvest in the fall. The company sent Reifschneider a written confirmation of the agreement with instructions to sign it and return it. In June, Reifschneider told the company that he would not sign the confirmation and that no contract existed between the parties. The company demanded that Reifschneider deliver the corn, but the demand was to no avail. The company sued Reifschneider for breach of contract, and the issue turned on whether Reifschneider was a "merchant" within the meaning of the UCC. How should the court rule? Discuss fully. [*Colorado-Kansas Grain Co. v. Reifschneider,* 817 P.2d 637 (Colo.App. 1991)]

15–8. Goods and Services Combined. Jane Pittsley contracted with Donald Houser, who was doing business as the Hilton Contract Carpet Co., for the installation of carpet in her home. Following installation, Pittsley complained to Hilton that some seams were visible, gaps appeared, the carpet did not lie flat in all areas, and the carpet failed to reach the wall in certain locations. Although Hilton made various attempts to fix the installation by stretching the carpet and other methods, Pittsley was not satisfied with the work and eventually sued Hilton to recover the $3,500 she had paid toward the $4,319.50 contract price for the carpet and its installation. Hilton paid the installers $700 for the work done in laying Pittsley's carpet. One of the issues before the court was whether the contract was a contract for the sale of goods or a contract for the sale of services. How should the court decide this issue? Discuss fully. [*Pittsley v. Houser,* 125 Idaho 820, 875 P.2d 232 (1994)]

15–9. Statute of Frauds. GPL Treatment, Ltd., orally agreed to sell a large quantity of cedar shakes to Louisiana-Pacific Corp. (L-P). GPL sent L-P order confirmation forms that stated the prices and quantities of shakes ordered. Each form also contained a "sign and return" clause, asking L-P to sign and return one copy. L-P did not sign or return any of the forms, but it also did not object to any of the terms. When L-P accepted only about 15 percent of the orders, GPL filed a suit in an Oregon state court against the buyer for breach of contract. Do GPL's confirmation forms satisfy the requirement of a writing under the Statute of Frauds? Are they enforceable against L-P? Discuss fully. [*GPL Treatment, Ltd. v. Louisiana-Pacific Corp.,* 323 Or. 116, 914 P.2d 682 (1996)]

15–10. Statute of Frauds. SNK, Inc., makes video arcade games and sells them to distributors, including Entertainment Sales, Inc. (ESI). Most sales between SNK and ESI were phone orders. Over one four-month period, ESI phoned in several orders for "Samurai Showdown" games. SNK did not fill the orders. ESI filed a suit against SNK and others, alleging, among other things, breach of contract. There was no written contract covering the orders. ESI claimed that it had faxed purchase orders for the games to SNK but did not offer proof that the faxes had been sent or received. SNK filed a motion for summary judgment. In whose favor will the court rule, and why? [*Entertainment Sales Co. v. SNK, Inc.,* 232 Ga.App. 669, 502 S.E.2d 263 (1998)]

A QUESTION OF ETHICS AND SOCIAL RESPONSIBILITY

15–11. John Schwanbeck entered into negotiations with Federal-Mogul Corp. to purchase Federal-Mogul's Vellumoid Division. The two parties drew up a letter of intent stating that "[n]o further obligation will arise until a definitive agreement is reduced to writing" and that it was the parties' intention "to proceed in good faith in the negotiation of such binding definitive agreement." At another place in the letter of intent were the following words: "Of course, this letter is not intended to create, nor do you or we presently have any binding legal obligation whatever in any way relating to such sale and purchase." Federal-Mogul eventually sold the Vellumoid Division to another party. Schwanbeck sued Federal-Mogul, alleging, among other things, that Federal-Mogul had breached an agreement to negotiate in good faith the proposed contract with Schwanbeck. Given these facts, consider the following questions. [*Schwanbeck v. Federal-Mogul Corp.*, 412 Mass. 703, 592 N.E.2d 1289 (1992)]

1. Did the letter of intent create a legally binding obligation, or was the letter merely an "agreement to agree" in the future? (You may wish to review the section on "Agreements to Agree" in Chapter 10 before you answer this question.)
2. Regardless of its legal duties, did Federal-Mogul have an ethical duty to proceed in negotiating a contract with Schwanbeck? Discuss.

FOR CRITICAL ANALYSIS

15–12. Why is the designation "merchant" or "nonmerchant" important?

Online Activities

ONLINE EXERCISE 15–1

Go to the "Internet Activities Book" on the Web site that accompanies this text, the URL for which is http://blt.westbuslaw.com. Select the following activity, and perform the exercise according to the instructions given there:

Activity 15–1: Is It a Contract?

Before the Test

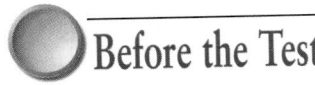

Go to the *Business Law Today* home page at http://blt.westbuslaw.com. Click on TestTutor.® You will find twenty interactive questions relating to this chapter.

CHAPTER 16

Title & Risk of Loss

"Now, it is of great moment that well-drawn laws should themselves define all the points they possibly can and leave as few as may be to the decision of the judges."

Aristotle, 384–322 B.C.E.
(Greek philosopher)

CONTENTS

LEARNING OBJECTIVES

After reading this chapter, you should be able to:

1. Indicate when title to goods passes from seller to buyer.
2. Explain the problems that can arise when persons who acquire goods with imperfect title attempt to resell the goods.
3. Define various contract terms that help to determine when the risk of loss passes from a seller or lessor to a buyer or lessee.
4. Identify who bears the risk of loss when a contract is breached.
5. Indicate when each party to a sales or lease contract has an insurable interest in the goods.

A sale of goods transfers ownership rights in (title to) the goods from the seller to the buyer. Often, a sales contract is signed before the actual goods are available. For example, a sales contract for oranges might be signed in May, but the oranges may not be ready for picking and shipment until October. Any number of things can happen between the time the sales contract is signed and the time the goods are actually transferred into the buyer's possession. Fire, flood, or frost may destroy the orange groves, or the oranges may be lost or damaged in transit. The same problems may occur under a lease contract. Because of these possibilities, it is important to know the rights and liabilities of the parties between the time the contract is formed and the time the goods are actually received by the buyer or lessee.

Before the creation of the Uniform Commercial Code (UCC), *title*—the right of ownership—was the central concept in sales law, controlling all issues of rights and remedies of the parties to a sales contract. In some situations, title is still relevant under the UCC, and the UCC has special rules for determining who has title. These rules will be discussed in the sections that follow. In most situations, however, the UCC has replaced the concept of title with three other concepts: (1) identification, (2) risk of loss, and (3) insurable interest. By breaking down the transfer of ownership into these three components, the drafters of the UCC have essentially followed Aristotle's advice in the chapter-opening quotation and created greater precision in the law governing sales—leaving as few points of law as possible "to the decision of the judges."

In lease contracts, of course, title to the goods is retained by the lessor-owner of the goods. Hence, the UCC's provisions relating to passage of title do not apply to leased goods. Other concepts discussed in this chapter, though, including identification, risk of loss, and insurable interest, relate to lease contracts as well as to sales contracts.

Identification

Before any interest in specific goods can pass from the seller or lessor to the buyer or lessee, two conditions must prevail: (1) the goods must be in existence, and (2) they must be identified as the specific goods designated in the contract. **Identification** is a designation of goods as the subject matter of a sales or lease contract. Title and risk of loss cannot pass from buyer to seller unless the goods are identified to the contract. (As mentioned, title to leased goods remains with the lessor—or, if the owner is a third party, with that party. The lessee does not acquire title to leased goods.) Identification is significant because it gives the buyer or lessee the right to insure (or to have an insurable interest in) the goods and the right to recover from third parties who damage the goods.

• **IDENTIFICATION**
In a sale of goods, the express designation of the goods provided for in the contract.

In their contract, the parties can agree on when identification will take place, but identification is effective to pass title and risk of loss to the buyer only after the goods are considered to be in existence. If they do not so specify, however, the UCC

A FREEZE CAN DESTROY AN ORANGE GROVE. IF A CONTRACT FOR A SALE OF THE ORANGES HAD ALREADY BEEN SIGNED, WHO WOULD SUFFER THE LOSS?

> **ON THE WEB**
> You can obtain information on current commercial law topics from the law firm of Hale and Dorr at **www.haledorr.com**.

provisions discussed here determine when identification takes place [UCC 2–501(1), 2A–217].

EXISTING GOODS

If the contract calls for the sale or lease of specific and ascertained goods that are already in existence, identification takes place at the time the contract is made. For example, you contract to purchase or lease a fleet of five cars by the serial numbers listed for the cars.

FUTURE GOODS

If a sale involves unborn animals to be born within twelve months after contracting, identification takes place when the animals are conceived. If a lease involves any unborn animals, identification occurs when the animals are conceived. If a sale involves crops that are to be harvested within twelve months (or the next harvest season occurring after contracting, whichever is longer), identification takes place when the crops are planted or begin to grow. In a sale or lease of any other future goods, identification occurs when the goods are shipped, marked, or otherwise designated by the seller or lessor as the goods to which the contract refers.

GOODS THAT ARE PART OF A LARGER MASS

As a general rule, goods that are part of a larger mass are identified when the goods are marked, shipped, or somehow designated by the seller or lessor as the particular goods to pass under the contract. • **EXAMPLE 16.1** A buyer orders 1,000 cases of beans from a 10,000-case lot. Until the seller separates the 1,000 cases of beans from the 10,000-case lot, title and risk of loss remain with the seller.•

A common exception to this rule deals with fungible goods. **Fungible goods** are goods that are alike by physical nature, by agreement, or by trade usage. Typical examples are specific grades or types of wheat, oil, and wine, usually stored in large containers. If these goods are held or intended to be held by owners as tenants in common (owners having shares undivided from the entire mass), a seller-owner can pass title and risk of loss to the buyer without an actual separation. The buyer replaces the seller as an owner in common [UCC 2–105(4)].

• **FUNGIBLE GOODS**
Goods that are alike by physical nature, by agreement, or by trade usage. Examples of fungible goods are wheat, oil, and wine that are identical in type and quality.

• **EXAMPLE 16.2** Anselm, Braudel, and Carpenter are farmers. They deposit, respectively, 5,000 bushels, 3,000 bushels, and 2,000 bushels of grain of the same grade and quality in a bin. The three become owners in common, with Anselm owning 50 percent of the 10,000 bushels, Braudel 30 percent, and Carpenter 20 percent. Anselm could contract to sell her 5,000 bushels of grain to Tareyton and, because the goods are fungible, pass title and risk of loss to Tareyton without physically separating 5,000 bushels. Tareyton now becomes an owner in common with Braudel and Carpenter.•

Passage of Title

Once goods exist and are identified, the provisions of UCC 2–401 apply to the passage of title. In virtually all subsections of UCC 2–401, the words "unless otherwise explicitly agreed" appear, meaning that any explicit understanding between the buyer and the seller determines when title passes. Unless an agreement is explicitly made, title passes to the buyer at the time and the place the seller performs the physical delivery of the goods [UCC 2–401(2)]. This rule is applied in the following case.

CASE 16.1 Synergistic Technologies, Inc. v. IDB Mobile Communications, Inc.

United States District Court,
District of Columbia, 1994.
871 F.Supp. 24.

HISTORICAL AND TECHNOLOGICAL SETTING *The former Soviet Union (now fifteen independent countries, of which the most important is Russia) launched the first artificial satellite, Sputnik I, into orbit around the earth in 1957. Today, several thousand artificial satellites circle our planet. They are used for weather forecasting, for communications, and for military, scientific, and other purposes. For example, the maritime and aviation industries use the International Maritime Satellite (INMARSAT) system for navigation and communication purposes. In the United States, one of the few providers of INMARSAT service is IDB Mobile Communications, Inc.*

BACKGROUND AND FACTS Synergistic Technologies, Inc. (SynTech), developed three computer software systems for IDB Mobile Communications, Inc., to provide IDB's customers with satellite voice and data communications services. SynTech installed the systems in IDB's computers under a "Statement of Work" negotiated between the two firms. During the installation, IDB discovered that the systems would not allow it to make back-up copies of the software. If IDB's computers crashed, a return to full operation would thus be delayed. When IDB hired another company to make back-up copies, SynTech filed a suit in a federal district court against IDB, seeking damages and other relief for, among other things, alleged infringement of SynTech's copyrights. IDB responded in part by filing a motion for summary judgment. One of the issues was whether IDB was the "owner" of the software.

IN THE WORDS OF THE COURT . . .
JOYCE HENS GREEN, District Judge.

* * * *

* * * The Statement of Work is not clear on the issue of transfer of ownership of the software. * * * If this matter turned solely on the Statement of Work, the Court would be unable to resolve the issue of ownership * * * .

However, this question is also governed by [Section] 2–401 of the Uniform Commercial Code, which provides that "[u]nless otherwise explicitly agreed title passes to the buyer at the time and place at which the seller completes his performance with reference to the physical delivery of the goods." The parties not having explicitly agreed otherwise, title to * * * the software passed to IDB at the time of delivery of the goods.

DECISION AND REMEDY The federal district court granted IDB's motion on this issue.

FOR CRITICAL ANALYSIS—Technological Consideration *Why would SynTech be concerned about the fact that its client was making back-up copies of the software?*

SHIPMENT AND DESTINATION CONTRACTS

Unless otherwise agreed, delivery arrangements can determine when title passes from the seller to the buyer. In a **shipment contract,** the seller is required or authorized to ship goods by carrier, such as a trucking company. Under a shipment contract, the seller is required only to deliver conforming goods into the hands of a carrier, and title passes to the buyer at the time and place of shipment [UCC 2–401(2)(a)]. Generally, *all contracts are assumed to be shipment contracts if nothing to the contrary is stated in the contract.*

• **SHIPMENT CONTRACT**
A contract for the sale of goods in which the seller is required or authorized to ship the goods by carrier. The seller assumes liability for any losses or damage to the goods until they are delivered to the carrier.

• **DESTINATION CONTRACT**
A contract for the sale of goods in which the seller is required or authorized to ship the goods by carrier and tender delivery of the goods at a particular destination. The seller assumes liability for any losses or damage to the goods until they are tendered at the destination specified in the contract.

In a **destination contract,** the seller is required to deliver the goods to a particular destination, usually directly to the buyer, but sometimes the buyer designates that the goods should be delivered to another party. Title passes to the buyer when the goods are *tendered* at that destination [UCC 2–401(2)(b)]. A tender of delivery is the seller's placing or holding of conforming goods at the buyer's disposition (with any necessary notice), enabling the buyer to take delivery [UCC 2–503(1)].

Delivery without Movement of the Goods

• **DOCUMENT OF TITLE**
Paper exchanged in the regular course of business that evidences the right to possession of goods (for example, a bill of lading or a warehouse receipt).

When the contract of sale does not call for the seller's shipment or delivery of the goods (when the buyer is to pick up the goods), the passage of title depends on whether the seller must deliver a **document of title,** such as a bill of lading or a warehouse receipt, to the buyer. A *bill of lading* is a receipt for goods that is signed by a carrier and that serves as a contract for the transportation of the goods. A *warehouse receipt* is a receipt issued by a warehouser for goods stored in a warehouse.

When a document of title is required, title passes to the buyer *when and where the document is delivered.* Thus, if the goods are stored in a warehouse, title passes to the buyer when the appropriate documents are delivered to the buyer. The goods never move. In fact, the buyer can choose to leave the goods at the same warehouse for a period of time, and the buyer's title to those goods will be unaffected.

ON THE WEB
To review bills of lading, access the following Web site: www.showtrans.com/bl.htm.

When no documents of title are required and delivery is made without moving the goods, title passes at the time and place the sales contract is made, if the goods have already been identified. If the goods have not been identified, title does not pass until identification occurs. • **Example 16.3** Rogers sells lumber to Bodan. It is agreed that Bodan will pick up the lumber at the lumberyard. If the lumber has been identified (segregated, marked, or in any other way distinguished from all other lumber), title passes to Bodan when the contract is signed. If the lumber is still in storage bins at the lumberyard, title does not pass to Bodan until the particular pieces of lumber to be sold under this contract are identified [UCC 2–401(3)].•

Sales or Leases by Nonowners

Problems occur when persons who acquire goods with imperfect titles attempt to sell or lease them. Sections 2–402 and 2–403 of the UCC deal with the rights of two parties who lay claim to the same goods, sold with imperfect titles. Generally, a buyer acquires at least whatever title the seller has to the goods sold.

The UCC also protects a person who leases such goods from the person who bought them. Of course, a lessee does not acquire whatever title the lessor has to the goods. A lessee acquires a right to possess and use the goods—that is, a *leasehold interest.* A lessee acquires whatever leasehold interest the lessor has or has the power to transfer, subject to the lease contract [UCC 2A–303, 2A–304, 2A–305].

¡REMEMBER!
Theft is a crime (larceny, embezzlement, and so on) and a tort (conversion). Receiving goods that the recipient knows were stolen is both a crime and a tort.

Void Title A buyer may unknowingly purchase goods from a seller who is not the owner of the goods. If the seller is a thief, the seller's title is *void*—legally, no title exists. Thus, the buyer acquires no title, and the real owner can reclaim the goods from the buyer. The same result would occur if the goods were only leased, because the lessor has no leasehold interest to transfer [UCC 2–403(1), 2A–305].

• **Example 16.4** If Jim steals diamonds owned by Maren, Jim has a *void title* to those diamonds. If Jim sells the diamonds to Shannon, Maren can reclaim them from Shannon even though Shannon acted in good faith and honestly was not aware that the goods were stolen.•

Voidable Title A seller has a *voidable title* if the goods that he or she is selling were obtained by fraud, paid for with a check that is later dishonored, purchased from a minor, or purchased on credit when the seller was insolvent. (Under the UCC, a person is **insolvent** when that person ceases to pay "his debts in the ordinary course of business or cannot pay his debts as they become due or is insolvent within the meaning of federal bankruptcy law" [UCC 1–201(23)].)

- **INSOLVENT**
Under the UCC, a term describing a person who ceases to pay "his debts in the ordinary course of business or cannot pay his debts as they become due or is insolvent within the meaning of federal bankruptcy law" [UCC 1–201(23)].

- **GOOD FAITH PURCHASER**
A purchaser who buys without notice of any circumstance that would put a person of ordinary prudence on inquiry as to whether the seller has valid title to the goods being sold.

In contrast to a seller with *void title,* a seller with *voidable title* has the power to transfer a good title to a good faith purchaser for value. A **good faith purchaser** is one who buys without knowledge of circumstances that would make a person of ordinary prudence inquire about the validity of the seller's title to the goods. One who purchases *for value* gives legally sufficient consideration (value) for the goods purchased. The real, or original, owner cannot recover goods from a good faith purchaser for value [UCC 2–403(1)].[1] If the buyer of the goods is not a good faith purchaser for value, then the actual owner of the goods can reclaim them from the buyer (or from the seller, if the goods are still in the seller's possession).

The same rules apply in circumstances involving leases. A lessor with voidable title has the power to transfer a valid leasehold interest to a good faith lessee for value. The real owner cannot recover the goods, except as permitted by the terms of the lease. The real owner can, however, receive all proceeds arising from the lease, as well as a transfer of all rights, title, and interest as lessor under the lease, including the lessor's interest in the return of the goods when the lease expires [UCC 2A–305(1)].

ON THE WEB

Law Journal EXTRA!, one of the largest and most comprehensive legal sites on the Internet, offers current articles on various topics relating to sales contracts. Go to www.ljx.com/practice/commercial/index.com.

ETHICAL ISSUE 16.1 ***Why does the UCC protect innocent persons (good faith purchasers) who buy goods from sellers with voidable title but not from sellers with void title?*** By now you must be asking yourself just this question. The answer is that the UCC attempts to protect not just innocent good faith purchasers but also the innocent true owners of goods. Consider the situation from the point of view of protecting true owners. If goods are stolen, normally the theft was not the fault of the true owner. In this situation, in which both the true owner and the person who purchases the stolen goods from the thief are innocent parties, the UCC tips the scales of justice in favor of the true owner. If goods are obtained from the true owner through fraud or in other ways so as to render the title to the goods voidable, however, the owner had at least some control over the transaction and might have avoided subsequent problems by exercising certain precautions. In the latter situation, the drafters of the UCC considered it fair to give the rights of the innocent good faith purchaser for value more weight than the rights of the true owner.

¡BE AWARE!

The purpose of most goods held in inventory is to turn those goods into cash by selling them. That is the reason for the entrustment rule.

The Entrustment Rule According to Section 2–403(2), entrusting goods to a merchant *who deals in goods of that kind* gives the merchant the power to transfer all rights to *a buyer in the ordinary course of business.* Entrusting includes both turning over the goods to the merchant and leaving the purchased goods with the merchant for later delivery or pickup [UCC 2–403(3)]. A buyer in the ordinary course of business is a person who, in good faith and without knowledge that the sale violates the ownership rights or security interest of a third party, buys in ordinary course from a person (other than a pawnbroker) in the business of selling goods of that kind [UCC 1–201(9)]. (A *security interest* is any interest in personal property that secures payment or the performance of an obligation—see Chapter 22.)

1. The real owner could, of course, sue the purchaser who initially obtained voidable title to the goods.

• **EXAMPLE 16.5** Jan leaves her watch with a jeweler to be repaired. The jeweler sells used watches. The jeweler sells Jan's watch to Kim, a customer, who does not know that the jeweler has no right to sell it. Kim, as a good faith buyer, gets good title against Jan's claim of ownership.[2] Kim, however, obtains only those rights held by the person entrusting the goods (here, Jan). Suppose that in fact Jan had stolen the watch from Greg and then left it with the jeweler to be repaired. The jeweler then sells it to Kim. In this situation, Kim gets good title against Jan, who entrusted the watch to the jeweler, but not against Greg (the real owner), who neither entrusted the watch to Jan nor authorized Jan to entrust it. •

Article 2A provides a similar rule for leased goods. If a lessor entrusts goods to a lessee-merchant who deals in goods of that kind, the lessee-merchant has the power to transfer all of the rights the lessor had in the goods to a buyer or sublessee in the ordinary course of business [UCC 2A–305(2)]. The following case involves an application of the entrustment doctrine.

2. Jan, of course, can sue the jeweler for the tort of trespass to personalty or conversion (see Chapter 4) for the equivalent money value of the watch.

CASE 16.2 DeWeldon, Ltd. v. McKean

United States Court of Appeals,
First Circuit, 1997.
125 F.3d 24.
www.law.emory.edu/1circuit/2nd-idx.html[a]

HISTORICAL AND SOCIAL SETTING *During World War II, after more than three years of fighting, U.S. forces invaded the island of Iwo Jima in February 1945. In the midst of the costly, month-long battle, five Marines and a Navy corpsman raised a U.S. flag on the peak of Mount Suribachi. A photograph of the flag raising epitomized the valor of the U.S. forces. Within days, work began on a statue to commemorate this courage. The United States Marine Corps Memorial took more than eight years to complete. Today, it is the world's tallest bronze statue. The sculptor was Felix DeWeldon.*

a. This is a page, within the Web site of the Emory University School of Law, that lists the published opinions of the U.S. Court of Appeals for the First Circuit since November 1995. Scroll down the list of cases to the *DeWeldon* case (included with the cases under the letter "M" for "McKean"). Click on the case name to access the opinion.

BACKGROUND AND FACTS Felix DeWeldon, a sculptor and an art collector, owned three paintings valued at $26,000 that were displayed in his home in Rhode Island. When he declared bankruptcy, DeWeldon, Ltd.,[b] bought all of his personal property from the bankruptcy trustee (a person appointed by the bankruptcy court to collect and distribute the debtor's assets—see Chapter 23) and entrusted the paintings to Felix. DeWeldon, Ltd., did not put signs on the premises or tags on the paintings to indicate that Felix no longer owned the paintings. Later, Felix paid for an option to repurchase the paintings and the right to retain their possession until the option expired. Within a year, Felix sold the paintings to Robert McKean for $50,000. DeWeldon, Ltd., claiming that Felix DeWeldon had no right to sell the paintings, sued in a federal district court to recover them. The court held that the entrustment doctrine applied and ruled in favor of McKean. DeWeldon, Ltd., appealed.

b. The abbreviation *Ltd.* stands for *Limited,* which is another word that can be used to designate a corporation.

IN THE WORDS OF THE COURT . . .
HILL, Senior Circuit Judge.

* * * *

* * * [T]he Uniform Commercial Code (UCC) as adopted by Rhode Island provides that an owner who entrusts items to a merchant who deals in goods of that kind gives him or her power to transfer all rights of the entruster to a buyer in the ordinary course of business. * * *

CASE 16.2—Continued

* * * McKean's purchase of the paintings is protected by the entrustment doctrine. First, DeWeldon, Ltd. entrusted the paintings to Felix DeWeldon. After DeWeldon, Ltd. purchased the paintings, it acquiesced in Felix DeWeldon's retention of them. * * *

Second, McKean was a buyer in the ordinary course of business. * * * McKean gave value for the paintings. * * *

McKean had no actual notice that Felix DeWeldon was no longer the true owner of the paintings. DeWeldon, Ltd. did nothing to shield the paintings in the cloak of its ownership. * * *

* * * *

Third, under the facts of this case, Felix DeWeldon acted as a merchant within the meaning of the [UCC]. * * *

* * * *

* * * Felix DeWeldon was a "well-known" artist whose work was for sale commercially and a "collector." There was art work all over Felix DeWeldon's home. He had recently sold paintings to a European buyer. By his occupation he held himself out as having knowledge and skill peculiar to art and the art trade.

DECISION AND REMEDY The U.S. Court of Appeals for the First Circuit affirmed the judgment of the lower court. The appellate court held that the entrustment doctrine protected McKean's purchase of the paintings.

FOR CRITICAL ANALYSIS—Ethical Consideration *Under the entrustment doctrine, when a person gives possession of his or her property to a merchant dealing in goods of the kind, that person assumes the risk that the merchant may sell the property to an innocent good faith purchaser for value. Is this fair?*

Risk of Loss

"This doing of something about disputes, this doing of it reasonably, is the business of law."

KARL N. LLEWELLYN, 1893–1962 (American legal scholar)

Under the UCC, risk of loss does not necessarily pass with title. When risk of loss passes from a seller or lessor to a buyer or lessee is generally determined by the contract between the parties. Sometimes, the contract states expressly when the risk of loss passes. At other times, it does not, and a court must interpret the performance and delivery terms of the contract to determine whether the risk has passed.

DELIVERY WITH MOVEMENT OF THE GOODS—CARRIER CASES

When there is no specification in the agreement, the following rules apply to cases involving movement of the goods (carrier cases).

Shipment Contracts In a shipment contract, if the seller or lessor is required or authorized to ship goods by carrier (but not required to deliver them to a particular final destination), risk of loss passes to the buyer or lessee when the goods are duly delivered to the carrier [UCC 2–319(1)(a), 2–509(1)(a), 2A–219(2)(a)].

• **EXAMPLE 16.6** A seller in Texas sells five hundred cases of grapefruit to a buyer in New York, F.O.B. Houston (free on board in Houston—that is, the buyer pays the transportation charges from Houston). The contract authorizes a shipment by carrier; it does not require that the seller tender the grapefruit in New York. Risk passes to the buyer when conforming goods are properly placed in the possession of the carrier. If the goods are damaged in transit, the loss is the buyer's. (Actually, buyers have recourse against carriers, subject to certain limitations, and buyers usually insure the goods from the time the goods leave the seller.) •

Destination Contracts In a destination contract, the risk of loss passes to the buyer or lessee when the goods are tendered to the buyer or lessee at the specified destination [UCC 2–319(1)(b), 2–509(1)(b), 2A–219(2)(b)]. In the preceding example, if the contract had been F.O.B. New York, risk of loss during transit to New York would have been the seller's.

Contract Terms Specific terms in the contract help determine when risk of loss passes to the buyer. These terms, which are listed and defined in Exhibit 16–1, relate generally to the determination of which party will bear the costs of delivery. Unless otherwise agreed, these terms also determine who has the risk of loss.

International Perspective • RISK OF LOSS IN INTERNATIONAL SALES CONTRACTS

The possibility that goods will be lost or damaged in transit or at some time before the buyer takes possession of the goods is enhanced when goods are shipped great distances, as is normally the situation with international sales contracts. Therefore, those who form international sales contracts should safeguard their interests by indicating in the contract the point at which risk of loss passes from the seller to the buyer. Note that the international sales contract between Starbucks Coffee Company and one of its coffee suppliers, shown in the fold-out exhibit included in Chapter 15, includes a specific (insurance) clause indicating when risk of loss will pass to the buyer (see annotation 18 to that exhibit).

The United Nations Convention on Contracts for the International Sale of Goods (CISG), which governs international sales contracts (see Chapter 15), contains provisions relating to risk of loss. Article 67 of the CISG provides that unless the contract requires the seller to hand the goods over at a particular place, the risk passes to the buyer when the goods identified to the contract "are handed over to the first carrier for transmission to the buyer in accordance with the contract of sale." In regard to goods sold in transit, Article 68 provides that risk of loss "passes to the buyer from the time of the conclusion of the contract." If the seller knew or should have known that the contract goods were lost or damaged, however, and failed to disclose this to the buyer, then the seller bears the risk.

FOR CRITICAL ANALYSIS
Why would buyers of goods that are to be shipped internationally ever agree to shipment contracts—which subject them to liability for any loss or damage to the goods while they are in transit?

EXHIBIT 16–1 • Contract Terms—Definitions

F.O.B. (free on board)—Indicates that the selling price of goods includes transportation costs (and that the seller carries the risk of loss) to the specific F.O.B. place named in the contract. The place can be either the place of initial shipment (for example, the seller's city or place of business) or the place of destination (for example, the buyer's city or place of business) [UCC 2–319(1)].
F.A.S. (free alongside)—Requires that the seller, at his or her own expense and risk, deliver the goods alongside the ship before risk passes to the buyer [UCC 2–319(2)].
C.I.F. or **C.&F.** (cost, insurance, and freight, or just cost and freight)—Requires, among other things, that the seller "put the goods in possession of a carrier" before risk passes to the buyer [UCC 2–320(2)]. (These are basically pricing terms, and the contracts remain shipment contracts, not destination contracts.)
Delivery ex-ship (delivery from the carrying ship)—Means that risk of loss does not pass to the buyer until the goods leave the ship or are otherwise properly unloaded [UCC 2–322].

IF THE GOODS ON BOARD THIS TRAIN WERE DAMAGED, WHAT DETERMINES WHO BEARS THE LOSS?

DELIVERY WITHOUT MOVEMENT OF THE GOODS

• **BAILEE**
Under the UCC, a party who, by a bill of lading, warehouse receipt, or other document of title, acknowledges possession of goods and/or contracts to deliver them.

The UCC also addresses situations in which the seller or lessor is required neither to ship nor to deliver the goods. Frequently, the buyer or lessee is to pick up the goods from the seller or lessor, or the goods are held by a bailee. Under the UCC, a **bailee** is a party who, by a bill of lading, warehouse receipt, or other document of title, acknowledges possession of goods and/or contracts to deliver them. A warehousing company, for example, or a trucking company that normally issues documents of title for the goods it receives is a bailee. (Bailments are discussed in detail in Chapter 40.)

Goods Held by the Seller If the goods are held by the seller, a document of title is usually not used. If the seller is a merchant, risk of loss to goods held by the seller passes to the buyer when the buyer *actually takes physical possession of the goods* [UCC 2–509(3)]. If the seller is not a merchant, the risk of loss to goods held by the seller passes to the buyer on tender of delivery [UCC 2–509(3)]. With respect to leases, the risk of loss passes to the lessee on the lessee's receipt of the goods if the lessor—or supplier, in a finance lease (see Chapter 15)—is a merchant. Otherwise, the risk passes to the lessee on *tender of delivery* [UCC 2A–219(c)].

¡COMPARE!
A merchant who is to make delivery at his or her own place has control of the goods and can be expected to insure his or her interest in them. The buyer has no control of the goods and will likely not carry insurance on goods that he or she does not possess.

Goods Held by a Bailee When a bailee is holding goods for a person who has contracted to sell them and the goods are to be delivered without being moved, the goods are usually represented by a negotiable or nonnegotiable document of title (a bill of lading or a warehouse receipt). Risk of loss passes to the buyer when (1) the buyer receives a negotiable document of title for the goods, (2) the bailee acknowledges the buyer's right to possess the goods, or (3) the buyer receives a nonnegotiable document of title *and* has had a *reasonable time* to present the document to the bailee and demand the goods. Obviously, if the bailee refuses to honor the document, the risk of loss remains with the seller [UCC 2–503(4)(b), 2–509(2)].

In respect to leases, if goods held by a bailee are to be delivered without being moved, the risk of loss passes to the lessee on acknowledgment by the bailee of the lessee's right to possession of the goods [UCC 2A–219(2)(b)].

CONDITIONAL SALES

Buyers and sellers sometimes form sales contracts that are conditioned either on the buyer's approval of the goods or on the buyer's resale of the goods. Under such contracts, the buyer is in possession of the goods. Sometimes, however, problems arise as to whether the buyer or seller should bear the loss if, for example, the goods are damaged or stolen while in the possession of the buyer.

• **SALE OR RETURN**
A type of conditional sale in which title and possession pass from the seller to the buyer; however, the buyer retains the option to return the goods during a specified period even though the goods conform to the contract.

Sale or Return A **sale or return** (sometimes called a *sale and return*) is a type of contract by which the seller actually sells a quantity of goods to the buyer but with the understanding that the buyer can set aside the sale by returning the goods or any portion of the goods. The buyer is required to pay for any goods *not* returned. When the buyer receives possession of the goods under a sale-or-return contract, the title and risk of loss pass to the buyer. Title and risk of loss remain with the buyer until the buyer returns the goods to the seller within the time period specified. If the buyer fails to return the goods within this time period, the sale is finalized. The return of the goods is made at the buyer's risk and expense. Goods held under a sale-or-return contract are subject to the claims of the buyer's creditors while they are in the buyer's possession (even if the buyer has not paid for the goods) [UCC 2–326, 2–327].

• **CONSIGNMENT**
A transaction in which an owner of goods (the consignor) delivers the goods to another (the consignee) for the consignee to sell. The consignee pays the consignor only for the goods that are sold by the consignee.

The UCC treats a **consignment** as a sale or return. Under a consignment, the owner of goods (the *consignor*) delivers them to another (the *consignee*) for the consignee to sell. If the consignee sells the goods, the consignee must pay the consignor for them. If the consignee does not sell the goods, they may simply be returned to the consignor. While the goods are in the possession of the consignee, the consignee holds title to them, and creditors of the consignee will prevail over the consignor in any action to repossess the goods [UCC 2–326(3)].[3]

• **SALE ON APPROVAL**
A type of conditional sale in which the buyer may take the goods on a trial basis. The sale becomes absolute only when the buyer approves of (or is satisfied with) the goods being sold.

Sale on Approval When a seller offers to sell goods to a buyer and permits the buyer to take the goods on a trial basis, a **sale on approval** is usually made. The term *sale* here is a misnomer, as only an *offer* to sell has been made, along with a *bailment* created by the buyer's possession. (A bailment is a temporary delivery of personal property into the care of another—see Chapter 36.)

Therefore, title and risk of loss (from causes beyond the buyer's control) remain with the seller until the buyer accepts (approves) the offer. Acceptance can be made expressly, by any act inconsistent with the *trial* purpose or the seller's ownership, or by the buyer's election not to return the goods within the trial period. If the buyer does not wish to accept, the buyer may notify the seller of that fact within the trial period, and the return is made at the seller's expense and risk [UCC 2–327(1)]. Goods held on approval are not subject to the claims of the buyer's creditors until acceptance.

3. UCC 2–326(3) states that this rule does not apply in certain circumstances. For example, if the consignor establishes that the consignee is generally known by his or her creditors to be "substantially engaged in selling the goods of others," then the consignor will prevail over the consignee's creditors in any action brought by those creditors to repossess the goods. The consignor will also prevail in such actions if he or she has a perfected security interest in the goods (see Chapter 22) or complies with an applicable law providing for a consignor's interest in the goods to be evidenced by a sign.

It is often difficult to determine from a particular transaction which exists—a contract for a sale on approval, a contract for a sale or return, or a contract for sale. The UCC states that (unless otherwise agreed) "if the goods are delivered primarily for use," the transaction is a sale on approval; "if the goods are delivered primarily for resale," the transaction is a sale or return [UCC 2–326(1)]. The court in the following case had to determine whether a particular transaction was a contract for a sale on approval or a contract for sale.

CASE 16.3 Houghton Wood Products, Inc. v. Badger Wood Products, Inc.

Court of Appeals of Wisconsin, 1995.
196 Wis.2d 457,
538 N.W.2d 621.
www.courts.state.wi.us/WCS/ca_opinion_search.html[a]

HISTORICAL AND SOCIAL SETTING *Small businesses make up over 90 percent of all nonagricultural businesses in the United States. They employ more than half of the work force in the private sector, make nearly half of the sales, and produce almost 40 percent of the annual national income. Over the last twenty years, the number of small businesses has increased by about 60 percent. Despite these inspiring statistics, however, small businesses also fail at a high rate.*

BACKGROUND AND FACTS Badger Wood Products, Inc., a manufacturer of cabinets and other wood products, owed Associated Bank Green Bay over $3.7 million. As collateral for the debt, Badger had pledged all of its raw materials and work in process as security. When Badger failed to repay the loan, it gave its assets to the bank, including three shipments of wood that had been delivered to Badger from Houghton Wood Products, Inc., but that had not been paid for. Houghton filed a suit in a Wisconsin state court against Badger and the bank, seeking the wood or the full purchase price of the wood. Houghton contended that it owned the wood because it was delivered pursuant to a sale on approval. The court agreed and issued a judgment in Houghton's favor. The bank appealed.

a. This is a page within the Wisconsin state courts' Web site maintained by the state of Wisconsin. In the "Docket Number" box, enter "950004" and click "Search." On the "Results" page, select the appropriate format and click "Download Marked Files" to load the case to your hard drive.

IN THE WORDS OF THE COURT . . .
MYSE, Judge.

* * * *

* * * [T]he wood delivered to Badger was to be made into cabinets that Badger would then sell to customers. Once the wood is made into cabinets, it undergoes substantial transformation and cannot be returned * * * . Yet, if the sale was on approval, title in the transformed wood would remain with Houghton until payment is made without regard to the transformation. It violates common sense and the rules of commerce to permit transformed goods to remain titled to the seller. We conclude that when a good is used in the manufacturing process where it undergoes transformation and is subsequently resold, it is not delivered for "use" as that term is used in the [UCC]. Because this transaction cannot be a delivery for "use," it was not a sale on approval.

DECISION AND REMEDY The Court of Appeals of Wisconsin reversed the lower court's ruling and remanded the case with an order to enter a judgment in the bank's favor.

FOR CRITICAL ANALYSIS—Economic Consideration *For what reasons would a seller ever agree to a sale on approval, given the fact that in a sale on approval the seller retains the risk of loss and is also responsible for the expenses involved in the buyer's returning of the goods?*

Risk of Loss When a Sales or Lease Contract Is Breached

There are many ways to breach a sales or lease contract, and the transfer of risk operates differently depending on which party breaches. Generally, the party in breach bears the risk of loss.

• **CURE** The right of a party who tenders nonconforming performance to correct his or her performance within the contract period [UCC 2–508(1)].

When the Seller or Lessor Breaches If the goods are so nonconforming that the buyer has the right to reject them, the risk of loss does not pass to the buyer until the defects are **cured** (that is, until the goods are repaired, replaced, or discounted in price by the seller) or until the buyer accepts the goods in spite of their defects (thus waiving the right to reject). • **EXAMPLE 16.7** A buyer orders ten white refrigerators from a seller, F.O.B. the seller's plant. The seller ships amber refrigerators instead. The amber refrigerators (nonconforming goods) are damaged in transit. The risk of loss falls on the seller. Had the seller shipped white refrigerators (conforming goods) instead, the risk would have fallen on the buyer [UCC 2–510(2)]. •

If a buyer accepts a shipment of goods and later discovers a defect, acceptance can be revoked. Revocation allows the buyer to pass the risk of loss back to the seller, at least to the extent that the buyer's insurance does not cover the loss [UCC 2–510(2)].

In regard to leases, Article 2A states a similar rule. If the lessor or supplier tenders goods that are so nonconforming that the lessee has the right to reject them, the risk of loss remains with the lessor or the supplier until cure or acceptance [UCC 2A–220(1)(a)]. If the lessee, after acceptance, revokes his or her acceptance of nonconforming goods, the revocation passes the risk of loss back to the seller or supplier, to the extent that the lessee's insurance does not cover the loss [UCC 2A–220(1)(b)].

In the following case, the buyer claimed that the seller should bear the risk of loss for nonconforming goods that were stolen before the buyer was able to return them to the seller.

CASE 16.4 Graybar Electric Co. v. Shook

Supreme Court of North Carolina, 1973.
283 N.C. 213,
195 S.E.2d 514.

HISTORICAL AND SOCIAL SETTING *The UCC clearly provides that a party who breaches a contract bears the risk of loss. There have been relatively few cases arising under this provision of the UCC. This is in part because it seems reasonable that, for example, a seller should bear the risk when he or she has delivered goods that are nonconforming or clearly defective.*

BACKGROUND AND FACTS Harold Shook agreed with Graybar Electric Company to purchase three reels of burial cable for use in Shook's construction work. When the reels were delivered, each carton was marked "burial cable," but two of the reels were in fact aerial cable. Shook accepted the conforming reel of cable and notified Graybar that he was rejecting the two reels of aerial cable. Because of a truckers' strike, Shook was unable to return the reels to Graybar. He stored the reels in a well-lighted space near a grocery store owner's dwelling, which was close to Shook's work site. About four months later, Shook noticed that one of the reels had been stolen. On the following day, he notified Graybar of the loss and, worried about the safety of the second reel, arranged to have it transported to a garage for storage. Before the second reel was transferred, however, it was also stolen, and Shook notified Graybar of the second theft. Graybar sued Shook in a North Carolina state court for the purchase price, claiming that Shook had agreed to return to Graybar the nonconforming reels and had failed to do so. Shook contended that he had agreed only to contact a trucking company to return the reels, and because he had contacted three trucking firms to no avail (owing to the strike), his obligation had been fulfilled. The trial court ruled for Shook, and Graybar appealed.

CASE 16.4—Continued

IN THE WORDS OF THE COURT . . .

HIGGINS, Justice.

* * * *

* * * [T]he defendant had not entered into a contract to return the nonconforming cable. * * *

* * * *

* * * [Under UCC 2–510(1)] "[w]here a tender or delivery of goods so fails to conform to the contract as to give a right of rejection the risk of their loss remains on the seller until cure or acceptance." The defendant did not accept the aerial cable. * * * [T]he defendant acted in accordance with the request of the owner in attempting to facilitate the return of that which the defendant rejected. The plaintiff with full notice of the place of storage which was at the place of delivery did nothing but sleep on its rights for more than three months.

DECISION AND REMEDY The Supreme Court of North Carolina affirmed the lower court's judgment in Shook's favor.

FOR CRITICAL ANALYSIS—Ethical Consideration *Did the fact that Graybar "did nothing but sleep on its rights for more than three months" have anything to do with the outcome of this case? Should it have?*

When the Buyer or Lessee Breaches The general rule is that when a buyer or lessee breaches a contract, the risk of loss immediately shifts to the buyer or lessee. There are three important limitations to this rule:

1. The seller or lessor must already have identified the contract goods.
2. The buyer or lessee bears the risk for only a commercially reasonable time after the seller has learned of the breach.
3. The buyer or lessee is liable only to the extent of any deficiency in the seller's insurance coverage [UCC 2–510(3), 2A–220(2)].

Insurable Interest

Parties to sales and lease contracts often obtain insurance coverage to protect against damage, loss, or destruction of goods. Any party purchasing insurance, however, must have a sufficient interest in the insured item to obtain a valid policy. Insurance laws—not the UCC—determine sufficiency. The UCC is helpful, however, because it contains certain rules regarding insurable interests in goods.

Insurable Interest of the Buyer or Lessee

INSURABLE INTEREST In regard to the sale or lease of goods, a property interest in the goods that is sufficiently substantial to permit a party to insure against damage to the goods.

A buyer or lessee has an **insurable interest** in identified goods. The moment the contract goods are identified by the seller or lessor, the buyer or lessee has a special property interest that allows the buyer or lessee to obtain necessary insurance coverage for those goods even before the risk of loss has passed [UCC 2–501(1), 2A–218(1)].

The rule stated in UCC 2–501(1)(c) is that such buyers obtain an insurable interest in crops by identification, which occurs when the crops are planted or otherwise become growing crops, provided that the contract is for "the sale of crops to be harvested within twelve months or the next normal harvest season after contracting,

"When the praying does no good, insurance does help."

BERTOLT BRECHT, 1898–1956
(German playwright and poet)

whichever is longer." • EXAMPLE 16.8 In March, a farmer sells a cotton crop he hopes to harvest in October. The buyer acquires an insurable interest in the crop when it is planted, because those goods (the cotton crop) are identified to the sales contract between the seller and the buyer. •

INSURABLE INTEREST OF THE SELLER OR LESSOR

A seller has an insurable interest in goods if he or she retains title to the goods. Even after title passes to a buyer, a seller who has a security interest in the goods (a right to secure payment—see Chapter 22) still has an insurable interest and can insure the goods [UCC 2–501(2)]. Hence, both a buyer and a seller can have an insurable interest in identical goods at the same time. Of course, the buyer or seller must sustain an actual loss to have the right to recover from an insurance company. In regard to leases, the lessor retains an insurable interest in leased goods until an option to buy has been exercised by the lessee and the risk of loss has passed to the lessee [UCC 2A–218(3)].

Bulk Transfers

Bulk transfers are the subject of UCC Article 6. A *bulk transfer* is defined as any transfer of a major part of the transferor's material, supplies, merchandise, or other inventory *not made in the ordinary course of the transferor's business* [UCC 6–102(1)]. Difficulties sometimes occur with bulk transfers. For example, when a business that owes debts to numerous creditors sells a substantial part of its equipment and inventories to a buyer, the business should use the proceeds to pay off the debts. What happens, though, if the merchant instead spends the funds on a vacation trip, leaving the creditors without payment? Can the creditors lay any claim to the goods that were transferred in bulk to the buyer?

GOODS, SUCH AS THESE B-52S AT AN AIR FORCE BASE IN ARIZONA, MUST BE DELIVERED FROM SELLER TO BUYER. WHAT DETERMINES WHICH PARTY HAS AN INSURABLE INTEREST IN THE GOODS BEFORE AND DURING DELIVERY?

The purpose of Article 6 is to protect creditors in such situations. UCC 6–104 and 6–105 provide that the following requirements must be met when a bulk transfer is undertaken:

1. The seller must furnish to the buyer a sworn list of his or her existing creditors. The list must include those whose claims are disputed and must state names, business addresses, and amounts due.
2. The buyer and the seller must prepare a schedule of the property that is to be transferred.
3. The buyer must preserve the list of creditors and the schedule of property for six months and permit inspection of the list by any creditor of the seller or must file the list and the schedule of property in a designated public office.
4. The buyer must give notice of the proposed bulk transfer to each of the seller's creditors at least ten days before the buyer takes possession of the goods or makes payments for them, whichever happens first.

¡WATCH OUT!

The notice provisions of Article 6 can sometimes interfere with and delay normal business transactions.

If these requirements are met, the buyer acquires title to the goods free of all claims by the seller's creditors. If the requirements are not met, goods in the possession of the buyer continue to be subject to the claims of the unpaid creditors of the seller for six months [UCC 6–111].

In 1988, the National Conference of Commissioners on Uniform State Laws recommended that those states that have adopted Article 6 repeal it, because changes in the business and legal contexts in which bulk sales are conducted have made their regulation unnecessary. For states disinclined to do so, Article 6 has been revised to provide creditors with better protection while reducing the burden imposed on good faith purchasers. To date, at least thirty-five states have repealed Article 6, and four states have opted for the revised version. The remainder of the states have retained Article 6 in its original form.

The revised Article 6 limits its application to bulk sales by sellers whose principal business is the sale of inventory from bulk stock. It does not apply to transactions involving property valued at less than $10,000 or more than $25 million. If a seller has more than two hundred creditors, a buyer, rather than having to send individual notice to each creditor, can give notice by public filing (for example, in the office of a state's secretary of state). The notice period is increased from ten to forty-five days, and the statute of limitations is extended from six months to one year.

APPLICATION

Law & the Seller or Buyer: Who Bears the Risk of Loss?*

A major aspect of commercial transactions involves the shipment of goods. Many issues arise when the unforeseen occurs, such as fire, theft, or other forms of damage to goods in transit. The UCC uses a three-part checklist to determine risk of loss:

1. If the contract includes terms allocating risk of loss, those terms are binding and must be applied.
2. If the contract is silent as to risk, and either party breaches the contract, the breaching party is liable for risk of loss.
3. When a contract makes no reference to risk, and neither party breaches, risk of loss is borne by the party having control over the goods.

If you are a seller of goods to be shipped, realize that as long as you have control over the goods, you are liable for any loss unless the buyer is in breach or the contract contains an

*This *Application* is not meant to substitute for the services of an attorney who is licensed to practice law in your state.

APPLICATION CONTINUED

explicit agreement to the contrary. When there is no explicit agreement, the UCC uses the delivery terms in your contract as a basis for determining control. Thus, "F.O.B. buyer's business" is a destination-delivery term, and risk of loss for goods shipped under these terms does not pass to the buyer until there is a tender of delivery at the point of destination. Any loss or damage in transit falls on the seller, because the seller has control until proper tender has been made.

From the buyer's point of view, it is important to remember that most sellers prefer "F.O.B. seller's business" as a delivery term. Under these terms, once the goods are delivered to the carrier, the buyer bears the risk of loss. Thus, if conforming goods are completely destroyed or lost in transit, the buyer not only suffers the loss but is obligated to pay the seller the contract price.

At the time of contract negotiation, both the seller and the buyer should determine the importance of risk of loss. In some circumstances, risk is relatively unimportant (such as when ten boxes of copier paper are being sold), and the delivery terms should simply reflect costs and price. In other circumstances, risk is extremely important (such as when a fragile piece of equipment is being sold), and the parties will need an express agreement as to the moment risk is to pass so that they can insure the goods accordingly. The point is that risk should be considered before the loss occurs, not after.

A major consideration relating to risk is when to insure goods against possible losses. Buyers and sellers should determine the point at which they have an insurable interest in the goods and obtain insurance coverage to protect them against loss from that point.

CHECKLIST F'OR THE SHIPMENT OF GOODS

1. Prior to entering a contract, determine the importance of risk of loss for a given sale.
2. If risk is extremely important, the contract should expressly state the moment risk of loss will pass from the seller to the buyer. This clause could even provide that risk will not pass until the goods are "delivered, installed, inspected, and tested (or in running order for a period of time)."
3. If an express clause is not agreed on, delivery terms determine passage of risk of loss.
4. When appropriate, either party or both parties should consider the need to procure insurance.

Key Terms

bailee 419

consignment 420

cure 422

destination contract 414

document of title 414

fungible goods 412

good faith purchaser 415

identification 411

insolvent 415

insurable interest 423

sale on approval 420

sale or return 420

shipment contract 413

Chapter Summary • Title and Risk of Loss

Shipment Contracts (See page 413.)	In the absence of an agreement, title and risk pass on the seller's or lessor's delivery of conforming goods to the carrier [UCC 2–319(1)(a), 2–401(2)(a), 2–509(1)(a), 2A–219(2)(a)].
Destination Contracts (See page 414.)	In the absence of an agreement, title and risk pass on the seller's or lessor's *tender* of delivery of conforming goods to the buyer or lessee at the point of destination [UCC 2–401(2)(b), 2–319(1)(b), 2–509(1)(b), 2A–219(2)(b)].
Delivery without Movement of the Goods (See pages 414 and 417–420.)	1. In the absence of an agreement, if the goods are not represented by a document of title: a. Title passes on the formation of the contract [UCC 2–401(3)(b)]. b. Risk passes to the buyer or lessee, if the seller or lessor (or supplier, in a finance lease) is a merchant, on the buyer's or lessee's receipt of the goods or, if the seller or lessor is a nonmerchant, on the seller's or lessor's *tender* of delivery of the goods [UCC 2–509(3), 2A–219(c)]. 2. In the absence of an agreement, if the goods are represented by a document of title: a. If the document is negotiable and the goods are held by a bailee, title and risk pass on the buyer's *receipt* of the document [UCC 2–401(3)(a), 2–509(2)(a)]. b. If the document is nonnegotiable and the goods are held by a bailee, title passes on the buyer's receipt of the document, but risk does *not* pass until the buyer, after receipt of the document, has had a reasonable time to present the document to demand the goods [UCC 2–401(3)(a), 2–509(2)(c), 2–503(4)(b)]. 3. In the absence of an agreement, if the goods are held by a bailee and no document of title is transferred, risk passes to the buyer when the bailee acknowledges the buyer's right to the possession of the goods [UCC 2–509(2)(b)]. 4. In respect to leases, if goods held by a bailee are to be delivered without being moved, the risk of loss passes to the lessee on acknowledgment by the bailee of the lessee's right to possession of the goods [UCC 2A–219(2)(b)].
Sales or Leases by Nonowners (See pages 414–417.)	Between the owner and a good faith purchaser or sublessee: 1. *Void title*—Owner prevails [UCC 2–403(1)]. 2. *Voidable title*—Buyer prevails [UCC 2–403(1)]. 3. *Entrusting to a merchant*—Buyer or sublessee prevails [UCC 2–403(2), (3); 2A–305(2)].
Sale-or-Return Contracts (See page 420.)	When the buyer receives possession of the goods, title and risk of loss pass to the buyer, with the buyer's option to return the goods to the seller. If the buyer returns the goods to the seller, title and risk of loss pass back to the seller [UCC 2–327(2)].
Sale-on-Approval Contracts (See pages 420–421.)	Title and risk of loss (from causes beyond the buyer's control) remain with the seller until the buyer approves (accepts) the offer [UCC 2–327(1)].
Risk of Loss When a Sales or Lease Contract Is Breached (See pages 422–423.)	1. If the seller or lessor breaches by tendering nonconforming goods that are rejected by the buyer or lessee, the risk of loss does not pass to the buyer or lessee until the defects are cured (unless the buyer or lessee accepts the goods in spite of their defects, thus waiving the right to reject) [UCC 2–510(1), 2A–220(1)]. 2. If the buyer or lessee breaches the contract, the risk of loss to identified goods immediately shifts to the buyer or lessee. Limitations to this rule are as follows [UCC 2–510(3), 2A–220(2)]: a. The seller or lessor must already have identified the contract goods. b. The buyer or lessee bears the risk for only a commercially reasonable time after the seller or lessor has learned of the breach. c. The buyer or lessee is liable only to the extent of any deficiency in the seller's or lessor's insurance coverage.

Chapter Summary • Title and Risk of Loss, Continued

Insurable Interest (See pages 423–424.)	1. Buyers and lessees have an insurable interest in goods the moment the goods are identified to the contract by the seller or the lessor [UCC 2–510(3), 2A–218(1)]. 2. Sellers have an insurable interest in goods as long as they have (1) title to the goods or (2) a security interest in the goods [UCC 2–501(2)]. Lessors have an insurable interest in leased goods until an option to buy has been exercised by the lessee and the risk of loss has passed to the lessee [UCC 2A–218(3)].
Bulk Transfers (See pages 424–425.)	1. In a bulk transfer of assets, in those states that have not repealed Article 6 of the UCC or replaced it with the revised Article 6, the buyer acquires title to the goods free of all claims of the seller's creditors if the following requirements are met: a. The transferor (seller) furnishes to the transferee (buyer) a sworn list of existing creditors, listing their names, business addresses, amounts due, and any disputed claims [UCC 6–104(1)(a)]. b. The buyer and seller prepare a schedule of the property to be transferred [UCC 6–104(1)(b)]. c. The buyer preserves the list of creditors and the schedule of property for six months, allowing any creditors of the seller to inspect it, or files the list and schedule of property in a designated public office [UCC 6–104(1)(c)]. d. Notice of the proposed bulk transfer is given by the buyer to each creditor of the seller at least ten days before the buyer takes possession of the goods or pays for them, whichever happens first [UCC 6–105]. 2. If these requirements are not met, goods in the possession of the buyer continue to be subject to the claims of the unpaid creditors of the seller for six months.

For Review

1 What is the significance of identifying goods to a contract?

2 If the parties to a contract do not expressly agree on when title to goods passes, what determines when title passes?

3 Risk of loss does not necessarily pass with title. If the parties to a contract do not expressly agree when risk passes and the goods are to be delivered without movement by the seller, when does risk pass?

4 Under what circumstances will the seller's title to goods being sold be void? Under what circumstances will a seller have voidable title? What is the legal effect on a good faith purchaser of the goods of the seller's having a void title versus a voidable title?

5 At what point does the buyer acquire an insurable interest in goods subject to a sales contract? Can the buyer and seller both have an insurable interest in the goods simultaneously?

Questions and Case Problems

16–1. Sales by Nonowners. In the following situations, two parties lay claim to the same goods sold. Discuss which of the parties would prevail in each situation.

(a) Terry steals Dom's television set and sells the set to Blake, an innocent purchaser, for value. Dom learns that Blake has the set and demands its return.

(b) Karlin takes her television set for repair to Orken, a merchant who sells new and used television sets. By accident, one of Orken's employees sells the set to Grady, an innocent purchaser-customer, who takes possession. Karlin wants her set back from Grady.

16–2. Risk of Loss. When will risk of loss pass from the seller to the buyer under each of the following contracts, assuming the parties have not expressly agreed on when risk of loss would pass?

(a) A New York seller contracts with a San Francisco buyer to ship goods to the buyer F.O.B. San Francisco.
(b) A New York seller contracts with a San Francisco buyer to ship goods to the buyer in San Francisco. There is no indication as to whether the shipment will be F.O.B. New York or F.O.B. San Francisco.
(c) A seller contracts with a buyer to sell goods located on the seller's premises. The buyer pays for the goods and makes arrangements to pick them up the next week at the seller's place of business.
(d) A seller contracts with a buyer to sell goods located in a warehouse.

16–3. Sales by Nonowners. Julian Makepeace, who had been declared mentally incompetent by a court, sold his diamond ring to Golding for value. Golding later sold the ring to Carmichael for value. Neither Golding nor Carmichael knew that Makepeace had been adjudged mentally incompetent by a court. Farrel, who had been appointed as Makepeace's guardian, subsequently learned that the diamond ring was in Carmichael's possession and demanded its return from Carmichael. Who has legal ownership of the ring? Why?

16–4. Risk of Loss. Alberto's Food Stores contracts to purchase from Giant Food Distributors, Inc., one hundred cases of Golden Rod corn to be shipped F.O.B. seller's warehouse by Janson Truck Lines. Giant Food Distributors, by mistake, delivers one hundred cases of Gold Giant corn to Janson Truck Lines. While in transit, the Gold Giant corn is stolen. Between Alberto's and Giant Food Distributors, who suffers the loss? Explain.

16–5. Sale on Approval. Chi Moy, a student, contracted to buy a television set from Ted's Electronics. Under the terms of the contract, Moy was to try out the set for thirty days, and if he liked it, he was to pay for the set at the end of the thirty-day period. If he did not want to purchase the set after thirty days, he could return the TV to Ted's Electronics with no obligation. Ten days after Moy took the set home, it was stolen from Moy's apartment, although Moy had not been negligent in his care of the set in any way. Ted's Electronics claimed that Moy had to pay for the stolen set. Moy argued that the risk of loss fell on Ted's Electronics. Which party will prevail?

16–6. Risk of Loss. Isis Foods, Inc., located in St. Louis, wanted to purchase a shipment of food from Pocasset Food Sales, Inc. The sale of food was initiated by a purchase order from Isis stating that the shipment was to be made "F.O.B. St. Louis." Pocasset made the shipment by delivery of the goods to the carrier. Pocasset's invoices contained a provision stating, "Our liability ceases upon delivery of merchandise to carrier." The shipment of food was destroyed before it reached St. Louis. Discuss which party bears the risk of loss, and why. [*In re Isis Foods, Inc.,* 38 Bankr. 48 (W.D.Mo. 1983)]

16–7. Sales by Nonowners. A new car owned by a New Jersey car-rental agency was stolen in 1967. The agency collected the full price of the car from its insurance company, Home Indemnity Co., and assigned all its interest in the automobile to the insurer. Subsequently, the thief sold the car to an automobile wholesaler, who in turn sold it to a retail car dealer. Schrier purchased the car from the dealer without knowledge of the theft. Home Indemnity sued Schrier to recover the car. Can Home Indemnity recover? [*Schrier v. Home Indemnity Co.,* 273 A.2d 248 (D.C. 1971)]

16–8. Entrustment Rule. Bobby Locke, the principal stockholder and chief executive officer (CEO) of Worthco Farm Center, Inc., hired Mr. Hobby as the company's manager. Subsequently, it was discovered that during the approximately thirteen months of Locke's tenure as CEO, Hobby had sold corn stored with Worthco to Arabi Grain & Elevator Co. and pocketed the proceeds. When Locke brought an action against Arabi to recover the corn, Arabi alleged, among other things, that Locke had entrusted the corn to Hobby and that because Arabi was a purchaser in the ordinary course of business, Hobby had transferred ownership rights in the corn to Arabi. Assuming that Arabi was a buyer in the ordinary course of business, how should the court rule? Discuss. [*Locke v. Arabi Grain & Elevator Co.,* 197 Ga.App. 854, 399 S.E.2d 705 (1991)]

16–9. Risk of Loss. Marilyn Thomas contracted with Sunkissed Pools for an "installed pool heater" for her home. One afternoon, Thomas noticed that a heating unit had been placed in her driveway. When Sunkissed returned to install the heater, it had been stolen. Thomas subsequently filed for personal bankruptcy. Sunkissed filed a claim for the price of the heater. Thomas objected. She argued that when she had noticed the heater in her driveway, she had called Sunkissed and told it that it needed to move the unit because the neighborhood was not safe. She said that the unit sat in her driveway for four days before it disappeared, after which she again called Sunkissed and was told "not to worry." Sunkissed's president testified that the firm did not receive any calls from Thomas and that he had gone to her home the day after the unit was left in her driveway and found that it was gone. In this situation, had the risk of loss of the pool heater passed from the seller to the buyer? Explain. [*In re Thomas,* 182 Bankr. 347 (S.D.Fla. 1995)]

16–10. Shipment and Destination Contracts. Roderick Cardwell owns Ticketworld, which sells tickets to entertainment and sporting events to be held at locations throughout the United States. Ticketworld's Massachusetts office sold tickets to an event in Connecticut to Mary Lou Lupovitch, a Connecticut resident, for $125 per ticket, although each ticket had a fixed price of $32.50. There was no agreement that Ticketworld would bear the risk of loss until the tickets were delivered to a specific location. Ticketworld gave the tickets to a carrier in Massachusetts who delivered the tickets to Lupovitch in Connecticut. The state of Connecticut brought an action against Cardwell in a Connecticut state court, charging in part a violation of a state statute that prohibited the sale of a ticket for more than $3 over its fixed price. Cardwell contended in part that the statute did not apply because the sale to Lupovitch involved a shipment contract that was formed outside the state. Is Cardwell correct? How will the court rule? Why? [*State v. Cardwell,* 246 Conn. 721, 718 A.2d 954 (1998)]

A QUESTION OF ETHICS AND SOCIAL RESPONSIBILITY

16–11. Toby and Rita Kahr accidentally included a small bag containing their sterling silver in a bag of used clothing that they had donated to Goodwill Industries, Inc. The silverware, which was valued at over $3,500, had been given to them twenty-seven years earlier by Rita's father as a wedding present and had great sentimental value for them. The Kahrs realized what had happened shortly after Toby returned from Goodwill, but when Toby called Goodwill, he was told that the silver had immediately been sold to a customer, Karon Markland, for $15. Although Goodwill called Markland and asked her to return the silver, Markland refused to return it. The Kahrs then brought an action against Markland to regain the silver, claiming that Markland did not have good title to it. In view of these circumstances, discuss the following issues. [*Kahr v. Markland,* 187 Ill.App.3d 603, 543 N.E.2d 579, 135 Ill.Dec. 196 (1989)]

1. Did Karon Markland act wrongfully in any way by not returning the silver to Goodwill Industries when requested to do so? What would you have done in her position?
2. Goodwill argued that the entrustment rule should apply. Why would Goodwill want the rule to be applied? How might Goodwill justify its argument from an ethical point of view?

FOR CRITICAL ANALYSIS

16–12. Under the UCC, passage of title does not always occur simultaneously with passage of risk of loss. Why is this? Give some examples of what might result if risk of loss and title always passed from the buyer to the seller at the same time.

Online Activities

ONLINE EXERCISE 16–1

Go to the "Internet Activities Book" on the Web site that accompanies this text, the URL for which is http://blt.westbuslaw.com. Select the following activity, and perform the exercise according to the instructions given there:

Activity 16–1: Passage of Title

Before the Test

Go to the *Business Law Today* home page at http://blt.westbuslaw.com. Click on TestTutor.® You will find twenty interactive questions relating to this chapter.

CHAPTER 17

Performance & Breach of Sales & Lease Contracts

"It has been uniformly laid down . . . , as far back as we can remember, that good faith is the basis of all mercantile transactions."

J. Buller, 1746–1800
(British jurist)

CONTENTS

LEARNING OBJECTIVES

After reading this chapter, you should be able to:

1. Outline the performance obligations of sellers and lessors under the UCC.
2. State the perfect tender rule, and identify and discuss its exceptions.
3. Describe the performance obligations of buyers and lessees under the UCC.
4. Point out the options available in the event that one of the parties to a sales or lease contract repudiates the contract prior to the time for performance.
5. List and discuss the remedies available to the nonbreaching party when a sales or lease contract is breached.

The performance that is required of the parties under a sales or lease contract consists of the duties and obligations each party has under the terms of the contract. Keep in mind that "duties and obligations" under the terms of the contract include those specified by the agreement, by custom, and by the Uniform Commercial Code (UCC). In this chapter, we examine the basic performance obligations of the parties under a sales or lease contract.

Sometimes circumstances make it difficult for a person to carry out the promised performance, in which case the contract may be breached. When breach occurs, the aggrieved party looks for remedies—which we deal with in the second half of the chapter.

Performance Obligations

As discussed in previous chapters and stressed in the opening quotation to this chapter, the standards of good faith and commercial reasonableness are read into every contract. These standards provide a framework in which the parties can specify particulars of performance. Thus, when one party delays specifying particulars of performance for an unreasonable period of time or fails to cooperate with the other party, the innocent party is excused from any resulting delay in performance. The innocent party can proceed to perform in any reasonable manner, and the other party's failure to specify particulars or to cooperate can be treated as a breach of contract. Good faith is a question of fact for the jury. (For an example of the importance of good faith in sales contracts, see this chapter's *Business Law in Action.*)

In the performance of a sales or lease contract, the basic obligation of the seller or lessor is to *transfer and deliver conforming goods.* The basic obligation of the buyer or lessee is to *accept and pay for conforming goods* in accordance with the contract [UCC 2–301, 2A-516(1)]. Overall performance of a sales or lease contract is controlled by the agreement between the parties. When the contract is unclear and disputes arise, the courts look to the UCC.

Obligations of the Seller or Lessor

The major obligation of the seller or lessor under a sales or lease contract is to tender conforming goods to the buyer or lessee.

TENDER OF DELIVERY

"It is only when merchants dispute about their own rules that they invoke the law."

J. BRETT, 1815–1899
(British jurist)

Tender of delivery requires that the seller or lessor have and hold *conforming goods* at the disposal of the buyer or lessee and give the buyer or lessee whatever notification is reasonably necessary to enable the buyer or lessee to take delivery [UCC 2–503(1), 2A–508(1)].

Tender must occur at a *reasonable hour* and in a *reasonable manner.* In other words, a seller cannot call the buyer at 2:00 A.M. and say, "The goods are ready. I'll give you twenty minutes to get them." Unless the parties have agreed otherwise, the goods must be tendered for delivery at a reasonable time and kept available for a reasonable period of time to enable the buyer to take possession of them [UCC 2–503(1)(a)].

All goods called for by a contract must be tendered in a single delivery unless the parties agree otherwise or the circumstances are such that either party can rightfully request delivery in lots [UCC 2–307, 2–612, 2A–510]. Hence, an order for 1,000 shirts cannot be delivered 2 shirts at a time. If, however, the seller and the buyer contemplate that the shirts will be delivered in four orders of 250 each, as they are produced (for summer, fall, winter, and spring stock), and the price can be apportioned accordingly, it may be commercially reasonable to deliver the shirts in this way.

PLACE OF DELIVERY

The UCC provides for the place of delivery pursuant to a contract if the contract does not. Of course, the parties may agree on a particular destination, or their contract's terms or the circumstances may indicate the place of delivery.

Business Law in Action • FOLLOWING THE LETTER OF A CONTRACT MAY NOT BE ENOUGH

Most companies believe that if they assiduously follow the "letter" of a contract in every detail, they will always be on safe ground. In some instances, however, a party's strict compliance with the words of a contract may not be enough—particularly if the party does not exercise good faith. A recent decision by the New Jersey Supreme Court confirms the importance of exercising good faith in sales contracts.

The case was brought by a company called Sons of Thunder, a clam supplier, against Borden, Inc., a major food-processing firm. Sons of Thunder had contracted with Borden to supply a specified minimum number of clams to Borden every week "for a period of one (1) year, after which this contract shall automatically be renewed for a period up to five years." The contract also stated that either party "may cancel this contract by giving prior notice of said cancellation in writing ninety (90) days prior to the effective cancellation date."

Borden encouraged Sons of Thunder to buy two large clamming boats, costing over $1 million, and a Borden representative told the bank that gave credit to Sons of Thunder that Borden expected to renew the contract for five years. Borden failed to purchase the minimum number of clams specified by the contract. Borden also charged Sons of Thunder for equipment that it provided to the clamming boats, even though this was not anticipated in the contract. Borden created further difficulties for Sons of Thunder by, for example, sending the Sons of Thunder boats out only in bad weather. Sons of Thunder, facing financial difficulties for these and other reasons, suffered the final blow from Borden when, after one year, Borden cancelled the contract.

The New Jersey trial court concluded that Borden had breached the contract by refusing to buy as many clams as it had agreed to and awarded $362,000 in damages for breach of the contract (Borden did not appeal this part of the trial court's decision). The court also awarded Sons of Thunder $412,000 for Borden's "breach of the implied covenant of good faith and fair dealing" under the UCC. When the case reached the New Jersey Supreme Court, a central issue was whether Borden's termination of the contract after one year evidenced bad faith on Borden's part.

Borden argued that it had every right to cancel the contract. After all, the contract itself stated that either party could cancel the contract by giving notice ninety days prior to the effective cancellation date. According to the state supreme court, however, there was sufficient evidence to indicate that Borden was not "honest in fact," as required by the UCC. The "bad faith" award was not due to Borden's cancellation of the contract; rather, it was for Borden's bad faith during the performance of the contract, including the events surrounding the termination of the contract.[a]

What is significant about this case is the court's conclusion that "a party can violate the implied covenant of good faith and fair dealing without violating an express term of a contract." The message for parties to sales contracts is clear: strict adherence to the terms of a contract may not be enough—good faith contract performance is also required.

FOR CRITICAL ANALYSIS

The lawyer for Borden criticized the court's judgment, claiming that it "casts a cloud over the reliability of clear contract language." What did he mean by this statement?

a. *Sons of Thunder, Inc. v. Borden, Inc.*, 148 N.J. 396, 690 A.2d 575 (1997).

Noncarrier Cases If the contract does not designate the place of delivery for the goods, and the buyer is expected to pick them up, the place of delivery is the *seller's place of business* or, if the seller has none, the seller's residence [UCC 2–308]. If the contract involves the sale of *identified goods*, and the parties know when they enter into the contract that these goods are located somewhere other than at the seller's place of business (such as at a warehouse), then *the location of the goods* is the place for their delivery [UCC 2–308].

• **EXAMPLE 17.1** Rogers and Aguirre live in San Francisco. In San Francisco, Rogers contracts to sell Aguirre five used trucks, which both parties know are located in a Chicago warehouse. If nothing more is specified in the contract, the place of delivery for the trucks is Chicago.● The seller may tender delivery by either giving the buyer a *negotiable or nonnegotiable document of title* or obtaining the *bailee's (warehouser's) acknowledgment* that the buyer is entitled to possession.[1]

¡KEEP IN MIND!
If goods never arrive, the buyer usually has at least some recourse against the carrier. Also, a buyer normally insures the goods from the time they leave the seller's possession.

Carrier Cases In many instances, attendant circumstances or delivery terms in the contract make it apparent that the parties intend that a carrier be used to move the goods. There are two ways a seller can complete performance of the obligation to deliver the goods in carrier cases—through a shipment contract and through a destination contract.

Shipment Contracts. Recall from Chapter 16 that a shipment contract requires or authorizes the seller to ship goods by a carrier. The contract does not require that the seller deliver the goods at a particular destination [UCC 2–319, 2–509]. Under a *shipment contract,* unless otherwise agreed, the seller must do the following:

1. Put the goods into the hands of the carrier.
2. Make a contract for their transportation that is reasonable according to the nature of the goods and their value. (For example, certain types of goods need refrigeration in transit.)
3. Obtain and promptly deliver or tender to the buyer any documents necessary to enable the buyer to obtain possession of the goods from the carrier.
4. Promptly notify the buyer that shipment has been made [UCC 2–504].

If the seller fails to notify the buyer that shipment has been made or fails to make a proper contract for transportation, the buyer can treat the contract as breached and reject the goods, but only if a *material loss* of the goods or a significant *delay* results.

¡DON'T FORGET!
Documents of title include bills of lading, warehouse receipts, and any other documents that, in the regular course of business, entitle a person holding these documents to obtain possession of and title to the goods covered.

Destination Contracts. Under a *destination contract,* the seller agrees to see that conforming goods will be duly tendered to the buyer at a particular destination. The goods must be tendered at a reasonable hour and held at the buyer's disposal for a reasonable length of time. The seller must also give the buyer any appropriate notice that is necessary to enable the buyer to take delivery. In addition, the seller must provide the buyer with any documents of title necessary to enable the buyer to obtain delivery from the carrier [UCC 2–503].

The Perfect Tender Rule

As previously noted, the seller or lessor has an obligation to ship or tender conforming goods, and the buyer or lessee is required to accept and pay for the goods according to the terms of the contract. Under the common law, the seller was obligated to deliver goods in conformity with the terms of the contract in every detail. This was called the *perfect tender doctrine.* The UCC preserves the perfect tender doctrine by stating that if goods or tender of delivery fail *in any respect* to conform to the contract, the buyer or lessee has the right to accept the goods, reject the entire shipment, or accept part and reject part [UCC 2–601, 2A–509].

1. If the seller delivers a nonnegotiable document of title or merely writes instructions to the bailee to release the goods to the buyer without the bailee's *acknowledgment* of the buyer's rights, this is also a sufficient tender, unless the buyer objects [UCC 2–503(4)]. Risk of loss, however, does not pass until the buyer has a reasonable amount of time in which to present the document or to give the bailee instructions for delivery.

ON THE WEB

To view the UCC provisions discussed in this chapter, go to www.law.cornell.edu/uniform.

• **EXAMPLE 17.2** A lessor contracts to lease fifty Vericlear monitors to be delivered at the lessee's place of business on or before October 1. On September 28, the lessor discovers that there are only thirty Vericlear monitors in inventory, but there will be another forty Vericlear monitors within the next two weeks. The lessor tenders delivery of the thirty Vericlear monitors on October 1, with the promise that the other monitors will be delivered within three weeks. Because the lessor failed to make a perfect tender of fifty Vericlear monitors, the lessee has the right to reject the entire shipment and hold the lessor in breach. •

EXCEPTIONS TO PERFECT TENDER

Because of the rigidity of the perfect tender rule, several exceptions to the rule have been created, some of which are discussed here.

Agreement of the Parties Exceptions to the perfect tender rule may be established by agreement. If the parties have agreed, for example, that defective goods or parts will not be rejected if the seller or lessor is able to repair or replace them within a reasonable period of time, the perfect tender rule does not apply.

Cure The UCC does not specifically define the term *cure,* but it refers to the right of the seller or lessor to repair, adjust, or replace defective or nonconforming goods [UCC 2–508, 2A–513]. When any tender of delivery is rejected because of nonconforming goods and the time for performance has not yet expired, the seller or lessor can notify the buyer or lessee promptly of the intention to cure and can then do so *within the contract time for performance* [UCC 2–508(1), 2A–513(1)]. Once the time for performance has expired, the seller or lessor can still, for a reasonable time, exercise the right to cure with respect to the rejected goods if he or she, at the time of delivery, had *reasonable grounds to believe that the nonconforming tender would be acceptable to the buyer or lessee* [UCC 2–508(2), 2A–513(2)].

> "It is the duty of a judge to inquire not only into the matter but into the circumstances of the matter."
>
> OVID, 43 B.C.E.–17 C.E. (Roman poet)

Sometimes, a seller or lessor will tender nonconforming goods with some type of price allowance. The allowance serves as the "reasonable grounds" for the seller or lessor to believe that the nonconforming tender will be acceptable to the buyer or lessee. Other reasons might also serve as the basis for the assumption that a buyer or lessee will accept a nonconforming tender. • **EXAMPLE 17.3** Suppose that in the past a buyer, an office-supply store, frequently accepted blue pens when the seller did not have black pens in stock. In this context, the seller has reasonable grounds to believe the store will again accept such a substitute. If the store rejects the substituted goods (blue pens) on a particular occasion, the seller nonetheless had reasonable grounds to believe that the blue pens would be acceptable. Therefore, the seller can cure within a reasonable time, even though the delivery of black pens will occur after the time limit for performance allowed under the contract. •

The right to cure means that the buyer or lessee must give notice to the seller or lessor of a particular defect in order to reject goods. For example, if a lessee refuses a tender of goods as nonconforming but does not disclose the nature of the defect to the lessor, the lessee cannot later assert the defect as a defense if the defect is one that the lessor could have cured. Generally, buyers and lessees must act in good faith and state specific reasons for refusing to accept goods [UCC 2–605, 2A–514].

Substitution of Carriers When an agreed-on manner of delivery (such as which carrier will be used to transport the goods) becomes impracticable or unavailable through no fault of either party, but a commercially reasonable substitute is available, the seller

COMPETITORS' TRUCKS TRAVEL THE SAME ROUTE. WHEN IS IT ACCEPTABLE TO SUBSTITUTE ONE CARRIER FOR ANOTHER SPECIFIED IN A CONTRACT?

must use this substitute performance, which is sufficient tender to the buyer [UCC 2–614(1)]. • **EXAMPLE 17.4** A sales contract calls for the delivery of a large generator to be shipped by Roadway Trucking Corporation on or before June 1. The contract terms clearly state the importance of the delivery date. The employees of Roadway Trucking go on strike. The seller is required to make a reasonable substitute tender, perhaps by rail, if one is available. Note that the seller here will normally be held responsible for any additional shipping costs, unless contrary arrangements have been made in the sales contract. •

• **INSTALLMENT CONTRACT**
Under the UCC, a contract that requires or authorizes delivery in two or more separate lots to be accepted and paid for separately.

Installment Contracts An **installment contract** is a single contract that requires or authorizes delivery in two or more separate lots to be accepted and paid for separately. In an installment contract, a buyer or lessee can reject an installment *only if the nonconformity substantially impairs the value* of the installment and cannot be cured [UCC 2–612(2), 2–307, 2A–510(1)].

Unless the contract provides otherwise, the entire installment contract is breached only when one or more nonconforming installments *substantially* impair the value of the *whole contract.* If the buyer or lessee subsequently accepts a nonconforming installment and fails to notify the seller or lessor of cancellation, however, the contract is reinstated [UCC 2–612(3), 2A–510(2)].

A major issue to be determined is what constitutes substantial impairment of the "value of the whole contract." • **EXAMPLE 17.5** Consider an installment contract for the sale of twenty carloads of plywood. The first carload does not conform to the contract because 9 percent of the plywood deviates from the thickness specifications. The buyer cancels the contract, and immediately thereafter the second and third carloads of conforming plywood arrive at the buyer's place of business. If a lawsuit ensued, the court would have to grapple with the question of whether the 9 percent of nonconforming plywood substantially impaired the value of the whole.[2] •

The point to remember is that the UCC significantly alters the right of the buyer or lessee to reject the entire contract if the contract requires delivery to be made in several installments. The UCC strictly limits rejection to cases of *substantial* nonconformity.

"Inability suspends the law."
(LEGAL MAXIM)

Commercial Impracticability As mentioned in Chapter 13, occurrences unforeseen by either party when a contract was made may make performance commercially impracticable. When this occurs, the rule of perfect tender no longer holds. According to UCC 2–615(a) and 2A–405(a), delay in delivery or nondelivery in whole or in part is not a breach when performance has been made impracticable "by the occurrence of a contingency the nonoccurrence of which was a basic assumption on which the contract was made." The seller or lessor must, however, notify the buyer or lessee as soon as practicable that there will be a delay or nondelivery.

Foreseeable versus Unforeseeable Contingencies. An increase in cost resulting from inflation does not in and of itself excuse performance, as this kind of risk is ordinarily assumed by a seller or lessor conducting business. The unforeseen contingency must be one that would have been impossible to contemplate in a given business situation. • **EXAMPLE 17.6** A major oil company that receives its supplies from the Middle East has a contract to supply a buyer with 100,000 gallons of oil. Because of

2. *Continental Forest Products, Inc. v. White Lumber Sales, Inc.,* 256 Or. 466, 474 P.2d 1 (1970). The court held that the deviation did not substantially impair the value of the whole contract. Additionally, the court stated that the nonconformity could be cured by an adjustment in the price.

an oil embargo by the Organization of Petroleum Exporting Countries (OPEC), the seller is prevented from securing oil supplies to meet the terms of the contract. Because of the same embargo, the seller cannot secure oil from any other source. This situation comes fully under the commercial-impracticability exception to the perfect tender doctrine. •

Can unanticipated increases in a seller's costs, which make performance "impracticable," constitute a valid defense to performance on the basis of commercial impracticability? The court dealt with this question in the following case.

CASE 17.1 Maple Farms, Inc. v. City School District of Elmira

Supreme Court of New York, 1974.
76 Misc.2d 1080,
352 N.Y.S.2d 784.

HISTORICAL AND ECONOMIC SETTING *In 1972, the former Soviet Union suffered its worst drought in ten years, forcing it to buy American grain, including 25 percent of the U.S. wheat crop. This led to higher U.S. grain prices, which consequently forced up the prices of other food, including dairy products. In response, U.S. farmers planted more grain. Nevertheless, food prices continued to rise. Consumers organized boycotts in protest. On June 13, 1973, President Richard Nixon ordered a temporary freeze on all retail prices, including those for food. On June 27, Nixon ordered a temporary embargo on soybean exports. The embargo shocked foreign buyers. Although the embargo was lifted after five days, amounts due under previous contracts were cut 40 to 50 percent. Fearing that further controls would be applied, foreign buyers doubled their purchases of U.S. grain. In response, U.S. farmers held back their crops as prices were bid up.*

BACKGROUND AND FACTS On June 15, 1973, Maple Farms, Inc., formed an agreement with the city school district of Elmira, New York, to supply the school district with milk for the 1973–1974 school year. The agreement was in the form of a requirements contract, under which Maple Farms would sell to the school district all the milk the district required at a fixed price—which was the June market price of milk. By December 1973, the price of raw milk had increased by 23 percent over the price specified in the contract. This meant that if the terms of the contract were fulfilled, Maple Farms would lose $7,350. Because it had similar contracts with other school districts, Maple Farms stood to lose a great deal if it was held to the price stated in the contracts. When the school district would not agree to release Maple Farms from its contract, Maple Farms brought an action in a New York state court for a declaratory judgment (a determination of the parties' rights under a contract). Maple Farms contended that the substantial increase in the price of raw milk was an event not contemplated by the parties when the contract was formed and that, given the increased price, performance of the contract was commercially impracticable.

IN THE WORDS OF THE COURT . . .

CHARLES B. SWARTWOOD, Justice.

* * * *

* * * [The doctrine of commercial impracticability requires that] a contingency—something unexpected—must have occurred. Second, the risk of the unexpected occurrence must not have been allocated either by agreement or by custom. * * *

* * * [H]ere we find that the contingency causing the increase of the price of raw milk was not totally unexpected. The price from the low point in the year 1972 to the price on the date of the award of the contract in June 1973 had risen nearly 10%. And any businessman should have been aware of the general inflation in this country during the previous years * * * .

* * * Here the very purpose of the contract was to guard against fluctuation of price of half pints of milk as a basis for the school budget. Surely had the price of raw milk fallen substantially, the defendant could not be excused from performance. We can reasonably assume that the plaintiff had to be aware of escalating inflation.

(Continued)

CASE 17.1—Continued

It is chargeable with knowledge of the substantial increase of the price of raw milk from the previous year's low. * * * It nevertheless entered into this agreement with that knowledge. It did not provide in the contract any exculpatory clause to excuse it from performance in the event of a substantial rise in the price of raw milk. On these facts the risk of a substantial or abnormal increase in the price of raw milk can be allocated to the plaintiff.

DECISION AND REMEDY The New York trial court ruled that performance in this case was not impracticable and granted summary judgment in favor of the school district.

FOR CRITICAL ANALYSIS—Economic Consideration *What would be the result for society if courts routinely allowed parties to avoid their contractual obligations because of steep price increases?*

Partial Performance. Sometimes, an unforeseen event only *partially* affects the capacity of the seller or lessor to perform, and the seller or lessor is thus able to fulfill the contract *partially* but cannot tender total performance. In this event, the seller or lessor is required to allocate in a fair and reasonable manner any remaining production and deliveries among those to whom it is contractually obligated to deliver the goods, and this allocation may take into account its regular customers [UCC 2–615(b), 2A–405(b)]. The buyer or lessee must receive notice of the allocation and has the right to accept or reject the allocation [UCC 2–615(c), 2A–405(c)].

• **EXAMPLE 17.7** A Florida orange grower, Best Citrus, Inc., contracts to sell this season's production to a number of customers, including Martin's grocery chain. Martin's contracts to purchase two thousand crates of oranges. Best Citrus has sprayed some of its orange groves with a chemical called Karmoxin. The Department of Agriculture discovers that persons who eat products sprayed with Karmoxin may develop cancer. The department issues an order prohibiting the sale of these products. Best Citrus picks all of the oranges not sprayed with Karmoxin, but the quantity does not fully meet all the contracted-for deliveries. In this situation, Best Citrus is required to allocate its production, and it notifies Martin's that it cannot deliver

A FLOOD CAN DESTROY A FARMER'S CROP. IF A CONTRACT FOR A SALE OF THE CROP HAD ALREADY BEEN SIGNED, WOULD THE FARMER BE IN BREACH OF THE CONTRACT?

the full quantity agreed on in the contract and specifies the amount it will be able to deliver under the circumstances. Martin's can either accept or reject the allocation, but Best Citrus has no further contractual liability. •

Destruction of Identified Goods The UCC provides that when an unexpected event, such as a fire, totally destroys *goods identified at the time the contract is formed* through no fault of either party and *before risk passes to the buyer or lessee,* the parties are excused from performance [UCC 2–613, 2A–221]. If the goods are only partially destroyed, however, the buyer or lessee can inspect them and either treat the contract as void or accept the goods with a reduction of the contract price.

• **EXAMPLE 17.8** Atlas Sporting Equipment agrees to lease to River Bicycles sixty bicycles of a particular model that has been discontinued. No other bicycles of that model are available. River specifies that it needs the bicycles to rent to tourists. Before Atlas can deliver the bikes, they are destroyed by a fire. In this situation, Atlas is not liable to River for failing to deliver the bikes. The goods were destroyed through no fault of either party, before the risk of loss passed to the lessee. The loss was total, so the contract is avoided. Clearly, Atlas has no obligation to tender the bicycles, and River has no obligation to pay for them. •

Obligations of the Buyer or Lessee

Once the seller or lessor has adequately tendered delivery, the buyer or lessee is obligated to accept the goods and pay for them according to the terms of the contract. In the absence of any specific agreements, the buyer or lessee must make payment at the time and place the buyer or lessee receives the goods [UCC 2–310(a), 2A–516(1)].

PAYMENT

When a sale is made on credit, the buyer is obliged to pay according to the specified credit terms (for example, 60, 90, or 120 days), not when the goods are received. The credit period usually begins on the *date of shipment* [UCC 2–310(d)]. Under a lease contract, a lessee must pay the lease payment that was specified in the contract [2A–516(1)].

Payment can be made by any means agreed on between the parties—cash or any other method generally acceptable in the commercial world. If the seller demands cash when the buyer offers a check, credit card, or the like, the seller must permit the buyer reasonable time to obtain legal tender [UCC 2–511].

RIGHT OF INSPECTION

"The buyer needs a hundred eyes, the seller not one."
GEORGE HERBERT, 1593–1633
(English poet)

Unless otherwise agreed, or for C.O.D. (collect on delivery) transactions, the buyer or lessee has an absolute right to inspect the goods. This right allows the buyer or lessee to verify, before making payment, that the goods tendered or delivered are what were contracted for or ordered. If the goods are not what the buyer or lessee ordered, the buyer or lessee has no duty to pay. *An opportunity for inspection is therefore a condition precedent to the right of the seller or lessor to enforce payment* [UCC 2–513(1), 2A–515(1)].

Unless otherwise agreed, inspection can take place at any reasonable place and time and in any reasonable manner. Generally, what is reasonable is determined by custom of the trade, past practices of the parties, and the like. Costs of inspecting conforming goods are borne by the buyer unless otherwise agreed [UCC 2–513(2)].

C.O.D. Shipments If a seller ships goods to a buyer C.O.D. (or under similar terms) and the buyer has not agreed to a C.O.D. shipment in the contract, the buyer can rightfully *reject* the goods. This is because a C.O.D. shipment does not permit inspection before payment, which is a denial of the buyer's right of inspection. When the buyer has agreed to a C.O.D. shipment in the contract, however, or has agreed to pay for the goods upon the presentation of a bill of lading, no right of inspection exists, because it was negated by the agreement [UCC 2–513(3)].

Payment Due—Documents of Title Under certain contracts, payment is due on the receipt of the required documents of title even though the goods themselves may not have arrived at their destination. With C.I.F. and C.&F. contracts (see Exhibit 16–1 in Chapter 16), payment is required on receipt of the documents unless the parties have agreed otherwise. Thus, payment may be required prior to inspection, and payment must be made unless the buyer knows that the goods are nonconforming [UCC 2–310(b), 2–513(3)].

ACCEPTANCE

A buyer or lessee can manifest assent to the delivered goods in the following ways, each of which constitutes acceptance:

1. The buyer or lessee can expressly accept the shipment by words or conduct. For example, there is an acceptance if the buyer or lessee, after having had a reasonable opportunity to inspect the goods, signifies agreement to the seller or lessor that the goods are either conforming or are acceptable despite their nonconformity [UCC 2–606(1)(a), 2A–515(1)(a)].
2. Acceptance is presumed if the buyer or lessee has had a reasonable opportunity to inspect the goods and has failed to reject them within a reasonable period of time [UCC 2–606(1)(b), 2–602(1), 2A–515(1)(b)].

Additionally, in sales contracts, the buyer will be deemed to have accepted the goods if he or she performs any act that would indicate that the seller no longer owns the goods. For example, any use or resale of the goods generally constitutes an acceptance. Limited use for the sole purpose of testing or inspecting the goods is not an acceptance, however [UCC 2–606(1)(c)].

If some of the goods delivered do not conform to the contract and the seller or lessor has failed to cure, the buyer or lessee can make a *partial* acceptance [UCC 2–601(c), 2A–509(1)]. The same is true if the nonconformity was not reasonably discoverable before acceptance. (In the latter situation, the buyer or lessee may be able to revoke the acceptance, as will be discussed later in this chapter.) A buyer or lessee cannot accept less than a single commercial unit, however. A *commercial unit* is defined by the UCC as a unit of goods that, by commercial usage, is viewed as a "single whole" for purposes of sale, division of which would materially impair the character of the unit, its market value, or its use [UCC 2–105(6), 2A–103(1)(c)]. A commercial unit can be a single article (such as a machine), a set of articles (such as a suite of furniture or an assortment of sizes), a quantity (such as a bale, a gross, or a carload), or any other unit treated in the trade as a single whole.

In the following case, the court considered whether a buyer's actions, in regard to goods shipped to it by the seller, were "inconsistent with the seller's ownership" so as to constitute acceptance under UCC 2–606(1)(c).

CASE 17.2 Industria de Calcados Martini Ltda.[a] v. Maxwell Shoe Co.

Appeals Court of Massachusetts, 1994.
36 Mass.App.Ct. 268,
630 N.E.2d 299.

HISTORICAL AND SOCIAL SETTING *In the middle of the nineteenth century, New England was the shoe capital of the United States. Except for expensive, custom-made footwear, men's and women's shoes were essentially all the same: black and functional. Near the end of the century, shoemakers in the Midwest began to mass-produce more fashionable dress shoes. The new lines met with instant success. Then, during the 1980s, more casual shoes (tennis shoes, sneakers, and the like), often made out of canvas and other material, became popular. Indeed, sales of all athletic-type footwear soared. Traditional leather-shoe manufacturing in the United States saw a concomitant decline. Today, most shoes sold in the United States are manufactured elsewhere.*

a. *Ltda.* is an abbreviation for *Limitada,* a business organization form involving limited liability for the owners.

BACKGROUND AND FACTS The Maxwell Shoe Company agreed to buy 12,042 pairs of shoes from Industria de Calcados Martini Ltda. (Martini), a Brazilian shoe manufacturer. Maxwell paid part of the price with a check. When the shoes arrived, they were cracked and peeling. Maxwell stopped payment on the check and told Martini that it was rejecting the shoes. Martini did not respond. Two months later, Maxwell shipped the shoes to Maine to have them refinished, sold the refinished shoes, and kept the money. Martini filed a suit in a Massachusetts state court against Maxwell for, among other things, breach of contract. The court held in part that Maxwell had accepted the shoes when it shipped them to Maine to be refinished, "on the grounds that an alteration or repair of a defect in goods is an act inconsistent with the seller's ownership" under UCC 2–606(1)(c). The court awarded damages to Martini, reduced by the amount that Maxwell had paid for the refinishing. Both parties appealed.

IN THE WORDS OF THE COURT . . .
PORADA, Justice.

* * * *

* * * Maxwell received no * * * instructions from Martini. Instead, it acted on its own in sending the shoes for refinishing and then selling them and retaining the proceeds for its own benefit. * * * Accordingly, we do not think the judge's ruling * * * was clearly erroneous.

DECISION AND REMEDY The Court of Appeals of Massachusetts affirmed the lower court's decision.

FOR CRITICAL ANALYSIS—Economic Consideration *What might have been Maxwell's recovery if, instead of refinishing and reselling the shoes, Maxwell had simply sent them back?*

Anticipatory Repudiation

What if, before the time for contract performance, one party clearly communicates to the other the intention not to perform? As discussed in Chapter 13, such an action is a breach of the contract by anticipatory repudiation.[3] When anticipatory repudiation occurs, the nonbreaching party has a choice of two responses. He or she can treat the repudiation as a final breach by pursuing a remedy; or he or she can wait, hoping that the repudiating party will decide to honor the obligations required

3. This doctrine was first enunciated in an English case decided in 1853, *Hochster v. De La Tour,* 2 Ellis and Blackburn Reports 678 (1853).

by the contract despite the avowed intention to renege [UCC 2–610, 2A–402]. In either situation, the nonbreaching party may suspend performance.

Should the latter course be pursued, the UCC permits the breaching party (subject to some limitations) to "retract" his or her repudiation. This can be done by any method that clearly indicates an intent to perform. Once retraction is made, the rights of the repudiating party under the contract are reinstated [UCC 2–611, 2A–403].

Remedies of the Seller or Lessor

"Life is so terrifyingly dependent on the law."
KARL N. LLEWELLYN, 1893–1962
(American legal scholar)

There are numerous remedies available under the UCC to a seller or lessor when the buyer or lessee is in breach. Generally, the remedies available to the seller or lessor depend on the circumstances existing at the time of the breach, such as which party has possession of the goods, whether the goods are in transit, whether the buyer or lessee has rejected or accepted the goods, and so on.

WHEN THE GOODS ARE IN THE POSSESSION OF THE SELLER OR LESSOR

Under the UCC, if the buyer or lessee breaches the contract before the goods have been delivered to the buyer or lessee, the seller or lessor has the right to pursue the remedies discussed here.

¡NOTE!
A buyer or lessee breaches a contract by wrongfully rejecting the goods, revoking acceptance, refusing to pay, or repudiating the contract.

The Right to Cancel the Contract One of the options available to a seller or lessor when the buyer or lessee breaches the contract is simply to cancel (rescind) the contract [UCC 2–703(f), 2A–523(1)(a)]. The seller must notify the buyer or lessee of the cancellation, and at that point all remaining obligations of the seller or lessor are discharged. The buyer or lessee is not discharged from all remaining obligations, however; he or she is in breach, and the seller or lessor can pursue remedies available under the UCC for breach.

The Right to Withhold Delivery In general, sellers and lessors can withhold or discontinue performance of their obligations under sales or lease contracts when the buyers or lessees are in breach. If a buyer or lessee has wrongfully rejected or revoked acceptance of contract goods (rejection and revocation of acceptance will be discussed later), failed to make proper and timely payment, or repudiated a part of the contract, the seller or lessor can withhold delivery of the goods in question [UCC 2–703(a), 2A–523(1)(c)]. If the breach results from the buyer's or the lessee's insolvency (inability to pay debts as they become due), the seller or lessor can refuse to deliver the goods unless the buyer or lessee pays in cash [UCC 2–702(1), 2A–525(1)].

The Right to Resell or Dispose of the Goods When a buyer or lessee breaches or repudiates a sales contract while the seller or lessor is still in possession of the goods, the seller or lessor can resell or dispose of the goods. The seller can retain any profits made as a result of the sale and can hold the buyer or lessee liable for any loss [UCC 2–703(d), 2–706(1), 2A–523(1)(e), 2A–527(1)].

When the goods contracted for are unfinished at the time of breach, the seller or lessor can do one of two things: (1) cease manufacturing the goods and resell them for scrap or salvage value or (2) complete the manufacture and resell or dispose of them, holding the buyer or lessee liable for any deficiency. In choosing between these two alternatives, the seller or lessor must exercise reasonable commercial judgment in order to mitigate the loss and obtain maximum value from the unfinished goods [UCC 2–704(2), 2A–524(2)]. Any resale of the goods must be made in good faith and in a commercially reasonable manner.

In sales transactions, the seller can recover any deficiency between the resale price and the contract price, along with **incidental damages,** defined as those costs to the seller resulting from the breach [UCC 2–706(1), 2–710]. The resale can be private or public, and the goods can be sold as a unit or in parcels. The seller must give the original buyer reasonable notice of the resale, unless the goods are perishable or will rapidly decline in value [UCC 2–706(2), (3)]. A good faith purchaser in a resale takes the goods free of any of the rights of the original buyer, even if the seller fails to comply with these requirements of the UCC [UCC 2–706(5)].

• **INCIDENTAL DAMAGES**
Damages resulting from a breach of contract, including all reasonable expenses incurred because of the breach.

In lease transactions, the lessor may lease the goods to another party and recover from the original lessee, as damages, any unpaid lease payments up to the beginning date of the lease term under the new lease. The lessor can also recover any deficiency between the lease payments due under the original lease contract and under the new lease contract, along with incidental damages [UCC 2A–527(2)].

The Right to Recover the Purchase Price or Lease Payments Due Under the UCC, an unpaid seller or lessor can bring an action to recover the purchase price or payments due under the lease contract, plus incidental damages, if the seller or lessor is unable to resell or dispose of the goods [UCC 2–709(1), 2A–529(1)].

• EXAMPLE 17.9 Suppose that Southern Realty contracts with Gem Point, Inc., to purchase one thousand pens with Southern Realty's name inscribed on them. Gem Point tenders delivery of the one thousand pens, but Southern Realty wrongfully refuses to accept them. In this situation, Gem Point has, as a proper remedy, an action for the purchase price. Gem Point tendered delivery of conforming goods, and Southern Realty, because it failed to accept the goods, is in breach. Gem Point obviously cannot sell to anyone else the pens inscribed with the buyer's business name, so this situation falls under UCC 2–709. •

If a seller or lessor sues for the contract price of, or lease payments for, goods that he or she has been unable to resell or dispose of, the goods must be held for the buyer or lessee. The seller or lessor can resell or dispose of the goods at any time prior to collection (of the judgment) from the buyer or lessee, but the net proceeds from the sale must be credited to the buyer or lessee. This is an example of the duty to mitigate damages.

The Right to Recover Damages If a buyer or lessee repudiates a contract or wrongfully refuses to accept the goods, a seller or lessor can maintain an action to recover the damages that were sustained. Ordinarily, the amount of damages equals the difference between the contract price or lease payments and the market price or lease payments (at the time and place of tender of the goods), plus incidental damages [UCC 2–708(1), 2A–528(1)]. The time and place of tender are frequently given by such terms as F.O.B., F.A.S., C.I.F., and the like, which determine whether there is a shipment or destination contract.

When the Goods Are in Transit

If the seller or lessor has delivered the goods to a carrier or a bailee but the buyer or lessee has not as yet received them, the goods are said to be in transit. If, while the goods are in transit, the seller or lessor learns that the buyer or lessee is insolvent, the seller or lessor can stop the carrier or bailee from delivering the goods, regardless of the quantity of goods shipped. If the buyer or lessee is in breach but is not insolvent, the seller or lessor can stop the goods in transit only if the quantity shipped is at least a carload, a truckload, a planeload, or a larger shipment [UCC 2–705(1), 2A–526(1)].

To stop delivery, the seller or lessor must *timely notify* the carrier or other bailee that the goods are to be returned or held for the seller or lessor. If the carrier has sufficient time to stop delivery, the goods must be held and delivered according to the instructions of the seller or lessor, who is liable to the carrier for any additional costs incurred [UCC 2–705(3), 2A–526(3)].

UCC 2–705(2) and 2A–526(2) provide that the right of the seller or lessor to stop delivery of goods in transit is lost when any of the following events occur:

1. The buyer or lessee obtains possession of the goods.
2. The carrier acknowledges the rights of the buyer or lessee by reshipping or storing the goods for the buyer or lessee.
3. A bailee of the goods other than a carrier acknowledges that he or she is holding the goods for the buyer or lessee.

Additionally, in sales transactions, the seller loses the right to stop delivery of goods in transit when a negotiable document of title covering the goods has been negotiated (properly transferred, giving the buyer ownership rights in the goods) to the buyer [UCC 2–705(2)].

Once the seller or lessor reclaims the goods in transit, he or she can pursue the remedies allowed to sellers and lessors when the goods are in their possession. In other words, the seller or lessor who has reclaimed goods may do the following:

1. Cancel (rescind) the contract.
2. Resell the goods and recover any deficiency.
3. Sue for any deficiency between the contract price (or lease payments due) and the market price (or market lease payments), plus incidental damages.
4. Sue to recover the purchase price or lease payments due if the goods cannot be resold, plus incidental damages.
5. Sue to recover damages.

¡RECALL!
Incidental damages include all reasonable expenses incurred because of a breach of contract.

WHEN THE GOODS ARE IN THE POSSESSION OF THE BUYER OR LESSEE

When the buyer or lessee breaches a sales or lease contract and the goods are in the buyer's or lessee's possession, the UCC gives the seller or lessor the following limited remedies.

The Right to Recover the Purchase Price or Payments Due under the Lease Contract If the buyer or lessee has accepted the goods but refuses to pay for them, the seller or lessor can sue for the purchase price of the goods or for the lease payments due, plus incidental damages [UCC 2–709(1), 2A–529(1)].

The Right to Reclaim the Goods In regard to sales contracts, if a seller discovers that the buyer has received goods on credit and is insolvent, the seller can demand return of the goods, if the demand is made within ten days of the buyer's receipt of the goods. The seller can demand and reclaim the goods at any time if the buyer misrepresented his or her solvency in writing within three months prior to the delivery of the goods [UCC 2–702(2)]. The seller's right to reclaim the goods, however, is subject to the rights of a good faith purchaser or other subsequent buyer in the ordinary course of business who purchases the goods from the buyer before the seller reclaims.

Under the UCC, a seller seeking to exercise the right to reclaim goods receives preferential treatment over the buyer's other creditors—the seller need only demand the return of the goods within ten days after the buyer has received them.[4] Because of this preferential treatment, the UCC provides that reclamation *bars* the seller from pursuing any other remedy as to these goods [UCC 2–702(3)].

In regard to lease contracts, if the lessee is in default (fails to make payments that are due, for example), the lessor may reclaim the leased goods that are in the possession of the lessee [UCC 2A–525(2)].

Remedies of the Buyer or Lessee

¡NOTE!

A seller or lessor breaches a contract by wrongfully failing to deliver the goods, delivering nonconforming goods, making an improper tender of the goods, or repudiating the contract.

Under the UCC, there are numerous remedies available to the buyer or lessee when the seller or lessor breaches the contract. As with the remedies available to sellers and lessors, the remedies of buyers and lessees depend on the circumstances existing at the time of the breach.

When the Seller or Lessor Refuses to Deliver the Goods

If the seller or lessor refuses to deliver the goods or the buyer or lessee has rejected the goods, the remedies available to the buyer or lessee include those discussed here.

The Right to Cancel the Contract When a seller or lessor fails to make proper delivery or repudiates the contract, the buyer or lessee can cancel, or rescind, the contract. On notice of cancellation, the buyer or lessee is relieved of any further obligations under the contract but retains all rights to other remedies against the seller [UCC 2–711(1), 2A–508(1)(a)].

The Right to Recover the Goods If a buyer or lessee has made a partial or full payment for goods that remain in the possession of the seller or lessor, the buyer or lessee can recover the goods if the seller or lessor is insolvent or becomes insolvent within ten days after receiving the first payment and if the goods are identified to the contract. To exercise this right, the buyer or lessee must tender to the seller any unpaid balance of the purchase price [UCC 2–502, 2A–522].

The Right to Obtain Specific Performance A buyer or lessee can obtain specific performance when the goods are unique and when the remedy at law is inadequate [UCC 2–716(1), 2A–521(1)]. Ordinarily, a successful suit for money damages is sufficient to place a buyer or lessee in the position he or she would have occupied if the seller or lessor had fully performed. When the contract is for the purchase of a particular work of art or a similarly unique item, however, money damages may not be sufficient. Under these circumstances, equity will require that the seller or lessor perform exactly by delivering the particular goods identified to the contract (a remedy of specific performance).

4. A seller who has delivered goods to an insolvent buyer also receives preferential treatment if the buyer enters into bankruptcy proceedings (discussed in Chapter 23).

The Right of Cover In certain situations, buyers and lessees can protect themselves by obtaining **cover**—that is, by purchasing other goods to substitute for those that were due under the contract. This option is available when the seller or lessor repudiates the contract or fails to deliver the goods, or when a buyer or lessee has rightfully rejected goods or revoked acceptance.

• **COVER**
Under the UCC, a remedy that allows the buyer or lessee, on the seller's or lessor's breach, to purchase the goods, in good faith and within a reasonable time, from another seller or lessor and substitute them for the goods due under the contract. If the cost of cover exceeds the cost of the contract goods, the breaching seller or lessor will be liable to the buyer or lessee for the difference, plus incidental and consequential damages.

In obtaining cover, the buyer or lessee must act in good faith and without unreasonable delay [UCC 2–712, 2A–518]. After purchasing or leasing substitute goods, the buyer or lessee can recover from the seller or lessor the difference between the cost of cover and the contract price (or lease payments), plus incidental and consequential damages, less the expenses (such as delivery costs) that were saved as a result of the breach [UCC 2–712, 2–715, 2A–518]. Consequential damages are any losses suffered by the buyer or lessee that the seller or lessor could have foreseen (had reason to know about) at the time of contract formation and any injury to the buyer's or lessee's person or property proximately resulting from the contract's breach [UCC 2–715(2), 2A–520(2)].

Buyers and lessees are not required to cover, and failure to do so will not bar them from using any other remedies available under the UCC. A buyer or lessee who fails to cover, however, may *not* be able to collect consequential damages that could have been avoided had he or she purchased or leased substitute goods.

If, by obtaining cover, a buyer is able to recoup some of his or her loss from a source other than the breaching party, should the buyer's recovery under UCC 2–712 be reduced? This was the issue confronting the court in the following case.

CASE 17.3 Terex Corp. v. Ingalls Shipbuilding, Inc.

Supreme Court of Mississippi, 1996.
671 So.2d 1316.

HISTORICAL AND ECONOMIC SETTING *The drafters of the Uniform Commercial Code were aware that the cost of cover in the marketplace, on a seller's breach of contract, is usually greater than the price in the seller's contract for the undelivered goods. Sometimes, however, assessing damages requires more than simply subtracting the amount of cover from the contract price. Determining damages can be complicated by such costs as construction, design, modifications, and options. Another potential complication is the cost of product testing. Any of these costs can affect the ultimate amount of damages—positively, negatively, or both.*

BACKGROUND AND FACTS Terex Corporation agreed to sell two five-ton diesel forklifts to Ingalls Shipbuilding, Inc., for $208,546, with an option for four more at $432,074. The forklifts were to be installed on a U.S. Navy ship according to specific criteria. Terex did not deliver, and Ingalls covered by purchasing substitute forklifts from Windham Power Lifts for $166,000, plus $270,000 for testing. Ingalls also bought four more forklifts from Windham for $336,000. Ingalls filed a suit in a Mississippi state court against Terex, alleging, among other things, breach of contract. Ingalls sought to recover $227,454, the difference between Terex's price for the first two forklifts and the cost of the first two Windham forklifts. The court awarded Ingalls what it asked, and Terex appealed.

IN THE WORDS OF THE COURT . . .
SMITH, Justice, for the Court:

* * * *

* * * Miss. Code Ann. Section 75-2-712 [UCC 2–712] * * * states:

(2) The buyer may recover from the seller as damages the difference between the cost of cover and the contract price together with any incidental or consequential damages as hereinafter defined [UCC 2–715], but less expenses saved in consequence of the seller's breach.

* * * *

CASE 17.3—Continued

In the present case, the numbers show that Ingalls, as a consequence of the breach by Terex, in the end, did not pay as much as it would have had Terex honored the contract. * * * This is a situation where the mathematics reveals that Ingalls did actually benefit as a consequence of the breach. * * *

* * * Ingalls saved $96,074 by dealing with Windham. * * * The jury award as it stands is $227,454. This Court grants a remittitur [an order to the plaintiff to remit a portion of the award] in the amount of $96,074, lowering the damage award to $131,380, which is a more accurate assessment of what Ingalls actually lost as a consequence of Terex's breach of contract.

DECISION AND REMEDY The Supreme Court of Mississippi held that when a buyer uses the remedy of cover, the amount that the buyer saves, as a consequence of the seller's breach, reduces the amount of damages. The court reduced the amount of the damages awarded by the lower court to $131,380.

FOR CRITICAL ANALYSIS—Economic Consideration
Is it fair for a breaching party to receive the benefit of a bargain struck by an innocent party who uses the remedy of cover?

The Right to Replevy Goods Buyers and lessees also have the right to replevy goods. **Replevin**[5] is an action to recover specific goods in the hands of a party who is wrongfully withholding them from the other party. Outside the UCC, the term *replevin* refers to a *prejudgment process* (a proceeding that takes place prior to a court's judgment) that permits the seizure of specific personal property in which a party claims a right or an interest. Under the UCC, the buyer or lessee can replevy goods subject to the contract if the seller or lessor has repudiated or breached the contract. To maintain an action to replevy goods, usually buyers and lessees must show that they are unable to cover for the goods after a reasonable effort [UCC 2–713, 2A–519].

• **REPLEVIN**
An action to recover identified goods in the hands of a party who is wrongfully withholding them from the other party. Under the UCC, this remedy is usually available only if the buyer is unable to cover.

The Right to Recover Damages If a seller or lessor repudiates the sales contract or fails to deliver the goods, or the buyer or lessee has rightfully rejected or revoked acceptance of the goods, the buyer or lessee can sue for damages. The measure of recovery is the difference between the contract price (or lease payments) and the market price of (or lease payments that could be obtained for) the goods at the time the buyer (or lessee) *learned* of the breach. The market price or market lease payments are determined at the place where the seller or lessor was supposed to deliver the goods. The buyer or lessee can also recover incidental and consequential damages, less the expenses that were saved as a result of the breach [UCC 2–713, 2A–519].

¡RECALL!
Consequential damages compensate for a loss (such as lost profits) that is not direct but that is reasonably foreseeable at the time of the breach.

• **EXAMPLE 17.10** Schilling orders ten thousand bushels of wheat from Valdone for $5 a bushel, with delivery due on June 14 and payment due on June 20. Valdone does not deliver on June 14. On June 14, the market price of wheat is $5.50 per bushel. Schilling chooses to do without the wheat. He sues Valdone for damages for nondelivery. Schilling can recover $0.50 × 10,000, or $5,000, plus any expenses the breach may have caused him. The measure of damages is the market price less the contract price on the day Schilling was to have received delivery. (Any expenses Schilling saved by the breach would be deducted from the damages.) •

5. Pronounced ruh-*pleh*-vun.

When the Seller or Lessor Delivers Nonconforming Goods

When the seller or lessor delivers nonconforming goods, the buyer or lessee has several remedies available under the UCC.

The Right to Reject the Goods If either the goods or the tender of the goods by the seller or lessor fails to conform to the contract *in any respect,* the buyer or lessee can reject the goods. If some of the goods conform to the contract, the buyer or lessee can keep the conforming goods and reject the rest [UCC 2–601, 2A–509]. If the buyer or lessee rejects the goods, he or she may then obtain cover, cancel the contract, or sue for damages for breach of contract, just as if the seller or lessor had refused to deliver the goods (see the earlier discussion of these remedies).

> **ON THE WEB**
> The Boeing Company has posted online a summary of the contract rights and duties of parties forming sales contracts with that company. Go to www.boeing.com/companyoffices/doingbiz/tcmdhs/sect7_97.htm#c.

Timeliness and Reason for Rejection Required. The buyer or lessee must reject the goods within a reasonable amount of time, and the seller or lessor must be notified seasonably—that is, in a timely fashion or at the proper time [UCC 2–602(1), 2A–509(2)]. If the buyer or lessee fails to reject the goods within a reasonable amount of time, acceptance will be presumed. Furthermore, the buyer or lessee must designate defects that would have been apparent to the seller or lessor on reasonable inspection. Failure to do so precludes the buyer or lessee from using such defects to justify rejection or to establish breach when the seller could have cured the defects if they had been stated seasonably [UCC 2–605, 2A–514].

Duties of Merchant Buyers and Lessees When Goods Are Rejected. If a merchant buyer or lessee rightfully rejects goods, and the seller or lessor has no agent or business at the place of rejection, the buyer or lessee is required to follow any reasonable instructions received from the seller or lessor with respect to the goods controlled by the buyer or lessee. The buyer or lessee is entitled to reimbursement for the care and cost entailed in following the instructions [UCC 2–603, 2A–511]. The same requirements hold if the buyer or lessee rightfully revokes his or her acceptance of the goods at some later time [UCC 2–608(3), 2A–517(5)]. (Revocation of acceptance will be discussed shortly.)

If no instructions are forthcoming and the goods are perishable or threaten to decline in value quickly, the buyer can resell the goods in good faith, taking the appropriate reimbursement from the proceeds. In addition, the buyer is entitled to a selling commission (not to exceed 10 percent of the gross proceeds) [UCC 2–603(1), (2); 2A–511(1)]. If the goods are not perishable, the buyer or lessee may store them for the seller or lessor or reship them to the seller or lessor [UCC 2–604, 2A–512].

Buyers who rightfully reject goods that remain in their possession or control have a *security interest* in the goods (basically, a legal claim to the goods to the extent necessary to recover expenses, costs, and the like—see Chapter 22). The security interest encompasses any payments the buyer has made for the goods, as well as any expenses incurred with regard to inspection, receipt, transportation, care, and custody of the goods [UCC 2–711(3)]. A buyer with a security interest in the goods is a "person in the position of a seller." This gives the buyer the same rights as an unpaid seller. Thus, the buyer can resell, withhold delivery of, or stop delivery of the goods. A buyer who chooses to resell must account to the seller for any amounts received in excess of the security interest [UCC 2–711, 2–706(6)].

ETHICAL ISSUE 17.1 ***What if a seller believes that the buyer has wrongfully rejected contract goods?*** What happens if the seller suspects that the buyer is wrongfully rejecting contract goods? Does the seller have any recourse? This question becomes important when a seller never sees the goods because they are shipped directly from a third party to the buyer. For example, in a recent case J. R. Cousin Industries, Inc., a hardware importer, arranged to have sinks and other items shipped from a Mexico manufacturer directly to Menard, Inc., a seller of home-improvement products. The contract between Cousin and Menard allowed Menard to destroy (and not pay for) any units that were either defective or returned by customers. When the purchaser returns claimed by Menard seemed unusually high, Cousin informed Menard that it wanted to inspect the returned goods before they were destroyed. Menard refused to cooperate, and Cousin sued Menard for $72,000—the amount Menard had deducted from its payment to Cousin for returned (rejected) goods. Normally, the right of inspection is a concern of the buyer, but does a seller also have such a right? A federal appellate court said yes. The court pointed to UCC 2–515(a), which allows either party to a contract, on reasonable notification to the other "and for the purpose of ascertaining the facts and preserving evidence," to inspect the goods in the possession of the other party. The court concluded that Cousin had a right to inspect the goods and was entitled to be paid for all returned units destroyed by Menard after Menard refused to allow Cousin to inspect the returned items.[6]

Revocation of Acceptance Acceptance of the goods precludes the buyer or lessee from exercising the right of rejection, but it does not necessarily preclude the buyer or lessee from pursuing other remedies. In certain circumstances, a buyer or lessee is permitted to *revoke* his or her acceptance of the goods. Acceptance of a lot or a commercial unit can be revoked if the nonconformity *substantially* impairs the value of the lot or unit and if one of the following factors is present:

1. If acceptance was predicated on the reasonable assumption that the nonconformity would be cured, and it has not been cured within a reasonable period of time [UCC 2–608(1)(a), 2A–517(1)(a)].
2. If the buyer or lessee did not discover the nonconformity before acceptance, either because it was difficult to discover before acceptance or because assurances made by the seller or lessor that the goods were conforming kept the buyer or lessee from inspecting the goods [UCC 2–608(1)(b), 2A–517(1)(b)].

Revocation of acceptance is not effective until notice is given to the seller or lessor, which must occur within a reasonable time after the buyer or lessee either discovers *or should have discovered* the grounds for revocation. Additionally, revocation must occur before the goods have undergone any substantial change (such as spoilage) not caused by their own defects [UCC 2–608(2), 2A–517(4)].

The Right to Recover Damages for Accepted Goods A buyer or lessee who has accepted nonconforming goods may also keep the goods and recover damages caused by the breach. The buyer or lessee, however, must notify the seller or lessor of the breach within a reasonable time after the defect was or should have been discovered. Failure of the buyer or lessee to give notice of the defects (breach) to the seller or lessor bars the buyer or lessee from pursuing any remedy [UCC 2–607(3),

6. *J. R. Cousin Industries, Inc. v. Menard, Inc.*, 127 F.3d 580 (7th Cir. 1997).

2A–516(3)]. In addition, the parties to a sales or lease contract can insert a provision requiring that the buyer or lessee give notice of any defects in the goods within a prescribed period.

When the goods delivered and accepted are not as promised, the measure of damages equals the difference between the value of the goods as accepted and their value if they had been delivered as promised [UCC 2–714(2), 2A–519(4)]. For this and other types of breaches in which the buyer or lessee has accepted the goods, the buyer or lessee is entitled to recover for any loss "resulting in the ordinary course of events . . . as determined in any manner which is reasonable" [UCC 2–714(1), 2A–519(3)]. The UCC also permits the buyer or lessee, with proper notice to the seller or lessor, to deduct all or any part of the damages from the price or lease payments still due and payable to the seller or lessor [UCC 2–717, 2A–516(1)]. To be effective, the buyer or lessee should notify the seller or lessor that the payment being tendered is considered to constitute full accord and satisfaction of contract obligations (for a further discussion of the concept of accord and satisfaction, see Chapter 13).

International Perspective • THE CISG'S APPROACH TO REVOCATION OF ACCEPTANCE

Under the UCC, a buyer or lessee who has accepted goods may be able to revoke acceptance under the circumstances just mentioned. Provisions of the United Nations Convention on Contracts for the International Sale of Goods (CISG) similarly allow buyers to rescind their contracts after they have accepted the goods. The CISG, however, takes a somewhat different—and more direct—approach to the problem than the UCC does. Circumstances that would permit a buyer to revoke acceptance under the UCC would, under the CISG, allow the buyer simply to declare that the seller has *fundamentally* breached the contract, thus allowing the buyer to sue the seller for breach of contract. Article 25 of the CISG states that a "breach of contract committed by one of the parties is fundamental if it results in such detriment to the other party as substantially to deprive him of what he is entitled to expect under the contract."

FOR CRITICAL ANALYSIS

What is the essential difference between revocation of acceptance and bringing a suit for breach of contract?

Statute of Limitations

An action for breach of contract under the UCC must be commenced *within four years after the cause of action accrues*—that is, within four years after the breach occurs. In addition to filing suit within the four-year period, an aggrieved party who has accepted nonconforming goods usually must notify the breaching party of the breach within a reasonable time, or the buyer or lessee is barred from pursuing any remedy [UCC 2–607(3)(a), 2A–516(3)]. By agreement in the contract, the parties can reduce this period to not less than one year but cannot extend it beyond four years [UCC 2–725(1), 2A–506(1)]. A cause of action accrues for breach of warranty when the seller or lessor tenders delivery. This is the rule even if the aggrieved party is unaware that the cause of action has accrued [UCC 2–725(2), 2A–506(2)].

International Perspective • NOTICE REQUIREMENTS UNDER THE CISG

The United Nations Convention on Contracts for the International Sale of Goods (CISG), like the UCC, establishes notice requirements for international sales transactions. In other words, before a buyer can recover damages for defective goods, the buyer must notify the seller that the goods are defective within a reasonable time. The CISG's notice requirements are not as strict as those imposed by the UCC, however. The CISG requires notice by the buyer only when the seller is reasonably unaware that the goods that were shipped did not conform to the contract. Thus, the lack of prompt notice of nonconformity need not necessarily defeat a buyer's claim.

FOR CRITICAL ANALYSIS

What purpose is served by the UCC's requirement that, to be entitled to recover damages or pursue other remedies, the buyer must notify the seller of the breach within a reasonable time—even if the seller knew that the goods were nonconforming?

Limitation of Remedies

ON THE WEB

For an example of a warranty providing for an exclusive remedy, see the "Warranty and Limited Remedy" of 3M Company, which is online at www.mmm.com/promote/warranty.htm.

The parties to a sales or lease contract can vary their respective rights and obligations by contractual agreement. For example, a seller and buyer can expressly provide for remedies in addition to those provided in the UCC. They can also provide remedies in lieu of those provided in the UCC, or they can change the measure of damages. The seller can provide that the buyer's only remedy on breach of warranty will be repair or replacement of the item, or the seller can limit the buyer's remedy to return of the goods and refund of the purchase price. In sales and lease contracts, an agreed-on remedy is in addition to those provided in the UCC unless the parties expressly agree that the remedy is exclusive of all others [UCC 2–719(1), 2A–503(1)].

If the parties state that a remedy is exclusive, then it is the sole remedy. When circumstances cause an exclusive remedy to fail in its essential purpose, however, it is

The Letter of the Law — THE CASE OF THE EXPLODING TV

Sometimes, defective goods can spread disaster far and wide, as Arthur and Kathy Nelson learned when their TV exploded. The TV, which was relatively new, burst into flames that set fire to the drapes, the rug, the furniture, and ultimately the house. The Nelsons sued the seller from whom they had purchased the TV, seeking to recover, among other things, consequential damages for breach of warranty. The problem was, the warranty excluded consequential damages for property damage and limited recovery to the replacement of parts, service, labor, and the like. Was this exclusion unconscionable? The Nelsons thought so and took their case all the way to the Georgia Supreme Court. That court, however, pointed out that while Section 2–719(3) of the UCC provides that a "limitation of consequential damages for injury to the person in the case of consumer goods is *prima facie* unconscionable," it does not say anything about damages for harm to consumer *property*. Said the court: "The legislature could have provided that a limitation on consequential property damages in the case of consumer goods is *prima facie* unconscionable, as it did with consequential damages for personal injuries, but it chose not to do so."[a]

THE BOTTOM LINE

Parties to contracts should not be surprised when a court applies the letter of the law to their claims.

a. *NEC Technologies, Inc. v. Nelson*, 267 Ga. 390, 478 S.E.2d 769 (1996).

no longer exclusive [UCC 2–719(2), 2A–503(2)]. For example, a sales contract that limits the buyer's remedy to repair or replacement fails in its essential purpose if the item cannot be repaired and no replacements are available.

A contract can limit or exclude consequential damages, provided the limitation is not unconscionable. When the buyer or lessee is a consumer, the limitation of consequential damages for personal injuries resulting from nonconforming goods is *prima facie* (on its face) unconscionable. (Note that this consumer provision refers to "personal injuries" and not property damage—a distinction underscored in this chapter's *The Letter of the Law.*) The limitation of consequential damages is not necessarily unconscionable, however, when the loss is commercial in nature—for example, if the loss consists of lost profits and property damage [UCC 2–719(3), 2A–503(3)]. In the following case, the court had to decide whether a contract clause that excluded liability for consequential damages was unconscionable.

CASE 17.4 Transport Corp. of America, Inc. v. International Business Machines Corp.

United States Court of Appeals,
Eighth Circuit, 1994.
30 F.3d 953.
www.badsoftware.com/cases/trnsport.htm[a]

COMPANY PROFILE *Transport Corporation of America, Inc. (TCA), provides a wide range of services to its customers, which include Ford Motor Company, General Mills, 3M Company, and Sears, Roebuck & Company. From ten regional centers, with a fleet of more than 1,100 tractors and 2,600 trailers, TCA provides temperature-controlled trailers, multistop loading and unloading, and time-definite pickup and delivery. In 1994, at a cost of more than $1.5 million, TCA began to develop a more sophisticated computer information system. The system was to combine operational data, through satellite communications, with information such as maintenance, billing, and accounting.*

a. This is a page within the Web site of the Law Office of Cem Kaner in Santa Clara, California.

BACKGROUND AND FACTS Innovative Computing Corporation (ICC) sold an International Business Machines Corporation (IBM) computer to TCA. As part of the deal, TCA expressly agreed to a disclaimer that stated, in part, "IN NO EVENT SHALL ICC BE LIABLE FOR ANY * * * CONSEQUENTIAL DAMAGES * * * IN CONNECTION WITH * * * THIS AGREEMENT." One year later, the computer failed. The downtime was nearly thirty-four hours. TCA spent more than $4,500 to replace lost data and purportedly lost nearly $470,000 in income while the computer was down. TCA filed a suit in a Minnesota state court against IBM and ICC, alleging, among other things, breach of warranty. The case was moved to a federal district court, and IBM and ICC filed a motion for summary judgment. The court granted the motion, based in part on the disclaimer. TCA appealed, arguing in part that the disclaimer was unconscionable.

IN THE WORDS OF THE COURT . . .
McMILLIAN, Circuit Judge.

* * * *

* * * The U.C.C. encourages negotiated agreements in commercial transactions, including warranties and limitations. It is at the time of contract formation that experienced parties define the product, identify the risks, and negotiate a price of the goods that reflects the relative benefits and risks to each. An exclusion of consequential damages set forth in advance in a commercial agreement between experienced business parties represents a bargained-for allocation of risk that is conscionable as a matter of law.

* * * *

We agree with the district court that the disclaimer of consequential damages was not unconscionable and that the damages claimed by TCA, for business interruption losses and replacement media, were consequential damages. Furthermore, TCA and

CASE 17.4—Continued

ICC were sophisticated business entities of relatively equal bargaining power. ICC's disclaimer was not unconscionable and TCA is therefore precluded from recovering consequential damages.

DECISION AND REMEDY The U.S. Court of Appeals for the Eighth Circuit affirmed the lower court's decision.

FOR CRITICAL ANALYSIS—Social Consideration *Why is a limitation on consequential damages considered unconscionable when one of the parties is a consumer but not when both parties are business entities?*

APPLICATION

Law & the Seller or Buyer: Breach of Contract*

A contract for the sale of goods has been breached. Can such a breach be settled without a trip to court? The answer depends on the willingness of the parties to agree on an appropriate remedy. First, the parties by contract may already have agreed on the remedy applicable in the event of a breach. This may take the form of a contract provision restricting or expanding remedies provided for under the Uniform Commercial Code [UCC 2–719].

Consider an example. When defective goods are delivered and accepted, usually it is preferable for the buyer and seller to reach an agreement on a reduced purchase price. Practically speaking, the buyer may be unable to obtain a partial refund from the seller. UCC 2–717 allows the buyer in such circumstances to give notice of the intention to deduct the damages from any part of the purchase price not yet paid. If you are a buyer who has accepted defective goods and has not yet paid in full, it may be appropriate for you to exercise your rights under UCC 2–717 and not pay in full when you make your final payment.

If there is nothing in your agreement to cover a breach of contract and you are the nonbreaching party, the UCC gives you a variety of alternatives. What you need to do is analyze the remedies that would be available if you were to go to court, put these remedies in order of priority, and then predict how successful you might be in pursuing each remedy. Next, look at the position of the breaching party to determine the basis for negotiating a settlement, including whether it is actually worth your trouble to go to court. Remember that most breaches of contract do not end up in court—they are settled beforehand.

CHECKLIST FOR THE NONBREACHING PARTY TO A CONTRACT

1. Ascertain if a remedy is explicitly written into your contract. Use that remedy, if possible, to avoid litigation.
2. If no specific remedy is available, look to the UCC.
3. Assess how successful you might be in pursuing a remedy if you went to court.
4. Analyze the position of the breaching party.
5. Determine whether a negotiated settlement is preferable to a lawsuit, which is best done by consulting your attorney.

*This *Application* is not meant to substitute for the services of an attorney who is licensed to practice law in your state.

Key Terms

cover 446

incidental damages 443

installment contract 436

replevin 447

Chapter Summary • Performance and Breach of Sales and Lease Contracts

REQUIREMENTS OF PERFORMANCE	
Obligations of the Seller or Lessor (See pages 432–439.)	1. The seller or lessor must tender *conforming* goods to the buyer. Tender must take place at a *reasonable hour* and in a *reasonable manner.* Under the perfect tender doctrine, the seller or lessor must tender goods that exactly conform to the terms of the contract [UCC 2–503(1), 2A–508(1)]. 2. If the seller or lessor tenders nonconforming goods prior to the performance date and the buyer or lessee rejects them, the seller or lessor may *cure* (repair or replace the goods) within the contract time for performance [UCC 2–508(1), 2A–513(1)]. If the seller or lessor has reasonable grounds to believe the buyer or lessee would accept the tendered goods, on the buyer's or lessee's rejection the seller or lessor has a reasonable time to substitute conforming goods without liability [UCC 2–508(2), 2A–513(2)]. 3. If the agreed-on means of delivery becomes impracticable or unavailable, the seller must substitute an alternative means (such as a different carrier) if one is available [UCC 2–614(1)]. 4. If a seller or lessor tenders nonconforming goods in any one installment under an installment contract, the buyer or lessee may reject the installment only if its value is substantially impaired and cannot be cured. The entire installment contract is breached when one or more installments *substantially* impair the value of the *whole* contract [UCC 2–612, 2A–510]. 5. When performance becomes commercially impracticable owing to circumstances unforeseen when the contract was formed, the perfect tender rule no longer holds [UCC 2–615, 2A–405].
Obligations of the Buyer or Lessee (See pages 439–441.)	1. On tender of delivery by the seller, the buyer or lessee must pay for the goods at the time and place the buyer or lessee *receives* the goods, even if the place of shipment is the place of delivery, unless the sale is made on credit. Payment may be made by any method generally acceptable in the commercial world unless the seller demands cash [UCC 2–310, 2–511]. In lease contracts, the lessee must pay lease payments in accordance with the contract [UCC 2A–516(1)]. 2. Unless otherwise agreed, the buyer or lessee has an absolute right to inspect the goods before acceptance [UCC 2–513(1), 2A–515(1)]. 3. The buyer or lessee can manifest acceptance of delivered goods expressly in words or by conduct or by failing to reject the goods after a reasonable period of time following inspection or after having had a reasonable opportunity to inspect them [UCC 2–606(1), 2A–515(1)]. A buyer will be deemed to have accepted goods if he or she performs any act inconsistent with the seller's ownership [UCC 2–606(1)(c)]. 4. Following the acceptance of delivered goods, the buyer or lessee may revoke acceptance only if the nonconformity *substantially* impairs the value of the unit or lot and if one of the following factors is present: a. Acceptance was predicated on the reasonable assumption that the nonconformity would be cured and it was not cured within a reasonable time [UCC 2–608(1)(a), 2A–517(1)(a)]. b. The buyer or lessee did not discover the nonconformity before acceptance, either because it was difficult to discover before acceptance or because the seller's or lessor's assurance that the goods were conforming kept the buyer or lessee from inspecting the goods [UCC 2–608(1)(b), 2A–517(1)(b)].
Anticipatory Repudiation (See pages 441–442.)	If, before the time for performance, either party clearly indicates to the other an intention not to perform, under UCC 2–610 and 2A–402 the aggrieved party may do the following: 1. Await performance by the repudiating party for a commercially reasonable time. 2. Resort to any remedy for breach. 3. In either situation, suspend performance.

Chapter Summary • Performance and Breach of Sales and Lease Contracts, Continued

REMEDIES FOR BREACH OF CONTRACT	
Remedies of the Seller or Lessor (See pages 442–445.)	1. *When the goods are in the possession of the seller or lessor*—The seller or lessor may do the following: a. Cancel the contract [UCC 2–703(f), 2A–523(1)(a)]. b. Withhold delivery [UCC 2–703(a), 2A–523(1)(c)]. c. Resell or dispose of the goods [UCC 2–703(d), 2–706(1), 2A–523(1)(e), 2A–527(1)]. d. Sue to recover the purchase price or lease payments due [UCC 2–703(e), 2–709(1), 2A–529(1)]. e. Sue to recover damages [UCC 2–703(e), 2–708, 2A–528]. 2. *When the goods are in transit*—The seller may stop the carrier or bailee from delivering the goods [UCC 2–705, 2A–526]. 3. *When the goods are in the possession of the buyer or lessee*—The seller may do the following: a. Sue to recover the purchase price or lease payments due [UCC 2–709(1), 2A–529(1)]. b. Reclaim the goods. A seller may reclaim goods received by an insolvent buyer if the demand is made within ten days of receipt (reclaiming goods excludes all other remedies) [UCC 2–702]; a lessor may repossess goods if the lessee is in default [UCC 2A–525(2)].
Remedies of the Buyer or Lessee (See pages 445–450.)	1. *When the seller or lessor refuses to deliver the goods*—The buyer or lessee may do the following: a. Cancel the contract [UCC 2–711(1), 2A–508(1)(a)]. b. Recover the goods if the seller or lessor becomes insolvent within ten days after receiving the first payment and the goods are identified to the contract [UCC 2–502, 2A–522]. c. Obtain specific performance (when the goods are unique or when the remedy at law is inadequate) [UCC 2–716(1), 2A–521(1)]. d. Obtain cover [UCC 2–712, 2A–518]. e. Replevy the goods (if cover is unavailable) [UCC 2–716(3), 2A–521(3)]. f. Sue to recover damages [UCC 2–713, 2A–519]. 2. *When the seller or lessor delivers or tenders delivery of nonconforming goods*—The buyer or lessee may do the following: a. Reject the goods [UCC 2–601, 2A–509]. b. Revoke acceptance (in certain circumstances) [UCC 2–608, 2A–517]. c. Accept the goods and recover damages [UCC 2–607, 2–714, 2–717, 2A–519].
Statute of Limitations (See page 450.)	The UCC has a four-year statute of limitations for actions involving breach of contract. By agreement, the parties to a sales or lease contract can reduce this period to not less than one year, but they cannot extend it beyond four years [UCC 2–725(1), 2A–506(1)].
Limitation of Remedies (See pages 451–453.)	Remedies may be limited in sales or lease contracts by agreement of the parties. If the contract states that a remedy is exclusive, then that is the sole remedy—unless the remedy fails in its essential purpose. Sellers and lessors can also limit the rights of buyers and lessees to consequential damages—unless the limitation is unconscionable [UCC 2–719, 2A–503].

For Review

1. What are the respective obligations of the parties under a contract for the sale or lease of goods?
2. What is the perfect tender rule? What are some important exceptions to this rule that apply to sales and lease contracts?
3. What options are available to the nonbreaching party when the other party to a sales or lease contract repudiates the contract prior to the time for performance?
4. What remedies are available to a seller or lessor when the buyer or lessee breaches the contract? What remedies are available to a buyer or lessee if the seller or lessor breaches the contract?
5. In contracts subject to the UCC, are parties free to limit the remedies available to the nonbreaching party on a breach of contract? If so, in what ways?

Questions and Case Problems

17–1. Revocation of Acceptance. What events or circumstances must occur before a buyer can rightfully revoke his or her acceptance of a sales contract?

17–2. Remedies. Genix, Inc., has contracted to sell Larson five hundred washing machines of a certain model at list price. Genix is to ship the goods on or before December 1. Genix produces one thousand washing machines of this model but has not yet prepared Larson's shipment. On November 1, Larson repudiates the contract. Discuss the remedies available to Genix in this situation.

17–3. Right of Inspection. Cummings ordered two Model-X Super Fidelity speakers from Jamestown Wholesale Electronics, Inc. Jamestown shipped the speakers via United Parcel Service, C.O.D. (collect on delivery), although Cummings had not requested or agreed to a C.O.D. shipment of the goods. When the speakers were delivered, Cummings refused to accept them because he would not be able to inspect them before payment. Jamestown claimed that Cummings had breached their contract, because Jamestown had shipped conforming goods. Had Cummings breached the contract? Explain.

17–4. Anticipatory Repudiation. Moore contracted in writing to sell her 1996 Ford Taurus to Hammer for $8,500. Moore agreed to deliver the car on Wednesday, and Hammer promised to pay the $8,500 on the following Friday. On Tuesday, Hammer informed Moore that he would not be buying the car after all. By Friday, Hammer had changed his mind again and tendered $8,500 to Moore. Moore, although she had not sold the car to another party, refused the tender and refused to deliver. Hammer claimed that Moore had breached their contract. Moore contended that Hammer's repudiation released her from her duty to perform under the contract. Who is correct, and why?

17–5. Remedies. Rodriguez is an antique car collector. He contracts to purchase spare parts for a 1938 engine from Gerrard. These parts are not made anymore and are scarce. To get the contract with Gerrard, Rodriguez has to pay 50 percent of the purchase price in advance. On May 1, Rodriguez sends the required payment, which is received on May 2. On May 3, Gerrard, having found another buyer willing to pay substantially more for the parts, informs Rodriguez that he will not deliver as contracted. That same day, Rodriguez learns that Gerrard is insolvent. Gerrard has the parts, and Rodriguez wants them. Discuss fully any remedies available to Rodriguez.

17–6. Notice of Defect. Rachel Hebron bought an Isuzu Trooper four-wheel-drive sports vehicle from American Isuzu Motors, Inc. Their contract required her to give notice of any defects in the car within two years of their discovery. In June 1991, Hebron was driving the Trooper when another vehicle pulled in front of her. She swerved to avoid hitting it, and the Trooper rolled over, causing her permanent injuries. Hebron waited, for no apparent reason, until July 1993 to file a suit in a federal district court against American, seeking damages for alleged defects in the car. She had already disposed of the Trooper, without notifying American. American filed a motion for summary judgment based on the contract requirement of notice within two years. How should the court rule? Discuss fully. [*Hebron v. American Isuzu Motors, Inc.*, 60 F.3d 1095 (4th Cir. 1995)]

17–7. Limitation of Remedies. Wilk Paving, Inc., bought a street-paving asphalt roller from Southworth-Milton, Inc. In large capital letters, on the front of the contract, was printed, "ADDITIONAL TERMS AND CONDITIONS ON REVERSE SIDE." A clause on the back stated that "under no circumstances shall seller . . . be held liable for any . . . consequential damages." In a hurry to close the deal, Wilk's representative did not notice this clause, and Southworth's representative did not call attention to it. Within sixty days, the roller needed the first of what became continuous repairs for mechanical problems. Wilk asked Southworth for its money back. When Southworth refused, Wilk sued Southworth, seeking the purchase price and consequential damages. Was the clause limiting damages enforceable in these circumstances? Explain. [*Wilk Paving, Inc. v. Southworth-Milton, Inc.*, 649 A.2d 778 (Vt. 1995)]

17–8. Remedies of the Buyer or Lessee. McCalif Grower Supplies, Inc., provides for the supply and shipping of plants from growers to wholesale greenhouses. Wilbur Reed operates a small greenhouse in Missoula, Montana. Reed ordered poinsettias from McCalif. When the poinsettias were delivered, Reed discovered that many of them were ruined because they had not been packed properly. Reed refused to pay for any of the plants. McCalif filed an action in a Montana state court against Reed for the money. Reed claimed that McCalif owed him damages for, among other things, the nonconforming goods. The court awarded McCalif an amount to cover the cost of the plants that had not been damaged and awarded Reed nothing. What will result on appeal? Explain. [*McCalif Grower Supplies, Inc. v. Reed,* 272 Mont. 254, 900 P.2d 800 (1995)]

17–9. Nonconforming Goods. Moore & Moore General Contractors, Inc., contracted to build a Red Lobster restaurant. Basepoint, Inc., agreed to supply and install plywood cabinets for the bar, the food service area, the office, and the rest rooms. Instead of plywood, Basepoint supplied cabinets made of particle board. Moore's on-site supervisors accepted the nonconforming cabinets and had them installed, believing that the restaurant owner would not know the difference. The owner did know the difference, however, and insisted that the cabinets be replaced. Moore replaced the cabinets and refused to pay Basepoint. Basepoint filed a suit in a Virginia state court against Moore to recover its price. Moore counterclaimed for the replacement expense, contending that it had a right to return the nonconforming cabinets. Who should pay whom, and why? [*Moore & Moore General Contractors, Inc. v. Basepoint, Inc.,* 253 Va. 304, 485 S.E.2d 131 (1997)]

17–10. Commercial Impracticability. E+E (US) Inc., Manley-Regan Chemicals Division, agreed to sell to Rockland Industries, Inc., three containers of antimony oxide for $1.80 per pound. At the time, both parties knew that there was a global shortage of the chemical, with rising prices, and that Manley-Regan would obtain its supply from GFI Chemicals, Inc. When GFI could not deliver, Manley-Regan told Rockland that it could not fulfill the contract. Rockland bought an equivalent amount of the chemical elsewhere at an increased price and filed a suit in a federal district court against Manley-Regan to recover the difference between the cost of the cover and the contract price. Manley-Regan argued that the failure of GFI, its sole source for the oxide, excused its failure to perform on the ground of commercial impracticability. Will the court agree? Why or why not? [*Rockland Industries, Inc. v. E+E (US) Inc., Manley-Regan Chemicals Division,* 991 F.Supp. 468 (D.Md. 1998)]

A QUESTION OF ETHICS AND SOCIAL RESPONSIBILITY

17–11. Bobby Murray Chevrolet, Inc., contracted to supply 1,200 school bus chassis to local school boards. The contract stated that "products of any manufacturer may be offered," but Bobby Murray submitted its orders exclusively to General Motors Corp. (GMC). When a shortage in automatic transmissions occurred, GMC informed the dealer that it could not fill the orders. Bobby Murray told the school boards, which then bought the chassis from another dealer. The boards sued Bobby Murray for breach of contract. The dealer responded that its obligation to perform was excused under the doctrine of commercial impracticability, in part because of GMC's failure to fill its orders. Given these facts, answer the following questions. [*Alamance County Board of Education v. Bobby Murray Chevrolet, Inc.,* 121 N.C.App. 222, 465 S.E.2d 306 (1996)]

1. How will the court likely decide this issue? What factors will the court consider in making its decision? Discuss fully.
2. If the decision were yours to make, would you excuse Bobby Murray from its performance obligations in these circumstances? Would your decision be any different if Bobby Murray had specified in its contract that GMC would be the exclusive source of supply instead of stating that "products of any manufacturer may be offered"?
3. Generally, how does the doctrine of commercial impracticability attempt to balance the rights of both parties to a contract?

FOR CRITICAL ANALYSIS

17–12. What are the circumstances under which courts should not allow fully informed contracting parties to agree to limit remedies?

Online Activities

ONLINE EXERCISE 17-1

Access the Fred Korematsu Law Library's Web site at

allrise.com/LAW/CONTRACTS/Ferguson8.html

This page summarizes three cases involving the doctrine of anticipatory repudiation. Read through the case summaries, and then answer the questions listed below. Note that the author uses various letters to refer to parties or items—including *P* for "plaintiff"; *D* for "defendant"; and *K* for "contract."

- What is the rationale for the doctrine of anticipatory repudiation according to the summary of *Hochster v. De La Tour,* an English case decided in 1853 (see footnote 3 in this chapter)?
- According to the author of this page, how does the doctrine of anticipatory repudiation lead to economic efficiency?
- What three UCC provisions are listed on this page? Why would the author include a hyperlink to UCC 2–609? Does that UCC provision have anything to do with the doctrine of anticipatory repudiation? If so, in what way?

Before the Test

Go to the *Business Law Today* home page at http://blt.westbuslaw.com. Click on TestTutor.® You will find twenty interactive questions relating to this chapter.

CHAPTER 18

Warranties & Product Liability

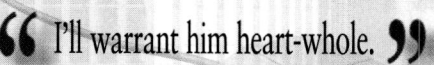

> "I'll warrant him heart-whole."
>
> William Shakespeare, 1564–1616
> (English dramatist and poet)

CONTENTS

LEARNING OBJECTIVES

After reading this chapter, you should be able to:

1. Describe the types of warranties that may arise in a sales or lease transaction.
2. Indicate how warranties may be disclaimed and the legal effect of warranty disclaimers.
3. Discuss how negligence and misrepresentation can provide a basis for a product liability action.
4. List the requirements for an action in strict product liability.
5. Summarize the defenses that can be raised against product liability claims.

Warranty is an age-old concept. In sales and lease law, a warranty is an assurance by one party of the existence of a fact on which the other party can rely. Just as William Shakespeare's character warranted his friend "heart-whole" in the play *As You Like It,* so sellers and lessors warrant to those who purchase or lease their goods that the goods are as represented or will be as promised.

The Uniform Commercial Code (UCC) has numerous rules governing the concept of product warranty as it occurs in sales and lease contracts. That will be the subject matter of the first part of this chapter. A natural addition to the discussion is *product liability:* Who is liable to consumers, users, and bystanders for physical harm and property damage caused by a particular good or the use thereof? Product liability encompasses the contract theory of warranty, as well as the tort theories of negligence and strict liability (discussed in Chapter 4).

Warranties

Article 2 (on sales) and Article 2A (on leases) of the UCC designate several types of warranties that can arise in a sales or lease contract, including warranties of title, express warranties, and implied warranties.

WARRANTIES OF TITLE

Title warranty arises automatically in most sales contracts. The UCC imposes three types of warranties of title.

Good Title In most cases, sellers warrant that they have good and valid title to the goods sold and that transfer of the title is rightful [UCC 2–312(1)(a)]. • **EXAMPLE 18.1** Sharon steals goods from Miguel and sells them to Carrie, who does not know that the goods are stolen. If Miguel reclaims the goods from Carrie, which he has a right to do, Carrie can then sue Sharon for breach of warranty. When Sharon sold Carrie the goods, Sharon *automatically* warranted to her that the title conveyed was valid and that its transfer was rightful. Because this was not in fact the case, Sharon breached the warranty of title imposed by UCC 2–312(1)(a) and became liable to the buyer for the appropriate damages. •

• **LIEN**
An encumbrance on a property to satisfy a debt or protect a claim for payment of a debt.

No Liens A second warranty of title provided by the UCC protects buyers who are *unaware* of any encumbrances (claims, charges, or liabilities—usually called **liens**[1]) against goods at the time the contract was made [UCC 2–312(1)(b)]. This warranty protects buyers who, for example, unknowingly purchase goods that are subject to a creditor's security interest (see Chapter 22). If a creditor legally repossesses the goods from a buyer *who had no actual knowledge of the security interest,* the buyer can recover from the seller for breach of warranty.

Article 2A affords similar protection for lessees. Section 2A–211(1) provides that during the term of the lease, no claim of any third party will interfere with the lessee's enjoyment of the leasehold interest.

No Infringements A merchant is also deemed to warrant that the goods delivered are free from any copyright, trademark, or patent claims of a third person[2] [UCC 2–312(3), 2A–211(2)]. If this warranty is breached and the buyer is sued by the party holding copyright, trademark, or patent rights in the goods, the buyer must notify the seller of the litigation within a reasonable time to enable the seller to decide whether to defend the lawsuit. If the seller states in writing that he or she has decided to defend and agrees to bear all expenses, including that of an adverse judgment, then the buyer must let the seller undertake litigation; otherwise, the buyer loses all rights against the seller if any infringement liability is established [UCC 2–607(3)(b), 2–607(5)(b)].

Article 2A provides for the same notice of litigation in situations that involve leases rather than sales [UCC 2A–516(3)(b), 2A–516(4)(b)]. There is an exception for leases to individual consumers for personal, family, or household purposes. A consumer who fails to notify the lessor within a reasonable time does not lose his or

1. Pronounced *leens.*
2. Recall from Chapter 15 that a *merchant* is defined in UCC 2–104(1) as a person who deals in goods of the kind involved in the sales contract or who, by occupation, presents himself or herself as having knowledge or skill peculiar to the goods involved in the transaction.

her remedy against the lessor for any liability established in the litigation [UCC 2A–516(3)(b)].

Disclaimer of Title Warranty In an ordinary sales transaction, the title warranty can be disclaimed or modified only by *specific language* in the contract [UCC 2–312(2)]. For example, sellers can assert that they are transferring only such rights, title, and interest as they have in the goods. In a lease transaction, the disclaimer must "be specific, be by a writing, and be conspicuous" [UCC 2A–214(4)].

EXPRESS WARRANTIES

• **EXPRESS WARRANTY**
A seller's or lessor's oral or written promise, ancillary to an underlying sales or lease agreement, as to the quality, description, or performance of the goods being sold or leased.

A seller or lessor can create an **express warranty** by making representations concerning the quality, condition, description, or performance potential of the goods. Under UCC 2–313 and 2A–210, express warranties arise when a seller or lessor indicates any of the following:

1. That the goods conform to any affirmation or promise of fact that the seller or lessor makes to the buyer or lessee about the goods. Such affirmations or promises are usually made during the bargaining process. Statements such as "these drill bits will penetrate stainless steel—and without dulling" are express warranties.
2. That the goods conform to any description of them. For example, a label that reads "Crate contains one 150-horsepower diesel engine" or a contract that calls for the delivery of a "camel's-hair coat" creates an express warranty.
3. That the goods conform to any sample or model of the goods shown to the buyer or lessee.

"Cheat me in the price, but not in the goods."
THOMAS FULLER, 1608–1661
(English clergyman)

Basis of the Bargain To create an express warranty, a seller or lessor does not have to use formal words such as *warrant* or *guarantee* [UCC 2–313(2), 2A–210(2)]. The UCC requires that for an express warranty to be created, the affirmation, promise, description, or sample must become part of the "basis of the bargain" [UCC 2–313(1), 2A–210(1)]. Just what constitutes the basis of the bargain is hard to say. The UCC does not define the concept, and it is a question of fact in each case whether a representation was made at such a time and in such a way that it induced the buyer or lessee to enter into the contract.

Statements of Opinion Statements of fact create express warranties. If the seller or lessor merely makes a statement that relates to the supposed value or worth of the goods, or makes a statement of opinion or recommendation about the goods, however, the seller or lessor is not creating an express warranty [UCC 2–313(2), 2A–210(2)].

• EXAMPLE 18.2 A seller claims that "this is the best used car to come along in years; it has four new tires and a 350-horsepower engine just rebuilt this year." The seller has made several *affirmations of fact* that can create a warranty: the automobile has an engine; it has a 350-horsepower engine; it was rebuilt this year; there are four tires on the automobile; and the tires are new. The seller's *opinion* that the vehicle is "the best used car to come along in years," however, is known as "puffing" and creates no warranty. (*Puffing* is the expression of opinion by a seller or lessor that is not made as a representation of fact.) •

A statement relating to the value of the goods, such as "it's worth a fortune" or "anywhere else you'd pay $10,000 for it," does not usually create a warranty. If the seller or lessor is an expert and gives an opinion as an expert to a layperson, though, then a warranty may be created.

It is not always easy to determine what constitutes an express warranty and what constitutes puffing. The reasonableness of the buyer's or lessee's reliance appears to be the controlling criterion in many cases. For example, a salesperson's statements that a ladder "will never break" and will "last a lifetime" are so clearly improbable that no reasonable buyer should rely on them. Additionally, the context within which a statement is made might be relevant in determining the reasonableness of the buyer's or lessee's reliance. For example, a reasonable person is more likely to rely on a written statement made in an advertisement than on a statement made orally by a salesperson. In a case discussed in this chapter's *Business Law in Action*, the criterion used by the court was whether a seller's statements went to the "basis of the bargain."

Business Law in Action • SOMETIMES, "PUFFERY" BECOMES THE "BASIS OF THE BARGAIN"

It could be said that every salesperson would like every statement that he or she makes to be deemed puffery, whereas every consumer would like every statement made by a salesperson to constitute an express warranty. The UCC sets forth the kind of statements that will constitute express warranties [UCC 2–313(1)]. The UCC also states that "an affirmation merely of the value of the goods or a statement purporting to be merely the seller's opinion or commendation of the goods does not create a warranty" [UCC 2–313(2)]. The latter provision has been called the "puffing" exception to UCC 2–313. In the real world, however, there is often no bright line that separates statements that amount to mere puffery and statements that form express warranties.

Consider the statements made by an Illinois used-car dealer to Michael and Carla Weng about a used car that they ultimately purchased. The salesperson assured the Wengs that the car was "in good condition," was "a good reliable car," was "mechnically sound," and had "no problems." The salesperson later stated that he was merely giving his opinion. The Wengs, however, believed that his words constituted an express warranty, and when the car proved not to be in good condition, reliable, or mechanically sound, the Wengs sued the dealer for breach of warranty.

A CAR SALESPERSON AND POTENTIAL BUYERS REVIEW THE TERMS OF A DEAL. DOES EVERYTHING A SALESPERSON SAYS ABOUT A PRODUCT CONSTITUTE PART OF THE "BASIS OF THE BARGAIN"?

At trial, the Wengs lost. The trial court concluded that the Wengs should have realized that the salesperson's statements were mere puffery. After all, the car cost only $800, was ten years old, and had almost 100,000 miles on it. On appeal, however, the Wengs prevailed. The reviewing court believed that the salesperson's statement that the car was "in good condition" was an affirmation of fact and therefore created an express warranty. The court reasoned that the salesperson's statements, even if the buyers had not relied on them, became "part of the basis of the bargain." Therefore, stated the appellate court, "It is not necessary . . . for the buyer to show reasonable reliance upon the seller's affirmations in order to make the affirmations part of the basis of the bargain . . . . This burden is upon the seller to establish by clear, affirmative proof that the affirmations *did not become part of the basis of the bargain.*" [Emphasis added] According to the court, the seller did not meet this burden of proof.[a]

FOR CRITICAL ANALYSIS

In reading the court's words, is there really a clear line between language considered to be mere puffing and language considered to create an express warranty?

a. *Weng v. Allison*, 287 Ill.App.3d 535, 678 N.E.2d 1254, 223 Ill.Dec. 123 (1997).

IMPLIED WARRANTIES

• **IMPLIED WARRANTY**
A warranty that the law derives by implication or inference from the nature of the transaction or the relative situation or circumstances of the parties.

An **implied warranty** is one that *the law derives* by implication or inference from the nature of the transaction or the relative situation or circumstances of the parties. In an action based on breach of implied warranty, it is necessary to show that an implied warranty existed and that the breach of the warranty proximately caused the damage sustained. We look here at some of the implied warranties that arise under the UCC. (See also this chapter's *Technology and the Year 2000 Problem* for a discussion of how year 2000 problems have given rise to lawsuits for breach of implied warranties.)

Technology and the Year 2000 Problem

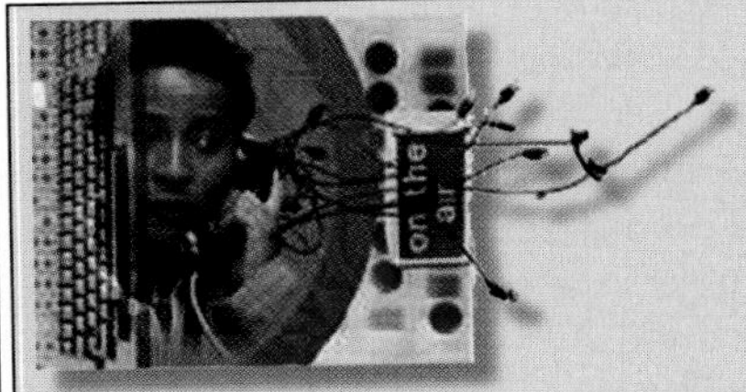

Quite a few years ago, when computers had very little capacity, programmers looked every which way to save "space." Rather than write out the year 1980, for example, they would simply leave two-digit spaces and put in 80. The system worked without a hitch until the mid-1990s, when people began to realize that in a very short time the year 2000 (or Y2K, as the year 2000 is referred to among programmers and businesses) would be upon us—and the last two digits in computer software would then be 00. This meant that software programmed with a two-digit number space for years could malfunction when the year turns to 2000.

For example, without a Y2K "fix," computer equipment designed to accept credit cards would not recognize credit cards with expiration dates after 1999. Legal analysts familiar with the Y2K problem argued that anything with an electronic component, including paper shredders and fax machines, has the potential for such a problem. Consequently, every sales contract would be affected.

Should sellers of software and electronic equipment who did not anticipate this Y2K problem be liable for breach of an implied warranty when the problem causes the buyer to incur damages? Yes, according to literally hundreds of lawyers who have filed Y2K lawsuits. The first suit was initiated by attorney Brian Parker on behalf of Sam Katz, the owner of the Produce Palace Grocery Store in Warren, Michigan. Katz's computer equipment failed in early 1998 when customers used credit cards with year 2000 expiration dates. The number of similar lawsuits has continued to rise. The first class-action suit was filed on behalf of Atlas International Limited in December 1997 against Software Business Technologies, Inc. The plaintiffs alleged, among other things, breach of warranty. The plaintiffs contended that Software Business had been forcing customers to buy an expensive new version of its accounting software to correct the Y2K problem instead of providing a free "patch" to resolve the issue. Other class-action suits have been brought against manufacturers of accounting and antivirus software.

Some analysts estimate that the total damages for Y2K problems could run as high as $100 billion.[a] Others estimate that such damages could reach $1 trillion.[b] The damages will occur because financial software may make errors relating to billing, interest, and payroll calculations. For example, a company's billing software may calculate that a bill was due to be paid one hundred years ago, instead of in the year 2000, and add interest charges accordingly. Additionally, manufacturers' computerized ordering systems may fail, causing delays. Some computer chips may malfunction. The result may be faulty security systems as well as faulty mechanical equipment, including elevators.

Defendants in Y2K suits for breach of contract and breach of warranty have argued that the Y2K problem is an event similar to a *force majeure* (a French term loosely defined as an "act of God"—see Chapter 43). To date, most courts have rejected this argument, because the coming of the year 2000 was fully anticipated.

Generally, lawsuits against computer companies based on Y2K claims will decrease in number once the year 2000 has come and gone. Most computer companies have already agreed to fix the problem. Only in cases where the "fix" was unsuccessful will such lawsuits continue to be brought.

FOR CRITICAL ANALYSIS

Do those who are sued for Y2K problems have any valid defense?

a. *Lawyers Weekly USA,* May 18, 1998, p. 20.
b. Rajiv Chandrasekaran, "Responsibility for the 'Millennium Bug' Puts a Gleam in Lawyers' Eyes," *International Herald Tribune,* May 4, 1998, p. 2.

INTERNET CONNECT

Implied Warranty of Merchantability Every sale or lease of goods made *by a merchant* who deals in goods of the kind sold or leased automatically gives rise to an **implied warranty of merchantability** [UCC 2–314, 2A–212]. Thus, a merchant who is in the business of selling ski equipment makes an implied warranty of merchantability every time the merchant sells a pair of skis, but a neighbor selling his or her skis at a garage sale does not.

• IMPLIED WARRANTY OF MERCHANTABILITY
A warranty that goods being sold or leased are reasonably fit for the general purpose for which they are sold or leased, are properly packaged and labeled, and are of proper quality. The warranty automatically arises in every sale or lease of goods made by a merchant who deals in goods of the kind sold or leased.

Merchantable Goods. Goods that are *merchantable* are "reasonably fit for the ordinary purposes for which such goods are used." They must be of at least average, fair, or medium-grade quality. The quality must be comparable to a level that will pass without objection in the trade or market for goods of the same description. To be merchantable, the goods must also be adequately packaged and labeled as provided by the agreement, and they must conform to the promises or affirmations of fact made on the container or label, if any.

An implied warranty of merchantability also imposes on the merchant liability for the safe performance of the product. It makes no difference whether the merchant knew of or could have discovered a defect that makes the product unsafe—he or she is liable in either situation. Of course, merchants are not absolute insurers against all accidents arising in connection with the goods. For example, a bar of soap is not unmerchantable merely because a user could slip and fall by stepping on it.

Merchantable Food. The UCC recognizes the serving of food or drink to be consumed on or off the premises as a sale of goods subject to the implied warranty of merchantability [UCC 2–314(1)]. "Merchantable" food means food that is fit to eat. Courts generally determine whether food is fit to eat on the basis of consumer expectations. For example, the courts assume that consumers should reasonably expect to find on occasion bones in fish fillets, cherry pits in cherry pie, a nutshell in a package of shelled nuts, and so on—because such substances are natural incidents of the food. In contrast, consumers would not reasonably expect to find an inchworm in a can of peas or a piece of glass in a soft drink—because these substances are not natural to the food product.[3] In the following classic case, the court had to determine whether a fish bone was a substance that one should reasonably expect to find in fish chowder.

3. See, for example, *Mexicali Rose v. Superior Court,* 1 Cal.4th 617, 4 Cal.Rptr.2d 145, 822 P.2d 1292 (1992).

CASE 18.1 Webster v. Blue Ship Tea Room, Inc.

Supreme Judicial Court of Massachusetts, 1964.
347 Mass. 421,
198 N.E.2d 309.

HISTORICAL AND CULTURAL SETTING *Chowder, a soup or stew made with fresh fish, possibly originated in the fishing villages of Brittany (a French province located west of Paris) and was probably carried to Canada and New England by Breton fishermen. In the nineteenth century and earlier, recipes for chowder did not call for the removal of the fish bones. Chowder recipes in the first half of the twentieth century remained as they had in previous centuries, sometimes specifying that the fish head, tail, and backbone were to be broken in pieces and boiled, with the "liquor thus produced * * * added to the balance of the chowder."[a] By the mid–twentieth century, there was a considerable body of case law concerning implied warranties and foreign and natural substances in food. It was perhaps inevitable that sooner or later, a consumer injured by a fish bone in chowder would challenge the merchantability of chowder containing fish bones.*

a. Fannie Farmer, *The Boston Cooking School Cook Book* (Boston: Little Brown Co., 1937), p. 166.

CASE 18.1—Continued

BACKGROUND AND FACTS Blue Ship Tea Room, Inc., was located in Boston in an old building overlooking the ocean. Webster, who had been born and raised in New England, went to the restaurant and ordered fish chowder. The chowder was milky in color. After three or four spoonfuls, she felt something lodged in her throat. As a result, she underwent two esophagoscopies; in the second esophagoscopy, a fish bone was found and removed. Webster filed suit against the restaurant in a Massachusetts state court for breach of the implied warranty of merchantability. The jury rendered a verdict for Webster, and the restaurant appealed to the state's highest court.

IN THE WORDS OF THE COURT . . .
REARDON, Justice.

* * * *

We must decide whether a fish bone lurking in a fish chowder * * * constitutes a breach of implied warranty under applicable provisions of the Uniform Commercial Code * * * .

* * * [T]he joys of life in New England include the ready availability of fresh fish chowder. We should be prepared to cope with the hazards of fish bones, the occasional presence of which in chowders is, it seems to us, to be anticipated, and which, in the light of a hallowed tradition, do not impair their fitness or merchantability.

DECISION AND REMEDY The Supreme Judicial Court of Massachusetts entered a judgment for the defendant, Blue Ship Tea Room.

FOR CRITICAL ANALYSIS—Cultural Consideration *If the fish chowder had been served in a restaurant located in, say, Nebraska, instead of a restaurant in New England, would the outcome of this case have been different? Should it have?*

• **IMPLIED WARRANTY OF FITNESS FOR A PARTICULAR PURPOSE**
A warranty that goods sold or leased are fit for a particular purpose. The warranty arises when any seller or lessor knows the particular purpose for which a buyer or lessee will use the goods and knows that the buyer or lessee is relying on the skill and judgment of the seller or lessor to select suitable goods.

Implied Warranty of Fitness for a Particular Purpose The **implied warranty of fitness for a particular purpose** arises when any seller or lessor (merchant or nonmerchant) knows the particular purpose for which a buyer or lessee will use the goods and knows that the buyer or lessee is relying on the skill and judgment of the seller or lessor to select suitable goods [UCC 2–315, 2A–213].

A "particular purpose" of the buyer or lessee differs from the "ordinary purpose for which goods are used" (merchantability). Goods can be merchantable but unfit for a particular purpose. • **EXAMPLE 18.3** Suppose that you need a gallon of paint to match the color of your living room walls—a light shade somewhere between coral and peach. You take a sample to your local hardware store and request a gallon of paint of that color. Instead, you are given a gallon of bright blue paint. Here, the salesperson has not breached any warranty of implied merchantability—the bright blue paint is of high quality and suitable for interior walls—but he or she has breached an implied warranty of fitness for a particular purpose.•

A seller or lessor does not need to have actual knowledge of the buyer's or lessee's particular purpose. It is sufficient if a seller or lessor "has reason to know" the purpose. The buyer or lessee, however, must have *relied* on the skill or judgment of the seller or lessor in selecting or furnishing suitable goods for an implied warranty to be created.

• **EXAMPLE 18.4** For example, Bloomberg leases a computer from Future Tech, a lessor of technical business equipment. Bloomberg tells the clerk that she wants a computer that will run a complicated new engineering graphics program at a realistic speed. Future Tech leases Bloomberg an Architex One computer with a CPU speed of only 133 megahertz, even though a speed of at least 400 megahertz would be required to run Bloomberg's graphics program at a "realistic speed." Bloomberg, after realizing that it takes her forever to run her program, wants her money back. Here, because Future Tech has breached the implied warranty of fitness for a particular purpose, Bloomberg normally will be able to recover. The clerk knew specifically that Bloomberg wanted a computer with enough speed to run certain software. Furthermore, Bloomberg relied on the clerk to furnish a computer that would fulfill this purpose. Because Future Tech did not do so, the warranty was breached. •

Other Implied Warranties Implied warranties can also arise (or be excluded or modified) as a result of course of dealing, course of performance, or usage of trade [UCC 2–314(3), 2A–212(3)]. In the absence of evidence to the contrary, when both parties to a sales or lease contract have knowledge of a well-recognized trade custom, the courts will infer that both parties intended for that trade custom to apply to their contract. For example, if an industry-wide custom is to lubricate a new car before it is delivered and a dealer fails to do so, the dealer can be held liable to a buyer for damages resulting from the breach of an implied warranty. This, of course, would also be negligence on the part of the dealer.

OVERLAPPING WARRANTIES

¡BE AWARE!
Express and implied warranties do not necessarily displace each other. More than one warranty can cover the same goods in the same transaction.

Sometimes two or more warranties are made in a single transaction. An implied warranty of merchantability, an implied warranty of fitness for a particular purpose, or both, can exist in addition to an express warranty. For example, when a sales contract for a new car states that "this car engine is warranted to be free from defects for 36,000 miles or thirty-six months, whichever occurs first," there is an express warranty against all defects and an implied warranty that the car will be fit for normal use.

The rule under the UCC is that express and implied warranties are construed as *cumulative* if they are consistent with one another [UCC 2–317, 2A–215]. If the warranties are inconsistent, the courts usually hold as follows:

1. *Express* warranties displace inconsistent *implied* warranties, except for implied warranties of fitness for a particular purpose.
2. Samples take precedence over inconsistent general descriptions.
3. Technical specifications displace inconsistent samples or general descriptions.

In the example described earlier, suppose that when Bloomberg leases the computer from Future Tech, the contract contains an express warranty concerning the speed of the CPU and the application programs that the computer is capable of running. Bloomberg does not realize that the speed expressly warranted in the contract is insufficient for her needs. Bloomberg later claims that Future Tech has breached the implied warranty of fitness for a particular purpose. Here, although the express warranty would take precedence over any implied warranty of merchantability, it normally would not take precedence over an implied warranty of fitness for a particular purpose. Bloomberg therefore has a good claim for the breach of implied warranty of fitness for a particular purpose, because she made it clear that she was leasing the computer to perform certain tasks.

THIRD PARTY BENEFICIARIES OF WARRANTIES

One of the general principles of contract law is that unless you are one of the parties to a contract, you have no rights under the contract. In other words, *privity of contract* must exist between a plaintiff and a defendant before any action based on a contract can be maintained. Two notable exceptions to the rule of privity are assignments and third party beneficiary contracts (these topics were discussed in Chapter 13). Another exception is made under warranty laws so that third parties can recover for harms suffered as a result of breached warranties.

There has been sharp disagreement among state courts as to how far warranty liability should extend, however. In view of this disagreement, the UCC offers three alternatives for liability to third parties [UCC 2–318, 2A–216]. All three alternatives are intended to eliminate the privity requirement with respect to certain enumerated types of injuries (personal versus property) for certain beneficiaries (for example, household members or bystanders).

WARRANTY DISCLAIMERS

Because each type of warranty is created in a special way, the manner in which warranties can be disclaimed or qualified by a seller or lessor varies depending on the type of warranty.

Express Warranties As already stated, any affirmation of fact or promise, description of the goods, or use of samples or models by a seller or lessor creates an express warranty. Obviously, then, express warranties can be excluded if the seller or lessor carefully refrains from making any promise or affirmation of fact relating to the goods, describing the goods, or using a sample or model.

The UCC does permit express warranties to be negated or limited by specific and unambiguous language, provided that this is done in a manner that protects the buyer or lessee from surprise. Therefore, a written disclaimer in language that is clear and conspicuous, and called to a buyer's or lessee's attention, could negate all oral express warranties not included in the written sales contract [UCC 2–316(1), 2A–214(1)]. This allows the seller or lessor to avoid false allegations that oral warranties were made, and it ensures that only representations made by properly authorized individuals are included in the bargain.

Note, however, that a buyer or lessee must be made aware of any warranty disclaimers or modifications *at the time the contract is formed*. In other words, any oral or written warranties—or disclaimers—made during the bargaining process as part of a contract's formation cannot be modified at a later time by the seller or lessor.

> **ON THE WEB**
> For an example of an "as is" clause, see the warranty disclaimer provided by the University of Minnesota for one of its research software products at **www.cmrr.drad.umn.edu/stimulate/stimUsersGuide/node7.html**.

Implied Warranties Generally speaking, unless circumstances indicate otherwise, the implied warranties of merchantability and fitness are disclaimed by the expressions "as is," "with all faults," and other similar expressions that in common understanding call the buyer's or lessee's attention to the fact that there are no implied warranties [UCC 2–316(3)(a), 2A–214(3)(a)].

The UCC also permits a seller or lessor to specifically disclaim an implied warranty either of fitness or of merchantability [UCC 2–316(2), 2A–214(2)]. To disclaim an implied warranty of fitness for a particular purpose, the disclaimer *must* be in writing and be conspicuous. The word *fitness* does not have to be mentioned in the writing; it is sufficient if, for example, the disclaimer states, "THERE ARE NO WARRANTIES THAT EXTEND BEYOND THE DESCRIPTION ON THE FACE HEREOF."

A merchantability disclaimer must be more specific; it must mention the word *merchantability*. It need not be written; but if it is, the writing must be conspicuous [UCC 2–316(2), 2A–214(4)]. According to UCC 1–201(10),

A term or clause is conspicuous when it is so written that a reasonable person against whom it is to operate ought to have noticed it. A printed heading in capitals . . . is conspicuous. Language in the body of a form is conspicuous if it is in larger or other contrasting type or color.

• **EXAMPLE 18.5** Forbes, a merchant, sells Maves a particular lawn mower selected by Forbes with the characteristics clearly requested by Maves. At the time of the sale, Forbes orally tells Maves that he does not warrant the merchantability of the mower, as it is last year's model and has been used extensively as a demonstrator. If the mower proves to be defective and does not work, Maves can hold Forbes liable for breach of the warranty of fitness for a particular purpose but not for breach of the warranty of merchantability. Forbes's oral disclaimer mentioning the word *merchantability* is a proper disclaimer. For Forbes to have disclaimed the implied warranty of fitness for a particular purpose, however, a conspicuous writing would have been required. Because he made no written disclaimer, Forbes can still be held liable. •

The conspicuousness of a disclaimer of implied warranties was at issue in the following case.

CASE 18.2 Borden, Inc. v. Advent Ink Co.

Superior Court of Pennsylvania, 1997.
701 A.2d 255.

HISTORICAL AND TECHNOLOGICAL SETTING *Printing inks have two essential components: one that provides color and one that transports the color from the ink fountain (where the ink is stored) to the substrate (which comes into contact with the plates used to transfer the image). The component that transports the color is a liquid base. This liquid can be a solvent, but environmental regulations have caused printers to rely more on water. Water-based inks can be difficult to work with on some substrates, however. Brief exposure to the air can dry water-based ink quickly, affecting the printing equipment and requiring more frequent cleaning.*

BACKGROUND AND FACTS Borden, Inc., sold Aquablak, a dispersion ingredient used in water-based inks, to Advent Ink Company. On the front of the sales invoice, in red capital letters, was the phrase "SEE REVERSE SIDE." On the reverse side was a list of nineteen conditions of sale, the first of which was a disclaimer of warranties, including the implied warranty of merchantability. On the Aquablak label, beneath Borden's name, phone number, advertising slogan, and other brief statements, was another disclaimer of all warranties. Advent used the Aquablak to make ink that caused problems in the printing equipment of one of its customers. Advent lost the customer's account, which cost the firm over $1 million in lost profits and caused it to go out of business. When Advent did not pay for the Aquablak, Borden filed a suit in a Pennsylvania state court against Advent to recover the amount. Advent counterclaimed that the Aquablak had not complied with the implied warranties of merchantability and fitness for a particular purpose. Against this claim, Borden filed a motion for summary judgment, pointing to its disclaimers. Advent responded that the disclaimers were not sufficiently conspicuous. The court granted the motion in favor of Borden. Advent appealed.

IN THE WORDS OF THE COURT . . .

SAYLOR, Judge:

* * * *

* * * [T]he print on the reverse side of the invoice is no larger than one-sixteenth inch in height. All of the type appears to be bold-faced. Although the disclaimer of warranties is the first of nineteen numbered paragraphs, * * * nevertheless there is nothing to indicate that the first paragraph is any more significant than, for example, the seventh ("WEIGHTS") * * * .

CASE 18.2—Continued

Even more important, the reference on the front of the invoice to the terms on the reverse side is even less informative * * * . The reference * * * simply states "SEE REVERSE SIDE"; there is absolutely no indication that among the terms on the reverse side is an exclusion of warranties, including * * * the implied warranty of merchantability * * * so commonly taken for granted that its exclusion from a contract is recognized as a matter threatening surprise * * * .

* * * *

* * * Finally, while the heading "DISCLAIMER" and the disclaimer itself are printed in capitals, so too are the preceding lines of text, and they are printed in larger sizes of type. Taking into account all of these factors, we conclude that this disclaimer, like that on the invoice, is inconspicuous and therefore ineffective.

DECISION AND REMEDY The Superior Court of Pennsylvania held that the disclaimers were so inconspicuous as to be ineffective. The court affirmed the lower court's decision on other grounds, however.

FOR CRITICAL ANALYSIS—Economic Consideration *With regard to the conspicuousness of a disclaimer, should a merchant-buyer be held to a different standard than a nonmerchant?*

Buyer's or Lessee's Refusal to Inspect If a buyer or lessee actually examines the goods (or a sample or model) as fully as desired before entering into a contract, or if the buyer or lessee refuses to examine the goods on the seller's or lessor's demand that he or she do so, *there is no implied warranty with respect to defects that a reasonable examination would reveal or defects that are actually found* [UCC 2–316(3)(b), 2A–214(2)(b)].

• **EXAMPLE 18.6** Suppose that Joplin buys an ax at Gershwin's Hardware Store. No express warranties are made. Joplin, even after Gershwin requests that she inspect the ax, refuses to inspect it before buying it. Had she done so, she would have noticed that the handle of the ax was obviously cracked. If she is later injured by the defective ax, she normally will not be able to hold Gershwin liable for breach of the warranty of merchantability, because she would have spotted the defect during an inspection. •

¡WATCH OUT!
Courts generally view warranty disclaimers unfavorably, especially when consumers are involved.

Warranty Disclaimers and Unconscionability The UCC sections dealing with warranty disclaimers do not refer specifically to unconscionability as a factor. Ultimately, however, the courts will test warranty disclaimers with reference to the UCC's unconscionability standards [UCC 2–302, 2A–108]. Such things as lack of bargaining position, "take-it-or-leave-it" choices, and a buyer's or lessee's failure to understand or know of a warranty disclaimer will become relevant to the issue of unconscionability.

MAGNUSON-MOSS WARRANTY ACT

The Magnuson-Moss Warranty Act of 1975[4] was designed to prevent deception in warranties by making them easier to understand. The act is mainly enforced by the Federal Trade Commission (FTC). Additionally, the attorney general or a consumer who has been injured can enforce the act if informal procedures for settling disputes prove to be ineffective. The act modifies UCC warranty rules to some extent when consumer transactions are involved. The UCC, however, remains the primary codification of warranty rules for industrial and commercial transactions.

4. 15 U.S.C. Sections 2301–2312.

A TELEVISION'S LIMITED WARRANTY SETS OUT ITS TERMS. WHAT DISTINGUISHES A *LIMITED WARRANTY* FROM A *FULL WARRANTY?*

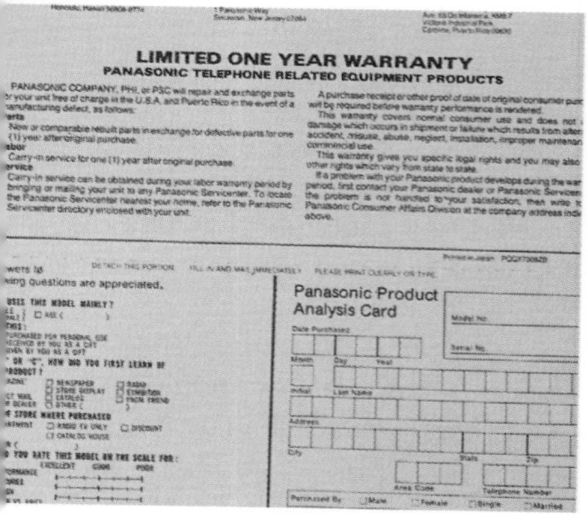

Under the Magnuson-Moss Act, no seller or lessor is required to give an express written warranty for consumer goods sold. If a seller or lessor chooses to make an express written warranty, however, and the cost of the consumer goods is more than $10, the warranty must be labeled as "full" or "limited." In addition, if the cost of the goods is more than $15, by FTC regulation, the warrantor must make certain disclosures fully and conspicuously in a single document in "readily understood language." This disclosure must state the names and addresses of the warrantor(s), what specifically is warranted, procedures for enforcement of the warranty, any limitations on warranty relief, and that the buyer has legal rights.

Full Warranty Although a *full warranty* may not cover every aspect of the consumer product sold, what it covers ensures some type of consumer satisfaction in case the product is defective. A full warranty requires free repair or replacement of any defective part; if the product cannot be repaired within a reasonable time, the consumer has the choice of either a refund or a replacement without charge. The full warranty frequently does not have a time limit on it. Any limitation on consequential damages must be *conspicuously* stated. Additionally, the warrantor need not perform warranty services if the problem with the product was caused by the consumer's unreasonable use of the product.

¡REMEMBER!

When a buyer or lessee is a consumer, a limitation on consequential damages for personal injuries resulting from nonconforming goods is *prima facie* unconscionable.

Limited Warranty A *limited warranty* arises when the written warranty fails to meet one of the minimum requirements of a full warranty. The fact that only a limited warranty is being given must be conspicuously designated. If it is only a time limitation that distinguishes a limited warranty from a full warranty, the Magnuson-Moss Warranty Act allows the warrantor to identify the warranty as a full warranty by such language as "full twelve-month warranty."

Implied Warranties Implied warranties do not arise under the Magnuson-Moss Warranty Act; they continue to be created according to UCC provisions. Implied warranties may not be disclaimed under the Magnuson-Moss Warranty Act, however. Although a warrantor can impose a time limit on the duration of an implied warranty, it has to correspond to the duration of the express warranty.[5]

Lemon Laws

Some purchasers of defective automobiles—called "lemons"—found that the remedies provided by the UCC, after limitations had been imposed by the seller, were inadequate. In response to the frustrations of these buyers, all of the states have enacted *lemon laws*. Basically, lemon laws provide that if an automobile under warranty possesses a defect that significantly affects the vehicle's value or use, and the defect has not been remedied by the seller within a specified number of opportunities (usually four), the buyer is entitled to a new car, replacement of defective parts, or return of all consideration paid.

"The biggest corporation, like the humblest private citizen, must be held to strict compliance with the will of the people."

THEODORE ROOSEVELT, 1858–1919
(Twenty-sixth president of the United States, 1901–1909)

In most states, lemon laws require an aggrieved new-car owner to notify the dealer or manufacturer of the problem and to provide the dealer or manufacturer with an opportunity to solve it. If the problem remains, the owner must then submit complaints to the arbitration program specified in the manufacturer's warranty

5. The time limit on an implied warranty occurring by virtue of the warrantor's express warranty must, of course, be reasonable, conscionable, and set forth in clear and conspicuous language on the face of the warranty.

before taking the case to court. Decisions by arbitration panels are binding on the manufacturer (that is, cannot be appealed by the manufacturer to the courts) but are not usually binding on the purchaser.

Most major automobile companies use their own arbitration panels. Some companies, however, subscribe to independent arbitration services, such as those provided by the Better Business Bureau. Although arbitration boards must meet state and/or federal standards of impartiality, industry-sponsored arbitration boards have been criticized for not being truly impartial in their decisions. In response to this criticism, some states have established mandatory, government-sponsored arbitration programs for lemon-law disputes.

ON THE WEB

For a discussion of "Lemon Law Basics," as well as information about other warranty laws, go to Car Talk's Web site at www.cartalk.cars.com/Got-A-Car/Lemon/lemon_general.html.

Product Liability

Manufacturers, sellers, and lessors of goods can be held liable to consumers, users, and bystanders for physical harm or property damage that is caused by the goods. This is called **product liability.** Product liability may be based on the warranty theories just discussed, as well as on the theories of negligence, misrepresentation, and strict liability. We look here at product liability based on negligence and misrepresentation.

• **PRODUCT LIABILITY**
The legal liability of manufacturers, sellers, and lessors of goods to consumers, users, and bystanders for injuries or damages that are caused by the goods.

NEGLIGENCE

Chapter 4 defined *negligence* as the failure to exercise the degree of care that a reasonable, prudent person would have exercised under the circumstances. If a manufacturer fails to exercise "due care" to make a product safe, a person who is injured by the product may sue the manufacturer for negligence.

Due care must be exercised in designing the product, in selecting the materials, in using the appropriate production process, in assembling the product, and in placing adequate warnings on the label informing the user of dangers of which an ordinary person might not be aware. The duty of care also extends to the inspection and testing of any purchased products that are used in the final product sold by the manufacturer.

A product liability action based on negligence does not require privity of contract between the injured plaintiff and the negligent defendant-manufacturer. Section 395 of the *Restatement (Second) of Torts* states as follows:

> A manufacturer who fails to exercise reasonable care in the manufacture of a chattel [movable good] which, unless carefully made, he should recognize as involving an unreasonable risk of causing physical harm to those who lawfully use it for a purpose for which the manufacturer should expect it to be used and to those whom he should expect to be endangered by its probable use, is subject to liability for physical harm caused to them by its lawful use in a manner and for a purpose for which it is supplied.

In other words, a manufacturer is liable for its failure to exercise due care to any person who sustained an injury proximately caused by a negligently made (defective) product, regardless of whether the injured person is in privity of contract with the negligent defendant-manufacturer or lessor. Relative to the long history of the common law, this exception to the privity requirement is a fairly recent development, dating to the early part of the twentieth century. A leading case in this respect is *MacPherson v. Buick Motor Co.*, which we present as this chapter's *Landmark in the Law.*

¡RECALL!
The elements of negligence include a duty of care, a breach of the duty, and an injury to the plaintiff proximately caused by the breach.

ON THE WEB

Law Journal EXTRA! has articles on current cases and issues in the area of product liability, as well as proposed legislation, at www.ljx.com/practice/productliability/index.html.

Landmark in the Law • MACPHERSON v. BUICK MOTOR CO. (1916)

In the landmark case of *MacPherson v. Buick Motor Co.*,[a] the New York Court of Appeals—New York's highest court—dealt with the liability of a manufacturer that failed to exercise reasonable care in manufacturing a finished product. The case was brought by Donald MacPherson, who suffered injuries while riding in a Buick automobile that suddenly collapsed because one of the wheels was made of defective wood. The spokes crumbled into fragments, throwing MacPherson out of the vehicle and injuring him.

MacPherson had purchased the car from a Buick dealer, but he brought suit against the manufacturer, Buick Motor Company. The wheel itself had not been made by Buick; it had been bought from another manufacturer. There was evidence, though, that the defects could have been discovered by reasonable inspection by Buick and that no such inspection had taken place. MacPherson charged Buick with negligence for putting a human life in imminent danger. The major issue before the court was whether Buick owed a duty of care to anyone except the immediate purchaser of the car (that is, the Buick dealer).

In deciding the issue, Justice Benjamin Cardozo stated that "[i]f the nature of a thing is such that it is reasonably certain to place life and limb in peril when negligently made, it is then a thing of danger. . . . If to the element of danger there is added knowledge that the thing will be used by persons other than the purchaser, and used without new tests, then, irrespective of contract, the manufacturer of this thing of danger is under a duty to make it carefully." The court concluded that "[b]eyond all question, the nature of an automobile gives warning of probable danger if its construction is defective. This automobile was designed to go 50 miles an hour. Unless its wheels were sound and strong, injury was almost certain."

Although Buick had not manufactured the wheel itself, the court held that Buick had a duty to inspect the wheels and that Buick "was responsible for the finished product." Therefore, Buick was liable to MacPherson for the injuries he sustained when he was thrown from the car.

a. 217 N.Y. 382, 111 N.E. 1050 (1916).

FOR CRITICAL ANALYSIS
To what extent, if any, have technological developments contributed to the courts' placing less emphasis on the doctrine of *caveat emptor* ("let the buyer beware") and more emphasis on the doctrine of *caveat venditor* ("let the seller beware")?

"One may smile, and smile, and be a villain."

WILLIAM SHAKESPEARE, 1564–1616
(English dramatist and poet)

MISREPRESENTATION

When a fraudulent misrepresentation has been made to a user or consumer, and that misrepresentation ultimately results in an injury, the basis of liability may be the tort of fraud. For example, the intentional mislabeling of packaged cosmetics and the intentional concealment of a product's defects would constitute fraudulent misrepresentation.

Strict Product Liability

Under the doctrine of strict liability (discussed in Chapter 4), people may be liable for the results of their acts regardless of their intentions or their exercise of reasonable care. Under this doctrine, liability does not depend on privity of contract. The injured party does not have to be the buyer or a third party beneficiary, as required under contract warranty theory. Indeed, this type of liability in law is not governed by the provisions of the UCC because it is a tort doctrine, not a principle of the law relating to sales contracts.

"The assault upon the citadel of privity [of contract] is proceeding in these days apace."

BENJAMIN CARDOZO, 1870–1938
(Associate justice of the United States Supreme Court, 1932–1938)

STRICT PRODUCT LIABILITY AND PUBLIC POLICY

Strict product liability is imposed by law as a matter of public policy. This policy rests on the threefold assumption that (1) consumers should be protected against unsafe products; (2) manufacturers and distributors should not escape liability for faulty products simply because they are not in privity of contract with the ultimate user of those products; and (3) manufacturers, sellers, and lessors of products are generally in a better position than consumers to bear the costs associated with injuries caused by their products—costs that they can ultimately pass on to all consumers in the form of higher prices.

California was the first state to impose strict product liability in tort on manufacturers. In the landmark decision that follows, the California Supreme Court sets out the reason for applying tort law rather than contract law to cases in which consumers are injured by defective products.

CASE 18.3 Greenman v. Yuba Power Products, Inc.

Supreme Court of California, 1962.
59 Cal.2d 57,
377 P.2d 897,
27 Cal.Rptr. 697.
mcs.newpaltz.edu/~zuckerman/cases/green1.htm[a]

HISTORICAL AND SOCIAL SETTING *From the earliest days of the common law, English courts applied a doctrine of strict liability. Often, persons whose conduct resulted in the injury of another were held liable for damages, even if they had not intended to injure anyone and had exercised reasonable care. This approach was abandoned around 1800 in favor of the fault approach, in which an action was considered tortious only if it was wrongful or blameworthy in some respect. Strict liability began to be reapplied to manufactured goods in several landmark cases in the 1960s, a decade during which many traditional assumptions were being challenged.*

a. This case is included within the Web site for an "Introduction to Law" course taught by Paul Zuckerman, a professor with the State University of New York at New Platz.

BACKGROUND AND FACTS The plaintiff, Greenman, wanted a Shopsmith—a combination power tool that could be used as a saw, drill, and wood lathe—after seeing a Shopsmith demonstrated by a retailer and studying a brochure prepared by the manufacturer. The plaintiff's wife bought and gave him one for Christmas. More than a year later, a piece of wood flew out of the lathe attachment of the Shopsmith while the plaintiff was using it, inflicting serious injuries on him. About ten and a half months later, the plaintiff filed suit in a California state court against both the retailer and the manufacturer for breach of warranties and negligence. The trial court jury found for the plaintiff. The case was ultimately appealed to the Supreme Court of California.

IN THE WORDS OF THE COURT . . .
TRAYNOR, Justice.

* * * *

Plaintiff introduced substantial evidence that his injuries were caused by defective design and construction of the Shopsmith. * * * The jury could therefore reasonably have concluded that the manufacturer negligently constructed the Shopsmith. The jury could also reasonably have concluded that statements in the manufacturer's brochure were untrue, that they constituted express warranties, and that plaintiff's injuries were caused by their breach.

* * * *

(Continued)

CASE 18.3—Continued

[But] to impose strict liability on the manufacturer under the circumstances of this case, it was not necessary for plaintiff to establish an express warranty * * * . A manufacturer is strictly liable in tort when an article he places on the market, knowing that it is to be used without inspection for defects, proves to have a defect that causes injury to a human being. * * *

* * * *

* * * The purpose of such liability is to insure that the costs of injuries resulting from defective products are borne by the manufacturers * * * rather than by the injured persons who are powerless to protect themselves.

DECISION AND REMEDY The Supreme Court of California upheld the jury verdict for the plaintiff. The manufacturer was held strictly liable in tort for the harm caused by its unsafe product.

FOR CRITICAL ANALYSIS—Ethical Consideration *What ethical doctrine underlies the doctrine of strict liability?*

REQUIREMENTS FOR STRICT LIABILITY

Section 402A of the *Restatement (Second) of Torts* indicates how it was envisioned that the doctrine of strict liability should be applied. It was issued in 1964, and during the decade following its release it became a widely accepted statement of the liabilities of sellers of goods (including manufacturers, processors, assemblers, packagers, bottlers, wholesalers, distributors, retailers, and lessors). Section 402A states as follows:

> (1) One who sells any product in a defective condition unreasonably dangerous to the user or consumer or to his property is subject to liability for physical harm thereby caused to the ultimate user or consumer or to his property, if
> (a) the seller is engaged in the business of selling such a product, and
> (b) it is expected to and does reach the user or consumer without substantial change in the condition in which it is sold.
> (2) The rule stated in Subsection (1) applies although
> (a) the seller has exercised all possible care in the preparation and sale of his product, and
> (b) the user or consumer has not bought the product from or entered into any contractual relation with the seller.

IF A CHILD IS INJURED BY A TOY, DOES HE OR SHE HAVE A CAUSE OF ACTION AGAINST THE MANUFACTURER?

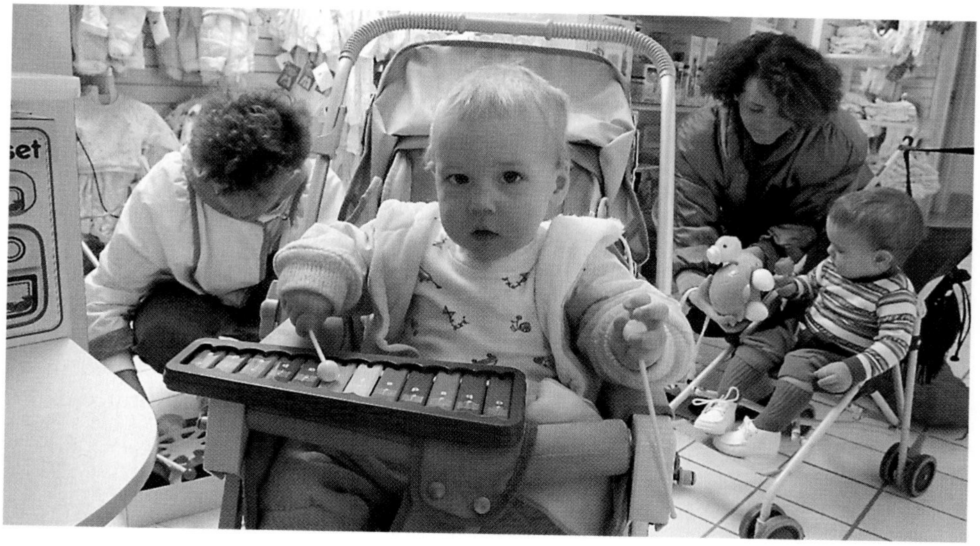

The bases for an action in strict liability as set forth in Section 402A of the *Restatement (Second) of Torts,* and as the doctrine came to be commonly applied, can be summarized as a series of six requirements, which are listed here. Depending on the jurisdiction, if these requirements were met, a manufacturer's liability to an injured party could be virtually unlimited.[6]

1. The product must be in a defective condition when the defendant sells it.
2. The defendant must normally be engaged in the business of selling (or otherwise distributing) that product.
3. The product must be unreasonably dangerous to the user or consumer because of its defective condition (in most states).
4. The plaintiff must incur physical harm to self or property by use or consumption of the product.
5. The defective condition must be the proximate cause of the injury or damage.
6. The goods must not have been substantially changed from the time the product was sold to the time the injury was sustained.

Thus, under these requirements, in any action against a manufacturer, seller, or lessor, the plaintiff does not have to show why or in what manner the product became defective. To recover damages, however, the plaintiff must show that the product was so "defective" as to be "unreasonably dangerous"; that the product caused the plaintiff's injury; and that at the time the injury was sustained, the condition of the product was essentially the same as when it left the hands of the defendant manufacturer, seller, or lessor.

A court could consider a product so defective as to be an **unreasonably dangerous product** if either (1) the product was dangerous beyond the expectation of the ordinary consumer or (2) a less dangerous alternative was economically feasible for the manufacturer, but the manufacturer failed to produce it. As will be discussed in the next section, a product may be unreasonably dangerous due to a flaw in the manufacturing process, a design defect, or an inadequate warning.

• UNREASONABLY DANGEROUS PRODUCT
In product liability, a product that is defective to the point of threatening a consumer's health and safety. A product will be considered unreasonably dangerous if it is dangerous beyond the expectation of the ordinary consumer or if a less dangerous alternative was economically feasible for the manufacturer, but the manufacturer failed to produce it.

Market-Share Liability

Generally, in all cases involving product liability, a plaintiff must prove that the defective product that caused his or her injury was the product of a specific defendant. In the last decade or so, in cases in which plaintiffs could not prove which of many distributors of a harmful product supplied the particular product that caused the plaintiffs' injuries, courts have dropped this requirement.

This has occurred in several cases involving DES (diethylstilbestrol), a drug administered in the past to prevent miscarriages. DES's harmful character was not realized until, a generation later, daughters of the women who had taken DES developed health problems, including vaginal carcinoma, that were linked to the drug. Partly because of the passage of time, a plaintiff-daughter often could not prove which pharmaceutical company—out of as many as three hundred—had marketed the DES her mother had ingested. In these cases, some courts applied market-share liability, holding that all firms that manufactured and distributed DES during the period in question were liable for the plaintiffs' injuries in proportion to the firms' respective shares of the market.[7]

6. Some states have enacted what are called *statutes of repose.* Basically, these statutes provide that after a specific statutory period of time from the date of manufacture or sale, a plaintiff is precluded from pursuing a cause of action for injuries or damages sustained from a product, even though the product is defective. The states of Illinois, Indiana, Alabama, Tennessee, Florida, Texas, and Nebraska are illustrative.
7. See, for example, *Martin v. Abbott Laboratories,* 102 Wash.2d 581, 689 P.2d 368 (1984).

Market-share liability has also been applied in other situations. • **EXAMPLE 18.7** In one case, a plaintiff who was a hemophiliac received injections of a blood protein known as antihemophiliac factor (AHF) concentrate. The plaintiff later tested positive for the AIDS (acquired immune deficiency syndrome) virus. Because it was not known which manufacturer was responsible for the particular AHF received by the plaintiff, the court held that all of the manufacturers of AHF could be held liable under a market-share theory of liability.[8] •

OTHER APPLICATIONS OF STRICT LIABILITY

Although the drafters of the *Restatement (Second) of Torts,* Section 402A, did not take a position on bystanders, all courts extend the strict liability of manufacturers and other sellers to injured bystanders. • **EXAMPLE 18.8** In one case, an automobile manufacturer was held liable for injuries caused by the explosion of a car's motor. A cloud of steam that resulted from the explosion caused multiple collisions because other drivers could not see well.[9] •

The rule of strict liability also is applicable to suppliers of component parts. • **EXAMPLE 18.9** General Motors buys brake pads from a subcontractor and puts them in Chevrolets without changing their composition. If those pads are defective, both the supplier of the brake pads and General Motors will be held strictly liable for the damages caused by the defects. •

Restatement (Third) of Torts: Products Liability

Because Section 402A of the *Restatement (Second) of Torts* did not clearly define such terms as "defective" and "unreasonably dangerous," they have been subject to different interpretations by different courts. Also, over the years, issues that had not even been imagined when Section 402A was written became points of contention and debate in the courts. These circumstances led to complex and confusing legal principles in the area of product liability and made it difficult to predict how a court might decide a certain case.

In the early 1990s, the American Law Institute (ALI) began drafting a new restatement of the principles and policies underlying product liability law. In particular, the ALI attempted to respond to questions that had not been part of the legal landscape thirty-five years before. The result was the *Restatement (Third) of Torts: Products Liability.* The final draft of the new *Restatement* was released in 1997, after five years of planning, drafting, and debating. The question now is whether state courts will adopt this new *Restatement* as rapidly as they did the *Restatement (Second) of Torts,* which spread the doctrine of strict liability throughout the United States in the late 1960s and early 1970s.

The law categorizes product defects into three types: manufacturing defects, design defects, and warning defects—each of which will be discussed shortly. The *Restatement (Third) of Torts: Products Liability* defines the three types of defects and integrates the applicable legal principles into the definitions. By defining defects in such a way, the new *Restatement* does away with some of the hard-to-understand distinctions that developed when different theories of liability were applied to the same defects.

8. *Smith v. Cutter Biological, Inc.,* 72 Haw. 416, 823 P.2d 717 (1991).
9. *Giberson v. Ford Motor Co.,* 504 S.W.2d 8 (Mo. 1974).

For example, in one case a court upheld a verdict that found a product "not defective" on a theory of strict liability but its manufacturer liable for harm caused by the product on a theory of breach of warranty.[10] The court based its decision on the different tests that exist under the different legal theories. The new *Restatement* sets out a single test for each type of defect to be applied regardless of the type of legal claim.

MANUFACTURING DEFECTS

According to Section 2(a) of the new *Restatement,* a product "contains a manufacturing defect when the product departs from its intended design even though all possible care was exercised in the preparation and marketing of the product." This statement imposes liability on the manufacturer (and on the wholesaler and retailer) whether or not the manufacturer acted "reasonably." This is strict liability, or liability without fault.

DESIGN DEFECTS

A determination that a product has a design defect (or a warning defect, discussed later in this chapter) can affect all of the units of a product. A product "is defective in design when the foreseeable risks of harm posed by the product could have been reduced or avoided by the adoption of a reasonable alternative design by the seller or other distributor, or a predecessor in the commercial chain of distribution, and the omission of the alternative design renders the product not reasonably safe."[11]

Different states have applied different tests to determine whether a product has a design defect under the *Restatement (Second) of Torts,* Section 402A. There has been much controversy about the different tests, particularly over one that focused on the "consumer expectations" concerning a product. The test prescribed by the *Restatement (Third) of Torts: Products Liability* focuses on a product's actual design and the reasonableness of that design.

To succeed in a product liability suit alleging a design defect, a plaintiff has to show that there is a reasonable alternative design. In other words, a manufacturer or other defendant is liable only when the harm was reasonably preventable. According to the Official Comments accompanying the new *Restatement,* factors that a court may consider on this point include

> the magnitude and probability of the foreseeable risks of harm, the instructions and warnings accompanying the product, and the nature and strength of consumer expectations regarding the product, including expectations arising from product portrayal and marketing. The relative advantages and disadvantages of the product as designed and as it alternatively could have been designed may also be considered. Thus, the likely effects of the alternative design on production costs; the effects of the alternative design on product longevity, maintenance, repair, and esthetics; and the range of consumer choice among products are factors that may be taken into account.

Note that "consumer expectations," instead of being the whole test, is only one factor taken into consideration. Another factor is the warning that accompanies a product. Can a warning insulate a manufacturer from liability for the harm caused by a design defect? That was the issue in the following case.

---

10. See, for example, *Denny v. Ford Motor Co.,* 87 N.Y.2d 248, 662 N.E.2d 730, 639 N.Y.S.2d 250 (1995). The *Restatement* has not eliminated all of these distinctions, however, because in some cases they may be necessary.

11. *Restatement (Third) of Torts: Products Liability,* Section 2(b).

CASE 18.4 Rogers v. Ingersoll-Rand Co.

U.S Court of Appeals,
District of Columbia Circuit, 1998.
144 F.3d 841.
laws.findlaw.com/DC/977131A.html[a]

COMPANY PROFILE *Ingersoll-Rand Company is a manufacturer of air compressors, construction and mining equipment, bearings and precision components, tools, locks and architectural hardware, and industrial machinery. The company also makes Bobcat skid-steer loaders, Blaw-Knox pavers, Club Car golf carts and light utility vehicles, and Thermo King transport temperature control systems. In joint ventures with other firms, Ingersoll-Rand is a supplier of pumps and hydrocarbon processing equipment and services. Ingersoll-Rand distributes its products in more than one hundred countries. Forty percent of its sales are outside the United States.*

a. This is a page within the Web site of FindLaw, a resource for Internet legal sources.

BACKGROUND AND FACTS Among the equipment that Ingersoll-Rand makes is a milling machine. In the maintenance manual that accompanies the machine are warnings that users should stay ten feet away from the rear of the machine when it is operating, verify that the back-up alarm is working, and check the area for the presence of others. There is also a sign on the machine that tells users to stay ten feet away. While using the machine to strip asphalt from a road being repaved, Terrill Wilson backed up. The alarm did not sound, and Cosandra Rogers, who was standing with her back to the machine, was run over and maimed. Rogers filed a suit in a federal district court against Ingersoll-Rand, alleging in part strict liability on the basis of a design defect. The jury awarded Rogers $10.2 million in compensatory damages and $6.5 million in punitive damages. Ingersoll-Rand appealed, emphasizing the adequacy of its warnings.

IN THE WORDS OF THE COURT . . .
SENTELLE, Justice.

* * * *

* * * Under [a risk-utility balancing] test [in a defective design case], a plaintiff must show the risks, costs and benefits of the product in question and alternative designs, and that the magnitude of the danger from the product outweighed the costs of avoiding danger. * * *

[Ingersoll-Rand argues that] the adequacy of its warnings [should be] the sole consideration in the risk-utility analysis. As Ingersoll-Rand would have it, once the jury evaluates the milling machine's warnings and finds them adequate, its job is over; it "should find for [the] defendant." * * * [T]he "warnings" defense would have instructed the jury that adequate warnings trump all other factors—including the "magnitude of the danger from the product" * * * .

* * * *

We do not mean to dispute that warnings may tip the balance in a manufacturer's favor in individual cases. On the other hand, warnings need not be the dispositive factor in every case. Here, for example, it seems reasonably foreseeable that a worker with her back to a milling machine would be in no position to "heed" a sign on the machine instructing her to keep ten feet away. Under these circumstances, a manufacturer may have a heightened responsibility to incorporate additional safety features to guard against foreseeable harm.

DECISION AND REMEDY The U.S. Court of Appeals for the District of Columbia Circuit upheld the jury's award. The court held that an adequate warning cannot immunize a manufacturer from any liability caused by a defectively designed product.

FOR CRITICAL ANALYSIS—Technological Consideration *What other safety features might a manufacturer in these circumstances use?*

WARNING DEFECTS

Product warnings and instructions alert consumers to the risks of using a product. A "reasonableness" test applies to this material. A product "is defective because of inadequate instructions or warnings when the foreseeable risks of harm posed by the product could have been reduced or avoided by the provision of reasonable instructions or warnings by the seller or other distributor, or a predecessor in the commercial chain of distribution, and the omission of the instructions or warnings renders the product not reasonably safe."[12]

Important factors for a court to consider under the *Restatement (Third) of Torts: Products Liability* include the risks of a product, the "content and comprehensibility" and "intensity of expression" of warnings and instructions, and the "characteristics of expected user groups."[13] For example, children would likely respond more readily to bright, bold, simple warning labels, while educated adults might need more detailed information.

There is no duty to warn about risks that are obvious or commonly known. Warnings about such risks do not add to the safety of a product and could even detract from it by making other warnings seem less significant. The obviousness of a risk and a user's decision to proceed in the face of that risk may be a defense in a product liability suit based on a warning defect. (This defense and other defenses in product liability suits are discussed later in this chapter.)

Generally, a seller must warn those who purchase its product of the harm that can result from the foreseeable misuse of the product as well. The key is the *foreseeability* of the misuse. According to the Official Comments accompanying the new *Restatement,* sellers "are not required to foresee and take precautions against every conceivable mode of use and abuse to which their products might be put."

Most states already apply the test outlined here to product warnings and instructions. Generally, everyone also agrees that despite the duty to warn, some risk is unavoidable and the users of a product bear some responsibility to prevent injury or damage. The difficult question, as noted in Chapter 4, has always been where to draw the line between the seller's liability and the user's responsibility.

ETHICAL ISSUE 18.1 ***Should consumers be warned that hot coffee can cause severe burns?*** In the last few years, a number of plaintiffs who have sustained burns due to coffee spills have alleged that the sellers of the coffee should have warned customers about the dangers of hot coffee. The problem is, what would such a warning entail? Should the warning state that coffee is served hot, or that hot coffee can cause burns? Coffee drinkers are already aware of these dangers, and plaintiffs in several coffee cases have conceded that they seek out hot coffee, know it can burn, and take precautions as a result.[14] What is not commonly known, though, is just how severe burns caused by coffee spills can be. Should manufacturers of coffee makers and sellers of hot coffee warn consumers of the severity of burns that can be caused by hot coffee? In one case addressing this issue, the court pointed out that such a warning would be self-defeating. In addition to having to deliver a "medical education" with every cup of coffee served, said the court, the warning would have to address such things as " the risk of burns in real life, starting with the number of cups of coffee sold annually, the number of these that spill (broken down by

---

12. *Restatement (Third) of Torts: Products Liability,* Section 2(c).
13. *Restatement (Third) of Torts: Products Liability,* Section 2, Comment h.
14. See, for example, *Greene v. Boddie-Noell Enterprises, Inc.,* 966 F.Supp. 416 (W.D.Va. 1997); and *Barnett v. Leiserv, Inc.,* 9137 F.3d 1356 (11th Cir. 1998).

location, such as home, restaurant, and car), and the probability that any given spill will produce a severe (as opposed to a mild or average) burn." According to the court, such a detailed warning, which would be equivalent to the package insert that comes with drugs, would only obscure the principal point—that precautions should be taken to avoid spills.[15]

Defenses to Product Liability

There are several defenses that manufacturers, sellers, or lessors can raise to avoid liability for harms caused by their products. We look at some of these defenses here.

Assumption of Risk

Assumption of risk can sometimes be used as a defense in a product liability action. For example, if a buyer fails to heed a product recall by the seller, a court might conclude that the buyer assumed the risk caused by the defect that led to the recall. To establish such a defense, the defendant must show that (1) the plaintiff knew and appreciated the risk created by the product defect and (2) the plaintiff voluntarily assumed the risk, even though it was unreasonable to do so. (See Chapter 4 for a more detailed discussion of assumption of risk.)

Product Misuse

Similar to the defense of voluntary assumption of risk is that of misuse of the product. Here, the injured party *does not know that the product is dangerous for a particular use* (contrast this with assumption of risk), but the use is not the one for which the product was designed. The courts have severely limited this defense, however. Even if the injured party does not know about the inherent danger of using the product in a wrong way, if the misuse is foreseeable, the seller must take measures to guard against it.

Comparative Negligence

Developments in the area of comparative negligence (discussed in Chapter 4) have even affected the doctrine of strict liability—the most extreme theory of product liability. Whereas previously the plaintiff's conduct was not a defense to strict liability, today many jurisdictions consider the negligent or intentional actions of both the plaintiff and the defendant in the apportionment of liability and damages. This means that even if a product was misused by the plaintiff, the plaintiff may nonetheless be able to recover at least some damages for injuries caused by the defendant's defective product.

Commonly Known Dangers

The dangers associated with certain products (such as sharp knives and guns) are so commonly known that manufacturers need not warn users of those dangers. If a defendant succeeds in convincing the court that a plaintiff's injury resulted from a *commonly known danger,* the defendant normally will not be liable.

15. *McMahon v. Bunn-O-Matic Corp.*, 150 F.3d 651 (7th Cir. 1998).

• **EXAMPLE 18.10** A classic case on this issue involved a plaintiff who was injured when an elastic exercise rope that she had purchased slipped off her foot and struck her in the eye, causing a detachment of the retina. The plaintiff claimed that the manufacturer should be liable because it had failed to warn users that the exerciser might slip off a foot in such a manner. The court stated that to hold the manufacturer liable in these circumstances "would go beyond the reasonable dictates of justice in fixing the liabilities of manufacturers." After all, stated the court, "[a]lmost every physical object can be inherently dangerous or potentially dangerous in a sense. . . . A manufacturer cannot manufacture a knife that will not cut or a hammer that will not mash a thumb or a stove that will not burn a finger. The law does not require [manufacturers] to warn of such common dangers."[16] •

A related defense is the *knowledgeable user* defense. If a particular danger (such as electrical shock) is or should be commonly known by particular users of the product (such as electricians), the manufacturer of electrical equipment need not warn these users of the danger. The following case illustrates this concept.

16. *Jamieson v. Woodward & Lothrop*, 247 F.2d 23, 101 D.C.App. 32 (1957).

CASE 18.5 Travelers Insurance Co. v. Federal Pacific Electric Co.

Supreme Court of New York,
Appellate Division, First Department, 1995.
211 A.D.2d 40,
625 N.Y.S.2d 121.

COMPANY PROFILE *Federal Pacific Electric Company makes electrical equipment, including Stab-Lok circuit breakers. Reliance Electric Company bought Federal from UV Industries Liquidating Trust, Inc., in 1979. In 1980, Federal revealed that it had obtained Underwriters Laboratories (UL) certification for its Stab-Lok circuit breakers by cheating on UL tests. Reliance sued UV Industries. A cash settlement ended the lawsuit in 1984. Two years later, Reliance sold Federal to the Challenger Electric Equipment Corporation. The federal Consumer Product Safety Commission later concluded that the Stab-Lok circuit breakers "did not present a serious risk of injury."*

BACKGROUND AND FACTS A water pipe burst, flooding a switchboard at the offices of RCA Global Communications, Inc. This tripped the switchboard circuit breakers. RCA employees assigned to reactivate the switchboard included an electrical technician with twelve years of on-the-job training, a licensed electrician, and an electrical engineer with twenty years of experience who had studied power engineering in college. The employees attempted to switch one of the circuit breakers back on without testing for short circuits, which they later admitted they knew how to do and should have done. The circuit breaker failed to engage but ignited an explosive fire. RCA filed a claim with its insurer, the Travelers Insurance Company. Travelers paid the claim and filed a suit in a New York state court against, among others, the Federal Pacific Electric Company, the supplier of the circuit breakers. Travelers alleged that Federal had been negligent in failing to give RCA adequate warnings and instructions regarding the circuit breakers. The court apportioned 15 percent of the responsibility for the fire to Federal. Federal appealed.

IN THE WORDS OF THE COURT . . .

NARDELLI, Justice.

* * * *

* * * [T]here is "no necessity to warn a customer already aware—through common knowledge or learning—of a specific hazard" and, in the proper case, the court can decide as a matter of law that there is no duty to warn or that the duty has been discharged. * * *

* * * *

(Continued)

CASE 18.5—Continued

Given the * * * common knowledge of the minimal accepted practices in the field and the level of expertise, training and experience of the RCA electricians which encompassed the specific situation they faced, the * * * court should have found that there was no necessity on the part of Federal to warn RCA, which was already aware of the specific hazard, and the court should have granted Federal's motion entering judgment in its favor * * * .

DECISION AND REMEDY The Supreme Court of New York, Appellate Division, reversed the judgment of the lower court and dismissed the complaint against Federal.

FOR CRITICAL ANALYSIS—Technological Consideration *What might have been the result in this case if the training, experience, and expertise of the employees dispatched to check the circuit breakers had been with a different, out-of-date technology?*

OTHER DEFENSES

A defendant can also defend against product liability by showing that there is no basis for the plaintiff's claim. Suppose that a plaintiff alleges that a seller breached an implied warranty. If the seller can prove that he or she effectively disclaimed all implied warranties, the plaintiff cannot recover. Similarly, in a product liability case based on negligence, a defendant who can show that the plaintiff has not met the requirements (such as causation) for an action in negligence will not be liable. In regard to strict product liability, a defendant could claim that the plaintiff failed to meet one of the requirements for an action in strict liability. If the defendant establishes that the goods have been subsequently altered, the defendant will not be held liable.

APPLICATION

Law & the Seller: The Creation of Warranties*

Warranties are important in both commercial and consumer purchase transactions. There are three types of product warranties: express warranties, implied warranties of merchantability, and implied warranties of fitness for a particular purpose. If you are a seller of products, you can make or create any one of these warranties, which are available to both consumers and commercial purchasers.

First and foremost, sellers and buyers need to know whether warranties have been created. Express warranties do not have to be labeled as such, but statements of simple opinion generally do not constitute express warranties. Express warranties can be made by descriptions of the goods. Express warranties can be found in a seller's advertisement, brochure, or promotional materials or can be made orally or in an express writing. A sales representative should use care in describing the merits of a product; otherwise, the seller could be held to an express warranty. If an express warranty is not intended, the sales pitch should not promise too much.

In most sales, because the seller is a merchant, the purchased goods carry the implied warranty of merchantability. If you are a seller, you must also be aware of the importance of the implied warranty of fitness for a particular purpose. Assume that a customer comes to your sales representative, describes the job to be done in detail, and says, "I really need something that can do the job." Your sales representative

*This *Application* is not meant to serve as a substitute for the services of an attorney who is licensed to practice law in your state.

APPLICATION CONTINUED

replies, "This product will do the job." An implied warranty that the product is fit for that particular purpose has been created.

Many sellers, particularly in commercial sales, try to limit or disclaim warranties. The Uniform Commercial Code permits all warranties, including express warranties, to be excluded or negated. Conspicuous statements—such as "THERE ARE NO WARRANTIES WHICH EXTEND BEYOND THE DESCRIPTION ON THE FACE HEREOF" or "THERE ARE NO IMPLIED WARRANTIES OF FITNESS FOR A PARTICULAR PURPOSE OR MERCHANTABILITY WHICH ACCOMPANY THIS SALE"—can be used to disclaim the implied warranties of fitness and merchantability. Used goods are sometimes sold "as is" or "with all faults" so that implied warranties of fitness and merchantability are disclaimed. Whenever these warranties are disclaimed, a purchaser should be aware that the product may not be of even average quality.

CHECKLIST FOR THE SALESPERSON

1. If you wish to limit warranties, do so by means of a carefully worded and prominently placed written or printed provision that a reasonable person would understand and accept.
2. As a seller, you might wish to have the buyer sign a statement certifying that he or she has read all of your warranty disclaimer provisions.
3. If you do not intend to make an express warranty, do not make a promise or an affirmation of fact concerning the performance or quality of a product you are selling.

Key Terms

express warranty 461

implied warranty 463

implied warranty of fitness for a particular purpose 465

implied warranty of merchantability 464

lien 460

product liability 471

unreasonably dangerous product 475

Chapter Summary • Warranties and Product Liability

WARRANTIES	
Warranties of Title (See pages 460–461.)	The UCC provides for the following warranties of title [UCC 2–312, 2A–211]: 1. *Good title*—A seller warrants that he or she has the right to pass good and rightful title to the goods. 2. *No liens*—A seller warrants that the goods sold are free of any encumbrances (claims, charges, or liabilities—usually called *liens*). A lessor warrants that the lessee will not be disturbed in his or her possession of the goods by the claims of a third party. 3. *No infringements*—A merchant seller warrants that the goods are free of infringement claims (claims that a patent, trademark, or copyright has been infringed) by third parties. Lessors make similar warranties.
Express Warranties (See pages 461–462.)	1. *Under the UCC*—An express warranty arises under the UCC when a seller or lessor indicates, as part of the basis of the bargain, any of the following: a. An affirmation or promise of fact. b. A description of the goods. c. A sample shown as conforming to the contract goods [UCC 2–313, 2A–210].

Chapter Summary • Warranties and Product Liability, Continued

Express Warranties—continued	2. *Under the Magnuson-Moss Warranty Act*—Express written warranties covering consumer goods priced at more than $10, *if made,* must be labeled as one of the following: a. Full warranty—Free repair or replacement of defective parts; refund or replacement for goods if they cannot be repaired in a reasonable time. b. Limited warranty—When less than a full warranty is being offered.
Implied Warranty of Merchantability (See pages 464–465.)	When a seller or lessor is a merchant who deals in goods of the kind sold or leased, the seller or lessor warrants that the goods sold or leased are properly packaged and labeled, are of proper quality, and are reasonably fit for the ordinary purposes for which such goods are used [UCC 2–314, 2A–212].
Implied Warranty of Fitness for a Particular Purpose (See pages 465–466.)	Arises when the buyer's or lessee's purpose or use is expressly or impliedly known by the seller or lessor, and the buyer or lessee purchases or leases the goods in reliance on the seller's or lessor's selection [UCC 2–315, 2A–213].
Other Implied Warranties (See page 466.)	Other implied warranties can arise as a result of course of dealing, course of performance, or usage of trade [UCC 2–314(3), 2A–212(3)].
	PRODUCT LIABILITY
Liability Based on Negligence (See pages 471–472.)	1. Due care must be used by the manufacturer in designing the product, selecting materials, using the appropriate production process, assembling and testing the product, and placing adequate warnings on the label or product. 2. Privity of contract is not required. A manufacturer is liable for failure to exercise due care to any person who sustains an injury proximately caused by a negligently made (defective) product.
Liability Based on Misrepresentation (See page 472.)	Fraudulent misrepresentation of a product may result in product liability based on the tort of fraud.
Strict Liability—Requirements (See pages 474–475.)	1. The defendant must sell the product in a defective condition. 2. The defendant must normally be engaged in the business of selling that product. 3. The product must be unreasonably dangerous to the user or consumer because of its defective condition (in most states). 4. The plaintiff must incur physical harm to self or property. 5. The defective condition must be the proximate cause of the injury or damage. 6. The goods must not have been substantially changed from the time the product was sold to the time the injury was sustained.
Market-Share Liability (See pages 475–476.)	In cases in which plaintiffs cannot prove which of many distributors of a defective product supplied the particular product that caused the plaintiffs' injuries, some courts have applied market-share liability. All firms that manufactured and distributed the harmful product during the period in question are then held liable for the plaintiffs' injuries in proportion to the firms' respective shares of the market, as directed by the court.
Other Applications of Strict Liability (See page 476.)	1. Manufacturers and other sellers are liable for harms suffered by injured bystanders due to defective products. 2. Suppliers of component parts are strictly liable for defective parts that, when incorporated into a product, cause injuries to users.

Chapter Summary • Warranties and Product Liability, Continued

Strict Liability—Product Defect (See pages 476–480.)	There are three basic ways in which a product may be defective: 1. In its manufacture. 2. In its design. 3. In the instructions or warnings that come with it.
Defenses to Product Liability (See pages 480–482.)	1. *Assumption of risk*—The user or consumer knew of the risk of harm and voluntarily assumed it. 2. *Product misuse*—The user or consumer misused the product in a way unforeseeable by the manufacturer. 3. *Comparative negligence and liability*—Liability may be distributed between plaintiff and defendant under the doctrine of comparative negligence if the plaintiff's misuse of the product contributed to the risk of injury. 4. *Commonly known dangers*— If a defendant succeeds in convincing the court that a plaintiff's injury resulted from a commonly known danger, such as the danger associated with using a sharp knife, the defendant will not be liable. 5. *Other defenses*—A defendant can also defend against a strict liability claim by showing that there is no basis for the plaintiff's claim (that the plaintiff has not met the requirements for an

For Review

1. What factors determine whether a seller's or lessor's statement constitutes an express warranty or merely "puffing"?
2. What implied warranties arise under the UCC?
3. Discuss whether a manufacturer can be held liable to any person who suffers an injury proximately caused by the manufacturer's negligently made product.
4. What are the elements of a cause of action in strict product liability?
5. What defenses to liability can be raised in a product liability lawsuit?

Questions and Case Problems

18–1. Product Liability. Under what contract theory can a seller be held liable to a consumer for physical harm or property damage that is caused by the goods sold? Under what tort theories can the seller be held liable?

18–2. Product Liability. Carmen buys a television set manufactured by AKI Electronics. She is going on vacation, so she takes the set to her mother's house for her mother to use. Because the set is defective, it explodes, causing considerable damage to her mother's house. Carmen's mother sues AKI for the damages to her house. Discuss the theories under which Carmen's mother can recover from AKI.

18–3. Warranty Disclaimers. Tandy purchased a washing machine from Marshall Appliances. The sales contract included a provision explicitly disclaiming all express or implied warranties, including the implied warranty of merchantability. The disclaimer was printed in the same size and color as the rest of the contract. The machine turned out to be a "lemon" and never functioned properly. Tandy sought a refund of the purchase price, claiming that Marshall had breached the implied warranty of merchantability. Can Tandy recover her money, notwithstanding the warranty disclaimer in the contract? Explain.

18–4. Implied Warranties. Sam, a farmer, needs to place a two-thousand-pound piece of equipment in his barn. The equipment must be lifted thirty feet into a hayloft. Sam goes to Durham Hardware and tells Durham that he needs some heavy-duty rope to be used on his farm. Durham recommends a one-inch-thick nylon rope, and Sam purchases two hundred feet of it. Sam ties the rope around the piece of equipment, puts it through a pulley, and with the aid of a tractor lifts the equipment off the ground. Suddenly the rope breaks. In the crash to the ground, the equipment is extensively damaged. Sam files suit against Durham for breach of the implied warranty of fitness for a particular purpose. Discuss how successful Sam will be with his suit.

18–5. Product Liability. George Nesselrode lost his life in an airplane crash. The plane had been manufactured by Beech Aircraft Corp. and sold to Executive Beechcraft, Inc. Shortly before the crash occurred, Executive Beechcraft had conducted a routine inspection of the plane and found that some of the parts needed to be replaced. The new parts were supplied by Beech Aircraft but installed by Executive Beechcraft. These particular airplane parts could be installed backward, and if they were, the plane would crash. Nesselrode's crash resulted from just such an incorrect installation of the airplane parts. Nesselrode's wife, Jane, and three daughters sued Executive Beechcraft, Beech Aircraft, and Gerald Hultgren, the pilot who had flown the plane, for damages. Beech Aircraft claimed that it was not at fault because it had not installed the parts. Will Beech Aircraft be held liable for Nesselrode's death? Discuss. [*Nesselrode v. Executive Beechcraft, Inc.,* 707 S.W.2d 371 (Mo. 1986)]

18–6. Strict Liability. Embs was buying some groceries at Stamper's Cash Market. Unnoticed by her, a carton of 7-Up was sitting on the floor at the edge of the produce counter about one foot from where she was standing. Several of the 7-Up bottles exploded. Embs's leg was injured severely enough that she had to be taken to the hospital by a managing agent of the store. Embs sued the manufacturer of 7-Up, Pepsi-Cola Bottling Co. of Lexington, Kentucky, Inc., claiming that the manufacturer should be held strictly liable for the harm caused by its products. The trial court dismissed her claim. On appeal, what will the court decide? Discuss fully. [*Embs v. Pepsi-Cola Bottling Co. of Lexington, Kentucky, Inc.,* 528 S.W.2d 703 (Ky.App. 1975)]

18–7. Defenses to Product Liability. The Campbell Soup Co. manufactured, sold, and shipped packages of chicken-flavored Campbell's Ramen Noodle Soup to a distributor. The distributor sold and shipped the packages to Associated Grocers. Associated Grocers shipped the packages to Warehouse Foods, a retail grocer. Six weeks after Campbell first shipped the soup to the distributor, Warehouse Foods sold a packet of the soup to Kathy Jo Gates. Gates prepared the soup. Halfway through eating her second bowl, she discovered beetle larvae in the noodles. She filed a product liability suit against Campbell and others. Gates argued, in effect, that the mere presence of the bugs in the soup was sufficient to hold Campbell strictly liable. How might Campbell defend itself? [*Campbell Soup Co. v. Gates,* 319 Ark. 54, 889 S.W.2d 750 (1994)]

18–8. Product Liability. John Whitted bought a Chevrolet Nova from General Motors Corp. (GMC). Six years later, Whitted crashed the Nova into two trees. During the impact, the seat belt broke, and Whitted was thrust against the steering wheel, which broke, and the windshield, which shattered. He suffered fractures in his left arm and cuts to his forehead. Whitted sued GMC and the manufacturer, asserting, among other things, that because the seat belt broke, the defendants were strictly liable for his injuries. What does Whitted have to show in order to prove his case? [*Whitted v. General Motors Corp.,* 58 F.3d 1200 (7th Cir. 1995)]

18–9. Implied Warranty of Merchantability. Marilyn Keaton entered an A.B.C. Drug store to buy a half-gallon bottle of liquid bleach. The bottles were stacked at a height above her eye level. She reached up, grasped the handle of one of the bottles, and began pulling it down from the shelf. The cap was loose, however, causing bleach to splash into her face, injuring her eye. Keaton filed a suit in a Georgia state court against A.B.C., alleging, in part, breach of the implied warranty of merchantability. She claimed that the bleach had not been adequately packaged. A.B.C. argued, in part, that Keaton had failed to exercise care for her own safety. Had A.B.C. breached the implied warranty of merchantability? Discuss. [*Keaton v. A.B.C. Drug Co.,* 266 Ga. 385, 467 S.E.2d 558 (1996)]

18–10. Failure to Warn. When Mary Bresnahan drove her Chrysler LeBaron, she sat very close to the steering wheel—less than a foot away from the steering-wheel enclosure of the driver's side air bag. At the time, Chrysler did not provide any warning that a driver should not sit close to the air bag. In an accident with another car, Bresnahan's air bag deployed. The bag caused her elbow to strike the windshield pillar and fracture in three places, resulting in repeated surgery and physical therapy. Bresnahan filed a suit in a California state court against Chrysler to recover for her injuries, alleging in part that they were caused by Chrysler's failure to warn consumers about sitting near the air bag. At the trial, an expert testified that the air bag was not intended to prevent arm injuries, which were "a predictable, incidental consequence" of the bag's deploying. Should Chrysler pay for Bresnahan's injuries? Why or why not? [*Bresnahan v. Chrysler Corp.,* 76 Cal.Rptr.2d 804, 65 Cal.App.4th 1149 (1998)]

A QUESTION OF ETHICS AND SOCIAL RESPONSIBILITY

18–11. Three-year-old Randy Welch, the son of Steve and Teresa Griffith, climbed up to a shelf and obtained a disposable butane cigarette lighter. Randy then used the lighter to ignite a flame, which set fire to his pajama top. Welch and his parents sued the lighter's manufacturer, Scripto-Tokai Corp., for damages, alleging that the lighter was defective and unreasonably dangerous because it was not child resistant. In view of this factual background, consider the following questions. [*Welch v. Scripto-Tokai Corp.,* 651 N.E.2d 810 (Ind.App. 1995)]

1. One of the questions raised in this case was whether the risks attending the lighter were sufficiently "open and obvious" that the manufacturer did not need to warn of those

risks. If you were the judge, how would you decide this issue? Explain your reasoning.
2. If a product is not dangerous to an extent beyond that contemplated by the ordinary consumer, should the manufacturer nonetheless be held liable if it could have made the product safer? Explain.
3. How can a court decide what kinds of risks should be open and obvious for the ordinary consumer?

FOR CRITICAL ANALYSIS

18–12. The United States has the strictest product liability laws in the world today. Why do you think many other countries, particularly developing countries, are more lax with respect to holding manufacturers liable for product defects?

Online Activities

ONLINE EXERCISE 18–1

Go to the "Internet Activities Book" on the Web site that accompanies this text, the URL for which is http://blt.westbuslaw.com. Select the following activities, and perform the exercises according to the instructions given there:

Activity 18–1: Product Liability
Activity 18–2: Warranties

Before the Test

Go to the *Business Law Today* home page at http://blt.westbuslaw.com. Click on TestTutor.® You will find twenty interactive questions relating to this chapter.

Unit Three • Cumulative Business Hypothetical

Sonja owns a bakery in San Francisco. To accommodate the growing demand for her products, she orders two new Model X23 McIntyre ovens from a local company, Western Heating Appliances. The purchase price of the two ovens is $4,000.

1. Sonja and Western Heating agreed orally, via the telephone, that Western would deliver the ovens within two weeks and that Sonja would pay for the ovens when they were delivered. Two days later, Sonja receives a fax from Western confirming her order. Shortly thereafter, but before Western delivers the ovens, Sonja learns that she can obtain Model X23 McIntyre ovens from another company at a much lower price. Sonja asks Western if she can cancel her order, but Western states that it intends to enforce the contract. Is the contract enforceable against Sonja? Explain.
2. After Western receives Sonja's order, it learns that McIntyre no longer manufactures ovens and that the Model X23 ovens are virtually unobtainable anywhere in the country. Western immediately notifies Sonja that it will not be able to fulfill her order. Sonja, who stands to lose a significant amount in profits if the ovens are not delivered on time, sues Western for breach of contract. Western raises the doctrine of commercial impracticability as a defense. Will Western succeed in this defense? Explain.
3. Assume that Western does have two Model X23 McIntyre ovens in stock. Unbeknownst to the sales representative who formed the contract with Sonja, the two ovens have already been purchased by another customer, Tony Garcia. Western is holding the ovens for Garcia until he returns from a business trip to France. The sales representative who dealt with Sonja has the two ovens delivered to Sonja's bakery. Shortly after the ovens are installed at Sonja's bakery, Western calls Sonja and explains that a mistake was made and that Garcia is demanding the two ovens, which cannot be obtained anywhere else. What are Sonja's legal options in this situation? What are Garcia's rights? What legal consequences might Western face as a result of its "mistake"?
4. One day, Sonja was baking a batch of croissants. When she opened the door to one of the new ovens, part of the door became detached from the oven. As she struggled with the door, Sonja's hands became badly burned, and she was unable to do any baking for several months. Sonja later learned that the hinge mechanism on the door had been improperly installed. Sonja wants to sue the oven's manufacturer to recover damages, including consequential damages for lost profits. In a product liability suit against the manufacturer, under what legal principles and doctrines might Sonja be able to recover damages? Discuss fully.

UNIT THREE • EXTENDED CASE STUDY: THE LAW IN CONTEXT

Uniroyal Goodrich Tire Co. v. Martinez

In Chapter 18, we discussed the common law principles of product liability. In this extended case study, we examine Uniroyal Goodrich Tire Co. v. Martinez,[1] *a recent decision that follows the principles set out in the* Restatement (Third) of Torts: Products Liability.

CASE BACKGROUND

Attached to a tire manufactured by Uniroyal Goodrich Tire Company was a prominent warning label containing yellow and red highlights and an illustration of a worker being thrown into the air by an exploding tire. The label stated conspicuously:

> **DANGER**
> **NEVER MOUNT A 16" SIZE DIAMETER TIRE ON A 16.5" RIM.** Mounting a 16" tire on a 16.5" rim can cause severe injury or death.

Ignoring these warnings, Roberto Martinez, a mechanic, attempted to mount a 16" Goodrich tire on a 16.5" rim. The tire exploded, putting Martinez in a coma and causing permanent brain damage. Martinez and others filed a suit a Texas state court against Uniroyal and others. Martinez did not claim that the warnings were inadequate, but in part that Goodrich was strictly liable for designing and manufacturing a defective tire and rim. Martinez argued that the tire was defective because it failed to incorporate a safer alternative design that was used by other tire manufacturers and would have kept this tire from exploding. Goodrich responded that Martinez's failure to heed the product's warnings was a complete defense to his claim. The jury found in part that the tire was defective, and the court awarded Martinez more than $10.2 million. Goodrich appealed, and the case was eventually heard by the Texas Supreme Court.

MAJORITY OPINION

PHILLIPS, Chief Justice, delivered the opinion of the Court * * * .

* * * *

Goodrich urges this Court to * * * [follow] certain language from Comment j of the *Restatement (Second) of Torts,* [which] provides in part:

> Where warning is given, the seller may reasonably assume that it will be read and heeded; and a product bearing such a warning, which is safe for use if it is followed, is not in defective condition, nor is it unreasonably dangerous.

The new *Restatement (Third) of Torts: Product Liability,* however, expressly rejects [this] approach [in Comment l]:

> Reasonable designs and instructions or warnings both play important roles in the production and distribution of reasonably safe products. In general, when a safer design can reasonably be implemented and risks can reasonably be designed out of a product, adoption of the safer design is required over a warning that leaves a significant residuum [leftover amount] of such risks. For example, instructions and warnings may be ineffective because users of the product may not be adequately reached, may be likely to be inattentive, or may be insufficiently motivated to follow the instructions or heed the warnings. However, when an alternative design to avoid risks cannot reasonably be implemented, adequate instructions and warnings will normally be sufficient to render the product reasonably safe. * * * Warnings are not, however, a substitute for the provision of a reasonably safe design.

The Reporters' Notes in the new *Restatement* refer to Comment j [of the *Restatement (Second) of Torts*] as "unfortunate language" that "has elicited heavy criticism from a host of commentators." Similarly, this Court has indicated that the fact that a danger is open and obvious (and thus need not be warned against) does not preclude a finding of product defect when a safer, reasonable alternative design exists.

The drafters of the new *Restatement* provide the following illustration for why courts have overwhelmingly rejected Comment j:

1. 977 S.W.2d 328 (Tex.Sup.Ct. 1998).

Jeremy's foot was severed when caught between the blade and compaction chamber of a garbage truck on which he was working. The injury occurred when he lost his balance while jumping on the back step of the garbage truck as it was moving from one stop to the next. The garbage truck, manufactured by XYZ Motor Co., has a warning in large red letters on both the left and right rear panels that reads "DANGER—DO NOT INSERT ANY OBJECT WHILE COMPACTION CHAMBER IS WORKING—KEEP HANDS AND FEET AWAY." The fact that adequate warning was given does not preclude Jeremy from seeking to establish a design defect * * *. The possibility that an employee might lose his balance and thus encounter the shear point was a risk that a warning could not eliminate and that might require a safety guard. * * *

For these reasons we refuse to adopt the approach of Comment j of the superseded *Restatement (Second) of Torts,* Section 402A.

DISSENTING OPINION

HECHT, Justice, * * * dissenting:

* * * *

I do not agree * * * that the Court correctly reads or follows Comment l. Comment l limits but does not foreclose the role of warnings in making products reasonably safe, even when there is a safer alternative design. The Court stresses the last sentence of Comment l and brushes past the first sentence. Taken as a whole, the Comment says, correctly, I think, that a safer alternative design that eliminates a risk is required over a warning that leaves a significant residuum of risk because product users may not get the warning, may be inattentive, or may not be motivated to heed the warning. The illustration accompanying Comment l is of a worker whose foot is severed by a garbage truck's blade and compaction chamber when he loses his balance jumping onto the back of the truck. A warning on the truck, "keep hands and feet away", does little to protect against a worker's foreseeable inadvertence or misstep in the usual discharge of his job. But the warning might well be adequate admonishment to the merely curious, even if the garbage truck could be designed to be safer, if the residuum of risk were insignificant. Even if the risk that a worker will lose his balance and slip is significant enough to warrant designing additional protections in the truck, the risk that someone will intentionally stick his hand in a place where it obviously may be hurt when he is effectively warned not to do so may not warrant design changes.

MEDIA COVERAGE

The court's ruling in this case was a surprise, at least in Texas. Here we present excerpts from an article titled "Court Gives Consumers Rare Wins" by Mary Flood that appeared in the *Wall Street Journal* on July 8, 1998.

"Some court-watchers believe that the pro-consumer outcome of the ruling * * * reflects a willingness of a majority of the court to side with plaintiffs in product-liability cases when the result is well within the mainstream of U.S. tort law.

* * * *

'In an effort to bolster the idea that this court isn't deviant from the mainstream,' says Corpus Christi appellate lawyer Rusty McMains, 'it may seek refuge in national documents [or trends].' He says national trends, especially in product-liability cases, may be 'not quite as conservative as the Texas court has otherwise been.'

But Republican [State] Supreme Court Justice Greg Abbott says in an interview that he disagrees that the court would look to its image in deciding cases and says each case is considered on its individual merit.

* * * *

The outcome came as a surprise to the lawyers who handled the [appeal] on behalf of Mr. Martinez * * *. 'I was shocked to win * * *,' says Steve Hastings, a Corpus Christi attorney who * * * argued the tire case before the Supreme Court.

* * * *

'There is some new blood on the court,' says Mr. Hastings, 'and perhaps those judges are more willing to follow traditional Texas law than be hard-liner [conservatives].'"

GOING ONLINE

The *Business Law Today,* Fifth Edition, Web site, at **http://blt.westbuslaw.com**, provides a link through which you can access other court opinions in product liability cases.

QUESTIONS FOR ANALYSIS

1. **Law.** What was the defendant's major argument? Why did the court conclude that it was invalid?
2. **International Dimensions.** How might the new *Restatement* affect the decision of a foreign seller to do business in the United States?
3. **Implications for the Business Manager.** Under the new *Restatement,* can a manufacturer ever avoid liability by providing a warning when a safer, alternative design is available?

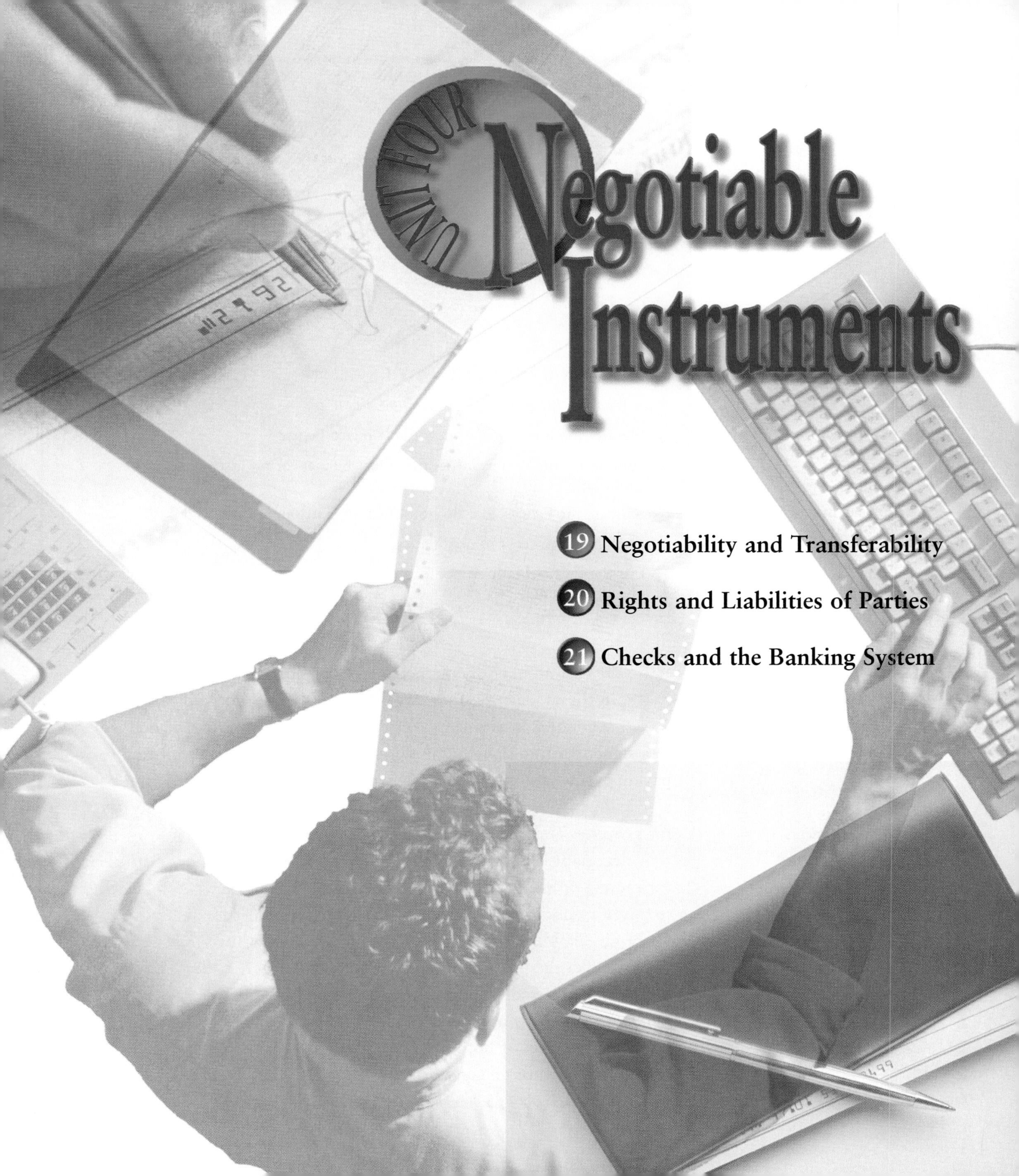

UNIT FOUR

Negotiable Instruments

CHAPTER 19

Negotiability & Transferability

"Convenience is the basis of mercantile law."

Lord Mansfield, 1705–1793
(British jurist)

CONTENTS

LEARNING OBJECTIVES

After reading this chapter, you should be able to:

1. Identify the four types of negotiable instruments.
2. Summarize the requirements that must be met for an instrument to be negotiable.
3. Indicate the factors that do not affect an instrument's negotiability.
4. Explain the process of negotiation.
5. List the types of indorsements, and describe the legal effect of each type of indorsement.

The vast number of commercial transactions that take place daily in the modern business world would be inconceivable without negotiable instruments. A **negotiable instrument** can be defined as a signed writing that contains an unconditional promise or order to pay an exact sum of money on demand or at a specified future time to a specific person or order, or to bearer. The checks you write to pay for groceries and other items are negotiable instruments.

A negotiable instrument can function in two ways—as a substitute for money or as an extension of credit. When a buyer writes a check to pay for goods, the check serves as a substitute for money. When a buyer gives a seller a promissory note in which the buyer promises to pay the seller the purchase price within sixty days, the seller has essentially extended credit to the buyer for a sixty-day period. For a negotiable instrument to operate *practically* as either a substitute for money or a credit device, or both, it is essential that the instrument be easily transferable without danger of being uncollectible. This is an essential

• **NEGOTIABLE INSTRUMENT**
A signed writing that contains an unconditional promise or order to pay an exact sum of money on demand or at an exact future time to a specific person or order, or to bearer.

function of negotiable instruments. Each rule described in the following pages can be examined in light of this function.

In the opening quotation, Lord Mansfield stresses the element of convenience in the evolution of mercantile law, and the law governing negotiable instruments did indeed grow out of commercial necessity. In the medieval world, merchants dealing in foreign trade used negotiable instruments to finance and conduct their affairs. Problems in transportation and in the safekeeping of gold or coins had prompted this practice. Because the English king's courts of those times did not recognize the validity of negotiable instruments, the merchants had to develop their own rules governing their use, and these rules were enforced by "fair" or "borough" courts. Eventually, these decisions formed a distinct set of laws that became known as the *Lex Mercatoria* (Law Merchant).

The Law Merchant was codified in England in the Bills of Exchange Act of 1882. In 1896, in the United States, the National Conference of Commissioners (NCC) on Uniform State Laws drafted the Uniform Negotiable Instruments Law (NIL), which was modeled on the British 1882 act and adopted by all of the states over the next three decades. By the 1940s, it was apparent that the NIL needed to be revised to address then-current business practices. As a part of a movement to create a set of uniform laws to govern commercial business transactions generally, the NCC eventually drafted the Uniform Commercial Code (UCC), Article 3 of which replaced the NIL.

Article 3 of the UCC

Negotiable instruments must meet special requirements relating to form and content. These requirements, which are imposed by Article 3 of the Uniform Commercial Code (UCC), will be discussed at length in this chapter. When an instrument is negotiable, its transfer from one person to another is also governed by Article 3. Indeed, UCC 3–104(b) defines *instrument* as a "negotiable instrument." For that reason, whenever the term *instrument* is used in this book, it refers to a negotiable instrument.

> **ON THE WEB**
>
> To find Article 3 of the UCC as adopted by a particular state, go to the Web site of Cornell University's Law School at www.law.cornell.edu/ucc/ucc.table.html.

In 1990, a revised version of Article 3 was issued for adoption by the states. Many of the changes to Article 3 simply clarified old sections; some significantly altered the former UCC Article 3 provisions. Because almost all of the states have adopted the revised article, references to Article 3 in this chapter and in the following two chapters are to the *revised* Article 3. When the revised Article 3 has made important changes in the law, however, we discuss the previous law in footnotes.

Article 4 of the UCC, which governs bank deposits and collections (discussed in Chapter 21), was also revised in 1990. In part, these changes were necessary to reflect changes in Article 3 that affect Article 4 provisions. The revised Articles 3 and 4 are included in their entirety in Appendix B.

Types of Instruments

The UCC specifies four types of negotiable instruments: *drafts, checks, promissory notes,* and *certificates of deposit* (CDs). These instruments are frequently divided into the two classifications that we will discuss in the following subsections: *orders to pay* (drafts and checks) and *promises to pay* (promissory notes and CDs).

Negotiable instruments may also be classified as either demand instruments or time instruments. A *demand instrument* is payable on demand; that is, it is payable immediately after it is issued and thereafter for a reasonable period of time. All checks are demand instruments, because by definition, they must be payable on demand. A *time instrument* is payable at a future date.

• **DRAFT**
Any instrument drawn on a drawee that orders the drawee to pay a certain sum of money, usually to a third party (the payee), on demand or at a definite future time.

• **DRAWER**
The party that initiates a draft (such as a check), thereby ordering the drawee to pay.

• **DRAWEE**
The party that is ordered to pay a draft or check. With a check, a bank or a financial institution is always the drawee.

• **PAYEE**
A person to whom an instrument is made payable.

• **TRADE ACCEPTANCE**
A draft that is drawn by a seller of goods ordering the buyer to pay a specified sum of money to the seller, usually at a stated time in the future. The buyer accepts the draft by signing the face of the draft, thus creating an enforceable obligation to pay the draft when it comes due. On a trade acceptance, the seller is both the drawer and the payee.

DRAFTS AND CHECKS (ORDERS TO PAY)

A **draft** (bill of exchange) is an unconditional written order that involves three parties. The party creating the draft (the **drawer**) orders another party (the **drawee**) to pay money, usually to a third party (the **payee**). A *time draft* is payable at a definite future time. A *sight draft* (or demand draft) is payable on sight—that is, when it is presented for payment. A draft can be both a time and a sight draft; such a draft is one payable at a stated time after sight.

Exhibit 19–1 shows a typical time draft. The drawee must be obligated to the drawer either by agreement or through a debtor-creditor relationship for the drawee to be obligated to the drawer to honor the order. • EXAMPLE 19.1 On November 16, the Bank of Ourtown orders $1,000 worth of office supplies from Eastman Supply Company, with payment due January 16. On December 16, Eastman borrows $1,000 from the First National Bank of Whiteacre, with payment also due January 16. The First National Bank of Whiteacre will usually accept a draft drawn by Eastman on the Bank of Ourtown as payment for the loan.•

A **trade acceptance** is a type of draft that is frequently used in the sale of goods. The seller is both the drawer and the payee on this draft. Essentially, the draft orders the buyer to pay a specified sum of money to the seller, usually at a stated time in the future. (If the draft orders the buyer's bank to pay, it is called a *banker's acceptance*.) • EXAMPLE 19.2 Jackson River Fabrics sells fabric priced at $50,000 to Comfort Creations, Inc., each fall on terms requiring payment to be made in ninety days. One year Jackson River needs cash, so it draws a *trade acceptance* (see Exhibit 19–2) that orders Comfort Creations to pay $50,000 to the order of Jackson River Fabrics ninety days hence. Jackson River presents the paper to Comfort Creations. Comfort

EXHIBIT 19–1 • A Typical Time Draft

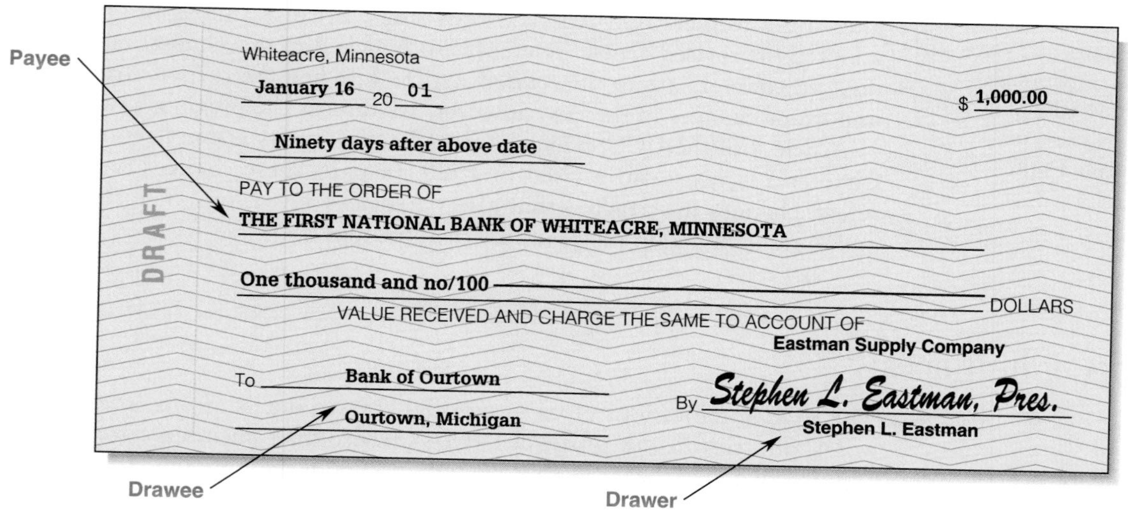
Payee
Whiteacre, Minnesota
January 16 20 01
$ 1,000.00
Ninety days after above date
PAY TO THE ORDER OF
THE FIRST NATIONAL BANK OF WHITEACRE, MINNESOTA
DRAFT
One thousand and no/100
DOLLARS
VALUE RECEIVED AND CHARGE THE SAME TO ACCOUNT OF
Eastman Supply Company
To Bank of Ourtown
Ourtown, Michigan
By Stephen L. Eastman, Pres.
Stephen L. Eastman
Drawee
Drawer

EXHIBIT 19–2 • A Typical Trade Acceptance

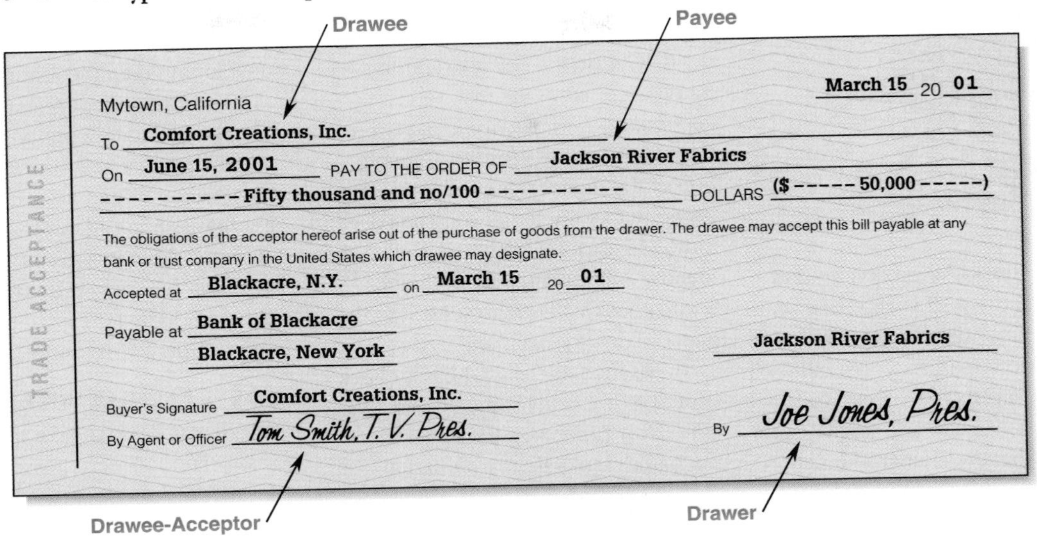

TRADE ACCEPTANCE

Mytown, California

March 15 20 01

To Comfort Creations, Inc.

On June 15, 2001 PAY TO THE ORDER OF Jackson River Fabrics

----------Fifty thousand and no/100---------- DOLLARS ($-----50,000-----)

The obligations of the acceptor hereof arise out of the purchase of goods from the drawer. The drawee may accept this bill payable at any bank or trust company in the United States which drawee may designate.

Accepted at Blackacre, N.Y. on March 15 20 01

Payable at Bank of Blackacre
Blackacre, New York

Jackson River Fabrics

Buyer's Signature Comfort Creations, Inc.
By Agent or Officer Tom Smith, T.V. Pres.

By Joe Jones, Pres.

Creations *accepts* the draft, by signing on the face of the draft, and returns it to Jackson River Fabrics. The acceptance by Comfort Creations creates an enforceable obligation to pay the draft when it comes due in ninety days. Jackson River can then immediately sell the trade acceptance in the commercial money market for cash.•

• **CHECK**
A draft drawn by a drawer ordering the drawee bank or financial institution to pay a certain amount of money to the holder on demand.

The most commonly used type of draft is a **check.** The writer of the check is the drawer, the bank on which the check is drawn is the drawee, and the person to whom the check is payable is the payee. As mentioned earlier, checks, because they are payable on demand, are demand instruments.

Checks will be discussed more fully in Chapter 21, but it should be noted here that with certain types of checks, such as *cashier's checks,* the bank is both the drawer and the drawee. The bank customer purchases a cashier's check from the bank—that is, pays the bank the amount of the check—and indicates to whom the check should be made payable. The bank, not the customer, is the drawer of the check—as well as the drawee. (For a discussion of how digital checks can be used in a way similar to cashier's checks, see this chapter's *Technology and Digital Checks.*)

Promissory Notes and Certificates of Deposit (Promises to Pay)

• **PROMISSORY NOTE**
A written promise made by one person (the maker) to pay a fixed amount of money to another person (the payee or a subsequent holder) on demand or on a specified date.

• **MAKER**
One who promises to pay a fixed amount of money to the holder of a promissory note or a certificate of deposit (CD).

A **promissory note** is a written promise made by one person (the **maker** of the promise to pay) to another (the payee, or the one to whom the promise is made). A promissory note, which is often referred to simply as a *note,* can be made payable at a definite time or on demand. It can name a specific payee or merely be payable to bearer (bearer instruments are discussed later in this chapter). • **EXAMPLE 19.3** On April 30, Laurence and Margaret Roberts sign a writing unconditionally promising to pay "to the order of" the First National Bank of Whiteacre $3,000 (with 8 percent interest) on or before June 29. This writing is a promissory note.• A typical promissory note is shown in Exhibit 19–3 on page 496.

Notes are used in a variety of credit transactions and often carry the name of the transaction involved. For example, a note that is secured by personal property, such

Technology and Digital Checks

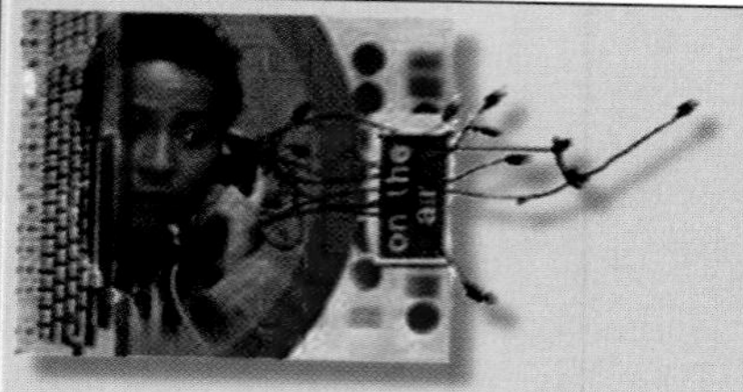

Paper checks have been around for hundreds of years. They still constitute a major type of negotiable instrument. More than sixty-five billion checks are processed each year. Today, in principle, banks can offer digital bank checks that are similar in function to paper checks. An electronic form identifies the payee, the payor, the amount of the payment, and the time and date of the transaction. All of the parties to the digital check must sign it digitally. A public key encryption system (described in the feature *Technology and Electronic Signatures* in Chapter 12) allows for the authentication of the digital signature necessary to properly identify the payor. The payee in turn uses its public key to ascertain the identity and authenticity of the electronic check when it presents it to the payor's bank for payment.

In essence, the digital bank check is similar to a cashier's check. The user effectively purchases the check from the bank. Banks that issue digital checks must similarly guarantee payment. Each such bank check has a unique identification number and can be redeemed only once.

The same system is available for developing digital coupons, which are similar to paper coupons (cents-off coupons). Digital coupons, which are somewhat similar to traveler's checks, have value only in a transaction involving the issuing organization. These coupons are relatively easy to create because they only require the issuing company's digital signature and some form of identifying serial number.

FOR CRITICAL ANALYSIS

Are digital bank checks similar to cash? (Hint: Which provides more anonymity?)

INTERNET CONNECT

• **CERTIFICATE OF DEPOSIT (CD)**
A note of a bank in which a bank acknowledges a receipt of money from a party and promises to repay the money, with interest, to the party on a certain date.

as an automobile, is called a *collateral note,* because the property pledged as security for the satisfaction of the debt is called collateral (see Chapter 22). A note payable in installments, such as for payment for a suite of furniture over a twelve-month period, is called an *installment note.*

A **certificate of deposit** (CD) is a type of note. A CD is issued when a party deposits funds with a bank that the bank promises to repay, with interest, on a certain date [UCC 3–104(j)]. The bank is the maker of the note, and the depositor is the payee. • **EXAMPLE 19.4** On February 15, Sara Levin deposits $5,000 with the

EXHIBIT 19–3 • A Typical Promissory Note

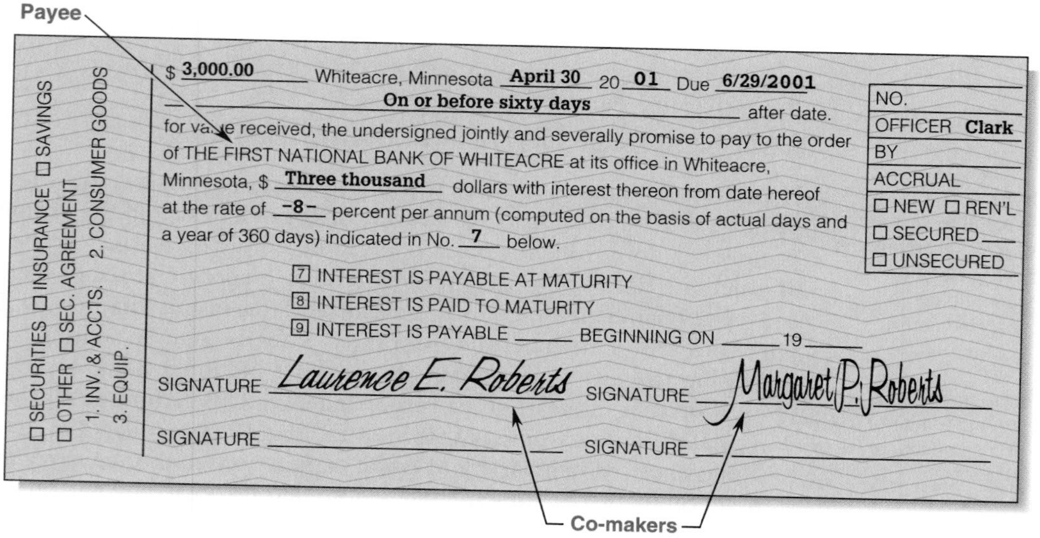
Payee

$ 3,000.00 Whiteacre, Minnesota April 30 20 01 Due 6/29/2001

On or before sixty days after date.

for value received, the undersigned jointly and severally promise to pay to the order of THE FIRST NATIONAL BANK OF WHITEACRE at its office in Whiteacre, Minnesota, $ Three thousand dollars with interest thereon from date hereof at the rate of -8- percent per annum (computed on the basis of actual days and a year of 360 days) indicated in No. 7 below.

7 INTEREST IS PAYABLE AT MATURITY
8 INTEREST IS PAID TO MATURITY
9 INTEREST IS PAYABLE ____ BEGINNING ON ____ 19____

SIGNATURE Laurence E. Roberts SIGNATURE Margaret P. Roberts

SIGNATURE ____ SIGNATURE ____

NO.
OFFICER Clark
BY
ACCRUAL
☐ NEW ☐ REN'L
☐ SECURED
☐ UNSECURED

☐ SECURITIES ☐ INSURANCE ☐ SAVINGS
☐ OTHER ☐ SEC. AGREEMENT
1. INV. & ACCTS. 2. CONSUMER GOODS
3. EQUIP.

Co-makers

"A negotiable bill or note is a courier without luggage."

JOHN B. GIBSON, 1780–1853
(American jurist)

First National Bank of Whiteacre. The bank issues a CD, in which it promises to repay the $5,000, plus 5 percent interest, on August 15.●

Certificates of deposit in small denominations (for amounts up to $100,000) are often sold by savings and loan associations, savings banks, and commercial banks. Certificates of deposit for amounts over $100,000 are called large (or jumbo) CDs. Exhibit 19–4 shows a typical small CD.

Requirements for Negotiability

For an instrument to be negotiable, it must meet the following requirements:

1. Be in writing.
2. Be signed by the maker or the drawer.
3. Be an unconditional promise or order to pay.
4. State a fixed amount of money.
5. Be payable on demand or at a definite time.
6. Be payable to order or to bearer, unless it is a check.

WRITTEN FORM

Negotiable instruments must be in written form [UCC 3–103(a)(6)]. This is because negotiable instruments must possess the quality of certainty that only formal, written expression can give. The writing must have the following qualities:

ON THE WEB

British author A. P. Herbert has some fun with the "written form" requirement for a negotiable instrument in his humorous (and fictitious) story titled "The Negotiable Cow," which can be found online at **www.kmoser.com/herb04.htm**.

1. The writing must be on material that lends itself to permanence. Instruments carved in blocks of ice or recorded on other impermanent surfaces would not qualify as negotiable instruments. Suppose that Suzanne writes in the sand, "I promise to pay $500 to the order of Jack." This cannot be a negotiable instrument because, although it is in writing, it lacks permanence.
2. The writing must also have portability. Although this is not a spelled-out legal requirement, if an instrument is not movable, it obviously cannot meet the requirement that it be freely transferable. For example, Charles writes on the side of a cow, "I promise to pay $500 to the order of Jason." Technically, this meets the requirements of a negotiable instrument, but as a cow cannot easily be transferred in the ordinary course of business, the "instrument" is nonnegotiable.

EXHIBIT 19–4 • A Typical Small CD

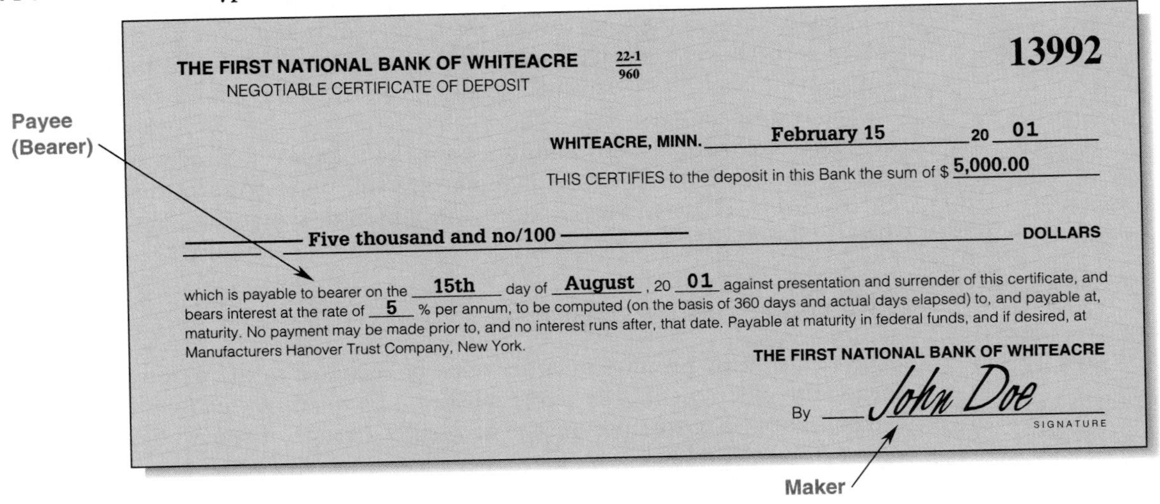
THE FIRST NATIONAL BANK OF WHITEACRE 22-1/960
NEGOTIABLE CERTIFICATE OF DEPOSIT
13992
WHITEACRE, MINN. February 15 20 01
THIS CERTIFIES to the deposit in this Bank the sum of $ 5,000.00
Five thousand and no/100 DOLLARS
which is payable to bearer on the 15th day of August, 20 01 against presentation and surrender of this certificate, and bears interest at the rate of 5 % per annum, to be computed (on the basis of 360 days and actual days elapsed) to, and payable at, maturity. No payment may be made prior to, and no interest runs after, that date. Payable at maturity in federal funds, and if desired, at Manufacturers Hanover Trust Company, New York.
THE FIRST NATIONAL BANK OF WHITEACRE
By John Doe
SIGNATURE

The Letter of the Law: What Is a Negotiable Instrument?

The UCC leaves a lot of room for imagination when it comes to negotiable instruments. Bearer instruments, for example, need not always be written to "cash" or to "bearer." They can be written to "Merry Christmas" or "Happy New Year" or just about any nonexistent or inanimate object. Even more extraordinary is the UCC's lack of specificity as to the form of a negotiable instrument. When we think of a check, for example, we normally envision a preprinted form with the "normal" terms and phrases on it, including the bank's name and address, "Pay to the order of," and so on. The UCC, however, says nothing to indicate that negotiable instruments must be typed or printed or placed on any specific kind of material. The UCC only stipulates that a negotiable instrument must be in writing, the writing must lend itself to permanence, and the writing must be portable.

THE BOTTOM LINE

As might be imagined, this lack of specificity has led to some extraordinary negotiable instruments. Checks and notes have been written on napkins, menus, tablecloths, shirts, and a variety of other materials—including a tractor fender, an eggshell, a watermelon, underwear, and a tamale.

SIGNATURES

For an instrument to be negotiable, it must be signed by (1) the maker, if it is a note or a certificate of deposit, or (2) the drawer, if it is a draft or a check [UCC 3–103(a)(3)]. If a person signs an instrument as an authorized agent of the maker or drawer, the maker or drawer has effectively signed the instrument. (Agents' signatures will be discussed in Chapter 20.)

• **SIGNATURE**
Under the UCC, "any symbol executed or adopted by a party with a present intention to authenticate a writing."

The UCC grants extreme latitude in regard to what constitutes a signature. UCC 1–201(39) provides that a **signature** may include "any symbol executed or adopted by a party with present intention to authenticate a writing." UCC 3–401(b) expands on this by stating that a "signature may be made (i) manually or by means of a device or machine, and (ii) by the use of any name, including a trade or assumed name, or by a word, mark, or symbol executed or adopted by a person with present intention to authenticate a writing." Thus, initials, an X (if the writing is signed by a witness), or a thumbprint will normally suffice as a signature. A trade name or an assumed name is also sufficient. Signatures that are placed onto instruments by means of rubber stamps are permitted and frequently used in the business world. If necessary, parol evidence (discussed in Chapter 12) is admissible to identify the signer. When the signer is identified, the signature becomes effective.

The location of the signature on the document is unimportant, although the usual place is the lower right-hand corner. A *handwritten* statement on the body of the instrument, such as "I, Jerome Cavallo, promise to pay Elaine Grant," is sufficient to act as a signature.

There are virtually no limitations on the manner in which a signature can be made, but one should be careful about receiving an instrument that has been signed in an unusual way. Furthermore, an unusual signature clearly decreases the *marketability* of an instrument, because it creates uncertainty.

UNCONDITIONAL PROMISE OR ORDER TO PAY

¡REMEMBER! Negotiable instruments are classified as promises to pay and orders to pay.

The terms of the promise or order must be included in the writing on the face of a negotiable instrument. The terms must also be *unconditional*—that is, they cannot be conditioned on the occurrence or nonoccurrence of some other event or agreement [UCC 3–104(a)].

Promise or Order For an instrument to be negotiable, it must contain an express order or promise to pay. A mere acknowledgment of the debt, which might logically *imply* a promise, is not sufficient under the UCC, because the promise must be an affirmative (express) undertaking [UCC 3–103(a)(9)]. The traditional I.O.U. is only an acknowledgment of indebtedness. Although the I.O.U. might logically imply a promise, it is not a negotiable instrument, because it does not contain an express promise to repay the debt.

A certificate of deposit is exceptional in this respect. No express promise is required in a CD, because the bank's acknowledgment of the deposit and the other terms of the instrument clearly indicate a promise by the bank to repay the sum of money [UCC 3–104(j)].

An *order* is associated with three-party instruments, such as trade acceptances, checks, and drafts. An order directs a third party to pay the instrument as drawn. In the typical check, for example, the word *pay* (to the order of a payee) is a command to the drawee bank to pay the check when presented, and thus it is an order. The order is mandatory even if it is written in a courteous form with such words as "Please pay" or "Kindly pay." Generally, precise language must be used. An order stating "I wish you would pay" does not fulfill the requirement of precision. The order to the drawee may be addressed to one person or to more than one person, either jointly ("to A *and* B") or alternatively ("to A *or* B") [UCC 3–103(a)(6)].

Unconditionality of Promise or Order A negotiable instrument's utility as a substitute for money or as a credit device would be dramatically reduced if it had conditional promises attached to it. • **EXAMPLE 19.5** Andrew promises in a note to pay Frances $10,000 only on the condition that a certain ship reaches port. No one could safely purchase the promissory note without first investigating whether the ship had arrived. Even then, the facts disclosed by the investigation might be incorrect.• To avoid such problems, the UCC provides that only unconditional promises or orders can be negotiable [UCC 3–104(a)].

A promise or order is conditional (and *not* negotiable) if it states (1) an express condition to payment, (2) that the promise or order is subject to or governed by another writing, or (3) that the rights or obligations with respect to the promise or order are stated in another writing. A reference to another writing, however, does not of itself make the promise or order conditional [UCC 3–106(a)]. For example, the words "As per contract" or "This debt arises from the sale of goods X and Y" do not render an instrument nonnegotiable.

Similarly, a statement in the instrument that payment can be made only out of a particular fund or source will not render the instrument nonnegotiable [UCC 3–106(b)(ii)].[1] • **EXAMPLE 19.6** Suppose that the terms in a note include the statement that payment will be made out of the proceeds of next year's cotton crop. This will not make the note nonnegotiable—although the payee of such a note may find the note commercially unacceptable and refuse to take it.•

Finally, a simple statement in an otherwise negotiable note indicating that the note is secured by a mortgage does not destroy its negotiability. Realize, though, that the statement that a note is secured by a mortgage must not stipulate that the maker's promise to pay is *subject* to the terms and conditions of the mortgage.

In the following case, the court had to decide whether a loan guaranty contained an unconditional promise to pay and therefore constituted a negotiable instrument.

1. Section 3–105(2)(b) of the unrevised Article 3 provided just the opposite: an instrument with a term providing that payment could be made only out of a particular fund or source rendered the instrument nonnegotiable.

CASE 19.1 Federal Deposit Insurance Corp. v. F.S.S.S.

United States District Court,
District of Alaska, 1993.
829 F.Supp. 317.

HISTORICAL AND ECONOMIC SETTING *Banks often fail because of too many bad loans. When a federally insured bank fails, the Federal Deposit Insurance Corporation (FDIC) normally pays off each depositor, up to $100,000, and then sells the bank's assets to obtain some repayment. Sometimes, the FDIC is repaid a percentage of what it pays out by negotiating another bank's acquisition of the failed bank. To arrange a deal, the FDIC may subsidize the acquisition. To obtain other funds, the FDIC may also attempt to collect on some of the failed bank's outstanding loans.*

BACKGROUND AND FACTS Thomas Fink, Donald Schroer, David Swanson, and Marie Swanson—doing business as F.S.S.S., a partnership—signed two promissory notes to borrow money from the Alaska Mutual Bank (AMB), providing the same real estate as security for both loans. Patricia Fink and LaVonne Schroer signed guaranties of repayment for the second note. AMB failed. The first note ended up in the hands of the First Interstate Bank of Oregon. The second fell into the possession of the Federal Deposit Insurance Corporation (FDIC). When Fink, Schroer, and the Swansons were unable to repay the first note, the Oregon bank agreed to accept a lesser amount if the FDIC would approve. The FDIC refused and filed a suit in a federal district court against the Finks, the Schroers, and the Swansons to collect the money due on the note that the FDIC now owned. On the FDIC's motion for summary judgment, one of the issues was whether Patricia and LaVonne's guaranties were negotiable instruments. If so, Patricia and LaVonne could have asserted a defense under which they might have been able to avoid liability.

IN THE WORDS OF THE COURT . . .
SEDWICK, District Judge.

* * * *

* * * To constitute a negotiable instrument, a document must be signed by the maker, contain an unconditional promise to pay * * * , be payable on demand or at a definite time, and be payable to order or bearer.

* * * Patricia Fink and LaVonne Schroer executed separate documents apart from the promissory notes that they guaranteed. Importantly, the promissory notes do not reference or incorporate the guaranties. Neither guaranty at issue contains an unconditional promise to pay a sum certain. Neither guaranty is a negotiable instrument.

DECISION AND REMEDY The federal district court granted the FDIC's motion for summary judgment.

FOR CRITICAL ANALYSIS—Economic Consideration *If the defendants in this case had avoided the repayment of their note to the FDIC, who would have ultimately had to pay for their default?*

A Fixed Amount of Money

Negotiable instruments must state with certainty a fixed amount of money to be paid at any time the instrument is payable [UCC 3–104(a)]. This requirement promises clarity and certainty in determining the value of the instrument.

Fixed Amount The term *fixed amount* means an amount that is ascertainable from the face of the instrument. A demand note payable with 8 percent interest meets the requirement of a fixed amount[2] because its amount can be determined at the time

2. Under Section 3–104(1)(b) of the unrevised Article 3, the amount to be paid was called a *sum certain.*

International Perspective • INSTRUMENTS WITH VARIABLE INTEREST RATES

During the 1980s, variable-rate mortgages became increasingly popular. This led to problems, because Article 3, prior to the 1990 revision, stated that an amount or rate of interest could be determined only from the instrument without reference to any outside source. The 1990 revision of Article 3 brought the UCC into line with current business practices by providing that notes tied to a variable interest rate can be negotiable. As part of an ongoing effort to make international law consistent for negotiable instruments, the United Nations Convention on International Bills of Exchange and International Promissory Notes (CIBN) has established rules to govern international transactions. The CIBN, like revised Article 3 of the UCC, considers an instrument with a variable interest rate to be negotiable.

FOR CRITICAL ANALYSIS

Can you think of any reasons why an instrument with a variable interest rate should not be negotiable?

it is payable or at any time thereafter [UCC 3–104(a)]. The rate of interest also may be determined with reference to information that is not contained in the instrument but that is readily ascertainable by reference to a formula or a source described in the instrument [UCC 3–112(b)].[3] For example, when an instrument is payable at the *legal rate of interest* (a rate of interest fixed by statute), the instrument is negotiable. Mortgage notes tied to a variable rate of interest (a rate that fluctuates as a result of market conditions) can also be negotiable. The requirement that to be negotiable a writing must contain a promise or order to pay a fixed amount applies only to the principal [UCC 3–104(a)].

Payable in Money UCC 3–104(a) provides that a fixed amount is to be *payable in money.* The UCC defines money as "a medium of exchange authorized or adopted by a domestic or foreign government as a part of its currency" [UCC 1–201(24)]. • **EXAMPLE 19.7** Suppose that the maker of a note promises "to pay on demand $1,000 in U.S. gold." Because gold is not a medium of exchange adopted by the U.S. government, the note is not payable in money. The same result would occur if the maker promises "to pay $1,000 and fifty bottles of 1990 Château Lafite-Rothschild wine," because the instrument is not payable *entirely* in money. An instrument payable in government bonds or in shares of IBM stock is not negotiable, because neither is a medium of exchange recognized by the U.S. government. •

The statement "Payable in $1,000 U.S. currency or an equivalent value in gold" would render the instrument nonnegotiable if the maker reserved the option of paying in money or gold. If the option were left to the payee, some legal scholars argue that the instrument would be negotiable. Any instrument payable in the United States with a face amount stated in a foreign currency is negotiable and can be paid in the foreign money or in the equivalent in U.S. dollars [UCC 3–107].

3. This was not possible under the unrevised Article 3, which required that an amount or rate of interest could be determined only from the instrument without reference to any outside source [UCC 3–106].

PAYABLE ON DEMAND OR AT A DEFINITE TIME

• ACCEPTOR
A drawee that promises to pay an instrument when the instrument is presented later for payment.

A negotiable instrument must "be payable on demand or at a definite time" [UCC 3–104(a)(2)]. Clearly, to ascertain the value of a negotiable instrument, it is necessary to know when the maker, drawee, or acceptor (an **acceptor** is a drawee that promises to pay an instrument when it is presented later for payment) is required to pay. It is also necessary to know when the obligations of secondary parties, such as indorsers[4] (to be discussed later in this chapter), will arise. Furthermore, it is necessary to know when an instrument is due in order to calculate when the statute of limitations may apply [UCC 3–118(a)]. Finally, with an interest-bearing instrument, it is necessary to know the exact interval during which the interest will accrue to determine the present value of the instrument.

• PRESENTMENT
The act of presenting an instrument to the party liable on the instrument to collect payment; presentment also occurs when a person presents an instrument to a drawee for a required acceptance.

Payable on Demand Instruments that are payable on demand include those that contain the words "Payable at sight" or "Payable upon presentment." **Presentment** occurs when a person presents an instrument to the party liable on the instrument to collect payment; presentment also occurs when a person presents an instrument to a drawee for acceptance (see the discussion of trade acceptances earlier in this chapter).

The very nature of the instrument may indicate that it is payable on demand. For example, a check, by definition, is payable on demand [UCC 3–104(f)]. If no time for payment is specified and the person responsible for payment must pay on the instrument's presentment, the instrument is payable on demand [UCC 3–108(a)].

Payable at a Definite Time If an instrument is not payable on demand, to be negotiable it must be payable at a definite time. An instrument is payable at a definite time if it states that it is payable (1) on a specified date, (2) within a definite period of time (such as thirty days) after sight or acceptance, or (3) on a date or time readily ascertainable at the time the promise or order is issued [UCC 3–108(b)]. The maker or drawee is under no obligation to pay until the specified time.

• **EXAMPLE 19.8** Suppose that an instrument dated June 1, 2000, states, "One year after the death of my grandfather, Henry Adams, I promise to pay to the order of James Harmon $5,000. [Signed] Jacqueline Wells." This instrument is nonnegotiable. Because the date of the grandfather's death is uncertain, the instrument is not payable at a definite time. •

¡BE AWARE!
Interest payable on an instrument normally cannot exceed the maximum limit on interest under a state's usury statute.

When an instrument is payable by the maker or drawer on or before a stated date, it is clearly payable at a definite time, although the maker or drawer has the option of paying before the stated maturity date. If the maker or drawer does not pay early, the holder can still rely on payment being made before the maturity date. Thus, the option to pay early does not violate the definite-time requirement. • **EXAMPLE 19.9** Suppose that Levine gives Hirsch an instrument dated November 1, 1999, that indicates on its face that it is payable on or before November 1, 2001. This instrument satisfies the requirement. • In contrast, an instrument that is undated and made payable "one month after date" is clearly nonnegotiable. There is no way to determine the maturity date from the face of the instrument.

The issue in the following case was whether a particular promissory note, on which the "date" blanks had not been filled in, was payable at a definite time.

4. We should note here that because the UCC uses the spelling indorse (indorsement, and so on), rather than endorse (endorsement, and so on), we adopt that spelling here and in other chapters in the text.

CASE 19.2 Barclays Bank PLC[a] v. Johnson

Court of Appeals of North Carolina, 1998.
129 N.C.App. 370,
499 S.E.2d 768.
www.aoc.state.nc.us/www/public/html/opinions.htm[b]

COMPANY PROFILE *Barclays PLC is one of the largest financial services companies in the United Kingdom (UK) and offers banking and investment services in other countries worldwide. Through Barclays Bank PLC and Barclays's other divisions, the company is involved in consumer and business banking (with nearly two thousand branches in the UK and one thousand branches in seventy-six other countries), credit cards, mortgage lending, factoring, leasing services, and travel agency services. Barclays also sells life insurance, manages pensions, and offers private banking services.*

a. *PLC* is an abbreviation for "Public Limited Company," a company in the United Kingdom with more than fifty shareholders that offers its shares for sale to the public but whose shareholders are not liable for company debts beyond the amount of their investments.
b. This page, within the Web site of the North Carolina state courts, contains links to some of the courts' opinions. Click on "Slip Opinions" or "Reported Decisions—1998," and on the page that opens, scroll down the list (or use your browser's "Find" function) to locate this case. Click on the link to access the opinion.

BACKGROUND AND FACTS Mark Johnson signed a promissory note for $28,979.15 in favor of Healthco International, Inc., as part of Johnson's purchase of supplies from Healthco for his dental practice. The note stated that it was payable as follows:

> Payable in ____ Successive Monthly Installments of $ ________ Each, and in 11 Successive Monthly Installments of $2,414.92 Each thereafter, and in a final payment of $2,415.03 thereafter. The first installment being payable on the __ day of _____ 19 __, and the remaining installments on the same date of each month thereafter until paid.

The blanks were never filled in. Barclays Bank PLC bought the note. When Johnson defaulted on the note, Barclays filed a complaint in a North Carolina state court against Johnson. Johnson responded in part that he had not paid off the note because he had not received all of the supplies. Concluding that the note was not negotiable because it was not payable at a definite time, the court issued a summary judgment in Johnson's favor. Barclays appealed.

IN THE WORDS OF THE COURT . . .
McGEE, Judge.

* * * *

Barclays Bank argues that the note is a negotiable instrument even though it does not state that it is payable on demand or at a definite time. We disagree. Historically, our courts have required strict compliance with the requirements set out under the Uniform Commercial Code defining negotiable instruments. The drafters of the Code encouraged the courts to strictly interpret the definitional requirements to the extent that "in doubtful cases the [court's] decision should be against negotiability." In this case it is undisputed that the note did not state either that it was payable on demand or at a definite time. For this reason, we hold that the note does not meet the requirements of [the UCC] for negotiability. Accordingly, Barclays Bank does not qualify as a holder in due course of a negotiable instrument and is not immune from the defense of failure of consideration.

DECISION AND REMEDY The Court of Appeals of North Carolina affirmed the judgment of the lower court. The state intermediate appellate court held that to be negotiable, an instrument must state that it is payable on demand or at a definite time.

FOR CRITICAL ANALYSIS—Economic Consideration *Why are the requirements for negotiability strictly enforced?*

• **ACCELERATION CLAUSE**
A clause that allows a payee or other holder of a time instrument to demand payment of the entire amount due, with interest, if a certain event occurs, such as a default in the payment of an installment when due.

• **HOLDER**
Any person in the possession of an instrument drawn, issued, or indorsed to him or her, to his or her order, to bearer, or in blank.

Acceleration Clause An **acceleration clause** allows a payee or other holder of a time instrument to demand payment of the entire amount due, with interest, if a certain event occurs, such as a default in the payment of an installment when due. (A **holder** is any person in the possession of an instrument drawn, issued, or indorsed to him or her, to his or her order, to bearer, or in blank [see UCC 1–201(20)]. (The terms *indorse, bearer,* and *in blank* will be explained later in the chapter.) Reasons for acceleration that are stated in the instrument do not affect the instrument's negotiability. For an acceleration clause to be enforced, however, there must be a good faith belief that payment will not be made.

• EXAMPLE 19.10 Assume that Martin lends $1,000 to Ruth. Ruth makes a negotiable note promising to pay $100 per month for eleven months. The note contains an acceleration provision that permits Martin or any holder to demand at once all of the remaining payments plus the interest owed to date if Ruth fails to pay an installment in any given month. If, for example, Ruth fails to make the third payment, the note will be due and payable in full. If Martin accelerates the unpaid balance, Ruth will owe Martin the remaining principal plus any unpaid interest.•

Under the UCC, instruments that include acceleration clauses are negotiable, because (1) the exact value of the instrument can be ascertained and (2) the instrument will be payable on a specified date if the event allowing acceleration does not occur [UCC 3–108(b)(ii)]. Thus, the specified date is the outside limit used to determine the value and negotiability of the instrument.

• **EXTENSION CLAUSE**
A clause in a time instrument that allows the instrument's date of maturity to be extended into the future.

Extension Clause The reverse of an acceleration clause is an **extension clause,** which allows the date of maturity to be extended into the future [UCC 3–108(b)(iii), (iv)]. To keep the instrument negotiable, the interval of the extension must be specified if the right to extend is given to the maker of the instrument. If, however, the holder of the instrument can extend it, the extended maturity date does not have to be specified.

• EXAMPLE 19.11 Suppose that a note reads, "The maker has the right to postpone the time of payment of this note beyond its definite maturity date of January 1, 2001. This extension, however, shall be for no more than a reasonable time." A note with this language is not negotiable, because it does not satisfy the definite-time requirement. The right to extend is the maker's, and the maker has not indicated when the note will become due after the extension. In contrast, a note that reads, "The holder of this note at the date of maturity, January 1, 2001, can extend the time of payment until the following June 1 or later, if the holder so wishes," is a negotiable instrument. The length of the extension does not have to be specified, because the option to extend is solely that of the holder. After January 1, 2001, the note is, in effect, a demand instrument.•

PAYABLE TO ORDER OR TO BEARER

Because one of the functions of a negotiable instrument is to serve as a substitute for money, freedom to transfer an instrument to another person is an essential requirement. To assure a proper transfer, the instrument must be "payable to order or to bearer" at the time it is issued or first comes into the possession of the holder [UCC 3–104(a)(1)]. This is no longer required for a check to be negotiable, however [UCC 3–104(c)]. Thus, a bank could eliminate the words "the order of" in the familiar phrase "Pay to the order of," and the check would still be negotiable. All other instruments, however, will not be negotiable unless they meet this requirement.

• **ORDER INSTRUMENT**
A negotiable instrument that is payable "to the order of an identified person" or "to an identified person or order."

Order Instruments An **order instrument** is an instrument that is payable (1) "to the order of an identified person" or (2) "to an identified person or order" [UCC

3–109(b)]. An identified person is the person "to whom the instrument is initially payable" as determined by the intent of the maker or drawer [UCC 3–110(a)]. The identified person, in turn, may transfer the instrument to whomever he or she wishes. Thus, the maker or drawer is agreeing to pay either the person specified on the instrument or whomever that person might designate. In this way, the instrument retains its transferability. • **EXAMPLE 19.12** Suppose an instrument states, "Payable to the order of Rocky Reed" or "Pay to Rocky Reed or order." Clearly, the maker or drawer has indicated that a payment will be made to Reed or to whomever Reed designates. The instrument is negotiable.•

• INDORSEMENT
A signature placed on an instrument for the purpose of transferring one's ownership rights in the instrument.

Except for bearer instruments (explained in the following paragraph), the person specified must be named with *certainty*, because the transfer of an order instrument requires an indorsement. (An **indorsement** is a signature placed on an instrument, such as on the back of a check, for the purpose of transferring one's ownership rights in the instrument.) • **EXAMPLE 19.13** If an instrument states, "Payable to the order of my kissing cousin," the instrument is nonnegotiable. This is because a holder could not be sure that the person who indorsed the instrument was actually the "kissing cousin" who was supposed to have indorsed it.•

• BEARER INSTRUMENT
Any instrument that is not payable to a specific person, including instruments payable to the bearer or to "cash."

• BEARER
A person in the possession of an instrument payable to bearer or indorsed in blank.

Bearer Instruments A **bearer instrument** is an instrument that does not designate a specific payee [UCC 3–109(a)]. The term **bearer** refers to a person in the possession of an instrument that is payable to bearer or indorsed in blank (with a signature only, as will be discussed shortly) [UCC 1–201(5), 3–109(a), 3–109(c)]. This means that the maker or drawer agrees to pay anyone who presents the instrument for payment. Any instrument containing the following terms is a bearer instrument:

- "Payable to the order of bearer."
- "Payable to Rocky Reed or bearer."
- "Payable to bearer."
- "Pay cash."
- "Pay to the order of cash."

In addition, an instrument that "indicates that it is not payable to an identified person" is bearer paper [UCC 3–109(a)(3)]. Thus, an instrument "payable to X" or "payable to Batman" can be negotiated as bearer paper, as though it were payable to cash. The UCC does not accept an instrument issued to a nonexistent organization as payable to bearer, however [UCC 3–109, Comment 2]. An instrument "payable to the order of the Camrod Company," if no such company exists, therefore would not be bearer paper.

¡NOTE!
An instrument that purports to be payable both to order and bearer is a contradiction in terms. Such an instrument is a bearer instrument.

Factors That Do Not Affect Negotiability

Certain ambiguities or omissions will not affect the negotiability of an instrument. The UCC's rules for clearing up ambiguous terms are the following:

1. Unless the date of an instrument is necessary to determine a definite time for payment, the fact that an instrument is undated does not affect its negotiability. A typical example is an undated check [UCC 3–113(b)].
2. Postdating or antedating an instrument does not affect the instrument's negotiability [UCC 3–113(a)].
3. Handwritten terms outweigh typewritten and printed terms (preprinted terms on forms, for example), and typewritten terms outweigh printed terms [UCC 3–114]. For example, if your check is printed, "Pay to the order of," and in handwriting you

insert in the blank, "Anita Delgado or bearer," the check is a bearer instrument. ❹ Words outweigh figures unless the words are ambiguous [UCC 3–114]. This rule is important when the numerical amount and written amount on a check differ. ❺ When a particular interest rate is not specified but the instrument simply states "with interest," the interest rate is the *judgment rate of interest* (a rate of interest fixed by statute that is applied to a monetary judgment awarded by a court until the judgment is paid or terminated) [UCC 3–112(b)].

Transfer of Instruments

Once issued, a negotiable instrument can be transferred by *assignment* or by *negotiation.*

TRANSFER BY ASSIGNMENT

Recall from Chapter 13 that an assignment is a transfer of rights under a contract. Under general contract principles, a transfer by assignment to an assignee gives the assignee only those rights that the assignor possessed. Any defenses that can be raised against an assignor can normally be raised against the assignee. This same principle applies when an instrument, such as a promissory note, is transferred by assignment. The transferee is then an *assignee* rather than a *holder.* Sometimes, a transfer fails to qualify as a negotiation because it fails to meet one or more of the requirements of a negotiable instrument, discussed above. When this occurs, the transfer becomes an assignment.

TRANSFER BY NEGOTIATION

• **NEGOTIATION**
The transfer of an instrument in such form that the transferee (the person to whom the instrument is transferred) becomes a holder.

Negotiation is the transfer of an instrument in such form that the transferee (the person to whom the instrument is transferred) becomes a holder [UCC 3–201(a)]. Under UCC principles, a transfer by negotiation creates a holder who, at the very least, receives the rights of the previous possessor [UCC 3–203(b)]. Unlike an assignment, a transfer by negotiation can make it possible for a holder to receive more rights in the instrument than the prior possessor had [UCC 3–202(b), 3–305, 3–306]. A holder who receives greater rights is known as a *holder in due course,* a concept we discuss in Chapter 20.

There are two methods of negotiating an instrument so that the receiver becomes a holder. The method used depends on whether the instrument is order paper or bearer paper.

Negotiating Order Instruments An order instrument contains the name of a payee capable of indorsing it, as in "Pay to the order of Lloyd Sorenson." An order instrument is also an instrument that has as its last or only indorsement a *special* indorsement, as in "Pay to Sorenson. [Signed] Adams." (Special indorsements are discussed in more detail later in this chapter.) If the instrument is an order instrument, it is negotiated by delivery with any necessary indorsements. • **EXAMPLE 19.14** National Express Corporation issues a payroll check "to the order of Lloyd Sorenson." Sorenson takes the check to the supermarket, signs his name on the back (an indorsement), gives it to the cashier (a delivery), and receives cash. Sorenson has *negotiated* the check to the supermarket [UCC 3–201(b)].•

¡RECALL!
A person convicted of theft may be sued for conversion. Conversion is the civil side of crimes of theft.

Negotiating Bearer Instruments If an instrument is payable to bearer, it is negotiated by delivery—that is, by transfer into another person's possession. Indorsement is not necessary [UCC 3–201(b)]. The use of bearer instruments thus involves more risk through loss or theft than the use of order instruments.

• **EXAMPLE 19.15** Assume that Richard Kray writes a check "payable to cash" and hands it to Jessie Arnold (a delivery). Kray has issued the check (a bearer instrument) to Arnold. Arnold places the check in her wallet, which is subsequently stolen. The thief has possession of the check. At this point, the thief has no rights to the check. If the thief "delivers" the check to an innocent third person, however, negotiation has occurred. All rights to the check will be passed absolutely to that third person, and Arnold will lose all rights to recover the proceeds of the check from him or her [UCC 3–306]. Of course, Arnold could attempt to recover the money from the thief if the thief can be found.•

> "Money has little value to its possessor unless it also has value to others."
>
> LELAND STANFORD, 1824–1893
> (U.S. senator and founder of Stanford University)

Converting Order Instruments to Bearer Instruments and Vice Versa The method used for negotiation depends on the character of the instrument at the time the negotiation takes place. • **EXAMPLE 19.16** Suppose that a check that was originally payable to "cash" was subsequently indorsed with the words "Pay to Arnold." This instrument must be negotiated as an order instrument (by indorsement and delivery), even though it was previously a bearer instrument [UCC 3–205(a)].•

An instrument payable to the order of a named payee and indorsed in blank (by the holder's signature only, as will be discussed shortly) becomes a bearer instrument [UCC 3–205(b)]. • **EXAMPLE 19.17** A check made payable to the order of Jessie Arnold is issued to Arnold, and Arnold indorses it by signing her name on the back. The instrument, which is now a bearer instrument, can be negotiated by delivery without indorsement. Arnold can negotiate the check to whomever she wishes merely by delivery, and that person can negotiate by delivery without indorsement. If Arnold loses the check after she indorses it, then a finder can negotiate it further.• Exhibit 19–5 illustrates how indorsements can convert an order instrument into a bearer instrument and vice versa.

EXHIBIT 19–5 • Converting an Order Instrument to a Bearer Instrument and Vice Versa

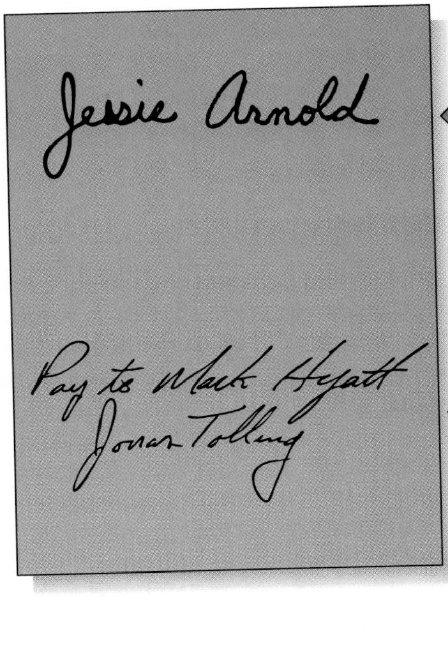

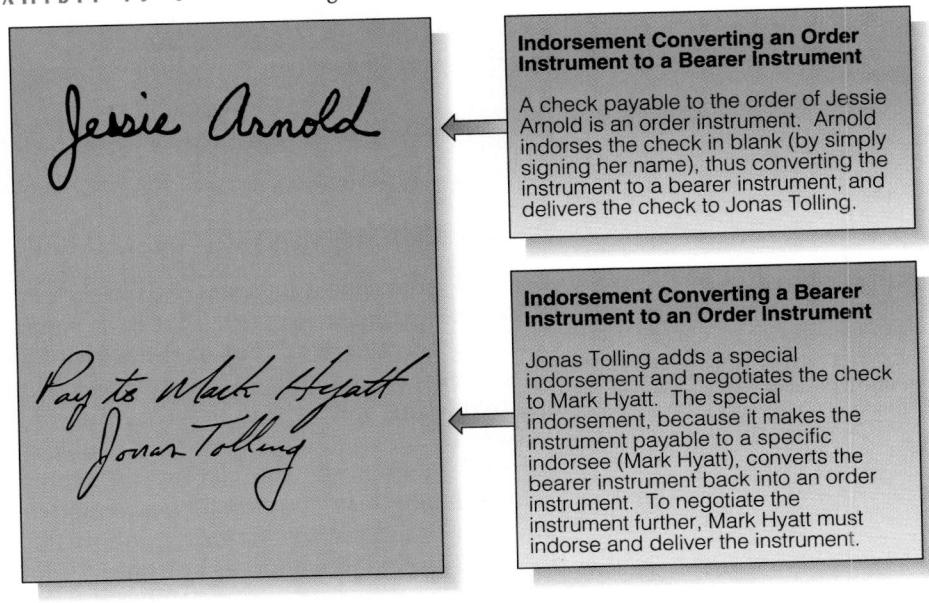

Indorsement Converting an Order Instrument to a Bearer Instrument

A check payable to the order of Jessie Arnold is an order instrument. Arnold indorses the check in blank (by simply signing her name), thus converting the instrument to a bearer instrument, and delivers the check to Jonas Tolling.

Indorsement Converting a Bearer Instrument to an Order Instrument

Jonas Tolling adds a special indorsement and negotiates the check to Mark Hyatt. The special indorsement, because it makes the instrument payable to a specific indorsee (Mark Hyatt), converts the bearer instrument back into an order instrument. To negotiate the instrument further, Mark Hyatt must indorse and deliver the instrument.

Indorsements

Indorsements are required whenever the instrument being negotiated is classified as an order instrument. An *indorsement* is a signature with or without additional words or statements. It is most often written on the back of the instrument itself. If there is no room on the instrument, indorsements can be written on a separate piece of paper, called an **allonge.**[5] The allonge must be "so firmly affixed [to the instrument] as to become a part thereof" [UCC 3–204(a)]. Pins or paper clips will not suffice. Most courts hold that staples are sufficient.

• **ALLONGE**
A piece of paper firmly attached to a negotiable instrument, on which transferees can make indorsements if there is no room left on the instrument itself.

A person who transfers an instrument by signing (indorsing) it and delivering it to another person is an **indorser.** The person to whom the check is indorsed and delivered is the **indorsee.** • EXAMPLE 19.18 Martha receives a graduation check for $500. She can transfer the check to her mother (or to anyone) by signing it on the back and delivering it. Martha is an indorser. If Martha indorses the check by writing "Pay to Mary Grimes," Mary Grimes is the indorsee. •

• **INDORSER**
A person who transfers an instrument by signing (indorsing) it and delivering it to another person.

• **INDORSEE**
The person to whom a negotiable instrument is transferred by indorsement.

One purpose of an indorsement is to effect the negotiation of order paper. Sometimes the transferee of a bearer instrument will request the holder-transferor to indorse the instrument in such a way as to to impose liability on the indorser (the liability of indorsers will be discussed in Chapter 20), although the UCC does not require bearer instruments to be indorsed.

We examine here four categories of indorsements: blank indorsements, special indorsements, qualified indorsements, and restrictive indorsements.

Blank Indorsements

A **blank indorsement** specifies no particular indorsee and can consist of a mere signature [UCC 3–205(b)]. Hence, a check payable "to the order of Alan Luberda" can be indorsed in blank simply by having Luberda's signature written on the back of the check. An instrument payable to order and indorsed in blank becomes a bearer instrument and can be negotiated by delivery alone, as already discussed. Exhibit 19–6 shows a blank indorsement.

• **BLANK INDORSEMENT**
An indorsement that specifies no particular indorsee and that can consist of a mere signature. An order instrument that is indorsed in blank becomes a bearer instrument.

EXHIBIT 19–6 • A Blank Indorsement

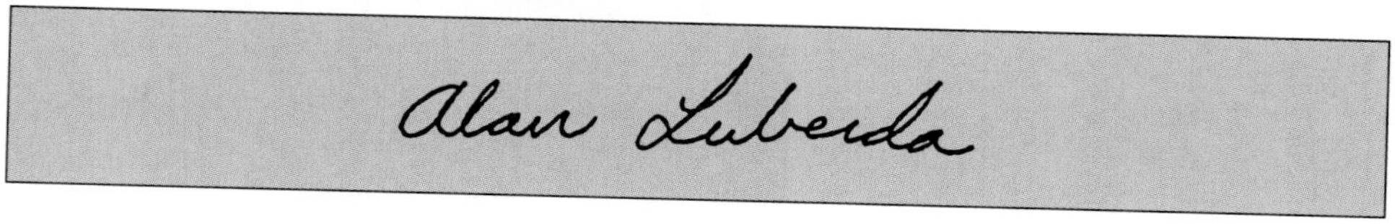

Special Indorsements

A **special indorsement** indicates the specific person to whom the indorser intends to make the instrument payable; that is, it names the indorsee [UCC 3–205(a)]. For example, words such as "Pay to the order of Storr" or "Pay to Storr," followed by the signature of the indorser, create a special indorsement. When an instrument is indorsed in this way, it is an order instrument.

• **SPECIAL INDORSEMENT**
An indorsement on an instrument that indicates the specific person to whom the indorser intends to make the instrument payable; that is, it names the indorsee.

To avoid the risk of loss from theft, a holder may convert a blank indorsement to a special indorsement. This changes the bearer instrument back to an order instrument. A holder may "convert a blank indorsement that consists only of a signature into a special indorsement by writing, above the signature of the indorser, words identifying the person to whom the instrument is made payable" [UCC 3–205(c)].

5. Pronounced uh-*lohnj*.

• **EXAMPLE 19.19** A check is made payable to Arthur Rabe. He indorses his name in blank (signs his name only) on the back of the check and delivers the check to Anthony Alfonso. Anthony, not wishing to cash the check immediately, wants to avoid any risk should he lose the check. He therefore writes "Pay to Anthony Alfonso" above Arthur's blank indorsement (see Exhibit 19–7). In this manner, Anthony has converted Arthur's blank indorsement into a special indorsement. Further negotiation now requires Anthony Alfonso's indorsement plus delivery. •

EXHIBIT 19–7 • A Special Indorsement

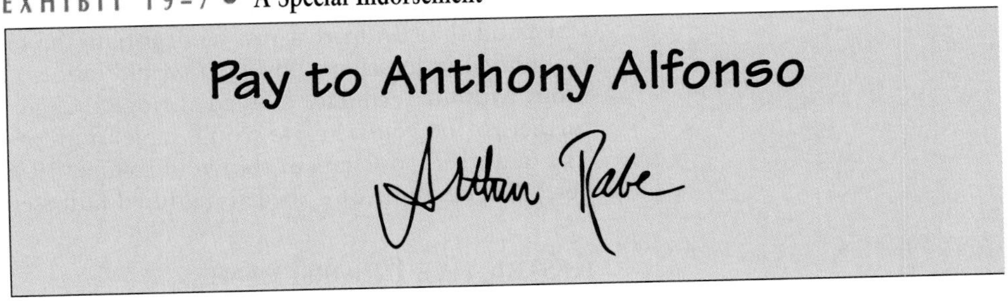

QUALIFIED INDORSEMENTS

Generally, an indorser, *merely by indorsing,* impliedly promises to pay the holder, or any subsequent indorser, the amount of the instrument in the event that the drawer or maker defaults on the payment [UCC 3–415(b)]. An indorser can use a **qualified indorsement** to disclaim this contract liability on the instrument. The notation "without recourse" is commonly used to create a qualified indorsement, such as the one shown in Exhibit 19–8.

• **QUALIFIED INDORSEMENT**
An indorsement on a negotiable instrument in which the indorser disclaims any contract liability on the instrument; the notation "without recourse" is commonly used to create a qualified indorsement.

EXHIBIT 19–8 • A Qualified Indorsement

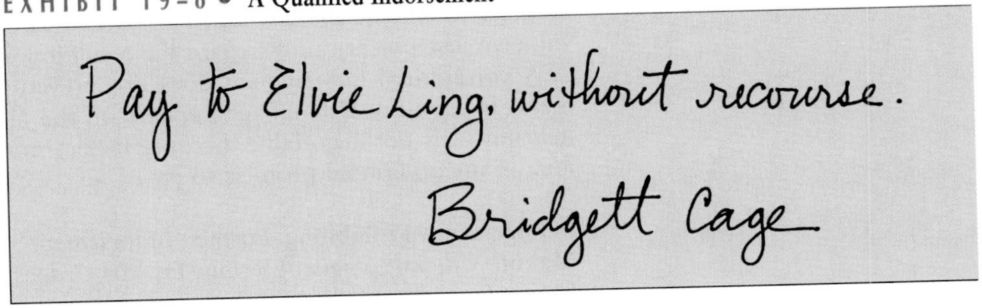

Qualified indorsements are often used by persons acting in a representative capacity. • **EXAMPLE 19.20** Insurance agents sometimes receive checks payable to them that are really intended as payment to the insurance company. The agent is merely indorsing the payment through to the insurance company and should not be required to make good on the check if it is later dishonored. The "without recourse" indorsement relieves the agent from any contract liability on a check. If the instrument is dishonored, the holder cannot obtain recovery from the agent who indorsed "without recourse" unless the indorser has breached one of the transfer warranties discussed in Chapter 20, which relate to good title, authorized signature, no material alteration, and so forth. •

Usually, then, blank and special indorsements are *unqualified indorsements*. That is, the blank or special indorser is guaranteeing payment of the instrument in addition to transferring title to it. The qualified indorser is not guaranteeing payment. Nonetheless, an instrument bearing a qualified indorsement can be negotiated.

A qualified indorsement is accompanied by either a special indorsement or a blank indorsement that determines further negotiation. Accordingly, a special qualified indorsement makes the instrument an order instrument, and it requires an indorsement plus delivery for negotiation. A blank qualified indorsement makes the instrument a bearer instrument, and only delivery is required for negotiation.

• **EXAMPLE 19.21** Assume that a check is made payable to the order of Bridgett Cage and that Bridgett wants to negotiate the check specifically to Elvie Ling with a qualified indorsement. Bridgett would indorse the check as follows: "Pay to Elvie Ling, without recourse. [Signed] Bridgett Cage." For Elvie to negotiate the check further to Joe Nantz, Elvie would have to indorse the check and deliver it to Joe.• The qualified indorsement shown in Exhibit 19–8 above, which was referred to earlier, is an example of a special qualified indorsement.

RESTRICTIVE INDORSEMENTS

• **RESTRICTIVE INDORSEMENT** Any indorsement on a negotiable instrument that requires the indorsee to comply with certain instructions regarding the funds involved. A restrictive indorsement does not prohibit the further negotiation of the instrument.

The **restrictive indorsement** requires indorsees to comply with certain instructions regarding the funds involved. A restrictive indorsement does not prohibit the further negotiation of an instrument [UCC 3–206(a)]. Restrictive indorsements come in many forms, some of which we discuss here.

Conditional Indorsements When payment depends on the occurrence of some event specified in the indorsement, the instrument has a conditional indorsement [UCC 3–205(a)]. For example, if Ken Barton indorses a check, "Pay to Lars Johansen if he completes the renovation of my kitchen by June 1, 2000. [Signed] Ken Barton," Barton has created a conditional indorsement. Article 3, however, states that an indorsement conditioning the right to receive payment "does not affect the right of the indorsee to enforce the instrument" [UCC 3–206(b)]. A person paying or taking for value an instrument can disregard the condition without liability.[6]

A conditional indorsement does not prevent further negotiation of the instrument. If conditional language appears on the *face* of an instrument, however, the instrument is not negotiable, because it does not meet the requirement that it contain an unconditional promise to pay.

Indorsements Prohibiting Further Indorsement An indorsement such as "Pay to Makoto Chi only. [Signed] Jerome Edelman" does not destroy transfer by negotiation. Chi can negotiate the instrument to a holder just as if it had read "Pay to Makoto Chi. [Signed] Jerome Edelman" [UCC 3–206(a)]. If the holder gives value to Chi, this type of restrictive indorsement has the same legal effect as a special indorsement.

Indorsements for Deposit or Collection A common type of restrictive indorsement is one that makes the indorsee (almost always a bank) a collecting agent of the indorser [UCC 3–206(c)]. For example, if Stephanie Mallak wants to deposit a check she has received into her checking account at the bank, she could indorse the check "For deposit only. [Signed] Stephanie Mallak." (See Exhibit 19–9.) A "Pay any bank or

6. Under the unrevised Article 3, neither the indorsee nor any subsequent holder had the right to enforce payment against an indorser who indorsed a check conditionally until the specified condition was met [UCC 3–206(3)].

banker" or "For deposit" indorsement has the effect of locking the instrument into the bank collection process, and thus prohibits further negotiation except by a bank. Following this indorsement, only a bank can acquire the rights of a holder.

EXHIBIT 19–9 • For Deposit/For Collection Indorsements

• **TRUST INDORSEMENT**
An indorsement for the benefit of the indorser or a third person; also known as an agency indorsement. The indorsement results in legal title vesting in the original indorsee.

Trust Indorsements An indorsement indicating that the indorsee is to hold or use the funds for the benefit of the indorser or a third party is called a **trust indorsement** (also known as an *agency indorsement*) [UCC 3–206(d)]. • EXAMPLE 19.22 Assume that Robert Emerson asks his accountant, Ada Johnson, to pay some bills for his invalid wife, Sarah, while he is out of the country. He indorses a check as follows: "Pay to Ada Johnson as Agent for Sarah Emerson." This agency indorsement obligates Johnson to use the funds only for the benefit of Sarah Emerson.• The fiduciary restrictions (restrictions mandated by a relationship involving trust and loyalty) on the instrument do not reach beyond the original indorsee [UCC 3–206(d), (e)]. Exhibit 19–10 shows sample trust indorsements.

EXHIBIT 19–10 • Trust Indorsements

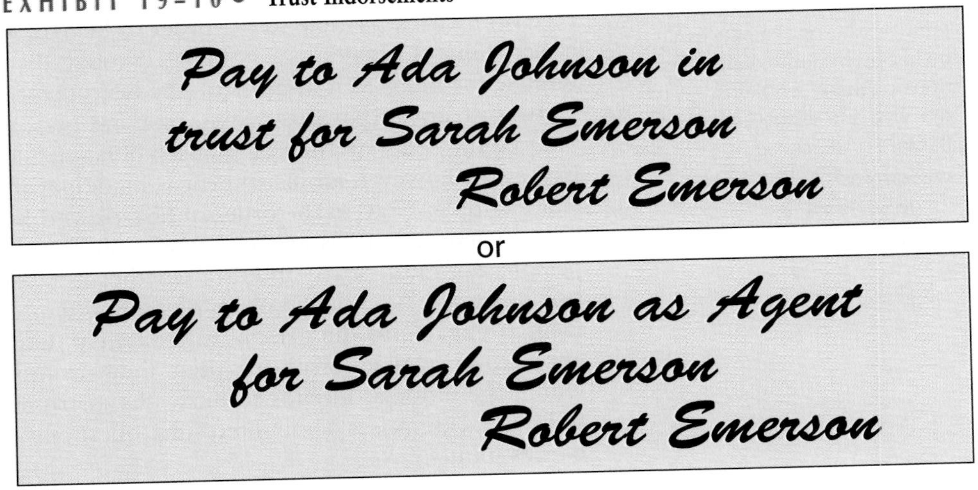

The result of a trust indorsement is that legal rights in the instrument are transferred to the original indorsee (Ada Johnson, in the example just given). To the extent that the original indorsee pays or applies the proceeds consistently with the indorsement (for example, "in trust for Sarah Emerson"), the indorsee is a holder and can become a holder in due course (described in Chapter 20).

ETHICAL ISSUE 19.1 ***Why should fiduciary restrictions on an instrument apply only to the original indorsee?*** Article 3 gives the force of law to the ethical duties of an indorsee on a trust instrument to use the funds in accordance with the wishes of the indorser. Yet what if the original indorsee disregards the fiduciary restrictions on a trust instrument and then transfers it to another person? In this situation, according to Article 3, the subsequent purchaser has no obligation to verify that the fiduciary requirements were met by the original indorsee. Although this may seem unfair, consider the alternative. If all subsequent holders were obligated to verify that the terms of the trust indorsement were fulfilled, it would impair the ease with which instruments could be transferred—and thus impair their function as substitutes for money. By holding only the original indorsee to the fiduciary restrictions on an instrument with a trust indorsement, the UCC furthers one of its basic goals—to encourage the free flow of commerce by making the laws practical and reasonable. Article 3's provisions relating to trust indorsements provide just one example of the many ways in which the UCC balances this goal against other ethical principles.

Miscellaneous Indorsement Problems

Of course, a significant problem in relation to indorsements occurs when an indorsement is forged or unauthorized. The UCC rules concerning unauthorized or forged signatures and indorsements will be discussed in Chapter 20, in the context of signature liability, and again in Chapter 21, in the context of the bank's liability for payment of an instrument over an unauthorized signature. Two other problems that may arise with indorsements concern misspelled names and multiple payees.

> **ON THE WEB**
>
> For a discussion of some of the problems that can arise when negotiable instruments have joint or alternative payees, including hypothetical illustrations of these problems, go to the Web site of the Community Bankers' Advisor at **www.minot.com/~obl/news.html**.

An indorsement should be identical to the name that appears on the instrument. The payee or indorsee whose name is misspelled can indorse with the misspelled name, the correct name, or both [UCC 3–204(d)]. For example, if Sheryl Kruger receives a check payable to the order of Sherrill Krooger, she can indorse the check either "Sheryl Kruger" or "Sherrill Krooger," or both. The usual practice is to indorse the name as it appears on the instrument and follow it by the correct name.

An instrument payable to two or more persons *in the alternative* (for example, "Pay to the order of Tuan or Johnson") requires the indorsement of only one of the payees. If, however, an instrument is made payable to two or more persons *jointly* (for example, "Pay to the order of Sharrie and Bob Covington"), all of the payees' indorsements are necessary for negotiation. If an instrument payable to two or more persons does not clearly indicate whether it is payable in the alternative or jointly (for example, "Pay to the order of John and/or Sara Fitzgerald"), then the instrument is payable to the persons alternatively [UCC 3–110(d)]. The same principles apply to special indorsements that indicate more than one identified person to whom the indorser intends to make the instrument payable [UCC 3–205(a)]. The following case raises some interesting questions concerning checks payable to two parties jointly.

CASE 19.3 General Motors Acceptance Corp. v. Abington Casualty Insurance Co.

Supreme Judicial Court of Massachusetts, 1992.
413 Mass. 583,
602 N.E.2d 1085.

COMPANY PROFILE *One of the major divisions of the General Motors Corporation (GM) is the General Motors Acceptance Corporation (GMAC). Created by William Durant, the founder of General Motors and president of GM before he resigned in 1920, GMAC originally loaned money only to buyers of GM vehicles. Over time, however, GMAC became the second largest mortgage banker in the United States. In the 1980s, GMAC was sometimes more profitable than the GM automotive divisions. By the late 1990s, GMAC held outstanding loans worth nearly $100 billion. This was more than was held by any commercial bank in the United States except Citibank, a division of Citigroup.*

BACKGROUND AND FACTS Abington Casualty Insurance Company issued an insurance policy to Robert Azevedo. The policy covered Azevedo's 1984 Jeep. GMAC held a security interest in the vehicle, and the insurance policy named GMAC as the beneficiary. In other words, if the Jeep was damaged and a claim submitted, Abington was to pay GMAC for the amount of appraised damages. The Jeep was later damaged, and Abington appraised the loss and issued a check payable jointly "to the order of Robert A. Azevedo and G.M.A.C." The check was delivered to Azevedo, who then indorsed the check and presented it to the bank. The bank accepted the check, which had not been indorsed by GMAC, and Azevedo received full payment. GMAC never received the funds. GMAC filed suit in a Massachusetts state court against the drawer of the check, Abington, to recover the insurance payment it should have received. The trial court dismissed the action, and GMAC appealed.

IN THE WORDS OF THE COURT . . .
NOLAN, Justice.

* * * *

* * * [T]he delivery of a negotiable instrument to one joint payee constitutes delivery to all joint payees. * * * [S]ince under Massachusetts law a person must seek the [i]ndorsements of every payee to negotiate, transfer, or discharge a negotiable instrument, delivery of the instrument to one payee does not jeopardize the rights of other payees. We hold, therefore, that Abington's delivery of the check to only one joint payee, Azevedo, nevertheless constitutes delivery to the remaining joint payee, GMAC.

* * * *

* * * However, * * * where there are copayees * * * , a negotiable instrument cannot be discharged by the actions of only one payee. [The UCC] expressly prohibits the discharge of an instrument except by all the payees. * * * Without this rule, there would be no assurance that all the joint payees would receive payment and that the drawer's underlying obligation would be fully discharged.

DECISION AND REMEDY The Supreme Judicial Court of Massachusetts held that although GMAC had received delivery, it had not been paid. The court reversed the lower court's dismissal of GMAC's complaint. The case was remanded to the trial court.

FOR CRITICAL ANALYSIS—Ethical Consideration *The general principle in negotiable instruments law is that the loss should fall on the party in the best position to prevent it. In the case just presented, which party was in the best position to prevent the loss?*

APPLICATION

Law and the Businessperson: Writing & Indorsing Checks*

As a businessperson (or as a consumer), you will certainly be writing and receiving checks. There are pitfalls involved in both activities.

The danger in signing a blank check is clear. Anyone can write in an unauthorized amount and cash the check. Although you may be able to assert lack of authorization against the person who filled in the unauthorized amount, subsequent holders of the properly indorsed check may be able to enforce the check as completed. While you are haggling with the person who inserted the unauthorized figure and who may not be able to repay the amount, you will also have to honor the check for the unauthorized amount to a subsequent holder in due course (see Chapter 20).

* This *Application* is not meant to substitute for the services of an attorney who is licensed to practice law in your state.

It is equally dangerous to write out and sign a check payable to "cash" until you are actually at the bank. Remember that checks payable to "cash" are bearer instruments. This means that if you lose or misplace the check, anybody who finds it can present it to the bank for payment.

Just as a check signed in blank or payable to cash may be dangerous, a negotiable instrument with a blank indorsement also has dangers, because as a bearer instrument, it is as easily transferred as cash. When you make a bank deposit, therefore, you should sign (indorse) the back of the check in blank only in the presence of a teller. If you choose to sign it ahead of time, make sure you insert the words "For deposit only" before you sign your name. As a precaution, you should consider obtaining an indorsement stamp from your bank. Then, when a check is received payable to your business, you can indorse it immediately. The stamped indorsement will indicate that the check is for deposit only to your business account specified by the number.

Checklist for the Use of Negotiable Instruments

1. A good rule of thumb is never to sign a blank check.
2. Another good rule of thumb is never to write and sign a check payable to "cash" until you are actually at the bank.
3. Be wary of indorsing a check in blank unless a bank teller is simultaneously giving you a receipt for your deposit.
4. Consider obtaining an indorsement stamp from your bank so that when you receive checks you can immediately indorse them "For deposit only" to your account.

Key Terms

acceleration clause 504
acceptor 502
allonge 508
bearer 505
bearer instrument 505
blank indorsement 508
certificate of deposit (CD) 496
check 495
draft 494
drawee 494
drawer 494
extension clause 504
holder 504
indorsee 508
indorsement 505
indorser 508
maker 495
negotiable instrument 492
negotiation 506
order instrument 504
payee 494
presentment 502
promissory note 495
qualified indorsement 509
restrictive indorsement 510
signature 498
special indorsement 508
trade acceptance 494
trust indorsement 511

Chapter Summary • Negotiability and Transferability

Article 3 of the UCC (See page 493.)	Article 3 of the Uniform Commercial Code governs the negotiability and transferability of negotiable instruments. Article 3 was significantly revised in 1990. Almost all of the states have adopted the revised article.
Types of Instruments (See pages 493–497.)	The UCC specifies four types of negotiable instruments: drafts, checks, promissory notes, and certificates of deposit (CDs). These instruments fall into two basic classifications: 1. *Demand instruments versus time instruments*—A demand instrument is payable on demand (when the holder presents it to the maker or drawer). A time instrument is payable at a future date. 2. *Orders to pay versus promises to pay*—Checks and drafts are *orders* to pay. Promissory notes and certificates of deposit (CDs) are *promises* to pay.
Requirements for Negotiability (See pages 497–505.)	To be negotiable, an instrument must meet the following requirements: 1. Be in writing. 2. Be signed by the maker or drawer. 3. Be an unconditional promise or order to pay. 4. State a fixed amount of money. 5. Be payable on demand or at a definite time. 6. Be payable to order or bearer.
Factors That Do Not Affect Negotiability (See pages 505–506.)	1. The fact that an instrument is undated does not affect its negotiability unless the date is necessary to determine a definite time for payment. 2. Postdating or antedating an instrument does not affect negotiability. 3. Handwritten terms take priority over typewritten and printed terms. 4. Words outweigh figures unless the words are ambiguous. 5. An instrument that states "with interest" but that does not state the interest rate is payable at the judgment rate of interest.
Transfer of Instruments (See pages 506–507.)	1. *Transfer by assignment*— A transfer by assignment to an assignee gives the assignee only those rights that the assignor possessed. Any defenses against payment that can be raised against an assignor can normally be raised against the assignee. 2. *Transfer by negotiation*—An order instrument is negotiated by indorsement and delivery; a bearer instrument is negotiated by delivery only.
Indorsements (See pages 508–512.)	1. *Blank* (for example, "Alan Luberda"). 2. *Special* (for example, "Pay to Anthony Alfonso. [Signed] Arthur Rabe"). 3. *Qualified* (for example, "Without recourse. [Signed] Bridgett Cage"). 4. *Restrictive* (for example, "For deposit only. [Signed] Stephanie Mallak" or "Pay to Ada Johnson in trust for Sarah Emerson. [Signed] Robert Emerson").
Miscellaneous Indorsement Problems (See pages 512–513.)	1. A payee or indorsee whose name is misspelled can indorse with the misspelled name, the correct name, or both. 2. An instrument payable to two or more persons in the alternative requires the indorsement of only one of the payees. 3. An instrument payable to two or more persons jointly requires all of the payees' indorsements for negotiation. 4. If an instrument payable to two or more persons does not clearly indicate whether it is payable in the alternative or jointly, it is payable to the persons alternatively. The same principle applies to special indorsements that contain multiple indorsees.

For Review

1 What are the four types of negotiable instruments with which Article 3 of the UCC is concerned? Which of these instruments are *orders* to pay, and which of these instruments are *promises* to pay?

2 What requirements must an instrument meet to be negotiable?

3 To whom is a bearer instrument payable?

4 What is the difference between an indorsement in blank and a special indorsement?

5 What is a restrictive indorsement? Does a restrictive indorsement prohibit further negotiation of the instrument? Discuss.

Questions and Case Problems

19–1. Parties to Negotiable Instruments. A note has two original parties. What are these parties called? A check has three original parties. What are these parties called?

19–2. Indorsements. Bertram writes a check for $200, payable to "cash." He puts the check in his pocket and drives to the bank to cash the check. As he gets out of his car in the bank's parking lot, the check slips out of his pocket and falls to the pavement. Jerrod walks by moments later, picks up the check, and later that day delivers it to Amber, to whom he owes $200. Amber indorses the check "For deposit only. [Signed] Amber Dowel" and deposits it into her checking account. In light of these circumstances, answer the following questions:

(a) Is the check a bearer instrument or an order instrument?

(b) Did Jerrod's delivery of the check to Amber constitute a valid negotiation? Why or why not?

(c) What type of indorsement did Amber make?

(d) Does Bertram have a right to recover the $200 from Amber? Explain.

19–3. Requirements for Negotiability. The following note is written by Muriel Evans on the back of an envelope: "I, Muriel Evans, promise to pay Karen Marvin or bearer $100 on demand." Is this a negotiable instrument? Discuss fully.

19–4. Requirements for Negotiability. The following instrument was written on a sheet of paper by Jeff Nolan: "I, the undersigned, do hereby acknowledge that I owe Stephanie Craig one thousand dollars, with interest, payable out of the proceeds of the sale of my horse, Swiftfoot, next month. Payment is to be made on or before six months from date." Discuss specifically why this instrument is not negotiable.

19–5. Indorsements. A check drawn by David for $500 is made payable to the order of Matthew and issued to Matthew. Matthew owes his landlord $500 in rent and transfers the check to his landlord with the following indorsement: "For rent paid. [Signed] Matthew." Matthew's landlord has contracted to have Juarez do some landscaping on the property. When Juarez insists on immediate payment, the landlord transfers the check to Juarez without indorsement. Later, to pay for some palm trees purchased from Green's Nursery, Juarez transfers the check with the following indorsement: "Pay to Green's Nursery, without recourse. [Signed] Juarez." Green's Nursery sends the check to its bank indorsed "For deposit only. [Signed] Green's Nursery."

(a) Classify each of these indorsements.

(b) Was the transfer from Matthew's landlord to Juarez, without indorsement, an assignment or a negotiation? Explain.

19–6. Undated Instruments. During a three-year period, Appliances, Inc., performed electrical heating and plumbing work for Yost Construction worth approximately $7,000. Yost never paid Appliances for any of these jobs. Yost, in both his capacity as president of the construction company and his individual capacity, signed an undated ninety-day promissory note in favor of Appliances to reduce Yost Construction's debt and to have Appliances perform services for Yost as an individual. Neither Yost in his individual capacity nor Yost Construction paid the note, and Appliances filed suit. The trial court held that the undated note was unenforceable. Should Appliances prevail on appeal by arguing that the note was negotiable? [*Appliances, Inc. v. Yost,* 181 Conn. 207, 435 A.2d 1 (1980)]

19–7. Words versus Figures. Eugene Kindy, a seller of diesel engine parts, agreed to buy four diesel engines from Tony Hicks. Kindy transferred $6,500 by wire and issued a check for the remainder of the purchase price. Kindy placed two different amounts on the check, because he did not want the check honored until Hicks had delivered the engine parts. Using a check-imprinting machine, Kindy imprinted $5,550 on the check in the space where the dollar amount is normally written in words, but he wrote $6,550 in figures in the box usually reserved for numbers. An employee of Galatia Community State Bank, noticing the discrepancy, altered the figures in the box to read "$5,550," initialed the change, and accepted the check. The check was returned to Galatia by Kindy's bank at his request, because Hicks had not delivered the engine parts. In the litigation that followed, a key issue was whether the machine-imprinted figure took precedence over the handwritten figure. What should the court decide on this issue? Discuss. [*Galatia Community State Bank v. Kindy,* 807 Ark. 467, 821 S.W.2d 765 (1991)]

19–8. Fixed Amount of Money. William Bailey and William Vaught, as officers for Bailey, Vaught, Robertson, and Co. (BVR), signed a promissory note to borrow $34,000 from the Forestwood National Bank. The interest rate was variable: "the lender's published prime rate" plus 1 percent. Forestwood National Bank went out of business, and ultimately, the note was acquired by Remington Investments, Inc. When BVR failed to make payments, Remington filed a suit in a Texas state court against BVR. BVR contended in part that the note was not negotiable because after Forestwood closed, there was no "published lender's prime rate" to use to calculate the interest. Did the note provide for payment of a "fixed amount of money"? [*Bailey, Vaught, Robertson, and Co. v. Remington Investments, Inc.*, 888 S.W.2d 860 (Tex.App.—Dallas, 1994)]

19–9. Indorsements. Universal Premium Acceptance Corp. issued more than $1 million in drafts, intending the payee to be Great American Insurance Co. When the drafts were issued, they were nonnegotiable instruments. Walter Talbot, an insurance agent, intercepted the drafts, forged Great American's indorsements in blank, and deposited the drafts in a phony account at York Bank & Trust Co. After Talbot was caught and convicted, Universal filed a suit in a federal district court against York to recover some of its losses. One of the issues was whether Talbot's indorsements converted the nonnegotiable drafts into negotiable bearer instruments. Did they? Why or why not? [*Universal Premium Acceptance Corp. v. York Bank & Trust Co.*, 69 F.3d 695 (3d Cir. 1995)]

19–10. Requirements for Negotiability. Walter Peffer loaned $125,000 to the Pefferoni Pizza Company. The note included a clause that allowed the maker (Pefferoni Pizza) to renegotiate the terms of repayment at any time and then extend the time for repayment by up to eighty-four months. Later, Peffer borrowed money from Northern Bank, using the Pefferoni Pizza note as collateral. When Peffer failed to repay his loan, the bank tried to collect on the collateral note, but the pizza company failed to pay. The bank filed a suit in a Nebraska state court against Pefferoni Pizza to recover on the collateral note. Pefferoni Pizza argued in part that its note was not a negotiable instrument because under the renegotiation clause, it was not payable at a definite time. Was the note a negotiable instrument? Explain. [*Northern Bank v. Pefferoni Pizza Co.*, 5 Neb.App. 50, 555 N.W.2d 338 (1996)]

A QUESTION OF ETHICS AND SOCIAL RESPONSIBILITY

19–11. Richard Caliendo, an accountant, prepared tax returns for various clients. To satisfy their tax liabilities, the clients issued checks payable to various state taxing entities and gave them to Caliendo. Between 1977 and 1979, Caliendo forged indorsements on these checks, deposited them in his own bank account, and subsequently withdrew the proceeds. In 1983, after learning of these events and after Caliendo's death, the state brought an action against Barclays Bank of New York, N.A., the successor to Caliendo's bank, to recover the amount of the checks. Barclays moved for dismissal on the ground that because the checks had never been delivered to the state, the state never acquired the status of holder and therefore never acquired any rights in the instruments. The trial court held for the state, but the appellate court reversed. The state then appealed the case to the state's highest court. That court ruled that the state could not recover the amount of the checks from the bank because, although the state was the named payee on the checks, the checks had never been delivered to the payee. [*State v. Barclays Bank of New York, N.A.*, 561 N.Y.2d 533, 563 N.E.2d 11, 561 N.Y.S.2d 697 (1990)]

1. If you were deciding this case, would you make an exception to the rule and let the state collect the funds from Barclays Bank? Why or why not? What ethical policies must be balanced in this situation?
2. Under agency law, which will be discussed in Chapter 24, delivery to the agent of a given individual or entity constitutes delivery to that person or entity. The court deemed that Caliendo was not an agent of the state but an agent of the taxpayers. Does it matter that the taxpayers may not have known this principle of agency law and might have thought that, by delivering their checks to Caliendo, they were delivering them to the state?

FOR CRITICAL ANALYSIS

19–12. The UCC requirements for negotiable instruments are generally strict. In regard to what constitutes a signature on an instrument, however, the UCC grants extreme latitude—X marks, initials, and rubber-stamped signatures are all permitted. Given the potential for forgery of these kinds of signatures, why does the UCC permit them?

Online Activities

ONLINE EXERCISE 19-1

Access the Web site of the American Bankers Association (ABA) at www.aba.com, and select "ABA on the Issues." Click on "Payments Systems," and you will be linked to an article entitled "ABA Payments Systems Task Force Executive Summary." Read through the article, and then answer the following questions:

- What are the four broad themes around which the report is structured?
- According to the report, how does electronic banking affect the interests of banks and consumers, respectively?

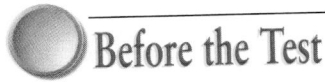

Before the Test

Go to the *Business Law Today* home page at http://blt.westbuslaw.com. Click on TestTutor.® You will find twenty interactive questions relating to this chapter.

CHAPTER 20 Rights & Liabilities of Parties

> "Wealth, in a commercial age, is made up largely of promises."
>
> Roscoe Pound, 1870–1964
> (American jurist)

CONTENTS

LEARNING OBJECTIVES

After reading this chapter, you should be able to:

1. Summarize the requirements for HDC status.
2. Explain the liability of parties who sign negotiable instruments.
3. Describe the effect of forged or unauthorized signatures on the liability of those persons whose names are signed.
4. Identify the defenses that can be raised to avoid liability for payment on negotiable instruments.
5. Indicate how liability on a negotiable instrument is discharged.

As pointed out in Chapter 19, negotiable instruments function as substitutes for money; they also function as extensions of credit. Any note in which a person promises to pay another a sum of money creates a debtor (the one promising) and a creditor (the one to be paid). As the eminent jurist Roscoe Pound indicated in this chapter's opening quotation, wealth "is made up largely of promises." The extensive exchange of negotiable instruments that takes place daily in the United States is predicated, ultimately, on the existence of law and a government capable of enforcing the promises made by parties to negotiable instruments.

The outcome of litigation concerning negotiable instruments usually turns on whether a holder is entitled to obtain payment on an instrument when it is due. Often, whether a holder is entitled to obtain payment will depend on whether the holder is a *holder in due course (HDC)*, a concept we examine in the opening pages of this chapter. We then discuss the liability of the parties to negotiable instruments. In the remainder of the chapter, we consider the defenses available for avoiding liability and, briefly, the ways in which a person can be discharged from an obligation on a negotiable instrument.

Holder versus Holder in Due Course (HDC)

As pointed out in Chapter 19, the Uniform Commercial Code (UCC) defines a *holder* as a person in the possession of an instrument drawn, issued, or indorsed to him or her, to his or her order, or to bearer or in blank [UCC 1–201(20)]. An ordinary holder obtains only those rights that the transferor had in the instrument. In this respect, a holder has the same status as an assignee (see Chapter 13). Like an assignee, a holder normally is subject to the same defenses that could be asserted against the transferor.

• **HOLDER IN DUE COURSE (HDC)**
A holder who acquires a negotiable instrument for value; in good faith; and without notice that the instrument is overdue, that it has been dishonored, that any person has a defense against it or a claim to it, or that the instrument contains unauthorized signatures, alterations, or is so irregular or incomplete as to call into question its authenticity.

In contrast, a **holder in due course (HDC)** is a holder who, by meeting certain acquisition requirements (to be discussed shortly), takes the instrument *free* of most of the defenses and claims that could be asserted against the transferor. Stated another way, an HDC can normally acquire a higher level of immunity than can an ordinary holder in regard to defenses against payment on the instrument or ownership claims to the instrument by other parties.

• **EXAMPLE 20.1** Marcia Cambry signs a $1,000 note payable to Alex Jerrod in payment for some ancient Roman coins. Jerrod negotiates the note to Alicia Larson, who promises to pay Jerrod for it in thirty days. During the next month, Larson learns that Jerrod has breached his contract with Cambry by delivering coins that were not from the Roman era, as promised, and that for this reason Cambry will not honor the $1,000 note. Whether Larson can hold Cambry liable on the note depends on whether Larson has met the requirements for HDC status. If Larson has met these requirements and thus has HDC status, Larson is entitled to payment on the note. If Larson has not met these requirements, she has the status of an ordinary holder, and Cambry's defense of breach of contract against payment to Jerrod will also be effective against Larson. •

Requirements for HDC Status

The basic requirements for attaining HDC status are set forth in UCC 3–302. A holder of a negotiable instrument is an HDC if he or she takes the instrument (1) for value; (2) in good faith; and (3) without notice that it is overdue, that it has been dishonored, that any person has a defense against it or a claim to it, or that the instrument contains unauthorized signatures, alterations, or is so irregular or incomplete as to call into question its authenticity. We now examine each of these requirements.

Taking for Value

An HDC must have given *value* for the instrument [UCC 3–302(a)(2)(i)]. A person who receives an instrument as a gift or who inherits it has not met the requirement of value. In these situations, the person becomes an ordinary holder and does not possess the rights of an HDC.

The concept of value in the law of negotiable instruments is not the same as the concept of *consideration* in the law of contracts. A promise to give value in the future is clearly sufficient consideration to support a contract [UCC 1–201(44)]. A promise to give value in the future, however, normally does not constitute value suf-

ON THE WEB
To find Article 4 of the UCC as adopted by a particular state, go to the Web site of Cornell University's Law School at www.law.cornell.edu/ucc/ucc.table.html.

ficient to make one an HDC. A holder takes an instrument for value only to the extent that the promise has been performed [UCC 3–303(a)(1)]. Therefore, if the holder plans to pay for the instrument later or plans to perform the required services at some future date, the holder has not yet given value. In that situation, the holder is not yet an HDC.

In the Larson-Cambry example presented earlier, Larson is not an HDC, because she did not take the instrument (Cambry's note) for value—she had not yet paid Jerrod for the note. Thus, Cambry's defense of breach of contract is valid not only against Jerrod but also against Larson. If Larson had paid Jerrod for the note at the time of transfer (which would mean she had given value for the instrument), she would be an HDC. As an HDC, she could hold Cambry liable on the note even though Cambry has a valid defense against Jerrod on the basis of breach of contract. Exhibit 20–1 illustrates these concepts.

Under UCC 3–303(a), a holder can take an instrument for value in one of five ways:

1. By performing the promise for which the instrument was issued or transferred.
2. By acquiring a security interest or other lien in the instrument, excluding a lien obtained by a judicial proceeding. (Security interests and liens are discussed in Chapters 22 and 23.)
3. By taking an instrument in payment of (or as security for) a preexisting debt.
4. By giving a negotiable instrument as payment.
5. By giving an irrevocable commitment as payment.

Taking in Good Faith

The second requirement for HDC status is that the holder take the instrument in *good faith* [UCC 3–302(a)(2)(ii)]. This means that the holder must have acted honestly in the process of acquiring the instrument. UCC 3–103(4) defines *good faith* as "honesty in fact and the observance of reasonable commercial standards of fair dealing." The good faith requirement applies only to the *holder*. It is immaterial whether the transferor acted in good faith. Thus, even a person who in good faith takes a negotiable instrument from a thief may become an HDC.

Because of the good faith requirement, one must ask whether the purchaser, when acquiring the instrument, honestly believed that the instrument was not defective. If a person purchases a $10,000 note for $300 from a stranger on a street corner, the issue

EXHIBIT 20–1 • Taking for Value

By exchanging defective goods for the note, Jerrod breached his contract with Cambry. Cambry could assert this defense if Jerrod presented the note to her for payment. Jerrod exchanged the note for Larson's promise to pay in thirty days, however. Because Larson did not take the note for value, she is not a holder in due course. Thus, Cambry can assert against Larson the defense of Jerrod's breach when Larson submits the note to Cambry for payment. If Larson had taken the note for value, Cambry could not assert that defense and would be liable to pay the note.

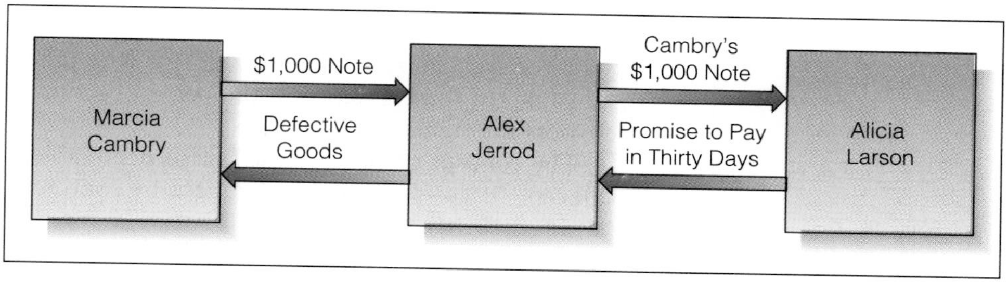

of good faith can be raised on the grounds of both the suspicious circumstances and the grossly inadequate consideration (value). In the following case, the court considered whether a casino fulfilled the good faith requirement to qualify as an HDC.

CASE 20.1 Adamar of New Jersey, Inc. v. Chase Lincoln First Bank, N.A.[a]

Supreme Court of New York,
Appellate Division,
Fourth Department, 1994.
615 N.Y.S.2d 550.

HISTORICAL AND ECONOMIC SETTING *Gambling is a multibillion-dollar industry that enjoyed tremendous growth in the 1990s. Currently, Americans wager about $500 billion each year. Most of this amount was wagered in twenty-seven states in casinos built in the previous decade. Cities and towns with casinos have generally experienced increases in crime, even while the crime rate for the United States as a whole has been dropping. Gambling's new frontier is the Internet, with hundreds of gambling-related sites on the World Wide Web. Because such services probably violate U.S. law, however, online casinos are based elsewhere—on islands in the Caribbean, for example. (For a further discussion of gambling on the Internet, see the feature entitled* Technology and Online Gambling Operations *in Chapter 11.)*

a. The initials *N.A.* stand for National Association.

BACKGROUND AND FACTS Joseph Thomas stole two signed blank cashier's checks from a loan officer's desk at Chase Lincoln First Bank, N.A. Thomas wrote $200,000 as the amount of one check and $300,000 as the amount of the other, and made them payable to the order of his brother-in-law. Posing as his brother-in-law, Thomas presented the checks to the Tropicana Casino. A casino employee who contacted Chase was told that the $200,000 check was "good," that there were adequate funds to cover it, and that there was no stop-payment order on the $300,000 check. Thomas gambled away most of the money before Chase stopped payment on the checks. The owner of the Tropicana, Adamar of New Jersey, Inc., filed a suit in a New York state court against the bank to recover the $500,000. When the court denied Adamar's motion for summary judgment, Adamar appealed.

IN THE WORDS OF THE COURT . . .
BOEHM, Justice.

* * * *

The * * * question is whether plaintiff had "knowledge of some fact which would prevent a commercially honest individual from taking up the instruments."
* * *

* * * [T]he Casino did not violate [state] gaming regulations or its own internal procedures in verifying Thomas's identity or the validity of the checks. * * * The statement by a Chase employee in response to inquiries from the Casino that the $200,000 check was "good" and that there were adequate funds to cover it, satisfied the requirement of [state regulations] that, "[p]rior to acceptance of any cash equivalent from a patron, the general cashier shall determine the validity of such cash equivalent by performing the necessary verification for each type of cash equivalent * * * ." Additionally, the Casino was expressly informed that there was no stop payment on the $300,000 check.

DECISION AND REMEDY The Supreme Court of New York, Appellate Division, held that the casino was entitled to payment.

FOR CRITICAL ANALYSIS—Ethical Consideration *Why should good faith be a requirement to attain HDC status?*

Taking without Notice

The final requirement for HDC status involves *notice* [UCC 3–302]. A person will not be afforded HDC protection if he or she acquires an instrument and is *on notice* (knows or has reason to know) that it is defective in any one of the following ways [UCC 3–302(a)]:

1. It is overdue.
2. It has been previously dishonored.
3. There is an uncured (uncorrected) default with respect to another instrument issued as part of the same series.
4. The instrument contains an unauthorized signature or has been altered.
5. There is a defense against the instrument or a claim to the instrument.
6. The instrument is so irregular or incomplete as to call into question the instrument's authenticity.

International Perspective • "PROTECTED HOLDER" STATUS

Good faith is an issue not only in domestic transactions involving negotiable instruments but also internationally. Under the United Nations Convention on International Bills of Exchange and International Promissory Notes (CIBN), the equivalent of a holder in due course is known as a "protected holder." As under the UCC, the protected holder is afforded greater protection than an ordinary holder. The CIBN, however, unlike the UCC, does not provide any objective test by which to measure good faith. Article 3 of the UCC, as revised in 1990, added to the subjective definition of *good faith* (which was defined under the unrevised Article 3 as simply "honesty in fact") the phrase, "and the observance of reasonable commercial standards of fair dealing." Thus, courts applying the UCC can have some objective guidelines as to what constitutes good faith. The CIBN, in contrast, simply qualifies someone as a protected holder if he or she was "without knowledge" of a fraud or other defense against the instrument.

FOR CRITICAL ANALYSIS
What might be a reason why the CIBN contains only a very broad and subjective definition of good faith?

What Constitutes Notice? Notice of a defective instrument is given whenever the holder (1) has actual knowledge of the defect; (2) has received a notice of the defect (such as a bank's receipt of a letter listing the serial numbers of stolen bearer instruments); or (3) has reason to know that a defect exists, given all the facts and circumstances known at the time in question [UCC 1–201(25)]. The holder must also have received the notice "at a time and in a manner that gives a reasonable opportunity to act on it" [UCC 3–302(f)]. A purchaser's knowledge of certain facts, such as insolvency proceedings against the maker or drawer of the instrument, does not constitute notice that the instrument is defective [UCC 3–302(b)].

Overdue Instruments What constitutes notice that an instrument is overdue depends on whether it is a demand instrument (payable on demand) or a time instrument (payable at a definite time). For example, a purchaser has notice that a *demand instrument* is overdue if he or she takes the instrument an unreasonable length of time after its issue. A "reasonable time" for the taking of a check is ninety days, but for other demand instruments, what will be considered a reasonable time depends on the circumstances [UCC 3–304(a)].[1]

¡REMEMBER!
Demand instruments are payable immediately. Time instruments are payable at a future date.

A holder of a *time instrument* who takes the instrument at any time after its expressed due date is on notice that it is overdue [UCC 3–304(b)(2)]. Nonpayment by the due date should indicate to any purchaser that the instrument may be defective. Thus, a promissory note due on May 15 must be acquired before midnight on May 15. If it is purchased on May 16, the purchaser will be an ordinary holder, not an HDC.

Sometimes, an instrument reads, "Payable in thirty days." A promissory note dated December 1 that is payable in thirty days is due by midnight on December 31. If the payment date falls on a Sunday or holiday, the instrument is payable on the next business day. If a debt is to be paid in installments or through a series of notes,

1. Under the unrevised Article 3, a reasonable time for the taking of a domestic check was *presumed* to be thirty days [UCC 3–304(3)(c)].

the maker's default on any installment of principal (not interest) or on any one note of the series will constitute notice to the purchaser that the instrument is overdue [UCC 3–304(b)(1)].

Dishonored Instruments An instrument is *dishonored* when the party to which the instrument is presented refuses to pay it. If a holder has actual knowledge that an instrument has been dishonored or has knowledge of facts that would lead him or her to suspect that an instrument has been dishonored, the holder is on notice [UCC 3–302(a)(2)].

• **EXAMPLE 20.2** Condor holds a demand note dated September 1 made by JWB Enterprises, Inc., a local business firm. On September 17, Condor demands payment, and JWB refuses to pay (that is, JWB dishonors the instrument). On September 22, Condor negotiates the note to Bream, a purchaser who lives in another state. Bream does not know, and has no reason to know, that the note has been dishonored, so Bream is *not* put on notice and therefore can become an HDC. •

Notice of Claims or Defenses A holder cannot become an HDC if he or she has notice of any claim to the instrument or any defense against it [UCC 3–302(a)]. Knowledge of claims or defenses can be imputed to the purchaser if these claims or defenses are apparent on the face of the instrument or if the purchaser otherwise had reason to know of them from facts surrounding the transaction.

A purchaser cannot expect to become an HDC of an instrument so incomplete on its face that an element of negotiability is lacking (for example, the amount is not filled in). Minor omissions (such as the omission of the date—see Chapter 19) are permissible, because these do not call into question the validity of the instrument. Similarly, when a person accepts an instrument that has been completed without knowing that it was incomplete when issued, that person can take it as an HDC.

> ¡NOTE!
> A difference between the handwriting in the body of a check and the handwriting in the signature does not affect the validity of the check.

• **EXAMPLE 20.3** Carrie asks Barron to buy a textbook for her at the campus bookstore. Carrie writes a check payable to the bookstore, leaves the amount blank, and tells Barron to fill in the price of the textbook. The cost of the textbook is $45. If Barron fills in the check for $75 before he gets to the bookstore, the bookstore cashier sees only a properly completed instrument. Therefore, because the bookstore had no notice that the check was incomplete when it was issued, the bookstore can take the check for $75 and become an HDC. •

Any irregularity on the face of an instrument (such as an obvious forgery or alteration) that calls into question its validity or terms of ownership, or that creates an ambiguity as to the party to pay, will bar HDC status. A careful forgery of a signature, however, or the careful alteration of an instrument can go undetected by reasonable examination; therefore, the purchaser can qualify as an HDC.

Holder through an HDC

A person who does not qualify as an HDC but who derives his or her title through an HDC can acquire the rights and privileges of an HDC. According to UCC 3–203(b),

> Transfer of an instrument, whether or not the transfer is a negotiation, vests in the transferee any right of the transferor to enforce the instrument, including any right as a holder in due course, but the transferee cannot acquire rights of a holder in due course by a transfer, directly or indirectly, from a holder in due course if the transferee engaged in fraud or illegality affecting the instrument.

Under this rule, which is sometimes called the **shelter principle,** anyone—no matter how far removed from an HDC—who can trace his or her title ultimately back to an HDC may acquire the rights of an HDC.

• **SHELTER PRINCIPLE**
The principle that the holder of a negotiable instrument who cannot qualify as a holder in due course (HDC), but who derives his or her title through an HDC, acquires the rights of an HDC.

"Most men are admirers of justice—when justice happens to be on their side."

RICHARD WHATELY, 1787–1863 (English theologian and logician)

There are some limitations on the shelter principle, however. Certain persons who formerly held instruments cannot improve their positions by later reacquiring the instruments from HDCs [UCC 3–203(b)]. Thus, if a holder was a party to fraud or illegality affecting the instrument or if, as a prior holder, he or she had notice of a claim or defense against an instrument, that holder is not allowed to improve his or her status by repurchasing from a later HDC.

Signature Liability

The key to liability on a negotiable instrument is a *signature*.[2] The general rule is as follows: Every party, except a qualified indorser,[3] who signs a negotiable instrument is either primarily or secondarily liable for payment of that instrument when it comes due. The following subsections discuss these two types of liability, as well as the conditions that must be met before liability can arise.

PRIMARY LIABILITY

ON THE WEB

For a brief history of the significance of signatures on documents, including negotiable instruments, go to sacam.oren.ortn.edu/~wooten/Esig/node3.html.

A person who is primarily liable on a negotiable instrument is absolutely required to pay the instrument—unless, of course, he or she has a valid defense to payment [UCC 3–305]. Only *makers* and *acceptors* of instruments are primarily liable.

The maker of a promissory note promises to pay the note. It is the maker's promise to pay that makes the note a negotiable instrument. The words "I promise to pay" embody the maker's obligation to pay the instrument according to the terms as written at the time of the signing. If the instrument is incomplete when the maker signs it, then the maker's obligation is to pay it to an HDC according to the terms written when it is completed [UCC 3–115, 3–407(a), 3–412].

A drawee that promises to pay an instrument when it is presented later for payment is called an *acceptor,* as discussed in Chapter 19. A drawee's acceptance of a draft, which it makes by signing the draft, guarantees that the drawee will pay the draft when it is presented in the future for payment [UCC 3–409(a)]. A drawee that refuses to accept a draft that *requires* the drawee's acceptance (such as a trade acceptance or a draft payable thirty days after acceptance) has dishonored the instrument. Acceptance of a check is called *certification* (discussed in Chapter 21). Certification is not necessary on checks, and a bank is under no obligation to certify checks. On certification, however, the drawee bank occupies the position of an acceptor and is primarily liable on the check to any holder [UCC 3–409(d)].

SECONDARY LIABILITY

¡RECALL!

A guarantor is liable on a contract to pay the debt of another only if the party who is primarily liable fails to pay.

Drawers and indorsers are secondarily liable. Secondary liability on a negotiable instrument is similar to the liability of a guarantor in a simple contract (described in Chapter 13) in the sense that it is *contingent liability.* In other words, a drawer or an indorser will be liable only if the party that is primarily liable on the instrument dishonors it by nonpayment or, in regard to drafts and checks, the drawee fails to pay or to accept the instrument, whichever is required [UCC 3–412, 3–415].

Dishonor of an instrument thus triggers the liability of parties who are secondarily liable on the instrument—that is, the drawer and *unqualified* indorsers. For example, Nina Lee writes a check on her account at Universal Bank payable to the order

2. See Chapter 19 for a discussion of how the UCC defines a *signature*.

3. A qualified indorser—one who indorses "without recourse"—undertakes no contractual obligation to pay. A qualified indorser merely assumes warranty liability, which is discussed later in this chapter.

of Stephen Miller. Universal Bank refuses to pay the check when Miller presents it for payment, thus dishonoring the check. In this situation, Lee will be liable to Miller on the basis of her secondary liability. Drawers are secondarily liable on drafts unless they disclaim their liability by drawing the instruments "without recourse" (if the draft is a check, however, a drawer cannot disclaim liability) [UCC 3–414(e)].

Parties that are secondarily liable on a negotiable instrument promise to pay on that instrument only if the following events occur:[4]

1. The instrument is properly and timely presented.
2. The instrument is dishonored.
3. Timely notice of dishonor is given to the secondarily liable party.

Proper and Timely Presentment The UCC requires that presentment by a holder must be made to the proper person, must be made in a proper manner, and must be timely [UCC 3–414(f), 3–415(e), 3–501]. The party to whom the instrument must be presented depends on what type of instrument is involved. A note or certificate of deposit (CD) must be presented to the maker for payment. A draft is presented by the holder to the drawee for acceptance, payment, or both, whichever is required. A check is presented to the drawee for payment [UCC 3–501(a), 3–502(b)].

Presentment can be properly made in any of the following ways, depending on the type of instrument involved [UCC 3–501(b)]:

1. By any commercially reasonable means, including oral, written, or electronic communication (but presentment is not effective until the demand for payment or acceptance is received).
2. Through a clearinghouse procedure used by banks, such as for deposited checks (see Chapter 21).
3. At the place specified in the instrument for acceptance or payment.

One of the most crucial criteria for proper presentment is timeliness [UCC 3–414(f), 3–415(e), 3–501(b)(4)]. Failure to present on time is the most common reason for improper presentment and results in the complete discharge of unqualified indorsers from secondary liability. For checks, failure to properly present a check discharges the drawer's secondary liability only to the extent that the drawee is deprived of the funds required to pay the check. The time for proper presentment for different types of instruments is shown in Exhibit 20–2.

4. These requirements are necessary for a secondarily liable party to have signature liability on a negotiable instrument, but they are not necessary for a secondarily liable party to have warranty liability (to be discussed later in the chapter).

EXHIBIT 20–2 • Time for Proper Presentment

TYPE OF INSTRUMENT	FOR ACCEPTANCE	FOR PAYMENT
Time	On or before due date.	On due date.
Demand	Within a reasonable time (after date of issue or after secondary party becomes liable on the instrument).	
Check	Not applicable.	Within thirty days of its date, to hold drawer secondarily liable. Within thirty days of indorsement to hold indorser secondarily liable.[a]

a. Under the unrevised Article 3, these periods were *presumed* to be thirty days to hold the drawer secondarily liable, and seven days to hold the indorser secondarily liable.

Dishonor An instrument is dishonored when the required acceptance or payment is refused or cannot be obtained within the prescribed time, or when required presentment is excused (as it would be, for example, if the maker had died) and the instrument is not properly accepted or paid [UCC 3–502(e), 3–504].

Proper Notice Once an instrument has been dishonored, proper notice must be given to secondary parties for them to be held contractually liable. Notice may be given in any reasonable manner. This includes oral notice, written notice (including notice by fax, e-mail, and the like), and notice written or stamped on the instrument itself. Any necessary notice must be given by a bank before its midnight deadline (midnight of the next banking day after receipt). Notice by any party other than a bank must be given within thirty days following the day of dishonor or the day on which the person who is secondarily liable receives notice of dishonor [UCC 3–503].[5]

ACCOMMODATION PARTIES

• **ACCOMMODATION PARTY**
A person who signs an instrument for the purpose of lending his or her name as credit to another party on the instrument.

An **accommodation party** is one who signs an instrument for the purpose of lending his or her name as credit to another party on the instrument [UCC 3–419(a)]. Accommodation parties are one form of security against nonpayment on a negotiable instrument. • EXAMPLE 20.4 Frank Huston applies to Northeast Bank for a $1,000 loan. The bank wants some reasonable assurance that if it loans Huston the funds, the debt will be paid. If Huston's financial condition is uncertain, the bank may be reluctant to rely solely on Huston's ability to pay. To reduce the risk of nonpayment, the bank can require the joining of a third person as an accommodation party on Huston's promissory note.• When one person (such as a parent) cosigns a promissory note with the maker (such as the parent's son or daughter), the cosigner is an accommodation party.

If the accommodation party signs on behalf of the *maker,* he or she becomes an *accommodation maker* and is primarily liable on the instrument. If the accommo-

5. Under the revised Article 3, notice by a person other than a bank has to be given "before midnight of the third business day after dishonor or receipt of notice of dishonor" [UCC 3–508(2)].

A FAMILY LOOKS AT A VAN ON A DEALER'S LOT. IF, AS PROSPECTIVE BORROWERS, THE FAMILY'S FINANCIAL CONDITION WERE UNCERTAIN, HOW COULD AN ACCOMMODATION PARTY HELP THE FAMILY OBTAIN THE MONEY TO PAY FOR THE VAN?

dation party indorses an instrument on behalf of a *payee or other holder* (usually to make the instrument more marketable), he or she is an *accommodation indorser* and is secondarily liable.

If the accommodation party pays the instrument, he or she has a right of recourse against the party accommodated [UCC 3–419(e)]. If the *accommodated party* pays the instrument, however, does he or she have a right of recourse (contribution) against the accommodation party? That was the issue in the following case.

CASE 20.2 Quality Wash Group V, Ltd. v. Shawkat Hallak

California Court of Appeal, Fourth District, Division 1, 1996.
58 Cal.Rptr.2d 592.

HISTORICAL AND ECONOMIC SETTING *A self-service car wash with seven bays (including an equipment room) can cost an average of about $450,000, which includes the costs of the land, the building, and the equipment. There are several ways to structure the financing. For example, a bank or the Small Business Administration may provide a loan, several investors could form a partnership, or an outside investor might lend the funds. As with any business, the most important decision is where to locate. For a car wash, if the population within a three-mile radius is too low or the passing traffic is too light, business will likely be bad. When that happens, the only recourse may be to sell the car wash.*

BACKGROUND AND FACTS Harvey and Patricia Allan built a car wash that was sold to Shawkat and Nahida Hallak. As part of the purchase price, the Hallaks signed a promissory note in favor of the Allans. The Hallaks subsquently sold the car wash to Quality Wash Group V, Limited. As part of their deal, Quality and the Hallaks signed an amendment to the Allan note under which Quality assumed primary liability on the note. When Quality stopped making payments on the note, the Allans filed a suit in a California state court against Quality and the Hallaks to collect. Quality paid off the note and then filed a claim against the Hallaks. The court ruled in part that the Hallaks were not liable, and Quality appealed.

IN THE WORDS OF THE COURT . . .
PATE, Associate Justice.

* * * *

* * * [As a result of signing the amendment to the Allan note,] the Hallaks fall within the definition of "accommodation party" under [UCC 3–419(a)], which provides: "If an instrument is issued for value given for the benefit of a party to the instrument ('accommodated party') and another party to the instrument ('accommodation party') signs the instrument for the purpose of incurring liability on the instrument without being a direct beneficiary of the value given for the instrument, the instrument is signed by the accommodation party 'for accommodation.'" Having assumed the Allan note as part of the purchase price of the car wash, Quality was the direct beneficiary of the value given for the note and, therefore, was the "accommodated party."

[UCC 3–419(e)] provides: "* * * An accommodated party who pays the instrument has no right of recourse against, and is not entitled to contribution from, an accommodation party." Accordingly, as an accommodated party to the Allan note who paid the note, Quality has no right of recourse against, and is not entitled to contribution from[,] the Hallaks, who are accommodation parties under the note.

DECISION AND REMEDY The state appellate court affirmed the part of the judgment that denied Quality the right to recover from the Hallaks.

FOR CRITICAL ANALYSIS—Ethical Consideration *Why would it be unfair to allow an accommodated party who pays an instrument to recover from the accommodation party?*

AGENTS' SIGNATURES

• **AGENT**
A person who agrees to represent or act for another, called the principal.

• **PRINCIPAL**
In agency law, a person who agrees to have another, called the agent, act on his or her behalf.

The general law of agency, covered in Chapter 24, applies to negotiable instruments. An **agent** is a person who agrees to represent or act for another, called the **principal.** Agents can sign negotiable instruments and thereby bind their principals [UCC 3–401(a)(ii), 3–402(a)]. Without such a rule, all corporate commercial business would stop—as every corporation can and must act through its agents.

Authorized Agent Generally, an *authorized* agent does not bind a principal on an instrument unless the agent *clearly names* the principal in his or her signature. The agent may or may not add his or her own name, but if the signature shows clearly that it is made on behalf of the principal, the agent is not liable on the instrument. • **EXAMPLE 20.5** Either of the following two signatures by Joan Collingsworth as agent for Brian Peterson would bind Peterson on the instrument, and Collingsworth would not be personally liable for payment on it:

1. Peterson, by Collingsworth, agent.
2. Peterson.

If Collingsworth (the agent) signed just her own name, however, she would be personally liable to an HDC who has no notice of her agency status. In respect to other holders, the agent can escape liability if the agent proves that the original parties did not intend the agent to be liable on the instrument [UCC 3–402(a), 3–402(b)(2)]. In either situation, the principal is bound if the party entitled to enforce the instrument can prove the agency relationship.[6] •

There are two other situations in which an authorized agent can be held personally liable on a negotiable instrument. When the instrument is signed in both the agent's name and the principal's name (for example, "Collingsworth, Peterson"), but nothing on the instrument indicates the agency relationship (so the agent cannot be distinguished from the principal), the agent may be held personally liable. An agent may also be held personally liable when the agent indicates agency status in signing a negotiable instrument but fails to name the principal (for example, "Joan Collingsworth, agent") [UCC 3–402(b)(2)]. (What if an agent is the payee on a note and the maker of the note defaults? Does the principal, whose name does not appear on the instrument, have standing to enforce payment? This question is explored in this chapter's *Business Law in Action.*)

An important exception to the above rules is made for checks that are signed by agents. If an agent signs his or her own name on a check that is *payable from the account of the principal,* and the principal is identified on the check, the agent will not be personally liable on the check [UCC 3–402(c)]. • **EXAMPLE 20.6** Suppose that Collingsworth, who is authorized to draw checks on Peterson Company's account, signs a check that is preprinted with Peterson Company's name. The signature reads simply "Joan Collingsworth." In this situation, Collingsworth would not be personally liable on the check. •

UNAUTHORIZED SIGNATURES

People normally are not liable to pay on negotiable instruments unless their signatures appear on the instruments. As already stated, the general rule is that an unauthorized signature is wholly inoperative and will not bind the person whose name is

6. Under the unrevised Article 3, a principal is not liable on an instrument unless his or her signature appears on it, even if the parties are aware of the agency relationship [UCC 3–401(1)].

Business Law in Action • Promissory Notes Payable to Agents

As discussed in Chapter 19, a negotiable instrument must include the terms of the instrument on its face. It cannot be governed by a separate writing that spells out the rights and obligations of the parties with respect to the instrument. If it could, the note would become conditional—that is, not an "unconditional order or promise to pay" as required by the UCC. With respect to agents' signatures, this requirement means that an agent who signs a negotiable instrument without indicating his or her representative capacity (agency status) on the instrument itself may be held personally liable on the instrument. Does the requirement also mean that when an agent is the payee on a note, only the agent is entitled to sue to enforce the note if the maker defaults?

This question was at issue in *Kane Plaza Associates v. Chadwick,*[a] a case that involved a $40,000 promissory note made by Bruce Chadwick and payable to J. M. Kane & Company "or order." The note was executed in conjunction with an agreement to assume a lease, and the note referred to the accompanying agreement. The lease agreement clearly stated that Kane & Company was acting as an agent for Kane Plaza in the transaction. When Chadwick defaulted on the note, Kane Plaza brought an action against Chadwick to enforce payment. A North Carolina trial court dismissed Kane Plaza's action on the ground that Kane Plaza did not have standing to enforce the note—because it was not the named payee and lacked the status of a holder. Said the court, "The court is of the opinion that the plaintiff is not a holder . . . and the complaint fails to allege that the plaintiff is the transferee . . . by endorsement or otherwise."

The appellate court viewed the matter differently and reversed the trial court's decision. The appellate court pointed out that under UCC 3–119 (carried over into the 1990 revision of Article 3 as UCC 3–117), the terms of a promissory note may be modified by a separate writing "as between the obligor and immediate obligee," providing that the separate writing is executed as part of the same transaction. The court held that in this case the separate writing (the lease agreement) was referred to in the note, and the note was executed as part of the lease transaction. The note thus modified the instrument so as to make Kane Plaza an "immediate obligee" under the note, which entitled Kane Plaza to seek payment from Chadwick.

a. 126 N.C.App. 661, 486 S.E.2d 465 (1997).

FOR CRITICAL ANALYSIS

Would the application of UCC 3–117 also permit Kane Plaza to transfer the instrument to a third party?

forged. • **EXAMPLE 20.7** Parra finds Dolby's checkbook lying on the street, writes out a check to himself, and forges Dolby's signature. If a bank fails to ascertain that Dolby's signature is not genuine (which banks normally have a duty to do) and cashes the check for Parra, the bank will generally be liable to Dolby for the amount.• (The liability of banks for paying over forged signatures is discussed further in Chapter 21.) There are two exceptions to this general rule:

1. Any unauthorized signature will bind the person whose name is forged if the person whose name is signed ratifies (affirms) it [UCC 3–403(a)]. For example, a mother may ratify her daughter's forgery of the mother's name so that her daughter will not be prosecuted for forgery. A person may be precluded from denying the effectiveness of an unauthorized signature, however, if the person's negligence led to the forgery [UCC 3–115, 3–406, 4–401(d)(2)]. • **EXAMPLE 20.8** Suppose that Jonathan leaves a blank check in a public place. If someone else finds the check, fills it out, and forges Jonathan's signature, Jonathan can be estopped (prevented), on the basis of negligence, from denying liability for payment of the check.•
2. An unauthorized signature operates as the signature of the unauthorized signer in favor of an HDC. A person who forges a check, for example, can be held personally liable for payment by an HDC [UCC 3–403(a)].

"*Life is* unfair."

MILTON FRIEDMAN,
1912–
(American economist)

SPECIAL RULES FOR UNAUTHORIZED INDORSEMENTS

Generally, when there is a forged or unauthorized indorsement, the burden of loss falls on the first party to take the instrument with the forged or unauthorized indorsement. If the indorsement was made by an imposter or by a fictitious payee, however, the loss falls on the maker or drawer. We look at these two situations here.

• IMPOSTER
One who, by use of the mails, telephone, or personal appearance, induces a maker or drawer to issue an instrument in the name of an impersonated payee. Indorsements by imposters are treated as authorized indorsements under Article 3 of the UCC.

Imposters An **imposter** is one who, by use of the mails, telephone, or personal appearance, induces a maker or drawer to issue an instrument in the name of an impersonated payee. If the maker or drawer believes the imposter to be the named payee at the time of issue, the indorsement by the imposter is not treated as unauthorized when the instrument is transferred to an innocent party. This is because the maker or drawer intended the imposter to receive the instrument. In this situation, under the UCC's *imposter rule,* the imposter's indorsement will be effective—that is, not considered a forgery—insofar as the drawer or maker is concerned [UCC 3–404(a)].

• FICTITIOUS PAYEE
A payee on a negotiable instrument whom the maker or drawer does not intend to have an interest in the instrument. Indorsements by fictitious payees are treated as authorized indorsements under Article 3 of the UCC.

Fictitious Payees Another situation in which an unauthorized indorsement will be effective is when a person causes an instrument to be issued to a payee who will have *no interest* in the instrument [UCC 3–404(b), 3–405]. In this situation, the payee is referred to as a **fictitious payee.** Situations involving fictitious payees most often arise when (1) a dishonest employee deceives the employer into signing an instrument payable to a party with no right to receive payment on the instrument or (2) a dishonest employee or agent has the authority to issue an instrument on behalf of the employer. Under the UCC's *fictitious payee rule,* the payee's indorsement is not treated as a forgery, and the employer can be held liable on the instrument by an innocent holder or a party (such as a bank) that pays the instrument in good faith.

• **EXAMPLE 20.9** Flair Industries, Inc., gives its bookkeeper, Axel Ford, general authority to issue checks in the company name drawn on First State Bank so that Ford can pay employees' wages and other corporate bills. Ford decides to cheat Flair Industries out of $10,000 by issuing a check payable to Erica Nied, an old acquaintance. Neither Flair nor Ford intends Nied to receive any of the money, and Nied is not an employee or creditor of the company. Ford indorses the check in Nied's name, naming himself as indorsee. He then cashes the check at a local bank, which collects payment from the drawee bank, First State Bank. First State Bank charges the Flair Industries account $10,000. Flair Industries discovers the fraud and demands that the account be recredited.

> **ON THE WEB**
> The editors of *Lawyers Weekly USA* include a number of court opinions on the *Lawyers Weekly* Web site. For a case involving the fictitious payee rule, go to **www.lweekly.com/vasc1971463.htm**.

Who bears the loss? UCC 3–404(b)(2) provides the answer. Neither the local bank that first accepted the check nor First State Bank is liable. Because Ford's indorsement in the name of a payee with no interest in the instrument is "effective," there is no "forgery." Hence, the collecting bank is protected in paying on the check, and the drawee bank is protected in charging Flair's account. It is the employer-drawer, Flair Industries, that bears the loss. Of course, Flair Industries has recourse against Axel Ford. •

Regardless of whether a dishonest employee actually signs the check or merely supplies his or her employer with names of fictitious creditors (or with true names of creditors having fictitious debts), the UCC makes no distinction in result. • **EXAMPLE 20.10** Nathan Holtz draws up the payroll list from which employees' salary checks are written. He fraudulently adds the name Sally Slight (a fictitious person) to the payroll, and the employer signs checks to be issued to her. Again, it is the employer-drawer who bears the loss. •

ETHICAL ISSUE 20.1 ***Should a bank that acts in "bad faith" be precluded from raising the fictitious payee rule as a defense?*** Remember from previous chapters that the requirement of good faith underlies all transactions governed by the UCC. Does this mean that a bank, to avoid liability for paying instruments with forged indorsements involving fictitious payees, must have acted in good faith when accepting the deposits? Yes, according to a number of courts. Recently, a Pennsylvania appellate court held that to assert the rule "the bank must have acted in good faith when paying the instrument." The bank in this case had accepted 882 payroll checks generated and indorsed by Dorothy Heck, a payroll clerk employed by Pavex, Inc. The checks were made payable to various current and former Pavex employees, indorsed by Heck with the payees' names, and deposited into Heck's personal checking account at her bank. In spite of its policy that indorsements on checks must match exactly the names of the payees, the bank never refused any of Heck's deposited checks on which the indorsements did not match the payees' names. Furthermore, even though bank personnel discussed Heck's check-depositing activities on more than one occasion, they never contacted her employer to see if Heck was authorized to deposit third-party payroll checks. Given the bank's choice of ignoring perceived irregularities in Heck's transactions, the trial court jury had concluded that the bank had acted in bad faith and was therefore liable for approximately $170,000 of the $250,000 loss suffered by Pavex. The appellate court affirmed the trial court's decision.[7]

Warranty Liability

In addition to the signature liability discussed in the preceding pages, transferors make certain implied warranties regarding the instruments that they are negotiating. Liability under these warranties is not subject to the conditions of proper presentment, dishonor, or notice of dishonor. These warranties arise even when a transferor does not indorse the instrument (as in the delivery of a bearer instrument) [UCC 3–416, 3–417].

Warranties fall into two categories: those that arise on the *transfer* of a negotiable instrument and those that arise on *presentment.* Both transfer and presentment warranties attempt to shift liability back to a wrongdoer or to the person who dealt face to face with the wrongdoer and thus was in the best position to prevent the wrongdoing.

TRANSFER WARRANTIES

• **TRANSFER WARRANTIES**
Implied warranties, made by any person who transfers an instrument for consideration to subsequent transferees and holders who take the instrument in good faith, that (1) the transferor is entitled to enforce the instrument, (2) all signatures are authentic and authorized, (3) the instrument has not been altered, (4) the instrument is not subject to a defense or claim of any party that can be asserted against the transferor, and (5) the transferor has no knowledge of any insolvency proceedings against the maker, the acceptor, or the drawer of the instrument.

The UCC describes five **transfer warranties** [UCC 3–416]. These warranties provide that any person who transfers an instrument *for consideration* makes the following warranties to all subsequent transferees and holders who take the instrument in good faith (with some exceptions, as will be noted shortly):

1. The transferor is entitled to enforce the instrument.
2. All signatures are authentic and authorized.
3. The instrument has not been altered.
4. The instrument is not subject to a defense or claim of any party that can be asserted against the transferor.[8]
5. The transferor has no knowledge of any insolvency proceedings against the maker, the acceptor, or the drawer of the instrument.

7. *Pavex, Inc. v. York Federal Savings and Loan Association,* 716 A.2d 640 (Pa.Super.Ct. 1998).
8. Under the unrevised Article 3, a qualified indorser who indorses an instrument "without recourse" limits this warranty to a warranty that he or she has "no knowledge" of such a defense (rather than that there is no defense). This limitation does not apply under the revised Article 3.

The manner of transfer and the negotiation that is used determine how far and to whom a transfer warranty will run. Transfer of order paper, for consideration, by indorsement and delivery extends warranty liability to any subsequent holder who takes the instrument in good faith. The warranties of a person who transfers *without indorsement* (by the delivery of a bearer instrument), however, will extend the transferor's warranties only to the immediate transferee [UCC 3–416(a)].

• **EXAMPLE 20.11** Abraham forges Peter's name as a maker of a promissory note. The note is made payable to Abraham. Abraham indorses the note in blank, negotiates it to Carla, and then leaves the country. Carla, without indorsement, delivers the note to Frank for consideration. Frank, in turn without indorsement, delivers the note to Ricardo for consideration. On Ricardo's presentment of the note to Peter, the forgery is discovered. Ricardo can hold Frank (the immediate transferor) liable for breach of the transfer warranty that all signatures are genuine. Ricardo cannot hold Carla liable, because the transfer warranties made by Carla, who negotiated the bearer instrument by delivery only, extend only to Frank, the immediate transferee. •

Note that if Abraham had added a special indorsement ("Payable to Carla") instead of a blank indorsement, the instrument would have remained an order instrument. In that situation, to negotiate the instrument to Frank, Carla would have had to indorse the instrument, and her transfer warranties would extend to all subsequent holders, including Ricardo. This example shows the importance of the distinction between a transfer by indorsement and delivery (of an order instrument) and a transfer by delivery only, without indorsement (of a bearer instrument).

PRESENTMENT WARRANTIES

Any person who presents an instrument for payment or acceptance makes the following **presentment warranties** to any other person who in good faith pays or accepts the instrument [UCC 3–417(a), 3–417(d)]:

• **PRESENTMENT WARRANTIES**
Implied warranties, made by any person who presents an instrument for payment or acceptance, that (1) the person obtaining payment or acceptance is entitled to enforce the instrument or is authorized to obtain payment or acceptance on behalf of a person who is entitled to enforce the instrument, (2) the instrument has not been altered, and (3) the person obtaining payment or acceptance has no knowledge that the signature of the drawer of the instrument is unauthorized.

1. The person obtaining payment or acceptance is entitled to enforce the instrument or is authorized to obtain payment or acceptance on behalf of a person who is entitled to enforce the instrument. (This is, in effect, a warranty that there are no missing or unauthorized indorsements.)
2. The instrument has not been altered.
3. The person obtaining payment or acceptance has no knowledge that the signature of the issuer of the instrument is unauthorized.

These warranties are referred to as presentment warranties because they protect the person to whom the instrument is presented. The second and third warranties do not apply to makers, acceptors, and drawers. It is assumed, for example, that a drawer or a maker will recognize his or her own signature and that a maker or an acceptor will recognize whether an instrument has been materially altered.

Defenses to Liability

Persons who would otherwise be liable on negotiable instruments may be able to avoid liability by raising certain defenses. There are two general categories of defenses—*universal defenses* and *personal defenses.*

• **UNIVERSAL DEFENSES**
Defenses that are valid against all holders of a negotiable instrument, including holders in due course (HDCs) and holders with the rights of HDCs.

UNIVERSAL DEFENSES

Universal defenses (also called *real defenses*) are valid against *all* holders, including HDCs and holders who take through an HDC. Universal defenses include those described here.

Forgery Forgery of a maker's or drawer's signature cannot bind the person whose name is used unless that person ratifies (approves or validates) the signature or is precluded from denying it (because the forgery was made possible by the maker's or drawer's negligence, for example) [UCC 3–403(a)]. Thus, when a person forges an instrument, the person whose name is forged normally has no liability to pay any holder or any HDC the value of the forged instrument.

Fraud in the Execution If a person is deceived into signing a negotiable instrument, believing that he or she is signing something other than a negotiable instrument (such as a receipt), *fraud in the execution,* or fraud in the inception, is committed against the signer [UCC 3–305(a)(1)]. • EXAMPLE 20.12 A salesperson asks a customer to sign a paper, which the salesperson says is a receipt for the delivery of goods that the customer is picking up from the store. In fact, the paper is a promissory note, but the customer, who is unfamiliar with the English language, does not realize this. In this situation, even if the note is negotiated to an HDC, the customer has a valid defense against payment.•

The defense of fraud in the execution cannot be raised, however, if a reasonable inquiry would have revealed the nature and terms of the instrument.[9] Thus, the signer's age, experience, and intelligence are relevant, because they frequently determine whether the signer should have known the nature of the transaction before signing.

Material Alteration An alteration is material if it changes the contract terms between any two parties in any way. Examples of material alterations include completing an incomplete instrument, adding words or numbers to an instrument, or making any other change to an instrument in an unauthorized manner that affects the obligation of a party to the instrument [UCC 3–407(a)].

Thus, cutting off part of the paper of a negotiable instrument; adding clauses; or making any change in the amount, the date, or the rate of interest—even if the change is only one penny, one day, or 1 percent—is material. It is not a material alteration, however, to correct the maker's address, for example, or to change the figures on a check so that they agree with the written amount (recall from Chapter 19 that words outweigh figures if there is a conflict between the written amount and the amount given in figures). If the alteration is not material, any holder is entitled to enforce the instrument according to its terms.

Material alteration is a *complete defense* against an ordinary holder. An ordinary holder can recover nothing on an instrument if it has been materially altered [UCC 3–407(b)]. Material alteration, however, may be only a *partial defense* against an HDC. When the holder is an HDC, if an original term, such as the monetary amount payable, has been *altered,* the HDC can enforce the instrument against the maker or drawer according to the original terms but not for the altered amount. If the instrument was originally incomplete and was later completed in an unauthorized manner, however, alteration no longer can be claimed as a defense against an HDC, and the HDC can enforce the instrument as completed [UCC 3–407(b)]. This is because the drawer or maker of the instrument, by issuing an incomplete instrument, will normally be held responsible for the alteration, which could have been avoided by the exercise of greater care. If the alteration is readily apparent, then obviously the holder has notice of some defect or defense and therefore cannot be an HDC [UCC 3–302(a)(1)].

Discharge in Bankruptcy Discharge in bankruptcy is an absolute defense on any instrument regardless of the status of the holder, because the purpose of bankruptcy is to settle finally all of the insolvent party's debts [UCC 3–305(a)(1)].

9. *Burchett v. Allied Concord Financial Corp.*, 74 N.M. 575, 396 P.2d 186 (1964).

¡CONTRAST!
Minority, illegality, mental incapacity, and duress can be universal defenses or personal defenses, depending in some cases on state law other than the UCC.

Minority Minority, or infancy, is a universal defense only to the extent that state law recognizes it as a defense to a simple contract (see Chapter 11). Because state laws on minority vary, so do determinations of whether minority is a universal defense against an HDC [UCC 3–305(a)(1)(i)].

Illegality Certain types of illegality constitute universal defenses. Other types constitute personal defenses—that is, defenses that are effective against ordinary holders but not against HDCs. The difference lies in the state statutes or ordinances that make the transactions illegal. If a statute provides that an illegal transaction is void, then the defense is universal—that is, absolute against both an ordinary holder and an HDC. If the law merely makes the instrument voidable, then the illegality is still a defense against an ordinary holder but not against an HDC [UCC 3–305(a)(1)(ii)].

Mental Incapacity If a person is adjudged mentally incompetent by state proceedings, then any instrument issued by that person thereafter is void. The instrument is *void ab initio* (void from the beginning) and unenforceable by any holder or HDC [UCC 3–305(a)(1)(ii)]. Mental incapacity in these circumstances is thus a universal defense. If a person has not been adjudged mentally incompetent by state proceedings, mental incapacity operates as a defense against an ordinary holder but not against an HDC.

Extreme Duress When a person signs and issues a negotiable instrument under such extreme duress as an immediate threat of force or violence (for example, at gunpoint), the instrument is void and unenforceable by any holder or HDC [UCC 3–305(a)(1)(ii)]. (Ordinary duress is a defense against ordinary holders but not against HDCs.)

Personal Defenses

• **PERSONAL DEFENSES**
Defenses that can be used to avoid payment to an ordinary holder of a negotiable instrument but not a holder in due course (HDC) or a holder with the rights of an HDC.

Personal defenses (sometimes called limited defenses), such as those described here, can be used to avoid payment to an ordinary holder of a negotiable instrument, but not an HDC or a holder with the rights of an HDC.

Breach of Contract or Breach of Warranty When there is a breach of the underlying contract for which the negotiable instrument was issued, the maker of a note can refuse to pay it, or the drawer of a check can order his or her bank to stop payment on the check. Breach of warranty can also be claimed as a defense to liability on the instrument. • EXAMPLE 20.13 Rhodes agrees to purchase several sets of imported china from Livingston. The china is to be delivered in four weeks. Rhodes gives Livingston a promissory note for $2,000, which is the price of the china. The china arrives, but many of the pieces are broken, and several others are chipped or cracked. Rhodes refuses to pay the note on the basis of breach of contract and breach of warranty. (Under sales law, a seller impliedly promises that the goods are at least merchantable—see Chapter 18.) Livingston cannot enforce payment on the note because of the breach of contract and breach of warranty. If Livingston has negotiated the note to a third party, however, and the third party is an HDC, Rhodes will not be able to use breach of contract or warranty as a defense against liability on the note. •

Lack or Failure of Consideration The absence of consideration (value) may be a successful personal defense in some instances [UCC 3–303(b), 3–305(a)(2)]. • EXAMPLE 20.14 Tara gives Clem, as a gift, a note that states "I promise to pay you $100,000." Clem accepts the note. Because there is no consideration for Tara's promise, a court will not enforce the promise. •

Fraud in the Inducement (Ordinary Fraud) A person who issues a negotiable instrument based on false statements by the other party will be able to avoid payment on that instrument, unless the holder is an HDC. • **EXAMPLE 20.15** Jerry agrees to purchase Howard's used tractor for $24,500. Howard, knowing his statements to be false, tells Jerry that the tractor is in good working order and that it has been used for only one harvest. In addition, he tells Jerry that he owns the tractor free and clear of all claims. Jerry pays Howard $4,500 in cash and issues a negotiable promissory note for the balance. As it turns out, Howard still owes the original seller $10,000 on the purchase of the tractor. In addition, the tractor is three years old and has been used in three harvests. Jerry can refuse to pay the note if it is held by an ordinary holder. If Howard has negotiated the note to an HDC, however, Jerry must pay the HDC. (Of course, Jerry can then sue Howard to recover the money.) •

Illegality As mentioned, if a statute provides that an illegal transaction is void, a universal defense exists. If, however, the statute provides that an illegal transaction is voidable, the defense is personal. The effect that a void contract might have on a check issued in payment under that contract is at issue in the following case.

CASE 20.3 Kedzie and 103rd Street Currency Exchange, Inc. v. Hodge

Supreme Court of Illinois, 1993.
156 Ill.2d 112,
619 N.E.2d 732,
189 Ill.Dec. 31.

HISTORICAL AND ETHICAL SETTING *There are always those who view federal, state, and local administrative regulations with disdain. This is particularly true with local and state regulations concerning home repairs and construction. Some people believe that they are qualified to construct or repair a house, for example, without first passing a test or obtaining a license that a local ordinance, state law, or federal law requires. Some of those with whom they do business agree. These customers are fully aware that their contractors are not licensed, but they expect to get the work done cheaply or quickly. Other customers have no idea whether their contractors are unlicensed and simply trust that whoever they hire will perform the work satisfactorily.*

BACKGROUND AND FACTS Beulah Hodge made out a check to Fred Fentress for $500 as a partial payment in advance for plumbing services at her home. When Fentress failed to appear on the date work was to begin, Hodge ordered her bank to stop payment on the check. Fentress, however, had already cashed the check at Kedzie and 103rd Street Currency Exchange, Inc. When the check was returned to Kedzie marked "payment stopped," Kedzie filed a suit in an Illinois state court against Hodge to recover the amount of the check. In the meantime, Hodge discovered that Fentress was not a licensed plumber and that under state law, engaging in the plumbing trade without a license was a crime. Hodge filed a motion to dismiss Kedzie's claim on the ground that the plumbing contract was illegal and void. The court granted Hodge's motion, the appellate court affirmed, and Kedzie appealed to the Supreme Court of Illinois.

IN THE WORDS OF THE COURT . . .
Justice *FREEMAN* delivered the opinion of the court:

* * * *

* * * [A] holder in due course is an innocent third party. Such a holder is without knowledge of the circumstances of the contract upon which the instrument was initially exchanged. * * *

* * * *

* * * Unless the instrument arising from a contract or transaction is, itself, made void by statute, the "illegality" defense under [UCC] 3–305 is not available to bar the claim of a holder in due course.

* * * *

* * * It is relevant only to determine whether the Illinois Plumbing License Law provides that any obligation arising from a contract for plumbing services made in violation of its requirements is void. It does not.

DECISION AND REMEDY The Supreme Court of Illinois reversed the lower court's ruling.

FOR CRITICAL ANALYSIS—Economic Consideration *How could Hodge have avoided this situation?*

Mental Incapacity As mentioned, if a maker or drawer has been declared by a court to be mentally incompetent, any instrument issued by the maker or drawer is void. Hence, mental incapacity can serve as a universal defense [UCC 3–305(a)(1)(ii)]. If a maker or drawer issues a negotiable instrument while mentally incompetent but before a formal court hearing has declared him or her to be so, however, the instrument is voidable. In this situation, mental incapacity can serve only as a personal defense.

Other Personal Defenses Other personal defenses can be used to avoid payment to an ordinary holder of a negotiable instrument, including the following:

1. Discharge by payment or cancellation [UCC 3–601(b), 3–602(a), 3–603, 3–604].
2. Unauthorized completion of an incomplete instrument [UCC 3–115, 3–302, 3–407, 4–401(d)(2)].
3. Nondelivery of the instrument [UCC 1–201(14), 3–105(b), 3–305(a)(2)].
4. Ordinary duress or undue influence rendering the contract voidable [UCC 3–305(a)(1)(ii)].

Federal Limitations on the Rights of HDCs

The effects of the HDC doctrine on consumers can sometimes be harsh. • **EXAMPLE 20.16** A consumer purchases a used car under express warranty from an automobile dealer. The consumer pays $1,000 down and signs a promissory note to the dealer for the remaining $5,000 due on the car. The dealer sells the bank this promissory note, which is a negotiable instrument, and the bank then becomes the creditor, to whom the consumer makes payments. The car does not perform as warranted. The consumer returns the car and requests return of the down payment and cancellation of the contract. Even if the dealer refunded the $1,000, however, under the traditional HDC rule, the consumer would normally still owe the remaining $5,000, because the consumer's claim of breach of warranty is a personal defense, and the bank is a holder in due course. Thus, the traditional HDC rule leaves consumers who have purchased defective products liable to HDCs.•

¡WATCH OUT! Under the UCC, a holder in due course has no right to the enforcement of an instrument that complies with the FTC rule.

To protect consumers, the Federal Trade Commission issued a rule in 1976 that effectively abolished the HDC doctrine in consumer transactions. This rule, because of its significance in curbing the rights of HDCs, is presented here as this chapter's *Landmark in the Law.*

Landmark in the Law •

FTC RULE 433

In 1976, the Federal Trade Commission (FTC) issued Rule 433,[a] which severely limited the rights of HDCs who purchase instruments arising out of *consumer credit* transactions. The rule, entitled "Preservation of Consumers' Claims and Defenses," applies to any seller or lessor of goods or services who takes or receives a consumer credit contract. The rule also applies to a seller or lessor who accepts as full or partial payment for a sale or lease the proceeds of any purchase-money loan[b] made in connection with any consumer credit con-

a. 16 C.F.R. Section 433.2. The rule was enacted pursuant to the FTC's authority under the Federal Trade Commission Act, 15 U.S.C. Sections 41–58.

b. A purchase-money loan is one in which a seller or lessor advances money to a buyer or lessee, through a credit contract, to purchase or lease goods. See Chapter 22.

tract. Under the rule, these parties must include in the consumer credit contract the following provision:

NOTICE

ANY HOLDER OF THIS CONSUMER CREDIT CONTRACT IS SUBJECT TO ALL CLAIMS AND DEFENSES WHICH THE DEBTOR COULD ASSERT AGAINST THE SELLER OF GOODS OR SERVICES OBTAINED PURSUANT HERETO OR WITH THE PROCEEDS HEREOF. RECOVERY HEREUNDER BY THE DEBTOR SHALL NOT EXCEED AMOUNTS PAID BY THE DEBTOR HEREUNDER.

Thus, a consumer who is party to a consumer credit transaction can now bring any defense he or she has against the seller of a product against a subsequent holder as well. In essence, the FTC rule places a holder in due course of the negotiable instrument in the position of a contract assignee. The rule makes the buyer's duty to pay conditional on the seller's full performance of the contract. Finally, the rule clearly reduces the degree of transferability of negotiable instruments resulting from consumer credit contracts.

What if the seller does not include the notice in a promissory note and then sells the note to a third party, such as a bank? While the seller has violated the rule, the bank has not. Because the FTC rule does not prohibit third parties from purchasing notes or credit contracts that do *not* contain the required provision, the third party does not become subject to the buyer's defenses against the seller. Thus, a few consumers remain unprotected by the FTC rule.

FOR CRITICAL ANALYSIS
How has FTC Rule 433 affected the ease with which consumer credit instruments can be negotiated?

Discharge from Liability

Discharge from liability on an instrument can occur in several ways. The liability of all parties to an instrument is discharged when the party primarily liable on it pays to the holder the amount due in full [UCC 3–602, 3–603]. Payment by any other party discharges only the liability of that party and subsequent parties.

Intentional cancellation of an instrument discharges the liability of all parties [UCC 3–604]. Intentionally writing "Paid" across the face of an instrument cancels it. Intentionally tearing up an instrument cancels it. If a holder intentionally crosses out a party's signature, that party's liability and the liability of subsequent indorsers who have already indorsed the instrument are discharged. Materially altering an instrument may discharge the liability of any party affected by the alteration, as previously discussed [UCC 3–407(b)]. (An HDC may be able to enforce a materially altered instrument against its maker or drawer according to the instrument's original terms, however.)

Discharge of liability can also occur when a party's right of recourse is impaired [UCC 3–605]. A *right of recourse* is a right to seek reimbursement. Ordinarily, when a holder collects the amount of an instrument from an indorser, the indorser has a right of recourse against prior indorsers, the maker or drawer, and accommodation parties. If the holder has adversely affected the indorser's right to seek reimbursement from these other parties, however, the indorser is not liable on the instrument. This occurs when, for example, the holder releases or agrees not to sue a party against whom the indorser has a right of recourse.

APPLICATION: Law & the Purchaser of a Negotiable Instrument*

Negotiable instruments are transferred every business day of the year. Most purchasers of negotiable instruments do not encounter any problems in further negotiating and transferring the instruments or in collecting payment on them if they are time instruments. Potential problems exist, however, and purchasers should take precautions against them.

For example, suppose that you wish to purchase a demand instrument as a holder in due course (HDC). By definition, such an instrument has no stated time for payment and therefore may be overdue—that is, payment may have been demanded by the payee but not made, or a reasonable amount of time may have passed. (With checks, a reasonable amount of time is presumed to be ninety days from the date on the check.) If you have any doubt about whether a demand instrument is overdue, you should investigate.

With any negotiable instrument, as a prospective holder, you cannot afford to ignore a defect in the instrument. A four-month-old date on a check, for example, constitutes notice that the instrument is overdue. Whenever a defect in an instrument exists, you will not qualify as an HDC, and you may be unable to obtain payment. In other words, it is prudent to determine whether the instrument is complete and in some cases whether the transfer is such as to qualify you for HDC status.

CHECKLIST FOR THE PURCHASER OF NEGOTIABLE INSTRUMENTS

1. Make sure that a demand instrument is not overdue before purchasing it.
2. Make sure that the negotiable instrument has no obvious defects—look for signs indicating whether the maker or drawer of the instrument might have a valid reason for refusing to pay.

*This *Application* is not meant to substitute for the services of an attorney who is licensed to practice law in your state.

Key Terms

accommodation party 526
agent 528
fictitious payee 530
holder in due course (HDC) 519
imposter 530
personal defense 534
presentment warranty 532
principal 528
shelter principle 523
transfer warranty 531
universal defense 532

Chapter Summary • Rights and Liabilities of Parties

Holder versus Holder in Due Course (HDC) (See page 519.)	1. *Holder*—A person in the possession of an instrument drawn, issued, or indorsed to him or her, to his or her order, or to bearer or in blank. A holder obtains only those rights that the transferor had in the instrument. 2. *Holder in due course (HDC)*—A holder who, by meeting certain acquisition requirements (summarized next), takes the instrument free of most defenses and claims to which the transferor was subject.
Requirements for HDC Status (See pages 519–523.)	To be an HDC, a holder must take the instrument: 1. *For value*—A holder can take an instrument for value in one of five ways [UCC 3–303]: a. By the complete or partial performance of the promise for which the instrument was issued or transferred. b. By acquiring a security interest or other lien in the instrument, excluding a lien obtained by a judicial proceeding. c. By taking an instrument in payment of (or as security for) an antecedent debt. d. By giving a negotiable instrument as payment. e. By giving an irrevocable commitment as payment. 2. *In good faith*—Good faith is defined as "honesty in fact and the observance of reasonable commercial standards of fair dealing" [UCC 3–103(a)(4)]. 3. *Without notice*—To be an HDC, a holder must not be on notice that the instrument is defective in any of the following ways [UCC 3–302, 3–304]: a. It is overdue. b. It has been dishonored. c. There is an uncured (uncorrected) default with respect to another instrument issued as part of the same series. d. The instrument contains an unauthorized signature or has been altered. e. There is a defense against the instrument or a claim to the instrument. f. The instrument is so irregular or incomplete as to call into question its authenticity.
Holder through an HDC (See pages 523–524.)	A holder who cannot qualify as an HDC has the *rights* of an HDC if he or she derives title through an HDC unless the holder engaged in fraud or illegality affecting the instrument [UCC 3–203(b)].
Signature Liability (See pages 524–531.)	Every party (except a qualified indorser) who signs a negotiable instrument is either primarily or secondarily liable for payment of the instrument when it comes due. 1. *Primary liability*—Makers and acceptors are primarily liable (an acceptor is a drawee that promises in writing to pay an instrument when it is presented for payment at a later time) [UCC 3–115, 3–407, 3–409, 3–412]. 2. *Secondary liability*—Drawers and indorsers are secondarily liable [UCC 3–412, 3–414, 3–415, 3–501, 3–502, 3–503]. Parties who are secondarily liable on an instrument promise to pay on that instrument if the following events occur: a. The instrument is properly and timely presented. b. The instrument is dishonored. c. Timely notice of dishonor is given to the secondarily liable party. 3. *Accommodation parties*—An accommodation party is one who signs his or her name as credit to another party on an instrument [UCC 3–419]. Accommodation *makers* are primarily liable; accommodation *indorsers* are secondarily liable.

Chapter Summary • Rights and Liabilities of Parties, Continued

Signature Liability—continued	4. *Agents' signatures*—An *agent* is a person who agrees to represent or act for another, called the *principal.* Agents can sign negotiable instruments and thereby bind their principals. Liability on an instrument signed by an agent depends on whether the agent is authorized and on whether the agent's representative capacity and the principal's identity are both indicated on the instrument [UCC 3–401, 3–402, 3–403]. Agents need not indicate their representative capacity on *checks*—provided the checks clearly identify the principal and are drawn on the principal's account. 5. *Unauthorized signatures*—An unauthorized signature is wholly inoperative *unless:* a. The person whose name is signed ratifies (affirms) it or is precluded from denying it [UCC 3–115, 3–401, 3–403, 3–406]. b. The instrument has been negotiated to an HDC [UCC 3–403]. 6. *Special rules for unauthorized indorsements*—An unauthorized indorsement will not bind the maker or drawer except in the following circumstances: a. When an imposter induces the maker or drawer of an instrument to issue it to the imposter (imposter rule) [UCC 3–404(a)]. b. When a person signs as or on behalf of a maker or drawer, intending that the payee will have no interest in the instrument, or when an agent or employee of the maker or drawer has supplied him or her with the name of the payee, also intending the payee to have no such interest (fictitious payee rule) [UCC 3–404(b), 3–405].
Warranty Liability (See pages 531–532.)	1. *Transfer warranties*—Any person who transfers an instrument for consideration makes the following warranties to all subsequent transferees and holders who take the instrument in good faith (but when a bearer instrument is transferred by delivery only, the transferor's warranties extend only to the immediate transferee) [UCC 3–416]: a. The transferor is entitled to enforce the instrument. b. All signatures are authentic and authorized. c. The instrument has not been altered. d. The instrument is not subject to a defense or claim of any party that can be asserted against the transferor. e. The transferor has no knowledge of any insolvency proceedings against the maker, the acceptor, or the drawer of the instrument. 2. *Presentment warranties*—Any person who presents an instrument for payment or acceptance makes the following warranties to any other person who in good faith pays or accepts the instrument [UCC 3–417(a), 3–417(d)]: a. The person obtaining payment or acceptance is entitled to enforce the instrument or is authorized to obtain payment or acceptance on behalf of a person who is entitled to enforce the instrument. (This is, in effect, a warranty that there are no missing or unauthorized indorsements.) b. The instrument has not been altered. c. The person obtaining payment or acceptance has no knowledge that the signature of the drawer of the instrument is unauthorized.
Defenses to Liability (See pages 532–536.)	1. *Universal (real) defenses*—The following defenses are valid against all holders, including HDCs and holders with the rights of HDCs [UCC 3–305, 3–401, 3–403, 3–407]: a. Forgery. b. Fraud in the execution.

Chapter Summary • Rights and Liabilities of Parties, Continued

Defenses to Liability—continued	c. Material alteration. d. Discharge in bankruptcy. e. Minority—if the contract is voidable under state law. f. Illegality, mental incapacity, or extreme duress—if the contract is void under state law. 2. *Personal (limited) defenses*—The following defenses are valid against ordinary holders but not against HDCs or holders with the rights of HDCs [UCC 3–105, 3–115, 3–302, 3–305, 3–306, 3–407, 3–601, 3–602, 3–603, 3–604, 4–401]: a. Breach of contract or breach of warranty. b. Lack or failure of consideration (value). c. Fraud in the inducement. d. Illegality and mental incapacity—if the contract is voidable. e. Previous payment of the instrument. f. Unauthorized completion of the instrument. g. Nondelivery of the instrument. h. Ordinary duress or undue influence that renders the contract voidable.
Federal Limitations on the Rights of HDCs (See pages 536–537.)	Rule 433 of the Federal Trade Commission, issued in 1976, limits the rights of HDCs who purchase instruments arising out of consumer credit transactions. Under the rule, a consumer who is a party to a consumer credit transaction is permitted to bring any defense he or she has against the seller against a subsequent holder as well, even if the subsequent holder is an HDC.
Discharge from Liability (See page 537.)	All parties to a negotiable instrument will be discharged when the party primarily liable on it pays to a holder the amount due in full. Discharge can also occur in other circumstances (if the instrument has been canceled, materially altered, and so on) [UCC 3–601 through 3–606].

For Review

❶ What are the requirements for attaining HDC status?
❷ How can a person who does not qualify as an HDC acquire the rights and privileges of an HDC?
❸ What is the key to liability on a negotiable instrument? What is the difference between signature liability and warranty liability?
❹ Certain defenses are valid against all holders, including HDCs. What are these defenses called? Name four defenses that fall within this category.
❺ Certain defenses can be used to avoid payment to an ordinary holder of a negotiable instrument but are not effective against an HDC. What are these defenses called? Name four defenses that fall within this category.

Questions and Case Problems

20–1. Unauthorized Indorsements. What are the exceptions to the rule that a bank will be liable for paying a check over an unauthorized indorsement?

20–2. Agents' Signatures. Karen Thorpe is a purchasing agent for GymNast, Inc., a manufacturer of sports equipment. Karen has authority to sign checks in payment of purchases made by GymNast. Karen makes out three checks to suppliers and signs each one differently, as follows:

(a) GymNast, Inc., by Karen Thorpe, purchasing agent.
(b) Karen Thorpe, purchasing agent.
(c) Karen Thorpe.

Discuss briefly whether Karen is personally liable on each signature and whether parol evidence is admissible to hold GymNast, Inc., liable.

20–3. Defenses. Jules sold Alfred a small motorboat for

$1,500; Jules maintained to Alfred that the boat was in excellent condition. Alfred gave Jules a check for $1,500, which Jules indorsed and gave to Sherry for value. When Alfred took the boat for a trial run, he discovered that the boat leaked, needed to be painted, and needed a new motor. Alfred stopped payment on his check, which had not yet been cashed. Jules has disappeared. Can Sherry recover from Alfred as a holder in due course? Discuss.

20–4. Defenses. Fox purchased a used car from Emerson for $1,000. Fox paid for the car with a check, written in pencil, payable to Emerson for $1,000. Emerson, through careful erasures and alterations, changed the amount on the check to read $10,000 and negotiated the check to Sanderson. Sanderson took the check for value, in good faith, and without notice of the alteration and thus met the UCC requirements for HDC status. Can Fox successfully raise the universal defense of material alteration to avoid payment on the check? Explain.

20–5. Signature Liability. Marion makes a promissory note payable to the order of Perry. Perry indorses the note by writing "without recourse, Perry" and transfers the note for value to Steven. Steven, in need of cash, negotiates the note to Harriet by indorsing it with the words "Pay to Harriet, [signed] Steven." On the due date, Harriet presents the note to Marion for payment, only to learn that Marion has filed for bankruptcy and will have all debts (including the note) discharged in bankruptcy. Discuss fully whether Harriet can hold Marion, Perry, or Steven liable on the note.

20–6. HDC Status. An employee of Epicycle Corp. cashed a payroll check at Money Mart Check Cashing Center, Inc. Money Mart deposited the check, with others, into its bank account. When the check was returned marked "Payment stopped," Money Mart sought to recover from Epicycle for the value of the check. Money Mart claimed that it was a holder in due course on the instrument because it had taken the check for value, in good faith, and without notice that a stop-payment order had been made. Epicycle argued that Money Mart was not a holder in due course, because it had failed to verify that the check was good before it cashed the check. Did Money Mart's failure to inquire into the validity of the check preclude it from being a holder in due course? Explain. [*Money Mart Check Cashing Center, Inc. v. Epicycle Corp.*, 667 P.2d 1372 (Colo. 1983)]

20–7. Imposter Rule. Edward Bauerband contacted Minster State Bank by phone and requested a $25,000 loan, purportedly on behalf of himself and his wife, Michelle. The Bauerbands had a long-standing relationship with the bank, and the request was not so unusual as to put the bank on notice. The bank mailed a promissory note to Edward to be signed by both him and his wife. Edward forged his wife's signature on the note, signed it himself, and returned the note and other loan documents to the bank. On its receipt of the documents, the bank issued a cashier's check in the amount of $25,000, payable to Edward and Michelle jointly, and mailed the check to the Bauerbands' home. Edward indorsed the check in his name, forged his wife's indorsement, and deposited the check in his business account at another bank, Baybank Middlesex. Michelle knew nothing about the loan transaction or the check. Ultimately, the forgery was discovered, and Minster State Bank sued Baybank Middlesex to recover the funds. Baybank contended that it was precluded from liability under the UCC's "imposter rule." Was it? Explain. [*Minster State Bank v. Bauerband,* 1992 Mass.App.Div. 61 (1992)]

20–8. Unauthorized Indorsements. Nancy Gabbard was the office manager at Golden Years Nursing Home (No. 2), Inc. She was given a signature stamp to issue checks to the nursing home's employees for up to $100 as advances on their pay. The checks were drawn on Golden Years's account at the First National Bank. Over a seven-year period, Gabbard wrote a number of checks to employees exclusively for the purpose of embezzling the money. She forged the employees' indorsements on the checks, signed her name as a second indorser, and deposited the checks in her personal account at Star Bank. First National paid Star Bank for the deposited checks. The employees whose names were on the checks never actually requested them. When the scheme was uncovered, Golden Years filed a suit in an Ohio state court against Gabbard, Star Bank, and others to recover the money. Which party, Golden Years or Star Bank, will bear the loss in this situation? Why? [*Golden Years Nursing Home (No. 2), Inc. v. Gabbard,* 640 N.E.2d 1186 (Ohio App. 1994)]

20–9. Discharge. Mary Ann McClusky and her husband Curtis borrowed $75,000 and signed a note payable to Francis and Thomas Gardner. As collateral, Mary Ann gave the Gardners a mortgage on a farm owned in her name only. After the McCluskys divorced, Mary Ann found, in a file in the basement of her house, the note with the word "Paid" written across it. When the Gardners refused to cancel the mortgage, she filed a suit in an Indiana state court against them. During the trial, she testified that she did not know how the note came to be in her basement or who wrote "Paid" across it. The Gardners testified that they had not surrendered it. Should the court presume that the note had been discharged, given that it was in Mary Ann's possession and had the word "Paid" written across it? Discuss. [*Gardner v. McClusky,* 647 N.E.2d 1 (Ind.App. 1995)]

A QUESTION OF ETHICS AND SOCIAL RESPONSIBILITY

20–10. One day, while Ort, a farmer, was working alone in his field, a stranger approached him. The stranger said he was the state agent for a manufacturer of iron posts and wire fence. Eventually the stranger persuaded Ort to accept a township-wide agency for the same manufacturer. The stranger then asked Ort to sign a document that purportedly was an agency agreement. Because Ort did not have his glasses with him and could read only with great difficulty, he asked the stranger to read what the document said. The stranger then pretended to read the document to Ort, not mentioning that it was a promissory note. Both men signed the note, and Ort assumed that he was signing a document of agency. The stranger later negotiated the note to a good faith purchaser for value. When that person sued Ort, Ort attempted to defend on the basis of fraud in the execution. In view of these facts, consider the following questions. [*Ort v. Fowler,* 31 Kan. 478, 2 P. 580 (1884)]

1. Although this classic case was decided long before the UCC was drafted, the court applied essentially the same rule that would apply under Article 3. What is this rule, and how would it be applied to Ort's attempted defense on the ground of fraud in the execution?
2. This case provides a clear example of a situation in which one of two innocent parties (Ort and the purchaser of the note) must bear the loss caused by a third party (the stranger, who was the perpetrator of the fraud). Under Article 3, which party should bear the loss, and why?

FOR CRITICAL ANALYSIS

20–11. How does the concept of holder in due course further Article 3's general goal of encouraging the negotiability of instruments? How does it further Article 3's goal of balancing the rights of parties to negotiable instruments?

Online Activities

ONLINE EXERCISE 20-1

Go to the "Internet Activities Book" on the Web site that accompanies this text, the URL for which is http://blt.westbuslaw.com. Select the following activities, and perform the exercises according to the instructions given there:

Activity 20–1: Review of Negotiable Instruments
Activity 20–2: Check Fraud

Before the Test

Go to the *Business Law Today* home page at http://blt.westbuslaw.com. Click on TestTutor.® You will find twenty interactive questions relating to this chapter.

CHAPTER 21 Checks & the Banking System

> "Money is just what we use to keep tally."
>
> Henry Ford, 1863–1947
> (American automobile manufacturer)

CONTENTS

LEARNING OBJECTIVES

After reading this chapter, you should be able to:

1. Identify the different types of checks.
2. Indicate when a bank may dishonor a customer's check without liability to the customer.
3. Outline a bank's responsibilities regarding stale checks, stop-payment orders, and forged or altered checks.
4. Describe how banks collect payment on checks deposited by their customers.
5. Explain the laws governing consumer electronic fund transfers and commercial fund transfers.

Checks are the most common type of negotiable instruments regulated by the Uniform Commercial Code (UCC). It is estimated that over sixty-five billion personal and commercial checks are written each year in the United States. Checks are more than a daily convenience; they are an integral part of the American economic system. They serve as substitutes for money and thus, as Henry Ford said in the chapter-opening quotation, help us to "keep tally."

Issues relating to checks are governed by Article 3 and Article 4 of the UCC. Recall from Chapters 19 and 20 that Article 3 establishes the requirements that all negotiable instruments, including checks, must meet. Article 3 also sets forth the rights and liabilities of parties to negotiable instruments. Article 4 of the UCC governs the relationships of banks with one another as they process checks for payment, and it establishes a framework for deposit and checking agreements between a bank and its customers. A check therefore may fall within the scope of Article 3 and yet be subject to the provisions of Article 4 while the check is in the course of collection. If a conflict between Article 3 and Article 4 arises, Article 4 controls [UCC 4–102(a)].

In this chapter, we first identify the legal characteristics of checks and the legal duties and liabilities that arise when a check is issued. Then we examine the collection process—that is, the actual procedure by which the checks deposited into bank accounts move through banking channels, causing the underlying funds to be shifted from one bank account to another. Increasingly, credit cards, debit cards, and other devices and methods to transfer funds electronically are being used to pay for goods and services. In the latter part of this chapter, we look at the law governing electronic fund transfers.

Checks

• **CHECK**
A draft drawn by a drawer ordering the drawee bank or financial institution to pay a fixed amount of money to the holder on demand.

A **check** is a special type of draft that is drawn on a bank, ordering the bank to pay a fixed amount of money on demand [UCC 3–104(f)]. Article 4 defines a bank as "a person engaged in the business of banking, including a savings bank, savings and loan association, credit union or trust company" [UCC 4–105(1)]. If any other institution (such as a brokerage firm) handles a check for payment or for collection, the check is not covered by Article 4.

Recall from the discussion of negotiable instruments in Chapters 19 and 20 that a person who writes a check is called the drawer. The drawer is a depositor in the bank on which the check is drawn. The person to whom the check is payable is the payee. The bank or financial institution on which the check is drawn is the drawee. If Anita Cruzak writes a check from her checking account to pay her college tuition, she is the drawer, her bank is the drawee, and her college is the payee. We now look at some special types of checks.

Cashier's Checks

Checks are usually three-party instruments, but on certain types of checks, the bank can serve as both the drawer and the drawee. For example, when a bank draws a check on itself, the check is called a **cashier's check** and is a negotiable instrument on issue (see Exhibit 21–1) [UCC 3–104(g)]. Normally, a cashier's check indicates a specific payee. In effect, with a cashier's check, the bank assumes responsibility for paying the check, thus making the check more readily acceptable as a substitute for cash.

• **CASHIER'S CHECK**
A check drawn by a bank on itself.

• **Example 21.1** Kramer needs to pay a moving company $8,000 for moving his household goods to a new home in another state. The moving company requests payment in the form of a cashier's check. Kramer goes to a bank (he need not have an

EXHIBIT 21–1 • A Cashier's Check

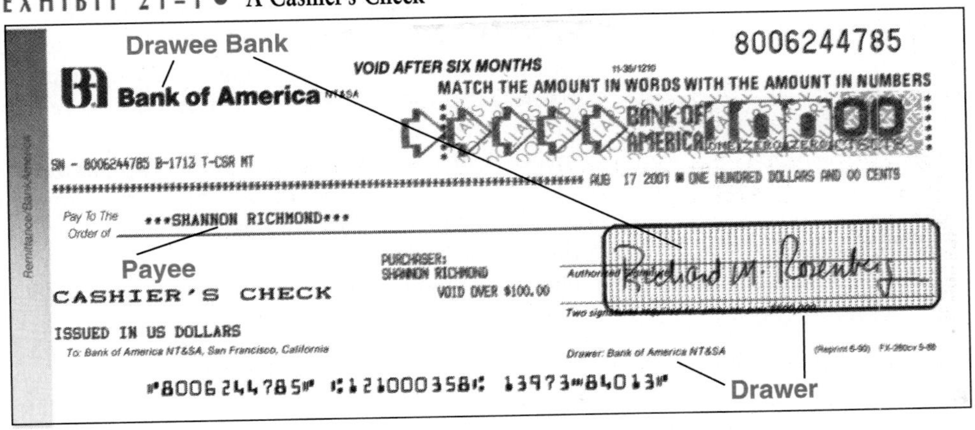

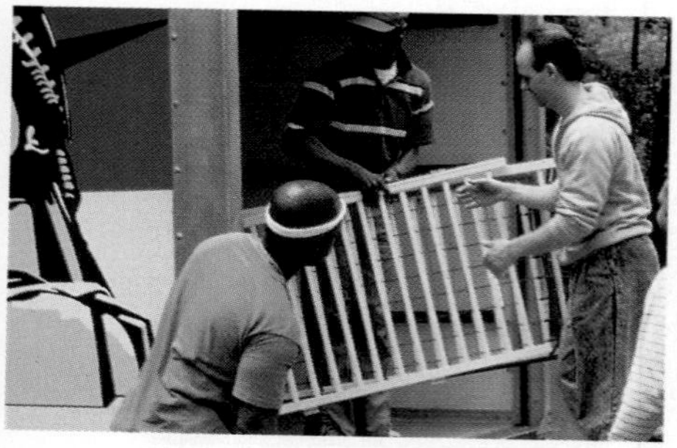

WORKERS LOAD FURNITURE ONTO A MOVING VAN. HOW WOULD THE OWNERS OF THE FURNITURE OBTAIN A CASHIER'S CHECK TO PAY THE MOVING COMPANY?

account at the bank) and purchases a cashier's check, payable to the moving company, in the amount of $8,000. Kramer has to pay the bank the $8,000 for the check, plus a small service fee. He then gives the check to the moving company. ●

Cashier's checks are sometimes used in the business community as nearly the equivalent of cash. Except in very limited circumstances, the issuing bank must honor its cashier's checks when they are presented for payment. If a bank wrongfully dishonors a cashier's check, a holder can recover from the bank all expenses incurred, interest, and consequential damages [UCC 3–411]. This same rule applies if a bank wrongfully dishonors a certified check (to be discussed shortly) or a teller's check. (A *teller's check* is a check drawn by a bank on another bank or, when drawn on a nonbank, payable at or through a bank [UCC 3–104(h)]). In the following case, the court considered whether a bank could legitimately refuse to honor its own cashier's checks.

CASE 21.1 First Railroad Community Federal Credit Union v. Columbia County Bank

United States District Court,
Middle District of Florida,
Jacksonville Division, 1994.
849 F.Supp. 780.

HISTORICAL AND ECONOMIC SETTING *In the 1980s, the share of the U.S. auto market held by U.S. automakers declined by 10 percent relative to imports. With sales dropping, U.S. manufacturers closed plants, replaced blue-collar workers with robots, substituted computers for white-collar workers, and sometimes used creative bookkeeping to satisfy their shareholders. Domestic auto dealers began to sell foreign models. Instead of selling only Chevrolets, for example, dealers also began to sell Mazdas, Hondas, or BMWs. A few dealers, however, were unable to meet the challenges resulting from declining profits and engaged in criminal schemes to bolster their finances.*

BACKGROUND AND FACTS Clark Crapps operated two automobile dealerships with bank accounts in the First Railroad Community Federal Credit Union and the Columbia County Bank. On one occasion, checks drawn on the account with First Railroad were deposited into the Columbia account. Unaware that the First Railroad account did not have enough funds to pay the checks, Columbia credited the account in its bank and issued two cashier's checks, each for $300,000, based on the credit. Both checks were immediately deposited into the First Railroad account. When Columbia learned of the financial misdealings, it refused to honor the cashier's checks. Seeking payment, First Railroad filed a suit in a federal district court against Columbia. Both parties filed motions for summary judgment.

IN THE WORDS OF THE COURT . . .
SCHLESINGER, District Judge.

* * * *

* * * Parties using cashier's checks in place of ordinary checks or instruments do so because cashier's checks do not carry the risk of litigation costs or insolvency. A cashier's check, unlike an ordinary check, stands on its own foundation as an independent, unconditional, and primary obligation of the bank. People accept a cashier's check as a substitute for cash because the bank stands behind the check, rather than an individual. When used in place of a personal check or other negotiable instrument, the parties' expectation is that the cashier's check will remove doubt as to whether the instrument will be returned to the holder unpaid due to insufficient funds in the account, a stop payment order, or insolvency.

* * * [T]he only inquiry a bank may make upon presentment of a cashier's check is whether or not the payee or endorsee is in fact a legitimate holder, i.e., whether the cashier's check is being presented by a thief or one who simply found a lost check, or whether the check has been materially altered.

DECISION AND REMEDY The federal district court held that First Railroad was entitled to payment and granted summary judgment in its favor.

FOR CRITICAL ANALYSIS—Economic Consideration *Why are the grounds on which a bank can refuse to pay a cashier's check so limited?*

EXHIBIT 21–2 • A Traveler's Check

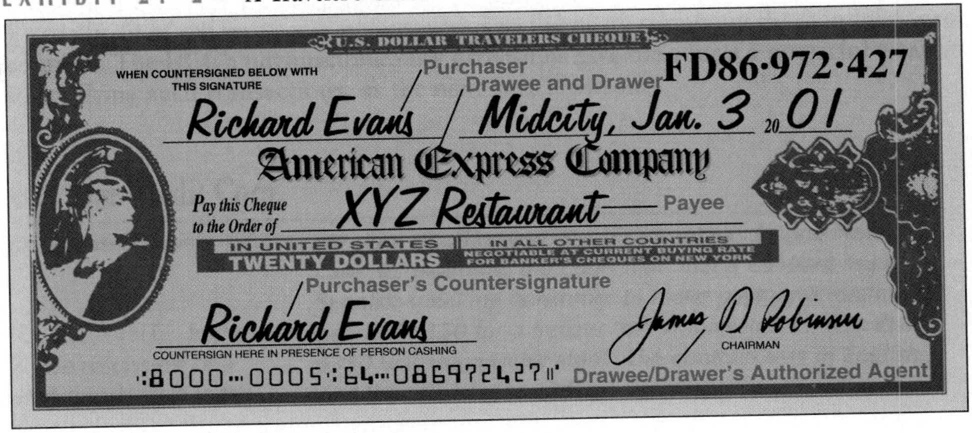

TRAVELER'S CHECKS

• **TRAVELER'S CHECK**
A check that is payable on demand, drawn on or payable through a financial institution (bank), and designated as a traveler's check.

A **traveler's check** has the characteristics of a teller's check. It is an instrument that is payable on demand, drawn on or payable at or through a financial institution (bank), and designated as a traveler's check. The institution is directly obligated to accept and pay its traveler's check according to the check's terms. The purchaser is required to sign the check at the time it is bought and again at the time it is used [UCC 3–104(i)]. Exhibit 21–2 shows an example of a traveler's check.

CERTIFIED CHECKS

• **CERTIFIED CHECK**
A check that has been accepted in writing by the bank on which it is drawn. Essentially, the bank, by certifying (accepting) the check, promises to pay the check at the time the check is presented.

A **certified check** is a check that has been *accepted* in writing by the bank on which it is drawn [UCC 3–409(d)]. When a drawee bank *certifies* (accepts) a check, it immediately charges the drawer's account with the amount of the check and transfers those funds to its own certified check account. In effect, the bank is agreeing in advance to accept that check when it is presented for payment and to make payment from those funds reserved in the certified check account. Essentially, certification prevents the bank from denying liability. It is a promise that sufficient funds are on deposit *and have been set aside* to cover the check. Exhibit 21–3 shows a sample certified check.

EXHIBIT 21–3 • A Certified Check

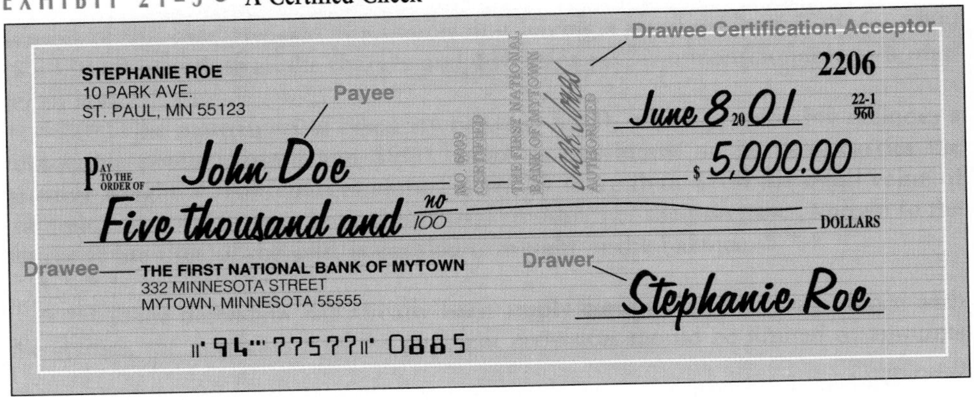

A drawee bank is not obligated to certify a check, and failure to do so is not a dishonor of the check [UCC 3–409(d)]. If a bank does certify a check, however, the bank should write on the check the amount that it will pay. If the certification does not state an amount, and the amount is later increased and the instrument negotiated to a holder in due course (HDC), the obligation of the certifying bank is the amount of the instrument when it was taken by the HDC [UCC 3–413(b)].

Certification may be requested by a holder (to ensure that the check will not be dishonored for insufficient funds) or by the drawer. In either circumstance, on certification the drawer and any prior indorsers are completely discharged from liability on the instrument [UCC 3–414(c), 3–415(d)].[1]

The Bank-Customer Relationship

The bank-customer relationship begins when the customer opens a checking account and deposits funds that the bank will use to pay for checks written by the customer. The rights and duties of the bank and the customer are contractual and depend on the nature of the transaction.

ON THE WEB

Cornell University's Legal Information Institute provides an overview of banking, as well as a "menu of sources" of federal and state statutes and court decisions relating to banking transactions. To access this information, go to www.law.cornell.edu/topics/banking.html.

A creditor-debtor relationship is created between a customer and a bank when, for example, the customer makes cash deposits into a checking account. When a customer makes a deposit, the customer becomes a creditor, and the bank a debtor, for the amount deposited. (What if a customer makes a deposit in the bank's night depository, but the bank claims it never received it? Has a debtor-creditor relationship—and the rights and duties accompanying that relationship—come into existence with respect to those funds? This question is answered in this chapter's *Business Law in Action.*)

An agency relationship also arises between the customer and the bank when the customer writes a check on his or her account. In effect, the customer is ordering the bank to pay the amount specified on the check to the holder when the holder presents the check to the bank for payment. In this situation, the bank becomes the customer's agent and is obligated to honor the customer's request. Similarly, if the customer deposits a check into his or her account, the bank, as the customer's agent, is obligated to collect payment on the check from the bank on which the check was drawn. To transfer checkbook funds among different banks, each bank acts as the agent of collection for its customer [UCC 4–201(a)].

Whenever a bank-customer relationship is established, certain contractual rights and duties arise. The respective rights and duties of banks and their customers are discussed in detail in the following pages.

Bank's Duty to Honor Checks

When a commercial bank provides checking services, it agrees to honor the checks written by its customers with the usual stipulation that there be sufficient funds available in the account to pay each check [UCC 4–401(a)]. The customer is generally obligated to keep sufficient funds on deposit to cover all checks written. The customer is liable to the payee or to the holder of a check in a civil suit if a check is

1. Under Section 3–411 of the unrevised Article 3, the legal liability of a drawer varies according to whether certification is requested by the drawee or a holder. The drawer who obtains certification remains *secondarily liable* on the instrument if the certifying bank does not honor the check when it is presented for payment. If the check is certified at the request of a holder, the drawer and anyone who indorses the check before certification are completely discharged.

Business Law in Action • The Deposit That Disappeared

Most banks provide night depositories for their customers—secured facilities into which customers can drop their deposits while the bank is closed. But what happens if the customer deposits checks into a night depository and the bank claims it never received them? Certainly, if the bank later finds the checks, it will be liable for any damages caused to the customer due to the bank's negligence. If, however, the checks never turn up and it is evident that the bank exercised due care in handling all deposits dropped into its night depository, does the customer have any recourse?

This question came before a New York court in *Epic Security Corp. v. Banco Popular (New York)*.[a] The case arose after Lane Bryant, a customer of Banco Popular, claimed that the bank had not credited to its account deposits contained in a night depository bag. Lane Bryant's agent, Epic Security Corporation, stated that it had deposited the bag in the night depository chute at Banco Popular's branch location in Brooklyn, New York. After investigating the matter, Banco Popular determined that all of the proper procedures had been followed by the bank's personnel at that branch and that the bag had not been deposited in the chute.

The court noted that the usual legal relationship between a customer and its bank is a creditor-debtor relationship, which creates an obligation on the part of the bank to pay funds deposited by the customer on the customer's demand for payment. The court concluded that, in this case, no creditor-debtor relationship had arisen. According to the court, "the view has been taken, particularly as to night deposits, that the relationship of debtor and creditor between the bank and the depositor does not arise until the official crediting of the deposit to the customer's account during regular banking hours."

The fact was, there was simply no evidence that the bag had been delivered to the bank. The bank was able to provide documentary evidence and affidavits to the court that it had, indeed, followed proper procedures in handling night deposits. In contrast, all that Epic Security could offer was its word that it had actually deposited the bag in the chute on the night in question. The court held that this was not enough and granted summary judgment in favor of the bank. "To hold otherwise," said the court, "would be sheer folly and permit unrestrained and unlimited suits against banks simply on the bare assertion of an individual that he made a deposit."

The message in this case for businesspersons (and others) is clear. Although night depositories may be convenient, they are not totally risk free.

FOR CRITICAL ANALYSIS

What if a bank required its customers to agree, in a signed writing, not to hold the bank liable for any missing night deposits? Would such an agreement be enforceable? Explain.

a. 1997 WL 823591 (N.Y.Civ.Ct. 1997).

dishonored for insufficient funds. If intent to defraud can be proved, the customer can also be subject to criminal prosecution for writing a bad check.

When the bank properly dishonors a check for insufficient funds, it has no liability to the customer. When a drawee bank *wrongfully* fails to honor a customer's check, however, it is liable to its customer for damages resulting from its refusal to pay [UCC 4–402].

Clearly, the bank's duty to honor its customers' checks is not absolute. As noted, the bank is under no duty to honor a check when there are insufficient funds in the customer's account. There are other circumstances in which the bank may rightfully make payment or refuse payment on a customer's check. We look here at the rights and duties of both the bank and its customers in relation to specific situations.

Overdrafts

When the bank receives an item properly payable from its customer's checking account but there are insufficient funds in the account to cover the amount of the check, the bank has two options. It can either (1) dishonor the item or (2) pay the

• **OVERDRAFT**
A check that is written on a checking account in which there are insufficient funds to cover the check and that is paid by the bank.

item and charge the customer's account, thus creating an **overdraft,** providing that the customer has authorized the payment and the payment does not violate any bank-customer agreement [UCC 4–401(a)].[2] The bank can subtract the difference (plus a service charge) from the customer's next deposit or eventually from other deposits made by the customer, because the check carries with it an enforceable implied promise to reimburse the bank.

A bank can expressly agree with a customer to accept overdrafts through what is sometimes called an "overdraft protection agreement." If such an agreement is formed, any failure of the bank to honor a check because it would create an overdraft breaches this agreement and is treated as wrongful dishonor [UCC 4–402(a)].

When a check "bounces," a holder can resubmit the check, hoping that at a later date sufficient funds will be available to pay it. The holder must notify any indorsers on the check of the first dishonor, however; otherwise, they will be discharged from their signature liability.

POSTDATED CHECKS

A bank may also charge a postdated check against a customer's account, unless the customer notifies the bank, in a timely manner, not to pay the check until the stated date. The notice of postdating must be given in time to allow the bank to act on the notice before the bank commits itself to pay on the check. The UCC states that the bank should treat a notice of postdating the same as a stop-payment order—to be discussed shortly. Generally, if the bank receives timely notice from the customer and nonetheless charges the customer's account before the date on the postdated check, the bank may be liable for any damages incurred by the customer as a result [UCC 4–401(c)].[3]

STALE CHECKS

• **STALE CHECK**
A check, other than a certified check, that is presented for payment more than six months after its date.

Commercial banking practice regards a check that is presented for payment more than six months from its date as a **stale check.** A bank is not obligated to pay an uncertified check presented more than six months from its date [UCC 4–404]. When receiving a stale check for payment, the bank has the option of paying or not paying the check. The bank may consult the customer before paying the check. If a bank pays a stale check in good faith without consulting the customer, however, the bank has the right to charge the customer's account for the amount of the check.

STOP-PAYMENT ORDERS

• **STOP-PAYMENT ORDER**
An order by a bank customer to his or her bank not to pay or certify a certain check.

A **stop-payment order** is an order by a customer to his or her bank not to pay or certify a certain check. Only a customer or a person authorized to draw on the account can order the bank not to pay the check when it is presented for payment [UCC 4–403(a)]. For a deceased customer, any person claiming a legitimate interest in the account may issue a stop-payment order [UCC 4–405]. A customer has no

2. If there is a joint account, the bank cannot hold any joint-account customer liable for payment of an overdraft unless the customer has signed the check or has benefited from the proceeds of the check [UCC 4–401(b)].

3. Under the UCC, postdating does not affect the negotiability of a check. Instead of treating postdated checks as checks payable on demand, however, some courts treated them as time drafts. Thus, regardless of whether the customer notified the bank of the postdating, a bank could not charge a customer's account for a postdated check without facing potential liability for the payment of later checks. Under the automated check-collection system in use today, however, a check is usually paid without respect to its date. Thus, today the bank can ignore the postdate on the check (treat it as a demand instrument) unless it has received notice of the postdate.

right to stop payment on a check that has been certified or accepted by a bank, however. Also, a stop-payment order must be received within a reasonable time and in a reasonable manner to permit the bank to act on it [UCC 4–403(a)]. Although a stop-payment order can be given orally, usually by phone, it is binding on the bank for only fourteen calendar days unless confirmed in writing.[4] A written stop-payment order (see Exhibit 21–4) or an oral order confirmed in writing is effective for six months, at which time it must be renewed in writing [UCC 4–403(b)].

If the bank pays the check over the customer's properly instituted stop-payment order, the bank will be obligated to recredit the customer's account—but only for the amount of the actual loss suffered by the drawer because of the wrongful payment [UCC 4–403(c)]. • **EXAMPLE 21.2** Arlene Drury orders six bamboo palms from a local nursery at $50 each and gives the nursery a check for $300. Later that day, the nursery tells Drury that it will not deliver the palms as arranged. Drury immediately calls her bank and stops payment on the check. If the bank nonetheless honors the check, the bank will be liable to Drury for the full $300. The result would be different, however, if the nursery had delivered five palms. In that situation, Drury would owe the nursery $250 for the delivered palms, and her actual losses would be only $50. Consequently, the bank would be liable to Drury for only $50. •

A stop-payment order has its risks for a customer. The customer-drawer must have *a valid legal ground* for issuing such an order; otherwise, the holder can sue the drawer for payment. Moreover, defenses sufficient to refuse payment against a payee may not be valid grounds to prevent payment against a subsequent holder in due course [UCC 3–305, 3–306]. A person who wrongfully stops payment on a check not only will be liable to the payee for the amount of the check but also may be liable for consequential damages incurred by the payee as a result of the wrongful stop-payment order.

At issue in the following case was whether a bank wrongfully honored a check by making payment on the check after its customer had given the bank a stop-payment order.

4. Some states do not recognize oral stop-payment orders; they must be in writing.

EXHIBIT 21–4 • A Stop-Payment Order

Bank of America

Checking Account Stop Payment Order

To: Bank of America NT&SA
I want to stop payment on the following check(s).

ACCOUNT NUMBER: ______ – ______

SPECIFIC STOP

*ENTER DOLLAR AMOUNT: ______ *CHECK NUMBER: ______

THE CHECK WAS SIGNED BY: ______

THE CHECK IS PAYABLE TO: ______

THE REASON FOR THIS STOP PAYMENT IS: ______

STOP RANGE (Use for lost or stolen check(s) only.)

DOLLAR AMOUNT: 000

*ENTER STARTING CHECK NUMBER: ______ *END CHECK NUMBER: ______

THE REASON FOR THIS STOP PAYMENT IS: ______

I agree that this order (1) is effective only if the above check(s) has (have) not yet been cashed or paid against my account, (2) will end six months from the date it is delivered to you unless I renew it in writing, and (3) is not valid if the check(s) was (were) accepted on the strength of my Bank of America courtesy-check guarantee card by a merchant participating in that program. I also agree (1) to notify you immediately to cancel this order if the reason for the stop payment no longer exists or (2) that closing the account on which the check(s) is (are) drawn automatically cancels this order.

IF ANOTHER BRANCH OF THIS BANK OR ANOTHER PERSON OR ENTITY BECOMES A "HOLDER IN DUE COURSE" OF THE ABOVE CHECK, I UNDERSTAND THAT PAYMENT MAY BE ENFORCED AGINST THE CHECK'S MAKER (SIGNER).

*I CERTIFY THE AMOUNT AND CHECK NUMBER(S) ABOVE ARE CORRECT.

☐ I have written a replacement check (number and date of check).

(Optional—please circle one: Mr., Ms., Mrs., Miss) CUSTOMER'S SIGNATURE **X** ______ DATE ______

BANK USE ONLY

TRANCODE:

☐ 21—ENTER STOP PAYMENT (SEE OTHER SIDE TO REMOVE)

NON READS: ______

UNPROC. STMT HIST: ______

PRIOR STMT CYCLE: ______

HOLDS ON COOLS: ______

REJECTED CHKS: ______

LARGE ITEMS: ______

FEE COLLECTED: ______

DATE ACCEPTED: ______

TIME ACCEPTED: ______

CASE 21.2 Thomas v. Marine Midland Tinkers National Bank

Civil Court of the City of New York, 1976.
86 Misc.2d 284,
381 N.Y.S.2d 797.

HISTORICAL AND TECHNOLOGICAL SETTING *Changing conditions constantly call for new procedures. Between 1950 and 2000, the volume of checks written grew from less than seven billion annually to more than sixty-five billion annually. Banks could not have handled this increase if they had not developed in the 1950s and 1960s an automated system for check processing based on encoding checks according to the Magnetic Ink Character Recognition (MICR) system. During the same decades, banks began to computerize their operations. Of course, computerized transactions are not always flawless. In the mid-1970s, banks had not yet designed and implemented software to identify and stop payment on checks from a specific account simply by account number and dollar amount.*

BACKGROUND AND FACTS On December 8, 1973, the plaintiff (Thomas) gave Ralph Gallo a check for $2,500 as a down payment on two rugs that Thomas was purchasing from Gallo. The check was postdated December 10 and drawn on the Marine Midland Tinkers National Bank. Having changed his mind about the purchase, Thomas went to the Marine Midland bank on the morning of December 10 and arranged with a bank officer whom he knew to have a stop-payment order placed on the check. Thomas gave the bank officer all the required information but described the check as #22 instead of #221, the correct number. On the afternoon of the following day, the check was presented for payment at the same bank, and the bank cashed it and debited the plaintiff's account in the amount of the $2,500. When Thomas called Gallo, demanding the return of the $2,500, Gallo refused to pay and threatened to enforce the purchase agreement. Thomas then brought an action in a New York court against the bank for wrongful payment. The bank moved for dismissal of the charge on the basis of the incorrect information (the erroneous check number) given by Thomas on the stop-payment order.

IN THE WORDS OF THE COURT . . .
SHANLEY N. EGETH, Judge.

* * * *

* * * A day and one half is more than reasonable notice to enforce a stop order on a check presented at the very same branch, and payment of the item by the bank thereafter constitutes a breach of its obligations to honor the stop order. The normal problem of reasonable computer lag when dealing with a great number of other branches of a large bank has no relevancy to the facts at bar, where all transactions occurred in a single branch. The single digital mistake in describing the check in the stop order is deemed trivial, and insignificant. Enough information was supplied to the bank to reasonably provide it with sufficient information to comply with the stop payment order. The bank is therefore held responsible for its act of improperly making payment upon the check.

DECISION AND REMEDY The New York trial court held the bank responsible for its act of improperly making payment on the check.

FOR CRITICAL ANALYSIS—Economic Consideration *If Thomas did not have a legally sufficient reason to stop payment on the check, would that circumstance affect the court's decision that the bank had improperly paid the check? Should it?*

DEATH OR INCOMPETENCE OF A CUSTOMER

A customer's death or incompetence does not affect the bank's authority to honor a check until the bank knows of the situation and has had a reasonable period of time to act on the information. Article 4 provides that if, at the time a check is issued or its collection has been undertaken, a bank does not know of an adjudication of incompetence or of the death of its customer, an item can be paid, and the bank will not incur liability.

Even when a bank knows of the death of its customer, for ten days after the *date of death,* it can pay or certify checks drawn on or before the date of death—unless a person claiming an interest in that account, such as an heir, orders the bank to stop payment [UCC 4–405]. Without this provision, banks would constantly be required to verify the continued life and competence of their drawers.

FORGED DRAWERS' SIGNATURES

When a bank pays a check on which the drawer's signature is forged, generally the bank is liable. A bank, however, may be able to recover at least some of the loss from the customer (if the customer's negligence contributed to the making of the forgery), from the forger of the check (if he or she can be found), or from the holder who presented the check for payment (if the holder knew that the signature was forged).

The General Rule A forged signature on a check has no legal effect as the signature of a drawer [UCC 3–403(a)]. For this reason, banks require signature cards from each customer who opens a checking account. Signature cards allow the bank to verify whether the signatures on their customers' checks are genuine. The general rule is that the bank must recredit the customer's account when it pays a check with a forged signature.

International Perspective • LIABILITY FOR FORGED INSTRUMENTS

Attempts by the United Nations to form an international law for negotiable instruments have proved to be complicated, because different legal traditions handle liability for forged instruments differently. In the United States, for example, forgery is a universal defense. In other words, the person whose signature is forged normally will not be liable for paying on the note even if the holder is a holder in due course. In civil law systems, however, such as that of France, a good faith taker of a forged instrument is protected by the rule that the person whose signature is forged is liable on the instrument.

FOR CRITICAL ANALYSIS

Who benefits most under the French rule?

Customer Negligence When the customer's negligence substantially contributes to the forgery, the bank will not normally be obligated to recredit the customer's account for the amount of the check [UCC 3–406]. The customer's liability may be reduced, however, by the amount of loss caused by negligence on the part of the bank (or other "person") paying the instrument or taking it for value if the negligence substantially contributes to the loss [UCC 3–406(b)].[5]

• **EXAMPLE 21.3** Gemco Corporation uses special check-writing equipment to write its payroll and business checks. Gemco discovers that one of its employees used the equipment to write himself a check for $10,000 and that the bank subsequently honored it. Gemco requests the bank to recredit $10,000 to its account for improperly paying the forged check. If the bank can show that Gemco failed to take reasonable care in controlling access to the check-writing equipment, the bank will not be required to recredit Gemco's account for the amount of the forged check. If Gemco can show that negligence on the part of the bank (or another person) contributed substantially to the loss, however, then Gemco's liability may be reduced proportionately. •

5. The unrevised Article 4 does not include a similar provision.

Timely Examination of Bank Statements Required. Banks typically send their customers monthly statements detailing activity on their checking accounts. Banks are not obligated to include the canceled checks themselves with the statement sent to the customer. If the bank does not send the canceled checks (or photocopies of the canceled checks), however, it must provide the customer with information (check number, amount, and date of payment) on the statement that will allow the customer to reasonably identify the checks that the bank has paid [UCC 4–406(a), 4–406(b)]. If the bank retains the canceled checks, it must keep the checks—or legible copies of the checks—for a period of seven years [UCC 4–406(b)]. The customer may obtain a check (or a copy of the check) during this period of time.

The customer has a duty to examine bank statements (and canceled checks or photocopies, if they are included with the statements) promptly and with reasonable care, and to report any alterations or forged signatures promptly [UCC 4–406(c)]. This includes forged signatures of indorsers, to be discussed later. If the customer fails to fulfill this duty and the bank suffers a loss as a result, the customer will be liable for the loss [UCC 4–406(d)]. Even if the customer can prove that he or she took reasonable care against forgeries, the UCC provides that discovery of such forgeries and notice to the bank must take place within specific time frames in order for the customer to require the bank to recredit his or her account.

Consequences of Failing to Detect Forgeries. When a series of forgeries by the same wrongdoer has taken place, the UCC provides that the customer, to recover for all the forged items, must have discovered and reported the first forged check to the bank within thirty calendar days of the receipt of the bank statement (and canceled checks or copies, if they are included) [UCC 4–406(d)(2)].[6] Failure to notify the bank within this period of time discharges the bank's liability for all forged checks that it pays prior to notification. The court in the following case was asked to apply the rules pronounced by UCC 4–406.

6. The unrevised Article 4 limits the period for examining and reporting to *fourteen* days [UCC 4–406(2)(b)].

CASE 21.3 Marx v. Whitney National Bank

Supreme Court of Louisiana, 1998.
713 So.2d 1142.

HISTORICAL AND SOCIAL SETTING *Before the adoption of the Uniform Commercial Code, common law rules shifted the risk of loss on certain forgeries to a customer who failed to give notice to the bank. Out of the duty imposed on the customer to review his or her statement grew the rule that when successive forgeries result from the failure of the customer to discover and report the initial forgery, the customer should bear the loss. The Official Comment to UCC 4–406 explains that "[o]ne of the most serious consequences of failure of the customer to comply with the requirements of [UCC 4–406(c)] is the opportunity to the wrongdoer to repeat the misdeeds."*

OUND AND FACTS David Marx had a ccount at Whitney National Bank. He did not statements for the account for January through April, which showed seventeen forged checks totaling almost $13,000. In April, he added two of his children, Stanley Marx and Maxine Goodman, as joint owners of the account. On the May statement, Stanley discovered five forged checks. David reported the forgeries to the bank and identified the forger as his grandson, Joel Goodman. David admitted that he was negligent for failing to review the January through April statements, but he asked the bank to credit the account for the amount of the forgeries on the May statement. The bank refused. David, Stanley, and Maxine filed a suit in a Louisiana state court, claiming that the bank was obligated to restore the funds. The bank argued that David's failure to discover and report the initial forgeries precluded recovery for the subsequent forgeries. The court issued a summary judgment in David's favor, the state intermediate appellate court affirmed, and the bank appealed to the Louisiana Supreme Court.

CASE 21.3—Continued

IN THE WORDS OF THE COURT . . .

MARCUS, Justice.

* * * *

* * * [UCC 4–406] provides in pertinent part:

(c) If a bank sends or makes available a statement of account * * * , the customer must exercise reasonable promptness in examining the statement * * * to determine whether any payment was not authorized because * * * a purported signature by or on behalf of the customer was not authorized. * * * [T]he customer must promptly notify the bank of the relevant facts.

(d) If the bank proves that the customer failed, with respect to an item, to comply with the duties imposed on the customer by Subsection (c), the customer is precluded from asserting against the bank: * * *

(2) the customer's unauthorized signature * * * by the same wrongdoer on any other item paid in good faith by the bank if the payment was made before the bank received notice from the customer of the unauthorized signature * * * and after the customer had been afforded a reasonable period of time * * * in which to examine the * * * statement of account and notify the bank.

The rule stated in Subsection (d)(2) imposes on the customer the risk of loss on all subsequent forgeries by the same wrongdoer after the customer had a reasonable time to detect an initial forgery if the bank has honored subsequent forgeries prior to notice. * * *

* * * *

In this case, * * * David Marx did not review the January * * * statement for his account and * * * if he had done so the unauthorized signature of his grandson on several checks would have been detected. Since he did not do so, plaintiffs are precluded from asserting against the bank all subsequent forgeries by the same unauthorized signatory.

DECISION AND REMEDY The Louisiana Supreme Court reversed the judgment of the lower court. The state supreme court held that David, Stanley, and Maxine could not recover from the bank for any of the forged checks.

FOR CRITICAL ANALYSIS—Social Consideration *What might have been the result in this case if the bank had not acted reasonably in paying the forged checks?*

¡KEEP IN MIND!

If a bank is forced to recredit a customer's account, the bank may recover from the forger or from the party that cashed the check (usually a different customer or a collecting bank).

When the Bank Is Also Negligent. There is one situation in which a bank customer can escape liability, at least in part, for failing to notify the bank of forged or altered checks promptly or within the required thirty-day period. If the customer can prove that the bank was also negligent—that is, that the bank failed to exercise ordinary care—then the bank will also be liable, and an allocation of the loss between the bank and the customer will be made on the basis of comparative negligence [UCC 4–406(e)].[7] In other words, even though a customer may have been negligent, the bank may still have to recredit the customer's account for a portion of the loss if the bank failed to exercise ordinary care.

Regardless of the degree of care exercised by the customer or the bank, the UCC places an absolute time limit on the liability of a bank for paying a check with a forged customer signature. A customer who fails to report a forged signature within one year from the date that the statement was made available for inspection loses the legal right to have the bank recredit his or her account [UCC 4–406(f)].

7. Under the unrevised Article 4, if both parties are negligent, then the bank is wholly liable [UCC 4–406(3)].

ETHICAL ISSUE 21.1 ***Does a bank fail to exercise ordinary care if it fails to examine every signature on every check?*** Prior to the 1990 revision of Article 3, bank customers whose own negligence contributed to forgeries sometimes sought to avoid liability by claiming that their banks were also negligent—that is, customers claimed that the banks' failure to examine every signature on the checks they paid constituted a breach of the banks' duty to exercise ordinary care. Some courts agreed; others did not. The revised Article 3 put an end to the problem by clarifying the meaning of ordinary care in the context of today's banking system. UCC 3–103(a)(7) of the revised Article 3 defines ordinary care to mean the "observance of reasonable commercial standards, prevailing in the area in which [a] person is located, with respect to the business in which that person is engaged." It is customary in the banking industry to manually examine signatures only on checks over a certain amount (such as $1,000, $2,500, or some higher amount). Thus, if a bank, in accordance with prevailing banking standards, fails to examine a signature on a particular check, the bank has not breached its duty to exercise ordinary care.

FORGED INDORSEMENTS

A bank that pays a customer's check bearing a forged indorsement must recredit the customer's account or be liable to the customer-drawer for breach of contract. • **EXAMPLE 21.4** Suppose that Brian issues a $50 check "to the order of Antonio." Jimmy steals the check, forges Antonio's indorsement, and cashes the check. When the check reaches Brian's bank, the bank pays it and debits Brian's account. The bank must recredit the $50 to Brian's account because it failed to carry out Brian's order to pay "to the order of Antonio" [UCC 4–401(a)]. Of course, Brian's bank can in turn recover—under breach of warranty principles (see Chapter 20)—from the bank that paid the check when Jimmy presented it [UCC 4–207(a)(2)]. •

Eventually, the loss usually falls on the first party to take the instrument bearing the forged indorsement, because, as discussed in Chapter 20, a forged indorsement does not transfer title. Thus, whoever takes an instrument with a forged indorsement cannot become a holder.

¡COMPARE! Three years is also the limit for bringing actions for breach of warranty and to enforce other obligations, duties, and rights under Article 3.

In any event, the customer has a duty to examine the returned checks (or copies of the checks) and statements received from the bank and to report forged indorsements promptly. A customer's failure to report forged indorsements within a three-year period after the forged items have been made available to the customer relieves the bank of liability [UCC 4–111].

A BANK TELLER VERIFIES A CUSTOMER'S SIGNATURE. IF A FORGED INDORSEMENT WERE PART OF THIS TRANSACTION, WHY SHOULD THE BANK SUFFER THE LOSS?

ALTERED CHECKS

The customer's instruction to the bank is to pay the exact amount on the face of the check to the holder. The bank has a duty to examine each check before making final payment. If it fails to detect an alteration, it is liable to its customer for the loss, because it did not pay as the customer ordered. The loss is the difference between the original amount of the check and the amount actually paid [UCC 4–401(d)(1)]. • **EXAMPLE 21.5** Suppose that a check written for $11 is raised to $111. The customer's account will be charged $11 (the amount the customer ordered the bank to pay). The bank will normally be responsible for the $100.•

The bank is entitled to recover the amount of loss from the transferor, who, by presenting the check for payment, warrants that the check has not been materially altered. If the bank is the drawer (as it is on a cashier's check and a teller's check), however, it cannot recover on this ground from the presenting party if the party is an HDC acting in good faith [UCC 3–417(a)(2), 4–208(a)(2)]. The reason is that an instrument's drawer is in a better position than an HDC to know whether the instrument has been altered.

Similarly, an HDC, acting in good faith in presenting a certified check for payment, will not be held liable under warranty principles if the check was altered before the HDC acquired it [UCC 3–417(a)(2), 4–207(a)(2)]. • **EXAMPLE 21.6** Jordan draws a check for $500 payable to Deffen. Deffen alters the amount to $5,000. The First National Bank of Whiteacre, the drawee bank, certifies the check for $5,000. Deffen negotiates the check to Evans, an HDC. The drawee bank pays Evans $5,000. On discovering the mistake, the bank cannot recover from Evans the $4,500 paid by mistake, even though the bank was not in a superior position to detect the alteration. This is in accord with the purpose of certification, which is to obtain the definite obligation of a bank to honor a definite instrument.•

"Opportunity makes the thief."
THOMAS FULLER, 1608–1661
(English clergyman and writer)

As in a situation involving a forged drawer's signature, when payment is made on an altered check, a customer's negligence can shift the loss (unless the bank was also negligent). A common example occurs when a person carelessly writes a check and leaves large gaps around the numbers and words so that additional numbers and words can be inserted (see Exhibit 21–5). Similarly, a person who signs a check and leaves the dollar amount for someone else to fill in is barred from protesting when the bank unknowingly and in good faith pays whatever amount is shown [UCC 4–401(d)(2)]. Finally, if the bank can trace its loss on successive altered checks to the customer's failure to discover the initial alteration, then the bank can reduce its liability for reimbursing the customer's account [UCC 4–406]. The law governing the customer's duty to examine monthly statements and canceled checks (or copies), and to discover and report unauthorized signatures to the drawee bank, applies to altered instruments as well as forgeries.

EXHIBIT 21–5 • A Poorly Filled-Out Check

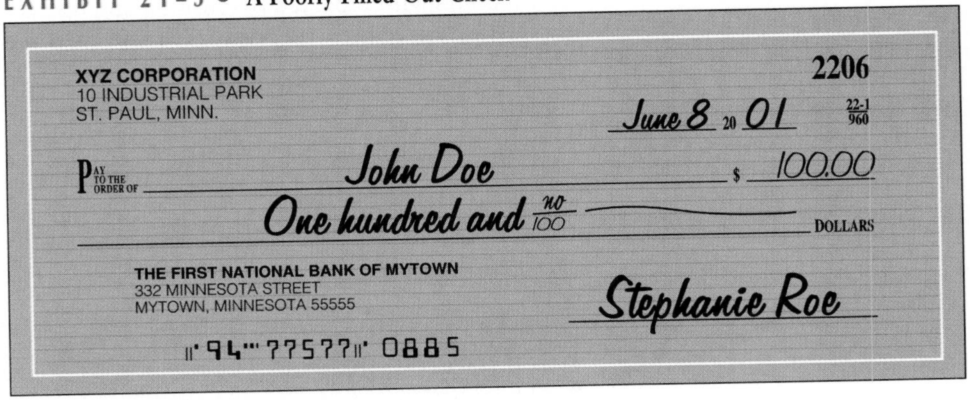

Bank's Duty to Accept Deposits

A bank has a duty to its customer to accept the customer's deposits of cash and checks. When checks are deposited, the bank must make the funds represented by those checks available within certain time frames. A bank also has a duty to collect payment on any checks payable or indorsed to its customers and deposited by them into their accounts. Cash deposits made in U.S. currency are received into customers' accounts without being subject to further collection procedures.

AVAILABILITY SCHEDULE FOR DEPOSITED CHECKS

The Expedited Funds Availability Act of 1987[8] and Regulation CC,[9] which was issued by the Federal Reserve Board of Governors (the Federal Reserve System will be discussed shortly) to implement the act, require that any local check deposited must be available for withdrawal by check or as cash within one business day from the date of deposit. A check is classified as a local check if the first bank to receive the check for payment and the bank on which the check is drawn are located in the same check-processing region (check-processing regions are designated by the Federal Reserve Board of Governors). For nonlocal checks, the funds must be available for withdrawal within not more than five business days.

In addition, the act requires the following:

1. That funds be available on the next business day for cash deposits and wire transfers, government checks, the first $100 of a day's check deposits, cashier's checks, certified checks, and checks for which the depositary and payor banks are branches of the same institution.
2. That the first $100 of any deposit be available for cash withdrawal on the opening of the next business day after deposit. If a local check is deposited, the next $400 is to be available for withdrawal by no later than 5:00 P.M. the next business day. If, for example, you deposit a local check for $500 on Monday, you can withdraw $100 in cash at the opening of the business day on Tuesday, and an additional $400 must be available for withdrawal by no later than 5:00 P.M. on Wednesday.

A different availability schedule applies to deposits made at nonproprietary automated teller machines (ATMs). These are ATMs that are not owned or operated by the depositary institution. Basically, a five-day hold is permitted on all deposits, including cash deposits, made at nonproprietary ATMs.

Other exceptions also exist. A depository institution has eight days to make funds available in new accounts (those open less than thirty days). It has an extra four days on deposits over $5,000 (except deposits of government and cashier's checks), on accounts with repeated overdrafts, and on checks of questionable collectibility (if the institution tells the depositor it suspects fraud or insolvency).

> **ON THE WEB**
> You can find answers to "Frequently Asked Questions" about the banking industry at the American Bankers Association's Web site, the URL for which is **www.aba.com**.

THE COLLECTION PROCESS

Usually, deposited checks involve parties who do business at different banks, but sometimes checks are written between customers of the same bank. Either situation brings into play the bank collection process as it operates within the statutory framework of Article 4 of the UCC.

8. 12 U.S.C. Sections 4001–4010.
9. 12 C.F.R. Sections 229.1–229.42.

• **DEPOSITARY BANK**
The first bank to receive a check for payment.

• **PAYOR BANK**
The bank on which a check is drawn (the drawee bank).

• **COLLECTING BANK**
Any bank handling an item for collection, except the payor bank.

• **INTERMEDIARY BANK**
Any bank to which an item is transferred in the course of collection, except the depositary or payor bank.

Designations of Banks Involved in the Collection Process The first bank to receive a check for payment is the **depositary bank.**[10] For example, when a person deposits an IRS tax-refund check into a personal checking account at the local bank, that bank is the depositary bank. The bank on which a check is drawn (the drawee bank) is called the **payor bank.** Any bank except the payor bank that handles a check during some phase of the collection process is a **collecting bank.** Any bank except the payor bank or the depositary bank to which an item is transferred in the course of this collection process is called an **intermediary bank.**

During the collection process, any bank can take on one or more of the various roles of depositary, payor, collecting, and intermediary bank. • EXAMPLE 21.7 A buyer in New York writes a check on her New York bank and sends it to a seller in San Francisco. The seller deposits the check in her San Francisco bank account. The seller's bank is both a *depositary bank* and a *collecting bank*. The buyer's bank in New York is the *payor bank*. As the check travels from San Francisco to New York, any collecting bank handling the item in the collection process (other than the ones acting as a depositary bank and a payor bank) is also called an *intermediary bank*.• Exhibit 21–6 illustrates how various banks function in the collection process.

10. All definitions in this section are found in UCC 4–105. The terms *depositary* and *depository* have different meanings in the banking context. A depository bank refers to a *physical place* (a bank or other institution) in which deposits or funds are held or stored.

EXHIBIT 21–6 • The Collection Process

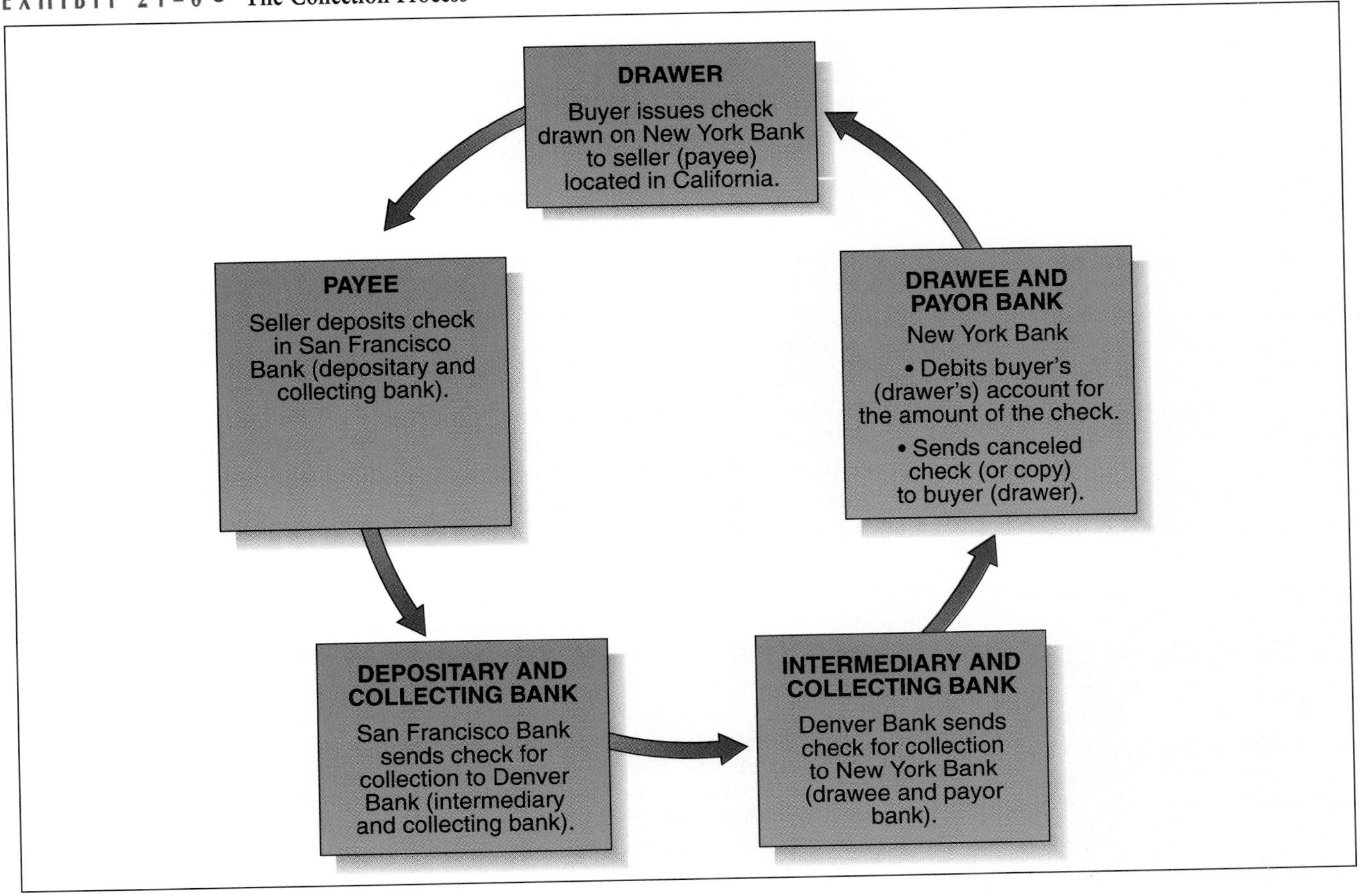

Check Collection between Customers of the Same Bank An item that is payable by the depositary bank (also the payor bank) that receives it is called an "on-us item." If the bank does not dishonor the check by the opening of the second banking day following its receipt, the check is considered paid [UCC 4–215(e)(2)]. • **EXAMPLE 21.8** Williams and Merkowitz both have checking accounts at State Bank. On Monday morning, Merkowitz deposits into his own checking account a $300 check drawn by Williams. That same day, State Bank issues Merkowitz a "provisional credit" for $300. When the bank opens on Wednesday, Williams's check is considered honored, and Merkowitz's provisional credit becomes a final payment. •

Check Collection between Customers of Different Banks Once a depositary bank receives a check, it must arrange to present it either directly or through intermediary banks to the appropriate payor bank. Each bank in the collection chain must pass the check on before midnight of the next banking day following its receipt [UCC 4–202(b)].[11] A "banking day" is any part of a day that the bank is open to carry on substantially all of its banking functions. Thus, if a bank has only its drive-through facilities open, a check deposited on Saturday would not trigger a bank's midnight deadline until the following Monday. When the check reaches the payor bank, unless the payor bank dishonors the check or returns it by midnight on the next banking day following receipt, the payor bank is accountable for the face amount of the check [UCC 4–302].[12]

Because of this deadline and because banks need to maintain an even work flow in the many items they handle daily, the UCC permits what is called *deferred posting*. According to UCC 4–108, "a bank may fix an afternoon hour of 2:00 P.M. or later as a cutoff hour for the handling of money and items and the making of entries on its books." Any checks received after that hour "may be treated as being received at the opening of the next banking day." Thus, if a bank's "cutoff hour" is 3:00 P.M., a check received by a payor bank at 4:00 P.M. on Monday would be deferred for posting until Tuesday. In this situation, the payor bank's deadline would be midnight Wednesday.

• **FEDERAL RESERVE SYSTEM**
A network of twelve district banks and related branches located around the country and headed by the Federal Reserve Board of Governors. Most banks in the United States have Federal Reserve accounts.

• **CLEARINGHOUSE**
A system or place where banks exchange checks and drafts drawn on each other and settle daily balances.

How the Federal Reserve System Clears Checks The **Federal Reserve System** is our nation's central bank. It consists of twelve district banks and related branches located around the country and is headed by the Federal Reserve Board of Governors. Most banks in the United States have Federal Reserve accounts. The Federal Reserve System has greatly simplified the check-collection process by acting as a **clearinghouse**—a system or a place where banks exchange checks and drafts drawn on each other and settle daily balances.

• **EXAMPLE 21.9** Suppose that Pamela Moy of Philadelphia writes a check to Jeanne Sutton in San Francisco. When Sutton receives the check in the mail, she deposits it in her bank. Her bank then deposits the check in the Federal Reserve Bank of San Francisco, which transfers it to the Federal Reserve Bank of Philadelphia. That Federal Reserve bank then sends the check to Moy's bank, which deducts the amount of the check from Moy's account. • Exhibit 21–7 illustrates this process.

ON THE WEB
You can access the Federal Reserve Bank's home page as well as extensive information about "the Fed" at woodrow.mpls.frb.fed.us/info/policy.

Electronic Check Presentment In the past, most checks were processed manually—the employees of each bank in the collection chain would physically handle each check

11. A bank may take a "reasonably longer time," such as when the bank's computer system is down due to a power failure, but the bank must show that it is still timely [UCC 4–202(b)].
12. Most checks are cleared by a computerized process, and communication and computer facilities may fail because of weather, equipment malfunction, or other conditions. If such conditions arise and a bank fails to meet its midnight deadline, the bank is "excused" from liability if the bank has exercised "such diligence as the circumstances require" [UCC 4–109(d)].

EXHIBIT 21–7 • How a Check Is Cleared

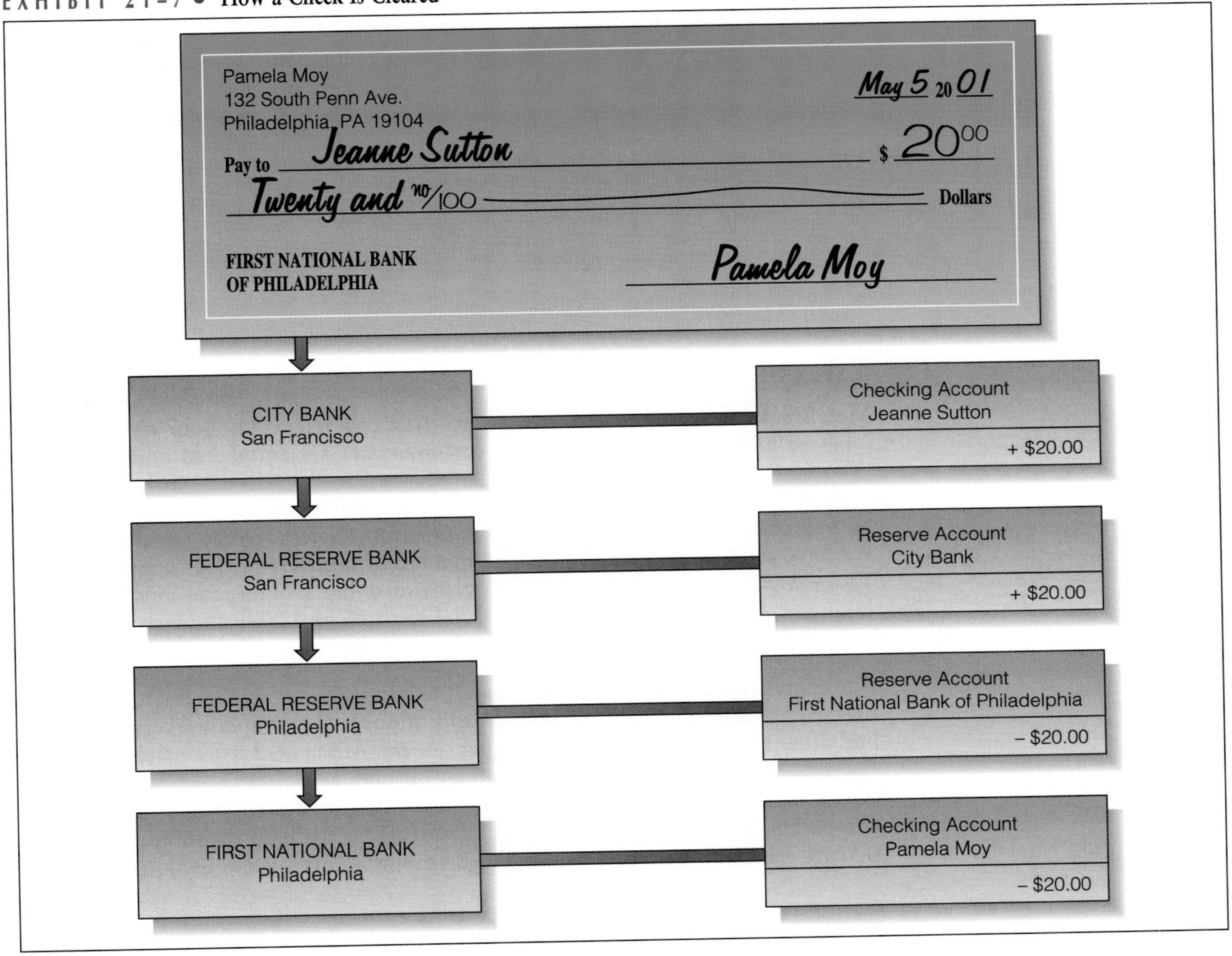

that passed through the bank for collection or payment. Today, however, most checks are processed electronically. In contrast to manual check processing, which can take days, *electronic check presentment* can be done on the day of the deposit. With electronic check presentment, items may be encoded with information (such as the amount of the check) that is read and processed by other banks' computers. In some situations, a check may be retained at its place of deposit, and only its image or information describing it is presented for payment under a Federal Reserve agreement, clearinghouse rule, or truncation agreement [UCC 4–110]. The term *truncation* refers to presentment by notice rather than by delivery.

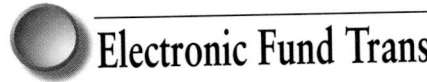

Electronic Fund Transfers

The application of computer technology to banking, in the form of electronic fund transfer systems, helped to relieve banking institutions of the burden of having to

• **ELECTRONIC FUND TRANSFER (EFT)** A transfer of funds with the use of an electronic terminal, a telephone, a computer, or magnetic tape.

move mountains of paperwork to process fund transfers. An **electronic fund transfer (EFT)** is a transfer of funds made by the use of an electronic terminal, a telephone, a computer, or magnetic tape.

The benefits of electronic banking are obvious. Automatic payments, direct deposits, and other fund transfers are now made electronically; no physical transfers of cash, checks, or other negotiable instruments are involved. Not surprisingly, though, electronic banking also poses difficulties on occasion, including the following:

1. It is difficult to issue stop-payment orders.
2. Fewer records are available to prove or disprove that a transaction took place.
3. The possibilities for tampering (with a resulting decrease in privacy) are increased.
4. The time between the writing of a check and its deduction from an account (float time) is lost.

TYPES OF EFT SYSTEMS

Most banks today offer EFT services to their customers. The four most common types of EFT systems used by bank customers are (1) automated teller machines, (2) point-of-sale systems, (3) systems handling direct deposits and withdrawals, and (4) pay-by-telephone systems. We look here at each of these types of EFT systems. Not surprisingly, technology has led to new forms of electronic payment systems. We look at some emerging forms of online fund transfers in this chapter's feature, *Technology and Digital Banking*. In terms of dollar volume, the most significant fund transfers are those between financial institutions. These commercial transfers of funds will be discussed later in the chapter.

"Money is human happiness in the abstract."

ARTHUR SCHOPENHAUER, 1788–1860 (German philosopher)

Automated Teller Machines Automated teller machines (ATMs) are located either on the bank's premises or at convenient locations such as supermarkets, drugstores and other stores, airports, and shopping centers. Automated teller machines receive deposits, dispense funds from checking or savings accounts, make credit-card advances, and receive payments. The devices are connected online to the banks' computers. To access an account through an ATM, the bank customer uses a plastic card (debit card, access card), issued to him or her by the bank, plus a secret

THE ADVANTAGES OF USING AN AUTOMATED TELLER MACHINE ARE OBVIOUS. ARE THERE ANY DISADVANTAGES?

Technology and Digital Banking

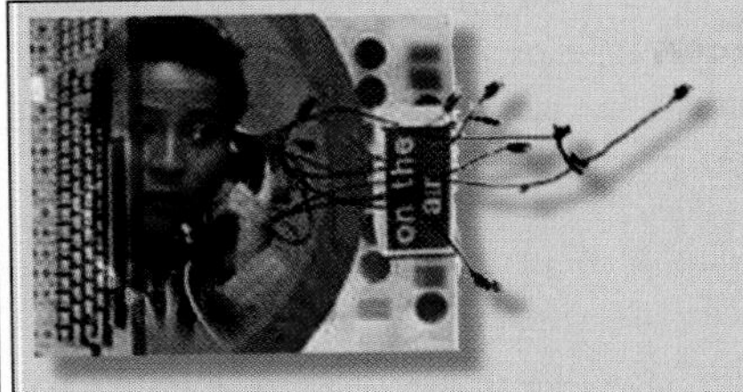

The era of digital banking is upon us. Within less than a minute, virtually anybody with the proper software can access his or her account, transfer money, write "checks," pay bills, check investments, and often even buy and sell stocks. Much of the online banking software today even talks to you. The benefit of online banking for banks is significant. A paper check costs over a dollar to process. Processing a payment transaction using the Internet costs about one cent.

Regular online banking that also may allow automatic bill-payment mechanisms is taking off rapidly. Citibank, First Union Bank, Wells Fargo, and a number of other banks all offer some form of online banking. Consider Securities First Network Bank (SFNB), which allows depositors to open accounts online and to bill payments to those accounts electronically. SFNB is a member of the Federal Deposit Insurance Corporation (FDIC), and thus its accounts are federally insured up to $100,000. Whenever the party receiving an electronic payment is unable to process it, SFNB produces a paper check and sends it.

Special forms of online banking are also emerging that are designed specifically for products that are sold online, such as software and videos. For example, First Virtual Holdings has developed a system that is similar to a credit-card payment process—but it is all done online. A person who wishes to make a purchase provides his or her First Virtual account number to the seller. The seller then forwards to First Virtual all of the essential information, including the buyer's First Virtual account number, the date and time of the sale, and the dollar value of the purchase. First Virtual then sends an e-mail message to the purchaser asking for confirmation. If a confirming e-mail is returned, First Virtual processes the transaction. Without the confirming e-mail, no purchase will be processed. The cost of such a system is relatively low. The one-time registration fee for the buyer is only $2; for the seller, it is $10. For each transaction the seller pays about 30 cents plus 2 percent of the value of the sale. First Virtual's approach does not use any encryption because of the verification process via e-mail.

As discussed in Chapter 7, forms of digital cash, or "e-money," are also emerging. A number of companies are experimenting with a type of system in which a person who opens an online account can download digital currency to his or her personal computer's hard drive. The company then issues and certifies the value of the currency. Each "customer" must use the company's proprietary software, and so, too, must all retailers who accept its e-money. The customer does not have to open an account with the retailer. Such a system uses a public key encryption mechanism (discussed in Chapter 12) for security.

FOR CRITICAL ANALYSIS

What are some of the potential problems with online banking and digital cash?

INTERNET CONNECT

personal identification number (PIN). The PIN protects the customer from someone else's use of a lost or stolen access card.

Point-of-Sale Systems Point-of-sale systems allow consumers to transfer funds to merchants to pay for purchases. Online terminals are located in, for example, grocery stores. When a purchase is made, the customer's *debit card* (issued by the bank to the customer) is inserted into the terminal, which reads the data encoded on it. The computer at the customer's bank verifies that the card and identification code are valid and that there are enough funds in the customer's account to cover the purchase. After the purchase is made, the customer's account is debited for the amount of the purchase.

Direct Deposits and Withdrawals A direct deposit may be made to a customer's account through an electronic terminal when the customer has authorized the deposit in advance. The federal government often uses this type of EFT to deposit Social Security payments directly into beneficiaries' accounts. Similarly, an employer may agree to make payroll and pension payments directly into an employee's account at specified intervals.

A customer may also authorize the bank (or other financial institution at which the customer's funds are on deposit) to make automatic payments at regular, recurrent intervals to a third party. For example, insurance premiums, utility bills, and automobile installment loan payments may often be made automatically.

Pay-by-Telephone Systems When it is undesirable to arrange in advance for an automatic payment—as, for example, when the amount of a regular payment varies—some financial institutions permit customers to pay bills through a pay-by-telephone system. This allows the customer to access the institution's computer system by telephone and direct a transfer of funds. Customers frequently pay utility bills directly using pay-by-telephone systems. Customers may also be permitted to transfer funds between accounts—for example, to withdraw funds from a savings account and make a deposit in a checking account—in this way.

CONSUMER FUND TRANSFERS

Consumer fund transfers are governed by the Electronic Fund Transfer Act (EFTA)[13] of 1978. This act provides a basic framework for the rights, liabilities, and responsibilities of users of EFT systems. Additionally, the act gave the Federal Reserve Board authority to issue rules and regulations to help implement the act's provisions. The Federal Reserve Board's implemental regulation is called Regulation E.

The EFTA governs financial institutions that offer electronic fund transfers involving consumer accounts. The types of accounts covered include checking accounts, savings accounts, and any other asset accounts established for personal, family, or household purposes. Note that telephone transfers are covered by the EFTA only if they are made in accordance with a prearranged plan under which periodic or recurring transfers are contemplated.[14]

Because of its importance in establishing the rights of consumers who engage in EFT transactions, the EFTA is presented as this chapter's *Landmark in the Law*. In the subsections that follow the *Landmark*, we look more closely at the act's provisions concerning two important issues: unauthorized transfers and error resolution.

13. 15 U.S.C. Sections 1693 *et seq.* The EFTA is Title IX of the Consumer Credit Protection Act.
14. *Kashanchi v. Texas Commerce Medical Bank, N.A.*, 703 F.2d 936 (5th Cir. 1983).

Landmark in the Law •

THE ELECTRONIC FUND TRANSFER ACT (1978)

Congress stated in 1978 that the use of electronic systems to transfer funds promised to provide substantial benefits for consumers. At the same time, Congress acknowledged that existing laws provided inadequate protection for consumers with respect to electronic fund transfers. Thus, Congress passed the Electronic Fund Transfer Act (EFTA) "to provide a basic framework establishing the rights, liabilities, and responsibilities of participants in electronic fund transfers." The EFTA is designed to protect consumers. It is not concerned with commercial electronic fund transfers—transfers between businesses or between businesses and financial institutions. (Commercial fund transfers are governed by Article 4A of the UCC.)

The EFTA is essentially a disclosure law benefiting consumers. The act requires financial institutions to inform consumers of their rights and responsibilities, including those listed here, with respect to EFT systems.

1. If a customer's debit card is lost or stolen and used without his or her permission, the customer may be required to pay no more than $50. The customer, however, must notify the bank of the loss or theft within two days of learning about it. Otherwise, the liability increases to $500. The customer may be liable for more than $500 if he or she does not report the unauthorized use within sixty days after it appears on the customer's statement. (If a customer voluntarily gives his or her debit card to another, who then uses it improperly, the protections just mentioned do not apply.)

2. The customer must discover any error on the monthly statement within sixty days, and he or she must notify the bank. The bank then has ten days to investigate and must report its conclusions to the customer in writing. If the bank takes longer than ten days, it must return the disputed amount of money to the customer's account until it finds the error. If there is no error, the customer has to give the money back to the bank.

3. The bank must furnish receipts for transactions made through computer terminals, but it is not obligated to do so for telephone transfers.

4. The bank must make a monthly statement for every month in which there is an electronic transfer of funds. Otherwise, the bank must make statements every quarter. The statement must show the amount and date of the transfer, the names of the retailers or other third parties involved, the location or identification of the terminal, and the fees. Additionally, the statement must give an address and a phone number for inquiries and error notices.

5. Any authorized prepayment for utility bills and insurance premiums can be stopped three days before the scheduled transfer.

FOR CRITICAL ANALYSIS

Few individuals are required to use electronic transfer systems, but many do. Why?

¡BE CAREFUL!

The EFTA does not provide for the reversal of an electronic transfer of funds once it has occurred.

Unauthorized Electronic Fund Transfers Unauthorized electronic fund transfers are one of the hazards of electronic banking. A paper check leaves visible evidence of a transaction, and a customer can easily detect a forgery or an alteration on a check with ordinary vigilance. Evidence of an electronic transfer, however, is in many cases only an entry in a computer printout of the various debits and credits made to a particular account during a specified time period.

Because of the vulnerability of EFT systems to fraudulent activities, the EFTA of 1978 clearly defined what constitutes an unauthorized transfer. Under the act, a transfer is unauthorized if (1) it is initiated by a person other than the consumer who has no actual authority to initiate the transfer; (2) the consumer receives no benefit from it; and (3) the consumer did not furnish the person "with the card, code, or other means of access" to his or her account.

Error Resolution and Damages Banks must strictly follow the error-resolution procedures prescribed by the EFTA and described briefly in the *Landmark in the Law*. If a bank fails to investigate an error and report its conclusion promptly to the customer, in the specific manner designated by the EFTA, it will be in violation of the act and subject to civil liability. Its liability extends to any actual damages sustained by a customer and to all the costs of a successful action brought against the bank by a customer, including attorneys' fees. In addition, the bank may be liable for punitive damages ranging from $100 to $1,000 for each individual action. Failure to investigate an error in good faith makes the bank liable for treble damages. Even when a customer has sustained no actual damage, the bank may be liable for legal costs and punitive damages if it fails to follow the proper procedures outlined by the EFTA in regard to error resolution.

COMMERCIAL TRANSFERS

The transfer of funds "by wire" between commercial parties is another way in which funds are transferred electronically. In fact, the dollar volume of payments by wire transfer is more than $1 trillion a day—an amount that far exceeds the dollar volume of payments made by other means. The two major wire payment systems are the Federal Reserve wire transfer network (Fedwire) and the New York Clearing House Interbank Payments Systems (CHIPS).

Unauthorized wire transfers are obviously possible and, indeed, have become a problem. If an imposter, for example, succeeds in having funds wired from another's account, the other party will bear the loss (unless he or she can recover from the imposter). In the past, any disputes arising as a result of unauthorized or incorrectly made transfers were settled by the courts under the common law principles of tort law or contract law. To clarify the rights and liabilities of parties involved in fund transfers not subject to the EFTA or other federal or state statutes, Article 4A of the UCC was promulgated in 1989. Almost all of the states have adopted this article.

> **¡NOTE!**
> If any part of an electronic fund transfer is covered by the EFTA, the entire transfer is excluded from UCC Article 4A.

The type of fund transfer covered by Article 4A is illustrated in the following example. • **EXAMPLE 21.10** Jellux, Inc., owes $5 million to Perot Corporation. Instead of sending Perot a check or some other instrument that would enable Perot to obtain payment, Jellux tells its bank, East Bank, to credit $5 million to Perot's account in West Bank. East Bank forwards this instruction to West Bank via a wire message. In more complex transactions, additional banks would be involved. •

In these and similar circumstances, ordinarily a financial institution's instruction is transmitted electronically. Any means may be used, however, including first-class mail. To reflect this fact, Article 4A uses the term *funds transfer* rather than wire transfer to describe the overall payment transaction. The full text of Article 4A is included in Appendix C, following Article 4 of the Uniform Commercial Code.

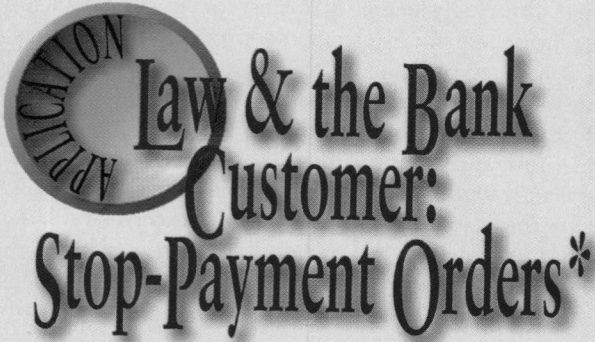

APPLICATION: Law & the Bank Customer: Stop-Payment Orders*

For a variety of reasons, a drawer should not misuse stop-payment orders. One reason is monetary: the bank's charges for stop-payment orders (which usually range between $15 and $25) are not small in relation to checks written for small amounts. Another reason is the risk attached to the issuing of a stop-payment order for any drawer-customer. The bank is entitled to take a reasonable amount of time to put your stop-payment order into effect before it has liability for improper payment. Hence, the payee or another holder may be able to cash the check despite your stop-payment order if he or she acts quickly. Indeed, you could be writing out a stop-payment order in the bank lobby while the payee or holder cashes the check in the drive-in facility next door. In addition, even if a bank pays over your proper stop-payment order, the bank is only liable to the drawer-customer for the amount of loss the drawer suffers from the improper payment.

Remember that a drawer, to avoid liability, must have a legal reason for issuing a stop-payment order. You cannot stop payment on a check simply because you have had a change of heart about the wisdom of your purchase. Generally, you can safely stop payment if you clearly did not get what you paid for or were fraudulently induced to make a purchase. You can also stop payment if a "cooling-off" law governs the transaction—that is, if you legally have a few days in which to change your mind about a purchase. Any wrongful stop order subjects the *drawer* to liability to the payee or a holder, and this liability may include special damages that resulted from the order. When all is considered, it may be unwise to order a stop payment hastily on a check because of a minor dispute with the payee.

CHECKLIST FOR STOP-PAYMENT ORDERS

1. Compare the stop-payment fee with the disputed sum to make sure it is worthwhile to issue a stop-payment order.
2. Make sure that your stop-payment order will be honored by your bank prior to the time the payee cashes the check.
3. Make sure that you have a legal reason for issuing the stop-payment order.

*This *Application* is not meant to substitute for the services of an attorney who is licensed to practice law in your state.

Key Terms

Chapter Summary • Checks and the Banking System

Checks (See pages 545–548.)	1. *Cashier's check*—A check drawn by a bank on itself (the bank is both the drawer and the drawee) and purchased by a customer. In effect, the bank lends its credit to the purchaser of the check, thus making the funds available for immediate use in banking circles. 2. *Traveler's check*—An instrument on which a financial institution is both the drawer and the drawee. The purchaser must provide his or her signature as a countersignature for a traveler's check to become a negotiable instrument. 3. *Certified check*—A check for which the drawee bank certifies in writing that it will set aside funds in the drawer's account to ensure payment of the check on presentation. On certification, the drawer and all prior indorsers are completely discharged from liability on the check.
The Bank-Customer Relationship (See page 548.)	1. *Contractual relationship*—The bank's relationship with its customer is contractual; both the bank and the customer assume certain contractual duties when a customer opens a bank account. 2. *Creditor-debtor relationship*—The relationship is also a creditor-debtor relationship (the bank is the creditor, because it holds the customer's funds on deposit). 3. *Agency relationship*—Because a bank must act in accordance with the customer's orders in regard to the customer's deposited money, an agency relationship also arises—the bank is the agent for the customer, who is the principal.
Bank's Duty to Honor Checks (See pages 548–557.)	Generally, a bank has a duty to honor its customers' checks, provided that the customers have sufficient funds on deposit to cover the checks [UCC 4–401(a)]. The bank is liable to its customers for actual damages proved to be due to wrongful dishonor. The bank's duty to honor its customers' checks is not absolute. The following list summarizes the rights and liabilities of the bank and the customer in various situations. 1. *Overdrafts*—The bank has the right to charge a customer's account for any item properly payable, even if the charge results in an overdraft [UCC 4–401(a)]. 2. *Postdated checks*—A bank may charge a postdated check against a customer's account as a demand instrument, unless the customer notifies the bank of the postdating in time to allow the bank to act on the notice before the bank commits itself to pay on the check [UCC 4–401(c)]. 3. *Stale checks*—The bank is not obligated to pay an uncertified check presented more than six months after its date, but it may do so in good faith without liability [UCC 4–404]. 4. *Stop-payment orders*—The customer must make a stop-payment order in time for the bank to have a reasonable opportunity to act. Oral orders are binding for only fourteen days unless they are confirmed in writing. Written orders are effective for only six months unless renewed in writing. The bank is liable for wrongful payment over a timely stop-payment order, but only to the extent of the loss suffered by the drawer-customer [UCC 4–403].

Chapter Summary • Checks and the Banking System, Continued

Bank's Duty to Honor Checks—continued	5. *Death or incompetence of a customer*—So long as the bank does not know of the death or incompetence of a customer, the bank can pay an item without liability to the customer's estate. Even with knowledge of a customer's death, a bank can honor or certify checks (in the absence of a stop-payment order) for ten days after the date of the customer's death [UCC 4–405]. 6. *Forged drawers' signatures, forged indorsements, and altered checks*—The customer has a duty to examine account statements with reasonable care on receipt and to notify the bank promptly of any forged signatures, forged or unauthorized indorsements, or alterations. On a series of unauthorized signatures or alterations by the same wrongdoer, examination and report must occur within thirty calendar days of receipt of the statement. Failure to notify the bank releases the bank from any liability unless the bank failed to exercise ordinary care. Regardless of care or lack of care, the customer is estopped from holding the bank liable after one year for unauthorized customer signatures or alterations and after three years for unauthorized indorsements [UCC 3–403, 4–111, 4–401(a), 4–406].
Bank's Duty to Accept Deposits (See pages 558–561.)	A bank has a duty to accept deposits made by its customers into their accounts. Funds represented by checks deposited must be made available to customers according to a schedule mandated by the Expedited Funds Availability Act of 1987 and Regulation CC. A bank also has a duty to collect payment on any checks deposited by its customers. When checks deposited by customers are drawn on other banks, as they often are, the check-collection process comes into play (summarized next). 1. *Definitions of banks*—UCC 4–105 provides the following definitions of banks involved in the collection process: a. Depositary bank—The first bank to accept a check for payment. b. Payor bank—The bank on which a check is drawn. c. Collecting bank—Any bank except the payor bank that handles a check during the collection process. d. Intermediary bank—Any bank except the payor bank or the depositary bank to which an item is transferred in the course of the collection process. 2. *Check collection between customers of the same bank*—A check payable by the depositary bank that receives it is an "on-us item"; if the bank does not dishonor the check by the opening of the second banking day following its receipt, the check is considered paid [UCC 4–215(e)(2)]. 3. *Check collection between customers of different banks*—Each bank in the collection process must pass the check on to the next appropriate bank before midnight of the next banking day following its receipt [UCC 4–108, 4–202(b), 4–302]. 4. *How the Federal Reserve System clears checks*—The Federal Reserve System facilitates the check-clearing process by serving as a clearinghouse for checks. 5. *Electronic check presentment*—When checks are presented electronically, items may be encoded with information (such as the amount of the check) that is read and processed by other banks' computers. In some situations, a check may be retained at its place of deposit, and only its image or information describing it is presented for payment under a Federal Reserve agreement, clearinghouse rule, or other agreement [UCC 4–110].
Electronic Fund Transfers (See pages 561–566.)	1. *Types of EFT systems*— a. Automated teller machines (ATMs). b. Point-of-sale systems. c. Direct deposits and withdrawals. d. Pay-by-telephone systems.

Chapter Summary • Checks and the Banking System, Continued

Electronic Fund Transfers—continued	2. *Consumer fund transfers*—Consumer fund transfers are governed by the Electronic Fund Transfer Act (EFTA) of 1978. The EFTA is basically a disclosure law that sets forth the rights and duties of the bank and the customer in respect to electronic fund transfer systems. Banks must comply strictly with EFTA requirements. 3. *Commercial transfers*—Disputes arising as a result of unauthorized or incorrectly made fund transfers between financial institutions are not covered under the EFTA. Article 4A of the UCC, which has been adopted by almost all of the states, governs fund transfers not subject to the EFTA or other federal or state statutes.

For Review

1. Checks are usually three-party instruments. On what type of check, however, does a bank serve as both the drawer and the drawee? What type of check does a bank agree in advance to accept when the check is presented for payment?
2. When may a bank properly dishonor a customer's check without liability to the customer?
3. In what circumstances might a bank not be liable for payment of a check containing a forged signature of the drawer?
4. Under the Electronic Fund Transfer Act, under what conditions will a bank be liable for an unauthorized fund transfer? When will the consumer be liable?
5. Are commercial electronic fund transfers between businesses governed by the Electronic Fund Transfer Act? If not, what law governs commercial fund transfers?

Questions and Case Problems

21–1. Error Resolution. Sheridan has a checking account at Gulf Bank. She frequently uses her access card to obtain money from the automatic teller machines. She always withdraws $50 when she makes a withdrawal, but she never withdraws more than $50 in any one day. When she received the April statement on her account, she noticed that on April 13 two withdrawals for $50 each had been made from the account. Believing this to be a mistake, she went to her bank on May 10 to inform the bank of the error. A bank officer told her that the bank would investigate and inform her of the result. On May 26, the bank officer called her and said that bank personnel were having trouble locating the error but would continue to try to find it. On June 20, the bank sent her a full written report advising her that no error had been made. Sheridan, unhappy with the bank's explanation, filed suit against the bank, alleging that it had violated the Electronic Fund Transfer Act. What was the outcome of the suit? Would it matter if the bank could show that on the day in question it had deducted $50 from Sheridan's account to cover a check that Sheridan had written to a local department store and that had cleared the bank on that day?

21–2. Forged Signatures. Gary goes grocery shopping and carelessly leaves his checkbook in his shopping cart. Dolores steals his checkbook, which has two blank checks remaining. On May 5, Dolores forges Gary's name on a check for $100 and cashes the check at Gary's bank, Citizens Bank of Middletown. Gary has not reported the theft of his blank checks to his bank. On June 1, Gary receives his monthly bank statement and canceled checks from Citizens Bank, including the forged check, but he does not examine the canceled checks. On June 20, Dolores forges Gary's last check. This check is for $1,000 and is cashed at Eastern City Bank, a bank with which Dolores has previously done business. Eastern City Bank puts the check through the collection process, and Citizens Bank honors it. On July 1, Gary receives his bank statement and canceled checks. On July 4, Gary discovers both forgeries and immediately notifies Citizens Bank. Dolores cannot be found. Gary claims that Citizens Bank must recredit his account for both checks, as his signature was forged. Discuss fully Gary's claim.

21–3. Death of Bank Customer/Stale Checks. Brian, on January 5, drafts a check for $3,000 drawn on the Southern Marine Bank payable to his assistant, Shanta. Brian puts last year's date on the check by mistake. On January 7, before Shanta has had a chance to go to the bank, Brian is killed in an automobile accident. Southern Marine is aware of Brian's death. On January 10, Shanta presents the check to the bank, and the bank honors the check by payment to Shanta. Brian's widow, Joyce, claims that the bank wrongfully paid Shanta, because it knew of Brian's death and also paid a check that was by date over one year old. Joyce, as executor of Brian's estate and sole heir by his will, demands that Southern Marine recredit Brian's estate for the check paid to Shanta. Discuss fully Southern Marine's liability in light of Joyce's demand.

21–4. Overdrafts. In September 1976, Edward and Christine McSweeney opened a joint checking account with the United States Trust Co. of New York. Between April 1978 and July 1978, 195 checks totaling $99,063 were written. In July 1978, activity in the account ceased. Christine wrote 95 of the 195 checks, totaling $16,811, and Edward wrote the rest of the checks. After deposits were credited for that period, the checks created a cumulative overdraft of $75,983. Can a bank knowingly honor a check when payment creates an overdraft, or must the bank dishonor the check? If the bank pays a check and thereby creates an overdraft, can the bank collect the amount of the overdraft (plus a service charge) from its customer? [*United States Trust Co. of New York v. McSweeney,* 91 A.D.2d 7, 457 N.Y.S.2d 276 (1982)]

21–5. Unauthorized Transfers. Parviz Haghighi Abyaneh and Iran Haghighi were co-owners of a savings account at First State Bank. On May 23, 1984, a person identifying himself as Abyaneh entered the Raleigh, North Carolina, office of Citizens Savings and Loan Association of Rocky Mount and opened a savings account. He then called First State Bank and asked a bank employee to transfer funds from Abyaneh's First State account into the newly created account. As a result, $53,825.66 was transferred to the new account, and subsequently the funds were withdrawn. When the true owners of the First State Bank account learned of the transfer, they filed suit against Merchants Bank, North, successor by merger to First State Bank, for violating the Electronic Fund Transfer Act. Discuss whether Abyaneh will be able to recover the $53,825.66. [*Abyaneh v. Merchants Bank, North,* 670 F.Supp. 1298 (M.D.Pa. 1987)]

21–6. Commercial Transfers. Dr. As'ad M. Masri and his wife borrowed $150,000 from First Virginia Bank–Colonial (FVBC). Masri then signed a wire-transfer request directing FVBC to transfer the funds to the Amro Bank in Amsterdam. The request also stated that the funds were to be deposited to the Lenex Corporation's account in that bank. FVBC transferred the funds to the Bank of Nova Scotia, an intermediary bank, and sent disbursal instructions directly to Amro. The following day, the funds were credited to the Lenex account at the Amro Bank. They were withdrawn, however, by someone other than the person intended by Masri to do so. When the Masris later defaulted on the loan, FVBC sought full repayment. The Masris claimed that FVBC breached the wire-transfer agreement. Has FVBC breached the transfer agreement? Where does FVBC's responsibility end? Discuss fully. [*First Virginia Bank–Colonial v. Masri, M.D.,* 245 Va. 461, 428 S.E.2d 903 (1993)]

21–7. Stale Checks. RPM Pizza, Inc., issued a $96,000 check to Systems Marketing but immediately placed a written stop-payment order on the check. Three weeks after the order expired, Systems cashed the check. Bank One Cambridge, RPM's bank, paid the check with funds from RPM's account. Because the check was more than six months old, it was stale and thus, according to standard banking procedures as well as Bank One's own procedures, the signature on the check should have been specially verified. RPM filed a suit in a federal district court against Bank One to recover the amount of the check. What should the court consider in deciding whether the bank's payment of the check violated the UCC? [*RPM Pizza, Inc. v. Bank One Cambridge,* 69 F.Supp. 517 (E.D.Mich. 1994)]

21–8. Article 3 versus Article 4. Gary Morgan Chevrolet and Oldsmobile, Inc., issued four checks payable to General Motors Acceptance Corp. (GMAC) on Morgan's account with the Bank of Richmondville. There were insufficient funds in Morgan's account, and the bank gave GMAC oral notice of dishonor. The bank returned the checks two days later. GMAC filed a suit against the bank in a New York state court, claiming that the bank failed to dishonor the checks before its midnight deadline, because notice of dishonor must be in writing under Article 4. The bank countered that notice of dishonor may be made orally under Article 3. Which article controls when there is such a conflict? [*General Motors Acceptance Corp. v. Bank of Richmondville,* 203 A.D.2d 851, 611 N.Y.S.2d 338 (1994)]

21–9. Forged Checks. Roy Supply, Inc., and R.M.R. Drywall, Inc., had checking accounts at Wells Fargo Bank. Both accounts required all checks to carry two signatures—that of Edward Roy and that of Twila June Moore, both of whom were executive officers of both companies. Between January 1989 and March 1991, the bank honored hundreds of checks on which Roy's signature was forged by Moore. On January 31, 1992, Roy and the two corporations notified the bank of the forgeries and then filed a suit in a California state court against the bank, alleging negligence. Who is liable for the amounts of the forged checks? Why? [*Roy Supply, Inc. v. Wells Fargo Bank, N.A.,* 39 Cal.App.4th, 46 Cal.Rptr.2d 309 (1995)]

21–10. Customer Negligence. Clem Macke Bindery hired Vincent Jones without investigating his background. At Clem Macke, blank checks were kept in a safe that was unlocked during working hours. Jones surreptitiously obtained two checks on which he forged Clem Macke's signature. The checks were made payable to a fictitious "Larry Pope," whose name Jones signed on the back. Jones cashed the checks at The Provident Bank, which did not ask for identification. Clem Macke assigned its claim against the bank for the amount of the checks to Atlantic Mutual Insurance Company, which filed a suit in an Ohio state court against the bank, alleging negligence. The bank responded that the employer had been negligent in hiring and failing to monitor Jones. If the court finds that both parties in this case were negligent, which party will bear the loss? Would the result be the same if the unrevised Article 3 were applied? Explain. [*Atlantic Mutual Insurance Co. v. The Provident Bank,* 79 Ohio Misc.2d 5, 669 N.E.2d 90 (1996)]

A QUESTION OF ETHICS AND SOCIAL RESPONSIBILITY

21–11. Lorine Daniels worked as a bookkeeper for Wilder Binding Co., which had a checking account with Oak Park Trust and Savings Bank. Among Daniels's responsibilities was the reconciliation of the bank statements with the firm's checkbook each month. Daniels forged signatures on forty-two checks, each for an amount under $1,000, which she made payable to herself. Over a six-month period, she embezzled a total of $25,254.78 in this way. When the forgeries were discovered, Wilder demanded that the bank recredit Wilder's account with the $25,254.78. In the lawsuit that followed, a key issue was whether the bank's custom of manually verifying signatures only on checks drawn for more than $1,000 constituted a breach of its duty of ordinary care. The bank testified that such policies and procedures were customary and routine and that its adherence to the policies and procedures therefore did not violate its duty of care. Given these facts, consider the following questions. [*Wilder Binding Co. v. Oak Park Trust and Savings Bank*, 135 Ill.2d 121, 552 N.E.2d 783, 142 Ill.Dec. 1192 (1990)]

1. This case was decided under Article 3 before it was revised in 1990. The court held that whether the bank had breached its duty of care was a question of fact for the jury. How would a court decide this issue under the revised Article 3?
2. Does the fact that a practice is "customary and routine" in a certain industry, such as the banking industry, mean that it is necessarily ethical?

FOR CRITICAL ANALYSIS

21–12. Under the 1990 revision of Article 4, banks are not required to send, with their monthly statements to customers, the customers' canceled checks. Banks may simply itemize the checks (by number, date, and amount) or, in addition to this itemization, also provide photocopies of the checks. Often, even when photocopies are included, the photocopies are reduced in size, so they are harder to read than the original canceled checks would be. What implications do the revised rules have for bank customers in terms of liability for unauthorized signatures and indorsements?

Online Activities

• **ONLINE EXERCISE 21–1**

Go to the "Internet Activities Book" on the Web site that accompanies this text, the URL for which is http://blt.westbuslaw.com. Select the following activity, and perform the exercise according to the instructions given there:

Activity 21–1: The Payments System

Before the Test

Go to the *Business Law Today* home page at http://blt.westbuslaw.com. Click on TestTutor.® You will find twenty interactive questions relating to this chapter.

Unit Four • Cumulative Business Hypothetical

Eve Anderson works as an accounts payable clerk for Future Tech, Inc., a software development and marketing firm. Eve, who has worked for the firm for years, is authorized to sign company checks, on which Future Tech's name and address are printed.

1 Future Tech pays its employees every two weeks. Eve gets her paycheck from her employer, indorses the back ("Eve Anderson"), and, on her lunch hour, goes to cash it at Future Tech's bank, United First Bank. On the street, in a crowd, she loses the check. Frank Smith finds it. Has the check been negotiated to Frank? Frank signs the back of the check beneath Eve's signature and cashes it. The check goes through the regular banking collection process, and United First Bank debits Future Tech's account for the amount. Future Tech refuses to issue another check to Eve to cover her loss. What might Eve have done to avoid this loss?

2 To pay her current bills, Eve asks her employer, Future Tech, to loan her the funds. Future Tech agrees if Eve will sign an instrument regarding the debt. What language do the parties need to include on that instrument to make it negotiable? Future Tech loans Eve the amount that she wants, and she signs a negotiable note to Future Tech due one year from the date signed. Six months later, Future Tech negotiates the note to Commercial Credit Corp. for 75 percent of the face amount in cash and a check for the rest. Is Commercial Credit a holder in due course of the note? To what extent?

3 To pay E-Systems, Inc., a Future Tech supplier, Eve issues a check in the amount due to E-Systems. The check is drawn on United First Bank. An E-Systems employee, with authorization, indorses the check and transfers it to E-Systems's financial institution, Western National Bank. Western National puts the check into the regular bank collection process. If United First refuses to cash the check, who will ultimately suffer the loss? Could Future Tech be subject to criminal prosecution if United First refuses to cash the check?

4 Alice works for Future Tech's accounts payable department with Eve but does not have the authority to sign company checks. Alice steals a blank Future Tech check from Eve's desk, forges Eve's signature, and cashes the check at Friendly Services, Inc., a check-cashing service. Friendly Services, which does not know that Eve's signature was forged, presents the check for payment to United First Bank. United First cashes the check. When the check is returned with Future Tech's bank statement, Eve discovers the forgery. Future Tech tells United First to recredit its account. Can United First legally refuse? If not, can United First recover the amount that it paid to Friendly Services?

UNIT FOUR • EXTENDED CASE STUDY: THE LAW IN CONTEXT

Triffin v. Dillabough

In Chapters 19, 20, and 21, we discussed the requirements for negotiability and for attaining the status of a holder in due course (HDC), the defenses against payment of a negotiable instrument to an HDC, and the bank collection process. In this extended case study, we examine Triffin v. Dillabough,[1] *a decision that applies these principles in the context of stolen money orders.*

CASE BACKGROUND

American Express Travel Related Services Company sells money orders. The money orders contain the preprinted signature of the chairman of American Express, who was, at one time, Louis Gerstner. A legend on the back of each money order provides, "THIS MONEY ORDER WILL NOT BE PAID IF IT HAS BEEN ALTERED OR STOLEN OR IF AN ENDORSEMENT IS MISSING OR FORGED."

Stacey Anne Dillabough presented two American Express money orders for payment to Chuckie Enterprises, Inc., a check-cashing service in Philadelphia. The money orders listed Dillabough as the payee. Robert Lynn presented an American Express money order to Chuckie's. The money order listed Lynn as the payee. Charles Giunta, the owner of Chuckie's, recognized Dillabough and Lynn, who also provided photo identification and indorsed the money orders. Giunta paid the amounts of the money orders to Dillabough and Lynn.

Giunta was unaware that the money orders were stolen. After being cashed, the money orders traveled the regular bank collection routes and were presented for payment to United Bank of Grand Junction, Colorado. Because American Express had already told the bank that the money orders were stolen, they were returned unpaid to Chuckie's bearing the stamp "REPORTED LOST OR STOLEN—DO NOT REDEPOSIT." Chuckie's sold the money orders to Robert Triffin and assigned all of its rights in the money orders to Triffin.

Triffin filed a suit in Pennsylvania state court against Dillabough, Lynn, and American Express, seeking payment. The court issued judgments against Dillabough and Lynn, but entered a verdict in favor of American Express. On Triffin's appeal, the state intermediate appellate court reversed the decision of the lower court, holding that the money orders were negotiable instruments and that Triffin had the status of a holder in due course. American Express appealed to the Supreme Court of Pennsylvania.

1. 552 Pa. 550, 716 A.2d 605 (1998).

MAJORITY OPINION

NEWMAN, Justice.

* * * *

The first requisite of negotiability, a signature by the drawer or maker, includes any symbol executed or adopted by a party with present intention to authenticate a writing. * * * American Express does not argue that Gerstner's signature was affixed to the money orders for any reason other than to authenticate them. Accordingly, the money orders satisfy the first requisite for negotiability.

The second requisite, [an unconditional promise or order to pay,] American Express argues is lacking * * * .

According to American Express, [the] legend [on the back of each money order] renders the order to pay conditional on the money order not being altered, stolen, unendorsed or forged and destroys the negotiability of the instrument.

* * * [This] legend * * * did not convert the money order into a conditional promise to pay, but merely operated as a warning to the party cashing the money order to protect himself against fraud. * * *

* * * *

The third requisite, that the writing be payable on demand or at a definite time, and the fourth requisite, that the writing be payable to order or bearer, are clear from the face of the money orders * * * . Thus, the American Express money orders qualify as negotiable instruments * * * .

* * * *

* * * [The UCC] provides that the defense of unauthorized completion discharges a party from liability to any person other than the holder in due course. "A subsequent holder in due course may in all cases * * * when an incomplete instrument has been completed, * * * enforce it as completed."* * *

* * * The loss should fall upon the party whose conduct

in signing blank paper has made the fraud possible, rather than upon the innocent purchaser. * * * The next question, then, is whether Triffin has the rights of a holder in due course who can enforce the negotiable money orders.

* * * *

* * * Triffin could acquire the status of a holder in due course from Chuckie's * * * if Chuckie's was a holder in due course because a transferee acquires whatever rights the tranferor had, even if the transferee is aware of the defenses to enforcement. * * * Therefore, the focus of our inquiry is whether Chuckie's was a holder in due course.

The parties do not dispute that Chuckie's took the money order for value. Giunta * * * paid Dillabough and Lynn the face value of the money orders * * * . American Express does not argue that Chuckie's failed to act in good faith. Based on Giunta's actions, we cannot say that * * * Chuckie's [did not act] in good faith. * * * [T]here was no evidence presented that Chuckie's had any notice that the Dillabough and Lynn money orders were stolen when he cashed them. Accordingly, * * * Chuckie's was a holder in due course. Because Triffin stands in Chuckie's shoes as its assignee, Triffin has attained the status of a holder in due course.

* * * Because Triffin has attained holder in due course status through the assignment of the money orders from Chuckie's, American Express cannot enforce the defenses against him. Accordingly, American Express is liable to Triffin for the face value of the money orders.

DISSENTING OPINION

CASTILLE, Justice, dissents.

* * * [S]ince the money orders at issue contained express conditional language which precluded negotiability under the relevant statute, I must respectfully dissent from the majority's conclusion.

* * * *

[The UCC] clearly distinguishes between language which creates an implied condition and language which creates an express condition. The latter renders a promise or order non-negotiable while the former does not * * * .

Here, the operative language in the money orders at issue clearly created an "express" condition and thereby rendered the money orders non-negotiable. * * *

This language explicitly conditions payments on the money orders' not being altered or stolen and the endorsements' not being missing or forged. The use of the word "if" renders the condition an express one, since "if" * * * means "on condition that; in case that; supposing that."

* * * *

Finally, the majority * * * contends that the language at issue amounts merely to a restatement of appellant's statutory defenses against payment * * * . The majority overlooks the fact that all of these statutory defenses are, by their own terms, ineffective against holders in due course. On the other hand, the language at issue here—which categorically states that the money order will not be paid if it was stolen—is operative even against holders who have taken in due course.

GOING ONLINE

The *Business Law Today,* Fifth Edition, Web site, at **http://blt.westbuslaw.com**, provides a link through which you can access other court opinions in cases involving negotiable instruments. Also Cornell University's Legal Information Institute at **www.law.cornell.edu/topics/negotiable.html** provides links to online resources for cases and other materials involving negotiable instruments.

QUESTIONS FOR ANALYSIS

1. **Law.** Why wasn't Dillabough and Lynn's filling in the blanks of the stolen money orders enough to absolve American Express of liability?
2. **Law.** How might American Express change what it prints on its money orders to avoid liability in future cases with similar circumstances?
3. **Ethics.** Should a party in the position of Triffin be endowed with the status of a holder in due course (HDC) simply because, when acquiring an instrument, the party is also "assigned" all of the "rights" of a previous HDC?
4. **International Dimensions.** Would the result in this case have been the same if American Express or Chuckie's were not a U.S. company or if Dillabough, Lynn, Giunta, or Triffin were not U.S. citizens?
5. **Implications for the Business Manager.** What lessons does the holding in this case have for businesspersons who accept money orders and other checks in payment for goods and services?

Unit Five
Debtor-Creditor Relationships

CHAPTER 22

Secured Transactions

"Article 9 is clearly the most novel and probably the most important article in the Code . . . and covers the entire range of transactions in which the debts are secured by personal property."

Walter D. Malcom, 1904–1979
(President of the National Conference of Commissioners on Uniform State Laws, 1963–1966)

CONTENTS

LEARNING OBJECTIVES

After reading this chapter, you should be able to:

1. List and define the various terms used in secured transactions.
2. State what is necessary to create an enforceable security interest.
3. Explain how and why security interests are perfected.
4. Indicate how priority disputes among creditors are decided.
5. Discuss the remedies available to a secured creditor when the debtor defaults.

Whenever the payment of a debt is guaranteed, or *secured,* by personal property owned by the debtor or in which the debtor has a legal interest, the transaction becomes known as a **secured transaction.** The concept of the secured transaction is as basic to modern business practice as the concept of credit. Logically, sellers and lenders do not want to risk nonpayment, so they usually will not sell goods or lend funds unless the promise of payment is somehow guaranteed. Indeed, business as we know it could not exist without laws permitting and governing secured transactions.

The significance of Article 9 of the Uniform Commercial Code (UCC), which governs secured transactions, is related in the *Landmark in the Law* on the following page. As will become evident, the law of secured transactions tends to favor the rights of creditors; but to a lesser extent, it offers debtors some protection, too.

• **SECURED TRANSACTION**
Any transaction in which the payment of a debt is guaranteed, or secured, by personal property owned by the debtor or in which the debtor has a legal interest.

Landmark in the Law • ARTICLE 9 SECURITY INTEREST

Prior to the drafting and adoption by the states of Article 9 of the Uniform Commercial Code, secured transactions were governed by a patchwork of security devices. These devices were replete with variations that, according to many, made no logical sense. Additionally, each device had its own jargon. Depending on the device used, for example, a debtor could be called variously a pledgor, a mortgagor, a conditional vendee, an assignor, or a borrower.

One of the earliest security devices, historically, is the pledge. A *pledge* is a possessory security interest in which the secured party acquires or holds possession of the property involved, called the *collateral,* to secure the payment or performance of the secured obligation. The pledge has existed since at least the fourth or fifth century. One security device that developed from the pledge concept involved obtaining a security interest in goods that could not be conveniently moved from the debtor's property. In such a situation, the creditor would have an independent warehouser establish a warehouse on the debtor's premises to obtain possession of the goods. This was called a field warehouse and dates from about 1900.

There were many other types of security devices. Nonetheless, creditors still faced several legal problems. For example, in many states, a security interest could not be taken in inventory or a stock in trade, such as cars for a car dealer or chocolate for a candy manufacturer. Sometimes, highly technical limitations were placed on the use of a particular security device. If a court determined that a particular security device was not appropriate for a given transaction, it might void the security interest entirely.

The drafters of Article 9 concluded that the two elements common to all security devices were (1) the objective of conferring on a creditor or secured party priority in certain property (the collateral) against the risk of the debtor's nonpayment of the debt or the debtor's insolvency or bankruptcy and (2) a means of notifying other creditors of this prior security interest. With these two elements in mind, the drafters created a new, simplified security device with a single set of terms to cover all situations. What is this security device called? It is called, simply, an Article 9 security interest.

Although the law of secured transactions still remains far from simple, it is now—thanks to the drafters of Article 9—far more rational and uniform than it was in the days prior to the UCC.

ON THE WEB
To find Article 9 of the UCC as adopted by a particular state, go to the Web site of Cornell University's Law School at www.law.cornell.edu/ucc/ucc.table.html.

FOR CRITICAL ANALYSIS
Clearly, creditors benefit from secured transactions. How do debtors also benefit from secured transactions?

The Terminology of Secured Transactions

The UCC's terminology is now uniformly adopted in all documents used in situations involving secured transactions. A brief summary of the UCC's definitions of terms relating to secured transactions follows.

1. A **security interest** is any interest "in personal property or fixtures which secures payment or performance of an obligation" [UCC 1–201(37)].
2. A **secured party** is a lender, a seller, or any person in whose favor there is a security interest, including a person to whom accounts or *chattel paper* (any writing evidencing a debt secured by personal property) has been sold [UCC 9–105(1)(m)]. The terms *secured party* and *secured creditor* are frequently used interchangeably.
3. A **debtor** is the party who owes payment or performance of the secured obligation, whether or not that party actually owns or has rights in the collateral [UCC 9–105(1)(d)].

• **SECURITY INTEREST**
Any interest "in personal property or fixtures which secures payment or performance of an obligation" [UCC 1–201(37)].

• **SECURED PARTY**
A lender, seller, or any other person in whose favor there is a security interest, including a person to whom accounts or chattel paper has been sold.

• **DEBTOR**
Under Article 9 of the UCC, a debtor is any party who owes payment or performance of a secured obligation, whether or not the party actually owns or has rights in the collateral.

• **SECURITY AGREEMENT**
An agreement that creates or provides for a security interest between the debtor and a secured party.

• **COLLATERAL**
Under Article 9 of the UCC, the property subject to a security interest, including accounts and chattel paper that have been sold.

4 A **security agreement** is the agreement that creates or provides for a security interest between the debtor and a secured party [UCC 9–105(1)(*l*)].
5 **Collateral** is the property subject to a security interest, including accounts and chattel paper that have been sold [UCC 9–105(1)(c)].

These basic definitions form the concept under which a debtor-creditor relationship becomes a secured transaction relationship (see Exhibit 22–1).

Creating and Perfecting a Security Interest

• **DEFAULT**
The failure to observe a promise or discharge an obligation. The term is commonly used to mean the failure to pay a debt when it is due.

A creditor has two main concerns if the debtor **defaults** (fails to pay the debt as promised): (1) satisfaction of the debt through the possession and (usually) sale of the collateral and (2) priority over any other creditors or buyers who may have rights in the same collateral. We look here at how these two concerns are met through the creation and perfection of a security interest.

CREATING A SECURITY INTEREST

To become a secured party, the creditor must obtain a security interest in the collateral of the debtor. Three requirements must be met for a creditor to have an enforceable security interest:

1 Either (a) the collateral must be in the possession of the secured party in accordance with an agreement, or (b) there must be a written security agreement describing the collateral and signed by the debtor.
2 The secured party must give value.
3 The debtor must have rights in the collateral.

• **ATTACHMENT**
In a secured transaction, the process by which a security interest in the property of another becomes enforceable.

Once these requirements have been met, the creditor's rights are said to attach to the collateral. **Attachment** gives the creditor an enforceable security interest in the collateral [UCC 9–203].

Written Security Agreement When the collateral is not in the possession of the secured party, a security agreement must be in writing to be enforceable. To be effective, (1) the security agreement must be signed by the debtor, (2) it must contain a description of the collateral, and (3) the description must reasonably identify the collateral [UCC 9–203(1), 9–110]. See Exhibit 22–2 for a sample security agreement.

EXHIBIT 22–1 • Secured Transactions—Concept and Terminology
In a security agreement, a debtor and creditor agree that the creditor will have a security interest in collateral in which the debtor has rights. In essence, the collateral secures the loan and ensures the creditor of payment should the debtor default.

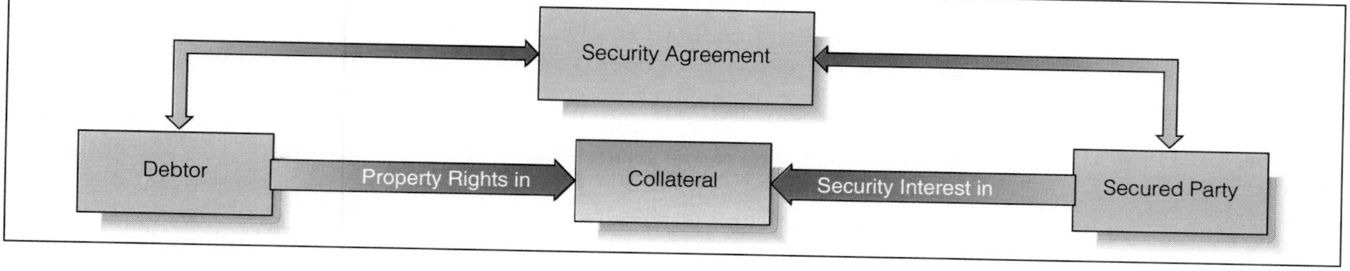

EXHIBIT 22–2 • A Sample Security Agreement

____
Date

____
Name No. and Street City County State

(hereinafter called Debtor) hereby grants to ______________________
Name

____
No. and Street City County State

(hereinafter called Secured Party) a security interest in the following property (here-inafter called the Collateral): ______________________

to secure payment and performance of obligations identified or set out as follows (here-inafter called the Obligations): ______________________

Default in payment or performance of any of the Obligations or default under any agreement evidencing any of the Obligations is a default under this agreement. Upon such default Secured Party may declare all Obligations immediately due and payable and shall have the remedies of a secured party under the __________ Uniform Com- mercial Code.

Signed in (duplicate) triplicate.

Debtor	Secured Party
By ______________	By ______________

At issue in the following case was whether a security agreement had reasonably identified the collateral and had, in fact, been signed by the debtor.

CASE 22.1 In re Ziluck

United States District Court,
Southern District of Florida, 1992.
139 Bankr. 44.

HISTORICAL AND SOCIAL SETTING *According to UCC 9–110, a description of collateral is sufficient "whether or not it is specific if it reasonably identifies what is described." In cases decided before Article 9 of the UCC was adopted, courts often held that descriptions were insufficient unless they were "of the most exact and detailed nature, the so-called 'serial number' test." In the Comment to UCC 9–110, the drafters of the UCC recognized that a description is sufficient if it does "the job assigned to it—that it make possible the identification of the thing described." Of course, in some situations, only a specific description—such as a serial number—will reasonably identify the collateral. In holding that a description is too general, a court may believe that it is protecting a debtor against a clause that would otherwise subject much of his or her property to the claim of a single creditor.*

BACKGROUND AND FACTS David Ziluck applied for a Radio Shack credit card. The front of the application contained blanks for various personal and employment information and a space for the applicant to sign. Above the signature line was the following statement: "I have read the Radio Shack Credit Account and Security Agreement, including the notice provisions in the last paragraph, and it contains no blanks or blank spaces. I agree to the terms of the Agreement and acknowledge a copy of the agreement." The back of the application contained a "Radio Shack Credit Account and Security Agreement," which stated in

(Continued)

CASE 22.1—Continued

part, "We retain a security interest under the Uniform Commercial Code in all merchandise charged to your Account. If you do not make payments on your Account as agreed, the security interest allows us to repossess only the merchandise that has not been paid in full." When Ziluck later filed for bankruptcy protection, the bankruptcy court had to decide whether the application form constituted a valid security agreement. The court concluded that it did not, for two reasons. First, Ziluck's signature was not effective, because it was not on the back side of the form, which stated the terms of the security agreement. Second, the security agreement's description of the collateral ("all merchandise charged to your Account") was not sufficiently descriptive. The bankruptcy court's decision was appealed.

IN THE WORDS OF THE COURT . . .
GONZALEZ, District Judge.

* * * *

Turning first to the signature issue, the Court finds that Ziluck did in fact sign the security agreement. Ziluck signed the front of the credit card application on a line provided. Directly above the signature line in clear, bold print appeared the following language: "I have read the Radio Shack Credit Account and Security Agreement, including the notice provision in the last paragraph thereof, and it contains no blanks or blank spaces. I agree to the terms of the Agreement and acknowledge receipt of a copy of the Agreement." * * *

The Court also finds that the bankruptcy court erred in finding that the description of the collateral in the security agreement was insufficient. [UCC 9–110] provides that "any description of personal property * * * is sufficient whether or not it is specific if it reasonably identifies what is described." The Court believes that the language in * * * the security agreement, " * * * all merchandise charged to your account," reasonably identifies the property subject to the security interest—namely any property purchased with the subject credit card.

DECISION AND REMEDY The federal district court held that Ziluck had effectively signed the security agreement and that the security agreement's description of the collateral was sufficient. The court reversed the bankruptcy court's decision and remanded the case.

FOR CRITICAL ANALYSIS—Ethical Consideration *Should the court have considered whether Ziluck had actually read the full agreement?*

Secured Party Must Give Value The secured party must give value. Value, according to UCC 1–201(44), is any consideration that supports a simple contract, security given for a preexisting (antecedent) obligation, or any binding commitment to extend credit. Normally, the value given by a secured party is in the form of a direct loan, or it involves a commitment to sell goods on credit.

Debtor Must Have Rights in the Collateral The debtor must have rights in the collateral; that is, the debtor must have some ownership interest or right to obtain possession of that collateral. The debtor's rights can represent either a current or a future legal interest in the collateral. For example, a retail seller-debtor can give a secured party a security interest not only in existing inventory owned by the retailer but also in *future* inventory to be acquired by the retailer.

• **PERFECTION**
The legal process by which secured parties protect themselves against the claims of third parties who may wish to have their debts satisfied out of the same collateral; usually accomplished by the filing of a financing statement with the appropriate government official.

PERFECTING A SECURITY INTEREST

Perfection represents the legal process by which secured parties protect themselves against the claims of third parties who may wish to have their debts satisfied out of the same collateral. Usually, perfection is accomplished by the filing of a financing

EXHIBIT 22–3 • Types of Collateral and Methods of Perfection

TYPE OF COLLATERAL	DEFINITION	PERFECTION METHOD	UCC SECTIONS
Tangible	All things that are *movable* at the time the security interest attaches or that are *fixtures* [UCC 9–105(1)(h)]. This includes timber to be cut, growing crops, and unborn animals.		
1. Consumer Goods	Goods used or bought primarily for personal, family, or household purposes—for example, household furniture [UCC 9–109(1)].	For purchase-money security interest, attachment is sufficient; for boats, motor vehicles, and trailers, there is a requirement of filing or compliance with a certificate-of-title statute; for other consumer goods, general rules of filing or possession apply.	9–302(1)(d), (3), (4); 9–305
2. Equipment	Goods bought for or used primarily in business—for example, a delivery truck [UCC 9–109(2)].	Filing or (rarely) possession by secured party.	9–302(1); 9–305
3. Farm Products	Crops, livestock, and supplies used or produced in a farming operation in the possession of a farmer-debtor. This includes products of crops or livestock—for example, milk, eggs, maple syrup, and ginned cotton [UCC 9–109(3)].	Filing or (rarely) possession by secured party.	9–302(1); 9–305
4. Inventory	Goods held for sale or lease and materials used or consumed in the course of business—for example, raw materials or floor stock of a retailer [UCC 9–109(4)].	Filing or (rarely) possession by secured party.	9–302(1); 9–305
5. Fixtures	Goods that become so affixed to realty that an interest in them arises under real estate law—for example, a central air-conditioning unit [UCC 9–313(1)(a)].	Filing only.	9–313(1)
Intangible	Nonphysical property that exists only in connection with something else.		
1. Chattel Paper	Any writing that evidences both a *monetary obligation and a security interest*—for example, a thirty-six-month-payment retail security agreement signed by a buyer to purchase a car [UCC 9–105(1)(b)].	Filing or possession by secured party.	9–304(1); 9–305
2. Documents of Title	Papers that entitle the person in possession to hold, receive, or dispose of the paper or goods the documents cover—for example, bills of lading, warehouse receipts, and dock warrants [UCC 9–105(1)(f), 1–201(15), 7–201].	Filing or possession by secured party.	9–304(1), (3); 9–305
3. Instruments	Any writing that evidences a right to payment of money that is not a security agreement or lease, and any negotiable instrument or certificated security that in the ordinary course of business is transferred by delivery with any necessary indorsement or assignment—for example, stock certificates, promissory notes, and certificates of deposit [UCC 9–105(1)(i), 3–104, 8–102(1)(a)].	Except for temporary perfected status, possession only.	9–304(1), (4) (5); 9–305
4. Accounts	Any right to payment for goods sold or leased or for services *rendered* that is not evidenced by an instrument or chattel paper—for example, accounts receivable and contract right payments [UCC 9–106].	Filing required (with exceptions).	9–302(1) (e), (g)
5. General Intangibles	Any personal property other than that defined above—for example, a patent, a copyright, goodwill, or a trademark [UCC 9–106].	Filing only; for copyrights, with the U.S. Copyright Office.	9–302(1)

• **FINANCING STATEMENT**
A document prepared by a secured creditor, and filed with the appropriate state or local official, to give notice to the public that the creditor has a security interest in collateral belonging to the debtor named in the statement. The financing statement must be signed by the debtor, contain the addresses of both the debtor and the creditor, and describe the collateral by type or item.

statement with the office of the appropriate government official. In some circumstances, however, a security interest becomes perfected without the filing of a financing statement. The classification of collateral is important in determining the proper method of perfection and where the financing statement should be filed. Note that the debtor's primary use of (or intended use of) the collateral determines how the collateral is classified. Thus, a computer purchased on credit from a retailer for use in the home is classified as consumer goods. If the computer is purchased for use in an office, however, it is classified as equipment. Exhibit 22–3 summarizes the various classifications of collateral and the methods of perfecting a security interest in them.

Perfection by Filing A secured party can perfect a security interest by filing a financing statement (or the security agreement) with the appropriate state or local official. The UCC requires a **financing statement** to contain (1) the signature of the debtor, (2) the addresses of both the debtor and the secured party, and (3) a description of the collateral by type or item [UCC 9–402(1)]. Filing is the most common means of perfection to use. A sample financing statement is shown in Exhibit 22–4. (For an example of a financing statement that failed to meet these requirements, see the feature, *The Letter of the Law: A Walk on the Dark Side.*)

The Letter of the Law — A Walk on the Dark Side

Creditors contemplating a loan to a debtor, if they search through the filing records, may change their minds about making the loan if they come across a filing statement filed under that debtor's name. In other words, debtors listed on filing statements may have difficulty obtaining loans. There is nothing unfair about imposing this burden on debtors—assuming, of course, that the filed financial statement is rooted in an actual credit transaction. But what if the filed statement is phony? Until the "debtor" can arrange to have the filing statement removed (which can be far from easy), his or her creditworthiness may be damaged in the eyes of potential creditors.

The idea of using a phony financing statement as a weapon against one's enemies is a novel one, to be sure, but at least one person has resorted to such a tactic. A prisoner who had been convicted and sentenced to seventeen years in prison for various crimes, including conspiracy to commit murder, filed a phony financing statement against one of the U.S. attorneys that prosecuted his case to "get even" with the attorney. The financing statement asserted a claim against the "debtor" for $1,000,000 for violating the prisoner's "commercial, constitutional and civil rights." Needless to say, the U.S. attorney in question knew exactly what to do: he filed a motion with the court to have the financing statement canceled. The court granted the petition, noting, among other things, that the statement was invalid because it had not been signed by the "debtor."[a]

THE BOTTOM LINE

If one decides to misuse or abuse the law, it is probably not a good idea to target an attorney as one's victim.

a. *United States v. Lopez,* 1997 WL 835419 (N.Y.Sup. 1997).

An improper filing reduces a secured party's claim in bankruptcy to that of an unsecured creditor. If the debtor's name on the financing statement is inaccurate, for example, or the collateral is not sufficiently described on the statement, the filing may not be effective. In addition, a subsequently perfected security interest in the same collateral would have priority over the debtor's collateral in the event that the debtor defaults.

¡NOTE!
To create a security interest in a fixture, the description of real estate to which the fixture is attached does not need to be the same as the description in a deed or mortgage. Such a description provides a familiar form of notice, however, to those searching the records.

The Debtor's Name. The UCC requires that a financing statement be filed under the name of the debtor [UCC 9–402(1)]. If the debtor is an individual, the financing statement must be filed under the name of the individual, but if the debtor is a partnership or a corporation, the financing statement must be filed under the partnership or corporate name [UCC 9–402(7)]. If a financing statement identifies the debtor by an incorrect name, the statement may be ineffective to perfect a security interest.

EXHIBIT 22-4 • A Sample Financing Statement

This FINANCING STATEMENT is presented for filing pursuant to the California Uniform Commercial Code.

1. DEBTOR (LAST NAME FIRST—IF AN INDIVIDUAL)		**1A.** SOCIAL SECURITY OR FEDERAL TAX NO.
1B. MAILING ADDRESS	**1C.** CITY, STATE	**1D.** ZIP CODE
2. ADDITIONAL DEBTOR (IF ANY) (LAST NAME FIRST—IF AN INDIVIDUAL)		**2A.** SOCIAL SECURITY OR FEDERAL TAX NO.
2B. MAILING ADDRESS	**2C.** CITY, STATE	**2D.** ZIP CODE
3. DEBTOR'S TRADE NAMES OR STYLES (IF ANY)		**3A.** FEDERAL TAX NUMBER
4. SECURED PARTY NAME MAILING ADDRESS CITY STATE ZIP CODE		**4A.** SOCIAL SECURITY NO., FEDERAL TAX NO. OR BANK TRANSIT AND A.B.A. NO.
5. ASSIGNEE OF SECURED PARTY (IF ANY) NAME MAILING ADDRESS CITY STATE ZIP CODE		**5A.** SOCIAL SECURITY NO., FEDERAL TAX NO. OR BANK TRANSIT AND A.B.A. NO.

6. This FINANCING STATEMENT covers the following types or items of property **(include description of real property on which located and owner of record when required by instruction 4).**
As security for and in consideration of all present and any future advances or other obligations debtor hereby grants United California Bank a security interest in all of the following types or items of property ("Collateral" herein) in which the debtor now has or hereafter acquires any right, title, or interest, or rights present and future, wheresoever located and whether in the possession of the debtor, a warehouseman, bailee, trustee or any other person, and all increases, therein and replacements, products, and proceeds thereof. Proceeds include but are not limited to inventory, returned merchandise, accounts, chattel paper, general intangibles, insurance proceeds, documents, money, goods, equipment, instruments, and any other tangible or intangible property arising under the sale, lease or other disposition of collateral:

7. CHECK IF APPLICABLE ☒	**7A.** ☐ PRODUCTS OF COLLATERAL ARE ALSO COVERED	**7B.** DEBTOR(S) SIGNATURE NOT REQUIRED IN ACCORDANCE WITH INSTRUCTION 5(c) ITEM: ☐ (1) ☐ (2) ☐ (3) ☐ (4)
8. CHECK IF APPLICABLE ☒	☐ DEBTOR IS A "TRANSMITTING UTILITY" IN ACCORDANCE WITH UCC § 9105 (1) (n)	

9. DATE:

▶ SIGNATURE(S) of DEBTOR(S)

TYPE OR PRINT NAME(S) OF DEBTOR(S)

▶ SIGNATURE(S) OF SECURED PARTY(IES)

TYPE OR PRINT NAME(S) OF SECURED PARTY(IES)

11. *Return copy to:*

NAME
ADDRESS
CITY
STATE
ZIP CODE

CODE 1 2 3 4 5 6 7 8 9 0

10. THIS SPACE FOR USE OF FILING OFFICER (DATE, TIME, FILE NUMBER AND FILING OFFICER)

(1) FILING OFFICER COPY

FORM UCC-1—FILING FEE $3.00
Approved by the Secretary of State

MS-336 10-78

ON THE WEB
The Web site of Cornell University's Legal Information Institute offers an overview and menu of sources on legal materials relating to secured transactions at **www.law.cornell.edu/topics/secured_transactions.html.**

Description of the Collateral. The UCC requires that both the security agreement and the financing statement contain a description of the collateral in which the secured party has a security interest. The security agreement must include a description of the collateral because no security interest in goods can exist unless the parties agree on which goods are subject to the security interest. The financing statement must include a description of the collateral because the purpose of filing the statement is to give public notice of the fact that certain goods in the debtor's possession are subject to a security interest. Other parties who might later wish to lend money to the debtor or buy the collateral can thus learn of the security interest by checking with the state or local office in which a financing statement for that type of collateral would be filed.

Sometimes, the descriptions in the two documents vary, with the description in the security agreement being more precise and the description in the financing statement more general. For example, a security agreement for a commercial loan to a manufacturer may list all of the manufacturer's equipment subject to the loan by serial number, whereas the financing statement may simply state "all equipment owned or hereafter acquired." To avoid problems arising from such variations in descriptions, a secured party may repeat exactly the security agreement's description in the financing statement or file the security agreement itself as a financing statement—assuming the security agreement meets the previously discussed criteria. Alternatively, where permitted, the secured party might file a combination security agreement–financing statement form. If the financing statement is too general or vague, a court may find it insufficient to perfect a security interest.

Where to File. Depending on how collateral is classified, filing is done either centrally with the secretary of state, locally with the county clerk or other official, or both, according to state law. According to UCC 9–401, a state may choose one of three alternatives.[1] In general, financing statements for consumer goods should be filed with the county clerk. Other kinds of collateral require filing with the secretary of state [UCC 9–401].

Perfection without Filing In two types of situations, security interests can be perfected without filing a financing statement. First, when the collateral is transferred into the possession of the secured party, the secured party's security interest in the collateral is perfected. Second, a purchase-money security interest in consumer goods and an assignment of a beneficial interest in a trust or a decedent's estate are perfected automatically.

Perfection by Possession. Under the common law, as discussed in this chapter's *Landmark in the Law,* one of the most common means of obtaining financing was to **pledge** certain collateral as security for the debt and transfer the collateral into the creditor's possession. When the debt was paid, the collateral would be returned to the debtor. Usually, the transfer of collateral was accompanied by a written security agreement, but the agreement did not have to be in writing. In other words, an oral security agreement was effective as long as the secured party possessed the collateral. Article 9 of the UCC retained the common law pledge and the principle that the security agreement need not be in writing to be enforceable if the collateral is transferred to the secured party [UCC 9–203(1)(a)].

• **PLEDGE**
A common law security device (retained in Article 9 of the UCC) in which personal property is turned over to the creditor as security for the payment of a debt and retained by the creditor until the debt is paid.

For most collateral, possession by the secured party is impractical because it denies the debtor the right to use or derive income from the property to pay off the debt.

1. See UCC 9–401 in Appendix C for these three alternatives. Approximately half the states have adopted the second alternative. Filing fees range from as low as $3 to as high as $25.

For example, if a farmer took out a loan to finance the purchase of a piece of heavy farm equipment, using the equipment as collateral, the purpose of the purchase would be defeated if the farmer transferred the collateral into the creditor's possession. Certain items, however, such as stocks, bonds, and jewelry, are commonly transferred into the creditor's possession when they are used as collateral for loans. With respect to negotiable instruments, transferable nonnegotiable instruments, and certain securities (such as stocks and bonds), with a few exceptions, the only way to properly perfect a security interest is through possession by the secured party.

"I will pay you some, and, as most debtors do, promise you infinitely."

WILLIAM SHAKESPEARE, 1564–1616 (English dramatist)

If a secured party is in possession of the collateral, he or she must use reasonable care in preserving it. Otherwise, the secured party is liable to the debtor [UCC 9–207(1), 9–207(3)].

Purchase-Money Security Interest. Often, sellers of consumer goods (defined as goods bought or used by the debtor primarily for personal, family, or household purposes) agree to extend credit for part or all of the purchase price of those goods. Additionally, financial institutions that are not in the business of selling such goods often agree to lend consumers much of the purchase price for goods. The security interest that the seller or the lender obtains when such a transaction occurs is called a **purchase-money security interest (PMSI),** because the lender or seller has essentially provided a buyer with the "purchase money" to buy goods [UCC 9–107].

• **PURCHASE-MONEY SECURITY INTEREST (PMSI)**
A security interest that arises when a seller or lender extends credit for part or all of the purchase price of goods purchased by a buyer.

• **EXAMPLE 22.1** Suppose that Jamie wants to purchase a new hot tub from ABC Pool and Spa Company. The purchase price is $5,500. Not being able to pay the entire amount in cash, Jamie signs a purchase agreement to pay $3,000 down and $200 per month until the balance plus interest is fully paid. ABC Pool and Spa is to retain a security interest in the purchased goods until full payment has been made. Because the security interest was created as part of the purchase agreement, it is a PMSI. •

A PMSI in consumer goods is perfected automatically at the time of a credit sale—that is, at the time that the PMSI is created. The seller in this situation need do nothing more to protect his or her interest. There are exceptions to this rule, however, that cover security interests in fixtures and in motor vehicles [UCC 9–302(1)(d)]. In a few states, a PMSI in farm equipment under a certain statutory value may also be perfected automatically by attachment.

Perfection of Security Interests in Motor Vehicles Most states require a certificate of title for any motor vehicle, boat, or motor home. The normal methods described above for the perfection of a security interest typically do not apply to such vehicles. Rather, the perfection of a security interest only occurs when a notation of such an interest appears on the certificate of title that covers the vehicle.

• **EXAMPLE 22.2** Suppose that your commercial bank lends you 80 percent of the money necessary to purchase a new BMW. You live in a state that requires certificates of title for all automobiles. If your bank fails to have its security interest noted on the certificate of title, its interest is not perfected. That means that a good faith purchaser of your BMW could take it free of the bank's interest. • In most states, purchasers of motor vehicles can buy vehicles with the confidence that no security interest exists that is not disclosed on the certificate of title.[2]

Collateral Moved to Another Jurisdiction Obviously, collateral may be moved by the debtor from one jurisdiction (state) to another. In general, a properly perfected security interest in collateral moved into a new jurisdiction continues to be perfected

2. In the few states that do not require title registration of motor vehicles, one must examine the appropriate statutes to determine the priority of conflicting security interests.

in the new jurisdiction for priority purposes (priority disputes will be examined later in the chapter) for a period of up to four months from the date the collateral was moved into the new jurisdiction or for the period of time remaining under the perfection in the original jurisdiction, whichever expires first [UCC 9–103(1)(d), 9–103(3)(e)]. Collateral moved from county to county within a state (if local filing is required), rather than from one state to another, however, may not have a four-month limitation [UCC 9–403(3)].

• **EXAMPLE 22.3** On January 1, Wheeler secures a loan from a Nebraska bank by putting up all his road-building equipment as security. The Nebraska bank files the security interest centrally with the secretary of state. In June, Wheeler has an opportunity to build roads in South Dakota and moves his equipment into that state on June 15. Under the UCC, the Nebraska bank's perfection remains effective in South Dakota for a period of four months from June 15. If the Nebraska bank wishes to retain its perfection priority, the bank must perfect properly in South Dakota during this four-month period. Should the bank fail to do so, its perfection would be lost after four months, and any subsequent perfected security interest in the same collateral in South Dakota would prevail. •

Among mobile goods, automobiles pose one of the biggest problems. If the original jurisdiction does not require a certificate of title as part of its perfection process for an automobile, perfection automatically ends four months after the automobile is moved into another jurisdiction. When a security interest exists on an automobile in a state in which title registration is required and when the security interest is noted on the certificate of title, the perfection of the security interest continues after the automobile is moved to another state requiring a certificate of title until the automobile is registered in the new state [UCC 9–103(2)]. This rule protects the secured party against anyone purchasing the car in the new state prior to the new registration. Moreover, because each certificate-of-title state requires that the old certificate of title be surrendered to obtain a new one, and because the secured party typically holds the certificate, the secured party usually is able to ensure that the security interest is noted on the new certificate of title.

• **CONTINUATION STATEMENT**
A statement that, if filed within six months prior to the expiration date of the original financing statement, continues the perfection of the original security interest for another five years. The perfection of a security interest can be continued in the same manner indefinitely.

Effective Time of Perfection A financing statement is effective for five years from the date of filing [UCC 9–403(2)]. If a **continuation statement** is filed within six months *prior to* the expiration date, the effectiveness of the original statement is continued for another five years, starting with the expiration date of the first five-year period [UCC 9–403(3)]. The effectiveness of the statement can be continued in the same manner indefinitely.

The Scope of a Security Interest

In addition to covering collateral already in the debtor's possession, a security agreement can cover various other types of property, including the proceeds of the sale of collateral, after-acquired property, and future advances.

PROCEEDS

• **PROCEEDS**
Under Article 9 of the UCC, whatever is received when the collateral is sold or otherwise disposed of, such as by exchange.

Proceeds include whatever is received when collateral is sold or disposed of in some other way. A secured party's security interest in the collateral includes a security interest in the proceeds of the sale of that collateral. For example, suppose that a bank has a perfected security interest in the inventory of a retail seller of heavy farm machinery. The retailer sells a tractor out of this inventory to a farmer, a buyer in the ordinary course of business. The farmer agrees, in a retail security agreement, to pay monthly payments for a period of twenty-four months. If the retailer should go into default on the loan from the bank, the bank is entitled to the remaining payments the farmer owes to the retailer as proceeds.

A security interest in proceeds perfects automatically on perfection of the secured party's security interest in the collateral and remains perfected for ten days after receipt of the proceeds by the debtor. One way to extend the ten-day automatic period is to provide for such extended coverage in the original security agreement. This is typically done when the collateral is the type that is likely to be sold, such as a retailer's inventory—for example, of snowboards or DVD players. The UCC provides that in the following circumstances the security interest in proceeds remains perfected for longer than ten days after the receipt of the proceeds by the debtor:

1. When a filed financing statement covers the original collateral and the proceeds are collateral in which a security interest may be perfected by a filing in the office or offices with which the financing statement has been filed. Furthermore, a secured party's interest automatically perfects in property that the debtor acquires with cash proceeds, if the original filing would have been effective as to that property and the financing statement indicates that type of property [UCC 9–306(3)(a)]. Thus, in the farm equipment example above, if the retailer used the farmer's monthly payments to acquire additional inventory, the bank would have a security interest in that additional inventory, providing that the bank's original filing was effective as to that property and the financing statement indicated that type of property.
2. Whenever there is a filed financing statement that covers the original collateral and the proceeds are identifiable cash proceeds [UCC 9–306(3)(b)].
3. Whenever the security interest in the proceeds is perfected before the expiration of the ten-day period [UCC 9–306(3)(c)].

AFTER-ACQUIRED PROPERTY

• **AFTER-ACQUIRED PROPERTY**
Property of the debtor that is acquired after the execution of a security agreement.

After-acquired property of the debtor is property acquired after the execution of the security agreement. The security agreement may provide for a security interest in after-acquired property [UCC 9–204(1)]. This is particularly useful for inventory financing arrangements, because a secured party whose security interest is in existing inventory knows that the debtor will sell that inventory, thereby reducing the collateral subject to the security interest. Generally, the debtor will purchase new inventory to replace the inventory sold. The secured party wants this newly acquired inventory to be subject to the original security interest. Thus, the after-acquired property clause continues the secured party's claim to any inventory acquired thereafter. This is not to say that the original security interest will be superior to the rights of all other creditors with regard to this after-acquired inventory, as will be discussed later.

• **EXAMPLE 22.4** Amato buys factory equipment from Bronson on credit, giving as security an interest in all of her equipment—both what she is buying and what she already owns. The security interest with Bronson contains an after-acquired property clause. Six months later, Amato pays cash to another seller of factory equipment for more equipment. Six months after that, Amato goes out of business before she has paid off her debt to Bronson. Bronson has a security interest in all of Amato's equipment, even the equipment bought from the other seller. •

FUTURE ADVANCES

Often, a debtor will arrange with a bank to have a *continuing line of credit* under which the debtor can borrow funds intermittently. Advances against lines of credit can be subject to a properly perfected security interest in certain collateral. The security agreement may provide that any future advances made against that line of credit are also subject to the security interest in the same collateral [UCC 9–204(3)].

• **EXAMPLE 22.5** Stroh is the owner of a small manufacturing plant with equipment valued at $1 million. He has an immediate need for $50,000 of working capital, so he obtains a loan from Midwestern Bank and signs a security agreement, putting up all of his equipment as security. The security agreement provides that Stroh can borrow up to $500,000 in the future, using the same equipment as collateral for any future advances. In this situation, Stroh does not have to execute a new security agreement and perfect a security interest in the collateral each time an advance is made up to a cumulative total of $500,000. •

THE FLOATING-LIEN CONCEPT

• **FLOATING LIEN**
A security interest in proceeds, after-acquired property, or property purchased under a line of credit (or all three); a security interest in collateral that is retained even when the collateral changes in character, classification, or location.

A security agreement that provides for a security interest in proceeds, in after-acquired property, or in property purchased under a line of credit (or in all three) is often characterized as a **floating lien.** This type of security interest continues in the collateral or proceeds even if the collateral is sold, exchanged, or otherwise disposed of, unless the disposition was authorized by the secured party [UCC 9–306(2)]. Floating liens commonly arise in the financing of inventories. A creditor is not interested in specific pieces of inventory, because they are constantly changing, so the lien "floats" from one item to another, as the inventory changes.

• **EXAMPLE 22.6** Suppose that Cascade Sports, Inc., a cross-country ski dealer, has a line of credit with Portland First Bank to finance an inventory of cross-country skis. Cascade and Portland First enter into a security agreement that provides for coverage of proceeds, after-acquired inventory, present inventory, and future advances. This security interest in inventory is perfected by filing centrally (with the office of the secretary of state). One day, Cascade sells a new pair of the latest cross-country skis, for which it receives a used pair in trade. That same day, it purchases two new pairs of cross-country skis from a local manufacturer with an additional amount of funds obtained from Portland First. Portland First gets a perfected security interest in the used pair of skis under the proceeds clause, has a perfected security interest in the two new pairs of skis purchased from the local manufacturer under the after-acquired property clause, and has the new amount of funds advanced to Cascade secured by the future-advances clause. All of this is accomplished under the original perfected security agreement. The various items in the inventory have changed, but Portland First still has a perfected security interest in Cascade's inventory, and hence it has a floating lien on the inventory. •

The concept of the floating lien can also apply to a shifting stock of goods. Under UCC 9–205, the lien can start with raw materials; follow them as they become finished goods and inventories; and continue as the goods are sold and are turned into accounts receivable, chattel paper, or cash.

Priorities among Security Interests

Whether a secured party's security interest is perfected or unperfected may have serious consequences for the secured party if the debtor defaults on the debt or files for bankruptcy. For example, what if the debtor has borrowed money from two different creditors, using the same property as collateral for both loans? If the debtor defaults on both loans, which of the two creditors has first rights to the collateral? In this situation, the creditor with a perfected security interest will prevail. Generally, the following UCC rules apply when more than one creditor claims rights in the same collateral:

¡KEEP IN MIND! Secured creditors—perfected or not—have priority over unsecured creditors.

1 *Conflicting perfected security interests.* When two or more secured parties have perfected security interests in the same collateral, generally the first to perfect (file or take possession of the collateral) has priority [UCC 9–312(5)(a)].
2 *Conflicting unperfected security interests.* When two conflicting security interests are unperfected, the first to attach has priority [UCC 9–312(5)(b)].
3 *Conflicting perfected security interests in commingled or processed goods.* When goods to which two or more perfected security interests attach are so manufactured or commingled that they lose their identities into a product or mass, the perfected parties' security interests attach to the new product or mass "according to the ratio that the cost of goods to which each interest originally attached bears to the cost of the total product or mass" [UCC 9–315(2)].

Under certain circumstances, on the debtor's default, the perfection of a security interest will not protect a secured party against certain other third parties having claims to the collateral. For example, the UCC provides that under certain conditions a PMSI, properly perfected,[3] will prevail over another security interest in after-acquired collateral, even though the other was perfected first [UCC 9–312].

• EXAMPLE 22.7 Suppose that Smith borrows funds from West Bank, signing a security agreement in which she puts up all of her present and after-acquired equipment as security. On May 1, West Bank perfects this security interest (which is not a PMSI). On July 1, Smith purchases a new piece of equipment from XYZ Company, paying 20 percent in cash and signing a security agreement in which she puts up the new equipment as security for the balance. The delivery date for the new piece of equipment is August 1. If Smith defaults on her payments to both West Bank and XYZ, which party has priority to the new piece of equipment, West Bank or XYZ? Generally, West Bank would have priority because it was perfected first in time. In this situation, however, XYZ has a PMSI, and if it perfects its interest by filing before Smith takes possession on August 1, or within ten days (twenty days, in many states) after that date, XYZ has priority. •

Because buyers should not be required to find out if there is an outstanding security interest in, for example, a merchant's inventory, the UCC also provides that a person who buys "in the ordinary course of business" will take the goods free from any security interest created by the seller in the purchased collateral.[4] This is so even if the security interest is perfected and *even if the buyer knows of its existence* [UCC 9–307(1)]. The UCC defines a *buyer in the ordinary course of business* as any person who in good faith, and without knowledge that the sale is in violation of the ownership rights or security interest of a third party in the goods, buys in ordinary course from a person in the business of selling goods of that kind [UCC 1–201(9)]. The priority of claims to a debtor's collateral is detailed in Exhibit 22–5.

Rights and Duties of Debtors and Creditors

"Let us live in a small circle as we will, we are either debtors or creditors before we have had time to look round."
JOHANN WOLFGANG VON GOETHE, 1749–1832
(German poet and dramatist)

The security agreement itself determines most of the rights and duties of the debtor and the secured party. The UCC, however, imposes some rights and duties that are applicable in the absence of a security agreement to the contrary.

3. Remember that, with some exceptions (such as motor vehicles), a PMSI in consumer goods is automatically perfected—no filing is necessary.
4. Under the Food Security Act of 1985, buyers in the ordinary course of business include buyers of farm products from a farmer. Under this act, these buyers are protected from prior perfected security interests unless the secured parties perfected centrally by a special form called an effective financing statement (EFS) or the buyers received proper notice.

EXHIBIT 22–5 • Priority of Claims to a Debtor's Collateral

PARTIES	PRIORITY
Unperfected Secured Party	Prevails over unsecured creditors and creditors who have obtained judgments against the debtor but who have not begun the legal process to collect on those judgments [UCC 9–301].
Purchaser of Debtor's Collateral	1. Goods purchased in the ordinary course of the seller's business—Purchaser prevails over a secured party's security interest, even if perfected and even if the purchaser knows of the security interest [UCC 9–307(1)]. 2. Consumer goods purchased out of the ordinary course of business—Purchaser prevails over a secured party's interest, even if perfected by attachment, providing purchaser purchased as follows: a. For value. b. Without actual knowledge of the security interest. c. For use as a consumer good. d. Prior to secured party's perfection by *filing* [UCC 9–307(2)].
Perfected Secured Parties to Same Collateral	Between two perfected secured parties in the same collateral, the general rule is that first in time of perfection is first in right to the collateral [UCC 9–312(5)]. Exceptions follow: 1. Crops—New value to produce crops given within three months of planting has priority over prior six-month perfected interest [UCC 9–312(2)]. 2. Purchase-money security interest—Even if second in time of perfection, it has priority, providing the following: a. Inventory—PMSI is perfected and proper written notice is given to the other security-interest holder *on* or *before* the time that debtor takes possession [UCC 9–312(3)]. b. Other collateral—PMSI has priority, providing it is perfected within ten days (twenty days, in many states) after debtor receives possession [UCC 9–312(4)].

Information Requests

Under UCC 9–407(1), a secured party has the option, when making the filing, of furnishing a *copy* of the financing statement being filed to the financing officer and requesting the filing officer to make a note of the file number, the date, and the hour of the original filing on the furnished copy. The filing officer must send this copy to the person making the request. Under UCC 9–407(2), a filing officer must also give information to a person who is contemplating obtaining a security interest from a prospective debtor. The filing officer must issue a certificate that provides information on possible perfected financing statements with respect to the named debtor. The filing officer will charge a fee for the certification and for any information copies provided.

Assignment, Amendment, and Release

Whenever desired, a secured party of record can release part or all of the collateral described in a filed financing statement. This ends his or her security interest in the released collateral [UCC 9–406]. A secured party can assign part or all of the security interest to another, called the assignee. That assignee becomes the secured party of record if, for example, he or she either makes a notation of the assignment somewhere on the financing statement or files a written statement of assignment [UCC 9–405(2)].

It is also possible to amend a financing statement that has already been filed. The amendment must be signed by both parties. The debtor signs the security agreement, the original financing statement, and the amendments [UCC 9–402]. All other secured transaction documents, such as releases, assignments, continuations of perfection, perfections of collateral moved into another jurisdiction, and termination statements, need only be signed by the secured party.

THE STATUS OF THE DEBT

At any time that the secured debt is outstanding, the debtor may wish to know the status of the debt. If so, the debtor need only sign a statement that indicates the aggregate amount of the unpaid debt at a specific date (and perhaps a list of the collateral covered by the security agreement) and send the statement to the secured party for approval or correction. The secured party (creditor) must then approve or correct this statement in writing. The creditor must comply with the request within two weeks of receipt; otherwise, the creditor is liable for any loss caused to the debtor by the failure to comply [UCC 9–208(2)]. One such request is allowed without charge every six months. For each additional request, the secured party—the creditor—can require a fee not exceeding $10 per request [UCC 9–208(3)].

TERMINATION STATEMENT

When a secured debt is paid, the secured party may send a termination statement to the debtor or file such a statement with the filing officer to whom the original financing statement was given. If the financing statement covers consumer goods, the termination statement must be filed by the secured party within one month after the debt is paid, or—if the debtor requests the termination statement in writing—it must be filed within ten days of receipt of such request after the debt is paid, whichever is earlier [UCC 9–404(1)].

In all other circumstances, the termination statement must be filed or furnished to the debtor within ten days after a written request is made by the debtor. If the affected secured party fails to file such a termination statement, as required by UCC 9–404(1), or fails to send the termination statement within ten days after proper demand, the secured party will be liable to the debtor for $100. Additionally, the secured party will be liable for any loss caused to the debtor.

Default

Article 9 defines the rights, duties, and remedies of the secured party and of the debtor on the debtor's default. Should the secured party fail to comply with his or her duties, the debtor is afforded particular rights and remedies.

"Nothing so cements and holds together all the parts of society as faith or credit, which can never be kept up unless men are under some force or necessity of honestly paying what they owe."

CICERO,
106–43 B.C.E.
(Roman politician, orator, and philosopher)

The topic of default is one of great concern to secured lenders and to the lawyers who draft security agreements. What constitutes default is not always clear. In fact, Article 9 does not define the term. Consequently, parties are encouraged in practice and by the UCC to include in their security agreements certain standards to be applied in determining when default occurs. In so doing, parties can stipulate the conditions that will constitute a default [UCC 9–501(1)]. Typically, because of the disparity in bargaining position between a debtor and a creditor, these critical terms are shaped by the creditor in an attempt to provide the maximum protection possible. The ultimate terms, however, are not allowed to go beyond the limitations imposed by the good faith requirement of UCC 1–203 and the unconscionability doctrine.

Although any breach of the terms of the security agreement can constitute default, default occurs most commonly when the debtor fails to meet the scheduled payments that the parties have agreed on or when the debtor becomes bankrupt.

BASIC REMEDIES

A secured party's remedies can be divided into two basic categories:

• **EXECUTION**
An action to carry into effect the directions in a court decree or judgment.

• **LEVY**
The obtaining of money by legal process through the seizure and sale of property, usually done after a writ of execution has been issued.

1. A secured party can relinquish a security interest and proceed to judgment on the underlying debt, followed by execution and levy. (**Execution** is the implementation of a court's decree or judgment. **Levy** is the obtaining of funds by legal process through the seizure and sale of property, usually done after a writ of execution has been issued.) Execution and levy are rarely undertaken unless the collateral is no longer in existence or its value has been reduced greatly below the amount of the debt and the debtor has other assets available that may be legally seized to satisfy the debt [UCC 9–501(1)].[5]
2. A secured party can take possession of the collateral covered by the security agreement [UCC 9–503]. On taking possession, the secured party may either retain the collateral for satisfaction of the debt [UCC 9–505(2)] or resell the goods and apply the proceeds toward the debt [UCC 9–504].

The rights and remedies under UCC 9–501(1) are *cumulative*. Therefore, if a creditor is unsuccessful in enforcing rights by one method, he or she can pursue another method.[6]

When a security agreement covers both real and personal property, the secured party can proceed against the personal property in accordance with the remedies of Article 9. Alternatively, the secured party can proceed against the entire collateral under procedures set down by local real estate law, in which case the UCC does not apply [UCC 9–501(4)]. Determining whether particular collateral is personal or real property at times can prove difficult, especially in dealing with fixtures—things affixed to real property. Under certain circumstances, the UCC allows the removal of fixtures on default; such removal, however, is subject to the provisions of Article 9 [UCC 9–313].

REPOSSESSION OF COLLATERAL

UCC 9–503 states that "[u]nless otherwise agreed, a secured party has on default the right to take possession of the collateral. In taking possession, a secured party may proceed without judicial process if this can be done without a breach of the peace." The underlying rationale for this "self-help" provision of Article 9 is that it simplifies the process of repossession for creditors and reduces the burden on the courts. Because the UCC does not define *breach of the peace,* however, it is not always easy to predict what will or will not constitute a breach of the peace.

Generally, the secured party or the secured party's agent cannot take the collateral by force or enter a debtor's house, garage, or place of business without permission. The latter action would constitute a trespass. Consider a situation in which an automobile is collateral. If the repossessing party walks onto the debtor's premises, proceeds up the driveway, enters the vehicle without entering the garage, and drives off, it probably will not amount to a breach of the peace. In some states, however, an action for wrongful trespass could start a cause of action for breach of the peace or other tortious action.

¡RECALL!
A trespass to land occurs when a person, without permission, enters onto another's land.

5. Some assets are exempt from creditors' claims—see Chapter 23.
6. See James J. White and Robert S. Summers, *Uniform Commercial Code,* 4th ed. (St. Paul: West Publishing Co., 1995), pp. 908–909.

ETHICAL ISSUE 22.1 ***Do the benefits of the "self-help" provision of Article 9 outweigh its potential harm?*** The "self-help" provision of Article 9 has generated substantial controversy because of its potential adverse consequences for both creditors and debtors. If a repossession attempt results in a "breach of the peace," the creditor may be barred from recovering the remainder of the debt from the debtor, and the breach may result in tort liability as well. A breach of the peace can, in turn, be emotionally distressful for the debtor. For example, suppose that a creditor (or someone hired by the creditor) appears on the debtor's property in the middle of the night to repossess collateral. A debtor in this situation may logically assume that someone is trying to steal his or her property; thus, violence and a "breach of the peace" may ensue. Additionally, in some cases, creditors (or persons hired by creditors) have engaged in outrageous conduct when repossessing collateral, which again may result in a breach of the peace (see, for example, the *Question of Ethics and Social Responsibility* at the end of this chapter). Finally, the "self-help" provision implicitly gives debtors a motive for resorting to violence and forcing a confrontation when collateral is being repossessed—because if the creditor breaches the peace, the creditor may be barred from recovering the rest of the debt.

DISPOSITION OF COLLATERAL

Once default has occurred and the secured party has obtained possession of the collateral, the secured party may sell, lease, or otherwise dispose of the collateral in any commercially reasonable manner [UCC 9–504(1)]. Any sale is always subject to procedures established by state law.

Retention of Collateral by the Secured Party The UCC acknowledges that parties are sometimes better off if they do not sell the collateral. Therefore, a secured party may retain collateral unless the collateral consists of consumer goods subject to a PMSI when the debtor has paid 60 percent or more of the purchase price or debt—as will be discussed shortly. This general right, however, is subject to several conditions. The secured party must send written notice of the proposal to the debtor if the debtor has not signed a statement renouncing or modifying his or her rights *after default*. If the collateral is consumer goods, the secured party does not need to give any other notice. In all other situations, the secured party must also send notice to any other secured party from whom the secured party has received written notice of a claim of interest in the collateral in question.

If within twenty-one days after the notice is sent, the secured party receives an objection in writing from a person entitled to receive notification, then the secured party must sell or otherwise dispose of the collateral in accordance with the provisions of UCC 9–504 (disposition procedures under UCC 9–504 will be discussed shortly). If no such written objection is forthcoming, the secured party can retain the collateral in full satisfaction of the debtor's obligation [UCC 9–505(2)].

Consumer Goods When the collateral is consumer goods with a PMSI and the debtor has paid 60 percent or more of the debt or the purchase price, then the secured party must sell or otherwise dispose of the repossessed collateral in accordance with the provisions of UCC 9–504 within ninety days. Failure to comply opens the secured party to an action for conversion or other liability under UCC 9–507(1) unless the consumer-debtor signed a written statement *after default* renouncing or modifying the right to demand the sale of the goods [UCC 9–505(1)].

¡REMEMBER!
Conversion is a tort that consists of an act depriving an owner of personal property without the owner's permission.

Disposition Procedures A secured party who does not choose to retain the collateral or who is required to sell it must resort to the disposition procedures prescribed under

UCC 9–504. The UCC allows a great deal of flexibility with regard to disposition. The only real limitations are that (1) the sale must be accomplished in a commercially reasonable manner, and (2) normally, the debtor must be notified of the sale.

What Qualifies as a Commercially Reasonable Sale? A secured party is not compelled to resort to public sale to dispose of the collateral. The party is given latitude under the UCC to seek out the best terms possible in a private sale. Generally, no specific time requirements must be met; however, the time must ultimately meet the standard of commercial reasonableness. Additionally, UCC 9–507(2) states as follows:

> The fact that a better price could have been obtained by a sale at a different time or in a different method from that selected by the secured party is not of itself sufficient to establish that the sale was not made in a commercially reasonable manner. If the secured party either sells the collateral in the usual manner in any recognized market therefor or if he sells at the price current in such a market at the time of sale or if he has otherwise sold in conformity with reasonable commercial practices among dealers in the type of property sold, he has sold in a commercially reasonable manner.

In the following case, the court had to decide whether a sale was conducted in a commercially reasonable manner. (See this chapter's *Business Law in Action* for a further discussion of this issue.)

CASE 22.2 First Westside Bank v. For-Med, Inc.

Supreme Court of Nebraska, 1995.
247 Neb. 641,
529 N.W.2d 66.

HISTORICAL AND SOCIAL SETTING *In the 1950s, the United States began building its interstate highway system. Wally Byam, known as "Mr. Trailer," organized caravans of cars and trailers to tour the new roads and to journey into Canada, Mexico, Central America, Europe, Africa, and the Middle East. Twenty years later, trailers had evolved into motor homes. Blue Bird motor homes have been described as the top of the line. There is a limited supply of Blue Birds, because the manufacturer does not want to saturate the market. Nationwide, there are less than a dozen Blue Bird dealers. A new Blue Bird can cost up to $200,000, depending on equipment, but depreciates at about 8 percent a year for the first decade.*

BACKGROUND AND FACTS David Anderson and For-Med, Inc., signed a security agreement with the First Westside Bank for $79,924.89, plus interest. The collateral for the loan was Anderson's Blue Bird motor home. Anderson and For-Med defaulted, and the bank took possession of the Blue Bird. The bank solicited bids for the motor home by word of mouth from other financial institutions, Blue Bird dealers, and some of its customers. Ultimately, the bank sold the motor home to a bank customer for $60,000. The buyer repaired the motor home at a cost of $22,000 and sold it two and a half years later for $58,000. Meanwhile, the bank sued For-Med and Anderson in a Nebraska state court for the difference between the amount due on the loan and the proceeds from the Blue Bird's sale. The court entered a judgment in favor of the bank. For-Med and Anderson appealed, acknowledging that although the price in the bank's sale had not been "wholly unreasonable," the sale had not been commercially reasonable, because it had not been advertised sufficiently.

IN THE WORDS OF THE COURT . . .
CAPORALE, Justice.

* * * *

* * * [I]t is the secured party's duty to the debtor to use all fair and reasonable means to obtain the best price under the circumstances, but the creditor need not use extraordinary means.

* * * *

* * * [U]nder particular circumstances, a sale may be commercially reasonable notwithstanding the lack of advertising.

Among the other factors to be considered in determining whether a sale of collateral was commercially reasonable is the adequacy or insufficiency of the price at

CASE 22.2—Continued

which it was sold. Here, the collateral was resold 2½ years after the purchaser acquired it, for an amount far less than he had invested in its purchase and repair. In light of that circumstance and the admission of For-Med and Anderson that the price at which the collateral was sold was not "wholly unreasonable," it cannot be said that the [lower] court's finding that the sale was commercially reasonable is clearly wrong.

DECISION AND REMEDY The Supreme Court of Nebraska affirmed the lower court's decision.

FOR CRITICAL ANALYSIS—Economic Consideration *Why should a court consider what the buyer of collateral does with it, or sells it for, after the secured party has disposed of it?*

Notice to the Debtor. The secured party normally must send to the debtor notice of any sale if the debtor has not signed a statement renouncing or modifying the right to notification of the sale *after default*. Except for the sale of consumer goods, notification also must be sent to any other secured party from whom the secured party has received written notice of a claim of interest in the collateral [UCC 9–504(3)]. Such notice is not necessary, however, when the collateral is perishable

Business Law in Action • CHALLENGING THE RESALE PRICE

As you will read later in this chapter, when a secured creditor sells repossessed collateral for a price lower than the amount of the secured debt, the creditor is entitled to collect the difference (deficiency) from the debtor. But what if the debtor believes that the creditor could have sold the collateral at a higher price, thus reducing the "deficiency" that the debtor is obligated to pay? Does the debtor have any recourse? Yes and no, according to Article 9 of the UCC.

Article 9 requires that a secured creditor, when disposing of repossessed collateral by sale, must conduct the sale in a "commercially reasonable" manner. If the debtor can show that the creditor has not complied with this requirement, the debtor may be able to reduce the deficiency. The problem here is that Article 9 does not define precisely what constitutes a "commercially reasonable" sale. As a result, the courts generally decide this issue on a case-by-case basis.

At the same time, Article 9 states that "[t]he fact that a better price could have been obtained by a sale at a different time or in a different method from that selected by the secured party is not of itself sufficient to establish that the sale was not made in a commercially reasonable manner" [UCC 9–507(2)]. Time and again, this provision has come into play when debtors assert that a better price for repossessed goods could have been obtained.

Consider a case brought by Claudia Prince in an Arkansas state court against R&T Motors, Inc., from whom she had purchased a Chevy Blazer. When Prince defaulted on her payments, R&T repossessed the Blazer and sold it, at a public sale, to another dealer for $8,500. R&T then sued Prince, who still owed R&T Motors $16,992.98 for the Blazer, for the deficiency. Prince argued that R&T could have obtained a much higher price for the Blazer. She contended that its value, as set out in the *Used Truck and Van Guide,* was over $12,000. In Prince's mind, R&T's sale of a van worth $12,000 for only $8,500 was not "commercially reasonable."

The court, however, concluded that the "bare assertion that a better price might have been realized" was not sufficient to show that the sale had violated Article 9's requirements. The court also noted that Prince "made no challenge to any other aspect of the repossession and sale." In a word, Prince lost out completely in her challenge. The court granted summary judgment for R&T Motors for the deficiency, as well as for prejudgment interest in the amount of $2,394.21, interest from the date of judgment at 10 percent, and attorneys' fees in the amount of $3,500.[a]

FOR CRITICAL ANALYSIS

Are Article 9 requirements relating to the resale of collateral slanted too heavily in favor of creditors?

a. *Prince v. R&T Motors, Inc.*, 59 Ark.App. 16, 953 S.W.2d 62 (1997).

or threatens to decline speedily in value, or when it is of a type customarily sold on a recognized market. Generally, notice of the place, time, and manner of the sale is required if the sale is to be classified as a sale conducted in a commercially reasonable manner.

How accurate should such a notice be in terms of informing a debtor of the amount owed, the date of the sale, and other details? The court addressed this question in the following case.

CASE 22.3 Fielder v. Credit Acceptance Corp.

United States District Court,
Western District of Missouri, 1998.
19 F.Supp.2d 966.

COMPANY PROFILE *For more than twenty-five years, Credit Acceptance Corporation (CAC) has helped thousands of auto dealers in the United States, Canada, and the United Kingdom obtain funds for used-car loans to people who have difficulty obtaining credit with other lenders. CAC's services include accounts management, payment collection, and staff training. The firm also provides credit life and disability insurance, vehicle protection insurance, vehicle service contracts, and risk-assessment and fraud-alert services.*

BACKGROUND AND FACTS Marvin Fielder and others signed contracts with Northeast Auto Credit, Inc. (NAC), and others to buy used cars. The sellers assigned the contracts to Credit Acceptance Corporation (CAC), which had supplied the contract forms to the sellers. When the buyers defaulted on the loans, CAC repossessed the cars and sent notices that they would be sold. Some of the notices overstated the amounts needed to redeem the vehicles (redemption rights are discussed later in this chapter) without indicating that the figures might be wrong. Others misstated the redemption dates or the dates of the sales. When CAC sold the cars for less than was owed under the contracts, it attempted to collect the difference. Fielder and other buyers filed a suit against CAC and NAC, charging in part that the notices violated UCC 9–504(3). Both sides filed motions for summary judgment in a federal district court.

IN THE WORDS OF THE COURT . . .
SMITH, District Judge.

* * * *

* * * [S]ome of the notices are deficient because the balance figures are overstated and the notices do not discuss [other] charges at all. * * * The Court finds that some of the notices in this case violated the statute because CAC's figures were not only incorrect but were unreasonably misleading as to the principal debt and the notices did not inform the debtors that the stated balance might be inaccurate. * * * Therefore, the debtors did not have reasonable notification of the sale because such notice is designed to ensure the debtors are aware of their rights which include redemption. Plaintiffs are granted summary judgment for those notices that contain inflated figures and no reference to the [other charges] * * * .

* * * *

Lastly, Plaintiffs claim that the pre-sale notices suffer from a host of other defects. Some of the notices contained dates of sale that were prior to the actual date of the notice. One notice was blank as to any date of sale. Another notice shows that payment to redeem must be made three days before the scheduled sale and yet others provide less notice than provided for in the contracts. All of these pre-sale notices violate section [UCC 9–504] and Plaintiffs' motion for summary judgment is granted.

DECISION AND REMEDY The court issued a summary judgment in the plaintiffs' favor for notices that contained inflated figures, without indicating that possibility, and for notices that misstated the redemption or sale dates. The court reasoned that these notices violated UCC 9–504(3).

FOR CRITICAL ANALYSIS—Social Consideration
How could CAC have avoided the result in this case?

International Perspective • THE ENFORCEABILITY OF A DEBTOR'S WAIVER OF NOTICE RIGHTS

To prevent challenges to the reasonability of sales of collateral, banks have sought to include clauses in loan contracts that essentially constitute waivers of this important right of debtors. In other words, a clause might state that if the debtor defaults and the bank chooses to repossess and sell the collateral, the debtor waives any right to be notified of the sale. In some countries, such as England, such waivers are enforceable. In the United States, however, they are generally not enforceable, because they are inconsistent with the UCC's requirement that the debtor be notified of any sale of collateral. Thus, a statement in a security agreement that the debtor waives the UCC notice requirement is null and void. To be enforceable, such a waiver must be made in a signed writing and only after the debtor's default.

FOR CRITICAL ANALYSIS
How does Article 9's requirement that the debtor be notified of any sale of the collateral benefit the debtor?

Proceeds from Disposition Proceeds from the disposition of collateral after default on the underlying debt must be applied in the following order:

1. Reasonable expenses stemming from the retaking, holding, or preparing for sale are paid first. When authorized by law and if provided for in the agreement, these can include reasonable attorneys' fees and other legal expenses.
2. Satisfaction of the balance of the debt owed to the secured party is then made.
3. Creditors with subordinate security interests whose written demands have been received prior to the completion of distribution of the proceeds are then entitled to receive the remaining proceeds from the sale [UCC 9–504(1)].
4. Unless the collateral consists of accounts or chattel paper, any surplus goes to the debtor.

Deficiency Judgment Often, after proper disposition of the collateral, the secured party has not collected all that the debtor still owes. Unless otherwise agreed, the debtor is liable for any deficiency, and the creditor can obtain a **deficiency judgment** from a court to collect the deficiency. Note, however, that if the underlying transaction was a sale of accounts or of chattel paper, the debtor is entitled to any surplus or is liable for any deficiency only if the security agreement so provides [UCC 9–504(2)].

• **DEFICIENCY JUDGMENT**
A judgment against a debtor for the amount of a debt remaining unpaid after collateral has been repossessed and sold.

Redemption Rights At any time before the secured party disposes of the collateral or enters into a contract for its disposition, or before the debtor's obligation has been discharged through the secured party's retention of the collateral, the debtor or any other secured party can exercise the right of *redemption* of the collateral. The debtor or other secured party can do this by tendering performance of all obligations secured by the collateral and by paying the expenses reasonably incurred by the secured party in retaking and maintaining the collateral [UCC 9–506].

APPLICATION

Law & the Creditor: Perfecting Your Security Interest*

The importance of perfecting your security interest cannot be overemphasized, particularly when the debt is large and you wish to maximize the priority of your security interest in the debtor's collateral. Failure to perfect or to perfect properly may result in your becoming the equivalent of an unsecured creditor.

The filing of a financing statement, either locally or centrally with the secretary of state, is the most common method of perfection. Generally, the moment the filing takes place, your priority over the other creditors is established, as well as your priority over some purchasers of the collateral and a subsequent trustee in bankruptcy.

When you create a financing statement, describe the collateral in terms that are specific enough to put third parties on notice of your security interest in that collateral. If your description is too general, your security interest will not be perfected.

Sometimes, credit transactions occur outside normal business relationships. You may be asked, for example, to aid an associate, a relative, or a friend. At that moment, you should reflect on your need for security for any debt that will be owed to you. If there is a need for security, then you should perfect your security interest, even if you believe this is an unnecessary action because the debtor is a friend or a relative. That particular friendship or blood relationship is irrelevant should he or she ever be forced into bankruptcy. Bankruptcy law does not allow friends or relatives to be paid ahead of nonfriends or nonrelatives. You will end up standing in line with the other unsecured creditors if you have not perfected your security interest in the collateral. The best way to protect your security interest by perfection is to have your friend, relative, or associate transfer to your possession the collateral—stocks, bonds, jewelry, or whatever. By possessing such collateral, you can keep the transaction private but still have security for the loan.

*This *Application* is not meant to substitute for the services of an attorney who is licensed to practice law in your state.

Checklist for Perfecting Your Security Interest

1. File a financing statement promptly.
2. Describe the collateral adequately—it is better to err by giving too much detail than by giving too little detail.
3. Even with friends, relatives, or associates, be sure to perfect your security interest, perhaps by having the debtor transfer the collateral to your possession.

Key Terms

after-acquired property 587
attachment 578
collateral 578
continuation statement 586
debtor 577
default 578
deficiency judgment 597
execution 592
financing statement 582
floating lien 588
levy 592
perfection 580
pledge 584
proceeds 586
purchase-money security interest (PMSI) 585
secured party 577
secured transaction 576
security agreement 578
security interest 577

Chapter Summary • Secured Transactions

Creating a Security Interest (See pages 578–580.)	1. Unless the creditor has possession of the collateral, there must be an agreement in writing, signed by the debtor, describing and reasonably identifying the collateral. 2. The secured party must give value to the debtor. 3. The debtor must have rights in the collateral—some ownership interest or right to obtain possession of the specified collateral.
Perfecting a Security Interest (See pages 580–586.)	1. *Perfection by filing*—The most common method of perfection is by filing a financing statement containing the names and addresses of the secured party and the debtor and describing the collateral by type or item. The financing statement must be signed by the debtor. a. State laws determine where the financing statement is to be filed—with the secretary of state, county clerk (or other local official), or both. b. Classification of collateral determines whether filing is necessary and where to file (see Exhibit 21–3). 2. *Perfection without filing*— a. By transfer of collateral—The debtor can transfer possession of the collateral to the secured party. This type of transfer is called a *pledge*. b. By attachment of a purchase-money security interest in consumer goods—If the secured party has a purchase-money security interest in consumer goods (goods bought or used by the debtor for personal, family, or household purposes), the secured party's security interest is perfected automatically. Exceptions: security interests in fixtures or motor vehicles.
The Scope of a Security Interest (See pages 586–588.)	A security agreement can cover the following types of property: 1. *Collateral in the present possession or control of the debtor.* 2. *Proceeds from a sale, exchange, or disposition of secured collateral.* 3. *After-acquired property*—A security agreement may provide that property acquired after the execution of the security agreement will also be secured by the agreement. This provision often accompanies security agreements covering a debtor's inventory. 4. *Future advances*—A security agreement may provide that any future advances made against a line of credit will be subject to the initial security interest in the same collateral.
Priorities among Security Interests (See pages 588–590.)	See Exhibit 22–5.
Rights and Duties of Debtors and Creditors (See pages 589–591.)	1. *Information requests*—On request by any person, the filing officer must send a statement listing the file number, the date, and the hour of the filing of financing statements and other documents covering collateral of a particular debtor; a fee is charged. 2. *Assignment, amendment, and release*—A secured party may (a) release part or all of the collateral described in a filed financing statement, thus ending the creditor's security interest; (b) assign part or all of the security interest to another party; and (3) amend a filed financing statement. 3. *The status of the debt*—If a debtor wishes to know the status of a secured debt, he or she may sign a descriptive statement of the amount of the unpaid debt (and a list of the covered collateral) as of a specific date and send the statement to the secured party for approval or correction. The creditor must then approve or correct this statement in writing within two weeks of receipt or be liable for any loss caused to the debtor by failure to do so. Only one request without charge is permitted per six-month period.

Chapter Summary • Secured Transactions, Continued

Rights and Duties of Debtors and Creditors—continued	4. *Termination statement*—When a debt is paid, the secured party generally must send to the debtor or file with the filing officer to whom the original financing statement was given a *termination statement.* Failure to comply results in the secured party's liability to the debtor for $100 plus any loss caused to the debtor. a. If the financing statement covers consumer goods, the termination statement must be filed by the secured party within one month after the debt is paid, or if the debtor requests the termination statement in writing, it must be filed within ten days of the request after the debt is paid—whichever is earlier. b. In all other cases, the termination statement must be filed or furnished to the debtor within ten days after a written request is made by the debtor.
Default (See pages 591–597.)	On the debtor's default, the secured party may do either of the following: 1. Relinquish the security interest and proceed to judgment on the underlying debt, followed by execution and levy on the nonexempt assets of the debtor. This remedy is rarely pursued. 2. Take possession (peacefully or by court order) of the collateral covered by the security agreement and then pursue one of two alternatives: a. Retain the collateral (unless the secured party has a purchase-money security interest in consumer goods and the debtor has paid 60 percent or more of the selling price or loan), in which case the secured party— (1) Must give written notice to the debtor if the debtor has not signed a statement renouncing or modifying his or her rights after default. With consumer goods, no other notice is necessary. (2) Must send notice to any other secured party who has given written notice of a claim to the same collateral. If an objection is received from the debtor or any other secured party within twenty-one days, in writing, the creditor must dispose of the collateral according to the requirements of UCC 9–504. Otherwise, the creditor may retain the collateral in full satisfaction of the debt. b. Sell the collateral, in which case the secured party— (1) Must sell the goods in a commercially reasonable manner at a public or private sale. (2) Must notify the debtor and (except in sales of consumer goods) other secured parties who have given written notice of claims to the collateral to be sold (unless the collateral is perishable or will decline rapidly in value). (3) Must apply the proceeds in the following order: (a) Expenses incurred by the sale (which may include reasonable attorneys' fees and other legal expenses). (b) Balance of the debt owed to the secured party. (c) Subordinate security interests of creditors whose written demands have been received prior to the completion of the distribution of the proceeds. (d) Surplus to the debtor (unless the collateral consists of accounts or chattel paper).

For Review

1. What is a security interest? Who is a secured party? What is a security agreement? What is a financing statement?
2. What three requirements must be met to create an enforceable security interest?
3. What is the most common method of perfecting a security interest under Article 9?
4. If two secured parties have perfected security interests in the collateral of the debtor, which party has priority to the collateral on the debtor's default?
5. What rights does a secured creditor have on the debtor's default?

Questions and Case Problems

22–1. Priority Disputes. Redford is a seller of electric generators. He purchases a large quantity of generators from a manufacturer, Mallon Corp., by making a down payment and signing an agreement to make the balance of payments over a period of time. The agreement gives Mallon Corp. a security interest in the generators and the proceeds. Mallon Corp. files a financing statement on its security interest centrally. Redford receives the generators and immediately sells one of them to Garfield on an installment contract, with payment to be made in twelve equal installments. At the time of sale, Garfield knows of Mallon's security interest. Two months later Redford goes into default on his payments to Mallon. Discuss Mallon's rights against purchaser Garfield in this situation.

22–2. Oral Security Agreements. Marsh has a prize horse named Arabian Knight. Marsh is in need of working capital. She borrows $5,000 from Mendez, with Mendez's taking possession of Arabian Knight as security for the loan. No written agreement is signed. Discuss whether, in the absence of a written agreement, Mendez has a security interest in Arabian Knight. If Mendez does have a security interest, is it a perfected security interest?

22–3. Default. Delgado is a retail seller of television sets. He sells a color television set to Cummings for $600. Cummings cannot pay cash, so she signs a security agreement, paying $100 down and agreeing to pay the balance in twelve equal installments of $50 each. The security agreement gives Delgado a security interest in the television set sold. Cummings makes six payments on time; then she goes into default because of unexpected financial problems. Delgado repossesses the set and wants to keep it in full satisfaction of the debt. Discuss Delgado's rights and duties in this matter.

22–4. The Scope of a Security Interest. Edward owned a retail sporting goods shop. A new ski resort was being created in his area, and to take advantage of the potential business, Edward decided to expand his operations. He borrowed a large sum of money from his bank, which took a security interest in his present inventory and any after-acquired inventory as collateral for the loan. The bank properly perfected the security interest by filing a financing statement. Edward's business is profitable, and he doubles his inventory. A year later, just a few months after the ski resort had opened, an avalanche destroyed the ski slope and lodge. Edward's business consequently took a turn for the worse, and he defaulted on his debt to the bank. The bank sought possession of his entire inventory, even though the inventory was now twice as large as it had been when the loan was made. Edward claimed that the bank only had rights to half his inventory. Is Edward correct? Explain.

22–5. Oral Security Agreements. John and Melody Fish bought various pieces of expensive jewelry, including a diamond ring, a diamond necklace, and a wedding band, from Odom's Jewelers. The Fishes agreed to make monthly installment payments to Odom's until the purchase price was paid in full. In 1988, the Fishes fell behind in their monthly payments on the account. The Fishes and Odom's orally agreed that the Fishes would return the jewelry to Odom's and that Odom's would hold the items for the Fishes until the account was paid. In 1991, the Fishes filed for bankruptcy protection. The jewelry was still in the possession of Odom's. One of the issues before the bankruptcy court was whether Odom's had a security interest in the jewelry. Did it? Explain. [*In re Fish,* 128 Bankr. 468 (N.D.Okla. 1991)]

22–6. Purchase-Money Security Interest. Barbara Wiegert and her daughter, Darcie Wiegert, went shopping at Sears, and Darcie bought a mattress and box spring for $396.11. Barbara later purchased from Sears a television set for $239.96. Both purchases were charged to the Sears credit card of Barbara (and her husband, Harold). On both credit slips was printed the following statement: "I grant Sears a security interest or lien in this merchandise, unless prohibited by law, until paid in full." When the Wiegerts filed their bankruptcy petition, the balance due to Sears was $587.26, plus interest. The Wiegerts claimed that Sears was an unsecured creditor. Sears claimed that it had a purchase-money security interest in the goods and that the security interest was perfected. Was Sears correct in making these claims? Discuss fully. [*In the Matter of Wiegert,* 145 Bankr. 621 (D.Neb. 1991)]

22–7. Perfection. Richard E. Walker, Kelly E. Walker, and Kenneth W. Walker were partners in the Walker Brothers Dairy, a general partnership located in Florida. The Walkers purchased a "Model 2955 utility tractor, a round bale saw, and a feed mixer box" from the John Deere Co. John Deere took a security interest in the equipment. The security agreement stated that the debtor was a partnership known as "Walker Brothers Dairy." John Deere filed a financing statement, however, that listed the debtors as "Richard Walker, Kelly Walker, and Kenneth Wendell Walker." Each of the three partners signed the statement. Their signatures were followed by a typewritten statement indicating that the partners were doing business as "Walker Brothers Dairy." When Walker Brothers Dairy voluntarily filed for bankruptcy, John Deere sought to repossess the equipment. The issue before the court was whether the financing statement, which listed as debtors the partners rather than the partnership, was sufficient to perfect John Deere's security interest in the partnership equipment. What should the court decide? Discuss. [*In re Walker,* 142 Bankr. 482 (M.D.Fla. 1992)]

22–8. Sale of Collateral. To pay for the purchases of several aircraft, Robert Wall borrowed funds from the Cessna Finance Corp., using the aircraft as collateral. Wall defaulted on the loans. Cessna took possession of the collateral (the aircraft) and sold it. Cessna filed a suit in a federal district court against Wall for the difference between the amount due on the loans and the amount received from the sale of the aircraft. Wall claimed that he could have obtained a higher price for the aircraft if he had sold it himself. What effect does the issue concerning whether a better price could have been obtained have on whether the sale was commercially reasonable? Discuss. [*Cessna Finance Corp. v. Wall,* 876 F.Supp. 273 (M.D.Ga. 1994)]

22–9. Debtor's Name. Cambria Fuel Oil Co. sold its business to 306 Fuel Oil Corp. As part of the deal, Cambria Fuel took a security interest in 306 Fuel's assets and filed a financing statement that identified 306 Fuel as the debtor. Six weeks later, 306 Fuel changed its name to Cambria Petroleum Co. Cambria Fuel did not file a new financing statement. Fleet Factors Corp. loaned money to Cambria Petroleum and took a security interest in the same assets as those subject to Cambria Fuel's security interest. When Cambria Petroleum failed to repay the loan, Fleet Factors filed suit in a New York state court to foreclose its security interest. Cambria Fuel claimed that its interest had priority. Whose security interest has priority? Why? [*Fleet Factors Corp. v. Bandolene Industries Corp.,* 86 N.Y.2d 519, 658 N.E.2d 202, 634 N.Y.S.2d 425 (1995)]

22–10. Repossession. Leroy Headspeth bought a car under an installment sales contract that expressly permitted the creditor to repossess the car if the debtor defaulted on the payments. The seller assigned the contract to Mercedes-Benz Credit Corp. (MBCC). When Headspeth defaulted on the payments, an agent of Laurel Adjustment Bureau, Inc. (LAB), went onto Headspeth's property and repossessed the car on MBCC's behalf. Headspeth filed a suit against MBCC and LAB, contending in part that LAB trespassed onto his property to retake the car and that therefore the repossession was wrongful. Headspeth admitted that the repossession occurred without confrontation. Can a secured creditor legally retake possession of collateral, on the debtor's default, by entering onto the debtor's land, or would that be an illegal breach of the peace? How will the court rule? Explain. [*Headspeth v. Mercedes-Benz Credit Corp.,* 709 A.2d 717 (D.C.App. 1998)]

A QUESTION OF ETHICS AND SOCIAL RESPONSIBILITY

22–11. Raymond and Joan Massengill borrowed money from Indiana National Bank (INB) to purchase a van. Toward the end of the loan period, the Massengills were notified by mail that they were delinquent on their last two loan payments. Joan called INB and said that she and her husband would go to the bank the following Monday morning and take care of the matter. In the meantime, INB had made arrangements for the van to be repossessed. At 1:30 A.M. Sunday morning, two men appeared at the Massengills' driveway and began to hook up the van to a tow truck. Raymond, assuming that the van was being stolen, went outside to intervene and did so vociferously. During the course of events, Massengill became entangled in machinery at the rear of the tow truck and was dragged down the street and then run over by his towed van. The "repo men"—those hired by INB to repossess the van—knew of Raymond's plight but sped away. The trial court granted summary judgment for the bank, ruling that the bank was not liable for the injuries caused by the repossession company. On appeal, however, the court ruled that the bank could be liable for the acts of the repossession company and remanded the case for the determination of damages. [*Massengill v. Indiana National Bank,* 550 N.E.2d 97 (Ind.App.1st Dist. 1990)]

1. Frequently, courts must decide, as in this case, whether the secured party should be held liable for the wrongful acts of persons hired by the secured party to undertake an actual repossession effort. Is it fair to hold the secured party liable for acts that the creditor did not commit? Why or why not?
2. Given the potential for violence during repossession efforts, why do you think Article 9 permits secured parties to resort to "self-help" repossessions?
3. Should repossession companies be prohibited from taking collateral from debtors' property during the middle of the night, when debtors are more likely to conclude that the activity is wrongful?

FOR CRITICAL ANALYSIS

22–12. Review the three requirements for an enforceable security interest. Why is each of these requirements necessary?

Online Activities

ONLINE EXERCISE 22-1

Access the Federal Trade Commission's "Consumer Protection" Web page at the following site:

www.ftc.gov/ftc/consumer.htm

Select "Automobiles," and read the article on "Vehicle Repossession." Then answer the following questions:

- If someone defaults on an automobile loan, can the creditor repossess the car at any time, even without prior notice to the debtor? Do state laws differ in this respect?
- What can the creditor do with the automobile, once it has been repossessed?
- Is the creditor allowed to sell any items of personal property that were in the car at the time of the repossession and apply the proceeds toward the debt owed?

ONLINE EXERCISE 22-2

Go to the following site, which is part of the Web site of Cornell University's Legal Information Institute:

www.law.cornell.edu/topics/debtor_creditor.html

- Look at the items listed in the right-hand column of this page. What federal statutes pertain to this area of the law?
- Look at one of the "Recent Decisions" on debtor-creditor law, and summarize the facts and issue involved in the case. How did the court decide the issue?

Before the Test

Go to the *Business Law Today* home page at http://blt.westbuslaw.com. Click on TestTutor.® You will find twenty interactive questions relating to this chapter.

CHAPTER 23

Creditors' Rights & Bankruptcy

> "Creditors are . . . great observers of set days and times."
>
> Benjamin Franklin, 1706–1790
> (American diplomat, author, and scientist)

CONTENTS

LEARNING OBJECTIVES

After reading this chapter, you should be able to:

1. Summarize the various remedies available to creditors, and indicate how and when creditors use these remedies to collect debts.
2. Differentiate between suretyship and guaranty arrangements.
3. Outline the typical steps in a bankruptcy proceeding.
4. Describe what property constitutes a debtor's estate in a bankruptcy proceeding and what property is exempt.
5. Compare and contrast the types of relief available under Chapter 7, Chapter 11, Chapter 12, and Chapter 13 of the Bankruptcy Code.

America's font of practical wisdom, Benjamin Franklin, observed a truth known to all debtors—that creditors do observe "set days and times" and will expect to recover their money at the agreed-on times. Historically, debtors and their families have been subjected to punishment, including involuntary servitude and imprisonment, for their inability to pay debts. The modern legal system, however, has moved away from a punishment philosophy in dealing with debtors. In fact, many observers say that it has moved too far in the other direction, to the detriment of creditors.

Normally, creditors have no problem collecting the debts owed to them. When disputes arise over the amount owed, however, or when the debtor defaults, what remedies are available to creditors? We have already discussed, in Chapter 22, the remedies available to secured creditors under Article 9 of the Uniform Commercial Code (UCC). In the first part of this chapter, we focus on other laws that assist the debtor and creditor in resolving their disputes without the debtor's having to resort to bankruptcy. The second part of this chapter discusses bankruptcy as a last resort in resolving debtor-creditor problems.

Laws Assisting Creditors

Both the common law and statutory laws create various rights and remedies for creditors. We discuss here some of these rights and remedies.

PAINTERS FINISH THE TRIM ON A HOUSE. IF THE HOMEOWNER DOES NOT PAY FOR THE WORK, WHAT CAN THE PAINTERS DO TO COLLECT WHAT THEY ARE OWED?

• **MECHANIC'S LIEN**
A statutory lien on the real property of another, created to ensure payment for work performed and materials furnished in the repair or improvement of real property, such as a building.

• **ARTISAN'S LIEN**
A possessory lien given to a person who has made improvements and added value to another person's personal property as security for payment for services performed.

"Creditors: One of a tribe of savages dwelling beyond the Financial Straits and dreaded for their desolating incursions."

AMBROSE BIERCE, 1842–1914
(American writer)

LIENS

As discussed in Chapter 18, a *lien* is an encumbrance on (claim against) property to satisfy a debt or protect a claim for the payment of a debt. Creditors' liens include mechanic's, artisan's, innkeeper's, and judicial liens.

Mechanic's Lien When a person contracts to provide labor, services, or materials for the purpose of making improvements or repairs on real property (land and things attached to the land, such as buildings and trees—see Chapter 41) but does not immediately pay for the improvements, the creditor can file a **mechanic's lien** on the property. This creates a special type of debtor-creditor relationship in which the real estate itself becomes security for the debt.

• EXAMPLE 23.1 A painter agrees to paint a house for a homeowner for an agreed-on price to cover labor and materials. If the homeowner refuses to pay for the work or pays only a portion of the charges, the painter can file a mechanic's lien against the property. The painter is the lienholder, and the real property is encumbered (burdened) with a mechanic's lien for the amount owed. If the homeowner does not pay the lien, the property can be sold to satisfy the debt. Notice of the foreclosure (the process by which the creditor deprives the debtor of his or her property) and sale must be given to the debtor in advance, however. •

Note that state law governs mechanic's liens. The time period within which a mechanic's lien must be filed is usually within 60 to 120 days from the last date labor or materials were provided.

Artisan's Lien An **artisan's lien** is a security device created at common law through which a creditor can recover payment from a debtor for labor and materials furnished in the repair or improvement of personal property. For example, if Cindy leaves her diamond ring at the jeweler's to be repaired and fails to pay for the repairs when they are completed, unless otherwise agreed the jeweler has a lien on Cindy's ring for the amount of the bill and normally can sell the ring in satisfaction of the lien.

In contrast to a mechanic's lien, an artisan's lien is possessory. The lienholder ordinarily must have retained possession of the property and have expressly or impliedly agreed to provide the services on a cash, not a credit, basis. When this occurs, the lien remains in existence as long as the lienholder maintains possession, and the lien is terminated once possession is voluntarily surrendered—unless the surrender is only temporary. If it is a temporary surrender, there must be an agreement that the property will be returned to the lienholder. Even with such an agreement, if a third party obtains rights in that property while it is out of the possession of the lienholder, the lien is lost. In a few situations, if state law so permits, a lienholder can protect a lien and surrender possession at the same time by recording notice of the lien in accordance with state lien and recording statutes.

Most statutes permit the holder of an artisan's lien to foreclose and sell the property subject to the lien to satisfy payment of the debt. As with the mechanic's lien, the holder of an artisan's lien is required to give notice to the owner of the property prior to foreclosure and sale. The sale proceeds are used to pay the debt and the costs of the legal proceedings, and the surplus, if any, is paid to the former owner.

• INNKEEPER'S LIEN
A possessory lien placed on the luggage of hotel guests for hotel charges that remain unpaid.

Innkeeper's Lien An **innkeeper's lien** is another possessory security device created at common law. An innkeeper's lien is placed on the baggage of guests for the agreed-on hotel charges that remain unpaid. If no express agreement has been made concerning the amount of those charges, then the lien will be for the reasonable value of the accommodations furnished. The innkeeper's lien is terminated either by the guest's payment of the hotel charges or by the innkeeper's surrender of the baggage to the guest, unless the surrender is temporary. Additionally, the lien is terminated by the innkeeper's foreclosure and sale of the property.

Judicial Liens When a debt is past due, a creditor can bring a legal action against the debtor to collect the debt. If a creditor is successful in the action, the court awards the creditor a judgment against the debtor (usually for the amount of the debt plus any interest and legal costs incurred in obtaining the judgment). Frequently, however, the creditor is unable to collect the awarded amount.

To ensure that a judgment in the creditor's favor will be collectible, creditors are permitted to request that certain nonexempt property of the debtor be seized to satisfy the debt. (As will be discussed later in this chapter, under state or federal statutes, certain property is exempt from seizure by creditors.) If the court orders the debtor's property to be seized prior to a judgment in the creditor's favor, the court's order is referred to as a *writ of attachment.* If the court orders the debtor's property to be seized following a judgment in the creditor's favor, the court's order is referred to as a *writ of execution.*

• ATTACHMENT
In the context of judicial liens, a court-ordered seizure and taking into custody of property prior to the securing of a judgment for a past-due debt.

Attachment. Recall from Chapter 22 that *attachment,* in the context of secured transactions, refers to the process through which a security interest in a debtor's collateral becomes enforceable. In the context of judicial liens, this word has another meaning: **attachment** is a court-ordered seizure and taking into custody of property prior to the securing of a judgment for a past-due debt. Attachment rights are created by state statutes. Attachment is a *prejudgment* remedy, because it occurs either at the time of default or immediately after the commencement of a lawsuit and before the entry of a final judgment. By statute, the restrictions and requirements for a creditor to attach before judgment are specific and limited. The due process clause of the Fourteenth Amendment to the Constitution limits the courts' power to authorize seizure of a debtor's property without notice to the debtor or a hearing on the facts.

• WRIT OF ATTACHMENT
A court's order, prior to a trial to collect a debt, directing the sheriff or other officer to seize nonexempt property of the debtor; if the creditor prevails at trial, the seized property can be sold to satisfy the judgment.

• WRIT OF EXECUTION
A court's order, after a judgment has been entered against the debtor, directing the sheriff to seize (levy) and sell any of the debtor's nonexempt real or personal property. The proceeds of the sale are used to pay off the judgment, accrued interest, and costs of the sale; any surplus is paid to the debtor.

To use attachment as a remedy, the creditor must have an enforceable right to payment of the debt under law, and the creditor must follow certain procedures. Otherwise, the creditor can be liable for damages for wrongful attachment. He or she must file with the court an *affidavit* (a written or printed statement, made under oath or sworn to) stating that the debtor is in default and stating the statutory grounds under which attachment is sought. The creditor must also post a bond to cover at least court costs, the value of the loss of use of the good(s) suffered by the debtor, and the value of the property attached. When the court is satisfied that all the requirements have been met, it issues a **writ of attachment,** which directs the sheriff or other officer to seize nonexempt property. If the creditor prevails at trial, the seized property can be sold to satisfy the judgment.

Writ of Execution. If the debtor will not or cannot pay the judgment, the creditor is entitled to go back to the court and obtain a court order, directing the sheriff to seize (levy) and sell any of the debtor's nonexempt real or personal property that is within the court's geographical jurisdiction (usually the county in which the courthouse is located). This order is called a **writ of execution.** The proceeds of the sale are used to pay off the judgment, accrued interest, and the costs of the sale. Any excess is paid to the debtor. The debtor can pay the judgment and redeem the nonexempt property any time before the sale takes place. (Because of exemption laws and bankruptcy laws, however, many judgments are virtually uncollectible.)

GARNISHMENT

• **GARNISHMENT**
A legal process used by a creditor to collect a debt by seizing property of the debtor (such as wages) that is being held by a third party (such as the debtor's employer).

Garnishment occurs when a creditor is permitted to collect a debt by seizing property of the debtor that is being held by a third party. Property held by a third party that is owed to the debtor may include the debtor's savings or checking-account funds held by a bank or wages held by an employer. Typically, a garnishment judgment is served on a debtor's employer so that part of the debtor's usual paycheck will be paid to the creditor. As a result of a garnishment proceeding, the court orders the debtor's employer to turn over a portion of the debtor's wages to pay the debt.

The legal proceeding for a garnishment action is governed by state law, and garnishment operates differently from state to state. According to the laws in some states, the creditor needs to obtain only one order of garnishment, which will then continuously apply to the debtor's weekly wages until the entire debt is paid. In other states, the creditor must go back to court for a separate order of garnishment for each pay period. Garnishment is usually a postjudgment remedy, but it can be a prejudgment remedy with a proper hearing by a court.

ON THE WEB
For an example of one state's (South Dakota's) laws on garnishment, go to
www.state.sd.us/state/legis/lrc/statutes/21/18/211800h.htm.

Both federal laws and state laws limit the amount of money that can be garnished from a debtor's weekly take-home pay.[1] Federal law provides a framework to protect debtors from suffering unduly when paying judgment debts.[2] State laws also provide dollar exemptions, and these amounts are often larger than those provided by federal law. Under federal law, garnishment of an employee's wages for any one indebtedness cannot be a ground for dismissal of an employee.

CREDITORS' COMPOSITION AGREEMENTS

• **CREDITORS' COMPOSITION AGREEMENT**
An agreement formed between a debtor and his or her creditors in which the creditors agree to accept a lesser sum than that owed by the debtor in full satisfaction of the debt.

Creditors may contract with the debtor for discharge of the debtor's liquidated debts (debts that are definite, or fixed, in amount) on payment of a sum less than that owed. These agreements are called **creditors' composition agreements,** or simply *composition agreements,* and are usually held to be enforceable.

MORTGAGE FORECLOSURE

• **MORTGAGEE**
Under a mortgage agreement, the creditor who takes a security interest in the debtor's real property.

• **MORTGAGOR**
Under a mortgage agreement, the debtor who gives the creditor a security interest in the debtor's real property in return for a mortgage loan.

Mortgage holders have the right to foreclose on mortgaged property in the event of a debtor's default. The usual method of foreclosure is by judicial sale of the property, although the statutory methods of foreclosure vary from state to state. If the proceeds of the foreclosure sale are more than sufficient to cover both the costs of the foreclosure and the mortgaged debt, the debtor receives any surplus. If the sale proceeds are insufficient to cover the foreclosure costs and the mortgaged debt, however, the **mortgagee** (the creditor-lender) can seek to recover the difference from the **mortgagor** (the debtor) by obtaining a deficiency judgment representing the

1. Some states (for example, Texas) do not permit garnishment of wages by private parties except under a child-support order.
2. For example, the federal Consumer Credit Protection Act of 1968, 15 U.S.C. Sections 1601–1693r, provides that a debtor can retain either 75 percent of the disposable earnings per week or the sum equivalent to thirty hours of work paid at federal minimum wage rates, whichever is greater.

difference between the mortgaged debt and the amount actually received from the proceeds of the foreclosure sale.

The mortgagee obtains a deficiency judgment in a separate legal action that he or she pursues subsequent to the foreclosure action. The deficiency judgment entitles the mortgagee to recover the amount of the deficiency from other nonexempt property owned by the debtor.

SURETYSHIP AND GUARANTY

When a third person promises to pay a debt owed by another in the event the debtor does not pay, either a *suretyship* or a *guaranty* relationship is created. Suretyship and guaranty have a long history under the common law and provide creditors with the right to seek payment from the third party if the primary debtor defaults on his or her obligations. Exhibit 23–1 illustrates the relationship between a suretyship or guaranty party and the creditor.

• **STRICT SURETYSHIP**
An express contract in which a third party to a debtor-creditor relationship (the surety) promises to be primarily responsible for the debtor's obligation. The surety has a right to be reimbursed by the co-debtor.

• **SURETY**
A person, such as a cosigner on a note, who agrees to be primarily responsible for the debt of another.

Surety A contract of **strict suretyship** is a promise made by a third person (the **surety**) to be primarily liable to a creditor, but by agreement with the principal debtor (co-debtor) can seek full reimbursement from the co-debtor if the surety pays the debt. It is an express contract between the surety (the third party) and the creditor, and it need not be in writing to be enforceable. The surety is primarily liable for the debt of the principal debtor. The creditor need not exhaust all legal remedies against the principal debtor before holding the surety responsible for payment. The creditor can demand payment from the surety from the moment the debt is due.

• **EXAMPLE 23.2** Robert Delmar wants to borrow money from the bank to buy a used car. Because Robert is still in college, the bank will not lend him the funds

EXHIBIT 23–1 • Suretyship and Guaranty Parties
In a suretyship or guaranty arrangement, a third party promises to be responsible for a debtor's obligations. A third party who agrees to be *primarily* liable for the debt (that is, liable even if the principal debtor does not default) is known as a surety; a third party who agrees to be *secondarily* liable for the debt (that is, liable only if the principal debtor defaults) is known as a guarantor. As noted in Chapter 12, normally a promise of guaranty (a collateral, or secondary, promise) must be in writing to be enforceable.

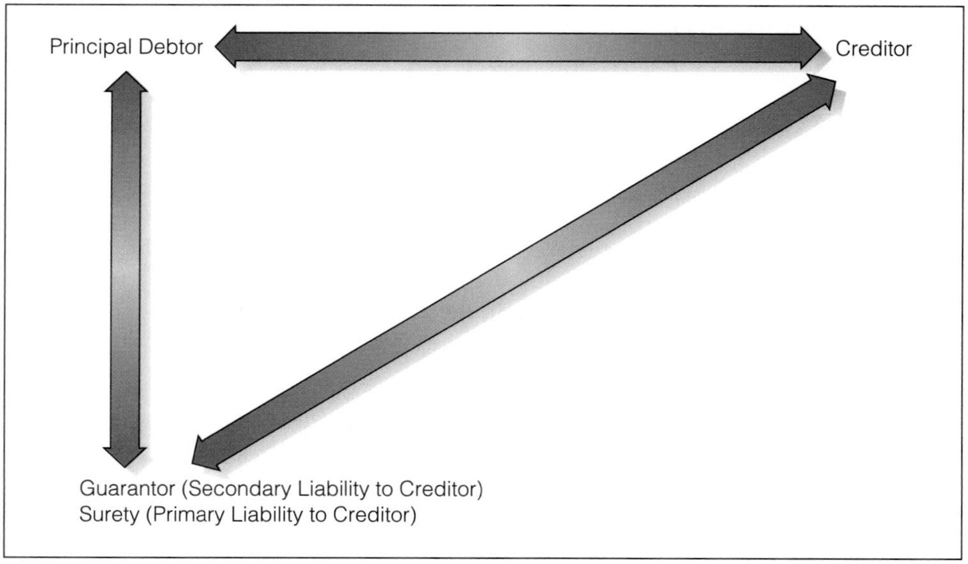

unless his father, Joseph Delmar, who has dealt with the bank before, will cosign the note (add his signature to the note, thereby becoming a surety and thus jointly liable for payment of the debt). When Joseph Delmar cosigns the note, he becomes primarily liable to the bank. By agreement between Robert and Joseph, if Joseph pays the debt, then he, as the surety, will be entitled to be reimbursed by Robert. On the note's due date, the bank has the option of seeking payment from either Robert or Joseph Delmar, or both jointly.●

Guaranty A guaranty contract is similar to a suretyship contract in that it includes a promise to answer for the debt or default of another. With a guaranty arrangement, the **guarantor**—the third person making the guaranty—is *secondarily* liable. The guarantor can be required to pay the obligation *only after the principal debtor defaults,* and default usually takes place only after the creditor has made an attempt to collect from the debtor.

• **GUARANTOR**
A person who agrees to satisfy the debt of another (the debtor) only after the principal debtor defaults; a guarantor's liability is thus secondary.

● EXAMPLE 23.3 A small corporation, BX Enterprises, needs to borrow money to meet its payroll. The bank is skeptical about the creditworthiness of BX and requires Dawson, its president, who is a wealthy businessperson and the owner of 70 percent of BX Enterprises, to sign an agreement making himself personally liable for payment if BX does not pay off the loan. As a guarantor of the loan, Dawson cannot be held liable until BX Enterprises is in default.●

The Statute of Frauds requires that a guaranty contract between the guarantor and the creditor must be in writing to be enforceable unless the *main purpose* exception applies. As discussed in Chapter 12, this exception provides that if the main purpose of the guaranty agreement is to benefit the guarantor, then the contract need not be in writing to be enforceable.

Defenses of the Surety and the Guarantor The defenses of the surety and the guarantor are basically the same. Therefore, the following discussion applies to both, although it refers only to the surety.

Certain actions will release the surety from the obligation. For example, any binding material modification in the terms of the original contract made between the principal debtor and the creditor—including a binding agreement to extend the time for making payment—without first obtaining the consent of the surety will discharge a gratuitous surety completely and a compensated surety to the extent that the surety suffers a loss. (An example of a gratuitous surety is a father who agrees to assume responsibility for his daughter's obligation; an example of a compensated surety is a venture capitalist who will profit from a loan made to the principal debtor.)

Naturally, if the principal obligation is paid by the debtor or by another person on behalf of the debtor, the surety is discharged from the obligation. Similarly, if valid tender of payment is made, and the creditor rejects it with knowledge of the surety's existence, then the surety is released from any obligation on the debt.

Generally, the surety can use any defenses available to a principal debtor to avoid liability on the obligation to the creditor. Defenses available to the principal debtor that the surety *cannot* use include the principal debtor's incapacity or bankruptcy and the statute of limitations. The ability of the surety to assert any defenses the debtor may have against the creditor is the most important concept in suretyship, because most of the defenses available to the surety are also those of the debtor.

Obviously, a surety may also have his or her own defenses—for example, incapacity or bankruptcy. If the creditor fraudulently induced the surety to guarantee the debt of the debtor, the surety can assert fraud as a defense. In most states, the creditor has a legal duty to inform the surety, prior to the formation of the suretyship contract, of material facts known by the creditor that would substantially increase the surety's risk. Failure to do so is presumed to constitute fraud and makes the suretyship obligation voidable. In addition, if a creditor surrenders the collateral to the debtor or impairs the collateral while knowing of the surety and without the surety's consent, the surety is released to the extent of any loss suffered from the creditor's actions. The primary reason for this requirement is to protect the surety who agreed to become obligated only because the debtor's collateral was in the possession of the creditor.

Rights of the Surety and the Guarantor The rights of the surety and the guarantor are basically the same. Therefore, again, the following discussion applies to both.

When the surety pays the debt owed to the creditor, the surety is entitled to certain rights. First, the surety has the legal **right of subrogation.** Simply stated, this means that any right the creditor had against the debtor now becomes the right of the surety. Included are creditor rights in bankruptcy, rights to collateral possessed by the creditor, and rights to judgments secured by the creditor. In short, the surety now stands in the shoes of the creditor and may pursue any remedies that were available to the creditor against the debtor.

• **RIGHT OF SUBROGATION**
The right of a person to stand in the place of (be substituted for) another, giving the substituted party the same legal rights that the original party had.

• **RIGHT OF REIMBURSEMENT**
The legal right of a person to be restored, repaid, or indemnified for costs, expenses, or losses incurred or expended on behalf of another.

Second, the surety has the **right of reimbursement** from the debtor. Basically, the surety is entitled to receive from the debtor all outlays made on behalf of the suretyship arrangement. Such outlays can include expenses incurred as well as the actual amount of the debt paid to the creditor.

• **CO-SURETY**
A joint surety; a person who assumes liability jointly with another surety for the payment of an obligation.

• **RIGHT OF CONTRIBUTION**
The right of a co-surety who pays more than his or her proportionate share on a debtor's default to recover the excess paid from other co-sureties.

Third, in the case of **co-sureties** (two or more sureties on the same obligation owed by the debtor), a surety who pays more than his or her proportionate share on a debtor's default is entitled to recover from the co-sureties the amount paid above the surety's obligation. This is the **right of contribution.** Generally, a co-surety's liability either is determined by agreement or, in the absence of agreement between the co-sureties, can be specified in, or inferred from, the suretyship contract itself.

• EXAMPLE 23.4 Assume that two co-sureties are obligated under a suretyship contract to guarantee the debt of a debtor. Together, the sureties' maximum liability is \$25,000. As specified in the suretyship contract, surety A's maximum liability is \$15,000, and surety B's is \$10,000. The debtor owes \$10,000 and is in default. Surety A pays the creditor the entire \$10,000. In the absence of any agreement between the two co-sureties, it is implied that the right of contribution is based on the ratio of maximum liability. Thus, surety A can recover \$4,000 from surety B (\$10,000/\$25,000 × \$10,000 = \$4,000). •

Laws Assisting Debtors

The law protects debtors as well as creditors. Certain property of the debtor, for example, is exempt from creditors' actions. Probably the most familiar of these exemptions is the homestead exemption. Each state permits the debtor to retain the family home, either in its entirety or up to a specified dollar amount, free from the claims of judgment creditors or trustees in bankruptcy. The purpose of the **homestead exemption** is to ensure that the debtor will retain some form of shelter.

• **HOMESTEAD EXEMPTION**
A law permitting a debtor to retain the family home, either in its entirety or up to a specified dollar amount, free from the claims of unsecured creditors or trustees in bankruptcy.

• EXAMPLE 23.5 Suppose that Van Cleave owes Acosta \$40,000. The debt is the subject of a lawsuit, and the court awards Acosta a judgment of \$40,000 against Van Cleave. Van Cleave's home is valued at \$50,000, and the state exemption on homesteads is \$25,000. There are no outstanding mortgages or other liens. To satisfy the judgment debt, Van Cleave's family home is sold at public auction for \$45,000. The proceeds of the sale are distributed as follows:

1. Van Cleave is given \$25,000 as his homestead exemption.

A NOTICE ANNOUNCES THE AUCTION OF A HOUSE. IF THE SALE IS TO PAY A DEBT, WHY SHOULDN'T THE CREDITOR BE PAID IN FULL BEFORE THE DEBTOR RECEIVES ANY PROCEEDS?

Public Notice
By order of the 8th District Court of Alameda, this property will be sold at public
AUCTION
Saturday, May 3 - Noon
All bids must be supported by bank certified check for at least 20% of the bid amount. Remainder of bid must be paid with certified check within 48 hours of bid.

❷ Acosta is paid $20,000 toward the judgment debt, leaving a $20,000 deficiency judgment that can be satisfied from any other nonexempt property (personal or real) that Van Cleave may have.●

State exemption statutes usually include both real and personal property. Personal property that is most often exempt from satisfaction of judgment debts includes the following:

❶ Household furniture up to a specified dollar amount.
❷ Clothing and certain personal possessions, such as family pictures or a Bible.
❸ A vehicle (or vehicles) for transportation (up to a specified dollar amount).
❹ Certain classified animals, usually livestock but including pets.
❺ Equipment that the debtor uses in a business or trade, such as tools or professional instruments, up to a specified dollar amount.

Consumer protection statutes (see Chapter 36) also protect debtors' rights. Of course, bankruptcy laws, which are discussed in the next section, are designed specifically to assist debtors in need of relief from their debts.

Bankruptcy and Reorganization

At one time, debtors who could not pay their debts as they came due faced harsh consequences, including imprisonment and involuntary servitude. Today, in contrast, debtors have numerous rights. Some of these rights have already been mentioned. We now look at another significant right of debtors: the right to petition for bankruptcy relief under federal law.

Bankruptcy law in the United States has two goals—to protect a debtor by giving him or her a fresh start, free from creditors' claims; and to ensure equitable treatment to creditors who are competing for a debtor's assets. Bankruptcy law is federal law, but state laws on secured transactions, liens, judgments, and exemptions also play a role in federal bankruptcy proceedings.

Current bankruptcy law is based on the Bankruptcy Reform Act of 1978, as amended. In this chapter, we refer to this act, as amended, as the Bankruptcy Code (or, more simply, the Code). The following *Landmark in the Law* traces the historical evolution of bankruptcy law and the importance of the 1978 Bankruptcy Reform Act.

"How often have I been able to trace bankruptcies and insolvencies to some lawsuit, . . . the costs of which have mounted up to large sums."

HENRY PETER BROUGHAM, 1778–1868
(English politician)

Landmark in the Law •

THE BANKRUPTCY REFORM ACT OF 1978

Article I, Section 8, of the U.S. Constitution gives Congress the power to establish "uniform Laws on the subject of Bankruptcies throughout the United States." Congress exercised this power in 1800, when the first bankruptcy law was enacted as a result of the business crisis created by restraints imposed on American trade by the British and French. In 1803, the law was repealed, and during the rest of the century—always in response to some crisis—Congress periodically enacted (and later repealed) other bankruptcy legislation. The National Bankruptcy Act of 1898, however, was not repealed, and since that time the United States has had ongoing federal statutory laws concerning bankruptcy. The 1898 act allowed only for *liquidation* in bankruptcy proceedings (which occurs when the debtor's assets are sold and the proceeds are distributed to creditors). Some relief through reorganization was first allowed by amendments to the 1898 act in the 1930s.

Modern bankruptcy law is based on the Bankruptcy Reform Act of 1978, which repealed the 1898 act and represented a major overhaul of federal bankruptcy law. The 1978 act attempted to remedy previous abuses of bankruptcy law and introduced more clarity into bankruptcy procedures. A major organizational change in the 1978 act was the establishment of a new system of bankruptcy courts, in which each federal judicial district would have an adjunct bankruptcy court with exclusive jurisdiction over bankruptcy cases. The act also specified that, in contrast to the lifetime terms of judges in other federal courts, bankruptcy court judges would have a fourteen-year term.

The 1978 act, referred to now simply as the Bankruptcy Code, has been amended several times since its passage. Amendments to the Code have created additional bankruptcy judgeships, placed bankruptcy court judges under the authority of the U.S. district courts, extended the bankruptcy trustee system nationally, granted more power to bankruptcy trustees in the handling of bankruptcy matters, and added a new chapter to the Bankruptcy Code (Chapter 12) to aid financially troubled farmers. The most significant amendments to the Bankruptcy Code were made by the Bankruptcy Reform Act of 1994. Among the many important changes of the 1994 act was the creation of a "fast-track" procedure for small-business debtors (those not involved in owning or managing real estate and with debts of less than $2 million) under Chapter 11 of the Code.

The 1978 act, which generally made it easier for debtors to obtain bankruptcy relief, has been criticized for making it too easy for debtors to discharge their debts in bankruptcy. Since 1980, the number of bankruptcy filings per year have climbed from less than 300,000 to over 1.4 million. This steep rise in the number of personal bankruptcy filings, which has continued even when the economy is booming, has caused Congress to again consider far-reaching bankruptcy reform measures. Bills currently before Congress would, among other things, make it more difficult to discharge certain debts in bankruptcy.

FOR CRITICAL ANALYSIS
The Code no longer refers to persons who file for bankruptcy as "bankrupts" but simply as "debtors." What does this change in terminology signify, if anything?

BANKRUPTCY COURTS

¡RECALL!
Congress regulates the jursidiction of the federal courts, within the limits set by the Constitution. Congress can expand or reduce the number of federal courts at any time.

Bankruptcy proceedings are held in federal bankruptcy courts. A bankruptcy court's primary function is to hold *core proceedings*[3] dealing with the procedures required to administer the estate of the debtor in bankruptcy. Bankruptcy courts are under the authority of U.S. district courts (see the chart showing the federal court system in Exhibit 3–2 in Chapter 3), and rulings from bankruptcy courts can be appealed to the district courts. Fundamentally, a bankruptcy court fulfills the role of an

3. Core proceedings are procedural functions, such as allowance of claims, decisions on preferences, automatic-stay proceedings, confirmation of bankruptcy plans, discharge of debts, and so on. These terms and procedures are defined and discussed in the following sections of this chapter.

administrative court for the district court concerning matters in bankruptcy. A bankruptcy court can conduct a jury trial if the appropriate district court has authorized it and if the parties to the bankruptcy consent to a jury trial.

TYPES OF BANKRUPTCY RELIEF

• **LIQUIDATION**
The sale of all of the nonexempt assets of a debtor and the distribution of the proceeds to the debtor's creditors. Chapter 7 of the Bankruptcy Code provides for liquidation bankruptcy proceedings.

The Bankruptcy Code, which is contained in Title 11 of the U.S. Code (U.S.C.), is divided into a series of "chapters." Chapters 1, 3, and 5 of the Code include general definitional provisions and provisions governing case administration and procedures, creditors, the debtor, and the estate. These three chapters of the Code apply generally to all types of bankruptcies. The next five chapters set forth the different types of relief that debtors may seek. Chapter 7 provides for **liquidation** proceedings (the selling of all nonexempt assets and the distribution of the proceeds to the debtor's creditors). Chapter 9 governs the adjustment of the debts of municipalities. Chapter 11 governs reorganizations. Chapter 12 (for family farmers) and Chapter 13 (for individuals) provide for adjustment of the debts of parties with regular income.[4]

In the following pages, we deal first with liquidation proceedings under Chapter 7 of the Code. We then examine the procedures required to obtain relief under Chapter 11, Chapter 12, and Chapter 13 of the Bankruptcy Code.

Chapter 7—Liquidation

• **DISCHARGE**
In bankruptcy proceedings, the extinction of the debtor's dischargeable debts.

Liquidation is the most familiar type of bankruptcy proceeding and is often referred to as an *ordinary,* or *straight, bankruptcy.* Put simply, debtors in straight bankruptcies state their debts and turn their assets over to trustees. The trustees sell the nonexempt assets and distribute the proceeds to creditors. With certain exceptions, the remaining debts are then **discharged** (extinguished), and the debtors are relieved of the obligation to pay the debts.

Any "person"—defined as including individuals, partnerships, and corporations—may be a debtor under Chapter 7. Railroads, insurance companies, banks, savings and loan associations, investment companies licensed by the Small Business Administration, and credit unions *cannot* be Chapter 7 debtors, however. Other chapters of the Code or other federal or state statutes apply to them. A husband and wife may file jointly for bankruptcy under a single petition.

FILING THE PETITION

• **PETITION IN BANKRUPTCY**
The document that is filed with a bankruptcy court to initiate bankruptcy proceedings. The official forms required for a petition in bankruptcy must be completed accurately, sworn to under oath, and signed by the debtor.

• **CONSUMER-DEBTOR**
An individual whose debts are primarily for purchases made for personal or household use.

A straight bankruptcy may be commenced by the filing of either a voluntary or an involuntary **petition in bankruptcy**—the document that is filed with a bankruptcy court to initiate bankruptcy proceedings.

Voluntary Bankruptcy A voluntary petition is brought by the debtor, who files official forms designated for that purpose in the bankruptcy court. A **consumer-debtor** (defined as an individual whose debts were incurred primarily for personal or family reasons) who has selected Chapter 7 must state in the petition, at the time of filing, that he or she understands the relief available under other chapters and has chosen to proceed under Chapter 7. If the consumer-debtor is represented by an attorney, the attorney must file an affidavit stating that he or she has informed the

4. There are no Chapters 2, 4, 6, 8, or 10 in Title 11. Such "gaps" are not uncommon in the U.S.C. This is because chapter numbers (or other subdivisional unit numbers) are sometimes reserved for future use when a statute is enacted. (A gap may also appear if a law has been repealed.)

debtor of the relief available under each chapter. Any debtor who is liable on a claim held by a creditor can file a voluntary petition. The debtor does not even have to be insolvent to do so.[5] The voluntary petition contains the following schedules:

1. A list of both secured and unsecured creditors, their addresses, and the amount of debt owed to each.
2. A statement of the financial affairs of the debtor.
3. A list of all property owned by the debtor, including property claimed by the debtor to be exempt.
4. A listing of current income and expenses.

The official forms must be completed accurately, sworn to under oath, and signed by the debtor. To conceal assets or knowingly supply false information on these schedules is a crime under the bankruptcy laws. If the voluntary petition for bankruptcy is found to be proper, the filing of the petition will itself constitute an order for relief. An **order for relief** relieves the debtor of the immediate obligation to pay the debts listed in the petition. Once a consumer-debtor's voluntary petition has been filed, the clerk of the court (or person directed) must give the trustee and creditors mailed notice of the order for relief not more than twenty days after the entry of the order.

• **ORDER FOR RELIEF**
A court's grant of assistance to a complainant. In bankruptcy proceedings, the order relieves the debtor of the immediate obligation to pay the debts listed in the bankruptcy petition.

As mentioned previously, debtors do not have to be insolvent to file for voluntary bankruptcy. Debtors do not have unfettered access to Chapter 7 bankruptcy proceedings, however. Section 707(b) of the Bankruptcy Code allows a bankruptcy court to dismiss a petition for relief under Chapter 7 if the granting of relief would constitute "substantial abuse" of Chapter 7.

• **EXAMPLE 23.6** Howard Rock, a consumer-debtor, petitions for Chapter 7 relief. The court might determine, after evaluating Rock's schedule listing current income and expenses, that Rock would be able to pay his creditors a reasonable amount from future income. In this situation, the court might conclude that it would be a substantial abuse of Chapter 7 to allow Rock to have his or her debts completely discharged. The court might dismiss Rock's Chapter 7 petition after a hearing and encourage Rock to file a repayment plan under Chapter 13 of the Code, if that would result in a substantial improvement in the creditors' receipt of payments. • In the following case, the court had to decide whether granting a Chapter 7 discharge to the debtor would constitute substantial abuse.

ON THE WEB

For information on bankruptcy law, including current articles and court cases on this topic, go to the Web site of the American Bankruptcy Institute at www.abiworld.org.

5. The inability to pay debts as they become due is known as *equitable* insolvency. A *balance-sheet* insolvency, which exists when a debtor's liabilities exceed assets, is not the test. Thus, it is possible for debtors to petition voluntarily for bankruptcy even though their assets far exceed their liabilities. This situation may occur when a debtor's cash-flow problems become severe.

CASE 23.1 Matter of Blair

United States Bankruptcy Court,
Northern District of Alabama,
Eastern Division, 1995.
180 Bankr. 656.

HISTORICAL AND POLITICAL SETTING *In the early 1980s, retailers and consumer lenders complained to Congress of an increasing number of Chapter 7 discharges being granted to debtors who creditors felt could actually afford to pay their debts. In response, Congress enacted the substantial abuse provision. The provision illustrates the tension between two principles underlying bankruptcy law: to give debtors the opportunity for a fresh start and to help creditors thwart the abuse of consumer credit. An indication of this tension is the fact that Congress did not define "substantial abuse" but left the task to the courts.*

BACKGROUND AND FACTS James Blair, Jr., owed primarily consumer debts of less than $7,000, and his income exceeded his living expenses by more than $200 a month. When he filed a petition for relief under Chapter 7, the court concluded that if he were to file a repayment plan under Chapter 13, his debts would be paid off in forty months. The bankruptcy administrator filed a motion to dismiss Blair's petition.

CASE 23.1—Continued

IN THE WORDS OF THE COURT . . .
JAMES S. SLEDGE, Bankruptcy Judge.

* * * *

* * * [T]he substantial abuse determination must be made on a case by case basis, in light of the totality of the circumstances. * * * [F]actors [that] should be considered * * * [include:] (1) Whether the bankruptcy petition was filed because of sudden illness, calamity, disability, or unemployment; (2) Whether the debtor incurred cash advances and made consumer purchases far in excess of his ability to pay; (3) Whether the debtor's proposed family budget is excessive or unreasonable; (4) Whether the debtor's schedules and statement of current income and expenses reasonably and accurately reflect the true financial condition; and (5) Whether the petition was filed in good faith.

* * * *

* * * [T]his Court concludes that granting this debtor relief under Chapter 7 would be a substantial abuse of the provisions of the chapter as well as perverting the purpose of the Bankruptcy Code: to give a fresh start to the honest but unfortunate debtor.

DECISION AND REMEDY The court dismissed Blair's petition.

FOR CRITICAL ANALYSIS—Economic Consideration *The court also stated that granting Blair relief under Chapter 7 would be "perverting the purpose of the Bankruptcy Code." What did the court mean by this statement?*

Involuntary Bankruptcy An involuntary bankruptcy occurs when the debtor's creditors force the debtor into bankruptcy proceedings. An involuntary case cannot be commenced against a farmer[6] or a charitable institution (or those entities not eligible for Chapter 7 relief—mentioned earlier), however. For an involuntary action to be filed against debtors, the following requirements must be met: If the debtor has twelve or more creditors, three or more of those creditors having unsecured claims totaling at least $10,775 must join in the petition. If a debtor has fewer than twelve creditors, one or more creditors having a claim of $10,775 may file.

A STORE ADVERTISES A COURT-ORDERED BANKRUPTCY SALE. ON WHAT BASIS MIGHT A COURT ENTER AN ORDER FOR RELIEF IN AN INVOLUNTARY BANKRUPTCY PROCEEDING INITIATED BY THE STORE'S CREDITORS?

If the debtor challenges the involuntary petition, a hearing will be held, and the debtor's challenge will fail if the bankruptcy court finds either of the following:

1. That the debtor is generally not paying debts as they become due.
2. That a general receiver, custodian, or assignee took possession of, or was appointed to take charge of, less than substantially all of the debtor's property within 120 days before the filing of the petition.

If the court allows the bankruptcy to proceed, the debtor will be required to supply the same information in the bankruptcy schedules as in a voluntary bankruptcy.

An involuntary petition should not be used as an everyday debt-collection device, and the Code provides penalties for the filing of frivolous (unjustified) petitions against debtors. Judgment may be granted against the petitioning creditors for the costs and attorneys' fees incurred by the debtor in defending against an involuntary petition that is dismissed by the court. If the petition is filed in bad faith, damages can be awarded for injury to the debtor's reputation. Punitive damages may also be awarded.

---

6. *Farmers* are defined as persons who receive more than 80 percent of their gross income from farming operations, such as tilling the soil; dairy farming; ranching; or the production or raising of crops, poultry, or livestock. Corporations and partnerships, as well as individuals, can be farmers.

AUTOMATIC STAY

• **AUTOMATIC STAY**
In bankruptcy proceedings, the suspension of virtually all litigation and other action by creditors against the debtor or the debtor's property; the stay is effective the moment the debtor files a petition in bankruptcy.

The filing of a petition, either voluntary or involuntary, operates as an **automatic stay** on (suspension of) virtually all litigation and other action by creditors against the debtor or the debtor's property. In other words, once a petition is filed, creditors cannot commence or continue most legal actions against the debtor to recover claims or to repossess property in the hands of the debtor. A secured creditor, however, may petition the bankruptcy court for relief from the automatic stay in certain circumstances, such as when a creditor seeks "adequate protection" against the possible loss or deterioration of the secured property. The automatic stay also does not apply to paternity, alimony, or family maintenance and support debts.

A creditor's failure to abide by an automatic stay imposed by the filing of a petition can be costly. If a creditor *knowingly* violates the automatic-stay provision (a willful violation), any party injured is entitled to recover actual damages, costs, and attorneys' fees and may also be entitled to recover punitive damages.

CREDITORS' MEETING AND CLAIMS

¡BE AWARE!
In most cases, creditors' meetings take only five or ten minutes. But a debtor who lies, commits bribery, conceals assets, uses a false name, or makes false claims is subject to a $5,000 fine and up to five years in prison.

Within a reasonable time after the order of relief is granted (not less than ten days or more than thirty days), the bankruptcy court must call a meeting of the creditors listed in the schedules filed by the debtor. The bankruptcy judge does not attend this meeting. The debtor must attend this meeting (unless excused by the court) and submit to an examination under oath. Failure to appear or making false statements under oath may result in the debtor's being denied a discharge of bankruptcy. At the meeting, the trustee ensures that the debtor is advised of the potential consequences of bankruptcy and of his or her ability to file under a different chapter.

In a bankruptcy case in which the debtor has no assets (called a "no-asset" case), creditors are notified of the debtor's petition for bankruptcy but are instructed not to file a claim. In such a situation, the creditors will receive no payment, and most, if not all, of the debtor's debts will be discharged.

If there are sufficient assets to be distributed to creditors, however, each creditor must normally file a *proof of claim* with the bankruptcy court clerk within ninety days of the creditors' meeting to be entitled to receive a portion of the debtor's estate. The proof of claim lists the creditor's name and address, as well as the amount that the creditor asserts is owed to the creditor by the debtor. If a creditor fails to file a proof of claim, the bankruptcy court or trustee may file the proof of claim on the creditor's behalf but is not obligated to do so. If a claim is for a disputed amount, the bankruptcy court will set the value of the claim.

Creditors' claims are automatically allowed unless contested by the trustee, the debtor, or another creditor. The Code, however, does not allow claims for breach of employment contracts or real estate leases for terms longer than one year. These claims are limited to one year's wages or rent, despite the remaining length of either contract in breach.

PROPERTY OF THE ESTATE

• **ESTATE IN PROPERTY**
In bankruptcy proceedings, all of the debtor's legal and equitable interests in property presently held, wherever located, together with certain jointly owned property, property transferred in transactions voidable by the trustee, proceeds and profits from the property of the estate, and certain property interests to which the debtor becomes entitled within 180 days after filing for bankruptcy.

On the commencement of a liquidation proceeding under Chapter 7, an **estate in property** is created. The estate consists of all the debtor's legal and equitable interests in property presently held, wherever located, together with certain jointly owned property, property transferred in transactions voidable by the trustee, proceeds and profits from the property of the estate, and certain after-acquired property. Interests in certain property—such as gifts, inheritances, property settlements (resulting from divorce), or life insurance death proceeds—to which the debtor becomes *entitled within 180 days after filing* may also become part of the estate. Thus, the filing of a bankruptcy petition generally fixes a dividing line: property acquired prior to the filing becomes property of the estate, and property acquired after the filing, except as just noted, remains the debtor's.

The issue in the following case was whether payments made under a covenant not to compete should be included in a debtor's estate. The covenant was entered into *before* the petition was filed, but the payments were due *after* the filing.

CASE 23.2 In re Andrews

United States Court of Appeals,
Fourth Circuit, 1996.
80 F.3d 906.
www.law.emory.edu/4circuit[a]

COMPANY PROFILE *John Andrews worked in the ready-mix concrete business most of his life. In 1974, he and various partners formed a ready-mix concrete company in Herndon, Virginia. The company, which ultimately came to be known as AMAX Corporation, grew to be successful, with annual sales of approximately $30 million. By expanding the customer contacts he developed at AMAX, in 1980 Andrews formed a real estate development company, which participated in joint ventures with builders and developers. In 1989, the owners of AMAX began negotiations with Tarmac Acquisition, Inc., for the purchase of AMAX. Experts valued the assets at about $9 million. AMAX's customer list, which represented the goodwill of the company, was valued at an additional $1 million.*

a. This Web page, which is part of a Web site maintained by Emory University School of Law, provides access to published opinions of the U.S. Court of Appeals for the Fourth Circuit. Click on "1996" and then on the "April" link. When that page opens, scroll down the list of cases to *Andrews v. Riggs National Bank of Washington.* Click on the case name to access this opinion.

BACKGROUND AND FACTS Tarmac Acquisition, Inc., bought AMAX Corporation, a ready-mix concrete company. As part of the deal, the AMAX owners, including John Andrews, signed agreements not to compete with Tarmac. Andrews was to receive $1 million, payable in quarterly installments over a five-year period. Three years later, Andrews filed a bankruptcy petition. He asked the federal bankruptcy court not to include, in the property of his estate (which would ultimately be distributed to creditors), any future installments. The court refused, and a federal district court affirmed this decision. Andrews appealed to the U.S. Court of Appeals for the Fourth Circuit.

IN THE WORDS OF THE COURT . . .
ELLIS, District Judge:

* * * *

* * * Pre-petition assets, like the NCA [noncompetition agreement] payments, are those assets rooted in the debtor's pre-petition activities, including any proceeds that may flow from those assets in the future. These assets belong to the estate and ultimately to the creditors. Post-petition assets are those that result from the debtor's post-petition activities and are his to keep free and clear of the bankruptcy proceeding.

* * * *

Seen in this light, the NCA payments due Andrews fall clearly on the pre-bankruptcy or "past" side of the bright line. These payments are plainly rooted in, and grow out of, Andrews's pre-petition activities. * * * [B]ut for the [AMAX] sale, there would have been no NCA and no quarterly payments to Andrews. * * * Given this close connection between the NCA and the pre-petition sale of the debtor's share in the concrete business, we are persuaded that the payments were well rooted in the pre-bankruptcy past. * * * [T]hey should be included in Andrews's estate.

DECISION AND REMEDY The U.S. Court of Appeals for the Fourth Circuit affirmed the lower court's decision.

FOR CRITICAL ANALYSIS—Ethical Consideration *How can you reconcile the court's decision with the rule that certain property interests to which the debtor becomes entitled within 180 days after filing a bankruptcy petition are a part of the debtor's estate?*

ON THE WEB

An excellent source for information on bankruptcy, including laws and court cases involving bankruptcy proceedings, is the Legal Information Institute (LII) at Cornell University. You can access the LII's Web page on this topic at www.law.cornell.edu/topics/bankruptcy.html.

Exempted Property

Any individual debtor is entitled to exempt certain property from the property of the estate. The Bankruptcy Code establishes a federal exemption scheme under which the following property is exempt:[7]

1. Up to $16,150 in equity in the debtor's residence and burial plot (the homestead exemption).
2. Interest in a motor vehicle up to $2,575.
3. Interest in household goods and furnishings, wearing apparel, appliances, books, animals, crops, and musical instruments up to $425 in a particular item but limited to $8,625 in total.
4. Interest in jewelry up to $1,075.
5. Any other property worth up to $850, plus any unused part of the $16,150 homestead exemption up to an amount of $8,075.
6. Interest in any tools of the debtor's trade, up to $1,625.
7. Certain life insurance contracts owned by the debtor.
8. Certain interests in accrued dividends or interests under life insurance contracts owned by the debtor.
9. Professionally prescribed health aids.
10. The right to receive Social Security and certain welfare benefits, alimony and support payments, and certain pension benefits.
11. The right to receive certain personal injury and other awards, up to $16,150.

Individual states have the power to pass legislation precluding debtors in their states from using the federal exemptions. At least thirty-four states have done this. In those states, debtors may use only state (not federal) exemptions. In the rest of the states, an individual debtor (or husband and wife who file jointly) may choose between the exemptions provided under state law and the federal exemptions. State laws may provide significantly greater protection for debtors than federal law. For example, Florida and Texas traditionally have provided for generous exemptions for homeowners. State laws may also define the property coming within an exemption differently than the federal law.

The Trustee's Role

• **U.S. TRUSTEE**
A government official who performs certain administrative tasks that a bankruptcy judge would otherwise have to perform.

Promptly after the order for relief has been entered, an interim, or provisional, trustee is appointed by the **U.S. trustee** (a government official who performs certain administrative tasks that a bankruptcy judge would otherwise have to perform). The interim trustee administers the debtor's estate until the first meeting of creditors, at which time either a permanent trustee is elected or the interim trustee becomes the permanent trustee. Trustees are entitled to compensation for services rendered, plus reimbursement for expenses.

The basic duty of the trustee is to collect the debtor's available estate and reduce it to money for distribution, preserving the interests of both the debtor and unsecured creditors. In other words, the trustee is accountable for administering the debtor's estate. To enable the trustee to accomplish this duty, the Code gives him or her certain powers, stated in both general and specific terms.

Trustee's Powers The trustee has the power to require persons holding the debtor's property at the time the petition is filed to deliver the property to the trustee. To

7. The dollar amounts stated in the Bankruptcy Code were adjusted automatically on April 1, 1998, and will be adjusted every three years thereafter based on changes in the Consumer Price Index.

enable the trustee to implement this power, the Code provides that the trustee occupies a position equivalent in rights to that of certain other parties. For example, in some situations, the trustee has the same rights as creditors and can obtain a judicial lien or levy execution on the debtor's property. This means that a trustee has priority over an unperfected secured party to the debtor's property. The trustee also has rights equivalent to those of the debtor.

In addition, the trustee has the power to avoid (cancel) certain types of transactions, including those transactions that the debtor could otherwise rightfully avoid, *preferences,* certain statutory *liens,* and *fraudulent transfers* by the debtor. Avoidance powers must be exercised within two years of the order for relief (the period runs even if a trustee has not been appointed). These powers of the trustee are discussed in more detail in the following subsections.

Voidable Rights A trustee steps into the shoes of the debtor. Thus, any reason that a debtor can use to obtain the return of his or her property can be used by the trustee as well. These grounds (for recovery) include fraud, duress, incapacity, and mutual mistake.

• **EXAMPLE 23.7** Rob sells his boat to Inga. Inga gives Rob a check, knowing that there are insufficient funds in her bank account to cover the check. Inga has committed fraud. Rob has the right to avoid that transfer and recover the boat from Inga. If Rob has filed for bankruptcy, once an order for relief has been entered for Rob, the trustee can exercise the same right to recover the boat from Inga. If the trustee does not take action, Rob is still able to enforce that right.[8] •

• **PREFERENCE**
In bankruptcy proceedings, property transfers or payments made by the debtor that favor (give preference to) one creditor over others. The bankruptcy trustee is allowed to recover payments made both voluntarily and involuntarily to one creditor in preference over another.

Preferences A debtor is not permitted to transfer property or to make a payment that favors—or gives a **preference** to—one creditor over others. The trustee is allowed to recover payments made both voluntarily and involuntarily to one creditor in preference over another.

To have made a preferential payment that can be recovered, an *insolvent* debtor generally must have transferred property, for a *preexisting* debt, during the *ninety days* prior to the filing of the petition in bankruptcy. The transfer must give the creditor more than the creditor would have received as a result of the bankruptcy proceedings. The trustee does not have to prove insolvency, as the Code provides that the debtor is presumed to be insolvent during this ninety-day period.

Sometimes the creditor receiving the preference is an insider—an individual, a partner, a partnership, or an officer or a director of a corporation (or a relative of one of these) who has a close relationship with the debtor. If this is the case, the avoidance power of the trustee is extended to transfers made within *one year* before filing; however, the *presumption* of insolvency is confined to the ninety-day period. Therefore, the trustee must prove that the debtor was insolvent at the time of an earlier transfer.

Not all transfers are preferences. To be a preference, the transfer must be made for something other than current consideration. Therefore, it is generally assumed by most courts that payment for services rendered within ten to fifteen days prior to the payment of the current consideration is not a preference. If a creditor receives payment in the ordinary course of business, such as payment of last month's telephone bill, the payment cannot be recovered by the trustee in bankruptcy. To be recoverable, a preference must be a transfer for an antecedent (preexisting) debt, such as a year-old printing bill. In addition, the Code permits a consumer-debtor to transfer

8. In a Chapter 11 reorganization (to be discussed later), for which generally no trustee exists, the debtor has the same avoiding powers as a trustee in a Chapter 7 liquidation. In repayment plans under Chapters 12 and 13 (also to be discussed later), a trustee must be appointed.

¡NOTE!
What the trustee does with property recovered as a preference, in most cases, is to sell it and distribute the proceeds to the debtor's creditors.

any property to a creditor up to a total value of $600, without the transfer's constituting a preference. Also, payments of certain other debts, including alimony and child support, are not preferences. If a preferred creditor has sold the property to an innocent third party, the trustee cannot recover the property from the innocent party.

Liens on Debtor's Property The trustee is permitted to avoid the fixing of certain statutory liens, such as a mechanic's lien, on property of the debtor. Liens that first become effective on the date that the bankruptcy petition was filed are also voidable by the trustee.

Fraudulent Transfers The trustee may avoid fraudulent transfers or obligations if they were made within one year of the filing of the petition or if they were made with actual intent to hinder, delay, or defraud a creditor. Transfers made for less than a reasonably equivalent consideration are also voidable if the debtor thereby became insolvent, was left engaged in business with an unreasonably small amount of capital, or intended to incur debts that would be beyond his or her ability to pay. When a fraudulent transfer is made outside the Code's one-year limit, creditors may seek alternative relief under state laws. State laws often allow creditors to recover for transfers made up to three years prior to the filing of a petition.

Property Distribution

Creditors are either secured or unsecured. As discussed in Chapter 22, a *secured* creditor has a security interest in collateral that secures the debt. An *unsecured* creditor does not have any security interest.

Secured Creditors The Code provides that a consumer-debtor, within thirty days of the filing of a Chapter 7 petition or before the date of the first meeting of the creditors (whichever is first), must file with the clerk a statement of intention with respect to the secured collateral. The statement must indicate whether the debtor will retain the collateral or surrender it to the secured party. Additionally, if applicable, the debtor must specify whether the collateral will be claimed as exempt property and whether the debtor intends to redeem the property or reaffirm the debt secured by the collateral. The trustee is obligated to enforce the debtor's statement within forty-five days after the statement is filed.

If the collateral is surrendered to the perfected secured party, the secured creditor can enforce the security interest either by accepting the property in full satisfaction of the debt or by foreclosing on the collateral and using the proceeds to pay off the debt. Thus, the secured party has priority over unsecured parties to the proceeds from the disposition of the secured collateral. Indeed, the Code provides that if the value of the secured collateral exceeds the secured party's claim, the secured party also has priority to the proceeds in an amount that will cover reasonable fees (including attorneys' fees, if provided for in the security agreement) and costs incurred because of the debtor's default. Any excess over this amount is used by the trustee to satisfy the claims of unsecured creditors. Should the secured collateral be insufficient to cover the secured debt owed, the secured creditor becomes an unsecured creditor for the remainder of the debt.

Unsecured Creditors Bankruptcy law establishes an order or priority for classes of debts owed to *unsecured* creditors, and they are paid in the order of their priority. Each class of debt must be fully paid before the next class is entitled to any of the proceeds—if there are sufficient funds to pay the entire class. If not, the proceeds are distributed *proportionately* to each creditor in the class, and all classes lower in priority on the list receive nothing. The order of priority among classes of unsecured creditors is as follows:

1. Administrative expenses—including court costs, trustee fees, and bankruptcy attorneys' fees.
2. In an involuntary bankruptcy, expenses incurred by the debtor in the ordinary course of business from the date of the filing of the petition up to the appointment of the trustee or the issuance by the court of an order for relief.
3. Unpaid wages, salaries, and commissions earned within ninety days of the filing of the petition, limited to $4,300 per claimant. Any claim in excess of $4,300 is treated as a claim of a general creditor (listed as number 9 below).
4. Unsecured claims for contributions to be made to employee benefit plans, limited to services performed during 180 days prior to the filing of the bankruptcy petition and $4,300 per employee.
5. Claims by farmers and fishers, up to $4,300, against debtor operators of grain storage or fish storage or processing facilities.
6. Consumer deposits of up to $1,950 given to the debtor before the petition was filed in connection with the purchase, lease, or rental of property or the purchase of services that were not received or provided. Any claim in excess of $1,950 is treated as a claim of a general creditor (listed as number 9 below).
7. Paternity, alimony, maintenance, and support debts.
8. Certain taxes and penalties due to government units, such as income and property taxes.
9. Claims of general creditors.

If any amount remains after the priority classes of creditors have been satisfied, it is turned over to the debtor.

DISCHARGE

From the debtor's point of view, the purpose of a liquidation proceeding is to obtain a fresh start through the discharge of debts.[9] Certain debts, however, are not dischargeable in a liquidation proceeding. Also, certain debtors may not qualify—because of their conduct—to have all debts discharged in bankruptcy.

¡BE AWARE!
Often, a discharge in bankruptcy—even under Chapter 7—does not free a debtor of *all* of his or her debts.

Exceptions to Discharge Claims that are not dischargeable under Chapter 7 of the Bankruptcy Code include the following:

1. Claims for back taxes accruing within three years prior to bankruptcy.
2. Claims for amounts borrowed by the debtor to pay federal taxes.
3. Claims against property or funds obtained by the debtor under false pretenses or by false representations.
4. Claims by creditors who were not notified of the bankruptcy; these claims did not appear on the schedules the debtor was required to file.
5. Claims based on fraud or misuse of funds by the debtor while he or she was acting in a fiduciary capacity or claims involving the debtor's embezzlement or larceny. (See this chapter's *Business Law in Action* for a further discussion of exceptions to discharge based on fraud.)
6. Alimony, child support, and (with certain exceptions) property settlements.
7. Claims based on willful or malicious conduct by the debtor toward another or the property of another.

9. Discharges are granted under Chapter 7 only to *individuals,* not to corporations or partnerships. The latter may use Chapter 11, or they may terminate their existence under state law.

Business Law in Action • Credit-Card Fraud—The Intent Factor

Today, it is relatively easy to obtain credit cards. It is also relatively easy, as many consumers have learned, to go heavily into debt by using credit cards. Indeed, sometimes consumers have taken advances on their credit cards even though they were aware that they probably would not be able to meet their credit-card payments. At issue in a number of bankruptcy cases is whether debtors who run up credit-card bills, knowing that they lack the ability to pay them, have engaged in fraud. How the courts decide this issue is important for both debtors and creditors because if such activity amounts to fraud, then the debt will not be dischargeable in bankruptcy.

Fraud, of course, requires intent. So a central question in bankruptcy cases dealing with this issue is whether a debtor's inability to pay a debt equates to fraud. In the past, many lower courts held that it did. This assumption seems to be changing, however. Consider a case that came before the Sixth Circuit Court of Appeals. In that case, Benethel Rembert, a woman who took $11,600 in cash advances on her credit cards to finance her gambling habit, was allowed to discharge the debt in bankruptcy. Rembert testified that she had hoped to repay the debt out of her gambling winnings, even though she realized that there was no reasonable expectation of being able to do this. Nonetheless, said the court, there was no fraud, because the debtor *intended* to repay the debt. According to the court, "To measure a debtor's intention to repay by her ability to do so, without more, would be contrary to one of the main reasons consumers use credit cards: because they often lack the ability to pay in full at the time they desire credit."

In determining a debtor's subjective intent, stated the court, it is necessary to look at the "totality of the circumstances." In Rembert's case, no evidence was presented to the bankruptcy court that indicated that Rembert used the credit cards without intending to repay the credit-card companies. Furthermore, Rembert had previously taken out a second mortgage on her home in the amount of $28,000 and used almost all of that amount to pay credit-card bills. She continued to make payments on her credit-card debts whenever she could. According to the court, "These facts indicate that Rembert subjectively intended to repay her debts. The fact that Rembert later admitted that it probably was not reasonable to believe that she would win enough money to repay the [debts] does not indicate a subjective intent not to repay her debts in this case."[a]

In making its determination, the court cited a previous case decided by the U.S. Court of Appeals for the Ninth Circuit, the only other federal appellate court to address this issue. That court had concluded that the "hopeless state of a debtor's financial condition should never become a substitute for an actual finding of bad faith."[b]

These rulings, while they may be good news for debtors, are not so for creditors. According to attorney Robert Markoff of Chicago, "Creditors are faced with a real uphill battle. If the debtor says she intended to pay, you're pretty much stuck."[c]

FOR CRITICAL ANALYSIS

What steps might creditors take to protect themselves against such problems?

a. *In re Rembert,* 141 F.3d 277 (6th Cir. 1998).
b. *In re Anastas,* 94 F.3d 1280 (9th Cir. 1996).
c. As quoted in Jake Halpern, "Credit Cards Easier to Discharge," *Lawyers Weekly USA,* May 4, 1998, p. 19.

8. Certain government fines and penalties.
9. Certain student loans, unless payment of the loans imposes an undue hardship on the debtor and the debtor's dependents.
10. Consumer debts of more than $1,075 for luxury goods or services owed to a single creditor incurred within sixty days of the order for relief. This denial of discharge is a rebuttable presumption (that is, the denial may be challenged by the debtor), however, and any debts reasonably incurred to support the debtor or dependents are not classified as luxuries.
11. Cash advances totaling more than $1,075 that are extensions of open-end consumer credit obtained by the debtor within sixty days of the order for relief. A denial of discharge of these debts is also a rebuttable presumption.
12. Judgments or consent decrees against a debtor as a result of the debtor's operation of a motor vehicle while intoxicated.

The Letter of the Law A LOAN BY ANY OTHER NAME . . .

Sometimes, debtors' attempts to get around the student-loan exception to discharge in bankruptcy can be quite creative. Consider the argument put forth by LeAnna Johnson, to whom Missouri Baptist College had extended credit in the amount of $5,892.49 for tuition, books, and other expenses. Because Johnson never received any funds from the college, just credit, she asserted that her debt to the college did not qualify as a "loan"; therefore, the debt should be dischargeable. Johnson failed to convince the bankruptcy court (or, on appeal, a bankruptcy appellate panel) of the soundness of her reasoning, however. The appellate panel, after a thorough discussion of case law bearing on the issue of what constitutes a loan and after checking various dictionary definitions of the term, affirmed the bankruptcy court's decision: the college's extension of credit to Johnson was definitely a student loan and, as such, not dischargeable in bankruptcy.[a]

THE BOTTOM LINE

As Johnson learned, a student loan by any other name is still a student loan.

a. *In re Johnson,* 218 Bankr. 449 (B.A.P. [Bankruptcy Appellate Panel] 8th Cir. 1998).

ETHICAL ISSUE 23.1 ***Should punitive damages for fraud be dischargeable in bankruptcy?*** As stated earlier, claims based on fraud are not dischargeable in bankruptcy. Often, a claim based on fraud consists of damages that were awarded to the creditor by a court in a lawsuit against the debtor for fraud. A question that sometimes comes before the courts is whether punitive damages, as well as actual damages, should be nondischargeable. How this question is answered depends on how a court interprets the language of the Bankruptcy Code with respect to fraud-based claims. Section 523(a)(2)(A) of the Code denies discharge in bankruptcy for "any debt . . . for money, property, services, or an extension, renewal, or refinancing of credit, to the extent obtained by . . . false pretenses, a false representation, or actual fraud." To resolve conflicting interpretations of this provision by the lower courts, the United States Supreme Court recently addressed the issue. In making its decision, the Court emphasized that the Bankruptcy Code "has long prohibited debtors from discharging liabilities incurred on account of their fraud, embodying a basic policy animating the Code of affording relief only to an 'honest but unfortunate debtor.'" According to the high court, when read in the historical context of bankruptcy law and other provisions of the current Bankruptcy Code, the relevant provision of the Code should be interpreted to mean that punitive damages for fraud are nondischargeable.[10]

In the following case, the debtor sought to have her student loans discharged in bankruptcy. The question before the court was whether payment of the loan would constitute an "undue hardship" for the debtor.

10. *Cohen v. De La Cruz,* __U.S.__, 118 S.Ct. 1212, 140 L.Ed.2d 341 (1998).

CASE 23.3 In re Baker

United States Bankruptcy Court, Eastern District of Tennessee, 1981.
10 Bankr. 870.

HISTORICAL AND SOCIAL SETTING *In 1980, about 53 percent of married women in the United States were working, compared with about 41 percent ten years earlier. More than 60 percent of wives who were separated from their husbands worked outside the home in 1980, compared with about 52 percent in 1970; for divorced women, the figures were about 74 percent and 72 percent, respectively. On average, however, in 1980, women earned only 62 cents for every dollar that men earned. In American families, husbands averaged nearly $21,000 in earnings and wives, $8,600. At the same time, of mothers who were*

(Continued)

CASE 23.3—Continued

entitled to child support, less than 75 percent actually received any payments. Of mothers living below the poverty line, more than 60 percent received nothing at all.

BACKGROUND AND FACTS Mary Lou Baker attended three different institutions of higher learning. At these three schools, she received educational loans totaling $6,635. After graduation, she was employed, but her monthly take-home pay was less than $650. Monthly expenses for herself and her three children were approximately $925. Her husband had left town and provided no child or other financial support. She received no public aid and had no other income. In January 1981, just prior to this action, Baker's church paid her gas bill so that she and her children could have heat in their home. One child had reading difficulty, and another required expensive shoes. Baker had not been well and had been unable to pay her medical bills. She filed for bankruptcy. In her petition, she sought a discharge of her educational loans based on the hardship provision.

IN THE WORDS OF THE COURT . . .
Ralph H. KELLEY, Bankruptcy Judge.

* * * *

* * * The restriction [against discharge of student loans] was designed to remedy an abuse by students who, immediately upon graduation, would file bankruptcy to secure a discharge of educational loans. These students often had no other indebtedness and could easily pay their debts from future wages.

* * * *

The court concludes that under the circumstances of this case, requiring the debtor to repay the debts * * * would impose upon her and her dependents an undue hardship. In passing [the restriction against discharge of student loans], Congress intended to correct an abuse. It did not intend to deprive those who have truly fallen on hard times of the "fresh start" policy of the new Bankruptcy Code.

DECISION AND REMEDY The debtor's student loans were discharged. Given the fact that she had "truly fallen on hard times," Baker should be allowed to have her debts discharged in bankruptcy to avoid undue hardship.

FOR CRITICAL ANALYSIS—Economic Consideration *Why does the Bankruptcy Code generally prohibit the discharge of student loans, such as those obtained through government-guaranteed educational loan programs?*

Objections to Discharge In addition to the exceptions to discharge previously listed, the following circumstances (relating to the debtor's conduct and not the debt) will cause a discharge to be denied:

1. The debtor's concealment or destruction of property with the intent to hinder, delay, or defraud a creditor.
2. The debtor's fraudulent concealment or destruction of financial records.
3. The debtor's discharge in bankruptcy within six years of the filing of the petition.[11]

When a discharge is denied under these circumstances, the assets of the debtor are still distributed to the creditors, but the debtor remains liable for the unpaid portions of all claims.

Effect of Discharge The primary effect of a discharge is to void, or set aside, any judgment on a discharged debt and prohibit any action to collect a discharged debt. A discharge does not affect the liability of a co-debtor.

Revocation of Discharge The Code provides that a debtor's discharge may be revoked. On petition by the trustee or a creditor, the bankruptcy court may, within one year, revoke the discharge decree if it is discovered that the debtor was fraudu-

11. A discharge under Chapter 13 of the Code within six years of the filing of the petition does not bar a subsequent Chapter 7 discharge when a good faith Chapter 13 plan paid at least 70 percent of all allowed unsecured claims and was the debtor's "best effort."

lent or dishonest during the bankruptcy proceedings. The revocation renders the discharge void, allowing creditors not satisfied by the distribution of the debtor's estate to proceed with their claims against the debtor.

Reaffirmation of Debt A debtor may voluntarily agree to pay off a debt—for example, a debt owed to a family member, close friend, or any creditor—notwithstanding the fact that the debt could be discharged in bankruptcy. An agreement to pay a debt dischargeable in bankruptcy is referred to as a *reaffirmation agreement.*

To be enforceable, reaffirmation agreements must be made before a debtor is granted a discharge, and they must be filed with the court. If the debtor is represented by an attorney, court approval is not required if the attorney files a declaration or affidavit stating that (1) the debtor has been fully informed of the consequences of the agreement (and a default under the agreement), (2) the agreement is made voluntarily, and (3) the agreement does not impose undue hardship on the debtor or the debtor's family. If the debtor is not represented by an attorney, court approval is required, and the agreement will be approved only if the court finds that the agreement will result in no undue hardship to the debtor and is in the best interest of the debtor.

The agreement must contain a clear and conspicuous statement advising the debtor that reaffirmation is not required. The debtor can rescind, or cancel, the agreement at any time prior to discharge or within sixty days of filing the agreement, *whichever is later.* This rescission period must be stated clearly and conspicuously in the reaffirmation agreement.

Chapter 11—Reorganization

"Debt rolls a man over and over, binding him hand and foot, and letting him hang upon the fatal mesh until the long-legged interest devours him."

HENRY WARD BEECHER, 1813–1887
(American clergyman, writer, and abolitionist)

The type of bankruptcy proceeding used most commonly by a corporate debtor is the Chapter 11 *reorganization.* In a reorganization, the creditors and the debtor formulate a plan under which the debtor pays a portion of his or her debts and the rest of the debts are discharged. The debtor is allowed to continue in business. Although this type of bankruptcy is commonly a corporate reorganization, any debtor (except a stockbroker or a commodities broker) who is eligible for Chapter 7 relief is eligible for relief under Chapter 11.[12] Railroads are also eligible.

The same principles that govern the filing of a liquidation petition apply to reorganization proceedings. The case may be brought either voluntarily or involuntarily. The same principles govern the entry of the order for relief. The automatic-stay provision is also applicable in reorganizations.

• **WORKOUT**
An out-of-court agreement between a debtor and his or her creditors in which the parties work out a payment plan or schedule under which the debtor's debts can be discharged.

In some instances, creditors may prefer private, negotiated debt-adjustment agreements, also known as **workouts,** to bankruptcy proceedings. Often these out-of-court workouts are much more flexible and thus more conducive to a speedy settlement. Speed is critical, because delay is one of the most costly elements in any bankruptcy proceeding. Another advantage of workouts is that they avoid the various administrative costs of bankruptcy proceedings.

A bankruptcy court, after notice and a hearing, may dismiss or suspend all proceedings in a case at any time if dismissal or suspension would better serve the interests of the creditors. The Code also allows a court, after notice and a hearing, to dismiss a case under reorganization "for cause." Cause includes the absence of a reasonable likelihood of rehabilitation, the inability to effect a plan, and an unreasonable delay by the debtor that is prejudicial to (may harm the interests of) creditors.[13] A debtor need not be insolvent to be entitled to Chapter 11 protection.[14]

12. *Toibb v. Radloff,* 501 U.S. 157, 111 S.Ct. 2197, 115 L.Ed.2d 145 (1991).
13. See 11 U.S.C. Section 1112(b).
14. *In re Johns-Manville Corp.,* 36 Bankr. 727 (S.D.N.Y. 1984).

DEBTOR IN POSSESSION

• **DEBTOR IN POSSESSION (DIP)**
In Chapter 11 bankruptcy proceedings, a debtor who is allowed to continue in possession of the property (the business) and to continue business operations.

On entry of the order for relief, the debtor generally continues to operate his or her business as a **debtor in possession (DIP).** The court, however, may appoint a trustee (often referred to as a *receiver*) to operate the debtor's business if gross mismanagement of the business is shown or if appointing a trustee is in the best interests of the estate.

The DIP's role is similar to that of a trustee in a liquidation. The DIP is entitled to avoid preferential payments made to creditors and fraudulent transfers of assets that occurred prior to the filing of the Chapter 11 petition. The DIP has the power to decide whether to cancel or assume obligations under executory contracts (contracts that have not yet been performed) that were made prior to the petition.

ETHICAL ISSUE 23.2 ***Should those who "bankrupt" a firm be allowed to continue to manage the firm as debtors in possession?*** Chapter 11 reorganizations have become the target of substantial criticism. One of the arguments against Chapter 11 is that it allows the very managers who "bankrupted" a firm to continue to manage the firm as debtors in possession while the firm is in Chapter 11 proceedings. According to some critics, the main beneficiaries of Chapter 11 corporate reorganizations are not the shareholder-owners of the corporations but attorneys and current management. Basically, these critics argue that reorganizations do not preserve companies' assets, because large firms must pay millions of dollars for attorneys and accountants during the reorganization process, which can take years to complete.

CREDITORS' COMMITTEES

As soon as practicable after the entry of the order for relief, a creditors' committee of unsecured creditors is appointed. The committee may consult with the trustee or the DIP concerning the administration of the case or the formulation of the reorganization plan. Additional creditors' committees may be appointed to represent special interest creditors. Orders affecting the estate generally will not be made without either the consent of the committee or a hearing in which the judge hears the position of the committee.

Businesses with debts of less than $2 million that do not own or manage real estate can avoid creditors' committees. In these cases, bankruptcy judges may enter orders without a committee's consent.

THE REORGANIZATION PLAN

A reorganization plan to rehabilitate the debtor is a plan to conserve and administer the debtor's assets in the hope of an eventual return to successful operation and solvency. The plan must be fair and equitable and must do the following:

1. Designate classes of claims and interests.
2. Specify the treatment to be afforded the classes. (The plan must provide the same treatment for each claim in a particular class.)
3. Provide an adequate means for execution.

Filing the Plan Only the debtor may file a plan within the first 120 days after the date of the bankruptcy court's order for relief. If the debtor does not meet the 120-day deadline, however, or if the debtor fails to obtain the required creditor consent (see below) within 180 days, any party may propose a plan. The plan need not provide for full repayment to unsecured creditors. Instead, unsecured creditors may receive a percentage of each dollar owed to them by the debtor. If a small-business debtor chooses to avoid creditors' committees, the time for the debtor's filing is shortened to 100 days, and any other party's plan must be filed within 160 days.

Acceptance and Confirmation of the Plan Once the plan has been developed, it is submitted to each class of creditors for acceptance. Each class must accept the plan unless the class is not adversely affected by the plan. A class has accepted the plan when a majority of the creditors, representing two-thirds of the amount of the total claim, vote to approve it. Even when all classes of claims accept the plan, the court may refuse to confirm it if it is not "in the best interests of the creditors." A spouse or child of the debtor can block the plan if it does not provide for payment of his or her maintenance, alimony, or support claims in cash.

• **CRAM-DOWN PROVISION**
A provision of the Bankruptcy Code that allows a court to confirm a debtor's Chapter 11 reorganization plan even though only one class of creditors has accepted it. To exercise the court's right under this provision, the court must demonstrate that the plan does not discriminate unfairly against any creditors and is fair and equitable.

Even if only one class of claims has accepted the plan, the court may still confirm the plan under the Code's so-called **cram-down provision.** In other words, the court may confirm the plan over the objections of a class of creditors. Before the court can exercise this right of cram-down confirmation, it must be demonstrated that the plan "does not discriminate unfairly" against any creditors and that the plan is "fair and equitable."

The plan is binding on confirmation. The debtor is given a reorganization discharge from all claims not protected under the plan. This discharge does not apply to any claims that would be denied discharge under liquidation.

Chapter 13—Repayment Plan

¡REMEMBER!
A secured debt is a debt in which a security interest in personal property or fixtures assures payment of the obligation.

Chapter 13 of the Bankruptcy Code provides for the "Adjustment of Debts of an Individual with Regular Income." Individuals (not partnerships or corporations) with regular income who owe fixed unsecured debts of less than $269,250 or fixed secured debts of less than $807,750 may take advantage of bankruptcy repayment plans. This includes salaried employees; individual proprietors; and individuals who live on welfare, Social Security, fixed pensions, or investment income. Many sole proprietors have a choice of filing under either Chapter 11 or Chapter 13. There are several advantages to repayment plans. One advantage is that they are less expensive and less complicated than reorganization proceedings or liquidation proceedings.

A Chapter 13 repayment plan can be initiated only by the filing of a voluntary petition by the debtor. Certain liquidation and reorganization cases may be converted to Chapter 13 with the consent of the debtor. A Chapter 13 repayment plan may be converted to a Chapter 7 liquidation at the request of either the debtor or, under certain circumstances, a creditor. A Chapter 13 repayment plan also may be converted to a Chapter 11 reorganization after a hearing. On the filing of a petition under Chapter 13, a trustee must be appointed. The automatic stay previously discussed also takes effect. Although the stay applies to all or part of a consumer debt, it does not apply to any business debt incurred by the debtor.

THE REPAYMENT PLAN

Shortly after the petition is filed, the debtor must file a repayment plan. This plan may provide either for payment of all obligations in full or for payment of a lesser amount. A plan of rehabilitation by repayment provides for the turnover to the trustee of such future earnings or income of the debtor as is necessary for execution of the plan. The time for payment under the plan may not exceed three years unless the court approves an extension. The term, with extension, may not exceed five years.

The Code requires the debtor to make "timely" payments, and the trustee is required to ensure that the debtor commences these payments. The debtor must begin making payments under the proposed plan within thirty days after the plan has been filed with the court. If the plan has not been confirmed, the trustee is instructed to retain the payments until the plan is confirmed and then distribute them accordingly. If the plan is denied, the trustee will return the payments to the debtor less any costs. Failure of the debtor to make timely payments or to begin payments within the thirty-day period will allow the court to convert the repayment plan to a liquidation bankruptcy or to dismiss the petition.

Confirmation of the Plan After the plan is filed, the court holds a confirmation hearing, at which interested parties may object to the plan. The court will confirm a plan with respect to each claim of a secured creditor under any of the following circumstances:

1. If the secured creditors have accepted the plan.
2. If the plan provides that creditors retain their claims against the debtor's property and if the value of the property to be distributed to the creditors under the plan is not less than the secured portion of their claims.
3. If the debtor surrenders the property securing the claim to the creditors.

Objection to the Plan Unsecured creditors do not have a vote to confirm a repayment plan, but they can object to it. The court can approve a plan over the objection of the trustee or any unsecured creditor only in either of the following situations:

1. When the value of the property to be distributed under the plan is at least equal to the amount of the claims.
2. When all the debtor's projected disposable income to be received during the three-year plan period will be applied to making payments. Disposable income is all income received less amounts needed to support the debtor and dependents and/or amounts needed to meet ordinary expenses to continue the operation of a business.

As emphasized by the decision in the following case, the timing of creditors' objections to a Chapter 13 plan is critical.

CASE 23.4 In re Andersen

United States Bankruptcy Appellate Panel,[a]
Tenth Circuit, 1998.
215 Bankr. 792.
www.utb.uscourts.gov/bap/bap.htm[b]

HISTORICAL AND SOCIAL SETTING *Resolving disputes as to the dischargeability of student loans has been a thorny issue for the courts. The Bankruptcy Code appears to require an all-or-nothing finding—that is, the entire amount of a student loan is either dischargeable or not. Most courts have agreed.*[c] *Frequently, a debtor may be able to pay part, but not all, of a loan, or may be able to pay the loan in full in the future when he or she is gainfully employed. In light of these variables, some courts allow more creative repayment plans, stating that only part of a debt is dischargeable or that repayment terms may be modified by the court.*

a. A bankruptcy appellate panel, with the consent of the parties, has jurisdiction to hear appeals from final judgments, orders, and decrees of bankruptcy judges.

b. This is the Web site for the U.S. Bankruptcy Court for the District of Utah. In the left-hand frame, click on the "Bankruptcy Appellate Panel" box. When the "United States Bankruptcy Appellate Panel for the Tenth Circuit" page opens in the right-hand box, click on the "Opinions" link. On that page, scroll down the list to the *Andersen* case (number 39), and click on the link to open it.

c. See, for example, *In re Shankwiler,* 208 Bankr. 701 (Bankr.C.D.Cal. 1997); and *In re Rivers,* 213 Bankr. 616 (Bankr.S.D.Ga. 1997).

Permitting debtors to use Chapter 13 to resolve a dispute about the dischargeability of a student loan can encourage the parties to find other inventive ways to compromise.

BACKGROUND AND FACTS Doreen Andersen had student loan obligations to a number of educational loan guaranty agencies and lending banks. She filed a Chapter 13 plan that contained the following information:

> All timely filed and allowed unsecured claims, including the claims of Higher Education Assistance Foundation [HEAF] and [other] government guaranteed education loans, shall be paid ten percent (10%) of each claim, and the balance of each claim shall be discharged. * * * [E]xcepting the aforementioned education loans from discharge will impose an undue hardship on the debtor and the debtor's dependents. Confirmation of debtor's plan shall constitute a finding to that effect and that said debt is dischargeable.

The lenders filed an objection to the treatment of their claims. Because the objection was untimely, however, the court denied it and confirmed the plan. Three years later, after Andersen fulfilled the plan, the court entered a discharge. When the lenders attempted to collect the balance of the loans, Andersen filed a suit in a bankruptcy court against them. The court held that the debts had not been discharged. Andersen appealed.

CASE 23.4—Continued

IN THE WORDS OF THE COURT . . .
MATHESON, Bankruptcy Judge.

* * * *

* * * The plan process, whether in a Chapter 11 or 12 or 13, is essentially consensual. It is carried on through a bargaining process. The Code allows a great deal of flexibility in devising the terms of these plans. It is important to remember that Chapter 13 imposes very few mandatory requirements as to the contents of a plan. Congress intended for debtors to have flexibility in dealing with their creditors. A plan that is filed and served is simply an offer to the creditors, one that may be deemed to have been accepted if the creditor does not object.

* * * [Andersen's] plan specifically stated the treatment to be accorded the [student] loans. No argument has been made that [the lenders were] not properly served with the plan and with notice, or that [they] lacked the opportunity either to object or to have a meaningful hearing. Indeed, [they] did respond and filed an objection, thereby indicating that [they] understood that the plan intended to grant relief affecting [their] interests. However, the objection was not timely filed and was denied for that reason, leading to confirmation of the plan. * * *

* * * *

* * * [Andersen's] plan does not purport to make a nondischargeable debt dischargeable. The plan, instead, resolved a potential controversy about whether payment of the student [loans] would result in an undue hardship to the debtor. Confirmation of the plan constituted a finding to that effect, thereby rendering the [loans] dischargeable. Thus the ultimate order of discharge properly discharged the balance of the student loan obligation.

DECISION AND REMEDY The bankruptcy appellate panel held that confirmation of the plan constituted a determination that payment of the student loans, beyond what was provided in the plan, would be an undue hardship for the debtor and made the loans dischargeable. The panel reversed the decision of the lower court and remanded the case for further proceedings, including the entry of a judgment that the unpaid student loans were discharged.

FOR CRITICAL ANALYSIS—Economic Consideration
How might the lenders have avoided the outcome in this case?

Modification of the Plan Prior to the completion of payments, the plan may be modified at the request of the debtor, the trustee, or an unsecured creditor. If any interested party has an objection to the modification, the court must hold a hearing to determine approval or disapproval of the modified plan.

DISCHARGE

After the completion of all payments, the court grants a discharge of all debts provided for by the repayment plan. Except for allowed claims not provided for by the plan, certain long-term debts provided for by the plan, and claims for alimony and child support, all other debts are dischargeable. A discharge of debts under a Chapter 13 repayment plan is sometimes referred to as a "superdischarge." One of the reasons for this is that the law allows a Chapter 13 discharge to include fraudulently incurred debt and claims resulting from malicious or willful injury. Therefore, a discharge under Chapter 13 may be much more beneficial to some debtors than a liquidation discharge under Chapter 7 might be.

Even if the debtor does not complete the plan, a hardship discharge may be granted if failure to complete the plan was due to circumstances beyond the debtor's control and if the value of the property distributed under the plan was greater than creditors would have received in a liquidation proceeding. A discharge can be revoked within one year if it was obtained by fraud.

Chapter 12—Family-Farmer Plan

The Bankruptcy Code defines a *family farmer* as one whose gross income is at least 50 percent farm dependent and whose debts are at least 80 percent farm related. The total debt must not exceed $1.5 million. A partnership or closely held corporation that is at least 50 percent owned by the farm family can also take advantage of Chapter 12.

The procedure for filing a family-farmer bankruptcy plan is very similar to the procedure for filing a repayment plan under Chapter 13. The farmer-debtor must file a plan not later than ninety days after the order for relief. The filing of the petition acts as an automatic stay against creditors' actions against the estate.

The content of a family-farmer plan is basically the same as that of a Chapter 13 repayment plan. The plan can be modified by the farmer-debtor but, except for cause, must be confirmed or denied within forty-five days of the filing of the plan.

Court confirmation of the plan is the same as for a repayment plan. In summary, the plan must provide for payment of secured debts at the value of the collateral. If the secured debt exceeds the value of the collateral, the remaining debt is unsecured. For unsecured debtors, the plan must be confirmed if either the value of the property to be distributed under the plan equals the amount of the claim or the plan provides that all of the farmer-debtor's disposable income to be received in a three-year period (or longer, by court approval) will be applied to making payments. Completion of payments under the plan discharges all debts provided for by the plan.

A farmer who has already filed a reorganization or repayment plan may convert the plan to a family-farmer plan. The farmer-debtor may also convert a family-farmer plan to a liquidation plan.

APPLICATION

Law & the Small-Business Owner: Preparing for Bankruptcy*

Chapter 11 of the Bankruptcy Code expresses the broad public policy of encouraging commerce. To this end, Chapter 11 allows financially troubled business firms to petition for reorganization in bankruptcy even while they are still solvent, so that the firms' business can continue. Small businesses, however, do not fare very well under Chapter 11. Although many megacorporations entering Chapter 11 emerge as functioning entities, very few smaller companies survive the process. The reason is that Chapter 11 proceedings are prolonged and extremely costly, and whether a firm survives is largely a matter of size. The greater the firm's assets, the greater the likelihood it will emerge from Chapter 11 intact.

If you ever are a small-business owner contemplating Chapter 11 reorganization, you can improve your chances of being among the survivors by planning ahead. You should take action before, not after, entering bankruptcy proceedings to ensure the greatest possibility of success. Your first step, of course, should be to do everything possible to avoid having to resort to Chapter 11. Discuss your financial troubles openly and cooperatively with creditors to see if you can agree on a workout or some other arrangement.

If it appears that you have no choice but to file for Chapter 11 protection, try to interest a lender in loaning you funds to see you through the bankruptcy. If your business is a small corporation, you might try to negotiate a favorable deal with a major investor. For example, you could offer to transfer stock ownership to the investor in return for a loan to pay the costs of the bankruptcy proceedings and an option to repurchase the stock when the firm becomes profitable again.

Most important, you should form a Chapter 11 plan prior to entering bankruptcy proceedings. Consult with creditors in advance to see what kind of a plan would be acceptable to them, and prepare your plan accordingly. Having an acceptable plan prepared before you file will help expedite the proceedings and thus save substantially on costs.

*This *Application* is not meant to substitute for the services of an attorney who is licensed to practice law in your state.

CHECKLIST FOR THE SMALL-BUSINESS OWNER

1. Try to negotiate workouts with creditors to avoid costly Chapter 11 proceedings.
2. If your business is a small corporation, see if a major investor will loan you funds to help you pay bankruptcy costs in return for stock ownership.
3. Consult with creditors in advance, and have an acceptable Chapter 11 plan prepared before filing in order to expedite bankruptcy proceedings and save on costs.

Key Terms

artisan's lien 605
attachment 606
automatic stay 616
consumer-debtor 613
co-surety 610
cram-down provision 627
creditors' composition agreement 607
debtor in possession (DIP) 626
discharge 613
estate in property 616
garnishment 607
guarantor 609
homestead exemption 610
innkeeper's lien 606
liquidation 613
mechanic's lien 605
mortgagee 607
mortgagor 607
order for relief 614
petition in bankruptcy 613
preference 619
right of contribution 610
right of reimbursement 610
right of subrogation 610
strict suretyship 608
surety 608
U.S. Trustee 618
workout 625
writ of attachment 606
writ of execution 606

Chapter Summary • Creditors' Rights and Bankruptcy

REMEDIES AVAILABLE TO CREDITORS	
Liens (See pages 605–607.)	1. *Mechanic's lien*—A nonpossessory, filed lien on an owner's real estate for labor, services, or materials furnished to or made on the realty. 2. *Artisan's lien*— A possessory lien on an owner's personal property for labor performed or value added. 3. *Innkeeper's lien*— A possessory lien on a hotel guest's baggage for hotel charges that remain unpaid. 4. *Judicial liens*— a. Attachment—A court-ordered seizure of property prior to a court's final determination of the creditor's rights to the property. Attachment is available only on the creditor's posting of a bond and in strict compliance with the applicable state statutes. b. Writ of execution—A court order directing the sheriff to seize (levy) and sell a debtor's nonexempt real or personal property to satisfy a court's judgment in the creditor's favor.
Garnishment (See page 607.)	A collection remedy that allows the creditor to attach a debtor's money (such as wages owed or bank accounts) and property that are held by a third person.
Creditors' Composition Agreement (See page 607.)	A contract between a debtor and his or her creditors by which the debtor's debts are discharged by payment of a sum less than the sum that is actually owed.
Mortgage Foreclosure (See page 607–608.)	On the debtor's default, the entire mortgage debt is due and payable, allowing the creditor to foreclose on the realty by selling it to satisfy the debt.
Suretyship or Guaranty (See pages 608–610.)	Under contract, a third person agrees to be primarily or secondarily liable for the debt owed by the principal debtor. A creditor can turn to this third person for satisfaction of the debt.
LAWS ASSISTING DEBTORS	
Exemptions (See pages 610–611.)	Numerous laws, including consumer protection statutes, assist debtors. Additionally, state laws exempt certain types of real and personal property from levy of execution or attachment. 1. *Real property*—Each state permits a debtor to retain the family home, either in its entirety or up to a specified dollar amount, free from the claims of judgment creditors or trustees in bankruptcy (homestead exemption).

Chapter Summary • Creditors' Rights and Bankruptcy, Continued

Exemptions—continued	2. *Personal property*—Personal property that is most often exempt from satisfaction of judgment debts includes the following: a. Household furniture up to a specified dollar amount. b. Clothing and certain personal possessions. c. Transportation vehicles up to a specified dollar amount. d. Certain classified animals, such as livestock and pets. e. Equipment used in a business or trade up to a specified dollar amount.

BANKRUPTCY—A COMPARISON OF CHAPTERS 7, 11, 12, AND 13

Issue	Chapter 7	Chapter 11	Chapters 12 and 13
Purpose	Liquidation.	Reorganization.	Adjustment.
Who Can Petition	Debtor (voluntary) or creditors (involuntary).	Debtor (voluntary) or creditors (involuntary).	Debtor (voluntary) only.
Who Can Be a Debtor	Any "person" (including partnerships and corporations) except railroads, insurance companies, banks, savings and loan institutions, investment companies licensed by the Small Business Administration, and credit unions. Farmers and charitable institutions cannot be involuntarily petitioned.	Any debtor eligible for Chapter 7 relief; railroads are also eligible.	*Chapter 12*—Any family farmer (one whose gross income is at least 50 percent farm dependent and whose debts are at least 80 percent farm related) or any partnership or closely held corporation at least 50 percent owned by a farm family, when total debt does not exceed $1.5 million. *Chapter 13*—Any individual (not partnerships or corporations) with regular income who owes fixed unsecured debts of less than $269,250 or fixed secured debts of less than $807,750.
Procedure Leading to Discharge	Nonexempt property is sold with proceeds to be distributed (in order) to priority groups. Dischargeable debts are terminated.	Plan is submitted; if it is approved and followed, the remaining debts are discharged.	Plan is submitted and must be approved if the debtor turns over disposable income for a three-year period; if the plan is followed, debts are discharged.
Advantages	On liquidation and distribution, most debts are discharged, and the debtor has an opportunity for a fresh start.	Debtor continues in business. Creditors can either accept the plan, or it can be "crammed down" on them. The plan allows for the reorganization and liquidation of debts over the plan period.	Debtor continues in business or possession of assets. If the plan is approved, most debts are discharged after a three-year period.

For Review

1. What is a prejudgment attachment? What is a writ of execution? How does a creditor use these remedies?
2. What is garnishment? When might a creditor undertake a garnishment proceeding?
3. In a bankruptcy proceeding, what constitutes the debtor's estate in property? What property is exempt from the estate under federal bankruptcy law?
4. What is the difference between an exception to discharge and an objection to discharge?
5. In a Chapter 11 reorganization, what is the role of the debtor in possession?

Questions and Case Problems

23–1. Creditors' Remedies. In what circumstances would a creditor resort to each of the following remedies when trying to collect on a debt?

(a) Mechanic's lien.
(b) Artisan's lien.
(c) Innkeeper's lien.
(d) Writ of attachment.
(e) Writ of execution.
(f) Garnishment.

23–2. Rights of the Surety. Meredith, a farmer, borrowed $5,000 from Farmer's Bank and gave the bank $4,000 in bearer bonds to hold as collateral for the loan. Meredith's neighbor, Peterson, who had known Meredith for years, signed as a surety on the note. Because of a drought, Meredith's harvest that year was only a fraction of what it normally was, and he was forced to default on his payments to Farmer's Bank. The bank did not immediately sell the bonds but instead requested $5,000 from Peterson. Peterson paid the $5,000 and then demanded that the bank give him the $4,000 in securities. Can Peterson enforce this demand? Explain.

23–3. Rights of the Guarantor. Sabrina is a student at Sunnyside University. In need of funds to pay for tuition and books, she attempts to secure a short-term loan from University Bank. The bank agrees to make a loan if Sabrina will have someone financially responsible guarantee the loan payments. Abigail, a well-known businessperson and a friend of Sabrina's family, calls the bank and agrees to pay the loan if Sabrina cannot. Because of Abigail's reputation, the bank makes the loan. Sabrina makes several payments on the loan, but because of illness she is not able to work for one month. She requests that University Bank extend the loan for three months. The bank agrees and raises the interest rate for the extended period. Abigail has not been notified of the extension (and therefore has not consented to it). One month later, Sabrina drops out of school. All attempts to collect from Sabrina have failed. University Bank wants to hold Abigail liable. Will the bank succeed? Explain.

23–4. Distribution of Property. Runyan voluntarily petitions for bankruptcy. He has three major claims against his estate. One is by Calvin, a friend who holds Runyan's negotiable promissory note for $2,500; one is by Kohak, an employee who is owed three months' back wages of $4,500; and one is by the First Bank of Sunny Acres on an unsecured loan of $5,000. In addition, Martinez, an accountant retained by the trustee, is owed $500, and property taxes of $1,000 are owed to Micanopa County. Runyan's nonexempt property has been liquidated, with the proceeds totaling $5,000. Discuss fully what amount each party will receive, and why.

23–5. Creditors' Remedies. Orkin owns a relatively old home valued at $45,000. He notices that the bathtubs and fixtures in both bathrooms are leaking and need to be replaced. He contracts with Pike to replace the bathtubs and fixtures. Pike replaces them and submits her bill of $4,000 to Orkin. Because of financial difficulties, Orkin does not pay the bill. Orkin's only asset is his home, which under state law is exempt up to $40,000 as a homestead. Discuss fully Pike's remedies in this situation.

23–6. Writ of Attachment. Topjian Plumbing and Heating, Inc., the plaintiff, sought prejudgment writs of attachment to satisfy an anticipated judgment in a contract action against Bruce Topjian, Inc., the defendant. The plaintiff did not petition the court for permission to attach the defendant's property but merely completed the forms, served them on the defendant and on the Fencers (the owners of a parcel of land that had previously belonged to the defendant), and recorded them at the registry of deeds. On what grounds might the court invalidate the attachments? [*Topjian Plumbing and Heating, Inc. v. Bruce Topjian, Inc.*, 129 N.H. 481, 529 A.2d 391 (1987)]

23–7. Preferences. Fred Currey purchased cattle from Itano Farms, Inc. As payment for the cattle, Currey gave Itano Farms worthless checks in the amount of $50,250. Currey was later convicted of passing bad checks, and the state criminal court ordered him to pay Itano Farms restitution in the amount of $50,250. About four months after this court order, Currey and his wife filed for Chapter 7 bankruptcy protection. During the ninety days prior to the filing of the petition, Currey had made three restitution payments to Itano, totaling $14,821. The Curreys sought to recover these payments as preferences. What should the court decide? Explain. [*In re Currey*, 144 Bankr. 490 (D.Ida. 1992)]

23–8. Dismissal of Chapter 7 Case. Ellis and Bonnie Jarrell filed a Chapter 7 petition. The reason for filing was not a calamity, sudden illness, disability, or unemployment—both Jarrells were employed. Their petition was full of inaccuracies that understated their income and overstated their obligations. For example, they declared as an expense a monthly contribution to an investment plan. The truth was that they had monthly income of $3,197.45 and expenses of $2,159.44. They were attempting to discharge a total of $15,391.64 in unsecured debts. Most of these were credit-card debts, at least half of which had been taken as cash advances. Should the court dismiss the petition? If so, why? Discuss. [*In re Jarrell,* 189 Bankr. 374 (M.D.N.C. 1995)]

23–9. Artisan's Lien. Air Ruidoso, Ltd., operated a commuter airline and air charter service between Ruidoso, New Mexico, and airports in Albuquerque and El Paso. Executive Aviation Center, Inc., provided services for airlines at the Albuquerque International Airport. When Air Rudioso failed to pay more than $10,000 that it owed for fuel, oil, and oxygen, Executive Aviation took possession of Air Ruidoso's plane. Executive Aviation claimed that it had a lien in the plane and filed a suit in a New Mexico state court to foreclose. Do supplies such as fuel, oil, and oxygen qualify as "materials" for the purpose of creating an artisan's lien? Why or why not? [*Air Ruidoso, Ltd. v. Executive Aviation Center, Inc.,* 122 N.M. 71, 920 P.2d 1025 (1996)]

23–10. Automatic Stay. David Sisco had about $600 in an account in Tinker Federal Credit Union. Sisco owed DPW Employees Credit Union a little more than $1,100. To collect on the debt, DPW obtained a garnishment judgment and served it on Tinker. The next day, Sisco filed a bankruptcy petition. Tinker then told DPW that, because of the bankruptcy filing, it could not pay the garnishment. DPW objected, and Tinker asked an Oklahoma state court to resolve the issue. What effect, if any, does Sisco's bankruptcy filing have on DPW's garnishment action? [*DPW Employees Credit Union v. Tinker Federal Credit Union,* 925 P.2d 93 (Okla.App.4th 1996)]

A QUESTION OF ETHICS AND SOCIAL RESPONSIBILITY

23–11. In September 1986, Edward and Debora Davenport pleaded guilty in a Pennsylvania court to welfare fraud and were sentenced to probation for one year. As a condition of their probation, the Davenports were ordered to make monthly restitution payments to the county probation department, which would forward the payments to the Pennsylvania Department of Public Welfare, the victim of the Davenports' fraud. In May 1987, the Davenports filed a petition for Chapter 13 relief and listed the restitution payments among their debts. The bankruptcy court held that the restitution obligation was a dischargeable debt. Ultimately, the United States Supreme Court reviewed the case. The Court noted that under the Bankruptcy Code, a debt is defined as a liability on a claim, and a claim is defined as a right to payment. Because the restitution obligations clearly constituted a right to payment, the Court held that the obligations were dischargeable in bankruptcy. [*Pennsylvania Department of Public Welfare v. Davenport,* 495 U.S. 552, 110 S.Ct. 2126, 109 L.Ed.2d 588 (1990)]

1. Critics of this decision contend that the Court adhered to the letter, but not the spirit, of bankruptcy law in arriving at its conclusion. In what way, if any, did the Court not abide by the "spirit" of bankruptcy law?
2. Do you think that Chapter 13 plans, which allow nearly all types of debts to be discharged, tip the scales of justice too far in favor of debtors?

FOR CRITICAL ANALYSIS

23–12. Has the Bankruptcy Code made it too easy for debtors to avoid their obligations by filing for bankruptcy? What are the implications of the increased number of bankruptcy filings for future potential debtors who seek to obtain credit?

Online Activities

ONLINE EXERCISE 23-1

Go to the "Internet Activities Book" on the Web site that accompanies this text, the URL for which is http://blt.westbuslaw.com. Select the following activities, and perform the exercises according to the instructions given there:

Activity 23–1: Bankruptcy Alternatives
Activity 23–2: Bankruptcy

ONLINE EXERCISE 23-2

Go to the Web site of the American Bankers Association at

www.aba.com.

Select "Consumer Connection," and then click on "Nonbusiness Bankruptcy Petitions." You will see a bar graph showing the number of nonbusiness bankruptcy petitions filed each year since 1980. Look over the graph, and then answer the following questions:

- Roughly, have nonbusiness bankruptcy petitions doubled, trebled, quadrupled, or quintupled between 1980 and 1998?
- Under which chapter of the Bankruptcy Code were most of these petitions filed?
- What source is given for this information?

Before the Test

Go to the *Business Law Today* home page at http://blt.westbuslaw.com. Click on TestTutor.® You will find twenty interactive questions relating to this chapter.

Unit Five • Cumulative Business Hypothetical

Java Jive, Inc., is a small chain of coffee shops. Adam is Java Jive's president.

1. Java Jive wants to borrow $40,000 from First National Bank to buy equipment. To secure the loan, First National could accept, as collateral, Java Jive's equipment. If so, how would First National let other potential creditors know of its interest? If First National secured its loan with the equipment, and Java Jive failed to repay the loan, what would be First National's alternatives, with respect to collecting the amount due?
2. Java Jive wants to borrow $30,000 from Eagle Credit Corp. to pay Java Jive employees. Java Jive believes that it will be able to repay the loan by the end of the month, which is when Marco Manufacturing Company agreed to pay Java Jive for its catering of Marco's facilities. Eagle agrees to make the loan if Adam will be personally liable for the amount. Under these circumstances, is Adam a guarantor, a surety, or neither? If Adam orally promises to assume personal liability if Java Jive defaults, but does not actually sign anything, could Eagle enforce the promise?
3. Java Jive borrows $20,000 from Ace Loan Company to make physical improvements to the Java Jive stores. Java Jive gives the money to Jones Construction, a contractor, to do the work. The amount represents only half of the cost, but when Jones finishes the work, Java Jive fails to pay the rest. Java Jive also does not repay Ace for the loan. What can Jones do to collect what it is owed? What can Ace do?
4. Ultimately, Java Jive is unable to pay its employees or to repay its creditors. The creditors include First National, whose loan is secured by Java Jive's equipment; Eagle, who loaned money to Java Jive to pay its employees without Adam's promise to repay the loan on Java Jive's default; Ace, who was not repaid for its loan to Java Jive to make physical improvements to its stores; and Jones Construction, the contractor who was not fully paid for its work. Java Jive, which also owes unpaid taxes, files a petition to declare bankruptcy. If the court grants the petition, will the creditors be paid? In what order?

UNIT FIVE • EXTENDED CASE STUDY: THE LAW IN CONTEXT

AmSouth Bank, N.A. v. J&D Financial Corp.

In Chapter 22, we discussed the priorities of secured parties on a debtor's default. In this extended case study, we examine AmSouth Bank, N.A. v. J&D Financial Corp.,[1] *a recent decision that applies these principles.*

CASE BACKGROUND

Presidential Financial Corporation held a security interest in the accounts receivable of Sweet Bonnie Sue, Inc. (SBS), a division of Lori & Me. Presidential had acquired its interest as part of a *factoring agreement* with SBS. Under this agreement, Presidential bought SBS's accounts receivable at a discount and then made a profit by collecting the full amount due directly from SBS's debtors. Later, AmSouth Bank, N.A., loaned $150,000 to SBS. As part of the loan, SBS granted a security interest to AmSouth that included "[a]ll . . . accounts of the Debtor." AmSouth perfected its security interest, which was subordinate to Presidential's interest.

After SBS defaulted in its obligation to AmSouth, SBS entered into a factoring agreement with J&D Financial Corporation, which perfected a security interest that included "[a]ll . . . accounts." As part of this agreement, Presidential agreed to subordinate its interest to J&D's. J&D then collected accounts receivable of SBS totaling $77,341.43.

AmSouth and Presidential each obtained judgments against SBS, which paid neither of them. AmSouth did collect $1,758 from creditors of Lori & Me, however, and filed a suit in an Alabama state court against J&D, claiming that AmSouth was entitled to the amount J&D had collected. The court issued a summary judgment in J&D's favor, holding that J&D was entitled to the amount it had collected, as well as the amount that AmSouth had collected. AmSouth appealed to the Alabama Supreme Court. The central issue on appeal was the effect of the agreement between Presidential and J&D on AmSouth's priority.

1. 679 So.2d 695 (Ala. 1996).

MAJORITY OPINION

PER CURIAM.

* * * *

* * * [H]e who holds a first lien and subordinates same to a third lien makes his lien inferior or subordinate to both second and third liens. This [principle] applies precisely to the situation before the court in this case. [Presidential] subordinated its first lien to [J&D], the third lienholder. [Presidential's] lien therefore became subordinate to both [AmSouth's] second lien and [J&D's] third lien. Obviously, [AmSouth's] lien then became superior to both [J&D's] lien and [Presidential's] lien:

Pre-Subordination	Post-Subordination
(1) [Presidential]	(1) [AmSouth]
(2) [AmSouth]	(2) [J&D]
(3) [J&D]	(3) [Presidential]

* * * Undoubtedly, [Presidential] could have transferred its interest to any inferior lienholder. If it had done so, the former inferior lienholder who purchased [Presidential's] interest would have succeeded to [Presidential's] superior priority position and stepped into its shoes on the priority ladder. However, that is not what occurred. [Presidential] merely subordinated its interest to that of [J&D]. [J&D's] interest was not made superior to the interest of any prior lienholder by virtue of [Presidential's] agreement to subordinate. Only [Presidential's] position on the priority ladder changed as a result of its subordination. * * * [W]e find [this] result * * * to be consistent with the definition of "subordination agreement":

> "An agreement by which one holding an otherwise senior lien * * * consents to a reduction in priority vis-a-vis another person holding an interest in the same [property]. An agreement by which the subordinating party agrees that its interest in [certain] property should have a lower priority than the interest to which it is being subordinated."

By definition, "subordination" contemplates a reduction in priority. Nothing in the definition contemplates raising a lower priority lienholder up to the position of the subordinating party.

DISSENTING OPINION

COOK, Justice (dissenting).

* * * *

* * * [T]he third lienholder should be able to succeed to that part of the interest that was subordinated by the first lienholder, so long as the second lienholder is neither burdened nor benefited by the subordination agreement. * * *

* * * Under the facts of this case, AmSouth has neither benefited from, nor been adversely affected by, Presidential's allowing J&D to move into first priority only to the extent of the amount of Presidential's lien. Had there been no agreement between Presidential and J&D, AmSouth would not have been entitled to the funds its now claims. Without question, those funds would have gone to Presidential. The obvious intent of the agreement between Presidential and J&D, in my opinion, was to allow J&D to move into first priority to the extent of Presidential's claim * * * .

MEDIA COVERAGE

The majority's ruling and the dissent's opinion show how the same agreement, when less than carefully phrased, can be subject to different interpretations. For a further discussion of this point, we present an excerpt from an article titled "U.C.C. Article 9: Personal Property Secured Transactions" by Steven O. Weise that appeared in *Business Lawyer* in November 1998 (Vol. 54, No. 1, pp. 307–344) (footnotes omitted).

"* * * In *AmSouth Bank, N.A. v. J&D Financial Corp.,* * * * [t]he dissent made the better argument—the court should have interpreted the agreement to have the holders of the first and third priority liens switch places, as there was no reason to give any benefit to the holder of the second priority lien.

AmSouth indicates the importance of careful drafting of subordination agreements. While there is little risk of this problem occurring when the holder of the first priority lien is absolutely confident that no interviewing liens (voluntary or involuntary) exist, an unfortunate result can occur when an interviewing lien does exist. The more prudent approach would be to have the holders of the first and third liens agree to maintain their respective priorities and to agree further that, to the extent the holder of the senior lien collects proceeds of the collateral, the holder of the senior lien will remit those proceeds to the third lien holder. The third lien holder would then agree to assign the benefits of its security interest to the first lien holder once the intermediate lien holder is paid in full. This procedure would permit the first lien holder to maintain its position ahead of the second lien holder at least to the extent that the amount secured by the first lien exceeded the amount the holder of the first lien paid to the holder of the third lien."

GOING ONLINE

The *Business Law Today,* Fifth Edition, Web site, at http://blt.westbuslaw.com, provides a link through which you can access other court opinions in cases involving secured transactions. Cornell University's Legal Information Institute at www.law.cornell.edu/uniform/ucc.html#a9 provides links to online resources for UCC Article 9, which covers secured transactions, including the most recent draft of Article 9's revisions and the states' individual versions of the statute.

QUESTIONS FOR ANALYSIS

1. **Law.** Should the facts in a case, and the application of the law to those facts, be subject to less interpretation by judges?
2. **Law.** What might the secured parties in this case have done before they dealt with SBS to avoid the negative consequences of those deals?
3. **Ethics.** Regardless of what might have been legally required, should J&D, or Presidential, have discussed with AmSouth what it intended to do?
4. **International Dimensions.** What further complications might have existed in this case if the parties had drafted their agreements in different languages? How might such problems be solved?
5. **Implications for the Business Manager.** What important lesson does the result in this case provide for businesspersons?

UNIT SIX Business Organizations

CHAPTER 24 Agency Relationships in Business

> "[It] is a universal principle in the law of agency, that the powers of the agent are to be exercised for the benefit of the principal only, and not of the agent or of third parties."
>
> Joseph Story, 1779–1845
> (Associate justice of the United States Supreme Court, 1811–1844)

CONTENTS

LEARNING OBJECTIVES

After reading this chapter, you should be able to:

1. Distinguish between employees and independent contractors.
2. Outline the ways in which an agency relationship can arise.
3. Specify the duties that agents and principals owe to each other.
4. Describe the liability of the principal and the agent with respect to third parties.
5. List the ways in which an agency relationship can be terminated.

One of the most common, important, and pervasive legal relationships is that of **agency.** As discussed in Chapter 20, in an agency relationship between two parties, one of the parties, called the *agent,* agrees to represent or act for the other, called the *principal.* The principal has the right to control the agent's conduct in matters entrusted to the agent, and the agent must exercise his or her powers "for the benefit of the principal only," as Justice Joseph Story indicated in the above quotation. By using agents, a principal can conduct multiple business operations simultaneously in various locations. Thus, for example, contracts that bind the principal can be made at different places with different persons at the same time.

Agency relationships permeate the business world. Indeed, agency law is essential to the existence and operation of a corporate entity, because only through its agents can a corporation function and enter into contracts. A familiar example of an agent is a corporate officer who serves in a representative capacity for the owners of the corporation. In this capacity, the officer has the authority to bind the principal (the corporation) to a contract.

• **AGENCY**
A relationship between two parties in which one party (the agent) agrees to represent or act for the other (the principal).

Agency Relationships

Section 1(1) of the *Restatement (Second) of Agency*[1] defines agency as "the fiduciary relation which results from the manifestation of consent by one person to another that the other shall act in his behalf and subject to his control, and consent by the other so to act." In other words, in a principal-agent relationship, the parties have agreed that the agent will act *on behalf and instead of* the principal in negotiating and transacting business with third persons.

The term **fiduciary** is at the heart of agency law. The term can be used both as a noun and as an adjective. When used as a noun, it refers to a person having a duty created by his or her undertaking to act primarily for another's benefit in matters connected with the undertaking. When used as an adjective, as in "fiduciary relationship," it means that the relationship involves trust and confidence.

• **FIDUCIARY**
As a noun, a person having a duty created by his or her undertaking to act primarily for another's benefit in matters connected with the undertaking. As an adjective, a relationship founded on trust and confidence.

Agency relationships commonly exist between employers and employees. Agency relationships may sometimes also exist between employers and independent contractors who are hired to perform special tasks or services.

EMPLOYER-EMPLOYEE RELATIONSHIPS

Normally, all employees who deal with third parties are deemed to be agents. A salesperson in a department store, for example, is an agent of the store's owner (the principal) and acts on the owner's behalf. Any sale of goods made by the salesperson to a customer is binding on the principal. Similarly, most representations of fact made by the salesperson with respect to the goods sold are binding on the principal.

> **ON THE WEB**
> For information on the *Restatements of the Law,* including planned revisions, go to the American Law Institute's Web site at www.ali.org.

Because employees who deal with third parties are normally deemed agents of their employers, agency law and employment law overlap considerably. Agency relationships, though, as will become apparent, can exist outside an employee-employer relationship and thus have a broader reach than employment laws do. Additionally, bear in mind that agency law is based on the common law. In the employment realm, many common law doctrines have been displaced by statutory law and government regulations governing employment relationships.

Employment laws (state and federal) apply only to the employer-employee relationship. Statutes governing Social Security, withholding taxes, workers' compensation, unemployment compensation, workplace safety, employment discrimination, and the like (see Chapters 37 and 38) are applicable only if there is employer-employee status. *These laws do not apply to the independent contractor.*

EMPLOYER–INDEPENDENT CONTRACTOR RELATIONSHIPS

Independent contractors are not employees, because by definition, those who hire them have no control over the details of their physical performance. Section 2 of the *Restatement (Second) of Agency* defines an **independent contractor** as follows:

• **INDEPENDENT CONTRACTOR**
One who works for, and receives payment from, an employer but whose working conditions and methods are not controlled by the employer. An independent contractor is not an employee but may be an agent.

> [An independent contractor is] a person who contracts with another to do something for him but who is not controlled by the other nor subject to the other's right to control with respect to his physical conduct in the performance of the undertaking. He may or may not be an agent.

Building contractors and subcontractors are independent contractors, and a property owner does not control the acts of either of these professionals. Truck

1. The *Restatement (Second) of Agency* is an authoritative summary of the law of agency and is often referred to by jurists in their decisions and opinions.

drivers who own their equipment and hire themselves out on a per-job basis are independent contractors, but truck drivers who drive company trucks on a regular basis are usually employees.

The relationship between a person or firm and an independent contractor may or may not involve an agency relationship. An owner of real estate who hires a real estate broker to negotiate a sale of his or her property not only has contracted with an independent contractor (the real estate broker) but also has established an agency relationship for the specific purpose of assisting in the sale of the property. Similarly, an insurance agent is both an independent contractor and an agent of the insurance company for which he or she sells policies. (Note that an insurance *broker,* in contrast to an insurance agent, normally is not an agent of the insurance company but of the person obtaining insurance.)

CRITERIA FOR DETERMINING EMPLOYEE STATUS

A question the courts frequently face in determining liability under agency law is whether a person hired by another to do a job is an employee or an independent contractor. Because employers are normally held liable as principals for the actions taken by their employee-agents within the scope of employment (as will be discussed later in this chapter), the court's decision as to employee versus independent-contractor status can be significant for the parties. In making this determination, courts often consider the following questions:

1. How much control can the employer exercise over the details of the work? (If an employer can exercise considerable control over the details of the work, this would indicate employee status.)
2. Is the worker engaged in an occupation or business distinct from that of the employer? (If not, this would indicate employee status.)
3. Is the work usually done under the employer's direction or by a specialist without supervision? (If the work is usually done under the employer's direction, this would indicate employee status.)
4. Does the employer supply the tools at the place of work? (If so, this would indicate employee status.)
5. For how long is the person employed? (If the person is employed for a long period of time, this would indicate employee status.)
6. What is the method of payment—by time period or at the completion of the job? (Payment by time period, such as once every two weeks or once a month, would indicate employee status.)
7. What degree of skill is required of the worker? (If little skill is required, this may indicate employee status.)

Often, the criteria for determining employee status are established by a statute or administrative agency regulation. The Internal Revenue Service (IRS), for example, establishes its own criteria for determining whether a worker is an independent contractor or an employee. In the past, these criteria consisted of a list of twenty factors. In 1996, however, these twenty factors were abolished in favor of rules that essentially encourage IRS examiners to look more closely at just one of the factors—the degree of control the business exercises over the worker.

The IRS tends to scrutinize closely a firm's classification of a worker as an independent contractor rather than an employee, because independent contractors can avoid certain tax liabilities by taking advantage of business organizational forms available to small businesses. Regardless of the firm's classification of a worker's status as an independent contractor, if the IRS decides that the worker should be classified as an employee, then the employer will be responsible for paying any applicable Social Security, withholding, and unemployment taxes.

Sometimes, it is advantageous to have employee status—to take advantage of laws protecting employees, for example. At other times, it may be advantageous to have independent-contractor status—for tax purposes, for example. The following case involves a dispute over ownership rights in a computer program. The outcome of the case hinged on whether the creator of the program, at the time it was created, was an employee or an independent contractor.

CASE 24.1 Graham v. James

United States Court of Appeals,
Second Circuit, 1998.
144 F.3d 229.
www.findlaw.com/casecode/courts/2nd.html[a]

HISTORICAL AND SOCIAL SETTING *Under the Copyright Act of 1976, any copyrighted work created by an employee within the scope of his or her employment at the request of the employer is a "work for hire," and the employer owns the copyright to the work. When an employer hires an independent contractor—a freelance artist, writer, or computer programmer, for example—the contractor owns the copyright unless the parties agree in writing that the work is a "work for hire" and the work falls into one of nine specific categories, including audiovisual and other works.*

a. This is a page with links to some of the opinions of the U.S. Court of Appeals for the Second Circuit. In the "1985" row, click on "May." When that page opens, scroll down the list of cases to the *Graham* case and click on the link to access it. This is part of the FindLaw Web site.

BACKGROUND AND FACTS Richard Graham marketed CD-ROM disks containing compilations of shareware, freeware, and public domain software.[b] With five to ten thousand programs per disk, Graham needed a file-retrieval program to allow users to access the software on the disks. Larry James agreed to create the program in exchange for, among other things, credit on the final product. James built into the final version of the program a notice attributing authorship and copyright to himself. Graham removed the notice, claiming that the program was a work for hire and the copyright was his. Graham used the program on several subsequent releases. James sold the program to another CD-ROM publisher. Graham filed a suit in a federal district court against James, alleging, among other things, copyright infringement. The court ruled that James was an independent contractor and that he owned the copyright. Graham appealed the ruling.

b. *Shareware* is software released to the public to sample, with the understanding that anyone using it will register with the author and pay a fee. *Freeware* is software available for free use. *Public domain software* is software unprotected by copyright.

IN THE WORDS OF THE COURT . . .
JACOBS, Circuit Judge.

* * * *

The Copyright Act provides, *inter alia* [among other things], that "a work prepared by an employee within the scope of his or her employment" is a work for hire. "[T]he employer or other person for whom the work [for hire] was prepared is considered the author" and the employer owns the copyright * * * .

* * * *

* * * [In determining whether a hired party is an employee, the important factors are:] (i) the hiring party's right to control the manner and means of creation; (ii) the skill required; (iii) the provision of employee benefits; (iv) the tax treatment of the hired party; and (v) whether the hiring party had the right to assign additional projects to the hired party. * * *

(Continued)

CASE 24.1—Continued

We are persuaded by the district court's conclusion that James was an independent contractor. Almost all of the * * * factors line up in favor of that conclusion: James is a skilled computer programmer, he was paid no benefits, no payroll taxes were withheld, and his engagement by Graham was project-by-project. The only * * * factor arguably favoring Graham is his general control over the work; but the district court has found, plausibly, that Graham's participation in the development of the [file-retrieval program] was minimal and that his instructions to James were very general.

DECISION AND REMEDY The U.S. Court of Appeals for the Second Circuit affirmed the lower court's judgment on this issue. The court agreed that James owned the copyright because he was an independent contractor when he developed the program.

FOR CRITICAL ANALYSIS—Economic Consideration *What are some other advantages of being an independent contractor? What might be some disadvantages?*

Agency Formation

Agency relationships normally are consensual; that is, they come about by voluntary consent and agreement between the parties. Generally, the agreement need not be in writing,[2] and consideration is not required.

A principal must have contractual capacity. A person who cannot legally enter into contracts directly should not be allowed to do so indirectly through an agent. Because an agent derives the authority to enter into contracts from the principal and because a contract made by an agent is legally viewed as a contract of the principal, it is immaterial whether the agent personally has the legal capacity to make that contract. Thus, a minor can be an agent but in some states cannot be a principal appointing an agent.[3] (When a minor is permitted to be a principal, however, any resulting contracts will be voidable by the minor principal but not by the adult third party.) In sum, any person can be an agent, regardless of whether he or she has the capacity to contract. Even a person who is legally incompetent can be appointed an agent.

An agency relationship can be created for any legal purpose. An agency relationship that is created for an illegal purpose or that is contrary to public policy is unenforceable. • **EXAMPLE 24.1** Suppose that Sharp (as principal) contracts with Blesh (as agent) to sell illegal narcotics. This agency relationship is unenforceable, because selling illegal narcotics is a felony and is contrary to public policy. • It is also illegal for medical doctors and other licensed professionals to employ unlicensed agents to perform professional actions.

ON THE WEB
An excellent source for information on agency, including court cases involving agency concepts, is the Legal Information Institute (LII) at Cornell University. You can access the LII's Web page on this topic at www.law.cornell.edu/topics/agency.html.

Generally, there are four ways in which an agency relationship can arise: by agreement of the parties, by ratification, by estoppel, and by operation of law. We look here at each of these possibilities.

2. There are two main exceptions to the statement that agency agreements need not be in writing: (1) Whenever agency authority empowers the agent to enter into a contract that the Statute of Frauds requires to be in writing, then the agent's authority from the principal must likewise be in writing (this is called the *equal dignity rule,* to be discussed later in this chapter). (2) A power of attorney, which confers authority to an agent, must be in writing.

3. Some courts have granted exceptions to allow a minor to appoint an agent for the limited purpose of contracting for the minor's necessities of life. See *Casey v. Kastel,* 237 N.Y. 305, 142 N.E. 671 (1924).

AGENCY BY AGREEMENT

Because an agency relationship is, by definition, normally consensual, normally it must be based on an express or implied agreement that the agent will act for the principal and the principal agrees to have the agent so act. An agency agreement can take the form of an express written contract. • EXAMPLE 24.2 Renato enters into a written agreement with Troy, a real estate agent, to sell Renato's house. An agency relationship exists between Renato and Troy for the sale of the house and is detailed in a document that both parties sign.•

Many express agency agreements are oral. • EXAMPLE 24.3 Suppose that Renato asks Cary, a gardener, to contract with others for the care of his lawn on a regular basis. Cary agrees. In this situation, an agency relationship exists between Renato and Cary for the lawn care.•

An agency agreement can also be implied by conduct. • EXAMPLE 24.4 A hotel expressly allows only Boris Koontz to park cars, but Boris has no employment contract there. The hotel's manager tells Boris when to work, as well as where and how to park the cars. The hotel's conduct amounts to a manifestation of its willingness to have Boris park its customers' cars, and Boris can infer from the hotel's conduct that he has authority to act as a parking valet. It can be inferred that Boris is an agent for the hotel, his purpose being to provide valet parking services for hotel guests.•

AGENCY BY RATIFICATION

• **RATIFICATION**
The act of accepting and giving legal force to an obligation that previously was not enforceable.

On occasion, a person who is in fact not an agent (or who is an agent acting outside the scope of his or her authority) may make a contract on behalf of another (a principal). If the principal approves or affirms that contract by word or by action, an agency relationship is created by **ratification.** Ratification is a question of intent, and intent can be expressed by either words or conduct. The basic requirements for ratification are discussed later in this chapter.

A PROPRIETOR REVIEWS THE INVENTORY IN HER CLOTHING STORE. UNDER WHAT CIRCUMSTANCES MIGHT A CLOTHING IMPORTER BE CONSIDERED TO ACT AS AN AGENT FOR THE STORE?

AGENCY BY ESTOPPEL

When a principal causes a third person to believe that another person is his or her agent, and the third person deals with the supposed agent, the principal is "estopped to deny" the agency relationship. In such a situation, the principal's actions create the *appearance* of an agency that does not in fact exist.

• EXAMPLE 24.5 Suppose that Andrew accompanies Charles, a seed sales representative, to call on a customer, Steve, the proprietor of the General Seed Store. Andrew has done independent sales work but has never signed an employment agreement with Charles. Charles boasts to Steve that he wishes he had three more assistants "just like Andrew." Steve has reason to believe from Charles's statements that Andrew is an agent for Charles. Steve then places seed orders with Andrew. If Charles does not correct the impression that Andrew is an agent, Charles will be bound to fill the orders just as if Andrew were really Charles's agent. Charles's representation to Steve created the impression that Andrew was Charles's agent and had authority to solicit orders.•

The acts or declarations of a purported *agent* in and of themselves do not create an agency by estoppel. Rather, it is the deeds or statements of the *principal* that create an agency by estoppel. • EXAMPLE 24.6 Suppose that Olivia walks into Dru's Dress Boutique and claims to be a sales agent for an exclusive Paris dress designer, Pierre Dumont. Dru has never had business relations with Pierre Dumont. Based on Olivia's claim, however, Dru gives Olivia an order and prepays 15 percent of the sales price. Olivia is not an agent, and the dresses are never delivered. Dru cannot hold Pierre Dumont liable. Olivia's acts and declarations alone do not create an agency by estoppel. ●

In addition, to assert the creation of an agency by estoppel, the third person must prove that he or she *reasonably* believed that an agency relationship existed and that the agent had authority. Facts and circumstances must show that an ordinary, prudent person familiar with business practice and custom would have been justified in concluding that the agent had authority.

The court in the following case considered whether an agency existed by estoppel between the owner of a jewelry cart in a mall and the seller of "The Only Completely Safe, Sterile Ear Piercing Method."

CASE 24.2 Williams v. Inverness Corp.

Supreme Judicial Court of Maine, 1995.
664 A.2d 1244.

COMPANY PROFILE *Inverness Corporation is the world's largest maker of body-piercing equipment. Sam Mann founded Inverness in 1975 with a design for piercing equipment that was more sterile and less threatening than the products then in use. The first year's sales totaled more than $750,000. Today, the company makes disposable ear-piercing kits, skin-care products, hair-removal waxes, electrolysis kits, and jewelry dips. Based in Fair Lawn, New Jersey, Inverness sells its products in fifty-two countries.*

BACKGROUND AND FACTS The Inverness Corporation markets the Inverness Ear Piercing System, which includes a training course, an "eye-catching assortment of selling aids" such as counter displays, and release forms that tout the system as "The Only Completely Safe, Sterile Ear Piercing Method." Margaret Barrera, the owner of a jewelry cart in a mall, bought the system, took the course, and set up the displays. Seventeen-year-old Angela Williams paid Barrera to pierce Williams's ear. The ear became infected, which led to complications. Williams's mother filed a suit on Angela's behalf in a Maine state court against Inverness and Barrera, claiming in part that Inverness was liable on a theory of agency by estoppel. When the court issued a judgment in Williams's favor, Inverness appealed to Maine's highest court.

IN THE WORDS OF THE COURT . . .
DANA, Justice.

* * * *

* * * There are critical pieces of evidence in the record that can fairly be interpreted as leading to an inference that Inverness did hold Barrera out as its agent. Most important, a jury reasonably could infer that Inverness knew, or should have known, that Barrera distributed Inverness's release forms * * * .

* * * A jury reasonably could infer * * * that Inverness knew, or should have known, that Barrera was using the Inverness Ear Piercing System, that she displayed Inverness's "eye-catching assortment of selling aids," and that she used Inverness's training program.

Finally, there was evidence that Angela believed that Barrera was Inverness's agent, that Angela relied on Inverness's manifestations of agency, and that Angela's reliance on Barrera's care and skill was justifiable. * * * The release form and display promote the Inverness Ear Piercing System as "The Only Completely Safe, Sterile Ear Piercing Method."

DECISION AND REMEDY The Supreme Judicial Court of Maine affirmed the lower court's judgment.

FOR CRITICAL ANALYSIS—Social Consideration
What are the policy reasons for holding a firm liable on a theory of agency by estoppel?

AGENCY BY OPERATION OF LAW

There are other situations in which the courts will find an agency relationship in the absence of a formal agreement. This may occur in family relationships. For example, suppose one spouse purchases certain basic necessaries and charges them to the other spouse's charge account. The courts will often rule that the latter is liable for payment for the necessaries, either because of a social policy of promoting the general welfare of the spouse or because of a legal duty to supply necessaries to family members.

Agency by operation of law may also occur in emergency situations, when the agent's failure to act outside the scope of his or her authority would cause the principal substantial loss. If the agent is unable to contact the principal, the courts will often grant this emergency power. For example, a railroad engineer may contract on behalf of his or her employer for medical care for an injured motorist hit by the train.

Duties of Agents and Principals

"I am 'in a fiduciary position'—which is always a ______ uncomfortable position."

FREDERIC W. MAITLAND, 1850–1906 (English jurist and historian)

The principal-agent relationship gives rise to duties that govern both parties' conduct. As discussed previously, an agency relationship is *fiduciary*—one of trust. In a fiduciary relationship, each party owes the other the duty to act with the utmost good faith.

We now examine the various duties of agents and principals. In general, for every duty of the principal, the agent has a corresponding right, and vice versa. When one party to the agency relationship violates his or her duty to the other party, the remedies available to the nonbreaching party arise out of contract and tort law. These remedies include monetary damages, termination of the agency relationship, injunction, and required accountings.

AGENT'S DUTIES TO THE PRINCIPAL

Generally, the agent owes the principal five duties—performance, notification, loyalty, obedience, and accounting.

Performance An implied condition in every agency contract is the agent's agreement to use reasonable diligence and skill in performing the work. When an agent fails to perform his or her duties entirely, liability for breach of contract normally will result. The degree of skill or care required of an agent is usually that expected of a reasonable person under similar circumstances. Generally, this is interpreted to mean ordinary care. An agent may, however, have represented himself or herself as possessing special skills (such as those that an accountant or attorney possesses). In these situations, the agent is expected to exercise the skill or skills claimed. Failure to do so constitutes a breach of the agent's duty.

¡BE AWARE! An agent's disclosure of confidential information could constitute the business tort of misappropriation of trade secrets.

Not all agency relationships are based on contract. In some situations, an agent acts gratuitously—that is, not for money. A gratuitous agent cannot be liable for breach of contract, as there is no contract; he or she is subject only to tort liability. Once a gratuitous agent has begun to act in an agency capacity, he or she has the duty to continue to perform in that capacity in an acceptable manner and is subject to the same standards of care and duty to perform as other agents.

Notification There is a maxim in agency law that notice to the agent is notice to the principal. An agent is thus required to notify the principal of all matters that

A REAL ESTATE AGENT STANDS BY A "FOR SALE" SIGN. IF THIS AGENT KNOWS A BUYER WHO IS WILLING TO PAY MORE THAN THE ASKING PRICE FOR THIS PROPERTY, WHAT DUTY WOULD THE AGENT BREACH IF HE BOUGHT THE PROPERTY AND SOLD IT AT A PROFIT TO THE BUYER?

come to his or her attention concerning the subject matter of the agency. This is the duty of notification. The law assumes that the principal knows of any information acquired by the agent that is relevant to the agency—regardless of whether the agent actually passes on this information to the principal.

Loyalty Loyalty is one of the most fundamental duties in a fiduciary relationship. Basically stated, the agent has the duty to act solely for the benefit of his or her principal and not in the interest of the agent or a third party. For example, an agent cannot represent two principals in the same transaction unless both know of the dual capacity and consent to it. The duty of loyalty also means that any information or knowledge acquired through the agency relationship is considered confidential. It would be a breach of loyalty to disclose such information either during the agency relationship or after its termination. Typical examples of confidential information are trade secrets and customer lists compiled by the principal.

In short, the agent's loyalty must be undivided. The agent's actions must be strictly for the benefit of the principal and must not result in any secret profit for the agent. • EXAMPLE 24.7 Suppose that Ryder contracts with Alton, a real estate agent, to sell Ryder's property. Alton knows that he can find a buyer who will pay substantially more for the property than Ryder is asking. If Alton secretly purchased Ryder's property, however, and then sold it at a profit to another buyer, Alton would breach his duty of loyalty as Ryder's agent. Alton has a duty to act in Ryder's best interests and can only become the purchaser in this situation with Ryder's knowledge and approval. •

ETHICAL ISSUE 24.1 ***What happens when the duty of loyalty conflicts with other duties?*** The duty of loyalty to one's employer-principal is a fundamental ethical duty that has been written into law. The duty is rooted in the principle that a person cannot serve two masters at the same time. In an agency relationship, the agent's loyalty must be undivided. There are times, however, when the ethical duty of loyalty may come into conflict with another duty, such as one's duty to society. For example, suppose that one's principal-employer is involved in an illegal activity. Or suppose that this employer is aware that a company product is dangerous but refuses to acknowledge consumer complaints or even act on its own studies showing that the product is defective. In either of these situations, must an agent-employee of the firm keep silent, out of loyalty to his or her employer? Or should the agent-employee disregard the duty of loyalty in these situations and "blow the whistle" on the employer's actions (by reporting them to a government official, for example, or to the press)? Some scholars have argued that many of the greatest "evils" in the past twenty-five years have been accomplished in the name of "duty" to the principal.

Obedience When an agent is acting on behalf of the principal, a duty is imposed on that agent to follow all lawful and clearly stated instructions of the principal. Any deviation from such instructions is a violation of this duty. During emergency situations, however, when the principal cannot be consulted, the agent may deviate from such instructions without violating this duty. Whenever instructions are not clearly stated, the agent can fulfill the duty of obedience by acting in good faith and in a manner reasonable under the circumstances.

ON THE WEB

For a discussion of significant cases decided by the New York Court of Appeals (that state's highest court) on fiduciary duties, go to the Web site of the *New York Law Journal* at **www.nylj.com/links/150sterk.html**, and scroll down the page to "Fiduciary Duties."

Accounting Unless an agent and a principal agree otherwise, the agent has the duty to keep and make available to the principal an account of all property and money received and paid out on behalf of the principal. This includes gifts from third persons in connection with the agency. For example, a gift from a customer to a salesperson for prompt deliveries made by the salesperson's firm, in the absence of a company policy to the contrary, belongs to the firm. The agent has a duty to maintain separate accounts for the principal's funds and for the agent's personal funds, and no intermingling of these accounts is allowed.

PRINCIPAL'S DUTIES TO THE AGENT

The principal also owes certain duties to the agent. These duties relate to compensation, reimbursement and indemnification, cooperation, and safe working conditions.

Compensation In general, when a principal requests certain services from an agent, the agent reasonably expects payment. The principal therefore has a duty to pay the agent for services rendered. For example, when an accountant or an attorney is asked to act as an agent, an agreement to compensate the agent for such service is implied. The principal also has a duty to pay that compensation in a timely manner. Except in a gratuitous agency relationship, in which an agent does not act for money, the principal must pay the agreed-on value for an agent's services. If no amount has been expressly agreed on, then the principal owes the agent the customary compensation for such services.

¡REMEMBER!

An agent who signs a negotiable instrument on behalf of a principal may be personally liable on the instrument. Liability depends in part on whether the identity of the principal is disclosed and whether the parties intend the agent to be bound.

Reimbursement and Indemnification Whenever an agent disburses sums of money to fulfill the request of the principal or to pay for necessary expenses in the course of a reasonable performance of his or her agency duties, the principal has the duty to reimburse the agent for these payments. Agents cannot recover for expenses incurred by their own misconduct or negligence, however.

Subject to the terms of the agency agreement, the principal has the duty to compensate, or *indemnify,* an agent for liabilities incurred because of authorized and lawful acts and transactions. For example, if the principal fails to perform a contract formed by the agent with a third party and the third party then sues the agent, the principal is obligated to compensate the agent for any costs incurred in defending against the lawsuit.

Additionally, the principal must indemnify (pay) the agent for the value of benefits that the agent confers on the principal. The amount of indemnification is usually specified in the agency contract. If it is not, the courts will look to the nature of the business and the type of loss to determine the amount.

Cooperation A principal has a duty to cooperate with the agent and to assist the agent in the agent's performance of his or her duties. The principal must do nothing to prevent such performance.

● **EXAMPLE 24.8** Suppose that Akers (the principal) grants Johnson (the agent) an exclusive territory within which Johnson may sell Akers's products, thus creating an exclusive agency. In this situation, Akers cannot compete with Johnson within that territory—or appoint or allow another agent to so compete—because this would violate the exclusive agency. If Akers did so, he would be exposed to liability for Johnson's lost sales or profits. ●

Safe Working Conditions The common law requires the principal to provide safe working premises, equipment, and conditions for all agents and employees. The principal has a duty to inspect working conditions and to warn agents and employees about any unsafe areas. When the agency is one of employment, the employer's liability and the safety standards with which the employer must comply normally are covered by federal and state statutes and regulations (see Chapter 37).

Agent's Authority

An agent's authority to act can be either *actual* (express or implied) or *apparent.* If an agent contracts outside the scope of his or her authority, the principal may still become liable by ratifying the contract.

Actual Authority

• **EQUAL DIGNITY RULE**
In most states, a rule stating that express authority given to an agent must be in writing if the contract to be made on behalf of the principal is required to be in writing.

As indicated, an agent's actual authority can be express or implied. *Express authority* is authority declared in clear, direct, and definite terms. Express authority can be given orally or in writing. The **equal dignity rule** in most states requires that if the contract being executed is or must be in writing, then the agent's authority must also be in writing.[4] Failure to comply with the equal dignity rule can make a contract voidable *at the option of the principal.* The law regards the contract at that point as a mere offer. If the principal decides to accept the offer, acceptance must be in writing.

• Example 24.9 Klee (the principal) orally asks Parkinson (the agent) to sell a ranch that Klee owns. Parkinson finds a buyer and signs a sales contract (a contract for an interest in realty must be in writing) on behalf of Klee to sell the ranch. The buyer cannot enforce the contract unless Klee subsequently ratifies Parkinson's agency status in *writing.* Once Parkinson's agency status is ratified, either party can enforce rights under the contract.•

The equal dignity rule does not apply when an agent acts in the presence of a principal or when the agent's act of signing is merely perfunctory. Thus, if Dickens (the principal) negotiates a contract but is called out of town the day it is to be signed and orally authorizes Santini to sign the contract, the oral authorization is sufficient.

• **POWER OF ATTORNEY**
A written document, which is usually notarized, authorizing another to act as one's agent; can be special (permitting the agent to do specified acts only) or general (permitting the agent to transact all business for the principal).

• **NOTARY PUBLIC**
A public official authorized to attest to the authenticity of signatures.

Giving an agent a **power of attorney** confers express authority.[5] The power of attorney normally is a written document and is usually notarized. (A document is notarized when a **notary public**—a public official authorized to attest to the authenticity of signatures—signs and dates the document and imprints it with his or her seal of authority.) A power of attorney can be special (permitting the agent to do specified acts only), or it can be general (permitting the agent to transact all business for the principal). An agent holding a power of attorney for a client is authorized to act *only* on the principal's behalf when exercising that power. An ordinary power of attorney terminates on the incapacity or death of the person giving the power.[6] Exhibit 24–1 on page 000 shows a sample power of attorney.

Implied authority can be (1) conferred by custom, (2) inferred from the position the agent occupies, or (3) inferred as being reasonably necessary to carry out express

4. An exception to the equal dignity rule exists in modern business practice. An executive officer of a corporation, when acting for the corporation in an ordinary business situation, is not required to obtain written authority from the corporation.

5. An agent who holds the power of attorney is called an *attorney-in-fact* for the principal. The holder does not have to be an attorney-at-law (and often is not).

6. A *durable* power of attorney, however, provides an agent with very broad powers to act and make decisions for the principal and specifies that it is not affected by the principal's incapacity. An elderly person, for example, might grant a durable power of attorney to provide for the handling of property and investments should he or she become incompetent.

authority. • **EXAMPLE 24.10** Mueller is employed by Al's Supermarket to manage one of its stores. Al's has not expressly stated that Mueller has authority to contract with third persons. In this situation, however, authority to manage a business implies authority to do what is reasonably required (as is customary or can be inferred from a manager's position) to operate the business. Reasonably required actions include creating contracts to hire employees, to buy merchandise and equipment, and to arrange for advertising the products sold in the store. •

The issue in the following case was whether it was reasonable for an attorney to believe that he had the authority to settle a case without the client's consent.

CASE 24.3 Gravens v. Auto-Owners Insurance Co.

Court of Appeals of Indiana, 1996.
666 N.E.2d 964.

HISTORICAL AND ETHICAL SETTING *Rule 1.2(a) of the Model Rules of Professional Conduct, a model ethical code drafted by the American Bar Association and adopted by many states, reads in part that "[a] lawyer shall abide by a client's decision concerning the objectives of representation * * * and shall consult with the client as to the means by which they are to be pursued. A lawyer shall abide by a client's decision whether to accept an offer of settlement of a matter." In other words, under this rule, an attorney must do what a client says, as long as it is within the law to do so. In every state and in every situation, an attorney has no authority to compromise a legal action merely by virtue of the attorney-client relationship.*[a]

a. Eunice A. Eichelberger, "Annotation: Authority of Attorney to Compromise Action—Modern Cases," 90 *A.L.R.4th* 326.

BACKGROUND AND FACTS James Gravens bought an insurance policy from Auto-Owners Insurance Company to cover his business, Pappy's Sunoco Service Station. The policy included a $20,000 limit on coverage of the contents of Pappy's, but when a burglary occurred on the premises, the loss exceeded the limit. Gravens hired an attorney to pursue a claim against Auto-Owners. He did not discuss with the attorney the amount for which he was willing to settle, and he did not give the attorney the authority to settle the claim without his consent. When the attorney agreed with Auto-Owners to settle the claim for $18,000, Gravens repudiated the agreement, hired a different attorney, and filed a suit in an Indiana state court against Auto-Owners. The court granted Auto-Owners a summary judgment. Gravens appealed.

IN THE WORDS OF THE COURT . . .
ROBERTSON, Judge.

* * * *

* * * [U]nder [the Model Rules of Professional Conduct, which govern the conduct of attorneys] a client has full authority over the decision whether or not to settle his case or proceed to trial. * * *

* * * [T]he requirement that an attorney must obtain his client's authority or consent to settle a case is implicit in the client's right to exercise ultimate authority over the settlement of a case * * * .

* * * *

Gravens did not authorize his original attorney to settle the case and immediately repudiated the settlement agreement purported to have been reached by that attorney. Under these circumstances, Gravens was not bound by his attorney's agreement * * * .

DECISION AND REMEDY The intermediate state appellate court reversed the lower court's decision and remanded the case.

FOR CRITICAL ANALYSIS—Ethical Consideration *What if Gravens had approved of the attorney's settlement? Would Gravens be bound by the agreement?*

EXHIBIT 24–1 • A Sample Power of Attorney

POWER OF ATTORNEY

GENERAL

Know All Men by These Presents: That I, ______________________________

____

the undersigned (jointly and severally, if more than one) hereby make, constitute and appoint ______________

____

as a true and lawful Attorney for me and in my name, place and stead and for my use and benefit:

(a) To ask, demand, sue for, recover, collect and receive each and every sum of money, debt, account, legacy, bequest, interest, dividend, annuity and demand (which now is or hereafter shall become due, owing or payable) belonging to or claimed by me, and to use and take any lawful means for the recovery thereof by legal process or otherwise, and to execute and deliver a satisfaction or release therefore, together with the right and power to compromise or compound any claim or demand;

(b) To exercise any or all of the following powers as to real property, any interest therein and/or any building thereon: To contract for, purchase, receive and take possession thereof and or evidence of title thereto; to lease the same for any term or purpose, including leases for business, residence, and oil and/or mineral development; to sell, exchange, grant or convey the same with or without warranty; and to mortgage, transfer in trust, or otherwise encumber or hypothecate the same to secure payment of a negotiable or non-negotiable note or performance of any obligation or agreement;

(c) To exercise any or all of the following powers as to all kinds of personal property and goods, wares and merchandise, choses in action and other property in possession or in action: To contract for, buy, sell, exchange, transfer and in any legal manner deal in and with the same; and to mortgage, transfer in trust, or otherwise encumber or hypothecate the same to secure payment of a negotiable or non-negotiable note or performance of any obligation or agreement;

(d) To borrow money and to execute and deliver negotiable or non-negotiable notes therefore with or without security; and to loan money and receive negotiable or non-negotiable notes therefore with such security as he shall deem proper;

(e) To create, amend, supplement and terminate any trust and to instruct and advise the trustee of any trust wherein I am or may be trustor or beneficiary; to represent and vote stock, exercise stock rights, accept and deal with any dividend, distribution or bonus, join in any corporate financing, reorganization, merger, liquidation, consolidation or other action and the extension, compromise, conversion, adjustment, enforcement or foreclosure, singly or in conjunction with others, of any corporate stock, bond, note, debenture or other security; to compound, compromise, adjust, settle and satisfy any obligation, secured or unsecured, owing by or to me and to give or accept any property and/or money whether or not equal to or less in value than the amount owing in payment, settlement or satisfaction thereof;

(f) To transact business of any kind or class and as my act and deed to sign, execute, acknowledge and deliver any deed, lease, assignment of lease, covenant, indenture, indemnity, agreement, mortgage, deed of trust, assignment of mortgage or of the beneficial interest under deed of trust, extension or renewal of any obligation, subordination or waiver of priority, hypothecation, bottomry, charter-party, bill of lading, bill of sale, bill, bond, note, whether negotiable or non-negotiable, receipt, evidence of debt, full or partial release or satisfaction of mortgage, judgment and other debt, request for partial or full reconveyance of deed of trust and such other instruments in writing of any kind or class as may be necessary or proper in the premises.

Giving and Granting unto my said Attorney full power and authority to do so and perform all and every act and thing whatsoever requisite, necessary or appropriate to be done in and about the premises as fully to all intents and purposes as I might or could do if personally present, hereby ratifying all that my said Attorney shall lawfully do or cause to be done by virtue of these presents. The powers and authority hereby conferred upon my said Attorney shall be applicable to all real and personal property or interests therein now owned or hereafter acquired by me and wherever situated.

My said Attorney is empowered hereby to determine in his sole discretion the time when, purpose for and manner in which any power herein conferred upon him shall be exercised, and the conditions, provisions and covenants of any instrument or document which may be executed by him pursuant hereto; and in the acquisition or disposition of real or personal property, my said Attorney shall have exclusive power to fix the terms thereof for cash, credit and/or property, and if on credit with or without security.

The undersigned, if a married woman, hereby further authorizes and empowers my said Attorney, as my duly authorized agent, to join in my behalf, in the execution of any instrument by which any community real property or any interest therein, now owned or hereafter acquired by my spouse and myself, or either of us, is sold, leased, encumbered, or conveyed.

When the context so requires, the masculine gender includes the feminine and/or neuter, and the singular number includes the plural.

WITNESS my hand this ____________ day of ____________________, 19____

______________________ ______________________

______________________ ______________________

State of California
County of ______________________ } ss.

On ______________________, before me, the undersigned, a Notary Public in and for said State, personally appeared ______________________

____

known to me to be the person ____________ whose name ______________________ subscribed to the within instrument and acknowledged that ______________________ executed the same.

Witness my hand and official seal. (Seal) ______________________

Notary Public in and for said State.

"The law is not a series of calculating machines where definitions and answers come tumbling out when the right levers are pushed."

WILLIAM O. DOUGLAS, 1898–1980
(Associate justice of the United States Supreme Court, 1939–1975)

APPARENT AUTHORITY

Actual authority arises from what the principal manifests *to the agent.* Apparent authority exists when the principal, by either words or actions, causes a *third party* reasonably to believe that an agent has authority to act, even though the agent has no express or implied authority. If the third party changes his or her position in reliance on the principal's representations, the principal may be *estopped* from denying that the agent had authority. Note that here, in contrast to agency formation by estoppel, the issue has to do with the apparent authority of an *agent,* not the apparent authority of a person who is in fact not an agent.

• **EXAMPLE 24.11** Suppose that a traveling salesperson, Anderson (the agent), is authorized to take customers' orders. Anderson, however, does not deliver the ordered goods and is not authorized to collect payments for the goods. A customer, Byron, pays Anderson for a solicited order. Anderson then takes the payment to the principal's accounting department, and an accountant accepts the payment and sends Byron a receipt. This procedure is thereafter followed for other orders solicited and paid for by Byron. Later, Anderson solicits an order, and Byron pays her as before. This time, however, Anderson absconds with the money. Can Byron claim that the payment to the agent was authorized and was thus, in effect, a payment to the principal?

The answer is normally yes, because the principal's *repeated* acts of accepting Byron's payment led Byron reasonably to expect that Anderson had authority to receive payments for goods solicited. Although Anderson did not have express or implied authority, the principal's conduct gave Anderson *apparent* authority to collect. In this situation, the principal would be estopped from denying that Anderson had authority to collect payments. •

RATIFICATION

As already mentioned, ratification is the affirmation of a previously unauthorized contract. Ratification can be either express or implied. If the principal does not ratify, there is no contract binding on the principal, and the third party's agreement with the agent is viewed merely as an unaccepted offer. The third party can revoke the offer at any time prior to the principal's ratification without liability. Death or incapacity of the third party before ratification will void an unauthorized contract.

¡BE AWARE! An agent who exceeds his or her authority to enter into a contract that the principal does not ratify may be liable to the third party on the ground of misrepresentation.

The requirements for ratification can be summarized as follows:

1. The purported agent must have acted on behalf of a principal who subsequently ratified the action.
2. The principal must know of all material facts involved in the transaction.
3. The agent's act must be affirmed in its entirety by the principal.
4. The principal must have the legal capacity to authorize the transaction at the time the agent engages in the act and at the time the principal ratifies.
5. The principal's affirmance must occur prior to the withdrawal of the third party from the transaction.
6. The principal must observe the same formalities when he or she approves the act purportedly done by the agent on his or her behalf as would have been required to authorize it initially.

Liability in Agency Relationships

Frequently, the issue arises as to which party, the principal or the agent, should be held liable for the contracts formed by the agent or for the torts or crimes committed by the agent. We look here at these aspects of agency law.

LIABILITY FOR CONTRACTS

An important consideration in determining liability for a contract formed by an agent is whether the third party knew the identity of the principal at the time the contract was made. The *Restatement (Second) of Agency,* Section 4, classifies principals as disclosed, partially disclosed, or undisclosed.

• **DISCLOSED PRINCIPAL**
A principal whose identity is known to a third party at the time the agent makes a contract with the third party.

• **PARTIALLY DISCLOSED PRINCIPAL**
A principal whose identity is unknown by a third person, but the third person knows that the agent is or may be acting for a principal at the time the agent and the third person form a contract.

Disclosed or Partially Disclosed Principal A principal whose identity is known to the third party at the time the agent makes the contract is a **disclosed principal.** For example, if an agent signs a contract with a third party for office supplies and indicates his or her status as purchasing agent for the owner of an office supply store, the principal—the store's owner—is fully disclosed.

The identity of a **partially disclosed principal** is not known by the third party, but the third party knows that the agent is or may be acting for a principal at the time the contract is made. • **EXAMPLE 24.12** Sarah has contracted with a real estate agent to sell certain property. She wishes to keep her identity a secret, but the agent can make it perfectly clear to a purchaser of the real estate that the agent is acting in an agency capacity for a principal. In this situation, Sarah is a partially disclosed principal.•

A disclosed or partially disclosed principal is liable to a third party for a contract made by an agent who is acting within the scope of his or her authority. Ordinarily, if the principal is disclosed or partially disclosed, the agent has no contractual liability if the principal or the third party does not perform the contract. If the agent *exceeds* the scope of his or her authority and the principal fails to ratify the contract, however, the third party cannot hold the principal liable for nonperformance. In such situations, the agent is generally liable unless the third party knew of the agent's lack of authority.

• **UNDISCLOSED PRINCIPAL**
A principal whose identity is unknown by a third person, and the third person has no knowledge that the agent is acting for a principal at the time the agent and the third person form a contract.

Undisclosed Principal The identity of an **undisclosed principal** is totally unknown to the third party. Furthermore, the third party has no knowledge that the agent is acting in an agency capacity at the time the contract is made.

When neither the fact of agency nor the identity of the principal is disclosed, a third party is deemed to be dealing with the agent personally, and the agent is liable as a party to the contract. If an agent has acted within the scope of his or her authority, the undisclosed principal is also liable as a party to the contract, just as if the principal had been fully disclosed at the time the contract was made. Conversely, the undisclosed principal can hold the third party to the contract, unless (1) the undisclosed principal was expressly excluded as a party in the contract, (2) the contract is a negotiable instrument signed by the agent with no indication of signing in a representative capacity, or (3) the performance of the agent is personal to the contract, allowing the third party to refuse the principal's performance.

One of the legal questions raised by the growth of online commerce has to do with the liability of principals for the actions of "intelligent agents." For a discussion of this issue, see this chapter's *Technology and "Intelligent Agents."*

LIABILITY FOR TORTS AND CRIMES

Obviously, an agent is liable for his or her own torts and crimes. Whether the principal can also be held liable depends on several factors, which we examine here. In some situations, a principal may be held liable not only for the torts of an agent but also for the torts committed by an independent contractor.

Technology and "Intelligent Agents"

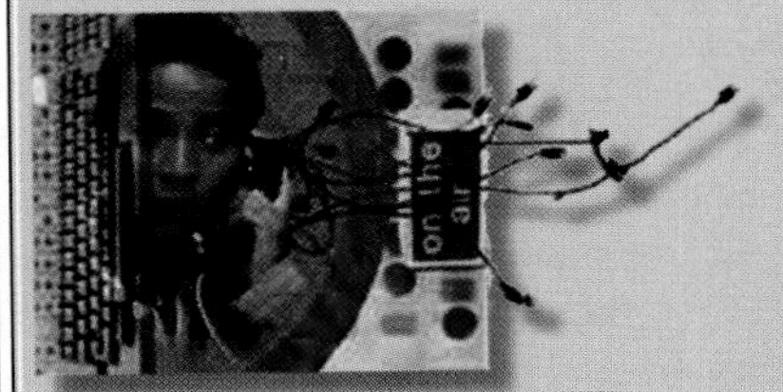

Intelligent agents are semiautonomous Internet computer programs that are capable of executing specific tasks. For example, intelligent agents can search through many databases on the Web and retrieve only relevant information for the user. Some intelligent agents are used to make purchases on the Internet. A user might use BargainFinder (Andersen Consulting, Chicago), for example, to search the many Web sites that offer compact discs (CDs) and seek out the lowest price for a particular CD. Once found, the intelligent agent links the user directly to the appropriate Web site. Other shopping agents locate other specific products in online catalogues and actually negotiate product acquisition, as well as delivery.

Agency principles have only applied to *human* agents, who have express or implied authority to enter into specific contracts. Many questions in agency law revolve around whether the human agent acted within the scope of his or her authority. What does this concept mean when dealing with an electronic intelligent agent? Consider an example. Software that an intelligent agent might find for its user ("principal") will undoubtedly involve a "click-on" agreement. Intelligent agents searching the Web may run into a wide variety of such "click-on" agreements, which, by necessity, contain many different terms and conditions. If the intelligent agent ignores the terms and conditions of a licensing agreement outlined in the "click-on" setting, is the user of the agent nonetheless bound by the agreement?

To avoid problems created by the use of intelligent agents, some online stores have blocked intelligent agents from accessing pricing information. Other online stores are developing click-on agreements that can be understood by a computer and that are therefore more appropriate for intelligent agents.

The National Conference of Commissioners on Uniform State Laws has drafted a proposed Article 2B, entitled "Software Contracts and Licenses of Information," for the Uniform Commercial Code (UCC). This proposed UCC article addresses the issue of intelligent agents. According to the Reporters' Notes, any company or individual that creates and sets out or adopts the intelligent agent ultimately takes responsibility for its conduct and is bound by its performances and messages. Unfortunately, no distinction is made between the person or business that developed and programmed the intelligent agent and the user. As currently used, most electronic agents are automatically agreeing to whatever terms are included in a click-on contract.

FOR CRITICAL ANALYSIS

What are the costs and benefits of using an intelligent shopping agent?

• ***RESPONDEAT SUPERIOR***
In Latin, "Let the master respond." A doctrine under which a principal or an employer is held liable for the wrongful acts committed by agents or employees while acting within the course and scope of their agency or employment.

¡NOTE!

An agent-employee going to or from work or meals is not usually considered to be within the scope of employment. An agent-employee whose job requires travel, however, is considered to be within the scope of employment for the entire trip, including the return.

Liability for Agent's Torts As mentioned, an agent is liable for his or her own torts. A principal may also be liable for an agent's torts under the doctrine of ***respondeat superior,***[7] a Latin term meaning "let the master respond." This doctrine, which is discussed in the following *Landmark in the Law,* is similar to the theory of strict liability discussed in Chapter 4. The doctrine imposes vicarious (indirect) liability on the employer without regard to the personal fault of the employer for torts committed by an employee in the course or scope of employment.

Scope of Employment. The key to determining whether a principal may be liable for the torts of the agent under the doctrine of *respondeat superior* is whether the torts are committed within the scope of the agency or employment. The *Restatement (Second) of Agency,* Section 229, indicates the factors that courts will consider in determining whether or not a particular act occurred within the course and scope of employment. These factors are as follows:

7. Pronounced ree-*spahn*-dee-uht soo-*peer*-ee-your.

Landmark in the Law • THE DOCTRINE OF *RESPONDEAT SUPERIOR*

The idea that a master (employer) must respond to third persons for losses negligently caused by the master's servant (employee) first appeared in Lord Holt's opinion in *Jones v. Hart* (1698).[a] By the early nineteenth century, this maxim had been adopted by most courts and was referred to as the doctrine of *respondeat superior.*

The vicarious (indirect) liability of the master for the acts of the servant has been supported primarily by two theories. The first theory rests on the issue of *control,* or *fault:* the master has control over the acts of the servant and is thus responsible for injuries arising out of such service. The second theory is economic in nature: because the master takes the benefits or profits of the servant's service, he or she should also suffer the losses; moreover, the master is better able than the servant to absorb such losses.

The *control* theory is clearly recognized in the *Restatement (Second) of Agency,* in which the master is defined as "a principal who employs an agent to perform service in his affairs and who controls, or has the right to control, the physical conduct of the other in the performance of the service." Accordingly, a servant is defined as "an agent employed by a master to perform service in his affairs whose physical conduct in his performance of the service is controlled, or is subject to control, by the master."

There are limitations on the master's liability for the acts of the servant, however. An employer (master) is only responsible for the wrongful conduct of an employee (servant) that occurs in "the scope of employment." The criteria used by the courts in determining whether an employee is acting within the scope of employment are set forth in the *Restatement (Second) of Agency* and will be discussed shortly. Generally, the act must be of a kind the servant was employed to do; must have occurred within "authorized time and space limits"; and must have been "activated, at least in part, by a purpose to serve the master."

The courts have accepted the doctrine of *respondeat superior* for nearly two centuries. This theory of vicarious liability is laden with practical implications in all situations in which a principal-agent (master-servant, employer-employee) relationship exists. The small-town grocer with one clerk and the multinational corporation with thousands of employees are equally subject to the doctrinal demand of "let the master respond."

FOR CRITICAL ANALYSIS
How does the doctrine of *respondeat superior* relate to the doctrine of strict product liability?

a. K.B. 642, 90 Eng. Reprint 1255 (1698).

A TRUCK LIES ON ITS SIDE FOLLOWING AN ACCIDENT. IF THE DRIVER HAD STOPPED AT A BAR DURING WORKING HOURS AND BECOME INEBRIATED, AND THIS ACCIDENT WAS CAUSED BY THE DRIVER'S INEBRIATED STATE, WHO WOULD BE HELD RESPONSIBLE FOR THE DAMAGE?

1. Whether the act was authorized by the employer.
2. The time, place, and purpose of the act.
3. Whether the act was one commonly performed by employees on behalf of their employers.
4. The extent to which the employer's interest was advanced by the act.
5. The extent to which the private interests of the employee were involved.
6. Whether the employer furnished the means or instrumentality (for example, a truck or a machine) by which the injury was inflicted.
7. Whether the employer had reason to know that the employee would do the act in question and whether the employee had ever done it before.
8. Whether the act involved the commission of a serious crime.

A useful insight into the "scope of employment" concept may be gained from Baron Parke's classic distinction between a "detour" and a "frolic" in the case of *Joel v. Morison* (1834).[8] In this case, the English court held that if a servant merely

8. 6 Car. & P. 501, 172 Eng. Reprint 1338 (1834).

took a detour from his master's business, the master will be responsible. If, however, the servant was on a "frolic of his own" and not in any way "on his master's business," the master will not be liable. At issue in the following case was whether a truck driver's actions fell within the scope of employment or constituted a "frolic of his own."

CASE 24.4 McNair v. Lend Lease Trucks, Inc.

United States Court of Appeals,
Fourth Circuit, 1995.
62 F.3d 651.
www.law.emory.edu/4circuit/sept96/index.html[a]

HISTORICAL AND SOCIAL SETTING *The illegal use of controlled substances and the misuse of alcohol in particular have long had terrible consequences on U.S. highways. Sometimes, the abusers are professional drivers of large trucks and other commercial vehicles. To curb this abuse, Congress enacted the Omnibus Transportation Employee Testing Act of 1991, which went into effect in 1996. The law requires all employers to test for drugs and alcohol whomever they hire to operate a commercial motor vehicle. Of course, the tests are too late for the millions who have already died on our nation's highways.*

a. This page, which is part of the Web site maintained by the Emory University School of Law in Atlanta, Georgia, provides access to published opinions of the U.S. Court of Appeals for the Fourth Circuit for September 1996. On the list of cases, find the *McNair* case. Click on the name to access the opinion.

BACKGROUND AND FACTS Lend Lease Trucks, Inc., employed Thomas Jones as an interstate truck driver. While on an assignment, Jones parked on the shoulder of U.S. Highway 301 near Kenly, North Carolina, and crossed the highway to the Dry Dock Lounge. In the lounge, Jones drank enough liquor for his blood-alcohol level to rise to dramatically above the level at which he could legally drive his truck. After a few hours, Jones left the lounge. As he started across the highway to his truck, he darted into the path of a motorcycle driven by Edward McNair. In the collision, Jones and McNair were killed. McNair's wife, Catherine, filed a suit in a North Carolina state court against Lend Lease Trucks, Inc., and others, claiming in part that Jones was acting within the scope of employment at the time of the accident. The case was removed to a federal district court. Lend Lease filed a motion to dismiss, the court granted the motion, and Catherine appealed.

IN THE WORDS OF THE COURT . . .
PHILLIPS, Senior Circuit Judge:

* * * *

* * * [G]enerally, an employee can go "on a frolic of his own" * * * by engaging in conduct which * * * is in no way "about," or "in furtherance of," "his master's business."

* * * [A] truck-driver employee who while en route on an assigned trip takes a three to four hour * * * break during which he consumes sufficient alcohol to make it illegal for him to drive his truck further, has thereby departed from the course and scope of his employment. * * *

* * * *

* * * [Jones's departure from the scope of his employment] could only have ceased * * * when his blood-alcohol content dropped at least to the legal limit for performing his duty. That obviously had not occurred by the time of the collision.

DECISION AND REMEDY The U.S. Court of Appeals for the Fourth Circuit affirmed the order of the lower court.

FOR CRITICAL ANALYSIS—Social Consideration *What effect might it have had on the outcome of this case if, during his break, Jones had not "consume[d] sufficient alcohol to make it illegal for him to drive his truck"?*

Misrepresentation. A principal is exposed to tort liability whenever a third person sustains a loss due to the agent's misrepresentation. The principal's liability depends on whether or not the agent was actually or apparently authorized to make representations and whether such representations were made within the scope of the agency. The principal is always directly responsible for an agent's misrepresentation made within the scope of the agent's authority, whether the misrepresentation was made fraudulently or simply by the agent's mistake or oversight.

International Perspective • ISLAMIC LAW AND *RESPONDEAT SUPERIOR*

The doctrine of *respondeat superior* is well established in the legal systems of the United States and most Western countries. Middle Eastern countries, however, do not employ the principle. Islamic law, codified in the *Shari'a,* holds to a strict principle that responsibility for human actions lies with the individual and cannot be vicariously extended to others. This principle and other concepts of Islamic law are based on the sayings of Mohammed, the seventh-century prophet and founder of Islam.

FOR CRITICAL ANALYSIS

How would American society be affected if employers could not be held vicariously liable for their employees' torts?

Liability for Independent Contractor's Torts Generally, the principal is not liable for physical harm caused to a third person by the negligent act of an independent contractor in the performance of the contract. This is because the employer does not have the *right to control* the details of an independent contractor's performance. Exceptions to this rule are made in certain situations, however, as when exceptionally hazardous activities are involved. Examples of such activities include blasting operations, the transportation of highly volatile chemicals, or the use of poisonous gases. In these situations, a principal cannot be shielded from liability merely by using an independent contractor. Strict liability is imposed on the principal as a matter of law and, in some states, by statute. (For a discussion of other exceptions to the general rule, see this chapter's *Business Law in Action.*)

Liability for Agent's Crimes An agent is liable for his or her own crimes. A principal or employer is not liable for an agent's crime even if the crime was committed within the scope of authority or employment—unless the principal participated by conspiracy or other action. In some jurisdictions, under specific statutes, a principal may be liable for an agent's violation, in the course and scope of employment, of regulations, such as those governing sanitation, prices, weights, and the sale of liquor.

Agency Termination

Agency law is similar to contract law in that both an agency and a contract can be terminated by an act of the parties or by operation of law. Once the relationship between the principal and the agent has ended, the agent no longer has the right to bind the principal. For an agent's apparent authority to be terminated, however, third persons may also need to be notified when the agency has been terminated.

Business Law in Action • SOMETIMES, EXCEPTIONS ARE THE RULE

As a general rule, an employer is not liable for the torts committed by an independent contractor. As one court pointed out, however, this rule is so riddled with exceptions that the "exceptions . . . have practically subsumed the rule."[a] In fact, the *Restatement (Second) of Torts*, in Comment b to Section 409, states that the exceptions to the rule "are so numerous, and they have so far eroded the 'general rule,' that it can now be said to be 'general' only in the sense that it is applied where no good reason is found for departing from it."

Exceptions to the general rule come in many forms. For example, in one case a woman sued a shopping mall owner to recover for injuries she sustained when she fell on a snow-covered entryway to the mall. The mall owner asserted that it was not liable for the injuries because the entryway was maintained by an independent contractor. At trial, the mall owner prevailed. When the case reached the Supreme Court of New Hampshire, however, that court held that when an owner of business premises employs an independent contractor to maintain the premises, the owner is subject to vicarious liability for the independent contractor's negligence.

In support of its decision, the court cited Section 425 of the *Restatement (Second) of Torts,* which provides that a possessor (owner or tenant) of business premises who employs an independent contractor "to maintain in safe condition land which he holds open to the entry of the public as his place of business" is subject to liability for injuries caused by the contractor's "negligent failure to maintain the land in reasonably safe condition." According to the court, the duty owed by possessors of business premises to those whom they invite onto those premises simply cannot be delegated to others.[b]

In a number of other cases, courts have held that certain duties imposed by statute are nondelegable. Consider the "self-help" provision of Article 9 of the Uniform Commercial Code. As you read in Chapter 22, this provision allows a secured creditor, on the debtor's default, to repossess collateral in the debtor's possession so long as the repossession does not cause a "breach of the peace." But what if the secured party hires an independent contractor to repossess the collateral, such as a vehicle, and the independent contractor, during the repossession, breaches the peace or otherwise acts wrongfully or unlawfully? In these circumstances, courts have often held that even though the statutory violation or wrongful action was committed by an independent contractor, the secured party nonetheless is liable—because the secured party has a nondelegable duty not to breach the peace.[c]

FOR CRITICAL ANALYSIS

What policy interest is furthered by imposing liability on employers for the torts of their independent contractors?

a. *Rowley v. City of Baltimore,* 305 Md. 456, 505 A.2d 494 (1986).

b. *Valenti v. Net Properties Management, Inc.,* 142 N.H. 633, 710 A.2d 399 (1998).

c. See, for example, *Sanchez v. MBank of El Paso,* 792 S.W.2d 530 (Tex.App.—El Paso 1990); and *Williamson v. Fowler Toyota, Inc.,* 956 P.2d 858 (Okla. 1998).

TERMINATION BY ACT OF THE PARTIES

An agency may be terminated by act of the parties in several ways, including those discussed here.

Lapse of Time An agency agreement may specify the time period during which the agency relationship will exist. If so, the agency ends when that time period expires. For example, if the parties agree that the agency will begin on January 1, 1999, and end on December 31, 2000, the agency is automatically terminated on December 31, 2000. If no definite time is stated, then the agency continues for a reasonable time and can be terminated at will by either party. What constitutes a "reasonable time" depends, of course, on the circumstances and the nature of the agency relationship.

Purpose Achieved An agent can be employed to accomplish a particular objective, such as the purchase of stock for a cattle rancher. In that situation, the agency automatically ends after the cattle have been purchased. If more than one agent is employed to accomplish the same purpose, such as the sale of real estate, the first agent to complete the sale automatically terminates the agency relationship for all the others.

Occurrence of a Specific Event An agency can be created to terminate on the happening of a certain event. If Posner appoints Rubik to handle his business affairs while he is away, the agency automatically terminates when Posner returns.

Mutual Agreement Recall from the chapters on contract law that parties can cancel (rescind) a contract by mutually agreeing to terminate the contractual relationship. The same holds true under agency law regardless of whether the agency contract is in writing or whether it is for a specific duration.

Termination by One Party As a general rule, either party can terminate the agency relationship. The agent's act is called a *renunciation of authority.* The principal's act is referred to as a *revocation of authority.* Although both parties have the power to terminate the agency, however, they may not possess the right.

Wrongful termination can subject the canceling party to a suit for damages. • **EXAMPLE 24.13** Rawlins has a one-year employment contract with Munro to act as an agent in return for $35,000. Munro can discharge Rawlins before the contract period expires (Munro has the power to breach the contract); however, Munro will be liable to Rawlins for money damages, because Munro has no *right* to breach the contract. •

A special rule applies in an *agency coupled with an interest.* This type of agency is not an agency in the usual sense, because it is created for the agent's benefit instead of for the principal's benefit. • **EXAMPLE 24.14** Suppose that Julie borrows $5,000 from Rob, giving Rob some of her jewelry and signing a letter giving Rob the power to sell the jewelry as her agent if she fails to repay the loan. Julie, after she has received the $5,000 from Rob, then attempts to revoke Rob's authority to sell the jewelry as her agent. Julie would not succeed in this attempt, because a principal cannot revoke an agency created for the agent's benefit. •

Notice of Termination If the parties themselves have terminated the agency, it is the principal's duty to inform any third parties who know of the existence of the agency that it has been terminated (although notice of the termination may be given by others).

An agent's authority continues until the agent receives some notice of termination. Notice to third parties follows the general rule that an agent's *apparent* authority continues until the third person receives notice (from any source of information) that such authority has been terminated. The principal is expected to notify directly any third person who the principal knows has dealt with the agent. For third persons who have heard about the agency but have not yet dealt with the agent, *constructive* notice is sufficient.[9]

No particular form is required for notice of agency termination to be effective. The principal can actually notify the agent, or the agent can learn of the termination through some other means. • **EXAMPLE 24.15** Manning bids on a shipment of

9. Constructive notice is information or knowledge of a fact imputed by law to a person if he or she could have discovered the fact by proper diligence. Constructive notice is often accomplished by newspaper publication.

steel, and Stone is hired as an agent to arrange transportation of the shipment. When Stone learns that Manning has lost the bid, Stone's authority to make the transportation arrangement terminates.•

If the agent's authority is written, it must be revoked in writing, and the writing must be shown to all people who saw the original writing that established the agency relationship. Sometimes, a written authorization (such as a power of attorney) contains an expiration date. The passage of the expiration date is sufficient notice of termination for third parties.

TERMINATION BY OPERATION OF LAW

Termination of an agency by operation of law occurs in the circumstances discussed here. Note that when an agency terminates by operation of law, there is no duty to notify third persons.

Death or Insanity The general rule is that the death or mental incompetence of either the principal or the agent automatically and immediately terminates the ordinary agency relationship. Knowledge of the death is not required. • EXAMPLE 24.16 Suppose that Geer sends Pyron to China to purchase a rare painting. Before Pyron makes the purchase, Geer dies. Pyron's agent status is terminated at the moment of Geer's death, even though Pyron does not know that Geer has died.• Some states, however, have changed this common law rule by statute, and death does not terminate an agency coupled with an interest.

An agent's transactions that occur after the death of the principal are not binding on the principal's estate.[10] • EXAMPLE 24.17 Assume that Carson is hired by Perry to collect a debt from Thomas (a third party). Perry dies, but Carson, not knowing of Perry's death, still collects the money from Thomas. Thomas's payment to Carson is no longer legally sufficient to discharge Thomas's debt to Perry, because Carson's authority to collect the money ended on Perry's death. If Carson absconds with the money, Thomas is still liable for the debt to Perry's estate.•

Impossibility When the specific subject matter of an agency is destroyed or lost, the agency terminates. • EXAMPLE 24.18 Bullard employs Gonzalez to sell Bullard's house. Prior to the sale, the premises are destroyed by fire. In this situation, Gonzalez's agency and authority to sell Bullard's house terminate.• The agency also terminates when it is impossible for the agent to perform the agency lawfully.

Changed Circumstances When an event occurs that has such an unusual effect on the subject matter of the agency that the agent can reasonably infer that the principal will not want the agency to continue, the agency terminates. • EXAMPLE 24.19 Roberts hires Mullen to sell a tract of land for $20,000. Subsequently, Mullen learns that there is oil under the land and that the land is worth $1 million. The agency and Mullen's authority to sell the land for $20,000 are terminated.•

Bankruptcy and War Bankruptcy of the principal or the agent usually terminates the agency relationship. When the principal's country and the agent's country are at war with each other, the agency is terminated or at least suspended.

10. There is an exception to this rule in banking under which the bank, as the agent of the customer, can continue to exercise specific types of authority even after the customer has died or become mentally incompetent unless it has knowledge of the death or incompetence [UCC 4–405]. Even with knowledge of the customer's death, the bank has authority for ten days following the customer's death to honor checks in the absence of a stop-payment order.

APPLICATION

Law & the Employer: Using Independent Contractors*

As an employer, you may at some time consider hiring an independent contractor. One reason for using an independent contractor is that it may reduce your susceptibility to tort liability. If, however, an independent contractor's words or conduct leads another party to believe that the independent contractor is your employee, you may not escape liability for the contractor's tort.

To minimize the possibility of your being legally liable for negligence on the part of an independent contractor, you should, prior to hiring that contractor, inquire about his or her qualifications. The degree to which you should investigate depends, of course, on the nature of the work. A more thorough investigation is necessary when there is a potential danger to the public from the contractor's activities (as in delivering explosives).

Generally, it is a good idea to have the independent contractor assume, in a written contract, liability for harms caused to third parties by the independent contractor's negligence. You should also require the independent contractor to purchase liability insurance to cover the costs of potential lawsuits for harms caused to third persons by the independent contractor's hazardous activities or negligence.

Another reason for hiring an independent contractor is that you need not pay or deduct Social Security and unemployment taxes on behalf of such individuals. The independent contractor is the party responsible for paying these taxes. Additionally, the independent contractor is not eligible for any retirement or medical plans or other fringe benefits that you have for yourself and your employees, and this is a cost saving to you.

*This *Application* is not meant to substitute for the services of an attorney who is licensed to practice law in your state.

A word of caution, though: simply designating a person as an independent contractor does not make him or her one. Under Internal Revenue Service (IRS) rules, an individual will be treated as an employee if he or she is "in fact" an employee, regardless of any classification that you might have made. For example, an office assistant will not be treated by the IRS as an independent contractor simply because you designate him or her as such. If, however, you contract with an employment service, the assistant is an employee of the service and not your employee directly. In this situation, even though you are utilizing an independent contractor (the employment service), you still retain the right to supervise and inspect work to make sure that it meets your contract specifications.

If you improperly designate an employee as an independent contractor, the penalty may be high. Usually, you will be liable for back Social Security and unemployment taxes, plus interest and penalties. When in doubt, seek professional assistance in such matters.

Checklist for Using Independent Contractors

1. Check the qualifications of any independent contractor you plan to use to reduce the potential for negligent actions.
2. It is best to require in any contract with an independent contractor that the contractor assume liability for harm to a third person caused by the contractor's negligence.
3. Require that independent contractors working for you carry liability insurance. Examine the policy to make sure that it is current, particularly when the contractor will be undertaking actions that are more than normally hazardous to the public.
4. Make sure that independent contractors do not represent themselves as your employees to the rest of the world.
5. Regularly inspect the work of the independent contractor to make sure that it is being performed in accordance with contract specifications. Such supervision on your part will not change the worker's status as an independent contractor.

Key Terms

agency 640
disclosed principal 654
equal dignity rule 650
fiduciary 641
independent contractor 641
notary public 650
partially disclosed principal 654
power of attorney 650
ratification 645
respondeat superior 655
undisclosed principal 654

Chapter Summary • Agency Relationships in Business

Agency Relationships (See pages 641–644.)	In a *principal-agent* relationship, an agent acts on behalf of and instead of the principal in dealing with third parties. An employee who deals with third parties is normally an agent. An independent contractor is not an employee, and the employer has no control over the details of physical performance. The independent contractor is not usually an agent.
Agency Formation (See pages 644–647.)	1. *By agreement*—Through express consent (oral or written) or implied by conduct. 2. *By ratification*—The principal, either by act or agreement, ratifies the conduct of an agent who acted outside the scope of authority or the conduct of a person who is in fact not an agent. 3. *By estoppel*—When the principal causes a third person to believe that another person is his or her agent, and the third person deals with the supposed agent in reasonable reliance on the agency's existence, the principal is "estopped to deny" the agency relationship. 4. *By operation of law*—Based on a social duty (such as the need to support family members) or created in emergency situations when the agent is unable to contact the principal.
Duties of Agents and Principals (See pages 647–650.)	1. *Duties of the agent*— a. Performance—The agent must use reasonable diligence and skill in performing his or her duties or use the special skills that the agent has represented to the principal that the agent possesses. b. Notification—The agent is required to notify the principal of all matters that come to his or her attention concerning the subject matter of the agency. c. Loyalty—The agent has a duty to act solely for the benefit of his or her principal and not in the interest of the agent or a third party. d. Obedience—The agent must follow all lawful and clearly stated instructions of the principal. e. Accounting—The agent has a duty to make available to the principal records of all property and money received and paid out on behalf of the principal. 2. *Duties of the principal*— a. Compensation—Except in a gratuitous agency relationship, the principal must pay the agreed-on value (or reasonable value) for an agent's services. b. Reimbursement and indemnification—The principal must reimburse the agent for all sums of money disbursed at the request of the principal and for all sums of money the agent disburses for necessary expenses in the course of reasonable performance of his or her agency duties. c. Cooperation—A principal must cooperate with and assist an agent in performing his or her duties. d. Safe working conditions—A principal must provide safe working conditions for the agent-employee.
Agent's Authority (See pages 650–653.)	1. *Express authority*—Can be oral or in writing. Authorization must be in writing if the agent is to execute a contract that must be in writing. 2. *Implied authority*—Authority customarily associated with the position of the agent or authority that is deemed necessary for the agent to carry out expressly authorized tasks. 3. *Apparent authority*—Exists when the principal, by word or action, causes a third party reasonably to believe that an agent has authority to act, even though the agent has no express or implied authority. 4. *Ratification*—The affirmation by the principal of an agent's unauthorized action or promise. For the ratification to be effective, the principal must be aware of all material facts.

Chapter Summary • Agency Relationships in Business, Continued

Liability in Agency Relationships (See pages 653–658.)	1. *Liability for contracts*—If the principal's identity is disclosed or partially disclosed at the time the agent forms a contract with a third party, the principal is liable to the third party under the contract if the agent acted within the scope of his or her authority. If the principal's identity is undisclosed at the time of contract formation, the agent is personally liable to the third party, but if the agent acted within the scope of authority, the principal is also bound by the contract. 2. *Liability for agent's torts*—Under the doctrine of *respondeat superior,* the principal is liable for any harm caused to another through the agent's torts if the agent was acting within the scope of his or her employment at the time the harmful act occurred. The principal is also liable for an agent's misrepresentation, whether made knowingly or by mistake. 3. *Liability for independent contractor's torts*—A principal is not liable for harm caused by an independent contractor's negligence, unless hazardous activities are involved (in which situation the principal is strictly liable for any resulting harm) or other exceptions apply. 4. *Liability for agent's crimes*—An agent is responsible for his or her own crimes, even if the crimes were committed while the agent was acting within the scope of authority or employment. A principal will be liable for an agent's crime only if the principal participated by conspiracy or other action or (in some jurisdictions) if the agent violated certain government regulations in the course of employment.
Agency Termination (See pages 658–661.)	1. *By act of the parties*— a. Lapse of time (when a definite time for the duration of the agency was agreed on when the agency was established). b. Purpose achieved. c. Occurrence of a specific event. d. Mutual rescission (requires mutual consent of principal and agent). e. Termination by act of either the principal (revocation) or the agent (renunciation). (A principal cannot revoke an agency coupled with an interest.) f. When an agency is terminated by act of the parties, all third persons who have previously dealt with the agency must be directly notified; constructive notice will suffice for all other third parties. 2. *By operation of law*— a. Death or mental incompetence of either the principal or the agent (except in an agency coupled with an interest). b. Impossibility (when the purpose of the agency cannot be achieved because of an event beyond the parties' control). c. Changed circumstances (in which it would be inequitable to require that the agency be continued). d. Bankruptcy of the principal or the agent, or war between the principal's and agent's countries. e. When an agency is terminated by operation of law, no notice to third parties is required.

For Review

1. What formalities are required to create an agency relationship?
2. What duties does the agent owe to the principal? What duties does the principal owe to the agent?
3. How does an agent's apparent authority differ from an agent's actual authority? If an agent acts outside the scope of his or her authority, how might a principal still be held liable for the act?
4. If an agent, acting within the scope of authority, forms a contract with a third party on behalf of an undisclosed principal, explain whether the principal can be held liable on the contract.
5. Under what doctrine can a principal-employer be held liable for the torts committed by an agent-employee?

Questions and Case Problems

24–1. Agency Formation. Pete Gaffrey is a well-known, wealthy financier living in the city of Takima. Alan Winter, Gaffrey's friend, tells Til Borge that he (Winter) is Gaffrey's agent for the purchase of rare coins. Winter even shows Borge a local newspaper clipping mentioning Gaffrey's interest in coin collecting. Borge, knowing of Winter's friendship with Gaffrey, contracts with Winter to sell to Gaffrey a rare coin valued at $25,000. Winter takes the coin and disappears with it. On the date of contract payment, Borge seeks to collect from Gaffrey, claiming that Winter's agency made Gaffrey liable. Gaffrey does not deny that Winter was a friend, but he claims that Winter was never his agent. Discuss fully whether an agency was in existence at the time the contract for the rare coin was made.

24–2. Ratification by Principal. Springer was a political candidate running for congressional office. He was operating on a tight budget and instructed his campaign staff not to purchase any campaign materials without his explicit authorization. In spite of these instructions, one of his campaign workers ordered Dubychek Printing Co. to print some promotional materials for Springer's campaign. When the printed materials were received, Springer did not return them but instead used them during his campaign. When Dubychek failed to obtain payment from Springer for the materials, he sued for recovery of the price. Springer contended that he was not liable on the sales contract, because he had not authorized his agent to purchase the printing services. Dubychek argued that the campaign worker was Springer's agent and that the worker had authority to make the printing contract. Additionally, Dubychek claimed that even if the purchase was unauthorized, Springer's use of the materials constituted ratification of his agent's unauthorized purchase. Is Dubychek correct? Explain.

24–3. Agent's Duties to Principal. Iliana is a traveling sales agent. Iliana not only solicits orders but also delivers the goods and collects payments from her customers. Iliana places all payments in her private checking account and at the end of each month draws sufficient cash from her bank to cover the payments made. Giberson Corp., Iliana's employer, is totally unaware of this procedure. Because of a slowdown in the economy, Giberson tells all its sales personnel to offer 20 percent discounts on orders. Iliana solicits orders, but she offers only 15 percent discounts, pocketing the extra 5 percent paid by customers. Iliana has not lost any orders by this practice, and she is rated as one of Giberson's top salespersons. Giberson now learns of Iliana's actions. Discuss fully Giberson's rights in this matter.

24–4. Liability for Agent's Contracts. Michael Mosely works as a purchasing agent for Suharto Coal Supply, a partnership. Mosely has authority to purchase the coal needed by Suharto to satisfy the needs of its customers. While Mosely is leaving a coal mine from which he has just purchased a large quantity of coal, his car breaks down. He walks into a small roadside grocery store for help. While there, he runs into Wiley, who owns 360 acres back in the mountains with all mineral rights. Wiley, in need of money, offers to sell Mosely the property at $1,500 per acre. On inspection, Mosely concludes that the subsurface may contain valuable coal deposits. Mosely contracts to purchase the property for Suharto, signing the contract, "Suharto Coal Supply, Michael Mosely, agent." The closing date is set for August 1. Mosely takes the contract to the partnership. The managing partner is furious, as Suharto is not in the property business. Later, just before August 1, both Wiley and the partnership learn that the value of the land is at least $15,000 per acre. Discuss the rights of Suharto and Wiley concerning the land contract.

24–5. Agent's Duties to Principal. Sam Kademenos was about to sell a $1 million life insurance policy to a prospective customer when he resigned from his position with Equitable Life Assurance Society. Before resigning from the company, he had expended substantial amounts of company money and had utilized Equitable's medical examiners to procure the $1 million sale. After resigning, Kademenos joined a competing insurance firm, Jefferson Life Insurance Co., and made the sale through it. Has he breached any duty to Equitable? Explain. [*Kademenos v. Equitable Life Assurance Society,* 513 F.2d 1073 (3d Cir. 1975)]

24–6. Ratification by Principal. Fred Hash worked for Van Stavern Construction Co. as a field supervisor in charge of constructing a new plant facility. Hash entered into a contract with Sutton's Steel & Supply, Inc., to supply steel to the construction site in several installments. Hash gave the name of B. D. Van

Stavern, the president and owner of the construction firm, instead of the firm's name as the party for whom he was acting. The contract and the subsequent invoices all had B. D. Van Stavern's name on them. Sutton delivered several loads. All of the invoices were signed by Van Stavern employees, and corporate checks were made out to Sutton. When Sutton Steel later sued Van Stavern personally for unpaid debts totaling $40,437, it claimed that Van Stavern had ratified the acts of his employee, Hash, by allowing payment on previous invoices. Although Van Stavern had had no knowledge of the unauthorized arrangement, had he legally ratified the agreement by his silence? Explain. [*Sutton's Steel & Supply, Inc. v. Van Stavern,* 496 So.2d 1360 (La.App.3d 1986)]

24–7. *Respondeat Superior.* Justin Jones suffered from genital herpes and sought treatment from Dr. Steven Baisch of Region West Pediatric Services. A nurse's assistant, Jeni Hallgren, who was a Region West employee, told her friends and some of Jones's friends about Jones's condition. This was a violation of the Region West employee handbook, which required employees to maintain the confidentiality of patients' records. Jones filed a suit in a federal district court against Region West, among others, alleging that Region West should be held liable for its employee's actions on the basis of *respondeat superior.* On what basis might the court hold that Region West is not liable for Hallgren's acts? Discuss fully. [*Jones v. Baisch, M.D.,* 40 F.3d 252 (8th Cir. 1994)]

24–8. Employee versus Independent Contractor. Stephen Hemmerling was a driver for the Happy Cab Co. Hemmerling paid certain fixed expenses and abided by a variety of rules relating to the use of the cab, the hours that could be worked, the solicitation of fares, and so on. Rates were set by the state. Happy Cab did not withhold taxes from Hemmerling's pay. While driving the cab, Hemmerling was injured in an accident and filed a claim against Happy Cab in a Nebraska state court for workers' compensation benefits. Such benefits are not available to independent contractors. On what basis might the court hold that Hemmerling is an employee? Explain. [*Hemmerling v. Happy Cab Co.,* 247 Neb. 919, 530 N.W.2d 916 (1995)]

24–9. Undisclosed Principal. John Dunning was the sole officer of the R. B. Dunning Company and was responsible for the management and operation of the business. When the company rented a warehouse from Samuel and Ruth Saliba, Dunning did not say that he was acting for the firm. The parties did not have a written lease. Business faltered, and the firm stopped paying rent. Eventually, it went bankrupt and vacated the property. The Salibas filed a suit in a Maine state court against Dunning personally, seeking to recover the unpaid rent. Dunning claimed the debt belonged to the company because he had only been acting as its agent. Who is liable for the rent, and why? [*Estate of Saliba v. Dunning,* 682 A.2d 224 (Me. 1996)]

24–10. Liability for Employee's Acts. Federated Financial Reserve Corp. leases consumer and business equipment. As part of its credit approval and debt-collection practices, Federated hires credit collectors, whom it authorizes to obtain credit reports on its customers. Janice Caylor, a Federated collector, used this authority to obtain a report on Karen Jones, who was not a Federated customer but who was the ex-wife of Caylor's roommate, Randy Lind. When Jones discovered that Lind had her address and how he had obtained it, she filed a suit in a federal district court against Federated and others. Jones claimed in part that they had violated the Fair Credit Reporting Act, the goal of which is to protect consumers from the improper use of credit reports. Under what theory might an employer be held liable for an agent-employee's violation of a statute? Does that theory apply in this case? Explain. [*Jones v. Federated Financial Reserve Corp.,* 144 F.3d 961 (6th Cir. 1998)]

A QUESTION OF ETHICS AND SOCIAL RESPONSIBILITY

24–11. Kimberly Sierra, suffering from a severe asthma attack, went to Southview Hospital & Family Health Center. She was treated in the emergency room by Dr. Thomas Mucci. At the time, as a result of statements by Southview administrators, brochures, and ads, Sierra believed that the physicians at Southview were "hospital doctors." In fact, however, Mucci's contract with Southview stated, "The relationship between [Southview and Mucci] shall be that of independent contractor." Within a few hours, Sierra was pronounced dead. Sierra's mother, Edna Clark, filed a suit in an Ohio state court against Southview and others, alleging, in part, negligent medical care. Southview argued that it was not responsible for the acts of its independent contractors. Ultimately, the Supreme Court of Ohio heard the case and held that Southview was liable, under the doctrine of agency by estoppel, based primarily on its "hold[ing] itself out to the public as a provider of medical services." [*Clark v. Southview Hospital & Family Health Center,* 68 Ohio St.3d 435, 628 N.E.2d 46 (1994)]

1. Could Southview have avoided liability if Sierra had known that Mucci was an independent contractor? If so, would a sign in the emergency room have been enough? If not, how might Southview have avoided liability? Is it ethical for a hospital to attempt to avoid such responsibility?
2. Some department stores rent space in their stores to vendors of individual lines of products, such as cosmetics. In doing so, does a department store hold itself out to the public as a "provider" of cosmetics, subjecting itself to liability for the negligent acts of the independent contractors on its premises? Should the holding in the *Southview* case be applied in such contexts?

FOR CRITICAL ANALYSIS

24–12. What policy is served by the law that employers do not have copyright ownership in works created by independent contractors (unless there is a written "work for hire" agreement)?

Online Activities

ONLINE EXERCISE 24–1

Go to the "Internet Activities Book" on the Web site that accompanies this text, the URL for which is http://blt.westbuslaw.com. Select the following activities, and perform the exercises according to the instructions given there:

Activity 24–1: Agency
Activity 24–2: Intelligent Electronic Agents

Before the Test

Go to the *Business Law Today* home page at http://blt.westbuslaw.com. Click on TestTutor.® You will find twenty interactive questions relating to this chapter.

CHAPTER 25

Sole Proprietorships & Partnerships

> “[E]veryone thirsteth after gaine.”
>
> Sir Edward Coke, 1552–1634
> (English jurist and politician)

CONTENTS

LEARNING OBJECTIVES

After reading this chapter, you should be able to:

1. Summarize the advantages and disadvantages of doing business as a sole proprietorship.
2. Identify the essential elements of a partnership.
3. Outline the rights, duties, and powers of partners.
4. Point out how general principles of agency apply to partnerships.
5. Explain how a partnership can be terminated.

Many Americans would agree with Sir Edward Coke that most people, at least, “thirsteth after gaine.” Certainly, an entrepreneur’s primary motive for undertaking a business enterprise is to make profits. An *entrepreneur* is by definition one who initiates and *assumes the financial risks* of a new enterprise and undertakes to provide or control its management.

One of the questions faced by any entrepreneur who wishes to start up a business is what form of business organization he or she should choose for the business endeavor. In making this determination, a number of factors need to be considered. Four important factors are (1) ease of creation, (2) the liability of the owners, (3) tax considerations, and (4) the need for capital. In studying this unit on business organizations, keep these factors in mind as you read about the various business organizational forms available to entrepreneurs.

Traditionally, entrepreneurs have used three major forms to structure their business enterprises—the sole proprietorship, the partnership, and the corporation. In this chapter, we examine the first two of these forms. The third major traditional form—the corporation—is discussed in detail in Chapters 27 through 31. Two relatively new forms of business enterprise—limited liability companies (LLCs) and limited liability partnerships (LLPs)—offer special advantages to businesspersons, particularly with respect to taxation and liability. We look at these business forms, which are coming into widespread use, in Chapter 32. In Chapter 33, we describe a number of other forms of business organization as well as private franchises.

Sole Proprietorships

• **SOLE PROPRIETORSHIP**
The simplest form of business, in which the owner is the business; the owner reports business income on his or her personal income tax return and is legally responsible for all debts and obligations incurred by the business.

The simplest form of business is a **sole proprietorship.** In this form, the owner is the business; thus, anyone who does business without creating a separate business organization has a sole proprietorship. Sole proprietorships constitute over two-thirds of all American businesses. They are also usually small enterprises—about 99 percent of the sole proprietorships existing in the United States have revenues of less than $1 million per year. Sole proprietors can own and manage any type of business from an informal, home-office undertaking to a large restaurant or construction firm.

A major advantage of the sole proprietorship is that the proprietor receives all of the profits (because he or she assumes all of the risk). In addition, it is often easier and less costly to start a sole proprietorship than to start any other kind of business, as few legal forms are involved. This type of business organization also entails more flexibility than does a partnership or a corporation. The sole proprietor is free to make any decision he or she wishes concerning the business—whom to hire, when to take a vacation, what kind of business to pursue, and so on. A sole proprietor pays only personal income taxes on profits, which are reported as personal income on the proprietor's personal income tax return. Sole proprietors are also allowed to establish tax-exempt retirement accounts in the form of Keogh plans.[1]

WHAT ARE THE ADVANTAGES OF DOING BUSINESS AS A SOLE PROPRIETORSHIP?

The major disadvantage of the sole proprietorship is that, as sole owner, the proprietor alone bears the burden of any losses or liabilities incurred by the business enterprise. In other words, the sole proprietor has unlimited liability, or legal responsibility, for all obligations incurred in doing business. This unlimited liability is a major factor to be considered in choosing a business form. The sole proprietorship also has the disadvantage of lacking continuity on the death of the proprietor. When the owner dies, so does the business—it is automatically dissolved. If the business is transferred to family members or other heirs, a new proprietorship is created.

Another disadvantage is that the proprietor's opportunity to raise capital is limited to personal funds and the funds of those who are willing to make loans. If the owner wishes to expand the business significantly, one way to raise more capital to finance the expansion is to join forces with another entrepreneur and establish a partnership or form a corporation.

The Law Governing Partnerships

When two or more persons agree to do business as partners, they enter into a special relationship with one another. To an extent, their relationship is similar to an

1. A *Keogh plan* is a retirement program designed for self-employed persons by which a certain percentage of their income can be contributed to the plan, and interest earnings will not be taxed until funds are withdrawn from the plan.

"Many forms of conduct permissible in a workaday world for those acting at arm's length, are forbidden to those bound by fiduciary ties."

BENJAMIN CARDOZO, 1870–1938
(Associate justice of the United States Supreme Court, 1932–1938)

agency relationship, because each partner is deemed to be the agent of the other partners and of the partnership. The common law agency concepts outlined in Chapter 24 thus apply—specifically, the imputation of knowledge of, and responsibility for, acts done within the scope of the partnership relationship. In their relations with one another, partners, like agents, are bound by fiduciary ties.

In one important way, however, partnership law is distinct from agency law. A partnership is based on a voluntary contract between two or more competent persons who agree to place financial capital, labor, and skill in a business with the understanding that profits and losses will be shared. In a nonpartnership agency relationship, the agent usually does not have an ownership interest in the business, nor is he or she obliged to bear a portion of the ordinary business losses.

ON THE WEB

For a brief summary of the UPA and RUPA and their significance, as well as some hypothetical applications of particular provisions of these acts, go to the following Web page, which is part of the Web site of Aspen Publishers: www.aspenpub.com/lawsch/law/ee1.htm.

Partnerships are also governed by statutory law. The Uniform Partnership Act (UPA) governs the operation of partnerships *in the absence of express agreement* and has done much to reduce controversies in the law relating to partnerships. Except for Louisiana, all of the states, as well as the District of Columbia, have adopted the UPA. The UPA is presented in Appendix C of this book. A revised version of the UPA, known as the Revised Uniform Partnership Act (RUPA), was formally adopted by the National Conference of Commissioners on Uniform State Laws in 1992 and has already been adopted in several states. The RUPA significantly changes some of the rules governing partnerships.

In the pages that follow, we look at the legal definition of a partnership and at the laws governing the formation, operation, and termination of general partnerships. Whenever relevant, we include bracketed references to specific UPA provisions. Additionally, if the RUPA has significantly changed particular UPA provisions, we indicate these changes in footnotes. (Special types of partnerships, including the limited partnership, or LP, and the limited liability partnership, or LLP, will be examined in Chapter 32.)

Definition of Partnership

Conflicts commonly arise over whether a business enterprise is legally a partnership, especially in the absence of a formal, written partnership agreement. The UPA defines a **partnership** as "an association of two or more persons to carry on as co-owners a business for profit" [UPA 6(1)]. The intent to associate is a key element of a partnership, and one cannot join a partnership unless all other partners consent [UPA 18(g)].

• **PARTNERSHIP**
An agreement by two or more persons to carry on, as co-owners, a business for profit.

PARTNERSHIP STATUS

In resolving disputes over whether partnership status exists, courts will usually look for the following three essential elements, which are implicit in the UPA's definition of a partnership:

1. A sharing of profits and losses.
2. A joint ownership of the business.
3. An equal right in the management of the business.

¡KEEP IN MIND!
Two or more persons are required to form a partnership. Many other forms of business can be organized by a single individual.

If the evidence in a particular case is insufficient to establish all three factors, the UPA provides a set of guidelines to be used. For example, the sharing of profits and losses from a business is considered *prima facie* ("on the face of it") evidence that a partnership has been created. No such inference is made, however, if the profits were received as payment of any of the following [UPA 7(4)]:

1. A debt by installments or interest on a loan.
2. Wages of an employee.
3. Rent to a landlord.
4. An annuity to a widow or representative of a deceased partner.
5. A sale of goodwill of a business or property.

Joint ownership of property, obviously, does not in and of itself create a partnership. Therefore, if persons own real property as joint tenants or as tenants in common (forms of joint ownership, to be discussed in Chapter 40), this does not mean that they are partners in a partnership. In fact, the sharing of gross returns and even profits from such ownership is usually not enough to create a partnership [UPA 7(2), (3)]. • **EXAMPLE 25.1** Suppose that Ablat and Burke jointly own a piece of rural property. They lease the land to a farmer, with the understanding that they will receive a share of the profits from the farming operation conducted by the farmer in lieu of set rental payments. This arrangement normally would not make Ablat, Burke, and the farmer partners. Note, though, that although the sharing of profits does not prove the existence of a partnership, sharing *both profits and losses* usually does. •

In the following case, two brothers and their mother bought a ranch that for many years the brothers operated together. After the mother disclaimed her interest and one brother stopped participating in ranch activities, a question arose as to whether the brothers were ever partners.

CASE 25.1 Tarnavsky v. Tarnavsky

United States Court of Appeals,
Eighth Circuit, 1998.
147 F.3d 674.
ls.wustl.edu/cgi-bin/8th_byname.pl[a]

HISTORICAL AND SOCIAL SETTING *In the 1700s, 90 percent of the U.S. work force was in agriculture. Today, that figure is less than 3 percent, but operating a farm or ranch has become far more of an exact science. To run a successful agribusiness today, a farmer or rancher must have knowledge of computers, economics, financial management, government regulation, human resources, marketing, and risk management. A farmer or rancher must be—or have access to—an accountant, an insurance agent, a lawyer, a stockbroker, and must have a connection to his or her representative in Congress. Despite this situation, which would seem to favor agriconglomerates, about 90 percent of U.S. farms are individual or family operations, which account for about two-thirds of total agricultural production.*

BACKGROUND AND FACTS In 1967, Mary Tarnavsky and her sons Morris and Thomas (who was known as T.R.) bought a ranch known as the Christ place. T.R. and Morris opened a bank account into which they deposited their shares of the ranch's proceeds, which were used to make payments on the property, to pay property taxes, and to buy cattle, equipment, supplies, and services. For the ranch, the brothers took out joint loans, and jointly purchased cattle and machinery. They reported their activities on state and federal partnership income tax returns. Morris handled the livestock. T.R. handled the bookkeeping. In 1980, Mary disclaimed her interest in proceeds from the ranch. Eight years later, T.R. stopped doing the bookkeeping and began spending little time on ranch activities. Morris sent T.R. a "Notice of Dissolution of Partnership." After unsuccessful attempts to arrive at a settlement, T.R. filed a suit in a federal district court, requesting payment for his share of the partnership assets. The court ordered a payment of $220,000 to T.R. Morris appealed, arguing in part that there was no partnership.

a. From this page, a search can be launched, based on a party's name, for a recent opinion of the U.S. Court of Appeals for the Eighth Circuit. In the "Search String" box, type "Tarnavsky" and then click on "Begin Search." From the search results, click on the appropriate link to access the case. This database is maintained by the Washington University School of Law.

IN THE WORDS OF THE COURT . . .
JOHN R. GIBSON, Circuit Judge.

* * * *

(Continued)

CASE 25.1—Continued

* * * [C]ertain elements are critical to the existence of a partnership. These elements are: (1) an intention to be partners; (2) co-ownership of the business; and (3) profit motive.

* * * *

* * * T.R. and Morris reported their farming activities on state and federal partnership income tax returns * * * . Morris and T.R. opened a joint bank account * * * . From this account, they made the Christ place property payments, purchased cattle, seed, and related supplies. * * * These actions by Morris and T.R. evidence their intent to be partners.

Co-ownership, the second element necessary for a partnership, includes the sharing of profits and losses as well as the power of control in the management of the business.

* * * [A]fter completing a sale of cattle or grain, the brothers would deposit their share of the income in their joint account. From this account, the brothers jointly paid expenses * * * . [J]ointly purchasing land and machinery with profits is a form of profit sharing. * * * [A]t the end of each year, Morris and T.R. would allocate the year's profits on the partnership income tax return equally between themselves * * * . This sharing of profits is further evidence that Morris and T.R. were partners.

* * * *

* * * [B]oth T.R. and Morris handled "marketing the cattle" and performed various administrative functions, such as the discussion of rations. * * * Morris was "in charge" of livestock production and "administered" equipment purchases, and * * * T.R. was "in charge" of paperwork and finances. This is strong evidence that T.R. and Morris both had the power of control over management of the business. * * * Control, when combined with profit sharing, strongly suggests the existence of a partnership.

The final critical element of a partnership is profit motive, and there is no dispute that the farming business was operated with such motive.

DECISION AND REMEDY The U.S. Court of Appeals for the Eighth Circuit affirmed the lower court's order. Morris and T.R. were partners.

FOR CRITICAL ANALYSIS—Economic Consideration *Why would Morris want to argue that there was no partnership between the brothers?*

ENTITY VERSUS AGGREGATE

A partnership is sometimes called a *firm* or a *company,* terms that connote an entity separate and apart from its aggregate members. Sometimes the law of partnership recognizes a partnership as an independent entity, but for most other purposes, the law treats it as an *aggregate of the individual partners.*

At common law, a partnership was never treated as a separate legal entity. Thus, at common law a suit could never be brought by or against the firm in its own name; each individual partner had to sue or be sued. Today, most states provide specifically that the partnership can be treated as an entity for certain purposes. For example, a partnership usually can sue or be sued, collect judgments, and have all accounting procedures in the name of the partnership entity. In addition, the UPA recognizes that partnership property may be held in the name of the partnership rather than in the names of the individual partners. Finally, federal procedural laws frequently permit the partnership to be treated as an entity in such matters as suits in federal courts, bankruptcy proceedings, and informational federal tax returns.

When the partnership is not regarded as a separate legal entity, it is treated as an aggregate of the individual partners. For example, for federal income tax purposes, a partnership is not a tax-paying entity. The income and losses it incurs are passed through the partnership framework and attributed to the partners on their individual tax returns.

Partnership Formation

"Mr. Morgan buys his partners; I grow my own."
ANDREW CARNEGIE, 1835–1918
(American industrialist and philanthropist)

A partnership is ordinarily formed by an explicit agreement among the parties. The law does recognize another form of partnership, however, called *partnership by estoppel,* which arises when persons who are not partners represent themselves as partners when dealing with third parties. This section will describe the requirements for the creation of a partnership, including references to liability with respect to *alleged* partners.

International Perspective • DOING BUSINESS WITH FOREIGN PARTNERS

American businesspersons who wish to operate a partnership in another country need to check to see what that country requires in terms of local participation. If a country requires local participation, this means that a specific share of the business must be owned by nationals of the host country. In other words, the American businesspersons would need to admit to the partnership a partner or partners who live in the host country.

Sometimes, Americans seeking to establish partnerships in a country that requires local participation are reluctant to do so. This is because the technology and expertise developed by the partnership business may end up in the hands of a future competitor if the partnership breaks up—and the American parties may have little recourse against their former partners' use of their intellectual property under the host country's law.

FOR CRITICAL ANALYSIS
Do local participation rules benefit countries in the long run?

THE PARTNERSHIP AGREEMENT

Agreements to form a partnership can be oral, written, or implied by conduct. Some partnership agreements, however, must be in writing to be legally enforceable within the Statute of Frauds (discussed in Chapter 12). For example, a partnership agreement that, by its terms, is to continue for more than one year must be evidenced by a sufficient writing.

• **ARTICLES OF PARTNERSHIP**
A written agreement that sets forth each partner's rights and obligations with respect to the partnership.

A partnership agreement, called **articles of partnership,** usually specifies the name and location of the business, the duration of the partnership, the purpose of the business, each partner's share of the profits, how the partnership will be managed, how assets will be distributed on dissolution, and other provisions. As mentioned, the UPA applies only in the absence of the parties' agreement on a particular issue. The partnership agreement is thus binding on the parties, even if certain provisions, such as the distribution of profits, seem to be unfair. A sample partnership agreement is shown in Exhibit 25–1.[2]

2. The RUPA provides for the voluntary filing of a partnership statement, containing such information as the agency authority of the partners, with the secretary of state. The statement must be executed by at least two partners, a copy must be sent to all of the partners, and a certified copy must be filed in the office for recording transfers of real property (in most states, in the county in which the property is located).

EXHIBIT 25–1 • A Sample Partnership Agreement

PARTNERSHIP AGREEMENT

This agreement, made and entered into as of the __________, by and among __________ __________________ (hereinafter collectively sometimes referred to as "Partners").

WITNESSETH:

Whereas, the Parties hereto desire to form a General Partnership (hereinafter referred to as the "Partnership"), for the term and upon the conditions hereinafter set forth;

Now, therefore, in consideration of the mutual covenants hereinafter contained, it is agreed by and among the Parties hereto as follows:

Article I
BASIC STRUCTURE

Form. The Parties hereby form a General Partnership pursuant to the Laws of __________ ______________.

Name. The business of the Partnership shall be conducted under the name of __________ ______________.

Place of Business. The principle office and place of business of the Partnership shall be located at ____________________, or such other place as the Partners may from time to time designate.

Term. The Partnership shall commence on __________, and shall continue for _____ years, unless earlier terminated in the following manner: (a) By the completion of the purpose intended, or (b) Pursuant to this Agreement, or (c) By applicable ______________ law, or (d) By death, insanity, bankruptcy, retirement, withdrawal, resignation, expulsion, or disability of all of the then Partners.

Purpose—General. The purpose for which the Partnership is organized is ____________ ____

Article II
FINANCIAL ARRANGEMENTS

Each Partner has contributed to the initial capital of the Partnership property in the amount and form indicated on Schedule A attached hereto and made a part hereof. Capital contributions to the Partnership shall not earn interest. An individual capital account shall be maintained for each Partner. If at any time during the existence of the Partnership it shall become necessary to increase the capital with which the said Partnership is doing business, then (upon the vote of the Managing Partner[s]): each party to this Agreement shall contribute to the capital of this Partnership within ___ days notice of such need in an amount according to his then Percentage Share of Capital as called for by the Managing Partner(s).

The Percentage Share of Profits and Capital of each Partner shall be (unless otherwise modified by the terms of this Agreement) as follows:

Names	Initial Percentage Share of Profits and Capital
____________	________________
____________	________________
____________	________________

No interest shall be paid on any contribution to the capital of the Partnership. No Partner shall have the right to demand the return of his capital contributions except as herein provided. Except as herein provided, the individual Partners shall have no right to any priority over each other as to the return of capital contributions except as herein provided.

Distributions to the Partners of net operating profits of the Partnership, as hereinafter defined, shall be made at ______________________. Such distributions shall be made to the Partners simultaneously.

For the purpose of this Agreement, net operating profit for any accounting period shall mean the gross receipts of the Partnership for such period, less the sum of all cash expenses of operation of the Partnership, and such sums as may be necessary to establish a reserve for operating expenses. In determining net operating profit, deductions for depreciation, amortization, or other similar charges not requiring actual current expenditures of cash shall *not* be taken into account in accordance with generally accepted accounting principles.

(Continued)

EXHIBIT 25-1 • A Sample Partnership Agreement—Continued

No partner shall be entitled to receive any compensation from the Partnership, nor shall any Partner receive any drawing account from the Partnership.

Article III
MANAGEMENT

The Managing Partner(s) shall be ______________________.

The Managing Partner(s) shall have the right to vote as to the management and conduct of the business of the Partnership as follows:

Names	Vote
____________	____________
____________	____________
____________	____________

Article IV
DISSOLUTION

In the event that the Partnership shall hereafter be dissolved for any reason whatsoever, a full and general account of its assets, liabilities and transactions shall at once be taken. Such assets may be sold and turned into cash as soon as possible and all debts and other amounts due the Partnership collected. The proceeds thereof shall thereupon be applied as follows:

(a) To discharge the debts and liabilities of the Partnership and the expenses of liquidation.

(b) To pay each Partner or his legal representative any unpaid salary, drawing account, interest or profits to which he shall then be entitled and in addition, to repay to any Partner his capital contributions in excess of his original capital contribution.

(c) To divide the surplus, if any, among the Partners or their representatives as follows:

(1) First (to the extent of each Partner's then capital account) in proportion to their then capital accounts. (2) Then according to each Partner's then Percentage Share of [*Capital/Income*].

No Partner shall have the right to demand and receive property in kind for his distribution.

Article V
MISCELLANEOUS

The Partnership's fiscal year shall commence on January 1st of each year and shall end on December 31st of each year. Full and accurate books of account shall be kept at such place as the Managing Partner(s) may from time to time designate, showing the condition of the business and finances of the Partnership; and each Partner shall have access to such books of account and shall be entitled to examine them at any time during ordinary business hours. At the end of each year, the Managing Partner(s) shall cause the Partnership's accountant to prepare a balance sheet setting forth the financial position of the Partnership as of the end of that year and a statement of operations (income and expenses) for that year. A copy of the balance sheet and statement of operations shall be delivered to each Partner as soon as it is available.

Each Partner shall be deemed to have waived all objections to any transaction or other facts about the operation of the Partnership disclosed in such balance sheet and/or statement of operations unless he shall have notified the Managing Partner(s) in writing of his objectives within thirty (30) days of the date on which such statement is mailed.

The Partnership shall maintain a bank account or bank accounts in the Partnership's name in a national or state bank in the State of ______________. Checks and drafts shall be drawn on the Partnership's bank account for Partnership purposes only and shall be signed by the Managing Partner(s) or their designated agent.

Any controversy or claim arising out of or relating to this Agreement shall only be settled by arbitration in accordance with the rules of the American Arbitration Association, one Arbitrator, and shall be enforceable in any court having competent jurisdiction.

Witnesses	Partners
____________	____________
____________	____________

Date: __________

ON THE WEB

The Small Business Administration offers an abundance of information for entrepreneurs who wish to start up businesses, including partnerships. For answers to "frequently asked questions" concerning business start-ups and when a partnership may be advantageous, go to www.sba.gov/starting/faq.

ETHICAL ISSUE 25.1 ***Why should partnership agreements be in writing?*** Time and again, disputes among partners come before the courts because of oral partnership agreements. For example, suppose that Turino and Crowder decide to create a partnership to sell tires. They orally agree that Turino will provide two-thirds of the capital to start up the business and will receive two-thirds of the profits in return. After the business is under way, Crowder claims that he is working harder at the business than Turino is, and thus at least one-half of the profits should be his. The dispute ends up in court, and Turino, because he has no evidence of the oral agreement, ends up with only one-half of the profits. This is because the law assumes that members of a partnership share profits and losses equally unless a partnership agreement provides otherwise, as will be discussed later in this chapter [UPA 18(a)]. Turino and Crowder could have avoided this problem by creating a written partnership agreement that specified how the profits would be shared.

PARTNERSHIP DURATION

The partnership agreement can specify the duration of the partnership in terms of a date or the completion of a particular project. A partnership that is specifically limited in duration is called a *partnership for a term.* A dissolution without the consent of all the partners prior to the expiration of the partnership term constitutes a breach of the agreement, and the responsible partner can be liable for any losses resulting from it. If no fixed duration is specified, the partnership is a *partnership at will.* This type of partnership can be dissolved at any time by any partner without violating the agreement and without incurring liability for losses to other partners resulting from the termination.

THE CORPORATION AS PARTNER

General partners are personally liable for the debts incurred by the partnership. If one of the general partners is a corporation, however, what does personal liability mean? Basically, the capacity of corporations to contract is a question of corporation law. Many states have restrictions on corporations becoming partners, although such restrictions have become less common over the years. The Revised Model Business Corporation Act (discussed in Chapter 27), however, generally allows corporations to make contracts and incur liabilities, and the UPA specifically permits a corporation to be a partner. By definition, "a partnership is an association of two or more persons," and the UPA defines *person* as including corporations [UPA 2].

PARTNERSHIP BY ESTOPPEL

Parties who are not partners sometimes represent themselves as such and cause third persons to rely on their representations. The law of partnership does not confer any partnership rights on these persons, but it may impose liability on them. This is also true when a partner represents, expressly or impliedly, that a nonpartner is a member of the firm. Whenever a third person has reasonably and detrimentally relied on the representation that a nonpartner was part of the partnership, partnership by estoppel is deemed to exist. When this occurs, the nonpartner is regarded as an agent whose acts are binding on the partnership. In the following case, an attorney's corporate client claimed to have relied on a representation that the attorney was a partner in a law firm.

CASE 25.2 Atlas Tack Corp. v. DiMasi

Appeals Court of Massachusetts,
Suffolk, 1994.
37 Mass.App.Ct. 66,
637 N.E.2d 230.

HISTORICAL AND SOCIAL SETTING *Professionals (accountants, attorneys, physicians, and others) commonly share office space with members of the same profession. They usually do not wish to share responsibility, however, for the wrongful acts of those with whom they share offices. To obtain the advantages of working near others in the same profession, professionals often form "professional associations." A professional association is a group of professionals organized to practice their profession together. This "association" need not be organized as a corporation or a partnership.*

BACKGROUND AND FACTS Attorneys Salvatore DiMasi, Ralph Donabed, and Stephen Karll shared office space, which they designated the "Law Offices of DiMasi, Donabed & Karll, A Professional Association." They also shared stationery that bore the same heading and that listed their names, along with the names of other attorneys, in the margin. Atlas Tack Corporation hired Donabed to handle a certain legal matter. All correspondence and invoices from Donabed to Atlas were on the "Law Offices" stationery, and Atlas's payment for the services was in the form of checks payable to "DiMasi, Donabed & Karll." Believing that Donabed had done something wrong in his handling of its matter, Atlas filed a suit in a Massachusetts state court against Donabed, DiMasi, and Karll. Donabed settled out of court, but Atlas maintained the suit against DiMasi and Karll, alleging that they were Donabed's partners and were thus liable for Donabed's acts. The court granted the defendants' motion for summary judgment, and Atlas appealed.

IN THE WORDS OF THE COURT . . .
PORADA, Justice.

* * * *

* * * [T]he defendants not only knew that Donabed was using stationery with the legend "DiMasi, Donabed & Karll" but they also knew and consented to his use of stationery that bore the legend after their names, "a professional association" and listed in the margin a roll of attorneys including themselves [and] Donabed * * * . In addition, the bills forwarded to the plaintiffs from Donabed came on stationery with this letterhead * * * . There is no indication on the bills that payment should be made to Donabed or that the bill was submitted by Donabed instead of the law office of DiMasi, Donabed & Karll. * * * [T]he use of the term "professional association" may well suggest a partnership to the public * * * . At the very least, the use of the term in the circumstances of this case presents a question of fact as to whether a partnership by estoppel exists.

DECISION AND REMEDY The Appeals Court of Massachusetts reversed the lower court's judgment and remanded the case for trial.

FOR CRITICAL ANALYSIS—Social Consideration *What could the members of a professional association do to avoid liability for the wrongful acts of other members?*

Rights among Partners

The rights and duties of partners are governed largely by the specific terms of their partnership agreement. In the absence of provisions to the contrary in the partnership agreement, the law imposes the rights and duties discussed here. The character and nature of the partnership business generally influence the application of these rights and duties.

INTEREST IN THE PARTNERSHIP

A partner's interest in the partnership is a personal asset consisting of a proportionate share of the profits earned [UPA 26] and a return of capital after the partnership is terminated. Each partner is entitled to the proportion of business profits and losses designated in the partnership agreement.

Profits and Losses If the agreement does not apportion profits or losses, the UPA provides that *profits shall be shared equally and losses shall be shared in the same ratio as profits* [UPA 18(a)]. • **EXAMPLE 25.2** The partnership agreement for Ponce and Brent provides for capital contributions of $6,000 from Ponce and $4,000 from Brent, but it is silent as to how Ponce and Brent will share profits or losses. In this situation, Ponce and Brent will share both profits and losses equally. If the partnership agreement provided for profits to be shared in the same ratio as capital contributions, however, 60 percent of the profits would go to Ponce, and 40 percent of the profits would go to Brent. If their partnership agreement was silent as to losses, losses would be shared in the same ratio as profits (60 percent to 40 percent).•

Assignment of Partnership Interest A partner may assign (transfer) his or her interest in the partnership to another party. When a partner's interest is assigned, the assignee (the person to whom the interest was transferred) has the right to receive the partner's share of the profits and, on the partnership's termination, the partner's capital contribution. The assignee, however, does not become a partner in the partnership and thus has no say in the management or administration of the partnership affairs and no right to inspect the partnership books. Rather, the partner who assigned his or her interest remains a partner with the full rights of a partner with respect to those rights that cannot be assigned.

Creditor's Lien on Partnership Interest A partner's interest is also subject to a judgment creditor's lien (described in Chapter 23). A judgment creditor can attach a partner's interest by petitioning the court that entered the judgment to grant the creditor a **charging order.** This order entitles the creditor to the profits of the partner and to any assets available to the partner on the firm's dissolution [UPA 28].

• **CHARGING ORDER**
In partnership law, an order granted by a court to a judgment creditor that entitles the creditor to attach profits or assets of a partner on the dissolution of the partnership.

MANAGEMENT RIGHTS

Under the UPA, all partners have equal rights in managing the partnership [UPA 18(e)]. Each partner has one vote in management matters *regardless of the proportional size of his or her interest in the firm.* Often, in a large partnership, partners will agree to delegate daily management responsibilities to a management committee made up of one or more of the partners.

"All partners have equal rights in the management and conduct of the partnership business."
UNIFORM PARTNERSHIP ACT, SECTION 18(e)

The majority rule controls decisions in ordinary matters connected with partnership business, unless otherwise specified in the agreement. Decisions to undertake any of the actions listed below, however, if they are to be binding on the partnership, require the *unanimous* consent of the partners. This is because these decisions significantly affect the nature of the partnership [UPA 9(3), 18(g), (h)].

1. To alter the essential nature of the firm's business as expressed in the partnership agreement or to alter the capital structure of the partnership.
2. To admit new partners or to enter a wholly new business.
3. To assign partnership property into a trust for the benefit of creditors.
4. To dispose of the partnership's goodwill.

• CONFESSION OF JUDGMENT
The act or agreement of a debtor in permitting a judgment to be entered against him or her by a creditor, for an agreed sum, without the institution of legal proceedings.

5. To confess judgment against the partnership or to submit partnership claims to arbitration. (A **confession of judgment** is the act of a debtor in permitting a judgment to be entered against him or her by a creditor, for an agreed sum, without the institution of legal proceedings.)
6. To undertake any act that would make further conduct of partnership business impossible.
7. To amend the articles of the partnership agreement.

COMPENSATION

A partner has a duty to expend time, skill, and energy on behalf of the partnership business, and such services are generally not compensable in the form of a salary. Rather, as mentioned, a partner's income from the partnership takes the form of a distribution of profits according to the partner's share in the business. Partners can, however, agree otherwise. For example, partners in a law firm often agree that the managing partner of the firm should receive a salary in addition to his or her share of profits for performing special administrative duties in office and personnel management. When a partnership must be terminated because a partner dies, a surviving partner is entitled to reasonable compensation for services relating to the final settlement (winding up) of partnership affairs (and reimbursement for expenses incurred in the process) above and apart from his or her share in the partnership profits [UPA 18(f)].

Each partner impliedly promises to subordinate his or her interests to those of the partnership. • **EXAMPLE 25.3** Assume that Hall, Banks, and Porter enter into a partnership. Porter undertakes independent consulting, in the same area in which the partnership specializes, for an outside firm without the consent of Hall and Banks. Porter's compensation from the outside firm is considered partnership income [UPA 21].• A partner cannot engage in any independent business that involves the partnership's time unless expressly agreed on by the partnership.

INSPECTION OF BOOKS

Partnership books and records must be kept accessible to all partners. Each partner has the right to receive (and each partner has the corresponding duty to produce) full and complete information concerning the conduct of all aspects of partnership business [UPA 20]. Each firm keeps books in which to record and preserve such information. Partners contribute the information, and a bookkeeper or an accountant typically has the duty to preserve it. The books must be kept at the firm's principal business office and cannot be removed without the consent of all of the partners [UPA 19]. Every partner, whether active or inactive, is entitled to inspect all books and records on demand and can make copies of the materials. The personal representative of a deceased partner's estate has the same right of access to partnership books and records that the decedent would have had.

ETHICAL ISSUE 25.2 ***Why is it important for partners to have the right to inspect partnership books?*** The right to inspect partnership books and records helps to ensure that partners abide by their fiduciary duties to one another. If one partner suspects that another partner is using the partnership assets for personal gain, for example, an inspection of the partnership records will help to either confirm or dispel the suspicion. If partners did not have the right of inspection, there would be no way for them to monitor the nature and types of business transactions undertaken by the partnership. Furthermore, the partner's interest in the partnership is essentially a property right—a right to own a share of partnership assets and profits. This right would be meaningless if the partner did not have access to information indicating how his or her property was being used.

ACCOUNTING OF ASSETS

An accounting of partnership assets or profits is required to determine the value of each partner's share in the partnership. An accounting can be performed voluntarily, or it can be compelled by a court. Under UPA 22, a partner has the right to a formal accounting in the following situations:

1. When the partnership agreement provides for a formal accounting.
2. When a partner is wrongfully excluded from the business or from the possession of its property, from access to the books, or both.
3. When any partner is withholding profits or benefits belonging to the partnership in breach of the fiduciary duty.
4. When circumstances "render it just and reasonable."

A formal accounting also occurs by right in connection with *dissolution* proceedings (discussed later in this chapter). Generally, the principal remedy of a partner against co-partners is a suit for dissolution, an accounting, or both. With minor exceptions, a partner cannot maintain an action against other firm members for damages until partnership affairs are settled and an accounting is done. This rule is necessary because legal disputes between partners invariably involve conflicting claims to shares in the partnership. Logically, the value of each partner's share must first be determined by an accounting.

PROPERTY RIGHTS

One of the property rights of partners—the right to a share of the profits made by the partnership—has already been discussed. A partner also has ownership rights in

BUSINESSPERSONS EXAMINE ACCOUNTING RECORDS. ARE THERE ANY RESTRICTIONS ON THE RIGHT OF A PARTNER TO INSPECT HIS OR HER FIRM'S BOOKS AND RECORDS? WHY OR WHY NOT?

any real or personal property owned by the partnership. Property owned by the partnership, or *partnership property,* is defined by the UPA as "all property originally brought into the partnership's stock or subsequently acquired, by purchase or otherwise, on account of the partnership" [UPA 8(1)].

For example, in the formation of a partnership, a partner may bring into the partnership any property that he or she owns as a part of his or her capital contribution. This property becomes partnership property even though title to it may still be in the name of the contributing partner. The intention that certain assets are to be partnership assets is the heart of the phrase "on account of the partnership." Thus, the more closely an asset is associated with the business operations of the partnership, the more likely it is to be a partnership asset.[3]

UPA 25(1) states that partners are tenants in partnership. This means that every partner is a co-owner with all other partners of specific partnership property, such as office equipment, paper supplies, and vehicles. Each partner has equal rights to possess partnership property for business purposes or in satisfaction of firm debts, but not for any other purpose without the consent of all the other partners. Tenancy in partnership has several important effects. If a partner dies, the surviving partners, not the heirs of the deceased partner, have the right of survivorship to the specific property. Although surviving partners are entitled to possession, they have a duty to account to the decedent's estate for the value of the deceased partner's interest in the property [UPA 25(2)(d), (e)].

A partner has no right to sell, assign, or in any way deal with a particular item of partnership property as an exclusive owner [UPA 25(2)(a), (b)]. Therefore, creditors cannot use partnership property to satisfy the personal debts of a partner. Partnership property is available only to satisfy partnership debts, to enhance the firm's credit, or to achieve other business purposes of the partnership.

Duties and Liabilities of Partners

"Of legal knowledge I acquired such a grip, that they took me into the partnership."

WILLIAM S. GILBERT, 1836–1911
(English playwright; Arthur Sullivan's collaborator in comic opera)

The duties and liabilities of partners are basically derived from agency law. Each partner is an agent of every other partner and acts as both a principal and an agent in any business transaction within the scope of the partnership agreement. Each partner is also a general agent of the partnership in carrying out the usual business of the firm.[4] Thus, every act of a partner concerning partnership business and every contract signed in the partnership name bind the firm [UPA 9(1)]. The UPA affirms general principles of agency law that pertain to the authority of a partner to bind a partnership in contract or tort.

We examine here the fiduciary duties of partners, the authority of partners, the joint and several liability that characterizes partnerships, and the limitations imposed on the liability of incoming partners for preexisting partnership debts.

FIDUCIARY DUTIES

Partners stand in a fiduciary relationship to one another just as principals and agents do. As indicated in Chapter 24, a fiduciary relationship is one of extraordi-

3. Under the RUPA, property that is not acquired in the name of the partnership is nonetheless partnership property if the instrument transferring title refers to (1) the person taking title as a partner or (2) indicates the existence of the partnership [RUPA 204(a)(2)]. Also, the property is still presumed to be partnership property if it is acquired with partnership funds [RUPA 204(c)]. If none of the above occurs, the property is presumed to be the property of individual partners, even if it is used in the partnership business [RUPA 204(d)].

4. The RUPA adds "or business of the kind carried on by the partnership" [RUPA 301(1)]. Basically, this addition gives added protection to third persons who deal with an unfamiliar partnership.

nary trust and loyalty. Each partner has a fiduciary duty to act in good faith and for the benefit of the partnership. Each partner must also subordinate his or her personal interests to those of the partnership if a conflict of interests arises.[5]

This fiduciary duty underlies the entire body of law pertaining to partnership and agency. From it, certain other duties are commonly implied. Thus, a partner must account to the partnership for personal profits or benefits derived from any partnership transaction that is undertaken without the consent of all of the partners.[6]

AUTHORITY OF PARTNERS

Agency concepts relating to actual (express and implied) authority, apparent authority, and ratification are also applicable to partnerships. In an ordinary partnership, firm members can exercise all implied powers reasonably necessary and customary to carry on that particular business. Some customarily implied powers include the authority to make warranties on goods in the sales business, the power to convey real property in the firm's name when such conveyances are part of the ordinary course of partnership business, the power to enter into contracts consistent with the firm's regular course of business, and the power to make admissions and representations concerning partnership affairs [UPA 11].

When a partner acts within the scope of authority, the partnership is bound to third parties by these acts. For example, a partner's authority to sell partnership products carries with it the implied authority to transfer title and to make the usual warranties. Hence, in a partnership that operates a retail tire store, any partner negotiating a contract with a customer for the sale of a set of tires can warrant that "each tire will be warranted for normal wear for 40,000 miles."

This same partner, however, does not have the authority to sell office equipment, fixtures, or the partnership office building without the consent of all of the other partners. In addition, because partnerships are formed to create profits, a partner does not generally have the authority to make charitable contributions without the consent of the other partners. Such actions are not binding on the partnership unless they are ratified by all of the other partners.

As in the law of agency, the law of partnership imputes one partner's knowledge to all other partners, because members of a partnership stand in a fiduciary relationship to one another. This relationship implies that each partner will fully disclose to every other partner all information pertaining to the business of the partnership [UPA 12].

JOINT LIABILITY

• **JOINT LIABILITY**
Shared liability. In partnership law, partners incur joint liability for partnership obligations and debts. For example, if a third party sues a partner on a partnership debt, the partner has the right to insist that the other partners be sued with him or her.

In most states, partners are subject to joint liability on partnership debts and contracts [UPA 15(b)]. **Joint liability** means that if a third party sues a partner on, for example, a partnership debt, the partner has the right to insist that the other partners be sued with him or her. If the third party does not sue all of the partners, the partners sued cannot be required to pay a judgment, and the assets of the partnership cannot be used to satisfy the judgment. (Similarly, a release of one partner releases all partners.) In other words, to bring a successful claim against the partnership on a debt or contract, a plaintiff must name all the partners as defendants.

---

5. The RUPA states that partners may pursue their own interests without automatically violating their fiduciary duties [RUPA 404(e)].

6. In this sense, to account to the partnership means not only to divulge the information but also to determine the value of any benefits or profits derived and to hold that money or property in trust on behalf of the partnership.

To simplify this rule, some states, such as California, have enacted statutes providing that a partnership may be sued in its own name and that a judgment will bind the partnership's and the individual partners' property even though not all the partners are named in the complaint. If the third party is successful, he or she may collect on the judgment against the assets of one or more of the partners. Otherwise stated, each partner is liable and may be required to pay the entire amount of the judgment. When one partner pays the entire amount, the partnership is required to indemnify that partner [UPA 18(b)]. If the partnership cannot do so, the obligation falls on the other partners.

JOINT AND SEVERAL LIABILITY

In some states, partners are both jointly liable and severally, or individually, liable for partnership debts and contracts. In all states, partners are jointly and severally liable for torts and breaches of trust [UPA 15(a)].[7] **Joint and several[8] liability** means that a third party may sue any one or more of the partners without suing all of them or the partnership itself. In other words, a third party may sue one or more of the partners separately (severally) or all of the partners together (jointly), at his or her option. This is true even if the partner did not participate in, ratify, or know about whatever it was that gave rise to the cause of action.[9]

• **JOINT AND SEVERAL LIABILITY**
In partnership law, a doctrine under which a plaintiff may sue, and collect a judgment from, one or more of the partners separately (severally, or individually) or all of the partners together (jointly). This is true even if one of the partners sued did not participate in, ratify, or know about whatever it was that gave rise to the cause of action.

A judgment against one partner on his or her several liability does not extinguish the others' liability. (Similarly, a release of one partner discharges the partners' joint but not several liability.) Thus, those not sued in the first action may be sued subsequently. The first action, however, may have been conclusive on the question of liability. If, for example, in an action against one partner, the court held that the partnership was in no way liable, the third party cannot bring an action against another partner and succeed on the issue of the partnership's liability.

If the third party is successful in a suit against a partner or partners, he or she may collect on the judgment only against the assets of those partners named as defendants. The partner who committed the tort is required to indemnify the partnership for any damages it pays.

LIABILITY OF INCOMING PARTNER

A newly admitted partner to an existing partnership normally has limited liability for whatever debts and obligations the partnership incurred prior to the new partner's admission. The new partner's liability can be satisfied only from partnership assets [UPA 17]. This means that the new partner usually has no personal liability for these debts and obligations, but any capital contribution made by him or her to the partnership is subject to these debts.

In cases involving old debts and new partners, there are two dates of great significance: the date on which the debt arose and the date on which the partner joined the firm. The court in the following case had to determine the date on which a partnership debt arose.

7. Under the RUPA, partners' liability is joint and several for all debts [RUPA 306].

8. The term *several* stems from the medieval English term *severall,* which meant "separately," or "severed from" one another. As used here, *several* liability means *separate* liability.

9. The RUPA prevents creditors from bringing an action to collect debts from the partners of a non-bankrupt partnership without first attempting unsuccessfully to collect from the partnership (or convincing a court that the attempt would be unsuccessful) [RUPA 307(d)].

CASE 25.3 Citizens Bank of Massachusetts v. Parham-Woodman Medical Associates

United States District Court,
Eastern District of Virginia, Richmond Division, 1995.
874 F.Supp. 705.

HISTORICAL AND ECONOMIC SETTING *Some of the most talented professionals do not have any special competence outside their fields. For example, the history of business is full of stories concerning brilliant artists, architects, dentists, and other professionals who made poor choices when investing their money. In the 1980s, many of these unwise investments were in real estate and construction projects. At the time, some of the most expert businesspersons and financial institutions also made wrong choices in deciding where and in what to invest and nearly put themselves out of business.*

BACKGROUND AND FACTS The Citizens Bank of Massachusetts agreed to lend Parham-Woodman Medical Associates, a partnership, $2 million to construct a new office building. Their agreement, which was signed on April 30, 1985, provided for the money to be disbursed in installments. Most of the funds had been disbursed before Richard Hunley, Nada Tas, and Joseph Tas joined the firm. When the partnership failed to repay the loan, the bank sold the building and obtained a deficiency judgment for more than $1.2 million. The bank filed a suit in a federal district court against the firm and the partners to recover this amount. Hunley and the Tases acknowledged that they joined the firm before all of the money was disbursed, but argued that was after the date of the loan, and thus they were not liable for the debt beyond the amount of their interests in partnership assets.

IN THE WORDS OF THE COURT . . .
PAYNE, District Judge.

* * * *

[UPA] Section 17 makes an incoming partner liable for "all the obligations of the partnership arising before his admission," but provides that "this liability shall be satisfied only out of partnership property." * * * [A] partnership obligation arises, within the meaning of Section 17, when the creditor extends the credit to the partnership. In this instance, that occurred on April 30, 1985 and not on the occasion when the bank disbursed each advance.

* * * *

Here the documents were executed long before Dr. Hunley and the Tases joined Parham-Woodman and, upon execution, they were binding obligations on both Citizens Bank and the partnership. That is not changed merely because the passage of part of the consideration was delayed pursuant to a schedule which also was set before Dr. Hunley and the Tases became partners.

DECISION AND REMEDY The federal district court held that Hunley and the Tases were liable only to the extent of the partnership property.

FOR CRITICAL ANALYSIS—Economic Consideration
Does the rule of UPA 17 favor debtors or creditors? Why?

Partnership Termination

Any change in the relations of the partners that demonstrates unwillingness or inability to carry on partnership business dissolves the partnership, resulting in termination [UPA 29]. If one of the partners wishes to continue the business, he or she is free to reorganize into a new partnership with the remaining members.

• **DISSOLUTION**
The formal disbanding of a partnership or a corporation. It can take place by (1) acts of the partners or, in a corporation, of the shareholders and board of directors; (2) the death of a partner; (3) the expiration of a time period stated in a partnership agreement or a certificate of incorporation; or (4) judicial decree.

• **WINDING UP**
The second of two stages involved in the termination of a partnership or corporation. Once the firm is dissolved, it continues to exist legally until the process of winding up all business affairs (collecting and distributing the firm's assets) is complete.

The termination of a partnership has two stages, both of which must take place before termination is complete. The first stage, **dissolution,** occurs when any partner (or partners) indicates an intention to disassociate from the partnership. The second stage, **winding up,**[10] is the actual process of collecting and distributing the partnership assets.

DISSOLUTION

Dissolution of a partnership can be brought about by the acts of the partners, by the operation of law, and by judicial decree. Each of these events will be discussed here.

Dissolution by Acts of Partners Dissolution of a partnership may come about through the acts of the partners in several ways. First, the partnership can be dissolved by the partners' agreement. For example, when a partnership agreement expresses a fixed term or a particular business objective to be accomplished, the passing of the date or the accomplishment of the objective dissolves the partnership.

Second, because a partnership is a voluntary association, a partner has the power to disassociate himself or herself from the partnership at any time and thus dissolve the partnership. (See this chapter's *Business Law in Action* for a discussion of a problem facing many law firms today—partners who leave the firm and take their clients with them.) Any change in the partnership, whether by the withdrawal of a partner or by the admission of a new partner, results in dissolution.[11] In practice, this is modified by the provision that the remaining or new partners may continue in the firm's business. Nonetheless, a new partnership arises. Creditors of the prior partnership become creditors of the new partnership [UPA 41].

Finally, the UPA provides that neither a voluntary assignment of a partner's interest nor an involuntary sale of a partner's interest for the benefit of creditors [UPA 27, 28] by itself dissolves the partnership. Either occurrence, however, can ultimately lead to judicial dissolution of the partnership (judicial dissolution will be discussed shortly).

Dissolution by Operation of Law If one of the partners dies, the partnership is dissolved by operation of law, even if the partnership agreement provides for carrying on the business with the executor of the decedent's estate.[12] The bankruptcy of a partner will also dissolve a partnership, and naturally, the bankruptcy of the firm itself will result in dissolution [UPA 31(4), (5)].

Additionally, any event that makes it unlawful for the partnership to continue its business or for any partner to carry on in the partnership will result in dissolution [UPA 31(3)]. Note, however, that even if the illegality of the partnership business is a cause for dissolution, the partners can decide to change the nature of their business and continue in the partnership. When the illegality applies to an individual partner, then dissolution is mandatory. • EXAMPLE 25.4 Suppose that a state legislature passes a law making it illegal for judges in that state to engage in the practice of law.

10. Although "winding down" would seem to describe more accurately the process of settling accounts and liquidating the assets of a partnership, "winding up" has been traditionally used in English and U.S. statutory and case law to denote this final stage of a partnership's existence.

11. The RUPA distinguishes the withdrawal of a partner that causes a breakup of a partnership from a withdrawal that causes only the end of a partner's participation in the business (and results in a buyout of that partner's interest) [RUPA 601, 701, 801]. Dissolution results only if the partnership must be liquidated [RUPA 801].

12. Under the RUPA, the death of a partner represents that partner's "dissociation" from the partnership, but it is not an automatic ground for the partnership's dissolution [RUPA 601].

Business Law in Action • Fiduciary Duties and Departing Partners

An ongoing problem faced by partnerships is that of departing partners who take their clients with them. There is nothing in the model ethical rules governing attorney conduct that expressly prohibits departing attorneys from soliciting business from clients with whom they have had an ongoing relationship. Yet the courts have placed some limits on what attorneys may or may not do when leaving their firms. Consider a case that came before the Illinois Supreme Court.

The case arose after two partners in a law firm left the firm to set up their own partnership. They took with them a major client of the firm, an insurance company whose business accounted for 58 percent of the firm's income, or approximately $6 million a year. The departing partners also took with them some of the firm's best paralegals and secretaries. Additionally, before they notified the firm that they were leaving, they had obtained a business loan, leased office space, furnished it, and arranged for telephone service. The law firm sued the partners, claiming that they had breached their fiduciary duties to the other partners by secretly undertaking these actions before they had notified the other partners that they were leaving.

When the case reached the Illinois Supreme Court, the court remanded the case for fact finding on whether the departing partners had solicited the major client's business before or after they announced that they were leaving—the parties disputed this issue. The court also set forth some broad guidelines on what kind of behavior might constitute a breach of a law partner's fiduciary duties.

The court noted that departing attorneys are involved in a delicate venture. On the one hand, common sense dictates that an attorney who is dissatisfied with the existing association should take steps to locate alternative office space and associations—and do so confidentially. The court also noted that it is permissible for departing partners "to inform clients with whom they have a prior professional relationship about their impending withdrawal and new practice, and to remind the client of its freedom to retain counsel of its choice." On the other hand, departing partners must take care not to breach their fiduciary obligations to the other partners. The court stated that "secretly attempting to lure firm clients . . . to the new association . . . and abandoning the firm on short notice (taking clients and files) would not be consistent with a partner's fiduciary duties."[a]

According to the court, then, departing partners have fairly wide latitude in making preparations for departure, even in secret. The one thing they may not do is solicit the firm's clients before leaving—or at least before notifying the partners of their intention to withdraw from the partnership.

FOR CRITICAL ANALYSIS

Is there any way a law firm can avoid the problems created by withdrawing partners who take their clients with them?

a. *Dowd & Dowd v. Gleason,* 181 Ill.2d 460, 693 N.E.2d 358, 230 Ill.Dec. 229 (1998).

If Gerald Fowler, an attorney in a law firm, is appointed or elected to a judgeship, then Fowler must leave the law firm, and the partnership must be dissolved.•

Dissolution by Judicial Decree For dissolution of a partnership by judicial decree to occur, an application or petition must be made in an appropriate court. The court then either denies the petition or grants a decree of dissolution. UPA 32 cites situations in which a court can dissolve a partnership. One situation occurs when a partner is adjudicated mentally incompetent or is shown to be of unsound mind. Another situation arises when a partner appears incapable of performing his or her duties under the partnership agreement. If the incapacity is likely to be permanent and to affect substantially the partner's ability to discharge his or her duties to the firm, a court will dissolve the partnership by decree.

Dissolution may also be ordered by a court when it becomes obviously impractical for the firm to continue—for example, if the business can only be operated at a loss. Additionally, a partner's impropriety involving partnership business (for example, fraud perpetrated on the other partners) or improper behavior reflecting unfavorably on the firm may provide grounds for a judicial decree of dissolution. Finally, if dissension between partners becomes so persistent and harmful as to undermine the confidence and cooperation necessary to carry on the firm's business, dissolution may also be granted.

Notice of Dissolution The intent to dissolve or to withdraw from a firm must be communicated clearly to each partner. A partner can express this notice of intent by either actions or words. All partners will share liability for the acts of any partner who continues conducting business for the firm without knowing that the partnership has been dissolved. Dissolution of a partnership by the act of a partner requires notice to all affected third persons as well. Any third person who has extended credit to the firm must receive actual notice (notice given to the party directly and personally). For all others, constructive notice (a newspaper announcement or similar public notice) is sufficient [UPA 35]. Dissolution resulting from the operation of law generally requires no notice to third parties.[13]

WINDING UP

¡DON'T FORGET! Secured creditors have priority over unsecured creditors to any assets that serve as collateral for a partnership's debts.

Once dissolution occurs and the partners have been notified, the partners cannot create new obligations on behalf of the partnership. Their only authority is to complete transactions begun but not finished at the time of dissolution and to wind up the business of the partnership [UPA 33, 37]. *Winding up* includes collecting and preserving partnership assets, discharging liabilities (paying debts), and accounting to each partner for the value of his or her interest in the partnership.

Both creditors of the partnership and creditors of the individual partners can make claims on the partnership's assets. In general, creditors of the partnership have priority over creditors of individual partners in the distribution of partnership assets; the converse priority is usually followed in the distribution of individual partner assets, except under bankruptcy law. The priorities in the distribution of a partnership's assets are as follows [UPA 40]:[14]

1. Payment of third party debts.
2. Refund of advances (loans) made to or for the firm by a partner.
3. Return of capital contribution to a partner.
4. Distribution of the balance, if any, to partners in accordance with their respective shares in the profits.

If the partnership's liabilities are greater than its assets, the partners bear the losses—in the absence of a contrary agreement—in the same proportion in which they shared the profits (rather than, for example, in proportion to their contributions to the partnership's capital). Partners continue in their fiduciary relationship until the winding-up process is completed.

Partnerships—Advantages and Disadvantages

As with a sole proprietorship, one of the advantages of a partnership is that it can be organized fairly easily and inexpensively. Additionally, the partnership form of

13. *Childers v. United States*, 442 F.2d 1299 (5th Cir. 1971).
14. Under the RUPA, partner creditors are included among creditors who take first priority [RUPA 808]. Capital contributions and profits or losses are then calculated together to determine the amounts that the partners receive or the amounts that they must pay.

> **ON THE WEB**
> For further information on the taxation of partnerships, as compared to other forms of business organizations, see the article by Dennis D'Annunzio in the *Sunbelt Business Journal*, which is online at **www.sunbeltnetwork.com/Journal/Current/D970804dsd.html**.

business offers important tax advantages. The partnership itself files only an informational tax return with the Internal Revenue Service. In other words, the firm itself pays no taxes. A partner's profit from the partnership (whether distributed or not) is taxed as individual income to the individual partner.

A partnership may also allow for greater capital contributions to the business than is possible in a sole proprietorship. Two or more persons can invest in the business, and lenders may be more willing to make loans to a partnership than they would be to a sole proprietorship.

The main disadvantage of the partnership form of business is that the partners are subject to personal liability for partnership obligations. If the partnership cannot pay its debts, the personal assets of the partners are subject to creditors' claims. This disadvantage of the partnership is one of the major reasons that many entrepreneurs choose to form a corporation. As will be discussed in the following chapters, in the corporate form of business the owners' liability is limited to the amount of their investments in the business. The limited liability companies and partnerships discussed in Chapter 32 are additional business forms that allow business owners to limit their personal liability for business debts and obligations.

Key Terms

Chapter Summary • Sole Proprietorships and Partnerships

Sole Proprietorships (See page 669.)	The simplest form of business; used by anyone who does business without creating an organization. The owner is the business. The owner pays personal income taxes on all profits and is personally liable for all business debts.
Partnerships (See pages 669–688.)	1. Created by agreement of the parties. 2. Not treated as an entity except for limited purposes. 3. Partners have unlimited liability for partnership debts. 4. Each partner has an equal voice in management unless otherwise provided for in the partnership agreement. 5. In the absence of an agreement, partners share profits equally and share losses in the same ratio as they share profits. 6. The capital contribution of each partner is determined by agreement. 7. Each partner pays a proportionate share of income taxes on the net profits of the partnership, whether or not they are distributed; the partnership files only an information return with the Internal Revenue Service. 8. Terminated by agreement or can be dissolved by action of the partners (withdrawal), operation of law (death or bankruptcy), or court decree.

For Review

1. What advantages and disadvantages are associated with the sole proprietorship?
2. List the three essential elements of a partnership.
3. Summarize the rights and duties of partners.
4. What is meant by joint and several liability? Why is this often considered to be a disadvantage of the partnership form of business?
5. Can a partner continue the business of a terminated partnership if he or she wishes to do so? How?

Questions and Case Problems

25–1. Distribution of Partnership Assets. Shawna and David formed a partnership. At the time of the partnership's formation, Shawna's capital contribution was $10,000, and David's was $15,000. Later, Shawna made a $10,000 loan to the partnership when it needed working capital. The partnership agreement provided that profits were to be shared, 40 percent for Shawna and 60 percent for David. The partnership was dissolved by David's death. At the end of the dissolution and the winding up of the partnership, the partnership's assets were $50,000, and the partnership's debts were $8,000. Discuss fully how the assets should be distributed.

25–2. Partnership Property. Schwartz and Zenov were partners in an accounting firm. Because business was booming and profits were better than ever, they decided to invest some of the firm's profits in Munificent Corp. stock. The investment turned out to be a good one, as the stock continued to increase in value. On Schwartz's death several years later, Zenov assumed full ownership of the business, including the Munificent Corp. stock, a partnership asset. Schwartz's daughter Rosalie, however, claimed a 50 percent ownership interest in the Munificent Corp. stock as Schwartz's sole heir. Can Rosalie enforce her claim? Explain.

25–3. Partner's Property Rights. Maruta, Samms, and Ortega were partners in a business firm. The firm's business equipment included several expensive computers. One day, Maruta borrowed one of the computers for use in his home, but he never bothered to return it. When the other partners asked him about it, Maruta claimed that because the computer represented less than one-third of the computers owned by the partnership, and because he owned one-third of the business, he had a right to keep the equipment. Was he right? Explain.

25–4. Rights among Partners. Jebeles and Costellos were partners in "Dino's Hot Dogs," doing business on the Montgomery Highway in Alabama. From the outset, Costellos worked at the business full-time, while Jebeles involved himself only to a small extent in the actual running of the business. Jebeles was married to Costellos's sister, and when marital difficulties developed between Jebeles and his wife, Costellos barred Jebeles from the premises. Jebeles sued for an accounting of the partnership's profits and for dissolution of the partnership, claiming a partnership at will and that the relationship between the partners made it impossible to conduct partnership business. Will the court grant the petition? Explain. [*Jebeles v. Costellos,* 391 So.2d 1024 (Ala. 1980)]

25–5. Partnership Dissolution. Carola and Grogan were partners in a law firm. The partnership began business in 1974 and was created by an oral agreement. On September 6, 1976, Carola withdrew from the partnership some of its files, furniture, and books, along with various other items of office equipment. The next day, Carola informed Grogan he had withdrawn from the partnership. Discuss whether Carola's actions on September 6, 1976, constituted effective notice of dissolution to Grogan. [*Carola v. Grogan,* 102 A.D.2d 934, 477 N.Y.S.2d 525 (1984)]

25–6. Distribution of Assets. Robert Lowther, Fred Riggleman, and Granville Zopp were equal partners in the Four Square Partnership. The partnership was created to acquire and develop real estate for commercial retail use. In the course of the partnership, Riggleman loaned $30,000 to the partnership, and Zopp loaned the partnership $50,000. Donald H. Lowther, Robert's brother and not a partner in the firm, loaned Four Square $80,000 and took a promissory note signed by the three partners. Four Square encountered financial difficulties shortly after the commercial venture began and eventually defaulted on payments due on a construction loan it had received from a bank. The bank foreclosed on the property securing the debt. The proceeds of the subsequent foreclosure sale satisfied the bank's interest and left a surplus of $87,783 to be returned to the partnership. In the meantime, the partnership had been dissolved and was in the process of winding up its affairs. Donald H. Lowther maintained that, as a nonpartner creditor, his claim against the firm's assets took priority over those of Riggleman and Zopp. Is Lowther correct? Explain. [*Lowther v. Riggleman,* 189 W.Va. 68, 428 S.E.2d 49 (1993)]

25–7. Rights among Partners. B&R Communications was a general partner in Amarillo CellTelco. Under the partnership agreement, each partner had the right to inspect partnership records "at reasonable times during business hours," so long as the inspection did not "unreasonably interfere with the operation of the partnership." B&R believed that the managers of the firm were using partnership money to engage in lawsuits that were too costly. B&R and other general partners filed a suit in a Texas state court against the managers. B&R wanted to inspect the firm's records to discover information about the lawsuits, but the court denied B&R's request. B&R asked a state appellate court to order the trial judge to grant the request. On what ground did the appellate court issue the order? [*B&R Communications v. Lopez,* 890 S.W.2d 224 (Tex.App.—Amarillo 1994)]

25–8. Liability of Incoming Partner. Conklin Farm sold land to LongView Estates, a general partnership, to build condominiums. LongView gave a promissory note to Conklin for $9 million as payment. A few years later, Doris Leibowitz joined LongView as a general partner. Leibowitz left the firm before the note came due, but while she was a partner, interest accrued on the balance. The condominium project failed, and LongView went out of business. Conklin filed a suit in a New Jersey state court against Leibowitz to recover some of the interest on the note. Conklin acknowledged that Leibowitz was not liable for debt incurred before she joined the firm but argued that the interest that accrued while she was a partner was "new" debt for which she was personally liable. To what extent, if any, is Leibowitz liable to Conklin? [*Conklin Farm v. Leibowitz,* 140 N.J. 417, 658 A.2d 1257 (1995)]

25–9. Liability of Partners. Frank Kolk was the manager of Triples American Grill, a sports bar and restaurant. Kolk and John Baines opened bank accounts in the name of the bar, each signing the account signature cards as "owner." Baines was often at the bar and had free access to its office. Baines told others that he was "an owner" and "a partner." Kolk told Steve Mager, the president of Cheesecake Factory, Inc., that Baines was a member of a partnership that owned Triples. On this basis, Cheesecake delivered its goods to Triples on credit. In fact, the bar was owned by a corporation. When the unpaid account totaled more than $20,000, Cheesecake filed a suit in a New Mexico state court against Baines to collect. On what basis might Baines be liable to Cheesecake? What does Cheesecake have to show to win its case? [*Cheesecake Factory, Inc. v. Baines,* 964 P.2d 183 (N.M.App. 1998)]

A QUESTION OF ETHICS AND SOCIAL RESPONSIBILITY

25–10. David Murphy and James Canion formed a general partnership to conduct real estate business. Their partnership agreement provided that both partners would devote their full-time efforts to conducting partnership business, that all personal earnings from personal services would be included as partnership income, and that any real estate or other partnership business conducted by either partner during the term of the partnership agreement should be for the joint account of the partnership. Through his business associates and contacts, Canion learned of several profitable real estate opportunities and secretly took advantage of them for his own gain. When Murphy found out about Canion's activities, he told Canion that he was canceling the partnership under a clause in the partnership agreement that allowed termination by a partner with ninety days' notice. In the lawsuit that followed, Murphy alleged that Canion had breached the partnership agreement and his fiduciary duty to the partnership. The trial court agreed with Murphy and awarded him damages, which the court held to be proximately caused by Canion's wrongful appropriation of partnership business opportunities. On appeal, Canion contended, among other things, that his breach of his fiduciary duty did not proximately cause any damages to Murphy, because the income generated by Canion's "secret" projects was received after the partnership had terminated. [*Murphy v. Canion,* 797 S.W.2d 944 (Tex.App.—Houston [14th Dist.] 1990)]

1. Should Murphy be entitled, in the form of damages, to a share of the profits made by Canion through his secret dealings, in view of the fact that Canion received the income *after* the partnership had terminated? If you were the judge, how would you decide this issue, and on what legal basis? From an ethical point of view, what solution would be the fairest?
2. What ethical considerations are involved in the rule that partners have a fiduciary duty to subordinate their personal interests to the mutual welfare of all of the partners? Do you think that a partnership would be a viable form of business organization if partners were not held to such a fiduciary duty?

FOR CRITICAL ANALYSIS

25–11. Given the extensive liability of partners, why would any entrepreneur choose to do business with another, or others, as a partnership?

Online Activities

ONLINE EXERCISE 25-1

Go to the "Internet Activities Book" on the Web site that accompanies this text, the URL for which is http://blt.westbuslaw.com. Select the following activity, and perform the exercise according to the instructions given there:

Activity 25–1: Partnerships

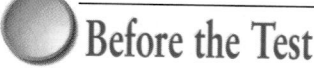

Before the Test

Go to the *Business Law Today* home page at http://blt.westbuslaw.com. Click on TestTutor.® You will find twenty interactive questions relating to this chapter.

CHAPTER 26

Partners & Joint Ventures

"There would be little for diplomats to do if the world consisted of partners, enjoying political intimacy, and responding to common appeals."

Walter Lippmann, 1899–1974
(American journalist)

CONTENTS

LEARNING OBJECTIVES

After reading this chapter, you should be able to:

1. Identify different classifications of partners and partnerships.
2. Summarize the effect of recognizing a partnership as a legal entity separate from the partners.
3. State the rights of innocent partners when a partner's violation of the partnership agreement causes the dissolution of the firm.
4. List the duties and liabilities of the members of a joint venture.
5. Identify the liability of an unincorporated association.

As Walter Lippmann implies in the opening quotation, partners get together to achieve a common goal. A *partnership* is an association of two or more persons to carry on as co-owners a business for profit. Persons who desire to start a partnership do not have to satisfy any formal requirements. In fact, a simple sharing of profits gives an inference that there is a partnership even between persons who did not intend to form a partnership at all. (Of course, if it becomes an issue, proof can be offered to show that a partnership does, or does not, actually exist.)

Many of the important topics concerning partnerships are discussed in Chapter 25. This chapter considers some additional details on partners, partnerships, and joint ventures.

Partners

ON THE WEB

The 'Lectric Law Library's "Business Law Lounge" page is "[d]edicated to matters of interest to businesses and the folks running them." This page can be found at **www.lectlaw.com/bus.html**.

Partners combine their capital, their skill, and their efforts to do business without having to comply with state incorporation statutes. Partners also form partnerships for tax benefits, as mentioned in Chapter 25. Consequently, partners can influence the flow of their income and losses in a way that the owners of a corporation ordinarily cannot.

CLASSIFICATIONS OF PARTNERS AND PARTNERSHIPS

General partners have the right to participate in the management and profits of a partnership and have unlimited liability to its creditors. *Limited partners* contribute capital to a partnership but do not participate in its management. The liability of the limited partners is limited to the amount of the capital that they contribute. If they participate in its management, they assume unlimited liability for the debts of the partnership.

General partners or limited partners may also be dormant partners, silent partners, or secret partners. A *dormant partner* is a partner who has the right to participate in management but who generally does not exercise the right, in contrast to those partners who actively conduct the business of the firm. A *silent partner* is a partner whose identity is undisclosed and who does not participate in the management of the partnership. • EXAMPLE 26.1 John's name does not appear in the name of the partnership in which he is a partner, nor does he participate in its management. John is a silent partner. • A *secret partner* is a partner whose identity is undisclosed but who participates in the management of the partnership. A partnership with secret partners is known as a *secret partnership*.

A *general partnership* is an ordinary partnership that consists only of general partners. A *limited partnership* is a special partnership that consists of one or more general partners and one or more limited partners. A general or limited partnership may also be a *family partnership*, which is a partnership in the control of the members of the same family. A *tiered partnership* is a partnership in which one partnership (the first tier) is a partner in one or more other partnerships (the second tier).

A partnership may also be classified according to its business. • EXAMPLE 26.2 A *mining partnership* is an association of the owners of a source of minerals or other natural resource, such as oil or gas, who cooperate to develop the property. A different type of partnership is a *commercial*, or *trading*, *partnership*, which is a partnership that participates in the business of buying and selling. A *nontrading partnership* is organized for some other purpose, such as the practice of law or accounting. •

WHO MAY BECOME A PARTNER

Any person having the capacity to enter a contract can become a partner. A partnership contract entered into with a minor as a partner is voidable and can be disaffirmed by the minor (see Chapter 12 for details). Lack of legal capacity due to insanity at the time of the agreement likewise allows the purported partner either to avoid the agreement or to enforce it. If a partner is adjudicated mentally incompetent during the course of the partnership, the partnership is not automatically dissolved, but dissolution can be decreed by a court on a petition. A partnership can also become a partner in another partnership, if all of the partners agree to the arrangement.[1] Even a corporation may become a partner [UPA 2].

1. Note, however, that a single partner cannot make another person a partner in a partnership merely by transferring his or her interest to that person [UPA 27].

Partners as Fiduciaries

Partners are fiduciaries in their relationships with each other. Among other aspects of their fiduciary duty, each partner holds in trust for all of the other partners all funds realized from transactions connected with the business of the partnership. A partner must also account to the other partners for the use of all of the assets of the partnership [UPA 21(1)].

A partner's fiduciary duty requires the highest degree of good faith and fair dealing. This is particularly true when a partner makes a partnership decision that affects him or her personally. Suppose a partner lends the partnership boat to a friend for a weekend party for $500. This partner holds the $500 in trust for the benefit of all of the partners. This principle of fiduciary duty is illustrated in the following case.

CASE 26.1 Starr v. Fordham

Supreme Judicial Court of Massachusetts, 1995.
420 Mass. 178,
648 N.E.2d 1261.

HISTORICAL AND ECONOMIC SETTING *Fifty years ago, many lawyers made good incomes but practicing law was not considered the same path to wealth that entering business was. As lawyers' incomes increased, however, particularly in the 1970s and 1980s, the number of attorneys also increased. This led to greater competition for business, which in turn caused frequent start-ups and breakups of law firms, with attorneys joining and quitting different partnerships at an unprecedented rate.*

BACKGROUND AND FACTS Ian Starr was a partner in the law firm of Fordham & Starrett. Under the partnership agreement, Laurence Fordham and Loyd Starrett (the "founding partners") determined each partner's share of the firm's profits. The first year, the two divided the profits equally. Starr quit the firm on the last day of the second year. Fordham came up with a list of negative factors for determining Starr's share of the second year's profits and paid him less than half an equal share. Starr filed a suit in a Massachusetts state court against the partners, alleging, among other things, breach of fiduciary duty. The court awarded Starr an additional share of the profits. The partners appealed this award to the state's highest court, the Supreme Judicial Court of Massachusetts.

IN THE WORDS OF THE COURT . . .
NOLAN, Justice.

* * * *

* * * The judge found that the plaintiff had produced [business] that constituted * * * 15% * * * of the total * * * dollar amounts for all of the partners as a group. The judge noted, however, that the founding partners distributed only 6.3% of the firm's * * * profits to the plaintiff. * * * The judge determined that this * * * was unfair * * * . The judge also noted that Fordham had fabricated a list of negative factors that the founding partners had used in determining the plaintiff's share of the firm's profits. As a result, the judge concluded that the founding partners had violated their respective fiduciary duties to the plaintiff * * * .

Having examined the record, all 127 exhibits, and the judge's own findings of fact and rulings of law, we * * * cannot conclude that the judge committed a mistake in finding that the founding partners had violated * * * their fiduciary duties to the plaintiff * * * .

DECISION AND REMEDY The Supreme Judicial Court of Massachusetts affirmed the judgment of the lower court.

FOR CRITICAL ANALYSIS—Social Consideration *Do partners who violate their fiduciary duty also violate the implied covenant of good faith and fair dealing?*

ACCOUNTING FOR PARTNERSHIP FUNDS

As noted in Chapter 25, an accounting of partnership assets or funds determines the value of each partner's share in the partnership. A formal accounting can be performed voluntarily, or it can be compelled by a court. It may be part of the termination of a partnership—part of the process of dissolution and winding up—or it may take place while a partnership is ongoing [UPA 22].

At issue in the following case was the date for an accounting. One partner claimed that it should have been the day he withdrew from the partnership. The other partners argued that it should have been the day the partnership affairs were finally wound up—more than eight years after the partner withdrew.

CASE 26.2 Centerre Bank of Kansas City, National Association v. Angle

Missouri Court of Appeals,
Western District, 1998.
976 S.W.2d 608.

HISTORICAL AND ETHICAL SETTING *Professionals of many callings are governed by state ethics codes. A failure to comply with a code is a ground for suspending or revoking the professional's license to practice his or her occupation and may determine whether that professional can practice in other states. Some professionals are not permitted to practice their occupations through partnerships, corporations, or other forms of business organizations with nonprofessionals. One of the reasons for this restriction is that it is believed a professional's judgment should not be subject to the direction or control of anyone other than a client.*

BACKGROUND AND FACTS Darrell Angle, who was a dentist, asked Bill Bright and Frank Hunter, who were not dentists, to invest in his dental practice. They formed ABH Investments, a partnership. ABH borrowed $50,000 from Centerre Bank of Kansas City to invest in an office, which it leased to Angle & Associates, Inc., a corporation formed to engage in dentistry. Angle, Bright, and Hunter owned the firm's stock. Less than a year later, the Missouri Dental Board told Angle that he could not practice dentistry through a corporation in which nondentists were shareholders. As a result, in October 1986, Angle withdrew from ABH, sold his dental practice, and moved to Oregon. Centerre Bank filed a suit in a Missouri state court against Angle, Bright, and Hunter for default on the loan. Bright and Hunter paid the claim and filed a cross-claim against Angle. After several years of litigation, the court ordered an accounting—setting February 1995, when ABH's affairs were finally wound up, as the date—and determined in part that Angle owed Hunter more than $38,000. Angle appealed, arguing in part that the accounting should have been figured as of October 1986.

IN THE WORDS OF THE COURT . . .
LAURA DENVIR STITH, Judge.

* * * *

In determining what date * * * should have been used in making the accounting, it is important to distinguish between dissolution and termination of a partnership. The dissolution of a partnership is the change in the relation of the partners caused by any partner ceasing to be associated in the carrying on, as distinguished from the winding up, of the business. * * *

Winding up involves the administration of the partnership assets in order to terminate the business and discharge the obligations of the partnership to its members. While it is unusual for the winding up period to be as long as it was in this case, there is no set period of time within which a winding up must be accomplished. * * *

* * * Where, as here, the partnership business was wound up rather than continued, then each partner's net interest is determined upon the winding up of the

CASE 26.2—Continued

partnership and the accounting must encompass the life of the partnership down to and including the winding up of the business. * * * ABH partnership was dissolved in 1986 when Angle withdrew from the partnership. The partnership had a number of financial and contractual obligations that continued despite the fact the partnership was no longer engaged in establishing dental offices; however, these were not wound up until February 28, 1995. If this Court were to follow Angle's suggestion and fix the appropriate date of accounting as 1986, Bright and Hunter would be penalized for their efforts in winding up the partnership, and these post-dissolution activities would not be included in the accounting.

DECISION AND REMEDY The Missouri Court of Appeals affirmed the lower court's order. It would not have been fair to the partners who wound up the partnership's affairs to have used an earlier date for the accounting.

FOR CRITICAL ANALYSIS—Technological Consideration *Are there any methods of recording revenues and expenses that might make a formal accounting easier and possibly unnecessary?*

LIABILITY FOR PARTNER'S FRAUD

The liability of partners for the acts of other partners in the same partnership is derived from the principles of agency law. As noted in Chapter 25, each partner is an agent of every other partner and acts as both a principal and an agent in any transaction within the scope of the partnership. The UPA affirms that the general principles of agency law relate to the authority of a partner to bind a partnership [UPA 9(1)].

For a partner to be liable for another partner's wrongful act, must the act have been intended to benefit the partnership? That was one of the questions in the following case.

CASE 26.3 Kansallis Finance Ltd. v. Fern

Supreme Judicial Court of Massachusetts, 1996.
421 Mass. 659,
659 N.E.2d 731.

HISTORICAL AND ETHICAL SETTING *It is a virtual certainty that everyone will, at some point in their lives, be asked to do something dishonest. The right answer is, of course, "no," but there will be some who say "yes." This is not a new fact, but in some contexts, there is increasing concern about the conduct of those who cut ethical corners.*

BACKGROUND AND FACTS Stephen Jones, Daniel Fern, and three other attorneys were partners in a law firm. Kansallis Finance Limited asked Jones for advice in connection with a loan. Jones responded in a letter that defrauded Kansallis of $880,000. Jones was convicted of criminal charges, and Kansallis filed a suit in a federal district court against the other partners to recover the loss. The court found that Jones had no authority to write the letter and concluded that the other partners were not liable. Kansallis appealed. Before issuing a judgment, the U.S. Court of Appeals for the First Circuit asked the Supreme Judicial Court of Massachusetts (Massachusetts' highest court) to decide, among other things, whether an act, to fall within the scope of a partnership, must be done with the intent to benefit the partnership.

IN THE WORDS OF THE COURT . . .
FRIED, Justice.

* * * *

* * * The Uniform Partnership Act provides as general principles that: * * * an act of the partner which is not apparently for the carrying on of the business of the partnership in the usual way does not bind it unless authorized. * * *

* * * *

(Continued)

CASE 26.3—Continued

Accordingly, * * * the answer [to the question] is "no." * * * If the partner has apparent authority to do the act, that will be sufficient to ground * * * liability, whether or not he acted to benefit the partnership.

DECISION AND REMEDY The Supreme Judicial Court of Massachusetts concluded in part that, because Jones did not have authority to write the letter, "the District Court's judgment for the defendants * * * accords with our [state law]."

FOR CRITICAL ANALYSIS—Social Consideration *If a partner who does not have authority commits a wrongful act with the intent to benefit the partnership, should the other partners be held liable?*

Business Law in Action • Fraud and the Innocent Partner

Partners are responsible for the actions other partners commit within the scope of the partnership. This responsibility is the reason that all general partners are given an equal right in the management of a partnership. Partners should always look for warnings of potential problems. Regular management and financial reports, copies of loan documents and correspondence with lenders and contractors, and partnership budgets should be subject to an ongoing review. Partners should observe their right to attend meetings, to inspect the books, and to review partnership contracts. No general partner can afford to take these responsibilities or these rights lightly.

Perhaps no one is more aware of these duties than Dr. J. Gregg Sikes. Sikes was a partner with Thomas Ledford in a partnership formed to build condominiums in Nashville, Tennessee. Ledford managed the business; Sikes took no part in day-to-day operations.

BancBoston lent the partnership $1.6 million to buy the land on which the project was to be built and agreed to lend the partnership construction funds of $4.625 million. The construction loan was contingent on the partnership's submission of contracts for the purchase of at least fourteen condominiums. Eventually, Ledford submitted fourteen contracts, but several of them were subject to undisclosed side agreements that violated the terms of the loan. For example, two of the contracts were signed as an accommodation to Ledford—one by a Ledford employee and the other by a friend of an employee, neither of whom had any intention of actually going through with a purchase. Without checking the contracts, the bank gave the money to the partnership. By the time the condominiums were built, the contracts had expired. The partnership defaulted on the loans, and the two partners filed for bankruptcy, asking the court to discharge the loans.

Ledford had clearly committed fraud, and the court refused to discharge the loans as to him. Sikes contended that his indebtedness on the construction loan was dischargeable because he had not known of Ledford's fraud. BancBoston argued that because the construction loan had been procured through fraud, it was not dischargeable.

No one disputed that Sikes was liable for the full amount of the partnership's debt to BancBoston. What Sikes asserted was that some culpability on his part was required if BancBoston's claim against him for the construction money was to be held nondischargeable in bankruptcy. On appeal, the court's reasoning was simple: Ledford perpetrated his fraud while acting on behalf of the partnership in the ordinary course of the partnership's business. Sikes shared in the monetary benefits of the fraud. The funds were used for partnership purposes; they financed a condominium project from which Sikes stood to profit. Therefore, the court held that Sikes would remain responsible, even after a declaration of bankruptcy, for the entire amount of the partnership debt, including the construction loan.[a]

FOR CRITICAL ANALYSIS
What might Sikes have done to prevent Ledford's fraud in the first place?

a. *BancBoston Mortgage Corp. v. Ledford*, 970 F.2d 1556 (6th Cir. 1992).

Partnerships

> **ON THE WEB**
>
> *How to Start a Business* is the title of a book on the Web at **www.inreach.com/sbdc/book.**
>
> Besides an index with links to pages within this Web site, the text includes similar links, as well as links to other Internet resources on related topics.

The classification of partnerships as *general* or *limited* is noted above, and their characteristics and differences are discussed in detail in Chapter 25. In addition, a partnership may also be classified as an *aggregate* or an *entity.* The effects of this distinction are defined briefly in Chapter 25. The ramifications of classifying a partnership as an entity are discussed next.

Regardless of the classifications applied to a partnership, its dissolution can result in the liquidation of its assets and the discharge of its liabilities, resulting in its termination. Aspects of the termination of a partnership are also examined.

THE FIRM NAME

A partnership does not need to have a name. Partners may, however, adopt any name, including a fictitious name. It cannot be the same, or even deceptively similar to, the name of another business entity if the purpose is to attract the same clientele. In some states, the name of a partnership may not include such words as "company."

In most states, the name of a partnership can be registered with the state. This registration is generally considered to be notice to the public that the firm is a partnership. Must a supplier with whom a firm does business check a state's registration records on an ongoing basis to confirm the partnership status of its customer? This was one of the issues in the following case.

CASE 26.4 Horizon Hobby Distributors v. Gurriero

Supreme Court of New York,
Trial/Special Term, Suffolk County, 1994.
161 Misc.2d 221,
613 N.Y.S.2d 550.

HISTORICAL AND ECONOMIC SETTING *The number of partnerships engaged in the wholesale and retail business declined in the 1980s. The number that suffered net losses remained fairly constant, but those that showed profits were slashed by nearly a third. Over the same period, the dollar value of such partnerships' total assets almost doubled. The same years saw increases in the number of new incorporations and in the number of corporate failures. No form of business guarantees financial success.*

BACKGROUND AND FACTS Salvatore Gurriero and David Hoffman filed a certificate with the New York secretary of state to do business as a partnership, "Island Hobbies & Raceway of Suffolk." The firm opened an account with Horizon Hobby Distributors. Less than two years later, the partnership filed a new certificate with the state to convert to a corporation. Horizon was not informed, and Island Hobbies continued to use its account as if the partnership still existed. When Island Hobbies did not pay its bill, Horizon filed a suit in a New York state court against Gurriero and Hoffman. They claimed that Horizon was suing the wrong parties. Horizon claimed that the two concealed the status of their business, and thus, it was suing the right parties. Both sides filed motions for summary judgment.

IN THE WORDS OF THE COURT . . .
MARY M. WERNER, Justice.

* * * *

* * * [S]ince defendants opened an account with plaintiff as a partnership, plaintiff would have no reason to check the files of the Secretary of State to determine the status of the store. To require the public to continually check the filings to

(Continued)

CASE 26.4—Continued

determine the status of the persons they are doing business with would place an onerous burden upon the public. Plaintiff had a right to rely on the status of Island Hobbies when it opened the account. In this case simply filing the [incorporation] certificate * * * would be insufficient to place plaintiff on notice that [Island Hobbies] was part of a corporation.

DECISION AND REMEDY The court denied the defendants' motion for summary judgment. The court also denied the plaintiff's motion, because there was a dispute as to whether Horizon actually received notice of the firm's change. The court set the case for trial.

FOR CRITICAL ANALYSIS—Social Consideration *What might Horizon have done when Island Hobbies opened its account to have avoided the problem in this case?*

Partnership as an Entity

A partnership is an aggregate of its members, and for most purposes and under the Uniform Partnership Act (UPA), the law concerning partnerships recognizes this characteristic. At other times, however, the law concerning partnerships recognizes a partnership as a separate legal entity. • **Example 26.3** Able, Bernacky, and Smith form a partnership called ABS Associates. ABS can purchase property in the partnership name rather than in the names of the individual partners. Also, the partnership can be sued in its name (ABS) rather than in the names of the partners. •

Legal Capacity States vary on whether a partnership is viewed as an entity or an aggregate of individual partners in a legal suit. Some permit a partnership to sue and be sued in the firm name. Others allow a partnership to be sued as an entity, but the partners must be named in the suit to be held liable individually. Federal courts recognize the partnership as an entity that can sue or be sued when a federal question is involved. Otherwise, federal courts follow the practice adopted by the state in which the federal court is located.

Judgments Partnership liability is first paid out of partnership assets when a judgment is rendered *against the firm name.* In a general partnership, the personal assets of the individual members are subject to liability if the partnership's assets are inadequate. Even in limited partnerships, at least one of the partners—the general partner—subjects his or her personal assets to liability for the partnership's obligations. Good legal practice dictates that when state law permits a firm to be sued, the partners should be included as parties to the suit. This ensures that a wide range of assets will be available for paying the judgment.

Under UPA Section 15, partners are jointly liable for debts and contracts of the partnership, and they are jointly and severally (individually) liable for torts and breaches of trust. In most states, however, a judgment creditor of a partnership (a creditor in whose favor a money judgment has been entered by a court) can execute the judgment against the partners either jointly or severally. In some states, the judgment creditor must exhaust the remedies against partnership property before proceeding to execute against the individual property of the partners. This is referred to as the doctrine of **marshalling assets.**

• **MARSHALLING ASSETS**
The arrangement or ranking of assets in a certain order toward the payment of debts. When two creditors have recourse to the same property of a debtor, but one has recourse to other property of the debtor, that creditor must resort first to those assets of the debtor available to the other creditor.

Marshalling Assets The arrangement or ranking of assets in a certain order toward the payment of debts outstanding is involved in marshalling assets. Marshalling assets is a common law equitable doctrine; it is not statutory. In particular, when there are two classes of assets and some creditors can enforce their claims against both whereas others can enforce their claims against only one, then the creditors of the former class are compelled to exhaust the assets against which they alone have a claim before they can have recourse to the other assets. This provides for the settlement of as many claims as possible.

As applied to a partnership, the doctrine of marshalling assets requires that the partnership's creditors have first priority to the partnership's assets and that personal creditors of the individual partners have first priority to the individual assets of each partner. When the partnership's assets are insufficient to satisfy a partnership creditor, that creditor does not have access to the assets of any individual partner until the personal creditors of that partner have been satisfied from such assets. This doctrine does not apply to partnerships that are in Chapter 7 proceedings in bankruptcy (see Chapter 23).

Bankruptcy In federal court, an adjudication of bankruptcy *in the firm name* applies only to the partnership entity. It does not constitute personal bankruptcy for the partners. Similarly, the personal bankruptcy of an individual partner does not bring the partnership entity or its assets into bankruptcy.

The doctrine of marshalling assets is modified when a partnership is granted an order of relief in bankruptcy. In such situations, if partnership assets are insufficient to cover debts owed to partnership creditors, each general partner becomes *personally* liable to the bankruptcy trustee for the amount of the deficiency.

Conveyance of Property The title to real or personal property can be held in the partnership's firm name. In other words, the partnership as an entity can own property apart from that owned by its individual members [UPA 8(3)]. Thus, the property held in the firm name can be conveyed (transferred) without each individual partner's joining in the transaction.

At common law, title to real estate could not be held in a partnership's firm name. Each partner was regarded as a co-owner and had to join in all conveyances (transfers of rights in the real estate).[2] Although the modern rule of partnership property ownership disregards the need for aggregate action to convey property, there are some practical difficulties to consider.

Most states do not require that public records include lists of members of a partnership. Thus, in determining the validity of a conveyance in a partnership's name, it may be impossible to tell whether the person executing the deed is actually a partner and has authority to convey. Some states, however, have passed laws requiring firms to file a statement of partnership. This list names members of the firm authorized to execute conveyances on behalf of the firm.

> **ON THE WEB**
> Information about starting, owning, operating, passing on, and terminating a family business is available on the Web at **www.fambiz.com**.
>
> Resources at this Web site include a unique search engine.

Termination of a Partnership

As discussed in Chapter 25, any change in the relationship of the partners caused by a partner's ceasing to be associated with the carrying on of partnership business is a ground for the dissolution of the partnership. A partnership does not terminate on its dissolution. Instead, it continues until the winding up of the partnership is finished.

2. The UPA retained this concept in UPA 25(1). Property may be held in the name of the partnership, but partners are still regarded as co-owners. The RUPA, however, states simply that "[a] partner is not a co-owner of partnership property" [RUPA 501]. Further, "[p]roperty acquired by a partnership is property of the partnership and not of the partners individually" [RUPA 203].

Dissolution Dissolution has a variety of causes, which can be divided into two categories: (1) those that result in the dissolution of a partnership according to the agreement of the partners and (2) those that result in the dissolution of the partnership by operation of law or by judicial decree [UPA 31]. The second category includes dissolution by judicial decree because of a partner's violation of the partnership agreement (see Case 26.5 below). The causes of dissolution generally are discussed in Chapter 25.

Winding Up The process of winding up a partnership's affairs involves an accounting of the partnership's assets and an applying of those assets against the partnership's liabilities. Every partner has the right to have any surplus applied in cash against amounts owed to him or her.

Dissolution resulting from the death of a partner vests all partnership assets in the surviving partners. The surviving partners act as fiduciaries in settling partnership affairs in a quick, practicable manner and in accounting to the estate of the deceased partner for the value of the decedent's interest in the partnership. The surviving partners are entitled to payment for their services in winding up the partnership, as well as to reimbursement for any costs incurred in the process [UPA 18(f)]. If all of the partners have died, the legal representative of the last surviving partner has the right to wind up the partnership business.

A partner who has committed a wrongful act or who is insolvent is barred from participating in the winding up process. Any other partner has the right to wind up the affairs of the firm, if the partnership agreement does not provide otherwise [UPA 37]. When dissolution is caused by a partner's act that violates the partnership agreement, the innocent partners may have rights to damages resulting from the dissolution [UPA 38(2)(a)]. The partnership in the following case was dissolved by a partner's violation of the partnership agreement.

CASE 26.5 Schrempp and Salerno v. Gross

Supreme Court of Nebraska, 1995.
247 Neb. 685,
529 N.W.2d 764.

HISTORICAL AND CULTURAL SETTING *In contrast to the mid–twentieth century, when long-term employment with a single employer was the norm, the U.S. work force in the 1990s became highly mobile. According to one source, the average U.S. worker can expect to change jobs as many as a dozen times over the course of his or her working life. For many workers, some of these job moves involve an entire change of career. Lawyers are as likely as the rest of the working population to change jobs, moving from a partnership to a sole proprietorship, for example.*

BACKGROUND AND FACTS Warren Schrempp, Joseph Gross, and Terrence Salerno formed a partnership to practice law. They agreed that if a partner withdrew, he or she would forfeit his or her interest in all "work in process" and client files. Gross left the firm, taking several clients' files with him. Two of the cases eventually earned about $126,000 in fees, which Gross refused to share. Schrempp and Salerno filed a suit against Gross in a Nebraska state court to obtain some of the money. The court ordered that the fees be distributed according to the partnership agreement. Gross appealed to the Supreme Court of Nebraska.

IN THE WORDS OF THE COURT . . .
FAHRNBRUCH, Justice.

* * * *

Because Gross acted in direct contravention of * * * the partnership agreement, he caused a dissolution of the partnership. * * *

(Continued)

CASE 26.5—Continued

* * * *

* * * Absent a contrary agreement, any income generated through the winding up of unfinished business of a partnership is allocated to the former partners according to their respective interests in the partnership.

* * * *

* * * Therefore, to finally wind up the Schrempp, Gross & Salerno partnership all that is necessary is the distribution of fees * * * in accordance with the partnership agreement.

DECISION AND REMEDY The Supreme Court of Nebraska held that Gross's withdrawal caused a dissolution of the firm, requiring a winding up of the partnership business. The court affirmed the order of the lower court.

FOR CRITICAL ANALYSIS—Social Consideration *How could the partners have avoided dissolution of the partnership in this case?*

Distribution of Assets The distribution of partnership assets begins with the subtraction of the partnership's total liabilities from its total assets (or vice versa, in the case of an insolvent partnership) [UPA 40(c)]. Liabilities include amounts owed to creditors, to partners for other than capital and profit, and to partners for their capital contributions. Amounts that remain after payment of the liabilities are distributed to the partners according to the profit-sharing ratio.

If a partnership's liabilities are greater than its assets, the partners bear the losses—in the absence of a contrary agreement—in the same proportion in which they shared the profits (rather than, for example, in proportion to their contributions to the partnership's capital) [UPA 40(d)]. If the partnership is insolvent, the partners must still contribute their respective shares. If one of the partners does not contribute, the other or others must provide the additional amounts necessary to pay the liabilities; but he, she, or they have a **right of contribution** against whoever has not paid his or her share [UPA 40(f)].[3]

• **RIGHT OF CONTRIBUTION**
The right of a partner who pays more than his or her proportionate share of a partnership's liabilities to recover the excess paid from other partners.

Joint Ventures

• **JOINT VENTURE**
A joint undertaking of a specific commercial enterprise by an association of persons. A joint venture is normally not a legal entity and is treated like a partnership for federal income tax purposes.

A **joint venture,** which is sometimes referred to as a *joint adventure,* is a relationship in which two or more persons combine their efforts or their property for a single transaction or project, or a related series of transactions or projects. • EXAMPLE 26.4 Several contractors—Anderson and Associates, Jones & Son Contractors, and Thomas Construction—combine their resources to build and sell houses in a single development. Their relationship is a joint venture.•

Large organizations often investigate new markets or new ideas by forming joint ventures with other enterprises. • EXAMPLE 26.5 General Motors Corporation and Volvo Truck Corporation were involved in a joint venture—Volvo GM—to manufacture heavy-duty trucks and market them in the United States.• At times, joint ventures that involve large corporations are themselves organized as jointly owned corporations with limited purposes. Despite the formation of a corporation, however, the enterprise is still a joint venture.

REMEMBER
An organization can be, in legal terms, a "person."

3. If an individual partner is insolvent and for that reason cannot pay his or her share of the loss, however, the solvent partner or partners will be unable to recover their additional contributions from the insolvent partner.

International Perspective • JOINT VENTURES IN JAPAN

Foreign investors sometimes view traditional Japanese business practices as obstacles to free competition. The members of Japanese business groups known as *keiretsus,* for example, often participate in group marketing, transportation, warehousing, and other business operations, and own stock in each others' companies. Membership in *keiretsus* is generally closed to foreign firms.

Such practices inhibit direct foreign investment in Japan. Many joint ventures between foreign investors and Japanese businesses, however, have been very successful. Hence, the joint venture has become one of the most popular forms of business organizations among foreign investors in Japan. For such enterprises, Japan has removed many of its legal restrictions and speeds the process for obtaining required permits and licenses.

FOR CRITICAL ANALYSIS
Other than forming a joint venture with a Japanese firm, how might a foreign investor compete successfully against a *keiretsu*?

ON THE WEB

"[A]n information toolbox with the ANSWERS you need for starting, running, and growing your small business," including a joint venture, is online at www.lowe.org.

The heart of this Web site is "a collection of over 4,000 documents, selected from government agencies" and other sources.

CHARACTERISTICS

A joint venture resembles a partnership. The essential difference is that a joint venture typically involves the pursuit of a single project or series of transactions and a partnership usually concerns an ongoing business. Of course, a partnership may be created to conduct a single transaction. For this reason, most courts apply the same principles to joint ventures as they apply to partnerships.[4] Exceptions to the application of partnership principles to joint ventures include the following.

1. If the members of a joint venture decide to organize a corporation to carry out the purposes of their enterprise, corporation law applies to the corporation.
2. The members of a joint venture have less implied and apparent authority than the partners in a partnership, because the activities of a joint venture are more limited than the business of a partnership.
3. Although the death of a partner terminates a partnership, the death of a joint venturer ordinarily does not terminate a joint venture.

DURATION

The members of a joint venture can specify its duration. If the members do not specify a duration, a joint venture normally terminates when the project or the transaction for which it was formed has been completed. • **EXAMPLE 26.6** The termination of the joint venture of Anderson and Associates, Jones & Son Contractors, and Thomas Construction to build and sell houses in a single development would occur once the houses were built and sold.• If the members do not specify a particular duration and the joint venture does not clearly relate to the achievement of a certain goal, a joint venture is terminable at the will of any of its members.

DUTIES, RIGHTS, AND LIABILITIES AMONG JOINT VENTURERS

The duties that joint venturers owe to each other are the same duties that partners owe to each other. • **EXAMPLE 26.7** The contractors in the previous example—Anderson and Associates, Jones & Son Contractors, and Thomas Construction—owe each other fiduciary duties. If Anderson and Jones secretly buy the land that

4. *626 Joint Venture v. Spinks,* 873 S.W.2d 73 (Tex.App.—Austin, 1993).

was to be acquired by the joint venture, Thomas may obtain damages in a suit against them for the breach of loyalty.●

When the members of a joint venture are ordinarily engaged in business operations that are similar to the activity of the joint venture, there are two areas of the law in which conflicts may develop. First, when the members of a joint venture are ordinarily competitors, each member may face a choice between disclosing trade secrets to a competitor and breaching the duty to disclose. Second, in those circumstances, there is also a potential for a violation of the antitrust laws (see Chapter 35). For both reasons, joint venturers should specify exactly the information that each will be required to disclose.

Each joint venturer has an equal right to manage the activities of the enterprise. Control of the operation may be given to no more than one of the members, however, without affecting the status of the relationship. ● **EXAMPLE 26.8** If Anderson and Associates, Jones & Son Contractors, and Thomas Construction agree that Anderson will serve as the general contractor to oversee the construction of the houses, it may appear that Anderson is the owner of the business, but this appearance does not affect the members' relationship as a joint venture.●

Each joint venturer is liable to third parties for the actions of the other members of the joint venture in pursuit of the goal of the enterprise. This is illustrated by the following case.

CASE 26.6 Fentress v. Triple Mining, Inc.

Appellate Court of Illinois,
Fourth District, 1994.
261 Ill.App.3d 930,
635 N.E.2d 102,
200 Ill.Dec. 1.

HISTORICAL AND TECHNOLOGICAL SETTING *Since prehistoric times, people have engaged in mining. Coal is mined for use in part as fuel. During the twentieth century, the use of coal as fuel declined until the so-called energy crisis of the 1970s, when the prices of oil and gas rose dramatically. Safer and more efficient computer-controlled ways of mining coal have replaced traditional methods.*

BACKGROUND AND FACTS John Henry, George Dolly, and Carl Bachtold were involved in a single coal venture with Bryan Perry Enterprises, Inc. Henry, Dolly, and Bachtold formed Triple Mining, Inc., which was soon dissolved. Before it dissolved, Bachtold signed a note, as a Triple Mining officer, for $10,000, payable to Forrest Fentress. When the money was not repaid, Fentress filed a suit in an Illinois state court against Triple Mining, Henry, Dolly, and Bachtold. Triple Mining was out of business, but the court concluded that Henry, Dolly, and Bachtold were joint venturers and ordered them to pay Fentress. Henry and Dolly appealed.

IN THE WORDS OF THE COURT . . .
Justice *GREEN* delivered the opinion of the court:

* * * *

* * * A joint venture can be implied by the circumstances and can be established by [an] association of * * * joint undertakers to carry out a single project for profit * * * . [E]very member of a joint venture can be held liable to a third party for acts of the other joint venturers done in the course of the enterprise.

Here, Henry, Dolly, and Bachtold were all involved for profit with the coal venture with Perry Enterprises * * * . That coal venture was the only coal business with which they were involved. * * * Henry, Dolly, and Bachtold were involved in a joint venture. The loan agreement with Fentress was clearly in furtherance of the joint venture.

(Continued)

CASE 26.6—Continued

DECISION AND REMEDY The Appellate Court of Illinois affirmed the order of the lower court. The parties were held to be involved in a joint venture and liable on the note.

FOR CRITICAL ANALYSIS—Ethical Consideration *Did Henry, Dolly, and Bachtold have an ethical obligation to repay the loan?*

Unincorporated Associations

• **UNINCORPORATED ASSOCIATION** An association of two or more persons to pursue a common objective. Unlike a partnership or a corporation, there is no particular form of organization.

An **unincorporated association** results when two or more persons join to pursue a common objective.[5] An agreement to associate or work together toward a common purpose is enough to create an unincorporated association. Conduct that indicates an intent to associate may be sufficient. In other words, unlike a partnership or corporation, there is no particular form of organization.

Examples of unincorporated associations include community groups that support local sports teams, such as recreational baseball, football, and softball teams. Members of communities also group together in unincorporated associations to support or oppose local developments, such as proposals to build or expand condominium complexes, sports arenas, or airports.

An unincorporated association is not an entity that is separate from its members. The members are not liable for an obligation of the association unless they authorize or ratify it. If a member does authorize or ratify such an obligation, however, his or her liability is unlimited.[6]

• EXAMPLE 26.9 Many businesses in Golden Valley are in favor of building a new sports complex to be called Gold Stadium. To show their support and gain publicity, the businesses agree to sponsor a rally. Some of the members order t-shirts printed with the slogan, "Go for the Gold!" These members can be held personally liable for the cost of the shirts, but the other members and the association itself cannot be held liable. •

That an association need not be a formal business entity to assume the attributes of other forms of business organizations is illustrated in the following case.

ON THE WEB

Articles about business law, including issues that can affect unincorporated associations, are available on the Web at www.abanet.org/buslaw/home.html.

This page is part of the Web site maintained by the American Bar Association.

5. *Four Way Plant Farm, Inc. v. National Council on Compensation Insurance,* 894 F.Supp. 1538 (M.D.Ala. 1995).

6. Volunteers who work for nonprofit organizations are protected from some liability by the Volunteer Protection Act of 1997.

CASE 26.7 Huett v. State

Court of Appeals of Texas,
Dallas, 1998.
970 S.W.2d 119.

HISTORICAL AND ENVIRONMENTAL SETTING *The oil industry is composed of companies that provide field equipment and services, install and maintain pipelines, operate refineries, and resell oil. Together, these firms produce the crude oil that is converted to gasoline, heating fuel, jet fuels, and other products. The leading companies—with such familiar brand names as Amoco, Chevron, and Texaco—explore for oil, refine it, and market it. There are about two dozen major oil producers and refiners in the United States, but hundreds of small, independent exploration and production firms account for about three-fourths of the oil wells.*

BACKGROUND AND FACTS Michael and Deborah Huett formed Offshore Resources Corporation (ORC) in

(Continued)

CASE 26.7—Continued

1979, but the firm was dissolved as a corporation in 1985. Nine years later, Harry Simon and Eric Kostbade invested in ORC. Deborah Huett, an ORC officer, told them that their money would be used solely for obtaining drilling leases and for developing those leases. Most of the funds were spent, however, with checks signed by Huett, to buy Rolls Royce and BMW automobiles, pay employees' salaries, make house payments, and obtain personal items. Mona Lisa Camarillo, an ORC employee, after seeing several hundred thousand dollars raised from investors used for purposes other than oil lease acquisitions, confronted Huett and demanded that future funds be put in escrow accounts. Huett stated that the funds were hers and that she could do with them what she wanted. Huett was indicted in Texas for misapplication of funds owned by ORC and convicted of the charge. She appealed, arguing in part that because ORC was not a legal corporation at the time of the alleged crime, it could not have been an "owner" of the funds.

IN THE WORDS OF THE COURT . . .
CHUCK MILLER, Justice.

* * * *

The penal code defines "owner" as an individual, corporation, or association that has title to the property, possession of the property, or a greater right to possession of the property than the actor * * * .

While ORC may not have been a legally chartered corporation during the time of the thefts, it certainly was, under the evidence, an association. An "association" is a body of persons acting together, without a charter, but on methods and forms used by corporations, and for prosecution of some common enterprise. It is a voluntary group of persons, without charter, formed by mutual consent, for purposes of promoting common enterprises or prosecuting common objectives.

* * * ORC was a business entity formed and operated by the Huetts. It was perhaps unchartered at the time of the events in question, but it operated with corporate methodology and terminology. It had a commercial checking account opened and operated in the name of Offshore Resources Corporation. ORC had a common publicized purpose and mission, to engage in the oil lease business. Under the name of Offshore Resources Corporation significant fund raising was done to accomplish ORC's enterprise. All of these factors combine to lead us to the inescapable conclusion that * * * ORC was an association as contemplated by the penal code.

DECISION AND REMEDY The Court of Appeals of Texas, Dallas, affirmed the judgment of the trial court. An association can be considered an owner of property even if it is not a formal business entity.

FOR CRITICAL ANALYSIS—Political Consideration *From a practical point of view, is there any other decision the court might have made in this case?*

APPLICATION Law & the International Joint Venture*

The members of an international joint venture come from different cultures with different business goals in different markets. Add to these different backgrounds such factors as unexpected political events, and it is easy to see that an international joint venture can be difficult to maintain.

Because so many such ventures fail, it is important for a business about to enter into such a relationship to consider some of the problems associated with termination. For example, in granting intellectual property rights to an international joint venture, a U.S firm should *license* (rather than assign) the rights. A license will automatically terminate if the U.S. firm withdraws or the venture ends.

*This *Application* is not meant to substitute for the services of an attorney who is licensed to practice law in your state.

A covenant not to compete in a joint venture agreement could bar a U.S. firm from entering a foreign market for a period of time after a joint venture in the market ends. Similarly, a clause that restricts firms from hiring the employees of former joint venturers may undercut business relationships once the venture ends. Thus, a business firm may wish to avoid such clauses in drafting the joint venture agreement.

A confidentiality clause should also be reviewed in light of the possibility that the joint venture will fail. The clause should provide that each member agrees to keep secret, even after the termination of the joint venture, whatever confidential information it learns.

CHECKLIST FOR JOINING AN INTERNATIONAL JOINT VENTURE

1. In anticipation of the possibility that the venture will fail, a U.S. firm granting intellectual property rights to the venture should consider licensing those rights.
2. A business firm may wish to avoid, in an international joint venture agreement, a covenant not to compete and an agreement not to hire the employees of former joint venturers.
3. An international joint venture agreement should provide that a confidentiality clause remains in force after the joint venture ends.

Key Terms

joint venture 701

marshalling assets 698

right of contribution 701

unincorporated association 704

Chapter Summary • Partners and Joint Ventures

Partners (See pages 692–696.)	1. General partners or limited partners may also be: a. *Dormant partners*—Partners who have the right to participate in management but who generally do not exercise the right. b. *Silent partners*—Dormant partners whose identities are not disclosed. c. *Secret partners*—Partners whose identities are not disclosed but who participate in the management of the partnership. 2. Partners are fiduciaries in their relationships with each other. 3. Partners must account to each other for their use of partnership funds.

Chapter Summary • Partners and Joint Ventures, Continued

Partnerships (See pages 697–701.)	1. For most purposes, a partnership is an aggregate of its members. 2. At times, the law recognizes a partnership as a separate legal entity. For example, a partnership can hold and convey real property in the partnership name, and some states allow a partnership to sue and be sued in the firm name; others allow a partnership to be sued but to hold individual partners liable, they must be named in the suit. Federal courts allow a partnership to sue or be sued in its firm name when a federal question is involved. 3. *Dissolution*—Results from any change in the relationship of the partners caused by a partner's ceasing to be associated with the carrying on of partnership business. A partner's violation of the partnership agreement is such an act.
Joint Ventures (See pages 701–704.)	1. *Joint venture*—Relationship in which two or more persons combine their efforts or property for a single transaction or project or a related series of transactions or projects. 2. The essential difference between a partnership and a joint venture is that the latter typically involves the pursuit of a single project or series of transactions and a partnership usually concerns an ongoing business.
Unincorporated Associations (See pages 704–705.)	Exist when two or more persons join to pursue a common objective. There is no particular form of organization.

For Review

❶ What is the difference between a dormant and a silent partner? A dormant and a secret partner? A silent and a secret partner?
❷ How does a partner's violation of the partnership agreement affect the partnership? What are the other partners' rights in such a situation?
❸ How are assets distributed on the termination of a partnership?
❹ What law generally applies to joint ventures?
❺ What is an unincorporated association?

Questions and Case Problems

26–1. Partnership as an Entity. Agatha wishes to purchase some real property owned by Tropical Gardens. She learns that Tropical Gardens is a partnership owned by Waldheim, Berry, and Lamont. She also learns that the partnership needs capital and that the need for capital is one of the major reasons the partners are selling their real property. Because Tropical Gardens is a partnership, Agatha has some concerns. Discuss fully each of the following of Agatha's concerns.

(a) Can the partnership convey the land in the name of Tropical Gardens?
(b) If there is a breach of contract, against whom must Agatha file a lawsuit?
(c) If Agatha obtains a judgment against Tropical Gardens, against whom can she execute it?

26–2. Dissolution by the Act of a Partner. Karen, Doug, and Charlie were partners in an accounting partnership. Without Karen and Charlie's consent, Doug told some of the firm's customers that he was starting his own firm and asked them to transfer their business. They agreed, and Doug quit the firm. When Karen and Charlie learned what Doug had done, they filed a suit against Doug for a share of the profits that Doug earned from former customers who transferred their business. Doug claimed that the firm dissolved when he quit, and thus the profits were his. On what basis might the court order Doug to pay a share of the profits from the unfinished business of the partnership to Karen and Charlie?

26–3. Partners as Fiduciaries. In 1974, Dunay, Weisglass, and Koenig formed a partnership at will (see Chapter 25) to engage in the brokerage business. They made no capital contributions to the partnership and agreed to share all revenue and expenses on an equal basis. The partnership entered into an agreement with Ladenburg, Thalmann & Co. to manage the latter's institutional investors services. The agreement did not provide any specific time limit. Each partner was appointed vice president of Ladenburg. Later, Dunay was appointed president of Ladenburg and was promised an additional share of profits for additional work on a year-to-year basis. Dunay contributed his salary as Ladenburg president and his additional share of profits to the partnership. On April 2, 1979, Weisglass and Koenig told Dunay that they wished to dissolve the partnership and did so immediately, forming their own partnership, W.K. Associates, the same day. Dunay received from the original partnership $15,044, the amount reflected on the partnership's records as his unpaid share of partnership income. Dunay remained with Ladenburg for a short period of time, leaving when the Ladenburg board of directors removed him as president and appointed in his place Weisglass on May 10. Dunay then filed a lawsuit, alleging, among other things, that Weisglass and Koenig had breached their fiduciary duty in dissolving the partnership and forming a new partnership. As part of the suit, Dunay sought some of the profits earned by Weisglass and Koenig after the dissolution. The defendants filed a motion to dismiss Dunay's complaint. In whose favor should the court rule, and why? Discuss fully. [*Dunay v. Ladenburg, Thalmann & Co.,* 170 A.D.2d 335, 565 N.Y.S.2d 819 (1991)]

26–4. Partner's Right to an Accounting. Oddo and Ries entered into a partnership agreement in March 1978 to create and publish a book describing how to restore F-100 pickup trucks. Oddo was to write the book and Ries was to provide the capital. Oddo supplied Ries with the manuscript, but Ries was dissatisfied and hired someone else to revise it. The book Ries finally published contained substantial amounts of Oddo's work. Ries did not account to Oddo for the profits on the book. On what basis can Oddo obtain a formal accounting for the profits and a dissolution of the partnership? [*Oddo v. Ries,* 743 F.2d 630 (9th Cir. 1984)]

26–5. Winding Up Partnership Affairs. Rex Thorne of Diesel Repower Systems, Inc., contracted to sell five diesel engines to C&S Sales Group, a partnership owned by Don Crosby and Dennis Stringer. C&S planned to resell the engines to Oregon Parts Co. Thorne provided Crosby with the serial numbers of the engines and agreed to have them ready for shipment no later than November 4, 1987. On October 19 and 28, C&S sent payments to Thorne to cover the $25,000 contract price for the engines. When Diesel Repower did not deliver the engines as promised, Stringer discovered that Thorne did not have the engines with the serial numbers he had provided. Instead, Thorne gave C&S three incomplete engines, including one that had been burned and could not be used. Oregon Parts sued C&S and received a judgment for $32,121.76. C&S dissolved as a partnership, but subsequently sued Thorne and Diesel Repower for the amount that C&S had been ordered to pay to Oregon Parts. The jury returned a verdict against Thorne, individually, for $32,121.76 in compensatory damages. The court entered a judgment on that verdict, and Thorne appealed. Thorne argued in part that C&S had lacked the capacity to file a complaint against him, because the C&S partnership had been dissolved before the complaint was filed. On what ground might the appellate court refuse to reverse the judgment of the trial court? [*Thorne v. C&S Sales Group,* 577 So.2d 1264 (Ala. 1991)]

26–6. Joint Ventures. Frank Hartman, Jr., and Robert Wiesner visited the site of a derailment of a Burlington Northern (BN) train near Ranchester, Wyoming, in February 1988, to consider a possible bid on the salvage of the lumber carried on nineteen of the derailed railway cars. Hartman had worked on other salvage operations and was to provide the expertise to do the work on this job. Wiesner had his own lumber-selling business and was to provide the expertise to sell the salvaged lumber. Hartman and Wiesner submitted a bid of $113,663, even though they did not have the cash available. BN accepted their bid on February 4, with payment due by 5:00 P.M. the next day. To obtain the cash, Hartman and Wiesner contacted Dave Anderson, who contacted Doug Feller, the managing partner of BBD Partnership. Hartman, Wiesner, Anderson, and Feller negotiated an agreement under which they agreed to share profits from the sale of the lumber. In accordance with the agreement, BBD borrowed the funds needed to pay BN and delivered a cashier's check for the full amount of the bid before the 5:00 P.M. deadline. BBD, through Feller, had promised to get involved only if it could own the lumber, however. Thus, at the last minute, on the bill of sale BN entered the names "Hartman Construction" and "Feller Associates," a sole proprietorship owned by Feller. BBD later sold its interest in the deal to another party. Two years later, Hartman, Wiesner, BBD, and Feller became involved in a lawsuit over the funds that BBD had borrowed to finance the lumber purchase. Was the transaction between the parties a joint venture or simply a loan from BBD to Hartman and the others? Discuss fully. [*Wiesner v. BBD Partnership,* 845 P.2d 120 (Mont. 1993)]

26–7. Joint Ventures. Windy City Balloon Port, Ltd., operated a balloon launching facility near Barrington Hills, Illinois, offering public commercial sightseeing flights in hot-air and helium balloons owned by third parties. Windy City sold tickets for the balloon rides for $100 to $150 per person per ride. The pilot of the balloon would receive $60 to $70 directly from Windy City for each ticket sold but otherwise received no consideration from Windy City. Although Windy City provided refueling and repair facilities for the balloons and canceled balloon flights when the weather conditions were unsafe, Windy City had no control over the balloons after they departed from the balloon launch. On August 15, 1981, a hot-air balloon piloted by James Bickett departed from a launching site at Windy City carrying five passengers—Kenneth Coleman, Jr., Terry Ritter, Brian Baker, William Keating, and Harry Evans. Shortly after takeoff, the balloon struck power lines and crashed to the ground, killing Bickett, Coleman, Ritter, Baker, and Keating. Evans survived, but sustained severe burns and injuries. On what basis might the court rule that Windy City and Bickett were involved in a joint venture? [*Coleman v. Charlesworth,* 240 Ill.App.3d 662, 608 N.E.2d 464, 181 Ill.Dec. 391 (1992)]

26–8. Joint Ventures. Arthur and Janet George agreed to buy a house from Opal Morgan, Arthur's step-grandmother, for $40,000. They asked Creative Capital Investment Bankers to help them obtain financing. The Creative representative mentioned only Capital South Mortgage Investments, Inc., as a source of funds and had the Georges execute a note for $60,000, claiming that Capital would not otherwise loan them $40,000. In the margin of the note, the Creative representative wrote an instruction to a Capital employee. Creative had Morgan assign the note to Capital, which assigned it to Elio Castanuela. Capital prepared the closing documents and arranged for $60,000 to be transferred from Castanuela to the closing agent, whom Capital told to give $32,000 to Morgan and the rest to Capital. Capital transferred this "overcharge" to Castanuela. At Capital's request, the Georges were not given any papers at the closing and were not told of the dispersal of the "overcharge" or of the assignments of the note. When the Georges discovered that they owed $60,000, they filed a suit in a Kansas state court against Creative, Capital, and Castanuela, alleging in part that the defendants engaged in a joint venture to commit fraud. What factors indicate the existence of a joint venture? Did Creative, Capital, and Castanuela engage in a joint venture? [*George v. Capital South Mortgage Investments, Inc.,* 265 Kan. 431, 961 P.2d 32 (Kan. 1998)]

A QUESTION OF ETHICS AND SOCIAL RESPONSIBILITY

26–9. Witten Productions, Inc., entered into a joint venture agreement with Bernard Bailey. Bailey was to produce various shows and concerts while Witten provided most of the financial backing. A separate contract was entered for each event promoted, and profits and losses were to be allocated on a pro rata basis. Bailey would inform Witten of the expenses incurred and receive a check for this amount. Bailey would deposit the check into an account from which creditors were to be paid. Finally, Bailey would calculate Witten's share of the profits and pay Witten this amount. Witten drew and delivered twenty-five checks totaling $953,251 to Bailey's company, Entertainers of America, Inc., for payment of expenses arising from the productions. All twenty-five checks were deposited into accounts controlled by Bailey in Bailey's bank, Republic Bank and Trust Co. Eighteen of the checks were made payable to "Republic Nat'l Bank & Ent. of America Escrow Acct." or "Republic Bank and Trust & Ent. of America Escrow Acct." The indorsement on these checks was a stamped "Entertainers." The remaining seven checks were made out to third parties. Two of these checks were indorsed by a stamped name similar to the payee's name. Five of the checks accepted for deposit by the bank were indorsed only by a stamped "For Deposit Only." Witten brought an action against the bank, alleging liability for its handling of these five checks. The trial court granted the bank's motion for summary judgment, and Witten appealed. The appellate court held that Witten bore the risk of loss for the checks, because of the agency relationship between Witten and Bailey as joint venturers. [*Witten Productions, Inc. v. Republic Bank & Trust Co.,* 401 S.E.2d 388 (N.C.App. 1991)]

1. When Bailey provided Witten with the payees' names for the five checks stamped "For Deposit Only," he intended that the named payees would have no interest in the checks. The court reasoned, in part, that Bailey was the intended payee and, thus, because the proceeds of the checks reached the intended payee, the bank incurred no liability for the checks' incomplete indorsements. What public policy considerations are expressed in this reasoning? Do you think such a conclusion is fair?
2. The case discussed above illustrates how carefully a joint venturer (or a partner) must supervise his or her agents, even if they are other joint venturers (or partners). What else might a joint venturer do to protect against such losses as those in this case?

FOR CRITICAL ANALYSIS

26–10. Why would two or more businesses opt to form a corporation as part of a joint venture? Are there any advantages to corporate status that would offset the expense and formality of setting up and operating a corporation to pursue a single transaction or project?

Online Activities

• **ONLINE EXERCISE 26–1**

Go to

www.pueblo.gsa.gov/smbuss.htm,

the "Small Business" page within the Web site of the Consumer Information Center maintained by the U.S. General Services Administration. Click on some of the links to determine what is available at this site and then answer the following questions:

• What help is provided for persons who want to start their own businesses?

- What information is available regarding the Small Business Administration's loan programs and services?
- Click on the "Additional Resources for the Topics of Small Business" link. What links are available on that page concerning small businesses?
- What links might you follow from these pages to determine how to sell (or buy) a small business?

• ONLINE EXERCISE 26-2

The Business Law Site! provides basic information concerning business law and other topics. Access this site at

members.aol.com/bmethven,

and then do the following:

- Click on the "Legal Checklists and Legal Forms" link, and browse through some of the links on that page. According to these sources, what forms are available to start a partnership or a joint venture? After an appropriate form has been filled out and signed, who should get a copy?
- On the "Raising Capital" page, click on some of the links to see what the sources offer. How might a partnership or a joint venture obtain capital to start or expand operations? What are the advantages and disadvantages of the different types of financing? What are the legal effects of the different types of financing on a business?

CHAPTER 27

Corporate Formation & Financing

> "A corporation is an artificial being, invisible, intangible, and existing only in contemplation of law."
>
> John Marshall, 1755–1835
> (Chief justice of the United States Supreme Court, 1801–1835)

CONTENTS

LEARNING OBJECTIVES

After reading this chapter, you should be able to:

1. Describe the basic characteristics of the corporate entity.
2. Identify the express and implied powers of a corporation.
3. Summarize the ways in which corporations are classified.
4. Outline the steps involved in forming a corporation, and point out the effects of improper incorporation.
5. Indicate how corporations are financed, and discuss the difference between stocks and bonds.

The corporation is a creature of statute. As John Marshall indicated in the opening quotation, a corporation is an artificial being, existing in law only and neither tangible nor visible. Its existence depends generally on state law, although some corporations, especially public organizations, can be created under state or federal law.

Each state has its own body of corporate law, and these laws are not entirely uniform. The Model Business Corporation Act (MBCA) is a codification of modern corporation law that has been influential in the drafting and revision of state corporation statutes. Today, the majority of state statutes are guided by the revised version of the MBCA, which is often referred to as the Revised Model Business Corporation Act (RMBCA). You should keep in mind, however, that there is considerable variation among the statutes of the states that have used the MBCA or the RMBCA as a basis for their statutes, and several states do not follow either act. Because of this, individual state corporation laws should be relied on rather than the MBCA or RMBCA.

The Nature of the Corporation

• **CORPORATION**
A legal entity formed in compliance with statutory requirements. The entity is distinct from its shareholder-owners.

A **corporation** is a legal entity created and recognized by state law. It can consist of one or more *natural* persons (as opposed to the artificial "person" of the corporation) identified under a common name. A corporation can be owned by a single person, or it can have hundreds, thousands, or even millions of owners (shareholders). The corporation substitutes itself for its shareholders in conducting corporate business and in incurring liability, yet its authority to act and the liability for its actions are separate and apart from the individuals who own it.

¡CONTRAST!
The death of a sole proprietor or the death of a partner can result in the dissolution of a business. The death of a corporate shareholder, however, rarely causes the dissolution of a corporation.

In a corporation, the responsibility for the overall management of the firm is entrusted to a *board of directors,* which is elected by the shareholders. The board of directors hires *corporate officers* and other employees to run the daily business operations of the corporation. When an individual purchases a share of stock in a corporation, that person becomes a *shareholder* and an owner of the corporation. Unlike the members in a partnership, the body of shareholders can change constantly without affecting the continued existence of the corporation. A shareholder can sue the corporation, and the corporation can sue a shareholder. Also, under certain circumstances, a shareholder can sue on behalf of a corporation. The rights and duties of corporate personnel will be examined in detail in Chapter 28.

The shareholder form of business organization developed in Europe at the end of the seventeenth century. Called *joint stock companies,* these organizations frequently collapsed because their organizers absconded with the funds or proved to be incompetent. Because of this history of fraud and collapse, organizations resembling corporations were regarded with suspicion in the United States during its early years. Although several business corporations were formed after the Revolutionary War, it was not until the nineteenth century that the corporation came into common use for private business. The *Landmark in the Law* that follows examines a leading case in the early development of private corporations in the United States.

Landmark in the Law • THE *DARTMOUTH COLLEGE* CASE (1819)

In 1819, the United States Supreme Court heard the case of *The Trustees of Dartmouth College v. Woodward.*[a] The decision by the Court in that case determined not only the continued private existence of the small college in New Hampshire but also the continued existence of private corporations in the United States.

Dartmouth College, named in honor of one of its wealthy patrons, the Earl of Dartmouth, had been founded by the Reverend Eleazar Wheelock, a young Connecticut minister who sought to establish a school to train both missionaries and Native Americans. In 1769, a corporate charter was obtained from the royal governor of New Hampshire. The charter made Wheelock and his English patrons who had donated capital to the college a self-perpetuating board of trustees for the project. When Wheelock died, his son became president of the college. Under the new, less experienced leadership, many disputes arose over the running of the institution, and the participants eventually divided along the prevailing political party lines of New Hampshire.

The Republican group[b] believed that the college ought to be under the control of the state and become a public rather than a sectarian institution. The Republicans persuaded the Republican-controlled New Hampshire Congress to pass legislation that significantly

a. 17 U.S. (4 Wheaton) 518, 4 L.Ed. 629 (1819).
b. The forerunner of the modern-day Democratic Party.

altered the composition of the board of trustees and added a board of overseers that had virtual authority to control the college.

The Federalist[c] board of trustees wanted to preserve the conservative, congregational character of the school and wanted to continue to govern the college without interference. They brought suit against William Woodward, the secretary-treasurer of the state-appointed board of overseers, alleging that the legislation violated the college's original charter. The trustees argued that the original grant of the charter, with its self-perpetuating board of trustees, was effectively a contract between the king and the board. Thus, the U.S. Constitution, which in Article I, Section 10, forbids states to pass legislation that would impair the obligation of contracts, prohibited the state from legislating changes in the self-governing structure of the board. The New Hampshire legislature was, therefore, without power to add trustees to the board, to create a board of overseers, or to alter the original charter in any manner.

Chief Justice Marshall delivered the opinion of the Court. He stated that the grant of the charter was a contract regarding private property within the meaning of Article I, Section 10, and that the legislative acts of New Hampshire, passed without the trustees' assent, were not binding on them. Justice Story, in a separate opinion, distinguished between public and private corporations. He stated that if the shareholders of a corporation were municipal or other public officials, then the corporation was a public corporation and therefore subject to continual public regulation. If the shareholders were private individuals, however, then quite a contrary situation prevailed. The corporation was private, regardless of whether it consequently was bound only by the terms of its original charter. Had the state reserved regulatory rights in the original grant of the charter, then the college would be subject to such control. In the absence of such reservations, the state of New Hampshire's legislative acts clearly impaired the original charter and thus violated the U.S. Constitution.

Story's opinion opened an avenue for the future regulation of new corporations, while at the same time creating vested rights in "private" corporations. Marshall and Story both made it clear that the United States Supreme Court would afford the property rights of private corporations the same protection afforded to other forms of property.

FOR CRITICAL ANALYSIS
Why did Justice Story's opinion open "an avenue for the future regulation of new corporations"?

c. The federalists were an early political group, or party, that advocated a strong national government.

The Constitutional Rights of Corporations

A corporation is recognized under state and federal law as a "person," and it enjoys many of the same rights and privileges that U.S. citizens enjoy. The Bill of Rights guarantees a person, as a citizen, certain protections, and corporations are considered persons in most instances. Accordingly, a corporation has the same right as a natural person to equal protection of the laws under the Fourteenth Amendment. It has the right of access to the courts as an entity that can sue or be sued. It also has the right of due process before denial of life, liberty, or property, as well as freedom from unreasonable searches and seizures (see Chapter 6 for a discussion of searches and seizures in the business context) and from double jeopardy.

Under the First Amendment, corporations are entitled to freedom of speech. As we pointed out in Chapter 2, however, commercial speech (such as advertising) and political speech (such as contributions to political causes or candidates) receive significantly less protection than noncommercial speech.

Only the corporation's individual officers and employees possess the Fifth Amendment right against self-incrimination.[1] Additionally, the privileges and

1. *In re Grand Jury No. 86–3 (Will Roberts Corp.)*, 816 F.2d 569 (11th Cir. 1987).

ON THE WEB

Corporate statutes for all but a few states are now online at fatty.law.cornell.edu/topics/state_statutes.html.

immunities clause of the Constitution (Article IV, Section 2) does not protect corporations, nor does it protect an unincorporated association.[2] This clause requires each state to treat citizens of other states equally with respect to access to courts, travel rights, and so forth.

THE LIMITED LIABILITY OF SHAREHOLDERS

One of the key advantages of the corporate form is the limited liability of its owners (shareholders). Corporate shareholders normally are not personally liable for the obligations of the corporation beyond the extent of their investments. In certain limited situations, however, the "corporate veil" can be pierced and liability for the corporation's obligations extended to shareholders—a concept that will be explained later in this chapter. Additionally, as discussed in this chapter's *Business Law in Action,* shareholders in small companies sometimes voluntarily assume personal liability, as guarantors, for corporate obligations in order to obtain credit.

2. *W. C. M. Window Co. v. Bernardi,* 730 F.2d 486 (7th Cir. 1984).

Business Law in Action • GUARANTIES BY SHAREHOLDERS

As mentioned elsewhere, one of the key advantages of the corporate form of business is the limited liability enjoyed by the corporation's owners (shareholders). Typically, though, if a corporation has relatively few shareholders, a bank or other lenders will require the shareholders to cosign or guarantee personally any loans made to the corporations precisely because of this limited liability. It is also fairly common for landlords to require a shareholder or shareholders in a small, newly incorporated business to assume personal responsibility for lease payments. In these situations, shareholders often voluntarily agree to become personally liable for corporate obligations if the firm cannot meet its debts or goes bankrupt.

Interestingly, in one case, even though a shareholder signed a personal guaranty in his representative capacity (as president of the corporation), the court held that the shareholder was personally liable for a corporate obligation. The shareholder was Anthony Riviera, the president of a small corporation, Tony Maroni's, Inc., that operated a retail business in Seattle. Maroni's leased commercial property for its business from Wilson Court Limited Partnership. As a condition of the lease, Wilson Court required Riviera to sign a personal guaranty (discussed in Chapter 23). Shortly after the lease and guaranty agreement were executed, Tony Maroni's filed for Chapter 11 bankruptcy protection. Wilson Court then brought an action against Riviera to enforce the guaranty agreement.

Riviera argued that he did not assume personal liability under the guaranty because he had written the description "President" following his name on the signature line of the agreement. Therefore, he had signed the agreement as an agent of the corporation, not in his personal capacity. The text of the guaranty agreement did little to clarify who was to be bound by the agreement, referring only to "the undersigned" or "Guarantor."

Nonetheless, the trial court found that Riviera was personally liable under the agreement, a decision upheld on appeal. The Washington Supreme Court, when it reviewed the case, cited several reasons for holding Riviera personally liable. Among other things, the court noted that "[a]s a matter of law, a party to a contract cannot guarantee its own contract. In the commercial setting, it would make no sense for Tony Maroni's to guarantee obligations it had already promised to undertake in the Lease." The court concluded that "a commercially reasonable approach to this case" required it to hold Riviera personally liable under the guaranty.[a]

FOR CRITICAL ANALYSIS

Would it ever be possible for a corporate officer to act as a guarantor for a corporate debt without becoming personally liable if the corporation defaults on the debt?

a. *Wilson Court Limited Partnership v. Tony Maroni's, Inc.,* 134 Wash.2d 692, 952 P.2d 590 (1998).

• **DIVIDEND**
A distribution to corporate shareholders of corporate profits or income, disbursed in proportion to the number of shares held.

• **RETAINED EARNINGS**
The portion of a corporation's profits that has not been paid out as dividends to shareholders.

• **CORPORATE CHARTER**
The document issued by a state agency or authority (usually the secretary of state) that grants a corporation legal existence and the right to function.

"The art of taxation consists in so plucking the goose as to obtain the largest amount of feathers with the smallest possible amount of hissing."

JEAN BAPTISTE COLBERT, 1619–1683
(French politician and financial reformer)

CORPORATE TAXATION

Corporate profits are taxed by state and federal governments. Corporations can do one of two things with corporate profits—retain them or pass them on to shareholders in the form of **dividends.** The corporation receives no tax deduction for dividends distributed to shareholders. Dividends are again taxable (except when they represent distributions of capital) as ordinary income to the shareholder receiving them. This double-taxation feature of the corporation is one of its major disadvantages.

Profits that are not distributed are retained by the corporation. These **retained earnings,** if invested properly, will yield higher corporate profits in the future and thus cause the price of the company's stock to rise. Individual shareholders can then reap the benefits of these retained earnings in the capital gains they receive when they sell their shares.

The consequences of a failure to pay corporate taxes can be severe. As will be discussed in Chapter 29, the state may dissolve a corporation for this reason. Alternatively, corporate status may be suspended until the taxes are paid. In the following case, the state had suspended a corporation's **corporate charter** (the document issued by a state agency or authority—usually the secretary of state—that grants a corporation legal existence and the right to function) because of the corporation's failure to pay certain taxes. The issue before the court was whether a shareholder who was unaware of the suspension could be held personally liable on a corporate contract.

CASE 27.1 Charles A. Torrence Co. v. Clary

Court of Appeals of North Carolina, 1995.
464 S.E.2d 502.
www.nando.net/insider/appeals/appeals95.html[a]

HISTORICAL AND POLITICAL SETTING *At one time, opening a small business was relatively simple in terms of the obligations to the government. Today, however, many businesspersons feel that there is an ocean of federal, state, and local laws that threatens to swamp even the least regulated of small businesses. For example, all states require proof of financial responsibility and compliance with other requirements before they issue a license to engage in particular businesses or occupations. Even a business that is exempt from state regulations may be required to obtain a county or city permit or license. Every level of government also imposes taxes and penalties for not paying them.*

a. This Web page includes opinions of the North Carolina Court of Appeals for 1995. In the list of cases for December 19, click on this case's name to access the opinion. This Web site is maintained by The Insider, the North Carolina State Government News Service.

BACKGROUND AND FACTS In 1989, the architectural firm of Clary, Martin, McMullen & Associates, Inc. (CMMA, Inc.), failed to pay its North Carolina franchise taxes,[b] and the state suspended its corporate charter. Between April 1991 and March 1992, the Charles A. Torrence Company provided graphics services for the firm. In September 1992, Moodye Clary—a shareholder, the president, and the director of marketing of CMMA, Inc.—learned that his firm's corporate charter had been suspended. When CMMA, Inc., failed to pay Torrence's bill, Torrence filed a suit in a North Carolina state court against CMMA, Inc., as well as against Moodye Clary personally, for the money. The court dismissed the claim against Moodye Clary, and Torrence appealed.

b. A *franchise tax* is an annual tax imposed for the privilege of doing business in a state.

IN THE WORDS OF THE COURT . . .
GREENE, Judge.

* * * *

* * * [T]he suspension was only designed to put "additional bite" into the collection of franchise taxes, but not to deprive the shareholders of the normal

(Continued)

CASE 27.1—Continued

protection of limited liability. * * * [D]irectors and officers are personally liable for corporate obligations incurred by them on behalf of the corporation, or by others with their acquiescence, if at that time they were aware that the corporate charter was suspended. * * *

In this case, the evidence is that the defendant * * * had no knowledge, at the time the debt was incurred on behalf of the Corporation, that the corporate charter was suspended.

DECISION AND REMEDY The Court of Appeals of North Carolina affirmed the lower court's decision.

FOR CRITICAL ANALYSIS—Social Consideration *Why wouldn't a court permit a shareholder who knows that the charter of his or her firm has been suspended to retain limited liability for corporate debts?*

"Did you expect a corporation to have a conscience, when it has no soul to be damned and no body to be kicked?"

EDWARD THURLOW, 1731–1806
(English jurist)

TORTS AND CRIMINAL ACTS

A corporation is liable for the torts committed by its agents or officers within the course and scope of their employment. This principle applies to a corporation exactly as it applies to the ordinary agency relationships discussed in Chapter 24. It follows the doctrine of *respondeat superior.*

As discussed in Chapter 6, under modern criminal law a corporation may be held liable for the criminal acts of its agents and employees, provided the punishment is one that can be applied to the corporation. Although corporations cannot be imprisoned, they can be fined. Of course, corporate directors and officers can be imprisoned, and in recent years, many have faced criminal penalties for their own actions or for the actions of employees under their supervision.

Recall from Chapter 6 that the U.S. Sentencing Commission, which was established by the Sentencing Reform Act of 1984, created standardized sentencing guidelines for federal crimes. These guidelines went into effect in 1987. The commission subsequently created specific sentencing guidelines for crimes committed by corporate employees (white-collar crimes). The net effect of the guidelines has been a fivefold to tenfold increase in criminal penalties for crimes committed by corporate personnel.

Corporate Powers

• **ARTICLES OF INCORPORATION**
The document filed with the appropriate governmental agency, usually the secretary of state, when a business is incorporated; state statutes usually prescribe what kind of information must be contained in the articles of incorporation.

• **BYLAWS**
A set of governing rules adopted by a corporation or other association.

When a corporation is created, the express and implied powers necessary to achieve its purpose also come into existence. The express powers of a corporation are found in its **articles of incorporation** (a document containing information about the corporation, including its organization and functions), in the law of the state of incorporation, and in the state and federal constitutions. Corporate **bylaws** (rules of management adopted by the corporation at its first organizational meeting) and the resolutions of the corporation's board of directors also grant or restrict certain powers. The following order of priority is used when conflicts arise among documents involving corporations:

1. The U.S. Constitution.
2. State constitutions.
3. State statutes.
4. The articles of incorporation.

5. Bylaws.
6. Resolutions of the board of directors.

Certain implied powers attach when a corporation is created. Barring express constitutional, statutory, or other prohibitions, the corporation has the implied power to perform all acts reasonably appropriate and necessary to accomplish its corporate purposes. For this reason, a corporation has the implied power to borrow funds within certain limits, to lend funds or to extend credit to those with whom it has a legal or contractual relationship, and to make charitable contributions.[3] To borrow money, the corporation acts through its board of directors to authorize the loan. Most often, the president or chief executive officer of the corporation will execute the necessary papers on behalf of the corporation. In so doing, corporate officers have the implied power to bind the corporation in matters directly connected with the *ordinary* business affairs of the enterprise.

• ***ULTRA VIRES***
A Latin term meaning "beyond the powers"; in corporate law, acts of a corporation that are beyond its express and implied powers to undertake.

The term ***ultra vires*** means "beyond the powers." In corporate law, acts of a corporation that are beyond its express and implied powers are *ultra vires* acts. Under Section 3.04 of the RMBCA, the following remedies are available for *ultra vires* acts:

1. The shareholders may sue on behalf of the corporation to obtain an injunction (to prohibit the corporation from engaging in the *ultra vires* transactions) or to obtain damages for the harm caused by the transactions.
2. The corporation itself can sue the officers and directors who were responsible for the *ultra vires* transactions to recover damages.
3. The attorney general of the state may institute a proceeding to obtain an injunction against the *ultra vires* transactions or to institute dissolution proceedings against the corporation for *ultra vires* acts.

In the following case, the court had to decide whether the board of directors of a cooperative housing corporation had exceeded its authority when it set minimum prices for the cooperative's housing units.

3. A corporation is prohibited from making political contributions in federal elections by the Federal Elections Campaign Act of 1974 (18 U.S.C. Section 321). Early law held that a corporation had no implied authority to make charitable contributions, because charitable activities were contrary to the primary purpose of the corporation to make a profit. Modern law, by statutes and court decisions, holds that a corporation has such implied authority.

CASE 27.2 Oakley v. Longview Owners, Inc.

Supreme Court of New York,
Westchester County, 1995.
165 Misc.2d 192,
628 N.Y.S.2d 468.

HISTORICAL AND ECONOMIC SETTING *Cooperative housing corporations are a special form of ownership of real property. A cooperative takes out a mortgage on, for example, an entire apartment building. Residents buy shares in the corporation representing their apartments (or units) and make payments to the cooperative to cover their proportionate share of the cooperative's mortgage payment. The board of directors of a cooperative housing corporation often has the power to disapprove sales of units to protect other residents' stake in the building. In the early 1990s, the prices for units in some New York cooperatives were dropping.*

BACKGROUND AND FACTS Dorothy Oakley owned shares in Longview Owners, Inc., a cooperative housing corporation in New York. When she tried to sell her shares—that is, her apartment—the Longview board of directors refused to approve the sale, in part because the price was less than a minimum price for the apartments set by the board two months earlier. The board set the minimum in a resolution without notifying the shareholder-owners or giving them the opportunity to vote on it.

(Continued)

CASE 27.2—Continued

Neither the Longview bylaws nor the certificate of incorporation gave the board the authority to set prices. Oakley filed a suit in a New York state court against the board, alleging that it had exceeded its authority in refusing to approve the sale. The board filed a motion to dismiss.

IN THE WORDS OF THE COURT . . .
DONALD N. SILVERMAN, Justice.

* * * *

* * * A cooperative board of directors may only act upon the authority which they are given. That authority may be found by looking to the by-laws of the corporation * * * and the certificate of incorporation.

Here, defendants are not granted by language expressed, or implied, authority to impose these restraints. In addition, there is no evidence that the shareholders of the corporation were ever given prior notice of this resolution and an opportunity to vote on this significant restriction affecting the stock of the corporation.

DECISION AND REMEDY The New York trial court denied the board's motion to dismiss and set the case for trial.

FOR CRITICAL ANALYSIS—Economic Consideration *Is it possible that the setting of a minimum sale price by the cooperative's board could help the owners of the cooperative?*

Classification of Corporations

The classification of a corporation depends on its purpose, ownership characteristics, and location.

• **DOMESTIC CORPORATION**
In a given state, a corporation that does business in, and is organized under the law of, that state.

• **FOREIGN CORPORATION**
In a given state, a corporation that does business in the state without being incorporated therein.

• **ALIEN CORPORATION**
A designation in the United States for a corporation formed in another country but doing business in the United States.

Domestic, Foreign, and Alien Corporations

A corporation is referred to as a **domestic corporation** by its home state (the state in which it incorporates). A corporation formed in one state but doing business in another is referred to in that other state as a **foreign corporation.** A corporation formed in another country—say, Mexico—but doing business in the United States is referred to in the United States as an **alien corporation.**

A corporation does not have an automatic right to do business in a state other than its state of incorporation. In some instances, it must obtain a *certificate of authority* in any state in which it plans to do business. Once the certificate has been issued, the powers conferred on a corporation by its home state generally can be exercised in the other state.

International Perspective • JURISDICTION OVER ALIEN CORPORATIONS

If a U.S. consumer is injured by a product manufactured by a corporation located in another country, can the consumer sue the corporation in a U.S. state court? In other words, may a U.S. state court exercise personal jurisdiction over an alien corporation? The answer depends on whether the defendant corporation has sufficient "contacts" with the state in which the lawsuit is filed. As discussed in Chapter 3, if the defendant corporation meets the "minimum-contacts" requirement, then the state court can exercise jurisdiction over the corporation. Generally, the minimum-contacts requirement is satisfied if a corporation does business within the state, advertises or sells its products within the state, or places its goods into the "stream of commerce" with the intent that the goods be sold in the state.

Alien corporations that are sued in U.S. courts sometimes claim that it is essentially unfair to force them to travel to the United States to defend against the suits—because the transportation of witnesses, documents, and other evidence can be very costly. In response to such arguments, U.S. courts generally hold that alien corporations, by marketing their goods in the United States, should expect to be "haled into court" in this country. As one court stated, any such inconvenience "must be weighed against a public policy which favors providing a forum for an injured resident to bring an action against a non-resident manufacturer."[a]

a. *Loral Fairchild Corp. v. Victor Co. of Japan, Ltd.*, 803 F.Supp. 626 (E.D.N.Y. 1992).

FOR CRITICAL ANALYSIS
Is there any way a foreign manufacturer that sells its products in the United States can avoid being "haled into court" in this country to defend against a product liability action?

Public and Private Corporations

A public corporation is one formed by the government to meet some political or governmental purpose. Cities and towns that incorporate are common examples. In addition, many federal government organizations, such as the U.S. Postal Service, the Tennessee Valley Authority, and AMTRAK, are public corporations. Note that a public corporation is not the same as a *publicly held* corporation. A publicly held corporation is any corporation whose shares are publicly traded in securities markets, such as the New York Stock Exchange or the over-the-counter market.

In contrast to public corporations, private corporations are created either wholly or in part for private benefit. Most corporations are private. Although they may serve a public purpose, as a public utility does, they are owned by private persons rather than by the government.[4]

¡NOTE!
A private corporation is a voluntary association, but a public corporation is not.

Nonprofit Corporations

Corporations formed without a profit-making purpose are called *nonprofit* or *not-for-profit corporations*. Private hospitals, educational institutions, charities, and

4. For a leading case on the distinction between private and public corporations, see this chapter's *Landmark in the Law*.

BMW AUTOMOBILES ARE INSPECTED AT A PLANT IN THE UNITED STATES. BMW IS CLASSIFIED AS AN ALIEN CORPORATION. WHAT IS THE DIFFERENCE BETWEEN AN ALIEN CORPORATION AND A FOREIGN CORPORATION?

religious organizations, for example, are frequently organized as nonprofit corporations. The nonprofit corporation is a convenient form of organization that allows various groups to own property and to form contracts without the individual members' being personally exposed to liability.

CLOSE CORPORATIONS

• CLOSE CORPORATION
A corporation whose shareholders are limited to a small group of persons, often including only family members. The rights of shareholders of a close corporation usually are restricted regarding the transfer of shares to others.

Most corporate enterprises in the United States fall into the category of close corporations. A **close corporation** is one whose shares are held by members of a family or by relatively few persons. Close corporations are also referred to as *closely held, family,* or *privately held* corporations. Usually, the members of the small group constituting a close corporation are personally known to each other. Because the number of shareholders is so small, there is no trading market for the shares.

Some states have enacted special statutory provisions that apply to close corporations. These provisions expressly permit close corporations to depart significantly from certain formalities required by traditional corporation law.[5] Additionally, Section 7.32 of the RMBCA, a provision added to the RMBCA in 1991 and adopted in several states, gives close corporations a substantial amount of flexibility in determining the rules by which they will operate. Under Section 7.32, if all of the shareholders of a corporation agree in writing, the corporation can operate without directors, bylaws, annual or special shareholders' or directors' meetings, stock certificates, or formal records of shareholders' or directors' decisions.[6]

Management of Close Corporations The close corporation has a single shareholder or a closely knit group of shareholders, who usually hold the positions of directors and officers. Management of a close corporation resembles that of a sole proprietorship or a partnership.

To prevent a majority shareholder from dominating a close corporation, the corporation may require that action can be taken by the board only on approval of more than a simple majority of the directors. Typically, this would not be required for ordinary business decisions but only for extraordinary actions, such as changing the amount of dividends or dismissing an employee-shareholder.

ETHICAL ISSUE 27.1 ***What if, in a close, family-owned corporation, one family member (shareholder) is treated unfairly by the others?*** Close corporations that are owned by family members may face severe problems when relations among the family members deteriorate. For example, suppose that two sisters and their brother are equal shareholders in a close corporation. Each shareholder is both a director and an officer of the corporation. Disagreements over how the corporation should be operated arise, and the two sisters, as the majority on the board of directors, vote to fire the brother from his position as corporate president. Although the brother remains a shareholder and a member of the board, he is deprived of his job (and his salary), which may have important economic consequences. Furthermore, he may be prevented by the corporate articles or by a shareholder agreement (to be discussed shortly) from selling his shares and investing his money elsewhere.

5. For example, in some states (such as Maryland), the close corporation need not have a board of directors.

6. Shareholders cannot agree, however, to eliminate certain rights of shareholders, such as the right to inspect corporate books and records or the right to bring derivative actions (lawsuits on behalf of the corporation—see Chapter 28).

What can the brother do? Often, the only option in this kind of situation is to petition a court to dissolve the corporation or force the majority shareholders to buy the minority shareholder's shares. Although courts generally are reluctant to interfere with corporate decisions, they have held, in some cases, that majority shareholders owe a fiduciary duty to minority shareholders (see Chapter 28). A breach of this duty may cause a court to order the majority shareholders to buy out the minority shareholder's interest in the firm or, as a last resort, to dissolve the corporation.

Transfer of Shares in Close Corporations Because, by definition, a close corporation has a small number of shareholders, the transfer of one shareholder's shares to someone else can cause serious management problems. The other shareholders may find themselves required to share control with someone they do not know or like.

• **EXAMPLE 27.1** Three brothers, Terry, Damon, and Henry Johnson, are the only shareholders of Johnson's Car Wash, Inc. Terry and Damon do not want Henry to sell his shares to an unknown third person. To avoid this situation, the articles of incorporation could restrict the transferability of shares to outside persons by stipulating that shareholders offer their shares to the corporation or the other shareholders before selling them to an outside purchaser. In fact, a few states have statutes under which close corporation shares cannot be transferred unless certain persons—including shareholders, family members, and the corporation—are first given the opportunity to purchase the shares for the same price.•

Another way that control of a close corporation can be stabilized is through the use of a shareholder agreement. A shareholder agreement can provide that when one of the original shareholders dies, his or her shares of stock in the corporation will be divided in such a way that the proportionate holdings of the survivors, and thus their proportionate control, will be maintained. Courts are generally reluctant to interfere with private agreements, including shareholder agreements.

S Corporations

The Subchapter S Revision Act of 1982 was passed "to permit the incorporation and operation of certain small businesses without the incidence of income taxation at both the corporate and shareholder level."[7] Additionally, Congress divided corporations into two groups: **S corporations,** which have elected Subchapter S treatment, and *C corporations*, which are all other corporations. Certain close corporations can choose to qualify under Subchapter S of the Internal Revenue Code to avoid the imposition of income taxes at the corporate level while retaining many of the advantages of a corporation, particularly limited liability.

• **S CORPORATION**
A close business corporation that has met certain requirements as set out by the Internal Revenue Code and thus qualifies for special income tax treatment. Essentially, an S corporation is taxed the same as a partnership, but its owners enjoy the privilege of limited liability.

Qualification Requirements for S Corporations Among the numerous requirements for S corporation status, the following are the most important:

1. The corporation must be a domestic corporation.
2. The corporation must not be a member of an affiliated group of corporations.
3. The shareholders of the corporation must be individuals, estates, or certain trusts. Partnerships and nonqualifying trusts cannot be shareholders. Corporations can be shareholders under certain circumstances.
4. The corporation must have seventy-five or fewer shareholders.

7. Senate Report No. 640, 97th Congress, 1st Session (1981).

5. The corporation must have only one class of stock, although not all shareholders need have the same voting rights.
6. No shareholder of the corporation may be a nonresident alien.

Benefits of S Corporations At times, it is beneficial for a regular corporation to elect S corporation status. Benefits include the following:

1. When the corporation has losses, the S election allows the shareholders to use the losses to offset other income.
2. When the stockholder's tax bracket is lower than the corporation's tax bracket, the S election causes the corporation's pass-through net income to be taxed in the shareholder's bracket. This is particularly attractive when the corporation wants to accumulate earnings for some future business purpose.

Because of these tax benefits, many close corporations have opted for S corporation status. In fact, today there are almost as many S corporations as regular corporations. Most S corporations (over 80 percent) are small enterprises with only one or two shareholders.

PROFESSIONAL CORPORATIONS

¡CONTRAST! Unlike the shareholders of most other corporations, the shareholders of professional corporations must generally be licensed professionals.

Professional persons such as physicians, lawyers, dentists, and accountants can incorporate. Professional corporations are typically identified by the letters *S.C.* (service corporation), *P.C.* (professional corporation), or *P.A.* (professional association). In general, the laws governing professional corporations are similar to those governing ordinary business corporations, but three basic areas of liability deserve special attention.

First, some courts, for liability purposes, regard the professional corporation as a partnership in which each partner can be held liable for whatever malpractice liability is incurred by the others within the scope of the partnership. Second, a shareholder in a professional corporation is protected from the liability imposed because of any torts (unrelated to malpractice) committed by other members. Third, many professional corporation statutes retain personal liability of professional persons for their acts and the professional acts performed under their supervision.

Corporate Formation

Up to this point, we have discussed some of the general characteristics of corporations. We now examine the process in which corporations come into existence. Generally, this process involves two steps: (1) preliminary organizational and promotional undertakings—particularly, obtaining capital for the future corporation; and (2) the legal process of incorporation.

Note that one of the most common reasons for changing from a sole proprietorship or a partnership to a corporation is the need for additional capital to finance expansion. A sole proprietor can seek partners who will bring capital with them. The partnership might be able to secure more funds from potential lenders than could the sole proprietor. When a firm wants to expand greatly, however, simply increasing the number of partners can result in too many partners and make it difficult for the firm to operate effectively. Therefore, incorporation might be the best choice for an expanding business organization because a corporation can obtain more capital by issuing shares of stock. (See the feature *Technology and Locating Potential Investors* for a discussion of how potential investors may be located

Technology and Locating Potential Investors

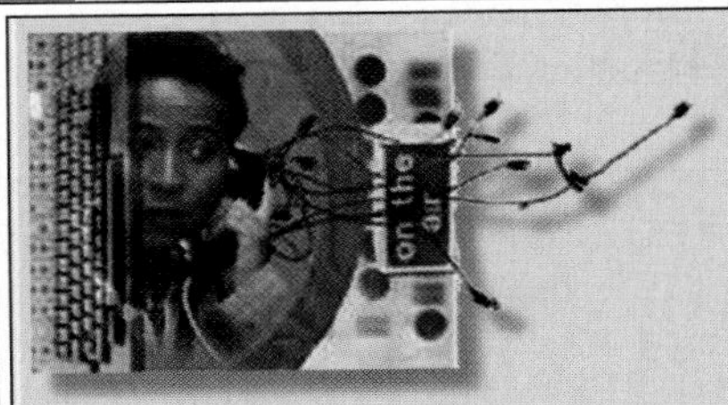

Technology via the Internet has allowed promoters and others to access, easily and inexpensively, a large number of potential investors. Today, there are several online "matching services." These services specialize in matching potential investors with companies or future companies that are seeking investors. A corporate promoter or a small company seeking capital investment could pay a fee to a service provider, which would then include a description of the company in a list that it makes available to investors—also for a fee.

For example, the American Venture Capital Exchange, or AVCE (at www.avce.com), lists hundreds of companies that seek financing. Some of these companies are just starting up, while others are existing firms that wish to expand their businesses. For each company listed, AVCE provides a summary of its business plan for potential investors to review. Potential investors can then contact the companies in which they are interested. A similar service is offered by garage.com™ (at www.garage.com). This service provides a list of start-up companies and summaries of their business plans in the "Garage" area of its site and a list of potential investors in the "Heaven" area. Potential investors who are interested in one of the listed start-up companies may contact those companies directly.

Matching services are not new. For decades, several companies have provided such services by using computerized databases to match business firms' investment needs with potential investors. What is new is that many of these service providers are now online and have expanded the geographical scope of their operations. For example, AVCE's listings include not only companies or start-ups in the United States but also in Canada, Europe, Russia, Mexico, South America, Asia, and Australia.

FOR CRITICAL ANALYSIS

How can investors who use online matching services protect themselves against fraud?

INTERNET CONNECT

online.) The original owners will find that, although their proportionate ownership of the company is reduced, they are able to expand much more rapidly by selling shares in the company.

PROMOTIONAL ACTIVITIES

• **PROMOTER**
A person who takes the preliminary steps in organizing a corporation, including (usually) issuing a prospectus, procuring stock subscriptions, making contract purchases, securing a corporate charter, and the like.

• **PROSPECTUS**
A document required by federal or state securities laws that describes the financial operations of the corporation, thus allowing investors to make informed decisions.

Before a corporation becomes a reality, **promoters**—those who, for themselves or others, take the preliminary steps in organizing a corporation—frequently make contracts with investors and others on behalf of the future corporation. One of the tasks of the promoter is to issue a prospectus. A **prospectus** is a document required by federal or state securities laws (discussed in Chapter 31) that describes the financial operations of the corporation, thus allowing investors to make informed decisions. The promoter also secures the corporate charter. In addition, a promoter may purchase or lease property with a view to selling or transferring it to the corporation when the corporation is formed. A promoter may also enter into contracts with attorneys, accountants, architects, or other professionals whose services will be needed in planning for the proposed corporation. Finally, a promoter induces people to purchase stock in the corporation.

Promoter's Liability As a general rule, a promoter is held personally liable on preincorporation contracts. Courts simply hold that promoters are not agents when a corporation has yet to come into existence. If, however, the promoter secures the contracting party's agreement to hold only the corporation (and not the promoter)

"A man to carry on a successful business must have imagination. He must see things as in a vision, a dream of the whole thing."

CHARLES M. SCHWAB, 1862–1939
(American industrialist)

liable on the contract, the promoter will not be liable in the event of any breach of contract. Basically, the personal liability of the promoter continues even after incorporation unless the third party *releases* the promoter. In most states, this rule is applied whether or not the promoter made the agreement in the name of, or with reference to, the proposed corporation.

Once the corporation is formed (the charter issued), the promoter remains personally liable until the corporation assumes the preincorporation contract by *novation* (discussed in Chapter 13). Novation releases the promoter and makes the corporation liable for performing the contractual obligations. In some situations, the corporation *adopts* the promoter's contract by undertaking to perform it. Most courts hold that adoption in and of itself does not discharge the promoter from contractual liability. A corporation cannot normally *ratify* a preincorporation contract, as no principal was in existence at the time the contract was made.

¡RECALL! Most offers to form a contract can be revoked, without liability, before they are accepted. Exceptions include option contracts, merchants' firm offers, and offers on which the offerees have changed their positions in justifiable reliance.

Subscribers and Subscriptions Prior to the actual formation of the corporation, the promoter can contact potential individual investors, and they can agree to purchase capital stock in the future corporation. This agreement is often called a *subscription agreement,* and the potential investor is called a *subscriber.* Depending on state law, subscribers become shareholders as soon as the corporation is formed or as soon as the corporation accepts the agreement.

Most courts view preincorporation subscriptions as continuing offers to purchase corporate stock. On or after its formation, the corporation can choose to accept the offer to purchase stock. Many courts also treat a subscription offer as irrevocable except with the consent of all of the subscribers. A subscription is irrevocable for a period of six months unless the subscription agreement provides otherwise or unless all the subscribers agree to the revocation of the subscription [RMBCA 6.20]. In some courts and jurisdictions, the preincorporation subscriber can revoke the offer to purchase before acceptance without liability, however.

INCORPORATION PROCEDURES

Exact procedures for incorporation differ among states, but the basic requirements are similar.

ON THE WEB For further information on incorporation, including a list of "frequently asked questions" on this topic, go to www.bizfilings.com.

State Chartering The first step in the incorporation procedure is to select a state in which to incorporate. Because state incorporation laws differ, individuals have found some advantage in looking for the states that offer the most advantageous tax or incorporation provisions. Delaware has historically had the least restrictive laws. Consequently, many corporations, including a number of the largest, have incorporated there. Delaware's statutes permit firms to incorporate in Delaware and carry out business and locate operating headquarters elsewhere. Most other states now permit this, as well. Note, though, that closely held corporations, particularly those of a professional nature, generally incorporate in the state in which their principal shareholders live and work.

Articles of Incorporation The primary document needed to begin the incorporation process is called the *articles of incorporation* (see Exhibit 27–1). The articles include basic information about the corporation and serve as a primary source of authority for its future organization and business functions. The person or persons who execute the articles are called *incorporators.* Generally, the articles of incorporation should include the elements discussed in the following subsections.

EXHIBIT 27-1 • Articles of Incorporation

ARTICLE ONE

The name of the corporation is ____.

ARTICLE TWO

The period of its duration is ________ (may be a number of years or until a certain date).

ARTICLE THREE

The purpose (or purposes) for which the corporation is organized is (are) ____
____.

ARTICLE FOUR

The aggregate number of shares that the corporation shall have authority to issue is ________ of the par value of ________ dollar(s) each (or without par value).

ARTICLE FIVE

The corporation will not commence business until it has received for the issuance of its shares consideration of the value of $1,000 (can be any sum not less that $1,000).

ARTICLE SIX

The address of the corporation's registered office is ____, New Pacum, and the name of its registered agent at such address is ____
____.

(Use the street or building or rural address of the registered office, not a post office box number.)

ARTICLE SEVEN

The number of initial directors is ____________________, and the names and addresses of the directors are
____
____.

ARTICLE EIGHT

The name and address of the incorporator is ____
____.

(signed) ____

Incorporator

Sworn to on ____________________ by the above-named incorporator.
(date)

____

Notary Public ________ County, New Pacum

(Notary Seal)

Corporate Name. The choice of a corporate name is subject to state approval to ensure against duplication or deception. State statutes usually require that the secretary of state run a check on the proposed name in the state of incorporation. Some states require that the incorporators, at their own expense, run a check on the proposed name for the newly formed corporation. Once cleared, a name can be reserved for a short time, for a fee, pending the completion of the articles of incorporation. All corporate statutes require the corporation name to include the word *Corporation, Incorporated, Company,* or *Limited,* or abbreviations of these terms.

A corporate name is prohibited from being the same as (or deceptively similar to) the name of an existing corporation doing business within the state. • **EXAMPLE 27.2** Suppose that there is an existing corporation named General Dynamics, Inc. The state will not allow another corporation to be called General Dynamic, Inc.—because that name is deceptively similar to the first, and it impliedly transfers a part of the goodwill established by the first corporate user to the second corporation. • Note that if a future firm contemplates doing business in other states, the incorporators also need to do a check on existing corporate names in those states as well. Otherwise, if the firm does business under a name that is the same as or deceptively similar to an existing company's name, it may be liable for trade name infringement.

Duration. A corporation can have perpetual existence under most state corporate statutes. A few states, however, prescribe a maximum duration, after which the corporation must formally renew its existence.

Nature and Purpose. The articles must specify the intended business activities of the corporation, and naturally, these activities must be lawful. A general statement of corporate purpose is usually sufficient to give rise to all of the powers necessary to carry out the purpose of the organization. The articles of incorporation can state, for example, that the corporation is organized "to engage in the production and sale of agricultural products." There is a trend toward allowing corporate articles to state that the corporation is organized for "any legal business," with no mention of specifics, to avoid unnecessary future amendments to the corporate articles.

Capital Structure. The articles generally set forth the capital structure of the corporation. A few state statutes require a relatively small capital investment (for example, $1,000) for ordinary business corporations but a greater capital investment for those engaged in insurance or banking. The articles must outline the number of shares of stock authorized for issuance; their valuation; the various types or classes of stock authorized for issuance; and other relevant information concerning equity, capital, and credit.

¡KEEP IN MIND!
Unlike the articles of incorporation, bylaws do not need to be filed with a state official.

Internal Organization. The articles should describe the internal management structure of the corporation, although this can be included in bylaws adopted after the corporation is formed. The articles of incorporation commence the corporation; the bylaws are formed after commencement by the board of directors. Bylaws cannot conflict with the incorporation statute or the corporation's charter [RMBCA 2.06].

Under the RMBCA, shareholders may amend or repeal bylaws. The board of directors may also amend or repeal bylaws unless the articles of incorporation or provisions of the incorporation statute reserve this power to shareholders exclusively [RMBCA 10.20]. Typical bylaw provisions describe such things as voting requirements for shareholders, the election of the board of directors, the methods of replacing directors, and the manner and time of scheduling shareholder and board meetings (these corporate activities will be discussed in Chapter 28).

ON THE WEB
For an example of one state's (Florida's) statute governing corporations, go to
www.ilrg.com/whatsnews/statute.html
and scroll down the page to "Corporations."

Registered Office and Agent. The corporation must indicate the location and address of its registered office within the state. Usually, the registered office is also the principal office of the corporation. The corporation must give the name and address of a specific person who has been designated as an *agent* and who can receive legal documents (such as orders to appear in court) on behalf of the corporation.

Incorporators. Each incorporator must be listed by name and must indicate an address. An incorporator is a person—often, the corporate promoter—who applies to the state on behalf of the corporation to obtain its corporate charter. The incorporator need not be a subscriber and need not have any interest at all in the corporation. Many states do not impose residency or age requirements for incorporators. States vary on the required number of incorporators; it can be as few as one or as many as three. Incorporators are required to sign the articles of incorporation when they are submitted to the state; often this is their only duty. In some states, they participate at the first organizational meeting of the corporation.

Certificate of Incorporation Once the articles of incorporation have been prepared, signed, and authenticated by the incorporators, they are sent to the appropriate state official, usually the secretary of state, along with the required filing fee. In many states, the secretary of state then issues a **certificate of incorporation** representing the state's authorization for the corporation to conduct business. (This may be called the *corporate charter.*) The certificate and a copy of the articles are returned to the incorporators.

• **CERTIFICATE OF INCORPORATION** The primary document that evidences corporate existence (referred to as articles of incorporation in some states).

First Organizational Meeting The first organizational meeting is provided for in the articles of incorporation but is held after the charter has actually been granted. At this meeting, the incorporators elect the first board of directors and complete the routine business of incorporation (pass bylaws and issue stock, for example). Sometimes, the meeting is held after the election of the board, and the business transacted depends on the requirements of the state's incorporation statute, the nature of the business, the provisions made in the articles, and the desires of the promoters. Adoption of bylaws—the internal rules of management for the corporation—is probably the most important function of the meeting. The shareholders, directors, and officers must abide by the bylaws in conducting corporate business.

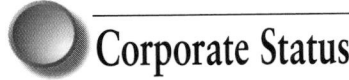

Corporate Status

The procedures for incorporation are very specific. If they are not followed precisely, others may be able to challenge the existence of the corporation.

Errors in the incorporation procedures can become important when, for example, a third person who is attempting to enforce a contract or bring suit for a tort injury learns of them. On the basis of improper incorporation, the plaintiff could seek to make the would-be shareholders personally liable. Additionally, when the corporation seeks to enforce a contract against a defaulting party, if the defaulting party learns of a defect in the incorporation procedure, he or she may be able to avoid liability on that ground.

To prevent injustice, courts will sometimes attribute corporate status to an improperly formed corporation by holding it to be a *de jure* corporation or a *de facto* corporation. Occasionally, a corporation may be held to exist by estoppel. Additionally, in certain circumstances involving abuse of the corporate form, a court may disregard the corporate entity and hold the shareholders personally liable.

De Jure and *De Facto* Corporations

In the event of substantial compliance with all conditions precedent to incorporation, the corporation is said to have *de jure* (rightful and lawful) existence. In most states and under the RMBCA, the certificate of incorporation is viewed as evidence that all mandatory statutory provisions have been met. This means that the corporation is properly formed, and neither the state nor a third party can attack its existence. If, for example, an incorporator's address was incorrectly listed, this would technically mean that the corporation was improperly formed; but the law does not regard such inconsequential procedural defects as detracting from substantial compliance, and courts will uphold the *de jure* status of the corporate entity.

Sometimes, there is a defect in complying with statutory mandates—for example, the corporation charter may have expired. Under these circumstances, the corporation may have *de facto* (actual) status, meaning that the corporation in fact exists, even if not rightfully or lawfully. A corporation with *de facto* status cannot be challenged by third persons (except for the state). The following elements are required for *de facto* status:

1. There must be a state statute under which the corporation can be validly incorporated.
2. The parties must have made a good faith attempt to comply with the statute.
3. The enterprise must already have undertaken to do business as a corporation.

Corporation by Estoppel

If an association that is neither an actual corporation nor a *de facto* or *de jure* corporation holds itself out as being a corporation, it normally will be estopped from denying corporate status in a lawsuit by a third party. This usually occurs when a third party contracts with an association that claims to be a corporation but does not hold a certificate of incorporation. When the third party brings suit naming the so-called corporation as the defendant, the association may not escape from liability on the ground that no corporation exists. When justice requires, the courts treat an alleged corporation as if it were an actual corporation for the purpose of determining the rights and liabilities involved in a particular situation. Corporation by estoppel is thus determined by the situation. It does not extend recognition of corporate status beyond the resolution of the problem at hand.

Disregarding the Corporate Entity

Occasionally, the owners use a corporate entity to perpetuate a fraud, circumvent the law, or in some other way accomplish an illegitimate objective. In these situations, the court will ignore the corporate structure by "piercing the corporate veil" and exposing the shareholders to personal liability. The following are some of the factors that frequently cause the courts to pierce the corporate veil:

1. A party is tricked or misled into dealing with the corporation rather than the individual.
2. The corporation is set up never to make a profit or always to be insolvent, or it is too "thinly" capitalized—that is, it has insufficient capital at the time of formation to meet its prospective debts or potential liabilities.
3. Statutory corporate formalities, such as holding required corporation meetings, are not followed.
4. Personal and corporate interests are **commingled** (mixed together) to the extent that the corporation has no separate identity.

• COMMINGLE
To mix together. To put funds or goods together into one mass so that the funds or goods are so mixed that they no longer have separate identities. In corporate law, if personal and corporate interests are commingled to the extent that the corporation has no separate identity, a court may "pierce the corporate veil" and expose the shareholders to personal liability.

To elaborate on the fourth factor in the preceding list, consider a close corporation that is formed according to law by a single person or by a few family members. In such a situation, the separate status of the corporate entity and the sole stockholder (or family-member stockholders) must be carefully preserved. Certain practices invite trouble for the one-person or family-owned corporation: the commingling of corporate and personal funds, the failure to hold and record minutes of board of directors' meetings, or the shareholders' continuous personal use of corporate property (for example, vehicles).

Corporation laws usually do not specifically prohibit a stockholder from lawfully lending money to his or her corporation. When an officer or director lends the corporation money and takes back security in the form of corporate assets, however, the courts will scrutinize the transaction closely. Any such transaction must be made in good faith and for fair value.

When the corporate privilege is abused for personal benefit or when the corporate business is treated in such a careless manner that the corporation and the shareholder in control are no longer separate entities, the court usually will require an owner to assume personal liability to creditors for the corporation's debts. In short, when the facts show that great injustice would result from the use of a corporation to avoid individual responsibility, a court of equity will look behind the corporate structure to the individual stockholder.

The following case illustrates a situation in which a corporation did business under an assumed name that was not registered with the state. The issue was whether the president of the corporation could be held personally liable for corporate debts incurred under the assumed name.

CASE 27.3 Hoskins Chevrolet, Inc. v. Hochberg

Appellate Court of Illinois,
First District,
First Division, 1998.
294 Ill.App.3d 550,
691 N.E.2d 28,
229 Ill.Dec. 92.
www.state.il.us/court/default.htm[a]

HISTORICAL AND SOCIAL SETTING *The corporate form of business organization permits the owners and operators of a business to avoid personal liability for corporate debts. To take advantage of this feature, corporate agents must comply with the applicable state statutory corporation formalities. For many small businesses, the formalities may seem excessive. Holding official, annual corporate meetings, for example, may seem superfluous when corporate officers and directors are spouses and co-workers. Requiring compliance to the letter of the law may thus sometimes seem to be laughable, but it is no joke when business goes bad, corporate debts go unpaid, and creditors go after corporate officers.*

a. This is a page within a Web site that includes recent "Opinions of the First District of the Appellate Court" of Illinois. Scroll down the list of 1998 cases to January 1998 and then to *Hoskins.* Click on the link to access the opinion. This site is maintained by the state of Illinois.

BACKGROUND AND FACTS Ronald Hochberg is the president of Diamond Auto Body & Repair, Inc. Under the name "Diamond Auto Construction," Hochberg ordered and received auto parts from Hoskins Chevrolet, Inc. Hoskins Chevrolet sent invoices to "Diamond Auto Construction." Hochberg paid some of the invoices with checks drawn on the bank account of "Diamond Auto Construction." When the unpaid invoices totaled more than $40,000, Hoskins Chevrolet filed a suit in an Illinois state court to collect from Hochberg individually. Hochberg asserted that he did business with Hoskins Chevrolet only as the president of a corporation. Hoskins Chevrolet responded that "Diamond Auto Construction" was not registered with the state as the name of a corporation. The court granted summary judgment in favor of Hoskins Chevrolet. Hochberg appealed.

IN THE WORDS OF THE COURT . . .
Presiding Justice *BUCKLEY* delivered the opinion of the court:

* * * *

The [Illinois] Business Corporations Act (the Act) permits a corporation to elect to adopt an assumed name provided that certain procedures are followed. Where

(Continued)

CASE 27.3—Continued

those procedures are not followed, the corporation is required to conduct business under its corporate name. * * *

* * * Diamond Auto Body & Repair, Inc., used the assumed name of Diamond Auto Construction without complying with * * * the Act. Further, the record contains no evidence that while using the assumed name in his dealings with plaintiff, defendant also disclosed the corporate name * * * . Accordingly, we find no error in the trial court's determination that under the Act, Diamond Auto Construction was neither a corporation nor the assumed name of a corporation for purposes of establishing contract liability in anyone other than defendant.

DECISION AND REMEDY The state intermediate appellate court affirmed the lower court's judgment. A person who incurs corporate debts under an unregistered corporate name is personally liable for those debts.

FOR CRITICAL ANALYSIS—Social Consideration *Why couldn't "Diamond Auto Construction" qualify as a* de facto *corporation?*

Corporate Financing

Part of the process of corporate formation involves corporate financing. Corporations are financed by the issuance and sale of corporate securities. *Securities* (stocks and bonds) evidence the obligation to pay money or the right to participate in earnings and the distribution of corporate property. **Stocks,** or *equity securities,* represent the purchase of ownership in the business firm. **Bonds** (debentures), or *debt securities,* represent the borrowing of money by firms (and governments). Of course, not all debt is in the form of debt securities. For example, some debt is in the form of accounts payable and notes payable. Accounts and notes payable are typically short-term debts. Bonds are simply a way for the corporation to split up its long-term debt so that it can market it more easily.

• **STOCK**
An equity (ownership) interest in a corporation, measured in units of shares.

• **BOND**
A certificate that evidences a corporate (or government) debt. It is a security that involves no ownership interest in the issuing entity.

Bonds

Bonds are issued by business firms and by governments at all levels as evidence of the funds they are borrowing from investors. Bonds normally have a designated *maturity date*—the date when the principal, or face, amount of the bond is returned to the investor. They are sometimes referred to as *fixed-income securities* because their owners (that is, the creditors) receive fixed-dollar interest payments during the period of time prior to maturity, usually semiannually.

Because debt financing represents a legal obligation on the part of the corporation, various features and terms of a particular bond issue are specified in a lending agreement called a **bond indenture.** A corporate trustee, often a commercial bank trust department, represents the collective well-being of all bondholders in ensuring that the corporation meets the terms of the bond issue. The bond indenture specifies the maturity date of the bond and the pattern of interest payments until maturity. The different types of corporate bonds are described in Exhibit 27–2.

• **BOND INDENTURE**
A contract between the issuer of a bond and the bondholder.

Stocks

Issuing stocks is another way that corporations can obtain financing. The ways in which stocks differ from bonds are summarized in Exhibit 27–3. Basically, as mentioned, stocks represent ownership in a business firm, whereas bonds represent borrowing by the firm.

EXHIBIT 27–2 • Types of Corporate Bonds

Debenture Bonds	Bonds for which no specific assets of the corporation are pledged as backing. Rather, they are backed by the general credit rating of the corporation, plus any assets that can be seized if the corporation allows the debentures to go into default.
Mortgage Bonds	Bonds that pledge specific property. If the corporation defaults on the bonds, the bondholders can take the property.
Convertible Bonds	Bonds that can be exchanged for a specified number of shares of common stock under certain conditions.
Callable Bonds	Bonds that may be called in and the principal repaid at specified times or under conditions specified in the bond when it is issued.

The most important characteristics of stockholders are as follows:

1. They need not be paid back.
2. The stockholder receives dividends only when so voted by the directors.
3. Stockholders are the last investors to be paid off on dissolution.
4. Stockholders vote for management and on major issues.

Exhibit 27–4 summarizes the types of stocks issued by corporations. We look now at the two major types of stock—*common stock* and *preferred stock*.

EXHIBIT 27–3 • How Do Stocks and Bonds Differ?

STOCKS	BONDS
1. Stocks represent ownership.	1. Bonds represent debt.
2. Stocks (common) do not have a fixed dividend rate.	2. Interest on bonds must always be paid, whether or not any profit is earned.
3. Stockholders can elect a board of directors, which controls the corporation.	3. Bondholders usually have no voice in, or control over, management of the corporation.
4. Stocks do not have a maturity date; the corporation does not usually repay the stockholder.	4. Bonds have a maturity date, when the corporation is to repay the bondholder the face value of the bond.
5. All corporations issue or offer to sell stocks. This is the usual definition of a corporation.	5. Corporations do not necessarily issue bonds.
6. Stockholders have a claim against the property and income of a corporation after all creditors' claims have been met.	6. Bondholders have a claim against the property and income of a corporation that must be met before the claims of stockholders.

EXHIBIT 27–4 • Types of Stocks

Common Stock	Voting shares that represent ownership interest in a corporation. Common stock has the lowest priority with respect to payment of dividends and distribution of assets on the corporation's dissolution.
Preferred Stock	Shares of stock that have priority over common-stock shares as to payment of dividends and distribution of assets on dissolution. Dividend payments are usually a fixed percentage of the face value of the share.
Cumulative Preferred Stock	Required dividends not paid in a given year must be paid in a subsequent year before any common-stock dividends are paid.
Participating Preferred Stock	Stock entitling the owner to receive the preferred-stock dividend and additional dividends if the corporation has paid dividends on common stock.
Convertible Preferred Stock	Stock entitling the owners to convert their shares into a specified number of common shares either in the issuing corporation or, sometimes, in another corporation.
Redeemable, or Callable, Preferred Stock	Preferred shares issued with the express condition that the issuing corporation has the right to repurchase the shares as specified.

Common Stock The true ownership of a corporation is represented by **common stock.** Common stock provides a proportionate interest in the corporation with regard to (1) control, (2) earnings, and (3) net assets. A shareholder's interest is generally in proportion to the number of shares he or she owns out of the total number of shares issued.

• **COMMON STOCK**
Shares of ownership in a corporation that give the owner of the stock a proportionate interest in the corporation with regard to control, earnings, and net assets; shares of common stock are lowest in priority with respect to payment of dividends and distribution of the corporation's assets on dissolution.

Voting rights in a corporation apply to the election of the firm's board of directors and to any proposed changes in the ownership structure of the firm. For example, a holder of common stock generally has the right to vote in a decision on a proposed merger, as mergers can change the proportion of ownership. State corporation law specifies the types of actions for which shareholder approval must be obtained.

Firms are not obligated to return a principal amount per share to each holder of common stock, because no firm can ensure that the market price per share of its common stock will not decline over time. The issuing firm also does not have to guarantee a dividend; indeed, some corporations never pay dividends.

"There are two times in a man's life when he should not speculate: when he can't afford it and when he can."

SAMUEL CLEMENS (MARK TWAIN), 1835–1910
(American author and humorist)

Holders of common stock are a group of investors who assume a *residual* position in the overall financial structure of a business. In terms of receiving payment for their investments, they are last in line. The earnings to which they are entitled are those left after preferred stockholders, bondholders, suppliers, employees, and other groups have been paid. Once those groups are paid, however, the owners of common stock may be entitled to *all* the remaining earnings as dividends. (The board of directors is not normally under any duty to declare the remaining earnings as dividends, however.)

Preferred Stock **Preferred stock** is stock with *preferences*. Usually, this means that holders of preferred stock have priority over holders of common stock as to dividends and as to payment on dissolution of the corporation. Holders of preferred stock may or may not have the right to vote.

• **PREFERRED STOCK**
Classes of stock that have priority over common stock both as to payment of dividends and distribution of assets on the corporation's dissolution.

EXHIBIT 27-5 • Cumulative Convertible Preferred-Stock Certificate

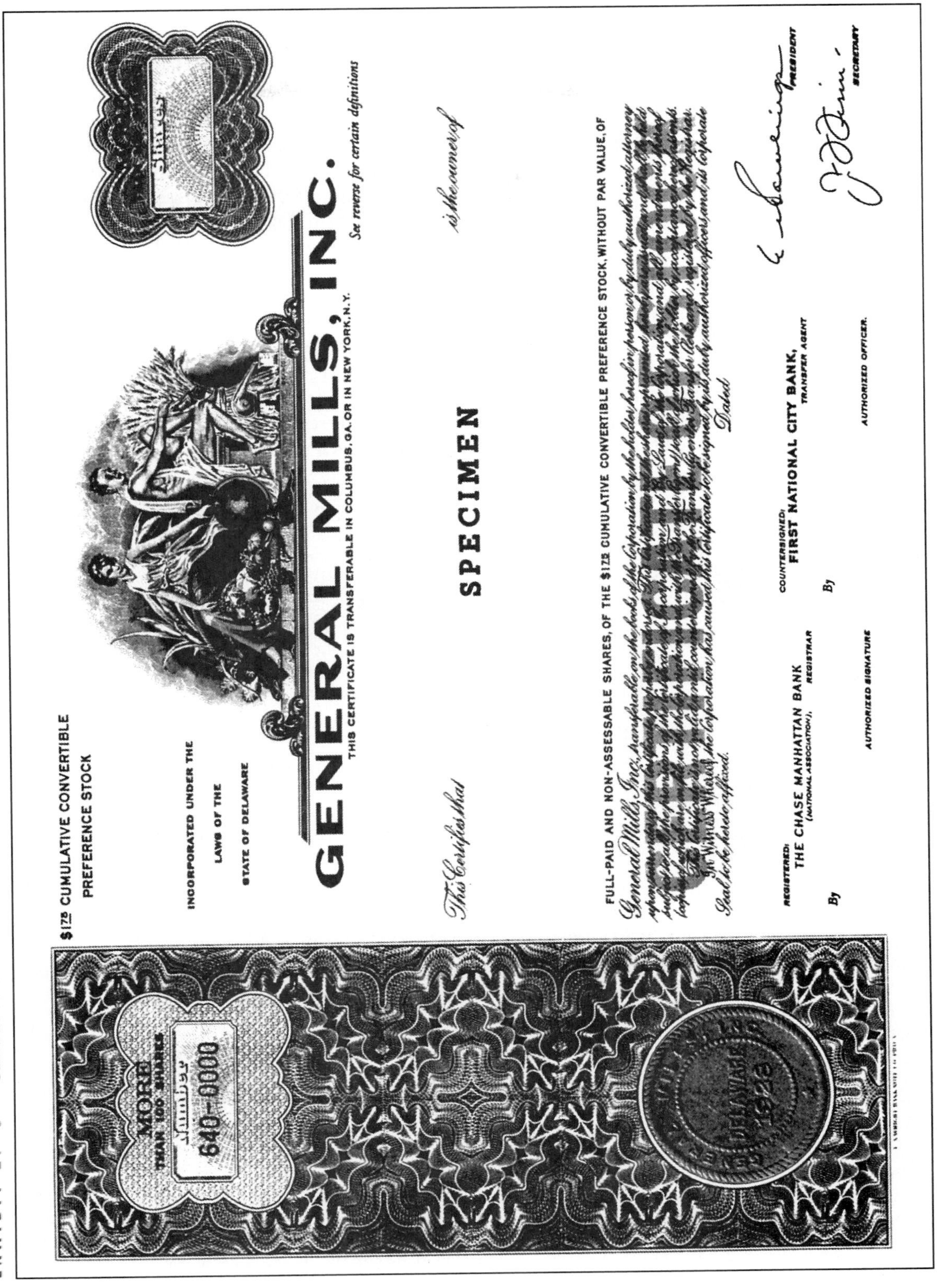

Preferred stock is not included among the liabilities of a business, because it is equity. Like other equity securities, preferred shares have no fixed maturity date on which the firm must pay them off. Although occasionally firms buy back preferred stock, they are not legally obligated to do so. A sample cumulative convertible preferred-stock certificate is shown in Exhibit 27–5.

Holders of preferred stock are investors who have assumed a rather cautious position in their relationship to the corporation. They have a stronger position than common shareholders with respect to dividends and claims on assets, but as a result, they will not share in the full prosperity of the firm if it grows successfully over time. This is because the value of preferred shares will not rise as rapidly as that of common shares during a period of financial success. Preferred stockholders do receive fixed dividends periodically, however, and they may benefit to some extent from changes in the market price of the shares.

The return and the risk for preferred stock lie somewhere between those for bonds and those for common stock. Preferred stock is more similar to bonds than to common stock, even though preferred stock appears in the ownership section of the firm's balance sheet. As a result, preferred stock is often categorized with corporate bonds as a fixed-income security, even though the legal status is not the same.

Application: Law & the Entrepreneur: How to Incorporate*

Incorporation generally involves a very modest investment in legal fees and filing fees. Indeed, just about anybody can form a corporation for any lawful purpose in any state. The requirements differ from state to state. You do not have to form your corporation in the state in which you live or the state in which you are doing business, however. In fact, many individuals obtain their corporate charters from the state of Delaware, because it has the fewest legal restrictions on corporate formation and operation.

Traditionally, Delaware has also been the state most often chosen for "mail-order incorporation." Perhaps you have even seen the ads—"You, too, can incorporate"—in various national and regional magazines. Those ads are usually generated by organizations in Delaware that have preprinted incorporation forms for you to fill out and send back with a small fee. The employees of these organizations send or take your forms to the appropriate state office in Delaware to obtain your certificate of incorporation.

Today, more than one hundred companies offer incorporation services, and most of these firms are now online. Some of the major companies offer a wide array of services. For example, at the Web site of The Company Corporation (TCC) of Delaware (www.companycorporation.com), you can find information on the advantages and disadvantages of incorporating your business, the cost of incorporating in your state (or in any other state), and the various types of corporate entities that are available. If you wish to use TCC's services, you can fill out incorporation forms provided online, and TCC will file the forms with the appropriate state office and obtain a certificate of incorporation (corporate charter) for you. Optional TCC services include making arrangements for a registered agent for your corporation, mail-forwarding services, obtaining a tax ID number, and obtaining a domain name registration for your business.

Such "do-it-yourself" incorporating may be sufficient for those who are interested in starting small businesses but who have no serious aspirations that their companies will grow much larger. If you believe that the business in which you are going to engage has growth potential and may require significant financing in the future, though, you are best advised to contact a local lawyer to take you through the necessary steps in incorporating your business.

Checklist of Factors to Discuss with an Attorney Concerning Incorporation

1. Tax considerations.
2. The initial cost of incorporation and any continuing costs.
3. The formalities that are necessary.
4. The amount of record keeping that will be required.
5. What should be included in the bylaws.

*This *Application* is not meant to substitute for the services of an attorney who is licensed to practice law in your state.

Key Terms

alien corporation 718
articles of incorporation 716
bond 730
bond indenture 730
bylaws 716
certificate of incorporation 727
close corporation 720
commingle 728
common stock 732
corporate charter 715
corporation 712
dividend 715
domestic corporation 718
foreign corporation 718
preferred stock 732
promoter 723
prospectus 723
retained earnings 715
S corporation 721
stock 730
ultra vires 717

Chapter Summary • Corporate Formation and Financing

The Nature of the Corporation (See pages 712–716.)	A corporation is a legal entity distinct from its owners. Formal statutory requirements, which vary somewhat from state to state, must be followed in forming a corporation. The corporation can have perpetual existence or be chartered for a specific period of time. 1. *Corporate parties*—The shareholders own the corporation. They elect a board of directors to govern the corporation. The board of directors hires corporate officers and other employees to run the daily business of the firm. 2. *Corporate taxation*—The corporation pays income tax on net profits; shareholders pay income tax on the disbursed dividends that they receive from the corporation (double-taxation feature). 3. *Torts and criminal acts*—The corporation is liable for the torts committed by its agents or officers within the course and scope of their employment (under the doctrine of *respondeat superior*). In some circumstances, a corporation can be held liable (and be fined) for the criminal acts of its agents and employees. In certain situations, corporate officers may be held personally liable for corporate crimes.
Corporate Powers (See pages 716–718.)	1. *Express powers*—The express powers of a corporation are granted by the following laws and documents (listed according to their priority): federal constitution, state constitutions, state statutes, articles of incorporation, bylaws, and resolutions of the board of directors. 2. *Implied powers*—Barring express constitutional, statutory, or other prohibitions, the corporation has the implied power to do all acts reasonably appropriate and necessary to accomplish its corporate purposes. 3. *Ultra vires doctrine*—Any act of a corporation that is beyond its express or implied powers to undertake is an *ultra vires* act. a. *Ultra vires* contracts may or may not be enforced by the courts, depending on the circumstances. b. The corporation (or shareholders on behalf of the corporation) may sue to enjoin or recover damages for *ultra vires* acts of corporate officers or directors. In addition, the state attorney general may bring an action either to institute an injunction against the transaction or to institute dissolution proceedings against the corporation for *ultra vires* acts.

Chapter Summary • Corporate Formation and Financing, Continued

Classification of Corporations (See pages 718–722.)	1. *Domestic, foreign, and alien corporations*—A corporation is referred to as a *domestic corporation* within its home state (the state in which it incorporates). A corporation is referred to as a *foreign corporation* by any state that is not its home state. A corporation is referred to as an *alien corporation* if it originates in another country but does business in the United States. 2. *Public and private corporations*—A public corporation is one formed by government (for example, cities, towns, and public projects). A private corporation is one formed wholly or in part for private benefit. Most corporations are private corporations. 3. *Nonprofit corporations*—Corporations formed without a profit-making purpose (for example, charitable, educational, and religious organizations and hospitals). 4. *Close corporations*—Corporations owned by a family or a relatively small number of individuals; transfer of shares is usually restricted, and the corporation cannot make a public offering of its securities. 5. *S corporations*—Small domestic corporations (must have seventy-five or fewer shareholders as members) that, under Subchapter S of the Internal Revenue Code, are given special tax treatment. These corporations allow shareholders to enjoy the limited legal liability of the corporate form but avoid its double-taxation feature (taxes are paid by shareholders as personal income, and the S corporation is not taxed separately). 6. *Professional corporations*—Corporations formed by professionals (for example, doctors and lawyers) to obtain the benefits of incorporation (such as tax benefits and limited liability). In most situations, the professional corporation is treated as other corporations, but sometimes the courts will disregard the corporate form and treat the shareholders as partners.
Corporate Formation (See pages 722–727.)	1. *Promotional activities*—A corporate promoter is one who takes the preliminary steps in organizing a corporation (issues prospectus, secures charter, interests investors in the purchase of corporate stock, forms subscription agreements, makes contracts with third parties so that the corporation can immediately begin doing business on its formation, and so on). 2. *Incorporation procedures*— a. A state in which to incorporate is selected. b. The articles of incorporation are prepared and filed. The articles generally should include the corporate name, duration, nature and purpose, capital structure, internal organization, registered office and agent, and incorporators. c. The certificate of incorporation (or charter), which authorizes the corporation to conduct business, is received from the appropriate state office (usually the secretary of state) after the articles of incorporation have been filed. d. The first organizational meeting is held after the charter is granted. The board of directors is elected and other business completed (bylaws passed, stock issued, and so on).
Corporate Status (See pages 727–730.)	1. *De jure or de facto corporation*—If a corporation has been improperly incorporated, courts will sometimes impute corporate status to the firm by holding that the firm is a *de jure* corporation (cannot be challenged by the state or third persons) or a *de facto* corporation (can be challenged by the state but not by third persons). 2. *Corporation by estoppel*—If a firm is neither a *de jure* nor *de facto* corporation but represents itself to be a corporation and is sued as such by a third party, it may be held to be a corporation by estoppel. 3. *Disregarding the corporate entity*—To avoid injustice, courts may "pierce the corporate veil" and hold a shareholder or shareholders personally liable for a judgment against the corporation. This usually occurs only when the corporation was established to circumvent the

Chapter Summary • Corporate Formation and Financing, Continued

Corporate Status—continued	law, when the corporate form is used for an illegitimate or fraudulent purpose, or when the controlling shareholder commingles his or her own interests with those of the corporation to such an extent that the corporation no longer has a separate identity.
Corporate Financing—Bonds (See page 730.)	Corporate bonds are securities representing *corporate debt*—money borrowed by a corporation. See Exhibit 27–2 for a list describing the various types of corporate bonds.
Corporate Financing—Stocks (See pages 730–734.)	Stocks are equity securities issued by a corporation that represent the purchase of ownership in the business firm. 1. *Important characteristics of stockholders*— a. They need not be paid back. b. The stockholder receives dividends only when so voted by the directors. c. Stockholders are the last investors to be paid on dissolution. d. Stockholders vote for management and on major issues. 2. *Types of stock (see Exhibit 27–4 for details)*— a. Common stock—Represents the true ownership of the firm. Holders of common stock share in the control, earning capacity, and net assets of the corporation. Common stockholders carry more risk than preferred stockholders but, if the corporation is successful, are compensated for this risk by greater returns on their investments. b. Preferred stock—Stock whose holders have a preferred status. Preferred stockholders have a stronger position than common shareholders with respect to dividends and claims on assets, but as a result, they will not share in the full prosperity of the firm if it grows successfully over time. The return and risk for preferred stock lie somewhere between those for bonds and those for common stock.

For Review

❶ What are the express and implied powers of corporations? On what sources are these powers based?
❷ What are the steps for bringing a corporation into existence? Who is liable for preincorporation contracts?
❸ What is the difference between a *de jure* corporation and a *de facto* corporation?
❹ In what circumstances might a court disregard the corporate entity ("pierce the corporate veil") and hold the shareholders personally liable?
❺ How are corporations financed? What is the difference between stocks and bonds?

Questions and Case Problems

27–1. Corporate Status. Three brothers inherited a small paper-supply business from their father, who had operated the business as a sole proprietorship. The brothers decided to incorporate under the name of Gomez Corp. and retained an attorney to draw up the necessary documents. The attorney drew up the papers and had the brothers sign them but neglected to send the application for a corporate charter to the secretary of state's office. The brothers assumed that all necessary legal work had been taken care of, and they proceeded to do business as Gomez Corp. One day, a Gomez Corp. employee, while making a delivery to one of Gomez's customers, negligently ran a red light and caused a car accident. Baxter, the driver of the other vehicle, was injured as a result and sued Gomez Corp. for damages. Baxter then learned that no state charter had ever been issued to Gomez Corp., so he sued each of the brothers personally for damages. Can the brothers avoid personal liability for the tort of their employee? Explain.

27–2. Liability for Preincorporation Contracts. Christy, Briggs, and Dobbs are recent college graduates who want to form a corporation to manufacture and sell personal computers. Perez tells them that he will set in motion the formation of their corporation. Perez first makes a contract with Oliver for the purchase of a parcel of land for $25,000. Oliver does not know of the prospective corporate formation at the time the contract is signed. Perez then makes a contract with Kovac to build a small plant on the property being purchased. Kovac's contract is conditional on the corporation's formation. Perez secures all necessary subscription agreements and capitalization, and he files the articles of incorporation. A charter is issued.

(a) Discuss whether the newly formed corporation or Perez (or both) is liable on the contracts with Oliver and Kovac.
(b) Discuss whether the corporation, on coming into legal existence, is automatically liable to Kovac.

27–3. Corporate Powers. Kora Nayenga and two business associates formed a corporation called Nayenga Corp. for the purpose of selling computer services. Kora, who owned 50 percent of the corporate shares, served as the corporation's president. Kora wished to obtain a personal loan from his bank for $250,000, but the bank required the note to be cosigned by a third party. Kora cosigned the note in the name of the corporation. Later, Kora defaulted on the note, and the bank sued the corporation for payment. The corporation asserted, as a defense, that Kora had exceeded his authority when he cosigned the note. Had he? Explain.

27–4. Liability of Shareholders. Charles Wolfe was the sole shareholder and president of Wolfe & Co., a firm that leased tractor-trailers. The corporation had no separate bank account. Banking transactions were conducted through Wolfe's personal accounts, and employees were paid from them. Wolfe never consulted with any other corporate directors. During the tax years 1974–1976, the corporation incurred $114,472.91 in federal tax liabilities. The government held Wolfe personally liable for the taxes. Wolfe paid the tax bill and then brought an action against the government for disregarding his corporate entity. Discuss whether the government can "pierce the corporate veil" in Wolfe's case and hold Wolfe personally liable for corporate taxes. [*Wolfe v. United States,* 798 F.2d 1241 (9th Cir. 1961)]

27–5. Liability for Preincorporation Contracts. Skandinavia, Inc., manufactured and sold polypropylene underwear. Following two years of poor sales, Skandinavia entered into negotiations to sell the business to Odilon Cormier, an individual who was an experienced textile manufacturer. Skandinavia and Cormier agreed that Cormier would take Skandinavia's underwear inventory and use it in a new corporation, which would be called Polypro, Inc. In return, Skandinavia would receive a commission on future sales from Polypro. Polypro was subsequently established and began selling the underwear. Skandinavia, however, having never received any commissions from the sales, sued Polypro and Cormier to recover its promised commissions. Is Cormier personally liable for the contract he signed in the course of setting up a new corporation? Discuss. [*Skandinavia, Inc. v. Cormier,* 128 N.H. 215, 214 A.2d 1250 (1986)]

27–6. Professional Corporations. Cohen, Stracher & Bloom, P.C., a law firm organized as a professional corporation under New York law, entered into an agreement with We're Associates Co. for the lease of office space located in Lake Success, New York. The lease was signed for We're Associates by one of the partners of that company and for the professional corporation by Paul J. Bloom, as vice president. Bloom, Cohen, and Stracher were the sole officers, directors, and shareholders of the professional corporation. The corporation became delinquent in paying its rent, and We're Associates brought an action to recover rents and other charges of approximately $9,000 alleged to be due under the lease. The complaint was filed against the professional corporation and each individual shareholder of the corporation. The individual shareholders moved to dismiss the action against them individually. Will the court grant their motion? Discuss. [*We're Associates Co. v. Cohen, Stracher & Bloom, P.C.,* 103 A.D.2d 130, 478 N.Y.S.2d 670 (1984)]

27–7. Liability of Shareholders. Moseley Group Management Co. (MGM) provided management services to apartment complexes. MGM's only assets were equipment worth $500 and a bank account with an average balance of $1,500. Richard Moseley ran the company and owned half of the stock. MGM contracted with Property Tax Research Co. (PTR) to obtain a lower property tax assessment on one of its complexes. PTR performed, but MGM refused to pay and transferred its assets and employees to Terrace Management, Inc., a corporation controlled by Moseley. PTR filed a suit in a Missouri state court against Moseley and others to recover the unpaid fees. Should the court pierce the corporate veil and hold Moseley personally liable for the debt? If so, on what basis? [*Sansone v. Moseley,* 912 S.W.2d 666 (Mo.App., W.D. 1995)]

27–8. Corporate Powers. Soda Dispensing Systems, Inc., was owned by two shareholders, each of whom owned half of the stock. One shareholder was the president of the corporation, and the other was vice president. Their shareholder agreement stated that neither shareholder could "encumber any corporate property . . . without the written consent of the other." When Soda Dispensing went out of business, the two shareholders agreed to sell the assets, split the proceeds, and pay $9,900 to their accountants, Cooper, Selvin & Strassberg. Later, the president committed Soda Dispensing to pay Cooper, Selvin more than $24,000, claiming that he had the authority, as president, to make that commitment. When the accountants tried to collect, the vice president objected, asserting that the president exceeded his authority. Will the court order Soda Dispensing to pay? Explain. [*Cooper, Selvin & Strassberg v. Soda Dispensing Systems, Inc.,* 212 A.D.2d 498, 622 N.Y.S.2d 312 (1995)]

27–9. Corporate Status. Cecil Hill was in the construction trade. He did business as "C&M Builders, Inc.," although there was no such corporation. County Concrete Co. supplied "C&M Builders, Inc." with over $50,000 worth of concrete for which it was not paid. The supplier filed a suit in a Maryland state court against Hill personally. Hill argued that because the supplier thought it was doing business with a corporate entity, C&M was a *de facto* corporation, and thus Hill was not personally liable. Should Hill be allowed to avoid liability on this basis? Why or why not? [*Hill v. County Concrete Co.,* 108 Md.App. 527, 672 A.2d 667 (1996)]

27–10. Disregarding the Corporate Entity. Steven and Janis Gimbert leased a warehouse to a manufacturing business owned by Manzar Zuberi. Zuberi signed the lease as the purported representative of "ATM Manufacturing, Inc.," which was a nonexistent corporation. Zuberi was actually the president of two existing corporations, ATM Enterprises, Inc., and Ameri-Pak International. Under the Ameri-Pak name, Zuberi manufactured a household cleaning product in the Gimberts' warehouse. The use of hydrochloric acid in the operations severely damaged the premises, and the Gimberts filed a suit in a Georgia state court against Zuberi personally to collect for the damage. On what basis might Zuberi be held personally liable? Discuss fully. [*Zuberi v. Gimbert,* 230 Ga.App. 471, 496 S.E.2d 741 (1998)]

A QUESTION OF ETHICS AND SOCIAL RESPONSIBILITY

27–11. On November 3, 1981, Garry Fox met with a representative of Coopers & Lybrand (Coopers), a national accounting firm, to obtain tax advice and other accounting services on behalf of a corporation Fox was in the process of forming. Coopers agreed to perform the services. The new corporation, G. Fox and Partners, Inc., was incorporated on December 4, 1981. Coopers had completed its work by mid-December and billed G. Fox and Partners for $10,827 for its accounting services. When neither the new corporation nor Fox paid the bill, Coopers sued Garry Fox personally for the amount. Coopers claimed that Fox had breached express and implied contracts and that, as a corporate promoter, Fox was liable for the unpaid debt. Fox argued that Coopers had agreed to look solely to the corporation for payment. The trial court found that there was no agreement, either express or implied, that would obligate Fox individually to pay Coopers's fee, because Coopers failed to prove the existence of any such agreement. On appeal, however, the trial court's judgment was reversed. Fox was held liable as a corporate promoter for the unpaid debt. [*Coopers & Lybrand v. Fox,* 758 P.2d 683 (Colo. 1988)]

1. In view of the fact that Coopers & Lybrand knew that Fox was acting on behalf of a future corporation, do you think that it is fair that Fox should be held personally liable for the contract?
2. Undertaking preliminary organization and promotion is an essential step in the process of corporate formation. Do you think that imposing risks on promoters by holding them personally liable for preincorporation contracts counters the public policy of promoting business enterprises?

FOR CRITICAL ANALYSIS

27–12. What are some of the ways in which the limited liability of corporate shareholders serves the public interest? Can you think of any ways in which this limited liability is harmful to the public interest? Explain.

Online Activities

ONLINE EXERCISE 27–1

Go to the "Internet Activities Book" on the Web site that accompanies this text, the URL for which is http://blt.westbuslaw.com. Select the following activities, and perform the exercises according to the instructions given there:

Activity 26–1: Companies Online
Activity 26–2: Financing a Business

Before the Test

Go to the *Business Law Today* home page at http://blt.westbuslaw.com. Click on TestTutor.® You will find twenty interactive questions relating to this chapter.

CHAPTER 28

Corporate Directors, Officers, & Shareholders

> "They [corporations] cannot commit treason, nor be outlawed nor excommunicated, because they have no soul."
>
> Sir Edward Coke, 1552–1634
> (English jurist and legal scholar)

CONTENTS

LEARNING OBJECTIVES

After reading this chapter, you should be able to:

1. Describe the role of corporate directors and officers.
2. Summarize the duties owed to the corporation by directors and officers.
3. Explain the effect of the business judgment rule on directors' liability for their decisions.
4. Identify the rights of shareholders, including the right to bring a derivative suit.
5. Discuss the liability of shareholders and the duties owed by majority shareholders.

Sir Edward Coke's observation that a corporation has no "soul" is based on the fact that a corporation is not a "natural" person but a legal fiction. No one individual shareholder or director bears sole responsibility for the corporation and its actions. Rather, a corporation joins the efforts and resources of a large number of individuals for the purpose of producing returns greater than the returns those persons could have obtained individually.

Sometimes, actions that benefit the corporation as a whole do not coincide with the separate interests of the individuals making up the corporation. In such situations, it is important to know the rights and duties of all participants in the corporate enterprise. This chapter focuses on the rights and duties of directors, officers, and shareholders and the ways in which conflicts among them are resolved.

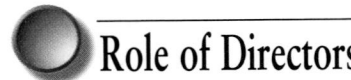

Role of Directors

A corporation typically is governed by a board of directors. A director occupies a position of responsibility unlike that of other corporate personnel. Directors are sometimes inappropriately characterized as *agents* because they act on behalf of the corporation. No *individual* director, however, can act as an agent to bind the corporation; and as a group, directors collectively control the corporation in a way that no agent is able to control a principal. Directors are often incorrectly characterized as *trustees* because they occupy positions of trust and control over the corporation. Unlike trustees, however, they do not own or hold title to property for the use and benefit of others.

> **ON THE WEB**
> One of the best sources on the Web for information on corporations, including their directors, is the "EDGAR" database of the Securities and Exchange Commission (SEC) at www.sec.gov/edgarhp.htm.

ELECTION OF DIRECTORS

Subject to statutory limitations, the number of directors is set forth in the corporation's articles or bylaws. Historically, the minimum number of directors has been three, but today many states permit fewer. Indeed, the Revised Model Business Corporation Act (RMBCA), in Section 8.01, permits corporations with fewer than fifty shareholders to eliminate the board of directors.

The first board of directors is normally appointed by the incorporators on the creation of the corporation, or directors are named by the corporation itself in the articles. The first board serves until the first annual shareholders' meeting. Subsequent directors are elected by a majority vote of the shareholders.

The term of office for a director is usually one year—from annual meeting to annual meeting. Longer and staggered terms are permissible under most state statutes. A common practice is to elect one-third of the board members each year for a three-year term. In this way, there is greater management continuity.

A director can be removed *for cause* (that is, for failing to perform a required duty), either as specified in the articles or bylaws or by shareholder action. Even the board of directors itself may be given power to remove a director for cause, subject to shareholder review. In most states, unless the shareholders have reserved the right at the time of election, a director cannot be removed without cause.

> **¡BE AWARE!**
> The articles of incorporation may provide that a director can be removed only for cause.

Vacancies can occur on the board of directors because of death or resignation, or when a new position is created through amendment of the articles or bylaws. In these situations, either the shareholders or the board itself can fill the position, depending on state law or on the provisions of the bylaws.

DIRECTORS' QUALIFICATIONS AND COMPENSATION

Few legal requirements exist concerning directors' qualifications. Only a handful of states impose minimum age and residency requirements. A director is sometimes a shareholder, but this is not a necessary qualification—unless, of course, statutory provisions or corporate articles or bylaws require ownership.

Compensation for directors is ordinarily specified in the corporate articles or bylaws. Because directors have a fiduciary relationship to the shareholders and to the corporation, an express agreement or provision for compensation often is necessary for them to receive money income from the funds that they control and for which they have responsibilities.

BOARD OF DIRECTORS' MEETINGS

The board of directors conducts business by holding formal meetings with recorded minutes. The date on which regular meetings are held is usually established in the articles or bylaws or by board resolution, and no further notice is customarily required. Special meetings can be called, with notice sent to all directors.

• **QUORUM**
The number of members of a decision-making body that must be present before business may be transacted.

Quorum requirements can vary among jurisdictions. (A **quorum** is the minimum number of members of a body of officials or other group that must be present in order for business to be validly transacted.) Many states leave the decision as to quorum requirements to the corporate articles or bylaws. In the absence of specific state statutes, most states provide that a quorum is a majority of the number of directors authorized in the articles or bylaws. Voting is done in person (unlike voting at shareholders' meetings, which can be done by proxy, as discussed later in this chapter).[1] The rule is one vote per director. Ordinary matters generally require a simple majority vote; certain extraordinary issues may require a greater-than-majority vote.

RIGHTS OF DIRECTORS

A director of a corporation has a number of rights, including the rights of participation, inspection, compensation, and indemnification.

Participation and Inspection A corporate director must have certain rights to function properly in that position. The main right is one of participation—meaning that the director must be notified of board of directors' meetings so as to participate in them. As pointed out earlier in this chapter, regular board meetings are usually established by the bylaws or by board resolution, and no notice of these meetings is required. If special meetings are called, however, notice is required unless waived by the director.

A director must have access to all of the corporate books and records to make decisions and to exercise the necessary supervision over corporate officers and employees. This right of inspection is virtually absolute and cannot be restricted.

Compensation and Indemnification Historically, directors have had no inherent right to compensation for their services as directors. Nominal sums are often paid as honorariums to directors, however. In many corporations, directors are also chief corporate officers (president or chief executive officer, for example) and receive compensation in their managerial positions. Most directors, however, gain through indirect benefits, such as business contacts, prestige, and other rewards, such as stock options. There is a trend toward providing more than nominal compensation for directors, especially in large corporations in which directorships can be enormous burdens in terms of time, work, effort, and risk. Many states permit the corporate articles or bylaws to authorize compensation for directors, and in some cases the board can set its own compensation unless the articles or bylaws provide otherwise.

Corporate directors may become involved in lawsuits by virtue of their positions and their actions as directors. Most states (and RMBCA 8.51) permit a corporation to indemnify (guarantee reimbursement to) a director for legal costs, fees, and judgments involved in defending corporation-related suits. Many states specifically permit a corporation to purchase liability insurance for the directors and officers to cover indemnification. When the statutes are silent on this matter, the power to purchase such insurance is usually considered to be part of the corporation's implied power.

1. Except in Louisiana, which allows a director to vote by proxy under certain circumstances. Some states, such as Michigan and Texas, and Section 8.20 of the RMBCA permit telephone conferences for board of directors' meetings.

MANAGEMENT RESPONSIBILITIES

Directors have responsibility for all policymaking decisions necessary to the management of corporate affairs. Just as shareholders cannot act individually to bind the corporation, the directors must act as a body in carrying out routine corporate business. The general areas of responsibility of the board of directors include the following:

1. The declaration and payment of corporate dividends to shareholders.
2. The authorization for major corporate policy decisions—for example, the initiation of proceedings for the sale or lease of corporate assets outside the regular course of business, the determination of new product lines, and the overseeing of major contract negotiations and major management-labor negotiations.
3. The appointment, supervision, and removal of corporate officers and other managerial employees and the determination of their compensation.
4. Financial decisions, such as the decision to issue authorized shares and bonds.

The board of directors can delegate some of its functions to an executive committee or to corporate officers. In doing so, the board is not relieved of its overall responsibility for directing the affairs of the corporation, but corporate officers and managerial personnel are empowered to make decisions relating to ordinary, daily corporate affairs within well-defined guidelines.

Role of Corporate Officers and Executives

¡CONTRAST!
Shareholders own a corporation and directors make policy decisions, but officers who run the daily business of the corporation often have significant decision-making power.

The officers and other executive employees are hired by the board of directors or, in rare instances, by the shareholders. In addition to carrying out the duties articulated in the bylaws, corporate and managerial officers act as agents of the corporation, and the ordinary rules of agency (discussed in Chapter 24) normally apply to their employment. The qualifications required of officers and executive employees are determined at the discretion of the corporation and are included in the articles or bylaws. In most states, a person can hold more than one office and can be both an officer and a director of the corporation.

The rights of corporate officers and other high-level managers are defined by employment contracts, because these persons are employees of the company. Corporate officers normally can be removed by the board of directors at any time with or without cause and regardless of the terms of the employment contracts—although in so doing, the corporation may be liable for breach of contract. The duties of corporate officers are the same as those of directors, because both groups are involved in decision making and are in similar positions of control. Hence, officers are viewed as having the same fiduciary duties of care and loyalty in their conduct of corporate affairs as directors have, a subject to which we now turn.

Duties of Directors and Officers

Directors and officers are deemed *fiduciaries* of the corporation, because their relationship with the corporation and its shareholders is one of trust and confidence. The fiduciary duties of the directors and officers include the duty of care and the duty of loyalty.

CORPORATE EXECUTIVES DISCUSS THE BUSINESS OF THEIR FIRM. HOW DO THE RIGHTS AND DUTIES OF CORPORATE OFFICERS DIFFER FROM THOSE OF CORPORATE DIRECTORS?

DUTY OF CARE

"It is not the crook in modern business that we fear but the honest man who does not know what he is doing."

OWEN D. YOUNG, 1874–1962 (American corporate executive and public official)

Directors and officers must exercise due care in performing their duties. The standard of *due care* has been variously described in judicial decisions and codified in many corporation codes. Generally, a director or officer is expected to act in good faith, to exercise the care that an ordinarily prudent person would exercise in similar circumstances, and to act in what he or she considers to be the best interests of the corporation.[2] Directors and officers who have not exercised the required duty of care can be held liable for the harms suffered by the corporation as a result of their negligence.

Duty to Make Informed and Reasonable Decisions Directors and officers are expected to be informed on corporate matters. To be informed, the director or officer must do what is necessary to become informed: attend presentations, ask for information from those who have it, read reports, review other written materials such as contracts—in other words, carefully study a situation and its alternatives. Depending on the nature of the business, directors and officers are often expected to act in accordance with their own knowledge and training. Most states (and Section 8.30 of the RMBCA), however, allow a director to make decisions in reliance on information furnished by competent officers or employees, professionals such as attorneys and accountants, or even an executive committee of the board without being accused of acting in bad faith or failing to exercise due care if such information turns out to be faulty.

Directors are also expected to make reasonable decisions. For example, a director should not accept a **tender offer** (an offer to purchase shares in the company that is made by another company directly to the shareholders, sometimes referred to as a "takeover" bid) with only a moment's consideration based solely on the market price of the corporation's shares.

• **TENDER OFFER**
An offer to purchase shares made by one company directly to the shareholders of another (target) company; often referred to as a "takeover bid."

Duty to Exercise Reasonable Supervision Directors are also expected to exercise a reasonable amount of supervision when they delegate work to corporate officers

2. RMBCA 8.30.

and employees. • **EXAMPLE 28.1** Suppose that a corporate bank director fails to attend any board of directors' meetings for five years, never inspects any of the corporate books or records, and generally fails to supervise the efforts of the bank president and the loan committee. Meanwhile, a corporate officer, the bank president, makes various improper loans and permits large overdrafts. In this situation, the corporate director may be held liable to the corporation for losses resulting from the unsupervised actions of the bank president and the loan committee. •

Dissenting Directors Directors are expected to attend board of directors' meetings, and their votes should be entered into the minutes of corporate meetings. Unless a dissent is entered, the director is presumed to have assented. Directors who dissent are rarely held individually liable for mismanagement of the corporation. For this reason, a director who is absent from a given meeting sometimes registers with the secretary of the board a dissent to actions taken at the meeting.

DUTY OF LOYALTY

"It is not within the lawful powers of a board of directors to shape and conduct the affairs of a corporation for the merely incidental benefit of the shareholders."

RUSSELL C. OSTRANDER, 1851–1919 (Michigan jurist)

Loyalty can be defined as faithfulness to one's obligations and duties. In the corporate context, the duty of loyalty requires directors and officers to subordinate their personal interests to the welfare of the corporation. This means, among other things, that directors may not use corporate funds or confidential corporate information for personal advantage. Similarly, they must refrain from self-dealing. For example, a director should not oppose a tender offer that is in the corporation's best interest simply because its acceptance may cost the director his or her position. Cases dealing with fiduciary duty typically involve one or more of the following:

1. Competing with the corporation.
2. Usurping (taking advantage of) a corporate opportunity.
3. Having an interest that conflicts with the interest of the corporation.
4. Engaging in insider trading (using information that is not public to make a profit trading securities, as discussed in Chapter 31).
5. Authorizing a corporate transaction that is detrimental to minority shareholders.
6. Using corporate facilities for personal business.

The usurping of a corporate opportunity occurs when an officer or director, for his or her personal gain, takes advantage of a business opportunity that is financially within the corporation's reach, is in line with the firm's business, is to the firm's practical advantage, and is one in which the corporation has an interest.

Whether buying certain corporate property constitutes the violation of two directors' fiduciary duties to their corporation was at issue in the following case.

CASE 28.1 Stokes v. Bruno

Court of Appeal of Louisiana,
Third Circuit, 1998.
720 So.2d 388.

HISTORICAL AND SOCIAL SETTING *A nonstock corporation is a corporation whose ownership is not recognized by stock but by a membership charter or agreement. Membership might be created according to a particular attribute, such as the ownership of land within the corporation's geographic reach. A corporation organized for other than a profit-making purpose is a nonprofit corporation. No part of the income of a nonprofit corporation is distributable to the directors, officers, or members. An example of a nonstock, nonprofit corporation might be a homeowner's association that is organized in a corporate form.*

BACKGROUND AND FACTS Point Cotile Parks Association, Inc. (PCPA), is a nonstock, nonprofit

(Continued)

CASE 28.1—Continued

corporation whose members are limited to owners of lots or building sites within the Point Cotile Subdivision. The board of directors, including Gerald Bruno and Michael Wright, adopted resolutions that effectively granted Bruno and Wright the authority to sell certain "common ground" on PCPA's behalf. The board designated lots and set prices, based on professional appraisals. Six years later, when some of the lots had not sold for their original prices, Bruno and Wright sold to themselves, and to Bruno's wife, 5.45 acres of the "common ground." The sale included lots with timber that had not been previously offered for sale. On their own appraisal, Bruno and Wright set the price for the acreage lower than the board had set for the individual lots. When the board learned of the sale, Craig Stokes and other PCPA members filed a suit in a Louisiana state court against Bruno and Wright. The court declared the sale *ultra vires* and void. Bruno appealed.

IN THE WORDS OF THE COURT . . .
DECUIR, Judge.

* * * *

* * * This apparently was a clear case of self dealing. * * * [Bruno] should have a duty to disclose to the Corporation several items. First that the sale consummated was the whole tract, not just the first lots as had been offered in prior sales. * * * Next he had a duty to disclose to the Corporation the potential for sales of timber, as well as the fact that the revised values he was negotiating with himself on behalf of the Corporation were based on his own determinations and no outside source. Once he took the position of evaluator of the land, he would be barred by fiduciary duty from consummating the sale without disclosing the reduction in price, offering an opportunity for other [PCPA] members to purchase, or make an effort to market the entire tract of land, as opposed to just the front lots. * * * Mr. Bruno and Mr. Wright owed a fiduciary [duty] to the Corporation to maximize the return and the mere fact that a portion of the property had not sold at the original requested prices did not give them the unilateral authorization to add more land, reduce the price and then purchase themselves without disclosure.

DECISION AND REMEDY The state intermediate appellate court affirmed the lower court's judgment. The sale of PCPA property under these circumstances was a breach of Bruno and Wright's fiduciary duty to the corporation. The appellate court ordered a rescission of the sale.

FOR CRITICAL ANALYSIS—Ethical Consideration
Under what circumstances might a sale by a director of corporate property to himself or herself be justified?

CONFLICTS OF INTEREST

The duty of loyalty also requires officers and directors to disclose fully to the board of directors any possible conflict of interest that might occur in conducting corporate transactions. The various state statutes contain different standards, but a contract will generally *not* be voidable if it was fair and reasonable to the corporation at the time it was made, if there was a full disclosure of the interest of the officers or directors involved in the transaction, and if the contract was approved by a majority of the disinterested directors or shareholders.

• **EXAMPLE 28.2** Southwood Corporation needs office space. Lambert Alden, one of its five directors, owns the building adjoining the corporation's main office building. He negotiates a lease with Southwood for the space, making a full disclosure to Southwood and the other four board directors. The lease arrangement is fair and reasonable, and it is unanimously approved by the corporation's board of directors. In this situation, Alden has not breached his duty of loyalty to the corporation, and the contract is thus valid. If it were otherwise, directors would be prevented from ever giving financial assistance to the corporations they serve. •

ETHICAL ISSUE 28.1 ***What happens to the duty of loyalty when a director sits on the boards of two corporations?*** Corporate directors often have many business affiliations, and they may even sit on the board of more than one corporation. (Of course, directors generally are precluded from sitting on the boards of directors of competing companies.) The duty of loyalty can become cloudy when corporate directors sit on the board of more than one corporation. Because of the potential for abuse in transactions negotiated between corporations whose boards have some members in common, courts tend to scrutinize such actions closely.

For example, suppose that four individuals own a total of 70 percent of the shares of Company A and 100 percent of the shares of Company B. All four of these shareholders sit on the boards of directors of both corporations. Company A decides to purchase all of Company B's stock for $6 million, when in fact it is worth only $3 million. The shareholder-directors of both firms have not breached their duty to Company B, because the $6 million price is beneficial to that company. A court would likely hold that the directors breached their duty to the other shareholders of Company A (who owned the remaining 30 percent of Company A's shares), however, because these other shareholders had nothing to gain by the transaction and much to lose by Company A's purchase of Company B at an inflated price.[3]

Liability of Directors and Officers

"All business proceeds on beliefs, or judgments of probabilities, and not on certainties."

CHARLES ELIOT, 1834–1936
(American educator and editor)

Directors and officers are exposed to liability on many fronts. Corporate directors and officers may be held liable for the crimes and torts committed by themselves or by corporate employees under their supervision, as discussed in Chapter 6 and Chapter 24, respectively. Additionally, shareholders may perceive that the corporate directors are not acting in the best interests of the corporation and may sue the directors, in what is called a *shareholder's derivative suit,* on behalf of the corporation. (This type of action is discussed later in this chapter, in the context of shareholders' rights.) Here, we examine the **business judgment rule,** under which a corporate director or officer may be able to avoid liability to the corporation or to its shareholders for poor business judgments.

• **BUSINESS JUDGMENT RULE**
A rule that immunizes corporate management from liability for actions that result in corporate losses or damages if the actions are undertaken in good faith and are within both the power of the corporation and the authority of management to make.

Directors and officers are expected to exercise due care and to use their best judgment in guiding corporate management, but they are not insurers of business success. Honest mistakes of judgment and poor business decisions on their part do not make them liable to the corporation for resulting damages. The business judgment rule generally immunizes directors and officers from liability for the consequences of a decision that is within managerial authority, as long as the decision complies with management's fiduciary duties and as long as acting on the decision is within the powers of the corporation. Consequently, if there is a reasonable basis for a business decision, it is unlikely that the court will interfere with that decision, even if the corporation suffers as a result.

To benefit from the rule, directors and officers must act in good faith, in what they consider to be the best interests of the corporation, and with the care that an ordinarily prudent person in a similar position would exercise in similar circumstances. This requires an informed decision, with a rational basis, and with no conflict between the decision maker's personal interest and the interest of the corporation.

3. See, for example, *Gries Sports Enterprises, Inc. v. Cleveland Browns Football Co.,* 26 Ohio St.3d 15, 496 N.E.2d 959 (1986).

Business Law in Action • Testing the Limits of the Business Judgment Rule

Employment contracts that provide for severance pay and other benefits on termination of employment are not uncommon. Yet what if severance benefits turn out to be worth approximately $140 million? Do directors who form a contract providing for such extensive benefits violate their fiduciary duties to the corporation by "wasting" corporate assets? Shareholders of the Walt Disney Company thought so, when the company's president, Michael Ovitz, left the company and became entitled to severance benefits valued at about $140 million.

Two shareholders brought a derivative suit against the company, seeking to recover for the corporation a sizeable portion of the severance pay. The shareholders argued that the directors had breached their fiduciary duties by, among other things, approving the employment agreement with Ovitz when he joined the company.

Understandably, the case received significant media attention because of the sheer dollar amount involved. As the Delaware court deciding the case stated, "This is a noteworthy case because the severance payment is large—larger than even the expert hired by the Disney Board to explain the contract imagined it to be, larger than almost anyone anywhere will receive in the lifetime of any of the parties, and perhaps larger than any ever paid." The court, however, found no reason to rule in favor of the shareholders merely because of the dollar amount of the severance package. Said the court: "Nature does not sink a ship merely because of its size, and neither do courts overrule a board's decision to approve and later honor a severance package, merely because of its size."

MICHAEL OVITZ SPEAKS PUBLICLY. WHEN OVITZ LEFT THE WALT DISNEY COMPANY, HE WAS ENTITLED TO OVER $140 MILLION IN SEVERANCE BENEFITS. WHY MIGHT A COURT UPHOLD AN EMPLOYMENT CONTRACT THAT INCLUDED SUCH A SEVERANCE PACKAGE?

In its analysis of the claim, the court explained that unless the shareholders "can plead with specificity facts that rebut the presumption of the business judgment rule . . . then the Board's decision will stand." To rebut the presumption of the business judgment rule, the shareholders would have to show that "the Board was corrupted and could not make a decision fairly and independently, in the best interests of the Corporation." In the court's eyes, the shareholders failed to meet this challenge.

There was no indication that the directors had sought personal gain or acted against the corporation's best interests in forming the contract with Ovitz. The court noted that in order to entice Ovitz—referred to by some as the "most powerful man in Hollywood" —to come to work for the Walt Disney Company, the directors had to include significant severance benefits in the employment contract. Furthermore, stated the court, had the directors failed to honor the contract on Ovitz's departure, Disney would have become involved in protracted and costly litigation with Ovitz over his rights under the employment agreement.[a]

FOR CRITICAL ANALYSIS

Generally, what factors might be considered in determining how large the dollar amount of a severance package should be?

a. *In re the Walt Disney Company Derivative Litigation,* 1998 WL 731587 (Del.Ch. 1998).

(See this chapter's *Business Law in Action* for a discussion of a case in which the business judgment rule was applied to decisions made by corporate directors.)

Role of Shareholders

The acquisition of a share of stock makes a person an owner and shareholder in a corporation. Shareholders thus own the corporation. Although they have no legal

¡BE AWARE! Shareholders are not normally agents of the corporation.

title to corporate property, such as buildings and equipment, they do have an equitable (ownership) interest in the firm.

As a general rule, shareholders have no responsibility for the daily management of the corporation, although they are ultimately responsible for choosing the board of directors, which does have such control. Ordinarily, corporate officers and other employees owe no direct duty to individual shareholders. Their duty is to the corporation as a whole. A director, however, is in a fiduciary relationship to the corporation and therefore serves the interests of the shareholders. Generally, there is no legal relationship between shareholders and creditors of the corporation. Shareholders can, in fact, be creditors of the corporation and thus have the same rights of recovery against the corporation as any other creditor.

In this section, we look at the powers and voting rights of shareholders, which are generally established in the articles of incorporation and under the state's general incorporation law.

SHAREHOLDERS' POWERS

Shareholders must approve fundamental corporate changes before the changes can be effected. Hence, shareholders are empowered to amend the articles of incorporation (charter) and bylaws, approve a merger or the dissolution of the corporation, and approve the sale of all or substantially all of the corporation's assets. Some of these powers are subject to prior board approval.

Directors are elected to (and removed from) the board of directors by a vote of the shareholders. The first board of directors is either named in the articles of incorporation or chosen by the incorporators to serve until the first shareholders' meeting. From that time on, the selection and retention of directors are exclusively shareholder functions.

Directors usually serve their full terms; if they are unsatisfactory, they are simply not reelected. Shareholders have the inherent power, however, to remove a director from office *for cause* (breach of duty or misconduct) by a majority vote.[4] Some state statutes (and some corporate charters) even permit removal of directors without cause by the vote of a majority of the holders of outstanding shares entitled to vote.

"There is no such thing . . . as an innocent stockholder. He may be innocent in fact, but socially he cannot be held innocent. He accepts the benefits of the system. It is his business and his obligation to see that those who represent him carry out a policy which is consistent with the public welfare."

LOUIS BRANDEIS, 1856–1941
(Associate justice of the United States Supreme Court, 1916–1938)

SHAREHOLDERS' MEETINGS

Shareholders' meetings must occur at least annually, and additional, special meetings can be called as needed to take care of urgent matters.

Notice of Meetings Each shareholder must receive written notice of the date, time, and place of a shareholders' meeting.[5] The notice must be received within a reasonable length of time prior to the date of the meeting. Notice of a special meeting must include a statement of the purpose of the meeting, and business transacted at the meeting is limited to that purpose.

Proxies and Proxy Materials Because it is usually not practical for owners of only a few shares of stock of publicly traded corporations to attend shareholders'

4. A director can often demand court review of removal for cause.

5. The shareholder can waive the requirement of written notice by signing a waiver form. In some states, a shareholder who does not receive written notice, but who learns of the meeting and attends without protesting the lack of notice, is said to have waived notice by such conduct. State statutes and corporate bylaws typically set forth the time within which notice must be sent, what methods can be used, and what the notice must contain.

SHAREHOLDERS MEET TO VOTE ON CORPORATE ISSUES. WHAT ISSUES MUST BE PUT BEFORE SHAREHOLDERS FOR THEIR VOTE?

• **PROXY**
In corporation law, a written agreement between a stockholder and another under which the stockholder authorizes the other to vote the stockholder's shares in a certain manner.

meetings, such stockholders normally give third parties written authorization to vote their shares at the meeting. This authorization is called a **proxy** (from the Latin *procurare,* "to manage, take care of"). Proxies are often solicited by management, but any person can solicit proxies to concentrate voting power. Proxies have been used by a group of shareholders as a device for taking over a corporation (corporate takeovers are discussed in Chapter 29). Proxies are normally revocable (that is, they can be withdrawn), unless they are specifically designated as irrevocable. Under RMBCA 7.22(c), proxies last for eleven months, unless the proxy agreement provides for a longer period.

When shareholders want to change a company policy, they can put their idea up for a shareholder vote. They can do this by submitting a shareholder proposal to the board of directors and asking the board to include the proposal in the proxy materials that are sent to all shareholders before meetings. The Securities and Exchange Commission (SEC), which regulates the purchase and sale of securities (see Chapter 31), has special provisions relating to proxies and shareholder proposals. SEC Rule 14a-8 requires that when a company sends proxy materials to its shareholders, the company must also include whatever proposals will be considered at the meeting and provide shareholders with the opportunity to vote on the proposals by marking and returning their proxy cards. SEC Rule 14a-8 provides that all shareholders who own stock worth at least $1,000 are eligible to submit proposals for inclusion in corporate proxy material. Only those proposals that relate to significant policy considerations must be included, however. A corporation is not required to include in proxy materials proposals that relate to "ordinary business operations."

ETHICAL ISSUE 28.2 ***Must shareholder proposals concerning equal employment opportunity be included in proxy materials?*** If a shareholder submits a proposal calling for the establishment of equal employment opportunity or an affirmative action policy, must the proposal be included in proxy materials? The answer to this question, which has significant ethical implications, depends on whether the proposal relates to important policy considerations. If it does, then it must be included in the proxy materials. If it does not—that is, if it relates to "ordinary business" decisions—the proposal may be excluded. It is often difficult, however, to draw a line between these two classifications, as the SEC has learned over the years. For example, in a 1976 ruling, the SEC stated that shareholder proposals concerning equal opportunity and affirmative action relate to significant policy issues on which shareholders should be allowed to vote. In 1992, however, the SEC reversed its position and ruled that all employment-related shareholder proposals would be automatically omittable under the "ordinary business" exclusion, even if they raised social policy concerns. In the wake of substantial criticism of its 1992 rule, the SEC again changed its stance. In 1998, the SEC issued a rule that essentially allows such decisions to be made on a case-by-case basis.

ON THE WEB

For more information on the SEC's rulings on proxy materials, go to the SEC's Web site at www.sec.gov.

SHAREHOLDER VOTING

Shareholders exercise ownership control through the power of their votes. Each shareholder is entitled to one vote per share, although the voting techniques that will be discussed shortly all enhance the power of the shareholder's vote. The articles of incorporation can exclude or limit voting rights, particularly for certain classes of shares. For example, owners of preferred shares are usually denied the right to vote.

¡BE CAREFUL!
Once a quorum is present, a vote can be taken even if some shareholders leave without casting their votes.

Quorum Requirements For shareholders to act during a meeting, a quorum must be present. Generally, a quorum exists when shareholders holding more than 50 percent of the outstanding shares are present. Corporate business matters are presented in the form of *resolutions,* which shareholders vote to approve or disapprove. Some state statutes have set forth specific voting requirements, and corporations' articles or bylaws must abide by these statutory requirements. Some states provide that the unanimous written consent of shareholders is a permissible alternative to holding a shareholders' meeting. Once a quorum is present, a majority vote of the shares represented at the meeting is usually required to pass resolutions.

• EXAMPLE 28.3 Assume that Novo Pictures, Inc., has 10,000 outstanding shares of voting stock. Its articles of incorporation set the quorum at 50 percent of outstanding shares and provide that a majority vote of the shares present is necessary to pass resolutions concerning ordinary matters. Therefore, for this firm, a quorum of shareholders representing 5,000 outstanding shares must be present at a shareholders' meeting to conduct business. If exactly 5,000 shares are represented at the meeting, a vote of at least 2,501 of those shares is needed to pass a resolution. If 6,000 shares are represented, a vote of 3,001 will be required, and so on. •

At times, a larger-than-majority vote will be required either by a statute or by the corporate charter. Extraordinary corporate matters, such as a merger, consolidation, or dissolution of the corporation (see Chapter 28), require a higher percentage of the representatives of all corporate shares entitled to vote, not just a majority of those present at that particular meeting.

Voting Lists Voting lists are prepared by the corporation prior to each meeting of the shareholders. Persons whose names appear on the corporation's shareholder records as owners are the ones ordinarily entitled to vote.[6] The voting list contains the name and address of each shareholder as shown on the corporate records on a given cutoff date, or record date. (Under RMBCA 7.07, the record date may be as much as seventy days before the meeting.) The voting list also includes the number of voting shares held by each owner. The list is usually kept at the corporate headquarters and is available for shareholder inspection.

Cumulative Voting Most states permit or even require shareholders to elect directors by *cumulative voting,* a method of voting designed to allow minority shareholders representation on the board of directors.[7] When cumulative voting is allowed or required, the number of members of the board to be elected is multiplied by the total number of voting shares. The result equals the number of votes a shareholder has, and this total can be cast for one or more nominees for director. All nominees stand for election at the same time. When cumulative voting is not required either by statute or under the articles, the entire board can be elected by a simple majority of shares at a shareholders' meeting.

Cumulative voting can best be understood by an example. • EXAMPLE 28.4 Suppose that a corporation has 10,000 shares issued and outstanding. One group of shareholders (the minority shareholders) holds only 3,000 shares, and the other group of shareholders (the majority shareholders) holds the other 7,000 shares. Three members of the board are to be elected. The majority shareholders' nominees are Acevedo, Barkley, and Craycik. The minority shareholders' nominee is Drake. Can Drake be elected by the minority shareholders?

6. When the legal owner is deceased, bankrupt, incompetent, or in some other way under a legal disability, his or her vote can be cast by a person designated by law to control and manage the owner's property.
7. See, for example, California Corporate Code Section 708. Under RMBCA 7.28, however, no cumulative voting rights exist unless the articles of incorporation so provide.

If cumulative voting is allowed, the answer is yes. The minority shareholders have 9,000 votes among them (the number of directors to be elected times the number of shares held by the minority shareholders equals 3 times 3,000, which equals 9,000 votes). All of these votes can be cast to elect Drake. The majority shareholders have 21,000 votes (3 times 7,000 equals 21,000 votes), but these votes have to be distributed among their three nominees. The principle of cumulative voting is that no matter how the majority shareholders cast their 21,000 votes, they will not be able to elect all three directors if the minority shareholders cast all of their 9,000 votes for Drake, as illustrated in Exhibit 28–1.•

Other Voting Techniques A group of shareholders can agree in writing prior to a shareholders' meeting, in a *shareholder voting agreement,* to vote their shares together in a specified manner. Such agreements usually are held to be valid and enforceable. A shareholder can also appoint a voting agent and vote by proxy. As mentioned, a proxy is a written authorization to cast the shareholder's vote, and a person can solicit proxies from a number of shareholders in an attempt to concentrate voting power.

• **VOTING TRUST**
An agreement (trust contract) under which legal title to shares of corporate stock is transferred to a trustee who is authorized by the shareholders to vote the shares on their behalf.

Another technique is for shareholders to enter into a **voting trust,** which is an agreement (a trust contract) under which legal title (record ownership on the corporate books) is transferred to a trustee who is responsible for voting the shares. The agreement can specify how the trustee is to vote, or it can allow the trustee to use his or her discretion. The trustee takes physical possession of the stock certificate and in return gives the shareholder a voting trust certificate. The shareholder retains all of the rights of ownership (for example, the right to receive dividend payments) except for the power to vote the shares.

Rights of Shareholders

Shareholders possess numerous rights. A significant right—the right to vote their shares—has already been discussed. We now look at some additional rights of shareholders.

Stock Certificates

• **STOCK CERTIFICATE**
A certificate issued by a corporation evidencing the ownership of a specified number of shares in the corporation.

A **stock certificate** is a certificate issued by a corporation that evidences ownership of a specified number of shares in the corporation. In jurisdictions that require the issuance of stock certificates, shareholders have the right to demand that the corporation issue certificates. In most states and under RMBCA 6.26, boards of directors may provide that shares of stock be uncertificated—that is, that physical stock certificates need not be issued. In that circumstance, the corporation may be required

EXHIBIT 28–1 • Results of Cumulative Voting
This exhibit illustrates how cumulative voting gives minority shareholders a greater chance of electing a director of their choice. By casting all of their 9,000 votes for one candidate (Drake), the minority shareholders will succeed in electing Drake to the board of directors.

BALLOT	MAJORITY SHAREHOLDERS' VOTES			MINORITY SHAREHOLDERS' VOTES	DIRECTORS ELECTED
	Acevedo	Barkley	Craycik	Drake	
1	10,000	10,000	1,000	9,000	Acevedo/Barkley/Drake
2	9,001	9,000	2,999	9,000	Acevedo/Barkley/Drake
3	6,000	7,000	8,000	9,000	Barkley/Craycik/Drake

STOCK CERTIFICATES ARE DISPLAYED. TO BE A SHAREHOLDER, IS IT NECESSARY TO HAVE PHYSICAL POSSESSION OF A CERTIFICATE? WHY OR WHY NOT?

to send the holders of uncertificated shares letters or some other form of notice containing the same information as that included on stock certificates.

Stock is intangible personal property, and the ownership right exists independently of the certificate itself. A stock certificate may be lost or destroyed, but ownership is not destroyed with it. A new certificate can be issued to replace one that has been lost or destroyed.[8] Notice of shareholders' meetings, dividends, and operational and financial reports are all distributed according to the recorded ownership listed in the corporation's books, not on the basis of possession of the certificate.

PREEMPTIVE RIGHTS

A **preemptive right** is a common law concept under which a preference is given to shareholders over all other purchasers to subscribe to or purchase shares of a new issue of stock in proportion to the percentage of total shares they already hold. This allows each shareholder to maintain his or her portion of control, voting power, or financial interest in the corporation. Most statutes either (1) grant preemptive rights but allow them to be negated in the corporation's articles or (2) deny preemptive rights except to the extent that they are granted in the articles. The result is that the articles of incorporation determine the existence and scope of preemptive rights. Generally, preemptive rights apply only to additional, newly issued stock sold for cash, and the preemptive rights must be exercised within a specified time period, which is usually thirty days.

• EXAMPLE 28.5 Detering Corporation authorizes and issues 1,000 shares of stock. Lebow purchases 100 shares, making her the owner of 10 percent of the company's stock. Subsequently, Detering, by vote of the shareholders, authorizes the issuance of another 1,000 shares (by amending the articles of incorporation). This increases its capital stock to a total of 2,000 shares. If preemptive rights have been provided, Lebow can purchase one additional share of the new stock being issued for each share she currently owns—or 100 additional shares. Thus, she can own 200 of the 2,000 shares outstanding, and she will maintain her relative position as a shareholder. If preemptive rights are not allowed, her proportionate control and voting power may be diluted from that of a 10 percent shareholder to that of a 5 percent shareholder because of the issuance of the additional 1,000 shares.•

• PREEMPTIVE RIGHTS
Rights held by shareholders that entitle them to purchase newly issued shares of a corporation's stock, equal in percentage to shares presently held, before the stock is offered to any outside buyers. Preemptive rights enable shareholders to maintain their proportionate ownership and voice in the corporation.

• STOCK WARRANT
A certificate that grants the owner the option to buy a given number of shares of stock, usually within a set time period.

Preemptive rights can be very important for shareholders in close corporations. This is because of the relatively small number of shares and the substantial interest that each shareholder controls in a close corporation. Without preemptive rights, it would be possible for a shareholder to lose his or her proportionate control over the firm.

STOCK WARRANTS

Usually, when preemptive rights exist and a corporation is issuing additional shares, each shareholder is given **stock warrants,** which are transferable options to acquire a given number of shares from the corporation at a stated price. Warrants are often publicly traded on securities exchanges. When the option to purchase is in effect for a short period of time, the stock warrants are usually referred to as *rights*.

DIVIDENDS

As mentioned in Chapter 27, a *dividend* is a distribution of corporate profits or

8. For a lost or destroyed certificate to be reissued, a shareholder normally must furnish an indemnity bond to protect the corporation against potential loss should the original certificate reappear at some future time in the hands of a bona fide purchaser [UCC 8–302, 8–405(2)].

income *ordered by the directors* and paid to the shareholders in proportion to their respective shares in the corporation. Dividends can be paid in cash, property, stock of the corporation that is paying the dividends, or stock of other corporations.[9]

State laws vary, but each state determines the general circumstances and legal requirements under which dividends are paid. State laws also control the sources of revenue to be used; only certain funds are legally available for paying dividends. Depending on state law, dividends may be paid from the following sources:

1. *Retained earnings.* All state statutes allow dividends to be paid from the undistributed net profits earned by the corporation, including capital gains from the sale of fixed assets. The undistributed net profits are called *retained earnings.*
2. *Net profits.* A few state statutes allow dividends to be issued from current net profits without regard to deficits in prior years.
3. *Surplus.* A number of statutes allow dividends to be paid out of any surplus.

Illegal Dividends A dividend paid while the corporation is insolvent is automatically an illegal dividend, and shareholders may be liable for returning the payment to the corporation or its creditors. Furthermore, as just discussed, dividends are generally required by statute to be distributed only from certain authorized corporate accounts. Sometimes dividends are improperly paid from an unauthorized account, or their payment causes the corporation to become insolvent. Generally, in such cases, shareholders must return illegal dividends only if they knew that the dividends were illegal when they received them. Whenever dividends are illegal or improper, the board of directors can be held personally liable for the amount of the payment. When directors can show that a shareholder knew that a dividend was illegal when it was received, however, the directors are entitled to reimbursement from the shareholder.

Directors' Failure to Declare a Dividend When directors fail to declare a dividend, shareholders can ask a court to compel the directors to meet and to declare a dividend. For the shareholders to succeed, they must show that the directors have acted so unreasonably in withholding the dividend that the directors' conduct is an abuse of their discretion.

Often, large money reserves are accumulated for a bona fide purpose, such as expansion, research, or other legitimate corporate goals. The mere fact that sufficient corporate earnings or surplus is available to pay a dividend is not enough to compel directors to distribute funds that, in the board's opinion, should not be paid. The courts are circumspect about interfering with corporate operations and will not compel directors to declare dividends unless abuse of discretion is clearly shown. In the following classic case, the shareholders brought a court action to compel Ford Motor Company to declare a dividend.

9. Technically, dividends paid in stock are not dividends. They maintain each shareholder's proportional interest in the corporation. On one occasion, a distillery declared and paid a "dividend" in bonded whiskey.

CASE 28.2 Dodge v. Ford Motor Co.

Supreme Court of Michigan, 1919.
204 Mich. 459,
170 N.W. 668.

HISTORICAL AND ETHICAL SETTING *Corporations are owned by shareholders but run by directors and officers. Practical and ethical problems are inevitable. Directors are supposed to act in the best interests of the corporation, which is presumed to be the same as the best interests of the shareholders. Directors and shareholders may have different views about the corporation's best interests, however. Directors who look toward long-term growth and future profitability may want to reinvest profits in the firm. Shareholders may be more interested in receiving those profits as current dividends.*

CASE 28.2—Continued

BACKGROUND AND FACTS Henry Ford was the president and major shareholder of Ford Motor Company. In the company's early years, business expanded rapidly, and in addition to regular quarterly dividends, special dividends were often paid. By 1916, surplus above capital was still $111,960,907. That year, however, Henry Ford declared that the company would no longer pay special dividends but would put back into the business all the earnings of the company above the regular dividend of 5 percent. According to the court, Ford stated as follows: "My ambition is to employ still more men, to spread the benefits of this industrial system to the greatest possible number, to help them build up their lives and their homes. To do this, we are putting the greatest share of our profits back into the business." The minority shareholders (who owned 10 percent of the stock) filed a lawsuit in a Michigan state court against Ford and others to force the declaration of a dividend. The court ordered the Ford directors to declare a dividend, and the case was appealed.

IN THE WORDS OF THE COURT . . .
OSTRANDER, Chief Justice.

* * * *

* * * Courts of equity will not interfere in the management of the directors unless it is clearly made to appear that they are guilty of fraud or misappropriation of the corporate funds, or refuse to declare a dividend when the corporation has a surplus of net profits which it can, without detriment to its business, divide among its stockholders, and when a refusal to do so would amount to such an abuse of discretion as would constitute a fraud, or breach of that good faith which they are bound to exercise towards the stockholders.

* * * *

Defendants say, and it is true, that a considerable cash balance must be at all times carried by such a concern [as Ford]. But * * * there was a large daily, weekly, monthly, receipt of cash. The output was practically continuous and was continuously, and within a few days, turned into cash. Moreover, the contemplated expenditures were not to be immediately made. * * * So that, without going further, it would appear that, accepting and approving the plan of the directors, it was their duty to distribute * * * a very large sum of money to stockholders.

DECISION AND REMEDY The Supreme Court of Michigan ordered Ford Motor Company to declare a dividend. The court held that, in view of the firm's large capital surplus, to withhold a dividend would violate the directors' duty to the shareholders.

FOR CRITICAL ANALYSIS—Social Consideration
Generally, how can a court determine when directors should pay dividends?

INSPECTION RIGHTS

Shareholders in a corporation enjoy both common law and statutory inspection rights.[10] The shareholder's right of inspection is limited, however, to the inspection and copying of corporate books and records for a *proper purpose*, provided the request is made in advance. The shareholder can inspect in person, or an attorney, agent, accountant, or other type of assistant can do so. The RMBCA requires the corporation to maintain an alphabetical voting list of shareholders with addresses and number of shares owned; this list must be kept open at the annual meeting for inspection by any shareholder of record [RMBCA 7.20].

The power of inspection is fraught with potential abuses, and the corporation is allowed to protect itself from them. For example, a shareholder can properly be denied access to corporate records to prevent harassment or to protect trade secrets

10. See, for example, *Schwartzman v. Schwartzman Packing Co.*, 99 N.M. 436, 659 P.2d 888 (1983).

or other confidential corporate information. Some states require that a shareholder must have held his or her shares for a minimum period of time immediately preceding the demand to inspect or must hold a minimum number of outstanding shares. The RMBCA provides, however, that every shareholder is entitled to examine specified corporate records [RMBCA 16.02].

Transfer of Shares

Stock certificates generally are negotiable and freely transferable by indorsement and delivery. Transfer of stock in closely held corporations, however, usually is restricted by the bylaws, by a restriction stamped on the stock certificate, or by a shareholder agreement (see Chapter 27). The existence of any restrictions on transferability must always be noted on the face of the stock certificate, and these restrictions must be reasonable.

Sometimes, corporations or their shareholders restrict transferability by reserving the option to purchase any shares offered for resale by a shareholder. This **right of first refusal** remains with the corporation or the shareholders for only a specified time or a reasonable time. Variations on the purchase option are possible. For example, a shareholder might be required to offer the shares to other shareholders first or to the corporation first.

• **RIGHT OF FIRST REFUSAL**
The right to purchase personal or real property—such as corporate shares or real estate—before the property is offered for sale to others.

When shares are transferred, a new entry is made in the corporate stock book to indicate the new owner. Until the corporation is notified and the entry is complete, the current record owner has the right to be notified of (and attend) shareholders' meetings, the right to vote the shares, the right to receive dividends, and all other shareholder rights.

Corporate Dissolution

When a corporation is dissolved and its outstanding debts and the claims of its creditors have been satisfied, the remaining assets are distributed to the shareholders in proportion to the percentage of shares owned by each shareholder. Certain classes of preferred stock can be given priority. If no preferences to distribution of assets on liquidation are given to any class of stock, then the shareholders are entitled to the remaining assets.

In some circumstances, shareholders may petition a court to have the corporation dissolved. Suppose, for example, that a minority shareholder knows that the board of directors is mishandling corporate assets. The minority shareholder is not powerless to intervene. He or she can petition a court to appoint a **receiver**—who will wind up corporate affairs and liquidate the business assets of the corporation.

• **RECEIVER**
In a corporate dissolution, a court-appointed person who winds up corporate affairs and liquidates corporate assets.

The RMBCA permits any shareholder to initiate such an action in any of the following circumstances [RMBCA 14.30]:

1. The directors are deadlocked in the management of corporate affairs. The shareholders are unable to break that deadlock, and irreparable injury to the corporation is being suffered or threatened.
2. The acts of the directors or those in control of the corporation are illegal, oppressive, or fraudulent.
3. Corporate assets are being misapplied or wasted.
4. The shareholders are deadlocked in voting power and have failed, for a specified period (usually two annual meetings), to elect successors to directors whose terms have expired or would have expired with the election of successors.

When the shareholders themselves are deadlocked, a court may order the dissolution of a corporation. This was the circumstance in the following case.

CASE 28.3 Black v. Graham

Supreme Court of Georgia, 1996.
464 S.E.2d 814.

HISTORICAL AND ECONOMIC SETTING *Despite the continued expansion of the economy in the early 1990s, there was negative growth in the market for construction materials. At the time, there were nearly 72,000 building materials and garden supplies establishments. In contrast, there were more than 500,000 construction contractors. Most contractors and building supplies firms are small businesses. In the construction industry, a business is classified as small if it has gross annual receipts between $7 million and $15 million.*

BACKGROUND AND FACTS Black and Graham each owned 50 percent of the stock of a building supplies corporation; they also served as the corporation's directors. When the two shareholder-directors deadlocked over differences of opinion on how to run their business, Graham filed a petition in a Georgia state court to dissolve the corporation. The parties agreed to the appointment of a custodian to run their firm while the court considered Graham's petition. Ultimately, the court ordered each shareholder to offer to buy the other out. This attempt to resolve the matter failed. The court then converted the custodian into a receiver, directed him to wind up the affairs of the business, and told him to liquidate the corporation. Both parties appealed to the Supreme Court of Georgia.

IN THE WORDS OF THE COURT . . .
HINES, Justice.

* * * *

* * * A deadlock occurs "[w]here stock of [a] corporation is owned in equal shares by two contending parties, which condition threatens to result in destruction of business, and it appears that [the] parties cannot agree upon management of [the] business, and under existing circumstances neither one is authorized to impose its views upon the other, * * * ." The evidence in this case portrays a classic situation of deadlock. Black and Graham as sole and equal shareholders functioned as *de facto* directors who were wholly unable to agree on the management of the business. Neither had the authority to prevail in his view and the hostile and static situation threatened irreparable injury to the corporation. Under these circumstances, the appointment of a receiver and dissolution was warranted.

DECISION AND REMEDY The Supreme Court of Georgia affirmed the orders of the lower court.

FOR CRITICAL ANALYSIS—Political Consideration *What steps might a corporation with an even number of shareholders and directors take to avoid a deadlock?*

THE SHAREHOLDER'S DERIVATIVE SUIT

When those in control of a corporation—the corporate directors—fail to sue in the corporate name to redress a wrong suffered by the corporation, shareholders are permitted to do so "derivatively" in what is known as a **shareholder's derivative suit.** Some wrong must have been done to the corporation, and before a derivative suit can be brought, the shareholders must first state their complaint to the board of directors. Only if the directors fail to solve the problem or take appropriate action can the derivative suit go forward.

• **SHAREHOLDER'S DERIVATIVE SUIT** A suit brought by a shareholder to enforce a corporate cause of action against a third person.

The right of shareholders to bring a derivative action is especially important when the wrong suffered by the corporation results from the actions of corporate directors or officers. This is because the directors and officers would probably want to prevent any action against themselves.

The shareholder's derivative suit is singular in that those suing are not pursuing rights or benefits for themselves personally but are acting as guardians of the corporate entity. Therefore, any damages recovered by the suit normally go into the corporation's treasury, not to the shareholders personally.

International Perspective • DERIVATIVE ACTIONS IN OTHER NATIONS

In the United States, the 1980s and early 1990s saw a dramatic increase in the number of shareholder suits brought against directors and officers for alleged breaches of duties. Today, most of the claims brought against directors and officers are those alleged in shareholders' derivative suits. Other nations, however, are more restrictive in regard to the use of such suits. In Germany, for example, there is no provision for derivative litigation, and a corporation's duty to its employees is just as significant as its duty to the shareholder-owners of the company. The United Kingdom has no statute authorizing derivative actions, which are permitted only to challenge directors' actions that the shareholders could not legally ratify. Japan authorizes derivative actions but also permits a company to sue the shareholder-plaintiff for damages if the action is unsuccessful.

FOR CRITICAL ANALYSIS
Do corporations benefit from shareholders' derivative suits? If so, how?

Liability of Shareholders

One of the hallmarks of the corporate organization is that shareholders are not personally liable for the debts of the corporation. If the corporation fails, shareholders can lose their investments, but that is generally the limit of their liability. As discussed in Chapter 27, in certain instances of fraud, undercapitalization, or careless observance of corporate formalities, a court will pierce the corporate veil (disregard the corporate entity) and hold the shareholders individually liable. These situations are the exception, however, not the rule. Although they are rare, certain other instances arise where a shareholder can be personally liable. One relates to illegal dividends, which were discussed previously. Two others relate to stock subscriptions and watered stock, which we discuss here.

Sometimes stock-subscription agreements—written contracts by which one agrees to buy capital stock of a corporation—exist prior to incorporation. Normally, these agreements are treated as continuing offers and are irrevocable (for up to six months under RMBCA 6.20). Once the corporation has been formed, it can sell shares to shareholder investors. In either situation, once the subscription agreement or stock offer is accepted, a binding contract is formed. Any refusal to pay constitutes a breach resulting in the personal liability of the shareholder.

• **PAR-VALUE SHARES**
Corporate shares that have a specific face value, or formal cash-in value, written on them, such as one dollar.

• **NO-PAR SHARES**
Corporate shares that have no face value—that is, no specific dollar amount is printed on their face.

• **WATERED STOCK**
Shares of stock issued by a corporation for which the corporation receives, as payment, less than the stated value of the shares.

Shares of stock can be paid for by property or by services rendered instead of cash. They cannot be purchased with promissory notes, however. The general rule is that for **par-value shares** (shares that have a specific face value, or formal cash-in value, written on them, such as one penny or one dollar), the corporation must receive a value at least equal to the par-value amount. For **no-par shares** (shares that have no face value—no specific amount printed on their face), the corporation must receive the value of the shares as determined by the board or the shareholders when the stock was issued. When the corporation issues shares for less than these stated values, the shares are referred to as **watered stock.**[11] Usually, the shareholder who

11. The phrase *watered stock* was originally used to describe cattle that—kept thirsty during a long drive—were allowed to drink large quantities of water just prior to their sale. The increased weight of the "watered stock" allowed the seller to reap a higher profit.

> **ON THE WEB**
> A leading case on the duties owed by majority shareholders to minority shareholders is discussed online at www.nylj.com/links/150sterk.html.

receives watered stock must pay the difference to the corporation (the shareholder is personally liable). In some states, the shareholder who receives watered stock may be liable to creditors of the corporation for unpaid corporate debts.

• **EXAMPLE 28.6** Suppose that during the formation of a corporation, Gomez, one of the incorporators, transfers his property, Sunset Beach, to the corporation for ten thousand shares of stock. The stock has a par value of $100 per share, and thus the total price of the ten thousand shares is $1 million. After the property is transferred and the shares are issued, Sunset Beach is carried on the corporate books at a value of $1 million. On appraisal, it is discovered that the market value of the property at the time of transfer was only $500,000. The shares issued to Gomez are therefore watered stock, and he is liable to the corporation for the difference. •

Duties of Majority Shareholders

In some cases, a majority shareholder is regarded as having a fiduciary duty to the corporation and to the minority shareholders. This occurs when a single shareholder (or a few shareholders acting in concert) owns a sufficient number of shares to exercise *de facto* control over the corporation. In these situations, majority shareholders owe a fiduciary duty to the minority shareholders when they sell their shares, because such a sale would be, in fact, a transfer of control of the corporation.

APPLICATION Law & the Corporation: Developing an Electronic & Paper Document-Retention Policy*

If a corporation becomes the target of a civil lawsuit or criminal investigation, the company may be required to turn over any documents in its files relating to the matter during the discovery stage of litigation. These documents may consist of legal documents, contracts, e-mail, faxes, letters, interoffice memorandums, notebooks, diaries, and other materials, even if they are kept in personal files in the homes of directors or officers.

*This *Application* is not meant to substitute for the services of an attorney who is licensed to practice law in your state.

At one time, document-retention policies referred only to paper documents. Today, a document-retention policy must also take into consideration electronic documents and data. Under the current Federal Rules of Civil Procedure, which govern civil litigation procedures (see Chapter 3), a defendant in a lawsuit must disclose all relevant electronic data compilations and documents, as well as all relevant paper documents. Although certain documents or data might free a company of any liability arising from a claim, others might serve to substantiate a civil claim or criminal charge. It is also possible that information contained in a document—an interoffice e-mail memo, for example (or even a memo referring to that memo)—could be used to convince a jury that the company or its directors or officers condoned a certain action when they denied condoning it.

To be fully prepared in the event of a lawsuit or criminal investigation, many companies today have created document-retention policies to determine what paper and electronic documents to keep. How does a company decide which documents should be retained and which should be destroyed? By law, corporations are required to keep certain types of documents, such as those documents specified in the Code of Federal Regulations and in regulations issued by government agencies, such as the Occupational Safety and Health Administration. Generally, any records that the company is not legally required to keep or that the company is sure it will have no legal need for should be removed from the files and destroyed. A joint-venture agreement, for example, should be kept. A memo about last year's company picnic, however, should be removed from the files and destroyed; obviously, it is just taking up storage space.

APPLICATION CONTINUED

If the company becomes the target of an investigation, it usually must modify its document-retention policy until the investigation has been completed. Company officers, after receiving a subpoena to produce specific types of documents, should instruct the appropriate employees not to destroy relevant papers that would otherwise be disposed of as part of the company's normal document-retention program.

Generally, company officials must always exercise good faith in deciding what documents should or should not be destroyed when attempting to comply with a subpoena to avoid being charged with the obstruction of justice. The specter of criminal prosecution would appear to encourage the retention of even those documents that are only remotely related to the dispute—at least until it has been resolved.

CHECKLIST FOR A DOCUMENT-RETENTION POLICY

1. Find out which documents must be retained under the Code of Federal Regulations and under other government agency regulations to which your corporation is subject.
2. Retain other paper and electronic documents only if the retention is in the corporation's interest.
3. If certain corporate documents are subpoenaed, modify your document-retention policy to retain any document that is even remotely related to the dispute until the legal action has been resolved.

Key Terms

business judgment rule 747
no-par share 758
par-value share 758
preemptive right 753
proxy 750
quorum 742
receiver 756
right of first refusal 756
shareholder's derivative suit 757
stock certificate 752
stock warrant 753
tender offer 744
voting trust 752
watered stock 758

Chapter Summary • Corporate Directors, Officers, and Shareholders

Role of Directors (See pages 741–743.)	1. *Election of directors*—The first board of directors is usually appointed by the incorporators; thereafter, directors are elected by the shareholders. Directors usually serve a one-year term, although the term can be longer and staggered terms are permitted under most state statutes. 2. *Directors' qualifications and compensation*—Few qualifications are required; a director can be a shareholder but is not required to be. Compensation is usually specified in the corporate articles or bylaws. 3. *Board of directors' meetings*—The board of directors conducts business by holding formal meetings with recorded minutes. The date of regular meetings is usually established in the corporate articles or bylaws; special meetings can be called, with notice sent to all directors. Quorum requirements vary from state to state; usually, a quorum is a majority of the corporate directors. Voting must usually be done in person, and in ordinary matters only a majority vote is required. 4. *Rights of directors*—Directors' rights include the rights of participation, inspection, compensation, and indemnification. 5. *Directors' management responsibilities*—Directors are responsible for declaring and paying corporate dividends to shareholders; authorizing major corporate decisions; appointing, supervising, and removing corporate officers and other managerial employees; determining employees' compensation; making financial decisions necessary to the management of corporate affairs; and issuing authorized shares and bonds. Directors may delegate some of their responsibilities to executive committees and corporate officers and executives.

Chapter Summary • Corporate Directors, Officers, and Shareholders, Continued

Role of Corporate Officers and Executives (See page 743.)	Corporate officers and other executive employees are normally hired by the board of directors. In most states, a person can hold more than one office and can be both an officer and a director of a corporation. The rights of corporate officers and executives are defined by employment contracts. The duties of corporate officers are the same as those of directors.
Duties of Directors and Officers (See pages 743–747.)	1. *Duty of care*—Directors are obligated to act in good faith, to use prudent business judgment in the conduct of corporate affairs, and to act in the corporation's best interests. If a director fails to exercise this duty of care, he or she can be answerable to the corporation and to the shareholders for breaching the duty. 2. *Duty of loyalty*—Directors have a fiduciary duty to subordinate their own interests to those of the corporation in matters relating to the corporation. 3. *Conflicts of interest*—To fulfill their duty of loyalty, directors and officers must make a full disclosure of any potential conflicts of interest between their personal interests and those of the corporation.
Liability of Directors and Officers (See page 747–748.)	Corporate directors and officers are personally liable for their own torts and crimes; additionally, they may be held personally liable for the torts and crimes committed by corporate personnel under their direct supervision (see Chapters 6 and 24). The *business judgment rule* immunizes a director from liability for a corporate decision as long as the decision was within the powers of the corporation and the authority of the director to make and was an informed, reasonable, and loyal decision.
Role of Shareholders (See pages 748–752.)	1. *Shareholders' powers*—Shareholders' powers include the approval of all fundamental changes affecting the corporation and the election of the board of directors. 2. *Shareholders' meetings*—Shareholders' meetings must occur at least annually; special meetings can be called when necessary. Notice of the date, time, and place of the meeting (and its purpose, if it is specially called) must be sent to shareholders. Shareholders may vote by proxy (authorizing someone else to vote their shares) and may submit proposals to be included in the company's proxy materials sent to shareholders before meetings. 3. *Shareholder voting*—Shareholder voting requirements and procedures are as follows: a. A minimum number of shareholders (a quorum—generally, more than 50 percent of shares held) must be present at a meeting for business to be conducted; resolutions are passed (usually) by simple majority vote. b. The corporation must prepare voting lists of shareholders on record prior to each shareholders' meeting. c. Cumulative voting may or may not be required or permitted. Cumulative voting gives minority shareholders a better chance to be represented on the board of directors. d. A shareholder voting agreement (an agreement of shareholders to vote their shares together) is usually held to be valid and enforceable. e. A shareholder may appoint a proxy (substitute) to vote his or her shares. f. A shareholder may enter into a voting trust agreement by which title (record ownership) of his or her shares is given to a trustee, and the trustee votes the shares in accordance with the trust agreement.
Rights of Shareholders (See pages 752–758.)	Shareholders have numerous rights, which may include the following: 1. The right to a stock certificate, preemptive rights, and the right to stock warrants (depending on the corporate charter). 2. The right to obtain a dividend (at the discretion of the directors). 3. Voting rights. 4. The right to inspect the corporate records.

Chapter Summary • Corporate Directors, Officers, and Shareholders, Continued

Rights of Shareholders—continued	5. The right to transfer shares (this right may be restricted in close corporations). 6. The right to a share of corporate assets when the corporation is dissolved. 7. The right to sue on behalf of the corporation (bring a shareholder's derivative suit) when the directors fail to do so.
Liability of Shareholders (See page 758–759.)	Shareholders may be liable for the retention of illegal dividends, for breach of a stock-subscription agreement, and for the value of watered stock.
Duties of Majority Shareholders (See page 759.)	In certain situations, majority shareholders may be regarded as having a fiduciary duty to minority shareholders and will be liable if that duty is breached.

For Review

1 What are the duties of the directors and officers of a corporation?

2 Directors are expected to use their best judgment in managing the corporation. What must directors do to avoid liability for honest mistakes of judgment and poor business decisions?

3 What is a voting proxy? What is cumulative voting?

4 If a group of shareholders perceives that the corporation has suffered a wrong and the directors refuse to take action, can the shareholders compel the directors to act? If so, how?

5 From what sources may dividends be paid legally? In what circumstances is a dividend illegal? What happens if a dividend is illegally paid?

Questions and Case Problems

28–1. Rights of Shareholders. Dmitri has acquired one share of common stock of a multimillion-dollar corporation with over 500,000 shareholders. Dmitri's ownership is so small that he is questioning what his rights are as a shareholder. For example, he wants to know whether this one share entitles him to attend and vote at shareholders' meetings, inspect the corporate books, and receive periodic dividends. Discuss Dmitri's rights in these matters.

28–2. Voting Techniques. Algonquin Corp. has issued and has outstanding 100,000 shares of common stock. Four stockholders own 60,000 of these shares, and for the past six years they have nominated a slate of people for membership on the board, all of whom have been elected. Sergio and twenty other shareholders, owning 20,000 shares, are dissatisfied with corporate management and want a representative on the board who shares their views. Explain under what circumstances Sergio and the minority shareholders can elect their representative to the board.

28–3. Duties of Directors. Starboard, Inc., has a board of directors consisting of three members (Ellsworth, Green, and Morino) and approximately five hundred shareholders. At a regular meeting of the board, the board selects Tyson as president of the corporation by a two-to-one vote, with Ellsworth dissenting. The minutes of the meeting do not register Ellsworth's dissenting vote. Later, during an audit, it is discovered that Tyson is a former convict and has openly embezzled $500,000 from Starboard. This loss is not covered by insurance. The corporation wants to hold directors Ellsworth, Green, and Morino liable. Ellsworth claims no liability. Discuss the personal liability of the directors to the corporation.

28–4. Liability of Shareholders. Mallard has made a preincorporation subscription agreement to purchase 500 shares of a newly formed corporation. The shares have a par value of $100 per share. The corporation is formed, and it accepts Mallard's subscription. Mallard transfers a piece of land he owns to the corporation as payment for 250 of the shares, and the corporation issues 250 shares for it. Mallard pays for the other 250 shares with cash. One year later, with the corporation in serious financial difficulty, the board declares and pays a $5-per-share dividend. It is now learned that the land transferred by Mallard had a market value of $18,000. Discuss any liability that shareholder Mallard has to the corporation or to the creditors of the corporation.

28–5. Duties of Directors. Overland Corp. is negotiating with Wharton Construction Co. for the renovation of Overland's corporate headquarters. Wharton, the owner of Wharton Construction, is also one of the five members of the board of directors of Overland. The contract terms are standard for this type of contract. Wharton has previously informed two of the other Overland directors of his interest in the construction company. Overland's board approves the contract on a three-to-two vote, with Wharton voting with the majority. Discuss whether this contract is binding on the corporation.

28–6. Duties of Directors and Officers. Klinicki and Lundgren formed Berlinair, a closely held Oregon corporation, to provide air transportation out of West Germany. Klinicki, who owned 33 percent of the company stock, was the vice president and a director. Lundgren, who also owned 33 percent of the stock, was the president and a director. Lelco, Inc., a corporation owned by Lundgren and his family, owned 33 percent of Berlinair, and Berlinair's attorney owned the last 1 percent of stock. One of the goals of Berlinair was to obtain a contract with BFR, a West German consortium of travel agents, to provide BFR with air charter service. Later, Lundgren learned that the BFR contract might become available. Lundgren then incorporated Air Berlin Charter Co., of which he was the sole owner, and bid for the BFR contract. Lundgren won the BFR contract for Air Berlin while using Berlinair working time, staff, money, and facilities without the knowledge of Klinicki. Has Lundgren breached any fiduciary duty to Berlinair or to Klinicki? If so, what duty, and how was it breached? Explain. [*Klinicki v. Lundgren,* 67 Or.App. 160, 678 P.2d 1250 (1984)]

28–7. Duties of Directors and Officers. While working for Veco Corp., an Illinois financial services company, officers Robert Babcock and Margaret Michails, after discussions with other employees, prepared a business plan for their own financial services company, CorMac, Inc. The plan listed other Veco employees who would join CorMac and detailed the "taking over" of an important Veco client. Veco's founder and sole shareholder, David Vear, discovered what Babcock had done and fired him. Michails and other Veco employees quit to work for CorMac. As a result, Veco was left with no personnel who were experienced in handling one of its major accounts. Veco sued Babcock and Michails, alleging that they had breached their fiduciary duties to Veco. Had they breached any fiduciary duty? If so, what duty had they breached? How should the court rule on this issue? [*Veco Corp. v. Babcock,* 243 Ill.App.3d 153, 611 N.E.2d 1054, 183 Ill.Dec. 406 (1993)]

28–8. Rights of Shareholders. Melissa and Gary Callicoat each owned 50 percent of Callicoat, Inc. They were also Callicoat's only directors. They could not agree on the day-to-day management of the firm. They also could not agree on whether a debt owed to Arthur Baz was a personal or corporate debt. Melissa suggested that they dissolve the corporation. Gary refused and shut her out from the operations of the firm. Melissa filed a petition in an Ohio state court against Gary and Callicoat, asking the court to disolve the corporation. On what basis might the court order the dissolution? [*Callicoat v. Callicoat,* 73 Ohio Misc.2d 38, 657 N.E.2d 874 (1994)]

28–9. Duty of Loyalty. Mackinac Cellular Corp. offered to sell Robert Broz a license to operate a cellular phone system in Michigan. Broz was a director of Cellular Information Systems, Inc. (CIS). CIS, as a result of bankruptcy proceedings, was in the process of selling its cellular holdings. Broz did not formally present the opportunity to the CIS board, but he told some of the firm's officers and directors, who replied that CIS was not interested. At the time, PriCellular, Inc., a firm that was interested in the Michigan license, was attempting to buy CIS. Without telling PriCellular, Broz bought the license himself. After PriCellular took over CIS, the company filed a suit in a Delaware state court against Broz, alleging that he had usurped a corporate opportunity. For what reasons might a court decide that Broz had done nothing wrong? Discuss. [*Broz v. Cellular Information Systems, Inc.,* 673 A.2d 148 (Del. 1996)]

28–10. Business Judgment Rule. The board of directors of Baltimore Gas and Electric Company (BGE) recommended a merger with Potomac Electric Power Company (PEPCO). After full disclosure, the BGE shareholders approved the merger. On the ground that each BGE director stood a chance of being named to the new company's board, Janice Wittman, a BGE shareholder, filed a suit in a Maryland state court against the directors, alleging, among other things, that they were prohibited from deciding whether to recommend the merger. Did the directors breach their duty of care by voting in favor of the merger? How should the court rule? Discuss. [*Wittman v. Crooke,* 120 Md.App. 369, 707 A.2d 422 (1998)]

A QUESTION OF ETHICS AND SOCIAL RESPONSIBILITY

28–11. McQuade was the manager of the New York Giants baseball team. McQuade and John McGraw purchased shares in the National Exhibition Co., the corporation that owned the Giants, from Charles Stoneham, who owned a majority of National Exhibition's stock. As part of the transaction, each of the three agreed to use his best efforts to ensure that the others continued as directors and officers of the organization. Stoneham and McGraw, however, subsequently failed to use their best efforts to ensure that McQuade continued as the treasurer and a director of the corporation, and McQuade sued to compel specific performance of the agreement. A court reviewing the matter noted that McQuade had been "shabbily" treated by the others but refused to grant specific performance on the ground that the agreement was void because it interfered with the duty of the others as directors to do what was best for all the shareholders. Although shareholders may join to elect corporate directors, they may not join to limit the directors' discretion in managing the business affairs of an organization; the directors must retain their independent judgment. Consider the implications of the case, and address the following questions. [*McQuade v. Stoneham,* 263 N.Y. 323, 189 N.E. 234 (1934)]

1. Given that even the court sympathized with McQuade, was it ethical to put the business judgment of the directors ahead of an otherwise valid promise they had made?
2. Are there practical considerations that support the court's decision? How can directors perform the tasks dictated to

them if their judgment is constrained by earlier agreements with some of the shareholders?

FOR CRITICAL ANALYSIS

28–12. In general, courts are reluctant to grant shareholders' petitions for corporate dissolution in all but the most extreme circumstances, as when corporate directors or shareholders are deadlocked and the corporation suffers as a result. Rather, a court will attempt to "save" the corporate entity whenever possible. Why is this?

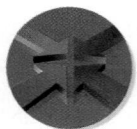

Online Activities

ONLINE EXERCISE 28–1

Go to the "Internet Activities Book" on the Web site that accompanies this text, the URL for which is http://blt.westbuslaw.com. Select the following activity, and perform the exercise according to the instructions given there:

Activity 27–1: Liability of Directors and Officers

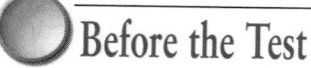

Before the Test

Go to the *Business Law Today* home page at http://blt.westbuslaw.com. Click on TestTutor.® You will find twenty interactive questions relating to this chapter.

CHAPTER 29

Corporate Merger, Consolidation, & Termination

> "Business is a combination of war and sport."
>
> André Maurois, 1885–1967
> (French author and historian)

CONTENTS

LEARNING OBJECTIVES

After reading this chapter, you should be able to:

1. Summarize the procedures involved in a merger or a consolidation.
2. Indicate what appraisal rights are and how they function.
3. Analyze the effects of a corporation's purchase of all or substantially all of another corporation's assets.
4. Discuss the effects of a corporation's purchase of a substantial number of voting shares of another corporation's stock.
5. Explain the phases of corporate termination.

Corporations increase the size of their operations for a number of reasons. During the 1980s, the acquisition of corporations by other corporations became a common phenomenon, and corporate takeovers will likely continue into the twenty-first century. Observers of the numerous corporate takeovers occurring in the business world today might well conclude, as André Maurois did, that business is indeed a "combination of war and sport."

A corporation typically extends its operations by combining with another corporation through a merger, a consolidation, a purchase of assets, or a purchase of a controlling interest in the other corporation. This chapter will examine these four types of corporate expansion. Dissolution and liquidation are the combined processes by which a corporation terminates its existence. The last part of this chapter will discuss the typical reasons for—and methods used in—terminating a corporation's existence.

Merger and Consolidation

The terms *merger* and *consolidation* often are used interchangeably, but they refer to two legally distinct proceedings. The rights and liabilities of the corporation, its shareholders, and its creditors are the same for both, however.

MERGER

• **MERGER**
A contractual and statutory process in which one corporation (the surviving corporation) acquires all of the assets and liabilities of another corporation (the merged corporation). The shareholders of the merged corporation receive either payment for their shares or shares in the surviving corporation.

A **merger** involves the legal combination of two or more corporations in such a way that only one of the corporations continues to exist. • EXAMPLE 29.1 Corporation A and Corporation B decide to merge. It is agreed that A will absorb B, so on merging, B ceases to exist as a separate entity, and A continues as the *surviving corporation.* Exhibit 29–1 graphically illustrates this process.•

After the merger, A is recognized as a single corporation, possessing all the rights, privileges, and powers of itself and B. It automatically acquires all of B's property and assets without the necessity of formal transfer. Additionally, A becomes liable for all of B's debts and obligations. Finally, A's articles of incorporation are deemed amended to include any changes that are stated in the *articles of merger* (a document setting forth the terms and conditions of the merger that is filed with the secretary of state).

In a merger, the surviving corporation inherits the disappearing corporation's preexisting legal rights and obligations. For example, if the disappearing corporation had a right of action against a third party, the surviving corporation can bring suit after the merger to recover the disappearing corporation's damages. The corporation statutes of many states provide that a successor (surviving) corporation inherits a **chose[1] in action** (a right to sue for a debt or sum of money) from a merging corporation as a matter of law. The common law similarly recognizes that, following a merger, a chose in action to enforce a property right will vest with the successor (surviving) corporation, and no right of action will remain with the disappearing corporation.

• **CHOSE IN ACTION**
A right that can be enforced in court to recover a debt or to obtain damages.

1. The word *chose* is French for "thing."

EXHIBIT 29–1 • Merger
In this illustration, Corporation A and Corporation B decide to merge. They agree that A will absorb B, so after the merger, B no longer exists as a separate entity, and A continues as the surviving corporation.

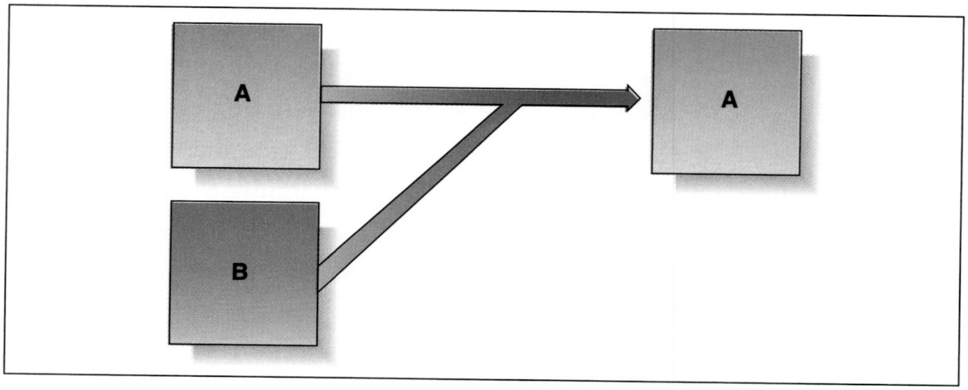

FRANK AND EARNEST BY BOB THAVES

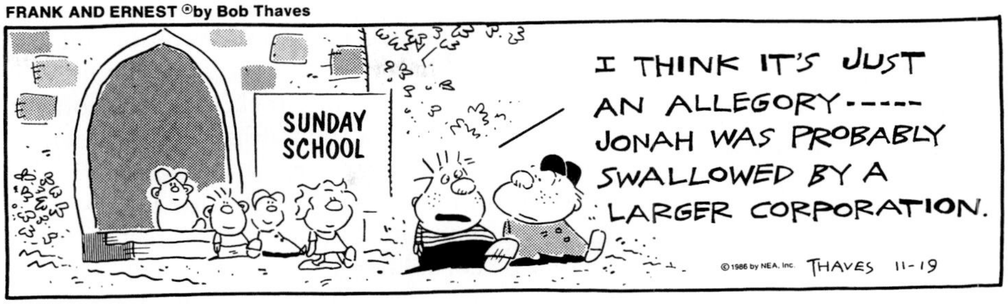

PRINTED WITH PERMISSION OF BOB THAVES.

CONSOLIDATION

• **CONSOLIDATION**
A contractual and statutory process in which two or more corporations join to become a completely new corporation. The original corporations cease to exist, and the new corporation acquires all their assets and liabilities.

In a **consolidation,** two or more corporations combine in such a way that each corporation ceases to exist and a new one emerges. • EXAMPLE 29.2 Corporation A and Corporation B consolidate to form an entirely new organization, Corporation C. In the process, A and B both terminate, and C comes into existence as an entirely new entity.• Exhibit 29–2 graphically illustrates this process.

As a result of the consolidation, C is recognized as a new corporation and a single entity; A and B cease to exist. C inherits all of the rights, privileges, and powers that A and B previously held. Title to any property and assets owned by A and B passes to C without formal transfer. C assumes liability for all of the debts and obligations owed by A and B. The terms and conditions of the consolidation are set forth in the *articles of consolidation,* which are filed with the secretary of state. These articles *take the place of* A's and B's original corporate articles and are thereafter regarded as C's corporate articles.

PROCEDURE FOR MERGER OR CONSOLIDATION

All states have statutes authorizing mergers and consolidations for domestic (in-state) corporations, and most states allow the combination of domestic and foreign (out-of-state) corporations. Although the procedures vary somewhat among jurisdictions, the basic requirements for a merger or a consolidation are as follows:

EXHIBIT 29–2 • Consolidation
In this illustration, Corporation A and Corporation B consolidate to form an entirely new organization, Corporation C. In the process, A and B terminate, and C comes into existence as an entirely new entity.

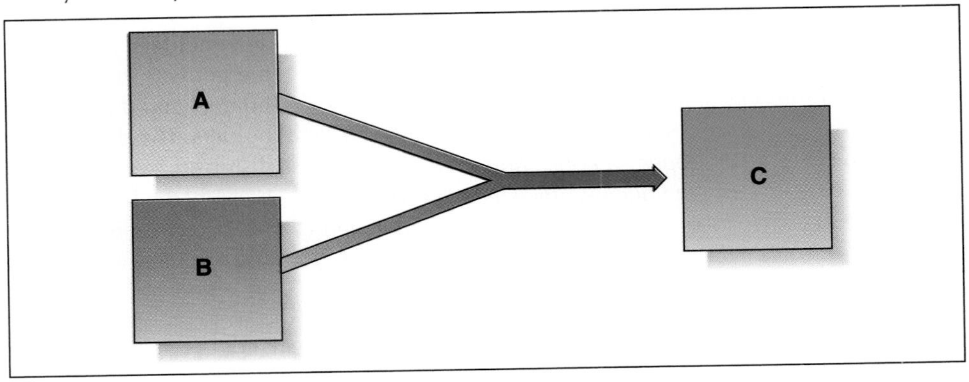

ON THE WEB

You may be able to find your state's statutory requirements for mergers and consolidations procedures at **fatty.law.cornell.edu/topics/state_statutes.html**.

1. The board of directors of each corporation involved must approve a merger or consolidation plan.
2. The shareholders of each corporation must approve the plan, by vote, at a shareholders' meeting. Most state statutes require the approval of two-thirds of the outstanding shares of voting stock, although some states require only a simple majority, and others require a four-fifths vote. Frequently, statutes require that each class of stock approve the merger; thus, the holders of nonvoting stock must also approve. A corporation's bylaws can provide for a stricter requirement.
3. Once approved by all of the directors and shareholders, the plan (articles of merger or consolidation) is filed, usually with the secretary of state.
4. When state formalities are satisfied, the state issues a certificate of merger to the surviving corporation or a certificate of consolidation to the newly consolidated corporation.

• SHORT-FORM MERGER
A merger between a subsidiary corporation and a parent corporation that owns at least 90 percent of the outstanding shares of each class of stock issued by the subsidiary corporation. Short-form mergers can be accomplished without the approval of the shareholders of either corporation.

RMBCA 11.04 provides for a simplified procedure for the merger of a substantially owned subsidiary corporation into its parent corporation. Under these provisions, a **short-form merger** can be accomplished *without the approval of the shareholders* of either corporation. The short-form merger can be used only when the parent corporation owns at least 90 percent of the outstanding shares of each class of stock of the subsidiary corporation. The simplified procedure requires that a plan for the merger be approved by the board of directors of the parent corporation before it is filed with the state. A copy of the merger plan must be sent to each shareholder of record of the subsidiary corporation. In the following case, a minority group of shareholders objected to a short-form merger undertaken to "cash out" public shareholders (including the plaintiffs in this case).

CASE 29.1 Roland International Corp. v. Najjar

Supreme Court of Delaware, 1979.
407 A.2d 1032.

HISTORICAL AND SOCIAL SETTING *Corporate property belongs to all shareholders, and those in control of a corporation are accountable to all owners of the corporate property. These concepts underlie the rule that majority shareholders—who have the power to control corporate property—owe a fiduciary duty to minority shareholders. This duty is violated when those who control a corporation's voting machinery use that power to exclude minority shareholders from continued participation in the corporate life for no reason other than to eliminate them. In a case decided in 1977, the Supreme Court of Delaware held that "when a freeze-out of minority stockholders on a cash-out basis is alleged to be [a merger's] sole purpose," and it is alleged that "the purpose is improper," a court must consider the allegation "because of the fiduciary obligation owed to the minority."[a] The case involved a regular merger. Undecided at that time was whether the same rule applied to a short-form merger.*

a. *Singer v. Magnavox Co.,* 380 A.2d 969 (Del.Sup. 1977).

BACKGROUND AND FACTS Roland International Corporation was 97.6 percent owned by Hyatt Corporation and others. This controlling group of shareholders created Landro Corporation for the purpose of merging it with Roland. All of the statutory requirements for a short-form merger were met, and the minority (public) shareholders were offered $5.25 per share for each share of Roland stock that they owned. If this price was not acceptable, the minority group could have their shares evaluated under the Delaware appraisal statute. Najjar brought a class-action suit in a Delaware state court on behalf of the minority shareholders, seeking damages. Najjar claimed that the merger was simply an effort to eliminate the public shareholders and that it had been grossly unfair to those shareholders. The defendants (the majority group) moved for dismissal, contending that a proper purpose is conclusively presumed when the conditions of the short-form merger statutes are met; thus the plaintiffs had no cause of action. The trial court denied the motion, and the defendants appealed.

CASE 29.1—Continued

IN THE WORDS OF THE COURT . . .
DUFFY, Justice:

* * * *

* * * [D]efendants say that * * * a parent corporation must show a bona fide purpose for effecting a long-form merger with a subsidiary, but that [the short-form merger statute] conclusively presumes a proper purpose for a short-form merger. * * *

That argument misses the point * * * . As we have attempted to make plain, the [law of fiduciary] duty arises from long-standing principles of equity and is superimposed on many sections of the Corporation Law, including, we think, [the short-form merger statute]. * * *

* * * *

* * * [T]he purpose of [the short-form merger statute] is to provide the parent with a means of eliminating minority shareholders in the subsidiary but * * * a merger [may not be] accomplished solely to freeze-out the minority without a valid business purpose. * * *

* * * *

* * * [T]o this extent, the complaint does state a cause of action for breach of fiduciary duty.

DECISION AND REMEDY The Supreme Court of Delaware affirmed the trial court's denial of the defendants' motion to dismiss.

FOR CRITICAL ANALYSIS—Economic Consideration *Why do state laws allow short-form mergers to be undertaken without shareholder approval?*

Shareholder Approval

¡REMEMBER! State statutes, articles of incorporation, and corporate bylaws can require the approval of more than a majority of shares for some extraordinary matters.

Shareholders invest in a corporate enterprise with the expectation that the board of directors will manage the enterprise and will approve ordinary business matters. Actions taken on extraordinary matters must be authorized by the board of directors and the shareholders. Often, modern statutes require that the shareholders approve certain types of extraordinary matters—such as the sale, lease, or exchange of all or substantially all corporate assets outside of the corporation's regular course of business. Other examples of matters requiring shareholder approval include amendments to the articles of incorporation, transactions concerning merger or consolidation, and dissolution.

Hence, when any extraordinary matter arises, the corporation must proceed as authorized by law to obtain the approval of the shareholders and the board of directors. Sometimes, a transaction can be characterized in such a way as not to require shareholder approval, but in that event, a court will use its equity powers to require such approval. To determine the nature of the transaction, the courts will look not only to the details of the transaction but also to its consequences.

ETHICAL ISSUE 29.1 ***Why should shareholders be required to approve certain types of corporate actions?*** The rule requiring shareholder approval for certain types of corporate actions protects the shareholders' interests in the corporate enterprise. Clearly, the shareholder-owners have a stake in the corporation's survival and profitability. Sometimes, corporate directors and officers may take certain actions—such as selling various corporate assets—over a period of time so that the shareholders do not realize how significantly the total number of assets is dwindling. In such a situation, however, a court normally will use its equity powers to require the approval of the shareholders. For example, in one case, a corporation was formed for the purpose of engaging in the restaurant business. One of the three shareholders, who was the corporate president, sold off the assets of the company until only one restaurant remained. When the president entered into a contract to sell this remaining asset, the other two shareholders sought to have a court issue an injunction prohibiting the sale. The court did so, in accordance with state law, which prohibited the sale of all or substantially all of a corporation's assets without shareholder approval. The court stated that the purpose of the law was "to protect the shareholders from . . . the destruction of the means to accomplish the purpose or objects for which the corporation was incorporated and actually performs."[2]

APPRAISAL RIGHTS

What if a shareholder disapproves of a merger or a consolidation but is outvoted by the other shareholders? The law recognizes that a dissenting shareholder should not be forced to become an unwilling shareholder in a corporation that is new or different from the one in which the shareholder originally invested. The shareholder has the right to dissent and may be entitled to be paid the fair value for the number of shares held on the date of the merger or consolidation. This right is referred to as the shareholder's **appraisal right.**

APPRAISAL RIGHT
The right of a dissenting shareholder, if he or she objects to an extraordinary transaction of the corporation (such as a merger or a consolidation), to have his or her shares appraised and to be paid the fair value of his or her shares by the corporation.

Appraisal rights are available only when a state statute specifically provides for them. Appraisal rights normally extend to regular mergers, consolidations, short-form mergers, and sales of substantially all of the corporate assets not in the ordinary course of business.

Shareholders may lose their appraisal rights if they do not follow precisely the elaborate statutory procedures. Whenever they lose the right to an appraisal, dissenting shareholders must go along with the transaction despite their objections. One of the usual basic requirements is a written notice of dissent filed by dissenting shareholders prior to the vote of the shareholders on the proposed transaction. This notice of dissent is also basically a notice to all shareholders of the costs that dissenting shareholders may impose should the merger or consolidation be approved. In addition, after approval, the dissenting shareholders must make a written demand for payment and for the fair value of their shares.

"The greatest of all gifts is the power to estimate things at their true worth."
FRANÇOIS LA ROCHEFOUCAULD, 1613–1680
(French writer and moralist)

Once a dissenting shareholder elects appraisal rights under a statute, in some jurisdictions, the shareholder loses his or her shareholder status. Without that status, a shareholder cannot vote, receive dividends, or sue to enjoin whatever action prompted his or her dissent. In some of those jurisdictions, statutes provide, or courts have held, that shareholder status may be reinstated during the appraisal process (for example, if the shareholder decides to withdraw from the process and the corporation approves). In other jurisdictions, shareholder status may not be reinstated until the appraisal is concluded. Even if an individual loses his or her shareholder status, courts may allow the individual to sue on the ground of fraud or other illegal conduct associated with the merger.

Valuation of shares is often a point of contention between the dissenting shareholder and the corporation. RMBCA 13.01 provides that the "fair value of shares" normally is the value on the day prior to the date on which the vote was taken. The corporation must make a written offer to purchase a dissenting shareholder's stock, accompanying the offer with a current balance sheet and income statement for the corporation. If the shareholder and the corporation do not agree on the fair value, a court will determine it. How the fair value of shares should be determined was at issue in the following case.

2. *Schwadel v. Uchitel*, 455 So.2d 401 (Fla.App. 1984).

CASE 29.2 Chokel v. First National Supermarkets, Inc.

Supreme Judicial Court of Massachusetts,
Suffolk, 1996.
421 Mass. 631,
660 N.E.2d 644.

HISTORICAL AND SOCIAL SETTING *Over the past fifty years, the number of small grocery stores has declined steadily. At the same time, the number of "supersized" supermarkets has increased to more than 30,000. Although these supermarkets make up less than 20 percent of the total number of stores, their share of the market is more than 75 percent. The top ten supermarket chains make almost half of all grocery sales.*

BACKGROUND AND FACTS The management of First National Supermarkets, Inc., wanted to buy the company and offered the shareholders $24.45 per share. Most of the shareholders voted to accept the offer, but Jeffrey Chokel voted against it. Chokel later filed a suit in a Massachusetts state court to obtain an appraisal of his shares. The judge appraised the value at $29.78 per share, based in part on a price-earnings ratio of 20.[a] First National appealed to the Supreme Judicial Court of Massachusetts, the state's highest court, arguing in part that the price-earnings ratio was too high.

a. A price-earnings ratio is calculated by dividing a stock's market price (per share) by its income (per share).

IN THE WORDS OF THE COURT . . .
ABRAMS, Justice.

* * * *

* * * The price-earnings ratio reflects the prospective financial condition of the corporation and the risk factor inherent in the corporation and the industry. It is usually selected by looking to the price-earnings ratios of comparable corporations.

* * * *

* * * [On the date for determining the price of Chokel's shares, the] average for the supermarket industry was 12.75. The trial judge, rather than relying on the average * * * , chose to compare First National with the four comparable companies with the highest percentage growth in five-year projected earnings. With a projected 249% growth in five-year projected earnings, First National would have ranked second. The comparable companies with available price-earnings ratios all had * * * price-earnings ratios near twenty. * * *

Given First National's projections and the price-earnings ratios of the most directly comparable companies, we believe the trial judge's choice of twenty as the price-earnings ratio to be "within the range of reason."

DECISION AND REMEDY The Supreme Judicial Court of Massachusetts affirmed the decision of the lower court.

FOR CRITICAL ANALYSIS—Ethical Consideration *Appraisal rights are the exclusive remedy for shareholders who are dissatisfied with the valuation of the corporation's shares. Is this fair? Why or why not?*

Purchase of Assets

When a corporation acquires all or substantially all of the assets of another corporation by direct purchase, the purchasing, or *acquiring,* corporation simply extends its ownership and control over more physical assets. Because no change in the legal entity occurs, the acquiring corporation is not required to obtain shareholder approval for the purchase.[3]

3. If the acquiring corporation plans to pay for the assets with its own corporate stock and not enough authorized unissued shares are available, the shareholders must vote to approve issuance of additional shares by amendment of the corporate articles. Additionally, acquiring corporations whose stock is traded in a national stock exchange can be required to obtain their own shareholders' approval if they plan to issue a significant number of shares, such as a number equal to 20 percent or more of the outstanding shares.

Although the acquiring corporation may not be required to obtain shareholder approval for such an acquisition, the U.S. Department of Justice and the Federal Trade Commission have issued guidelines that significantly constrain and often prohibit mergers that could result from a purchase of assets, including takeover bids. These guidelines are discussed in Chapter 35, in the context of federal antitrust laws.

Business Law in Action • Purchases of Assets and Product Liability

When a corporation sells all of its assets, the general rule is that the acquiring corporation does not acquire the selling corporation's liabilities as well. As just discussed, four exceptions to this rule are sometimes made, depending on the circumstances. In a few states, courts have adopted yet another exception, known as the "product-line exception." If the corporate successor (the acquiring corporation) continues to manufacture and sell the same product as the predecessor (the selling corporation), the successor may be held liable for injuries caused by products marketed by the predecessor.

To understand the rationale underlying the product-line exception, consider a case that came before the Supreme Court of New Mexico. The case was brought by Altagracia Garcia, whose husband was killed in an accident at the fiberboard manufacturing plant where he worked. The husband was cleaning up wood chips near a conveyor belt and inadvertently came into contact with the belt while it was stopped for a brief period. On restarting, the conveyor pulled him underneath a roller, crushing him to death. Mrs. Garcia claimed, among other things, that the equipment was defective and unreasonably dangerous because it lacked a shield or guard that would have prevented her husband from being pulled underneath the roller.

Garcia could not bring a product liability suit against the manufacturer of the equipment, Washington Iron Works (WIW), because that company had gone out of business. Prior to the accident, WIW had sold all of its assets—including the fiberboard manufacturing equipment, its customer lists, and general goodwill—to Coe Manufacturing Company. Garcia thus sued Coe Manufacturing, which continued to produce and sell the same equipment. The trial court applied the general rule that a corporation that purchases the assets of another company is not responsible for the liabilities of the selling company. Finding that none of the four exceptions to the rule applied to the circumstances in Garcia's case, the court granted summary judgment for Coe Manufacturing.

At issue before the New Mexico Supreme Court was whether it should adopt the product-line exception to the general rule of successor corporation liability. The court decided to do so, reasoning that if plaintiffs, such as Garcia, could not sue successor corporations in these types of circumstances, they would be left virtually without a remedy for product-related injuries. The court also reasoned that adopting the product-line exception was consistent with the policy underlying strict liability—that manufacturers are in a better position than consumers to bear the costs of injuries. The court stated that the "manufacturer's successor, carrying over the experience and expertise of the manufacturer, is likewise in a better position than the consumer to gauge the risks and the costs of meeting them. The successor knows the product, is as able to calculate the risk of defects as the predecessor, is in a position to insure [against such costs] and reflect such [costs] in sale negotiations, and is the only entity capable of improving the quality of the product."[a]

To date, only a few other states, including California, New York, and New Jersey, have adopted the product-line exception. According to the compilers of the *Restatement (Third) of Torts: Products Liability,* a majority of courts have concluded that adopting this exception would be unfair and wasteful, while not benefiting very many tort plaintiffs. For one thing, a more expansive liability rule would depress the price of corporate assets. Companies would end up buying and selling assets on a piecemeal basis, so that the buyers would not be subject to liability for the sellers' defective products.[b]

For Critical Analysis

Why would a more expansive liability rule depress (lower) the price of corporate assets?

a. *Garcia v. Coe Manufacturing Co.,* 123 N.M. 34, 933 P.2d 243 (1997).

b. *Restatement (Third) of Torts: Products Liability,* Section 12, Comment b.

Note that the corporation that is selling all its assets is substantially changing its business position and perhaps its ability to carry out its corporate purposes. For that reason, the corporation whose assets are acquired must obtain the approval of both the board of directors and the shareholders. In most states and under RMBCA 13.02, a dissenting shareholder of the selling corporation can demand appraisal rights.

¡RECALL!
In a merger or consolidation, the surviving corporation inherits the disappearing corporation's rights *and* obligations.

Generally, a corporation that purchases the assets of another corporation is not responsible for the liabilities of the selling corporation. Exceptions to this rule are made in the following circumstances:

1. When the purchasing corporation impliedly or expressly assumes the seller's liabilities.
2. When the sale amounts to what in fact is a merger or consolidation.
3. When the purchaser continues the seller's business and retains the same personnel (same shareholders, directors, and officers).
4. When the sale is fraudulently executed to escape liability.

In any of these situations, the acquiring corporation will be held to have assumed both the assets and the liabilities of the selling corporation. (For another exception to the general rule, see this chapter's *Business Law in Action.*)

In the following case, the court was asked to determine whether a transfer of assets between two corporations was for the fraudulent purpose of escaping liability.

CASE 29.3 Eagle Pacific Insurance Co. v. Christensen Motor Yacht Corp.

Supreme Court of Washington, 1998.
135 Wash.2d 894,
959 P.2d 1052.

HISTORICAL AND SOCIAL SETTING *When one corporation sells all of its assets to another, common ownership of the two corporations casts a suspicion on the transaction that it is fraudulent, and liability may be imposed for any obligations that might otherwise be avoided. As early as 1933, the Washington Supreme Court said, "Undoubtedly, it is the general rule that mere common ownership of the capital stock or interlocking directorates, or like evidences of close association, will not justify the courts in disregarding corporate identities, but where * * * the identities are so confused and intermingled as to result in probable fraud upon third persons dealing with the corporations or either of them, whether fraud be actually intended or not, then the * * * rule will apply."*[a]

BACKGROUND AND FACTS Christensen Motor Yacht Corporation (CMYC) was organized to build yachts. Eagle Pacific Insurance Company issued workers' compensation policies to CMYC but canceled the policies when CMYC failed to pay the premiums. CMYC had several contracts with buyers, but the yachts had not been completed. CMYC thus lacked the ability to pay its debts. David Christensen, the chief executive officer and sole shareholder of CMYC, created a new corporation, Christensen Shipyards, Limited (CSL), to complete the boats. CMYC transferred its employees, facilities, and contracts to CSL. Meanwhile, claims had been filed against the Eagle policies, and Eagle filed a suit in a Washington state court against CMYC to collect the unpaid premiums. The court awarded Eagle $268,443. Because CMYC was insolvent, Eagle sought to recover the debt from others, including CSL as a successor corporation to CMYC. Christensen testified that he had effected the transfer between CMYC and CSL to avoid creditors and "save the business." The court ruled that CSL was liable for CMYC's debt to Eagle as a successor corporation. A state intermediate appellate court upheld the ruling. CSL appealed to the Washington Supreme Court.

a. *Associated Oil Co. v. Seiberling Rubber Co.*, 172 Wash. 204, 19 P.2d 940 (1933).

IN THE WORDS OF THE COURT . . .
DOLLIVER, Justice.

* * * *

* * * CMYC's principal business purpose was the construction of yachts. In the course of the construction of the three yachts, CMYC incurred debts which it could

(Continued)

CASE 29.3—Continued

not pay. With the transfer of the three yacht contracts to CSL, and CMYC's surrender of its employees and facilities to CSL, CMYC was stripped of its main potential source for future revenues. Christensen admits the yacht contracts were transferred to CSL to allow the continuation of construction on the yachts unhampered by creditors' efforts to collect unpaid bills.

Christensen's admitted reason for the transfer of assets from CMYC to CSL fits the definition of a fraudulent transfer. * * *

* * * *

* * * Transferring assets to another corporation to hinder or delay creditors is by definition a fraudulent transfer. * * * In the course of conducting business and building yachts, CMYC incurred debts which Christensen sought to avoid by transferring the business to CSL. Because the assets were transferred to CSL to avoid the reach of the creditors, the transaction is fraudulent and successor liability attaches to CSL. The fact that the transaction was designed to "save the business" does not defeat imposition of successor liability.

DECISION AND REMEDY The Washington Supreme Court affirmed the lower court's judgment. The state supreme court held that the transfer of assets from CMYC to CSL fit the definition of a fraudulent transfer.

FOR CRITICAL ANALYSIS—Ethical Consideration *If, after completing the boats, Christensen had paid all of the creditors of both corporations, would the transfer of assets from CMYC to CSL have been more acceptable?*

Purchase of Stock

An alternative to the purchase of another corporation's assets is the purchase of a substantial number of the voting shares of its stock. This enables the acquiring corporation to control the acquired corporation. The acquiring corporation deals directly with the target company's shareholders in seeking to purchase the shares they hold. It does this by making a *tender offer* to all of the shareholders of the corporation to be acquired, or the **target corporation.** The tender offer is publicly advertised and addressed to all shareholders of the target company. The price of the stock in the tender offer is generally higher than the market price of the target stock prior to the announcement of the tender offer. The higher price induces shareholders to tender their shares to the acquiring firm.

• **TARGET CORPORATION**
The corporation to be acquired in a corporate takeover; a corporation to whose shareholders a tender offer is submitted.

The tender offer can be conditioned on the receipt of a specified number of outstanding shares by a specified date. The offering corporation can make an *exchange tender offer* in which it offers target stockholders its own securities in exchange for their target stock. In a *cash tender offer,* the offering corporation offers the target stockholders cash in exchange for their target stock.

Federal securities laws strictly control the terms, duration, and circumstances under which most tender offers are made. In addition, a majority of states have passed takeover statutes that impose additional regulations on tender offers.

A firm may respond to a tender offer in numerous ways. Sometimes, a target firm's board of directors will see a tender offer as favorable and will recommend to the shareholders that they accept it. To resist a takeover, a target company may make a *self-tender,* which is an offer to acquire stock from its own shareholders and thereby retain corporate control. Alternatively, a target corporation might resort to one of several other tactics to resist a takeover (see Exhibit 29–3). One commonly used tactic is known as the "poison pill"—a target company gives its shareholders rights to purchase additional shares at low prices when there is a takeover attempt. The use of poison pills prevents takeovers by making them prohibitively expensive.

ON THE WEB
For an article on new takeover tactics, as well as other information on mergers and acquisitions, go to the Web site of Law Journal EXTRA! at www.ljx.com/practice/mergers/index.html.

EXHIBIT 29–3 • The Terminology of Takeover Defenses

TERM	DEFINITION
Crown Jewel	When threatened with a takeover, management makes the company less attractive to the raider by selling to a third party the company's most valuable asset (hence the term *crown jewel*).
Golden Parachute	When a takeover is successful, top management is usually changed. With this in mind, a company may establish special termination or retirement benefits that must be paid to top management if they are "retired." In other words, a departing high-level manager's parachute will be "golden" when he or she is forced to "bail out" of the company.
Greenmail	To regain control, a target company may pay a higher-than-market price to repurchase the stock that the acquiring corporation bought. When a takeover is attempted through a gradual accumulation of target stock rather than a tender offer, the intent may be to get the target company to buy back the accumulated shares at a premium price—a concept similar to blackmail.
Lobster Trap	Lobster traps are designed to catch large lobsters but to allow small lobsters to escape. In the "lobster trap" defense, holders of convertible securities (corporate bonds or stock that is convertible into common shares) are prohibited from converting the securities into common shares if the holders already own, or would own after conversion, 10 percent or more of the voting shares of stock.
Pac-Man	Named after the Atari video game, this is an aggressive defense by which the target corporation attempts its own takeover of the acquiring corporation.
Poison Pill	The target corporation gives its stockholders the right to purchase additional shares at low prices when there is a takeover attempt. This makes the takeover undesirably or even prohibitively expensive for the acquiring corporation.
Scorched Earth	The target corporation sells off assets or divisions or takes out loans that it agrees to repay in the event of a takeover, thus making itself less financially attractive to the acquiring corporation.
Shark Repellent	To make a takeover more difficult, a target company may change its articles of incorporation or bylaws. For example, the bylaws may be amended to require that a large number of shareholders approve the firm's combination. This tactic casts the acquiring corporation in the role of a shark that must be repelled.
White Knight	The target corporation solicits a merger with a third party, which then makes a better (often simply a higher) tender offer to the target's shareholders. The third party that "rescues" the target is the "white knight."

ETHICAL ISSUE 29.2 ***Should shareholders be allowed to eliminate poison pills by amending the corporate bylaws?*** Once a target company's directors put a "poison-pill" rights plan in place, the plan remains in effect until the directors nullify it—which may never happen. Clearly, poison pills benefit corporate directors and officers, who are able to retain their positions and their control over the company. Yet what if the shareholders would like to sell out to an acquiring corporation that offers above-market prices for their shares? In effect, their hands are tied by the poison pill. Some have suggested that shareholders should be allowed to amend the corporate bylaws to give shareholders the right to vote on whether a poison pill should be retained when a takeover bid is made. After all, claim those who support such "shareholder-rights bylaws," state laws specifically give shareholders the power to adopt, amend, and repeal corporate bylaws. Others, however, point out that giving shareholders such rights would essentially involve shareholders in corporate management—an area specifically reserved for directors under state laws. It is not yet known how the courts will decide this issue. The Supreme Court of Delaware, whose rulings on corporate law are followed in many states, has generally given great deference to directors' decisions in response to takeover proposals. In any event, as one legal scholar noted, the validity of such bylaws "will probably be the next major battleground in takeover struggles."[4]

Termination

• **DISSOLUTION**
The formal disbanding of a partnership or a corporation. Dissolution of a corporation can take place by (1) an act of the state legislature, (2) agreement of the shareholders and the board of directors, (3) the expiration of a time period stated in the certificate of incorporation, or (4) court order.

• **LIQUIDATION**
In regard to corporations, the process by which corporate assets are converted into cash and distributed among creditors and shareholders according to specific rules of preference.

The termination of a corporation's existence has two phases. **Dissolution** is the legal death of the artificial "person" of the corporation. **Liquidation** is the process by which corporate assets are converted into cash and distributed among creditors and shareholders according to specific rules of preference (see Chapter 27).

DISSOLUTION

Dissolution of a corporation can be brought about in any of the following ways:

1. An act of a legislature in the state of incorporation.
2. Expiration of the time provided in the certificate of incorporation.
3. Voluntary approval of the shareholders and the board of directors.
4. Unanimous action by all shareholders.[5]
5. A court decree brought about by the attorney general of the state of incorporation for any of the following reasons: (a) the failure to comply with administrative requirements (for example, failure to pay annual franchise taxes, to submit an annual report, or to have a designated registered agent), (b) the procurement of a corporation charter through fraud or misrepresentation on the state, (c) the abuse of corporate powers (*ultra vires* acts), (d) the violation of the state criminal code after the demand to discontinue has been made by the secretary of state, (e) the fail-

4. Marc B. Tucker, "Takeover Bylaws: A Wrench in the Proxy Works," *The National Law Journal*, April 13, 1998, p. A20.
5. This is permitted under Delaware law—see Delaware Code Section 275(c)—but not under the RMBCA.

A STORE ADVERTISES A LIQUIDATION SALE. WHEN A CORPORATE LIQUIDATION IS VOLUNTARY, WHO ACTS AS THE TRUSTEE OF THE CORPORATE ASSETS? WHO ACTS AS THE TRUSTEE IF THE LIQUIDATION IS INVOLUNTARY?

ure to commence business operations, or (f) the abandonment of operations before starting up [RMBCA 14.20].

As discussed in Chapter 28, sometimes a shareholder or a group of shareholders petitions a court for corporate dissolution. For example, the board of directors may be deadlocked. Courts hesitate to order involuntary dissolution in such circumstances unless there is specific statutory authorization to do so. If the deadlock cannot be resolved by the shareholders and if it will irreparably injure the corporation, however, the court will proceed with an involuntary dissolution. Courts can also dissolve a corporation in other circumstances, such as when the controlling shareholders or directors are committing fraudulent or oppressive acts or when management is misapplying or wasting corporate assets [RMBCA 14.30].

"Lots of folks confuse bad management with destiny."

KIN (F. MCKINNEY) HUBBARD, 1868–1930 (American humorist and journalist)

LIQUIDATION

When dissolution takes place by voluntary action, the members of the board of directors act as trustees of the corporate assets. As trustees, they are responsible for winding up the affairs of the corporation for the benefit of corporate creditors and shareholders. This makes the board members personally liable for any breach of their fiduciary trustee duties.

Liquidation can be accomplished without court supervision unless the members of the board do not wish to act as trustees of the corporate assets, or unless shareholders or creditors can show cause to the court why the board should not be permitted to assume the trustee function. In either situation, the court will appoint a receiver to wind up the corporate affairs and liquidate corporate assets. A receiver is always appointed by the court if the dissolution is involuntary.

¡CONTRAST!

Except during liquidation, directors do not act as trustees of the corporate assets. Although they are in positions of control over the corporation, they do not hold title to its property.

Key Terms

appraisal right 770
chose in action 766
consolidation 767
dissolution 776
liquidation 776
merger 766
short-form merger 768
target corporation 774

Chapter Summary • Corporate Merger, Consolidation, and Termination

Merger and Consolidation (See pages 766–771.)	1. *Merger*—The legal combination of two or more corporations, the result of which is that the surviving corporation acquires all the assets and obligations of the other corporation, which then ceases to exist. 2. *Consolidation*—The legal combination of two or more corporations, the result of which is that each corporation ceases to exist and a new one emerges. The new corporation assumes all the assets and obligations of the former corporations. 3. *Procedure*—Determined by state statutes. Basic requirements are the following: a. The board of directors of each corporation involved must approve the merger or consolidation plan. b. The shareholders of each corporation must approve the merger or consolidation plan at a shareholders' meeting.

Chapter Summary • Corporate Merger, Consolidation, and Termination, Continued

Merger and Consolidation—continued	c. Articles of merger or consolidation (the plan) must be filed, usually with the secretary of state. d. The state issues a certificate of merger (or consolidation) to the surviving (or newly consolidated) corporation. 4. *Short-form merger (parent-subsidiary merger)*—Possible when the parent corporation owns at least 90 percent of the outstanding shares of each class of stock of the subsidiary corporation. a. Shareholder approval is not required. b. The merger must be approved only by the board of directors of the parent corporation. c. A copy of the merger plan must be sent to each shareholder of record. d. The merger plan must be filed with the state. 5. *Appraisal rights*—Rights of dissenting shareholders (given by state statute) to receive the *fair value* for their shares when a merger or consolidation takes place. If the shareholder and the corporation do not agree on the fair value, a court will determine it.
Purchase of Assets (See pages 771–774.)	A purchase of assets occurs when one corporation acquires all or substantially all of the assets of another corporation. 1. *Acquiring corporation*—The acquiring (purchasing) corporation is not required to obtain shareholder approval; the corporation is merely increasing its assets, and no fundamental business change occurs. 2. *Acquired corporation*—The acquired (purchased) corporation is required to obtain the approval of both its directors and its shareholders for the sale of its assets, because this creates a substantial change in the corporation's business position.
Purchase of Stock (See pages 774–776.)	A purchase of stock occurs when one corporation acquires a substantial number of the voting shares of the stock of another (target) corporation. 1. *Tender offer*—A public offer to all shareholders of the target corporation to purchase its stock at a price generally higher than the market price of the target stock prior to the announcement of the tender offer. Federal and state securities laws strictly control the terms, duration, and circumstances under which most tender offers are made. 2. *Target responses*—Ways in which target corporations respond to takeover bids. These include self-tender (the target firm's offer to acquire its own shareholders' stock), the Pac-Man defense (the target firm's takeover of the acquiring corporation), and numerous other strategies (see Exhibit 29–3).
Termination (See pages 776–777.)	The termination of a corporation involves the following two phases: 1. *Dissolution*—The legal death of the artificial "person" of the corporation. Dissolution can be brought about in any of the following ways: a. An act of a legislature in the state of incorporation. b. Expiration of the time provided in the corporate charter. c. Voluntary approval of the shareholders and the board of directors. d. Unanimous action by all shareholders. e. Court decree. 2. *Liquidation*—The process by which corporate assets are converted into cash and distributed to creditors and shareholders according to specified rules of preference. May be supervised by members of the board of directors (when dissolution is voluntary) or by a receiver appointed by the court to wind up corporate affairs.

For Review

❶ What is the difference between a corporate merger and a corporate consolidation?
❷ What are the four steps of the merger or consolidation procedure?
❸ Under what circumstances is a corporation that purchases the assets of another corporation responsible for the liabilities of the selling corporation?
❹ A target corporation can use a number of defenses to resist a takeover. Name five such defenses.
❺ What are the two ways in which a corporation can be voluntarily dissolved? Under what circumstances might a corporation be involuntarily dissolved by state action?

Questions and Case Problems

29–1. Consolidations. Determine which of the following situations describes a consolidation:

(a) Arkon Corp. purchases all of the assets of Botrek Co.
(b) Arkon Corp. and Botrek Co. combine their firms, with Arkon Corp. as the surviving corporation.
(c) Arkon Corp. and Botrek Co. agree to combine their assets, dissolve their old corporations, and form a new corporation under a new name.
(d) Arkon Corp. agrees to sell all its accounts receivable to Botrek Co.

29–2. Corporate Combinations. Jolson is chairman of the board of directors of Artel, Inc., and Douglas is chairman of the board of directors of Fox Express, Inc. Artel is a manufacturing corporation, and Fox Express is a transportation corporation. Jolson and Douglas meet to consider the possibility of combining their corporations and activities into a single corporate entity. They consider two alternative courses of action: Artel could acquire all of the stock and assets of Fox Express, or the corporations could combine to form a new corporation, called A&F Enterprises, Inc. Both chairmen are concerned about the necessity of a formal transfer of property, liability for existing debts, and the problem of amending the articles of incorporation. Discuss what the two proposed combinations are called and the legal effect each has on the transfer of property, the liabilities of the combined corporations, and the need to amend the articles of incorporation.

29–3. Mergers. Tally Ho Co. was merged into Perfecto Corp., with Perfecto being the surviving corporation in the merger. Hanjo, a creditor of Tally Ho, brought suit against Perfecto Corp. for payment of the debt. The directors of Perfecto refused to pay, stating that Tally Ho no longer existed and that Perfecto had never agreed to assume any of Tally Ho's liabilities. Discuss fully whether Hanjo will be able to recover from Perfecto.

28–4. Purchase of Assets. Fuju Enterprises, Inc., purchased all the assets of Grosmont Corp. The directors of both corporations approved the sale, and 80 percent of Grosmont's shareholders approved. The shareholders of Fuju Enterprises, however, were never consulted. Some of these shareholders claimed that the purchase was invalid. Are they correct?

29–5. Corporate Dissolution. Two brothers, Albert and Raymond Martin, each owned 50 percent of the stock in Martin's News Service, Inc. Albert and Raymond had difficulty working together and communicated only through their accountant. For ten years, there were no corporate meetings, elections to the board of directors, or other corporate formalities. During that time, Raymond operated the business much as a sole proprietorship, failing to consult Albert on any matter and making all of the decisions himself. The corporation, however, was a viable concern that had grown successfully through the years. Albert sued to have the corporation dissolved. Should he succeed? Discuss. [*Martin v. Martin's News Service, Inc.*, 9 Conn.App. 304, 518 A.2d 951 (1986)]

29–6. Mergers and Consolidations. Edward Antar and William Markowitz were the sole stockholders and directors of E.B.M., Inc., a corporation formed for the purpose of buying and managing real estate. Antar and Markowitz were also the controlling shareholders and directors of Acousti-Phase, Inc., a corporation that manufactured and sold stereo speakers. In 1982, Acousti-Phase was effectively shut down when a fire destroyed the manufacturing and storage facility that it was renting from E.B.M. Shortly after the fire, E.B.M. contracted with a New York firm to assemble the speakers, affix the Acousti-Phase name, and sell the final product, primarily to former customers of Acousti-Phase. At the time of the fire, Acousti-Phase owed $26,470 to Cab-Tek, Inc., a corporation that supplied it with cabinet housings for its stereo speakers. In 1985, Cab-Tek sued E.B.M. to recover the debt owed by Acousti-Phase. Discuss fully whether E.B.M. can be held liable for Acousti-Phase's debt. [*Cab-Tek, Inc. v. E.B.M., Inc.*, 153 Vt. 432, 571 A.2d 671 (1990)]

29–7. Purchase of Assets. MRS Manufacturing, Inc., manufactured tractors, which it sold to Glades Equipment, Inc. Glades Equipment sold one of the tractors to the U.S. Sugar Corp. Later, Glade and Grove Supply, Inc., bought the Glades Equipment dealership under a contract that stated the sale covered only such property "as [Glades Equipment] has on hand at the time of the . . . sale." Daniel Brown, an employee of the U.S. Sugar Corp., was operating an MRS tractor when it rolled over and killed him. His wife, Patricia, filed a product liability suit against, among others, Glade and Grove. What factors will the court consider in determining whether Glade and Grove is liable? [*Brown v. Glade and Grove Supply, Inc.,* 647 So.2d 1033 (Fla.App. 1994)]

29–8. Appraisal Rights. Travelers Corp. announced that it would merge with Primerica Corp. At a special shareholders' meeting, a vote of the Travelers shareholders revealed that 95 percent approved of the merger. Robert Brandt and other shareholders who did not approve of the merger sued Travelers and others, complaining that the defendants had not obtained "the highest possible price for shareholders." Travelers asked the court to dismiss the suit, contending that Brandt and the others had, as a remedy for their complaint, their statutory appraisal rights. On what basis might the court dismiss the suit? Discuss. [*Brandt v. Travelers Corp.,* 44 Conn.Supp. 12, 665 A.2d 616 (1995)]

29–9. Corporate Dissolution. Jerry Yarmouth incorporated J&R Interiors, Inc., and was its president, secretary, and sole shareholder. J&R failed to file annual reports and pay annual fees, however, and was involuntarily dissolved by the state. More than a year later, Yarmouth bought a workbench in J&R's name from Equipto Division of Aurora Equipment Co. When the price was not paid, Equipto filed a suit in a Washington state court against Yarmouth, claiming that he was personally liable for payment. Yarmouth argued that he was not personally liable because he had acted as an agent for J&R. Does a corporation continue to exist after it is dissolved? If so, can it continue to conduct business? In whose favor should the court rule in this case, and why? [*Equipto Division Aurora Equipment Co. v. Yarmouth,* 83 Wash.App. 817, 924 P.2d 405 (1996)]

29–10. Purchase of Assets. Ernie Gross and his brother started Sealomatic Electronics Corp. in the 1940s, later changing the name to Solidyne Corp. Sealomatic became a division of Solidyne, which continued to make heat-sealing machines under the brand name Sealomatic. Gross bought other heat-sealing equipment makers, including Thermex and Thermatron, which became other divisions of Solidyne. After the brothers died in 1981, Solidyne was sold and its heat-sealing equipment divisions were consolidated into a single division, Thermex-Thermatron. The new division, with its assets and liabilities, was resold to TTI Acquisitions, which merged to become Thermex-Thermatron, Inc. Thermex-Thermatron continued to use Solidyne customer lists. The names of former Solidyne divisions were on the window of Thermex-Thermatron's public sales office. Listings in phone directories maintained and paid for by Thermex-Thermatron continued to use the names of Solidyne and its former divisions. Meanwhile, Solidyne was completely dissolved. Juanita Rosales, an employee of Perfect Plastics Products, was using a Solidyne Sealomatic machine made in 1969 when it collapsed on her hand. She was seriously injured. She filed a suit in a California state court against Thermex-Thermatron and others. Is Thermex-Thermatron liable for her injury? If so, on what basis? If not, why not? How should the court rule? Explain. [*Rosales v. Thermex-Thermatron, Inc.,* 67 Cal.App.4th 187, 78 Cal.Rptr.2d 861 (1998)]

A QUESTION OF ETHICS AND SOCIAL RESPONSIBILITY

29–11. In a corporate merger, Diamond Shamrock retained its corporate identity, and Natomas Corp. was absorbed into Diamond's corporate hierarchy. Five inside directors (directors who are also officers of the corporation) of Natomas had "golden parachutes," which were incorporated into the merger agreement. The terms of the parachute agreements provided that each of the five individuals would receive a payment equal to three years' compensation in the event that they left their positions at Natomas at any time for any reason other than termination for just cause. Three of the five voluntarily left their positions after three years. Under the terms of their parachute agreements, they collected over $10 million. A suit challenging the golden parachutes was brought by Gaillard, a Natomas shareholder. A trial court granted the defendants' motion for summary judgment; the court sustained the golden parachutes on the ground that the directors were protected by the business judgment rule in effecting the agreement. The appellate court held that the business judgment rule does not apply in a review of the conduct of inside directors and remanded the case for trial. [*Gaillard v. Natomas,* 208 Cal.App.3d 1250, 256 Cal.Rptr. 702 (1989)]

1. Regardless of the legal issues, are golden parachutes ethical in a general sense? Discuss.
2. What practical considerations would lead a corporation to want to grant its top management such seemingly one-sided agreements?
3. In the *Gaillard* case, how would your views be affected by evidence showing that the golden parachutes had been developed and presented to the board by the very individuals who were the beneficiaries of the agreements—that is, by the five inside directors?

FOR CRITICAL ANALYSIS

29–12. A corporation that purchases the assets of another corporation generally is not liable for the obligations and duties of the predecessor corporation. Exceptions to this rule are made in certain circumstances, such as when the purchasing corporation assumes the liabilities, fraud is involved, or the transaction is actually a merger or merely a change of name. Why are these exceptions made?

Online Activities

ONLINE EXERCISE 29–1

Go to the "Internet Activities Book" on the Web site that accompanies this text, the URL for which is http://blt.westbuslaw.com. Select the following activity, and perform the exercise according to the instructions given there:

Activity 28–1: Big Business

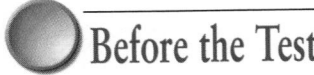

Before the Test

Go to the *Business Law Today* home page at http://blt.westbuslaw.com. Click on TestTutor.® You will find twenty interactive questions relating to this chapter.

CHAPTER 30

Additional Shareholders' Rights & Takeovers

"Business underlies everything in our national life."

Woodrow Wilson, 1856–1924
(Twenty-eighth president of the United States, 1912–1920)

CONTENTS

LEARNING OBJECTIVES

After reading this chapter, you should be able to:

1. Identify the requirements for a person to exercise shareholders' inspection rights.
2. State on what basis a company could exclude a shareholder proposal from proxy materials.
3. Explain when shareholders may exercise their appraisal rights.
4. Summarize several tactics that an acquiring corporation might use in an attempted takeover and defenses that a target corporation might use against an attempted takeover.
5. Outline provisions of federal and state laws that are directed toward disclosing and discouraging takeover attempts.

Woodrow Wilson's assertion in the opening quotation that business underlies everything in our national life points to the importance of corporations, which are the dominant form of business organization in the United States. Large corporations are a product of the Industrial Revolution (1830–1880) and a phenomenon of the last hundred years, but they have gone through more changes in the last two decades than in perhaps any other period in their history. Some of these changes have been brought about by the corporations' owners—the shareholders—according to the methods outlined in previous chapters and discussed in more detail here.

In this chapter, we add to our earlier discussion of shareholders' inspection rights and appraisal rights. We also include an explanation of the right of shareholders to be informed, when they are sent proxy materials, of any proposals to be considered at the shareholders' meetings. Finally, we expand on our previous outline of the framework of takeovers—the deals and the upheavals that have characterized the most recent period of corporate history.

Shareholders' Inspection Rights

ON THE WEB

"The Virtual Chase" Web site is "A Research Site for Legal Professionals." This site is sponsored by Ballard, Spahr, Andrews and Ingersoll, a law firm in Philadelphia. Included is a page with an eight-step guide to Web links for uncovering company information that may be of interest to shareholders and others. This page can be found at www.virtualchase.com/coinfo/index.htm.

Directors and shareholders have a right to inspect corporate books and records in certain circumstances. Directors have a virtually absolute right to examine all corporate books and records. Directors have been denied inspection rights, however, when it was clear that they were acting with an improper purpose.

The right of a shareholder to inspect the corporate books and records is narrower than the right of directors. Some of these rights are discussed in Chapter 28. Under the Revised Model Business Corporation Act (RMBCA), Sections 16.01 and 16.02, shareholders have an unrestricted right to inspect certain corporate records—articles of incorporation, bylaws, board resolutions creating classes of stock, minutes of shareholders' meetings, annual reports, and so on—which must be kept at the corporation's principal office. But shareholders can inspect and copy other corporate records, such as corporate accounting records, only on showing a "proper purpose" and good faith. In addition, the shareholders' list for the annual meeting must be available for shareholders' inspection [RMBCA 7.20].

A shareholder who is denied the right of inspection can seek a court order to compel the inspection. The court in the following case considered whether a person who does not own shares in a corporation could obtain an order to compel an inspection of the corporate books.

CASE 30.1 Shaw v. Agri-Mark, Inc.

Supreme Court of Delaware, 1995.
663 A.2d 464.

HISTORICAL AND SOCIAL SETTING *The salaries of officers and directors of corporations have skyrocketed since 1980. In some instances, employees, shareholders, and others who have an interest in a corporation have protested the high pay. In part, they assert that the funds could be spent in other ways to benefit their corporation. To protest—or support—the level of executive salaries, however, those who are interested must first discover how much the pay is.*

BACKGROUND AND FACTS Agri-Mark, Inc., was incorporated in Delaware. Agri-Mark handles dairy products under exclusive contracts with farmers. The farmers are considered "members" of the corporation, but only its directors are shareholders. Karen Shaw and other members filed a suit in a federal district court against Agri-Mark, seeking to inspect its books and records. They sought in part salary information concerning the five highest-paid executives. When the court ruled in their favor, Agri-Mark appealed to the U.S. Court of Appeals for the Second Circuit. The appellate court asked the Supreme Court of Delaware whether the right of inspection of corporate books and records under Delaware law is exclusively reserved to shareholders.

IN THE WORDS OF THE COURT . . .
WALSH, Justice:

* * * *

* * * While the appellants may assert certain rights arising out of the fiduciary relationship between themselves [as members] * * * and those who manage the

(Continued)

CASE 30.1—Continued

affairs of the corporation, those rights do not extend to or include the attributes of record stockholders. Our corporate law has traditionally limited the rights of stockholders to stockholders of record. * * *

* * * *

In this case, appellants are not stockholders of Agri-Mark, let alone stockholders of record. * * * As the only stockholders of Agri-Mark, the directors exclusively enjoy the rights incident to their share ownership, including the right of inspection * * * .

DECISION AND REMEDY The Supreme Court of Delaware held that a person must be a "stockholder of record"—his or her name must be listed in the corporate stock ledger—to be entitled to inspect the books and records of the corporation.

FOR CRITICAL ANALYSIS—Political Consideration *If the court had not drawn a line at "stockholder of record," how might other shareholder rights have been affected?*

Shareholder Proposals in Proxy Materials

Most shareholders do not personally attend shareholders' meetings. A *proxy* is a means by which a shareholder authorizes another person to represent him or her and vote his or her shares at a meeting [RMBCA 7.22]. Proxies are an indispensable part of corporate governance because under state law, a quorum of the shares eligible to vote must be represented at a meeting to elect directors and transact other corporate business. Without the proxy mechanism, corporations effectively would be unable to elect directors and take other actions.

To vote by proxy on proposals for corporate action, shareholders must be informed. SEC Rule 14a-8 requires that when a company sends proxy materials to its shareholders, the company must also include whatever proposals will be considered at the meeting and provide shareholders with the opportunity to vote on the proposals by marking and returning their proxy cards, or by submitting their votes electronically. A corporation does not have to include a proposal that relates to "ordinary business operations," unless the proposal concerns significant policy considerations.

> **ON THE WEB**
> To review some of the proposed and final rules of the Securities and Exchange Commission (SEC), visit the "Current SEC Rulemaking" page at www.sec.gov/rulemake.htm, which is within the SEC's Web site.

As mentioned in Chapter 28, in 1976, the SEC recognized that employment discrimination is a significant policy consideration.[1] In 1992, however, the SEC stated, in response to a corporation that wanted to exclude a discrimination-related proposal from its proxy materials, that such proposals could be excluded because the line "between policies implicating broad social issues and the conduct of day-to-day business [is] simply too hard to draw" in the area of employment.[2] This statement was included in a "no-action letter," so called because it stated that the SEC would take no action if the corporation left the proposal out.

In 1998, however, the SEC amended SEC Rule 14a-8 to reverse this "no-action" position. Under the new amendments, the SEC will not routinely allow companies to exclude from their proxy materials employment-related proposals raising significant social policy issues.[3]

1. *Adoption of Amendments Relating to Proposals by Security Holders,* Exchange Act Release No. 12999, 41 Fed.Reg. 52,994 (December 3, 1976).
2. *Cracker Barrel Old Country Stores, Inc.,* SEC No-Action Letter, 1992 W.L. 289095 (October 13, 1992). This position was upheld in *New York City Employees' Retirement System v. Securities and Exchange Commission,* 45 F.3d 7 (2d Cir. 1995).
3. See 17 C.F.R. Section 240.14a-8.

Shareholders' Appraisal Rights

ON THE WEB

A variety of legal forms, including general business forms such as Stock Purchase Agreements, can be found at a page within the 'Lectric Law Library Web site. The page can be found at www.lectlaw.com/formb.htm.

As explained in Chapter 29, in certain circumstances, shareholders may have a right to dissent from a corporate transaction and be paid the fair value of their shares [RMBCA 13.02]. This is known as an *appraisal right.* Available only when granted by statute, appraisal rights may exist in such transactions as mergers, consolidations, short-form mergers, sales of substantially all of the corporate assets not in the ordinary course of business, and corporate reorganizations. When there is an exchange of shares in one corporation for shares in another corporation, the right may also exist for a shareholder who owns shares in the corporation whose shares are being acquired, if the shareholder is entitled to vote on the transaction.

The following case involves one aspect of the problem of determining the fair value of shares when the shareholder of a close corporation exercises his or her appraisal rights.

CASE 30.2 Lawson Mardon Wheaton Inc. v. Smith

Superior Court of New Jersey,
Appellate Division, 1998.
315 N.J.Super. 32,
716 A.2d 550.
lawlibrary.rutgers.edu/search.shtml[a]

COMPANY PROFILE *Theodore Wheaton founded Wheaton Glass Company in 1888. Wheaton produces glass and plastic containers, closures, and components, as well as tubing products, molded rubber products, and aluminum seals. The company serves the cosmetic, food, medical, personal care, pharmaceutical, and scientific industries. For more than a century, Wheaton was a privately held, family-controlled business. As shares passed from generation to generation, the number of shareholders increased to 159 and the number of shares to over five million. Wheaton had its best year in 1989, but by 1991, the company was experiencing financial problems, in part because of declining sales in its plastics division and fraud uncovered at one of its subsidiaries.*

a. On this page, in the "search dialog" box, type "lawson w/1 mardon" and click on "search." In the list of results, click on the appropriate link to access the opinion for this case. This Web site is maintained by Rutgers University School of Law—Camden in New Jersey.

BACKGROUND AND FACTS Some Wheaton shareholders wanted to sell their shares, but not at what they felt to be a low price, and asked Wheaton's board of directors to do something to increase it. The board proposed an "initial public offering" (IPO) of a limited number of additional shares, which would help to boost the price of the current shares. To prepare for the IPO, the board approved a plan to restructure the firm. The shareholders voted in favor of the plan. Twenty-six of the shareholders who had asked the board to act to increase the share price took advantage of the restructuring plan to dissent and demand payment of fair value for their shares. An appraiser retained by the company valued the shares between $52.65 and $56.70 per share and then reduced this by 25 percent—a "lack of marketability" discount to reflect that Wheaton was a close corporation. The board offered the dissenters $41.50 per share, but they refused. Wheaton asked a New Jersey state court to determine fair value. Meanwhile, in part because of the dissenters' actions, the board dropped the IPO plan. The court upheld the use of the discount. The dissenters appealed.

IN THE WORDS OF THE COURT . . .
CUFF, J.A.D. [Judge, Appellate Division]

* * * *

In general, the concept of a marketability discount stems from the fact that marketability problems often affect shares of closely-held corporations, and that as a result, a discount should be applied to reflect the illiquidity of such shares. This illiquidity is the result of the fact that there is no large pool of potential buyers for these businesses when they come on the market; consequently, the longer it takes to sell an asset, the lower its ultimate value will be and such businesses must be sold at a substantial discount in order to attract buyers. * * *

(Continued)

CASE 30.2—Continued

* * * *

* * * [M]arketability discounts have been viewed as especially inapplicable to intra-family transfers in closely-held companies, as in this case. In family businesses, the members do not want outsiders to have ownership interests. Thus, the lack of marketability can actually enhance the value of the stock. * * *

* * * *

* * * [A] marketability discount should be applied only in extraordinary circumstances. * * * [A] court should apply this exception only when it finds that the dissenting shareholder has held out in order to exploit the transaction giving rise to appraisal so as to divert value to itself that could not be made available proportionately to other shareholders. * * *

* * * *

* * * [Here] defendants opportunistically exploited a minor corporate structural change to further their quest for liquidity without regard to the impact of their dissent on the company * * * .

DECISION AND REMEDY The state intermediate appellate court affirmed the judgment of the lower court. When a close corporation is being asked to buy its own shares, a marketability discount applies in extraordinary circumstances, such as in this case.

FOR CRITICAL ANALYSIS—Ethical Consideration
Why is it left to a court, rather than a shareholder or a company, to determine the value of stock under statutory appraisal rights?

Business Law in Action • Timing Isn't Everything—In a Takeover, It's the Only Thing

Minority shareholders often find themselves outnumbered, outvoted, and cashed out when there is a merger or other takeover acquisition. The law allows minority shareholders to have a transaction reviewed by a court when, for example, a merger at a specific price per share is approved by a majority of shareholders and a minority of shareholders believes that the deal is not fair or the price per share is too low. Despite the minority's opinion, however, it is not always certain that a court will agree—and it may disagree—about the fairness of the transaction and the price.

Consider, for example, the decision facing minority shareholders of Lynch Communications Systems, Inc., when, as a result of a cash-out merger between Lynch and another corporation, they were given notice that they could either accept the offered price of $15.50 per share or prepare for "an unfriendly tender at a lower price." An independent committee, formed by the Lynch board of directors, voted to recommend the approval of the $15.50 cash-per-share merger. Taking a cue from one committee member who felt that the price was unfair, some of the minority shareholders opted to challenge the deal. They filed a suit against Lynch and others, including Alcatel, USA, Inc., the acquiring corporation. Alcatel was also Lynch's parent corporation, its majority shareholder, and the party who had chosen the time for the merger. The minority alleged that "Alcatel timed its merger offer, with a thinly-veiled threat of using its controlling position to force the result, to take advantage of the opportunity to buy Lynch on the cheap."

The court, however, disagreed. "Alcatel is not to be faulted for taking advantage of the objective reality of Lynch's financial situation," which was affected by "difficult and rapidly changing competitive" circumstances. As for the member of the committee who thought the price per share was unfair, "there is no requirement of unanimity in such matters," at the committee level or even at the board level. Evidence that the minority offered as proof that the merger price was unfair was not sufficient, the court concluded.[a]

FOR CRITICAL ANALYSIS
What steps might the minority shareholders have taken to discourage the takeover before it started?

a. *Kahn v. Lynch Communications Systems, Inc.*, 669 A.2d 79 (Del.Sup. 1995).

Takeovers

"The strategy is really to be a bigger fish in a strong pond."

BERT ELLIS, 1953–
(American entrepreneur and president, Ellis Communications, Inc.)

• **TAKEOVER**
Acquiring control of a corporation through a merger, consolidation, or purchase of a substantial number of voting shares or the assets of the corporation.

• **AGGRESSOR**
An individual, group, or firm seeking to obtain control of a target corporation in a takeover attempt.

The control of a corporation may be acquired through a merger, a consolidation, or a purchase of the corporation's assets. The most direct way to acquire the control of a corporation is through a **takeover.** The basic outlines of a takeover are described in Chapter 29: a takeover is accomplished through the purchase of a substantial number of the voting shares of a firm. The majority shareholder can thus control the acquired corporation's assets and dictate its business policies. In effecting a takeover, the acquiring firm deals directly with the shareholders of the corporation whose control is being sought. The following sections provide additional details concerning takeovers.

Takeovers are of two types: friendly and hostile. A *friendly takeover* occurs when the management of the firm being acquired welcomes the acquisition. A *hostile takeover,* by contrast, occurs when the management of the firm being acquired opposes the acquisition. In both cases, the individual, group, or firm seeking to take over a target corporation is often referred to as the **aggressor.**

TAKEOVER TACTICS

> **ON THE WEB**
> The "SEC Pathfinder" Web site, sponsored by the University of Texas at Austin, assists business researchers who need SEC information. Background information and links relating to mergers, acquisitions, and tender offers are within the site on a page at **porsche.gslis.utexas.edu/bres/grouppr/mergers.htm**.

A takeover, especially one opposed by the management of the target firm (a hostile takeover), can be a complicated process. Sometimes, a takeover may begin as a proposed merger, with a public offer to buy shares from the shareholders of the target corporation. Other times, the takeover of a publicly traded corporation may begin with an anonymous purchase of shares on an open stock exchange.

During the "merger mania" that swept Wall Street during the 1980s, corporate takeovers often resembled open warfare. Takeover battles were sometimes launched in a manner comparable to an army's surprise invasion of another country. Corporate "raiders" went to great lengths to keep from tipping opposing management to the fact that its company was "in play." • **EXAMPLE 30.1** ABC Holding Company wants to take over International Manufacturing, Inc. (IM), without alerting IM's management. To counter rumors of an impending takeover attempt, ABC sends decoy raiders of another company, with considerable publicity, to distant cities, while ABC masterminds meet in seclusion with their investment advisers and lawyers to map out battle plans.• Some takeover experts have figured out yet another way to hide their plans. • **EXAMPLE 30.2** Smith & Jones Investments, Inc., wants to take control of Technical Products Corporation. Smith & Jones uses several *dummy corporations*—with different names such as S&JCo, Smith & Associates Corporation, Jones & Co. Investments, and so on—to buy Technical shares, thus keeping the name of Smith & Jones Investments secret.[4]•

Many of these tactics tested the limits of what was legally permissible in waging a takeover battle, and in some instances the limits were exceeded: by the close of the 1980s, a number of prominent investment bankers and financiers were behind bars or awaiting sentencing for violations of federal securities laws.

In the 1990s, the number of mergers increased, but the character and purpose of takeovers changed. Many takeovers were not as hostile as the battles of the 1980s.

4. Secrecy may be carried only so far under federal securities laws. Under the Williams Act (discussed later in this chapter), anyone acquiring over 5 percent of any class of a corporation's securities must file a statement with the SEC detailing certain information, such as the source of the funds used for the acquisition, any plans for the corporation which the acquiring party may have in purchasing the securities, and any contracts or agreements the acquiring party may have with the corporation.

Also, unlike the leveraged buyouts of the previous decade (leveraged buyouts are discussed below), mergers in the 1990s represented attempts to increase profits by expanding market share or reducing costs. Many of these were in the telecommunications sector.

• **BEACHHEAD ACQUISITION**
The gradual accumulation of a bloc of a target corporation's shares by an aggressor during an attempt to obtain control of the corporation.

• **PROXY FIGHT**
A conflict between an individual, group, or firm attempting to take control of a corporation and the corporation's management for the votes of the shareholders.

Beachhead Acquisitions and Proxy Fights An attempted takeover may begin with a gradual accumulation of a target corporation's shares. Having established a *beachhead* (hence the name, **beachhead acquisition**) with a bloc of shares, the purchaser of the shares may then launch a *proxy fight* for control of the corporation.

A **proxy fight** resembles a political campaign in that the individual or group seeking control of the target must secure the proxies of other shareholders. As explained in Chapter 28, a proxy entitles the holder to cast votes on behalf of the party conferring the proxy. A proxy may be obtained for each share that may be voted. If the voting shares owned and the proxies obtained equal enough votes to outvote all of the other shareholders, effective control of the corporation will have been gained. The controlling group usually exercises control by using its majority vote to elect a board of directors that supports its views.

To wage a successful proxy contest, an aggressor must obtain a list of shareholders so that the shareholders may be contacted and their proxies solicited. Federal securities laws require that a target corporation's management provide only minimal assistance to an aggressor. Management may resist providing a list of shareholders; if so, costly litigation may result. Even when an aggressor obtains a list of shareholders, it must pay the costs associated with contacting the shareholders and mailing the proxy requests. In contrast, management's solicitations to the shareholders may be charged to the corporation—at least insofar as the contest between the group seeking control and the incumbent management is based on issues of corporate policy, rather than being a personality contest between two opposing factions. Most courts have allowed management to charge to the corporation reasonable expenses of educating the shareholders about the policy issues that are raised in a particular proxy fight.

The rules of solicitation and other aspects of a proxy contest are slanted in favor of the incumbent management. Also, the solicitation process can be lengthy and expensive. Thus, more recently, other takeover strategies have been favored over the proxy contest. Nonetheless, there are some factors that may lessen the one-sidedness of a proxy fight. One factor is the increased importance of the institutional investor in financial markets. Obtaining the support of a handful of institutional investors that hold large blocs of shares obviates the need to contact a multitude of individual investors, each of whom may hold only a small fraction of a corporation's voting shares. In addition, a successful aggressor may recoup the expense of its efforts by having the corporation approve a reimbursement out of corporate funds; again, however, the legality of this action turns on whether the contest involved policy issues rather than personalities.

• **LEVERAGED BUY-OUT (LBO)**
A corporate takeover financed by loans secured by the acquired corporation's assets or by the issuance of corporate bonds, resulting in a high debt load for the corporation.

Leveraged Buy-outs (LBOs) In the last twenty years, a number of corporations have arranged to "go private" through so-called **leveraged buyouts (LBOs).** In an LBO, the management of a corporation—or any other group, such as the employees, but management is usually included—purchases all outstanding corporate stock held by the public and in this way gains control over the corporate enterprise. The LBO is financed by money borrowed against the assets of the corporation, which may include real estate or plant and equipment. The borrowing may take the form of the issuance of bonds, a straight bank loan, or a loan from an investment bank.

Technology and the Proxy

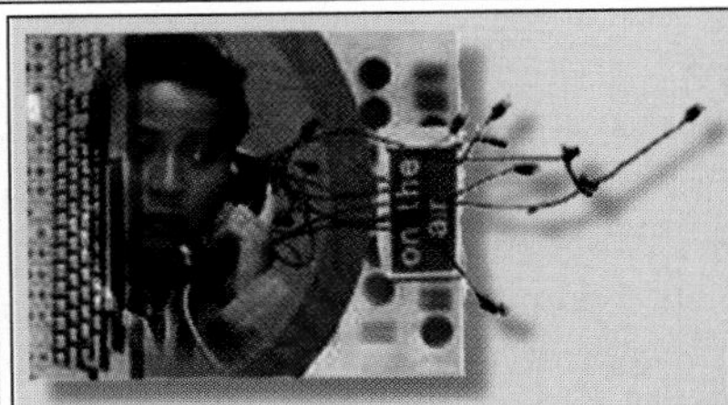

The technology revolution is having profound effects on corporate practices. Nowhere has this been more significant than in proxy procedures. Faxes, electronic mail, and other nontraditional means of submitting proxies and casting shareholder votes has changed the process forever.

As has often been the case, Delaware was one of the first states to respond to these changes. Under 8 Del. Code Section 212, Delaware allows proxies in virtually any form. The essential requirement is that a proxy be "submitted with information from which it can be determined that . . . [the] electronic transmission was authorized by the stockholder." Faxes are permitted as long as they are complete and accurate.

The American Bar Association's Committee on Corporate Laws has responded to these developments by issuing changes to the Revised Model Business Corporation Act (RMBCA). The amendments relate to the section that deals with proxies. RMBCA Section 7.22 was changed to specifically authorize the transmission of proxy appointments by electronic means (or other means not "directly involving the physical transfer of paper"), as long as the transmission includes, or is accompanied by, information from which it can be "reasonably verified" that the shareholder authorized it. An Official Comment added to the RMBCA makes it clear that proxy forms can be sent by fax, so long as the fax is a complete reproduction of the entire form.[a]

FOR CRITICAL ANALYSIS

When shareholder votes are accepted by modem, how can forgeries and other unauthorized acts be prevented?

a. The Securities and Exchange Commission (SEC) provides guidance in the use of electronic media for the delivery of information under the federal securities laws. Electronic media includes audiotapes, videotapes, faxes, CD-ROMs, e-mail, electronic bulletin boards, Internet Web sites, and computer networks. See *Use of Electronic Media for Delivery Purposes,* Securities Act Release No. 7233, 1 Fed.Sec.L.Rep. (CCH) ¶ 3200 (Oct. 6, 1995).

Because an LBO often results in a high debt load for the corporation, the interest payments on the debt may become so burdensome that the corporation cannot survive.

TAKEOVER DEFENSES

"The mouse that hath but one hole is quickly taken."
GEORGE HERBERT
1593–1633
(English clergyman and poet)

As explained in Chapter 28, the directors of a corporation owe a fiduciary duty to its shareholders. In the context of a tender offer, this duty requires that the directors carefully consider the offer and make a good faith recommendation as to whether the shareholders should accept or reject the offer. To resist a takeover, a target company may use a variety of tactics. Many of these defenses—the *self-tender,* the *white knight defense,* the *Pac-Man defense, scorched earth tactics,* the *shark repellant defense,* and the *poison pill*—are defined in Chapter 29. Alternatively, a target corporation might resort to one of the following tactics.

Crown Jewel Defense Virtually every corporation, and certainly every conglomerate (a firm owning two or more unrelated businesses), possesses a variety of assets. Some, of course, are more valuable than others. When a corporation is threatened with an imminent takeover, management may seek to prevent the takeover by making the firm less attractive to the aggressor. One way to do so is to sell off its valuable assets. • **EXAMPLE 30.3** Diversified Properties, Inc., owns an aging mining operation in Reno and an extremely valuable piece of real estate in downtown Manhattan. In an attempt to thwart a takeover, the firm sells its Manhattan real estate. By selling the valuable asset and retaining the undesirable one, the firm becomes less of a prize in a potential takeover.● This defense is referred to as the **crown jewel defense** because the firm attempts to avoid a takeover by selling off its most valuable asset—that is, its *crown jewel.*

● **CROWN JEWEL DEFENSE**
Selling off a corporation's most valuable asset to a third party to make the corporation less attractive to individuals, groups, or firms who are attempting to gain control of the corporation.

Lobster Trap Defense Another way in which the target firm may effect a corporate change that makes a takeover more difficult is by preventing the aggressor from acquiring more than 10 percent of the voting shares. The firm may accomplish this by prohibiting the conversion of *convertible securities* into common shares if the holders already own, or would own after conversion, 10 percent or more of the outstanding voting shares. (Convertible securities are corporate bonds or nonvoting, preferred stock that may be converted into common shares.) Because this tactic applies only to holders of large blocs, it is referred to as the **lobster trap defense;** a lobster trap is designed to catch the larger lobsters while allowing the smaller ones to escape.

● **LOBSTER TRAP DEFENSE**
Prohibiting holders of convertible securities (stocks or bonds that can be converted into common shares) from converting the securities into common shares if the holders already own, or would own after conversion, 10 percent or more of the voting shares of stock.

Limitations on Takeover Defenses The ultimate responsibility for deciding whether to accept or resist a takeover attempt rests with the target corporation's directors. In making their decision, the directors must meet the standards imposed under their fiduciary duty to the corporation's shareholders. If the directors decide to resist the takeover attempt, they must still meet high standards of loyalty and care. Indeed, because the directors—especially inside directors, who also serve as officers of the target corporation—may fear being replaced after a successful takeover, the degree of scrutiny used in assessing whether the directors met their standard of duty and care in trying to fend off a takeover is often greater than the degree of scrutiny applied to directors who do not resist a takeover.

Shareholders often benefit from the efforts of an aggressor through an improvement in management or as a result of having the opportunity to sell their shares for a premium to a corporate suitor. Directors may fear being replaced, however. Thus, there is a potential for conflict between the interests of the shareholders and the interests of the directors. This potential conflict may limit the directors' efforts in resisting a takeover attempt.

The court in the following case considered whether the board of a target corporation that adopted defensive measures in response to a tender offer acted in the best interests of the shareholders.

CASE 30.3 Moore Corp. Ltd. v. Wallace Computer Services, Inc.

United States District Court,
District of Delaware, 1995.
907 F.Supp. 1545.

HISTORICAL AND TECHNOLOGICAL SETTING *In the 1990s, the technology revolution provided many opportunities for profitable applications to the needs of businesses. Development of new applications has not been cheap, however. For example, Wallace Computer Services, Inc., invested $34 million into developing the Wallace Information Network (WIN). WIN is a set of computer programs that enables businesses to consolidate certain recordkeeping systems at a low cost. By August 1995, sales indicated that the WIN system was superior to, and preferred over, its competitors' products.*

BACKGROUND AND FACTS In the summer and fall of 1995, the board of Wallace Computer Systems, Inc., learned that its company's investment in the WIN system was beginning to generate profits that exceeded all predictions. At the same time, Moore Corporation Limited made a tender offer to Wallace shareholders as part of a takeover attempt. The Wallace board adopted antitakeover measures. Moore filed a suit in a federal district court against Wallace and its directors, claiming that the defensive actions violated the directors' fiduciary duty to the shareholders. Moore asked the court to block the antitakeover measures.

CASE 30.3—Continued

IN THE WORDS OF THE COURT . . .
MURRAY M. SCHWARTZ, Senior District Judge.

* * * *

* * * The favorable results from the [Wallace] Board's past actions are now beginning to be translated into financial results which even surpass management and financial analyst projections, and the financial data which manifest these results are facts only known to them. * * * Moore's tender offer poses a threat to Wallace that shareholders, because they are uninformed, will cash out before realizing the fruits of the substantial technological innovations achieved by Wallace. * * *

* * * *

* * * [T]he Wallace Board reasonably believed that the shareholders were entitled to protection from what they considered to be a "low ball" offer. * * * Given this situation, the Wallace Board's response can hardly be deemed unreasonable.

DECISION AND REMEDY The court refused to block the antitakeover steps taken by the Wallace board.

FOR CRITICAL ANALYSIS—Social Consideration *Should the result in this case have been the same if the shareholders had been aware of WIN's success?*

Antitrust Law as a Takeover Defense A target corporation may also seek an injunction against an aggressor on the ground that an attempted takeover violates antitrust laws, which are intended to prevent the illegal restraint of competition (discussed in Chapter 35). This defense may succeed if the takeover would, in the eyes of a court, result in a substantial increase in an acquiring corporation's market power. Because antitrust laws are designed to protect competition rather than competitors, incumbent managers who are able to avoid a takeover by resorting to the use of private antitrust actions are unintended beneficiaries of the laws. Antitrust challenges to mergers may also be brought by the government rather than private parties. Hence, the antitrust considerations involved in a proposed takeover can exist apart from the consideration of defense tactics.

FINANCIAL CONSIDERATIONS

One of the factors that have propelled the unprecedented number and magnitude of takeovers and mergers over the last twenty years—indeed, perhaps the most important one—is the innovation in corporate financing that has taken place during this same period. Financial instruments and methods of raising capital that once would have been considered unorthodox—if not unsound—are now common among investment bankers and corporate financial officers.

Junk Bonds One of the most important and most controversial innovations in corporate finance has been the so-called junk bond. Similar to other bonds, a junk bond is a promise to pay a certain amount to investors after or during a specific period. **Junk bonds** are unique in that they are subject to a high degree of risk—the risk that the borrower will not be able to pay the lender under the terms of the bond. Because the bonds are subject to high risk, they are called *junk*. The high degree of risk, however, means that investors must be compensated for taking on the risk; thus, the bonds yield high returns. In theory, because only a fraction of the bonds will go into default (be unpaid in the full amount on schedule), junk bonds can be an attractive investment when included in a portfolio that is diversified (a diverse package of different securities).

• **JUNK BOND**
A bond that represents a promise to pay a certain amount to investors after or during a specific period but that is subject to a higher degree of risk than other bonds—the risk that the issuer will be unable to pay according to the terms of the bonds.

Bonds have often been employed to finance takeovers; the investors have been promised that they would be repaid by the aggressor's selling off some of the target corporation's assets after the acquisition has been completed. Because a takeover attempt's success is uncertain, and because even if a takeover succeeds, the value of the assets may not be sufficient to repay the debt holders, the bonds issued to finance the attempt have often been sold as junk bonds—high-risk, high-yield bonds. For a time, the junk-bond market seemed to offer an unlimited supply of funds to finance takeover bids. Eventually, however, some of the deals proved too risky, and some proved to be ill advised for reasons other than the mode of financing.

These events, with the decline of the stock market in October 1987, cooled the takeover fever that had raged throughout the 1980s. Nonetheless, reports of the demise of the junk-bond market proved to be exaggerated. Junk bonds remain a feature of corporate finance. Thus, there remains a possibility that even the largest, most well-established firm could become the target of a small, unknown aggressor.

Two-Tier Financing In a two-tier financing process, the aggressor first acquires a controlling interest in the target by making a very attractive purchase offer to the shareholders of the target corporation. After obtaining a sufficient number of shares through its initial offer to achieve a controlling interest, the aggressor then merges the acquired firm into one of the aggressor's subsidiaries. The minority shareholders in the target firm (those who elected not to accept the tender offer) are usually helpless to oppose the merger. They are paid less for their shares and are thus eliminated at a lower price. • **EXAMPLE 30.4** U.S. Steel Corporation (now called USX Corporation) acquired a controlling interest in Marathon Oil Corporation by making a tender offer of $125 per share to the Marathon shareholders. After acquiring its controlling interest, U.S. Steel instigated a merger according to the terms of which Marathon's minority shareholders were given U.S. Steel stock worth $76 per share. In subsequent litigation, the actions under this two-tier plan were held to have been lawful.[5] •

THE WILLIAMS ACT OF 1970

> **ON THE WEB**
> Recent news articles about events in the field of mergers and acquisitions, which includes such federal securities laws as the Securities Exchange Act of 1934 and the Williams Act of 1970, can be found within the Web site of "Law Journal Extra!" on a page at **www.ljextra.com/practice/mergers/index.html**.

The significant role played by federal securities law in the area of corporate finance extends to takeovers. One of the most important pieces of federal legislation concerning takeovers is the Williams Act of 1970. The act amended Sections 13 and 14 of the Securities Exchange Act of 1934. The Williams Act regulates offers to buy stock, specifically tender offers. The provisions of the act apply to all offers to buy more than 5 percent of a corporation's securities.

Purposes of the Act One of the purposes of the Williams Act is to create a level playing field for both the target and the aggressor. The act is also intended to protect shareholders against unfair and deceptive practices in the securities market. Many economists contend that the act is misguided and perhaps counterproductive. Others contend that federal protection is necessary to safeguard less powerful interests and unsophisticated investors. Because so many different groups with divergent interests are affected, the regulation of takeovers is often influenced more by political considerations than by economic ones. As discussed in the subsequent section, this tendency is even more pronounced at the state level.

Provisions of the Act The important provisions of the Williams Act impose disclosure requirements on aggressors and targets. In addition, the act's provisions establish the basic framework for making a tender offer.

5. *Radol v. Thomas*, 772 F.2d 244 (6th Cir. 1985).

Section 13(d) of the Williams Act focuses on open-market and privately negotiated acquisitions. Under Section 13(d), any person who acquires more than 5 percent of the securities of a corporation registered under Section 12 of the Securities Exchange Act (the section pertaining to reporting requirements) must file a statement of ownership with the Securities and Exchange Commission (SEC). The filing must have been made within ten days after the 5 percent ownership level is reached. The statement must include information about the individual or organization making the purchase and the details of any financial arrangements behind the purchase. The statement must disclose the purchaser's intentions regarding the corporation whose stock has been acquired, such as whether or not a tender offer is anticipated and whether or not a merger or consolidation is intended. A purchaser may simply state that the purchase is solely for investment purposes, if that is the intention of the purchase. Section 13(d) is intended to alert a target's shareholders and management to an imminent takeover attempt.

Section 14(d) of the Williams Act pertains to tender offers. As with Section 13(d) of the act, Section 14(d) applies to all securities subject to the reporting requirements of the Securities Exchange Act of 1934. With regard to such securities, Section 14(d) requires that any person planning to make a tender offer file with the SEC all solicitations, advertisements, and any other material to be used in making the tender offer. The tender offeror must also disclose such information as the financial arrangements and the future intentions concerning the target, as in a Section 13(d) disclosure. The filings and disclosure must precede the distribution of the tender offer materials. Anyone planning to oppose or support the tender offer must also file materials relating to the offer before distributing the materials.

Section 14(f) of the Williams Act requires that a public disclosure be made of the identities of persons to be elected to the board and any agreements affecting the directors of the target during the transfer of management control should the tender offer succeed.

If a takeover proceeds uncontested, the target company's directors must make one of the following declarations to the shareholders within ten days of the announcement of the tender offer: (1) that it recommends that the shareholders accept the offer or that they reject it; (2) that it has no opinion on the offer; or (3) that it is unable to take a position concerning the offer.

State Law Restrictions

Managers and directors are not the only corporate personnel who have reason to fear a takeover. A company's rank and file also face potential hardship from corporate changes. Indeed, the rank and file may have even more to fear than others. Shareholders often walk away from a takeover having sold their shares to the aggressor at a substantial premium. As discussed earlier, the target corporation's directors and top managers may also find a takeover profitable: many either stay on in the new organization or leave after collecting the benefits contained in their *golden parachutes* (agreements by which they will receive payments and other benefits in the event of demotion or layoff because of a takeover). Often, the rank and file do not fare as well.

Local and Regional Concerns When the acquired corporation has served as the major employer in a community, the effects of a takeover or merger can extend beyond the employees of the company. Businesses that relied on the patronage of the acquired corporation's employees also suffer. Indeed, the closing of a major plant or division of the acquired company can be a death warrant for an entire community.

Most thoughtful observers recognize that the gains from active competition for corporate assets are essential to a modern, dynamic economy. Corporate takeovers and mergers are a necessary component of competition. Without the threat of being replaced by more aggressive, entrepreneurial-minded managers, a company's leaders may become complacent. Without competition for corporate assets, there is no guarantee that labor and capital will be allocated to their most valuable uses.

Still, though, when a takeover or merger affects your job, your family, and your community, it is easy to lose sight of the "big picture." What is indisputably beneficial for the overall economy may seem to be an inequitable burden for the individual worker. Moreover, the adverse effects of takeovers and mergers sometimes fall disproportionately on local communities where plant closings and layoffs have occurred. Because state governments are inevitably more concerned with regional and local matters than with the broader issues, state governments have been the most hostile to unrestrained competition for corporate assets. Over several decades, various states have launched direct legislative assaults on takeovers and mergers. The rationale apparently has been that the best strategy for mitigating the hardships wrought by corporate acquisitions is the outright elimination of takeovers and mergers.

States' Responses Over a thirty-year period, states have enacted at least two types of antitakeover statutes that have been upheld by the courts. • **EXAMPLE 30.5** Indiana enacted a statute that provides the aggressor's shares in the target firm lose their voting power unless either the target's directors approve the acquisition or the shareholders not affiliated with the aggressor or management authorize restoration of the shares' voting power. The United States Supreme Court upheld the law, finding no inconsistency between the state law and federal law because the Indiana statute allowed any aggressor to acquire shares unhindered.[6] • The Indiana statute makes the shares of Indiana corporations less attractive, but it does not interfere with the process of bidding for shares in an attempted acquisition. The Court held that the law does not violate the commerce clause. The Court instead found that the law deals only with the internal affairs of a corporation and that the statute may benefit shareholders because it allows investors to avoid coercion from two-tier bids and similar takeover tactics.

• **EXAMPLE 30.6** Laws in Wisconsin (and other states) require an aggressor to wait three years after buying shares in the target corporation before merging with the company or acquiring more than 5 percent of its assets, unless the directors of the target agree in advance to an earlier takeover. •

The following case involved a challenge to both types of antitakeover statutes.

6. *CTS Corp. v. Dynamics Corp. of America,* 481 U.S. 69, 107 S.Ct. 1637, 95 L.Ed.2d 67 (1987).

CASE 30.4 WLR Foods, Inc. v. Tyson Foods, Inc.

United States Court of Appeals,
Fourth Circuit, 1995.
65 F.3d 1172.
www.law.emory.edu/4circuit/sept95/index.html[a]

a. This is a page, within the Web site of the Emory University School of Law, that lists the published opinions of the U.S. Court of Appeals for the Fourth Circuit for September 1995. Scroll down the list of cases to the *WLR Foods* case. Click on the case name to access the opinion.

COMPANY PROFILE *During the Depression of the 1930s, John Tyson supported his family by buying, transporting, and selling vegetables and poultry. Today, Tyson Foods, Inc., controls nearly 20 percent of the U.S. chicken market and 70 percent of the market for U.S. chickens exported to Japan (which is only one of more than forty countries to which Tyson exports its products). Half of Tyson's sales are to food services, including caterers and restaurants such as KFC and McDonald's.*

CASE 30.4—Continued

BACKGROUND AND FACTS When Tyson Foods, Inc., attempted to acquire WLR Foods, Inc., a Virginia corporation, the WLR board took defensive measures, such as adopting a "poison pill" shareholder rights plan (see Chapter 29). WLR filed a suit in a federal district court against Tyson, seeking a declaration that its actions were valid. Tyson asserted its own claims, challenging WLR's tactics. The court ruled in WLR's favor. Tyson appealed, arguing in part that Virginia statutes that allow companies to take defensive actions against takeover attempts violate the Williams Act.

IN THE WORDS OF THE COURT . . .
MURNAGHAN, Circuit Judge:

* * * *

* * * [T]he purpose of the Williams Act is to protect independent investors from bidders and management by ensuring that the investors have access to information. * * * [T]he Williams Act is simply not designed to protect a company in Tyson's position; the Williams Act does not create a right to profit from the business of making tender offers.

The * * * Virginia statutes may work to give target management an advantage in the tender offer context. The * * * question we address here, however, is whether Virginia's decision to allow management access to a set of defensive mechanisms in the takeover situation frustrates the Williams Act's goal of investor protection. We hold that it does not.

DECISION AND REMEDY The U.S. Court of Appeals for the Fourth Circuit affirmed the lower court's ruling.

FOR CRITICAL ANALYSIS—Social Consideration *If an acquiring corporation has no plans to close down any part of a target corporation, why might the target wish to oppose a takeover?*

ETHICAL ISSUE 30.1 ***Can an outsider be liable for trading on inside information?*** Federal law prohibits investors from using inside information to profit in the trading of shares of stock in the corporation from which the information was gleaned. Even a *tippee* (an outsider) can be liable for insider trading under securities law if the tippee's acquisition of inside information followed from an officer's or director's breach of his or her fiduciary duties. Tippees of tippees (remote tippees) can also be held liable if they knew, or should have known, that they were trading on improperly obtained inside information. For example, suppose that a manager passes inside information about a corporate merger to a friend's stockbroker, who passes the information to a third party, who shares the information with his brother, who recommends to his friend—Alice—that she buy certain securities. Alice buys the securities and profits. Can Alice, who was never told (and never asked about) the source of the information, be liable for insider trading as a remote tippee? Yes. Her liability would be founded on the fact that she *should have known* that she was trading on improperly acquired inside information. Thus, even if she consciously avoided knowledge about the source of the information, she would not be protected from liability.

APPLICATION Law & the Small Business: Issuing Stock in Foreign Markets*

For a company to issue stock in the United States, there is the potentially expensive and lengthy process of registering the issue with the Securities and Exchange Commission (SEC). Attorneys and underwriters (marketing professionals) must be consulted, certain forms must be filed, the SEC must review the offer, and so on. (The requirements for stock offerings are discussed in more detail in Chapter 31.) Even without the expense, a small company that needs capital quickly could be out of business before the process is complete.

In 1990, the SEC adopted Regulation S (Reg S) to allow U.S. companies to sell stock in foreign markets without going through the time-consuming registration process. The SEC does not need to review the offer before it is made. A U.S. company issuing stock in a foreign market under Reg S need only disclose the offering in its quarterly reports. This speeds the process of issuing the stock and makes it less expensive, which makes it possible for the company to seek a lower amount of capital.

Reg S also makes it attractive for foreign investors to buy stock in American companies. Under previous law, foreign investors could not resell the stock for two years. Under Reg S, they can sell it after forty days. There is always a risk that the price of the stock could go down within those forty days. Thus, the issuer usually offers the stock at a discount to offset that risk.

CHECKLIST FOR REG S ISSUES

A Reg S issue—offering stock for sale in foreign markets—should be considered under the following circumstances:

1. A U.S. company wants to attract foreign investors.
2. A U.S. company needs to raise more funds than it has been able to get in U.S. markets.
3. A U.S. company does not have time to go through the lengthy SEC registration process for domestic issues.

*This *Application* is not meant to substitute for the services of an attorney who is licensed to practice law in your state.

Key Terms

aggressor 787
beachhead acquisition 788
crown jewel defense 790
junk bonds 791
leveraged buy-out (LBO) 788
lobster trap defense 790
proxy fight 788
takeover 787

Chapter Summary • Additional Shareholders' Rights and Takeovers

Shareholders' Inspection Rights (See pages 783–784.)	1. *Unrestricted rights*—Shareholders have an unrestricted right to inspect certain records (articles of incorporation, bylaws, board resolutions creating classes of stock, minutes of shareholders' meetings, annual reports, and so on). 2. *Limited rights*—Shareholders can inspect and copy other records only on showing a "proper purpose" and good faith. The records must be connected to that purpose.
Shareholder Proposals in Proxy Materials (See page 784.)	When a company sends proxy materials to its shareholders, it must include whatever proposals will be considered at the shareholders' meeting. A proposal does not have to be included if it relates to ordinary business operations, unless it also relates to significant policy considerations.

Chapter Summary • Additional Shareholders' Rights and Takeovers, Continued

Shareholders' Appraisal Rights (See pages 785–786.)	Shareholders may have a right, under a state statute, to dissent from a corporate transaction (merger, consolidation, short-form merger, reorganization, or sale of substantially all of the corporate assets not in the ordinary course of business) and be paid the fair value of their shares. A shareholder may also exercise the right when shares in one corporation are exchanged for shares in another corporation if (1) the shareholder owns shares in the corporation whose shares are being acquired and (2) the shareholder is entitled to vote on the transaction.
Takeovers (See pages 787–795.)	1. The purpose of a takeover is to gain control of a firm. A takeover is usually accomplished through the purchase of a substantial number of the voting shares of a firm. A majority shareholder can control a corporation's assets and dictate its business policies. A *friendly takeover* occurs when the management of the firm being acquired welcomes the acquisition. A *hostile takeover* occurs when the management of the firm being acquired opposes the acquisition. 2. *Takeover tactics* include: a. Beachhead acquisition— Acquisition of the first bloc of shares of a target corporation. b. Proxy fight—Fight between the aggressor and the target to gain the right to cast votes on behalf of the shareholders. If the aggressor's voting shares owned and the proxies obtained equal enough votes to outvote the other shareholders, effective control of the corporation will have been gained. c. Leveraged buyout (LBO)—Buyout in which the management of a corporation (or any other group) purchases all outstanding corporate stock held by the public and in this way gains control over the corporation. The LBO is financed by money borrowed against the assets of the corporation. 3. *Takeover defenses* include— a. Crown jewel defense—Selling a firm's most valuable asset and retaining an undesirable one, making the firm less of a prize in a potential takeover. b. Lobster trap defense—Preventing an aggressor from acquiring more than 10 percent of the target's voting shares by prohibiting the conversion of convertible securities into common shares if the holders already own, or would own after conversion, 10 percent or more of the outstanding voting shares. c. Antitrust laws—A target corporation may seek an injunction against an aggressor on the ground that an attempted takeover violates antitrust laws. 4. *Williams Act of 1970*—Intended to protect shareholders against unfair and deceptive practices in the securities market. Provisions include: a. Any person who acquires more than 5 percent of the securities of a corporation registered under Section 12 of the Securities Exchange Act (the section pertaining to reporting requirements) must file a statement of ownership with the Securities and Exchange Commission. b. Any person planning to make a tender offer must file with the SEC all solicitations, advertisements, and other material to be used. The offeror must disclose such information as the financial arrangements and the future intentions concerning the target. 5. *State law restrictions*—State statutes may discourage takeover attempts by limiting an aggressor's options to dictate the course of the target's business once the firm is taken over.

For Review

1. On what grounds can a shareholder inspect and copy corporate records?
2. On what basis does a shareholder proposal have to be included in proxy materials sent to all shareholders before a shareholders' meeting?
3. Under what circumstances can a shareholder dissent from a corporate transaction and be paid the fair value of his or her shares in the corporation?
4. How might an acquiring corporation accomplish a takeover of a target corporation? How might a target corporation defeat a takeover attempt?
5. What federal and state laws help shareholders guard against unwanted corporate takeovers? How do those laws protect shareholders' interests?

Questions and Case Problems

30–1. Appraisal Rights. Ann owns 10,000 shares of Ajax Corp. Her shares represent a 10 percent ownership in Ajax. Zeta Corp. is interested in acquiring Ajax in a merger, and the board of directors of each corporation has approved the merger. The shareholders of Zeta have already approved the acquisition, and Ajax has called for a shareholders' meeting to approve the merger. Ann disapproves of the merger and does not want to accept Zeta shares for the Ajax shares she holds. The market price of Ajax shares is $20 per share the day before the shareholder vote and drops to $16 on the day the shareholders of Ajax approve the merger. Discuss Ann's rights in this matter, beginning with notice of the proposed merger.

30–2. Takeover Tactics. Under what circumstances do defense tactics employed by a corporation's board of directors against a takeover attempt represent a breach of the fiduciary duty owed by the directors to the corporation's shareholders?

30–3. Takeover Tactics. Alitech Corp. is a small midwestern business that owns a valuable patent. Alitech has approximately 1,000 shareholders with 100,000 authorized and outstanding shares. Block Corp. would like to have use of the patent, but Alitech refuses to give Block a license. Block has tried to acquire Alitech by purchasing Alitech's assets, but Alitech's board of directors has refused to approve the acquisition. Alitech's shares are presently selling for $5 per share. Discuss how Block Corp. might proceed to gain the control and use of Alitech's patent.

30–4. Shareholder Proposals. Chlorofluorocarbons (CFCs) and other synthetic chemicals are suspected of harming the earth's ozone layer. In 1990, Congress called for CFC production to cease by January 1, 2000. E. I. du Pont de Nemours & Co. manufactures CFCs. In early 1991, Du Pont's policy was to phase out CFC production according to the government's schedule or "as soon as possible." Amelia Roosevelt, a Du Pont shareholder, was concerned with the company's CFC-production policy. On Roosevelt's behalf, the Friends of the Earth Oceanic Society submitted to Du Pont a shareholder proposal seeking, among other things, Du Pont's phaseout of the production of CFCs by the end of 1994. The Friends of the Earth asked that the proposal be included in Du Pont's proxy materials before the 1991 annual shareholder meeting. Du Pont was opposed to the idea and told the Securities and Exchange Commission (SEC) that it would not include the proposal in its proxy materials. The SEC supported Du Pont's decision. Roosevelt filed a complaint in federal district court. The court agreed with the SEC and ruled that Du Pont could omit Roosevelt's proposal. The court noted that Du Pont had already spent more than $240 million developing alternatives to CFCs and had shut down the world's largest CFC plant. Roosevelt appealed. Meanwhile, Du Pont announced that it would phase out CFC production by the end of 1995. On what ground might the appellate court uphold the lower court's ruling, which was based on the SEC's decision? [*Roosevelt v. E. I. du Pont de Nemours & Co.*, 958 F.2d 416 (D.C. Cir. 1992)]

30–5. Shareholder Proposals. Ohio Edison Co. is a public utility. Ohio Edison's articles of incorporation vest the authority to make capital expenditures solely in the board of directors. Since 1982, the company's capital expenditures have averaged $595 million per year. C. L. Grimes, a shareholder in Ohio Edison, proposed that the company amend its articles of incorporation to require shareholder approval of certain capital expenditures in excess of $300 million. In other words, under Grimes's proposal, once the spending threshold of $300 million was reached, each expenditure, including such routine expenditures as the purchase of a typewriter or a new desk, would require shareholder approval. On October 23, 1990, Grimes asked Ohio Edison to enclose his proposal in the proxy materials for the next shareholders' meeting. Ohio Edison submitted the proposal to the Securities and Exchange Commission (SEC) for an opinion as to whether it needed to be included with the proxy materials. The SEC ruled that the proposal could be omitted. When Ohio Edison distributed proxy materials for the meeting without mentioning Grimes's proposal, Grimes filed suit. Grimes contended that Ohio Edison violated SEC rules by failing to include his proposal in its proxy materials and by failing to inform its shareholders that he would offer his proposal at the meeting (which, Grimes argued, made the proxy materials "false and misleading"). Ohio Edison responded with a motion to dismiss the complaint. The court granted the motion. Grimes appealed. On what grounds might the appellate court uphold the lower court's judgment, which was based in part on the SEC's ruling? [*Grimes v. Ohio Edison Co.*, 992 F.2d 455 (2d Cir. 1993)]

30–6. Appraisal Rights. Mi-Tech makes high-density metal products and electrical contacts produced from powdered metals. In 1979, Mi-Tech hired Ed Freeland to serve as manufacturing manager. Freeland was murdered in 1989. A few months later, Ted Leslie and the other Mi-Tech directors concluded that "Freeland's tragic death caused Mi-Tech to be extremely vulnerable." The board proposed a merger with another company, Birco, Inc. Most of the shareholders approved. Patricia Settles and Freeland's other heirs, who had inherited his shares of Mi-Tech stock, filed a notice of dissent. The board told the heirs what steps to take to exercise their statutory appraisal rights. The heirs did not follow those steps but filed a suit against Mi-Tech in an Indiana state court, asserting, among other things, breach of fiduciary duty and asking for payment of fair value for their shares. Mi-Tech filed a motion for summary judgment. Will the court grant the motion? Why or why not? [*Settles v. Leslie*, 701 N.E.2d 849 (Ind.App. 1998)]

30–7. Antitrust Law as a Takeover Defense. Anago, Inc., and Tecnol Medical Products, Inc., make disposable hospital supplies. Both companies service hospitals, and, together, share a large percentage of the market for their products. Anago is smaller than Tecnol and privately held. Tecnol is publicly held. In 1991, Tecnol began efforts to buy Anago and eventually succeeded in purchasing all of Anago's preferred stock. After reaching agreements to purchase the common stock of several Anago shareholders, Tecnol publicly proposed a friendly merger. Anago immediately sued Tecnol for violations of the Williams Act, and filed a motion for an injunction under Section 7 of the Clayton Act (an antitrust law). Anago offered evidence that a takeover would substantially decrease competition and raise prices in the market for disposable hospital supplies. Anago also offered proof that it would lose its power of independent decision making if Tecnol bought its operations. Anago argued that this established an antitrust injury. The district court denied Anago's claims. Anago appealed the ruling concerning its request for an injunction. On what basis might Anago's claim defeat Tecnol's attempted takeover? Will the appellate court affirm the lower court's ruling? [*Anago, Inc. v. Tecnol Medical Products, Inc.*, 976 F.2d 248 (5th Cir. 1992)]

30–8. Williams Act. On August 16, 1991, Computer Associates International, Inc. (CA), and On-Line Software announced that CA had made an offer, which On-Line's management had accepted, to purchase all outstanding shares of On-Line stock for $15.75 in cash per share. The offer was subject to the approval of the boards of directors of both companies. The terms of the offer were set forth in two documents, dated August 22 and August 23. On August 21, Jack Berdy, a senior On-Line officer, and Anthony Wang, a senior CA officer, executed an agreement that provided, among other things, for the payment to Berdy of $5 million over the amount he would receive for his On-Line shares in exchange for Berdy's agreement not to compete with On-Line or CA for five years. Joel Gerber, on behalf of On-Line shareholders, filed a suit against CA and others, alleging violations of various securities laws. Gerber charged in part that the agreement with Berdy was part of the tender offer and that the $5 million payment to Berdy represented higher, additional consideration. Under Section 14(d) of the Williams Act, a party making a tender offer must pay the same consideration to all holders of the same stock. Thus, if increased consideration is offered to one shareholder, it must be offered to all shareholders. The key is the time at which the tender offer commences. Gerber claimed that the offer was made when it was announced on August 16. CA argued that under the "totality of the circumstances," the offer did not commence until August 22. CA filed a motion to dismiss. On what basis might the court deny the motion? [*Gerber v. Computer Associates International, Inc.*, 812 F.Supp. 361 (E.D.N.Y. 1993)]

A QUESTION OF ETHICS AND SOCIAL RESPONSIBILITY

30–9. Two couples, the Kimmelmans and the Zauderers, held approximately two-thirds of the outstanding shares of 79 Realty Corp., a Madison Avenue firm. Alpert and three other shareholders (the Alpert group) owned 26 percent of the outstanding shares. Madison 28 Associates, a limited partnership, bought the shares of the Kimmelmans and the Zauderers. Once Madison 28 Associates was in control, four of the Madison partners were appointed to the board of 79 Realty Corp. The new directors, who now controlled 79 Realty, approved a plan to merge 79 Realty Corp. with 28 Williams Street Corp., with 28 Williams Street being the surviving corporation. A shareholders' meeting was called to approve the plan, with proper notice being sent to all shareholders as to the purpose of the meeting, and the merger was approved by a two-thirds vote of the shareholders. The Alpert group sued Madison 28 Associates, alleging that the merger was illegal because it was undertaken for the sole benefit of the Madison group, and since the Madison group controlled both firms involved in the merger, there was a clear conflict of interest. The Madison group defended on the basis that the merger was beneficial to 79 Realty's corporate interests because it advanced proper business interests: more capital would be available for necessary renovations of the 79 Realty building, and more tax advantages could be gained. [*Alpert v. 28 Williams Street Corp.*, 63 N.Y.2d 557, 473 N.E.2d 19, 483 N.Y.S.2d 667 (1984)]

1. Was the proposed merger unethical? Would it benefit all of the shareholders of 79 Realty?
2. Did the Madison group's control of both firms constitute a clear conflict of interest?
3. Do you think that the Alpert group's suit was reasonable?

FOR CRITICAL ANALYSIS

30–10. When an aggressor takes over a target corporation, some of the target's assets may be sold and some of its personnel may be discharged. Thus, among the reasons for resisting a takeover attempt is that a takeover may not be in the best interests of the personnel of the target firm. What are the benefits that result from these changes? Consequently, what are the costs and benefits of the laws that restrict takeovers?

Online Activities

• ONLINE EXERCISE 30-1

Go to

www.CEOexpress.com,

the "CEO Express!" page maintained by ExpressCompany.com, Inc. Click on some of the links to determine what resources are available from this site and then answer the following questions:

- What resources might provide individuals, groups, or firms with background information on business firms that they may want to acquire?
- What information is available online to any business firm regarding the firm's market and its competitors?
- In the "Business Research" box, in the "Small/Family Business" category, click on the "SCORE" link. What is available on that Web site concerning small businesses?
- What links might you follow from these pages to read a business firm's annual reports and other shareholder communications?

• ONLINE EXERCISE 30-2

The U.S. Business Advisor Web site provides links to government information concerning business law and other topics. The site is maintained by the National Technical Information Service. Access this site at

www.business.gov,

and then do the following:

- Click on the "How To . . ." link, and browse through some of the links on that page. As a potential shareholder or investor seeking investment opportunities, which links might be most useful? As an aggressor seeking a takeover target, which resources might you want to use?
- From the main page, click on the "Common Questions," "Search," and "Browse" links to see what the sources offer. From which link or links might you find more information about the laws and regulations governing shareholders and securities?

CHAPTER 31 Investor Protection

> "It shall be unlawful for any person in the offer or sale of any security . . . to engage in any transaction, practice, or course of business which operates or would operate as a fraud or deceit upon the purchaser."
>
> Securities Act of 1933, Section 17

CONTENTS

LEARNING OBJECTIVES

After reading this chapter, you should be able to:

1. Define what is meant by the term *securities*.
2. Describe the purpose and provisions of the Securities Act of 1933.
3. Explain the purpose and provisions of the Securities Exchange Act of 1934.
4. Identify federal laws that specifically regulate investment companies.
5. Point out some of the features of state securities laws.

After the stock market crash of 1929, many members of Congress argued in favor of regulating securities markets. Basically, legislation for such regulation was enacted to provide investors with more information to help them make buying and selling decisions about **securities**—generally defined as any documents evidencing corporate ownership (stock) or debts (bonds)—and to prohibit deceptive, unfair, and manipulative practices. Today, the sale and transfer of securities are heavily regulated by federal and state statutes and by government agencies.

• **SECURITY**
Generally, a stock certificate, bond, note, debenture, warrant, or other document given as evidence of an ownership interest in a corporation or as a promise of repayment by a corporation.

This chapter will discuss the nature of federal securities regulations and their effects on the business world. First, though, it is necessary to understand the paramount role played by the Securities and Exchange Commission (SEC) in the regulation of federal securities laws. Because of its importance in this area, we examine the origin and functions of the SEC in the following *Landmark in the Law*.

Landmark in the Law •

THE SECURITIES AND EXCHANGE COMMISSION

In 1931, the Senate passed a resolution calling for an extensive investigation of securities trading. The investigation led, ultimately, to the passage by Congress of the Securities Act of 1933, which is also known as the *truth-in-securities* bill. In the following year, Congress passed the Securities Exchange Act. This 1934 act created the Securities and Exchange Commission as an independent regulatory agency whose function was to administer the 1933 and 1934 acts. Its major responsibilities in this respect are as follows:

1. Requiring disclosure of facts concerning offerings of securities listed on national securities exchanges and of certain securities traded over the counter (OTC).
2. Regulating the trade in securities on the thirteen national and regional securities exchanges and in the over-the-counter markets.
3. Investigating securities fraud.
4. Regulating the activities of securities brokers, dealers, and investment advisers and requiring their registration.
5. Supervising the activities of mutual funds.
6. Recommending administrative sanctions, injunctive remedies, and criminal prosecution against those who violate securities laws. (The SEC can bring enforcement actions for civil violations of federal securities laws. The Fraud Section of the Criminal Division of the Department of Justice prosecutes criminal violations.)

Since its creation, the SEC's regulatory functions have gradually been increased by legislation granting it authority in different areas. We look at the expanding powers of the SEC later in the chapter.

FOR CRITICAL ANALYSIS
What is the source of the national government's authority to regulate the securities industry?

Securities Act of 1933

The Securities Act of 1933[1] was designed to prohibit various forms of fraud and to stabilize the securities industry by requiring that all relevant information concerning the issuance of securities be made available to the investing public. Essentially, the purpose of this act is to require disclosure.

¡NOTE! Congress intended the federal securities laws to protect the public from unethical business practices.

ON THE WEB
The Center for Corporate Law at the University of Cincinnati College of Law examines all of the acts discussed in this chapter. Go to www.law.uc.edu/CCL.

WHAT IS A SECURITY?

Section 2(1) of the Securities Act states that securities include the following:

> [A]ny note, stock, treasury stock, bond, debenture, evidence of indebtedness, certificate of interest or participation in any profit-sharing agreement, collateral-trust certificate, preorganization certificate or subscription, transferable share, investment contract, voting-trust certificate, certificate of deposit for a security, fractional undivided interest in oil, gas, or other mineral rights, or, in general, any interest or instrument commonly known as a "security," or any certificate of interest or participation in, temporary or interim certificate for, receipt for, guarantee of, or warrant or right to subscribe to or purchase, any of the foregoing.[2]

Generally, the courts have interpreted the Securities Act's definition of what constitutes a security[3] to mean that a security exists in any transaction in which a person

1. 15 U.S.C. Sections 77–77aa.
2. 15 U.S.C. Section 77b(1). Amendments in 1982 added stock options.
3. See 15 U.S.C. Section 77b(a)(1).

"Spending and investing differ only in degree, depending on the length of time elapsing between the expenditure and the enjoyment."

IRVING FISHER, 1867–1947
(U.S. economist)

(1) invests (2) in a common enterprise (3) reasonably expecting profits (4) derived *primarily* or *substantially* from others' managerial or entrepreneurial efforts.[4]

For our purposes, it is probably most convenient to think of securities in their most common forms—stocks and bonds issued by corporations. Bear in mind, however, that securities can take many forms and have been held to include whiskey, cosmetics, worms, beavers, boats, vacuum cleaners, muskrats, and cemetery lots, as well as investment contracts in condominiums, franchises, limited partnerships, oil or gas or other mineral rights, and farm animals accompanied by care agreements.

REGISTRATION STATEMENT

¡DON'T FORGET!
The purpose of the Securities Act of 1933 is disclosure—the SEC does not consider whether a security is worth the investment.

Section 5 of the Securities Act of 1933 broadly provides that if a security does not qualify for an exemption, that security must be *registered* before it is offered to the public either through the mails or through any facility of interstate commerce, including securities exchanges. Issuing corporations must file a *registration statement* with the SEC. Investors must be provided with a prospectus that describes the security being sold, the issuing corporation, and the investment or risk attaching to the security. In principle, the registration statement and the prospectus supply sufficient information to enable unsophisticated investors to evaluate the financial risk involved.

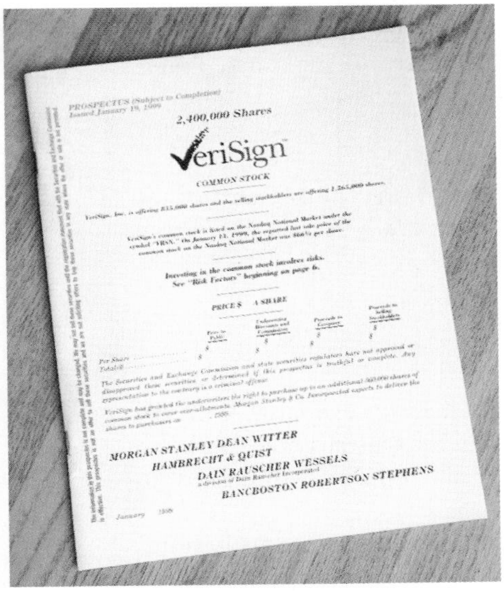

A REGISTRATION STATEMENT DISCUSSES A SECURITY THAT IS BEING OFFERED TO THE PUBLIC. WHAT ARE THE MAJOR CONTENTS OF A REGISTRATION STATEMENT?

Contents of the Registration Statement The registration statement must include the following:

1. A description of the significant provisions of the security offered for sale, including the relationship between that security and the other capital securities of the registrant. Also, the corporation must disclose how it intends to use the proceeds of the sale.
2. A description of the registrant's properties and business.
3. A description of the management of the registrant and its security holdings; remuneration; and other benefits, including pensions and stock options. Any interests of directors or officers in any material transactions with the corporation must be disclosed.
4. A financial statement certified by an independent public accounting firm.
5. A description of pending lawsuits.

Those who register securities offerings with the SEC should realize that as of 1998, the SEC requires certain documents, or portions of documents, to be written in "plain English." See this chapter's *The Letter of the Law* for more information on this topic.

Other Requirements Before filing the registration statement and the prospectus with the SEC, the corporation is allowed to obtain an *underwriter*—a company that agrees to purchase the new issue of securities for resale to the public. There is a twenty-day waiting period (which can be accelerated by the SEC) after registration before the sale can take place. During this period, oral offers between interested investors and the issuing corporation concerning the purchase and sale of the proposed securities may take place, and very limited written advertising is allowed. At this time, the so-called **red herring** prospectus may be distributed. It gets its name from the red legend printed across it stating that the registration has been filed but has not become effective.

• **RED HERRING**
A preliminary prospectus that can be distributed to potential investors after the registration statement (for a securities offering) has been filed with the Securities and Exchange Commission. The name derives from the red legend printed across the prospectus stating that the registration has been filed but has not become effective.

4. *SEC v. W. J. Howey Co.*, 328 U.S. 293, 66 S.Ct. 1100, 90 L.Ed. 1244 (1946).

The Letter of the Law — SECURITIES OFFERINGS IN PLAIN ENGLISH

The letter of the law with respect to securities offerings is becoming clearer, thanks to a "plain-English" rule adopted by the SEC in 1998.[a] The rule requires companies to use plain English in their securities offerings documents. For example, in any prospectus filed with the SEC, a company must utilize plain-English principles in the language and in the design of the cover page, summary, and risk-factor sections of the prospectus. Agency officials have indicated that they do not act as "grammar police," but they do evaluate certain documents filed with the SEC to determine the clarity of communication. The SEC has also taken steps to get rid of the "gobbledegook" in its existing and new rules. At one point, it even held a contest among its employees to see who could do the best job of translating either an SEC document or a document submitted to the agency into plain English.[b]

a. The SEC has published its *Plain English Handbook* on its Web site at **www.sec.gov**.

THE BOTTOM LINE

Informing investors in "plain English" about the nature of—and the risks involved in—securities investments is considered by the SEC to be consistent with the disclosure goals of both the 1933 Securities Act and the 1934 Securities Exchange Act.

b. *BNA's Corporate Counsel Weekly,* Vol. 13, No. 4 (January 28, 1998), p. 1.

After the waiting period, the registered securities can be legally bought and sold. Written advertising is allowed in the form of a **tombstone ad,** so named because historically the format resembles a tombstone. Such ads simply tell the investor where and how to obtain a prospectus. Normally, any other type of advertising is prohibited.

• **TOMBSTONE AD**
An advertisement, historically in a format resembling a tombstone, of a securities offering. The ad informs potential investors of where and how they may obtain a prospectus.

EXEMPT SECURITIES

A number of specific securities are exempt from the registration requirements of the Securities Act of 1933. These securities—which can also generally be resold without being registered—include the following:[5]

1. All bank securities sold prior to July 27, 1933.
2. Commercial paper, if the maturity date does not exceed nine months.
3. Securities of charitable organizations.
4. Securities resulting from a corporate reorganization issued for exchange with the issuer's existing security holders and certificates issued by trustees, receivers, or debtors in possession under the bankruptcy laws (bankruptcy is discussed in Chapter 23).
5. Securities issued exclusively for exchange with the issuer's existing security holders, provided no commission is paid (for example, stock dividends and stock splits).
6. Securities issued to finance the acquisition of railroad equipment.
7. Any insurance, endowment, or annuity contract issued by a state-regulated insurance company.
8. Government-issued securities.
9. Securities issued by banks, savings and loan associations, farmers' cooperatives, and similar institutions subject to supervision by governmental authorities.
10. In consideration of the "small amount involved,"[6] an issuer's offer of up to $5 million in securities in any twelve-month period.

¡BE AWARE!
The issuer of an exempt security does not have to disclose the same information that other issuers do.

For the last exemption, under Regulation A,[7] the issuer must file with the SEC a notice of the issue and an offering circular, which must also be provided to investors

5. 15 U.S.C. Section 77c.
6. 15 U.S.C. Section 77c(b).
7. 17 C.F.R. Sections 230.251–230.263.

before the sale. This is a much simpler and less expensive process than the procedures associated with full registration. Companies are allowed to "test the waters" for potential interest before preparing the offering circular. To test the waters means to determine potential interest without actually selling any securities or requiring any commitment on the part of those who are interested. Small-business issuers (companies with less than $25 million in annual revenues and less than $25 million in outstanding voting stock) can also use an integrated registration and reporting system that uses simpler forms than the full registration system.

Exhibit 31–1 summarizes the securities and transactions (discussed next) that are exempt from the registration requirements under the Securities Act of 1933 and SEC regulations.

EXEMPT TRANSACTIONS

An issuer of securities that are not exempt under one of the ten categories listed in the previous subsection can avoid the high cost and complicated procedures associated with registration by taking advantage of certain transaction exemptions. An offering may qualify for more than one exemption. These exemptions are very broad, and thus many sales occur without registration. Because there is some overlap in the coverage of the exemptions, an offering may qualify for more than one.

EXHIBIT 31–1 • Exemptions under the 1933 Securities Act

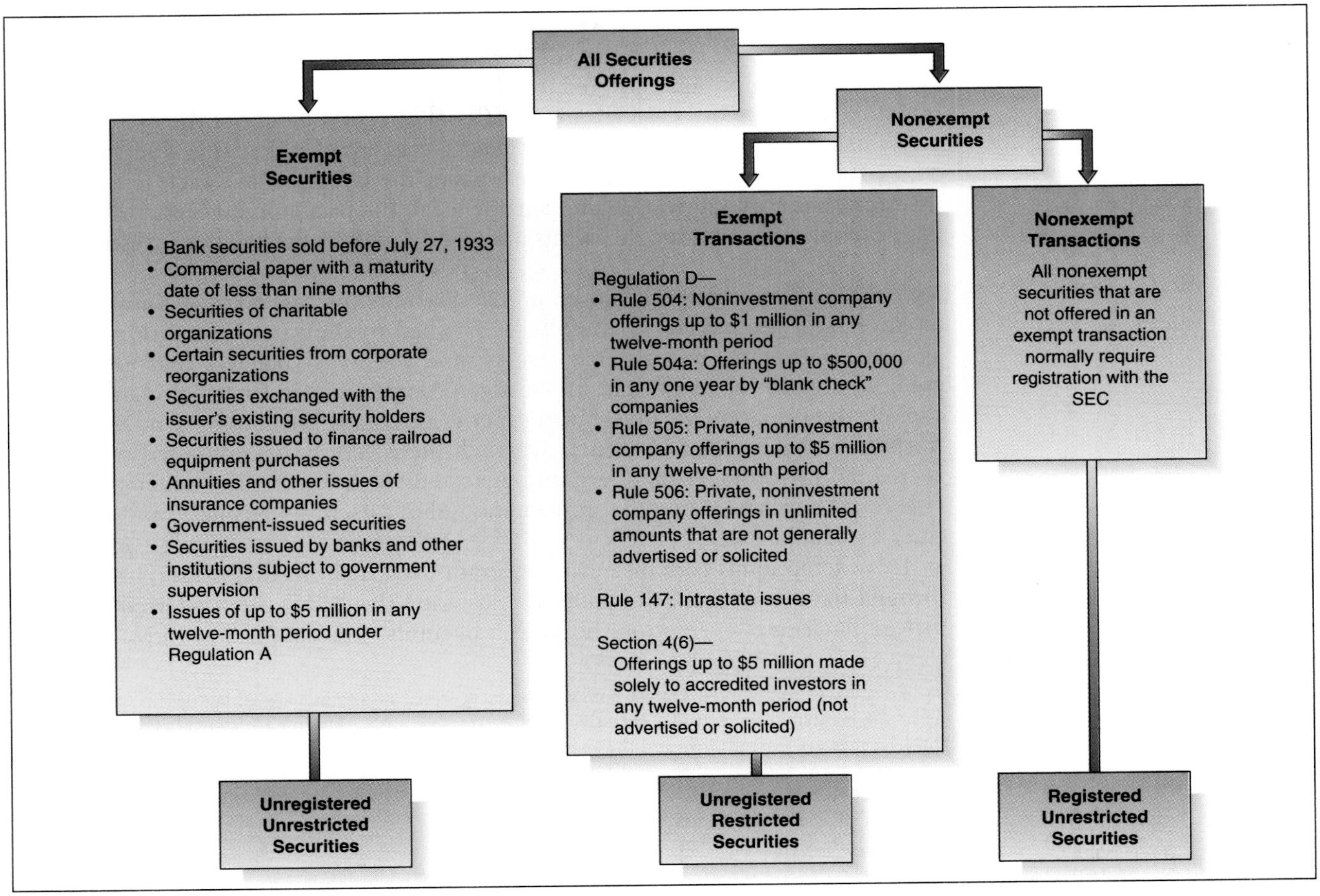

Small Offerings—Regulation D The SEC's Regulation D contains four separate exemptions from registration requirements for limited offers (offers that either involve a small amount of money or are made in a limited manner). Regulation D provides that any of these offerings made during any twelve-month period are exempt from the registration requirements.

Rule 504. Noninvestment company offerings up to $1 million in any one year are exempt. In contrast to investment companies (discussed later in this chapter), noninvestment companies are firms that are not engaged primarily in the business of investing or trading in securities.

Rule 504a. Offerings up to $500,000 in any one year by so-called blank check companies—companies with no specific business plans except to locate and acquire presently unknown businesses or opportunities—are exempt if no general solicitation or advertising is used; the SEC is notified of the sales; and precaution is taken against nonexempt, unregistered resales.[8] The limits on advertising and unregistered resales do not apply if the offering is made solely in states that provide for registration and disclosure and the securities are sold in compliance with those provisions.[9]

• **ACCREDITED INVESTORS**
In the context of securities offerings, "sophisticated" investors, such as banks, insurance companies, investment companies, the issuer's executive officers and directors, and persons whose income or net worth exceeds certain limits.

Rule 505. Private, noninvestment company offerings up to $5 million in any twelve-month period are exempt, regardless of the number of **accredited investors** (banks, insurance companies, investment companies, the issuer's executive officers and directors, and persons whose income or net worth exceeds certain limits), so long as there are no more than thirty-five unaccredited investors; no general solicitation or advertising is used; the SEC is notified of the sales; and precaution is taken against nonexempt, unregistered resales. If the sale involves any unaccredited investors, *all* investors must be given material information about the offering company, its business, and the securities before the sale. Unlike Rule 506 (discussed next), Rule 505 includes no requirement that the issuer believe each unaccredited investor "has such knowledge and experience in financial and business matters that he is capable of evaluating the merits and the risks of the prospective investment."[10]

Rule 506. Private offerings in unlimited amounts that are not generally solicited or advertised are exempt if the SEC is notified of the sales; precaution is taken against nonexempt, unregistered resales; and the issuer believes that each unaccredited investor has sufficient knowledge or experience in financial matters to be capable of evaluating the investment's merits and risks. There may be no more than thirty-five unaccredited investors, although there may be an unlimited number of accredited investors. If there are *any* unaccredited investors, the issuer must provide to *all* purchasers material information about itself, its business, and the securities before the sale.[11]

This exemption is perhaps most important to those firms that want to raise funds through the sale of securities without registering them. It is often referred to as the *private placement* exemption, because it exempts "transactions not involving any

¡KEEP IN MIND!
An investor can be "sophisticated" by virtue of his or her education and experience or by investing through a knowledgeable, experienced representative.

8. Precautions to be taken against nonexempt, unregistered resales include asking the investor whether he or she is buying the securities for others; before the sale, disclosing to each purchaser in writing that the securities are unregistered and thus cannot be resold, except in an exempt transaction, without first being registered; and indicating on the certificates that the securities are unregistered and restricted.
9. 17 C.F.R. Section 230.504a.
10. 17 C.F.R. Section 230.505.
11. 17 C.F.R. Section 230.506.

public offering."[12] This provision applies to private offerings to a limited number of persons who are sufficiently sophisticated and in a sufficiently strong bargaining position to be able to assume the risk of the investment (and who thus have no need for federal registration protection), as well as to private offerings to similarly situated institutional investors.

Small Offerings—Section 4(6) Under Section 4(6) of the Securities Act of 1933, an offer made *solely* to accredited investors is exempt if its amount is not more than $5 million. Any number of accredited investors may participate, but no unaccredited investors may do so. No general solicitation or advertising may be used; the SEC must be notified of all sales; and precaution must be taken against nonexempt, unregistered resales. Precaution is necessary because these are *restricted* securities and may be resold only by registration or in an exempt transaction.[13] (The securities purchased and sold by most people who deal in stock are called, in contrast, *unrestricted* securities.)

Intrastate Issues—Rule 147 Also exempt are intrastate transactions involving purely local offerings.[14] This exemption applies to most offerings that are restricted to residents of the state in which the issuing company is organized and doing business. For nine months after the last sale, virtually no resales may be made to nonresidents, and precautions must be taken against this possibility. These offerings remain subject to applicable laws in the state of issue.

Resales Most securities can be resold without registration (although some resales may be subject to restrictions, which are discussed above in connection with specific exemptions). The Securities Act of 1933 provides exemptions for resales by most persons other than issuers or underwriters. The average investor who sells shares of stock does not have to file a registration statement with the SEC. Resales of restricted securities acquired under Rule 504a, Rule 505, Rule 506, or Section 4(6), however, trigger the registration requirements unless the party selling them complies with Rule 144 or Rule 144A. These rules are sometimes referred to as "safe harbors."

Rule 144. Rule 144 exempts restricted securities from registration on resale if there is adequate current public information about the issuer, the person selling the securities has owned them for at least two years, they are sold in certain limited amounts in unsolicited brokers' transactions, and the SEC is given notice of the resale.[15] "Adequate current public information" consists of the reports that certain companies are required to file under the Securities Exchange Act of 1934. A person who has owned the securities for at least three years is subject to none of these requirements, unless the person is an affilate. An *affiliate* is one who controls, is controlled by, or is in common control with the issuer. Sales of *nonrestricted* securities by an affiliate are also subject to the requirements for an exemption under Rule 144 (except that the affiliate need not have owned the securities for at least two years).

Rule 144A. Securities that at the time of issue are not of the same class as securities listed on a national securities exchange or quoted in a U.S. automated interdealer quotation system may be resold under Rule 144A.[16] They may be sold only to a qualified institutional buyer (an institution, such as an insurance company, an

12. 15 U.S.C. Section 77d(2).
13. 15 U.S.C. Section 77d(6).
14. 15 U.S.C. Section 77c(a)(11); 17 C.F.R. Section 230.147.
15. 17 C.F.R. Section 230.144.
16. 17 C.F.R. Section 230.144A.

¡CONTRAST! Securities do not have to be held for two years to be exempt from registration on a resale under Rule 144A, as they do under Rule 144.

investment company, or a bank, that owns and invests at least $100 million in securities). The seller must take reasonable steps to ensure that the buyer knows that the seller is relying on the exemption under Rule 144A. A sample restricted stock certificate is shown in Exhibit 31–2.

VIOLATIONS OF THE 1933 ACT

As mentioned, the SEC has the power to investigate and bring civil enforcement actions against companies that violate federal securities laws, including the Securities Act of 1933. Criminal violations are prosecuted by the Department of Justice. Violators may be penalized by fines up to $10,000, imprisonment for up to five years, or both. Private parties may also bring suits against those who violate federal securities laws. Those who purchase securities and suffer harm as a result of false or omitted statements, or other violations, may bring a suit in a federal court to recover their losses and other damages.

Securities Exchange Act of 1934

The Securities Exchange Act of 1934 provides for the regulation and registration of securities exchanges; brokers; dealers; and national securities associations, such as the National Association of Securities Dealers (NASD). The SEC regulates the

EXHIBIT 31–2 • A Sample Restricted Stock Certificate

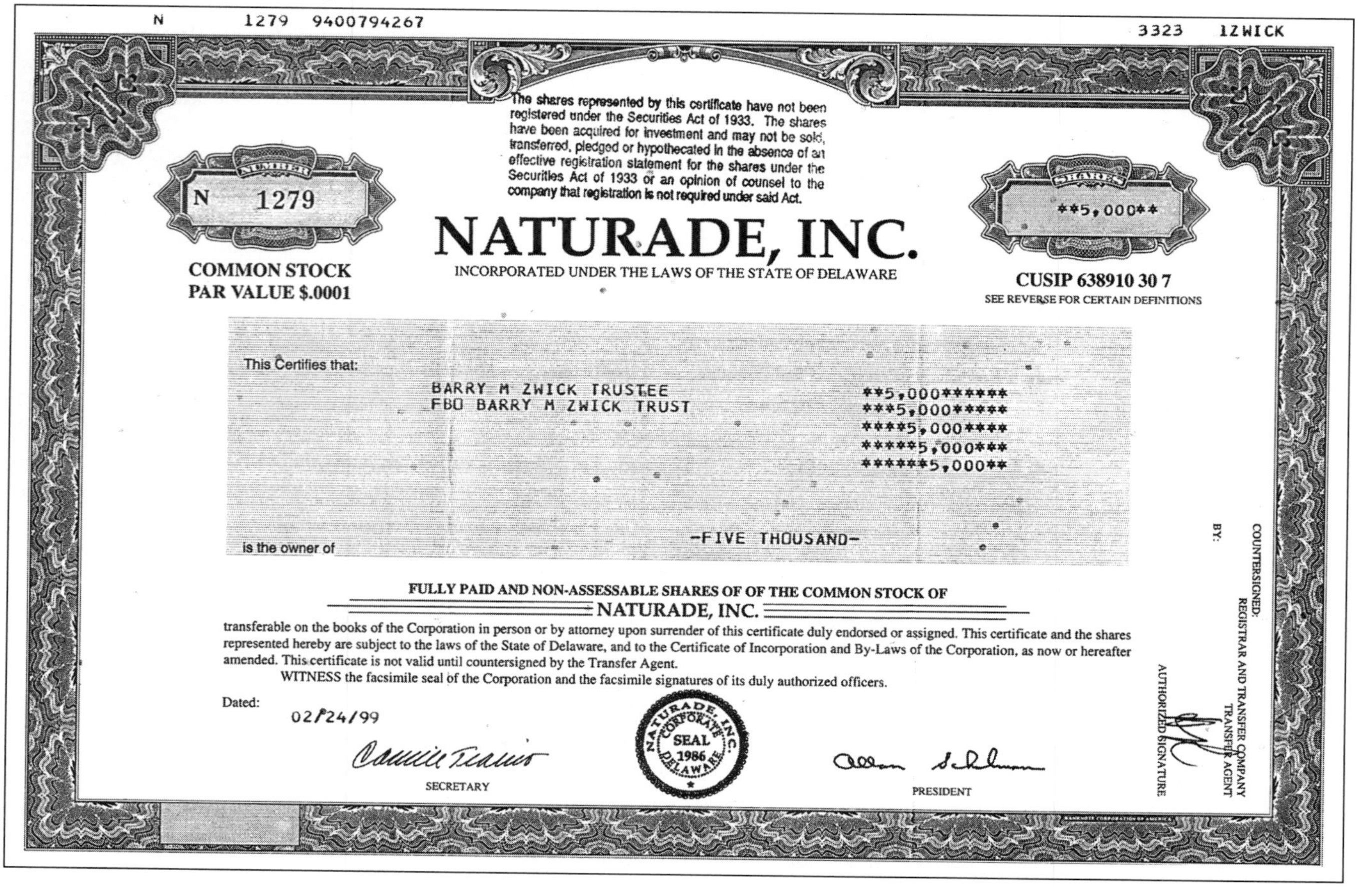
N 1279 9400794267 3323 1ZWICK

The shares represented by this certificate have not been registered under the Securities Act of 1933. The shares have been acquired for investment and may not be sold, transferred, pledged or hypothecated in the absence of an effective registration statement for the shares under the Securities Act of 1933 or an opinion of counsel to the company that registration is not required under said Act.

NUMBER N 1279

SHARES **5,000**

NATURADE, INC.

INCORPORATED UNDER THE LAWS OF THE STATE OF DELAWARE

COMMON STOCK
PAR VALUE $.0001

CUSIP 638910 30 7
SEE REVERSE FOR CERTAIN DEFINITIONS

This Certifies that:
BARRY M ZWICK TRUSTEE
FBO BARRY M ZWICK TRUST

5,000****
5,000**
****5,000****
*****5,000***
******5,000**

is the owner of -FIVE THOUSAND-

FULLY PAID AND NON-ASSESSABLE SHARES OF OF THE COMMON STOCK OF
NATURADE, INC.

transferable on the books of the Corporation in person or by attorney upon surrender of this certificate duly endorsed or assigned. This certificate and the shares represented hereby are subject to the laws of the State of Delaware, and to the Certificate of Incorporation and By-Laws of the Corporation, as now or hereafter amended. This certificate is not valid until countersigned by the Transfer Agent.

WITNESS the facsimile seal of the Corporation and the facsimile signatures of its duly authorized officers.

Dated: 02/24/99

NATURADE, INC. CORPORATE SEAL 1986 DELAWARE

SECRETARY PRESIDENT

COUNTERSIGNED: REGISTRAR AND TRANSFER COMPANY TRANSFER AGENT
BY:
AUTHORIZED SIGNATURE

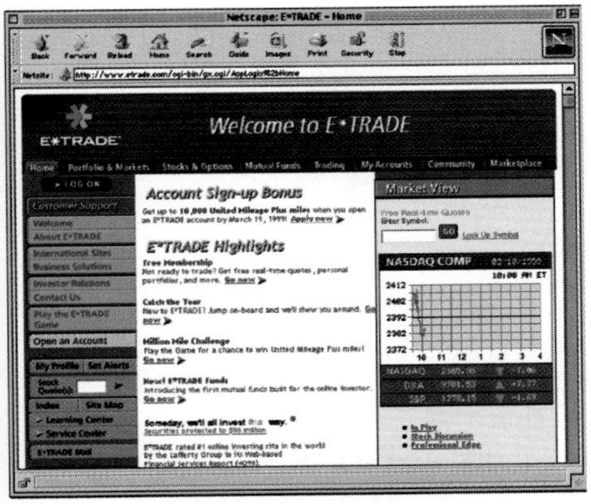

E*TRADE DISPLAYS ITS HOME PAGE. ONLINE TRADING THROUGH A FIRM SUCH AS E*TRADE DOES NOT INVOLVE PERSONAL CONTACT WITH A BROKER. DOES THIS MEAN THAT ONLINE TRADING IS UNREGULATED?

• **SEC RULE 10b-5**
A rule of the Securities and Exchange Commission that makes it unlawful, in connection with the purchase or sale of any security, to make any untrue statement of a material fact or to omit a material fact if such omission causes the statement to be misleading.

• **INSIDER TRADING**
The purchase or sale of securities on the basis of information that has not been made available to the public.

markets in which securities are traded by maintaining a continuous disclosure system for all corporations with securities on the securities exchanges and for those companies that have assets in excess of $10 million and five hundred or more shareholders. These corporations are referred to as Section 12 companies, because they are required to register their securities under Section 12 of the 1934 act.

The act regulates proxy solicitation for voting (discussed in Chapter 28) and allows the SEC to engage in market surveillance to regulate undesirable market practices such as fraud, market manipulation, and misrepresentation.

SECTION 10(b), SEC RULE 10b-5, AND INSIDER TRADING

Section 10(b) is one of the most important sections of the Securities Exchange Act of 1934. This section proscribes the use of "any manipulative or deceptive device or contrivance in contravention of such rules and regulations as the [SEC] may prescribe." Among the rules that the SEC has promulgated pursuant to the 1934 act is **SEC Rule 10b-5,** which prohibits the commission of fraud in connection with the purchase or sale of any security.

One of the most important purposes of Section 10(b) and SEC Rule 10b-5 relates to so-called **insider trading.** Because of their positions, corporate directors and officers often obtain advance inside information that can affect the future market value of the corporate stock. Obviously, their positions can give them a trading advantage over the general public and shareholders. The 1934 Securities Exchange Act defines inside information and extends liability to officers and directors for taking advantage of such information in their personal transactions when they know that it is unavailable to the persons with whom they are dealing.

Section 10(b) of the 1934 act and SEC Rule 10b-5 cover not only corporate officers, directors, and majority shareholders but also any persons having access to or receiving information of a nonpublic nature on which trading is based.

In the following classic case, a shareholder alleged that a corporate officer and a corporate director had breached their fiduciary duties by trading corporate shares on the basis of nonpublic information.

CASE 31.1 Diamond v. Oreamuno

Court of Appeals of New York, 1969.
24 N.Y.2d 494,
248 N.E.2d 910,
301 N.Y.S.2d 78.

HISTORICAL AND ETHICAL SETTING *Officers and directors owe fiduciary duties to their corporation and its shareholders with respect to corporate business and property. Shares in the corporation are private property, however, and trading in those shares is not usually a corporate transaction. Thus, at common law a century ago, directors and officers were considered to owe no fiduciary duties when they traded in the shares of their corporations. Directors or officers with inside information could trade with impunity without disclosing the information (as long as they avoided outright fraud). Today, in contrast, the law holds that officers and directors owe a fiduciary duty to their corporation not to engage in the trading of shares in the corporation on the basis of inside information.*

BACKGROUND AND FACTS The defendants in this case were the chairman of the board (Oreamuno) and president (Gonzalez) of Management Assistance, Inc. (MAI), a corporation that bought and leased computers, with maintenance services being provided by IBM. The defendants learned that IBM was going to increase its maintenance prices dramatically, to such an extent that MAI's profits would be cut by 75 percent per month. Just before the IBM maintenance price increase was announced, the defendants sold their MAI stock for $28 per share. After IBM publicly announced its price increase, MAI stock fell to $11 per share. A shareholder of the corporation (Diamond) brought

(Continued)

CASE 31.1—Continued

a shareholder's derivative lawsuit in a New York state court on behalf of MAI to recover the profits the defendants had made by selling their shares at the higher price. The trial court granted the defendants' motion to dismiss, and Diamond appealed.

IN THE WORDS OF THE COURT . . .
FULD, Chief Judge.

* * * *

Accepting the truth of the complaint's allegations, there is no question but that the defendants were guilty of withholding material information from the purchasers of the shares and, indeed, the defendants acknowledge that the facts asserted constitute a violation of rule 10b-5. * * * Of course, any individual purchaser, who could prove an injury as a result of a rule 10b-5 violation can bring his own action for rescission but we have not been referred to a single case in which such an action has been successfully prosecuted where the public sale of securities is involved. The reason for this is that sales of securities, whether through a stock exchange or over-the-counter, are characteristically anonymous transactions, usually handled through brokers, and the matching of the ultimate buyer with the ultimate seller presents virtually insurmountable obstacles. * * *

In view of the practical difficulties inherent in an action under the Federal law, the desirability of creating an effective common-law remedy is manifest. * * * There is ample room in a situation such as is here presented for a "private Attorney General" to come forward and enforce proper behavior on the part of corporate officials through the medium of the derivative action brought in the name of the corporation. Only by sanctioning such a cause of action will there be any effective method to prevent the type of abuse of corporate office complained of in this case.

DECISION AND REMEDY The court of appeals held that when corporate fiduciaries have breached their duty to the corporation by the use of nonpublic information, a shareholder may bring a derivative action for any profit resulting from the breach of duty.

FOR CRITICAL ANALYSIS—Economic Consideration *What is the difference between a suit brought by an individual investor-shareholder and a shareholder's derivative suit? (HINT: Review the discussion of the shareholder's derivative suit in Chapter 28.)*

"There are three kinds of lies: lies, damned lies, and statistics."
BENJAMIN DISRAELI, 1804–1881
(British prime minister, 1868, 1874–1880)

Disclosure under SEC Rule 10b-5 Any material omission or misrepresentation of material facts in connection with the purchase or sale of a security may violate not only Section 11 of the Securities Act of 1933 but also the antifraud provisions of Section 10(b) and SEC Rule 10b-5 of the 1934 act. The key to liability (which can be civil or criminal) under Section 10(b) and SEC Rule 10b-5 is whether the insider's information is *material.* The following are some examples of material facts calling for a disclosure under the rule:

1. A new ore discovery.
2. Fraudulent trading in the company stock by a broker-dealer.
3. A dividend change (whether up or down).
4. A contract for the sale of corporate assets.
5. A new discovery (process or product).
6. A significant change in the firm's financial condition.

Ironically, one of the effects of SEC Rule 10b-5 was to deter the disclosure of material information. • **EXAMPLE 31.1** A company announces that its projected earnings in a certain time period will be X amount. It turns out that the forecast is wrong. The earnings are in fact much lower, and the price of the company's stock is affected—negatively. The shareholders then bring a class-action suit against the company, alleging that the directors violated SEC Rule 10b-5 by disclosing misleading financial information. ●

In an attempt to rectify this problem and promote disclosure, Congress passed the Private Securities Litigation Reform Act of 1995. Among other things, the act provides a "safe harbor" for publicly held companies that make forward-looking statements, such as financial forecasts. Those who make such statements are protected against liability for securities fraud as long as the statements are accompanied by "meaningful cautionary statements identifying important factors that could cause actual results to differ materially from those in the forward-looking statement."[17]

The following is one of the landmark cases interpreting SEC Rule 10b-5. The SEC sued Texas Gulf Sulphur Company for issuing a misleading press release. The release underestimated the magnitude and the value of a mineral discovery. The SEC also sued several of Texas Gulf Sulphur's directors, officers, and employees under SEC Rule 10b-5 for purchasing large amounts of the corporate stock prior to the announcement of the corporation's rich ore discovery.

> **ON THE WEB**
>
> For information on investor protection, including answers to frequently asked questions on the topic of securities fraud, go to **www.securitieslaw.com**.

17. 15 U.S.C. Sections 77z-2, 78u-5.

CASE 31.2 SEC v. Texas Gulf Sulphur Co.

United States Court of Appeals,
Second Circuit, 1968.
401 F.2d 833.

HISTORICAL AND ENVIRONMENTAL SETTING *No court has ever held that every buyer or seller is entitled to all of the information relating to all of the circumstances in every stock transaction. By the mid-1950s, however, significant understatement of the value of the assets of a company had been held to be materially misleading.*[a] *In 1957, the Texas Gulf Sulphur Company (TGS) began exploring for minerals in eastern Canada. In March 1959, aerial geophysical surveys were conducted over more than fifteen thousand square miles of the area. The operations revealed numerous and extraordinary variations in the conductivity of the rock, which indicated a remarkable concentration of commercially exploitable minerals. One site of such variations was near Timmins, Ontario. On October 29 and 30, 1963, a ground survey of the site near Timmins indicated a need to drill for further evaluation.*

BACKGROUND AND FACTS The Texas Gulf Sulphur Company drilled a hole on November 12, 1963, that appeared to yield a core with an exceedingly high mineral content. TGS kept secret the results of the core sample. Officers and employees of the company made substantial purchases of TGS's stock or accepted stock options after learning of the ore discovery, even though further drilling was necessary to establish whether there was enough ore to be mined commercially. On April 11, 1964, an unauthorized report of the mineral find appeared in the newspapers. On the following day, April 12, TGS issued a press release that played down the discovery and stated that it was too early to tell whether the ore finding would be a significant one. Later on, TGS announced a strike of at least twenty-five million tons of ore, substantially driving up the price of TGS stock. The SEC brought suit in a federal district court against the officers and employees of TGS for violating the insider-trading prohibition of SEC Rule 10b-5. The officers and employees argued that the prohibition did not apply. They reasoned that the information on which they had traded was not material, as the mine had not been commercially proved. The court held that most of the defendants had not violated SEC Rule 10b-5, and the SEC appealed.

a. *Speed v. Transamerica Corp.*, 99 F.Supp. 808 (D.Del. 1951).

IN THE WORDS OF THE COURT . . .
WATERMAN, Circuit Judge.

* * * *

* * * [W]hether facts are material within Rule 10b-5 when the facts relate to a particular event and are undisclosed by those persons who are knowledgeable

(Continued)

CASE 31.2—Continued

thereof will depend at any given time upon a balancing of both the indicated probability that the event will occur and the anticipated magnitude of the event in light of the totality of the company activity. Here, * * * knowledge of the possibility, which surely was more than marginal, of the existence of a mine of the vast magnitude indicated by the remarkably rich drill core located rather close to the surface (suggesting mineability by the less expensive openpit method) within the confines of a large anomaly (suggesting an extensive region of mineralization) might well have affected the price of TGS stock and would certainly have been an important fact to a reasonable * * * investor in deciding whether he should buy, sell, or hold. After all, this first drill core was "unusually good and * * * excited the interest and speculation of those who knew about it."

* * * *

* * * [A] major factor in determining whether the * * * discovery was a material fact is the importance attached to the drilling results by those who knew about it. * * * [T]he timing by those who knew of it of their stock purchases and their purchases of *short-term* calls [rights to buy shares at a specified price within a specified time period]—purchases in some cases by individuals who had never before purchased calls or even TGS stock—virtually compels the inference that the insiders were influenced by the drilling results.

* * * *

We hold, therefore, that all transactions in TGS stock or calls by individuals apprised of the drilling results * * * were made in violation of Rule 10b-5.

DECISION AND REMEDY The U.S. Court of Appeals for the Second Circuit ruled in favor of the SEC. All of the trading by insiders who knew of the mineral find violated Rule 10b-5.

FOR CRITICAL ANALYSIS—Economic Consideration *Who is hurt by insider trading?*

Applicability of SEC Rule 10b-5 SEC Rule 10b-5 applies in virtually all cases concerning the trading of securities, whether on organized exchanges, in over-the-counter markets, or in private transactions. The rule covers notes, bonds, certificates of interest and participation in any profit-sharing agreement, agreements to form a corporation, and joint venture agreements; in short, it covers just about any form of security. It is immaterial whether a firm has securities registered under the 1933 act for the 1934 act to apply.

Although SEC Rule 10b-5 is applicable only when the requisites of federal jurisdiction—such as the use of the mails, of stock exchange facilities, or of any instrumentality of interstate commerce—are present, virtually no commercial transaction can be completed without such contact. In addition, the states have corporate securities laws, many of which include provisions similar to SEC Rule 10b-5.

ETHICAL ISSUE 31.1 ***Should insider trading be legal?*** SEC Rule 10b-5 has broad applicability. As will be discussed shortly, the rule covers not only corporate insiders but even "outsiders"—those who receive and trade on tips received from insiders. Investigating and prosecuting violations of SEC Rule 10b-5 is costly, both for the government and for those accused of insider trading. Some people doubt that such extensive regulation is necessary and even contend that insider trading should be legal. Would there be any benefit from the legalization of insider trading? To evaluate this question, review the facts in *SEC v. Texas Gulf Sulphur Co.* (Case 31.2 in this chapter). If insider trading were legal, the discovery of the ore sample would probably have caused many more company insiders to purchase stock. Consequently, the price of Texas Gulf's stock would have increased fairly quickly. These increases presumably would have attracted the attention of outside investors, who would have learned sooner that something positive had happened to the company and would thus have had the opportunity to purchase the stock. The higher demand for the stock would have more quickly translated into higher prices for the stock and hence, perhaps, a more efficient capital market.

Outsiders and SEC Rule 10b-5 The traditional insider-trading case involves true insiders—corporate officers, directors, and majority shareholders who have access to (and trade on) inside information. Increasingly, liability under Section 10(b) of the 1934 act and SEC Rule 10b-5 has been extended to include certain "outsiders"—those persons who trade on inside information acquired indirectly. Two theories have been developed under which outsiders may be held liable for insider trading: the *tipper/tippee theory* and the *misappropriation theory.*

TIPPEE
A person who receives inside information.

Tipper/Tippee Theory. Anyone who acquires inside information as a result of a corporate insider's breach of his or her fiduciary duty can be liable under SEC Rule 10b-5. This liability extends to **tippees** (those who receive "tips" from insiders) and even remote tippees (tippees of tippees).

The key to liability under this theory is that the inside information be obtained as a result of someone's breach of a fiduciary duty to the corporation whose shares are involved in the trading. Unless there is a breach of a duty not to disclose inside information, the disclosure was in exchange for personal benefit, and the tippee knows of this breach (or should know of it) and benefits from it, there is no liability under this theory.[18] Is the offering of a tip as a gift of profits to someone with whom the insider has a close relationship enough to infer that the insider realized a personal benefit? That was an issue in the following case.

18. See, for example, *Chiarella v. United States,* 445 U.S. 222, 100 S.Ct. 1108, 63 L.Ed.2d 348 (1980); and *Dirks v. SEC,* 463 U.S. 646, 103 S.Ct. 3255, 77 L.Ed.2d 911 (1983).

CASE 31.3 SEC v. Warde

United States Court of Appeals,
Second Circuit, 1998.
151 F.3d 42.
www.tourolaw.edu/2ndcircuit/July98[a]

HISTORICAL AND SOCIAL SETTING *In 1983, the United States Supreme Court considered a case involving alleged insider trading by a financial analyst named Raymond Dirks. In that case, the Court held that for a recipient of material, nonpublic information to be liable for insider trading, the person who disclosed the information must benefit from the disclosure.*[b] *In subsequent cases, the Securities and Exchange Commission (SEC) often found it difficult to prove that the tipper benefited from passing on inside information.*

BACKGROUND AND FACTS Edward Downe was a close friend of Fred Sullivan, chairman of Kidde, Inc. At Sullivan's request, Downe became a director of Kidde. Thomas Warde was a good friend of Downe. In June 1987, Sullivan learned that Kidde was the target of a takeover attempt by Hanson Trust PLC, a British firm.

a. This page provides access to opinions of the U.S. Court of Appeals for the Second Circuit decided in July 1998. Scroll down the list of cases to the *Warde* case and click on the link to access the opinion.

b. *Dirks v. SEC,* 463 U.S. 646, 103 S.Ct. 3255, 77 L.Ed.2d 911 (1983).

(Continued)

CASE 31.3—Continued

After negotiations, the Kidde board announced in August that it would merge with Hanson. The price of Kidde stock increased, and warrants for the shares, which had been priced at $1 in June, went to $26.50.[c] Between learning about the takeover attempt in June and the merger in August, Downe and Warde bought and sold warrants several times, earning very large profits. The SEC filed a suit in a federal district court against Warde and others, alleging insider trading in violation, in part, of Section 10(b). Warde contended that his purchases were based on market savvy, rumor, and public information. The jury found him liable. The court ordered him to pay more than $3 million in penalties and interest. Warde appealed to the U.S. Court of Appeals for the Second Circuit.

c. A warrant is an agreement to buy stock at a certain price before a certain date. If, before the warrant is exercised, the price goes up, the buyer profits. If the price never exceeds the level in the warrant, the warrant is worthless.

IN THE WORDS OF THE COURT . . .

LEVAL, Circuit Judge:

* * * *

To affirm Warde's liability as a tippee * * *, we must find sufficient evidence to permit a reasonable finding that * * * Downe benefitted by the disclosure to Warde. * * *

* * * *

* * * [In *Dirks v. SEC*, 463 U.S. 646, 103 S.Ct. 3255, 77 L.Ed.2d 911 (1983), the United States] Supreme Court * * * made plain that to prove a Section 10(b) violation, the SEC need not show that the tipper expected or received a specific or tangible benefit in exchange for the tip. Rather, the "benefit" element of Section 10(b) is satisfied when the tipper "intend[s] to benefit the * * * recipient" or "makes a gift of confidential information to a trading relative or friend."

Under this standard, Downe clearly benefitted from Warde's inside trades. Warde's trades "resemble[d] trading by the insider himself followed by a gift of the profits to the recipient." The close friendship between Downe and Warde suggests that Downe's tip was "inten[ded] to benefit" Warde, and therefore allows a jury finding that Downe's tip breached a duty under Section 10(b).

DECISION AND REMEDY The U.S. Court of Appeals for the Second Circuit affirmed the lower court's decision, concluding that the SEC presented sufficient evidence to support every element necessary to hold Warde liable. Warde was ordered to pay the fines, with interest.

FOR CRITICAL ANALYSIS—Social Consideration *How does the decision in this case make it easier for the SEC to win in other insider-trading cases?*

Misappropriation Theory. Liability for insider trading may also be established under the misappropriation theory. This theory holds that if an individual wrongfully obtains (misappropriates) inside information and trades on it for his or her personal gain, then the individual should be held liable because, in essence, the individual stole information rightfully belonging to another.

The misappropriation theory has been controversial because it significantly extends the reach of SEC Rule 10b-5 to outsiders who would not ordinarily be deemed fiduciaries of the corporations in whose stock they trade. In the following case, the United States Supreme Court addressed the issue of whether liability under Rule 10b-5 can be based on the misappropriation theory.

CASE 31.4 United States v. O'Hagan

Supreme Court of the United States, 1997.
521 U.S. 642,
117 S.Ct. 2199,
138 L.Ed.2d 724.
supct.law.cornell.edu/supct[a]

COMPANY PROFILE *The law firm of Dorsey & Whitney LLP (Limited Liability Partnership) was founded in 1912. Today, Dorsey & Whitney is one of the forty largest law firms in the United States, with more than five hundred lawyers and seven hundred support staff. The firm is based in Minneapolis, Minnesota, with offices in a dozen other U.S. cities and in London, Brussels, and Hong Kong. The firm's attorneys have included Harry Blackmun, a former United States Supreme Court justice, and Walter Mondale, a former vice president of the United States and ambassador to Japan. The firm is organized into two large groups, each of which is broken down into smaller "practice" groups. These smaller groups include "Mergers & Acquisitions," the members of which, according to the firm's Web site at* ***www.dorseylaw.com****, "have extensive experience in all types of mergers and acquisitions work."*

BACKGROUND AND FACTS James O'Hagan was a partner in the law firm of Dorsey & Whitney. Grand Metropolitan PLC (Grand Met), a United Kingdom firm, hired Dorsey & Whitney to assist in a takeover of the Pillsbury Company. Before Grand Met made its tender offer, O'Hagan bought shares of Pillsbury stock. When the tender offer was announced, the price of Pillsbury stock increased by more than 35 percent. O'Hagan sold his shares for a profit of over $4 million. The Securities and Exchange Commission (SEC) prosecuted O'Hagan for, among other things, securities fraud in violation of Rule 10b-5 under the misappropriation theory. The SEC contended that O'Hagan breached his fiduciary duties to his law firm and to Grand Met. When O'Hagan was convicted, he appealed to the U.S. Court of Appeals for the Eighth Circuit, which reversed the convictions. The SEC appealed to the United States Supreme Court.

a. This page provides access to some of the published opinions of the United States Supreme Court. In the right-hand column, in the "From 1990–1998, by party name" list, in the "1997" row, click on "2nd party." When that page opens, find the *O'Hagan* case name and click on the link. From that page, click on the appropriate link to access the Court's opinion.

IN THE WORDS OF THE COURT . . .
JUSTICE GINSBURG delivered the opinion of the Court.

* * * *

* * * [M]isappropriation * * * satisfies [Section] 10(b)'s requirement that chargeable conduct involve a "deceptive device or contrivance" used "in connection with" the purchase or sale of securities. * * * [M]isappropriators * * * deal in deception. A fiduciary who pretends loyalty to the principal while secretly converting the principal's information for personal gain dupes or defrauds the principal.

* * * *

* * * [T]he fiduciary's fraud is consummated * * * when, without disclosure to his principal, he uses the information to purchase or sell securities. * * *

* * * *

* * * An investor's informational disadvantage *vis-a-vis* a misappropriator with material, nonpublic information stems from contrivance, not luck; it is a disadvantage that cannot be overcome with research or skill.

DECISION AND REMEDY The United States Supreme Court held that liability under Rule 10b-5 can be based on the misappropriation theory, reversed the judgment, and remanded the case.

FOR CRITICAL ANALYSIS—Ethical Consideration *If a nonlawyer employee of Dorsey & Whitney, such as a paralegal, learned about the tender offer and traded profitably on the inside information, could the employee be held liable under the misappropriation theory? Why or why not?*

INSIDER REPORTING AND TRADING—SECTION 16(b)

Officers, directors, and certain large stockholders[19] of Section 12 corporations (corporations that are required to register their securities under Section 12 of the 1934 act) must file reports with the SEC concerning their ownership and trading of the corporations' securities.[20] To discourage such insiders from using nonpublic information about their companies for their personal benefit in the stock market, Section 16(b) of the 1934 act provides for the recapture by the corporation of all profits realized by an insider on any purchase and sale or sale and purchase of the corporation's stock within any six-month period.[21] It is irrelevant whether the insider actually uses inside information; all such short-swing profits must be returned to the corporation.

Section 16(b) applies not only to stock but to warrants, options, and securities convertible into stock. In addition, the courts have fashioned complex rules for determining profits. Corporate insiders are wise to seek specialized counsel prior to trading in the corporation's stock. Exhibit 31–3 compares the effects of SEC Rule 10b-5 and Section 16(b).

---

19. Those stockholders owning 10 percent of the class of equity securities registered under Section 12 of the 1934 act.
20. 15 U.S.C. Section 78*l*.
21. When a decline is predicted in the market for a particular stock, one can realize profits by "selling short"—selling at a high price and repurchasing later at a lower price to cover the "short sale."

EXHIBIT 31–3 • Comparison of Coverage, Application, and Liabilities under SEC Rule 10b-5 and Section 16(b)

AREAS OF COMPARISON	SEC RULE 10b-5	SECTION 16(b)
What is the subject matter of the transaction?	Any security (does not have to be registered).	Any security (does not have to be registered).
What transactions are covered?	Purchase or sale.	Short-swing purchase and sale or short-swing sale and purchase.
Who is subject to liability?	Virtually anyone with inside information under a duty to disclose—including officers, directors, controlling stockholders, and tippees.	Officers, directors, and certain 10 percent stockholders.
Is omission or misrepresentation necessary for liability?	Yes.	No.
Are there any exempt transactions?	No.	Yes, there are a variety of exemptions.
Is direct dealing with the party necessary?	No.	No.
Who may bring an action?	A person transacting with an insider, the SEC, or a purchaser or seller damaged by a wrongful act.	A corporation or a shareholder by derivative action.

PROXY STATEMENTS

Section 14(a) of the Securities Exchange Act of 1934 regulates the solicitation of proxies from shareholders of Section 12 companies. The SEC regulates the content of proxy statements. As discussed in Chapter 28, a proxy statement is a statement that is sent to shareholders by corporate officials who are requesting authority to vote on behalf of the shareholders in a particular election on specified issues. Whoever solicits a proxy must fully and accurately disclose in the proxy statement all of the facts that are pertinent to the matter on which the shareholders are to vote. SEC Rule 14a-9 is similar to the antifraud provisions of SEC Rule 10b-5. Remedies for violation are extensive; they range from injunctions that prevent a vote from being taken to monetary damages.

VIOLATIONS OF THE 1934 ACT

Violations of Section 10(b) of the Securities Exchange Act of 1934 and SEC Rule 10b-5 include insider trading. This is a criminal offense, with criminal penalties. Violators of these laws may also be subject to civil liability. For any sanctions to be imposed, however, there must be *scienter*—the violator must have had an intent to defraud or knowledge of his or her misconduct (see Chapter 12). *Scienter* can be proved by showing that a defendant made false statements or wrongfully failed to disclose material facts. (For a further discussion of *scienter* and liability for insider trading, see this chapter's *Business Law in Action*.)

Violations of Section 16(b) include the sale by insiders of stock acquired less than six months before the sale. These violations are subject to civil sanctions. Liability under Section 16(b) is strict liability. *Scienter* is not required.

Criminal Penalties For violations of Section 10(b) and Rule 10b-5, an individual may be fined up to $1 million, imprisoned for up to ten years, or both. A partnership or a corporation may be fined up to $2.5 million.

Civil Sanctions Both the SEC and private parties can bring actions to seek civil sanctions against violators of the 1934 act.

The Insider Trading Sanctions Act of 1984 permits the SEC to bring suit in a federal district court against anyone violating or aiding in a violation of the 1934 act or SEC rules by purchasing or selling a security while in the possession of material nonpublic information.[22] The violation must occur on or through the facilities of a national securities exchange or from or through a broker or dealer. Transactions pursuant to a public offering by an issuer of securities are excepted. The court may assess as a penalty as much as triple the profits gained or the loss avoided by the guilty party. Profit or loss is defined as "the difference between the purchase or sale price of the security and the value of that security as measured by the trading price of the security at a reasonable period of time after public dissemination of the nonpublic information."[23]

The Insider Trading and Securities Fraud Enforcement Act of 1988 enlarged the class of persons who may be subject to civil liability for insider-trading violations. This act also gave the SEC authority to award **bounty payments** (rewards given by

• **BOUNTY PAYMENT**
A reward (payment) given to a person or persons who perform a certain service—such as informing legal authorities of illegal actions.

22. 15 U.S.C. Section 78u(d)(2)(A).
23. 15 U.S.C. Section 78u(d)(2)(C).

Business Law in Action • INSIDER TRADING: THE USE-POSSESSION DEBATE

An emerging issue in insider-trading cases has to do with the *scienter* requirement for insider-trading liability. As discussed elsewhere, *scienter* requires an intent to defraud or to deceive another. The question is this: Does the mere *possession* of inside information while trading in securities establish an intent to defraud, or must the trader actually *use* the inside information for intent to be established?

On one side of this possession-use debate are the government and the SEC, which have adopted the position that the intent to defraud can be inferred when a person trades in securities while in the possession of inside information. This position was bolstered by a 1993 case decided by the U.S. Court of Appeals for the Second Circuit, *United States v. Teicher.*[a] In that case, the court suggested that proof of the possession of inside information is "sufficient to sustain an insider-trading prosecution and that the government need not affirmatively prove that the investor used the information in formulating his trade." Among other things, the court noted that inside information has a subtle, and perhaps unconscious effect, on traders: "Unlike a loaded weapon which may stand ready but unused, material information cannot lay idle in the human brain."

On the other side of the debate are those who maintain that for liability for insider trading to be established, the government must show that the trading was actually based on the information. In *United States v. Smith,*[b] one of the few court decisions to squarely address this issue, the U.S. Court of Appeals for the Ninth Circuit came down firmly on the "use" side of the debate. The court noted that the Supreme Court, in *O'Hagan* as well as in earlier decisions,[c] stressed that a violation of Rule 10b-5 requires an intent to deceive or defraud investors. In the opinion of the Ninth Circuit, the SEC's "possession" standard was inconsistent with the Supreme Court's position because the standard was too broad—it extended beyond situations involving actual fraud. "For instance," said the court, "an investor who has a preexisting plan to trade, and who carries through with that plan after coming into possession of material nonpublic information, does not intend to defraud or deceive; he simply intends to implement his pre-possession financial strategy."

The Ninth Circuit stated that it did "not take lightly" the SEC's argument that a "use" requirement poses difficulties of proof. The court, however, concluded that the difficulties were not insurmountable and that various types of circumstantial evidence might be used to demonstrate use. "Suppose, for instance, that an individual who has never before invested comes into possession of material nonpublic information and the very next day invests a significant sum of money." The court was "confident that the government would have little trouble demonstrating 'use' in such a situation, or in other situations in which unique trading patterns or unusually large trading quantities suggest that an investor had used inside information."

FOR CRITICAL ANALYSIS

Does anyone who unwittingly acquires inside information face a legal risk?

a. 987 F.2d 112 (2d Cir. 1993).

b. 155 F.3d 1051 (9th Cir. 1998).

c. See, for example, *Dirks v. SEC,* 463 U.S. 646, 103 S.Ct. 3255, 77 L.Ed.2d 911 (1983).

government officials for acts beneficial to the state) to persons providing information leading to the prosecution of insider-trading violations.[24]

Private parties may also sue violators of Section 10(b) and Rule 10b-5. A private party may obtain rescission of a contract to buy securities or damages to the extent of the violator's illegal profits. Those found liable have a right to seek contribution from those who share responsibility for the violations, including accountants, attorneys, and corporations.[25] For violations of Section 16(b), a corporation can bring an action to recover the short-swing profits.

24. 15 U.S.C. Section 78u-1.

25. Note that a private cause of action under Section 10(b) and SEC Rule 10b-5 cannot be brought against accountants, attorneys, and others who "aid and abet" violations of the act. Only the SEC can bring actions against so-called aiders and abettors. See *SEC v. Fehn,* 97 F.3d 1276 (9th Cir. 1996).

The Expanded Powers of the SEC

> **ON THE WEB**
>
> The SEC's Electronic Data Gathering Analysis and Retrieval system (EDGAR) contains information about the SEC's operations, the statutes it implements, its proposed and final rules, and its enforcement actions, as well as corporate financial information. Go to www.sec.gov/edgarhp.htm.

From the time of its creation until the present, the SEC's regulatory functions have gradually been increased by legislation granting it authority in different areas. In the last decade, for example, Congress has passed several acts that have significantly expanded the SEC's powers.

To further curb securities fraud, the Securities Enforcement Remedies and Penny Stock Reform Act[26] of 1990 amended existing securities laws to expand greatly the types of securities violation cases that SEC administrative law judges can hear and the SEC's enforcement options. The act also provides that courts can bar persons who have engaged in securities fraud from serving as officers and directors of publicly held corporations.

The 1990 Securities Acts Amendments[27] authorized the SEC to seek sanctions against those who violate foreign securities laws. These amendments increase the ability of the SEC to cooperate in international securities law enforcement. Under the Market Reform Act of 1990,[28] the SEC can suspend trading in securities in the event that the prices rise and fall excessively in a short period of time.

The National Securities Markets Improvement Act of 1996 expanded the power of the SEC to exempt persons, securities, and transactions from the requirements of the securities laws.[29] (This part of the act is also known as the Capital Markets Efficiency Act.) The act also limited the authority of the states to regulate certain securities transactions, as well as certain investment advisory firms.[30]

Currently, both Congress and the SEC are in the process of making fundamental changes in the regulatory framework applying to securities transactions. Over the years, as more and more SEC rules were issued, the body of regulations governing securities transactions became increasingly cumbersome and complex. Congress and the SEC are eliminating some rules, revising others, and generally attempting to streamline the regulatory process to make it more efficient and more relevant to today's securities trading practices. The SEC is also making it easy for the public to access information on securities law and trading by posting such information on its Web site. For a further discussion of this topic, see the feature *Technology and Securities Law.*

The Regulation of Investment Companies

• **INVESTMENT COMPANY**
A company that acts on behalf of many smaller shareholders/owners by buying a large portfolio of securities and professionally managing that portfolio.

• **MUTUAL FUND**
A specific type of investment company that continually buys or sells to investors shares of ownership in a portfolio.

Investment companies, and mutual funds in particular, grew rapidly after World War II. **Investment companies** act on behalf of many smaller shareholders by buying a large portfolio of securities and professionally managing that portfolio. A **mutual fund** is a specific type of investment company that continually buys or sells to investors shares of ownership in a portfolio. Such companies are regulated by the Investment Company Act of 1940,[31] which provides for SEC regulation of their activities. The act was expanded by the 1970 amendments to the Investment Company Act. Further minor changes were made in the Securities Act Amendments of 1975 and in later years.

26. 15 U.S.C. Section 77g.
27. 15 U.S.C. Section 78a.
28. 15 U.S.C. Section 78a.
29. 15 U.S.C. Sections 77z-3, 78mm.
30. 15 U.S.C. Section 80b-3a.
31. 15 U.S.C. Sections 80a-1 to 64.

Technology and Securities Law

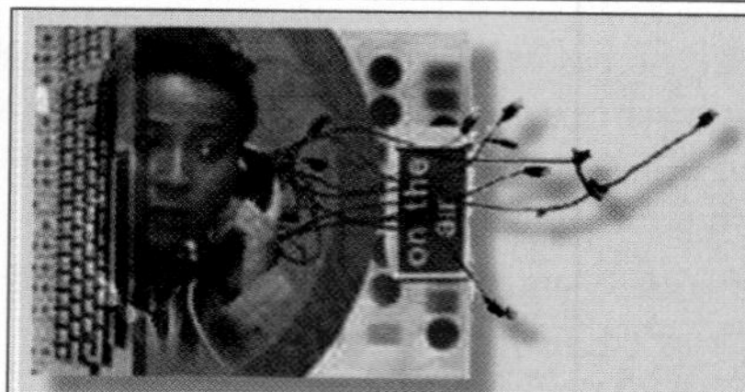

We have emphasized elsewhere how technological advances have affected business practices as well as the law governing those practices. Not surprisingly, technology is also affecting practices in the securities industry—and securities law. More than ever before, today's investors have access to information that can help them make informed decisions. Information on the Internet, for example, ranges from data concerning the financial performance of various companies to all securities laws and regulations.

As the Web has become more sophisticated, so too has the Web site of the Securities and Exchange Commission (SEC), the URL for which is www.sec.gov. From its home page, you can access significant information, including new SEC rules, recent announcements, enforcement actions, the SEC's new "Plain English Handbook," and the EDGAR (Electronic Data Gathering, Analysis, and Retrieval) database. This database includes initial public offerings, proxy statements, annual corporate reports, registration statements, and other documents that have been filed with the SEC. EDGAR also provides public access to information regarding securities trading suspensions and current class-action suits for securities fraud.

In 1996, when the SEC allowed Spring Street Brewing Company to trade its shares via its Web site without registering as a broker-dealer, many people looked to the Internet as the stock market of tomorrow—but we are going to have to wait a few more years for that. Offerings by small, nonpublic companies have been limited in scope, mainly because of regulatory restraints. To a large extent, any company wishing to make an initial public offering (IPO) of securities over the Internet has to comply with federal and state law filing requirements. Such filings are costly and time consuming. Typically, only those companies that are exempt from registration requirements have gone to the Internet to raise capital. Another problem relates to the lack of secondary markets for IPO shares sold directly on the Internet.

One of the questions raised by Internet transactions has to do with securities offerings by foreign companies. Today, anybody in the world can offer shares of stock worldwide via the Web without any additional cost. Traditionally, foreign companies have not been able to offer new shares to the U.S. public without first registering them with the Securities and Exchange Commission. How can these requirements be enforced for offerings made using the Internet?

In 1998, the SEC issued an interpretive release to address this question and similar concerns. The SEC stated that foreign issuers must implement measures to avoid targeting U.S. investors. For example, a foreign company offering shares of stock on the Internet must add a disclaimer on its Web site stating that it has not gone through the registration procedure in the United States. If the SEC believes that a Web site's offering of foreign securities has been targeted at U.S. persons, it will pursue that company in an attempt to require it to register in the United States.[a] Given that some Web site prospectuses for new security offerings have full audio and downloadable video, the investing public will probably become more interested in such Web sites. This means that the SEC's job of policing these Web sites will become increasingly difficult.

FOR CRITICAL ANALYSIS

Will state securities regulators find Internet securities transactions more or less difficult to police? Why?

a. International Series Release #1125, March 23, 1998. See also Arthur B. Laby, "The SEC Has Issued an Interpretive Release Delineating the Instances When an Offshore Offering of Securities Made on the Internet Must be Registered," *The National Law Journal,* April 20, 1998, p. B6.

INTERNET CONNECT

The 1940 act requires that every investment company register with the SEC and imposes restrictions on the activities of these companies and persons connected with them. For the purposes of the act, an investment company is defined as any entity that (1) is engaged primarily "in the business of investing, reinvesting, or trading in securities" or (2) is engaged in such business and has more than 40 percent of its assets in investment securities. Excluded from coverage by the act are banks, insurance companies, savings and loan associations, finance companies, oil and gas drilling firms, charitable foundations, tax-exempt pension funds, and other special types of institutions, such as closely held corporations.

All investment companies must register with the SEC by filing a notification of registration. Each year, registered investment companies must file reports with the SEC. To safeguard company assets, all securities must be held in the custody of a bank or stock exchange member, and that bank or stock exchange member must follow strict procedures established by the SEC.

No dividends may be paid from any source other than accumulated, undistributed net income. Furthermore, there are some restrictions on investment activities. For example, investment companies are not allowed to purchase securities on the margin (pay only part of the total price, borrowing the rest), sell short (sell shares not yet owned), or participate in joint trading accounts.

State Securities Laws

¡BE AWARE! Federal securities laws do not supersede state securities laws.

Today, all states have their own corporate securities laws, or "blue sky laws," that regulate the offer and sale of securities within individual state borders.[32] (As mentioned in Chapter 11, the phrase *blue sky laws* dates to a 1917 decision by the United States Supreme Court in which the Court declared that the purpose of such laws was to prevent "speculative schemes which have no more basis than so many feet of 'blue sky.' ")[33] Article 8 of the Uniform Commercial Code, which has been adopted by all of the states, also imposes various requirements relating to the purchase and sale of securities. State securities laws apply only to intrastate transactions. Since the adoption of the 1933 and 1934 federal securities acts, the state and federal governments have regulated securities concurrently. Issuers must comply with both federal and state securities laws, and exemptions from federal law are not exemptions from state laws.

There are differences in philosophy among state statutes, but certain features are common to all state blue sky laws. Typically, state laws have disclosure requirements and antifraud provisions, many of which are patterned after Section 10(b) of the Securities Exchange Act of 1934 and SEC Rule 10b-5. State laws also provide for the registration or qualification of securities offered or issued for sale within the state and impose disclosure requirements. Unless an applicable exemption from registration is found, issuers must register or qualify their stock with the appropriate state official, often called a *corporations commissioner*. Additionally, most state securities laws regulate securities brokers and dealers. The Uniform Securities Act, which has been adopted in part by several states, was drafted to be acceptable to states with differing regulatory philosophies.

32. These laws are catalogued and annotated in the *Blue Sky Law Reports*, a loose-leaf service provided by CCH, Inc.
33. *Hall v. Geiger-Jones Co.*, 242 U.S. 539, 37 S.Ct. 217, 61 L.Ed. 480 (1917).

Key Terms

accredited investor 806
bounty payment 817
insider trading 809
investment company 819
mutual fund 819
red herring 803
SEC Rule 10b-5 809
security 801
tippee 813
tombstone ad 804

Chapter Summary • Investor Protection

The Securities Act of 1933 (See pages 802–808.)	Prohibits fraud and stabilizes the securities industry by requiring disclosure of all essential information relating to the issuance of stocks to the investing public. 1. *Registration requirements*—Securities, unless exempt, must be registered with the SEC before being offered to the public through the mails or any facility of interstate commerce (including securities exchanges). The *registration statement* must include detailed financial information about the issuing corporation; the intended use of the proceeds of the securities being issued; and certain disclosures, such as interests of directors or officers and pending lawsuits. 2. *Prospectus*—A *prospectus* must be provided to investors, describing the security being sold, the issuing corporation, and the risk attaching to the security. 3. *Exemptions*—The SEC has exempted certain offerings from the requirements of the Securities Act of 1933. Exemptions may be determined on the basis of the size of the issue, whether the offering is private or public, and whether advertising is involved. Exemptions are summarized in Exhibit 31–1.
The Securities Exchange Act of 1934 (See pages 808–819.)	Provides for the regulation and registration of securities exchanges, brokers, dealers, and national securities associations (such as the NASD). Maintains a continuous disclosure system for all corporations with securities on the securities exchanges and for those companies that have assets in excess of $5 million and five hundred or more shareholders (Section 12 companies). 1. *SEC Rule 10b-5 [under Section 10(b) of the 1934 act]*— a. Applies to insider trading by corporate officers, directors, majority shareholders, and any persons receiving information not available to the public who base their trading on this information. b. Liability for violation can be civil or criminal. c. May be violated by failing to disclose "material facts" that must be disclosed under this rule. d. Applies in virtually all cases concerning the trading of securities—a firm does not have to have its securities registered under the 1933 act for the 1934 act to apply. e. Liability may be based on the tipper-tippee or misappropriation theory. f. Applies only when the requisites of federal jurisdiction (such as use of the mails, stock exchange facilities, or any facility of interstate commerce) are present. 2. *Insider trading [under Section 16(b) of the 1934 act]*—To prevent corporate officers and directors from taking advantage of inside information (information not available to the investing public), the 1934 act requires officers, directors, and shareholders owning 10 percent or more of the issued stock of a corporation to turn over to the corporation all short-term profits (called short-swing profits) realized from the purchase and sale or sale and purchase of corporate stock within any six-month period. 3. *Proxies [under Section 14(a) of the 1934 act]*—The SEC regulates the content of proxy statements sent to shareholders by corporate managers of Section 12 companies who are requesting authority to vote on behalf of the shareholders in a particular election on specified issues. Section 14(a) is essentially a disclosure law, with provisions similar to the antifraud provisions of SEC Rule 10b-5.
Regulation of Investment Companies (See pages 819–821.)	The Investment Company Act of 1940 provides for SEC regulation of investment company activities. It was altered and expanded by the amendments of 1970 and 1975.
State Securities Laws (See page 821.)	All states have corporate securities laws (*blue sky laws*) that regulate the offer and sale of securities within state borders; designed to prevent "speculative schemes which have no more basis than so many feet of 'blue sky.' " States regulate securities concurrently with the federal government.

For Review

❶ What is the essential purpose of the Securities Act of 1933? What is the essential purpose of the Securities Exchange Act of 1934?

❷ What is a registration statement? What must a registration statement include? What is a prospectus?

❸ Basically, what constitutes a security under the Securities Act of 1933?

❹ What is SEC Rule 10b-5? What is the key to liability under this rule? To what kinds of transactions does SEC Rule 10b-5 apply?

❺ Discuss two theories under which "outsiders" can be held liable for violating SEC Rule 10b-5.

Questions and Case Problems

31–1. Registration Requirements. Langley Brothers, Inc., a corporation incorporated and doing business in Kansas, decides to sell no-par common stock worth $1 million to the public. The stock will be sold only within the state of Kansas. Joseph Langley, the chairman of the board, says the offering need not be registered with the SEC. His brother, Harry, disagrees. Who is right? Explain.

31–2. Registration Requirements. Huron Corp. had 300,000 common shares outstanding. The owners of these outstanding shares lived in several different states. Huron decided to split the 300,000 shares two for one. Will Huron Corp. have to file a registration statement and prospectus on the 300,000 new shares to be issued as a result of the split? Explain.

31–3. Definition of a Security. The W. J. Howey Co. (Howey) owned large tracts of citrus acreage in Lake County, Florida. For several years, it planted about five hundred acres annually, keeping half of the groves itself and offering the other half to the public to help finance additional development. Howey-in-the-Hills Service, Inc., was a service company engaged in cultivating and developing these groves, including the harvesting and marketing of the crops. Each prospective customer was offered both a land sales contract and a service contract, after being told that it was not feasible to invest in a grove unless service arrangements were made. Of the acreage sold by Howey, 85 percent was sold with a service contract with Howey-in-the-Hills Service. Howey did not register with the SEC or meet the other administrative requirements that issuers of securities must fulfill. The SEC sued to enjoin Howey from continuing to offer the land sales and service contracts. Howey responded that no SEC violation existed, because no securities had been issued. Evaluate the definition of a security given in this chapter, and then determine which party should prevail in court, Howey or the SEC. [*SEC v. W. J. Howey Co.*, 328 U.S. 293, 66 S.Ct. 1100, 90 L.Ed. 1244 (1946)]

31–4. Definition of a Security. U.S. News & World Report, Inc., set up a profit-sharing plan in 1962 that allotted to certain employees specially issued stock known as bonus or anniversary stock. The stock was given to the employees for past services and could not be traded or sold to anyone other than the corporate issuer, U.S. News. This special stock was issued only to employees and for no other purpose than as bonuses. Because there was no market for the stock, U.S. News hired an independent appraiser to estimate the fair value of the stock so that the employees could redeem the shares. Charles Foltz and several other employees held stock through this plan and sought to redeem the shares with U.S. News, but Foltz disputed the value set by the appraisers. Foltz sued U.S. News for violation of securities regulations. What defense would allow U.S. News to resist successfully Foltz's claim? [*Foltz v. U.S. News & World Report, Inc.*, 627 F.Supp. 1143 (D.D.C. 1986)]

31–5. Short-Swing Profits. Emerson Electric Co. purchased 13.2 percent of Dodge Manufacturing Co.'s stock in an unsuccessful takeover attempt in June 1967. Less than six months later, when Dodge merged with Reliance Electric Co., Emerson decided to sell its shares. To avoid being subject to the short-swing profit restrictions of Section 16(b) of the Securities Exchange Act of 1934, Emerson decided on a two-step selling plan. First, it sold off sufficient shares to reduce its holdings to 9.96 percent [owners with less than 10 percent are exempt from Section 16(b)], and then it sold the remaining stock—all within a six-month period. Emerson in this way succeeded in avoiding Section 16(b) requirements. Reliance demanded that Emerson return the profits made on both sales. Emerson sought a declaratory judgment from the court that it was not liable, arguing that because at the time of the second sale it had not owned 10 percent of Dodge stock, Section 16(b) did not apply. Does Section 16(b) of the Securities Exchange Act of 1934 apply to Emerson's transactions, and is Emerson liable to Reliance for its profits? Discuss fully. [*Reliance Electric Co. v. Emerson Electric Co.*, 404 U.S. 418, 92 S.Ct. 596, 30 L.E.2d 575 (1972)]

31–6. SEC Rule 10b-5. In early 1985, FMC Corp. made plans to buy some of its own stock as part of a restructuring of its balance statement. Unknown to FMC management, the brokerage firm FMC employed—Goldman, Sachs & Co.—disclosed information on the stock purchase that found its way to Ivan Boesky. FMC was one of the seven major corporations in whose stock Boesky allegedly traded using inside information. Boesky made purchases of FMC's stock between February 18 and February 21, 1986, and between March 12 and April 4, 1986. Boesky's purchases amounted to a substantial portion of the total volume of FMC stock traded during these periods. The price of FMC stock increased from $71.25 on February 20, 1986, to $97.00 on April 25, 1986. As a result, FMC paid substantially more for the repurchase of its own stock than anticipated. When FMC discovered Boesky's knowledge of its recapitalization plan, FMC sued Boesky for the excess price it had paid—approximately $220 million. Discuss whether FMC should recover under Section 10(b) of the Securities Exchange Act and SEC Rule 10b-5. [*In re Ivan F. Boesky Securities Litigation,* 36 F.3d 255 (2d Cir. 1994)]

31–7. SEC Rule 10b-5. Louis Ferraro was the chairman and president of Anacomp, Inc. In June 1988, Ferraro told his good friend Michael Maio that Anacomp was negotiating a tender offer for stock in Xidex Corp. Maio passed on the information to Patricia Ladavac, a friend of both Ferraro and Maio. Maio and Ladavac immediately purchased shares in Xidex stock. On the day that the tender offer was announced—an announcement that caused the price of Xidex shares to increase—Maio and Ladavac sold their Xidex stock and made substantial profits (Maio made $211,000 from the transactions, and Ladavac gained $78,750). The SEC brought an action against the three individuals, alleging that they had violated, among other laws, SEC Rule 10b-5. Maio and Ladavac claimed that they had done nothing illegal. They argued that they had no fiduciary duty either to Anacomp or to Xidex, and therefore they had no duty to disclose or abstain from trading in the stock of those corporations. Had Maio and Ladavac violated SEC Rule 10b-5? Discuss fully. [*SEC v. Maio,* 51 F.3d 623 (7th Cir. 1995)]

31–8. Definition of a Security. Life Partners, Inc. (LPI), facilitates the sale of life insurance policies that are owned by persons suffering from AIDS (acquired immune deficiency syndrome) to investors at a discount. The investors pay LPI, and LPI pays the policyholder. Typically, the policyholder, in turn, assigns the policy to LPI, which also obtains the right to make LPI's president the beneficiary of the policy. On the policyholder's death, LPI receives the proceeds of the policy and pays the investor. In this way, the terminally ill sellers secure much-needed income in the final years of life, when employment is unlikely and medical bills are often staggering. The SEC sought to enjoin (prevent) LPI from engaging in further transactions on the ground that the investment contracts were securities, which LPI had failed to register with the SEC in violation of securities laws. Do the investment contracts meet the definition of a security discussed in this chapter? Discuss fully. [*SEC v. Life Partners, Inc.,* 87 F.3d 536 (D.C.Cir. 1996)]

31–9. Section 10(b). Joseph Jett worked for Kidder, Peabody & Co., a financial services firm owned by General Electric Co. (GE). Over a three-year period, Jett allegedly engaged in a scheme to generate false profits at Kidder, Peabody to increase his performance-based bonuses. When the scheme was discovered, Daniel Chill and other GE shareholders who had bought stock in the previous year filed a suit in a federal district court against GE. The shareholders alleged that GE had engaged in securities fraud in violation of Section 10(b). They claimed that GE's interest in justifying its investment in Kidder, Peabody gave GE "a motive to willfully blind itself to facts casting doubt on Kidder's purported profitability." On what basis might the court dismiss the shareholders' complaint? Discuss fully. [*Chill v. General Electric Co.,* 101 F.3d 263 (2d Cir. 1996)]

31–10. SEC Rule 10b-5. Grand Metropolitan PLC (Grand Met) planned to make a tender offer as part of an attempted takeover of the Pillsbury Company. Grand Met hired Robert Falbo, an independent contractor, to complete electrical work as part of security renovations to its offices to prevent leaks of information concerning the planned tender offer. Falbo was given a master key to access the executive offices. When an executive secretary told Falbo that a takeover was brewing, he used his key to access the offices and eavesdrop on conversations to learn that Pillsbury was the target. Falbo bought thousands of shares of Pillsbury stock for less than $40 per share. Within two months, Grand Met made an offer for all outstanding Pillsbury stock at $60 per share and ultimately paid up to $66 per share. Falbo made over $165,000 in profit. The Securities and Exchange Commission (SEC) filed a suit in a federal district court against Falbo and others for alleged violations of, among other things, SEC Rule 10b-5. Under what theory might Falbo be liable? Do the circumstances of this case meet all of the requirements for liability under that theory? Explain. [*SEC v. Falbo,* 14 F.Supp.2d 508 (S.D.N.Y. 1998)]

A QUESTION OF ETHICS AND SOCIAL RESPONSIBILITY

31–11. Susan Waldbaum was a niece of the president and controlling shareholder of Waldbaum, Inc. Susan's mother (the president's sister) told Susan that the company was going to be sold at a favorable price and that a tender offer was soon to be made. She told Susan not to tell anyone except her husband, Keith Loeb, about the sale. (Loeb did not work for the company and was never brought into the family's inner circle, in which family members discussed confidential business information.) The next day, Susan told her husband of the sale and cautioned him not to tell anyone, because "it could possibly ruin the sale." The day after he learned of the sale, Loeb told Robert Chestman, his broker, about the sale, and Chestman purchased shares of the company for both Loeb and himself. Chestman was later convicted by a jury of, among other things, trading on misappropriated inside information in violation of SEC Rule 10b-5. [*United States v. Chestman,* 947 F.2d 551 (2d Cir. 1991)]

1. On appeal, the central question was whether Chestman had acquired the inside information about the tender offer as a result of an insider's breach of a fiduciary duty. Could Loeb—the "tipper" in this case—be considered an insider?
2. If Loeb was not an insider, did he owe any fiduciary (legal) duty to his wife or his wife's family to keep the information confidential? Would it be fair of the court to impose such a legal duty on Loeb?

FOR CRITICAL ANALYSIS

31–12. Do you think that the tipper/tippee and misappropriation theories extend liability under SEC Rule 10b-5 too far? Why or why not?

Online Activities

ONLINE EXERCISE 31–1

Go to the "Internet Activities Book" on the Web site that accompanies this text, the URL for which is http://blt.westbuslaw.com. Select the following activities, and perform the exercises according to the instructions given there:

Activity 29–1: The SEC's Role
Activity 29–2: Securities Arbitration

Before the Test

Go to the *Business Law Today* home page at http://blt.westbuslaw.com. Click on TestTutor.® You will find twenty interactive questions relating to this chapter.

CHAPTER 32 Limited Liability Companies & Partnerships

> "All gains . . . are the fruit of venturing."
>
> Herodotus, fifth century B.C.E. (Greek historian)

CONTENTS

LEARNING OBJECTIVES

After reading this chapter, you should be able to:

1. Indicate why limited liability companies and partnerships are attractive to businesspersons.
2. Describe what a limited liability company is and how it operates.
3. Give some examples of how limited liability partnerships limit the tort liability of partners.
4. Explain what a family limited liability partnership is and when it is an appropriate business organizational choice.
5. Summarize the ways in which a limited partnership differs from a general partnership.

The two most common forms of business organization selected by two or more persons entering into business together are the partnership and the corporation. As explained in previous chapters, each form has distinct advantages and disadvantages. For partnerships, the advantage is that partnership income is taxed only once (all income is "passed through" the partnership entity to the partners themselves, who are taxed only as individuals); the disadvantage is the personal liability of the partners. For corporations, the advantage is the limited liability of shareholders; the disadvantage is the double taxation of corporate income. For many entrepreneurs and investors, the ideal business form would combine the tax advantages of the partnership form of business with the limited liability of the corporate enterprise.

• **LIMITED LIABILITY COMPANY (LLC)** A hybrid form of business enterprise that offers the limited liability of the corporation but the tax advantages of a partnership.

A relatively new form of business organization, the **limited liability company (LLC),** is a hybrid form of business enterprise that meets these needs by offering the limited liability of the corporation and the tax advantages of a partnership. Increasingly, LLCs are becoming an organizational form of choice among businesspersons, a trend encouraged by state statutes permitting their use. As the chapter-opening quotation indicates, all gains are the "fruit of venturing," and LLCs—to the extent they encourage business ventures— contribute to those gains.

In this chapter, we begin by examining the LLC, the origins and evolution of which are discussed in this chapter's *Landmark in the Law.* We then look at a similar type of entity that is also relatively new—the limited liability partnership (LLP). The chapter concludes with a discussion of the limited partnership, a special type of partnership in which some of the partners have limited liability, and the limited liability limited partnership (LLLP).

Landmark in the Law • LIMITED LIABILITY COMPANY (LLC) STATUTES

In 1977, Wyoming became the first state to pass legislation authorizing the creation of a limited liability company (LLC). Although LLCs emerged in the United States only in 1977, they have been in existence for over a century in other areas, including several European and South American nations. For example, the South American *limitada* is a form of business organization that operates more or less as a partnership but provides limited liability for the owners.

In the United States, after Wyoming's adoption of an LLC statute, it still was not known how the Internal Revenue Service (IRS) would treat the LLC for tax purposes. In 1988, however, the IRS ruled that Wyoming LLCs would be taxed as partnerships instead of as corporations, providing that certain requirements were met. Prior to this ruling, only one other state—Florida, in 1982—had authorized LLCs. The 1988 ruling encouraged other states to enact LLC statutes, and in less than a decade, all states had done so.

New IRS rules that went into effect on January 1, 1997, encouraged even more widespread use of LLCs in the business world. These rules provide that any unincorporated business will automatically be taxed as a partnership unless it indicates otherwise on the tax form. The exceptions involve publicly traded companies, companies formed under a state incorporation statute, and certain foreign-owned companies. If a business chooses to be taxed as a corporation, it can indicate this choice by checking a box on the IRS form.

Part of the impetus behind creating LLCs in this country is that foreign investors are allowed to become LLC members. Generally, in an era increasingly characterized by global business efforts and investments, the LLC offers U.S. firms and potential investors from other countries flexibility and opportunities greater than those available through partnerships or corporations.

FOR CRITICAL ANALYSIS
Given the fact that the tax and liability characteristics of partnerships and corporations have long been in existence, why is it that LLC statutes have emerged only relatively recently?

Limited Liability Companies

• **MEMBER** The term used to designate a person who has an ownership interest in a limited liability company.

• **ARTICLES OF ORGANIZATION** The document filed with a designated state official by which a limited liability company is formed.

Like the corporation, an LLC must be formed and operated in compliance with state law. About one-fourth of the states specifically require LLCs to have at least two owners, called **members.** In the rest of the states, although some LLC statutes are silent on this issue, one-member LLCs are usually permitted.

To form an LLC, **articles of organization** must be filed with a central state agency—usually the secretary of state's office. Typically, the articles are required to set forth such information as the name of the business, its principal address, the

> **ON THE WEB**
> You can find information on how to form an LLC, including the fees charged in each state for filing LLC articles of organization, at the Web site of BIZCORP International, Inc. Go to www.bizcorp.com.

name and address of a registered agent, the names of the owners, and information on how the LLC will be managed. The business's name must include the words "Limited Liability Company" or the initials "LLC." In addition to filing the articles of organization, a few states require that a notice of the intention to form an LLC be published in a local newspaper.

Note that although the LLC, like the corporation, is a legal entity apart from its owners, for federal jurisdictional purposes an LLC is treated differently than a corporation. The federal jurisdiction statute provides that a corporation is deemed to be a citizen of the state in which it is incorporated and in which it maintains its principal place of business. The statute does not mention the citizenship of partnerships and other unincorporated associations, but courts have tended to regard these entities as citizens of every state of which their members are citizens.

The citizenship of LLCs may come into play when a party sues an LLC based on diversity of citizenship. Remember from Chapter 3 that in some circumstances, such as when parties to a lawsuit are from different states, a federal court can exercise diversity jurisdiction in cases in which the amount in controversy exceeds $75,000. *Complete* diversity of citizenship must exist, however. For example, a citizen of New York will not be able to bring a suit in federal court—on the basis of diversity jurisdiction—against multiple defendants if one of the defendants is also a citizen of New York.

One of the issues in the following case concerned the state citizenship of a limited liability company. Was there diversity of citizenship between the parties so that a federal court could exercise jurisdiction?

CASE 32.1 Cosgrove v. Bartolotta

United States Court of Appeals,
Seventh Circuit, 1998.
150 F.3d 729.
www.findlaw.com/casecode/courts/7th.html[a]

HISTORICAL AND SOCIAL SETTING *Whenever there is an "unconventional party"—someone other than a natural person suing in his or her own, rather than a representative, capacity or some entity other than a corporation—a jurisdictional warning flag goes up. In the case of a corporation, the owners' state of citizenship is irrelevant as to whether there is the required diversity of citizenship for a federal court to hear the case. In the case of a partnership, however, the owners' state of citizenship is crucial. The citizenship of a partnership is the citizenship of its partners. Thus, in a case in which a partnership is a defendant, if even one of the partners is a citizen of the same state as the plaintiff, the suit cannot be brought as a diversity suit.*[b]

BACKGROUND AND FACTS Joseph Bartolotta wanted to open a restaurant. He asked Barry Cosgrove, his friend and an experienced corporate attorney, for a $100,000 loan, plus Cosgrove's business and legal advice. Bartolotta promised, among other things, to give Cosgrove a 19 percent ownership interest in the restaurant. In reliance on this promise, Cosgrove helped Bartolotta negotiate a lease for the restaurant premises and advised Bartolotta to organize the venture as a limited liability company (LLC). Bartolotta formed Mary-Bart, LLC, and with Cosgrove's help, obtained other financing. Then, before Cosgrove made his loan, Bartolotta cut him out of the deal. The restaurant, "Bartolotta's Lake Park Bistro," proved to be a success. Cosgrove filed a suit in a federal district court against Bartolotta and Mary-Bart, based in part on diversity of citizenship (Cosgrove and Bartolotta were residents of different states). The jury awarded Cosgrove $135,000, but the judge reduced the award, and both sides appealed.

a. This is a page, within the FindLaw Web site, that provides access to recent opinions of the U.S. Court of Appeals for the Seventh Circuit. In the "1998" row, click on the "July" link. When that page opens, scroll down the list of cases to the *Cosgrove* case. Click on the name to access the opinion.

b. *Carden v. Arkoma Associates,* 494 U.S. 185, 110 S.Ct. 1015, 108 L.Ed.2d 157 (1990).

CASE 32.1—Continued

IN THE WORDS OF THE COURT . . .

POSNER, Chief Judge.

* * * *

Mary-Bart is neither a partnership nor a corporation, but a "limited liability company." This animal is like a limited partnership; the principal difference is that it need have no equivalent to a general partner, that is, an owner who has unlimited personal liability for the debts of the firm. Given the resemblance between an LLC and a limited partnership, * * * we conclude that the citizenship of an LLC for purposes of the diversity jurisdiction is the citizenship of its members. That does not defeat jurisdiction in this case, however, because Mary-Bart, LLC has only one member—Mr. Bartolotta, who is not a citizen of the same state as the plaintiff.

DECISION AND REMEDY The U.S. Court of Appeals for the Seventh Circuit ruled that a federal court could exercise jurisdiction in this case. For purposes of federal court jurisdiction, the citizenship of an LLC is the citizenship of its members. The court also remanded the case with orders to reinstate the award to Cosgrove.

FOR CRITICAL ANALYSIS—Political Consideration *Why is the rule concerning the citizenship of a business entity different for corporations than it is for unincorporated entities, including LLCs?*

ADVANTAGES AND DISADVANTAGES OF LLCS

A key advantage of the LLC is that the liability of members is limited to the amount of their investments. Another significant advantage is that an LLC with two or more members can choose whether to be taxed as a partnership or a corporation.

LLCs that want to distribute profits to the members may prefer to be taxed as a partnership, to avoid the "double taxation" characteristic of the corporate entity. Remember that in the corporate form of business, the corporation as an entity pays income taxes on its profits, and the shareholders pay personal income taxes on profits distributed as dividends. Unless the LLC indicates that it wishes to be taxed as a corporation, it is automatically taxed as a partnership by the Internal Revenue Service (IRS). This means that the LLC as an entity pays no taxes; rather, as in a partnership, profits are "passed through" the LLC and paid personally by the members. If LLC members want to reinvest profits in the business, however, rather than distribute the profits to members, they may prefer to be taxed as a corporation if corporate income tax rates are lower than personal tax rates. Part of the attractiveness of the LLC for businesspersons is this flexibility with respect to taxation options.

¡ REMEMBER!
A uniform law is a "model" law. It does not become the law of any state until the state legislature adopts it, either in part or in its entirety.

For federal income tax purposes, one-member LLCs are automatically taxed as sole proprietorships unless they indicate that they wish to be taxed as corporations. With respect to state taxes, most states follow the IRS rules. Still another advantage of the LLC for businesspersons is the flexibility it offers in terms of business operations and management—as will be discussed shortly.

The disadvantages of the LLC are relatively few. Some of the initial disadvantages with respect to uncertainties over how LLCs would be taxed no longer exist. The only remaining disadvantage of the LLC is that state statutes are not yet uniform. In an attempt to promote some uniformity among the states in respect to LLC statutes, the National Conference of Commissioners on Uniform State Laws drafted a Uniform Limited Liability Company Act for submission to the states to consider for adoption. Until all of the states have adopted the uniform law, however, an LLC in one state will have to check the rules in the other states in which the firm does business to ensure that it retains its limited liability.

The LLC Operating Agreement

• OPERATING AGREEMENT In a limited liability company, an agreement in which the members set forth the details of how the business will be managed and operated. State statutes typically give the members wide latitude in deciding for themselves the rules that will govern their organization.

The LLC is also a flexible business entity in another important way. In an LCC, the members themselves can decide how to operate the various aspects of the business by forming an **operating agreement.** Operating agreements typically contain provisions relating to management, how profits will be divided, the transfer of membership interests, whether the LLC will be dissolved on the death or departure of a member, and other important issues.

Operating agreements need not be in writing, and indeed they need not even be formed for an LLC to exist. Generally, though, LLC members should protect their interests by forming a written operating agreement. As with any business arrangement, disputes may arise over any number of issues. If there is no agreement covering the topic being disputed, such as how profits will be divided, the state LLC statute will govern the outcome. For example, most LLC statutes provide that if the members have not specified how profits will be divided among the members, they will be divided equally.

Generally, with respect to issues not covered by an operating agreement or by an LLC statute, the principles of partnership law are applied. At issue in the following case was whether partnership law should apply to a dispute between LLC members as to how business receipts were to be divided on the firm's dissolution.

CASE 32.2 Hurwitz v. Padden

Court of Appeals of Minnesota, 1998.
581 N.W.2d 359.
www.courts.state.mn.us/library/archive/capgi.html[a]

HISTORICAL AND SOCIAL SETTING *The law has long recognized that a partnership is based on mutual trust and confidence.*[b] *In their dealings with one another, partners are subject to the highest standards of good faith and integrity. This is also true of the officers and shareholders of close corporations.*[c] *In fact, reasoning that many close corporations are partnerships under a different name, some courts have even applied partnership principles to enforce the fiduciary duty among the shareholders of close corporations.*[d]

a. This page includes a partial list of Minnesota Court of Appeals opinions available in the Minnesota State Law Library online database. The last name of the parties in these cases begins with the letter G, H, or I. Scroll down the list to the *Hurwitz* name and click on the link to read the case.

b. *Prince v. Sonnesyn,* 222 Minn. 528, 25 N.W.2d 468 (1946).

c. *Evans v. Blesi,* 345 N.W.2d 775 (Minn.App. 1984), review denied (Minn. 1984).

d. See, for example, *Harris v. Mardan Business Systems, Inc.,* 421 N.W.2d 350 (Minn.App. 1988).

BACKGROUND AND FACTS Thomas Hurwitz and Michael Padden formed a two-person law firm as a partnership without a written agreement. They shared all proceeds on a fifty-fifty basis and reported all income as partnership income. Less than eighteen months later, Hurwitz filed articles of organization with the state of Minnesota to establish the firm as an LLC. More than three years later, Padden told Hurwitz that he wanted to dissolve their professional relationship. They resolved all business issues between them, except for a division of fees from several of the firm's cases. Hurwitz filed a suit in a Minnesota state court against Padden, seeking, among other things, a distribution of the fees on a fifty-fifty basis. The court applied the principles of partnership law, ruled that the fees should be divided equally, and entered a judgment in favor of Hurwitz for $101,750. Padden appealed, arguing in part that these principles of partnership law should not apply to an LLC.

IN THE WORDS OF THE COURT . . .
SHORT, Judge.

* * * *

* * * [T]he Minnesota Limited Liability Company Act specifically incorporates the definition and use of the term "dissolution" from the Uniform Partnership Act

CASE 32.2—Continued

[UPA]. Under both statutes, the entity is not terminated upon dissolution, but continues until all business issues are resolved. Thus, the UPA provides guidance when examining the end stages of either entity's life. * * *

It is undisputed: (1) the firm had no written or oral agreement regarding the division of * * * fees upon dissolution; (2) the firm existed for approximately five-and-a-half years before Padden requested dissolution; (3) a little over five months elapsed between the date of dissolution and the date the parties [filed a suit] to settle the firm's remaining issues; (4) the firm's [disputed] fee cases were acquired before the firm's dissolution; (5) prior to its dissolution, the firm divided fees equally between the parties; and (6) at the time the parties filed suit, the firm was in a winding-up phase. Under these circumstances, partnership principles * * * govern the division of fees obtained from pre-dissolution * * * files. Thus, the * * * fees obtained from pre-dissolution case files must be divided equally between the parties, which is consistent with the pre-dissolution method of allocation.

DECISION AND REMEDY The state intermediate appellate court affirmed the decision of the lower court. The state intermediate appellate court concluded that the disputed fees should be divided equally, as the receipts were divided before the dissolution.

FOR CRITICAL ANALYSIS—Social Consideration *Should the principles of partnership law apply to other forms of business entities?*

MANAGEMENT OF AN LLC

"One cannot manage too many affairs: Like pumpkins in the water, one pops up while you try to hold down the other."

(CHINESE PROVERB)

ON THE WEB

Nolo Press provides information on LLCs and how they are operated at www.nolo.com/Runs/index.html.

Basically, there are two options with respect to the management of an LLC. The members may decide in their operating agreement to be either a "member-managed" LLC or a "manager-managed" LLC.

In a *member-managed* LLC, all of the members participate in management. In a *manager-managed* LLC, the members designate a group of persons to manage the firm. The management group may consist of only members, both members and nonmembers, or only nonmembers. Most LLC statutes provide that unless the members agree otherwise, all members of the LLC will participate in management. (Note that membership interests in LLCs, particularly in manager-managed LLCs, may be defined as securities—see this chapter's *Business Law in Action* for a further discussion of this topic.)

The members of an LLC can also set forth in their operating agreement provisions governing decision-making procedures. For example, the agreement can indicate what procedures are to be followed for choosing or removing managers, an issue on which most LLC statutes are silent. The members are also free to include in the agreement provisions designating when and for what purposes formal members' meetings will be held. In contrast to state laws governing corporations, LLC statutes in most states have no provisions regarding members' meetings. Members may also specify in their agreement how voting rights will be apportioned. If they do not, LLC statutes in most states provide that voting rights are apportioned according to the capital contributions made by each member. Some states provide that, in the absence of an agreement to the contrary, each member has one vote.

• LIMITED LIABILITY PARTNERSHIP (LLP)
A business organizational form that is similar to the LCC but that is designed more for professionals who normally do business as partners in a partnership. The LLP is a pass-through entity for tax purposes, like the general partnership, but it limits the personal liability of the partners.

Limited Liability Partnerships

The **limited liability partnership (LLP)** is similar to the LLC. The difference between an LLP and an LLC is that the LLP is designed more for professionals who normally

Business Law in Action • Are LLC Memberships Securities?

Businesspersons who plan to form an LLC should be aware that ownership interests in the LLC may be considered securities in some circumstances. To some extent, whether LLC memberships will be treated as securities depends on how the LLC is managed. To date, the courts have tended to hold that interests in an LLC that is managed by all of its members are not securities. If an LLC is managed by just some of the members, or by some of the members and/or nonmembers, however, ownership interests in the firm are more likely to be deemed securities—and thus subject to securities laws.

Remember from Chapter 29 that the United States Supreme Court has held that a security exists in any transaction in which a person (1) invests (2) in a common enterprise (3) reasonably expecting profits (4) derived *primarily* or *substantially* from others' managerial or entrepreneurial efforts.[a] Thus, if a person becomes a member of (invests in) an LLC, does not participate in the firm's management, and reasonably expects to make profits derived primarily from the efforts of the LLC's management group, it is very possible that the member's interest in the LLC will qualify as a security.

Consider a case that came before an Arizona appellate court. The question before the court was whether membership interests in several LLCs involved in a telecommunications network were securities. A key player in forming the LLCs was Albert Koenigsberg, the president and member-owner of SMR Advisory Group, a Texas LLC. In 1994, Koenigsberg began forming numerous LLCs in Texas and marketing interests in them. The LLCs were organized to construct, maintain, and operate an integrated communications network that would extend over several states. In each LLC, the initial members were SMR and an individual who held a certain type of radio license issued by the Federal Communications Commission (FCC). For each LLC, an operating agreement gave the FCC licensee ultimate control over the operation of the system and designated Koenigsberg as the "managing member."

SMR and the other initial members, through extensive marketing efforts, were able to collect over $10.4 million from over nine hundred investors, some of whom lived in Arizona. These investors had nothing to do with the management of the LLCs. SMR combined the investors' funds into a single administrative account and used the funds to purchase communications equipment and pay other expenses. SMR then charged the expenses to the respective LLCs involved. Koenigsberg was the sole signatory on this account.

In 1995, the Arizona Corporation Commission ruled that the membership interests in the LLCs constituted securities and charged Koenigsberg and the other LLC organizers with violating Arizona securities laws by, among other things, selling unregistered securities. Ultimately, the Arizona Court of Appeals upheld this ruling. The court concluded that the agreements formed by the LLCs prior to the marketing of the membership interest prevented the new members from exercising any control over the firms. Not only were the investor-members deprived of any opportunity to decide on how the firms would be managed, but most of them lacked the technical expertise that would allow them to participate in managerial decision making. Because the investors expected to make a profit primarily derived from the managerial efforts of others, particularly Koenigsberg, the LLC membership interests were securities.[b]

FOR CRITICAL ANALYSIS

Would the outcome in this case have been any different if all of the investor-members did have the technical expertise to run the companies?

a. *SEC v. W. J. Howey Co.*, 328 U.S. 293, 66 S.Ct. 1100, 90 L.Ed. 1244 (1946). Because state securities laws closely parallel the federal acts, this definition of a security is widely used by courts in determining whether a certain transaction is a security under state law.

b. *Nutek Information Systems, Inc. v. Arizona Corporation Commission*, 1998 WL 767176 (Ariz.App.Div.1 1998).

do business as partners in a partnership. The major advantage of the LLP is that it allows a partnership to continue as a pass-through entity for tax purposes but limits the personal liability of the partners.

The first state to enact an LLP statute was Texas, in 1991. Other states quickly followed suit, and by 1997, virtually all of the states had enacted LLP statutes. Like LLCs, LLPs must be formed and operated in compliance with state statutes. The appropriate

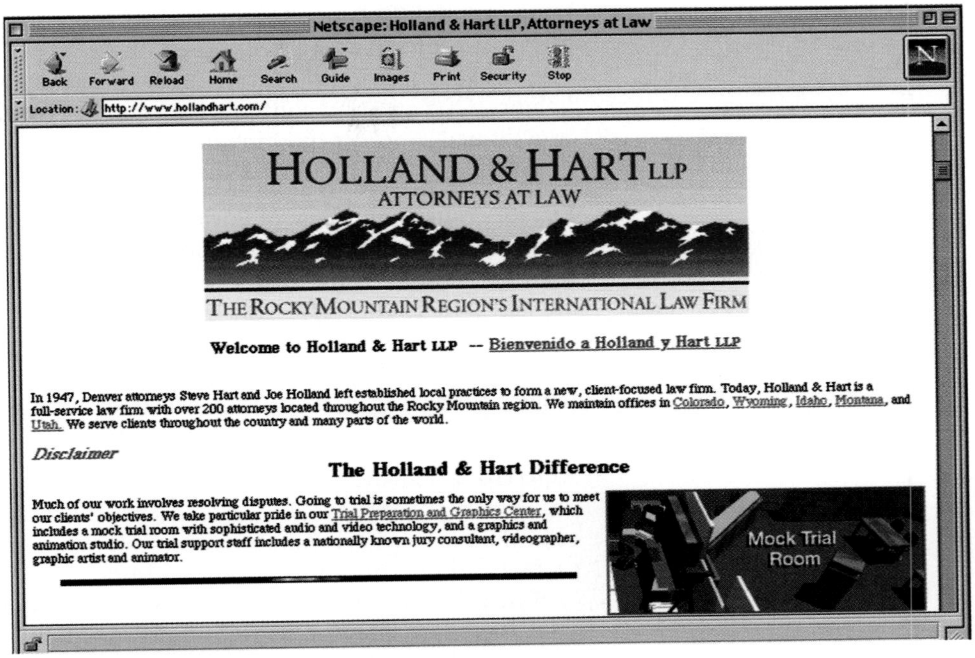

ATTORNEYS ADVERTISE THEIR AFFILIATION AS A LIMITED LIABILITY PARTNERSHIP (LLP). WHAT ADVANTAGES AND DISADVANTAGES DO THE PARTNERS IN AN LLP HAVE OVER THE PARTICIPANTS IN OTHER FORMS OF BUSINESS ORGANIZATIONS?

form must be filed with a central state agency, usually the secretary of state's office, and the business's name must include either "Limited Liability Partnership" or "LLP."

In most states, it is relatively easy to convert a traditional partnership into an LLP because the firm's basic organizational structure remains the same. Additionally, all of the statutory and common law rules governing partnerships still apply (apart from those modified by the LLP statute). Normally, LLP statutes are simply amendments to a state's already existing partnership law.

The LLP is especially attractive for two categories of businesses: professional services and family businesses. Professional service firms include law firms and accounting firms. Family limited liability partnerships are basically business organizations in which all of the partners are related.

LIABILITY IN AN LLP

Many professionals, such as attorneys and accountants, work together using the business form of the partnership. Remember from Chapter 25 that a major disadvantage of the partnership is the unlimited personal liability of its owner-partners. Partners are also subject to joint and several (individual) liability for partnership obligations. • EXAMPLE 32.1 A group of lawyers is operating as a partnership. A client sues one of the attorneys for malpractice and wins a large judgment, and the firm's malpractice insurance is insufficient to cover the obligation. When the attorney's personal assets are exhausted, the personal assets of the other, innocent partners can be used to satisfy the judgment.•

The LLP allows professionals to avoid personal liability for the malpractice of other partners. Although LLP statutes vary from state to state, generally each state statute limits in some way the liability of partners. For example, Delaware law protects each innocent partner from the "debts and obligations of the partnership arising from negligence, wrongful acts, or misconduct." In North Carolina, Texas, and Washington, D.C., the statutes protect innocent partners from obligations arising from "errors, omissions, negligence, incompetence, or malfeasance." Although the

ON THE WEB

For an example of a state law (that of Florida) governing limited liability partnerships, go to the Internet Legal Resource Guide's Web page at www.ilrg.com/whatsnews/statute.html and scroll down the page to "Registered Limited Liability Partnerships" language of these statutes may seem to apply specifically to attorneys, virtually any group of professionals can use the LLP.

Questions remain, however, concerning the exact limits of this exemption from liability. One question concerns limits on liability outside the state in which the LLP was formed. Another question involves whether liability should be imposed to some extent on a negligent partner's supervising partner.

Liability outside the State of Formation Because state LLP statutes are not uniform, a question arises when an LLP formed in one state does business in another state. If the LLP statutes in the two states provide different liability protection, which law applies? Most states apply the law of the state in which the LLP was formed, even when the firm does business in another state. Some states, though, do not expressly recognize foreign LLPs (that is, LLPs formed in another state), and others do not require foreign LLPs to register before doing business.[1] In these states, there have been no cases to date, but disputes will likely arise over which law should apply.

Supervising Partner's Liability A partner who commits a wrongful act, such as negligence, is liable for the results of the act. Also liable is the partner who supervises the party who commits a wrongful act. This is generally true for all types of partners and partnerships, including LLPs.

When the partners are members of an LLP and more than one member is negligent, there is a question as to how liability is to be shared. Is each partner jointly and severally liable for the entire result, as a general partner would be in most states? Some states provide for proportionate liability—that is, for separate determinations of the negligence of the partners.[2] The American Institute of Certified Public Accountants supports the enactment of proportionate liability statutes.[3]

• EXAMPLE 32.2 Imagine that accountants Don and Jane are partners in an LLP, with Don supervising Jane. Jane negligently fails to file tax returns for their client, Centaur Tools. Centaur files a suit against Don and Jane. In a state that does not allow for proportionate liability, Don can be held liable for the entire loss. Under a proportionate liability statute, Don will be liable for no more than his portion of the responsibility for the missed tax deadline. (Even if Jane settles the case quickly, Don will still be liable for his portion.) •

FAMILY LIMITED LIABILITY PARTNERSHIPS

• **FAMILY LIMITED LIABILITY PARTNERSHIP (FLLP)**
A type of limited liability partnership owned by family members or fiduciaries of family members.

A **family limited liability partnership** (FLLP) is a limited liability partnership in which the majority of the partners are persons related to each other, essentially as spouses, parents, grandparents, siblings, cousins, nephews, or nieces. A person acting in a fiduciary capacity for persons so related can also be a partner. All of the partners must be natural persons or persons acting in a fiduciary capacity for the benefit of natural persons.

Probably the most significant use of the FLLP form of business organization is in agriculture. Family-owned farms sometimes find this form to their benefit. The FLLP has the same advantages as other LLPs with some additional advantages, such as, in Iowa, an exemption from real estate transfer taxes when partnership real estate is transferred among partners.[4]

---

1. For example, Delaware and Texas do not expressly recognize foreign LLPs, and Utah does not require the registration of foreign LLPs.
2. See, for example, Colorado Revised Statutes Annotated Section 13-21-111.5(1) and Utah Code Annotated Section 78-27-39.
3. Public Oversight Board of the SEC Practice Section, AICPA, *In the Public Interest: Issues Confronting the Accounting Profession* (New York: AICPA, March 5, 1993), Recommendation I-1.
4. Iowa Statutes Section 428A.

Limited Partnerships

To this point, we have been discussing relatively new forms of limited liability business organizations. We now look at an older business organizational form that limits the liability of some of its owners—the limited partnership. Limited partnerships originated in medieval Europe and have been existence in the United States since the early 1800s. In many ways, limited partnerships are like the general partnerships discussed in Chapter 25, but they differ from general partnerships in several ways. Because of this, they are sometimes referred to as *special partnerships.*

EXHIBIT 32–1 • A Comparison of General Partnerships and Limited Partnerships

CHARACTERISTIC	GENERAL PARTNERSHIP (UPA)	LIMITED PARTNERSHIP (RULPA)
Creation	By agreement of two or more persons to carry on a business as co-owners for profit.	By agreement of two or more persons to carry on a business as co-owners for profit. Must include one or more general partners and one or more limited partners. Filing of a certificate with the secretary of state is required.
Sharing of Profits and Losses	By agreement; or, in the absence of agreement, profits are shared equally by the partners, and losses are shared in the same ratio as profits.	Profits are shared as required in the certificate agreement, and losses are shared likewise, up to the amount of the limited partners' capital contributions. In the absence of a provision in the certificate agreement, profits and losses are shared on the basis of percentages of capital contributions.
Liability	Unlimited personal liability of all partners.	Unlimited personal liability of all general partners; limited partners liable only to the extent of their capital contributions.
Capital Contribution	No minimum or mandatory amount; set by agreement.	Set by agreement.
Management	By agreement, or in the absence of agreement, all partners have an equal voice.	General partners by agreement, or else each has an equal voice. Limited partners have no voice or else are subject to liability as general partners (but *only* if a third party has reason to believe that the limited partner is a general partner). A limited partner may act as an agent or employee of the partnership and vote on amending the certificate or on the sale or dissolution of the partnership.
Duration	By agreement, or can be dissolved by action of the partners (withdrawal), operation of law (death or bankruptcy), or court decree.	By agreement in the certificate or by withdrawal, death, or mental incompetence of a general partner in the absence of the right of the other general partners to continue the partnership. Death of a limited partner, unless he or she is the only remaining limited partner, does not terminate the partnership.
Distribution of Assets on Liquidation—Order of Priorities	1. Outside creditors. 2. Partner creditors. 3. Partners, according to capital contributions. 4. Partners, according to profits.	1. Outside creditors and partner creditors. 2. Partners and former partners entitled to distributions before withdrawal under the agreement or the RULPA. 3. Partners, according to capital contributions. 4. Partners, according to profits.

• LIMITED PARTNERSHIP
A partnership consisting of one or more general partners (who manage the business and are liable to the full extent of their personal assets for debts of the partnership) and one or more limited partners (who contribute only assets and are liable only up to the extent of their contributions).

• GENERAL PARTNER
In a limited partnership, a partner who assumes responsibility for the management of the partnership and liability for all partnership debts.

• LIMITED PARTNER
In a limited partnership, a partner who contributes capital to the partnership but who has no right to participate in the management and operation of the business. The limited partner assumes no liability for partnership debts beyond the capital contributed.

• CERTIFICATE OF LIMITED PARTNERSHIP
The basic document filed with a designated state official by which a limited partnership is formed.

A **limited partnership** consists of at least one **general partner** and one or more **limited partners.** A general partner assumes management responsibility for the partnership and so has full responsibility for the partnership and for all debts of the partnership. A limited partner contributes cash or other property and owns an interest in the firm but does not undertake any management responsibilities and is not personally liable for partnership debts beyond the amount of his or her investment. A limited partner can forfeit limited liability by taking part in the management of the business. A comparison of the basic characteristics of general partnerships and limited partnerships appears in Exhibit 32–1 on the previous page.[5]

Until 1976, the law governing limited partnerships in all states except Louisiana was the Uniform Limited Partnership Act (ULPA). Since 1976, most states and the District of Columbia have adopted the revised version of the ULPA, known as the Revised Uniform Limited Partnership Act (RULPA). Because the RULPA is the dominant law governing limited partnerships in the United States, we will refer to the RULPA in the following discussion of limited partnerships.

FORMATION

Compared with the informal, private, and voluntary agreement that usually suffices for a general partnership, the formation of a limited partnership is a public and formal proceeding that must follow statutory requirements. A limited partnership must have at least one general partner and one limited partner, as mentioned previously. Additionally, the partners must sign a **certificate of limited partnership,** which requires information similar to that found in a corporate charter (see Chapter 27). The certificate must be filed with the designated state official—under the RULPA, the secretary of state. The certificate is usually open to public inspection.

The following case illustrates the importance of complying carefully with the formal statutory requirements imposed on limited partnerships.

5. Under the RUPA, a general partnership can be converted into a limited partnership and vice versa [RUPA 902, 903]. The RUPA also provides for the merger of a general partnership with one or more general or limited partnerships under rules that are similar to those governing corporate mergers [RUPA 905].

CASE 32.3 Miller v. Department of Revenue, State of Oregon

Supreme Court of Oregon, 1998.
327 Or. 129,
958 P.2d 833.
www.ejsimmons.com/advanced.html[a]

HISTORICAL AND ECONOMIC SETTING *Oregon statutes provide that "[i]t is the intent of the [Oregon] Legislative Assembly * * * to make the Oregon personal income tax law identical in effect to the provisions of the federal Internal Revenue Code relating to the measurement of taxable income of individuals." Oregon applies federal tax laws and federal court interpretations of those laws in resolving the issues raised by taxpayers. Under federal law, taxes are to be based on the "objective economic realities of a transaction rather than * * * the particular form [that] the parties employed."[b] Under state law, a taxpayer has the burden of proving by a preponderance of the evidence that a claimed deduction is allowable.[c]*

BACKGROUND AND FACTS Robert Loverin and Paul Miller bought a low-income housing project and retained Rockwood Development Corporation to manage it. For the project, Loverin and Miller formed a limited partnership. The certificate and articles of limited partnership identified Loverin and Miller as general partners and Rockwood as

a. This page provides access to opinions of the Oregon Supreme Court decided between July 1997 and December 3, 1998. In the "Query" box, type "Loverin" and click on "Submit Query." When the results appear, click on the "full" link to access the opinion. This site is maintained by attorney E. J. Simmons.

b. *Frank Lyon Co. v. United States,* 435 U.S. 561, 98 S.Ct. 1291, 55 L.Ed.2d 550 (1978).

c. *Reed v. Department of Revenue,* 310 Or. 260, 798 P.2d 235 (1990).

CASE 32.3—Continued

the only limited partner. It allocated 2 percent of the profits and losses to the general partners and 98 percent to the limited partner. Eventually, twenty-one investors became limited partners, but none of them signed the articles or the certificate. When American Properties Corporation (APC) replaced Rockwood as a limited partner, Loverin, Miller, and the president of APC signed a document that purported to amend the articles. The document provided in part that the partners could reallocate profits and losses as they "may agree." On their income tax returns, Loverin and Miller allocated 99.9 percent of the losses to themselves. The Oregon Department of Revenue reallocated the losses according to the provisions in the original articles—2 percent to general partners and 98 percent to limited partners. Miller and others appealed to the Oregon state tax court. The court upheld the assessment, and the plaintiffs appealed to the Oregon Supreme Court.

IN THE WORDS OF THE COURT . . .
LEESON, Justice.

* * * *

* * * [Oregon Revised Statute (ORS)] 69.180(1) describes the procedure required for forming a limited partnership * * * . It provides, in part, that when two or more persons desire to form a limited partnership they shall "[s]ign and verify a certificate" and shall "[f]ile one copy of such certificate in the office of the Corporation Commissioner." Taxpayers followed that procedure with respect to the [original] articles * * * . ORS 69.410(1) describes the procedure required to amend a certificate of limited partnership to change a limited partnership's composition. That statute provides that the writing to amend a certificate of limited partnership shall: "Be signed and verified by all partners. * * * "

The only evidence regarding the amended articles that taxpayers submitted to the Tax Court was a document signed by taxpayers and the president of APC. There is no evidence in this record that the amended articles were signed by the 21 [other] limited partners * * * . Thus, the amended articles were not properly executed. Consequently, taxpayers were not entitled to rely on * * * the amended articles for the purposes of allocating profits and losses * * * . The only document that conforms to the statutory requirements and that is binding is the [original] articles. * * * [Those] articles unambiguously allocate two percent of the losses to the general partners and 98 percent of the losses to the limited partners.

DECISION AND REMEDY The Oregon Supreme Court affirmed the lower court's decision, concluding that Loverin and Miller were not entitled to allocate 99.9 percent of the losses to themselves. The fact that none of the investing limited partners signed the purported amendments rendered them invalid.

FOR CRITICAL ANALYSIS—Economic Consideration
How might a power of attorney have been used to avoid the outcome in this case?

RIGHTS AND LIABILITIES OF PARTNERS

General partners, unlike limited partners, are personally liable to the partnership's creditors; thus, at least one general partner is necessary in a limited partnership so that someone has personal liability. This policy can be circumvented in states that allow a corporation to be the general partner in a partnership. Because the corporation has limited liability by virtue of corporate laws, if a corporation is the general partner, no one in the limited partnership has personal liability.

Rights of Limited Partners Subject to the limitations that will be discussed here, limited partners have essentially the same rights as general partners, including the right of access to partnership books and the right to other information regarding partnership business. On dissolution, limited partners are entitled to a return of their contributions in accordance with the partnership certificate [RULPA 201(a)(10)]. They can also assign their interests subject to the certificate [RULPA 702, 704].

The RULPA provides a limited partner with the right to sue an outside party on behalf of the firm if the general partners with authority to do so have refused to file suit [RULPA 1001]. In addition, investor protection legislation, such as securities laws (discussed in Chapter 31), may give some protection to limited partners.

Liabilities of Limited Partners In contrast to the personal liability of general partners, the liability of a limited partner is limited to the capital that he or she contributes or agrees to contribute to the partnership [RULPA 502].

> ¡NOTE! A limited partner is also liable to the extent of any contribution that he or she made to the partnership but later took back from the firm.

A limited partnership is formed by good faith compliance with the requirements for signing and filing the certificate, even if it is incomplete or defective. When a limited partner discovers a defect in the formation of the limited partnership, he or she can avoid future liability by causing an appropriate amendment or certificate to be filed or by renouncing an interest in the profits of the partnership [RULPA 304]. If the limited partner takes neither of these actions on the discovery of the defect, however, the partner can be held personally liable by the firm's creditors. Liability for false statements in a partnership certificate runs in favor of persons relying on the false statements and against members who know of the falsity but still sign the certificate [RULPA 207].

International Perspective • LIABILITY OF LIMITED PARTNERS IN ARGENTINA

Many nations permit businesspersons to establish limited partnerships. In Argentina, the limited partnership is called a *sociedad en comandita* and is closely regulated by the government. Limited partners, known as "sleeping partners," have limited liability so long as they do not participate in management. Argentinian law, however, does permit limited partners to inspect the books, express their views to managers, and offer advice at partnership meetings.

FOR CRITICAL ANALYSIS

What might happen if a limited partner in the United States offered advice to the general partners at partnership meetings?

Limited Partners and Management Limited partners enjoy limited liability so long as they do not participate in management [RULPA 303]. A limited partner who participates in management will be just as liable as a general partner to any creditor who transacts business with the limited partnership and believes, based on a limited partner's conduct, that the limited partner is a general partner [RULPA 303]. How much actual review and advisement a limited partner can engage in before being exposed to liability is an unsettled question.[6] A limited partner who knowingly permits his or her name to be used in the name of the limited partnership is liable to creditors who extend credit to the limited partnership without knowledge that the limited partner is not a general partner [RULPA 102, 303(d)].

6. It is an unsettled question partly because there are differences among the laws in different states. Factors to be considered under RULPA are listed in RULPA 303(b), (c).

Despite the restriction on the participation of limited partners in the management of a firm, all of the partners continue to have a fiduciary obligation to the other partners. In the following case, two limited partners filed suit against a general partner of the limited partnership. The issue before the court was whether the general partner breached his fiduciary obligation to the other partners.

CASE 32.4 Drucker v. Mige Associates II

Supreme Court, Appellate Division,
First Department, 1996.
639 N.Y.S.2d 365.

HISTORICAL AND ECONOMIC SETTING *One of the greatest fortunes in U.S. real estate had its start in 1789, when John Jacob Astor, a German immigrant, bought his first parcel of property in New York City. By buying one lot at a time, Astor eventually acquired huge sections of Manhattan. By 1830, he was the wealthiest man in North America. Investment in real estate became a route to riches for many other immigrants. The Lefrak Organization, for example, which was founded at the turn of the twentieth century by penniless immigrant Harry Lefrak, today owns nearly sixty-five thousand apartments and millions of square feet of commercial space in New York and New Jersey.*

BACKGROUND AND FACTS Mige Associates II was a limited partnership. Mige owned an apartment building that could have been converted into a cooperative (a housing complex jointly owned by the residents) at a substantial profit. The conversion required, under the voting provisions of the partnership agreement, the consent of Jon Meadow, one of the general partners. Before consenting, Meadow demanded that he receive more money than the other general partners. When his demand was rejected, he blocked the conversion. Ronald Drucker and Ronald Schaffer, two of the limited partners, filed a suit in a New York state court against Meadow. The court ruled in Meadow's favor. Drucker and Schaffer appealed.

IN THE WORDS OF THE COURT . . .
MEMORANDUM DECISION.

* * * *

* * * Meadow breached his fiduciary responsibility to the general and limited partners of Mige II Associates. Meadow effectively derailed the profitable conversion of the partnership's building into a cooperative apartment through his unwarranted demands * * * . Meadow's conduct was neither economically nor otherwise justified and can only fairly be viewed as an attempt to use the voting provisions of the partnership agreement for personal gain in contravention of the fundamental implied covenant of good faith and fair dealing governing the partners' fiduciary obligations to one another, and as a threat of irreparable harm to his own as well as plaintiffs' partnership interests.

* * * *

* * * Accordingly, while the court-ordered removal of a partner or judicial dissolution of a partnership are rarely invoked remedies, the totality of the circumstances lead us to conclude that the interests of the partnership would be best served by Meadow's removal as a general partner * * * .

DECISION AND REMEDY The New York state appellate court terminated Meadow's rights as a general partner.

FOR CRITICAL ANALYSIS—Economic Consideration *The court pointed out that the courts rarely order the removal of a partner or the dissolution of a partnership as a remedy when partners are in disagreement. Why is this?*

DISSOLUTION

A limited partnership is dissolved in much the same way as an ordinary partnership. The retirement, death, or mental incompetence of a general partner can dissolve the

EXHIBIT 33–2 • Major Forms of Business Compared

CHARACTERISTIC	SOLE PROPRIETORSHIP	PARTNERSHIP	CORPORATION
Method of Creation	Created at will by owner.	Created by agreement of the parties.	Charter issued by state—created by statutory authorization.
Legal Position	Not a separate entity; owner is the business.	Not a separate legal entity in many states.	Always a legal entity separate and distinct from its owners—a legal fiction for the purposes of owning property and being a party to litigation.
Liability	Unlimited liability.	Unlimited liability.	Limited liability of shareholders—shareholders are not liable for the debts of the corporation.
Duration	Determined by owner; automatically dissolved on owner's death.	Terminated by agreement of the partners, by the death of one or more of the partners, by withdrawal of a partner, by bankruptcy, and so on.	Can have perpetual existence.
Transferability of Interest	Interest can be transferred, but individual's proprietorship then ends.	Although partnership interest can be assigned, assignee does not have full rights of a partner.	Shares of stock can be transferred.
Management	Completely at owner's discretion.	Each general partner has a direct and equal voice in management unless expressly agreed otherwise in the partnership agreement.	Shareholders elect directors, who set policy and appoint officers.
Taxation	Owner pays personal taxes on business income.	Each partner pays pro rata share of income taxes on net profits, whether or not they are distributed.	Double taxation—corporation pays income tax on net profits, with no deduction for dividends, and shareholders pay income tax on disbursed dividends they receive.
Organizational Fees, Annual License Fees, and Annual Reports	None.	None.	All required.
Transaction of Business in Other States	Generally no limitation.	Generally no limitation.[a]	Normally must qualify to do business and obtain certificate of authority.

a. A few states have enacted statutes requiring that foreign partnerships qualify to do business there.

EXHIBIT 32–2 • Major Forms of Business Compared—Continued

CHARACTERISTIC	LIMITED PARTNERSHIP	LIMITED LIABILITY COMPANY	LIMITED LIABILITY PARTNERSHIP
Method of Creation	Created by agreement to carry on a business for a profit. At least one party must be a general partner and the other(s) limited partner(s). Certificate of limited partnership is filed. Charter must be issued by the state.	Created by an agreement of the owner-members of the company. Articles of organization are filed. Charter must be issued by the state.	Created by agreement of the partners. Certificate of a limited liability partnership is filed. Charter must be issued by state.
Legal Position	Treated as a legal entity.	Treated as a legal entity.	Generally, treated same as a general partnership.
Liability	Unlimited liability of all general partners; limited partners are liable only to the extent of capital contributions.	Member-owners' liability is limited to the amount of capital contributions or investment.	Varies from state to state but usually limits liability of a partner for certain acts committed by other partners.
Duration	By agreement in certificate, or by termination of the last general partner (withdrawal, death, and so on) or last limited partner.	Unless a single-member LLC, can have perpetual existence (same as a corporation).	Terminated by agreement of partners, by death or withdrawal of a partner, or by law (such as bankruptcy).
Transferability of Interest	Interest can be assigned (same as general partnership), but if assignee becomes a member with consent of other partners, certificate must be amended.	Member interests are freely transferable.	Interest can be assigned same as in a general partnership.
Management	General partners have equal voice or by agreement. Limited partners may not retain limited liability if they actively participate in management.	Member-owners can fully participate in management, or management is selected by owner-members who manage on behalf of the members.	Same as a general partnership.
Taxation	Generally taxed as a partnership.	LLC is not taxed, and members are taxed personally on profits "passed through" the LCC.	Same as a general partnership.
Organizational Fees, Annual License Fees, and Annual Reports	Organizational fee required; usually not others.	Organizational fee required; others vary with states.	Organizational fee required (such as a set amount per partner); usually not others.
Transaction of Business in Other States	Generally, no limitations.	Generally, no limitation but may vary depending on state.	Generally, no limitation, but state laws vary as to formation and limitation of liability.

partnership, but not if the business can be continued by one or more of the other general partners in accordance with their certificate or by the consent of all of the members [RULPA 801]. The death or assignment of interest of a limited partner does not dissolve the limited partnership [RULPA 702, 704, 705]. A limited partnership can be dissolved by court decree [RULPA 802].

Bankruptcy or the withdrawal of a general partner dissolves a limited partnership. Bankruptcy of a limited partner, however, does not dissolve the partnership unless it causes the bankruptcy of the limited partnership. The retirement of a general partner causes a dissolution unless the members consent to a continuation by the remaining general partners or unless this contingency is provided for in the certificate.

On dissolution, creditors' rights, including those of partners who are creditors, take first priority. Then partners and former partners receive unpaid distributions of partnership assets and, except as otherwise agreed, amounts representing returns on their contributions and amounts proportionate to their shares of the distributions [RULPA 804].

Limited Liability Limited Partnerships

• **LIMITED LIABILITY LIMITED PARTNERSHIP (LLLP)**
A type of limited partnership in which the liability of all of the partners, including general partners, is limited to the amount of their investments.

A **limited liability limited partnership** (LLLP) is a type of limited partnership. The difference between a limited partnership and an LLLP is that the liability of a general partner in an LLLP is the same as the liability of a limited partner. That is, the liability of all partners is limited to the amount of their investments in the firm.

A few states provide expressly for LLLPs.[7] In states that do not provide for LLLPs but do allow for limited partnerships and limited liability partnerships, a limited partnership should probably still be able to register with the state as an LLLP.

Major Business Forms Compared

ON THE WEB
The law firm of Wordes, Wilshin, Goren & Conner offers a comparison of the advantages and disadvantages of major business forms with respect to various factors, including ease of formation, management, and ability to raise capital, at its Web site. Go to www.wwgc.com/wwgc-be1.htm.

As mentioned in Chapter 25, when deciding which form of business organization would be most appropriate, businesspersons normally take several factors into consideration. These factors include ease of creation, the liability of the owners, tax considerations, and the need for capital. Each major form of business organization offers distinct advantages and disadvantages with respect to these and other factors. Exhibit 32–2 on pages 840 and 841 summarizes the essential advantages and disadvantages of each of the forms of business organization discussed in Chapters 25 through 31, as well as in this chapter.

7. See, for example, Colorado Revised Statutes Annotated Section 7-62-109. Other states that provide expressly for limited liability limited partnerships include Delaware, Florida, Missouri, Pennsylvania, Texas, and Virginia.

APPLICATION

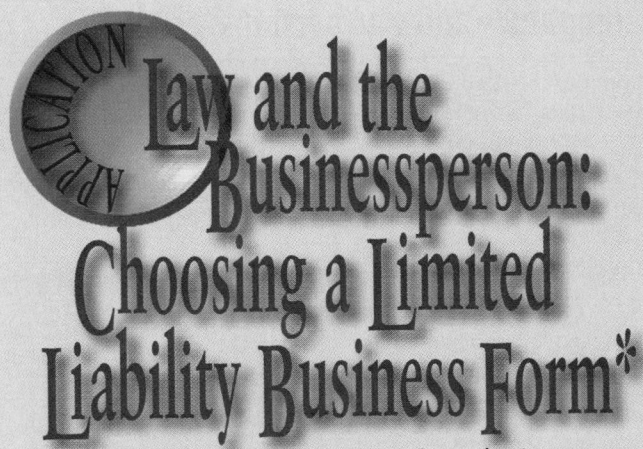

Law and the Businessperson: Choosing a Limited Liability Business Form*

One of the most important decisions that a businessperson makes is the selection of the form in which to do business. To make the best decision, a businessperson should understand all of the aspects of the variety of forms, including the legal, tax, licensing, and business considerations. It is also important that all of the participants in the business understand their actual relationship, regardless of the organizational structure.

During the last decade, new forms of business organizations, including limited liability partnerships (LLPs) and limited liability companies (LLCs), have been added to the options for business entities. An initial consideration in choosing between these forms is the number of participants. An LLP must have two or more partners, but in many states, an LLC can be limited to a single member (owner).

The members of an LLC are not liable for the obligations of the organization. The liability of the partners in an LLP varies from state to state. About half of the states exempt the partners from liability for any obligation of the firm. In some states, the partners are individually liable for the contractual obligations of the firm but not liable for obligations arising from the torts of others. In either situation, each partner may be on his or own with respect to liability unless the other partners decide to help.

Members and partners are generally paid by allowing them to withdraw funds from the firm against their share of the profits. In many states, a member of an LLC must repay so-called "wrongful distributions" even if he or she did not know that the distributions were wrongful. Under most LLP statutes, by contrast, the partners must repay only distributions that were fraudulent.

Both LLPs and LLCs can set up whatever management structure the participants desire to have. Also, all unincorporated business organizations, including LLPs and LLCs, are treated as partnerships for federal income tax purposes (unless an LLC elects to be treated as a corporation[a]). This means that the entities are not taxed at the firm level. Their income is passed through to the partners or members who must report it on their individual income tax returns. Some states impose additional taxes on LLCs.

The business in which a firm engages is another factor to consider in choosing a business form. For example, with a few exceptions, professionals—accountants, attorneys, physicians, and so on—may organize as either an LLP or an LLC in any state. In many states, however, the ownership of an entity that engages in a certain profession and the liability of the owners are prescribed by state law.

Despite their importance, the legal consequences of choosing a business form are often secondary considerations to the financial and personal relationships among the participants. Work effort, motivation, ability, and other personal attributes can be significant factors, as may be fundamental business concerns such as the expenses and debts of the firm. Other practical factors to consider include the willingness of others to do business with an LLP or an LLC. A supplier, for example, may not be willing to extend credit to a firm whose partners or members will not accept personal liability for the debt.

CHECKLIST FOR CHOOSING A LIMITED LIABILITY BUSINESS FORM

1. Determine the number of participants, which forms a state allows, and what a state provides for the participants in terms of liability.
2. Evaluate the tax considerations.
3. Consider the business in which a firm engages, or will engage, and any restrictions that exist on that type of business.
4. Weigh such practical concerns as the financial and personal relationships among the participants, and among the participants and those with whom a firm will deal.

*This *Application* is not meant to substitute for the services of an attorney who is licensed to practice law in your state.

a. The chief benefits of electing corporate status for tax purposes are that the members are not generally subject to self-employment taxes, and fringe benefits may be provided to employee-members on a tax-reduced basis. The tax laws are complicated, however, and a professional should be consulted about the details.

Key Terms

articles of organization 827
certificate of limited partnership 836
family limited liability partnership (FLLP) 834
general partner 836
limited liability company (LLC) 827
limited liability limited partnership (LLLP) 842
limited liability partnership (LLP) 831
limited partner 836
limited partnership 836
member 827
operating agreement 830

Chapter Summary • Limited Liability Companies and Partnerships

Limited Liability Companies (LLCs) (See pages 827–831.)	1. *Formation*—Articles of organization must be filed with the appropriate state office—usually the office of the secretary of state—setting forth the name of the business, its principal address, the names of the owners (called *members*), and other relevant information. 2. *Advantages and disadvantages of the LLC*—Advantages of the LLC include limited liability, the option to be taxed as a partnership or as a corporation, and flexibility in deciding how the business will be managed and operated. 3. *Operating agreement*—When an LLC is formed, the members decide, in an operating agreement, how the business will be managed and what rules will apply to the organization. 4. *Management*—An LLC may be managed by members only, by some members and some nonmembers, or by nonmembers only.
Limited Liability Partnerships (LLPs) (See pages 831–834.)	1. *Formation*—Articles must be filed with the appropriate state agency, usually the secretary of state's office. Typically, an LLP is formed by professionals who work together as partners in a partnership. Under most state LLP statutes, it is relatively easy to convert a traditional partnership into an LLP. 2. *Liability of partners*—LLP statutes vary, but generally they allow professionals to avoid personal liability for the malpractice of other partners. The extent to which partners' limited liability will be recognized when the partnership does business in another state depends on the other state's laws. Partners in an LLP continue to be liable for their own wrongful acts and for the wrongful acts of those whom they supervise. 3. *Family limited liability partnership (FLLP)*—A form of LLP in which all of the partners are family members or fiduciaries of family members; the most significant use of the FLLP is by families engaged in agricultural enterprises.
Limited Partnerships (See pages 835–842.)	1. *Formation*—A certificate of limited partnership must be filed with the secretary of state's office or other designated state official. The certificate must include information about the business, similar to the information included in a corporate charter. The partnership consists of one or more general partners and one or more imited partners. 2. *Rights and liabilities of partners*—With some exceptions, the rights of partners are the same as the rights of partners in a general partnership. General partners have unlimited liability for partnership obligations; limited partners are liable only to the extent of their contributions. 3. *Limited partners and management*—Only general partners can participate in management. Limited partners have no voice in management; if they do participate in management activities, they risk having general-partner liability. 4. *Dissolution*—Generally, a limited partnership can be dissolved in much the same way as an ordinary partnership. The death or assignment of interest of a limited partner does not dissolve the partnership; bankruptcy of a limited partner will also not dissolve the partnership unless it causes the bankruptcy of the firm.
Limited Liability Limited Partnerships (LLLPs) (See page 842.)	A special type of limited partnership in which the liability of all partners, including general partners, is limited to the amount of their investments.

For Review

❶ What advantages do limited liability companies and partnerships offer to businesspersons that are not offered by general partnerships or the corporate form of business?
❷ How are limited liability companies formed, and who decides how they will be managed and operated?
❸ What is the difference between limited liability companies and limited liability partnerships?
❹ What is a family limited liability partnership?
❺ What are the key differences between the rights and liabilities of general partners and limited partners?

Questions and Case Problems

32–1. Limited Liability Companies. John, Lesa, and Trevor form an LLC. John contributes 60 percent of the capital, and Lesa and Trevor each contribute 20 percent. Nothing is decided about how profits will be divided. John assumes that he will be entitled to 60 percent of the profits, in accordance with his contribution. Lesa and Trevor, however, assume that the profits will be divided equally. A dispute over the issue arises, and ultimately a court has to decide the issue. What law will the court apply? In most states, what will result? How could this dispute have been avoided in the first place? Discuss fully.

32–2. Liability of Limited Partners. Asher and Breem form a limited partnership with Asher as the general partner and Breem as the limited partner. Breem puts up $15,000, and Asher contributes some office equipment that he owns. A certificate of limited partnership is properly filed, and business is begun. One month later, Asher becomes ill. Instead of hiring someone to manage the business, Breem takes over complete management himself. While Breem is in control, he makes a contract with Thaler involving a large sum of money. Asher returns to work. Because of other commitments, Asher and Breem breach the Thaler contract. Thaler contends that Asher and Breem will be personally liable for damages caused by the breach if the damages cannot be satisfied out of the assets of the limited partnership. Discuss this contention.

32–3. Limited Partnerships. Dorinda, Lois, and Elizabeth form a limited partnership. Dorinda is a general partner, and Lois and Elizabeth are limited partners. Consider each of the separate events below, and discuss fully which event or events constitute a dissolution of the limited partnership.

(a) Lois assigns her partnership interest to Ashley.
(b) Elizabeth is petitioned into involuntary bankruptcy.
(c) Dorinda dies.

32–4. Liability of Limited Partners. Combat Associates was formed as a limited partnership to promote an exhibition boxing match between Lyle Alzado (a professional football player) and Muhammad Ali. Alzado and others had formed Combat Promotions; this organization was to be the general partner and Blinder, Robinson & Co. (Blinder), the limited partner in Combat Associates. The general partner's contribution consisted of assigning all contracts pertaining to the match, and the limited partner's contribution was a $250,000 letter of credit to ensure Ali's compensation. Alzado personally guaranteed to repay Blinder for any amount of loss if the proceeds of the match were less than $250,000. In preparation for the match, at Alzado's request, Blinder's president participated in interviews and a promotional rally, and the company sponsored parties and allowed its local office to be used as a ticket sales outlet. The proceeds of the match were insufficient, and Blinder sued Alzado on his guaranty. Alzado counterclaimed by asserting that Blinder had taken an active role in the control and management of Combat Associates and should be held liable as a general partner. How did the court rule on Alzado's counterclaim? Discuss. [*Blinder, Robinson & Co. v. Alzado,* 713 P.2d 1314 (Colo.App. 1985)]

32–5. Liability of General Partners. Pat McGowan, Val Somers, and Brent Roberson were general partners in Vermont Place, a limited partnership formed to construct duplexes on a tract of land in Fort Smith, Arkansas. In 1984, the partnership mortgaged the property so that it could build there. McGowan owned a separate company, Advance Development Corp., which was hired by the partnership to develop the project. On September 3, 1984, Somers and Roberson discovered that McGowan had not been paying the suppliers to the project, including National Lumber Co., and had not been making the mortgage payments. The suppliers and the bank sued the partnership and the general partners individually. Discuss whether Somers and Roberson could be held individually liable for the debts incurred by McGowan. [*National Lumber Co. v. Advance Development Corp.,* 293 Ark. 1, 732 S.W.2d 840 (1987)]

32–6. Limited Partners. Caton Avenue Associates was a limited partnership that owned rental property. Caton paid Theodore Dalmazio, one of the general partners, a management fee to manage the property. Dalmazio paid his employees with Caton's money. Dalmazio billed Caton for services that are normally performed by property management firms at no cost and also billed Caton at an hourly rate for work that is normally billed per rental unit. Alfred Friedman and the other limited partners filed a suit on Caton's behalf in a New York state court against Dalmazio and the other general partner to recover damages. On what basis might the court rule in favor of the limited partners? Explain. [*Friedman v. Dalmazio,* 644 N.Y.S.2d 548 (App.Div. 1996)]

32–7. Foreign Limited Liability Companies. Page, Scrantom, Sprouse, Tucker & Ford, a Georgia law firm, entered into a lease of office equipment in Georgia. The lessor assigned the lease to Danka Funding Company (DFC), a New York limited liability company (LLC) with its principal place of business in New Jersey. DFC was registered as a foreign LLC in New Jersey for almost two years before the registration lapsed or was withdrawn. Under the applicable statute, a foreign LLC "may not maintain any action . . . in this State until it has registered." When Page defaulted on the lease, DFC filed a complaint in a New Jersey state court against Page for more than $100,000. In its response, Page pointed out that DFC was not registered as a foreign LLC. DFC reregistered. Asserting that DFC had not been registered when it filed its suit, Page asked a federal district court to dismiss it. Should the court grant this request? Why or why not? [*Danka Funding, L.L.C. v. Page, Scrantom, Sprouse, Tucker & Ford, P.C.*, 21 F.Supp.2d 465 (D.N.J. 1998)]

32–8. Limited Liability Partnerships. Mudge Rose Guthrie Alexander & Ferdon, a law firm, was organized as a general partnership but converted into a limited liability partnership (LLP). Mudge's principal place of business was New York, where it was organized, but some of its members were citizens of Maryland. The firm filed a suit in a federal district court to recover unpaid legal fees from Robert Pickett and other citizens of Maryland. The defendants filed a motion to dismiss on the ground that there was not complete diversity of citizenship, because some of the LLC members were Maryland citizens also. Mudge argued that an LLP was like a corporation, and therefore the citizenship of the firm's members was irrelevant. How should the court rule? Explain. [*Mudge Rose Guthrie Alexander & Ferdon v. Pickett*, 11 F.Supp.2d 449 (S.D.N.Y. 1998)]

A QUESTION OF ETHICS AND SOCIAL RESPONSIBILITY

32–9. Mt. Hood Meadows Oregon, Ltd., was a limited partnership established to carry on the business of constructing and operating a winter sports development in the Hood River area of Oregon. Elizabeth Brooke and two of the other limited partners were dissatisfied because, for all the years in which profits were earned after 1974, the general partner distributed only 50 percent of the limited partners' taxable profits. The remaining profits were retained and reinvested in the business. Each of the limited partners was taxed on his or her distributable share of the profits, however, regardless of whether the cash was actually distributed. Brooke and the others brought an action to compel the general partner to distribute all of the limited partnership's profits. The court held that, in the absence of a limited partnership agreement concerning the distribution of profits, the decision to reinvest profits was strictly a managerial one. Unless the limited partners could prove that the general partner's conduct was inappropriate or violated a fiduciary duty, the decision of the general partner was binding on the limited partners. [*Brooke v. Mt. Hood Meadows Oregon, Ltd.*, 81 Ore.App. 387, 725 P.2d 925 (1986)]

1. The major attraction of limited partnerships is that the investors, as limited partners, are not liable for partnership obligations beyond the amount that they have invested. The "price" paid for this limited liability, however, is that limited partners have no say in management—as is well illustrated by the case described here. What ethical considerations are expressed in the rule that limited partners cannot participate in management? Do you think such a rule is fair?
2. This case also illustrates how relatively helpless the limited partners are when faced with a general partner whose actions do not correspond to the limited partners' wishes. Apart from selling their partnership shares to others (and at times, buyers are hard to find) or participating in management (and losing their limited liability as a result), limited partners have little recourse against the decisions of general partners so long as the general partners have not violated their fiduciary duties or the partnership agreement. Do you think that, because limited partners cannot participate in management, general partners have ethical duties to limited partners that go beyond those prescribed by law? If not, why not? If so, how would you describe or define such duties?

FOR CRITICAL ANALYSIS

32–10. Although a limited liability entity may be the best choice of form for most businesses, a significant number of firms may be better off as a corporation or some other organization. What effect does the fact that most of the limited liability entities are new forms for doing business have on the reasons for choosing another form of organization in which to do business? Explain.

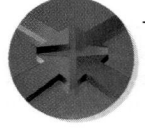

Online Activities

ONLINE EXERCISE 32-1

Go to the "Internet Activities Book" on the Web site that accompanies this text, the URL for which is http://blt.westbuslaw.com. Select the following activity, and perform the exercise according to the instructions given there:

Activity 30–1: Limited Liability Companies and Partnerships

Before the Test

Go to the *Business Law Today* home page at http://blt.westbuslaw.com. Click on TestTutor.® You will find twenty interactive questions relating to this chapter.

CHAPTER 33

Special Business Forms & Private Franchises

"Nothing contributes so much to the prosperity and happiness of a country as high profits."

David Ricardo, 1772–1823
(English economist)

CONTENTS

LEARNING OBJECTIVES

After reading this chapter, you should be able to:

1. Describe the major characteristics of the following business organizational forms: joint ventures, syndicates, joint stock companies, business trusts, and cooperatives.
2. Explain how a franchising relationship arises and define the terms *franchise, franchisor,* and *franchisee.*
3. Give examples of how federal and state laws govern franchising arrangements.
4. Summarize some of the major concerns of franchisors and franchisees with respect to franchise contracts.
5. Identify the circumstances in which franchisors may be liable under agency law.

Few would argue with David Ricardo's statement that high profits contribute to the "prosperity and happiness of a country." Certainly, this assumption is the basis for this country's public policy of encouraging trade and commerce. To promote commerce and profit-making activities, our government, among other things, allows entrepreneurs to choose from a variety of business organizational forms when undertaking their business ventures.

We have examined in the preceding chapters some of the most significant business forms—including sole proprietorships, partnerships, corporations, and limited liability companies and partnerships. In this chapter, after first describing a number of forms that can be used for special types of business ventures, we look in detail at private franchises. Although the franchise is not really a business organizational form, the franchising arrangement has become widely used by those seeking to make profits.

Special Business Forms

¡CONTRAST!
A partnership involves a continuing relationship of the partners. A joint venture is essentially a one-time association.

Besides the business forms discussed in previous chapters, there are several other forms that can be used to organize a business. For the most part, these other business forms are hybrid organizations—that is, they have characteristics similar to those of partnerships or corporations or combine features of both. These forms include joint ventures, syndicates, joint stock companies, business trusts, and cooperatives.

JOINT VENTURES

• **JOINT VENTURE**
A joint undertaking of a specific commercial enterprise by an association of persons. A joint venture is normally not a legal entity and is treated like a partnership for federal income tax purposes.

A **joint venture** is an enterprise in which two or more persons or business entities combine their efforts or their property for a single transaction or project, or a related series of transactions or projects. For example, when several contractors combine their resources to build and sell houses in a single development, their relationship is a joint venture. The joint venture is treated much like a partnership, but it differs in that it is created in contemplation of a limited activity or a single transaction. Joint ventures are taxed like partnerships, and, unless otherwise agreed, joint venturers share profits and losses equally.

Members of a joint venture usually have limited powers to bind their co-venturers. A joint venture is normally not a legal entity and therefore cannot be sued as such, but its members can be sued individually. Joint ventures range in size from very small activities to huge, multimillion-dollar joint actions engaged in by some of the world's largest corporations.

SYNDICATES

• **SYNDICATE**
An investment group of persons or firms brought together for the purpose of financing a project that they would not or could not undertake independently.

A group of individuals getting together to finance a particular project, such as the building of a shopping center or the purchase of a professional basketball franchise, is called a **syndicate** or an *investment group*. The form of such groups varies considerably. A syndicate may exist as a corporation or as a general or limited partnership. In some cases, the members merely purchase and own property jointly but have no legally recognized business arrangement.

A HOUSING DEVELOPMENT PUBLICIZES THAT IT OFFERS NEW HOUSES FOR SALE. WHEN THE BUSINESS FIRM BEHIND A HOUSING DEVELOPMENT IS ORGANIZED AS A JOINT VENTURE, WHAT HAPPENS TO THE JOINT VENTURE AFTER THE LAST HOUSE IS SOLD?

Joint Stock Companies

• **JOINT STOCK COMPANY**
A hybrid form of business organization that combines characteristics of a corporation and a partnership. Usually, the joint stock company is regarded as a partnership for tax and other legally related purposes.

A **joint stock company** is a true hybrid of a partnership and a corporation. It has many characteristics of a corporation in that (1) its ownership is represented by transferable shares of stock, (2) it is usually managed by directors and officers of the company or association, and (3) it can have a perpetual existence. Most of its other features, however, are more characteristic of a partnership, and it is usually treated like a partnership. As with a partnership, it is formed by agreement (not statute), property is usually held in the names of the members, shareholders have personal liability, and generally the company is not treated as a legal entity for purposes of a lawsuit. In a joint stock company, however, shareholders are not considered to be agents of each other, as would be the case if the company were a true partnership (see Chapter 25).

Business Trusts

• **BUSINESS TRUST**
A form of business organization in which investors (trust beneficiaries) transfer cash or property to trustees in exchange for trust certificates that represent their investment shares. The certificate holders share in the trust's profits but have limited liability.

A **business trust** is created by a written trust agreement that sets forth the interests of the beneficiaries and the obligations and powers of the trustees. With a business trust, legal ownership and management of the property of the business stay with one or more of the trustees, and the profits are distributed to the beneficiaries.

The business trust was started in Massachusetts in an attempt to obtain the limited liability advantage of corporate status while avoiding certain restrictions on a corporation's ownership and development of real property. The business trust resembles a corporation in many respects. Beneficiaries of the trust, for example, are not personally responsible for the debts or obligations of the business trust. In fact, in a number of states, business trusts must pay corporate taxes.

Cooperatives

• **COOPERATIVE**
An association, which may or may not be incorporated, that is organized to provide an economic service to its members. Unincorporated cooperatives are often treated like partnerships for tax and other legally related purposes. Examples of cooperatives are consumer purchasing cooperatives, credit cooperatives, and farmers' cooperatives.

• **FRANCHISE**
Any arrangement in which the owner of a trademark, trade name, or copyright licenses another to use that trademark, trade name, or copyright in the selling of goods and services.

A **cooperative** is an association, which may or may not be incorporated, that is organized to provide an economic service, without profit, to its members (or shareholders). An incorporated cooperative is subject to state laws governing nonprofit corporations. It will make distributions of dividends, or profits, to its owners on the basis of their transactions with the cooperative rather than on the basis of the amount of capital they contributed. Cooperatives that are unincorporated are often treated like partnerships. The members have joint liability for the cooperative's acts.

This form of business is generally adopted by groups of individuals who wish to pool their resources to gain some advantage in the marketplace. Consumer purchasing co-ops are formed to obtain lower prices through quantity discounts. Seller marketing co-ops are formed to control the market and thereby obtain higher sales prices from consumers. Often cooperatives are exempt from certain federal laws, such as antitrust laws (laws prohibiting anticompetitive practices—see Chapter 35), because of their special status.

Private Franchises

Many entrepreneurs, instead of setting up a business form through which to market their own products or services, opt to purchase a franchise. A **franchise** is defined as any arrangement in which the owner of a trademark, a trade name, or a copyright licenses others to use the trademark, trade name, or copyright in the selling of goods

• **FRANCHISEE**
One receiving a license to use another's (the franchisor's) trademark, trade name, or copyright in the sale of goods and services.

• **FRANCHISOR**
One licensing another (the franchisee) to use his or her trademark, trade name, or copyright in the sale of goods or services.

¡KEEP IN MIND!
Because a franchise involves the licensing of a trademark, a trade name, or a copyright, the law governing intellectual property may apply in some cases.

or services. A **franchisee** (a purchaser of a franchise) is generally legally independent of the **franchisor** (the seller of the franchise). At the same time, the franchisee is economically dependent on the franchisor's integrated business system. In other words, a franchisee can operate as an independent businessperson but still obtain the advantages of a regional or national organization.

The franchising boom was launched by Ray Kroc, the late founder of McDonald's, nearly forty years ago. Today, over a third of all retail transactions and an increasing percentage of the total annual national output of the United States are generated by private franchises. Well-known franchises include McDonald's, KFC, and Burger King.

Types of Franchises

Because the franchising industry is so extensive and so many different types of businesses sell franchises, it is difficult to summarize the many types of franchises that now exist. Generally, though, the majority of franchises fall into one of the following three classifications: distributorships, chain-style business operations, or manufacturing or processing-plant arrangements. We briefly describe these types of franchises here.

Distributorship A *distributorship* arises when a manufacturer (franchisor) licenses a dealer (franchisee) to sell its product. Often, a distributorship covers an exclusive territory. An example of this type of franchise is an automobile dealership.

Chain-Style Business Operation A *chain-style business operation* exists when a franchise operates under a franchisor's trade name and is identified as a member of a select group of dealers that engages in the franchisor's business. Often, the franchisor requires that the franchisee maintain certain standards of operation. In addition, sometimes the franchisee is obligated to deal exclusively with the franchisor to obtain materials and supplies. Examples of this type of franchise are McDonald's and most other fast-food chains.

Manufacturing or Processing-Plant Arrangement A *manufacturing or processing-plant arrangement* exists when the franchisor transmits to the franchisee the essential ingredients or formula to make a particular product. The franchisee then markets the product either at wholesale or at retail in accordance with the franchisor's standards. Examples of this type of franchise are Coca-Cola and other soft-drink bottling companies.

Laws Governing Franchising

Because a franchise relationship is primarily a contractual relationship, it is governed by contract law. If the franchise exists primarily for the sale of products manufactured by the franchisor, the law governing sales contracts as expressed in Article 2 of the Uniform Commercial Code applies (see Chapters 15 through 18). Additionally, the federal government and most states have enacted laws governing certain aspects of franchising. Generally, these laws are designed to protect prospective franchisees from dishonest franchisors and to prohibit franchisors from terminating franchises without good cause.

FAMILIAR FRANCHISES COMPETE FOR BUSINESS. WHAT LAWS GOVERN THE RELATIONSHIP BETWEEN FRANCHISORS AND FRANCHISEES?

Federal Regulation of Franchising Automobile dealership franchisees are protected from automobile manufacturers' bad faith termination of their franchises by the Automobile Dealers' Franchise Act[1]—also known as the Automobile Dealers' Day in Court Act—of 1965. If a manufacturer-franchisor terminates a franchise because of a dealer-franchisee's failure to comply with unreasonable demands (for example, failure to attain an unrealistically high sales quota), the manufacturer may be liable for damages.

Another federal statute is the Petroleum Marketing Practices Act (PMPA)[2] of 1979, which prescribes the grounds and conditions under which a franchisor may terminate or decline to renew a gasoline station franchise. Federal antitrust laws (discussed in Chapter 35), which prohibit certain types of anticompetitive agreements, may also apply in certain circumstances.

Additionally, regulations were issued by the Federal Trade Commission (FTC) that require franchisors to disclose material facts necessary to a prospective franchisee's making an informed decision concerning the purchase of a franchise.

> **ON THE WEB**
> For information on the FTC regulations on franchising, as well as state laws regulating franchising, go to **www.ftc.gov/bcp/franchise/netfran.htm**.

State Regulation of Franchising State legislation tends to be similar to federal statutes and the FTC's regulations. To protect franchisees, a state law might require the disclosure of information that is material to making an informed decision regarding the purchase of a franchise. This could include such information as the actual costs of operation, recurring expenses, and profits earned, along with facts substantiating these figures. The law may also require that certain procedures be followed in terminating a franchising relationship to protect franchisees against arbitrary or bad faith terminations. State deceptive trade practices acts may also prohibit certain types of actions on the part of franchisors.

In response to the need for a uniform franchise law, the National Conference of Commissioners on Uniform State Laws drafted a model law that standardizes the various state franchise regulations. Because the uniform law represents a compromise of so many diverse interests, it has met with little success in being adopted as law by the various states.

ETHICAL ISSUE 33.1 ***Why should the government protect franchisees?*** A franchising relationship is based on a contract, and contract law thus applies. Why, then, has the government deemed it necessary to enact laws to protect franchisees from the consequences of contracts into which they have voluntarily entered? One reason is that a franchisee often relies heavily on information about the business provided by the franchisor when deciding to purchase a franchise. Disclosure requirements mandated by the FTC and state statutes help to ensure that prospective franchisees have accurate information when deciding whether to enter into a franchise contract.

Another reason is that the purchaser of a franchise often has little bargaining power relative to the franchisor and little say in the contract provisions. Additionally, franchise contracts are typically lengthy documents, consisting of perhaps fifty pages. A franchisee who is relatively inexperienced in business may not realize the economic and legal consequences of ambiguous clauses in the contract or of the absence of certain clauses—such as a clause granting the franchisee exclusive rights to sell the franchisor's products in a particular territory.

1. 15 U.S.C. Sections 1221 *et seq.*
2. 15 U.S.C. Sections 2801 *et seq.*

THE FRANCHISE CONTRACT

> **ON THE WEB**
> A good source of information on the purchase and sale of franchises is Franchising.org, which is online at **www.franchsing.org**.

The franchise relationship is defined by a contract between the franchisor and the franchisee. The franchise contract specifies the terms and conditions of the franchise and spells out the rights and duties of the franchisor and the franchisee. If either party fails to perform the contractual duties, that party may be subject to a lawsuit for breach of contract. Generally, the statutory and case law governing franchising tend to emphasize the importance of good faith and fair dealing in franchise relationships.

Because each type of franchise relationship has its own characteristics, it is difficult to describe the broad range of details a franchising contract may include. In the remaining pages of this chapter, we look at some of the major issues that typically are addressed in a franchise contract.

Payment for the Franchise The franchisee ordinarily pays an initial fee or lump-sum price for the franchise license (the privilege of being granted a franchise). This fee is separate from the various products that the franchisee purchases from or through the franchisor. In some industries, the franchisor relies heavily on the initial sale of the franchise for realizing a profit. In other industries, the continued dealing between the parties brings profit to both. In most situations, the franchisor will receive a stated percentage of the annual sales or annual volume of business done by the franchisee. The franchise agreement may also require the franchisee to pay a percentage of advertising costs and certain administrative expenses.

Business Premises The franchise agreement may specify whether the premises for the business must be leased or purchased outright. In some cases, construction of a building is necessary to meet the terms of the agreement. The agreement usually will specify whether the franchisor supplies equipment and furnishings for the premises or whether this is the responsibility of the franchisee.

Location of the Franchise Typically, the franchisor will determine the territory to be served. Some franchise contracts will give the franchisee exclusive rights, or "territorial rights," to a certain geographical area. Other franchise contracts, while

The Letter of the Law — WHAT HAPPENED TO GOOD FAITH AND FAIR DEALING?

Zuri Barnes operated a Burger King restaurant in Los Angeles. The franchise contract required Barnes to pay 3.5 percent of his gross sales in royalties to Burger King and to operate the restaurant at the specified location for twenty years. Three years after he started up the business, Burger King allowed another franchisee to set up a competing business five blocks away. Although Burger King's action did not violate the franchise contract, which did not give Barnes exclusive territorial rights, Barnes complained that the new franchise would cause a 50 percent decline in his gross sales, a prediction that later came true. Burger King, though, was not concerned and told Barnes that his fears were unjustified. When Barnes closed his business and ceased paying royalties to Burger King, Burger King sued him for breach of contract to recover "lost profits"—that is, the estimated royalties for the remaining seventeen years under the contract. The royalties were based on the gross sales during the three years prior to Barnes's breach. Barnes tried to convince the court that the damages were too speculative, but to no avail. After all was said and done, Barnes was ordered to pay Burger King over $275,000 in damages.[a]

THE BOTTOM LINE

Franchisees should be prepared to pay the consequences of entering into a franchise contract that does not allow for exclusive territorial rights. Not all courts, including the court in this case, will give good faith and fair dealing priority over the words of a written contract.

a. *Burger King Corp. v. Barnes,* 1 F.Supp.2d 1367 (S.D.Fla. 1998).

they define the territory allotted to a particular franchise, either specifically state that the franchise is nonexclusive or are silent on the issue of territorial rights.

Many franchise cases involve disputes over territorial rights, and this is one area of franchising in which the implied covenant of good faith and fair dealing often comes into play. For example, suppose that a franchisee is not given exclusive territorial rights in the franchise contract, or the contract is silent on the issue. If the franchisor allows a competing franchise to be established nearby, the franchisee may suffer a significant loss in profits. In this situation, a court may hold that the franchisor's actions breached an implied covenant of good faith and fair dealing. (Then again, a court may not—see, for example, the feature *The Letter of the Law* on the previous page.)

In the following case, the franchisee did not have any exclusive territorial rights under the franchise contract. When the franchisor built a competing operation nearby, the franchisee sued the franchisor. At issue in the case was whether the franchisor had breached an implied covenant of good faith and fair dealing.

CASE 33.1 Camp Creek Hospitality Inns, Inc. v. Sheraton Franchise Corp.

United States Court of Appeals,
Eleventh Circuit, 1998.
139 F.3d 1396.
www.findlaw.com/casecode/courts/11th.html[a]

HISTORICAL AND ECONOMIC SETTING *Before 1950, travel was often slow, at best. By the end of the 1950s, airlines had established regular routes between American and European cities, and the travel industry began to change dramatically. Thirty years later, the federal government relaxed the tight control it maintained over U.S. air routes. Over the next decade, travel became even more common, frequent weekend trips replaced the standard two-week family vacation, and business travelers filled more than half of the hotel rooms in the United States. Despite these trends, the hotel industry suffered losses in the late 1980s and the early 1990s.*

a. This page contains links to recent opinions of the U.S. Court of Appeals for the Eleventh Circuit. In the "1998" row, click on the "April" link. When the results appear, click on the *Camp Creek* case name to access the opinion. This Web site is maintained by FindLaw.

BACKGROUND AND FACTS In 1990, Camp Creek Hospitality Inns, Inc., entered into a contract with Sheraton Franchise Corporation (a subsidiary of ITT Sheraton Corporation) to operate a Sheraton Inn franchise west of the Atlanta airport. Because another franchisee, the Sheraton Hotel Atlanta Airport, already served that market, Sheraton named Camp Creek's facility "Sheraton Inn Hartsfield-West, Atlanta Airport." Three years later, ITT Sheraton bought a Hyatt hotel in the vicinity of the Atlanta airport and gave it the name "Sheraton Gateway Hotel, Atlanta Airport." The presence of three Sheraton properties in the same market caused some customer confusion. Also, the Inn and the Gateway competed for the same customers, which caused the Inn to suffer a decrease in the growth of its business. Camp Creek filed a suit in a federal district court against Sheraton and others, alleging in part that by establishing the Gateway, ITT Sheraton denied Camp Creek the fruits of its contract in breach of the implied covenant of good faith and fair dealing. The court issued a summary judgment in favor of the defendants. Camp Creek appealed to the U.S. Court of Appeals for the Eleventh Circuit.

IN THE WORDS OF THE COURT . . .
BIRCH, Circuit Judge:

* * * *

* * * [T]he contract, as executed, says nothing about whether or where Sheraton could establish a competing hotel. * * * Camp Creek had no contractual right to expect the Sheraton Franchise to refrain from licensing the Sheraton name to additional franchises beyond the site of the Inn. By the express terms of the contract, therefore, Sheraton could have authorized a competing franchise directly across the street from the Inn, and Camp Creek would have little recourse.

(Continued)

CASE 33.1—Continued

Sheraton, however, did not establish such a franchise in this case; instead, it purchased and operated the Gateway on its own behalf. * * *

As a result, we must determine whether the implied covenant of good faith and fair dealing permits the Sheraton to establish its own hotel in the same vicinity as the Inn. * * *

* * * Sheraton emphasizes that the Inn has been more profitable every year since the Gateway opened. Camp Creek, however, * * * describe[d] a number of trends present in the market for hotel rooms in the Atlanta area, both before and after Sheraton began operating the Gateway, and present[ed] credible theories and measures of damages attributable to the additional intra-brand competition associated with the Gateway's entry to the market. We hold that Camp Creek's evidence is sufficient to withstand Sheraton's motion for summary judgment on this claim.

DECISION AND REMEDY The U.S. Court of Appeals for the Eleventh Circuit held that unless a franchise contract expressly provides otherwise, it could violate the implied covenant of good faith and fair dealing for a franchisor to compete against a franchisee in the same market for the same customers. The court reversed the judgment of the lower court and remanded the case for trial.

FOR CRITICAL ANALYSIS—Economic Consideration *Why would a franchisor compete directly with its franchisee?*

Business Organization of the Franchisee The business organization of the franchisee is of great concern to the franchisor. Depending on the terms of the franchise agreement, the franchisor may specify particular requirements for the form and capital structure of the business. The franchise agreement may also provide that standards of operation—relating to such aspects of the business as sales quotas, quality, and record keeping—be met by the franchisee. Furthermore, a franchisor may wish to retain stringent control over the training of personnel involved in the operation and over administrative aspects of the business.

¡RECALL!
Under the doctrine of *respondeat superior,* an employer may be liable for the torts of his or her employees if they occur within the scope of employment, without regard to the personal fault of the employer.

Quality Control by the Franchisor Although the day-to-day operation of the franchise business is normally left up to the franchisee, the franchise agreement may provide for the amount of supervision and control agreed on by the parties. When the franchise is a service operation, such as a motel, the contract often provides that the franchisor will establish certain standards for the facility. Typically, the contract will provide that the franchisor is permitted to make periodic inspections to ensure that the standards are being maintained in order to protect the franchise's name and reputation.

As a general rule, the validity of a provision permitting the franchisor to establish and enforce certain quality standards is unquestioned. Because the franchisor has a legitimate interest in maintaining the quality of the product or service to protect its name and reputation, it can exercise greater control in this area than would otherwise be tolerated. Increasingly, however, franchisors are finding that if they exercise too much control over the operations of their franchisees, they may incur liability under agency theory for the acts of their franchisees' employees—as the following case illustrates. (A franchisee may even be held to be an employee of the franchisor—see this chapter's *Business Law in Action* for a discussion of this topic.)

CASE 33.2 Miller v. D. F. Zee's, Inc.

United States District Court,
District of Oregon, 1998.
31 F.Supp.2d 792.

COMPANY PROFILE *Based in South Carolina, Flagstar Corporation franchised or owned Denny's restaurants, as well as the Carrows, Coco's, El Pollo Loco, Hardee's, and*

CASE 33.2—Continued

Quincy's Family Steakhouse chains. In the early 1990s, Denny's was the defendant in two civil rights class-action suits brought by African American customers who claimed that some restaurants refused to seat or serve them. Denny's paid more than $54 million to settle those suits and responded "quickly, decisively, and sincerely" to, among other things, hire and promote more minorities.[a] *In the mid-1990s, Flagstar declared bankruptcy, sold the Hardee's and Quincy's chains, and renamed itself Advantica Restaurant Group, Inc. By the late 1990s, Advantica's annual sales approached $3 billion, with about 2 percent annual growth.*

BACKGROUND AND FACTS D. F. Zee's, Inc., owns a Denny's restaurant in Tualatin, Oregon. Under the franchise agreement, Zee's agreed to train and supervise employees in accordance with Denny's Operations and Food Service Standards Manuals. Denny's regularly sent inspectors to assess compliance and reserved the right to terminate the franchise for noncompliance. The Denny's logo was displayed throughout the restaurant, and there was no indication that its owners were other than "Denny's." Christine Miller worked as a server at the restaurant. After several incidents of sexually inappropriate comments and conduct by her co-workers, Miller complained to Stanley Templeton, the manager. When her complaints were unavailing, Miller contacted the manager of another Denny's restaurant, who referred her to the district franchise manager for Denny's, who referred the complaint to Zee's. Templeton resigned, but the harassment continued. Finally, Miller and three other employees filed a suit in a federal district court against Zee's, Denny's, and others. Denny's filed a motion for summary judgment, contending in part that a franchisor cannot be held liable for harassment by franchise employees.

a. Anne Faircloth, "Guess Who's Coming to Denny's," *Fortune*, August 3, 1998.

IN THE WORDS OF THE COURT . . .
AIKEN, J.

* * * *

Here, Denny's is responsible for acts of harassment by employees at the Tualatin Denny's because employees of the Tualatin Denny's are agents of [Denny's].

* * * [A]n agency results from the manifestation of consent by one person to another so that the other will act on his or her behalf and "subject" to his or her control, and consent by the other to so act. An agency relationship may be evidenced by an express agreement between the parties, or it may be implied from the circumstances and conduct of the parties. The principal's consent and "right to control" are the essential elements of an agency relationship. * * *

* * * *

Here, * * * the franchise agreement requires adherence to comprehensive, detailed [Franchise Operations and Food Service Standards] manuals for the operation of the restaurant. * * *

Here, * * * defendants enforce the use of these methods by regularly sending inspectors into the restaurant to assess compliance and by its retained power to cancel the agreement.

Further, the Franchise Operations Manual provides that the defendants had the right to control their franchisees in the precise parts of the franchisee's business that allegedly resulted in plaintiffs' injuries—training and discipline of employees.

DECISION AND REMEDY The court denied Denny's motion for summary judgment. The court held that a franchisor may be held vicariously liable under an agency theory for intentional acts of discrimination by the employees of a franchisee.

FOR CRITICAL ANALYSIS—Ethical Consideration *Should a franchisor be allowed to control the operation of its franchisee without liability for the franchisee's conduct?*

Business Law in Action • Is It a Franchise . . . or Not?

A series of court decisions in the late 1990s has put businesspersons on notice that what will or will not be deemed a franchise may not always be determined by private contracts. For example, in one case a franchisee of a West Sanitation Services, Inc., a commercial sanitation company, was deemed to be employee of the company even though he was designated as a franchisee in a franchise contract with the company.

The franchisee, Glenroy Francis, began working for West in 1986 as an employee. As an employee, he serviced commercial customers in a certain area. In 1987, West initiated a franchise program, in which some of its service employees, including Francis, became franchisees. When West later terminated its franchising arrangement with Francis for cause, Francis applied for unemployment insurance benefits.

The state labor department, after investigating Francis's working relationship with West, decided that an employment relationship existed because of the degree of direction and control exercised by West over Francis's work schedule and activities. The department ruled that Francis, as a former "employee," was entitled to unemployment benefits. The department further ruled that West was liable for unemployment insurance contributions, based on the amount West had paid to Francis and the other franchisees.

Ultimately, a New York appellate court upheld the labor department's ruling, concluding that "the franchise agreement vested West with substantial control over claimant's activities."[a]

In another case, the National Labor Relations Board ruled that some five hundred drivers for a New York company that provided limousine services should be considered as employees for labor law purposes, despite their franchise contracts with the company. Again, the decision was based on the extensive control exercised by the company over the drivers' activities.[b]

In yet other cases, courts have gone in the opposite direction—they have found franchising relationships to exist even though the parties had *not* formed franchise contracts. In a number of states, if a business arrangement meets the definition of a franchising relationship under state law, it may be held to be a *de facto* franchise in that state. These cases typically arise because one of the parties wants to take advantage of a state franchising statute that offers certain protections to franchisees that would not be available under other types of contractual arrangements. For example, in one case a Mitsubishi subsidiary terminated its relationship with one of its distributors. The distributor sued for wrongful termination under the state franchising law and received $1.5 million in damages.[c]

FOR CRITICAL ANALYSIS

Under what common law concept is the degree of control over a worker's activities a significant factor in determining employee status?

a. *West Sanitation Services, Inc. v. Francis,* 1998 WL 11023 (N.Y.Sup.Ct.App.Div. 1998).
b. *In re Elite Limousine Plus, Inc.,* 324 NLRB No. 182 (November 6, 1997).
c. *To-Am Equipment Co. v. Mitsubishi Caterpillar Forklift America, Inc.,* 953 F.Supp. 987 (N.D.Ill. 1997).

Pricing Arrangements Franchises provide the franchisor with an outlet for the firm's goods and services. Depending on the nature of the business, the franchisor may require the franchisee to purchase certain supplies from the franchisor at an established price.[3] A franchisor who sets the prices at which the franchisee will resell the goods may violate state or federal antitrust laws, or both, however.

3. Although a franchisor can require franchisees to purchase supplies from it, requiring a franchisee to purchase exclusively from the franchisor may violate federal antitrust laws (see Chapter 35). For two landmark cases in these areas, see *United States v. Arnold, Schwinn & Co.,* 388 U.S. 365, 87 S.Ct. 1956, 18 L.Ed.2d (1967), and *Fortner Enterprises, Inc. v. U.S. Steel Corp.,* 394 U.S. 495, 89 S.Ct. 1252, 22 L.Ed.2d 495 (1969).

ON THE WEB

At the Web site of Law Journal EXTRA!, you can find articles and other information on franchising, including links to numerous sources on this topic. Go to www.ljx.com/franchising.

Termination of the Franchise The duration of the franchise is a matter to be determined between the parties. Generally, a franchise will start out for a short period, such as a year, so that the franchisee and the franchisor can determine whether they want to stay in business with one another. Usually, the franchise agreement will specify that termination must be "for cause," such as death or disability of the franchisee, insolvency of the franchisee, breach of the franchise agreement, or failure to meet specified sales quotas. Most franchise contracts provide that notice of termination must be given. If no set time for termination is specified, then a reasonable time, with notice, will be implied. A franchisee must be given reasonable time to wind up the business—that is, to do the accounting and return the copyright or trademark or any other property of the franchisor.

Because a franchisor's termination of a franchise often has adverse consequences for the franchisee, much franchise litigation involves claims of wrongful termination. Generally, the termination provisions of contracts are more favorable to the franchisor. This means that the franchisee, who normally invests a substantial amount of time and funds in the franchise operation to make it successful, may receive little or nothing for the business on termination. The franchisor owns the trademark and hence the business.

It is in this area that statutory and case law become important. The federal and state laws discussed earlier attempt, among other things, to protect franchisees from the arbitrary or unfair termination of their franchises by the franchisors. Generally, both statutory and case law emphasize the importance of good faith and fair dealing in terminating a franchise relationship.

In determining whether a franchisor has acted in good faith when terminating a franchise agreement, the courts generally try to balance the rights of both parties. If a court perceives that a franchisor has arbitrarily or unfairly terminated a franchise, the franchisee will be provided with a remedy for wrongful termination. If a franchisor's decision to terminate a franchise was made in the normal course of the franchisor's business operations, however, and reasonable notice of termination was given to the franchisee, normally a court would not consider such a termination wrongful. At issue in the following case was whether Domino's Pizza, Inc., had acted wrongfully when it terminated one of its franchises.

CASE 33.3 Bennett Enterprises, Inc. v. Domino's Pizza, Inc.

United States Court of Appeals,
District of Columbia Circuit, 1995.
45 F.3d 493.
www.findlaw.com/casecode/courts/dc.html[a]

HISTORICAL AND ECONOMIC SETTING *Pizza was originally an Italian dish, but its popularity exploded in the United States as part of the fast-food revolution that began in the 1950s. Today, the American appetite for pizza is more than eight pounds per person per year. U.S. pizza franchisors have spread their operations overseas to open pizza stores and restaurants in more than fifty countries. Pizza Hut, Inc., is the leader in sales in pizza restaurants. Domino's Pizza, Inc., is number one in pizza delivery sales.*

BACKGROUND AND FACTS Bennett Enterprises, Inc., entered into a franchise agreement with Domino's Pizza, Inc., to operate a Domino's pizza store. The agreement stated that Domino's had the right to terminate the franchise if Bennett failed to comply with any provision,

(Continued)

a. This page, which is part of FindLaw's Web site, provides access to some of the opinions of the U.S. Court of Appeals for the District of Columbia Circuit. In the "1995" row, click on "Feb". On the page that opens, scroll down the list to the *Bennett* case and click on the link to access the opinion.

CASE 33.3—Continued

including a promise to comply with "all applicable laws." For most of its first year in business, Bennett did not turn a profit and did not pay any taxes. Domino's told Bennett that if it did not resolve its tax problems, Domino's would terminate the franchise. Bennett did not pay the taxes or work out a payment plan with the government, but instead sold the franchise and filed a suit against Domino's in a federal district court. Bennett charged Domino's with, among other things, breach of contract, on the ground that the franchise agreement did not entitle Domino's to declare Bennett in default on the basis of unpaid taxes. The court ruled in Bennett's favor. Domino's appealed.

IN THE WORDS OF THE COURT . . .
SENTELLE, Circuit Judge:

* * * *

The language of [the franchise agreement] is not ambiguous * * * because it is not reasonably or fairly susceptible to an interpretation that does not encompass compliance with state and federal tax laws. * * * [A]ny reasonable construction of the language "all applicable laws" in a business franchise agreement must include tax statutes at the very minimum. To that extent the contract is unambiguous, and that is the only extent with which we are concerned. * * * Under the franchise agreement Domino's had the right to place Bennett in default for failure to pay taxes.

DECISION AND REMEDY The U.S. Court of Appeals for the District of Columbia Circuit reversed the lower court's judgment.

FOR CRITICAL ANALYSIS—Economic Consideration *Would violations of other laws, such as parking ordinances or speed limits, have been sufficient grounds for Domino's to terminate Bennett's franchise?*

APPLICATION Law & the Franchisee*

A franchise arrangement appeals to many prospective businesspersons for several reasons. Entrepreneurs who purchase franchises can operate independently and without the risks associated with products that have never been marketed before. Additionally, the franchisee can usually rely on the assistance and guidance of a management network that is regional or national in scope and that has been in place for some time.

Franchisees do face potential problems, however. Consider the franchise fee. Virtually all franchise contracts require a franchise fee payable up front or in installments. This fee often ranges between $10,000 and $50,000. For nationally known franchises, such as McDonald's, the fee may be $500,000 or more. The true cost of the franchise, however, must also include fees that are paid once the franchisee opens for business. For example, as a franchisee, you would probably pay royalties to the franchisor (for the use of the franchisor's trademark, for example) of anywhere from 2 to 8

*This *Application* is not meant to substitute for the services of an attorney who is licensed to practice law in your state.

APPLICATION CONTINUED

percent of your gross sales. Another 1 to 2 percent of gross sales might go to the franchisor to cover advertising costs. Although your business would benefit from the advertising, the cost of that advertising might exceed the benefits you would realize.

Another problem that many franchisees do not anticipate is the adverse effects on their businesses of so-called electronic encroachment. For example, suppose that a franchise contract gives the franchisee exclusive rights to operate a franchise in a certain territory. Nothing in the contract, though, indicates what will happen if the franchisor sells its products to customers located within the franchisee's territory via telemarketing methods, mail-order catalogues, or online services over the Internet. As a prospective franchisee, you should make sure that your franchise contract covers such contingencies and protects you against any losses you might incur if you face these types of competition in your area.

A major economic consequence, usually of a negative nature, will occur if the franchisor terminates your franchise agreement. Before you sign a franchise contract, make sure that the contract provisions regarding termination are reasonable and clearly specified.

Generally, to avoid potentially significant economic and legal problems, it is imperative that you obtain all relevant details about the business and that you have an attorney evaluate the franchise contract for possible pitfalls.

CHECKLIST FOR THE FRANCHISEE

1. Find out all you can about the franchisor: How long has the franchisor been in business? How profitable is the business? Is there a healthy market for the product?
2. Obtain the most recent financial statement from the franchisor and a complete description of the business.
3. Obtain a clear and complete statement of all fees that you will be required to pay.
4. Will the franchisor help you in training management and employees? With promotion and advertising? By supplying capital or credit? In finding a good location for your business?
5. Visit other franchisees in the same business. Ask them about their experiences with the product, the market, and the franchisor.
6. Evaluate your training and experience in the business on which you are about to embark. Are they sufficient to ensure success as a franchisee?
7. Carefully examine the franchise contract provisions relating to termination of the franchise agreement. Are they specific enough to allow you to sue for breach of contract in the event the franchisor wrongfully terminates the contract? Find out how many franchises have been terminated in the past several years.
8. Will you have an exclusive geographical territory and, if so, for how many years? What plans does the franchisor have in regard to telemarketing, electronic marketing, and mail-order sales to customers within the territory?
9. Finally, the most important way to protect yourself is to have an attorney familiar with franchise law examine the contract before you sign it.

Key Terms

business trust 849
cooperative 849
franchise 849
franchisee 850
franchisor 850
joint stock company 849
joint venture 848
syndicate 848

Chapter Summary • Special Business Forms and Private Franchises

Special Business Forms (See pages 848–849.)	1. *Joint venture*—An organization created by two or more persons in contemplation of a limited activity or a single transaction; otherwise, similar to a partnership. 2. *Syndicate*—An investment group that undertakes to finance a particular project; may exist as a corporation or as a general or limited partnership. 3. *Joint stock company*—A business form similar to a corporation in some respects (transferable shares of stock, management by directors and officers, perpetual existence) but otherwise resembling a partnership. 4. *Business trust*—Created by a written trust agreement that sets forth the interests of the beneficiaries and obligations and powers of the trustee(s). Similar to a corporation in many respects. Beneficiaries are not personally liable for the debts or obligations of the business trust. 5. *Cooperative*—An association organized to provide an economic service, without profit, to its members. May take the form of a corporation or a partnership.
Private Franchises (See pages 849–858.)	1. *Types of franchises*— a. Distributorship (for example, automobile dealerships). b. Chain-style operation (for example, fast-food chains). c. Manufacturing/processing-plant arrangement (for example, soft-drink bottling companies, such as Coca-Cola). 2. *Laws governing franchising*— a. Franchises are governed by contract law. b. Franchises are also governed by federal and state statutory and regulatory laws, as well as agency law. 3. *The franchise contract*— a. Ordinarily requires the franchisee (purchaser) to pay a price for the franchise license. b. Specifies the territory to be served by the franchisee's firm. c. May require the franchisee to purchase certain supplies from the franchisor at an established price. d. May require the franchisee to abide by certain standards of quality relating to the product or service offered but cannot set retail resale prices. e. Usually provides for the date and/or conditions of termination of the franchise arrangement. Both federal and state statutes attempt to protect certain franchisees from franchisors who unfairly or arbitrarily terminate franchises.

For Review

1. What are the essential characteristics of each of the following business forms: joint ventures, joint stock companies, syndicates, business trusts, and cooperatives?
2. What is a franchise? What are the most common types of franchises?
3. What laws govern a franchising relationship?
4. What terms and conditions are typically included in a franchise contract?
5. When might franchisors be liable under agency laws?

Questions and Case Problems

33–1. Business Forms and Liability. Assume that Faraway Corp. is considering entering into two contracts, one with a joint stock company that distributes home products east of the Mississippi River and the other with a business trust formed by a number of sole proprietors who are sellers of home products on the West Coast. Both contracts involve large capital outlays for Faraway, which will supply each business with soft-drink dispensers. In both business organizations, at least two shareholders or beneficiaries are personally wealthy, but each business organization has limited financial resources. The owner-managers of Faraway are not familiar with either form of business organization. Because each form resembles a corporation, they are concerned about whether they will be able to collect payments from the wealthy members of the business organizations in the event that either business organization breaches the contract by failing to make the payments. Discuss fully Faraway's concern.

33–2. Business Organizations. Alan, Jane, and Kyle organize a nonprofit business—AJK Markets, Inc.—to buy groceries from wholesalers and sell them to consumers who buy a membership in AJK. Because the firm is a nonprofit entity, it is able to sell the groceries for less than a commercial grocer could. What form of business organization is AJK Markets? Is it significant that AJK is incorporated?

33–3. Private Franchises. May, Paul, and Vicky are recent college graduates who would like to go into business for themselves. They are considering the idea of purchasing a franchise. If they entered into a franchising arrangement, they would have the support of a larger company to provide them with answers to questions they might have. Also, a firm that has been in business for many years would have experience with some of the problems that novice businesspersons would encounter. These and other attributes of franchises can lessen some of the risks of the marketplace. What other aspects of franchising—positive and negative—might May, Paul, and Vicky want to consider before committing themselves to a particular franchise?

33–4. Control of a Franchise. National Foods, Inc., sells franchises to its fast-food restaurants, known as Chicky-D's. Under the franchise agreement, franchisees agree to hire and train employees strictly according to Chicky-D's standards. Chicky-D's regional supervisors are required to approve all job candidates before they are hired and all general policies affecting those employees. Chicky-D's reserves the right to terminate a franchise for violating the franchisor's rules. In practice, however, Chicky-D's regional supervisors routinely approve new employees and individual franchisees' policies. After several incidents of racist comments and conduct by Tim, a recently hired assistant manager at a Chicky-D's, Sharon, a counterperson at the restaurant, resigns. Sharon files a suit in a federal district court against National. National files a motion for summary judgment, arguing that it is not liable for harassment by franchise employees. Will the court grant National's motion? Why or why not?

33–5. Joint Ventures. Gustave Peterson contacted his family doctor, Leland Reichelt, complaining of abdominal pain. The doctor recommended gallbladder surgery. Another doctor, George Fortier, performed the surgery, and Reichelt assisted. It was Reichelt's normal practice to refer patients to Fortier for surgery, and each doctor charged the patient separately for his services. During the operation, a metal clip was inadvertently left inside Peterson's abdominal cavity. It eventually formed a stone, which later caused Peterson to have chest and gastric pain. Peterson repeatedly complained to Reichelt, who diagnosed the problem as being related to either a hernia or stress. Peterson finally sought the advice of another physician, who, on performing surgery, discovered the metal clip. Peterson filed suit against both Reichelt and Fortier for malpractice under the theory that Fortier and Reichelt were engaged in a joint enterprise (joint venture). Discuss whether the two doctors were joint venturers. [*Peterson v. Fortier,* 406 N.W.2d 563 (Minn.App. 1987)]

33–6. Good Faith in Franchising Relationships. Ernst and Barbara Larese entered into a ten-year franchise agreement with Creamland Dairies, Inc. The agreement provided that the franchisee "shall not assign, transfer or sublet this franchise, or any of [the] rights under this agreement, without the prior written consent of Area Franchisor [Creamland] and Baskin Robbins, any such unauthorized assignment, transfer or subletting being null and without effect." The Lareses attempted to sell their franchise rights in February and August of 1979, but Creamland refused to consent to the sales. The Lareses brought suit, alleging that Creamland had interfered with their contractual relations with the prospective buyers by unreasonably withholding its consent; they claimed that Creamland had a duty to act in good faith and in a commercially reasonable manner when a franchisee sought to transfer its rights under the franchise agreement. Creamland contended that the contract gave it an unqualified right to refuse to consent to proposed sales of the franchise rights. Which party prevailed? Explain. [*Larese v. Creamland Dairies, Inc.,* 767 F.2d 716 (10th Cir. 1985)]

33–7. Franchise Termination. Ormsby Motors, Inc. (OMI), was a General Motors Corp. (GM) dealership. Their agreement provided for termination if OMI submitted "false . . . claims for any payment." Larry Kain was in charge of OMI's warranty claims. After several years of excessive claims, GM complained to OMI. When nothing changed, GM conducted a dealer audit. The audit uncovered, among other things, over eighty claims in one ten-day period for paint repair work that was never done. OMI denied knowledge of Kain's activities. GM terminated its dealership agreement with OMI. OMI asked a federal district court to stop the termination, arguing in part that GM did not have good cause. Did GM have good cause? Explain. [*Ormsby Motors, Inc. v. General Motors Corp.,* 842 F.Supp. 344 (N.D.Ill. 1994)]

33–8. Good Faith in Franchising Relationships. Barn-Chestnut, Inc. (BCI), entered into a franchise agreement with Grocers

Development Corp. (GDC) for a Convenient Food Mart "for as long as [BCI] . . . shall have a good and valid lease" to the property. GDC sold its interest in the franchise and the property to CFM Development Corp. When the lease was about to expire, CFM offered to enter into a new lease and franchise agreement with BCI at a significantly higher price. BCI refused. When CFM refused to make another deal, BCI filed a suit against CFM in a West Virginia state court on the ground that CFM had to offer BCI a lease because the franchise was contingent on a lease. The court did not agree. BCI then argued that the implied obligation of good faith required CFM to offer to renew the lease. Essentially, the question on appeal was whether a franchisor had an obligation to renew a franchise even though there was no clause in the contract requiring that the lease/franchise be renewed. Is BCI correct in contending that the franchisor does have such an obligation? Explain. [*Barn-Chestnut, Inc. v. CFM Development Corp.*, 193 W.Va. 565, 457 S.E.2d 502 (1995)]

33–9. The Franchise Contract. Kubis & Perszyk Associates, Inc., was in business as Entre Computer. As a franchise, Entre sold, among other products, computer systems marketed by Sun Microsystems, Inc. Entre's agreement with Sun included a forum-selection clause that provided that any suit between the parties had to be filed in a California court. When Sun terminated its relationship with Entre, Entre filed a suit in a New Jersey state court. Sun asked the court to dismiss the suit on the basis of the forum-selection clause. Entre argued that the clause violated state franchise law, which invalidated such clauses in auto dealership franchises. On what basis might the court extend this law to cover Entre's franchise? Discuss. [*Kubis & Perszyk Associates, Inc. v. Sun Microsystems, Inc.*, 146 N.J. 176, 680 A.2d 618 (1996)]

33–10. Franchise Termination. C. B. Management Co. operated McDonald's restaurants in Cleveland, Ohio, under a franchise agreement with McDonald's Corp. The agreement required C. B. to make monthly payments of, among other things, certain percentages of the gross sales to McDonald's. If any payment was more than thirty days late, McDonald's had the right to terminate the franchise. The agreement stated, "No waiver by [McDonald's] of any breach . . . shall constitute a waiver of any subsequent breach." McDonald's sometimes accepted C. B.'s late payments, but when C. B. defaulted on the payments in July 1997 McDonald's gave notice of thirty days to comply or surrender possession of the restaurants. C. B. missed the deadline. McDonald's demanded that C. B. vacate the restaurants. C. B. refused. McDonald's filed a suit in a federal district court against C. B., alleging violations of the franchise agreement. C. B. counterclaimed in part that McDonald's had breached the implied covenant of good faith and fair dealing. McDonald's filed a motion to dismiss C. B.'s counterclaim. On what did C. B. base its claim? Will the court agree? Why or why not? [*McDonald's Corp. v. C. B. Management Co.*, 13 F.Supp.2d 705 (N.D.Ill. 1998)]

A QUESTION OF ETHICS AND SOCIAL RESPONSIBILITY

33–11. Graham Oil Co. (Graham) had been a distributor of ARCO gasoline in Coos Bay, Oregon, for nearly forty years under successive distributorship agreements. ARCO notified Graham that it intended to terminate the franchise because Graham had not been purchasing the minimum amount of gasoline required under their most recent agreement. Graham sought a preliminary injunction against ARCO, arguing that ARCO had violated the Petroleum Marketing Practices Act (PMPA) by deliberately raising its prices so that Graham would be unable to meet the minimum gasoline requirements; thus, ARCO should not be allowed to terminate the agreement. The court ordered Graham to submit the claim to arbitration, in accordance with an arbitration clause in the distributorship agreement. Graham refused to do so, and the court granted summary judgment for ARCO. On appeal, Graham claimed that the arbitration clause was invalid because it forced him to forfeit rights given to franchisees under the PMPA, including the right to punitive damages and attorneys' fees. The appellate court agreed with Graham and remanded the case for trial. In view of these facts, answer the following questions. [*Graham Oil Co. v. Arco Products Co., A Division of Atlantic Richfield Co.*, 43 F.3d 1244 (9th Cir. 1994)]

1. Do you agree with Graham and the appellate court that statutory rights cannot be forfeited contractually, through an arbitration clause?
2. Review the discussion of arbitration in Chapter 3. Does the decision in the above case conflict with any established public policy concerning arbitration? Is the decision in the case consistent with other court decisions on arbitration discussed in Chapter 3, including decisions of the United States Supreme Court?

FOR CRITICAL ANALYSIS

33–12. The law permits individuals to exercise the option of organizing their business enterprises in many different forms. What policy interests are served by granting entrepreneurs these options? Would it be better if the law required that everyone organize his or her business in the same form? Discuss.

Online Activities

ONLINE EXERCISE 33–1

Go to the "Internet Activities Book" on the Web site that accompanies this text, the URL for which is http://blt.westbuslaw.com. Select the following activity, and perform the exercise according to the instructions given there:

Activity 31–1: Franchises

Before the Test

Go to the *Business Law Today* home page at http://blt.westbuslaw.com. Click on TestTutor.® You will find twenty interactive questions relating to this chapter.

Unit Six • Cumulative Business Hypothetical

John leases an office and buys computer equipment. Initially, to pay for the lease and the equipment, he goes into the business of designing Web pages. He has an idea for a new software product, however, on which he works whenever he has time and which he hopes will be more profitable than designing Web pages.

1 After six months, Mary and Paul come to work in the office to help develop John's idea. John continues to pay the rent and other expenses, including salaries for Mary and Paul. John does not expect to make a profit at least until the software is developed, which could be months, and there may be very little profit if the product is not marketed successfully. John believes that if the product is successful, however, the firm will be able to follow up with other products. In choosing a form of business organization for this firm, what are the important considerations? What are the advantages and disadvantages of each basic option?

2 It is decided that an organizational form for this firm should include limited liability for its owners. The owners will include John, Mary, Paul, and some members of their respective families. One of the features of the corporate form is limited liability. Ordinarily, however, corporate income is taxed at the corporate level and at the shareholder level. Which corporate form could the firm use to avoid this double taxation? Which other forms of business organization feature limited liability? What factors, other than liability and taxation, influence a firm's choice among these forms?

3 The firm is incorporated as Digital Software, Inc. (DSI). The software is developed and marketed successfully, and DSI prospers. John, Mary, and Paul become directors of DSI. For the marketing of DSI's next product, Paul makes a proposal that John and Mary approve at a board meeting. Implementing the proposal causes a drop in profits for DSI. If the shareholders accuse Paul of breaching his fiduciary duty to DSI, what is Paul's most likely defense? If the shareholders accuse John and Mary of the same breach, what is their best defense? In either case, if the shareholders file a suit, how is a court likely to rule?

4 International Investments, Inc., makes a public offer to buy the stock of DSI. The price of the offer is higher than the market price of the stock, but DSI's board believes that the offer should not be accepted and that International's attempt to take over DSI should be resisted. What steps can DSI take to resist the attempt?

5 Mary and Paul withdraw from DSI to set up their own firm. To obtain operating capital, they solicit investors who agree to become "general partners." Mary and Paul designate themselves "managing partners." The investors are spread over a wide area geographically and do not know anything about Mary and Paul's business until they are contacted. Are Mary and Paul truly soliciting partners, or are they selling securities? What are the criteria for determining whether an investment is a security? What are the advantages and disadvantages of selling securities compared to soliciting partners?

UNIT SIX • EXTENDED CASE STUDY: THE LAW IN CONTEXT

Henkels & McCoy, Inc. v. Adochio

We discussed the principles of agency law in Chapter 24 and the principles of partnership law in Chapter 25. We also discussed, in Chapter 32, limited partnerships and, in Chapter 33, joint ventures. We examine, in this extended case study, Henkels & McCoy, Inc. v. Adochio,[1] *a recent decision that involved the application of the principles of agency and partnership law to the liability of limited partners, whose firm was part of a joint venture.*

CASE BACKGROUND

G&A Development Corporation was the general partner of Red Hawk North Associates, L.P. (limited partnership), which also had twenty limited partners. Section 12(a)(iv) of the partnership agreement provided that before any receipts were distributed to the partners, G&A was to use the firm's "Cash Receipts derived from the operation of the Property" to establish a reserve fund to pay creditors.

Red Hawk entered into a joint venture—the Chestnut Woods Partnership—with Cedar Ridge Development Corporation to build and sell houses. Red Hawk was to provide the funding. Cedar Ridge was to provide the land and act as manager and general contractor.

As the general contractor, Cedar Ridge entered into a contract with Henkels & McCoy, Inc. The contract required Henkels to install storm and sanitary sewer systems for Chestnut Woods. Cedar Ridge agreed to pay Henkels $300,270. Henkels completed the work, but Cedar Ridge paid Henkels only $96,053. Meanwhile, Red Hawk, which never established a reserve fund, distributed capital that it withdrew from another project, which it had abandoned, to its limited partners as a return of capital contributions.

Henkels filed a suit in a federal district court against Cedar Ridge, Red Hawk, and G&A and won default judgments, but the defendants did not pay. Henkels then filed a suit in the same court against Robert Adochio and Red Hawk's other limited partners, seeking, among other things, the amount of the distributions made by Red Hawk to its limited partners. The court entered a judgment in favor of Henkels. The limited partners appealed to the U.S. Court of Appeals for the Third Circuit.

1. 138 F.3d 491 (3d Cir. 1998).

MAJORITY OPINION

ROSENN, Circuit Judge.

* * * *

* * * [F]undamental principles of agency and partnership law * * * control the outcome of this case. * * * [I]t is elementary that [e]very partner is an agent of the partnership for the purpose of its business, and the act of every partner * * * binds the partnership, unless the partner so acting has in fact no authority to act for the partnership in the particular matter. * * *

Here, it is undisputed that Red Hawk was a partner with Cedar Ridge in the Chestnut Woods Partnership, that Cedar Ridge had actual authority to enter into the contract with Henkels, that the sewer systems were being installed for the benefit of the Chestnut Woods Partnership, and that Cedar Ridge was entitled to reimbursement from Chestnut Woods for all monies paid by Cedar Ridge to Henkels. * * * [A]lthough indirect, a creditor relationship existed between Red Hawk and Henkels based on the contract signed by Red Hawk's partner in the Chestnut Woods Partnership, Cedar Ridge.

* * * *

* * * [T]he Red Hawk general partner's failure to establish any reserves in the face of the fixed obligation and imminent payments due under the contract with Henkels and the operations of the Chestnut Woods development was callous and not reasonable.

* * * *

* * * The Partners are therefore obligated to return the improper capital distributions to Red Hawk. Because the plaintiff stands in the shoes of Red Hawk for the purpose of recovering these funds on behalf of the partnership, and because of the multiple suits it already has been compelled to undergo to enforce collection of its debt, judicial resources will be conserved and economies of time and expenses effectuated, to hold the Partners directly liable to Henkels.

DISSENTING OPINION

STAPLETON, Circuit Judge, Dissenting:

The critical issue posed by this appeal is one of intent—the intent of the Red Hawk partners when they negotiated their partnership agreement. * * *

* * * *

In my view, the court errs for at least five reasons: (1) In context, Section 12(a)(iv) was intended for the protection of the limited partners, not as a creditor protection device even for creditors of Red Hawk; (2) Section 12(a)(iv), even if viewed as a creditor protection provision, was not intended for the protection of joint venture creditors for whom the joint ventures were to make other provision; (3) the challenged distributions were a return of capital that the partners had agreed to devote to an abandoned venture, and it is not reasonable to find an intent in Section 12(a)(iv) to commit that capital contribution to the creditors of a different * * * venture; (4) Section 12(a)(iv) permits the general partner to retain reserves only from "Cash Receipts derived from the operations of the Property" and the challenged distributions did not come from funds generated by operations; and (5) even if Section 12(a)(iv) could reasonably be read to require Red Hawk's general partner to set aside funds for creditors in Henkels' position whenever a reasonable general partner exercising business judgment would do so, this record provides no basis for a conclusion that the failure of Red Hawk's general partner to set aside funds for Henkels * * * was a decision beyond the bounds of business judgment.

Going Online

The *Business Law Today*, Fifth Edition, Web site, the URL for which is http://blt.westbuslaw.com, provides a link through which you can access other court opinions in cases involving secured transactions. FindLaw, at smallbiz.findlaw.com/text/P07_2011.stm, provides links to discussions of some of the issues that can determine a business's selection of its organizational form, including partnerships and limited liability entities.

Questions for Analysis

1. **Law.** If any of the business entities in this case had been a limited liability company, would the outcome have been different?
2. **Law.** How did the court in this case apply the principles of contract interpretation discussed in Chapter 9 to the limited partnership agreement?
3. **Ethics.** Is it ethical to devise an interrelated maze of business organizations in an attempt to avoid liability for those firms' business obligations?
4. **International Dimensions.** What are the implications of the decision in this case for business firms that enter into joint ventures with foreign business entities?
5. **Implications for the Business Manager.** How much attention should be given to the drafting of such business documents as partnership and joint venture agreements?

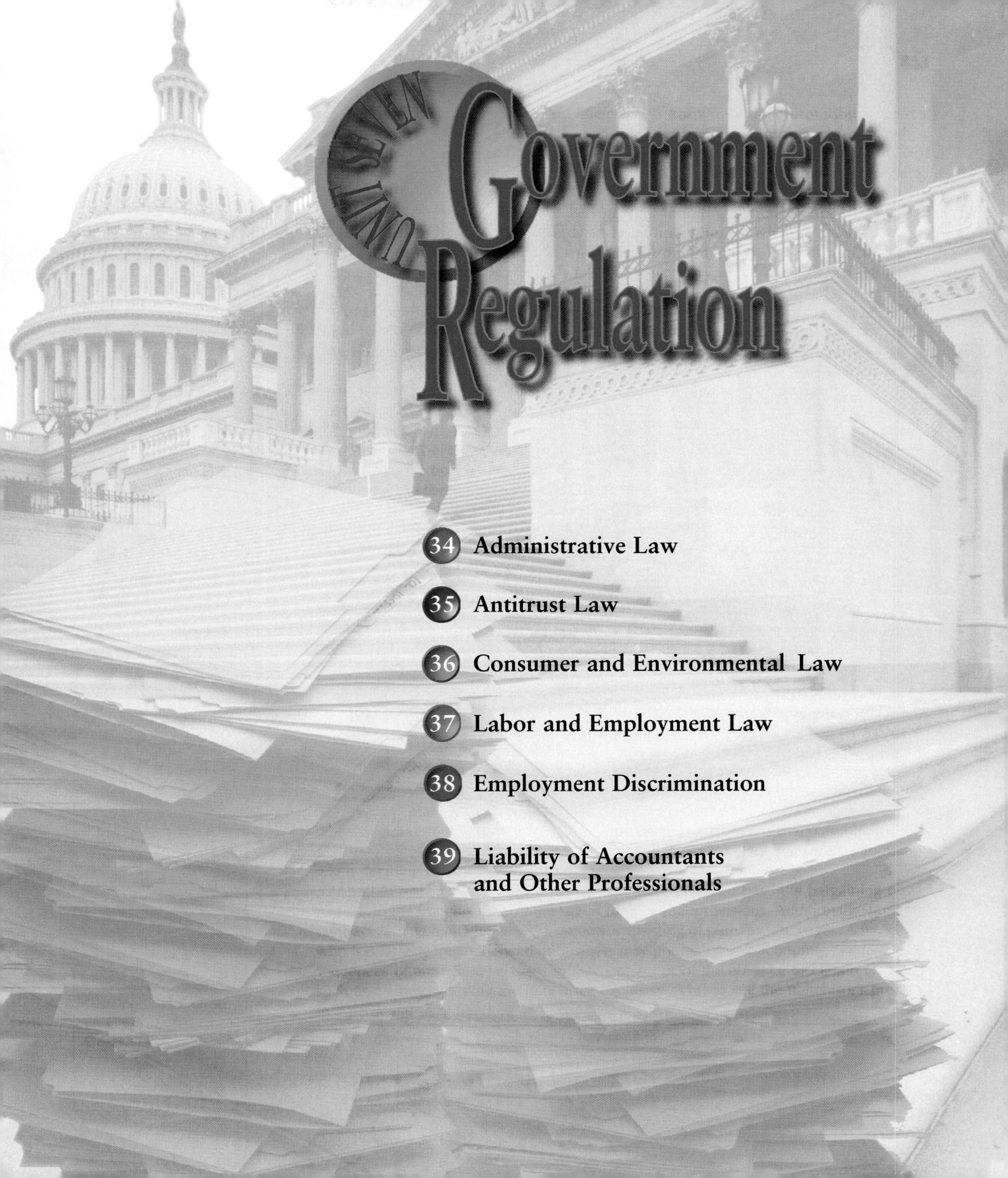

UNIT SEVEN Government Regulation

CHAPTER 34

Administrative Law

"[P]erhaps more values today are affected by [administrative] decisions than by those of all the courts."

Robert H. Jackson, 1892–1954
(Associate justice of the United States Supreme Court, 1941–1954)

CONTENTS

LEARNING OBJECTIVES

After reading this chapter, you should be able to:

1. Explain the rulemaking function of administrative agencies.
2. Describe the investigation and adjudication functions of agencies.
3. Identify how agency authority is held in check.
4. List laws that make agencies more accountable to the public.
5. Discuss the relation between state and federal agencies.

As the opening quotation suggests, government agencies established to administer the law have a tremendous impact on the day-to-day operation of the government and the economy. In the early years of our nation, the United States had a relatively simple, nonindustrial economy that required little regulation. Because administrative agencies often create and enforce such regulations, there were relatively few such agencies. Today, however, there are rules covering virtually every aspect of a business's operation. Consequently, agencies have multiplied. • **EXAMPLE 34.1** At the federal level, the Securities and Exchange Commission regulates the firm's capital structure and financing, as well as its financial reporting. The National Labor Relations Board oversees relations between the firm and any unions with which it may deal. The Equal Employment Opportunity Commission also regulates employment relationships. The Environmental Protection Agency and the Occupational Safety and Health Administration affect the way the firm manufactures its products. The Federal Trade Commission affects the way it markets these products. •

Added to this layer of federal regulation is a second layer of state regulation that, when not preempted by federal legislation, may cover many of the same activities or regulate independently those activities not covered by federal regulation. Finally, agency regulations at the county or municipal level also affect certain types of business activities.

Administrative agencies issue rules, orders, and decisions. These regulations make up the body of *administrative law*. You were introduced briefly to some of the main principles of administrative law in Chapter 1. In the following pages, these principles are presented in much greater detail.

Agency Creation and Powers

ON THE WEB

Information on federal and state administrative law, links to federal and state administrative procedure acts, and other resources relating to administrative law can be found at law.fsu.edu/library/admin.

This is a Web site maintained by the American Bar Association and the Florida State University College of Law.

Congress creates federal administrative agencies. Because Congress cannot possibly oversee the actual implementation of all the laws it enacts, it must delegate such tasks to others, particularly when the issues relate to highly technical areas, such as air and water pollution. By delegating some of its authority to make and implement laws, Congress can monitor indirectly a particular area in which it has passed legislation without becoming bogged down in the details relating to enforcement—details that are often best left to specialists.

Enabling Legislation

• ENABLING LEGISLATION Statutes enacted by Congress that authorize the creation of an administrative agency and specify the name, composition, and powers of the agency being created.

To create an administrative agency, Congress passes **enabling legislation,** which specifies the name, purposes, functions, and powers of the agency being created. Federal administrative agencies may exercise only those powers that Congress has delegated to them in enabling legislation. Through similar enabling acts, state legislatures create state administrative agencies.

For example, Congress created the Federal Trade Commission (FTC) in the Federal Trade Commission Act of 1914.[1] The act prohibits unfair and deceptive trade practices. It also describes the procedures that the agency must follow to charge persons or organizations with violations of the act, and it provides for judicial review of agency orders. The act grants the FTC the power to

- Create "rules and regulations for the purpose of carrying out the Act."
- Conduct investigations of business practices.
- Obtain reports from interstate corporations concerning their business practices.
- Investigate possible violations of federal antitrust statutes.[2]
- Publish findings of its investigations.
- Recommend new legislation.
- Hold trial-like hearings to resolve certain kinds of trade disputes that involve FTC regulations or federal antitrust laws.

The commission that heads the FTC is composed of five members, each of whom the president appoints, with the advice and consent of the Senate, for a term of seven years. The president designates one of the commissioners to be chairperson. Various offices and bureaus of the FTC undertake different administrative activities for the agency. The organization of the FTC is illustrated in Exhibit 34–1.

1. 15 U.S.C. Sections 41–58.
2. The FTC shares this task with the Antitrust Division of the U.S. Department of Justice.

EXHIBIT 34–1 • Organization of the Federal Trade Commission

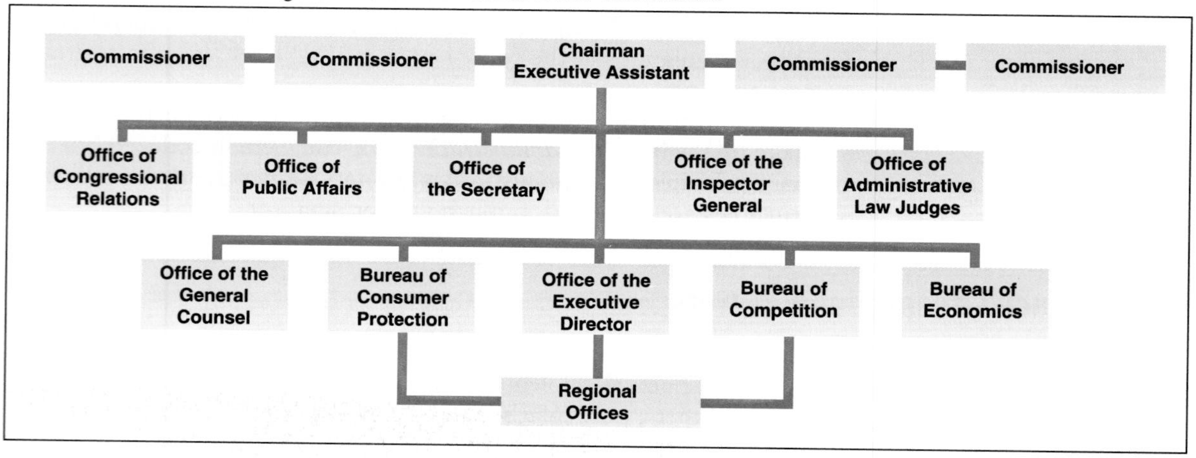

TYPES OF AGENCIES

There are two basic types of administrative agencies: executive agencies and independent regulatory agencies. Federal **executive agencies** include the cabinet departments of the executive branch, which were formed to assist the president in carrying out executive functions, and the subagencies within the cabinet departments. The Occupational Safety and Health Administration, for example, is a subagency within the Department of Labor. Exhibit 34–2 lists the cabinet departments and their most important subagencies.

• **EXECUTIVE AGENCY**
An administrative agency that is either a cabinet department or a subagency within a cabinet department. Executive agencies fall under the authority of the president, who has the power to appoint and remove federal officers.

• **INDEPENDENT REGULATORY AGENCY**
An administrative agency that is not considered part of the government's executive branch and is not subject to the authority of the president. Agency officials cannot be removed without cause.

All administrative agencies are part of the executive branch of government, but **independent regulatory agencies** are outside the major executive departments. The Federal Trade Commission and the Securities and Exchange Commission are examples of independent regulatory agencies. These and other selected independent regulatory agencies, as well as their principal functions, are listed in Exhibit 34–3.

The significant difference between the two types of agencies lies in the accountability of the regulators. Agencies that are considered part of the executive branch are subject to the authority of the president, who has the power to appoint and remove federal officers. In theory, this power is less pronounced in regard to independent agencies, whose officers serve for fixed terms and cannot be removed without just cause. In practice, however, the president's power to exert influence over independent agencies is often considerable.

ON THE WEB

The Federal Web Locator permits searches for the names of federal administrative agencies and links to agency-related information on the Internet. The Federal Web Locator can be found on a site maintained by the Villanova University School of Law at www.law.vill.edu/Fed-Agency/fedwebloc.html.

AGENCY POWERS AND THE CONSTITUTION

Administrative agencies occupy an unusual niche in the American legal scheme, because they exercise powers that are normally divided among the three branches of government. • **EXAMPLE 34.2** In the FTC's enabling legislation discussed above, the FTC's grant of power incorporates functions associated with the legislature (rulemaking), the executive branch (enforcement of the rules), and the courts (adjudication, or the formal resolution of disputes). •

The constitutional principle of *checks and balances* allows each branch of government to act as a check on the actions of the other two branches. Furthermore, the Constitution authorizes only the legislative branch to create laws. Yet

EXHIBIT 34–2 • Executive Departments and Important Subagencies

DEPARTMENT	DATE FORMED	IMPORTANT SUBAGENCIES
State	1789	Passport Office; Bureau of Diplomatic Security; Foreign Service; Bureau of Human Rights and Humanitarian Affairs; Bureau of Consular Affairs; Bureau of Intelligence and Research
Treasury	1789	Internal Revenue Service; Bureau of Alcohol, Tobacco, and Firearms; U.S. Secret Service; U.S. Mint; Customs Service
Interior	1849	U.S. Fish and Wildlife Service; National Park Service; Bureau of Indian Affairs; Bureau of Land Management
Justice	1870[a]	Federal Bureau of Investigation; Drug Enforcement Administration; Bureau of Prisons; U.S. Marshals Service; Immigration and Naturalization Service
Agriculture	1889	Soil Conservation Service; Agricultural Research Service; Food Safety and Inspection Service; Federal Crop Insurance Corporation; Farmers Home Administration
Commerce	1913[b]	Bureau of the Census; Bureau of Economic Analysis; Minority Business Development Agency; Patent and Trademark Office; National Oceanic and Atmospheric Administration; U.S. Travel and Tourism Administration
Labor	1913[b]	Occupational Safety and Health Administration; Bureau of Labor Statistics; Employment Standards Administration; Office of Labor-Management Standards; Employment and Training Administration
Defense	1949[c]	National Guard; Defense Investigative Service; National Security Agency; Joint Chiefs of Staff; Departments of the Air Force, Navy, Army
Housing and Urban Development	1965	Assistant Secretary for Community Planning and Development; Government National Mortgage Association; Assistant Secretary for Housing—Federal Housing Commissioner; Assistant Secretary for Fair Housing and Equal Opportunity
Transportation	1967	Federal Aviation Administration; Federal Highway Administration; National Highway Traffic Safety Administration; U.S. Coast Guard; Federal Transit Administration
Energy	1977	Office of Civilian Radioactive Waste Management; Bonneville Power Administration; Office of Nuclear Energy; Energy Information Administration; Office of Conservation and Renewable Energy
Health and Human Services	1980[d]	Food and Drug Administration; Health Care Financing Administration; Public Health Service
Education	1980[e]	Office of Special Education and Rehabilitation Services; Office of Elementary and Secondary Education; Office of Postsecondary Education; Office of Vocational and Adult Education
Veterans' Affairs	1989	Veterans Health Administration; Veterans Benefits Administration; National Cemetery System

a. Formed from the Office of the Attorney General (created in 1789).
b. Formed from the Department of Commerce and Labor (created in 1903).
c. Formed from the Department of War (created in 1789) and the Department of the Navy (created in 1798).
d. Formed from the Department of Health, Education, and Welfare (created in 1953).
e. Formed from the Department of Health, Education, and Welfare (created in 1953).

EXHIBIT 34–3 • Selected Independent Regulatory Agencies

NAME	DATE FORMED	PRINCIPAL DUTIES
Federal Reserve System Board of Governors (Fed)	1913	Determines policy with respect to interest rates, credit availability, and the money supply.
Federal Trade Commission (FTC)	1914	Prevents businesses from engaging in unfair trade practices; stops the formation of monopolies in the business sector; protects consumer rights.
Securities and Exchange Commission (SEC)	1934	Regulates the nation's stock exchanges, in which shares of stock are bought and sold; enforces the securities laws, which require full disclosure of the financial profiles of companies that wish to sell stock and bonds to the public.
Federal Communications Commission (FCC)	1934	Regulates all communications by telegraph, cable, telephone, radio, satellite, and television.
National Labor Relations Board (NLRB)	1935	Protects employees' rights to join unions and bargain collectively with employers; attempts to prevent unfair labor practices by both employers and unions.
Equal Employment Opportunity Commission (EEOC)	1964	Works to eliminate discrimination in employment based on religion, sex, race, color, disability, national origin, or age; investigates claims of discrimination.
Environmental Protection Agency (EPA)	1970	Undertakes programs aimed at reducing air and water pollution; works with state and local agencies to help fight environmental hazards. (It has been suggested recently that its status be elevated to that of a department.)
Nuclear Regulatory Commission (NRC)	1975	Ensures that electricity-generating nuclear reactors in the United States are built and operated safely; regularly inspects operations of such reactors.

administrative agencies, to which the Constitution does not specifically refer, make **legislative rules,** or *substantive rules,* that are as legally binding as laws that Congress passes.

Courts generally hold that Article I of the U.S. Constitution authorizes delegating such powers to administrative agencies. In fact, courts generally hold that Article I is the basis for all administrative law. Section 1 of that article grants all legislative powers to Congress and requires Congress to oversee the implementation of all laws. Article I, Section 8, gives Congress the power to make all laws necessary for executing its specified powers. The courts interpret these passages, under what is known as the **delegation doctrine,** as granting Congress the power to establish administrative agencies that can create rules for implementing those laws.

The three branches of government exercise certain controls over agency powers and functions, as is discussed later in this chapter, but in many ways administrative agencies function independently. For this reason, administrative agencies, which constitute the **bureaucracy,** are sometimes referred to as the "fourth branch" of the American government.

• **LEGISLATIVE RULE**
An administrative agency rule that carries the same weight as a congressionally enacted statute.

• **DELEGATION DOCTRINE**
A doctrine based on Article I, Section 8, of the U.S. Constitution, which has been construed to allow Congress to delegate some of its power to make and implement laws to administrative agencies.

• **BUREAUCRACY**
The organizational structure, consisting of government bureaus and agencies, through which the government implements and enforces the laws.

Administrative Process

ON THE WEB

The text of the Administrative Procedure Act of 1946 can be viewed on a Web site maintained by the Legal Information Institute, which is part of Cornell Law School. The Web address is www.law.cornell.edu/uscode/5/ch5/html.

The three functions mentioned previously—rulemaking, enforcement, and adjudication—make up what is called the administrative process. **Administrative process** involves the administration of law by administrative agencies, in contrast to **judicial process,** which involves the administration of law by the courts.

The Administrative Procedure Act (APA) of 1946[3] imposes procedural requirements that all federal agencies must follow in their rulemaking, adjudication, and other functions. The APA is such an integral part of the administrative process that its application will be examined as we go through the basic functions carried out by administrative agencies.

• **ADMINISTRATIVE PROCESS**
The procedure used by administrative agencies in the administration of law.

• **JUDICIAL PROCESS**
The procedures relating to, or connected with, the administration of justice through the judicial system.

• **RULEMAKING**
The actions undertaken by administrative agencies when formally adopting new regulations or amending old ones. Under the Administrative Procedure Act, rulemaking includes notifying the public of proposed rules or changes and receiving and considering the public's comments.

• **NOTICE-AND-COMMENT RULEMAKING**
A procedure in agency rulemaking that requires (1) notice, (2) opportunity for comment, and (3) a published draft of the final rule.

RULEMAKING

A major function of an administrative agency is **rulemaking**—the formulation of new regulations. In an agency's enabling legislation, Congress confers the agency's power to make rules. • **EXAMPLE 34.3** The Occupational Safety and Health Act of 1970 authorized the Occupational Health and Safety Administration (OSHA) to develop and issue rules governing safety in the workplace. In 1991, OSHA deemed it in the public interest to issue a new rule regulating the health-care industry to prevent the spread of such diseases as acquired immune deficiency syndrome (AIDS). OSHA created a rule specifying various standards—on how contaminated instruments should be handled, for example—with which employers in that industry must comply. •

In formulating rules, administrative agencies follow specific rulemaking procedures required under the APA. We look here at the most common rulemaking procedure, called **notice-and-comment rulemaking.** This procedure involves three basic steps: notice of the proposed rulemaking, a comment period, and the final rule.

Notice of the Proposed Rulemaking When a federal agency decides to create a new rule, the agency publishes a notice of the proposed rulemaking proceedings in the *Federal Register,* a daily publication of the executive branch that prints government orders, rules, and regulations. The notice states where and when the proceedings will be held, the agency's legal authority for making the rule (usually its enabling legislation), and the terms or subject matter of the proposed rule.

Comment Period Following the publication of the notice of the proposed rulemaking proceedings, the agency must allow ample time for persons to comment in writing on the proposed rule. The purpose of this comment period is to give interested parties the opportunity to express their views on the proposed rule in an effort to influence agency policy. The comments may be in writing or, if a hearing is held, may be given orally. The agency need not respond to all comments, but it must respond to any significant comments that bear directly on the proposed rule. The agency responds by either modifying its final rule or explaining, in a statement accompanying the final rule, why it did not make any changes. In some circumstances, particularly when the procedure being used in a specific instance is less formal, an agency may accept comments after the comment period is closed. The agency should summarize these *ex parte* comments for possible review.

"In some respects matters of procedure constitute the very essence of ordered liberty under the Constitution."

WILEY B. RUTLEDGE, 1894–1949
(Associate justice of the United States Supreme Court, 1943–1949)

The Final Rule After the agency reviews the comments, it drafts the final rule and publishes it in the *Federal Register.* Exhibit 34–4 shows a sample page from a rule

3. 5 U.S.C. Sections 551–706.

EXHIBIT 34–4 • A Page from the Federal Register

ENVIRONMENTAL PROTECTION AGENCY
40 CFR Part 50
[AD-FRL-5659-5]
RIN 2060-AE66
National Ambient Air Quality Standards for Particulate Matter: Proposed Decision
Friday, December 13, 1996
AGENCY: Environmental Protection Agency (EPA).
ACTION: Proposed rule.

SUMMARY: In accordance with sections 108 and 109 of the Clean Air Act (Act), EPA has reviewed the air quality criteria and national ambient air quality standards (NAAQS) for particulate matter (PM) and for ozone (O sub3). Based on these reviews, EPA proposes to change the standards for both classes of pollutants. This document describes EPA's proposed changes with respect to the NAAQS for PM. The EPA's proposed actions with respect to O sub3 are being proposed elsewhere in today's Federal Register.

With respect to PM, EPA proposes to revise the current primary PM sub10 standards by adding two new primary PM sub2.5 standards set at 15 MUg/m 3 , annual mean, and 50 MUg/m super3, 24-hour average, to provide increased protection against a wide range of PM-related health effects, including premature mortality and increased hospital admissions and emergency room visits (primarily in the elderly and individuals with cardiopulmonary disease); increased respiratory symptoms and disease (in children and individuals with cardiopulmonary disease such as asthma); decreased lung function (particularly in children and individuals with asthma); and alterations in lung tissue and structure and in respiratory tract defense mechanisms. The proposed annual PM sub2.5 standard would be based on the 3-year average of the annual arithmetic mean PM sub2.5 concentrations, spatially averaged across an area. The proposed 24-hour PM sub2.5 standard would be based on the 3-year average of the 98th percentile of 24-hour PM sub2.5 concentrations at each monitor within an area. The EPA also solicits comment on two alternative approaches for selecting the levels of PM sub2.5 standards. The EPA proposes to revise the current 24-hour primary PM sub10 standard of 150 MUg/m super3 by replacing the 1-expected-exceedance form with a 98th percentile form, averaged over 3 years at each monitor within an area, and solicits comment on an alternative proposal to revoke the 24-hour PM sub10 standard. The EPA also proposes to retain the current annual primary PM sub10 standard of 50 mg/m super3. Further, EPA proposes new data handling conventions for calculating 98th percentile values and spatial averages (Appendix K), proposes to revise the reference method for monitoring PM as PM sub10 (Appendix J), and proposes a new reference method for monitoring PM as PM sub2.5 (Appendix L).

The EPA proposes to revise the current secondary standards by making them identical to the suite of proposed primary standards. In the Administrator's judgment, these standards, in conjunction with the establishment of a regional haze program under section 169A of the Act, would provide appropriate protection against PM-related public welfare effects including soiling, material damage, and visibility impairment.

DATES: Written comments on this proposed rule must be received by February 18, 1997.

ADDRESSES: Submit comments in duplicate if possible on the proposed action to: Office of Air and Radiation Docket and Information Center (6102), Attention: Docket No. A-95-54, U.S. Environmental Protection Agency, 401 M St., SW., Washington, DC 20460.

PUBLIC HEARINGS: The EPA will announce in a separate Federal Register document the date, time, and address of the public hearing on this proposed rule.

FOR FURTHER INFORMATION CONTACT: Ms. Patricia Koman, MD-15, Air Quality Strategies and Standards Division, Office of Air Quality Planning and Standards, U.S. Environmental Protection Agency, Research Triangle Park, North Carolina 27711, telephone: (919) 541-5170.

> **ON THE WEB**
>
> The Internet Law Library, which is sponsored by the U.S. House of Representatives, contains links to federal and state regulatory materials, including the *Code of Federal Regulations.* This page can be found at law.house.gov.

published in the *Federal Register.* The final rule is later compiled with the rules and regulations of other federal administrative agencies in the *Code of Federal Regulations* (CFR). Final rules have binding legal effect unless the courts later overturn them.

In the following case, AT&T Corporation and other established local telephone service providers asked the United State Supreme Court to overturn a Federal Communications Commission (FCC) rule issued to implement part of the Telecommunications Act of 1996. The Court considered the FCC's interpretation of certain terms in the act that the agency made in formulating its rule. This illustrates the interpretation and application of statutory terms that any agency must make in its rulemaking.

CASE 34.1 AT&T Corp. v. Iowa Utilities Board

Supreme Court of the United States, 1999.
__ U.S. __,
119 S.Ct. 721,
142 L.Ed.2d 835.
supct.law.cornell.edu/supct/supct.January.1999.html[a]

HISTORICAL AND SOCIAL SETTING *Until the 1990s, local phone service was thought to be a natural monopoly. States typically granted an exclusive franchise in each local service area to a local exchange carrier (LEC), which owns, among other things, the local loops (wires connecting telephones to switches), the switches (equipment directing calls to their destinations), and the transport trunks (wires carrying calls between switches) that constitute a local exchange network. When technological advances made competition among multiple providers of local service seem possible, however, Congress enacted the Telecommunications Act of 1996 to end the state-sanctioned monopolies.*

BACKGROUND AND FACTS The act required existing LECs to, among other things, share elements of their networks (loops, switches, and trunks) with their new competitors. The act ordered the Federal Communications Commission (FCC) to issue rules to implement this requirement. In deciding which elements to make available, the FCC was directed to consider whether access to each element was "necessary" and whether a lack of access would "impair" a competitor's ability to provide service. The FCC concluded that access was "necessary" even if a competitor could substitute an element from another source, and that "impairment" occurred if access was denied and a competitor had *any* increase in cost or decrease in quality. The FCC issued Rule 319, requiring the LECs to give their new competitors access to seven specific network elements.[b] The LECs, including AT&T Corporation, and others filed suits in courts across the United States to challenge the FCC's new rules, including Rule 319. The suits were combined into a single case in the U.S. Court of Appeals for the Eighth Circuit, which held, among other things, that the FCC's interpretations of "necessary" and "impair" were reasonable. The LECs appealed to the United States Supreme Court.

a. On this page, click on the case title to access the opinion. This page is part of the database of United States Supreme Court opinions maintained by the Legal Information Institute of Cornell Law School.

b. 47 C.F.R. Section 51.319. The seven elements included "the local loop, the network interface device, switching capability, interoffice transmission facilities, signaling networks and call-related databases, operations support systems functions, and operator services and directory assistance."

IN THE WORDS OF THE COURT . . .
Justice *SCALIA* delivered the opinion of the Court.

* * * *

* * * [T]he [Telecommunications] Act requires the FCC to apply some limiting standard, rationally related to the goals of the Act, which it has simply failed to do. * * * [I]t is hard to imagine when [an LEC's] failure to give access to the element[s] would not constitute an "impairment" under [the FCC's] standard. * * * [T]hat judgment allows [competitors], rather than the [FCC], to determine whether access

(Continued)

CASE 34.1—Continued

to [the] elements is necessary, and whether the failure to obtain access to [the] elements would impair the ability to provide services. The [FCC] cannot, consistent with the statute, [ignore] the availability of elements outside the [LEC's] network. That failing alone would require [Rule 319] to be set aside. In addition, however, the [FCC's] assumption that any increase in cost (or decrease in quality) imposed by denial of a network element renders access to that element "necessary," and causes the failure to provide that element to "impair" the [competitor's] ability to furnish its desired services, is simply not in accord with the ordinary and fair meaning of those terms. [A competitor] whose anticipated annual profits from the proposed service are reduced [by only 1 percent] of [its] investment has perhaps been "impaired" in its ability to amass earnings, but has not * * * been "impair[ed] * * * in its ability to provide the services it seeks to offer"; and it cannot realistically be said that the network element enabling it to [increase] its profits [by 1 percent] is "necessary." In a world of perfect competition, in which all carriers are providing their service at marginal [incremental] cost, the [FCC's] total equating of increased cost (or decreased quality) with "necessity" and "impairment" might be reasonable; but it has not established the existence of such an ideal world.

DECISION AND REMEDY The United States Supreme Court concluded that the FCC did not interpret the terms of the Telecommunications Act in a "reasonable fashion" and vacated Rule 319. The Court indicated that the FCC should consider the availability, to competitors, of elements outside the LECs' networks.

FOR CRITICAL ANALYSIS—Political Consideration *Why doesn't Congress always define specifically what an administrative agency is to consider when making rules?*

The Letter of the Law — GRIST FOR THE MILL

Is the growth in government regulations stifling business? Health, safety, and environmental regulations have generally made the United States healthier, safer, and cleaner. But the administrative obsession with detailed regulations, which may be genuinely worthwhile in some areas, such as airplane safety, can be extreme when applied to other businesses and workplaces.

For example, consider the regulatory dilemma facing the Bradley family over their corn-grinding mill, located near Tallahassee, the capital of Florida. The Bradleys opened the mill in the 1920s and offered everyone in the area the opportunity to bring their corn on Sundays, hitch their horses to the grinding wheel, and make meal. Soon, the Bradleys opened a store near the mill to sell farm supplies and their own brand of grits, ground in their mill.

For nearly seventy years, no one complained. In 1993, however, an inspector for the Florida Department of Agriculture concluded that the mill, built of wood and stone, was in violation of state regulations concerning food-processing equipment. There was no known health problem, nor had anyone ever gotten sick from eating the Bradleys' grits. Nonetheless, the Bradleys were ordered to bring the mill up to current standards.

The mill, however, is on the National Register of Historic Places. Under the law governing such sites, the millhouse could not be changed. Thus, to comply with one rule, the Bradleys would have to violate another. Their only choice was to shut down the mill.

One of the Bradleys' regular customers was Lawton Chiles, the governor of Florida. When Chiles heard of the Bradleys' predicament, he got involved. With the governor on their side, a compromise was soon reached. The Bradleys were allowed to enclose the mill with screening and stay in business. Meanwhile, the governor set a goal of cutting in half the number of Florida's administrative regulations.

THE BOTTOM LINE

There may be more than one government agency with the authority to apply its rules in a particular situation.

INVESTIGATION

Administrative agencies conduct investigations of the entities that they regulate. Agencies investigate a wide range of activities, including coal mining, automobile manufacturing, and the industrial discharge of pollutants into the environment. A typical agency investigation occurs during the rulemaking process to obtain information about a certain individual, firm, or industry. The purpose of such an investigation is to avoid issuing a rule that is arbitrary and capricious and instead to issue a rule based on a consideration of relevant factors. After final rules are issued, agencies conduct investigations to monitor compliance with those rules. A typical agency investigation of this kind might begin when a citizen reports a possible violation.

Inspections and Tests Many agencies gather information through on-site inspections. Sometimes, inspecting an office, a factory, or some other business facility is the only way to obtain the evidence needed to prove a regulatory violation. At other times, an inspection or test is used in place of a formal hearing to show the need to correct or prevent an undesirable condition. Administrative inspections and tests cover a wide range of activities, including safety inspections of underground coal mines, safety tests of commercial equipment and automobiles, and environmental monitoring of factory emissions. An agency may also ask a firm or individual to submit certain documents or records to the agency for examination.

Normally, business firms comply with agency requests to inspect facilities or business records, because it is in any firm's interest to maintain a good relationship with regulatory bodies. In some instances, however, such as when a firm thinks an agency's request is unreasonable and may be detrimental to the firm's interest, the firm may refuse to comply with the request. In such situations, an agency may resort to the use of a subpoena or a search warrant.

Subpoenas There are two basic types of subpoenas. The subpoena *ad testificandum* ("to testify") is the technical term for an ordinary subpoena. It is a writ, or order, compelling a witness to appear at an agency hearing. The subpoena *duces tecum* ("bring it with you") compels an individual or organization to hand over books, papers, records, or documents to the agency. An administrative agency may use either type of subpoena to obtain testimony or documents.

There are limits on what an agency can demand. To determine whether an agency is abusing its discretion in its pursuit of information as part of an investigation, a court may consider such factors as the following:

- The purpose of the investigation. An investigation must have a legitimate purpose. An improper purpose is, for example, harassment.
- The relevancy of the information being sought. Information is relevant if it reveals that the law is being violated or if it assures the agency that the law is not being violated.
- The specificity of the demand for testimony or documents. A subpoena must, for example, adequately describe the material being sought.
- The burden of the demand on the party from whom the information is sought. In responding to a request for information, a party must bear the costs of, for example, copying the documents that must be handed over, but a business is generally protected from revealing such information as trade secrets.

In the following case, former bank directors challenged the right of an administrative agency to subpoena their personal financial records. The court considered the extent of the agency's investigative powers.

CASE 34.2 Federal Deposit Insurance Corp. v. Wentz

United States Court of Appeals,
Third Circuit, 1995.
55 F.3d 905.

HISTORICAL AND ECONOMIC SETTING *Congress created the Federal Deposit Insurance Corporation (FDIC) in 1933 to help prevent commercial bank failures and to protect bank customers' accounts. In 1992, nearly five hundred banks failed. More than half of all bank failures can be attributed to agricultural loans, when the failure of farms leads to default on the loans. Fraud also often plays a role, particularly in nonagricultural states. When a bank fails, the FDIC covers each depositor's loss up to $100,000 and then sells the bank's assets, or takes other steps, to regain some of those funds.*

BACKGROUND AND FACTS Sidney Wentz and Natalie Koether were directors of The Howard Savings Bank of Livingston, New Jersey, when it was declared insolvent in October 1992. The Federal Deposit Insurance Corporation (FDIC) was appointed receiver. In April 1993, the FDIC issued subpoenas *duces tecum* to Wentz, Koether, and others, seeking, among other things, their personal financial records. The directors refused to comply. The FDIC asked a federal district court to enforce the subpoenas, arguing that the records were needed to assess any bank losses that might be due to any breach of the directors' fiduciary duties. The court ordered the directors to produce only those records showing additions to or reductions in their assets. The directors appealed, contending that this order intruded on their privacy.

IN THE WORDS OF THE COURT . . .
WEIS, Circuit Judge.

* * * *

When personal documents of individuals, as contrasted with business records of corporations, are the subject of an administrative subpoena, privacy concerns must be considered. * * * [R]elevant factors [include] such matters as the type of record requested, the information that it might contain, the potential for harm and subsequent nonconsensual disclosure, the adequacy of safeguards to prevent unauthorized disclosure, the degree of need for access, * * * and the presence of recognizable public interests justifying access.

* * * *

In applying [these] factors * * * , there is a significant public interest in promptly resolving the affairs of insolvent banks on behalf of their creditors and depositors, many of whom have lost significant sums of money and are often left with little hope for recovery. * * *

The FDIC has shown a reasonable need for gaining access to the directors' records in order to determine whether they reveal breaches of fiduciary duties through the improper channeling of bank funds for personal benefit. Moreover, the directors have not produced any evidence to show that the information contained in their personal financial records "is of such a high degree of sensitivity that the intrusion could be considered severe or that the [directors] are likely to suffer any adverse effects from disclosure to [FDIC] personnel." Finally, we observe that regulatory provisions have been promulgated to guard against subsequent unauthorized disclosure of the subpoenaed information.

DECISION AND REMEDY The U.S. Court of Appeals for the Third Circuit affirmed the district court's order.

FOR CRITICAL ANALYSIS—Economic Consideration *If the FDIC covers most of the customers' losses, why would anyone care whether the bank directors channeled some bank funds for their personal benefit?*

Search Warrants The Fourth Amendment protects against unreasonable searches and seizures by requiring that in most instances a physical search for evidence must be conducted under the authority of a search warrant. An agency's search warrant is an order directing law enforcement officials to search a specific place for a specific item and present it to the agency. Although it was once thought that administrative inspections were exempt from the warrant requirement, the United States Supreme Court held in *Marshall v. Barlow's, Inc.*,[4] that the requirement does apply to the administrative process.

Agencies can conduct warrantless searches in several situations. Warrants are not required to conduct searches in highly regulated industries. Firms that sell firearms or liquor, for example, are automatically subject to inspections without warrants. Sometimes, a statute permits warrantless searches of certain types of hazardous operations, such as coal mines. Also, a warrantless inspection in an emergency situation is normally considered reasonable.

ADJUDICATION

After conducting an investigation of a suspected rule violation, an agency may begin to take administrative action against an individual or organization. Most administrative actions are resolved through negotiated settlements at their initial stages, without the need for formal **adjudication** (the resolution of the dispute through a hearing conducted by the agency).

• **ADJUDICATION**
The act of rendering a judicial decision. In an administrative process, the proceeding in which an administrative law judge hears and decides on issues that arise when an administrative agency charges a person or a firm with violating a law or regulation enforced by the agency.

Negotiated Settlements Depending on the agency, negotiations may take the form of a simple conversation or a series of informal conferences. Whatever form the negotiations take, their purpose is to rectify the problem to the agency's satisfaction and eliminate the need for additional proceedings.

Settlement is an appealing option to firms for two reasons. First, regulated industries often do not want to appear to the regulating agency to be uncooperative. Second, litigation can be very expensive. To conserve their own resources and avoid formal actions, administrative agencies devote a great deal of effort to giving advice and negotiating solutions to problems.

Formal Complaints If a settlement cannot be reached, the agency may issue a formal complaint against the suspected violator. • **EXAMPLE 34.4** The Environmental Protection Agency (EPA) finds that Acme Manufacturing, Inc., is polluting groundwater in violation of federal pollution laws. The EPA issues a complaint against the violator in an effort to bring the plant into compliance with federal regulations. • This complaint is a public document, and a press release may accompany it. The party charged in the complaint responds by filing an *answer* to the allegations. If the charged party and the agency cannot agree on a settlement, the case is heard in a trial-like setting before an **administrative law judge (ALJ)**. The formal adjudication process is described below and illustrated graphically in Exhibit 34–5.

• **ADMINISTRATIVE LAW JUDGE (ALJ)**
One who presides over an administrative agency hearing and who has the power to administer oaths, take testimony, rule on questions of evidence, and make determinations of fact.

The Role of the Administrative Law Judge The ALJ presides over the hearing and has the power to administer oaths, take testimony, rule on questions of evidence, and make determinations of fact. Although formally the ALJ works for the agency prosecuting the case, the law requires an ALJ to be an unbiased adjudicator (judge).

Certain safeguards prevent bias on the part of the ALJ and promote fairness in the proceedings. For example, the Administrative Procedure Act requires that the

4. 436 U.S. 307, 98 S.Ct. 1816, 56 L.Ed.2d 305 (1978).

EXHIBIT 34–5 • The Process of Formal Administrative Adjudication

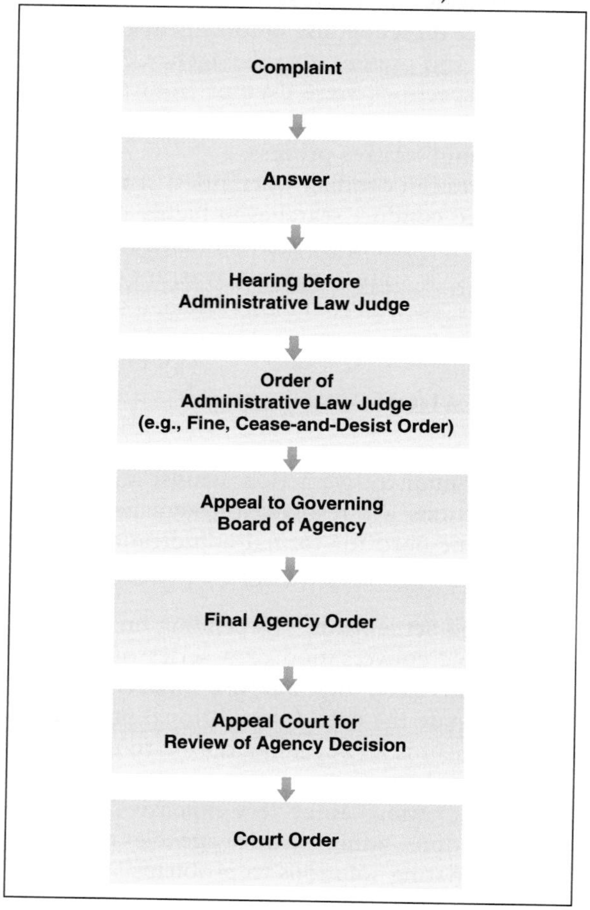

ALJ be separate from the agency's investigative and prosecutorial staff. The APA also prohibits *ex parte* (private) communications between the ALJ and any party to an agency proceeding, including a party charged with a complaint and the agency itself. Finally, provisions of the APA protect the ALJ from agency disciplinary actions unless the agency can show good cause for such an action.

Hearing Procedures Hearing procedures vary widely from agency to agency. Administrative agencies generally can exercise substantial discretion over the type of hearing procedures that will be used. Frequently, disputes are resolved through informal adjudication proceedings. • EXAMPLE 34.5 The Federal Trade Commission (FTC) charges Good Foods, Inc., with deceptive advertising. Representatives of Good Foods and of the FTC, their counsel, and the ALJ meet at a table in a conference room to resolve the dispute informally. •

A formal adjudicatory hearing, in contrast, resembles a trial in many respects. Prior to the hearing, the parties are permitted to undertake extensive discovery proceedings (involving depositions, interrogatories, and requests for documents or other information, as described in Chapter 3). During the hearing, the parties may give testimony, present other evidence, and cross-examine adverse witnesses.

A significant difference between a trial and an administrative agency hearing, though, is that normally, much more information, including hearsay (secondhand information offered for its truth), can be introduced as evidence during an administrative hearing.

• **INITIAL ORDER**
In the context of administrative law, an agency's disposition in a matter other than a rulemaking. An administrative law judge's initial order becomes final unless it is appealed.

• **FINAL ORDER**
The final decision of an administrative agency on an issue. If no appeal is taken, or if the case is not reviewed or considered anew by the agency commission, the administrative law judge's initial order becomes the final order of the agency.

Agency Orders Following a hearing, the ALJ renders an **initial order,** or decision, on the case. Either party may appeal the ALJ's decision to the board or commission that governs the agency. • **EXAMPLE 34.6** National Warehouse Corporation is charged with violations of the Occupational Safety and Health Act, and an ALJ from the Occupational Health and Safety Administration (OSHA) imposes penalties on National Warehouse. If the firm is dissatisfied with the ALJ's decision, it may appeal the decision to the commission that governs OSHA. If the firm is dissatisfied with the commission's decision, it may appeal the decision to a federal court of appeals. • If no party appeals the case, the ALJ's decision becomes the **final order** of the agency. If a party does appeal the case, the final order comes from the commission's decision or that of the reviewing court. If a party appeals and the commission and the court decline to review the case, the ALJ's decision also becomes final. This point, as well as the role of common sense in an administrative decision, is illustrated in the following case.

CASE 34.3 Buck Creek Coal, Inc. v. Federal Mine Safety and Health Administration

United States Court of Appeals,
Seventh Circuit, 1995.
52 F.3d 133.

HISTORICAL AND ENVIRONMENTAL SETTING *Historically, three fossil fuels—coal, oil, and natural gas—have accounted for the bulk of U.S. energy production. Of those three fuels, coal accounted for the largest share of energy production in the 1980s. It is estimated that U.S. coal production could be sustained at present levels for more than two hundred years. Some of the richest U.S. coal deposits are in the Appalachian Mountains and in the southern half of Indiana.*

BACKGROUND AND FACTS Buck Creek Coal, Inc., operates a coal mine in Sullivan County, Indiana. When James Holland, an inspector for the Mine Safety and Health Administration (MSHA), inspected the mine, he noted an accumulation of loose coal and coal dust in the feeder area, where mined coal is transferred from mine shuttle cars to conveyor belts. Holland issued a citation, charging Buck Creek with violations of federal regulations that require mine operators to keep feeder areas clean. After hearing evidence from both sides, an ALJ found that the evidence supported Holland's conclusions and fined Buck Creek $2,000. Buck Creek asked the Federal Mine Safety and Health Review Commission to review the ALJ's conclusions. When the Commission declined, Buck Creek sought review in the courts.

IN THE WORDS OF THE COURT . . .
ILANA DIAMOND ROVNER, Circuit Judge.

* * * *

* * * [The ALJ] made these findings, based primarily on the testimony of Inspector Holland: "[T]here were substantial accumulations of loose coal, coal fines and float coal dust, in the feeder area * * * . A heated roller turning in that combustible material could easily be an ignition source which could in turn cause a fire. * * * [I]n the event of a fire, smoke and gas inhalation by miners in the area would cause a reasonably serious injury requiring medical attention." * * * [N]o further evidence was necessary to support the ALJ's conclusion. First, * * * Inspector Holland [is] a federal mine inspector with 32 years of mining experience who specializes in mine ventilation.

(Continued)

CASE 34.3—Continued

Nor was anything more than Inspector Holland's opinion necessary to support the common sense conclusion that a fire burning in an underground coal mine would present a serious risk of smoke and gas inhalation to miners who are present. * * * [F]ire is one of the primary safety concerns that has motivated federal regulation of the coal mining industry.

Nor has Buck Creek identified any evidence that tends to undermine the ALJ's conclusion. * * * Buck Creek has relied mainly on * * * testimony [that] pertained to Buck Creek's fire safety systems. * * * The fact that Buck Creek has safety measures in place * * * does not mean that fires do not pose a serious safety risk to miners. Indeed, the precautions are * * * in place * * * precisely because of the significant dangers associated with coal mine fires.

DECISION AND REMEDY The U.S. Court of Appeals for the Seventh Circuit denied Buck Creek's petition for review. The ALJ's conclusions became the final order for the agency.

FOR CRITICAL ANALYSIS—Social Consideration *What role does common sense play in the application and review of administrative rulings?*

Limitations on Agency Powers

"Absolute discretion . . . is more destructive of freedom than any of man's other inventions."

WILLIAM O. DOUGLAS, 1892–1954
(Associate justice of the United States Supreme Court, 1939–1975)

Combining the functions normally divided among the three branches of government into an administrative agency concentrates considerable power in a single organization. Because of this concentration of authority, one of the major policy objectives of the government is to control the risks of arbitrariness and overreaching by administrative agencies without hindering the effective use of agency power to deal with particular problem areas, as Congress intends.

The judicial branch of the government exercises control over agency powers through the courts' review of agency actions. The executive and legislative branches of government also exercise control over agency authority.

JUDICIAL CONTROLS

The APA provides for judicial review of most agency decisions. As discussed above, if a charged party is dissatisfied with an agency's order, it can appeal the decision to a federal appeals court. Agency actions are not automatically subject to judicial review, however. Parties seeking review must demonstrate that they meet certain requirements, including those listed here:

- The action must be *reviewable* by the court. The APA creates a presumption that agency actions are reviewable, making this requirement easy to satisfy.
- The party must have *standing to sue* the agency (the party must have a direct stake in the outcome of the judicial proceeding).
- The party must have *exhausted all possible administrative remedies*. Each agency has its "chain of review," and the party must follow agency appeal procedures before a court will deem that administrative remedies have been exhausted.
- There must be an *actual controversy* at issue. Courts will not review cases before it is necessary to decide them.

Recall from Chapter 3 that appellate courts normally defer to the decisions of trial courts on questions of fact. In reviewing administrative actions, the courts are similarly reluctant to review the factual findings of agencies. In most cases, the courts accept the facts as found in the agency proceedings. Normally, when a court reviews an administrative agency decision, the court considers the following types of issues:

- Whether the agency has exceeded its authority under its enabling legislation.
- Whether the agency has properly interpreted laws applicable to the agency action under review.
- Whether the agency has violated any constitutional provisions.
- Whether the agency has acted in accordance with procedural requirements of the law.
- Whether the agency's actions were arbitrary, capricious, or an abuse of discretion.
- Whether any conclusions drawn by the agency are not supported by substantial evidence.

The issue in the following case was whether an agency's action was arbitrary and capricious.

CASE 34.4 Sierra Club v. Thomas

United States Court of Appeals,
Sixth Circuit, 1997.
105 F.3d 248.
www.law.emory.edu/6circuit/jan97/index.html[a]

HISTORICAL AND POLITICAL SETTING *Congress enacted the National Forest Management Act of 1976*[b] *out of concern that timber production was becoming the dominant policy of the U.S. Forest Service. Congress believed that, if left unregulated, the Forest Service would manage the national forests as "tree farms." The act required the Forest Service to develop formal "Land and Resource Management Plans" for the national forests. Congress hoped that this would inhibit agency discretion and ensure forest preservation and productivity. Among other things, the act imposed limitations on timber harvesting by restricting the use of clearcutting unless that was the optimum method for harvesting. Clearcutting involves the removal of all trees within areas ranging in size from fifteen to thirty acres.*

a. This is a page, within the Web site of the Emory University School of Law, that lists the published opinions of the U.S. Court of Appeals for the Sixth Circuit for January 1997. Scroll down the list of cases to the *Sierra Club* case. Click on the case name to access the opinion.
b. 16 U.S.C. Sections 1600–1614.

BACKGROUND AND FACTS The Forest Service issued a plan for cutting timber from the Wayne National Forest. Most of the cutting was to be done by a technique known as even-aged management, which requires clearcutting. The Sierra Club challenged the plan in an appeal to Jack Ward Thomas, chief of the Forest Service. When Thomas affirmed the plan, the Sierra Club and others filed a suit in a federal district court against Thomas and others, arguing that the plan was arbitrary and capricious because, in making it, the Forest Service had not complied with the National Forest Management Act. The court granted the Forest Service's motion for summary judgment, and the Sierra Club appealed.

IN THE WORDS OF THE COURT . . .
BOYCE F. MARTIN, JR., Chief Judge.

* * * *

* * * The Forest Service argues that its even-aged management plan is based on evidence that timbering will provide new opportunities for recreation that will, in turn, preserve and enhance the diversity of plant and animal communities in the Wayne National Forest. Most recreation does not require timber harvesting, however. Further, as the Forest Service's own records reflect, the Wayne is surrounded by and intermingled with privately-held land which already contains an abundance of diverse plant and animal life. Timbering simply does not promote the kind of recreational activities that are in demand in the Wayne; in fact, recreation like fishing and hiking is harmed by clearcutting. The planners also failed to recognize that cutting is unlikely to stimulate new and valuable forms of recreation because much of the Wayne has already been cut or developed. In that particular environment, clearcutting loses its value.

(Continued)

CASE 34.4—Continued

* * * The National Forest Management Act * * * contemplates that even-aged management techniques will be used only in exceptional circumstances. Yet, the defendants would utilize even-aged management logging as if it were the statutory rule, rather than the exception. By arbitrarily undervaluing the recreational value of wilderness, the Forest Service created a very distorted picture of the Wayne National Forest. Based on false premises such as these, the Forest Service improperly concluded that clearcutting was necessary.

DECISION AND REMEDY The U.S. Court of Appeals for the Sixth Circuit concluded that the Forest Service plan was arbitrary and capricious. The court reversed the lower court's decision and remanded the case.

FOR CRITICAL ANALYSIS—Economic Consideration *Why isn't every agency action subject to automatic judicial review?*

Business Law in Action • BUSINESS OPPORTUNITY SCAMS

This is how it starts: a promise of big income for a few hours of easy work—"No Experience Necessary!" The promise appears in an ad in a newspaper or a magazine, or a commercial on television or radio, urging you to "Act Now!" The work may be said to take "only a little of your spare time" tending video games or pay phones, or stocking vending machines or display racks for anything from car wax and cookies to herbal pills and pizza. It sounds too good to be true—and it is. Such deals cost innocent investors more than $100 million a year.

If you agree to take advantage of one of these so-called "opportunities," it may end up taking advantage of you. To obtain the display racks and inventory, for example, you may be asked to make a large down payment or to buy a large amount of start-up product. To convince you of the "Easy Money!" claims, a seller may cite a government report or include testimonials from "satisfied dealers." The promises of profitability are usually empty—the report may not exist and the testimonials will be hand-picked for what they say.

One item that a scam-artist will not provide is the document that the Federal Trade Commission (FTC) requires under its business opportunity disclosure rule.[a] Basically, this rule applies to deals that cost an investor $500 or more in the first six months and in which the seller agrees to handle such matters as finding locations. The document must include an audited financial statement and must cover, among other things, the seller's business history. If an ad claims that a product will be profitable, a prospective buyer is entitled to written proof. The document must also state the following: "To protect you, we've required your [seller] to give you this information. We haven't checked it, and don't know if it's correct. * * * If you find anything you think may be wrong or anything important that's been left out, you should let us know about it. It may be against the law."

Such information might have helped the individual who invested $12,000 in popcorn vending machines that return less than $30 per month. It might have helped the person who invested more than $13,000 in video games that broke down in less than ninety days, or the two investors who lost $72,000 in hot-pizza vending machines. Other buyers have lost as much as $40,000 each in display-rack frauds involving such items as greeting cards and CD-ROM disks.

In response to an astounding increase in such bogus money-making schemes, the FTC initiated Project Telesweep in 1995. A team of FTC employees, pretending to be potential entrepreneurs, began answering the ads that boasted big returns on such business "opportunities" as those listed above. After identifying the frauds and accumulating evidence, the FTC joined the U.S. Department of Justice, the North American Securities Administrators Association, and the attorneys general of twenty states to bring legal actions against more than one hundred business opportunity scams for violations of state and federal law, including the FTC disclosure rule.

FOR CRITICAL ANALYSIS
What should a potential entrepreneur do to protect himself or herself from fraudulent business opportunities?

a. 16 C.F.R. Section 436.1.

EXECUTIVE CONTROLS

The executive branch of government exercises control over agencies both through the president's powers to appoint federal officers and through the president's veto powers. The president may veto enabling legislation presented by Congress or congressional attempts to modify an existing agency's authority.

LEGISLATIVE CONTROLS

Congress also exercises authority over agency powers. Through enabling legislation, Congress gives power to an agency. Of course, an agency may not exceed the power that Congress delegates to it. Through subsequent legislation, Congress can take away that power or even abolish an agency altogether. Legislative authority is required to fund an agency, and enabling legislation usually sets certain time and monetary limits relating to the funding of particular programs. Congress can always revise these limits.

In addition to its power to create and fund agencies, Congress has the authority to investigate the implementation of its laws and the agencies that it has created. Individual legislators may also affect agency policy through their "casework" activities, which involve attempts to help their constituents deal with agencies.

Congress also has the power to "freeze" the enforcement of most federal regulations before the regulations take effect. Under the Small Business Regulatory Enforcement Fairness Act of 1996,[5] all federal agencies must submit final rules to Congress before the rules become effective. If, within sixty days, Congress passes a joint resolution of disapproval concerning a rule, enforcement of the regulation is frozen while the rule is reviewed by congressional committees.

Other legislative checks on agency actions include the Administrative Procedure Act, discussed earlier in this chapter, and the laws discussed in the next section.

Public Accountability

"Law . . . is a human institution, created by human agents to serve human ends."

HARLAN F. STONE, 1872–1946
(Chief justice of the United States Supreme Court, 1941–1946)

As a result of growing public concern over the powers exercised by administrative agencies, Congress passed several laws to make agencies more accountable through public scrutiny. We discuss here the most significant of these laws.

FREEDOM OF INFORMATION ACT

Enacted in 1966, the Freedom of Information Act (FOIA)[6] requires the federal government to disclose certain "records" to "any person" on request, even without any reason being given for the request. The FOIA exempts certain types of records. For other records, though, a request that complies with the FOIA procedures need only contain a reasonable description of the information sought (see Exhibit 34–6). An agency's failure to comply with a request may be challenged in a federal district court. The media, industry trade associations, public-interest groups, and even companies seeking information about competitors rely on these FOIA provisions to obtain information from government agencies.

5. 5 U.S.C. Sections 801–808.
6. 5 U.S.C. Section 552.

EXHIBIT 34–6 • Sample Letter Requesting Information from an Executive Department or Agency

Date

Agency Head or FOIA Officer
Title
Name of Agency
Address of Agency
City, State, Zip

Re: Freedom of Information Act Request.

Dear ______________ :

Under the provisions of the Freedom of Information Act, 5 U.S.C. Section 552, I am requesting access to
____
[identify the records as clearly as possible].

[Optional] I am requesting this information because
____
____
[state the reason for your request if you think it will assist you in obtaining the information].

If there are any fees for searching for, or copying, the records I have requested, please inform me before you fill the request [or:] please supply the records without informing me if the fees do not exceed $ __________ .

[or:] As you know, the act permits you to reduce or waive fees when the release of the information is considered as "primarily benefiting the public." I believe that this request fits that category, and I therefore ask that you waive any fees.

If all or any part of this request is denied, please cite the specific exemption(s) that you think justifies your refusal to release the information, and inform me of the appeal procedures available to me under the law.

I would appreciate your handling this request as quickly as possible, and I look forward to hearing from you within 10 days, as the law stipulates.

Sincerely,
[Signature]
Name
Address
City, State, Zip

Source: U.S. Congress, House Committee on Government Operations, *A Citizen's Guide on How to Use the Freedom of Information Act and the Privacy Act Requesting Government Documents,* 95th Congress, 1st session, 1977.

GOVERNMENT-IN-THE-SUNSHINE ACT

Congress passed the Government-in-the-Sunshine Act,[7] or open meeting law, in 1976. It requires that "every portion of every meeting of an agency" be open to "public observation." The act also requires procedures to ensure that the public is provided with adequate advance notice of the agency's scheduled meeting and agenda. As with the FOIA, the Sunshine Act contains certain exceptions. Closed meetings are permitted when (1) the subject of the meeting concerns accusing any

7. 5 U.S.C. Section 552b.

person of a crime, (2) open meetings would frustrate implementation of future agency actions, or (3) the subject of the meeting involves matters relating to future litigation or rulemaking. Courts interpret these exceptions to allow open access whenever possible.

REGULATORY FLEXIBILITY ACT

Concern over the effects of regulation on the efficiency of businesses, particularly smaller ones, led Congress to pass the Regulatory Flexibility Act in 1980.[8] Under this act, whenever a new regulation will have a "significant impact upon a substantial number of small entities," the agency must conduct a regulatory flexibility analysis. The analysis must measure the cost that the rule would impose on small businesses and must consider less burdensome alternatives. The act also contains provisions to alert small businesses about forthcoming regulations. The act relieved some record-keeping burdens for small businesses, especially with regard to hazardous waste management.

SMALL BUSINESS REGULATORY ENFORCEMENT FAIRNESS ACT

As mentioned above, the Small Business Regulatory Enforcement Fairness Act (SBREFA) of 1996 allows Congress to review new federal regulations for at least sixty days before they take effect. This period gives opponents of the rules time to present their arguments to Congress.

The SBREFA also authorizes the courts to enforce the Regulatory Flexibility Act. This helps to ensure that federal agencies, such as the Internal Revenue Service, consider ways to reduce the economic impact of new regulations on small businesses. Federal agencies are required to prepare guides that explain in "plain English" how small businesses can comply with federal regulations.

At the Small Business Administration, the SBREFA set up the National Enforcement Ombudsman to receive comments from small businesses about their dealings with federal agencies. Based on these comments, Regional Small Business Fairness Boards rate the agencies and publicize their findings.

Finally, the SBREFA allows small businesses to recover their expenses and legal fees from the government when an agency makes demands for fines or penalties that a court considers excessive.

State Administrative Agencies

> **ON THE WEB**
>
> The State Web Locator provides links to information on state administrative agencies. The State Web Locator can be found on a site maintained by the Villanova University School of Law at www.law.vill.edu/State-Agency/statewebloc.html.

Although much of this chapter deals with federal administrative agencies, state agencies also play a significant role in regulating activities within the states. Many of the factors that encouraged the proliferation of federal agencies also fostered the growing presence of state agencies. For example, the reasons for the growth of administrative agencies at all levels of government include the inability of Congress and state legislatures to oversee the actual implementation of their laws and the greater technical competence of the agencies.

PARALLEL AGENCIES

Commonly, a state creates an agency as a parallel to a federal agency to provide similar services on a more localized basis. • **EXAMPLE 34.7** The Pennsylvania Department

8. 5 U.S.C. Sections 601–612.

of Public Welfare shoulders some of the same responsibilities at the state level as the Social Security Administration does at the federal level. The New York Department of Taxation and Finance performs, on a statewide basis, duties that resemble those performed by the Internal Revenue Service on a nationwide basis. The Minnesota Pollution Control Agency parallels the federal Environmental Protection Agency. • Not all federal agencies have parallel state agencies, however. For example, the Federal Bureau of Investigation and the Nuclear Regulatory Commission have no parallel agencies at the state level.

CONFLICTS BETWEEN PARALLEL AGENCIES

If the actions of parallel state and federal agencies conflict, the actions of the federal agency will prevail. • **EXAMPLE 34.8** The Federal Aviation Administration (FAA) specifies the hours during which airplanes may land at and depart from airports. A California state agency issues inconsistent regulations governing the same activities. In a proceeding initiated by Interstate Distribution Corporation, an air transport company, to challenge the state rules, the FAA regulations would be held to prevail. • The priority of federal law over conflicting state laws is based on the supremacy clause of the U.S. Constitution. This clause, which is found in Article VI of the Constitution, states that the Constitution and "the Laws of the United States which shall be made in Pursuance thereof . . . shall be the supreme Law of the Land."

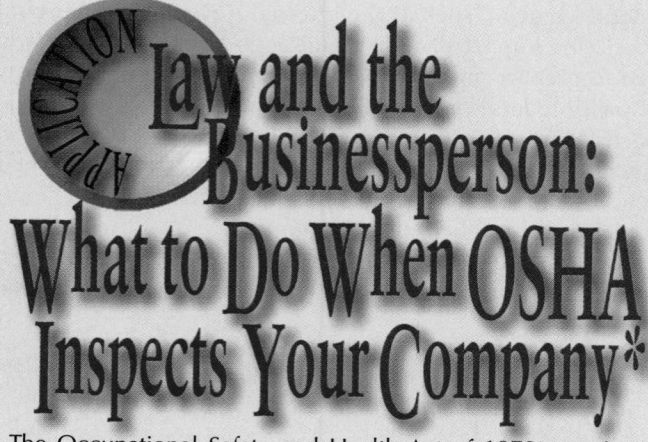

APPLICATION Law and the Businessperson: What to Do When OSHA Inspects Your Company*

The Occupational Safety and Health Act of 1970[a] requires employers to furnish a workplace free of hazards likely to cause death or serious injury and to comply with safety and health regulations that the Occupational Safety and Health Administration (OSHA) issues. There are literally hundreds of OSHA standards covering all aspects of the workplace: ladders, stairs, exits, noise, safety devices, and so on.

To determine whether an employer is complying with the standards, an OSHA inspector can enter a workplace at any reasonable time. The employer may refuse to permit the inspector to enter, but a refusal only postpones the inevitable—the inspector can obtain a search warrant and return.

When an OSHA inspector arrives, he or she must show official credentials, including identification with a serial number and his or her photograph. Normally, an inspector will explain the purpose of a visit and give the employer a copy of any employee complaints.

What the inspector looks at, where in the workplace he or she goes, and how long he or she is there is up to the inspector. Typically, an inspector reviews an employer's records of deaths, injuries, and illnesses—records that the employer is required to keep. An inspector may tour the workplace, checking the display of OSHA posters and other materials and looking for compliance with other regulations.

An employer can choose anyone—typically a manager or supervisor—to accompany an OSHA inspector during an inspection. A representative of the employees can also accompany the inspector. The inspector may talk with employees about working conditions, but work disruptions must be minimal. Also, trade secrets and business conditions are confidential under both state and federal law. Any such information that an inspector discovers cannot be disclosed outside OSHA and the workplace.

If an inspector finds a violation, he or she may informally discuss it with the employer or issue a formal citation. Even a violation that can be corrected immediately may be the basis for a citation and a penalty. A citation—which may be issued

*Remember that "He who is his own lawyer has a fool for a client." This *Application* is not meant to substitute for the services of an attorney who is licensed to practice law in your state.

a. 29 U.S.C. Sections 651–678.

APPLICATION CONTINUED

any time within ninety days of an inspection—normally includes an allegation of a violation, a proposed penalty, and a deadline for correcting the violation.

A citation must be posted in the area of the violation for at least three days. Violations must be corrected, and OSHA must be notified of the corrections. If an employer decides to fight a citation, a penalty, or a correction deadline, he or she has fifteen business days after receipt of the citation to advise OSHA. An appeal may be made to the Occupational Safety and Health Review Commission (OSHRC).

The OSHRC may grant the employer a temporary variance for up to a year (which may be renewed twice) or a permanent variance. The employer must show that it cannot make a correction because of a lack of personnel, materials, equipment, or a need to alter facilities. The employer must also show that what it is doing is safe and healthful.

CHECKLIST FOR OSHA INSPECTIONS

1. Insist on proper identification, which should include a serial number and a photograph of the OSHA inspector. If a person who claims to be an OSHA inspector attempts to collect a penalty or sell a product, he or she is *not* an official OSHA inspector.
2. Designate a company manager or supervisor to accompany the OSHA inspector.
3. If a citation is issued, post it, but if a correction is not possible, or if the condition is already safe and healthful, seek a variance from compliance.

Key Terms

adjudication 879

administrative law judge (ALJ) 879

administrative process 873

bureaucracy 872

delegation doctrine 872

enabling legislation 869

executive agency 870

final order 881

independent regulatory agency 870

initial order 881

judicial process 873

legislative rule 872

notice-and-comment rulemaking 873

rulemaking 873

Chapter Summary • Administrative Law

Creation and Powers of Administrative Agencies (See pages 869–872.)	1. Under the U.S. Constitution, Congress may delegate the task of implementing its laws to government agencies. By delegating the task, Congress may indirectly monitor an area in which it has passed legislation without becoming bogged down in the details relating to enforcement of the legislation. 2. Administrative agencies are created by enabling legislation, which usually specifies the name, composition, and powers of the agency. 3. Administrative agencies exercise enforcement, rulemaking, and adjudicatory powers.
Administrative Process—Rulemaking (See pages 873–876.)	1. Agencies are authorized to create new regulations—their rulemaking function. This power is conferred on an agency in the enabling legislation. 2. Agencies may create legislative rules, which are as important as formal acts of Congress. 3. *Notice-and-comment rulemaking*—The most common rulemaking procedure. Begins with the publication of the proposed regulation in the *Federal Register.* Publication of the notice is followed by a comment period to allow private parties to comment on the proposed rule.

Chapter Summary • Administrative Law, Continued

Administrative Process—Investigation (See pages 877–879.)	1. Administrative agencies investigate the entities that they regulate. Investigations are conducted during the rulemaking process to obtain information and after rules are issued to monitor compliance. 2. The most important investigative tools available to an agency are the following: a. *Inspections and tests*—Used to gather information and to correct or prevent undesirable conditions. b. *Subpoenas*—Orders that direct individuals to appear at a hearing or to hand over specified documents. 3. Limits on administrative investigations include the following: a. The investigation must be for a legitimate purpose. b. The information sought must be relevant, and the investigative demands must be specific and not unreasonably burdensome. c. The Fourth Amendment protects companies and individuals from unreasonable searches and seizures by requiring search warrants in most instances.
Administrative Process—Adjudication (See pages 879–882.)	1. After a preliminary investigation, an agency may initiate an administrative action against an individual or organization by filing a complaint. Most such actions are resolved at this stage before they go through the formal adjudicatory process. 2. If there is no settlement, the case is presented to an administrative law judge (ALJ) in a proceeding similar to a trial. 3. After a case is concluded, the ALJ renders an initial order that may be appealed by either party in federal appeals court. If no appeal is taken or the case is not reviewed, then the order becomes the final order of the agency. It may order the charged party to pay damages, or it may forbid the party from carrying on some specified activity.
Limitations on Agency Powers (See pages 882–885.)	1. *Judicial controls*—Administrative agencies are subject to the judicial review of the courts. A court may review whether— a. An agency has exceeded the scope of its enabling legislation. b. An agency has properly interpreted the laws. c. An agency has violated the U.S. Constitution. d. An agency has complied with all applicable procedural requirements. e. An agency's actions are arbitrary or capricious, or an abuse of discretion. f. An agency's conclusions are not supported by substantial evidence. 2. *Executive controls*—The president can control administrative agencies through appointments of federal officers and through vetoes of legislation creating or affecting agency powers. 3. *Legislative controls*—Congress can give power to an agency, take it away, increase or decrease the agency's finances, or abolish the agency. The Administrative Procedure Act of 1946 also limits agencies.
Public Accountability (See pages 885–887.)	1. *Freedom of Information Act of 1966*—Requires the government to disclose records to "any person" on request. 2. *Government-in-the-Sunshine Act of 1976*—Requires the following: a. "[E]very portion of every meeting of an agency" must be open to "public observation." b. Procedures must be implemented to ensure that the public is provided with adequate advance notice of the agency's scheduled meeting and agenda.

Chapter Summary • Administrative Law, Continued

Public Accountability —continued	3. *Regulatory Flexibility Act of 1980*—Requires a regulatory flexibility analysis whenever a new regulation will have a "significant impact upon a substantial number of small entities." 4. *Small Business Regulatory Enforcement Fairness Act of 1996*—Allows Congress to review new federal regulations. Requires federal agencies to explain in "plain English" how to comply with regulations. Established Regional Small Business Fairness Boards to rate agencies from a small-business perspective. Provides for the recovery of expenses and fees when an agency imposes an excessive penalty.
State Administrative Agencies (See pages 887–888.)	1. States create agencies that parallel federal agencies to provide similar services on a more localized basis. 2. If the actions of parallel state and federal agencies conflict, the actions of the federal agency will prevail.

For Review

1. How are federal administrative agencies created?
2. What are the three operations that make up the basic functions of most administrative agencies?
3. What sequence of events must normally occur before an agency rule becomes law?
4. How do administrative agencies enforce their rules?
5. How do the three branches of government limit the power of administrative agencies?

Questions and Case Problems

34–1. Rulemaking Procedures. Assume that the Securities and Exchange Commission (SEC) has a policy not to enforce rules prohibiting insider trading except when the insiders make monetary profits for themselves. Then the SEC modifies this policy by a determination that the agency has the statutory authority to bring an enforcement action against an individual even if he or she does not personally profit from the insider trading. In modifying the policy, the SEC does not conduct a rulemaking but simply announces its new decision. A securities organization objects and says that the policy was unlawfully developed without opportunity for public comment. In a lawsuit challenging the new policy, should the policy be overruled under the Administrative Procedure Act? Discuss.

34–2. Rulemaking Procedures. Assume that the Food and Drug Administration (FDA), using proper procedures, adopts a rule describing its future investigations. This new rule covers all future cases in which the FDA wants to regulate food additives. Under the new rule, the FDA says that it will not regulate food additives without giving food companies an opportunity to cross-examine witnesses. Some time later, the FDA wants to regulate methylisocyanate, a food additive. In doing so, the FDA undertakes an informal rulemaking procedure, without cross-examination, and regulates methylisocyanate. Producers protest, saying that the FDA promised cross-examination. The FDA responds that the Administrative Procedure Act does not require such cross-examination and that it could freely withdraw the promise made in its new rule. If the producers challenge the FDA in a court, on what basis would the court rule in their favor?

34–3. Rulemaking and Adjudication Powers. For decades, the Federal Trade Commission (FTC) resolved fair trade and advertising disputes through individual adjudications. In the 1960s, the FTC began promulgating rules that defined fair and unfair trade practices. In cases involving violations of these rules, the due process rights of participants were more limited and did not include cross-examination. This was because, although anyone found violating a rule would receive a full adjudication, the legitimacy of the rule itself could not be challenged in the adjudication. Any party charged with violating a rule was almost certain to lose the adjudication. Affected parties complained to a court, arguing that their rights before the FTC were unduly limited by the new rules. What will the court examine to determine whether to uphold the new rules?

34–4. Rulemaking Procedures. The Atomic Energy Commission (AEC) was engaged in rulemaking proceedings for nuclear reactor safety. An environmental group sued the commission, arguing that its proceedings were inadequate. The commission had carefully complied with all requirements of the Administrative Procedure Act. The environmentalists argued, however, that the very hazardous and technical nature of the reactor safety issue required elaborate procedures above and beyond those of the act. A federal court of appeals agreed and overturned the AEC rules. The commission appealed the case to the United States Supreme Court. Under what circumstances should an agency have to do more than comply with the Administrative Procedure Act? [*Vermont Yankee Nuclear Power Corp. v. Natural Resources Defense Council, Inc.,* 435 U.S. 519, 98 S.Ct. 1197, 55 L.Ed.2d 460 (1978)]

34–5. Executive Controls. In 1982, the president of the United States appointed Matthew Chabal, Jr., to the position of U.S. marshal. U.S. marshals are assigned to the federal courts. In the fall of 1985, Chabal received an unsatisfactory annual performance rating, and he was fired shortly thereafter by the president. Given that U.S. marshals are assigned to the federal courts, are these appointees members of the executive branch? Did the president have the right to fire Chabal without consulting Congress about the decision? [*Chabal v. Reagan,* 841 F.2d 1216 (3d Cir. 1988)]

34–6. Agency Investigations. A state statute required vehicle dismantlers—persons whose business includes dismantling automobiles and selling the parts—to be licensed and to keep records regarding the vehicles and parts in their possession. The statute also authorized warrantless administrative inspections; that is, without first obtaining a warrant, agents of the state department of motor vehicles or police officers could inspect a vehicle dismantler's license and records, as well as vehicles on the premises. Pursuant to this statute, police officers entered an automobile junkyard and asked to see the owner's license and records. The owner replied that he did not have the documents. The officers inspected the premises and discovered stolen vehicles and parts. Charged with possession of stolen property and unregistered operation as a vehicle dismantler, the junkyard owner argued that the warrantless inspection statute was unconstitutional under the Fourth Amendment. The trial court disagreed, reasoning that the junkyard business was a highly regulated industry. On appeal, the highest state court concluded that the statute had no truly administrative purpose and impermissibly authorized searches only to discover stolen property. The state appealed to the United States Supreme Court. Should the Court uphold the statute? Discuss. [*New York v. Burger,* 482 U.S. 691, 107 S.Ct. 2636, 96 L.Ed.2d 601 (1987)]

34–7. *Ex Parte* Comments. In 1976, the Environmental Protection Agency (EPA) proposed a rule establishing new standards for coal-fired steam generators. The agency gave notice and received comments in the manner prescribed by the Administrative Procedure Act. After the public comments had been received, the EPA received informal suggestions from members of Congress and other federal officials. In 1979, the EPA published its final standards. Several environmental groups protested these standards, arguing that they were too lax. As part of this protest, the groups complained that political influence from Congress and other federal officials had encouraged the EPA to relax the proposed standards. The groups went on to argue that these *ex parte* comments were themselves illegal or that such comments at least should have been summarized in the record. What will the court decide? Discuss fully. [*Sierra Club v. Costle,* 657 F.2d 298 (D.C.Cir. 1981)]

34–8. Arbitrary and Capricious Test. In 1977, the Department of Transportation (DOT) adopted a passive-restraint standard (known as Standard 208) that required new cars to have either air bags or automatic seat belts. By 1981, it had become clear that all the major auto manufacturers would install automatic seat belts to comply with this rule. The DOT determined that most purchasers of cars would detach their automatic seat belts, thus making them ineffective. Consequently, the department repealed the regulation. State Farm Mutual Automobile Insurance Co. and other insurance companies sued in the District of Columbia Circuit Court of Appeals for a review of the DOT's repeal of the regulation. That court held that the repeal was arbitrary and capricious because the DOT had reversed its rule without sufficient support. The motor vehicle manufacturers then appealed this decision to the United States Supreme Court. What will result? Discuss. [*Motor Vehicle Manufacturers Association v. State Farm Mutual Automobile Insurance Co.,* 463 U.S. 29, 103 S.Ct. 2856, 77 L.Ed.2d 443 (1983)]

34–9. Judicial Review. American Message Centers (AMC) provides answering services to retailers. Calls to a retailer are automatically forwarded to AMC, which pays for the calls. AMC obtains telephone service at a discount from major carriers, including Sprint. Sprint's tariff (a public document setting out rates and rules relating to Sprint's services) states that the "subscriber shall be responsible for the payment of all charges for service." When AMC learned that computer hackers had obtained the access code for AMC's lines and had made nearly $160,000 in long-distance calls, it asked Sprint to absorb the cost. Sprint refused. AMC filed a complaint with the Federal Communications Commission (FCC), claiming in part that Sprint's tariff was vague and ambiguous, in violation of the Communications Act of 1934 and FCC rules. These laws require that a carrier's tariff "clearly and definitely" specify any "exceptions or conditions which in any way affect the rates named in the tariff." The FCC rejected AMC's complaint. AMC appealed the FCC's decision to a federal appellate court, claiming that the FCC's decision to reject AMC's complaint was arbitrary and capricious. What should the court decide? Discuss fully. [*American Message Centers v. Federal Communications Commission,* 50 F.3d 35 (D.C.Cir. 1995)]

A QUESTION OF ETHICS AND SOCIAL RESPONSIBILITY

34–10. The Marine Mammal Protection Act was enacted in 1972 to reduce incidental killing and injury of marine mammals during commercial fishing operations. Under the act, commercial fishing vessels are required to allow an employee of the

National Oceanic and Atmospheric Administration (NOAA) to accompany the vessels to conduct research and observe operations. In December 1986, after NOAA had adopted a new policy of recruiting female as well as male observers, NOAA notified Caribbean Marine Services Co. that female observers would be assigned to accompany two of the company's fishing vessels on their next voyages. The owners and crew members of the ships (the plaintiffs) moved for an injunction against the implementation of the NOAA directive. The plaintiffs contended that the presence of a female on board a fishing vessel would be very awkward, because the female would have to share the crew's quarters, and crew members enjoyed little or no privacy with respect to bodily functions. Further, they alleged that the presence of a female would be disruptive to fishing operations, because some of the crew members were "crude" men with little formal education who might harass or sexually assault a female observer, and the officers would therefore have to devote time to protecting the female from the crew. Finally, the plaintiffs argued that the presence of a female observer could destroy morale and distract the crew, thus affecting the crew's efficiency and decreasing the vessel's profits. [*Caribbean Marine Services Co. v. Baldrige,* 844 F.2d 668 (9th Cir. 1988)]

1. In general, do you think that the public policy of promoting equal employment opportunity should override the concerns of the vessel owners and crew? If you were the judge, would you grant the injunction? Why or why not?
2. The plaintiffs pointed out that fishing voyages could last three months or longer. Would the length of a particular voyage affect your answer to the preceding question?
3. The plaintiffs contended that even if the indignity of sharing bunk rooms and toilet facilities with a female observer could be overcome, the observer's very presence in the common areas of the vessel, such as the dining area, would unconstitutionally infringe on the crew members' right to privacy in these areas. Evaluate this claim.

FOR CRITICAL ANALYSIS

34–11. Does Congress delegate too much power to federal administrative agencies? Do the courts defer too much to Congress in its grant of power to those agencies? What are the alternatives to the agencies that we encounter in every facet of our lives?

Online Activities

ONLINE EXERCISE 34–1

Go to

www.doc.gov,

a Web site maintained by the U.S. Department of Commerce. Click on some of the links to determine what is available on this site and at linked locations. Then answer the following questions:

- What is the purpose of the U.S. Department of Commerce? What does the agency do?
- What is the National Technical Information Service (NTIS)? What is available from the NTIS?
- What might a business firm find useful on this site? Which businesses might find this site most useful?
- How could this site be improved?

CHAPTER 35 Antitrust Law

> "Free competition is worth more to society than it costs."
>
> Oliver Wendell Holmes, Jr., 1841–1935
> (Associate justice of the United States Supreme Court, 1902–1932)

CONTENTS

LEARNING OBJECTIVES

After reading this chapter, you should be able to:

1. Explain the purpose of antitrust laws and identify the major federal antitrust statutes.
2. Summarize the types of activities prohibited by Sections 1 and 2 of the Sherman Act, respectively.
3. Indicate why the Clayton Act was passed and summarize the types of activities prohibited by this act.
4. Describe how the antitrust laws are enforced.
5. Name several exemptions from the antitrust laws.

Today's antitrust laws are the direct descendants of common law actions intended to limit *restraints on trade* (agreements between firms that have the effect of reducing competition in the marketplace). Such actions date to the fifteenth century in England. In America, concern over monopolistic practices arose following the Civil War with the growth of large corporate enterprises and their attempts to reduce or eliminate competition. To thwart competition, they legally tied themselves together in business trusts. As discussed in Chapter 33, business trusts are forms of business organization in which trustees hold title to property for the benefit of others. The most powerful of these trusts, the Standard Oil trust, is examined in this chapter's *Landmark in the Law.*

Many states attempted to control such monopolistic behavior by enacting statutes outlawing the use of trusts. That is why all of the laws that regulate economic competition today are referred to as **antitrust laws.** At the national level, Congress passed the Sherman Antitrust Act in 1890. In 1914, Congress passed the Clayton Act and the Federal Trade Commission Act to further curb anticompetitive or unfair business practices. Since their passage, the 1914 acts have been amended by Congress to broaden and strengthen their coverage.

• **ANTITRUST LAWS**
Laws protecting commerce from unlawful restraints.

This chapter examines these major antitrust statutes, focusing particularly on the Sherman Act and the Clayton Act, as amended, and the types of activities prohibited by those acts. Remember in reading this chapter that the basis of antitrust legislation is the desire to foster competition. Antitrust legislation was initially created—and continues to be enforced—because of our belief that competition leads to lower prices, generates more product information, and results in a better distribution of wealth between consumers and producers. As Oliver Wendell Holmes, Jr., indicated in the opening quotation, free competition is worth more to our society than the cost we pay for it. The cost is, of course, government regulation of business behavior.

The Sherman Antitrust Act

In 1890, Congress passed "An Act to Protect Trade and Commerce against Unlawful Restraints and Monopolies"—commonly known as the Sherman Antitrust Act or, more simply, as the Sherman Act. The Sherman Act was and remains one of the government's most powerful weapons in the struggle to maintain a competitive economy. Because of the act's significance, we examine its passage more closely in the following *Landmark in the Law.*

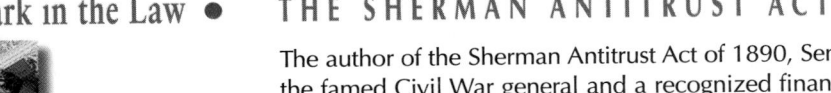

Landmark in the Law • THE SHERMAN ANTITRUST ACT OF 1890

The author of the Sherman Antitrust Act of 1890, Senator John Sherman, was the brother of the famed Civil War general and a recognized financial authority. Sherman had been concerned for years with the diminishing competition within American industry. This concern led him to introduce into Congress in 1888, in 1889, and again in 1890 bills designed to destroy the large combinations of capital that were, he felt, creating a lack of balance within the nation's economy. He told Congress that the Sherman Act "does not announce a new principle of law, but applies old and well-recognized principles of the common law."[a]

The common law regarding trade regulation was not always consistent. Certainly it was not very familiar to the legislators of the Fifty-first Congress of the United States. The public concern over large business integrations and trusts was familiar, however. By 1890, the Standard Oil trust had become the foremost petroleum manufacturing and marketing combination in the United States. Streamlined, integrated, and centrally and efficiently controlled, its monopoly over the industry could not be disputed. Standard Oil controlled 90 percent of the U.S. market for refined petroleum products, and small manufacturers were incapable of competing with such an industrial leviathan.

The increasing consolidation occurring in American industry, and particularly the Standard Oil trust, did not escape the attention of the American public. In March 1881, Henry Demarest Lloyd, a young journalist from Chicago, published an article in the *Atlantic Monthly* entitled "The Story of a Great Monopoly," which discussed the success of the Standard Oil Company. The article brought to the public's attention for the first time the fact that the petroleum industry in America was dominated by one firm—Standard Oil. Lloyd's article, which was so popular that the issue was reprinted six times, marked the beginning of the American public's growing awareness of, and concern over, the growth of monopolies, a concern that eventually prompted Congress to pass the Sherman Act in 1890.

In the pages that follow, we look closely at the major provisions of this act. Generally, the act prohibits business combinations and conspiracies that restrain trade and commerce, as well as certain monopolistic practices.

a. 21 Congressional Record 2456 (1890).

FOR CRITICAL ANALYSIS
Is monopoly power (the ability to control a particular market) necessarily harmful to society's interests?

"As a charter of freedom, the [Sherman] Act has a generality and adaptability comparable to that found to be desirable in constitutional provisions."

CHARLES EVANS HUGHES, 1862–1948
(Associate justice of the United States Supreme Court, 1930–1941)

MAJOR PROVISIONS OF THE SHERMAN ACT

Sections 1 and 2 contain the main provisions of the Sherman Act:

> **1:** Every contract, combination in the form of trust or otherwise, or conspiracy, in restraint of trade or commerce among the several States, or with foreign nations, is hereby declared to be illegal [and is a felony punishable by fine and/or imprisonment].
>
> **2:** Every person who shall monopolize, or attempt to monopolize, or combine or conspire with any other person or persons, to monopolize any part of the trade or commerce among the several States, or with foreign nations, shall be deemed guilty of a felony [and is similarly punishable].

These two sections of the Sherman Act are quite different. Violation of Section 1 requires two or more persons, as a person cannot contract or combine or conspire alone. Thus, the essence of the illegal activity is *the act of joining together.* Section 2 applies both to several people who have joined together and to individual persons, because it specifies "[e]very person who . . . ." Thus, unilateral conduct can result in a violation of Section 2.

The cases brought to court under Section 1 of the Sherman Act differ from those brought under Section 2. Section 1 cases are often concerned with finding an agreement (written or oral) that leads to a restraint of trade. Section 2 cases deal with the structure of a monopoly that already exists in the marketplace. The term **monopoly** is generally used to describe a market in which there is a single or a limited number of sellers. Whereas Section 1 focuses on agreements that are restrictive—that is, agreements that have a wrongful purpose—Section 2 looks at the so-called misuse of **monopoly power** in the marketplace. Monopoly power exists when a firm has an extremely great amount of **market power**—the power to affect the market price of its product. We return to a discussion of these two sections of the Sherman Act after we look at the act's jurisdictional requirements.

• **MONOPOLY**
A term generally used to describe a market in which there is a single seller or a limited number of sellers.

• **MONOPOLY POWER**
The ability of a monopoly to dictate what takes place in a given market.

• **MARKET POWER**
The power of a firm to control the market price of its product. A monopoly has the greatest degree of market power.

JURISDICTIONAL REQUIREMENTS

Because Congress can regulate only interstate commerce, the Sherman Act applies only to restraints that affect interstate commerce. As discussed in Chapter 2, courts have construed the meaning of *interstate commerce* broadly, bringing even local activities within the regulatory power of the national government. In regard to the Sherman Act, courts have generally held that any activity that substantially affects interstate commerce is covered by the act. The Sherman Act also extends to nationals abroad who are engaged in activities that have an effect on U.S. foreign commerce. (The extraterritorial application of U.S. antitrust laws will be discussed in this chapter's *International Perspective* as well as in Chapter 43.)

Section 1 of the Sherman Act

The underlying assumption of Section 1 of the Sherman Act is that society's welfare is harmed if rival firms are permitted to join in an agreement that consolidates their market power or otherwise restrains competition. The types of trade restraints that Section 1 of the Sherman Act prohibits generally fall into two broad categories: *horizontal restraints* and *vertical restraints.* Some restraints are so blatantly and substantially anticompetitive that they are deemed ***per se* violations**—illegal *per se* (on their face, or inherently)—under Section 1. Other agreements, however, even though they result in enhanced market power, do not *unreasonably* restrain trade.

• ***PER SE* VIOLATION**
A type of anticompetitive agreement—such as a horizontal price-fixing agreement—that is considered to be so injurious to the public that there is no need to determine whether it actually injures market competition; rather, it is in itself (*per se*) a violation of the Sherman Act.

• **RULE OF REASON**
A test by which a court balances the positive effects (such as economic efficiency) of an agreement against its potentially anticompetitive effects. In antitrust litigation, many practices are analyzed under the rule of reason.

Under what is called the **rule of reason,** anticompetitive agreements that allegedly violate Section 1 of the Sherman Act are analyzed with the view that they may, in fact, constitute reasonable restraints on trade.

PER SE VIOLATIONS VERSUS THE RULE OF REASON

The need for a rule-of-reason analysis of some agreements in restraint of trade is obvious—if the rule of reason had not been developed, virtually any business agreement could conceivably be held to violate the Sherman Act. Justice Louis Brandeis effectively phrased this sentiment in *Chicago Board of Trade v. United States,* a case decided in 1918:

> Every agreement concerning trade, every regulation of trade, restrains. To bind, to restrain, is of their very essence. The true test of legality is whether the restraint imposed is such as merely regulates and perhaps thereby promotes competition or whether it is such as may suppress or even destroy competition.[1]

ON THE WEB
The Web site of Cornell University's Legal Information Institute contains the text of federal statutes relating to commerce and trade, including the Sherman Act, at www4.law.cornell.edu/uscode/15/1.html.

When analyzing an alleged Section 1 violation under the rule of reason, a court will consider several factors. These factors include the purpose of the agreement, the parties' power to implement the agreement to achieve that purpose, and the effect or potential effect of the agreement on competition. Yet another factor that a court might consider is whether the parties could have relied on less restrictive means to achieve their purpose.

The dividing line between agreements that constitute *per se* violations and agreements that should be judged under a rule of reason is seldom clear. Moreover, in some cases, the United States Supreme Court has stated that it is applying a *per se* rule, and yet a careful reading of the Court's analysis suggests that the Court is weighing benefits against harms under a rule of reason. Perhaps the most that can be said with certainty is that although the distinction between the two rules seems clear in theory, in the actual application of antitrust laws, the distinction has not always been so clear.

SECTION 1—HORIZONTAL RESTRAINTS

• **HORIZONTAL RESTRAINT**
Any agreement that in some way restrains competition between rival firms competing in the same market.

The term **horizontal restraint** is encountered frequently in antitrust law. A horizontal restraint is any agreement that in some way restrains competition between rival firms competing in the same market. In the following subsections, we look at several types of horizontal restraints.

• **PRICE-FIXING AGREEMENT**
An agreement between competitors in which the competitors agree to fix the prices of products or services at a certain level.

Price Fixing Any agreement among competitors to fix prices constitutes a *per se* violation of Section 1. Perhaps the definitive case regarding **price-fixing agreements** remains the 1940 case *of United States v. Socony-Vacuum Oil Co.*[2] In that case, a group of independent oil producers in Texas and Louisiana were caught between falling demand due to the Great Depression of the 1930s and increasing supply from newly discovered oil fields in the region. In response to these conditions, a group of the major refining companies agreed to buy "distress" gasoline (excess supplies) from the independents so as to dispose of it in an "orderly manner." Although there was no explicit agreement as to price, it was clear that the purpose of the agreement was to limit the supply of gasoline on the market and thereby raise prices.

The United States Supreme Court recognized the dangerous effects that such an agreement could have on open and free competition. The Court held that the asserted reasonableness of a price-fixing agreement is never a defense; any agreement that

1. 246 U.S. 231, 38 S.Ct. 242, 62 L.Ed. 683 (1918).
2. 310 U.S. 150, 60 S.Ct. 811, 84 L.Ed.2d 1129 (1940).

restricts output or artificially fixes price is a *per se* violation of Section 1. The rationale of the *per se* rule was best stated in what is now the most famous portion of the Court's opinion—footnote 59. In that footnote, Justice William O. Douglas compared a freely functioning price system to a body's central nervous system, condemning price-fixing agreements as threats to "the central nervous system of the economy."

• **GROUP BOYCOTT**
The refusal to deal with a particular person or firm by a group of competitors; prohibited by the Sherman Act.

Group Boycotts A **group boycott** is an agreement by two or more sellers to boycott, or refuse to deal with, a particular person or firm. Such group boycotts have been held to constitute *per se* violations of Section 1 of the Sherman Act. Section 1 has been violated if it can be demonstrated that the boycott or joint refusal to deal was undertaken with the intention of eliminating competition or preventing entry into a given market. Some boycotts, such as group boycotts against a supplier for political reasons, may be protected under the First Amendment right to freedom of expression, however.

Horizontal Market Division It is a *per se* violation of Section 1 of the Sherman Act for competitors to divide up territories or customers. • **EXAMPLE 35.1** Manufacturers A, B, and C compete against each other in the states of Kansas, Nebraska, and Iowa. By agreement, A sells products only in Kansas; B sells only in Nebraska; and C sells only in Iowa. This concerted action not only reduces marketing costs but also allows all three (assuming there is no other competition) to raise the price of the goods sold in their respective states. The same violation would take place if A, B, and C simply agreed that A would sell only to institutional purchasers (such as school districts, universities, state agencies and departments, and municipalities) in all three states, B only to wholesalers, and C only to retailers.•

In the following case, after a partnership's dissolution, the former partners agreed to restrict future advertising to certain geographical regions. At issue was whether the agreement constituted a *per se* violation of Section 1 of the Sherman Act.

CASE 35.1 Blackburn v. Sweeney

United States Court of Appeals,
Seventh Circuit, 1995.
53 F.3d 825.

HISTORICAL AND SOCIAL SETTING *Disagreements over the allocation of funds often lead to the breakup of partnerships and other business associations. Perhaps the most common mistake of partners—including lawyers who practice law together—is failing to adopt the common-sense approach of putting their partnership agreement in writing when business begins. It is the wrong time to attempt to come to an agreement after relations have become hostile, especially if the partnership has already dissolved.*

BACKGROUND AND FACTS Thomas Blackburn, Raymond Green, Charles Sweeney, and Daniel Pfeiffer practiced law together as partners, relying on advertising to attract clients. When they came to a disagreement over the use of partnership funds, they split into separate partnerships—Blackburn and Green, and Sweeney and Pfeiffer. After the split, they negotiated and signed an agreement that restricted, for an indefinite time, the geographical area within which each partnership could advertise. Less than a year later, the Blackburn firm filed a suit in a federal district court against the Sweeney firm, alleging in part that the restriction on advertising was a *per se* violation of the Sherman Act. The court ruled in favor of Sweeney, and Blackburn appealed.

IN THE WORDS OF THE COURT . . .
CUMMINGS, Circuit Judge.

* * * *

* * * The purpose of the advertising Agreement was, as testified to by defendant Sweeney, to "really trade markets * * * . We, in effect, said that'll be your market."

CASE 35.1—Continued

Both parties in this case * * * rely heavily on advertising as their primary source of clients. * * * [T]he reciprocal Agreement to limit advertising to different geographical regions was intended to be, and sufficiently approximates an agreement to allocate markets so that the *per se* rule of illegality applies.

DECISION AND REMEDY The U.S. Court of Appeals for the Seventh Circuit reversed the ruling of the lower court and remanded the case for the entry of a judgment in favor of the Blackburn firm.

FOR CRITICAL ANALYSIS—Ethical Consideration *Why didn't the court see the agreement to limit advertising as a reasonable covenant not to compete?*

Trade Associations Businesses in the same general industry or profession frequently organize trade associations to pursue common interests. A trade association's activities may include facilitating exchanges of information, representing members' business interests before governmental bodies, conducting advertising campaigns, and setting regulatory standards to govern the industry or profession.

Generally, the rule of reason is applied to many of these horizontal actions. If a court finds that a trade association practice or agreement that restrains trade is sufficiently beneficial both to the association and to the public, it may deem the restraint reasonable. Other trade association agreements may have such substantially anticompetitive effects that the court will consider them to be in violation of Section 1 of the Sherman Act. • EXAMPLE 35.2 In *National Society of Professional Engineers v. United States*,[3] it was held that the society's code of ethics—which prohibited members from discussing prices with a potential customer until after the customer had chosen an engineer—was a Section 1 violation. The United States Supreme Court found that this ban on competitive bidding was "nothing less than a frontal assault on the basic policy of the Sherman Act." •

ON THE WEB

The Federal Trade Commission (FTC) offers an abundance of information on antitrust law, including "A Plain English Guide to Antitrust Laws," at its Web site. Go to www.ftc.gov/ftc/antitrust.htm.

Joint Ventures Joint ventures undertaken by competitors are also subject to antitrust laws. As discussed in Chapter 33, a *joint venture* is an undertaking by two or more individuals or firms for a specific purpose. If a joint venture does not involve price fixing or market divisions, the agreement will be analyzed under the rule of reason. Whether the venture will then be upheld under Section 1 depends on an overall assessment of the purposes of the venture, a strict analysis of the potential benefits relative to the likely harms, and—in some cases—an assessment of whether there are less restrictive alternatives for achieving the same goals.[4]

SECTION 1—VERTICAL RESTRAINTS

• **VERTICAL RESTRAINT**
Any restraint on trade created by agreements between firms at different levels in the manufacturing and distribution process.

A **vertical restraint** of trade is one that results from an agreement between firms at different levels in the manufacturing and distribution process. In contrast to horizontal relationships, which occur at the same level of operation, vertical relationships encompass the entire chain of production: the purchase of inventory, basic manufacturing, distribution to wholesalers, and eventual sale of a product at the retail level. For some products, these distinct phases may be carried out by different firms. If a single firm carries out two or more of the different functional phases involved in bringing a product to the final consumer, the firm is considered to be a **vertically integrated firm.**

• **VERTICALLY INTEGRATED FIRM**
A firm that carries out two or more functional phases (manufacture, distribution, retailing, and so on) of a product.

3. 453 U.S. 679, 98 S.Ct. 1355, 55 L.Ed.2d 637 (1978).
4. See, for example, *United States v. Morgan*, 118 F.Supp. 621 (S.D.N.Y. 1953). This case is often cited as a classic example of how to judge joint ventures under the rule of reason.

Even though firms operating at different functional levels are not in direct competition with one another, they are in competition with other firms. Thus, agreements between firms standing in a vertical relationship do significantly affect competition.

Territorial or Customer Restrictions In arranging for the distribution of its product, a manufacturing firm often wishes to insulate dealers from direct competition with other dealers selling the product. To this end, it may institute territorial restrictions, or it may attempt to prohibit wholesalers or retailers from reselling the product to certain classes of buyers, such as competing retailers. There may be legitimate, procompetitive reasons for imposing such territorial or customer restrictions. • EXAMPLE 35.3 A computer manufacturer may wish to prevent a dealer from cutting costs and undercutting rivals by providing computers without promotion or customer service, while relying on nearby dealers to provide these services. This is an illustration of the "free rider" problem. •

Vertical territorial and customer restrictions are judged under a rule of reason. In *United States v. Arnold, Schwinn & Co.*,[5] a case decided in 1967, the Supreme Court had held that vertical territorial and customer restrictions were *per se* violations of Section 1 of the Sherman Act. Ten years later, however, in *Continental T.V., Inc. v. GTE Sylvania, Inc.*,[6] the Court overturned the *Schwinn* decision and held that such vertical restrictions should be judged under the rule of reason. The *Continental* case marked a definite shift from rigid characterization of these kinds of vertical restraints to a more flexible, economic analysis of the restraints under the rule of reason.

• RESALE PRICE MAINTENANCE AGREEMENT
An agreement between a manufacturer and a retailer in which the manufacturer specifies what the retail price of its products must be.

Resale Price Maintenance Agreements An agreement between a manufacturer and a distributor or retailer in which the manufacturer specifies what the retail prices of its products must be is referred to as a **resale price maintenance agreement.** This type of agreement may violate Section 1 of the Sherman Act.

5. 388 U.S. 365, 87 S.Ct. 1856, 18 L.Ed.2d 1249 (1967).
6. 433 U.S. 36, 97 S.Ct. 2549, 53 L.Ed.2d 568 (1977).

A RETAIL STORE DISPLAYS A WELL-KNOWN DESIGNER'S CLOTHING. IS AN AGREEMENT BETWEEN THE MANUFACTURER AND AN INDEPENDENT RETAILER TO SELL THE CLOTHING AT A CERTAIN PRICE CONSIDERED A VIOLATION OF THE SHERMAN ACT?

In a 1968 case, *Albrecht v. Herald Co.,*[7] the United States Supreme Court held that these vertical price-fixing agreements constituted *per se* violations of Section 1 of the Sherman Act. In the following case, which involved an agreement that set a maximum price for the resale of products supplied by a wholesaler to a dealer, the Supreme Court reevaluated its approach in *Albrecht.* At issue was whether such price-fixing arrangements should continue to be deemed *per se* violations of Section 1 of the Sherman Act or whether the rule of reason should be applied.

7. 390 U.S. 145, 88 S.Ct. 869, 19 L.Ed.2d 998 (1968).

CASE 35.2 State Oil Co. v. Khan

Supreme Court of the United States, 1997.
522 U.S. 3,
118 S.Ct. 275,
139 L.Ed.2d 199.
www.findlaw.com/casecode/supreme.html[a]

HISTORICAL AND SOCIAL SETTING *For more than thirty years, it was illegal for a supplier and a distributor to set the price that the distributor could charge its customers. It did not matter whether the price was intended to be the maximum or the minimum price. Such vertical price-fixing agreements were held to be* per se *violations in the same category as horizontal price-fixing agreements (agreements between competitors).*[b] *The decision of the United States Supreme Court that established this rule was much criticized by other courts and by many commentators. There are circumstances, the critics contended, when vertical maximum price-fixing can be procompetitive.*

a. This page, which is part of a Web site maintained by FindLaw, contains links to opinions of the United States Supreme Court. In the "Party Name Search" box, type "Khan" and click "Search." When the results appear, click on the case name to access the opinion.
b. *Albrecht v. Herald Co.,* 390 U.S. 145, 88 S.Ct. 869, 19 L.Ed.2d 998 (1968).

BACKGROUND AND FACTS Barkat Khan leased a gas station under a contract with State Oil Company, which also agreed to supply gas to Khan for resale. Under the contract, State Oil would set a suggested retail price and sell gas to Khan for 3.25 cents per gallon less than that price. Khan could sell the gas at a higher price, but he would then be required to pay State Oil the difference (which would equal the entire profit Khan realized from raising the price). Khan failed to pay some of the rent due under the lease, and State Oil terminated the contract. Khan filed a suit in a federal district court against State Oil, alleging, among other things, price fixing in violation of the Sherman Act. The U.S. Court of Appeals for the Seventh Circuit reversed this judgment, and State Oil appealed to the United States Supreme Court.

IN THE WORDS OF THE COURT . . .
Justice *O'CONNOR* delivered the opinion of the Court.

* * * *

* * * Our analysis is * * * guided by our general view that the primary purpose of the antitrust laws is to protect interbrand competition. * * * [C]ondemnation of practices resulting in lower prices to consumers is especially costly because cutting prices in order to increase business often is the very essence of competition.

* * * [W]e find it difficult to maintain that vertically-imposed maximum prices could harm consumers or competition to the extent necessary to justify their *per se* invalidation. * * *

* * * *

* * * [T]he *per se* rule * * * could in fact exacerbate problems related to the unrestrained exercise of market power by monopolist-dealers. Indeed, both courts and antitrust scholars have noted that [the *per se*] rule may actually harm consumers and manufacturers. * * *

(Continued)

CASE 35.2—Continued

* * * *

* * *[V]ertical maximum price fixing, like the majority of commercial arrangements subject to the antitrust laws, should be evaluated under the rule of reason. In our view, rule-of-reason analysis can effectively identify those situations in which vertical maximum price fixing amounts to anticompetitive conduct.

DECISION AND REMEDY The United States Supreme Court vacated the decision of the appellate court and remanded the case. The Supreme Court held that vertical price-fixing is not a *per se* violation of the Sherman Act but should be evaluated under the rule of reason.

FOR CRITICAL ANALYSIS—Economic Consideration *Should all "commercial arrangements subject to the antitrust laws" be evaluated under the rule of reason?*

Refusals to Deal As discussed previously, joint refusals to deal (group boycotts) are subject to close scrutiny under Section 1 of the Sherman Act. A single manufacturer acting unilaterally, however, is generally free to deal, or not to deal, with whomever it wishes. In vertical arrangements, even though a manufacturer cannot set retail prices for its products, it can refuse to deal with retailers or dealers that cut prices to levels substantially below the manufacturer's suggested retail prices. In *United States v. Colgate & Co.*,[8] for example, the United States Supreme Court held that a manufacturer's advance announcement that it would not sell to price cutters was not a violation of the Sherman Act.

There are instances, however, in which a unilateral refusal to deal will violate antitrust laws. These instances involve offenses proscribed under Section 2 of the Sherman Act and occur only if (1) the firm refusing to deal has—or is likely to acquire—monopoly power and (2) the refusal is likely to have an anticompetitive effect on a particular market.

Section 2 of the Sherman Act

• **PREDATORY PRICING**
The pricing of a product below cost with the intent to drive competitors out of the market.

Section 1 of the Sherman Act proscribes certain concerted, or joint, activities that restrain trade. In contrast, Section 2 condemns "every person who shall monopolize, or attempt to monopolize." There are two distinct types of behavior that are subject to sanction under Section 2: *monopolization* and *attempts to monopolize*. A tactic that may be involved in either offense is **predatory pricing.** Predatory pricing involves an attempt by one firm to drive its competitors from the market by selling its product at prices substantially *below* the normal costs of production; once the competitors are eliminated, the firm will attempt to recapture its losses and go on to earn very high profits by driving prices up far above their competitive levels.

MONOPOLIZATION

• **MONOPOLIZATION**
The possession of monopoly power in the relevant market and the willful acquisition or maintenance of the power, as distinguished from growth or development as a consequence of a superior product, business acumen, or historic accident.

In *United States v. Grinnell Corp.*,[9] the United States Supreme Court defined the offense of **monopolization** as involving the following two elements: "(1) the possession of monopoly power in the relevant market and (2) the willful acquisition or maintenance of the power as distinguished from growth or development as a consequence of a superior product, business acumen, or historic accident." A violation

8. 250 U.S. 300, 39 S.Ct. 465, 63 L.Ed. 992 (1919).
9. 384 U.S. 563, 86 S.Ct. 1698, 16 L.Ed.2d 778 (1966).

of Section 2 requires that both these elements—monopoly power and an intent to monopolize—be established.

"A rule of such a nature as to bring all trade or traffic into the hands of one company, or one person, and to exclude all others, is illegal."

SIR EDWARD COKE, 1552–1634
(British jurist and legal scholar)

Monopoly Power The Sherman Act does not define *monopoly.* In economic parlance, monopoly refers to control by a single entity. It is well established in antitrust law, however, that a firm may be a monopolist even though it is not the sole seller in a market. Additionally, size alone does not determine whether a firm is a monopoly. For example, a "mom and pop" grocery located in an isolated desert town is a monopolist if it is the only grocery serving that particular market. Size in relation to the market is what matters, because monopoly involves the power to affect prices and output. *Monopoly power,* as mentioned earlier in this chapter, exists when a firm has an extremely great amount of market power. If a firm has sufficient market power to control prices and exclude competition, that firm has monopoly power.

• MARKET-SHARE TEST
The primary measure of monopoly power. A firm's market share is the percentage of a market that the firm controls.

As difficult as it is to define market power precisely, it is even more difficult to measure it. Courts often use the so-called **market-share test**[10]—a firm's percentage share of the "relevant market"—in determining the extent of the firm's market power. A firm may be considered to have monopoly power if its share of the relevant market is 70 percent or more. This is merely a rule of thumb, however; it is not a binding principle of law. In some cases, a smaller share may be held to constitute monopoly power.[11]

The relevant market consists of two elements: (1) a relevant product market and (2) a relevant geographical market. What should the relevant product market include? No doubt, it must include all products that, although produced by different firms, have identical attributes, such as sugar. Products that are not identical, however, may sometimes be substituted for one another. Coffee may be substituted for tea, for example. In defining the relevant product market, the key issue is the degree of interchangeability between products. If one product is a sufficient substitute for another, the two products are considered to be part of the same product market.

The second component of the relevant market is the geographical boundaries of the market. For products that are sold nationwide, the geographical boundaries of the market encompass the entire United States. If a producer and its competitors sell in only a limited area (one in which customers have no access to other sources of the product), then the geographical market is limited to that area. A national firm may thus compete in several distinct areas and have monopoly power in one area but not in another.

¡KEEP IN MIND!
Section 2 of the Sherman Act essentially condemns the act of monopolizing, not the possession of monopoly power.

The Intent Requirement Monopoly power, in and of itself, does not constitute the offense of monopolization under Section 2 of the Sherman Act. The offense also requires an *intent* to monopolize. A dominant market share may be the result of business acumen or the development of a superior product. It may simply be the result of historical accident. In these situations, the acquisition of monopoly power is not an antitrust violation. Indeed, it would be contrary to society's interest to condemn every firm that acquired a position of power because it was well managed, efficient, and marketed a product desired by consumers.

If, however, a firm possesses market power as a result of carrying out some purposeful act to acquire or maintain that power through anticompetitive means, then it

10. Other measures of market power have been devised, but the market-share test is the most widely used.
11. This standard was first articulated by Judge Learned Hand in *United States v. Aluminum Co. of America,* 148 F.2d 416 (2d Cir. 1945). A 90 percent share was held to be clear evidence of monopoly power. Anything less than 64 percent, said Judge Hand, made monopoly power doubtful, and anything less than 30 percent was clearly not monopoly power.

is in violation of Section 2. In most monopolization cases, intent may be inferred from evidence that the firm had monopoly power and engaged in anticompetitive behavior.

ATTEMPTS TO MONOPOLIZE

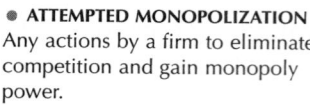

• **ATTEMPTED MONOPOLIZATION** Any actions by a firm to eliminate competition and gain monopoly power.

Section 2 also prohibits **attempted monopolization** of a market. Any action challenged as an attempt to monopolize must have been specifically intended to exclude competitors and garner monopoly power. In addition, the attempt must have had a "dangerous" probability of success—only *serious* threats of monopolization are condemned as violations. The probability cannot be dangerous unless the alleged offender possesses some degree of market power. (See this chapter's *Technology and Protecting Competition in Cyberspace* for a discussion of the widely publicized case brought against Microsoft Corporation for alleged violations of antitrust laws, including monopolization and attempted monopolization.)

The Clayton Act

"The commerce of the world is conducted by the strong, and usually it operates against the weak."

HENRY WARD BEECHER, 1813–1887
(American abolitionist leader)

In 1914, Congress attempted to strengthen federal antitrust laws by enacting the Clayton Act. The Clayton Act was aimed at specific anticompetitive or monopolistic practices that the Sherman Act did not cover. The substantive provisions of the act deal with four distinct forms of business behavior, which are declared illegal but not criminal. With regard to each of the four provisions, the act's prohibitions are qualified by the general condition that the behavior is illegal only if it substantially tends to lessen competition or tends to create monopoly power. The major offenses under the Clayton Act are set out in Sections 2, 3, 7, and 8 of the act.

SECTION 2—PRICE DISCRIMINATION

• **PRICE DISCRIMINATION** Setting prices in such a way that two competing buyers pay two different prices for an identical product or service.

Section 2 of the Clayton Act prohibits **price discrimination,** which occurs when a seller charges different prices to competitive buyers for identical goods. Because businesses frequently circumvented Section 2 of the act, Congress strengthened this section by amending it with the passage of the Robinson-Patman Act in 1936.

As amended, Section 2 prohibits price discrimination that cannot be justified by differences in production costs, transportation costs, or cost differences due to other reasons. To violate Section 2, the seller must be engaged in interstate commerce, and the effect of the price discrimination must be to substantially lessen competition or create a competitive injury. Under Section 2, as amended, a seller is prohibited from reducing a price to one buyer below the price charged to that buyer's competitor. (Even offering goods to different customers at the same price but with different delivery arrangements may violate Section 2 in some circumstances—see, for example, the case discussed in this chapter's *Business Law in Action.*)

"Combinations are no less unlawful because they have not as yet resulted in restraint."

HUGO L. BLACK, 1886–1971
(Associate justice of the United States Supreme Court, 1937–1971)

An exception is made if the seller can justify the price reduction by demonstrating that he or she charged the lower price temporarily and in good faith to meet another seller's equally low price to the buyer's competitor. To be predatory, a seller's pricing policies must also include a reasonable prospect of the seller's recouping its losses.[12]

12. See, for example, *Brooke Group, Ltd. v. Brown & Williamson Tobacco Corp.,* 509 U.S. 209, 113 S.Ct. 2578, 125 L.Ed.2d 168 (1993), in which the Supreme Court held that a seller's price-cutting policies could not be predatory "[g]iven the market's realities"—the size of the seller's market share, the expanding output by other sellers, plus other factors.

Technology and Protecting Competition in Cyberspace

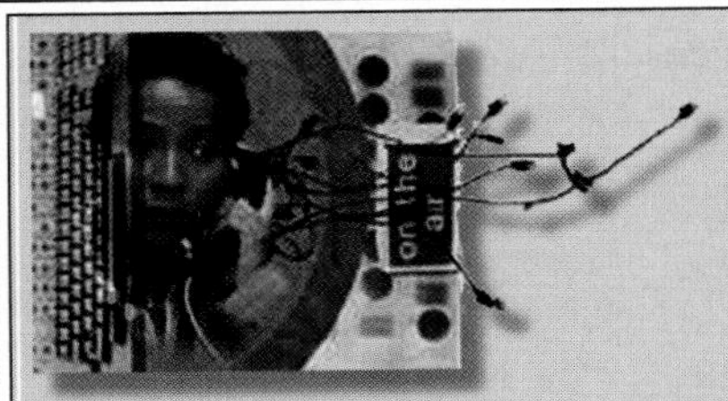

In the United States, competition between businesses is seen as a primary factor for the success of our economy. It is believed that those who violate laws protecting competition—antitrust laws—cause us to pay higher prices for products of lower quality. Violations of antitrust laws can also block new advances in technology.

To date, there are very few cases involving the application of antitrust law in cyberspace. One court has held that it likely was *not* a violation of antitrust law for an Internet service provider, America Online, Inc. (AOL), to refuse to transmit e-mail ads to its subscribers for free.[a]

Currently, the most well-known instance involving cyberspace technology and antitrust law is the ongoing litigation between the U.S. Department of Justice and twenty states' attorneys general, and Microsoft Corporation. The plaintiffs charge, in part, that Microsoft committed such violations of antitrust law as the following.

- Unreasonably restrained competition by "tying" its Internet browser to Windows 98, by entering into "exclusive-dealing" arrangements with various Internet providers, and by imposing start-up screen restrictions on computer manufacturers. (The elements of these and other violations of antitrust law are discussed in more detail in this chapter.)
- Illegally maintained a monopoly in its operating system software.
- Attempted to monopolize the market for Internet browsers.
- Unlawfully used its operating system monopoly to obtain a competitive advantage in the browser market.

a. *Cyber Promotions, Inc. v. America Online, Inc.*, 948 F.Supp. 456 (E.D.Pa. 1996).

BILL GATES, THE FOUNDER OF MICROSOFT CORPORATION, TESTIFIES BEFORE THE SENATE JUDICIARY COMMITTEE DURING THE ANTITRUST LITIGATION INVOLVING MICROSOFT. WHY DO SOME CRITICS OF THIS LITIGATION THINK THAT THE CASE AGAINST MICROSOFT HAS LITTLE MERIT?

While the government hit hard against Microsoft during the trial, there are numerous problems with the case. The first one concerns the fact that the prices of all Microsoft products, and certainly its operating system, have been falling over time. Most economists would argue that such is not the typical picture of a firm that has long-run monopoly power. Indeed, economists arguing in favor of the defendant Microsoft showed that a real monopolist would have charged considerably more than $50 to $75 for its operating system.

Another problem with the case against Microsoft occurred during the trial. AOL bought Netscape (the maker of the Navigator browser) in a multibillion-dollar deal. Today there is a real powerhouse confronting Microsoft in the Internet browser field. Moreover, new browsers, some free, are starting to take hold in the marketplace.

Finally, even if the government ultimately wins its case against Microsoft, no one knows what it should then do. Should it break up Microsoft into component parts? Should it regulate Microsoft and all other software producers? Even the Department of Justice has been quiet on this necessary last step of a successful prosecution.

FOR CRITICAL ANALYSIS

How is it possible to define the relevant market in the case of Internet products?

INTERNET CONNECT

SECTION 3—EXCLUSIONARY PRACTICES

Under Section 3 of the Clayton Act, sellers or lessors cannot sell or lease goods "on the condition, agreement or understanding that the . . . purchaser or lessee thereof shall not use or deal in the goods . . . of a competitor or competitors of the seller." In effect, this section prohibits two types of vertical agreements involving exclusionary practices—exclusive-dealing contracts and tying arrangements.

Business Law in Action • A CLOSER LOOK AT THE "PRICE" IN PRICE DISCRIMINATION

Suppose that a seller charges two customers the same price for a specific product but provides free delivery services to one customer but not the other. Is this a form of price discrimination? Jack and Bob Bell thought so when they faced a similar situation. The Bell brothers purchased feed from Fur Breeders Agricultural Cooperative for use in their fur-breeding business. The price they paid was the same as that paid by every other member. The cooperative, however, offered free delivery services to all of its members except the Bells, who had to pick up the feed.

The Bells sued the cooperative in a federal district court, alleging that the cooperative's actions constituted price discrimination in violation of the Robinson-Patman Act, which amended Section 2 of the Clayton Act. The Bells argued that the added costs they had to incur in picking up the feed effectively raised the "price" they paid for the feed relative to the other members. According to the Bells, the fur-breeding industry is an intensively competitive one in which it is difficult to make significant profits. Because of the cooperative's actions, the Bells were at a competitive disadvantage. They claimed that the cost over time of picking up their feed caused them to reap lower profits relative to their competitors.

The cooperative made a motion to dismiss the case on the ground that all members were charged the same "price," and therefore there could be no "price" discrimination. Furthermore, claimed the cooperative, even if the different treatment with respect to delivery services amounted to price discrimination, the Bells had not proved that this different treatment caused their lower profits.

The court refused to dismiss the case, holding that the Bells had stated a valid claim of price discrimination in violation of the Robinson Patman Act. To the court, it seemed "obvious" that a plaintiff's "competitive opportunities may be harmed when it is forced to incur $16,000–$17,000 in costs each year to pick up feed that its competitors have delivered at no cost. This is clearly the type of competitive injury the Robinson-Patman Act was designed to discourage and prevent."[a]

FOR CRITICAL ANALYSIS

Suppose that a business offered free delivery services to customers within a certain geographical area but not to customers located outside that area. Would this practice constitute price discrimination?

a. *Bell v. Fur Breeders Agricultural Cooperative,* 3 F.Supp.2d 1241 (D.Utah 1998).

• **EXCLUSIVE-DEALING CONTRACT**
An agreement under which a seller forbids a buyer to purchase products from the seller's competitors.

Exclusive-Dealing Contracts A contract under which a seller forbids a buyer to purchase products from the seller's competitors is called an **exclusive-dealing contract.** A seller is prohibited from making an exclusive-dealing contract under Section 3 if the effect of the contract is "to substantially lessen competition or tend to create a monopoly."

• **EXAMPLE 35.4** In *Standard Oil Co. of California v. United States,*[13] a leading case decided by the United States Supreme Court in 1949, the then-largest gasoline seller in the nation made exclusive-dealing contracts with independent stations in seven western states. The contracts involved 16 percent of all retail outlets, whose sales were approximately 7 percent of all retail sales in that market. The Court noted that the market was substantially concentrated because the seven largest gasoline suppliers all used exclusive-dealing contracts with their independent retailers and together controlled 65 percent of the market. Looking at market conditions after the arrangements were instituted, the Court found that market shares were extremely stable, and entry into the market was apparently restricted. Thus, the Court held that Section 3 of the Clayton Act had been violated, because competition was "foreclosed in a substantial share" of the relevant market. •

13. 37 U.S. 293, 69 S.Ct. 1051, 93 L.Ed. 1371 (1949).

• **TYING ARRANGEMENT**
An agreement between a buyer and a seller in which the buyer of a specific product or service becomes obligated to purchase additional products or services from the seller.

Tying Arrangements When a seller conditions the sale of a product (the tying product) on the buyer's agreement to purchase another product (the tied product) produced or distributed by the same seller, a **tying arrangement,** or *tie-in sales agreement,* results. The legality of a tie-in agreement depends on many factors, particularly the purpose of the agreement and the agreement's likely effect on competition in the relevant markets (the market for the tying product and the market for the tied product).

• **EXAMPLE 35.5** In 1936, the United States Supreme Court held that International Business Machines and Remington Rand had violated Section 3 of the Clayton Act by requiring the purchase of their own machine cards (the tied product) as a condition to the leasing of their tabulation machines (the tying product). Because only these two firms sold completely automated tabulation machines, the Court concluded that each possessed market power sufficient to "substantially lessen competition" through the tying arrangements.[14] •

Section 3 of the Clayton Act has been held to apply only to commodities, not to services. Tying arrangements, however, also can be considered agreements that restrain trade in violation of Section 1 of the Sherman Act. Thus, those cases involving tying arrangements of services have been brought under Section 1 of the Sherman Act. Traditionally, the courts have held tying arrangements brought under the Sherman Act to be illegal *per se.* In recent years, however, courts have shown a willingness to look at factors that are important in a rule-of-reason analysis.

What if a tying arrangement affects only one customer? Can the arrangement nonetheless violate Section 1 of the Sherman Act? The following case addresses this issue.

14. *International Business Machines Corp. v. United States,* 298 U.S. 131, 56 S.Ct. 701, 80 L.Ed. 1085 (1936).

CASE 35.3 Datagate, Inc. v. Hewlett-Packard Co.

United States Court of Appeals,
Ninth Circuit, 1995.
60 F.3d 1421.
www.findlaw.com/casecode/courts/9th.html[a]

HISTORICAL AND TECHNOLOGICAL SETTING *Military investment in the 1940s fueled the growth of the electronics industry. Computers made at this time weighed several tons and required the space of a warehouse to store operating components. With the advent of smaller components in the 1960s, computers and other technological equipment became more compact. The Hewlett-Packard Company (HP) produced the first hand-held scientific calculator in 1972. In the decades since then, the growth of the electronics and computer industries has seemed unstoppable. Today, HP makes a variety of electronic products, including computer hardware and software.*

a. This page, which is part of a Web site maintained by FindLaw, contains links to recent opinions of the U.S. Court of Appeals for the Ninth Circuit. In the "Browsing" section, click on the "1995" link. When that page opens, scroll down the list of cases to the *Datagate* case and click on the case name to access the opinion.

BACKGROUND AND FACTS Datagate, Inc., provided repair service for computer hardware made by the Hewlett-Packard Company (HP). HP offered the same service. HP also offered support for those who used its software, but the company refused to provide software support to those who did not buy its hardware service. Datagate filed a suit in a federal district court against HP, claiming in part that HP's practice constituted an illegal tying arrangement. The arrangement had been imposed on only one HP customer, Rockwell International, but the Rockwell hardware service contract was worth $100,000 per year. The court held that one customer was not enough and entered a judgment in favor of HP. Datagate appealed.

(Continued)

CASE 35.3—Continued

IN THE WORDS OF THE COURT . . .

BEEZER, Circuit Judge:

* * * *

[One of the] elements [that] must be satisfied to establish that a tying arrangement is illegal *per se* [is that] the tying arrangement affects a not insubstantial volume of commerce. * * *

* * * *

* * * The * * * requirement can be satisfied by the foreclosure of a single purchaser, so long as the purchaser represents a "not insubstantial" dollar-volume of sales.

* * * *

* * * [T]he Rockwell hardware service contract at issue was worth approximately $100,000 per year. * * *

This amount is sufficient.

DECISION AND REMEDY The U.S. Court of Appeals for the Ninth Circuit reversed the decision of the lower court and remanded the case for trial.

FOR CRITICAL ANALYSIS—Economic Consideration *Did Rockwell International have an alternative to the tying arrangement required by HP?*

SECTION 7—MERGERS

Under Section 7 of the Clayton Act, a person or business organization cannot hold stock and/or assets in another entity "where the effect . . . may be to substantially lessen competition." Section 7 is the statutory authority for preventing mergers or acquisitions that could result in monopoly power or a substantial lessening of competition in the marketplace. Section 7 applies to three specific types of mergers: horizontal mergers, vertical mergers, and conglomerate mergers. We discuss each type of merger in the following subsections.

• **MARKET CONCENTRATION**
The percentage of a particular firm's market sales in a relevant market area.

A crucial consideration in most merger cases is the **market concentration** of a product or business. Determining market concentration involves allocating percentage market shares among the various companies in the relevant market. When a small number of companies share a larger part of the market, the market is concentrated. For example, if the four largest grocery stores in Chicago accounted for 80 percent of all retail food sales, the market clearly would be concentrated in those four firms. Competition, however, is not necessarily diminished solely as a result of market concentration, and other factors will be considered in determining whether a merger will violate Section 7. One factor of particular importance in evaluating the effects of a merger is whether the merger will make it more difficult for potential competitors to enter the relevant market.

• **HORIZONTAL MERGER**
A merger between two firms that are competing in the same marketplace.

Horizontal Mergers Mergers between firms that compete with each other in the same market are called **horizontal mergers.** If a horizontal merger creates an entity with anything other than a small percentage market share, the merger will be presumed illegal. This is because of the United States Supreme Court's interpretation that Congress, in amending Section 7 of the Clayton Act in 1950, intended to prevent mergers that increase market concentration.[15] Three other factors that the courts also consider in analyzing the legality of a horizontal merger are overall concentration of the relevant product market, the relevant market's history of tending toward concentration, and whether the apparent design of the merger is to establish market power or to restrict competition.

15. *Brown Shoe v. United States,* 370 U.S. 294, 82 S.Ct. 1502, 8 L.Ed.2d 510 (1962).

The Federal Trade Commission (FTC) and the Department of Justice (DOJ) have established guidelines indicating which mergers will be challenged. Under the guidelines, the first factor to be considered in determining whether a merger will be challenged is the degree of concentration in the relevant market.

• HERFINDAHL-HIRSCHMAN INDEX (HHI)
An index of market power used to calculate whether a merger of two businesses will result in sufficient monopoly power to violate antitrust laws.

In determining market concentration, the FTC and DOJ employ what is known as the **Herfindahl-Hirschman Index (HHI)**. The HHI is the sum of the squares of the percentage market shares of the firms in the relevant market. For example, if there are four firms with shares of 30 percent, 30 percent, 20 percent, and and 20 percent, respectively, then the HHI equals 2,600 ($30^2 + 30^2 + 20^2 + 20^2 = 2{,}600$).

If the premerger HHI is less than 1,000, then the market is unconcentrated, and the merger will not likely be challenged. If the premerger HHI is between 1,000 and 1,800, the industry is moderately concentrated, and the merger will be challenged only if it increases the HHI by 100 points or more. If the premerger HHI is greater than 1,800, the market is highly concentrated. In a highly concentrated market, a merger that produces an increase in the HHI between 50 and 100 points raises significant competitive concerns. Mergers that produce an increase in the HHI of more than 100 points in a highly concentrated market are deemed likely to enhance the market power of the surviving corporation. Thus, any attempted merger by the above four firms would be challenged by the FTC or the DOJ.

The FTC and the DOJ will also look at a number of other factors, including the ease of entry into the relevant market, economic efficiency, the financial condition of the merging firms, the nature and price of the product or products involved, and so on. If a firm is a leading one—having at least a 35 percent share and twice that of the next leading firm—any merger with a firm having as little as a 1 percent share will probably be challenged.

• VERTICAL MERGER
The acquisition by a company at one level in a marketing chain of a company at a higher or lower level in the chain (such as a company merging with one of its suppliers or retailers).

Vertical Mergers A **vertical merger** occurs when a company at one stage of production acquires a company at a higher or lower stage of production. An example of a vertical merger is a company merging with one of its suppliers or retailers. Courts in the past have almost exclusively focused on "foreclosure" in assessing vertical mergers. Foreclosure occurs because competitors of the merging firms lose opportunities to either sell or buy products from the merging firms.

• EXAMPLE 35.6 In *United States v. E. I. du Pont de Nemours & Co.*,[16] du Pont was challenged for acquiring a considerable amount of General Motors (GM) stock. In holding that the transaction was illegal, the United States Supreme Court noted that stock acquisition would enable du Pont to prevent other sellers of fabrics and finishes from selling to GM, which then accounted for 50 percent of all auto fabric and finishes purchases. •

Today, whether a vertical merger will be deemed illegal generally depends on several factors, including market concentration, barriers to entry into the market, and the apparent intent of the merging parties. Mergers that do not prevent competitors of either of the merging firms from competing in a segment of the market will not be condemned as "foreclosing" competition and are legal.

• CONGLOMERATE MERGER
A merger between firms that do not compete with each other because they are in different markets (as opposed to horizontal and vertical mergers).

Conglomerate Mergers There are three general types of **conglomerate mergers:** market-extension, product-extension, and diversification mergers. A market-extension merger occurs when a firm seeks to sell its product in a new market by merging with a firm already established in that market. A product-extension merger occurs when a firm seeks to add a closely related product to its existing line by merging with a firm already producing that product. For example, a manufacturer might

16. 353 U.S. 586, 77 S.Ct. 872, 1 L.Ed.2d 1057 (1957).

seek to extend its line of household products to include floor wax by acquiring a leading manufacturer of floor wax. Diversification occurs when a firm merges with another firm that offers a product or service wholly unrelated to the first firm's existing activities. An example of a diversification merger is an automobile manufacturer's acquisition of a motel chain.

Although in a conglomerate merger no firm is removed from the marketplace, conglomerate mergers can be challenged under Section 7 of the Clayton Act. In deciding whether the act has been violated, the courts usually evaluate (1) whether the merger will allow the acquiring firm to shift assets and revenue to the acquired firm to potentially drive out businesses who compete with the acquired firm, and (2) whether the merger creates a barrier, keeping other firms from entering the relevant market.

SECTION 8—INTERLOCKING DIRECTORATES

¡CONTRAST!
Section 5 of the Federal Trade Commission Act is broader than the other antitrust laws. It covers virtually all anticompetitive behavior, including conduct that does not violate either the Sherman Act or the Clayton Act.

Section 8 of the Clayton Act deals with *interlocking directorates*—that is, the practice of having individuals serve as directors on the boards of two or more competing companies simultaneously. Specifically, no person may be a director in two or more competing corporations at the same time if either of the corporations has capital, surplus, or undivided profits aggregating more than $15,308,000 or competitive sales of $1,530,800 or more. The threshold amounts are adjusted each year by the Federal Trade Commission (FTC). (The amounts given here are those announced by the FTC in 1999.)

The Federal Trade Commission Act

The Federal Trade Commission Act was enacted in 1914, the same year the Clayton Act was written into law. Section 5 is the sole substantive provision of the act. It provides, in part, as follows: "Unfair methods of competition in or affecting commerce, and unfair or deceptive acts or practices in or affecting commerce are hereby declared illegal." Section 5 condemns all forms of anticompetitive behavior that are not covered under other federal antitrust laws. The act also created the Federal Trade Commission to implement the act's provisions.

Enforcement of Antitrust Laws

The federal agencies that enforce the federal antitrust laws are the U.S. Department of Justice (DOJ) and the Federal Trade Commission (FTC). The DOJ can prosecute violations of the Sherman Act as either criminal or civil violations. Violations of the Clayton Act are not crimes, and the DOJ can enforce that statute only through civil proceedings. The various remedies that the DOJ has asked the courts to impose include **divestiture** (making a company give up one or more of its operating functions) and dissolution. The DOJ might force a group of meat packers, for example, to divest itself of control or ownership of butcher shops.

• **DIVESTITURE**
The act of selling one or more of a company's parts, such as a subsidiary or plant; often mandated by the courts in merger or monopolization cases.

The FTC also enforces the Clayton Act (but not the Sherman Act) and has sole authority to enforce violations of Section 5 of the Federal Trade Commission Act. FTC actions are effected through administrative orders, but if a firm violates an FTC order, the FTC can seek court sanctions for the violation.

A private party can sue for treble damages and attorneys' fees under Section 4 of the Clayton Act if the party is injured as a result of a violation of any of the federal antitrust laws, except Section 5 of the Federal Trade Commission Act. In some instances, private parties may also seek injunctive relief to prevent antitrust violations. The courts have determined that the ability to sue depends on the directness of the injury suffered by the would-be plaintiff. Thus, a person wishing to sue under the Sherman Act must prove (1) that the antitrust violation either caused or was a substantial factor in causing the injury that was suffered and (2) that the unlawful actions of the accused party affected business activities of the plaintiff that were protected by the antitrust laws.

In recent years, more than 90 percent of all antitrust actions have been brought by private plaintiffs. One reason for this is, of course, that successful plaintiffs may recover three times the damages that they have suffered as a result of the violation. Such recoveries by private plaintiffs for antitrust violations have been rationalized as encouraging people to act as "private attorneys general" who will vigorously pursue antitrust violators on their own initiative.

ON THE WEB

You can find links to the home pages for federal government agencies, including the Department of Justice and the Federal Trade Commission, at **www.fedworld.gov**.

International Perspective • THE EXTRATERRITORIAL APPLICATION OF ANTITRUST LAWS

As mentioned earlier in this chapter, the reach of U.S. antitrust laws extends beyond the territorial borders of the United States. The U.S. government (the DOJ or the FTC) and private parties may bring an action against a foreign party that has violated Section 1 of the Sherman Act. The FTC act may also be applied to foreign trade. Foreign mergers, if Section 7 of the Clayton Act applies, may also be brought within the jurisdiction of U.S. courts. Before U.S. courts will exercise jurisdiction and apply antitrust laws to actions occurring in other countries, however, normally it must be shown that the alleged violation had a substantial effect on U.S. commerce. (See Chapter 43 for a further discussion of the extraterritorial application of U.S. antitrust laws.)

In the past, companies usually only had to be concerned with U.S. antitrust laws. Today, however, many countries have adopted antitrust laws. The European Union has antitrust provisions that are broadly analogous to Sections 1 and 2 of the Sherman Act, as well as laws governing mergers. Japanese antitrust laws prohibit unfair trade practices, monopolization, and restrictions that unreasonably restrain trade. Several southeastern nations, including Vietnam, Indonesia, and Malaysia, have either enacted anticompetitive statutes or are in the process of considering them for adoption. Argentina, Peru, Brazil, Chile, and several other Latin American countries have adopted modern antitrust laws as well. Most of the antitrust laws apply extraterritorially, as U.S. antitrust laws do. This means that a U.S. company may be subject to another nation's antitrust laws if the company's conduct has a substantial affect on that nation's commerce.

FOR CRITICAL ANALYSIS

Do antitrust laws place too great a burden on commerce in the global marketplace?

Exemptions from Antitrust Laws

There are many legislative and constitutional limitations on antitrust enforcement. Most statutory and judicially created exemptions to the antitrust laws apply to the following areas or activities:

1. *Labor.* Section 6 of the Clayton Act generally permits labor unions to organize and bargain without violating antitrust laws. Section 20 of the Clayton Act specifies that strikes and other labor activities are not violations of any law of the United States. A union can lose its exemption, however, if it combines with a nonlabor group rather than acting simply in its own self-interest.

❷ *Agricultural associations and fisheries.* Section 6 of the Clayton Act (along with the Capper-Volstead Act of 1922) exempts agricultural cooperatives from the antitrust laws. The Fisheries Cooperative Marketing Act of 1976 exempts from antitrust legislation individuals in the fishing industry who collectively catch, produce, and prepare for market their products. Both exemptions allow members of such co-ops to combine and set prices for a particular product, but they do not allow them to engage in exclusionary practices or restraints of trade directed at competitors.
❸ *Insurance.* The McCarran-Ferguson Act of 1945 exempts the insurance business from the antitrust laws whenever state regulation exists. This exemption does not cover boycotts, coercion, or intimidation on the part of insurance companies.
❹ *Foreign trade.* Under the provisions of the 1918 Webb-Pomerene Act, American exporters may engage in cooperative activity to compete with similar foreign associations. This type of cooperative activity may not, however, restrain trade within the United States or injure other American exporters. The Export Trading Company Act of 1982 broadened the Webb-Pomerene Act by permitting the Department of Justice to certify properly qualified export trading companies. Any activity within the scope described by the certificate is exempt from public prosecution under the antitrust laws.
❺ *Professional baseball.* In 1922, the United States Supreme Court held that professional baseball was not within the reach of federal antitrust laws because it did not involve "interstate commerce."[17] Some of the effects of this decision, however, were modified by the Curt Flood Act of 1998. (See the *Ethical Issue* below for a further discussion of the baseball exemption.)
❻ *Oil marketing.* The 1935 Interstate Oil Compact allows states to determine quotas on oil that will be marketed in interstate commerce.
❼ *Cooperative research and production.* Cooperative research among small business firms is exempt under the Small Business Administration Act of 1958, as amended. Research or production of a product, process, or service by joint ventures consisting of competitors is exempt under special federal legislation, including the National Cooperative Research Act of 1984 and the National Cooperative Production Amendments of 1993.
❽ *Joint efforts by businesspersons to obtain legislative or executive action.* This is often referred to as the Noerr-Pennington doctrine.[18] For example, video producers might jointly lobby Congress to change the copyright laws, or a video-rental company might sue another video-rental firm, without being held liable for attempting to restrain trade. Though selfish rather than purely public-minded conduct is permitted, there is an exception: an action will not be protected if it is clear that the action is "objectively baseless in the sense that no reasonable [person] could reasonably expect success on the merits" and it is an attempt to make anticompetitive use of government processes.[19]
❾ *Other exemptions.* Other activities exempt from antitrust laws include activities approved by the president in furtherance of the defense of our nation (under the Defense Production Act of 1950, as amended); state actions, when the state policy is clearly articulated and the policy is actively supervised by the state;[20] and activities of

¡ NOTE!
State actions include the regulation of public utilities, whose rates may be set by the states in which they do business.

17. *Federal Baseball Club of Baltimore, Inc. v. National League of Professional Baseball Clubs,* 259 U.S. 200, 42 S.Ct. 465, 66 L.Ed. 898 (1922).
18. See *United Mine Workers of America v. Pennington,* 381 U.S. 657, 89 S.Ct. 1585, 14 L.Ed.2d 626 (1965), and *Eastern Railroad Presidents Conference v. Noerr Motor Freight, Inc.,* 365 U.S. 127, 81 S.Ct. 523, 5 L.Ed.2d 464 (1961).
19. *Professional Real Estate Investors Inc. v. Columbia Pictures Industries Inc.,* 508 U.S. 49, 113 S.Ct. 1920, 123 L.Ed.2d 611 (1993).
20. See *Parker v. Brown,* 347 U.S. 341, 63 S.Ct. 307, 87 L.Ed. 315 (1943).

regulated industries (such as the communication and banking industries) when federal commissions, boards, or agencies (such as the Federal Communications Commission and the Federal Maritime Commission) have primary regulatory authority.

ETHICAL ISSUE 35.1 ***Should the baseball exemption from antitrust laws be completely abolished?*** The fact that until recently, baseball remained totally exempt from antitrust laws not only seemed unfair to many but also defied logic: Why was an exemption made for baseball but not for other professional sports? The answer to this perfectly reasonable question has always been the same: baseball was exempt because the United States Supreme Court, in 1922, said that it was. The Court held that baseball was a sport played only locally by local players. Because the activity purportedly did not involve interstate commerce, it did not meet the requirement for federal jurisdiction. The exemption was challenged in the early 1970s, but the Supreme Court ruled that it was up to Congress, not the Court, to overturn the exemption. In 1998, Congress did address the issue and passed the Curt Flood Act—named for the St. Louis Cardinals' star outfielder who challenged the exemption in the early 1970s. Essentially, the act allows players the option of suing team owners for anticompetitive practices if, for example, the owners collude to "blacklist" players, hold down players' salaries, or force players to play for specific teams. Although the act's sponsors, including Senator Orrin Hatch of Utah, claim that the statute brings the rule of antitrust law to baseball, in fact the act did not overturn the 1922 Supreme Court decision but only limited some of the effects of baseball's exempt status. Baseball is still not subject to antitrust laws to the extent that football, basketball, and other professional sports are. Critics of the act claim that the exemption should be completely abolished because it simply makes no sense to continue to treat a $2-billion-a-year enterprise as a "local" activity.

APPLICATION Law and the Businessperson: Avoiding Antitrust Problems*

Business managers need to be aware of how antitrust legislation may affect their activities. In addition to federal antitrust laws covered in this chapter, numerous state antitrust laws also exist. States also now have the power to bring civil suits to enforce federal antitrust laws. Additionally, antitrust law is subject to various interpretations by the courts. Unless a businessperson exercises caution, a court may decide that his or her actions are in violation of a federal or state statute.

If you are a business manager or owner, you should thus be careful when communicating with a direct competitor that offers products or services that are similar to those of your own company. If you know that such communications might cause problems in your line of business, you should probably arrange for the appropriate employees to attend a seminar given by professionals who will let your employees know what is legal and what is not in dealing with competitors. Generally, any businessperson who is worried about potential antitrust violations should seek counsel from a competent

*This *Application* is not meant to substitute for the services of an attorney who is licensed to practice law in your state.

CHECKLIST FOR AVOIDING ANTITRUST PROBLEMS

1. Exercise caution when communicating and dealing with competitors.
2. Seek the advice of an attorney specializing in antitrust law to assure that your business practices and agreements do not violate antitrust laws.
3. If you conduct business ventures in other countries, you should obtain the advice of an attorney who is familiar with the antitrust laws of those nations.

Key Terms

Chapter Summary • Antitrust Law

Sherman Antitrust Act (1890) (See pages 895–904.)	1. *Major provisions—* a. Section 1—Prohibits contracts, combinations, and conspiracies in restraint of trade. (1) Horizontal restraints subject to Section 1 include price-fixing agreements, group boycotts (joint refusals to deal), horizontal market division, trade association agreements, and joint ventures. (2) Vertical restraints subject to Section 1 include resale price maintenance agreements, territorial or customer restrictions, and refusals to deal. b. Section 2—Prohibits monopolies and attempts to monopolize. 2. *Jurisdictional requirements—*The Sherman Act applies only to activities that have a significant impact on interstate commerce. 3. *Interpretative rules—* a. *Per se* rule—Applied to restraints on trade that are so inherently anticompetitive that they cannot be justified and are deemed illegal as a matter of law. b. Rule of reason—Applied when an anticompetitive agreement may be justified by legitimate benefits. Under the rule of reason, the lawfulness of a trade restraint will be determined by the purpose and effects of the restraint.
Clayton Act (1914) (See pages 904–910.)	The major provisions are as follows: 1. *Section 2—*As amended in 1936 by the Robinson-Patman Act, prohibits price discrimination that substantially lessens competition and prohibits a seller engaged in interstate commerce from selling to two or more buyers goods of similar grade and quality at different prices when the result is a substantial lessening of competition or the creation of a competitive injury. 2. *Section 3—*Prohibits exclusionary practices, such as exclusive-dealing contracts and tying arrangements, when the effect may be to substantially lessen competition. 3. *Section 7—*Prohibits mergers when the effect may be to substantially lessen competition or to tend to create a monopoly.

Chapter Summary • Antitrust Law, Continued

Clayton Act (1914)—continued	a. Horizontal mergers—The acquisition by merger or consolidation of a competing firm engaged in the same relevant market. Will be unlawful only if a merger results in the merging firms' holding a disproportionate share of the market, resulting in a substantial lessening of competition, and if the merger does not enhance consumer welfare by increasing efficiency of production or marketing. b. Vertical mergers—The acquisition by a seller of one of its buyers or vice versa. Will be unlawful if the merger prevents competitors of either merging firm from competing in a segment of the market that otherwise would be open to them, resulting in a substantial lessening of competition. c. Conglomerate mergers—The acquisition of a noncompeting business. 4. *Section 8*—Prohibits interlocking directorates.
Federal Trade Commission Act (1914) (See page 910.)	Prohibits unfair methods of competition; established and defined the powers of the Federal Trade Commission.
Enforcement of Antitrust Laws (See pages 910–911.)	Antitrust laws are enforced by the Department of Justice, by the Federal Trade Commission, and in some cases by private parties, who may be awarded treble damages and attorneys' fees.
Exemptions from Antitrust Laws (See pages 911–913.)	1. Labor unions (under Section 6 of the Clayton Act of 1914). 2. Agricultural associations and fisheries (under Section 6 of the Clayton Act of 1914, the Capper-Volstead Act of 1922, and the Fisheries Cooperative Marketing Act of 1976). 3. Insurance—when state regulation exists (under the McCarran-Ferguson Act of 1945). 4. Export trading companies (under the Webb-Pomerene Act of 1918 and the Export Trading Company Act of 1982). 5. Professional baseball (by a 1922 judicial decision), although modified by a 1998 federal statute. 6. Oil marketing (under the Interstate Oil Compact of 1935). 7. Cooperative research and production (under various acts, including the Small Business Administration Act of 1958, as amended, the National Cooperative Research Act of 1984, and the National Cooperative Production Amendments of 1993). 8. Joint efforts by businesspersons to obtain legislative or executive action (under the *Noerr-Pennington* doctrine). 9. Other activities, including certain national defense actions, state actions, and actions of certain regulated industries.

For Review

1 What is a monopoly? What is market power? How do these concepts relate to each other?

2 What type of activity is prohibited by Section 1 of the Sherman Act? What type of activity is prohibited by Section 2 of the Sherman Act?

3 What are the four major provisions of the Clayton Act, and what types of activities do these provisions prohibit?

4 What agencies of the federal government enforce the federal antitrust laws?

5 Name four activities that are exempt from the antitrust laws.

Questions and Case Problems

35–1. Sherman Act. An agreement that is blatantly and substantially anticompetitive is deemed a *per se* violation of Section 1 of the Sherman Act. Under what rule is an agreement analyzed if it appears to be anticompetitive but is not a *per se* violation? In making this analysis, what factors will a court consider?

35–2. Antitrust Laws. Allitron, Inc., and Donovan, Ltd., are interstate competitors selling similar appliances, principally in the states of Indiana, Kentucky, Illinois, and Ohio. Allitron and Donovan agree that Allitron will no longer sell in Ohio and Indiana and that Donovan will no longer sell in Kentucky and Illinois. Have Allitron and Donovan violated any antitrust laws? If so, which law? Explain.

35–3. Antitrust Laws. The partnership of Alvaredo and Parish is engaged in the oil-wellhead service industry in the states of New Mexico and Colorado. The firm presently has about 40 percent of the market for this service. Webb Corp. competes with the Alvaredo-Parish partnership in the same state area. Webb has approximately 35 percent of the market. Alvaredo and Parish acquire the stock and assets of the Webb Corp. Do the antitrust laws prohibit the type of action undertaken by Alvaredo and Parish? Discuss fully.

35–4. Horizontal Restraints. Jorge's Appliance Corp. was a new retail seller of appliances in Sunrise City. Because of its innovative sales techniques and financing, Jorge's caused a substantial loss of sales from the appliance department of No-Glow Department Store, a large chain store with a great deal of buying power. No-Glow told a number of appliance manufacturers that if they continued to sell to Jorge's, No-Glow would discontinue its large volume of purchases from them. The manufacturers immediately stopped selling appliances to Jorge's. Jorge's filed suit against No-Glow and the manufacturers, claiming that their actions constituted an antitrust violation. No-Glow and the manufacturers were able to prove that Jorge's was a small retailer with a small portion of the market. They claimed that because the relevant market was not substantially affected, they were not guilty of restraint of trade. Discuss fully whether there was an antitrust violation.

35–5. Exclusionary Practices. Instant Foto Corp. is a manufacturer of photography film. At the present time, Instant Foto has approximately 50 percent of the market. Instant Foto advertises that the purchase price for Instant Foto film includes photo processing by Instant Foto Corp. Instant Foto claims that its film processing is specially designed to improve the quality of photos taken with Instant Foto film. Is Instant Foto's combination of film purchase and film processing an antitrust violation? Explain.

35–6. Sherman Act, Section 1. Harcourt Brace Jovanovich Legal and Professional Publications (HBJ), the nation's largest provider of bar review materials and lecture services, began offering a Georgia bar review course in 1976. It was in direct, and often intense, competition with BRG of Georgia, Inc., the other main provider of bar review courses in Georgia, from 1977 to 1979. In early 1980, HBJ and BRG entered into an agreement that gave BRG the exclusive right to market HBJ's materials in Georgia and to use its trade name, Bar/Bri. The parties agreed that HBJ would not compete with BRG in Georgia and that BRG would not compete with HBJ outside of Georgia. Immediately after the 1980 agreement, the price of BRG's course was increased from $150 to over $400. Jay Palmer, a former law student, brought an action against the two firms, alleging that the 1980 agreement violated Section 1 of the Sherman Act. What will the court decide? Discuss fully. [*Palmer v. BRG of Georgia, Inc.*, 498 U.S. 46, 111 S.Ct. 401, 112 L.Ed.2d 349 (1990)]

35–7. Tying Arrangements. Eastman Kodak Co. has about a 20 percent share of the highly competitive market for high-volume photocopiers and microfilm equipment and controls nearly the entire market for replacement parts for its equipment (which are not interchangeable with parts for other manufacturers' equipment). Prior to 1985, Kodak sold replacement parts for its equipment without significant restrictions. As a result, a number of independent service organizations (ISOs) purchased Kodak parts to use when repairing and servicing Kodak copiers. In 1985, Kodak changed its policy to prevent the ISOs from competing with Kodak's own service organizations. It ceased selling parts to ISOs and refused to sell replacement parts to its customers unless they agreed not to have their equipment serviced by ISOs. In 1987, Image Technical Services, Inc., and seventeen other ISOs sued Kodak, alleging that Kodak's policy was a tying arrangement in violation of Section 1 of the Sherman Act. Assuming that Kodak does not have market power in the market for photocopying and microfilm equipment, does Kodak's restrictive policy constitute an illegal tying arrangement? Does it violate antitrust laws in any way? Discuss fully. [*Eastman Kodak Co. v. Image Technical Services, Inc.*, 504 U.S. 451, 112 S.Ct. 2072, 119 L.Ed.2d 265 (1992)]

35–8. Clayton Act, Section 2. Stelwagon Manufacturing Co. agreed with Tarmac Roofing Systems, Inc., to promote and develop a market for Tarmac's products in the Philadelphia area. In return, Tarmac promised not to sell its products to other area distributors. In 1991, Stelwagon learned that Tarmac had been selling its products to Stelwagon's competitors—the Standard Roofing Co. and the Celotex Corp.—at substantially lower prices. Stelwagon filed a suit against Tarmac in a federal district court. What is the principal factor in determining whether Tarmac violated Section 2 of the Clayton Act, as amended. Did Tarmac violate the act? [*Stelwagon Manufacturing Co. v. Tarmac Roofing Systems, Inc.*, 63 F.3d 1267 (3d Cir. 1995)]

35–9. Antitrust Laws. Great Western Directories, Inc. (GW), is an independent publisher of telephone directory Yellow Pages. GW buys information for its listings from Southwestern Bell Telephone Co. (SBT). Southwestern Bell Corp. owns SBT and Southwestern Bell Yellow Pages (SBYP), which publishes a directory in competition with GW. In June 1988, in some markets, SBT raised the price for its listing information, and SBYP lowered the price for advertising in its Yellow Pages. GW feared that these companies would do the same thing in other local markets, and it would then be too expensive to compete in those markets. Because of this fear, GW left one market and declined to compete in another. Consequently, SBYP had a monopoly in those markets. GW and another independent publisher filed a suit in a federal district court against Southwestern Bell Corp. What antitrust law, if any, did Southwestern Bell Corp. violate? Should the independent companies be entitled to damages? [*Great Western Directories, Inc. v. Southwestern Bell Telephone Co.,* 74 F.3d 613 (5th Cir. 1996)]

35–10. Restraint of Trade. The National Collegiate Athletic Association (NCAA) coordinates the intercollegiate athletic programs of its members by issuing rules and setting standards governing, among other things, the coaching staffs. The NCAA set up a "Cost Reduction Committee" to consider ways to cut the costs of intercollegiate athletics while maintaining competition. The committee included financial aid personnel, intercollegiate athletic administrators, college presidents, university faculty members, and a university chancellor. It was felt that "only a collaborative effort could reduce costs while maintaining a level playing field." The committee proposed a rule to restrict the annual compensation of certain coaches to $16,000. The NCAA adopted the rule. Basketball coaches affected by the rule filed a suit in a federal district court against the NCAA, alleging a violation of Section 1 of the Sherman Antitrust Act. Is the rule a *per se* violation of the Sherman Act, or should it be evaluated under the rule of reason? If it is subject to the rule of reason, is it an illegal restraint of trade? Discuss fully. [*Law v. National Collegiate Athletic Association,* 134 F.3d 1010 (10th Cir. 1998)]

A QUESTION OF ETHICS AND SOCIAL RESPONSIBILITY

35–11. A group of lawyers in the District of Columbia regularly acted as court-appointed attorneys for indigent defendants in District of Columbia criminal cases. At a meeting of the Superior Court Trial Lawyers Association (SCTLA), the attorneys agreed to stop providing this representation until the district increased their compensation. Their subsequent boycott had a severe impact on the district's criminal justice system, and the District of Columbia gave in to the lawyers' demands for higher pay. After the lawyers had returned to work, the Federal Trade Commission filed a complaint against the SCTLA and four of its officers and, after an investigation, ruled that the SCTLA's activities constituted an illegal group boycott in violation of antitrust laws. [*Federal Trade Commission v. Superior Court Trial Lawyers Association,* 493 U.S. 411, 110 S.Ct. 768, 107 L.Ed.2d 851 (1990)]

1. The SCTLA obviously was aware of the negative impact its decision would have on the district's criminal justice system. Given this fact, do you think the lawyers behaved ethically?
2. On appeal, the SCTLA claimed that its boycott was undertaken to publicize the fact that the attorneys were underpaid and that the boycott thus constituted an expression protected by the First Amendment. Do you agree with this argument?
3. Labor unions have the right to strike when negotiations between labor and management fail to result in agreement. Is it fair to prohibit members of the SCTLA from "striking" against their employer, the District of Columbia, simply because the SCTLA is a professional organization and not a labor union?

FOR CRITICAL ANALYSIS

35–12. Critics of antitrust law claim that in the long run, competitive market forces will eliminate private monopolies unless they are fostered by government regulation. Do you agree with these critics? Why or why not?

Online Activities

ONLINE EXERCISE 35–1

Go to the "Internet Activities Book" on the Web site that accompanies this text, the URL for which is http://blt.westbuslaw.com. Select the following activity, and perform the exercise according to the instructions given there:

Activity 32–1: Vertical Restraints and the Rule of Reason

Before the Test

Go to the *Business Law Today* home page at http://blt.westbuslaw.com. Click on TestTutor.® You will find twenty interactive questions relating to this chapter.

CHAPTER 36

Consumer & Environmental Law

> "Subject to specific constitutional limitations, when the legislature has spoken, the public interest has been declared in terms well nigh conclusive."
>
> William O. Douglas, 1898–1980
> (Associate justice of the United States Supreme Court, 1939–1975)

CONTENTS

LEARNING OBJECTIVES

After reading this chapter, you should be able to:

1. Summarize the major consumer protection laws.
2. Indicate some specific ways in which consumers are protected against deceptive advertising and sales practices.
3. Explain how the government protects consumers who are involved in credit transactions.
4. List and describe the major statutes that regulate environmental pollution.
5. Identify the purpose and functions of Superfund.

The "public interest" referred to by Justice William O. Douglas in the opening quotation was evident during the 1960s and 1970s in what has come to be known as the consumer movement. Some have labeled the 1960s and 1970s "the age of the consumer," because so much legislation was passed to protect consumers against purportedly unfair practices and unsafe products of sellers. Since the 1980s, the impetus driving the consumer movement has lessened, to a great extent because so many of its goals have been achieved. *Consumer law* consists of all of the statutes, administrative agency rules, and judicial decisions that serve to protect the interests of consumers.

In the first part of this chapter, we examine some of the sources and some of the major issues of consumer protection. We then turn to a discussion of *environmental law*—which consists of all of the laws and regulations designed to protect and preserve our environmental resources.

Consumer Law

Sources of consumer protection exist at all levels of government. At the federal level, a number of laws have been passed to define the duties of sellers and the rights of consumers. Exhibit 36–1 lists the major federal consumer protection statutes. Federal administrative agencies, such as the Federal Trade Commission (FTC), also provide an important source of consumer protection. Nearly every agency and

EXHIBIT 36–1 • Selected Federal Consumer Protection Statutes

STATUTE OR REGULATION	PURPOSE
ADVERTISING	
Federal Trade Commission Act (1914)	Prohibits deceptive and unfair trade practices.
Public Health Cigarette Smoking Act (1970)	Prohibits radio and TV cigarette advertising; requires labels warning of possible health hazards associated with the smoking of cigarettes.
Smokeless Tobacco Health Education Act (1986)	Prohibits radio and TV advertising of smokeless tobacco products; requires special labeling to warn consumers of potential health hazards associated with smokeless tobacco.
Telephone Consumer Protection Act (1991)	Prohibits telephone solicitation using an automatic telephone dialing system or a prerecorded voice; prohibits the transmission of advertisements by fax machine without the permission of the recipient.
Telemarketing and Consumer Fraud and Abuse Prevention Act (1994)	Directed the Federal Trade Commission to establish rules governing telemarketing.
CREDIT	
Consumer Credit Protection Act (Truth-in-Lending Act) (1968)	Offers comprehensive protection covering all phases of credit transactions.
Fair Credit Reporting Act (1970)	Protects consumers' credit reputations.
Equal Credit Opportunity Act (1974)	Prohibits discrimination in the extending of credit.
Fair Credit Billing Act (1974)	Protects consumers from credit-card billing errors and in other disputes.
Fair Debt Collection Practices Act (1977)	Prohibits debt collectors' abuses.
Counterfeit Access Device and Computer Fraud and Abuse Act (1984)	Prohibits the production, use, and sale of counterfeit credit cards or other access devices used to obtain funds, goods, services, or other things of value.
Fair Credit and Charge Card Disclosure Act (1988)	Requires full disclosure of terms and conditions in credit-card and charge-card applications and solicitations.
Consumer Leasing Act (1988)	Amended the Truth-in-Lending Act to provide protection for consumers who lease automobiles and other goods.
Home Ownership and Equity Protection Act (1994)	Requires home equity lenders to make written disclosures to borrowers of payment amounts, of the consequences of default, and of the borrowers' right to cancel loans within a certain time period.

(Continued)

EXHIBIT 36–1 • Selected Federal Consumer Protection Statutes—Continued

STATUTE OR REGULATION	PURPOSE
HEALTH AND SAFETY	
Pure Food and Drugs Act (1906)	Prohibits the adulteration and mislabeling of food and drugs.
Meat Inspection Act (1906)	Provides for the inspection of meat.
Federal Food, Drug and Cosmetic Act (1938)	Protects consumers from unsafe food products and from unsafe and/or ineffective drugs.
Flammable Fabrics Act (1953)	Prohibits the sale of highly flammable clothing.
Poultry Products Inspection Act (1957)	Provides for the inspection of poultry.
Wholesome Meat Act (1967)	Updated the Meat Inspection Act of 1906 to provide for stricter standards for plants where red-meat animals are slaughtered.
Child Protection and Toy Safety Act (1969)	Requires childproof devices and special labeling.
Consumer Product Safety Act (1972)	Established the Consumer Product Safety Commission to regulate all potentially hazardous consumer products.
Department of Transportation Rule on Passive Restraints in Automobiles (1984)	Requires automatic restraint systems in all new cars sold after September 1, 1990.
Toy Safety Act (1984)	Allows the Consumer Product Safety Commission to recall toys and other articles intended for use by children that present a substantial risk of injury.
Drug-Price Competition and Patent-Term Restoration Act (Generic Drug Act) (1984)	Speeds up and simplifies the Food and Drug Administration's approval of generic versions of drugs on which patents have expired.
LABELING AND PACKAGING	
Wool Products Labeling Act (1939)	Requires accurate labeling of wool products.
Fur Products Labeling Act (1951)	Prohibits misbranding of fur products.
Textile Fiber Products Identification Act (1958)	Prohibits false labeling and advertising of textile products; requires that fiber contents be identified on labels.
Federal Hazardous Substances Act (1960)	Requires warning labels on all items containing dangerous chemicals.
Cigarette Labeling and Advertising Act (1965)	Requires labels warning of the possible health hazards associated with smoking cigarettes.
Fair Packaging and Labeling Act (1966)	Requires that accurate names, quantities, and weights be given on product labels.
Child Protection and Toy Safety Act (1969)	Requires childproof devices and special labeling.
Smokeless Tobacco Health Education Act (1986)	Requires labels disclosing possible health hazards of smokeless tobacco; prohibits radio and TV advertising of smokeless tobacco products.
Nutrition Labeling and Education Act (1990)	Requires standard nutrition facts (for example, fat content) on food labels; regulates the use of such terms as *fresh* and *low-fat;* and subject to the Food and Drug Administration's approval, authorizes certain health claims.

EXHIBIT 36–1 • Selected Federal Consumer Protection Statutes—Continued

STATUTE OR REGULATION	PURPOSE
SALES AND WARRANTIES	
Interstate Land Sales Full Disclosure Act (1968)	Requires disclosure in interstate land sales.
Odometer Act (1972)	Protects consumers against odometer fraud in used-car sales.
Real Estate Settlement Procedures Act (1974)	Requires disclosure of home-buying costs.
FTC Mail Order Rule (1975)	Federal Trade Commission rule providing protection for consumers who purchase goods through the mails.
Magnuson-Moss Warranty Act (1975)	Provides rules governing the content of express warranties for consumer goods.
FTC Mail or Telephone Order Merchandise Rule (1993)	Federal Trade Commission rule amending the FTC Mail Order Rule of 1975 to provide specific protections for consumers who purchase goods via phone lines, as well as through the mails.

department of the federal government has an office of consumer affairs, and most states have one or more such offices, including the offices of state attorneys general, to assist consumers.

Because of the wide variation among state consumer protection laws, our primary focus here will be on federal legislation—specifically, on legislation governing deceptive advertising, telemarketing and electronic advertising, labeling and packaging, sales, health protection, product safety, and credit protection. Realize, though, that state laws often provide more sweeping and significant protections for the consumer than do federal laws. State consumer protection laws will be discussed later in this section.

Deceptive Advertising

One of the earliest—and still one of the most important—federal consumer protection laws is the Federal Trade Commission Act of 1914 (discussed in Chapter 35). The act created the FTC to carry out the broadly stated goal of preventing unfair and deceptive trade practices, including deceptive advertising, within the meaning of Section 5 of the act.

• **DECEPTIVE ADVERTISING**
Advertising that misleads consumers, either by unjustified claims concerning a product's performance or by the omission of a material fact concerning the product's composition or performance.

Defining Deceptive Advertising Generally, **deceptive advertising** occurs if a reasonable consumer would be misled by the advertising claim. Vague generalities and obvious exaggerations are permissible. These claims are known as *puffing*. When a claim takes on the appearance of literal authenticity, however, it may create problems. Advertising that would *appear* to be based on factual evidence but that in fact is scientifically untrue will be deemed deceptive. A classic example is provided by a 1944 case in which the claim that a skin cream would restore youthful qualities to aged skin was deemed deceptive.[1]

Some advertisements contain "half-truths," meaning that the presented information is true but incomplete, and it leads consumers to a false conclusion. • **EXAMPLE 36.1** The makers of Campbell's soups advertised that "most" Campbell's soups were low in fat and cholesterol and thus were helpful in fighting heart disease. What the ad did not

1. *Charles of the Ritz Distributing Corp. v. Federal Trade Commission*, 143 F.2d 676 (2d Cir. 1944).

say was that Campbell's soups are high in sodium, and high-sodium diets may increase the risk of heart disease. The FTC ruled that Campbell's claims were thus deceptive.• Advertising that contains an endorsement by a celebrity may be deemed deceptive if the celebrity actually makes no use of the product.

Bait-and-Switch Advertising The FTC has promulgated rules to govern specific forms of advertising. One of the more important rules is contained in the FTC's "Guides on Bait Advertising."[2] The rule is designed to prohibit what is referred to as **bait-and-switch advertising**—that is, advertising a very low price for a particular item that will likely be unavailable to the consumer, who will then be encouraged to purchase a more expensive item. The low price is the "bait" to lure the consumer into the store. The salesperson is instructed to "switch" the consumer to a different item. According to the FTC guidelines, bait-and-switch advertising occurs if the seller refuses to show the advertised item, fails to have reasonable quantities of it available, fails to promise to deliver the advertised item within a reasonable time, or discourages employees from selling the item.

• **BAIT-AND-SWITCH ADVERTISING**
Advertising a product at a very attractive price (the "bait") and then informing the consumer, once he or she is in the store, that the advertised product is either not available or is of poor quality; the customer is then urged to purchase ("switched" to) a more expensive item.

FTC Actions against Deceptive Advertising The FTC receives complaints from many sources, including competitors of alleged violators, consumers, consumer organizations, trade associations, Better Business Bureaus, government organizations, and state and local officials. If enough consumers complain and the complaints are widespread, the FTC will investigate the problem and perhaps take action. If, after its investigations, the FTC believes that a given advertisement is unfair or deceptive, it drafts a formal complaint, which it sends to the alleged offender. The company may agree to settle the complaint without further proceedings.

If the company does not agree to settle a complaint, the FTC can conduct a hearing—which is similar to a trial—in which the company can present its defense. The hearing is held before an administrative law judge (ALJ) instead of a federal district court judge (see the discussion of administrative law in Chapter 34). If the FTC succeeds in proving that an advertisement is unfair or deceptive, it usually issues a **cease-and-desist order** requiring that the challenged advertising be stopped. It might also impose a sanction known as **counteradvertising** by requiring the company to advertise anew—in print, on radio, and on television—to inform the public about the earlier misinformation.

• **CEASE-AND-DESIST ORDER**
An administrative or judicial order prohibiting a person or business firm from conducting activities that an agency or court has deemed illegal.

• **COUNTERADVERTISING**
New advertising that is undertaken pursuant to a Federal Trade Commission order for the purpose of correcting earlier false claims that were made about a product.

When an ALJ rules against a company, the company can appeal to the full commission. The FTC commissioners listen to the parties' arguments and may uphold, modify, or reverse the ALJ's decision. If the commission rules against a company, the company can appeal the FTC's order through judicial channels, but a reviewing court generally accords great weight to the FTC's judgment. This is because the court recognizes that the FTC, as the administrative agency that deals continually with such claims, is often in a better position than the courts to determine when a practice is deceptive within the meaning of the Federal Trade Commission Act.

TELEMARKETING AND ELECTRONIC ADVERTISING

The pervasive use of the telephone to market goods and services to the home and other businesses led to the passage in 1991 of the Telephone Consumer Protection Act (TCPA).[3] The act prohibits telephone solicitation using an automatic telephone

¡REMEMBER!
Changes in technology often require changes in the law.

2. 16 C.F.R. Section 288.
3. 47 U.S.C. Sections 227 *et seq.*

dialing system or a prerecorded voice. Most states also have laws regulating telephone solicitation.[4]

> **ON THE WEB**
> You can find current articles concerning consumer issues at the Alexander Law Firm's "Consumer Law Page." Go to **consumerlawpage.com/intro.html**.

Not surprisingly, the widespread use of fax machines has led to the use of faxes as a tool for direct marketing. Advertising by fax is less expensive than mailing a letter, and faxes normally receive greater attention than "junk mail." At the same time, unsolicited fax messages tie up the recipient's fax machine and impose a cost on the recipient, who must pay for fax paper, toner, and other supplies. The TCPA also makes it illegal to transmit ads via fax without first obtaining the recipient's permission. (Similar issues have arisen with respect to junk e-mail, called "spam"; see Chapter 7 for a discussion of this topic.)

The act is enforced by the Federal Communications Commission and also provides for a private right of action. Consumers can recover any actual monetary loss resulting from a violation of the act or receive $500 in damages for each violation, whichever is greater. If a court finds that a defendant willfully or knowingly violated the act, the court has the discretion to treble the damages awarded.

The Telemarketing and Consumer Fraud and Abuse Prevention Act[5] of 1994 directed the FTC to establish rules governing telemarketing and to bring actions against fraudulent telemarketers. The FTC's Telemarketing Sales Rule[6] of 1995 requires telemarketers, before making a sales pitch, to inform recipients that the call is a sales call and to identify the seller's name and the product being sold. The rule makes it illegal for telemarketers to misrepresent information (including facts about their goods or services, earnings potential, profitability, the risk attending an investment, or the nature of a prize). Additionally, telemarketers must inform the people they call of the total cost of the goods being sold, any restrictions on obtaining or using them, and whether a sale will be considered to be final and nonrefundable.

A major challenge in today's legal environment has to do with the advertising of products and services over the Internet. See this chapter's *Technology and Consumer Protection* for a discussion of this topic.

LABELING AND PACKAGING

In addition to broadly restricting advertising, a number of federal and state laws deal specifically with the information given on labels and packages. The restrictions are designed to provide accurate information about the product and to warn about possible dangers from its use or misuse. In general, labels must be accurate. That is, they must use words that are understood by the ordinary consumer. For example, a box of cereal cannot be labeled "giant" if it would exaggerate the amount of cereal contained in the box. In some instances, labels must specify the raw materials used in the product, such as the percentage of cotton, nylon, or other fibers used in a garment. In other instances, the products must carry a warning. Cigarette packages and advertising, for example, must include one of several warnings about the health hazards associated with smoking.[7]

Federal laws regulating the labeling and packaging of products include the Wool Products Labeling Act of 1939,[8] the Fur Products Labeling Act of 1951,[9] the

4. For a discussion of the constitutionality of the TCPA, which some plaintiffs have alleged goes too far in restricting free speech, see *Moser v. FCC*, 46 F.3d 970 (9th Cir. 1995); *cert.* denied, 515 U.S. 1161, 115 S.Ct. 2615, 132 L.Ed.2d 857 (1995).
5. 15 U.S.C. Sections 6101–6108.
6. 16 C.F.R. Sections 310.1–310.8.
7. 15 U.S.C. Sections 1331 *et seq.*
8. 15 U.S.C. Section 68.
9. 15 U.S.C. Section 69.

Technology and Consumer Protection

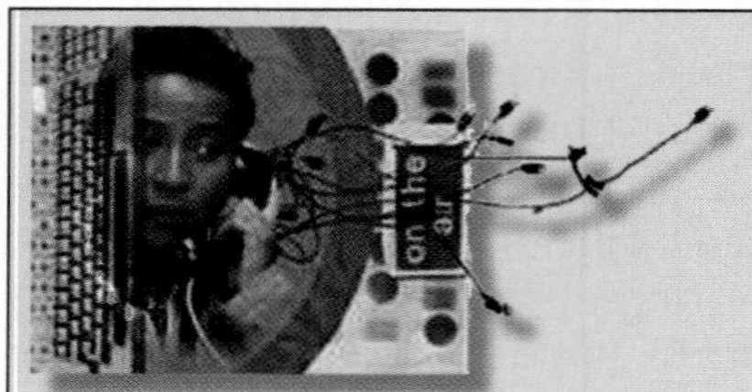

Since the beginning of 1996, the Federal Trade Commission (FTC) has filed dozens of cases under existing consumer protection statutes concerning use of the Internet. The FTC also is currently considering whether to regulate the collection of information about visitors to Web sites. (The FTC's actions concerning privacy can be accessed at the FTC's Web site at www.ftc.gov.) Also, the FTC, which for years has fought deceptive advertising in printed materials and in radio and television broadcasts, has announced that in the future it will spend more of its resources to monitor deceptive advertising on the Internet.

Already, the FTC has brought several enforcement actions against entities that apparently had made false or unsubstantiated claims in their Internet ads. The FTC has moved particularly quickly on commercial Internet fraud schemes. It has even provided "hot links" on Web sites that it has targeted. A hot link takes the user to the FTC's own Web site, on which the complaint, restraining order, and other documents in the case can be read and downloaded.

Other federal agencies have also taken action with respect to consumer fraud. The Securities and Exchange Commission (SEC), for example, has been active in prosecuting online scams. One fraudulent scheme involved twenty thousand investors, who lost more than $3 million in all. Other cases have involved false claims about the earnings potential of home business programs, such as the claim that one could "earn $4,000 or more each month."

The Department of Transportation (DOT) has also brought actions against purported online violators of advertising and disclosure laws. The DOT fined Virgin Airlines for failing to disclose the true price of a flight that it advertised on the Web. Additionally, the Consumer Product Safety Commission has decided to present relevant information to consumers. At its Web site at www.consumer.gov, it provides information from the Food and Drug Administration, its own commissioners, the National Highway Traffic Safety Administration, and other federal agencies. This so-called one-stop Web site provides information that will allow consumers to avoid the most obvious fraud problems on the Web and elsewhere.

Consumers themselves have also taken action to curb online fraud. For example, the National Consumers League has developed Web pages to help consumers, as well as lawyers who deal in Internet consumer fraud. At its Web site at www.fraud.org/ifw.htm, it lists the ten most common scams. The National Consumers League receives hundreds of scam complaints per month. The most frequent complaints of Internet fraud concern undelivered services, damaged or defective goods, undelivered merchandise, and pyramid and multilevel marketing schemes.

Various states are also setting up information sites to help consumers protect themselves. One of the most well-designed sites is the state of

Flammable Fabrics Act of 1953,[10] the Fair Packaging and Labeling Act of 1966,[11] and the Smokeless Tobacco Health Education Act of 1986.[12] The Smokeless Tobacco Health Education Act, for example, requires that producers, packagers, and importers of smokeless tobacco label their product with one of several warnings about the health hazards associated with the use of smokeless tobacco; the warnings are similar to those contained on cigarette packages.

The Fair Packaging and Labeling Act requires that products possess labels that identify the product; the net quantity of the contents, as well as the quantity of servings, if the number of servings is stated; the manufacturer; and the packager or distributor. The act also provides authority to add requirements concerning words used to describe packages, terms that are associated with savings claims, information disclosures for ingredients in nonfood products, and standards for the partial filling of

10. 15 U.S.C. Section 1191.
11. 15 U.S.C. Sections 4401–4408.
12. 15 U.S.C. Sections 1451 *et seq.*

Technology and Consumer Protection, Continued

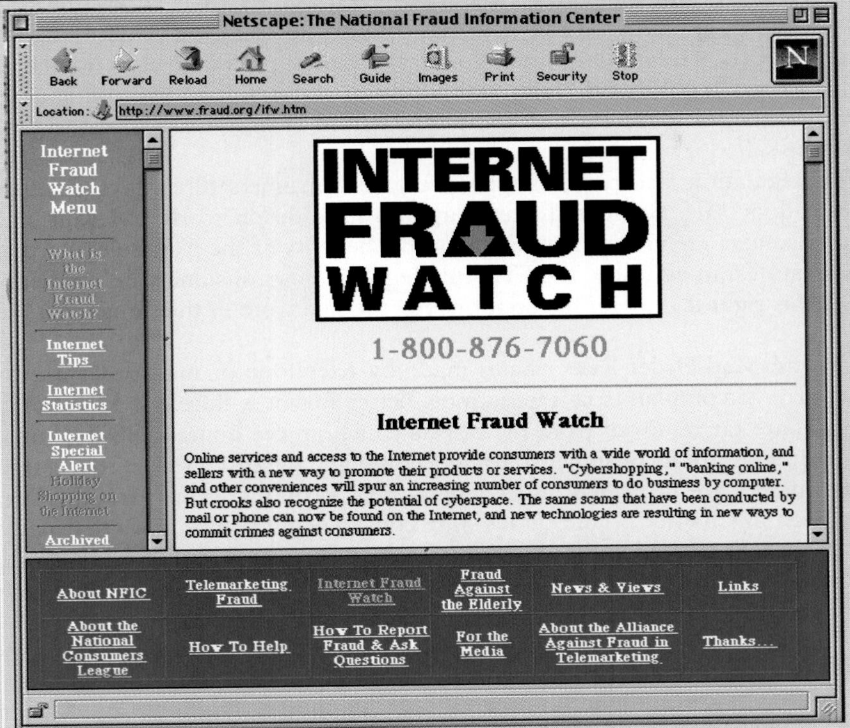

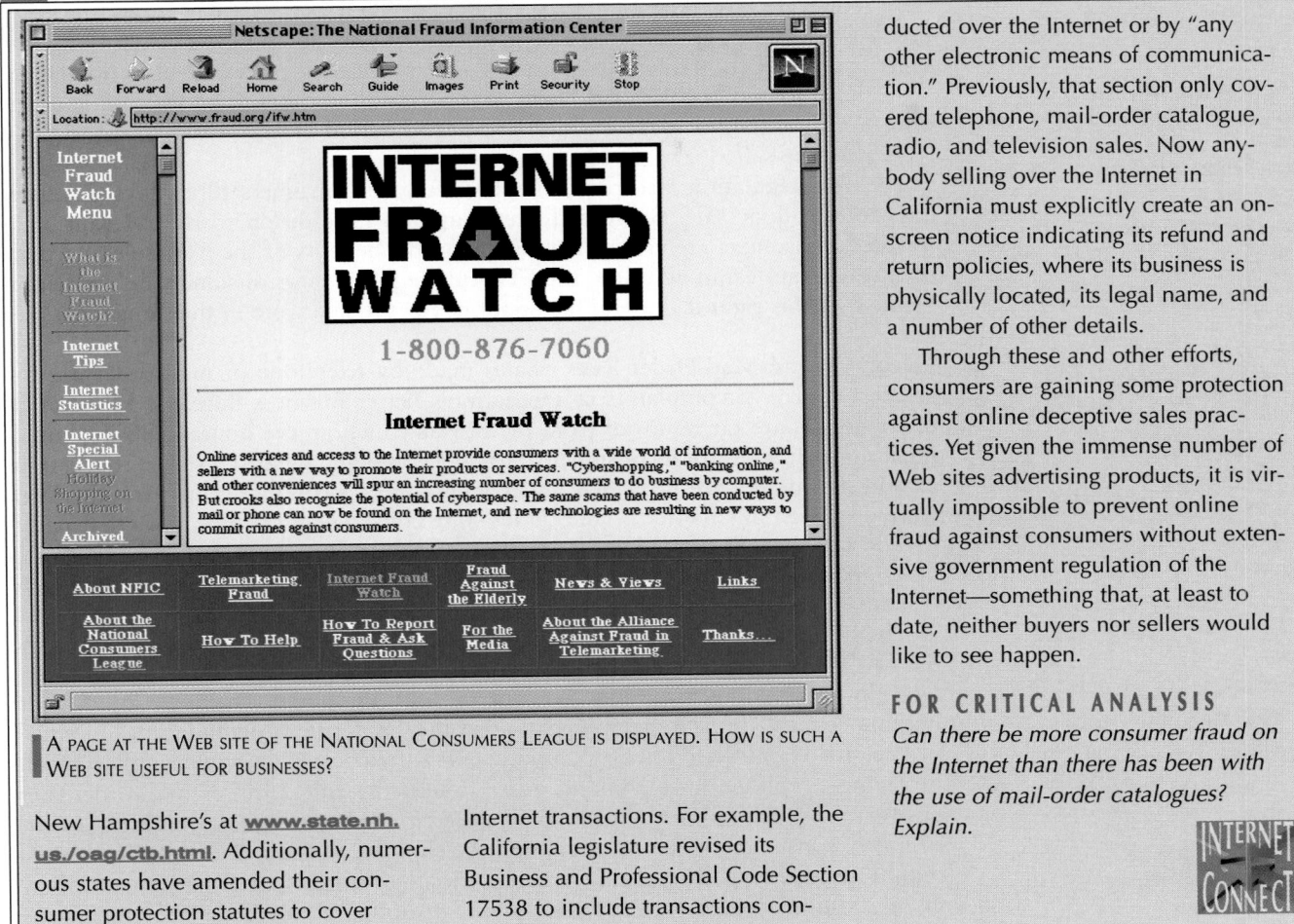

A PAGE AT THE WEB SITE OF THE NATIONAL CONSUMERS LEAGUE IS DISPLAYED. HOW IS SUCH A WEB SITE USEFUL FOR BUSINESSES?

New Hampshire's at **www.state.nh.us./oag/ctb.html**. Additionally, numerous states have amended their consumer protection statutes to cover Internet transactions. For example, the California legislature revised its Business and Professional Code Section 17538 to include transactions conducted over the Internet or by "any other electronic means of communication." Previously, that section only covered telephone, mail-order catalogue, radio, and television sales. Now anybody selling over the Internet in California must explicitly create an on-screen notice indicating its refund and return policies, where its business is physically located, its legal name, and a number of other details.

Through these and other efforts, consumers are gaining some protection against online deceptive sales practices. Yet given the immense number of Web sites advertising products, it is virtually impossible to prevent online fraud against consumers without extensive government regulation of the Internet—something that, at least to date, neither buyers nor sellers would like to see happen.

FOR CRITICAL ANALYSIS

Can there be more consumer fraud on the Internet than there has been with the use of mail-order catalogues? Explain.

INTERNET CONNECT

packages. Food products must bear labels detailing nutrition, including how much fat a product contains and what kind of fat it is. These restrictions are enforced by the Department of Health and Human Services, as well as the Federal Trade Commission.

SALES

A number of statutes that protect the consumer in sales transactions concern the disclosure of certain terms in sales and provide rules governing home or door-to-door sales, mail-order transactions, referral sales, and unsolicited merchandise. The Federal Reserve Board of Governors, for example, has issued **Regulation Z,** which governs credit provisions associated with sales contracts, and numerous states have passed laws governing the remedies available to consumers in home sales. Furthermore, states have provided a number of consumer protection provisions, such as implied warranties, through the adoption of the Uniform Commercial Code. In some states, the Uniform Consumer Credit Code's requirements, including disclosure requirements, also protect consumers in credit transactions.

• **REGULATION Z**
A set of rules promulgated by the Federal Reserve Board to implement the provisions of the Truth-in-Lending Act.

Door-to-Door Sales Door-to-door sales are singled out for special treatment in the laws of most states. This special treatment stems in part from the nature of the sales transaction. Because repeat purchases are not as likely as they are in stores, the seller has less incentive to cultivate the goodwill of the purchaser. Furthermore, the seller is unlikely to present alternative products and their prices. Thus, a number of states have passed **"cooling-off" laws** that permit the buyers of goods sold door-to-door to cancel their contracts within a specified period of time, usually two to three days after the sale.

• **"COOLING-OFF" LAWS**
Laws that allow buyers a period of time, such as three days, in which to cancel door-to-door sales contracts.

An FTC regulation also requires sellers to give consumers three days to cancel any door-to-door sale. Because this rule applies in addition to the relevant state statutes, consumers are given the most favorable benefits of the FTC rule and their own state statutes. In addition, the FTC rule requires that consumers be notified in Spanish of this right if the oral negotiations for the sale were in that language.

ON THE WEB
To learn more about the FTC's Cooling-Off Rule, go to **www.ftc.gov/bcp/conline/pubs/buying/cooling.htm**.

Telephone and Mail-Order Sales Sales made by telephone or mail order are the greatest source of complaints to the nation's Better Business Bureaus. Many mail-order houses are far removed from the buyers to whom the houses sell, thus making it more difficult for a consumer to bring a complaint against a seller. To a certain extent, consumers are protected under federal laws prohibiting mail fraud, which were discussed in Chapter 6, and under state consumer protection laws that parallel and supplement the federal laws. (Refer back to this chapter's *Technology and Consumer Protection* feature for a discussion of how the FTC is responding to fraudulent online sales transactions involving consumers.)

¡DON'T FORGET!
A seller's puffery—his or her opinion about the goods—is not a legally binding warranty or promise, nor is it a deceptive advertisement.

The FTC "Mail or Telephone Order Merchandise Rule" of 1993, which amended the FTC "Mail Order Rule" of 1975,[13] provides specific protections for consumers who purchase goods via phone lines or through the mails. The 1993 rule, which became effective in March 1994, extended the 1975 rule to include sales in which orders are transmitted using computers, fax machines, or some similar means involving telephone lines. Among other things, the rule requires mail-order merchants to ship orders within the time promised in their catalogues or advertisements, to notify consumers when orders cannot be shipped on time, and to issue a refund within a specified period of time when a consumer cancels an order.

In addition, the Postal Reorganization Act of 1970[14] provides that unsolicited merchandise sent by U.S. mail may be retained, used, discarded, or disposed of in any manner the recipient deems appropriate, without the recipient's incurring any obligation to the sender.

HEALTH AND SAFETY PROTECTION

Laws discussed earlier regarding the labeling and packaging of products go a long way toward promoting consumer health and safety. There is a significant distinction, however, between regulating the information dispensed about a product and regulating the content of the actual product. The classic example is tobacco products. Tobacco products have not been altered by regulation or banned outright despite their obvious hazards. What has been regulated are the warnings that producers are required to give consumers about the hazards of tobacco.[15] We now examine various laws that regulate the actual products made available to consumers.

13. 16 C.F.R. Sections 435.1–435.2.
14. 39 U.S.C. Section 3009.
15. We are ignoring recent civil litigation concerning the liability of tobacco product manufacturers for injuries that arise from the use of tobacco.

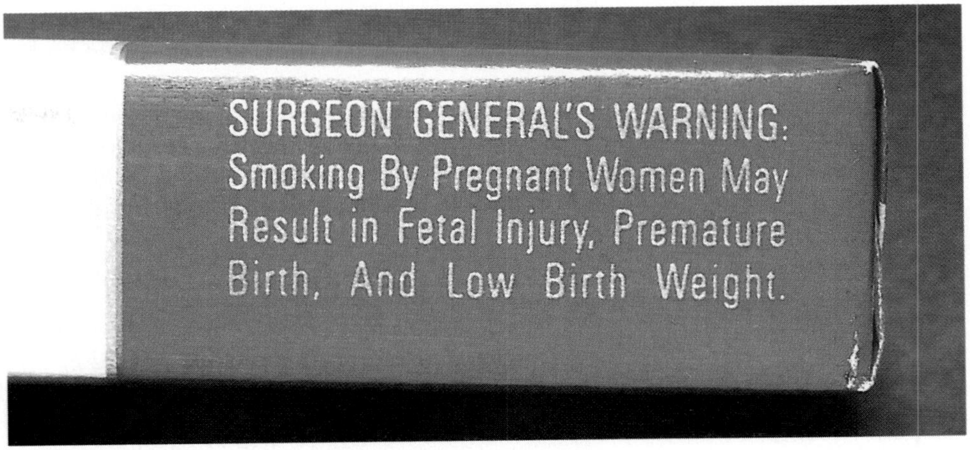

A WARNING APPEARS ON A PACKAGE OF CIGARETTES, AS REQUIRED BY FEDERAL LAW. WHY IS CONGRESS CONCERNED WITH PROTECTING CONSUMERS AGAINST PURPORTEDLY UNSAFE PRODUCTS?

¡BE AWARE!

The Food and Drug Administration is authorized to obtain, among other things, orders for the recall and seizure of certain products.

Foods and Drugs The first federal legislation regulating food and drugs was enacted in 1906 as the Pure Food and Drugs Act.[16] That law, as amended in 1938, exists presently as the Federal Food, Drug and Cosmetic Act (FFDCA).[17] The act protects consumers against adulterated and misbranded foods and drugs. More recent amendments have added additional substantive and procedural requirements to the act. In its present form, the act establishes food standards, specifies safe levels of potentially hazardous food additives, and sets classifications of food and food advertising.

Most of these statutory requirements are monitored and enforced by the Food and Drug Administration (FDA). Under an extensive set of procedures established by the FDA, drugs must be shown to be effective as well as safe before they may be marketed to the public, and the use of some food additives suspected of being carcinogenic is prohibited. A 1975 amendment to the FFDCA[18] authorizes the FDA to regulate medical devices, such as pacemakers and other health devices or equipment, and to withdraw from the market any such device that is mislabeled.

Consumer Product Safety Consumer product-safety legislation began in 1953 with the enactment of the Flammable Fabrics Act, which prohibits the sale of highly flammable clothing or materials. Over the next two decades, Congress enacted legislation regarding the design or composition of specific classes of products. Then in 1972, Congress, by enacting the Consumer Product Safety Act,[19] created a comprehensive scheme of regulation over matters concerning consumer safety. The act also established far-reaching authority over consumer safety by creating the Consumer Product Safety Commission (CPSC).

The CPSC conducts research on the safety of individual products, and it maintains a clearinghouse on the risks associated with different consumer products. The Consumer Product Safety Act authorizes the CPSC to set standards for consumer products and to ban the manufacture and sale of any product that the commission deems to be potentially hazardous to consumers. The CPSC also has authority to remove from the market any products it believes to be imminently hazardous and to require manufacturers to report on any products already sold or intended for sale if

16. 21 U.S.C. Sections 1–5, 7–15.
17. 21 U.S.C. Section 301.
18. 21 U.S.C. Sections 360(c) *et seq.*
19. 15 U.S.C. Section 2051.

the products have proved to be hazardous. Additionally, the CPSC administers other product-safety legislation, such as the Child Protection and Toy Safety Act of 1969,[20] the Federal Hazardous Substances Act of 1960,[21] and the Flammable Fabrics Act.

The CPSC's authority is sufficiently broad to allow it to ban any product that the CPSC believes poses merely an "unreasonable risk" to the consumer. Some of the products that the CPSC has banned include various types of fireworks, cribs, and toys, as well as many products containing asbestos or vinyl chloride.

Credit Protection

Because of the extensive use of credit by American consumers, credit protection is one of the more important areas regulated by consumer protection legislation. One of the most significant statutes regulating the credit and credit-card industry is the Truth-in-Lending Act (TILA), the name commonly given to Title 1 of the Consumer Credit Protection Act (CCPA),[22] which was passed by Congress in 1968.

Truth in Lending The TILA is basically a *disclosure law.* The TILA is administered by the Federal Reserve Board and requires sellers and lenders to disclose credit terms or loan terms so that individuals can shop around for the best financing arrangements. TILA requirements apply only to persons who, in the ordinary course of business, lend funds, sell on credit, or arrange for the extension of credit. Thus, sales or loans made between two consumers do not come under the protection of the act. Additionally, only debtors who are *natural* persons (as opposed to the artificial "person" of the corporation) are protected by this law; other legal entities are not.

¡NOTE! The Federal Reserve Board is part of the Federal Reserve System, which influences the lending and investing activities of commercial banks and the cost and availability of credit.

The disclosure requirements are found in Regulation Z, which, as mentioned earlier in this chapter, was promulgated by the Federal Reserve Board. If the contracting parties are subject to the TILA, the requirements of Regulation Z apply to any transaction involving an installment sales contract in which payment is to be made in more than four installments. Transactions subject to Regulation Z typically include installment loans, retail and installment sales, car loans, home-improvement loans, and certain real estate loans if the amount of financing is less than $25,000.

Under the provisions of the TILA, all of the terms of a credit instrument must be clearly and conspicuously disclosed. The TILA provides for contract rescission (cancellation) if a creditor fails to follow exactly the procedures required by the act.[23] TILA requirements are strictly enforced (see this chapter's feature *The Letter of the Law* on this topic).

Equal Credit Opportunity. In 1974, Congress enacted, as an amendment to the TILA, the Equal Credit Opportunity Act (ECOA).[24] The ECOA prohibits the denial of credit solely on the basis of race, religion, national origin, color, gender, marital status, or age. The act also prohibits credit discrimination on the basis of whether an individual receives certain forms of income, such as public-assistance benefits.

Under the ECOA, a creditor may not require the signature of an applicant's spouse, other than a joint applicant, on a credit instrument if the applicant qualifies

20. 15 U.S.C. Section 1262(e).
21. 15 U.S.C. Sections 1261–1273.
22. 15 U.S.C. Sections 1601–1693r. The act was amended in 1980 by the Truth-in-Lending Simplification and Reform Act.
23. Note, however, that amendments to the TILA enacted in 1995 prevent borrowers from rescinding loans for minor clerical errors in closing documents [15 U.S.C. Sections 1605, 1631, 1635, 1640, and 1641].
24. 15 U.S.C. Section 1643.

The Letter of the Law — CONSUMER LAWS ARE STRICTLY ENFORCED

Generally, the courts adhere strictly to the letter of the law when enforcing the Truth-in-Lending Act (TILA), as well as other consumer legislation. This is true even in cases in which consumers have obviously taken unfair advantage of the TILA's requirements to avoid genuine obligations that they voluntarily assumed. For example, under the TILA, borrowers are allowed three business days to rescind, without penalty, a consumer loan that uses their principal dwelling as security. The lender must state specifically the last day on which the borrower can rescind the agreement. If the lender inadvertently fails to do so, the borrower can rescind the loan within three years after it was made. The courts reason that, overall, consumers will benefit from strict compliance requirements, even though some consumers may abuse the act.

THE BOTTOM LINE

In essence, the TILA is a "strict liability" statute (this is generally true of most consumer protection statutes). In other words, intention normally is irrelevant in determining whether a consumer protection statute has been violated.

under the creditor's standards of creditworthiness for the amount and terms of the credit request. Creditors are permitted to request any information from a credit applicant except that which would be used for the type of discrimination covered in the act or its amendments. In the following case, the issue concerned whether a creditor had violated the ECOA by requesting a spouse to cosign a loan guaranty.

CASE 36.1 Federal Deposit Insurance Corp. v. Medmark, Inc.

United States District Court,
District of Kansas, 1995.
897 F.Supp. 511.

HISTORICAL AND ECONOMIC SETTING *The health-care industry is the largest single industry in the United States. Some major corporations, such as Abbott Laboratories, Inc., and Johnson & Johnson, have sold medical equipment and other health-care products to doctors and hospitals for more than one hundred years. The industry is made up primarily of new, small firms, however, as well as private doctors and hospitals. Probably the most difficult problem that such small organizations face is a lack of capital.*

BACKGROUND AND FACTS Bruce Shalberg was a director of Medmark, Inc., a small medical equipment supply company. As a condition of a loan to Medmark, the Merchants Bank asked Shalberg—whom the bank found to be independently creditworthy—to sign a guaranty of repayment. Later, for another loan, the bank required Shalberg's wife, Mary—who had nothing to do with Medmark—to sign the guaranty. When the bank failed, the Federal Deposit Insurance Corporation (FDIC) took over its assets. The FDIC filed a suit in a federal district court against Medmark and the Shalbergs to recover the amount of the loans. Mrs. Shalberg filed a motion for summary judgment, contending that the bank, in requiring her to sign the guaranty, had violated the Equal Credit Opportunity Act (ECOA).

IN THE WORDS OF THE COURT . . .
VRATIL, District Judge.

* * * *

[A regulation issued under the ECOA] specifically provides that a creditor may not require the signature of an applicant's spouse if the applicant qualifies under the creditor's standards of creditworthiness for the amount and terms of the credit requested. The FDIC argues that the Bank "obviously" did not believe Mr. Shalberg to be independently creditworthy * * * . [But the] record contains no evidence that Mr. Shalberg was not creditworthy, in his own right, in the Bank's eyes. Summary judgment in favor of Mrs. Shalberg is therefore appropriate.

(Continued)

CASE 36.1—Continued

DECISION AND REMEDY The federal district court issued a summary judgment in favor of Mrs. Shalberg, relieving her from any obligation on the loans.

FOR CRITICAL ANALYSIS—Political Consideration *Why does the ECOA prohibit lenders from requiring a spouse's signature on a credit application if the applicant independently qualifies for the credit?*

Credit-Card Rules. The TILA also contains provisions regarding credit cards. One provision limits the liability of a cardholder to $50 per card for unauthorized charges made before the creditor is notified that the card has been lost. Another provision prohibits a credit-card company from billing a consumer for any unauthorized charges if the credit card was improperly issued by the company. For example, if a consumer receives an unsolicited credit card in the mail and the card is later stolen and used by the thief to make purchases, the consumer to whom the card was sent will not be liable for the unauthorized charges.

Further provisions of the act concern billing disputes related to credit-card purchases. If a debtor thinks that an error has occurred in billing or wishes to withhold payment for a faulty product purchased by credit card, the act outlines specific procedures for both the consumer and the credit-card company in settling the dispute.

Consumer Leases. The Consumer Leasing Act (CLA) of 1988[25] amended the TILA to provide protection for consumers who lease automobiles and other goods. The CLA applies to those who lease or arrange to lease consumer goods in the ordinary course of their business. The act only applies if the goods are priced at $25,000 or less and if the lease term exceeds four months. The CLA and its implementing regulation, Regulation M,[26] requires lessors to disclose in writing all of the material terms of the lease.

Fair Credit Reporting In 1970, to protect consumers against inaccurate credit reporting, Congress enacted the Fair Credit Reporting Act (FCRA).[27] The act provides that consumer credit reporting agencies may issue credit reports to users only for specified purposes, including the extension of credit, the issuance of insurance policies, compliance with a court order, and compliance with a consumer's request for a copy of his or her own credit report. The act further provides that any time a consumer is denied credit or insurance on the basis of the consumer's credit report, or is charged more than others ordinarily would be for credit or insurance, the consumer must be notified of that fact and of the name and address of the credit reporting agency that issued the credit report.

Under the act, consumers may request the source of any information being given out by a credit agency, as well as the identity of anyone who has received an agency's report. Consumers are also permitted to have access to the information contained about them in a credit reporting agency's files. If a consumer discovers that a credit reporting agency's files contain inaccurate information about the consumer's credit standing, the agency, on the consumer's written request, must investigate the matter and delete any unverifiable or erroneous information within a reasonable period of time. The following case illustrates the potential liability exposure of companies that maintain credit reports and ratings.

25. 15 U.S.C. Sections 1667–1667e.
26. 12 C.F.R. Part 213.
27. 15 U.S.C. Sections 1681 *et seq.*

CASE 36.2 Guimond v. Trans Union Credit Information Co.

United States Court of Appeals,
Ninth Circuit, 1995.
45 F.3d 1329.

HISTORICAL AND ECONOMIC SETTING *A credit report reflects a consumer's bill-paying history. It lists the consumer's creditors and whether he or she has made payments on time. Inaccurate information can keep an individual from obtaining credit, through a creditor's denial of it or the consumer's decision not to apply for it out of fear it will be denied. The major credit reporting agencies are Equifax, Inc.; TRW, Inc.; and the Trans Union Credit Information Company.*

BACKGROUND AND FACTS Renie Guimond learned that the Trans Union Credit Information Company had inaccurate information in its file on her. She notified Trans Union, which told her the file would be corrected; however, it was not corrected for a year. Guimond filed a suit in a federal district court against Trans Union, in part to recover damages under the Fair Credit Reporting Act (FCRA) for the company's failure to correct the information more quickly. Trans Union countered that Guimond had no claim, because she had not been denied credit before the information was corrected. The court ruled in favor of Trans Union, and Guimond appealed.

IN THE WORDS OF THE COURT . . .
FONG, District Judge:

* * * *

[The FCRA] states: Whenever a consumer reporting agency prepares a consumer report it shall follow reasonable procedures to assure maximum possible accuracy of the information * * * .

* * * *

Liability * * * is predicated on the reasonableness of the credit reporting agency's procedures * * * .

* * * [T]he focus should not have been on Guimond's damage claims. Rather the inquiry should have centered on whether Trans Union's procedures for preparing Guimond's file contained reasonable procedures to prevent inaccuracies. Guimond has made out a *prima facie* case under [the FCRA] by showing that there were inaccuracies in her credit report. The district court was then required to consider whether Trans Union was liable under [the FCRA] before it determined that Guimond had suffered no recoverable damages.

DECISION AND REMEDY The U.S. Court of Appeals for the Ninth Circuit reversed this part of the lower court's ruling and remanded the case for trial.

FOR CRITICAL ANALYSIS—Social Consideration *How do the policies underlying the FCRA support the court's interpretation of the statute in Guimond's case?*

Fair Debt-Collection Practices In 1977, Congress enacted the Fair Debt Collection Practices Act (FDCPA)[28] in an attempt to curb what were perceived to be abuses by collection agencies. The act applies only to specialized debt-collection agencies that, usually for a percentage of the amount owed, regularly attempt to collect debts on behalf of someone else. Creditors who attempt to collect debts are not covered by the act unless, by misrepresenting themselves to debtors, they cause the debtor to believe they are collection agencies. The act explicitly prohibits a collection agency from using any of the following tactics:

1. Contacting the debtor at the debtor's place of employment if the debtor's employer objects.

28. 15 U.S.C. Section 1692.

2. Contacting the debtor during inconvenient or unusual times (for example, calling the debtor at three o'clock in the morning) or at any time if the debtor is being represented by an attorney.
3. Contacting third parties other than the debtor's parents, spouse, or financial adviser about payment of a debt unless a court authorizes such action.
4. Using harassment or intimidation (for example, using abusive language or threatening violence), or employing false and misleading information (for example, posing as a police officer).
5. Communicating with the debtor at any time after receiving notice that the debtor is refusing to pay the debt, except to advise the debtor of further action to be taken by the collection agency.

The FDCPA also requires collection agencies to include a "validation notice" whenever they initially contact a debtor for payment of a debt or within five days of that initial contact. The notice must state that the debtor has thirty days within which to dispute the debt and to request a written verification of the debt from the collection agency. The debtor's request for debt validation must be in writing. The FDCPA provides that a debt collector who fails to comply with the act is liable for actual damages, plus additional damages not to exceed $1,000[29] and attorneys' fees.

Cases brought under the FDCPA often raise questions as to who qualifies as a debt collector or debt-collecting agency subject to the act. For example, for several years it was not clear whether attorneys who attempted to collect debts owed to their clients were subject to the FDCPA's provisions. In 1995, the United States Supreme Court addressed this issue to resolve conflicting opinions in the lower courts. The Court held that an attorney who regularly tries to obtain payment of consumer debts through legal proceedings meets the FDCPA's definition of "debt collector."[30]

Another question that sometimes arises in the context of FDCPA litigation has to do with what, exactly, constitutes a "debt." In the following case, the court considered whether a dishonored check constituted a "debt" within the meaning of the FDCPA.

29. According to the U.S. Court of Appeals for the Sixth Circuit, the $1,000 limit on damages applies to each lawsuit, not to each violation. See *Wright v. Finance Service of Norwalk, Inc.*, 22 F.3d 647 (6th Cir. 1994).

30. *Heintz v. Jenkins*, 514 U.S. 291, 115 S.Ct. 1489, 131 L.Ed.2d 395 (1995).

CASE 36.3 Snow v. Jesse L. Riddle, P.C.

United States Court of Appeals,
Tenth Circuit, 1998.
143 F.3d 1350.
www.washlaw.edu/ca10/caselist/caselist.htm[a]

HISTORICAL AND SOCIAL SETTING *The FDCPA defines debt as "any obligatory or alleged obligation of a consumer to pay money arising out of a transaction in which the money, property, insurance, or services which are the subject of the transaction are primarily for personal, family, or household purposes, whether or not such obligation has been reduced to judgment."*[b] *At one time, it was generally held that the type of transaction giving rise to a debt, within this definition, is the same type of transaction that is dealt with in all other parts of the Consumer Credit Protection Act: a transaction that involves an offer or extension of credit to a consumer. By the time the U.S. Court of Appeals for the Tenth Circuit decided this case, however, this view had changed.*

BACKGROUND AND FACTS At a Circle-K store, Alan Snow paid for merchandise with his personal check in the amount of $23.12. Circle-K deposited the check at its bank, but the check was dishonored because of insufficient funds. Circle-K sent the returned check to its attorney, Jesse L. Riddle, P.C., for collection. In a letter to Snow, Riddle wrote

a. This page contains links to opinions of the U.S. Court of Appeals for the Tenth Circuit. Scroll down the list of cases and click on the *Snow* case name to access the opinion. This Web site is maintained by the Washburn University School of Law.

b. 15 U.S.C. Section 1692a(5).

CASE 36.3—Continued

that "the check amount, along with a service fee of $15, must be paid within seven (7) days of this notice. If it is not paid, . . . [a] suit [will] be filed." Snow paid the check and then filed a suit in a federal district court against Riddle. Snow alleged in part that Riddle's letter violated the FDCPA because it did not contain a "validation notice." Riddle filed a motion to dismiss on the ground that the FDCPA does not cover a dishonored check because it is not an "offer or extension of credit." The court granted the motion, and Snow appealed to the U.S. Court of Appeals for the Tenth Circuit.

IN THE WORDS OF THE COURT . . .
McWILLIAMS, Senior Circuit Judge.

* * * *

[The FDCPA] provides as follows:

* * * Abusive debt collection practices contribute to the number of personal bankruptcies, to marital instability, to the loss of jobs, and to invasions of individual privacy. * * * It is the purpose of [the FDCPA] to eliminate abusive debt collection practices by debt collectors * * * .

* * * *

* * * [A] payment obligation arising from a dishonored check create[s] a "debt" triggering the protections of the [FDCPA].* * * [A]n offer or extension of credit is not required for a payment obligation to constitute a "debt" under the [FDCPA]. * * *

* * * *

* * * Under the "plain meaning" test, it would seem to us that a "debt" is created where one obtains goods and gives a dishonored check in return therefor.

DECISION AND REMEDY The U.S. Court of Appeals for the Tenth Circuit reversed the decision of the lower court and remanded the case. The appellate court held that a dishonored check constitutes a debt within the meaning of the FDCPA.

FOR CRITICAL ANALYSIS—Political Consideration *Should those who write bad checks to pay for consumer goods or services be protected by the FDCPA?*

STATE CONSUMER PROTECTION LAWS

Thus far, our primary focus has been on federal legislation. State laws, however, often provide more extensive protections for consumers than do federal laws. The warranty and unconscionability provisions of the Uniform Commercial Code (discussed in Chapters 15 through 18) offer important protections for consumers against unfair practices on the part of sellers. Far less widely adopted than the UCC is the Uniform Consumer Credit Code (UCCC), which has provisions concerning truth in lending, maximum credit ceilings, door-to-door sales, fine-print clauses, and other practices affecting consumer transactions.

Virtually all states have specific consumer protection acts, often titled "deceptive trade practices acts." Although state consumer protection statutes vary widely in their provisions, a common thread runs through most of them. Typically, state consumer protection laws are directed at sellers' deceptive practices, such as providing false or misleading information to consumers. As just mentioned, some of the legislation provides broad protection for consumers. One example is the Texas Deceptive Trade Practices Act of 1973, which forbids a seller from selling to a buyer anything that the buyer does not need or cannot afford.

Environmental Law

"Man, however much he may like to pretend the contrary, is part of nature."

RACHEL CARSON, 1907–1964
(American writer and conservationist)

To this point, this chapter has dealt with government regulation of business in the interest of protecting consumers. We now turn to a discussion of the various ways in which businesses are regulated by the government in the interest of protecting the environment. Concern over the degradation of the environment has increased over time in response to the environmental effects of population growth, urbanization, and industrialization. Environmental protection is not without a price, however. For many businesses, the costs of complying with environmental regulations are high, and for some they are too high. There is a constant tension between the desirability of increasing profits and productivity and the need to attain a higher quality in the environment.

To a great extent, environmental law consists of statutes passed by federal, state, or local governments and regulations issued by administrative agencies. Before examining statutory and regulatory environmental laws, however, we look at the remedies available under the common law against environmental pollution.

COMMON LAW ACTIONS

Common law remedies against environmental pollution originated centuries ago in England. Those responsible for operations that created dirt, smoke, noxious odors, noise, or toxic substances were sometimes held liable under common law theories of nuisance or negligence. Today, injured individuals continue to rely on the common law to obtain damages and injunctions against business polluters.

• **NUISANCE**
A common law doctrine under which persons may be held liable for using their property in a manner that unreasonably interferes with others' rights to use or enjoy their own property.

Nuisance Under the common law doctrine of **nuisance,** persons may be held liable if they use their property in a manner that unreasonably interferes with others' rights to use or enjoy their own property. In these situations, the courts commonly balance the equities between the harm caused by the pollution and the costs of stopping it.

Courts have often denied injunctive relief on the ground that the hardships to be imposed on the polluter and on the community are relatively greater than the hardships to be suffered by the plaintiff. • **EXAMPLE 36.2** A factory that causes neighboring landowners to suffer from smoke, dirt, and vibrations may be left in operation if it is the core of a local economy. The injured parties may be awarded only their money damages. These damages may include compensation for the decreased value of the neighbors' property that results from the factory's operation. •

"A nuisance may be merely a right thing in the wrong place, like a pig in the parlor instead of the barnyard."

GEORGE SUTHERLAND, 1862–1942
(American jurist)

A property owner may be given relief from pollution in situations in which he or she can identify a distinct harm separate from that affecting the general public. This is referred to as a "private" nuisance. Under the common law, citizens were denied standing (access to the courts—see Chapter 3) unless they suffered a harm distinct from the harm suffered by the public at large. Some states still require this. Therefore, a group of citizens who wished to stop a new development that would cause significant water pollution was denied access to the courts on the ground that the harm to them did not differ from the harm to the general public.[31] A public authority (such as a state's attorney general) can sue to abate a "public" nuisance.

Negligence and Strict Liability An injured party may sue a business polluter in tort under the negligence and strict liability theories discussed in Chapter 4. The basis for a negligence action is the business's alleged failure to use reasonable care toward the party whose injury was foreseeable and, of course, caused by the lack of rea-

31. *Save the Bay Committee, Inc. v. Mayor of City of Savannah,* 227 Ga. 436, 181 S.E.2d 351 (1971).

A FACTORY RELEASES EFFLUENTS INTO THE ATMOSPHERE. ON WHAT BASIS MIGHT A BUSINESS OWNER FILE A SUIT TO OBTAIN RELIEF FROM ANY DAMAGE CAUSED BY POLLUTION?

sonable care. For example, employees might sue an employer whose failure to use proper pollution controls contaminated the air and caused the employees to suffer respiratory illnesses. A developing area of tort law involves *toxic torts*—actions against toxic polluters.

Businesses that engage in ultrahazardous activities—such as the transportation of radioactive materials—are strictly liable for whatever injuries the activities cause. In a strict liability action, the injured party does not need to prove that the business failed to exercise reasonable care.

STATE AND LOCAL REGULATION

Many states regulate the degree to which the environment may be polluted. Thus, for example, even when state zoning laws permit a business's proposed development, the proposal may have to be altered to change the development's impact on the environment. State laws may restrict a business's discharge of chemicals into the air or water or regulate its disposal of toxic wastes. States may also regulate the disposal or recycling of other wastes, including glass, metal, and plastic containers and paper. Additionally, states may restrict the emissions from motor vehicles.

City, county, and other local governments control some aspects of the environment. For instance, local zoning laws control some land use. These laws may be designed to inhibit or direct the growth of cities and suburbs or to protect the natural environment. Other aspects of the environment may be subject to local regulation for other reasons. Methods of waste and garbage removal and disposal, for example, can have a substantial impact on a community. The appearance of buildings and other structures, including advertising signs and billboards, may affect traffic safety, property values, or local aesthetics. Noise generated by a business or its customers may be annoying, disruptive, or damaging to neighbors. The location and condition of parks, streets, and other publicly used land subject to local control affect the environment and can also affect business.

FEDERAL REGULATION

Congress has passed a number of statutes to control the impact of human activities on the environment. Some of these have been passed to improve the quality of air and water. Some of them specifically regulate toxic chemicals—including pesticides, herbicides, and hazardous wastes.

Environmental Regulatory Agencies Much of the body of federal law governing business activities consists of the regulations issued and enforced by administrative agencies. The most well known of the agencies regulating environmental law is, of course, the Environmental Protection Agency (EPA), which was created in 1970 to coordinate federal environmental responsibilities. Other federal agencies with authority for regulating specific environmental matters include the Department of the Interior, the Department of Defense, the Department of Labor, the Food and Drug Administration, and the Nuclear Regulatory Commission. These regulatory agencies—and all other agencies of the federal government—must take environmental factors into consideration when making significant decisions.

Most federal environmental laws provide that citizens can sue to enforce environmental regulations if government agencies fail to do so—or if agencies go too far in their enforcement actions. Typically, a threshold hurdle in such suits is meeting the requirements for standing to sue—a topic discussed in this chapter's *Business Law in Action*.

Business Law in Action • CAN CITIZENS SUE THE GOVERNMENT FOR "OVERREGULATING" THE ENVIRONMENT?

As already mentioned, there is a constant tension between the two policy goals of economic productivity and environmental protection. This tension was highlighted in a case brought by two Oregon ranchers—Brad Bennett and Mario Giordano—and two Oregon irrigation districts (collectively, the Bennett group) against the Fish and Wildlife Service (FWS) and the secretary of the Department of the Interior.

The case originated after the FWS proposed that the minimum water levels in two reservoirs be increased to protect two endangered species of fish. If the proposal were implemented, less water could be drawn from the reservoirs for irrigation and other purposes, which would have a serious economic impact on the ranchers' businesses. In a citizens' suit against the FWS, the Bennett group claimed that the agency neglected to use the best available scientific and commercial data in making its decision, as required under the Endangered Species Act (ESA) of 1973; nor did the FWS take into account the economic impact of its water-level recommendations.

At issue in the case, which ultimately reached the United States Supreme Court, was whether the ranchers had standing to sue under the ESA. The question was significant because the Bennett group was not seeking to protect the environment but to protect their economic interests. Both a federal district court and a federal appellate court held that the group did not have standing to sue because its claim did not fall within the "zone of interests" protected by the ESA, which was to protect species. The zone-of-interests test has long been applied by the federal courts in determining whether a party has standing to sue under a specific law. Basically, to have standing under this test, a plaintiff must show that the interest that he or she seeks to protect is the kind of interest protected by that specific law.

The Supreme Court, however, unanimously reversed the appellate court's decision. In applying the zone-of-interests test, the Court looked to the citizen-suit language of the ESA, which gives "any person" the right to sue. According to the Court, this language was expansive enough to include the economic interests of the Bennett group.

Moreover, the Court held that in determining whether a party has standing, the courts must look not to the overall purpose of an act but to the particular provision of an act on which the party based his or her complaint. In this case, the Bennett group alleged that the FWS failed to abide by a specific ESA provision that requires an agency to use the "best scientific and commercial data available." The Court noted that while this provision "no doubt serves to advance the ESA's overall goal of species preservation, we think it readily apparent that another objective (if not indeed the primary one) is to avoid needless economic dislocation produced by agency officials zealously but unintelligently pursuing their environmental objectives."[a]

FOR CRITICAL ANALYSIS

What are some implications of this decision for other businesses whose economic interests are harmed by environmental laws?

a. *Bennett v. Spear,* 520 U.S. 154, 117 S.Ct. 1154, 137 L.Ed.2d 281 (1997).

Assessing the Environmental Impact of Agency Actions The National Environmental Policy Act (NEPA) of 1969[32] requires that for every major federal action that significantly affects the quality of the environment, an **environmental impact statement (EIS)** must be prepared. An action qualifies as "major" if it involves a substantial commitment of resources (monetary or otherwise). An action is "federal" if a federal agency has the power to control it. Construction by a private developer of a ski resort on federal land, for example, may require an EIS.[33] Building or operat-

• **ENVIRONMENTAL IMPACT STATEMENT (EIS)**
A statement required by the National Environmental Policy Act for any major federal action that will significantly affect the quality of the environment. The statement must analyze the action's impact on the environment and explore alternative actions that might be taken.

32. 42 U.S.C. Sections 4321–4370d.

33. *Robertson v. Methow Valley Citizens' Council,* 490 U.S. 332, 109 S.Ct. 1835, 104 L.Ed.2d 351 (1989).

ing a nuclear plant, which requires a federal permit,[34] or constructing a dam as part of a federal project would require an EIS.[35] If an agency decides that an EIS is unnecessary, it must issue a statement supporting this conclusion.

An EIS must analyze (1) the impact on the environment that the action will have, (2) any adverse effects on the environment and alternative actions that might be taken, and (3) irreversible effects the action might generate. EISs have become instruments for private citizens, consumer interest groups, businesses, and others to challenge federal agency actions on the basis that the actions improperly threaten the environment.

AIR POLLUTION

Federal involvement with air pollution goes back to the 1950s, when Congress authorized funds for air-pollution research. In 1963, the federal government passed the Clean Air Act,[36] which focused on multistate air pollution and provided assistance to states. Various amendments, particularly in 1970, 1977, and 1990, strengthened the government's authority to regulate the quality of air. These laws provide the basis for issuing regulations to control pollution coming primarily from mobile sources and stationary sources.

> **ON THE WEB**
> The Virtual Law Library of the Indiana University School of Law provides numerous links to online environmental law sources. Go to www.law.indiana.edu.

Mobile Sources of Pollution Regulations governing air pollution from automobiles and other mobile sources specify pollution standards and time schedules for meeting the standards. For example, the 1970 Clean Air Act required a reduction of 90 percent in the amount of carbon monoxide and other pollutants emitted by automobiles by 1975. (This did not happen, however, and the 1977 amendments extended the deadline to 1983. Generally, automobile manufacturers met the 90 percent reduction goal by installing catalytic converters on automobiles.) Under the 1990 amendments, automobile manufacturers must cut new automobiles' exhaust emission of nitrogen oxide by 60 percent and emission of other pollutants by 35 percent. By 1998, all new automobiles had to do so. Another set of emission controls may be ordered after 2000.

Service stations are also subject to environmental regulations. The 1990 amendments required that beginning in 1992, service stations had to sell gasoline with a higher oxygen content in forty-one cities that experienced carbon monoxide pollution in the winter. Beginning in 1995, service stations were required to sell even cleaner burning gasoline in Los Angeles and another eight of the most polluted urban areas.

The EPA attempts to update pollution-control standards when new scientific information becomes available. In light of evidence that very small particles (2.5 microns, or millionths of a meter) of soot affect our health as significantly as larger particles, the EPA issued new particulate standards for motor vehicle exhaust systems and other sources of pollution. The EPA also increased the acceptable standard for ozone, which is formed when sunlight combines with pollutants from cars and other sources. Ozone is the basic ingredient of smog.

> **ON THE WEB**
> For information on EPA standards, guidelines, and regulations, go to the EPA's Web site at www.epa.gov.

Stationary Sources of Pollution The Clean Air Act authorizes the EPA to establish air-quality standards for stationary sources (such as manufacturing plants) but

34. *Calvert Cliffs Coordinating Committee v. Atomic Energy Commission,* 449 F.2d 1109 (D.C. Cir. 1971).
35. *Marsh v. Oregon Natural Resources Council,* 490 U.S. 360, 109 S.Ct. 1851, 104 L.Ed.2d 377 (1989).
36. 42 U.S.C. Sections 7401 *et seq.*

recognizes that the primary responsibility for preventing and controlling air pollution rests with state and local governments. The EPA sets primary and secondary levels of ambient standards—that is, the maximum levels of certain pollutants—and the states formulate plans to achieve those standards. The plans are to provide for the attainment of primary standards within three years and secondary standards within a reasonable time. For economic, political, and technological reasons, however, the deadlines are often subject to change.

Different standards apply to sources of pollution in clean areas and sources in polluted areas. Different standards also apply to existing sources of pollution and major new sources. Major new sources include existing sources modified by a change in a method of operation that increases emissions. Performance standards for major sources require use of the *maximum achievable control technology,* or MACT, to reduce emissions from the combustion of fossil fuels (coal and oil). The EPA issues guidelines as to what equipment meets this standard.

Under the 1990 amendments to the Clean Air Act, 110 of the oldest coal-burning power plants in the United States had to cut their emissions by 40 percent by the year 2001 to reduce acid rain. Utilities were granted "credits" to emit certain amounts of sulfur dioxide, and those that emit less than the allowed amounts can sell their credits to other polluters. Controls on other factories and businesses are intended to reduce ground-level ozone pollution in ninety-six cities to healthful levels by 2005 (except Los Angeles, which has until 2010). Industrial emissions of 189 hazardous air pollutants had to be reduced by 90 percent by 2000. By 2002, the production of chlorofluorocarbons, carbon tetrachloride, and methyl chloroform—used in air conditioning, refrigeration, and insulation and linked to depletion of the ozone layer—must stop.

Hazardous Air Pollutants Hazardous air pollutants are those likely to cause an increase in mortality or in serious irreversible or incapacitating illness. As noted, there are 189 of these pollutants, including asbestos, benzene, beryllium, cadmium, mercury, and vinyl chloride. These pollutants may cause cancer as well as neurological and reproductive damage. They are emitted from stationary sources by a variety of business activities, including smelting, dry cleaning, house painting, and commercial baking. Instead of establishing specific emissions standards for each hazardous air pollutant, the 1990 amendments to the Clean Air Act require industry to use pollution-control equipment that represents the maximum achievable control technology.

In recent years, the EPA has become increasingly concerned with the hazardous air pollutants emitted by landfills. In the past, when environmental regulators considered the pollution caused by landfilling, they generally focused only on groundwater contamination. By the 1990s, however, it had become apparent that emissions from landfills, including hazardous air pollutants, constituted a significant source of air pollution. In 1996, the EPA issued a new rule to regulate these emissions. The rule requires landfills constructed after May 30, 1991, that emit more than a specified amount of pollutants to install landfill gas collection and control systems. The rule also requires the states to impose the same requirements on landfills constructed before May 30, 1991, if they accepted waste after November 8, 1987.[37]

Violations of the Clean Air Act For violations of emission limits under the Clean Air Act, the EPA can assess civil penalties of up to $25,000 per day. Additional fines of up to $5,000 per day can be assessed for other violations, such as failing to maintain the required records. To penalize those for whom it is more cost effective to violate

37. 40 C.F.R. Sections 60.750–759.

the act than to comply with it, the EPA is authorized to obtain a penalty equal to the violator's economic benefits from noncompliance. Persons who provide information about violators may be paid up to $10,000. Private citizens can also sue violators.

Those who knowingly violate the act may be subject to criminal penalties, including fines of up to $1 million and imprisonment for up to two years (for false statements or failures to report violations). Corporate officers are among those who may be subject to these penalties.

WATER POLLUTION

"Among the treasures of our land is water—fast becoming our most valuable, most prized, most critical resource."

DWIGHT D. EISENHOWER, 1890–1969 (Thirty-fourth president of the United States, 1953–1961)

The major sources of water pollution are industrial, municipal, and agricultural. Pollutants entering streams, lakes, and oceans include organic wastes, heated water, sediments from soil runoff, nutrients (including detergents, fertilizers, and human and animal wastes), and toxic chemicals and other hazardous substances. We look here at laws and regulations governing water pollution.

Navigable Waters Federal regulations governing the pollution of water can be traced back to the Rivers and Harbors Appropriations Act of 1899.[38] These regulations required a permit for discharging or depositing refuse in navigable waterways. In 1948, Congress passed the Federal Water Pollution Control Act (FWPCA),[39] but its regulatory system and enforcement powers proved to be inadequate.

In 1972, amendments to the FWPCA—known as the Clean Water Act—established the following goals: (1) make waters safe for swimming, (2) protect fish and wildlife, and (3) eliminate the discharge of pollutants into the water. The amendments set forth specific time schedules, which were extended by amendment in 1977 and by the Water Quality Act of 1987.[40] Under these schedules, the EPA establishes limitations for discharges of types of pollutants based on the technology available for controlling them. The 1972 amendments also required municipal and industrial polluters to apply for permits before discharging wastes into navigable waters.

Under the act, violators are subject to a variety of civil and criminal penalties. Civil penalties for each violation range from $10,000 per day to as much as $25,000 per day or per violation. Criminal penalties range from a fine of $2,500 per day and imprisonment of up to one year to a fine of $1 million and fifteen years' imprisonment. Injunctive relief and damages can also be imposed. The polluting party can be required to clean up the pollution or pay for the cost of doing so.

• **WETLANDS**
Areas of land designated by government agencies (such as the Army Corps of Engineers or the Environmental Protection Agency) as protected areas that support wildlife and that therefore cannot be filled in or dredged by private contractors or parties.

The Clean Water Act prohibits the filling or dredging of **wetlands** unless a permit is obtained from the Army Corps of Engineers. The EPA defines *wetlands* as "those areas that are inundated or saturated by surface or ground water at a frequency and duration sufficient to support, and that under normal circumstances do support, a prevalence of vegetation typically adapted for life in saturated soil conditions." In recent years, federal regulatory policy in regard to wetlands has elicited substantial controversy because of the broad interpretation of what constitutes a wetland subject to the regulatory authority of the federal government.

Drinking Water Another statute governing water pollution is the Safe Drinking Water Act of 1974.[41] This act requires the EPA to set maximum levels for pollutants in public water systems. Public water system operators must come as close as pos-

38. 33 U.S.C. Sections 401–418.
39. 33 U.S.C. Sections 1251–1387.
40. This act amended 33 U.S.C. Section 1251.
41. 42 U.S.C. Sections 300f to 300j–25.

sible to meeting the EPA's standards by using the best available technology that is economically and technologically feasible. The EPA is particularly concerned with contamination from underground sources. Pesticides and wastes leaked from landfills or disposed of in underground injection wells are among the more than two hundred pollutants known to exist in groundwater used for drinking in at least thirty-four states. The act was amended in 1996 to give the EPA more flexibility in setting regulatory standards.

Ocean Dumping The Marine Protection, Research, and Sanctuaries Act of 1972[42] (popularly known as the Ocean Dumping Act), as amended in 1983, regulates the transportation and dumping of material into ocean waters. It prohibits entirely the ocean dumping of radiological, chemical, and biological-warfare agents and high-level radioactive waste. A violation of any provision may result in a civil penalty of $50,000, and a knowing violation is a criminal offense that may result in a $50,000 fine, imprisonment for not more than a year, or both.

Oil Spills In 1989, the supertanker *Exxon Valdez* caused the worst oil spill in North American history in the waters of Alaska's Prince William Sound. A quarter of a million barrels of crude oil—more than ten million gallons—leaked out of the ship's broken hull. In response to the *Exxon Valdez* oil spill disaster, Congress passed the Oil Pollution Act of 1990.[43] Any onshore or offshore oil facility, oil shipper, vessel owner, or vessel operator that discharges oil into navigable waters or onto an adjoining shore may be liable for clean-up costs, as well as damages.

The act provides for civil penalties of $1,000 per barrel spilled or $25,000 for each day of the violation. The party held responsible for the clean-up costs can bring a civil suit, however, for contribution from other potentially liable parties. The act also created a $1 billion oil clean-up and economic compensation fund and decreed that by the year 2011, oil tankers using U.S. ports must be double hulled to limit the severity of accidental spills.

Noise Pollution

Regulations concerning noise pollution include the Noise Control Act of 1972.[44] This act directed the EPA to establish noise-emission standards (maximum noise levels below which no harmful effects occur due to interference with speech or other activity). The standards must be achievable by the best available technology, and they must be economically within reason. Violations of provisions of the Noise Control Act can result in penalties of not more than $50,000 per day and imprisonment for not more than two years.

Toxic Chemicals

Originally, most environmental clean-up efforts were directed toward reducing smog and making water safe for fishing and swimming. Over time, some scientists argued that chemicals released into the environment in relatively small amounts could pose a threat to human life and health. Control of these toxic chemicals has become an important part of environmental law.

42. 16 U.S.C. Sections 1401–1445.
43. 33 U.S.C. Sections 2701–2761.
44. 42 U.S.C. Sections 4901–4918.

Pesticides and Herbicides The federal statute regulating pesticides and herbicides is the Federal Insecticide, Fungicide, and Rodenticide Act (FIFRA) of 1947.[45] Under FIFRA, pesticides and herbicides must be (1) registered before they can be sold, (2) certified and used only for approved applications, and (3) used in limited quantities when applied to food crops. If a substance is identified as harmful, the EPA can cancel its registration after a hearing. If the harm is imminent, the EPA can suspend registration pending the hearing. The EPA, or state officers or employees, may also inspect factories in which these chemicals are manufactured.

Under 1996 amendments to FIFRA, for a pesticide to remain on the market, there must be a "reasonable certainty of no harm" to people from exposure to the pesticide.[46] This means that there must be no more than a one-in-a-million risk to people of developing cancer from exposure in any way, including eating food that contains residues from the pesticide. Pesticide residues are in nearly all fruits and vegetables and processed foods. Under the 1996 amendments, the EPA must distribute to grocery stores brochures on high-risk pesticides that are in food, and the stores must display these brochures for consumers.

It is a violation of FIFRA to sell a pesticide or herbicide that is unregistered, a pesticide or herbicide with a registration that has been canceled or suspended, or a pesticide or herbicide with a false or misleading label. For example, it is an offense to sell a substance that is adulterated (that has a chemical strength different from the concentration declared on the label). It is also an offense to destroy or deface any labeling required under the act. The act's labeling requirements include directions for the use of the pesticide or herbicide, warnings to protect human health and the environment, a statement of treatment in the case of poisoning, and a list of the ingredients.

A commercial dealer who violates FIFRA may be imprisoned for up to one year and fined up to $25,000. Farmers and other private users of pesticides or herbicides who violate the act are subject to a $1,000 fine and incarceration for up to thirty days.

Toxic Substances The first comprehensive law covering toxic substances was the Toxic Substances Control Act of 1976.[47] The act was passed to regulate chemicals and chemical compounds that are known to be toxic—such as asbestos and polychlorinated biphenyls, popularly known as PCBs—and to institute investigation of any possible harmful effects from new chemical compounds. The regulations authorize the EPA to require that manufacturers, processors, and other organizations planning to use chemicals first determine their effects on human health and the environment. The EPA can regulate substances that potentially pose an imminent hazard or an unreasonable risk of injury to health or the environment. The EPA may require special labeling, limit the use of a substance, set production quotas, or prohibit the use of a substance altogether.

HAZARDOUS WASTE DISPOSAL

Some industrial, agricultural, and household wastes pose more serious threats than others. If not properly disposed of, these toxic chemicals may present a substantial danger to human health and the environment. If released into the environment, they may contaminate public drinking water resources.

"All property in this country is held under the implied obligation that the owner's use of it shall not be injurious to the community."

JOHN HARLAN, 1899–1971
(Associate justice of the United States Supreme Court, 1955–1971)

45. 7 U.S.C. Sections 135–136y.
46. 21 U.S.C. Section 346a.
47. 15 U.S.C. Sections 2601–2692.

Resource Conservation and Recovery Act In 1976, Congress passed the Resource Conservation and Recovery Act (RCRA)[48] in reaction to an ever-increasing concern over the effects of hazardous waste materials on the environment. The RCRA required the EPA to establish regulations to monitor and control hazardous waste disposal and to determine which forms of solid waste should be considered hazardous and thus subject to regulation. The EPA has promulgated various technical requirements for limited types of facilities for storage and treatment of hazardous waste. The act also requires all producers of hazardous waste materials to label and package properly any hazardous waste to be transported.

The RCRA was amended in 1984 and 1986 to add several new regulatory requirements to those already monitored and enforced by the EPA.[49] The basic aims of the amendments were to decrease the use of land containment in the disposal of hazardous waste and to require compliance with the act by some generators of hazardous waste—such as those generating less than 1,000 kilograms (2,200 pounds) a month—that had previously been excluded from regulation under the RCRA.

Under the RCRA, a company may be assessed a civil penalty based on the seriousness of the violation, the probability of harm, and the extent to which the violation deviates from RCRA requirements. The assessment may be up to $25,000 for each violation.[50] Criminal penalties include fines up to $50,000 for each day of violation, imprisonment for up to two years (in most instances), or both.[51] Criminal fines and the time of imprisonment can be doubled for certain repeat offenders.

Superfund In 1980, Congress passed the Comprehensive Environmental Response, Compensation, and Liability Act (CERCLA),[52] commonly known as Superfund. The basic purpose of Superfund is to regulate the clean-up of leaking hazardous waste disposal sites. A special federal fund was created for that purpose. Because of its impact on the business community, the act is presented here as this chapter's *Landmark in the Law.*

48. 42 U.S.C. Sections 6901 *et seq.*
49. 42 U.S.C. Sections 6901 *et seq.*
50. 42 U.S.C. Section 6929(g).
51. 42 U.S.C. Section 6929(d).
52. 42 U.S.C. Sections 9601–9675.

Landmark in the Law • SUPERFUND

The origins of the Comprehensive Environmental Response, Compensation, and Liability Act (CERCLA) of 1980, which is commonly referred to as Superfund, can be traced to drafts that the Environmental Protection Agency (EPA) started to circulate in 1978. EPA officials emphasized the political necessity of new legislation by pointing to what they thought were "ticking time bombs"—dump sites around the country that were ready to explode and injure the public with toxic fumes.

The popular press also gave prominence to hazardous waste dump sites at the time. The New York Love Canal disaster began to make the headlines in 1978 after residents in the area complained about health problems, contaminated sludge oozing into their basements, and chemical "volcanoes" erupting in their yards as a result of Hooker Chemical's dumping of approximately 21,000 tons of chemicals into the canal from 1942 to 1953. The Love Canal situation made the national news virtually every day from the middle of May to the middle of June in 1980.

The basic purpose of CERCLA, which was amended in 1986 by the Superfund Amendments and Reauthorization Act, is to regulate the clean-up of leaking hazardous waste disposal sites. The act has four primary elements:

- It established an information-gathering and analysis system that allows federal and state governments to characterize chemical dump sites and to develop priorities for appropriate action.
- It authorized the EPA to respond to hazardous substance emergencies and to clean up leaking sites directly through contractors or through cooperative agreements with the states if the persons responsible for the problem fail to clean up the site.
- It created a Hazardous Substance Response Trust Fund (Superfund) to pay for the clean-up of hazardous sites. Monies for the fund are obtained through taxes on certain businesses, including those processing or producing petroleum and chemical feedstock.
- It allowed the government to recover the cost of clean-up from the persons who were (even remotely) responsible for hazardous substance releases.

FOR CRITICAL ANALYSIS
Must *all* of the contamination be removed from a hazardous waste site to ensure that it no longer poses any threat of harm to life? Would some lesser amount satisfy a reasonable degree of environmental quality?

Potentially Responsible Parties under Superfund. Superfund provides that when a release or a threatened release of hazardous chemicals from a site occurs, the EPA can clean up the site and recover the cost of the clean-up from the following persons: (1) the person who generated the wastes disposed of at the site, (2) the person who transported the wastes to the site, (3) the person who owned or operated the site at the time of the disposal, or (4) the current owner or operator. A person falling within one of these categories is referred to as a **potentially responsible party (PRP).**

• POTENTIALLY RESPONSIBLE PARTY (PRP)
A party liable under the Comprehensive Environmental Response, Compensation, and Liability Act (CERCLA). Any person who generated the hazardous waste, transported the hazardous waste, owned or operated a waste site at the time of disposal, or currently owns or operates a site may be responsible for some or all of the clean-up costs involved in removing the hazardous chemicals.

ETHICAL ISSUE 36.1 ***Who should be a potentially responsible party under Superfund?*** Deciding who qualifies as a potentially responsible party (PRP) under Superfund is not always easy; nor are the results of such decisions always necessarily fair. Successor corporations (see Chapter 29) have been held liable for their predecessors' polluting activities. In some cases, courts have even "pierced the corporate veil" to hold corporate shareholder-officers personally liable because of the degree of control they exercised over their corporations. Should parent companies be liable for their subsidiaries' polluting activities? One argument in favor of imposing liability on parent companies is, of course, that parent companies may have "deeper pockets" than their subsidiaries—that is, they can better afford to pay the clean-up costs. In 1998, the United States Supreme Court resolved a split among the lower courts on this issue by holding that a parent company can be liable as a PRP under Superfund *only* if it was directly involved in running the polluting facility.[53] Decisions as to who qualifies as a PRP have important ramifications, because liability under Superfund can be extensive.

Joint and Several Liability under Superfund. Liability under Superfund is usually joint and several—that is, a person who generated only a fraction of the hazardous waste disposed of at the site may nevertheless be liable for all of the clean-up costs. CERCLA authorizes a party who has incurred clean-up costs to bring a "contribution action" against any other person who is liable or potentially liable for a percentage of the costs.

53. *United States v. Best Foods*, ___U.S. ___, 118 S.Ct. 1876, 141 L.Ed.2d 43 (1998).

APPLICATION Law and the Businessperson: Keeping Abreast of Environmental Laws*

Businesspersons today increasingly face the threat of severe civil or criminal penalties if they violate environmental laws and regulations. It therefore is necessary that every person in the business world be aware of what those laws and regulations are and how to monitor changes in them. At a minimum, knowledge of the changing and complex nature of environmental law will help a businessperson to know when to contact an attorney during the normal course of business.

Consider some areas of concern that affect businesses. Businesspersons often purchase business property. When engaging in such purchases, you must keep in mind the environmental problems that may arise. Realize that it is up to you as a purchaser of the property to raise environmental issues. This is because sellers, title insurance companies, and real estate brokers will rarely pursue such matters. (A bank financing the property may worry about the potential environmental hazards of the property, however.)

As a purchaser of business property, you should learn whether there are any restrictions regarding the use of the land, such as whether the land can be cleared of trees for construction purposes. The most prominent environmental concern, however, is whether the property has been contaminated by hazardous wastes created by the previous owners.

There seems to be an unending number of ways in which those who purchase property can be held liable under the Comprehensive Environmental Response, Compensation, and Liability Act (CERCLA) of 1980 for the clean-up of hazardous wastes dumped by previous property owners. Although it is true that current property owners who are sued under CERCLA for clean-up costs can sue the previous owners, such litigation is uncertain and usually costly. Clearly, a more prudent course when purchasing property is to investigate the history of the use of the land. If you purchase business property, you would be well advised to hire a private environmental site inspector to determine, at a minimum, whether the land has any obvious signs of former contamination.

There is also an incentive for today's companies to discover their own environmental wrongdoings. As mentioned in Chapter 6, the federal sentencing guidelines encourage companies to promptly detect, disclose, and correct wrongdoing, including environmental crimes. Companies that do so are subject to lighter penalties for violations of environmental laws. Under the guidelines, a company that regularly conducts comprehensive audits of its compliance with environmental requirements, immediately reports a violation to the government, disciplines the responsible people within the corporation, and provides their names to the government should qualify for leniency.

Small businesses will find it particularly advantageous to investigate and correct environmental violations. Under current EPA guidelines, the EPA will waive all fines if a company corrects environmental violations within 180 days (or 360 days if pollution-prevention techniques are involved). The EPA's policy applies to companies with one hundred or fewer employees. The policy does not apply to criminal violations of environmental laws or to actions that pose a significant threat to public health, safety, or the environment.

*This *Application* is not meant to substitute for the services of an attorney who is licensed to practice law in your state.

CHECKLIST FOR THE BUSINESSPERSON

1. If you are in business or plan to open a business that is going to purchase real estate, use land, or engage in activities that might cause environmental damage, check with your attorney immediately.
2. If you want to avoid liability for violating environmental regulations or statutes, conduct environmental compliance audits on a regular basis. To learn whether you are doing so appropriately, check with your attorney.
3. If you are ever charged with violating an environmental regulation or law, you must check with your attorney.
4. In general: environmental law is sufficiently complex that you should never attempt to deal with it without the help of an attorney.

Key Terms

bait-and-switch advertising 922
cease-and-desist order 922
"cooling-off" laws 926
counteradvertising 922
deceptive advertising 921
environmental impact statement (EIS) 936
nuisance 934
potentially responsible party (PRP) 943
Regulation Z 925
wetlands 939

Chapter Summary • Consumer and Environmental Law

CONSUMER LAW	
Deceptive Advertising (See pages 921–922.)	1. *Definition of deceptive advertising*—Generally, an advertising claim will be deemed deceptive if it would mislead a reasonable consumer. 2. *Bait-and-switch advertising*—Advertising a lower-priced product (the "bait") when the intention is not to sell the advertised product but to lure consumers into the store and convince them to buy a higher-priced product (the "switch") is prohibited by the FTC. 3. *FTC actions against deceptive advertising*— a. Cease-and-desist orders—Requiring the advertiser to stop the challenged advertising. b. Counteradvertising—Requiring the advertiser to advertise to correct the earlier misinformation.
Telemarketing and Electronic Advertising (See pages 922–923.)	The Telephone Consumer Protection Act of 1991 prohibits telephone solicitation using an automatic telephone dialing system or a prerecorded voice, as well as the transmission of advertising materials via fax without first obtaining the recipient's permission to do so.
Labeling and Packaging (See pages 923–925.)	Manufacturers must comply with labeling or packaging requirements for their specific products. In general, all labels must be accurate and not misleading.
Sales (See pages 925–926.)	1. *Door-to-door sales*—The FTC requires all door-to-door sellers to give consumers three days (a "cooling-off" period) to cancel any sale. States also provide for similar protection. 2. *Telephone and mail-order sales*—Federal and state statutes and regulations govern certain practices of sellers who solicit over the telephone or through the mails and prohibit the use of the mails to defraud individuals.
Health and Safety Protection (See pages 926–928.)	1. *Food and drugs*—The Federal Food, Drug and Cosmetic Act of 1938, as amended, protects consumers against adulterated and misbranded foods and drugs. The act establishes food standards, specifies safe levels of potentially hazardous food additives, and sets classifications of food and food advertising. 2. *Consumer product safety*—The Consumer Product Safety Act of 1972 seeks to protect consumers from risk of injury from hazardous products. The Consumer Product Safety Commission has the power to remove products that are deemed imminently hazardous from the market and to ban the manufacture and sale of hazardous products.
Credit Protection (See pages 928–933.)	1. *Consumer Credit Protection Act, Title I (Truth-in-Lending Act, or TILA)*—A disclosure law that requires sellers and lenders to disclose credit terms or loan terms in certain transactions, including retail and installment sales and loans, car loans, home-improvement loans, and certain real estate loans. Additionally, the TILA provides for the following: a. Equal credit opportunity—Creditors are prohibited from discriminating on the basis of race, religion, marital status, gender, and so on. b. Credit-card protection—Credit-card users may withhold payment for a faulty product sold, or for an error in billing, until the dispute is resolved; liability of cardholders for unauthorized charges is limited to $50, providing notice requirements are met; consumers are not liable for unauthorized charges made on unsolicited credit cards. c. Consumer leases—The Consumer Leasing Act (CLA) of 1988 protects consumers who lease automobiles and other goods priced at $25,000 or less if the lease term exceeds four months. 2. *Fair Credit Reporting Act*—Entitles consumers to request verification of the accuracy of a credit report and to have unverified or false information removed from their files.

Chapter Summary • Consumer and Environmental Law, Continued

Credit Protection—continued	3. *Fair Debt Collection Practices Act*—Prohibits debt collectors from using unfair debt-collection practices, such as contacting the debtor at his or her place of employment if the employer objects or at unreasonable times, contacting third parties about the debt, harassing the debtor, and so on.
State Consumer Protection Laws (See page 933.)	State laws often provide for greater consumer protection against deceptive trade practices than do federal laws. In addition, the warranty and unconscionability provisions of the Uniform Commercial Code protect consumers against sellers' deceptive practices. The Uniform Consumer Credit Code, which has not been widely adopted by the states, provides credit protection for consumers.
ENVIRONMENTAL LAW	
Common Law Actions (See pages 934–935.)	1. *Nuisance*—A common law doctrine under which actions against pollution-causing activities may be brought. An action is permissible only if an individual suffers a harm separate and distinct from that of the general public. 2. *Negligence and strict liability*—Parties may recover damages for injuries sustained as a result of pollution-causing activities of a firm if it can be demonstrated that the harm was a foreseeable result of the firm's failure to exercise reasonable care (negligence); businesses engaging in ultrahazardous activities are liable for whatever injuries the activities cause, regardless of whether the firms exercise reasonable care.
State and Local Regulation (See page 935.)	Activities affecting the environment are controlled at the local and state levels through regulations relating to land use, the disposal and recycling of garbage and waste, and pollution-causing activities in general.
Federal Regulation (See pages 935–943.)	1. *Environmental protection agencies*—The most well known of the agencies regulating environmental law is the federal Environmental Protection Agency (EPA), which was created in 1970 to coordinate federal environmental programs. The EPA administers most federal environmental policies and statutes. 2. *Assessing environmental impact*—The National Environmental Policy Act of 1969 imposes environmental responsibilities on all federal agencies and requires for every major federal action the preparation of an environmental impact statement (EIS). An EIS must analyze the action's impact on the environment, its adverse effects and possible alternatives, and its irreversible effects on environmental quality. 3. *Important areas regulated by the federal government*—In addition to fish and wildlife (regulated by the Fish and Wildlife Coordination Act of 1958) and endangered species (regulated under the Endangered Species Act of 1973), important areas regulated by the federal government include the following: a. Air pollution—Regulated under the authority of the Clean Air Act of 1963 and its amendments, particularly those of 1970, 1977, and 1990. b. Water pollution—Regulated under the authority of the Rivers and Harbors Appropriation Act of 1899, as amended, and the Federal Water Pollution Control Act of 1948, as amended by the Clean Water Act of 1972. c. Noise pollution—Regulated by the Noise Control Act of 1972. d. Toxic chemicals and hazardous waste—Pesticides and herbicides, toxic substances, and hazardous waste are regulated under the authority of the Federal Insecticide, Fungicide, and Rodenticide Act of 1947, the Toxic Substances Control Act of 1976, and the Resource Conservation and Recovery Act of 1976, respectively. The Comprehensive Environmental Response, Compensation, and Liability Act (CERCLA) of 1980, as amended, regulates the clean-up of hazardous waste disposal sites.

For Review

1 When will advertising be deemed deceptive?
2 How does the Federal Food, Drug and Cosmetic Act protect consumers? What are the major federal statutes providing for consumer protection in credit transactions?
3 Under what common law theories may polluters be held liable?
4 What is an environmental impact statement, and who must file one? What does the Environmental Protection Agency do?
5 What major federal statutes regulate air and water pollution? What is Superfund? To what categories of persons does liability under Superfund extend?

Questions and Case Problems

36–1. Clean Air Act. Current scientific knowledge indicates that there is no safe level of exposure to a cancer-causing agent. In theory, even one molecule of such a substance has the potential for causing cancer. Section 112 of the Clean Air Act requires that all cancer-causing substances be regulated to ensure a margin of safety. Some environmental groups have argued that all emissions of such substances must be eliminated in order for such a margin of safety to be reached. Such a total elimination would likely shut down many major U.S. industries. Should the Environmental Protection Agency totally eliminate all emissions of cancer-causing chemicals? Discuss.

36–2. Environmental Laws. Fruitade, Inc., is a processor of a soft drink called Freshen Up. Fruitade uses returnable bottles and uses a special acid to clean its bottles for further beverage processing. The acid is diluted with water and then allowed to pass into a navigable stream. Fruitade crushes its broken bottles and also throws the crushed glass into the stream. Discuss fully any environmental laws that Fruitade has violated.

36–3. Sales. On June 28, a sales representative for Renowned Books called on the Guevaras at their home. After listening to a very persuasive sales pitch, the Guevaras agreed in writing to purchase a twenty-volume set of historical encyclopedias from Renowned Books for a total price of $299. An initial down payment of $35 was required, with the remainder of the price to be paid in monthly payments over a one-year period. Two days later, the Guevaras, having second thoughts about the purchase, contacted the book company and stated that they had decided to rescind the contract. Renowned Books said this would be impossible. Has Renowned Books violated any consumer law by not allowing the Guevaras to rescind their contract? Explain.

36–4. Credit Protection. Maria Ochoa receives two new credit cards on May 1. She had solicited one of them from Midtown Department Store, and the other had arrived unsolicited from High-Flying Airlines. During the month of May, Ochoa makes numerous credit-card purchases from Midtown Store, but she does not use the High-Flying Airlines card. On May 31, a burglar breaks into Ochoa's home and steals both credit cards, along with other items. Ochoa notifies the Midtown Department Store of the theft on June 2, but she fails to notify High-Flying Airlines. Using the Midtown credit card, the burglar makes a $500 purchase on June 1 and a $200 purchase on June 3. The burglar then charges a vacation flight on the High-Flying Airlines card for $1,000 on June 5. Ochoa receives the bills for these charges and refuses to pay them. Discuss Ochoa's liability in these situations.

36–5. Deceptive Advertising. Dennis and Janice Geiger saw an advertisement in a newspaper for a Kimball Whitney spinet piano on sale for $699 at McCormick Piano & Organ Co. Because the style of the piano drawn in the advertisement matched their furniture, the Geigers were particularly interested in the Kimball. When they went to McCormick Piano & Organ, however, they learned that the drawing closely resembled another, more expensive Crest piano and that the Kimball spinet looked quite different from the piano sketched in the drawing. The salesperson told the Geigers that she was unable to order the spinet piano in the style requested by the Geigers. When the Geigers asked for the names of other customers who had purchased the advertised pianos, the salesperson became hysterical and said she would not, under any circumstances, sell the Geigers a piano. The Geigers then brought suit against the piano store, alleging that the store had engaged in deceptive advertising in violation of Indiana law. Had McCormick Piano & Organ Co. engaged in deceptive advertising? Explain. [*McCormick Piano & Organ Co. v. Geiger,* 412 N.E.2d 842 (Ind.App. 1980)]

36–6. Deceptive Advertising. Thompson Medical Co. marketed a new cream, called Aspercreme, which was supposed to help people with arthritis and others suffering from minor aches. Aspercreme contained no aspirin. Thompson's television advertisements stated that the product provided "the strong relief of aspirin right where you hurt" and showed the announcer holding up aspirin tablets, as well as a tube of Aspercreme. The Federal Trade Commission held that the advertisements were misleading, because they led consumers to believe that Aspercreme contained aspirin. Thompson Medical Co. appealed this decision and argued that the advertisements never actually stated that its product contained aspirin. How should the court rule? Discuss. [*Thompson Medical Co. v. Federal Trade Commission,* 791 F.2d 189 (D.C. Cir. 1986)]

36–7. Superfund. During the 1970s, a number of chemical companies disposed of their wastes at a facility maintained by

South Carolina Recycling and Disposal, Inc. Hazardous chemical wastes were stored rather haphazardly; some leaked into the ground, and fires occurred on several occasions. Eventually, the Environmental Protection Agency (EPA) conducted clean-up operations under Superfund and sued companies that had used the site for the costs of the clean-up. Five of the defendant companies claimed that they should not be liable for the clean-up costs because there was no evidence that their waste materials had contributed in any way to the leakage problem or to any other hazard posed by the site. The EPA asserted that causation was not required for the companies' liability, only evidence that the companies had sent waste to the site. Will the EPA succeed in its claim? Discuss. [*United States v. South Carolina Recycling and Disposal, Inc.,* 653 F.Supp. 984 (D.S.C. 1986)]

36–8. Equal Credit Opportunity. The Riggs National Bank of Washington, D.C., loaned more than $11 million to Samuel Linch and Albert Randolph. To obtain the loan, Linch and Randolph provided personal financial statements. Linch's statement included substantial assets that he owned jointly with his wife, Marcia. As a condition of the loan, Riggs required that Marcia, as well as Samuel and Albert, sign a personal guaranty for repayment. When the borrowers defaulted, Riggs filed a suit in a federal district court to recover its funds, based on the personal guaranties. The court ruled against the borrowers, who appealed. On what basis might the borrowers argue that Riggs violated the Equal Credit Opportunity Act (ECOA)? [*Riggs National Bank of Washington, D.C. v. Linch,* 36 F.3d 370 (4th Cir. 1994)]

36–9. Debt Collection. Equifax A.R.S., a debt-collection agency, sent Donna Russell a notice about one of her debts. The front of the notice stated that "[i]f you do not dispute this claim (see reverse side) and wish to pay it within the next 10 days we will not post this collection to your file." The reverse side set out Russell's rights under the Fair Debt Collection Practices Act (FDCPA), including that she had thirty days to decide whether to contest the claim. Russell filed a suit in a federal district court against Equifax. The court ruled against Russell, who appealed. On what basis might Russell argue that Equifax violated the FDCPA? [*Russell v. Equifax A.R.S.,* 74 F.3d 30 (2d Cir. 1996)]

36–10. Fair Debt Collection Practices Act (FDCPA). Rancho Santa Margarita Recreation and Landscape Corp., a condominium association, attempted unsuccessfully to collect an assessment fee from Andrew Ladick. The association referred the matter to the Law Offices of Gerald J. Van Gemert. Van Gemert sent Ladick a letter demanding payment of the fee. The letter did not include an FDCPA "validation notice" nor did it disclose that Van Gemert was attempting to collect a debt and that any information obtained would be used for that purpose. Ladick filed a suit in a federal district court against Van Gemert and his office, alleging violations of the FDCPA. Van Gemert filed a motion for summary judgment on the ground that the assessment was not a "debt," as defined by the FDCPA, in part because there was no "transaction," as required by the FDCPA definition, out of which Ladick's obligation arose. Will the court agree with Van Gemert? Why or why not? [*Ladick v. Van Gemert,* 146 F.3d 1205 (10th Cir. 1998)]

A QUESTION OF ETHICS AND SOCIAL RESPONSIBILITY

36–11. The Endangered Species Act of 1973 makes it unlawful for any person to "take" endangered or threatened species. The act defines *take* to mean to "harass, harm, pursue," "wound," or "kill." The secretary of the Interior (Bruce Babbitt) issued a regulation that further defined harm to include "significant habitat modification or degradation where it actually kills or injures wildlife." A group of businesses and individuals involved in the timber industry brought an action against the secretary of the Interior and others. The group complained that the application of the "harm" regulation to the red-cockaded woodpecker and the northern spotted owl had injured the group economically, because it prevented logging operations (habitat modification) in Pacific Northwest forests containing these species. The group challenged the regulation's validity, contending that Congress did not intend the word *take* to include habitat modification. The case ultimately reached the United States Supreme Court, which held that the secretary reasonably construed Congress's intent when he defined harm to include habitat modification. [*Babbitt v. Sweet Home Chapter of Communities for a Great Oregon,* 515 U.S. 687, 115 S.Ct. 2407, 132 L.Ed.2d 597 (1995)]

1. Traditionally, the term *take* has been used to refer to the capture or killing of wildlife, usually for private gain. Is the secretary's regulation prohibiting habitat modification consistent with this definition?
2. One of the issues in this case was whether Congress intended to protect existing generations of species or future generations. How do the terms *take* and *habitat modification* relate to this issue?
3. Three dissenting Supreme Court justices contended that construing the act as prohibiting habitat modification "imposes unfairness to the point of financial ruin—not just upon the rich, but upon the simplest farmer who finds his land conscripted to national zoological use." Should private parties be required to bear the burden of preserving habitats for wildlife?
4. Generally, should the economic welfare of private parties be taken into consideration when creating and applying environmental statutes and regulations?

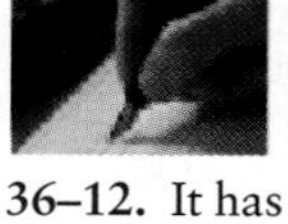

FOR CRITICAL ANALYSIS

36–12. It has been estimated that for every dollar spent cleaning up hazardous waste sites, administrative agencies spend seven dollars in overhead. Can you think of any way to trim the administrative costs associated with the clean-up of contaminated sites?

Online Activities

ONLINE EXERCISE 36–1

Go to the "Internet Activities Book" on the Web site that accompanies this text, the URL for which is http://blt.westbuslaw.com. Select the following activities, and perform the exercises according to the instructions given there:

Activity 33–1: Internet Fraud Watch
Activity 33–2: Consumer Information Center
Activity 33–3: Environmental Law

Before the Test

Go to the *Business Law Today* home page at http://blt.westbuslaw.com. Click on TestTutor.® You will find twenty interactive questions relating to this chapter.

CHAPTER 37

Labor & Employment Law

> "Show me the country in which there are no strikes, and I'll show you the country in which there is no liberty."
>
> Samuel Gompers, 1850–1924
> (American labor leader)

CONTENTS

LEARNING OBJECTIVES

After reading this chapter, you should be able to:

1. Discuss the employment-at-will doctrine.
2. Identify the leading federal statute governing wages and working hours.
3. List and summarize the major laws governing labor unions.
4. Describe the major laws relating to health and safety in the workplace.
5. Summarize the laws governing the rights of employees in regard to pension plans, family and medical leave, and privacy.

Until the early 1900s, most employer-employee relationships were governed by the common law. Under the doctrine of **employment at will,** either party may terminate the employment relationship at any time and for any reason—provided, of course, that the employment termination does not violate the provisions of an employment contract. Other common law concepts governing employment relationships were those of contract, agency, and tort law.

In the 1930s, during the Great Depression, both state and federal governments began to regulate employment relationships. Legislation during the 1930s and subsequent decades established the right of employees to form labor unions. At the heart of labor rights is the right to unionize and bargain with management for improved working conditions, salaries, and benefits. The ultimate weapon of labor is, of course, the strike. As noted in the opening quotation, the labor leader Samuel Gompers concluded that without the right to strike, there could be no liberty. A succession of other laws during and since the 1930s provided further protection for employees. Today's employers

• **EMPLOYMENT AT WILL**
A common law doctrine under which either party may terminate an employment relationship at any time for any reason, unless a contract specifies otherwise.

must comply with a myriad of laws and regulations to ensure that employee rights are protected.

In this chapter, we look at the most significant laws regulating employment relationships. We deal with other important laws regulating the workplace—those that prohibit employment discrimination—in the next chapter.

Wage-Hour Laws

In the 1930s, Congress enacted several laws regulating the wages and working hours of employees. In 1931, Congress passed the Davis-Bacon Act,[1] which requires the payment of "prevailing wages" to employees of contractors and subcontractors working on government construction projects. In 1936, the Walsh-Healey Act[2] was passed. This act requires that a minimum wage, as well as overtime pay of time and a half, be paid to employees of manufacturers or suppliers entering into contracts with agencies of the federal government.

In 1938, Congress passed the Fair Labor Standards Act[3] (FLSA). This act extended wage-hour requirements to cover all employers engaged in interstate commerce or engaged in the production of goods for interstate commerce, plus selected types of businesses. We examine here the FLSA's provisions in regard to child labor, maximum hours, and minimum wages.

CHILD LABOR

The FLSA prohibits oppressive child labor. Children under fourteen years of age are allowed to do certain types of work, such as deliver newspapers, work for their parents, and work in the entertainment and (with some exceptions) agricultural areas. Children who are fourteen or fifteen years of age are allowed to work, but not in hazardous occupations. Most states require persons under sixteen years of age to obtain work permits. There are also numerous restrictions on how many hours per day and per week they can work. • **EXAMPLE 37.1** Children in this age group cannot work during school hours, for more than three hours on a school day (or eight hours on a nonschool day), for more than eighteen hours during a school week (or forty hours during a nonschool week), or before 7 A.M. or after 7 P.M. (9 P.M. during the summer).•

Persons between the ages of sixteen and eighteen do not face such restrictions on working times and hours, but they cannot be employed in hazardous jobs or in jobs detrimental to their health and well-being. Persons over the age of eighteen are not affected by any of the above-mentioned restrictions.

CHILDREN TAKE A BREAK FROM THEIR WORK IN A COAL MINE IN THE EARLY TWENTIETH CENTURY. WHAT RESTRICTIONS DO EMPLOYERS FACE IN EMPLOYING CHILDREN TODAY?

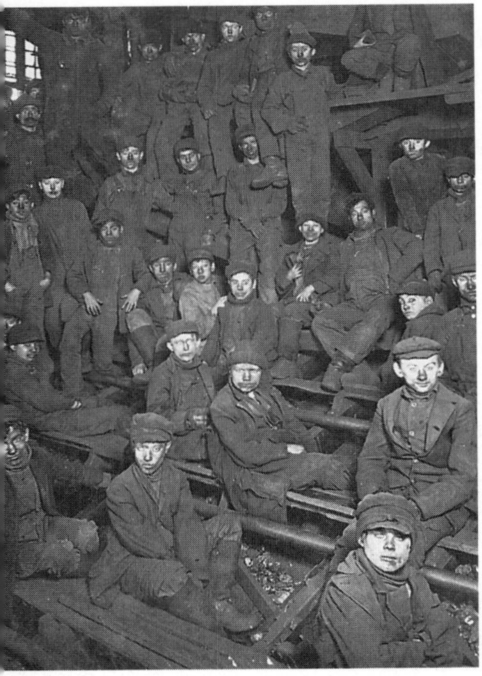

HOURS AND WAGES

Under the FLSA, any employee who agrees to work more than forty hours per week must be paid no less than one and a half times his or her regular pay for all hours over forty. Note that the FLSA overtime provisions only apply after an employee has worked more than forty hours per *week*. Thus, employees who work for ten hours a day, four days per week, are not entitled to overtime pay because they do not work more than forty hours a week.

Certain employees are exempt from the overtime provisions of the act. Exempt employees fall into four categories: executives, administrative employees, profes-

1. 40 U.S.C. Sections 276a–276a-5.
2. 41 U.S.C. Sections 35–45.
3. 29 U.S.C. Sections 201–260.

sional employees, and outside salespersons. Generally, to fall into one of these categories, an employee must earn more than a specified amount of income per week and devote a certain percentage of work time to the performance of specific types of duties, as determined by the FLSA. To qualify as an outside salesperson, the employee must regularly engage in sales work away from the office and spend no more than 20 percent of work time per week performing duties other than sales.

• **MINIMUM WAGE**
The lowest wage, either by government regulation or union contract, that an employer may pay an hourly worker.

The FLSA provides that a **minimum wage** of a specified amount (currently, $5.15 per hour) must be paid to employees in covered industries. Congress periodically revises such minimum wages. Under the FLSA, the term *wages* includes the reasonable cost of the employer in furnishing employees with board, lodging, and other facilities if they are customarily furnished by that employer.

Labor Unions

In the 1930s, in addition to wage-hour laws, the government also enacted the first of several labor laws. These laws protect employees' rights to join labor unions, to bargain with management over the terms and conditions of employment, and to conduct strikes.

¡BE CAREFUL!
To check for compliance with safety standards without being cited for violations, an employer can often obtain advice from an insurer, a trade association, or a state agency.

FEDERAL LABOR LAWS

Federal labor laws governing union-employer relations have developed considerably since the first law was enacted in 1932. Initially, the laws were concerned with protecting the rights and interests of workers. Subsequent legislation placed some restraints on unions and granted rights to employers. We look here at four major federal statutes regulating union-employer relations.

Norris-LaGuardia Act Congress protected peaceful strikes, picketing, and boycotts in 1932 in the Norris-LaGuardia Act.[4] The statute restricted federal courts in their power to issue injunctions against unions engaged in peaceful strikes. In effect, this act declared a national policy permitting employees to organize.

National Labor Relations Act One of the foremost statutes regulating labor is the National Labor Relations Act (NLRA) of 1935.[5] This act established the rights of employees to engage in collective bargaining and to strike. The act also specifically defined a number of employer practices as unfair to labor:

ON THE WEB
An excellent site for up-to-date information on labor and employment law is that of Law Journal EXTRA! at www.ljx.com/practice.

1. Interference with the efforts of employees to form, join, or assist labor organizations or interference with the efforts of employees to engage in concerted activities for their mutual aid or protection.
2. An employer's domination of a labor organization or contribution of financial or other support to it.
3. Discrimination based on union affiliation in the hiring or awarding of tenure to employees.
4. Discrimination against employees for filing charges under the act or giving testimony under the act.
5. Refusal to bargain collectively with the duly designated representative of the employees.

The act also created the National Labor Relations Board (NLRB) to oversee union elections and to prevent employers from engaging in unfair and illegal union

4. 29 U.S.C. Sections 101–110, 113–115.
5. 20 U.S.C. Section 151.

activities and unfair labor practices. The purpose of the NLRA was to secure for employees the rights to organize; to bargain collectively through representatives of their own choosing; and to engage in concerted activities for organizing, collective bargaining, and other purposes.

The NLRB has the authority to investigate employees' charges of unfair labor practices and to serve complaints against employers in response to these charges. The NLRB may also issue cease-and-desist orders—orders compelling employers to cease engaging in the unfair practices—when violations are found. Cease-and-desist orders can be enforced by a circuit court of appeals if necessary. Arguments over alleged unfair labor practices are first decided by the NLRB and may then be appealed to a federal court.

To be protected under the NLRA, an individual must be an "employee," as that term is defined in the statute. Courts have long held that job applicants fall within the definition (otherwise, the NLRA's ban on discrimination in regard to hiring would mean nothing). In the following case, the United States Supreme Court considered whether an individual may be a company's "employee" if, at the same time, a union pays the individual to organize the company.

CASE 37.1 National Labor Relations Board v. Town & Country Electric, Inc.

Supreme Court of the United States, 1995.
516 U.S. 85,
116 S.Ct. 450,
133 L.Ed.2d 371.
www.findlaw.com/casecode/supreme.html[a]

HISTORICAL AND ECONOMIC SETTING *Over the last two decades, the percentage of private-sector workers who are union members has declined. Perhaps this is due, at least in part, to a popular belief that unions represent only a level of interference between a company's making profits and the workers' getting paid. In the public sector, however, unions are becoming more popular and are growing in force. Unions themselves are consolidating and still attempting to organize workers.*

a. This page contains links to opinions of the United States Supreme Court. In the "Party Name Search" box, type "Town & Country Electric" and click "Search." When the results appear, click on the case name to access the opinion. This Web site is maintained by FindLaw.

BACKGROUND AND FACTS Town & Country Electric, Inc., advertised for job applicants but refused to interview ten of eleven applicants who were members of a union, the International Brotherhood of Electrical Workers. The applicants were union "salts"—persons paid by the union to apply for a job with a company and then, when hired, to unionize the company (in this case, Town & Country's work force). The applicants filed a complaint with the National Labor Relations Board (NLRB), alleging that the company had committed an unfair labor practice by discriminating against the applicants on the basis of union membership. The issue turned on whether job applicants paid by a union to organize a company could be considered "employees" under the National Labor Relations Act (NLRA). The NLRB determined that the applicants were employees and ruled in their favor. Town & Country appealed, and the U.S. Court of Appeals for the Eighth Circuit reversed. The applicants appealed to the United States Supreme Court.

IN THE WORDS OF THE COURT . . .
Justice *BREYER* delivered the opinion of the Court.

* * * *

* * * [T]he Board's decision is consistent with the broad language of the [NLRA] * * * . The ordinary dictionary definition of "employee" includes any "person who works for another in return for financial or other compensation." The phrasing of the [NLRA] seems to reiterate the breadth of the ordinary dictionary definition, for it says "[t]he term 'employee' shall include any employee." * * *

(Continued)

CASE 37.1—Continued

For another thing, the Board's broad, literal interpretation of the word "employee" is consistent with several of the [NLRA's] purposes, such as protecting "the right of employees to organize for mutual aid without employer interference" * * * .

DECISION AND REMEDY The United States Supreme Court reversed the decision of the appellate court and remanded the case.

FOR CRITICAL ANALYSIS—Economic Consideration *How would the relationship between labor and management be affected if job applicants did not have rights under the NLRA?*

• **CLOSED SHOP**
A firm that requires union membership by its workers as a condition of employment. The closed shop was made illegal by the Labor-Management Relations Act of 1947.

• **UNION SHOP**
A place of employment in which all workers, once employed, must become union members within a specified period of time as a condition of their continued employment.

• **RIGHT-TO-WORK LAW**
A state law providing that employees are not to be required to join a union as a condition of obtaining or retaining employment.

• **SECONDARY BOYCOTT**
A union's refusal to work for, purchase from, or handle the products of a secondary employer, with whom the union has no dispute, for the purpose of forcing that employer to stop doing business with the primary employer, with whom the union has a labor dispute.

• **HOT-CARGO AGREEMENT**
An agreement in which employers voluntarily agree with unions not to handle, use, or deal in nonunion-produced goods of other employers; a type of secondary boycott explicitly prohibited by the Labor-Management Reporting and Disclosure Act of 1959.

Labor-Management Relations Act The Labor-Management Relations Act (LMRA) of 1947[6] was passed to proscribe certain unfair union practices, such as the *closed shop*. A **closed shop** requires union membership by its workers as a condition of employment. Although the act made the closed shop illegal, it preserved the legality of the union shop. A **union shop** does not require membership as a prerequisite for employment but can, and usually does, require that workers join the union after a specified amount of time on the job.

The LMRA also prohibited unions from refusing to bargain with employers, engaging in certain types of picketing, and featherbedding (causing employers to hire more employees than necessary). The act also allowed individual states to pass their own **right-to-work laws**—laws making it illegal for union membership to be required for *continued* employment in any establishment. Thus, union shops are technically illegal in states with right-to-work laws.

Labor-Management Reporting and Disclosure Act The Labor-Management Reporting and Disclosure Act (LMRDA) of 1959[7] established an employee bill of rights and reporting requirements for union activities. The act strictly regulates internal union business procedures. Union elections, for example, are regulated by the LMRDA, which requires that regularly scheduled elections of officers occur and that secret ballots be used. Ex-convicts and Communists are prohibited from holding union office. Moreover, union officials are accountable for union property and funds. Members have the right to attend and to participate in union meetings, to nominate officers, and to vote in most union proceedings.

The act made all secondary boycotts illegal. A **secondary boycott** is a union's refusal to work for, purchase from, or handle the products of a secondary employer, with whom the union has no dispute, for the purpose of forcing that employer to stop doing business with the primary employer, with whom the union has a labor dispute. The act also outlawed **hot-cargo agreements**—agreements in which employers voluntarily agree with unions not to handle, use, or deal in nonunion-produced goods of other employers.

UNION ORGANIZATION

Suppose that the workers of a particular firm want to join a union. How is a union formed? Typically, the first step in the process is to have the workers sign authorization cards. An authorization card usually states that the worker desires to have a certain union, such as the American Federation of Labor and Congress of Industrial Organizations (AFL-CIO), represent the work force. If those in favor of the union can obtain authorization cards from a majority of the workers, they may present the cards to the employer and ask the employer to recognize the union formally. If the

6. 29 U.S.C. Sections 141 *et seq.*
7. 29 U.S.C. Sections 401 *et seq.*

employer refuses to do so, the union organizers (unionizers) can petition the NLRB for an election.

Union Elections For an election to be held, the unionizers must demonstrate that at least 30 percent of the workers to be represented support a union or an election on unionization. The NLRB supervises the election and ensures secret voting and voter eligibility. If the election is a fair one and if the proposed union receives majority support, the NLRB certifies the union as the bargaining representative for the employees.

Union Election Campaigns Many labor-management disputes arise during union election campaigns. Generally, the employer has control over unionizing activities that take place on company property and during working hours. Employers may thus limit the campaign activities of union supporters. For example, an employer may prohibit all solicitations and pamphlets on company property as long as the employer has a legitimate business reason for doing so. An owner of a department store, for instance, can prohibit all solicitation in areas of the store open to the public because union campaign activities in these circumstances could seriously interfere with the store's business. The employer may not, however, discriminate in its prohibition against solicitation in the workplace. For example, the employer could not prohibit union solicitation but allow solicitation for charitable causes.

An employer may also campaign among its workers against the union, but the NLRB carefully monitors and regulates campaign tactics by management. Otherwise, management might use its economic power to coerce the workers into voting against unionization. For example, an employer might tell its workers, "If the union wins, you'll all be fired." The NLRB prohibits employers from making such threats. If the employer issues threats or engages in other unfair labor practices, the NLRB may certify the union even though it lost the election. Alternatively, the NLRB may ask a court to order a new election.

COLLECTIVE BARGAINING

If a fair election is held and the union wins, the NLRB will certify the union as the *exclusive bargaining representative* of the workers. The central legal right of a union is to engage in collective bargaining on the members' behalf. **Collective bargaining** can be defined as the process by which labor and management negotiate the terms and conditions of employment, including wages, benefits, working conditions, and other matters. Collective bargaining allows union representatives to be elected by union members and to speak on behalf of the members at the bargaining table.

• **COLLECTIVE BARGAINING**
The process by which labor and management negotiate the terms and conditions of employment, including working hours and workplace conditions.

When a union is officially recognized, it may make a demand to bargain with the employer and negotiate new terms or conditions of employment. In collective bargaining, as in most other business negotiations, each side uses its economic power to pressure or persuade the other side to grant concessions.

Bargaining is a somewhat vague term. Bargaining does not mean that one side must give in to the other or that compromises must be made. It does mean that a demand to bargain with the employer must be taken seriously and that both sides must bargain in "good faith." Good faith bargaining means that management, for example, must be willing to meet with union representatives and consider the union's wishes when negotiating a contract. Examples of bad faith bargaining on the part of management include engaging in a campaign among workers to undermine the union, constantly shifting positions on disputed contract terms, and sending bargainers who lack authority to commit the company to a contract. If an employer (or a union) refuses to bargain in good faith without justification, it has committed an unfair labor practice, and the other party may petition the NLRB for an order requiring good faith bargaining.

STRIKING WORKERS PICKET TO PUBLICIZE THEIR LABOR DISPUTE. WHY IS THE RIGHT TO STRIKE IMPORTANT TO UNIONS?

STRIKES

Even when labor and management have bargained in good faith, they may be unable to reach a final agreement. When extensive collective bargaining has been conducted and an impasse results, the union may call a strike against the employer to pressure it into making concessions. A **strike** occurs when the unionized workers leave their jobs and refuse to work. The workers also typically picket the plant, standing outside the facility with signs that complain of management's unfairness.

A strike is an extreme action. Striking workers lose their rights to be paid, and management loses production and may lose customers, whose orders cannot be filled. Labor law regulates the circumstances and conduct of strikes. Most strikes take the form of "economic strikes," which are initiated because the union wants a better contract. A union may also strike when the employer has engaged in unfair labor practices.

• **STRIKE**
An action undertaken by unionized workers when collective bargaining fails; the workers leave their jobs, refuse to work, and (typically) picket the employer's workplace.

The right to strike is guaranteed by the NLRA, within limits, and strike activities, such as picketing, are protected by the free speech guarantee of the First Amendment to the Constitution. Nonworkers have a right to participate in picketing an employer. The NLRA also gives workers the right to refuse to cross a picket line of fellow workers who are engaged in a lawful strike. Employers are permitted to hire replacement workers to substitute for the workers who are on strike.

An important issue concerns the rights of strikers after a strike ends. In a typical economic strike over working conditions, the strikers have no right to return to their jobs. If satisfactory replacement workers are found, the strikers may find themselves out of work. The law does prohibit the employer from discriminating against former strikers, however. Employers must give former strikers preferential rights to any new vacancies that arise and also retain their seniority rights. Different rules apply when a union strikes because the employer has engaged in unfair labor practices. In this situation, the employer may still hire replacements but must give the strikers back their jobs once the strike is over.

Worker Health and Safety

Under the common law, employees injured on the job had to rely on tort law or contract law theories in suits they brought against their employers. Additionally, workers had some recourse under the common law governing agency relationships (discussed in Chapter 24), which imposes a duty on a principal-employer to provide a safe workplace for his or her agent-employee. Today, numerous state and federal statutes protect employees and their families from the risk of accidental injury, death, or disease resulting from their employment. This section discusses the primary federal statute governing health and safety in the workplace, along with state workers' compensation acts.

ON THE WEB
A good source for information relating to workplace health and safety is OSHA's Web site, which includes, among other things, the text of the Occupational Safety and Health Act of 1970, OSHA's regulatory standards and regulations, and instructions on how to file OSHA complaints. Go to www.osha.gov.

THE OCCUPATIONAL SAFETY AND HEALTH ACT

At the federal level, the primary legislation for employee health and safety protection is the Occupational Safety and Health Act of 1970.[8] Congress passed this act in an attempt to ensure safe and healthful working conditions for practically every employee in the country. The act provides for specific standards that employers must meet, plus a general duty to keep workplaces safe.

8. 29 U.S.C. Sections 553, 651–678.

Enforcement Agencies Three federal agencies develop and enforce the standards set by the Occupational Safety and Health Act. The Occupational Safety and Health Administration (OSHA) is part of the Department of Labor and has the authority to promulgate standards, make inspections, and enforce the act. OSHA has safety standards governing many workplace details, such as the structural stability of ladders and the requirements for railings. OSHA also establishes standards that protect employees against exposure to substances that may be harmful to their health.

The National Institute for Occupational Safety and Health is part of the Department of Health and Human Services. Its main duty is to conduct research on safety and health problems and to recommend standards for OSHA to adopt. Finally, the Occupational Safety and Health Review Commission is an independent agency set up to handle appeals from actions taken by OSHA administrators.

Procedures and Violations OSHA compliance officers may enter and inspect facilities of any establishment covered by the Occupational Safety and Health Act.[9] Employees may also file complaints of violations. Under the act, an employer cannot discharge an employee who files a complaint or who, in good faith, refuses to work in a high-risk area if bodily harm or death might result.

Employers with eleven or more employees are required to keep occupational injury and illness records for each employee. Each record must be made available for inspection when requested by an OSHA inspector. Whenever a work-related injury or disease occurs, employers must make reports directly to OSHA. Whenever an employee is killed in a work-related accident or when five or more employees are hospitalized in one accident, the employer must notify the Department of Labor within forty-eight hours. If the company fails to do so, it will be fined. Following the accident, a complete inspection of the premises is mandatory.

Criminal penalties for willful violation of the Occupational Safety and Health Act are limited. Employers may be prosecuted under state laws, however. In other words, the act does not preempt state and local criminal laws.[10] In the following case, an employer argued that it should not be penalized by OSHA for violating a regulation of which the employer was ignorant.

9. In the past, warrantless inspections were conducted. In 1978, however, the United States Supreme Court held that warrantless inspections violated the warrant clause of the Fourth Amendment to the Constitution. See *Marshall v. Barlow's, Inc.*, 436 U.S. 307, 98 S.Ct. 1816, 56 L.Ed.2d 305 (1978).
10. *Pedraza v. Shell Oil Co.*, 942 F.2d 48 (1st Cir. 1991); cert. denied, *Shell Oil Co. v. Pedraza*, 502 U.S. 1082, 112 S.Ct. 993, 117 L.Ed.2d 154 (1992).

CASE 37.2 Valdak Corp. v. Occupational Safety and Health Review Commission

United States Court of Appeals,
Eighth Circuit, 1996.
73 F.3d 1466.
ls.wustl.edu/8th.cir/opinions.html[a]

a. This page contains links to some of the opinions of the U.S. Court of Appeals for the Eighth Circuit. Click on the "Party Name" link. In the "Search string" box, type "Valdak" and click "Begin Search." When the results appear, click on the case number to access the opinion. This Web site is maintained by Washington University School of Law in St. Louis, Missouri.

HISTORICAL AND SOCIAL SETTING *Since the Occupational Safety and Health Act was enacted in 1970, the rates of deaths and injuries in the workplace have been cut in half. In 1970, for example, eighteen of every one hundred thousand workers were killed on the job. In 1996, the rate was eight per one hundred thousand. To prevent accidental injuries and deaths, employers often impose safety measures. Such measures are particularly important*

(Continued)

CASE 37.2—Continued

when an employer's work force is young and inexperienced, as in many restaurants, retail establishments, and car washes.

BACKGROUND AND FACTS The Valdak Corporation operates a car wash that uses an industrial dryer to spin-dry towels. The dryer was equipped with a device that was supposed to keep it locked while it spun, but the device often did not work. An employee reached into the dryer while it was spinning, and his arm was cut off above the elbow. OSHA cited Valdak for, among other things, a willful violation of a machine-guarding regulation and assessed a $28,000 penalty. Valdak appealed to the Occupational Safety and Health Review Commission, which upheld the penalty. Valdak appealed to the U.S. Court of Appeals for the Eighth Circuit, arguing in part that it did not know about the specific regulation.

IN THE WORDS OF THE COURT . . .

JOHN R. GIBSON, Circuit Judge.

* * * *

Valdak's claimed ignorance of the OSHA standard does not negate a finding of willfulness. Willfulness can be proved by "plain indifference" to the [Occupational Safety and Health Act's] requirements. Plain indifference to the machine guarding requirement is amply demonstrated by the facts that the dryer was equipped with an interlocking device, the interlocking device did not work, and Valdak continued to use the dryer with the broken interlock device. * * *

DECISION AND REMEDY The U.S. Court of Appeals for the Eighth Circuit upheld the agency's finding.

FOR CRITICAL ANALYSIS—Ethical Consideration *For what policy reasons might an employer set up a formal safety program or issue a written safety manual?*

Workers' Compensation

• **WORKERS' COMPENSATION LAWS** State statutes establishing an administrative procedure for compensating workers' injuries that arise out of—or in the course of—their employment, regardless of fault.

State **workers' compensation laws** establish an administrative procedure for compensating workers injured on the job. Instead of suing, an injured worker files a claim with the administrative agency or board that administers the local workers' compensation claims.

Most workers' compensation statutes are similar. No state covers all employees. Typically excluded are domestic workers, agricultural workers, temporary employees, and employees of common carriers (companies that provide transportation services to the public). Typically, the statutes cover minors. Usually, the statutes allow employers to purchase insurance from a private insurer or a state fund to pay workers' compensation benefits in the event of a claim. Most states also allow employers to be self-insured—that is, employers who show an ability to pay claims do not need to buy insurance.

In general, the right to recover benefits is predicated wholly on the existence of an employment relationship and the fact that the injury was *accidental* and *occurred on the job or in the course of employment,* regardless of fault. Intentionally inflicted self-injury, for example, would not be considered accidental and hence would not be covered. If an injury occurred while an employee was commuting to or from work, it would not usually be considered to have occurred on the job or in the course of employment and hence would not be covered.

An employee must notify his or her employer promptly (usually within thirty days) of an injury. Generally, an employee also must file a workers' compensation claim with the appropriate state agency or board within a certain period (sixty days to two years) from the time the injury is first noticed, rather than from the time of the accident.

An employee's acceptance of workers' compensation benefits bars the employee from suing for injuries caused by the employer's negligence. By barring lawsuits for negligence, workers' compensation laws also bar employers from raising common law defenses to negligence, such as contributory negligence, assumption of risk, or injury caused by a "fellow servant" (another employee). A worker may sue an employer who *intentionally* injures the worker, however.

The court in the following case considered whether an employee's injury in an automobile accident arose out of and in the course of employment for purposes of workers' compensation.

CASE 37.3 Rogers v. Pacesetter Corp.

Missouri Court of Appeals,
Eastern District,
Division 4, 1998.
972 S.W.2d 540.
www.osca.state.mo.us/courts/pubopinions.nsf[a]

COMPANY PROFILE *Pacesetter Corporation, which has been in the home-improvement business since 1962, calls itself "America's Leading Home Improvement Company!" Pacesetter sells a range of building supplies, including cabinet refacing, doors, siding, windows, and patio awnings and covers. The company designs, manufactures, finances the purchase of, installs, guarantees, and services its products, which are advertised as durable and energy efficient.*

a. This page contains links to some of the opinions of the Missouri state courts. Click on "Eastern District." When that page opens, click on "Search." In the "Search for the following word(s)" box, type "Pacesetter." From the results, click on the *Rogers* case name to access the opinion. This Web site is maintained by the Missouri Office of State Courts Administrator.

BACKGROUND AND FACTS Sean Rogers was a manager for Pacesetter Corporation. He worked at the Pacesetter offices from 9:00 A.M. to 9:00 P.M. Mondays through Fridays and 10:00 A.M. to 4:00 P.M. Saturdays. He also worked at home, drafting ads and conducting performance reviews, because he did not have enough time to do all of his work at the office. At the invitation of Rogers's supervisor, Rogers and the supervisor met at the River Port Club, a bar, to discuss a promotion. It was a Monday, when Rogers normally conducted performance reviews at home, which he planned to do after leaving the bar. While driving home, Rogers was injured in an automobile accident. He filed a claim for workers' compensation with the Missouri Division of Workers' Compensation. After a hearing, the administrative law judge awarded Rogers temporary compensation for a permanent partial disability. Pacesetter appealed to the Missouri Labor and Industrial Relations Commission, which reversed the award. Rogers appealed to a Missouri state court.

IN THE WORDS OF THE COURT . . .

ROBERT G. DOWD, Jr., Presiding Judge.

* * * *

An employee's injuries arise out of his employment if they are a natural and reasonable incident thereof, and they are in the course of employment if the accident occurs within the period of employment at a place where the employee may reasonably be fulfilling the duties of employment. * * *

* * * *

* * * [C]ompensation for injuries while traveling home may be proper * * * when it can genuinely * * * be said that the home has become part of the employment premises. * * * [A]n employee demonstrates this by showing a clear business use of the home at the end of the specific journey during which the accident occurred.

* * * *

(Continued)

CASE 37.3—Continued

* * * Here, Claimant [Rogers] regularly worked twelve hours, Monday through Friday, and six hours each Saturday. Claimant also regularly did work for his employer at home * * * . The night of the accident was a Monday and it was Claimant's practice to do performance reviews * * * on Monday evenings in order that on Tuesday mornings he could discuss [the employees'] performance with them. Claimant testified it was necessary to conduct these performance reviews at home because * * * "there was insufficient time to perform [his duties] during regular office hours." Moreover, * * * the work performed at home by Claimant was an integral part of the conduct of his employer's business, and not only a convenience to Claimant. Clearly a benefit accrued to employer by Claimant conducting these performance reviews at home. We conclude that * * * Claimant demonstrated that the demands of his employment created the expectation that work needed to be done at home for the benefit of his employer.

DECISION AND REMEDY The court reversed the decision of the commission and remanded the case for the entry of an award of compensation. The court held that Rogers's injury arose out of and in the course of employment for purposes of workers' compensation.

FOR CRITICAL ANALYSIS—Social Consideration *Should workers' compensation be denied to a worker who is injured off the employer's premises, regardless of the reason the worker is off the premises?*

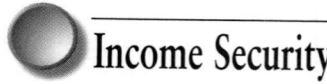

Income Security

Federal and state governments participate in insurance programs designed to protect employees and their families by covering the financial impact of retirement, disability, death, hospitalization, and unemployment. The key federal law on this subject is the Social Security Act of 1935.[11]

Social Security and Medicare

The Social Security Act provides for old age (retirement), survivors, and disability insurance. The act is therefore often referred to as OASDI. Both employers and employees must "contribute" under the Federal Insurance Contributions Act (FICA)[12] to help pay for the employees' loss of income on retirement. The basis for the employee's and the employer's contribution is the employee's annual wage base—the maximum amount of the employee's wages that are subject to the tax. The employer withholds the employee's FICA contribution from the employee's wages and then matches this contribution. (In 1999, employers were required to withhold 6.2 percent of each employee's wages, up to a maximum wage base of $72,600, and to match this contribution.)

Retired workers are then eligible to receive monthly payments from the Social Security Administration, which administers the Social Security Act. Social Security benefits are fixed by statute but increase automatically with increases in the cost of living.

¡BE AWARE! Social Security currently covers almost all jobs in the United States. Nine out of ten workers contribute to this protection for themselves and their families.

Medicare, a health-insurance program, is administered by the Social Security Administration for people sixty-five years of age and older and for some under the age of sixty-five who are disabled. It has two parts, one pertaining to hospital costs and the other to nonhospital medical costs, such as visits to doctors' offices. People who have Medicare hospital insurance can also obtain additional federal medical insurance

11. 42 U.S.C. Sections 301–1397e.
12. 26 U.S.C. Sections 3101–3125.

if they pay small monthly premiums, which increase as the cost of medical care increases. As with Social Security contributions, both the employer and the employee contribute to Medicare. Currently, 2.9 percent of the amount of *all* wages and salaries paid to employees goes toward financing Medicare. Unlike Social Security contributions, there is no cap on the amount of wages subject to the Medicare tax.

Private Pension Plans

There has been significant legislation to regulate employee retirement plans set up by employers to supplement Social Security benefits. The major federal act covering these retirement plans is the Employee Retirement Income Security Act (ERISA) of 1974.[13] This act empowers the Labor Management Services Administration of the Department of Labor to enforce its provisions governing employers who have private pension funds for their employees. ERISA does not require an employer to establish a pension plan. When a plan exists, however, ERISA establishes standards for its management.

• **VESTING**
The creation of an absolute or unconditional right or power.

A key provision of ERISA concerns vesting. **Vesting** gives an employee a legal right to receive pension benefits at some future date when he or she stops working. Before ERISA was enacted, some employees who had worked for companies for as long as thirty years received no pension benefits when their employment terminated, because those benefits had not vested. ERISA establishes complex vesting rules. Generally, however, all employee contributions to pension plans vest immediately, and employee rights to employer pension-plan contributions vest after five years of employment.

In an attempt to prevent mismanagement of pension funds, ERISA has established rules on how they must be invested. Pension managers must be cautious in their investments and refrain from investing more than 10 percent of the fund in securities of the employer. ERISA also contains detailed record-keeping and reporting requirements.

Unemployment Insurance

¡WATCH OUT!
A state government can place a lien on the property of an employer who does not pay unemployment taxes.

The United States has a system of unemployment insurance in which employers pay into a fund, the proceeds of which are paid out to qualified unemployed workers. The Federal Unemployment Tax Act (FUTA) of 1935[14] created a state-administered system that provides unemployment compensation to eligible individuals. The FUTA and state laws require employers that fall under the provisions of the act to pay unemployment taxes at regular intervals.

COBRA

Federal legislation also addresses the issue of health insurance for workers whose jobs have been terminated—and who are thus no longer eligible for group health-insurance plans. The Consolidated Omnibus Budget Reconciliation Act (COBRA) of 1985[15] prohibits the elimination of a worker's medical, optical, or dental insurance coverage on the voluntary or involuntary termination of the worker's employment. Employers, with some exceptions, must comply with COBRA if they employ twenty or more workers and provide a benefit plan to those workers. They must inform an employee of COBRA's provisions when a group health plan is established

13. 29 U.S.C. Sections 1001 *et seq.*
14. 26 U.S.C. Sections 3301–3310.
15. 29 U.S.C. Sections 1161–1169.

and if that worker faces termination or a reduction of hours that would affect his or her eligibility for coverage under the plan.

The worker has sixty days (beginning with the date that the group coverage would stop) to decide whether to continue with the employer's group insurance plan. If the worker chooses to discontinue the coverage, then the employer has no further obligation. If the worker chooses to continue coverage, however, the employer is obligated to keep the policy active for up to eighteen months. If the worker is disabled, the employer must extend coverage up to twenty-nine months. The coverage provided must be the same as that enjoyed by the worker prior to the termination or reduction of work. If family members were originally included, for example, COBRA would prohibit their exclusion. This is not a free ride for the worker, however. To receive continued benefits, he or she may be required to pay all of the premium, as well as a 2 percent administrative charge.

The employer is relieved of the responsibility to provide benefit coverage if it completely eliminates its group benefit plan. An employer is also relieved of responsibility when the worker becomes eligible for Medicare, becomes covered under a spouse's health plan, becomes insured under a different plan (with a new employer, for example), or fails to pay the premium. An employer that does not comply with COBRA risks substantial penalties, such as a tax of up to 10 percent of the annual cost of the group plan or $500,000, whichever is less.[16]

Family and Medical Leave

"It is the job of the legislature to follow the spirit of the nation, provided it is not contrary to the principles of government."

CHARLES-LOUIS DE SECONDAT, BARON DE MONTESQUIEU, 1689–1755 (French philosopher and jurist)

In 1993, Congress passed the Family and Medical Leave Act (FMLA)[17] to allow employees to take time off work for family or medical reasons. A majority of the states also have legislation allowing for a leave from employment for family or medical reasons, and many employers maintain private family-leave plans for their workers.

Coverage and Applicability of the FMLA The FMLA requires employers who have fifty or more employees to provide employees with up to twelve weeks of unpaid family or medical leave during any twelve-month period. During the employee's leave, the employer must continue the worker's health-care coverage and guarantee employment in the same position or a comparable position when the employee returns to work. An important exception to the FMLA, however, allows the employer to avoid reinstatement of a *key employee*—defined as an employee whose pay falls within the top 10 percent of the firm's work force. Additionally, the act does not apply to employees who have worked less than one year or less than twenty-five hours a week during the previous twelve months.

Generally, an employee may take family leave when he or she wishes to care for a newborn baby, an adopted child, or a foster child.[18] An employee may take medical leave when the employee or the employee's spouse, child, or parent has a "serious health condition" requiring care. For most absences, the employee must demonstrate that the health condition requires continued treatment by a health-care provider and includes a period of incapacity of more than three days.

Under regulations issued by the Department of Labor (DOL) in 1995, employees suffering from certain chronic health conditions may take FMLA leave for their own

16. Health-care legislation proposed by the Clinton administration may supersede COBRA.
17. 29 U.S.C. Sections 2601, 2611–2619, 2651–2654.
18. The foster care must be state sanctioned before such an arrangement falls within the coverage of the FMLA.

incapacities that require absences of less than three days. For example, an employee who has asthma or diabetes may have periodic episodes of illness, rather than episodes continuing over an extended period of time. Similarly, pregnancy may involve periodic visits to a health-care provider and episodes of morning sickness. According to the DOL's regulations, employees with such conditions are covered by the FMLA.

> **ON THE WEB**
> An excellent Web site for information on employee benefits—including the full text of relevant statutes, such as the FMLA or COBRA, as well as case law and current articles—is BenefitsLink. Go to **www.benefitslink.com/index.html**.

Violations of the FMLA Employers who violate the FMLA may be held liable for damages to compensate employees for unpaid wages (or salary), lost benefits, denied compensation, and actual monetary losses (such as the cost of providing for care) up to an amount equivalent to the employee's wages for twelve weeks. The employer may also be required to reinstate an employee in his or her job or grant a promotion that had been denied. A successful plaintiff is also entitled to court costs; attorneys' fees; and in cases involving bad faith on the part of the employer, double damages.

The FMLA defines an "employer" as "any person who acts, directly or indirectly, in the interest of an employer to any of the employees of such employer." Because of this broad definition, supervisors may be subject to personal liability, as employers, for violations of the act.[19]

ETHICAL ISSUE 37.1 ***Should the coverage of the FMLA be broadened?*** Now that the Family and Medical Leave Act (FMLA) has been in effect for some years, members of Congress and others are taking stock. For employees who face major illnesses or family emergencies, the FMLA has meant that they can take care of these problems without losing their jobs. Some employers even claim that they have benefited by the act. According to a study conducted by the Families and Work Institute, about 84 percent of employers regard the act has having had a positive impact on their workplaces, and nearly 25 percent of employers grant even more leave than the FMLA requires with respect to pregnancy leave.[20] Supporters of the FMLA have concluded that a problem with the act is that it does not go far enough. As it is, the act applies only to employers with fifty or more employees. This means that more than half of the work force in the private sector does not fall under the protection of the act. Congress is currently considering legislation that would broaden coverage of the law to cover employers with twenty-five or more employees and to provide leave for school-related purposes.

Employee Privacy Rights

> "We are rapidly entering the age of no privacy, where everyone is open to surveillance at all times; where there are no secrets."
>
> WILLIAM O. DOUGLAS, 1898–1980
> (Associate justice of the United States Supreme Court, 1939–1975)

Recall from Chapter 2 that there is no provision in the U.S. Constitution that guarantees a right to privacy. A personal right to privacy, however, has been inferred from other constitutional guarantees provided by the First, Third, Fourth, Fifth, and Ninth Amendments to the Constitution. In the last two decades, concerns about the privacy rights of employees have arisen in response to the sometimes invasive tactics used by employers in their efforts to monitor and screen workers. Lie-detector tests, drug tests, and other practices have increasingly been subject to challenge as violations of employee privacy rights.

19. See, for example, *Rupnow v. TRC, Inc.*, 999 F.Supp. 1046 (N.D.Ohio 1998).
20. "Five Years after Its Passage, FMLA Remains a Hot Issue," *BNA's Corporate Counsel Weekly*, September 16, 1998, p. 8.

A MAN TAKES A POLYGRAPH TEST. WHY ARE MOST EMPLOYERS PROHIBITED, IN MOST CIRCUMSTANCES, FROM REQUIRING THEIR EMPLOYEES TO TAKE POLYGRAPH TESTS?

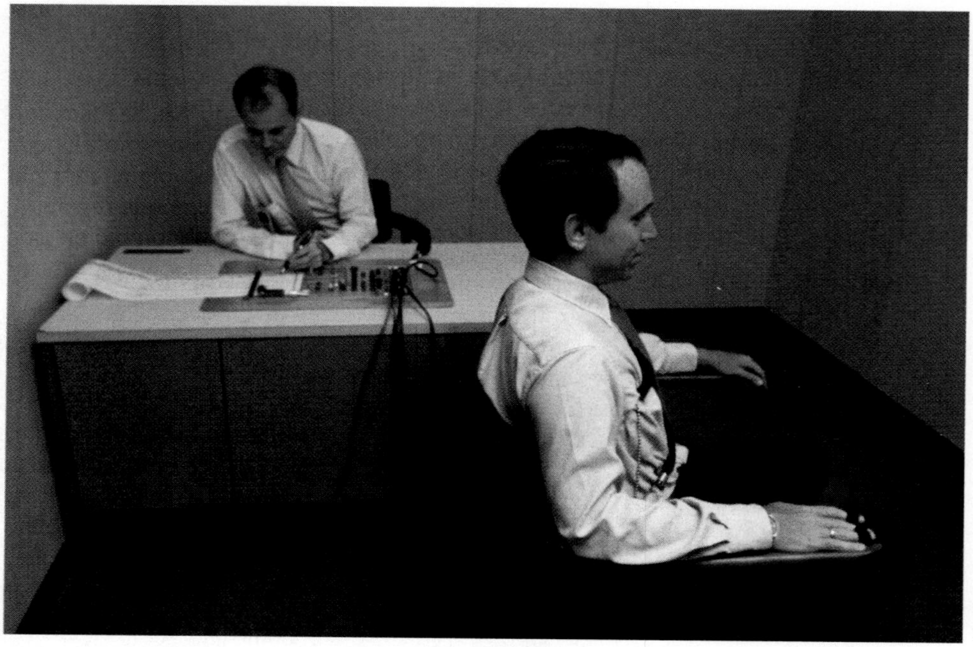

LIE-DETECTOR TESTS

At one time, many employers required employees or job applicants to take polygraph examinations (lie-detector tests) in connection with their employment. To protect the privacy interests of employees and job applicants, in 1988 Congress passed the Employee Polygraph Protection Act.[21] The act prohibits employers from (1) requiring or causing employees or job applicants to take lie-detector tests or suggesting or requesting that they do so; (2) using, accepting, referring to, or asking about the results of lie-detector tests taken by employees or applicants; and (3) taking or threatening negative employment-related action against employees or applicants based on results of lie-detector tests or on their refusal to take the tests.

Employers excepted from these prohibitions include federal, state, and local government employers; certain security service firms; and companies manufacturing and distributing controlled substances. Other employers may use polygraph tests when investigating losses attributable to theft—including embezzlement and the theft of trade secrets.

DRUG TESTING

In the interests of public safety and to reduce unnecessary costs, many of today's employers, including the government, require their employees to submit to drug testing. State laws relating to the privacy rights of private-sector employees vary from state to state. Some state constitutions may prohibit private employers from testing for drugs, and state statutes may restrict drug testing by private employers in any number of ways. A collective bargaining agreement may also provide protection against drug testing. In some instances, employees have brought an action against the employer for the tort of invasion of privacy (discussed in Chapter 4).

21. 29 U.S.C. Sections 2001 *et seq.*

Constitutional limitations apply to the testing of government employees. The Fourth Amendment provides that individuals have the right to be "secure in their persons" against "unreasonable searches and seizures" conducted by government agents. Drug tests have been held constitutional, however, when there was a reasonable basis for suspecting government employees of using drugs. Additionally, when drug use in a particular government job could threaten public safety, testing has been upheld. For example, a Department of Transportation rule that requires employees engaged in oil and gas pipeline operations to submit to random drug testing was upheld, even though the rule did not require that before being tested the individual must have been suspected of drug use.[22] The court held that the government's interest in promoting public safety in the pipeline industry outweighed the employees' privacy interests.

AIDS Testing

An increasing number of employers are testing their workers for acquired immune deficiency syndrome (AIDS). Few public issues are more controversial than this practice. Some state laws restrict AIDS testing, and federal statutes offer some protection to employees or job applicants who have AIDS or have tested positive for the AIDS virus. The federal Americans with Disabilities Act of 1990[23] (discussed in Chapter 38), for example, prohibits discrimination against persons with disabilities and the term *disability* has been broadly defined to include those individuals with diseases such as AIDS. The law also requires employers to reasonably accommodate the needs of persons with disabilities. As a rule, although the law may not prohibit AIDS testing, it may prohibit the discharge of employees based on the results of those tests.

Electronic Performance Monitoring

A particularly troublesome privacy issue concerns employers' monitoring of their employees' computer files, voice mail, e-mail, or other electronic communications. Electronic monitoring by employers may violate the Electronic Communications Privacy Act (ECPA) of 1986.[24] This act amended existing federal wiretapping law to cover electronic forms of communications, such as communications via cellular telephones or e-mail. The ECPA prohibits the intentional interception of any wire or electronic communication or the intentional disclosure or use of the information obtained by the interception.

The act excludes from coverage, however, any electronic communications through devices that are "furnished to the subscriber or user by a provider of wire or electronic communication service" and that are being used by the subscriber or user, or by the provider of the service, "in the ordinary course of its business." This "business-extension exception" to the ECPA permits employers to monitor employee electronic communications in the ordinary course of their businesses. It does not, however, permit employers to monitor employees' personal communications. Under another exception to the ECPA, employers may also avoid liability under the act if the employees consent to having their electronic communications intercepted by the employer.

Generally, there is little specific government regulation of monitoring activities, and an employer may be able to avoid what laws do exist by simply requiring employees to sign forms indicating that they consent to such monitoring. Then, if employees later challenge the monitoring practice, the employer can claim that the

22. *Electrical Workers Local 1245 v. Skinner,* 913 F.2d 1454 (9th Cir. 1990).
23. 42 U.S.C. Sections 12102–12118.
24. 18 U.S.C. Sections 2510–2521.

EXCEPTIONS BASED ON CONTRACT THEORY

Some courts have held that an *implied* employment contract exists between the employer and the employee. If the employee is fired outside the terms of the implied contract, he or she may succeed in an action for breach of contract even though no written employment contract exists. • **EXAMPLE 37.2** An employer's manual or personnel bulletin may state that, as a matter of policy, workers will be dismissed only for good cause. If the employee is aware of this policy and continues to work for the

Business Law in Action • THE AT-WILL DOCTRINE IS ALIVE AND WELL

Remember from Chapter 1 that the common law applies to all disputes that are not governed by statutory law. In the employment context, employment statutes and agency regulations have significantly narrowed the applicability of the common law doctrine of employment at will. In addition to the laws described in this chapter, a host of laws prohibiting various forms of employment discrimination also apply to the workplace, as you will read in Chapter 38. Even when the common law is applicable to a dispute, courts often make exceptions to the at-will doctrine, as discussed elsewhere in this chapter.

Because of these exceptions and the extensive array of statutory protections for workers, Americans often lose sight of the fact that approximately 85 percent of American workers have the legal status of "employees at will." In all states but Montana, an employer may fire employees for any reason or no reason if they do not have employment contracts—unless, of course, the employees fall under the protection of a state or federal statute.[a]

A problem faced by many at-will employees is that not all employers are covered by federal and state statutes regulating the workplace. For example, as already mentioned, the Family and Medical Leave Act only applies to employers that have fifty or more workers. As you will read in Chapter 38, the major federal law prohibiting employment discrimination applies only to firms with fifteen or more employees. Similarly, state laws apply only to firms with over a certain number of employees, such as eight or ten employees. Even if an employer is subject to such statutes, these laws do not apply to many types of employment disputes, such as whether or not an employment contract was formed.

Consider the situation faced by Lewis Kurtzman when he was terminated from his job with Applied Analytical Industries, Inc. (AAI). Kurtzman had worked in the pharmaceutical industry for over twenty years when he was contacted by AAI. AAI offered Kurtzman a job as director of sales for the company, which was located in Wilmington, North Carolina. Kurtzman, concerned about job security, later stated that AAI representatives made such statements as "If you do your job, you'll have a job"; "This is a long-term growth opportunity for you"; "This is a secure position"; and "We're offering you a career position." Relying on these assurances, Kurtzman and his family sold their home in Massachusetts and moved to Wilmington. Seven months after he began working for AAI, he was fired "without cause."

Kurtzman sued AAI in a North Carolina court, alleging, among other things, that AAI had breached an implied employment contract under which his employment could not be terminated without some showing of cause. The trial jury found in favor of Kurtzman and awarded him $350,000 in damages, and a state appellate court upheld the verdict. The Supreme Court of North Carolina, however, reversed the lower courts' rulings. The state's highest court stated that "[t]he employment-at-will doctrine has prevailed in this state for a century. The narrow exceptions to it have been grounded in considerations of public policy." According to the court, the facts in this case did not "present policy concerns of this nature. Rather, they are representative of negotiations and circumstances characteristically associated with traditional at-will employment situations."[b]

FOR CRITICAL ANALYSIS

Surveys indicate that a majority of Americans (66 percent) believe that it would be unlawful for an employer to discharge an employee at will, even though an employment handbook specifically reserves this right to the employer. Why is this?

a. Pauline Kim of Washington University's School of Law, as cited in Matt Seigel, "Yes, They *Can* Fire You," *Fortune*, October 26, 1998, p. 301.

b. *Kurtzman v. Applied Analytical Industries, Inc.*, 347 N.C. 329, 493 S.E.2d 420 (1997).

¡ REMEMBER!
An implied contract may exist if a party furnishes a service expecting to be paid, and the other party, who knows (or should know) of this expectation, has a chance to reject the service and does not.

employer, a court may find that there is an implied contract based on the terms stated in the manual or bulletin.●

Promises that an employer makes to employees regarding discharge policy may also be considered part of an implied contract. If the employer fires a worker in a manner contrary to the manner promised, a court may hold that the employer has violated the implied contract and is liable for damages. Most state courts will consider this claim and judge it by traditional contract standards.

A few states have gone further and held that all employment contracts contain an implied covenant of good faith. This means that both sides promise to abide by the contract in good faith. If an employer fires an employee for an arbitrary or unjustified reason, the employee can claim that the covenant of good faith was breached and the contract violated.

In the following case, one of the issues was whether there existed between an employer and its employees an implied-in-fact contract not to demote the employees without good cause.

CASE 37.4 Scott v. Pacific Gas and Electric Co.

Supreme Court of California, 1995.
11 Cal.4th 454,
904 P.2d 834,
46 Cal.Rptr.2d 427.

HISTORICAL AND ECONOMIC SETTING *Faced with more regulations than they believe they can afford to enforce and supported by the popular belief that fewer regulations help businesses prosper, many states are attempting to deregulate some industries. California is leading the way in the deregulation of the power industry. For this reason, utilities in California are facing increased competition. In response, utility firms are cutting costs to increase efficiency. Some of these cuts involve the elimination of jobs. Others involve the investigation of possible employee misconduct, such as time card fraud and conflict of interest.*

BACKGROUND AND FACTS The Pacific Gas and Electric Company (PG&E) had a system called "Positive Discipline" that, according to its personnel manual, was to apply to all employees. The basic principle was to discipline employees only for good cause. Byron Scott and Al Johnson were engineers working for PG&E as senior managers when they were demoted, allegedly for a conflict of interest from their outside consulting practice. They filed a suit in a California state court against PG&E, claiming that there was no good cause for the demotions. The court issued a judgment in their favor, and PG&E appealed. The state appellate court reversed, and the engineers appealed to the Supreme Court of California.

IN THE WORDS OF THE COURT . . .

MOSK, Justice.

* * * *

* * * PG&E had adopted a detailed system of "Positive Discipline" that was to apply to all employees * * * . PG&E employees had a reasonable expectation that the company would follow its own human resources policy, which had as its basic premise the disciplining of its employees only for good cause.

* * * Scott and Johnson committed no significant conflict of interest violations * * * . PG&E, pursuant to its personnel policies, was obliged to afford Scott and Johnson the opportunity to cure [any] relatively minor offenses through the positive discipline process, but * * * failed to do so * * * . The [trial court] therefore reasonably concluded that PG&E had breached its implied contractual agreement by wrongfully demoting Scott and Johnson.

(Continued)

CASE 37.4—Continued

DECISION AND REMEDY The Supreme Court of California reversed the decision of the intermediate appellate court and remanded the case.

FOR CRITICAL ANALYSIS—Political Consideration *What incentives do employers have to use basic principles of due process in disciplining employees?*

EXCEPTIONS BASED ON TORT THEORY

In a few cases, the discharge of an employee may give rise to an action for wrongful discharge under tort theories. Abusive discharge procedures may result in intentional infliction of emotional distress or defamation. • **EXAMPLE 37.3** In one case, a restaurant had suffered some thefts of supplies, and the manager announced that he would start firing waitresses alphabetically until the thief was identified. The first waitress fired said that she suffered great emotional distress as a result. The state's highest court upheld her claim as stating a valid cause of action.[29] •

EXCEPTIONS BASED ON PUBLIC POLICY

The most widespread common law exception to the employment-at-will doctrine is an exception made on the basis of public policy. Courts may apply this exception when an employer fires a worker for reasons that violate a fundamental public policy of the jurisdiction. For example, a court may prevent an employer from firing a worker who serves on a jury and therefore cannot work during his or her normally scheduled working hours.

Sometimes, an employer will direct an employee to do something that violates the law. If the employee refuses to perform the illegal act, the employer might decide to fire the worker. Similarly, employees who "blow the whistle" on the wrongdoing of their employers often find themselves disciplined or even out of a job. **Whistleblowing** occurs when an employee tells a government official, upper-management authorities, or the press that his or her employer is engaged in some unsafe or illegal activity. Whistleblowers on occasion have been protected from wrongful discharge for reasons of public policy. For example, a bank was held to have wrongfully discharged an employee who pressured the employer to comply with state and federal consumer credit laws.[30]

• **WHISTLEBLOWING**
An employee's disclosure to government, the press, or upper-management authorities that the employer is engaged in unsafe or illegal activities.

ETHICAL ISSUE 37.2 ***Does discrimination by small firms violate public policy?*** Employees of small businesses are often precluded from seeking protection under federal or state laws prohibiting employment discrimination. This is because, as already mentioned, these statutes typically restrict their coverage to employers that have a specified number of workers. If a small business with, say, only five or six employees discriminates against an employee, does that employee have any recourse under the common law? According to a number of courts, yes. For example, in one case a woman was fired from a veterinary clinic that had fewer than eight employees, allegedly because she became pregnant. She sued the employer for wrongful discharge on the ground that her employer's action violated the public policy against discrimination. The court held that her case could go forward because, even though the state statute prohibiting gender discrimination applied only to firms with eight or more employees, it reflected a broad public policy against gender dis-

29. *Agis v. Howard Johnson Co.*, 371 Mass. 140, 355 N.E.2d 315 (1976).
30. *Harless v. First National Bank in Fairmont*, 162 W.Va. 116, 246 S.E.2d 270 (1978).

crimination.[31] Increasingly, the courts are allowing employees in similar situations to recover damages for discrimination on public-policy grounds.

Whistleblower Statutes

To encourage workers to report employer wrongdoing, such as fraud, a number of states have enacted so-called whistleblower statutes.[32] These statutes protect whistleblowers from subsequent retaliation on the part of employers. On the federal level, the Whistleblower Protection Act of 1989[33] protects federal employees who blow the whistle on their employers from their employers' retaliatory actions. Whistleblower statutes may also provide an incentive to disclose information by providing the whistleblower with a monetary reward. For example, the federal False Claims Reform Act of 1986[34] requires that a whistleblower who has disclosed information relating to a fraud perpetrated against the U.S. government receive between 15 and 25 percent of the proceeds if the government brings suit against the wrongdoer.

31. *Roberts v. Dudley, D.V.M.*, 92 Wash.App. 652, 966 P.2d 377 (1998).
32. At least thirty-seven states now have whistleblower statutes.
33. 5 U.S.C. Section 1201.
34. 31 U.S.C. Sections 3729–3733. This act amended the False Claims Act of 1863.

International Perspective • PROTECTION FOR WHISTLEBLOWERS IN ENGLAND

England also provides legal protection for whistleblowers to some extent. The English Parliament has passed legislation protecting workers who report health and safety violations by their employers. In one case, a company dismissed a worker who reported unsafe levels of a chemical, lindane, and called in a health and safety inspector. After the company fired the worker, the worker sued the employer for violating the law protecting whistleblowers and recovered approximately $12,000 in damages.

FOR CRITICAL ANALYSIS

Why might a government be reluctant to come to the aid of all whistleblowers at all times?

APPLICATION

Law & the Employer: Establishing an E-Mail Policy*

Employers that make electronic communications systems (such as access to the Internet and e-mail) available to their employees face some obvious risks. One risk is that e-mail could be used to harass employees. Another risk is that employees could subject the employer to liability by reproducing, without authorization, copyright-protected materials on the Internet. Still another risk is that confidential information contained in e-mail messages transmitted via the Internet could be intercepted by an outside party. Finally, those employers who monitor employees' e-mail in an attempt to avoid these risks face yet another risk: the risk of being held liable for violating the employees' privacy rights.

If you are an employer and find it prudent to monitor employees' e-mail messages, you should take certain precautions. First, you should establish a comprehensive e-mail policy statement. The statement should indicate to employees why you will be monitoring their e-mail and what methods you will use in doing so. The statement should also include specific instructions concerning the form and content of e-mail messages. You might advise your employees, for example, that e-mail may only be used for business communications and that they should use the same degree of care in drafting e-mail messages as they do when drafting communications printed on company letterhead.

*This *Application* is not meant to substitute for the services of an attorney who is licensed to practice law in your state.

To underscore the importance of this rule, you can point out that e-mail messages may be subject to discovery in litigation. To avoid liability for copyright infringement, you might inform your employees that they should regard all information available on the Internet as protected by copyright.

Second, to protect yourself as fully as possible against liability under the Electronic Communications Privacy Act (ECPA) of 1986, you should have each employee sign a consent form indicating that he or she consents to have his or her e-mail messages monitored. As stated in this chapter, the ECPA prohibits the intentional and unauthorized interception of electronic communications, including e-mail, and imposes both civil and criminal liability on violators. An exception to the act is made, however, when electronic interception, or monitoring, is conducted with the employees' consent.

Finally, you should realize that state laws relating to privacy issues vary widely. Furthermore, new federal or state statutes may give more specific guidance to employers on the extent to which they can monitor their employees' communications. Additionally, case law interpreting existing state and federal statutes may change over time. For these reasons, to protect your interests fully and make sure your actions are legal, you should discuss your proposed monitoring policy with an attorney before implementing it.

CHECKLIST FOR THE EMPLOYER

1. Develop a comprehensive policy statement indicating how e-mail should and should not be used, why employees' e-mail messages are being monitored, and the methods used for monitoring.
2. Obtain employees' consent to having their electronic communications monitored.
3. Discuss your proposed monitoring policy with an attorney to make sure you fully protect your interests and stay within the limits allowed by law.

Key Terms

closed shop 954
collective bargaining 955
employment at will 950
hot-cargo agreement 954
minimum wage 952
right-to-work law 954
secondary boycott 954
strike 956
union shop 954
vesting 961
whistleblowing 970
workers' compensation laws 958
wrongful discharge 967

Chapter Summary • Employment Relationships

Wage-Hour Laws (See pages 951–952.)	1. *Davis-Bacon Act (1931)*—Requires the payment of "prevailing wages" to employees of contractors and subcontractors working on federal government construction projects. 2. *Walsh-Healey Act (1936)*—Requires that a minimum wage and overtime pay be paid to employees of firms that contract with federal agencies. 3. *Fair Labor Standards Act (1938)*—Extended wage-hour requirements to cover all employers whose activities affect interstate commerce plus certain businesses. The act has specific requirements in regard to child labor, maximum hours, and minimum wages.
Labor Unions (See pages 952–956.)	1. *Federal labor laws*— a. Norris-LaGuardia Act (1932)—Protects peaceful strikes, picketing, and primary boycotts. b. National Labor Relations Act (1935)—Established the rights of employees to engage in collective bargaining and to strike; also defined specific employer practices as unfair to labor. The National Labor Relations Board (NLRB) was created to administer and enforce the act. c. Labor-Management Relations Act (1947)—Proscribes certain unfair union practices, such as the closed shop. d. Labor-Management Reporting and Disclosure Act (1959)—Established an employee bill of rights and reporting requirements for union activities. 2. *Union organization*—Union campaign activities and elections must comply with the requirements established by federal labor laws and the NLRB. 3. *Collective bargaining*—The process by which labor and management negotiate the terms and conditions of employment (wages, benefits, working conditions, and so on). The central legal right of a labor union is to engage in collective bargaining on the members' behalf. 4. *Strikes*—When collective bargaining reaches an impasse, union members may use their ultimate weapon in labor-management struggles—the strike. A strike occurs when unionized workers leave their jobs and refuse to work.
Worker Health and Safety (See pages 956–960.)	1. The Occupational Safety and Health Act of 1970 requires employers to meet specific safety and health standards that are established and enforced by the Occupational Safety and Health Administration (OSHA). 2. State workers' compensation laws establish an administrative procedure for compensating workers who are injured in accidents that occur on the job, regardless of fault.
Income Security (See pages 960–961.)	1. *Social Security and Medicare*—The Social Security Act of 1935 provides for old-age (retirement), survivors, and disability insurance. Both employers and employees must make contributions under the Federal Insurance Contributions Act (FICA) to help pay for the employees' loss of income on retirement. The Social Security Administration administers Medicare, a health-insurance program for older or disabled persons. 2. *Private pension plans*—The federal Employee Retirement Income Security Act (ERISA) of 1974 establishes standards for the management of employer-provided pension plans. 3. *Unemployment insurance*—The Federal Unemployment Tax Act of 1935 created a system that provides unemployment compensation to eligible individuals. Covered employers are taxed to help cover the costs of unemployment compensation.
COBRA (See pages 961–962.)	The Consolidated Omnibus Budget Reconciliation Act (COBRA) of 1985 requires employers to give employees, on termination of employment, the option of continuing their medical, optical, or dental insurance coverage for a certain period.

Chapter Summary • Employment Relationships, Continued

Family and Medical Leave (See pages 962–963.)	The Family and Medical Leave Act (FMLA) of 1993 requires employers with fifty or more employees to provide their employees (except for key employees) with up to twelve weeks of unpaid family or medical leave during any twelve-month period for the following reasons: 1. *Family leave*—May be taken to care for a newborn baby, an adopted child, or a foster child. 2. *Medical leave*—May be taken when the employee or the employee's spouse, child, or parent has a serious health condition requiring care.
Privacy Rights of Employees (See pages 963–967.)	A right to privacy has been inferred from guarantees provided by the First, Third, Fourth, Fifth, and Ninth Amendments to the U.S. Constitution. State laws may also provide for privacy rights. Employer practices that are often challenged by employees as invasive of their privacy rights include lie-detector tests, drug testing, AIDS testing, performance monitoring, and screening procedures.
Employment-Related Immigration Laws (See page 967.)	1. *Immigration Reform and Control Act (1986)*—Prohibits employers from hiring illegal immigrants; administered by the U.S. Immigration and Naturalization Service. 2. *Immigration Act (1990)*—Limits the number of legal immigrants entering the United States by capping the number of visas (entry permits) that are issued each year.
Wrongful Discharge (See pages 967–971.)	Wrongful discharge occurs whenever an employer discharges an employee in violation of the law or of an employment contract. To protect employees from some of the harsh results of the common law employment-at-will doctrine (under which employers may hire or fire employees "at will" unless a contract indicates to the contrary), courts have made exceptions to the doctrine on the basis of contract theory, tort theory, and public policy.
Whistleblower Statutes (See page 971.)	Most states have passed whistleblower statutes specifically to protect employees who "blow the whistle" on their employers from subsequent retaliation by those employers. The federal Whistleblower Protection Act of 1989 protects federal employees who report their employers' wrongdoing. The federal False Claims Reform Act of 1986 provides monetary rewards for whistleblowers who disclosed information relating to fraud perpetrated against the U.S. government.

For Review

1. What is the employment-at-will doctrine? When and why are exceptions to this doctrine made?
2. What federal statute governs working hours and wages? What federal statutes govern labor unions and collective bargaining?
3. What federal act was enacted to protect the health and safety of employees? What are workers' compensation laws?
4. Under the Family and Medical Leave Act of 1993, under what circumstances may an employee take family or medical leave?
5. Does drug testing violate employees' privacy rights? What other types of activities undertaken by employers might violate the privacy rights of employees?

Questions and Case Problems

37–1. Labor Laws. Calzoni Boating Co. is an interstate business engaged in manufacturing and selling boats. The company has five hundred nonunion employees. Representatives of these employees are requesting a four-day, ten-hours-per-day workweek, and Calzoni is concerned that this would require paying time and a half after eight hours per day. Which federal act is

Calzoni thinking of that might require this? Will the act in fact require paying time and a half for all hours worked over eight hours per day if the employees' proposal is accepted? Explain.

37–2. Health and Safety Regulations. Denton and Carlo were employed at an appliance plant. Their job required them to do occasional maintenance work while standing on a wire mesh twenty feet above the plant floor. Other employees had fallen through the mesh, one of whom had been killed by the fall. When Denton and Carlo were asked by their supervisor to do work that would likely require them to walk on the mesh, they refused due to their fear of bodily harm or death. Because of their refusal to do the requested work, the two employees were fired from their jobs. Was their discharge wrongful? If so, under what federal employment law? To what federal agency or department should they turn for assistance?

37–3. Unfair Labor Practices. Suppose that Consolidated Stores is undergoing a unionization campaign. Prior to the union election, management says that the union is unnecessary to protect workers. Management also provides bonuses and wage increases to the workers during this period. The employees reject the union. Union organizers protest that the wage increases during the election campaign unfairly prejudiced the vote. Should these wage increases be regarded as an unfair labor practice? Discuss.

37–4. Workers' Compensation. Galvin Strang worked for a tractor company in one of its factories. Near his work station there was a conveyor belt that ran through a large industrial oven. Sometimes, the workers would use the oven to heat their meals. Thirty-inch-high flasks containing molds were fixed at regular intervals on the conveyor and were transported into the oven. Strang had to walk between the flasks to get to his work station. One day, the conveyor was not moving, and Strang used the oven to cook a frozen pot pie. As he was removing the pot pie from the oven, the conveyor came on. One of the flasks struck Strang and seriously injured him. Strang sought recovery under the state workers' compensation law. Should he recover? Why or why not?

37–5. Health and Safety Regulations. At an REA Express, Inc., shipping terminal, a conveyor belt was inoperative because an electrical circuit had shorted out. The manager called a licensed electrical contractor. When the contractor arrived, REA's maintenance supervisor was in the circuit breaker room. The floor was wet, and the maintenance supervisor was using sawdust to try to soak up the water. While the licensed electrical contractor was standing on the wet floor and attempting to fix the short circuit, he was electrocuted. Simultaneously, REA's maintenance supervisor, who was standing on a wooden platform, was burned and knocked unconscious. The Occupational Safety and Health Administration (OSHA) sought to fine REA Express $1,000 for failure to furnish a place of employment free from recognized hazards. Will the court uphold OSHA's decision? Discuss fully. [*REA Express, Inc. v. Brennan,* 495 F.2d 822 (2d Cir. 1974)]

37–6. Workers' Compensation. Linda Kidwell, employed as a state traffic officer by the California Highway Patrol (CHP), suffered an injury at home, off duty, while practicing the standing long jump. The jump is part of a required test during the CHP's annual physical performance program fitness test. Kidwell filed a claim for workers' compensation benefits. The CHP and the California workers' compensation appeals board denied her claim. Kidwell appealed to a state appellate court. What is the requirement for granting a workers' compensation claim? Should Kidwell's claim be granted? [*Kidwell v. Workers' Compensation Appeals Board,* 33 Cal.App.4th 1130, 39 Cal.Rptr.2d 540 (1995)]

37–7. Privacy Rights. The city of Los Angeles requires a polygraph examination for police officers who ask to be promoted or transferred into a few specialized divisions where the work is unusually sensitive and requires a high level of integrity. Generally, those who fail the test are not promoted or transferred, but neither are they demoted or otherwise penalized. The Los Angeles Protective League filed a suit against the city in a California state court, asking the court, among other things, to order the city to stop the testing. On what basis might the court grant the league's request? On what basis might it refuse to do so? [*Los Angeles Protective League v. City of Los Angeles,* 35 Cal.App.4th 1535, 42 Cal.Rptr.2d 23 (1995)]

37–8. Whistleblowing. Barbara Kraus was vice president of nursing at the New Rochelle Hospital Medical Center. She learned that a certain doctor had written on the charts of some patients that he had performed procedures for them that he had not performed, and in fact, he had not obtained consent forms from the patients to perform those procedures. She reported this to the doctor's superiors, who took little action against the doctor. Some time later, Kraus was terminated. She filed a suit in a New York state court against the hospital in order to recover damages for wrongful termination. What is required for the court to rule in Kraus's favor? [*Kraus v. New Rochelle Hospital Medical Center,* 628 N.Y.S.2d 360 (1995)]

37–9. Performance Monitoring. The Communications Operations Division (COD) of the Milwaukee Police Department (MPD) received incoming emergency calls and coordinated the dispatch of officers. All incoming emergency calls were taped. The taping system was in a glass case in the middle of the COD work area. Also, the employees knew that their supervisors might monitor their calls for evaluation and training purposes. Cynthia Griffin, a COD telecommunicator, filed a suit in a federal district court against the MPD and her supervisors, alleging that they had illegally monitored her personal calls. For what reasons might the court rule in favor of the defendants? [*Griffin v. City of Milwaukee,* 74 F.3d 824 (7th Cir. 1996)]

37–10. Wrongful Discharge. Stephen Fredrick, a pilot for Simmons Airlines, Inc., criticized the safety of the aircraft that Simmons used on many of its flights and warned the airline about the possible safety problems. Simmons took no action. After one of the planes crashed, Fredrick appeared on the television program *Good Morning America* to discuss his safety concerns. The same day, Fredrick refused to allow employees of Simmons to search his personal bags before a flight that he was scheduled to work. Claiming insubordination, the airline terminated Fredrick. Fredrick filed a suit in a federal district court against Simmons, claiming, among other things, retaliatory discharge for his public criticism of the safety of Simmons's aircraft and that this discharge violated the public policy of providing for safe air travel. Simmons responded that an employee who "goes public" with his or her concerns should not be protected by the law. Will the court agree with Simmons? Explain. [*Fredrick v. Simmons Airlines Corp.*, 144 F.3d 500 (7th Cir. 1998)]

A QUESTION OF ETHICS AND SOCIAL RESPONSIBILITY

37–11. Keith Cline worked for Wal-Mart Stores, Inc., as a night maintenance supervisor. When he suffered a recurrence of a brain tumor, he took a leave from work, which was covered by the Family and Medical Leave Act (FMLA) of 1993 and authorized by his employer. When he returned to work, his employer refused to allow him to continue his supervisory job and demoted him to the status of a regular maintenance worker. A few weeks later, the company fired him, ostensibly because he "stole" company time by clocking in thirteen minutes early for a company meeting. Cline sued Wal-Mart, alleging, among other things, that Wal-Mart had violated the FMLA by refusing to return him to his prior position when he returned to work. In view of these facts, answer the following questions. [*Cline v. Wal-Mart Stores, Inc.*, 144 F.3d 294 (4th Cir. 1998)]

1. Did Wal-Mart violate the FMLA by refusing to return Cline to his prior position when he returned to work?
2. From an ethical perspective, the FMLA has been viewed as a choice on the part of society to shift to the employer family burdens caused by changing economic and social needs. What "changing" needs does the act meet? In other words, why did Congress feel that workers should have the right to family and medical leave in 1993, but not in 1983, or 1973, or earlier?
3. "Congress should amend the FMLA, which currently applies to employers with fifty or more employees, so that it applies to employers with twenty-five or more employees." Do you agree with this statement? Why or why not?

FOR CRITICAL ANALYSIS

37–12. Employees have a right to privacy, but employers also have a right to create and maintain an efficient and safe workplace. Do you think that existing laws strike an appropriate balance between employers' rights and employees' rights?

Online Activities

ONLINE EXERCISE 37–1

Go to the "Internet Activities Book" on the Web site that accompanies this text, the URL for which is http://blt.westbuslaw.com. Select the following activities, and perform the exercises according to the instructions given there:

Activity 34–1: Family and Medical Leave
Activity 34–2: Wrongful Discharge and Whistleblowing

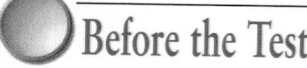

Before the Test

Go to the *Business Law Today* home page at http://blt.westbuslaw.com. Click on TestTutor.® You will find twenty interactive questions relating to this chapter.

CHAPTER 38

Employment Discrimination

"Nor shall any State . . . deny to any person within its jurisdiction the equal protection of the laws."

The Fourteenth Amendment to the U.S. Constitution

CONTENTS

LEARNING OBJECTIVES

After reading this chapter, you should be able to:

1. Indicate what types of discrimination are prohibited by federal laws.
2. List and describe the three major federal statutes that prohibit employment discrimination.
3. Distinguish between disparate-treatment discrimination and disparate-impact discrimination.
4. Summarize the remedies available to victims of employment discrimination.
5. Discuss how employers can defend against claims of employment discrimination.

During the early 1960s we, as a nation, focused our attention on the civil rights of all Americans, including our rights under the Fourteenth Amendment to the equal protection of the laws. Out of this movement to end racial and other forms of discrimination grew a body of law protecting workers against discrimination in the workplace. This protective legislation further eroded the employment-at-will doctrine, which was discussed in the previous chapter. In the past several decades, judicial decisions, administrative agency actions, and legislation have restricted the ability of employers, as well as unions, to discriminate against workers on the basis of race, color, religion, national origin, gender, age, or disability. A class of persons defined by one or more of these criteria is known as a **protected class.**

• **PROTECTED CLASS**
A group of persons protected by specific laws because of the group's defining characteristics. Under laws prohibiting employment discrimination, these characteristics include race, color, religion, national origin, gender, age, or disability.

Several federal statutes prohibit discrimination in the employment context against members of protected classes. The most important statute is Title VII of the Civil Rights Act of 1964.[1] Title VII prohibits discrimination on the basis of race, color, religion, national origin, and

1. 42 U.S.C. Sections 2000e–2000e-17.

gender at any stage of employment. Discrimination on the basis of age and disability are prohibited by the Age Discrimination in Employment Act of 1967[2] and the Americans with Disabilities Act of 1990,[3] respectively.

The focus of this chapter is on the kinds of discrimination prohibited by these federal statutes. Note, however, that discrimination against employees on the basis of any of the above-mentioned criteria may also violate state human rights statutes or other state laws or public policies prohibiting discrimination.

Title VII of the Civil Rights Act of 1964

• **EMPLOYMENT DISCRIMINATION** Treating employees or job applicants unequally on the basis of race, color, national origin, religion, gender, age, or disability; prohibited by federal statutes.

Title VII of the Civil Rights Act of 1964 and its amendments prohibit **employment discrimination** against employees, applicants, and union members on the basis of race, color, national origin, religion, and gender at any stage of employment. Title VII applies to employers with fifteen or more employees, labor unions with fifteen or more members, labor unions that operate hiring halls (to which members go regularly to be rationed jobs as they become available), employment agencies, and state and local governing units or agencies. A special section of the act prohibits discrimination in most federal government employment.

ON THE WEB

You can find the complete text of Title VII and information about the activities of the EEOC at that agency's Web site. Go to www.eeoc.gov.

THE EQUAL EMPLOYMENT OPPORTUNITY COMMISSION

Compliance with Title VII is monitored by the Equal Employment Opportunity Commission (EEOC). A victim of alleged discrimination, before bringing a suit against the employer, must first file a claim with the EEOC. The EEOC may investigate the dispute and attempt to obtain the parties' voluntary consent to an out-of-court settlement. If voluntary agreement cannot be reached, the EEOC may then file a suit against the employer on the employee's behalf. If the EEOC decides not to investigate the claim, the victim may bring his or her own lawsuit against the employer.

The EEOC does not investigate every claim of employment discrimination, regardless of the merits of the claim. In accordance with its 1996 "National Enforcement Plan," the EEOC investigates only "priority cases." The plan contains a list of the types of cases that the EEOC wants to investigate and take to litigation and those that it does not. Generally, priority cases are cases that affect many workers, cases involving retaliatory discharge (firing an employee in retaliation for submitting a claim to the EEOC), and cases involving types of discrimination that are of particular concern to the EEOC.

TYPES OF DISCRIMINATION

• **DISPARATE-TREATMENT DISCRIMINATION** A form of employment discrimination that results when an employer intentionally discriminates against employees who are members of protected classes.

Title VII prohibits both intentional and unintentional discrimination. Intentional discrimination by an employer against an employee is known as **disparate-treatment discrimination.** Because intent may sometimes be difficult to prove, courts have established certain procedures for resolving disparate-treatment cases. Suppose that a woman applies for employment with a construction firm and is rejected. If she sues on the basis of disparate-treatment discrimination in hiring, she must show that (1) she is a member of a protected class, (2) she applied and was qualified for the job in question, (3) she was rejected by the employer, and (4) the employer continued to seek applicants for the position or filled the position with a person not in a protected class.

2. 29 U.S.C. Sections 621–634.
3. 42 U.S.C. Sections 12102–12118.

• *PRIMA FACIE* CASE
A case in which the plaintiff has produced sufficient evidence of his or her conclusion that the case can go to a jury; a case in which the evidence compels the plaintiff's conclusion if the defendant produces no affirmative defense or evidence to disprove it.

If the woman can meet these relatively easy requirements, she makes out a ***prima facie* case** of illegal discrimination. Making out a *prima facie* case of discrimination means that the plaintiff has met her initial burden of proof and will win in the absence of a legally acceptable employer defense (defenses to claims of employment discrimination will be discussed later in this chapter). The burden then shifts to the employer-defendant, who must articulate a legal reason for not hiring the plaintiff. To prevail, the plaintiff must then show that the employer's reason is a *pretext* (not the true reason) and that discriminatory intent actually motivated the employer's decision.

• DISPARATE-IMPACT DISCRIMINATION
A form of employment discrimination that results from certain employer practices or procedures that, although not discriminatory on their face, have a discriminatory effect.

Employers often find it necessary to use interviews and testing procedures to choose from among a large number of applicants for job openings. Minimum educational requirements are also common. Employer practices, such as those involving educational requirements, may have an unintended discriminatory impact on a protected class. **Disparate-impact discrimination** occurs when, as a result of educational or other job requirements or hiring procedures, an employer's work force does not reflect the percentage of nonwhites, women, or members of other protected classes that characterizes qualified individuals in the local labor market. If a person challenging an employment practice having a discriminatory effect can show a connection between the practice and the disparity, he or she makes out a *prima facie* case, and no evidence of discriminatory intent needs to be shown. Disparate-impact discrimination can also occur when an educational or other job requirement or hiring procedure excludes members of a protected class from an employer's work force at a substantially higher rate than nonmembers, regardless of the racial balance in the employer's work force.

DISCRIMINATION BASED ON RACE, COLOR, AND NATIONAL ORIGIN

If a company's standards or policies for selecting or promoting employees have the effect of discriminating against employees or job applicants on the basis of race, color, or national origin, they are illegal—unless (except for race) they have a substantial, demonstrable relationship to realistic qualifications for the job in question. Discrimination against these protected classes in regard to employment conditions and benefits is also illegal. In the following case, the court had to decide whether an employer's decision to promote one employee over another constituted race-based discrimination.

CASE 38.1 McCullough v. Real Foods, Inc.

United States Court of Appeals,
Eighth Circuit, 1998.
140 F.3d 1123.
ls.wustl.edu/8th.cir/opinions.html[a]

HISTORICAL AND TECHNOLOGICAL SETTING *In grocery stores, cash registers have been replaced with scanning systems that automatically register prices, compute totals, and keep running inventories to help a grocery store maintain its stock. Some stores provide hand-held scanners to customers so that the customers can record their purchases as they shop. Many retailers use electronic benefit transfer systems to process food stamps and other forms of government welfare. Magnetic readers read e-cards to automatically deduct discounts and print out coupons based on purchases. These technological innovations contrast sharply with human attitudes, which sometimes seem slow to change.*

BACKGROUND AND FACTS In 1992, Cynthia McCullough, an African American woman with a college degree in urban affairs, began working at a deli in Chubb's Finer Foods (Real Foods, Inc.), a grocery store owned and managed by Ron Meredith. More than a year later, Meredith hired Kathy Craven, a white woman, to work at

(Continued)

a. This page contains links to opinions of the U.S. Court of Appeals for the Eighth Circuit. Click on the "Party Name" link. In the "Search string" box, type "Real Foods" and click "Begin Search." When the results appear, click on the case number to access the opinion. This Web site is maintained by Washington University School of Law in St. Louis, Missouri.

CASE 38.1—Continued

the deli. Craven had no prior deli experience, only a sixth-grade education, and poor reading and math skills. For example, Craven could not calculate prices or read recipes. McCullough and Craven were the only deli employees. Three months after Craven's arrival, Meredith appointed her "deli manager." Meredith later said that he did not promote McCullough because he "understood" that she would not work past 3:00 P.M., that she felt she was overeducated for the position, that she spoke of quitting, and that she would not accept a managerial job for the salary he was willing to pay. Denying all of what Meredith "understood," McCullough filed a suit in a federal district court against Real Foods, alleging discrimination on the basis of race. The court granted a summary judgment in favor of Real Foods, and McCullough appealed to the U.S. Court of Appeals for the Eighth Circuit.

IN THE WORDS OF THE COURT . . .
HANSEN, Circuit Judge.

* * * *

* * * McCullough had 15 months more hands-on experience working in the deli than did Craven, * * * [and] McCullough's objective educational qualifications greatly exceeded those of Craven. * * * [W]hen McCullough's education and experience are contrasted with Craven's poor reading, writing, and math skills—as evidenced by her inability to read recipes or calculate prices—a reasonable inference arises that Meredith promoted a substantially less qualified white woman over a substantially better qualified black woman. We believe it is common business practice to pick the best qualified candidate for promotion. When that is not done, a reasonable inference arises that the employment decision was based on something other than the relative qualifications of the applicants.

Critical to our analysis in this case is the extremely subjective nature of the employer's stated promotion criteria. * * * [S]ubjective criteria for promotions are particularly easy for an employer to invent in an effort to sabotage a plaintiff's *prima facie* case and mask discrimination. * * *

* * * [W]hen the employer's asserted nondiscriminatory reasons are essentially checkmated by McCullough's denials that she ever made the statements the employer advances as its nondiscriminatory reasons, the failure to promote the objectively better qualified black woman raises a reasonable, nonspeculative inference that the decision to promote the less qualified white woman was based on an impermissible consideration—in this case race.

DECISION AND REMEDY The U.S. Court of Appeals for the Eighth Circuit reversed the lower court's judgment and remanded the case for trial. The court held McCullough raised an inference that Real Foods's articulated reasons for promoting Craven were a pretext and that the real reason was illegal discriminatory intent.

FOR CRITICAL ANALYSIS—Social Consideration *When applying Title VII in cases such as McCullough's, do you think that courts are acting as "super-personnel departments reviewing the wisdom or fairness of the business judgments made by employers"?*

DISCRIMINATION BASED ON RELIGION

Title VII of the Civil Rights Act of 1964 also prohibits government employers, private employers, and unions from discriminating against persons because of their religion. An employer must "reasonably accommodate" the religious practices of its employees, unless to do so would cause undue hardship to the employer's business. For example, if an employee's religion prohibits him or her from working on a certain day of the week or at a certain type of job, the employer must make a reasonable attempt to accommodate these religious requirements. Employers must reasonably accommodate an employee's religious belief even if the belief is not based on the tenets or dogma of a particular church, sect, or denomination. The only requirement is that the belief be sincerely held by the employee.[4]

DISCRIMINATION BASED ON GENDER

"A sign that says 'men only' looks very different on a bathroom door than a courthouse door."

THURGOOD MARSHALL, 1908–1993
(Associate justice of the United States Supreme Court, 1967–1991)

Under Title VII, as well as other federal acts, employers are forbidden to discriminate against employees on the basis of gender. Employers are prohibited from classifying jobs as male or female and from advertising in help-wanted columns that are designated male or female unless the employer can prove that the gender of the applicant is essential to the job. Furthermore, employers cannot have separate male and female seniority lists.

Generally, to succeed in a suit for gender discrimination, a plaintiff must demonstrate that gender was a determining factor in the employer's decision to hire, fire, or promote him or her. Typically, this involves looking at all of the surrounding circumstances.

The Pregnancy Discrimination Act of 1978,[5] which amended Title VII, expanded the definition of gender discrimination to include discrimination based on pregnancy. Women affected by pregnancy, childbirth, or related medical conditions must be treated—for all employment-related purposes, including the receipt of benefits under employee-benefit programs—the same as other persons not so affected but similar in ability to work.

In the following case, the plaintiff charged the defendant with gender discrimination. The plaintiff made out a *prima facie* case, and the defendant presented a nondiscriminatory reason as a defense. Was the defendant's reason a pretext covering a discriminatory motive? That was the question before the court.

4. *Frazee v. Illinois Department of Employment Security,* 489 U.S. 829, 109 S.Ct. 1514, 103 L.Ed.2d 914 (1989).
5. 42 U.S.C. Section 2000e(k).

CASE 38.2 Carey v. Mount Desert Island Hospital

United States Court of Appeals,
First Circuit, 1998.
156 F.3d 31.
www.law.emory.edu/1circuit/aug98[a]

COMPANY PROFILE *Mount Desert Island Hospital (MDI) is a forty-nine-bed facility in Bar Harbor, Maine, with a medical staff that specializes in family practice, general surgery, internal medicine, ophthalmology, pathology, and radiology. A consulting staff includes practitioners of other medical specialties. MDI also operates an occupational health service, community health education, and affiliated health centers: Community Health Center in Southwest Harbor; Family Health Center, Women's Health Center, Breast Center, and High Street Health Center in Bar Harbor; and Northeast Harbor Clinic, open seasonally in Northeast Harbor. MDI is licensed by the state of Maine and fully accredited by the Joint Commission on Accreditation of Healthcare Organizations.*

BACKGROUND AND FACTS Michael Carey was a vice president in charge of the finance department for Mount Desert Island Hospital (MDI). When the position of chief executive officer (CEO) opened up, Carey applied, and his application was endorsed by Dan Hobbs, the acting CEO. At the time, an audit of the finance department revealed some deficiencies, but the auditor concluded that the department was "already attacking the problem." MDI's board offered the CEO post to Leslie Hawkins, a woman, who accepted. Less than a year later, Hawkins terminated

(Continued)

a. This page contains links to opinions of the U.S. Court of Appeals for the First Circuit decided in August 1998. Click on the *Carey* case name to access the opinion. This Web site is maintained by Emory University School of Law in Atlanta, Georgia.

CASE 38.2—Continued

Carey, giving as reasons the problems cited in the audit and "lack of confidence" in Carey. Carey filed a suit in a federal district court against MDI for gender discrimination in violation of Title VII and other laws. Evidence introduced during the trial included a statement by one female executive that "we have different standards for men and women," with regard to discipline and termination; and a statement by another female executive that "it's about time that we get a woman for this [CEO] position." The court awarded Carey more than $300,000 in damages. MDI appealed to the U.S. Court of Appeals for the First Circuit.

IN THE WORDS OF THE COURT . . .
COFFIN, Senior Circuit Judge.

* * * *

* * * [T]his was a case with much to say on either side, involving the always difficult question of probing the wellsprings of human motivation. * * *

* * * *

In a case such as this, where a plaintiff must rely on circumstantial as opposed to direct evidence of gender discrimination, the evidence will necessarily be composed of bits and pieces, which may or may not point to an atmosphere of gender discrimination. While an employer should not find itself in jeopardy by reason of occasional stray remarks by ordinary employees, circumstantial evidence of a discriminatory atmosphere at a plaintiff's place of employment is relevant to the question of motive in considering a discrimination claim * * * .

* * * *

* * * [Based on the record, we] hold that there was sufficient evidence to support a finding that deficiencies in Carey's handling of financial controls were not the real reason for his discharge but instead covered an action stemming from gender discrimination.

DECISION AND REMEDY The U.S. Court of Appeals for the First Circuit affirmed the lower court's judgment. The court held that that there was sufficient evidence to support a finding that the reason for Carey's discharge was gender discrimination.

FOR CRITICAL ANALYSIS—Cultural Consideration
Is it possible for jurors and judges to overcome their own prejudices in deciding cases in which gender plays a key role?

SEXUAL HARASSMENT

• **SEXUAL HARASSMENT**
In the employment context, the granting of job promotions or other benefits in return for sexual favors, or language or conduct that is so sexually offensive that it creates a hostile working environment.

Title VII also protects employees against **sexual harassment** in the workplace. Sexual harassment has often been classified as either *quid pro quo* harassment or hostile-environment harassment. *Quid pro quo* is a Latin phrase that is often translated to mean "something in exchange for something else." *Quid pro quo* harassment occurs when job opportunities, promotions, salary increases, and so on are given in return for sexual favors. According to the United States Supreme Court, hostile-environment harassment occurs when "the workplace is permeated with discriminatory intimidation, ridicule, and insult, that is sufficiently severe or pervasive to alter the conditions of the victim's employment and create an abusive working environment."[6]

Generally, the courts apply this Supreme Court guideline on a case-by-case basis. Some courts have held that just one incident of sexually offensive conduct—such as a sexist remark by a co-worker or a photo on an employer's desk of his bikini-clad

6. *Harris v. Forklift Systems*, 510 U.S. 17, 114 S.Ct. 367, 126 L.Ed.2d 295 (1993).

wife—can create a hostile environment.[7] At least one court has held that a worker may recover damages under Title VII because *other* persons were harassed sexually in the workplace.[8] According to some employment specialists, employers should assume that hostile-environment harassment has occurred if an employee claims that it has. (See this chapter's feature entitled *Technology and Online Sexual Harassment* on the previous page for a discussion of how e-mail and online communications may create a hostile environment.)

ON THE WEB

The law firm of Arent Fox discusses current issues in the area of employment law, including sexual harassment, in its online newsletter, "Arent Fox Employment News," at www.arentfox.com/newslett/employ.htm.

7. For other examples, see *Radtke v. Everett*, 442 Mich. 368, 501 N.W.2d 155 (1993); and *Nadeau v. Rainbow Rugs, Inc.*, 675 A.2d 973 (Me. 1996).
8. *Leibovitz v. New York City Transit Authority*, 4 F.Supp.2d 144 (E.D.N.Y. 1998).

Technology and Online Sexual Harassment

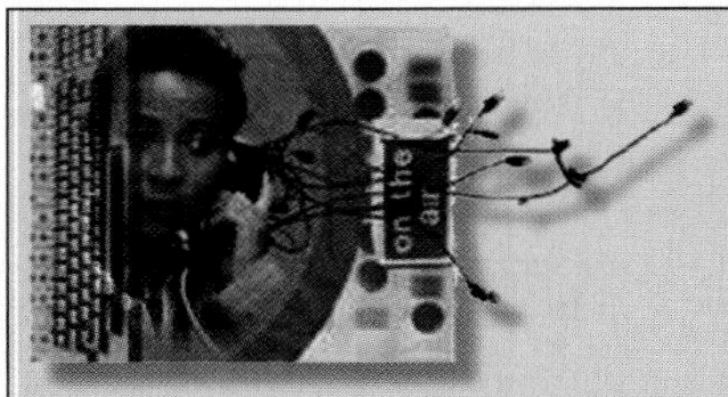

Today's "wired" workplace has made life easier in many ways for employers and employees alike, but it also has presented some problems. A significant problem is that employees who access Web sites containing sexually explicit materials, racist cartoons, and pornographic images can create a hostile environment for their co-workers. For example, a woman may walk by a co-worker's desk and see some images on that worker's computer screen that she finds objectionable. An employee may download materials from a pornographic site to the company's computer system, which another employee accidentally views. A worker might print out a sexually explicit image and forget to remove it from the printer before a co-worker happens to see it.

Racial jokes, ethnic slurs, or other comments contained in e-mail may also be the basis for a claim of hostile-environment harassment or other form of discrimination. In one case, for example, Chevron Corporation had to pay $2.2 million to four female employees who claimed that they had been sexually harassed by e-mail messages.[a]

Just one successful suit for harassment against a small company can bankrupt that firm. Even if a worker does not succeed in the suit, the legal fees incurred by defending against the claim—and the possible harm to the firm's reputation—could be devastating for the firm's profits. Not surprisingly, many employers are establishing workplace policies for their employees' Internet use. As discussed in Chapter 37, some companies use special software to block employees' access to certain Web sites. Others prohibit their employees from using the Internet at all or allow employees to use it only for business purposes. A number of companies also monitor their employees' use of the Internet, including their e-mail, in an attempt to increase worker productivity as well as to minimize the risk of lawsuits for harassment.

Generally, employers who want to avoid online harassment in the workplace seem to be caught between the proverbial "rock and a hard place." On the one hand, if they do not take effective steps to curb such harassment, they may face liability for violating Title VII. On the other hand, if they monitor their employees' communications, they may face liability under other laws—for invading their employees' privacy, for example. Additionally, there are constitutional rights to be considered. As one federal appellate court noted, "Where pure expression is involved, Title VII steers into the territory of the First Amendment. . . . [W]hen Title VII is applied to sexual-harasssment claims based solely on verbal insults or pictorial or literary matter, the statute imposes content-based . . . restrictions on speech."[b] In another case, an Oregon court held that religious speech that unintentionally creates a hostile environment is constitutionally protected.[c]

FOR CRITICAL ANALYSIS

Can you think of any ways, other than those mentioned above, in which Internet use in the workplace could create a hostile environment?

a. Tamar Lewin, "Chevron Settles Sexual Harassment Charges," *The New York Times*, February 21, 1995, p. A14. See also *Owens v. Morgan Stanley & Co.*, 1997 WL 793004 (S.D.N.Y. 1997).

b. *De Angelis v. El Paso Municipal Police Officers Association*, 51 F.3d 591 (5th Cir. 1995).

c. *Meltebeke v. B.O.L.I.*, 903 P.2d 351 (Ore. 1995).

Harassment by Supervisors and Co-Workers What if an employee is harassed by a manager or supervisor of a large firm, and the firm itself (the "employer") is not aware of the harassment? Should the employer be held liable for the harassment nonetheless? For some time, the courts were in disagreement on this issue. Typically, employers were held liable for Title VII violations by the firm's managerial or supervisory personnel in *quid pro quo* harassment cases regardless of whether the employer knew about the harassment. In hostile-environment cases, the majority of courts tended to hold employers liable only if the employer knew or should have known of the harassment and failed to take prompt remedial action. In 1998, the Supreme Court addressed this issue and set forth some significant guidelines (see this chapter's *Business Law in Action* for details).

Often, employees alleging harassment complain that the actions of co-workers, not supervisors, are responsible for creating a hostile working environment. In such cases, the employee still has a cause of action against the employer. Normally, though, the employer will be held liable only if it knew, or should have known, about the harassment and failed to take immediate remedial action.

International Perspective • SEXUAL HARASSMENT IN OTHER NATIONS

The problem of sexual harassment in the workplace is not confined to the United States. Indeed, it is a worldwide problem for women workers. In Egypt, Turkey, Argentina, Brazil, and many other countries, there is no legal protection against any form of employment discrimination. Even in those countries that do have laws prohibiting discriminatory employment practices, including gender-based discrimination, those laws often do not specifically include sexual harassment as a discriminatory practice. Several countries have attempted to remedy this omission by passing new laws or amending others to specifically prohibit sexual harassment in the workplace. Japan, for example, has amended its Equal Employment Opportunity Law to include a provision making sexual harassment illegal. The revised law went into effect in 1999. In 1998, Thailand passed its first sexual-harassment law. The European Union, which some years ago outlawed gender-based discrimination, is considering a proposal that would specifically identify sexual harassment as a form of discrimination. In the meantime, old traditions die hard. Women's support groups throughout Europe contend that corporations in European countries tend to view sexual harassment with "quiet tolerance." They contrast this attitude with that of most U.S. corporations, which have implemented specific procedures to deal with harassment claims.

FOR CRITICAL ANALYSIS
Why do you think U.S. corporations are more aggressive than European companies in taking steps to prevent sexual harassment in the workplace?

Harassment by Nonemployees Employers may also be liable for harassment by *nonemployees* in certain circumstances. • **EXAMPLE 38.1** If a restaurant owner or manager knows that a certain customer repeatedly harasses a waitress and permits the harassment to continue, the restaurant owner may be liable under Title VII even though the customer is not an employee of the restaurant. The issue turns on the control that the employer exerts over a nonemployee. In one case, an owner of a Pizza Hut franchise was held liable for the harassment of a waitress by two male customers because no steps were taken to prevent the harassment.[9] •

Same-Gender Harassment The courts have also had to address the issue of whether men who are harassed by other men, or women who are harassed by other

9. *Lockard v. Pizza Hut, Inc.*, 162 F.3d 1062 (10th Cir. 1998).

Business Law in Action • SUPREME COURT GUIDELINES ON LIABILITY FOR SEXUAL HARASSMENT

In 1998, in two separate cases, the United States Supreme Court issued some significant guidelines relating to the liability of employers for their supervisors' harassment of employees in the workplace.

In one case, *Faragher v. City of Boca Raton*,[a] the issue was whether the employer could be held liable for a supervisor's harassment of employees even though the employer was unaware of the behavior. The case was brought by Beth Faragher, who, while working as a lifeguard for the city of Boca Raton, Florida, had allegedly been sexually harassed by male supervisors. When Faragher complained to a supervising captain about the harassment, the captain said that there was nothing he could do about it. When the case reached the Supreme Court, the Court ruled that the city could be held liable in these circumstances even though it was unaware of the behavior. The Court reached this conclusion primarily because, although the city had a written policy against sexual harassment, the policy had not been distributed to city employees. Additionally, the city had not established any procedures that could be followed by employees who felt that they were victims of sexual harassment.

In the other case, *Burlington Industries, Inc. v. Ellerth*,[b] the Court focused on whether a company could be held liable for the harassment of an employee by one of its vice presidents even though the employee suffered no adverse job consequences. The case was brought by Kimberly Ellerth, who claimed that she had been subjected to offensive sexual advances by a company vice president when she worked for Burlington Industries, Inc. Ellerth never complained to Burlington's human resources department about the behavior, and her refusal to accommodate the vice president's sexual wishes never caused her to be fired or demoted—in fact, she was promoted before leaving the company and bringing her harassment suit. Burlington argued that before it could be held liable, Ellerth would have to prove that she was fired or demoted because she did not submit to the vice president's sexual advances. The Supreme Court ruled that an employer could be liable for sexual harassment even if the employee did not suffer any adverse job consequences. (For excerpts from the Court's opinion in this case, see the *Extended Case Study* that follows this chapter.)

These two cases established some common-sense guidelines on liability for workplace harassment that will be helpful to employers and employees alike. On the one hand, employees benefit by the ruling that employers may be held liable for their supervisors' harassment even though they were unaware of the actions and even though the employees suffered no adverse job consequences. On the other hand, the Court made it clear in both decisions that employers have an affirmative defense against liability for their supervisors' harassment of employees if they can show that (1) they have taken "reasonable care to prevent and correct promptly any sexually harassing behavior" (by establishing effective harassment policies and complaint procedures, for example), and (2) the employee suing for harassment failed to follow these policies and procedures.

FOR CRITICAL ANALYSIS

The Court indicated at one point that an employer's potential liability for sexual harassment in the workplace might be considered just one of the "costs of doing business." Is it fair to impose such a burden on businesses? Would it be fair not to do so?

a. ___ U.S. ___, 118 S.Ct. 2275, 141 L.Ed.2d 662 (1998).

b. 524 U.S. 742 , 118 S.Ct. 2257, 141 L.Ed.2d 633 (1998).

women, are also protected by laws that prohibit gender-based discrimination in the workplace. For example, what if the male president of a firm demands sexual favors from a male employee? Does this action qualify as sexual harassment? For some time, the courts were widely split on this issue. In 1998, in *Oncale v. Sundowner Offshore Services, Inc.*,[10] the Supreme Court resolved the issue by holding that Title VII protection extended to situations in which individuals are harassed by members of the same sex.

10. 523 U.S. 75, 118 S.Ct. 998, 140 L.Ed.2d 207 (1998).

REMEDIES UNDER TITLE VII

Employer liability under Title VII may be extensive. If the plaintiff successfully proves that unlawful discrimination occurred, he or she may be awarded reinstatement, back pay, retroactive promotions, and damages. Prior to the Civil Rights Act of 1991, damages were not available under Title VII. Plaintiffs alleging racial discrimination therefore often brought actions under 42 U.S.C. Section 1981. Section 1981, which was enacted as part of the Civil Rights Act of 1866, prohibits discrimination on the basis of race or ethnicity in the formation or enforcement of contracts. The 1991 Civil Rights Act allowed compensatory damages to be awarded in cases brought under other employment laws, such as Title VII, thus significantly broadening the rights of victims of employment discrimination.

Under the 1991 act, compensatory damages are available only in cases of intentional discrimination. The statute also stipulates that compensatory damages shall not include back pay, interest on back pay, or other relief already available under Title VII. Punitive damages may be recovered against a private employer only if the employer acted with malice or reckless indifference to an individual's rights. The sum of the amount of compensatory and punitive damages is limited by the statute to specific amounts against specific employers—ranging from $50,000 against employers with one hundred or fewer employees to $300,000 against employers with more than five hundred employees.

ETHICAL ISSUE 38.1 ***Should employees be deprived of statutory remedies because of arbitration clauses in their contracts?*** An ongoing issue in employment relationships concerns arbitration clauses in employment contracts. On the one hand, public policy, as expressed in the Federal Arbitration Act of 1925 and various state statutes, favors arbitration or some other method of alternative dispute resolution in the settlement of employment disputes. Remember from Chapter 3 that the Supreme Court, in *Gilmer v. Interstate Johnson/Lane Corp.,*[11] held that arbitration agreements will be enforced even though an employee claims protection under a specific federal statute governing employees. In *Gilmer,* the relevant statute was the Age Discrimination in Employment Act (ADEA) of 1967. On the other hand, critics of this policy (and of the Supreme Court's decision in *Gilmer*) claim that all employees, even those who sign contracts containing arbitration clauses, should be allowed to pursue remedies for employment discrimination provided by Title VII, the ADEA, and the Americans with Disabilities Act of 1990. Some recent court decisions indicate a similar concern. In a 1998 case reviewed by the Eleventh Circuit Court of Appeals, for example, the court refused to compel the arbitration of a Title VII claim because the arbitration clause at issue provided that damages could be awarded only for breach of contract.[12] Even more significantly, the United States Supreme Court recently held, in *Wright v. Universal Maritime Services Corp.,*[13] that an arbitration clause in a union contract was not binding because it did not "contain a clear and unmistakable waiver" of the right of union members to sue. According to Justice Scalia, "The right to a federal judicial forum is of sufficient importance" that it cannot be casually waived.

11. 500 U.S. 20, 111 S.Ct. 1647, 114 L.Ed.2d 26 (1991).
12. *Paladino v. Avnet Computer Technologies, Inc.,* 134 F.3d 1054 (11th Cir. 1998).
13. ___U.S. ___, 119 S.Ct. 391, 142 L.Ed.2d 361 (1998).

Equal Pay Act of 1963

The Equal Pay Act of 1963 was enacted as an amendment to the Fair Labor Standards Act of 1938. Basically, the act prohibits gender-based discrimination in the wages paid for equal work on jobs when their performance requires equal skill, effort, and responsibility under similar conditions. It is job content rather than job description that controls in all cases. To determine whether the Equal Pay Act has been violated, a court will thus look to the primary duties of the two jobs. The jobs of a barber and a beautician, for example, are considered essentially "equal." So, too, are those of a tailor and a seamstress. For the equal pay requirements to apply, the act requires that male and female employees must work at the same establishment.

A wage differential for equal work is justified if it is shown to be because of (1) seniority, (2) merit, (3) a system that pays according to quality or quantity of production, or (4) any factor other than gender. Small differences in job content, however, do not justify higher pay for one gender.

Discrimination Based on Age

Age discrimination is potentially the most widespread form of discrimination, because anyone—regardless of race, color, national origin, or gender—could be a victim at some point in life. The Age Discrimination in Employment Act (ADEA) of 1967, as amended, prohibits employment discrimination on the basis of age against individuals forty years of age or older. An amendment to the act prohibits mandatory retirement for nonmanagerial workers. For the act to apply, an employer must have twenty or more employees, and the employer's business activities must affect interstate commerce.

¡REMEMBER! The Fourteenth Amendment prohibits any state from denying any person "the equal protection of the laws." This prohibition applies to the *federal* government through the due process clause of the Fifth Amendment.

The burden-shifting procedure under the ADEA is similar to that under Title VII. If a plaintiff can establish that he or she (1) was a member of the protected age group, (2) was qualified for the position from which he or she was discharged, and (3) was discharged under circumstances that give rise to an inference of discrimination, the plaintiff has established a *prima facie* case of unlawful age discrimination. The burden then shifts to the employer, who must articulate a legitimate reason for the discrimination. If the plaintiff can prove that the employer's reason is only a pretext and that the plaintiff's age was a determining factor in the employer's decision, the employer will be held liable under the ADEA.

Numerous cases of alleged age discrimination have been brought against employers who, to cut costs, replaced older, higher-salaried employees with younger, lower-salaried workers. Whether a firing is discriminatory or simply part of a rational business decision to prune the company's ranks is not always clear. Companies generally defend a decision to discharge a worker by asserting that the worker could no longer perform his or her duties or that the worker's skills were no longer needed. The employee must prove that the discharge was motivated, at least in part, by age bias. Proof that qualified older employees are generally discharged before younger employees or that co-workers continually made unflattering age-related comments about the discharged worker may be enough.

In the past, courts had sometimes held that to establish a *prima facie* case of age discrimination, the plaintiff must also prove that he or she was replaced by a person outside the protected class—that is, by a person under the age of forty years. In 1996, however, in *O'Connor v. Consolidated Coin Caterers Corp.*,[14] the United

14. 517 U.S. 308, 116 S.Ct 1307, 134 L.Ed.2d 433 (1996).

States Supreme Court held that a cause of action for age discrimination under the ADEA does not require the replacement worker to be outside the protected class. Rather, the issue in all ADEA cases turns on whether age discrimination has, in fact, occurred, regardless of the age of the replacement worker. In the following case, the court had to decide whether there was sufficient evidence to support a jury's finding of discrimination on the basis of age.

CASE 38.3 Rhodes v. Guiberson Oil Tools

United States Court of Appeals,
Fifth Circuit, 1996.
75 F.3d 989.

HISTORICAL AND ECONOMIC SETTING *Exploring and drilling for oil is an expensive operation; drills, pipes, pumps, testing and measuring equipment, trucks, tankers, helicopters, and a variety of services are utilized. Suppliers of these products and services depend entirely on the activities of oil companies in the field. If no one is drilling for oil, the suppliers are out of business. In 1986, the oil industry was in the throes of a severe economic downturn.*

BACKGROUND AND FACTS Calvin Rhodes sold oil field equipment for Guiberson Oil Tools. When he was discharged in 1986 at age fifty-six, he was told that the discharge was part of a reduction in the work force (RIF), and that he would be considered for reemployment. Within six weeks, Guiberson hired a forty-two-year-old person to do the same job. Rhodes filed a suit in a federal district court against Guiberson under the Age Discrimination in Employment Act. At the trial, Guiberson officials testified that they had not told Rhodes the truth about why they discharged him and that they had intended to replace him. Guiberson offered as a defense Rhodes's "poor work performance" but did not present any company sales records or goals. Rhodes countered with customers' testimony about his expertise and diligence. The jury found that Rhodes was discharged because of his age. Guiberson appealed to the U.S. Court of Appeals for the Fifth Circuit.

IN THE WORDS OF THE COURT . . .
W. EUGENE DAVIS and *DUHE*, Circuit Judges:

* * * *

Based on this evidence, the jury was entitled to find that the reasons given for Rhodes' discharge were pretexts for age discrimination. The jury was entitled to find that Guiberson's stated reason for discharging Rhodes—RIF—was false. Additionally, the reason for discharge that Guiberson Oil proffered in court * * * was countered with evidence from which the jury could have found that Rhodes was an excellent salesman who met Guiberson Oil's legitimate productivity expectations. * * * [A] reasonable jury could have found that Guiberson Oil discriminated against Rhodes on the basis of his age.

DECISION AND REMEDY The U.S. Court of Appeals for the Fifth Circuit affirmed the jury's finding.

FOR CRITICAL ANALYSIS—Ethical Consideration *If age is not the sole reason for an adverse employment decision, how significant a factor do you think it should be to support a finding of discrimination?*

Discrimination Based on Disability

The Americans with Disabilities Act (ADA) of 1990 is designed to eliminate discriminatory employment practices that prevent otherwise qualified workers with disabilities from fully participating in the national labor force. Prior to 1990, the major federal law providing protection to those with disabilities was the Rehabilitation Act of 1973. That act covered only federal government employees and those employed under federally funded programs. The ADA extends federal protection against disability-based discrimination to all workplaces with fifteen or more workers. Basically, the ADA requires that employers "reasonably accommodate" the needs of persons with disabilities unless to do so would cause the employer to suffer an "undue hardship."

To prevail on a claim under the ADA, a plaintiff must show that he or she (1) has a disability, (2) is otherwise qualified for the employment in question, and (3) was excluded from the employment solely because of the disability. As in Title VII cases, a claim alleging violation of the ADA may be commenced only after the plaintiff has pursued the claim through the EEOC. Plaintiffs may sue for many of the same remedies available under Title VII. They may seek reinstatement, back pay, a limited amount of compensatory and punitive damages (for intentional discrimination), and certain other forms of relief. Repeat violators may be ordered to pay fines of up to $100,000.

WHAT IS A DISABILITY?

The ADA is broadly drafted to define persons with disabilities as persons with a physical or mental impairment that "substantially limits" their everyday activities. More specifically, the ADA defines *disability* as "(1) a physical or mental impairment that substantially limits one or more of the major life activities of such individuals; (2) a record of such impairment; or (3) being regarded as having such an impairment."

Generally, the determination of whether an individual has a disability as defined by the ADA is made on a case-by-case basis. Unlike plaintiffs in cases brought under Title VII or the ADEA, who clearly either are or are not members of the classes protected by those acts, a plaintiff suing under the ADA must *prove* that he or she has a disability—and thus falls under the protection of the ADA. Meeting this first requirement for a case of disability-based discrimination is sometimes difficult.

CO-WORKERS DISCUSS BUSINESS MATTERS. WHICH WORKERS WITH DISABILITIES ARE PROTECTED FROM EMPLOYMENT DISCRIMINATION BY THE AMERICANS WITH DISABILITIES ACT?

Health conditions that have been considered disabilities under federal law include blindness, alcoholism, heart disease, cancer, muscular dystrophy, cerebral palsy, paraplegia, diabetes, acquired immune deficiency syndrome (AIDS), and morbid obesity (defined as existing when an individual's weight is two times that of the normal person).[15] The ADA excludes from coverage certain conditions, such as kleptomania.

One issue that frequently arises in ADA cases is whether a person whose disability is controlled by medication still qualifies for protection under the ADA. For example, a federal appellate court recently reviewed a case involving a person who suffers from high blood pressure but functions "normally" when the problem is controlled by medication. According to the court, in these circumstances the person could not be considered "disabled."[16] Generally, however, the courts are divided on this issue.

For some time, the courts were split on another issue: Should a person who is infected with the human immunodeficiency virus (HIV) but who has no symptoms of AIDS come under the protection of the ADA as a person with a disability? In 1998, the Supreme Court resolved this issue by holding that an HIV infection is a disability even if the infection has not yet progressed to the symptomatic phase.[17]

15. *Cook v. Rhode Island Department of Mental Health*, 10 F.3d 17 (1st Cir. 1993).
16. *Murphy v. United Parcel Service, Inc.*, 141 F.3d 1185 (10th Cir. 1998).
17. *Bragdon v. Abbott*, __U.S.__, 118 S.Ct. 2196, 141 L.Ed.2d 540 (1998). This case is presented as the sample court case in Chapter 1.

> **ON THE WEB**
> An abundance of helpful information on disability-based discrimination, including the text of the ADA, can be found online at janweb.icdi.wvu.edu/kinder.

Reasonable Accommodation

The ADA does not require that *unqualified* applicants with disabilities be hired or retained. Therefore, employers are not obligated to accommodate the needs of job applicants or employees with disabilities who are not otherwise qualified for the work. If a job applicant or an employee with a disability, with reasonable accommodation, can perform essential job functions, however, then the employer must make the accommodation. Required modifications may include installing ramps for a wheelchair, establishing more flexible working hours, creating or modifying job assignments, and creating or improving training materials and procedures.

Generally, employers should give primary consideration to employees' preferences in deciding what accommodations should be made. What happens if a job applicant or employee does not indicate to the employer how his or her disability can be accommodated so that the employee can perform essential job functions? In this situation, the employer may avoid liability for failing to hire or retain the individual on the ground that the applicant or employee has failed to meet the "otherwise qualified" requirement.[18]

ETHICAL ISSUE 38.2 ***Who should decide when a person with disabilities is "otherwise qualified" for a particular job?*** A significant issue concerning the ADA has to do with the determination of whether a person with disabilities is "otherwise qualified" for a particular job. Consider just one example: Should a freight company or airline be required to hire job candidates with monocular vision—persons who are blind in one eye? According to some federal courts, the answer to this question is yes. For example, in one case, a federal appellate court held that a truck driver who was blind in one eye was "disabled" and thus could sue an employer who refused to hire him under the ADA.[19] In another case, a federal appellate court held that a pilot with vision in only one eye was entitled to sue Aloha Islandair, a passenger airline, for refusing to hire him.[20] These are just two of several examples of situations in which courts have held that employers can be liable for failing to accommodate employees with visual impairments. Such cases raise the question of whether such decisions should be left up to the employer, who may face substantial liability in the event of an accident, or to the courts, who are charged with the responsibility of upholding the mandates of the ADA.

Employers who do not accommodate the needs of persons with disabilities must demonstrate that the accommodations will cause "undue hardship." Generally, the law offers no uniform standards for identifying what is an undue hardship other than the imposition of a "significant difficulty or expense" on the employer.

Usually, the courts decide whether an accommodation constitutes an undue hardship on a case-by-case basis. In one case, the court decided that paying for a parking space near the office for an employee with a disability was not an undue hardship.[21] In another case, the court held that accommodating the request of an employee with diabetes for indefinite leave until his disease was under control would create an undue hardship for the employer, because the employer would not know when the employee

18. See, for example, *Beck v. University of Wisconsin Board of Regents,* 75 F.3d 1130 (7th Cir. 1996); and *White v. York International Corp.,* 45 F.3d 357 (10th Cir. 1995).
19. *Kirkingburg v. Albertson's, Inc.,* 143 F.3d 1228 (9th Cir. 1998).
20. *Aloha Islandair, Inc. v. Tseu,* 128 F.3d 1301 (9th Cir. 1998).
21. See *Lyons v. Legal Aid Society,* 68 F.3d 1512 (2d Cir. 1995).

was returning to work. The court stated that reasonable accommodation under the ADA means accommodation so that the employee can perform the job now or "in the immediate future" rather than at some unspecified distant time.[22]

We now look at some specific requirements of the ADA in regard to the extent to which employers must reasonably accommodate the needs of employees with disabilities.

¡DON'T FORGET! Preemployment screening procedures must be applied carefully in regard to all job applicants.

Job Applications and Preemployment Physical Exams Employers must modify their job-application process so that those with disabilities can compete for jobs with those who do not have disabilities. • EXAMPLE 38.2 A job announcement that only has a phone number would discriminate against potential job applicants with hearing impairments. Thus, the job announcement must also provide an address. •

Employers are restricted in the kinds of questions they may ask on job-application forms and during preemployment interviews (see the *Application* at the end of this chapter for guidelines on this topic). Furthermore, they cannot require persons with disabilities to submit to preemployment physicals unless such exams are required of all other applicants. Employers can condition an offer of employment on the employee's successfully passing a medical examination, but disqualifications must result from the discovery of problems that render the applicant unable to perform the job for which he or she is to be hired.

Dangerous Workers Employers are not required to hire or retain workers who, because of their disabilities, pose a "direct threat to the health or safety" of their co-workers or the public. This danger must be substantial and immediate; it cannot be speculative. In the wake of the AIDS epidemic, many employers are concerned about hiring or continuing to employ a worker who has AIDS under the assumption that the worker might pose a direct threat to the health or safety of others in the workplace. Courts have generally held, however, that AIDS is not so contagious as to disqualify employees in most jobs. Therefore, employers must reasonably accommodate job applicants or employees who have AIDS or who test positive for the human immunodeficiency virus (HIV), the virus that causes AIDS.

Health-Insurance Plans Workers with disabilities must be given equal access to any health insurance provided to other employees. Employers can exclude from coverage preexisting health conditions and certain types of diagnostic or surgical procedures, however. An employer can also put a limit, or cap, on health-care payments in its particular group-health policy—as long as such caps are "applied equally to all insured employees" and do not "discriminate on the basis of disability." Whenever a group health-care plan makes a disability-based distinction in its benefits, the plan violates the ADA. The employer must then be able to justify the distinction by proving one of the following:

1. That limiting coverage of certain ailments is required to keep the plan financially sound.
2. That coverage of certain ailments would cause a significant increase in premium payments or their equivalent such that the plan would be unappealing to a significant number of workers.
3. That the disparate treatment is justified by the risks and costs associated with a particular disability.

22. *Myers v. Hase,* 50 F.3d 278 (4th Cir. 1995).

A DISCUSSION OCCURS AT A MEETING OF ALCOHOLICS ANONYMOUS. SHOULD EMPLOYERS BE ALLOWED TO DISCRIMINATE AGAINST PERSONS SUFFERING FROM ALCOHOLISM?

The ADA and Substance Abusers Drug addiction is a disability under the ADA, because drug addiction is a substantially limiting impairment. Those who are currently using illegal drugs are not protected by the act. The ADA only protects persons with *former* drug addictions—those who have completed a supervised drug-rehabilitation program or who are currently in a supervised rehabilitation program. Individuals who have used drugs casually in the past are not protected under the act. They are not considered addicts and therefore do not have a disability (addiction).

People recovering from alcoholism are protected by the ADA. Employers cannot legally discriminate against employees simply because they are suffering from alcoholism and must treat them in the same way as they treat other employees. In other words, an employee suffering from alcoholism cannot be disciplined any differently than anyone else simply because he or she was drinking the night before and came to work late. Of course, employers have the right to prohibit the use of alcohol in the workplace and can require that employees not be under the influence of alcohol while working. Employers can also fire or refuse to hire a person suffering from alcoholism if he or she poses a substantial risk of harm to either himself or herself or to others and the risk cannot be reduced by reasonable accommodation. (See the feature *The Letter of the Law* for an ironic outcome resulting from the ADA's requirements with respect to recovering alcoholics.)

The Letter of the Law — EXXON—ADRIFT ON A SEA OF REGULATIONS?

When the supertanker *Exxon Valdez* hit a reef in Prince William Sound, Alaska, in 1989, it caused one of the worst oil spills in history. Exxon faced extensive liability under environmental laws (see Chapter 36) for this polluting disaster and ultimately had to pay billions of dollars in fines and clean-up costs. It was widely believed that the captain of the tanker was intoxicated at the time of the accident. To reduce the chances of such a disaster happening in the future, Exxon established a policy of not allowing anyone with a history of alcohol abuse to be a tanker captain or to work in certain other safety-sensitive positions. It turned out that Exxon's policy, designed to minimize accidents and shield the company from liability under environmental laws, violated another law—the Americans with Disabilities Act (ADA). In a suit against Exxon, the Equal Employment Opportunity Commission (EEOC) claimed that Exxon had violated the ADA by discriminating against some fifty employees who were "rehabilitated substance abusers." The federal court agreed and held that Exxon could not discriminate against such employees unless it could show that they posed a direct threat to the health or safety of others.[a]

THE BOTTOM LINE

Companies sometimes find, as Exxon did, that in attempting to comply with one law, they end up violating another.

a. *Equal Employment Opportunity Commission v. Exxon Corp.*, 1 F.Supp.2d 635 (N.D. Tex. 1998).

Defenses to Employment Discrimination

The first line of defense for an employer charged with employment discrimination is, of course, to assert that the plaintiff has failed to meet his or her initial burden of proof—proving that discrimination in fact occurred. As noted, plaintiffs bringing cases under the ADA sometimes find it difficult to meet this initial burden, because they must prove that their alleged disabilities are disabilities covered by the ADA. Furthermore, plaintiffs in ADA cases must prove that they were otherwise qualified for the job and that the reason they were not hired or were fired was solely because of their disabilities.

Once a plaintiff succeeds in proving that discrimination occurred, then the burden shifts to the employer to justify the discriminatory practice. Often, employers attempt to justify the discrimination by claiming that it was a result of a business necessity, a bona fide occupational qualification, or a seniority system. As mentioned in this chapter's *Business Law in Action,* in some cases an effective anti-harassment policy and prompt remedial action when harassment occurs also may shield employers from liability under Title VII for sexual harassment.

BUSINESS NECESSITY

• BUSINESS NECESSITY
A defense to allegations of employment discrimination in which the employer demonstrates that an employment practice that discriminates against members of a protected class is related to job performance.

An employer may defend against a claim of discrimination by asserting that a practice that has a discriminatory effect is a **business necessity.** • EXAMPLE 38.3 If requiring a high school diploma is shown to have a discriminatory effect, an employer might argue that a high school education is required for workers to perform the job at a required level of competence. If the employer can demonstrate to the court's satisfaction that there exists a definite connection between a high school education and job performance, then the employer will succeed in this business necessity defense.•

BONA FIDE OCCUPATIONAL QUALIFICATION

• BONA FIDE OCCUPATIONAL QUALIFICATION (BFOQ))
Identifiable characteristics reasonably necessary to the normal operation of a particular business. These characteristics can include gender, national origin, and religion, but not race.

Another defense applies when discrimination against a protected class is essential to a job—that is, when a particular trait is a **bona fide occupational qualification (BFOQ).** For example, a men's fashion magazine might legitimately hire only male models. Similarly, the Federal Aviation Administration can legitimately impose age limits for airline pilots. Race, however, can never be a BFOQ. Generally, courts have restricted the BFOQ defense to instances in which the employee's gender is essential to the job. In 1991, the United States Supreme Court held that even a fetal-protection policy that was adopted to protect the unborn children of female employees from the harmful effects of exposure to lead was an unacceptable BFOQ.[23]

SENIORITY SYSTEMS

• SENIORITY SYSTEM
In regard to employment relationships, a system in which those who have worked longest for the company are first in line for promotions, salary increases, and other benefits; they are also the last to be laid off if the work force must be reduced.

An employer with a history of discrimination may have no members of protected classes in upper-level positions. Even if the employer now seeks to be unbiased, it may face a lawsuit seeking an order that minorities be promoted ahead of schedule to compensate for past discrimination. If no present intent to discriminate is shown, and promotions or other job benefits are distributed according to a fair **seniority system** (in which workers with more years of service are promoted first, or laid off last), however, the employer has a good defense against the suit.

AFTER-ACQUIRED EVIDENCE IS NO DEFENSE

In some situations, employers have attempted to avoid liability for employment discrimination on the basis of "after-acquired evidence" of an employee's misconduct. • EXAMPLE 38.4 Suppose that an employer fires a worker, and the employee sues the employer for employment discrimination. During pretrial investigation, the employer learns that the employee made material misrepresentations on his or her

23. *United Auto Workers v. Johnson Controls, Inc.,* 113 U.S. 158, 111 S.Ct. 1196, 113 L.Ed.2d 158 (1991).

employment application—misrepresentations that, had the employer known about them, would have served as a ground to fire the individual. •

Can such after-acquired evidence be used as a defense? The United States Supreme Court addressed this question in *McKennon v. Banner Publishing Co.*,[24] a case decided in 1995. The Court stated that both Title VII and the ADEA share a common purpose: "the elimination of discrimination in the workplace." The Court held that allowing employers to avoid liability for discrimination on the basis of after-acquired evidence did "not accord" with this purpose. After-acquired evidence of wrongdoing should not operate, "in every instance, to bar all relief for an earlier violation of the Act." Since this decision, the courts have generally held that after-acquired evidence cannot be used to shield employers from liability for employment discrimination, although it may be a factor in determining the amount of damages awarded to plaintiffs.

Affirmative Action

• **AFFIRMATIVE ACTION**
Job-hiring policies that give special consideration to members of protected classes in an effort to overcome present effects of past discrimination.

Federal statutes and regulations providing for equal opportunity in the workplace were designed to reduce or eliminate discriminatory practices with respect to hiring, retaining, and promoting employees. **Affirmative action** programs go a step further and attempt to "make up" for past patterns of discrimination by giving members of protected classes preferential treatment in hiring or promotion.

Affirmative action programs have caused much controversy, particularly when they result in what is frequently called "reverse discrimination"—discrimination against "majority" workers, such as white males (or discrimination against other minority groups that may not be given preferential treatment under a particular affirmative action program). At issue is whether affirmative action programs, because of their inherently discriminatory nature, violate the equal protection clause of the Fourteenth Amendment to the Constitution.

THE *BAKKE* CASE

An early case addressing this issue, *Regents of the University of California v. Bakke*,[25] involved an affirmative action program implemented by the University of California at Davis. Allan Bakke, who had been turned down for medical school at the Davis campus, sued the university for reverse discrimination after he discovered that his academic record was better than those of some of the minority applicants who had been admitted to the program.

The United States Supreme Court held that affirmative action programs were subject to "intermediate scrutiny." Recall from the discussion of the equal protection clause in Chapter 2 that any law or action evaluated under a standard of intermediate scrutiny, to be constitutionally valid, must be substantially related to important government objectives. Applying this standard, the Court held that the university could give favorable weight to minority applicants as part of a plan to increase minority enrollment so as to achieve a more culturally diverse student body. The Court stated, however, that the use of a quota system, in which a certain number of places is explicitly reserved for minority applicants, violated the equal protection clause of the Fourteenth Amendment.

24. 573 U.S. 352, 115 S.Ct. 879, 130 L.Ed.2d 852 (1995).
25. 438 U.S. 265, 98 S.Ct. 2733, 57 L.Ed.2d 750 (1978).

THE *ADARAND* CASE

Although the *Bakke* case and later court decisions alleviated the harshness of the quota system, during the 1990s courts went even further in questioning the constitutional validity of affirmative action programs. For example, in *Adarand Constructors, Inc. v. Peña,*[26] a case decided by the United States Supreme Court in 1995, the plaintiff (Adarand Constructors, Inc.) was not awarded a federal highway construction project even though it had submitted the lowest bid. Instead, the project went to an Hispanic-owned firm pursuant to a federal program designed to give at least 5 percent of highway construction projects to disadvantaged business enterprises. Adarand sued Federico Peña, the secretary of the Transportation Department, alleging that the federal program violated the equal protection clause.

The Supreme Court held that any federal, state, or local affirmative action program that uses racial or ethnic classifications as the basis for making decisions is subject to "strict scrutiny" by the courts. As discussed in Chapter 2, under a strict-scrutiny analysis, to be constitutional, a discriminatory law or action must be narrowly tailored to meet a *compelling* government interest. In effect, the Court's opinion in *Adarand* means that an affirmative action program cannot make use of quotas or preferences for unqualified persons, and once the program has succeeded, it must be changed or dropped.

SUBSEQUENT DEVELOPMENTS

Since the *Adarand* decision, the lower courts have followed the Supreme Court's lead in subjecting affirmative action programs to strict scrutiny. In several cases, the lower courts have held that the affirmative action programs being challenged do violate the equal protection clause.

The first federal appellate ruling on the issue, in *Hopwood v. State of Texas,*[27] involved two white law school applicants who sued the University of Texas School of Law in Austin, alleging that they were denied admission because of the school's affirmative action program. The program allowed admitting officials to take racial and other factors into consideration when determining which students would be admitted. The Court of Appeals for the Fifth Circuit held that the program violated the equal protection clause because it discriminated in favor of minority applicants. Significantly, the court directly challenged the *Bakke* decision by stating that the use of race even as a means of achieving diversity on college campuses "undercuts the Fourteenth Amendment."

While these decisions do not directly relate to affirmative action programs in the employment context, they indicate a trend that will affect employers' affirmative action programs as well. Additionally, in 1996 California voters amended their state constitution to ban affirmative action policies in state employment, education, and contracting.[28] Similar movements are currently under way in other states.

The question in the following case was whether an employer's voluntary affirmative action policy of "racial diversity" violated Title VII of the Civil Rights Act of 1964. The decision presented below was appealed further to the United States Supreme Court, which granted *certiorari.* The case received a significant amount of publicity in 1998, because many hoped that the Court would use this case to make

26. 575 U.S. 200, 115 S.Ct. 2097, 132 L.Ed.2d. 158 (1995).

27. 84 F.3d. 720 (5th Cir. 1996).

28. The constitutionality of this amendment was upheld in *Coalition for Economic Equity v. Wilson,* 110 F.3d 1431 (9th Cir. 1997).

a definitive decision on the legality of affirmative action programs. Before the Court decided the case, however, the parties reached a settlement. Interestingly, about 70 percent of the $433,500 settlement received by the plaintiff, Shirley Taxman, was paid by civil rights groups. These groups feared that if the Supreme Court decided the issue, the Court might hold in favor of Taxman, thus virtually ending similar affirmative action programs throughout the nation.

CASE 38.4 Taxman v. Board of Education of the Township of Piscataway

United States Court of Appeals,
Third Circuit, 1996.
91 F.3d 1547.

HISTORICAL AND SOCIAL SETTING *In the 1970s, the New Jersey State Board of Education directed local school boards to adopt affirmative action programs that would "ensure equal opportunity to all persons regardless of race, color, creed, religion, sex or national origin." In response, in 1975 the Board of Education of the Township of Piscataway developed an "Affirmative Action Program" to apply to employment decisions. The program required that in all cases, including layoffs, when persons appeared to be of equal qualification, members of groups identified as minorities by the state department of education were to be "recommended" for employment. These groups included African Americans. At the time, the percentage of African American teachers in the Piscataway School District exceeded the percentage of African Americans in the available work force.*

BACKGROUND AND FACTS The Board of Education of the Township of Piscataway, New Jersey, decided to reduce the teaching staff at Piscataway High School by one. Between two teachers of equal seniority and qualifications but different races, the board chose to lay off the white teacher, Sharon Taxman. Minority teachers were not underrepresented in the school district work force. The board based its decision on an affirmative action policy that was designed not to remedy discrimination but to promote "racial diversity." Taxman and others filed a suit in a federal district court against the board, challenging the policy as a violation of Title VII of the Civil Rights Act of 1964. The court granted a summary judgment in favor of the plaintiffs. The case was appealed to the U.S. Court of Appeals for the Third Circuit.

IN THE WORDS OF THE COURT . . .
MANSMANN, Circuit Judge.

* * * *

Title VII was enacted to further two primary goals: to end discrimination on the basis of race, color, religion, sex or national origin, thereby guaranteeing equal opportunity in the workplace, and to remedy the segregation and underrepresentation of minorities that discrimination has caused in our Nation's work force.

* * * *

* * * [T]he Board's sole purpose in applying its affirmative action policy in this case was to obtain an educational benefit which it believed would result from a racially diverse faculty. While the benefits flowing from diversity in the educational context are significant * * * , the Board does not even attempt to show that its affirmative action plan was adopted to remedy past discrimination or as the result of a manifest imbalance in the employment of minorities * * * .

* * * *

* * * [T]he Board's policy, devoid of goals and standards, is governed entirely by the Board's whim, leaving the Board free, if it so chooses, to grant racial preferences that do not promote even the policy's claimed purpose. Indeed, under the terms of this policy, the Board, in pursuit of a "racially diverse" work force, could use affirmative action to discriminate against those whom Title VII was enacted to protect.

CASE 38.4—Continued

DECISION AND REMEDY The U.S. Court of Appeals for the Third Circuit affirmed the lower court's judgment in favor of the plaintiffs and awarded Taxman 100 percent of her back pay.

FOR CRITICAL ANALYSIS—Ethical Consideration *Is it possible to create a racially diverse work force without an affirmative action policy?*

State Statutes

Although the focus of this chapter has been on federal legislation, most states also have statutes that prohibit employment discrimination. Generally, the kinds of discrimination prohibited under federal legislation are also prohibited by state laws. In addition, state statutes often provide protection for certain individuals who are not protected under federal laws. For example, a New Jersey appellate court has held that anyone over the age of eighteen was entitled to sue for age discrimination under the state law, which specified no threshold age limit.[29] Furthermore, as mentioned in Chapter 37, state laws prohibiting discrimination may apply to firms with fewer employees than the threshold number required under federal statutes, thus offering protection to a broader number of workers. Finally, state laws may provide additional damages, such as damages for emotional distress, that are not provided for under federal statutes.

29. *Bergen Commercial Bank v. Sisler,* 307 N.J.Super. 333, 704 A.2d 1017 (1998).

APPLICATION

Law & the Employer: Interviewing Workers with Disabilities*

Many employers have been held liable under the Americans with Disabilities Act (ADA) of 1990 simply because they asked the wrong questions when interviewing job applicants with disabilities. If you are an employer, you can do several things to avoid violating the ADA.

As a preliminary matter, you should become familiar with the guidelines on job interviews issued by the Equal Employment Opportunity Commission (EEOC). These guidelines indicate the kinds of questions that employers may—and may not—ask job applicants with disabilities. Often, the line between permissible and impermissible questions is a fine one. Consider these examples:

- *Ability to perform the job:* As an employer, you may ask a job applicant, "Can you do the job?" You may also ask whether the applicant can perform specific tasks related to the job. You may not ask the candidate, "How would you do the job?"—*unless* the disability is obvious, the applicant brings up the subject during the interview, or you ask the question of all applicants.
- *Absenteeism:* You may ask, "Can you meet our attendance requirements?" or "How many days were you absent last year?" You may not ask, "How many days were you sick last year?"
- *Drug use:* Generally, employers may ask about the current or past use of illegal drugs but not about drug addiction. Therefore, as an employer, you may ask, "Have you ever used illegal drugs?" or "Have you done so in the last six months?" You may not ask, "How often did you use illegal drugs?" or "Have you been treated for drug abuse?"

*This *Application* is not meant to substitute for the services of an attorney who is licensed to practice law in your state.

APPLICATION CONTINUED

• *Alcohol use:* Generally, employers may ask about a candidate's drinking habits but not about alcoholism. Therefore, you may ask, "Do you drink alcohol?" or "Have you been arrested for driving while intoxicated?" but you may not ask, "How often do you drink?"

• *History of job-related injuries:* Employers may not ask a job candidate with a disability any questions about the applicant's previous job-related injuries or about workers' compensation claims submitted in the past.

Once you have made a job offer, however, you may ask the applicant questions concerning his or her disability, including questions about previous workers' compensation claims or about the extent of a drinking problem. You may also ask for medical documents verifying the nature of the applicant's disability. Generally, though, you should ask such questions only if you ask them of all applicants or if they are follow-up questions concerning the applicant's disability that he or she already disclosed during a job interview.

To avoid liability under the ADA, the wisest thing you can do is consult with an attorney. You should inform the attorney of the kinds of questions you typically ask job applicants during interviews or following employment offers. Then, you should work with the attorney in modifying these questions so that they are consistent with the EEOC's guidelines on permissible and impermissible questions. Finally, you should make sure that anyone on your staff who interviews job applicants receives thorough instructions on what questions may and may not be asked of candidates with disabilities. You might also remind your staff that under the ADA, the words and phraseology the interviewer uses may result in a violation of the ADA regardless of the interviewer's intentions.

Checklist for the Employer

1. Familiarize yourself with the EEOC's guidelines indicating what questions are and are not permissible while interviewing job applicants with disabilities.
2. Work with an attorney to create a list of particular types of questions that are or are not permissible under the EEOC's guidelines with respect to job candidates with disabilities.
3. Make sure that everyone in your firm who interviews job applicants is thoroughly instructed as to the types of questions that they may and may not ask when interviewing job applicants with disabilities.

Key Terms

affirmative action 994
bona fide occupational qualification (BFOQ) 993
business necessity 993
disparate-impact discrimination 979
disparate-treatment discrimination 978
employment discrimination 978
***prima facie* case 979**
protected class 977
seniority system 993
sexual harassment 982

Chapter Summary • Employment Discrimination

Title VII of the Civil Rights Act of 1964 (See pages 978–986.)	Title VII prohibits employment discrimination based on race, color, national origin, religion, or gender. 1. *Procedures*—Employees must file a claim with the Equal Employment Opportunity Commission (EEOC). The EEOC may sue the employer on the employee's behalf; if not, the employee may sue the employer directly. 2. *Types of discrimination*—Title VII prohibits both intentional (disparate-treatment) and unintentional (disparate-impact) discrimination. Disparate-impact discrimination occurs when an employer's practice, such as hiring only persons with a certain level of education, has the effect of discriminating against a class of persons protected by Title VII. 3. *Remedies for discrimination under Title VII*—If a plaintiff proves that unlawful discrimination occurred, he or she may be awarded reinstatement, back pay, and retroactive promotions. Damages (both compensatory and punitive) may be awarded for intentional discrimination.

Chapter Summary • Employment Discrimination, Continued

Discrimination Based on Age (See pages 987–988.)	The Age Discrimination in Employment Act (ADEA) of 1967 prohibits employment discrimination on the basis of age against individuals forty years of age or older. Procedures for bringing a case under the ADEA are similar to those for bringing a case under Title VII.
Discrimination Based on Disability (See pages 988–992.)	The Americans with Disabilities Act (ADA) of 1990 prohibits employment discrimination against persons with disabilities who are otherwise qualified to perform the essential functions of the jobs for which they apply. 1. *Procedures and remedies*—To prevail on a claim under the ADA, the plaintiff must show that he or she has a disability, is otherwise qualified for the employment in question, and was excluded from the employment solely because of the disability. Procedures under the ADA are similar to those required in Title VII cases; remedies are also similar to those under Title VII. 2. *Definition of disability*—The ADA defines the term *disability* as a physical or mental impairment that substantially limits one or more major life activities; a record of such impairment; or being regarded as having such an impairment. 3. *Reasonable accommodation*—Employers are required to reasonably accommodate the needs of persons with disabilities. Reasonable accommodations may include altering job-application procedures, modifying the physical work environment, and permitting more flexible work schedules. Employers are not required to accommodate the needs of all workers with disabilities. For example, employers need not accommodate workers who pose a definite threat to health and safety in the workplace or those who are not otherwise qualified for their jobs.
Defenses to Employment Discrimination (See pages 992–994.)	If a plaintiff proves that employment discrimination occurred, employers may avoid liability by successfully asserting certain defenses. Employers may assert that the discrimination was required for reasons of business necessity, to meet a bona fide occupational qualification, or to maintain a legitimate seniority system. Evidence of prior employee misconduct acquired after the employee has been fired is not a defense to discrimination.
Affirmative Action (See pages 994–997.)	Affirmative action programs attempt to "make up" for past patterns of discrimination by giving members of protected classes preferential treatment in hiring or promotion. Increasingly, such programs are being strictly scrutinized by the courts, and state-sponsored affirmative action has been banned in California.
State Statutes (See page 997.)	Generally, the kinds of discrimination prohibited by federal statutes are also prohibited by state laws. State laws may provide for more extensive protection and remedies than federal laws.

For Review

1. Generally, what kind of conduct is prohibited by Title VII of the Civil Rights Act of 1964, as amended?
2. What is the difference between disparate-treatment discrimination and disparate-impact discrimination?
3. What remedies are available under Title VII of the 1964 Civil Rights Act, as amended?
4. What federal acts prohibit discrimination based on age and discrimination based on disability?
5. Name and discuss three defenses to claims of employment discrimination.

Questions and Case Problems

38–1. Title VII Violations. Discuss fully whether any of the following actions would constitute a violation of Title VII of the 1964 Civil Rights Act, as amended:

(a) Tennington, Inc., is a consulting firm and has ten employees. These employees travel on consulting jobs in seven states. Tennington has an employment record of hiring only white males.

(b) Novo Films, Inc., is making a film about Africa and needs to employ approximately one hundred extras for this picture. Novo advertises in all major newspapers in southern California for the hiring of these extras. The ad states that only African Americans need apply.

38–2. Discrimination Based on Age. Tavo Jones had worked since 1974 for Westshore Resort, where he maintained golf carts. During the first decade, he received positive job evaluations and numerous merit pay raises. He was promoted to the position of supervisor of golf-cart maintenance at three courses. Then a new employee, Ben Olery, was placed in charge of the golf courses. He demoted Jones, who was over the age of forty, to running only one of the three cart facilities, and he froze Jones's salary indefinitely. Olery also demoted five other men over the age of forty. Another cart facility was placed under the supervision of Blake Blair. Later, the cart facilities for the three courses were again consolidated, but Blair—not Jones—was put in charge. At the time, Jones was still in his forties, and Blair was in his twenties. Jones overheard Blair say that "we are going to have to do away with these . . . old and senile" men. Jones quit and sued Westshore for employment discrimination. Should he prevail? Explain.

38–3. Disparate-Impact Discrimination. Chinawa, a major processor of cheese sold throughout the United States, employs one hundred workers at its principal processing plant. The plant is located in Heartland Corners, which has a population that is 50 percent white and 25 percent African American, with the balance Hispanic American, Asian American, and others. Chinawa requires a high school diploma as a condition of employment for its cleaning crew. Three-fourths of the white population complete high school, compared with only one-fourth of those in the minority groups. Chinawa has an all-white cleaning crew. Has Chinawa violated Title VII of the Civil Rights Act of 1964? Explain.

38–4. Discrimination Based on Gender. Beginning in June 1966, Corning Glass Works started to open up jobs on the night shift to women. The previously separate male and female seniority lists were consolidated, and the women became eligible to exercise their seniority on the same basis as men and to bid for higher-paid night inspection jobs as vacancies occurred. On January 20, 1969, however, a new collective bargaining agreement went into effect; it established a new job evaluation system for setting wage rates. This agreement abolished (for the future) separate base wages for night-shift and day-shift inspectors and imposed a uniform base wage for inspectors that exceeded the wage rate previously in effect for the night shift. The agreement, though, did allow for a higher "red circle" rate for employees hired prior to January 20, 1969, when they were working as inspectors on the night shift. This "red circle" wage served essentially to perpetuate the differential in base wages between day and night inspectors. Had Corning violated Title VII of the Civil Rights Act of 1964? Discuss. [*Corning Glass Works v. Brennan,* 417 U.S. 188, 94 S.Ct. 2223, 41 L.Ed.2d 1 (1974)]

38–5. Defenses to Employment Discrimination. Dorothea O'Driscoll had worked as a quality control inspector for Hercules, Inc., for six years when her employment was terminated in 1986. O'Driscoll, who was over forty years of age, sued Hercules for age discrimination in violation of the Age Discrimination in Employment Act of 1967. While preparing for trial, Hercules learned that O'Driscoll had made several misrepresentations when she applied for the job. Among other things, she misrepresented her age, did not disclose a previous employer, falsely represented that she had never applied for work with Hercules before, and falsely stated that she had completed two quarters of study at a technical college. Additionally, on her application for group insurance coverage, she misrepresented the age of her son, who would otherwise have been ineligible for coverage as her dependent. Hercules defended against O'Driscoll's claim of age discrimination by stating that had it known of this misconduct, it would have terminated her employment anyway. What should the court decide? Discuss fully. [*O'Driscoll v. Hercules, Inc.,* 12 F.3d 176 (10th Cir. 1994)]

38–6. Discrimination Based on National Origin. Phanna Xieng was sent by the Cambodian government to the United States in 1974 for "advanced military training." When the Cambodian government fell in 1975, Xieng remained in the United States and eventually was employed by Peoples National Bank of Washington in 1979. In performance appraisals from 1980 through 1985, Xieng was rated by his supervisors as "capable of dealing effectively with customers" and qualified for promotion, although in each appraisal it was noted that Xieng might improve his communication skills to maximize his possibilities for future advancement. Xieng sought job promotions on numerous occasions but was never promoted. In 1986, he filed a complaint against the bank, alleging employment discrimination based on national origin. The employer argued that its refusal to promote Xieng because of his accent or communication skills did not amount to discrimination based on national origin. Is it possible to separate discrimination based on an employee's accent and communication skills from discrimination based on national origin? How should the court rule on this issue? [*Xieng v. Peoples National Bank of Washington,* 120 Wash.2d 512, 844 P.2d 389 (1993)]

38–7. Disparate-Impact Discrimination. Local 1066 of the Steamship Clerks Union accepted only new members who were sponsored by existing members. All of the existing members were white. During a six-year period, the local admitted thirty new members, all of whom were relatives of present members and also white. The Equal Employment Opportunity Commission filed a suit in a federal district court against the union, alleging that this practice constituted disparate-impact discrimination under Title VII. The union argued that it was only continuing a family tradition. What does each party have to prove to win its case? Should the union be required to change its practice? [*EEOC v. Steamship Clerks Union, Local 1066,* 48 F.3d 594 (1st Cir. 1995)]

38–8. Discrimination Based on Disability. When the University of Maryland Medical System Corp. learned that one of its surgeons was HIV positive, the university offered him transfers to positions that did not involve surgery. The surgeon refused, and the university terminated him. The surgeon filed a suit in a federal district court against the university, alleging in part a violation of the Americans with Disabilities Act. The surgeon claimed that he was "otherwise qualified" for his former position. What does he have to prove to win his case? Should he be reinstated? [*Doe v. University of Maryland Medical System Corp.,* 50 F.3d 1261 (4th Cir. 1995)]

38–9. Discrimination Based on Race. Theodore Rosenblatt, a white attorney, worked for the law firm of Bivona & Cohen, P.C. When Bivona & Cohen terminated Rosenblatt's employment, he filed a suit in a federal district court against the firm. Rosenblatt claimed that he had been discharged because he was married to an African American and that a discharge for such a reason violated Title VII and other laws. The firm filed a motion for summary judgment, arguing that he was alleging discrimination against his wife, not himself, and thus did not have standing to sue under Title VII for racial discrimination. Should the court grant or deny the motion? Explain. [*Rosenblatt v. Bivona & Cohen, P.C.,* 946 F.Supp. 298 (S.D.N.Y. 1996)]

38–10. Religious Discrimination. Mary Tiano, a devout Roman Catholic, worked for Dillard Department Stores, Inc. (Dillard's), in Phoenix, Arizona. Dillard's considered Tiano a productive employee because her sales exceeded $200,000 a year. At the time, the store gave its managers the discretion to grant unpaid leave to employees but prohibited vacations or leave during the holiday season—October through December. Tiano felt that she had a "calling" to go on a "pilgrimage" in October 1988 to Medjugorje, Yugoslavia, where some persons claimed to have had visions of the Virgin Mary. The Catholic Church had not designated the site an official pilgrimage site, the visions were not expected to be stronger in October, and tours were available at other times. The store managers denied Tiano's request for leave, but she had a nonrefundable ticket and left anyway. Dillard's terminated her employment. For a year, Tiano searched for a new job and did not attain the level of her Dillard's salary for four years. She filed a suit in a federal district court against Dillard's, alleging religious discrimination in violation of Title VII. Can Tiano establish a *prima facie* case of religious discrimination? Explain. [*Tiano v. Dillard Department Stores, Inc.,* 139 F.3d 679 (9th Cir. 1998)]

A QUESTION OF ETHICS AND SOCIAL RESPONSIBILITY

38–11. Luz Long and three other Hispanic employees (the plaintiffs) worked as bank tellers for the Culmore branch of the First Union Corp. of Virginia. The plaintiffs often conversed with one another in Spanish, their native language. In 1992, the Culmore branch manager adopted an "English-only" policy, which required all employees to speak English during working hours unless they had to speak another language to assist customers. The plaintiffs refused to cooperate with the new policy and were eventually fired. In a suit against the bank, the plaintiffs alleged that the English-only policy discriminated against them on the basis of their national origin. The court granted the bank's motion for summary judgment, concluding that "[t]here is nothing in Title VII which . . . provides that an employee has a right to speak his or her native tongue while on the job." [*Long v. First Union Corp. of Virginia,* 894 F.Supp. 933 (E.D.Va. 1995)]

1. The bank argued that the policy was implemented in response to complaints made by fellow employees that the Spanish-speaking employees were creating a hostile environment by speaking Spanish among themselves in the presence of other employees. From an ethical perspective, is this a sufficient reason to institute an English-only policy?
2. Is it ever ethically justifiable for employers to deny bilingual employees the opportunity to speak their native language while on the job?
3. Might there be situations in which English-only policies are necessary to promote worker health and safety?
4. Generally, what are the pros and cons of English-only policies in the workplace?

FOR CRITICAL ANALYSIS

38–12. Why has the federal government limited the application of the statutes discussed in this chapter only to firms with a specified number of employees, such as fifteen or twenty? Should these laws apply to all employers, regardless of size?

Online Activities

ONLINE EXERCISE 38–1

Go to the "Internet Activities Book" on the Web site that accompanies this text, the URL for which is http://blt.westbuslaw.com. Select the following activities, and perform the exercises according to the instructions given there:

Activity 35–1: Americans with Disabilities Act
Activity 35–2: Equal Employment Opportunity

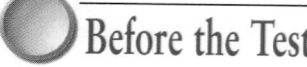

Before the Test

Go to the *Business Law Today* home page at http://blt.westbuslaw.com. Click on TestTutor.® You will find twenty interactive questions relating to this chapter.

CHAPTER 39

Liability of Accountants & Other Professionals

"A member should observe the profession's technical and ethical standards, strive continually to improve competence and the quality of services, and discharge professional responsibility to the best of the member's ability."

Article V, *Code of Professional Conduct,* American Institute of Certified Public Accountants

CONTENTS

LEARNING OBJECTIVES

After reading this chapter, you should be able to:

1. Summarize areas in which professionals may be liable at common law.
2. Outline liability that may be imposed on accountants under the securities laws.
3. Identify accountants' potential criminal liability.
4. State professionals' privileges concerning working papers.
5. Explain the protection of professionals and their clients for their communications.

The standard of due care to which the members of the American Institute of Certified Public Accountants are expected to adhere is stated in the opening quotation. Accountants, attorneys, physicians, and other professionals have found themselves increasingly subject to liability in the past decade or so. This more extensive liability has resulted in large part from a greater public awareness of the fact that professionals are required to deliver competent services and are obligated to adhere to standards of performance commonly accepted within their professions.

Considering the many potential sources of legal liability that may be imposed on them, accountants, attorneys, and other professionals should be well aware of their legal obligations. In the first part of this chapter, we look at the potential common law liability of professionals and then examine the potential liability of accountants under securities laws and the Internal Revenue Code. The chapter concludes with a brief examination of the relationship of professionals, particularly accountants and attorneys, with their clients.

Potential Common Law Liability to Clients

Under the common law, professionals may be liable to clients for breach of contract, negligence, or fraud.

ON THE WEB

The Web site of the Institute of Management Accountants (IMA) contains, among its pages, links to "Information Resources." These other sources of accounting information include a link to a "Student Web Site" with information on accounting careers and technology. The IMA site can be found at

www.rutgers.edu/Accounting/raw/ima/ima.htm.

LIABILITY FOR BREACH OF CONTRACT

Accountants and other professionals face liability for any breach of contract under the common law. A professional owes a duty to his or her client to honor the terms of the contract and to perform the contract within the stated time period. If the professional fails to perform as agreed in the contract, then he or she has breached the contract, and the client has the right to recover damages from the professional. A professional may be held liable for expenses incurred by his or her client in securing another professional to provide the contracted-for services, for penalties imposed on the client for failure to meet time deadlines, and for any other reasonable and foreseeable monetary losses that arise from the professional's breach.

LIABILITY FOR NEGLIGENCE

Accountants and other professionals may also be held liable under the common law for negligence in the performance of their services. As with any negligence claim, the elements that must be proved to establish negligence on the part of a professional are as follows:

1. A duty of care existed.
2. That duty of care was breached.
3. The plaintiff suffered an injury.
4. The injury was proximately caused by the defendant's breach of the duty of care.

All professionals are subject to standards of conduct established by codes of professional ethics, by state statutes, and by judicial decisions. They are also governed by the contracts they enter into with their clients. In their performance of contracts, professionals must exercise the established standard of care, knowledge, and judgment generally accepted by members of their professional group. We look below at the duty of care owed by two groups of professionals that frequently perform services for business firms: accountants and attorneys.

Accountant's Duty of Care Accountants play a major role in a business's financial system. Accountants have the necessary expertise and experience in establishing and maintaining accurate financial records to design, control, and audit record-keeping systems; to prepare reliable statements that reflect an individual's or a business's financial status; and to give tax advice and prepare tax returns.

• **GENERALLY ACCEPTED ACCOUNTING PRINCIPLES (GAAP)**
The conventions, rules, and procedures necessary to define accepted accounting practices at a particular time. The source of the principles is the Financial Accounting Standards Board.

• **GENERALLY ACCEPTED AUDITING STANDARDS (GAAS)**
Standards concerning an auditor's professional qualities and the judgment exercised by him or her in the performance of an examination and report. The source of the standards is the American Institute of Certified Public Accountants.

GAAP and GAAS. In the performance of their services, accountants must comply with **generally accepted accounting principles (GAAP)** and **generally accepted auditing standards (GAAS)**. The Financial Accounting Standards Board (FASB, usually pronounced "faz-bee") determines what accounting conventions, rules, and procedures constitute GAAP at a given point in time. GAAS are standards concerning an auditor's professional qualities and the judgment that he or she exercises in performing an audit and report. GAAS are established by the American Institute of Certified Public Accountants. As long as an accountant conforms to generally accepted accounting principles and acts in good faith, he or she will not be held liable to the client for incorrect judgment. As a general rule, an accountant is not required to discover every impropriety, **defalcation** (embezzlement), or fraud in his or her client's books.[1] If, however, the impropriety, defalcation, or fraud has gone undiscovered because of an accountant's negligence or failure to perform an express or implied duty, the accountant will be liable for any resulting losses suffered by his or her client. Therefore, an accountant who uncovers suspicious financial transactions and fails to investigate the matter fully or to inform his or her client of the discovery can be held liable to the client for the resulting loss.

• **DEFALCATION**
Embezzlement; the misappropriation of funds held by a party, such as a corporate officer or a public official, in a fiduciary relationship with another.

A violation of GAAP and GAAS will be considered *prima facie* evidence of negligence on the part of the accountant. Compliance with GAAP and GAAS, however, does not *necessarily* relieve an accountant from potential legal liability. An accountant may be held to a higher standard of conduct established by state statute and by judicial decisions.

ON THE WEB

"The mission of the Financial Accounting Standards Board is to establish and improve standards of financial accounting and reporting for the guidance and education of the public, including issuers, auditors, and users of financial information," according to its Web site, which can be found at

www.rutgers.edu/Accounting/raw/fasb.

Defenses to Negligence. If an accountant is deemed guilty of negligence, the client may collect damages for losses that arose from the accountant's negligence. An accountant, however, is not without possible defenses to a cause of action for damages based on negligence. Possible defenses include the following allegations:

1. The accountant was not negligent.
2. If the accountant was negligent, this negligence was not the proximate cause of the client's losses.
3. The client was negligent (depending on whether state law allows contributory negligence as a defense).

Unaudited Financial Statements. Sometimes accountants are hired to prepare unaudited financial statements. (A financial statement is considered unaudited if no auditing procedures have been used in its preparation or if insufficient procedures have been used to justify an opinion.) Accountants may be subject to liability for failing, in accordance with standard accounting procedures, to delineate a balance sheet as "unaudited." An accountant will also be held liable for failure to disclose to a client facts or circumstances that give reason to believe that misstatements have been made or that a fraud has been committed.

Attorney's Duty of Care The conduct of attorneys is governed by rules established by each state and by the American Bar Association's Code of Professional Responsibility and Model Rules of Professional Conduct. All attorneys owe a duty to provide competent and diligent representation. In judging an attorney's performance, the standard used will normally be that of a reasonably competent general practitioner of ordinary skill, experience, and capacity. If the attorney holds himself or herself out as having expertise in a special area of law, the standard is that of a reasonably competent specialist of ordinary skill, experience, and capacity in that area of the law. Attorneys are required to be familiar with well-settled principles of law applicable to a case and to discover law that can be found through a reasonable amount of research. The lawyer also must investigate and discover facts that could materially affect the client's legal rights.

When an attorney fails to exercise reasonable care and professional judgment, he or she breaches the duty of care. The plaintiff must then prove that the breach actually

1. The word *defalcation* originated in the fifteenth century. Its roots are two Latin words that loosely translate to "a lopping off" or "a cutting off."

caused him or her some injury. • **EXAMPLE 39.1** John Jones, an attorney, allows the statute of limitations to lapse on the claim of Karen Anderson, a client. Jones can be held liable for **malpractice** (professional negligence)—because Anderson can no longer file a cause of action in this case and has lost a potential award of damages. •

• **MALPRACTICE**
Professional misconduct or unreasonable lack of skill. The failure of a professional to use the skills and learning common to the average reputable members of the profession or those the professional claims to possess, resulting in injury, loss, or damage to those relying on the professional.

Traditionally, to establish causation, the client normally had to show that "but for" the attorney's negligence, the client would not have suffered the injury. In recent years, however, several courts have held that plaintiffs in malpractice cases only need show that the defendant's negligence was a "substantial factor" in causing the plaintiff's injury. In the following case, the Supreme Court of New Jersey addresses the issue of what standard should be applied in determining whether an attorney's malpractice was the proximate cause of the plaintiffs' injuries.

CASE 39.1 Conklin v. Hannoch Weisman

Supreme Court of New Jersey, 1996.
145 N.J. 395,
678 A.2d 1060.
lawlibrary.rutgers.edu/citefind.html[a]

HISTORICAL AND SOCIAL SETTING *Dissatisfaction with attorneys' efforts has existed as long as there have been attorneys. When a client is dissatisfied, he or she has several alternatives. For example, if a client loses his or her case and is unhappy that he or she must still pay the attorney's fees, the client can discuss the situation with the attorney. If a client believes the attorney mishandled the case, the client can file a complaint with the state bar association or the disciplinary board of the state supreme court. If these attempts do not bring the result that the client seeks, he or she can file a malpractice suit.*

BACKGROUND AND FACTS The Conklins hired the law firm of Hannoch Weisman, Professional Corporation, to represent them in a sale of one hundred acres of their farm to Longview Estates. The purchase price of the land was $12 million. Longview made a $3 million down payment and gave the Conklins a mortgage for the balance. The mortgage, however, was subordinate (second in priority) to a mortgage held by another lender: if Longview defaulted on its payments, the other lender would be paid first. When Longview defaulted, the other lender took the land and the Conklins got nothing. They filed a suit in a New Jersey state court against Hannoch Weisman, claiming that the firm had not explained completely the risks of a subordinate mortgage. The jury was charged (instructed) to hold the firm liable only if the Conklins proved that their loss would not have occurred "but for" the firm's negligence. The jury issued a verdict in favor of the firm, but the judge decided that the jury charge was unclear and ordered a new trial. Hannoch Weisman appealed. The intermediate state appellate court affirmed the order of the trial judge (calling for a new trial), and the law firm appealed to the Supreme Court of New Jersey.

a. On this page, enter the appropriate numbers for the citation to the *Conklin* case in the *New Jersey Reports*. Click on "Submit Form" to access the opinion. This Web site is maintained by Rutgers School of Law in Camden, New Jersey

IN THE WORDS OF THE COURT . . .
O'HERN, J [Justice].

* * * *

In reality, there is usually no such thing as a risk-free deal. The best that a lawyer can do is to control the risks to help the clients to achieve their financial objectives. * * * Through advice and negotiating the terms of the contract, the parties and their lawyers control the risks of the deal. The Conklins wanted a specific price—twelve million dollars. They made a poor deal and sustained a grave loss. The question is whether the lack of adequate advice was a substantial factor in causing the Conklins' exposure to an unwanted risk of harm.

* * * *

* * * [T]he jury charge * * * could have confused the jury and led to an unjust result * * * . [T]he traditional jury charge [in which liability is subject to the "but for" test] * * * is inapt [inappropriate] for legal malpractice cases in which there are

CASE 39.1—Continued

concurrent independent causes of harm and * * * a jury in such cases must be instructed to determine whether the negligence was a substantial factor in bringing about the ultimate harm.

DECISION AND REMEDY The Supreme Court of New Jersey affirmed the judgment of the lower court. A new trial was ordered because the jury was given erroneous instructions in the applicable law. The law in New Jersey (and other states) provides that to recover in a legal malpractice case, a plaintiff needs to show only that the lawyer's negligence was a "substantial factor" in causing the harm.

FOR CRITICAL ANALYSIS—Social Consideration *Should lawyers be subject to higher legal and ethical standards than other professionals?*

PROFESSIONALS' LIABILITY FOR FRAUD

Actual fraud and constructive fraud present two different circumstances under which an accountant may be found liable. Recall from Chapter 12 that fraud, or misrepresentation, consists of the following elements:

1. A misrepresentation of a material fact has occurred.
2. There exists an intent to deceive.
3. The innocent party has justifiably relied on the misrepresentation.
4. For damages, the innocent party must have been injured.

A professional may be held liable for *actual fraud* when he or she intentionally misstates a material fact to mislead his or her client and the client justifiably relies on the misstated fact to his or her injury. A material fact is one that a reasonable person would consider important in deciding whether to act. In contrast, a professional may be held liable for *constructive fraud* whether or not he or she acted with

Technology and Attorney Advertising

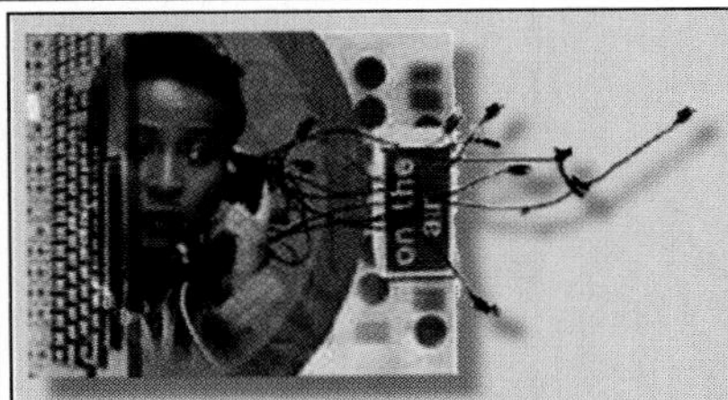

Do the rules of professional conduct that govern attorneys apply to the Internet? This is a question of growing importance because more and more attorneys are establishing home pages on the World Wide Web. Still, ethical as well as legal issues have inhibited many attorneys from creating Web pages or from otherwise becoming part of the Internet world.

Typically, law firms and solo practitioners that do have sites on the Web avoid ethical and legal problems by posting, in large print, a disclaimer indicating that the Web site is to provide general information, which is intended but not guaranteed to be correct or up to date. The disclaimer may also indicate that the site is not intended to give legal advice or solicit business. Therefore, no attorney-client relationship can be established by accessing the site.

It is illegal in all states to engage in the unauthorized practice of law, which occurs when an attorney practices law in a state but is not licensed by that particular state to do so. The Internet presents a serious problem because any advice given, for example, by an attorney in New York to a resident of Texas may constitute the unauthorized practice of law in Texas.

Another issue involves an implicit waiver of the attorney-client privilege. For example, consider the exchange of e-mail between an attorney and his or her client. Given that e-mail normally is not a secure communications medium, does its use constitute an implied waiver of the attorney-client privilege?

FOR CRITICAL ANALYSIS

Given that attorney codes of conduct are established by state law, how can they apply to Internet activities by lawyers, such as advertising?

fraudulent intent. • **EXAMPLE 39.2** In conducting an audit of National Computing Company (NCC), Paula, the auditor, accepts the explanations of Ron, an NCC officer, regarding certain financial irregularities, despite evidence that contradicts those explanations and indicates that the irregularities may be illegal. Paula's conduct could be characterized as an intentional failure to perform a duty in reckless disregard of the consequences of such a failure. This would constitute gross negligence and could be held to be constructive fraud. • Both actual and constructive fraud are potential sources of legal liability under which a client may bring an action against an accountant or other professional.

When a client is dissatisfied with the performance of an accounting or legal firm, he or she will often sue on several theories. In the following case, which deals with accountants, the court had to sift through claims for negligence, breach of contract, and constructive fraud. The court concluded that only the last theory presented a ground for going forward to trial.

CASE 39.2 Barger v. McCoy Hillard & Parks

Court of Appeals of North Carolina, 1995.
120 N.C.App. 326,
462 S.E.2d 252.

HISTORICAL AND TECHNOLOGICAL SETTING *Since at least the movie* 2001: A Space Odyssey *in 1968, it has been surmised that one day computers will replace human intelligence. In fact, as advanced as a computer may be at this stage of the technological revolution, it can only retrieve, analyze, and report the data that are entered into it. When people enter the data, mistakes are sometimes made. Because of the widely held notion that computers are infallible, however, whatever a computer does with data is generally accepted. This can turn what may have been a small error into a major blunder.*

BACKGROUND AND FACTS Jerry Barger, Wayne Kennerly, and Harry Young were the shareholders and directors of The Furniture House of North Carolina, Inc. (TFH). They asked David McCoy of the accounting firm of McCoy Hillard & Parks to determine the financial health of TFH. A misapplication of computer data resulted in an overstatement of sales and an understatement of liabilities. Based on these statements, McCoy assured Barger and the others that TFH could repay certain loans. Consequently, Barger and the others personally guaranteed the loans. Ultimately, TFH filed for bankruptcy and the guarantors were forced to repay the loans with their own money. They filed a suit against the accountants in a North Carolina state court, alleging, in part, fraud. The court granted the accountants' motion for summary judgment. Barger and the others appealed.

IN THE WORDS OF THE COURT . . .
JOHN C. MARTIN, Judge.

* * * *

For a constructive fraud claim, plaintiffs must allege the facts and circumstances (1) which created the relation of trust and confidence, and (2) led up to and surrounded the consummation of the transaction in which defendant is alleged to have taken advantage of his position of trust to the hurt of plaintiff. * * *

* * * [T]he record as to plaintiffs' * * * fraud claims arising from the personal guarantees does reflect a genuine issue of material fact when considered in the light most favorable to plaintiffs. It is possible to infer that defendant McCoy was aware plaintiffs would rely on his opinion in personally guaranteeing loans for TFH, and that the parties may have had a relationship of trust which defendants breached to the detriment of plaintiffs.

DECISION AND REMEDY The Court of Appeals of North Carolina reversed the lower court's grant of summary judgment on this issue and remanded the case for trial.

FOR CRITICAL ANALYSIS—Technological Consideration *How might the losses in this case have been avoided?*

Auditors' Liability to Third Parties

Traditionally, an accountant or other professional did not owe any duty to a third person with whom he or she had no direct contractual relationship—that is, to any person not in *privity of contract* with the professional. A professional's duty was only to his or her client. Violations of statutory laws, fraud, and other intentional or reckless acts of wrongdoing were the only exceptions to this general rule.

Today, numerous third parties—including investors, shareholders, creditors, corporate managers and directors, regulatory agencies, and others—rely on professional opinions, such as those of auditors, when making decisions. In view of this extensive reliance, many courts have all but abandoned the privity requirement in regard to accountants' liability to third parties.

In this section, we focus on the potential liability of auditors to third parties. Understanding an auditor's common law liability to third parties is critical, because often, when a business fails, its independent auditor (accountant) may be one of the few potentially solvent defendants. The majority of courts now hold that auditors can be held liable to third parties for negligence, but the standard for the imposition of this liability varies. There are generally three different views of accountants' liability to third parties, each of which we discuss below.

THE *ULTRAMARES* RULE

The traditional rule regarding an accountant's liability to third parties was enunciated by Chief Judge Benjamin Cardozo in *Ultramares Corp. v. Touche,* a case decided in 1931.[2] In *Ultramares,* Fred Stern & Company (Stern) hired the public accounting firm of Touche, Niven & Company (Touche) to review Stern's financial records and prepare a balance sheet for the year ending December 31, 1923.[3] Touche prepared the balance sheet and supplied Stern with thirty-two certified copies. According to the certified balance sheet, Stern had a net worth (assets less liabilities) of $1,070,715.26. In reality, however, Stern was insolvent—the company's records had been falsified by Stern's insiders to reflect a positive net worth. In reliance on the certified balance sheets, a lender, Ultramares Corporation, loaned substantial amounts to Stern. After Stern was declared bankrupt, Ultramares brought an action against Touche for negligence in an attempt to recover damages.

The New York Court of Appeals (that state's highest court) refused to impose liability on the accountants and concluded that they owed a duty of care only to those persons for whose "primary benefit" the statements were intended. In this case, Stern was the only person for whose primary benefit the statements were intended. The court held that in the absence of privity or a relationship "so close as to approach that of privity," a party could not recover from an accountant.

The court's requirement of privity or near privity has since been referred to as the *Ultramares* rule, or the New York rule. The rule was restated and somewhat modified in a 1985 New York case, *Credit Alliance Corp. v. Arthur Andersen & Co.*[4] In that case, the court held that if a third party has a sufficiently close relationship or nexus (link or connection) with an accountant, then the *Ultramares* privity requirement may

2. 255 N.Y. 170, 174 N.E. 441 (1931).

3. A balance sheet is often relied on by banks, creditors, stockholders, purchasers, or sellers as a basis for making decisions relating to a company's business.

4. 65 N.Y.2d 536, 483 N.E.2d 110 (1985): A "relationship sufficiently intimate to be equated with privity" is sufficient for a third party to sue another's accountant for negligence.

be satisfied without establishing an accountant-client relationship. The rule enunciated in *Credit Alliance* is often referred to as the "near privity" rule. Only a minority of states have adopted this rule of accountants' liability to third parties.

THE *RESTATEMENT* RULE

In the past several years, the *Ultramares* rule has been severely criticized. Auditors perform much of their work for use by persons who are not parties to the contract; and thus, it is asserted that they owe a duty to these third parties. Consequently, there has been an erosion of the *Ultramares* rule, and accountants have been exposed to potential liability to third parties.

The majority of courts have adopted the position taken by the *Restatement (Second) of Torts,* which states that accountants are subject to liability for negligence not only to their clients but also to *foreseen,* or *known,* users—or classes of users—of their reports or financial statements. Under Section 552(2) of the *Restatement (Second) of Torts,* an accountant's liability extends to those persons for whose benefit and guidance the accountant "intends to supply the information or knows that the recipient intends to supply it" and to those persons whom the accountant "intends the information to influence or knows that the recipient so intends." • **EXAMPLE 39.3** Steve, an accountant, prepares a financial statement for Tech Software, Inc., a client, knowing that the client will submit that statement to First National Bank to secure a loan. If Steve makes negligent misstatements or omissions in the statement, he may be held liable by the bank—because he knew that the bank would rely on his work product when deciding whether to make the loan. •

LIABILITY TO REASONABLY FORESEEABLE USERS

A small minority of courts hold accountants liable to any users whose reliance on an accountant's statements or reports was *reasonably foreseeable.* This standard has been criticized as extending liability too far. • **EXAMPLE 39.4** In *Raritan River Steel Co. v. Cherry, Bekaert & Holland,* the North Carolina Supreme Court stated that "in fairness accountants should not be liable in circumstances where they are unaware of the use to which their opinions will be put. Instead, their liability should be commensurate with those persons or classes of persons whom they know will rely on their work. With such knowledge the auditor can, through purchase of liability insurance, setting fees, and adopting other protective measures appropriate to the risk, prepare accordingly."[5] •

It is the view of the majority of the courts that the *Restatement's* approach is the more reasonable because it allows accountants to control their exposure to liability. Liability is "fixed by the accountants' particular knowledge at the moment the audit is published," not by the foreseeability of the harm that might occur to a third party after the report is released.[6]

Even the California courts, which for several years had relied on reasonable foreseeability as the standard for determining an auditor's liability to third parties, have recently changed their position. In a 1992 case, the California Supreme Court held that an accountant "owes no general duty of care regarding the conduct of an audit to persons other than the client." The court went on to say that if third parties rely on an auditor's opinion, "there is no liability even though the [auditor] should reasonably have foreseen such a possibility."[7]

5. 322 N.C. 200, 367 S.E.2d 609 (1988).
6. *Bethlehem Steel Corp. v. Ernst & Whinney,* 822 S.W.2d 592 (1991).
7. *Bily v. Arthur Young & Co.,* 3 Cal.4th 370, 834 P.2d 745, 11 Cal.Rptr.2d 51 (1992).

Business Law in Action • A Limit to Auditors' Liability

Osborne Computer Corporation manufactured the first portable personal computer. Why isn't the name "Osborne" on everyone's laptop? Because simultaneously, International Business Machines, Inc. (IBM), introduced its first personal computer. IBM's entry devastated Osborne, and Osborne's sales plummeted. The company also experienced manufacturing problems with its new computer and consequently filed for bankruptcy in September 1983. No one was more disappointed than those who had invested in Osborne. The investors filed a suit in a California state court against Osborne's independent auditor, Arthur Young & Company, for, among other things, professional negligence.

An *auditor* is hired by a company to conduct an independent inspection of the company's accounting records. After inspecting the records, the auditor reviews the company's financial statements, which summarize its financial situation. The auditor may then issue an *audit opinion,* which endorses, criticizes, or disclaims the fairness of the financial statements. At one time, if an auditor committed professional negligence in conducting an audit, the auditor was liable only to the client. As audits circulated more widely among lenders and investors, however, the courts began to make it easier for others to sue. Auditors argue that they did not intend or expect many of these parties to rely on their work and that these plaintiffs are simply looking for a "deep pocket."

In the case of the Osborne investors' lawsuit, Arthur Young & Company had issued unqualified, "clean" opinions on Osborne's financial statements. The jury assessed $4.3 million in damages against Young on the professional negligence claim. Young appealed.

At the time, the law in California on the issue of auditor liability to third parties focused on foreseeability. That is, accountants were potentially liable to any third party who might reasonably have relied on the auditor's opinion regarding a company's financial statements. In this case, however, the California Supreme Court interpreted the *Restatement (Second) of Torts,* Section 552, to limit the liability of auditors to third parties. The court believed that the jury's award "raises the spectre of multibillion-dollar professional liability that is distinctly out of proportion" to fault. "[A]n auditor owes no general duty of care regarding the conduct of an audit to persons other than the client." In other words, "[i]f others become aware of the representation and act upon it, there is no liability even though the [auditor] should reasonably have foreseen such a possibility."[a]

Did the court leave third parties with no alternatives but to accept their losses? No. The court left open the possibility of suing an auditor for negligent misrepresentation to "those persons who act in reliance upon those misrepresentations in a transaction which the auditor intended to influence." Also, "reasonably foreseeable third persons" can sue an auditor for *intentional* fraud.

FOR CRITICAL ANALYSIS

What are policy reasons for not holding auditors liable to third parties who were not "reasonably foreseeable"?

a. *Bily v. Arthur Young & Co.,* 3 Cal.4th 370, 834 P.2d 745, 11 Cal.Rptr.2d 51 (1992).

International Perspective • ACCOUNTANTS' LIABILITY IN ENGLAND

After a long history of requiring privity, English courts began permitting foreseeable third parties to sue accountants for negligence. This produced a backlash, and a 1990 decision restricted such third party liability. The court described the "frightening" extent of accountants' liability in the United States and stressed that English courts should "demonstrate a greater concern for equity."

FOR CRITICAL ANALYSIS

What policy considerations might motivate a government to restrict the liability of accountants to third parties?

Liability of Attorneys to Third Parties

Like accountants, attorneys may also be held liable under the common law to third parties who rely on legal opinions to their detriment. Generally, an attorney is not liable to a nonclient unless there is fraud (or malicious conduct) by the attorney. The liability principles stated in Section 552 of the *Restatement (Second) of Torts*, however, may apply to attorneys just as they may apply to accountants. This is illustrated in the following case.

CASE 39.3 Mehaffy, Rider, Windholz & Wilson v. Central Bank Denver, N.A.

Supreme Court of Colorado, 1995.
892 P.2d 230.

HISTORICAL AND POLITICAL SETTING *Based on the ancient principle that "the King can do no wrong," a government can be sued only when it consents. This is known as sovereign immunity. Congress has enacted laws that, in most cases, waive the federal government's sovereign immunity. State and local governments have waived their immunity only in various degrees, however. For example, when a school district sells bonds to finance the construction of a new school but defaults on repayment, a buyer of the bonds might not be able to collect from the district because it may be immune from suit.*

BACKGROUND AND FACTS To raise money for a new parking garage, the town of Winter Park, Colorado, issued over $5 million in bonds. In a suit challenging the garage, the law firm of Mehaffy, Rider, Windholz & Wilson represented Winter Park. Central Bank Denver was considering a purchase of the bonds and asked Mehaffy, Rider, and other law firms, for "opinion letters" as to whether the suit had any merit. The law firms said no. The bank bought the bonds. When the case came to trial, however, the judge voided the town's plan. Central Bank filed a suit in a Colorado state court against the law firms, alleging, among other things, negligent misrepresentation. The court dismissed the suit. Central Bank appealed, the state intermediate appellate court reversed, and the law firms appealed to the Supreme Court of Colorado.

IN THE WORDS OF THE COURT . . .
Justice *ERICKSON* delivered the Opinion of the Court.

* * * *

The tort of negligent misrepresentation provides a remedy when money is lost due to misrepresentation in a business transaction. * * *

Professionals other than attorneys are subject to liability to third persons for negligent misrepresentation in Colorado. A theory of negligent misrepresentation is proper where a professional knows that its representation will be relied upon by a non-client for business purposes.

* * * *

In the present case, respondent [Central Bank] requested * * * opinion letters because of the potential damage of the lawsuit on [Winter Park's] ability to pay off the * * * Bonds. [Mehaffy, Rider's] opinion letters were prepared for the benefit of respondent and most of the letters were addressed to the respondent. The letters assured respondent that the lawsuit did not have merit. The opinion letters were not issued in the context of an adversarial relationship, but were issued in order to secure respondent's participation in a business relationship that would mutually benefit the Town * * * and respondent. Accordingly, by issuing legal opinion letters for the purpose of inducing respondent to purchase the * * * Bonds, petitioners may be liable to respondent for negligent misrepresentation.

CASE 39.3—Continued

DECISION AND REMEDY The Supreme Court of Colorado affirmed the appellate court's decision and remanded the case for trial.

FOR CRITICAL ANALYSIS—Social Consideration *When this case is returned to the lower court for a trial, what will the plaintiff have to prove to win?*

Potential Statutory Liability of Accountants

Both civil and criminal liability may be imposed on accountants under the Securities Act of 1933 and the Securities Exchange Act of 1934.[8]

LIABILITY UNDER THE SECURITIES ACT OF 1933

The Securities Act of 1933 requires registration statements to be filed with the Securities and Exchange Commission (SEC) prior to an offering of securities (see Chapter 31).[9] Accountants frequently prepare and certify the issuer's financial statements that are included in the registration statement.

Liability under Section 11 Section 11 of the Securities Act of 1933 imposes civil liability on accountants for misstatements and omissions of material facts in registration statements. Therefore, an accountant may be found liable if he or she prepared any financial statements included in the registration statement that "contained an untrue statement of a material fact or omitted to state a material fact required to be stated therein or necessary to make the statements therein not misleading."[10]

Liability to Purchasers of Securities. Under Section 11, an accountant's liability for a misstatement or omission of a material fact in a registration statement extends to anyone who acquires a security covered by the registration statement. A purchaser of a security need only demonstrate that he or she has suffered a loss on the security. Proof of reliance on the materially false statement or misleading omission is not ordinarily required. Nor is there a requirement of privity between the accountant and the security purchasers.

• **DUE DILIGENCE**
A required standard of care that certain professionals, such as accountants, must meet to avoid liability for securities violations.

The Due Diligence Standard. Section 11 imposes a duty on accountants to use **due diligence** in the preparation of financial statements included in the filed registration statements. After the purchaser has proved the loss on the security, the accountant bears the burden of showing that he or she exercised due diligence in the preparation of the financial statements. To avoid liability, the accountant must show that he or she had, "after reasonable investigation, reasonable grounds to believe and did believe, at the time such part of the registration statement became effective, that the statements therein were true and that there was no omission of a material fact required to be stated therein or necessary to make the statements therein not misleading."[11] Further, the failure to follow GAAP and GAAS is also proof of a lack of due diligence.

8. Other potential sources of civil and criminal liability that may be imposed on accountants and other professionals include provisions of the Racketeer Influenced and Corrupt Organizations Act (RICO). RICO is discussed in Chapter 5.
9. Many securities and transactions are expressly exempted from the 1933 act.
10. 15 U.S.C. Section 77k(a).
11. 15 U.S.C. Section 77k(b)(3).

In particular, the due diligence standard places a burden on accountants to verify information furnished by a corporation's officers and directors. The burden of proving due diligence requires an accountant to demonstrate that he or she is free from negligence or fraud. Merely asking questions is not always sufficient to satisfy the requirement of due diligence. • **EXAMPLE 39.5** In *Escott v. BarChris Construction Corp.*,[12] accountants were held liable for failing to detect danger signals in documents furnished by corporate officers that, under GAAS, required further investigation under the circumstances. •

Defenses to Liability. Besides proving that he or she has acted with due diligence, an accountant may raise the following defenses to Section 11 liability:

1. There were no misstatements or omissions.
2. The misstatements or omissions were not of material facts.
3. The misstatements or omissions had no causal connection to the plaintiff's loss.
4. The plaintiff purchaser invested in the securities knowing of the misstatements or omissions.

Another defense is that an alleged misstatement or omission was not part of a financial statement that the accountant prepared or certified. Whether an accountant prepared or certified a particular statement is not always as obvious as it might seem, as illustrated by the following case.

12. 283 F.Supp. 643 (S.D.N.Y. 1968).

CASE 39.4 Endo v. Arthur Andersen & Co.

United States Court of Appeals,
Seventh Circuit, 1999.
163 F.3d 463.
www.findlaw.com/casecode/courts/7th.html[a]

HISTORICAL AND SOCIAL SETTING *Sometimes, a financial statement prepared by an auditor in a previous year is republished. When the auditor who certified the previous statement is not the current auditor, sound accounting practice requires the former auditor to check with its successor to make sure that nothing has been discovered that would falsify the previous statement.*[b] *It has been a common and unquestioned practice to revise the footnotes on the basis of new information provided by the current auditor.*

BACKGROUND AND FACTS Arthur Andersen & Company audited the financial statements of Fruit of the Loom, Inc. (FOL), for 1985. The statements included a footnote that said FOL was contesting, in federal court, $105 million in deficiencies assessed by the Internal Revenue Service (IRS). The footnote warned that the ultimate payment to the IRS could, with interest, exceed $105 million. This warning did not appear in FOL's 1986 financial statements, which were audited by Ernst & Young. In 1987, FOL made a stock offering that required the firm to disclose its 1985 financial statements. FOL asked Andersen to consent to a republication of its 1985 report without the warning in the footnote. Andersen checked with Ernst & Young, which certified that nothing had been discovered to warrant changing the data in the 1985 statements. Andersen consented to the republication. Within a year, FOL was ordered to pay the IRS more than $105 million. The price of the FOL stock dropped by 33 percent. Investors who lost money filed a suit in a federal district court against Andersen and others, alleging in part that omitting the warning from the footnote in the republished report violated Section 11 of the Securities Act of 1933. The court granted a summary judgment in Andersen's favor. The plaintiffs appealed to the U.S. Court of Appeals for the Seventh Circuit.

a. This is a page, within the FindLaw Web site, that provides access to some of the opinions of the U.S. Court of Appeals for the Seventh Circuit. In the "1999" row, click on the "Jan" link. When that page opens, scroll down the list of cases to the *Endo* case. Click on the case name to access the opinion.
b. Statements on Auditing Standards No. 37, 1 American Institute of Certified Public Accountants, AICPA Professional Standards AU Section 711.11 (1996).

CASE 39.4—Continued

IN THE WORDS OF THE COURT . . .
POSNER, Chief Judge.

* * * *

* * * The investor who reads the documentation accompanying FOL's [stock offering] sees a column for the company's 1985 financial results, a column for its 1986 results, a set of footnotes dealing with contingent [potential] liabilities not reflected in the columns, and notations that Andersen audited the 1985 results and continues to stand by them and that Ernst & Young audited the 1986 results. * * *

The footnotes are, it is true, a part of the financial statements. But remember that an accountant's liability for misleading representations in a registration statement is limited to the portion of any financial statements which purports to have been prepared or certified by him. Andersen did not purport to certify the footnotes to Fruit of the Loom's 1986 financial statements * * * . Nor would any reasonable investor have thought otherwise.

* * * *

* * * The investor does not expect the same financial data and estimates to be audited by two separate audit companies. He expects the current data, including the current estimates of contingent liabilities, to be audited by the current auditor, and data for periods prior to the hiring of this auditor to be audited by a former auditor. Ernst & Young did not audit the 1985 financials; Andersen did. Andersen did not audit the 1986 predictions; Ernst & Young did.[c]

DECISION AND REMEDY The U.S. Court of Appeals for the Seventh Circuit affirmed the judgment of the lower court. The omitted warning was a past prediction about a future event as to which Andersen's successor had more current information. A reasonable investor would expect current data, including estimates of tax liability, to be audited by the current auditor.

FOR CRITICAL ANALYSIS—Social Consideration *If the court had held that old audits could be republished only with unrevised footnotes, what would happen to the documents that accompany stock offerings?*

c. The investors also filed a suit against Ernst & Young, which settled out of court.

Liability under Section 12(2) Section 12(2) of the Securities Act of 1933 imposes civil liability for fraud on anyone offering or selling a security.[13] Liability is based on the communication to an investor, whether orally or in the written prospectus,[14] of an untrue statement or omission of a material fact.

Before 1994, some courts applied Section 12(2) to accountants who *aided and abetted* the seller or the offeror of the securities in violating Section 12(2). In those jurisdictions that apply Section 12(2) to accountants for aiding and abetting, the accountant might have been liable if he or she knew, or should have known, that an untrue statement or omission of material fact existed in the offer or sale. In light of the United States Supreme Court's decision in *Central Bank of Denver, N.A. v. First Interstate Bank of Denver, N.A.*[15] (discussed later in this chapter), regarding liability for aiding and abetting under Section 10(b), accountants are unlikely to be held liable in the future, in suits by private individuals, for aiding and abetting their clients' Section 12(2) violations.

13. 15 U.S.C. Section 77*l*.

14. As discussed in Chapter 31, a *prospectus* contains financial disclosures about the corporation for the benefit of potential investors.

15. 511 U.S. 164, 114 S.Ct. 1439, 128 L.Ed.2d 119 (1994).

LIABILITY UNDER THE SECURITIES EXCHANGE ACT OF 1934

Under Sections 18 and 10(b) of the Securities Exchange Act of 1934 and Rule 10b-5 of the Securities and Exchange Commission, an accountant may be found liable for fraud. A plaintiff has a substantially heavier burden of proof under the 1934 act than under the 1933 act. Unlike the 1933 act, the 1934 act provides that an accountant need not prove due diligence to escape liability.

Liability under Section 18 Section 18 of the 1934 act imposes civil liability on an accountant who makes or causes to be made in any application, report, or document a statement that at the time and in light of the circumstances was false or misleading with respect to any material fact.[16]

Section 18 liability is narrow in that it applies only to applications, reports, documents, and registration statements filed with the SEC. This remedy is further limited in that it applies only to sellers and purchasers. Under Section 18, a seller or purchaser must prove one of the following:

1. That the false or misleading statement affected the price of the security.
2. That the purchaser or seller relied on the false or misleading statement in making the purchase or sale and was not aware of the inaccuracy of the statement.

Even if a purchaser or seller proves these two elements, an accountant can be exonerated of liability on proof of "good faith" in the preparation of the financial statement. To demonstrate good faith, an accountant must show that he or she had no knowledge that the financial statement was false and misleading. Acting in good faith requires the total absence of an intention on the part of the accountant to seek an unfair advantage over, or to defraud, another party. Proving a lack of intent to deceive, manipulate, or defraud is frequently referred to as proving a lack of *scienter* (knowledge on the part of a misrepresenting party that material facts have been misrepresented or omitted with an intent to deceive).

Absence of good faith can be demonstrated not only by proof of *scienter* but also by the accountant's reckless conduct and gross negligence. (Note that "mere" negligence in the preparation of a financial statement does not constitute liability under the 1934 act. This differs from provisions of the 1933 act, under which an accountant is liable for all negligent acts.) In addition to the good faith defense, accountants have available as a defense the buyer's or seller's knowledge that the financial statement was false and misleading.

A court, under Section 18 of the 1934 act, also has the discretion to assess reasonable costs, including attorneys' fees, against accountants.[17] Sellers and purchasers may maintain a cause of action "within one year after the discovery of the facts constituting the cause of action and within three years after such cause of action accrued."[18]

Liability under Section 10(b) and Rule 10b-5 The Securities Exchange Act of 1934 further subjects accountants to potential legal liability in its antifraud provisions. Section 10(b) of the 1934 act and SEC Rule 10b-5 contain the antifraud provisions. As stated in *Herman & MacLean v. Huddleston,* "a private right of action under Section 10(b) of the 1934 act and Rule 10b-5 has been consistently recognized for more than 35 years."[19]

16. 15 U.S.C. Section 78r(a).
17. 15 U.S.C. Section 78r(a).
18. 15 U.S.C. Section 78r(c).
19. 459 U.S. 375, 103 S.Ct. 683, 74 L.Ed.2d 548 (1983).

Section 10(b) makes it unlawful for any person, including accountants, to use, in connection with the purchase or sale of any security, any manipulative or deceptive device or contrivance in contravention of SEC rules and regulations.[20] Rule 10b-5 further makes it unlawful for any person, by use of any means or instrumentality of interstate commerce, to do the following:

1. To employ any device, scheme, or artifice to defraud.
2. To make any untrue statement of a material fact or to omit to state a material fact necessary to make the statements made, in light of the circumstances, not misleading.
3. To engage in any act, practice, or course of business that operates or would operate as a fraud or deceit on any person, in connection with the purchase or sale of any security.[21]

Accountants may be held liable only to sellers or purchasers under Section 10(b) and Rule 10b-5.[22] The scope of these antifraud provisions is extremely wide. Privity is not necessary for a recovery. Under these provisions, an accountant may be found liable not only for fraudulent misstatements of material facts in written material filed with the SEC but also for any fraudulent oral statements or omissions made in connection with the purchase or sale of any security.

***The Requirement of* Scienter.** For a plaintiff to recover from an accountant under the antifraud provisions of the 1934 act, he or she must, in addition to establishing status as a purchaser or seller, prove *scienter,*[23] a fraudulent action or deception, reliance, materiality, and causation. A plaintiff who fails to establish these elements cannot recover damages from an accountant under Section 10(b) or Rule 10b-5.

Liability of Aiders and Abettors. A significant issue in recent years concerns whether accountants (and others) may be held liable in private actions for "aiding and abetting" violations of various provisions of the securities laws, including Section 10(b) and Rule 10b-5. In a 1994 case, *Central Bank of Denver, N.A. v. First Interstate Bank of Denver, N.A.,*[24] the United States Supreme Court held that private parties could not bring actions against accountants for aiding and abetting violations of Section 10(b) of the 1934 act. The Court stated that "none of the express causes of action in the 1934 Act further imposes liability on one who aids or abets a violation." It was not clear from the Court's opinion, however, whether the logic of *Central Bank* should extend to injunctive actions brought by the Securities and Exchange Commission (SEC) against aiders and abettors of Section 10(b) violations. We will examine this issue further in the next subsection.

The Private Securities Litigation Reform Act of 1995

The Private Securities Litigation Reform Act of 1995 made some changes to the potential liability of accountants and other professionals in securities fraud cases.[25] Among other things, the act imposed a new statutory obligation on accountants. An auditor must use adequate procedures in an audit to detect any illegal acts of the

20. 15 U.S.C. Section 78j(b).
21. 17 C.F.R. Section 240.10b-5.
22. See *Blue Chip Stamps v. Manor Drug Stores,* 421 U.S. 723, 95 S.Ct. 1917, 44 L.Ed.2d 539 (1975).
23. See *Ernst & Ernst v. Hochfelder,* 425 U.S. 185, 96 S.Ct. 1375, 47 L.Ed.2d 668 (1976).
24. 511 U.S. 164, 114 S.Ct. 1439, 128 L.Ed.2d 119 (1994).
25. Some parties attempted to bypass the new law by filing their suits in state, rather than federal, courts. Congress acted to block such suits by passing the Securities Litigation Uniform Standards Act of 1998.

company being audited. If something illegal is detected, the auditor must disclose it to the company's board of directors, the audit committee, or the SEC, depending on the circumstances.[26]

In terms of liability, the 1995 act provides that in most situations, a party is liable only for that proportion of damages for which he or she is responsible.[27] • **EXAMPLE 39.6** Marcos, an accountant, knowingly helps the officers of Interstate Transportation Corporation (ITC) draft financial statements that misrepresent ITC's financial condition. This is actual participation in the defrauding of investors. Marcos could be held liable for the entire loss. • An accountant who does not participate in, and is unaware of, illegal conduct may not be liable for an entire loss caused by the illegality. • **EXAMPLE 39.7** Nina, an accountant, helps the president and owner of Midstate Trucking Company draft financial statements that misrepresent the financial state of Midstate, but Nina is not actually aware of the fraud. Nina might be held liable, but the amount of her liability could be proportionately less than the entire loss. •

The act also stated that aiding and abetting a violation of the Securities Exchange Act of 1934 is a violation in itself. The following case addresses this provision of the 1995 act. The case arose after the SEC issued an injunctive order against an attorney for aiding and abetting violations of Section 10(b) of the 1934 act. The order was issued just two weeks after the Supreme Court had rendered its opinion in the *Central Bank* case. The attorney appealed the order, claiming that the Supreme Court's decision in *Central Bank* precluded the SEC from bringing a civil injunctive action for aiding and abetting securities fraud. A central issue in the case had to do with whether the 1995 Private Securities Litigation Reform Act reversed any impact that *Central Bank* might have had on the SEC's power to enjoin aiding and abetting of Section 10(b).

26. 15 U.S.C. Section 78j-1.
27. 15 U.S.C. Section 78u-4(g).

CASE 39.5 SEC v. Fehn

United States Court of Appeals,
Ninth Circuit, 1996.
97 F.3d 1276.
www.law.vill.edu/fed-ct/Circuit/9th/October96.html[a]

HISTORICAL AND SOCIAL SETTING *In the late 1980s and early 1990s, there seemed to be an increasing number of lawsuits against professionals and financial institutions on what many observers considered to be somewhat flimsy bases. Liability expanded as courts allowed diverse actions founded on tort, contract, and statutory grounds. It was as if the defendants were being told to focus, not so much on the bottom line, but in-between the lines, with a high level of responsibility. These suits led to the* Central Bank *decision, which did not, however, bring an end to them.*

a. This page lists opinions issued by the U.S. Court of Appeals for the Ninth Circuit in October 1996. Scroll down the list of cases and click on the *Fehn* case name to access the opinion. This Web site is maintained by the Center for Information Law and Policy at Villanova University School of Law.

BACKGROUND AND FACTS CTI Technical, Inc., issued stock in a public offering that violated federal securities laws. The Securities and Exchange Commission (SEC) began an investigation. Thomas Fehn, an attorney who represented CTI during the investigation, prepared certain required reports for CTI and sent them to the SEC. The reports contained material misrepresentations related to the securities violations. The SEC filed a suit in a federal district court against Fehn, charging him with aiding and abetting securities fraud. The court issued an injunction barring Fehn from aiding and abetting any future securities fraud. Fehn appealed to the U.S. Court of Appeals for the Ninth Circuit. Fehn argued, among other things, that the United States Supreme Court's decision in *Central Bank* prevented the SEC from filing suits for aiding and abetting securities violations.

CASE 39.5—Continued

IN THE WORDS OF THE COURT . . .
MICHAEL DALY HAWKINS, Circuit Judge:

* * * *

By its clear terms, [the Private Securities Litigation Reform Act of 1995] provides that aiding and abetting a violation of [federal securities laws] is itself a violation, and as such is subject to injunctive actions and civil actions for money penalties by the SEC. * * *

Legislative history confirms that [the Private Securities Litigation Reform Act of 1995] was intended to override *Central Bank's* apparent elimination of the SEC's power to enjoin the aiding and abetting of securities law violations. Discussion of the proposed legislation is contained in Senate Banking Committee Report No. 104-98. That report makes clear the drafters' intent to authorize the SEC to enjoin those who aid and abet such violations: "Prior to the Supreme Court's decision in *Central Bank,* courts of appeals had recognized that private parties could bring actions against persons who 'aided and abetted' primary violators of the securities laws. In *Central Bank,* the Court held that there was no aiding and abetting liability for private lawsuits involving violations of the securities antifraud provisions. * * * The Committee does, however, grant the SEC express authority to bring actions seeking injunctive relief or money damages against persons who knowingly aid and abet primary violators of the securities laws."

DECISION AND REMEDY The U.S. Court of Appeals for the Ninth Circuit affirmed the lower court's injunction barring Fehn from participating in any future securities fraud. The Private Securities Litigation Reform Act of 1995 precluded the extension of the Supreme Court's decision in *Central Bank* to SEC actions.

FOR CRITICAL ANALYSIS—Economic Consideration *If there were a private cause of action for "aiding and abetting," what effect might that have on newer and smaller companies?*

Potential Criminal Liability

ON THE WEB

Federal tax forms and federal tax information is available from the Internal Revenue Service at its Web site, which can be found at

www.irs.ustreas.gov.

An accountant may be found criminally liable for violations of the Securities Act of 1933, the Securities Exchange Act of 1934, the Internal Revenue Code, and both state and federal criminal codes. Under both the 1933 act and the 1934 act, accountants may be subject to criminal penalties for *willful* violations—imprisonment of up to ten years and/or a fine of up to $10,000 under the 1933 act and up to $100,000 under the 1934 act.

The Internal Revenue Code, Section 7206(2),[28] makes aiding or assisting in the preparation of a false tax return a felony punishable by a fine of $100,000 ($500,000 in the case of a corporation) and imprisonment for up to three years. Those who prepare tax returns for others also may face liability under the Internal Revenue Code. Note that one does not have to be an accountant to be subject to liability for tax-preparer penalties. The Internal Revenue Code defines a tax preparer as any person who prepares for compensation, or who employs one or more persons to prepare for compensation, all or a substantial portion of a tax return or a claim for a tax refund.[29]

28. 26 U.S.C. Section 7206(2).
29. 26 U.S.C. Section 7701(a)(36).

Section 6694[30] of the Internal Revenue Code imposes on the tax preparer a penalty of $250 per return for negligent understatement of his or her client's tax liability and a penalty of $1,000 for willful understatement of tax liability or reckless or intentional disregard of rules or regulations. A tax preparer may also be subject to penalties under Section 6695[31] for failing to furnish the taxpayer with a copy of the return, failing to sign the return, or failing to furnish the appropriate tax identification numbers.

Section 6701[32] of the Internal Revenue Code imposes a penalty of $1,000 per document for aiding and abetting an individual's understatement of tax liability (the penalty is increased to $10,000 in corporate cases). The tax preparer's liability is limited to one penalty per taxpayer per tax year. If this penalty is imposed, no penalty can be imposed under Section 6694 with respect to the same document.

In most states, criminal penalties may be imposed for such actions as knowingly certifying false or fraudulent reports; falsifying, altering, or destroying books of account; and obtaining property or credit through the use of false financial statements.

Working Papers

• **WORKING PAPERS**
The various documents used and developed by an accountant during an audit. Working papers include notes, computations, memoranda, copies, and other papers that make up the work product of an accountant's services to a client.

Performing an audit for a client involves an accumulation of **working papers**—the various documents used and developed during the audit. These include notes, computations, memoranda, copies, and other papers that make up the work product of an accountant's services to a client. Under the common law, which in this instance has been codified in a number of states, working papers remain the accountant's property. It is important for accountants to retain such records in the event that they need to defend against lawsuits for negligence or other actions in which their competence is challenged. Because an accountant's working papers reflect his or her client's financial situation, however, the client has a right of access to them. (An accountant must return to his or her client any of the client's records or journals on the client's request, and failure to do so may result in liability.)

The client must give permission before working papers can be transferred to another accountant. Without the client's permission or a valid court order, the contents of working papers are not to be disclosed. Disclosure would constitute a breach of the accountant's fiduciary duty to the client. On the ground of unauthorized disclosure, the client could initiate a malpractice suit. The accountant's best defense would be that the client gave permission for the papers' release.

Confidentiality and Privilege

Professionals are restrained by the ethical tenets of their professions to keep all communications with their clients confidential. The confidentiality of attorney-client communications is also protected by law, which confers a privilege on such communications. This privilege is granted because of the need for full disclosure to the attorney of the facts of a client's case. To encourage frankness, confidential attorney-client communications relating to representation are normally held in strictest confidence and protected by law. The attorney and his or her employees may not discuss the client's case with anyone—even under court order—without the client's permission. The client holds the privilege, and only the client may waive it.

30. 26 U.S.C. Section 6694.
31. 26 U.S.C. Section 6695.
32. 26 U.S.C. Section 6701.

• **EXAMPLE 39.8** Jane consults with Larry, an attorney, regarding her potential liability in an upcoming lawsuit. Jane discusses the suit with some of her co-workers and friends. By disclosing otherwise privileged information to someone outside the privilege, Jane has waived it. •

In a few states, accountant-client communications are privileged by state statute. In these states, accountant-client communications may not be revealed even in court or in court-sanctioned proceedings without the client's permission. The majority of states, however, abide by the common law, which provides that, if a court so orders, an accountant must disclose information about his or her client to the court. Physicians and other professionals may similarly be compelled to disclose in court information given to them in confidence by patients or clients.

Professional-client communications—other than those between an attorney and his or her client—are not privileged under federal law. In cases involving federal law, state-provided rights to confidentiality of accountant-client communications are not recognized. • **EXAMPLE 39.9** Greg, an accountant, has a client, Mary, who is involved in a case brought in a federal court against Mary by the Internal Revenue Service claiming that she filed false federal tax returns. In that case, in response to a court order, Greg must provide the information sought. •

Limiting Professionals' Liability

As mentioned earlier in this chapter, accountants (and other professionals) can limit their liability to some extent by disclaiming it. Depending on the circumstances, a disclaimer that does not meet certain requirements will not be effective, and in some situations, a disclaimer may not be effective at all.

Professionals may be able to limit their liability for the misconduct of other professionals with whom they work by organizing their business as a professional corporation (PC) or a limited liability partnership (LLP). In some states, a professional who is a member of a PC is not personally liable for a co-member's misconduct unless he or she participated in it or supervised the member who acted wrongly. The innocent professional is liable only to the extent of his or her interest in the assets of the firm. This is also true for professionals who are partners in an LLP. PCs are discussed in more detail in Chapter 27. LLPs are covered in Chapter 32.

APPLICATION Law and the Businessperson: Avoiding Fraudulent Financial Reporting*

*This *Application* is not meant to substitute for the services of an attorney who is licensed to practice law in your state.

Fraudulent financial reporting occurs when the management of a company intentionally overstates the company's assets or recognizes revenue that the company does not have. Fraudulent financial reporting results in materially misleading financial statements. These statements may involve the misapplication of generally accepted accounting principles, inflated evaluations of assets, or the omission of material information. For example, exaggerating company records to overstate inventory, show nonexistent transactions, and inflate earnings is fraudulent financial reporting.

When these misrepresentations come to light, a company is forced to issue new, more accurate financial statements. Because the fraudulent statements exaggerated the financial status of the company, the truer statements typically result in a decrease in the market price of the company's stock. This can serve as the motivation for a lawsuit. Shareholders may allege that the board of directors, the company's officers, and

APPLICATION CONTINUED

an independent auditing firm prepared and made public materially false and misleading financial statements.

What should a company do to avoid fraudulent financial reporting? First, a company can establish an audit committee, composed of directors, that nominates the independent auditor and works with the auditing firm. More importantly, however, the committee should review and evaluate the company's financial statements and accounting policies in accord with generally accepted accounting principles.

The responsibilities of this committee, or of the company's management in the absence of a committee, should include reviewing the company's financial reporting process and the internal controls that are intended to thwart fraud. The committee can also act as a mediator should any problems develop with the auditing firm. Lawyers might also be employed to help recognize early symptoms that could lead to liability for fraudulent financial reporting. Finally, the committee should review carefully all financial statements and press releases concerning the financial situation of the company before they are issued.

Checklist for the Businessperson

1. Establish an audit committee composed of directors to nominate an independent auditor and to work with the auditing firm.
2. Review and evaluate your company's financial statements and accounting policies in accord with generally accepted accounting principles.
3. Review your company's financial reporting process and its internal controls that are intended to thwart fraud.
4. Hire lawyers or other outsiders to help recognize early symptoms that could lead to liability for fraudulent reporting.
5. Review all financial statements and press releases concerning the financial situation of the company carefully before they are issued.

Key Terms

defalcation 1005

due diligence 1013

generally accepted accounting principles (GAAP) 1004

generally accepted auditing standards (GAAS) 1004

malpractice 1006

working papers 1020

Chapter Summary • Liability of Accountants and Other Professionals

	COMMON LAW LIABILITY
Liability to Client (See pages 1005–1008.)	1. *Breach of contract*—An accountant or other professional who fails to perform according to his or her contractual obligations can be held liable for breach of contract and resulting damages. 2. *Negligence*—An accountant or other professional, in performance of his or her duties, must use the care, knowledge, and judgment generally used by professionals in the same or similar circumstances. Failure to do so is negligence. An accountant's violation of generally accepted accounting principles and generally accepted auditing standards is *prima facie* evidence of negligence. An accountant who reveals confidential information or the contents of working papers without the client's permission or a court order can be held liable for malpractice. 3. *Fraud*—Actual intent to misrepresent a material fact to a client, when the client relies on the misrepresentation, is fraud. Gross negligence in performance of duties is constructive fraud.
Liability to Third Parties (See pages 1009–1013.)	An accountant may be liable for negligence to any third person the accountant knows or should have known will benefit from the accountant's work. The standard for imposing this liability varies, but generally courts follow one of the following three rules:

Chapter Summary • Liability of Accountants and Other Professionals

Liability to Third Parties—continued	1. Ultramares *rule*—Liability will be imposed only if the accountant is in privity, or near privity, with the third party. 2. Restatement *rule*—Liability will be imposed only if the third party's reliance is foreseen, or known, or if the third party is among a class of foreseeable, or known, users. The majority of courts adopt this rule. 3. *"Reasonably foreseeable user" rule*—Liability will be imposed if the third party's use was reasonably foreseeable.
STATUTORY LIABILITY	
Securities Act of 1933, Section 11 (See pages 1013–1015.)	An accountant who makes a false statement or omits a material fact in audited financial statements required for registration of securities under the law may be liable to anyone who acquires securities covered by the registration statement. The accountant's defense is basically the use of due diligence and the reasonable belief that the work was complete and correct. The burden of proof is on the accountant. Willful violations of this act may be subject to criminal penalties.
Securities Act of 1933, Section 12(2) (See page 1015.)	In some jurisdictions, an accountant may be liable for aiding and abetting the seller or offeror of securities when a prospectus or communication presented to an investor contained an untrue statement or omission of material fact. To be liable, the accountant must have known, or at least should have known, that an untrue statement or omission of material fact existed in the offer to sell the security.
Securities Exchange Act of 1934, Sections 10(b) and 18 (See pages 1016–1019.)	Accountants are held liable for false and misleading applications, reports, and documents required under the act. The burden is on the plaintiff, and the accountant has numerous defenses, including good faith and lack of knowledge that what was submitted was false. Willful violations of this act may be subject to criminal penalties.
Internal Revenue Code (See pages 1019–1020.)	1. Aiding or assisting in the preparation of a false tax return is a felony. Aiding and abetting an individual's understatement of tax liability is a separate crime. 2. Tax preparers who negligently or willfully understate a client's tax liability or who recklessly or intentionally disregard Internal Revenue rules or regulations are subject to criminal penalties. 3. Tax preparers who fail to provide a taxpayer with a copy of the return, fail to sign the return, or fail to furnish the appropriate tax identification numbers may also be subject to criminal penalties.

For Review

1. What are the common law theories under which professionals may be liable to clients?
2. What are the rules concerning an auditor's liability to third parties?
3. How might an accountant violate federal securities laws?
4. What crimes might an accountant commit under the Internal Revenue Code?
5. What restrains professionals to keep communications with their clients confidential?

Questions and Case Problems

39–1. *Ultramares* Rule. Larkin, Inc., retains Howard Perkins to manage its books and prepare its financial statements. Perkins, a certified public accountant, lives in Indiana and practices there. After twenty years, Perkins has become a bit bored with the format of generally accepted accounting principles and has become creative in his accounting methods. Now, though, Perkins has a problem, as he is being sued by Molly Tucker, one of Larkin's creditors. Tucker alleges that Perkins either knew or should have known that Larkin's financial statements would be distributed to various individuals. Furthermore, she asserts that these financial statements were negligently prepared and seriously inaccurate. What are the consequences of Perkins's failure to adopt generally accepted accounting principles? Under the traditional *Ultramares* rule, can Tucker recover damages from Perkins? Explain.

39–2. Accountant's Liability to Third Parties and Public Policy. The accounting firm of Goldman, Walters, Johnson & Co. prepared financial statements for Lucy's Fashions, Inc. After reviewing the various financial statements, Happydays State Bank agreed to loan Lucy's Fashions $35,000 for expansion. When Lucy's Fashions declared bankruptcy under Chapter 11 six months later, Happydays State Bank promptly filed an action against Goldman, Walters, Johnson & Co., alleging negligent preparation of financial statements. Assuming that the court has abandoned the *Ultramares* approach, what is the result? What are the policy reasons for holding accountants liable to third parties with whom they are not in privity?

39–3. Accountant's Liability under Rule 10b-5. In early 1995, Bennett, Inc., offered a substantial number of new common shares to the public. Harvey Helms had a long-standing interest in Bennett because his grandfather had once been president of the company. On receiving a prospectus prepared and distributed by Bennett, Helms was dismayed by the pessimism it embodied. Helms decided to delay purchasing stock in the company. Later, Helms asserted that the prospectus prepared by the accountants was overly pessimistic and contained materially misleading statements. Discuss fully how successful Helms would be in bringing a cause of action under Rule 10b-5 against the accountants of Bennett, Inc.

39–4. Negligence. Robert Potts was a partner at the accounting firm of Touche Ross and its successor, Deloitte & Touche. Potts was the concurring partner for 1988 and 1989 audits of Kahler Corp., which owned and managed the University Park Hotel. According to the American Institute of Certified Public Accountants (AICPA), a concurring partner assures that an audited company's financial statements conform with generally accepted accounting principles (GAAP) and generally accepted auditing standards (GAAS). In 1988 and 1989, the hotel lost money, but Kahler showed a gain in 1988 by accounting for the hotel as an asset held for sale. Under GAAP, certain conditions must be met to account for property as an asset held for sale. Despite evidence that Kahler did not meet the conditions, Potts approved the audits. Potts also agreed to Kahler's valuation of the hotel, despite evidence that it was worth less than Kahler said. The Securities and Exchange Commission (SEC) filed a complaint against Potts, alleging that he acted negligently. Will the court agree? Why or why not? [*Potts v. SEC,* 151 F.3d 810 (8th Cir. 1998)]

39–5. Auditors' Liability to Third Parties. Max Mitchell, a certified public accountant and president of Max Mitchell & Co., went to First Florida Bank to negotiate a $500,000 unsecured line of credit for C. M. Systems, Inc. The audited financial statements that Mitchell gave the bank did not indicate that C. M. Systems owed any money. In fact, the company owed at least $750,000 to several banks. First Florida approved the loan, but C. M. Systems never repaid it. The bank filed a suit in a Florida state court against Mitchell and his firm, alleging negligence. Because there was no privity between Mitchell and the bank, the court granted Mitchell summary judgment. The bank appealed. On what basis might the appellate court reverse? [*First Florida Bank, N.A. v. Max Mitchell & Co.,* 558 So.2d 9 (Fla. 1990)]

39–6. Accountant's Liability to Third Parties. Toro Co. was a major supplier of equipment and credit to Summit Power Equipment Distributors. Toro required audited reports from Summit to evaluate the distributor's financial condition. Summit supplied Toro with reports prepared by Krouse, Kern & Co., an accounting firm. The reports allegedly contained mistakes and omissions regarding Summit's financial condition. According to Toro, it extended and renewed large amounts of credit to Summit in reliance on the audited reports. Summit was unable to repay these amounts, and Toro brought a negligence action against the accounting firm and the individual accountants. Evidence produced at the trial showed that Krouse knew that the reports it furnished to Summit were to be used by Summit to induce Toro to extend credit, but no evidence was produced to show either a contractual relationship between Krouse and Toro or a link between these companies evidencing Krouse's understanding of Toro's actual reliance on the reports. The relevant state law follows the *Ultramares* rule. What was the result? [*Toro Co. v. Krouse, Kern & Co.,* 827 F.2d 155 (7th Cir. 1987)]

39–7. Accountant's Liability under Rule 10b-5. The accounting firm of Arthur Young & Co. was employed by DMI Furniture, Inc., to conduct a review of an audit prepared by Brown, Kraft & Co., certified public accountants, for Gillespie Furniture Co. DMI planned to purchase Gillespie and wished to determine its net worth. Arthur Young, by letter, advised DMI that Brown, Kraft had performed a high-quality audit and that Gillespie's inventory on the audit dates was fairly stated on the general ledger. Allegedly as a result of these representations, DMI went forward with its purchase of Gillespie. Subsequently, DMI charged Brown, Kraft & Co., Arthur Young, and Gillespie's former owners with violations of Section 10(b) of the Securities Exchange Act and SEC Rule 10b-5. DMI complained that Arthur Young's review had proved to be materially inaccurate and misleading, primarily because the inventory reflected in the balance sheet was grossly overstated. Arthur Young was charged "with acting recklessly in failing to detect, and thus failing to disclose, material omissions and reckless conduct on the part of Brown, Kraft, and in making affirmative misstatements in its letter" to DMI. Did DMI have a valid cause of action under either Section 10(b) or Rule 10b-5? Discuss. [*DMI Furniture, Inc. v. Brown, Kraft & Co.,* 644 F.Supp. 1517 (C.D.Cal. 1986)]

39–8. Attorney-Client Privilege. John and Christine Powell invested in a hotel-condominium development project. When legal problems with the project arose, the attorney representing the Powells was given access to certain documents and correspondence between the project developer, H. E. F. Partnership (HEF), and HEF's own legal counsel. When the project failed, the Powells sued HEF and others involved with the development scheme. In preparation for trial, the Powells sought discovery (see Chapter 4) of the documents and correspondence that HEF had released to them earlier. HEF refused to release the documents, alleging that they were confidential communications and protected under the attorney-client privilege. The Powells filed a motion with the court to compel discovery. How should the court rule on the motion to compel? Explain. [*Powell v. H.E.F. Partnership,* 835 F.Supp. 762 (D.Vt. 1993)]

39–9. Attorney's Duty of Care. Five members of the Hendry family owned property in Arlington, Virginia. When a dispute arose with a developer, the family hired attorney Francis Pelland to represent them. The mother wanted to continue to live in a house on the property. The son and the daughter wanted to preserve the trees on the property. The best interest of the two grandchildren was to maximize the property's long-term value. Pelland advised the family to settle with the developer for $1.5 million, which they did. Unhappy with this result, the Hendrys filed a suit in a federal district court against Pelland for breach of fiduciary duty, seeking in part a refund of the legal fees they had paid. On what basis might the court rule in the Hendrys' favor? Is there any basis on which a court could rule in Pelland's favor? [*Hendry v. Pelland,* 73 F.3d 397 (D.C.Cir. 1996)]

A QUESTION OF ETHICS AND SOCIAL RESPONSIBILITY

39–10. Crawford, a certified public accountant, prepared a financial statement for Erps Construction Co., which was seeking a loan from the First National Bank of Bluefield. Crawford knew at the time he prepared the statement that the bank would rely on the statement in making its decision on whether to extend credit to Erps. The loan was made and Erps defaulted. The bank sued Crawford, alleging that he had been professionally negligent in preparing the financial statement, on which the bank had relied in determining whether to give the construction company a loan. Crawford defended against the suit by asserting that he could not be liable to the bank because of lack of privity. The trial court ruled that in the absence of contractual privity between the parties, the bank could not recover from the accountant. On appeal, the appellate court adopted the rule enunciated by the *Restatement (Second) of Torts* in regard to a professional's liability to third parties. [*First National Bank of Bluefield v. Crawford,* 386 S.E.2d 310 (W.Va. 1989)]

1. What is the standard of an accountant's liability to third parties under the *Restatement (Second) of Torts*? What ethical reasoning underlies this standard?
2. Do you think that the standard of liability under the *Restatement* adequately balances the rights of accountants and the rights of third parties? Can you think of a fairer standard?
3. A few courts have adopted the principle that accountants should be liable for negligence to all persons who use and rely on their work products, provided that this use and reliance was foreseeable by the accountants at the time they prepared the documents relied on. Does such a standard of liability impose too great a burden on accountants and accounting firms? Why or why not?

FOR CRITICAL ANALYSIS

39–11. The savings and loan crisis, which developed in the 1980s and came to light in the 1990s, illustrates that a failure to provide accurate financial information can have a devastating effect on the economy. In cases in which third parties suffer losses in reliance on negligent misrepresentations in accountants' financial reports, the courts apply different standards to assess liability. Some courts impose liability only when there is privity between the accountant and the party who seeks recovery. Other courts impose liability under a foreseeability rule. What do you see as the implications of imposing liability on accountants for losses suffered by third parties on the basis

Online Activities

• ONLINE EXERCISE 39-1

Go to smallbiz.findlaw.com/tools/tools.stm, the "Business Tools" page within the "Small Business Center" database at the Web site of FindLaw. Click on some of the links to determine what is available at this site and then answer the following questions:

- What help is available on this page for persons who want to start their own businesses?
- What is the purpose of the "financial templates"? What links are provided within the templates?
- Click on the "Checklists" link. Who would want to use this information? In what circumstances would they want to use it? Why?

Unit Seven • Cumulative Business Hypothetical

Alpha Software, Inc., and Beta Products Corporation—both small firms—are competitors in the business of software research, development, and production.

1 Alpha and Beta form a joint venture to research, develop, and produce new software for a particular line of computers. Does this business combination violate the antitrust laws? If so, is it a *per se* violation or is it subject to the rule of reason? Alpha and Beta decide to merge. After the merger, Beta is the surviving firm. What aspect of this firm's presence in the market will be assessed to decide whether this merger is in violation of any antitrust laws?

2 To market its products profitably, Beta considers a number of advertising and labeling proposals. One proposal is that Beta suggest in its advertising that one of its software products has a certain function without specifying on its packaging that it does not actually have that capability. Another suggestion is that Beta place only half of a certain program in packaging that misleads the buyer into believing the entire program is included. To obtain the entire program, customers would need to buy a second product. Can Beta implement these suggestions or otherwise market its products any way it likes? If not, why not?

3 Beta generates hazardous waste from the production part of its operations. Gamma Transport Company transports the waste to Omega Waste Corporation, which owns and operates a hazardous waste disposal site. At the site, some containers leak hazardous waste, and the Environmental Protection Agency (EPA) cleans it up. From whom can the EPA recover the cost of the clean-up?

4 Beta provides health insurance for its two hundred employees, including Dan. For personal medical reasons, Dan takes twelve weeks' leave. During this period, can Dan continue his coverage under Beta's health-insurance plan? If so, at whose expense? After Dan returns to work, Beta closes Dan's division and terminates the employees, including Dan. Can Dan continue his coverage under Beta's health-insurance plan? If so, at whose expense?

5 Beta has a policy against sexual harassment that includes specific procedures for reporting, investigating, and resolving incidents of alleged harassment. Kay, a Beta employee, believes that she has been the object of her supervisor's sexual comments on the job and she perceives these comments as offensive. She reports the incident, and Beta follows up with an investigation but decides that there is no basis for disciplining the supervisor. Kay subsequently quits her job and eventually files a suit against Beta. What must Kay prove to win her case? What is Beta's best defense?

UNIT SEVEN • EXTENDED CASE STUDY: THE LAW IN CONTEXT

Burlington Industries, Inc. v. Ellerth

We discussed, in Chapter 38, employment discrimination and, in Chapter 24, employer liability for the acts of employees and agents. In this extended case study, we examine Burlington Industries, Inc. v. Ellerth,[1] *a recent decision that involved the application of the principles of agency law in the context of employment discrimination. Recall from Chapter 38's* Business Law in Action *that this is one of the two cases decided in 1998 in which the United States Supreme Court set forth some guidelines on liability for supervisors' harassment of employees in the workplace. In the* Burlington *case, the question was whether an employer could be held liable for its supervisor's harassment of a subordinate employee when the employer did not know about the harassment and the employee did not suffer any adverse job consequences.*

1. 524 U.S. 742, 118 S.Ct. 2257, 141 L.Ed.2d 633 (1998).

CASE BACKGROUND

Ted Slowik was a manager within a division of Burlington Industries, Inc., a national fabric manufacturer. Slowik had the authority to hire and promote employees, subject to his manager's approval. Kimberly Ellerth worked for the same Burlington division as a salesperson under Slowik's supervision. Slowik made repeated boorish and offensive remarks and gestures that included sexual advances and threats to deny Ellerth tangible job benefits if she did not comply. Ellerth refused all of Slowik's advances but suffered no tangible retaliation and was, in fact, promoted. Ellerth knew that Burlington had a policy against sexual harassment, but she never told anyone in authority about Slowik's conduct. She quit the job after fifteen months.

Ellerth filed a suit in a federal district court against Burlington, alleging sexual harassment and constructive discharge, in violation of Title VII of the Civil Rights Act of 1964. The court granted a summary judgment in Burlington's favor. Ellerth appealed to the U.S. Court of Appeals for the Seventh Circuit, which reversed the decision. Burlington appealed to the United States Supreme Court.

MAJORITY OPINION

KENNEDY, J. [Justice], delivered the opinion of the Court * * * .

* * * *

Tangible employment actions are the means by which the supervisor brings the official power of the enterprise to bear on subordinates. * * *

* * * *

* * * [A]gency principles constrain the imposition of vicarious liability in cases of supervisory harassment. * * *

* * * [O]ther considerations might be relevant as well. For example, Title VII is designed to encourage the creation of antiharassment policies and effective grievance mechanisms. Were employer liability to depend in part on an employer's effort to create such procedures, it would effect Congress' intention to promote conciliation rather than litigation in the Title VII context * * * .

In order to accommodate the agency principles of vicarious liability for harm caused by misuse of supervisory authority, as well as Title VII's equally basic policies of encouraging forethought by employers and saving action by objecting employees, we adopt the following holding in this case * * * . An employer is subject to vicarious liability to a victimized employee for an actionable hostile environment created by a supervisor with immediate (or successively higher) authority over the employee. When no tangible employment action is taken, a defending employer may raise an affirmative defense to liability or damages * * * . The defense comprises two necessary elements: (a) that the employer exercised reasonable care to prevent and correct promptly any sexually harassing behavior, and (b) that the plaintiff employee unreasonably failed to take advantage of any preventive or corrective opportunities provided by the employer or to avoid harm otherwise. While proof that an employer had promulgated an antiharassment policy with complaint procedure is not necessary in every instance as a matter of law, the need for a stated policy suitable to the employment circumstances may appropriately be addressed in any case when litigating the first element of the defense. And while proof that an employee failed to fulfill the corresponding obligation of reasonable care to avoid harm is not limited to showing any unreasonable failure to use any complaint procedure provided by the employer, a demonstration of such failure will normally suffice to satisfy the * * * second element of the defense. No affirmative defense is available, however, when the supervisor's harassment culminates in a tangible employment action, such as discharge, demotion, or undesirable reassignment.

DISSENTING OPINION

Justice *THOMAS,* with whom Justice SCALIA joins, dissenting.

* * * *

* * * [The majority] imposes a rule of vicarious employer liability, subject to a vague affirmative defense, for the acts of supervisors who wield no delegated authority in creating a hostile work environment. This rule is a whole-cloth creation that draws no support from the legal principles on which the Court claims it is based. Compounding its error, the Court fails to explain how employers can rely upon the affirmative defense, thus ensuring a continuing reign of confusion in this important area of the law.

* * * *

* * * [L]iability under [the principles of agency law] depends upon the plaintiff's belief that the agent acted in the ordinary course of business or within the scope of his apparent authority. In this day and age, no sexually harassed employee can reasonably believe that a harassing supervisor is conducting the official business of the company or acting on its behalf. * * *

Thus * * * [the majority's] holding is a product of willful policymaking, pure and simple. The only agency principle that justifies imposing employer liability in this context is the principle that a master will be liable for a servant's torts if the master was negligent or reckless in permitting them to occur; and * * * under a negligence standard, Burlington cannot be held liable.

* * * *

The Court's holding does guarantee one result: There will be more and more litigation to clarify applicable legal rules in an area in which both practitioners and the courts have long been begging for guidance.

MEDIA COVERAGE

The court's rulings in this case and in other recent sexual harassment cases have been controversial. Here we present excerpts from an article titled "Rewriting the Rules: For decades, American Society Has Grappled with Defining Sexual Harassment. Now It's the Supreme Court's Turn to Step into the Fray" by John Aloysius Farrell that appeared in *The Boston Globe* on February 7, 1999.

"It remains to be seen if American men and women will find clarity in the law or further strife. The court's recent actions have sent a tremor through the offices of the nation's corporate lawyers, who have moved zealously to protect their clients—drawing up lists of behavioral do's and don'ts, posting conduct codes for employees, calling for sensitivity seminars, and instructing managers to err on the side of caution. The court's critics contend that the warnings being posted across the country will actually serve to chill the workplace and spur new divisiveness at job sites, where men and women are already struggling to define the difference between flirtation and harassment, humor and humiliation.

* * * *

And yet millions of Americans—men and women—recognize the wrong in the kind of boorish macho conduct that forced * * * Kimberly Ellerth * * * to seek justice in court. In its attempts to draw bright lines in the mess of human sexual behavior, the Supreme Court * * * has forthrightly confronted a combustible issue. * * *

* * * *

* * * [S]ays [Catharine] MacKinnon [author of the book *Sexual Harassment of Working Women*], 'It is itself a victory that women are now able to speak out at all. These cases may be done right in court or they may be done wrong in court—but it is a victory that they are in court at all.'"

GOING ONLINE

The *Business Law Today*, Fifth Edition, Web site, at **http://blt.westbuslaw.com**, provides a link through which you can access other court opinions in cases involving sexual harrassment.

QUESTIONS FOR ANALYSIS

1. **Law.** Considering the decision in this case, can an employer ever avoid liability when its supervisor harasses a subordinate? If so, how?
2. **Law.** Does the attention paid to sexual harassment in the workplace detract from other, more important aspects of gender discrimination?
3. **Ethics.** Is it unethical for an employer *not* to adopt policies for employees regarding sexual harassment?
4. **International Dimensions.** To what extent, if any, should U.S. law regarding employment discrimination be imposed on foreign firms that do business in the United States?
5. **Implications for the Business Manager.** As an employer, what steps would you take to combat sexual harassment in the workplace?

UNIT EIGHT Property & Its Protection

CHAPTER 40

Personal Property & Bailments

> "The great . . . end . . . of men united into commonwealths, and putting themselves under government, is the preservation of their property."
>
> John Locke, 1632–1704
> (English political philosopher)

CONTENTS

LEARNING OBJECTIVES

After reading this chapter, you should be able to:

1. Distinguish between personal property and real property.
2. Discuss different types of property ownership and the ways in which property can be acquired.
3. Identify who has rights to mislaid, lost, or abandoned property.
4. List the elements of a bailment.
5. Outline the rights and duties of a bailee and a bailor.

Property consists of the legally protected rights and interests a person has in anything with an ascertainable value that is subject to ownership. Property would have little value (and the word would have little meaning) if the law did not define the right to use it, to sell or dispose of it, and to prevent trespass on it. Indeed, John Locke, as indicated in the opening quotation, considered the preservation of property to be the primary reason for the establishment of government.

Property is divided into real property and personal property. **Real property** (sometimes called *realty* or *real estate*) means the land and everything permanently attached to it. Everything else is **personal property,** or *personalty.* Attorneys sometimes refer to personal property as **chattel,** a term used under the common law to denote all forms of personal property. Personal property can be tangible or intangible. *Tangible* personal property, such as a TV set or a car, has physical substance. *Intangible* personal property represents some set of rights and interests but has no real physical existence. Stocks and bonds, patents, and copyrights are examples of intangible personal property.

PROPERTY
Legally protected rights and interests in anything with an ascertainable value that is subject to ownership.

REAL PROPERTY
Land and everything attached to it, such as foliage and buildings.

PERSONAL PROPERTY
Property that is movable; any property that is not real property.

CHATTEL
All forms of personal property.

In the first part of this chapter, we look at the ways in which title to property is held; the methods of acquiring ownership of personal property; and issues relating to mislaid, lost, and abandoned personal property. In the second part of the chapter, we examine bailment relationships. A *bailment* is created when personal property is temporarily delivered into the care of another without a transfer of title. This is the distinguishing characteristic of a bailment compared with a sale or a gift—there is no passage of title and no intent to transfer title.

Property Ownership

"Private property began the minute somebody had a mind of his own."

E. E. CUMMINGS, 1894–1962 (American poet)

Property ownership[1] can be viewed as a bundle of rights, including the right to possess property and to dispose of it—by sale, gift, lease, or other means.

FEE SIMPLE

• FEE SIMPLE
An absolute form of property ownership entitling the property owner to use, possess, or dispose of the property as he or she chooses during his or her lifetime. Upon death, the interest in the property descends to the owner's heirs.

A person who holds the entire bundle of rights to property is said to be the owner in **fee simple.** The owner in fee simple is entitled to use, possess, or dispose of the property as he or she chooses during his or her lifetime, and on this owner's death, the interests in the property descend to his or her heirs. We will return to this form of property ownership in Chapter 41, in the context of ownership rights in real property.

CONCURRENT OWNERSHIP

Persons who share ownership rights simultaneously in a particular piece of property are said to be *concurrent* owners. There are two principal types of concurrent ownership: tenancy in common and joint tenancy. Other types of concurrent ownership include tenancy by the entirety and community property.

• TENANCY IN COMMON
Co-ownership of property in which each party owns an undivided interest that passes to his or her heirs at death.

Tenancy in Common The term **tenancy in common** refers to a form of co-ownership in which each of two or more persons owns an *undivided* interest in the property. The interest is undivided because each tenant has rights in the *whole* property. • **EXAMPLE 40.1** Rosa and Chad own a rare-stamp collection as tenants in common. This does not mean that Rosa owns some particular stamps and Chad others. Rather, it means that Rosa and Chad each have rights in the entire collection. (If Rosa owned some stamps and Chad owned others, then the interest would be *divided.*) •

On the death of a tenant in common, that tenant's interest in the property passes to his or her heirs. • **EXAMPLE 40.2** Should Rosa die before Chad, a one-half interest in the stamp collection would become the property of Rosa's heirs. If Rosa sold her interest to Fred before she died, Fred and Chad would be co-owners as tenants in common. If Fred died, his interest in the personal property would pass to his heirs, and they in turn would own the property with Chad as tenants in common. •

• JOINT TENANCY
The joint ownership of property by two or more co-owners of property in which each co-owner owns an undivided portion of the property. On the death of one of the joint tenants, his or her interest automatically passes to the surviving joint tenants.

Joint Tenancy In a **joint tenancy,** each of two or more persons owns an undivided interest in the property, and a deceased joint tenant's interest passes to the surviving joint tenant or tenants. The rights of a surviving joint tenant to inherit a deceased joint tenant's ownership interest, which are referred to as *survivorship rights,* distinguish the joint tenancy from the tenancy in common. A joint tenancy can be terminated before a joint tenant's death by gift or by sale, in which situation the person who received the property as a gift or who purchased the property would become a tenant in common, not a joint tenant.

• **EXAMPLE 40.3** If, in the preceding example, Rosa and Chad held their stamp collection in a joint tenancy and if Rosa died before Chad, the entire collection

1. The principles discussed in this section apply equally to real property ownership, discussed in Chapter 41.

International Perspective • ISLAMIC LAW AND CONCURRENT OWNERSHIP

Islamic law, which is followed in Muslim countries, makes no provision for joint tenancy with rights of survivorship. Instead, concurrent owners of property are normally regarded as tenants in common. In regard to survivorship rights, Islamic law provides that an owner can transfer no more than one-third of an estate by will. The rest of the estate must be inherited by those who are designated as legal heirs under Islamic law.

FOR CRITICAL ANALYSIS

What policy considerations might motivate a government to restrict the transfer of property to legally designated heirs (such as spouses, children, and so on)?

would become the property of Chad; Rosa's heirs would receive absolutely no interest in the collection. If Rosa, while living, sold her interest to Fred, however, the sale would terminate the joint tenancy, and Fred and Chad would become owners as tenants in common. ●

• **TENANCY BY THE ENTIRETY**
The joint ownership of property by a husband and wife. Neither party can transfer his or her interest in the property without the consent of the other.

• **COMMUNITY PROPERTY**
A form of concurrent ownership of property in which each spouse technically owns an undivided one-half interest in property acquired during the marriage. This form of joint ownership occurs in only nine states and Puerto Rico.

Tenancy by the Entirety Concurrent ownership of property can also take the form of a **tenancy by the entirety**—a form of co-ownership between a husband and wife that is similar to a joint tenancy, except that a spouse cannot transfer his or her interest during his or her lifetime without the consent of the other spouse.

Community Property When property is held as **community property,** each spouse technically owns an undivided one-half interest in property acquired during the marriage. The community property form of ownership occurs in only nine states and Puerto Rico.

Acquiring Ownership of Personal Property

"In no country in the world is the love of property more active and more anxious than in the United States."

ALEXIS DE TOCQUEVILLE, 1805–1859 (French historian and statesman)

The most common way of acquiring personal property is by purchasing it. We have already discussed the purchase and sale of personal property (goods) in Chapters 15 through 18. Often, property is acquired by will or inheritance, a topic we cover in Chapter 42. Here we look at additional ways in which ownership of personal property can be acquired, including acquisition by possession, production, gift, accession, and confusion.

POSSESSION

One example of acquiring ownership by possession is the capture of wild animals. Wild animals belong to no one in their natural state, and the first person to take possession of a wild animal normally owns it. The killing of a wild animal amounts to assuming ownership of it. Merely being in hot pursuit does not give title, however. There are two exceptions to this basic rule. First, any wild animals captured by a trespasser are the property of the landowner, not the trespasser. Second, if wild animals are captured or killed in violation of wild-game statutes, the capturer does not obtain title to the animals; rather, the state does.

Those who find lost or abandoned property also can acquire ownership rights through mere possession of the property, as will be discussed later in the chapter. (Ownership rights in real property can also be acquired through possession, such as adverse possession—see Chapter 41.)

PRODUCTION

Production—the fruits of labor—is another means of acquiring ownership of personal property. For example, writers, inventors, and manufacturers all produce personal property and thereby acquire title to it. (In some situations, though, as when a researcher is hired to invent a new product or technique, the researcher-producer may not own what is produced—see Chapter 24.)

GIFTS

• **GIFT**
Any voluntary transfer of property made without consideration, past or present.

A **gift** is another fairly common means of acquiring and transferring ownership of real and personal property. A gift is essentially a voluntary transfer of property ownership for which no consideration is given. As discussed in Chapter 10, the presence of consideration is what distinguishes a contract from a gift. Certain conditions

Business Law in Action • WHO OWNS THE ENGAGEMENT RING?

Often, when a couple decides to marry, one party gives the other an engagement ring. If the engagement is called off, typically the engagement ring is returned. Yet what if the recipient of the ring refuses to return it, and a dispute over who owns the ring reaches a court? What law should apply in determining ownership rights in this particular form of personal property?

The Supreme Court of Kansas recently faced this question in a case brought by Jerod Heiman against Heather Parrish. When the couple became engaged, Jerod gave Heather an engagement ring. Later, Jerod broke the engagement and wanted the ring back. When Heather refused to return it, Jerod sued Heather to recover the ring.

The Kansas Supreme Court held that, by its very nature, an engagement ring is a "conditional gift" given in contemplation of marriage. Having established an engagement ring as a conditional gift, the court considered the question of whether ownership rights in the ring depended on who broke the engagement. The court noted that there is "a split of authority on this issue." Some jurisdictions determine the issue on the basis of fault. In other words, if an engagement has been "unjustifiably broken by the donor, the donor shall not recover the ring." If, however, the engagement is broken by mutual agreement or "unjustifiably by the donee," the ring should be returned to the donor.

The court contrasted this "fault-based" principle with the "no-fault" rule followed in a number of jurisdictions. Under the no-fault rule, once an engagement has been broken, the ring should be returned to the donor. The question of who broke the engagement and why—or who was "at fault"—is irrelevant. The lower court had adopted the no-fault rule and awarded the ring to Jerod, the donor. The state supreme court affirmed this decision, concluding that "[l]itigating fault for a broken engagement" would not further any public policy. Rather, it would only "intensify the hurt feelings and delay the parties' being able to get on with their lives."

A dissenting judge took issue with the majority opinion. The dissenting judge argued that the giving of an engagement ring is a valid gift. The judge noted that in the case before the court, all of the conditions for a valid gift were met: Jerod (the donor) intended to make the gift, the ring was delivered to Heather (the donee), and the donee accepted the gift. According to the dissent, "Those jurisdictions that rely on the analysis that an engagement ring is a conditional gift ignore general gift law, which holds that a gift is complete if there is intent, delivery, and acceptance."

The dissent also took issue with the view that an engagement ring is consideration for a contract, which had been suggested in the court's majority opinion. The dissenting judge found it difficult to accept this view. "If the parties have exchanged mutual promises," said the dissenting judge, "the consideration for the woman's promise to marry is the man's promise to marry. Under this analysis, the ring is transferred without consideration and is a gift."[a]

FOR CRITICAL ANALYSIS

In determining ownership rights in an engagement ring, should the courts take into consideration the monetary or sentimental value of the ring?

a. *Heiman v. Parrish,* 262 Kan. 926, 942 P.2d 6731 (1997).

> **ON THE WEB**
> Who owns a gift received by a married person—the spouse who received the gift or the husband and wife jointly? To learn the answer to this question, go to Scott Law Firm's Web page at **www.scottlawfirm.com/property.htm**.

must exist, however, before a gift will be deemed effective in the eyes of the law. The donor (the one making the gift) must intend to make the gift, the gift must be delivered to the donee (the recipient of the gift), and the donee must accept the gift. We examine each of these requirements here, as well as the requirements of a gift made in contemplation of imminent death. (Should the law governing gifts apply when one person "gives" an engagement ring to another? See this chapter's *Business Law in Action* on the previous page for an exploration of this question.)

Donative Intent When a gift is challenged in court, the court will determine whether donative intent exists by looking at the surrounding circumstances. • **EXAMPLE 40.4** A court may look at the relationship between the parties and the size of the gift in relation to the donor's other assets. A gift to a mortal enemy is viewed with suspicion. Similarly, when a gift represents a large portion of a person's assets, the courts scrutinize the transaction closely to determine the mental capacity of the donor and whether there is any element of fraud or duress present. •

• **DOMINION**
Ownership rights in property, including the right to possess and control the property.

• **CONSTRUCTIVE DELIVERY**
An act equivalent to the actual, physical delivery of property that cannot be physically delivered because of difficulty or impossibility; for example, the transfer of a key to a safe constructively delivers the contents of the safe.

Delivery The gift must be delivered to the donee. An effective delivery requires giving up complete control and **dominion** (ownership rights) over the subject matter of the gift. When a gift cannot be physically delivered, a symbolic, or *constructive*, delivery will be sufficient. **Constructive delivery** is an act that the law holds to be equivalent to an act of actual delivery. • **EXAMPLE 40.5** Suppose that you want to make a gift of various old rare coins that you have stored in a safe-deposit box. You certainly cannot deliver the box itself to the donee, and you do not want to take the coins out of the bank. In this situation, the delivery of the key to the safe-deposit box (along with appropriate instructions to the bank) constitutes a constructive delivery of the contents of the box. •

The delivery of intangible property—such as stocks, bonds, insurance policies, contracts, and so on—is always accomplished by symbolic, or constructive, delivery. This is because the documents represent rights and are not, in themselves, the true property.

Delivery may be accomplished by means of a third party. If the third party is the agent of the donor, the delivery is effective when the agent delivers the gift to the donee. If the third party is the agent of the donee, then the gift is effectively delivered when the donor delivers the property to the donee's agent.[2] Naturally, no delivery is necessary if the gift is already in the hands of the donee.

In the following case, the court focused on the requirement that a donor must give up complete control and dominion over property given to the donee before a gift can be effectively delivered.

2. *Bickford v. Mattocks*, 95 Me. 547, 50 A. 894 (1901).

CASE 40.1 In re Estate of Piper

Missouri Court of Appeals, 1984.
676 S.W.2d 897.

HISTORICAL AND CULTURAL SETTING *The rule that there must be a delivery for a gift to be valid originated at a time when handing over possession of an item was the only method of transferring it. The policy behind the rule is to protect alleged donors and their heirs from fraudulent claims based only on parol evidence. It is too easy for an alleged donee to claim that a gift was made when, in fact, it was not. For this reason, courts are wary of purported gifts that have not been delivered, except when the alleged donee is a member of the family.*

BACKGROUND AND FACTS Gladys Piper died intestate (without a will) in 1982. At her death, she owned miscellaneous personal property worth $5,000 and had in her purse $200 in cash and two diamond rings, known as the Andy Piper rings. The contents of her purse were taken by her niece Wanda Brown, allegedly to preserve them for the estate. Clara Kaufmann, a friend of Piper's, filed a claim against the estate for $4,800. From October 1974 until

CASE 40.1—Continued

Piper's death, Kaufmann had taken Piper to the doctor, beauty shop, and grocery store; had written her checks to pay her bills; and had helped her care for her home. Kaufmann maintained that Piper had promised to pay her for these services and had given her the diamond rings as a gift. A Missouri state trial court denied her request for payment; the court found that her services had been voluntary. Kaufmann then filed a petition for delivery of personal property, the rings, which was granted by the trial court. Brown, other heirs, and the administrator of Piper's estate appealed.

IN THE WORDS OF THE COURT . . .

GREENE, Judge.

* * * *

* * * Clara's petition claimed the rings belonged to her by reason of "a consummated gift long prior to the death of Gladys Piper." The only evidence of the gift issue came from two witnesses. * * *

There was no evidence of any actual delivery to Clara, at any time, of the rings. * * * The essentials of such a gift are (1) a present intention to make a gift on the part of the donor, (2) a delivery of the property by donor to donee, and (3) an acceptance by donee, whose ownership takes effect immediately and absolutely.

While no particular form is necessary to effect a delivery, and while the delivery may be actual, constructive, or symbolical, there must be some evidence to support a delivery theory. What we have here, at best, * * * was an intention on the part of Gladys, at some future time, to make a gift of the rings to Clara. Such an intention, no matter how clearly expressed, which has not been carried into effect, confers no ownership rights in the property in the intended donee.

DECISION AND REMEDY The Missouri appellate court reversed the judgment of the trial court. No effective gift of the rings had been made, because Piper had never delivered the rings to Kauffman.

FOR CRITICAL ANALYSIS—Social Consideration *What could Piper have done to ensure that Kaufmann received the rings on Piper's death?*

Acceptance The final requirement of a valid gift is acceptance by the donee. This rarely presents any problem, as most donees readily accept their gifts. The courts generally assume acceptance unless shown otherwise.

• **GIFT *INTER VIVOS***
A gift made during one's lifetime and not in contemplation of imminent death, in contrast to a gift *causa mortis.*

• **GIFT *CAUSA MORTIS***
A gift made in contemplation of death. If the donor does not die of that ailment, the gift is revoked.

Gifts *Causa Mortis* A gift made during one's lifetime is termed a **gift *inter vivos.*** **Gifts *causa mortis*** (so-called *deathbed gifts*), in contrast, are made in contemplation of imminent death. A gift *causa mortis* does not become absolute until the donor dies from the contemplated illness, and it is automatically revoked if the donor recovers from the illness. Moreover, the donee must survive to take the gift. To be effective, a gift *causa mortis* must also meet the three requirements discussed earlier—donative intent, delivery, and acceptance by the donee.

• **EXAMPLE 40.6** Suppose that Young is to be operated on for a cancerous tumor. Before the operation, he delivers an envelope to a close business associate. The envelope contains a letter saying, "I realize my days are numbered, and I want to give you this check for $1 million in the event of my death from this operation." The business associate cashes the check. The surgeon performs the operation and removes the tumor. Young recovers fully. Several months later, Young dies from a heart attack that is totally unrelated to the operation. If Young's personal representative (the party charged with administering Young's estate) tries to recover the $1 million, normally she will succeed. The gift *causa mortis* is automatically revoked if the donor recovers. The *specific event* that was contemplated in making the gift was death from a particular operation. Because Young's death was not the result of this event, the gift is revoked, and the $1 million passes to Young's estate.•

Accession

• **ACCESSION**
Occurs when an individual adds value to personal property by either labor or materials. In some situations, a person may acquire ownership rights in another's property through accession.

Accession, which means "adding on" to something, occurs when someone adds value to an item of personal property by either labor or materials. Generally, there is no dispute about who owns the property after accession has occurred, especially when the accession is accomplished with the owner's consent. When accession occurs without the permission of the owner, the courts will tend to favor the owner over the improver—the one who improves the property—provided that the accession was wrongful and undertaken in bad faith. In addition, many courts will deny the improver any compensation for the value added; for example, a car thief who puts new tires on the stolen car will obviously not be compensated for the value of the new tires.

If the accession is performed in good faith, however, even without the owner's consent, ownership of the improved item most often depends on whether the accession has increased the value of the property or changed its identity. The greater the increase in value, the more likely it is that ownership will pass to the improver. If ownership so passes, the improver obviously must compensate the original owner for the value of the property prior to the accession. If the increase in value is not sufficient for ownership to pass to the improver, most courts will require the owner to compensate the improver for the value added.

Confusion

• **CONFUSION**
The mixing together of goods belonging to two or more owners so that the separately owned goods cannot be identified.

Confusion is defined as the commingling (mixing together) of goods so that one person's personal property cannot be distinguished from another's. Confusion frequently occurs when the goods are *fungible,* meaning that each particle is identical to every other particle, as with grain and oil, and the goods are owned by two or more parties as tenants in common. For example, if two farmers put their Number 2–grade winter wheat into the same storage bin, confusion would occur.

If confusion of goods is caused by a person who wrongfully and willfully mixes the goods for the purpose of rendering them indistinguishable, the innocent party acquires title to the whole. If confusion occurs as a result of agreement, an honest mistake, or the act of some third party, the owners share ownership as tenants in common and will share any loss in proportion to their shares of ownership of the property.

Mislaid, Lost, and Abandoned Property

As already mentioned, one of the methods of acquiring ownership of property is to possess it. Simply finding something and holding onto it, however, does not necessarily give the finder any legal rights in the property. Different rules apply, depending on whether the property was mislaid, lost, or abandoned.

Mislaid Property

• **MISLAID PROPERTY**
Property with which the owner has voluntarily parted and then cannot find or recover.

Property that has been placed somewhere by the owner voluntarily and then inadvertently forgotten is **mislaid property.** Suppose that you go to the theater and leave your gloves on the concession stand. The gloves are mislaid property, and the theater owner is entrusted with the duty of reasonable care for them. When mislaid property is found, the finder does not obtain title to the goods. Instead, the owner

ON THE WEB

Some states and government agencies now post online a list of unclaimed property. For an example of the various types of property that may go unclaimed, go to the following Web page, which is part of the state of Delaware's Web site: www.state.de.us/revenue/escheat/escheat.htm.

of the place where the property was mislaid becomes the caretaker of the property, because it is highly likely that the true owner will return.[3]

LOST PROPERTY

• **LOST PROPERTY**
Property with which the owner has involuntarily parted and then cannot find or recover.

Property that is involuntarily left and forgotten is **lost property.** A finder of the property can claim title to the property against the whole world, *except the true owner.*[4] If the true owner demands that the lost property be returned, the finder must return it. If a third party takes possession of lost property from a finder, however, the third party cannot assert a better title than the finder. When a finder knows who the true owner of the property is and fails to return it to that person, the finder is guilty of the tort of *conversion* (the wrongful taking of another's property—see Chapter 4). Finally, many states require the finder to make a reasonably diligent search to locate the true owner of lost property.

• EXAMPLE 40.7 Suppose that Kormian works in a large library at night. In the courtyard on her way home, she finds a piece of gold jewelry set with stones that look like precious stones to her. She takes it to a jeweler to have it appraised. While pretending to weigh the jewelry, an employee of the jeweler removes several of the stones. If Kormian brings an action to recover the stones from the jeweler, she normally will win, because she found lost property and holds valid title against everyone *except the true owner.* Because the property was lost, rather than mislaid, the finder is not the caretaker of the jewelry. Instead, the finder acquires title good against the whole world (except the true owner). •

• **ESTRAY STATUTE**
A statute defining finders' rights in property when the true owners are unknown.

Many states have laws that encourage and facilitate the return of property to its true owner and then reward a finder for honesty if the property remains unclaimed. These laws, called **estray statutes,** provide an incentive for finders to report their discoveries by making it possible for them, after the passage of a specified period of time, to acquire legal title to the property they have found. The statute usually requires the county clerk to advertise the property in an attempt to enhance the opportunity of the owner to recover what has been lost. Some preliminary questions must always be resolved before the estray statute can be employed. The item must be lost property, not merely mislaid property. When the situation indicates that the property was probably lost and not mislaid or abandoned, loss is presumed as a matter of public policy, and the estray statute applies.

The law that finders of lost property may obtain good title to the property has a long history. The cases discussed in the following *Landmark in the Law* on the origin of the law of finders illustrate the doctrine of *relativity of title.* Under this doctrine, if two contestants are before the court, neither of whom can claim absolute title to the property, the one who can claim prior possession will likely have established sufficient rights to the property to win the case.

3. The finder of mislaid property is an involuntary bailee (to be discussed later in this chapter).
4. See *Armory v. Delamirie,* discussed in this chapter's *Landmark in the Law.*

Landmark in the Law • THE LAW OF FINDERS

The well-known children's adage, "Finders keepers, losers weepers," is actually written into law—provided that the loser (the rightful owner) cannot be found. A finder of lost property may acquire good title to found personal property *against everyone except the true owner.* A number of landmark cases have made this principle clear. An early English case, *Armory v. Delamirie,*[a] is considered a landmark in Anglo-American jurisprudence concerning finders' rights in property.

a. 93 Eng.Rep. 664 (K.B. [King's Bench] 1722).

(Continued)

¡BE AWARE!
A finder who appropriates the personal property of another, knowing who the true owner is, can be guilty of conversion.

The plaintiff in the case was Armory, a chimney sweep who found a jewel in its setting during the course of his work. He took the jewel to a goldsmith to have it appraised. The goldsmith refused to return the jewel to Armory, claiming that Armory was not the rightful owner of the property. The court held that the finder, as prior possessor of the item, had rights to the jewel superior to those of all others except the rightful owner. The court stated, "The finder of a jewel, though he does not by such finding acquire an absolute property or ownership, yet . . . has such a property as will enable him to keep it against all but the rightful owner."

A curious situation arises when goods wrongfully obtained by one person are in turn wrongfully obtained by another, and the two parties contest their rights to possession. In such a situation, does the *Armory* rule still apply—that is, does the first (illegal) possessor have more rights in the property than the second (illegal) possessor? In a case that came before the Minnesota Supreme Court in 1892, *Anderson v. Gouldberg,*[b] the court said yes.

In the Anderson case, the plaintiffs had trespassed on another's land and wrongfully cut timber. The defendants later took the logs from the mill site, allegedly in the name of the owner of the property on which the timber had been cut. The evidence at trial indicated that both parties had illegally acquired the property. The court instructed the jury that even if the plaintiffs were trespassers when they cut the logs, they were entitled to recover them from later possessors—except the true owner or an agent of the true owner. The jury found for the plaintiffs, a decision affirmed later by the Minnesota Supreme Court. The latter court held that the plaintiffs' possession, "though wrongfully obtained," justified an action to repossess the property from another who took it from them.

FOR CRITICAL ANALYSIS
As will be discussed in Chapter 38, if a person dies without a valid will and has no legal heirs, that person's property is transferred to the state. Why doesn't the state similarly claim ownership of found property when the property's true owner cannot be located?

b. 51 Minn. 294, 53 N.W. 636 (1892).

ABANDONED PROPERTY

• ABANDONED PROPERTY
Property with which the owner has voluntarily parted, with no intention of recovering it.

Property that has been discarded by the true owner, who has no intention of reclaiming title to it, is **abandoned property.** Someone who finds abandoned property acquires title to it, and such title is good against the whole world, *including the original owner.* The owner of lost property who eventually gives up any further attempt to find the lost property is frequently held to have abandoned the property. In situations in which the finder is trespassing on the property of another and finds abandoned property, title vests not in the finder but in the owner of the land. The following case involved a find of abandoned property that was embedded in the soil.

CASE 40.2 United States v. Shivers

United States Court of Appeals,
Fifth Circuit, 1996.
96 F.3d 120.
www.ca5.uscourts.gov/oparchive.cfm[a]

HISTORICAL AND ENVIRONMENTAL SETTING
Taking its name from the Angelina River in eastern Texas, Angelina National Forest is spread across parts of five Texas counties. Sam Rayburn Lake, the largest lake in the state with 570 miles of shoreline, is located in the heart of Angelina, but fishing, camping, boating, and water-skiing are possible at a number of lake and river recreation areas in the forest. Angelina's dense pine and hardwood forests offer opportunities for hunting, horseback riding, wilderness camping, and other backcountry activities. The Sawmill Hiking Trail links two recreation areas and passes an abandoned sawmill site, which was part of the great East Texas timber boom between 1890 and 1920.

a. This page provides access to some of the opinions of the U.S. Court of Appeals for the Fifth Circuit, which maintains this Web site. In the left frame, click on "by Docket Number." On that page, click on "1995," and when the list expands, click on "40000." Scroll down the list to "95-40748" and click on the number to access the opinion.

CASE 40.2—Continued

BACKGROUND AND FACTS Using a metal detector, Billy Ray Shivers found metal tokens at the site of an abandoned sawmill that once belonged to the Aldridge Lumber Company. The tokens were used fifty to a hundred years ago by the mill as payment for their workers. Because the site was in the Angelina National Forest, the federal government claimed ownership of the tokens and seized them. Shivers filed a motion in federal district court against the government, seeking to have the tokens returned. The court ruled in favor of the government, and Shivers appealed.

IN THE WORDS OF THE COURT . . .
EDITH H. JONES, Circuit Judge:

* * * *

* * * [T]he common law of finds generally assigns ownership of * * * abandoned property without regard to where the property is found. Two exceptions to the rule are recognized: First, when the abandoned property is embedded in the soil, it belongs to the owner of the soil; Second, when the owner of the land where the property is found (whether on or embedded in the soil) has constructive possession of the property such that the property is not "lost," it belongs to the owner of the land. * * * [T]he Aldridge tokens excavated by Shivers were buried in the soil of the Angelina National Forest. * * * [T]his soil belongs to the United States, and with it the embedded tokens * * * .

DECISION AND REMEDY The U.S. Court of Appeals for the Fifth Circuit affirmed the lower court's decision.

FOR CRITICAL ANALYSIS—Ethical Consideration *What argument might be used to justify the law that abandoned property embedded in the soil belongs to the owner of the soil?*

Bailments

• **BAILMENT**
A situation in which the personal property of one person (a bailor) is entrusted to another (a bailee), who is obligated to return the bailed property to the bailor or dispose of it as directed.

• **BAILOR**
One who entrusts goods to a bailee.

• **BAILEE**
One to whom goods are entrusted by a bailor.

A **bailment** is formed by the delivery of personal property, without transfer of title, by one person, called a **bailor,** to another, called a **bailee,** usually under an agreement for a particular purpose (for example, for storage, repair, or transportation). On completion of the purpose, the bailee is obligated to return the bailed property to the bailor or to a third person or to dispose of it as directed.

Bailments usually are created by agreement but not necessarily by contract, because in many bailments not all of the elements of a contract (such as mutual assent and consideration) are present. For example, if you loan your bicycle to a friend, a bailment is created, but not by contract, because there is no consideration. Many commercial bailments, such as the delivery of clothing to the cleaners for dry cleaning, are based on contract, however.

Virtually every individual or business is affected by the law of bailments at one time or another (and sometimes even on a daily basis). When individuals deal with bailments, whether they realize it or not, they are subject to the obligations and duties that arise from the bailment relationship. The number, scope, and importance of bailments created daily in the business community and in everyday life make it desirable for every person to understand the elements necessary for the creation of a bailment and to know what rights, duties, and liabilities flow from bailments.

ON THE WEB
For a discussion of the origins of the term *bailment* and how bailment relationships have been defined, go to www.lectlaw.com/def/b005.htm.

ELEMENTS OF A BAILMENT

Not all transactions involving the delivery of property from one person to another create a bailment. For such a transfer to become a bailment, three conditions must be met. We look here at each of these conditions.

Personal Property Bailment involves only personal property; there can be no bailment of persons. Although a bailment of your luggage is created when it is transported by an airline, as a passenger you are not the subject of a bailment. Additionally, you cannot bail realty; thus, leasing your house to a tenant does not create a bailment.

Delivery of Possession In a voluntary bailment, possession of the property must be transferred to the bailee in such a way that (1) the bailee is given exclusive possession and control over the property and (2) the bailee *knowingly* accepts the personal property. If either of these conditions for effective delivery of possession is lacking, there is no bailment relationship. • EXAMPLE 40.8 Suppose that you take a friend out to dinner at an expensive restaurant. When you enter the restaurant, your friend checks her coat. In the pocket of the coat is a $20,000 diamond necklace. The bailee, by accepting the coat, does not knowingly also accept the necklace; thus, a bailment of the coat exists—because the restaurant has exclusive possession and control over the coat and knowingly accepted it—but a bailment of the necklace does not exist. •

Two types of delivery—*physical* and *constructive*—will result in the bailee's exclusive possession of and control over the property. As discussed earlier, in the context of gifts, constructive delivery is a substitute, or symbolic, delivery. What is delivered to the bailee is not the actual property bailed (such as a car) but something so related to the property (such as the car keys) that the requirement of delivery is satisfied.

In certain unique situations, a bailment is found despite the apparent lack of the requisite elements of control and knowledge. In particular, the rental of a safe-deposit box is usually held to create a bailor-bailee relationship between the bank and its customer, despite the bank's lack of knowledge of the contents and its inability to have exclusive control of the property.[5] Another example of such a situation occurs when the bailee acquires the property accidentally or by mistake—as in finding someone else's lost or mislaid property. A bailment is created even though the bailor did not voluntarily deliver the property to the bailee. Such bailments are called *constructive* or *involuntary* bailments.

To what extent is a parking lot attendant responsible for undisclosed articles left in the trunk of a car placed in his or her care? This was the question in the following case.

5. By statute or by express contract, the rental of a safe-deposit box may be regarded as a lease of space or a license instead of a bailment.

CASE 40.3 Jack Boles Services, Inc. v. Stavely

Court of Appeals of Texas,
Austin, 1995.
906 S.W.2d 185.

HISTORICAL AND CULTURAL SETTING *The value of artwork fluctuates as much as the value of other investments. Vincent van Gogh, for example, sold less than a handful of his paintings in his lifetime in the 1800s, and those were sold for very low prices. Today, van Gogh's paintings are some of the most expensive works on the market; they cost as much as tens of millions of dollars each. Van Gogh is regarded as a master, but the price of other artists' work may have nothing to do with their importance to the art world.*

BACKGROUND AND FACTS Gerald Stavely entrusted a valuable painting to the care of Patricia Bolger. Bolger put the painting in the trunk of her husband's Cadillac. Her husband left the car at his country club in the care of a parking attendant who worked for Jack Boles Services, Inc. The car and painting were stolen. Bolger's car was eventually returned to him, but the painting was missing. Stavely filed a suit in a Texas state court against Jack Boles Services, Inc., arguing that the bailee was responsible for the theft. The court agreed. Boles appealed.

CASE 40.3—Continued

IN THE WORDS OF THE COURT . . .
ABOUSSIE, Justice.

* * * *

* * * [A] bailee accepts responsibility for unknown contents of a bailed automobile when the presence of those contents is reasonably foreseeable based on the factual circumstances surrounding the bailment of the automobile. * * *

* * * *

* * * It cannot be said * * * that a country club parking attendant should reasonably foresee the presence of valuable artwork in each member's car trunk. As such, Jack Boles cannot be charged with notice of a valuable painting contained within the trunk of the bailed Cadillac. It did not expressly or implicitly accept Stavely's painting as a bailed piece of property. Without acceptance, no bailor-bailee relationship existed in regard to the painting, and accordingly, Jack Boles had no duty of care in regard to the painting.

DECISION AND REMEDY The Texas appellate court reversed the lower court's judgment and awarded Stavely nothing.

FOR CRITICAL ANALYSIS—Economic Consideration *Why did Stavely file suit against Boles instead of against the parking attendant?*

Bailment Agreement A bailment agreement, or contract, can be express or implied. Although a written agreement is not required for bailments of less than one year (that is, the Statute of Frauds does not apply—see Chapter 12), it is a good idea to have one, especially when valuable property is involved.

The bailment agreement expressly or impliedly provides for the return of the bailed property to the bailor or to a third person, or it provides for disposal by the bailee. The agreement presupposes that the bailee will return the identical goods originally given by the bailor. In certain types of bailments, however, such as bailments of fungible goods, the property returned need only be equivalent property.

• **EXAMPLE 40.9** If Holman stores his grain (fungible goods) in Joe's Warehouse, a bailment is created. At the end of the storage period, however, the warehouse is not obligated to return to Holman exactly the same grain that he stored. As long as the warehouse returns goods of the same *type, grade,* and *quantity,* the warehouse—the bailee—has performed its obligation.•

ORDINARY BAILMENTS

Bailments are either *ordinary* or *special (extraordinary).* There are three types of ordinary bailments. The distinguishing feature among them is *which party receives a benefit from the bailment.* Ultimately, the courts may use this factor to determine the standard of care required of the bailee in possession of the personal property, and this factor will dictate the rights and liabilities of the parties. The three types of ordinary bailments are as follows:

1. *Bailment for the sole benefit of the bailor.* This is a gratuitous bailment (a bailment without consideration) for the convenience and benefit of the bailor. For example, if Allen asks his friend, Sumi, to store Allen's car in Sumi's garage, and Sumi agrees to do so, the bailment of the car would be for the sole benefit of the bailor (Allen).
2. *Bailment for the sole benefit of the bailee.* This type of bailment typically occurs when one person loans an item to another person (the bailee) solely for the bailee's convenience and benefit. For example, Allen asks his friend Sumi to borrow Sumi's

boat so that Allen can go sailing over the weekend. The bailment of the boat is for Allen's (the bailee's) sole benefit.

3 *Bailment for the mutual benefit of the bailee and the bailor.* This is the most common kind of bailment and involves some form of compensation for storing items or holding property while it is being serviced. It is a contractual bailment and is often referred to as a bailment for hire. For example, leaving your car at a service station for an oil change is a mutual-benefit bailment.

Rights of the Bailee Certain rights are implicit in the bailment agreement. A hallmark of the bailment agreement is that the bailee acquires the *right to control and possess the property temporarily.* The bailee's right of possession permits the bailee to recover damages from any third person for damage or loss of the property. If the property is stolen, the bailee has a legal right to regain possession of it or to obtain damages from any third person who has wrongfully interfered with the bailee's possessory rights. The bailee's right to regain possession of the property or to obtain damages is important because, as you will read shortly, a bailee is liable to the bailor for any loss or damage to bailed property resulting from the bailee's negligence.

Depending on the type of bailment and the terms of the bailment agreement, a bailee also may have a *right to use the bailed property.* • **EXAMPLE 40.10** If you borrow a friend's car to drive to the airport, you, as the bailee, would obviously be expected to use the car. In a bailment involving the long-term storage of a car, however, the bailee is not expected to use the car, because the ordinary purpose of a storage bailment does not include use of the property. •

Except in a gratuitous bailment, a bailee has a *right to be compensated* as provided for in the bailment agreement, a right to be reimbursed for costs and services rendered in the keeping of the bailed property, or both. Even in a gratuitous bailment, a bailee has a right to be reimbursed or compensated for costs incurred in the keeping of the bailed property. • **EXAMPLE 40.11** Margo loses her pet dog, which Judith finds. Judith takes Margo's dog to her home and feeds it. Even though she takes good care of the dog, it becomes ill, and she calls a veterinarian. Judith pays the bill for the veterinarian's services and the medicine. Judith normally will be entitled to be reimbursed by Margo for all reasonable costs incurred in the keeping of Margo's dog. •

To enforce the right of compensation, the bailee has a right to place a *possessory lien* (which entitles a creditor to retain possession of the debtor's goods until a debt is paid) on the specific bailed property until he or she has been fully compensated. This type of lien, sometimes referred to as an artisan's lien or a *bailee's lien,* was discussed in Chapter 23.

Ordinary bailees have the *right to limit their liability* as long as the limitations are called to the attention of the bailor and are not against public policy. It is essential that the bailor in some way know of the limitation. Even if the bailor has notice, certain types of disclaimers of liability have been considered to be against public policy and therefore illegal. For example, certain exculpatory clauses limiting a person's liability for his or her own wrongful acts are often scrutinized by the courts and, in the case of bailments, are routinely held to be illegal. This is particularly true in bailments for the mutual benefit of the bailor and the bailee.

Duties of the Bailee The bailee has two basic responsibilities: (1) to take proper care of the property and (2) to surrender to the bailor or dispose of the property in accordance with the bailor's instructions at the end of the bailment. The bailee must exercise reasonable care in preserving the bailed property. What constitutes reasonable care in a bailment situation normally depends on the nature and specific circumstances of the bailment. Traditionally, courts have determined the appropriate standard of care on the basis of the type of bailments involved. In a bailment for the sole benefit for the bailor, for example, the bailee need exercise only a slight degree of care. In a bailment for the sole benefit of the bailee, however, the bailee must exercise great care. In a mutual-benefit bailment, courts normally impose a reasonable standard of care—that is, the bailee must exercise the degree of care that a reasonable and prudent person would exercise in the same circumstances. Exhibit 40–1 illustrates these concepts.

ETHICAL ISSUE 40.1 ***Why do different standards of care apply to bailed goods?*** The standard of care expected of a bailee clearly illustrates how the law reflects ethical principles. For example, suppose that a friend asks to borrow your business law text for the weekend. You agree to loan your friend the book. In this situation, which is a bailment for the sole benefit of the bailee (your friend), most people would agree that your friend has an ethical obligation to take great care of your book. After all, if your friend lost your book, you would incur damages. You would have to purchase another one, and if you could not, you might find it difficult to do well in your homework assignments, examinations, and so on. It would be different if you had loaned your book to your friend totally for your own benefit. For example, suppose that you are leaving town during the summer, and a friend offers to store several boxes of books for you until you return in the fall. In this situation, a benefit for the sole benefit of the bailor (you) exists. If your books are destroyed while in the bailee's (your friend's) possession and you sue the bailee for damages, a court will likely take into consideration the fact that the bailee was essentially doing you a favor by storing the books. Although bailees generally have a duty to exercise reasonable care over bailed property, what constitutes reasonable care in a specific situation normally depends on the surrounding circumstances—including the reason for the bailment and who stood to benefit from the arrangement.

A bailee's failure to exercise appropriate care in handling the bailor's property results in tort liability. The duty to relinquish the property at the end of the bailment is grounded in both contract and tort law principles. Failure to return the property constitutes a breach of contract or the tort of conversion, and with one exception, the bailee is liable for damages. The exception is when the obligation is excused because the goods or chattels have been destroyed, lost, or stolen through no fault of the bailee (or claimed by a third party with a superior claim).

Under the law of bailments, a bailor's proof that damage or loss to the property has occurred will, in and of itself, raise a presumption that the bailee is guilty of negligence or conversion. In other words, whenever a bailee fails to return bailed property, the bailee's negligence will be presumed by the court.

EXHIBIT 40–1 • Degree of Care Required of a Bailee

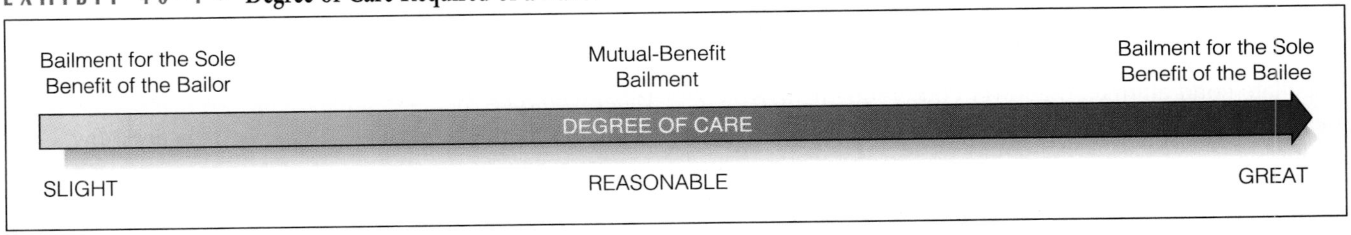

The court in the following case weighed the duty of a bailee to return bailed property to the bailor against charges that giving car keys to an intoxicated person was negligent entrustment, regardless of any bailment.

CASE 40.4 Umble v. Sandy McKie and Sons, Inc.

Appellate Court of Illinois,
Second District, 1998.
294 Ill.App.3d 449,
690 N.E.2d 157,
228 Ill.Dec. 848.

HISTORICAL AND SOCIAL SETTING *Sometimes, the question arises as to whether individuals have a duty to prevent an intoxicated driver from driving his or her vehicle. Consider an example. Edward Hoag went to the beach with several friends, including Ronald Niemeyer. After Hoag became intoxicated, Niemeyer drove Hoag's car to Niemeyer's house. Hoag then attempted to drive home but was involved in an accident in which Keith Lombardo was injured. Lombardo sued Hoag, and one of the questions in the suit was whether Neimeyer had a duty to prevent Hoag from driving Hoag's car while intoxicated. The court refused to impose such a duty on Niemeyer. The court explained that "[o]ne problem with * * * that particular form of a duty is that the standard is so broad that it would conceivably apply to gas station attendants, toll booth collectors, parking lot attendants, repair services, and onlookers who may have observed the participants get into a vehicle driven by an intoxicated person."* [a] *Most courts would agree.*

BACKGROUND AND FACTS Jerome Butzen brought his car to Sandy McKie & Sons, Inc., to fix a leaking tire and replace a burned-out headlight. Butzen was intoxicated, which was apparent to the McKie employees. The car was repaired, Butzen paid for the repairs, and McKie returned the car. Shortly afterwards, Butzen's car collided with one driven by Phillip Umble, who died in the collision. Mary Ellen Umble filed a suit in an Illinois state court against McKie, alleging in part that McKie was negligent in giving car keys to an obviously intoxicated driver. The court dismissed the suit, and Umble appealed.

a. *Lombardo v. Hoag,* 269 N.J.Super. 36, 634 A.2d 550 (1993).

IN THE WORDS OF THE COURT . . .
Justice *McLAREN* delivered the opinion of the court:

* * * *

* * * Negligent entrustment occurs where one entrusts to another something under the actor's control if the actor knows that the third person will use the thing to create an unreasonable risk of harm to others. Thus, an essential element of a negligent entrustment cause of action is that the person charged with liability have a superior right to control the property. * * *

* * * [A] majority of courts * * * have held that a bailee for hire is not liable for returning the property to the bailor. * * *

* * * *

In light of these precedents, defendant [McKie] was clearly a bailee for hire. Once Butzen paid for the repairs and demanded the return of his keys, defendant had no discretion to refuse without being found liable for conversion. Because Butzen already owned the car, defendant cannot be liable for negligently "entrusting" it to him.

DECISION AND REMEDY The state intermediate appellate court affirmed the lower court's judgment. A bailee is not liable for returning bailed property to the bailor.

FOR CRITICAL ANALYSIS—Cultural Consideration *What would be McKie's liability if Butzen had not paid for the repairs and McKie had not returned the car? Why?*

Duties of the Bailor It goes without saying that the rights of a bailor are essentially the same as the duties of a bailee. The major duty of the bailor is to provide the bailee with goods or chattels that are free from known defects that could cause injury to the bailee. In the case of a mutual-benefit bailment, the bailor must also notify the bailee of any hidden defects that the bailor could have discovered with reasonable diligence and proper inspection.

The bailor's duty to reveal defects is based on a negligence theory of tort law. A bailor who fails to give the appropriate notice is liable to the bailee and to any other person who might reasonably be expected to come into contact with the defective article. For example, if an equipment rental firm leases equipment with a *discoverable* defect, and the lessee (bailee) is not notified of such a defect and is harmed because of it, the rental firm is liable for negligence under tort law.

An exception to this rule exists if the bailment was created for the sole benefit of the bailee. Thus, if you loaned your car to a friend as a favor to your friend and not for any direct return benefit to yourself, you would be required to notify your friend of any *known* defect of the automobile that could cause injury but not of a defect of which you were unaware (even if it was a *discoverable* defect). If your friend was injured in an accident as a result of a defect unknown to you, you would normally not be liable.

A bailor can also incur *warranty liability* based on contract law (see Chapter 18) for injuries resulting from the bailment of defective articles. Property leased by a bailor must be *fit for the intended purpose of the bailment.* Warranties of fitness arise by law in sales contracts and leases and by judicial interpretation in the case of bailments for hire. Article 2A of the Uniform Commercial Code extends implied warranties of merchantability and fitness for a particular purpose to bailments whenever the bailments include rights to use the bailed goods.[6]

Special Types of Bailments

Up to this point, our discussion of bailments has been concerned with ordinary bailments—bailments in which bailees are expected to exercise ordinary care in the handling of bailed property. Some bailment transactions warrant special consideration. These include bailments in which the bailee's duty of care is *extraordinary*—that is, his or her liability for loss or damage to the property is absolute—as is generally true in cases involving common carriers and innkeepers. Warehouse companies have the same duty of care as ordinary bailees; but, like carriers, they are subject to extensive regulation under federal and state laws, including Article 7 of the Uniform Commercial Code (UCC).

Common Carriers Transportation providers that are publicly licensed to provide transportation services to the general public are referred to as **common carriers.** Common carriers are distinguished from private carriers, which operate transportation facilities for a select clientele. Whereas a private carrier is not bound to provide service to every person or company making a request, a common carrier must arrange carriage for all who apply, within certain limitations.[7]

• **COMMON CARRIER**
An owner of a truck, railroad, airline, ship, or other vehicle who is licensed to offer transportation services to the public, generally in return for compensation or a payment.

The delivery of goods to a common carrier creates a bailment relationship between the shipper (bailor) and the common carrier (bailee). Unlike ordinary

6. UCC 2A–212, 2A–213.
7. A common carrier is not required to take any and all property anywhere in all instances. Public regulatory agencies govern common carriers, and carriers can be restricted to geographical areas. They can also be limited to carrying certain kinds of goods or to providing only special types of transportation equipment.

A TRUCK TRAVELS A HIGHWAY. WHY ARE COMMON CARRIERS, SUCH AS MOST TRUCKING COMPANIES, SUBJECT TO STRICT LIABILITY WHILE ORDINARY BAILEES MUST EXERCISE ONLY "REASONABLE CARE"?

bailees, the common carrier is held to a standard of care based on *strict liability*, rather than reasonable care, in protecting the bailed personal property. This means that the common carrier is absolutely liable, regardless of due care, for all loss or damage to goods except damage caused by one of the following common law exceptions: (1) an act of God, (2) an act of a public enemy, (3) an order of a public authority, (4) an act of the shipper, or (5) the inherent nature of the goods.

Common carriers cannot contract away their liability for damaged goods. Subject to government regulations, however, they are permitted to limit their dollar liability to an amount stated on the shipment contract or rate filing.[8]

Warehouse Companies Warehousing is the business of providing storage of property for compensation.[9] A warehouse company is a professional bailee whose responsibility differs from an ordinary bailee's in two important aspects. First, a warehouse company is empowered to issue documents of title—in particular, warehouse receipts.[10] Second, warehouse companies are subject to an extraordinary network of state and federal statutes, including Article 7 of the UCC.

A warehouse company accepts goods for storage and issues a warehouse receipt describing the property and the terms of the bailment contract. The warehouse receipt can be negotiable or nonnegotiable, depending on how it is written. It is negotiable if its terms provide that the warehouse company will deliver the goods "to the bearer" of the receipt or "to the order of" a person named on the receipt.[11]

8. Federal laws require common carriers to offer shippers the opportunity to obtain higher dollar limits for loss by paying a higher fee for the transport.
9. UCC 7–102(h) defines the person engaged in the storing of goods for hire as a "warehouseman."
10. A document of title is defined in UCC 1–201(15) as any "document which in the regular course of business or financing is treated as adequately evidencing that the person in possession of it is entitled to receive, hold, and dispose of the document and the goods it covers. To be a document of title, a document must purport to be issued by or addressed to a bailee and purport to cover goods in the bailee's possession."
11. UCC 7–104.

The warehouse receipt serves multiple functions. It is a receipt for the goods stored; it is a contract of bailment; and it also represents the goods (that is, it indicates title) and hence has value and utility in financing commercial transactions. • EXAMPLE 40.12 Ossip, a processor and canner of corn, delivers 6,500 cases of corn to Shaneyfelt, the owner of a warehouse. Shaneyfelt issues a negotiable warehouse receipt payable "to bearer" and gives it to Ossip. Ossip sells and delivers the warehouse receipt to a large supermarket chain, Better Foods, Inc. Better Foods is now the owner of the corn and has the right to obtain the cases from Shaneyfelt. It will present the warehouse receipt to Shaneyfelt, who in return will release the cases of corn to the grocery chain.•

Like ordinary bailees, a warehouse company is liable for loss or damage to property resulting from *negligence* (and therefore does not have the same liability as a common carrier). As a professional bailee, however, it is expected to exercise a high degree of care to protect and preserve the goods. A warehouse company can limit the dollar amount of its liability, but the bailor must be given the option of paying an increased storage rate for an increase in the liability limit.

"All saints can do miracles, but few of them can keep a hotel."
SAMUEL CLEMENS (MARK TWAIN), 1835–1910
(American author and humorist)

Innkeepers At common law, innkeepers, hotel owners, and similar operators were held to the same strict liability as common carriers with respect to property brought into the rooms by guests. Today, only those who provide lodging to the public for compensation as a *regular* business are covered under this rule of strict liability. Moreover, the rule applies only to those who are guests, as opposed to lodgers. A lodger is a permanent resident of the hotel or inn, whereas a guest is a transient traveler.

In many states, innkeepers can avoid strict liability for loss of guests' valuables and funds by providing a safe in which to keep them. Each guest must be clearly notified of the availability of such a safe. Statutes often limit the liability of innkeepers with regard to articles that are not kept in the safe or that are of such a nature that they are not normally kept in a safe. These statutes may limit the amount of monetary damages or even provide for no liability in the absence of innkeeper negligence.

Suppose that Joyce stays for a night at the Harbor Hotel. When she returns from eating breakfast in the hotel restaurant, she discovers that the people in the room next door have forced the lock on the door between the two rooms and stolen her suitcase. Joyce claims that the hotel is liable for her loss. The hotel maintains that because it was not negligent, it is not liable. At common law, the hotel would have been liable, because innkeepers were actually insurers of the property of their guests. Today, however, state statutes limit strict liability by limiting the amount of monetary damages for which the innkeeper is liable or providing that the innkeeper has no liability in the absence of negligence. Most statutes require these limitations to be posted or the guest to be notified. Such postings, or notices, are frequently found on the doors of the rooms in the motel or hotel.

Normally, the innkeeper (a motel keeper, for example) assumes no responsibility for the safety of a guest's automobile, because the guest usually retains possession and control over it. If, however, the innkeeper provides parking facilities and the guest's car is entrusted to the innkeeper or to an employee, the innkeeper will be liable under the rules that pertain to parking-lot bailments (which are ordinary bailments).

APPLICATION

What to Do with Lost Property*

If you are walking down a street in New York City and chance upon a valuable diamond ring that is lying next to a gutter, what should you do with the ring? The tempting thing would be to keep it or sell it and enjoy the proceeds. That would be unethical, however; it would also be illegal under New York laws governing the finding of lost property. New York law defines *lost property* to include lost property, mislaid property, abandoned property, "waifs [goods to which all ownership rights have been waived, such as goods that are found but unclaimed] and treasure trove, and other property which is found." Property includes "money, goods, chattels and tangible personal property," with some exceptions. Generally, the finder of property worth $20 or more must deposit it with police authorities (or with the owner of the premises on which the property was found) within ten days. Failure to do so is a misdemeanor, subject to a fine of up to $100 and imprisonment for not more than six months.

Many states have enacted lost-property statutes. The statutes differ significantly from state to state, but typically, they eliminate the distinction between lost property, mislaid property, abandoned property, and treasure trove, as the New York statute does. Many statutes also require the finder to deposit found property with local authorities, although the penalty imposed for failure to do so may not be as severe as under New York's statute (in Illinois, for example, a finder who fails to comply with the requirements of that state's lost-property statute may be fined $10). Lost-property statutes also typically require the police to attempt to find the true owner, such as by calling the owner or person in charge of the premises on which the property was found. Sometimes, the finder must advertise, at the county court, the property and its discovery.

Generally, if the true owner cannot be located within a certain period of time, which varies depending on the value of the property and whether the property is perishable, the finder gets the property. If the finder does not appear after the period of time has lapsed, the property may be sold and the proceeds disposed of as specified by the statute. In California, for instance, the proceeds from such a sale go into a state abandoned-property fund (if the state police had custody of the lost property) or become the property of the city, county, town, or village (if other police had custody).

Every statute has exceptions, of course. In some situations, an employer may have rights to property found by an employee. Property found in a safe-deposit area in a bank may also be subject to different rules.

*This *Application* is not meant to substitute for the services of an attorney who is licensed to practice law in your state.

CHECKLIST FOR THE FINDER OF LOST PROPERTY

1. To maximize your chances of legally keeping lost property, take the found property to the nearest police station.

Key Terms

abandoned property 1038
accession 1036
bailee 1039
bailment 1039
bailor 1039
chattel 1030
common carrier 1045
community property 1032
confusion 1036
constructive delivery 1034
dominion 1034
estray statute 1037
fee simple 1031
gift 1033
gift *causa mortis* 1035
gift *inter vivos* 1035
joint tenancy 1031
lost property 1037
mislaid property 1036
personal property 1030
property 1030
real property 1030
tenancy by the entirety 1032
tenancy in common 1031

Chapter Summary • Personal Property and Bailments

PERSONAL PROPERTY	
Definition of Personal Property (See page 1030.)	Personal property (personalty) is considered to include all property not classified as real property (realty). Personal property can be tangible (such as a TV set or a car) or intangible (such as stocks or bonds). Personal property may be referred to legally as *chattel*—a term used under the common law to denote all forms of personal property.
Property Ownership (See pages 1031–1032.)	1. *Fee simple*—Exists when individuals have the right to use, possess, or dispose of the property as they choose during their lifetimes and to pass on the property to their heirs at death. 2. *Concurrent ownership*— a. Tenancy in common—Co-ownership in which two or more persons own an undivided interest in the property; on one tenant's death, the property interest passes to his or her heirs. b. Joint tenancy—Exists when two or more persons own an undivided interest in property; on the death of a joint tenant, the property interest transfers to the remaining tenant(s), not to the heirs of the deceased. c. Tenancy by the entirety—A form of co-ownership between a husband and wife that is similar to a joint tenancy, except that a spouse cannot transfer separately his or her interest during his or her lifetime without the consent of the other spouse. d. Community property—A form of co-ownership in which each spouse technically owns an undivided one-half interest in property acquired during the marriage. This type of ownership occurs in only a few states.
Acquiring Ownership of Personal Property (See pages 1032–1036.)	The most common means of acquiring ownership in personal property is by purchasing it (see Chapters 15 through 18). Another way in which personal property is often acquired is by will or inheritance (see Chapter 38). The following are additional methods of acquiring personal property: 1. *Possession*—Ownership may be acquired by possession if no other person has ownership title (for example, capturing wild animals or finding abandoned property). 2. *Production*—Any product or item produced by an individual (with minor exceptions) becomes the property of that individual. 3. *Gift*—An effective gift exists when the following conditions exist: a. There is evidence of *intent* to make a gift of the property in question. b. The gift is *delivered* (physically or constructively) to the donee or the donee's agent. c. The gift is *accepted* by the donee or the donee's agent. 4. *Accession*—When someone adds value to an item of personal property by labor or materials, the added value generally becomes the property of the owner of the original property (includes accessions made in bad faith or wrongfully). Good faith accessions that substantially increase the property's value or change the identity of the property may cause title to pass to the improver. 5. *Confusion*—In the case of fungible goods, if a person wrongfully and willfully commingles goods with those of another in order to render them indistinguishable, the innocent party acquires title to the whole. Otherwise, the owners become tenants in common of the commingled goods.
Mislaid, Lost, and Abandoned Property (See pages 1036–1039.)	1. *Mislaid property*—Property that is placed somewhere voluntarily by the owner and then inadvertently forgotten. A finder of mislaid property will not acquire title to the goods, and the owner of the place where the property was mislaid becomes a caretaker of the mislaid property. 2. *Lost property*—Property that is involuntarily left and forgotten. A finder of lost property can claim title to the property against the whole world *except the true owner.* 3. *Abandoned property*—Property that has been discarded by the true owner, who has no intention of claiming title to the property in the future. A finder of abandoned property can claim title to it against the whole world, *including the original owner.*

Chapter Summary • Personal Property and Bailments, Continued

BAILMENTS	
Elements of a Bailment (See pages 1039–1041.)	1. *Personal property*—Bailments involve only personal property. 2. *Delivery of possession*—For an effective bailment to exist, the bailee (the one receiving the property) must be given exclusive possession and control over the property, and in a voluntary bailment, the bailee must knowingly accept the personal property. 3. *The bailment agreement*—Expressly or impliedly provides for the return of the bailed property to the bailor or a third party, or for the disposal of the bailed property by the bailee.
Ordinary Bailments (See pages 1041–1045.)	1. *Types of bailments*— a. Bailment for the sole benefit of the bailor—A gratuitous bailment undertaken for the sole benefit of the bailor (for example, as a favor to the bailor). b. Bailment for the sole benefit of the bailee—A gratuitous loan of an article to a person (the bailee) solely for the bailee's benefit. c. Mutual-benefit (contractual) bailment—The most common kind of bailment; involves compensation between the bailee and bailor for the service provided. 2. *Rights of a bailee (duties of a bailor)*— a. The right of possession—Allows actions against third persons who damage or convert the bailed property and allows actions against the bailor for wrongful breach of the bailment. b. The right to be compensated and reimbursed for expenses—In the event of nonpayment, the bailee has the right to place a possessory (bailee's) lien on the bailed property. c. The right to limit liability—An ordinary bailee can limit his or her liability for loss or damage, provided proper notice is given and the limitation is not against public policy. In special bailments, limitations on liability for negligence or on types of losses are usually not allowed, but limitations on the monetary amount of liability are permitted. 3. *Duties of a bailee (rights of a bailor)*— a. A bailee must exercise appropriate care over property entrusted to him or her. What constitutes appropriate care normally depends on the nature and circumstances of the bailment. b. Bailed goods in a bailee's possession must be either returned to the bailor or disposed of according to the bailor's directions. A bailee's failure to return the bailed property creates a presumption of negligence and constitutes a breach of contract or the tort of conversion of goods.
Special Types of Bailments (See pages 1045–1047.)	1. *Common carriers*—Carriers that are publicly licensed to provide transportation services to the general public. The common carrier is held to a standard of care based on *strict liability* unless the bailed property is lost or destroyed due to (a) an act of God, (b) an act of a public enemy, (c) an order of a public authority, (d) an act of a shipper, or (e) the inherent nature of the goods. 2. *Warehouse companies*—Professional bailees that differ from ordinary bailees because they (a) can issue documents of title (warehouse receipts) and (b) are subject to state and federal statutes, including Article 7 of the UCC (as are common carriers). They must exercise a high degree of care over the bailed property and are liable for loss or damage of property if they fail to do so. 3. *Innkeepers (hotel operators)*—Those who provide lodging to the public for compensation as a *regular* business. The common law strict liability standard to which innkeepers were once held is limited today by state statutes, which vary from state to state.

For Review

1. What is real property? What is personal property?
2. What does it mean to own property in fee simple? What is the difference between a joint tenancy and a tenancy in common?
3. What are the three elements necessary for an effective gift? How else can property be acquired?
4. What are the three elements of a bailment?
5. What are the basic rights and duties of the bailee? What are the rights and duties of the bailor?

Questions and Case Problems

40–1. Duties of the Bailee. Discuss the standard of care traditionally required of the bailee for the bailed property in each of the following situations, and determine whether the bailee breached that duty.

(a) Ricardo borrows Steve's lawn mower because his own lawn mower needs repair. Ricardo mows his front yard. To mow the back yard, he needs to move some hoses and lawn furniture. He leaves the mower in front of his house while doing so. When he returns to the front yard, he discovers that the mower has been stolen.

(b) Alicia owns a valuable speedboat. She is going on vacation and asks her neighbor, Maureen, to store the boat in one stall of Maureen's double garage. Maureen consents, and the boat is moved into the garage. Maureen needs some grocery items for dinner and drives to the store. She leaves the garage door open while she is gone, as is her custom, and the speedboat is stolen during that time.

40–2. Gifts. Reineken, very old and ill, wanted to make a gift to his nephew, Gerald. He had a friend obtain $2,500 in cash for him from his bank account, placed this cash in an envelope, and wrote on the envelope, "This is for my nephew, Gerald." Reineken then placed the envelope in his dresser drawer. When Reineken died a month later, his family found the envelope, and Gerald got word of the intended gift. Gerald then demanded that Reineken's daughter, the executor of Reineken's estate (the person appointed by Reineken to handle his affairs after his death), turn over the gift to him. The daughter refused to do so. Discuss fully whether Gerald can successfully claim ownership rights to the $2,500.

40–3. Gifts. In 1968, Armando was about to be shipped to Vietnam for active duty with the U.S. Marines. Shortly before he left, he gave an expensive stereo set and other personal belongings to his girlfriend, Sara, saying, "I'll probably not return from this war, so I'm giving these to you." Armando returned eighteen months later and requested that Sara return the property. Sara said that because Armando had given her these items to keep, she was not required to return them. Was a gift made in this instance, and can Armando recover his property? Discuss fully.

40–4. Requirements of a Bailment. Calvin is an executive on a business trip to the West Coast. He has driven his car on this trip and checks into the Hotel Ritz. The hotel has a guarded underground parking lot. Calvin gives his car keys to the parking-lot attendant but fails to notify the attendant that his wife's $10,000 diamond necklace is in a box in the trunk. The next day, on checking out, he discovers that his car has been stolen. Calvin wants to hold the hotel liable for both the car and the necklace. Discuss the probable success of his claim.

40–5. Abandoned Property. Danny Smith and his brother discovered a sixteen-foot boat lying beside a roadway in Alabama. Smith informed the police, who immediately impounded the boat and stored it in a city warehouse. Although Smith acquiesced to the police action, he told the police that if the true owner did not claim the boat, he wanted it. When the true owner did not come forward, the police refused to relinquish the boat to Smith and instead told Smith that they planned to auction it to the highest bidder on behalf of the city. Smith sued for custody of the boat. Because Smith never physically held the boat but rather allowed the police to take possession, should Smith succeed in his claim to title as finder? Could Smith defeat a claim if the true owner sought to retake the boat? Discuss fully. [*Smith v. Purvis*, 474 So.2d 1131 (Ala.Civ.App. 1985)]

40–6. Gifts. William Yee and S. Hing Woo had been lovers for nearly twenty years. They held themselves out as husband and wife, and Woo wore a wedding band. Two days before his death, Yee told Woo that he felt "terribly bad" and believed he would die. He gave Woo three checks, for $42,700, $80,000, and $1,900, and told her that if he died, he wanted her "to be taken care of." After Yee's death, Woo cashed the $42,700 check and the $1,900 check. She never cashed the $80,000 check. The administrator of Yee's estate petitioned a Virginia state court to declare that Woo was not entitled to the funds represented by the checks. What will the court decide, and why? [*Woo v. Smart*, 247 Va. 365, 442 S.E.2d 690 (1994)]

40–7. Bailments. Jole Liddle, a high school student in Salem School District No. 600, played varsity basketball. A letter from Monmouth College of West Long Branch, New Jersey, addressed to Liddle in care of the coach, was delivered to Liddle's school a few days after it was mailed on July 18, 1990. The letter notified Liddle that he was being recruited for a basketball scholarship. The school, which had a policy of delivering promptly any mail sent to students in care of the school, did not deliver the letter to Liddle until seven months later. Because Monmouth College had not heard from Liddle, the college discontinued its efforts to recruit him. Liddle sued the school district, alleging that the coach was negligent in his duties as a bailee of the letter. The school district filed a motion to dismiss the case, arguing that the letter was not bailable property. Was the letter bailable property? Discuss fully. [*Liddle v. Salem School District No. 600*, 249 Ill.App.3d 768, 619 N.E.2d 530, 188 Ill.Dec. 905 (1993)]

40–8. Gratuitous Bailments. Raul Covarrubias, David Haro, and Javier Aguirre immigrated to the United States from Colima,

Mexico, to find jobs and help their families. When they learned that Francisco Alcaraz-Garcia planned to travel to Colima, they asked him to deliver various sums, totaling more than $25,000, to their families. During customs inspections at the border, Alcaraz told officers of the U.S. Customs Service that he was not carrying more than $10,000. In fact, he carried more than $35,000. He was charged with—and convicted of—criminal currency and customs violations, and the government seized most of the cash. Covarrubias, Haro, and Aguirre filed a petition for the return of their money, arguing that Alcaraz was a gratuitous bailee and that they still had title to the money. Are they right? Explain fully. [*United States v. Alcaraz-Garcia,* 79 F.3d 769 (9th Cir. 1996)]

40–9. Gifts. Hugh Chalmers issued a promissory note to his father in the amount of $50,000, plus interest. The note was secured by a deed of trust on certain real estate and was payable on demand or within sixty days of the father's death. More than seventeen years later, the father assigned the deed of trust to his wife, Nina. The existence of the note was mentioned in the assignment, which was recorded in the appropriate state office with the deed of trust. After the father died, Nina found the note in a safe-deposit box. On the back of the note, the father had indorsed the note to Nina. When Chalmers refused to pay the amount due, Nina filed a lawsuit in an Arkansas state court against him. Chalmers argued that the note had not been effectively delivered. What should the court hold? Discuss. [*Chalmers v. Chalmers,* 937 S.W.2d 171 (Ark. 1997)]

40–10. Gift *Inter Vivos*. Thomas Stafford owned four promissory notes. Payments on the notes were deposited into a bank account in the names of Stafford and his daughter June Zink "as joint tenants with right of survivorship." Stafford kept control of the notes and would not allow Zink to spend any of the proceeds. He also kept the interest on the account. On one note, Stafford endorsed "Pay to the order of Thomas J. Stafford or June S. Zink, or the survivor." The payee on each of the other notes was "Thomas J. Stafford and June S. Zink, or the survivor." When Stafford died, Zink took possession of the notes, claiming that she had been a joint tenant of the notes with her father. Stafford's son, also Thomas, filed a suit in a Virginia state court against Zink, claiming that the notes were partly his. The son argued that their father had not made a valid gift *inter vivos* of the notes to Zink. In whose favor will the court rule? Why? [*Zink v. Stafford,* 509 S.E.2d 833 (Va. 1999)]

A QUESTION OF ETHICS AND SOCIAL RESPONSIBILITY

40–11. George Cook stayed at a Day's Inn Motel in Nashville, Tennessee, while attending a trade show. At the trade show, Cook received orders for 225 cases of his firm's product, representing $17,336.25 in profits to the company. On the third day of his stay, Cook's room was burglarized while he was gone from the room. The burglar took Cook's order lists, as well as $174 in cash and medicine worth about $10. Cook sued the owner of the motel, Columbia Sussex Corp., alleging negligence. The motel defended by stating that it had posted a notice on the door of Cook's room informing guests of the fact that the motel would not be liable for any valuable property not placed in the motel safe for safekeeping. Given these circumstances, evaluate and answer the following questions. [*Cook v. Columbia Sussex Corp.,* 807 S.W.2d 567 (Tenn.App. 1990)]

1. The relevant state statute governing the liability of innkeepers allowed motels to disclaim their liability by posting a notice such as the one posted by Day's Inn, but the statute also required that the notice be posted "in a conspicuous manner." The notice posted by Day's Inn on the inside of the door to Cook's room was six-by-three inches in size. In your opinion, is the notice sufficiently conspicuous? If you were the guest, would you notice the disclaimer? Is it fair to guests to assume that they will notice such disclaimers? Discuss fully.
2. Should hotels or motels ever be allowed to disclaim liability by posting such notices? From a policy point of view, evaluate the implications of your answer.

FOR CRITICAL ANALYSIS

40–12. Suppose that a certificate of deposit (CD) owned by two joint tenants (with the right of survivorship) is given by one of the joint tenants as security for a loan (without the other joint tenant's knowledge). Further suppose that the joint tenant died after defaulting on the loan. Who has superior rights in the CD, the creditor or the other surviving joint tenant?

Online Activities

ONLINE EXERCISE 40–1

Go to the "Internet Activities Book" on the Web site that accompanies this text, the URL for which is http://blt.westbuslaw.com. Select the following activities, and perform the exercises according to the instructions given there:

Activity 36–1: Unclaimed Property
Activity 36–2: Bailments

Before the Test

Go to the *Business Law Today* home page at http://blt.westbuslaw.com. Click on TestTutor.® You will find twenty interactive questions relating to this chapter.

CHAPTER 41

Real Property

> "The right of property is the most sacred of all the rights of citizenship."
>
> Jean–Jacques Rousseau, 1712–1778
> (French writer and philosopher)

CONTENTS

LEARNING OBJECTIVES

After reading this chapter, you should be able to:

1. Distinguish among different types of possessory ownership interests in real property.
2. Identify three types of nonpossessory interests in real property.
3. Discuss how ownership interests in real property can be transferred.
4. Indicate what a leasehold estate is and how a landlord-tenant relationship comes into existence.
5. Outline the respective rights of landlords and tenants concerning the possession, use, and maintenance of leased property.

From earliest times, property has provided a means for survival. Primitive peoples lived off the fruits of the land, eating the vegetation and wildlife. Later, as the wildlife was domesticated and the vegetation cultivated, property provided pasturage and farmland. In the twelfth and thirteenth centuries, the power of feudal lords was determined by the amount of land that they held; the more land they held, the more powerful they were. After the age of feudalism passed, property continued to be an indicator of family wealth and social position. In the Western world, the protection of an individual's right to his or her property has become, in the words of Jean-Jacques Rousseau, one of the "most sacred of all the rights of citizenship."

In this chapter, we first examine closely the nature of real property. We then look at the various ways in which real property can be owned and at how ownership rights in real property are transferred from one person to another. We conclude the chapter with a discussion of leased property and landlord-tenant relationships.

The Nature of Real Property

Real property consists of land and the buildings, plants, and trees that it contains. Real property also includes subsurface and air rights, as well as personal property that has become permanently attached to real property. Whereas personal property is movable, real property—also called *real estate* or *realty*—is immovable.

LAND

ON THE WEB

For links to numerous online legal sources relating to real property, go to www.findlaw.com/01topics/index.html.

Land includes the soil on the surface of the earth and the natural or artificial structures that are attached to it. It further includes all the waters contained on or under the surface and much, but not necessarily all, of the airspace above it. The exterior boundaries of land extend down to the center of the earth and up to the farthest reaches of the atmosphere (subject to certain qualifications).

AIR AND SUBSURFACE RIGHTS

The owner of real property has relatively exclusive rights to the airspace above the land, as well as to the soil and minerals underneath it.

Air Rights Early cases involving air rights dealt with matters such as the right to run a telephone wire across a person's property when the wire did not touch any of the property[1] and whether a bullet shot over a person's land constituted trespass.[2] Today, disputes concerning air rights may involve the right of commercial and private planes to fly over property and the right of individuals and governments to seed clouds and produce rain artificially. Flights over private land do not normally violate the property owners' rights unless the flights are low and frequent enough to

1. *Butler v. Frontier Telephone Co.,* 186 N.Y. 486, 79 N.E. 716 (1906).
2. *Herrin v. Sutherland,* 74 Mont. 587, 241 P. 328 (1925). Shooting over a person's land constitutes trespass.

A PLANE FLIES LOW OVER A RESIDENTIAL AREA. ARE THE PROPERTY OWNERS' RIGHTS VIOLATED BY SUCH A LOW-FLYING PLANE?

cause a direct interference with the enjoyment and use of the land.[3] Leaning walls or buildings and projecting eave spouts or roofs may also violate the air rights of an adjoining property owner.

¡BE AWARE! If, during an excavation, a subsurface owner causes the land to subside, he or she may be liable to the owner of the surface.

Subsurface Rights In many states, the owner of the surface of a piece of land is not the owner of the subsurface, and hence the land ownership may be separated. Subsurface rights can be extremely valuable, as these rights include the ownership of minerals and, in most states, oil and natural gas. Water rights are also extremely valuable, especially in the West. When the ownership is separated into surface and subsurface rights, each owner can pass title to what he or she owns without the consent of the other owner. Each owner has the right to use the land owned, and in some cases a conflict arises between a surface owner's use and the subsurface owner's need to extract minerals, oil, and natural gas. When this occurs, one party's interest may become subservient to the other party's interest, either by statute or case decision.

Significant limitations on either air rights or subsurface rights normally have to be indicated on the deed transferring title at the time of purchase. (Deeds and the types of warranties they contain are discussed later in this chapter.)

PLANT LIFE AND VEGETATION

Plant life, both natural and cultivated, is also considered to be real property. In many instances, the natural vegetation, such as trees, adds greatly to the value of the realty. When a parcel of land is sold and the land has growing crops on it, the sale includes the crops, unless otherwise specified in the sales contract. When crops are sold by themselves, however, they are considered to be personal property or goods. Consequently, the sale of crops is a sale of goods, and therefore it is governed by the Uniform Commercial Code rather than by real property law.[4]

FIXTURES

• FIXTURE
A thing that was once personal property but that has become attached to real property in such a way that it takes on the characteristics of real property and becomes part of that real property.

Certain personal property can become so closely associated with the real property to which it is attached that the law views it as real property. Such property is known as a **fixture**—a thing *affixed* to realty, meaning it is attached to it by roots; embedded in it; permanently situated on it; or permanently attached by means of cement, plaster, bolts, nails, or screws. The fixture can be physically attached to real property, be attached to another fixture, or even be without any actual physical attachment to the land (such as a statue). As long as the owner intends the property to be a fixture, normally it will be a fixture.

Fixtures are included in the sale of land if the sales contract does not provide otherwise. The sale of a house includes the land and the house and the garage on the land, as well as the cabinets, plumbing, and windows. Because these are permanently affixed to the property, they are considered to be a part of it. Unless otherwise agreed, however, the curtains and throw rugs are not included. Items such as drapes and window-unit air conditioners are difficult to classify. Thus, a contract for the sale of a house or commercial realty should indicate which items of this sort are included in the sale. At issue in the following case was whether telephone poles, wires, and other communications equipment qualified as fixtures.

3. *United States v. Causby,* 328 U.S. 256, 66 S.Ct. 1062, 90 L.Ed. 1206 (1946).
4. See UCC 2–107(2).

CASE 41.1 New England Telephone and Telegraph Co. v. City of Franklin

Supreme Court of New Hampshire, 1996.
685 A.2d 913.
www.state.nh.us/courts/supreme/opinions/9611/netel.htm[a]

HISTORICAL AND TECHNOLOGICAL SETTING *Although telephone poles, wires, and underground conduits often have an expected life of at least forty years, the equipment is installed with its removal and relocation in mind. As a result, removal is normally not complicated or time consuming, and it does not harm the underlying real property or change its usefulness. In obtaining a state license, a property owner's consent, or an easement to install telecommunications equipment, the installer typically insists on maintaining ownership of it and refuses any requests to make it a permanent part of the real property. In fact, telecommunications office equipment is also usually portable and designed to permit easy removal and relocation. Technology changes quickly, and telecommunications companies want to be able to adapt.*

a. This page contains the opinion in this case. This opinion is part of a database on a Web site maintained by the New Hampshire state library for the New Hampshire state government.

BACKGROUND AND FACTS To obtain revenue, cities and towns tax the owners of real property within their jurisdictions. The tax is based on an assessment of the value of the property. New England Telephone and Telegraph Company (NETT) and other telephone companies filed a lawsuit in a New Hampshire state court against the City of Franklin and other municipalities, challenging the cities' property assessments. NETT and the other plaintiffs objected to the inclusion in their assessments of communications equipment, including telephone poles, wires, and central office equipment. They argued that the equipment was personal property and therefore should not have been taxed. The court granted the telephone companies' motion for summary judgment, and the cities appealed.

IN THE WORDS OF THE COURT . . .
HORTON, Justice.

* * * *

* * * [W]hether an item of property is properly classified as either personalty or a fixture turns on several factors, including: the item's nature and use; the intent of the party making the annexation; the degree and extent to which the item is specially adapted to the realty; the degree and extent of the item's annexation to the realty; and the relationship between the realty's owner and the person claiming the item. The central factors are the nature of the article and its use, as connected with the use of the underlying land, because these factors provide the basis for ascertaining the intent of the party who affixes or annexes the item in question.

In this case, the items of communications equipment did not constitute fixtures. * * * The poles, wires, and central office equipment, though placed in the ground or bolted to the buildings, were readily removable and transportable without affecting the utility of the underlying land, the buildings, or the equipment itself. * * * In addition, the very nature of telephone poles and wires, as well as their use by the [telephone companies] in connection with integrated telecommunications systems, belies the proposition that the equipment became a permanent and essential part of the underlying realty so as to pass by conveyance with it.

DECISION AND REMEDY The Supreme Court of New Hampshire affirmed the trial court's decision. The telephone poles, wires, and central equipment were not fixtures and thus not subject to taxation by the cities as real property.

FOR CRITICAL ANALYSIS—Social Consideration *Intent is an important factor in determining whether an item is a fixture, yet how can a court objectively decide whether someone did or did not intend an item to be a fixture?*

Ownership of Real Property

"Few . . . men own their property. The property owns them."
ROBERT G. INGERSOLL, 1833–1899
(American politician and lecturer)

Ownership of property is an abstract concept that cannot exist independently of the legal system. No one can actually possess or *hold* a piece of land, the air above it, the earth below it, and all the water contained on it. The legal system therefore recognizes certain rights and duties that constitute ownership interests in real property.

Recall from Chapter 40 that property ownership is often viewed as a bundle of rights. One who possesses the entire bundle of rights is said to hold the property in *fee simple,* which is the most complete form of ownership. When only some of the rights in the bundle are transferred to another person, the effect is to limit the ownership rights of both the one transferring the rights and the one receiving them.

OWNERSHIP IN FEE SIMPLE

• **FEE SIMPLE ABSOLUTE**
An ownership interest in land in which the owner has the greatest possible aggregation of rights, privileges, and power. Ownership in fee simple absolute is limited absolutely to a person and his or her heirs.

The most common type of property ownership today is the fee simple. Generally, the term *fee simple* is used to designate a **fee simple absolute,** in which the owner has the greatest possible aggregation of rights, privileges, and power. The fee simple is limited absolutely to a person and his or her heirs and is assigned forever without limitation or condition. The rights that accompany a fee simple include the right to use the land for whatever purpose the owner sees fit, subject to laws that prevent the owner from unreasonably interfering with another person's land and subject to applicable zoning laws. Furthermore, the owner has the rights of *exclusive* possession and use of the property. A fee simple is potentially infinite in duration and can be disposed of by deed or by will (by selling or giving away). When there is no will, the fee simple passes to the owner's legal heirs.

• **CONVEYANCE**
The transfer of a title to land from one person to another by deed; a document (such as a deed) by which an interest in land is transferred from one person to another.

• **FEE SIMPLE DEFEASIBLE**
An ownership interest in real property that can be taken away (by the prior grantor) upon the occurrence or nonoccurrence of a specified event.

Ownership in fee simple may become limited whenever a **conveyance,** or transfer of real property, is made to another party *conditionally.* When this occurs, the fee simple is known as a **fee simple defeasible** (the word *defeasible* means capable of being terminated or annulled). • **EXAMPLE 41.1** A conveyance "to A and his heirs as long as the land is used for charitable purposes" creates a fee simple defeasible, because ownership of the property is conditioned on the land's being used for charitable purposes. The original owner retains a *partial* ownership interest, because if the specified condition does not occur (if the land ceases to be used for charitable purposes), then the land reverts, or returns, to the original owner. If the original owner is not living at the time, the land passes to his or her heirs.•

LIFE ESTATES

• **LIFE ESTATE**
An interest in land that exists only for the duration of the life of some person, usually the holder of the estate.

A **life estate** is an estate that lasts for the life of some specified individual. A conveyance "to A for his life" creates a life estate.[5] In a life estate, the life tenant has fewer rights of ownership than the holder of a fee simple defeasible, because the rights necessarily cease to exist on the life tenant's death.

The life tenant has the right to use the land, provided that he or she commits no waste (injury to the land). In other words, the life tenant cannot injure the land in a manner that would adversely affect its value. The life tenant can use the land to harvest crops or, if mines and oil wells are already on the land, can extract minerals and oil from it, but the life tenant cannot exploit the land by creating new wells or

5. A less common type of life estate is created by the conveyance "to A for the life of B." This is known as an estate *pur autre vie,* or an estate for the duration of the life of another.

mines. The life tenant is entitled to any rents or royalties generated by the realty and has the right to mortgage the life estate and create liens, easements, and leases; but none can extend beyond the life of the tenant. In addition, with few exceptions, the owner of a life estate has an exclusive right to possession during his or her life.

Along with these rights, the life tenant also has some duties—to keep the property in repair and to pay property taxes. In short, the owner of the life estate has the same rights as a fee simple owner except that he or she must maintain the value of the property during his or her tenancy, less the decrease in value resulting from the normal use of the property allowed by the life tenancy.

FUTURE INTERESTS

When an owner in fee simple absolute conveys the estate conditionally to another (such as with a fee simple defeasible) or for a limited period of time (such as with a life estate), the original owner still retains an interest in the land. The owner retains the right to repossess ownership of the land if the conditions of the fee simple defeasible are not met or when the life of the life-estate holder ends. The interest in the property that the owner retains (or transfers to another) is called a **future interest,** because if it arises, it will only arise in the future.

FUTURE INTEREST
An interest in real property that is not at present possessory but will or may become possessory in the future.

REVERSIONARY INTEREST
A future interest in property retained by the original owner.

REMAINDER
A future interest in property held by a person other than the original owner.

EXECUTORY INTEREST
A future interest, held by a person other than the grantor, that begins after the termination of the preceding estate.

If the owner retains ownership of the future interest, then the future interest is described as a **reversionary interest,** because the property will revert to the original owner if the condition specified in a fee simple defeasible fails or when a life tenant dies. If, however, the owner of the future interest transfers ownership rights in that future interest to another, the future interest is described as a **remainder.** For example, a conveyance "to A for life, then to B" creates a life estate for A and a remainder (future interest) for B. An **executory interest** is a type of future interest very similar to a remainder, the difference being that an executory interest does not take effect immediately on the expiration of another interest, such as a life estate. For example, a conveyance "to A and his (or her) heirs, as long as the premises are used for charitable purposes, and if not so used for charitable purposes, then to B" creates an executory interest in the property for B.

NONPOSSESSORY INTERESTS

In contrast to the types of property interests just described, some interests in land do not include any rights to possess the property. These interests are thus known as *nonpossessory interests*. Three forms of nonpossessory interests are easements, profits, and licenses.

EASEMENT
A nonpossessory right to use another's property in a manner established by either express or implied agreement.

PROFIT
In real property law, the right to enter upon and remove things from the property of another (for example, the right to enter onto a person's land and remove sand and gravel therefrom).

An **easement** is the right of a person to make limited use of another person's real property without taking anything from the property. An easement, for example, can be the right to travel over another's property. In contrast, a **profit**[6] is the right to go onto land in possession of another and take away some part of the land itself or some product of the land. If Akmed, the owner of Sandy View, gives Carmen the right to go there and remove all the sand and gravel that she needs for her cement business, Carmen has a profit. Easements and profits can be classified as either appurtenant or in gross. Because easements and profits are similar and the same rules apply to both, they are discussed together.

6. The term *profit,* as used here, does not refer to the "profits" made by a business firm. Rather, it means a gain or an advantage.

Easement or Profit Appurtenant An easement or profit appurtenant arises when the owner of one piece of land has a right to go onto (or to remove things from) an *adjacent* piece of land owned by another. • **EXAMPLE 41.2** Suppose that Acosta, the owner of Juniper Hills, has a right to drive his car across Green's land, Greenacres, which is adjacent to Juniper Hills. This right-of-way over Green's property is an easement appurtenant to Juniper Hills and can be used only by the owner of Juniper Hills. Acosta can convey the easement when he conveys Juniper Hills. Now suppose that the highway is on the other side of Bancroft's property, which is on the other side of Green's property. To reach the highway, Acosta has easements across both Green's and Bancroft's properties. Juniper Hills and Bancroft's property are not adjacent, but Green's and Bancroft's properties are, so Acosta has an easement appurtenant.•

¡CONTRAST!
An easement appurtenant requires two adjacent pieces of land owned by two different persons, but an easement in gross needs only one piece of land owned by someone other than the owner of the easement.

Easement or Profit in Gross An easement or profit in gross exists when one's right to use or take things from another's land does not depend on one's owning an adjacent tract of land. • **EXAMPLE 41.3** Suppose that Avery owns a parcel of land with a marble quarry. Avery conveys to XYZ Corporation, which owns no land, the right to come onto his land and remove up to five hundred pounds of marble per day. XYZ Corporation owns a profit in gross.• When a utility company is granted an easement to run its power lines across another's property, it obtains an easement in gross.

Effect of a Sale of Property When a parcel of land that is *benefited* by an easement or profit appurtenant is sold, the property carries the easement or profit along with it. Thus, if Acosta sells Juniper Hills to Thomas and includes the appurtenant right-of-way across Green's property in the deed to Thomas, Thomas will own both the property and the easement that benefits it.

When a parcel of land that has the *burden* of an easement or profit appurtenant is sold, the new owner must recognize its existence only if he or she knew or should have known of it or if it was recorded in the appropriate office of the county. Thus, if Acosta records his easement across Green's property in the appropriate county office before Green conveys the land, the new owner of Green's property will have to allow Acosta, or any subsequent owner of Juniper Hills, to continue to use the path across Green's property.

A TICKET TO A CELEBRITY'S PERFORMANCE. IS THE HOLDER OF SUCH A TICKET CONSIDERED HAVE A PROPERTY INTEREST IN THE THEATER AT WHICH THE CELEBRITY IS TO PERFORM?

Creation of an Easement or Profit Easements and profits can be created by contract, by deed, by will, or by implication, necessity, or prescription. Two parties can create a contract in which they agree that one party has the right to an easement or profit on a portion of the other party's land. Creation by *deed* or *will* simply involves the delivery of a deed or a disposition in a will by the owner of an easement stating that the grantee (the person receiving the profit or easement) is granted the owner's rights in the easement or profit.

An easement or profit may be created by *implication* when the circumstances surrounding the division of a parcel of property imply its creation. If Barrow divides a parcel of land that has only one well for drinking water and conveys the half without a well to Jarad, a profit by implication arises, because Jarad needs drinking water.

An easement may also be created by *necessity.* An easement by necessity does not require division of property for its existence. A person who rents an apartment, for example, has an easement by necessity in the private road leading up to it.

Easements and profits by *prescription* are created in much the same way as title to property is obtained by *adverse possession* (discussed later in this chapter). An easement arises by prescription when one person exercises an easement, such as a right-of-way, on another person's land without the landowner's consent, and the use is apparent and continues for a period of time equal to the applicable statute of limitations.

Termination of an Easement or Profit An easement or profit can be terminated or extinguished in several ways. The simplest way is to deed it back to the owner of the land that is burdened by it. Another way is to abandon it and create evidence of intent to relinquish the right to use it. Mere nonuse will not extinguish an easement or profit *unless the nonuse is accompanied by an intent to abandon.* If the easement or profit is created merely by contract, the termination of the contract terminates the easement or profit. Finally, when the owner of an easement or profit becomes the owner of the property burdened by it, then it is merged into the property.

• **LICENSE**
A revocable right or privilege of a person to come on another person's land.

License A **license** is the revocable right of a person to come onto another person's land. It is a personal privilege that arises from the consent of the owner of the land and that can be revoked by the owner. A ticket to attend a movie at a theater is an example of a license. • **EXAMPLE 41.4** Assume that a Broadway theater owner issues to Carla a ticket to see a play. If Carla is refused entry into the theater because she is improperly dressed, she has no right to force her way into the theater. The ticket is only a revocable license, not a conveyance of an interest in property. •

Transfer of Ownership

Ownership of real property can pass from one person to another in a number of ways. Commonly, ownership interests in land are transferred by sale, in which case the terms of the transfer are specified in a real estate sales contract. When real property is sold or transferred as a gift, title to the property is conveyed by means of a **deed**—the instrument of conveyance of real property. We look here at transfers of real property by deed, as well as some other ways in which ownership rights in real property can be transferred.

• **DEED**
A document by which title to property (usually real property) is passed.

DEEDS

A valid deed must contain the following elements:

1. The names of the buyer (grantee) and seller (grantor).
2. Words evidencing an intent to convey the property (for example, "I hereby bargain, sell, grant, or give").
3. A legally sufficient description of the land.
4. The grantor's (and, sometimes, the spouse's) signature.

Additionally, to be valid, a deed must be delivered to the person to whom the property is being conveyed or to his or her agent.

• **WARRANTY DEED**
A deed in which the grantor assures (warrants to) the grantee that the grantor has title to the property conveyed in the deed, that there are no encumbrances on the property other than what the grantor has represented, and that the grantee will enjoy quiet possession of the property; a deed that provides the greatest amount of protection for the grantee.

Warranty Deeds Different types of deeds provide different degrees of protection against defects of title. A **warranty deed** warrants the greatest number of things and thus provides the greatest protection for the buyer, or grantee. In most states, special language is required to make a deed a general warranty deed; normally, the deed must include a written promise to protect the buyer against all claims of ownership of the property. A sample warranty deed is shown in Exhibit 41–1. Warranty deeds commonly include a number of *covenants,* or promises, that the grantor makes to the grantee.

A *covenant of seisin*[7] and a *covenant of the right to convey* warrant that the seller has title to the estate that the deed describes and the power to convey the estate, respectively. The covenant of seisin specifically assures the buyer that the grantor has the property in the purported quantity and quality.

A *covenant against encumbrances* is a covenant that the property being sold or conveyed is not subject to any outstanding rights or interests that will diminish the value of the land, except as explicitly stated. Examples of common encumbrances include mortgages, liens, profits, easements, and private deed restrictions on the use of the land.

A *covenant of quiet enjoyment* guarantees that the buyer will not be disturbed in his or her possession of the land by the seller or any third persons. • **EXAMPLE 41.5** Assume that Julio sells a two-acre lot and office building by warranty deed. Subsequently, a third person shows better title than Julio had and proceeds to evict the buyer. Here, the covenant of quiet enjoyment has been breached, and the buyer can sue to recover the purchase price of the land plus any other damages incurred as a result of the eviction. •

Quitclaim Deeds A **quitclaim deed** offers the least amount of protection against defects in the title. Basically, a quitclaim deed conveys to the grantee whatever interest the grantor had; so if the grantor had no interest, then the grantee receives no interest. Quitclaim deeds are often used when the seller, or grantor, is uncertain as to the extent of his or her rights in the property.

• **QUITCLAIM DEED**
A deed intended to pass any title, interest, or claim that the grantor may have in the property but not warranting that such title is valid. A quitclaim deed offers the least amount of protection against defects in the title.

Recording Statutes Every jurisdiction has **recording statutes,** which allow deeds to be recorded. Recording a deed gives notice to the public that a certain person is now the owner of a particular parcel of real estate. Thus, prospective buyers can check the public records to see whether there have been earlier transactions creating interests or rights in specific parcels of real property. Placing everyone on notice as to the identity of the true owner is intended to prevent the previous owners from fraudulently conveying the land to other purchasers. Deeds are recorded in the county in which the property is located. Many state statutes require that the grantor sign the deed in the presence of two witnesses before it can be recorded.

• **RECORDING STATUTES**
Statutes that allow deeds, mortgages, and other real property transactions to be recorded so as to provide notice to future purchasers or creditors of an existing claim on the property.

WILL OR INHERITANCE

Property that is transferred on an owner's death is passed either by will or by state inheritance laws. If the owner of land dies with a will, the land passes in accordance with the terms of the will. If the owner dies without a will, state inheritance statutes prescribe how and to whom the property will pass. Transfers of property by will or inheritance are examined in detail in Chapter 42.

ADVERSE POSSESSION

Adverse possession is a means of obtaining title to land without delivery of a deed. Essentially, when one person possesses the property of another for a certain statutory period of time (three to thirty years, with ten years being most common), that person, called the *adverse possessor,* acquires title to the land and cannot be removed from it by the original owner. The adverse possessor is vested with a perfect title just as if there had been a conveyance by deed.

• **ADVERSE POSSESSION**
The acquisition of title to real property by occupying it openly, without the consent of the owner, for a period of time specified by a state statute. The occupation must be actual, open, notorious, exclusive, and in opposition to all others, including the owner.

7. Pronounced *see*-zuhn.

EXHIBIT 41–1 • A Sample Warranty Deed

Date: May 31, 2001

Grantor: GAYLORD A. JENTZ AND WIFE, JOANN H. JENTZ

Grantor's Mailing Address (including county):
4106 North Loop Drive
Austin, Travis County, Texas

Grantee: DAVID F. FRIEND AND WIFE, JOAN E. FRIEND AS JOINT TENANTS WITH RIGHT OF SURVIVORSHIP

Grantee's Mailing Address (including county):
5929 Fuller Drive
Austin, Travis County, Texas

Consideration:
For and in consideration of the sum of Ten and No/100 Dollars ($10.00) and other valuable consideration to the undersigned paid by the grantees herein named, the receipt of which is hereby acknowledged, and for which no lien is retained, either express or implied.

Property (including any improvements):
Lot 23, Block "A", Northwest Hills, Green Acres Addition, Phase 4, Travis County, Texas, according to the map or plat of record in volume 22, pages 331-336 of the Plat Records of Travis County, Texas.

Reservations from and Exceptions to Conveyance and Warranty:

This conveyance with its warranty is expressly made subject to the following:

Easements and restrictions of record in Volume 7863, Page 53, Volume 8430, Page 35, Volume 8133, Page 152 of the Real Property Record of Travis County, Texas; Volume 22, Pages 335-339, of the Plat Records of Travis County, Texas; and to any other restrictions and easements affecting said property which are of record in Travis County, Texas.

Grantor, for the consideration and subject to the reservations from and exceptions to conveyance and warranty, grants, sells, and conveys to Grantee the property, together with all and singular the rights and appurtenances thereto in any wise belonging, to have and hold it to Grantee, Grantee's heirs, executors, administrators, successors, or assigns forever. Grantor binds Grantor and Grantor's heirs, executors, administrators, and successors to warrant and forever defend all and singular the property to Grantee and Grantee's heirs, executors, administrators, successors, and assigns against every person whomsoever lawfully claiming or to claim the same or any part thereof, except as to the reservations from and exceptions to conveyance and warranty.

When the context requires, singular nouns and pronouns include the plural.

BY: *Gaylord A. Jentz*
Gaylord A. Jentz

BY: *JoAnn H. Jentz*
JoAnn H. Jentz

(Acknowledgment)

STATE OF TEXAS
COUNTY OF TRAVIS

This instrument was acknowledged before me on the 31st day of May, 2001
by Gaylord A. and JoAnn H. Jentz

Rosemary Potter
Notary Public.State of Texas
Notary's name (printed): Rosemary Potter

Notary Seal

Notary's commission expires: 1/31/2004

For property to be held adversely, four elements must be satisfied:

1. Possession must be actual and exclusive; that is, the possessor must take sole physical occupancy of the property.
2. The possession must be open, visible, and notorious, not secret or clandestine. The possessor must occupy the land for all the world to see.
3. Possession must be continuous and peaceable for the required period of time. This requirement means that the possessor must not be interrupted in the occupancy by the true owner or by the courts.
4. Possession must be hostile and adverse. In other words, the possessor must claim the property as against the whole world. He or she cannot be living on the property with the permission of the owner.

ETHICAL ISSUE 41.1 ***What public policies underlie the doctrine of adverse possession?*** There are a number of public-policy reasons for the adverse possession doctrine. One reason is that it furthers society's interest in resolving boundary disputes in as fair a manner as possible. For example, suppose that a couple mistakenly assumes that they own a certain strip of land by their driveway. They plant grass and shrubs in the area, and maintain the property over the years. The shrubs contribute to the beauty of their lot and to the value of the property. Some thirty years later, their neighbors have a survey taken, and the results show that the strip of property actually belongs to them. In this situation, the couple could claim that they owned the property by adverse possession, and a court would likely agree.[8] The doctrine of adverse possession thus helps to determine ownership rights when title to property is in question. The doctrine also furthers the policies of rewarding possessors for putting land to productive use, keeping land in the stream of commerce, and not rewarding owners who sit on their rights too long.

EMINENT DOMAIN

Even ownership in real property in fee simple absolute is limited by a superior ownership. Just as in medieval England the king was the ultimate landowner, so in the United States the government has an ultimate ownership right in all land. This right is known as **eminent domain,** and it is sometimes referred to as the condemnation power of the government to take land for public use. It gives the government a right to acquire possession of real property in the manner directed by the Constitution and the laws of the state whenever the public interest requires it. Property may be taken only for public use.

• **EMINENT DOMAIN**
The power of a government to take land for public use from private citizens for just compensation.

When the government takes land owned by a private party for public use, it is referred to as a **taking,** and the government must compensate the private party. Under the so-called *takings clause* of the Fifth Amendment, the government may not take private property for public use without "just compensation."

• **TAKING**
The taking of private property by the government for public use. Under the Fifth Amendment to the Constitution, the government may not take private property for public use without "just compensation."

The power of eminent domain is generally invoked through condemnation proceedings. For example, when a new public highway is to be built, the government must decide where to build it and how much land to condemn. After the government determines that a particular parcel of land is necessary for public use, it brings a judicial proceeding to obtain title to the land. Then, in another proceeding, the court determines the *fair value* of the land, which is usually approximately equal to its market value.

8. In a case with similar facts, a Pennsylvania court held that the party that had maintained the strip of land for over thirty years acquired title to the land by adverse possession. See *Klos v. Molenda,* 355 Pa.Super. 399, 513 A.2d 490 (1986).

UNDEVELOPED SEASHORE STRETCHES INTO THE DISTANCE. SHOULD THE GOVERNMENT BE PERMITTED TO TAKE SUCH PROPERTY FROM PRIVATE CITIZENS FOR PUBLIC USE?

In an attempt to preserve the natural beauty and resources of the land, environmental laws have increasingly prohibited private parties from using certain lands (coastal lands, for example) in specific ways. Does imposing such limitations on landowners' rights constitute a taking by the government? This question is explored in this chapter's *Business Law in Action.*

Leasehold Estates

Often, real property is used by those who do not own it. A **lease** is a contract by which the owner of real property (the landlord, or lessor) grants to a person (the tenant, or lessee) an exclusive right to use and possess the property, usually for a specified period of time, in return for rent or some other form of payment. Property in the possession of a tenant is referred to as a **leasehold estate.**

The respective rights and duties of the landlord and tenant that arise under a lease agreement will be discussed shortly. Here we look at the types of leasehold estates, or tenancies, that can be created when real property is leased.

• **LEASE**
In real property law, a contract by which the owner of real property (the landlord, or lessor) grants to a person (the tenant, or lessee) an exclusive right to use and possess the property, usually for a specified period of time, in return for rent or some other form of payment.

• **LEASEHOLD ESTATE**
An estate in realty held by a tenant under a lease. In every leasehold estate, the tenant has a qualified right to possess and/or use the land.

TENANCY FOR YEARS

A **tenancy for years** is created by an express contract by which property is leased for a specified period of time, such as a day, a month, a year, or a period of years. For example, signing a one-year lease to occupy an apartment creates a tenancy for years. At the end of the period specified in the lease, the lease ends (without notice), and possession of the apartment returns to the lessor. If the tenant dies during the period of the lease, the lease interest passes to the tenant's heirs as personal property. Often, leases include renewal or extension provisions.

• **TENANCY FOR YEARS**
A type of tenancy under which property is leased for a specified period of time, such as a month, a year, or a period of years.

PERIODIC TENANCY

A **periodic tenancy** is created by a lease that does not specify how long it is to last but does specify that rent is to be paid at certain intervals. This type of tenancy is automatically renewed for another rental period unless properly terminated. For example, a periodic tenancy is created by a lease that states, "Rent is due on the

• **PERIODIC TENANCY**
A lease interest in land for an indefinite period involving payment of rent at fixed intervals, such as week to week, month to month, or year to year.

Business Law in Action • LAND-USE REGULATIONS AND THE TAKINGS CLAUSE

Environmental regulations and other legislation to control land use are prevalent throughout the United States. Generally, these laws reflect the public's interest in preserving the beauty and natural resources of the land and in allowing the public to have access to and enjoy limited natural resources, such as coastal areas. Although few would disagree with the rationale underlying these laws, the owners of the private property directly affected by the laws may feel that they should be compensated for the limitation imposed on their right to do as they wish with their land. Several cases have been brought by private-property owners who allege that regulations limiting their control over their own land essentially constitute a taking of private property in the public interest. Therefore, the property owners should receive the just compensation guaranteed under the Fifth Amendment.

For example, in one case the owners of ocean-front property in Monterey, California, applied to the city of Monterey several times for a permit to build a residential development. Del Monte Dunes at Monterey, Limited, bought the property and continued to seek a permit. Each time, the city denied the use of more of the property, until no part remained available for any use that would be inconsistent with leaving the property in its natural state. The city justified its actions by stating that it was seeking to protect various forms of wildlife that inhabit the coastal sand dunes, particularly the endangered Smith's blue butterfly. This butterfly, which is unique to the region and is nearly extinct, lays its eggs on the branches of a type of buckwheat plant that is native to the region's dunes.

Del Monte finally sold the property to the city and filed suit against the city in a federal district court. Del Monte claimed that the restrictions on use amounted to an unconstitutional taking without the "just compensation" required by the Fifth Amendment. The jury agreed and awarded Del Monte nearly $1.45 million in damages. The city appealed, but it fared no better in the federal appellate court, which affirmed the jury's award. The appellate court concluded that the evidence "supports the jury's finding that the City's actions denied all economically viable use of the Dunes." According to the appellate court, the city's restrictions on the use of the property amounted to an unconstitutional taking, and Del Monte was entitled to damages.[a]

An interesting aspect of this case is the city's claim that the issue of whether a taking had occurred should never have gone before a jury. Typically, lawsuits involving the power of eminent domain—such as when a local government takes private property to create a road—are heard by judges. The city argued that this case should also have been decided by a judge, as land-use cases usually are. For one thing, a judge is more knowledgeable than lay jurors are in the land-use regulations at issue and in the legal theory of regulatory takings. For another, if such actions were to be decided by jurors, who are more likely than judges to be sympathetic to the plaintiffs, more and more citizens would bring suits challenging zoning laws. The federal appellate court held that jury trials may be demanded at every step along the way.

The case is now before the United States Supreme Court, and this procedural question is one of the central issues that the Court will decide. Understandably, the case is being closely watched by regulatory bodies in other cities, counties, and states because its outcome may have a significant impact on land-use control throughout the nation. Thirty-one states and two hundred cities, including San Francisco and eighty-six other California cities, have filed briefs with the Court in support of the city of Monterey.

FOR CRITICAL ANALYSIS

In land-use cases, should juries be allowed to decide whether a taking has occurred, or should their role be limited to determining the amount of compensation that should be paid to a property owner if a judge rules that a taking has occurred?

a. *Del Monte Dunes at Monterey, Ltd. v. City of Monterey,* 95 F.3d 1422 (9th Cir. 1996).

tenth day of every month." This provision creates a tenancy from month to month. This type of tenancy can also extend from week to week or from year to year.

Under the common law, to terminate a periodic tenancy, the landlord or tenant must give at least one period's notice to the other party. If the tenancy extends from month to month, for example, one month's notice must be given prior to the last month's rent payment. State statutes may require a different period for notice of termination in a periodic tenancy, however.

Tenancy at Will

• **TENANCY AT WILL**
A type of tenancy under which either party can terminate the tenancy without notice; usually arises when a tenant who has been under a tenancy for years retains possession, with the landlord's consent, after the tenancy for years has terminated.

• **TENANCY AT SUFFERANCE**
A type of tenancy under which one who, after rightfully being in possession of leased premises, continues (wrongfully) to occupy the property after the lease has been terminated. The tenant has no rights to possess the property and occupies it only because the person entitled to evict the tenant has not done so.

Suppose that a landlord rents an apartment to a tenant "for as long as both agree." In such a situation, the tenant receives a leasehold estate known as a **tenancy at will.** Under the common law, either party can terminate the tenancy without notice (that is, "at will"). This type of estate usually arises when a tenant who has been under a tenancy for years retains possession after the termination date of that tenancy with the landlord's consent. Before the tenancy has been converted into a periodic tenancy (by the periodic payment of rent), it is a tenancy at will, terminable by either party without notice. Once the tenancy is treated as a periodic tenancy, termination notice must conform to the one already discussed for that type of tenancy. The death of either party or the voluntary commission of waste by the tenant will terminate a tenancy at will.

Tenancy at Sufferance

The mere possession of land without right is called a **tenancy at sufferance.** It is not a true tenancy. A tenancy at sufferance is not an estate, because it is created when a tenant *wrongfully* retains possession of property. Whenever a tenancy for years, periodic tenancy, or tenancy at will ends and the tenant continues to retain possession of the premises without the owner's permission, a tenancy at sufferance is created. When a tenancy at sufferance arises, the owner can immediately evict the tenant.

Landlord-Tenant Relationships

ON THE WEB
You can find online links to most uniform laws, including the URLTA, at www.lawsource.com.

In the past several decades, landlord-tenant relationships have become much more complex than they were before, as has the law governing them. Generally, the law has come to apply contract doctrines, such as those providing for implied warranties and unconscionability, to the landlord-tenant relationship. Increasingly, landlord-tenant relationships have become subject to specific state and local statutes and ordinances as well. In 1972, in an effort to create more uniformity in the law governing landlord-tenant relationships, the National Conference of Commissioners on Uniform State Laws issued the Uniform Residential Landlord and Tenant Act (URLTA). We look now at how a landlord-tenant relationship is created and at the respective rights and duties of landlords and tenants.

Creating the Landlord-Tenant Relationship

A landlord-tenant relationship is established by a lease contract. As mentioned, a lease contract arises when a property owner (landlord) agrees to give another party (the tenant) the exclusive right to possess the property—usually for a price and for a specified term.

Form of the Lease A lease contract may be oral or written. Under the common law, an oral lease is valid. As with most oral contracts, however, a party who seeks to enforce an oral lease may have difficulty proving its existence. In most states, statutes mandate that leases be in writing for some tenancies (such as those exceeding one year). To ensure the validity of a lease agreement, it should therefore be in writing and do the following:

1. Express an intent to establish the relationship.
2. Provide for the transfer of the property's possession to the tenant at the beginning of the term.
3. Provide for the landlord's reversionary interest, which entitles the property owner to retake possession at the end of the term.
4. Describe the property—for example, give its street address.
5. Indicate the length of the term, the amount of the rent, and how and when it is to be paid.

¡NOTE! Sound business practice dictates that a lease for commercial property should be written carefully and should clearly define the parties' rights and obligations.

Legal Requirements State or local law often dictates permissible lease terms. For example, a statute or ordinance might prohibit the leasing of a structure that is in a certain physical condition or is not in compliance with local building codes. Similarly, a statute may prohibit the leasing of property for a particular purpose. For instance, a state law might prohibit gambling houses. Thus, if a landlord and tenant intend that the leased premises be used only to house an illegal betting operation, their lease is unenforceable.

A property owner cannot legally discriminate against prospective tenants on the basis of race, color, national origin, religion, gender, or disability. Similarly, a tenant cannot legally promise to do something counter to laws prohibiting discrimination. A tenant, for example, cannot legally promise to do business only with members of a particular race. The public policy underlying these prohibitions is to treat all people equally. In the following case, a rental housing applicant claimed that her rental application had been denied because of her live-in boyfriend's race.

CASE 41.2 Osborn v. Kellogg

Court of Appeals of Nebraska, 1996.
4 Neb.App. 594,
547 N.W.2d 504.

HISTORICAL AND ENVIRONMENTAL SETTING *Since its founding as the village of Lancaster in 1859, Lincoln has grown to become the second largest city in Nebraska. Lincoln is the state capital and the home of the University of Nebraska. With a population of more than 200,000, Lincoln is often included on lists of the best cities in the United States in which to live. In the early 1990s, the average monthly apartment rental ranged from $275 to $500 and the average monthly house rental was between $350 and $700. The average cost of a house in the city was $75,000 to $100,000. Unemployment was less than 3 percent, and the typical wage for a manufacturing job was between $5 and $15 per hour.*

BACKGROUND AND FACTS Kristi Kellogg, her daughter Mindy, and her boyfriend James Greene attempted to lease half of a house. The house was owned by Keith Osborn and Pam Lyman, and managed, as rental property, by Keith's mother, Barbara Osborn. Kellogg was white. Greene was African American. The owners refused to rent to them, claiming, among other things, that three people were too many, Greene's income was too low, and Greene had not provided credit references. They later rented half of the house to the Li family, which had five members, and the other half to the Suggett family, which numbered three. Both the Li family and the Suggett family had less income than Kellogg and Greene. Kellogg had provided extensive credit references, but the Lis and the Suggetts had provided none. Kellogg filed a complaint with the Nebraska Equal Opportunity Commission (NEOC) against the Osborns and Lyman. The NEOC concluded that the defendants had discriminated against Kellogg in violation of state fair housing laws. A Nebraska state trial court adopted the NEOC's conclusion. The defendants appealed to an intermediate state appellate court.

(Continued)

CASE 41.2—Continued

IN THE WORDS OF THE COURT . . .

WARREN, District Judge * * *

* * * *

* * * While Kellogg is not a member of a racial minority, we note that she qualifies as * * * a person who claims to have been injured by a discriminatory housing practice. It is undisputed that Greene is a member of a racial minority. The evidence further shows that Kellogg applied for and was qualified to rent the house from the Osborns, as evidenced by the rental applications of the Lis and the Suggetts; that her application was rejected, which is undisputed; and that the housing opportunity remained available, which is also undisputed. * * *

* * * *

The NEOC hearing examiner found that Kellogg proved by a preponderance of the evidence that the Osborns' seemingly legitimate reasons for rejecting Kellogg were, in fact, a pretext for intentional discrimination. * * * [W]e conclude that competent evidence supports the NEOC hearing examiner's factual findings.

DECISION AND REMEDY The intermediate state appellate court affirmed the judgment of the lower court. The Osborns and Lyman had discriminated against Kellogg in violation of fair housing laws.

FOR CRITICAL ANALYSIS—Ethical Consideration *What if the Osborns and Lyman discriminated against Kellogg not because her boyfriend was African American but because they disapproved of cohabitation by unmarried couples? Should this form of discrimination be permissible?*

Rights and Duties

The rights and duties of landlords and tenants generally pertain to four broad areas of concern—the possession, use, and maintenance of leased property and, of course, rent.

> **ON THE WEB**
> Many Web sites now provide information on laws and other information relating to landlord-tenant relationships. One of them is TenantNet™ at www.tenant.net.

Possession Possession involves both the obligation of the landlord to deliver possession to the tenant at the beginning of the lease term and the right of the tenant to obtain possession and retain it until the lease expires.

The covenant of quiet enjoyment mentioned previously also applies to leased premises. Under this covenant, the landlord promises that during the lease term, neither the landlord nor anyone having a superior title to the property will disturb the tenant's use and enjoyment of the property. This covenant forms the essence of the landlord-tenant relationship, and if it is breached, the tenant can terminate the lease and sue for damages.

If the landlord deprives the tenant of the tenant's possession of the leased property or interferes with the tenant's use or enjoyment of it, an eviction occurs. An **eviction** occurs, for example, when the landlord changes the lock and refuses to give the tenant a new key. A **constructive eviction** occurs when the landlord wrongfully performs or fails to perform any of the undertakings the lease requires, thereby making the tenant's further use and enjoyment of the property exceedingly difficult or impossible. Examples of constructive eviction include a landlord's failure to provide heat in the winter, light, or other essential utilities.

• **EVICTION**
A landlord's act of depriving a tenant of possession of the leased premises.

• **CONSTRUCTIVE EVICTION**
A form of eviction that occurs when a landlord fails to perform adequately any of the undertakings (such as providing heat in the winter) required by the lease, thereby making the tenant's further use and enjoyment of the property exceedingly difficult or impossible.

Use and Maintenance of the Premises If the parties do not limit by agreement the uses to which the property may be put, the tenant may make any use of it, as long as the use is legal and reasonably relates to the purpose for which the property is adapted or ordinarily used and does not injure the landlord's interest.

The tenant is responsible for any damages to the premises that he or she causes, intentionally or negligently, and the tenant may be held liable for the cost of returning the property to the physical condition it was in at the lease's inception. Unless the parties have agreed otherwise, the tenant is not responsible for ordinary wear and tear and the property's consequent depreciation in value.

Usually, the landlord must comply with state statutes and city ordinances that delineate specific standards for the construction and maintenance of buildings. Typically, these codes contain structural requirements common to the construction, wiring, and plumbing of residential and commercial buildings. In some jurisdictions, landlords of residential property are required by statute to maintain the premises in good repair.

International Perspective • LANDLORD-TENANT LAW IN ENGLAND

Unlike the law in the United States governing landlord-tenant relationships, much of which evolved under the common law, English landlord-tenant law has been created, to a great extent, by statute. English law traditionally adhered to the principle of *caveat tenant* ("let the tenant beware"). In other words, tenants had little recourse against landlords who refused to keep the leased premises in good repair. In 1985, however, the English Parliament enacted the Landlord and Tenant Act. The act sets forth details related to the landlord's obligations to maintain and repair leased premises. The act also requires that leased premises be fit for human habitation, a concept similar to the implied warranty of habitability in some U.S. jurisdictions (to be discussed shortly). Although the English Landlord and Tenant Act applies mainly to dwellings rented for very low rates, it has improved, to some extent, the rights of all tenants in that country.

FOR CRITICAL ANALYSIS

Given that tenants in the United States have traditionally had rights under the common law, why has it been necessary to regulate landlord-tenant relationships in the United States so extensively by statutory law?

• **IMPLIED WARRANTY OF HABITABILITY**
An implied promise by a landlord that rented residential premises are fit for human habitation—that is, in a condition that is safe and suitable for people to live in.

Implied Warranty of Habitability The **implied warranty of habitability** requires a landlord who leases residential property to deliver the premises to the tenant in a habitable condition—that is, in a condition that is safe and suitable for people to live in—at the beginning of a lease term and to maintain them in that condition for the lease's duration. Some state legislatures have enacted this warranty into law. In other jurisdictions, courts have based the warranty on the existence of a landlord's statutory duty to keep leased premises in good repair, or they have simply applied it as a matter of public policy.

Generally, this warranty applies to major, or *substantial,* physical defects that the landlord knows or should know about and has had a reasonable time to repair—for example, a large hole in the roof. An unattractive or annoying feature, such as a crack in the wall, may be unpleasant, but unless the crack is a structural defect or affects the residence's heating capabilities, it is probably not sufficiently substantial to make the place uninhabitable.

At issue in the following case was whether the lack of a smoke detector constituted a violation of a statutory requirement that rental property be "in reasonable repair and fit for human habitation."

CASE 41.3 Schiernbeck v. Davis

U.S. Court of Appeals,
Eighth Circuit, 1998.
143 F.3d 434.
laws.findlaw.com/8th[a]

HISTORICAL AND TECHNOLOGICAL SETTING *Different smoke detectors come with a variety of capabilities. Some can detect flames with little smoke and can detect even "smokeless" fires. Other devices include strobe lights for alerting the hearing impaired, fixtures for lighting darkened areas, "hush" buttons for nuisance alarms, and buttons for testing the functions. A basic, battery-operated smoke detector, with an alarm only, can cost as little as $6. Some states require the installation of smoke detectors on property offered for rent. A missing smoke detector in residential rental property is a violation of some local building codes. Not every jurisdiction requires their use, however.*

BACKGROUND AND FACTS Linda Schiernbeck rented a house from Clark and Rosa Davis. A month after moving into the house, Schiernbeck noticed a discolored circular area where, she determined, a smoke detector had previously been attached to the wall. Schiernbeck later claimed that she told Clark Davis about the missing detector. Davis did not remember the conversation. He admitted, however, that he gave Schiernbeck a detector, which she denied. At any rate, when a fire in the house severely injured Schiernbeck, she filed a suit in a federal district court against the Davises, alleging negligence and breach of contract for failing to provide a detector. The Davises filed a motion for summary judgment, arguing that they had no duty to install a detector in a rental house. The court ruled in the Davises' favor, and Schiernbeck appealed to the U.S. Court of Appeals for the Eighth Circuit.

a. This page provides access to some of the opinions of the U.S. Court of Appeals for the Eighth Circuit. In the "Docket Number Search" box, type "97-3431" and click "Get It" to access the *Schiernbeck* opinion. This Web site is maintained by FindLaw.

IN THE WORDS OF THE COURT . . .
WATERS, District Judge.

* * * *

* * * South Dakota Codified Laws Section 43-32-8 requires that the lessor keep the leased premises "in reasonable repair and fit for human habitation * * * ." We do not believe that equipping the leased premises with a smoke detector constitutes keeping the premises in "reasonable repair." * * * [T]he accepted dictionary definition [of "repair" is:] "To restore to a sound or good state after decay, injury, dilapidation, or partial destruction." Schiernbeck cites an additional part of the dictionary's definition which states * * * "to supply * * * that which is lost or destroyed" to include replacing a missing smoke detector in the definition of repair. We conclude, however, that when reading the entire definition, the term "repair" does not encompass replacing a missing smoke detector.

* * * *

In addition, we do not believe that the Davises were required to replace the smoke detector in order to make the rental house "fit for human habitation." * * * Clearly, unstable stairs create a place that is unfit for human habitation, as does a lack of running water, heat, or electricity. We do not believe, however, that a lessor * * * is required to equip his or her residential premises with smoke detectors, fire extinguishers, carbon monoxide detectors, etc. in order to make the leased premises "fit for human habitation."

DECISION AND REMEDY The U.S. Court of Appeals for the Eighth Circuit held that a landlord's statutory duty to keep rental premises "in reasonable repair and fit for human habitation" does not include installing a smoke detector. The court affirmed the lower court's judgment.

FOR CRITICAL ANALYSIS—Ethical Consideration *What is a landlord's ethical duty with respect to keeping rental premises "fit for human habitation"?*

Rent *Rent* is the tenant's payment to the landlord for the tenant's occupancy or use of the landlord's real property. Generally, the tenant must pay the rent even if he or she refuses to occupy the property or moves out, as long as the refusal or the move is unjustifiable and the lease is in force.

Under the common law, destruction by fire or flood of a building leased by a tenant did not relieve the tenant of the obligation to pay rent and did not permit the termination of the lease. Today, however, state statutes have altered the common law rule. If the building burns down, apartment dwellers in most states are not continuously liable to the landlord for the payment of rent.

¡NOTE! Options that may be available to a tenant on a landlord's breach of the implied warranty of habitability include repairing the defect and deducting the amount from the rent, canceling the lease, and suing for damages.

In some situations, such as when a landlord breaches the implied warranty of habitability, a tenant is allowed to withhold rent as a remedy. When rent withholding is authorized under a statute (sometimes referred to as a "rent-strike" statute), the tenant must usually put the amount withheld into an *escrow account.* This account is held in the name of the depositor (in this case, the tenant) and an *escrow agent* (in this case, usually the court or a government agency), and the funds are returnable to the depositor if the third person (in this case, the landlord) fails to fulfill the escrow condition. Generally, the tenant may withhold an amount equal to the amount by which the defect rendering the premises unlivable reduces the property's rental value. How much that is may be determined in different ways, and the tenant who withholds more than is legally permissible is liable to the landlord for the excessive amount withheld.

TRANSFERRING RIGHTS TO LEASED PROPERTY

Either the landlord or the tenant may wish to transfer his or her rights to the leased property during the term of the lease.

Transferring the Landlord's Interest Just as any other real property owner can sell, give away, or otherwise transfer his or her property, so can a landlord—who is, of course, the leased property's owner. If complete title to the leased property is transferred, the tenant becomes the tenant of the new owner. The new owner may collect subsequent rent but must abide by the terms of the existing lease agreement.

Transferring the Tenant's Interest The tenant's transfer of his or her entire interest in the leased property to a third person is an *assignment of the lease.* A lease assignment is an agreement to transfer all rights, title, and interest in the lease to the assignee. It is a complete transfer. Many leases require that the assignment have the landlord's written consent, and an assignment that lacks consent can be avoided (nullified) by the landlord. A landlord who knowingly accepts rent from the assignee, however, will be held to have waived the requirement. An assignment does not terminate a tenant's liabilities under a lease agreement, however, because the tenant may assign rights but not duties. Thus, even though the assignee of the lease is required to pay rent, the original tenant is not released from the contractual obligation to pay the rent if the assignee fails to do so.

• **SUBLEASE** A lease executed by the lessee of real estate to a third person, conveying the same interest that the lessee enjoys but for a shorter term than that held by the lessee.

The tenant's transfer of all or part of the premises for a period shorter than the lease term is a **sublease.** The same restrictions that apply to an assignment of the tenant's interest in leased property apply to a sublease. • EXAMPLE 41.6 A student named Derek leases an apartment for a two-year period. Although Derek had planned on attending summer school, he is offered a job in Europe for the summer months and accepts. Because he does not wish to pay three months' rent for an unoccupied apartment, Derek subleases the apartment to Singleton, who becomes a sublessee. (Derek may have to obtain his landlord's consent for this sublease if the lease requires it.) Singleton is bound by the same terms of the lease as Derek, but as in a lease assignment, Derek remains liable for the obligations under the lease if Singleton fails to fulfill them. ●

Application: Law & the Entrepreneur: How to Negotiate a Favorable Lease

Generally, an entrepreneur first starting a business is well advised to lease rather than buy property, because the future success of the business is uncertain. By leasing instead of purchasing property, persons just starting out in business allow themselves some time to determine whether business profits will warrant the outright purchase of property.

One thing to keep in mind when leasing property is that lease contracts are usually form contracts that favor the landowner. That means that, as a prospective tenant, you need to think about negotiating terms more favorable to you. Before negotiating the terms of the lease, do some comparison shopping to see what the rent for other comparable properties in the area is. Usually, rental prices for business property are stated as so many dollars per square foot (per month or per year). In commercial leases to retail stores, it is common for part or all of the rent to consist of a percentage of the tenant's sales made on the premises during the term of the lease. Bear in mind, too, that the nature of your business should determine, to a great extent, the location of the leased premises.

*This *Application* is not meant to substitute for the services of an attorney who is licensed to practice law in your state.

If you are involved in a mail-order business, for example, you need not pay the extra price for a prime location that might be required for a restaurant business.

When negotiating a lease, you must also determine who will pay property taxes and insurance on the property and who will be responsible for repairs of the property and utility payments. These terms are generally negotiable, and depending on who takes responsibility, the rent payment may be adjusted accordingly. Generally, your success in negotiating favorable lease terms will depend on the market. If the rental market is "good" (that is, if you have numerous other rental options at favorable rates), you may be able to convince the landlord that he or she should be responsible for taxes, insurance, maintenance, and the like, and possibly for improvements to the property necessary for your business. Therefore, it is important to investigate the status of the market before you begin negotiations with a potential landlord.

Checklist for the Lessee of Business Property

1. When you are entering into business, leasing rather than buying property has advantages, because it reduces your liability in the event that your business is unsuccessful.
2. Realize that although lease contracts normally favor the landlord, you usually can negotiate favorable terms for your lease of the premises.
3. Make sure that the lease contract clearly indicates whether the landlord or tenant is to be responsible for taxes on the property, costs relating to necessary maintenance and repairs, and utility costs. By comparison shopping, you should be able to judge which lease terms are favorable and which are not.
4. To protect yourself in the event your business is unsuccessful, start with a short-term initial lease, perhaps with an option to renew the lease in the future.

Key Terms

adverse possession 1061
constructive eviction 1068
conveyance 1057
deed 1060
easement 1058
eminent domain 1063
eviction 1068
executory interest 1058
fee simple absolute 1057
fee simple defeasible 1057
fixture 1055
future interest 1058
implied warranty of habitability 1069
lease 1064
leasehold estate 1064
license 1060
life estate 1057
periodic tenancy 1064
profit 1058
quitclaim deed 1061
recording statutes 1061
remainder 1058
reversionary interest 1058
sublease 1071
taking 1063
tenancy at sufferance 1066
tenancy at will 1066
tenancy for years 1064
warranty deed 1060

Chapter Summary • Real Property

The Nature of Real Property (See pages 1054–1056.)	Real property (also called real estate or realty) is immovable. It includes land, subsurface and air rights, plant life and vegetation, and fixtures.
Ownership of Real Property (See pages 1057–1060.)	1. *Fee simple absolute*—The most complete form of ownership. 2. *Fee simple defeasible*—Ownership in fee simple that can end if a specified event or condition occurs. 3. *Life estate*—An estate that lasts for the life of a specified individual during which time the individual is entitled to possess, use, and benefit from the estate; ownership rights in a life estate are subject to the rights of the future-interest holder. 4. *Future interest*—A residuary interest not granted by the grantor in conveying an estate to another for life, for a specified period of time, or on the condition that a specific event does or does not occur. The grantor may retain the residuary interest (which is then called a reversionary interest) or transfer ownership rights in the future interest to another (the interest is then referred to as a remainder). 5. *Nonpossessory interest*—An interest that involves the right to use real property but not to possess it. Easements, profits, and licenses are nonpossessory interests.
Transfer of Ownership (See pages 1060–1064.)	1. *By deed*—When real property is sold or transferred as a gift, title to the property is conveyed by means of a deed. A deed must meet specific legal requirements. A *warranty deed* warrants the most extensive protection against defects of title. A *quitclaim deed* conveys to the grantee only whatever interest the grantor had in the property. A deed may be recorded in the manner prescribed by *recording statutes* in the appropriate jurisdiction to give third parties notice of the owner's interest. 2. *By will or inheritance*—If the owner dies after having made a valid will, the land passes as specified in the will. If the owner dies without having made a will, the heirs inherit according to state inheritance statutes. 3. *By adverse possession*—When a person possesses the property of another for a statutory period of time (three to thirty years, with ten years being the most common), that person acquires title to the property, provided the possession is actual and exclusive, open and visible, continuous and peaceable, and hostile and adverse (without the permission of the owner). 4. *By eminent domain*—The government can take land, for public use, with just compensation, when the public interest requires the taking.

Chapter Summary • Real Property, Continued

Leasehold Estates (See pages 1064–1066.)	A leasehold estate is an interest in real property that is held only for a limited period of time, as specified in the lease agreement. Types of tenancies relating to leased property include the following: 1. *Tenancy for years*—Tenancy for a period of time stated by express contract. 2. *Periodic tenancy*—Tenancy for a period determined by the frequency of rent payments; automatically renewed unless proper notice is given. 3. *Tenancy at will*—Tenancy for as long as both parties agree; no notice of termination is required. 4. *Tenancy at sufferance*—Possession of land without legal right.
Landlord-Tenant Relationships (See pages 1066–1072.)	1. *Lease agreement*—The landlord-tenant relationship is created by a lease agreement. State or local laws may dictate whether the lease must be in writing and what lease terms are permissible. 2. *Rights and duties*—The rights and duties that arise under a lease agreement generally pertain to the following areas: a. Possession—The tenant has an exclusive right to possess the leased premises, which must be available to the tenant at the agreed-on time. Under the covenant of quiet enjoyment, the landlord promises that during the lease term neither the landlord nor anyone having superior title to the property will disturb the tenant's use and enjoyment of the property. b. Use and maintenance of the premises—Unless the parties agree otherwise, the tenant may make any legal use of the property. The tenant is responsible for any damage that he or she causes. The landlord must comply with laws that set specific standards for the maintenance of real property. The implied warranty of habitability requires that a landlord furnish and maintain residential premises in a habitable condition (that is, in a condition safe and suitable for human life). c. Rent—The tenant must pay the rent as long as the lease is in force, unless the tenant justifiably refuses to occupy the property or withholds the rent because of the landlord's failure to maintain the premises properly. 3. *Transferring rights to leased property*— a. If the landlord transfers complete title to the leased property, the tenant becomes the tenant of the new owner. The new owner may then collect the rent but must abide by the existing lease. b. Generally, in the absence of an agreement to the contrary, tenants may assign their rights (but not their duties) under a lease contract to a third person. Tenants may also sublease leased property to a third person, but the original tenant is not relieved of any obligations to the landlord under the lease.

For Review

❶ What can a person who holds property in fee simple absolute do with the property? Explain whether a person who holds property as a life estate can do the same.
❷ What are the requirements for acquiring property by adverse possession?
❸ What limitations may be imposed on the rights of property owners?
❹ What is a leasehold estate? What types of leasehold estates, or tenancies, can be created when real property is leased?
❺ What are the respective duties of the landlord and tenant concerning the use and maintenance of leased property? Is the tenant responsible for all damages that he or she causes, intentionally or negligently? Explain.

Questions and Case Problems

41–1. Tenant's Rights and Responsibilities. You are a student in college and plan to attend classes for nine months. You sign a twelve-month lease for an apartment. Discuss fully each of the following situations:

(a) You have a summer job in another town and wish to assign the balance of your lease (three months) to a fellow student who will be attending summer school. Can you do so?
(b) You are graduating in May. The lease will have three months remaining. Can you terminate the lease without liability by giving a thirty-day notice to the landlord?

41–2. Property Ownership. Antonio is the owner of a lakeside house and lot. He deeds the house and lot "to my wife, Angela, for life, then to my son, Charles." Given these facts, answer the following questions:

(a) Does Antonio have any ownership interest in the lakeside house after making these transfers? Explain.
(b) What is Angela's interest called? Is there any limitation on her rights to use the property as she wishes?
(c) What is Charles's interest called? Why?

41–3. Property Ownership. Lorenz was a wanderer twenty-two years ago. At that time, he decided to settle down on an unoccupied, three-acre parcel of land that he did not own. People in the area indicated to him that they had no idea who owned the property. Lorenz built a house on the land, got married, and raised three children while living there. He fenced in the land, placed a gate with a sign above it that read "Lorenz's Homestead," and had trespassers removed. Lorenz is now confronted by Joe Reese, who has a deed in his name as owner of the property. Reese, claiming ownership of the land, orders Lorenz and his family off the property. Discuss who has the better "title" to the property.

41–4. Deeds. Wiley and Gemma are neighbors. Wiley's lot is extremely large, and his present and future use of it will not involve the entire area. Gemma wants to build a single-car garage and driveway along the present lot boundary. Because of ordinances requiring buildings to be set back fifteen feet from an adjoining property line, and because of the placement of her existing structures, Gemma cannot build the garage. Gemma contracts to purchase ten feet of Wiley's property along their boundary line for $3,000. Wiley is willing to sell but will give Gemma only a quitclaim deed, whereas Gemma wants a warranty deed. Discuss the differences between these deeds as they would affect the rights of the parties if the title to this ten feet of land later proved to be defective.

41–5. Leased Property. The landlord of an apartment building leased a building he owned nearby for use as a cocktail lounge. The residential tenants complained to the landlord about the late evening and early morning music and disturbances coming from the lounge. Although the lease for the lounge provided that entertainment had to be conducted so that it could not be heard outside the building and would not disturb the apartment tenants, the landlord was unsuccessful in remedying the problem. The tenants vacated their apartments. Was the landlord successful in his suit to collect rent from the tenants who vacated the premises? Discuss. [*Blackett v. Olanoff,* 371 Mass. 714, 358 N.E.2d 817 (1977)]

41–6. Adverse Possession. As the result of a survey in 1976, the Nolans discovered that their neighbor's garage extended more than a foot onto their property. Nolan requested that his neighbor, Naab, tear down the garage. The Naabs refused to do this, stating that the garage had been built in 1952 and had been on the property when the Naabs purchased it in 1973. In West Virginia, where these properties were located, there is a ten-year possessory requirement covering adverse possession of property. Were the Naabs able to claim title to the land on which the garage was situated by adverse possession? Explain. [*Naab v. Nolan,* 327 S.E.2d 151 (W.Va.1985)]

41–7. Easements. Merton Peterson owned a golf course, a supper club, and the parking lot between them. Both golfers and club patrons always parked in the lot. Peterson sold the club and the lot to the American Legion, which sold them to VBC, Inc. (owned by Richard Beck and others). When VBC demanded rent from Peterson for use of the lot, Peterson filed a suit in a South Dakota state court to determine title. On what basis might the court hold that Peterson has an easement for the use of the lot? Does Peterson have an easement? [*Peterson v. Beck,* 537 N.W.2d 375 (S.Dak. 1995)]

41–8. Habitability. James and Bernadine Winn rented a house from Rick and Cynthia McGeehan. Each month, the rent was either late or underpaid. When the McGeehans told the Winns that no further late payments would be accepted, the Winns complained of a number of habitability problems. The McGeehans made repairs. The Winns again failed to pay the rent on time. The McGeehans filed a suit in an Oregon state court to regain possession of the house. While the suit was pending, the Winns paid the rent to the court. The court held that the McGeehans were entitled to possession. The Winns appealed, claiming that they were entitled to possession. Who should have possession of the house, and why? [*Winn v. McGeehan,* 142 Or.App. 390, 921 P.2d 1337 (1996)]

41–9. Taking. Richard and Jaquelyn Jackson owned property in a residential subdivision near an airport operated by the Metropolitan Knoxville Airport Authority in Blount County, Tennessee. The Airport Authority considered extending a runway near the subdivision and undertook a study that found that the noise, vibration, and pollution from aircraft using the extension would render the Jacksons' property incompatible with residential use. The airport built the extension, bringing about the predicted results, and the Jacksons filed a suit against the Airport Authority, alleging a taking of their property. The Airport Authority responded that there was no taking because there were no direct flights over the Jacksons' property. In whose favor will the court rule, and why? [*Jackson v. Metropolitan Knoxville Airport Authority,* 922 S.W.2d 860 (Tenn. 1996)]

41–10. Warranty of Habitability. Three-year-old Nkenge Lynch fell from the window of her third-floor apartment and suffered serious and permanent injuries. There were no window stops or guards on the window. The use of window stops, even if installed, is optional with the tenant. Stanley James owned the apartment building. Zsa Zsa Kinsey, Nkenge's mother, filed a suit on Nkenge's behalf in a Massachusetts state court against James, alleging in part a breach of an implied warranty of habitability. The plaintiff did not argue that the absence of stops or guards made the apartment unfit for human habitation but that their absence "endangered and materially impaired her health and safety," and therefore the failure to install them was a breach of warranty. Should the court rule that the absence of window stops breached a warranty of habitability? Should the court mandate that landlords provide window guards? Why or why not? [*Lynch v. James,* 44 Mass.App.Ct. 448, 692 N.E.2d 81 (1998)]

A QUESTION OF ETHICS AND SOCIAL RESPONSIBILITY

41–11. John and Terry Hoffius own property in Jackson, Michigan, which they rent. Kristal McCready and Keith Kerr responded to the Hoffiuses' ad about the property. The Hoffiuses refused to rent to McCready and Kerr, however, when they learned that the two were single and intended to live together. John Hoffius told all prospective tenants that unmarried cohabitation violated his religious beliefs. McCready and others filed a suit in a Michigan state court against the Hoffiuses. They alleged in part that the Hoffiuses' actions violated the plaintiffs' civil rights under a state law that prohibits discrimination on the basis of "marital status." The Hoffiuses responded in part that forcing them to rent to unmarried couples in violation of the Hoffiuses' religious beliefs would be unconstitutional. [*McCready v. Hoffius,* 586 N.W.2d 723 (Mich. 1998)]

1. Was it the plaintiffs' "marital status" or their conduct to which the defendants objected? Did the defendants violate the plaintiffs' civil rights? Explain.
2. Should a court, in the interest of preventing discrimination in housing, compel a landlord to violate his or her conscience? In other words, whose rights should prevail in this case? Why?
3. Is there an objective rule that determines when civil rights or religious freedom, or any two similarly important principles, should prevail? If so, what is it? If not, should there be?

FOR CRITICAL ANALYSIS

41–12. Real property law dates back hundreds of years. What changes have occurred in society, including business and technological changes, that have affected the development and application of real property law? (Hint: Was airspace an issue three hundred years ago?)

Online Activities

ONLINE EXERCISE 41–1

Go to the "Internet Activities Book" on the Web site that accompanies this text, the URL for which is http://blt.westbuslaw.com. Select the following activities, and perform the exercises according to the instructions given there:

Activity 37–1: Real Estate Law
Activity 37–2: Fair Housing

Before the Test

Go to the *Business Law Today* home page at http://blt.westbuslaw.com. Click on TestTutor.® You will find twenty interactive questions relating to this chapter.

CHAPTER 42

Insurance, Wills & Trusts

"Insurance is part charity and part business, but all common sense."

Calvin Coolidge, 1872–1933
(Thirtieth president of the United States, 1923–1929)

CONTENTS

LEARNING OBJECTIVES

After reading this chapter, you should be able to:

1. Indicate when an insurable interest arises in regard to life and property insurance.
2. Distinguish between an insurance broker and an insurance agent.
3. Summarize some of the clauses that are typically included in insurance contracts.
4. Describe the requirements of a valid will.
5. Explain how property is transferred when a person dies without a valid will.

Most individuals insure both real and personal property (as well as their lives). As Calvin Coolidge asserted in the opening quotation above, insurance is "all common sense"—by insuring our property, we protect ourselves against damage and loss.

After discussing insurance, which is a foremost concern of all property owners, we examine how property is transferred on the death of its owner. Certainly, the laws of succession of property are a necessary corollary to the concept of private ownership of property. Our laws require that on death, title to the property of a decedent (one who has recently died) must be delivered in full somewhere. In this chapter we see that this can be done by will, through trusts, or through state laws prescribing distribution of property among heirs or next of kin.

Insurance

• **INSURANCE**
A contract in which, for a stipulated consideration, one party agrees to compensate the other for loss on a specific subject by a specified peril.

• **RISK**
A prediction concerning potential loss based on known and unknown factors.

Insurance is a contract by which the insurance company (the insurer) promises to pay a sum of money or give something of value to another (either the insured or the beneficiary) in the event that the insured is injured, dies, or sustains damage to his or her property as a result of particular, stated contingencies. Basically, insurance is an arrangement for *transferring and allocating risk*. In many cases, **risk** can be described as a prediction concerning potential loss based on known and unknown factors. Insurance, however, involves much more than a game of chance.

Many precautions may be taken to protect against the hazards of life. For example, an individual may wear a seat belt to protect against automobile injuries or install smoke detectors to guard against injury from the risk of fire. Of course, no one can predict whether an accident or a fire will ever occur, but individuals and businesses must establish plans to protect their personal and financial interests should some event threaten to undermine their security. This concept is known as **risk management.** The most common method of risk management is the transfer of certain risks from the individual to the insurance company.

• **RISK MANAGEMENT**
Planning that is undertaken to protect one's interest should some event threaten to undermine its security. In the context of insurance, risk management involves transferring certain risks from the insured to the insurance company.

Risk is transferred to an insurance company by a contractual agreement. The insurance contract and its provisions will be examined shortly. First, however, we look at the different types of insurance that can be obtained, insurance terminology, and the concept of insurable interest.

ETHICAL ISSUE 42.1 ***Does insurance coverage reduce a property owner's incentive to prevent losses?*** A major ethical concern in the area of insurance involves moral hazard. In the insurance industry, moral hazard occurs when insurance coverage reduces the incentive of individuals or companies to act cautiously or to guard against destruction or loss that will be paid for by their insurance companies. For example, the businessperson who takes out a large insurance policy on a building has less incentive to take care that the building is protected from fire than an individual without any insurance policy. Similarly, the property owner who takes out property insurance may have less incentive to install alarm systems, to pay for private patrol service, and so on. Additionally, the smaller the *deductible* (a specified amount that the policyholder must pay on a claim—for example, the first $250 of a claim) in an insurance policy, the less incentive the policy-holder has to prevent losses from fire or theft. Moral hazard exists with medical insurance as well. The smaller the deductible, the greater the incentive for the individual to be less worried about preventing health problems.

Classifications of Insurance

Insurance is classified according to the nature of the risk involved. For example, fire insurance, casualty insurance, life insurance, and title insurance apply to different types of risk. Furthermore, policies of these types differ in the persons and interests that they protect. This is reasonable, because the types of losses that are expected and the types that are foreseeable or unforeseeable vary with the nature of the activity. Exhibit 42–1 presents a list of insurance classifications. (For a relatively new type of insurance coverage, see the *Technology and Web Site Insurance Policies* on page 1080.)

Insurance Terminology

• **POLICY**
In insurance law, a contract between the insurer and the insured in which, for a stipulated consideration, the insurer agrees to compensate the insured for loss on a specific subject by a specified peril.

• **PREMIUM**
In insurance law, the price paid by the insured for insurance protection for a specified period of time.

• **UNDERWRITER**
In insurance law, the insurer, or the one assuming a risk in return for the payment of a premium.

An insurance contract is called a **policy;** the consideration paid to the insurer is called a **premium;** and the insurance company is sometimes called an **underwriter.**

EXHIBIT 42–1 • Insurance Classifications

TYPE OF INSURANCE	COVERAGE
Accident	Covers expenses, losses, and suffering incurred by the insured because of accidents causing physical injury and any consequent disability; sometimes includes a specified payment to heirs of the insured if death results from an accident.
All-risk	Covers all losses that the insured may incur except those resulting from fraud on the part of the insured.
Automobile	May cover damage to automobiles resulting from specified hazards or occurrences (such as fire, vandalism, theft, or collision); normally provides protection against liability for personal injuries and property damage resulting from the operation of the vehicle.
Casualty	Protects against losses that may be incurred by the insured as a result of being held liable for personal injuries or property damage sustained by others.
Credit	Pays to a creditor the balance of a debt on the disability, death, insolvency, or bankruptcy of the debtor; often offered by lending institutions.
Decreasing-term life	Provides life insurance; requires uniform payments over the life (term) of the policy, but with a decreasing face value (amount of coverage).
Employer's liability	Insures employers against liability for injuries or losses sustained by employees during the course of their employment; covers claims not covered under workers' compensation insurance.
Fidelity or guaranty	Provides indemnity against losses in trade or losses caused by the dishonesty of employees, the insolvency of debtors, or breaches of contract.
Fire	Covers losses caused to the insured as a result of fire.
Floater	Covers movable property, as long as the property is within the territorial boundaries specified in the contract.
Group	Provides individual life, medical, or disability insurance coverage but is obtainable through a group of persons, usually employees; the policy premium is paid either entirely by the employer or partially by the employer and partially by the employee.
Health	Covers expenses incurred by the insured resulting from physical injury or illness and other expenses relating to health and life maintenance.
Homeowners'	Protects homeowners against some or all risks of loss to their residences and the residences' contents or liability arising from the use of the property.
Key-person	Protects a business in the event of the death or disability of a key employee.
Liability	Protects against liability imposed on the insured resulting from injuries to the person or property of another.
Life	Covers the death of the policyholder. On the death of the insured, an amount specified in the policy is paid by the insurer to the insured's beneficiary.
Major medical	Protects the insured against major hospital, medical, or surgical expenses.
Malpractice	Protects professionals (doctors, lawyers, and others) against malpractice claims brought against them by their patients or clients; a form of liability insurance.
Marine	Covers movable property (including ships, freight, and cargo) against certain perils or navigation risks during a specific voyage or time period.
Mortgage	Covers a mortgage loan; the insurer pays the balance of the mortgage to the creditor on the death or disability of the debtor.
No-fault auto	Covers personal injury and (sometimes) property damage resulting from automobile accidents. The insured submits his or her claims to his or her own insurance company, regardless of who was at fault. A person may sue the party at fault or that party's insurer only in cases involving serious medical injury and consequent high medical costs. Governed by state "no-fault" statutes.
Term life	Provides life insurance for a specified period of time (term) with no cash surrender value; usually renewable.
Title	Protects against any defects in title to real property and any losses incurred as a result of existing claims against or liens on the property at the time of purchase.

Technology and Web Site Insurance Policies

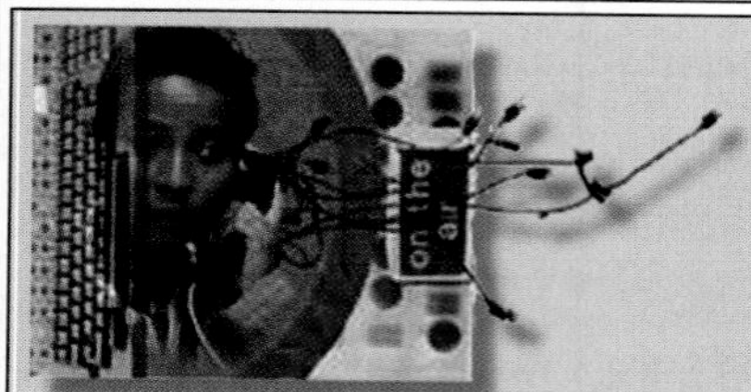

Internet transactions pose special risks for businesspersons, risks that are not covered by traditional types of insurance. For example, suppose that the XYZ Company sells its products via its Web site. The buyers purchase the products using their credit cards. A hacker accesses the business's server containing the customers' credit-card numbers and then uses those numbers to purchase goods. Consumers, of course, are protected against unauthorized use of their cards under federal law (see Chapter 36). The XYZ Company, however, may be liable to the credit-card companies for negligence if it failed to maintain appropriate security measures to protect the data from unauthorized access.

Not surprisingly, some companies are now offering insurance policies that are designed to cover such risks. For example, InsureSite is an insurance policy created specifically to cover injuries to commercial Web sites. The policy, which is underwritten by member companies of American International Group, Inc., covers three particular types of risks: liability for loss of electronic funds resulting from the operation of a Web business; exposure to suits for invastion of privacy; and losses due to damage to computer equipment or software as a result of vandalism or computer viruses.

In contrast to other types of insurance policies, Web site insurance premiums typically are determined by such factors as the number of pages on a Web site, the type of goods offered on the site, and so on. The premium depends on the extent of the risks involved. For an InsureSite policy, the minimum premium is $2,500 a year.

FOR CRITICAL ANALYSIS

How could an insurance company that sells Web site policies evaluate the extent of the risk posed by, say, computer viruses?

INTERNET CONNECT

The parties to an insurance policy are the *insurer* (the insurance company) and the *insured* (the person covered by the insurer's provisions or the holder of the policy). Insurance contracts are usually obtained through an *agent,* who ordinarily works for the insurance company, or through a *broker,* who is ordinarily an *independent contractor.* When a broker deals with an applicant for insurance, the broker is, in effect, the applicant's agent. In contrast, an insurance agent is an agent of the insurance company, not of the applicant. As a general rule, the insurance company is bound by the acts of its agents when they act within the agency relationship (discussed in Chapter 24). A broker, however, normally has no relationship with the insurance company and is an agent of the insurance applicant. In most situations, state law determines the status of all parties writing or obtaining insurance.

INSURABLE INTEREST

• INSURABLE INTEREST
An interest either in a person's life or well-being or in property that is sufficiently substantial that insuring against injury to (or the death of) the person or against damage to the property does not amount to a mere wagering (betting) contract.

A person can insure anything in which he or she has an **insurable interest.** Without this insurable interest, there is no enforceable contract, and a transaction to insure would have to be treated as a wager. In regard to real and personal property, an insurable interest exists when the insured derives a pecuniary benefit (a benefit consisting of or relating to money) from the preservation and continued existence of the property. Put another way, one has an insurable interest in property when one would sustain a pecuniary loss from its destruction. In regard to life insurance, a person must have a reasonable expectation of benefit from the continued life of another in order to have an insurable interest in that person's life. The benefit may be pecuniary (as with so-called *key-person insurance,* which insures the lives of important employees, usually in small companies), or it may be founded on the relationship between the parties (by blood or affinity).

For property insurance, the insurable interest must exist at the time the loss occurs but need not exist when the policy is purchased. In contrast, for life insurance, the insurable interest must exist at the time the policy is obtained. The existence of an insurable interest is a primary concern in determining liability under an insurance policy.

¡NOTE! The federal government has the power to regulate the insurance industry under the commerce clause of the U.S. Constitution. Instead of exercising this power itself, Congress allows the states to regulate insurance.

THE INSURANCE CONTRACT

An insurance contract is governed by the general principles of contract law, although the insurance industry is heavily regulated by each state. Several aspects of the insurance contract will be treated here, including the application for insurance, when the contract takes effect, important contract provisions, cancellation of the policy, and defenses that can be raised by insurance companies against payment on a policy.

Application The filled-in application form for insurance is usually attached to the policy and made a part of the insurance contract. Thus, an insurance applicant is bound by any false statements that appear in the application (subject to certain exceptions). Because the insurance company evaluates the risk factors based on the information included in the insurance application, misstatements or misrepresentations can void a policy, especially if the insurance company can show that it would not have extended insurance if it had known the true facts. (If an insurance applicant makes a misrepresentation on an application without intending to, will the policy still be declared void? See this chapter's *Business Law in Action* for a discussion of a case involving this issue.)

Business Law in Action • TO THE BEST OF MY KNOWLEDGE AND BELIEF . . .

Because any misstatement or misrepresentation of a material fact on an insurance application may void the policy, insurance applicants must be especially careful to answer all questions accurately and truthfully. Yet what if an applicant believes that he or she has answered the questions truthfully but in fact has not?

For example, when Harold Green applied for a health-insurance policy, he answered "no" to a question asking whether, within the last five years, he had, or had been told that he had, "kidney failure." A year later, Green made a claim against the policy after he had been hospitalized for kidney failure, among other things. The insurance company, after learning from Green's medical records that he had suffered for several years from chronic kidney failure, canceled the policy and returned to Green all of the premiums that he had paid for the policy.

Green sued the company to obtain reimbursement for the cost of his hospitalization, contending that his physician had never told him that he had kidney failure and that he had answered the question truthfully on the application. Green's physician testified that it was his regular practice to use layperson's terms, rather than medical terms, when informing patients of their conditions. The physician stated that he probably told Green that he had "some sluggish kidneys" or "slow kidneys."

The insurance company countered by stating that even though Green may have innocently misled the company, a state statute provided that an insurance company could deny recovery under a policy if the insured had made any material misrepresentation, innocently or otherwise, on the application that would alter the nature of the risk assumed by the insurer. Relying on this statutory authority, the trial court entered summary judgment in favor of the insurance company. On appeal, however, the state supreme court reversed that decision.

The state supreme court pointed to the following words in the application form, which appeared just above the signature line: "The answers given by me are full, true and complete to the best of my knowledge and belief." The court held that "truthful answers on an insurance application according to the best of the insured's 'knowledge and belief' do not constitute misstatements within the meaning of [the relevant statutory provision] and therefore cannot provide the grounds for the insurer's rescission of the insurance policy." The court emphasized that the insurance company, which drafted the application form, chose to include the words, "to the best of my knowledge and belief." By doing so, the company elected to bypass the "rigid statutory standards." "In essence," stated the court, the insurer "now seeks to repudiate its own contract and, as a fall back position, claim refuge in the stricter statutory standard, a method that disadvantages a good faith insured."[a]

FOR CRITICAL ANALYSIS

How can you explain the insurance company's decision to include the "knowledge and belief" language in its application form?

a. *Green v. Life & Health of America,* 704 So.2d 1386 (Fla. 1998).

Effective Date The effective date of an insurance contract is important. In some instances, the insurance applicant is not protected until a formal written policy is issued. In other situations, the applicant is protected between the time the application is received and the time the insurance company either accepts or rejects it. Four facts should be kept in mind:

1. A broker is merely the agent of an applicant. Therefore, until the broker obtains a policy, the applicant normally is not insured.
2. A person who seeks insurance from an insurance company's agent will usually be protected from the moment the application is made, provided—in the case of life insurance—that some form of premium has been paid. Between the time the application is received and either rejected or accepted, the applicant is covered (possibly subject to medical examination). Usually, the agent will write a memorandum, or **binder,** indicating that a policy is pending and stating its essential terms.
3. If the parties agree that the policy will be issued and delivered at a later time, the contract is not effective until the policy is issued and delivered or sent to the applicant, depending on the agreement. Thus, any loss sustained between the time of application and the delivery of the policy is not covered.
4. Parties may agree that a life insurance policy will be binding at the time the insured pays the first premium, or the policy may be expressly contingent on the applicant's passing a physical examination. In the latter situation, if the applicant pays the premium and passes the examination, then the policy coverage is in effect. If the applicant pays the premium but dies before having the physical examination, then to collect, the applicant's estate must show that the applicant would have passed the examination had he or she not died.

• **BINDER**
A written, temporary insurance policy.

In the following case, the court had to decide whether a policy that required an applicant to be "still insurable" on the effective date of the policy should prevent the beneficiary from recovering.

CASE 42.1 Life Insurance Co. of North America v. Cichowlas

District Court of Appeal of Florida,
Fourth District, 1995.
659 So.2d 1333.

HISTORICAL AND GLOBAL SETTING *The United States leads the world in insurance coverage. Over 3,500 U.S. companies sell property insurance, and more than 2,200 offer life insurance. Thirty-three of these companies have been selling insurance for more than one hundred years and control more than half of the insurance market. In the 1980s, some of these companies tripled the amount that they take in annually in premiums. Despite these glowing figures, some insurers claim that writing insurance in certain markets causes them to lose profits.*

BACKGROUND AND FACTS Waldemar Cichowlas applied to the Life Insurance Company of North America (LINA) for insurance naming his wife Ewa as beneficiary. The application asked if he had been hospitalized during the past five years and if he had ever been treated for lung disease. A yes answer would have affected his insurability. Waldemar truthfully answered no. The policy required that an applicant be "still insurable" on the effective date of the policy. Three weeks before the policy took effect, Waldemar was hospitalized with a lung disease. He did not tell LINA. When he died of other causes, LINA refused to pay Ewa. She filed a suit in a Florida state court against the insurer. The court ordered LINA to pay. The insurer appealed.

IN THE WORDS OF THE COURT . . .
PER CURIAM [by the entire court].

* * * *

* * * Clauses requiring that an applicant remain insurable between the filing of the application and the delivery of the policy have traditionally been approved by Florida courts. They are generally in the form of statements that the policy shall not take effect unless it is delivered during the continued insurability or sound health of

CASE 42.1—Continued

the applicant. Thus, as the evidence was uncontradicted that Mr. Cichowlas was not insurable on the effective date of the policy, the "still insurable" clause precluded recovery for [Ewa] pursuant to its terms.

DECISION AND REMEDY The District Court of Appeal of Florida reversed the judgment of the lower court and remanded the case.

FOR CRITICAL ANALYSIS—Ethical Consideration *What effect might it have had on the outcome of this case if the court had held that LINA had a continuing duty to ask about the health of its applicants?*

Coinsurance Clauses Often, when taking out fire insurance policies, property owners insure their property for less than full value. Part of the reason for this is that most fires do not result in a total loss. To encourage owners to insure their property for an amount as close to full value as possible, a standard provision of fire insurance policies is a coinsurance clause. Typically, a *coinsurance clause* provides that if the owner insures the property up to a specified percentage—usually 80 percent—of its value, he or she will recover any loss up to the face amount of the policy. If the insurance is for less than the fixed percentage, the owner is responsible for a proportionate share of the loss.

Coinsurance applies only in instances of partial loss. • **EXAMPLE 42.1** If the owner of property valued at $100,000 took out a policy in the amount of $40,000 and suffered a loss of $30,000, the recovery would be $15,000. The formula for calculating the recovery amount is as follows:

$$\frac{\text{amount of insurance } (\$40{,}000)}{\text{coinsurance percentage } (80\%) \times \text{property value } (\$100{,}000)} = \text{recovery percentage } (50\%)$$

$$\text{recovery percentage } (50\%) \times \text{amount of loss } (\$30{,}000) = \text{recovery amount } (\$15{,}000)$$

If the owner had taken out a policy in the amount of $80,000, then according to the same formula, the full loss would have been recovered. •

ON THE WEB

For a summary of the law governing insurance contracts in the United States, including rules of interpretation, go to **www.consumerlawpage.com/article/insureds.shtml**.

Other Provisions and Clauses Some other important provisions and clauses contained in insurance contracts are listed and defined in Exhibit 42–2. The courts are increasingly cognizant of the fact that most people do not have the special training necessary to understand the intricate terminology used in insurance policies. Thus, the words used in an insurance contract have their ordinary meanings. They are interpreted by the courts in light of the nature of the coverage involved.

When there is an ambiguity in the policy, the provision generally is interpreted against the insurance company. When the written policy has not been delivered and it is unclear whether an insurance contract actually exists, the uncertainty normally will be resolved against the insurance company. The court will presume that the policy is in effect unless the company can show otherwise. Similarly, an insurer must take care to make sure that the insured is adequately notified of any change in coverage under an existing policy.

Cancellation The insured can cancel a policy at any time, and the insurer can cancel under certain circumstances. When an insurance company can cancel its

EXHIBIT 42–2 • Insurance Contract Provisions and Clauses

Incontestability clause	An incontestability clause provides that after a policy has been in force for a specified length of time—usually two or three years—the insurer cannot contest statements made in the application.
Appraisal clause	Insurance policies frequently provide that if the parties cannot agree on the amount of a loss covered under the policy or the value of the property lost, an appraisal, or estimate, by an impartial and qualified third party can be demanded.
Arbitration clause	Many insurance policies include clauses that call for arbitration of disputes that may arise between the insurer and the insured concerning the settlement of claims.
Antilapse clause	An antilapse clause provides that the policy will not automatically lapse if no payment is made on the date due. Ordinarily, under such a provision, the insured has a *grace period* of thirty or thirty-one days within which to pay an overdue premium before the policy is canceled.
Cancellation	Cancellation of an insurance policy can occur for various reasons, depending on the type of insurance. When an insurance company can cancel its insurance contract, the policy or a state statute usually requires that the insurer give advance written notice of the cancellation. An insurer cannot cancel—or refuse to renew—a policy because of the national origin or race of an applicant or because the insured has appeared as a witness in a case against the company.

insurance contract, the policy or a state statute usually requires that the insurer give advance written notice of the cancellation to the insured.

The insurer may cancel an insurance policy for various reasons, depending on the type of insurance. For example, automobile insurance can be canceled for nonpayment of premiums or suspension of the insured's driver's license. Property insurance can be canceled for nonpayment of premiums or for other reasons, including the insured's fraud or misrepresentation, conviction for a crime that increases the hazard insured against, or gross negligence that increases the hazard insured against. Life and health policies can be canceled because of false statements made by the insured in the application. An insurer cannot cancel—or refuse to renew—a policy for discriminatory reasons or other reasons that violate public policy, or because the insured has appeared as a witness in a case against the company.

Defenses against Payment In attempting to avoid payment on a policy claim, an insurance company can raise any of the defenses that would be valid in any ordinary action on a contract, as well as some defenses that do not apply in ordinary contract actions. If the insurance company can show that the policy was procured by fraud, misrepresentation, or violation of warranties, it may have a valid defense for not paying on a claim. Improper actions, such as those that are against public policy or that are otherwise illegal, can also give the insurance company a defense against the payment of a claim or allow it to rescind the contract.

An insurance company can be prevented from asserting some defenses that are normally available, however. For example, if a company tells an insured that information requested on a form is optional, and the insured provides it anyway, the company cannot use the information to avoid its contractual obligation under the insurance contract. Similarly, incorrect statements as to the age of the insured normally do not allow the insurer to avoid payment on the death of the insured.

In the following case, an insurance company attempted to avoid payment under a policy for life and disability insurance by claiming that the policy owner did not have an insurable interest, thus rendering the policy void from the outset.

CASE 42.2 Paul Revere Life Insurance Co. v. Fima

United States Court of Appeals,
Ninth Circuit, 1997.
105 F.3d 490.
www.vcilp.org/Fed-Ct/Circuit/9th/January97.html[a]

COMPANY PROFILE *Disability insurance can replace part of the income that an individual loses after suffering a disabling accident or illness. The coverage may be offered by an insurance company through an employer or may be obtained from an insurer by an individual. Provident Companies, Inc., which calls itself "North America's leader in personal income protection," offers disability insurance, as well as other types of insurance, to employers and individuals. Based in Chattanooga, Tennessee, Provident traces its beginnings to 1887. Provident is the parent company of six insurance subsidiary companies, including Paul Revere Life Insurance Company.*

a. This page lists decisions of the U.S. Court of Appeals for the Ninth Circuit for January 1997. Scroll down the list to the *Fima* case and click on the link to access the opinion.

BACKGROUND AND FACTS Raoul Fima applied to Paul Revere Life Insurance Company for a disability policy. On the application, Fima stated his income as $105,000 for the previous year and $85,000 for the current year. Fima's actual income for those years was $21,603 and $6,320, respectively. The policy included the following incontestability clause: "After your policy has been in force for two years, . . . we cannot contest the statements in the application." Three years later, when Fima filed a claim under the policy, Revere discovered the truth regarding Fima's income. Revere filed a suit in a federal district court against Fima, seeking to have the policy declared void *ab initio* (from the beginning) on the ground that he lacked an insurable interest. The court denied the request. Revere appealed.

IN THE WORDS OF THE COURT . . .
BRUNETTI, Circuit Judge:

* * * *

Fima had an insurable interest under California Insurance Code [S]ection 10110 as a matter of law. Section 10110 states that "[e]very person has an insurable interest in the life and health of * * * [h]imself." Because Fima had an insurable interest under [S]ection 10110, his disability insurance policy was not void *ab initio.*

* * * *

* * * Because that policy is not void *ab initio* and because the period for contesting the policy has passed under the incontestability clause, Revere may not now challenge the terms of the policy or the extent of Fima's insurable interest.

DECISION AND REMEDY The U.S. Court of Appeals for the Ninth Circuit affirmed the judgment of the lower court. Every person has an insurable interest in his or her own life and health.

FOR CRITICAL ANALYSIS—Ethical Consideration *What is the underlying rationale for including inconstestability clauses in insurance contracts?*

Wills

• **WILL**
An instrument directing what is to be done with the testator's property on his or her death, made by the testator and revocable during his or her lifetime. No interests in the testator's property pass until the testator dies.

Private ownership of property leads logically to both the protection of that property by insurance coverage while the owner is alive and the transfer of that property on the death of the owner to those designated in the owner's will. A **will** is the final declaration of how a person desires to have his or her property disposed of after death. A will, because it is a person's "last will and testament," is referred to as a *testamentary disposition* of property. It is a formal instrument that must follow exactly the requirements of state law to be effective. The reasoning behind such a strict requirement is obvious. A will becomes effective only after death. No attempts to modify it after the death of the maker are allowed, because the court cannot ask the maker to confirm the attempted modifications. (Sometimes, however, the wording of the will must be "interpreted" by the courts.)

A will can serve other purposes besides the distribution of property. It can appoint a guardian for minor children or incapacitated adults. It can also appoint a personal representative to settle the affairs of the deceased. Exhibit 42–3 on the next page presents a copy of John Lennon's will.

A person who dies without having created a valid will is said to have died **intestate.** In this situation, state **intestacy laws** prescribe the distribution of the property among heirs or next of kin. If no heirs or kin can be found, title to the property will be transferred to the state.

• **INTESTATE**
As a noun, one who has died without having created a valid will; as an adjective, the state of having died without a will.

• **INTESTACY LAWS**
State statutes that specify how property will be distributed when a person dies intestate (without a valid will); also called statutes of descent and distribution.

TERMINOLOGY OF WILLS

A person who makes out a will is known as a **testator** (from the Latin *testari,* "to make a will"). The court responsible for administering any legal problems surrounding a will is called a *probate court,* as mentioned in Chapter 3. When a person dies, a personal representative administers the estate and settles finally all of the decedent's (deceased person's) affairs. An **executor** is a personal representative named in the will; an **administrator** is a personal representative appointed by the court for a decedent who dies without a will, who fails to name an executor in the will, who names an executor lacking the capacity to serve, or who writes a will that the court refuses to admit to probate.

A gift of real estate by will is generally called a **devise,** and a gift of personal property by will is called a **bequest,** or **legacy.** The recipient of a gift by will is a **devisee** or **legatee,** depending on whether the gift was a devise or a legacy.

• **TESTATOR**
One who makes and executes a will.

• **EXECUTOR**
A person appointed by a testator in a will to see that his or her will is administered appropriately.

• **ADMINISTRATOR**
One who is appointed by a court to handle the probate (disposition) of a person's estate if that person dies intestate (without a valid will) or if the executor named in the will cannot serve.

• **DEVISE**
To make a gift of real property by will.

• **BEQUEST**
A gift by will of personal property (from the verb *to bequeath*).

• **LEGACY**
A gift of personal property under a will.

• **DEVISEE**
One designated in a will to receive a gift of real property.

• **LEGATEE**
One designated in a will to receive a gift of personal property.

TYPES OF GIFTS

Gifts by will can be specific, general, or residuary. A *specific* devise or bequest (legacy) describes particular property (such as "Eastwood Estate" or "my gold pocket watch") that can be distinguished from all the rest of the testator's property. A *general* devise or bequest (legacy) uses less restrictive terminology. For example, "I devise all my lands" is a general devise. A general bequest often specifies a sum of money instead of a particular item of property, such as a watch or an automobile. For example, "I give to my nephew, Carleton, $30,000" is a general bequest.

If the assets of an estate are insufficient to pay in full all general bequests provided for in the will, an *abatement,* by which the legatees receive reduced benefits, takes place. If a legatee dies prior to the death of the testator or before the legacy is payable, a *lapsed legacy* results. At common law, the legacy failed. Today, the legacy may not lapse if the legatee is in a certain blood relationship to the testator (such as a child, grandchild, brother, or sister) and has left a child or other surviving descendant.

Sometimes a will provides that any assets remaining after specific gifts have been made and debts are paid—called the *residuum*—are to be distributed through a *residuary clause.* A residuary clause is used when the exact amount to be distributed cannot be determined until all of the other gifts and payouts have been made. A residuary clause can pose problems, however, when the will does not specifically name the beneficiaries to receive the residuum. In such a situation, if the court cannot determine the testator's intent, the residuum passes according to state laws of intestacy.

"If you want to see a man's true character, watch him divide an estate."

BENJAMIN FRANKLIN, 1706–1790
(American diplomat, author, and scientist)

EXHIBIT 42–3 • A Sample Will

LAST WILL AND TESTAMENT
OF
JOHN WINSTON ONO LENNON

I, JOHN WINSTON ONO LENNON, a resident of the County of New York, State of New York, which I declare to be my domicile do hereby make, publish and declare this to be my Last Will and Testament, hereby revoking all other Wills, Codicils and Testamentary dispositions by me at any time heretofore made.

FIRST: The expenses of my funeral and the administration of my estate, and all inheritance, estate or successions taxes, including interest and penalties, payable by reason of my death shall be paid out of and charged generally against the principal of my residuary estate without apportionment or proration. My Executor shall not seek contribution or reimbursement for any such payments.

SECOND: Should my wife survive me, I give, devise and bequeath to her absolutely, an amount equal to that portion of my residuary estate, the numerator and denominator of which shall be determined as follows:

1. The numerator shall be an amount equal to one-half (½) of my adjusted gross estate less the value of all other property included in my gross estate for Federal Estate Tax purposes and which pass or shall have passed to my wife either under any other provision of this Will or in any manner outside of this Will in such manner as to qualify for and be allowed as a marital deduction. The words "pass," "have passed," "marital deduction" and "adjusted gross estate" shall have the same meaning as said words have under those provisions of the United States Internal Revenue Code applicable to my estate.

2. The denominator shall be an amount representing the value of my residuary estate.

THIRD: I give, devise and bequeath all the rest, residue and remainder of my estate, wheresoever situate, to the Trustees under a Trust Agreement dated November 12, 1979, which I signed with my wife YOKO ONO, and ELI GARBER as Trustees, to be added to the trust property and held and distributed in accordance with the terms of that agreement and any amendments made pursuant to its terms before my death.

FOURTH: In the event that my wife and I die under such circumstances that there is not sufficient evidence to determine which of us has predeceased the other, I hereby declare it to be my will that it shall be deemed that I shall have predeceased her and that this, my Will, and any and all of its provisions shall be construed based upon that assumption.

FIFTH: I hereby nominate, constitute and appoint my beloved wife, YOKO ONO, to act as the Executor of this my Last Will and Testament. In the event that my beloved wife YOKO ONO shall predecease me or chooses not to act for any reason, I nominate and appoint ELI GARBER, DAVID WARMFLASH and CHARLES PETTIT, in the order named, to act in her place and stead.

SIXTH: I nominate, constitute and appoint my wife YOKO ONO, as the Guardian of the person and property of any children of the marriage who may survive me. In the event that she predeceases me, or for any reason she chooses not to act in that capacity, I nominate, constitute and appoint SAM GREEN to act in her place and stead.

SEVENTH: No person named herein to serve in any fiduciary capacity shall be required to file or post any bond for the faithful performance of his or her duties, in that capacity in this or in any other jurisdiction, any law to the contrary notwithstanding.

EIGHTH: If any legatee or beneficiary under this will or the trust agreement between myself as Grantor and YOKO ONO LENNON and ELI GARBER as Trustees, dated November 12, 1979 shall interpose objections to the probate of this Will, or institute or prosecute or be in any way interested or instrumental in the institution or prosecution of any action or proceeding for the purpose of setting aside or invalidating this Will, then and in each such case, I direct that such legatee or beneficiary shall receive nothing whatsoever under this Will or the aforementioned Trust.

IN WITNESS WHEREOF, I have subscribed and sealed and do publish and declare these presents as and for my Last Will and Testament, this 12th day of November, 1979.

/s/

John Winston Ono Lennon

THE FOREGOING INSTRUMENT consisting of four (4) typewritten pages, including this page, was on the 12th day of November, 1979, signed, sealed, published and declared by JOHN WINSTON ONO LENNON, the Testator therein named as and for his Last Will and Testament, in the presence of us, who at his request, and in his presence, and in the presence of each other, have hereunto set our names as witnesses.

(The names of the three witnesses are illegible.)

ON THE WEB
To learn more about wills and probate procedures, you can access the Uniform Probate Code online at **www.law.cornell.edu/uniform/probate.html**.

Probate Procedures

Laws governing wills come into play when a will is probated. To *probate* a will means to establish its validity and to carry the administration of the estate through a court process. Probate laws vary from state to state. In 1969, however, the American Bar Association and the National Conference of Commissioners on Uniform State Laws approved the Uniform Probate Code (UPC). The UPC codifies general principles and procedures for the resolution of conflicts in settling estates and relaxes some of the requirements for a valid will contained in earlier state laws. Nearly all of the states have adopted some part of the UPC. Because succession and inheritance laws vary widely among states, one should always check the particular laws of the state involved.[1] Typically, probate procedures vary, depending on the size of the decedent's estate.

Informal Probate For smaller estates, most state statutes provide for the distribution of assets without formal probate proceedings. Faster and less expensive methods are then used. For example, property can be transferred by affidavit (a written statement taken before a person who has authority to affirm it), and problems or questions can be handled during an administrative hearing. In addition, some state statutes provide that title to cars, savings and checking accounts, and certain other property can be passed merely by filling out forms.

A majority of states also provide for *family settlement agreements,* which are private agreements among the beneficiaries. Once a will is admitted to probate, the family members can agree to settle among themselves the distribution of the decedent's assets. Although a family settlement agreement speeds the settlement process, a court order is still needed to protect the estate from future creditors and to clear title to the assets involved. The use of these and other types of summary procedures in estate administration can save time and dollars.

"You cannot live without the lawyers, and certainly you cannot die without them."
JOSEPH H. CHOATE, 1832–1917
(American lawyer and diplomat)

Formal Probate For larger estates, normally formal probate proceedings are undertaken, and the probate court supervises every aspect of the settlement of the decedent's estate. Additionally, in some situations—such as when a guardian for minor children or for an incompetent person must be appointed, and a trust has been created to protect the minor or the incompetent person—more formal probate procedures cannot be avoided. Formal probate proceedings may take several months to complete, and as a result, a sizable portion of the decedent's assets (up to perhaps 10 percent or more) may have to go toward payment of court costs and fees charged by attorneys and personal representatives.

Property Transfers outside the Probate Process In the ordinary situation, a person can employ various will substitutes to avoid the cost of probate—for example, *inter vivos* trusts (discussed later in this chapter), life insurance policies with named beneficiaries, or joint-tenancy arrangements. Not all methods are suitable for every estate, but there are alternatives to complete probate administration.

Requirements for a Valid Will

A will must comply with statutory formalities designed to ensure that the testator understood his or her actions at the time the will was made. These formalities are intended to help prevent fraud. Unless they are followed, the will is declared void,

1. For example, California law differs substantially from the UPC.

and the decedent's property is distributed according to the laws of intestacy of that state. The requirements are not uniform among the jurisdictions. Most states, however, uphold certain basic requirements for executing a will. We now look at these requirements.

¡RECALL! In most states, the age of majority for contractual purposes is also eighteen years.

Testamentary Capacity For a will to be valid, the testator must have testamentary capacity—that is, the testator must be of legal age and sound mind *at the time the will is made.* The legal age for executing a will varies, but in most states and under the UPC the minimum age is eighteen years [UPC 2–501]. Thus, the will of a twenty-one-year-old decedent written when the person was sixteen is invalid if, under state law, the legal age for executing a will is eighteen.

The concept of "being of sound mind" refers to the testator's ability to formulate and to comprehend a personal plan for the disposition of property. Generally, a testator must (1) intend the document to be his or her last will and testament, (2) comprehend the kind and character of the property being distributed, and (3) comprehend and remember the "natural objects of his or her bounty" (usually, family members and persons for whom the testator has affection).

In the following case, the question before the court was whether the testator had the required testamentary capacity. As the court notes, testamentary capacity will be presumed unless sufficient evidence exists to call such capacity into question.

CASE 42.3 Bolan v. Bolan

Supreme Court of Alabama, 1993.
611 So.2d 1051.

HISTORICAL AND CULTURAL SETTING *In cases involving contested wills, English courts did not allow trial by jury. In actions of ejectment (in which a plaintiff seeks the removal of the defendant from land), English courts did allow trial by jury, even when one of the issues in the case was title to land that had been part of a testamentary disposition. When wills involving title to land came to be probated in the United States, it was believed that if those wills were contested, trial by jury should be allowed. Thus, trial by jury in will-contest cases came to be allowed in many states, including Alabama. Juries answer questions of fact. Incapacity is a question of fact. Because appellate courts do not generally consider questions of fact, an appellate court will normally not overturn the finding of a jury on the issue of incapacity as long as there is evidence to support the finding.*

BACKGROUND AND FACTS On Charley Bolan's death, he was survived by six children. His will left one dollar to each of three of his children and to each child of his deceased son ("the contestants") and the remainder of his estate to the other three children ("the proponents"). The contestants claimed that the will was invalid, alleging, among other things, that Charley lacked testamentary capacity at the time he made the will. The evidence before the court was conflicting. Witnesses present at the time the will was executed testified that Charley was in sound mental condition on that occasion, and other family members testified to the same effect. Other testimony, including statements made by the contestants, indicated that Charley was "in poor health before the date of execution; that he repeatedly held conversations with his dead wife; that he refused to bathe, change his clothes, or otherwise take care of himself; and that he had rigged up a dangerous spring-gun to protect himself from intruders when no real threat existed." The case was transferred from a probate court to an Alabama state trial court, and the trial jury held for the contestants. The proponents appealed.

IN THE WORDS OF THE COURT . . .
ALMON, Justice.

* * * *

* * * Every testator is presumed to have the capacity to make a will, * * * and the burden is on the contestant to prove the lack of testamentary capacity. The

(Continued)

CASE 42.3—Continued

contestant need not show that the testator suffered from permanent insanity; the contestant's burden may be carried by demonstrating that the testator lacked testamentary capacity at the time the will was executed.

* * * *

Although the evidence was conflicting, the contestants presented sufficient evidence of a lack of testamentary capacity to support the submission of the contest to the jury on this ground.

DECISION AND REMEDY The Supreme Court of Alabama affirmed the trial court's judgment.

FOR CRITICAL ANALYSIS—Social Consideration *What policy considerations underlie the courts' presumption that testamentary capacity exists?*

• **HOLOGRAPHIC WILL**
A will written entirely in the signer's handwriting and usually not witnessed.

• **NUNCUPATIVE WILL**
An oral will (often called a deathbed will) made before witnesses; usually limited to transfers of personal property.

Writing Requirements Generally, a will must be in writing. The writing itself can be informal as long as it substantially complies with the statutory requirements. In some states, a will can be handwritten in crayon or ink. It can be written on a sheet or scrap of paper, on a paper bag, or on a piece of cloth. A will that is completely in the handwriting of the testator is called a **holographic will** (sometimes referred to as an *olographic will*).

In some cases, oral wills are found valid. A **nuncupative will** is an oral will made before witnesses. It is not permitted in most states. Where authorized by statute, such wills are generally valid only if made during the last illness of the testator and are therefore sometimes referred to as *deathbed wills*. Normally, only personal property can be transferred by a nuncupative will. Statutes frequently permit soldiers and sailors to make nuncupative wills when on active duty.

Signature Requirements It is a fundamental requirement that the testator's signature appear, generally at the end of the will. Each jurisdiction dictates by statute and court decision what constitutes a signature. Initials, an X or other mark, and words such as "Mom" have all been upheld as valid when it was shown that the testators *intended* them to be signatures.

ON THE WEB
To find the wills of over one hundred famous people from 1493 to the present, go to www.ca-probate.com/wills.

Witness Requirements Unless a will is a holograph will, it must be attested (sworn to) by two, and sometimes three, witnesses. The number of witnesses, their qualifications, and the manner in which the witnessing must be done are generally set out in a statute. A witness can be required to be disinterested—that is, not a beneficiary under the will. The UPC, however, provides that a will is valid even if it is attested by an interested witness [UPC 2–505]. There are no age requirements for witnesses, but witnesses must be mentally competent.

The purpose of witnesses is to verify that the testator actually executed (signed) the will and had the requisite intent and capacity at the time. A witness does not have to read the contents of the will. Usually, the testator and all witnesses must sign in the sight or the presence of one another, but the UPC deems it sufficient if the testator acknowledges his or her signature to the witnesses [UPC 2–502]. The UPC does not require all parties to sign in the presence of one another.

Publication Requirements A will is *published* by an oral declaration by the maker to the witnesses that the document they are about to sign is his or her "last will and testament." Publication is becoming an unnecessary formality in most states, and it is not required under the UPC.

Undue Influence

> **¡DON'T FORGET!**
> Undue influence can also occur in the making of a contract. The essential feature in all situations is that the party of whom advantage is taken does not exercise free will.

A valid will is one that represents the maker's intention to transfer and distribute his or her property. When it can be shown that the decedent's plan of distribution was the result of improper pressure brought by another person, the will is declared invalid. Undue influence may be inferred by the court if the testator ignored blood relatives and named as beneficiary a nonrelative who was in constant close contact and in a position to influence the making of the will. For example, if a nurse or friend caring for the deceased at the time of death was named as beneficiary to the exclusion of all family members, the validity of the will might well be challenged on the basis of undue influence.

Revocation of Wills

An executed will is revocable by the maker at any time during the maker's lifetime. The maker may revoke a will by a physical act, such as tearing up the will, or by a subsequent writing. Wills can also be revoked by operation of law. Revocation can be partial or complete, and it must follow certain strict formalities.

Revocation by a Physical Act of the Maker A testator may revoke a will by intentionally burning, tearing, canceling, obliterating, or otherwise destroying it, or by having someone else do so in the presence of the maker and at the maker's direction.[2] In some states, partial revocation by physical act of the maker is recognized. Thus, those portions of a will lined out or torn away are dropped, and the remaining parts of the will are valid. In no circumstances, however, can a provision be crossed out and an additional or substitute provision written in. Such altered portions require reexecution (re-signing) and reattestation (rewitnessing).

To revoke a will by physical act, it is necessary to follow the mandates of a state statute exactly. When a state statute prescribes the exact methods for revoking a will by physical act, those are the only methods that will revoke the will.

• CODICIL
A written supplement or modification to a will. A codicil must be executed with the same formalities as a will.

Revocation by a Subsequent Writing A will may also be wholly or partially revoked by a **codicil,** a written instrument separate from the will that amends or revokes provisions in the will. A codicil eliminates the necessity of redrafting an entire will merely to add to it or amend it. It can also be used to revoke an entire will. The codicil must be executed with the same formalities required for a will, and it must refer expressly to the will. In effect, it updates a will, because the will is "incorporated by reference" into the codicil.

A new will (second will) can be executed that may or may not revoke the first or a prior will, depending on the language used. To revoke a prior will, the second will must use language specifically revoking other wills, such as, "This will hereby revokes all prior wills." If the second will is otherwise valid and properly executed, it will revoke all prior wills. If the express *declaration of revocation* is missing, then both wills are read together. If any of the dispositions made in the second will are inconsistent with the prior will, the second will controls.

Revocation by Operation of Law Revocation by *operation of law* occurs when marriage, divorce or annulment, or the birth of a child takes place after a will has

2. The destruction cannot be inadvertent. The maker's intent to revoke must be shown. Consequently, when a will has been burned or torn accidentally, it is normally recommended that the maker have a new document created so that it will not falsely appear that the maker intended to revoke the will.

been executed. In most states, when a testator marries after executing a will that does not include the new spouse, on the testator's death the spouse can still receive the amount he or she would have taken had the testator died intestate (how an intestate's property is distributed under state laws will be discussed shortly). In effect, this revokes the will to the point of providing the spouse with an intestate share. The rest of the estate is passed under the will [UPC 2–301, 2–508]. If, however, the new spouse is otherwise provided for in the will (or by transfer of property outside the will), the new spouse will not be given an intestate amount.

At common law and under the UPC, divorce does not necessarily revoke the entire will. A divorce or an annulment occurring after a will has been executed will revoke those dispositions of property made under the will to the former spouse [UPC 2–508].

If a child is born after a will has been executed and if it appears that the deceased parent would have made a provision for the child, then the child is entitled to receive whatever portion of the estate he or she is allowed under state laws providing for the distribution of an intestate's property. Most state laws allow a child to receive some portion of a parent's estate if no provision is made in the parent's will, unless it appears from the terms of the will that the testator intended to disinherit the child. Under the UPC, the rule is the same.

INTESTACY LAWS

"Land was never lost for want of an heir."

(ENGLISH PROVERB)

As mentioned, state intestacy laws determine how property will be distributed when a person dies intestate (without a valid will). These statutes are more formally known as *statutes of descent and distribution.* Intestacy laws attempt to carry out the likely intent and wishes of the decedent. These laws assume that deceased persons would have intended that their natural heirs (spouses, children, grandchildren, or other family members) inherit their property. Therefore, intestacy statutes set out rules and priorities under which these heirs inherit the property. If no heirs exist, the state will assume ownership of the property. The rules of descent vary widely from state to state.

Surviving Spouse and Children Usually, state statutes provide that first the debts of the decedent must be satisfied out of his or her estate, and then the remaining assets will pass to the surviving spouse and to the children. A surviving spouse usually receives only a share of the estate—one-half if there is also a surviving child and one-third if there are two or more children. Only if no children or grandchildren survive the decedent will a surviving spouse succeed to the entire estate.

• **EXAMPLE 42.2** Assume that Allen dies intestate and is survived by his wife, Della, and his children, Duane and Tara. Allen's property passes according to intestacy laws. After Allen's outstanding debts are paid, Della will receive the homestead (either in fee simple or as a life estate) and ordinarily a one-third interest in all other property. The remaining real and personal property will pass to Duane and Tara in equal portions. • Under most state intestacy laws and under the UPC, in-laws do not share in an estate. If a child dies before his or her parents, the child's spouse will not receive an inheritance on the parents' death. For example, if Duane died before his father (Allen), Duane's spouse would not inherit Duane's share of Allen's estate.

When there is no surviving spouse or child, the order of inheritance is grandchildren, then brothers and sisters, and in some states, parents of the decedent. These relatives are usually called *lineal descendants.* If there are no lineal descendants, then *collateral heirs*—nieces, nephews, aunts, and uncles of the decedent—make up the next group to share. If there are no survivors in any of these groups, most statutes provide for the property to be distributed among the next of kin of the collateral heirs.

Stepchildren, Adopted Children, and Illegitimate Children Under intestacy laws, stepchildren are not considered kin. Legally adopted children, however, are recognized as lawful heirs of their adoptive parents. Statutes vary from state to state in regard to the inheritance laws governing illegitimate children. Generally, an illegitimate child is treated as the child of the mother and can inherit from her and her relatives. The child is usually not regarded as the legal child of the father with the right of inheritance unless paternity is established through some legal proceeding prior to the father's death. The following *Landmark in the Law* discusses a leading case in regard to the rights of illegitimate children.

Landmark in the Law • *TRIMBLE v. GORDON* (1977)

At common law, the illegitimate child was regarded as a *filius nullius* (Latin for "child of no one") and had no right to inherit. Over time, this attitude changed. A landmark case in establishing the rights of illegitimate children in the United States was decided by the United States Supreme Court in 1977. In *Trimble v. Gordon,*[a] an illegitimate child sought to inherit property from her deceased natural father on the ground that an Illinois statute prohibiting inheritance by illegitimate children in the absence of a will was unconstitutional.

The child was Deta Mona Trimble, daughter of Jessie Trimble and Sherman Gordon. The paternity of the father had been established before a Cook County, Illinois, circuit court in 1973. Gordon died intestate in 1974. The mother filed a petition on behalf of the child in the probate division of the county circuit court; the petition was denied by the court on the basis of an Illinois law disallowing the child's inheritance because she was illegitimate. Had she been legitimate, she would have been her father's sole heir. The Illinois Supreme Court in 1975 affirmed the petition's dismissal.

When the case came before the United States Supreme Court in 1977, the Court acknowledged that the "judicial task here is the difficult one of vindicating constitutional rights without interfering unduly with the State's primary responsibility in this area . . . [a]nd the need for the States to draw 'arbitrary lines . . . to facilitate potentially difficult problems of proof.'" The Court held that the section of the Illinois Probate Act that forbade Deta Mona Trimble to inherit her father's property was unconstitutional, because it "cannot be squared with the command of the Equal Protection Clause of the Fourteenth Amendment." The Court "expressly considered and rejected the argument that a State may attempt to influence the actions of men and women by imposing sanctions on the children born of their illegitimate relationships."

By declaring the Illinois statute unconstitutional, the Court invalidated similar laws of several other states. That does not mean that all illegitimate children will have inheritance rights identical to those of legitimate children. Those state statutes that discriminate between the two classes for legitimate state purposes have been thus far allowed to stand, in the interests of each state's need to create an appropriate legal framework for the legal disposition of property at death.[b]

a. 430 U.S. 762, 97 S.Ct. 1459, 52 L.Ed.2d 31 (1977).
b. UPC 2–109; *White v. Randolph,* 59 Ohio St.2d 6, 391 N.E.2d 333 (1979).

FOR CRITICAL ANALYSIS
Can there ever be a legitimate state purpose for discriminating between legitimate and illegitimate children? Explain.

Distribution to Grandchildren When an intestate is survived by descendants of deceased children, a question arises as to what share these descendants (that is, grandchildren of the intestate) will receive. ***Per stirpes*** is a method of dividing an intestate share by which, within a class or group of distributees (for example, grandchildren), the children of any one descendant take the share that their deceased parent *would have been* entitled to inherit.

• ***PER STIRPES***
A Latin term meaning "by the roots." In the law governing estate distribution, a method of distributing an intestate's estate in which each heir in a certain class (such as grandchildren) takes the share to which his or her deceased ancestor (such as a mother or father) would have been entitled.

EXHIBIT 42–4 • *Per Stirpes* Distribution

Under this method of distribution, an heir takes the share that his or her deceased parent would have been entitled to inherit, had the parent lived. This may mean that a class of distributees—the grandchildren in this example—will not inherit in equal portions. Note that Becky and Holly only receive one-fourth of Michael's estate while Paul inherits one-half.

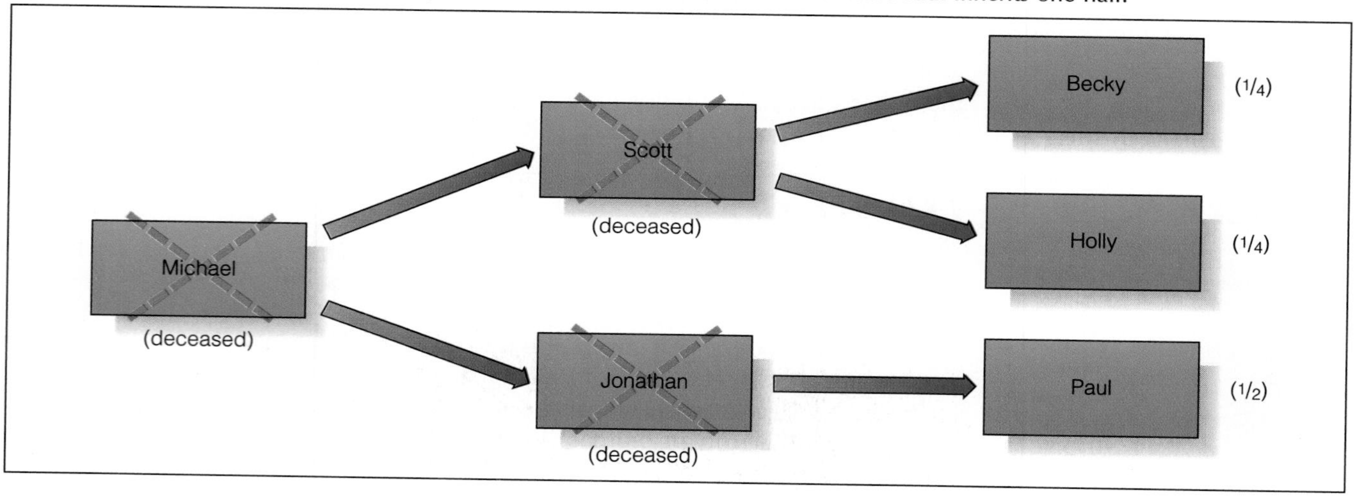

• **PER CAPITA**
A Latin term meaning "per person." In the law governing estate distribution, a method of distributing the property of an intestate's estate in which each heir in a certain class (such as grandchildren) receives an equal share.

• **EXAMPLE 42.3** Assume that Michael, a widower, has two children, Scott and Jonathan. Scott has two children (Becky and Holly), and Jonathan has one child (Paul). Scott and Jonathan die before their father, and then Michael dies. If Michael's estate is distributed *per stirpes,* Becky and Holly will each receive one-fourth of the estate (dividing Scott's one-half share). Paul will receive one-half of the estate (taking Jonathan's one-half share). Exhibit 42–4 illustrates the *per stirpes* method of distribution. •

An estate may also be distributed on a ***per capita*** basis, which means that each person in a class or group takes an equal share of the estate. If Michael's estate is distributed *per capita,* Becky, Holly, and Paul will each receive a one-third share. Exhibit 42–5 illustrates the *per capita* method of distribution.

Trusts

• **TRUST**
An arrangement in which title to property is held by one person (a trustee) for the benefit of another (a beneficiary).

"Put not your trust in money, but put your money in trust."
OLIVER WENDELL HOLMES, JR., 1841–1935
(Associate justice of the United States Supreme Court, 1902–1932)

A **trust** is any arrangement through which property is transferred from one person to a trustee to be administered for the transferor's or another party's benefit. It can also be defined as a right or property, real or personal, held by one party for the benefit of another. A trust can be created for any purpose that is not illegal or against public policy. Its essential elements are as follows:

1. A designated beneficiary.
2. A designated trustee.
3. A fund sufficiently identified to enable title to pass to the trustee.
4. Actual delivery by the settlor or grantor to the trustee with the intention of passing title.

If James conveys his farm to the First Bank of Minnesota to be held for the benefit of his daughters, he has created a trust. James is the settlor, the First Bank of Minnesota is the trustee, and James's daughters are the beneficiaries. This arrange-

EXHIBIT 42–5 • *Per Capita* Distribution

Under this method of distribution, all heirs in a certain class—in this case, the grandchildren—inherit equally. Note that Becky and Holly in this situation each inherit one-third, as does Paul.

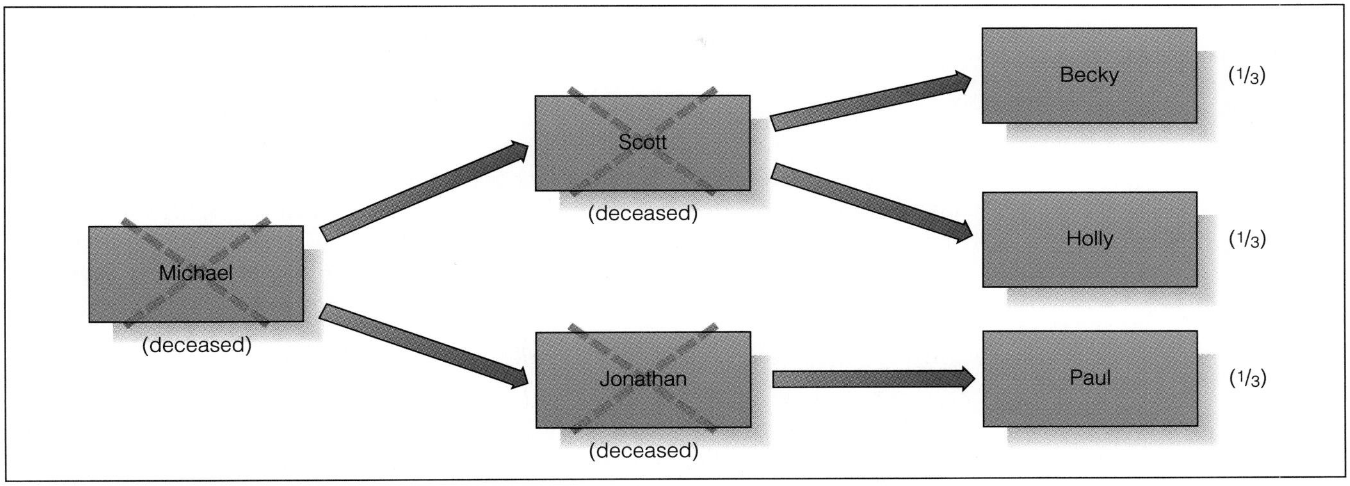

ment is illustrated in Exhibit 42–6. Numerous types of trusts can be established. In this section, we look at some of the major types of trusts and their characteristics.

Express Trusts

An *express trust* is one created or declared in explicit terms, usually in writing. Express trusts fall into two categories: *inter vivos* (living) *trusts* and *testamentary trusts* (trusts provided for in a last will and testament).

• ***INTER VIVOS* TRUST**
A trust created by the grantor (settlor) and effective during the grantor's lifetime; a trust not established by a will.

An ***inter vivos* trust** is a trust executed by a grantor during his or her lifetime. The grantor (settlor) executes a *trust deed,* and legal title to the trust property passes to the named trustee. The trustee has a duty to administer the property as directed by the grantor for the benefit and in the interest of the beneficiaries. The trustee must

EXHIBIT 42–6 • Trust Arrangement

In a trust, there is a separation of interests in the trust property. The trustee takes *legal* title, which is the complete ownership and possession but which does not include the right to receive any benefits from the property. The beneficiary takes *equitable* title, which is the right to receive benefits from the property.

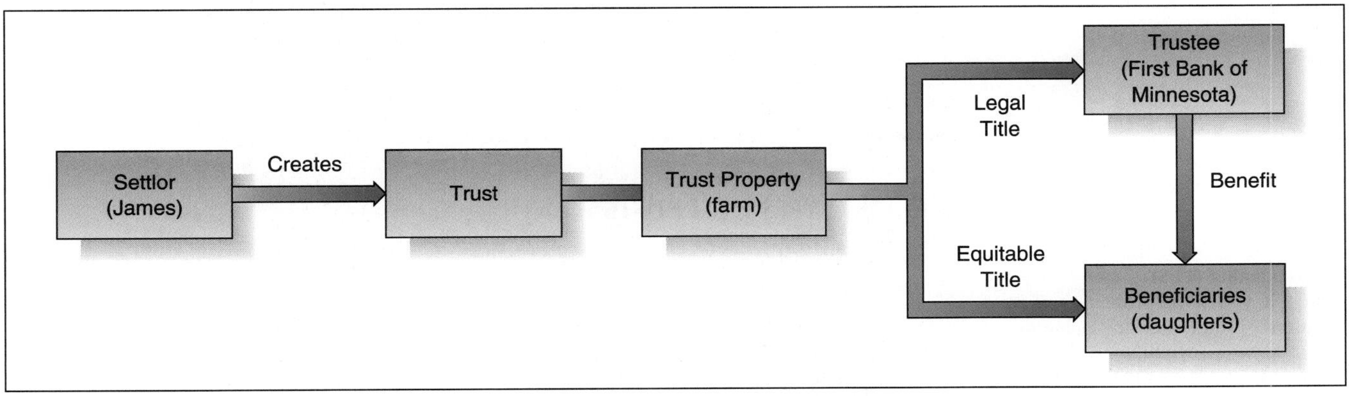

preserve the trust property, make it productive, and if required by the terms of the trust agreement, pay income to the beneficiaries, all in accordance with the terms of the trust. Once the *inter vivos* trust is created, the grantor has, in effect, given over the property for the benefit of the beneficiaries. Often, tax-related benefits exist in setting up this type of trust.

• **TESTAMENTARY TRUST**
A trust that is created by will and therefore does not take effect until the death of the testator.

A **testamentary trust** is a trust created by a will to come into existence on the settlor's death. Although a testamentary trust has a trustee who maintains legal title to the trust property, actions of the trustee are subject to judicial approval. This trustee can be named in the will or be appointed by the court. Thus, a testamentary trust does not fail because a trustee has not been named in the will. The legal responsibilities of the trustee are the same as in an *inter vivos* trust. If the will setting up a testamentary trust is invalid, then the trust will also be invalid. The property that was supposed to be in the trust will then pass according to intestacy laws, not according to the terms of the trust.

Implied Trusts

Sometimes, a trust will be imposed (implied) by law, even in the absence of an express trust. Implied trusts include resulting trusts and constructive trusts.

• **RESULTING TRUST**
An implied trust arising from the conduct of the parties. A trust in which a party holds the actual legal title to another's property but only for that person's benefit.

A **resulting trust** arises from the conduct of the parties. Here, the trust results, or is created, when circumstances raise an inference that the party holding legal title to the property does so for the benefit of another. • **Example 42.4** Suppose that Garrison wants to put one acre of land she owns on the market for sale. Because she is going out of the country for two years and would not be able to deed the property to a buyer during that period, Garrison conveys the property to her good friend Oswald. Oswald will attempt to sell the property while Garrison is gone. Because the intent of the transaction to convey the property to Oswald is neither a sale nor a gift, the property will be held in trust (a resulting trust) by Oswald for the benefit of Garrison. Therefore, on Garrison's return, Oswald will be required either to deed back the property to Garrison or, if the property has been sold, to turn over the proceeds (held in trust) to Garrison. Here, the trust arises (*results from*) the *apparent intention* of the parties. •

• **CONSTRUCTIVE TRUST**
An equitable trust that is imposed in the interests of fairness and justice when someone wrongfully holds legal title to property. A court may require the owner to hold the property in trust for the person or persons who rightfully should own the property.

A **constructive trust** is an equitable trust imposed in the interests of fairness and justice. If someone wrongfully holds legal title to property—for example, if the property was obtained through fraud or in breach of a legal duty—a court may require that owner to hold the property in trust for the person or persons who rightfully should own the property. • **Example 42.5** Suppose that Kraft is a partner in a partnership that purchases and develops real estate. Kraft learns in a partners' meeting that the partnership is considering the purchase of a vacant lot that will soon come on the market. Kraft secretly purchases the property in his own name, thus violating his fiduciary duty of loyalty to the partnership. If the partnership discovers what Kraft has done and brings a legal action against Kraft, a court may impose a constructive trust, thus requiring Kraft to hold the property in trust for the partnership. •

Special Types of Trusts

• **CHARITABLE TRUST**
A trust in which the property held by a trustee must be used for a charitable purpose, such as the advancement of health, education, or religion.

Certain trusts are created for special purposes. Three of these trusts that warrant discussion are charitable, spendthrift, and Totten trusts. A trust designed for the benefit of a segment of the public or of the public in general is a **charitable trust.** Usually, to be deemed a charitable trust, a trust must be created for charitable, educational, religious, or scientific purposes.

• SPENDTHRIFT TRUST
A trust created to protect the beneficiary from spending all the funds to which he or she is entitled. Only a certain portion of the total amount is given to the beneficiary at any one time, and most states prohibit creditors from attaching assets of the trust.

• TOTTEN TRUST
A trust created by the deposit of a person's own funds in his or her own name as a trustee for another. It is a tentative trust, revocable at will until the depositor dies or completes the gift in his or her lifetime by some unequivocal act or declaration.

A trust created to provide for the maintenance of a beneficiary by preventing his or her improvidence with the bestowed funds is a **spendthrift trust.** Essentially, the beneficiary is permitted to draw only a certain portion of the total amount to which he or she is entitled at any one time. The majority of states allow spendthrift trust provisions that prohibit creditors from attaching such trusts.

A **Totten trust**[3] is created when one person deposits funds in his or her own name as a trustee for another. This trust is tentative in that it is revocable at will until the depositor dies or completes the gift in his or her lifetime by some unequivocal act or declaration (for example, delivery of the funds to the intended beneficiary). If the depositor should die before the beneficiary dies and if the depositor has not revoked the trust expressly or impliedly, the beneficiary obtains property rights to the balance on hand.

3. This type of trust derives its unusual name from *In the Matter of Totten,* 179 N.Y. 112, 71 N.E. 748 (1904).

APPLICATION: Law & the Partner or Shareholder: Key-Person Insurance*

Life insurance on the lives of partners or shareholders may be a valuable tool for those who are partners in a partnership or shareholders in a closely held corporation. Typically, should one partner or co-shareholder die, the others will want to buy that person's interest, particularly if they wish to continue in the business. The partnership or corporation may wish to purchase key-person life insurance on each partner or shareholder to help fund the buyout. Problems arise, however, when the partners or co-shareholders are not all the same age or do not all have the same financial interest in the partnership or corporation. How does one arrange an insurance and buyout agreement that is fair to everyone?

If you are a partner or a shareholder in a close corporation, you must first determine the current value of the business and then provide a method for determining the value of the business when one of the owners dies. There are numerous ways to accomplish such a valuation. The important point is that all of the partners or shareholders agree on the method to be used. Each participant must be satisfied that if he or she is the first to die, the valuation method will provide a fair and equitable way to buy that interest from the estate.

*This *Application* is not meant to substitute for the services of an attorney who is licensed to practice law in your state.

Next, you must determine how much life insurance to purchase. Insurance can be used to fund the entire amount of the purchase price of the deceased's interest in the firm or just a part of that purchase price. Because the premiums for some of the owners may cost more (due to more advanced age or poorer health), an agreement may be reached to buy less insurance for them to reduce the current cost of the life insurance policy. The agreement could specify that the remaining part of the buyout purchase price would be paid to the deceased's heirs in the form of installments, including interest payments at current interest rates.

Owners can negotiate a variety of payment plans to fit the needs of each partner or shareholder in the event a buyout becomes necessary. For example, for an older partner, the payments may be spread over only a few years, and for younger partners, over a longer period of time. All of these points are negotiable. It should be possible to draft an agreement that provides for insurance and/or a buyout purchase plan that protects the interest of each person.

CHECKLIST FOR PARTNERS AND CLOSE CORPORATION SHAREHOLDERS

1. If anyone in your partnership or closely held corporation can be considered a key person, then you should probably buy key-person life insurance on that individual.
2. Estimate the amount of loss that the partnership or closely held corporation would suffer if a key person died or became incapacitated. Insure that person for only that amount (the partnership or close corporation should not benefit from a partner's or shareholder's death but rather be left in an equal financial position compared with its position prior to the death).
3. Establish a buyout purchase plan for the partnership or close corporation members in the event of one key person's death.

Key Terms

administrator 1086
bequest 1086
binder 1082
charitable trust 1096
codicil 1091
constructive trust 1096
devise 1086
devisee 1086
executor 1086
holographic will 1090
insurable interest 1080
insurance 1078
inter vivos trust 1095
intestacy laws 1086
intestate 1086
legacy 1086
legatee 1086
nuncupative will 1090
per capita 1094
per stirpes 1093
policy 1078
premium 1078
resulting trust 1096
risk 1078
risk management 1078
spendthrift trust 1097
testamentary trust 1096
testator 1086
Totten trust 1097
trust 1094
underwriter 1078
will 1085

Chapter Summary • Insurance, Wills, and Trusts

INSURANCE	
Classifications (See pages 1078–1079.)	See Exhibit 42–1.
Terminology (See pages 1078–1080.)	1. *Policy*—The insurance contract. 2. *Premium*—The consideration paid to the insurer for a policy. 3. *Underwriter*—The insurance company. 4. *Parties*—Include the insurer (the insurance company), the insured (the person covered by insurance), an agent (a representative of the insurance company) or a broker (ordinarily an independent contractor), and a beneficiary (a person to receive proceeds under the policy).
Insurable Interest (See page 1080.)	An insurable interest exists whenever an individual or entity benefits from the preservation of the health or life of the insured or the property to be insured. For life insurance, an insurable interest must exist at the time the policy is issued. For property insurance, an insurable interest must exist at the time of the loss.
The Insurance Contract (See pages 1081–1085.)	1. *Laws governing*—The general principles of contract law are applied; the insurance industry is also heavily regulated by the states. 2. *Application*—An insurance applicant is bound by any false statements that appear in the application (subject to certain exceptions), which is part of the insurance contract. Misstatements or misrepresentations may be grounds for voiding the policy. 3. *Effective date*—Coverage on an insurance policy can begin when the *binder* (a written memorandum indicating that a formal policy is pending and stating its essential terms) is written; when the policy is issued; at the time of contract formation; or depending on the terms of the contract, when certain conditions are met.

Chapter Summary • Insurance, Wills, and Trusts, Continued

The Insurance Contract—continued	4. *Provisions and clauses*—See Exhibit 42–2. Words will be given their ordinary meanings, and any ambiguity in the policy will be interpreted against the insurance company. When the written policy has not been delivered and it is unclear whether an insurance contract actually exists, the uncertainty will be determined against the insurance company. The court will presume that the policy is in effect unless the company can show otherwise. 5. *Defenses against payment to the insured*—Defenses include misrepresentation, fraud, or violation of warranties by the applicant.
	WILLS
Terminology (See pages 1085–1086.)	1. *Intestate*—One who dies without a valid will. 2. *Testator*—A person who makes out a will. 3. *Personal representative*—A person appointed in a will or by a court to settle the affairs of a decedent. A personal representative named in the will is an *executor;* a personal representative appointed by the court for an intestate decedent is an *administrator.* 4. *Devise*—A gift of real estate by will; may be general or specific. The recipient of a devise is a *devisee.* 5. *Bequest, or legacy*—A gift of personal property by will; may be general or specific. The recipient of a bequest (legacy) is a *legatee.*
Probate Procedures (See page 1088.)	To probate a will means to establish its validity and to carry the administration of the estate through a court process. Probate laws vary from state to state. Probate procedures may be informal or formal, depending on the size of the estate and other factors, such as whether a guardian for minor children must be appointed.
Requirements for a Valid Will (See pages 1088–1091.)	1. The testator must have testamentary capacity (be of legal age and sound mind at the time the will is made). 2. A will must be in writing (except for nuncupative wills). A holographic will is completely in the handwriting of the testator. 3. A will must be signed by the testator; what constitutes a signature varies from jurisdiction to jurisdiction. 4. A nonholographic will (an attested will) must be witnessed in the manner prescribed by state statute. 5. A will may have to be *published*—that is, the testator may be required to announce to witnesses that this is his or her "last will and testament." Not required under the UPC.
Revocation of Wills (See pages 1091–1092.)	1. *By physical act of the maker*—Tearing up, canceling, obliterating, or deliberately destroying part or all of a will. 2. *By subsequent writing*— a. Codicil—A formal, separate document to amend or revoke an existing will. b. Second will or new will—A new, properly executed will expressly revoking the existing will. 3. *By operation of law*— a. Marriage—Generally revokes part of a will written before the marriage. b. Divorce or annulment—Revokes dispositions of property made under a will to a former spouse. c. Subsequently born child—It is *implied* that the child is entitled to receive the portion of the estate granted under intestacy distribution laws.
Intestacy Laws (See pages 1092–1094.)	1. Vary widely from state to state. Usually, the law provides that the surviving spouse and children inherit the property of the decedent (after the decedent's debts are paid). The spouse usually will inherit the entire estate if there are no children, one-half of the estate if there is one child, and one-third of the estate if there are two or more children.

Chapter Summary, Continued

Intestacy Laws —continued	2. If there is no surviving spouse or child, then, in order, lineal descendants (grandchildren, brothers and sisters, and—in some states—parents of the decedent) inherit. If there are no lineal descendants, then collateral heirs (nieces, nephews, aunts, and uncles of the decedent) inherit.
	TRUSTS
Definition (See pages 1094–1095.)	A trust is any arrangement through which property is transferred from one person to be administered by a trustee for another party's benefit. The essential elements of a trust are (1) a designated beneficiary, (2) a designated trustee, (3) a fund sufficiently identified to enable title to pass to the trustee, and (4) actual delivery to the trustee with the intention of passing title.
Express Trusts (See pages 1095–1096.)	Express trusts are created by expressed terms, usually in writing, and fall into two categories: 1. *Inter vivos trust*—A trust executed by a grantor during his or her lifetime. 2. *Testamentary trust*—A trust created by will and coming into existence on the death of the grantor.
Implied Trusts (See page 1096.)	Implied trusts, which are imposed by law in the interests of fairness and justice, include the following: 1. *Resulting trust*—Arises from the conduct of the parties when an *apparent intention* to create a trust is present. 2. *Constructive trust*—Arises by operation of law whenever a transaction takes place in which the person who takes title to property is in equity not entitled to enjoy the beneficial interest therein.
Special Types of Trusts (See pages 1096–1097.)	1. *Charitable trust*—A trust designed for the benefit of a public group or the public in general. 2. *Spendthrift trust*—A trust created to provide for the maintenance of a beneficiary by allowing only a certain portion of the total amount to be received by the beneficiary at any one time. 3. *Totten trust*—A trust created when one person deposits funds in his or her own name as a trustee for another.

For Review

1 What is an insurable interest? To obtain life insurance, when must an insurable interest exist—at the time that the policy is obtained, at the time that the loss occurs, or both? To obtain property insurance, when must an insurable interest exist—at the time that the policy is obtained, at the time that the loss occurs, or both?

2 Is an insurance broker the agent of the insurance applicant or the agent of the insurer? If the broker accepts an applicant's initial premium but fails to obtain coverage, and the applicant is damaged as a result, who may be liable for the damage?

3 Who can make a will? What are the basic requirements for executing a will? How may a will be revoked?

4 What is the difference between a *per stirpes* and a *per capita* distribution of an estate to the grandchildren of the deceased?

5 What are the four essential elements of a trust? What is an express trust? How do implied trusts arise?

Questions and Case Problems

42–1. Timing of Insurance Coverage. On October 10, Joleen Vora applied for a $50,000 life insurance policy with Magnum Life Insurance Co.; she named her husband, Jay, as the beneficiary. Joleen paid the insurance company the first year's policy premium on making the application. Two days later, before she had a chance to take the physical examination required by the insurance company and before the policy was issued, Joleen was killed in an automobile accident. Jay submitted a claim to the insurance company for the $50,000. Can Jay collect? Explain.

42–2. Validity of Wills. Merlin Winters had three sons. Merlin and his youngest son, Abraham, had a falling out in 1994 and had not spoken to each other since. Merlin made a formal will in 1996, leaving all his property to the two older children and deliberately excluding Abraham. Merlin's health began to deteriorate, and by 1997 he was under the full-time care of a nurse, Julia. In 1998, he made a new will expressly revoking the 1996 will and leaving all his property to Julia. On Merlin's death, the two older children contested the 1998 will, claiming that Julia had exercised undue influence over their father. Abraham claimed that both wills were invalid, because the first one had been revoked by the second will, and the second will was invalid on the ground of undue influence. Is Abraham's contention correct? Explain.

42–3. Wills. Gary Mendel drew up a will in which he left his favorite car, a 1966 red Ferrari, to his daughter, Roberta. A year prior to his death, Mendel sold the 1966 Ferrari and purchased a 1969 Ferrari. Discuss whether Roberta will inherit the 1969 Ferrari under the terms of her father's will.

42–4. Estate Distribution. Benjamin is a widower who has two married children, Edward and Patricia. Patricia has two children, Perry and Paul. Edward has no children. Benjamin dies, and his typewritten will leaves all his property equally to his children, Edward and Patricia, and provides that should a child predecease him, the grandchildren are to take *per stirpes*. The will was witnessed by Patricia and by Benjamin's lawyer and was signed by Benjamin in their presence. Patricia has predeceased Benjamin. Edward claims the will is invalid.

(a) Discuss whether the will is valid.
(b) Discuss the distribution of Benjamin's estate if the will is invalid.
(c) Discuss the distribution of Benjamin's estate if the will is valid.

42–5. Validity of Wills. An elderly, childless widow had nine nieces and nephews. Her will divided her entire estate equally among two nieces and the husband of one of the nieces, who was also the attorney who drafted the will and the executor named in the will. The testator was definitely of sound mind when the will was executed. If you were one of the seven nieces or nephews omitted from the will, could you think of any way to have the will invalidated? [*Estate of Eckert*, 93 Misc.2d 677, 403 N.Y.S.2d 633 (Surrogate's Ct. 1978)]

42–6. Insurer's Defenses. Kirk Johnson applied for life insurance with New York Life Insurance Co. on October 7, 1986. In answer to a question about smoking habits, Johnson stated that he had not smoked in the past twelve months and that he had never smoked cigarettes. In fact, Johnson had smoked for thirteen years, and during the month prior to the insurance application, he was smoking approximately ten cigarettes per day. Johnson died on July 17, 1988, for reasons unrelated to smoking. Johnson's father, Lawrence Johnson, who was the beneficiary of the policy, filed a claim for the insurance proceeds. While investigating the claim, New York Life discovered Kirk Johnson's misrepresentation and denied the claim. The company canceled the policy and sent Lawrence Johnson a check for the premiums that had been paid. Lawrence Johnson refused to accept the check, and New York Life brought an action for a declaratory judgment (a court determination of a plaintiff's rights). What should the court decide? Discuss fully. [*New York Life Insurance Co. v. Johnson*, 923 F.2d 279 (3d Cir. 1991)]

42–7. Validity of Wills. In the last fourteen years of Evelyn Maheras's life, William Cook, a Baptist pastor, became her spiritual adviser and close personal friend. Cook—and no one else—actively participated in helping Maheras draft her will. He gave Maheras a church-sponsored booklet on will drafting, recommended an attorney (a church member) to do the drafting, and reviewed the terms of the will with Maheras. When Maheras died, she left most of her estate to Cook's church. Cook personally received nothing under the will. Maheras's nephew and only heir, Richard Suagee, filed a suit against Cook in an Oklahoma state court to contest the will, arguing that Cook unduly influenced Maheras. Can a party who receives nothing under a will be regarded as having exercised undue influence over the testator? What should the court in Maheras's case do? [*Estate of Maheras*, 897 P.2d 268 (Okla. 1995)]

42–8. Interpretation of an Insurance Contract's Terms. RLI Insurance Co. issued an insurance policy to Richard Brown to cover his aircraft. One provision of the policy excluded coverage for a "resident spouse." A different provision included coverage for "any passenger." Richard was piloting the aircraft, with his wife, Janet, as a passenger, when it crashed. Richard was killed, and Janet was injured. At the time, Janet and Richard had been living together. Janet filed a suit in a federal district court to collect under the policy for her injuries. RLI claimed that the policy clearly excluded Janet. Janet argued that the policy was ambiguous. What will the court decide? Why? [*RLI Insurance Co. v. Drollinger*, 97 F.3d 230 (8th Cir. 1996)]

42–9. Adopted Children. Gail MacCallum was the daughter of Anita Seymour. After the death of Gail's father, Anita married Richard Seymour, who adopted Gail the next year, when she was seven years old. The same year, Janet Seymour was born to Richard and Anita. Almost forty years later, when Richard's brother Philip died, both Gail and Janet sought to share in the estate. A Vermont state court concluded that Gail could not share in the estate because a state statute prohibited "inheritance between the person adopted . . . and collateral kin of the person or persons making the adoption." Gail appealed, arguing that the statute was unconstitutional. Will the court agree? Discuss fully. [*MacCallum v. Seymour*, 686 A.2d. 935 (Vt. 1996)]

42–10. Revocation. William Laneer urged his son, also William, to join the family business. The son, who was made partner, became suspicious of the handling of the business's finances. He filed a suit against the business and reported it to the Internal Revenue Service. Laneer then executed a will that disinherited his son, giving him one dollar and leaving the balance of the estate equally to Laneer's four daughters, including Bellinda Barrera. Until his death more than twenty years later, Laneer harbored ill feelings towards his son. After Laneer's death, his original copy of the will could not be found. A photocopy was found in his safe-deposit box, however, and his lawyer's original copy was entered for probate in an Arkansas state court. Barrera, who wanted her brother William to share an equal portion of the inheritance, filed a petition to contest the will. Barrera claimed, among other things, that Laneer had revoked the will, and that was why his original copy of the will could not be found. Was the will revoked? If so, to whom would the estate be distributed? [*Barrera v. Vanpelt,* 332 Ark. 482, 965 S.W.2d 780 (1998)]

A QUESTION OF ETHICS AND SOCIAL RESPONSIBILITY

42–11. Heber Burke and his wife Evelyn had been married for fifty-three years. Evelyn died, and about five months later, Heber married Lexie Damron, a widow who attended his church. Seven days after the marriage, Heber executed a will, which was drawn up by Lexie's attorney, in which he left all of his property to Lexie. Heber died three weeks later. Heber's children, Donald Burke and Beatrice Bates, contested the will, alleging that Heber lacked testamentary capacity and that Heber's will resulted from Lexie's undue influence over him. Friends and relatives of Heber testified that they had never known Heber to drink and that, although he seemed saddened by his first wife's death, he was not incapacitated by it. According to the children's witnesses, however, after Evelyn's death, Heber drank heavily and constantly, had frequent crying spells, repeatedly visited his wife's grave, tried to dig her up so that he could talk to her, and had hallucinations. The jury found the will to be invalid on the ground of undue influence, and Lexie appealed. [*Burke v. Burke,* 801 S.W.2d 691 (Ken.App. 1990)]

1. The appellate court had to weigh two conflicting policies in deciding this issue. What are these two policies, and what criteria should be used in resolving the issue?
2. Given the circumstances described above, would you infer undue influence on the part of Lexie if you were the judge? Would you conclude that Heber lacked testamentary capacity? What would be the fairest solution, in your opinion?
3. Heber's first wife, Evelyn, contributed substantially to the acquisition of the property subject to Heber's will. A natural assumption would be that Evelyn would want their children to inherit the jointly acquired property. If Heber were found to be of sound mind and not the victim of any undue influence, however, the court would allow him to disregard the children totally, if he wished, in his will. Is this fair to Evelyn's presumed intentions? To the children? Is there any solution to the possible unfairness that can result from giving people the right to disregard natural heirs in their wills?

FOR CRITICAL ANALYSIS

42–12. Statistics show that the extent of risk assumed by insurance companies varies depending on the gender of the insured. Many people contend that laws prohibiting gender-based insurance rates are thus fundamentally unfair. Do you agree with this contention? Why or why not?

Online Activities

ONLINE EXERCISE 42–1

Go to the "Internet Activities Book" on the Web site that accompanies this text, the URL for which is http://blt.westbuslaw.com. Select the following activities, and perform the exercises according to the instructions given there:

Activity 38–1: Employment Practices Insurance
Activity 38–2: Death and Taxes

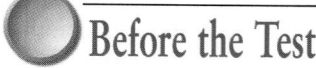

Before the Test

Go to the *Business Law Today* home page at http://blt.westbuslaw.com. Click on TestTutor.® You will find twenty interactive questions relating to this chapter.

Unit Eight • Cumulative Business Hypothetical

Dave graduates from State University with an engineering degree and goes into business as a self-employed computer programmer.

1 To advertise his services on the Internet, Dave creates and produces a short digital video. Hollywood Films, Inc., sees the video and hires Dave to program the special effects for a short sequence in a Hollywood movie. Their contract states that all rights to the sequence belong to Hollywood. Does the digital video, the movie sequence, or both, or neither, belong to Dave?

2 Dave leases an office in Carl's Riverside Plaza office building for a two-year term. What is Dave's obligation for the rent if he moves out before the end of the term? If Dave dies during the term, who is entitled to the possession of the office? What is Dave's obligation for the rent if Carl sells the building to Commercial Investments, Inc., before Dave's lease is up?

3 At the end of the term, Dave buys the office building from Carl, who gives Dave a warranty deed. Commercial Investments later challenges Dave's ownership of the building with its own allegedly valid deed. What will it mean if Dave is held to own the building in fee simple? If Commercial Investments is successful, can Dave recover anything from Carl?

4 Dave's programming business expands, and he hires Mary as an employee. Mary becomes invaluable to the business, and Dave obtains a key-person insurance policy on her life. She dies six years later. If it is discovered that Dave understated Mary's age, when applying for the policy (which includes an incontestability clause), can the insurer legitimately refuse payment? If, one year before Mary died, she resigned to start her own programming firm, can Dave collect payment under the policy?

5 Over time, Dave acquires other commercial property, which eventually becomes the most lucrative part of his business. Dave wants his adult children, Frank and Terry, to get the benefit of this property when he dies. Dave does not think that Frank and Terry can manage the property, however, because they are involved in their own lives in other locations. How can Dave provide for them to get the benefit of the property under someone else's management? In his will, Dave designates Hal, his attorney, executor. What does an executor do?

UNIT EIGHT • EXTENDED CASE STUDY: THE LAW IN CONTEXT

Santa Monica Beach, Ltd. v. Superior Court

We mentioned, in Chapter 41, that the takings clause of the Fifth Amendment of the U.S. Constitution prohibits the government from taking private property for a public use without paying "just compensation." In this extended case study, we examine Santa Monica Beach, Ltd. v. Superior Court,[1] *a recent decision that involved the issue of whether a city's rent control law violated this clause.*

CASE BACKGROUND

The City of Santa Monica, California, adopted a rent control law to set maximum rents. The preamble of the law stated its purpose:

> A growing shortage of housing units resulting in a low vacancy rate and rapidly rising rents exploiting this shortage constitute a serious housing problem affecting the lives of a substantial portion of those Santa Monica residents who reside in residential housing. In addition, speculation in the purchase and sale of existing residential housing units results in further rent increases. These conditions endanger the public health and welfare of Santa Monica tenants, especially the poor, minorities, students, young families, and senior citizens. The purpose of this [law], therefore, is to alleviate the hardship caused by this serious housing shortage by * * * regulat[ing] rentals in the City of Santa Monica so that rents will not be increased unreasonably and so that landlords will receive no more than a fair return.

Santa Monica Beach, Limited (SMB), owned a twelve-unit residential rental property in Santa Monica. When the city denied SMB's request to raise the rent of its units, the landlord filed a suit against the city in a California state court for compensation. SMB argued that the rent control law had failed to achieve its goal of providing affordable housing for low-income renters and had instead, according to statistics, caused "gentrification" (an exodus of low-income renters and an increase in high-income households). By failing to attain its goal, SMB contended, the law failed to advance a legitimate governmental purpose, and in SMB's situation, this violated SMB's rights under the takings clause of the Fifth Amendment.

The court ruled in favor of the city. SMB appealed, and the state intermediate appellate court set aside the trial court's judgment. The city appealed to the California Supreme Court.

1. 19 Cal.4th 952, 968 P. 2d 993, 81 Cal.Rptr.2d 93 (1999).

MAJORITY OPINION

MOSK, J. [Justice].

* * * *

* * * The notion that a court may invalidate legislation that it finds, after a trial, to have failed to live up to expectations, is indeed novel. * * *

* * * *

* * * [SMB] misperceives [the purpose of the rent control law] as only to help the poor, elderly, minorities, and families with children. The Rent Control Law's stated purpose is to help all Santa Monica tenants, not just those within the mentioned groups * * * .

Moreover, there is no constitutional requirement that the inquiry into whether the legislation substantially serves legitimate goals must be limited to stated goals, much less to only some of the stated goals. Legislative bodies have broad scope to experiment with economic problems * * * . [A]ny complex piece of social or economic legislation will often have unanticipated consequences that can be both beneficial and detrimental, and * * * the legislative body or the electorate that enacted the legislation must be entrusted to weigh whatever harms and benefits result from the legislation in determining whether that legislation should be amended or abrogated. There is simply no authority for the proposition that a piece of legislation that advances legitimate goals, but not precisely those goals specified in its preamble, may be struck down by a court as unconstitutional.

* * * *

Our adoption of SMB's position * * * would create formidable practical problems as well. How long would a court, or a litigant, have to wait to give the law a "fair chance" to work before declaring that it is a failure and therefore unconstitutional? There is no answer to this question that would not be arbitrary and would not put courts in a distinctively legislative role.

That is not to say that a change in conditions may never justify the constitutional invalidation of a once valid law. But the circumstances for such invalidation [do not exist in this case].

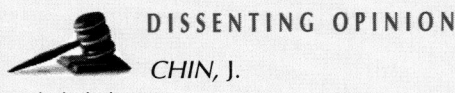

DISSENTING OPINION

CHIN, J.

* * * *

The majority decries as "novel" * * * "[t]he notion that a court may invalidate legislation that it finds, after a trial, to have failed to live up to expectations." * * * But [what the] plaintiff requests here is hardly a new idea. It is simply applying in the context of economic regulation practices that are already quite standard with respect to social and moral regulation.

* * * *

Far from being "novel" * * *, [SMB's claim] simply represents the unremarkable conclusion that, if a regulation deprives someone of private property without substantially advancing its purpose, the government should pay compensation.

MEDIA COVERAGE

The California Supreme Court's ruling in this case was controversial. Here we present excerpts from an article titled "State's High Court Upholds Cities' Rent Control Laws" by Maura Dolan that appeared in the *Los Angeles Times* on January 5, 1999.

"[T]he ruling was a broad victory for California city governments and a major defeat for conservative legal activists.

Sixty-five cities sided with Santa Monica at the court. They feared a decision against rent control could endanger all sorts of economic regulations by subjecting them to judicial second-guessing about whether they were effective in serving the public good.

'You probably heard a collective sigh of relief in city halls all across the state today,' said Loyola Law School professor Karl M. Manheim, who represented Santa Monica. '* * * [T]here have been similar cases filed around the country against * * * other land use regulations.'

* * * *

Conservative legal activists have had a long-standing campaign to strike down economic regulations. They have argued that regulations restricting what a person can do with his or her property should be reviewed by courts with the same level of scrutiny used when governments flatly require a person to give up the property.

'It's been a big campaign,' said John Echeverria, a professor at Georgetown University Law Center who specializes in property rights law. * * * 'This opinion appears to signal that that campaign has been defeated, at least in California.'

The Pacific Legal Foundation, a conservative public interest law firm that represented a Santa Monica landlord in the case, said it will ask the U.S. Supreme Court to review the case."

GOING ONLINE

The *Business Law Today,* Fifth Edition, Web site, at **http://blt.westbuslaw.com**, provides a link through which you can access other court opinions in case involving real property.

QUESTIONS FOR ANALYSIS

1. **Law.** Should the California Supreme Court in this case have taken this opportunity to rule on how to apply the takings clause to all rent control laws?
2. **Law.** Should the court, in its opinion in this case, have addressed the issue of how to apply the takings clause to other property regulations?
3. **Ethics.** What is the ethical basis for a government's regulation of property rights?
4. **International Dimensions.** What are the implications for business firms and investors outside the United States of the decision in this case?
5. **Implications for the Business Manager.** How do rent control ordinances and other price control laws benefit and harm business firms?

Unit Nine

The International Legal Environment

CHAPTER 43

International Law in a Global Economy

> “Our interests are those of the open door—a door of friendship and mutual advantage. This is the only door we care to enter.”
>
> Woodrow Wilson, 1856–1924
> (Twenty-eighth president of the United States, 1913–1921)

CONTENTS

LEARNING OBJECTIVES

After reading this chapter, you should be able to:

1. Identify and discuss some basic principles and doctrines that frame international business transactions.
2. Describe some ways in which U.S. businesspersons do business internationally.
3. Explain how parties to international contracts protect against various risks through contractual clauses and letters of credit.
4. Discuss how specific types of international business activities are regulated by governments.
5. Give examples of the extraterritorial application of certain U.S. laws.

Since ancient times, independent peoples and nations have traded their goods and wares with one another. In other words, international business transactions are not unique to the modern world, because people have always found that they can benefit from exchanging goods with others, as suggested by President Woodrow Wilson's statement in the opening quotation. What is new in our time is that, particularly since World War II, business has become increasingly *multinational.* It is not uncommon, for example, for a U.S. corporation to have investments or manufacturing plants in a foreign country, or for a foreign corporation to have operations within the United States.

Transacting business on an international level is considerably different from transacting business within the boundaries of just one nation. Buyers and sellers face far greater risks in the international marketplace than they do in a domestic context because the laws governing these transactions are more complex and uncertain. For example, the Uniform Commercial Code will govern many disputes that arise between U.S. buyers and sellers of goods unless they have provided otherwise in their contracts. What happens, however, if a U.S. buyer breaches a contract formed with a British seller? What law will govern the dispute—British or American? What if an investor owns substantial assets in a developing nation and the government of that nation decides to nationalize—assert its ownership over—the property? What recourse does the investor have against the actions of a foreign government? Questions such as these, which normally do not arise in a domestic context, can become critical in international business dealings.

Because the exchange of goods, services, and ideas on a global level is now a common activity, the student of business law should be familiar with the laws pertaining to international business transactions. In this chapter, we first examine the legal context of international business transactions. We then look at some selected areas relating to business activities in a global context, including international sales contracts, civil dispute resolution, letters of credit, and investment protection. We conclude the chapter with a discussion of the application of certain U.S. laws in a transnational setting.

International Principles and Doctrines

Recall from our discussion in Chapter 1 that *international law* is a body of written and unwritten laws that are observed by otherwise independent nations and that govern the acts of individuals as well as states. We also discussed in that chapter the major sources of international law, including international customs, treaties between nations, and international organizations and conferences. Here, we look at some other legal principles and doctrines that have evolved over time and that the courts of various nations have employed—to a greater or lesser extent—to resolve or reduce conflicts that involve a foreign element. The three important legal principles and doctrines discussed in the following sections are based primarily on courtesy and respect and are applied in the interests of maintaining harmonious relations among nations.

THE PRINCIPLE OF COMITY

• **COMITY**
A deference by which one nation gives effect to the laws and judicial decrees of another nation. This recognition is based primarily on respect.

Under what is known as the principle of **comity**, one nation will defer and give effect to the laws and judicial decrees of another country, as long as those laws and judicial decrees are consistent with the law and public policy of the accommodating nation. This recognition is based primarily on courtesy and respect.

• **EXAMPLE 43.1** Assume that a Swedish seller and an American buyer have formed a contract, which the buyer breaches. The seller sues the buyer in a Swedish court, which awards damages. The buyer's assets, however, are in the United States and cannot be reached unless the judgment is enforced by a U.S. court of law. In this situation, if it is determined that the procedures and laws applied in the Swedish court were consistent with U.S. national law and policy, a court in the United States will likely defer to (and enforce) the foreign court's judgment. •

THE ACT OF STATE DOCTRINE

• **ACT OF STATE DOCTRINE**
A doctrine that provides that the judicial branch of one country will not examine the validity of public acts committed by a recognized foreign government within its own territory.

The **act of state doctrine** is a judicially created doctrine that provides that the judicial branch of one country will not examine the validity of public acts committed by a recognized foreign government within its own territory. This doctrine is premised on the theory that the judicial branch should not "pass upon the validity of foreign acts when to do so would vex the harmony of our international relations with that foreign nation."[1]

The act of state doctrine can have important consequences for individuals and firms doing business with, and investing in, other countries. For example, this doctrine is frequently employed in cases involving expropriation or confiscation. **Expropriation** occurs when a government seizes a privately owned business or privately owned goods for a proper public purpose and awards just compensation. When a government seizes private property for an illegal purpose or without just compensation, the taking is referred to as a **confiscation.** The line between these two forms of taking is sometimes blurred because of differing interpretations of what is illegal and what constitutes just compensation.

• **EXPROPRIATION**
The seizure by a government of privately owned business or personal property for a proper public purpose and with just compensation.

• **CONFISCATION**
A government's taking of privately owned business or personal property without a proper public purpose or an award of just compensation.

• **EXAMPLE 43.2** Tim Flaherty, an American businessperson, owns a mine in Brazil. The government of Brazil seizes the mine for public use and claims that the profits that Tim has realized from the mine in preceding years constitute just compensation. Tim disagrees, but the act of state doctrine may prevent Tim's recovery in a U.S. court of law. •

When applicable, both the act of state doctrine and the doctrine of sovereign immunity (to be discussed next) tend to immunize foreign nations from the jurisdiction of U.S. courts. What this means is that firms or individuals who own property overseas often have little legal protection against government actions in the countries in which they operate.

The Doctrine of Sovereign Immunity

• **SOVEREIGN IMMUNITY**
A doctrine that immunizes foreign nations from the jurisdiction of U.S. courts when certain conditions are satisfied.

Under certain conditions, the doctrine of **sovereign immunity** immunizes (protects) foreign nations from the jurisdiction of the U.S. courts. In 1976, Congress codified this rule in the Foreign Sovereign Immunities Act (FSIA). The FSIA exclusively governs the circumstances in which an action may be brought in the United States against a foreign nation, including attempts to attach a foreign nation's property.

Section 1605 of the FSIA sets forth the major exceptions to the jurisdictional immunity of a foreign state or country. A foreign state is not immune from the jurisdiction of the courts of the United States when the state has "waived its immunity either explicitly or by implication" or when the action is "based upon a commercial activity carried on in the United States by the foreign state."[2]

Issues frequently arise as to what entities fall within the category of a foreign state. The question of what is a commercial activity has also been the subject of dispute. Under Section 1603 of the FSIA, a *foreign state* is defined to include both a political subdivision of a foreign state and an instrumentality of a foreign state. A *commercial activity* is broadly defined under Section 1603 to mean a commercial activity that is carried out by a foreign state within the United States. The act, however, does not define the particulars of what constitutes a commercial activity. Rather, it is left up to the courts to decide whether a particular activity is governmental or commercial in nature.

ON THE WEB
FindLaw's Web site includes an extensive array of links to international doctrines, treaties, and other nations' laws. Go to www.findlaw.com and select "International Law."

In the following case, a foreign government claimed immunity from the jurisdiction of U.S. courts on the basis of sovereign immunity. The issue turned on whether the actions of the foreign government were commercial activities.

1. *Libra Bank, Ltd. v. Banco Nacional de Costa Rica, S.A.*, 570 F.Supp. 870 (S.D.N.Y. 1983).
2. 28 U.S.C. Section 1605(a)(1), (2).

CASE 43.1 Holden v. Canadian Consulate

United States Court of Appeals,
Ninth Circuit, 1996.
92 F.3d 918.
www.vcilp.org/Fed-Ct/Circuit/9th/August96.html[a]

HISTORICAL AND INTERNATIONAL SETTING *In the early 1990s, the initiating of diplomatic services in more than twenty new countries, mostly in Eastern Europe, and governmental budget cuts forced many nations to reorganize their diplomatic offices. The governments of Australia and Sweden, for example, closed their consulates in Chicago. Similarly, actions by the Canadian government forced Canada's External Affairs Department to close its San Francisco consulate, an office that had been open for almost fifty years. The operations of the Canadian consul in San Francisco were transferred to Los Angeles. Canada continues to maintain its embassy in Washington, D.C., and consulates in eleven other U.S. cities.*

BACKGROUND AND FACTS Canada closed its consulate in San Francisco and laid off many employees, including Arlene Holden, who had worked for thirteen years as one of the consulate's commercial officers. In place of the consulate, Canada opened a small office staffed with only one commercial officer—Mark Ritchie, a man younger and less experienced than Holden. Holden filed a suit in a U.S. district court against the consulate, alleging, among other things, discrimination. The consulate asked the court to dismiss the suit based on sovereign immunity under the Foreign Sovereign Immunities Act (FSIA). The court concluded that the consulate's employment of Holden was a "commercial activity." The consulate appealed.

a. This page lists opinions issued by the U.S. Court of Appeals for the Ninth Circuit in August 1996. Scroll down the list of cases and click on the *Holden* case name to access the opinion in that case. This Web site is maintained by the Center for Information Law and Policy at the Villanova University School of Law.

IN THE WORDS OF THE COURT . . .
LEAVY, Circuit Judge:

* * * *

* * * [T]he [FSIA's] legislative history * * * provides a useful framework for analyzing [commercial activity.] The * * * House Report states, " * * * [A] government's * * * employment or engagement of laborers, clerical staff or public relations or marketing agents * * * would be among those [activities] included within the definition [of commercial activity]."

* * * *

The district court examined the nature of Holden's work to determine if she was a civil servant, and found that she was not. * * * Holden did not compete for any examination prior to being hired, was not entitled to tenure, was not provided the same benefits as foreign service officers and did not receive any civil service protections from the Canadian government. * * *

* * * *

Although Holden * * * was a part of the Consulate's staff, her work was not that of a diplomat. As the district court found, Holden's activities were primarily promoting and marketing and she was not involved in any policy making and was not privy to any governmental policy deliberations. She did not engage in any lobbying activity or legislative work for Canada, and she could not speak for the government. * * * Furthermore, as an American, she was not allowed in the Consulate unless in the company of a foreign service officer.

Her employment is more analogous to a marketing agent. * * * The nature of Holden's work, promotion of products, is regularly done by private persons. As such, her employment was a commercial activity, and thus the Consulate is not entitled to sovereign immunity under the FSIA.

(Continued)

CASE 43.1—Continued

DECISION AND REMEDY The U.S. Court of Appeals for the Ninth Circuit affirmed the lower court's ruling. The appellate court denied the consulate sovereign immunity on the ground that the consulate's employment of Holden was a commercial activity.

FOR CRITICAL ANALYSIS—Political Consideration *Does the "commercial activities" exception to the FSIA conflict with the act of state doctrine?*

Doing Business Internationally

A U.S. domestic firm can engage in international business transactions in a number of ways. The simplest way to engage in international business transactions is to seek out foreign markets for domestically produced products or services. In other words, U.S. firms can look abroad for **export** markets for their goods and services.

• **EXPORT**
To sell products to buyers located in other countries.

Alternatively, a U.S. firm can establish foreign production facilities so as to be closer to the foreign market or markets in which its products are sold. The advantages may include lower labor costs, fewer government regulations, and lower taxes and trade barriers. A domestic firm can obtain revenues through the licensing of technology to an existing foreign company. Yet another way to expand abroad is by selling franchises to overseas entities. The presence of McDonald's, Burger King, and KFC franchises throughout the world attests to the popularity of franchising.

"Commerce is the great equalizer. We exchange ideas when we exchange fabrics."
R. G. INGERSOLL, 1833–1899
(American lawyer and orator)

EXPORTING

The initial foray into international business by most U.S. companies is through exporting. Exporting can take two forms: direct exporting and indirect exporting. In *direct exporting,* a U.S. company signs a sales contract with a foreign purchaser that provides for the conditions of shipment and payment for the goods. (How payments are made in international transactions is discussed later in this chapter.) If business develops sufficiently in foreign countries, a U.S. corporation may develop a specialized marketing organization that, for example, sells directly to consumers in that country. Such *indirect exporting* can be undertaken by the appointment of a foreign agent or a foreign distributor.

ON THE WEB
If you are interested in learning more details on what is involved in exporting goods to other countries, go to the state of New Mexico's Web page on "How to Export" at **www.edd.state.nm.us/TRADE/HOWTO/howto.htm**.

Foreign Agent When a U.S. firm desires a limited involvement in an international market, it will typically establish an *agency relationship* with a foreign firm. In an agency relationship (discussed in Chapter 24), one person (the agent) agrees to act on behalf of another (the principal). The foreign agent is thereby empowered to enter into contracts in the agent's country on behalf of the U.S. principal.

• **DISTRIBUTION AGREEMENT**
A contract between a seller and a distributor of the seller's products setting out the terms and conditions of the distributorship.

• **EXCLUSIVE DISTRIBUTORSHIP**
A distributorship in which the seller and distributor of the seller's products agree that the distributor has the exclusive right to distribute the seller's products in a certain geographic area.

Foreign Distributor When a substantial market exists in a foreign country, a U.S. firm may wish to appoint a distributor located in that country. The U.S. firm and the distributor enter into a **distribution agreement,** which is a contract between the seller and the distributor setting out the terms and conditions of the distributorship—for example, price, currency of payment, availability of supplies, and method of payment. The terms and conditions primarily involve contract law. Disputes concerning distribution agreements may involve jurisdictional or other issues (discussed in detail later in this chapter). In addition, some **exclusive distributorships**—in which distributors agree to distribute only the sellers' goods—have raised antitrust problems.

MANUFACTURING ABROAD

An alternative to direct or indirect exporting is the establishment of foreign manufacturing facilities. Typically, U.S. firms want to establish manufacturing plants abroad if they believe that by doing so they will reduce costs—particularly for labor, shipping, and raw materials—and thereby be able to compete more effectively in foreign markets. Apple Computer, IBM, General Motors, and Ford are some of the many U.S. companies that have established manufacturing facilities abroad. Foreign firms have done the same in the United States. Sony, Nissan, and other Japanese manufacturers have established U.S. plants to avoid import duties that the U.S. Congress may impose on Japanese products entering this country.

There are several ways in which an American firm can manufacture goods in other countries. They include licensing and franchising, as well as investing in a wholly owned subsidiary or a joint venture.

• TECHNOLOGY LICENSING
Allowing another to use and profit from intellectual property (patents, copyrights, trademarks, innovative products or processes, and so on) for consideration. In the context of international business transactions, technology licensing is sometimes an attractive alternative to the establishment of foreign production facilities.

Licensing It is possible for U.S. firms to license their technologies to foreign manufacturers. **Technology licensing** may involve a process innovation that lowers the cost of production, or it may involve a product innovation that generates a superior product. Technology licensing may be an attractive alternative to establishing foreign production facilities, particularly if the process or product innovation has been patented, because the patent protects—at least to some extent—against the possibility that the innovation might be pirated. Like any licensing agreement, a licensing agreement with a foreign-based firm calls for a payment of royalties on some basis—such as so many cents per unit produced or a certain percentage of profits from units sold in a particular geographical territory.

In certain circumstances, even in the absence of a patent, a firm may be able to license the "know-how" associated with a particular manufacturing process—for example, a plant design or a secret formula. The foreign firm that agrees to sign the licensing agreement further agrees to keep the know-how confidential and to pay royalties. For example, the Coca-Cola Bottling Company licenses firms worldwide to use (and keep confidential) its secret formula for the syrup used in that soft drink, in return for a percentage of the income gained from the sale of Coca-Cola by those firms.

The licensing of technology benefits all parties to the transaction. Those who receive the license can take advantage of an established reputation for quality, and the firm that grants the license receives income from the foreign sales of the firm's products, as well as establishing a worldwide reputation. Additionally, once a firm's trademark is known worldwide, the demand for other products manufactured or sold by that firm may increase—obviously an important consideration.

ON THE WEB
For information on the legal requirements of doing business in other nations, a good source is the Internet Law Library's collection of laws of other nations. Go to law.house.gov/52.htm.

Franchising Franchising is a well-known form of licensing. Recall from Chapter 33 that a franchise can be defined as an arrangement in which the owner of a trademark, trade name, or copyright (the franchisor) licenses another (the franchisee) to use the trademark, trade name, or copyright—under certain conditions or limitations—in the selling of goods or services in exchange for a fee, usually based on a percentage of gross or net sales. Examples of international franchises include McDonald's, the Coca-Cola Bottling Company, Holiday Inn, Avis, and Hertz.

Investing in a Wholly Owned Subsidiary or a Joint Venture One way to expand into a foreign market is to establish a wholly owned subsidiary firm in a foreign country. The European subsidiary would likely take the form of the *société anonyme*

(S.A.), which is similar to a U.S. corporation. In German-speaking nations, it would be called an *Aktiengesellschaft* (A.G.). When a wholly owned subsidiary is established, the parent company, which remains in the United States, retains complete ownership of all the facilities in the foreign country, as well as complete authority and control over all phases of the operation.

The expansion of a U.S. firm into international markets can also take the form of a joint venture. In a joint venture, the U.S. company owns only part of the operation; the rest is owned either by local owners in the foreign country or by another foreign entity. In a joint venture, all of the firms involved share responsibilities, as well as profits and liabilities.

Commercial Contracts in an International Setting

¡RECALL!

The interpretation of the words in a contract can be the basis for a dispute even when both parties communicate in the same language.

Like all commercial contracts, an international contract should be in writing. For an example of an actual international sales contract, refer back to the fold-out contract in Chapter 15.

Language and legal differences among nations can create special problems for parties to international contracts when disputes arise. It is possible to avoid these problems by including in a contract special provisions designating the official language of the contract, the legal forum (court or place) in which disputes under the contract will be settled, and the substantive law that will be applied in settling any disputes. Parties to international contracts should also indicate in their contracts what acts or events will excuse the parties from performance under the contract and whether disputes under the contract will be arbitrated or litigated.

Business Law in Action • LIABILITY FOR HUMAN RIGHTS VIOLATIONS

An increasingly important consideration for American companies that have partners or subsidiaries in other countries concerns human rights violations. If a joint venturer located in another nation mistreats its workers, the American partner may be held liable for that mistreatment, even though it was unaware of it.

Consider the situation in which Unocal Corporation, an American corporation, found itself when its joint venturer in Burma (Myanmar) was accused of mistreating its workers. Unocal had entered into a joint venture with an agency of the Burmese government for the purpose of constructing a gas pipeline in Burma.

A group of Burmese workers sued the Burmese government and Unocal Corporation, alleging that these employers had violated human rights. The plaintiffs complained that they were the victims of rape, forced labor, involuntary relocation, and torture. A U.S. district court dismissed the claims against the Burmese government, holding that the claims against the Burmese government did not fall within the "commercial activities" exception to the Foreign Sovereign Immunities Act.[a]

In essence, this left Unocal Corporation as the only defendant in the case.

This decision, understandably, has led American companies to think twice about doing business with overseas partners. According to Robert Benson, an environmental law professor at Loyola Marymount University in Los Angeles, the decision means that "corporate capital is going to have to be responsible for the human rights consequences in the countries where it is going."[b]

FOR CRITICAL ANALYSIS

Should U.S. business owners be held liable for human rights violations even if they are unaware of such violations?

a. *John Doe I v. Unocal Corp.*, 963 F.Supp. 880 (C.D.Cal. 1997).

b. Gail Diane Cox, "Unocal May Be Liable for Partner's Acts," *The National Law Journal*, May 5, 1997, p. B1.

CHOICE OF LANGUAGE

A deal struck between a U.S. company and a company in another country normally involves two languages. The complex contractual terms involved may not be understood by one party in the other party's language. Typically, many phrases in one language are not readily translatable into another. To make sure that no disputes arise out of this language problem, an international sales contract should have a **choice-of-language clause** designating the official language by which the contract will be interpreted in the event of disagreement.

• **CHOICE-OF-LANGUAGE CLAUSE**
A clause in a contract designating the official language by which the contract will be interpreted in the event of a future disagreement over the contract's terms.

CHOICE OF FORUM

When several countries are involved, litigation may be sought in courts in different nations. There are no universally accepted rules regarding the jurisdiction of a particular court over subject matter or parties to a dispute. Consequently, parties to an international transaction should always include in the contract a **forum-selection clause** indicating what court, jurisdiction, or tribunal will decide any disputes arising under the contract. It is especially important to indicate specifically what court will have jurisdiction. The forum does not necessarily have to be within the geographical boundaries of either of the parties' nations.

• **FORUM-SELECTION CLAUSE**
A provision in a contract designating the court, jurisdiction, or tribunal that will decide any disputes arising under the contract.

International Perspective • LANGUAGE REQUIREMENTS IN FRANCE

In 1995, France implemented a law making the use of the French language mandatory in certain legal documents. Documents relating to securities offerings, such as prospectuses, for example, must be written in French. So must instruction manuals and warranties for goods and services offered for sale in France. Additionally, all agreements entered into with French state or local authorities, with entities controlled by state or local authorities, and with private entities carrying out a public service (such as providing utilities) must be written in French. The law has posed problems for some businesspersons because certain legal terms or phrases in documents governed by, say, U.S. or English law have no equivalent terms or phrases in the French legal system.

FOR CRITICAL ANALYSIS

How might language differences affect the meaning of certain terms or phrases in an international contract?

CHOICE OF LAW

A contractual provision designating the applicable law—such as the law of Germany or England or California—is called a **choice-of-law clause.** Every international contract typically includes a choice-of-law clause. At common law (and in European civil law systems), parties are allowed to choose the law that will govern their contractual relationship provided that the law chosen is the law of a jurisdiction that has a substantial relationship to the parties and to the international business transaction.

• **CHOICE-OF-LAW CLAUSE**
A clause in a contract designating the law (such as the law of a particular state or nation) that will govern the contract.

Under Section 1–105 of the Uniform Commercial Code, parties may choose the law that will govern the contract as long as the choice is "reasonable." Article 6 of the United Nations Convention on Contracts for the International Sale of Goods (discussed in Chapter 15), however, imposes no limitation on the parties in their choice of what law will govern the contract. The 1986 Hague Convention on the Law Applicable to Contracts for the International Sale of Goods—often referred to as the Choice-of-Law Convention—allows unlimited autonomy in the choice of law. The Hague Convention indicates that whenever a choice of law is not specified in a contract, the governing law is that of the country in which the *seller's* place of business is located.

FORCE MAJEURE CLAUSE

• ***FORCE MAJEURE* CLAUSE** A provision in a contract stipulating that certain unforeseen events—such as war, political upheavals, acts of God, or other events—will excuse a party from liability for nonperformance of contractual obligations.

Every contract, particularly those involving international transactions, should have a ***force majeure* clause.** *Force majeure* is a French term meaning "impossible or irresistible force"—which sometimes is loosely identified as "an act of God." In international business contracts, *force majeure* clauses commonly stipulate that in addition to acts of God, a number of other eventualities (such as governmental orders or regulations, embargoes, or shortages of materials) may excuse a party from liability for nonperformance.

CIVIL DISPUTE RESOLUTION

International contracts frequently include arbitration clauses. By means of such clauses, the parties agree in advance to be bound by the decision of a specified third party in the event of a dispute, as discussed in Chapter 3. The third party may be a neutral entity (such as the International Chamber of Commerce), a panel of individuals representing both parties' interests, or some other group or organization. (For an example of an arbitration clause in an international contract, refer to the fold-out exhibit in Chapter 15.) The United Nations Convention on the Recognition and Enforcement of Foreign Arbitral Awards (often referred to as the New York Convention) assists in the enforcement of arbitration clauses, as do provisions in specific treaties between nations. The New York Convention has been implemented in nearly one hundred countries, including the United States.

If no arbitration clause is contained in the sales contract, litigation may occur. If forum-selection and choice-of-law clauses are included in the contract, the lawsuit will be heard by a court in the forum specified and decided according to that forum's law. If no forum and choice of law have been specified, however, legal proceedings will be more complex and attended by much more uncertainty. For example, litigation may take place in two or more countries, with each country applying its own choice-of-law rules to determine which substantive law will be applied to the particular transactions.

Even if a plaintiff wins a favorable judgment in a lawsuit litigated in the plaintiff's country, there is no way to predict whether the court's judgment will be enforced by judicial bodies in the defendant's country. As discussed earlier in this chapter, under the principle of comity, the judgment may be enforced in the defendant's country, particularly if the defendant's country is the United States and the foreign court's decision is consistent with U.S. national law and policy. Other nations, however, may not be as accommodating as the United States in this respect.

Making Payment on International Transactions

Currency differences between nations and the geographical distance between parties to international sales contracts add a degree of complexity to international sales that does not exist within the domestic market. Because international contracts involve greater financial risks, special care should be taken in drafting these contracts to specify both the currency in which payment is to be made and the method of payment.

MONETARY SYSTEMS

While it is true that our national currency, the U.S. dollar, is one of the primary forms of international currency, any U.S. firm undertaking business transactions abroad must be prepared to deal with one or more other currencies. After all, just as a U.S. firm wants to be paid in U.S. dollars for goods and services sold abroad, so, too, does a Japanese firm want to be paid in Japanese yen for goods and services sold outside Japan. Both firms therefore must rely on the convertibility of currencies.

International Perspective • ARBITRATION VERSUS LITIGATION

One of the reasons many businesspersons find it advantageous to include arbitration clauses in their international contracts is because arbitration awards are usually easier to enforce than court judgments. As mentioned, the New York Convention provides for the enforcement of arbitration awards in those countries that have signed the convention. Enforcement of court judgments, though, normally depends on the principle of comity and bilateral agreements providing for such enforcement. How the principle of comity is applied, however, varies from one nation to another, and many countries have not agreed, in bilateral agreements, to enforce judgments rendered in U.S. courts. Furthermore, even in the United States a court might not enforce a foreign court's judgment if that judgment conflicts with U.S. laws or policies. For example, in one case the Court of Appeals of Maryland, that state's highest court, refused to enforce the judgment of a British court in a libel case. The Maryland court pointed out that the judgment was contrary to the public policy of Maryland and the United States generally, which "favors a much broader and more protective freedom of the press than [has] ever been provided for under English law."[a]

a. *Telnikoff v. Matusevitch,* 159 F.3d 636 (D.C. Cir. 1998).

FOR CRITICAL ANALYSIS
What might be some other advantages of arbitration in the context of international transactions? Are there any disadvantages?

Foreign Exchange Markets Currencies are convertible when they can be freely exchanged one for the other at some specified market rate in a **foreign exchange market.** Foreign exchange markets are a worldwide system for the buying and selling of foreign currencies. At any point in time, the foreign exchange rate is set by the forces of supply and demand in unrestricted foreign exchange markets. The foreign exchange rate is simply the price of a unit of one country's currency in terms of another country's currency. For example, if today's exchange rate is one hundred Japanese yen for one dollar, that means that anybody with one hundred yen can obtain one dollar, and vice versa.

• **FOREIGN EXCHANGE MARKET**
A worldwide system in which foreign currencies are bought and sold.

Correspondent Banking Frequently, a U.S. company can deal directly with its domestic bank, which will take care of the international funds-transfer problem. Commercial banks sometimes have **correspondent banks** in other countries. Correspondent banking is a major means of transferring funds internationally.

• **CORRESPONDENT BANK**
A bank in which another bank has an account (and vice versa) for the purpose of facilitating fund transfers.

• **EXAMPLE 43.3** Suppose that a customer of Citibank wishes to pay a bill in French francs to a company in Paris. Citibank can draw a bank check payable in francs on its account in Crédit Lyonnais, a Paris correspondent bank, and then send it to the French company to which its customer owes the funds. Alternatively, Citibank's customer can request a wire transfer of the funds to the French company.

Citibank instructs Crédit Lyonnais by wire to pay the necessary amount in French francs.•

The Clearinghouse Interbank Payment System (CHIPS) handles about 90 percent of both national and international interbank transfers of U.S. funds. In addition, the Society for Worldwide International Financial Telecommunications (SWIFT) is a communication system that provides banks with messages concerning transactions.

LETTERS OF CREDIT

Because buyers and sellers engaged in international business transactions are often separated by thousands of miles, special precautions are frequently taken to ensure performance under the contract. Sellers want to avoid delivering goods for which they might not be paid. Buyers desire the assurance that sellers will not be paid until there is evidence that the goods have been shipped. Thus, **letters of credit** are frequently used to facilitate international business transactions.

• **LETTER OF CREDIT**
A written instrument, usually issued by a bank on behalf of a customer or other person, in which the issuer promises to honor drafts or other demands for payment by third persons in accordance with the terms of the instrument.

In a simple letter-of-credit transaction, the issuer (a bank) agrees to issue a letter of credit and to ascertain whether the *beneficiary* (seller) performs certain acts. In return, the *account party* (buyer) promises to reimburse the issuer for the amount paid to the beneficiary. There may also be an *advising bank* that transmits information, and a *paying bank* may be involved to expedite payment under the letter of credit. Exhibit 43–1 below summarizes the "life cycle" of a letter of credit.

Under a letter of credit, the issuer is bound to pay the beneficiary (seller) when the beneficiary has complied with the terms and conditions of the letter of credit. The beneficiary looks to the issuer, not to the account party (buyer), when it presents the documents required by the letter of credit. Typically, the letter of credit will require that the beneficiary deliver to the issuing bank a *bill of lading* to prove that shipment has been made. Letters of credit assure beneficiaries (sellers) of payment while at the same time assuring account parties (buyers) that payment will not be made until the beneficiaries have complied with the terms and conditions of the letter of credit.

EXHIBIT 43–1 • The "Life Cycle" of a Letter of Credit

Although the letter of credit appears quite complex at first, it is not difficult to understand. This cycle merely involves the exchange of documents (and money) through intermediaries. The following steps depict the letter-of-credit procurement cycle.

Step 1: The buyer and seller agree on the terms of sale. The sales contract dictates that a letter of credit is to be used to finance the transaction.

Step 2: The buyer completes an application for a letter of credit and forwards it to his or her bank, which will issue the letter of credit.

Step 3: The issuing (buyer's) bank then forwards the letter of credit to a correspondent bank in the seller's country.

Step 4: The correspondent's bank relays the letter of credit to the seller.

Step 5: Having received assurance of payment, the seller makes the necessary shipping arrangements.

Step 6: The seller prepares the documents required under the letter of credit and delivers them to the correspondent bank.

Step 7: The correspondent bank examines the documents. If it finds them in order, it sends them to the issuing bank and pays the seller in accordance with the terms of the letter of credit.

Step 8: The issuing bank, having received the documents, examines them. If they are in order, the issuing bank will charge the buyer's account and send the documents on to the buyer or his or her customs broker. The issuing bank also will reimburse the correspondent bank.

Step 9: The buyer or broker receives the documents and picks up the merchandise from the shipper (carrier).

Source: National Association of Purchasing Management.

¡DON'T FORGET!
A letter of credit is independent of the underlying contract between the buyer and the seller.

The Value of a Letter of Credit The basic principle behind letters of credit is that payment is made against the documents presented by the beneficiary and not against the facts that the documents purport to reflect. Thus, in a letter-of-credit transaction, the issuer does not police the underlying contract; a letter of credit is independent of the underlying contract between the buyer and the seller. Eliminating the need for banks (issuers) to inquire into whether or not actual conditions have been satisfied greatly reduces the costs of letters of credit. Moreover, the use of a letter of credit protects both buyers and sellers.

Compliance with a Letter of Credit In a letter-of-credit transaction, generally at least three separate and distinct contracts are involved: the contract between the account party (buyer) and the beneficiary (seller); the contract between the issuer (bank) and the account party (buyer); and finally, the letter of credit itself, which involves the issuer (bank) and the beneficiary (seller). These contracts are separate and distinct, and the issuer's obligations under the letter of credit do not concern the underlying contract between the buyer and the seller. Rather, it is the issuer's duty to ascertain whether the documents presented by the beneficiary (seller) comply with the terms of the letter of credit.

If the documents presented by the beneficiary comply with the terms of the letter of credit, the issuer (bank) must honor the letter of credit. Sometimes, however, it is difficult to determine exactly what a letter of credit requires. Moreover, the courts are divided as to whether *strict* or *substantial* compliance with the terms of the letter of credit is required. Traditionally, courts required strict compliance with the terms of a letter of credit, but in recent years, some courts have moved to a standard of *reasonable* compliance.

If the issuing bank refuses to pay the seller (beneficiary) even though the seller has complied with all the requirements of the letter of credit, the seller can bring an action to enforce payment. In the international context, the fact that the issuing bank may be thousands of miles distant from the seller's business location can pose difficulties for the seller—as the following case illustrates.

CASE 43.2 Pacific Reliant Industries, Inc. v. Amerika Samoa Bank

United States Court of Appeals,
Ninth Circuit, 1990.
901 F.2d 735.
196 Va. 493,
84 S.E.2d 516.

HISTORICAL AND POLITICAL SETTING *Samoa, which was originally inhabited by Polynesians, is a group of islands 2,610 miles south of Hawaii. In 1899, the islands were divided into Western Samoa and American Samoa by the Treaty of Berlin, which was signed by Great Britain, Germany, and the United States. Thus, the United States acquired American Samoa. In 1960, American Samoa adopted a constitution, which it revised in 1967, but it remains a non-self-governing, unincorporated territory of the United States. Its currency is the U.S. dollar, its languages are Samoan and English, and it is administered by the U.S. Department of the Interior. The population of American Samoa is less than fifty thousand.*

BACKGROUND AND FACTS Pacific Reliant Industries, Inc., an Oregon company, sold building materials to Paradise Development Company, a company located in American Samoa. Pacific was reluctant to make several large deliveries, totaling more than $1 million in value, without some protection against nonpayment. Accordingly, representatives from Pacific, Paradise, and Amerika Samoa Bank (ASB) met in American Samoa on two occasions to discuss the supply contract and a letter of credit. Following these negotiations, ASB issued a letter of credit in favor of Pacific on Paradise's account. Later, alleging that ASB had wrongfully dishonored the letter of credit, Pacific brought

(Continued)

CASE 43.2—Continued

suit in the U.S. district court for the district of Oregon against ASB to recover payment. The court dismissed the suit for lack of personal jurisdiction, holding that ASB lacked sufficient "minimum contacts" (see Chapter 3) with the state of Oregon to subject it to a lawsuit in that state.[a] Pacific appealed, contending that this case was not typical of other letter-of-credit cases because ASB had participated in forming the underlying contract, had had personal contact with the beneficiary (Pacific), and had known that Pacific would not extend credit or ship goods from Oregon without the letter of credit.

a. State law governs some cases that may be brought in a federal court because the parties to the case are citizens of different states or are aliens. In such a case, the federal court normally applies the law of the state in which the court is located.

IN THE WORDS OF THE COURT . . .

CANBY, Circuit Judge:

* * * *

Here, both the negotiations for the underlying contract and the letter of credit occurred in American Samoa. * * * ASB did not initiate the transactions between itself, Paradise, or Pacific. Nor did ASB take any significant actions in Oregon. ASB did not invoke the benefits and protections of Oregon law and could not reasonably have expected to be haled into court there. We conclude that ASB's conduct as an issuing bank of a letter of credit does not subject it to suit in Oregon * * * .

DECISION AND REMEDY The U.S Court of Appeals for the Ninth Circuit affirmed the lower court's ruling. Pacific could not bring suit against ASB in Oregon.

FOR CRITICAL ANALYSIS—Political Consideration *If a court could exercise jurisdiction over a nonresident corporation that did not have minimum contacts with the jurisdiction in which the suit was brought, what might result?*

Regulation of Specific Business Activities

Doing business abroad can affect the economies, foreign policy, domestic politics, and other national interests of the countries involved. For this reason, nations impose laws to restrict or facilitate international business. Controls may also be imposed by international agreement. We discuss here how different types of international activities are regulated.

INVESTING

Investing in foreign nations involves a risk that the foreign government may take possession of the investment property. Expropriation, as already mentioned, occurs when property is taken and the owner is paid just compensation for what is taken. This does not violate generally observed principles of international law. Confiscation occurs when property is taken and no (or inadequate) compensation is paid. International legal principles are violated when property is confiscated. Few remedies are available for confiscation of property by a foreign government. Claims are often resolved by lump-sum settlements after negotiations between the United States and the taking nation.

To counter the deterrent effect that the possibility of confiscation may have on potential investors, many countries guarantee that foreign investors will be compensated if their property is taken. A guaranty can take the form of national constitutional or statutory laws or provisions in international treaties. As further protection for foreign investments, some countries provide insurance for their citizens' investments abroad.

EXPORT RESTRICTIONS AND INCENTIVES

¡NOTE! Most countries restrict exports for the same reasons: to protect national security, to protect foreign policy, to prevent the spread of nuclear weapons, and to preserve scarce commodities.

The U.S. Constitution provides in Article I, Section 9, that "No Tax or Duty shall be laid on Articles exported from any State." Thus, Congress cannot impose any export taxes. Congress can, however, use a variety of other devices to control exports. Congress may set export quotas on various items, such as grain being sold abroad. Under the Export Administration Act of 1979,[3] restrictions can be imposed on the flow of technologically advanced products and technical data.

Devices to stimulate exports and thereby aid domestic businesses include export incentives and subsidies. The Revenue Act of 1971,[4] for example, gave tax benefits to firms marketing their products overseas through certain foreign sales corporations, exempting income produced by the exports. Under the Export Trading Company Act of 1982,[5] U.S. banks are encouraged to invest in export trading companies. An export trading company consists of exporting firms joined to export a line of goods. The Export-Import Bank of the United States provides financial assistance, which consists primarily of credit guaranties given to commercial banks that in turn loan funds to U.S. exporting companies.

IMPORT RESTRICTIONS

"The notion dies hard that in some sort of way exports are patriotic but imports are immoral."

LORD HARLECH (DAVID ORMSLEY GORE), 1918–1985
(English writer)

All nations have restrictions on imports, and the United States is no exception. Restrictions include strict prohibitions, quotas, and tariffs. Under the Trading with the Enemy Act of 1917,[6] for example, no goods may be imported from nations that have been designated enemies of the United States. Other laws prohibit the importation of illegal drugs, books that urge insurrection against the United States, and agricultural products that pose dangers to domestic crops or animals.

Quotas and Tariffs Quotas are limits on the amounts of goods that can be imported. Tariffs are taxes on imports. A tariff is usually a percentage of the value of the import, but it can be a flat rate per unit (for example, per barrel of oil). Tariffs raise the prices of goods, which causes some consumers to purchase less expensive, domestically manufactured goods.

Dumping The United States has specific laws directed at what it sees as unfair international trade practices. **Dumping,** for example, is the sale of imported goods at "less than fair value." "Fair value" is usually determined by the price of those goods in the exporting country. Foreign firms that engage in dumping in the United States hope to undersell U.S. businesses to obtain a larger share of the U.S. market. To prevent this, an extra tariff—known as an antidumping duty—may be assessed on the imports.

• DUMPING
The selling of goods in a foreign country at a price below the price charged for the same goods in the domestic market.

Minimizing Trade Barriers Restrictions on imports are also known as trade barriers. The elimination of trade barriers is sometimes seen as essential to the world's economic well-being. Most of the world's leading trade nations are members of the

3. 50 U.S.C. Sections 2401–2420.
4. 26 U.S.C. Sections 991–994.
5. 15 U.S.C. Sections 4001, 4003.
6. 12 U.S.C. Section 95a.

• **MOST-FAVORED-NATION STATUS** A status granted in an international treaty by a provision stating that the citizens of the contracting nations may enjoy the privileges accorded by either party to citizens of the most favored nations. Generally, most-favored-nation clauses are designed to establish equality of international treatment.

World Trade Organization (WTO), which was established in 1995. To minimize trade barriers among nations, each member country of the WTO is required to grant **most-favored-nation status** to other member countries. This means each member is obligated to treat other members at least as well as it treats that country that receives its most favorable treatment with regard to imports or exports.

Various regional trade agreements, or associations, also help to minimize trade barriers between nations. The European Union (EU), for example, attempts to minimize or remove barriers to trade among European member countries. The EU is the result of negotiations undertaken by European nations since the 1950s. Currently, the EU is a single integrated European trading unit made up of fifteen European nations. Another important regional trade agreement is the North American Free Trade Agreement (NAFTA). NAFTA, which became effective on January 1, 1994, created a regional trading unit consisting of Mexico, the United States, and Canada. The primary goal of NAFTA is to eliminate tariffs among these three countries on substantially all goods over a period of fifteen to twenty years.

BRIBING FOREIGN OFFICIALS

Giving cash or in-kind benefits to foreign government officials to obtain business contracts and other favors is often considered normal practice. To reduce such bribery by representatives of U.S. corporations, Congress enacted the Foreign Corrupt Practices Act (FCPA) in 1977.[7] This act and its implications for American businesspersons engaged in international business transactions were discussed in detail in the *Landmark in the Law* in Chapter 8.

U.S. Laws in a Global Context

The internationalization of business raises questions of the extraterritorial effect of a nation's laws—that is, the effect of the country's laws outside the country. To what extent do U.S. domestic laws affect other nations' businesses? To what extent are U.S. businesses affected by domestic laws when doing business abroad? The following subsections discuss these questions in the context of U.S. antitrust law. We also look at the extraterritorial application of U.S. laws prohibiting employment discrimination.

U.S. ANTITRUST LAWS

U.S. antitrust laws (discussed in Chapter 35) have a wide application. They may *subject* persons in foreign nations to their provisions, as well as *protect* foreign consumers and competitors from violations committed by U.S. citizens. Consequently, *foreign persons,* a term that by definition includes foreign governments, may sue under U.S. antitrust laws in U.S. courts.

Section 1 of the Sherman Act provides for the extraterritorial effect of the U.S. antitrust laws. The United States is a major proponent of free competition in the global economy, and thus any conspiracy that has a *substantial effect* on U.S. commerce is within the reach of the Sherman Act. The violation may even occur outside the United States, and foreign governments as well as persons can be sued for violations of U.S. antitrust laws.

Before U.S. courts will exercise jurisdiction and apply antitrust laws, it must be shown that the alleged violation had a substantial effect on U.S. commerce. U.S. juris-

7. 15 U.S.C. Sections 78m–78ff.

diction is automatically invoked, however, when a *per se* violation occurs.[8] A *per se* violation may consist of resale price fixing and tying, or tie-in, contracts. • **EXAMPLE 43.4** If a domestic firm joins a foreign cartel to control the production, price, or distribution of goods, and this cartel has a *substantial restraining effect* on U.S. commerce, a *per se* violation may exist. Hence, both the domestic firm and the foreign cartel may be sued for violation of the U.S. antitrust laws. Likewise, if foreign firms doing business in the United States enter into a price-fixing or other anticompetitive agreement to control a portion of U.S. markets, a *per se* violation may exist.•

In the following case, the court considered whether a *criminal* prosecution under the Sherman Act could be based on price-fixing activities that took place entirely outside the United States but had a substantial effect in this country.

8. Certain types of restrictive contracts, such as price-fixing agreements, are deemed inherently anticompetitive and thus in restraint of trade as a matter of law. When such a restrictive contract is entered into, there is said to be a *per se* violation of the antitrust laws. See Chapter 35.

CASE 43.3 United States v. Nippon Paper Industries Co.

United States Court of Appeals,
First Circuit, 1997.
109 F.3d 1.

COMPANY PROFILE *In 1993, two Japanese paper companies merged to form Nippon Paper Industries Company. Nippon makes paper and paper products, operating tree plantations and lumber mills in Australia and Chile. In thirteen other countries, Nippon engages in import and export activities in the chemicals, cosmetics, food, and pharmaceuticals industries. Paper production, however, accounts for about three-quarters of the company's sales. In the late 1980s and early 1990s, one of Nippon's predecessors sold thermal fax paper for use in fax machines and medical printing equipment. In 1990, North American thermal fax paper sales by Japanese firms accounted for $120 million, of which $6 million went to Nippon's predecessor.*

BACKGROUND AND FACTS A federal grand jury issued a criminal indictment against Nippon Paper Industries Company (NPI) and others, charging the defendants with agreeing to fix the price of thermal fax paper throughout North America. The indictment alleged that the meetings to reach the agreement had occurred entirely in Japan but that the defendants had sold the paper through subsidiaries in the United States at above-normal prices. The indictment stated that these activities had had a substantial adverse effect on commerce in the United States and had unreasonably restrained trade in violation of Section 1 of the Sherman Act. NPI filed a motion to dismiss the indictment. The court granted the motion, declaring that a criminal antitrust prosecution could not be based on wholly extraterritorial conduct. The government appealed.

IN THE WORDS OF THE COURT . . .
SELYA, Circuit Judge.

* * * *

* * * [C]ivil antitrust actions predicated on wholly foreign conduct which has an intended and substantial effect in the United States come within Section One's jurisdictional reach. * * *

* * * *

* * * [I]n both criminal and civil cases, the claim that Section One applies extraterritorially is based on the same language in the same section of the same statute * * * .

* * * It is a fundamental interpretive principle that identical words or terms used in different parts of the same act are intended to have the same meaning. * * * It follows, therefore, that if the language upon which the indictment rests were the same as the language upon which civil liability rests but appeared in a different section of the Sherman Act, or in a different part of the same section, we would * * * construe the

(Continued)

CASE 43.3—Continued

two iterations [statements] of the language identically. Where, as here, the tie binds more tightly—that is, the text under consideration is not merely a duplicate appearing somewhere else in the statute, but is the original phrase in the original setting— * * * the case for reading the language in a [consistent] manner * * * is irresistible.

DECISION AND REMEDY The U.S. Court of Appeals for the First Circuit reversed the decision of the lower court. The criminal indictment under the Sherman Act would not be dismissed simply because the actions on which it was based occurred outside the United States.

FOR CRITICAL ANALYSIS—Economic Consideration *Why should the United States apply its antitrust laws to business firms owned by citizens or the government of another nation?*

DISCRIMINATION LAWS

As explained in Chapter 38, there are laws in the United States prohibiting discrimination on the basis of race, color, national origin, religion, gender, age, and disability. These laws, as they affect employment relationships, generally apply extraterritorially. Since 1984, for example, the Age Discrimination in Employment Act (ADEA) of 1967 has covered U.S. employees working abroad for U.S. employers. The Americans with Disabilities Act of 1990, which requires employers to accommodate the needs of workers with disabilities, also applies to U.S. nationals working abroad for U.S. firms.

For some time, it was uncertain whether the major U.S. law regulating discriminatory practices in the workplace, Title VII of the Civil Rights Act of 1964, applied extraterritorially. The Civil Rights Act of 1991 addressed this issue. The act provides that Title VII applies extraterritorially to all U.S. employees working for U.S. employers abroad. Generally, U.S. employers must abide by U.S. discrimination laws unless to do so would violate the laws of the country in which their workplaces are located. This "foreign laws exception" allows employers to avoid being subjected to conflicting laws.

Key Terms

Chapter Summary • International Law in a Global Economy

International Principles and Doctrines (See pages 1109–1112.)	1. *The principle of comity*—Under this principle, nations give effect to the laws and judicial decrees of other nations for reasons of courtesy and international harmony. 2. *The act of state doctrine*—A doctrine under which American courts avoid passing judgment on the validity of public acts committed by a recognized foreign government within its own territory. 3. *The doctrine of sovereign immunity*—When certain conditions are satisfied, foreign nations are immune from U.S. jurisdiction under the Foreign Sovereign Immunities Act of 1976. Exceptions are made (a) when the foreign state has "waived its immunity either explicitly or by implication" or (b) when the action is "based upon a commercial activity carried on in the United States by the foreign state."

Chapter Summary • International Law in a Global Economy, Continued

Doing Business Internationally (See pages 1112–1114.)	Ways in which U.S. domestic firms engage in international business transactions include (a) exporting, which may involve foreign agents or distributors, and (b) manufacturing abroad through licensing arrangements, franchising operations, wholly owned subsidiaries, or joint ventures.
Commercial Contracts in an International Setting (See pages 1114–1116.)	Choice-of-language, forum-selection, and choice-of-law clauses are often included in international business contracts to reduce the uncertainties associated with interpreting the language of the agreement and dealing with legal differences. *Force majeure* clauses are included in most domestic and international contracts. They commonly stipulate that certain events, such as floods, fire, accidents, labor strikes, and shortages, may excuse a party from liability for nonperformance of the contract. Arbitration clauses are also frequently found in international contracts.
Making Payment on International Transactions (See pages 1116–1120.)	1. *Currency conversion*—Because nations have different monetary systems, payment on international contracts requires currency conversion at a rate specified in a foreign exchange market. 2. *Correspondent banking*—Correspondent banks facilitate the transfer of funds from a buyer in one country to a seller in another. 3. *Letters of credit*—Letters of credit facilitate international transactions by ensuring payment to sellers and ensuring to buyers that payment will not be made until the sellers have complied with the terms of the letters of credit. Typically, compliance occurs when a bill of lading is delivered to the issuing bank.
Regulation of Specific Business Activities (See pages 1120–1122.)	In the interests of their economies, foreign policies, domestic policies, or other national priorities, nations impose laws that restrict or facilitate international business. Such laws regulate foreign investments; exporting and importing activities, and in the United States, the bribery of foreign officials to obtain favorable contracts. The General Agreement on Tariffs and Trade (now the World Trade Organization) attempts to minimize trade barriers among nations, as do regional trade agreements, including the European Union and the North American Free Trade Agreement.
U.S. Laws in a Global Context (See pages 1122–1124.)	1. *Antitrust laws*—U.S. antitrust laws may be applied beyond the borders of the United States. Any conspiracy that has a substantial effect on commerce within the United States may be subject to the Sherman Act, even if the violation occurs outside the United States. 2. *Discrimination laws*—The major U.S. laws prohibiting employment discrimination, including Title VII of the Civil Rights Act of 1964, the Age Discrimination in Employment Act of 1967, and the Americans with Disabilities Act of 1990, cover U.S. employees working abroad for U.S. firms—*unless* to apply the U.S. laws would violate the laws of the host country.

For Review

1. What is the principle of comity, and why do courts deciding disputes involving a foreign law or judicial decree apply this principle?
2. What is the act of state doctrine? In what circumstances is this doctrine applied?
3. A foreign nation is not immune from the jurisdiction of U.S. courts if the nation waives its immunity. Under the Foreign Sovereign Immunities Act of 1976, on what other basis might a foreign state be considered subject to the jurisdiction of U.S. courts?
4. In what circumstances will U.S. antitrust laws be applied extraterritorially?
5. Do U.S. laws prohibiting employment discrimination apply in all circumstances to U.S. employees working for U.S. employers abroad?

Questions and Case Problems

43–1. Letters of Credit. James Reynolds entered into an agreement to purchase dental supplies from Tooth-Tech, Inc. Reynolds also secured a letter of credit from Central Bank to pay for the supplies. Tooth-Tech placed sixty crates of dental supplies on board a steamship and received in return the invoices required under the letter of credit. The purchaser, Reynolds, subsequently learned that Tooth-Tech, Inc., had filled the sixty crates with rubbish, not dental supplies. Given the fact that an issuer's obligation under a letter of credit is independent of the underlying contract between the buyer and the seller, would the issuer be required to pay the seller in this situation? Explain.

43–2. Sovereign Immunity. Texas Trading & Milling Corp. and other companies brought an action for breach of contract against the Federal Republic of Nigeria and its central bank. Nigeria, a rapidly developing and oil-rich nation, had overbought huge quantities of cement from Texas Trading and others. Unable to accept delivery of the cement, Nigeria repudiated the contract, alleging immunity under the Foreign Sovereign Immunities Act of 1976. Because the buyer of the cement was the Nigerian government, did the doctrine of sovereign immunity remove the dispute from the jurisdiction of U.S. courts? [*Texas Trading & Milling Corp. v. Federal Republic of Nigeria,* 647 F.2d 300 (2d Cir. 1981)]

43–3. Letters of Credit. The Swiss Credit Bank issued a letter of credit in favor of Antex Industries to cover the sale of 92,000 electronic integrated circuits manufactured by Electronic Arrays. The letter of credit specified that the chips would be transported to Tokyo by ship. Antex shipped the circuits by air. Payment on the letter of credit was dishonored because the shipment by air did not fulfill the precise terms of the letter of credit. Should a court compel payment? Explain. [*Board of Trade of San Francisco v. Swiss Credit Bank,* 728 F.2d 1241 (9th Cir. 1984)]

43–4. Act of State Doctrine. Sabbatino, an American, contracted with a Cuban corporation that was largely owned by U.S. residents to buy Cuban sugar. When the Cuban government expropriated the corporation's property and rights in retaliation against a U.S. reduction of the Cuban sugar quota, Sabbatino entered into a new contract to make payment for the sugar to Banco Nacional de Cuba, a government-owned Cuban bank. Sabbatino refused to make the promised payment, and Banco subsequently filed an action in a U.S. district court seeking to recover payment for the sugar. The issue was whether the act of state doctrine should apply when a foreign state violates international law. (If the doctrine were applied, the Cuban government's action would be presumed valid, and thus Banco's claim would be legitimate.) Should the act of state doctrine be applied in these circumstances? Discuss. [*Banco Nacional de Cuba v. Sabbatino,* 376 U.S. 398, 84 S.Ct. 923, 11 L.Ed.2d 804 (1964)]

43–5. Antitrust Claims. Billy Lamb and Carmon Willis (the plaintiffs) were tobacco growers in Kentucky. Phillip Morris, Inc., and B.A.T. Industries, PLC, routinely purchased tobacco not only from Kentucky but also from producers in several foreign countries. In 1982, subsidiaries of Phillip Morris and B.A.T. (the defendants) entered into an agreement with La Fundacion Del Niño (the Children's Foundation) of Caracas, Venezuela, headed by the wife of the president of Venezuela. The agreement provided that the two subsidiaries would donate a total of approximately $12.5 million to the Children's Foundation, and in exchange, the subsidiaries would obtain price controls on Venezuelan tobacco, elimination of controls on retail cigarette prices in Venezuela, tax deductions for the donations, and assurances that existing tax rates applicable to tobacco companies would not be increased. The plaintiffs brought an action, alleging that the Venezuelan arrangement was an inducement designed to restrain trade in violation of U.S. antitrust laws. Such an arrangement, the plaintiffs contended, would result in the artificial depression of tobacco prices to the detriment of domestic tobacco growers, while ensuring lucrative retail prices for tobacco products sold abroad. The trial court held that the plaintiffs' claim was barred by the act of state doctrine. What will result on appeal? Discuss. [*Lamb v. Phillip Morris, Inc.,* 915 F.2d 1024 (6th Cir. 1990)]

43–6. Sovereign Immunity. The Bank of Jamaica, which is wholly owned by the government of Jamaica, contracted with Chisholm & Co. in January 1981 for Chisholm to arrange for lines of credit from various U.S. banks and to obtain $50 million in credit insurance from the Export-Import Bank of the United States. This Chisholm successfully did, but subsequently the Bank of Jamaica refused the deals arranged by Chisholm, and the bank refused to pay Chisholm for its services. Chisholm sued the bank in a federal district court for breach of an implied contract. The bank moved to dismiss the case, claiming, among other things, that it was immune from the jurisdiction of U.S. courts under the doctrine of sovereign immunity. What factors will the court consider in deciding whether the bank is immune from the jurisdiction of U.S. courts under the doctrine of sovereign immunity? Will the court agree? Discuss fully. [*Chisholm & Co. v. Bank of Jamaica,* 643 F.Supp. 1393 (S.D.Fla. 1986)]

43–7. Forum-Selection Clauses. Royal Bed and Spring Co., a Puerto Rican distributor of furniture products, entered into an exclusive distributorship agreement with Famossul Industria e Comercio de Moveis Ltda., a Brazilian manufacturer of furniture products. Under the terms of the contract, Royal Bed was to distribute in Puerto Rico the furniture products manufactured by Famossul in Brazil. The contract contained choice-of-forum and choice-of-law clauses, which designated the judicial district of Curitiba, State of Paraná, Brazil, as the judicial forum and the Brazilian Civil Code as the law to be applied in the event of any dispute. Famossul terminated the exclusive distributorship and suspended the shipment of goods without just cause. Under Puerto Rican law, forum-selection clauses providing for foreign venues are not enforced as a matter of public policy. In what jurisdiction should Royal Bed bring suit? Discuss fully. [*Royal Bed and Spring Co. v. Famossul Industria e Comercio de Moveis Ltda.,* 906 F.2d 45 (5th Cir. 1990)]

43–8. Discrimination Claims. Radio Free Europe and Radio Liberty (RFE/RL), a U.S. corporation doing business in Germany, employs more than three hundred U.S. citizens at its principal place of business in Munich, Germany. The concept of mandatory retirement is deeply embedded in German labor policy, and a contract formed in 1982 between RFE/RL and a German labor union contained a clause that required workers to be retired when they reach the age of sixty-five. When William Mahoney and other American employees (the plaintiffs) reached the age of sixty-five, RFE/RL terminated their employment as required under its contract with the labor union. The plaintiffs sued RFE/RL for discriminating against them on the basis of age, in violation of the Age Discrimination in Employment Act of 1967. Will the plaintiffs succeed in their suit? Discuss fully. [*Mahoney v. RFE/RL, Inc.*, 47 F.3d 447 (D.C. Cir. 1995)]

43–9. Sovereign Immunity. Reed International Trading Corp., a New York corporation, agreed to sell down jackets to Alink, a Russian business. Alink referred Reed to the Bank for Foreign and Economic Affairs of the Russian Federation for payment and gave Reed a letter of credit payable in New York. When Reed tried to collect, the bank refused to pay. Reed (and others) filed a suit in a federal district court against the bank (and others). The bank qualified as a "sovereign" under the Foreign Sovereign Immunities Act and thus claimed in part that it was immune from suit in U.S. courts. On what basis might the court hold that the bank was not immune? Explain. [*Reed International Trading Corp. v. Donau Bank, A.G.*, 866 F.Supp. 750 (S.D.N.Y. 1994)]

43–10. Sovereign Immunity. Nuovo Pignone, Inc., is an Italian company that designs and manufactures turbine systems. Nuovo sold a turbine system to Cabinda Gulf Oil Co. (CABGOC). The system was manufactured, tested, and inspected in Italy, then sent to Louisiana for mounting on a platform by CABGOC's contractor. Nuovo sent a representative to consult on the mounting. The platform went to a CABGOC site off the coast of West Africa. Marcus Pere, an instrument technician at the site, was killed when a turbine within the system exploded. Pere's widow filed a suit in a U.S. federal district court against Nuovo and others. Nuovo claimed sovereign immunity on the ground that its majority shareholder at the time of the explosion was Ente Nazionale Idrocaburi, which was created by the government of Italy to lead its oil and gas exploration and development. Is Nuovo exempt from suit under the doctrine of sovereign immunity? Is it subject to suit under the "commercial activity" exception? Why or why not? [*Pere v. Nuovo Pignone, Inc.*, 150 F.3d 477 (5th Cir. 1998)]

A QUESTION OF ETHICS AND SOCIAL RESPONSIBILITY

43–11. Ronald Riley, an American citizen, and Council of Lloyd's, a British insurance corporation with its principal place of business in London, entered into an agreement in 1980 that allowed Riley to underwrite insurance through Lloyd's. The agreement provided that if any dispute arose between Lloyd's and Riley, the courts of England would have exclusive jurisdiction, and the laws of England would apply. Over the next decade, some of the parties insured under policies that Riley underwrote experienced large losses, for which they filed claims. Instead of paying his share of the claims, Riley filed a lawsuit in a U.S. district court against Lloyd's and its managers and directors (all British citizens or entities), seeking, among other things, rescission of the 1980 agreement. Riley alleged that the defendants had violated the Securities Act of 1933, the Securities Exchange Act of 1934, and Rule 10b-5. The defendants asked the court to enforce the forum-selection clause in the agreement. Riley argued that if the clause was enforced, he would be deprived of his rights under the U.S. securities laws. The court held that the parties were to resolve their dispute in England. [*Riley v. Kingsley Underwriting Agencies, Ltd.*, 969 F.2d 953 (10th Cir. 1992)]

1. Did the court's decision fairly balance the rights of the parties? How would you argue in support of the court's decision in this case? How would you argue against it?
2. Should the fact that an international transaction may be subject to laws and remedies different from or less favorable than those of the United States be a valid basis for denying enforcement of forum-selection and choice-of-law clauses?
3. All parties to this litigation other than Riley were British. Should this fact be considered by the court in deciding this case?

FOR CRITICAL ANALYSIS

43–12. Business cartels and monopolies that are legal in some countries may engage in practices that violate U.S. antitrust laws. In view of this fact, what are some of the implications of applying U.S. antitrust laws extraterritorially?

Online Activities

ONLINE EXERCISE 43-1

Go to the "Internet Activities Book" on the Web site that accompanies this text, the URL for which is http://blt.westbuslaw.com. Select the following activity, and perform the exercise according to the instructions given there:

Activity 39–1: World Trade Organization

Before the Test

Go to the *Business Law Today* home page at http://blt.westbuslaw.com. Click on TestTutor.® You will find twenty interactive questions relating to this chapter.

Unit Nine • Cumulative Business Hypothetical

Macrotech, Inc., makes an innovative computer chip on which the firm obtains a patent and markets under the trademarked brand name "Flash."

1. Macrotech wants to sell the Flash chip to Nitron, Ltd., in Pacifica, a foreign country. Macrotech is concerned, however, that after an initial purchase, Nitron will duplicate the chip, pirate it, and sell the pirated version to computer manufacturers in Pacifica. To avoid this situation, Macrotech could establish its own manufacturing facility in Pacifica, but it does not want to do this. How can Macrotech, without establishing a manufacturing facility in Pacifica, protect against Flash being pirated by Nitron?
2. A representative of Pixel, S.A., in Raretania, a foreign country, contacts Macrotech, says that Pixel may be interested in buying a quantity of the Flash chips, and asks for a demonstration and a list of prices. Before Pixel makes a buy, Macrotech learns that there is a proposal in Congress to tax certain exports, including products such as Flash. Macrotech also learns of a proposal to impose restrictions on the export of Flash and similar products. Which of these proposals is most likely to be implemented, and why? If Congress wanted to stimulate, rather than restrict, the export of Flash, what steps might it take to do so?
3. Quaro Corp. and Selecta Corp., which are manufacturers in Techuan, a foreign country, make products that compete with the Flash chip. When Quaro and Selecta products seem to flood the U.S. market at low prices, Macrotech believes that its competitors have conspired to fix their prices. Can Macrotech file a suit against Quaro and Selecta in a U.S. court? If Quaro thought Macrotech was conspiring with other firms against it, could Quaro file a suit against Macrotech in a U.S. court? What could the U.S. government do if it found that Quaro and Selecta were selling their products in U.S. markets at "less than fair value"?

UNIT NINE • EXTENDED CASE STUDY: THE LAW IN CONTEXT

In re Simon

We discussed, in Chapter 43, the extraterritorial application of U.S. laws and the principle of comity as it applies in cases of international scope. In Chapter 3, we discussed in rem *jurisdiction, and in Chapter 23, we covered bankruptcy. In this extended case study, we examine* In re Simon,[1] *a recent decision that involved all of these topics.*

CASE BACKGROUND

Hong Kong and Shanghai Banking Corporation lent more than $37 million to Odyssey International Holdings, Limited. Hong Kong-Shanghai, incorporated in Hong Kong, frequently does business in the United States. Odyssey is an international company incorporated in the British Virgin Islands, with offices in Hong Kong. Later, in a separate deal, Hong Kong-Shanghai lent Odyssey more than $24 million. William Simon, Odyssey's major shareholder, personally guaranteed the second loan. In less than a year, with personal debts of over $200 million, Simon filed for personal bankruptcy in the United States under Chapter 7 of the U.S. Bankruptcy Code. Hong Kong-Shanghai filed a claim based on the $37 million loan, but did not file a claim based on Simon's guaranty of the $24 million loan and did not object to the discharge of his debts, which the court granted.

Hong Kong-Shanghai then filed a complaint, asking the bankruptcy court in part to declare that the discharge was not enforceable if the bank chose to ignore it to pursue collection proceedings outside the United States. The court dismissed the complaint. The bank appealed to a federal district court, which affirmed the bankruptcy court's decision. Hong Kong-Shanghai appealed to the U.S. Court of Appeals for the Ninth Circuit, primarily arguing that enforcing the discharge constituted an improper extraterritorial application of a statute (the U.S. Bankruptcy Code).

1. 153 F.3d 991 (9th Cir. 1998).

MAJORITY OPINION

THOMAS, Circuit Judge:

* * * *

* * * [T]he legislation of Congress, unless a contrary intent appears, is meant to apply only within the territorial jurisdiction of the United States. * * *

* * * *

* * * The filing of a bankruptcy petition under [the U.S. Bankruptcy Code] creates a bankruptcy estate. With certain exceptions, the estate is comprised of the debtor's legal or equitable interests in property "wherever located and by whomever held." The district court in which the bankruptcy case is commenced obtains exclusive *in rem* jurisdiction over all of the property in the estate. The court's exercise of "custody" over the debtor's property, via its exercise of *in rem* jurisdiction, essentially creates a fiction that the property—regardless of actual location—is legally located within the jurisdictional boundaries of the district in which the court sits. This includes property outside the territorial jurisdiction of the United States.

Given this clear expression of intent by Congress in the express language of the Bankruptcy Code, we conclude that Congress intended extraterritorial application of the Bankruptcy Code as it applies to property of the estate. * * *

* * * *

* * * By acceding to bankruptcy court jurisdiction so that it might recover a portion of the money it was owed, Hong Kong-Shanghai forfeited any right it had to claim that the court lacked the power to [issue a discharge and thereby] enjoin Hong Kong-Shanghai from commencing a post-bankruptcy collection proceeding against the debtor. * * * A sanction for violating that order is not an improper extraterritorial application of United States laws. * * *

* * * *

* * * [T]his case does not involve competing bankruptcy proceedings; indeed, there is no proceeding pending in Hong Kong. The sole, plenary [complete] insolvency proceeding was initiated in the United States without objection and with the participation of the appellant. Hong Kong-Shanghai cannot point to a single conflict which exists between Hong Kong and United States law on the issue in

question. In fact, the discharge * * * does not apply to the Hong Kong courts at all, but only to the creditor who enjoyed the benefits of participating in the United States bankruptcy. Under these circumstances, international comity does not dictate a result contrary to that reached by the district and bankruptcy courts.

DISSENTING OPINION

CYNTHIA HOLCOMB HALL, Circuit Judge, * * * dissenting in part * * * .

* * * The majority concludes that Congress clearly intended the extraterritorial application of the Bankruptcy Code as it applies to the property of the estate. The majority bases this conclusion on a single vague specification in [the Code] that the estate is comprised of the debtor's legal or equitable interests in property "wherever located and by whomever held." While this language may plausibly apply to property located within foreign jurisdictions, we do not simply apply statutes extraterritorially if it is plausible or even desirable to do so. We must assume that Congress legislates against the backdrop of the presumption against extraterritoriality. * * * If we were to permit possible, or even plausible, interpretations of language such as that involved here to override the presumption against extraterritorial application, there would be little left of the presumption.

MEDIA COVERAGE

The ruling of the U.S Court of Appeals for the Ninth Circuit addresses a question that is arising with increasing frequency in bankruptcy proceedings. Here, placing that ruling in context, are excerpts from an article titled "Foreign Creditors: Impact of Discharge Granted to Debtor" by John Rapasardi that appeared in the *New York Law Journal* on November 19, 1998 (vol. 220, no. 98, p. 3, col. 1).

"While the globalization of the marketplace has created increased international business opportunities, it has heightened the financial risks faced by multinational corporations and those entities or individuals that finance them. Despite the convergence in world markets brought about through a globalized economy, neither a uniform legal system governs nor a single international forum oversees cross-border liquidations and reorganizations. Consequently, conflicts frequently arise as to the policies of and actions permitted or enjoined by the insolvency laws of individual foreign jurisdictions.

One question commonly raised in the context of U.S. bankruptcy cases is what impact, if any, the discharge granted to a debtor has on foreign creditors. This issue most recently was addressed in part by the Ninth Circuit in *In re William Neil Simon*. The *Simon* court held that a foreign creditor was subject to bankruptcy court sanctions for pursuing foreign collection of a debt discharged in the debtor's U.S. bankruptcy case in which the foreign creditor had participated. Most important, the decision clarifies that foreign creditors cannot always rely on international comity in defeasance of [to undo] a bankruptcy discharge."

GOING ONLINE

The *Business Law Today,* Fifth Edition, Web site, at **http://blt.westbuslaw.com**, provides a link through which you can access other court opinions in cases involving international law.

QUESTIONS FOR ANALYSIS

1. **Law.** What might have been the effect, on the application of U.S. bankruptcy law in other cases, if the court in this case had allowed the creditor to proceed against the debtor despite the discharge in bankruptcy?
2. **Law.** Should there be an international bankruptcy law?
3. **Ethics.** What is the ethical basis for the principle of international comity?
4. **International Dimensions.** Would the principle of comity ever apply in a case like *In re Simon*, in which there was no real conflict between domestic and foreign law?
5. **Implications for the Business Manager.** What message does the holding in the *Simon* case have for foreign creditors?

APPENDIX A

The Constitution of The United States

Preamble

We the People of the United States, in Order to form a more perfect Union, establish Justice, insure domestic Tranquility, provide for the common defence, promote the general Welfare, and secure the Blessings of Liberty to ourselves and our Posterity, do ordain and establish this Constitution for the United States of America.

Article I

Section 1. All legislative Powers herein granted shall be vested in a Congress of the United States, which shall consist of a Senate and House of Representatives.

Section 2. The House of Representatives shall be composed of Members chosen every second Year by the People of the several States, and the Electors in each State shall have the Qualifications requisite for Electors of the most numerous Branch of the State Legislature.

No Person shall be a Representative who shall not have attained to the Age of twenty five Years, and been seven Years a Citizen of the United States, and who shall not, when elected, be an Inhabitant of that State in which he shall be chosen.

Representatives and direct Taxes shall be apportioned among the several States which may be included within this Union, according to their respective Numbers, which shall be determined by adding to the whole Number of free Persons, including those bound to Service for a Term of Years, and excluding Indians not taxed, three fifths of all other Persons. The actual Enumeration shall be made within three Years after the first Meeting of the Congress of the United States, and within every subsequent Term of ten Years, in such Manner as they shall by Law direct. The Number of Representatives shall not exceed one for every thirty Thousand, but each State shall have at Least one Representative; and until such enumeration shall be made, the State of New Hampshire shall be entitled to chuse three, Massachusetts eight, Rhode Island and Providence Plantations one, Connecticut five, New York six, New Jersey four, Pennsylvania eight, Delaware one, Maryland six, Virginia ten, North Carolina five, South Carolina five, and Georgia three.

When vacancies happen in the Representation from any State, the Executive Authority thereof shall issue Writs of Election to fill such Vacancies.

The House of Representatives shall chuse their Speaker and other Officers; and shall have the sole Power of Impeachment.

Section 3. The Senate of the United States shall be composed of two Senators from each State, chosen by the Legislature thereof, for six Years; and each Senator shall have one Vote.

Immediately after they shall be assembled in Consequence of the first Election, they shall be divided as equally as may be into three Classes. The Seats of the Senators of the first Class shall be vacated at the Expiration of the second Year, of the second Class at the Expiration of the fourth Year, and of the third Class at the Expiration of the sixth Year, so that one third may be chosen every second Year; and if Vacancies happen by Resignation, or otherwise, during the Recess of the Legislature of any State, the Executive thereof may make temporary Appointments until the next Meeting of the Legislature, which shall then fill such Vacancies.

No Person shall be a Senator who shall not have attained to the Age of thirty Years, and been nine Years a Citizen of the United States, and who shall not, when elected, be an Inhabitant of that State for which he shall be chosen.

The Vice President of the United States shall be President of the Senate, but shall have no Vote, unless they be equally divided.

The Senate shall chuse their other Officers, and also a President pro tempore, in the Absence of the Vice President, or when he shall exercise the Office of President of the United States.

The Senate shall have the sole Power to try all Impeachments. When sitting for that Purpose, they shall be on Oath or Affirmation. When the President of the United States is tried, the Chief Justice shall preside: And no Person shall be convicted without the Concurrence of two thirds of the Members present.

Judgment in Cases of Impeachment shall not extend further than to removal from Office, and disqualification to hold and enjoy any Office of honor, Trust, or Profit under the United States: but the Party convicted shall nevertheless be liable and subject to Indictment, Trial, Judgment, and Punishment, according to Law.

Section 4. The Times, Places and Manner of holding Elections for Senators and Representatives, shall be prescribed in each State by the Legislature thereof; but the Congress may at any time by Law make or alter such Regulations, except as to the Places of chusing Senators.

The Congress shall assemble at least once in every Year, and such Meeting shall be on the first Monday in December, unless they shall by Law appoint a different Day.

Section 5. Each House shall be the Judge of the Elections, Returns, and Qualifications of its own Members, and a Majority of each shall constitute a Quorum to do Business; but a smaller Number may adjourn from day to day, and may be authorized to compel the Attendance of absent Members, in such Manner, and under such Penalties as each House may provide.

Each House may determine the Rules of its Proceedings, punish its Members for disorderly Behavior, and, with the Concurrence of two thirds, expel a Member.

Each House shall keep a Journal of its Proceedings, and from time to time publish the same, excepting such Parts as may in their Judgment require Secrecy; and the Yeas and Nays of the Members of either House on any question shall, at the Desire of one fifth of those Present, be entered on the Journal.

Neither House, during the Session of Congress, shall, without the Consent of the other, adjourn for more than three days, nor to any other Place than that in which the two Houses shall be sitting.

Section 6. The Senators and Representatives shall receive a Compensation for their Services, to be ascertained by Law, and paid out of the Treasury of the United States. They shall in all Cases, except Treason, Felony and Breach of the Peace, be privileged from Arrest during their Attendance at the Session of their respective Houses, and in going to and returning from the same; and for any Speech or Debate in either House, they shall not be questioned in any other Place.

No Senator or Representative shall, during the Time for which he was elected, be appointed to any civil Office under the Authority of the United States, which shall have been created, or the Emoluments whereof shall have been increased during such time; and no Person holding any Office under the United States, shall be a Member of either House during his Continuance in Office.

Section 7. All Bills for raising Revenue shall originate in the House of Representatives; but the Senate may propose or concur with Amendments as on other Bills.

Every Bill which shall have passed the House of Representatives and the Senate, shall, before it become a Law, be presented to the President of the United States; If he approve he shall sign it, but if not he shall return it, with his Objections to the House in which it shall have originated, who shall enter the Objections at large on their Journal, and proceed to reconsider it. If after such Reconsideration two thirds of that House shall agree to pass the Bill, it shall be sent together with the Objections, to the other House, by which it shall likewise be reconsidered, and if approved by two thirds of that House, it shall become a Law. But in all such Cases the Votes of both Houses shall be determined by Yeas and Nays, and the Names of the Persons voting for and against the Bill shall be entered on the Journal of each House respectively. If any Bill shall not be returned by the President within ten Days (Sundays excepted) after it shall have been presented to him, the Same shall be a Law, in like Manner as if he had signed it, unless the Congress by their Adjournment prevent its Return in which Case it shall not be a Law.

Every Order, Resolution, or Vote, to which the Concurrence of the Senate and House of Representatives may be necessary (except on a question of Adjournment) shall be presented to the President of the United States; and before the Same shall take Effect, shall be approved by him, or being disapproved by him, shall be repassed by two thirds of the Senate and House of Representatives, according to the Rules and Limitations prescribed in the Case of a Bill.

Section 8. The Congress shall have Power To lay and collect Taxes, Duties, Imposts and Excises, to pay the Debts and provide for the common Defence and general Welfare of the United States; but all Duties, Imposts and Excises shall be uniform throughout the United States;

To borrow Money on the credit of the United States;

To regulate Commerce with foreign Nations, and among the several States, and with the Indian Tribes;

To establish an uniform Rule of Naturalization, and uniform Laws on the subject of Bankruptcies throughout the United States;

To coin Money, regulate the Value thereof, and of foreign Coin, and fix the Standard of Weights and Measures;

To provide for the Punishment of counterfeiting the Securities and current Coin of the United States;

To establish Post Offices and post Roads;

To promote the Progress of Science and useful Arts, by securing for limited Times to Authors and Inventors the exclusive Right to their respective Writings and Discoveries;

To constitute Tribunals inferior to the supreme Court;

To define and punish Piracies and Felonies committed on the high Seas, and Offenses against the Law of Nations;

To declare War, grant Letters of Marque and Reprisal, and make Rules concerning Captures on Land and Water;

To raise and support Armies, but no Appropriation of Money to that Use shall be for a longer Term than two Years;

To provide and maintain a Navy;

To make Rules for the Government and Regulation of the land and naval Forces;

To provide for calling forth the Militia to execute the Laws of the Union, suppress Insurrections and repel Invasions;

To provide for organizing, arming, and disciplining, the Militia, and for governing such Part of them as may be employed in the Service of the United States, reserving to the States respectively, the Appointment of the Officers, and the Authority of training the Militia according to the discipline prescribed by Congress;

To exercise exclusive Legislation in all Cases whatsoever, over such District (not exceeding ten Miles square) as may, by Cession of particular States, and the Acceptance of Congress, become the Seat of the Government of the United States, and to exercise like Authority over all Places purchased by the Consent of the Legislature of the State in which the Same shall be, for the Erection of Forts, Magazines, Arsenals, dock-Yards, and other needful Buildings;—And

To make all Laws which shall be necessary and proper for carrying into Execution the foregoing Powers, and all other Powers vested by this Constitution in the Government of the United States, or in any Department or Officer thereof.

Section 9. The Migration or Importation of such Persons as any of the States now existing shall think proper to admit, shall not be prohibited by the Congress prior to the Year one thousand eight hundred and eight, but a Tax or duty may be imposed on such Importation, not exceeding ten dollars for each Person.

The privilege of the Writ of Habeas Corpus shall not be suspended, unless when in Cases of Rebellion or Invasion the public Safety may require it.

No Bill of Attainder or ex post facto Law shall be passed.

No Capitation, or other direct, Tax shall be laid, unless in Proportion to the Census or Enumeration herein before directed to be taken.

No Tax or Duty shall be laid on Articles exported from any State.

No Preference shall be given by any Regulation of Commerce or Revenue to the Ports of one State over those of another: nor shall Vessels bound to, or from, one State be obliged to enter, clear, or pay Duties in another.

No Money shall be drawn from the Treasury, but in Consequence of Appropriations made by Law; and a regular Statement and Account of the Receipts and Expenditures of all public Money shall be published from time to time.

No Title of Nobility shall be granted by the United States: And no Person holding any Office of Profit or Trust under them, shall, without the Consent of the Congress, accept of any present, Emolument, Office, or Title, of any kind whatever, from any King, Prince, or foreign State.

Section 10. No State shall enter into any Treaty, Alliance, or Confederation; grant Letters of Marque and Reprisal; coin Money; emit Bills of Credit; make any Thing but gold and silver Coin a Tender in Payment of Debts; pass any Bill of Attainder, ex post facto Law, or Law impairing the Obligation of Contracts, or grant any Title of Nobility.

No State shall, without the Consent of the Congress, lay any Imposts or Duties on Imports or Exports, except what may be absolutely necessary for executing its inspection Laws: and the net Produce of all Duties and Imposts, laid by any State on Imports or Exports, shall be for the Use of the Treasury of the United States; and all such Laws shall be subject to the Revision and Controul of the Congress.

No State shall, without the Consent of Congress, lay any Duty of Tonnage, keep Troops, or Ships of War in time of Peace, enter into any Agreement or Compact with another State, or with a foreign Power, or engage in War, unless actually invaded, or in such imminent Danger as will not admit of delay.

ARTICLE II

Section 1. The executive Power shall be vested in a President of the United States of America. He shall hold his Office during the Term of four Years, and, together with the Vice President, chosen for the same Term, be elected, as follows:

Each State shall appoint, in such Manner as the Legislature thereof may direct, a Number of Electors, equal to the whole Number of Senators and Representatives to which the State may be entitled in the Congress; but no Senator or Representative, or Person holding an Office of Trust or Profit under the United States, shall be appointed an Elector.

The Electors shall meet in their respective States, and vote by Ballot for two Persons, of whom one at least shall not be an Inhabitant of the same State with themselves. And they shall make a List of all the Persons voted for, and of the Number of Votes for each; which List they shall sign and certify, and transmit sealed to the Seat of the Government of the United States, directed to the President of the Senate. The President of the Senate shall, in the Presence of the Senate and House of Representatives, open all the Certificates, and the Votes shall then be counted. The Person having the greatest Number of Votes shall be the President, if such Number be a Majority of the whole Number of Electors appointed; and if there be more than one who have such Majority, and have an equal Number of Votes, then the House of Representatives shall immediately chuse by Ballot one of them for President; and if no Person have a Majority, then from the five highest on the List the said House shall in like Manner chuse the President. But in chusing the President, the Votes shall be taken by States, the Representation from each State having one Vote; A quorum for this Purpose shall consist of a Member or Members from two thirds of the States, and a Majority of all the States shall be necessary to a Choice. In every Case, after the Choice of the President, the Person having the greater Number of Votes of the Electors shall be the Vice President. But if there should remain two or more who have equal Votes, the Senate shall chuse from them by Ballot the Vice President.

The Congress may determine the Time of chusing the Electors, and the Day on which they shall give their Votes; which Day shall be the same throughout the United States.

No person except a natural born Citizen, or a Citizen of the United States, at the time of the Adoption of this Constitution, shall be eligible to the Office of President; neither shall any Person be eligible to that Office who shall not have attained to the Age of thirty five Years, and been fourteen Years a Resident within the United States.

In Case of the Removal of the President from Office, or of his Death, Resignation or Inability to discharge the Powers and Duties of the said Office, the same shall devolve on the Vice President, and the Congress may by Law provide for the Case of Removal, Death, Resignation or Inability, both of the President and Vice President, declaring what Officer shall then act as President, and such Officer shall act accordingly, until the Disability be removed, or a President shall be elected.

The President shall, at stated Times, receive for his Services, a Compensation, which shall neither be increased nor diminished during the Period for which he shall have been elected, and he shall not receive within that Period any other Emolument from the United States, or any of them.

Before he enter on the Execution of his Office, he shall take the following Oath or Affirmation: "I do solemnly swear (or affirm) that I will faithfully execute the Office of President of the United States, and will to the best of my Ability, preserve, protect and defend the Constitution of the United States."

Section 2. The President shall be Commander in Chief of the Army and Navy of the United States, and of the Militia of the several States, when called into the actual Service of the United States; he may require the Opinion, in writing, of the principal Officer in each of the executive Departments, upon any Subject relating to the Duties of their respective Offices, and he shall have Power to grant Reprieves and Pardons for Offenses against the United States, except in Cases of Impeachment.

He shall have Power, by and with the Advice and Consent of the Senate to make Treaties, provided two thirds of the Senators present concur; and he shall nominate, and by and with the Advice and Consent of the Senate, shall appoint Ambassadors, other public Ministers and Consuls, Judges of the supreme Court, and all other Officers of the United States, whose Appointments are not herein otherwise provided for, and which shall be established by Law; but the Congress may by Law vest the Appointment of such inferior Officers, as they think proper, in the President alone, in the Courts of Law, or in the Heads of Departments.

The President shall have Power to fill up all Vacancies that may happen during the Recess of the Senate, by granting Commissions which shall expire at the End of their next Session.

Section 3. He shall from time to time give to the Congress Information of the State of the Union, and recommend to their Consideration such Measures as he shall judge necessary and expedient; he may, on extraordinary Occasions, convene both Houses, or either of them, and in Case of Disagreement between them, with Respect to the Time of Adjournment, he may adjourn them to such Time as he shall think proper; he shall receive Ambassadors and other public Ministers; he shall take Care that the Laws be faithfully executed, and shall Commission all the Officers of the United States.

Section 4. The President, Vice President and all civil Officers of the United States, shall be removed from Office on Impeachment for, and Conviction of, Treason, Bribery, or other high Crimes and Misdemeanors.

Article III

Section 1. The judicial Power of the United States, shall be vested in one supreme Court, and in such inferior Courts as the Congress may from time to time ordain and establish. The Judges, both of the supreme and inferior Courts, shall hold their Offices during good Behaviour, and shall, at stated Times, receive for their Services a Compensation, which shall not be diminished during their Continuance in Office.

Section 2. The judicial Power shall extend to all Cases, in Law and Equity, arising under this Constitution, the Laws of the United States, and Treaties made, or which shall be made, under their Authority;—to all Cases affecting Ambassadors, other public Ministers and Consuls;—to all Cases of admiralty and maritime Jurisdiction;—to Controversies to which the United States shall be a Party;—to Controversies between two or more States;—between a State and Citizens of another State;—between Citizens of different States;—between Citizens of the same State claiming Lands under Grants of different States, and between a State, or the Citizens thereof, and foreign States, Citizens or Subjects.

In all Cases affecting Ambassadors, other public Ministers and Consuls, and those in which a State shall be a Party, the supreme Court shall have original Jurisdiction. In all the other Cases before mentioned, the supreme Court shall have appellate Jurisdiction, both as to Law and Fact, with such Exceptions, and under such Regulations as the Congress shall make.

The Trial of all Crimes, except in Cases of Impeachment, shall be by Jury; and such Trial shall be held in the State where the said Crimes shall have been committed; but when not committed within any State, the Trial shall be at such Place or Places as the Congress may by Law have directed.

Section 3. Treason against the United States, shall consist only in levying War against them, or, in adhering to their Enemies, giving them Aid and Comfort. No Person shall be convicted of Treason unless on the Testimony of two Witnesses to the same overt Act, or on Confession in open Court.

The Congress shall have Power to declare the Punishment of Treason, but no Attainder of Treason shall work Corruption of Blood, or Forfeiture except during the Life of the Person attainted.

Article IV

Section 1. Full Faith and Credit shall be given in each State to the public Acts, Records, and judicial Proceedings of every other State. And the Congress may by general Laws prescribe the Manner in which such Acts, Records and Proceedings shall be proved, and the Effect thereof.

Section 2. The Citizens of each State shall be entitled to all Privileges and Immunities of Citizens in the several States.

A Person charged in any State with Treason, Felony, or other Crime, who shall flee from Justice, and be found in another State, shall on Demand of the executive Authority of the State from which he fled, be delivered up, to be removed to the State having Jurisdiction of the Crime.

No Person held to Service or Labour in one State, under the Laws thereof, escaping into another, shall, in Consequence of any Law or Regulation therein, be discharged from such Service or Labour, but shall be delivered up on Claim of the Party to whom such Service or Labour may be due.

Section 3. New States may be admitted by the Congress into this Union; but no new State shall be formed or erected within the Jurisdiction of any other State; nor any State be formed by the Junction of two or more States, or Parts of States, without the Consent of the Legislatures of the States concerned as well as of the Congress.

The Congress shall have Power to dispose of and make all needful Rules and Regulations respecting the Territory or other Property belonging to the United States; and nothing in this Constitution shall be so construed as to Prejudice any Claims of the United States, or of any particular State.

Section 4. The United States shall guarantee to every State in this Union a Republican Form of Government, and shall protect each of them against Invasion; and on Application of the Legislature, or of the Executive (when the Legislature cannot be convened) against domestic Violence.

ARTICLE V

The Congress, whenever two thirds of both Houses shall deem it necessary, shall propose Amendments to this Constitution, or, on the Application of the Legislatures of two thirds of the several States, shall call a Convention for proposing Amendments, which, in either Case, shall be valid to all Intents and Purposes, as part of this Constitution, when ratified by the Legislatures of three fourths of the several States, or by Conventions in three fourths thereof, as the one or the other Mode of Ratification may be proposed by the Congress; Provided that no Amendment which may be made prior to the Year One thousand eight hundred and eight shall in any Manner affect the first and fourth Clauses in the Ninth Section of the first Article; and that no State, without its Consent, shall be deprived of its equal Suffrage in the Senate.

ARTICLE VI

All Debts contracted and Engagements entered into, before the Adoption of this Constitution shall be as valid against the United States under this Constitution, as under the Confederation.

This Constitution, and the Laws of the United States which shall be made in Pursuance thereof; and all Treaties made, or which shall be made, under the Authority of the United States, shall be the supreme Law of the Land; and the Judges in every State shall be bound thereby, any Thing in the Constitution or Laws of any State to the Contrary notwithstanding.

The Senators and Representatives before mentioned, and the Members of the several State Legislatures, and all executive and judicial Officers, both of the United States and of the several States, shall be bound by Oath or Affirmation, to support this Constitution; but no religious Test shall ever be required as a Qualification to any Office or public Trust under the United States.

ARTICLE VII

The Ratification of the Conventions of nine States shall be sufficient for the Establishment of this Constitution between the States so ratifying the Same.

AMENDMENT I [1791]

Congress shall make no law respecting an establishment of religion, or prohibiting the free exercise thereof; or abridging the freedom of speech, or of the press; or the right of the people peaceably to assembly, and to petition the Government for a redress of grievances.

AMENDMENT II [1791]

A well regulated Militia, being necessary to the security of a free State, the right of the people to keep and bear Arms, shall not be infringed.

AMENDMENT III [1791]

No Soldier shall, in time of peace be quartered in any house, without the consent of the Owner, nor in time of war, but in a manner to be prescribed by law.

AMENDMENT IV [1791]

The right of the people to be secure in their persons, houses, papers, and effects, against unreasonable searches and seizures, shall not be violated, and no Warrants shall issue, but upon probable cause, supported by Oath or affirmation, and particularly describing the place to be searched, and the persons or things to be seized.

AMENDMENT V [1791]

No person shall be held to answer for a capital, or otherwise infamous crime, unless on a presentment or indictment of a Grand Jury, except in cases arising in the land or naval forces, or in the Militia, when in actual service in time of War or public danger; nor shall any person be subject for the same offence to be twice put in jeopardy of life or limb; nor shall be compelled in any criminal case to be a witness against himself, nor be deprived of life, liberty, or property, without due process of law; nor shall private property be taken for public use, without just compensation.

AMENDMENT VI [1791]

In all criminal prosecutions, the accused shall enjoy the right to a speedy and public trial, by an impartial jury of the State and district wherein the crime shall have been committed, which district shall have been previously ascertained by law, and to be informed of the nature and cause of the accusation; to be confronted with the witnesses against him; to have compulsory process for obtaining witnesses in his favor, and to have the Assistance of Counsel for his defence.

AMENDMENT VII [1791]

In Suits at common law, where the value in controversy shall exceed twenty dollars, the right of trial by jury shall be preserved, and no fact tried by jury, shall be otherwise re-examined in any Court of the United States, than according to the rules of the common law.

AMENDMENT VIII [1791]

Excessive bail shall not be required, nor excessive fines imposed, nor cruel and unusual punishments inflicted.

AMENDMENT IX [1791]

The enumeration in the Constitution, of certain rights, shall not be construed to deny or disparage others retained by the people.

AMENDMENT X [1791]

The powers not delegated to the United States by the Constitution, nor prohibited by it to the States, are reserved to the States respectively, or to the people.

AMENDMENT XI [1798]

The Judicial power of the United States shall not be construed to extend to any suit in law or equity, commenced or prosecuted against one of the United States by Citizens of another State, or by Citizens or Subjects of any Foreign State.

Amendment XII [1804]

The Electors shall meet in their respective states, and vote by ballot for President and Vice-President, one of whom, at least, shall not be an inhabitant of the same state with themselves; they shall name in their ballots the person voted for as President, and in distinct ballots the person voted for as Vice-President, and they shall make distinct lists of all persons voted for as President, and of all persons voted for as Vice-President, and of the number of votes for each, which lists they shall sign and certify, and transmit sealed to the seat of the government of the United States, directed to the President of the Senate;—The President of the Senate shall, in the presence of the Senate and House of Representatives, open all the certificates and the votes shall then be counted;—The person having the greatest number of votes for President, shall be the President, if such number be a majority of the whole number of Electors appointed; and if no person have such majority, then from the persons having the highest numbers not exceeding three on the list of those voted for as President, the House of Representatives shall choose immediately, by ballot, the President. But in choosing the President, the votes shall be taken by states, the representation from each state having one vote; a quorum for this purpose shall consist of a member or members from two-thirds of the states, and a majority of all states shall be necessary to a choice. And if the House of Representatives shall not choose a President whenever the right of choice shall devolve upon them, before the fourth day of March next following, then the Vice-President shall act as President, as in the case of the death or other constitutional disability of the President.—The person having the greatest number of votes as Vice-President, shall be the Vice-President, if such number be a majority of the whole number of Electors appointed, and if no person have a majority, then from the two highest numbers on the list, the Senate shall choose the Vice-President; a quorum for the purpose shall consist of two-thirds of the whole number of Senators, and a majority of the whole number shall be necessary to a choice. But no person constitutionally ineligible to the office of President shall be eligible to that of Vice-President of the United States.

Amendment XIII [1865]

Section 1. Neither slavery nor involuntary servitude, except as a punishment for crime whereof the party shall have been duly convicted, shall exist within the United States, or any place subject to their jurisdiction.

Section 2. Congress shall have power to enforce this article by appropriate legislation.

Amendment XIV [1868]

Section 1. All persons born or naturalized in the United States, and subject to the jurisdiction thereof, are citizens of the United States and of the State wherein they reside. No State shall make or enforce any law which shall abridge the privileges or immunities of citizens of the United States; nor shall any State deprive any person of life, liberty, or property, without due process of law; nor deny to any person within its jurisdiction the equal protection of the laws.

Section 2. Representatives shall be apportioned among the several States according to their respective numbers, counting the whole number of persons in each State, excluding Indians not taxed. But when the right to vote at any election for the choice of electors for President and Vice President of the United States, Representatives in Congress, the Executive and Judicial officers of a State, or the members of the Legislature thereof, is denied to any of the male inhabitants of such State, being twenty-one years of age, and citizens of the United States, or in any way abridged, except for participation in rebellion, or other crime, the basis of representation therein shall be reduced in the proportion which the number of such male citizens shall bear to the whole number of male citizens twenty-one years of age in such State.

Section 3. No person shall be a Senator or Representative in Congress, or elector of President and Vice President, or hold any office, civil or military, under the United States, or under any State, who having previously taken an oath, as a member of Congress, or as an officer of the United States, or as a member of any State legislature, or as an executive or judicial officer of any State, to support the Constitution of the United States, shall have engaged in insurrection or rebellion against the same, or given aid or comfort to the enemies thereof. But Congress may by a vote of two-thirds of each House, remove such disability.

Section 4. The validity of the public debt of the United States, authorized by law, including debts incurred for payment of pensions and bounties for services in suppressing insurrection or rebellion, shall not be questioned. But neither the United States nor any State shall assume or pay any debt or obligation incurred in aid of insurrection or rebellion against the United States, or any claim for the loss or emancipation of any slave; but all such debts, obligations and claims shall be held illegal and void.

Section 5. The Congress shall have power to enforce, by appropriate legislation, the provisions of this article.

Amendment XV [1870]

Section 1. The right of citizens of the United States to vote shall not be denied or abridged by the United States or by any State on account of race, color, or previous condition of servitude.

Section 2. The Congress shall have power to enforce this article by appropriate legislation.

Amendment XVI [1913]

The Congress shall have power to lay and collect taxes on incomes, from whatever source derived, without apportionment among the several States, and without regard to any census or enumeration.

Amendment XVII [1913]

Section 1. The Senate of the United States shall be composed of two Senators from each State, elected by the people thereof, for six years; and each Senator shall have one vote. The electors in each State shall have the qualifications requisite for electors of the most numerous branch of the State legislatures.

Section 2. When vacancies happen in the representation of any State in the Senate, the executive authority of such State shall issue writs of election to fill such vacancies: *Provided*, That the legislature of any State may empower the executive thereof to make temporary appointments until the people fill the vacancies by election as the legislature may direct.

Section 3. This amendment shall not be so construed as to affect the election or term of any Senator chosen before it becomes valid as part of the Constitution.

Amendment XVIII [1919]

Section 1. After one year from the ratification of this article the manufacture, sale, or transportation of intoxicating liquors within, the importation thereof into, or the exportation thereof from the United States and all territory subject to the jurisdiction thereof for beverage purposes is hereby prohibited.

Section 2. The Congress and the several States shall have concurrent power to enforce this article by appropriate legislation.

Section 3. This article shall be inoperative unless it shall have been ratified as an amendment to the Constitution by the legislatures of the several States, as provided in the Constitution, within seven years from the date of the submission hereof to the States by the Congress.

Amendment XIX [1920]

Section 1. The right of citizens of the United States to vote shall not be denied or abridged by the United States or by any State on account of sex.

Section 2. Congress shall have power to enforce this article by appropriate legislation.

Amendment XX [1933]

Section 1. The terms of the President and Vice President shall end at noon on the 20th day of January, and the terms of Senators and Representatives at noon on the 3d day of January, of the years in which such terms would have ended if this article had not been ratified; and the terms of their successors shall then begin.

Section 2. The Congress shall assemble at least once in every year, and such meeting shall begin at noon on the 3d day of January, unless they shall by law appoint a different day.

Section 3. If, at the time fixed for the beginning of the term of the President, the President elect shall have died, the Vice President elect shall become President. If the President shall not have been chosen before the time fixed for the beginning of his term, or if the President elect shall have failed to qualify, then the Vice President elect shall act as President until a President shall have qualified; and the Congress may by law provide for the case wherein neither a President elect nor a Vice President elect shall have qualified, declaring who shall then act as President, or the manner in which one who is to act shall be selected, and such person shall act accordingly until a President or Vice President shall have qualified.

Section 4. The Congress may by law provide for the case of the death of any of the persons from whom the House of Representatives may choose a President whenever the right of choice shall have devolved upon them, and for the case of the death of any of the persons from whom the Senate may choose a Vice President whenever the right of choice shall have devolved upon them.

Section 5. Sections 1 and 2 shall take effect on the 15th day of October following the ratification of this article.

Section 6. This article shall be inoperative unless it shall have been ratified as an amendment to the Constitution by the legislatures of three-fourths of the several States within seven years from the date of its submission.

Amendment XXI [1933]

Section 1. The eighteenth article of amendment to the Constitution of the United States is hereby repealed.

Section 2. The transportation or importation into any State, Territory, or possession of the United States for delivery or use therein of intoxicating liquors, in violation of the laws thereof, is hereby prohibited.

Section 3. This article shall be inoperative unless it shall have been ratified as an amendment to the Constitution by conventions in the several States, as provided in the Constitution, within seven years from the date of the submission hereof to the States by the Congress.

Amendment XXII [1951]

Section 1. No person shall be elected to the office of the President more than twice, and no person who has held the office of President, or acted as President, for more than two years of a term to which some other person was elected President shall be elected to the office of President more than once. But this Article shall not apply to any person holding the office of President when this Article was proposed by the Congress, and shall not prevent any person who may be holding the office of President, or acting as President, during the term within which this Article becomes operative from holding the office of President or acting as President during the remainder of such term.

Section 2. This article shall be inoperative unless it shall have been ratified as an amendment to the Constitution by the legislatures of three-fourths of the several States within seven years from the date of its submission to the States by the Congress.

Amendment XXIII [1961]

Section 1. The District constituting the seat of Government of the United States shall appoint in such manner as the Congress may direct:

A number of electors of President and Vice President equal to the whole number of Senators and Representatives in Congress to which the District would be entitled if it were a State, but in no event more than the least populous state; they shall be in addition to those appointed by the states, but they shall be considered, for the purposes of the election of President and Vice President, to be electors appointed by a state; and they shall meet in the District and perform such duties as provided by the twelfth article of amendment.

Section 2. The Congress shall have power to enforce this article by appropriate legislation.

Amendment XXIV [1964]

Section 1. The right of citizens of the United States to vote in any primary or other election for President or Vice President, for electors for President or Vice President, or for Senator or Representative in Congress, shall not be denied or abridged by the United States, or any State by reason of failure to pay any poll tax or other tax.

Section 2. The Congress shall have power to enforce this article by appropriate legislation.

Amendment XXV [1967]

Section 1. In case of the removal of the President from office or of his death or resignation, the Vice President shall become President.

Section 2. Whenever there is a vacancy in the office of the Vice President, the President shall nominate a Vice President who shall take office upon confirmation by a majority vote of both Houses of Congress.

Section 3. Whenever the President transmits to the President pro tempore of the Senate and the Speaker of the House of Representatives his written declaration that he is unable to discharge the powers and duties of his office, and until he transmits to them a written declaration to the contrary, such powers and duties shall be discharged by the Vice President as Acting President.

Section 4. Whenever the Vice President and a majority of either the principal officers of the executive departments or of such other body as Congress may by law provide, transmit to the President pro tempore of the Senate and the Speaker of the House of Representatives their written declaration that the President is unable to discharge the powers and duties of his office, the Vice President shall immediately assume the powers and duties of the office as Acting President.

Thereafter, when the President transmits to the President pro tempore of the Senate and the Speaker of the House of Representatives his written declaration that no inability exists, he shall resume the powers and duties of his office unless the Vice President and a majority of either the principal officers of the executive department or of such other body as Congress may by law provide, transmit within four days to the President pro tempore of the Senate and the Speaker of the House of Representatives their written declaration that the President is unable to discharge the powers and duties of his office. Thereupon Congress shall decide the issue, assembling within forty-eight hours for that purpose if not in session. If the Congress, within twenty-one days after receipt of the latter written declaration, or, if Congress is not in session, within twenty-one days after Congress is required to assemble, determines by two-thirds vote of both Houses that the President is unable to discharge the powers and duties of his office, the Vice President shall continue to discharge the same as Acting President; otherwise, the President shall resume the powers and duties of his office.

Amendment XXVI [1971]

Section 1. The right of citizens of the United States, who are eighteen years of age or older, to vote shall not be denied or abridged by the United States or by any State on account of age.

Section 2. The Congress shall have power to enforce this article by appropriate legislation.

Amendment XXVII [1992]

No law, varying the compensation for the services of the Senators and Representatives, shall take effect, until an election of Representatives shall have intervened.

Appendix B The Uniform Commercial Code

(Adopted in fifty-two jurisdictions; all fifty States, although Louisiana has adopted only Articles 1, 3, 4, 7, 8, and 9; the District of Columbia; and the Virgin Islands.)

The Code consists of the following articles:

Art.

1. General Provisions
2. Sales
2A. Leases
3. Commercial Paper
4. Bank Deposits and Collections
4A. Funds Transfers
5. Letters of Credit
6. Bulk Transfers (including Alternative B)
7. Warehouse Receipts, Bills of Lading and Other Documents of Title
8. Investment Securities
9. Secured Transactions: Sales of Accounts and Chattel Paper
10. Effective Date and Repealer
11. Effective Date and Transition Provisions

Article 1
GENERAL PROVISIONS

Part 1 Short Title, Construction, Application and Subject Matter of the Act

§ 1—101. Short Title.

This Act shall be known and may be cited as Uniform Commercial Code.

§ 1—102. Purposes; Rules of Construction; Variation by Agreement.

(1) This Act shall be liberally construed and applied to promote its underlying purposes and policies.

(2) Underlying purposes and policies of this Act are

(a) to simplify, clarify and modernize the law governing commercial transactions;

(b) to permit the continued expansion of commercial practices through custom, usage and agreement of the parties;

(c) to make uniform the law among the various jurisdictions.

(3) The effect of provisions of this Act may be varied by agreement, except as otherwise provided in this Act and except that the obligations of good faith, diligence, reasonableness and care prescribed by this Act may not be disclaimed by agreement but the parties may by agreement determine the standards by which the performance of such obligations is to be measured if such standards are not manifestly unreasonable.

(4) The presence in certain provisions of this Act of the words "unless otherwise agreed" or words of similar import does not imply that the effect of other provisions may not be varied by agreement under subsection (3).

(5) In this Act unless the context otherwise requires

(a) words in the singular number include the plural, and in the plural include the singular;

(b) words of the masculine gender include the feminine and the neuter, and when the sense so indicates words of the neuter gender may refer to any gender.

§ 1—103. Supplementary General Principles of Law Applicable.

Unless displaced by the particular provisions of this Act, the principles of law and equity, including the law merchant and the law relative to capacity to contract, principal and agent, estoppel, fraud, misrepresentation, duress, coercion, mistake, bankruptcy, or other validating or invalidating cause shall supplement its provisions.

§ 1—104. Construction Against Implicit Repeal.

This Act being a general act intended as a unified coverage of its subject matter, no part of it shall be deemed to be impliedly repealed by subsequent legislation if such construction can reasonably be avoided.

§ 1—105. Territorial Application of the Act; Parties' Power to Choose Applicable Law.

(1) Except as provided hereafter in this section, when a transaction bears a reasonable relation to this state and also to another state or nation the parties may agree that the law either of this state or of such other state or nation shall govern their rights and duties. Failing such agreement this Act applies to transactions bearing an appropriate relation to this state.

(2) Where one of the following provisions of this Act specifies the applicable law, that provision governs and a contrary agreement is effective only to the extent permitted by the law (including the conflict of laws rules) so specified:

Rights of creditors against sold goods. Section 2—402.

Applicability of the Article on Leases. Sections 2A—105 and 2A—106.

Applicability of the Article on Bank Deposits and Collections. Section 4—102.

Governing law in the Article on Funds Transfers. Section 4A—507.

Letters of Credit, Section 5—116.

Bulk sales subject to the Article on Bulk Sales. Section 6—103.

Applicability of the Article on Investment Securities. Section 8—106.

Perfection provisions of the Article on Secured Transactions. Section 9—103.

§ 1—106. Remedies to Be Liberally Administered.

(1) The remedies provided by this Act shall be liberally administered to the end that the aggrieved party may be put in as good a position as if the other party had fully performed but neither consequential or special nor penal damages may be had except as specifically provided in this Act or by other rule of law.

(2) Any right or obligation declared by this Act is enforceable by action unless the provision declaring it specifies a different and limited effect.

§ 1—107. Waiver or Renunciation of Claim or Right After Breach.

Any claim or right arising out of an alleged breach can be discharged in whole or in part without consideration by a written waiver or renunciation signed and delivered by the aggrieved party.

§ 1—108. Severability.

If any provision or clause of this Act or application thereof to any person or circumstances is held invalid, such invalidity shall not affect other provisions or applications of the Act which can be given effect without the invalid provision or application, and to this end the provisions of this Act are declared to be severable.

§ 1—109. Section Captions.

Section captions are parts of this Act.

Part 2 General Definitions and Principles of Interpretation

§ 1—201. General Definitions.

Subject to additional definitions contained in the subsequent Articles of this Act which are applicable to specific Articles or Parts thereof, and unless the context otherwise requires, in this Act:

(1) "Action" in the sense of a judicial proceeding includes recoupment, counterclaim, set-off, suit in equity and any other proceedings in which rights are determined.

(2) "Aggrieved party" means a party entitled to resort to a remedy.

(3) "Agreement" means the bargain of the parties in fact as found in their language or by implication from other circumstances including course of dealing or usage of trade or course of performance as provided in this Act (Sections 1—205 and 2—208). Whether an agreement has legal consequences is determined by the provisions of this Act, if applicable; otherwise by the law of contracts (Section 1—103). (Compare "Contract".)

(4) "Bank" means any person engaged in the business of banking.

(5) "Bearer" means the person in possession of an instrument, document of title, or certificated security payable to bearer or indorsed in blank.

(6) "Bill of lading" means a document evidencing the receipt of goods for shipment issued by a person engaged in the business of transporting or forwarding goods, and includes an airbill. "Airbill" means a document serving for air transportation as a bill of lading does for marine or rail transportation, and includes an air consignment note or air waybill.

(7) "Branch" includes a separately incorporated foreign branch of a bank.

(8) "Burden of establishing" a fact means the burden of persuading the triers of fact that the existence of the fact is more probable than its non-existence.

(9) "Buyer in ordinary course of business" means a person who in good faith and without knowledge that the sale to him is in violation of the ownership rights or security interest of a third party in the goods buys in ordinary course from a person in the business of selling goods of that kind but does not include a pawnbroker. All persons who sell minerals or the like (including oil and gas) at wellhead or minehead shall be deemed to be persons in the business of selling goods of that kind. "Buying" may be for cash or by exchange of other property or on secured or unsecured credit and includes receiving goods or documents of title under a pre-existing contract for sale but does not include a transfer in bulk or as security for or in total or partial satisfaction of a money debt.

(10) "Conspicuous": A term or clause is conspicuous when it is so written that a reasonable person against whom it is to operate ought to have noticed it. A printed heading in capitals (as: NON-NEGOTIABLE BILL OF LADING) is conspicuous. Language in the body of a form is "conspicuous" if it is in larger or other contrasting type or color. But in a telegram any stated term is "conspicuous". Whether a term or clause is "conspicuous" or not is for decision by the court.

(11) "Contract" means the total legal obligation which results from the parties' agreement as affected by this Act and any other applicable rules of law. (Compare "Agreement".)

(12) "Creditor" includes a general creditor, a secured creditor, a lien creditor and any representative of creditors, including an

assignee for the benefit of creditors, a trustee in bankruptcy, a receiver in equity and an executor or administrator of an insolvent debtor's or assignor's estate.

(13) "Defendant" includes a person in the position of defendant in a cross-action or counterclaim.

(14) "Delivery" with respect to instruments, documents of title, chattel paper, or certificated securities means voluntary transfer of possession.

(15) "Document of title" includes bill of lading, dock warrant, dock receipt, warehouse receipt or order for the delivery of goods, and also any other document which in the regular course of business or financing is treated as adequately evidencing that the person in possession of it is entitled to receive, hold and dispose of the document and the goods it covers. To be a document of title a document must purport to be issued by or addressed to a bailee and purport to cover goods in the bailee's possession which are either identified or are fungible portions of an identified mass.

(16) "Fault" means wrongful act, omission or breach.

(17) "Fungible" with respect to goods or securities means goods or securities of which any unit is, by nature or usage of trade, the equivalent of any other like unit. Goods which are not fungible shall be deemed fungible for the purposes of this Act to the extent that under a particular agreement or document unlike units are treated as equivalents.

(18) "Genuine" means free of forgery or counterfeiting.

(19) "Good faith" means honesty in fact in the conduct or transaction concerned.

(20) "Holder" with respect to a negotiable instrument, means the person in possession if the instrument is payable to bearer or, in the cases of an instrument payable to an identified person, if the identified person is in possession. "Holder" with respect to a document of title means the person in possession if the goods are deliverable to bearer or to the order of the person in possession.

(21) To "honor" is to pay or to accept and pay, or where a credit so engages to purchase or discount a draft complying with the terms of the credit.

(22) "Insolvency proceedings" includes any assignment for the benefit of creditors or other proceedings intended to liquidate or rehabilitate the estate of the person involved.

(23) A person is "insolvent" who either has ceased to pay his debts in the ordinary course of business or cannot pay his debts as they become due or is insolvent within the meaning of the federal bankruptcy law.

(24) "Money" means a medium of exchange authorized or adopted by a domestic or foreign government and includes a monetary unit of account established by an intergovernmental organization or by agreement between two or more nations.

(25) A person has "notice" of a fact when

(a) he has actual knowledge of it; or

(b) he has received a notice or notification of it; or

(c) from all the facts and circumstances known to him at the time in question he has reason to know that it exists.

A person "knows" or has "knowledge" of a fact when he has actual knowledge of it. "Discover" or "learn" or a word or phrase of similar import refers to knowledge rather than to reason to know. The time and circumstances under which a notice or notification may cease to be effective are not determined by this Act.

(26) A person "notifies" or "gives" a notice or notification to another by taking such steps as may be reasonably required to inform the other in ordinary course whether or not such other actually comes to know of it. A person "receives" a notice or notification when

(a) it comes to his attention; or

(b) it is duly delivered at the place of business through which the contract was made or at any other place held out by him as the place for receipt of such communications.

(27) Notice, knowledge or a notice or notification received by an organization is effective for a particular transaction from the time when it is brought to the attention of the individual conducting that transaction, and in any event from the time when it would have been brought to his attention if the organization had exercised due diligence. An organization exercises due diligence if it maintains reasonable routines for communicating significant information to the person conducting the transaction and there is reasonable compliance with the routines. Due diligence does not require an individual acting for the organization to communicate information unless such communication is part of his regular duties or unless he has reason to know of the transaction and that the transaction would be materially affected by the information.

(28) "Organization" includes a corporation, government or governmental subdivision or agency, business trust, estate, trust, partnership or association, two or more persons having a joint or common interest, or any other legal or commercial entity.

(29) "Party", as distinct from "third party", means a person who has engaged in a transaction or made an agreement within this Act.

(30) "Person" includes an individual or an organization (See Section 1—102).

(31) "Presumption" or "presumed" means that the trier of fact must find the existence of the fact presumed unless and until evidence is introduced which would support a finding of its non-existence.

(32) "Purchase" includes taking by sale, discount, negotiation, mortgage, pledge, lien, issue or re-issue, gift or any other voluntary transaction creating an interest in property.

(33) "Purchaser" means a person who takes by purchase.

(34) "Remedy" means any remedial right to which an aggrieved party is entitled with or without resort to a tribunal.

(35) "Representative" includes an agent, an officer of a corporation or association, and a trustee, executor or administrator of an estate, or any other person empowered to act for another.

(36) "Rights" includes remedies.

(37) "Security interest" means an interest in personal property or fixtures which secures payment or performance of an obligation. The retention or reservation of title by a seller of goods notwithstanding shipment or delivery to the buyer (Section 2—401) is limited in effect to a reservation of a "security interest". The term also includes any interest of a buyer of accounts or chattel paper which is subject to Article 9. The special property interest of a buyer of goods on identification of those goods to a contract for sale under Section 2—401 is not a "security interest", but a buyer may also acquire a "security interest" by complying with Article 9. Unless a consignment is intended as security, reservation of title thereunder is not a "security interest," but a consignment is in any event subject to the provisions on consignment sales (Section 2—326).

Whether a transaction creates a lease or security interest is determined by the facts of each case; however, a transaction creates a security interest if the consideration the lessee is to pay the lessor for the right to possession and use of the goods is an obligation for the term of the lease not subject to termination by the lessee, and

(a) the original term of the lease is equal to or greater than the remaining economic life of the goods,

(b) the lessee is bound to renew the lease for the remaining economic life of the goods or is bound to become the owner of the goods,

(c) the lessee has an option to renew the lease for the remaining economic life of the goods for no additional consideration or nominal additional consideration upon compliance with the lease agreement, or

(d) the lessee has an option to become the owner of the goods for no additional consideration or nominal additional consideration upon compliance with the lease agreement.

A transaction does not create a security interest merely because it provides that

(a) the present value of the consideration the lessee is obligated to pay the lessor for the right to possession and use of the goods is substantially equal to or is greater than the fair market value of the goods at the time the lease is entered into,

(b) the lessee assumes risk of loss of the goods, or agrees to pay taxes, insurance, filing, recording, or registration fees, or service or maintenance costs with respect to the goods,

(c) the lessee has an option to renew the lease or to become the owner of the goods,

(d) the lessee has an option to renew the lease for a fixed rent that is equal to or greater than the reasonably predictable fair market rent for the use of the goods for the term of the renewal at the time the option is to be performed, or

(e) the lessee has an option to become the owner of the goods for a fixed price that is equal to or greater than the reasonably predictable fair market value of the goods at the time the option is to be performed.

For purposes of this subsection (37):

(x) Additional consideration is not nominal if (i) when the option to renew the lease is granted to the lessee the rent is stated to be the fair market rent for the use of the goods for the term of the renewal determined at the time the option is to be performed, or (ii) when the option to become the owner of the goods is granted to the lessee the price is stated to be the fair market value of the goods determined at the time the option is to be performed. Additional consideration is nominal if it is less than the lessee's reasonably predictable cost of performing under the lease agreement if the option is not exercised;

(y) "Reasonably predictable" and "remaining economic life of the goods" are to be determined with reference to the facts and circumstances at the time the transaction is entered into; and

(z) "Present value" means the amount as of a date certain of one or more sums payable in the future, discounted to the date certain. The discount is determined by the interest rate specified by the parties if the rate is not manifestly unreasonable at the time the transaction is entered into; otherwise, the discount is determined by a commercially reasonable rate that takes into account the facts and circumstances of each case at the time the transaction was entered into.

(38) "Send" in connection with any writing or notice means to deposit in the mail or deliver for transmission by any other usual means of communication with postage or cost of transmission provided for and properly addressed and in the case of an instrument to an address specified thereon or otherwise agreed, or if there be none to any address reasonable under the circumstances. The receipt of any writing or notice within the time at which it would have arrived if properly sent has the effect of a proper sending.

(39) "Signed" includes any symbol executed or adopted by a party with present intention to authenticate a writing.

(40) "Surety" includes guarantor.

(41) "Telegram" includes a message transmitted by radio, teletype, cable, any mechanical method of transmission, or the like.

(42) "Term" means that portion of an agreement which relates to a particular matter.

(43) "Unauthorized" signature means one made without actual, implied or apparent authority and includes a forgery.

(44) "Value". Except as otherwise provided with respect to negotiable instruments and bank collections (Sections 3—303, 4—210 and 4—211) a person gives "value" for rights if he acquires them

(a) in return for a binding commitment to extend credit or for the extension of immediately available credit whether or not drawn upon and whether or not a chargeback is provided for in the event of difficulties in collection; or

(b) as security for or in total or partial satisfaction of a preexisting claim; or

(c) by accepting delivery pursuant to a preexisting contract for purchase; or

(d) generally, in return for any consideration sufficient to support a simple contract.

(45) "Warehouse receipt" means a receipt issued by a person engaged in the business of storing goods for hire.

(46) "Written" or "writing" includes printing, typewriting or any other intentional reduction to tangible form.

§1—202. Prima Facie Evidence by Third Party Documents.

A document in due form purporting to be a bill of lading, policy or certificate of insurance, official weigher's or inspector's certificate, consular invoice, or any other document authorized or required by the contract to be issued by a third party shall be prima facie evidence of its own authenticity and genuineness and of the facts stated in the document by the third party.

§ 1—203. Obligation of Good Faith.

Every contract or duty within this Act imposes an obligation of good faith in its performance or enforcement.

§ 1—204. Time; Reasonable Time; "Seasonably".

(1) Whenever this Act requires any action to be taken within a reasonable time, any time which is not manifestly unreasonable may be fixed by agreement.

(2) What is a reasonable time for taking any action depends on the nature, purpose and circumstances of such action.

(3) An action is taken "seasonably" when it is taken at or within the time agreed or if no time is agreed at or within a reasonable time.

§ 1—205. Course of Dealing and Usage of Trade.

(1) A course of dealing is a sequence of previous conduct between the parties to a particular transaction which is fairly to be regarded as establishing a common basis of understanding for interpreting their expressions and other conduct.

(2) A usage of trade is any practice or method of dealing having such regularity of observance in a place, vocation or trade as to justify an expectation that it will be observed with respect to the transaction in question. The existence and scope of such a usage are to be proved as facts. If it is established that such a usage is embodied in a written trade code or similar writing the interpretation of the writing is for the court.

(3) A course of dealing between parties and any usage of trade in the vocation or trade in which they are engaged or of which they are or should be aware give particular meaning to and supplement or qualify terms of an agreement.

(4) The express terms of an agreement and an applicable course of dealing or usage of trade shall be construed wherever reasonable as consistent with each other; but when such construction is unreasonable express terms control both course of dealing and usage of trade and course of dealing controls usage trade.

(5) An applicable usage of trade in the place where any part of performance is to occur shall be used in interpreting the agreement as to that part of the performance.

(6) Evidence of a relevant usage of trade offered by one party is not admissible unless and until he has given the other party such notice as the court finds sufficient to prevent unfair surprise to the latter.

§ 1—206. Statute of Frauds for Kinds of Personal Property Not Otherwise Covered.

(1) Except in the cases described in subsection (2) of this section a contract for the sale of personal property is not enforceable by way of action or defense beyond five thousand dollars in amount or value of remedy unless there is some writing which indicates that a contract for sale has been made between the parties at a defined or stated price, reasonably identifies the subject matter, and is signed by the party against whom enforcement is sought or by his authorized agent.

(2) Subsection (1) of this section does not apply to contracts for the sale of goods (Section 2—201) nor of securities (Section 8—113) nor to security agreements (Section 9—203).

§ 1—207. Performance or Acceptance Under Reservation of Rights.

(1) A party who with explicit reservation of rights performs or promises performance or assents to performance in a manner demanded or offered by the other party does not thereby prejudice the rights reserved. Such words as "without prejudice", "under protest" or the like are sufficient.

(2) Subsection (1) does not apply to an accord and satisfaction.

§ 1—208. Option to Accelerate at Will.

A term providing that one party or his successor in interest may accelerate payment or performance or require collateral or additional collateral "at will" or "when he deems himself insecure" or in words of similar import shall be construed to mean that he shall have power to do so only if he in good faith believes that the prospect of payment or performance is impaired. The burden of establishing lack of good faith is on the party against whom the power has been exercised.

§ 1—209. Subordinated Obligations.

An obligation may be issued as subordinated to payment of another obligation of the person obligated, or a creditor may subordinate his right to payment of an obligation by agreement with either the person obligated or another creditor of the person obligated. Such a subordination does not create a security interest as against either the common debtor or a subordinated creditor. This section shall be construed as declaring the law as it existed prior to the enactment of this section and not as modifying it. Added 1966.

Note: *This new section is proposed as an optional provision to make it clear that a subordination agreement does not create a security interest unless so intended.*

Article 2
SALES

Part 1 Short Title, General Construction and Subject Matter

§ 2—101. Short Title.

This Article shall be known and may be cited as Uniform Commercial Code—Sales.

§ 2—102. Scope; Certain Security and Other Transactions Excluded From This Article.

Unless the context otherwise requires, this Article applies to transactions in goods; it does not apply to any transaction which although in the form of an unconditional contract to sell or present sale is intended to operate only as a security transaction nor does this Article impair or repeal any statute regulating sales to consumers, farmers or other specified classes of buyers.

§ 2—103. Definitions and Index of Definitions.

(1) In this Article unless the context otherwise requires

(a) "Buyer" means a person who buys or contracts to buy goods.

(b) "Good faith" in the case of a merchant means honesty in fact and the observance of reasonable commercial standards of fair dealing in the trade.

(c) "Receipt" of goods means taking physical possession of them.

(d) "Seller" means a person who sells or contracts to sell goods.

(2) Other definitions applying to this Article or to specified Parts thereof, and the sections in which they appear are:

"Acceptance". Section 2—606.
"Banker's credit". Section 2—325.
"Between merchants". Section 2—104.
"Cancellation". Section 2—106(4).
"Commercial unit". Section 2—105.
"Confirmed credit". Section 2—325.
"Conforming to contract". Section 2—106.
"Contract for sale". Section 2—106.
"Cover". Section 2—712.
"Entrusting". Section 2—403.
"Financing agency". Section 2—104.
"Future goods". Section 2—105.
"Goods". Section 2—105.
"Identification". Section 2—501.
"Installment contract". Section 2—612.
"Letter of Credit". Section 2—325.
"Lot". Section 2—105.
"Merchant". Section 2—104.
"Overseas". Section 2—323.
"Person in position of seller". Section 2—707.
"Present sale". Section 2—106.
"Sale". Section 2—106.
"Sale on approval". Section 2—326.
"Sale or return". Section 2—326.
"Termination". Section 2—106.

(3) The following definitions in other Articles apply to this Article:

"Check". Section 3—104.
"Consignee". Section 7—102.
"Consignor". Section 7—102.
"Consumer goods". Section 9—109.
"Dishonor". Section 3—507.
"Draft". Section 3—104.

(4) In addition Article 1 contains general definitions and principles of construction and interpretation applicable throughout this Article.

§ 2—104. Definitions: "Merchant"; "Between Merchants"; "Financing Agency".

(1) "Merchant" means a person who deals in goods of the kind or otherwise by his occupation holds himself out as having knowledge or skill peculiar to the practices or goods involved in the transaction or to whom such knowledge or skill may be attributed by his employment of an agent or broker or other intermediary who by his occupation holds himself out as having such knowledge or skill.

(2) "Financing agency" means a bank, finance company or other person who in the ordinary course of business makes advances against goods or documents of title or who by arrangement with either the seller or the buyer intervenes in ordinary course to make or collect payment due or claimed under the contract for sale, as by purchasing or paying the seller's draft or making advances against it or by merely taking it for collection whether or not documents of title accompany the draft. "Financing agency" includes also a bank or other person who similarly intervenes between persons who are in the position of seller and buyer in respect to the goods (Section 2—707).

(3) "Between merchants" means in any transaction with respect to which both parties are chargeable with the knowledge or skill of merchants.

§ 2—105. Definitions: Transferability; "Goods"; "Future" Goods; "Lot"; "Commercial Unit".

(1) "Goods" means all things (including specially manufactured goods) which are movable at the time of identification to the contract for sale other than the money in which the price is to be paid, investment securities (Article 8) and things in action. "Goods" also includes the unborn young of animals and growing crops and other identified things attached to realty as described in the section on goods to be severed from realty (Section 2—107).

(2) Goods must be both existing and identified before any interest in them can pass. Goods which are not both existing and identified are "future" goods. A purported present sale of future goods or of any interest therein operates as a contract to sell.

(3) There may be a sale of a part interest in existing identified goods.

(4) An undivided share in an identified bulk of fungible goods is sufficiently identified to be sold although the quantity of the bulk is not determined. Any agreed proportion of such a bulk or any quantity thereof agreed upon by number, weight or other measure may to the extent of the seller's interest in the bulk be sold to the buyer who then becomes an owner in common.

(5) "Lot" means a parcel or a single article which is the subject matter of a separate sale or delivery, whether or not it is sufficient to perform the contract.

(6) "Commercial unit" means such a unit of goods as by commercial usage is a single whole for purposes of sale and division of which materially impairs its character or value on the market or in use. A commercial unit may be a single article (as a machine) or a set of articles (as a suite of furniture or an assortment of sizes) or a quantity (as a bale, gross, or carload) or any other unit treated in use or in the relevant market as a single whole.

§ 2—106. Definitions: "Contract"; "Agreement"; "Contract for Sale"; "Sale"; "Present Sale"; "Conforming" to Contract; "Termination"; "Cancellation".

(1) In this Article unless the context otherwise requires "contract" and "agreement" are limited to those relating to the present or future sale of goods. "Contract for sale" includes both a present sale of goods and a contract to sell goods at a future time. A "sale" consists in the passing of title from the seller to the buyer for a price (Section 2—401). A "present sale" means a sale which is accomplished by the making of the contract.

(2) Goods or conduct including any part of a performance are "conforming" or conform to the contract when they are in accordance with the obligations under the contract.

(3) "Termination" occurs when either party pursuant to a power created by agreement or law puts an end to the contract otherwise than for its breach. On "termination" all obligations which are still executory on both sides are discharged but any right based on prior breach or performance survives.

(4) "Cancellation" occurs when either party puts an end to the contract for breach by the other and its effect is the same as that of "termination" except that the cancelling party also retains any remedy for breach of the whole contract or any unperformed balance.

§ 2—107. Goods to Be Severed From Realty: Recording.

(1) A contract for the sale of minerals or the like (including oil and gas) or a structure or its materials to be removed from realty is a contract for the sale of goods within this Article if they are to be severed by the seller but until severance a purported present sale thereof which is not effective as a transfer of an interest in land is effective only as a contract to sell.

(2) A contract for the sale apart from the land of growing crops or other things attached to realty and capable of severance without material harm thereto but not described in subsection (1) or of timber to be cut is a contract for the sale of goods within this Article whether the subject matter is to be severed by the buyer or by the seller even though it forms part of the realty at the time of contracting, and the parties can by identification effect a present sale before severance.

(3) The provisions of this section are subject to any third party rights provided by the law relating to realty records, and the contract for sale may be executed and recorded as a document transferring an interest in land and shall then constitute notice to third parties of the buyer's rights under the contract for sale.

Part 2 Form, Formation and Readjustment of Contract

§ 2—201. Formal Requirements; Statute of Frauds.

(1) Except as otherwise provided in this section a contract for the sale of goods for the price of $500 or more is not enforceable by way of action or defense unless there is some writing sufficient to indicate that a contract for sale has been made between the parties and signed by the party against whom enforcement is sought or by his authorized agent or broker. A writing is not insufficient because it omits or incorrectly states a term agreed upon but the contract is not enforceable under this paragraph beyond the quantity of goods shown in such writing.

(2) Between merchants if within a reasonable time a writing in confirmation of the contract and sufficient against the sender is received and the party receiving it has reason to know its contents, its satisfies the requirements of subsection (1) against such party unless written notice of objection to its contents is given within ten days after it is received.

(3) A contract which does not satisfy the requirements of subsection (1) but which is valid in other respects is enforceable

(a) if the goods are to be specially manufactured for the buyer and are not suitable for sale to others in the ordinary course of the seller's business and the seller, before notice of repudiation is received and under circumstances which reasonably indicate that the goods are for the buyer, has made either a substantial beginning of their manufacture or commitments for their procurement; or

(b) if the party against whom enforcement is sought admits in his pleading, testimony or otherwise in court that a contract for sale was made, but the contract is not enforceable under this provision beyond the quantity of goods admitted; or

(c) with respect to goods for which payment has been made and accepted or which have been received and accepted (Sec. 2—606).

§ 2—202. Final Written Expression: Parol or Extrinsic Evidence.

Terms with respect to which the confirmatory memoranda of the parties agree or which are otherwise set forth in a writing intended by the parties as a final expression of their agreement with respect to such terms as are included therein may not be contradicted by evidence of any prior agreement or of a contemporaneous oral agreement but may be explained or supplemented

(a) by course of dealing or usage of trade (Section 1—205) or by course of performance (Section 2—208); and

(b) by evidence of consistent additional terms unless the court finds the writing to have been intended also as a complete and exclusive statement of the terms of the agreement.

§ 2—203. Seals Inoperative.

The affixing of a seal to a writing evidencing a contract for sale or an offer to buy or sell goods does not constitute the writing a sealed instrument and the law with respect to sealed instruments does not apply to such a contract or offer.

§ 2—204. Formation in General.

(1) A contract for sale of goods may be made in any manner sufficient to show agreement, including conduct by both parties which recognizes the existence of such a contract.

(2) An agreement sufficient to constitute a contract for sale may be found even though the moment of its making is undetermined.

(3) Even though one or more terms are left open a contract for sale does not fail for indefiniteness if the parties have intended to make a contract and there is a reasonably certain basis for giving an appropriate remedy.

§ 2—205. Firm Offers.

An offer by a merchant to buy or sell goods in a signed writing which by its terms gives assurance that it will be held open is not revocable, for lack of consideration, during the time stated or if no time is stated for a reasonable time, but in no event may such period of irrevocability exceed three months; but any such term of assurance on a form supplied by the offeree must be separately signed by the offeror.

§ 2—206. Offer and Acceptance in Formation of Contract.

(1) Unless other unambiguously indicated by the language or circumstances

(a) an offer to make a contract shall be construed as inviting acceptance in any manner and by any medium reasonable in the circumstances;

(b) an order or other offer to buy goods for prompt or current shipment shall be construed as inviting acceptance either by a prompt promise to ship or by the prompt or current shipment of conforming or nonconforming goods, but such a shipment of non-conforming goods does not constitute an acceptance if the seller seasonably notifies the buyer that the shipment is offered only as an accommodation to the buyer.

(2) Where the beginning of a requested performance is a reasonable mode of acceptance an offeror who is not notified of acceptance within a reasonable time may treat the offer as having lapsed before acceptance.

§ 2—207. Additional Terms in Acceptance or Confirmation.

(1) A definite and seasonable expression of acceptance or a written confirmation which is sent within a reasonable time operates as an acceptance even though it states terms additional to or different from those offered or agreed upon, unless acceptance is expressly made conditional on assent to the additional or different terms.

(2) The additional terms are to be construed as proposals for addition to the contract. Between merchants such terms become part of the contract unless:

(a) the offer expressly limits acceptance to the terms of the offer;

(b) they materially alter it; or

(c) notification of objection to them has already been given or is given within a reasonable time after notice of them is received.

(3) Conduct by both parties which recognizes the existence of a contract is sufficient to establish a contract for sale although the writings of the parties do not otherwise establish a contract. In such case the terms of the particular contract consist of those terms on which the writings of the parties agree, together with any supplementary terms incorporated under any other provisions of this Act.

§ 2—208. Course of Performance or Practical Construction.

(1) Where the contract for sale involves repeated occasions for performance by either party with knowledge of the nature of the performance and opportunity for objection to it by the other, any course of performance accepted or acquiesced in without objection shall be relevant to determine the meaning of the agreement.

(2) The express terms of the agreement and any such course of performance, as well as any course of dealing and usage of trade, shall be construed whenever reasonable as consistent with each other; but when such construction is unreasonable, express terms shall control course of performance and course of performance shall control both course of dealing and usage of trade (Section 1—205).

(3) Subject to the provisions of the next section on modification and waiver, such course of performance shall be relevant to show a waiver or modification of any term inconsistent with such course of performance.

§ 2—209. Modification, Rescission and Waiver.

(1) An agreement modifying a contract within this Article needs no consideration to be binding.

(2) A signed agreement which excludes modification or rescission except by a signed writing cannot be otherwise modified or rescinded, but except as between merchants such a requirement on a form supplied by the merchant must be separately signed by the other party.

(3) The requirements of the statute of frauds section of this Article (Section 2—201) must be satisfied if the contract as modified is within its provisions.

(4) Although an attempt at modification or rescission does not satisfy the requirements of subsection (2) or (3) it can operate as a waiver.

(5) A party who has made a waiver affecting an executory portion of the contract may retract the waiver by reasonable notification received by the other party that strict performance will be required of any term waived, unless the retraction would be unjust in view of a material change of position in reliance on the waiver.

§ 2—210. Delegation of Performance; Assignment of Rights.

(1) A party may perform his duty through a delegate unless otherwise agreed or unless the other party has a substantial interest in having his original promisor perform or control the acts required by the contract. No delegation of performance relieves the party delegating of any duty to perform or any liability for breach.

(2) Unless otherwise agreed all rights of either seller or buyer can be assigned except where the assignment would materially change the duty of the other party, or increase materially the burden or risk imposed on him by his contract, or impair materially his chance of obtaining return performance. A right to damages for breach of the whole contract or a right arising out of the assignor's due performance of his entire obligation can be assigned despite agreement otherwise.

(3) Unless the circumstances indicate the contrary a prohibition of assignment of "the contract" is to be construed as barring only the delegation to the assignee of the assignor's performance.

(4) An assignment of "the contract" or of "all my rights under the contract" or an assignment in similar general terms is an assignment of rights and unless the language or the circumstances (as in an assignment for security) indicate the contrary, it is a delegation of performance of the duties of the assignor and its acceptance by the assignee constitutes a promise by him to perform those duties. This promise is enforceable by either the assignor or the other party to the original contract.

(5) The other party may treat any assignment which delegates performance as creating reasonable grounds for insecurity and may without prejudice to his rights against the assignor demand assurances from the assignee (Section 2—609).

Part 3 General Obligation and Construction of Contract

§ 2—301. General Obligations of Parties.

The obligation of the seller is to transfer and deliver and that of the buyer is to accept and pay in accordance with the contract.

§ 2—302. Unconscionable Contract or Clause.

(1) If the court as a matter of law finds the contract or any clause of the contract to have been unconscionable at the time it was made the court may refuse to enforce the contract, or it may enforce the remainder of the contract without the unconscionable clause, or it may so limit the application of any unconscionable clause as to avoid any unconscionable result.

(2) When it is claimed or appears to the court that the contract or any clause thereof may be unconscionable the parties shall be afforded a reasonable opportunity to present evidence as to its commercial setting, purpose and effect to aid the court in making the determination.

§ 2—303. Allocations or Division of Risks.

Where this Article allocates a risk or a burden as between the parties "unless otherwise agreed", the agreement may not only shift the allocation but may also divide the risk or burden.

§ 2—304. Price Payable in Money, Goods, Realty, or Otherwise.

(1) The price can be made payable in money or otherwise. If it is payable in whole or in part in goods each party is a seller of the goods which he is to transfer.

(2) Even though all or part of the price is payable in an interest in realty the transfer of the goods and the seller's obligations with reference to them are subject to this Article, but not the transfer of the interest in realty or the transferor's obligations in connection therewith.

§ 2—305. Open Price Term.

(1) The parties if they so intend can conclude a contract for sale even though the price is not settled. In such a case the price is a reasonable price at the time for delivery if

(a) nothing is said as to price; or

(b) the price is left to be agreed by the parties and they fail to agree; or

(c) the price is to be fixed in terms of some agreed market or other standard as set or recorded by a third person or agency and it is not so set or recorded.

(2) A price to be fixed by the seller or by the buyer means a price for him to fix in good faith.

(3) When a price left to be fixed otherwise than by agreement of the parties fails to be fixed through fault of one party the other may at his option treat the contract as cancelled or himself fix a reasonable price.

(4) Where, however, the parties intend not to be bound unless the price be fixed or agreed and it is not fixed or agreed there is no contract. In such a case the buyer must return any goods already received or if unable so to do must pay their reasonable value at the time of delivery and the seller must return any portion of the price paid on account.

§ 2—306. Output, Requirements and Exclusive Dealings.

(1) A term which measures the quantity by the output of the seller or the requirements of the buyer means such actual output or requirements as may occur in good faith, except that no

quantity unreasonably disproportionate to any stated estimate or in the absence of a stated estimate to any normal or otherwise comparable prior output or requirements may be tendered or demanded.

(2) A lawful agreement by either the seller or the buyer for exclusive dealing in the kind of goods concerned imposes unless otherwise agreed an obligation by the seller to use best efforts to supply the goods and by the buyer to use best efforts to promote their sale.

§ 2—307. Delivery in Single Lot or Several Lots.

Unless otherwise agreed all goods called for by a contract for sale must be tendered in a single delivery and payment is due only on such tender but where the circumstances give either party the right to make or demand delivery in lots the price if it can be apportioned may be demanded for each lot.

§ 2—308. Absence of Specified Place for Delivery.

Unless otherwise agreed

(a) the place for delivery of goods is the seller's place of business or if he has none his residence; but

(b) in a contract for sale of identified goods which to the knowledge of the parties at the time of contracting are in some other place, that place is the place for their delivery; and

(c) documents of title may be delivered through customary banking channels.

§ 2—309. Absence of Specific Time Provisions; Notice of Termination.

(1) The time for shipment or delivery or any other action under a contract if not provided in this Article or agreed upon shall be a reasonable time.

(2) Where the contract provides for successive performances but is indefinite in duration it is valid for a reasonable time but unless otherwise agreed may be terminated at any time by either party.

(3) Termination of a contract by one party except on the happening of an agreed event requires that reasonable notification be received by the other party and an agreement dispensing with notification is invalid if its operation would be unconscionable.

§ 2—310. Open Time for Payment or Running of Credit; Authority to Ship Under Reservation.

Unless otherwise agreed

(a) payment is due at the time and place at which the buyer is to receive the goods even though the place of shipment is the place of delivery; and

(b) if the seller is authorized to send the goods he may ship them under reservation, and may tender the documents of title, but the buyer may inspect the goods after their arrival before payment is due unless such inspection is inconsistent with the terms of the contract (Section 2—513); and

(c) if delivery is authorized and made by way of documents of title otherwise than by subsection (b) then payment is due at the time and place at which the buyer is to receive the documents regardless of where the goods are to be received; and

(d) where the seller is required or authorized to ship the goods on credit the credit period runs from the time of shipment but post-dating the invoice or delaying its dispatch will correspondingly delay the starting of the credit period.

§ 2—311. Options and Cooperation Respecting Performance.

(1) An agreement for sale which is otherwise sufficiently definite (subsection (3) of Section 2—204) to be a contract is not made invalid by the fact that it leaves particulars of performance to be specified by one of the parties. Any such specification must be made in good faith and within limits set by commercial reasonableness.

(2) Unless otherwise agreed specifications relating to assortment of the goods are at the buyer's option and except as otherwise provided in subsections (1)(c) and (3) of Section 2—319 specifications or arrangements relating to shipment are at the seller's option.

(3) Where such specification would materially affect the other party's performance but is not seasonably made or where one party's cooperation is necessary to the agreed performance of the other but is not seasonably forthcoming, the other party in addition to all other remedies

(a) is excused for any resulting delay in his own performance; and

(b) may also either proceed to perform in any reasonable manner or after the time for a material part of his own performance treat the failure to specify or to cooperate as a breach by failure to deliver or accept the goods.

§ 2—312. Warranty of Title and Against Infringement; Buyer's Obligation Against Infringement.

(1) Subject to subsection (2) there is in a contract for sale a warranty by the seller that

(a) the title conveyed shall be good, and its transfer rightful; and

(b) the goods shall be delivered free from any security interest or other lien or encumbrance of which the buyer at the time of contracting has no knowledge.

(2) A warranty under subsection (1) will be excluded or modified only by specific language or by circumstances which give the buyer reason to know that the person selling does not claim title in himself or that he is purporting to sell only such right or title as he or a third person may have.

(3) Unless otherwise agreed a seller who is a merchant regularly dealing in goods of the kind warrants that the goods shall be delivered free of the rightful claim of any third person by way of infringement or the like but a buyer who furnishes specifications to the seller must hold the seller harmless against any such claim which arises out of compliance with the specifications.

§ 2—313. Express Warranties by Affirmation, Promise, Description, Sample.

(1) Express warranties by the seller are created as follows:

(a) Any affirmation of fact or promise made by the seller to the buyer which relates to the goods and becomes part of the basis of the bargain creates an express warranty that the goods shall conform to the affirmation or promise.

(b) Any description of the goods which is made part of the basis of the bargain creates an express warranty that the goods shall conform to the description.

(c) Any sample or model which is made part of the basis of the bargain creates an express warranty that the whole of the goods shall conform to the sample or model.

(2) It is not necessary to the creation of an express warranty that the seller use formal words such as "warrant" or "guarantee" or that he have a specific intention to make a warranty, but an affirmation merely of the value of the goods or a statement purporting to be merely the seller's opinion or commendation of the goods does not create a warranty.

§ 2—314. Implied Warranty: Merchantability; Usage of Trade.

(1) Unless excluded or modified (Section 2—316), a warranty that the goods shall be merchantable is implied in a contract for their sale if the seller is a merchant with respect to goods of that kind. Under this section the serving for value of food or drink to be consumed either on the premises or elsewhere is a sale.

(2) Goods to be merchantable must be at least such as

(a) pass without objection in the trade under the contract description; and

(b) in the case of fungible goods, are of fair average quality within the description; and

(c) are fit for the ordinary purposes for which such goods are used; and

(d) run, within the variations permitted by the agreement, of even kind, quality and quantity within each unit and among all units involved; and

(e) are adequately contained, packaged, and labeled as the agreement may require; and

(f) conform to the promises or affirmations of fact made on the container or label if any.

(3) Unless excluded or modified (Section 2—316) other implied warranties may arise from course of dealing or usage of trade.

§ 2—315. Implied Warranty: Fitness for Particular Purpose.

Where the seller at the time of contracting has reason to know any particular purpose for which the goods are required and that the buyer is relying on the seller's skill or judgment to select or furnish suitable goods, there is unless excluded or modified under the next section an implied warranty that the goods shall be fit for such purpose.

§ 2—316. Exclusion or Modification of Warranties.

(1) Words or conduct relevant to the creation of an express warranty and words or conduct tending to negate or limit warranty shall be construed wherever reasonable as consistent with each other; but subject to the provisions of this Article on parol or extrinsic evidence (Section 2—202) negation or limitation is inoperative to the extent that such construction is unreasonable.

(2) Subject to subsection (3), to exclude or modify the implied warranty of merchantability or any part of it the language must mention merchantability and in case of a writing must be conspicuous, and to exclude or modify any implied warranty of fitness the exclusion must be by a writing and conspicuous. Language to exclude all implied warranties of fitness is sufficient if it states, for example, that "There are no warranties which extend beyond the description on the face hereof."

(3) Notwithstanding subsection (2)

(a) unless the circumstances indicate otherwise, all implied warranties are excluded by expressions like "as is", "with all faults" or other language which in common understanding calls the buyer's attention to the exclusion of warranties and makes plain that there is no implied warranty; and

(b) when the buyer before entering into the contract has examined the goods or the sample or model as fully as he desired or has refused to examine the goods there is no implied warranty with regard to defects which an examination ought in the circumstances to have revealed to him; and

(c) an implied warranty can also be excluded or modified by course of dealing or course of performance or usage of trade.

(4) Remedies for breach of warranty can be limited in accordance with the provisions of this Article on liquidation or limitation of damages and on contractual modification of remedy (Sections 2—718 and 2—719).

§ 2—317. Cumulation and Conflict of Warranties Express or Implied.

Warranties whether express or implied shall be construed as consistent with each other and as cumulative, but if such construction is unreasonable the intention of the parties shall determine which warranty is dominant. In ascertaining that intention the following rules apply:

(a) Exact or technical specifications displace an inconsistent sample or model or general language of description.

(b) A sample from an existing bulk displaces inconsistent general language of description.

(c) Express warranties displace inconsistent implied warranties other than an implied warranty of fitness for a particular purpose.

§ 2—318. Third Party Beneficiaries of Warranties Express or Implied.

Note: If this Act is introduced in the Congress of the United States this section should be omitted. (States to select one alternative.)

Alternative A

A seller's warranty whether express or implied extends to any natural person who is in the family or household of his buyer or who is a guest in his home if it is reasonable to expect that such person may use, consume or be affected by the goods and who is injured in person by breach of the warranty. A seller may not exclude or limit the operation of this section.

Alternative B

A seller's warranty whether express or implied extends to any natural person who may reasonably be expected to use, consume or be affected by the goods and who is injured in person by breach of the warranty. A seller may not exclude or limit the operation of this section.

Alternative C

A seller's warranty whether express or implied extends to any person who may reasonably be expected to use, consume or be affected by the goods and who is injured by breach of the warranty. A seller may not exclude or limit the operation of this section with respect to injury to the person of an individual to whom the warranty extends. As amended 1966.

§ 2—319. F.O.B. and F.A.S. Terms.

(1) Unless otherwise agreed the term F.O.B. (which means "free on board") at a named place, even though used only in connection with the stated price, is a delivery term under which

(a) when the term is F.O.B. the place of shipment, the seller must at that place ship the goods in the manner provided in this Article (Section 2—504) and bear the expense and risk of putting them into the possession of the carrier; or

(b) when the term is F.O.B. the place of destination, the seller must at his own expense and risk transport the goods to that place and there tender delivery of them in the manner provided in this Article (Section 2—503);

(c) when under either (a) or (b) the term is also F.O.B. vessel, car or other vehicle, the seller must in addition at his own expense and risk load the goods on board. If the term is F.O.B. vessel the buyer must name the vessel and in an appropriate case the seller must comply with the provisions of this Article on the form of bill of lading (Section 2—323).

(2) Unless otherwise agreed the term F.A.S. vessel (which means "free alongside") at a named port, even though used only in connection with the stated price, is a delivery term under which the seller must

(a) at his own expense and risk deliver the goods alongside the vessel in the manner usual in that port or on a dock designated and provided by the buyer; and

(b) obtain and tender a receipt for the goods in exchange for which the carrier is under a duty to issue a bill of lading.

(3) Unless otherwise agreed in any case falling within subsection (1)(a) or (c) or subsection (2) the buyer must seasonably give any needed instructions for making delivery, including when the term is F.A.S. or F.O.B. the loading berth of the vessel and in an appropriate case its name and sailing date. The seller may treat the failure of needed instructions as a failure of cooperation under this Article (Section 2—311). He may also at his option move the goods in any reasonable manner preparatory to delivery or shipment.

(4) Under the term F.O.B. vessel or F.A.S. unless otherwise agreed the buyer must make payment against tender of the required documents and the seller may not tender nor the buyer demand delivery of the goods in substitution for the documents.

§ 2—320. C.I.F. and C. & F. Terms.

(1) The term C.I.F. means that the price includes in a lump sum the cost of the goods and the insurance and freight to the named destination. The term C. & F. or C.F. means that the price so includes cost and freight to the named destination.

(2) Unless otherwise agreed and even though used only in connection with the stated price and destination, the term C.I.F. destination or its equivalent requires the seller at his own expense and risk to

(a) put the goods into the possession of a carrier at the port for shipment and obtain a negotiable bill or bills of lading covering the entire transportation to the named destination; and

(b) load the goods and obtain a receipt from the carrier (which may be contained in the bill of lading) showing that the freight has been paid or provided for; and

(c) obtain a policy or certificate of insurance, including any war risk insurance, of a kind and on terms then current at the port of shipment in the usual amount, in the currency of the contract, shown to cover the same goods covered by the bill of lading and providing for payment of loss to the order of the buyer or for the account of whom it may concern; but the seller may add to the price the amount of the premium for any such war risk insurance; and

(d) prepare an invoice of the goods and procure any other documents required to effect shipment or to comply with the contract; and

(e) forward and tender with commercial promptness all the documents in due form and with any indorsement necessary to perfect the buyer's rights.

(3) Unless otherwise agreed the term C. & F. or its equivalent has the same effect and imposes upon the seller the same obligations and risks as a C.I.F. term except the obligation as to insurance.

(4) Under the term C.I.F. or C. & F. unless otherwise agreed the buyer must make payment against tender of the required documents and the seller may not tender nor the buyer demand delivery of the goods in substitution for the documents.

§ 2—321. C.I.F. or C. & F.: "Net Landed Weights"; "Payment on Arrival"; Warranty of Condition on Arrival.

Under a contract containing a term C.I.F. or C. & F.

(1) Where the price is based on or is to be adjusted according to "net landed weights", "delivered weights", "out turn" quantity or quality or the like, unless otherwise agreed the seller must reasonably estimate the price. The payment due on tender of the documents called for by the contract is the amount so estimated, but after final adjustment of the price a settlement must be made with commercial promptness.

(2) An agreement described in subsection (1) or any warranty of quality or condition of the goods on arrival places upon the seller the risk of ordinary deterioration, shrinkage and the like in transportation but has no effect on the place or time of identification to the contract for sale or delivery or on the passing of the risk of loss.

(3) Unless otherwise agreed where the contract provides for payment on or after arrival of the goods the seller must before payment allow such preliminary inspection as is feasible; but if the goods are lost delivery of the documents and payment are due when the goods should have arrived.

§ 2—322. Delivery "Ex-Ship".

(1) Unless otherwise agreed a term for delivery of goods "ex-ship" (which means from the carrying vessel) or in equivalent language is not restricted to a particular ship and requires delivery from a ship which has reached a place at the named port of destination where goods of the kind are usually discharged.

(2) Under such a term unless otherwise agreed

(a) the seller must discharge all liens arising out of the carriage and furnish the buyer with a direction which puts the carrier under a duty to deliver the goods; and

(b) the risk of loss does not pass to the buyer until the goods leave the ship's tackle or are otherwise properly unloaded.

§ 2—323. Form of Bill of Lading Required in Overseas Shipment; "Overseas".

(1) Where the contract contemplates overseas shipment and contains a term C.I.F. or C. & F. or F.O.B. vessel, the seller unless otherwise agreed must obtain a negotiable bill of lading stating that the goods have been loaded on board or, in the case of a term C.I.F. or C. & F., received for shipment.

(2) Where in a case within subsection (1) a bill of lading has been issued in a set of parts, unless otherwise agreed if the documents are not to be sent from abroad the buyer may demand tender of the full set; otherwise only one part of the bill of lading need be tendered. Even if the agreement expressly requires a full set

(a) due tender of a single part is acceptable within the provisions of this Article on cure of improper delivery (subsection (1) of Section 2—508); and

(b) even though the full set is demanded, if the documents are sent from abroad the person tendering an incomplete set may nevertheless require payment upon furnishing an indemnity which the buyer in good faith deems adequate.

(3) A shipment by water or by air or a contract contemplating such shipment is "overseas" insofar as by usage of trade or agreement it is subject to the commercial, financing or shipping practices characteristic of international deep water commerce.

§ 2—324. "No Arrival, No Sale" Term.

Under a term "no arrival, no sale" or terms of like meaning, unless otherwise agreed,

(a) the seller must properly ship conforming goods and if they arrive by any means he must tender them on arrival but he assumes no obligation that the goods will arrive unless he has caused the non-arrival; and

(b) where without fault of the seller the goods are in part lost or have so deteriorated as no longer to conform to the contract or arrive after the contract time, the buyer may proceed as if there had been casualty to identified goods (Section 2—613).

§ 2—325. "Letter of Credit" Term; "Confirmed Credit".

(1) Failure of the buyer seasonably to furnish an agreed letter of credit is a breach of the contract for sale.

(2) The delivery to seller of a proper letter of credit suspends the buyer's obligation to pay. If the letter of credit is dishonored, the seller may on seasonable notification to the buyer require payment directly from him.

(3) Unless otherwise agreed the term "letter of credit" or "banker's credit" in a contract for sale means an irrevocable credit issued by a financing agency of good repute and, where the shipment is overseas, of good international repute. The term "confirmed credit" means that the credit must also carry the direct obligation of such an agency which does business in the seller's financial market.

§ 2—326. Sale on Approval and Sale or Return; Consignment Sales and Rights of Creditors.

(1) Unless otherwise agreed, if delivered goods may be returned by the buyer even though they conform to the contract, the transaction is

(a) a "sale on approval" if the goods are delivered primarily for use, and

(b) a "sale or return" if the goods are delivered primarily for resale.

(2) Except as provided in subsection (3), goods held on approval are not subject to the claims of the buyer's creditors until acceptance; goods held on sale or return are subject to such claims while in the buyer's possession.

(3) Where goods are delivered to a person for sale and such person maintains a place of business at which he deals in goods of the kind involved, under a name other than the name of the person making delivery, then with respect to claims of creditors of the person conducting the business the goods are deemed to be on sale or return. The provisions of this subsection are applicable even though an agreement purports to reserve title to the person making delivery until payment or resale or uses such

words as "on consignment" or "on memorandum". However, this subsection is not applicable if the person making delivery

(a) complies with an applicable law providing for a consignor's interest or the like to be evidenced by a sign, or

(b) establishes that the person conducting the business is generally known by his creditors to be substantially engaged in selling the goods of others, or

(c) complies with the filing provisions of the Article on Secured Transactions (Article 9).

(4) Any "or return" term of a contract for sale is to be treated as a separate contract for sale within the statute of frauds section of this Article (Section 2—201) and as contradicting the sale aspect of the contract within the provisions of this Article on parol or extrinsic evidence (Section 2—202).

§ 2—327. Special Incidents of Sale on Approval and Sale or Return.

(1) Under a sale on approval unless otherwise agreed

(a) although the goods are identified to the contract the risk of loss and the title do not pass to the buyer until acceptance; and

(b) use of the goods consistent with the purpose of trial is not acceptance but failure seasonably to notify the seller of election to return the goods is acceptance, and if the goods conform to the contract acceptance of any part is acceptance of the whole; and

(c) after due notification of election to return, the return is at the seller's risk and expense but a merchant buyer must follow any reasonable instructions.

(2) Under a sale or return unless otherwise agreed

(a) the option to return extends to the whole or any commercial unit of the goods while in substantially their original condition, but must be exercised seasonably; and

(b) the return is at the buyer's risk and expense.

§ 2—328. Sale by Auction.

(1) In a sale by auction if goods are put up in lots each lot is the subject of a separate sale.

(2) A sale by auction is complete when the auctioneer so announces by the fall of the hammer or in other customary manner. Where a bid is made while the hammer is falling in acceptance of a prior bid the auctioneer may in his discretion reopen the bidding or declare the goods sold under the bid on which the hammer was falling.

(3) Such a sale is with reserve unless the goods are in explicit terms put up without reserve. In an auction with reserve the auctioneer may withdraw the goods at any time until he announces completion of the sale. In an auction without reserve, after the auctioneer calls for bids on an article or lot, that article or lot cannot be withdrawn unless no bid is made within a reasonable time. In either case a bidder may retract his bid until the auctioneer's announcement of completion of the sale, but a bidder's retraction does not revive any previous bid.

(4) If the auctioneer knowingly receives a bid on the seller's behalf or the seller makes or procures such as bid, and notice has not been given that liberty for such bidding is reserved, the buyer may at his option avoid the sale or take the goods at the price of the last good faith bid prior to the completion of the sale. This subsection shall not apply to any bid at a forced sale.

Part 4 Title, Creditors and Good Faith Purchasers

§ 2—401. Passing of Title; Reservation for Security; Limited Application of This Section.

Each provision of this Article with regard to the rights, obligations and remedies of the seller, the buyer, purchasers or other third parties applies irrespective of title to the goods except where the provision refers to such title. Insofar as situations are not covered by the other provisions of this Article and matters concerning title became material the following rules apply:

(1) Title to goods cannot pass under a contract for sale prior to their identification to the contract (Section 2—501), and unless otherwise explicitly agreed the buyer acquires by their identification a special property as limited by this Act. Any retention or reservation by the seller of the title (property) in goods shipped or delivered to the buyer is limited in effect to a reservation of a security interest. Subject to these provisions and to the provisions of the Article on Secured Transactions (Article 9), title to goods passes from the seller to the buyer in any manner and on any conditions explicitly agreed on by the parties.

(2) Unless otherwise explicitly agreed title passes to the buyer at the time and place at which the seller completes his performance with reference to the physical delivery of the goods, despite any reservation of a security interest and even though a document of title is to be delivered at a different time or place; and in particular and despite any reservation of a security interest by the bill of lading

(a) if the contract requires or authorizes the seller to send the goods to the buyer but does not require him to deliver them at destination, title passes to the buyer at the time and place of shipment; but

(b) if the contract requires delivery at destination, title passes on tender there.

(3) Unless otherwise explicitly agreed where delivery is to be made without moving the goods,

(a) if the seller is to deliver a document of title, title passes at the time when and the place where he delivers such documents; or

(b) if the goods are at the time of contracting already identified and no documents are to be delivered, title passes at the time and place of contracting.

(4) A rejection or other refusal by the buyer to receive or retain the goods, whether or not justified, or a justified revocation of acceptance revests title to the goods in the seller. Such revesting occurs by operation of law and is not a "sale".

§ 2—402. Rights of Seller's Creditors Against Sold Goods.

(1) Except as provided in subsections (2) and (3), rights of unsecured creditors of the seller with respect to goods which have been identified to a contract for sale are subject to the buyer's rights to recover the goods under this Article (Sections 2—502 and 2—716).

(2) A creditor of the seller may treat a sale or an identification of goods to a contract for sale as void if as against him a retention of possession by the seller is fraudulent under any rule of law of the state where the goods are situated, except that retention of possession in good faith and current course of trade by a merchant-seller for a commercially reasonable time after a sale or identification is not fraudulent.

(3) Nothing in this Article shall be deemed to impair the rights of creditors of the seller

(a) under the provisions of the Article on Secured Transactions (Article 9); or

(b) where identification to the contract or delivery is made not in current course of trade but in satisfaction of or as security for a pre-existing claim for money, security or the like and is made under circumstances which under any rule of law of the state where the goods are situated would apart from this Article constitute the transaction a fraudulent transfer or voidable preference.

§ 2—403. Power to Transfer; Good Faith Purchase of Goods; "Entrusting".

(1) A purchaser of goods acquires all title which his transferor had or had power to transfer except that a purchaser of a limited interest acquires rights only to the extent of the interest purchased. A person with voidable title has power to transfer a good title to a good faith purchaser for value. When goods have been delivered under a transaction of purchase the purchaser has such power even though

(a) the transferor was deceived as to the identity of the purchaser, or

(b) the delivery was in exchange for a check which is later dishonored, or

(c) it was agreed that the transaction was to be a "cash sale", or

(d) the delivery was procured through fraud punishable as larcenous under the criminal law.

(2) Any entrusting of possession of goods to a merchant who deals in goods of that kind gives him power to transfer all rights of the entruster to a buyer in ordinary course of business.

(3) "Entrusting" includes any delivery and any acquiescence in retention of possession regardless of any condition expressed between the parties to the delivery or acquiescence and regardless of whether the procurement of the entrusting or the possessor's disposition of the goods have been such as to be larcenous under the criminal law.

(4) The rights of other purchasers of goods and of lien creditors are governed by the Articles on Secured Transactions (Article 9), Bulk Transfers (Article 6) and Documents of Title (Article 7).

Part 5 Performance

§ 2—501. Insurable Interest in Goods; Manner of Identification of Goods.

(1) The buyer obtains a special property and an insurable interest in goods by identification of existing goods as goods to which the contract refers even though the goods so identified are non-conforming and he has an option to return or reject them. Such identification can be made at any time and in any manner explicitly agreed to by the parties. In the absence of explicit agreement identification occurs

(a) when the contract is made if it is for the sale of goods already existing and identified;

(b) if the contract is for the sale of future goods other than those described in paragraph (c), when goods are shipped, marked or otherwise designated by the seller as goods to which the contract refers;

(c) when the crops are planted or otherwise become growing crops or the young are conceived if the contract is for the sale of unborn young to be born within twelve months after contracting or for the sale of crops to be harvested within twelve months or the next normal harvest season after contracting whichever is longer.

(2) The seller retains an insurable interest in goods so long as title to or any security interest in the goods remains in him and where the identification is by the seller alone he may until default or insolvency or notification to the buyer that the identification is final substitute other goods for those identified.

(3) Nothing in this section impairs any insurable interest recognized under any other statute or rule of law.

§ 2—502. Buyer's Right to Goods on Seller's Insolvency.

(1) Subject to subsection (2) and even though the goods have not been shipped a buyer who has paid a part or all of the price of goods in which he has a special property under the provisions of the immediately preceding section may on making and keeping good a tender of any unpaid portion of their price recover them from the seller if the seller becomes insolvent within ten days after receipt of the first installment on their price.

(2) If the identification creating his special property has been made by the buyer he acquires the right to recover the goods only if they conform to the contract for sale.

§ 2—503. Manner of Seller's Tender of Delivery.

(1) Tender of delivery requires that the seller put and hold conforming goods at the buyer's disposition and give the buyer any notification reasonably necessary to enable him to take delivery. The manner, time and place for tender are determined by the agreement and this Article, and in particular

(a) tender must be at a reasonable hour, and if it is of goods they must be kept available for the period reasonably necessary to enable the buyer to take possession; but

(b) unless otherwise agreed the buyer must furnish facilities reasonably suited to the receipt of the goods.

(2) Where the case is within the next section respecting shipment tender requires that the seller comply with its provisions.

(3) Where the seller is required to deliver at a particular destination tender requires that he comply with subsection (1) and also in any appropriate case tender documents as described in subsections (4) and (5) of this section.

(4) Where goods are in the possession of a bailee and are to be delivered without being moved

(a) tender requires that the seller either tender a negotiable document of title covering such goods or procure acknowledgment by the bailee of the buyer's right to possession of the goods; but

(b) tender to the buyer of a non-negotiable document of title or of a written direction to the bailee to deliver is sufficient tender unless the buyer seasonably objects, and receipt by the bailee of notification of the buyer's rights fixes those rights as against the bailee and all third persons; but risk of loss of the goods and of any failure by the bailee to honor the non-negotiable document of title or to obey the direction remains on the seller until the buyer has had a reasonable time to present the document or direction, and a refusal by the bailee to honor the document or to obey the direction defeats the tender.

(5) Where the contract requires the seller to deliver documents

(a) he must tender all such documents in correct form, except as provided in this Article with respect to bills of lading in a set (subsection (2) of Section 2—323); and

(b) tender through customary banking channels is sufficient and dishonor of a draft accompanying the documents constitutes non-acceptance or rejection.

§ 2—504. Shipment by Seller.

Where the seller is required or authorized to send the goods to the buyer and the contract does not require him to deliver them at a particular destination, then unless otherwise agreed he must

(a) put the goods in the possession of such a carrier and make such a contract for their transportation as may be reasonable having regard to the nature of the goods and other circumstances of the case; and

(b) obtain and promptly deliver or tender in due form any document necessary to enable the buyer to obtain possession of the goods or otherwise required by the agreement or by usage of trade; and

(c) promptly notify the buyer of the shipment.

Failure to notify the buyer under paragraph (c) or to make a proper contract under paragraph (a) is a ground for rejection only if material delay or loss ensues.

§ 2—505. Seller's Shipment under Reservation.

(1) Where the seller has identified goods to the contract by or before shipment:

(a) his procurement of a negotiable bill of lading to his own order or otherwise reserves in him a security interest in the goods. His procurement of the bill to the order of a financing agency or of the buyer indicates in addition only the seller's expectation of transferring that interest to the person named.

(b) a non-negotiable bill of lading to himself or his nominee reserves possession of the goods as security but except in a case of conditional delivery (subsection (2) of Section 2—507) a non-negotiable bill of lading naming the buyer as consignee reserves no security interest even though the seller retains possession of the bill of lading.

(2) When shipment by the seller with reservation of a security interest is in violation of the contract for sale it constitutes an improper contract for transportation within the preceding section but impairs neither the rights given to the buyer by shipment and identification of the goods to the contract nor the seller's powers as a holder of a negotiable document.

§ 2—506. Rights of Financing Agency.

(1) A financing agency by paying or purchasing for value a draft which relates to a shipment of goods acquires to the extent of the payment or purchase and in addition to its own rights under the draft and any document of title securing it any rights of the shipper in the goods including the right to stop delivery and the shipper's right to have the draft honored by the buyer.

(2) The right to reimbursement of a financing agency which has in good faith honored or purchased the draft under commitment to or authority from the buyer is not impaired by subsequent discovery of defects with reference to any relevant document which was apparently regular on its face.

§ 2—507. Effect of Seller's Tender; Delivery on Condition.

(1) Tender of delivery is a condition to the buyer's duty to accept the goods and, unless otherwise agreed, to his duty to pay for them. Tender entitles the seller to acceptance of the goods and to payment according to the contract.

(2) Where payment is due and demanded on the delivery to the buyer of goods or documents of title, his right as against the seller to retain or dispose of them is conditional upon his making the payment due.

§ 2—508. Cure by Seller of Improper Tender or Delivery; Replacement.

(1) Where any tender or delivery by the seller is rejected because non-conforming and the time for performance has not yet expired, the seller may seasonably notify the buyer of his intention to cure and may then within the contract time make a conforming delivery.

(2) Where the buyer rejects a non-conforming tender which the seller had reasonable grounds to believe would be acceptable with or without money allowance the seller may if he seasonably notifies the buyer have a further reasonable time to substitute a conforming tender.

§ 2—509. Risk of Loss in the Absence of Breach.

(1) Where the contract requires or authorizes the seller to ship the goods by carrier

(a) if it does not require him to deliver them at a particular destination, the risk of loss passes to the buyer when the goods are duly delivered to the carrier even though the shipment is under reservation (Section 2—505); but

(b) if it does require him to deliver them at a particular destination and the goods are there duly tendered while in the possession of the carrier, the risk of loss passes to the buyer when the goods are there duly so tendered as to enable the buyer to take delivery.

(2) Where the goods are held by a bailee to be delivered without being moved, the risk of loss passes to the buyer

(a) on his receipt of a negotiable document of title covering the goods; or

(b) on acknowledgment by the bailee of the buyer's right to possession of the goods; or

(c) after his receipt of a non-negotiable document of title or other written direction to deliver, as provided in subsection (4)(b) of Section 2—503.

(3) In any case not within subsection (1) or (2), the risk of loss passes to the buyer on his receipt of the goods if the seller is a merchant; otherwise the risk passes to the buyer on tender of delivery.

(4) The provisions of this section are subject to contrary agreement of the parties and to the provisions of this Article on sale on approval (Section 2—327) and on effect of breach on risk of loss (Section 2—510).

§ 2—510. Effect of Breach on Risk of Loss.

(1) Where a tender or delivery of goods so fails to conform to the contract as to give a right of rejection the risk of their loss remains on the seller until cure or acceptance.

(2) Where the buyer rightfully revokes acceptance he may to the extent of any deficiency in his effective insurance coverage treat the risk of loss as having rested on the seller from the beginning.

(3) Where the buyer as to conforming goods already identified to the contract for sale repudiates or is otherwise in breach before risk of their loss has passed to him, the seller may to the extent of any deficiency in his effective insurance coverage treat the risk of loss as resting on the buyer for a commercially reasonable time.

§ 2—511. Tender of Payment by Buyer; Payment by Check.

(1) Unless otherwise agreed tender of payment is a condition to the seller's duty to tender and complete any delivery.

(2) Tender of payment is sufficient when made by any means or in any manner current in the ordinary course of business unless the seller demands payment in legal tender and gives any extension of time reasonably necessary to procure it.

(3) Subject to the provisions of this Act on the effect of an instrument on an obligation (Section 3—310), payment by check is conditional and is defeated as between the parties by dishonor of the check on due presentment.

§ 2—512. Payment by Buyer Before Inspection.

(1) Where the contract requires payment before inspection non-conformity of the goods does not excuse the buyer from so making payment unless

(a) the non-conformity appears without inspection; or

(b) despite tender of the required documents the circumstances would justify injunction against honor under the provisions of this Act (Section 5—114).

(2) Payment pursuant to subsection (1) does not constitute an acceptance of goods or impair the buyer's right to inspect or any of his remedies.

§ 2—513. Buyer's Right to Inspection of Goods.

(1) Unless otherwise agreed and subject to subsection (3), where goods are tendered or delivered or identified to the contract for sale, the buyer has a right before payment or acceptance to inspect them at any reasonable place and time and in any reasonable manner. When the seller is required or authorized to send the goods to the buyer, the inspection may be after their arrival.

(2) Expenses of inspection must be borne by the buyer but may be recovered from the seller if the goods do not conform and are rejected.

(3) Unless otherwise agreed and subject to the provisions of this Article on C.I.F. contracts (subsection (3) of Section 2—321), the buyer is not entitled to inspect the goods before payment of the price when the contract provides

(a) for delivery "C.O.D." or on other like terms; or

(b) for payment against documents of title, except where such payment is due only after the goods are to become available for inspection.

(4) A place or method of inspection fixed by the parties is presumed to be exclusive but unless otherwise expressly agreed it does not postpone identification or shift the place for delivery or for passing the risk of loss. If compliance becomes impossible, inspection shall be as provided in this section unless the place or method fixed was clearly intended as an indispensable condition failure of which avoids the contract.

§ 2—514. When Documents Deliverable on Acceptance; When on Payment.

Unless otherwise agreed documents against which a draft is drawn are to be delivered to the drawee on acceptance of the draft if it is payable more than three days after presentment; otherwise, only on payment.

§ 2—515. Preserving Evidence of Goods in Dispute.

In furtherance of the adjustment of any claim or dispute

(a) either party on reasonable notification to the other and for the purpose of ascertaining the facts and preserving evidence has the right to inspect, test and sample the goods including such of them as may be in the possession or control of the other; and

(b) the parties may agree to a third party inspection or survey to determine the conformity or condition of the goods and may agree that the findings shall be binding upon them in any subsequent litigation or adjustment.

Part 6 Breach, Repudiation and Excuse

§ 2—601. Buyer's Rights on Improper Delivery.

Subject to the provisions of this Article on breach in installment contracts (Section 2—612) and unless otherwise agreed under the sections on contractual limitations of remedy (Sections 2—718 and 2—719), if the goods or the tender of delivery fail in any respect to conform to the contract, the buyer may

(a) reject the whole; or

(b) accept the whole; or

(c) accept any commercial unit or units and reject the rest.

§ 2—602. Manner and Effect of Rightful Rejection.

(1) Rejection of goods must be within a reasonable time after their delivery or tender. It is ineffective unless the buyer seasonably notifies the seller.

(2) Subject to the provisions of the two following sections on rejected goods (Sections 2—603 and 2—604),

(a) after rejection any exercise of ownership by the buyer with respect to any commercial unit is wrongful as against the seller; and

(b) if the buyer has before rejection taken physical possession of goods in which he does not have a security interest under the provisions of this Article (subsection (3) of Section 2—711), he is under a duty after rejection to hold them with reasonable care at the seller's disposition for a time sufficient to permit the seller to remove them; but

(c) the buyer has no further obligations with regard to goods rightfully rejected.

(3) The seller's rights with respect to goods wrongfully rejected are governed by the provisions of this Article on Seller's remedies in general (Section 2—703).

§ 2—603. Merchant Buyer's Duties as to Rightfully Rejected Goods.

(1) Subject to any security interest in the buyer (subsection (3) of Section 2—711), when the seller has no agent or place of business at the market of rejection a merchant buyer is under a duty after rejection of goods in his possession or control to follow any reasonable instructions received from the seller with respect to the goods and in the absence of such instructions to make reasonable efforts to sell them for the seller's account if they are perishable or threaten to decline in value speedily. Instructions are not reasonable if on demand indemnity for expenses is not forthcoming.

(2) When the buyer sells goods under subsection (1), he is entitled to reimbursement from the seller or out of the proceeds for reasonable expenses of caring for and selling them, and if the expenses include no selling commission then to such commission as is usual in the trade or if there is none to a reasonable sum not exceeding ten per cent on the gross proceeds.

(3) In complying with this section the buyer is held only to good faith and good faith conduct hereunder is neither acceptance nor conversion nor the basis of an action for damages.

§ 2—604. Buyer's Options as to Salvage of Rightfully Rejected Goods.

Subject to the provisions of the immediately preceding section on perishables if the seller gives no instructions within a reasonable time after notification of rejection the buyer may store the rejected goods for the seller's account or reship them to him or resell them for the seller's account with reimbursement as provided in the preceding section. Such action is not acceptance or conversion.

§ 2—605. Waiver of Buyer's Objections by Failure to Particularize.

(1) The buyer's failure to state in connection with rejection a particular defect which is ascertainable by reasonable inspection precludes him from relying on the unstated defect to justify rejection or to establish breach

(a) where the seller could have cured it if stated seasonably; or

(b) between merchants when the seller has after rejection made a request in writing for a full and final written statement of all defects on which the buyer proposes to rely.

(2) Payment against documents made without reservation of rights precludes recovery of the payment for defects apparent on the face of the documents.

§ 2—606. What Constitutes Acceptance of Goods.

(1) Acceptance of goods occurs when the buyer

(a) after a reasonable opportunity to inspect the goods signifies to the seller that the goods are conforming or that he will take or retain them in spite of their nonconformity; or

(b) fails to make an effective rejection (subsection (1) of Section 2—602), but such acceptance does not occur until the buyer has had a reasonable opportunity to inspect them; or

(c) does any act inconsistent with the seller's ownership; but if such act is wrongful as against the seller it is an acceptance only if ratified by him.

(2) Acceptance of a part of any commercial unit is acceptance of that entire unit.

§ 2—607. Effect of Acceptance; Notice of Breach; Burden of Establishing Breach After Acceptance; Notice of Claim or Litigation to Person Answerable Over.

(1) The buyer must pay at the contract rate for any goods accepted.

(2) Acceptance of goods by the buyer precludes rejection of the goods accepted and if made with knowledge of a non-conformity cannot be revoked because of it unless the acceptance was on the reasonable assumption that the non-conformity would be seasonably cured but acceptance does not of itself impair any other remedy provided by this Article for non-conformity.

(3) Where a tender has been accepted

(a) the buyer must within a reasonable time after he discovers or should have discovered any breach notify the seller of breach or be barred from any remedy; and

(b) if the claim is one for infringement or the like (subsection (3) of Section 2—312) and the buyer is sued as a result of such a breach he must so notify the seller within a reasonable time after he receives notice of the litigation or be barred from any remedy over for liability established by the litigation.

(4) The burden is on the buyer to establish any breach with respect to the goods accepted.

(5) Where the buyer is sued for breach of a warranty or other obligation for which his seller is answerable over

(a) he may give his seller written notice of the litigation. If the notice states that the seller may come in and defend and that if the seller does not do so he will be bound in any action against him by his buyer by any determination of fact common to the two litigations, then unless the seller after seasonable receipt of the notice does come in and defend he is so bound.

(b) if the claim is one for infringement or the like (subsection (3) of Section 2—312) the original seller may demand in writing that his buyer turn over to him control of the litigation including settlement or else be barred from any remedy over and if he also agrees to bear all expense and to satisfy any adverse judgment, then unless the buyer after seasonable receipt of the demand does turn over control the buyer is so barred.

(6) The provisions of subsections (3), (4) and (5) apply to any obligation of a buyer to hold the seller harmless against infringement or the like (subsection (3) of Section 2—312).

§ 2—608. Revocation of Acceptance in Whole or in Part.

(1) The buyer may revoke his acceptance of a lot or commercial unit whose non-conformity substantially impairs its value to him if he has accepted it

(a) on the reasonable assumption that its nonconformity would be cured and it has not been seasonably cured; or

(b) without discovery of such non-conformity if his acceptance was reasonably induced either by the difficulty of discovery before acceptance or by the seller's assurances.

(2) Revocation of acceptance must occur within a reasonable time after the buyer discovers or should have discovered the ground for it and before any substantial change in condition of the goods which is not caused by their own defects. It is not effective until the buyer notifies the seller of it.

(3) A buyer who so revokes has the same rights and duties with regard to the goods involved as if he had rejected them.

§ 2—609. Right to Adequate Assurance of Performance.

(1) A contract for sale imposes an obligation on each party that the other's expectation of receiving due performance will not be impaired. When reasonable grounds for insecurity arise with respect to the performance of either party the other may in writing demand adequate assurance of due performance and until he receives such assurance may if commercially reasonable suspend any performance for which he has not already received the agreed return.

(2) Between merchants the reasonableness of grounds for insecurity and the adequacy of any assurance offered shall be determined according to commercial standards.

(3) Acceptance of any improper delivery or payment does not prejudice the party's right to demand adequate assurance of future performance.

(4) After receipt of a justified demand failure to provide within a reasonable time not exceeding thirty days such assurance of due performance as is adequate under the circumstances of the particular case is a repudiation of the contract.

§ 2—610. Anticipatory Repudiation.

When either party repudiates the contract with respect to a performance not yet due the loss of which will substantially impair the value of the contract to the other, the aggrieved party may

(a) for a commercially reasonable time await performance by the repudiating party; or

(b) resort to any remedy for breach (Section 2—703 or Section 2—711), even though he has notified the repudiating party that he would await the latter's performance and has urged retraction; and

(c) in either case suspend his own performance or proceed in accordance with the provisions of this Article on the seller's right to identify goods to the contract notwithstanding breach or to salvage unfinished goods (Section 2—704).

§ 2—611. Retraction of Anticipatory Repudiation.

(1) Until the repudiating party's next performance is due he can retract his repudiation unless the aggrieved party has since the repudiation cancelled or materially changed his position or otherwise indicated that he considers the repudiation final.

(2) Retraction may be by any method which clearly indicates to the aggrieved party that the repudiating party intends to perform, but must include any assurance justifiably demanded under the provisions of this Article (Section 2—609).

(3) Retraction reinstates the repudiating party's rights under the contract with due excuse and allowance to the aggrieved party for any delay occasioned by the repudiation.

§ 2—612. "Installment Contract"; Breach.

(1) An "installment contract" is one which requires or authorizes the delivery of goods in separate lots to be separately

accepted, even though the contract contains a clause "each delivery is a separate contract" or its equivalent.

(2) The buyer may reject any installment which is non-conforming if the non-conformity substantially impairs the value of that installment and cannot be cured or if the non-conformity is a defect in the required documents; but if the non-conformity does not fall within subsection (3) and the seller gives adequate assurance of its cure the buyer must accept that installment.

(3) Whenever non-conformity or default with respect to one or more installments substantially impairs the value of the whole contract there is a breach of the whole. But the aggrieved party reinstates the contract if he accepts a non-conforming installment without seasonably notifying of cancellation or if he brings an action with respect only to past installments or demands performance as to future installments.

§ 2—613. Casualty to Identified Goods.

Where the contract requires for its performance goods identified when the contract is made, and the goods suffer casualty without fault of either party before the risk of loss passes to the buyer, or in a proper case under a "no arrival, no sale" term (Section 2—324) then

(a) if the loss is total the contract is avoided; and

(b) if the loss is partial or the goods have so deteriorated as no longer to conform to the contract the buyer may nevertheless demand inspection and at his option either treat the contract as voided or accept the goods with due allowance from the contract price for the deterioration or the deficiency in quantity but without further right against the seller.

§ 2—614. Substituted Performance.

(1) Where without fault of either party the agreed berthing, loading, or unloading facilities fail or an agreed type of carrier becomes unavailable or the agreed manner of delivery otherwise becomes commercially impracticable but a commercially reasonable substitute is available, such substitute performance must be tendered and accepted.

(2) If the agreed means or manner of payment fails because of domestic or foreign governmental regulation, the seller may withhold or stop delivery unless the buyer provides a means or manner of payment which is commercially a substantial equivalent. If delivery has already been taken, payment by the means or in the manner provided by the regulation discharges the buyer's obligation unless the regulation is discriminatory, oppressive or predatory.

§ 2—615. Excuse by Failure of Presupposed Conditions.

Except so far as a seller may have assumed a greater obligation and subject to the preceding section on substituted performance:

(a) Delay in delivery or non-delivery in whole or in part by a seller who complies with paragraphs (b) and (c) is not a breach of his duty under a contract for sale if performance as agreed has been made impracticable by the occurrence of a contingency the nonoccurrence of which was a basic assumption on which the contract was made or by compliance in good faith with any applicable foreign or domestic governmental regulation or order whether or not it later proves to be invalid.

(b) Where the causes mentioned in paragraph (a) affect only a part of the seller's capacity to perform, he must allocate production and deliveries among his customers but may at his option include regular customers not then under contract as well as his own requirements for further manufacture. He may so allocate in any manner which is fair and reasonable.

(c) The seller must notify the buyer seasonably that there will be delay or non-delivery and, when allocation is required under paragraph (b), of the estimated quota thus made available for the buyer.

§ 2—616. Procedure on Notice Claiming Excuse.

(1) Where the buyer receives notification of a material or indefinite delay or an allocation justified under the preceding section he may by written notification to the seller as to any delivery concerned, and where the prospective deficiency substantially impairs the value of the whole contract under the provisions of this Article relating to breach of installment contracts (Section 2—612), then also as to the whole,

(a) terminate and thereby discharge any unexecuted portion of the contract; or

(b) modify the contract by agreeing to take his available quota in substitution.

(2) If after receipt of such notification from the seller the buyer fails so to modify the contract within a reasonable time not exceeding thirty days the contract lapses with respect to any deliveries affected.

(3) The provisions of this section may not be negated by agreement except in so far as the seller has assumed a greater obligation under the preceding section.

Part 7 Remedies

§ 2—701. Remedies for Breach of Collateral Contracts Not Impaired.

Remedies for breach of any obligation or promise collateral or ancillary to a contract for sale are not impaired by the provisions of this Article.

§ 2—702. Seller's Remedies on Discovery of Buyer's Insolvency.

(1) Where the seller discovers the buyer to be insolvent he may refuse delivery except for cash including payment for all goods theretofore delivered under the contract, and stop delivery under this Article (Section 2—705).

(2) Where the seller discovers that the buyer has received goods on credit while insolvent he may reclaim the goods upon demand made within ten days after the receipt, but if misrepresentation of solvency has been made to the particular seller in writing within three months before delivery the ten day limita-

tion does not apply. Except as provided in this subsection the seller may not base a right to reclaim goods on the buyer's fraudulent or innocent misrepresentation of solvency or of intent to pay.

(3) The seller's right to reclaim under subsection (2) is subject to the rights of a buyer in ordinary course or other good faith purchaser under this Article (Section 2—403). Successful reclamation of goods excludes all other remedies with respect to them.

§ 2—703. Seller's Remedies in General.

Where the buyer wrongfully rejects or revokes acceptance of goods or fails to make a payment due on or before delivery or repudiates with respect to a part or the whole, then with respect to any goods directly affected and, if the breach is of the whole contract (Section 2—612), then also with respect to the whole undelivered balance, the aggrieved seller may

(a) withhold delivery of such goods;

(b) stop delivery by any bailee as hereafter provided (Section 2—705);

(c) proceed under the next section respecting goods still unidentified to the contract;

(d) resell and recover damages as hereafter provided (Section 2—706);

(e) recover damages for non-acceptance (Section 2—708) or in a proper case the price (Section 2—709);

(f) cancel.

§ 2—704. Seller's Right to Identify Goods to the Contract Notwithstanding Breach or to Salvage Unfinished Goods.

(1) An aggrieved seller under the preceding section may

(a) identify to the contract conforming goods not already identified if at the time he learned of the breach they are in his possession or control;

(b) treat as the subject of resale goods which have demonstrably been intended for the particular contract even though those goods are unfinished.

(2) Where the goods are unfinished an aggrieved seller may in the exercise of reasonable commercial judgment for the purposes of avoiding loss and of effective realization either complete the manufacture and wholly identify the goods to the contract or cease manufacture and resell for scrap or salvage value or proceed in any other reasonable manner.

§ 2—705. Seller's Stoppage of Delivery in Transit or Otherwise.

(1) The seller may stop delivery of goods in the possession of a carrier or other bailee when he discovers the buyer to be insolvent (Section 2—702) and may stop delivery of carload, truckload, planeload or larger shipments of express or freight when the buyer repudiates or fails to make a payment due before delivery or if for any other reason the seller has a right to withhold or reclaim the goods.

(2) As against such buyer the seller may stop delivery until

(a) receipt of the goods by the buyer; or

(b) acknowledgment to the buyer by any bailee of the goods except a carrier that the bailee holds the goods for the buyer; or

(c) such acknowledgment to the buyer by a carrier by reshipment or as warehouseman; or

(d) negotiation to the buyer of any negotiable document of title covering the goods.

(3) (a) To stop delivery the seller must so notify as to enable the bailee by reasonable diligence to prevent delivery of the goods.

(b) After such notification the bailee must hold and deliver the goods according to the directions of the seller but the seller is liable to the bailee for any ensuing charges or damages.

(c) If a negotiable document of title has been issued for goods the bailee is not obliged to obey a notification to stop until surrender of the document.

(d) A carrier who has issued a non-negotiable bill of lading is not obliged to obey a notification to stop received from a person other than the consignor.

§ 2—706. Seller's Resale Including Contract for Resale.

(1) Under the conditions stated in Section 2—703 on seller's remedies, the seller may resell the goods concerned or the undelivered balance thereof. Where the resale is made in good faith and in a commercially reasonable manner the seller may recover the difference between the resale price and the contract price together with any incidental damages allowed under the provisions of this Article (Section 2—710), but less expenses saved in consequence of the buyer's breach.

(2) Except as otherwise provided in subsection (3) or unless otherwise agreed resale may be at public or private sale including sale by way of one or more contracts to sell or of identification to an existing contract of the seller. Sale may be as a unit or in parcels and at any time and place and on any terms but every aspect of the sale including the method, manner, time, place and terms must be commercially reasonable. The resale must be reasonably identified as referring to the broken contract, but it is not necessary that the goods be in existence or that any or all of them have been identified to the contract before the breach.

(3) Where the resale is at private sale the seller must give the buyer reasonable notification of his intention to resell.

(4) Where the resale is at public sale

(a) only identified goods can be sold except where there is a recognized market for a public sale of futures in goods of the kind; and

(b) it must be made at a usual place or market for public sale if one is reasonably available and except in the case of goods which are perishable or threaten to decline in value speedily the seller must give the buyer reasonable notice of the time and place of the resale; and

(c) if the goods are not to be within the view of those attending the sale the notification of sale must state the place where the goods are located and provide for their reasonable inspection by prospective bidders; and

(d) the seller may buy.

(5) A purchaser who buys in good faith at a resale takes the goods free of any rights of the original buyer even though the seller fails to comply with one or more of the requirements of this section.

(6) The seller is not accountable to the buyer for any profit made on any resale. A person in the position of a seller (Section 2—707) or a buyer who has rightfully rejected or justifiably revoked acceptance must account for any excess over the amount of his security interest, as hereinafter defined (subsection (3) of Section 2—711).

§ 2—707. "Person in the Position of a Seller".

(1) A "person in the position of a seller" includes as against a principal an agent who has paid or become responsible for the price of goods on behalf of his principal or anyone who otherwise holds a security interest or other right in goods similar to that of a seller.

(2) A person in the position of a seller may as provided in this Article withhold or stop delivery (Section 2—705) and resell (Section 2—706) and recover incidental damages (Section 2—710).

§ 2—708. Seller's Damages for Non-Acceptance or Repudiation.

(1) Subject to subsection (2) and to the provisions of this Article with respect to proof of market price (Section 2—723), the measure of damages for non-acceptance or repudiation by the buyer is the difference between the market price at the time and place for tender and the unpaid contract price together with any incidental damages provided in this Article (Section 2—710), but less expenses saved in consequence of the buyer's breach.

(2) If the measure of damages provided in subsection (1) is inadequate to put the seller in as good a position as performance would have done then the measure of damages is the profit (including reasonable overhead) which the seller would have made from full performance by the buyer, together with any incidental damages provided in this Article (Section 2—710), due allowance for costs reasonably incurred and due credit for payments or proceeds of resale.

§ 2—709. Action for the Price.

(1) When the buyer fails to pay the price as it becomes due the seller may recover, together with any incidental damages under the next section, the price

(a) of goods accepted or of conforming goods lost or damaged within a commercially reasonable time after risk of their loss has passed to the buyer; and

(b) of goods identified to the contract if the seller is unable after reasonable effort to resell them at a reasonable price or the circumstances reasonably indicate that such effort will be unavailing.

(2) Where the seller sues for the price he must hold for the buyer any goods which have been identified to the contract and are still in his control except that if resale becomes possible he may resell them at any time prior to the collection of the judgment. The net proceeds of any such resale must be credited to the buyer and payment of the judgment entitles him to any goods not resold.

(3) After the buyer has wrongfully rejected or revoked acceptance of the goods or has failed to make a payment due or has repudiated (Section 2—610), a seller who is held not entitled to the price under this section shall nevertheless be awarded damages for non-acceptance under the preceding section.

§ 2—710. Seller's Incidental Damages.

Incidental damages to an aggrieved seller include any commercially reasonable charges, expenses or commissions incurred in stopping delivery, in the transportation, care and custody of goods after the buyer's breach, in connection with return or resale of the goods or otherwise resulting from the breach.

§ 2—711. Buyer's Remedies in General; Buyer's Security Interest in Rejected Goods.

(1) Where the seller fails to make delivery or repudiates or the buyer rightfully rejects or justifiably revokes acceptance then with respect to any goods involved, and with respect to the whole if the breach goes to the whole contract (Section 2—612), the buyer may cancel and whether or not he has done so may in addition to recovering so much of the price as has been paid

(a) "cover" and have damages under the next section as to all the goods affected whether or not they have been identified to the contract; or

(b) recover damages for non-delivery as provided in this Article (Section 2—713).

(2) Where the seller fails to deliver or repudiates the buyer may also

(a) if the goods have been identified recover them as provided in this Article (Section 2—502); or

(b) in a proper case obtain specific performance or replevy the goods as provided in this Article (Section 2—716).

(3) On rightful rejection or justifiable revocation of acceptance a buyer has a security interest in goods in his possession or control for any payments made on their price and any expenses reasonably incurred in their inspection, receipt, transportation, care and custody and may hold such goods and resell them in like manner as an aggrieved seller (Section 2—706).

§ 2—712. "Cover"; Buyer's Procurement of Substitute Goods.

(1) After a breach within the preceding section the buyer may "cover" by making in good faith and without unreasonable

delay any reasonable purchase of or contract to purchase goods in substitution for those due from the seller.

(2) The buyer may recover from the seller as damages the difference between the cost of cover and the contract price together with any incidental or consequential damages as hereinafter defined (Section 2—715), but less expenses saved in consequence of the seller's breach.

(3) Failure of the buyer to effect cover within this section does not bar him from any other remedy.

§ 2—713. Buyer's Damages for Non-Delivery or Repudiation.

(1) Subject to the provisions of this Article with respect to proof of market price (Section 2—723), the measure of damages for non-delivery or repudiation by the seller is the difference between the market price at the time when the buyer learned of the breach and the contract price together with any incidental and consequential damages provided in this Article (Section 2—715), but less expenses saved in consequence of the seller's breach.

(2) Market price is to be determined as of the place for tender or, in cases of rejection after arrival or revocation of acceptance, as of the place of arrival.

§ 2—714. Buyer's Damages for Breach in Regard to Accepted Goods.

(1) Where the buyer has accepted goods and given notification (subsection (3) of Section 2—607) he may recover as damages for any non-conformity of tender the loss resulting in the ordinary course of events from the seller's breach as determined in any manner which is reasonable.

(2) The measure of damages for breach of warranty is the difference at the time and place of acceptance between the value of the goods accepted and the value they would have had if they had been as warranted, unless special circumstances show proximate damages of a different amount.

(3) In a proper case any incidental and consequential damages under the next section may also be recovered.

§ 2—715. Buyer's Incidental and Consequential Damages.

(1) Incidental damages resulting from the seller's breach include expenses reasonably incurred in inspection, receipt, transportation and care and custody of goods rightfully rejected, any commercially reasonable charges, expenses or commissions in connection with effecting cover and any other reasonable expense incident to the delay or other breach.

(2) Consequential damages resulting from the seller's breach include

(a) any loss resulting from general or particular requirements and needs of which the seller at the time of contracting had reason to know and which could not reasonably be prevented by cover or otherwise; and

(b) injury to person or property proximately resulting from any breach of warranty.

§ 2—716. Buyer's Right to Specific Performance or Replevin.

(1) Specific performance may be decreed where the goods are unique or in other proper circumstances.

(2) The decree for specific performance may include such terms and conditions as to payment of the price, damages, or other relief as the court may deem just.

(3) The buyer has a right of replevin for goods identified to the contract if after reasonable effort he is unable to effect cover for such goods or the circumstances reasonably indicate that such effort will be unavailing or if the goods have been shipped under reservation and satisfaction of the security interest in them has been made or tendered.

§ 2—717. Deduction of Damages From the Price.

The buyer on notifying the seller of his intention to do so may deduct all or any part of the damages resulting from any breach of the contract from any part of the price still due under the same contract.

§ 2—718. Liquidation or Limitation of Damages; Deposits.

(1) Damages for breach by either party may be liquidated in the agreement but only at an amount which is reasonable in the light of the anticipated or actual harm caused by the breach, the difficulties of proof of loss, and the inconvenience or nonfeasibility of otherwise obtaining an adequate remedy. A term fixing unreasonably large liquidated damages is void as a penalty.

(2) Where the seller justifiably withholds delivery of goods because of the buyer's breach, the buyer is entitled to restitution of any amount by which the sum of his payments exceeds

(a) the amount to which the seller is entitled by virtue of terms liquidating the seller's damages in accordance with subsection (1), or

(b) in the absence of such terms, twenty per cent of the value of the total performance for which the buyer is obligated under the contract or $500, whichever is smaller.

(3) The buyer's right to restitution under subsection (2) is subject to offset to the extent that the seller establishes

(a) a right to recover damages under the provisions of this Article other than subsection (1), and

(b) the amount or value of any benefits received by the buyer directly or indirectly by reason of the contract.

(4) Where a seller has received payment in goods their reasonable value or the proceeds of their resale shall be treated as payments for the purposes of subsection (2); but if the seller has notice of the buyer's breach before reselling goods received in part performance, his resale is subject to the conditions laid down in this Article on resale by an aggrieved seller (Section 2—706).

§ 2—719. Contractual Modification or Limitation of Remedy.

(1) Subject to the provisions of subsections (2) and (3) of this section and of the preceding section on liquidation and limitation of damages,

(a) the agreement may provide for remedies in addition to or in substitution for those provided in this Article and may limit or alter the measure of damages recoverable under this Article, as by limiting the buyer's remedies to return of the goods and repayment of the price or to repair and replacement of non-conforming goods or parts; and

(b) resort to a remedy as provided is optional unless the remedy is expressly agreed to be exclusive, in which case it is the sole remedy.

(2) Where circumstances cause an exclusive or limited remedy to fail of its essential purpose, remedy may be had as provided in this Act.

(3) Consequential damages may be limited or excluded unless the limitation or exclusion is unconscionable. Limitation of consequential damages for injury to the person in the case of consumer goods is prima facie unconscionable but limitation of damages where the loss is commercial is not.

§ 2—720. Effect of "Cancellation" or "Rescission" on Claims for Antecedent Breach.

Unless the contrary intention clearly appears, expressions of "cancellation" or "rescission" of the contract or the like shall not be construed as a renunciation or discharge of any claim in damages for an antecedent breach.

§ 2—721. Remedies for Fraud.

Remedies for material misrepresentation or fraud include all remedies available under this Article for non-fraudulent breach. Neither rescission or a claim for rescission of the contract for sale nor rejection or return of the goods shall bar or be deemed inconsistent with a claim for damages or other remedy.

§ 2—722. Who Can Sue Third Parties for Injury to Goods.

Where a third party so deals with goods which have been identified to a contract for sale as to cause actionable injury to a party to that contract

(a) a right of action against the third party is in either party to the contract for sale who has title to or a security interest or a special property or an insurable interest in the goods; and if the goods have been destroyed or converted a right of action is also in the party who either bore the risk of loss under the contract for sale or has since the injury assumed that risk as against the other;

(b) if at the time of the injury the party plaintiff did not bear the risk of loss as against the other party to the contract for sale and there is no arrangement between them for disposition of the recovery, his suit or settlement is, subject to his own interest, as a fiduciary for the other party to the contract;

(c) either party may with the consent of the other sue for the benefit of whom it may concern.

§ 2—723. Proof of Market Price: Time and Place.

(1) If an action based on anticipatory repudiation comes to trial before the time for performance with respect to some or all of the goods, any damages based on market price (Section 2—708 or Section 2—713) shall be determined according to the price of such goods prevailing at the time when the aggrieved party learned of the repudiation.

(2) If evidence of a price prevailing at the times or places described in this Article is not readily available the price prevailing within any reasonable time before or after the time described or at any other place which in commercial judgment or under usage of trade would serve as a reasonable substitute for the one described may be used, making any proper allowance for the cost of transporting the goods to or from such other place.

(3) Evidence of a relevant price prevailing at a time or place other than the one described in this Article offered by one party is not admissible unless and until he has given the other party such notice as the court finds sufficient to prevent unfair surprise.

§ 2—724. Admissibility of Market Quotations.

Whenever the prevailing price or value of any goods regularly bought and sold in any established commodity market is in issue, reports in official publications or trade journals or in newspapers or periodicals of general circulation published as the reports of such market shall be admissible in evidence. The circumstances of the preparation of such a report may be shown to affect its weight but not its admissibility.

§ 2—725. Statute of Limitations in Contracts for Sale.

(1) An action for breach of any contract for sale must be commenced within four years after the cause of action has accrued. By the original agreement the parties may reduce the period of limitation to not less than one year but may not extend it.

(2) A cause of action accrues when the breach occurs, regardless of the aggrieved party's lack of knowledge of the breach. A breach of warranty occurs when tender of delivery is made, except that where a warranty explicitly extends to future performance of the goods and discovery of the breach must await the time of such performance the cause of action accrues when the breach is or should have been discovered.

(3) Where an action commenced within the time limited by subsection (1) is so terminated as to leave available a remedy by another action for the same breach such other action may be commenced after the expiration of the time limited and within six months after the termination of the first action unless the termination resulted from voluntary discontinuance or from dismissal for failure or neglect to prosecute.

(4) This section does not alter the law on tolling of the statute of limitations nor does it apply to causes of action which have accrued before this Act becomes effective.

Article 2A
LEASES

Part 1 General Provisions

§ 2A—101. Short Title.

This Article shall be known and may be cited as the Uniform Commercial Code—Leases.

§ 2A—102. Scope.

This Article applies to any transaction, regardless of form, that creates a lease.

§ 2A—103. Definitions and Index of Definitions.

(1) In this Article unless the context otherwise requires:

(a) "Buyer in ordinary course of business" means a person who in good faith and without knowledge that the sale to him [or her] is in violation of the ownership rights or security interest or leasehold interest of a third party in the goods buys in ordinary course from a person in the business of selling goods of that kind but does not include a pawnbroker. "Buying" may be for cash or by exchange of other property or on secured or unsecured credit and includes receiving goods or documents of title under a pre-existing contract for sale but does not include a transfer in bulk or as security for or in total or partial satisfaction of a money debt.

(b) "Cancellation" occurs when either party puts an end to the lease contract for default by the other party.

(c) "Commercial unit" means such a unit of goods as by commercial usage is a single whole for purposes of lease and division of which materially impairs its character or value on the market or in use. A commercial unit may be a single article, as a machine, or a set of articles, as a suite of furniture or a line of machinery, or a quantity, as a gross or carload, or any other unit treated in use or in the relevant market as a single whole.

(d) "Conforming" goods or performance under a lease contract means goods or performance that are in accordance with the obligations under the lease contract.

(e) "Consumer lease" means a lease that a lessor regularly engaged in the business of leasing or selling makes to a lessee who is an individual and who takes under the lease primarily for a personal, family, or household "purpose [, if" the total payments to be made under the lease contract, excluding payments for options to renew or buy, do not exceed. . . .

(f) "Fault" means wrongful act, omission, breach, or default.

(g) "Finance lease" means a lease with respect to which:

(i) the lessor does not select, manufacture or supply the goods;

(ii) the lessor acquires the goods or the right to possession and use of the goods in connection with the lease; and

(iii) one of the following occurs:

(A) the lessee receives a copy of the contract by which the lessor acquired the goods or the right to possession and use of the goods before signing the lease contract;

(B) the lessee's approval of the contract by which the lessor acquired the goods or the right to possession and use of the goods is a condition to effectiveness of the lease contract;

(C) the lessee, before signing the lease contract, receives an accurate and complete statement designating the promises and warranties, and any disclaimers of warranties, limitations or modifications of remedies, or liquidated damages, including those of a third party, such as the manufacturer of the goods, provided to the lessor by the person supplying the goods in connection with or as part of the contract by which the lessor acquired the goods or the right to possession and use of the goods; or

(D) if the lease is not a consumer lease, the lessor, before the lessee signs the lease contract, informs the lessee in writing (a) of the identity of the person supplying the goods to the lessor, unless the lessee has selected that person and directed the lessor to acquire the goods or the right to possession and use of the goods from that person, (b) that the lessee is entitled under this Article to any promises and warranties, including those of any third party, provided to the lessor by the person supplying the goods in connection with or as part of the contract by which the lessor acquired the goods or the right to possession and use of the goods, and (c) that the lessee may communicate with the person supplying the goods to the lessor and receive an accurate and complete statement of those promises and warranties, including any disclaimers and limitations of them or of remedies.

(h) "Goods" means all things that are movable at the time of identification to the lease contract, or are fixtures (Section 2A—309), but the term does not include money, documents, instruments, accounts, chattel paper, general intangibles, or minerals or the like, including oil and gas, before extraction. The term also includes the unborn young of animals.

(i) "Installment lease contract" means a lease contract that authorizes or requires the delivery of goods in separate lots to be separately accepted, even though the lease contract contains a clause "each delivery is a eparate lease" or its equivalent.

(j) "Lease" means a transfer of the right to possession and use of goods for a term in return for consideration, but a sale, including a sale on approval or a sale or return, or retention or creation of a security interest is not a lease. Unless the context clearly indicates otherwise, the term includes a sublease.

(k) "Lease agreement" means the bargain, with respect to the lease, of the lessor and the lessee in fact as found in their language or by implication from other circumstances including course of dealing or usage of trade or course of performance as provided in this Article. Unless the context clearly indicates otherwise, the term includes a sublease agreement.

(l) "Lease contract" means the total legal obligation that results from the lease agreement as affected by this Article and any other applicable rules of law. Unless the context clearly indicates otherwise, the term includes a sublease contract.

(m) "Leasehold interest" means the interest of the lessor or the lessee under a lease contract.

(n) "Lessee" means a person who acquires the right to possession and use of goods under a lease. Unless the context clearly indicates otherwise, the term includes a sublessee.

(o) "Lessee in ordinary course of business" means a person who in good faith and without knowledge that the lease to him [or her] is in violation of the ownership rights or security interest or leasehold interest of a third party in the goods, leases in ordinary course from a person in the business of selling or leasing goods of that kind but does not include a pawnbroker. "Leasing" may be for cash or by exchange of other property or on secured or unsecured credit and includes receiving goods or documents of title under a pre-existing lease contract but does not include a transfer in bulk or as security for or in total or partial satisfaction of a money debt.

(p) "Lessor" means a person who transfers the right to possession and use of goods under a lease. Unless the context clearly indicates otherwise, the term includes a sublessor.

(q) "Lessor's residual interest" means the lessor's interest in the goods after expiration, termination, or cancellation of the lease contract.

(r) "Lien" means a charge against or interest in goods to secure payment of a debt or performance of an obligation, but the term does not include a security interest.

(s) "Lot" means a parcel or a single article that is the subject matter of a separate lease or delivery, whether or not it is sufficient to perform the lease contract.

(t) "Merchant lessee" means a lessee that is a merchant with respect to goods of the kind subject to the lease.

(u) "Present value" means the amount as of a date certain of one or more sums payable in the future, discounted to the date certain. The discount is determined by the interest rate specified by the parties if the rate was not manifestly unreasonable at the time the transaction was entered into; otherwise, the discount is determined by a commercially reasonable rate that takes into account the facts and circumstances of each case at the time the transaction was entered into.

(v) "Purchase" includes taking by sale, lease, mortgage, security interest, pledge, gift, or any other voluntary transaction creating an interest in goods.

(w) "Sublease" means a lease of goods the right to possession and use of which was acquired by the lessor as a lessee under an existing lease.

(x) "Supplier" means a person from whom a lessor buys or leases goods to be leased under a finance lease.

(y) "Supply contract" means a contract under which a lessor buys or leases goods to be leased.

(z) "Termination" occurs when either party pursuant to a power created by agreement or law puts an end to the lease contract otherwise than for default.

(2) Other definitions applying to this Article and the sections in which they appear are:

"Accessions". Section 2A—310(1).
"Construction mortgage". Section 2A—309(1)(d).
"Encumbrance". Section 2A—309(1)(e).
"Fixtures". Section 2A—309(1)(a).
"Fixture filing". Section 2A—309(1)(b).
"Purchase money lease". Section 2A—309(1)(c).

(3) The following definitions in other Articles apply to this Article:

"Accounts". Section 9—106.
"Between merchants". Section 2—104(3).
"Buyer". Section 2—103(1)(a).
"Chattel paper". Section 9—105(1)(b).
"Consumer goods". Section 9—109(1).
"Document". Section 9—105(1)(f).
"Entrusting". Section 2—403(3).
"General intangibles". Section 9—106.
"Good faith". Section 2—103(1)(b).
"Instrument". Section 9—105(1)(i).
"Merchant". Section 2—104(1).
"Mortgage". Section 9—105(1)(j).
"Pursuant to commitment". Section 9—105(1)(k).
"Receipt". Section 2—103(1)(c).
"Sale". Section 2—106(1).
"Sale on approval". Section 2—326.
"Sale or return". Section 2—326.
"Seller". Section 2—103(1)(d).

(4) In addition Article 1 contains general definitions and principles of construction and interpretation applicable throughout this Article.

As amended in 1990.

§ 2A—104. Leases Subject to Other Law.

(1) A lease, although subject to this Article, is also subject to any applicable:

(a) certificate of title statute of this State: (list any certificate of title statutes covering automobiles, trailers, mobile homes, boats, farm tractors, and the like);

(b) certificate of title statute of another jurisdiction (Section 2A—105); or

(c) consumer protection statute of this State, or final consumer protection decision of a court of this State existing on the effective date of this Article.

(2) In case of conflict between this Article, other than Sections 2A—105, 2A—304(3), and 2A—305(3), and a statute or decision referred to in subsection (1), the statute or decision controls.

(3) Failure to comply with an applicable law has only the effect specified therein.

As amended in 1990.

§ 2A—105. Territorial Application of Article to Goods Covered by Certificate of Title.

Subject to the provisions of Sections 2A—304(3) and 2A—305(3), with respect to goods covered by a certificate of title issued under a statute of this State or of another jurisdiction, compliance and the effect of compliance or noncompliance with a certificate of title statute are governed by the law (including the conflict of laws rules) of the jurisdiction issuing the certificate until the earlier of (a) surrender of the certificate, or (b) four months after the goods are removed from that jurisdiction and thereafter until a new certificate of title is issued by another jurisdiction.

§ 2A—106. Limitation on Power of Parties to Consumer Lease to Choose Applicable Law and Judicial Forum.

(1) If the law chosen by the parties to a consumer lease is that of a jurisdiction other than a jurisdiction in which the lessee resides at the time the lease agreement becomes enforceable or within 30 days thereafter or in which the goods are to be used, the choice is not enforceable.

(2) If the judicial forum chosen by the parties to a consumer lease is a forum that would not otherwise have jurisdiction over the lessee, the choice is not enforceable.

§ 2A—107. Waiver or Renunciation of Claim or Right After Default.

Any claim or right arising out of an alleged default or breach of warranty may be discharged in whole or in part without consideration by a written waiver or renunciation signed and delivered by the aggrieved party.

§ 2A—108. Unconscionability.

(1) If the court as a matter of law finds a lease contract or any clause of a lease contract to have been unconscionable at the time it was made the court may refuse to enforce the lease contract, or it may enforce the remainder of the lease contract without the unconscionable clause, or it may so limit the application of any unconscionable clause as to avoid any unconscionable result.

(2) With respect to a consumer lease, if the court as a matter of law finds that a lease contract or any clause of a lease contract has been induced by unconscionable conduct or that unconscionable conduct has occurred in the collection of a claim arising from a lease contract, the court may grant appropriate relief.

(3) Before making a finding of unconscionability under subsection (1) or (2), the court, on its own motion or that of a party, shall afford the parties a reasonable opportunity to present evidence as to the setting, purpose, and effect of the lease contract or clause thereof, or of the conduct.

(4) In an action in which the lessee claims unconscionability with respect to a consumer lease:

(a) If the court finds unconscionability under subsection (1) or (2), the court shall award reasonable attorney's fees to the lessee.

(b) If the court does not find unconscionability and the lessee claiming unconscionability has brought or maintained an action he [or she] knew to be groundless, the court shall award reasonable attorney's fees to the party against whom the claim is made.

(c) In determining attorney's fees, the amount of the recovery on behalf of the claimant under subsections (1) and (2) is not controlling.

§ 2A—109. Option to Accelerate at Will.

(1) A term providing that one party or his [or her] successor in interest may accelerate payment or performance or require collateral or additional collateral "at will" or "when he [or she] deems himself [or herself] insecure" or in words of similar import must be construed to mean that he [or she] has power to do so only if he [or she] in good faith believes that the prospect of payment or performance is impaired.

(2) With respect to a consumer lease, the burden of establishing good faith under subsection (1) is on the party who exercised the power; otherwise the burden of establishing lack of good faith is on the party against whom the power has been exercised.

Part 2 Formation and Construction of Lease Contract

§ 2A—201. Statute of Frauds.

(1) A lease contract is not enforceable by way of action or defense unless:

(a) the total payments to be made under the lease contract, excluding payments for options to renew or buy, are less than $1,000; or

(b) there is a writing, signed by the party against whom enforcement is sought or by that party's authorized agent, sufficient to indicate that a lease contract has been made between the parties and to describe the goods leased and the lease term.

(2) Any description of leased goods or of the lease term is sufficient and satisfies subsection (1)(b), whether or not it is specific, if it reasonably identifies what is described.

(3) A writing is not insufficient because it omits or incorrectly states a term agreed upon, but the lease contract is not enforceable under subsection (1)(b) beyond the lease term and the quantity of goods shown in the writing.

(4) A lease contract that does not satisfy the requirements of subsection (1), but which is valid in other respects, is enforceable:

(a) if the goods are to be specially manufactured or obtained for the lessee and are not suitable for lease or sale to others in the ordinary course of the lessor's business, and the lessor, before notice of repudiation is received and under circumstances that reasonably indicate that the goods are for the lessee, has made either a substantial beginning of their manufacture or commitments for their procurement;

(b) if the party against whom enforcement is sought admits in that party's pleading, testimony or otherwise in court that a lease contract was made, but the lease contract is not enforceable under this provision beyond the quantity of goods admitted; or

(c) with respect to goods that have been received and accepted by the lessee.

(5) The lease term under a lease contract referred to in subsection (4) is:

(a) if there is a writing signed by the party against whom enforcement is sought or by that party's authorized agent specifying the lease term, the term so specified;

(b) if the party against whom enforcement is sought admits in that party's pleading, testimony, or otherwise in court a lease term, the term so admitted; or

(c) a reasonable lease term.

§ 2A—202. Final Written Expression: Parol or Extrinsic Evidence.

Terms with respect to which the confirmatory memoranda of the parties agree or which are otherwise set forth in a writing intended by the parties as a final expression of their agreement with respect to such terms as are included therein may not be contradicted by evidence of any prior agreement or of a contemporaneous oral agreement but may be explained or supplemented:

(a) by course of dealing or usage of trade or by course of performance; and

(b) by evidence of consistent additional terms unless the court finds the writing to have been intended also as a complete and exclusive statement of the terms of the agreement.

§ 2A—203. Seals Inoperative.

The affixing of a seal to a writing evidencing a lease contract or an offer to enter into a lease contract does not render the writing a sealed instrument and the law with respect to sealed instruments does not apply to the lease contract or offer.

§ 2A—204. Formation in General.

(1) A lease contract may be made in any manner sufficient to show agreement, including conduct by both parties which recognizes the existence of a lease contract.

(2) An agreement sufficient to constitute a lease contract may be found although the moment of its making is undetermined.

(3) Although one or more terms are left open, a lease contract does not fail for indefiniteness if the parties have intended to make a lease contract and there is a reasonably certain basis for giving an appropriate remedy.

§ 2A—205. Firm Offers.

An offer by a merchant to lease goods to or from another person in a signed writing that by its terms gives assurance it will be held open is not revocable, for lack of consideration, during the time stated or, if no time is stated, for a reasonable time, but in no event may the period of irrevocability exceed 3 months. Any such term of assurance on a form supplied by the offeree must be separately signed by the offeror.

§ 2A—206. Offer and Acceptance in Formation of Lease Contract.

(1) Unless otherwise unambiguously indicated by the language or circumstances, an offer to make a lease contract must be construed as inviting acceptance in any manner and by any medium reasonable in the circumstances.

(2) If the beginning of a requested performance is a reasonable mode of acceptance, an offeror who is not notified of acceptance within a reasonable time may treat the offer as having lapsed before acceptance.

§ 2A—207. Course of Performance or Practical Construction.

(1) If a lease contract involves repeated occasions for performance by either party with knowledge of the nature of the performance and opportunity for objection to it by the other, any course of performance accepted or acquiesced in without objection is relevant to determine the meaning of the lease agreement.

(2) The express terms of a lease agreement and any course of performance, as well as any course of dealing and usage of trade, must be construed whenever reasonable as consistent with each other; but if that construction is unreasonable, express terms control course of performance, course of performance controls both course of dealing and usage of trade, and course of dealing controls usage of trade.

(3) Subject to the provisions of Section 2A—208 on modification and waiver, course of performance is relevant to show a waiver or modification of any term inconsistent with the course of performance.

§ 2A—208. Modification, Rescission and Waiver.

(1) An agreement modifying a lease contract needs no consideration to be binding.

(2) A signed lease agreement that excludes modification or rescission except by a signed writing may not be otherwise modified or rescinded, but, except as between merchants, such a requirement on a form supplied by a merchant must be separately signed by the other party.

(3) Although an attempt at modification or rescission does not satisfy the requirements of subsection (2), it may operate as a waiver.

(4) A party who has made a waiver affecting an executory portion of a lease contract may retract the waiver by reasonable notification received by the other party that strict performance will be required of any term waived, unless the retraction would be unjust in view of a material change of position in reliance on the waiver.

§ 2A—209. Lessee under Finance Lease as Beneficiary of Supply Contract.

(1) The benefit of the supplier's promises to the lessor under the supply contract and of all warranties, whether express or implied, including those of any third party provided in connection with or as part of the supply contract, extends to the lessee to the extent of the lessee's leasehold interest under a finance

lease related to the supply contract, but is subject to the terms warranty and of the supply contract and all defenses or claims arising therefrom.

(2) The extension of the benefit of supplier's promises and of warranties to the lessee (Section 2A–209(1)) does not: (i) modify the rights and obligations of the parties to the supply contract, whether arising therefrom or otherwise, or (ii) impose any duty or liability under the supply contract on the lessee.

(3) Any modification or rescission of the supply contract by the supplier and the lessor is effective between the supplier and the lessee unless, before the modification or rescission, the supplier has received notice that the lessee has entered into a finance lease related to the supply contract. If the modification or rescission is effective between the supplier and the lessee, the lessor is deemed to have assumed, in addition to the obligations of the lessor to the lessee under the lease contract, promises of the supplier to the lessor and warranties that were so modified or rescinded as they existed and were available to the lessee before modification or rescission.

(4) In addition to the extension of the benefit of the supplier's promises and of warranties to the lessee under subsection (1), the lessee retains all rights that the lessee may have against the supplier which arise from an agreement between the lessee and the supplier or under other law.

As amended in 1990.

§ 2A—210. Express Warranties.

(1) Express warranties by the lessor are created as follows:

(a) Any affirmation of fact or promise made by the lessor to the lessee which relates to the goods and becomes part of the basis of the bargain creates an express warranty that the goods will conform to the affirmation or promise.

(b) Any description of the goods which is made part of the basis of the bargain creates an express warranty that the goods will conform to the description.

(c) Any sample or model that is made part of the basis of the bargain creates an express warranty that the whole of the goods will conform to the sample or model.

(2) It is not necessary to the creation of an express warranty that the lessor use formal words, such as "warrant" or "guarantee," or that the lessor have a specific intention to make a warranty, but an affirmation merely of the value of the goods or a statement purporting to be merely the lessor's opinion or commendation of the goods does not create a warranty.

§ 2A—211. Warranties Against Interference and Against Infringement; Lessee's Obligation Against Infringement.

(1) There is in a lease contract a warranty that for the lease term no person holds a claim to or interest in the goods that arose from an act or omission of the lessor, other than a claim by way of infringement or the like, which will interfere with the lessee's enjoyment of its leasehold interest.

(2) Except in a finance lease there is in a lease contract by a lessor who is a merchant regularly dealing in goods of the kind a warranty that the goods are delivered free of the rightful claim of any person by way of infringement or the like.

(3) A lessee who furnishes specifications to a lessor or a supplier shall hold the lessor and the supplier harmless against any claim by way of infringement or the like that arises out of compliance with the specifications.

§ 2A—212. Implied Warranty of Merchantability.

(1) Except in a finance lease, a warranty that the goods will be merchantable is implied in a lease contract if the lessor is a merchant with respect to goods of that kind.

(2) Goods to be merchantable must be at least such as

(a) pass without objection in the trade under the description in the lease agreement;

(b) in the case of fungible goods, are of fair average quality within the description;

(c) are fit for the ordinary purposes for which goods of that type are used;

(d) run, within the variation permitted by the lease agreement, of even kind, quality, and quantity within each unit and among all units involved;

(e) are adequately contained, packaged, and labeled as the lease agreement may require; and

(f) conform to any promises or affirmations of fact made on the container or label.

(3) Other implied warranties may arise from course of dealing or usage of trade.

§ 2A—213. Implied Warranty of Fitness for Particular Purpose.

Except in a finance of lease, if the lessor at the time the lease contract is made has reason to know of any particular purpose for which the goods are required and that the lessee is relying on the lessor's skill or judgment to select or furnish suitable goods, there is in the lease contract an implied warranty that the goods will be fit for that purpose.

§ 2A—214. Exclusion or Modification of Warranties.

(1) Words or conduct relevant to the creation of an express warranty and words or conduct tending to negate or limit a warranty must be construed wherever reasonable as consistent with each other; but, subject to the provisions of Section 2A—202 on parol or extrinsic evidence, negation or limitation is inoperative to the extent that the construction is unreasonable.

(2) Subject to subsection (3), to exclude or modify the implied warranty of merchantability or any part of it the language must mention "merchantability", be by a writing, and be conspicuous. Subject to subsection (3), to exclude or modify any implied warranty of fitness the exclusion must be by a writing and be conspicuous. Language to exclude all implied warranties of fitness is sufficient if it is in writing, is conspicuous and states, for example, "There is no warranty that the goods will be fit for a particular purpose".

(3) Notwithstanding subsection (2), but subject to subsection (4),

(a) unless the circumstances indicate otherwise, all implied warranties are excluded by expressions like "as is" or "with all faults" or by other language that in common understanding calls the lessee's attention to the exclusion of warranties and makes plain that there is no implied warranty, if in writing and conspicuous;

(b) if the lessee before entering into the lease contract has examined the goods or the sample or model as fully as desired or has refused to examine the goods, there is no implied warranty with regard to defects that an examination ought in the circumstances to have revealed; and

(c) an implied warranty may also be excluded or modified by course of dealing, course of performance, or usage of trade.

(4) To exclude or modify a warranty against interference or against infringement (Section 2A—211) or any part of it, the language must be specific, be by a writing, and be conspicuous, unless the circumstances, including course of performance, course of dealing, or usage of trade, give the lessee reason to know that the goods are being leased subject to a claim or interest of any person.

§ 2A—215. Cumulation and Conflict of Warranties Express or Implied.

Warranties, whether express or implied, must be construed as consistent with each other and as cumulative, but if that construction is unreasonable, the intention of the parties determines which warranty is dominant. In ascertaining that intention the following rules apply:

(a) Exact or technical specifications displace an inconsistent sample or model or general language of description.

(b) A sample from an existing bulk displaces inconsistent general language of description.

(c) Express warranties displace inconsistent implied warranties other than an implied warranty of fitness for a particular purpose.

§ 2A—216. Third-Party Beneficiaries of Express and Implied Warranties.

Alternative A

A warranty to or for the benefit of a lessee under this Article, whether express or implied, extends to any natural person who is in the family or household of the lessee or who is a guest in the lessee's home if it is reasonable to expect that such person may use, consume, or be affected by the goods and who is injured in person by breach of the warranty. This section does not displace principles of law and equity that extend a warranty to or for the benefit of a lessee to other persons. The operation of this section may not be excluded, modified, or limited, but an exclusion, modification, or limitation of the warranty, including any with respect to rights and remedies, effective against the lessee is also effective against any beneficiary designated under this section.

Alternative B

A warranty to or for the benefit of a lessee under this Article, whether express or implied, extends to any natural person who may reasonably be expected to use, consume, or be affected by the goods and who is injured in person by breach of the warranty. This section does not displace principles of law and equity that extend a warranty to or for the benefit of a lessee to other persons. The operation of this section may not be excluded, modified, or limited, but an exclusion, modification, or limitation of the warranty, including any with respect to rights and remedies, effective against the lessee is also effective against the beneficiary designated under this section.

Alternative C

A warranty to or for the benefit of a lessee under this Article, whether express or implied, extends to any person who may reasonably be expected to use, consume, or be affected by the goods and who is injured by breach of the warranty. The operation of this section may not be excluded, modified, or limited with respect to injury to the person of an individual to whom the warranty extends, but an exclusion, modification, or limitation of the warranty, including any with respect to rights and remedies, effective against the lessee is also effective against the beneficiary designated under this section.

§ 2A—217. Identification.

Identification of goods as goods to which a lease contract refers may be made at any time and in any manner explicitly agreed to by the parties. In the absence of explicit agreement, identification occurs:

(a) when the lease contract is made if the lease contract is for a lease of goods that are existing and identified;

(b) when the goods are shipped, marked, or otherwise designated by the lessor as goods to which the lease contract refers, if the lease contract is for a lease of goods that are not existing and identified; or

(c) when the young are conceived, if the lease contract is for a lease of unborn young of animals.

§ 2A—218. Insurance and Proceeds.

(1) A lessee obtains an insurable interest when existing goods are identified to the lease contract even though the goods identified are nonconforming and the lessee has an option to reject them.

(2) If a lessee has an insurable interest only by reason of the lessor's identification of the goods, the lessor, until default or insolvency or notification to the lessee that identification is final, may substitute other goods for those identified.

(3) Notwithstanding a lessee's insurable interest under subsections (1) and (2), the lessor retains an insurable interest until an option to buy has been exercised by the lessee and risk of loss has passed to the lessee.

(4) Nothing in this section impairs any insurable interest recognized under any other statute or rule of law.

(5) The parties by agreement may determine that one or more parties have an obligation to obtain and pay for insurance covering the goods and by agreement may determine the beneficiary of the proceeds of the insurance.

§ 2A—219. Risk of Loss.

(1) Except in the case of a finance lease, risk of loss is retained by the lessor and does not pass to the lessee. In the case of a finance lease, risk of loss passes to the lessee.

(2) Subject to the provisions of this Article on the effect of default on risk of loss (Section 2A—220), if risk of loss is to pass to the lessee and the time of passage is not stated, the following rules apply:

(a) If the lease contract requires or authorizes the goods to be shipped by carrier

(i) and it does not require delivery at a particular destination, the risk of loss passes to the lessee when the goods are duly delivered to the carrier; but

(ii) if it does require delivery at a particular destination and the goods are there duly tendered while in the possession of the carrier, the risk of loss passes to the lessee when the goods are there duly so tendered as to enable the lessee to take delivery.

(b) If the goods are held by a bailee to be delivered without being moved, the risk of loss passes to the lessee on acknowledgment by the bailee of the lessee's right to possession of the goods.

(c) In any case not within subsection (a) or (b), the risk of loss passes to the lessee on the lessee's receipt of the goods if the lessor, or, in the case of a finance lease, the supplier, is a merchant; otherwise the risk passes to the lessee on tender of delivery.

§ 2A—220. Effect of Default on Risk of Loss.

(1) Where risk of loss is to pass to the lessee and the time of passage is not stated:

(a) If a tender or delivery of goods so fails to conform to the lease contract as to give a right of rejection, the risk of their loss remains with the lessor, or, in the case of a finance lease, the supplier, until cure or acceptance.

(b) If the lessee rightfully revokes acceptance, he [or she], to the extent of any deficiency in his [or her] effective insurance coverage, may treat the risk of loss as having remained with the lessor from the beginning.

(2) Whether or not risk of loss is to pass to the lessee, if the lessee as to conforming goods already identified to a lease contract repudiates or is otherwise in default under the lease contract, the lessor, or, in the case of a finance lease, the supplier, to the extent of any deficiency in his [or her] effective insurance coverage may treat the risk of loss as resting on the lessee for a commercially reasonable time.

§ 2A—221. Casualty to Identified Goods.

If a lease contract requires goods identified when the lease contract is made, and the goods suffer casualty without fault of the lessee, the lessor or the supplier before delivery, or the goods suffer casualty before risk of loss passes to the lessee pursuant to the lease agreement or Section 2A—219, then:

(a) if the loss is total, the lease contract is avoided; and

(b) if the loss is partial or the goods have so deteriorated as to no longer conform to the lease contract, the lessee may nevertheless demand inspection and at his [or her] option either treat the lease contract as avoided or, except in a finance lease that is not a consumer lease, accept the goods with due allowance from the rent payable for the balance of the lease term for the deterioration or the deficiency in quantity but without further right against the lessor.

Part 3 Effect Of Lease Contract

§ 2A—301. Enforceability of Lease Contract.

Except as otherwise provided in this Article, a lease contract is effective and enforceable according to its terms between the parties, against purchasers of the goods and against creditors of the parties.

§ 2A—302. Title to and Possession of Goods.

Except as otherwise provided in this Article, each provision of this Article applies whether the lessor or a third party has title to the goods, and whether the lessor, the lessee, or a third party has possession of the goods, notwithstanding any statute or rule of law that possession or the absence of possession is fraudulent.

§ 2A—303. Alienability of Party's Interest Under Lease Contract or of Lessor's Residual Interest in Goods; Delegation of Performance; Transfer of Rights.

(1) As used in this section, "creation of a security interest" includes the sale of a lease contract that is subject to Article 9, Secured Transactions, by reason of Section 9—102(1)(b).

(2) Except as provided in subsections (3) and (4), a provision in a lease agreement which (i) prohibits the voluntary or involuntary transfer, including a transfer by sale, sublease, creation or enforcement of a security interest, or attachment, levy, or other judicial process, of an interest of a party under the lease contract or of the lessor's residual interest in the goods, or (ii) makes such a transfer an event of default, gives rise to the rights and remedies provided in subsection (5), but a transfer that is prohibited or is an event of default under the lease agreement is otherwise effective.

(3) A provision in a lease agreement which (i) prohibits the creation or enforcement of a security interest in an interest of a party under the lease contract or in the lessor's residual interest in the goods, or (ii) makes such a transfer an event of default, is not enforceable unless, and then only to the extent that, there is an actual transfer by the lessee of the lessee's right of possession or use of the goods in violation of the provision or an actual delegation of a material performance of either party to the lease

contract in violation of the provision. Neither the granting nor the enforcement of a security interest in (i) the lessor's interest under the lease contract or (ii) the lessor's residual interest in the goods is a transfer that materially impairs the prospect of obtaining return performance by, materially changes the duty of, or materially increases the burden or risk imposed on, the lessee within the purview of subsection (5) unless, and then only to the extent that, there is an actual delegation of a material performance of the lessor.

(4) A provision in a lease agreement which (i) prohibits a transfer of a right to damages for default with respect to the whole lease contract or of a right to payment arising out of the transferor's due performance of the transferor's entire obligation, or (ii) makes such a transfer an event of default, is not enforceable, and such a transfer is not a transfer that materially impairs the prospect of obtaining return performance by, materially changes the duty of, or materially increases the burden or risk imposed on, the other party to the lease contract within the purview of subsection (5).

(5) Subject to subsections (3) and (4):

(a) if a transfer is made which is made an event of default under a lease agreement, the party to the lease contract not making the transfer, unless that party waives the default or otherwise agrees, has the rights and remedies described in Section 2A—501(2);

(b) if paragraph (a) is not applicable and if a transfer is made that (i) is prohibited under a lease agreement or (ii) materially impairs the prospect of obtaining return performance by, materially changes the duty of, or materially increases the burden or risk imposed on, the other party to the lease contract, unless the party not making the transfer agrees at any time to the transfer in the lease contract or otherwise, then, except as limited by contract, (i) the transferor is liable to the party not making the transfer for damages caused by the transfer to the extent that the damages could not reasonably be prevented by the party not making the transfer and (ii) a court having jurisdiction may grant other appropriate relief, including cancellation of the lease contract or an injunction against the transfer.

(6) A transfer of "the lease" or of "all my rights under the lease," or a transfer in similar general terms, is a transfer of rights and, unless the language or the circumstances, as in a transfer for security, indicate the contrary, the transfer is a delegation of duties by the transferor to the transferee. Acceptance by the transferee constitutes a promise by the transferee to perform those duties. The promise is enforceable by either the transferor or the other party to the lease contract.

(7) Unless otherwise agreed by the lessor and the lessee, a delegation of performance does not relieve the transferor as against the other party of any duty to perform or of any liability for default.

(8) In a consumer lease, to prohibit the transfer of an interest of a party under the lease contract or to make a transfer an event of default, the language must be specific, by a writing, and conspicuous.

As amended in 1990.

§ 2A—304. Subsequent Lease of Goods by Lessor.

(1) Subject to Section 2A—303, a subsequent lessee from a lessor of goods under an existing lease contract obtains, to the extent of the leasehold interest transferred, the leasehold interest in the goods that the lessor had or had power to transfer, and except as provided in subsection (2) and Section 2A—527(4), takes subject to the existing lease contract. A lessor with voidable title has power to transfer a good leasehold interest to a good faith subsequent lessee for value, but only to the extent set forth in the preceding sentence. If goods have been delivered under a transaction of purchase the lessor has that power even though:

(a) the lessor's transferor was deceived as to the identity of the lessor;

(b) the delivery was in exchange for a check which is later dishonored;

(c) it was agreed that the transaction was to be a "cash sale"; or

(d) the delivery was procured through fraud punishable as larcenous under the criminal law.

(2) A subsequent lessee in the ordinary course of business from a lessor who is a merchant dealing in goods of that kind to whom the goods were entrusted by the existing lessee of that lessor before the interest of the subsequent lessee became enforceable against that lessor obtains, to the extent of the leasehold interest transferred, all of that lessor's and the existing lessee's rights to the goods, and takes free of the existing lease contract.

(3) A subsequent lessee from the lessor of goods that are subject to an existing lease contract and are covered by a certificate of title issued under a statute of this State or of another jurisdiction takes no greater rights than those provided both by this section and by the certificate of title statute.

As amended in 1990.

§ 2A—305. Sale or Sublease of Goods by Lessee.

(1) Subject to the provisions of Section 2A—303, a buyer or sublessee from the lessee of goods under an existing lease contract obtains, to the extent of the interest transferred, the leasehold interest in the goods that the lessee had or had power to transfer, and except as provided in subsection (2) and Section 2A—511(4), takes subject to the existing lease contract. A lessee with a voidable leasehold interest has power to transfer a good leasehold interest to a good faith buyer for value or a good faith sublessee for value, but only to the extent set forth in the preceding sentence. When goods have been delivered under a transaction of lease the lessee has that power even though:

(a) the lessor was deceived as to the identity of the lessee;

(b) the delivery was in exchange for a check which is later dishonored; or

(c) the delivery was procured through fraud punishable as larcenous under the criminal law.

(2) A buyer in the ordinary course of business or a sublessee in the ordinary course of business from a lessee who is a merchant

dealing in goods of that kind to whom the goods were entrusted by the lessor obtains, to the extent of the interest transferred, all of the lessor's and lessee's rights to the goods, and takes free of the existing lease contract.

(3) A buyer or sublessee from the lessee of goods that are subject to an existing lease contract and are covered by a certificate of title issued under a statute of this State or of another jurisdiction takes no greater rights than those provided both by this section and by the certificate of title statute.

§ 2A—306. Priority of Certain Liens Arising by Operation of Law.

If a person in the ordinary course of his [or her] business furnishes services or materials with respect to goods subject to a lease contract, a lien upon those goods in the possession of that person given by statute or rule of law for those materials or services takes priority over any interest of the lessor or lessee under the lease contract or this Article unless the lien is created by statute and the statute provides otherwise or unless the lien is created by rule of law and the rule of law provides otherwise.

§ 2A—307. Priority of Liens Arising by Attachment or Levy on, Security Interests in, and Other Claims to Goods.

(1) Except as otherwise provided in Section 2A—306, a creditor of a lessee takes subject to the lease contract.

(2) Except as otherwise provided in subsections (3) and (4) and in Sections 2A—306 and 2A—308, a creditor of a lessor takes subject to the lease contract unless:

(a) the creditor holds a lien that attached to the goods before the lease contract became enforceable,

(b) the creditor holds a security interest in the goods and the lessee did not give value and receive delivery of the goods without knowledge of the security interest; or

(c) the creditor holds a security interest in the goods which was perfected (Section 9—303) before the lease contract became enforceable.

(3) A lessee in the ordinary course of business takes the leasehold interest free of a security interest in the goods created by the lessor even though the security interest is perfected (Section 9—303) and the lessee knows of its existence.

(4) A lessee other than a lessee in the ordinary course of business takes the leasehold interest free of a security interest to the extent that it secures future advances made after the secured party acquires knowledge of the lease or more than 45 days after the lease contract becomes enforceable, whichever first occurs, unless the future advances are made pursuant to a commitment entered into without knowledge of the lease and before the expiration of the 45-day period.

§ 2A—308. Special Rights of Creditors.

(1) A creditor of a lessor in possession of goods subject to a lease contract may treat the lease contract as void if as against the creditor retention of possession by the lessor is fraudulent under any statute or rule of law, but retention of possession in good faith and current course of trade by the lessor for a commercially reasonable time after the lease contract becomes enforceable is not fraudulent.

(2) Nothing in this Article impairs the rights of creditors of a lessor if the lease contract (a) becomes enforceable, not in current course of trade but in satisfaction of or as security for a pre-existing claim for money, security, or the like, and (b) is made under circumstances which under any statute or rule of law apart from this Article would constitute the transaction a fraudulent transfer or voidable preference.

(3) A creditor of a seller may treat a sale or an identification of goods to a contract for sale as void if as against the creditor retention of possession by the seller is fraudulent under any statute or rule of law, but retention of possession of the goods pursuant to a lease contract entered into by the seller as lessee and the buyer as lessor in connection with the sale or identification of the goods is not fraudulent if the buyer bought for value and in good faith.

§ 2A—309. Lessor's and Lessee's Rights When Goods Become Fixtures.

(1) In this section:

(a) goods are "fixtures" when they become so related to particular real estate that an interest in them arises under real estate law;

(b) a "fixture filing" is the filing, in the office where a mortgage on the real estate would be filed or recorded, of a financing statement covering goods that are or are to become fixtures and conforming to the requirements of Section 9—402(5);

(c) a lease is a "purchase money lease" unless the lessee has possession or use of the goods or the right to possession or use of the goods before the lease agreement is enforceable;

(d) a mortgage is a "construction mortgage" to the extent it secures an obligation incurred for the construction of an improvement on land including the acquisition cost of the land, if the recorded writing so indicates; and

(e) "encumbrance" includes real estate mortgages and other liens on real estate and all other rights in real estate that are not ownership interests.

(2) Under this Article a lease may be of goods that are fixtures or may continue in goods that become fixtures, but no lease exists under this Article of ordinary building materials incorporated into an improvement on land.

(3) This Article does not prevent creation of a lease of fixtures pursuant to real estate law.

(4) The perfected interest of a lessor of fixtures has priority over a conflicting interest of an encumbrancer or owner of the real estate if:

(a) the lease is a purchase money lease, the conflicting interest of the encumbrancer or owner arises before the goods become fixtures, the interest of the lessor is perfected by a fixture filing before the goods become fixtures or within ten days thereafter, and the lessee has an interest of record in the real estate or is in possession of the real estate; or

(b) the interest of the lessor is perfected by a fixture filing before the interest of the encumbrancer or owner is of record, the lessor's interest has priority over any conflicting interest of a predecessor in title of the encumbrancer or owner, and the lessee has an interest of record in the real estate or is in possession of the real estate.

(5) The interest of a lessor of fixtures, whether or not perfected, has priority over the conflicting interest of an encumbrancer or owner of the real estate if:

(a) the fixtures are readily removable factory or office machines, readily removable equipment that is not primarily used or leased for use in the operation of the real estate, or readily removable replacements of domestic appliances that are goods subject to a consumer lease, and before the goods become fixtures the lease contract is enforceable; or

(b) the conflicting interest is a lien on the real estate obtained by legal or equitable proceedings after the lease contract is enforceable; or

(c) the encumbrancer or owner has consented in writing to the lease or has disclaimed an interest in the goods as fixtures; or

(d) the lessee has a right to remove the goods as against the encumbrancer or owner. If the lessee's right to remove terminates, the priority of the interest of the lessor continues for a reasonable time.

(6) Notwithstanding paragraph (4)(a) but otherwise subject to subsections (4) and (5), the interest of a lessor of fixtures, including the lessor's residual interest, is subordinate to the conflicting interest of an encumbrancer of the real estate under a construction mortgage recorded before the goods become fixtures if the goods become fixtures before the completion of the construction. To the extent given to refinance a construction mortgage, the conflicting interest of an encumbrancer of the real estate under a mortgage has this priority to the same extent as the encumbrancer of the real estate under the construction mortgage.

(7) In cases not within the preceding subsections, priority between the interest of a lessor of fixtures, including the lessor's residual interest, and the conflicting interest of an encumbrancer or owner of the real estate who is not the lessee is determined by the priority rules governing conflicting interests in real estate.

(8) If the interest of a lessor of fixtures, including the lessor's residual interest, has priority over all conflicting interests of all owners and encumbrancers of the real estate, the lessor or the lessee may (i) on default, expiration, termination, or cancellation of the lease agreement but subject to the agreement and this Article, or (ii) if necessary to enforce other rights and remedies of the lessor or lessee under this Article, remove the goods from the real estate, free and clear of all conflicting interests of all owners and encumbrancers of the real estate, but the lessor or lessee must reimburse any encumbrancer or owner of the real estate who is not the lessee and who has not otherwise agreed for the cost of repair of any physical injury, but not for any diminution in value of the real estate caused by the absence of the goods removed or by any necessity of replacing them. A person entitled to reimbursement may refuse permission to remove until the party seeking removal gives adequate security for the performance of this obligation.

(9) Even though the lease agreement does not create a security interest, the interest of a lessor of fixtures, including the lessor's residual interest, is perfected by filing a financing statement as a fixture filing for leased goods that are or are to become fixtures in accordance with the relevant provisions of the Article on Secured Transactions (Article 9).

As amended in 1990.

§ 2A—310. Lessor's and Lessee's Rights When Goods Become Accessions.

(1) Goods are "accessions" when they are installed in or affixed to other goods.

(2) The interest of a lessor or a lessee under a lease contract entered into before the goods became accessions is superior to all interests in the whole except as stated in subsection (4).

(3) The interest of a lessor or a lessee under a lease contract entered into at the time or after the goods became accessions is superior to all subsequently acquired interests in the whole except as stated in subsection (4) but is subordinate to interests in the whole existing at the time the lease contract was made unless the holders of such interests in the whole have in writing consented to the lease or disclaimed an interest in the goods as part of the whole.

(4) The interest of a lessor or a lessee under a lease contract described in subsection (2) or (3) is subordinate to the interest of

(a) a buyer in the ordinary course of business or a lessee in the ordinary course of business of any interest in the whole acquired after the goods became accessions; or

(b) a creditor with a security interest in the whole perfected before the lease contract was made to the extent that the creditor makes subsequent advances without knowledge of the lease contract.

(5) When under subsections (2) or (3) and (4) a lessor or a lessee of accessions holds an interest that is superior to all interests in the whole, the lessor or the lessee may (a) on default, expiration, termination, or cancellation of the lease contract by the other party but subject to the provisions of the lease contract and this Article, or (b) if necessary to enforce his [or her] other rights and remedies under this Article, remove the goods from the whole, free and clear of all interests in the whole, but he [or she] must reimburse any holder of an interest in the whole who is not the lessee and who has not otherwise agreed for the cost of repair of any physical injury but not for any diminution in value of the whole caused by the absence of the goods removed or by any necessity for replacing them. A person entitled to reimbursement may refuse permission to remove until the party seeking removal gives adequate security for the performance of this obligation.

§ 2A—311. Priority Subject to Subordination.

Nothing in this Article prevents subordination by agreement by any person entitled to priority.

As added in 1990.

Part 4 Performance Of Lease Contract: Repudiated, Substituted And Excused

§ 2A—401. Insecurity: Adequate Assurance of Performance.

(1) A lease contract imposes an obligation on each party that the other's expectation of receiving due performance will not be impaired.

(2) If reasonable grounds for insecurity arise with respect to the performance of either party, the insecure party may demand in writing adequate assurance of due performance. Until the insecure party receives that assurance, if commercially reasonable the insecure party may suspend any performance for which he [or she] has not already received the agreed return.

(3) A repudiation of the lease contract occurs if assurance of due performance adequate under the circumstances of the particular case is not provided to the insecure party within a reasonable time, not to exceed 30 days after receipt of a demand by the other party.

(4) Between merchants, the reasonableness of grounds for insecurity and the adequacy of any assurance offered must be determined according to commercial standards.

(5) Acceptance of any nonconforming delivery or payment does not prejudice the aggrieved party's right to demand adequate assurance of future performance.

§ 2A—402. Anticipatory Repudiation.

If either party repudiates a lease contract with respect to a performance not yet due under the lease contract, the loss of which performance will substantially impair the value of the lease contract to the other, the aggrieved party may:

(a) for a commercially reasonable time, await retraction of repudiation and performance by the repudiating party;

(b) make demand pursuant to Section 2A—401 and await assurance of future performance adequate under the circumstances of the particular case; or

(c) resort to any right or remedy upon default under the lease contract or this Article, even though the aggrieved party has notified the repudiating party that the aggrieved party would await the repudiating party's performance and assurance and has urged retraction. In addition, whether or not the aggrieved party is pursuing one of the foregoing remedies, the aggrieved party may suspend performance or, if the aggrieved party is the lessor, proceed in accordance with the provisions of this Article on the lessor's right to identify goods to the lease contract notwithstanding default or to salvage unfinished goods (Section 2A—524).

§ 2A—403. Retraction of Anticipatory Repudiation.

(1) Until the repudiating party's next performance is due, the repudiating party can retract the repudiation unless, since the repudiation, the aggrieved party has cancelled the lease contract or materially changed the aggrieved party's position or otherwise indicated that the aggrieved party considers the repudiation final.

(2) Retraction may be by any method that clearly indicates to the aggrieved party that the repudiating party intends to perform under the lease contract and includes any assurance demanded under Section 2A—401.

(3) Retraction reinstates a repudiating party's rights under a lease contract with due excuse and allowance to the aggrieved party for any delay occasioned by the repudiation.

§ 2A—404. Substituted Performance.

(1) If without fault of the lessee, the lessor and the supplier, the agreed berthing, loading, or unloading facilities fail or the agreed type of carrier becomes unavailable or the agreed manner of delivery otherwise becomes commercially impracticable, but a commercially reasonable substitute is available, the substitute performance must be tendered and accepted.

(2) If the agreed means or manner of payment fails because of domestic or foreign governmental regulation:

(a) the lessor may withhold or stop delivery or cause the supplier to withhold or stop delivery unless the lessee provides a means or manner of payment that is commercially a substantial equivalent; and

(b) if delivery has already been taken, payment by the means or in the manner provided by the regulation discharges the lessee's obligation unless the regulation is discriminatory, oppressive, or predatory.

§ 2A—405. Excused Performance.

Subject to Section 2A—404 on substituted performance, the following rules apply:

(a) Delay in delivery or nondelivery in whole or in part by a lessor or a supplier who complies with paragraphs (b) and (c) is not a default under the lease contract if performance as agreed has been made impracticable by the occurrence of a contingency the nonoccurrence of which was a basic assumption on which the lease contract was made or by compliance in good faith with any applicable foreign or domestic governmental regulation or order, whether or not the regulation or order later proves to be invalid.

(b) If the causes mentioned in paragraph (a) affect only part of the lessor's or the supplier's capacity to perform, he [or she] shall allocate production and deliveries among his [or her] customers but at his [or her] option may include regular customers not then under contract for sale or lease as well as his [or her] own requirements for further manufacture. He [or she] may so allocate in any manner that is fair and reasonable.

(c) The lessor seasonably shall notify the lessee and in the case of a finance lease the supplier seasonably shall notify the lessor and the lessee, if known, that there will be delay or nondelivery and, if allocation is required under paragraph (b), of the estimated quota thus made available for the lessee.

§ 2A—406. Procedure on Excused Performance.

(1) If the lessee receives notification of a material or indefinite delay or an allocation justified under Section 2A—405, the lessee may by written notification to the lessor as to any goods involved, and with respect to all of the goods if under an installment lease contract the value of the whole lease contract is substantially impaired (Section 2A—510):

(a) terminate the lease contract (Section 2A—505(2)); or

(b) except in a finance lease that is not a consumer lease, modify the lease contract by accepting the available quota in substitution, with due allowance from the rent payable for the balance of the lease term for the deficiency but without further right against the lessor.

(2) If, after receipt of a notification from the lessor under Section 2A—405, the lessee fails so to modify the lease agreement within a reasonable time not exceeding 30 days, the lease contract lapses with respect to any deliveries affected.

§ 2A—407. Irrevocable Promises: Finance Leases.

(1) In the case of a finance lease that is not a consumer lease the lessee's promises under the lease contract become irrevocable and independent upon the lessee's acceptance of the goods.

(2) A promise that has become irrevocable and independent under subsection (1):

(a) is effective and enforceable between the parties, and by or against third parties including assignees of the parties, and

(b) is not subject to cancellation, termination, modification, repudiation, excuse, or substitution without the consent of the party to whom the promise runs.

(3) This section does not affect the validity under any other law of a covenant in any lease contract making the lessee's promises irrevocable and independent upon the lessee's acceptance of the goods.

As amended in 1990.

Part 5 Default

A. In General

§ 2A—501. Default: Procedure.

(1) Whether the lessor or the lessee is in default under a lease contract is determined by the lease agreement and this Article.

(2) If the lessor or the lessee is in default under the lease contract, the party seeking enforcement has rights and remedies as provided in this Article and, except as limited by this Article, as provided in the lease agreement.

(3) If the lessor or the lessee is in default under the lease contract, the party seeking enforcement may reduce the party's claim to judgment, or otherwise enforce the lease contract by self-help or any available judicial procedure or nonjudicial procedure, including administrative proceeding, arbitration, or the like, in accordance with this Article.

(4) Except as otherwise provided in Section 1–106(1) or this Article or the lease agreement, the rights and remedies referred to in subsections (2) and (3) are cumulative.

(5) If the lease agreement covers both real property and goods, the party seeking enforcement may proceed under this Part as to the goods, or under other applicable law as to both the real property and the goods in accordance with that party's rights and remedies in respect of the real property, in which case this Part does not apply.

As amended in 1990.

§ 2A—502. Notice After Default.

Except as otherwise provided in this Article or the lease agreement, the lessor or lessee in default under the lease contract is not entitled to notice of default or notice of enforcement from the other party to the lease agreement.

§ 2A—503. Modification or Impairment of Rights and Remedies.

(1) Except as otherwise provided in this Article, the lease agreement may include rights and remedies for default in addition to or in substitution for those provided in this Article and may limit or alter the measure of damages recoverable under this Article.

(2) Resort to a remedy provided under this Article or in the lease agreement is optional unless the remedy is expressly agreed to be exclusive. If circumstances cause an exclusive or limited remedy to fail of its essential purpose, or provision for an exclusive remedy is unconscionable, remedy may be had as provided in this Article.

(3) Consequential damages may be liquidated under Section 2A—504, or may otherwise be limited, altered, or excluded unless the limitation, alteration, or exclusion is unconscionable. Limitation, alteration, or exclusion of consequential damages for injury to the person in the case of consumer goods is prima facie unconscionable but limitation, alteration, or exclusion of damages where the loss is commercial is not prima facie unconscionable.

(4) Rights and remedies on default by the lessor or the lessee with respect to any obligation or promise collateral or ancillary to the lease contract are not impaired by this Article.

As amended in 1990.

§ 2A—504. Liquidation of Damages.

(1) Damages payable by either party for default, or any other act or omission, including indemnity for loss or diminution of anticipated tax benefits or loss or damage to lessor's residual interest, may be liquidated in the lease agreement but only at an amount or by a formula that is reasonable in light of the then anticipated harm caused by the default or other act or omission.

(2) If the lease agreement provides for liquidation of damages, and such provision does not comply with subsection (1), or such provision is an exclusive or limited remedy that circum-

stances cause to fail of its essential purpose, remedy may be had as provided in this Article.

(3) If the lessor justifiably withholds or stops delivery of goods because of the lessee's default or insolvency (Section 2A—525 or 2A—526), the lessee is entitled to restitution of any amount by which the sum of his [or her] payments exceeds:

(a) the amount to which the lessor is entitled by virtue of terms liquidating the lessor's damages in accordance with subsection (1); or

(b) in the absence of those terms, 20 percent of the then present value of the total rent the lessee was obligated to pay for the balance of the lease term, or, in the case of a consumer lease, the lesser of such amount or $500.

(4) A lessee's right to restitution under subsection (3) is subject to offset to the extent the lessor establishes:

(a) a right to recover damages under the provisions of this Article other than subsection (1); and

(b) the amount or value of any benefits received by the lessee directly or indirectly by reason of the lease contract.

§ 2A—505. Cancellation and Termination and Effect of Cancellation, Termination, Rescission, or Fraud on Rights and Remedies.

(1) On cancellation of the lease contract, all obligations that are still executory on both sides are discharged, but any right based on prior default or performance survives, and the cancelling party also retains any remedy for default of the whole lease contract or any unperformed balance.

(2) On termination of the lease contract, all obligations that are still executory on both sides are discharged but any right based on prior default or performance survives.

(3) Unless the contrary intention clearly appears, expressions of "cancellation," "rescission," or the like of the lease contract may not be construed as a renunciation or discharge of any claim in damages for an antecedent default.

(4) Rights and remedies for material misrepresentation or fraud include all rights and remedies available under this Article for default.

(5) Neither rescission nor a claim for rescission of the lease contract nor rejection or return of the goods may bar or be deemed inconsistent with a claim for damages or other right or remedy.

§ 2A—506. Statute of Limitations.

(1) An action for default under a lease contract, including breach of warranty or indemnity, must be commenced within 4 years after the cause of action accrued. By the original lease contract the parties may reduce the period of limitation to not less than one year.

(2) A cause of action for default accrues when the act or omission on which the default or breach of warranty is based is or should have been discovered by the aggrieved party, or when the default occurs, whichever is later. A cause of action for indemnity accrues when the act or omission on which the claim for indemnity is based is or should have been discovered by the indemnified party, whichever is later.

(3) If an action commenced within the time limited by subsection (1) is so terminated as to leave available a remedy by another action for the same default or breach of warranty or indemnity, the other action may be commenced after the expiration of the time limited and within 6 months after the termination of the first action unless the termination resulted from voluntary discontinuance or from dismissal for failure or neglect to prosecute.

(4) This section does not alter the law on tolling of the statute of limitations nor does it apply to causes of action that have accrued before this Article becomes effective.

§ 2A—507. Proof of Market Rent: Time and Place.

(1) Damages based on market rent (Section 2A—519 or 2A—528) are determined according to the rent for the use of the goods concerned for a lease term identical to the remaining lease term of the original lease agreement and prevailing at the times specified in Sections 2A–519 and 2A–528.

(2) If evidence of rent for the use of the goods concerned for a lease term identical to the remaining lease term of the original lease agreement and prevailing at the times or places described in this Article is not readily available, the rent prevailing within any reasonable time before or after the time described or at any other place or for a different lease term which in commercial judgment or under usage of trade would serve as a reasonable substitute for the one described may be used, making any proper allowance for the difference, including the cost of transporting the goods to or from the other place.

(3) Evidence of a relevant rent prevailing at a time or place or for a lease term other than the one described in this Article offered by one party is not admissible unless and until he [or she] has given the other party notice the court finds sufficient to prevent unfair surprise.

(4) If the prevailing rent or value of any goods regularly leased in any established market is in issue, reports in official publications or trade journals or in newspapers or periodicals of general circulation published as the reports of that market are admissible in evidence. The circumstances of the preparation of the report may be shown to affect its weight but not its admissibility.

As amended in 1990.

B. Default by Lessor

§ 2A—508. Lessee's Remedies.

(1) If a lessor fails to deliver the goods in conformity to the lease contract (Section 2A—509) or repudiates the lease contract (Section 2A—402), or a lessee rightfully rejects the goods (Section 2A—509) or justifiably revokes acceptance of the goods (Section 2A—517), then with respect to any goods involved, and with respect to all of the goods if under an installment lease contract the value of the whole lease contract is substantially impaired (Section 2A—510), the lessor is in default under the lease contract and the lessee may:

(a) cancel the lease contract (Section 2A—505(1));

(b) recover so much of the rent and security as has been paid and is just under the circumstances;

(c) cover and recover damages as to all goods affected whether or not they have been identified to the lease contract (Sections 2A—518 and 2A—520), or recover damages for nondelivery (Sections 2A—519 and 2A—520);

(d) exercise any other rights or pursue any other remedies provided in the lease contract..

(2) If a lessor fails to deliver the goods in conformity to the lease contract or repudiates the lease contract, the lessee may also:

(a) if the goods have been identified, recover them (Section 2A—522); or

(b) in a proper case, obtain specific performance or replevy the goods (Section 2A—521).

(3) If a lessor is otherwise in default under a lease contract, the lessee may exercise the rights and pursue the remedies provided in the lease contract, which may include a right to cancel the lease, and in Section 2A–519(3).

(4) If a lessor has breached a warranty, whether express or implied, the lessee may recover damages (Section 2A—519(4)).

(5) On rightful rejection or justifiable revocation of acceptance, a lessee has a security interest in goods in the lessee's possession or control for any rent and security that has been paid and any expenses reasonably incurred in their inspection, receipt, transportation, and care and custody and may hold those goods and dispose of them in good faith and in a commercially reasonable manner, subject to Section 2A—527(5).

(6) Subject to the provisions of Section 2A—407, a lessee, on notifying the lessor of the lessee's intention to do so, may deduct all or any part of the damages resulting from any default under the lease contract from any part of the rent still due under the same lease contract.

As amended in 1990.

§ 2A—509. Lessee's Rights on Improper Delivery; Rightful Rejection.

(1) Subject to the provisions of Section 2A—510 on default in installment lease contracts, if the goods or the tender or delivery fail in any respect to conform to the lease contract, the lessee may reject or accept the goods or accept any commercial unit or units and reject the rest of the goods.

(2) Rejection of goods is ineffective unless it is within a reasonable time after tender or delivery of the goods and the lessee seasonably notifies the lessor.

§ 2A—510. Installment Lease Contracts: Rejection and Default.

(1) Under an installment lease contract a lessee may reject any delivery that is nonconforming if the nonconformity substantially impairs the value of that delivery and cannot be cured or the nonconformity is a defect in the required documents; but if the nonconformity does not fall within subsection (2) and the lessor or the supplier gives adequate assurance of its cure, the lessee must accept that delivery.

(2) Whenever nonconformity or default with respect to one or more deliveries substantially impairs the value of the installment lease contract as a whole there is a default with respect to the whole. But, the aggrieved party reinstates the installment lease contract as a whole if the aggrieved party accepts a nonconforming delivery without seasonably notifying of cancellation or brings an action with respect only to past deliveries or demands performance as to future deliveries.

§ 2A—511. Merchant Lessee's Duties as to Rightfully Rejected Goods.

(1) Subject to any security interest of a lessee (Section 2A—508(5)), if a lessor or a supplier has no agent or place of business at the market of rejection, a merchant lessee, after rejection of goods in his [or her] possession or control, shall follow any reasonable instructions received from the lessor or the supplier with respect to the goods. In the absence of those instructions, a merchant lessee shall make reasonable efforts to sell, lease, or otherwise dispose of the goods for the lessor's account if they threaten to decline in value speedily. Instructions are not reasonable if on demand indemnity for expenses is not forthcoming.

(2) If a merchant lessee (subsection (1)) or any other lessee (Section 2A—512) disposes of goods, he [or she] is entitled to reimbursement either from the lessor or the supplier or out of the proceeds for reasonable expenses of caring for and disposing of the goods and, if the expenses include no disposition commission, to such commission as is usual in the trade, or if there is none, to a reasonable sum not exceeding 10 percent of the gross proceeds.

(3) In complying with this section or Section 2A—512, the lessee is held only to good faith. Good faith conduct hereunder is neither acceptance or conversion nor the basis of an action for damages.

(4) A purchaser who purchases in good faith from a lessee pursuant to this section or Section 2A—512 takes the goods free of any rights of the lessor and the supplier even though the lessee fails to comply with one or more of the requirements of this Article.

§ 2A—512. Lessee's Duties as to Rightfully Rejected Goods.

(1) Except as otherwise provided with respect to goods that threaten to decline in value speedily (Section 2A—511) and subject to any security interest of a lessee (Section 2A—508(5)):

(a) the lessee, after rejection of goods in the lessee's possession, shall hold them with reasonable care at the lessor's or the supplier's disposition for a reasonable time after the lessee's seasonable notification of rejection;

(b) if the lessor or the supplier gives no instructions within a reasonable time after notification of rejection, the lessee may store the rejected goods for the lessor's or the supplier's account or ship them to the lessor or the supplier or dispose of them for the lessor's or the supplier's account with reimbursement in the manner provided in Section 2A—511; but

(c) the lessee has no further obligations with regard to goods rightfully rejected.

(2) Action by the lessee pursuant to subsection (1) is not acceptance or conversion.

§ 2A—513. Cure by Lessor of Improper Tender or Delivery; Replacement.

(1) If any tender or delivery by the lessor or the supplier is rejected because nonconforming and the time for performance has not yet expired, the lessor or the supplier may seasonably notify the lessee of the lessor's or the supplier's intention to cure and may then make a conforming delivery within the time provided in the lease contract.

(2) If the lessee rejects a nonconforming tender that the lessor or the supplier had reasonable grounds to believe would be acceptable with or without money allowance, the lessor or the supplier may have a further reasonable time to substitute a conforming tender if he [or she] seasonably notifies the lessee.

§ 2A—514. Waiver of Lessee's Objections.

(1) In rejecting goods, a lessee's failure to state a particular defect that is ascertainable by reasonable inspection precludes the lessee from relying on the defect to justify rejection or to establish default:

(a) if, stated seasonably, the lessor or the supplier could have cured it (Section 2A—513); or

(b) between merchants if the lessor or the supplier after rejection has made a request in writing for a full and final written statement of all defects on which the lessee proposes to rely.

(2) A lessee's failure to reserve rights when paying rent or other consideration against documents precludes recovery of the payment for defects apparent on the face of the documents.

§ 2A—515. Acceptance of Goods.

(1) Acceptance of goods occurs after the lessee has had a reasonable opportunity to inspect the goods and

(a) the lessee signifies or acts with respect to the goods in a manner that signifies to the lessor or the supplier that the goods are conforming or that the lessee will take or retain them in spite of their nonconformity; or

(b) the lessee fails to make an effective rejection of the goods (Section 2A—509(2)).

(2) Acceptance of a part of any commercial unit is acceptance of that entire unit.

§ 2A—516. Effect of Acceptance of Goods; Notice of Default; Burden of Establishing Default after Acceptance; Notice of Claim or Litigation to Person Answerable Over.

(1) A lessee must pay rent for any goods accepted in accordance with the lease contract, with due allowance for goods rightfully rejected or not delivered.

(2) A lessee's acceptance of goods precludes rejection of the goods accepted. In the case of a finance lease, if made with knowledge of a nonconformity, acceptance cannot be revoked because of it. In any other case, if made with knowledge of a nonconformity, acceptance cannot be revoked because of it unless the acceptance was on the reasonable assumption that the nonconformity would be seasonably cured. Acceptance does not of itself impair any other remedy provided by this Article or the lease agreement for nonconformity.

(3) If a tender has been accepted:

(a) within a reasonable time after the lessee discovers or should have discovered any default, the lessee shall notify the lessor and the supplier, if any, or be barred from any remedy against the party notified;

(b) except in the case of a consumer lease, within a reasonable time after the lessee receives notice of litigation for infringement or the like (Section 2A—211) the lessee shall notify the lessor or be barred from any remedy over for liability established by the litigation; and

(c) the burden is on the lessee to establish any default.

(4) If a lessee is sued for breach of a warranty or other obligation for which a lessor or a supplier is answerable over the following apply:

(a) The lessee may give the lessor or the supplier, or both, written notice of the litigation. If the notice states that the person notified may come in and defend and that if the person notified does not do so that person will be bound in any action against that person by the lessee by any determination of fact common to the two litigations, then unless the person notified after seasonable receipt of the notice does come in and defend that person is so bound.

(b) The lessor or the supplier may demand in writing that the lessee turn over control of the litigation including settlement if the claim is one for infringement or the like (Section 2A—211) or else be barred from any remedy over. If the demand states that the lessor or the supplier agrees to bear all expense and to satisfy any adverse judgment, then unless the lessee after seasonable receipt of the demand does turn over control the lessee is so barred.

(5) Subsections (3) and (4) apply to any obligation of a lessee to hold the lessor or the supplier harmless against infringement or the like (Section 2A—211).

As amended in 1990.

§ 2A—517. Revocation of Acceptance of Goods.

(1) A lessee may revoke acceptance of a lot or commercial unit whose nonconformity substantially impairs its value to the lessee if the lessee has accepted it:

(a) except in the case of a finance lease, on the reasonable assumption that its nonconformity would be cured and it has not been seasonably cured; or

(b) without discovery of the nonconformity if the lessee's acceptance was reasonably induced either by the lessor's assurances or, except in the case of a finance lease, by the difficulty of discovery before acceptance.

(2) Except in the case of a finance lease that is not a consumer lease, a lessee may revoke acceptance of a lot or commercial unit if the lessor defaults under the lease contract and the default substantially impairs the value of that lot or commercial unit to the lessee.

(3) If the lease agreement so provides, the lessee may revoke acceptance of a lot or commercial unit because of other defaults by the lessor.

(4) Revocation of acceptance must occur within a reasonable time after the lessee discovers or should have discovered the ground for it and before any substantial change in condition of the goods which is not caused by the nonconformity. Revocation is not effective until the lessee notifies the lessor.

(5) A lessee who so revokes has the same rights and duties with regard to the goods involved as if the lessee had rejected them.

As amended in 1990.

§ 2A—518. Cover; Substitute Goods.

(1) After a default by a lessor under the lease contract of the type described in Section 2A—508(1), or, if agreed, after other default by the lessor, the lessee may cover by making any purchase or lease of or contract to purchase or lease goods in substitution for those due from the lessor.

(2) Except as otherwise provided with respect to damages liquidated in the lease agreement (Section 2A—504) or otherwise determined pursuant to agreement of the parties (Sections 1—102(3) and 2A—503), if a lessee's cover is by lease agreement substantially similar to the original lease agreement and the new lease agreement is made in good faith and in a commercially reasonable manner, the lessee may recover from the lessor as damages (i) the present value, as of the date of the commencement of the term of the new lease agreement, of the rent under the new lease agreement applicable to that period of the new lease term which is comparable to the then remaining term of the original lease agreement minus the present value as of the same date of the total rent for the then remaining lease term of the original lease agreement, and (ii) any incidental or consequential damages, less expenses saved in consequence of the lessor's default.

(3) If a lessee's cover is by lease agreement that for any reason does not qualify for treatment under subsection (2), or is by purchase or otherwise, the lessee may recover from the lessor as if the lessee had elected not to cover and Section 2A—519 governs.

As amended in 1990.

§ 2A—519. Lessee's Damages for Non-Delivery, Repudiation, Default, and Breach of Warranty in Regard to Accepted Goods.

(1) Except as otherwise provided with respect to damages liquidated in the lease agreement (Section 2A—504) or otherwise determined pursuant to agreement of the parties (Sections 1—102(3) and 2A—503), if a lessee elects not to cover or a lessee elects to cover and the cover is by lease agreement that for any reason does not qualify for treatment under Section 2A—518(2), or is by purchase or otherwise, the measure of damages for non-delivery or repudiation by the lessor or for rejection or revocation of acceptance by the lessee is the present value, as of the date of the default, of the then market rent minus the present value as of the same date of the original rent, computed for the remaining lease term of the original lease agreement, together with incidental and consequential damages, less expenses saved in consequence of the lessor's default.

(2) Market rent is to be determined as of the place for tender or, in cases of rejection after arrival or revocation of acceptance, as of the place of arrival.

(3) Except as otherwise agreed, if the lessee has accepted goods and given notification (Section 2A—516(3)), the measure of damages for non-conforming tender or delivery or other default by a lessor is the loss resulting in the ordinary course of events from the lessor's default as determined in any manner that is reasonable together with incidental and consequential damages, less expenses saved in consequence of the lessor's default.

(4) Except as otherwise agreed, the measure of damages for breach of warranty is the present value at the time and place of acceptance of the difference between the value of the use of the goods accepted and the value if they had been as warranted for the lease term, unless special circumstances show proximate damages of a different amount, together with incidental and consequential damages, less expenses saved in consequence of the lessor's default or breach of warranty.

As amended in 1990.

§ 2A—520. Lessee's Incidental and Consequential Damages.

(1) Incidental damages resulting from a lessor's default include expenses reasonably incurred in inspection, receipt, transportation, and care and custody of goods rightfully rejected or goods the acceptance of which is justifiably revoked, any commercially reasonable charges, expenses or commissions in connection with effecting cover, and any other reasonable expense incident to the default.

(2) Consequential damages resulting from a lessor's default include:

(a) any loss resulting from general or particular requirements and needs of which the lessor at the time of contracting had reason to know and which could not reasonably be prevented by cover or otherwise; and

(b) injury to person or property proximately resulting from any breach of warranty.

§ 2A—521. Lessee's Right to Specific Performance or Replevin.

(1) Specific performance may be decreed if the goods are unique or in other proper circumstances.

(2) A decree for specific performance may include any terms

and conditions as to payment of the rent, damages, or other relief that the court deems just.

(3) A lessee has a right of replevin, detinue, sequestration, claim and delivery, or the like for goods identified to the lease contract if after reasonable effort the lessee is unable to effect cover for those goods or the circumstances reasonably indicate that the effort will be unavailing.

§ 2A—522. Lessee's Right to Goods on Lessor's Insolvency.

(1) Subject to subsection (2) and even though the goods have not been shipped, a lessee who has paid a part or all of the rent and security for goods identified to a lease contract (Section 2A—217) on making and keeping good a tender of any unpaid portion of the rent and security due under the lease contract may recover the goods identified from the lessor if the lessor becomes insolvent within 10 days after receipt of the first installment of rent and security.

(2) A lessee acquires the right to recover goods identified to a lease contract only if they conform to the lease contract.

C. Default by Lessee

§ 2A—523. Lessor's Remedies.

(1) If a lessee wrongfully rejects or revokes acceptance of goods or fails to make a payment when due or repudiates with respect to a part or the whole, then, with respect to any goods involved, and with respect to all of the goods if under an installment lease contract the value of the whole lease contract is substantially impaired (Section 2A—510), the lessee is in default under the lease contract and the lessor may:

(a) cancel the lease contract (Section 2A—505(1));

(b) proceed respecting goods not identified to the lease contract (Section 2A—524);

(c) withhold delivery of the goods and take possession of goods previously delivered (Section 2A—525);

(d) stop delivery of the goods by any bailee (Section 2A—526);

(e) dispose of the goods and recover damages (Section 2A—527), or retain the goods and recover damages (Section 2A—528), or in a proper case recover rent (Section 2A—529)

(f) exercise any other rights or pursue any other remedies provided in the lease contract.

(2) If a lessor does not fully exercise a right or obtain a remedy to which the lessor is entitled under subsection (1), the lessor may recover the loss resulting in the ordinary course of events from the lessee's default as determined in any reasonable manner, together with incidental damages, less expenses saved in consequence of the lessee's default.

(3) If a lessee is otherwise in default under a lease contract, the lessor may exercise the rights and pursue the remedies provided in the lease contract, which may include a right to cancel the lease. In addition, unless otherwise provided in the lease contract:

(a) if the default substantially impairs the value of the lease contract to the lessor, the lessor may exercise the rights and pursue the remedies provided in subsections (1) or (2); or

(b) if the default does not substantially impair the value of the lease contract to the lessor, the lessor may recover as provided in subsection (2).

As amended in 1990.

§ 2A—524. Lessor's Right to Identify Goods to Lease Contract.

(1) After default by the lessee under the lease contract of the type described in Section 2A—523(1) or 2A—523(3)(a) or, if agreed, after other default by the lessee, the lessor may:

(a) identify to the lease contract conforming goods not already identified if at the time the lessor learned of the default they were in the lessor's or the supplier's possession or control; and

(b) dispose of goods (Section 2A—527(1)) that demonstrably have been intended for the particular lease contract even though those goods are unfinished.

(2) If the goods are unfinished, in the exercise of reasonable commercial judgment for the purposes of avoiding loss and of effective realization, an aggrieved lessor or the supplier may either complete manufacture and wholly identify the goods to the lease contract or cease manufacture and lease, sell, or otherwise dispose of the goods for scrap or salvage value or proceed in any other reasonable manner.

As amended in 1990.

§ 2A—525. Lessor's Right to Possession of Goods.

(1) If a lessor discovers the lessee to be insolvent, the lessor may refuse to deliver the goods.

(2) After a default by the lessee under the lease contract of the type described in Section 2A—523(1) or 2A—523(3)(a) or, if agreed, after other default by the lessee, the lessor has the right to take possession of the goods. If the lease contract so provides, the lessor may require the lessee to assemble the goods and make them available to the lessor at a place to be designated by the lessor which is reasonably convenient to both parties. Without removal, the lessor may render unusable any goods employed in trade or business, and may dispose of goods on the lessee's premises (Section 2A—527).

(3) The lessor may proceed under subsection (2) without judicial process if that can be done without breach of the peace or the lessor may proceed by action.

As amended in 1990.

§ 2A—526. Lessor's Stoppage of Delivery in Transit or Otherwise.

(1) A lessor may stop delivery of goods in the possession of a carrier or other bailee if the lessor discovers the lessee to be

insolvent and may stop delivery of carload, truckload, planeload, or larger shipments of express or freight if the lessee repudiates or fails to make a payment due before delivery, whether for rent, security or otherwise under the lease contract, or for any other reason the lessor has a right to withhold or take possession of the goods.

(2) In pursuing its remedies under subsection (1), the lessor may stop delivery until

(a) receipt of the goods by the lessee;

(b) acknowledgment to the lessee by any bailee of the goods, except a carrier, that the bailee holds the goods for the lessee; or

(c) such an acknowledgment to the lessee by a carrier via reshipment or as warehouseman.

(3) (a) To stop delivery, a lessor shall so notify as to enable the bailee by reasonable diligence to prevent delivery of the goods.

(b) After notification, the bailee shall hold and deliver the goods according to the directions of the lessor, but the lessor is liable to the bailee for any ensuing charges or damages.

(c) A carrier who has issued a nonnegotiable bill of lading is not obliged to obey a notification to stop received from a person other than the consignor.

§ 2A—527. Lessor's Rights to Dispose of Goods.

(1) After a default by a lessee under the lease contract of the type described in Section 2A—523(1) or 2A–523(3)(a) or after the lessor refuses to deliver or takes possession of goods (Section 2A—525 or 2A—526), or, if agreed, after other default by a lessee, the lessor may dispose of the goods concerned or the undelivered balance thereof by lease, sale, or otherwise.

(2) Except as otherwise provided with respect to damages liquidated in the lease agreement (Section 2A—504) or otherwise determined pursuant to agreement of the parties (Sections 1—102(3) and 2A—503), if the disposition is by lease agreement substantially similar to the original lease agreement and the new lease agreement is made in good faith and in a commercially reasonable manner, the lessor may recover from the lessee as damages (i) accrued and unpaid rent as of the date of the commencement of the term of the new lease agreement, (ii) the present value, as of the same date, of the total rent for the then remaining lease term of the original lease agreement minus the present value, as of the same date, of the rent under the new lease agreement applicable to that period of the new lease term which is comparable to the then remaining term of the original lease agreement, and (iii) any incidental damages allowed under Section 2A—530, less expenses saved in consequence of the lessee's default.

(3) If the lessor's disposition is by lease agreement that for any reason does not qualify for treatment under subsection (2), or is by sale or otherwise, the lessor may recover from the lessee as if the lessor had elected not to dispose of the goods and Section 2A—528 governs.

(4) A subsequent buyer or lessee who buys or leases from the lessor in good faith for value as a result of a disposition under this section takes the goods free of the original lease contract and any rights of the original lessee even though the lessor fails to comply with one or more of the requirements of this Article.

(5) The lessor is not accountable to the lessee for any profit made on any disposition. A lessee who has rightfully rejected or justifiably revoked acceptance shall account to the lessor for any excess over the amount of the lessee's security interest (Section 2A—508(5)).

As amended in 1990.

§ 2A—528. Lessor's Damages for Non-acceptance, Failure to Pay, Repudiation, or Other Default.

(1) Except as otherwise provided with respect to damages liquidated in the lease agreement (Section 2A—504) or otherwise determined pursuant to agreement of the parties (Section 1—102(3) and 2A—503), if a lessor elects to retain the goods or a lessor elects to dispose of the goods and the disposition is by lease agreement that for any reason does not qualify for treatment under Section 2A—527(2), or is by sale or otherwise, the lessor may recover from the lessee as damages for a default of the type described in Section 2A—523(1) or 2A—523(3)(a), or if agreed, for other default of the lessee, (i) accrued and unpaid rent as of the date of the default if the lessee has never taken possession of the goods, or, if the lessee has taken possession of the goods, as of the date the lessor repossesses the goods or an earlier date on which the lessee makes a tender of the goods to the lessor, (ii) the present value as of the date determined under clause (i) of the total rent for the then remaining lease term of the original lease agreement minus the present value as of the same date of the market rent as the place where the goods are located computed for the same lease term, and (iii) any incidental damages allowed under Section 2A—530, less expenses saved in consequence of the lessee's default.

(2) If the measure of damages provided in subsection (1) is inadequate to put a lessor in as good a position as performance would have, the measure of damages is the present value of the profit, including reasonable overhead, the lessor would have made from full performance by the lessee, together with any incidental damages allowed under Section 2A—530, due allowance for costs reasonably incurred and due credit for payments or proceeds of disposition.

As amended in 1990.

§ 2A—529. Lessor's Action for the Rent.

(1) After default by the lessee under the lease contract of the type described in Section 2A—523(1) or 2A—523(3)(a) or, if agreed, after other default by the lessee, if the lessor complies with subsection (2), the lessor may recover from the lessee as damages:

(a) for goods accepted by the lessee and not repossessed by or tendered to the lessor, and for conforming goods lost or damaged within a commercially reasonable time after risk of loss passes to the lessee (Section 2A—219), (i) accrued and unpaid rent as of the date of entry of judgment in favor of the lessor (ii) the present value as of the same date of the rent for the then remaining lease term of the lease agreement, and (iii) any incidental damages allowed under Section 2A—530, less expenses saved in consequence of the lessee's default; and

(b) for goods identified to the lease contract if the lessor is unable after reasonable effort to dispose of them at a reasonable price or the circumstances reasonably indicate that effort will be unavailing, (i) accrued and unpaid rent as of the date of entry of judgment in favor of the lessor, (ii) the present value as of the same date of the rent for the then remaining lease term of the lease agreement, and (iii) any incidental damages allowed under Section 2A—530, less expenses saved in consequence of the lessee's default.

(2) Except as provided in subsection (3), the lessor shall hold for the lessee for the remaining lease term of the lease agreement any goods that have been identified to the lease contract and are in the lessor's control.

(3) The lessor may dispose of the goods at any time before collection of the judgment for damages obtained pursuant to subsection (1). If the disposition is before the end of the remaining lease term of the lease agreement, the lessor's recovery against the lessee for damages is governed by Section 2A—527 or Section 2A—528, and the lessor will cause an appropriate credit to be provided against a judgment for damages to the extent that the amount of the judgment exceeds the recovery available pursuant to Section 2A—527 or 2A—528.

(4) Payment of the judgment for damages obtained pursuant to subsection (1) entitles the lessee to the use and possession of the goods not then disposed of for the remaining lease term of and in accordance with the lease agreement.

(5) After default by the lessee under the lease contract of the type described in Section 2A—523(1) or Section 2A—523(3)(a) or, if agreed, after other default by the lessee, a lessor who is held not entitled to rent under this section must nevertheless be awarded damages for non-acceptance under Sections 2A—527 and 2A—528.

As amended in 1990.

§ 2A—530. Lessor's Incidental Damages.

Incidental damages to an aggrieved lessor include any commercially reasonable charges, expenses, or commissions incurred in stopping delivery, in the transportation, care and custody of goods after the lessee's default, in connection with return or disposition of the goods, or otherwise resulting from the default.

§ 2A—531. Standing to Sue Third Parties for Injury to Goods.

(1) If a third party so deals with goods that have been identified to a lease contract as to cause actionable injury to a party to the lease contract (a) the lessor has a right of action against the third party, and (b) the lessee also has a right of action against the third party if the lessee:

(i) has a security interest in the goods;

(ii) has an insurable interest in the goods; or

(iii) bears the risk of loss under the lease contract or has since the injury assumed that risk as against the lessor and the goods have been converted or destroyed.

(2) If at the time of the injury the party plaintiff did not bear the risk of loss as against the other party to the lease contract and there is no arrangement between them for disposition of the recovery, his [or her] suit or settlement, subject to his [or her] own interest, is as a fiduciary for the other party to the lease contract.

(3) Either party with the consent of the other may sue for the benefit of whom it may concern.

§ 2A—532. Lessor's Rights to Residual Interest.

In addition to any other recovery permitted by this Article or other law, the lessor may recover from the lessee an amount that will fully compensate the lessor for any loss of or damage to the lessor's residual interest in the goods caused by the default of the lessee.

As added in 1990.

Revised Article 3
NEGOTIABLE INSTRUMENTS

Part 1 General Provisions and Definitions

§ 3—101. Short Title.

This Article may be cited as Uniform Commercial Code—Negotiable Instruments.

§ 3—102. Subject Matter.

(a) This Article applies to negotiable instruments. It does not apply to money, to payment orders governed by Article 4A, or to securities governed by Article 8.

(b) If there is conflict between this Article and Article 4 or 9, Articles 4 and 9 govern.

(c) Regulations of the Board of Governors of the Federal Reserve System and operating circulars of the Federal Reserve Banks supersede any inconsistent provision of this Article to the extent of the inconsistency.

§ 3—103. Definitions.

(a) In this Article:

(1) "Acceptor" means a drawee who has accepted a draft.

(2) "Drawee" means a person ordered in a draft to make payment.

(3) "Drawer" means a person who signs or is identified in a draft as a person ordering payment.

(4) "Good faith" means honesty in fact and the observance of reasonable commercial standards of fair dealing.

(5) "Maker" means a person who signs or is identified in a note as a person undertaking to pay.

(6) "Order" means a written instruction to pay money signed by the person giving the instruction. The instruc-

tion may be addressed to any person, including the person giving the instruction, or to one or more persons jointly or in the alternative but not in succession. An authorization to pay is not an order unless the person authorized to pay is also instructed to pay.

(7) "Ordinary care" in the case of a person engaged in business means observance of reasonable commercial standards, prevailing in the area in which the person is located, with respect to the business in which the person is engaged. In the case of a bank that takes an instrument for processing for collection or payment by automated means, reasonable commercial standards do not require the bank to examine the instrument if the failure to examine does not violate the bank's prescribed procedures and the bank's procedures do not vary unreasonably from general banking usage not disapproved by this Article or Article 4.

(8) "Party" means a party to an instrument.

(9) "Promise" means a written undertaking to pay money signed by the person undertaking to pay. An acknowledgment of an obligation by the obligor is not a promise unless the obligor also undertakes to pay the obligation.

(10) "Prove" with respect to a fact means to meet the burden of establishing the fact (Section 1—201(8)).

(11) "Remitter" means a person who purchases an instrument from its issuer if the instrument is payable to an identified person other than the purchaser.

(b);(c) [Other definitions' section references deleted.]

(d) In addition, Article 1 contains general definitions and principles of construction and interpretation applicable throughout this Article.

§ 3—104. Negotiable Instrument.

(a) Except as provided in subsections (c) and (d), "negotiable instrument" means an unconditional promise or order to pay a fixed amount of money, with or without interest or other charges described in the promise or order, if it:

(1) is payable to bearer or to order at the time it is issued or first comes into possession of a holder;

(2) is payable on demand or at a definite time; and

(3) does not state any other undertaking or instruction by the person promising or ordering payment to do any act in addition to the payment of money, but the promise or order may contain (i) an undertaking or power to give, maintain, or protect collateral to secure payment, (ii) an authorization or power to the holder to confess judgment or realize on or dispose of collateral, or (iii) a waiver of the benefit of any law intended for the advantage or protection of an obligor.

(b) "Instrument" means a negotiable instrument.

(c) An order that meets all of the requirements of subsection (a), except paragraph (1), and otherwise falls within the definition of "check" in subsection (f) is a negotiable instrument and a check.

(d) A promise or order other than a check is not an instrument if, at the time it is issued or first comes into possession of a holder, it contains a conspicuous statement, however expressed, to the effect that the promise or order is not negotiable or is not an instrument governed by this Article.

(e) An instrument is a "note" if it is a promise and is a "draft" if it is an order. If an instrument falls within the definition of both "note" and "draft," a person entitled to enforce the instrument may treat it as either.

(f) "Check" means (i) a draft, other than a documentary draft, payable on demand and drawn on a bank or (ii) a cashier's check or teller's check. An instrument may be a check even though it is described on its face by another term, such as "money order."

(g) "Cashier's check" means a draft with respect to which the drawer and drawee are the same bank or branches of the same bank.

(h) "Teller's check" means a draft drawn by a bank (i) on another bank, or (ii) payable at or through a bank.

(i) "Traveler's check" means an instrument that (i) is payable on demand, (ii) is drawn on or payable at or through a bank, (iii) is designated by the term "traveler's check" or by a substantially similar term, and (iv) requires, as a condition to payment, a countersignature by a person whose specimen signature appears on the instrument.

(j) "Certificate of deposit" means an instrument containing an acknowledgment by a bank that a sum of money has been received by the bank and a promise by the bank to repay the sum of money. A certificate of deposit is a note of the bank.

§ 3—105. Issue of Instrument.

(a) "Issue" means the first delivery of an instrument by the maker or drawer, whether to a holder or nonholder, for the purpose of giving rights on the instrument to any person.

(b) An unissued instrument, or an unissued incomplete instrument that is completed, is binding on the maker or drawer, but nonissuance is a defense. An instrument that is conditionally issued or is issued for a special purpose is binding on the maker or drawer, but failure of the condition or special purpose to be fulfilled is a defense.

(c) "Issuer" applies to issued and unissued instruments and means a maker or drawer of an instrument.

§ 3—106. Unconditional Promise or Order.

(a) Except as provided in this section, for the purposes of Section 3—104(a), a promise or order is unconditional unless it states (i) an express condition to payment, (ii) that the promise or order is subject to or governed by another writing, or (iii) that rights or obligations with respect to the promise or order are stated in another writing. A reference to another writing does not of itself make the promise or order conditional.

(b) A promise or order is not made conditional (i) by a reference to another writing for a statement of rights with respect to collateral, prepayment, or acceleration, or (ii) because payment is limited to resort to a particular fund or source.

(c) If a promise or order requires, as a condition to payment, a countersignature by a person whose specimen signature appears on the promise or order, the condition does not make the promise or order conditional for the purposes of Section 3—104(a). If the person whose specimen signature appears on an instrument fails to countersign the instrument, the failure to countersign is a defense to the obligation of the issuer, but the failure does not prevent a transferee of the instrument from becoming a holder of the instrument.

(d) If a promise or order at the time it is issued or first comes into possession of a holder contains a statement, required by applicable statutory or administrative law, to the effect that the rights of a holder or transferee are subject to claims or defenses that the issuer could assert against the original payee, the promise or order is not thereby made conditional for the purposes of Section 3—104(a); but if the promise or order is an instrument, there cannot be a holder in due course of the instrument.

§ 3—107. Instrument Payable in Foreign Money.

Unless the instrument otherwise provides, an instrument that states the amount payable in foreign money may be paid in the foreign money or in an equivalent amount in dollars calculated by using the current bank-offered spot rate at the place of payment for the purchase of dollars on the day on which the instrument is paid.

§ 3—108. Payable on Demand or at Definite Time.

(a) A promise or order is "payable on demand" if it (i) states that it is payable on demand or at sight, or otherwise indicates that it is payable at the will of the holder, or (ii) does not state any time of payment.

(b) A promise or order is "payable at a definite time" if it is payable on elapse of a definite period of time after sight or acceptance or at a fixed date or dates or at a time or times readily ascertainable at the time the promise or order is issued, subject to rights of (i) prepayment, (ii) acceleration, (iii) extension at the option of the holder, or (iv) extension to a further definite time at the option of the maker or acceptor or automatically upon or after a specified act or event.

(c) If an instrument, payable at a fixed date, is also payable upon demand made before the fixed date, the instrument is payable on demand until the fixed date and, if demand for payment is not made before that date, becomes payable at a definite time on the fixed date.

§ 3—109. Payable to Bearer or to Order.

(a) A promise or order is payable to bearer if it:

(1) states that it is payable to bearer or to the order of bearer or otherwise indicates that the person in possession of the promise or order is entitled to payment;

(2) does not state a payee; or

(3) states that it is payable to or to the order of cash or otherwise indicates that it is not payable to an identified person.

(b) A promise or order that is not payable to bearer is payable to order if it is payable (i) to the order of an identified person or (ii) to an identified person or order. A promise or order that is payable to order is payable to the identified person.

(c) An instrument payable to bearer may become payable to an identified person if it is specially indorsed pursuant to Section 3—205(a). An instrument payable to an identified person may become payable to bearer if it is indorsed in blank pursuant to Section 3—205(b).

§ 3—110. Identification of Person to Whom Instrument Is Payable.

(a) The person to whom an instrument is initially payable is determined by the intent of the person, whether or not authorized, signing as, or in the name or behalf of, the issuer of the instrument. The instrument is payable to the person intended by the signer even if that person is identified in the instrument by a name or other identification that is not that of the intended person. If more than one person signs in the name or behalf of the issuer of an instrument and all the signers do not intend the same person as payee, the instrument is payable to any person intended by one or more of the signers.

(b) If the signature of the issuer of an instrument is made by automated means, such as a check-writing machine, the payee of the instrument is determined by the intent of the person who supplied the name or identification of the payee, whether or not authorized to do so.

(c) A person to whom an instrument is payable may be identified in any way, including by name, identifying number, office, or account number. For the purpose of determining the holder of an instrument, the following rules apply:

(1) If an instrument is payable to an account and the account is identified only by number, the instrument is payable to the person to whom the account is payable. If an instrument is payable to an account identified by number and by the name of a person, the instrument is payable to the named person, whether or not that person is the owner of the account identified by number.

(2) If an instrument is payable to:

(i) a trust, an estate, or a person described as trustee or representative of a trust or estate, the instrument is payable to the trustee, the representative, or a successor of either, whether or not the beneficiary or estate is also named;

(ii) a person described as agent or similar representative of a named or identified person, the instrument is payable to the represented person, the representative, or a successor of the representative;

(iii) a fund or organization that is not a legal entity, the instrument is payable to a representative of the members of the fund or organization; or

(iv) an office or to a person described as holding an office, the instrument is payable to the named person, the incumbent of the office, or a successor to the incumbent.

(d) If an instrument is payable to two or more persons alternatively, it is payable to any of them and may be negotiated, discharged, or enforced by any or all of them in possession of the instrument. If an instrument is payable to two or more persons not alternatively, it is payable to all of them and may be negotiated, discharged, or enforced only by all of them. If an instrument payable to two or more persons is ambiguous as to whether it is payable to the persons alternatively, the instrument is payable to the persons alternatively.

§ 3—111. Place of Payment.

Except as otherwise provided for items in Article 4, an instrument is payable at the place of payment stated in the instrument. If no place of payment is stated, an instrument is payable at the address of the drawee or maker stated in the instrument. If no address is stated, the place of payment is the place of business of the drawee or maker. If a drawee or maker has more than one place of business, the place of payment is any place of business of the drawee or maker chosen by the person entitled to enforce the instrument. If the drawee or maker has no place of business, the place of payment is the residence of the drawee or maker.

§ 3—112. Interest.

(a) Unless otherwise provided in the instrument, (i) an instrument is not payable with interest, and (ii) interest on an interest-bearing instrument is payable from the date of the instrument.

(b) Interest may be stated in an instrument as a fixed or variable amount of money or it may be expressed as a fixed or variable rate or rates. The amount or rate of interest may be stated or described in the instrument in any manner and may require reference to information not contained in the instrument. If an instrument provides for interest, but the amount of interest payable cannot be ascertained from the description, interest is payable at the judgment rate in effect at the place of payment of the instrument and at the time interest first accrues.

§ 3—113. Date of Instrument.

(a) An instrument may be antedated or postdated. The date stated determines the time of payment if the instrument is payable at a fixed period after date. Except as provided in Section 4—401(c), an instrument payable on demand is not payable before the date of the instrument.

(b) If an instrument is undated, its date is the date of its issue or, in the case of an unissued instrument, the date it first comes into possession of a holder.

§ 3—114. Contradictory Terms of Instrument.

If an instrument contains contradictory terms, typewritten terms prevail over printed terms, handwritten terms prevail over both, and words prevail over numbers.

§ 3—115. Incomplete Instrument.

(a) "Incomplete instrument" means a signed writing, whether or not issued by the signer, the contents of which show at the time of signing that it is incomplete but that the signer intended it to be completed by the addition of words or numbers.

(b) Subject to subsection (c), if an incomplete instrument is an instrument under Section 3—104, it may be enforced according to its terms if it is not completed, or according to its terms as augmented by completion. If an incomplete instrument is not an instrument under Section 3—104, but, after completion, the requirements of Section 3—104 are met, the instrument may be enforced according to its terms as augmented by completion.

(c) If words or numbers are added to an incomplete instrument without authority of the signer, there is an alteration of the incomplete instrument under Section 3—407.

(d) The burden of establishing that words or numbers were added to an incomplete instrument without authority of the signer is on the person asserting the lack of authority.

§ 3—116. Joint and Several Liability; Contribution.

(a) Except as otherwise provided in the instrument, two or more persons who have the same liability on an instrument as makers, drawers, acceptors, indorsers who indorse as joint payees, or anomalous indorsers are jointly and severally liable in the capacity in which they sign.

(b) Except as provided in Section 3—419(e) or by agreement of the affected parties, a party having joint and several liability who pays the instrument is entitled to receive from any party having the same joint and several liability contribution in accordance with applicable law.

(c) Discharge of one party having joint and several liability by a person entitled to enforce the instrument does not affect the right under subsection (b) of a party having the same joint and several liability to receive contribution from the party discharged.

§ 3—117. Other Agreements Affecting Instrument.

Subject to applicable law regarding exclusion of proof of contemporaneous or previous agreements, the obligation of a party to an instrument to pay the instrument may be modified, supplemented, or nullified by a separate agreement of the obligor and a person entitled to enforce the instrument, if the instrument is issued or the obligation is incurred in reliance on the agreement or as part of the same transaction giving rise to the agreement. To the extent an obligation is modified, supplemented, or nullified by an agreement under this section, the agreement is a defense to the obligation.

§ 3—118. Statute of Limitations.

(a) Except as provided in subsection (e), an action to enforce the obligation of a party to pay a note payable at a definite time must be commenced within six years after the due date or dates stated in the note or, if a due date is accelerated, within six years after the accelerated due date.

(b) Except as provided in subsection (d) or (e), if demand for payment is made to the maker of a note payable on demand, an action to enforce the obligation of a party to pay the note must be commenced within six years after the demand. If no demand for payment is made to the maker, an action to enforce the note is barred if neither principal nor interest on the note has been paid for a continuous period of 10 years.

(c) Except as provided in subsection (d), an action to enforce the obligation of a party to an unaccepted draft to pay the draft must be commenced within three years after dishonor of the draft or 10 years after the date of the draft, whichever period expires first.

(d) An action to enforce the obligation of the acceptor of a certified check or the issuer of a teller's check, cashier's check, or traveler's check must be commenced within three years after demand for payment is made to the acceptor or issuer, as the case may be.

(e) An action to enforce the obligation of a party to a certificate of deposit to pay the instrument must be commenced within six years after demand for payment is made to the maker, but if the instrument states a due date and the maker is not required to pay before that date, the six-year period begins when a demand for payment is in effect and the due date has passed.

(f) An action to enforce the obligation of a party to pay an accepted draft, other than a certified check, must be commenced (i) within six years after the due date or dates stated in the draft or acceptance if the obligation of the acceptor is payable at a definite time, or (ii) within six years after the date of the acceptance if the obligation of the acceptor is payable on demand.

(g) Unless governed by other law regarding claims for indemnity or contribution, an action (i) for conversion of an instrument, for money had and received, or like action based on conversion, (ii) for breach of warranty, or (iii) to enforce an obligation, duty, or right arising under this Article and not governed by this section must be commenced within three years after the [cause of action] accrues.

§ 3—119. Notice of Right to Defend Action.

In an action for breach of an obligation for which a third person is answerable over pursuant to this Article or Article 4, the defendant may give the third person written notice of the litigation, and the person notified may then give similar notice to any other person who is answerable over. If the notice states (i) that the person notified may come in and defend and (ii) that failure to do so will bind the person notified in an action later brought by the person giving the notice as to any determination of fact common to the two litigations, the person notified is so bound unless after seasonable receipt of the notice the person notified does come in and defend.

Part 2 Negotiation, Transfer, and Indorsement

§ 3—201. Negotiation.

(a) "Negotiation" means a transfer of possession, whether voluntary or involuntary, of an instrument by a person other than the issuer to a person who thereby becomes its holder.

(b) Except for negotiation by a remitter, if an instrument is payable to an identified person, negotiation requires transfer of possession of the instrument and its indorsement by the holder. If an instrument is payable to bearer, it may be negotiated by transfer of possession alone.

§ 3—202. Negotiation Subject to Rescission.

(a) Negotiation is effective even if obtained (i) from an infant, a corporation exceeding its powers, or a person without capacity, (ii) by fraud, duress, or mistake, or (iii) in breach of duty or as part of an illegal transaction.

(b) To the extent permitted by other law, negotiation may be rescinded or may be subject to other remedies, but those remedies may not be asserted against a subsequent holder in due course or a person paying the instrument in good faith and without knowledge of facts that are a basis for rescission or other remedy.

§ 3—203. Transfer of Instrument; Rights Acquired by Transfer.

(a) An instrument is transferred when it is delivered by a person other than its issuer for the purpose of giving to the person receiving delivery the right to enforce the instrument.

(b) Transfer of an instrument, whether or not the transfer is a negotiation, vests in the transferee any right of the transferor to enforce the instrument, including any right as a holder in due course, but the transferee cannot acquire rights of a holder in due course by a transfer, directly or indirectly, from a holder in due course if the transferee engaged in fraud or illegality affecting the instrument.

(c) Unless otherwise agreed, if an instrument is transferred for value and the transferee does not become a holder because of lack of indorsement by the transferor, the transferee has a specifically enforceable right to the unqualified indorsement of the transferor, but negotiation of the instrument does not occur until the indorsement is made.

(d) If a transferor purports to transfer less than the entire instrument, negotiation of the instrument does not occur. The transferee obtains no rights under this Article and has only the rights of a partial assignee.

§ 3—204. Indorsement.

(a) "Indorsement" means a signature, other than that of a signer as maker, drawer, or acceptor, that alone or accompanied by other words is made on an instrument for the purpose of (i) negotiating the instrument, (ii) restricting payment of the instrument, or (iii) incurring indorser's liability on the instrument, but regardless of the intent of the signer, a signature and its accompanying words is an indorsement unless the accompanying words, terms of the instrument, place of the signature, or other circumstances unambiguously indicate that the signature was made for a purpose other than indorsement. For the purpose of determining whether a signature is made on an instrument, a paper affixed to the instrument is a part of the instrument.

(b) "Indorser" means a person who makes an indorsement.

(c) For the purpose of determining whether the transferee of an instrument is a holder, an indorsement that transfers a security interest in the instrument is effective as an unqualified indorsement of the instrument.

(d) If an instrument is payable to a holder under a name that is not the name of the holder, indorsement may be made by the holder in the name stated in the instrument or in the holder's name or both, but signature in both names may be required by a person paying or taking the instrument for value or collection.

§ 3—205. Special Indorsement; Blank Indorsement; Anomalous Indorsement.

(a) If an indorsement is made by the holder of an instrument, whether payable to an identified person or payable to bearer, and the indorsement identifies a person to whom it makes the instrument payable, it is a "special indorsement." When specially indorsed, an instrument becomes payable to the identified person and may be negotiated only by the indorsement of that person. The principles stated in Section 3—110 apply to special indorsements.

(b) If an indorsement is made by the holder of an instrument and it is not a special indorsement, it is a "blank indorsement." When indorsed in blank, an instrument becomes payable to bearer and may be negotiated by transfer of possession alone until specially indorsed.

(c) The holder may convert a blank indorsement that consists only of a signature into a special indorsement by writing, above the signature of the indorser, words identifying the person to whom the instrument is made payable.

(d) "Anomalous indorsement" means an indorsement made by a person who is not the holder of the instrument. An anomalous indorsement does not affect the manner in which the instrument may be negotiated.

§ 3—206. Restrictive Indorsement.

(a) An indorsement limiting payment to a particular person or otherwise prohibiting further transfer or negotiation of the instrument is not effective to prevent further transfer or negotiation of the instrument.

(b) An indorsement stating a condition to the right of the indorsee to receive payment does not affect the right of the indorsee to enforce the instrument. A person paying the instrument or taking it for value or collection may disregard the condition, and the rights and liabilities of that person are not affected by whether the condition has been fulfilled.

(c) If an instrument bears an indorsement (i) described in Section 4—201(b), or (ii) in blank or to a particular bank using the words "for deposit," "for collection," or other words indicating a purpose of having the instrument collected by a bank for the indorser or for a particular account, the following rules apply:

(1) A person, other than a bank, who purchases the instrument when so indorsed converts the instrument unless the amount paid for the instrument is received by the indorser or applied consistently with the indorsement.

(2) A depositary bank that purchases the instrument or takes it for collection when so indorsed converts the instrument unless the amount paid by the bank with respect to the instrument is received by the indorser or applied consistently with the indorsement.

(3) A payor bank that is also the depositary bank or that takes the instrument for immediate payment over the counter from a person other than a collecting bank converts the instrument unless the proceeds of the instrument are received by the indorser or applied consistently with the indorsement.

(4) Except as otherwise provided in paragraph (3), a payor bank or intermediary bank may disregard the indorsement and is not liable if the proceeds of the instrument are not received by the indorser or applied consistently with the indorsement.

(d) Except for an indorsement covered by subsection (c), if an instrument bears an indorsement using words to the effect that payment is to be made to the indorsee as agent, trustee, or other fiduciary for the benefit of the indorser or another person, the following rules apply:

(1) Unless there is notice of breach of fiduciary duty as provided in Section 3—307, a person who purchases the instrument from the indorsee or takes the instrument from the indorsee for collection or payment may pay the proceeds of payment or the value given for the instrument to the indorsee without regard to whether the indorsee violates a fiduciary duty to the indorser.

(2) A subsequent transferee of the instrument or person who pays the instrument is neither given notice nor otherwise affected by the restriction in the indorsement unless the transferee or payor knows that the fiduciary dealt with the instrument or its proceeds in breach of fiduciary duty.

(e) The presence on an instrument of an indorsement to which this section applies does not prevent a purchaser of the instrument from becoming a holder in due course of the instrument unless the purchaser is a converter under subsection (c) or has notice or knowledge of breach of fiduciary duty as stated in subsection (d).

(f) In an action to enforce the obligation of a party to pay the instrument, the obligor has a defense if payment would violate an indorsement to which this section applies and the payment is not permitted by this section.

§ 3—207. Reacquisition.

Reacquisition of an instrument occurs if it is transferred to a former holder, by negotiation or otherwise. A former holder who reacquires the instrument may cancel indorsements made after the reacquirer first became a holder of the instrument. If the cancellation causes the instrument to be payable to the reacquirer or to bearer, the reacquirer may negotiate the instrument. An indorser whose indorsement is canceled is discharged, and the discharge is effective against any subsequent holder.

Part 3 Enforcement of Instruments

§ 3—301. Person Entitled to Enforce Instrument.

"Person entitled to enforce" an instrument means (i) the holder of the instrument, (ii) a nonholder in possession of the instrument who has the rights of a holder, or (iii) a person not in possession of the instrument who is entitled to enforce the instrument pursuant to Section 3—309 or 3—418(d). A person may be a person entitled to enforce the instrument even though the person is not the owner of the instrument or is in wrongful possession of the instrument.

§ 3—302. Holder in Due Course.

(a) Subject to subsection (c) and Section 3—106(d), "holder in due course" means the holder of an instrument if:

(1) the instrument when issued or negotiated to the holder does not bear such apparent evidence of forgery or alteration or is not otherwise so irregular or incomplete as to call into question its authenticity; and

(2) the holder took the instrument (i) for value, (ii) in good faith, (iii) without notice that the instrument is overdue or has been dishonored or that there is an uncured default with respect to payment of another instrument issued as part of the same series, (iv) without notice that the instrument contains an unauthorized signature or has been altered, (v) without notice of any claim to the instrument described in Section 3—306, and (vi) without notice that any party has a defense or claim in recoupment described in Section 3—305(a).

(b) Notice of discharge of a party, other than discharge in an insolvency proceeding, is not notice of a defense under subsection (a), but discharge is effective against a person who became a holder in due course with notice of the discharge. Public filing or recording of a document does not of itself constitute notice of a defense, claim in recoupment, or claim to the instrument.

(c) Except to the extent a transferor or predecessor in interest has rights as a holder in due course, a person does not acquire rights of a holder in due course of an instrument taken (i) by legal process or by purchase in an execution, bankruptcy, or creditor's sale or similar proceeding, (ii) by purchase as part of a bulk transaction not in ordinary course of business of the transferor, or (iii) as the successor in interest to an estate or other organization.

(d) If, under Section 3—303(a)(1), the promise of performance that is the consideration for an instrument has been partially performed, the holder may assert rights as a holder in due course of the instrument only to the fraction of the amount payable under the instrument equal to the value of the partial performance divided by the value of the promised performance.

(e) If (i) the person entitled to enforce an instrument has only a security interest in the instrument and (ii) the person obliged to pay the instrument has a defense, claim in recoupment, or claim to the instrument that may be asserted against the person who granted the security interest, the person entitled to enforce the instrument may assert rights as a holder in due course only to an amount payable under the instrument which, at the time of enforcement of the instrument, does not exceed the amount of the unpaid obligation secured.

(f) To be effective, notice must be received at a time and in a manner that gives a reasonable opportunity to act on it.

(g) This section is subject to any law limiting status as a holder in due course in particular classes of transactions.

§ 3—303. Value and Consideration.

(a) An instrument is issued or transferred for value if:

(1) the instrument is issued or transferred for a promise of performance, to the extent the promise has been performed;

(2) the transferee acquires a security interest or other lien in the instrument other than a lien obtained by judicial proceeding;

(3) the instrument is issued or transferred as payment of, or as security for, an antecedent claim against any person, whether or not the claim is due;

(4) the instrument is issued or transferred in exchange for a negotiable instrument; or

(5) the instrument is issued or transferred in exchange for the incurring of an irrevocable obligation to a third party by the person taking the instrument.

(b) "Consideration" means any consideration sufficient to support a simple contract. The drawer or maker of an instrument has a defense if the instrument is issued without consideration. If an instrument is issued for a promise of performance, the issuer has a defense to the extent performance of the promise is due and the promise has not been performed. If an instrument is issued for value as stated in subsection (a), the instrument is also issued for consideration.

§ 3—304. Overdue Instrument.

(a) An instrument payable on demand becomes overdue at the earliest of the following times:

(1) on the day after the day demand for payment is duly made;

(2) if the instrument is a check, 90 days after its date; or

(3) if the instrument is not a check, when the instrument has been outstanding for a period of time after its date which is unreasonably long under the circumstances of the particular case in light of the nature of the instrument and usage of the trade.

(b) With respect to an instrument payable at a definite time the following rules apply:

(1) If the principal is payable in installments and a due date has not been accelerated, the instrument becomes overdue upon default under the instrument for nonpayment of an

installment, and the instrument remains overdue until the default is cured.

(2) If the principal is not payable in installments and the due date has not been accelerated, the instrument becomes overdue on the day after the due date.

(3) If a due date with respect to principal has been accelerated, the instrument becomes overdue on the day after the accelerated due date.

(c) Unless the due date of principal has been accelerated, an instrument does not become overdue if there is default in payment of interest but no default in payment of principal.

§ 3—305. Defenses and Claims in Recoupment.

(a) Except as stated in subsection (b), the right to enforce the obligation of a party to pay an instrument is subject to the following:

(1) a defense of the obligor based on (i) infancy of the obligor to the extent it is a defense to a simple contract, (ii) duress, lack of legal capacity, or illegality of the transaction which, under other law, nullifies the obligation of the obligor, (iii) fraud that induced the obligor to sign the instrument with neither knowledge nor reasonable opportunity to learn of its character or its essential terms, or (iv) discharge of the obligor in insolvency proceedings;

(2) a defense of the obligor stated in another section of this Article or a defense of the obligor that would be available if the person entitled to enforce the instrument were enforcing a right to payment under a simple contract; and

(3) a claim in recoupment of the obligor against the original payee of the instrument if the claim arose from the transaction that gave rise to the instrument; but the claim of the obligor may be asserted against a transferee of the instrument only to reduce the amount owing on the instrument at the time the action is brought.

(b) The right of a holder in due course to enforce the obligation of a party to pay the instrument is subject to defenses of the obligor stated in subsection (a)(1), but is not subject to defenses of the obligor stated in subsection (a)(2) or claims in recoupment stated in subsection (a)(3) against a person other than the holder.

(c) Except as stated in subsection (d), in an action to enforce the obligation of a party to pay the instrument, the obligor may not assert against the person entitled to enforce the instrument a defense, claim in recoupment, or claim to the instrument (Section 3—306) of another person, but the other person's claim to the instrument may be asserted by the obligor if the other person is joined in the action and personally asserts the claim against the person entitled to enforce the instrument. An obligor is not obliged to pay the instrument if the person seeking enforcement of the instrument does not have rights of a holder in due course and the obligor proves that the instrument is a lost or stolen instrument.

(d) In an action to enforce the obligation of an accommodation party to pay an instrument, the accommodation party may assert against the person entitled to enforce the instrument any defense or claim in recoupment under subsection (a) that the accommodated party could assert against the person entitled to enforce the instrument, except the defenses of discharge in insolvency proceedings, infancy, and lack of legal capacity.

§ 3—306. Claims to an Instrument.

A person taking an instrument, other than a person having rights of a holder in due course, is subject to a claim of a property or possessory right in the instrument or its proceeds, including a claim to rescind a negotiation and to recover the instrument or its proceeds. A person having rights of a holder in due course takes free of the claim to the instrument.

§ 3—307. Notice of Breach of Fiduciary Duty.

(a) In this section:

(1) "Fiduciary" means an agent, trustee, partner, corporate officer or director, or other representative owing a fiduciary duty with respect to an instrument.

(2) "Represented person" means the principal, beneficiary, partnership, corporation, or other person to whom the duty stated in paragraph (1) is owed.

(b) If (i) an instrument is taken from a fiduciary for payment or collection or for value, (ii) the taker has knowledge of the fiduciary status of the fiduciary, and (iii) the represented person makes a claim to the instrument or its proceeds on the basis that the transaction of the fiduciary is a breach of fiduciary duty, the following rules apply:

(1) Notice of breach of fiduciary duty by the fiduciary is notice of the claim of the represented person.

(2) In the case of an instrument payable to the represented person or the fiduciary as such, the taker has notice of the breach of fiduciary duty if the instrument is (i) taken in payment of or as security for a debt known by the taker to be the personal debt of the fiduciary, (ii) taken in a transaction known by the taker to be for the personal benefit of the fiduciary, or (iii) deposited to an account other than an account of the fiduciary, as such, or an account of the represented person.

(3) If an instrument is issued by the represented person or the fiduciary as such, and made payable to the fiduciary personally, the taker does not have notice of the breach of fiduciary duty unless the taker knows of the breach of fiduciary duty.

(4) If an instrument is issued by the represented person or the fiduciary as such, to the taker as payee, the taker has notice of the breach of fiduciary duty if the instrument is (i) taken in payment of or as security for a debt known by the taker to be the personal debt of the fiduciary, (ii) taken in a transaction known by the taker to be for the personal benefit of the fiduciary, or (iii) deposited to an account other than an account of the fiduciary, as such, or an account of the represented person.

§ 3—308. Proof of Signatures and Status as Holder in Due Course.

(a) In an action with respect to an instrument, the authenticity of, and authority to make, each signature on the instrument is admitted unless specifically denied in the pleadings. If the validity of a signature is denied in the pleadings, the burden of establishing validity is on the person claiming validity, but the signature is presumed to be authentic and authorized unless the action is to enforce the liability of the purported signer and the signer is dead or incompetent at the time of trial of the issue of validity of the signature. If an action to enforce the instrument is brought against a person as the undisclosed principal of a person who signed the instrument as a party to the instrument, the plaintiff has the burden of establishing that the defendant is liable on the instrument as a represented person under Section 3—402(a).

(b) If the validity of signatures is admitted or proved and there is compliance with subsection (a), a plaintiff producing the instrument is entitled to payment if the plaintiff proves entitlement to enforce the instrument under Section 3—301, unless the defendant proves a defense or claim in recoupment. If a defense or claim in recoupment is proved, the right to payment of the plaintiff is subject to the defense or claim, except to the extent the plaintiff proves that the plaintiff has rights of a holder in due course which are not subject to the defense or claim.

§ 3—309. Enforcement of Lost, Destroyed, or Stolen Instrument.

(a) A person not in possession of an instrument is entitled to enforce the instrument if (i) the person was in possession of the instrument and entitled to enforce it when loss of possession occurred, (ii) the loss of possession was not the result of a transfer by the person or a lawful seizure, and (iii) the person cannot reasonably obtain possession of the instrument because the instrument was destroyed, its whereabouts cannot be determined, or it is in the wrongful possession of an unknown person or a person that cannot be found or is not amenable to service of process.

(b) A person seeking enforcement of an instrument under subsection (a) must prove the terms of the instrument and the person's right to enforce the instrument. If that proof is made, Section 3—308 applies to the case as if the person seeking enforcement had produced the instrument. The court may not enter judgment in favor of the person seeking enforcement unless it finds that the person required to pay the instrument is adequately protected against loss that might occur by reason of a claim by another person to enforce the instrument. Adequate protection may be provided by any reasonable means.

§ 3—310. Effect of Instrument on Obligation for Which Taken.

(a) Unless otherwise agreed, if a certified check, cashier's check, or teller's check is taken for an obligation, the obligation is discharged to the same extent discharge would result if an amount of money equal to the amount of the instrument were taken in payment of the obligation. Discharge of the obligation does not affect any liability that the obligor may have as an indorser of the instrument.

(b) Unless otherwise agreed and except as provided in subsection (a), if a note or an uncertified check is taken for an obligation, the obligation is suspended to the same extent the obligation would be discharged if an amount of money equal to the amount of the instrument were taken, and the following rules apply:

(1) In the case of an uncertified check, suspension of the obligation continues until dishonor of the check or until it is paid or certified. Payment or certification of the check results in discharge of the obligation to the extent of the amount of the check.

(2) In the case of a note, suspension of the obligation continues until dishonor of the note or until it is paid. Payment of the note results in discharge of the obligation to the extent of the payment.

(3) Except as provided in paragraph (4), if the check or note is dishonored and the obligee of the obligation for which the instrument was taken is the person entitled to enforce the instrument, the obligee may enforce either the instrument or the obligation. In the case of an instrument of a third person which is negotiated to the obligee by the obligor, discharge of the obligor on the instrument also discharges the obligation.

(4) If the person entitled to enforce the instrument taken for an obligation is a person other than the obligee, the obligee may not enforce the obligation to the extent the obligation is suspended. If the obligee is the person entitled to enforce the instrument but no longer has possession of it because it was lost, stolen, or destroyed, the obligation may not be enforced to the extent of the amount payable on the instrument, and to that extent the obligee's rights against the obligor are limited to enforcement of the instrument.

(c) If an instrument other than one described in subsection (a) or (b) is taken for an obligation, the effect is (i) that stated in subsection (a) if the instrument is one on which a bank is liable as maker or acceptor, or (ii) that stated in subsection (b) in any other case.

§ 3—311. Accord and Satisfaction by Use of Instrument.

(a) If a person against whom a claim is asserted proves that (i) that person in good faith tendered an instrument to the claimant as full satisfaction of the claim, (ii) the amount of the claim was unliquidated or subject to a bona fide dispute, and (iii) the claimant obtained payment of the instrument, the following subsections apply.

(b) Unless subsection (c) applies, the claim is discharged if the person against whom the claim is asserted proves that the instrument or an accompanying written communication contained a conspicuous statement to the effect that the instrument was tendered as full satisfaction of the claim.

(c) Subject to subsection (d), a claim is not discharged under subsection (b) if either of the following applies:

(1) The claimant, if an organization, proves that (i) within a reasonable time before the tender, the claimant sent a conspicuous statement to the person against whom the claim is asserted that communications concerning disputed debts, including an instrument tendered as full satisfaction of a debt, are to be sent to a designated person, office, or place, and (ii) the instrument or accompanying communication was not received by that designated person, office, or place.

(2) The claimant, whether or not an organization, proves that within 90 days after payment of the instrument, the claimant tendered repayment of the amount of the instrument to the person against whom the claim is asserted. This paragraph does not apply if the claimant is an organization that sent a statement complying with paragraph (1)(i).

(d) A claim is discharged if the person against whom the claim is asserted proves that within a reasonable time before collection of the instrument was initiated, the claimant, or an agent of the claimant having direct responsibility with respect to the disputed obligation, knew that the instrument was tendered in full satisfaction of the claim.

§ 3—312. Lost, Destroyed, or Stolen Cashier's Check, Teller's Check, or Certified Check.

(a) In this section:

(1) "Check" means a cashier's check, teller's check, or certified check.

(2) "Claimant" means a person who claims the right to receive the amount of a cashier's check, teller's check, or certified check that was lost, destroyed, or stolen.

(3) "Declaration of loss" means a written statement, made under penalty of perjury, to the effect that (i) the declarer lost possession of a check, (ii) the declarer is the drawer or payee of the check, in the case of a certified check, or the remitter or payee of the check, in the case of a cashier's check or teller's check, (iii) the loss of possession was not the result of a transfer by the declarer or a lawful seizure, and (iv) the declarer cannot reasonably obtain possession of the check because the check was destroyed, its whereabouts cannot be determined, or it is in the wrongful possession of an unknown person or a person that cannot be found or is not amenable to service of process.

(4) "Obligated bank" means the issuer of a cashier's check or teller's check or the acceptor of a certified check.

(b) A claimant may assert a claim to the amount of a check by a communication to the obligated bank describing the check with reasonable certainty and requesting payment of the amount of the check, if (i) the claimant is the drawer or payee of a certified check or the remitter or payee of a cashier's check or teller's check, (ii) the communication contains or is accompanied by a declaration of loss of the claimant with respect to the check, (iii) the communication is received at a time and in a manner affording the bank a reasonable time to act on it before the check is paid, and (iv) the claimant provides reasonable identification if requested by the obligated bank. Delivery of a declaration of loss is a warranty of the truth of the statements made in the declaration. If a claim is asserted in compliance with this subsection, the following rules apply:

(1) The claim becomes enforceable at the later of (i) the time the claim is asserted, or (ii) the 90th day following the date of the check, in the case of a cashier's check or teller's check, or the 90th day following the date of the acceptance, in the case of a certified check.

(2) Until the claim becomes enforceable, it has no legal effect and the obligated bank may pay the check or, in the case of a teller's check, may permit the drawee to pay the check. Payment to a person entitled to enforce the check discharges all liability of the obligated bank with respect to the check.

(3) If the claim becomes enforceable before the check is presented for payment, the obligated bank is not obliged to pay the check.

(4) When the claim becomes enforceable, the obligated bank becomes obliged to pay the amount of the check to the claimant if payment of the check has not been made to a person entitled to enforce the check. Subject to Section 4—302(a)(1), payment to the claimant discharges all liability of the obligated bank with respect to the check.

(c) If the obligated bank pays the amount of a check to a claimant under subsection (b)(4) and the check is presented for payment by a person having rights of a holder in due course, the claimant is obliged to (i) refund the payment to the obligated bank if the check is paid, or (ii) pay the amount of the check to the person having rights of a holder in due course if the check is dishonored.

(d) If a claimant has the right to assert a claim under subsection (b) and is also a person entitled to enforce a cashier's check, teller's check, or certified check which is lost, destroyed, or stolen, the claimant may assert rights with respect to the check either under this section or Section 3—309.

Part 4 Liability of Parties

§ 3—401. Signature.

(a) A person is not liable on an instrument unless (i) the person signed the instrument, or (ii) the person is represented by an agent or representative who signed the instrument and the signature is binding on the represented person under Section 3—402.

(b) A signature may be made (i) manually or by means of a device or machine, and (ii) by the use of any name, including a trade or assumed name, or by a word, mark, or symbol executed or adopted by a person with present intention to authenticate a writing.

§ 3—402. Signature by Representative.

(a) If a person acting, or purporting to act, as a representative signs an instrument by signing either the name of the represented person or the name of the signer, the represented person is bound by the signature to the same extent the represented person would be bound if the signature were on a simple contract. If the represented person is bound, the signature of the representative is the "authorized signature of the represented person" and the represented person is liable on the instrument, whether or not identified in the instrument.

(b) If a representative signs the name of the representative to an instrument and the signature is an authorized signature of the represented person, the following rules apply:

(1) If the form of the signature shows unambiguously that the signature is made on behalf of the represented person who is identified in the instrument, the representative is not liable on the instrument.

(2) Subject to subsection (c), if (i) the form of the signature does not show unambiguously that the signature is made in a representative capacity or (ii) the represented person is not identified in the instrument, the representative is liable on the instrument to a holder in due course that took the instrument without notice that the representative was not intended to be liable on the instrument. With respect to any other person, the representative is liable on the instrument unless the representative proves that the original parties did not intend the representative to be liable on the instrument.

(c) If a representative signs the name of the representative as drawer of a check without indication of the representative status and the check is payable from an account of the represented person who is identified on the check, the signer is not liable on the check if the signature is an authorized signature of the represented person.

§ 3—403. Unauthorized Signature.

(a) Unless otherwise provided in this Article or Article 4, an unauthorized signature is ineffective except as the signature of the unauthorized signer in favor of a person who in good faith pays the instrument or takes it for value. An unauthorized signature may be ratified for all purposes of this Article.

(b) If the signature of more than one person is required to constitute the authorized signature of an organization, the signature of the organization is unauthorized if one of the required signatures is lacking.

(c) The civil or criminal liability of a person who makes an unauthorized signature is not affected by any provision of this Article which makes the unauthorized signature effective for the purposes of this Article.

§ 3—404. Impostors; Fictitious Payees.

(a) If an impostor, by use of the mails or otherwise, induces the issuer of an instrument to issue the instrument to the impostor, or to a person acting in concert with the impostor, by impersonating the payee of the instrument or a person authorized to act for the payee, an indorsement of the instrument by any person in the name of the payee is effective as the indorsement of the payee in favor of a person who, in good faith, pays the instrument or takes it for value or for collection.

(b) If (i) a person whose intent determines to whom an instrument is payable (Section 3—110(a) or (b)) does not intend the person identified as payee to have any interest in the instrument, or (ii) the person identified as payee of an instrument is a fictitious person, the following rules apply until the instrument is negotiated by special indorsement:

(1) Any person in possession of the instrument is its holder.

(2) An indorsement by any person in the name of the payee stated in the instrument is effective as the indorsement of the payee in favor of a person who, in good faith, pays the instrument or takes it for value or for collection.

(c) Under subsection (a) or (b), an indorsement is made in the name of a payee if (i) it is made in a name substantially similar to that of the payee or (ii) the instrument, whether or not indorsed, is deposited in a depositary bank to an account in a name substantially similar to that of the payee.

(d) With respect to an instrument to which subsection (a) or (b) applies, if a person paying the instrument or taking it for value or for collection fails to exercise ordinary care in paying or taking the instrument and that failure substantially contributes to loss resulting from payment of the instrument, the person bearing the loss may recover from the person failing to exercise ordinary care to the extent the failure to exercise ordinary care contributed to the loss.

§ 3—405. Employer's Responsibility for Fraudulent Indorsement by Employee.

(a) In this section:

(1) "Employee" includes an independent contractor and employee of an independent contractor retained by the employer.

(2) "Fraudulent indorsement" means (i) in the case of an instrument payable to the employer, a forged indorsement purporting to be that of the employer, or (ii) in the case of an instrument with respect to which the employer is the issuer, a forged indorsement purporting to be that of the person identified as payee.

(3) "Responsibility" with respect to instruments means authority (i) to sign or indorse instruments on behalf of the employer, (ii) to process instruments received by the employer for bookkeeping purposes, for deposit to an account, or for other disposition, (iii) to prepare or process instruments for issue in the name of the employer, (iv) to supply information determining the names or addresses of payees of instruments to be issued in the name of the employer, (v) to control the disposition of instruments to be issued in the name of the employer, or (vi) to act otherwise with respect to instruments in a responsible capacity. "Responsibility" does not include authority that merely allows an employee to have access to instruments or blank

or incomplete instrument forms that are being stored or transported or are part of incoming or outgoing mail, or similar access.

(b) For the purpose of determining the rights and liabilities of a person who, in good faith, pays an instrument or takes it for value or for collection, if an employer entrusted an employee with responsibility with respect to the instrument and the employee or a person acting in concert with the employee makes a fraudulent indorsement of the instrument, the indorsement is effective as the indorsement of the person to whom the instrument is payable if it is made in the name of that person. If the person paying the instrument or taking it for value or for collection fails to exercise ordinary care in paying or taking the instrument and that failure substantially contributes to loss resulting from the fraud, the person bearing the loss may recover from the person failing to exercise ordinary care to the extent the failure to exercise ordinary care contributed to the loss.

(c) Under subsection (b), an indorsement is made in the name of the person to whom an instrument is payable if (i) it is made in a name substantially similar to the name of that person or (ii) the instrument, whether or not indorsed, is deposited in a depositary bank to an account in a name substantially similar to the name of that person.

§ 3—406. Negligence Contributing to Forged Signature or Alteration of Instrument.

(a) A person whose failure to exercise ordinary care substantially contributes to an alteration of an instrument or to the making of a forged signature on an instrument is precluded from asserting the alteration or the forgery against a person who, in good faith, pays the instrument or takes it for value or for collection.

(b) Under subsection (a), if the person asserting the preclusion fails to exercise ordinary care in paying or taking the instrument and that failure substantially contributes to loss, the loss is allocated between the person precluded and the person asserting the preclusion according to the extent to which the failure of each to exercise ordinary care contributed to the loss.

(c) Under subsection (a), the burden of proving failure to exercise ordinary care is on the person asserting the preclusion. Under subsection (b), the burden of proving failure to exercise ordinary care is on the person precluded.

§ 3—407. Alteration.

(a) "Alteration" means (i) an unauthorized change in an instrument that purports to modify in any respect the obligation of a party, or (ii) an unauthorized addition of words or numbers or other change to an incomplete instrument relating to the obligation of a party.

(b) Except as provided in subsection (c), an alteration fraudulently made discharges a party whose obligation is affected by the alteration unless that party assents or is precluded from asserting the alteration. No other alteration discharges a party, and the instrument may be enforced according to its original terms.

(c) A payor bank or drawee paying a fraudulently altered instrument or a person taking it for value, in good faith and without notice of the alteration, may enforce rights with respect to the instrument (i) according to its original terms, or (ii) in the case of an incomplete instrument altered by unauthorized completion, according to its terms as completed.

§ 3—408. Drawee Not Liable on Unaccepted Draft.

A check or other draft does not of itself operate as an assignment of funds in the hands of the drawee available for its payment, and the drawee is not liable on the instrument until the drawee accepts it.

§ 3—409. Acceptance of Draft; Certified Check.

(a) "Acceptance" means the drawee's signed agreement to pay a draft as presented. It must be written on the draft and may consist of the drawee's signature alone. Acceptance may be made at any time and becomes effective when notification pursuant to instructions is given or the accepted draft is delivered for the purpose of giving rights on the acceptance to any person.

(b) A draft may be accepted although it has not been signed by the drawer, is otherwise incomplete, is overdue, or has been dishonored.

(c) If a draft is payable at a fixed period after sight and the acceptor fails to date the acceptance, the holder may complete the acceptance by supplying a date in good faith.

(d) "Certified check" means a check accepted by the bank on which it is drawn. Acceptance may be made as stated in subsection (a) or by a writing on the check which indicates that the check is certified. The drawee of a check has no obligation to certify the check, and refusal to certify is not dishonor of the check.

§ 3—410. Acceptance Varying Draft.

(a) If the terms of a drawee's acceptance vary from the terms of the draft as presented, the holder may refuse the acceptance and treat the draft as dishonored. In that case, the drawee may cancel the acceptance.

(b) The terms of a draft are not varied by an acceptance to pay at a particular bank or place in the United States, unless the acceptance states that the draft is to be paid only at that bank or place.

(c) If the holder assents to an acceptance varying the terms of a draft, the obligation of each drawer and indorser that does not expressly assent to the acceptance is discharged.

§ 3—411. Refusal to Pay Cashier's Checks, Teller's Checks, and Certified Checks.

(a) In this section, "obligated bank" means the acceptor of a certified check or the issuer of a cashier's check or teller's check bought from the issuer.

(b) If the obligated bank wrongfully (i) refuses to pay a cashier's check or certified check, (ii) stops payment of a teller's check, or (iii) refuses to pay a dishonored teller's check, the person asserting the right to enforce the check is entitled to compensation for expenses and loss of interest resulting from the nonpayment and may recover consequential damages if the obligated bank refuses to pay after receiving notice of particular circumstances giving rise to the damages.

(c) Expenses or consequential damages under subsection (b) are not recoverable if the refusal of the obligated bank to pay occurs because (i) the bank suspends payments, (ii) the obligated bank asserts a claim or defense of the bank that it has reasonable grounds to believe is available against the person entitled to enforce the instrument, (iii) the obligated bank has a reasonable doubt whether the person demanding payment is the person entitled to enforce the instrument, or (iv) payment is prohibited by law.

§ 3—412. Obligation of Issuer of Note or Cashier's Check.

The issuer of a note or cashier's check or other draft drawn on the drawer is obliged to pay the instrument (i) according to its terms at the time it was issued or, if not issued, at the time it first came into possession of a holder, or (ii) if the issuer signed an incomplete instrument, according to its terms when completed, to the extent stated in Sections 3—115 and 3—407. The obligation is owed to a person entitled to enforce the instrument or to an indorser who paid the instrument under Section 3—415.

§ 3—413. Obligation of Acceptor.

(a) The acceptor of a draft is obliged to pay the draft (i) according to its terms at the time it was accepted, even though the acceptance states that the draft is payable "as originally drawn" or equivalent terms, (ii) if the acceptance varies the terms of the draft, according to the terms of the draft as varied, or (iii) if the acceptance is of a draft that is an incomplete instrument, according to its terms when completed, to the extent stated in Sections 3—115 and 3—407. The obligation is owed to a person entitled to enforce the draft or to the drawer or an indorser who paid the draft under Section 3—414 or 3—415.

(b) If the certification of a check or other acceptance of a draft states the amount certified or accepted, the obligation of the acceptor is that amount. If (i) the certification or acceptance does not state an amount, (ii) the amount of the instrument is subsequently raised, and (iii) the instrument is then negotiated to a holder in due course, the obligation of the acceptor is the amount of the instrument at the time it was taken by the holder in due course.

§ 3—414. Obligation of Drawer.

(a) This section does not apply to cashier's checks or other drafts drawn on the drawer.

(b) If an unaccepted draft is dishonored, the drawer is obliged to pay the draft (i) according to its terms at the time it was issued or, if not issued, at the time it first came into possession of a holder, or (ii) if the drawer signed an incomplete instrument, according to its terms when completed, to the extent stated in Sections 3—115 and 3—407. The obligation is owed to a person entitled to enforce the draft or to an indorser who paid the draft under Section 3—415.

(c) If a draft is accepted by a bank, the drawer is discharged, regardless of when or by whom acceptance was obtained.

(d) If a draft is accepted and the acceptor is not a bank, the obligation of the drawer to pay the draft if the draft is dishonored by the acceptor is the same as the obligation of an indorser under Section 3—415(a) and (c).

(e) If a draft states that it is drawn "without recourse" or otherwise disclaims liability of the drawer to pay the draft, the drawer is not liable under subsection (b) to pay the draft if the draft is not a check. A disclaimer of the liability stated in subsection (b) is not effective if the draft is a check.

(f) If (i) a check is not presented for payment or given to a depositary bank for collection within 30 days after its date, (ii) the drawee suspends payments after expiration of the 30-day period without paying the check, and (iii) because of the suspension of payments, the drawer is deprived of funds maintained with the drawee to cover payment of the check, the drawer to the extent deprived of funds may discharge its obligation to pay the check by assigning to the person entitled to enforce the check the rights of the drawer against the drawee with respect to the funds.

§ 3—415. Obligation of Indorser.

(a) Subject to subsections (b), (c), and (d) and to Section 3—419(d), if an instrument is dishonored, an indorser is obliged to pay the amount due on the instrument (i) according to the terms of the instrument at the time it was indorsed, or (ii) if the indorser indorsed an incomplete instrument, according to its terms when completed, to the extent stated in Sections 3—115 and 3—407. The obligation of the indorser is owed to a person entitled to enforce the instrument or to a subsequent indorser who paid the instrument under this section.

(b) If an indorsement states that it is made "without recourse" or otherwise disclaims liability of the indorser, the indorser is not liable under subsection (a) to pay the instrument.

(c) If notice of dishonor of an instrument is required by Section 3—503 and notice of dishonor complying with that section is not given to an indorser, the liability of the indorser under subsection (a) is discharged.

(d) If a draft is accepted by a bank after an indorsement is made, the liability of the indorser under subsection (a) is discharged.

(e) If an indorser of a check is liable under subsection (a) and the check is not presented for payment, or given to a depositary bank for collection, within 30 days after the day the indorsement was made, the liability of the indorser under subsection (a) is discharged.

§ 3—416. Transfer Warranties.

(a) A person who transfers an instrument for consideration warrants to the transferee and, if the transfer is by indorsement, to any subsequent transferee that:

(1) the warrantor is a person entitled to enforce the instrument;

(2) all signatures on the instrument are authentic and authorized;

(3) the instrument has not been altered;

(4) the instrument is not subject to a defense or claim in recoupment of any party which can be asserted against the warrantor; and

(5) the warrantor has no knowledge of any insolvency proceeding commenced with respect to the maker or acceptor or, in the case of an unaccepted draft, the drawer.

(b) A person to whom the warranties under subsection (a) are made and who took the instrument in good faith may recover from the warrantor as damages for breach of warranty an amount equal to the loss suffered as a result of the breach, but not more than the amount of the instrument plus expenses and loss of interest incurred as a result of the breach.

(c) The warranties stated in subsection (a) cannot be disclaimed with respect to checks. Unless notice of a claim for breach of warranty is given to the warrantor within 30 days after the claimant has reason to know of the breach and the identity of the warrantor, the liability of the warrantor under subsection (b) is discharged to the extent of any loss caused by the delay in giving notice of the claim.

(d) A [cause of action] for breach of warranty under this section accrues when the claimant has reason to know of the breach.

§ 3—417. Presentment Warranties.

(a) If an unaccepted draft is presented to the drawee for payment or acceptance and the drawee pays or accepts the draft, (i) the person obtaining payment or acceptance, at the time of presentment, and (ii) a previous transferor of the draft, at the time of transfer, warrant to the drawee making payment or accepting the draft in good faith that:

(1) the warrantor is, or was, at the time the warrantor transferred the draft, a person entitled to enforce the draft or authorized to obtain payment or acceptance of the draft on behalf of a person entitled to enforce the draft;

(2) the draft has not been altered; and

(3) the warrantor has no knowledge that the signature of the drawer of the draft is unauthorized.

(b) A drawee making payment may recover from any warrantor damages for breach of warranty equal to the amount paid by the drawee less the amount the drawee received or is entitled to receive from the drawer because of the payment. In addition, the drawee is entitled to compensation for expenses and loss of interest resulting from the breach. The right of the drawee to recover damages under this subsection is not affected by any failure of the drawee to exercise ordinary care in making payment. If the drawee accepts the draft, breach of warranty is a defense to the obligation of the acceptor. If the acceptor makes payment with respect to the draft, the acceptor is entitled to recover from any warrantor for breach of warranty the amounts stated in this subsection.

(c) If a drawee asserts a claim for breach of warranty under subsection (a) based on an unauthorized indorsement of the draft or an alteration of the draft, the warrantor may defend by proving that the indorsement is effective under Section 3—404 or 3—405 or the drawer is precluded under Section 3—406 or 4—406 from asserting against the drawee the unauthorized indorsement or alteration.

(d) If (i) a dishonored draft is presented for payment to the drawer or an indorser or (ii) any other instrument is presented for payment to a party obliged to pay the instrument, and (iii) payment is received, the following rules apply:

(1) The person obtaining payment and a prior transferor of the instrument warrant to the person making payment in good faith that the warrantor is, or was, at the time the warrantor transferred the instrument, a person entitled to enforce the instrument or authorized to obtain payment on behalf of a person entitled to enforce the instrument.

(2) The person making payment may recover from any warrantor for breach of warranty an amount equal to the amount paid plus expenses and loss of interest resulting from the breach.

(e) The warranties stated in subsections (a) and (d) cannot be disclaimed with respect to checks. Unless notice of a claim for breach of warranty is given to the warrantor within 30 days after the claimant has reason to know of the breach and the identity of the warrantor, the liability of the warrantor under subsection (b) or (d) is discharged to the extent of any loss caused by the delay in giving notice of the claim.

(f) A [cause of action] for breach of warranty under this section accrues when the claimant has reason to know of the breach.

§ 3—418. Payment or Acceptance by Mistake.

(a) Except as provided in subsection (c), if the drawee of a draft pays or accepts the draft and the drawee acted on the mistaken belief that (i) payment of the draft had not been stopped pursuant to Section 4—403 or (ii) the signature of the drawer of the draft was authorized, the drawee may recover the amount of the draft from the person to whom or for whose benefit payment was made or, in the case of acceptance, may revoke the acceptance. Rights of the drawee under this subsection are not affected by failure of the drawee to exercise ordinary care in paying or accepting the draft.

(b) Except as provided in subsection (c), if an instrument has been paid or accepted by mistake and the case is not covered by subsection (a), the person paying or accepting may, to the extent permitted by the law governing mistake and restitution, (i) recover the payment from the person to whom or for whose benefit payment was made or (ii) in the case of acceptance, may revoke the acceptance.

(c) The remedies provided by subsection (a) or (b) may not be asserted against a person who took the instrument in good faith and for value or who in good faith changed position in reliance on the payment or acceptance. This subsection does not limit remedies provided by Section 3—417 or 4—407.

(d) Notwithstanding Section 4—215, if an instrument is paid or accepted by mistake and the payor or acceptor recovers payment or revokes acceptance under subsection (a) or (b), the instrument is deemed not to have been paid or accepted and is treated as dishonored, and the person from whom payment is recovered has rights as a person entitled to enforce the dishonored instrument.

§ 3—419. Instruments Signed for Accommodation.

(a) If an instrument is issued for value given for the benefit of a party to the instrument ("accommodated party") and another party to the instrument ("accommodation party") signs the instrument for the purpose of incurring liability on the instrument without being a direct beneficiary of the value given for the instrument, the instrument is signed by the accommodation party "for accommodation."

(b) An accommodation party may sign the instrument as maker, drawer, acceptor, or indorser and, subject to subsection (d), is obliged to pay the instrument in the capacity in which the accommodation party signs. The obligation of an accommodation party may be enforced notwithstanding any statute of frauds and whether or not the accommodation party receives consideration for the accommodation.

(c) A person signing an instrument is presumed to be an accommodation party and there is notice that the instrument is signed for accommodation if the signature is an anomalous indorsement or is accompanied by words indicating that the signer is acting as surety or guarantor with respect to the obligation of another party to the instrument. Except as provided in Section 3—605, the obligation of an accommodation party to pay the instrument is not affected by the fact that the person enforcing the obligation had notice when the instrument was taken by that person that the accommodation party signed the instrument for accommodation.

(d) If the signature of a party to an instrument is accompanied by words indicating unambiguously that the party is guaranteeing collection rather than payment of the obligation of another party to the instrument, the signer is obliged to pay the amount due on the instrument to a person entitled to enforce the instrument only if (i) execution of judgment against the other party has been returned unsatisfied, (ii) the other party is insolvent or in an insolvency proceeding, (iii) the other party cannot be served with process, or (iv) it is otherwise apparent that payment cannot be obtained from the other party.

(e) An accommodation party who pays the instrument is entitled to reimbursement from the accommodated party and is entitled to enforce the instrument against the accommodated party. An accommodated party who pays the instrument has no right of recourse against, and is not entitled to contribution from, an accommodation party.

§ 3—420. Conversion of Instrument.

(a) The law applicable to conversion of personal property applies to instruments. An instrument is also converted if it is taken by transfer, other than a negotiation, from a person not entitled to enforce the instrument or a bank makes or obtains payment with respect to the instrument for a person not entitled to enforce the instrument or receive payment. An action for conversion of an instrument may not be brought by (i) the issuer or acceptor of the instrument or (ii) a payee or indorsee who did not receive delivery of the instrument either directly or through delivery to an agent or a co-payee.

(b) In an action under subsection (a), the measure of liability is presumed to be the amount payable on the instrument, but recovery may not exceed the amount of the plaintiff's interest in the instrument.

(c) A representative, other than a depositary bank, who has in good faith dealt with an instrument or its proceeds on behalf of one who was not the person entitled to enforce the instrument is not liable in conversion to that person beyond the amount of any proceeds that it has not paid out.

Part 5 Dishonor

§ 3—501. Presentment.

(a) "Presentment" means a demand made by or on behalf of a person entitled to enforce an instrument (i) to pay the instrument made to the drawee or a party obliged to pay the instrument or, in the case of a note or accepted draft payable at a bank, to the bank, or (ii) to accept a draft made to the drawee.

(b) The following rules are subject to Article 4, agreement of the parties, and clearing-house rules and the like:

(1) Presentment may be made at the place of payment of the instrument and must be made at the place of payment if the instrument is payable at a bank in the United States; may be made by any commercially reasonable means, including an oral, written, or electronic communication; is effective when the demand for payment or acceptance is received by the person to whom presentment is made; and is effective if made to any one of two or more makers, acceptors, drawees, or other payors.

(2) Upon demand of the person to whom presentment is made, the person making presentment must (i) exhibit the instrument, (ii) give reasonable identification and, if presentment is made on behalf of another person, reasonable evidence of authority to do so, and (. . .) sign a receipt on the instrument for any payment made or surrender the instrument if full payment is made.

(3) Without dishonoring the instrument, the party to whom presentment is made may (i) return the instrument for lack of a necessary indorsement, or (ii) refuse payment or acceptance for failure of the presentment to comply with the terms of the instrument, an agreement of the parties, or other applicable law or rule.

(4) The party to whom presentment is made may treat presentment as occurring on the next business day after the day of presentment if the party to whom presentment is made has established a cut-off hour not earlier than 2 P.M. for the receipt and processing of instruments presented for pay-

ment or acceptance and presentment is made after the cut-off hour.

§ 3—502. Dishonor.

(a) Dishonor of a note is governed by the following rules:

(1) If the note is payable on demand, the note is dishonored if presentment is duly made to the maker and the note is not paid on the day of presentment.

(2) If the note is not payable on demand and is payable at or through a bank or the terms of the note require presentment, the note is dishonored if presentment is duly made and the note is not paid on the day it becomes payable or the day of presentment, whichever is later.

(3) If the note is not payable on demand and paragraph (2) does not apply, the note is dishonored if it is not paid on the day it becomes payable.

(b) Dishonor of an unaccepted draft other than a documentary draft is governed by the following rules:

(1) If a check is duly presented for payment to the payor bank otherwise than for immediate payment over the counter, the check is dishonored if the payor bank makes timely return of the check or sends timely notice of dishonor or nonpayment under Section 4—301 or 4—302, or becomes accountable for the amount of the check under Section 4—302.

(2) If a draft is payable on demand and paragraph (1) does not apply, the draft is dishonored if presentment for payment is duly made to the drawee and the draft is not paid on the day of presentment.

(3) If a draft is payable on a date stated in the draft, the draft is dishonored if (i) presentment for payment is duly made to the drawee and payment is not made on the day the draft becomes payable or the day of presentment, whichever is later, or (ii) presentment for acceptance is duly made before the day the draft becomes payable and the draft is not accepted on the day of presentment.

(4) If a draft is payable on elapse of a period of time after sight or acceptance, the draft is dishonored if presentment for acceptance is duly made and the draft is not accepted on the day of presentment.

(c) Dishonor of an unaccepted documentary draft occurs according to the rules stated in subsection (b)(2), (3), and (4), except that payment or acceptance may be delayed without dishonor until no later than the close of the third business day of the drawee following the day on which payment or acceptance is required by those paragraphs.

(d) Dishonor of an accepted draft is governed by the following rules:

(1) If the draft is payable on demand, the draft is dishonored if presentment for payment is duly made to the acceptor and the draft is not paid on the day of presentment.

(2) If the draft is not payable on demand, the draft is dishonored if presentment for payment is duly made to the acceptor and payment is not made on the day it becomes payable or the day of presentment, whichever is later.

(e) In any case in which presentment is otherwise required for dishonor under this section and presentment is excused under Section 3—504, dishonor occurs without presentment if the instrument is not duly accepted or paid.

(f) If a draft is dishonored because timely acceptance of the draft was not made and the person entitled to demand acceptance consents to a late acceptance, from the time of acceptance the draft is treated as never having been dishonored.

§ 3—503. Notice of Dishonor.

(a) The obligation of an indorser stated in Section 3—415(a) and the obligation of a drawer stated in Section 3—414(d) may not be enforced unless (i) the indorser or drawer is given notice of dishonor of the instrument complying with this section or (ii) notice of dishonor is excused under Section 3—504(b).

(b) Notice of dishonor may be given by any person; may be given by any commercially reasonable means, including an oral, written, or electronic communication; and is sufficient if it reasonably identifies the instrument and indicates that the instrument has been dishonored or has not been paid or accepted. Return of an instrument given to a bank for collection is sufficient notice of dishonor.

(c) Subject to Section 3—504(c), with respect to an instrument taken for collection by a collecting bank, notice of dishonor must be given (i) by the bank before midnight of the next banking day following the banking day on which the bank receives notice of dishonor of the instrument, or (ii) by any other person within 30 days following the day on which the person receives notice of dishonor. With respect to any other instrument, notice of dishonor must be given within 30 days following the day on which dishonor occurs.

§ 3—504. Excused Presentment and Notice of Dishonor.

(a) Presentment for payment or acceptance of an instrument is excused if (i) the person entitled to present the instrument cannot with reasonable diligence make presentment, (ii) the maker or acceptor has repudiated an obligation to pay the instrument or is dead or in insolvency proceedings, (iii) by the terms of the instrument presentment is not necessary to enforce the obligation of indorsers or the drawer, (iv) the drawer or indorser whose obligation is being enforced has waived presentment or otherwise has no reason to expect or right to require that the instrument be paid or accepted, or (v) the drawer instructed the drawee not to pay or accept the draft or the drawee was not obligated to the drawer to pay the draft.

(b) Notice of dishonor is excused if (i) by the terms of the instrument notice of dishonor is not necessary to enforce the obligation of a party to pay the instrument, or (ii) the party whose obligation is being enforced waived notice of dishonor. A waiver of presentment is also a waiver of notice of dishonor.

(c) Delay in giving notice of dishonor is excused if the delay was caused by circumstances beyond the control of the person giving the notice and the person giving the notice exercised reasonable diligence after the cause of the delay ceased to operate.

§ 3—505. Evidence of Dishonor.

(a) The following are admissible as evidence and create a presumption of dishonor and of any notice of dishonor stated:

(1) a document regular in form as provided in subsection (b) which purports to be a protest;

(2) a purported stamp or writing of the drawee, payor bank, or presenting bank on or accompanying the instrument stating that acceptance or payment has been refused unless reasons for the refusal are stated and the reasons are not consistent with dishonor;

(3) a book or record of the drawee, payor bank, or collecting bank, kept in the usual course of business which shows dishonor, even if there is no evidence of who made the entry.

(b) A protest is a certificate of dishonor made by a United States consul or vice consul, or a notary public or other person authorized to administer oaths by the law of the place where dishonor occurs. It may be made upon information satisfactory to that person. The protest must identify the instrument and certify either that presentment has been made or, if not made, the reason why it was not made, and that the instrument has been dishonored by nonacceptance or nonpayment. The protest may also certify that notice of dishonor has been given to some or all parties.

Part 6 Discharge and Payment

§ 3—601. Discharge and Effect of Discharge.

(a) The obligation of a party to pay the instrument is discharged as stated in this Article or by an act or agreement with the party which would discharge an obligation to pay money under a simple contract.

(b) Discharge of the obligation of a party is not effective against a person acquiring rights of a holder in due course of the instrument without notice of the discharge.

§ 3—602. Payment.

(a) Subject to subsection (b), an instrument is paid to the extent payment is made (i) by or on behalf of a party obliged to pay the instrument, and (ii) to a person entitled to enforce the instrument. To the extent of the payment, the obligation of the party obliged to pay the instrument is discharged even though payment is made with knowledge of a claim to the instrument under Section 3—306 by another person.

(b) The obligation of a party to pay the instrument is not discharged under subsection (a) if:

(1) a claim to the instrument under Section 3—306 is enforceable against the party receiving payment and (i) payment is made with knowledge by the payor that payment is prohibited by injunction or similar process of a court of competent jurisdiction, or (ii) in the case of an instrument other than a cashier's check, teller's check, or certified check, the party making payment accepted, from the person having a claim to the instrument, indemnity against loss resulting from refusal to pay the person entitled to enforce the instrument; or

(2) the person making payment knows that the instrument is a stolen instrument and pays a person it knows is in wrongful possession of the instrument.

§ 3—603. Tender of Payment.

(a) If tender of payment of an obligation to pay an instrument is made to a person entitled to enforce the instrument, the effect of tender is governed by principles of law applicable to tender of payment under a simple contract.

(b) If tender of payment of an obligation to pay an instrument is made to a person entitled to enforce the instrument and the tender is refused, there is discharge, to the extent of the amount of the tender, of the obligation of an indorser or accommodation party having a right of recourse with respect to the obligation to which the tender relates.

(c) If tender of payment of an amount due on an instrument is made to a person entitled to enforce the instrument, the obligation of the obligor to pay interest after the due date on the amount tendered is discharged. If presentment is required with respect to an instrument and the obligor is able and ready to pay on the due date at every place of payment stated in the instrument, the obligor is deemed to have made tender of payment on the due date to the person entitled to enforce the instrument.

§ 3—604. Discharge by Cancellation or Renunciation.

(a) A person entitled to enforce an instrument, with or without consideration, may discharge the obligation of a party to pay the instrument (i) by an intentional voluntary act, such as surrender of the instrument to the party, destruction, mutilation, or cancellation of the instrument, cancellation or striking out of the party's signature, or the addition of words to the instrument indicating discharge, or (ii) by agreeing not to sue or otherwise renouncing rights against the party by a signed writing.

(b) Cancellation or striking out of an indorsement pursuant to subsection (a) does not affect the status and rights of a party derived from the indorsement.

§ 3—605. Discharge of Indorsers and Accommodation Parties.

(a) In this section, the term "indorser" includes a drawer having the obligation described in Section 3—414(d).

(b) Discharge, under Section 3—604, of the obligation of a party to pay an instrument does not discharge the obligation of an indorser or accommodation party having a right of recourse against the discharged party.

(c) If a person entitled to enforce an instrument agrees, with or without consideration, to an extension of the due date of the obligation of a party to pay the instrument, the extension discharges an indorser or accommodation party having a right of recourse against the party whose obligation is extended to the extent the indorser or accommodation party proves that the extension caused loss to the indorser or accommodation party with respect to the right of recourse.

(d) If a person entitled to enforce an instrument agrees, with or without consideration, to a material modification of the obligation of a party other than an extension of the due date, the modification discharges the obligation of an indorser or accommodation party having a right of recourse against the person whose obligation is modified to the extent the modification causes loss to the indorser or accommodation party with respect to the right of recourse. The loss suffered by the indorser or accommodation party as a result of the modification is equal to the amount of the right of recourse unless the person enforcing the instrument proves that no loss was caused by the modification or that the loss caused by the modification was an amount less than the amount of the right of recourse.

(e) If the obligation of a party to pay an instrument is secured by an interest in collateral and a person entitled to enforce the instrument impairs the value of the interest in collateral, the obligation of an indorser or accommodation party having a right of recourse against the obligor is discharged to the extent of the impairment. The value of an interest in collateral is impaired to the extent (i) the value of the interest is reduced to an amount less than the amount of the right of recourse of the party asserting discharge, or (ii) the reduction in value of the interest causes an increase in the amount by which the amount of the right of recourse exceeds the value of the interest. The burden of proving impairment is on the party asserting discharge.

(f) If the obligation of a party is secured by an interest in collateral not provided by an accommodation party and a person entitled to enforce the instrument impairs the value of the interest in collateral, the obligation of any party who is jointly and severally liable with respect to the secured obligation is discharged to the extent the impairment causes the party asserting discharge to pay more than that party would have been obliged to pay, taking into account rights of contribution, if impairment had not occurred. If the party asserting discharge is an accommodation party not entitled to discharge under subsection (e), the party is deemed to have a right to contribution based on joint and several liability rather than a right to reimbursement. The burden of proving impairment is on the party asserting discharge.

(g) Under subsection (e) or (f), impairing value of an interest in collateral includes (i) failure to obtain or maintain perfection or recordation of the interest in collateral, (ii) release of collateral without substitution of collateral of equal value, (iii) failure to perform a duty to preserve the value of collateral owed, under Article 9 or other law, to a debtor or surety or other person secondarily liable, or (iv) failure to comply with applicable law in disposing of collateral.

(h) An accommodation party is not discharged under subsection (c), (d), or (e) unless the person entitled to enforce the instrument knows of the accommodation or has notice under Section 3—419(c) that the instrument was signed for accommodation.

(i) A party is not discharged under this section if (i) the party asserting discharge consents to the event or conduct that is the basis of the discharge, or (ii) the instrument or a separate agreement of the party provides for waiver of discharge under this section either specifically or by general language indicating that parties waive defenses based on suretyship or impairment of collateral.

ADDENDUM TO REVISED ARTICLE 3

Notes to Legislative Counsel

1. If revised Article 3 is adopted in your state, the reference in Section 2—511 to Section 3—802 should be changed to Section 3—310.

2. If revised Article 3 is adopted in your state and the Uniform Fiduciaries Act is also in effect in your state, you may want to consider amending Uniform Fiduciaries Act § 9 to conform to Section 3—307(b)(2)(iii) and (4)(iii). See Official Comment 3 to Section 3—307.

Revised Article 4
BANK DEPOSITS AND COLLECTIONS

Part 1 General Provisions and Definitions

§ 4—101. Short Title.

This Article may be cited as Uniform Commercial Code—Bank Deposits and Collections.

§ 4—102. Applicability.

(a) To the extent that items within this Article are also within Articles 3 and 8, they are subject to those Articles. If there is conflict, this Article governs Article 3, but Article 8 governs this Article.

(b) The liability of a bank for action or non-action with respect to an item handled by it for purposes of presentment, payment, or collection is governed by the law of the place where the bank is located. In the case of action or non-action by or at a branch or separate office of a bank, its liability is governed by the law of the place where the branch or separate office is located.

§ 4—103. Variation by Agreement; Measure of Damages; Action Constituting Ordinary Care.

(a) The effect of the provisions of this Article may be varied by agreement, but the parties to the agreement cannot disclaim a bank's responsibility for its lack of good faith or failure to exercise ordinary care or limit the measure of damages for the lack or failure. However, the parties may determine by agreement the standards by which the bank's responsibility is to be measured if those standards are not manifestly unreasonable.

(b) Federal Reserve regulations and operating circulars, clearing-house rules, and the like have the effect of agreements under subsection (a), whether or not specifically assented to by all parties interested in items handled.

(c) Action or non-action approved by this Article or pursuant to Federal Reserve regulations or operating circulars is the exercise of ordinary care and, in the absence of special instructions, action or non-action consistent with clearing-house rules and the like or with a general banking usage not disapproved by this Article, is prima facie the exercise of ordinary care.

(d) The specification or approval of certain procedures by this Article is not disapproval of other procedures that may be reasonable under the circumstances.

(e) The measure of damages for failure to exercise ordinary care in handling an item is the amount of the item reduced by an amount that could not have been realized by the exercise of ordinary care. If there is also bad faith it includes any other damages the party suffered as a proximate consequence.

§ 4—104. Definitions and Index of Definitions.

(a) In this Article, unless the context otherwise requires:

(1) "Account" means any deposit or credit account with a bank, including a demand, time, savings, passbook, share draft, or like account, other than an account evidenced by a certificate of deposit;

(2) "Afternoon" means the period of a day between noon and midnight;

(3) "Banking day" means the part of a day on which a bank is open to the public for carrying on substantially all of its banking functions;

(4) "Clearing house" means an association of banks or other payors regularly clearing items;

(5) "Customer" means a person having an account with a bank or for whom a bank has agreed to collect items, including a bank that maintains an account at another bank;

(6) "Documentary draft" means a draft to be presented for acceptance or payment if specified documents, certificated securities (Section 8—102) or instructions for uncertificated securities (Section 8—102), or other certificates, statements, or the like are to be received by the drawee or other payor before acceptance or payment of the draft;

(7) "Draft" means a draft as defined in Section 3—104 or an item, other than an instrument, that is an order;

(8) "Drawee" means a person ordered in a draft to make payment;

(9) "Item" means an instrument or a promise or order to pay money handled by a bank for collection or payment. The term does not include a payment order governed by Article 4A or a credit or debit card slip;

(10) "Midnight deadline" with respect to a bank is midnight on its next banking day following the banking day on which it receives the relevant item or notice or from which the time for taking action commences to run, whichever is later;

(11) "Settle" means to pay in cash, by clearing-house settlement, in a charge or credit or by remittance, or otherwise as agreed. A settlement may be either provisional or final;

(12) "Suspends payments" with respect to a bank means that it has been closed by order of the supervisory authorities, that a public officer has been appointed to take it over, or that it ceases or refuses to make payments in the ordinary course of business.

(b);(c) [Other definitions' section references deleted.]

(d) In addition, Article 1 contains general definitions and principles of construction and interpretation applicable throughout this Article.

§ 4—105. "Bank"; "Depositary Bank"; "Payor Bank"; "Intermediary Bank"; "Collecting Bank"; "Presenting Bank".

In this Article:

(1) "Bank" means a person engaged in the business of banking, including a savings bank, savings and loan association, credit union, or trust company;

(2) "Depositary bank" means the first bank to take an item even though it is also the payor bank, unless the item is presented for immediate payment over the counter;

(3) "Payor bank" means a bank that is the drawee of a draft;

(4) "Intermediary bank" means a bank to which an item is transferred in course of collection except the depositary or payor bank;

(5) "Collecting bank" means a bank handling an item for collection except the payor bank;

(6) "Presenting bank" means a bank presenting an item except a payor bank.

§ 4—106. Payable Through or Payable at Bank: Collecting Bank.

(a) If an item states that it is "payable through" a bank identified in the item, (i) the item designates the bank as a collecting bank and does not by itself authorize the bank to pay the item, and (ii) the item may be presented for payment only by or through the bank.

Alternative A

(b) If an item states that it is "payable at" a bank identified in the item, the item is equivalent to a draft drawn on the bank.

Alternative B

(b) If an item states that it is "payable at" a bank identified in the item, (i) the item designates the bank as a collecting bank and does not by itself authorize the bank to pay the item, and (ii) the item may be presented for payment only by or through the bank.

(c) If a draft names a nonbank drawee and it is unclear whether a bank named in the draft is a co-drawee or a collecting bank, the bank is a collecting bank.

§ 4—107. Separate Office of Bank.

A branch or separate office of a bank is a separate bank for the purpose of computing the time within which and determining the place at or to which action may be taken or notices or orders shall be given under this Article and under Article 3.

§ 4—108. Time of Receipt of Items.

(a) For the purpose of allowing time to process items, prove balances, and make the necessary entries on its books to determine its position for the day, a bank may fix an afternoon hour of 2 P.M. or later as a cutoff hour for the handling of money and items and the making of entries on its books.

(b) An item or deposit of money received on any day after a cutoff hour so fixed or after the close of the banking day may be treated as being received at the opening of the next banking day.

§ 4—109. Delays.

(a) Unless otherwise instructed, a collecting bank in a good faith effort to secure payment of a specific item drawn on a payor other than a bank, and with or without the approval of any person involved, may waive, modify, or extend time limits imposed or permitted by this [act] for a period not exceeding two additional banking days without discharge of drawers or indorsers or liability to its transferor or a prior party.

(b) Delay by a collecting bank or payor bank beyond time limits prescribed or permitted by this [act] or by instructions is excused if (i) the delay is caused by interruption of communication or computer facilities, suspension of payments by another bank, war, emergency conditions, failure of equipment, or other circumstances beyond the control of the bank, and (ii) the bank exercises such diligence as the circumstances require.

§ 4—110. Electronic Presentment.

(a) "Agreement for electronic presentment" means an agreement, clearing-house rule, or Federal Reserve regulation or operating circular, providing that presentment of an item may be made by transmission of an image of an item or information describing the item ("presentment notice") rather than delivery of the item itself. The agreement may provide for procedures governing retention, presentment, payment, dishonor, and other matters concerning items subject to the agreement.

(b) Presentment of an item pursuant to an agreement for presentment is made when the presentment notice is received.

(c) If presentment is made by presentment notice, a reference to "item" or "check" in this Article means the presentment notice unless the context otherwise indicates.

§ 4—111. Statute of Limitations.

An action to enforce an obligation, duty, or right arising under this Article must be commenced within three years after the [cause of action] accrues.

Part 2 Collection of Items: Depositary and Collecting Banks

§ 4—201. Status of Collecting Bank As Agent and Provisional Status of Credits; Applicability of Article; Item Indorsed "Pay Any Bank".

(a) Unless a contrary intent clearly appears and before the time that a settlement given by a collecting bank for an item is or becomes final, the bank, with respect to an item, is an agent or sub-agent of the owner of the item and any settlement given for the item is provisional. This provision applies regardless of the form of indorsement or lack of indorsement and even though credit given for the item is subject to immediate withdrawal as of right or is in fact withdrawn; but the continuance of ownership of an item by its owner and any rights of the owner to proceeds of the item are subject to rights of a collecting bank, such as those resulting from outstanding advances on the item and rights of recoupment or setoff. If an item is handled by banks for purposes of presentment, payment, collection, or return, the relevant provisions of this Article apply even though action of the parties clearly establishes that a particular bank has purchased the item and is the owner of it.

(b) After an item has been indorsed with the words "pay any bank" or the like, only a bank may acquire the rights of a holder until the item has been:

(1) returned to the customer initiating collection; or

(2) specially indorsed by a bank to a person who is not a bank.

§ 4—202. Responsibility for Collection or Return; When Action Timely.

(a) A collecting bank must exercise ordinary care in:

(1) presenting an item or sending it for presentment;

(2) sending notice of dishonor or nonpayment or returning an item other than a documentary draft to the bank's transferor after learning that the item has not been paid or accepted, as the case may be;

(3) settling for an item when the bank receives final settlement; and

(4) notifying its transferor of any loss or delay in transit within a reasonable time after discovery thereof.

(b) A collecting bank exercises ordinary care under subsection (a) by taking proper action before its midnight deadline following receipt of an item, notice, or settlement. Taking proper action within a reasonably longer time may constitute the exercise of ordinary care, but the bank has the burden of establishing timeliness.

(c) Subject to subsection (a)(1), a bank is not liable for the insolvency, neglect, misconduct, mistake, or default of another bank or person or for loss or destruction of an item in the possession of others or in transit.

§ 4—203. Effect of Instructions.

Subject to Article 3 concerning conversion of instruments (Section 3—420) and restrictive indorsements (Section 3—206), only a collecting bank's transferor can give instructions that affect the bank or constitute notice to it, and a collecting bank is not liable to prior parties for any action taken pursuant to the instructions or in accordance with any agreement with its transferor.

§ 4—204. Methods of Sending and Presenting; Sending Directly to Payor Bank.

(a) A collecting bank shall send items by a reasonably prompt method, taking into consideration relevant instructions, the nature of the item, the number of those items on hand, the cost of collection involved, and the method generally used by it or others to present those items.

(b) A collecting bank may send:

(1) an item directly to the payor bank;

(2) an item to a nonbank payor if authorized by its transferor; and

(3) an item other than documentary drafts to a nonbank payor, if authorized by Federal Reserve regulation or operating circular, clearing-house rule, or the like.

(c) Presentment may be made by a presenting bank at a place where the payor bank or other payor has requested that presentment be made.

§ 4—205. Depositary Bank Holder of Unindorsed Item.

If a customer delivers an item to a depositary bank for collection:

(1) the depositary bank becomes a holder of the item at the time it receives the item for collection if the customer at the time of delivery was a holder of the item, whether or not the customer indorses the item, and, if the bank satisfies the other requirements of Section 3—302, it is a holder in due course; and

(2) the depositary bank warrants to collecting banks, the payor bank or other payor, and the drawer that the amount of the item was paid to the customer or deposited to the customer's account.

§ 4—206. Transfer Between Banks.

Any agreed method that identifies the transferor bank is sufficient for the item's further transfer to another bank.

§ 4—207. Transfer Warranties.

(a) A customer or collecting bank that transfers an item and receives a settlement or other consideration warrants to the transferee and to any subsequent collecting bank that:

(1) the warrantor is a person entitled to enforce the item;

(2) all signatures on the item are authentic and authorized;

(3) the item has not been altered;

(4) the item is not subject to a defense or claim in recoupment (Section 3—305(a)) of any party that can be asserted against the warrantor; and

(5) the warrantor has no knowledge of any insolvency proceeding commenced with respect to the maker or acceptor or, in the case of an unaccepted draft, the drawer.

(b) If an item is dishonored, a customer or collecting bank transferring the item and receiving settlement or other consideration is obliged to pay the amount due on the item (i) according to the terms of the item at the time it was transferred, or (ii) if the transfer was of an incomplete item, according to its terms when completed as stated in Sections 3—115 and 3—407. The obligation of a transferor is owed to the transferee and to any subsequent collecting bank that takes the item in good faith. A transferor cannot disclaim its obligation under this subsection by an indorsement stating that it is made "without recourse" or otherwise disclaiming liability.

(c) A person to whom the warranties under subsection (a) are made and who took the item in good faith may recover from the warrantor as damages for breach of warranty an amount equal to the loss suffered as a result of the breach, but not more than the amount of the item plus expenses and loss of interest incurred as a result of the breach.

(d) The warranties stated in subsection (a) cannot be disclaimed with respect to checks. Unless notice of a claim for breach of warranty is given to the warrantor within 30 days after the claimant has reason to know of the breach and the identity of the warrantor, the warrantor is discharged to the extent of any loss caused by the delay in giving notice of the claim.

(e) A cause of action for breach of warranty under this section accrues when the claimant has reason to know of the breach.

§ 4—208. Presentment Warranties.

(a) If an unaccepted draft is presented to the drawee for payment or acceptance and the drawee pays or accepts the draft, (i) the person obtaining payment or acceptance, at the time of presentment, and (ii) a previous transferor of the draft, at the time of transfer, warrant to the drawee that pays or accepts the draft in good faith that:

(1) the warrantor is, or was, at the time the warrantor transferred the draft, a person entitled to enforce the draft or authorized to obtain payment or acceptance of the draft on behalf of a person entitled to enforce the draft;

(2) the draft has not been altered; and

(3) the warrantor has no knowledge that the signature of the purported drawer of the draft is unauthorized.

(b) A drawee making payment may recover from a warrantor damages for breach of warranty equal to the amount paid by the drawee less the amount the drawee received or is entitled to receive from the drawer because of the payment. In addition, the drawee is entitled to compensation for expenses and loss of interest resulting from the breach. The right of the drawee to recover damages under this subsection is not affected by any failure of the drawee to exercise ordinary care in making payment. If the drawee accepts the draft (i) breach of warranty is a defense to the obligation of the acceptor, and (ii) if the acceptor makes payment with respect to the draft, the acceptor is entitled to recover from a warrantor for breach of warranty the amounts stated in this subsection.

(c) If a drawee asserts a claim for breach of warranty under subsection (a) based on an unauthorized indorsement of the draft or an alteration of the draft, the warrantor may defend by proving that the indorsement is effective under Section 3—404 or 3—405 or the drawer is precluded under Section 3—406 or 4—406 from asserting against the drawee the unauthorized indorsement or alteration.

(d) If (i) a dishonored draft is presented for payment to the drawer or an indorser or (ii) any other item is presented for payment to a party obliged to pay the item, and the item is paid, the person obtaining payment and a prior transferor of the item warrant to the person making payment in good faith that the warrantor is, or was, at the time the warrantor transferred the item, a person entitled to enforce the item or authorized to obtain payment on behalf of a person entitled to enforce the item. The person making payment may recover from any warrantor for breach of warranty an amount equal to the amount paid plus expenses and loss of interest resulting from the breach.

(e) The warranties stated in subsections (a) and (d) cannot be disclaimed with respect to checks. Unless notice of a claim for breach of warranty is given to the warrantor within 30 days after the claimant has reason to know of the breach and the identity of the warrantor, the warrantor is discharged to the extent of any loss caused by the delay in giving notice of the claim.

(f) A cause of action for breach of warranty under this section accrues when the claimant has reason to know of the breach.

§ 4—209. Encoding and Retention Warranties.

(a) A person who encodes information on or with respect to an item after issue warrants to any subsequent collecting bank and to the payor bank or other payor that the information is correctly encoded. If the customer of a depositary bank encodes, that bank also makes the warranty.

(b) A person who undertakes to retain an item pursuant to an agreement for electronic presentment warrants to any subsequent collecting bank and to the payor bank or other payor that retention and presentment of the item comply with the agreement. If a customer of a depositary bank undertakes to retain an item, that bank also makes this warranty.

(c) A person to whom warranties are made under this section and who took the item in good faith may recover from the warrantor as damages for breach of warranty an amount equal to the loss suffered as a result of the breach, plus expenses and loss of interest incurred as a result of the breach.

§ 4—210. Security Interest of Collecting Bank in Items, Accompanying Documents and Proceeds.

(a) A collecting bank has a security interest in an item and any accompanying documents or the proceeds of either:

(1) in case of an item deposited in an account, to the extent to which credit given for the item has been withdrawn or applied;

(2) in case of an item for which it has given credit available for withdrawal as of right, to the extent of the credit given, whether or not the credit is drawn upon or there is a right of charge-back; or

(3) if it makes an advance on or against the item.

(b) If credit given for several items received at one time or pursuant to a single agreement is withdrawn or applied in part, the security interest remains upon all the items, any accompanying documents or the proceeds of either. For the purpose of this section, credits first given are first withdrawn.

(c) Receipt by a collecting bank of a final settlement for an item is a realization on its security interest in the item, accompanying documents, and proceeds. So long as the bank does not receive final settlement for the item or give up possession of the item or accompanying documents for purposes other than collection, the security interest continues to that extent and is subject to Article 9, but:

(1) no security agreement is necessary to make the security interest enforceable (Section 9—203(1)(a));

(2) no filing is required to perfect the security interest; and

(3) the security interest has priority over conflicting perfected security interests in the item, accompanying documents, or proceeds.

§ 4—211. When Bank Gives Value for Purposes of Holder in Due Course.

For purposes of determining its status as a holder in due course, a bank has given value to the extent it has a security interest in an item, if the bank otherwise complies with the requirements of Section 3—302 on what constitutes a holder in due course.

§ 4—212. Presentment by Notice of Item Not Payable by, Through, or at Bank; Liability of Drawer or Indorser.

(a) Unless otherwise instructed, a collecting bank may present an item not payable by, through, or at a bank by sending to the party to accept or pay a written notice that the bank holds the item for acceptance or payment. The notice must be sent in time to be received on or before the day when presentment is due and the bank must meet any requirement of the party to accept or pay under Section 3—501 by the close of the bank's next banking day after it knows of the requirement.

(b) If presentment is made by notice and payment, acceptance, or request for compliance with a requirement under Section 3—501 is not received by the close of business on the day after maturity or, in the case of demand items, by the close of business on the third banking day after notice was sent, the presenting bank may treat the item as dishonored and charge any drawer or indorser by sending it notice of the facts.

§ 4—213. Medium and Time of Settlement by Bank.

(a) With respect to settlement by a bank, the medium and time of settlement may be prescribed by Federal Reserve regulations or circulars, clearing-house rules, and the like, or agreement. In the absence of such prescription:

(1) the medium of settlement is cash or credit to an account in a Federal Reserve bank of or specified by the person to receive settlement; and

(2) the time of settlement is:

(i) with respect to tender of settlement by cash, a cashier's check, or teller's check, when the cash or check is sent or delivered;

(ii) with respect to tender of settlement by credit in an account in a Federal Reserve Bank, when the credit is made;

(iii) with respect to tender of settlement by a credit or debit to an account in a bank, when the credit or debit is made or, in the case of tender of settlement by authority to charge an account, when the authority is sent or delivered; or

(iv) with respect to tender of settlement by a funds transfer, when payment is made pursuant to Section 4A—406(a) to the person receiving settlement.

(b) If the tender of settlement is not by a medium authorized by subsection (a) or the time of settlement is not fixed by subsection (a), no settlement occurs until the tender of settlement is accepted by the person receiving settlement.

(c) If settlement for an item is made by cashier's check or teller's check and the person receiving settlement, before its midnight deadline:

(1) presents or forwards the check for collection, settlement is final when the check is finally paid; or

(2) fails to present or forward the check for collection, settlement is final at the midnight deadline of the person receiving settlement.

(d) If settlement for an item is made by giving authority to charge the account of the bank giving settlement in the bank receiving settlement, settlement is final when the charge is made by the bank receiving settlement if there are funds available in the account for the amount of the item.

§ 4—214. Right of Charge-Back or Refund; Liability of Collecting Bank: Return of Item.

(a) If a collecting bank has made provisional settlement with its customer for an item and fails by reason of dishonor, suspension of payments by a bank, or otherwise to receive settlement for the item which is or becomes final, the bank may revoke the settlement given by it, charge back the amount of any credit given for the item to its customer's account, or obtain refund from its customer, whether or not it is able to return the item, if by its midnight deadline or within a longer reasonable time after it learns the facts it returns the item or sends notification of the facts. If the return or notice is delayed beyond the bank's midnight deadline or a longer reasonable time after it learns the facts, the bank may revoke the settlement, charge back the credit, or obtain refund from its customer, but it is liable for any loss resulting from the delay. These rights to revoke, charge back, and obtain refund terminate if and when a settlement for the item received by the bank is or becomes final.

(b) A collecting bank returns an item when it is sent or delivered to the bank's customer or transferor or pursuant to its instructions.

(c) A depositary bank that is also the payor may charge back the amount of an item to its customer's account or obtain refund in accordance with the section governing return of an item received by a payor bank for credit on its books (Section 4—301).

(d) The right to charge back is not affected by:

(1) previous use of a credit given for the item; or

(2) failure by any bank to exercise ordinary care with respect to the item, but a bank so failing remains liable.

(e) A failure to charge back or claim refund does not affect other rights of the bank against the customer or any other party.

(f) If credit is given in dollars as the equivalent of the value of an item payable in foreign money, the dollar amount of any charge-back or refund must be calculated on the basis of the bank-offered spot rate for the foreign money prevailing on the day when the person entitled to the charge-back or refund learns that it will not receive payment in ordinary course.

§ 4—215. Final Payment of Item by Payor Bank; When Provisional Debits and Credits Become Final; When Certain Credits Become Available for Withdrawal.

(a) An item is finally paid by a payor bank when the bank has first done any of the following:

(1) paid the item in cash;

(2) settled for the item without having a right to revoke the settlement under statute, clearing-house rule, or agreement; or

(3) made a provisional settlement for the item and failed to revoke the settlement in the time and manner permitted by statute, clearing-house rule, or agreement.

(b) If provisional settlement for an item does not become final, the item is not finally paid.

(c) If provisional settlement for an item between the presenting and payor banks is made through a clearing house or by debits or credits in an account between them, then to the extent that provisional debits or credits for the item are entered in accounts between the presenting and payor banks or between the presenting and successive prior collecting banks seriatim, they become final upon final payment of the item by the payor bank.

(d) If a collecting bank receives a settlement for an item which is or becomes final, the bank is accountable to its customer for the amount of the item and any provisional credit given for the item in an account with its customer becomes final.

(e) Subject to (i) applicable law stating a time for availability of funds and (ii) any right of the bank to apply the credit to an obligation of the customer, credit given by a bank for an item in a customer's account becomes available for withdrawal as of right:

(1) if the bank has received a provisional settlement for the item, when the settlement becomes final and the bank has had a reasonable time to receive return of the item and the item has not been received within that time;

(2) if the bank is both the depositary bank and the payor bank, and the item is finally paid, at the opening of the bank's second banking day following receipt of the item.

(f) Subject to applicable law stating a time for availability of funds and any right of a bank to apply a deposit to an obligation of the depositor, a deposit of money becomes available for withdrawal as of right at the opening of the bank's next banking day after receipt of the deposit.

§ 4— 216. Insolvency and Preference.

(a) If an item is in or comes into the possession of a payor or collecting bank that suspends payment and the item has not been finally paid, the item must be returned by the receiver, trustee, or agent in charge of the closed bank to the presenting bank or the closed bank's customer.

(b) If a payor bank finally pays an item and suspends payments without making a settlement for the item with its customer or the presenting bank which settlement is or becomes final, the owner of the item has a preferred claim against the payor bank.

(c) If a payor bank gives or a collecting bank gives or receives a provisional settlement for an item and thereafter suspends payments, the suspension does not prevent or interfere with the settlement's becoming final if the finality occurs automatically upon the lapse of certain time or the happening of certain events.

(d) If a collecting bank receives from subsequent parties settlement for an item, which settlement is or becomes final and the bank suspends payments without making a settlement for the item with its customer which settlement is or becomes final, the owner of the item has a preferred claim against the collecting bank.

Part 3 Collection of Items: Payor Banks

§ 4—301. Deferred Posting; Recovery of Payment by Return of Items; Time of Dishonor; Return of Items by Payor Bank.

(a) If a payor bank settles for a demand item other than a documentary draft presented otherwise than for immediate payment over the counter before midnight of the banking day of receipt, the payor bank may revoke the settlement and recover the settlement if, before it has made final payment and before its midnight deadline, it

(1) returns the item; or

(2) sends written notice of dishonor or nonpayment if the item is unavailable for return.

(b) If a demand item is received by a payor bank for credit on its books, it may return the item or send notice of dishonor and may revoke any credit given or recover the amount thereof withdrawn by its customer, if it acts within the time limit and in the manner specified in subsection (a).

(c) Unless previous notice of dishonor has been sent, an item is dishonored at the time when for purposes of dishonor it is returned or notice sent in accordance with this section.

(d) An item is returned:

(1) as to an item presented through a clearing house, when it is delivered to the presenting or last collecting bank or to the clearing house or is sent or delivered in accordance with clearing-house rules; or

(2) in all other cases, when it is sent or delivered to the bank's customer or transferor or pursuant to instructions.

§ 4—302. Payor Bank's Responsibility for Late Return of Item.

(a) If an item is presented to and received by a payor bank, the bank is accountable for the amount of:

(1) a demand item, other than a documentary draft, whether properly payable or not, if the bank, in any case in which it is not also the depositary bank, retains the item beyond midnight of the banking day of receipt without settling for it or, whether or not it is also the depositary bank, does not pay or return the item or send notice of dishonor until after its midnight deadline; or

(2) any other properly payable item unless, within the time allowed for acceptance or payment of that item, the bank either accepts or pays the item or returns it and accompanying documents.

(b) The liability of a payor bank to pay an item pursuant to subsection (a) is subject to defenses based on breach of a presentment warranty (Section 4—208) or proof that the person seeking enforcement of the liability presented or transferred the item for the purpose of defrauding the payor bank.

§ 4—303. When Items Subject to Notice, Stop-Payment Order, Legal Process, or Setoff; Order in Which Items May Be Charged or Certified.

(a) Any knowledge, notice, or stop-payment order received by, legal process served upon, or setoff exercised by a payor bank comes too late to terminate, suspend, or modify the bank's right or duty to pay an item or to charge its customer's account for the item if the knowledge, notice, stop-payment order, or legal process is received or served and a reasonable time for the bank to act thereon expires or the setoff is exercised after the earliest of the following:

(1) the bank accepts or certifies the item;

(2) the bank pays the item in cash;

(3) the bank settles for the item without having a right to revoke the settlement under statute, clearing-house rule, or agreement;

(4) the bank becomes accountable for the amount of the item under Section 4—302 dealing with the payor bank's responsibility for late return of items; or

(5) with respect to checks, a cutoff hour no earlier than one hour after the opening of the next banking day after the banking day on which the bank received the check and no later than the close of that next banking day or, if no cutoff hour is fixed, the close of the next banking day after the banking day on which the bank received the check.

(b) Subject to subsection (a), items may be accepted, paid, certified, or charged to the indicated account of its customer in any order.

Part 4 Relationship Between Payor Bank and its Customer

§ 4—401. When Bank May Charge Customer's Account.

(a) A bank may charge against the account of a customer an item that is properly payable from the account even though the charge creates an overdraft. An item is properly payable if it is authorized by the customer and is in accordance with any agreement between the customer and bank.

(b) A customer is not liable for the amount of an overdraft if the customer neither signed the item nor benefited from the proceeds of the item.

(c) A bank may charge against the account of a customer a check that is otherwise properly payable from the account, even though payment was made before the date of the check, unless the customer has given notice to the bank of the postdating describing the check with reasonable certainty. The notice is effective for the period stated in Section 4—403(b) for stop-payment orders, and must be received at such time and in such manner as to afford the bank a reasonable opportunity to act on it before the bank takes any action with respect to the check described in Section 4—303. If a bank charges against the account of a customer a check before the date stated in the notice of postdating, the bank is liable for damages for the loss resulting from its act. The loss may include damages for dishonor of subsequent items under Section 4—402.

(d) A bank that in good faith makes payment to a holder may charge the indicated account of its customer according to:

(1) the original terms of the altered item; or

(2) the terms of the completed item, even though the bank knows the item has been completed unless the bank has notice that the completion was improper.

§ 4—402. Bank's Liability to Customer for Wrongful Dishonor; Time of Determining Insufficiency of Account.

(a) Except as otherwise provided in this Article, a payor bank wrongfully dishonors an item if it dishonors an item that is properly payable, but a bank may dishonor an item that would create an overdraft unless it has agreed to pay the overdraft.

(b) A payor bank is liable to its customer for damages proximately caused by the wrongful dishonor of an item. Liability is limited to actual damages proved and may include damages for an arrest or prosecution of the customer or other consequential damages. Whether any consequential damages are proximately caused by the wrongful dishonor is a question of fact to be determined in each case.

(c) A payor bank's determination of the customer's account balance on which a decision to dishonor for insufficiency of available funds is based may be made at any time between the time the item is received by the payor bank and the time that the payor bank returns the item or gives notice in lieu of return, and no more than one determination need be made. If, at the election of the payor bank, a subsequent balance determination is made for the purpose of reevaluating the bank's decision to dishonor the item, the account balance at that time is determinative of whether a dishonor for insufficiency of available funds is wrongful.

§ 4—403. Customer's Right to Stop Payment; Burden of Proof of Loss.

(a) A customer or any person authorized to draw on the account if there is more than one person may stop payment of any item drawn on the customer's account or close the account by an order to the bank describing the item or account with reasonable certainty received at a time and in a manner that affords the bank a reasonable opportunity to act on it before any action by the bank with respect to the item described in Section 4—303. If the signature of more than one person is required to draw on an account, any of these persons may stop payment or close the account.

(b) A stop-payment order is effective for six months, but it lapses after 14 calendar days if the original order was oral and was not confirmed in writing within that period. A stop-payment order may be renewed for additional six-month periods by a writing given to the bank within a period during which the stop-payment order is effective.

(c) The burden of establishing the fact and amount of loss resulting from the payment of an item contrary to a stop-payment order or order to close an account is on the customer. The loss from payment of an item contrary to a stop-payment order may include damages for dishonor of subsequent items under Section 4—402.

§ 4—404. Bank Not Obliged to Pay Check More Than Six Months Old.

A bank is under no obligation to a customer having a checking account to pay a check, other than a certified check, which is presented more than six months after its date, but it may charge its customer's account for a payment made thereafter in good faith.

§ 4—405. Death or Incompetence of Customer.

(a) A payor or collecting bank's authority to accept, pay, or collect an item or to account for proceeds of its collection, if otherwise effective, is not rendered ineffective by incompetence of a customer of either bank existing at the time the item is issued or its collection is undertaken if the bank does not know of an adjudication of incompetence. Neither death nor incompetence of a customer revokes the authority to accept, pay, collect, or account until the bank knows of the fact of death or of an adjudication of incompetence and has reasonable opportunity to act on it.

(b) Even with knowledge, a bank may for 10 days after the date of death pay or certify checks drawn on or before the date unless ordered to stop payment by a person claiming an interest in the account.

§ 4—406. Customer's Duty to Discover and Report Unauthorized Signature or Alteration.

(a) A bank that sends or makes available to a customer a statement of account showing payment of items for the account shall either return or make available to the customer the items paid or provide information in the statement of account sufficient to allow the customer reasonably to identify the items paid. The statement of account provides sufficient information if the item is described by item number, amount, and date of payment.

(b) If the items are not returned to the customer, the person retaining the items shall either retain the items or, if the items are destroyed, maintain the capacity to furnish legible copies of the items until the expiration of seven years after receipt of the items. A customer may request an item from the bank that paid the item, and that bank must provide in a reasonable time either the item or, if the item has been destroyed or is not otherwise obtainable, a legible copy of the item.

(c) If a bank sends or makes available a statement of account or items pursuant to subsection (a), the customer must exercise reasonable promptness in examining the statement or the items to determine whether any payment was not authorized because of an alteration of an item or because a purported signature by or on behalf of the customer was not authorized. If, based on the statement or items provided, the customer should reasonably have discovered the unauthorized payment, the customer must promptly notify the bank of the relevant facts.

(d) If the bank proves that the customer failed, with respect to an item, to comply with the duties imposed on the customer by subsection (c), the customer is precluded from asserting against the bank:

(1) the customer's unauthorized signature or any alteration on the item, if the bank also proves that it suffered a loss by reason of the failure; and

(2) the customer's unauthorized signature or alteration by the same wrongdoer on any other item paid in good faith by the bank if the payment was made before the bank received notice from the customer of the unauthorized signature or alteration and after the customer had been afforded a reasonable period of time, not exceeding 30 days, in which to examine the item or statement of account and notify the bank.

(e) If subsection (d) applies and the customer proves that the bank failed to exercise ordinary care in paying the item and that the failure substantially contributed to loss, the loss is allocated between the customer precluded and the bank asserting the preclusion according to the extent to which the failure of the customer to comply with subsection (c) and the failure of the bank to exercise ordinary care contributed to the loss. If the customer proves that the bank did not pay the item in good faith, the preclusion under subsection (d) does not apply.

(f) Without regard to care or lack of care of either the customer or the bank, a customer who does not within one year after the statement or items are made available to the customer (subsection (a)) discover and report the customer's unauthorized signature on or any alteration on the item is precluded from asserting against the bank the unauthorized signature or alteration. If there is a preclusion under this subsection, the payor bank may not recover for breach or warranty under Section 4—208 with respect to the unauthorized signature or alteration to which the preclusion applies.

§ 4—407. Payor Bank's Right to Subrogation on Improper Payment.

If a payor has paid an item over the order of the drawer or maker to stop payment, or after an account has been closed, or otherwise under circumstances giving a basis for objection by the drawer or maker, to prevent unjust enrichment and only to the extent necessary to prevent loss to the bank by reason of its payment of the item, the payor bank is subrogated to the rights

(1) of any holder in due course on the item against the drawer or maker;

(2) of the payee or any other holder of the item against the drawer or maker either on the item or under the transaction out of which the item arose; and

(3) of the drawer or maker against the payee or any other holder of the item with respect to the transaction out of which the item arose.

Part 5 Collection of Documentary Drafts

§ 4—501. Handling of Documentary Drafts; Duty to Send for Presentment and to Notify Customer of Dishonor.

A bank that takes a documentary draft for collection shall present or send the draft and accompanying documents for presentment and, upon learning that the draft has not been paid or accepted in due course, shall seasonably notify its customer of the fact even though it may have discounted or bought the draft or extended credit available for withdrawal as of right.

§ 4—502. Presentment of "On Arrival" Drafts.

If a draft or the relevant instructions require presentment "on arrival", "when goods arrive" or the like, the collecting bank need not present until in its judgment a reasonable time for arrival of the goods has expired. Refusal to pay or accept because the goods have not arrived is not dishonor; the bank must notify its transferor of the refusal but need not present the draft again until it is instructed to do so or learns of the arrival of the goods.

§ 4—503. Responsibility of Presenting Bank for Documents and Goods; Report of Reasons for Dishonor; Referee in Case of Need.

Unless otherwise instructed and except as provided in Article 5, a bank presenting a documentary draft:

(1) must deliver the documents to the drawee on acceptance of the draft if it is payable more than three days after presentment, otherwise, only on payment; and

(2) upon dishonor, either in the case of presentment for acceptance or presentment for payment, may seek and follow instructions from any referee in case of need designated in the draft or, if the presenting bank does not choose to utilize the referee's services, it must use diligence and good faith to ascertain the reason for dishonor, must notify its transferor of the dishonor and of the results of its effort to ascertain the reasons therefor, and must request instructions.

However, the presenting bank is under no obligation with respect to goods represented by the documents except to follow any reasonable instructions seasonably received; it has a right to reimbursement for any expense incurred in following instructions and to prepayment of or indemnity for those expenses.

§ 4—504. Privilege of Presenting Bank to Deal With Goods; Security Interest for Expenses.

(a) A presenting bank that, following the dishonor of a documentary draft, has seasonably requested instructions but does not receive them within a reasonable time may store, sell, or otherwise deal with the goods in any reasonable manner.

(b) For its reasonable expenses incurred by action under subsection (a) the presenting bank has a lien upon the goods or their proceeds, which may be foreclosed in the same manner as an unpaid seller's lien.

Article 4A
FUNDS TRANSFERS

Part 1 Subject Matter and Definitions

§ 4A—101. Short Title.

This Article may be cited as Uniform Commercial Code—Funds Transfers.

§ 4A—102. Subject Matter.

Except as otherwise provided in Section 4A—108, this Article applies to funds transfers defined in Section 4A—104.

§ 4A—103. Payment Order—Definitions.

(a) In this Article:

(1) "Payment order" means an instruction of a sender to a receiving bank, transmitted orally, electronically, or in writing, to pay, or to cause another bank to pay, a fixed or determinable amount of money to a beneficiary if:

(i) the instruction does not state a condition to payment to the beneficiary other than time of payment,

(ii) the receiving bank is to be reimbursed by debiting an account of, or otherwise receiving payment from, the sender, and

(iii) the instruction is transmitted by the sender directly to the receiving bank or to an agent, funds-transfer system, or communication system for transmittal to the receiving bank.

(2) "Beneficiary" means the person to be paid by the beneficiary's bank.

(3) "Beneficiary's bank" means the bank identified in a payment order in which an account of the beneficiary is to be credited pursuant to the order or which otherwise is to make payment to the beneficiary if the order does not provide for payment to an account.

(4) "Receiving bank" means the bank to which the sender's instruction is addressed.

(5) "Sender" means the person giving the instruction to the receiving bank.

(b) If an instruction complying with subsection (a)(1) is to make more than one payment to a beneficiary, the instruction is a separate payment order with respect to each payment.

(c) A payment order is issued when it is sent to the receiving bank.

§ 4A—104. Funds Transfer—Definitions.

In this Article:

(a) "Funds transfer" means the series of transactions, beginning with the originator's payment order, made for the purpose of making payment to the beneficiary of the order. The term includes any payment order issued by the originator's bank or an intermediary bank intended to carry out the originator's payment order. A funds transfer is completed by acceptance by the beneficiary's bank of a payment order for the benefit of the beneficiary of the originator's payment order.

(b) "Intermediary bank" means a receiving bank other than the originator's bank or the beneficiary's bank.

(c) "Originator" means the sender of the first payment order in a funds transfer.

(d) "Originator's bank" means (i) the receiving bank to which the payment order of the originator is issued if the originator is not a bank, or (ii) the originator if the originator is a bank.

§ 4A—105. Other Definitions.

(a) In this Article:

(1) "Authorized account" means a deposit account of a customer in a bank designated by the customer as a source of payment of payment orders issued by the customer to the bank. If a customer does not so designate an account, any account of the customer is an authorized account if payment of a payment order from that account is not inconsistent with a restriction on the use of that account.

(2) "Bank" means a person engaged in the business of banking and includes a savings bank, savings and loan association, credit union, and trust company. A branch or separate office of a bank is a separate bank for purposes of this Article.

(3) "Customer" means a person, including a bank, having an account with a bank or from whom a bank has agreed to receive payment orders.

(4) "Funds-transfer business day" of a receiving bank means the part of a day during which the receiving bank is open for the receipt, processing, and transmittal of payment orders and cancellations and amendments of payment orders.

(5) "Funds-transfer system" means a wire transfer network, automated clearing house, or other communication system of a clearing house or other association of banks through which a payment order by a bank may be transmitted to the bank to which the order is addressed.

(6) "Good faith" means honesty in fact and the observance of reasonable commercial standards of fair dealing.

(7) "Prove" with respect to a fact means to meet the burden of establishing the fact (Section 1—201(8)).

(b) Other definitions applying to this Article and the sections in which they appear are:

"Acceptance"	Section 4A—209
"Beneficiary"	Section 4A—103

"Beneficiary's bank"	Section 4A—103
"Executed"	Section 4A—301
"Execution date"	Section 4A—301
"Funds transfer"	Section 4A—104
"Funds-transfer system rule"	Section 4A—501
"Intermediary bank"	Section 4A—104
"Originator"	Section 4A—104
"Originator's bank"	Section 4A—104
"Payment by beneficiary's bank to beneficiary"	Section 4A—405
"Payment by originator to beneficiary"	Section 4A—406
"Payment by sender to receiving bank"	Section 4A—403
"Payment date"	Section 4A—401
"Payment order"	Section 4A—103
"Receiving bank"	Section 4A—103
"Security procedure"	Section 4A—201
"Sender"	Section 4A—103

(c) The following definitions in Article 4 apply to this Article:

"Clearing house"	Section 4—104
"Item"	Section 4—104
"Suspends payments"	Section 4—104

(d) In addition, Article 1 contains general definitions and principles of construction and interpretation applicable throughout this Article.

§ 4A—106. Time Payment Order Is Received.

(a) The time of receipt of a payment order or communication cancelling or amending a payment order is determined by the rules applicable to receipt of a notice stated in Section 1—201(27). A receiving bank may fix a cut-off time or times on a funds-transfer business day for the receipt and processing of payment orders and communications cancelling or amending payment orders. Different cut-off times may apply to payment orders, cancellations, or amendments, or to different categories of payment orders, cancellations, or amendments. A cut-off time may apply to senders generally or different cut-off times may apply to different senders or categories of payment orders. If a payment order or communication cancelling or amending a payment order is received after the close of a funds-transfer business day or after the appropriate cut-off time on a funds-transfer business day, the receiving bank may treat the payment order or communication as received at the opening of the next funds-transfer business day.

(b) If this Article refers to an execution date or payment date or states a day on which a receiving bank is required to take action, and the date or day does not fall on a funds-transfer business day, the next day that is a funds-transfer business day is treated as the date or day stated, unless the contrary is stated in this Article.

§ 4A—107. Federal Reserve Regulations and Operating Circulars.

Regulations of the Board of Governors of the Federal Reserve System and operating circulars of the Federal Reserve Banks supersede any inconsistent provision of this Article to the extent of the inconsistency.

§ 4A—108. Exclusion of Consumer Transactions Governed by Federal Law.

This Article does not apply to a funds transfer any part of which is governed by the Electronic Fund Transfer Act of 1978 (Title XX, Public Law 95—630, 92 Stat. 3728, 15 U.S.C. § 1693 et seq.) as amended from time to time.

Part 2 Issue and Acceptance of Payment Order

§ 4A—201. Security Procedure.

"Security procedure" means a procedure established by agreement of a customer and a receiving bank for the purpose of (i) verifying that a payment order or communication amending or cancelling a payment order is that of the customer, or (ii) detecting error in the transmission or the content of the payment order or communication. A security procedure may require the use of algorithms or other codes, identifying words or numbers, encryption, callback procedures, or similar security devices. Comparison of a signature on a payment order or communication with an authorized specimen signature of the customer is not by itself a security procedure.

§ 4A—202. Authorized and Verified Payment Orders.

(a) A payment order received by the receiving bank is the authorized order of the person identified as sender if that person authorized the order or is otherwise bound by it under the law of agency.

(b) If a bank and its customer have agreed that the authenticity of payment orders issued to the bank in the name of the customer as sender will be verified pursuant to a security procedure, a payment order received by the receiving bank is effective as the order of the customer, whether or not authorized, if (i) the security procedure is a commercially reasonable method of providing security against unauthorized payment orders, and (ii) the bank proves that it accepted the payment order in good faith and in compliance with the security procedure and any written agreement or instruction of the customer restricting acceptance of payment orders issued in the name of the customer. The bank is not required to follow an instruction that violates a written agreement with the customer or notice of which is not received at a time and in a manner affording the bank a reasonable opportunity to act on it before the payment order is accepted.

(c) Commercial reasonableness of a security procedure is a question of law to be determined by considering the wishes of the customer expressed to the bank, the circumstances of the customer known to the bank, including the size, type, and frequency of payment orders normally issued by the customer to the bank, alternative security procedures offered to the customer, and security procedures in general use by customers and receiving banks similarly situated. A security procedure is deemed to be commercially reasonable if (i) the security procedure was chosen by the customer after the bank offered, and the customer refused, a security procedure that was commercially reasonable for that customer, and (ii) the customer expressly agreed in writing to be bound by any payment order, whether or not authorized, issued in its name and accepted by the bank in compliance with the security procedure chosen by the customer.

(d) The term "sender" in this Article includes the customer in whose name a payment order is issued if the order is the authorized order of the customer under subsection (a), or it is effective as the order of the customer under subsection (b).

(e) This section applies to amendments and cancellations of payment orders to the same extent it applies to payment orders.

(f) Except as provided in this section and in Section 4A—203(a)(1), rights and obligations arising under this section or Section 4A—203 may not be varied by agreement.

§ 4A—203. Unenforceability of Certain Verified Payment Orders.

(a) If an accepted payment order is not, under Section 4A—202(a), an authorized order of a customer identified as sender, but is effective as an order of the customer pursuant to Section 4A—202(b), the following rules apply:

(1) By express written agreement, the receiving bank may limit the extent to which it is entitled to enforce or retain payment of the payment order.

(2) The receiving bank is not entitled to enforce or retain payment of the payment order if the customer proves that the order was not caused, directly or indirectly, by a person (i) entrusted at any time with duties to act for the customer with respect to payment orders or the security procedure, or (ii) who obtained access to transmitting facilities of the customer or who obtained, from a source controlled by the customer and without authority of the receiving bank, information facilitating breach of the security procedure, regardless of how the information was obtained or whether the customer was at fault. Information includes any access device, computer software, or the like.

(b) This section applies to amendments of payment orders to the same extent it applies to payment orders.

§ 4A—204. Refund of Payment and Duty of Customer to Report with Respect to Unauthorized Payment Order.

(a) If a receiving bank accepts a payment order issued in the name of its customer as sender which is (i) not authorized and not effective as the order of the customer under Section 4A—202, or (ii) not enforceable, in whole or in part, against the customer under Section 4A—203, the bank shall refund any payment of the payment order received from the customer to the extent the bank is not entitled to enforce payment and shall pay interest on the refundable amount calculated from the date the bank received payment to the date of the refund. However, the customer is not entitled to interest from the bank on the amount to be refunded if the customer fails to exercise ordinary care to determine that the order was not authorized by the customer and to notify the bank of the relevant facts within a reasonable time not exceeding 90 days after the date the customer received notification from the bank that the order was accepted or that the customer's account was debited with respect to the order. The bank is not entitled to any recovery from the customer on account of a failure by the customer to give notification as stated in this section.

(b) Reasonable time under subsection (a) may be fixed by agreement as stated in Section 1—204(1), but the obligation of a receiving bank to refund payment as stated in subsection (a) may not otherwise be varied by agreement.

§ 4A—205. Erroneous Payment Orders.

(a) If an accepted payment order was transmitted pursuant to a security procedure for the detection of error and the payment order (i) erroneously instructed payment to a beneficiary not intended by the sender, (ii) erroneously instructed payment in an amount greater than the amount intended by the sender, or (iii) was an erroneously transmitted duplicate of a payment order previously sent by the sender, the following rules apply:

(1) If the sender proves that the sender or a person acting on behalf of the sender pursuant to Section 4A—206 complied with the security procedure and that the error would have been detected if the receiving bank had also complied, the sender is not obliged to pay the order to the extent stated in paragraphs (2) and (3).

(2) If the funds transfer is completed on the basis of an erroneous payment order described in clause (i) or (iii) of subsection (a), the sender is not obliged to pay the order and the receiving bank is entitled to recover from the beneficiary any amount paid to the beneficiary to the extent allowed by the law governing mistake and restitution.

(3) If the funds transfer is completed on the basis of a payment order described in clause (ii) of subsection (a), the sender is not obliged to pay the order to the extent the amount received by the beneficiary is greater than the amount intended by the sender. In that case, the receiving bank is entitled to recover from the beneficiary the excess amount received to the extent allowed by the law governing mistake and restitution.

(b) If (i) the sender of an erroneous payment order described in subsection (a) is not obliged to pay all or part of the order, and (ii) the sender receives notification from the receiving bank that the order was accepted by the bank or that the sender's account was debited with respect to the order, the sender has a duty to exercise ordinary care, on the basis of information available to the sender, to discover the error with respect to the order and to advise the bank of the relevant facts within a reasonable time, not exceeding 90 days, after the bank's notification was received by the sender. If the bank proves that the sender failed to perform that duty, the sender is liable to the bank for the loss the bank proves it incurred as a result of the failure, but the liability of the sender may not exceed the amount of the sender's order.

(c) This section applies to amendments to payment orders to the same extent it applies to payment orders.

§ 4A—206. Transmission of Payment Order through Funds-Transfer or Other Communication System.

(a) If a payment order addressed to a receiving bank is transmitted to a funds-transfer system or other third party communication system for transmittal to the bank, the system is deemed to be an agent of the sender for the purpose of transmitting the payment order to the bank. If there is a discrepancy between the terms of the payment order transmitted to the system and the terms of the payment order transmitted by the system to the bank, the terms of the payment order of the sender are those transmitted by the system. This section does not apply to a funds-transfer system of the Federal Reserve Banks.

(b) This section applies to cancellations and amendments to payment orders to the same extent it applies to payment orders.

§ 4A—207. Misdescription of Beneficiary.

(a) Subject to subsection (b), if, in a payment order received by the beneficiary's bank, the name, bank account number, or other identification of the beneficiary refers to a nonexistent or unidentifiable person or account, no person has rights as a beneficiary of the order and acceptance of the order cannot occur.

(b) If a payment order received by the beneficiary's bank identifies the beneficiary both by name and by an identifying or bank account number and the name and number identify different persons, the following rules apply:

(1) Except as otherwise provided in subsection (c), if the beneficiary's bank does not know that the name and number refer to different persons, it may rely on the number as the proper identification of the beneficiary of the order. The beneficiary's bank need not determine whether the name and number refer to the same person.

(2) If the beneficiary's bank pays the person identified by name or knows that the name and number identify different persons, no person has rights as beneficiary except the person paid by the beneficiary's bank if that person was entitled to receive payment from the originator of the funds transfer. If no person has rights as beneficiary, acceptance of the order cannot occur.

(c) If (i) a payment order described in subsection (b) is accepted, (ii) the originator's payment order described the beneficiary inconsistently by name and number, and (iii) the beneficiary's bank pays the person identified by number as permitted by subsection (b)(1), the following rules apply:

(1) If the originator is a bank, the originator is obliged to pay its order.

(2) If the originator is not a bank and proves that the person identified by number was not entitled to receive payment from the originator, the originator is not obliged to pay its order unless the originator's bank proves that the originator, before acceptance of the originator's order, had notice that payment of a payment order issued by the originator might be made by the beneficiary's bank on the basis of an identifying or bank account number even if it identifies a person different from the named beneficiary. Proof of notice may be made by any admissible evidence. The originator's bank satisfies the burden of proof if it proves that the originator, before the payment order was accepted, signed a writing stating the information to which the notice relates.

(d) In a case governed by subsection (b)(1), if the beneficiary's bank rightfully pays the person identified by number and that person was not entitled to receive payment from the originator, the amount paid may be recovered from that person to the extent allowed by the law governing mistake and restitution as follows:

(1) If the originator is obliged to pay its payment order as stated in subsection (c), the originator has the right to recover.

(2) If the originator is not a bank and is not obliged to pay its payment order, the originator's bank has the right to recover.

§ 4A—208. Misdescription of Intermediary Bank or Beneficiary's Bank.

(a) This subsection applies to a payment order identifying an intermediary bank or the beneficiary's bank only by an identifying number.

(1) The receiving bank may rely on the number as the proper identification of the intermediary or beneficiary's bank and need not determine whether the number identifies a bank.

(2) The sender is obliged to compensate the receiving bank for any loss and expenses incurred by the receiving bank as a result of its reliance on the number in executing or attempting to execute the order.

(b) This subsection applies to a payment order identifying an intermediary bank or the beneficiary's bank both by name and an identifying number if the name and number identify different persons.

(1) If the sender is a bank, the receiving bank may rely on the number as the proper identification of the intermediary or beneficiary's bank if the receiving bank, when it executes the sender's order, does not know that the name and number identify different persons. The receiving bank need not determine whether the name and number refer to the same person or whether the number refers to a bank. The sender is obliged to compensate the receiving bank for any loss and expenses incurred by the receiving bank as a result of its reliance on the number in executing or attempting to execute the order.

(2) If the sender is not a bank and the receiving bank proves that the sender, before the payment order was accepted, had

notice that the receiving bank might rely on the number as the proper identification of the intermediary or beneficiary's bank even if it identifies a person different from the bank identified by name, the rights and obligations of the sender and the receiving bank are governed by subsection (b)(1), as though the sender were a bank. Proof of notice may be made by any admissible evidence. The receiving bank satisfies the burden of proof if it proves that the sender, before the payment order was accepted, signed a writing stating the information to which the notice relates.

(3) Regardless of whether the sender is a bank, the receiving bank may rely on the name as the proper identification of the intermediary or beneficiary's bank if the receiving bank, at the time it executes the sender's order, does not know that the name and number identify different persons. The receiving bank need not determine whether the name and number refer to the same person.

(4) If the receiving bank knows that the name and number identify different persons, reliance on either the name or the number in executing the sender's payment order is a breach of the obligation stated in Section 4A—302(a)(1).

§ 4A—209. Acceptance of Payment Order.

(a) Subject to subsection (d), a receiving bank other than the beneficiary's bank accepts a payment order when it executes the order.

(b) Subject to subsections (c) and (d), a beneficiary's bank accepts a payment order at the earliest of the following times:

(1) When the bank (i) pays the beneficiary as stated in Section 4A—405(a) or 4A—405(b), or (ii) notifies the beneficiary of receipt of the order or that the account of the beneficiary has been credited with respect to the order unless the notice indicates that the bank is rejecting the order or that funds with respect to the order may not be withdrawn or used until receipt of payment from the sender of the order;

(2) When the bank receives payment of the entire amount of the sender's order pursuant to Section 4A—403(a)(1) or 4A—403(a)(2); or

(3) The opening of the next funds-transfer business day of the bank following the payment date of the order if, at that time, the amount of the sender's order is fully covered by a withdrawable credit balance in an authorized account of the sender or the bank has otherwise received full payment from the sender, unless the order was rejected before that time or is rejected within (i) one hour after that time, or (ii) one hour after the opening of the next business day of the sender following the payment date if that time is later. If notice of rejection is received by the sender after the payment date and the authorized account of the sender does not bear interest, the bank is obliged to pay interest to the sender on the amount of the order for the number of days elapsing after the payment date to the day the sender receives notice or learns that the order was not accepted, counting that day as an elapsed day. If the withdrawable credit balance during that period falls below the amount of the order, the amount of interest payable is reduced accordingly.

(c) Acceptance of a payment order cannot occur before the order is received by the receiving bank. Acceptance does not occur under subsection (b)(2) or (b)(3) if the beneficiary of the payment order does not have an account with the receiving bank, the account has been closed, or the receiving bank is not permitted by law to receive credits for the beneficiary's account.

(d) A payment order issued to the originator's bank cannot be accepted until the payment date if the bank is the beneficiary's bank, or the execution date if the bank is not the beneficiary's bank. If the originator's bank executes the originator's payment order before the execution date or pays the beneficiary of the originator's payment order before the payment date and the payment order is subsequently cancelled pursuant to Section 4A—211(b), the bank may recover from the beneficiary any payment received to the extent allowed by the law governing mistake and restitution.

§ 4A—210. Rejection of Payment Order.

(a) A payment order is rejected by the receiving bank by a notice of rejection transmitted to the sender orally, electronically, or in writing. A notice of rejection need not use any particular words and is sufficient if it indicates that the receiving bank is rejecting the order or will not execute or pay the order. Rejection is effective when the notice is given if transmission is by a means that is reasonable in the circumstances. If notice of rejection is given by a means that is not reasonable, rejection is effective when the notice is received. If an agreement of the sender and receiving bank establishes the means to be used to reject a payment order, (i) any means complying with the agreement is reasonable and (ii) any means not complying is not reasonable unless no significant delay in receipt of the notice resulted from the use of the noncomplying means.

(b) This subsection applies if a receiving bank other than the beneficiary's bank fails to execute a payment order despite the existence on the execution date of a withdrawable credit balance in an authorized account of the sender sufficient to cover the order. If the sender does not receive notice of rejection of the order on the execution date and the authorized account of the sender does not bear interest, the bank is obliged to pay interest to the sender on the amount of the order for the number of days elapsing after the execution date to the earlier of the day the order is cancelled pursuant to Section 4A—211(d) or the day the sender receives notice or learns that the order was not executed, counting the final day of the period as an elapsed day. If the withdrawable credit balance during that period falls below the amount of the order, the amount of interest is reduced accordingly.

(c) If a receiving bank suspends payments, all unaccepted payment orders issued to it are are deemed rejected at the time the bank suspends payments.

(d) Acceptance of a payment order precludes a later rejection of the order. Rejection of a payment order precludes a later acceptance of the order.

§ 4A—211. Cancellation and Amendment of Payment Order.

(a) A communication of the sender of a payment order cancelling or amending the order may be transmitted to the receiving bank orally, electronically, or in writing. If a security procedure is in effect between the sender and the receiving bank, the communication is not effective to cancel or amend the order unless the communication is verified pursuant to the security procedure or the bank agrees to the cancellation or amendment.

(b) Subject to subsection (a), a communication by the sender cancelling or amending a payment order is effective to cancel or amend the order if notice of the communication is received at a time and in a manner affording the receiving bank a reasonable opportunity to act on the communication before the bank accepts the payment order.

(c) After a payment order has been accepted, cancellation or amendment of the order is not effective unless the receiving bank agrees or a funds-transfer system rule allows cancellation or amendment without agreement of the bank.

(1) With respect to a payment order accepted by a receiving bank other than the beneficiary's bank, cancellation or amendment is not effective unless a conforming cancellation or amendment of the payment order issued by the receiving bank is also made.

(2) With respect to a payment order accepted by the beneficiary's bank, cancellation or amendment is not effective unless the order was issued in execution of an unauthorized payment order, or because of a mistake by a sender in the funds transfer which resulted in the issuance of a payment order (i) that is a duplicate of a payment order previously issued by the sender, (ii) that orders payment to a beneficiary not entitled to receive payment from the originator, or (iii) that orders payment in an amount greater than the amount the beneficiary was entitled to receive from the originator. If the payment order is cancelled or amended, the beneficiary's bank is entitled to recover from the beneficiary any amount paid to the beneficiary to the extent allowed by the law governing mistake and restitution.

(d) An unaccepted payment order is cancelled by operation of law at the close of the fifth funds-transfer business day of the receiving bank after the execution date or payment date of the order.

(e) A cancelled payment order cannot be accepted. If an accepted payment order is cancelled, the acceptance is nullified and no person has any right or obligation based on the acceptance. Amendment of a payment order is deemed to be cancellation of the original order at the time of amendment and issue of a new payment order in the amended form at the same time.

(f) Unless otherwise provided in an agreement of the parties or in a funds-transfer system rule, if the receiving bank, after accepting a payment order, agrees to cancellation or amendment of the order by the sender or is bound by a funds-transfer system rule allowing cancellation or amendment without the bank's agreement, the sender, whether or not cancellation or amendment is effective, is liable to the bank for any loss and expenses, including reasonable attorney's fees, incurred by the bank as a result of the cancellation or amendment or attempted cancellation or amendment.

(g) A payment order is not revoked by the death or legal incapacity of the sender unless the receiving bank knows of the death or of an adjudication of incapacity by a court of competent jurisdiction and has reasonable opportunity to act before acceptance of the order.

(h) A funds-transfer system rule is not effective to the extent it conflicts with subsection (c)(2).

§ 4A—212. Liability and Duty of Receiving Bank Regarding Unaccepted Payment Order.

If a receiving bank fails to accept a payment order that it is obliged by express agreement to accept, the bank is liable for breach of the agreement to the extent provided in the agreement or in this Article, but does not otherwise have any duty to accept a payment order or, before acceptance, to take any action, or refrain from taking action, with respect to the order except as provided in this Article or by express agreement. Liability based on acceptance arises only when acceptance occurs as stated in Section 4A—209, and liability is limited to that provided in this Article. A receiving bank is not the agent of the sender or beneficiary of the payment order it accepts, or of any other party to the funds transfer, and the bank owes no duty to any party to the funds transfer except as provided in this Article or by express agreement.

Part 3 Execution of Sender's Payment Order by Receiving Bank

§ 4A—301. Execution and Execution Date.

(a) A payment order is "executed" by the receiving bank when it issues a payment order intended to carry out the payment order received by the bank. A payment order received by the beneficiary's bank can be accepted but cannot be executed.

(b) "Execution date" of a payment order means the day on which the receiving bank may properly issue a payment order in execution of the sender's order. The execution date may be determined by instruction of the sender but cannot be earlier than the day the order is received and, unless otherwise determined, is the day the order is received. If the sender's instruction states a payment date, the execution date is the payment date or an earlier date on which execution is reasonably necessary to allow payment to the beneficiary on the payment date.

§ 4A—302. Obligations of Receiving Bank in Execution of Payment Order.

(a) Except as provided in subsections (b) through (d), if the receiving bank accepts a payment order pursuant to Section 4A—209(a), the bank has the following obligations in executing the order:

(1) The receiving bank is obliged to issue, on the execution

date, a payment order complying with the sender's order and to follow the sender's instructions concerning (i) any intermediary bank or funds-transfer system to be used in carrying out the funds transfer, or (ii) the means by which payment orders are to be transmitted in the funds transfer. If the originator's bank issues a payment order to an intermediary bank, the originator's bank is obliged to instruct the intermediary bank according to the instruction of the originator. An intermediary bank in the funds transfer is similarly bound by an instruction given to it by the sender of the payment order it accepts.

(2) If the sender's instruction states that the funds transfer is to be carried out telephonically or by wire transfer or otherwise indicates that the funds transfer is to be carried out by the most expeditious means, the receiving bank is obliged to transmit its payment order by the most expeditious available means, and to instruct any intermediary bank accordingly. If a sender's instruction states a payment date, the receiving bank is obliged to transmit its payment order at a time and by means reasonably necessary to allow payment to the beneficiary on the payment date or as soon thereafter as is feasible.

(b) Unless otherwise instructed, a receiving bank executing a payment order may (i) use any funds-transfer system if use of that system is reasonable in the circumstances, and (ii) issue a payment order to the beneficiary's bank or to an intermediary bank through which a payment order conforming to the sender's order can expeditiously be issued to the beneficiary's bank if the receiving bank exercises ordinary care in the selection of the intermediary bank. A receiving bank is not required to follow an instruction of the sender designating a funds-transfer system to be used in carrying out the funds transfer if the receiving bank, in good faith, determines that it is not feasible to follow the instruction or that following the instruction would unduly delay completion of the funds transfer.

(c) Unless subsection (a)(2) applies or the receiving bank is otherwise instructed, the bank may execute a payment order by transmitting its payment order by first class mail or by any means reasonable in the circumstances. If the receiving bank is instructed to execute the sender's order by transmitting its payment order by a particular means, the receiving bank may issue its payment order by the means stated or by any means as expeditious as the means stated.

(d) Unless instructed by the sender, (i) the receiving bank may not obtain payment of its charges for services and expenses in connection with the execution of the sender's order by issuing a payment order in an amount equal to the amount of the sender's order less the amount of the charges, and (ii) may not instruct a subsequent receiving bank to obtain payment of its charges in the same manner.

§ 4A—303. Erroneous Execution of Payment Order.

(a) A receiving bank that (i) executes the payment order of the sender by issuing a payment order in an amount greater than the amount of the sender's order, or (ii) issues a payment order in execution of the sender's order and then issues a duplicate order, is entitled to payment of the amount of the sender's order under Section 4A—402(c) if that subsection is otherwise satisfied. The bank is entitled to recover from the beneficiary of the erroneous order the excess payment received to the extent allowed by the law governing mistake and restitution.

(b) A receiving bank that executes the payment order of the sender by issuing a payment order in an amount less than the amount of the sender's order is entitled to payment of the amount of the sender's order under Section 4A—402(c) if (i) that subsection is otherwise satisfied and (ii) the bank corrects its mistake by issuing an additional payment order for the benefit of the beneficiary of the sender's order. If the error is not corrected, the issuer of the erroneous order is entitled to receive or retain payment from the sender of the order it accepted only to the extent of the amount of the erroneous order. This subsection does not apply if the receiving bank executes the sender's payment order by issuing a payment order in an amount less than the amount of the sender's order for the purpose of obtaining payment of its charges for services and expenses pursuant to instruction of the sender.

(c) If a receiving bank executes the payment order of the sender by issuing a payment order to a beneficiary different from the beneficiary of the sender's order and the funds transfer is completed on the basis of that error, the sender of the payment order that was erroneously executed and all previous senders in the funds transfer are not obliged to pay the payment orders they issued. The issuer of the erroneous order is entitled to recover from the beneficiary of the order the payment received to the extent allowed by the law governing mistake and restitution.

§ 4A—304. Duty of Sender to Report Erroneously Executed Payment Order.

If the sender of a payment order that is erroneously executed as stated in Section 4A—303 receives notification from the receiving bank that the order was executed or that the sender's account was debited with respect to the order, the sender has a duty to exercise ordinary care to determine, on the basis of information available to the sender, that the order was erroneously executed and to notify the bank of the relevant facts within a reasonable time not exceeding 90 days after the notification from the bank was received by the sender. If the sender fails to perform that duty, the bank is not obliged to pay interest on any amount refundable to the sender under Section 4A—402(d) for the period before the bank learns of the execution error. The bank is not entitled to any recovery from the sender on account of a failure by the sender to perform the duty stated in this section.

§ 4A—305. Liability for Late or Improper Execution or Failure to Execute Payment Order.

(a) If a funds transfer is completed but execution of a payment order by the receiving bank in breach of Section 4A—302 results in delay in payment to the beneficiary, the bank is obliged to pay interest to either the originator or the beneficiary of the funds transfer for the period of delay caused by the improper execution. Except as provided in subsection (c), additional damages are not recoverable.

(b) If execution of a payment order by a receiving bank in breach of Section 4A—302 results in (i) noncompletion of the funds transfer, (ii) failure to use an intermediary bank designated by the originator, or (iii) issuance of a payment order that does not comply with the terms of the payment order of the originator, the bank is liable to the originator for its expenses in the funds transfer and for incidental expenses and interest losses, to the extent not covered by subsection (a), resulting from the improper execution. Except as provided in subsection (c), additional damages are not recoverable.

(c) In addition to the amounts payable under subsections (a) and (b), damages, including consequential damages, are recoverable to the extent provided in an express written agreement of the receiving bank.

(d) If a receiving bank fails to execute a payment order it was obliged by express agreement to execute, the receiving bank is liable to the sender for its expenses in the transaction and for incidental expenses and interest losses resulting from the failure to execute. Additional damages, including consequential damages, are recoverable to the extent provided in an express written agreement of the receiving bank, but are not otherwise recoverable.

(e) Reasonable attorney's fees are recoverable if demand for compensation under subsection (a) or (b) is made and refused before an action is brought on the claim. If a claim is made for breach of an agreement under subsection (d) and the agreement does not provide for damages, reasonable attorney's fees are recoverable if demand for compensation under subsection (d) is made and refused before an action is brought on the claim.

(f) Except as stated in this section, the liability of a receiving bank under subsections (a) and (b) may not be varied by agreement.

Part 4 Payment

§ 4A—401. Payment Date.

"Payment date" of a payment order means the day on which the amount of the order is payable to the beneficiary by the beneficiary's bank. The payment date may be determined by instruction of the sender but cannot be earlier than the day the order is received by the beneficiary's bank and, unless otherwise determined, is the day the order is received by the beneficiary's bank.

§ 4A—402. Obligation of Sender to Pay Receiving Bank.

(a) This section is subject to Sections 4A—205 and 4A—207.

(b) With respect to a payment order issued to the beneficiary's bank, acceptance of the order by the bank obliges the sender to pay the bank the amount of the order, but payment is not due until the payment date of the order.

(c) This subsection is subject to subsection (e) and to Section 4A—303. With respect to a payment order issued to a receiving bank other than the beneficiary's bank, acceptance of the order by the receiving bank obliges the sender to pay the bank the amount of the sender's order. Payment by the sender is not due until the execution date of the sender's order. The obligation of that sender to pay its payment order is excused if the funds transfer is not completed by acceptance by the beneficiary's bank of a payment order instructing payment to the beneficiary of that sender's payment order.

(d) If the sender of a payment order pays the order and was not obliged to pay all or part of the amount paid, the bank receiving payment is obliged to refund payment to the extent the sender was not obliged to pay. Except as provided in Sections 4A—204 and 4A—304, interest is payable on the refundable amount from the date of payment.

(e) If a funds transfer is not completed as stated in subsection (c) and an intermediary bank is obliged to refund payment as stated in subsection (d) but is unable to do so because not permitted by applicable law or because the bank suspends payments, a sender in the funds transfer that executed a payment order in compliance with an instruction, as stated in Section 4A—302(a)(1), to route the funds transfer through that intermediary bank is entitled to receive or retain payment from the sender of the payment order that it accepted. The first sender in the funds transfer that issued an instruction requiring routing through that intermediary bank is subrogated to the right of the bank that paid the intermediary bank to refund as stated in subsection (d).

(f) The right of the sender of a payment order to be excused from the obligation to pay the order as stated in subsection (c) or to receive refund under subsection (d) may not be varied by agreement.

§ 4A—403. Payment by Sender to Receiving Bank.

(a) Payment of the sender's obligation under Section 4A—402 to pay the receiving bank occurs as follows:

(1) If the sender is a bank, payment occurs when the receiving bank receives final settlement of the obligation through a Federal Reserve Bank or through a funds-transfer system.

(2) If the sender is a bank and the sender (i) credited an account of the receiving bank with the sender, or (ii) caused an account of the receiving bank in another bank to be credited, payment occurs when the credit is withdrawn or, if not withdrawn, at midnight of the day on which the credit is withdrawable and the receiving bank learns of that fact.

(3) If the receiving bank debits an account of the sender with the receiving bank, payment occurs when the debit is made to the extent the debit is covered by a withdrawable credit balance in the account.

(b) If the sender and receiving bank are members of a funds-transfer system that nets obligations multilaterally among participants, the receiving bank receives final settlement when settlement is complete in accordance with the rules of the system. The obligation of the sender to pay the amount of a payment order transmitted through the funds-transfer system may be satisfied, to the extent permitted by the rules of the system, by setting off and applying against the sender's obligation the right of the sender to receive payment from the receiving bank of the amount of any other payment order transmitted to the sender by the receiving bank through the funds-transfer system. The aggregate balance of obligations owed by each sender to each receiving bank in the funds-transfer system may be satisfied, to the extent permitted by the rules of the system, by setting off and applying against that balance the aggregate balance of obligations owed to the sender by other members of the system. The aggregate balance is determined after the right of setoff stated in the second sentence of this subsection has been exercised.

(c) If two banks transmit payment orders to each other under an agreement that settlement of the obligations of each bank to the other under Section 4A—402 will be made at the end of the day or other period, the total amount owed with respect to all orders transmitted by one bank shall be set off against the total amount owed with respect to all orders transmitted by the other bank. To the extent of the setoff, each bank has made payment to the other.

(d) In a case not covered by subsection (a), the time when payment of the sender's obligation under Section 4A—402(b) or 4A—402(c) occurs is governed by applicable principles of law that determine when an obligation is satisfied.

§ 4A—404. Obligation of Beneficiary's Bank to Pay and Give Notice to Beneficiary.

(a) Subject to Sections 4A—211(e), 4A—405(d), and 4A—405(e), if a beneficiary's bank accepts a payment order, the bank is obliged to pay the amount of the order to the beneficiary of the order. Payment is due on the payment date of the order, but if acceptance occurs on the payment date after the close of the funds-transfer business day of the bank, payment is due on the next funds-transfer business day. If the bank refuses to pay after demand by the beneficiary and receipt of notice of particular circumstances that will give rise to consequential damages as a result of nonpayment, the beneficiary may recover damages resulting from the refusal to pay to the extent the bank had notice of the damages, unless the bank proves that it did not pay because of a reasonable doubt concerning the right of the beneficiary to payment.

(b) If a payment order accepted by the beneficiary's bank instructs payment to an account of the beneficiary, the bank is obliged to notify the beneficiary of receipt of the order before midnight of the next funds-transfer business day following the payment date. If the payment order does not instruct payment to an account of the beneficiary, the bank is required to notify the beneficiary only if notice is required by the order. Notice may be given by first class mail or any other means reasonable in the circumstances. If the bank fails to give the required notice, the bank is obliged to pay interest to the beneficiary on the amount of the payment order from the day notice should have been given until the day the beneficiary learned of receipt of the payment order by the bank. No other damages are recoverable. Reasonable attorney's fees are also recoverable if demand for interest is made and refused before an action is brought on the claim.

(c) The right of a beneficiary to receive payment and damages as stated in subsection (a) may not be varied by agreement or a funds-transfer system rule. The right of a beneficiary to be notified as stated in subsection (b) may be varied by agreement of the beneficiary or by a funds-transfer system rule if the beneficiary is notified of the rule before initiation of the funds transfer.

§ 4A—405. Payment by Beneficiary's Bank to Beneficiary.

(a) If the beneficiary's bank credits an account of the beneficiary of a payment order, payment of the bank's obligation under Section 4A—404(a) occurs when and to the extent (i) the beneficiary is notified of the right to withdraw the credit, (ii) the bank lawfully applies the credit to a debt of the beneficiary, or (iii) funds with respect to the order are otherwise made available to the beneficiary by the bank.

(b) If the beneficiary's bank does not credit an account of the beneficiary of a payment order, the time when payment of the bank's obligation under Section 4A—404(a) occurs is governed by principles of law that determine when an obligation is satisfied.

(c) Except as stated in subsections (d) and (e), if the beneficiary's bank pays the beneficiary of a payment order under a condition to payment or agreement of the beneficiary giving the bank the right to recover payment from the beneficiary if the bank does not receive payment of the order, the condition to payment or agreement is not enforceable.

(d) A funds-transfer system rule may provide that payments made to beneficiaries of funds transfers made through the system are provisional until receipt of payment by the beneficiary's bank of the payment order it accepted. A beneficiary's bank that makes a payment that is provisional under the rule is entitled to refund from the beneficiary if (i) the rule requires that both the beneficiary and the originator be given notice of the provisional nature of the payment before the funds transfer is initiated, (ii) the beneficiary, the beneficiary's bank, and the originator's bank agreed to be bound by the rule, and (iii) the beneficiary's bank did not receive payment of the payment order that it accepted. If the beneficiary is obliged to refund payment to the beneficiary's bank, acceptance of the payment order by the beneficiary's bank is nullified and no payment by the originator of the funds transfer to the beneficiary occurs under Section 4A—406.

(e) This subsection applies to a funds transfer that includes a payment order transmitted over a funds-transfer system that (i) nets obligations multilaterally among participants, and (ii) has in effect a loss-sharing agreement among participants for the purpose of providing funds necessary to complete settlement of the obligations of one or more participants that do not meet their settlement obligations. If the beneficiary's bank in the funds transfer accepts a payment order and the system fails to complete settlement pursuant to its rules with respect to any payment order in the funds transfer, (i) the acceptance by the beneficiary's bank is nullified and no person has any right or obligation based on the acceptance, (ii) the beneficiary's bank is entitled to recover payment from the beneficiary, (iii) no payment by the originator to the beneficiary occurs under Section 4A—406, and (iv) subject to Section 4A—402(e), each sender in the funds transfer is excused from its obligation to pay its payment order under Section 4A—402(c) because the funds transfer has not been completed.

§ 4A—406. Payment by Originator to Beneficiary; Discharge of Underlying Obligation.

(a) Subject to Sections 4A—211(e), 4A—405(d), and 4A—405(e), the originator of a funds transfer pays the beneficiary of the originator's payment order (i) at the time a payment order for the benefit of the beneficiary is accepted by the beneficiary's bank in the funds transfer and (ii) in an amount equal to the amount of the order accepted by the beneficiary's bank, but not more than the amount of the originator's order.

(b) If payment under subsection (a) is made to satisfy an obligation, the obligation is discharged to the same extent discharge would result from payment to the beneficiary of the same amount in money, unless (i) the payment under subsection (a) was made by a means prohibited by the contract of the beneficiary with respect to the obligation, (ii) the beneficiary, within a reasonable time after receiving notice of receipt of the order by the beneficiary's bank, notified the originator of the beneficiary's refusal of the payment, (iii) funds with respect to the order were not withdrawn by the beneficiary or applied to a debt of the beneficiary, and (iv) the beneficiary would suffer a loss that could reasonably have been avoided if payment had been made by a means complying with the contract. If payment by the originator does not result in discharge under this section, the originator is subrogated to the rights of the beneficiary to receive payment from the beneficiary's bank under Section 4A—404(a).

(c) For the purpose of determining whether discharge of an obligation occurs under subsection (b), if the beneficiary's bank accepts a payment order in an amount equal to the amount of the originator's payment order less charges of one or more receiving banks in the funds transfer, payment to the beneficiary is deemed to be in the amount of the originator's order unless upon demand by the beneficiary the originator does not pay the beneficiary the amount of the deducted charges.

(d) Rights of the originator or of the beneficiary of a funds transfer under this section may be varied only by agreement of the originator and the beneficiary.

Part 5 Miscellaneous Provisions

§ 4A—501. Variation by Agreement and Effect of Funds-Transfer System Rule.

(a) Except as otherwise provided in this Article, the rights and obligations of a party to a funds transfer may be varied by agreement of the affected party.

(b) "Funds-transfer system rule" means a rule of an association of banks (i) governing transmission of payment orders by means of a funds-transfer system of the association or rights and obligations with respect to those orders, or (ii) to the extent the rule governs rights and obligations between banks that are parties to a funds transfer in which a Federal Reserve Bank, acting as an intermediary bank, sends a payment order to the beneficiary's bank. Except as otherwise provided in this Article, a funds-transfer system rule governing rights and obligations between participating banks using the system may be effective even if the rule conflicts with this Article and indirectly affects another party to the funds transfer who does not consent to the rule. A funds-transfer system rule may also govern rights and obligations of parties other than participating banks using the system to the extent stated in Sections 4A—404(c), 4A—405(d), and 4A—507(c).

§ 4A—502. Creditor Process Served on Receiving Bank; Setoff by Beneficiary's Bank.

(a) As used in this section, "creditor process" means levy, attachment, garnishment, notice of lien, sequestration, or similar process issued by or on behalf of a creditor or other claimant with respect to an account.

(b) This subsection applies to creditor process with respect to an authorized account of the sender of a payment order if the creditor process is served on the receiving bank. For the purpose of determining rights with respect to the creditor process, if the receiving bank accepts the payment order the balance in the authorized account is deemed to be reduced by the amount of the payment order to the extent the bank did not otherwise receive payment of the order, unless the creditor process is served at a time and in a manner affording the bank a reasonable opportunity to act on it before the bank accepts the payment order.

(c) If a beneficiary's bank has received a payment order for payment to the beneficiary's account in the bank, the following rules apply:

(1) The bank may credit the beneficiary's account. The amount credited may be set off against an obligation owed by the beneficiary to the bank or may be applied to satisfy creditor process served on the bank with respect to the account.

(2) The bank may credit the beneficiary's account and allow withdrawal of the amount credited unless creditor process with respect to the account is served at a time and in a manner affording the bank a reasonable opportunity to act to prevent withdrawal.

(3) If creditor process with respect to the beneficiary's account has been served and the bank has had a reasonable opportunity to act on it, the bank may not reject the payment order except for a reason unrelated to the service of process.

(d) Creditor process with respect to a payment by the originator to the beneficiary pursuant to a funds transfer may be served only on the beneficiary's bank with respect to the debt owed by that bank to the beneficiary. Any other bank served with the creditor process is not obliged to act with respect to the process.

§ 4A—503. Injunction or Restraining Order with Respect to Funds Transfer.

For proper cause and in compliance with applicable law, a court may restrain (i) a person from issuing a payment order to initiate a funds transfer, (ii) an originator's bank from executing the payment order of the originator, or (iii) the beneficiary's bank from releasing funds to the beneficiary or the beneficiary from withdrawing the funds. A court may not otherwise restrain a person from issuing a payment order, paying or receiving payment of a payment order, or otherwise acting with respect to a funds transfer.

§ 4A—504. Order in Which Items and Payment Orders May Be Charged to Account; Order of Withdrawals from Account.

(a) If a receiving bank has received more than one payment order of the sender or one or more payment orders and other items that are payable from the sender's account, the bank may charge the sender's account with respect to the various orders and items in any sequence.

(b) In determining whether a credit to an account has been withdrawn by the holder of the account or applied to a debt of the holder of the account, credits first made to the account are first withdrawn or applied.

§ 4A—505. Preclusion of Objection to Debit of Customer's Account.

If a receiving bank has received payment from its customer with respect to a payment order issued in the name of the customer as sender and accepted by the bank, and the customer received notification reasonably identifying the order, the customer is precluded from asserting that the bank is not entitled to retain the payment unless the customer notifies the bank of the customer's objection to the payment within one year after the notification was received by the customer.

§ 4A—506. Rate of Interest.

(a) If, under this Article, a receiving bank is obliged to pay interest with respect to a payment order issued to the bank, the amount payable may be determined (i) by agreement of the sender and receiving bank, or (ii) by a funds-transfer system rule if the payment order is transmitted through a funds-transfer system.

(b) If the amount of interest is not determined by an agreement or rule as stated in subsection (a), the amount is calculated by multiplying the applicable Federal Funds rate by the amount on which interest is payable, and then multiplying the product by the number of days for which interest is payable. The applicable Federal Funds rate is the average of the Federal Funds rates published by the Federal Reserve Bank of New York for each of the days for which interest is payable divided by 360. The Federal Funds rate for any day on which a published rate is not available is the same as the published rate for the next preceding day for which there is a published rate. If a receiving bank that accepted a payment order is required to refund payment to the sender of the order because the funds transfer was not completed, but the failure to complete was not due to any fault by the bank, the interest payable is reduced by a percentage equal to the reserve requirement on deposits of the receiving bank.

§ 4A—507. Choice of Law.

(a) The following rules apply unless the affected parties otherwise agree or subsection (c) applies:

(1) The rights and obligations between the sender of a payment order and the receiving bank are governed by the law of the jurisdiction in which the receiving bank is located.

(2) The rights and obligations between the beneficiary's bank and the beneficiary are governed by the law of the jurisdiction in which the beneficiary's bank is located.

(3) The issue of when payment is made pursuant to a funds transfer by the originator to the beneficiary is governed by the law of the jurisdiction in which the beneficiary's bank is located.

(b) If the parties described in each paragraph of subsection (a) have made an agreement selecting the law of a particular jurisdiction to govern rights and obligations between each other, the law of that jurisdiction governs those rights and obligations, whether or not the payment order or the funds transfer bears a reasonable relation to that jurisdiction.

(c) A funds-transfer system rule may select the law of a particular jurisdiction to govern (i) rights and obligations between participating banks with respect to payment orders transmitted or processed through the system, or (ii) the rights and obligations of some or all parties to a funds transfer any part of which is carried out by means of the system. A choice of law made pursuant to clause (i) is binding on participating banks. A choice of law made pursuant to clause (ii) is binding on the originator, other sender, or a receiving bank having notice that the funds-transfer system might be used in the funds transfer and of the choice of law by the system when the originator, other sender, or receiving bank issued or accepted a payment order. The beneficiary of a funds transfer is bound by the choice of law if, when the funds transfer is initiated, the beneficiary has notice that the funds-transfer system might be used in the funds transfer and of the choice of law by the system. The law of a jurisdiction selected pursuant to this subsection may govern, whether or not that law bears a reasonable relation to the matter in issue.

(d) In the event of inconsistency between an agreement under subsection (b) and a choice-of-law rule under subsection (c), the agreement under subsection (b) prevails.

(e) If a funds transfer is made by use of more than one funds-transfer system and there is inconsistency between choice-of-law rules of the systems, the matter in issue is governed by the law of the selected jurisdiction that has the most significant relationship to the matter in issue.

Article 5
LETTERS OF CREDIT

§ 5—101. Short Title.

This Article shall be known and may be cited as Uniform Commercial Code—Letters of Credit.

§ 5—102. Scope.

(1) This Article applies

(a) to a credit issued by a bank if the credit requires a documentary draft or a documentary demand for payment; and

(b) to a credit issued by a person other than a bank if the credit requires that the draft or demand for payment be accompanied by a document of title; and

(c) to a credit issued by a bank or other person if the credit is not within subparagraphs (a) or (b) but conspicuously states that it is a letter of credit or is conspicuously so entitled.

(2) Unless the engagement meets the requirements of subsection (1), this Article does not apply to engagements to make advances or to honor drafts or demands for payment, to authorities to pay or purchase, to guarantees or to general agreements.

(3) This Article deals with some but not all of the rules and concepts of letters of credit as such rules or concepts have developed prior to this act or may hereafter develop. The fact that this Article states a rule does not by itself require, imply or negate application of the same or a converse rule to a situation not provided for or to a person not specified by this Article.

§ 5—103. Definitions.

(1) In this Article unless the context otherwise requires

(a) "Credit" or "letter of credit" means an engagement by a bank or other person made at the request of a customer and of a kind within the scope of this Article (Section 5—102) that the issuer will honor drafts or other demands for payment upon compliance with the conditions specified in the credit. A credit may be either revocable or irrevocable. The engagement may be either an agreement to honor or a statement that the bank or other person is authorized to honor.

(b) A "documentary draft" or a "documentary demand for payment" is one honor of which is conditioned upon the presentation of a document or documents. "Document" means any paper including document of title, security, invoice, certificate, notice of default and the like.

(c) An "issuer" is a bank or other person issuing a credit.

(d) A "beneficiary" of a credit is a person who is entitled under its terms to draw or demand payment.

(e) An "advising bank" is a bank which gives notification of the issuance of a credit by another bank.

(f) A "confirming bank" is a bank which engages either that it will itself honor a credit already issued by another bank or that such a credit will be honored by the issuer or a third bank.

(g) A "customer" is a buyer or other person who causes an issuer to issue a credit. The term also includes a bank which procures issuance or confirmation on behalf of that bank's customer.

(2) Other definitions applying to this Article and the sections in which they appear are:

"Notation of Credit". Section 5—108.

"Presenter". Section 5—112(3).

(3) Definitions in other Articles applying to this Article and the sections in which they appear are:

"Accept" or "Acceptance". Section 3—410.

"Contract for sale". Section 2—106.

"Draft". Section 3—104.

"Holder in due course". Section 3—302.

"Midnight deadline". Section 4—104.

"Security". Section 8—102.

(4) In addition, Article 1 contains general definitions and principles of construction and interpretation applicable throughout this Article.

§ 5—104. Formal Requirements; Signing.

(1) Except as otherwise required in subsection (1)(c) of Section 5—102 on scope, no particular form of phrasing is required for a credit. A credit must be in writing and signed by the issuer and a confirmation must be in writing and signed by the confirming bank. A modification of the terms of a credit or confirmation must be signed by the issuer or confirming bank.

(2) A telegram may be a sufficient signed writing if it identifies its sender by an authorized authentication. The authentication may be in code and the authorized naming of the issuer in an advice of credit is a sufficient signing.

§ 5—105. Consideration.

No consideration is necessary to establish a credit or to enlarge or otherwise modify its terms.

§ 5—106. Time and Effect of Establishment of Credit.

(1) Unless otherwise agreed a credit is established

(a) as regards the customer as soon as a letter of credit is sent to him or the letter of credit or an authorized written advice of its issuance is sent to the beneficiary; and

(b) as regards the beneficiary when he receives a letter of credit or an authorized written advice of its issuance.

(2) Unless otherwise agreed once an irrevocable credit is established as regards the customer it can be modified or revoked only with the consent of the customer and once it is established as regards the beneficiary it can be modified or revoked only with his consent.

(3) Unless otherwise agreed after a revocable credit is established it may be modified or revoked by the issuer without notice to or consent from the customer or beneficiary.

(4) Notwithstanding any modification or revocation of a revocable credit any person authorized to honor or negotiate under the terms of the original credit is entitled to reimbursement for or honor of any draft or demand for payment duly honored or negotiated before receipt of notice of the modification or revocation and the issuer in turn is entitled to reimbursement from its customer.

§ 5—107. Advice of Credit; Confirmation; Error in Statement of Terms.

(1) Unless otherwise specified an advising bank by advising a credit issued by another bank does not assume any obligation to honor drafts drawn or demands for payment made under the credit but it does assume obligation for the accuracy of its own statement.

(2) A confirming bank by confirming a credit becomes directly obligated on the credit to the extent of its confirmation as though it were its issuer and acquires the rights of an issuer.

(3) Even though an advising bank incorrectly advises the terms of a credit it has been authorized to advise the credit is established as against the issuer to the extent of its original terms.

(4) Unless otherwise specified the customer bears as against the issuer all risks of transmission and reasonable translation or interpretation of any message relating to a credit.

§ 5—108. "Notation Credit"; Exhaustion of Credit.

(1) A credit which specifies that any person purchasing or paying drafts drawn or demands for payment made under it must note the amount of the draft or demand on the letter or advice of credit is a "notation credit".

(2) Under a notation credit

(a) a person paying the beneficiary or purchasing a draft or demand for payment from him acquires a right to honor only if the appropriate notation is made and by transferring or forwarding for honor the documents under the credit such a person warrants to the issuer that the notation has been made; and

(b) unless the credit or a signed statement that an appropriate notation has been made accompanies the draft or demand for payment the issuer may delay honor until evidence of notation has been procured which is satisfactory to it but its obligation and that of its customer continue for a reasonable time not exceeding thirty days to obtain such evidence.

(3) If the credit is not a notation credit

(a) the issuer may honor complying drafts or demands for payment presented to it in the order in which they are presented and is discharged pro tanto by honor of any such draft or demand;

(b) as between competing good faith purchasers of complying drafts or demands the person first purchasing his priority over a subsequent purchaser even though the later purchased draft or demand has been first honored.

§ 5—109. Issuer's Obligation to Its Customer.

(1) An issuer's obligation to its customer includes good faith and observance of any general banking usage but unless otherwise agreed does not include liability or responsibility

(a) for performance of the underlying contract for sale or other transaction between the customer and the beneficiary; or

(b) for any act or omission of any person other than itself or its own branch or for loss or destruction of a draft, demand or document in transit or in the possession of others; or

(c) based on knowledge or lack of knowledge of any usage of any particular trade.

(2) An issuer must examine documents with care so as to ascertain that on their face they appear to comply with the terms of the credit but unless otherwise agreed assumes no liability or responsibility for the genuineness, falsification or effect of any document which appears on such examination to be regular on its face.

(3) A non-bank issuer is not bound by any banking usage of which it has no knowledge.

§ 5—110. Availability of Credit in Portions; Presenter's Reservation of Lien or Claim.

(1) Unless otherwise specified a credit may be used in portions in the discretion of the beneficiary.

(2) Unless otherwise specified a person by presenting a documentary draft or demand for payment under a credit relinquishes upon its honor all claims to the documents and a person by transferring such draft or demand or causing such presentment authorizes such relinquishment. An explicit reservation of claim makes the draft or demand noncomplying.

§ 5—111. Warranties on Transfer and Presentment.

(1) Unless otherwise agreed the beneficiary by transferring or presenting a documentary draft or demand for payment warrants to all interested parties that the necessary conditions of the credit have been complied with. This is in addition to any warranties arising under Articles 3, 4, 7 and 8.

(2) Unless otherwise agreed a negotiating, advising, confirming, collecting or issuing bank presenting or transferring a draft or demand for payment under a credit warrants only the matters warranted by a collecting bank under Article 4 and any such bank transferring a document warrants only the matters warranted by an intermediary under Articles 7 and 8.

§ 5—112. Time Allowed for Honor or Rejection; Withholding Honor or Rejection by Consent; "Presenter".

(1) A bank to which a documentary draft or demand for payment is presented under a credit may without dishonor of the draft, demand or credit

(a) defer honor until the close of the third banking day following receipt of the documents; and

(b) further defer honor if the presenter has expressly or impliedly consented thereto.

Failure to honor within the time here specified constitutes dishonor of the draft or demand and of the credit [except as otherwise provided in subsection (4) of Section 5—114 on conditional payment].

Note: *The bracketed language in the last sentence of subsection (1) should be included only if the optional provisions of Section 5—114(4) and (5) are included.*

(2) Upon dishonor the bank may unless otherwise instructed fulfill its duty to return the draft or demand and the documents by holding them at the disposal of the presenter and sending him an advice to that effect.

(3) "Presenter" means any person presenting a draft or demand for payment for honor under a credit even though that person is a confirming bank or other correspondent which is acting under an issuer's authorization.

§ 5—113. Indemnities.

(1) A bank seeking to obtain (whether for itself or another) honor, negotiation or reimbursement under a credit may give an indemnity to induce such honor, negotiation or reimbursement.

(2) An indemnity agreement inducing honor, negotiation or reimbursement

(a) unless otherwise explicitly agreed applies to defects in the documents but not in the goods; and

(b) unless a longer time is explicitly agreed expires at the end of ten business days following receipt of the documents by the ultimate customer unless notice of objection is sent before such expiration date. The ultimate customer may send notice of objection to the person from whom he received the documents and any bank receiving such notice is under a duty to send notice to its transferor before its midnight deadline.

§ 5—114. Issuer's Duty and Privilege to Honor; Right to Reimbursement.

(1) An issuer must honor a draft or demand for payment which complies with the terms of the relevant credit regardless of whether the goods or documents conform to the underlying contract for sale or other contract between the customer and the beneficiary. The issuer is not excused from honor of such a draft or demand by reason of an additional general term that all documents must be satisfactory to the issuer, but an issuer may require that specified documents must be satisfactory to it.

(2) Unless otherwise agreed when documents appear on their face to comply with the terms of a credit but a required document does not in fact conform to the warranties made on negotiation or transfer of a document of title (Section 7—507) or of a certificated security (Section 8—306) or is forged or fraudulent or there is fraud in the transaction:

(a) the issuer must honor the draft or demand for payment if honor is demanded by a negotiating bank or other holder of the draft or demand which has taken the draft or demand under the credit and under circumstances which would make it a holder in due course (Section 3—302) and in an appropriate case would make it a person to whom a document of title has been duly negotiated (Section 7—502) or a bona fide purchaser of a certificated security (Section 8—302); and

(b) in all other cases as against its customer, an issuer acting in good faith may honor the draft or demand for payment despite notification from the customer of fraud, forgery or other defect not apparent on the face of the documents but a court of appropriate jurisdiction may enjoin such honor.

(3) Unless otherwise agreed an issuer which has duly honored a draft or demand for payment is entitled to immediate reimbursement of any payment made under the credit and to be put in effectively available funds not later than the day before maturity of any acceptance made under the credit.

[(4) When a credit provides for payment by the issuer on receipt of notice that the required documents are in the possession of a correspondent or other agent of the issuer

(a) any payment made on receipt of such notice is conditional; and

(b) the issuer may reject documents which do not comply with the credit if it does so within three banking days following its receipt of the documents; and

(c) in the event of such rejection, the issuer is entitled by charge back or otherwise to return of the payment made.]

[(5) In the case covered by subsection (4) failure to reject documents within the time specified in sub-paragraph (b) constitutes acceptance of the documents and makes the payment final in favor of the beneficiary.]

Note: *Subsections (4) and (5) are bracketed as optional. If they are included the bracketed language in the last sentence of Section 5—112(1) should also be included.*

§ 5—115. Remedy for Improper Dishonor or Anticipatory Repudiation.

(1) When an issuer wrongfully dishonors a draft or demand for payment presented under a credit the person entitled to honor has with respect to any documents the rights of a person in the position of a seller (Section 2—707) and may recover from the issuer the face amount of the draft or demand together with incidental damages under Section 2—710 on seller's incidental damages and interest but less any amount realized by resale or other use or disposition of the subject matter of the transaction. In the event no resale or other utilization is made the documents, goods or other subject matter involved in the transaction must be turned over to the issuer on payment of judgment.

(2) When an issuer wrongfully cancels or otherwise repudiates a credit before presentment of a draft or demand for payment drawn under it the beneficiary has the rights of a seller after anticipatory repudiation by the buyer under Section 2—610 if he learns of the repudiation in time reasonably to avoid procurement of the required documents. Otherwise the beneficiary has an immediate right of action for wrongful dishonor.

§ 5—116. Transfer and Assignment.

(1) The right to draw under a credit can be transferred or assigned only when the credit is expressly designated as transferable or assignable.

(2) Even though the credit specifically states that it is nontransferable or nonassignable the beneficiary may before performance of the conditions of the credit assign his right to proceeds. Such an assignment is an assignment of an account under Article 9 on Secured Transactions and is governed by that Article except that

(a) the assignment is ineffective until the letter of credit or advice of credit is delivered to the assignee which delivery constitutes perfection of the security interest under Article 9; and

(b) the issuer may honor drafts or demands for payment drawn under the credit until it receives a notification of the assignment signed by the beneficiary which reasonably identifies the credit involved in the assignment and contains a request to pay the assignee; and

(c) after what reasonably appears to be such a notification has been received the issuer may without dishonor refuse to accept or pay even to a person otherwise entitled to honor until the letter of credit or advice of credit is exhibited to the issuer.

(3) Except where the beneficiary has effectively assigned his right to draw or his right to proceeds, nothing in this section limits his right to transfer or negotiate drafts or demands drawn under the credit.

§ 5—117. Insolvency of Bank Holding Funds for Documentary Credit.

(1) Where an issuer or an advising or confirming bank or a bank which has for a customer procured issuance of a credit by another bank becomes insolvent before final payment under the credit and the credit is one to which this Article is made applicable by paragraphs (a) or (b) of Section 5—102(1) on scope, the receipt or allocation of funds or collateral to secure or meet obligations under the credit shall have the following results:

(a) to the extent of any funds or collateral turned over after or before the insolvency as indemnity against or specifically for the purpose of payment of drafts or demands for payment drawn under the designated credit, the drafts or demands are entitled to payment in preference over depositors or other general creditors of the issuer or bank; and

(b) on expiration of the credit or surrender of the beneficiary's rights under it unused any person who has given such funds or collateral is similarly entitled to return thereof; and

(c) a charge to a general or current account with a bank if specifically consented to for the purpose of indemnity against or payment of drafts or demands for payment drawn under the designated credit falls under the same rules as if the funds had been drawn out in cash and then turned over with specific instructions.

(2) After honor or reimbursement under this section the customer or other person for whose account the insolvent bank has acted is entitled to receive the documents involved.

Article 6
BULK TRANSFERS

§ 6—101. Short Title.

This Article shall be known and may be cited as Uniform Commercial Code—Bulk Transfers.

§ 6—102. "Bulk Transfers"; Transfers of Equipment; Enterprises Subject to This Article; Bulk Transfers Subject to This Article.

(1) A "bulk transfer" is any transfer in bulk and not in the ordinary course of the transferor's business of a major part of the materials, supplies, merchandise or other inventory (Section 9—109) of an enterprise subject to this Article.

(2) A transfer of a substantial part of the equipment (Section 9—109) of such an enterprise is a bulk transfer if it is made in connection with a bulk transfer of inventory, but not otherwise.

(3) The enterprises subject to this Article are all those whose principal business is the sale of merchandise from stock, including those who manufacture what they sell.

(4) Except as limited by the following section all bulk transfers of goods located within this state are subject to this Article.

§ 6—103. Transfers Excepted From This Article.

The following transfers are not subject to this Article:

(1) Those made to give security for the performance of an obligation;

(2) General assignments for the benefit of all the creditors of the transferor, and subsequent transfers by the assignee thereunder;

(3) Transfers in settlement or realization of a lien or other security interests;

(4) Sales by executors, administrators, receivers, trustees in bankruptcy, or any public officer under judicial process;

(5) Sales made in the course of judicial or administrative proceedings for the dissolution or reorganization of a corporation and of which notice is sent to the creditors of the corporation pursuant to order of the court or administrative agency;

(6) Transfers to a person maintaining a known place of business in this State who becomes bound to pay the debts of the transferor in full and gives public notice of that fact, and who is solvent after becoming so bound;

(7) A transfer to a new business enterprise organized to take over and continue the business, if public notice of the transaction is given and the new enterprise assumes the debts of the transferor and he receives nothing from the transaction except an interest in the new enterprise junior to the claims of creditors;

(8) Transfers of property which is exempt from execution.

Public notice under subsection (6) or subsection (7) may be given by publishing once a week for two consecutive weeks in a newspaper of general circulation where the transferor had its principal place of business in this state an advertisement including the names and addresses of the transferor and transferee and the effective date of the transfer.

§ 6—104. Schedule of Property, List of Creditors.

(1) Except as provided with respect to auction sales (Section 6—108), a bulk transfer subject to this Article is ineffective against any creditor of the transferor unless:

(a) The transferee requires the transferor to furnish a list of his existing creditors prepared as stated in this section; and

(b) The parties prepare a schedule of the property transferred sufficient to identify it; and

(c) The transferee preserves the list and schedule for six months next following the transfer and permits inspection of either or both and copying therefrom at all reasonable hours by any creditor of the transferor, or files the list and schedule in (a public office to be here identified).

(2) The list of creditors must be signed and sworn to or affirmed by the transferor or his agent. It must contain the names and business addresses of all creditors of the transferor, with the amounts when known, and also the names of all persons who are known to the transferor to assert claims against him even though such claims are disputed. If the transferor is the obligor of an outstanding issue of bonds, debentures or the like as to which there is an indenture trustee, the list of creditors need include only the name and address of the indenture trustee and the aggregate outstanding principal amount of the issue.

(3) Responsibility for the completeness and accuracy of the list of creditors rests on the transferor, and the transfer is not rendered ineffective by errors or omissions therein unless the transferee is shown to have had knowledge.

§ 6—105. Notice to Creditors.

In addition to the requirements of the preceding section, any bulk transfer subject to this Article except one made by auction sale (Section 6—108) is ineffective against any creditor of the transferor unless at least ten days before he takes possession of the goods or pays for them, whichever happens first, the transferee gives notice of the transfer in the manner and to the persons hereafter provided (Section 6—107).

§ 6—106. Application of the Proceeds.

In addition to the requirements of the two preceding sections:

(1) Upon every bulk transfer subject to this Article for which new consideration becomes payable except those made by sale at auction it is the duty of the transferee to assure that such consideration is applied so far as necessary to pay those debts of the transferor which are either shown on the list furnished by the transferor (Section 6—104) or filed in writing in the place stated in the notice (Section 6—107) within thirty days after the mailing of such notice. This duty of the transferee runs to all the holders of such debts, and may be enforced by any of them for the benefit of all.

(2) If any of said debts are in dispute the necessary sum may be withheld from distribution until the dispute is settled or adjudicated.

(3) If the consideration payable is not enough to pay all of the said debts in full distribution shall be made pro rata.]

Note: *This section is bracketed to indicate division of opinion as to whether or not it is a wise provision, and to suggest that this is a point on which State enactments may differ without serious damage to the principle of uniformity. In any State where this section is omitted, the following parts of sections, also bracketed in the text, should also be omitted, namely:*

Section 6—107(2)(e).
6—108(3)(c).
6—109(2).

In any State where this section is enacted, these other provisions should be also.

Optional Subsection (4)

[(4) The transferee may within ten days after he takes possession of the goods pay the consideration into the (specify court) in the county where the transferor had its principal place of business in this state and thereafter may discharge his duty under this section by giving notice by registered or certified mail to all the persons to whom the duty runs that the consideration has been paid into that court and that they should file their claims there. On motion of any interested party, the court may order the distribution of the consideration to the persons entitled to it.]

Note: Optional subsection (4) is recommended for those states which do not have a general statute providing for payment of money into court.

§ 6—107. The Notice.

(1) The notice to creditors (Section 6—105) shall state:

(a) that a bulk transfer is about to be made; and

(b) the names and business addresses of the transferor and transferee, and all other business names and addresses used by the transferor within three years last past so far as known to the transferee; and

(c) whether or not all the debts of the transferor are to be paid in full as they fall due as a result of the transaction, and if so, the address to which creditors should send their bills.

(2) If the debts of the transferor are not to be paid in full as they fall due or if the transferee is in doubt on that point then the notice shall state further:

(a) the location and general description of the property to be transferred and the estimated total of the transferor's debts;

(b) the address where the schedule of property and list of creditors (Section 6—104) may be inspected;

(c) whether the transfer is to pay existing debts and if so the amount of such debts and to whom owing;

(d) whether the transfer is for new consideration and if so the amount of such consideration and the time and place of payment; [and]

[(e) if for new consideration the time and place where creditors of the transferor are to file their claims.]

(3) The notice in any case shall be delivered personally or sent by registered or certified mail to all the persons shown on the list of creditors furnished by the transferor (Section 6—104) and to all other persons who are known to the transferee to hold or assert claims against the transferor.

§ 6—108. Auction Sales; "Auctioneer".

(1) A bulk transfer is subject to this Article even though it is by sale at auction, but only in the manner and with the results stated in this section.

(2) The transferor shall furnish a list of his creditors and assist in the preparation of a schedule of the property to be sold, both prepared as before stated (Section 6—104).

(3) The person or persons other than the transferor who direct, control or are responsible for the auction are collectively called the "auctioneer". The auctioneer shall:

(a) receive and retain the list of creditors and prepare and retain the schedule of property for the period stated in this Article (Section 6—104);

(b) give notice of the auction personally or by registered or certified mail at least ten days before it occurs to all persons shown on the list of creditors and to all other persons who are known to him to hold or assert claims against the transferor; [and]

[(c) assure that the net proceeds of the auction are applied as provided in this Article (Section 6—106).]

(4) Failure of the auctioneer to perform any of these duties does not affect the validity of the sale or the title of the purchasers, but if the auctioneer knows that the auction constitutes a bulk transfer such failure renders the auctioneer liable to the creditors of the transferor as a class for the sums owing to them from the transferor up to but not exceeding the net proceeds of the auction. If the auctioneer consists of several persons their liability is joint and several.

§ 6—109. What Creditors Protected; [Credit for Payment to Particular Creditors].

(1) The creditors of the transferor mentioned in this Article are those holding claims based on transactions or events occurring before the bulk transfer, but creditors who become such after notice to creditors is given (Sections 6—105 and 6—107) are not entitled to notice.

[(2) Against the aggregate obligation imposed by the provisions of this Article concerning the application of the proceeds (Section 6—106 and subsection (3)(c) of 6—108) the transferee or auctioneer is entitled to credit for sums paid to particular creditors of the transferor, not exceeding the sums believed in good faith at the time of the payment to be properly payable to such creditors.]

§ 6—110. Subsequent Transfers.

When the title of a transferee to property is subject to a defect by reason of his noncompliance with the requirements of this Article, then:

(1) a purchaser of any of such property from such transferee who pays no value or who takes with notice of such noncompliance takes subject to such defect, but

(2) a purchaser for value in good faith and without such notice takes free of such defect.

§ 6—111. Limitation of Actions and Levies.

No action under this Article shall be brought nor levy made more than six months after the date on which the transferee took possession of the goods unless the transfer has been concealed. If the transfer has been concealed, actions may be brought or levies made within six months after its discovery.

Note to Article 6: *Section 6—106 is bracketed to indicate division of opinion as to whether or not it is a wise provision, and to suggest that this is a point on which State enactments may differ without serious damage to the principle of uniformity.*

In any State where Section 6—106 is not enacted, the following parts of sections, also bracketed in the text, should also be omitted, namely:
Sec. 6—107(2)(e).
6—108(3)(c).
6—109(2).

In any State where Section 6—106 is enacted, these other provisions should be also.

Article 6
Alternative B*

§ 6—101. Short Title.

This Article shall be known and may be cited as Uniform Commercial Code—Bulk Sales.

§ 6—102. Definitions and Index of Definitions.

(1) In this Article, unless the context otherwise requires:

(a) "Assets" means the inventory that is the subject of a bulk sale and any tangible and intangible personal property used or held for use primarily in, or arising from, the seller's business and sold in connection with that inventory, but the term does not include:

(i) fixtures (Section 9—313(1)(a)) other than readily removable factory and office machines;

(ii) the lessee's interest in a lease of real property; or

(iii) property to the extent it is generally exempt from creditor process under nonbankruptcy law.

(b) "Auctioneer" means a person whom the seller engages to direct, conduct, control, or be responsible for a sale by auction.

(c) "Bulk sale" means:

(i) in the case of a sale by auction or a sale or series of sales conducted by a liquidator on the seller's behalf, a sale or series of sales not in the ordinary course of the seller's business of more than half of the seller's inventory, as measured by value on the date of the bulk-sale agreement, if on that date the auctioneer or liquidator has notice, or after reasonable inquiry would have had notice, that the seller will not continue to operate the same or a similar kind of business after the sale or series of sales; and

(ii) in all other cases, a sale not in the ordinary course of the seller's business of more than half the seller's

*Approved in substance by the National Conference of Commissioners on Uniform State Laws and The American Law Institute. States have the choice of adopting this alternative to the existing Article 6 or repealing Article 6 entirely (Alternative A).

inventory, as measured by value on the date of the bulk-sale agreement, if on that date the buyer has notice, or after reasonable inquiry would have had notice, that the seller will not continue to operate the same or a similar kind of business after the sale.

(d) "Claim" means a right to payment from the seller, whether or not the right is reduced to judgment, liquidated, fixed, matured, disputed, secured, legal, or equitable. The term includes costs of collection and attorney's fees only to the extent that the laws of this state permit the holder of the claim to recover them in an action against the obligor.

(e) "Claimant" means a person holding a claim incurred in the seller's business other than:

(i) an unsecured and unmatured claim for employment compensation and benefits, including commissions and vacation, severance, and sick-leave pay;

(ii) a claim for injury to an individual or to property, or for breach of warranty, unless:

(A) a right of action for the claim has accrued;

(B) the claim has been asserted against the seller; and

(C) the seller knows the identity of the person asserting the claim and the basis upon which the person has asserted it; and

(States to Select One Alternative)

Alternative A

[(iii) a claim for taxes owing to a governmental unit.]

Alternative B

[(iii) a claim for taxes owing to a governmental unit, if:

(A) a statute governing the enforcement of the claim permits or requires notice of the bulk sale to be given to the governmental unit in a manner other than by compliance with the requirements of this Article; and

(B) notice is given in accordance with the statute.]

(f) "Creditor" means a claimant or other person holding a claim.

(g)(i) "Date of the bulk sale" means:

(A) if the sale is by auction or is conducted by a liquidator on the seller's behalf, the date on which more than ten percent of the net proceeds is paid to or for the benefit of the seller; and

(B) in all other cases, the later of the date on which:

(I) more than ten percent of the net contract price is paid to or for the benefit of the seller; or

(II) more than ten percent of the assets, as measured by value, are transferred to the buyer.

(ii) For purposes of this subsection:

(A) delivery of a negotiable instrument (Section 3—104(1)) to or for the benefit of the seller in exchange for assets constitutes payment of the contract price pro tanto;

(B) to the extent that the contract price is deposited in an escrow, the contract price is paid to or for the benefit of the seller when the seller acquires the unconditional right to receive the deposit or when the deposit is delivered to the seller or for the benefit of the seller, whichever is earlier; and

(C) an asset is transferred when a person holding an unsecured claim can no longer obtain through judicial proceedings rights to the asset that are superior to those of the buyer arising as a result of the bulk sale. A person holding an unsecured claim can obtain those superior rights to a tangible asset at least until the buyer has an unconditional right, under the bulk-sale agreement, to possess the asset, and a person holding an unsecured claim can obtain those superior rights to an intangible asset at least until the buyer has an unconditional right, under the bulk-sale agreement, to use the asset.

(h) "Date of the bulk-sale agreement" means:

(i) in the case of a sale by auction or conducted by a liquidator (subsection (c)(i)), the date on which the seller engages the auctioneer or liquidator; and

(ii) in all other cases, the date on which a bulk-sale agreement becomes enforceable between the buyer and the seller.

(i) "Debt" means liability on a claim.

(j) "Liquidator" means a person who is regularly engaged in the business of disposing of assets for businesses contemplating liquidation or dissolution.

(k) "Net contract price" means the new consideration the buyer is obligated to pay for the assets less:

(i) the amount of any proceeds of the sale of an asset, to the extent the proceeds are applied in partial or total satisfaction of a debt secured by the asset; and

(ii) the amount of any debt to the extent it is secured by a security interest or lien that is enforceable against the asset before and after it has been sold to a buyer. If a debt is secured by an asset and other property of the seller, the amount of the debt secured by a security interest or lien that is enforceable against the asset is determined by multiplying the debt by a fraction, the numerator of which is the value of the new consideration for the asset on the date of the bulk sale and the denominator of which is the value of all property securing the debt on the date of the bulk sale.

(l) "Net proceeds" means the new consideration received for assets sold at a sale by auction or a sale conducted by a liquidator on the seller's behalf less:

(i) commissions and reasonable expenses of the sale;

(ii) the amount of any proceeds of the sale of an asset, to the extent the proceeds are applied in partial or total satisfaction of a debt secured by the asset; and

(iii) the amount of any debt to the extent it is secured by a security interest or lien that is enforceable against the asset before and after it has been sold to a buyer. If a debt is secured by an asset and other property of the seller, the amount of the debt secured by a security interest or lien that is enforceable against the asset is determined by multiplying the debt by a fraction, the numerator of which is the value of the new consideration for the asset on the date of the bulk sale and the denominator of which is the value of all property securing the debt on the date of the bulk sale.

(m) A sale is "in the ordinary course of the seller's business" if the sale comports with usual or customary practices in the kind of business in which the seller is engaged or with the seller's own usual or customary practices.

(n) "United States" includes its territories and possessions and the Commonwealth of Puerto Rico.

(o) "Value" means fair market value.

(p) "Verified" means signed and sworn to or affirmed.

(2) The following definitions in other Articles apply to this Article:

(a) "Buyer."	Section 2—103(1)(a).
(b) "Equipment."	Section 9—109(2).
(c) "Inventory."	Section 9—109(4).
(d) "Sale."	Section 2—106(1).
(e) "Seller."	Section 2—103(1)(d).

(3) In addition, Article 1 contains general definitions and principles of construction and interpretation applicable throughout this Article.

§ 6—103. Applicability of Article.

(1) Except as otherwise provided in subsection (3), this Article applies to a bulk sale if:

(a) the seller's principal business is the sale of inventory from stock; and

(b) on the date of the bulk-sale agreement the seller is located in this state or, if the seller is located in a jurisdiction that is not a part of the United States, the seller's major executive office in the United States is in this state.

(2) A seller is deemed to be located at his [or her] place of business. If a seller has more than one place of business, the seller is deemed located at his [or her] chief executive office.

(3) This Article does not apply to:

(a) a transfer made to secure payment or performance of an obligation;

(b) a transfer of collateral to a secured party pursuant to Section 9—503;

(c) a sale of collateral pursuant to Section 9—504;

(d) retention of collateral pursuant to Section 9—505;

(e) a sale of an asset encumbered by a security interest or lien if (i) all the proceeds of the sale are applied in partial or total satisfaction of the debt secured by the security interest or lien or (ii) the security interest or lien is enforceable against the asset after it has been sold to the buyer and the net contract price is zero;

(f) a general assignment for the benefit of creditors or to a subsequent transfer by the assignee;

(g) a sale by an executor, administrator, receiver, trustee in bankruptcy, or any public officer under judicial process;

(h) a sale made in the course of judicial or administrative proceedings for the dissolution or reorganization of an organization;

(i) a sale to a buyer whose principal place of business is in the United States and who:

(i) not earlier than 21 days before the date of the bulk sale, (A) obtains from the seller a verified and dated list of claimants of whom the seller has notice three days before the seller sends or delivers the list to the buyer or (B) conducts a reasonable inquiry to discover the claimants;

(ii) assumes in full the debts owed to claimants of whom the buyer has knowledge on the date the buyer receives the list of claimants from the seller or on the date the buyer completes the reasonable inquiry, as the case may be;

(iii) is not insolvent after the assumption; and

(iv) gives written notice of the assumption not later than 30 days after the date of the bulk sale by sending or delivering a notice to the claimants identified in subparagraph (ii) or by filing a notice in the office of the [Secretary of State];

(j) a sale to a buyer whose principal place of business is in the United States and who:

(i) assumes in full the debts that were incurred in the seller's business before the date of the bulk sale;

(ii) is not insolvent after the assumption; and

(iii) gives written notice of the assumption not later than 30 days after the date of the bulk sale by sending or delivering a notice to each creditor whose debt is assumed or by filing a notice in the office of the [Secretary of State];

(k) a sale to a new organization that is organized to take over and continue the business of the seller and that has its principal place of business in the United States if:

(i) the buyer assumes in full the debts that were incurred in the seller's business before the date of the bulk sale;

(ii) the seller receives nothing from the sale except an interest in the new organization that is subordinate to the claims against the organization arising from the assumption; and

(iii) the buyer gives written notice of the assumption

not later than 30 days after the date of the bulk sale by sending or delivering a notice to each creditor whose debt is assumed or by filing a notice in the office of the [Secretary of State];

(l) a sale of assets having:

(i) a value, net of liens and security interests, of less than $10,000. If a debt is secured by assets and other property of the seller, the net value of the assets is determined by subtracting from their value an amount equal to the product of the debt multiplied by a fraction, the numerator of which is the value of the assets on the date of the bulk sale and the denominator of which is the value of all property securing the debt on the date of the bulk sale; or

(ii) a value of more than $25,000,000 on the date of the bulk-sale agreement; or

(m) a sale required by, and made pursuant to, statute.

(4) The notice under subsection (3)(i)(iv) must state: (i) that a sale that may constitute a bulk sale has been or will be made; (ii) the date or prospective date of the bulk sale; (iii) the individual, partnership, or corporate names and the addresses of the seller and buyer; (iv) the address to which inquiries about the sale may be made, if different from the seller's address; and (v) that the buyer has assumed or will assume in full the debts owed to claimants of whom the buyer has knowledge on the date the buyer receives the list of claimants from the seller or completes a reasonable inquiry to discover the claimants.

(5) The notice under subsections (3)(j)(iii) and (3)(k)(iii) must state: (i) that a sale that may constitute a bulk sale has been or will be made; (ii) the date or prospective date of the bulk sale; (iii) the individual, partnership, or corporate names and the addresses of the seller and buyer; (iv) the address to which inquiries about the sale may be made, if different from the seller's address; and (v) that the buyer has assumed or will assume the debts that were incurred in the seller's business before the date of the bulk sale.

(6) For purposes of subsection (3)(l), the value of assets is presumed to be equal to the price the buyer agrees to pay for the assets. However, in a sale by auction or a sale conducted by a liquidator on the seller's behalf, the value of assets is presumed to be the amount the auctioneer or liquidator reasonably estimates the assets will bring at auction or upon liquidation.

§ 6—104. Obligations of Buyer.

(1) In a bulk sale as defined in Section 6—102(1)(c)(ii) the buyer shall:

(a) obtain from the seller a list of all business names and addresses used by the seller within three years before the date the list is sent or delivered to the buyer;

(b) unless excused under subsection (2), obtain from the seller a verified and dated list of claimants of whom the seller has notice three days before the seller sends or delivers the list to the buyer and including, to the extent known by the seller, the address of and the amount claimed by each claimant;

(c) obtain from the seller or prepare a schedule of distribution (Section 6—106(1));

(d) give notice of the bulk sale in accordance with Section 6—105;

(e) unless excused under Section 6—106(4), distribute the net contract price in accordance with the undertakings of the buyer in the schedule of distribution; and

(f) unless excused under subsection (2), make available the list of claimants (subsection (1)(b)) by:

(i) promptly sending or delivering a copy of the list without charge to any claimant whose written request is received by the buyer no later than six months after the date of the bulk sale;

(ii) permitting any claimant to inspect and copy the list at any reasonable hour upon request received by the buyer no later than six months after the date of the bulk sale; or

(iii) filing a copy of the list in the office of the [Secretary of State] no later than the time for giving a notice of the bulk sale (Section 6—105(5)). A list filed in accordance with this subparagraph must state the individual, partnership, or corporate name and a mailing address of the seller.

(2) A buyer who gives notice in accordance with Section 6—105(2) is excused from complying with the requirements of subsections (1)(b) and (1)(f).

§ 6—105. Notice to Claimants.

(1) Except as otherwise provided in subsection (2), to comply with Section 6—104(1)(d) the buyer shall send or deliver a written notice of the bulk sale to each claimant on the list of claimants (Section 6—104(1)(b)) and to any other claimant of which the buyer has knowledge at the time the notice of the bulk sale is sent or delivered.

(2) A buyer may comply with Section 6—104(1)(d) by filing a written notice of the bulk sale in the office of the [Secretary of State] if:

(a) on the date of the bulk-sale agreement the seller has 200 or more claimants, exclusive of claimants holding secured or matured claims for employment compensation and benefits, including commissions and vacation, severance, and sick-leave pay; or

(b) the buyer has received a verified statement from the seller stating that, as of the date of the bulk-sale agreement, the number of claimants, exclusive of claimants holding secured or matured claims for employment compensation and benefits, including commissions and vacation, severance, and sick-leave pay, is 200 or more.

(3) The written notice of the bulk sale must be accompanied by a copy of the schedule of distribution (Section 6—106(1)) and state at least:

(a) that the seller and buyer have entered into an agreement for a sale that may constitute a bulk sale under the laws of the State of ________;

(b) the date of the agreement;

(c) the date on or after which more than ten percent of the assets were or will be transferred;

(d) the date on or after which more than ten percent of the net contract price was or will be paid, if the date is not stated in the schedule of distribution;

(e) the name and a mailing address of the seller;

(f) any other business name and address listed by the seller pursuant to Section 6—104(1)(a);

(g) the name of the buyer and an address of the buyer from which information concerning the sale can be obtained;

(h) a statement indicating the type of assets or describing the assets item by item;

(i) the manner in which the buyer will make available the list of claimants (Section 6—104(1)(f)), if applicable; and

(j) if the sale is in total or partial satisfaction of an antecedent debt owed by the seller, the amount of the debt to be satisfied and the name of the person to whom it is owed.

(4) For purposes of subsections (3)(e) and (3)(g), the name of a person is the person's individual, partnership, or corporate name.

(5) The buyer shall give notice of the bulk sale not less than 45 days before the date of the bulk sale and, if the buyer gives notice in accordance with subsection (1), not more than 30 days after obtaining the list of claimants.

(6) A written notice substantially complying with the requirements of subsection (3) is effective even though it contains minor errors that are not seriously misleading.

(7) A form substantially as follows is sufficient to comply with subsection (3):

Notice of Sale

(1) ________, whose address is ________, is described in this notice as the "seller."

(2) ________, whose address is ________, is described in this notice as the "buyer."

(3) The seller has disclosed to the buyer that within the past three years the seller has used other business names, operated at other addresses, or both, as follows: ________________________________.

(4) The seller and the buyer have entered into an agreement dated ________, for a sale that may constitute a bulk sale under the laws of the State of ______.

(5) The date on or after which more than ten percent of the assets that are the subject of the sale were or will be transferred is ________, and [if not stated in the schedule of distribution] the date on or after which more than ten percent of the net contract price was or will be paid is ________.

(6) The following assets are the subject of the sale: ________________________________.

(7) [If applicable] The buyer will make available to claimants of the seller a list of the seller's claimants in the following manner: ________________________.

(8) [If applicable] The sale is to satisfy $ ________ of an antecedent debt owed by the seller to ________.

(9) A copy of the schedule of distribution of the net contract price accompanies this notice.

[End of Notice]

§ 6—106. Schedule of Distribution.

(1) The seller and buyer shall agree on how the net contract price is to be distributed and set forth their agreement in a written schedule of distribution.

(2) The schedule of distribution may provide for distribution to any person at any time, including distribution of the entire net contract price to the seller.

(3) The buyer's undertakings in the schedule of distribution run only to the seller. However, a buyer who fails to distribute the net contract price in accordance with the buyer's undertakings in the schedule of distribution is liable to a creditor only as provided in Section 6—107(1).

(4) If the buyer undertakes in the schedule of distribution to distribute any part of the net contract price to a person other than the seller, and, after the buyer has given notice in accordance with Section 6—105, some or all of the anticipated net contract price is or becomes unavailable for distribution as a consequence of the buyer's or seller's having complied with an order of court, legal process, statute, or rule of law, the buyer is excused from any obligation arising under this Article or under any contract with the seller to distribute the net contract price in accordance with the buyer's undertakings in the schedule if the buyer:

(a) distributes the net contract price remaining available in accordance with any priorities for payment stated in the schedule of distribution and, to the extent that the price is insufficient to pay all the debts having a given priority, distributes the price pro rata among those debts shown in the schedule as having the same priority;

(b) distributes the net contract price remaining available in accordance with an order of court;

(c) commences a proceeding for interpleader in a court of competent jurisdiction and is discharged from the proceeding; or

(d) reaches a new agreement with the seller for the distribution of the net contract price remaining available, sets forth the new agreement in an amended schedule of distribution, gives notice of the amended schedule, and distributes the net contract price remaining available in accordance with the buyer's undertakings in the amended schedule.

(5) The notice under subsection (4)(d) must identify the buyer and the seller, state the filing number, if any, of the original notice, set forth the amended schedule, and be given in accordance with subsection (1) or (2) of Section 6—105, whichever

is applicable, at least 14 days before the buyer distributes any part of the net contract price remaining available.

(6) If the seller undertakes in the schedule of distribution to distribute any part of the net contract price, and, after the buyer has given notice in accordance with Section 6—105, some or all of the anticipated net contract price is or becomes unavailable for distribution as a consequence of the buyer's or seller's having complied with an order of court, legal process, statute, or rule of law, the seller and any person in control of the seller are excused from any obligation arising under this Article or under any agreement with the buyer to distribute the net contract price in accordance with the seller's undertakings in the schedule if the seller:

(a) distributes the net contract price remaining available in accordance with any priorities for payment stated in the schedule of distribution and, to the extent that the price is insufficient to pay all the debts having a given priority, distributes the price pro rata among those debts shown in the schedule as having the same priority;

(b) distributes the net contract price remaining available in accordance with an order of court;

(c) commences a proceeding for interpleader in a court of competent jurisdiction and is discharged from the proceeding; or

(d) prepares a written amended schedule of distribution of the net contract price remaining available for distribution, gives notice of the amended schedule, and distributes the net contract price remaining available in accordance with the amended schedule.

(7) The notice under subsection (6)(d) must identify the buyer and the seller, state the filing number, if any, of the original notice, set forth the amended schedule, and be given in accordance with subsection (1) or (2) of Section 6—105, whichever is applicable, at least 14 days before the seller distributes any part of the net contract price remaining available.

§ 6—107. Liability for Noncompliance.

(1) Except as provided in subsection (3), and subject to the limitation in subsection (4):

(a) a buyer who fails to comply with the requirements of Section 6—104(1)(e) with respect to a creditor is liable to the creditor for damages in the amount of the claim, reduced by any amount that the creditor would not have realized if the buyer had complied; and

(b) a buyer who fails to comply with the requirements of any other subsection of Section 6—104 with respect to a claimant is liable to the claimant for damages in the amount of the claim, reduced by any amount that the claimant would not have realized if the buyer had complied.

(2) In an action under subsection (1), the creditor has the burden of establishing the validity and amount of the claim, and the buyer has the burden of establishing the amount that the creditor would not have realized if the buyer had complied.

(3) A buyer who:

(a) made a good faith and commercially reasonable effort to comply with the requirements of Section 6—104(1) or to exclude the sale from the application of this Article under Section 6—103(3); or

(b) on or after the date of the bulk-sale agreement, but before the date of the bulk sale, held a good faith and commercially reasonable belief that this Article does not apply to the particular sale

is not liable to creditors for failure to comply with the requirements of Section 6—104. The buyer has the burden of establishing the good faith and commercial reasonableness of the effort or belief.

(4) In a single bulk sale the cumulative liability of the buyer for failure to comply with the requirements of Section 6—104(1) may not exceed an amount equal to:

(a) if the assets consist only of inventory and equipment, twice the net contract price, less the amount of any part of the net contract price paid to or applied for the benefit of the seller or a creditor; or

(b) if the assets include property other than inventory and equipment, twice the net value of the inventory and equipment less the amount of the portion of any part of the net contract price paid to or applied for the benefit of the seller or a creditor which is allocable to the inventory and equipment.

(5) For the purposes of subsection (4)(b), the "net value" of an asset is the value of the asset less (i) the amount of any proceeds of the sale of an asset, to the extent the proceeds are applied in partial or total satisfaction of a debt secured by the asset and (ii) the amount of any debt to the extent it is secured by a security interest or lien that is enforceable against the asset before and after it has been sold to a buyer. If a debt is secured by an asset and other property of the seller, the amount of the debt secured by a security interest or lien that is enforceable against the asset is determined by multiplying the debt by a fraction, the numerator of which is the value of the asset on the date of the bulk sale and the denominator of which is the value of all property securing the debt on the date of the bulk sale. The portion of a part of the net contract price paid to or applied for the benefit of the seller or a creditor that is "allocable to the inventory and equipment" is the portion that bears the same ratio to that part of the net contract price as the net value of the inventory and equipment bears to the net value of all of the assets.

(6) A payment made by the buyer to a person to whom the buyer is, or believes he [or she] is, liable under subsection (1) reduces pro tanto the buyer's cumulative liability under subsection (4).

(7) No action may be brought under subsection (1)(b) by or on behalf of a claimant whose claim is unliquidated or contingent.

(8) A buyer's failure to comply with the requirements of Section 6—104(1) does not (i) impair the buyer's rights in or title to the assets, (ii) render the sale ineffective, void, or voidable, (iii) entitle a creditor to more than a single satisfaction of his [or her] claim, or (iv) create liability other than as provided in this Article.

(9) Payment of the buyer's liability under subsection (1) discharges pro tanto the seller's debt to the creditor.

(10) Unless otherwise agreed, a buyer has an immediate right of reimbursement from the seller for any amount paid to a creditor in partial or total satisfaction of the buyer's liability under subsection (1).

(11) If the seller is an organization, a person who is in direct or indirect control of the seller, and who knowingly, intentionally, and without legal justification fails, or causes the seller to fail, to distribute the net contract price in accordance with the schedule of distribution is liable to any creditor to whom the seller undertook to make payment under the schedule for damages caused by the failure.

§ 6—108. Bulk Sales by Auction; Bulk Sales Conducted by Liquidator.

(1) Sections 6—104, 6—105, 6—106, and 6—107 apply to a bulk sale by auction and a bulk sale conducted by a liquidator on the seller's behalf with the following modifications:

(a) "buyer" refers to auctioneer or liquidator, as the case may be;

(b) "net contract price" refers to net proceeds of the auction or net proceeds of the sale, as the case may be;

(c) the written notice required under Section 6—105(3) must be accompanied by a copy of the schedule of distribution (Section 6—106(1)) and state at least:

(i) that the seller and the auctioneer or liquidator have entered into an agreement for auction or liquidation services that may constitute an agreement to make a bulk sale under the laws of the State of ________;

(ii) the date of the agreement;

(iii) the date on or after which the auction began or will begin or the date on or after which the liquidator began or will begin to sell assets on the seller's behalf;

(iv) the date on or after which more than ten percent of the net proceeds of the sale were or will be paid, if the date is not stated in the schedule of distribution;

(v) the name and a mailing address of the seller;

(vi) any other business name and address listed by the seller pursuant to Section 6—104(1)(a);

(vii) the name of the auctioneer or liquidator and an address of the auctioneer or liquidator from which information concerning the sale can be obtained;

(viii) a statement indicating the type of assets or describing the assets item by item;

(ix) the manner in which the auctioneer or liquidator will make available the list of claimants (Section 6—104(1)(f)), if applicable; and

(x) if the sale is in total or partial satisfaction of an antecedent debt owed by the seller, the amount of the debt to be satisfied and the name of the person to whom it is owed; and

(d) in a single bulk sale the cumulative liability of the auctioneer or liquidator for failure to comply with the requirements of this section may not exceed the amount of the net proceeds of the sale allocable to inventory and equipment sold less the amount of the portion of any part of the net proceeds paid to or applied for the benefit of a creditor which is allocable to the inventory and equipment.

(2) A payment made by the auctioneer or liquidator to a person to whom the auctioneer or liquidator is, or believes he [or she] is, liable under this section reduces pro tanto the auctioneer's or liquidator's cumulative liability under subsection (1)(d).

(3) A form substantially as follows is sufficient to comply with subsection (1)(c):

Notice of Sale

(1) ________, whose address is ________, is described in this notice as the "seller."

(2) ______, whose address is ______, is described in this notice as the "auctioneer" or "liquidator."

(3) The seller has disclosed to the auctioneer or liquidator that within the past three years the seller has used other business names, operated at other addresses, or both, as follows: ________________.

(4) The seller and the auctioneer or liquidator have entered into an agreement dated ________ for auction or liquidation services that may constitute an agreement to make a bulk sale under the laws of the State of ________.

(5) The date on or after which the auction began or will begin or the date on or after which the liquidator began or will begin to sell assets on the seller's behalf is ________, and [if not stated in the schedule of distribution] the date on or after which more than ten percent of the net proceeds of the sale were or will be paid is ________.

(6) The following assets are the subject of the sale: ________________________________.

(7) [If applicable] The auctioneer or liquidator will make available to claimants of the seller a list of the seller's claimants in the following manner: ________.

(8) [If applicable] The sale is to satisfy $ ________ of an antecedent debt owed by the seller to ________.

(9) A copy of the schedule of distribution of the net proceeds accompanies this notice.

[End of Notice]

(4) A person who buys at a bulk sale by auction or conducted by a liquidator need not comply with the requirements of Section 6—104(1) and is not liable for the failure of an auctioneer or liquidator to comply with the requirements of this section.

§ 6—109. What Constitutes Filing; Duties of Filing Officer; Information from Filing Officer.

(1) Presentation of a notice or list of claimants for filing and tender of the filing fee or acceptance of the notice or list by the filing officer constitutes filing under this Article.

(2) The filing officer shall:

(a) mark each notice or list with a file number and with the date and hour of filing;

(b) hold the notice or list or a copy for public inspection;

(c) index the notice or list according to each name given for the seller and for the buyer; and

(d) note in the index the file number and the addresses of the seller and buyer given in the notice or list.

(3) If the person filing a notice or list furnishes the filing officer with a copy, the filing officer upon request shall note upon the copy the file number and date and hour of the filing of the original and send or deliver the copy to the person.

(4) The fee for filing and indexing and for stamping a copy furnished by the person filing to show the date and place of filing is $ ______ for the first page and $ ______ for each additional page. The fee for indexing each name beyond the first two is $ ________ .

(5) Upon request of any person, the filing officer shall issue a certificate showing whether any notice or list with respect to a particular seller or buyer is on file on the date and hour stated in the certificate. If a notice or list is on file, the certificate must give the date and hour of filing of each notice or list and the name and address of each seller, buyer, auctioneer, or liquidator. The fee for the certificate is $ ________ if the request for the certificate is in the standard form prescribed by the [Secretary of State] and otherwise is $ ________ . Upon request of any person, the filing officer shall furnish a copy of any filed notice or list for a fee of $ ________ .

(6) The filing officer shall keep each notice or list for two years after it is filed.

§ 6—110. Limitation of Actions.

(1) Except as provided in subsection (2), an action under this Article against a buyer, auctioneer, or liquidator must be commenced within one year after the date of the bulk sale.

(2) If the buyer, auctioneer, or liquidator conceals the fact that the sale has occurred, the limitation is tolled and an action under this Article may be commenced within the earlier of (i) one year after the person bringing the action discovers that the sale has occurred or (ii) one year after the person bringing the action should have discovered that the sale has occurred, but no later than two years after the date of the bulk sale. Complete noncompliance with the requirements of this Article does not of itself constitute concealment.

(3) An action under Section 6—107(11) must be commenced within one year after the alleged violation occurs.

Article 7

Warehouse Receipts, Bills of Lading and Other Documents of Title

Part 1 General

§ 7—101. Short Title.

This Article shall be known and may be cited as Uniform Commercial Code—Documents of Title.

§ 7—102. Definitions and Index of Definitions.

(1) In this Article, unless the context otherwise requires:

(a) "Bailee" means the person who by a warehouse receipt, bill of lading or other document of title acknowledges possession of goods and contracts to deliver them.

(b) "Consignee" means the person named in a bill to whom or to whose order the bill promises delivery.

(c) "Consignor" means the person named in a bill as the person from whom the goods have been received for shipment.

(d) "Delivery order" means a written order to deliver goods directed to a warehouseman, carrier or other person who in the ordinary course of business issues warehouse receipts or bills of lading.

(e) "Document" means document of title as defined in the general definitions in Article 1 (Section 1—201).

(f) "Goods" means all things which are treated as movable for the purposes of a contract of storage or transportation.

(g) "Issuer" means a bailee who issues a document except that in relation to an unaccepted delivery order it means the person who orders the possessor of goods to deliver. Issuer includes any person for whom an agent or employee purports to act in issuing a document if the agent or employee has real or apparent authority to issue documents, notwithstanding that the issuer received no goods or that the goods were misdescribed or that in any other respect the agent or employee violated his instructions.

(h) "Warehouseman" is a person engaged in the business of storing goods for hire.

(2) Other definitions applying to this Article or to specified Parts thereof, and the sections in which they appear are:

"Duly negotiate". Section 7—501.

"Person entitled under the document". Section 7—403(4).

(3) Definitions in other Articles applying to this Article and the sections in which they appear are:

"Contract for sale". Section 2—106.

"Overseas". Section 2—323.

"Receipt" of goods. Section 2—103.

(4) In addition Article 1 contains general definitions and principles of construction and interpretation applicable throughout this Article.

§ 7—103. Relation of Article to Treaty, Statute, Tariff, Classification or Regulation.

To the extent that any treaty or statute of the United States, regulatory statute of this State or tariff, classification or regulation filed or issued pursuant thereto is applicable, the provisions of this Article are subject thereto.

§ 7—104. Negotiable and Nonnegotiable Warehouse Receipt, Bill of Lading or Other Document of Title.

(1) A warehouse receipt, bill of lading or other document of title is negotiable

(a) if by its terms the goods are to be delivered to bearer or to the order of a named person; or

(b) where recognized in overseas trade, if it runs to a named person or assigns.

(2) Any other document is nonnegotiable. A bill of lading in which it is stated that the goods are consigned to a named person is not made negotiable by a provision that the goods are to be delivered only against a written order signed by the same or another named person.

§ 7—105. Construction Against Negative Implication.

The omission from either Part 2 or Part 3 of this Article of a provision corresponding to a provision made in the other Part does not imply that a corresponding rule of law is not applicable.

Part 2 Warehouse Receipts: Special Provisions

§ 7—201. Who May Issue a Warehouse Receipt; Storage Under Government Bond.

(1) A warehouse receipt may be issued by any warehouseman.

(2) Where goods including distilled spirits and agricultural commodities are stored under a statute requiring a bond against withdrawal or a license for the issuance of receipts in the nature of warehouse receipts, a receipt issued for the goods has like effect as a warehouse receipt even though issued by a person who is the owner of the goods and is not a warehouseman.

§ 7—202. Form of Warehouse Receipt; Essential Terms; Optional Terms.

(1) A warehouse receipt need not be in any particular form.

(2) Unless a warehouse receipt embodies within its written or printed terms each of the following, the warehouseman is liable for damages caused by the omission to a person injured thereby:

(a) the location of the warehouse where the goods are stored;

(b) the date of issue of the receipt;

(c) the consecutive number of the receipt;

(d) a statement whether the goods received will be delivered to the bearer, to a specified person, or to a specified person or his order;

(e) the rate of storage and handling charges, except that where goods are stored under a field warehousing arrangement a statement of that fact is sufficient on a nonnegotiable receipt;

(f) a description of the goods or of the packages containing them;

(g) the signature of the warehouseman, which may be made by his authorized agent;

(h) if the receipt is issued for goods of which the warehouseman is owner, either solely or jointly or in common with others, the fact of such ownership; and

(i) a statement of the amount of advances made and of liabilities incurred for which the warehouseman claims a lien or security interest (Section 7—209). If the precise amount of such advances made or of such liabilities incurred is, at the time of the issue of the receipt, unknown to the warehouseman or to his agent who issues it, a statement of the fact that advances have been made or liabilities incurred and the purpose thereof is sufficient.

(3) A warehouseman may insert in his receipt any other terms which are not contrary to the provisions of this Act and do not impair his obligation of delivery (Section 7—403) or his duty of care (Section 7—204). Any contrary provisions shall be ineffective.

§ 7—203. Liability for Nonreceipt or Misdescription.

A party to or purchaser for value in good faith of a document of title other than a bill of lading relying in either case upon the description therein of the goods may recover from the issuer damages caused by the nonreceipt or misdescription of the goods, except to the extent that the document conspicuously indicates that the issuer does not know whether any part or all of the goods in fact were received or conform to the description, as where the description is in terms of marks or labels or kind, quantity or condition, or the receipt or description is qualified by "contents, condition and quality unknown", "said to contain" or the like, if such indication be true, or the party or purchaser otherwise has notice.

§ 7—204. Duty of Care; Contractual Limitation of Warehouseman's Liability.

(1) A warehouseman is liable for damages for loss of or injury to the goods caused by his failure to exercise such care in regard to them as a reasonably careful man would exercise under like circumstances but unless otherwise agreed he is not liable for damages which could not have been avoided by the exercise of such care.

(2) Damages may be limited by a term in the warehouse receipt or storage agreement limiting the amount of liability in case of loss or damage, and setting forth a specific liability per article or item, or value per unit of weight, beyond which the warehouseman shall not be liable; provided, however, that such liability may on written request of the bailor at the time of signing such storage agreement or within a reasonable time after receipt of the warehouse receipt be increased on part or all of the goods thereunder, in which event increased rates may be charged based on such increased valuation, but that no such increase shall be permitted contrary to a lawful limitation of liability contained in the warehouseman's tariff, if any. No such limitation is effective with respect to the warehouseman's liability for conversion to his own use.

(3) Reasonable provisions as to the time and manner of presenting claims and instituting actions based on the bailment may be included in the warehouse receipt or tariff.

(4) This section does not impair or repeal . . .

Note: *Insert in subsection (4) a reference to any statute which imposes a higher responsibility upon the warehouseman or invalidates contractual limitations which would be permissible under this Article.*

§ 7—205. Title Under Warehouse Receipt Defeated in Certain Cases.

A buyer in the ordinary course of business of fungible goods sold and delivered by a warehouseman who is also in the business of buying and selling such goods takes free of any claim under a warehouse receipt even though it has been duly negotiated.

§ 7—206. Termination of Storage at Warehouseman's Option.

(1) A warehouseman may on notifying the person on whose account the goods are held and any other person known to claim an interest in the goods require payment of any charges and removal of the goods from the warehouse at the termination of the period of storage fixed by the document, or, if no period is fixed, within a stated period not less than thirty days after the notification. If the goods are not removed before the date specified in the notification, the warehouseman may sell them in accordance with the provisions of the section on enforcement of a warehouseman's lien (Section 7—210).

(2) If a warehouseman in good faith believes that the goods are about to deteriorate or decline in value to less than the amount of his lien within the time prescribed in subsection (1) for notification, advertisement and sale, the warehouseman may specify in the notification any reasonable shorter time for removal of the goods and in case the goods are not removed, may sell them at public sale held not less than one week after a single advertisement or posting.

(3) If as a result of a quality or condition of the goods of which the warehouseman had no notice at the time of deposit the goods are a hazard to other property or to the warehouse or to persons, the warehouseman may sell the goods at public or private sale without advertisement on reasonable notification to all persons known to claim an interest in the goods. If the warehouseman after a reasonable effort is unable to sell the goods he may dispose of them in any lawful manner and shall incur no liability by reason of such disposition.

(4) The warehouseman must deliver the goods to any person entitled to them under this Article upon due demand made at any time prior to sale or other disposition under this section.

(5) The warehouseman may satisfy his lien from the proceeds of any sale or disposition under this section but must hold the balance for delivery on the demand of any person to whom he would have been bound to deliver the goods.

§ 7—207. Goods Must Be Kept Separate; Fungible Goods.

(1) Unless the warehouse receipt otherwise provides, a warehouseman must keep separate the goods covered by each receipt so as to permit at all times identification and delivery of those goods except that different lots of fungible goods may be commingled.

(2) Fungible goods so commingled are owned in common by the persons entitled thereto and the warehouseman is severally liable to each owner for that owner's share. Where because of overissue a mass of fungible goods is insufficient to meet all the receipts which the warehouseman has issued against it, the persons entitled include all holders to whom overissued receipts have been duly negotiated.

§ 7—208. Altered Warehouse Receipts.

Where a blank in a negotiable warehouse receipt has been filled in without authority, a purchaser for value and without notice of the want of authority may treat the insertion as authorized. Any other unauthorized alteration leaves any receipt enforceable against the issuer according to its original tenor.

§ 7—209. Lien of Warehouseman.

(1) A warehouseman has a lien against the bailor on the goods covered by a warehouse receipt or on the proceeds thereof in his possession for charges for storage or transportation (including demurrage and terminal charges), insurance, labor, or charges present or future in relation to the goods, and for expenses necessary for preservation of the goods or reasonably incurred in their sale pursuant to law. If the person on whose account the goods are held is liable for like charges or expenses in relation to other goods whenever deposited and it is stated in the receipt that a lien is claimed for charges and expenses in relation to other goods, the warehouseman also has a lien against him for such charges and expenses whether or not the other goods have been delivered by the warehouseman. But against a person to whom a negotiable warehouse receipt is duly negotiated a warehouseman's lien is limited to charges in an amount or at a rate specified on the receipt or if no charges are so specified then to a reasonable charge for storage of the goods covered by the receipt subsequent to the date of the receipt.

(2) The warehouseman may also reserve a security interest against the bailor for a maximum amount specified on the receipt for charges other than those specified in subsection (1), such as for money advanced and interest. Such a security interest is governed by the Article on Secured Transactions (Article 9).

(3)(a) A warehouseman's lien for charges and expenses under subsection (1) or a security interest under subsection (2) is also effective against any person who so entrusted the bailor with possession of the goods that a pledge of them by him to a good faith purchaser for value would have been valid but is not effective against a person as to whom the document confers no right in the goods covered by it under Section 7—503.

(b) A warehouseman's lien on household goods for charges and expenses in relation to the goods under subsection (1) is also effective against all persons if the depositor was the legal possessor of the goods at the time of deposit. "Household goods" means furniture, furnishings and personal effects used by the depositor in a dwelling.

(4) A warehouseman loses his lien on any goods which he voluntarily delivers or which he unjustifiably refuses to deliver.

§ 7—210. Enforcement of Warehouseman's Lien.

(1) Except as provided in subsection (2), a warehouseman's lien may be enforced by public or private sale of the goods in bloc or in parcels, at any time or place and on any terms which are commercially reasonable, after notifying all persons known to claim an interest in the goods. Such notification must include a statement of the amount due, the nature of the proposed sale and the

time and place of any public sale. The fact that a better price could have been obtained by a sale at a different time or in a different method from that selected by the warehouseman is not of itself sufficient to establish that the sale was not made in a commercially reasonable manner. If the warehouseman either sells the goods in the usual manner in any recognized market therefor, or if he sells at the price current in such market at the time of his sale, or if he has otherwise sold in conformity with commercially reasonable practices among dealers in the type of goods sold, he has sold in a commercially reasonable manner. A sale of more goods than apparently necessary to be offered to ensure satisfaction of the obligation is not commercially reasonable except in cases covered by the preceding sentence.

(2) A warehouseman's lien on goods other than goods stored by a merchant in the course of his business may be enforced only as follows:

(a) All persons known to claim an interest in the goods must be notified.

(b) The notification must be delivered in person or sent by registered or certified letter to the last known address of any person to be notified.

(c) The notification must include an itemized statement of the claim, a description of the goods subject to the lien, a demand for payment within a specified time not less than ten days after receipt of the notification, and a conspicuous statement that unless the claim is paid within the time the goods will be advertised for sale and sold by auction at a specified time and place.

(d) The sale must conform to the terms of the notification.

(e) The sale must be held at the nearest suitable place to that where the goods are held or stored.

(f) After the expiration of the time given in the notification, an advertisement of the sale must be published once a week for two weeks consecutively in a newspaper of general circulation where the sale is to be held. The advertisement must include a description of the goods, the name of the person on whose account they are being held, and the time and place of the sale. The sale must take place at least fifteen days after the first publication. If there is no newspaper of general circulation where the sale is to be held, the advertisement must be posted at least ten days before the sale in not less than six conspicuous places in the neighborhood of the proposed sale.

(3) Before any sale pursuant to this section any person claiming a right in the goods may pay the amount necessary to satisfy the lien and the reasonable expenses incurred under this section. In that event the goods must not be sold, but must be retained by the warehouseman subject to the terms of the receipt and this Article.

(4) The warehouseman may buy at any public sale pursuant to this section.

(5) A purchaser in good faith of goods sold to enforce a warehouseman's lien takes the goods free of any rights of persons against whom the lien was valid, despite noncompliance by the warehouseman with the requirements of this section.

(6) The warehouseman may satisfy his lien from the proceeds of any sale pursuant to this section but must hold the balance, if any, for delivery on demand to any person to whom he would have been bound to deliver the goods.

(7) The rights provided by this section shall be in addition to all other rights allowed by law to a creditor against his debtor.

(8) Where a lien is on goods stored by a merchant in the course of his business the lien may be enforced in accordance with either subsection (1) or (2).

(9) The warehouseman is liable for damages caused by failure to comply with the requirements for sale under this section and in case of willful violation is liable for conversion.

Part 3 Bills of Lading: Special Provisions

§ 7—301. Liability for Nonreceipt or Misdescription; "Said to Contain"; "Shipper's Load and Count"; Improper Handling.

(1) A consignee of a nonnegotiable bill who has given value in good faith or a holder to whom a negotiable bill has been duly negotiated relying in either case upon the description therein of the goods, or upon the date therein shown, may recover from the issuer damages caused by the misdating of the bill or the nonreceipt or misdescription of the goods, except to the extent that the document indicates that the issuer does not know whether any part of all of the goods in fact were received or conform to the description, as where the description is in terms of marks or labels or kind, quantity, or condition or the receipt or description is qualified by "contents or condition of contents of packages unknown", "said to contain", "shipper's weight, load and count" or the like, if such indication be true.

(2) When goods are loaded by an issuer who is a common carrier, the issuer must count the packages of goods if package freight and ascertain the kind and quantity if bulk freight. In such cases "shipper's weight, load and count" or other words indicating that the description was made by the shipper are ineffective except as to freight concealed by packages.

(3) When bulk freight is loaded by a shipper who makes available to the issuer adequate facilities for weighing such freight, an issuer who is a common carrier must ascertain the kind and quantity within a reasonable time after receiving the written request of the shipper to do so. In such cases "shipper's weight" or other words of like purport are ineffective.

(4) The issuer may by inserting in the bill the words "shipper's weight, load and count" or other words of like purport indicate that the goods were loaded by the shipper; and if such statement be true the issuer shall not be liable for damages caused by the improper loading. But their omission does not imply liability for such damages.

(5) The shipper shall be deemed to have guaranteed to the issuer the accuracy at the time of shipment of the description, marks, labels, number, kind, quantity, condition and weight, as furnished

by him; and the shipper shall indemnify the issuer against damage caused by inaccuracies in such particulars. The right of the issuer to such indemnity shall in no way limit his responsibility and liability under the contract of carriage to any person other than the shipper.

§ 7—302. Through Bills of Lading and Similar Documents.

(1) The issuer of a through bill of lading or other document embodying an undertaking to be performed in part by persons acting as its agents or by connecting carriers is liable to anyone entitled to recover on the document for any breach by such other persons or by a connecting carrier of its obligation under the document but to the extent that the bill covers an undertaking to be performed overseas or in territory not contiguous to the continental United States or an undertaking including matters other than transportation this liability may be varied by agreement of the parties.

(2) Where goods covered by a through bill of lading or other document embodying an undertaking to be performed in part by persons other than the issuer are received by any such person, he is subject with respect to his own performance while the goods are in his possession to the obligation of the issuer. His obligation is discharged by delivery of the goods to another such person pursuant to the document, and does not include liability for breach by any other such persons or by the issuer.

(3) The issuer of such through bill of lading or other document shall be entitled to recover from the connecting carrier or such other person in possession of the goods when the breach of the obligation under the document occurred, the amount it may be required to pay to anyone entitled to recover on the document therefor, as may be evidenced by any receipt, judgment, or transcript thereof, and the amount of any expense reasonably incurred by it in defending any action brought by anyone entitled to recover on the document therefor.

§ 7—303. Diversion; Reconsignment; Change of Instructions.

(1) Unless the bill of lading otherwise provides, the carrier may deliver the goods to a person or destination other than that stated in the bill or may otherwise dispose of the goods on instructions from

(a) the holder of a negotiable bill; or

(b) the consignor on a nonnegotiable bill notwithstanding contrary instructions from the consignee; or

(c) the consignee on a nonnegotiable bill in the absence of contrary instructions from the consignor, if the goods have arrived at the billed destination or if the consignee is in possession of the bill; or

(d) the consignee on a nonnegotiable bill if he is entitled as against the consignor to dispose of them.

(2) Unless such instructions are noted on a negotiable bill of lading, a person to whom the bill is duly negotiated can hold the bailee according to the original terms.

§ 7—304. Bills of Lading in a Set.

(1) Except where customary in overseas transportation, a bill of lading must not be issued in a set of parts. The issuer is liable for damages caused by violation of this subsection.

(2) Where a bill of lading is lawfully drawn in a set of parts, each of which is numbered and expressed to be valid only if the goods have not been delivered against any other part, the whole of the parts constitute one bill.

(3) Where a bill of lading is lawfully issued in a set of parts and different parts are negotiated to different persons, the title of the holder to whom the first due negotiation is made prevails as to both the document and the goods even though any later holder may have received the goods from the carrier in good faith and discharged the carrier's obligation by surrender of his part.

(4) Any person who negotiates or transfers a single part of a bill of lading drawn in a set is liable to holders of that part as if it were the whole set.

(5) The bailee is obliged to deliver in accordance with Part 4 of this Article against the first presented part of a bill of lading lawfully drawn in a set. Such delivery discharges the bailee's obligation on the whole bill.

§ 7—305. Destination Bills.

(1) Instead of issuing a bill of lading to the consignor at the place of shipment a carrier may at the request of the consignor procure the bill to be issued at destination or at any other place designated in the request.

(2) Upon request of anyone entitled as against the carrier to control the goods while in transit and on surrender of any outstanding bill of lading or other receipt covering such goods, the issuer may procure a substitute bill to be issued at any place designated in the request.

§ 7—306. Altered Bills of Lading.

An unauthorized alteration or filling in of a blank in a bill of lading leaves the bill enforceable according to its original tenor.

§ 7—307. Lien of Carrier.

(1) A carrier has a lien on the goods covered by a bill of lading for charges subsequent to the date of its receipt of the goods for storage or transportation (including demurrage and terminal charges) and for expenses necessary for preservation of the goods incident to their transportation or reasonably incurred in their sale pursuant to law. But against a purchaser for value of a negotiable bill of lading a carrier's lien is limited to charges stated in the bill or the applicable tariffs, or if no charges are stated then to a reasonable charge.

(2) A lien for charges and expenses under subsection (1) on goods which the carrier was required by law to receive for transportation is effective against the consignor or any person entitled to the goods unless the carrier had notice that the consignor lacked authority to subject the goods to such charges and expenses. Any other lien under subsection (1) is effective against the consignor and any person who permitted the bailor to have control or possession of the goods unless the carrier had notice that the bailor lacked such authority.

(3) A carrier loses his lien on any goods which he voluntarily delivers or which he unjustifiably refuses to deliver.

§ 7—308. Enforcement of Carrier's Lien.

(1) A carrier's lien may be enforced by public or private sale of the goods, in bloc or in parcels, at any time or place and on any terms which are commercially reasonable, after notifying all persons known to claim an interest in the goods. Such notification must include a statement of the amount due, the nature of the proposed sale and the time and place of any public sale. The fact that a better price could have been obtained by a sale at a different time or in a different method from that selected by the carrier is not of itself sufficient to establish that the sale was not made in a commercially reasonable manner. If the carrier either sells the goods in the usual manner in any recognized market therefor or if he sells at the price current in such market at the time of his sale or if he has otherwise sold in conformity with commercially reasonable practices among dealers in the type of goods sold he has sold in a commercially reasonable manner. A sale of more goods than apparently necessary to be offered to ensure satisfaction of the obligation is not commercially reasonable except in cases covered by the preceding sentence.

(2) Before any sale pursuant to this section any person claiming a right in the goods may pay the amount necessary to satisfy the lien and the reasonable expenses incurred under this section. In that event the goods must not be sold, but must be retained by the carrier subject to the terms of the bill and this Article.

(3) The carrier may buy at any public sale pursuant to this section.

(4) A purchaser in good faith of goods sold to enforce a carrier's lien takes the goods free of any rights of persons against whom the lien was valid, despite noncompliance by the carrier with the requirements of this section.

(5) The carrier may satisfy his lien from the proceeds of any sale pursuant to this section but must hold the balance, if any, for delivery on demand to any person to whom he would have been bound to deliver the goods.

(6) The rights provided by this section shall be in addition to all other rights allowed by law to a creditor against his debtor.

(7) A carrier's lien may be enforced in accordance with either subsection (1) or the procedure set forth in subsection (2) of Section 7—210.

(8) The carrier is liable for damages caused by failure to comply with the requirements for sale under this section and in case of willful violation is liable for conversion.

§ 7—309. Duty of Care; Contractual Limitation of Carrier's Liability.

(1) A carrier who issues a bill of lading whether negotiable or nonnegotiable must exercise the degree of care in relation to the goods which a reasonably careful man would exercise under like circumstances. This subsection does not repeal or change any law or rule of law which imposes liability upon a common carrier for damages not caused by its negligence.

(2) Damages may be limited by a provision that the carrier's liability shall not exceed a value stated in the document if the carrier's rates are dependent upon value and the consignor by the carrier's tariff is afforded an opportunity to declare a higher value or a value as lawfully provided in the tariff, or where no tariff is filed he is otherwise advised of such opportunity; but no such limitation is effective with respect to the carrier's liability for conversion to its own use.

(3) Reasonable provisions as to the time and manner of presenting claims and instituting actions based on the shipment may be included in a bill of lading or tariff.

Part 4 Warehouse Receipts and Bills of Lading: General Obligations

§ 7—401. Irregularities in Issue of Receipt or Bill or Conduct of Issuer.

The obligations imposed by this Article on an issuer apply to a document of title regardless of the fact that

(a) the document may not comply with the requirements of this Article or of any other law or regulation regarding its issue, form or content; or

(b) the issuer may have violated laws regulating the conduct of his business; or

(c) the goods covered by the document were owned by the bailee at the time the document was issued; or

(d) the person issuing the document does not come within the definition of warehouseman if it purports to be a warehouse receipt.

§ 7—402. Duplicate Receipt or Bill; Overissue.

Neither a duplicate nor any other document of title purporting to cover goods already represented by an outstanding document of the same issuer confers any right in the goods, except as provided in the case of bills in a set, overissue of documents for fungible goods and substitutes for lost, stolen or destroyed documents. But the issuer is liable for damages caused by his overissue or failure to identify a duplicate document as such by conspicuous notation on its face.

§ 7—403. Obligation of Warehouseman or Carrier to Deliver; Excuse.

(1) The bailee must deliver the goods to a person entitled under the document who complies with subsections (2) and (3), unless and to the extent that the bailee establishes any of the following:

(a) delivery of the goods to a person whose receipt was rightful as against the claimant;

(b) damage to or delay, loss or destruction of the goods for which the bailee is not liable [, but the burden of establishing negligence in such cases is on the person entitled under the document];

Note: *The brackets in (1)(b) indicate that State enactments may differ on this point without serious damage to the principle of uniformity.*

(c) previous sale or other disposition of the goods in lawful enforcement of a lien or on warehouseman's lawful termination of storage;

(d) the exercise by a seller of his right to stop delivery pursuant to the provisions of the Article on Sales (Section 2—705);

(e) a diversion, reconsignment or other disposition pursuant to the provisions of this Article (Section 7—303) or tariff regulating such right;

(f) release, satisfaction or any other fact affording a personal defense against the claimant;

(g) any other lawful excuse.

(2) A person claiming goods covered by a document of title must satisfy the bailee's lien where the bailee so requests or where the bailee is prohibited by law from delivering the goods until the charges are paid.

(3) Unless the person claiming is one against whom the document confers no right under Sec. 7—503(1), he must surrender for cancellation or notation of partial deliveries any outstanding negotiable document covering the goods, and the bailee must cancel the document or conspicuously note the partial delivery thereon or be liable to any person to whom the document is duly negotiated.

(4) "Person entitled under the document" means holder in the case of a negotiable document, or the person to whom delivery is to be made by the terms of or pursuant to written instructions under a nonnegotiable document.

§ 7—404. No Liability for Good Faith Delivery Pursuant to Receipt or Bill.

A bailee who in good faith including observance of reasonable commercial standards has received goods and delivered or otherwise disposed of them according to the terms of the document of title or pursuant to this Article is not liable therefor. This rule applies even though the person from whom he received the goods had no authority to procure the document or to dispose of the goods and even though the person to whom he delivered the goods had no authority to receive them.

Part 5 Warehouse Receipts and Bills of Lading: Negotiation and Transfer

§ 7—501. Form of Negotiation and Requirements of "Due Negotiation".

(1) A negotiable document of title running to the order of a named person is negotiated by his indorsement and delivery. After his indorsement in blank or to bearer any person can negotiate it by delivery alone.

(2)(a) A negotiable document of title is also negotiated by delivery alone when by its original terms it runs to bearer.

(b) When a document running to the order of a named person is delivered to him the effect is the same as if the document had been negotiated.

(3) Negotiation of a negotiable document of title after it has been indorsed to a specified person requires indorsement by the special indorsee as well as delivery.

(4) A negotiable document of title is "duly negotiated" when it is negotiated in the manner stated in this section to a holder who purchases it in good faith without notice of any defense against or claim to it on the part of any person and for value, unless it is established that the negotiation is not in the regular course of business or financing or involves receiving the document in settlement or payment of a money obligation.

(5) Indorsement of a nonnegotiable document neither makes it negotiable nor adds to the transferee's rights.

(6) The naming in a negotiable bill of a person to be notified of the arrival of the goods does not limit the negotiability of the bill nor constitute notice to a purchaser thereof of any interest of such person in the goods.

§ 7—502. Rights Acquired by Due Negotiation.

(1) Subject to the following section and to the provisions of Section 7—205 on fungible goods, a holder to whom a negotiable document of title has been duly negotiated acquires thereby:

(a) title to the document;

(b) title to the goods;

(c) all rights accruing under the law of agency or estoppel, including rights to goods delivered to the bailee after the document was issued; and

(d) the direct obligation of the issuer to hold or deliver the goods according to the terms of the document free of any defense or claim by him except those arising under the terms of the document or under this Article. In the case of a delivery order the bailee's obligation accrues only upon acceptance and the obligation acquired by the holder is that the issuer and any indorser will procure the acceptance of the bailee.

(2) Subject to the following section, title and rights so acquired are not defeated by any stoppage of the goods represented by the document or by surrender of such goods by the bailee, and are not impaired even though the negotiation or any prior negotiation constituted a breach of duty or even though any person has been deprived of possession of the document by misrepresentation, fraud, accident, mistake, duress, loss, theft or conversion, or even though a previous sale or other transfer of the goods or document has been made to a third person.

§ 7—503. Document of Title to Goods Defeated in Certain Cases.

(1) A document of title confers no right in goods against a person who before issuance of the document had a legal interest or a perfected security interest in them and who neither

(a) delivered or entrusted them or any document of title covering them to the bailor or his nominee with actual or apparent authority to ship, store or sell or with power to obtain delivery under this Article (Section 7—403) or with power of disposition under this Act (Sections 2—403 and 9—307) or other statute or rule of law; nor

(b) acquiesced in the procurement by the bailor or his nominee of any document of title.

(2) Title to goods based upon an unaccepted delivery order is subject to the rights of anyone to whom a negotiable warehouse receipt or bill of lading covering the goods has been duly negotiated. Such a title may be defeated under the next section to the same extent as the rights of the issuer or a transferee from the issuer.

(3) Title to goods based upon a bill of lading issued to a freight forwarder is subject to the rights of anyone to whom a bill issued by the freight forwarder is duly negotiated; but delivery by the carrier in accordance with Part 4 of this Article pursuant to its own bill of lading discharges the carrier's obligation to deliver.

§ 7—504. Rights Acquired in the Absence of Due Negotiation; Effect of Diversion; Seller's Stoppage of Delivery.

(1) A transferee of a document, whether negotiable or nonnegotiable, to whom the document has been delivered but not duly negotiated, acquires the title and rights which his transferor had or had actual authority to convey.

(2) In the case of a nonnegotiable document, until but not after the bailee receives notification of the transfer, the rights of the transferee may be defeated

(a) by those creditors of the transferor who could treat the sale as void under Section 2—402; or

(b) by a buyer from the transferor in ordinary course of business if the bailee has delivered the goods to the buyer or received notification of his rights; or

(c) as against the bailee by good faith dealings of the bailee with the transferor.

(3) A diversion or other change of shipping instructions by the consignor in a nonnegotiable bill of lading which causes the bailee not to deliver to the consignee defeats the consignee's title to the goods if they have been delivered to a buyer in ordinary course of business and in any event defeats the consignee's rights against the bailee.

(4) Delivery pursuant to a nonnegotiable document may be stopped by a seller under Section 2—705, and subject to the requirement of due notification there provided. A bailee honoring the seller's instructions is entitled to be indemnified by the seller against any resulting loss or expense.

§ 7—505. Indorser Not a Guarantor for Other Parties.

The indorsement of a document of title issued by a bailee does not make the indorser liable for any default by the bailee or by previous indorsers.

§ 7—506. Delivery Without Indorsement: Right to Compel Indorsement.

The transferee of a negotiable document of title has a specifically enforceable right to have his transferor supply any necessary indorsement but the transfer becomes a negotiation only as of the time the indorsement is supplied.

§ 7—507. Warranties on Negotiation or Transfer of Receipt or Bill.

Where a person negotiates or transfers a document of title for value otherwise than as a mere intermediary under the next following section, then unless otherwise agreed he warrants to his immediate purchaser only in addition to any warranty made in selling the goods

(a) that the document is genuine; and

(b) that he has no knowledge of any fact which would impair its validity or worth; and

(c) that his negotiation or transfer is rightful and fully effective with respect to the title to the document and the goods it represents.

§ 7—508. Warranties of Collecting Bank as to Documents.

A collecting bank or other intermediary known to be entrusted with documents on behalf of another or with collection of a draft or other claim against delivery of documents warrants by such delivery of the documents only its own good faith and authority. This rule applies even though the intermediary has purchased or made advances against the claim or draft to be collected.

§ 7—509. Receipt or Bill: When Adequate Compliance With Commercial Contract.

The question whether a document is adequate to fulfill the obligations of a contract for sale or the conditions of a credit is governed by the Articles on Sales (Article 2) and on Letters of Credit (Article 5).

Part 6 Warehouse Receipts and Bills of Lading: Miscellaneous Provisions

§ 7—601. Lost and Missing Documents.

(1) If a document has been lost, stolen or destroyed, a court may order delivery of the goods or issuance of a substitute document and the bailee may without liability to any person comply with such order. If the document was negotiable the claimant must post security approved by the court to indemnify any person who may suffer loss as a result of non-surrender of the document. If the document was not negotiable, such security may be required at the discretion of the court. The court may also in its discretion order payment of the bailee's reasonable costs and counsel fees.

(2) A bailee who without court order delivers goods to a person claiming under a missing negotiable document is liable to any person injured thereby, and if the delivery is not in good faith becomes liable for conversion. Delivery in good faith is not conversion if made in accordance with a filed classification or tariff or, where no classification or tariff is filed, if the claimant posts security with the bailee in an amount at least double the value of the goods at the time of posting to indemnify any person injured by the delivery who files a notice of claim within one year after the delivery.

§ 7—602. Attachment of Goods Covered by a Negotiable Document.

Except where the document was originally issued upon delivery of the goods by a person who had no power to dispose of them, no lien attaches by virtue of any judicial process to goods in the possession of a bailee for which a negotiable document of title is outstanding unless the document be first surrendered to the bailee or its negotiation enjoined, and the bailee shall not be compelled to deliver the goods pursuant to process until the document is surrendered to him or impounded by the court. One who purchases the document for value without notice of the process or injunction takes free of the lien imposed by judicial process.

§ 7—603. Conflicting Claims; Interpleader.

If more than one person claims title or possession of the goods, the bailee is excused from delivery until he has had a reasonable time to ascertain the validity of the adverse claims or to bring an action to compel all claimants to interplead and may compel such interpleader, either in defending an action for nondelivery of the goods, or by original action, whichever is appropriate.

Revised (1994) Article 8 INVESTMENT SECURITIES

Part 1 Short Title and General Matters

§ 8—101. Short Title.

This Article may be cited as Uniform Commercial Code—Investment Securities.

§ 8—102. Definitions.

(a) In this Article:

(1) "Adverse claim" means a claim that a claimant has a property interest in a financial asset and that it is a violation of the rights of the claimant for another person to hold, transfer, or deal with the financial asset.

(2) "Bearer form," as applied to a certificated security, means a form in which the security is payable to the bearer of the security certificate according to its terms but not by reason of an indorsement.

(3) "Broker" means a person defined as a broker or dealer under the federal securities laws, but without excluding a bank acting in that capacity.

(4) "Certificated security" means a security that is represented by a certificate.

(5) "Clearing corporation" means:

(i) a person that is registered as a "clearing agency" under the federal securities laws;

(ii) a federal reserve bank; or

(iii) any other person that provides clearance or settlement services with respect to financial assets that would require it to register as a clearing agency under the federal securities laws but for an exclusion or exemption from the registration requirement, if its activities as a clearing corporation, including promulgation of rules, are subject to regulation by a federal or state governmental authority.

(6) "Communicate" means to:

(i) send a signed writing; or

(ii) transmit information by any mechanism agreed upon by the persons transmitting and receiving the information.

(7) "Entitlement holder" means a person identified in the records of a securities intermediary as the person having a security entitlement against the securities intermediary. If a person acquires a security entitlement by virtue of Section 8-501(b)(2) or (3), that person is the entitlement holder.

(8) "Entitlement order" means a notification communicated to a securities intermediary directing transfer or redemption of a financial asset to which the entitlement holder has a security entitlement.

(9) "Financial asset," except as otherwise provided in Section 8-103, means:

(i) a security;

(ii) an obligation of a person or a share, participation, or other interest in a person or in property or an enterprise of a person, which is, or is of a type, dealt in or traded on financial markets, or which is recognized in any area in which it is issued or dealt in as a medium for investment; or

(iii) any property that is held by a securities intermediary for another person in a securities account if the securities intermediary has expressly agreed with the other person that the property is to be treated as a financial asset under this Article.

As context requires, the term means either the interest itself or the means by which a person's claim to it is evidenced, including a certificated or uncertificated security, a security certificate, or a security entitlement.

(10) "Good faith," for purposes of the obligation of good faith in the performance or enforcement of contracts or duties within this Article, means honesty in fact and the observance of reasonable commercial standards of fair dealing.

(11) "Indorsement" means a signature that alone or accompanied by other words is made on a security certificate in registered form or on a separate document for the purpose of assigning, transferring, or redeeming the security or granting a power to assign, transfer, or redeem it.

(12) "Instruction" means a notification communicated to the issuer of an uncertificated security which directs that the transfer of the security be registered or that the security be redeemed.

(13) "Registered form," as applied to a certificated security, means a form in which:

(i) the security certificate specifies a person entitled to the security; and

(ii) a transfer of the security may be registered upon books maintained for that purpose by or on behalf of the issuer, or the security certificate so states.

(14) "Securities intermediary" means:

(i) a clearing corporation; or

(ii) a person, including a bank or broker, that in the ordinary course of its business maintains securities accounts for others and is acting in that capacity.

(15) "Security," except as otherwise provided in Section 8-103, means an obligation of an issuer or a share, participation, or other interest in an issuer or in property or an enterprise of an issuer:

(i) which is represented by a security certificate in bearer or registered form, or the transfer of which may be registered upon books maintained for that purpose by or on behalf of the issuer;

(ii) which is one of a class or series or by its terms is divisible into a class or series of shares, participations, interests, or obligations; and

(iii) which:

(A) is, or is of a type, dealt in or traded on securities exchanges or securities markets; or

(B) is a medium for investment and by its terms expressly provides that it is a security governed by this Article.

(16) "Security certificate" means a certificate representing a security.

(17) "Security entitlement" means the rights and property interest of an entitlement holder with respect to a financial asset specified in Part 5.

(18) "Uncertificated security" means a security that is not represented by a certificate.

(b) Other definitions applying to this Article and the sections in which they appear are:

Appropriate person	Section 8-107
Control	Section 8-106
Delivery	Section 8-301
Investment company security	Section 8-103
Issuer	Section 8-201
Overissue	Section 8-210
Protected purchaser	Section 8-303
Securities account	Section 8-501

(c) In addition, Article 1 contains general definitions and principles of construction and interpretation applicable throughout this Article.

(d) The characterization of a person, business, or transaction for purposes of this Article does not determine the characterization of the person, business, or transaction for purposes of any other law, regulation, or rule.

§ 8—103. Rules for Determining Whether Certain Obligations and Interests Are Securities or Financial Assets.

(a) A share or similar equity interest issued by a corporation, business trust, joint stock company, or similar entity is a security.

(b) An "investment company security" is a security. "Investment company security" means a share or similar equity interest issued by an entity that is registered as an investment company under the federal investment company laws, an interest in a unit investment trust that is so registered, or a face-amount certificate issued by a face-amount certificate company that is so registered. Investment company security does not include an insurance policy or endowment policy or annuity contract issued by an insurance company.

(c) An interest in a partnership or limited liability company is not a security unless it is dealt in or traded on securities exchanges or in securities markets, its terms expressly provide that it is a security governed by this Article, or it is an investment company security. However, an interest in a partnership or limited liability company is a financial asset if it is held in a securities account.

(d) A writing that is a security certificate is governed by this Article and not by Article 3, even though it also meets the requirements of that Article. However, a negotiable instrument governed by Article 3 is a financial asset if it is held in a securities account.

(e) An option or similar obligation issued by a clearing corporation to its participants is not a security, but is a financial asset.

(f) A commodity contract, as defined in Section 9-115, is not a security or a financial asset.

§ 8—104. Acquisition of Security or Financial Asset or Interest Therein.

(a) A person acquires a security or an interest therein, under this Article, if:

(1) the person is a purchaser to whom a security is delivered pursuant to Section 8-301; or

(2) the person acquires a security entitlement to the security pursuant to Section 8-501.

(b) A person acquires a financial asset, other than a security, or an interest therein, under this Article, if the person acquires a security entitlement to the financial asset.

(c) A person who acquires a security entitlement to a security or other financial asset has the rights specified in Part 5, but is a purchaser of any security, security entitlement, or other financial asset held by the securities intermediary only to the extent provided in Section 8-503.

(d) Unless the context shows that a different meaning is intended, a person who is required by other law, regulation, rule, or agreement to transfer, deliver, present, surrender, exchange, or otherwise put in the possession of another person a security or financial asset satisfies that requirement by causing the other person to acquire an interest in the security or financial asset pursuant to subsection (a) or (b)

§ 8—105. Notice of Adverse Claim.

(a) A person has notice of an adverse claim if:

(1) the person knows of the adverse claim;

(2) the person is aware of facts sufficient to indicate that there is a significant probability that the adverse claim exists and deliberately avoids information that would establish the existence of the adverse claim; or

(3) the person has a duty, imposed by statute or regulation, to investigate whether an adverse claim exists, and the investigation so required would establish the existence of the adverse claim.

(b) Having knowledge that a financial asset or interest therein is or has been transferred by a representative imposes no duty of inquiry into the rightfulness of a transaction and is not notice of an adverse claim. However, a person who knows that a representative has transferred a financial asset or interest therein in a transaction that is, or whose proceeds are being used, for the individual benefit of the representative or otherwise in breach of duty has notice of an adverse claim.

(c) An act or event that creates a right to immediate performance of the principal obligation represented by a security certificate or sets a date on or after which the certificate is to be presented or surrendered for redemption or exchange does not itself constitute notice of an adverse claim except in the case of a transfer more than:

(1) one year after a date set for presentment or surrender for redemption or exchange; or

(2) six months after a date set for payment of money against presentation or surrender of the certificate, if money was available for payment on that date.

(d) A purchaser of a certificated security has notice of an adverse claim if the security certificate:

(1) whether in bearer or registered form, has been indorsed "for collection" or "for surrender" or for some other purpose not involving transfer; or

(2) is in bearer form and has on it an unambiguous statement that it is the property of a person other than the transferor, but the mere writing of a name on the certificate is not such a statement.

(e) Filing of a financing statement under Article 9 is not notice of an adverse claim to a financial asset.

§ 8—106. Control.

(a) A purchaser has "control" of a certificated security in bearer form if the certificated security is delivered to the purchaser.

(b) A purchaser has "control" of a certificated security in registered form if the certificated security is delivered to the purchaser, and:

(1) the certificate is indorsed to the purchaser or in blank by an effective indorsement; or

(2) the certificate is registered in the name of the purchaser, upon original issue or registration of transfer by the issuer.

(c) A purchaser has "control" of an uncertificated security if:

(1) the uncertificated security is delivered to the purchaser; or

(2) the issuer has agreed that it will comply with instructions originated by the purchaser without further consent by the registered owner.

(d) A purchaser has "control" of a security entitlement if:

(1) the purchaser becomes the entitlement holder; or

(2) the securities intermediary has agreed that it will comply with entitlement orders originated by the purchaser without further consent by the entitlement holder.

(e) If an interest in a security entitlement is granted by the entitlement holder to the entitlement holder's own securities intermediary, the securities intermediary has control.

(f) A purchaser who has satisfied the requirements of subsection (c)(2) or (d)(2) has control even if the registered owner in the case of subsection (c)(2) or the entitlement holder in the case of subsection (d)(2) retains the right to make substitutions for the uncertificated security or security entitlement, to originate instructions or entitlement orders to the issuer or securities intermediary, or otherwise to deal with the uncertificated security or security entitlement.

(g) An issuer or a securities intermediary may not enter into an agreement of the kind described in subsection (c)(2) or (d)(2) without the consent of the registered owner or entitlement holder, but an issuer or a securities intermediary is not required to enter into such an agreement even though the registered owner or entitlement holder so directs. An issuer or securities intermediary that has entered into such an agreement is not required to confirm the existence of the agreement to another party unless requested to do so by the registered owner or entitlement holder.

§ 8—107. Whether Indorsement, Instruction, or Entitlement Order Is Effective.

(a) "Appropriate person" means:

(1) with respect to an indorsement, the person specified by a security certificate or by an effective special indorsement to be entitled to the security;

(2) with respect to an instruction, the registered owner of an uncertificated security;

(3) with respect to an entitlement order, the entitlement holder;

(4) if the person designated in paragraph (1), (2), or (3) is deceased, the designated person's successor taking under other law or the designated person's personal representative acting for the estate of the decedent; or

(5) if the person designated in paragraph (1), (2), or (3) lacks capacity, the designated person's guardian, conservator, or other similar representative who has power under other law to transfer the security or financial asset.

(b) An indorsement, instruction, or entitlement order is effective if:

(1) it is made by the appropriate person;

(2) it is made by a person who has power under the law of

agency to transfer the security or financial asset on behalf of the appropriate person, including, in the case of an instruction or entitlement order, a person who has control under Section 8-106(c)(2) or (d)(2); or

(3) the appropriate person has ratified it or is otherwise precluded from asserting its ineffectiveness.

(c) An indorsement, instruction, or entitlement order made by a representative is effective even if:

(1) the representative has failed to comply with a controlling instrument or with the law of the State having jurisdiction of the representative relationship, including any law requiring the representative to obtain court approval of the transaction; or

(2) the representative's action in making the indorsement, instruction, or entitlement order or using the proceeds of the transaction is otherwise a breach of duty.

(d) If a security is registered in the name of or specially indorsed to a person described as a representative, or if a securities account is maintained in the name of a person described as a representative, an indorsement, instruction, or entitlement order made by the person is effective even though the person is no longer serving in the described capacity.

(e) Effectiveness of an indorsement, instruction, or entitlement order is determined as of the date the indorsement, instruction, or entitlement order is made, and an indorsement, instruction, or entitlement order does not become ineffective by reason of any later change of circumstances.

§ 8—108. Warranties in Direct Holding.

(a) A person who transfers a certificated security to a purchaser for value warrants to the purchaser, and an indorser, if the transfer is by indorsement, warrants to any subsequent purchaser, that:

(1) the certificate is genuine and has not been materially altered;

(2) the transferor or indorser does not know of any fact that might impair the validity of the security;

(3) there is no adverse claim to the security;

(4) the transfer does not violate any restriction on transfer;

(5) if the transfer is by indorsement, the indorsement is made by an appropriate person, or if the indorsement is by an agent, the agent has actual authority to act on behalf of the appropriate person; and

(6) the transfer is otherwise effective and rightful.

(b) A person who originates an instruction for registration of transfer of an uncertificated security to a purchaser for value warrants to the purchaser that:

(1) the instruction is made by an appropriate person, or if the instruction is by an agent, the agent has actual authority to act on behalf of the appropriate person;

(2) the security is valid;

(3) there is no adverse claim to the security; and

(4) at the time the instruction is presented to the issuer:

(i) the purchaser will be entitled to the registration of transfer;

(ii) the transfer will be registered by the issuer free from all liens, security interests, restrictions, and claims other than those specified in the instruction;

(iii) the transfer will not violate any restriction on transfer; and

(iv) the requested transfer will otherwise be effective and rightful.

(c) A person who transfers an uncertificated security to a purchaser for value and does not originate an instruction in connection with the transfer warrants that:

(1) the uncertificated security is valid;

(2) there is no adverse claim to the security;

(3) the transfer does not violate any restriction on transfer; and

(4) the transfer is otherwise effective and rightful.

(d) A person who indorses a security certificate warrants to the issuer that:

(1) there is no adverse claim to the security; and

(2) the indorsement is effective.

(e) A person who originates an instruction for registration of transfer of an uncertificated security warrants to the issuer that:

(1) the instruction is effective; and

(2) at the time the instruction is presented to the issuer the purchaser will be entitled to the registration of transfer.

(f) A person who presents a certificated security for registration of transfer or for payment or exchange warrants to the issuer that the person is entitled to the registration, payment, or exchange, but a purchaser for value and without notice of adverse claims to whom transfer is registered warrants only that the person has no knowledge of any unauthorized signature in a necessary indorsement.

(g) If a person acts as agent of another in delivering a certificated security to a purchaser, the identity of the principal was known to the person to whom the certificate was delivered, and the certificate delivered by the agent was received by the agent from the principal or received by the agent from another person at the direction of the principal, the person delivering the security certificate warrants only that the delivering person has authority to act for the principal and does not know of any adverse claim to the certificated security.

(h) A secured party who redelivers a security certificate received, or after payment and on order of the debtor delivers the security certificate to another person, makes only the warranties of an agent under subsection (g).

(i) Except as otherwise provided in subsection (g), a broker acting for a customer makes to the issuer and a purchaser the warranties provided in subsections (a) through (f). A broker that delivers a security certificate to its customer, or causes its customer to be registered as the owner of an uncertificated security, makes to the customer the warranties provided in subsection (a) or (b), and has the rights and privileges of a purchaser under this section. The warranties of and in favor of the broker acting as an agent are in addition to applicable warranties given by and in favor of the customer.

§ 8—109. Warranties in Indirect Holding.

(a) A person who originates an entitlement order to a securities intermediary warrants to the securities intermediary that:

(1) the entitlement order is made by an appropriate person, or if the entitlement order is by an agent, the agent has actual authority to act on behalf of the appropriate person; and

(2) there is no adverse claim to the security entitlement.

(b) A person who delivers a security certificate to a securities intermediary for credit to a securities account or originates an instruction with respect to an uncertificated security directing that the uncertificated security be credited to a securities account makes to the securities intermediary the warranties specified in Section 8-108(a) or (b).

(c) If a securities intermediary delivers a security certificate to its entitlement holder or causes its entitlement holder to be registered as the owner of an uncertificated security, the securities intermediary makes to the entitlement holder the warranties specified in Section 8-108(a) or (b).

§ 8—110. Applicability; Choice of Law.

(a) The local law of the issuer's jurisdiction, as specified in subsection (d), governs:

(1) the validity of a security;

(2) the rights and duties of the issuer with respect to registration of transfer;

(3) the effectiveness of registration of transfer by the issuer;

(4) whether the issuer owes any duties to an adverse claimant to a security; and

(5) whether an adverse claim can be asserted against a person to whom transfer of a certificated or uncertificated security is registered or a person who obtains control of an uncertificated security.

(b) The local law of the securities intermediary's jurisdiction, as specified in subsection (e), governs:

(1) acquisition of a security entitlement from the securities intermediary;

(2) the rights and duties of the securities intermediary and entitlement holder arising out of a security entitlement;

(3) whether the securities intermediary owes any duties to an adverse claimant to a security entitlement; and

(4) whether an adverse claim can be asserted against a person who acquires a security entitlement from the securities intermediary or a person who purchases a security entitlement or interest therein from an entitlement holder.

(c) The local law of the jurisdiction in which a security certificate is located at the time of delivery governs whether an adverse claim can be asserted against a person to whom the security certificate is delivered.

(d) "Issuer's jurisdiction" means the jurisdiction under which the issuer of the security is organized or, if permitted by the law of that jurisdiction, the law of another jurisdiction specified by the issuer. An issuer organized under the law of this State may specify the law of another jurisdiction as the law governing the matters specified in subsection (a)(2) through (5).

(e) The following rules determine a "securities intermediary's jurisdiction" for purposes of this section:

(1) If an agreement between the securities intermediary and its entitlement holder specifies that it is governed by the law of a particular jurisdiction, that jurisdiction is the securities intermediary's jurisdiction.

(2) If an agreement between the securities intermediary and its entitlement holder does not specify the governing law as provided in paragraph (1), but expressly specifies that the securities account is maintained at an office in a particular jurisdiction, that jurisdiction is the securities intermediary's jurisdiction.

(3) If an agreement between the securities intermediary and its entitlement holder does not specify a jurisdiction as provided in paragraph (1) or (2), the securities intermediary's jurisdiction is the jurisdiction in which is located the office identified in an account statement as the office serving the entitlement holder's account.

(4) If an agreement between the securities intermediary and its entitlement holder does not specify a jurisdiction as provided in paragraph (1) or (2) and an account statement does not identify an office serving the entitlement holder's account as provided in paragraph (3), the securities intermediary's jurisdiction is the jurisdiction in which is located the chief executive office of the securities intermediary.

(f) A securities intermediary's jurisdiction is not determined by the physical location of certificates representing financial assets, or by the jurisdiction in which is organized the issuer of the financial asset with respect to which an entitlement holder has a security entitlement, or by the location of facilities for data processing or other record keeping concerning the account.

§ 8—111. Clearing Corporation Rules.

A rule adopted by a clearing corporation governing rights and obligations among the clearing corporation and its participants in the clearing corporation is effective even if the rule conflicts with this [Act] and affects another party who does not consent to the rule.

§ 8—112. Creditor's Legal Process.

(a) The interest of a debtor in a certificated security may be reached by a creditor only by actual seizure of the security certificate by the officer making the attachment or levy, except as otherwise provided in subsection (d). However, a certificated security for which the certificate has been surrendered to the issuer may be reached by a creditor by legal process upon the issuer.

(b) The interest of a debtor in an uncertificated security may be reached by a creditor only by legal process upon the issuer at its chief executive office in the United States, except as otherwise provided in subsection (d).

(c) The interest of a debtor in a security entitlement may be reached by a creditor only by legal process upon the securities intermediary with whom the debtor's securities account is maintained, except as otherwise provided in subsection (d).

(d) The interest of a debtor in a certificated security for which the certificate is in the possession of a secured party, or in an uncertificated security registered in the name of a secured party, or a security entitlement maintained in the name of a secured party, may be reached by a creditor by legal process upon the secured party.

(e) A creditor whose debtor is the owner of a certificated security, uncertificated security, or security entitlement is entitled to aid from a court of competent jurisdiction, by injunction or otherwise, in reaching the certificated security, uncertificated security, or security entitlement or in satisfying the claim by means allowed at law or in equity in regard to property that cannot readily be reached by other legal process.

§ 8—113. Statute of Frauds Inapplicable.

A contract or modification of a contract for the sale or purchase of a security is enforceable whether or not there is a writing signed or record authenticated by a party against whom enforcement is sought, even if the contract or modification is not capable of performance within one year of its making.

§ 8—114. Evidentiary Rules Concerning Certificated Securities.

The following rules apply in an action on a certificated security against the issuer:

(1) Unless specifically denied in the pleadings, each signature on a security certificate or in a necessary indorsement is admitted.

(2) If the effectiveness of a signature is put in issue, the burden of establishing effectiveness is on the party claiming under the signature, but the signature is presumed to be genuine or authorized.

(3) If signatures on a security certificate are admitted or established, production of the certificate entitles a holder to recover on it unless the defendant establishes a defense or a defect going to the validity of the security.

(4) If it is shown that a defense or defect exists, the plaintiff has the burden of establishing that the plaintiff or some person under whom the plaintiff claims is a person against whom the defense or defect cannot be asserted.

§ 8—115. Securities Intermediary and Others Not Liable to Adverse Claimant.

A securities intermediary that has transferred a financial asset pursuant to an effective entitlement order, or a broker or other agent or bailee that has dealt with a financial asset at the direction of its customer or principal, is not liable to a person having an adverse claim to the financial asset, unless the securities intermediary, or broker or other agent or bailee:

(1) took the action after it had been served with an injunction, restraining order, or other legal process enjoining it from doing so, issued by a court of competent jurisdiction, and had a reasonable opportunity to act on the injunction, restraining order, or other legal process; or

(2) acted in collusion with the wrongdoer in violating the rights of the adverse claimant; or

(3) in the case of a security certificate that has been stolen, acted with notice of the adverse claim.

§ 8—116. Securities Intermediary as Purchaser for Value.

A securities intermediary that receives a financial asset and establishes a security entitlement to the financial asset in favor of an entitlement holder is a purchaser for value of the financial asset. A securities intermediary that acquires a security entitlement to a financial asset from another securities intermediary acquires the security entitlement for value if the securities intermediary acquiring the security entitlement establishes a security entitlement to the financial asset in favor of an entitlement holder.

Part 2 Issue and Issuer

§ 8—201 Issuer.

(a) With respect to an obligation on or a defense to a security, an "issuer" includes a person that:

(1) places or authorizes the placing of its name on a security certificate, other than as authenticating trustee, registrar, transfer agent, or the like, to evidence a share, participation, or other interest in its property or in an enterprise, or to evidence its duty to perform an obligation represented by the certificate;

(2) creates a share, participation, or other interest in its property or in an enterprise, or undertakes an obligation, that is an uncertificated security;

(3) directly or indirectly creates a fractional interest in its rights or property, if the fractional interest is represented by a security certificate; or

(4) becomes responsible for, or in place of, another person described as an issuer in this section.

(b) With respect to an obligation on or defense to a security, a guarantor is an issuer to the extent of its guaranty, whether or not its obligation is noted on a security certificate.

(c) With respect to a registration of a transfer, issuer means a person on whose behalf transfer books are maintained.

§ 8—202. Issuer's Responsibility and Defenses; Notice of Defect or Defense.

(a) Even against a purchaser for value and without notice, the terms of a certificated security include terms stated on the certificate and terms made part of the security by reference on the certificate to another instrument, indenture, or document or to a constitution, statute, ordinance, rule, regulation, order, or the like, to the extent the terms referred to do not conflict with terms stated on the certificate. A reference under this subsection does not of itself charge a purchaser for value with notice of a defect going to the validity of the security, even if the certificate expressly states that a person accepting it admits notice. The terms of an uncertificated security include those stated in any instrument, indenture, or document or in a constitution, statute, ordinance, rule, regulation, order, or the like, pursuant to which the security is issued.

(b) The following rules apply if an issuer asserts that a security is not valid:

(1) A security other than one issued by a government or governmental subdivision, agency, or instrumentality, even though issued with a defect going to its validity, is valid in the hands of a purchaser for value and without notice of the particular defect unless the defect involves a violation of a constitutional provision. In that case, the security is valid in the hands of a purchaser for value and without notice of the defect, other than one who takes by original issue.

(2) Paragraph (1) applies to an issuer that is a government or governmental subdivision, agency, or instrumentality only if there has been substantial compliance with the legal requirements governing the issue or the issuer has received a substantial consideration for the issue as a whole or for the particular security and a stated purpose of the issue is one for which the issuer has power to borrow money or issue the security.

(c) Except as otherwise provided in Section 8-205, lack of genuineness of a certificated security is a complete defense, even against a purchaser for value and without notice.

(d) All other defenses of the issuer of a security, including nondelivery and conditional delivery of a certificated security, are ineffective against a purchaser for value who has taken the certificated security without notice of the particular defense.

(e) This section does not affect the right of a party to cancel a contract for a security "when, as and if issued" or "when distributed" in the event of a material change in the character of the security that is the subject of the contract or in the plan or arrangement pursuant to which the security is to be issued or distributed.

(f) If a security is held by a securities intermediary against whom an entitlement holder has a security entitlement with respect to the security, the issuer may not assert any defense that the issuer could not assert if the entitlement holder held the security directly.

§ 8—203. Staleness as Notice of Defect or Defense.

After an act or event, other than a call that has been revoked, creating a right to immediate performance of the principal obligation represented by a certificated security or setting a date on or after which the security is to be presented or surrendered for redemption or exchange, a purchaser is charged with notice of any defect in its issue or defense of the issuer, if the act or event:

(1) requires the payment of money, the delivery of a certificated security, the registration of transfer of an uncertificated security, or any of them on presentation or surrender of the security certificate, the money or security is available on the date set for payment or exchange, and the purchaser takes the security more than one year after that date; or

(2) is not covered by paragraph (1) and the purchaser takes the security more than two years after the date set for surrender or presentation or the date on which performance became due.

§ 8—204. Effect of Issuer's Restriction on Transfer.

A restriction on transfer of a security imposed by the issuer, even if otherwise lawful, is ineffective against a person without knowledge of the restriction unless:

(1) the security is certificated and the restriction is noted conspicuously on the security certificate; or

(2) the security is uncertificated and the registered owner has been notified of the restriction.

§ 8—205. Effect of Unauthorized Signature on Security Certificate.

An unauthorized signature placed on a security certificate before or in the course of issue is ineffective, but the signature is effective in favor of a purchaser for value of the certificated security if the purchaser is without notice of the lack of authority and the signing has been done by:

(1) an authenticating trustee, registrar, transfer agent, or other person entrusted by the issuer with the signing of the security certificate or of similar security certificates, or the immediate preparation for signing of any of them; or

(2) an employee of the issuer, or of any of the persons listed in paragraph (1), entrusted with responsible handling of the security certificate.

§ 8—206. Completion or Alteration of Security Certificate.

(a) If a security certificate contains the signatures necessary to its issue or transfer but is incomplete in any other respect:

(1) any person may complete it by filling in the blanks as authorized; and

(2) even if the blanks are incorrectly filled in, the security certificate as completed is enforceable by a purchaser who took it for value and without notice of the incorrectness.

(b) A complete security certificate that has been improperly altered, even if fraudulently, remains enforceable, but only according to its original terms.

§ 8—207. Rights and Duties of Issuer With Respect to Registered Owners.

(a) Before due presentment for registration of transfer of a certificated security in registered form or of an instruction requesting registration of transfer of an uncertificated security, the issuer or indenture trustee may treat the registered owner as the person exclusively entitled to vote, receive notifications, and otherwise exercise all the rights and powers of an owner.

(b) This Article does not affect the liability of the registered owner of a security for a call, assessment, or the like.

§ 8—208. Effect of Signature of Authenticating Trustee, Registrar, or Transfer Agent.

(a) A person signing a security certificate as authenticating trustee, registrar, transfer agent, or the like, warrants to a purchaser for value of the certificated security, if the purchaser is without notice of a particular defect, that:

(1) the certificate is genuine;

(2) the person's own participation in the issue of the security is within the person's capacity and within the scope of the authority received by the person from the issuer; and

(3) the person has reasonable grounds to believe that the certificated security is in the form and within the amount the issuer is authorized to issue.

(b) Unless otherwise agreed, a person signing under subsection (a) does not assume responsibility for the validity of the security in other respects.

§ 8—209. Issuer's Lien.

A lien in favor of an issuer upon a certificated security is valid against a purchaser only if the right of the issuer to the lien is noted conspicuously on the security certificate.

§ 8—210. Overissue.

(a) In this section, "overissue" means the issue of securities in excess of the amount the issuer has corporate power to issue, but an overissue does not occur if appropriate action has cured the overissue.

(b) Except as otherwise provided in subsections (c) and (d), the provisions of this Article which validate a security or compel its issue or reissue do not apply to the extent that validation, issue, or reissue would result in overissue.

(c) If an identical security not constituting an overissue is reasonably available for purchase, a person entitled to issue or validation may compel the issuer to purchase the security and deliver it if certificated or register its transfer if uncertificated, against surrender of any security certificate the person holds.

(d) If a security is not reasonably available for purchase, a person entitled to issue or validation may recover from the issuer the price the person or the last purchaser for value paid for it with interest from the date of the person's demand.

Part 3 Transfer of Certificated and Uncertificated Securities

§ 8—301. Delivery.

(a) Delivery of a certificated security to a purchaser occurs when:

(1) the purchaser acquires possession of the security certificate;

(2) another person, other than a securities intermediary, either acquires possession of the security certificate on behalf of the purchaser or, having previously acquired possession of the certificate, acknowledges that it holds for the purchaser; or

(3) a securities intermediary acting on behalf of the purchaser acquires possession of the security certificate, only if the certificate is in registered form and has been specially indorsed to the purchaser by an effective indorsement.

(b) Delivery of an uncertificated security to a purchaser occurs when:

(1) the issuer registers the purchaser as the registered owner, upon original issue or registration of transfer; or

(2) another person, other than a securities intermediary, either becomes the registered owner of the uncertificated security on behalf of the purchaser or, having previously become the registered owner, acknowledges that it holds for the purchaser.

§ 8—302. Rights of Purchaser.

(a) Except as otherwise provided in subsections (b) and (c), upon delivery of a certificated or uncertificated security to a purchaser, the purchaser acquires all rights in the security that the transferor had or had power to transfer.

(b) A purchaser of a limited interest acquires rights only to the extent of the interest purchased.

(c) A purchaser of a certificated security who as a previous holder had notice of an adverse claim does not improve its position by taking from a protected purchaser.

§ 8—303. Protected Purchaser.

(a) "Protected purchaser" means a purchaser of a certificated or uncertificated security, or of an interest therein, who:

(1) gives value;

(2) does not have notice of any adverse claim to the security; and

(3) obtains control of the certificated or uncertificated security.

(b) In addition to acquiring the rights of a purchaser, a protected purchaser also acquires its interest in the security free of any adverse claim.

§ 8—304. Indorsement.

(a) An indorsement may be in blank or special. An indorsement in blank includes an indorsement to bearer. A special indorsement specifies to whom a security is to be transferred or who has power to transfer it. A holder may convert a blank indorsement to a special indorsement.

(b) An indorsement purporting to be only of part of a security certificate representing units intended by the issuer to be separately transferable is effective to the extent of the indorsement.

(c) An indorsement, whether special or in blank, does not constitute a transfer until delivery of the certificate on which it appears or, if the indorsement is on a separate document, until delivery of both the document and the certificate.

(d) If a security certificate in registered form has been delivered to a purchaser without a necessary indorsement, the purchaser may become a protected purchaser only when the indorsement is supplied. However, against a transferor, a transfer is complete upon delivery and the purchaser has a specifically enforceable right to have any necessary indorsement supplied.

(e) An indorsement of a security certificate in bearer form may give notice of an adverse claim to the certificate, but it does not otherwise affect a right to registration that the holder possesses.

(f) Unless otherwise agreed, a person making an indorsement assumes only the obligations provided in Section 8-108 and not an obligation that the security will be honored by the issuer.

§ 8—305. Instruction.

(a) If an instruction has been originated by an appropriate person but is incomplete in any other respect, any person may complete it as authorized and the issuer may rely on it as completed, even though it has been completed incorrectly.

(b) Unless otherwise agreed, a person initiating an instruction assumes only the obligations imposed by Section 8-108 and not an obligation that the security will be honored by the issuer.

§ 8—306. Effect of Guaranteeing Signature, Indorsement, or Instruction.

(a) A person who guarantees a signature of an indorser of a security certificate warrants that at the time of signing:

(1) the signature was genuine;

(2) the signer was an appropriate person to indorse, or if the signature is by an agent, the agent had actual authority to act on behalf of the appropriate person; and

(3) the signer had legal capacity to sign.

(b) A person who guarantees a signature of the originator of an instruction warrants that at the time of signing:

(1) the signature was genuine;

(2) the signer was an appropriate person to originate the instruction, or if the signature is by an agent, the agent had actual authority to act on behalf of the appropriate person, if the person specified in the instruction as the registered owner was, in fact, the registered owner, as to which fact the signature guarantor does not make a warranty; and

(3) the signer had legal capacity to sign.

(c) A person who specially guarantees the signature of an originator of an instruction makes the warranties of a signature guarantor under subsection (b) and also warrants that at the time the instruction is presented to the issuer:

(1) the person specified in the instruction as the registered owner of the uncertificated security will be the registered owner; and

(2) the transfer of the uncertificated security requested in the instruction will be registered by the issuer free from all liens, security interests, restrictions, and claims other than those specified in the instruction.

(d) A guarantor under subsections (a) and (b) or a special guarantor under subsection (c) does not otherwise warrant the rightfulness of the transfer.

(e) A person who guarantees an indorsement of a security certificate makes the warranties of a signature guarantor under subsection (a) and also warrants the rightfulness of the transfer in all respects.

(f) A person who guarantees an instruction requesting the transfer of an uncertificated security makes the warranties of a special signature guarantor under subsection (c) and also warrants the rightfulness of the transfer in all respects.

(g) An issuer may not require a special guaranty of signature, a guaranty of indorsement, or a guaranty of instruction as a condition to registration of transfer.

(h) The warranties under this section are made to a person taking or dealing with the security in reliance on the guaranty, and the guarantor is liable to the person for loss resulting from their breach. An indorser or originator of an instruction whose signature, indorsement, or instruction has been guaranteed is liable to a guarantor for any loss suffered by the guarantor as a result of breach of the warranties of the guarantor.

§ 8—307. Purchaser's Right to Requisites for Registration of Transfer.

Unless otherwise agreed, the transferor of a security on due demand shall supply the purchaser with proof of authority to transfer or with any other requisite necessary to obtain registration of the transfer of the security, but if the transfer is not for value, a transferor need not comply unless the purchaser pays the necessary expenses. If the transferor fails within a reasonable time to comply with the demand, the purchaser may reject or rescind the transfer.

Part 4 Registration

§ 8—401. Duty of Issuer to Register Transfer.

(a) If a certificated security in registered form is presented to an issuer with a request to register transfer or an instruction is presented to an issuer with a request to register transfer of an uncertificated security, the issuer shall register the transfer as requested if:

(1) under the terms of the security the person seeking registration of transfer is eligible to have the security registered in its name;

(2) the indorsement or instruction is made by the appropriate person or by an agent who has actual authority to act on behalf of the appropriate person;

(3) reasonable assurance is given that the indorsement or instruction is genuine and authorized (Section 8-402);

(4) any applicable law relating to the collection of taxes has been complied with;

(5) the transfer does not violate any restriction on transfer imposed by the issuer in accordance with Section 8-204;

(6) a demand that the issuer not register transfer has not become effective under Section 8-403, or the issuer has complied with Section 8-403(b) but no legal process or indemnity bond is obtained as provided in Section 8-403(d); and

(7) the transfer is in fact rightful or is to a protected purchaser.

(b) If an issuer is under a duty to register a transfer of a security, the issuer is liable to a person presenting a certificated security or an instruction for registration or to the person's principal for loss resulting from unreasonable delay in registration or failure or refusal to register the transfer.

§ 8—402. Assurance That Indorsement or Instruction Is Effective.

(a) An issuer may require the following assurance that each necessary indorsement or each instruction is genuine and authorized:

(1) in all cases, a guaranty of the signature of the person making an indorsement or originating an instruction including, in the case of an instruction, reasonable assurance of identity;

(2) if the indorsement is made or the instruction is originated by an agent, appropriate assurance of actual authority to sign;

(3) if the indorsement is made or the instruction is originated by a fiduciary pursuant to Section 8-107(a)(4) or (a)(5), appropriate evidence of appointment or incumbency;

(4) if there is more than one fiduciary, reasonable assurance that all who are required to sign have done so; and

(5) if the indorsement is made or the instruction is originated by a person not covered by another provision of this subsection, assurance appropriate to the case corresponding as nearly as may be to the provisions of this subsection.

(b) An issuer may elect to require reasonable assurance beyond that specified in this section.

(c) In this section:

(1) "Guaranty of the signature" means a guaranty signed by or on behalf of a person reasonably believed by the issuer to be responsible. An issuer may adopt standards with respect to responsibility if they are not manifestly unreasonable.

(2) "Appropriate evidence of appointment or incumbency" means:

(i) in the case of a fiduciary appointed or qualified by a court, a certificate issued by or under the direction or supervision of the court or an officer thereof and dated within 60 days before the date of presentation for transfer; or

(ii) in any other case, a copy of a document showing the appointment or a certificate issued by or on behalf of a person reasonably believed by an issuer to be responsible or, in the absence of that document or certificate, other evidence the issuer reasonably considers appropriate.

§ 8—403. Demand That Issuer Not Register Transfer.

(a) A person who is an appropriate person to make an indorsement or originate an instruction may demand that the issuer not register transfer of a security by communicating to the issuer a notification that identifies the registered owner and the issue of which the security is a part and provides an address for communications directed to the person making the demand. The demand is effective only if it is received by the issuer at a time and in a manner affording the issuer reasonable opportunity to act on it.

(b) If a certificated security in registered form is presented to an issuer with a request to register transfer or an instruction is presented to an issuer with a request to register transfer of an uncertificated security after a demand that the issuer not register transfer has become effective, the issuer shall promptly communicate to (i) the person who initiated the demand at the address provided in the demand and (ii) the person who presented the security for registration of transfer or initiated the instruction requesting registration of transfer a notification stating that:

(1) the certificated security has been presented for registration of transfer or the instruction for registration of transfer of the uncertificated security has been received;

(2) a demand that the issuer not register transfer had previously been received; and

(3) the issuer will withhold registration of transfer for a period of time stated in the notification in order to provide the person who initiated the demand an opportunity to obtain legal process or an indemnity bond.

(c) The period described in subsection (b)(3) may not exceed 30 days after the date of communication of the notification. A shorter period may be specified by the issuer if it is not manifestly unreasonable.

(d) An issuer is not liable to a person who initiated a demand that the issuer not register transfer for any loss the person suffers as a result of registration of a transfer pursuant to an effective indorsement or instruction if the person who initiated the demand does not, within the time stated in the issuer's communication, either:

(1) obtain an appropriate restraining order, injunction, or other process from a court of competent jurisdiction enjoining the issuer from registering the transfer; or

(2) file with the issuer an indemnity bond, sufficient in the issuer's judgment to protect the issuer and any transfer agent, registrar, or other agent of the issuer involved from any loss it or they may suffer by refusing to register the transfer.

(e) This section does not relieve an issuer from liability for registering transfer pursuant to an indorsement or instruction that was not effective.

§ 8—404. Wrongful Registration.

(a) Except as otherwise provided in Section 8-406, an issuer is liable for wrongful registration of transfer if the issuer has registered a transfer of a security to a person not entitled to it, and the transfer was registered:

(1) pursuant to an ineffective indorsement or instruction;

(2) after a demand that the issuer not register transfer became effective under Section 8-403(a) and the issuer did not comply with Section 8-403(b);

(3) after the issuer had been served with an injunction, restraining order, or other legal process enjoining it from registering the transfer, issued by a court of competent jurisdiction, and the issuer had a reasonable opportunity to act on the injunction, restraining order, or other legal process; or

(4) by an issuer acting in collusion with the wrongdoer.

(b) An issuer that is liable for wrongful registration of transfer under subsection (a) on demand shall provide the person entitled to the security with a like certificated or uncertificated security, and any payments or distributions that the person did not receive as a result of the wrongful registration. If an overissue would result, the issuer's liability to provide the person with a like security is governed by Section 8-210.

(c) Except as otherwise provided in subsection (a) or in a law relating to the collection of taxes, an issuer is not liable to an owner or other person suffering loss as a result of the registration of a transfer of a security if registration was made pursuant to an effective indorsement or instruction.

§ 8-405. Replacement of Lost, Destroyed, or Wrongfully Taken Security Certificate.

(a) If an owner of a certificated security, whether in registered or bearer form, claims that the certificate has been lost, destroyed, or wrongfully taken, the issuer shall issue a new certificate if the owner:

(1) so requests before the issuer has notice that the certificate has been acquired by a protected purchaser;

(2) files with the issuer a sufficient indemnity bond; and

(3) satisfies other reasonable requirements imposed by the issuer.

(b) If, after the issue of a new security certificate, a protected purchaser of the original certificate presents it for registration of transfer, the issuer shall register the transfer unless an overissue would result. In that case, the issuer's liability is governed by Section 8-210. In addition to any rights on the indemnity bond, an issuer may recover the new certificate from a person to whom it was issued or any person taking under that person, except a protected purchaser.

§ 8—406. Obligation to Notify Issuer of Lost, Destroyed, or Wrongfully Taken Security Certificate.

If a security certificate has been lost, apparently destroyed, or wrongfully taken, and the owner fails to notify the issuer of that fact within a reasonable time after the owner has notice of it and the issuer registers a transfer of the security before receiving notification, the owner may not assert against the issuer a claim for registering the transfer under Section 8- 404 or a claim to a new security certificate under Section 8-405.

§ 8—407. Authenticating Trustee, Transfer Agent, and Registrar.

A person acting as authenticating trustee, transfer agent, registrar, or other agent for an issuer in the registration of a transfer of its securities, in the issue of new security certificates or uncertificated securities, or in the cancellation of surrendered security certificates has the same obligation to the holder or owner of a certificated or uncertificated security with regard to the particular functions performed as the issuer has in regard to those functions.

Part 5 Security Entitlements

§ 8—501. Securities Account; Acquisition of Security Entitlement From Securities Intermediary.

(a) "Securities account" means an account to which a financial asset is or may be credited in accordance with an agreement under which the person maintaining the account undertakes to treat the person for whom the account is maintained as entitled to exercise the rights that comprise the financial asset.

(b) Except as otherwise provided in subsections (d) and (e), a person acquires a security entitlement if a securities intermediary:

(1) indicates by book entry that a financial asset has been credited to the person's securities account;

(2) receives a financial asset from the person or acquires a financial asset for the person and, in either case, accepts it for credit to the person's securities account; or

(3) becomes obligated under other law, regulation, or rule to credit a financial asset to the person's securities account.

(c) If a condition of subsection (b) has been met, a person has a security entitlement even though the securities intermediary does not itself hold the financial asset.

(d) If a securities intermediary holds a financial asset for another person, and the financial asset is registered in the name of, payable to the order of, or specially indorsed to the other person, and has not been indorsed to the securities intermediary or in blank, the other person is treated as holding the financial asset directly rather than as having a security entitlement with respect to the financial asset.

(e) Issuance of a security is not establishment of a security entitlement.

§ 8—502. Assertion of Adverse Claim Against Entitlement Holder.

An action based on an adverse claim to a financial asset, whether framed in conversion, replevin, constructive trust, equitable lien, or other theory, may not be asserted against a person who acquires a security entitlement under Section 8-501 for value and without notice of the adverse claim.

§ 8—503. Property Interest of Entitlement Holder in Financial Asset Held by Securities Intermediary.

(a) To the extent necessary for a securities intermediary to satisfy all security entitlements with respect to a particular financial asset, all interests in that financial asset held by the securities intermediary are held by the securities intermediary for the entitlement holders, are not property of the securities intermediary, and are not subject to claims of creditors of the securities intermediary, except as otherwise provided in Section 8-511.

(b) An entitlement holder's property interest with respect to a particular financial asset under subsection (a) is a pro rata property interest in all interests in that financial asset held by the securities intermediary, without regard to the time the entitlement holder acquired the security entitlement or the time the securities intermediary acquired the interest in that financial asset.

(c) An entitlement holder's property interest with respect to a particular financial asset under subsection (a) may be enforced against the securities intermediary only by exercise of the entitlement holder's rights under Sections 8-505 through 8-508.

(d) An entitlement holder's property interest with respect to a particular financial asset under subsection (a) may be enforced against a purchaser of the financial asset or interest therein only if:

(1) insolvency proceedings have been initiated by or against the securities intermediary;

(2) the securities intermediary does not have sufficient interests in the financial asset to satisfy the security entitlements of all of its entitlement holders to that financial asset;

(3) the securities intermediary violated its obligations under Section 8-504 by transferring the financial asset or interest therein to the purchaser; and

(4) the purchaser is not protected under subsection (e).

The trustee or other liquidator, acting on behalf of all entitlement holders having security entitlements with respect to a particular financial asset, may recover the financial asset, or interest therein, from the purchaser. If the trustee or other liquidator elects not to pursue that right, an entitlement holder whose security entitlement remains unsatisfied has the right to recover its interest in the financial asset from the purchaser.

(e) An action based on the entitlement holder's property interest with respect to a particular financial asset under subsection (a), whether framed in conversion, replevin, constructive trust, equitable lien, or other theory, may not be asserted against any purchaser of a financial asset or interest therein who gives value, obtains control, and does not act in collusion with the securities intermediary in violating the securities intermediary's obligations under Section 8-504.

§ 8—504. Duty of Securities Intermediary to Maintain Financial Asset.

(a) A securities intermediary shall promptly obtain and thereafter maintain a financial asset in a quantity corresponding to the aggregate of all security entitlements it has established in favor of its entitlement holders with respect to that financial asset. The securities intermediary may maintain those financial assets directly or through one or more other securities intermediaries.

(b) Except to the extent otherwise agreed by its entitlement holder, a securities intermediary may not grant any security interests in a financial asset it is obligated to maintain pursuant to subsection (a).

(c) A securities intermediary satisfies the duty in subsection (a) if:

(1) the securities intermediary acts with respect to the duty as agreed upon by the entitlement holder and the securities intermediary; or

(2) in the absence of agreement, the securities intermediary exercises due care in accordance with reasonable commercial standards to obtain and maintain the financial asset.

(d) This section does not apply to a clearing corporation that is itself the obligor of an option or similar obligation to which its entitlement holders have security entitlements.

§ 8—505. Duty of Securities Intermediary With Respect to Payments and Distributions.

(a) A securities intermediary shall take action to obtain a payment or distribution made by the issuer of a financial asset. A securities intermediary satisfies the duty if:

(1) the securities intermediary acts with respect to the duty as agreed upon by the entitlement holder and the securities intermediary; or

(2) in the absence of agreement, the securities intermediary exercises due care in accordance with reasonable commercial standards to attempt to obtain the payment or distribution.

(b) A securities intermediary is obligated to its entitlement holder for a payment or distribution made by the issuer of a financial asset if the payment or distribution is received by the securities intermediary.

§ 8—506. Duty of Securities Intermediary to Exercise Rights as Directed by Entitlement Holder.

A securities intermediary shall exercise rights with respect to a financial asset if directed to do so by an entitlement holder. A securities intermediary satisfies the duty if:

(1) the securities intermediary acts with respect to the duty as agreed upon by the entitlement holder and the securities intermediary; or

(2) in the absence of agreement, the securities intermediary either places the entitlement holder in a position to exercise the rights directly or exercises due care in accordance with reasonable commercial standards to follow the direction of the entitlement holder.

§ 8—507. Duty of Securities Intermediary to Comply With Entitlement Order.

(a) A securities intermediary shall comply with an entitlement order if the entitlement order is originated by the appropriate person, the securities intermediary has had reasonable opportunity to assure itself that the entitlement order is genuine and authorized, and the securities intermediary has had reasonable opportunity to comply with the entitlement order. A securities intermediary satisfies the duty if:

(1) the securities intermediary acts with respect to the duty as agreed upon by the entitlement holder and the securities intermediary; or

(2) in the absence of agreement, the securities intermediary exercises due care in accordance with reasonable commercial standards to comply with the entitlement order.

(b) If a securities intermediary transfers a financial asset pursuant to an ineffective entitlement order, the securities intermediary shall reestablish a security entitlement in favor of the person entitled to it, and pay or credit any payments or distributions that the person did not receive as a result of the wrongful transfer. If the securities intermediary does not reestablish a security entitlement, the securities intermediary is liable to the entitlement holder for damages.

§ 8—508. Duty of Securities Intermediary to Change Entitlement Holder's Position to Other Form of Security Holding.

A securities intermediary shall act at the direction of an entitlement holder to change a security entitlement into another available form of holding for which the entitlement holder is eligible, or to cause the financial asset to be transferred to a securities account of the entitlement holder with another securities intermediary. A securities intermediary satisfies the duty if:

(1) the securities intermediary acts as agreed upon by the entitlement holder and the securities intermediary; or

(2) in the absence of agreement, the securities intermediary exercises due care in accordance with reasonable commercial standards to follow the direction of the entitlement holder.

§ 8—509. Specification of Duties of Securities Intermediary by Other Statute or Regulation; Manner of Performance of Duties of Securities Intermediary and Exercise of Rights of Entitlement Holder.

(a) If the substance of a duty imposed upon a securities intermediary by Sections 8-504 through 8-508 is the subject of other statute, regulation, or rule, compliance with that statute, regulation, or rule satisfies the duty.

(b) To the extent that specific standards for the performance of the duties of a securities intermediary or the exercise of the rights of an entitlement holder are not specified by other statute, regulation, or rule or by agreement between the securities intermediary and entitlement holder, the securities intermediary shall perform its duties and the entitlement holder shall exercise its rights in a commercially reasonable manner.

(c) The obligation of a securities intermediary to perform the duties imposed by Sections 8-504 through 8-508 is subject to:

(1) rights of the securities intermediary arising out of a security interest under a security agreement with the entitlement holder or otherwise; and

(2) rights of the securities intermediary under other law, regulation, rule, or agreement to withhold performance of its duties as a result of unfulfilled obligations of the entitlement holder to the securities intermediary.

(d) Sections 8-504 through 8-508 do not require a securities intermediary to take any action that is prohibited by other statute, regulation, or rule.

§ 8—510. Rights of Purchaser of Security Entitlement From Entitlement Holder.

(a) An action based on an adverse claim to a financial asset or security entitlement, whether framed in conversion, replevin, constructive trust, equitable lien, or other theory, may not be asserted against a person who purchases a security entitlement, or an interest therein, from an entitlement holder if the purchaser gives value, does not have notice of the adverse claim, and obtains control.

(b) If an adverse claim could not have been asserted against an entitlement holder under Section 8-502, the adverse claim cannot be asserted against a person who purchases a security entitlement, or an interest therein, from the entitlement holder.

(c) In a case not covered by the priority rules in Article 9, a purchaser for value of a security entitlement, or an interest therein, who obtains control has priority over a purchaser of a security entitlement, or an interest therein, who does not obtain control. Purchasers who have control rank equally, except that a securities intermediary as purchaser has priority over a conflicting purchaser who has control unless otherwise agreed by the securities intermediary.

§ 8—511. Priority Among Security Interests and Entitlement Holders.

(a) Except as otherwise provided in subsections (b) and (c), if a securities intermediary does not have sufficient interests in a particular financial asset to satisfy both its obligations to entitlement holders who have security entitlements to that financial asset and its obligation to a creditor of the securities intermediary who has a security interest in that financial asset, the claims of entitlement holders, other than the creditor, have priority over the claim of the creditor.

(b) A claim of a creditor of a securities intermediary who has a security interest in a financial asset held by a securities intermediary has priority over claims of the securities intermediary's entitlement holders who have security entitlements with respect to that financial asset if the creditor has control over the financial asset.

(c) If a clearing corporation does not have sufficient financial assets to satisfy both its obligations to entitlement holders who have security entitlements with respect to a financial asset and its obligation to a creditor of the clearing corporation who has a security interest in that financial asset, the claim of the creditor has priority over the claims of entitlement holders.

Part 6 Transition Provisions for Revised Article 8

§ 8—601. Effective Date.

This [Act] takes effect ....

§ 8—602. Repeals.

This [Act] repeals ....

§ 8—603. Savings Clause.

(a) This [Act] does not affect an action or proceeding commenced before this [Act] takes effect.

(b) If a security interest in a security is perfected at the date this [Act] takes effect, and the action by which the security interest was perfected would suffice to perfect a security interest under this [Act], no further action is required to continue perfection. If a security interest in a security is perfected at the date this [Act] takes effect but the action by which the security interest was perfected would not suffice to perfect a security interest under this [Act], the security interest remains perfected for a period of four months after the effective date and continues perfected thereafter if appropriate action to perfect under this [Act] is taken within that period. If a security interest is perfected at the date this [Act] takes effect and the security interest can be perfected by filing under this [Act], a financing statement signed by the secured party instead of the debtor may be filed within that period to continue perfection or thereafter to perfect.

Article 9
SECURED TRANSACTIONS; SALES OF ACCOUNTS AND CHATTEL PAPER

Note: *The adoption of this Article should be accompanied by the repeal of existing statutes dealing with conditional sales, trust receipts, factor's liens where the factor is given a nonpossessory lien, chattel mortgages, crop mortgages, mortgages on railroad equipment, assignment of accounts and generally statutes regulating security interests in personal property.*

Where the state has a retail installment selling act or small loan act, that legislation should be carefully examined to determine what changes in those acts are needed to conform them to this Article. This Article primarily sets out rules defining rights of a secured party against persons dealing with the debtor; it does not prescribe regulations and controls which may be necessary to curb abuses arising in the small loan business or in the financing of consumer purchases on credit. Accordingly there is no intention to repeal existing regulatory acts in those fields by enactment or re-enactment of Article 9. See Section 9—203(4) and the Note thereto.

Part 1 Short Title, Applicability and Definitions

§ 9—101. Short Title.

This Article shall be known and may be cited as Uniform Commercial Code—Secured Transactions.

§ 9—102. Policy and Subject Matter of Article.

(1) Except as otherwise provided in Section 9—104 on excluded transactions, this Article applies

(a) to any transaction (regardless of its form) which is intended to create a security interest in personal property or fixtures including goods, documents, instruments, general intangibles, chattel paper or accounts; and also

(b) to any sale of accounts or chattel paper.

(2) This Article applies to security interests created by contract including pledge, assignment, chattel mortgage, chattel trust, trust deed, factor's lien, equipment trust, conditional sale, trust receipt, other lien or title retention contract and lease or consignment intended as security. This Article does not apply to statutory liens except as provided in Section 9—310.

(3) The application of this Article to a security interest in a secured obligation is not affected by the fact that the obligation is itself secured by a transaction or interest to which this Article does not apply.

§ 9—103. Perfection of Security Interest in Multiple State Transactions.

(1) Documents, instruments and ordinary goods.

(a) This subsection applies to documents, instruments, rights to proceeds of written letters of credit, and goods other than those covered by a certificate of title described in subsection (2), mobile goods described in subsection (3), and minerals described in subsection (5).

(b) Except as otherwise provided in this subsection, perfection and the effect of perfection or non-perfection of a security interest in collateral are governed by the law of the jurisdiction where the collateral is when the last event occurs on which is based the assertion that the security interest is perfected or unperfected.

(c) If the parties to a transaction creating a purchase money security interest in goods in one jurisdiction understand at the time that the security interest attaches that the goods will be kept in another jurisdiction, then the law of the other jurisdiction governs the perfection and the effect of perfection or non-perfection of the security interest from the time it attaches until thirty days after the debtor receives possession of the goods and thereafter if the goods are taken to the other jurisdiction before the end of the thirty-day period.

(d) When collateral is brought into and kept in this state while subject to a security interest perfected under the law of the jurisdiction from which the collateral was removed, the security interest remains perfected, but if action is required by Part 3 of this Article to perfect the security interest,

(i) if the action is not taken before the expiration of the period of perfection in the other jurisdiction or the end of four months after the collateral is brought into this state, whichever period first expires, the security interest becomes unperfected at the end of that period and is thereafter deemed to have been unperfected as against a person who became a purchaser after removal;

(ii) if the action is taken before the expiration of the period specified in subparagraph (i), the security interest continues perfected thereafter;

(iii) for the purpose of priority over a buyer of consumer goods (subsection (2) of Section 9—307), the period of the effectiveness of a filing in the jurisdiction from which the collateral is removed is governed by the rules with respect to perfection in subparagraphs (i) and (ii).

(2) Certificate of title.

(a) This subsection applies to goods covered by a certificate of title issued under a statute of this state or of another jurisdiction under the law of which indication of a security interest on the certificate is required as a condition of perfection.

(b) Except as otherwise provided in this subsection, perfection and the effect of perfection or non-perfection of the security interest are governed by the law (including the conflict of laws rules) of the jurisdiction issuing the certificate until four months after the goods are removed from that jurisdiction and thereafter until the goods are registered in another jurisdiction, but in any event not beyond surrender of the certificate. After the expiration of that period, the goods are not covered by the certificate of title within the meaning of this section.

(c) Except with respect to the rights of a buyer described in the next paragraph, a security interest, perfected in another jurisdiction otherwise than by notation on a certificate of title, in goods brought into this state and thereafter covered by a certificate of title issued by this state is subject to the rules stated in paragraph (d) of subsection (1).

(d) If goods are brought into this state while a security interest therein is perfected in any manner under the law of the jurisdiction from which the goods are removed and a certificate of title is issued by this state and the certificate does not show that the goods are subject to the security interest or that they may be subject to security interests not shown on the certificate, the security interest is subordinate to the rights of a buyer of the goods who is not in the business of selling goods of that kind to the extent that he gives value and receives delivery of the goods after issuance of the certificate and without knowledge of the security interest.

(3) Accounts, general intangibles and mobile goods.

(a) This subsection applies to accounts (other than an account described in subsection (5) on minerals) and general intangibles (other than uncertificated securities) and to goods which are mobile and which are of a type normally used in more than one jurisdiction, such as motor vehicles, trailers, rolling stock, airplanes, shipping containers, road building and construction machinery and commercial harvesting machinery and the like, if the goods are equipment or are inventory leased or held for lease by the debtor to others, and are not covered by a certificate of title described in subsection (2).

(b) The law (including the conflict of laws rules) of the jurisdiction in which the debtor is located governs the perfection and the effect of perfection or non-perfection of the security interest.

(c) If, however, the debtor is located in a jurisdiction which is not a part of the United States, and which does not provide for perfection of the security interest by filing or recording in that jurisdiction, the law of the jurisdiction in the United States in which the debtor has its major executive office in the United States governs the perfection and the effect of perfection or non-perfection of the security interest through filing. In the alternative, if the debtor is located in a jurisdiction which is not a part of the United States or Canada and the collateral is accounts or general intangibles for money due or to become due, the security interest may be perfected by notification to the account debtor. As used in this paragraph, "United States" includes its territories and possessions and the Commonwealth of Puerto Rico.

(d) A debtor shall be deemed located at his place of business if he has one, at his chief executive office if he has more than one place of business, otherwise at his residence. If, however, the debtor is a foreign air carrier under the Federal Aviation Act of 1958, as amended, it shall be deemed located at the designated office of the agent upon whom service of process may be made on behalf of the foreign air carrier.

(e) A security interest perfected under the law of the jurisdiction of the location of the debtor is perfected until the expiration of four months after a change of the debtor's location to another jurisdiction, or until perfection would have ceased by the law of the first jurisdiction, whichever period first expires. Unless perfected in the new jurisdiction before the end of that period, it becomes unperfected thereafter and is deemed to have been unperfected as against a person who became a purchaser after the change.

(4) Chattel paper.

The rules stated for goods in subsection (1) apply to a possessory security interest in chattel paper. The rules stated for accounts in subsection (3) apply to a nonpossessory security interest in chattel paper, but the security interest may not be perfected by notification to the account debtor.

(5) Minerals.

Perfection and the effect of perfection or non-perfection of a security interest which is created by a debtor who has an interest in minerals or the like (including oil and gas) before extraction and which attaches thereto as extracted, or which attaches to an account resulting from the sale thereof at the wellhead or minehead are governed by the law (including the conflict of laws rules) of the jurisdiction wherein the wellhead or minehead is located.

(6) Investment property.

(a) This subsection applies to investment property.

(b) Except as otherwise provided in paragraph (f), during the time that a security certificate is located in a jurisdiction, perfection of a security interest, the effect of perfection or non-perfection, and the priority of a security interest in the certificated security represented thereby are governed by the local law of that jurisdiction.

(c) Except as otherwise provided in paragraph (f), perfection of a security interest, the effect of perfection or non-perfection, and the priority of a security interest in an uncertificated security are governed by the local law of the issuer's jurisdiction as specified in Section 8—110(d).

(d) Except as otherwise provided in paragraph (f), perfection of a security interest, the effect of perfection or non-perfection, and the priority of a security interest in a security entitlement or securities account are governed by the local law of the securities intermediary's jurisdiction as specified in Section 8—110(e).

(e) Except as otherwise provided in paragraph (f), perfection of a security interest, the effect of perfection or non-perfection, and the priority of a security interest in a commodity contract or commodity account are governed by the local law of the commodity intermediary's jurisdiction. The following rules determine a "commodity intermediary's jurisdiction" for purposes of this paragraph:

(i) If an agreement between the commodity intermediary and commodity customer specifies that it is governed by the law of a particular jurisdiction, that jurisdiction is the commodity intermediary's jurisdiction.

(ii) If an agreement between the commodity intermediary and commodity customer does not specify the governing law as provided in subparagraph (i), but expressly specifies that the commodity account is maintained at an office in a particular jurisdiction, that jurisdiction is the commodity intermediary's jurisdiction.

(iii) If an agreement between the commodity intermediary and commodity customer does not specify a jurisdiction as provided in subparagraphs (i) or (ii), the commodity intermediary's jurisdiction is the jurisdiction in which is located the office identified in an account statement as the office serving the commodity customer's account.

(iv) If an agreement between the commodity intermediary and commodity customer does not specify a jurisdiction as provided in subparagraphs (i) or (ii) and an account statement does not identify an office serving the commodity customer's account as provided in subparagraph (iii), the commodity intermediary's jurisdiction is the jurisdiction in which is located the chief executive office of the commodity intermediary.

(f) Perfection of a security interest by filing, automatic perfection of a security interest in investment property granted by a broker or securities intermediary, and automatic perfection of a security interest in a commodity contract or commodity account granted by a commodity intermediary are governed by the local law of the jurisdiction in which the debtor is located.

§ 9—104. Transactions Excluded From Article.

This Article does not apply

(a) to a security interest subject to any statute of the United States, to the extent that such statute governs the rights of parties to and third parties affected by transactions in particular types of property; or

(b) to a landlord's lien; or

(c) to a lien given by statute or other rule of law for services or materials except as provided in Section 9—310 on priority of such liens; or

(d) to a transfer of a claim for wages, salary or other compensation of an employee; or

(e) to a transfer by a government or governmental subdivision or agency; or

(f) to a sale of accounts or chattel paper as part of a sale of the business out of which they arose, or an assignment of accounts or chattel paper which is for the purpose of collection only, or a transfer of a right to payment under a contract to an assignee who is also to do the performance under the contract or a transfer of a single account to an assignee in whole or partial satisfaction of a preexisting indebtedness; or

(g) to a transfer of an interest in or claim in or under any policy of insurance, except as provided with respect to proceeds (Section 9—306) and priorities in proceeds (Section 9—312); or

(h) to a right represented by a judgment (other than a judgment taken on a right to payment which was collateral); or

(i) to any right of set-off; or

(j) except to the extent that provision is made for fixtures in Section 9—313, to the creation or transfer of an interest in or lien on real estate, including a lease or rents thereunder; or

(k) to a transfer in whole or in part of any claim arising out of tort; or

(*l*) to a transfer of an interest in any deposit account (subsection (1) of Section 9—105), except as provided with respect to proceeds (Section 9—306) and priorities in proceeds (Section 9—312).

(m) to a transfer of an interest in a letter of credit other than the rights to proceeds of a written letter of credit.

§ 9—105. Definitions and Index of Definitions.

(1) In this Article unless the context otherwise requires:

(a) "Account debtor" means the person who is obligated on an account, chattel paper or general intangible;

(b) "Chattel paper" means a writing or writings which evidence both a monetary obligation and a security interest in or a lease of specific goods, but a charter or other contract involving the use or hire of a vessel is not chattel paper. When a transaction is evidenced both by such a security agreement or a lease and by an instrument or a series of instruments, the group of writings taken together constitutes chattel paper;

(c) "Collateral" means the property subject to a security interest, and includes accounts and chattel paper which have been sold;

(d) "Debtor" means the person who owes payment or other performance of the obligation secured, whether or not he owns or has rights in the collateral, and includes the seller of accounts or chattel paper. Where the debtor and the owner of the collateral are not the same person, the term "debtor" means the owner of the collateral in any provision of the Article dealing with the collateral, the obligor in any provision dealing with the obligation, and may include both where the context so requires;

(e) "Deposit account" means a demand, time, savings, passbook or like account maintained with a bank, savings and loan association, credit union or like organization, other than an account evidenced by a certificate of deposit;

(f) "Document" means document of title as defined in the general definitions of Article 1 (Section 1—201), and a receipt of the kind described in subsection (2) of Section 7—201;

(g) "Encumbrance" includes real estate mortgages and other liens on real estate and all other rights in real estate that are not ownership interests;

(h) "Goods" includes all things which are movable at the time the security interest attaches or which are fixtures (Section 9—313), but does not include money, documents, instruments, investment property, commodity contracts accounts, chattel paper, general intangibles, or minerals or the like (including oil and gas) before extraction. "Goods" also includes standing timber which is to be cut and removed under a conveyance or contract for sale, the unborn young of animals, and growing crops;

(i) "Instrument" means a negotiable instrument (defined in Section 3—104), or any other writing which evidences a right to the payment of money and is not itself a security agreement or lease and is of a type which is in ordinary course of business transferred by delivery with any necessary indorsement or assignment. The term does not include investment property.

(j) "Mortgage" means a consensual interest created by a real estate mortgage, a trust deed on real estate, or the like;

(k) An advance is made "pursuant to commitment" if the secured party has bound himself to make it, whether or not a subsequent event of default or other event not within his control has relieved or may relieve him from his obligation;

(*l*) "Security agreement" means an agreement which creates or provides for a security interest;

(m) "Secured party" means a lender, seller or other person in whose favor there is a security interest, including a person to whom accounts or chattel paper have been sold. When the holders of obligations issued under an indenture of trust, equipment trust agreement or the like are represented by a trustee or other person, the representative is the secured party;

(n) "Transmitting utility" means any person primarily engaged in the railroad, street railway or trolley bus business, the electric or electronics communications transmission business, the transmission of goods by pipeline, or the transmission or the production and transmission of electricity, steam, gas or water, or the provision of sewer service.

(2) Other definitions applying to this Article and the sections in which they appear are:

"Account". Section 9—106.

"Attach". Section 9—203.

"Commodity contract". Section 9—115.

"Commodity customer". Section 9—115.

"Commodity intermediary". Section 9—115.

"Construction mortgage". Section 9—313(1).

"Consumer goods". Section 9—109(1).

"Control". Section 9—115.

"Equipment". Section 9—109(2).

"Farm products". Section 9—109(3).

"Fixture". Section 9—313(1).

"Fixture filing". Section 9—313(1).

"General intangibles". Section 9—106.

"Inventory". Section 9—109(4).

"Investment property". Section 9—115.

"Lien creditor". Section 9—301(3).

"Proceeds". Section 9—306(1).

"Purchase money security interest". Section 9—107.

"United States". Section 9—103.

(3) The following definitions in other Articles apply to this Article:

"Broker". Section. 8—102.

"Certified security". Section 8—102.

"Check". Section 3—104.

"Clearing corporation". Section 8—102.

"Contract for sale". Section 2—106.

"Control". Section 8—106.

"Delivery". Section 8—301.

"Entitlement holder". Section 8—102.

"Financial asset". Section 8—102.

"Holder in due course". Section 3—302.

"Letter of credit". Section 5—102.

"Note". Section 3—104.

"Proceeds of a letter of credit". Section 5—114(a).

"Sale". Section 2—106.

"Securities intermediary". Section 8—102.

"Security". Section 8—102.

"Security certificate". Section 8—102.

"Security entitlement". Section 8—102.

"Uncertertificated security". Section 8—102.

(4) In addition Article 1 contains general definitions and principles of construction and interpretation applicable throughout this Article.

§ 9—106. Definitions: "Account"; "General Intangibles".

"Account" means any right to payment for goods sold or leased or for services rendered which is not evidenced by an instrument or chattel paper, whether or not it has been earned by performance. "General intangibles" means any personal property (including things in action) other than goods, accounts, chattel paper, documents, instruments, investment property, rights to proceeds of written letters of credit, and money. All rights to payment earned or unearned under a charter or other contract involving the use or hire of a vessel and all rights incident to the charter or contract are accounts.

§ 9—107. Definitions: "Purchase Money Security Interest".

A security interest is a "purchase money security interest" to the extent that it is

(a) taken or retained by the seller of the collateral to secure all or part of its price; or

(b) taken by a person who by making advances or incurring an obligation gives value to enable the debtor to acquire rights in or the use of collateral if such value is in fact so used.

§ 9—108. When After-Acquired Collateral Not Security for Antecedent Debt.

Where a secured party makes an advance, incurs an obligation, releases a perfected security interest, or otherwise gives new value which is to be secured in whole or in part by after-acquired property his security interest in the after-acquired collateral shall be deemed to be taken for new value and not as security for an antecedent debt if the debtor acquires his rights in such collateral either in the ordinary course of his business or under a contract of purchase made pursuant to the security agreement within a reasonable time after new value is given.

§ 9—109. Classification of Goods; "Consumer Goods"; "Equipment"; "Farm Products"; "Inventory".

Goods are

(1) "consumer goods" if they are used or bought for use primarily for personal, family or household purposes;

(2) "equipment" if they are used or bought for use primarily in business (including farming or a profession) or by a debtor who is a non-profit organization or a governmental subdivision or agency or if the goods are not included in the definitions of inventory, farm products or consumer goods;

(3) "farm products" if they are crops or livestock or supplies used or produced in farming operations or if they are products of crops or livestock in their unmanufactured states (such as ginned cotton, wool-clip, maple syrup, milk and eggs), and if they are in the possession of a debtor engaged in raising, fattening, grazing or other farming operations. If goods are farm products they are neither equipment nor inventory;

(4) "inventory" if they are held by a person who holds them for sale or lease or to be furnished under contracts of service or if he has so furnished them, or if they are raw materials, work in process or materials used or consumed in a business. Inventory of a person is not to be classified as his equipment.

§ 9—110. Sufficiency of Description.

For purposes of this Article any description of personal property or real estate is sufficient whether or not it is specific if it reasonably identifies what is described.

§ 9—111. Applicability of Bulk Transfer Laws.

The creation of a security interest is not a bulk transfer under Article 6 (see Section 6—103).

§ 9—112. Where Collateral Is Not Owned by Debtor.

Unless otherwise agreed, when a secured party knows that collateral is owned by a person who is not the debtor, the owner of the collateral is entitled to receive from the secured party any surplus under Section 9—502(2) or under Section 9—504(1), and is not liable for the debt or for any deficiency after resale, and he has the same right as the debtor

(a) to receive statements under Section 9—208;

(b) to receive notice of and to object to a secured party's proposal to retain the collateral in satisfaction of the indebtedness under Section 9—505;

(c) to redeem the collateral under Section 9—506;

(d) to obtain injunctive or other relief under Section 9—507(1); and

(e) to recover losses caused to him under Section 9—208(2).

§ 9—113. Security Interests Arising Under Article on Sales or Under Article on Leases.

A security interest arising solely under the Article on Sales (Article 2) or the Article on Leases is subject to the provisions of this Article except that to the extent that and so long as the debtor does not have or does not lawfully obtain possession of the goods

(a) no security agreement is necessary to make the security interest enforceable; and

(b) no filing is required to perfect the security interest; and

(c) the rights of the secured party on default by the debtor are governed (i) by the Article on Sales (Article 2) in the case of a security interest arising solely under such Article or (ii) by the Article on Leases (Article 2A) in the case of a security interest arising solely under such Article.

§ 9—114. Consignment.

(1) A person who delivers goods under a consignment which is not a security interest and who would be required to file under this Article by paragraph (3)(c) of Section 2—326 has priority over a secured party who is or becomes a creditor of the consignee and who would have a perfected security interest in the goods if they were the property of the consignee, and also has priority with respect to identifiable cash proceeds received on or before delivery of the goods to a buyer, if

(a) the consignor complies with the filing provision of the Article on Sales with respect to consignments (paragraph (3)(c) of Section 2—326) before the consignee receives possession of the goods; and

(b) the consignor gives notification in writing to the holder of the security interest if the holder has filed a financing statement covering the same types of goods before the date of the filing made by the consignor; and

(c) the holder of the security interest receives the notification within five years before the consignee receives possession of the goods; and

(d) the notification states that the consignor expects to deliver goods on consignment to the consignee, describing the goods by item or type.

(2) In the case of a consignment which is not a security interest and in which the requirements of the preceding subsection have not been met, a person who delivers goods to another is subordinate to a person who would have a perfected security interest in the goods if they were the property of the debtor.

§ 9—115. Investment Property.

(1) In this Article:

(a) "Commodity account" means an account maintained by a commodity intermediary in which a commodity contract is carried for a commodity customer.

(b) "Commodity contract" means a commodity futures contract, an option on a commodity futures contract, a commodity option, or other contract that, in each case, is:

(i) traded on or subject to the rules of a board of trade that has been designated as a contract market for such a contract pursuant to the federal commodities laws; or

(ii) traded on a foreign commodity board of trade, exchange, or market, and is carried on the books of a commodity intermediary for a commodity customer.

(c) "Commodity customer" means a person for whom a commodity intermediary carries a commodity contract on its books.

(d) "Commodity intermediary" means:

(i) a person who is registered as a futures commission merchant under the federal commodities laws; or

(ii) a person who in the ordinary course of its business provides clearance or settlement services for a board of trade that has been designated as a contract market pursuant to the federal commodities laws.

(e) "Control" with respect to a certificated security, uncertificated security, or security entitlement has the meaning specified in Section 8—106. A secured party has control over a commodity contract if by agreement among the commodity customer, the commodity intermediary, and the secured party, the commodity intermediary has agreed that it will apply any value distributed on account of the commodity contract as directed by the secured party without further consent by the commodity customer. If a commodity customer grants a security interest in a commodity contract to its own commodity intermediary, the commodity intermediary as secured party has control. A secured party has control over a securities account or commodity account if the secured party has control over all security entitlements or commodity contracts carried in the securities account or commodity account.

(f) "Investment property" means:

(i) a security, whether certificated or uncertificated;

(ii) a security entitlement;

(iii) a securities account;

(iv) a commodity contract; or

(v) a commodity account.

(2) Attachment or perfection of a security interest in a securities account is also attachment or perfection of a security interest in all security entitlements carried in the securities account. Attachment or perfection of a security interest in a commodity account is also attachment or perfection of a security interest in all commodity contracts carried in the commodity account.

(3) A description of collateral in a security agreement or financing statement is sufficient to create or perfect a security interest in a certificated security, uncertificated security, security entitlement, securities account, commodity contract, or commodity account whether it describes the collateral by those terms, or as

investment property, or by description of the underlying security, financial asset, or commodity contract. A description of investment property collateral in a security agreement or financing statement is sufficient if it identifies the collateral by specific listing, by category, by quantity, by a computational or allocational formula or procedure, or by any other method, if the identity of the collateral is objectively determinable.

(4) Perfection of a security interest in investment property is governed by the following rules:

(a) A security interest in investment property may be perfected by control.

(b) Except as otherwise provided in paragraphs (c) and (d), a security interest in investment property may be perfected by filing.

(c) If the debtor is a broker or securities intermediary a security interest in investment property is perfected when it attaches. The filing of a financing statement with respect to a security interest in investment property granted by a broker or securities intermediary has no effect for purposes of perfection or priority with respect to that security interest.

(d) If a debtor is a commodity, intermediary, a security interest in a commodity contract or a commodity account is perfected when it attaches. The filing of a financing statement with respect to a security interest in a commodity contract or a commodity account granted by a commodity intermediary has no effect for purposes of perfection or priority with respect to that security interest.

(5) Priority between conflicting security interests in the same investment property is governed by the following rules:

(a) A security interest of a secured party who has control over investment property has priority over a security interest of a secured party who does not have control over the investment property.

(b) Except as otherwise provided in paragraphs (c) and (d), conflicting security interests of secured parties each of whom has control rank equally.

(c) Except as otherwise agreed by the securities intermediary, a security interest in a security entitlement or a securities account granted to the debtor's own securities intermediary has priority over any security interest granted by the debtor to another secured party.

(d) Except as otherwise agreed by the commodity intermediary, a security interest in a commodity contract or a commodity account granted to the debtor's own commodity intermediary has priority over any security interest granted by the debtor to another secured party.

(e) Conflicting security interests granted by a broker, a securities intermediary, or a commodity intermediary which are perfected without control rank equally.

(f) In all other cases, priority between conflicting security interests in investment property is governed by Section 9—312(5), (6), and (7). Section 9—312(4) does not apply to investment property.

(6) If a security certificate in registered form is delivered to a secured party pursuant to agreement, a written security agreement is not required for attachment or enforceability of the security interest, delivery suffices for perfection of the security interest, and the security interest has priority over a conflicting security interest perfected by means other than control, even if a necessary indorsement is lacking.

§ 9—116. Security Interest Arising in Purchase or Delivery of Financial Asset.

(1) If a person buys a financial asset through a securities intermediary in a transaction in which the buyer is obligated to pay the purchase price to the securities intermediary at the time of the purchase, and the securities intermediary credits the financial asset to the buyer's securities account before the buyer pays the securities intermediary, the securities intermediary has a security interest in the buyer's security entitlement securing the buyer's obligation to pay. A security agreement is not required for attachment or enforceability of the security interest, and the security interest is automatically perfected.

(2) If a certificated security, or other financial asset represented by a writing which in the ordinary course of business is transferred by delivery with any necessary indorsement or assignment is delivered pursuant to an agreement between persons in the business of dealing with such securities or financial assets and the agreement calls for delivery versus payment, the person delivering the certificate or other financial asset has a security interest in the certificated security or other financial asset securing the seller's right to receive payment. A security agreement is not required for attachment or enforceability of the security interest, and the security interest is automatically perfected.

Part 2 Validity of Security Agreement and Rights of Parties Thereto

§ 9—201. General Validity of Security Agreement.

Except as otherwise provided by this Act a security agreement is effective according to its terms between the parties, against purchasers of the collateral and against creditors. Nothing in this Article validates any charge or practice illegal under any statute or regulation thereunder governing usury, small loans, retail installment sales, or the like, or extends the application of any such statute or regulation to any transaction not otherwise subject thereto.

§ 9—202. Title to Collateral Immaterial.

Each provision of this Article with regard to rights, obligations and remedies applies whether title to collateral is in the secured party or in the debtor.

§ 9—203. Attachment and Enforceability of Security Interest; Proceeds; Formal Requisites.

(1) Subject to the provisions of Section 4—210 on the security interest of a collecting bank, Sections 9—115 and 9—116 on

security interests in investment property, and Section 9—113 on a security interest arising under the Articles on Sales and Leases, a security interest is not enforceable against the debtor or third parties with respect to the collateral and does not attach unless:

(a) the collateral is in the possession of the secured party pursuant to agreement, the collateral is investment property and the secured party has control pursuant to agreement, or the debtor has signed a security agreement which contains a description of the collateral and in addition, when the security interest covers crops growing or to be grown or timber to be cut, a description of the land concerned;

(b) value has been given; and

(c) the debtor has rights in the collateral.

(2) A security interest attaches when it becomes enforceable against the debtor with respect to the collateral. Attachment occurs as soon as all of the events specified in subsection (1) have taken place unless explicit agreement postpones the time of attaching.

(3) Unless otherwise agreed a security agreement gives the secured party the rights to proceeds provided by Section 9—306.

(4) A transaction, although subject to this Article, is also subject to . . . .*, and in the case of conflict between the provisions of this Article and any such statute, the provisions of such statute control. Failure to comply with any applicable statute has only the effect which is specified therein.

Note: *At * in subsection (4) insert reference to any local statute regulating small loans, retail installment sales and the like.*

The foregoing subsection (4) is designed to make it clear that certain transactions, although subject to this Article, must also comply with other applicable legislation.

This Article is designed to regulate all the "security" aspects of transactions within its scope. There is, however, much regulatory legislation, particularly in the consumer field, which supplements this Article and should not be repealed by its enactment. Examples are small loan acts, retail installment selling acts and the like. Such acts may provide for licensing and rate regulation and may prescribe particular forms of contract. Such provisions should remain in force despite the enactment of this Article. On the other hand if a retail installment selling act contains provisions on filing, rights on default, etc., such provisions should be repealed as inconsistent with this Article except that inconsistent provisions as to deficiencies, penalties, etc., in the Uniform Consumer Credit Code and other recent related legislation should remain because those statutes were drafted after the substantial enactment of the Article and with the intention of modifying certain provisions of this Article as to consumer credit.

§ 9—204. After-Acquired Property; Future Advances.

(1) Except as provided in subsection (2), a security agreement may provide that any or all obligations covered by the security agreement are to be secured by after-acquired collateral.

(2) No security interest attaches under an after-acquired property clause to consumer goods other than accessions (Section 9—314) when given as additional security unless the debtor acquires rights in them within ten days after the secured party gives value.

(3) Obligations covered by a security agreement may include future advances or other value whether or not the advances or value are given pursuant to commitment (subsection (1) of Section 9—105).

§ 9—205. Use or Disposition of Collateral Without Accounting Permissible.

A security interest is not invalid or fraudulent against creditors by reason of liberty in the debtor to use, commingle or dispose of all or part of the collateral (including returned or repossessed goods) or to collect or compromise accounts or chattel paper, or to accept the return of goods or make repossessions, or to use, commingle or dispose of proceeds, or by reason of the failure of the secured party to require the debtor to account for proceeds or replace collateral. This section does not relax the requirements of possession where perfection of a security interest depends upon possession of the collateral by the secured party or by a bailee.

§ 9—206. Agreement Not to Assert Defenses Against Assignee; Modification of Sales Warranties Where Security Agreement Exists.

(1) Subject to any statute or decision which establishes a different rule for buyers or lessees of consumer goods, an agreement by a buyer or lessee that he will not assert against an assignee any claim or defense which he may have against the seller or lessor is enforceable by an assignee who takes his assignment for value, in good faith and without notice of a claim or defense, except as to defenses of a type which may be asserted against a holder in due course of a negotiable instrument under the Article on Negotiable Instruments (Article 3). A buyer who as part of one transaction signs both a negotiable instrument and a security agreement makes such an agreement.

(2) When a seller retains a purchase money security interest in goods the Article on Sales (Article 2) governs the sale and any disclaimer, limitation or modification of the seller's warranties.

§ 9—207. Rights and Duties When Collateral is in Secured Party's Possession

(1) A secured party must use reasonable care in the custody and preservation of collateral in his possession. In the case of an instrument or chattel paper reasonable care includes taking necessary steps to preserve rights against prior parties unless otherwise agreed.

(2) Unless otherwise agreed, when collateral is in the secured party's possession

(a) reasonable expenses (including the cost of any insurance and payment of taxes or other charges) incurred in the custody, preservation, use or operation of the collateral are chargeable to the debtor and are secured by the collateral;

(b) the risk of accidental loss or damage is on the debtor to the extent of any deficiency in any effective insurance coverage;

(c) the secured party may hold as additional security any increase or profits (except money) received from the collateral, but money so received, unless remitted to the debtor, shall be applied in reduction of the secured obligation;

(d) the secured party must keep the collateral identifiable but fungible collateral may be commingled;

(e) the secured party may repledge the collateral upon terms which do not impair the debtor's right to redeem it.

(3) A secured party is liable for any loss caused by his failure to meet any obligation imposed by the preceding subsections but does not lose his security interest.

(4) A secured party may use or operate the collateral for the purpose of preserving the collateral or its value or pursuant to the order of a court of appropriate jurisdiction or, except in the case of consumer goods, in the manner and to the extent provided in the security agreement.

§ 9—208. Request for Statement of Account or List of Collateral.

(1) A debtor may sign a statement indicating what he believes to be the aggregate amount of unpaid indebtedness as of a specified date and may send it to the secured party with a request that the statement be approved or corrected and returned to the debtor. When the security agreement or any other record kept by the secured party identifies the collateral a debtor may similarly request the secured party to approve or correct a list of the collateral.

(2) The secured party must comply with such a request within two weeks after receipt by sending a written correction or approval. If the secured party claims a security interest in all of a particular type of collateral owned by the debtor he may indicate that fact in his reply and need not approve or correct an itemized list of such collateral. If the secured party without reasonable excuse fails to comply he is liable for any loss caused to the debtor thereby; and if the debtor has properly included in his request a good faith statement of the obligation or a list of the collateral or both the secured party may claim a security interest only as shown in the statement against persons misled by his failure to comply. If he no longer has an interest in the obligation or collateral at the time the request is received he must disclose the name and address of any successor in interest known to him and he is liable for any loss caused to the debtor as a result of failure to disclose. A successor in interest is not subject to this section until a request is received by him.

(3) A debtor is entitled to such a statement once every six months without charge. The secured party may require payment of a charge not exceeding $10 for each additional statement furnished.

Part 3 Rights of Third Parties; Perfected and Unperfected Security Interests; Rules of Priority

§ 9—301. Persons Who Take Priority Over Unperfected Security Interests; Rights of "Lien Creditor".

(1) Except as otherwise provided in subsection (2), an unperfected security interest is subordinate to the rights of

(a) persons entitled to priority under Section 9—312;

(b) a person who becomes a lien creditor before the security interest is perfected;

(c) in the case of goods, instruments, documents, and chattel paper, a person who is not a secured party and who is a transferee in bulk or other buyer not in ordinary course of business or is a buyer of farm products in ordinary course of business, to the extent that he gives value and receives delivery of the collateral without knowledge of the security interest and before it is perfected;

(d) in the case of accounts, general intangibles, and investment property a person who is not a secured party and who is a transferee to the extent that he gives value without knowledge of the security interest and before it is perfected.

(2) If the secured party files with respect to a purchase money security interest before or within ten days after the debtor receives possession of the collateral, he takes priority over the rights of a transferee in bulk or of a lien creditor which arise between the time the security interest attaches and the time of filing.

(3) A "lien creditor" means a creditor who has acquired a lien on the property involved by attachment, levy or the like and includes an assignee for benefit of creditors from the time of assignment, and a trustee in bankruptcy from the date of the filing of the petition or a receiver in equity from the time of appointment.

(4) A person who becomes a lien creditor while a security interest is perfected takes subject to the security interest only to the extent that it secures advances made before he becomes a lien creditor or within 45 days thereafter or made without knowledge of the lien or pursuant to a commitment entered into without knowledge of the lien.

§ 9—302. When Filing Is Required to Perfect Security Interest; Security Interests to Which Filing Provisions of This Article Do Not Apply.

(1) A financing statement must be filed to perfect all security interests except the following:

(a) a security interest in collateral in possession of the secured party under Section 9—305;

(b) a security interest temporarily perfected in instruments, certificated securities, or documents without delivery under Section 9—304 or in proceeds for a 10 day period under Section 9—306;

(c) a security interest created by an assignment of a beneficial interest in a trust or a decedent's estate;

(d) a purchase money security interest in consumer goods; but filing is required for a motor vehicle required to be registered; and fixture filing is required for priority over conflicting interests in fixtures to the extent provided in Section 9—313;

(e) an assignment of accounts which does not alone or in conjunction with other assignments to the same assignee transfer a significant part of the outstanding accounts of the assignor;

(f) a security interest of a collecting bank (Section 4—210) or arising under the Articles on Sales and Leases (see Section 9—113) or covered in subsection (3) of this section;

(g) an assignment for the benefit of all the creditors of the transferor, and subsequent transfers by the assignee thereunder.

(h) a security interest in investment property which is perfected without filing under Section 9—115 or Section 9—116.

(2) If a secured party assigns a perfected security interest, no filing under this Article is required in order to continue the perfected status of the security interest against creditors of and transferees from the original debtor.

(3) The filing of a financing statement otherwise required by this Article is not necessary or effective to perfect a security interest in property subject to

(a) a statute or treaty of the United States which provides for a national or international registration or a national or international certificate of title or which specifies a place of filing different from that specified in this Article for filing of the security interest; or

(b) the following statutes of this state; [list any certificate of title statute covering automobiles, trailers, mobile homes, boats, farm tractors, or the like, and any central filing statute.]; but during any period in which collateral is inventory held for sale by a person who is in the business of selling goods of that kind, the filing provisions of this Article (Part 4) apply to a security interest in that collateral created by him as debtor; or

(c) a certificate of title statute of another jurisdiction under the law of which indication of a security interest on the certificate is required as a condition of perfection (subsection (2) of Section 9—103).

(4) Compliance with a statute or treaty described in subsection (3) is equivalent to the filing of a financing statement under this Article, and a security interest in property subject to the statute or treaty can be perfected only by compliance therewith except as provided in Section 9—103 on multiple state transactions. Duration and renewal of perfection of a security interest perfected by compliance with the statute or treaty are governed by the provisions of the statute or treaty; in other respects the security interest is subject to this Article.

§ 9—303. When Security Interest Is Perfected; Continuity of Perfection.

(1) A security interest is perfected when it has attached and when all of the applicable steps required for perfection have been taken. Such steps are specified in Sections 9—115, 9—302, 9—304, 9—305 and 9—306. If such steps are taken before the security interest attaches, it is perfected at the time when it attaches.

(2) If a security interest is originally perfected in any way permitted under this Article and is subsequently perfected in some other way under this Article, without an intermediate period when it was unperfected, the security interest shall be deemed to be perfected continuously for the purposes of this Article.

§ 9—304. Perfection of Security Interest in Instruments, Documents, Proceeds of a Written Letter of Credit, and Goods Covered by Documents; Perfection by Permissive Filing; Temporary Perfection Without Filing or Transfer of Possession.

(1) A security interest in chattel paper or negotiable documents may be perfected by filing. A security interest in the rights to proceeds of a written letter of credit can be perfected only by the secured party's taking possession of the letter of credit. A security interest in money or instruments (other than instruments which constitute part of chattel paper) can be perfected only by the secured party's taking possession, except as provided in subsections (4) and (5) of this section and subsections (2) and (3) of Section 9—306 on proceeds.

(2) During the period that goods are in the possession of the issuer of a negotiable document therefor, a security interest in the goods is perfected by perfecting a security interest in the document, and any security interest in the goods otherwise perfected during such period is subject thereto.

(3) A security interest in goods in the possession of a bailee other than one who has issued a negotiable document therefor is perfected by issuance of a document in the name of the secured party or by the bailee's receipt of notification of the secured party's interest or by filing as to the goods.

(4) A security interest in instruments, certificated securities, or negotiable documents is perfected without filing or the taking of possession for a period of 21 days from the time it attaches to the extent that it arises for new value given under a written security agreement.

(5) A security interest remains perfected for a period of 21 days without filing where a secured party having a perfected security interest in an instrument, a certificated security, a negotiable document or goods in possession of a bailee other than one who has issued a negotiable document therefor

(a) makes available to the debtor the goods or documents representing the goods for the purpose of ultimate sale or exchange or for the purpose of loading, unloading, storing, shipping, transshipping, manufacturing, processing or otherwise dealing with them in a manner preliminary to their sale or exchange, but priority between conflicting security interests in the goods is subject to subsection (3) of Section 9—312; or

(b) delivers the instrument or certificated security to the debtor for the purpose of ultimate sale or exchange or of presentation, collection, renewal or registration of transfer.

(6) After the 21 day period in subsections (4) and (5) perfection depends upon compliance with applicable provisions of this Article.

§ 9—305. When Possession by Secured Party Perfects Security Interest Without Filing.

A security interest in goods, instruments, money, negotiable documents, or chattel paper may be perfected by the secured party's taking possession of the collateral. A security interest in the right to proceeds of a written letter of credit may be perfected by the secured party's taking possession of the letter of credit. If such collateral other than goods covered by a negotiable document is held by a bailee, the secured party is deemed to have possession from the time the bailee receives notification of the secured party's interest. A security interest is perfected by possession from the time possession is taken without a relation back and continues only so long as possession is retained, unless otherwise specified in this Article. The security interest may be otherwise perfected as provided in this Article before or after the period of possession by the secured party.

§ 9—306. "Proceeds"; Secured Party's Rights on Disposition of Collateral.

(1) "Proceeds" includes whatever is received upon the sale, exchange, collection or other disposition of collateral or proceeds. Insurance payable by reason of loss or damage to the collateral is proceeds, except to the extent that it is payable to a person other than a party to the security agreement. Any payments or distributions made with respect to investment property collateral are proceeds. Money, checks, deposit accounts, and the like are "cash proceeds". All other proceeds are "noncash proceeds".

(2) Except where this Article otherwise provides, a security interest continues in collateral notwithstanding sale, exchange or other disposition thereof unless the disposition was authorized by the secured party in the security agreement or otherwise, and also continues in any identifiable proceeds including collections received by the debtor.

(3) The security interest in proceeds is a continuously perfected security interest if the interest in the original collateral was perfected but it ceases to be a perfected security interest and becomes unperfected ten days after receipt of the proceeds by the debtor unless

(a) a filed financing statement covers the original collateral and the proceeds are collateral in which a security interest may be perfected by filing in the office or offices where the financing statement has been filed and, if the proceeds are acquired with cash proceeds, the description of collateral in the financing statement indicates the types of property constituting the proceeds; or

(b) a filed financing statement covers the original collateral and the proceeds are identifiable cash proceeds; or

(c) the original collateral was investment property and the proceeds are identifiable cash proceeds; or

(d) the security interest in the proceeds is perfected before the expiration of the ten day period.

Except as provided in this section, a security interest in proceeds can be perfected only by the methods or under the circumstances permitted in this Article for original collateral of the same type.

(4) In the event of insolvency proceedings instituted by or against a debtor, a secured party with a perfected security interest in proceeds has a perfected security interest only in the following proceeds:

(a) in identifiable noncash proceeds and in separate deposit accounts containing only proceeds;

(b) in identifiable cash proceeds in the form of money which is neither commingled with other money nor deposited in a deposit account prior to the insolvency proceedings;

(c) in identifiable cash proceeds in the form of checks and the like which are not deposited in a deposit account prior to the insolvency proceedings; and

(d) in all cash and deposit accounts of the debtor in which proceeds have been commingled with other funds, but the perfected security interest under this paragraph (d) is

(i) subject to any right to set-off; and

(ii) limited to an amount not greater than the amount of any cash proceeds received by the debtor within ten days before the institution of the insolvency proceedings less the sum of (I) the payments to the secured party on account of cash proceeds received by the debtor during such period and (II) the cash proceeds received by the debtor during such period to which the secured party is entitled under paragraphs (a) through (c) of this subsection (4).

(5) If a sale of goods results in an account or chattel paper which is transferred by the seller to a secured party, and if the goods are returned to or are repossessed by the seller or the secured party, the following rules determine priorities:

(a) If the goods were collateral at the time of sale, for an indebtedness of the seller which is still unpaid, the original security interest attaches again to the goods and continues as a perfected security interest if it was perfected at the time when the goods were sold. If the security interest was originally perfected by a filing which is still effective, nothing further is required to continue the perfected status; in any other case, the secured party must take possession of the returned or repossessed goods or must file.

(b) An unpaid transferee of the chattel paper has a security interest in the goods against the transferor. Such security interest is prior to a security interest asserted under paragraph (a) to the extent that the transferee of the chattel paper was entitled to priority under Section 9—308.

(c) An unpaid transferee of the account has a security interest in the goods against the transferor. Such security interest is subordinate to a security interest asserted under paragraph (a).

(d) A security interest of an unpaid transferee asserted under paragraph (b) or (c) must be perfected for protection against creditors of the transferor and purchasers of the returned or repossessed goods.

§ 9—307. Protection of Buyers of Goods.

(1) A buyer in ordinary course of business (subsection (9) of Section 1—201) other than a person buying farm products from

a person engaged in farming operations takes free of a security interest created by his seller even though the security interest is perfected and even though the buyer knows of its existence [subject to the Food Security Act of 1985 (7 U.S.C. Section 1631)].

(2) In the case of consumer goods, a buyer takes free of a security interest even though perfected if he buys without knowledge of the security interest, for value and for his own personal, family or household purposes unless prior to the purchase the secured party has filed a financing statement covering such goods.

(3) A buyer other than a buyer in ordinary course of business (subsection (1) of this section) takes free of a security interest to the extent that it secures future advances made after the secured party acquires knowledge of the purchase, or more than 45 days after the purchase, whichever first occurs, unless made pursuant to a commitment entered into without knowledge of the purchase and before the expiration of the 45 day period.

§ 9—308. Purchase of Chattel Paper and Instruments.

A purchaser of chattel paper or an instrument who gives new value and takes possession of it in the ordinary course of his business has priority over a security interest in the chattel paper or instrument

(a) which is perfected under Section 9—304 (permissive filing and temporary perfection) or under Section 9—306 (perfection as to proceeds) if he acts without knowledge that the specific paper or instrument is subject to a security interest; or

(b) which is claimed merely as proceeds of inventory subject to a security interest (Section 9—306) even though he knows that the specific paper or instrument is subject to the security interest.

§ 9—309. Protection of Purchasers of Instruments, Documents and Securities.

Nothing in this Article limits the rights of a holder in due course of a negotiable instrument (Section 3—302) or a holder to whom a negotiable document of title has been duly negotiated (Section 7—501) or a bona fide purchaser of a security (Section 8—302) and the holders or purchasers take priority over an earlier security interest even though perfected. Filing under this Article does not constitute notice of the security interest to such holders or purchasers.

§ 9—310. Priority of Certain Liens Arising by Operation of Law.

When a person in the ordinary course of his business furnishes services or materials with respect to goods subject to a security interest, a lien upon goods in the possession of such person given by statute or rule of law for such materials or services takes priority over a perfected security interest unless the lien is statutory and the statute expressly provides otherwise.

§ 9—311. Alienability of Debtor's Rights: Judicial Process.

The debtor's rights in collateral may be voluntarily or involuntarily transferred (by way of sale, creation of a security interest, attachment, levy, garnishment or other judicial process) notwithstanding a provision in the security agreement prohibiting any transfer or making the transfer constitute a default.

§ 9—312. Priorities Among Conflicting Security Interests in the Same Collateral.

(1) The rules of priority stated in other sections of this Part and in the following sections shall govern when applicable: Section 4—208 with respect to the security interests of collecting banks in items being collected, accompanying documents and proceeds; Section 9—103 on security interests related to other jurisdictions; Section 9—114 on consignments.

(2) A perfected security interest in crops for new value given to enable the debtor to produce the crops during the production season and given not more than three months before the crops become growing crops by planting or otherwise takes priority over an earlier perfected security interest to the extent that such earlier interest secures obligations due more than six months before the crops become growing crops by planting or otherwise, even though the person giving new value had knowledge of the earlier security interest.

(3) A perfected purchase money security interest in inventory has priority over a conflicting security interest in the same inventory and also has priority in identifiable cash proceeds received on or before the delivery of the inventory to a buyer if

(a) the purchase money security interest is perfected at the time the debtor receives possession of the inventory; and

(b) the purchase money secured party gives notification in writing to the holder of the conflicting security interest if the holder had filed a financing statement covering the same types of inventory (i) before the date of the filing made by the purchase money secured party, or (ii) before the beginning of the 21 day period where the purchase money security interest is temporarily perfected without filing or possession (subsection (5) of Section 9—304); and

(c) the holder of the conflicting security interest receives the notification within five years before the debtor receives possession of the inventory; and

(d) the notification states that the person giving the notice has or expects to acquire a purchase money security interest in inventory of the debtor, describing such inventory by item or type.

(4) A purchase money security interest in collateral other than inventory has priority over a conflicting security interest in the same collateral or its proceeds if the purchase money security interest is perfected at the time the debtor receives possession of the collateral or within ten days thereafter.

(5) In all cases not governed by other rules stated in this section (including cases of purchase money security interests which do not qualify for the special priorities set forth in subsections (3) and (4) of this section), priority between conflicting security interests in the same collateral shall be determined according to the following rules:

(a) Conflicting security interests rank according to priority in time of filing or perfection. Priority dates from the time a filing is first made covering the collateral or the time the security interest is first perfected, whichever is earlier, provided that there is no period thereafter when there is neither filing nor perfection.

(b) So long as conflicting security interests are unperfected, the first to attach has priority.

(6) For the purposes of subsection (5) a date of filing or perfection as to collateral is also a date of filing or perfection as to proceeds.

(7) If future advances are made while a security interest is perfected by filing, the taking of possession, or under Section 8—321 on securities, the security interest has the same priority for the purposes of subsection (5) with respect to the future advances as it does with respect to the first advance. If a commitment is made before or while the security interest is so perfected, the security interest has the same priority with respect to advances made pursuant thereto. In other cases a perfected security interest has priority from the date the advance is made.

§ 9—313. Priority of Security Interests in Fixtures.

(1) In this section and in the provisions of Part 4 of this Article referring to fixture filing, unless the context otherwise requires

(a) goods are "fixtures" when they become so related to particular real estate that an interest in them arises under real estate law

(b) a "fixture filing" is the filing in the office where a mortgage on the real estate would be filed or recorded of a financing statement covering goods which are or are to become fixtures and conforming to the requirements of subsection (5) of Section 9—402

(c) a mortgage is a "construction mortgage" to the extent that it secures an obligation incurred for the construction of an improvement on land including the acquisition cost of the land, if the recorded writing so indicates.

(2) A security interest under this Article may be created in goods which are fixtures or may continue in goods which become fixtures, but no security interest exists under this Article in ordinary building materials incorporated into an improvement on land.

(3) This Article does not prevent creation of an encumbrance upon fixtures pursuant to real estate law.

(4) A perfected security interest in fixtures has priority over the conflicting interest of an encumbrancer or owner of the real estate where

(a) the security interest is a purchase money security interest, the interest of the encumbrancer or owner arises before the goods become fixtures, the security interest is perfected by a fixture filing before the goods become fixtures or within ten days thereafter, and the debtor has an interest of record in the real estate or is in possession of the real estate; or

(b) the security interest is perfected by a fixture filing before the interest of the encumbrancer or owner is of record, the security interest has priority over any conflicting interest of a predecessor in title of the encumbrancer or owner, and the debtor has an interest of record in the real estate or is in possession of the real estate; or

(c) the fixtures are readily removable factory or office machines or readily removable replacements of domestic appliances which are consumer goods, and before the goods become fixtures the security interest is perfected by any method permitted by this Article; or

(d) the conflicting interest is a lien on the real estate obtained by legal or equitable proceedings after the security interest was perfected by any method permitted by this Article.

(5) A security interest in fixtures, whether or not perfected, has priority over the conflicting interest of an encumbrancer or owner of the real estate where

(a) the encumbrancer or owner has consented in writing to the security interest or has disclaimed an interest in the goods as fixtures; or

(b) the debtor has a right to remove the goods as against the encumbrancer or owner. If the debtor's right terminates, the priority of the security interest continues for a reasonable time.

(6) Notwithstanding paragraph (a) of subsection (4) but otherwise subject to subsections (4) and (5), a security interest in fixtures is subordinate to a construction mortgage recorded before the goods become fixtures if the goods become fixtures before the completion of the construction. To the extent that it is given to refinance a construction mortgage, a mortgage has this priority to the same extent as the construction mortgage.

(7) In cases not within the preceding subsections, a security interest in fixtures is subordinate to the conflicting interest of an encumbrancer or owner of the related real estate who is not the debtor.

(8) When the secured party has priority over all owners and encumbrancers of the real estate, he may, on default, subject to the provisions of Part 5, remove his collateral from the real estate but he must reimburse any encumbrancer or owner of the real estate who is not the debtor and who has not otherwise agreed for the cost of repair of any physical injury, but not for any diminution in value of the real estate caused by the absence of the goods removed or by any necessity of replacing them. A person entitled to reimbursement may refuse permission to remove until the secured party gives adequate security for the performance of this obligation.

§ 9—314. Accessions.

(1) A security interest in goods which attaches before they are installed in or affixed to other goods takes priority as to the goods installed or affixed (called in this section "accessions") over the claims of all persons to the whole except as stated in subsection (3) and subject to Section 9—315(1).

(2) A security interest which attaches to goods after they become part of a whole is valid against all persons subsequently acquiring interests in the whole except as stated in subsection (3) but is invalid against any person with an interest in the

whole at the time the security interest attaches to the goods who has not in writing consented to the security interest or disclaimed an interest in the goods as part of the whole.

(3) The security interests described in subsections (1) and (2) do not take priority over

(a) a subsequent purchaser for value of any interest in the whole; or

(b) a creditor with a lien on the whole subsequently obtained by judicial proceedings; or

(c) a creditor with a prior perfected security interest in the whole to the extent that he makes subsequent advances

if the subsequent purchase is made, the lien by judicial proceedings obtained or the subsequent advance under the prior perfected security interest is made or contracted for without knowledge of the security interest and before it is perfected. A purchaser of the whole at a foreclosure sale other than the holder of a perfected security interest purchasing at his own foreclosure sale is a subsequent purchaser within this section.

(4) When under subsections (1) or (2) and (3) a secured party has an interest in accessions which has priority over the claims of all persons who have interests in the whole, he may on default subject to the provisions of Part 5 remove his collateral from the whole but he must reimburse any encumbrancer or owner of the whole who is not the debtor and who has not otherwise agreed for the cost of repair of any physical injury but not for any diminution in value of the whole caused by the absence of the goods removed or by any necessity for replacing them. A person entitled to reimbursement may refuse permission to remove until the secured party gives adequate security for the performance of this obligation.

§ 9—315. Priority When Goods Are Commingled or Processed.

(1) If a security interest in goods was perfected and subsequently the goods or a part thereof have become part of a product or mass, the security interest continues in the product or mass if

(a) the goods are so manufactured, processed, assembled or commingled that their identity is lost in the product or mass; or

(b) a financing statement covering the original goods also covers the product into which the goods have been manufactured, processed or assembled.

In a case to which paragraph (b) applies, no separate security interest in that part of the original goods which has been manufactured, processed or assembled into the product may be claimed under Section 9—314.

(2) When under subsection (1) more than one security interest attaches to the product or mass, they rank equally according to the ratio that the cost of the goods to which each interest originally attached bears to the cost of the total product or mass.

§ 9—316. Priority Subject to Subordination.

Nothing in this Article prevents subordination by agreement by any person entitled to priority.

§ 9—317. Secured Party Not Obligated on Contract of Debtor.

The mere existence of a security interest or authority given to the debtor to dispose of or use collateral does not impose contract or tort liability upon the secured party for the debtor's acts or omissions.

§ 9—318. Defenses Against Assignee; Modification of Contract After Notification of Assignment; Term Prohibiting Assignment Ineffective; Identification and Proof of Assignment.

(1) Unless an account debtor has made an enforceable agreement not to assert defenses or claims arising out of a sale as provided in Section 9—206 the rights of an assignee are subject to

(a) all the terms of the contract between the account debtor and assignor and any defense or claim arising therefrom; and

(b) any other defense or claim of the account debtor against the assignor which accrues before the account debtor receives notification of the assignment.

(2) So far as the right to payment or a part thereof under an assigned contract has not been fully earned by performance, and notwithstanding notification of the assignment, any modification of or substitution for the contract made in good faith and in accordance with reasonable commercial standards is effective against an assignee unless the account debtor has otherwise agreed but the assignee acquires corresponding rights under the modified or substituted contract. The assignment may provide that such modification or substitution is a breach by the assignor.

(3) The account debtor is authorized to pay the assignor until the account debtor receives notification that the amount due or to become due has been assigned and that payment is to be made to the assignee. A notification which does not reasonably identify the rights assigned is ineffective. If requested by the account debtor, the assignee must seasonably furnish reasonable proof that the assignment has been made and unless he does so the account debtor may pay the assignor.

(4) A term in any contract between an account debtor and an assignor is ineffective if it prohibits assignment of an account or prohibits creation of a security interest in a general intangible for money due or to become due or requires the account debtor's consent to such assignment or security interest.

Part 4 Filing

§ 9—401. Place of Filing; Erroneous Filing; Removal of Collateral.

First Alternative Subsection (1)

(1) The proper place to file in order to perfect a security interest is as follows:

(a) when the collateral is timber to be cut or is minerals or the like (including oil and gas) or accounts subject to subsection (5) of Section 9—103, or when the financing statement is filed as a fixture filing (Section 9—313) and the collateral is goods which are or are to become fixtures, then in the office where a mortgage on the real estate would be filed or recorded;

(b) in all other cases, in the office of the [Secretary of State].

Second Alternative Subsection (1)

(1) The proper place to file in order to perfect a security interest is as follows:

(a) when the collateral is equipment used in farming operations, or farm products, or accounts or general intangibles arising from or relating to the sale of farm products by a farmer, or consumer goods, then in the office of the . . . . in the county of the debtor's residence or if the debtor is not a resident of this state then in the office of the . . . . in the county where the goods are kept, and in addition when the collateral is crops growing or to be grown in the office of the . . . . in the county where the land is located;

(b) when the collateral is timber to be cut or is minerals or the like (including oil and gas) or accounts subject to subsection (5) of Section 9—103, or when the financing statement is filed as a fixture filing (Section 9—313) and the collateral is goods which are or are to become fixtures, then in the office where a mortgage on the real estate would be filed or recorded;

(c) in all other cases, in the office of the [Secretary of State].

Third Alternative Subsection (1)

(1) The proper place to file in order to perfect a security interest is as follows:

(a) when the collateral is equipment used in farming operations, or farm products, or accounts or general intangibles arising from or relating to the sale of farm products by a farmer, or consumer goods, then in the office of the . . . . in the county of the debtor's residence or if the debtor is not a resident of this state then in the office of the . . . . in the county where the goods are kept, and in addition when the collateral is crops growing or to be grown in the office of the . . . . in the county where the land is located;

(b) when the collateral is timber to be cut or is minerals or the like (including oil and gas) or accounts subject to subsection (5) of Section 9—103, or when the financing statement is filed as a fixture filing (Section 9—313) and the collateral is goods which are or are to become fixtures, then in the office where a mortgage on the real estate would be filed or recorded;

(c) in all other cases, in the office of the [Secretary of State] and in addition, if the debtor has a place of business in only one county of this state, also in the office of . . . . of such county, or, if the debtor has no place of business in this state, but resides in the state, also in the office of . . . . of the county in which he resides.

Note: *One of the three alternatives should be selected as subsection (1).*

(2) A filing which is made in good faith in an improper place or not in all of the places required by this section is nevertheless effective with regard to any collateral as to which the filing complied with the requirements of this Article and is also effective with regard to collateral coered by the financing statement against any person who has knowledge of the contents of such financing statement.

(3) A filing which is made in the proper place in this state continues effective even though the debtor's residence or place of business or the location of the collateral or its use, whichever controlled the original filing, is thereafter changed.

Alternative Subsection (3)

[(3) A filing which is made in the proper county continues effective for four months after a change to another county of the debtor's residence or place of business or the location of the collateral, whichever controlled the original filing. It becomes ineffective thereafter unless a copy of the financing statement signed by the secured party is filed in the new county within said period. The security interest may also be perfected in the new county after the expiration of the four-month period; in such case perfection dates from the time of perfection in the new county. A change in the use of the collateral does not impair the effectiveness of the original filing.]

(4) The rules stated in Section 9—103 determine whether filing is necessary in this state.

(5) Notwithstanding the preceding subsections, and subject to subsection (3) of Section 9—302, the proper place to file in order to perfect a security interest in collateral, including fixtures, of a transmitting utility is the office of the [Secretary of State]. This filing constitutes a fixture filing (Section 9—313) as to the collateral described therein which is or is to become fixtures.

(6) For the purposes of this section, the residence of an organization is its place of business if it has one or its chief executive office if it has more than one place of business.

Note: *Subsection (6) should be used only if the state chooses the Second or Third Alternative Subsection (1).*

§ 9—402. Formal Requisites of Financing Statement; Amendments; Mortgage as Financing Statement.

(1) A financing statement is sufficient if it gives the names of the debtor and the secured party, is signed by the debtor, gives an address of the secured party from which information concerning the security interest may be obtained, gives a mailing address of the debtor and contains a statement indicating the types, or describing the items, of collateral. A financing statement may be filed before a security agreement is made or a security interest otherwise attaches. When the financing statement covers crops growing or to be grown, the statement must also contain a description of the real estate concerned. When the financing statement covers timber to be cut or covers minerals or the like (including oil and gas) or accounts subject to subsection (5) of Section 9—103, or when the financing statement is filed as a fixture filing (Section 9—313) and the collateral is

goods which are or are to become fixtures, the statement must also comply with subsection (5). A copy of the security agreement is sufficient as a financing statement if it contains the above information and is signed by the debtor. A carbon, photographic or other reproduction of a security agreement or a financing statement is sufficient as a financing statement if the security agreement so provides or if the original has been filed in this state.

(2) A financing statement which otherwise complies with subsection (1) is sufficient when it is signed by the secured party instead of the debtor if it is filed to perfect a security interest in

(a) collateral already subject to a security interest in another jurisdiction when it is brought into this state, or when the debtor's location is changed to this state. Such a financing statement must state that the collateral was brought into this state or that the debtor's location was changed to this state under such circumstances; or

(b) proceeds under Section 9—306 if the security interest in the original collateral was perfected. Such a financing statement must describe the original collateral; or

(c) collateral as to which the filing has lapsed; or

(d) collateral acquired after a change of name, identity or corporate structure of the debtor (subsection (7)).

(3) A form substantially as follows is sufficient to comply with subsection (1):

Name of debtor (or assignor) . . . .
Address . . . .
Name of secured party (or assignee) . . . .
Address . . . .
1. This financing statement covers the following types (or items) of property:
(Describe) . . . .
2. (If collateral is crops) The above described crops are growing or are to be grown on:
(Describe Real Estate) . . . .
3. (If applicable) The above goods are to become fixtures on *

*Where appropriate substitute either "The above timber is standing on . . . ." or "The above minerals or the like (including oil and gas) or accounts will be financed at the wellhead or minehead of the well or mine located on . . . ."

(Describe Real Estate) . . . .
and this financing statement is to be filed [for record] in the real estate records. (If the debtor does not have an interest of record) The name of a record owner is
. . . .
4. (If products of collateral are claimed) Products of the collateral are also covered.

(use whichever	. . . . Signature of Debtor (or Assignor)
is applicable)	. . . . Signature of Secured Party (or Assignee)

(4) A financing statement may be amended by filing a writing signed by both the debtor and the secured party. An amendment does not extend the period of effectiveness of a financing statement. If any amendment adds collateral, it is effective as to the added collateral only from the filing date of the amendment. In this Article, unless the context otherwise requires, the term "financing statement" means the original financing statement and any amendments.

(5) A financing statement covering timber to be cut or covering minerals or the like (including oil and gas) or accounts subject to subsection (5) of Section 9—103, or a financing statement filed as a fixture filing (Section 9—313) where the debtor is not a transmitting utility, must show that it covers this type of collateral, must recite that it is to be filed [for record] in the real estate records, and the financing statement must contain a description of the real estate [sufficient if it were contained in a mortgage of the real estate to give constructive notice of the mortgage under the law of this state]. If the debtor does not have an interest of record in the real estate, the financing statement must show the name of a record owner.

(6) A mortgage is effective as a financing statement filed as a fixture filing from the date of its recording if

(a) the goods are described in the mortgage by item or type; and

(b) the goods are or are to become fixtures related to the real estate described in the mortgage; and

(c) the mortgage complies with the requirements for a financing statement in this section other than a recital that it is to be filed in the real estate records; and

(d) the mortgage is duly recorded.

No fee with reference to the financing statement is required other than the regular recording and satisfaction fees with respect to the mortgage.

(7) A financing statement sufficiently shows the name of the debtor if it gives the individual, partnership or corporate name of the debtor, whether or not it adds other trade names or names of partners. Where the debtor so changes his name or in the case of an organization its name, identity or corporate structure that a filed financing statement becomes seriously misleading, the filing is not effective to perfect a security interest in collateral acquired by the debtor more than four months after the change, unless a new appropriate financing statement is filed before the expiration of that time. A filed financing statement remains effective with respect to collateral transferred by the debtor even though the secured party knows of or consents to the transfer.

(8) A financing statement substantially complying with the requirements of this section is effective even though it contains minor errors which are not seriously misleading.

Note: *Language in brackets is optional.*

Note: *Where the state has any special recording system for real estate other than the usual grantor-grantee index (as, for instance, a tract system or a title registration or Torrens system) local adaptations of sub-*

section (5) and Section 9—403(7) may be necessary. See Mass.Gen.Laws Chapter 106, Section 9—409.

§ 9—403. What Constitutes Filing; Duration of Filing; Effect of Lapsed Filing; Duties of Filing Officer.

(1) Presentation for filing of a financing statement and tender of the filing fee or acceptance of the statement by the filing officer constitutes filing under this Article.

(2) Except as provided in subsection (6) a filed financing statement is effective for a period of five years from the date of filing. The effectiveness of a filed financing statement lapses on the expiration of the five year period unless a continuation statement is filed prior to the lapse. If a security interest perfected by filing exists at the time insolvency proceedings are commenced by or against the debtor, the security interest remains perfected until termination of the insolvency proceedings and thereafter for a period of sixty days or until expiration of the five year period, whichever occurs later. Upon lapse the security interest becomes unperfected, unless it is perfected without filing. If the security interest becomes unperfected upon lapse, it is deemed to have been unperfected as against a person who became a purchaser or lien creditor before lapse.

(3) A continuation statement may be filed by the secured party within six months prior to the expiration of the five year period specified in subsection (2). Any such continuation statement must be signed by the secured party, identify the original statement by file number and state that the original statement is still effective. A continuation statement signed by a person other than the secured party of record must be accompanied by a separate written statement of assignment signed by the secured party of record and complying with subsection (2) of Section 9—405, including payment of the required fee. Upon timely filing of the continuation statement, the effectiveness of the original statement is continued for five years after the last date to which the filing was effective whereupon it lapses in the same manner as provided in subsection (2) unless another continuation statement is filed prior to such lapse. Succeeding continuation statements may be filed in the same manner to continue the effectiveness of the original statement. Unless a statute on disposition of public records provides otherwise, the filing officer may remove a lapsed statement from the files and destroy it immediately if he has retained a microfilm or other photographic record, or in other cases after one year after the lapse. The filing officer shall so arrange matters by physical annexation of financing statements to continuation statements or other related filings, or by other means, that if he physically destroys the financing statements of a period more than five years past, those which have been continued by a continuation statement or which are still effective under subsection (6) shall be retained.

(4) Except as provided in subsection (7) a filing officer shall mark each statement with a file number and with the date and hour of filing and shall hold the statement or a microfilm or other photographic copy thereof for public inspection. In addition the filing officer shall index the statement according to the name of the debtor and shall note in the index the file number and the address of the debtor given in the statement.

(5) The uniform fee for filing and indexing and for stamping a copy furnished by the secured party to show the date and place of filing for an original financing statement or for a continuation statement shall be $. . . . . . . if the statement is in the standard form prescribed by the [Secretary of State] and otherwise shall be $. . . . . . ., plus in each case, if the financing statement is subject to subsection (5) of Section 9—402, $. . . . . . . The uniform fee for each name more than one required to be indexed shall be $. . . . . . . The secured party may at his option show a trade name for any person and an extra uniform indexing fee of $. . . . . . . shall be paid with respect thereto.

(6) If the debtor is a transmitting utility (subsection (5) of Section 9—401) and a filed financing statement so states, it is effective until a termination statement is filed. A real estate mortgage which is effective as a fixture filing under subsection (6) of Section 9—402 remains effective as a fixture filing until the mortgage is released or satisfied of record or its effectiveness otherwise terminates as to the real estate.

(7) When a financing statement covers timber to be cut or covers minerals or the like (including oil and gas) or accounts subject to subsection (5) of Section 9—103, or is filed as a fixture filing, [it shall be filed for record and] the filing officer shall index it under the names of the debtor and any owner of record shown on the financing statement in the same fashion as if they were the mortgagors in a mortgage of the real estate described, and, to the extent that the law of this state provides for indexing of mortgages under the name of the mortgagee, under the name of the secured party as if he were the mortgagee thereunder, or where indexing is by description in the same fashion as if the financing statement were a mortgage of the real estate described.

Note: *In states in which writings will not appear in the real estate records and indices unless actually recorded the bracketed language in subsection (7) should be used.*

§ 9—404. Termination Statement.

(1) If a financing statement covering consumer goods is filed on or after . . . ., then within one month or within ten days following written demand by the debtor after there is no outstanding secured obligation and no commitment to make advances, incur obligations or otherwise give value, the secured party must file with each filing officer with whom the financing statement was filed, a termination statement to the effect that he no longer claims a security interest under the financing statement, which shall be identified by file number. In other cases whenever there is no outstanding secured obligation and no commitment to make advances, incur obligations or otherwise give value, the secured party must on written demand by the debtor send the debtor, for each filing officer with whom the financing statement was filed, a termination statement to the effect that he no longer claims a security interest under the financing statement, which shall be identified by file number. A termination statement signed by a person other than the secured party of record must be accompanied by a separate written statement of assignment signed by the secured party of record complying with subsection (2) of Section 9—405, including payment of the required fee. If the affected secured party fails

to file such a termination statement as required by this subsection, or to send such a termination statement within ten days after proper demand therefor, he shall be liable to the debtor for one hundred dollars, and in addition for any loss caused to the debtor by such failure.

(2) On presentation to the filing officer of such a termination statement he must note it in the index. If he has received the termination statement in duplicate, he shall return one copy of the termination statement to the secured party stamped to show the time of receipt thereof. If the filing officer has a microfilm or other photographic record of the financing statement, and of any related continuation statement, statement of assignment and statement of release, he may remove the originals from the files at any time after receipt of the termination statement, or if he has no such record, he may remove them from the files at any time after one year after receipt of the termination statement.

(3) If the termination statement is in the standard form prescribed by the [Secretary of State], the uniform fee for filing and indexing the termination statement shall be $. . . . ., and otherwise shall be $. . . . ., plus in each case an additional fee of $. . . . . for each name more than one against which the termination statement is required to be indexed.

Note: *The date to be inserted should be the effective date of the revised Article 9.*

§ 9—405. Assignment of Security Interest; Duties of Filing Officer; Fees.

(1) A financing statement may disclose an assignment of a security interest in the collateral described in the financing statement by indication in the financing statement of the name and address of the assignee or by an assignment itself or a copy thereof on the face or back of the statement. On presentation to the filing officer of such a financing statement the filing officer shall mark the same as provided in Section 9—403(4). The uniform fee for filing, indexing and furnishing filing data for a financing statement so indicating an assignment shall be $. . . . . if the statement is in the standard form prescribed by the [Secretary of State] and otherwise shall be $. . . . ., plus in each case an additional fee of $. . . . . for each name more than one against which the financing statement is required to be indexed.

(2) A secured party may assign of record all or part of his rights under a financing statement by the filing in the place where the original financing statement was filed of a separate written statement of assignment signed by the secured party of record and setting forth the name of the secured party of record and the debtor, the file number and the date of filing of the financing statement and the name and address of the assignee and containing a description of the collateral assigned. A copy of the assignment is sufficient as a separate statement if it complies with the preceding sentence. On presentation to the filing officer of such a separate statement, the filing officer shall mark such separate statement with the date and hour of the filing. He shall note the assignment on the index of the financing statement, or in the case of a fixture filing, or a filing covering timber to be cut, or covering minerals or the like (including oil and gas) or accounts subject to subsection (5) of Section 9—103, he shall index the assignment under the name of the assignor as grantor and, to the extent that the law of this state provides for indexing the assignment of a mortgage under the name of the assignee, he shall index the assignment of the financing statement under the name of the assignee. The uniform fee for filing, indexing and furnishing filing data about such a separate statement of assignment shall be $. . . . . . if the statement is in the standard form prescribed by the [Secretary of State] and otherwise shall be $. . . . . ., plus in each case an additional fee of $. . . . . . for each name more than one against which the statement of assignment is required to be indexed. Notwithstanding the provisions of this subsection, an assignment of record of a security interest in a fixture contained in a mortgage effective as a fixture filing (subsection (6) of Section 9—402) may be made only by an assignment of the mortgage in the manner provided by the law of this state other than this Act.

(3) After the disclosure or filing of an assignment under this section, the assignee is the secured party of record.

§ 9—406. Release of Collateral; Duties of Filing Officer; Fees.

A secured party of record may by his signed statement release all or a part of any collateral described in a filed financing statement. The statement of release is sufficient if it contains a description of the collateral being released, the name and address of the debtor, the name and address of the secured party, and the file number of the financing statement. A statement of release signed by a person other than the secured party of record must be accompanied by a separate written statement of assignment signed by the secured party of record and complying with subsection (2) of Section 9—405, including payment of the required fee. Upon presentation of such a statement of release to the filing officer he shall mark the statement with the hour and date of filing and shall note the same upon the margin of the index of the filing of the financing statement. The uniform fee for filing and noting such a statement of release shall be $. . . . . . if the statement is in the standard form prescribed by the [Secretary of State] and otherwise shall be $. . . . . ., plus in each case an additional fee of $. . . . . . for each name more than one against which the statement of release is required to be indexed.

§ 9—407. Information From Filing Officer.

[(1) If the person filing any financing statement, termination statement, statement of assignment, or statement of release, furnishes the filing officer a copy thereof, the filing officer shall upon request note upon the copy the file number and date and hour of the filing of the original and deliver or send the copy to such person.]

[(2) Upon request of any person, the filing officer shall issue his certificate showing whether there is on file on the date and hour stated therein, any presently effective financing statement naming a particular debtor and any statement of assignment thereof and if there is, giving the date and hour of filing of each such statement and the names and addresses of each secured party therein. The uniform fee for such a certificate shall be $. . . . . .

if the request for the certificate is in the standard form prescribed by the [Secretary of State] and otherwise shall be $. . . . . . . Upon request the filing officer shall furnish a copy of any filed financing statement or statement of assignment for a uniform fee of $. . . . . . per page.]

Note: *This section is proposed as an optional provision to require filing officers to furnish certificates. Local law and practices should be consulted with regard to the advisability of adoption.*

§ 9—408. Financing Statements Covering Consigned or Leased Goods.

A consignor or lessor of goods may file a financing statement using the terms "consignor," "consignee," "lessor," "lessee" or the like instead of the terms specified in Section 9—402. The provisions of this Part shall apply as appropriate to such a financing statement but its filing shall not of itself be a factor in determining whether or not the consignment or lease is intended as security (Section 1—201(37)). However, if it is determined for other reasons that the consignment or lease is so intended, a security interest of the consignor or lessor which attaches to the consigned or leased goods is perfected by such filing.

Part 5 Default

§ 9—501. Default; Procedure When Security Agreement Covers Both Real and Personal Property.

(1) When a debtor is in default under a security agreement, a secured party has the rights and remedies provided in this Part and except as limited by subsection (3) those provided in the security agreement. He may reduce his claim to judgment, foreclose or otherwise enforce the security interest by any available judicial procedure. If the collateral is documents the secured party may proceed either as to the documents or as to the goods covered thereby. A secured party in possession has the rights, remedies and duties provided in Section 9—207. The rights and remedies referred to in this subsection are cumulative.

(2) After default, the debtor has the rights and remedies provided in this Part, those provided in the security agreement and those provided in Section 9—207.

(3) To the extent that they give rights to the debtor and impose duties on the secured party, the rules stated in the subsections referred to below may not be waived or varied except as provided with respect to compulsory disposition of collateral (subsection (3) of Section 9—504 and Section 9—505) and with respect to redemption of collateral (Section 9—506) but the parties may by agreement determine the standards by which the fulfillment of these rights and duties is to be measured if such standards are not manifestly unreasonable:

(a) subsection (2) of Section 9—502 and subsection (2) of Section 9—504 insofar as they require accounting for surplus proceeds of collateral;

(b) subsection (3) of Section 9—504 and subsection (1) of Section 9—505 which deal with disposition of collateral;

(c) subsection (2) of Section 9—505 which deals with acceptance of collateral as discharge of obligation;

(d) Section 9—506 which deals with redemption of collateral; and

(e) subsection (1) of Section 9—507 which deals with the secured party's liability for failure to comply with this Part.

(4) If the security agreement covers both real and personal property, the secured party may proceed under this Part as to the personal property or he may proceed as to both the real and the personal property in accordance with his rights and remedies in respect of the real property in which case the provisions of this Part do not apply.

(5) When a secured party has reduced his claim to judgment the lien of any levy which may be made upon his collateral by virtue of any execution based upon the judgment shall relate back to the date of the perfection of the security interest in such collateral. A judicial sale, pursuant to such execution, is a foreclosure of the security interest by judicial procedure within the meaning of this section, and the secured party may purchase at the sale and thereafter hold the collateral free of any other requirements of this Article.

§ 9—502. Collection Rights of Secured Party.

(1) When so agreed and in any event on default the secured party is entitled to notify an account debtor or the obligor on an instrument to make payment to him whether or not the assignor was theretofore making collections on the collateral, and also to take control of any proceeds to which he is entitled under Section 9—306.

(2) A secured party who by agreement is entitled to charge back uncollected collateral or otherwise to full or limited recourse against the debtor and who undertakes to collect from the account debtors or obligors must proceed in a commercially reasonable manner and may deduct his reasonable expenses of realization from the collections. If the security agreement secures an indebtedness, the secured party must account to the debtor for any surplus, and unless otherwise agreed, the debtor is liable for any deficiency. But, if the underlying transaction was a sale of accounts or chattel paper, the debtor is entitled to any surplus or is liable for any deficiency only if the security agreement so provides.

§ 9—503. Secured Party's Right to Take Possession After Default.

Unless otherwise agreed a secured party has on default the right to take possession of the collateral. In taking possession a secured party may proceed without judicial process if this can be done without breach of the peace or may proceed by action. If the security agreement so provides the secured party may require the debtor to assemble the collateral and make it available to the secured party at a place to be designated by the secured party which is reasonably convenient to both parties. Without removal a secured party may render equipment unusable, and may dispose of collateral on the debtor's premises under Section 9—504.

§ 9—504. Secured Party's Right to Dispose of Collateral After Default; Effect of Disposition.

(1) A secured party after default may sell, lease or otherwise dispose of any or all of the collateral in its then condition or following any commercially reasonable preparation or processing. Any sale of goods is subject to the Article on Sales (Article 2). The proceeds of disposition shall be applied in the order following to

(a) the reasonable expenses of retaking, holding, preparing for sale or lease, selling, leasing and the like and, to the extent provided for in the agreement and not prohibited by law, the reasonable attorneys' fees and legal expenses incurred by the secured party;

(b) the satisfaction of indebtedness secured by the security interest under which the disposition is made;

(c) the satisfaction of indebtedness secured by any subordinate security interest in the collateral if written notification of demand therefor is received before distribution of the proceeds is completed. If requested by the secured party, the holder of a subordinate security interest must seasonably furnish reasonable proof of his interest, and unless he does so, the secured party need not comply with his demand.

(2) If the security interest secures an indebtedness, the secured party must account to the debtor for any surplus, and, unless otherwise agreed, the debtor is liable for any deficiency. But if the underlying transaction was a sale of accounts or chattel paper, the debtor is entitled to any surplus or is liable for any deficiency only if the security agreement so provides.

(3) Disposition of the collateral may be by public or private proceedings and may be made by way of one or more contracts. Sale or other disposition may be as a unit or in parcels and at any time and place and on any terms but every aspect of the disposition including the method, manner, time, place and terms must be commercially reasonable. Unless collateral is perishable or threatens to decline speedily in value or is of a type customarily sold on a recognized market, reasonable notification of the time and place of any public sale or reasonable notification of the time after which any private sale or other intended disposition is to be made shall be sent by the secured party to the debtor, if he has not signed after default a statement renouncing or modifying his right to notification of sale. In the case of consumer goods no other notification need be sent. In other cases notification shall be sent to any other secured party from whom the secured party has received (before sending his notification to the debtor or before the debtor's renunciation of his rights) written notice of a claim of an interest in the collateral. The secured party may buy at any public sale and if the collateral is of a type customarily sold in a recognized market or is of a type which is the subject of widely distributed standard price quotations he may buy at private sale.

(4) When collateral is disposed of by a secured party after default, the disposition transfers to a purchaser for value all of the debtor's rights therein, discharges the security interest under which it is made and any security interest or lien subordinate thereto. The purchaser takes free of all such rights and interests even though the secured party fails to comply with the requirements of this Part or of any judicial proceedings

(a) in the case of a public sale, if the purchaser has no knowledge of any defects in the sale and if he does not buy in collusion with the secured party, other bidders or the person conducting the sale; or

(b) in any other case, if the purchaser acts in good faith.

(5) A person who is liable to a secured party under a guaranty, indorsement, repurchase agreement or the like and who receives a transfer of collateral from the secured party or is subrogated to his rights has thereafter the rights and duties of the secured party. Such a transfer of collateral is not a sale or disposition of the collateral under this Article.

§ 9—505. Compulsory Disposition of Collateral; Acceptance of the Collateral as Discharge of Obligation.

(1) If the debtor has paid sixty per cent of the cash price in the case of a purchase money security interest in consumer goods or sixty per cent of the loan in the case of another security interest in consumer goods, and has not signed after default a statement renouncing or modifying his rights under this Part a secured party who has taken possession of collateral must dispose of it under Section 9—504 and if he fails to do so within ninety days after he takes possession the debtor at his option may recover in conversion or under Section 9—507(1) on secured party's liability.

(2) In any other case involving consumer goods or any other collateral a secured party in possession may, after default, propose to retain the collateral in satisfaction of the obligation. Written notice of such proposal shall be sent to the debtor if he has not signed after default a statement renouncing or modifying his rights under this subsection. In the case of consumer goods no other notice need be given. In other cases notice shall be sent to any other secured party from whom the secured party has received (before sending his notice to the debtor or before the debtor's renunciation of his rights) written notice of a claim of an interest in the collateral. If the secured party receives objection in writing from a person entitled to receive notification within twenty-one days after the notice was sent, the secured party must dispose of the collateral under Section 9—504. In the absence of such written objection the secured party may retain the collateral in satisfaction of the debtor's obligation. Amended in 1972.

§ 9—506. Debtor's Right to Redeem Collateral.

At any time before the secured party has disposed of collateral or entered into a contract for its disposition under Section 9—504 or before the obligation has been discharged under Section 9—505(2) the debtor or any other secured party may unless otherwise agreed in writing after default redeem the collateral by tendering fulfillment of all obligations secured by the collateral as well as the expenses reasonably incurred by the secured party in retaking, holding and preparing the collateral for disposition, in arranging for the sale, and to the extent provided in the agreement and not prohibited by law, his reasonable attorneys' fees and legal expenses.

§ 9—507. Secured Party's Liability for Failure to Comply With This Part.

(1) If it is established that the secured party is not proceeding in accordance with the provisions of this Part disposition may be ordered or restrained on appropriate terms and conditions. If the disposition has occurred the debtor or any person entitled to notification or whose security interest has been made known to the secured party prior to the disposition has a right to recover from the secured party any loss caused by a failure to comply with the provisions of this Part. If the collateral is consumer goods, the debtor has a right to recover in any event an amount not less than the credit service charge plus ten per cent of the principal amount of the debt or the time price differential plus 10 per cent of the cash price.

(2) The fact that a better price could have been obtained by a sale at a different time or in a different method from that selected by the secured party is not of itself sufficient to establish that the sale was not made in a commercially reasonable manner. If the secured party either sells the collateral in the usual manner in any recognized market therefor or if he sells at the price current in such market at the time of his sale or if he has otherwise sold in conformity with reasonable commercial practices among dealers in the type of property sold he has sold in a commercially reasonable manner. The principles stated in the two preceding sentences with respect to sales also apply as may be appropriate to other types of disposition. A disposition which has been approved in any judicial proceeding or by any bona fide creditors' committee or representative of creditors shall conclusively be deemed to be commercially reasonable, but this sentence does not indicate that any such approval must be obtained in any case nor does it indicate that any disposition not so approved is not commercially reasonable.

APPENDIX C

The Uniform Partnership Act

(Adopted in forty-nine states [all of the states except Louisiana], the District of Columbia, the Virgin Islands, and Guam. The adoptions by Alabama and Nebraska do not follow the official text in every respect, but they are substantially similar, with local variations.)

The Act consists of 7 Parts as follows:

I. Preliminary Provisions

II. Nature of Partnership

III. Relations of Partners to Persons Dealing with the Partnership

IV. Relations of Partners to One Another

V. Property Rights of a Partner

VI. Dissolution and Winding Up

VII. Miscellaneous Provisions

An Act to make uniform the Law of Partnerships

Be it enacted, etc.:

Part I Preliminary Provisions

Sec. 1. Name of Act

This act may be cited as Uniform Partnership Act.

Sec. 2. Definition of Terms

In this act, "Court" includes every court and judge having jurisdiction in the case.

"Business" includes every trade, occupation, or profession.

"Person" includes individuals, partnerships, corporations, and other associations.

"Bankrupt" includes bankrupt under the Federal Bankruptcy Act or insolvent under any state insolvent act.

"Conveyance" includes every assignment, lease, mortgage, or encumbrance.

"Real property" includes land and any interest or estate in land.

Sec. 3. Interpretation of Knowledge and Notice

(1) A person has "knowledge" of a fact within the meaning of this act not only when he has actual knowledge thereof, but also when he has knowledge of such other facts as in the circumstances shows bad faith.

(2) A person has "notice" of a fact within the meaning of this act when the person who claims the benefit of the notice:

(a) States the fact to such person, or

(b) Delivers through the mail, or by other means of communication, a written statement of the fact to such person or to a proper person at his place of business or residence.

Sec. 4. Rules of Construction

(1) The rule that statutes in derogation of the common law are to be strictly construed shall have no application to this act.

(2) The law of estoppel shall apply under this act.

(3) The law of agency shall apply under this act.

(4) This act shall be so interpreted and construed as to effect its general purpose to make uniform the law of those states which enact it.

(5) This act shall not be construed so as to impair the obligations of any contract existing when the act goes into effect, nor to affect any action or proceedings begun or right accrued before this act takes effect.

Sec. 5. Rules for Cases Not Provided for in This Act.

In any case not provided for in this act the rules of law and equity, including the law merchant, shall govern.

Part II Nature of Partnership

Sec. 6. Partnership Defined

(1) A partnership is an association of two or more persons to carry on as co-owners a business for profit.

(2) But any association formed under any other statute of this state, or any statute adopted by authority, other than the authority of this state, is not a partnership under this act, unless such association would have been a partnership in this state prior to the adoption of this act; but this act shall apply to limited partnerships except in so far as the statutes relating to such partnerships are inconsistent herewith.

Sec. 7. Rules for Determining the Existence of a Partnership

In determining whether a partnership exists, these rules shall apply:

(1) Except as provided by Section 16 persons who are not partners as to each other are not partners as to third persons.

(2) Joint tenancy, tenancy in common, tenancy by the entireties, joint property, common property, or part ownership does not of

itself establish a partnership, whether such co-owners do or do not share any profits made by the use of the property.

(3) The sharing of gross returns does not of itself establish a partnership, whether or not the persons sharing them have a joint or common right or interest in any property from which the returns are derived.

(4) The receipt by a person of a share of the profits of a business is prima facie evidence that he is a partner in the business, but no such inference shall be drawn if such profits were received in payment:

(a) As a debt by installments or otherwise,

(b) As wages of an employee or rent to a landlord,

(c) As an annuity to a widow or representative of a deceased partner,

(d) As interest on a loan, though the amount of payment vary with the profits of the business,

(e) As the consideration for the sale of a good-will of a business or other property by installments or otherwise.

Sec. 8. Partnership Property

(1) All property originally brought into the partnership stock or subsequently acquired by purchase or otherwise, on account of the partnership, is partnership property.

(2) Unless the contrary intention appears, property acquired with partnership funds is partnership property.

(3) Any estate in real property may be acquired in the partnership name. Title so acquired can be conveyed only in the partnership name.

(4) A conveyance to a partnership in the partnership name, though without words of inheritance, passes the entire estate of the grantor unless a contrary intent appears.

Part III Relations of Partners to Persons Dealing with the Partnership

Sec. 9. Partner Agent of Partnership as to Partnership Business

(1) Every partner is an agent of the partnership for the purpose of its business, and the act of every partner, including the execution in the partnership name of any instrument, for apparently carrying on in the usual way the business of the partnership of which he is a member binds the partnership, unless the partner so acting has in fact no authority to act for the partnership in the particular matter, and the person with whom he is dealing has knowledge of the fact that he has no such authority.

(2) An act of a partner which is not apparently for the carrying on of the business of the partnership in the usual way does not bind the partnership unless authorized by the other partners.

(3) Unless authorized by the other partners or unless they have abandoned the business, one or more but less than all the partners have no authority to:

(a) Assign the partnership property in trust for creditors or on the assignee's promise to pay the debts of the partnership,

(b) Dispose of the good-will of the business,

(c) Do any other act which would make it impossible to carry on the ordinary business of a partnership,

(d) Confess a judgment,

(e) Submit a partnership claim or liability to arbitration or reference.

(4) No act of a partner in contravention of a restriction on authority shall bind the partnership to persons having knowledge of the restriction.

Sec. 10. Conveyance of Real Property of the Partnership

(1) Where title to real property is in the partnership name, any partner may convey title to such property by a conveyance executed in the partnership name; but the partnership may recover such property unless the partner's act binds the partnership under the provisions of paragraph (1) of section 9, or unless such property has been conveyed by the grantee or a person claiming through such grantee to a holder for value without knowledge that the partner, in making the conveyance, has exceeded his authority.

(2) Where title to real property is in the name of the partnership, a conveyance executed by a partner, in his own name, passes the equitable interest of the partnership, provided the act is one within the authority of the partner under the provisions of paragraph (1) of section 9.

(3) Where title to real property is in the name of one or more but not all the partners, and the record does not disclose the right of the partnership, the partners in whose name the title stands may convey title to such property, but the partnership may recover such property if the partners' act does not bind the partnership under the provisions of paragraph (1) of section 9, unless the purchaser or his assignee, is a holder for value, without knowledge.

(4) Where the title to real property is in the name of one or more or all the partners, or in a third person in trust for the partnership, a conveyance executed by a partner in the partnership name, or in his own name, passes the equitable interest of the partnership, provided the act is one within the authority of the partner under the provisions of paragraph (1) of section 9.

(5) Where the title to real property is in the names of all the partners a conveyance executed by all the partners passes all their rights in such property.

Sec. 11. Partnership Bound by Admission of Partner

An admission or representation made by any partner concerning partnership affairs within the scope of his authority as conferred by this act is evidence against the partnership.

Sec. 12. Partnership Charged with Knowledge of or Notice to Partner

Notice to any partner of any matter relating to partnership affairs, and the knowledge of the partner acting in the particular matter, acquired while a partner or then present to his mind, and the knowledge of any other partner who reasonably could and should have communicated it to the acting partner, operate as notice to or knowledge of the partnership, except in the case of a fraud on the partnership committed by or with the consent of that partner.

Sec. 13. Partnership Bound by Partner's Wrongful Act

Where, by any wrongful act or omission of any partner acting in the ordinary course of the business of the partnership or with the authority of his co-partners, loss or injury is caused to any person, not being a partner in the partnership, or any penalty is incurred, the partnership is liable therefor to the same extent as the partner so acting or omitting to act.

Sec. 14. Partnership Bound by Partner's Breach of Trust

The partnership is bound to make good the loss:

(a) Where one partner acting within the scope of his apparent authority receives money or property of a third person and misapplies it; and

(b) Where the partnership in the course of its business receives money or property of a third person and the money or property so received is misapplied by any partner while it is in the custody of the partnership.

Sec. 15. Nature of Partner's Liability

All partners are liable

(a) Jointly and severally for everything chargeable to the partnership under sections 13 and 14.

(b) Jointly for all other debts and obligations of the partnership; but any partner may enter into a separate obligation to perform a partnership contract.

Sec. 16. Partner by Estoppel

(1) When a person, by words spoken or written or by conduct, represents himself, or consents to another representing him to any one, as a partner in an existing partnership or with one or more persons not actual partners, he is liable to any such person to whom such representation has been made, who has, on the faith of such representation, given credit to the actual or apparent partnership, and if he has made such representation or consented to its being made in a public manner he is liable to such person, whether the representation has or has not been made or communicated to such person so giving credit by or with the knowledge of the apparent partner making the representation or consenting to its being made.

(a) When a partnership liability results, he is liable as though he were an actual member of the partnership.

(b) When no partnership liability results, he is liable jointly with the other persons, if any, so consenting to the contract or representation as to incur liability, otherwise separately.

(2) When a person has been thus represented to be a partner in an existing partnership, or with one or more persons not actual partners, he is an agent of the persons consenting to such representation to bind them to the same extent and in the same manner as though he were a partner in fact, with respect to persons who rely upon the representation. Where all the members of the existing partnership consent to the representation, a partnership act or obligation results; but in all other cases it is the joint act or obligation of the person acting and the persons consenting to the representation.

Sec. 17. Liability of Incoming Partner

A person admitted as a partner into an existing partnership is liable for all the obligations of the partnership arising before his admission as though he had been a partner when such obligations were incurred, except that this liability shall be satisfied only out of partnership property.

Part IV Relations of Partners to One Another

Sec. 18. Rules Determining Rights and Duties of Partners

The rights and duties of the partners in relation to the partnership shall be determined, subject to any agreement between them, by the following rules:

(a) Each partner shall be repaid his contributions, whether by way of capital or advances to the partnership property and share equally in the profits and surplus remaining after all liabilities, including those to partners, are satisfied; and must contribute towards the losses, whether of capital or otherwise, sustained by the partnership according to his share in the profits.

(b) The partnership must indemnify every partner in respect of payments made and personal liabilities reasonably incurred by him in the ordinary and proper conduct of its business, or for the preservation of its business or property.

(c) A partner, who in aid of the partnership makes any payment or advance beyond the amount of capital which he agreed to contribute, shall be paid interest from the date of the payment or advance.

(d) A partner shall receive interest on the capital contributed by him only from the date when repayment should be made.

(e) All partners have equal rights in the management and conduct of the partnership business.

(f) No partner is entitled to remuneration for acting in the partnership business, except that a surviving partner is entitled to reasonable compensation for his services in winding up the partnership affairs.

(g) No person can become a member of a partnership without the consent of all the partners.

(h) Any difference arising as to ordinary matters connected with the partnership business may be decided by a majority of the partners; but no act in contravention of any agreement between the partners may be done rightfully without the consent of all the partners.

Sec. 19. Partnership Books

The partnership books shall be kept, subject to any agreement between the partners, at the principal place of business of the partnership, and every partner shall at all times have access to and may inspect and copy any of them.

Sec. 20. Duty of Partners to Render Information

Partners shall render on demand true and full information of all things affecting the partnership to any partner or the legal representative of any deceased partner or partner under legal disability.

Sec. 21. Partner Accountable as a Fiduciary

(1) Every partner must account to the partnership for any benefit, and hold as trustee for it any profits derived by him without the consent of the other partners from any transaction connected with the formation, conduct, or liquidation of the partnership or from any use by him of its property.

(2) This section applies also to the representatives of a deceased partner engaged in the liquidation of the affairs of the partnership as the personal representatives of the last surviving partner.

Sec. 22. Right to an Account

Any partner shall have the right to a formal account as to partnership affairs:

(a) If he is wrongfully excluded from the partnership business or possession of its property by his co-partners,

(b) If the right exists under the terms of any agreement,

(c) As provided by section 21,

(d) Whenever other circumstances render it just and reasonable.

Sec. 23. Continuation of Partnership beyond Fixed Term

(1) When a partnership for a fixed term or particular undertaking is continued after the termination of such term or particular undertaking without any express agreement, the rights and duties of the partners remain the same as they were at such termination, so far as is consistent with a partnership at will.

(2) A continuation of the business by the partners or such of them as habitually acted therein during the term, without any settlement or liquidation of the partnership affairs, is prima facie evidence of a continuation of the partnership.

Part V Property Rights of a Partner

Sec. 24. Extent of Property Rights of a Partner

The property rights of a partner are (1) his rights in specific partnership property, (2) his interest in the partnership, and (3) his right to participate in the management.

Sec. 25. Nature of a Partner's Right in Specific Partnership Property

(1) A partner is co-owner with his partners of specific partnership property holding as a tenant in partnership.

(2) The incidents of this tenancy are such that:

(a) A partner, subject to the provisions of this act and to any agreement between the partners, has an equal right with his partners to possess specific partnership property for partnership purposes; but he has no right to possess such property for any other purpose without the consent of his partners.

(b) A partner's right in specific partnership property is not assignable except in connection with the assignment of rights of all the partners in the same property.

(c) A partner's right in specific partnership property is not subject to attachment or execution, except on a claim against the partnership. When partnership property is attached for a partnership debt the partners, or any of them, or the representatives of a deceased partner, cannot claim any right under the homestead or exemption laws.

(d) On the death of a partner his right in specific partnership property vests in the surviving partner or partners, except where the deceased was the last surviving partner, when his right in such property vests in his legal representative. Such surviving partner or partners, or the legal representative of the last surviving partner, has no right to possess the partnership property for any but a partnership purpose.

(e) A partner's right in specific partnership property is not subject to dower, curtesy, or allowances to widows, heirs, or next of kin.

Sec. 26. Nature of Partner's Interest in the Partnership

A partner's interest in the partnership is his share of the profits and surplus, and the same is personal property.

Sec. 27. Assignment of Partner's Interest

(1) A conveyance by a partner of his interest in the partnership does not of itself dissolve the partnership, nor, as against the other partners in the absence of agreement, entitle the assignee, during the continuance of the partnership, to interfere in the management or administration of the partnership business or affairs, or to require any information or account of partnership transactions, or to inspect the partnership books; but it merely entitles the assignee to receive in accordance with his contract the profits to which the assigning partner would otherwise be entitled.

(2) In case of a dissolution of the partnership, the assignee is entitled to receive his assignor's interest and may require an account from the date only of the last account agreed to by all the partners.

Sec. 28. Partner's Interest Subject to Charging Order

(1) On due application to a competent court by any judgment creditor of a partner, the court which entered the judgment, order, or decree, or any other court, may charge the interest of the debtor partner with payment of the unsatisfied amount of such judgment debt with interest thereon; and may then or later appoint a receiver of his share of the profits, and of any other money due or to fall due to him in respect of the partnership, and make all other orders, directions, accounts and inquiries which the debtor partner might have made, or which the circumstances of the case may require.

(2) The interest charged may be redeemed at any time before foreclosure, or in case of a sale being directed by the court may be purchased without thereby causing a dissolution:

(a) With separate property, by any one or more of the partners, or

(b) With partnership property, by any one or more of the partners with the consent of all the partners whose interests are not so charged or sold.

(3) Nothing in this act shall be held to deprive a partner of his right, if any, under the exemption laws, as regards his interest in the partnership.

Part VI Dissolution and Winding up

Sec. 29. Dissolution Defined

The dissolution of a partnership is the change in the relation of the partners caused by any partner ceasing to be associated in the carrying on as distinguished from the winding up of the business.

Sec. 30. Partnership not Terminated by Dissolution

On dissolution the partnership is not terminated, but continues until the winding up of partnership affairs is completed.

Sec. 31. Causes of Dissolution

Dissolution is caused:

(1) Without violation of the agreement between the partners,

(a) By the termination of the definite term or particular undertaking specified in the agreement,

(b) By the express will of any partner when no definite term or particular undertaking is specified,

(c) By the express will of all the partners who have not assigned their interests or suffered them to be charged for their separate debts, either before or after the termination of any specified term or particular undertaking,

(d) By the expulsion of any partner from the business bona fide in accordance with such a power conferred by the agreement between the partners;

(2) In contravention of the agreement between the partners, where the circumstances do not permit a dissolution under any other provision of this section, by the express will of any partner at any time;

(3) By any event which makes it unlawful for the business of the partnership to be carried on or for the members to carry it on in partnership;

(4) By the death of any partner;

(5) By the bankruptcy of any partner or the partnership;

(6) By decree of court under section 32.

Sec. 32. Dissolution by Decree of Court

(1) On application by or for a partner the court shall decree a dissolution whenever:

(a) A partner has been declared a lunatic in any judicial proceeding or is shown to be of unsound mind,

(b) A partner becomes in any other way incapable of performing his part of the partnership contract,

(c) A partner has been guilty of such conduct as tends to affect prejudicially the carrying on of the business,

(d) A partner wilfully or persistently commits a breach of the partnership agreement, or otherwise so conducts himself in matters relating to the partnership business that it is not reasonably practicable to carry on the business in partnership with him,

(e) The business of the partnership can only be carried on at a loss,

(f) Other circumstances render a dissolution equitable.

(2) On the application of the purchaser of a partner's interest under sections 28 or 29 [should read 27 or 28];

(a) After the termination of the specified term or particular undertaking,

(b) At any time if the partnership was a partnership at will when the interest was assigned or when the charging order was issued.

Sec. 33. General Effect of Dissolution on Authority of Partner

Except so far as may be necessary to wind up partnership affairs or to complete transactions begun but not then finished, dissolution terminates all authority of any partner to act for the partnership,

(1) With respect to the partners,

(a) When the dissolution is not by the act, bankruptcy or death of a partner; or

(b) When the dissolution is by such act, bankruptcy or death of a partner, in cases where section 34 so requires.

(2) With respect to persons not partners, as declared in section 35.

Sec. 34. Rights of Partner to Contribution from Copartners after Dissolution

Where the dissolution is caused by the act, death or bankruptcy of a partner, each partner is liable to his copartners for his share of any liability created by any partner acting for the partnership as if the partnership had not been dissolved unless

(a) The dissolution being by act of any partner, the partner acting for the partnership had knowledge of the dissolution, or

(b) The dissolution being by the death or bankruptcy of a partner, the partner acting for the partnership had knowledge or notice of the death or bankruptcy.

Sec. 35. Power of Partner to Bind Partnership to Third Persons after Dissolution

(1) After dissolution a partner can bind the partnership except as provided in Paragraph (3).

(a) By any act appropriate for winding up partnership affairs or completing transactions unfinished at dissolution;

(b) By any transaction which would bind the partnership if dissolution had not taken place, provided the other party to the transaction

(I) Had extended credit to the partnership prior to dissolution and had no knowledge or notice of the dissolution; or

(II) Though he had not so extended credit, had nevertheless known of the partnership prior to dissolution, and, having no knowledge or notice of dissolution, the fact of dissolution had not been advertised in a newspaper of general circulation in the place (or in each place if more than one) at which the partnership business was regularly carried on.

(2) The liability of a partner under paragraph (1b) shall be satisfied out of partnership assets alone when such partner had been prior to dissolution

(a) Unknown as a partner to the person with whom the contract is made; and

(b) So far unknown and inactive in partnership affairs that the business reputation of the partnership could not be said to have been in any degree due to his connection with it.

(3) The partnership is in no case bound by any act of a partner after dissolution

(a) Where the partnership is dissolved because it is unlawful to carry on the business, unless the act is appropriate for winding up partnership affairs; or

(b) Where the partner has become bankrupt; or

(c) Where the partner has no authority to wind up partnership affairs; except by a transaction with one who

(I) Had extended credit to the partnership prior to dissolution and had no knowledge or notice of his want of authority; or

(II) Had not extended credit to the partnership prior to dissolution, and, having no knowledge or notice of his want of authority, the fact of his want of authority has not been advertised in the manner provided for advertising the fact of dissolution in paragraph (1bII).

(4) Nothing in this section shall affect the liability under Section 16 of any person who after dissolution represents himself or consents to another representing him as a partner in a partnership engaged in carrying on business.

Sec. 36. Effect of Dissolution on Partner's Existing Liability

(1) The dissolution of the partnership does not of itself discharge the existing liability of any partner.

(2) A partner is discharged from any existing liability upon dissolution of the partnership by an agreement to that effect between himself, the partnership creditor and the person or partnership continuing the business; and such agreement may be inferred from the course of dealing between the creditor having knowledge of the dissolution and the person or partnership continuing the business.

(3) Where a person agrees to assume the existing obligations of a dissolved partnership, the partners whose obligations have been assumed shall be discharged from any liability to any creditor of the partnership who, knowing of the agreement, consents to a material alteration in the nature or time of payment of such obligations.

(4) The individual property of a deceased partner shall be liable for all obligations of the partnership incurred while he was a partner but subject to the prior payment of his separate debts.

Sec. 37. Right to Wind Up

Unless otherwise agreed the partners who have not wrongfully dissolved the partnership or the legal representative of the last surviving partner, not bankrupt, has the right to wind up the partnership affairs; provided, however, that any partner, his legal representative or his assignee, upon cause shown, may obtain winding up by the court.

Sec. 38. Rights of Partners to Application of Partnership Property

(1) When dissolution is caused in any way, except in contravention of the partnership agreement, each partner, as against his copartners and all persons claiming through them in respect of their interests in the partnership, unless otherwise agreed, may have the partnership property applied to discharge its liabilities, and the surplus applied to pay in cash the net amount owing to the respective partners. But if dissolution is caused by expulsion of a partner, bona fide under the partnership agreement and if the expelled partner is discharged from all partnership liabilities, either by payment or agreement under section 36(2), he shall receive in cash only the net amount due him from the partnership.

(2) When dissolution is caused in contravention of the partnership agreement the rights of the partners shall be as follows:

(a) Each partner who has not caused dissolution wrongfully shall have,

(I) All the rights specified in paragraph (1) of this section, and

(II) The right, as against each partner who has caused the dissolution wrongfully, to damages for breach of the agreement.

(b) The partners who have not caused the dissolution wrongfully, if they all desire to continue the business in the same name, either by themselves or jointly with others, may do so, during the agreed term for the partnership and for that purpose may possess the partnership property, provided they secure the payment by bond approved by the court, or pay to any partner who has caused the dissolution wrongfully, the value of his interest in the partnership at the dissolution, less any damages recoverable under clause (2a II) of the section, and in like manner indemnify him against all present or future partnership liabilities.

(c) A partner who has caused the dissolution wrongfully shall have:

(I) If the business is not continued under the provisions of paragraph (2b) all the rights of a partner under paragraph (1), subject to clause (2a II), of this section,

(II) If the business is continued under paragraph (2b) of this section the right as against his co-partners and all claiming through them in respect of their interests in the partnership, to have the value of his interest in the partnership, less any damages caused to his co-partners by the dissolution, ascertained and paid to him in cash, or the payment secured by bond approved by the court, and to be released from all existing liabilities of the partnership; but in ascertaining the value of the partner's interest the value of the good-will of the business shall not be considered.

Sec. 39. Rights Where Partnership Is Dissolved for Fraud or Misrepresentation

Where a partnership contract is rescinded on the ground of the fraud or misrepresentation of one of the parties thereto, the party entitled to rescind is, without prejudice to any other right, entitled,

(a) To a lien on, or right of retention of, the surplus of the partnership property after satisfying the partnership liabilities to third persons for any sum of money paid by him for the purchase of an interest in the partnership and for any capital or advances contributed by him; and

(b) To stand, after all liabilities to third persons have been satisfied, in the place of the creditors of the partnership for any payments made by him in respect of the partnership liabilities; and

(c) To be indemnified by the person guilty of the fraud or making the representation against all debts and liabilities of the partnership.

Sec. 40. Rules for Distribution

In settling accounts between the partners after dissolution, the following rules shall be observed, subject to any agreement to the contrary:

(a) The assets of the partnership are:

(I) The partnership property,

(II) The contributions of the partners necessary for the payment of all the liabilities specified in clause (b) of this paragraph.

(b) The liabilities of the partnership shall rank in order of payment, as follows:

(I) Those owing to creditors other than partners,

(II) Those owing to partners other than for capital and profits,

(III) Those owing to partners in respect of capital,

(IV) Those owing to partners in respect of profits.

(c) The assets shall be applied in the order of their declaration in clause (a) of this paragraph to the satisfaction of the liabilities.

(d) The partners shall contribute, as provided by section 18(a) the amount necessary to satisfy the liabilities; but if any, but not all, of the partners are insolvent, or, not being subject to process, refuse to contribute, the other partners shall contribute their share of the liabilities, and, in the relative proportions in which they share the profits, the additional amount necessary to pay the liabilities.

(e) An assignee for the benefit of creditors or any person appointed by the court shall have the right to enforce the contributions specified in clause (d) of this paragraph.

(f) Any partner or his legal representative shall have the right to enforce the contributions specified in clause (d) of this paragraph, to the extent of the amount which he has paid in excess of his share of the liability.

(g) The individual property of a deceased partner shall be liable for the contributions specified in clause (d) of this paragraph.

(h) When partnership property and the individual properties of the partners are in possession of a court for distribution, partnership creditors shall have priority on partnership property and separate creditors on individual property, saving the rights of lien or secured creditors as heretofore.

(i) Where a partner has become bankrupt or his estate is insolvent the claims against his separate property shall rank in the following order:

(I) Those owing to separate creditors,

(II) Those owing to partnership creditors,

(III) Those owing to partners by way of contribution.

Sec. 41. Liability of Persons Continuing the Business in Certain Cases

(1) When any new partner is admitted into an existing partnership, or when any partner retires and assigns (or the representative of the deceased partner assigns) his rights in partnership property to two or more of the partners, or to one or more of the partners and one or more third persons, if the business is continued without liquidation of the partnership affairs, creditors of the first or dissolved partnership are also creditors of the partnership so continuing the business.

(2) When all but one partner retire and assign (or the representative of a deceased partner assigns) their rights in partnership property to the remaining partner, who continues the business without liquidation of partnership affairs, either alone or with others, creditors of the dissolved partnership are also creditors of the person or partnership so continuing the business.

(3) When any partner retires or dies and the business of the dissolved partnership is continued as set forth in paragraphs (1) and (2) of this section, with the consent of the retired partners or the representative of the deceased partner, but without any assignment of his right in partnership property, rights of creditors of the dissolved partnership and of the creditors of the person or partnership continuing the business shall be as if such assignment had been made.

(4) When all the partners or their representatives assign their rights in partnership property to one or more third persons

who promise to pay the debts and who continue the business of the dissolved partnership, creditors of the dissolved partnership are also creditors of the person or partnership continuing the business.

(5) When any partner wrongfully causes a dissolution and the remaining partners continue the business under the provisions of section 38(2b), either alone or with others, and without liquidation of the partnership affairs, creditors of the dissolved partnership are also creditors of the person or partnership continuing the business.

(6) When a partner is expelled and the remaining partners continue the business either alone or with others, without liquidation of the partnership affairs, creditors of the dissolved partnership are also creditors of the person or partnership continuing the business.

(7) The liability of a third person becoming a partner in the partnership continuing the business, under this section, to the creditors of the dissolved partnership shall be satisfied out of partnership property only.

(8) When the business of a partnership after dissolution is continued under any conditions set forth in this section the creditors of the dissolved partnership, as against the separate creditors of the retiring or deceased partner or the representative of the deceased partner, have a prior right to any claim of the retired partner or the representative of the deceased partner against the person or partnership continuing the business, on account of the retired or deceased partner's interest in the dissolved partnership or on account of any consideration promised for such interest or for his right in partnership property.

(9) Nothing in this section shall be held to modify any right of creditors to set aside any assignment on the ground of fraud.

(10) The use by the person or partnership continuing the business of the partnership name, or the name of a deceased partner as part thereof, shall not of itself make the individual property of the deceased partner liable for any debts contracted by such person or partnership.

Sec. 42. Rights of Retiring or Estate of Deceased Partner When the Business Is Continued

When any partner retires or dies, and the business is continued under any of the conditions set forth in section 41 (1, 2, 3, 5, 6), or section 38(2b) without any settlement of accounts as between him or his estate and the person or partnership continuing the business, unless otherwise agreed, he or his legal representative as against such persons or partnership may have the value of his interest at the date of dissolution ascertained, and shall receive as an ordinary creditor an amount equal to the value of his interest in the dissolved partnership with interest, or, at his option or at the option of his legal representative, in lieu of interest, the profits attributable to the use of his right in the property of the dissolved partnership; provided that the creditors of the dissolved partnership as against the separate creditors, or the representative of the retired or deceased partner, shall have priority on any claim arising under this section, as provided by section 41(8) of this act.

Sec. 43. Accrual of Actions

The right to an account of his interest shall accrue to any partner, or his legal representative, as against the winding up partners or the surviving partners or the person or partnership continuing the business, at the date of dissolution, in the absence of any agreement to the contrary.

Part VII Miscellaneous Provisions

Sec. 44. When Act Takes Effect

This act shall take effect on the ___ day of ___ one thousand nine hundred and ___.

Sec. 45. Legislation Repealed

All acts or parts of acts inconsistent with this act are hereby repealed.

APPENDIX D The Revised Model Business Corporation Act (Excerpts)

Chapter 2. INCORPORATION

§ 2.01 Incorporators

One or more persons may act as the incorporator or incorporators of a corporation by delivering articles of incorporation to the secretary of state for filing.

§ 2.02 Articles of Incorporation

(a) The articles of incorporation must set forth:

(1) a corporate name * * * ;

(2) the number of shares the corporation is authorized to issue;

(3) the street address of the corporation's initial registered office and the name of its initial registered agent at that office; and

(4) the name and address of each incorporator.

(b) The articles of incorporation may set forth:

(1) the names and addresses of the individuals who are to serve as the initial directors;

(2) provisions not inconsistent with law regarding:

(i) the purpose or purposes for which the corporation is organized;

(ii) managing the business and regulating the affairs of the corporation;

(iii) defining, limiting, and regulating the powers of the corporation, its board of directors, and shareholders;

(iv) a par value for authorized shares or classes of shares;

(v) the imposition of personal liability on shareholders for the debts of the corporation to a specified extent and upon specified conditions;

(3) any provision that under this Act is required or permitted to be set forth in the bylaws; and

(4) a provision eliminating or limiting the liability of a director to the corporation or its shareholders for money damages for any action taken, or any failure to take any action, as a director, except liability for (A) the amount of a financial benefit received by a director to which he is not entitled; (B) an intentional infliction of harm on the corporation or the shareholders; (C) [unlawful distributions]; or (D) an intentional violation of criminal law.

(c) The articles of incorporation need not set forth any of the corporate powers enumerated in this Act.

§ 2.03 Incorporation

(a) Unless a delayed effective date is specified, the corporate existence begins when the articles of incorporation are filed.

(b) The secretary of state's filing of the articles of incorporation is conclusive proof that the incorporators satisfied all conditions precedent to incorporation except in a proceeding by the state to cancel or revoke the incorporation or involuntarily dissolve the corporation.

§ 2.04 Liability for Preincorporation Transactions

All persons purporting to act as or on behalf of a corporation, knowing there was no incorporation under this Act, are jointly and severally liable for all liabilities created while so acting.

§ 2.05 Organization of Corporation

(a) After incorporation:

(1) if initial directors are named in the articles of incorporation, the initial directors shall hold an organizational meeting, at the call of a majority of the directors, to complete the organization of the corporation by appointing officers, adopting bylaws, and carrying on any other business brought before the meeting;

(2) if initial directors are not named in the articles, the incorporator or incorporators shall hold an organizational meeting at the call of a majority of the incorporators:

(i) to elect directors and complete the organization of the corporation; or

(ii) to elect a board of directors who shall complete the organization of the corporation.

(b) Action required or permitted by this Act to be taken by incorporators at an organizational meeting may be taken without a meeting if the action taken is evidenced by one or more written consents describing the action taken and signed by each incorporator.

(c) An organizational meeting may be held in or out of this state.

* * * *

Chapter 3.
PURPOSES AND POWERS

§ 3.01 Purposes

(a) Every corporation incorporated under this Act has the purpose of engaging in any lawful business unless a more limited purpose is set forth in the articles of incorporation.

(b) A corporation engaging in a business that is subject to regulation under another statute of this state may incorporate under this Act only if permitted by, and subject to all limitations of, the other statute.

§ 3.02 General Powers

Unless its articles of incorporation provide otherwise, every corporation has perpetual duration and succession in its corporate name and has the same powers as an individual to do all things necessary or convenient to carry out its business and affairs, including without limitation power:

(1) to sue and be sued, complain and defend in its corporate name;

(2) to have a corporate seal, which may be altered at will, and to use it, or a facsimile of it, by impressing or affixing it or in any other manner reproducing it;

(3) to make and amend bylaws, not inconsistent with its articles of incorporation or with the laws of this state, for managing the business and regulating the affairs of the corporation;

(4) to purchase, receive, lease, or otherwise acquire, and own, hold, improve, use, and otherwise deal with, real or personal property, or any legal or equitable interest in property, wherever located;

(5) to sell, convey, mortgage, pledge, lease, exchange, and otherwise dispose of all or any part of its property;

(6) to purchase, receive, subscribe for, or otherwise acquire; own, hold, vote, use, sell, mortgage, lend, pledge, or otherwise dispose of; and deal in and with shares or other interests in, or obligations of, any other entity;

(7) to make contracts and guarantees, incur liabilities, borrow money, issue its notes, bonds, and other obligations (which may be convertible into or include the option to purchase other securities of the corporation), and secure any of its obligations by mortgage or pledge of any of its property, franchises, or income;

(8) to lend money, invest and reinvest its funds, and receive and hold real and personal property as security for repayment;

(9) to be a promoter, partner, member, associate, or manager of any partnership, joint venture, trust, or other entity;

(10) to conduct its business, locate offices, and exercise the powers granted by this Act within or without this state;

(11) to elect directors and appoint officers, employees, and agents of the corporation, define their duties, fix their compensation, and lend them money and credit;

(12) to pay pensions and establish pension plans, pension trusts, profit sharing plans, share bonus plans, share option plans, and benefit or incentive plans for any or all of its current or former directors, officers, employees, and agents;

(13) to make donations for the public welfare or for charitable, scientific, or educational purposes;

(14) to transact any lawful business that will aid governmental policy;

(15) to make payments or donations, or do any other act, not inconsistent with law, that furthers the business and affairs of the corporation.

* * * *

Chapter 5.
OFFICE AND AGENT

§ 5.01 Registered Office and Registered Agent

Each corporation must continuously maintain in this state:

(1) a registered office that may be the same as any of its places of business; and

(2) a registered agent, who may be:

(i) an individual who resides in this state and whose business office is identical with the registered office;

(ii) a domestic corporation or not-for-profit domestic corporation whose business office is identical with the registered office; or

(iii) a foreign corporation or not-for-profit foreign corporation authorized to transact business in this state whose business office is identical with the registered office.

* * * *

§ 5.04 Service on Corporation

(a) A corporation's registered agent is the corporation's agent for service of process, notice, or demand required or permitted by law to be served on the corporation.

(b) If a corporation has no registered agent, or the agent cannot with reasonable diligence be served, the corporation may be served by registered or certified mail, return receipt requested, addressed to the secretary of the corporation at its principal office. Service is perfected under this subsection at the earliest of:

(1) the date the corporation receives the mail;

(2) the date shown on the return receipt, if signed on behalf of the corporation; or

(3) five days after its deposit in the United States Mail, if mailed postpaid and correctly addressed.

(c) This section does not prescribe the only means, or necessarily the required means, of serving a corporation.

Chapter 6.
SHARES AND DISTRIBUTIONS

* * * *

Subchapter B. Issuance of Shares

* * * *

§ 6.21 Issuance of Shares

(a) The powers granted in this section to the board of directors may be reserved to the shareholders by the articles of incorporation.

(b) The board of directors may authorize shares to be issued for consideration consisting of any tangible or intangible property or benefit to the corporation, including cash, promissory notes, services performed, contracts for services to be performed, or other securities of the corporation.

(c) Before the corporation issues shares, the board of directors must determine that the consideration received or to be received for shares to be issued is adequate. That determination by the board of directors is conclusive insofar as the adequacy of consideration for the issuance of shares relates to whether the shares are validly issued, fully paid, and nonassessable.

(d) When the corporation receives the consideration for which the board of directors authorized the issuance of shares, the shares issued therefor are fully paid and nonassessable.

(e) The corporation may place in escrow shares issued for a contract for future services or benefits or a promissory note, or make other arrangements to restrict the transfer of the shares, and may credit distributions in respect of the shares against their purchase price, until the services are performed, the note is paid, or the benefits received. If the services are not performed, the note is not paid, or the benefits are not received, the shares escrowed or restricted and the distributions credited may be cancelled in whole or part.

* * * *

§ 6.27 Restriction on Transfer or Registration of Shares and Other Securities

(a) The articles of incorporation, bylaws, an agreement among shareholders, or an agreement between shareholders and the corporation may impose restrictions on the transfer or registration of transfer of shares of the corporation. A restriction does not affect shares issued before the restriction was adopted unless the holders of the shares are parties to the restriction agreement or voted in favor of the restriction.

(b) A restriction on the transfer or registration of transfer of shares is valid and enforceable against the holder or a transferee of the holder if the restriction is authorized by this section and its existence is noted conspicuously on the front or back of the certificate or is contained in the information statement [sent to the shareholder]. Unless so noted, a restriction is not enforceable against a person without knowledge of the restriction.

(c) A restriction on the transfer or registration of transfer of shares is authorized:

(1) to maintain the corporation's status when it is dependent on the number or identity of its shareholders;

(2) to preserve exemptions under federal or state securities law;

(3) for any other reasonable purpose.

(d) A restriction on the transfer or registration of transfer of shares may:

(1) obligate the shareholder first to offer the corporation or other persons (separately, consecutively, or simultaneously) an opportunity to acquire the restricted shares;

(2) obligate the corporate or other persons (separately, consecutively, or simultaneously) to acquire the restricted shares;

(3) require the corporation, the holders of any class of its shares, or another person to approve the transfer of the restricted shares, if the requirement is not manifestly unreasonable;

(4) prohibit the transfer of the restricted shares to designated persons or classes of persons, if the prohibition is not manifestly unreasonable.

(e) For purposes of this section, "shares" includes a security convertible into or carrying a right to subscribe for or acquire shares.

* * * *

Chapter 7. SHAREHOLDERS

Subchapter A. Meetings

§ 7.01 Annual Meeting

(a) A corporation shall hold annually at a time stated in or fixed in accordance with the bylaws a meeting of shareholders.

(b) Annual shareholders' meetings may be held in or out of this state at the place stated in or fixed in accordance with the bylaws. If no place is stated in or fixed in accordance with the bylaws, annual meetings shall be held at the corporation's principal office.

(c) The failure to hold an annual meeting at the time stated in or fixed in accordance with a corporation's bylaws does not affect the validity of any corporate action.

* * * *

§ 7.05 Notice of Meeting

(a) A corporation shall notify shareholders of the date, time, and place of each annual and special shareholders' meeting no fewer than 10 nor more than 60 days before the meeting date. Unless this Act or the articles of incorporation require otherwise, the corporation is required to give notice only to shareholders entitled to vote at the meeting.

(b) Unless this Act or the articles of incorporation require otherwise, notice of an annual meeting need not include a description of the purpose or purposes for which the meeting is called.

(c) Notice of a special meeting must include a description of the purpose or purposes for which the meeting is called.

(d) If not otherwise fixed * * *, the record date for determining shareholders entitled to notice of and to vote at an annual or special shareholders' meeting is the day before the first notice is delivered to shareholders.

(e) Unless the bylaws require otherwise, if an annual or special shareholders' meeting is adjourned to a different date, time, or place, notice need not be given of the new date, time, or place if the new date, time, or place is announced at the meeting before adjournment. * * *

* * * *

§ 7.07 Record Date

(a) The bylaws may fix or provide the manner of fixing the record date for one or more voting groups in order to determine the shareholders entitled to notice of a shareholders' meeting, to demand a special meeting, to vote, or to take any other action. If the bylaws do not fix or provide for fixing a record date, the board of directors of the corporation may fix a future date as the record date.

(b) A record date fixed under this section may not be more than 70 days before the meeting or action requiring a determination of shareholders.

(c) A determination of shareholders entitled to notice of or to vote at a shareholders' meeting is effective for any adjournment of the meeting unless the board of directors fixes a new record date, which it must do if the meeting is adjourned to a date more than 120 days after the date fixed for the original meeting.

(d) If a court orders a meeting adjourned to a date more than 120 days after the date fixed for the original meeting, it may provide that the original record date continues in effect or it may fix a new record date.

Subchapter B. Voting

§ 7.20 Shareholders' List for Meeting

(a) After fixing a record date for a meeting, a corporation shall prepare an alphabetical list of the names of all its shareholders who are entitled to notice of a shareholders' meeting. The list must be arranged by voting group (and within each voting group by class or series of shares) and show the address of and number of shares held by each shareholder.

(b) The shareholders' list must be available for inspection by any shareholder, beginning two business days after notice of the meeting is given for which the list was prepared and continuing through the meeting, at the corporation's principal office or at a place identified in the meeting notice in the city where the meeting will be held. A shareholder, his agent, or attorney is entitled on written demand to inspect and, subject to the requirements of section 16.02(c), to copy the list, during regular business hours and at his expense, during the period it is available for inspection.

(c) The corporation shall make the shareholders' list available at the meeting, and any shareholder, his agent, or attorney is entitled to inspect the list at any time during the meeting or any adjournment.

(d) If the corporation refuses to allow a shareholder, his agent, or attorney to inspect the shareholders' list before or at the meeting (or copy the list as permitted by subsection (b)), the [name or describe] court of the county where a corporation's principal office (or, if none in this state, its registered office) is located, on application of the shareholder, may summarily order the inspection or copying at the corporation's expense and may postpone the meeting for which the list was prepared until the inspection or copying is complete.

(e) Refusal or failure to prepare or make available the shareholders' list does not affect the validity of action taken at the meeting.

* * * *

§ 7.22 Proxies

(a) A shareholder may vote his shares in person or by proxy.

(b) A shareholder may appoint a proxy to vote or otherwise act for him by signing an appointment form, either personally or by his attorney-in-fact.

(c) An appointment of a proxy is effective when received by the secretary or other officer or agent authorized to tabulate votes. An appointment is valid for 11 months unless a longer period is expressly provided in the appointment form.

* * * *

§ 7.28 Voting for Directors; Cumulative Voting

(a) Unless otherwise provided in the articles of incorporation, directors are elected by a plurality of the votes cast by the shares entitled to vote in the election at a meeting at which a quorum is present.

(b) Shareholders do not have a right to cumulate their votes for directors unless the articles of incorporation so provide.

(c) A statement included in the articles of incorporation that "[all] [a designated voting group of] shareholders are entitled to cumulate their votes for directors" (or words of similar import) means that the shareholders designated are entitled to multiply the number of votes they are entitled to cast by the number of directors for whom they are entitled to vote and cast the product for a single candidate or distribute the product among two or more candidates.

(d) Shares otherwise entitled to vote cumulatively may not be voted cumulatively at a particular meeting unless:

(1) the meeting notice or proxy statement accompanying the notice states conspicuously that cumulative voting is authorized; or

(2) a shareholder who has the right to cumulate his votes gives notice to the corporation not less than 48 hours before the time set for the meeting of his intent to cumulate his votes during the meeting, and if one shareholder gives this notice all other shareholders in the same voting group participating in the election are entitled to cumulate their votes without giving further notice.

* * * *

Subchapter D. Derivative Proceedings

* * * *

§ 7.41 Standing

A shareholder may not commence or maintain a derivative proceeding unless the shareholder:

(1) was a shareholder of the corporation at the time of the act or omission complained of or became a shareholder through transfer by operation of law from one who was a shareholder at that time; and

(2) fairly and adequately represents the interests of the corporation in enforcing the right of the corporation.

§ 7.42 Demand

No shareholder may commence a derivative proceeding until:

(1) a written demand has been made upon the corporation to take suitable action; and

(2) 90 days have expired from the date the demand was made unless the shareholder has earlier been notified that the demand has been rejected by the corporation or unless irreparable injury to the corporation would result by waiting for the expiration of the 90 day period.

* * * *

Chapter 8. DIRECTORS AND OFFICERS

Subchapter A. Board of Directors

* * * *

§ 8.02 Qualifications of Directors

The articles of incorporation or bylaws may prescribe qualifications for directors. A director need not be a resident of this state or a shareholder of the corporation unless the articles of incorporation or bylaws so prescribe.

§ 8.03 Number and Election of Directors

(a) A board of directors must consist of one or more individuals, with the number specified in or fixed in accordance with the articles of incorporation or bylaws.

(b) If a board of directors has power to fix or change the number of directors, the board may increase or decrease by 30 percent or less the number of directors last approved by the shareholders, but only the shareholders may increase or decrease by more than 30 percent the number of directors last approved by the shareholders.

(c) The articles of incorporation or bylaws may establish a variable range for the size of the board of directors by fixing a minimum and maximum number of directors. If a variable range is established, the number of directors may be fixed or changed from time to time, within the minimum and maximum, by the shareholders or the board of directors. After shares are issued, only the shareholders may change the range for the size of the board or change from a fixed to a variable-range size board or vice versa.

(d) Directors are elected at the first annual shareholders' meeting and at each annual meeting thereafter unless their terms are staggered under section 8.06.

* * * *

§ 8.08 Removal of Directors by Shareholders

(a) The shareholders may remove one or more directors with or without cause unless the articles of incorporation provide that directors may be removed only for cause.

(b) If a director is elected by a voting group of shareholders, only the shareholders of that voting group may participate in the vote to remove him.

(c) If cumulative voting is authorized, a director may not be removed if the number of votes sufficient to elect him under cumulative voting is voted against his removal. If cumulative voting is not authorized, a director may be removed only if the number of votes cast to remove him exceeds the number of votes cast not to remove him.

(d) A director may be removed by the shareholders only at a meeting called for the purpose of removing him and the meeting notice must state that the purpose, or one of the purposes, of the meeting is removal of the director.

* * * *

Subchapter B. Meetings and Action of the Board

§ 8.20 Meetings

(a) The board of directors may hold regular or special meetings in or out of this state.

(b) Unless the articles of incorporation or bylaws provide otherwise, the board of directors may permit any or all directors to participate in a regular or special meeting by, or conduct the meeting through the use of, any means of communication by which all directors participating may simultaneously hear each other during the meeting. A director participating in a meeting by this means is deemed to be present in person at the meeting.

* * * *

§ 8.22 Notice of Meeting

(a) Unless the articles of incorporation or bylaws provide otherwise, regular meetings of the board of directors may be held without notice of the date, time, place, or purpose of the meeting.

(b) Unless the articles of incorporation or bylaws provide for a longer or shorter period, special meetings of the board of directors must be preceded by at least two days' notice of the date, time, and place of the meeting. The notice need not describe the purpose of the special meeting unless required by the articles of incorporation or bylaws.

* * * *

§ 8.24 Quorum and Voting

(a) Unless the articles of incorporation or bylaws require a greater number, a quorum of a board of directors consists of:

(1) a majority of the fixed number of directors if the corporation has a fixed board size; or

(2) a majority of the number of directors prescribed, or if no number is prescribed the number in office immediately

before the meeting begins, if the corporation has a variable-range size board.

(b) The articles of incorporation or bylaws may authorize a quorum of a board of directors to consist of no fewer than one-third of the fixed or prescribed number of directors determined under subsection (a).

(c) If a quorum is present when a vote is taken, the affirmative vote of a majority of directors present is the act of the board of directors unless the articles of incorporation or bylaws require the vote of a greater number of directors.

(d) A director who is present at a meeting of the board of directors or a committee of the board of directors when corporate action is taken is deemed to have assented to the action taken unless: (1) he objects at the beginning of the meeting (or promptly upon his arrival) to holding it or transacting business at the meeting; (2) his dissent or abstention from the action taken is entered in the minutes of the meeting; or (3) he delivers written notice of his dissent or abstention to the presiding officer of the meeting before its adjournment or to the corporation immediately after adjournment of the meeting. The right of dissent or abstention is not available to a director who votes in favor of the action taken.

* * * *

Subchapter C. Standards of Conduct

§ 8.30 General Standards for Directors

(a) A director shall discharge his duties as a director, including his duties as a member of a committee:

(1) in good faith;

(2) with the care an ordinarily prudent person in a like position would exercise under similar circumstances; and

(3) in a manner he reasonably believes to be in the best interests of the corporation.

(b) In discharging his duties a director is entitled to rely on information, opinions, reports, or statements, including financial statements and other financial data, if prepared or presented by:

(1) one or more officers or employees of the corporation whom the director reasonably believes to be reliable and competent in the matters presented;

(2) legal counsel, public accountants, or other persons as to matters the director reasonably believes are within the person's professional or expert competence; or

(3) a committee of the board of directors of which he is not a member if the director reasonably believes the committee merits confidence.

(c) A director is not acting in good faith if he has knowledge concerning the matter in question that makes reliance otherwise permitted by subsection (b) unwarranted.

(d) A director is not liable for any action taken as a director, or any failure to take any action, if he performed the duties of his office in compliance with this section.

* * * *

Subchapter D. Officers

* * * *

§ 8.41 Duties of Officers

Each officer has the authority and shall perform the duties set forth in the bylaws or, to the extent consistent with the bylaws, the duties prescribed by the board of directors or by direction of an officer authorized by the board of directors to prescribe the duties of other officers.

§ 8.42 Standards of Conduct for Officers

(a) An officer with discretionary authority shall discharge his duties under that authority:

(1) in good faith;

(2) with the care an ordinarily prudent person in a like position would exercise under similar circumstances; and

(3) in a manner he reasonably believes to be in the best interests of the corporation.

(b) In discharging his duties an officer is entitled to rely on information, opinions, reports, or statements, including financial statements and other financial data, if prepared or presented by:

(1) one or more officers or employees of the corporation whom the officer reasonably believes to be reliable and competent in the matters presented; or

(2) legal counsel, public accountants, or other persons as to matters the officer reasonably believes are within the person's professional or expert competence.

(c) An officer is not acting in good faith if he has knowledge concerning the matter in question that makes reliance otherwise permitted by subsection (b) unwarranted.

(d) An officer is not liable for any action taken as an officer, or any failure to take any action, if he performed the duties of his office in compliance with this section.

* * * *

Chapter 11.
MERGER AND SHARE EXCHANGE

§ 11.01 Merger

(a) One or more corporations may merge into another corporation if the board of directors of each corporation adopts and its shareholders (if required * * *) approve a plan of merger.

(b) The plan of merger must set forth:

(1) the name of each corporation planning to merge and the name of the surviving corporation into which each other corporation plans to merge;

(2) the terms and conditions of the merger; and

(3) the manner and basis of converting the shares of each corporation into shares, obligations, or other securities of the surviving or any other corporation or into cash or other property in whole or part.

(c) The plan of merger may set forth:

(1) amendments to the articles of incorporation of the surviving corporation; and

(2) other provisions relating to the merger.

* * * *

§ 11.04 Merger of Subsidiary

(a) A parent corporation owning at least 90 percent of the outstanding shares of each class of a subsidiary corporation may merge the subsidiary into itself without approval of the shareholders of the parent or subsidiary.

(b) The board of directors of the parent shall adopt a plan of merger that sets forth:

(1) the names of the parent and subsidiary; and

(2) the manner and basis of converting the shares of the subsidiary into shares, obligations, or other securities of the parent or any other corporation or into cash or other property in whole or part.

(c) The parent shall mail a copy or summary of the plan of merger to each shareholder of the subsidiary who does not waive the mailing requirement in writing.

(d) The parent may not deliver articles of merger to the secretary of state for filing until at least 30 days after the date it mailed a copy of the plan of merger to each shareholder of the subsidiary who did not waive the mailing requirement.

(e) Articles of merger under this section may not contain amendments to the articles of incorporation of the parent corporation (except for amendments enumerated in section 10.02).

* * * *

§ 11.06 Effect of Merger or Share Exchange

(a) When a merger takes effect:

(1) every other corporation party to the merger merges into the surviving corporation and the separate existence of every corporation except the surviving corporation ceases;

(2) the title to all real estate and other property owned by each corporation party to the merger is vested in the surviving corporation without reversion or impairment;

(3) the surviving corporation has all liabilities of each corporation party to the merger;

(4) a proceeding pending against any corporation party to the merger may be continued as if the merger did not occur or the surviving corporation may be substituted in the proceeding for the corporation whose existence ceased;

(5) the articles of incorporation of the surviving corporation are amended to the extent provided in the plan of merger; and

(6) the shares of each corporation party to the merger that are to be converted into shares, obligations, or other securities of the surviving or any other corporation or into cash or other property are converted and the former holders of the shares are entitled only to the rights provided in the articles of merger or to their rights under chapter 13.

(b) When a share exchange takes effect, the shares of each acquired corporation are exchanged as provided in the plan, and the former holders of the shares are entitled only to the exchange rights provided in the articles of share exchange or to their rights under chapter 13.

* * * *

Chapter 13.
DISSENTERS' RIGHTS

Subchapter A. Right to Dissent and Obtain Payment for Shares

* * * *

§ 13.02 Right to Dissent

(a) A shareholder is entitled to dissent from, and obtain payment of the fair value of his shares in the event of, any of the following corporate actions:

(1) consummation of a plan of merger to which the corporation is a party (i) if shareholder approval is required for the merger by [statute] or the articles of incorporation and the shareholder is entitled to vote on the merger or (ii) if the corporation is a subsidiary that is merged with its parent under section 11.04;

(2) consummation of a plan of share exchange to which the corporation is a party as the corporation whose shares will be acquired, if the shareholder is entitled to vote on the plan;

(3) consummation of a sale or exchange of all, or substantially all, of the property of the corporation other than in the usual and regular course of business, if the shareholder is entitled to vote on the sale or exchange, including a sale in dissolution, but not including a sale pursuant to court order or a sale for cash pursuant to a plan by which all or substantially all of the net proceeds of the sale will be distributed to the shareholders within one year after the date of sale;

(4) an amendment of the articles of incorporation that materially and adversely affects rights in respect of a dissenter's shares because it:

(i) alters or abolishes a preferential right of the shares;

(ii) creates, alters, or abolishes a right in respect of redemption, including a provision respecting a sinking fund for the redemption or repurchase, of the shares;

(iii) alters or abolishes a preemptive right of the holder of the shares to acquire shares or other securities;

(iv) excludes or limits the right of the shares to vote on any matter, or to cumulate votes, other than a limitation by dilution through issuance of shares or other securities with similar voting rights; or

(v) reduces the number of shares owned by the shareholder to a fraction of a share if the fractional share so created is to be acquired for cash * * *; or

(5) any corporate action taken pursuant to a shareholder vote to the extent the articles of incorporation, bylaws, or a

resolution of the board of directors provides that voting or nonvoting shareholders are entitled to dissent and obtain payment for their shares.

(b) A shareholder entitled to dissent and obtain payment for his shares under this chapter may not challenge the corporate action creating his entitlement unless the action is unlawful or fraudulent with respect to the shareholder or the corporation.

* * * *

Subchapter B. Procedure for Exercise of Dissenters' Rights

* * * *

§ 13.21 Notice of Intent to Demand Payment

(a) If proposed corporate action creating dissenters' rights under section 13.02 is submitted to a vote at a shareholders' meeting, a shareholder who wishes to assert dissenters' rights (1) must deliver to the corporation before the vote is taken written notice of his intent to demand payment for his shares if the proposed action is effectuated and (2) must not vote his shares in favor of the proposed action.

(b) A shareholder who does not satisfy the requirements of subsection (a) is not entitled to payment for his shares under this chapter.

* * * *

§ 13.25 Payment

(a) * * * [A]s soon as the proposed corporate action is taken, or upon receipt of a payment demand, the corporation shall pay each dissenter * * * the amount the corporation estimates to be the fair value of his shares, plus accrued interest.

* * * *

§ 13.28 Procedure If Shareholder Dissatisfied with Payment or Offer

(a) A dissenter may notify the corporation in writing of his own estimate of the fair value of his shares and amount of interest due, and demand payment of his estimate (less any payment under section 13.25) * * * if:

(1) the dissenter believes that the amount paid under section 13.25 * * * is less than the fair value of his shares or that the interest due is incorrectly calculated;

(2) the corporation fails to make payment under section 13.25 within 60 days after the date set for demanding payment; or

(3) the corporation, having failed to take the proposed action, does not return the deposited certificates or release the transfer restrictions imposed on uncertificated shares within 60 days after the date set for demanding payment.

(b) A dissenter waives his right to demand payment under this section unless he notifies the corporation of his demand in writing under subsection (a) within 30 days after the corporation made or offered payment for his shares.

* * * *

Chapter 14. DISSOLUTION

Subchapter A. Voluntary Dissolution

* * * *

§ 14.02 Dissolution by Board of Directors and Shareholders

(a) A corporation's board of directors may propose dissolution for submission to the shareholders.

(b) For a proposal to dissolve to be adopted:

(1) the board of directors must recommend dissolution to the shareholders unless the board of directors determines that because of conflict of interest or other special circumstances it should make no recommendation and communicates the basis for its determination to the shareholders; and

(2) the shareholders entitled to vote must approve the proposal to dissolve as provided in subsection (e).

(c) The board of directors may condition its submission of the proposal for dissolution on any basis.

(d) The corporation shall notify each shareholder, whether or not entitled to vote, of the proposed shareholders' meeting in accordance with section 7.05. The notice must also state that the purpose, or one of the purposes, of the meeting is to consider dissolving the corporation.

(e) Unless the articles of incorporation or the board of directors (acting pursuant to subsection (c)) require a greater vote or a vote by voting groups, the proposal to dissolve to be adopted must be approved by a majority of all the votes entitled to be cast on that proposal.

* * * *

§ 14.05 Effect of Dissolution

(a) A dissolved corporation continues its corporate existence but may not carry on any business except that appropriate to wind up and liquidate its business and affairs, including:

(1) collecting its assets;

(2) disposing of its properties that will not be distributed in kind to its shareholders;

(3) discharging or making provision for discharging its liabilities;

(4) distributing its remaining property among its shareholders according to their interests; and

(5) doing every other act necessary to wind up and liquidate its business and affairs.

(b) Dissolution of a corporation does not:

(1) transfer title to the corporation's property;

(2) prevent transfer of its shares or securities, although the authorization to dissolve may provide for closing the corporation's share transfer records;

(3) subject its directors or officers to standards of conduct different from those prescribed in chapter 8;

(4) change quorum or voting requirements for its board of directors or shareholders; change provisions for selection, resignation, or removal of its directors or officers or both; or change provisions for amending its bylaws;

(5) prevent commencement of a proceeding by or against the corporation in its corporate name;

(6) abate or suspend a proceeding pending by or against the corporation on the effective date of dissolution; or

(7) terminate the authority of the registered agent of the corporation.

* * * *

Subchapter C. Judicial Dissolution

§ 14.30 Grounds for Judicial Dissolution

The [name or describe court or courts] may dissolve a corporation:

(1) in a proceeding by the attorney general if it is established that:

(i) the corporation obtained its articles of incorporation through fraud; or

(ii) the corporation has continued to exceed or abuse the authority conferred upon it by law;

(2) in a proceeding by a shareholder if it is established that:

(i) the directors are deadlocked in the management of the corporate affairs, the shareholders are unable to break the deadlock, and irreparable injury to the corporation is threatened or being suffered, or the business and affairs of the corporation can no longer be conducted to the advantage of the shareholders generally, because of the deadlock;

(ii) the directors or those in control of the corporation have acted, are acting, or will act in a manner that is illegal, oppressive, or fraudulent;

(iii) the shareholders are deadlocked in voting power and have failed, for a period that includes at least two consecutive annual meeting dates, to elect successors to directors whose terms have expired; or

(iv) the corporate assets are being misapplied or wasted;

(3) in a proceeding by a creditor if it is established that:

(i) the creditor's claim has been reduced to judgment, the execution on the judgment returned unsatisfied, and the corporation is insolvent; or

(ii) the corporation has admitted in writing that the creditor's claim is due and owing and the corporation is insolvent; or

(4) in a proceeding by the corporation to have its voluntary dissolution continued under court supervision.

* * * *

Chapter 16. RECORDS AND REPORTS

Subchapter A. Records

§ 16.01 Corporate Records

(a) A corporation shall keep as permanent records minutes of all meetings of its shareholders and board of directors, a record of all actions taken by the shareholders or board of directors without a meeting, and a record of all actions taken by a committee of the board of directors in place of the board of directors on behalf of the corporation.

(b) A corporation shall maintain appropriate accounting records.

(c) A corporation or its agent shall maintain a record of its shareholders, in a form that permits preparation of a list of the names and addresses of all shareholders, in alphabetical order by class of shares showing the number and class of shares held by each.

(d) A corporation shall maintain its records in written form or in another form capable of conversion into written form within a reasonable time.

(e) A corporation shall keep a copy of the following records at its principal office:

(1) its articles or restated articles of incorporation and all amendments to them currently in effect;

(2) its bylaws or restated bylaws and all amendments to them currently in effect;

(3) resolutions adopted by its board of directors creating one or more classes or series of shares, and fixing their relative rights, preferences, and limitations, if shares issued pursuant to those resolutions are outstanding;

(4) the minutes of all shareholders' meetings, and records of all action taken by shareholders without a meeting, for the past three years;

(5) all written communications to shareholders generally within the past three years, including the financial statements furnished for the past three years * * *;

(6) a list of the names and business addresses of its current directors and officers; and

(7) its most recent annual report delivered to the secretary of state * * *.

§ 16.02 Inspection of Records by Shareholders

(a) Subject to section 16.03(c), a shareholder of a corporation is entitled to inspect and copy, during regular business hours at the corporation's principal office, any of the records of the corporation described in section 16.01(e) if he gives the corporation written notice of his demand at least five business days before the date on which he wishes to inspect and copy.

(b) A shareholder of a corporation is entitled to inspect and copy, during regular business hours at a reasonable location specified by the corporation, any of the following records of the corporation if the shareholder meets the requirements of subsection (c) and gives the corporation written notice of his demand at least five business days before the date on which he wishes to inspect and copy:

(1) excerpts from minutes of any meeting of the board of directors, records of any action of a committee of the board of directors while acting in place of the board of directors on behalf of the corporation, minutes of any meeting of the shareholders, and records of action taken by the shareholders or board of directors without a meeting, to the extent not subject to inspection under section 16.02(a);

(2) accounting records of the corporation; and

(3) the record of shareholders.

(c) A shareholder may inspect and copy the records identified in subsection (b) only if:

(1) his demand is made in good faith and for a proper purpose;

(2) he describes with reasonable particularity his purpose and the records he desires to inspect; and

(3) the records are directly connected with his purpose.

(d) The right of inspection granted by this section may not be abolished or limited by a corporation's articles of incorporation or bylaws.

(e) This section does not affect:

(1) the right of a shareholder to inspect records under section 7.20 or, if the shareholder is in litigation with the corporation, to the same extent as any other litigant;

(2) the power of a court, independently of this Act, to compel the production of corporate records for examination.

(f) For purposes of this section, "shareholder" includes a beneficial owner whose shares are held in a voting trust or by a nominee on his behalf.

APPENDIX E The Uniform Limited Liability Company Act (Excerpts)

[ARTICLE] 2. ORGANIZATION

Section 201. Limited liability company as legal entity.

A limited liability company is a legal entity distinct from its members.

Section 202. Organization.

(a) One or more persons may organize a limited liability company, consisting of one or more members, by delivering articles of organization to the office of the [Secretary of State] for filing.

(b) Unless a delayed effective date is specified, the existence of a limited liability company begins when the articles of organization are filed.

(c) The filing of the articles of organization by the [Secretary of State] is conclusive proof that the organizers satisfied all conditions precedent to the creation of a limited liability company.

Section 203. Articles of organization.

(a) Articles of organization of a limited liability company must set forth:

(1) the name of the company;

(2) the address of the initial designated office;

(3) the name and street address of the initial agent for service of process;

(4) the name and address of each organizer;

(5) whether the company is to be a term company and, if so, the term specified;

(6) whether the company is to be manager-managed, and, if so, the name and address of each initial manager; and

(7) whether one or more of the members of the company are to be liable for its debts and obligations under Section 303(c).

(b) Articles of organization of a limited liability company may set forth:

(1) provisions permitted to be set forth in an operating agreement; or

(2) other matters not inconsistent with law.

(c) Articles of organization of a limited liability company may not vary the nonwaivable provisions of Section 103(b). As to all other matters, if any provision of an operating agreement is inconsistent with the articles of organization:

(1) the operating agreement controls as to managers, members, and members' transferees; and

(2) the articles of organization control as to persons, other than managers, members and their transferees, who reasonably rely on the articles to their detriment.

* * * *

Section 208. Certificate of existence or authorization.

(a) A person may request the [Secretary of State] to furnish a certificate of existence for a limited liability company or a certificate of authorization for a foreign limited liability company.

(b) A certificate of existence for a limited liability company must set forth:

(1) the company's name;

(2) that it is duly organized under the laws of this State, the date of organization, whether its duration is at-will or for a specified term, and, if the latter, the period specified;

(3) if payment is reflected in the records of the [Secretary of State] and if nonpayment affects the existence of the company, that all fees, taxes, and penalties owed to this State have been paid;

(4) whether its most recent annual report required by Section 211 has been filed with the [Secretary of State];

(5) that articles of termination have not been filed; and

(6) other facts of record in the office of the [Secretary of State] which may be requested by the applicant.

(c) A certificate of authorization for a foreign limited liability company must set forth:

(1) the company's name used in this State;

(2) that it is authorized to transact business in this State;

(3) if payment is reflected in the records of the [Secretary of State] and if nonpayment affects the authorization of the company, that all fees, taxes, and penalties owed to this State have been paid;

(4) whether its most recent annual report required by Section 211 has been filed with the [Secretary of State];

(5) that a certificate of cancellation has not been filed; and

(6) other facts of record in the office of the [Secretary of State] which may be requested by the applicant.

(d) Subject to any qualification stated in the certificate, a certificate of existence or authorization issued by the [Secretary of State] may be relied upon as conclusive evidence that the domestic or foreign limited liability company is in existence or is authorized to transact business in this State.

* * * *

[ARTICLE] 3. RELATIONS OF MEMBERS AND MANAGERS TO PERSONS DEALING WITH LIMITED LIABILITY COMPANY

* * * *

Section 303. Liability of members and managers.

(a) Except as otherwise provided in subsection (c), the debts, obligations, and liabilities of a limited liability company, whether arising in contract, tort, or otherwise, are solely the debts, obligations, and liabilities of the company. A member or manager is not personally liable for a debt, obligation, or liability of the company solely by reason of being or acting as a member or manager.

(b) The failure of a limited liability company to observe the usual company formalities or requirements relating to the exercise of its company powers or management of its business is not a ground for imposing personal liability on the members or managers for liabilities of the company.

(c) All or specified members of a limited liability company are liable in their capacity as members for all or specified debts, obligations, or liabilities of the company if:

(1) a provision to that effect is contained in the articles of organization; and

(2) a member so liable has consented in writing to the adoption of the provision or to be bound by the provision.

* * * *

[ARTICLE] 4. RELATIONS OF MEMBERS TO EACH OTHER AND TO LIMITED LIABILITY COMPANY

* * * *

Section 404. Management of limited liability company.

(a) In a member-managed company:

(1) each member has equal rights in the management and conduct of the company's business; and

(2) except as otherwise provided in subsection (c) or in Section 801(b)(3)(i), any matter relating to the business of the company may be decided by a majority of the members.

(b) In a manager-managed company:

(1) each manager has equal rights in the management and conduct of the company's business;

(2) except as otherwise provided in subsection (c) or in Section 801(b)(3)(i), any matter relating to the business of the company may be exclusively decided by the manager or, if there is more than one manager, by a majority of the managers; and

(3) a manager:

(i) must be designated, appointed, elected, removed, or replaced by a vote, approval, or consent of a majority of the members; and

(ii) holds office until a successor has been elected and qualified, unless the manager sooner resigns or is removed.

(c) The only matters of a member or manager-managed company's business requiring the consent of all of the members are:

(1) the amendment of the operating agreement under Section 103;

(2) the authorization or ratification of acts or transactions under Section 103(b)(2)(ii) which would otherwise violate the duty of loyalty;

(3) an amendment to the articles of organization under Section 204;

(4) the compromise of an obligation to make a contribution under Section 402(b);

(5) the compromise, as among members, of an obligation of a member to make a contribution or return money or other property paid or distributed in violation of this [Act];

(6) the making of interim distributions under Section 405(a), including the redemption of an interest;

(7) the admission of a new member;

(8) the use of the company's property to redeem an interest subject to a charging order;

(9) the consent to dissolve the company under Section 801(b)(2);

(10) a waiver of the right to have the company's business wound up and the company terminated under Section 802(b);

(11) the consent of members to merge with another entity under Section 904(c)(1); and

(12) the sale, lease, exchange, or other disposal of all, or substantially all, of the company's property with or without goodwill.

(d) Action requiring the consent of members or managers under this [Act] may be taken without a meeting.

(e) A member or manager may appoint a proxy to vote or otherwise act for the member or manager by signing an appointment instrument, either personally or by the member's or manager's attorney-in-fact.

* * * *

APPENDIX F Restatement (Second) of Torts (Excerpts)

Section 402 A. Special liability of seller of product for physical harm to user or consumer.

(1) One who sells any product in a defective condition unreasonably dangerous to the consumer or to his property is subject to liability for physical harm thereby caused to the ultimate user or consumer, or to his property, if

(a) the seller is engaged in the business of selling such a product, and

(b) it is expected to and does reach the user or consumer without substantial change in the condition in which it is sold.

(2) The rule stated in Subsection (1) applies although

(a) the seller has exercised all possible care in the preparation and sale of his product, and

(b) the user or consumer has not bought the product from or entered into any contractual relation with the seller.

Section 402 B. Misrepresentation by seller of chattels to consumer.

One engaged in the business of selling chattels who, by advertising, labels, or otherwise, makes to the public a misrepresentation of a material fact concerning the character or quality of a chattel sold by him is subject to liability for physical harm to a consumer of the chattel caused by justifiable reliance upon the misrepresentation, even though

(a) it is not made fraudulently or negligently, and

(b) the consumer has not bought the chattel from or entered into any contractual relations with the seller.

APPENDIX G Restatement (Third) of Torts: Products Liability (Excerpts)

Section 2. CATEGORIES OF PRODUCT DEFECT

A product is defective when, at the time of sale or distribution, it contains a manufacturing defect, is defective in design, or is defective because of inadequate instructions or warnings. A product:

(a) contains a manufacturing defect when the product departs from its intended design even though all possible care was exercised in the preparation and marketing of the product;

(b) is defective in design when the foreseeable risks of harm posed by the product could have been reduced or avoided by the adoption of a reasonable alternative design by the seller or other distributor, or a predecessor in the commercial chain of distribution, and the omission of the alternative design renders the product not reasonably safe;

(c) is defective because of inadequate instructions or warnings when the foreseeable risks of harm posed by the product could have been reduced or avoided by the provision of reasonable instructions or warnings by the seller or other distributor, or a predecessor in the commercial chain of distribution, and the omission of the instructions or warnings renders the product not reasonably safe.

* * * *

Section 10. LIABILITY OF COMMERCIAL PRODUCT SELLER OR DISTRIBUTOR FOR HARM CAUSED BY POST-SALE FAILURE TO WARN

(a) One engaged in the business of selling or otherwise distributing products is subject to liability for harm to persons or property caused by the seller's failure to provide a warning after the time of sale or distribution of a product if a reasonable person in the seller's position would provide such a warning.

(b) A reasonable person in the seller's position would provide a warning after the time of sale if:

(1) the seller knows or reasonably should know that the product poses a substantial risk of harm to persons or property; and

(2) those to whom a warning might be provided can be identified and can reasonably be assumed to be unaware of the risk of harm; and

(3) a warning can be effectively communicated to and acted on by those to whom a warning might be provided; and

(4) the risk of harm is sufficiently great to justify the burden of providing a warning.

* * * *

Section 17. APPORTIONMENT OF RESPONSIBILITY BETWEEN OR AMONG PLAINTIFF, SELLERS AND DISTRIBUTORS OF DEFECTIVE PRODUCTS, AND OTHERS

(a) A plaintiff's recovery of damages for harm caused by a product defect may be reduced if the conduct of the plaintiff combines with the product defect to cause the harm and the plaintiff's conduct fails to conform to generally applicable rules establishing appropriate standards of care.

(b) The manner and extent of the reduction under Subsection (a) and the apportionment of plaintiff's recovery among multiple defendants are governed by generally applicable rules apportioning responsibility.

APPENDIX H

Sherman Antitrust Act of 1890 (Excerpts)

Section. 1 Every contract, combination in the form of trust or otherwise, or conspiracy, in restraint of trade or commerce among the several States, or with foreign nations, is hereby declared to be illegal. Every person who shall make any such contract or engage in any such combination or conspiracy shall be deemed guilty of a felony, and, on conviction thereof, shall be punished by fine not exceeding one million dollars if a corporation, or, if any other person, one hundred thousand dollars or by imprisonment not exceeding three years, or by both said punishments in the discretion of the court.

Section 2. Every person who shall monopolize, or attempt to monopolize, or conspire with any other person or persons, to monopolize any part of the trade or commerce among the several States, or with foreign nations, shall be deemed guilty of a felony, and, on conviction thereof, shall be punished by fine not exceeding one million dollars if a corporation, or, if any other person, one hundred thousand dollars or by imprisonment not exceeding three years, or by both said punishments, in the discretion of the court.

APPENDIX I Securities Act of 1933 (Excerpts)

Definitions

Section 2. When used in this title, unless the context requires—

(1) The term "security" means any note, stock, treasury stock, bond, debenture, evidence of indebtedness, certificate of interest or participation in any profit-sharing agreement, collateral-trust certificate, preorganization certificate or subscription, transferable share, investment contract, voting-trust certificate, certificate of deposit for a security, fractional undivided interest in oil, gas, or other mineral rights, any put, call, straddle, option, or privilege on any security, certificate of deposit, or group or index of securities (including any interest therein or based on the value thereof), or any put, call, straddle, option, or privilege entered into on a national securities exchange relating to foreign currency, or, in general, any interest or participation in, temporary or interim certificate for, receipt for, guarantee of, or warrant or right to subscribe to or purchase, any of the foregoing.

Exempted Securities

Section 3. (a) Except as hereinafter expressly provided the provisions of this title shall not apply to any of the following classes of securities:

* * * *

(2) Any security issued or guaranteed by the United States or any territory thereof, or by the District of Columbia, or by any State of the United States, or by any political subdivision of a State or Territory, or by any public instrumentality of one or more States or Territories, or by any person controlled or supervised by and acting as an instrumentality of the Government of the United States pursuant to authority granted by the Congress of the United States; or any certificate of deposit for any of the foregoing; or any security issued or guaranteed by any bank; or any security issued by or representing an interest in or a direct obligation of a Federal Reserve Bank. * * *

(3) Any note, draft, bill of exchange, or banker's acceptance which arises out of a current transaction or the proceeds of which have been or are to be used for current transactions, and which has a maturity at the time of issuance of not exceeding nine months, exclusive of days of grace, or any renewal thereof the maturity of which is likewise limited;

(4) Any security issued by a person organized and operated exclusively for religious, educational, benevolent, fraternal, charitable, or reformatory purposes and not for pecuniary profit, and no part of the net earnings of which inures to the benefit of any person, private stockholder, or individual;

* * * *

(11) Any security which is a part of an issue offered and sold only to persons resident within a single State or Territory, where the issuer of such security is a person resident and doing business within, or, if a corporation, incorporated by and doing business within, such State or Territory.

(b) The Commission may from time to time by its rules and regulations and subject to such terms and conditions as may be described therein, add any class of securities to the securities exempted as provided in this section, if it finds that the enforcement of this title with respect to such securities is not necessary in the public interest and for the protection of investors by reason of the small amount involved or the limited character of the public offering; but no issue of securities shall be exempted under this subsection where the aggregate amount at which such issue is offered to the public exceeds $5,000,000.

Exempted Transactions

Section 4. The provisions of section 5 shall not apply to—

(1) transactions by any person other than an issuer, underwriter, or dealer.

(2) transactions by an issuer not involving any public offering.

(3) transactions by a dealer (including an underwriter no longer acting as an underwriter in respect of the security involved in such transactions), except—

(A) transactions taking place prior to the expiration of forty days after the first date upon which the security was bona fide offered to the public by the issuer or by or through an underwriter.

(B) transactions in a security as to which a registration statement has been filed taking place prior to the expiration of forty days after the effective date of such registration statement or prior to the expiration of forty days after the first date upon which the security was bona fide offered to the public by the issuer or by or through an underwriter after such effective date, whichever is later (excluding in the computation of such forty days any time during which a stop order issued under section 8 is in effect as to the security), or such shorter period as the Commission may specify by rules and regulations or order, and

(C) transactions as to the securities constituting the whole or a part of an unsold allotment to or subscription by such dealer as a participant in the distribution of such securities by the issuer or by or through an underwriter.

With respect to transactions referred to in clause (B), if securities of the issuer have not previously been sold pursuant to an earlier effective registration statement the applicable period, instead of forty days, shall be ninety days, or such shorter period as the Commission may specify by rules and regulations or order.

(4) brokers' transactions, executed upon customers' orders on any exchange or in the over-the-counter market but not the solicitation of such orders.

* * * *

(6) transactions involving offers or sales by an issuer solely to one or more accredited investors, if the aggregate offering price of an issue of securities offered in reliance on this paragraph does not exceed the amount allowed under Section 3(b) of this title, if there is no advertising or public solicitation in connection with the transaction by the issuer or anyone acting on the issuer's behalf, and if the issuer files such notice with the Commission as the Commission shall prescribe.

Prohibitions Relating to Interstate Commerce and the Mails

Section 5. (a) Unless a registration statement is in effect as to a security, it shall be unlawful for any person, directly or indirectly—

(1) to make use of any means or instruments of transportation or communication in interstate commerce or of the mails to sell such security through the use or medium of any prospectus or otherwise; or

(2) to carry or cause to be carried through the mails or in interstate commerce, by any means or instruments of transportation, any such security for the purpose of sale or for delivery after sale.

(b) It shall be unlawful for any person, directly or indirectly—

(1) to make use of any means or instruments of transportation or communication in interstate commerce or of the mails to carry or transmit any prospectus relating to any security with respect to which a registration statement has been filed under this title, unless such prospectus meets the requirements of section 10, or

(2) to carry or to cause to be carried through the mails or in interstate commerce any such security for the purpose of sale or for delivery after sale, unless accompanied or preceded by a prospectus that meets the requirements of subsection (a) of section 10.

(c) It shall be unlawful for any person, directly, or indirectly, to make use of any means or instruments of transportation or communication in interstate commerce or of the mails to offer to sell or offer to buy through the use or medium of any prospectus or otherwise any security, unless a registration statement has been filed as to such security, or while the registration statement is the subject of a refusal order or stop order or (prior to the effective date of the registration statement) any public proceeding of examination under section 8.

APPENDIX J Securities Exchange Act of 1934 (Excerpts)

Definitions and Application of Title

Section 3. (a) When used in this title, unless the context otherwise requires—

* * * *

(4) The term "broker" means any person engaged in the business of effecting transactions in securities for the account of others, but does not include a bank.

(5) The term "dealer" means any person engaged in the business of buying and selling securities for his own account, through a broker or otherwise, but does not include a bank, or any person insofar as he buys or sells securities for his own account, either individually or in some fiduciary capacity, but not as part of a regular business.

* * * *

(7) The term "director" means any director of a corporation or any person performing similar functions with respect to any organization, whether incorporated or unincorporated.

(8) The term "issuer" means any person who issues or proposes to issue any security; except that with respect to certificates of deposit for securities, voting-trust certificates, or collateral-trust certificates, or with respect to certificates of interest or shares in an unincorporated investment trust not having a board of directors or the fixed, restricted management, or unit type, the term "issuer" means the person or persons performing the acts and assuming the duties of depositor or manager pursuant to the provisions of the trust or other agreement or instrument under which such securities are issued; and except that with respect to equipment-trust certificates or like securities, the term "issuer" means the person by whom the equipment or property is, or is to be, used.

(9) The term "person" means a natural person, company, government, or political subdivision, agency, or instrumentality of a government.

Regulation of the Use of Manipulative and Deceptive Devices

Section 10. It shall be unlawful for any person, directly or indirectly, by the use of any means or instrumentality of interstate commerce or of the mails, or of any facility of any national securities exchange—

(a) To effect a short sale, or to use or employ any stop-loss order in connection with the purchase or sale, of any security registered on a national securities exchange, in contravention of such rules and regulations as the Commission may prescribe as necessary or appropriate in the public interest or for the protection of investors.

(b) To use or employ, in connection with the purchase or sale of any security registered on a national securities exchange or any security not so registered, any manipulative or deceptive device or contrivance in contravention of such rules and regulations as the Commission may prescribe as necessary or appropriate in the public interest or for the protection of investors.

APPENDIX K Title VII of the Civil Rights Act of 1964 (Excerpts)

Section 703. Unlawful Employment Practices. (a) It shall be an unlawful employment practice for an employer—

(1) to fail or refuse to hire or to discharge any individual, or otherwise to discriminate against any individual with respect to his compensation, terms, conditions, or privileges of employment, because of such individual's race, color, religion, sex, or national origin; or

(2) to limit, segregate, or classify his employees or applicants for employment in any way which would deprive or tend to deprive any individual of employment opportunities or otherwise adversely affect his status as an employee, because of such individual's race, color, religion, sex, or national origin.

(b) It shall be an unlawful employment practice for an employment agency to fail or refuse to refer for employment, or otherwise to discriminate against, any individual because of his race, color, religion, sex, or national origin, or to classify or refer for employment any individual on the basis or his race, color, religion, sex, or national origin.

(c) It shall be an unlawful employment practice for a labor organization—

(1) to exclude or to expel from its membership, or otherwise to discriminate against, any individual because of his race, color, religion, sex, or national origin;

(2) to limit, segregate, or classify its membership or applicants for membership, or to classify or fail or refuse to refer for employment any individual, in any way which would deprive or tend to deprive any individual of employment opportunities, or would limit such employment opportunities or otherwise adversely affect his status as an employee or as an applicant for employment, because of such individual's race, color, religion, sex, or national origin; or

(3) to cause or attempt to cause an employer to discriminate against an individual in violation of this section.

(d) It shall be an unlawful employment practice for any employer, labor organization, or joint labor-management committee controlling apprenticeship or other training or retraining, including on-the-job training programs to discriminate against any individual because of his race, color, religion, sex, or national origin in admission to, or employment in, any program established to provide apprenticeship or other training.

(e) Notwithstanding any other provision of this subchapter—

(1) it shall not be an unlawful employment practice for an employer to hire and employ employees, for an employment agency to classify, or refer for employment any individual, for a labor organization to classify its membership or to classify or refer for employment any individual, or for an employer, labor organization, or joint labor-management committee controlling apprenticeship or other training or retraining programs to admit or employ any individual in any such program, on the basis of his religion, sex, or national origin in those certain instances where religion, sex, or national origin is a bona fide occupational qualification reasonably necessary to the normal operation of that particular business or enterprise, and

(2) it shall not be an unlawful employment practice for a school, college, university, or other educational institution or institution of learning to hire and employ employees of a particular religion if such school, college, university, or other educational institution or institution of learning is, in whole or in substantial part, owned, supported, controlled, or managed by a particular religion or by a particular religious corporation, association, or society, or if the curriculum of such school, college, university, or other educational institution or institution of learning is directed toward the propagation of a particular religion.

(f) As used in this subchapter, the phrase "unlawful employment practice" shall not be deemed to include any action or measure taken by an employer, labor organization, joint labor-management committee, or employment agency with respect to an individual who is a member of the Communist Party of the United States or of any other organization required to register as a Communist-action or Communist-front organization. * * *

(g) Notwithstanding any other provision of this subchapter, it shall not be an unlawful employment practice for an employer to fail or refuse to hire and employ any individual for any position, for an employer to discharge any individual from any position, or for an employment agency to fail or refuse to refer any individual for employment in any position, or for a labor organization to fail or refuse to refer any individual for employment in any position, if—

(1) the occupancy of such position, or access to the premises in or upon which any part of the duties of such position is performed or is to be performed, is subject to any requirement

imposed in the interest of the national security of the United States * * * and

(2) such individual has not fulfilled or has ceased to fulfill that requirement.

(h) Notwithstanding any other provision of this subchapter, it shall not be an unlawful employment practice for an employer to apply different standards of compensation, or different terms, conditions, or privileges of employment pursuant to a bona fide seniority or merit system, or a system which measures earnings by quantity or quality of production or to employees who work in different locations, provided that such differences are not the result of an intention to discriminate because of race, color, religion, sex, or national origin, nor shall it be an unlawful employment practice for an employer to give and act upon the results of any professionally developed ability test provided that such test, its administration or action upon the results is not designed, intended or used to discriminate because of race, color, religion, sex, or national origin. * * *

(j) Nothing contained in this subchapter shall be interpreted to require any employer, employment agency, labor organization, or joint labor-management committee subject to this subchapter to grant preferential treatment to any individual or to any group because of the race, color, religion, sex, or national origin of such individual or group on account of an imbalance which may exist with respect to the total number or percentage of persons of any race, color, religion, sex, or national origin employed by any employer, referred or classified for employment by any employment agency or labor organization, or admitted to, or employed in, any apprenticeship or other training program, in comparison with the total number or percentage of persons of such race, color, religion, sex, or national origin in any community, State, section, or other area, or in the available work force in any community, State, section, or other area.

* * * *

Section 704. Other Unlawful Employment Practices. (a) It shall be an unlawful employment practice for an employer to discriminate against any of his employees or applicants for employment, for an employment agency, or joint labor-management committee controlling apprenticeship or other training or retraining, including on-the-job training programs, to discriminate against any individual, or for a labor organization to discriminate against any member thereof or applicant for membership, because he has opposed any practice made an unlawful employment practice by this subchapter, or because he has made a charge, testified, assisted, or participated in any manner in an investigation, proceeding, or hearing under this subchapter.

(b) It shall be an unlawful employment practice for an employer, labor organization, employment agency, or joint labor-management committee controlling apprenticeship or other training or retraining, including on-the-job training programs, to print or publish or cause to be printed or published any notice or advertisement relating to employment by such an employer or membership or any classification or referral for employment by such a labor organization, or relating to any classification or referral for employment by such an employment agency, or relating to admission to, or employment in, any program established to provide apprenticeship or other training by such a joint-labor-management committee, indicating any preference, limitation, specification, or discrimination, based on race, color, religion, sex, or national origin, except that such a notice or advertisement may indicate a preference, limitation, specification, or discrimination based on religion, sex or national origin when religion, sex, or national origin is a bona fide occupational qualification for employment.

APPENDIX L Americans with Disabilities Act of 1990 (Excerpts)

Title I—EMPLOYMENT

Sec. 101. Definitions.

As used in this title: * * *

(8) **Qualified individual with a disability.**—The term "qualified individual with a disability" means an individual with a disability who, with or without reasonable accommodation, can perform the essential functions of the employment position that such individual holds or desires. For the purposes of this title, consideration shall be given to the employer's judgment as to what functions of a job are essential, and if an employer has prepared a written description before advertising or interviewing applicants for the job, this description shall be considered evidence of the essential functions of the job.

(9) **Reasonable accommodation.**—The term "reasonable accommodation" may include—

(A) making existing facilities used by employees readily accessible to and usable by individuals with disabilities; and

(B) job restructuring, part-time or modified work schedules, reassignment to a vacant position, acquisition or modification of equipment or devices, appropriate adjustment or modifications of examinations, training materials or policies, the provision of qualified readers or interpreters, and other similar accommodations for individuals with disabilities.

(10) **Undue Hardship.**—

(A) **In general.**—The term "undue hardship" means an action requiring significant difficulty or expense, when considered in light of the factors set forth in subparagraph (B).

(B) **Factors to be considered.**—In determining whether an accommodation would impose an undue hardship on a covered entity, factors to be considered include—

(i) the nature and cost of accommodation needed under this Act;

(ii) the overall financial resources of the facility or facilities involved in the provision of the reasonable accommodation; the number of persons employed at such facility; the effect on expenses and resources, or the impact otherwise of such accommodation upon the operation of the facility;

(iii) the overall financial resources of the covered entity; the overall size of the business of a covered entity with respect to the number of its employees; the number, type, and location of its facilities; and

(iv) the type of operation or operations of the covered entity, including the composition, structure, and functions of the workforce of such entity; the geographic separateness, administrative, or fiscal relationship of the facility or facilities in question to the covered entity.

Sec. 102. Discrimination.

(a) **General Rule.**—No covered entity shall discriminate against a qualified individual with a disability because of the disability of such individual in regard to job application procedures, the hiring, advancement, or discharge of employees, employee compensation, job training, and other terms, conditions, and privileges of employment.

(b) **Construction.**—As used in subsection (a), the term "discriminate" includes—

(1) limiting, segregating, or classifying a job applicant or employee in a way that adversely affects the opportunities or status of such applicant or employee because of the disability of such applicant or employee;

(2) participating in a contractual or other arrangement or relationship that has the effect of subjecting a covered entity's qualified applicant or employee with a disability to the discrimination prohibited by this title (such relationship includes a relationship with an employment or referral agency, labor union, an organization providing fringe benefits to an employee of the covered entity, or an organization providing training and apprenticeship programs);

(3) utilizing standards, criteria, or methods of administration—

(A) that have the effect of discrimination on the basis of disability; or

(B) that perpetuate the discrimination of others who are subject to common administrative control;

(4) excluding or otherwise denying equal jobs or benefits to a qualified individual because of the known disability of an individual with whom the qualified individual is known to have a relationship or association;

(5)

(A) not making reasonable accommodations to the known physical or mental limitations of an otherwise qualified individual with a disability who is an applicant or employee, unless such covered entity can demonstrate that the accommodation would impose an undue hardship on the operation of the business of such covered entity; or

(B) denying employment opportunities to a job applicant or employee who is an otherwise qualified individual with a disability, if such denial is based on the need of such covered entity to make reasonable accommodation to the physical or mental impairments of the employee or applicant;

(6) using qualification standards, employment tests or other selection criteria that screen out or tend to screen out an individual with a disability or a class of individuals with disabilities unless the standard, test or other selection criteria, as used by the covered entity, is shown to be job-related for the position in question and is consistent with business necessity; and

(7) failing to select and administer tests concerning employment in the most effective manner to ensure that, when such test is administered to a job applicant or employee who has a disability that impairs sensory, manual, or speaking skills, such test results accurately reflect the skills, aptitude, or whatever other factor of such applicant or employee that such test purports to measure, rather than reflecting the impaired sensory, manual, or speaking skills of such employee or applicant (except where such skills are the factors that the test purports to measure). * * *

Sec. 104. Illegal Use of Drugs and Alcohol. * * *

(b) **Rules of Construction.**—Nothing in subsection (a) shall be construed to exclude as a qualified individual with a disability an individual who—

(1) has successfully completed a supervised drug rehabilitation program and is no longer engaging in the illegal use of drugs, or has otherwise been rehabilitated successfully and is no longer engaging in such use;

(2) is participating in a supervised rehabilitation program and is no longer engaging in such use; or

(3) is erroneously regarded as engaging in such use, but is not engaging in such use; except that it shall not be a violation of this Act for a covered entity to adopt or administer reasonable policies or procedures, including but not limited to drug testing, designed to ensure that an individual described in paragraph (1) or (2) is no longer engaging in the illegal use of drugs. * * *

Sec. 107. Enforcement.

(a) **Powers, Remedies, and Procedures.**—The powers, remedies, and procedures set forth in sections 705, 706, 707, 709, and 710 of the Civil Rights Act of 1964 (42 U.S.C. 2000e-4, 2000e-5, 2000e-6, 2000e-8, and 2000e-9) shall be the powers, remedies, and procedures this title provides to the Commission, to the Attorney General, or to any person alleging discrimination on the basis of disability in violation of any provision of this Act, or regulations promulgated under section 106, concerning employment.

(b) **Coordination.**—The agencies with enforcement authority for actions which allege employment discrimination under this title and under the Rehabilitation Act of 1973 shall develop procedures to ensure that administrative complaints filed under this title and under the Rehabilitation Act of 1973 are dealt with in a manner that avoids duplication of effort and prevents imposition of inconsistent or conflicting standards for the same requirements under this title and the Rehabilitation Act of 1973. The Commission, the Attorney General, and the Office of Federal Contract Compliance Programs shall establish such coordinating mechanisms (similar to provisions contained in the joint regulations promulgated by the Commission and the Attorney General at part 42 of title 28 and part 1691 of title 29, Code of Federal Regulations, and the Memorandum of Understanding between the Commission and the Office of Federal Contract Compliance Programs dated January 16, 1981 (46 Fed. Reg. 7435, January 23, 1981)) in regulations implementing this title and Rehabilitation Act of 1973 not later than 18 months after the date of enactment of this Act.

Sec. 108. Effective Date.

This title shall become effective 24 months after the date of enactment.

APPENDIX M Civil Rights Act of 1991 (Excerpts)

Section 3. Purposes.

The purposes of this Act are—

(1) to provide appropriate remedies for intentional discrimination and unlawful harassment in the workplace;

(2) to codify the concepts of "business necessity" and "job related" enunciated by the Supreme Court in *Griggs v. Duke Power Co.*, 401 U.S. 424 (1971), and in the other Supreme Court decisions prior to *Wards Cove Packing Co. v. Atonio*, 490 U.S. 642 (1989);

(3) to confirm statutory authority and provide statutory guidelines for the adjudication of disparate impact suits under title VII of the Civil Rights Act of 1964 (42 U.S.C. 2000e *et seq.*); and

(4) to respond to recent decisions of the Supreme Court by expanding the scope of relevant civil rights statutes in order to provide adequate protection to victims of discrimination.

Section 101. Prohibition against All Racial Discrimination in the Making and Enforcement of Contracts.

Section 1977 of the Revised Statutes (42 U.S.C. 1981) is amended * * * by adding at the end the following new subsections:

(b) For purposes of this section, the term "make and enforce contracts" includes the making, performance, modification, and termination of contracts, and the enjoyment of all benefits, privileges, terms, and conditions of the contractual relationship.

(c) The rights protected by this section are protected against impairment by nongovernmental discrimination and impairment under color of State law.

Section 102. Damages in Cases of Intentional Discrimination.

The Revised Statutes are amended by inserting after section 1977 (42 U.S.C.1981) the following new section:

Section 1977A. Damages in Cases of Intentional Discrimination in Employment.

(a) Right of Recovery.—

(1) Civil Rights.—In an action brought by a complaining party under section 706 or 717 of the Civil Rights Act of 1964 (42 U.S.C. 2000e-5) against a respondent who engaged in unlawful intentional discrimination (not an employment practice that is unlawful because of its disparate impact) prohibited under section 703, 704, or 717 of the Act (42 U.S.C. 2000e-2 or 2000e-3), and provided that the complaining party cannot recover under section 1977 of the Revised Statutes (42 U.S.C.1981), the complaining party may recover compensatory and punitive damages as allowed in subsection (b), in addition to any relief authorized by section 706(g) of the Civil Rights Act of 1964, from the respondent.

* * * *

(b) Compensatory and Punitive Damages.—

(1) Determination of Punitive Damages.—A complaining party may recover punitive damages under this section against a respondent (other than a government, government agency or political subdivision) if the complaining party demonstrates that the respondent engaged in a discriminatory practice or discriminatory practices with malice or with reckless indifference to the federally protected rights of an aggrieved individual.

(2) Exclusions from Compensatory Damages. Compensatory damages awarded under this section shall not include backpay, interest on backpay, or any other type of relief authorized under section 706(g) of the Civil Rights Act of 1964.

(3) Limitations.—The sum of the amount of compensatory damages awarded under this section for future pecuniary losses, emotional pain, suffering, inconvenience, mental anguish, loss of enjoyment of life, and other nonpecuniary losses, and the amount of punitive damages awarded under this section, shall not exceed, for each complaining party—

(A) in the case of a respondent who has more than 14 and fewer than 101 employees in each of 20 or more calendar weeks in the current or preceding calendar year, $50,000;

(B) in the case of a respondent who has more than 100 and fewer than 201 employees in each of 20 or more calendar weeks in the current or preceding calendar year, $100,000; and

(C) in the case of a respondent who has more than 200 and fewer than 501 employees in each of 20 or more calendar weeks in the current or preceding calendar year, $200,000; and

(D) in the case of a respondent who has more than 500 employees in each of 20 or more calendar weeks in the current or preceding calendar year, $300,000.

* * * *

Section 105. Burden of Proof in Disparate Impact Cases.

(a) Section 703 of the Civil Rights Act of 1964 (42 U.S.C. 2000e-2) is amended by adding at the end the following new [subsections to 703(k)(1)]—

(A) An unlawful employment practice based on disparate impact is established under this title only if—

(i) a complaining party demonstrates that a respondent uses a particular employment practice that causes a disparate impact on the basis of race, color, religion, sex, or national origin and the respondent fails to demonstrate that the challenged practice is job related for the position in question and consistent with business necessity; or

(ii) the complaining party makes the demonstration described in subparagraph (C) with respect to an alternative employment practice and the respondent refuses to adopt such alternative employment practice.

* * * *

(C) The demonstration referred to by subparagraph (A)(ii) shall be in accordance with the law as it existed on June 4, 1989, with respect to the concept of "alternative employment practice."

* * * *

Section 107. Clarifying Prohibition against Impermissible Consideration of Race, Color, Religion, Sex, or National Origin in Employment Practices.

(a) In General.—Section 703 of the Civil Rights Act of 1964 (42 U.S.C. 2000e-2) (as amended by sections 105 and 106) is further amended by adding at the end the following new subsection:

(m) Except as otherwise provided in this title, an unlawful employment practice is established when the complaining party demonstrates that race, color, religion, sex, or national origin was a motivating factor for any employment practice, even though other factors also motivated the practice.

* * * *

Section 109. Protection of Extraterritorial Employment.

(a) Definition of Employee.—Section 701(f) of the Civil Rights Act of 1964 (42 U.S.C. 2000e(f)) and section 101(4) of the Americans with Disabilities Act of 1990 (42 U.S.C. 12111(4)) are each amended by adding at the end the following: "With respect to employment in a foreign country, such term includes an individual who is a citizen of the United States."

APPENDIX N The United Nations Convention on Contracts for the International Sale of Goods (Excerpts)

Part I. SPHERE OF APPLICATION AND GENERAL PROVISIONS

* * * *

Chapter II—General Provisions

* * * *

Article 8

(1) For the purposes of this Convention statements made by and other conduct of a party are to be interpreted according to his intent where the other party knew or could not have been unaware what that intent was.

(2) If the preceding paragraph is not applicable, statements made by and other conduct of a party are to be interpreted according to the understanding that a reasonable person of the same kind as the other party would have had in the same circumstances.

(3) In determining the intent of a party or the understanding a reasonable person would have had, due consideration is to be given to all relevant circumstances of the case including the negotiations, any practices which the parties have established between themselves, usages and any subsequent conduct of the parties.

Article 9

(1) The parties are bound by any usage to which they have agreed and by any practices which they have established between themselves.

(2) The parties are considered, unless otherwise agreed, to have impliedly made applicable to their contract or its formation a usage of which the parties knew or ought to have known and which in international trade is widely known to, and regularly observed by, parties to contracts of the type involved in the particular trade concerned.

* * * *

Article 11

A contract of sale need not be concluded in or evidenced by writing and is not subject to any other requirement as to form. It may be proved by any means, including witnesses.

* * * *

Part II. FORMATION OF THE CONTRACT

Article 14

(1) A proposal for concluding a contract addressed to one or more specific persons constitutes an offer if it is sufficiently definite and indicates the intention of the offeror to be bound in case of acceptance. A proposal is sufficiently definite if it indicates the goods and expressly or implicitly fixes or makes provision for determining the quantity and the price.

(2) A proposal other than one addressed to one or more specific persons is to be considered merely as an invitation to make offers, unless the contrary is clearly indicated by the person making the proposal.

Article 15

(1) An offer becomes effective when it reaches the offeree.

(2) An offer, even if it is irrevocable, may be withdrawn if the withdrawal reaches the offeree before or at the same time as the offer.

Article 16

(1) Until a contract is concluded an offer may be revoked if the revocation reaches the offeree before he has dispatched an acceptance.

(2) However, an offer cannot be revoked:

(a) If it indicates, whether by stating a fixed time for acceptance or otherwise, that it is irrevocable; or

(b) If it was reasonable for the offeree to rely on the offer as being irrevocable and the offeree has acted in reliance on the offer.

Article 17

An offer, even if it is irrevocable, is terminated when a rejection reaches the offeror.

Article 18

(1) A statement made by or other conduct of the offeree indicating assent to an offer is an acceptance. Silence or inactivity does not in itself amount to acceptance.

(2) An acceptance of an offer becomes effective at the moment the indication of assent reaches the offeror. An acceptance is not effective if the indication of assent does not reach the offeror within the time he has fixed or, if no time is fixed, within a reasonable time, due account being taken of the circumstances of the transaction, including the rapidity of the means of communication employed by the offeror. An oral offer must be accepted immediately unless the circumstances indicate otherwise.

(3) However, if, by virtue of the offer or as a result of practices which the parties have established between themselves or of usage, the offeree may indicate assent by performing an act, such as one relating to the dispatch of the goods or payment of the price, with-

out notice to the offeror, the acceptance is effective at the moment the act is performed, provided that the act is performed within the period of time laid down in the preceding paragraph.

Article 19

(1) A reply to an offer which purports to be an acceptance but contains additions, limitations or other modifications is a rejection of the offer and constitutes a counter-offer.

(2) However, a reply to an offer which purports to be an acceptance but contains additional or different terms which do not materially alter the terms of the offer constitutes an acceptance, unless the offeror, without undue delay, objects orally to the discrepancy or dispatches a notice to that effect. If he does not so object, the terms of the contract are the terms of the offer with the modifications contained in the acceptance.

(3) Additional or different terms relating, among other things, to the price, payment, quality and quantity of the goods, place and time of delivery, extent of one party's liability to the other or the settlement of disputes are considered to alter the terms of the offer materially.

* * * *

Article 22

An acceptance may be withdrawn if the withdrawal reaches the offeror before or at the same time as the acceptance would have become effective.

* * * *

Part III. SALE OF GOODS

Chapter I—General Provisions

Article 25

A breach of contract committed by one of the parties is fundamental if it results in such detriment to the other party as substantially to deprive him of what he is entitled to expect under the contract, unless the party in breach did not foresee and a reasonable person of the same kind in the same circumstances would not have foreseen such a result.

* * * *

Article 28

If, in accordance with the provisions of this Convention, one party is entitled to require performance of any obligation by the other party, a court is not bound to enter a judgment for specific performance unless the court would do so under its own law in respect of similar contracts of sale not governed by this Convention.

Article 29

(1) A contract may be modified or terminated by the mere agreement of the parties.

(2) A contract in writing which contains a provision requiring any modification or termination by agreement to be in writing may not be otherwise modified or terminated by agreement. However, a party may be precluded by his conduct from asserting such a provision to the extent that the other party has relied on that conduct.

* * * *

Chapter II—Obligations of the Seller

* * * *

Section II. Conformity of the Goods and Third Party Claims

Article 35

(1) The seller must deliver goods which are of the quantity, quality and description required by the contract and which are contained or packaged in the manner required by the contract.

(2) Except where the parties have agreed otherwise, the goods do not conform with the contract unless they:

(a) Are fit for the purposes for which goods of the same description would ordinarily be used;

(b) Are fit for any particular purpose expressly or impliedly made known to the seller at the time of the conclusion of the contract, except where the circumstances show that the buyer did not rely, or that it was unreasonable for him to rely, on the seller's skill and judgment;

(c) Possess the qualities of goods which the seller has held out to the buyer as a sample or model;

(d) Are contained or packaged in the manner usual for such goods or, where there is no such manner, in a manner adequate to preserve and protect the goods.

(3) The seller is not liable under subparagraphs (a) to (d) of the preceding paragraph for any lack of conformity of the goods if at the time of the conclusion of the contract the buyer knew or could not have been unaware of such lack of conformity.

* * * *

Article 64

(1) The seller may declare the contract avoided:

(a) If the failure by the buyer to perform any of his obligations under the contract or this Convention amounts to a fundamental breach of contract; or

(b) If the buyer does not, within the additional period of time fixed by the seller in accordance with paragraph (1) of article 63, perform his obligation to pay the price or take delivery of the goods, or if he declares that he will not do so within the period so fixed.

(2) However, in cases where the buyer has paid the price, the seller loses the right to declare the contract avoided unless he does so:

(a) In respect of late performance by the buyer, before the seller has become aware that performance has been rendered; or

(b) In respect of any breach other than late performance by the buyer, within a reasonable time:

(i) After the seller knew or ought to have known of the breach; or

(ii) After the expiration of any additional period of time fixed by the seller in accordance with paragraph (1) of article 63, or after the buyer has declared that he will not perform his obligations within such an additional period.

* * * *

Chapter IV—Passing of Risk

* * * *

Article 67

(1) If the contract of sale involves carriage of the goods and the seller is not bound to hand them over at a particular place, the risk passes to the buyer when the goods are handed over to the first carrier for transmission to the buyer in accordance with the contract of sale. If the seller is bound to hand the goods over to a carrier at a particular place, the risk does not pass to the buyer until the goods are handed over to the carrier at that place. The fact that the seller is authorized to retain documents controlling the disposition of the goods does not affect the passage of the risk.

(2) Nevertheless, the risk does not pass to the buyer until the goods are clearly identified to the contract, whether by markings on the goods, by shipping documents, by notice given to the buyer or otherwise.

* * * *

Chapter V—Provisions Common to the Obligations of the Seller and of the Buyer

Section I. Anticipatory Breach and Instalment Contracts

Article 71

(1) A party may suspend the performance of his obligations if, after the conclusion of the contract, it becomes apparent that the other party will not perform a substantial part of his obligations as a result of:

(a) A serious deficiency in his ability to perform or in his creditworthiness; or

(b) His conduct in preparing to perform or in performing the contract.

(2) If the seller has already dispatched the goods before the grounds described in the preceding paragraph become evident, he may prevent the handing over of the goods to the buyer even though the buyer holds a document which entitles him to obtain them. The present paragraph relates only to the rights in the goods as between the buyer and the seller.

(3) A party suspending performance, whether before or after dispatch of the goods, must immediately give notice of the suspension to the other party and must continue with performance if the other party provides adequate assurance of his performance.

Article 72

(1) If prior to the date for performance of the contract it is clear that one of the parties will commit a fundamental breach of contract, the other party may declare the contract avoided.

(2) If time allows, the party intending to declare the contract avoided must give reasonable notice to the other party in order to permit him to provide adequate assurance of his performance.

(3) The requirements of the preceding paragraph do not apply if the other party has declared that he will not perform his obligations.

Article 73

(1) In the case of a contract for delivery of goods by instalments, if the failure of one party to perform any of his obligations in respect of any instalment constitutes a fundamental breach of contract with respect to that instalment, the other party may declare the contract avoided with respect to that instalment.

(2) If one party's failure to perform any of his obligations in respect of any instalment gives the other party good grounds to conclude that a fundamental breach of contract will occur with respect to future instalments, he may declare the contract avoided for the future, provided that he does so within a reasonable time.

(3) A buyer who declares the contract avoided in respect of any delivery may, at the same time, declare it avoided in respect of deliveries already made or of future deliveries if, by reason of their interdependence, those deliveries could not be used for the purpose contemplated by the parties at the time of the conclusion of the contract.

Section II. Damages

Article 74

Damages for breach of contract by one party consist of a sum equal to the loss, including loss of profit, suffered by the other party as a consequence of the breach. Such damages may not exceed the loss which the party in breach foresaw or ought to have foreseen at the time of the conclusion of the contract, in the light of the facts and matters of which he then knew or ought to have known, as a possible consequence of the breach of contract.

Article 75

If the contract is avoided and if, in a reasonable manner and within a reasonable time after avoidance, the buyer has bought goods in replacement or the seller has resold the goods, the party claiming damages may recover the difference between the contract price and the price in the substitute transaction as well as any further damages recoverable under article 74.

Article 76

(1) If the contract is avoided and there is a current price for the goods, the party claiming damages may, if he has not made a purchase or resale under article 75, recover the difference between the price fixed by the contract and the current price at the time of avoidance as well as any further damages recoverable under article 74. If, however, the party claiming damages has avoided the contract after taking over the goods, the current price at the time of such taking over shall be applied instead of the current price at the time of avoidance.

(2) For the purposes of the preceding paragraph, the current price is the price prevailing at the place where delivery of the goods should have been made or, if there is no current price at that place, the price at such other place as serves as a reasonable substitute, making due allowance for differences in the cost of transporting the goods.

Article 77

A party who relies on a breach of contract must take such measures as are reasonable in the circumstances to mitigate the loss, including loss of profit, resulting from the breach. If he fails to take such measures, the party in breach may claim a reduction in the damages in the amount by which the loss should have been mitigated.

APPENDIX O

Spanish Equivalents for Important Legal Terms in English

Abandoned property: bienes abandonados
Acceptance: aceptación; consentimiento; acuerdo
Acceptor: aceptante
Accession: toma de posesión; aumento; accesión
Accommodation indorser: avalista de favor
Accommodation party: firmante de favor
Accord: acuerdo; convenio; arregio
Accord and satisfaction: transacción ejecutada
Act of state doctrine: doctrina de acto de gobierno
Administrative law: derecho administrativo
Administrative process: procedimiento o metódo administrativo
Administrator: administrador (-a)
Adverse possession: posesión de hecho susceptible de proscripción adquisitiva
Affirmative action: acción afirmativa
Affirmative defense: defensa afirmativa
After-acquired property: bienes adquiridos con posterioridad a un hecho dado
Agency: mandato; agencia
Agent: mandatorio; agente; representante
Agreement: convenio; acuerdo; contrato
Alien corporation: empresa extranjera
Allonge: hojas adicionales de endosos
Answer: contestación de la demande; alegato
Anticipatory repudiation: anuncio previo de las partes de su imposibilidad de cumplir con el contrato
Appeal: apelación; recurso de apelación
Appellate jurisdiction: jurisdicción de apelaciones
Appraisal right: derecho de valuación
Arbitration: arbitraje
Arson: incendio intencional
Articles of partnership: contrato social
Artisan's lien: derecho de retención que ejerce al artesano
Assault: asalto; ataque; agresión
Assignment of rights: transmisión; transferencia; cesión
Assumption of risk: no resarcimiento por exposición voluntaria al peligro
Attachment: auto judicial que autoriza el embargo; embargo

Bailee: depositario
Bailment: depósito; constitución en depósito
Bailor: depositante
Bankruptcy trustee: síndico de la quiebra
Battery: agresión; física
Bearer: portador; tenedor
Bearer instrument: documento al portador
Bequest or legacy: legado (de bienes muebles)
Bilateral contract: contrato bilateral
Bill of lading: conocimiento de embarque; carta de porte
Bill of Rights: declaración de derechos
Binder: póliza de seguro provisoria; recibo de pago a cuenta del precio
Blank indorsement: endoso en blanco
Blue sky laws: leyes reguladoras del comercio bursátil
Bond: título de crédito; garantía; caución
Bond indenture: contrato de emisión de bonos; contrato del ampréstito
Breach of contract: incumplimiento de contrato
Brief: escrito; resumen; informe
Burglary: violación de domicilio
Business judgment rule: regla de juicio comercial
Business tort: agravio comercial

Case law: ley de casos; derecho casuístico
Cashier's check: cheque de caja
Causation in fact: causalidad en realidad
Cease-and-desist order: orden para cesar y desistir
Certificate of deposit: certificado de depósito
Certified check: cheque certificado
Charitable trust: fideicomiso para fines benéficos
Chattel: bien mueble
Check: cheque
Chose in action: derecho inmaterial; derecho de acción
Civil law: derecho civil
Close corporation: sociedad de un solo accionista o de un grupo restringido de accionistas
Closed shop: taller agremiado (emplea solamente a miembros de un gremio)
Closing argument: argumento al final
Codicil: codicilo
Collateral: guarantía; bien objeto de la guarantía real
Comity: cortesía; cortesía entre naciones
Commercial paper: instrumentos negociables; documentos a valores commerciales
Common law: derecho consuetudinario; derecho común; ley común
Common stock: acción ordinaria
Comparative negligence: negligencia comparada
Compensatory damages: daños y perjuicios reales o compensatorios
Concurrent conditions: condiciones concurrentes
Concurrent jurisdiction: competencia concurrente de varios tribunales para entender en una misma causa
Concurring opinion: opinión concurrente
Condition: condición
Condition precedent: condición suspensiva
Condition subsequent: condición resolutoria
Confiscation: confiscación
Confusion: confusión; fusión
Conglomerate merger: fusión de firmas que operan en distintos mercados

Consent decree: acuerdo entre las partes aprobado por un tribunal
Consequential damages: daños y perjuicios indirectos
Consideration: consideración; motivo; contraprestación
Consolidation: consolidación
Constructive delivery: entrega simbólica
Constructive trust: fideicomiso creado por aplicación de la ley
Consumer protection law: ley para proteger el consumidor
Contract: contrato
Contract under seal: contrato formal o sellado
Contributory negligence: negligencia de la parte actora
Conversion: usurpación; conversión de valores
Copyright: derecho de autor
Corporation: sociedad anómina; corporación; persona juridica
Co-sureties: cogarantes
Counterclaim: reconvención; contrademanda
Counteroffer: contraoferta
Course of dealing: curso de transacciones
Course of performance: curso de cumplimiento
Covenant: pacto; garantía; contrato
Covenant not to sue: pacto or contrato a no demandar
Covenant of quiet enjoyment: garantía del uso y goce pacífico del inmueble
Creditors' composition agreement: concordato preventivo
Crime: crimen; delito; contravención
Criminal law: derecho penal
Cross-examination: contrainterrogatorio
Cure: cura; cuidado; derecho de remediar un vicio contractual
Customs receipts: recibos de derechos aduaneros

Damages: daños; indemnización por daños y perjuicios
Debit card: tarjeta de dé bito
Debtor: deudor
Debt securities: seguridades de deuda
Deceptive advertising: publicidad engañosa
Deed: escritura; título; acta translativa de domino
Defamation: difamación
Delegation of duties: delegación de obligaciones
Demand deposit: depósito a la vista
Depositions: declaración de un testigo fuera del tribunal
Devise: legado; deposición testamentaria (bienes inmuebles)
Directed verdict: veredicto según orden del juez y sin participación activa del jurado
Direct examination: interrogatorio directo; primer interrogatorio
Disaffirmance: repudiación; renuncia; anulación
Discharge: descargo; liberación; cumplimiento
Disclosed principal: mandante revelado
Discovery: descubrimiento; producción de la prueba
Dissenting opinion: opinión disidente
Dissolution: disolución; terminación
Diversity of citizenship: competencia de los tribunales federales para entender en causas cuyas partes intervinientes son cuidadanos de distintos estados
Divestiture: extinción premature de derechos reales
Dividend: dividendo
Docket: orden del día; lista de causas pendientes
Domestic corporation: sociedad local
Draft: orden de pago; letrade cambio
Drawee: girado; beneficiario
Drawer: librador
Duress: coacción; violencia

Easement: servidumbre
Embezzlement: desfalco; malversación
Eminent domain: poder de expropiación
Employment discrimination: discriminación en el empleo
Entrepreneur: empresario
Environmental law: ley ambiental
Equal dignity rule: regla de dignidad egual
Equity security: tipo de participación en una sociedad
Estate: propiedad; patrimonio; derecho
Estop: impedir; prevenir
Ethical issue: cuestión ética
Exclusive jurisdiction: competencia exclusiva
Exculpatory clause: cláusula eximente
Executed contract: contrato ejecutado
Execution: ejecución; cumplimiento
Executor: albacea
Executory contract: contrato aún no completamente consumado
Executory interest: derecho futuro
Express contract: contrato expreso
Expropriation: expropriación

Federal question: caso federal
Fee simple: pleno dominio; dominio absoluto
Fee simple absolute: dominio absoluto
Fee simple defeasible: dominio sujeta a una condición resolutoria
Felony: crimen; delito grave
Fictitious payee: beneficiario ficticio
Fiduciary: fiduciaro
Firm offer: oferta en firme
Fixture: inmueble por destino, incorporación a anexación
Floating lien: gravamen continuado
Foreign corporation: sociedad extranjera; U.S. sociedad constituída en otro estado
Forgery: falso; falsificación
Formal contract: contrato formal
Franchise: privilegio; franquicia; concesión
Franchisee: persona que recibe una concesión
Franchisor: persona que vende una concesión
Fraud: fraude; dolo; engaño
Future interest: bien futuro

Garnishment: embargo de derechos
General partner: socio comanditario
General warranty deed: escritura translativa de domino con garantía de título
Gift: donación
Gift *causa mortis*: donación por causa de muerte
Gift *inter vivos*: donación entre vivos
Good faith: buena fe
Good faith purchaser: comprador de buena fe

Holder: tenedor por contraprestación
Holder in due course: tenedor legítimo
Holographic will: testamento olográfico
Homestead exemption laws: leyes que exceptúan las casas de familia de ejecución por duedas generales
Horizontal merger: fusión horizontal

Identification: identificación
Implied-in-fact contract: contrato implícito en realidad
Implied warranty: guarantía implícita
Implied warranty of merchantability: garantía implícita de vendibilidad
Impossibility of performance: imposibilidad de cumplir un contrato

Imposter: imposter
Incidental beneficiary: beneficiario incidental; beneficiario secundario
Incidental damages: daños incidentales
Indictment: auto de acusación; acusación
Indorsee: endorsatario
Indorsement: endoso
Indorser: endosante
Informal contract: contrato no formal; contrato verbal
Information: acusación hecha por el ministerio público
Injunction: mandamiento; orden de no innovar
Innkeeper's lien: derecho de retención que ejerce el posadero
Installment contract: contrato de pago en cuotas
Insurable interest: interés asegurable
Intended beneficiary: beneficiario destinado
Intentional tort: agravio; cuasi-delito intenciónal
International law: derecho internaciónal
Interrogatories: preguntas escritas sometidas por una parte a la otra o a un testigo
***Inter vivos* trust:** fideicomiso entre vivos
Intestacy laws: leyes de la condición de morir intestado
Intestate: intestado
Investment company: compañia de inversiones
Issue: emisión

Joint tenancy: derechos conjuntos en un bien inmueble en favor del beneficiario sobreviviente
Judgment *n.o.v.*: juicio no obstante veredicto
Judgment rate of interest: interés de juicio
Judicial process: acto de procedimiento; proceso jurídico
Judicial review: revisión judicial
Jurisdiction: jurisdicción

Larceny: robo; hurto
Law: derecho; ley; jurisprudencia
Lease: contrato de locación; contrato de alquiler
Leasehold estate: bienes forales
Legal rate of interest: interés legal
Legatee: legatario
Letter of credit: carta de crédito
Levy: embargo; comiso
Libel: libelo; difamación escrita
Life estate: usufructo
Limited partner: comanditario
Limited partnership: sociedad en comandita
Liquidation: liquidación; realización
Lost property: objetos perdidos

Majority opinion: opinión de la mayoría
Maker: persona que realiza u ordena; librador
Mechanic's lien: gravamen de constructor
Mediation: mediación; intervención
Merger: fusión
Mirror image rule: fallo de reflejo
Misdemeanor: infracción; contravención
Mislaid property: bienes extraviados
Mitigation of damages: reducción de daños
Mortgage: hypoteca
Motion to dismiss: excepción parentoria
Mutual fund: fondo mutual

Negotiable instrument: instrumento negociable
Negotiation: negociación
Nominal damages: daños y perjuicios nominales
Novation: novación
Nuncupative will: testamento nuncupativo

Objective theory of contracts: teoria objetiva de contratos
Offer: oferta
Offeree: persona que recibe una oferta
Offeror: oferente
Order instrument: instrumento o documento a la orden
Original jurisdiction: jurisdicción de primera instancia
Output contract: contrato de producción

Parol evidence rule: regla relativa a la prueba oral
Partially disclosed principal: mandante revelado en parte
Partnership: sociedad colectiva; asociación; asociación de participación
Past consideration: causa o contraprestación anterior
Patent: patente; privilegio
Pattern or practice: muestra o práctica
Payee: beneficiario de un pago
Penalty: pena; penalidad
***Per capita*:** por cabeza
Perfection: perfeción
Performance: cumplimiento; ejecución
Personal defenses: excepciones personales
Personal property: bienes muebles
***Per stirpes*:** por estirpe
Plea bargaining: regateo por un alegato
Pleadings: alegatos
Pledge: prenda
Police powers: poders de policia y de prevención del crimen
Policy: póliza
Positive law: derecho positivo; ley positiva
Possibility of reverter: posibilidad de reversión
Precedent: precedente
Preemptive right: derecho de prelación
Preferred stock: acciones preferidas
Premium: recompensa; prima
Presentment warranty: garantía de presentación
Price discrimination: discriminación en los precios
Principal: mandante; principal
Privity: nexo jurídico
Privity of contract: relación contractual
Probable cause: causa probable
Probate: verificación; verificación del testamento
Probate court: tribunal de sucesiones y tutelas
Proceeds: resultados; ingresos
Profit: beneficio; utilidad; lucro
Promise: promesa
Promisee: beneficiario de una promesa
Promisor: promtente
Promissory estoppel: impedimento promisorio
Promissory note: pagaré; nota de pago
Promoter: promotor; fundador
Proximate cause: causa inmediata o próxima
Proxy: apoderado; poder
Punitive, or exemplary, damages: daños y perjuicios punitivos o ejemplares

Qualified indorsement: endoso con reservas
Quasi contract: contrato tácito o implícito
Quitclaim deed: acto de transferencia de una propiedad por finiquito, pero sin ninguna garantía sobre la validez del título transferido

Ratification: ratificación
Real property: bienes inmuebles
Reasonable doubt: duda razonable
Rebuttal: refutación
Recognizance: promesa; compromiso; reconocimiento

Recording statutes: leyes estatales sobre registros oficiales
Redress: reporacíon
Reformation: rectificación; reforma; corrección
Rejoinder: dúplica; contrarréplica
Release: liberación; renuncia a un derecho
Remainder: substitución; reversión
Remedy: recurso; remedio; reparación
Replevin: acción reivindicatoria; reivindicación
Reply: réplica
Requirements contract: contrato de suministro
Rescission: rescisión
Res judicata: cosa juzgada; res judicata
Respondeat superior: responsabilidad del mandante o del maestro
Restitution: restitución
Restrictive indorsement: endoso restrictivo
Resulting trust: fideicomiso implícito
Reversion: reversión; sustitución
Revocation: revocación; derogación
Right of contribution: derecho de contribución
Right of reimbursement: derecho de reembolso
Right of subrogation: derecho de subrogación
Right-to-work law: ley de libertad de trabajo
Robbery: robo
Rule 10b-5: Regla 10b-5

Sale: venta; contrato de compreventa
Sale on approval: venta a ensayo; venta sujeta a la aprobación del comprador
Sale or return: venta con derecho de devolución
Sales contract: contrato de compraventa; boleto de compraventa
Satisfaction: satisfacción; pago
***Scienter*:** a sabiendas
S corporation: S corporación
Secured party: acreedor garantizado
Secured transaction: transacción garantizada
Securities: volares; titulos; seguridades
Security agreement: convenio de seguridad
Security interest: interés en un bien dado en garantía que permite a quien lo detenta venderlo en caso de incumplimiento
Service mark: marca de identificación de servicios
Shareholder's derivative suit: acción judicial entablada por un accionista en nombre de la sociedad
Signature: firma; rúbrica
Slander: difamación oral; calumnia
Sovereign immunity: immunidad soberana
Special indorsement: endoso especial; endoso a la orden de una person en particular
Specific performance: ejecución precisa, según los términos del contrato
Spendthrift trust: fideicomiso para pródigos
Stale check: cheque vencido
Stare decisis: acatar las decisiones, observar los precedentes
Statutory law: derecho estatutario; derecho legislado; derecho escrito
Stock: acciones
Stock warrant: certificado para la compra de acciones
Stop-payment order: orden de suspensión del pago de un cheque dada por el librador del mismo
Strict liability: responsabilidad uncondicional
Summary judgment: fallo sumario

Tangible property: bienes corpóreos
Tenancy at will: inguilino por tiempo indeterminado (según la voluntad del propietario)
Tenancy by sufferance: posesión por tolerancia
Tenancy by the entirety: locación conyugal conjunta
Tenancy for years: inguilino por un término fijo
Tenancy in common: specie de copropiedad indivisa
Tender: oferta de pago; oferta de ejecución
Testamentary trust: fideicomiso testamentario
Testator: testador (-a)
Third party beneficiary contract: contrato para el beneficio del tercero-beneficiario
Tort: agravio; cuasi-delito
Totten trust: fideicomiso creado por un depósito bancario
Trade acceptance: letra de cambio aceptada
Trademark: marca registrada
Trade name: nombre comercial; razón social
Traveler's check: cheque del viajero
Trespass to land: ingreso no authorizado a las tierras de otro
Trespass to personal property: violación de los derechos posesorios de un tercero con respecto a bienes muebles
Trust: fideicomiso; trust

Ultra vires: ultra vires; fuera de la facultad (de una sociedad anónima)
Unanimous opinion: opinión unámine
Unconscionable contract or clause: contrato leonino; cláusula leonino
Underwriter: subscriptor; asegurador
Unenforceable contract: contrato que no se puede hacer cumplir
Unilateral contract: contrato unilateral
Union shop: taller agremiado; empresa en la que todos los empleados son miembros del gremio o sindicato
Universal defenses: defensas legitimas o legales
Usage of trade: uso comercial
Usury: usura

Valid contract: contrato válido
Venue: lugar; sede del proceso
Vertical merger: fusión vertical de empresas
Voidable contract: contrato anulable
Void contract: contrato nulo; contrato inválido, sin fuerza legal
Voir dire: examen preliminar de un testigo a jurado por el tribunal para determinar su competencia
Voting trust: fideicomiso para ejercer el derecho de voto

Waiver: renuncia; abandono
Warranty of habitability: garantía de habitabilidad
Watered stock: acciones diluídos; capital inflado
White-collar crime: crimen administrativo
Writ of attachment: mandamiento de ejecución; mandamiento de embargo
Writ of *certiorari*: auto de avocación; auto de certiorari
Writ of execution: auto ejecutivo; mandamiento de ejecutión
Writ of mandamus: auto de mandamus; mandamiento; orden judicial

Glossary

A

Abandoned Property Property with which the owner has voluntarily parted, with no intention of recovering it.

Acceleration clause A clause that allows a payee or other holder of a time instrument to demand payment of the entire amount due, with interest, if a certain event occurs, such as a default in the payment of an installment when due.

Acceptance A voluntary act by the offeree that shows assent, or agreement, to the terms of an offer; may consist of words or conduct.

Acceptor A drawee that promises to pay an instrument when the instrument is presented later for payment.

Accession Occurs when an individual adds value to personal property by either labor or materials. In some situations, a person may acquire ownership rights in another's property through accession.

Accord and Satisfaction A common means of settling a claim, in which a debtor offers to pay a lesser amount than the creditor purports to be owed. The creditor's acceptance of the offer creates an accord (agreement), and when the accord is executed, satisfaction occurs.

Accredited Investors In the context of securities offerings, "sophisticated" investors, such as banks, insurance companies, investment companies, the issuer's executive officers and directors, and persons whose income or net worth exceeds certain limits.

Act of State Doctrine A doctrine that provides that the judicial branch of one country will not examine the validity of public acts committed by a recognized foreign government within its own territory.

Actionable Capable of serving as the basis of a lawsuit. An actionable claim can be pursued in a lawsuit or other court action.

Actual Malice Real and demonstrable evil intent. In a defamation suit, a statement made about a public figure normally must be made with actual malice (with either knowledge of its falsity or a reckless disregard of the truth) for liability to be incurred.

Adhesion Contract A "standard-form" contract, such as that between a large retailer and a consumer, in which the stronger party dictates the terms.

Adjudication The act of rendering a judicial decision. In an administrative process, the proceeding in which an administrative law judge hears and decides on issues that arise when an administrative agency charges a person or a firm with violating a law or regulation enforced by the agency.

Adjudicate To render a judicial decision. In the administrative process, the proceeding in which an administrative law judge hears and decides on issues that arise when an administrative agency charges a person or a firm with violating a law or regulation enforced by the agency.

Administrative Agency A federal or state government agency established to perform a specific function. Administrative agencies are authorized by legislative acts to make and enforce rules to administer and enforce the acts.

Administrative Law The body of law created by administrative agencies (in the form of rules, regulations, orders, and decisions) in order to carry out their duties and responsibilities.

Administrative Law Judge (ALJ) One who presides over an administrative agency hearing and who has the power to administer oaths, take testimony, rule on questions of evidence, and make determinations of fact.

Administrative Process The procedure used by administrative agencies in the administration of law.

Administrator One who is appointed by a court to handle the probate (disposition) of a person's estate if that person dies intestate (without a valid will) or if the executor named in the will cannot serve.

Adverse Possession The acquisition of title to real property by occupying it openly, without the consent of the owner, for a period of time specified by a state statute. The occupation must be actual, open, notorious, exclusive, and in opposition to all others, including the owner.

Affirmative Action Job-hiring policies that give special consideration to members of protected classes in an effort to overcome present effects of past discrimination.

After-Acquired Property Property of the debtor that is acquired after the execution of a security agreement.

Agency A relationship between two parties in which one party (the agent) agrees to represent or act for the other (the principal).

Agent A person who agrees to represent or act for another, called the principal.

Aggressor An individual, group, or firm seeking to obtain control of a target corporation in a takeover attempt.

Agreement A meeting of two or more minds in regard to the terms of a contract; usually broken down into two events—an offer by one party to form a contract, and an acceptance of the offer by the person to whom the offer is made.

Alien Corporation A designation in the United States for a corporation formed in another country but doing business in the United States.

Alienation A term used to define the process of transferring land out of one's possession (thus "alienating" the land from oneself).

Allonge (pronounced uh-*lohnj*) A piece of paper firmly attached to a negotiable instrument, on which transferees can make indorsements if there is no room left on the instrument itself.

Alternative Dispute Resolution (ADR) The resolution of disputes in ways other than those involved in the traditional judicial process. Negotiation, mediation, and arbitration are examples of ADR methods.

Answer Procedurally, a defendant's response to the plaintiff's complaint.

Anticipatory Repudiation An assertion or action by a party indicating that he or she will not perform an obligation that the party is contractually obligated to perform at a future time.

Antitrust Laws Laws protecting commerce from unlawful restraints.

Appraisal Right The right of a dissenting shareholder, if he or she objects to an extraordinary transaction of the corporation (such as a merger or a consolidation), to have his or her shares appraised and to be paid the fair value of his or her shares by the corporation.

Appropriation In tort law, the use by one person of another person's name, likeness, or other identifying characteristic without permission and for the benefit of the user.

Arbitration The settling of a dispute by submitting it to a disinterested third party (other than a court), who renders a decision that is (most often) legally binding.

Arbitration Clause A clause in a contract that provides that, in case of a dispute, the parties will submit the dispute to arbitration rather than litigate the dispute in court.

Arson The intentional burning of another's dwelling. Some statutes have expanded this to include any real property regardless of ownership and the destruction of property by other means—for example, by explosion.

Articles of Incorporation The document filed with the appropriate governmental agency, usually the secretary of state, when a business is incorporated; state statutes usually prescribe what kind of information must be contained in the articles of incorporation.

Articles of Partnership A written agreement that sets forth each partner's rights and obligations with respect to the partnership.

Articles of Organization The document filed with a designated state official by which a limited liability company is formed.

Artisan's Lien A possessory lien given to a person who has made improvements and added value to another person's personal property as security for payment for services performed.

Assault Any word or action intended to make another person fearful of immediate physical harm; a reasonably believable threat.

Assignment The act of transferring to another all or part of one's rights arising under a contract.

Assumption of Risk A doctrine whereby a plaintiff may not recover for injuries or damages suffered from risks he or she knows of and assents to. A defense against negligence that can be used when the plaintiff has knowledge of and appreciates a danger and voluntarily exposes himself or herself to the danger.

Attachment In a secured transaction, the process by which a security interest in the property of another becomes enforceable. In the context of judicial liens, a court-ordered seizure and taking into custody of property prior to the securing of a judgment for a past-due debt.

Attempted Monopolization Any actions by a firm to eliminate competition and gain monopoly power.

Automatic Stay In bankruptcy proceedings, the suspension of virtually all litigation and other action by creditors against the debtor or the debtor's property; the stay is effective the moment the debtor files a petition in bankruptcy.

Award The amount of money awarded to a plaintiff in a civil lawsuit as damages.

B

Bailee One to whom goods are entrusted by a bailor. Under the UCC, a party who, by a bill of lading, warehouse receipt, or other document of title, acknowledges possession of goods and/or contracts to deliver them.

Bailment A situation in which the personal property of one person (a bailor) is entrusted to another (a bailee), who is obligated to return the bailed property to the bailor or dispose of it as directed.

Bailor One who entrusts goods to a bailee.

Bait-and-Switch Advertising Advertising a product at a very attractive price (the "bait") and then informing the consumer, once he or she is in the store, that the advertised product is either not available or is of poor quality; the customer is then urged to purchase ("switched" to) a more expensive item.

Bankruptcy Court A federal court of limited jurisdiction that handles only bankruptcy proceedings. Bankruptcy proceedings are governed by federal bankruptcy law.

Battery The unprivileged, intentional touching of another.

Beachhead acquisition The gradual accumulation of a bloc of a target corporation's shares by an aggressor during an attempt to obtain control of the corporation.

Bearer A person in the possession of an instrument payable to bearer or indorsed in blank.

Bearer Instrument Any instrument that is not payable to a specific person, including instruments payable to the bearer or to "cash."

Bequest A gift by will of personal property (from the verb to bequeath).

Beyond a Reasonable Doubt The standard of proof used in criminal cases. If there is any reasonable doubt that a criminal defendant did not commit the crime with which he or she has been charged, then the verdict must be "not guilty."

Bilateral Contract A type of contract that arises when a promise is given in exchange for a return promise.

Bill of Rights The first ten amendments to the U.S. Constitution.

Binder A written, temporary insurance policy.

Binding Authority Any source of law that a court must follow when deciding a case. Binding authorities include constitutions, statutes, and regulations that govern the issue being decided, as well as court decisions that are controlling precedents within the jurisdiction.

Blank Indorsement An indorsement that specifies no particular indorsee and that can consist of a mere signature. An order instrument that is indorsed in blank becomes a bearer instrument.

Blue Laws State or local laws that prohibit the performance of certain types of commercial activities on Sunday.

Blue Sky Laws State laws that regulate the offer and sale of securities.

Bona Fide Occupational Qualification (BFOQ) Identifiable characteristics reasonably necessary to the normal operation of a particular business. These characteristics can include gender, national origin, and religion, but not race.

Bond A certificate that evidences a corporate (or government) debt. It is a security that involves no ownership interest in the issuing entity.

Bond Indenture A contract between the issuer of a bond and the bondholder.

Bounty Payment A reward (payment) given to a person or persons who perform a certain service—such as informing legal authorities of illegal actions.

Breach of Contract The failure, without legal excuse, of a promisor to perform the obligations of a contract.

Brief A formal legal document submitted by the attorney for the appellant or the appellee (in answer to the appellant's brief) to an appellate court when a case is appealed. The appellant's brief outlines the facts and issues of the case, the judge's rulings or jury's findings that should be reversed or modified, the applicable law, and the arguments on the client's behalf.

Bureaucracy The organizational structure, consisting of government bureaus and agencies, through which the government implements and enforces the laws.

Burglary The unlawful entry or breaking into a building with the intent to commit a felony. (Some state statutes expand this to include the intent to commit any crime.)
Business Ethics Ethics in a business context; a consensus of what constitutes right or wrong behavior in the world of business and the application of moral principles to situations that arise in a business setting.
Business Invitees Those people, such as customers or clients, who are invited onto business premises by the owner of those premises for business purposes.
Business Judgment Rule A rule that immunizes corporate management from liability for actions that result in corporate losses or damages if the actions are undertaken in good faith and are within both the power of the corporation and the authority of management to make.
Business Tort The wrongful interference with another's business rights.
Business Necessity A defense to allegations of employment discrimination in which the employer demonstrates that an employment practice that discriminates against members of a protected class is related to job performance.
Business Trust A form of business organization in which investors (trust beneficiaries) transfer cash or property to trustees in exchange for trust certificates that represent their investment shares. The certificate holders share in the trust's profits but have limited liability.
Bylaws A set of governing rules adopted by a corporation or other association.

C

Case Law The rules of law announced in court decisions. Case law includes the aggregate of reported cases that interpret judicial precedents, statutes, regulations, and constitutional provisions.
Cashier's Check A check drawn by a bank on itself.
Categorical Imperative A concept developed by the philosopher Immanuel Kant as an ethical guideline for behavior. In deciding whether an action is right or wrong, or desirable or undesirable, a person should evaluate the action in terms of what would happen if everybody else in the same situation, or category, acted the same way.
Causation in Fact An act or omission without which an event would not have occurred.
Cease-and-Desist Order An administrative or judicial order prohibiting a person or business firm from conducting activities that an agency or court has deemed illegal.
Certificate of Deposit (CD) A note of a bank in which a bank acknowledges a receipt of money from a party and promises to repay the money, with interest, to the party on a certain date.
Certificate of Incorporation The primary document that evidences corporate existence (referred to as articles of incorporation in some states).
Certificate of Limited Partnership The basic document filed with a designated state official by which a limited partnership is formed.
Certified Check A check that has been accepted in writing by the bank on which it is drawn. Essentially, the bank, by certifying (accepting) the check, promises to pay the check at the time the check is presented.
Charging Order In partnership law, an order granted by a court to a judgment creditor that entitles the creditor to attach profits or assets of a partner on the dissolution of the partnership.
Charitable Trust A trust in which the property held by a trustee must be used for a charitable purpose, such as the advancement of health, education, or religion.
Check A draft drawn by a drawer ordering the drawee bank or financial institution to pay a fixed amount of money to the holder on demand.
Checks and Balances The national government is composed of three separate branches: the executive, the legislative, and the judicial branches. Each branch of the government exercises a check on the actions of the others.
Choice-of-Language Clause A clause in a contract designating the official language by which the contract will be interpreted in the event of a future disagreement over the contract's terms.
Choice-of-Law Clause A clause in a contract designating the law (such as the law of a particular state or nation) that will govern the contract.
Chose in Action A right that can be enforced in court to recover a debt or to obtain damages.
Citation A reference to a publication in which a legal authority—such as a statute or a court decision—or other source can be found.
Civil Law The branch of law dealing with the definition and enforcement of all private or public rights, as opposed to criminal matters.
Civil Law System A system of law derived from that of the Roman Empire and based on a code rather than case law; the predominant system of law in the nations of continental Europe and the nations that were once their colonies. In the United States, Louisiana, because of its historical ties to France, has in part a civil law system.
Clearinghouse A system or place where banks exchange checks and drafts drawn on each other and settle daily balances.
Close Corporation A corporation whose shareholders are limited to a small group of persons, often including only family members. The rights of shareholders of a close corporation usually are restricted regarding the transfer of shares to others.
Closed Shop A firm that requires union membership by its workers as a condition of employment. The closed shop was made illegal by the Labor-Management Relations Act of 1947.
Co-Surety A joint surety; a person who assumes liability jointly with another surety for the payment of an obligation.
Codicil A written supplement or modification to a will. A codicil must be executed with the same formalities as a will.
Collateral Under Article 9 of the UCC, the property subject to a security interest, including accounts and chattel paper that have been sold.
Collateral Promise A secondary promise that is ancillary (subsidiary) to a principal transaction or primary contractual relationship, such as a promise made by one person to pay the debts of another if the latter fails to perform. A collateral promise normally must be in writing to be enforceable.
Collecting Bank Any bank handling an item for collection, except the payor bank.
Collective Bargaining The process by which labor and management negotiate the terms and conditions of employment, including working hours and workplace conditions.
Comity A deference by which one nation gives effect to the laws and judicial decrees of another nation. This recognition is based primarily on respect.
Commerce Clause The provision in Article I, Section 8, of the

U.S. Constitution that gives Congress the power to regulate interstate commerce.

Commingle To mix together. To put funds or goods together into one mass so that the funds or goods are so mixed that they no longer have separate identities. In corporate law, if personal and corporate interests are commingled to the extent that the corporation has no separate identity, a court may "pierce the corporate veil" and expose the shareholders to personal liability.

Common Carrier An owner of a truck, railroad, airline, ship, or other vehicle who is licensed to offer transportation services to the public, generally in return for compensation or a payment.

Common Law That body of law developed from custom or judicial decisions in English and U.S. courts, not attributable to a legislature.

Common Stock Shares of ownership in a corporation that give the owner of the stock a proportionate interest in the corporation with regard to control, earnings, and net assets; shares of common stock are lowest in priority with respect to payment of dividends and distribution of the corporation's assets on dissolution.

Community Property A form of concurrent ownership of property in which each spouse technically owns an undivided one-half interest in property acquired during the marriage. This form of joint ownership occurs in only nine states and Puerto Rico.

Comparative Negligence A theory in tort law under which the liability for injuries resulting from negligent acts is shared by all persons who were guilty of negligence (including the injured party), on the basis of each person's proportionate carelessness.

Compensatory Damages A money award equivalent to the actual value of injuries or damages sustained by the aggrieved party.

Complaint The pleading made by a plaintiff alleging wrongdoing on the part of the defendant; the document that, when filed with a court, initiates a lawsuit.

Computer Crime Any act that is directed against computers and computer parts, that uses computers as instruments of crime, or that involves computers and constitutes abuse.

Concurrent Conditions Conditions that must occur or be performed at the same time; they are mutually dependent. No obligations arise until these conditions are simultaneously performed.

Concurrent Jurisdiction Jurisdiction that exists when two different courts have the power to hear a case. For example, some cases can be heard in a federal or a state court.

Condition A qualification, provision, or clause in a contractual agreement, the occurrence of which creates, suspends, or terminates the obligations of the contracting parties.

Condition Precedent In a contractual agreement, a condition that must be met before a party's promise becomes absolute.

Condition Subsequent A condition in a contract that, if not fulfilled, operates to terminate a party's absolute promise to perform.

Confession of Judgment The act or agreement of a debtor in permitting a judgment to be entered against him or her by a creditor, for an agreed sum, without the institution of legal proceedings.

Confiscation A government's taking of privately owned business or personal property without a proper public purpose or an award of just compensation.

Confusion The mixing together of goods belonging to two or more owners so that the separately owned goods cannot be identified.

Conglomerate Merger A merger between firms that do not compete with each other because they are in different markets (as opposed to horizontal and vertical mergers).

Consent Voluntary agreement to a proposition or an act of another. A concurrence of wills.

Consequential Damages Special damages that compensate for a loss that does not directly or immediately result from the breach (for example, lost profits). The special damages must have been reasonably foreseeable at the time the breach or injury occurred in order for the plaintiff to collect them.

Consideration Generally, the value given in return for a promise. The consideration, which must be present to make the contract legally binding, must result in a detriment to the promisee (something of legally sufficient value and bargained for) or a benefit to the promisor.

Consignment A transaction in which an owner of goods (the consignor) delivers the goods to another (the consignee) for the consignee to sell. The consignee pays the consignor only for the goods that are sold by the consignee.

Consolidation A contractual and statutory process in which two or more corporations join to become a completely new corporation. The original corporations cease to exist, and the new corporation acquires all their assets and liabilities.

Constitutional Law Law based on the U.S. Constitution and the constitutions of the various states.

Constructive Delivery An act equivalent to the actual, physical delivery of property that cannot be physically delivered because of difficulty or impossibility; for example, the transfer of a key to a safe constructively delivers the contents of the safe.

Constructive Eviction A form of eviction that occurs when a landlord fails to perform adequately any of the undertakings (such as providing heat in the winter) required by the lease, thereby making the tenant's further use and enjoyment of the property exceedingly difficult or impossible.

Constructive Trust An equitable trust that is imposed in the interests of fairness and justice when someone wrongfully holds legal title to property. A court may require the owner to hold the property in trust for the person or persons who rightfully should own the property.

Consumer-Debtor An individual whose debts are primarily for purchases made for personal or household use.

Continuation Statement A statement that, if filed within six months prior to the expiration date of the original financing statement, continues the perfection of the original security interest for another five years. The perfection of a security interest can be continued in the same manner indefinitely.

Contract An agreement that can be enforced in court; formed by two or more competent parties who agree, for consideration, to perform or to refrain from performing some legal act now or in the future.

Contractual Capacity The threshold mental capacity required by law for a party who enters into a contract to be bound by that contract.

Contributory Negligence A theory in tort law under which a complaining party's own negligence contributed to or caused his or her injuries. Contributory negligence is an absolute bar to recovery in a minority of jurisdictions.

Conversion The wrongful taking or retaining possession of a person's personal property and placing it in the service of another.

Conveyance The transfer of a title to land from one person to another by deed; a document (such as a deed) by which an interest in land is transferred from one person to another.

"Cooling-Off" Laws Laws that allow buyers a period of time, such as three days, in which to cancel door-to-door sales contracts.
Cooperative An association, which may or may not be incorporated, that is organized to provide an economic service to its members. Unincorporated cooperatives are often treated like partnerships for tax and other legally related purposes. Examples of cooperatives are consumer purchasing cooperatives, credit cooperatives, and farmers' cooperatives.
Copyright The exclusive right of "authors" to publish, print, or sell an intellectual production for a statutory period of time. A copyright has the same monopolistic nature as a patent or trademark, but it differs in that it applies exclusively to works of art, literature, and other works of authorship (including computer programs).
Corporate Charter The document issued by a state agency or authority (usually the secretary of state) that grants a corporation legal existence and the right to function.
Corporate Social Responsibility The concept that corporations can and should act ethically and be accountable to society for their actions.
Corporation A legal entity formed in compliance with statutory requirements. The entity is distinct from its shareholder-owners.
Correspondent Bank A bank in which another bank has an account (and vice versa) for the purpose of facilitating fund transfers.
Cost-Benefit Analysis A decision-making technique that involves weighing the costs of a given action against the benefits of the action.
Counteradvertising New advertising that is undertaken pursuant to a Federal Trade Commission order for the purpose of correcting earlier false claims that were made about a product.
Counterclaim A claim made by a defendant in a civil lawsuit against the plaintiff. In effect, the defendant is suing the plaintiff.
Counteroffer An offeree's response to an offer in which the offeree rejects the original offer and at the same time makes a new offer.
Course of Dealing Prior conduct between parties to a contract that establishes a common basis for their understanding.
Course of Performance The conduct that occurs under the terms of a particular agreement; such conduct indicates what the parties to an agreement intended it to mean.
Covenant Not to Sue An agreement to substitute a contractual obligation for some other type of legal action based on a valid claim.
Cover Under the UCC, a remedy that allows the buyer or lessee, on the seller's or lessor's breach, to purchase the goods, in good faith and within a reasonable time, from another seller or lessor and substitute them for the goods due under the contract. If the cost of cover exceeds the cost of the contract goods, the breaching seller or lessor will be liable to the buyer or lessee for the difference, plus incidental and consequential damages.
Cram-Down Provision A provision of the Bankruptcy Code that allows a court to confirm a debtor's Chapter 11 reorganization plan even though only one class of creditors has accepted it. To exercise the court's right under this provision, the court must demonstrate that the plan does not discriminate unfairly against any creditors and is fair and equitable.
Creditors' Composition Agreement An agreement formed between a debtor and his or her creditors in which the creditors agree to accept a lesser sum than that owed by the debtor in full satisfaction of the debt.
Crime A wrong against society proclaimed in a statute and, if committed, punishable by society through fines, removal from public office, and/or imprisonment—and, in some cases, death.
Criminal Law Law that defines and governs actions that constitute crimes. Generally, criminal law has to do with wrongful actions committed against society for which society demands redress.
Crown jewel defense Selling off a corporation's most valuable asset to a third party to make the corporation less attractive to individuals, groups, or firms who are attempting to gain control of the corporation.
Cure The right of a party who tenders nonconforming performance to correct his or her performance within the contract period [UCC 2–508(1)].
Cyber Crime A crime that occurs online, in the virtual community of the Internet, as opposed to the physical world.
Cyber Hate Speech Extreme hate speech on the Internet. Racist materials and Holocaust denials disseminated on the Web are examples.
Cyber Mark A trademark in cyberspace.
Cyber Stalker A person who commits the crime of stalking in cyberspace. Generally, stalking consists of harassing a person and putting that person in reasonable fear for his or her safety or the safety of the person's immediate family.
Cyber Terrorist A hacker whose purpose is to exploit a target computer for a serious impact, such as the corruption of a program to sabotage a business.
Cyber Tort A tort committed in cyberspace.
Cyberlaw An informal term used to refer to all laws governing electronic communications and transactions, particularly those conducted via the Internet.

D

Damages Money sought as a remedy for a breach of contract or a tortious action.
Debtor Under Article 9 of the UCC, a debtor is any party who owes payment or performance of a secured obligation, whether or not the party actually owns or has rights in the collateral.
Debtor in Possession (DIP) In Chapter 11 bankruptcy proceedings, a debtor who is allowed to continue in possession of the property (the business) and to continue business operations.
Deceptive Advertising Advertising that misleads consumers, either by unjustified claims concerning a product's performance or by the omission of a material fact concerning the product's composition or performance.
Deed A document by which title to property (usually real property) is passed.
Defalcation Embezzlement; the misappropriation of funds held by a party, such as a corporate officer or a public official, in a fiduciary relationship with another.
Defamation Anything published or publicly spoken that causes injury to another's good name, reputation, or character.
Default The failure to observe a promise or discharge an obligation. The term is commonly used to mean the failure to pay a debt when it is due.
Default Judgment A judgment entered by a court against a defendant who has failed to appear in court to answer or defend against the plaintiff's claim.
Defendant One against whom a lawsuit is brought; the accused person in a criminal proceeding.

Defense That which a defendant offers and alleges in an action or suit as a reason why the plaintiff should not recover or establish what he or she seeks.

Deficiency Judgment A judgment against a debtor for the amount of a debt remaining unpaid after collateral has been repossessed and sold.

Delegation Doctrine A doctrine based on Article I, Section 8, of the U.S. Constitution, which has been construed to allow Congress to delegate some of its power to make and implement laws to administrative agencies.

Delegation of Duties The act of transferring to another all or part of one's duties arising under a contract.

Depositary Bank The first bank to receive a check for payment.

Deposition The testimony of a party to a lawsuit or a witness taken under oath before a trial.

Destination Contract A contract for the sale of goods in which the seller is required or authorized to ship the goods by carrier and tender delivery of the goods at a particular destination. The seller assumes liability for any losses or damage to the goods until they are tendered at the destination specified in the contract.

Devise To make a gift of real property by will.

Devisee One designated in a will to receive a gift of real property.

Disaffirmance The legal avoidance, or setting aside, of a contractual obligation.

Discharge The termination of an obligation. In contract law, discharge occurs when the parties have fully performed their contractual obligations or when events, conduct of the parties, or operation of the law releases the parties from performance. In bankruptcy proceedings, the extinction of the debtor's dischargeable debts.

Disclosed Principal A principal whose identity is known to a third party at the time the agent makes a contract with the third party.

Discovery A phase in the litigation process during which the opposing parties may obtain information from each other and from third parties prior to trial.

Disparagement of Property An economically injurious falsehood made about another's product or property. A general term for torts that are more specifically referred to as slander of quality or slander of title.

Disparate-Impact Discrimination A form of employment discrimination that results from certain employer practices or procedures that, although not discriminatory on their face, have a discriminatory effect.

Disparate-Treatment Discrimination A form of employment discrimination that results when an employer intentionally discriminates against employees who are members of protected classes.

Dissolution The formal disbanding of a partnership or a corporation. It can take place by (1) acts of the partners or, in a corporation, of the shareholders and board of directors; (2) the death of a partner; (3) the expiration of a time period stated in a partnership agreement or a certificate of incorporation; or (4) judicial decree.

Distribution Agreement A contract between a seller and a distributor of the seller's products setting out the terms and conditions of the distributorship.

Diversity of Citizenship Under Article III, Section 2, of the Constitution, a basis for federal district court jurisdiction over a lawsuit between (1) citizens of different states, (2) a foreign country and citizens of a state or of different states, or (3) citizens of a state and citizens or subjects of a foreign country. The amount in controversy must be more than $75,000 before a federal district court can take jurisdiction in such cases.

Divestiture The act of selling one or more of a company's parts, such as a subsidiary or plant; often mandated by the courts in merger or monopolization cases.

Dividend A distribution to corporate shareholders of corporate profits or income, disbursed in proportion to the number of shares held.

Docket The list of cases entered on a court's calendar and thus scheduled to be heard by the court.

Document of Title Paper exchanged in the regular course of business that evidences the right to possession of goods (for example, a bill of lading or a warehouse receipt).

Domestic Corporation In a given state, a corporation that does business in, and is organized under the law of, that state.

Dominion Ownership rights in property, including the right to possess and control the property.

Double Jeopardy A situation occurring when a person is tried twice for the same criminal offense; prohibited by the Fifth Amendment to the Constitution.

Draft Any instrument drawn on a drawee that orders the drawee to pay a certain sum of money, usually to a third party (the payee), on demand or at a definite future time.

Dram Shop Acts State statutes that impose liability on the owners of bars and taverns, as well as those who serve alcoholic drinks to the public, for injuries resulting from accidents caused by intoxicated persons when the sellers or servers of alcoholic drinks contributed to the intoxication.

Drawee The party that is ordered to pay a draft or check. With a check, a bank or a financial institution is always the drawee.

Drawer The party that initiates a draft (such as a check), thereby ordering the drawee to pay.

Due Diligence A required standard of care that certain professionals, such as accountants, must meet to avoid liability for securities violations.

Due Process Clause The provisions of the Fifth and Fourteenth Amendments to the Constitution that guarantee that no person shall be deprived of life, liberty, or property without due process of law. Similar clauses are found in most state constitutions.

Dumping The selling of goods in a foreign country at a price below the price charged for the same goods in the domestic market.

Duress Unlawful pressure brought to bear on a person, causing the person to perform an act that he or she would not otherwise perform.

Duty of Care The duty of all persons, as established by tort law, to exercise a reasonable amount of care in their dealings with others. Failure to exercise due care, which is normally determined by the "reasonable person standard," constitutes the tort of negligence.

E

E-Commerce Business transacted in cyberspace.

E-Contract A contract that is entered into in cyberspace and is evidenced only by electronic impulses (such as those that make up a computer's memory), rather than, for example, a typewritten form.

E-Money Prepaid funds recorded on a computer or a card (such as a smart card).

Early Neutral Case Evaluation A form of alternative dispute resolution in which a neutral third party evaluates the strengths and weakness of the disputing parties' positions; the evaluator's opinion forms the basis for negotiating a settlement.
Easement A nonpossessory right to use another's property in a manner established by either express or implied agreement.
Electronic Fund Transfer (EFT) A transfer of funds with the use of an electronic terminal, a telephone, a computer, or magnetic tape.
Emancipation In regard to minors, the act of being freed from parental control; occurs when a child's parent or legal guardian relinquishes the legal right to exercise control over the child. Normally, a minor who leaves home to support himself or herself is considered emancipated.
Embezzlement The fraudulent appropriation of funds or other property by a person to whom the funds or property has been entrusted.
Eminent Domain The power of a government to take land for public use from private citizens for just compensation.
Employment at Will A common law doctrine under which either party may terminate an employment relationship at any time for any reason, unless a contract specifies otherwise.
Employment Discrimination Treating employees or job applicants unequally on the basis of race, color, national origin, religion, gender, age, or disability; prohibited by federal statutes.
Enabling Legislation A statute enacted by Congress that authorizes the creation of an administrative agency and specifies the name, composition, purpose, and powers of the agency being created.
Encryption The process by which a message (plaintext) is transformed into something (ciphertext) that the sender and receiver intend third parties not to understand.
Entrapment In criminal law, a defense in which the defendant claims that he or she was induced by a public official—usually an undercover agent or police officer—to commit a crime that he or she would otherwise not have committed.
Environmental Impact Statement (EIS) A statement required by the National Environmental Policy Act for any major federal action that will significantly affect the quality of the environment. The statement must analyze the action's impact on the environment and explore alternative actions that might be taken.
Equal Dignity Rule In most states, a rule stating that express authority given to an agent must be in writing if the contract to be made on behalf of the principal is required to be in writing.
Equal Protection Clause The provision in the Fourteenth Amendment to the Constitution that guarantees that no state will "deny to any person within its jurisdiction the equal protection of the laws." This clause mandates that the state governments treat similarly situated individuals in a similar manner.
Equitable Principles and Maxims General propositions or principles of law that have to do with fairness (equity).
Establishment Clause The provision in the First Amendment to the Constitution that prohibits Congress from creating any law "respecting an establishment of religion."
Estate in Property In bankruptcy proceedings, all of the debtor's legal and equitable interests in property presently held, wherever located, together with certain jointly owned property, property transferred in transactions voidable by the trustee, proceeds and profits from the property of the estate, and certain property interests to which the debtor becomes entitled within 180 days after filing for bankruptcy.
Estopped Barred, impeded, or precluded.
Estray Statute A statute defining finders' rights in property when the true owners are unknown.
Ethics Moral principles and values applied to social behavior.
Eviction A landlord's act of depriving a tenant of possession of the leased premises.
Exclusionary Rule In criminal procedure, a rule under which any evidence that is obtained in violation of the accused's constitutional rights guaranteed by the Fourth, Fifth, and Sixth Amendments, as well as any evidence derived from illegally obtained evidence, will not be admissible in court.
Exclusive-Dealing Contract An agreement under which a seller forbids a buyer to purchase products from the seller's competitors.
Exclusive Distributorship A distributorship in which the seller and distributor of the seller's products agree that the distributor has the exclusive right to distribute the seller's products in a certain geographic area.
Exclusive Jurisdiction Jurisdiction that exists when a case can be heard only in a particular court or type of court.
Exculpatory Clause A clause that releases a contractual party from liability in the event of monetary or physical injury, no matter who is at fault.
Executed Contract A contract that has been completely performed by both parties.
Execution An action to carry into effect the directions in a court decree or judgment.
Executive Agency An administrative agency that is either a cabinet department or a subagency within a cabinet department. Executive agencies fall under the authority of the president, who has the power to appoint and remove federal officers.
Executor A person appointed by a testator in a will to see that his or her will is administered appropriately.
Executory Contract A contract that has not as yet been fully performed.
Executory Interest A future interest, held by a person other than the grantor, that begins after the termination of the preceding estate.
Export To sell products to buyers located in other countries.
Express Contract A contract in which the terms of the agreement are fully and explicitly stated in words, oral or written.
Express Warranty A seller's or lessor's oral or written promise, ancillary to an underlying sales or lease agreement, as to the quality, description, or performance of the goods being sold or leased.
Expropriation The seizure by a government of privately owned business or personal property for a proper public purpose and with just compensation.
Extension Clause A clause in a time instrument that allows the instrument's date of maturity to be extended into the future.

F

Family Limited Liability Partnership (FLLP) A type of limited liability partnership owned by family members or fiduciaries of family members.
Federal Form of Government A system of government in which the states form a union and the sovereign power is divided between a central government and the member states.

Federal Question A question that pertains to the U.S. Constitution, acts of Congress, or treaties. A federal question provides a basis for federal jurisdiction.
Federal Reserve System A network of twelve district banks and related branches located around the country and headed by the Federal Reserve Board of Governors. Most banks in the United States have Federal Reserve accounts.
Fee Simple An absolute form of property ownership entitling the property owner to use, possess, or dispose of the property as he or she chooses during his or her lifetime. Upon death, the interest in the property descends to the owner's heirs.
Fee Simple Absolute An ownership interest in land in which the owner has the greatest possible aggregation of rights, privileges, and power. Ownership in fee simple absolute is limited absolutely to a person and his or her heirs.
Fee Simple Defeasible An ownership interest in real property that can be taken away (by the prior grantor) upon the occurrence or nonoccurrence of a specified event.
Felony A crime—such as arson, murder, rape, or robbery—that carries the most severe sanctions, which range from one year in a state or federal prison to the death penalty.
Fictitious Payee A payee on a negotiable instrument whom the maker or drawer does not intend to have an interest in the instrument. Indorsements by fictitious payees are treated as authorized indorsements under Article 3 of the UCC.
Fiduciary As a noun, a person having a duty created by his or her undertaking to act primarily for another's benefit in matters connected with the undertaking. As an adjective, a relationship founded on trust and confidence.
Filtering Software A computer program that includes a pattern through which data are passed. When designed to block access to certain Web sites, the pattern blocks the retrieval of a site whose URL or key words are on a list within the program.
Final order The final decision of an administrative agency on an issue. If no appeal is taken, or if the case is not reviewed or considered anew by the agency commission, the administrative law judge's initial order becomes the final order of the agency.
Financing Statement A document prepared by a secured creditor, and filed with the appropriate state or local official, to give notice to the public that the creditor has a security interest in collateral belonging to the debtor named in the statement. The financing statement must be signed by the debtor, contain the addresses of both the debtor and the creditor, and describe the collateral by type or item.
Firm Offer An offer (by a merchant) that is irrevocable without consideration for a stated period of time or, if no definite period is stated, for a reasonable time (neither period to exceed three months). A firm offer by a merchant must be in writing and must be signed by the offeror.
Fixture A thing that was once personal property but that has become attached to real property in such a way that it takes on the characteristics of real property and becomes part of that real property.
Flame An online message in which one party attacks another in harsh, often personal terms.
Floating Lien A security interest in proceeds, after-acquired property, or property purchased under a line of credit (or all three); a security interest in collateral that is retained even when the collateral changes in character, classification, or location.
Force Majeure **(pronounced mah-*zhure*) Clause** A provision in a contract stipulating that certain unforeseen events—such as war, political upheavals, acts of God, or other events—will excuse a party from liability for nonperform-ance of contractual obligations.
Foreign Corporation In a given state, a corporation that does business in the state without being incorporated therein.
Foreign Exchange Market A worldwide system in which foreign currencies are bought and sold.
Forgery The fraudulent making or altering of any writing in a way that changes the legal rights and liabilities of another.
Formal Contract A contract that by law requires for its validity a specific form, such as executed under seal.
Forum-Selection Clause A provision in a contract designating the court, jurisdiction, or tribunal that will decide any disputes arising under the contract.
Franchise Any arrangement in which the owner of a trademark, trade name, or copyright licenses another to use that trademark, trade name, or copyright in the selling of goods and services.
Franchisee One receiving a license to use another's (the franchisor's) trademark, trade name, or copyright in the sale of goods and services.
Franchisor One licensing another (the franchisee) to use his or her trademark, trade name, or copyright in the sale of goods or services.
Fraudulent Misrepresentation Any misrepresentation, either by misstatement or omission of a material fact, knowingly made with the intention of deceiving another and on which a reasonable person would and does rely to his or her detriment.
Free Exercise Clause The provision in the First Amendment to the Constitution that prohibits Congress from making any law "prohibiting the free exercise" of religion.
Fungible Goods Goods that are alike by physical nature, by agreement, or by trade usage. Examples of fungible goods are wheat, oil, and wine that are identical in type and quality.
Future Interest An interest in real property that is not at present possessory but will or may become possessory in the future.

G

Garnishment A legal process used by a creditor to collect a debt by seizing property of the debtor (such as wages) that is being held by a third party (such as the debtor's employer).
General Partner In a limited partnership, a partner who assumes responsibility for the management of the partnership and liability for all partnership debts.
Generally Accepted Accounting Principles (GAAP) The conventions, rules, and procedures necessary to define accepted accounting practices at a particular time. The source of the principles is the Financial Accounting Standards Board.
Generally Accepted Auditing Standards (GAAS) Standards concerning an auditor's professional qualities and the judgment exercised by him or her in the performance of an examination and report. The source of the standards is the American Institute of Certified Public Accountants.
Gift Any voluntary transfer of property made without consideration, past or present.
Gift *Causa Mortis* A gift made in contemplation of death. If the donor does not die of that ailment, the gift is revoked.
Gift *Inter Vivos* A gift made during one's lifetime and not in contemplation of imminent death, in contrast to a gift causa mortis.
Good Faith Purchaser A purchaser who buys without notice of any

circumstance that would put a person of ordinary prudence on inquiry as to whether the seller has valid title to the goods being sold.
Good Samaritan Statutes State statutes that provide that persons who provide emergency services to, or rescue, others in peril—unless they do so recklessly, thus causing further harm—cannot be sued for negligence.
Grand Jury A group of citizens called to decide, after hearing the state's evidence, whether a reasonable basis (probable cause) exists for believing that a crime has been committed and whether a trial ought to be held.
Group Boycott The refusal to deal with a particular person or firm by a group of competitors; prohibited by the Sherman Act.
Guarantor A person who agrees to satisfy the debt of another (the debtor) only after the principal debtor defaults; a guarantor's liability is thus secondary.

H

Hacker A person who uses one computer to break into another. Professional computer programmers refer to such persons as "crackers."
Herfindahl-Hirschman Index (HHI) An index of market power used to calculate whether a merger of two businesses will result in sufficient monopoly power to violate antitrust laws.
Holder Any person in the possession of an instrument drawn, issued, or indorsed to him or her, to his or her order, to bearer, or in blank.
Holder in Due Course (HDC) A holder who acquires a negotiable instrument for value; in good faith; and without notice that the instrument is overdue, that it has been dishonored, that any person has a defense against it or a claim to it, or that the instrument contains unauthorized signatures, alterations, or is so irregular or incomplete as to call into question its authenticity.
Holographic Will A will written entirely in the signer's handwriting and usually not witnessed.
Homestead Exemption A law permitting a debtor to retain the family home, either in its entirety or up to a specified dollar amount, free from the claims of unsecured creditors or trustees in bankruptcy.
Horizontal Merger A merger between two firms that are competing in the same marketplace.
Horizontal Restraint Any agreement that in some way restrains competition between rival firms competing in the same market.
Hot-Cargo Agreement An agreement in which employers voluntarily agree with unions not to handle, use, or deal in nonunion-produced goods of other employers; a type of secondary boycott explicitly prohibited by the Labor-Management Reporting and Disclosure Act of 1959.

I

Identification In a sale of goods, the express designation of the goods provided for in the contract.
Implied Warranty of Fitness for a Particular Purpose A warranty that goods sold or leased are fit for a particular purpose. The warranty arises when any seller or lessor knows the particular purpose for which a buyer or lessee will use the goods and knows that the buyer or lessee is relying on the skill and judgment of the seller or lessor to select suitable goods.
Implied Warranty of Merchantability A warranty that goods being sold or leased are reasonably fit for the general purpose for which they are sold or leased, are properly packaged and labeled, and are of proper quality. The warranty automatically arises in every sale or lease of goods made by a merchant who deals in goods of the kind sold or leased.
Implied Warranty of Habitability An implied promise by a landlord that rented residential premises are fit for human habitation—that is, in a condition that is safe and suitable for people to live in.
Implied-in-Fact Contract A contract formed in whole or in part from the conduct of the parties (as opposed to an express contract).
Impossibility of Performance A doctrine under which a party to a contract is relieved of his or her duty to perform when performance becomes objectively impossible or totally impracticable (through no fault of either party).
Imposter One who, by use of the mails, telephone, or personal appearance, induces a maker or drawer to issue an instrument in the name of an impersonated payee. Indorsements by imposters are treated as authorized indorsements under Article 3 of the UCC.
Incidental Beneficiary A third party who incidentally benefits from a contract but whose benefit was not the reason the contract was formed; an incidental beneficiary has no rights in a contract and cannot sue to have the contract enforced.
Incidental Damages Damages resulting from a breach of contract, including all reasonable expenses incurred because of the breach.
Independent Contractor One who works for, and receives payment from, an employer but whose working conditions and methods are not controlled by the employer. An independent contractor is not an employee but may be an agent.
Independent Regulatory Agency An administrative agency that is not considered part of the government's executive branch and is not subject to the authority of the president. Independent agency officials cannot be removed without cause.
Indictment (pronounced in-*dyte*-ment) A charge by a grand jury that a named person has committed a crime.
Indorsee The person to whom a negotiable instrument is transferred by indorsement.
Indorsement A signature placed on an instrument for the purpose of transferring one's ownership rights in the instrument.
Indorser A person who transfers an instrument by signing (indorsing) it and delivering it to another person.
Informal Contract A contract that does not require a specified form or formality in order to be valid.
Information A formal accusation or complaint (without an indictment) issued in certain types of actions (usually criminal actions involving lesser crimes) by a law officer, such as a magistrate.
Initial Order In the context of administrative law, an agency's disposition in a matter other than a rulemaking. An administrative law judge's initial order becomes final unless it is appealed.
Innkeeper's Lien A possessory lien placed on the luggage of hotel guests for hotel charges that remain unpaid.
Insider Trading The purchase or sale of securities on the basis of information that has not been made available to the public.
Insolvent Under the UCC, a term describing a person who ceases to pay "his debts in the ordinary course of business or cannot pay his debts as they become due or is insolvent within the meaning of federal bankruptcy law" [UCC 1–201(23)].
Installment Contract Under the UCC, a contract that requires or authorizes delivery in two or more separate lots to be accepted and paid for separately.

Insurable Interest An interest either in a person's life or well-being or in property that is sufficiently substantial that insuring against injury to (or the death of) the person or against damage to the property does not amount to a mere wagering (betting) contract.

Insurance A contract in which, for a stipulated consideration, one party agrees to compensate the other for loss on a specific subject by a specified peril.

Integrated Contract A written contract that constitutes the final expression of the parties' agreement. If a contract is integrated, evidence extraneous to the contract that contradicts or alters the meaning of the contract in any way is inadmissible.

Intellectual Property Property resulting from intellectual, creative processes.

Intended Beneficiary A third party for whose benefit a contract is formed; an intended beneficiary can sue the promisor if such a contract is breached.

Intentional Tort A wrongful act knowingly committed.

***Inter Vivos* Trust** A trust created by the grantor (settlor) and effective during the grantor's lifetime; a trust not established by a will.

Intermediary Bank Any bank to which an item is transferred in the course of collection, except the depositary or payor bank.

International Law The law that governs relations among nations. National laws, customs, treaties, and international conferences and organizations are generally considered to be the most important sources of international law.

Interrogatories A series of written questions for which written answers are prepared and then signed under oath by a party to a lawsuit, usually with the assistance of the party's attorney.

Intestacy Laws State statutes that specify how property will be distributed when a person dies intestate (without a valid will); also called statutes of descent and distribution.

Intestate As a noun, one who has died without having created a valid will; as an adjective, the state of having died without a will.

Investment Company A company that acts on behalf of many smaller shareholders/owners by buying a large portfolio of securities and professionally managing that portfolio.

J

Joint and Several Liability In partnership law, a doctrine under which a plaintiff may sue, and collect a judgment from, one or more of the partners separately (severally, or individually) or all of the partners together (jointly). This is true even if one of the partners sued did not participate in, ratify, or know about whatever it was that gave rise to the cause of action.

Joint Liability Shared liability. In partnership law, partners incur joint liability for partnership obligations and debts. For example, if a third party sues a partner on a partnership debt, the partner has the right to insist that the other partners be sued with him or her.

Joint Stock Company A hybrid form of business organization that combines characteristics of a corporation and a partnership. Usually, the joint stock company is regarded as a partnership for tax and other legally related purposes.

Joint Tenancy The joint ownership of property by two or more co-owners of property in which each co-owner owns an undivided portion of the property. On the death of one of the joint tenants, his or her interest automatically passes to the surviving joint tenants.

Joint Venture A joint undertaking of a specific commercial enterprise by an association of persons. A joint venture is normally not a legal entity and is treated like a partnership for federal income tax purposes.

Judicial Process The procedures relating to, or connected with, the administration of justice through the judicial system.

Judicial Review The process by which a court decides on the constitutionality of legislative enactments and actions of the executive branch.

Junk bond A bond that represents a promise to pay a certain amount to investors after or during a specific period but that is subject to a higher degree of risk than other bonds—the risk that the issuer will be unable to pay according to the terms of the bonds.

Jurisdiction The authority of a court to hear and decide a specific action.

Jurisprudence The science or philosophy of law.

Justiciable (pronounced jus-*tish*-a-bul) Controversy A controversy that is not hypothetical or academic but real and substantial; a requirement that must be satisfied before a court will hear a case.

L

Larceny The wrongful taking and carrying away of another person's personal property with the intent to permanently deprive the owner of the property. Some states classify larceny as either grand or petit, depending on the property's value.

Law A body of enforceable rules governing relationships among individuals and between individuals and their society.

Lease Agreement In regard to the lease of goods, an agreement in which one person (the lessor) agrees to transfer the right to the possession and use of property to another person (the lessee) in exchange for rental payments.

Lease In real property law, a contract by which the owner of real property (the landlord, or lessor) grants to a person (the tenant, or lessee) an exclusive right to use and possess the property, usually for a specified period of time, in return for rent or some other form of payment.

Leasehold Estate An estate in realty held by a tenant under a lease. In every leasehold estate, the tenant has a qualified right to possess and/or use the land.

Legacy A gift of personal property under a will.

Legal Positivism A school of legal thought centered on the assumption that there is no law higher than the laws created by the government. Laws must be obeyed, even if they are unjust, to prevent anarchy.

Legal Realism A school of legal thought of the 1920s and 1930s that generally advocated a less abstract and more realistic approach to the law, an approach that takes into account customary practices and the circumstances in which transactions take place. The school left a lasting imprint on American jurisprudence.

Legatee One designated in a will to receive a gift of personal property.

Legislative Rule An administrative agency rule that carries the same weight as a congressionally enacted statute.

Lessee A person who acquires the right to the possession and use of another's goods in exchange for rental payments.

Lessor A person who sells the right to the possession and use of goods to another in exchange for rental payments.

Letter of Credit A written instrument, usually issued by a bank on behalf of a customer or other person, in which the issuer promises to honor drafts or other demands for payment by third persons in accordance with the terms of the instrument.

Leveraged Buy-Out (LBO) A corporate takeover financed by loans secured by the acquired corporation's assets or by the issuance of corporate bonds, resulting in a high debt load for the corporation.

Levy The obtaining of money by legal process through the seizure and sale of property, usually done after a writ of execution has been issued.

Libel Defamation in writing or other form (such as in a videotape) having the quality of permanence.

License A revocable right or privilege of a person to come on another person's land.

Lien (pronounced *leen*) An encumbrance on a property to satisfy a debt or protect a claim for payment of a debt.

Life Estate An interest in land that exists only for the duration of the life of some person, usually the holder of the estate.

Limited Liability Company (LLC) A hybrid form of business enterprise that offers the limited liability of the corporation but the tax advantages of a partnership.

Limited Liability Limited Partnership (LLLP) A type of limited partnership in which the liability of all of the partners, including general partners, is limited to the amount of their investments.

Limited Liability Partnership (LLP) A business organizational form that is similar to the LCC but that is designed more for professionals who normally do business as partners in a partnership. The LLP is a pass-through entity for tax purposes, like the general partnership, but it limits the personal liability of the partners.

Limited Partner In a limited partnership, a partner who contributes capital to the partnership but who has no right to participate in the management and operation of the business. The limited partner assumes no liability for partnership debts beyond the capital contributed.

Limited Partnership A partnership consisting of one or more general partners (who manage the business and are liable to the full extent of their personal assets for debts of the partnership) and one or more limited partners (who contribute only assets and are liable only up to the extent of their contributions).

Liquidated Damages An amount, stipulated in the contract, that the parties to a contract believe to be a reasonable estimation of the damages that will occur in the event of a breach.

Liquidation In regard to bankruptcy, the sale of all of the nonexempt assets of a debtor and the distribution of the proceeds to the debtor's creditors. Chapter 7 of the Bankruptcy Code provides for liquidation bankruptcy proceedings. In regard to corporations, the process by which corporate assets are converted into cash and distributed among creditors and shareholders according to specific rules of preference.

Litigation The process of resolving a dispute through the court system.

Lobster Trap Defense Prohibiting holders of convertible securities (stocks or bonds that can be converted into common shares) from converting the securities into common shares if the holders already own, or would own after conversion, 10 percent or more of the voting shares of stock.

Long Arm Statute A state statute that permits a state to obtain personal jurisdiction over nonresident defendants. A defendant must have certain "minimum contacts" with that state for the statute to apply.

Lost Property Property with which the owner has involuntarily parted and then cannot find or recover.

M

Mailbox Rule A rule providing that an acceptance of an offer becomes effective on dispatch (on being placed in an official mailbox), if mail is, expressly or impliedly, an authorized means of communication of acceptance to the offeror.

Maker One who promises to pay a fixed amount of money to the holder of a promissory note or a certificate of deposit (CD).

Malpractice Professional misconduct or unreasonable lack of skill. The failure of a professional to use the skills and learning common to the average reputable members of the profession or those the professional claims to possess, resulting in injury, loss, or damage to those relying on the professional.

Market Concentration The percentage of a particular firm's market sales in a relevant market area.

Market Power The power of a firm to control the market price of its product. A monopoly has the greatest degree of market power.

Market-Share Test The primary measure of monopoly power. A firm's market share is the percentage of a market that the firm controls.

Marshalling Assets The arrangement or ranking of assets in a certain order toward the payment of debts. When two creditors have recourse to the same property of a debtor, but one has recourse to other property of the debtor, that creditor must resort first to those assets of the debtor available to the other creditor.

Mechanic's Lien A statutory lien on the real property of another, created to ensure payment for work performed and materials furnished in the repair or improvement of real property, such as a building.

Mediation A method of settling disputes outside of court by using the services of a neutral third party, who acts as a communicating agent between the parties and assists the parties in negotiating a settlement.

Member The term used to designate a person who has an ownership interest in a limited liability company.

Merchant A person who is engaged in the purchase and sale of goods. Under the UCC, a person who deals in goods of the kind involved in the sales contract or who holds himself or herself out as having skill or knowledge peculiar to the practice or use of the goods being purchased or sold. For definitions, see UCC 2–104.

Merger A contractual and statutory process in which one corporation (the surviving corporation) acquires all of the assets and liabilities of another corporation (the merged corporation). The shareholders of the merged corporation receive either payment for their shares or shares in the surviving corporation.

Meta Tags Words inserted into a Web site's key words field to increase the site's appearance in search engine results.

Mini-trial A private proceeding in which each party to a dispute argues its position before the other side and vice versa. A neutral third party may be present and act as an adviser if the parties fail to reach an agreement.

Minimum Wage The lowest wage, either by government regulation or union contract, that an employer may pay an hourly worker.

Mirror Image Rule A common law rule that requires, for a valid contractual agreement, that the terms of the offeree's acceptance adhere exactly to the terms of the offeror's offer.

Misdemeanor A lesser crime than a felony, punishable by a fine or incarceration in a jail for up to one year.

Mislaid Property Property with which the owner has voluntarily parted and then cannot find or recover.

Mitigation of Damages A rule requiring a plaintiff to have done whatever was reasonable to minimize the damages caused by the defendant.

Money Laundering Falsely reporting income that has been obtained through criminal activity as income obtained through a legitimate business enterprise—in effect, "laundering" the "dirty money."

Monopolization The possession of monopoly power in the relevant market and the willful acquisition or maintenance of the power, as distinguished from growth or development as a consequence of a superior product, business acumen, or historic accident.
Monopoly A term generally used to describe a market in which there is a single seller or a limited number of sellers.
Monopoly Power The ability of a monopoly to dictate what takes place in a given market.
Moral Rights The rights of an author to proclaim or disclaim authorship, and to object to any change to the author's work that would injure his or her reputation. These rights are personal to the author and cannot be taken away or abridged.
Mortgagee Under a mortgage agreement, the creditor who takes a security interest in the debtor's real property.
Mortgagor Under a mortgage agreement, the debtor who gives the creditor a security interest in the debtor's real property in return for a mortgage loan.
Most-Favored-Nation Status A status granted in an international treaty by a provision stating that the citizens of the contracting nations may enjoy the privileges accorded by either party to citizens of the most favored nations. Generally, most-favored-nation clauses are designed to establish equality of international treatment.
Motion for a Directed Verdict In a jury trial, a motion for the judge to take the decision out of the hands of the jury and direct a verdict for the moving party on the ground that the other party has not produced sufficient evidence to support his or her claim.
Motion for a New Trial A motion asserting that the trial was so fundamentally flawed (because of error, newly discovered evidence, prejudice, or other reason) that a new trial is necessary to prevent a miscarriage of justice.
Motion for Judgment *N.O.V.* A motion requesting the court to grant judgment in favor of the party making the motion on the ground that the jury verdict against him or her was unreasonable and erroneous.
Motion for Judgment on the Pleadings A motion by either party to a lawsuit at the close of the pleadings requesting the court to decide the issue solely on the pleadings without proceeding to trial. The motion will be granted only if no facts are in dispute.
Motion for Summary Judgment A motion requesting the court to enter a judgment without proceeding to trial. The motion can be based on evidence outside the pleadings and will be granted only if no facts are in dispute.
Motion to Dismiss A pleading in which a defendant asserts that the plaintiff's claim fails to state a cause of action (that is, has no basis in law) or that there are other grounds on which a suit should be dismissed.
Mutual Fund A specific type of investment company that continually buys or sells to investors shares of ownership in a portfolio.

N

National Law Law that pertains to a particular nation (as opposed to international law).
Natural Law The belief that government and the legal system should reflect universal moral and ethical principles that are inherent in human nature. The natural law school is the oldest and one of the most significant schools of legal thought.
Necessaries Necessities required for life, such as food, shelter, clothing, and medical attention; may include whatever is believed to be necessary to maintain a person's standard of living or financial and social status.
Negligence The failure to exercise the standard of care that a reasonable person would exercise in similar circumstances.
Negligence *Per Se* An action or failure to act in violation of a statutory requirement.
Negotiation A process in which parties attempt to settle their dispute informally, with or without attorneys to represent them. The transfer of an instrument in such form that the transferee (the person to whom the instrument is transferred) becomes a holder.
No-Par Shares Corporate shares that have no face value—that is, no specific dollar amount is printed on their face.
Nominal Damages A small monetary award (often one dollar) granted to a plaintiff when no actual damage was suffered.
Notary Public A public official authorized to attest to the authenticity of signatures.
Notice-and-Comment Rulemaking A procedure in agency rulemaking that requires (1) notice, (2) opportunity for comment, and (3) a published draft of the final rule.
Novation The substitution, by agreement, of a new contract for an old one, with the rights under the old one being terminated. Typically, there is a substitution of a new person who is responsible for the contract and the removal of the original party's rights and duties under the contract.
Nuisance A common law doctrine under which persons may be held liable for using their property in a manner that unreasonably interferes with others' rights to use or enjoy their own property.
Nuncupative Will An oral will (often called a deathbed will) made before witnesses; usually limited to transfers of personal property.

O

Objective Theory of Contracts A theory under which the intent to form a contract will be judged by outward, objective facts (what the party said when entering into the contract, how the party acted or appeared, and the circumstances surrounding the transaction) as interpreted by a reasonable person, rather than by the party's own secret, subjective intentions.
Offer A promise or commitment to perform or refrain from performing some specified act in the future.
Offeree A person to whom an offer is made.
Offeror A person who makes an offer.
Operating Agreement In a limited liability company, an agreement in which the members set forth the details of how the business will be managed and operated. State statutes typically give the members wide latitude in deciding for themselves the rules that will govern their organization.
Option Contract A contract under which the offeror cannot revoke his or her offer for a stipulated time period, and the offeree can accept or reject the offer during this period without fear that the offer will be made to another person. The offeree must give consideration for the option (the irrevocable offer) to be enforceable.
Order for Relief A court's grant of assistance to a complainant. In bankruptcy proceedings, the order relieves the debtor of the immediate obligation to pay the debts listed in the bankruptcy petition.
Order Instrument A negotiable instrument that is payable "to the order of an identified person" or "to an identified person or order."
Output Contract An agreement in which a seller agrees to sell

and a buyer agrees to buy all or up to a stated amount of what the seller produces.
Overdraft A check that is written on a checking account in which there are insufficient funds to cover the check and that is paid by the bank.

P

Par-Value Shares Corporate shares that have a specific face value, or formal cash-in value, written on them, such as one dollar.
Parol Evidence Rule A substantive rule of contracts, as well as a procedural rule of evidence, under which a court will not receive into evidence the parties' prior negotiations, prior agreements, or contemporaneous oral agreements if that evidence contradicts or varies the terms of the parties' written contract.
Partially Disclosed Principal A principal whose identity is unknown by a third person, but the third person knows that the agent is or may be acting for a principal at the time the agent and the third person form a contract.
Partnership An agreement by two or more persons to carry on, as co-owners, a business for profit.
Past Consideration An act done before the contract is made, which ordinarily, by itself, cannot be consideration for a later promise to pay for the act.
Patent A government grant that gives an inventor the exclusive right or privilege to make, use, or sell his or her invention for a limited time period.
Payee A person to whom an instrument is made payable.
Payor Bank The bank on which a check is drawn (the drawee bank).
Penalty A sum inserted into a contract, not as a measure of compensation for its breach but rather as punishment for a default. The agreement as to the amount will not be enforced, and recovery will be limited to actual damages.
Per Capita A Latin term meaning "per person." In the law governing estate distribution, a method of distributing the property of an intestate's estate in which each heir in a certain class (such as grandchildren) receives an equal share.
Per Stirpes A Latin term meaning "by the roots." In the law governing estate distribution, a method of distributing an intestate's estate in which each heir in a certain class (such as grandchildren) takes the share to which his or her deceased ancestor (such as a mother or father) would have been entitled.
***Per Se* Violation** A type of anticompetitive agreement—such as a horizontal price-fixing agreement—that is considered to be so injurious to the public that there is no need to determine whether it actually injures market competition; rather, it is in itself (*per se*) a violation of the Sherman Act.
Perfection The legal process by which secured parties protect themselves against the claims of third parties who may wish to have their debts satisfied out of the same collateral; usually accomplished by the filing of a financing statement with the appropriate government official.
Performance In contract law, the fulfillment of one's duties arising under a contract with another; the normal way of discharging one's contractual obligations.
Periodic Tenancy A lease interest in land for an indefinite period involving payment of rent at fixed intervals, such as week to week, month to month, or year to year.
Personal Defenses Defenses that can be used to avoid payment to an ordinary holder of a negotiable instrument but not a holder in due course (HDC) or a holder with the rights of an HDC.
Persuasive Authority Any legal authority or source of law that a court may look to for guidance but on which it need not rely in making its decision. Persuasive authorities include cases from other jurisdictions and secondary sources of law.
Petition in Bankruptcy The document that is filed with a bankruptcy court to initiate bankruptcy proceedings. The official forms required for a petition in bankruptcy must be completed accurately, sworn to under oath, and signed by the debtor.
Petty Offense In criminal law, the least serious kind of criminal offense, such as a traffic or building-code violation.
Plaintiff One who initiates a lawsuit.
Plea Bargaining The process by which a criminal defendant and the prosecutor in a criminal case work out a mutually satisfactory disposition of the case, subject to court approval; usually involves the defendant's pleading guilty to a lesser offense in return for a lighter sentence.
Pleadings Statements made by the plaintiff and the defendant in a lawsuit that detail the facts, charges, and defenses involved in the litigation; the complaint and answer are part of the pleadings.
Pledge A common law security device (retained in Article 9 of the UCC) in which personal property is turned over to the creditor as security for the payment of a debt and retained by the creditor until the debt is paid.
Police Powers Powers possessed by states as part of their inherent sovereignty. These powers may be exercised to protect or promote the public order, health, safety, morals, and general welfare.
Policy In insurance law, a contract between the insurer and the insured in which, for a stipulated consideration, the insurer agrees to compensate the insured for loss on a specific subject by a specified peril.
Positive Law The body of conventional, or written, law of a particular society at a particular point in time.
Potentially Responsible Party (PRP) A party liable under the Comprehensive Environmental Response, Compensation, and Liability Act (CERCLA). Any person who generated the hazardous waste, transported the hazardous waste, owned or operated a waste site at the time of disposal, or currently owns or operates a site may be responsible for some or all of the clean-up costs involved in removing the hazardous chemicals.
Power of Attorney A written document, which is usually notarized, authorizing another to act as one's agent; can be special (permitting the agent to do specified acts only) or general (permitting the agent to transact all business for the principal).
Precedent A court decision that furnishes an example or authority for deciding subsequent cases involving identical or similar facts.
Predatory Behavior Business behavior, such as the entry into business, that is undertaken with the intention of unlawfully driving competitors out of the market.
Predatory Pricing The pricing of a product below cost with the intent to drive competitors out of the market.
Preemption A doctrine under which certain federal laws preempt, or take precedence over, conflicting state or local laws.
Preemptive Rights Rights held by shareholders that entitle them to purchase newly issued shares of a corporation's stock, equal in percentage to shares presently held, before the stock is offered to any outside buyers. Preemptive rights enable shareholders to maintain their proportionate ownership and voice in the corporation.

Preference In bankruptcy proceedings, property transfers or payments made by the debtor that favor (give preference to) one creditor over others. The bankruptcy trustee is allowed to recover payments made both voluntarily and involuntarily to one creditor in preference over another.
Preferred Stock Classes of stock that have priority over common stock both as to payment of dividends and distribution of assets on the corporation's dissolution.
Premium In insurance law, the price paid by the insured for insurance protection for a specified period of time.
Prenuptial Agreement An agreement made before marriage that defines each partner's ownership rights in the other partner's property. Prenuptial agreements must be in writing to be enforceable.
Presentment The act of presenting an instrument to the party liable on the instrument to collect payment; presentment also occurs when a person presents an instrument to a drawee for a required acceptance.
Presentment Warranties Implied warranties, made by any person who presents an instrument for payment or acceptance, that (1) the person obtaining payment or acceptance is entitled to enforce the instrument or is authorized to obtain payment or acceptance on behalf of a person who is entitled to enforce the instrument, (2) the instrument has not been altered, and (3) the person obtaining payment or acceptance has no knowledge that the signature of the drawer of the instrument is unauthorized.
Price-Fixing Agreement An agreement between competitors in which the competitors agree to fix the prices of products or services at a certain level.
***Prima Facie* Case** A case in which the plaintiff has produced sufficient evidence of his or her conclusion that the case can go to a jury; a case in which the evidence compels the plaintiff's conclusion if the defendant produces no affirmative defense or evidence to disprove it.
Primary Source of Law A document that establishes the law on a particular issue, such as a constitution, a statute, an administrative rule, or a court decision.
Principal In agency law, a person who agrees to have another, called the agent, act on his or her behalf.
Privilege In tort law, the ability to act contrary to another person's right without that person's having legal redress for such acts. Privilege may be raised as a defense to defamation.
Probable Cause Reasonable grounds to believe the existence of facts warranting certain actions, such as the search or arrest of a person.
Probate Court A state court of limited jurisdiction that conducts proceedings relating to the settlement of a deceased person's estate.
Procedural Law Law that establishes the methods of enforcing the rights established by substantive law.
Proceeds Under Article 9 of the UCC, whatever is received when the collateral is sold or otherwise disposed of, such as by exchange.
Product Liability The legal liability of manufacturers, sellers, and lessors of goods to consumers, users, and bystanders for injuries or damages that are caused by the goods.
Profit In real property law, the right to enter upon and remove things from the property of another (for example, the right to enter onto a person's land and remove sand and gravel therefrom).
Promise A declaration that something either will or will not happen in the future.
Promisee A person to whom a promise is made.
Promisor A person who makes a promise.
Promissory Estoppel A doctrine that applies when a promisor makes a clear and definite promise on which the promisee justifiably relies; such a promise is binding if justice will be better served by the enforcement of the promise.
Promissory Note A written promise made by one person (the maker) to pay a fixed amount of money to another person (the payee or a subsequent holder) on demand or on a specified date.
Promoter A person who takes the preliminary steps in organizing a corporation, including (usually) issuing a prospectus, procuring stock subscriptions, making contract purchases, securing a corporate charter, and the like.
Prospectus A document required by federal or state securities laws that describes the financial operations of the corporation, thus allowing investors to make informed decisions.
Protected Class A group of persons protected by specific laws because of the group's defining characteristics. Under laws prohibiting employment discrimination, these characteristics include race, color, religion, national origin, gender, age, or disability.
Proximate Cause Legal cause; exists when the connection between an act and an injury is strong enough to justify imposing liability.
Proxy In corporation law, a written agreement between a stockholder and another under which the stockholder authorizes the other to vote the stockholder's shares in a certain manner.
Proxy Fight A conflict between an individual, group, or firm attempting to take control of a corporation and the corporation's management for the votes of the shareholders.
Puffery A salesperson's often exaggerated claims concerning the quality of property offered for sale. Such claims involve opinions rather than facts and are not considered to be legally binding promises or warranties.
Punitive Damages Money damages that may be awarded to a plaintiff to punish the defendant and deter future similar conduct.
Purchase-Money Security Interest (PMSI) A security interest that arises when a seller or lender extends credit for part or all of the purchase price of goods purchased by a buyer.

Q

Qualified Indorsement An indorsement on a negotiable instrument in which the indorser disclaims any contract liability on the instrument; the notation "without recourse" is commonly used to create a qualified indorsement.
Quasi Contract A fictional contract imposed on parties by a court in the interests of fairness and justice; usually, quasi contracts are imposed to avoid the unjust enrichment of one party at the expense of another.
Quitclaim Deed A deed intended to pass any title, interest, or claim that the grantor may have in the property but not warranting that such title is valid. A quitclaim deed offers the least amount of protection against defects in the title.
Quorum The number of members of a decision-making body that must be present before business may be transacted.

R

Ratification The act of accepting and giving legal force to an obligation that previously was not enforceable.
Reasonable Person Standard The standard of behavior expected of a hypothetical "reasonable person." The standard against which negligence is measured and that must be observed to avoid liability for negligence.

Receiver In a corporate dissolution, a court-appointed person who winds up corporate affairs and liquidates corporate assets.
Recording Statutes Statutes that allow deeds, mortgages, and other real property transactions to be recorded so as to provide notice to future purchasers or creditors of an existing claim on the property.
Red Herring A preliminary prospectus that can be distributed to potential investors after the registration statement (for a securities offering) has been filed with the Securities and Exchange Commission. The name derives from the red legend printed across the prospectus stating that the registration has been filed but has not become effective.
Reformation A court-ordered correction of a written contract so that it reflects the true intentions of the parties.
Regulation Z A set of rules promulgated by the Federal Reserve Board to implement the provisions of the Truth-in-Lending Act.
Release A contract in which one party forfeits the right to pursue a legal claim against the other party.
Remainder A future interest in property held by a person other than the original owner.
Remedy The relief given to an innocent party to enforce a right or compensate for the violation of a right.
Replevin (pronounced ruh-*pleh*-vin) An action to recover identified goods in the hands of a party who is wrongfully withholding them from the other party. Under the UCC, this remedy is usually available only if the buyer is unable to cover.
Reply Procedurally, a plaintiff's response to a defendant's answer.
Requirements Contract An agreement in which a buyer agrees to purchase and the seller agrees to sell all or up to a stated amount of what the buyer needs or requires.
Resale Price Maintenance Agreement An agreement between a manufacturer and a retailer in which the manufacturer specifies what the retail price of its products must be.
Rescission (pronounced reh-*sih*-zhen) A remedy whereby a contract is canceled and the parties are returned to the positions they occupied before the contract was made; may be effected through the mutual consent of the parties, by their conduct, or by court decree.
Res Ipsa Loquitur A doctrine under which negligence may be inferred simply because an event occurred, if it is the type of event that would not occur in the absence of negligence. Literally, the term means "the facts speak for themselves."
***Respondeat Superior* (pronounced ree-*spahn*-dee-uht soo-*peer*-ee-your)** In Latin, "Let the master respond." A doctrine under which a principal or an employer is held liable for the wrongful acts committed by agents or employees while acting within the course and scope of their agency or employment.
Restitution An equitable remedy under which a person is restored to his or her original position prior to loss or injury, or placed in the position he or she would have been in had the breach not occurred.
Restrictive Indorsement Any indorsement on a negotiable instrument that requires the indorsee to comply with certain instructions regarding the funds involved. A restrictive indorsement does not prohibit the further negotiation of the instrument.
Resulting Trust An implied trust arising from the conduct of the parties. A trust in which a party holds the actual legal title to another's property but only for that person's benefit.
Retained Earnings The portion of a corporation's profits that has not been paid out as dividends to shareholders.
Reversionary Interest A future interest in property retained by the original owner.
Revocation In contract law, the withdrawal of an offer by an offeror; unless the offer is irrevocable, it can be revoked at any time prior to acceptance without liability.
Right of Contribution The right of a co-surety who pays more than his or her proportionate share on a debtor's default to recover the excess paid from other co-sureties. Also, the right of a partner who pays more than his or her proportionate share of a partnership's liabilities to recover the excess paid from other partners.
Right of First Refusal The right to purchase personal or real property—such as corporate shares or real estate—before the property is offered for sale to others.
Right of Reimbursement The legal right of a person to be restored, repaid, or indemnified for costs, expenses, or losses incurred or expended on behalf of another.
Right of Subrogation The right of a person to stand in the place of (be substituted for) another, giving the substituted party the same legal rights that the original party had.
Right-to-Work Law A state law providing that employees are not to be required to join a union as a condition of obtaining or retaining employment.
Risk A prediction concerning potential loss based on known and unknown factors.
Risk Management Planning that is undertaken to protect one's interest should some event threaten to undermine its security. In the context of insurance, risk management involves transferring certain risks from the insured to the insurance company.
Robbery The act of forcefully and unlawfully taking personal property of any value from another; force or intimidation is usually necessary for an act of theft to be considered a robbery.
Rulemaking The actions undertaken by administrative agencies when formally adopting new regulations or amending old ones. Under the Administrative Procedure Act, rulemaking includes notifying the public of proposed rules or changes and receiving and considering the public's comments.
Rule of Four A rule of the United States Supreme Court under which the Court will not issue a writ of certiorari unless at least four justices approve of the decision to issue the writ.
Rule of Reason A test by which a court balances the positive effects (such as economic efficiency) of an agreement against its potentially anticompetitive effects. In antitrust litigation, many practices are analyzed under the rule of reason.
Rulemaking The process undertaken by an administrative agency when formally adopting a new regulation or amending an old one. Rulemaking involves notifying the public of a proposed rule or change and receiving and considering the public's comments.

S

S Corporation A close business corporation that has met certain requirements as set out by the Internal Revenue Code and thus qualifies for special income tax treatment. Essentially, an S corporation is taxed the same as a partnership, but its owners enjoy the privilege of limited liability.
Sale The passing of title to property from the seller to the buyer for a price.
Sale on Approval A type of conditional sale in which the buyer may take the goods on a trial basis. The sale becomes absolute

only when the buyer approves of (or is satisfied with) the goods being sold.

Sale or Return A type of conditional sale in which title and possession pass from the seller to the buyer; however, the buyer retains the option to return the goods during a specified period even though the goods conform to the contract.

Scienter **(pronounced sy-*en*-ter)** Knowledge by the misrepresenting party that material facts have been falsely represented or omitted with an intent to deceive.

Search Warrant An order granted by a public authority, such as a judge, that authorizes law enforcement personnel to search particular premises or property.

Seasonably Within a specified time period, or, if no period is specified, within a reasonable time.

SEC Rule 10b-5 A rule of the Securities and Exchange Commission that makes it unlawful, in connection with the purchase or sale of any security, to make any untrue statement of a material fact or to omit a material fact if such omission causes the statement to be misleading.

Secondary Boycott A union's refusal to work for, purchase from, or handle the products of a secondary employer, with whom the union has no dispute, for the purpose of forcing that employer to stop doing business with the primary employer, with whom the union has a labor dispute.

Secondary Source of Law A publication that summarizes or interprets the law, such as a legal encyclopedia, a legal treatise, or an article in a law review.

Secured Party A lender, seller, or any other person in whose favor there is a security interest, including a person to whom accounts or chattel paper has been sold.

Secured Transaction Any transaction in which the payment of a debt is guaranteed, or secured, by personal property owned by the debtor or in which the debtor has a legal interest.

Security Generally, a stock certificate, bond, note, debenture, warrant, or other document given as evidence of an ownership interest in a corporation or as a promise of repayment by a corporation.

Security Agreement An agreement that creates or provides for a security interest between the debtor and a secured party.

Security Interest Any interest "in personal property or fixtures which secures payment or performance of an obligation" [UCC 1–201(37)].

Self-Defense The legally recognized privilege to protect one's self or property against injury by another. The privilege of self-defense protects only acts that are reasonably necessary to protect oneself, one's property, or another person.

Self-Incrimination The giving of testimony that may subject the testifier to criminal prosecution. The Fifth Amendment to the Constitution protects against self-incrimination by providing that no person "shall be compelled in any criminal case to be a witness against himself."

Seniority System In regard to employment relationships, a system in which those who have worked longest for the company are first in line for promotions, salary increases, and other benefits; they are also the last to be laid off if the work force must be reduced.

Service Mark A mark used in the sale or the advertising of services, such as to distinguish the services of one person from the services of others. Titles, character names, and other distinctive features of radio and television programs may be registered as service marks.

Sexual Harassment In the employment context, the granting of job promotions or other benefits in return for sexual favors, or language or conduct that is so sexually offensive that it creates a hostile working environment.

Shareholder's Derivative Suit A suit brought by a shareholder to enforce a corporate cause of action against a third person.

Shelter Principle The principle that the holder of a negotiable instrument who cannot qualify as a holder in due course (HDC), but who derives his or her title through an HDC, acquires the rights of an HDC.

Shipment Contract A contract for the sale of goods in which the seller is required or authorized to ship the goods by carrier. The seller assumes liability for any losses or damage to the goods until they are delivered to the carrier.

Short-Form Merger A merger between a subsidiary corporation and a parent corporation that owns at least 90 percent of the outstanding shares of each class of stock issued by the subsidiary corporation. Short-form mergers can be accomplished without the approval of the shareholders of either corporation.

Signature Under the UCC, "any symbol executed or adopted by a party with a present intention to authenticate a writing."

Slander Defamation in oral form.

Slander of Quality (Trade Libel) The publication of false information about another's product, alleging that it is not what its seller claims.

Slander of Title The publication of a statement that denies or casts doubt on another's legal ownership of any property, causing financial loss to that property's owner.

Small Claims Courts Special courts in which parties may litigate small claims (usually, claims involving $5,000 or less). Attorneys are not required in small claims courts, and in many states attorneys are not allowed to represent the parties.

Smart Card Prepaid funds recorded on a microprocessor chip embedded on a card. One type of e-money.

Sole Proprietorship The simplest form of business, in which the owner is the business; the owner reports business income on his or her personal income tax return and is legally responsible for all debts and obligations incurred by the business.

Sovereign Immunity A doctrine that immunizes foreign nations from the jurisdiction of U.S. courts when certain conditions are satisfied.

Spam Bulk, unsolicited ("junk") e-mail.

Special Indorsement An indorsement on an instrument that indicates the specific person to whom the indorser intends to make the instrument payable; that is, it names the indorsee.

Specific Performance An equitable remedy requiring exactly the performance that was specified in a contract; usually granted only when money damages would be an inadequate remedy and the subject matter of the contract is unique (for example, real property).

Spendthrift Trust A trust created to protect the beneficiary from spending all the funds to which he or she is entitled. Only a certain portion of the total amount is given to the beneficiary at any one time, and most states prohibit creditors from attaching assets of the trust.

Stale Check A check, other than a certified check, that is presented for payment more than six months after its date.

Standing to Sue The requirement that an individual must have a sufficient stake in a controversy before he or she can bring a lawsuit. The plaintiff must demonstrate that he or she either has been injured or threatened with injury.

***Stare Decisis* (pronounced *ster*-ay dih-*si*-ses)** A common law doctrine under which judges are obligated to follow the precedents established in prior decisions.

Statutory Law The body of law enacted by legislative bodies (as opposed to constitutional law, administrative law, or case law).

Stock An equity (ownership) interest in a corporation, measured in units of shares.

Stock Certificate A certificate issued by a corporation evidencing the ownership of a specified number of shares in the corporation.

Stock Warrant A certificate that grants the owner the option to buy a given number of shares of stock, usually within a set time period.

Stop-Payment Order An order by a bank customer to his or her bank not to pay or certify a certain check.

Strict Liability Liability regardless of fault. In tort law, strict liability is imposed on a merchant who introduces into commerce a good that is unreasonably dangerous when in a defective condition.

Strict Suretyship An express contract in which a third party to a debtor-creditor relationship (the surety) promises to be primarily responsible for the debtor's obligation. The surety has a right to be reimbursed by the co-debtor.

Strike An action undertaken by unionized workers when collective bargaining fails; the workers leave their jobs, refuse to work, and (typically) picket the employer's workplace.

Sublease A lease executed by the lessee of real estate to a third person, conveying the same interest that the lessee enjoys but for a shorter term than that held by the lessee.

Substantive Law Law that defines, describes, regulates, and creates legal rights and obligations.

Summary Jury Trial (SJT) A method of settling disputes used in many federal courts in which a trial is held, but the jury's verdict is not binding. The verdict acts only as a guide to both sides in reaching an agreement during the mandatory negotiations that immediately follow the summary jury trial.

Summons A document informing a defendant that a legal action has been commenced against him or her and that the defendant must appear in court on a certain date to answer the plaintiff's complaint. The document is delivered by a sheriff or any other person so authorized.

Supremacy Clause The provision in Article VI of the Constitution that provides that the Constitution, laws, and treaties of the United States are "the supreme Law of the Land." Under this clause, state and local laws that directly conflict with federal law will be rendered invalid.

Surety A person, such as a cosigner on a note, who agrees to be primarily responsible for the debt of another.

Symbolic Speech Nonverbal expressions of beliefs. Symbolic speech, which includes gestures, movements, and articles of clothing, is given substantial protection by the courts.

Syndicate An investment group of persons or firms brought together for the purpose of financing a project that they would not or could not undertake independently.

T

Tag A key word in a document that can serve as an index reference to the document. On the Web, search engines return results based, in part, on the tags in Web documents.

Takeover Acquiring control of a corporation through a merger, consolidation, or purchase of a substantial number of voting shares or the assets of the corporation.

Taking The taking of private property by the government for public use. Under the Fifth Amendment to the Constitution, the government may not take private property for public use without "just compensation."

Tangible Property Property that has physical existence and can be distinguished by the senses of touch, sight, and so on. A car is tangible property; a patent right is intangible property.

Target Corporation The corporation to be acquired in a corporate takeover; a corporation to whose shareholders a tender offer is submitted.

Technology Licensing Allowing another to use and profit from intellectual property (patents, copyrights, trademarks, innovative products or processes, and so on) for consideration. In the context of international business transactions, technology licensing is sometimes an attractive alternative to the establishment of foreign production facilities.

Tenancy at Sufferance A type of tenancy under which one who, after rightfully being in possession of leased premises, continues (wrongfully) to occupy the property after the lease has been terminated. The tenant has no rights to possess the property and occupies it only because the person entitled to evict the tenant has not done so.

Tenancy at Will A type of tenancy under which either party can terminate the tenancy without notice; usually arises when a tenant who has been under a tenancy for years retains possession, with the landlord's consent, after the tenancy for years has terminated.

Tenancy by the Entirety The joint ownership of property by a husband and wife. Neither party can transfer his or her interest in the property without the consent of the other.

Tenancy for Years A type of tenancy under which property is leased for a specified period of time, such as a month, a year, or a period of years.

Tenancy in Common Co-ownership of property in which each party owns an undivided interest that passes to his or her heirs at death.

Tender An unconditional offer to perform an obligation by a person who is ready, willing, and able to do so.

Tender Offer An offer to purchase shares made by one company directly to the shareholders of another (target) company; often referred to as a "takeover bid."

Testamentary Trust A trust that is created by will and therefore does not take effect until the death of the testator.

Testator One who makes and executes a will.

Third Party Beneficiary One for whose benefit a promise is made in a contract but who is not a party to the contract.

Tippee A person who receives inside information.

Tombstone Ad An advertisement, historically in a format resembling a tombstone, of a securities offering. The ad informs potential investors of where and how they may obtain a prospectus.

Tort A civil wrong not arising from a breach of contract. A breach of a legal duty that proximately causes harm or injury to another.

Tortfeasor One who commits a tort.

Totten Trust A trust created by the deposit of a person's own funds in his or her own name as a trustee for another. It is a tentative trust, revocable at will until the depositor dies or completes the gift in his or her lifetime by some unequivocal act or declaration.

Trade Acceptance A draft that is drawn by a seller of goods ordering the buyer to pay a specified sum of money to the seller, usually at a stated time in the future. The buyer accepts the draft by signing the face of the draft, thus creating an enforceable obligation to pay the draft when it comes due. On a trade acceptance, the seller is both the drawer and the payee.

Trade Dress The image and overall appearance of a product—for example, the distinctive decor, menu, layout, and style of service of a particular restaurant. Basically, trade dress is subject to the same protection as trademarks.

Trade Name A term that is used to indicate part or all of a business's name and that is directly related to the business's reputation and goodwill. Trade names are protected under the common law (and under trademark law, if the name is the same as the firm's trademarked property).

Trade Secrets Information or processes that give a business an advantage over competitors who do not know the information or processes.

Trademark A distinctive mark, motto, device, or emblem that a manufacturer stamps, prints, or otherwise affixes to the goods it produces so that they may be identified on the market and their origins made known. Once a trademark is established (under the common law or through registration), the owner is entitled to its exclusive use.

Transfer Warranties Implied warranties, made by any person who transfers an instrument for consideration to subsequent transferees and holders who take the instrument in good faith, that (1) the transferor is entitled to enforce the instrument, (2) all signatures are authentic and authorized, (3) the instrument has not been altered, (4) the instrument is not subject to a defense or claim of any party that can be asserted against the transferor, and (5) the transferor has no knowledge of any insolvency proceedings against the maker, the acceptor, or the drawer of the instrument.

Traveler's Check A check that is payable on demand, drawn on or payable through a financial institution (bank), and designated as a traveler's check.

Trespass to Land The entry onto, above, or below the surface of land owned by another without the owner's permission or legal authorization.

Trespass to Personal Property The unlawful taking or harming of another's personal property; interference with another's right to the exclusive possession of his or her personal property.

Trust An arrangement in which title to property is held by one person (a trustee) for the benefit of another (a beneficiary).

Trust Indorsement An indorsement for the benefit of the indorser or a third person; also known as an agency indorsement. The indorsement results in legal title vesting in the original indorsee.

Tying Arrangement An agreement between a buyer and a seller in which the buyer of a specific product or service becomes obligated to purchase additional products or services from the seller.

U

U.S. Trustee A government official who performs certain administrative tasks that a bankruptcy judge would otherwise have to perform.

Ultra Vires **(pronounced *uhl*-trah *vye*-reez)** A Latin term meaning "beyond the powers"; in corporate law, acts of a corporation that are beyond its express and implied powers to undertake.

Unconscionable (pronounced un-*kon*-shun-uh-bul) Contract (or Unconscionable Clause) A contract or clause that is void on the basis of public policy because one party, as a result of his or her disproportionate bargaining power, is forced to accept terms that are unfairly burdensome and that unfairly benefit the dominating party.

Underwriter In insurance law, the insurer, or the one assuming a risk in return for the payment of a premium.

Undisclosed Principal A principal whose identity is unknown by a third person, and the third person has no knowledge that the agent is acting for a principal at the time the agent and the third person form a contract.

Unenforceable Contract A valid contract rendered unenforceable by some statute or law.

Unilateral Contract A contract that results when an offer can only be accepted by the offeree's performance.

Unincorporated association An association of two or more persons to pursue a common objective. Unlike a partnership or a corporation, there is no particular form of organization.

Union Shop A place of employment in which all workers, once employed, must become union members within a specified period of time as a condition of their continued employment.

Universal Defenses Defenses that are valid against all holders of a negotiable instrument, including holders in due course (HDCs) and holders with the rights of HDCs.

Unreasonably Dangerous Product In product liability, a product that is defective to the point of threatening a consumer's health and safety. A product will be considered unreasonably dangerous if it is dangerous beyond the expectation of the ordinary consumer or if a less dangerous alternative was economically feasible for the manufacturer, but the manufacturer failed to produce it.

Usage of Trade Any practice or method of dealing having such regularity of observance in a place, vocation, or trade as to justify an expectation that it will be observed with respect to the transaction in question.

Usury Charging an illegal rate of interest.

Utilitarianism An approach to ethical reasoning in which ethically correct behavior is not related to any absolute ethical or moral values but to an evaluation of the consequences of a given action on those who will be affected by it. In utilitarian reasoning, a "good" decision is one that results in the greatest good for the greatest number of people affected by the decision.

V

Valid Contract A contract that results when the elements necessary for contract formation (agreement, consideration, legal purpose, and contractual capacity) are present.

Venue (pronounced *ven*-yoo) The geographical district in which an action is tried and from which the jury is selected.

Vertical Merger The acquisition by a company at one level in a marketing chain of a company at a higher or lower level in the chain (such as a company merging with one of its suppliers or retailers).

Vertical Restraint Any restraint on trade created by agreements between firms at different levels in the manufacturing and distribution process.

Vertically Integrated Firm A firm that carries out two or more functional phases (manufacture, distribution, retailing, and so on) of a product.

Vesting The creation of an absolute or unconditional right or power.

Virtual Courtroom A courtroom that is conceptual and not physical. In the context of cyberspace, a virtual courtroom could be a location on the Internet at which judicial proceedings take place.

Virtual Property Property that, in the context of cyberspace, is conceptual, as opposed to physical. Intellectual property that exists on the Internet is virtual property.

Void Contract A contract having no legal force or binding effect.

Voidable Contract A contract that may be legally avoided (canceled, or annulled) at the option of one or both of the parties.

***Voir Dire* (pronounced vwahr-*deehr*)** French verbs that mean, literally, "to see" and "to speak." In jury trials, the phrase refers to the process in which the attorneys question prospective jurors to determine whether they are biased or have any connection with a party to the action or with a prospective witness.

Voting Trust An agreement (trust contract) under which legal title to shares of corporate stock is transferred to a trustee who is authorized by the shareholders to vote the shares on their behalf.

W

Warranty Deed A deed in which the grantor assures (warrants to) the grantee that the grantor has title to the property conveyed in the deed, that there are no encumbrances on the property other than what the grantor has represented, and that the grantee will enjoy quiet possession of the property; a deed that provides the greatest amount of protection for the grantee.

Watered Stock Shares of stock issued by a corporation for which the corporation receives, as payment, less than the stated value of the shares.

Wetlands Areas of land designated by government agencies (such as the Army Corps of Engineers or the Environmental Protection Agency) as protected areas that support wildlife and that therefore cannot be filled in or dredged by private contractors or parties.

Whistleblowing An employee's disclosure to government, the press, or upper-management authorities that the employer is engaged in unsafe or illegal activities.

White-Collar Crime Nonviolent crime committed by individuals or corporations to obtain a personal or business advantage.

Will An instrument directing what is to be done with the testator's property on his or her death, made by the testator and revocable during his or her lifetime. No interests in the testator's property pass until the testator dies.

Winding Up The second of two stages involved in the termination of a partnership or corporation. Once the firm is dissolved, it continues to exist legally until the process of winding up all business affairs (collecting and distributing the firm's assets) is complete.

Workers' Compensation Laws State statutes establishing an administrative procedure for compensating workers' injuries that arise out of—or in the course of—their employment, regardless of fault.

Workout An out-of-court agreement between a debtor and his or her creditors in which the parties work out a payment plan or schedule under which the debtor's debts can be discharged.

Writ of Attachment A court's order, prior to a trial to collect a debt, directing the sheriff or other officer to seize nonexempt property of the debtor; if the creditor prevails at trial, the seized property can be sold to satisfy the judgment.

Writ of *Certiorari* (pronounced sur-shee-uh-*rah*-ree) A writ from a higher court asking the lower court for the record of a case.

Writ of Execution A court's order, after a judgment has been entered against the debtor, directing the sheriff to seize (levy) and sell any of the debtor's nonexempt real or personal property. The proceeds of the sale are used to pay off the judgment, accrued interest, and costs of the sale; any surplus is paid to the debtor.

Wrongful Discharge An employer's termination of an employee's employment in violation of the law.

Table of Cases

The principal cases (those presented within the chapters) are in bold type. Cases cited or discussed within the text or in case problems are in roman type.

C

D

E

F

G

H

I

J

K

L

M

N

S

T

U

V

W

X

Y

Z

Index

D

F

J

K

L

M

O

P

T

U

Y

Z

PHOTO CREDITS

All chapter and unit opener montages are comprised of PhotoDisc images. **5** From the painting by Benjamin Ferrers in National Portrait Gallery, Photo Corbis-Bettmann; **9** © Michael Evans, Sygma; **10** © Spencer Grant, PhotoEdit; **12** © Spencer Grant, PhotoEdit; **31** © PhotoDisc **40** © Matthew McVay, Tony Stone Images; **44** © Chris Brown, Stock Boston; **46** © Amy C. Etra, PhotoEdit **48** © A. Ramey, PhotoEdit **62** © Bettmann **72** © Photo by Richard Strauss, Smithsonian Institution, Collection of the Supreme Court of the United States **75** © Aaron Haupt, Stock Boston; **105** © Frederick D. Bodlin, Stock Boston; **113** © Steve Myerson, International Stock; **129** © C.E. Mitchell, Black Star **132** © Mike Mazzaschi, Stock Boston; **157** © Michael Keller, FPG; **167** © Michael Newman, PhotoEdit **170** © Reprinted with permsission of the *Daily Breeze* © 1995 **184** © Mary Kate Denny, PhotoEdit; **189** © Jan Sonnemair, Aurora; **213** © Ted Horowitz, The Stock Market; **219** © Vincent DeWitt, Stock Boston **225** © Barbara Alper, Stock Boston; **228** © A. Ramey, Stock Boston; **243** © Ron Chapple, FPG; **245** © Billy E. Barnes, PhotoEdit; **261** © Steve Benbow, Stock Boston; **267** © Bob Daemmrich, Stock Boston; **272** © Michael Newman, PhotoEdit; **288** © Michael Newman, PhotoEdit; **293** © M. Borchi, Photo Researchers; **312** (top) © Mark Mellett, Stock Boston, (bottom) © Tony Freeman, PhotoEdit; **316** © Ewing Galloway, Inc.; **334** © David Young-Wolff, PhotoEdit; **343** © Joseph Nettis, Stock Boston; **350** © Dick Luria, FPG; **360** © Associated Press; **364** © Elizabeth Simpson, FPG; **384** © Telegraph Colour Library, FPG; **398** © Bryce Flynn, Stock Boston; **404** © Andy Sacks, Tony Stone Images; **411** © Wayne Eastep, Tony Stone Images; **419** © Rick Friedman, Black Star; **424** © Joseph Sohm, Tony Stone Images; **436** © Tony Freeman, PhotoEdit; **438** © Phillip Wallick, The Stock Market; **462** © Mark Richards, PhotoEdit; **470** © Michael Newman, PhotoEdit; **474** © Steve Leonard, Black Star; **526** © Index Stock Photography, Inc.; **546** © Robert Brenner, PhotoEdit; **556** © Bob Daemmrich, Stock Boston; **562** © Tony Freeman, PhotoEdit; **605** Myrleen Ferguson, PhotoEdit; **611** © Tony Freeman, PhotoEdit; **615** © Tony Freeman, PhotoEdit; **645** © Comstock; **648** © Amy C. Etra, PhotoEdit; **656** © Michael Newman, PhotoEdit; **669** © Phil Borden, PhotoEdit; **680** © Jose L. Palaez, The Stock Market; **719** © McIntyre, Photo Researchers; **744** © John Terence Turner, FPG; **748** © Rhonda Birndorf, Associated Press; **750** © Tom Carroll, International Stock; **753** © Amy C. Etra, PhotoEdit; **776** © Robert Brenner, PhotoEdit; **803** © David Young-Wolff, PhotoEdit; **848** © Michael Newman, PhotoEdit; **850** © Day Williams, Photo Researchers; **900** © John Coletti, Stock Boston; **905** © Joe Marquette, Associated Press; **927** © PhotoEdit; **935** © PhotoDisc; **951** © The Library of Congress; **956** © Jonathan Nourak, PhotoEdit; **964** © Conklin, Monkmeyer Press; **989** © Johnny Stockshooter, International Stock; **992** © John Boykin, PhotoEdit; **1048** © Peter Vadnai, The Stock Market; **1056** © Jonathan Nourok, PhotoEdit; **1066** © Vic Bider, PhotoEdit.